TROUBLESHOOTING THE PC
With A+ Preparation

Third Edition

Patrick Regan

Upper Saddle River, New Jersey
Columbus, Ohio

Library of Congress Cataloging-in-Publication Data

Regan, Patrick E.
Troubleshooting the PC : with A+ preparation / Patrick E. Regan.—3rd ed.
p. cm.
ISBN 0-13-119467-4 (paperback)
1. Microcomputers—Maintenance and repair. I. Title.

TK7887.R44 2006
004.16—dc22

2004060045

Assistant Vice President and Publisher: Charles E. Stewart, Jr.
Production Editor: Alexandrina Benedicto Wolf
Production Coordination: Carlisle Publishers Services
Design Coordinator: Diane Ernsberger
Cover Designer: Jason Moore
Cover Art: Index Stock
Production Manager: Matt Ottenweller
Marketing Manager: Ben Leonard

This book was set in Times by Carlisle Communications, Ltd. It was printed and bound by Banta Book Group. The cover was printed by The Lehigh Press, Inc.

Pearson Education Ltd.
Pearson Education Singapore, Pte. Ltd.
Pearson Education Canada, Ltd.
Pearson Education—Japan
Pearson Education Australia Pty. Limited
Pearson Education North Asia Ltd.
Pearson Educación de Mexico, S.A. de C.V.
Pearson Education Malaysia, Pte. Ltd.

10 9 8 7 6 5 4 3 2 1
0-13-119467-4

"Dedicated to my father, who was always there when I needed him."

Brief Contents

Contents

CHAPTER 5 RAM 142

CHAPTER 6 Motherboards 168

CHAPTER 17 Serial Ports and Modems 478

CHAPTER 18 Parallel Ports and Printers 504

CHAPTER 19 The DOS Interface 532

Preface

Computers are a fast-paced technology that requires constant learning. People who learn how to fix computers must be familiar with new and old technology to become effective technicians.

This book is intended for the basic computer user who wants to be a successful PC technician and who may desire to pass the A+ PC technician exam and/or the Microsoft Desktop Technician for Windows XP. For more information on these exams, see Appendix E. It is assumed that users of this book are familiar with the computer, know how to use the computer, have a general understanding of Windows, and have basic word processing and spreadsheet skills.

Each chapter typically begins with basic concepts and ends with a troubleshooting section that includes questions to check understanding, emphasize troubleshooting skills, and prepare the reader to take the A+ test. Each chapter also includes hands-on exercises to reinforce basic skills and troubleshooting practices.

When planning a computer curriculum, it is often difficult for a group of computer professionals to agree on the order of topics. In this book, the basic hardware components (processor, motherboard, RAM, and drives) are covered first, followed by the add-on peripherals. The book ends with the operating systems. Depending on the students' experience, instructors may choose a different order.

As you go through the book, you will notice that a lot of information is repeated. This allows the chapters to be taught out of order and helps complete the overall picture. In addition, I have found that the best way to teach this material is to repeat the information several times and combine it with hands-on exercises.

I have included important websites that are necessary to become a successful computer technician. Some of the hands-on exercises include finding patches, drivers, jumper settings, and technical information on the Internet.

About the Author

Patrick Regan has been a PC technician and network administrator/engineer for the past 14 years. He has also taught many computer and network classes at Sacramento local colleges (Heald Colleges and MTI College), conducted considerable formal and informal training while an IT administrator (Heald Colleges) and a product support engineer for the Intel Corporation Customer Service, and participated in and led many projects (Heald Colleges and Intel Corporation). For his teaching accomplishments, he received the Teacher of the Year award from Heald Colleges; in addition, he received several recognition awards from Intel. Currently, he is a network engineer for Virtual Alert supporting the BioTerrorism Readiness suite. He holds many certifications, including Microsoft's MCSE, MCSA, and MCT; CompTIA's A+, Network+, Server+, Linux+, Security+, and CTT+; Cisco's CCNA; and Novell's CNE.

You can write to the author with questions and comments at patrick_regan@hotmail.com. (Because of the high volume of mail, every message may not receive a reply.)

Introduction

IT PROFESSIONALS

Everyone will agree that computers and the Internet are here to stay. In addition, the need is still great to connect computers to form a network and to connect computers at home and in businesses to the Internet. Even if you don't choose a career in computers and technology, the reality of today's workplace is that you're going to be using computers, whatever your job.

There are education, sales, training, managerial, and customer service jobs in the computers and technology industry. For these jobs you don't have to know programming or electronic design. Liberal arts graduates, business majors, and many others find careers in computers and technology. Of course, it does help if you've been bitten by the "computer bug" and find technology fascinating.

Most workers in the field of computers and technology earn considerably higher salaries than the average U.S. worker. Salaries vary with the job performed, the experience, the location, the amount of responsibility, and other factors, but many computer and technology jobs start in the $20,000 to $40,000 range and go much higher with experience. (Note: Although money is important to many people, you should always choose a career that you know you will enjoy.)

It is an established fact that computers and networking provide a fast-paced environment. Therefore, employees who work in information technology (IT) must learn to keep up with the ever-changing technology and have the ability to learn new technology. It is said that a person in IT must be able to learn or retrain him- or herself every 1 to 1 1/2 years.

Most jobs require a combination of technical and people skills. Today, being able to speak well, write well, and relate to other people (frequently people less technically savvy than you are) is very important. Every day brings something new in the field of computers and technology. If you want to be part of that process, if you're up to the challenge of constantly pushing the boundaries of new technology and harnessing it for useful work, there's a place for you in computers and technology.

According to *Certification Magazine* (http://www.certmag.com), the successful IT worker must:

- Be proficient in two or more technical specialties
- Be able to wear multiple hats
- Be business-oriented because hiring managers will be looking for employees who see the big picture of profit, loss, competitive advantage, and customer retention and understand that IT fits into this picture
- Be able to work easily with nontechnical personnel
- Have soft skills of good listening, problem solving, and effective written and verbal communication

In addition, there is a demand for those who can demonstrate expertise in IT project management. Those moving to a mid- to high-level position will have a mix of academic credentials and industry certifications, as well as increasing levels of responsibility.

Today, technical certifications are highly valuable. Depending on which certification or certifications an individual has, they can allow a user to begin as an entry-level technician or administrator. They also demonstrate the knowledge and capabilities of a current technician or administrator. Technical companies may see technical certifications as just as valuable as a college degree, whereas nontechnical companies might consider them a little less valuable than a college degree.

In 2001, researchers from Gartner Consulting surveyed nearly 18,000 IT managers, certified professionals, and certification candidates. They reported that:

- IT professionals seek certification to increase compensation, find employment, or boost productivity.
- Of those certified, 66 percent of certified professionals received an increase in salary after becoming certified, and 83 percent reported that certification helped them gain a new position.
- Although most certification candidates combine several study methods, printed materials designed for self-study and instructor-led training were reported as the most useful preparation methods.

From the employer's perspective, although many managers (42 percent) feared that certified employees would move on to another organization, 71 percent of IT professionals gaining certification stay put. IT managers cited a higher level of service, competitive advantage, and increased productivity as key benefits of having certified staff. Of course, the drawbacks include cost of training and testing.

The economy may have hiccupped in 2001 and 2002, but the need for technically trained people is still as important as ever. Job growth is projected to increase in computers and technology. In addition, although new studies find that employers will attempt to fill many new IT jobs, many of these positions will go unfilled because of a lack of applicants with the requisite technical and nontechnical skills.

Recently in the United States, there has been some concern about technical jobs being outsourced overseas since these jobs can be filled at a lower cost. Whereas this may affect some technical jobs, there will still be a need for well-rounded, multidisciplined technical professionals who also understand the business aspects of designing, implementing, and maintaining technology.

This book covers two certifications, CompTIA's A+ certification and Microsoft's Desktop Support Technician (DST), each of which consists of two exams. Both certifications will help you get jobs as computer technicians. The A+ exam covers hardware and Windows, whereas the Desktop Support Technician exam covers Windows XP and Microsoft Office. See Appendix E for more information.

LOOKING FOR A JOB

Once you have learned the necessary knowledge and skills, earned any necessary certificates, and reached a comfort level with computers or networks, you are going to have to look for a job. Awhile ago, a network engineer certification was thought to be a job guarantee. Unfortunately, many people looking to change jobs purchased and studied practice tests, passed the certification tests without ever installing a network operating system, and then looked for a job. This devalued the whole certification process because those people did not have hands-on experience. Today, the process is a bit different. Once you earn a certification, many potential employers are still looking for one year of experience. But after you get that one year of experience, your job opportunities increase greatly.

So, what do you need to do? First, you will have to prepare at least two resumes. The resume is a document that describes your knowledge, skills, and experiences. The reason for at least two resumes is you will need one that is formatted with fonts and styles such as boldface, italics, and underlines, whereas the other one will be a plain text document with no formatting. You will use the formatted resume when you go on interviews or when you send email. You will post the unformatted document on job websites.

Of course, in either case, you want the resume to be readable and well organized. In addition, you should make sure that you are using correct grammar and spelling. Remember that your resume represents you; if the resume is not organized well, then the reader may also assume that you are not well organized. Being organized is a valuable trait when working in IT. Your proficiency in grammar and spelling will show your ability to communicate and attention to detail.

When you are applying for a job via the mail or email, you should also create a cover letter. Whereas the resume tells the reader your qualifications for a job, the cover letter should tell the reader why you are a good fit for the specific job. I would even recommend listing each of the requirements that the company posted for the job, and explaining why you are qualified for this job.

Eventually, you will get someone's attention and you will be asked to go for an interview. First, you should dress well. That does not necessarily mean dressing in formal attire. Men should wear a nice shirt and tie; women should dress in appropriate business attire. Many IT jobs have a relaxed dress code; however, you should dress a bit more formally to show your professionalism. Of course, make sure that your clothes are neat and in good repair.

When you go for the interview, be friendly and attentive. Don't be afraid to smile. If the interviewer asks you a question and you really don't know the answer, say that you don't know the answer. When the interview is done, you should immediately send a thank-you letter thanking him or her for the time. In addition, if there were questions asked to which you did not know the answers, you should research them and include them in your cover letter. This shows that you really want the job and that you can find the answers when you need them. Of course, in IT jobs you will not know all of the answers, but how quickly you find the answers will make or break a network administrator.

The next question is, where do you find a job? First, you should check the newspaper. When an IT job is posted in a newspaper, many people will apply for the job who are not qualified. So you need to make sure that your cover letter and resume show that you are more than qualified.

If you don't find any good leads in the newspaper, you might want to try job agencies—specifically, job agencies that handle technical jobs. These agencies will have permanent jobs and most likely will have temporary jobs as well. A temporary job allows you to try out a company, but it also allows the company, to try you out before permanently hiring you. It is also the agency's job to find and screen qualified applicants, especially since many jobs go on for long periods of time because the company cannot find qualified applicants.

Another option is to use the Internet. If there is a particular company that you want to work for, go to the website and find out what jobs are available and where you can send your resume. For a wider scale search, look for job websites that focus on technology. This is where you can get the most job leads. Of course, how you fill out your profile on the web page is just as important as your resume. In addition, this is where you can post your resume, most likely the unformatted resume.

Some good job websites include:

Dice

http://www.dice.com/

Monster

http://www.monster.com/
http://technology.monster.com/

Hot Jobs

http://www.hotjobs.com/index.html
http://www.hotjobs.com/htdocs/channels/tech/

Tech-Engine

http://www.tech-engine.com/

Computer Jobs

http://www.computerjobs.com

Careerbuilder.com

http://www.careerbuilder.com/
http://informationtechnology.careerbuilder.com

Techies.com

http://www.techies.com/

Career Mag

http://www.careermag.com/

ManPower Inc.

http://www.manpower.com
http://www.manpower.com/mpcom/JobSearch.jsp

Another important source of jobs is not through any advertisement, but through networking. In this context, networking is meeting people and making contacts. You may get a job because of who you know. Of course, in most cases you will still need to show that you have the necessary skills and experience for the new position. But you will get opportunities that would not be open to the general public.

Good luck with your career as an IT professional.

CHAPTER 1

A PC Overview

Topics Covered in This Chapter

Introduction

Before you can do any troubleshooting, you must learn the components of the personal computer, or PC. These include the case, monitor, and keyboard. In addition, you must be familiar with the operating system and application software and have a basic understanding of how they interact with hardware. This chapter introduces you to the primary basic components of the computer, the most common operating systems, and the application software packages used today.

Objectives

1. Explain the differences among a personal computer, a minicomputer, and a mainframe computer.
2. Differentiate between hardware and software.
3. Understand the importance of data.
4. Identify major PC components.
5. Recognize the purpose of all major PC components.
6. Given the size and density of a floppy disk, state its capacity.
7. List the purpose and function of the operating system.
8. Compare and contrast the common PC operating systems.
9. Explain the difference between an operating system and an operating environment.
10. Define the de jure standard and the de facto standard and explain how they differ.
11. Explain how software interacts with hardware.

1.1 COMPUTERS

A **computer** is a machine composed of electronic devices used to process data. **Data** is the raw facts, numbers, letters, or symbols that the computer processes into meaningful information. Examples of data include a letter to a company or a client, a report for your boss, a budget proposal for a large project, or an address book of your friends' and business associates' addresses. Whatever the data, once it is saved (or written to disk), it can be retrieved at any time, printed on paper, or sent to someone else over the telephone lines.

Computers can be classified into four main groups: personal computers, minicomputers, mainframe computers, and supercomputers. This book focuses on the first type, the personal computer, sometimes known as the **PC**. It is based on the Intel (or Intel-compatible) microprocessor (the microprocessor is the "brain" of the computer).

A **personal computer** is a computer that is meant to be used by one person. It usually consists of a case that contains the essential electronic and mechanical parts of the computer, a monitor so that you can output (display) data, and a keyboard so that you can input (insert) data.

Personal computers can be divided into desktop models and portable computers. See figure 1.1. Desktop computers are small enough to fit on a desk but are too big to carry with you. Portable computers (including laptops, notebooks, and subnotebooks) are fully functional computers that can be carried with you. Desktop computers tend to be more powerful and more flexible than portable computers.

Minicomputers, mainframe computers, and supercomputers use a single central computer. These computers, which are much more powerful than any single PC, are designed for many people to use at the same time through dumb terminals. A dumb terminal has a keyboard and a monitor that allows the user to input and view data, but it does not have a microprocessor or RAM (a type of memory) to process data. Therefore, although a PC does its own processing, dumb terminals rely on a central computer to perform tasks. These computers are considered noninteractive because they usually run in batch mode, where tasks are submitted as individual jobs by the users.

As personal computers became popular and more powerful, people wanted to connect personal computers together to form a network. A network can share data files, application programs, and expensive printers, as well as provide communication capabilities such as connecting to the Internet.

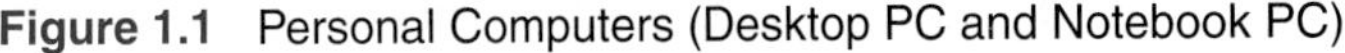

Figure 1.1 Personal Computers (Desktop PC and Notebook PC)

When discussing computers in detail, you must break the computer into three major elements:

1. Hardware
2. Software
3. User

Hardware is defined as the physical components that make up the personal computer. If you can touch and carry an item, the item is hardware. The major hardware components consist of the system unit (usually containing a motherboard, RAM chips, expansion cards, floppy drives, and a hard drive), the monitor, and the keyboard.

Software, also known as a program or an application, is a series of instructions that are loaded into the computer's memory. These instructions tell the computer what to do and when to do it. It controls the hardware and manipulates data.

When you buy a software package, the instructions are written on a floppy disk or a compact disk (CD-ROM). Although the instructions are written on the disk, the disk is considered to be a hardware item because it is something that you can touch and carry. The instructions themselves represent software.

The **user** is the computer operator who tells the computer what to do. Typically, the user gives a command or performs an action and the commands or actions are interpreted by the computer to perform the specified task. Some of the commands and tasks may start another program, delete a file from your hard drive, print a document, or email a message using your modem.

Because data represent hours of work that may consist of irreplaceable information, it is the most valuable element to the user. Therefore, all efforts must be made to protect it. This includes ensuring that the hardware is working properly; that the user is developing good work habits that will enhance data protection; and that the user is making extra copies of the important data, also known as **backing up** the data.

1.2 PC HISTORY

The first personal computer was introduced in 1975 by a company called MITS. Its computer, the Altair, included an Intel 8080 microprocessor, a power supply, a number of lights, and 256 bytes of memory. If you don't understand what some of these items are, don't worry, because they will all be explained to you. For now, let us say that by today's standard, this computer would be nothing more than a toy with lights.

IBM's first attempt at the personal computer market was a computer that had 16 kilobytes (abbreviated KB or K) of memory, a display (to view the software and data), and a tape drive (to store the software and data). Unfortunately for IBM, it never became successful because of its $9,000 price tag in 1975.

In 1976, Apple introduced the Apple I computer, which consisted of a circuit board screwed into a piece of plywood. The following year, Apple introduced the now-classic Apple II computer, which represented the first affordable personal computer. Its general design was used in later designs of other personal computers.

In 1981, IBM introduced the original **IBM PC** (model 5150), which quickly became the personal computer standard. It contained an Intel 8088 microprocessor, 16 KB of RAM, a 63.5-watt (W) power supply, a monochrome monitor, and one 320 or 360 KB disk drive. One of the popular features of the IBM PC was that it was expandable. With this feature, you could upgrade to new technology as it became available without replacing the whole computer.

Since technology has changed so rapidly through the years, today the IBM PC is an extremely outdated machine. Today's average personal computer would have at least a Pentium 4 microprocessor, 512 megabytes (MB) of RAM, a 40-gigabyte (GB) hard drive, one 1.44 MB floppy disk drive, a 300 W power supply, a color Super VGA monitor, a sound card, and a CD-ROM drive. Again, if you don't understand these terms, don't worry; they will be explained throughout the book.

1.3 PARTS OF THE COMPUTER

The computer is divided into three main parts: the case, the monitor, and the keyboard. Most of what makes up the computer is located in the case, such as the processor, motherboard, RAM, floppy disk drives, and hard drive. The case is designed to protect these components. In addition, other **peripherals** (external devices attached to the computer) may be added. Peripherals include printers, external disk drives, monitors, keyboards, mice, and external modems. See table 1.1, figure 1.2 and figure 1.3. Today, most motherboards are integrated because they include built-in video, sound, modem and Ethernet network devices.

1.3.1 Motherboards and Microprocessors

The computer is built around an integrated chip called the **processor.** The processor is sometimes referred to as the **central processing unit (CPU).** See figure 1.2. It is considered the "brain" of the computer because all the instructions it performs are mathematical calculations and logical comparisons. IBM and IBM-compatible computers use Intel, Cyrix, and AMD microprocessors, whereas Apple computers use Motorola microprocessors. The Intel processors found in the IBM and IBM-compatible computers are the 8088, 8086, 80286, 80386DX, 80386SX, 80486DX, 80486SX, Pentium, Pentium Pro, Pentium II, Pentium III, and Pentium 4.

The speed of the processor is usually expressed in megahertz (MHz). One megahertz is equal to 1 million cycles per second and 1 gigahertz (GHz) is equal to 1 billion cycles per second. During each cycle, a circuit will react in a predictable way. These reactions make the computer do what it does.

The processor is the central component of the computer. It is plugged into a large circuit board called the **motherboard,** or **system board.** The motherboard allows the microprocessor to branch out and communicate with all the other computer components; it can be considered the nervous system of the PC. Daughter boards, commonly called **expansion cards,** are used to expand the motherboard.

1.3.2 Memory

RAM, or **random access memory,** is the computer's short-term or temporary memory. Program instructions and data are stored on the RAM chips, which the microprocessor accesses directly. The more RAM you have, the more instructions and data you can load. The amount of RAM greatly affects the performance of the PC. Unfortunately, if power is discontinued to the RAM, as when you shut off your PC, the contents of the RAM disappear. This is why we use disks (floppy disks and hard disks) for long-term storage.

Another type of memory used in the PC is **ROM,** or **read-only memory.** ROM contains instructions and data that the microprocessor accesses directly. It differs from RAM in that ROM instructions are permanent and cannot be changed or erased by normal means. The instructions in ROM chips can be thought of as the instincts of the computer. Instructions that control much of the computer's input/output functions, such as communicating with disks, RAM, and the monitor, are stored in the ROM chips and are known as the **BIOS (basic input/output system).**

Table 1.1 PC Components

Component	Purpose
Case	The case is the box that most of the computer components rest in, and it is designed to protect these components. It contains the power supply (supplies DC power to the rest of the computer), motherboard, floppy drives, hard drive, expansion cards (including the sound card), CD-ROM drive, and RAM. (See chapter 8.)
Floppy drive	Floppy drives enable you to read and write data to and from floppy disks, small, thin plastic disks used for long-term storage of files. The storage capacity of a disk is very limited, but the disk can easily be taken to another computer. (See chapter 10.)
Hard drive	The hard drive (sometimes called a hard disk or fixed disk) is the principal device for storing programs and data. It usually has a large capacity and is much quicker than the floppy disk drive. Generally, it is not removed from the computer. (See chapter 9.)
Keyboard	The keyboard is a device similar to a typewriter by which the user inputs instructions and data into the computer. The keyboard is the main input device. (See chapter 15.)
Monitor	The monitor is a device similar to a television. The monitor is the computer's main output device. It is also called a display or video. (See chapter 14.)
Motherboard and microprocessor	The motherboard is the circuit board, which is the central core of the computer. (See chapter 6.) On the motherboard, there is a microprocessor (also known as a CPU). The microprocessor does most of the computer's work. (See chapter 4.) The motherboard is expandable using expansion cards. (See chapter 7.)
RAM (random access memory)	The RAM chips are integrated chips used for short-term memory. RAM holds program instructions and data, which the microprocessor directly accesses. RAM chips are volatile, meaning they immediately lose their data when the computer is shut off. (See chapter 5.)
ROM (read-only memory)	The ROM chips contain encoded progam instructions and data that the microprocessor accesses directly. Unlike RAM, ROM instructions are permanent and generally cannot be changed or erased. (See chapter 6.)
Printer	The printer is a common output device used with computers. This device produces images of text and graphics on paper. Some printers can also produce color images. (See chapter 18.)
Modem	*Modem* stands for *mo*dulator/*dem*odulator. This device is communication hardware that enables transmission of data through telephone lines. (See chapter 17.)
Pointing devices (mice and trackballs)	Mice and trackballs are devices that can move the cursor back and forth on the screen (assuming the software supports pointing devices). Using these devices is easy and sometimes quicker than using the keyboard, which can improve productivity. Note: Pointing devices are enhancements to a keyboard, not replacements. (See chapter 15.)
CD and/or DVD drive	Compact disks (CDs) and digital video disks (DVDs) store large quantities of data that are accessed using a CD-ROM drive. CDs and DVDs are similar to hard drives and floppy disks; however, CD-ROMs and DVDs are designed to provide read-only data. Today, many CD drives are also CDRW, which can create and write to CDs, and some CD drives are combined CDRW and DVD drives. (See chapter 11.)
Network card	The network card (or port) allows you to connect to a local area network. The most common network card or port is the Ethernet card. (See chapter 25.)
Sound card	The sound card adds music, speech, and sound effects to the PC. (See chapter 16.)

Figure 1.2 Motherboard with CPU and RAM

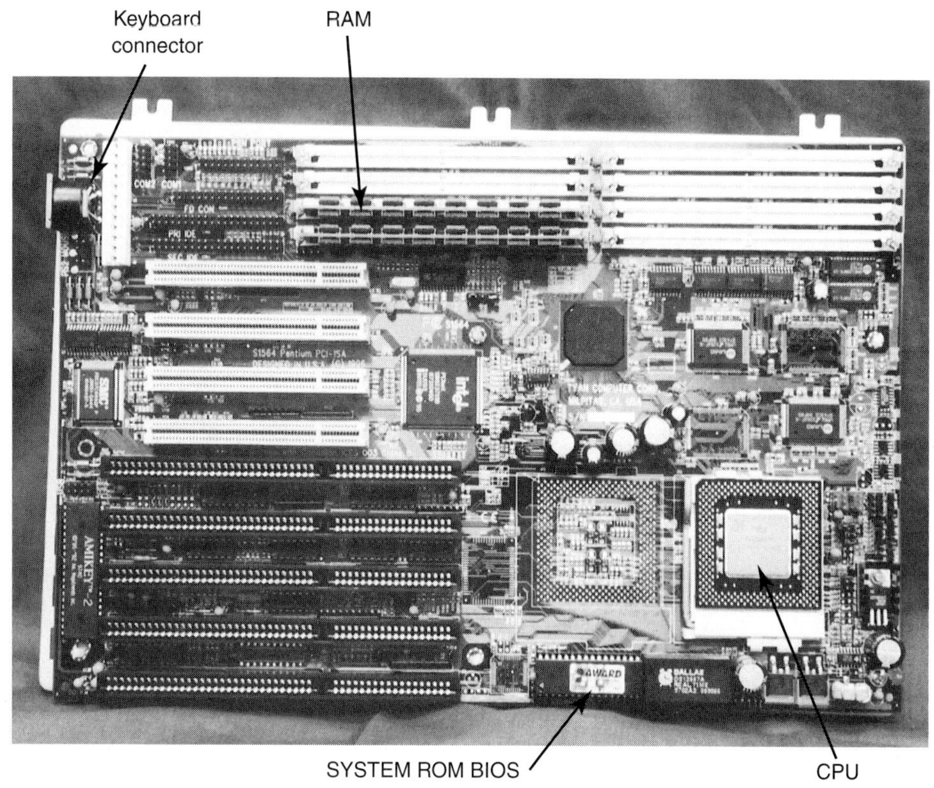

Figure 1.3 Motherboard Connected to Power Supply, Hard Drive, and Floppy Drive

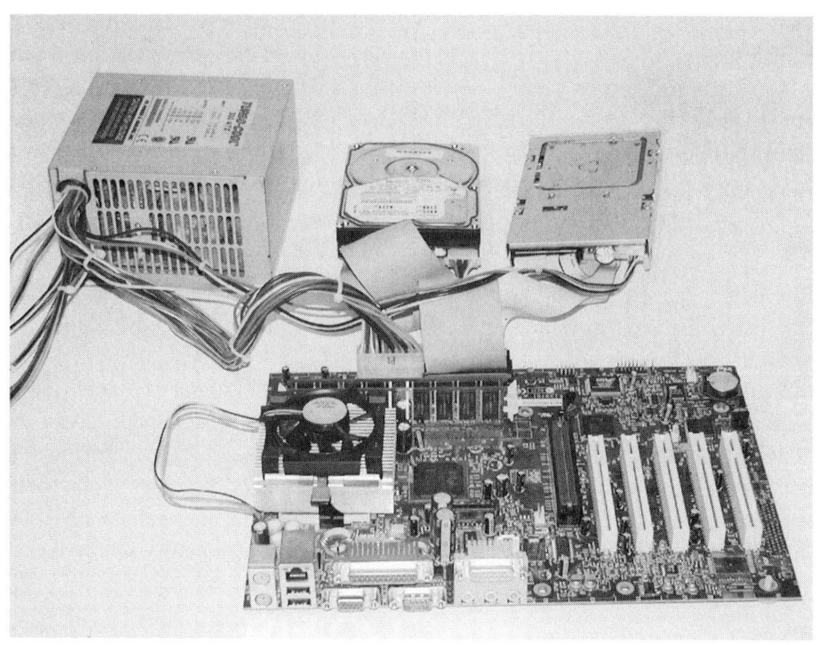

Figure 1.4 Floppy Disks (3 1/2-inch)

Table 1.2 Floppy Disk Capacity

Size	DS/DD	DS/HD	DS/ED
3½-in.	720 KB	1.44 MB	2.88 MB

1.3.3 Hard Drives and Floppy Disk Drives

Disks are half-electronic, half-mechanical devices that store magnetic fields on rotating platters. The magnetic fields represent the data. Disks are usually classified as hard disks or floppy disks. Floppy disks do not hold as much information as hard disks, but they can be easily transported from one computer to another. Hard disks, on the other hand, are much faster than floppy disks and have a greater storage capacity.

Today, floppy disks come in one size: 3½-in. diameter. See figure 1.4. There are three different densities for floppy disks: double density (DD), high density (HD), and extra density (ED). All the floppy disks today are double-sided (DS), which means that the disk drive reads both sides of the floppy disk. See table 1.2. Today the disks are DS/HD 3½-in. disks, which can hold 1.44 MB of data. (The 3½-in. DS/ED disks, which can hold 2.88 MB of data, were never widely accepted. Although they hold more than the 1.44 MB disks, their size is still too limiting for today's large files.)

NOTE: Since floppy disks are considered to be a legacy device, some systems are being sold without floppy disks.

Today, it is very easy to create a large document or picture that is several megabytes in size. Therefore, it is easy to see that floppy disks are too small to store these large files. Currently, there are several companies that make high-capacity removable magneto-optical disk drives. Some of these are designed to replace the floppy disk drive. These include an LS-120 drive, which can store up to 750 MB, the Iomega Zip Drive, which can hold 100 MB, 250 MB, or 750 MB, depending on the model you purchase, and the Iomega Jazz drive, which can store up to 2 GB. More recently, there have been a large range of portable drives available, including portable hard drives, portable CD writers, and USB flash drives.

1.3.4 Monitors

The **monitor** is the standard output device, similar to a television. Monitors are characterized by their size and resolution. The size of a monitor is measured diagonally across the screen. Typical monitors range from 14 in. to 21 in.

The **resolution** of a computer monitor is determined by the number of **pixels** (picture elements) or dots going across the screen and the number of pixels or dots going down the screen. A typical resolution for a standard VGA monitor is 640 pixels across the screen and 480 pixels down, giving it a resolution of 640 × 480. At this resolution, the standard VGA displays 16 colors at one time. A Super VGA monitor has a higher resolution, such as 800 × 600 or 1024 × 768, and can use up to 16 million colors or more on the screen at the same time, allowing for photographic-quality screen output.

1.3.5 Keyboards

The **keyboard** is the primary input device. It is used to input or enter letters, numbers, symbols, punctuation, and commands into the computer. It includes the same keys as a typewriter. Most keyboards include a numeric keypad, cursor-movement keys, and 12 function keys. Today, most keyboards are 101-, 102-, or 104-key keyboards. Of course, the name is derived from the number of keys on the keyboard.

1.3.6 Printers

The **printer** is an output device that allows the user to take information from the computer and print it on paper. Just as there are many types of computers and monitors, there are many different types of printers. Most printers connect directly to the computer through the parallel port, or USB port connectors located at the back of the computer. See table 3.1. The port is a device that can communicate eight bits at a time. (A bit is a binary digit based on 0s and 1s. Eight bits are equal to one byte of data, which represents a single character.)

Printers can be divided into impact and nonimpact printers. Impact printers have movable parts that strike an ink ribbon against a sheet of paper. Impact printers include daisy wheel/ball printers and dot-matrix printers. See figure 1.5. Their disadvantages are that they are slow and noisy, and their output is not considered to be high quality or "letter-perfect," except for the wheel/ball printers. In addition, the availability of dot-matrix printers is very limited since they lost their popularity.

Instead of striking the paper, nonimpact printers use other methods to print. Nonimpact printers include ink-jet printers, laser printers, and thermal printers. The ink-jet and laser printers are the most commonly used.

Ink-jet printers spray ink through a small hole. They are superior to dot-matrix printers in that they have better print quality and are much quieter. Today an ink-jet printer costs about the same as a dot-matrix printer and they both operate at the same speed. See figure 1.6.

Figure 1.5 Dot-Matrix Printer

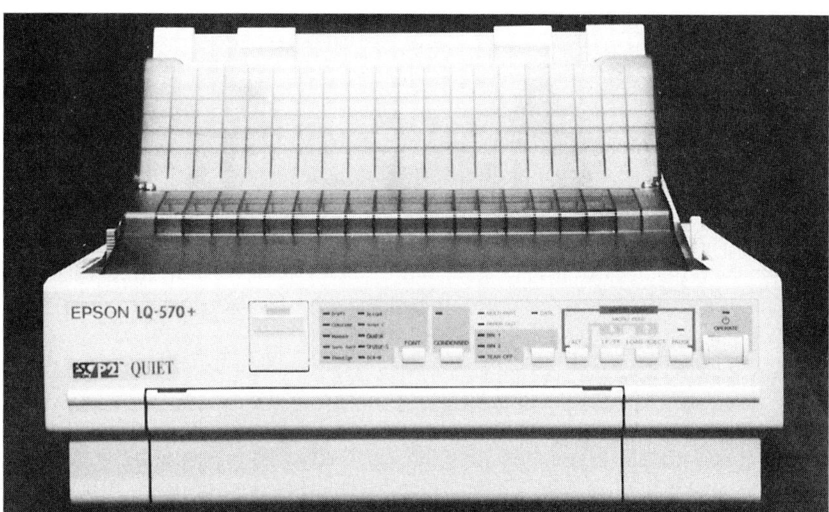

Figure 1.6 Ink-Jet Printer

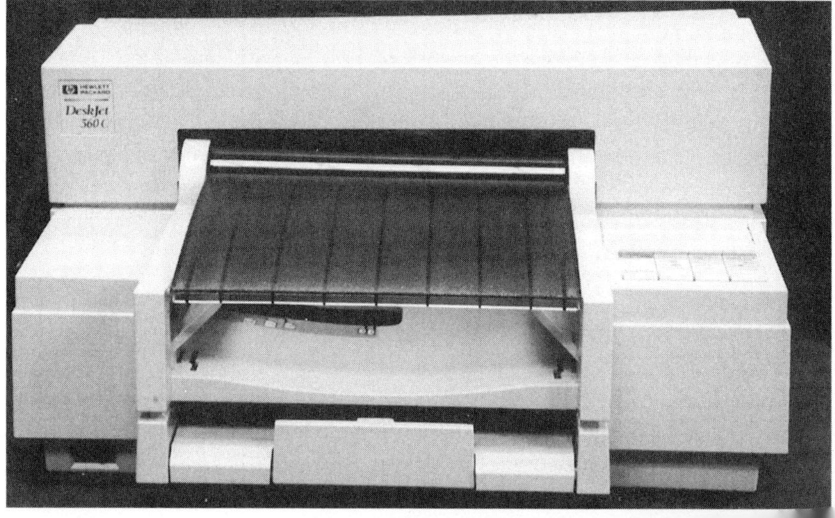

Figure 1.7 Laser Printer

The best-looking print comes from a laser printer. See figure 1.7. The printer works similar to a photocopy machine using fine toner powder to transfer images to paper. By heating (fusing) the toner, it becomes permanent on the paper. The laser printer is of extremely high quality with a wide range of fonts and graphics. It is also quiet and fast. Of course, it is more expensive than other types of printers. The most popular laser printers are produced by Hewlett-Packard.

1.3.7 Serial Devices

Serial devices are devices that can communicate one bit at a time. They are often connected to a serial port. See table 3.1. The most popular serial device is the pointing device, such as a mouse or trackball. See figure 1.8. A **mouse** is a small device that fits in your hand. A ball is located on the bottom of the device. When you run the ball along a surface, you are able to easily move an arrow (mouse pointer) on the screen. With this arrow, you can perform certain actions quickly and more precisely than with the keyboard. This includes line drawing, deleting words, or running applications. The **trackball** is similar to a mouse except that the ball is on the top of the device. You use your fingers to roll the ball. As the ball moves, the mouse pointer moves.

As computers became more popular, connectivity was added to the PC so that it could communicate with other computers. One of the more common peripherals used to enable PCs to communicate with other PCs is the **modem,** which actually stands for *mo*dulator/*dem*odulator. It allows users to "talk" to other computers through a telephone line. By using a modem, you can connect to the Internet, call up bulletin boards (BBS), and use other telephone services. You can access online encyclopedias and informational databases, make airline reservations, and do shopping and banking. Today, most modems also have fax (facsimile transmission) capabilities.

1.3.8 Multimedia Peripherals

A computer system that combines text, graphics, animation, and sound is known as a **multimedia system.** A **sound card** is used to add digitized sound to the PC. A video-interface card allows you to take a television signal and display it on your computer screen. To add pictures into your documents, you can create them with a draw or paint program or scan them in with a **scanner.**

Figure 1.8 Mouse and Trackball

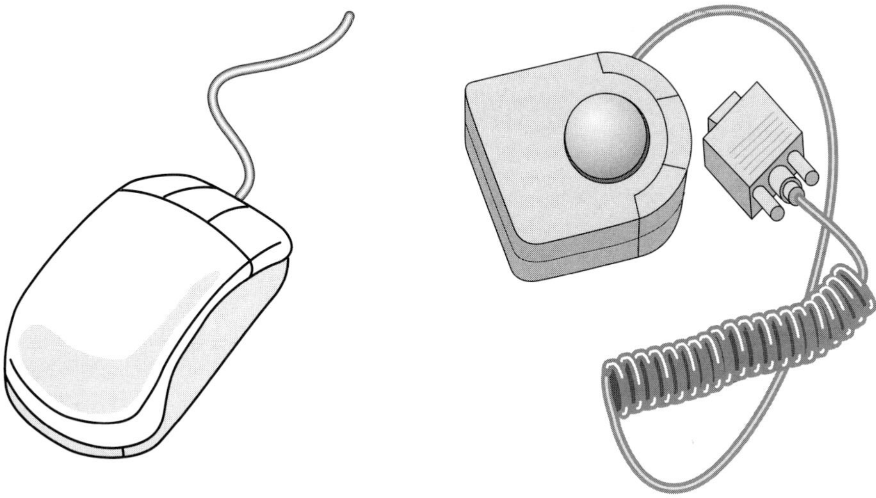

Figure 1.9 Compact Disk

The **compact disk (CD)** is one of the newer additions to the PC. See figure 1.9. Information is stored on the compact disk using laser light. This newer technology allows a single disk to hold enormous amounts of information (for instance, 650 MB of data, or approximately the equivalent of 450 floppy disks). A PC's CD-ROM drive can read CD-ROM data disks, music CDs, and photo CDs. Though most CDs are designed to be read-only (CD-ROM), today rewritable compact disks are very common.

Digital video disks (DVDs) are the newest type of compact disk that have the capability to store massive computer applications such as a full multimedia encyclopedia, or a feature-length movie on one disk. Today, the DVD can store up to 17 GB using both sides. Eventually, rewritable DVDs will be common on PCs.

1.4 SOFTWARE

As you have seen with hardware, the computer has many parts, and each component is designed for a particular function. Software is very similar. It can be divided into two primary categories—application software and system software.

Software is designed by programmers. A programmer or group of programmers writes the instructions using a programming language resembling English. Some of these languages include BASIC language, C language, and assembly language. Because the computer cannot understand English, it must first translate the English commands into machine language (commands understood by the CPU) written in binary code, consisting of combinations of the numbers 1 and 0. (This corresponds to the bipolar, or on/off, state of electrical components, where "on" equals 1 and "off" equals 0.) Translating the commands into binary code is called compiling a program, which is completed by system software known as a compiler.

Figure 1.10 Word Processor

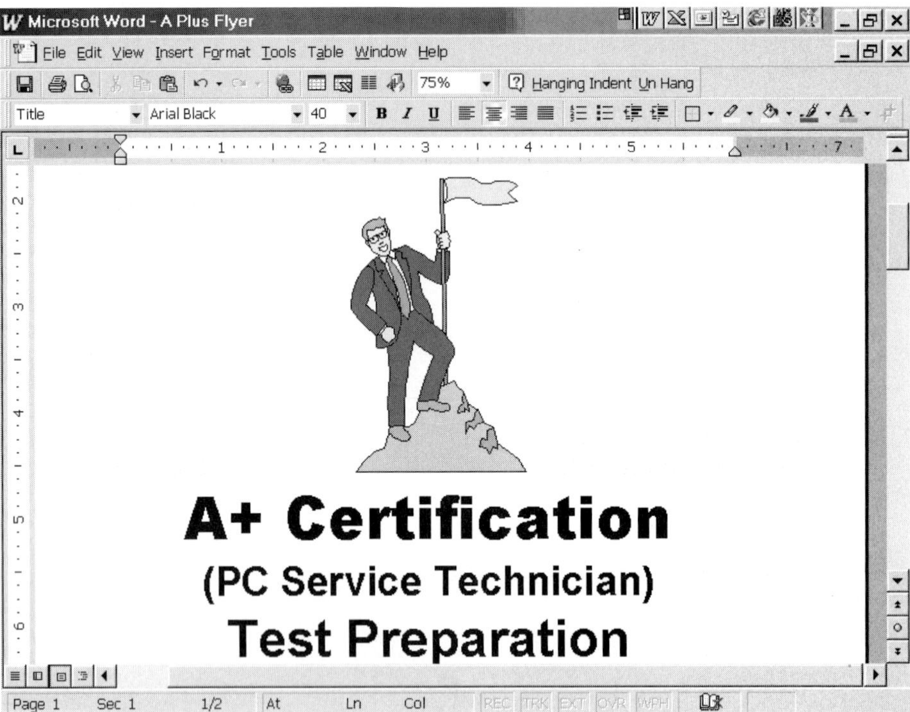

1.4.1 Application Software

Application software allows a user to input, process, and output data to create usable information. It is this type of software that allows the user to create a letter, report, budget, chart, graph, or database.

The most common application software is the **word processor**. See figure 1.10. Word processing software allows you to type a document, much like a typewriter. Additional features include a spell checker, a grammar checker, a find-and-replace function, and the ability to move text. The most popular word processing programs include Microsoft Word and Corel WordPerfect.

Another type of application software is **spreadsheet** software. Most people think of spreadsheets as tables of numbers or financial models. If the spreadsheet is created using formulas and a value is changed, the entire spreadsheet is automatically recalculated. Today spreadsheets do a lot more than "number crunching." They sort numbers, create graphs, and perform data analysis. The two most popular spreadsheet programs are Microsoft Excel and Lotus 1-2-3.

Database application software allows users to work with files of related data. An address book or employee records are examples of database files. The data can be organized and quickly retrieved. The most popular database application is Microsoft Access.

There are many other types of application software. Graphics programs allow you to create graphs and pictures. **Desktop publishing programs** allow you to combine graphics and text to create newsletters and reports. **Draw** and **paint programs** allow you to become an artist using the mouse or other input devices instead of a pencil, pen, or brush.

Finally, there are computer games and educational software packages. Unlike early games and text-based tutorials, these packages are complex, sophisticated software consisting of exciting graphics, sound, and animation.

1.4.2 Operating System Software

Although application software is the best-known software, it is not the only type of software. The **system software** directs the entire system. Operating systems and compilers make up most of the system software. The only system software that this book will discuss in detail is that of the operating system.

Table 1.3 Operating Systems

Operating System	Interface	Comments
DOS	Command-driven	First PC operating system
UNIX (including Linux)	Command-driven/GUI	PC operating system usually associated with local area networks (LANs) and the Internet Note: Linux uses X Window to provide a GUI interface.
OS/2	GUI	IBM's graphical user interface
Microsoft Windows 95, Microsoft Windows 98, Microsoft Windows Me	GUI	Microsoft's replacements for DOS and the Windows 3.XX operating environment
Microsoft Windows NT, Microsoft Windows 2000, Microsoft Windows XP, Windows Server 2003	GUI	Microsoft's newest graphical user interface OS
System 6, System 7, System 8, System 9, Mac OS X	GUI	Macintosh's operating systems

The **operating system (OS)** is the computer's most important software. It coordinates the actions of the hardware, the software, and the user so that they can work as one. Table 1.3 shows today's common operating systems.

The operating system is essential to the computer. During **boot-up,** the operating system is loaded (copied) from the boot disk (typically the hard disk) to RAM. It provides an interface to the user so that he or she can start other programs by entering a command at the keyboard or by using the mouse to perform an action. Of course, depending on the actions of the user and the instructions specified in the software, the operating system directs the computer's hardware. When you save a file to a disk, the OS automatically records the location so that you can find and access the file in the future and so that the operating system will not accidentally write over it with another file.

Operating systems have one of two types of interface, command-driven or icon-driven. The command-driven operating systems, such as DOS and UNIX/Linux, require that you type in commands from the keyboard. With the command-driven interface, you must know the correct spelling, syntax, parameters, and punctuation for each command. If you have one character that is wrong or out of place, you will receive an error message or an incorrect response. Mastering a command-driven OS requires memorization of the correct way to type each command.

The other type of interface is icon-driven. Icon-driven operating systems (such as Windows 95, Windows 98, and Windows NT) are known as *graphical interfaces* because they use small pictures known as icons to represent a function or application. The programs are started by using a mouse or trackball to move an arrow to an icon and then pressing a button on the mouse. Since the operating system uses icons, it requires a much smaller learning curve than a command-driven system. Operating systems that use icons are known to have a **graphical user interface (GUI).** Most people like the look and feel of an icon-driven operating system and consider it user-friendly. **User-friendly** is a term indicating that computer equipment or software is easy to understand and operate. Today most operating systems use a graphical interface.

Another characteristic of an operating system is that of single tasking versus multitasking. Single tasking allows one application to work at one time, while multitasking allows more than one application to work at one time. Depending upon the application programs and the type of operating system, you can run two or more programs, share information, and switch back and forth between the different applications. Today's PC can process jobs in the background (i.e., printing or complicated calculations) while you work on something else (i.e., typing a report). When an operating system has a GUI, it is usually multitasking.

Figure 1.11 DOS (A Command-Driven Operating System)

1.4.3 MS-DOS and Microsoft Windows

The first operating system that began with the IBM PC was **Microsoft DOS** (commonly known as MS-DOS or just DOS). DOS stands for disk operating system. While today DOS is found only on old computers, the DOS environment is still used for troubleshooting. See figure 1.11.

Most machines that have DOS also have Microsoft Windows 3.XX. XX represents any of the version numbers released as improvements to Microsoft Windows 3.0. Although Windows 3.XX provides a GUI to DOS, Windows 3.XX cannot boot the computer. Instead, the computer is booted using DOS, and Windows is loaded on top of DOS. Therefore, Windows 3.XX is an **operating environment,** not an operating system. Windows 3.XX is a 16-bit operating environment that runs 16-bit applications.

Operating System/2 (OS/2) began as an effort by IBM and Microsoft to replace MS-DOS. It is an icon-driven, multitasking operating system requiring a 386 machine. Due to a fallout between the two companies, IBM owns OS/2 and Microsoft developed **Microsoft Windows NT, Microsoft Windows 95, Microsoft Windows 98, Microsoft Windows Me, Windows NT, Microsoft Windows 2000, Microsoft Windows XP,** and **Windows Server 2003. Microsoft Windows 95** and **Microsoft Windows 98** are the operating systems that eventually replaced DOS and Windows 3.XX. See figure 1.12. Microsoft Windows can run most Windows 3.XX applications and DOS applications.

NOTE: While Windows 9X and Windows NT can be found on older machines, today's modern machines will have Windows 2000 or Windows XP.

1.5 SOFTWARE VERSIONS

Since the original IBM PC was introduced, IBM has produced many versions of the personal computer. Usually the major changes were based on the introduction of a new Intel processor or other new technology.

Like hardware, software has to change to make use of the new technology. To signify these changes, software companies number their software with a version number. To display the version in DOS, you would enter the VER command at the DOS prompt. Windows list the version number in the System icon/applet in the Control Panel. By knowing the version number, it will help you determine the software's capabilities, determine when it is appropriate to purchase an upgrade, and find patches or other updates. You will also need to know the version number when talking to a manufacturer's technical support person.

When a software package releases a new version, its version number increases. If it increases by a whole number, it usually means major changes (updates) to the program. When it increases by .1, it indicates moderate changes. When it increases by only .01, it indicates minor changes. Microsoft Windows NT 3.51, which included the older Windows 3.XX interface, was upgraded to Windows NT 4.0 when its Windows 3.XX interface was replaced with the Windows 95 interface.

Not all software companies use the version number scheme. To help simplify the system, many companies are now using the year to indicate the version. Microsoft Windows 95, Windows 98, Office 95, and Office 97 are good examples of this system. This is not always a perfect system because some

Figure 1.12 Windows XP

companies introduce several versions within the same year or might not make any significant changes from one year's version to the next year's version. For these situations, companies may assign or change a letter. For example, Windows 95 was introduced in 1995. After loading a service pack to fix some bugs within the operating system, the newer version was known as Windows 95a. Later, after fixing some minor problems and adding some new features, Windows 95b (OSR2) was introduced, followed by Windows 95b (OSR2.5).

1.6 STANDARDS

To overcome compatibility issues, hardware and software often follow **standards** (specifications that either are dictated by the computer industry or are the most common in the industry). Standards exist for operating systems, data formats, communication protocols, and electrical interfaces. If a product does not follow a widely used standard, it is usually not widely accepted in the computer market and often causes problems with your PC. As far as the user is concerned, standards help you determine what hardware and software to purchase, and they allow you to customize a system made of components from different manufacturers.

As new technology is introduced, manufacturers are usually rushing to get their product out so that it has a better chance of becoming the standard. Often, competing computer manufacturers introduce similar technology at the same time. Until one is designated as the standard, other companies and customers are sometimes forced to take sides. Because it is sometimes difficult to determine what will emerge as the true standard because the technology sometimes needs to mature, it is best to wait to see what happens before making an expensive purchase.

There are two main types of standards. The first standard is called the de jure standard. The **de jure standard,** or the "by law" standard, is a standard that has been dictated by an appointed committee, such as the International Organization for Standardization (ISO). Some of the more common standard

Table 1.4 Common Standards Committees

Committee	Description
American National Standards Institute (ANSI) http://www.ansi.org	ANSI is primarily concerned with software. ANSI has defined standards for a number of programming languages, including C language and the SCSI interface.
Comité Consultatif Internationale Télégraphique et Téléphonique (CCITT)	CCITT defines international standards, particularly communications protocols.
Institute of Electrical and Electronic Engineers (IEEE) http://www.ieee.org/	IEEE sets standards for most types of electrical interfaces, including RS-232C (serial communication interface) and network communications.
International Organization for Standardization (ISO) http://www.iso.ch/	ISO is an international standard for communications and information exchange.
Video Electronics Standards Association (VESA) http://www.vesa.org	VESA is an organization that standardized Super VGA video systems and other video specifications.

committees are shown in table1.4. The other type of standard is the de facto standard. The **de facto standard,** or the "from the fact" standard, is a standard that has been accepted by the industry just because it is the most common. These standards are not recognized by a standards committee. For example, the de facto for microprocessors is those produced by Intel, while the de facto for sound cards is those produced by Creative Labs.

When a system or standard has an **open architecture,** it indicates that the specifications of the system or standard are public. This includes approved standards as well as privately designed architecture whose specifications are made public by the designers. The advantage of an open architecture is that anyone can design products based on the architecture and design add-on products for it. Of course, this also allows other manufacturers to duplicate the product.

The opposite of an open architecture is a **proprietary system.** A proprietary system is privately owned and controlled by a company that has not divulged specifications that would allow other companies to duplicate the product. Proprietary architectures often do not allow mixing and matching products from different manufacturers and may cause hardware and software compatibility problems.

1.7 SOFTWARE AND HARDWARE TOGETHER

When you turn on the computer, the processor does a quick power check to make sure that the power supply can supply enough power to all the PC components. When the power check is complete, the microprocessor then goes to the instructions in the system ROM BIOS and starts executing them. The instructions tell the microprocessor to test and initialize the major PC components. Next, the processor looks for other ROM BIOS chips so that it can get more instructions on how to initialize devices not specified in the system ROM BIOS.

Still following the instructions in the system ROM BIOS, the processor starts looking for a boot device (typically, the A drive followed by the C drive). On the boot device, it will find additional instructions on how to boot, or load, the operating system into RAM.

While the operating system is loading, the operating system instructions tell the processor to find and load (copy into RAM) drivers from the disk. The drivers contain instructions on initializing the hardware not specified in the ROM BIOS chips, and they specify how the OS is to interface with the hardware. In addition, the drivers load instructions for the operating system interface and configure the operating system environment.

The operating system waits until the user performs a task or enters a command. When the user performs a task, such as double-clicking on an icon or entering a command to start a program, the microprocessor receives signals from the input device (pointing device or keyboard) telling the microprocessor

Figure 1.13 The User Interacting with the Computer

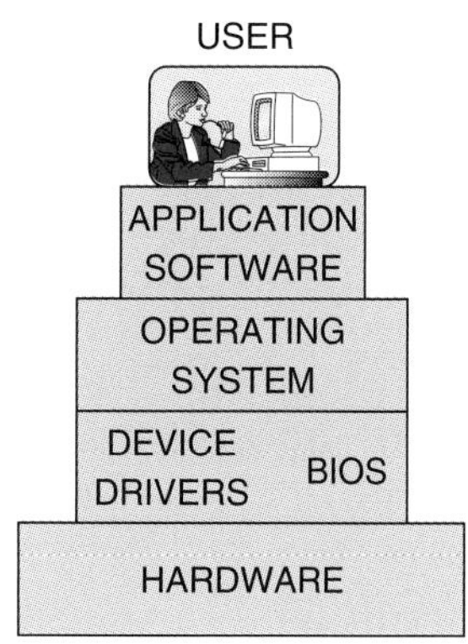

that it has a task to process. The microprocessor then processes instructions that are already in RAM to interpret the tasks or command and performs the designated function. Often, the instructions will tell the microprocessor to open additional files from disk and copy more instructions into RAM.

If you create a new document using a software program, the program tells the microprocessor to designate a memory area in RAM to hold the document. As the user inputs data into the document, the data is stored in the designated memory area. If the user decides to open a file that has already been created, the memory area is designated and the data is copied from a file on the disk into RAM. During this process, the microprocessor has to access instructions from RAM and the ROM BIOS on how to access certain hardware components. See figure 1.13.

After the document has been created, the user may decide to save his or her document to the hard drive. Again, the mouse or keyboard is used to issue commands from the application software. The application software relays those commands to the operating system, which then tells the hardware to copy the document from RAM to the hard drive. If the user decides to perform a spell check or grammar check, change the appearance of text, or add a picture to the document, the necessary instructions are executed by the microprocessor. Additional instructions are often loaded from the disk into RAM. Since the microprocessor accesses the data and instructions that are in RAM, the amount of RAM determines the amount of instructions and data that the microprocessor can have open (ready to be accessed in RAM) at once.

1.8 DECIMAL, BINARY, AND HEXADECIMAL NUMBER SYSTEMS

The most commonly used numbering system is the **decimal number system.** There are 10 different possible digits for each position in the decimal numbering system. Because there are 10 different possible digits—the digits are 0, 1, 2, 3, 4, 5, 6, 7, 8, and 9—the decimal number system is said to have numbers with *base 10.* In order to count values larger than 9, each position going away from the decimal point increases in value by a multiple of 10. (See table 1.5.)

A number system defines a set of values used to represent quantity. In number systems, you should think of recurring sets, where a set of values is repeated over and over again. When it gets to the largest digit, it will increment the next place holder and restart the digit. This basic set is repeated over and over, creating large numbers. Numbers that contain three digits is bigger than numbers that contain two digits, which are bigger than number that contains only one digit. Typically, number systems are written with largest value on the left of the number.

Table 1.5 Decimal Number System

7th place	6th Place	5th Place	4th Place	3rd Place	2nd Place	1st Place
10^6	10^5	10^4	10^3	10^2	10^1	10^0
1,000,000	100,000	10,000	1,000	100	10	1

Example 1.1:

The value of decimal number 234 is shown by the following:

2	3	4
2×10^2	3×10^1	4×10^0
200	30	4

Therefore, the value is $200 + 30 + 4 = 234$.

1.8.1 Binary Number System

The **binary number system** is another way of counting. The binary system is less complicated than the decimal system because it has only two digits, a zero (0) and a one (1). A computer represents a binary value with the electronic switch known as a transistor. If the switch is on, it allows current to flow through a wire or metal trace to represent a binary value of one (1). If the switch is off, it does not allow current to flow through a wire and represents a value of zero (0). See table 1.6. The on switch is also referred to as a *high* signal, whereas the off switch is referred to as a *low* signal.

If two switches are used to represent binary data, the first switch can be on or off and the second switch can be on or off, giving a total of four combinations or four binary values. See table 1.7. If four switches are used to represent data, 16 different binary values can be represented. See table 1.8.

Because each switch represents two values, each switch used doubles the number of binary values. Therefore, the number of binary values can be expressed with the following equation:

$$\text{Number of binary numbers} = 2^{\text{Number of binary digits}}$$

Therefore, one wire allows $2^1 = 2$ binary numbers, 0 and 1. Two wires allow $2^2 = 4$ binary numbers, 0, 1, 2, and 3. Four wires allow $2^4 = 16$ binary numbers.

Question:

How many values can 1 byte represent?

Answer:

Because a byte has eight binary digits, a byte can represent $2^8 = 256$ different characters.

Table 1.6 One-Digit Binary Number

Switch 1	Binary Equivalent	Decimal Equivalent
Off	0	0
On	1	1

Table 1.7 Two-Digit Binary Number

Switch 1	Switch 2	Binary Equivalent	Decimal Equivalent
Off	Off	00	0
Off	On	01	1
On	Off	10	2
On	On	11	3

Table 1.8 Four-Digit Binary Number

Switch 1	Switch 2	Switch 3	Switch 4	Binary Equivalent	Decimal Equivalent
Off	Off	Off	Off	0000	0
Off	Off	Off	On	0001	1
Off	Off	On	Off	0010	2
Off	Off	On	On	0011	3
Off	On	Off	Off	0100	4
Off	On	Off	On	0101	5
Off	On	On	Off	0110	6
Off	On	On	On	0111	7
On	Off	Off	Off	1000	8
On	Off	Off	On	1001	9
On	Off	On	Off	1010	10
On	Off	On	On	1011	11
On	On	Off	Off	1100	12
On	On	Off	On	1101	13
On	On	On	Off	1110	14
On	On	On	On	1111	15

Table 1.9 Binary Number System

8th Place	7th Place	6th Place	5th Place	4th Place	3rd Place	2nd Place	1st Place
2^7	2^6	2^5	2^4	2^3	2^2	2^1	2^0
128	64	32	16	8	4	2	1

Much like decimal numbers, the binary digits have placeholders that represent certain values, as shown in table 1.9.

Example 1.2:

Convert the binary number 11101010 to a decimal number.

1	1	1	0	1	0	1	0
1×2^7	1×2^6	1×2^5	0×2^4	1×2^3	0×2^2	1×2^1	0×2^0
128	64	32	0	8	0	2	0

Therefore, the binary number 11101010 is equal to the decimal number $128 + 64 + 32 + 8 + 2 = 234$.

Example 1.3:

Convert the decimal number 234 to a binary number.
Referring to table 1.9, you can see that the largest power of 2 that will fit into 234 is 2^7 (128). This leaves the value 234 − 128 = 106. The next largest power of 2 that will fit into 106 is 2^6 (64). This leaves the value 106 − 64 = 42. The next largest power of 2 that will fit into 42 is 2^5 (32), which gives us 42 − 32 = 10. The next largest power of 2 that will fit into 10 is 2^3 (8), which gives us 10 − 8 = 2. The next largest power of 2 that will fit into 2 is 2^1 (2), which gives us 2 − 2 = 0.

234	
−128	2^7
106	
−64	2^6
42	
−32	2^5
−10	
−8	2^3
2	
−2	2^1
0	

Therefore, the binary equivalent of 234 is 11101010.

1	1	1	0	1	0	1	0
2^7	2^6	2^5	2^4	2^3	2^2	2^1	2^0

In computers, one of these digits is known as a **bit.** When several bits are combined, they can signify a letter, a number, a punctuation mark, a special graphical character, or a computer instruction. Eight bits make up a **byte.**

Because a byte is such a small unit, it is more convenient to use kilobytes (KB), megabytes (MB), and gigabytes (GB). The prefix *kilo-* indicates one thousand, *mega-* indicates one million, *giga-* indicates one billion, and *tera-* indicates one trillion. These measurements are not exact, however. A kilobyte is actually 1,024 bytes, not 1,000. This is because 2^{10} is equal to 1,024. A megabyte is 1,024 kilobytes, a gigabyte is 1,024 megabytes, and a terabyte is 1,024 gigabytes.

1 kilobyte = 1,024 bytes
1 megabyte = 1,024 kilobytes = 1,048,576 bytes
1 gigabyte = 1,024 megabytes = 1,048,576 kilobytes = 1,073,741,824 bytes

1.8.2 Hexadecimal Number System

The **hexadecimal number system** has 16 digits. One hexadecimal digit is equivalent to a four-digit binary number (4 bits, or a *nibble*), and two hexadecimal digits are used to represent a byte (8 bits). Therefore, it is very easy to translate between hexadecimal and binary, and the hexadecimal system is used primarily as a "shorthand" way of displaying binary numbers. See table 1.10. A number that represents a hexadecimal number will often end with the letter *H.* In order to count values larger than 15 in the hexadecimal system, each position going away from the decimal point in a decimal number increases in value by a multiple of 16. See table 1.11.

Question:

What is the hexadecimal number that represents the binary number 1001 1010?

Answer:

1001 is equivalent to 9 and 1010 is equivalent to A, so the hexadecimal equivalent is 9AH.

To convert a hexadecimal number to a decimal number, you could first convert the hexadecimal number to binary and then convert the binary number to decimal. Another way to convert is to multiply the decimal value of each hexadecimal digit by its place and then take the sum of these products.

Table 1.10 Hexadecimal Digit

Decimal	Binary	Hexadecimal
0	0000	0
1	0001	1
2	0010	2
3	0011	3
4	0100	4
5	0101	5
6	0110	6
7	0111	7
8	1000	8
9	1001	9
10	1010	A
11	1011	B
12	1100	C
13	1101	D
14	1110	E
15	1111	F

Table 1.11 Hexadecimal Number System

7th Place	6th Place	5th Place	4th Place	3rd Place	2nd Place	1st Place
16^6	16^5	16^4	16^3	16^2	16^1	16^0
16777216	1048576	65536	4096	256	16	1

Example 1.4:

To convert EAH to a decimal number, you would multiply A by 16^0 and E by 16^1 and then add up the totals.

E	A
$E \times 16^1 = 14 \times 16^1 = 14 \times 16$	$A \times 16^0 = 10 \times 16^0 = 10 \times 1$
224	10

Therefore, the hexadecimal number EA is equal to the decimal number $224 + 10 = 234$.

Example 1.5:

To convert the decimal number of 234 to a hexadecimal number, refer to table 1.11 to see that the largest power of 16 that will fit into 234 is 16^1 (16). 16 goes into 234 a total of 14 (E) times, leaving a 10 (A).

$$234/16 = \mathbf{14}.625$$
$$234 - (\mathbf{14} \times 16) = 10$$
$$\mathbf{14} = \text{EH}$$

16^1	16^0
14×16^1	10×16^0
E	A

Table 1.12 A Partial List of the ASCII Character Set

DEC	BIN	HEX	ASCII	DEC	BIN	HEX	ASCII	DEC	BIN	HEX	ASCII
32	00100000	20	space	64	01000000	40	@	96	01100000	60	`
33	00100001	21	!	65	01000001	41	A	97	01100001	61	a
34	00100010	22	"	66	01000010	42	B	98	01100010	62	b
35	00100011	23	#	67	01000011	43	C	99	01100011	63	c
36	00100100	24	$	68	01000100	44	D	100	01100100	64	d
37	00100101	25	%	69	01000101	45	E	101	01100101	65	e
38	00100110	26	&	70	01000110	46	F	102	01100110	66	f
39	00100111	27	'	71	01000111	47	G	103	01100111	67	g
40	00101000	28	(	72	01001000	48	H	104	01101000	68	h
41	00101001	29	)	73	01001001	49	I	105	01101001	69	i
42	00101010	2A	*	74	01001010	4A	J	106	01101010	6A	j
43	00101011	2B	+	75	01001011	4B	K	107	01101011	6B	k
44	00101100	2C	,	76	01001100	4C	L	108	01101100	6C	l
45	00101101	2D	-	77	01001101	4D	M	109	01101101	6D	m
46	00101110	2E	.	78	01001110	4E	N	110	01101110	6E	n
47	00101111	2F	/	79	01001111	4F	O	111	01101111	6F	o
48	00110000	30	0	80	01010000	50	P	112	01110000	70	p
49	00110001	31	1	81	01010001	51	Q	113	01110001	71	q
50	00110010	32	2	82	01010010	52	R	114	01110010	72	r
51	00110011	33	3	83	01010011	53	S	115	00111011	73	s
52	00110100	34	4	84	01010100	54	T	116	01110100	74	t
53	00110101	35	5	85	01010101	55	U	117	01110101	75	u
54	00110110	36	6	86	01010110	56	V	118	01110110	76	v
55	00110111	37	7	87	01010111	57	W	119	01110111	77	w
56	00111000	38	8	88	01011000	58	X	120	01111000	78	x
57	00111001	39	9	89	01011001	59	Y	121	01111001	79	y
58	00111010	3A	:	90	01011010	5A	Z	122	01111010	7A	z
59	00111011	3B	;	91	01011011	5B	[	123	01111011	7B	{
60	00111100	3C	<	92	01011100	5C	\	124	01111100	7C	|
61	00111101	3D	=	93	01011101	5D	]	125	01111101	7D	}
62	00111110	3E	>	94	01011110	5E	^	126	01111110	7E	~
63	00111111	3F	?	95	01011111	5F	—	127	01111111	7F	Delete

Figure 1.14 A Byte Representing an ASCII Character

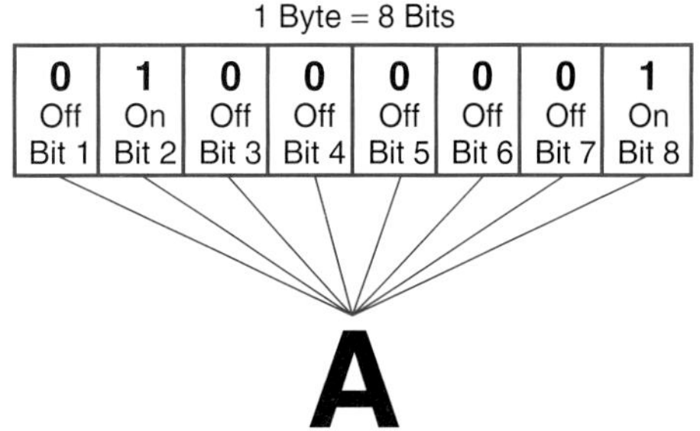

1.8.3 Character Sets

In order to communicate, you need numbers, letters, punctuation, and other symbols. In the computer, an alphanumeric code represents these characters and various instructions necessary for conveying information. A character set (charset) is a defined list of characters recognized by the computer hardware and software. Each character is represented by a binary number.

One commonly used character code is the **American Standard Code for Information Interchange (ASCII) character set,** pronounced *ask-ee.* ASCII is a code for representing English characters as numbers, with each letter assigned a number from 0 to 127. Since there are 128 different characters, it uses 7 bits for each character.

Extended ASCII is based on 8 bits, so there are 256 different possible combinations of 0s and 1s, allowing 256 ($2^8 = 256$) different characters. A partial listing of the ASCII characters is shown in table 1.12. The entire ASCII chart is shown in appendix A. For example, if a byte had the binary code 01000001, the byte would represent capital letter *A* (see figure 1.14); 01100001 would represent lowercase *a.* The extra characters represent characters from foreign languages and special symbols for drawing pictures.

Extended Binary-Coded Decimal Interchange Code (EBCDIC), pronounced *eb-sih-dik,* was IBM code for representing characters as numbers. Similar to ASCII, in an EBCDIC file, each alphabetic or numeric character is represented with an 8-bit binary number (a string of eight 0s or 1s). A total of 256 possible characters (letters of the alphabet, numerals, and special characters) are defined. Although it is widely used on large IBM computers, most other computers, including PCs and Macintoshes, use ASCII codes.

A more universal standard is the **ISO Latin-1** set of characters, which is used by many operating systems, as well as web browsers. Standardized as ISO-8859-1, ISO Latin-1 is a standard character set developed by the International Organization for Standardization (ISO). It is a superset of the ASCII character set and is very similar to the ANSI character set used in Windows, though the two are not identical. Both the HTTP and HTML protocols used on the World Wide Web are based on ISO Latin-1. This means that to represent non-ASCII characters on a web page, you need to use the corresponding ISO Latin-1 code.

Unicode is another standard for representing characters as integers. Unlike ASCII, which uses 7 or 8 bits for each character, Unicode uses 16 bits, which means that it can represent more than 65,000 unique characters. Since Unicode uses 2 bytes to identify each character, it is also known as the **double-byte character set.** While this may be more than enough for English and Western European languages, it is necessary for some languages such as Greek, Chinese, and Japanese. Many analysts believe that as the software industry becomes increasingly global, Unicode will eventually replace ASCII as the standard character coding format. Currently, the Unicode standard contains 34,168 distinct coded characters derived from 24 supported language scripts. These characters cover the principal written languages of the world. Additional work is under way to add the few modern languages not yet included.

A binary file is stored in binary format that is computer-readable but not human-readable. All executable programs are stored in binary files, as are most numeric data files. If you open these files with a text editor, they will look like garbage, yet the OS or program that created them knows how to read them. In contrast, text files are stored in a form (usually ASCII) that is human-readable.

SUMMARY

1. A computer is a machine composed of electronic devices used to process data.
2. Data is the raw facts, numbers, letters, or symbols that the computer processes into meaningful information.
3. A personal computer is a computer meant to be used by one person.
4. Software is a series of instructions that tell the computer what to do and when to do it.
5. A processor is an integrated chip that the computer is built around. It is often thought of as the "brain" of the computer.
6. RAM, or random access memory, is the short-term memory for the computer. All data stored in RAM is lost when the computer is shut off.
7. ROM, or ready-only memory, contains instructions and data that the processor accesses directly. Different from the RAM, ROM instructions are permmnent and cannot be changed or erased by normal means.
8. Instructions that control much of the computer's input/output functions, such as communicating with disks, RAM, and the monitor, are kept in the ROM chips and are known as the BIOS (basic input/output system).
9. Disks are half-electronic, half-mechanical devices that store magnetic fields on rotating platters.
10. A DS/HD 3 1/2-in. floppy disk stores up to 1.44 MB of data.
11. The computer display, commonly known as the monitor, is the PC's most commonly used output divice.
12. The keyboard is the primary input device and is arranged much like a typewriter.
13. Application software lets a user apply the knowledge and available information to create or edit a document or report.
14. The operating system coordinates the actions of the hardware, software, and the user.
15. DOS is a common command-driven operating system found on older PCs.
16. Newer operating systems, such as Windows 95/98 and Windows 2000/XP, use graphical interfaces.
17. Software programs consist of programming language code that is converted to machine code by a programmer using a compiler.
18. Much like hardware, software is frequently improved.
19. To overcome compatibility issues, hardware and software often follow standards or dictated specifications.
20. The de jure standard or by law standard is a standard that has been dictated by an appointed committee.
21. The de facto standard or from the fact standard is a standard that has been accepted by the industry just because it is the most common.
22. The most commonly used numbering system is the decimal number system, which consists of 10 different possible digits (0, 1, 2, 3, 4, 5, 6, 7, 8, and 9).
23. The binary number system is less complicated than the decimal number system because it has only two digits, a zero (0) and a one (1). One of these digits is known as a bit.
24. A computer represents a binary value with the electronic switch known as a transistor. An on switch represents a 1 and an off switch represents a 0.
25. Eight bits equal one byte.
26. Because a byte is such a small unit, it is more convenient to use kilobytes (KB), megabytes (MB), and gigabytes (GB).
27. The hexadecimal number system has 16 digits. One hexadecimal digit is equivalent to a four-digit binary number.
28. American Standard Code for Information Interchange (ASCII) character set is based on 8 bits to represent one of 256 different possible characters.

QUESTIONS

1. Which of the following is designed to be used by one person?
   a. personal computer
   b. mainframe computer
   c. minicomputer
   d. midrange computer
   e. supercomputer
2. You have a CD-ROM that contains the Microsoft Windows NT installation program. The instructions written on the disk are
   a. hardware.
   b. software.
   c. RAM.
   d. electrical signals.

3. The screen display is made up of an arrangement of dots called
   a. graphics. b. resolution.
   c. pixels. d. VGA.
4. Which component is the computer built around?
   a. the RAM
   b. the hard drive
   c. the monitor
   d. the microprocessor
   e. the BIOS
5. Which instructions control much of the computer's input/output functions, such as communicating with disks, RAM, and the monitor?
   a. BIOS b. microcode
   c. CMOS d. temporary
6. Which of the following is the primary input device?
   a. keyboard b. monitor
   c. printer d. mouse
   e. modem f. disk
7. Which of the following is the primary output device?
   a. keyboard b. monitor
   c. printer d. mouse
   e. modem f. disk
8. Which device allows you to communicate with another computer by using the phone lines?
   a. keyboard b. monitor
   c. printer d. mouse
   e. modem f. disk
9. Software that allows the user to input information to create or edit a document or report is
   a. operating system software.
   b. application software.
   c. a software utility.
   d. a software diagnostic package.
10. The most common application software that allows the user to type letters and reports is a
    a. word processing package.
    b. spreadsheet package.
    c. database package.
    d. desktop publishing package.
11. The PC's most important software, which coordinates the hardware, software, and the user, is
    a. utility software.
    b. device drivers software.
    c. operating system software.
    d. integrated software.
    e. none of the above.
12. Which of the following operating systems is *not* icon-driven?
    a. Microsoft Windows NT
    b. OS/2
    c. DOS
    d. System 7
    e. Microsoft Windows 95
13. Which standard is a standard because it the most commonly used?
    a. de jure standard
    b. de facto standard
    c. your company standard
    d. the one that you prefer
14. The microprocessor executes instructions kept in (choose two answers)
    a. RAM.
    b. ROM.
    c. the hard drive.
    d. the keyboard.
    e. the monitor.
15. Instructions to initialize and control hardware not specified in the BIOS are called
    a. ROM. b. drivers.
    c. utilities. d. compilers.
16. Convert the decimal value 6 to binary.
    a. 00000101 b. 00001111
    c. 00000111 d. 01010101
    e. 00000110
17. Convert the decimal value of 68 to binary.
    a. 10101010 b. 00001111
    c. 01000010 d. 11110000
    e. 01010101 f. 01000100
18. Convert the binary value of 10101010 to decimal.
    a. 170 b. 165
    c. 224 d. 128
19. Convert the hexadecimal number of FH to binary.
    a. 1000 b. 1110
    c. 1111 d. 1010
    e. 0001
20. The ASCII character (standard + extended) set contains __________ characters.
    a. 8 b. 256
    c. 64 d. 512
    e. 128 f. 1,024
21. The most basic format in which data and programs are stored in a computer is the __________ format.
    a. ASCII b. octal
    c. binary d. hexadecimal
22. How many bits are represented by a single hexadecimal digit?
    a. 1 b. 2
    c. 4 d. 8
    e. 16 f. 32
23. You have a file that is 2.2 megabytes in size. Exactly how many bytes is 2.2 megabytes?
    a. 22000000.0
    b. 2252.8
    c. 2252800.0
    d. 2306867
    e. none of the above

CHAPTER 2

The PC Technician

Topics Covered in This Chapter

Introduction

As a computer technician, consultant, or support person, you are a detective in the PC world. When the computer fails for any reason, it is your job to find the problem and correct it quickly with a minimum loss of data. Finding the problem is not always the easiest thing to do. However, if you possess a working knowledge of the PC, combined with a little technique and a little patience, no problem will be too difficult to solve.

Objectives

1. List and describe the different computer problem classifications.
2. Identify the steps in troubleshooting a problem.
3. List places to go to find additional help.
4. Research a topic on the Internet.
5. Given a scenario, determine if a software piracy is occurring.
6. List the common tools needed to effectively troubleshoot and fix a PC.
7. Install and run a software diagnostic package.
8. Create a boot/rescue disk with the most common operating system files used to fix a computer.
9. Test an AC power wall outlet.
10. Use a voltmeter to measure the voltage of an electronic device.
11. Use an ohmmeter to measure the resistance of an electronic device including a wire.
12. Define *electrostatic electricity.*
13. List the ways to avoid electrostatic electricity.

2.1 COMPUTER PROBLEMS

When a computer has a problem, the user's first response is, "Oh no, not now!" I am sure that you will agree that there is no good time for a computer to break down. See figure 2.1. Of course, with some good maintenance, excellent backup procedures, and a little bit of knowledge, you can easily minimize computer failure and data loss.

Figure 2.1 Sick PC

NOTE: When troubleshooting PC problems, it is recommended to limit the time used to troubleshoot and fix computers. Most repair shops charge $45 per hour or more to fix computer problems, and many components inside a computer cost less than $50. In addition, for older computers, it may be best to save the contents of the hard drive to a newer system. Of course, you can try to reuse some of the components of the older system such as the monitor, keyboard, and mouse.

2.1.1 Before You Troubleshoot

When encountering a computer problem, you should follow certain guidelines. First, your mind must be clear and rested. You must be able to concentrate on the problem. Concentration is key to troubleshooting. If not, you may overlook something that was obvious, such as the power cord not being plugged in.

Next, don't panic, don't get frustrated, and allow enough time to do the job right. If you panic, you may do something that will make the situation worse. If you start to get frustrated, take a break. You will be amazed at how 5 or 10 minutes away from the problem will clear your mind and will allow you to look at the problem a little differently when you come back. Finally, make sure that you have enough time to properly analyze the problem, fix the problem, and properly test the system after the repair. Again, if you rush a job, you may make the problem worse or you may overlook something simple.

2.1.2 Types of Problems

When troubleshooting the PC, you must keep an open mind about the cause of the problem. It could be a hardware failure, a compatibility problem, an improper configuration, a software glitch, an environmental factor, or a user error. See table 2.1. Some problems could be due to a faulty component, such as a hard drive, floppy drive, power supply, cable, or modem. In addition, problems can be caused by viruses, software that is not compatible with a screen saver, BIOS setup program settings, power management features, Control Panel settings, software drivers, hardware settings, power fluctuations, or electromagnetic interference.

Table 2.1 Computer Problem Classifications

Reason for Failure	Description
Hardware failure	One or more components fail inside the computer.
Hardware incompatibility	One component is not compatible with another component. Note: This error may appear to be a hardware failure.
Improper hardware configuration	The hardware has not been installed or configured properly. This often happens when the user does not read the manual or lacks the knowledge to make use of the manual. Note: This error often appears to be a hardware failure.
Improper software configuration	The software (operating system or application software) is not installed or configured properly. This often happens when the user does not read the manual or lacks the knowledge to make use of the manual. Note: This error may appear to be a hardware failure.
Software failure	There is a glitch in the software. This can range from corrupted data to a flaw in the programming. Note: This error may appear to be a hardware failure.
Software incompatibility	The software is not compatible with the hardware or other software. Note: This error may appear to be a hardware failure.
Poor environment	The location of the computer and its environment (i.e., temperature, air flow, electromagnetic interference, magnetic fields) may affect the reliability of the PC and have a direct impact on the PC's life. Note: This problem may appear to be a hardware failure.
User error	This is a very common situation where the user hits the wrong keys or is not familiar with the computer or software. It could be something as simple as the user hitting the zero (0) key rather than the letter *O* key.

Today, the PC technician must also know how to troubleshoot network problems where one computer communicates with another computer using copper cables or wireless technology. The PC could be part of an organization's network or it could be connected to the Internet using a dial-up modem, a digital subscriber line (DSL), or a cable model or some other technology.

A network problem would include problems with the medium that connects a server and/or client to the network and anything else the medium connects to. For example, most computers are connected to a network through a cable that is connected to a hub or switch. Then the smaller networks can be connected together to form a larger network by using routers. Therefore, in the event of a problem, the cables, the hub or switch, or the router could be faulty—a cable may not be connected properly, or a hub, switch, or router may not be configured properly.

In addition, for a computer and a server to operate properly, the computer's protocol has to be configured correctly. Also, permission must be given to use a network resource. A network may require services provided by other servers—perhaps a DNS server provides name resolution for your network to function properly. For example, when you type in http://www.acme.com, a DNS server will look up the IP address for www.acme.com so that it knows how to contact that web server. Also, network communications can be interrupted by external environmental factors such as electromagnetic interference.

In a network running Active Directory on a Windows NT Server, Windows 2000 Server, or Windows Server 2003, a domain is a collection of computers and users that share a common directory database and set of security policies. Each user, identified by the user name and password, is assigned rights and permissions that specify what they the user access on the network and in what way. From a support standpoint, users in a domain may be affected by the rights and permissions that they are assigned. You may also need to look at profile and security policies for the user and start-up scripts. Of course, anytime you are troubleshooting possible network problems, you need to determine the extent of the network problem. Is the problem isolated to or one person's PC, or is it affecting other users and their PCs? Can the user(s) access other network resources?

2.1.3 General Troubleshooting Strategy

The Computing Technology Industry Association (CompTIA) is a nonprofit organization that represents more than 8,000 computing and communications companies. The main goal is to develop vendor neutral certifications, such as the CompTIA A+, Network+ and Security+ exams, to provide credibility, recognition of achievement and quality assurance.

CompTIA uses a general troubleshooting strategy that consists of the following eight steps:

1. Establish symptoms.
2. Identify the affected area.
3. Establish what has changed.
4. Select the most probable cause.
5. Implement a solution.
6. Test the result.
7. Recognize the potential effects of the solution.
8. Document the solution.

If you are fixing a computer for someone else, you must determine the problem from the owner or the computer. Then while you investigate the problem, ask lots of questions, but try to keep the questions relevant to the problem. When talking to the user, make sure you speak at the user's level so that he or she will understand and so that you don't insult the user's knowledge. Of course, be courteous and give the person an opportunity to explain everything.

Some of the things that you should determine include:

- Determine what type of computer the user has and what operating system (if the information is relevant) he or she is using.
- Establish the symptoms of the problem. What are the circumstances? What is happening or not happening? When did it start occurring? Does the problem follow a certain pattern (such as after a particular action or after the computer has been on for a while) or does the problem occur randomly?
- Determine if the user tried to restart the machine to see if the problem still exists.

- Can you duplicate the problem? If you cannot duplicate the problem, can the user duplicate the problem so that you can see if it is a user problem?
- What changes have been made recently to the hardware or the software? You should explain carefully what you mean by recent changes to the system. Many times, servicing or changes can cause other problems. Of course, this is one of the main reasons you should have a service log.

Most modern operating systems also have error or system logs available that record problems and inconsistencies that they find during their operations. When problems occur with the operating systems and the applications and services that run on the operating system, check these logs to give you as much information as possible. If a problem appears within the log, check to see if it occurred before in the logs and if there are any other errors or messages that appear at the same time as the problem. For Windows, the system log is the event viewer.

The more difficult problems are the intermittent problems. Since the intermittent errors do not happen on a regular basis, the computer may work fine when you test it, but as soon as the customer takes it home, it will fail again. When dealing with intermittent problems, you make a change that might fix the system. You must then thoroughly test the system over a period of time to see if the problem actually goes away.

When gathering information, you must be observant by using four of your five senses. For example:

Seeing—Are all the components present and are they connected properly? Are there any burn marks on any of the components, or is the cable physically damaged?

Hearing—Do you hear any excessive noise or electrical noises? In addition, do you not hear noises that you typically would hear, such as the fan or the hard drive spinning?

Smelling—Do you smell anything abnormal, such as something burning?

Feeling—Does the case feel excessively warm? Can you feel the hard drive spin?

After the problem has been repeated and verified, you need to test the system further to see the extent of the problem. For example, if your system doesn't boot properly, can you boot from the floppy drive and access the hard drive? If you can't print from a particular program, can you print using another program? If the mouse doesn't work in one environment, such as Windows, does it work at a command prompt or Windows safe mode.

You can gather additional information by trying to use software utilities to test your system and by using a **digital multimeter (DMM)** to measure certain electrical characteristics of the computer. Some of the utilities include software to test the computer components, check for viruses, look for formatting errors on a disk, or check software configuration.

Lastly, just because you have seen this problem a hundred times before does not mean it is the same thing in this case. Experience gives you a broader range of scenarios to test out, but it does not give you the answer before you touch the computer. Even if you think you know the solution, test it out. Assumptions lead to rigidity in your response, and you need to be flexible and open-minded when you are troubleshooting. Many symptoms have many different causes in similar or different machines. As soon as you think you know everything, a computer somewhere will be waiting to stump you.

After you have gathered as much information as you can, you are now ready to make the repair or fix. Sometimes you will know exactly what to change or replace. Other times, you will have it narrowed down to several causes that will require you to isolate the problem. If you suspect a faulty component, you can replace the component with a known good component. If the system works with the new component, the problem was the item that you just removed.

NOTE: When a new item is taken off the shelf, it does not mean that the item is always good.

In addition, you can try "reverse swapping," which is trying a suspected faulty component with a second working system that is known to be compatible. If the component does not work in either one, you suspect that the component is faulty. If the product works in the second system but does not work in the first system, you would suspect a compatibility problem, a configuration problem, a BIOS setting, or a driver problem.

Other solutions include reconfiguring the software or hardware; reloading the operating system, application software, or drivers; or making changes to the CMOS setup program. Whatever course of action you choose, you should make only one change at a time. If the problem still exists, you will then make another change until the problem no longer exists. When determining which item to check or swap, you should first try to check items that are most likely to cause the problem and that are the easiest and quickest to check.

NOTE: If the computer or device is under warranty, you should let the vendor fix the problem. If you open and try to repair a computer that is under warranty, you may void the warranty.

After you fix the problem, you should always thoroughly test the computer before returning it to the customer or client. This will make sure that the problem did go away and that you did not cause another problem while fixing the first problem.

In addition, you should keep a log of changes made to a system and list any problems you encounter, as well as their solutions. The log can tell you if the system has gone through any recent changes, especially if you work for a department that has several PC support people. The log will also help you look for trends so that in the future you can make plans to minimize the problem and have the resources available when the problem occurs.

2.2 WHERE TO GET HELP WHEN NEEDED

When dealing with computer problems, there is no way that you are going to know everything about computers, nor are you expected to. What is expected is that you understand computers well enough to investigate and isolate problems, know when you need to find more information, and know how to get the information in a timely manner so that you can fix the problem. Some of the common places to find help include:

1. Documentation for the computer, device, or software package
2. HELP files, README files, and other text files
3. Fellow colleagues
4. Books
5. Popular computer magazines
6. The Internet
7. Computer and product technical support people

The documentation that comes with a computer, a device, or a software package usually contains valuable installation, configuration, and troubleshooting information. Software packages also often contain HELP files, README files, or other informational files describing installation procedures, troubleshooting problems, and last-minute changes to the documentation. If you lose the documentation to a computer, device, or software package, the documentation can often be found on the manufacturer's website.

When working within a computer or information system (IS) department, you will be part of a team. An effective team uses teamwork. Since a colleague will have certain experiences and you will have certain experiences, it is common for colleagues to ask each other for help. Another source is to contact the company's technical support.

NOTE: Not all technical support services are free. In addition, you may need to provide information such as the product license number, serial number or OEM number, the type of computer, and the type of software that is on the system.

Other sources of information are books, magazines, and the Internet. If you ever go into a large bookstore, you will usually find many PC books and magazines. Some of these include sections on installation, configuring, optimizing, troubleshooting, standards, and emerging technology. The Internet provides an easy way to find product documentation, software patches and fixes, tips, and troubleshooting utilities. See figure 2.2. The most common Internet services are shown in table 2.2 and some useful websites are listed in table 2.3.

For example, Microsoft has a huge website that includes tons of information. One of the more useful tools in troubleshooting is Microsoft's Knowledge Base (KB), a database of past incidents and solutions that is created and added to by gathering information from service requests. The Knowledge Base articles are identified by Knowledge Base Article ID Number.

A comprehensive technical resource for installing, configuring, and supporting Windows 2000 and Windows XP are the Windows Resource Kits. Although these are purchased in a book/box set with CDs that contain resource kit utilities, the resource kit can be accessed from the Microsoft website.

Figure 2.2 Internet Web Page Showing the Jumper Settings for a Hard Drive (Courtesy of Western Digital Corporation)

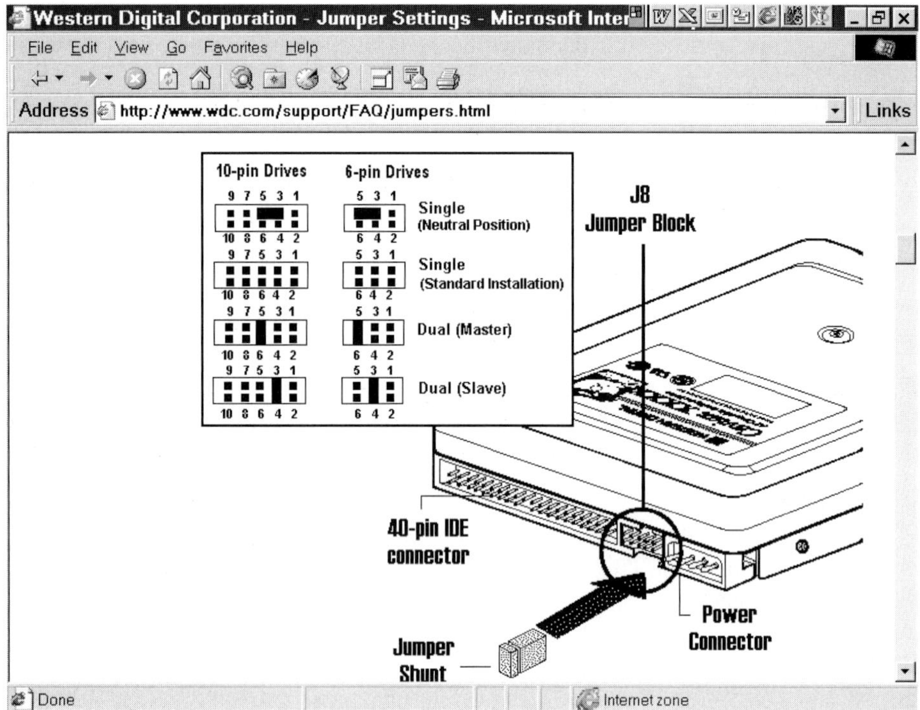

Table 2.2 Internet Services

Service	Description
Electronic Mail (Email)	Mail that can be sent to and from other Internet users.
Telnet	Remote logins to other machines on the Internet that allow you to work on the remote system or to try software.
File Transfer Protocol (FTP)	File transfer between machines that allows you to download software, graphics, and other files. Although hypertext transfer protocol (HTTP) can also download files, FTP specializes in downloading files.
World Wide Web (WWW)	A graphical information service. Usually uses HTTP to navigate web pages and to choose options.
Usenet Newsgroups	A set of bulletin boards for conversations on many different subjects, including computers.
Search Engines	An information search system.

Microsoft Help and Support

http://support.microsoft.com/default.aspx

Microsoft Knowledge Base

http://support.microsoft.com/default.aspx?scid=fh;EN-US;KBHOWTO

Microsoft Downloads and Updates

http://support.microsoft.com/default.aspx?scid=fh;EN-US;DOWNLOADOVER&style=home

Microsoft Product Support Centers (FAQs)

http://support.microsoft.com/default.aspx?scid=fh;EN-US;FAQS

Table 2.3 Useful Computer Troubleshooting Websites

Website	Name or Sponsor	Content
http://www.cnet.com	CNET: The Computer Network	Offers update news, tips, and software downloads
http://www.modems.com	Zoom Telephonics, Inc.	Valuable information on modems and related technology
http://www.webopedia.com	PC Webopedia	An encyclopedia of computer and computer-related terms with many links to related sites
http://www.pcworld.com	*PC World Magazine*	Offers reviews, tips, and software downloads
http://www.tomshardware.com	Tom's Hardware Guide	Valuable technical information about major PC components
http://www.zdnet.com	Ziff-Davis, Inc., publisher of *PC Magazine, PC Computing,* and other magazines	Offers reviews, tips, and software downloads (Note: To search their magazines, use http://xlink.zdnet.com/cgi-bin/texis/xlink/xlink/search.html.)
http://pcmech.pair.com	PC Mechanic	Online source for do-it-yourself computing
http://www.driverzone.com	The Driver's Zone	Provides easy access to find most drivers, as well as a search engine to identify a manufacturer by the product's FCC number
http://www.windrivers.com	WinDrivers.Com	Provides drivers, troubleshooting information, and identification information
http://www.rojakpot.com/Speed_Demonz/BIOS_Guide/BIOS_Guide_Index.htm	The BIOS Optimization Guide	Valuable information about configuring the CMOS setup program
http://www.pcguide.com	The PC Guide	Offers detailed PC reference information

Microsoft Windows 2000 Professional Resource Kit

http://www.microsoft.com/windows2000/techinfo/reskit/enus/default.asp?url=/windows2000/techinfo/reskit/en-us/Pro.asp

Microsoft Windows XP Resource Kit

http://www.microsoft.com/resources/documentation/Windows/XP/all/reskit/en-us/Default.asp?url=/resources/documentation/Windows/XP/all/reskit/en-us/prork_overview.asp

2.3 BACKUP

As a computer technician, you should always emphasize to your customers that they must back up all important files. A **backup** of a system is extra copies of data and programs. Unfortunately, it is often ignored by most people, and they do not think about doing it until it is too late.

Question:

Why do a backup?

Answer:

As you use the computer more and learn how the computer works, you will understand that the data generated by the computer and stored on disk is the user's most valuable item within the computer. The data usually represents hours of work and is sometimes irreplaceable.

As a computer technician or consultant, you may be the one that selects and installs the equipment, performs the actual backup, or trains other people in doing the backup. You need to make sure to select the equipment and method that will ensure that the backup is completed on a regular basis. Remember that even if you have the best equipment and software, yet no one completes the backup, the equipment and software are wasted. Backup equipment and methods will be discussed in chapter 14.

2.4 SOFTWARE PIRACY

Software can be categorized into three categories—retail, freeware, and shareware. Retail software is software that is purchased from the software company or an authorized vendor. When purchasing retail software, a license is included in the user manual or on a separate piece of paper stating the legal use of the software. Freeware, or public domain software, is free software. Therefore, you can copy, install, and distribute it freely. Shareware is software that can be installed on your computer and tried for a time to see if you like it. If you decide to keep using the software, you are supposed to purchase it. See figure 2.3.

As a computer technician or consultant, you need to be aware of software piracy and its consequences. Software piracy (theft of intellectual property) is the illegal copying, distribution, or installation of software. It is copyright infringement. Some examples include:

1. Purchasing a software package that comes with a single-user license and loading it onto multiple computers or a network server.
2. Making, distributing, or selling copies that appear to be from an unauthorized source.
3. Distributing or selling software that has been unbundled from the products for which it was intended.
4. Downloading software from the Internet or bulletin boards without permission from the copyright holder.
5. Using a software package, purchasing an upgrade, and giving or selling the original software package to someone else.

If you are sued for civil copyright infringement, the penalty is up to $100,000 per title infringed. If charged with a criminal violation, the fine is up to $250,000 per title infringed and up to 5 years' imprisonment.

The Software and Information Industry Association (SIIA), formerly the Software Publishers Association (SPA), is an organization made up of software companies. One of its primary functions is to educate the public about software piracy and to catch companies and individuals pirating software. To accomplish this, they offer:

1. Easy ways to report software piracy by calling 1-800-388-7478 or sending an email to piracy@siia.net.
2. Recommended software policy and employed usage guidelines, which can be utilized and adapted as needed. (http://www.spa.org/piracy/corporate.asp)
3. Several evaluation audit programs that can conduct hardware and software audits on network and stand-alone machines.

Since Microsoft is the largest software company, it is, of course, concerned about piracy. For more information about Microsoft and software piracy, or to download software to perform inventory of Microsoft software and ways to contact Microsoft about piracy, visit http://www.microsoft.com/piracy.

Figure 2.3 You should not pirate software

2.5 DEALING WITH THE CUSTOMER

When repairing computers, you may be repairing the computer for someone that works within the same company as you or for a customer who contacted you. One of your main responsibilities is to satisfy the customer or client. Your job or business depends on the customers, so you must be skilled at dealing with people.

As a PC technician, you are a vital contact between you and your customers. You could be part of customer service, which deals mostly with external customers, or you could be part of the Information Technology (IT) department that supports internal customers (other employees within your organization). In either case, your customers expect reliability, availability, and security of their PCs, their information, and the network services that they use such as email or accessing network resources. They expect knowledgeable people who are familiar with their product or system are able to handle hardware and software installation tasks, perform system maintenance, and monitor PC and network performance. Of course, PC technicians will not know all of the answers; therefore, they will need to understand where to get those answers and redirect the end users when necessary. If the answer still cannot be found, they must know when and how to escalate to people who would know the answer. At all times, PC technicians must be resourceful and organized in everything that they do.

You will find a wide range of computer users. Some of these people will be very knowledgeable about computers, and other people can barely turn them on. Some people will be easy to work with, and others will be more difficult. Although you can show some people how to use the computer properly, you may find it is sometimes harder to fix people's attitudes than it is to fix a hardware or software problem.

When dealing with customers, you should follow certain guidelines:

1. Always be courteous. Try to smile and say positive things to the customer whenever you can.
2. Focus on the customer and don't get distracted.
3. Be concerned about the customer's needs.
4. Don't belittle a customer, a customer's knowledge, or a customer's choice of hardware or software.
5. Don't complain to the customer and don't make excuses.
6. Stay calm. Don't get angry.
7. If you give a customer a component that appears to be defective or faulty, offer an immediate replacement.
8. Be professional. Dress appropriately for the environment. Don't take over a person's workspace without asking.
9. Follow proper personal hygiene.
10. Be honest, especially if you caused a problem or you don't know the answer.
11. Be dependable and follow up on the service. If you will miss an appointment or will be late, call the customer to let him or her know.
12. Allow the customer to complain.
13. Allow the customer to explain the problem, and listen carefully.
14. Don't do anything until you have interviewed the user.
15. Always ask permission first.
16. Keep things neat, tidy, and out of the client's way.
17. Explain how to prevent future problems without condescension and disrespect.
18. If a customer is unhappy with you, your company, or a product, an apology can go a long way. If it is not your fault, you can still apologize for the situation. In addition, find out how you can make things better.

With the complexity of PCs, there has been a growing need for companies to provide phone and email support for their internal and external customers. Different from meeting someone in person, phone support requires more interaction with customers. You must give clear instructions and you must be able to visualize what the customer is seeing on his or her computer. This usually takes patience. If you get disconnected, be sure to call back immediately. If you have to put someone on hold, be sure to say how long he or she will be on hold. If it is a long time, you may consider calling back the customer. If you cannot solve the problem and you need to escalate the problem, be sure you know the proper procedures for your organization. You should also make sure that you follow up if necessary.

When you begin a phone support call, you should first identify yourself and your organization. You should then record the customer's name and phone number and his or her business (if applicable). Depending on your organization, you may also have to retrieve licensing or warranty information so that you can determine if the customer is eligible for support or you will have to gather credit card information or other method of payment. You will then allow the customer to describe the problem. If you do a lot of phone support, you should use a phone headset so that it frees up your hands to work on the computer or use printed material; it also reduces ear or neck strain. Lastly, make sure that you have completed the call to the customer's satisfaction and that you thank him or her for the call.

Most PC repair jobs start out as a service request, either by phone call, by email, relayed through a ticket system or in person. In any case, all service requests must be logged within your organization or department's help desk system. Then, as the problem is worked on and solved, the results must be recorded in the help desk system. By recording this information you will be able to look for trends that will help keep track of any growing problems, and determine how much staffing and other resources were needed to fix these problems.

In any case, whether you are fixing a PC in person or by phone or email, you have to solve the problem in a timely manner and as specified in a service level agreement (SLA). The SLA is a document that identifies the type of support the customer has purchased from your organization (or department), as well as the support functions your organization (or department) is obligated to perform. For a PC technician, it is important to understand a customer's SLA. Sometimes certain issues are not covered in the SLA. In these cases, the SLA defines the limits on how far you can go to support the customer.

Some other definitions that you should know include:

- A problem is an unknown cause of an incident.
- An incident is any occurrence that is not part of normal hardware or software performance and that diminishes or stops that performance.
- A major incident is an incident that has a high or potentially high impact upon a large number of customers and requires significantly more resources to resolve than a normal incident.
- A known error is a hardware or software problem with a known cause and a temporary resolution. The problem remains a known error until a permanent fix is released.

Example 2.1:

You are working for a help desk. At 8:45 A.M., you get a call from a customer saying that the printer he just bought from your company is not working.

When dealing with customers over the telephone, first gather certain information, such as the name of the company (if any), the name of the customer, a phone number to reach the customer, the type of hardware or software (in this case, the type of printer), and the nature of the problem. When the customer is done explaining the problem, you can then follow up with some of your own questions to gather more information. Next, you can ask the customer to check certain things, such as the printer connections and computer configuration. The customer's knowledge will determine the level at which you should communicate. For people who are not knowledgeable about computers, your explanations and directions need to be in easy-to-understand terms. If you can fix the problem over the phone, the customer will not have to bring the printer or system into your service department and you will not have to send someone to the customer.

If the customer cannot understand your directions, you can ask if there is anyone else to talk to, or you can get someone else from your department to talk to the customer. Don't be rude to the customer; stay calm. Whatever you do, don't yell at the customer and don't hang up on the customer.

Example 2.2:

After talking to the customer in example 2.1, the help desk personnel cannot fix the problem over the telephone. Therefore, they decide to send a service person to the customer's company. You are supposed to arrive at 11:30 A.M.

If the appointment is at 11:30 A.M., you need to show up at 11:30 A.M. If you can't make the appointment time because you are still finishing another service call, you need to call the customer to let her know what time you can make the appointment and apologize for the inconvenience. When you show up for the service call, you should be dressed appropriately for the environment. You should arrive with all the tools, test equipment, and software that is needed to effectively troubleshoot the problem. Don't take over the customer's work area and don't use the customer's telephone without permission. If you can't fix the problem because the printer is faulty, replace the printer immediately.

Example 2.3:

A customer brings in a computer saying that the computer will not turn on. What do you tell the customer when you cannot repeat or duplicate the problem?

If you cannot duplicate the problem, your people skills will be put to the test. First, you have to explain to the customer that you could not find anything wrong. This kind of news does not please most people. They feel that you do not know what you are doing, or they are angry with themselves for bringing in a system to be repaired that wasn't broken. In either case, they will usually be charged for the time and effort that you put into checking the machine.

To ease the customer's pain, show the customer what you did to try to duplicate the problem. Next, show the customer that the system is running properly. After assuring him that all is well, have the customer show you what he did when the computer failed. If the customer is able to duplicate the problem, you can then see the problem. If the user is causing the error by typing the wrong key or doing something out of order, you can then show him the correct way to run the PC. In any case, you gave the customer excellent service.

ANECDOTES IN COMPUTER ILLITERACY

The next few stories will demonstrate some of the computer-illiterate people that you might deal with. Although these are extreme cases, they are all true stories. The first four anecdotes are based on stories that originally appeared in the *Wall Street Journal* and can be found throughout the Internet. The last story was told to me by a student of mine. Some of these stories might have happened to you when you were learning to use the computer!

Story #1—Many companies provide computer support over the telephone. One time, a customer was asked to send a copy of a defective disk. A few days later an envelope arrived from the customer with a photocopy of the disk.

Story #2—An exasperated caller to tech support could not get her new computer to turn on. After ensuring the computer was plugged in, the technician asked her what happened when she pushed the power button. Her response was, "I pushed and pushed on this foot pedal and nothing happens." The "foot pedal" turned out to be the computer's mouse.

Story #3—Technical support had a caller complaining that her mouse was hard to control with the dust cover on. The cover turned out to be the plastic bag the mouse was packaged in.

Story #4—A person called technical support on how to get his cup holder repaired because it broke off. The support person was puzzled and asked whether the cup holder was part of some special sales promotion or if it had any trademarks on it. The customer stated that he didn't know about any sales promotions and that it only had "4X" on it. Finally, the technician discovered that the customer broke off the load drawer of the CD-ROM drive.

Story #5—The last story is about a person who worked at a temporary service. The person's job was to fill out a form and fax the form to the central office. While sending the forms in a machine next to the computer, the temporary worker noticed that small strands came out the other side of the machine. When the owner discovered what the temporary worker did repeatedly, the owner asked, "Didn't you see the shredded paper?" The temporary worker's only response was, "Yes, but I thought that the paper was being shrunken down to fit through the wire."

2.6 PC TECHNICIAN TOOL KIT

To get a better understanding of what makes up a PC, you must first learn how to disassemble and reassemble a computer. To accomplish this, you will need a few basic tools. Many of these can be bought in a small tool kit made for PC technicians that sells for about $20. See figure 2.4. The most common tools are described in table 2.4. Other useful tools include a flashlight, wire cutters, tamper-proof Torx drivers, file, electrical tape, can of compressed air, and lint-free cloth. A flashlight will help you identify PC components, especially in those hard-to-reach places. Wire cutters are useful for making or repairing cables or wiring. The Torx drivers are used to remove hex screws with a tamper-resistant pin in the center. A file is used to smooth rough or sharp edges. A roll of black electrical tape is used to wrap wire ends and insulate components.

Figure 2.4 Tool Kit

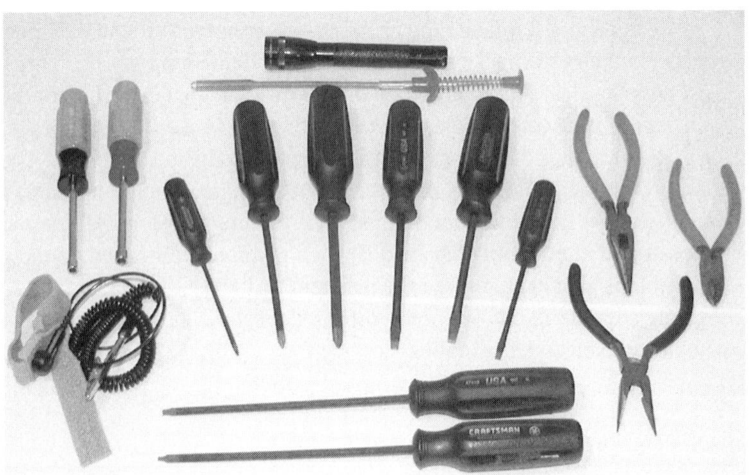

Table 2.4 PC Technician's Tool Kit

Tool	Usage
Medium Phillips screwdriver (#2 head)	Probably the most commonly used tool. It is used to open most PCs and remove expansion cards, power supplies, motherboards, and drives.
Medium flat-edge screwdriver	
Small Phillips screwdriver	
Small flat-edge screwdriver	Can be used to pry chips from the motherboard. When using this tool to remove chips, take extreme care so that you do not bend or break any pins on the chips.
3/16-inch nut driver and 1/4-inch nut driver	Used to remove hexagonal-headed screws. These screws are used to secure the computer cover and expansion cards. Although you could use the screwdriver for most of these screws, a nut driver is easier and quicker to use.
Needlenose pliers	Useful for straightening pins on chips, changing jumper settings, crimping cables, or grabbing small parts.
Tweezers	Used to grab small parts.
Claw-type parts grabber	Used to grab small parts in tight places.
Chip puller (chip extractor)	Used to discharge NiCad (nickel-cadmium) batteries when needed or to remove keyboard key caps. Do not use the chip puller to remove chips since it will usually result in bent or broken pins.

You can use mild detergent and a damp cloth to clean the outside of the computer. To clean the monitor screen, use a damp cloth or special antistatic wipes. To reduce the risk of component failure and to allow for better system cooling you can use a small brush, a can of compressed air or a vacuum cleaner. A can of compressed air is better than a vacuum cleaner because the compressed air can be directed more accurately and provides more cleaning power.

NOTE: The brush, can of compressed air, and vacuum cleaner must be designed not to generate electrostatic discharge. To clean the electrical contacts inside the computer, use metal contact cleaner or isopropyl alcohol with a cotton swab.

When using special cleaners or other chemicals, you should be aware of the proper usage, storage, and disposal of the chemicals and their impact on the environment. This information is usually found on the cleaner's container or on the Material Safety Directions Sheet (MSDS) that comes with the container or from the vendor.

2.7 ELECTRICITY AND ELECTRONIC COMPONENTS

Atoms, which make up everything, consist of three particles. In the center of the atom, there are protons (positive-charged particles) and neutrons (neutral-charged particles), which make up the nucleus. Orbiting the nucleus, there are electrons (negative-charged particles). Under certain conditions, the electrons can move from one atom to another. The rate of flow of electrons is known as **current** (electricity), which is measured in **amperes amps** (A). See figure 2.5.

The electronic devices are made of a conductor, insulator, and semiconductor material. A **conductor** is material in which current can flow easily. Most metals are good conductors including silver and copper. Copper wire is commonly used as a conductor in electric circuits because it is inexpensive and a good conductor. An **insulator** is a poor conductor of electric current. In fact, insulators, like rubber, are used to prevent current where it is not wanted. See figure 2.6.

Figure 2.5 The Atom

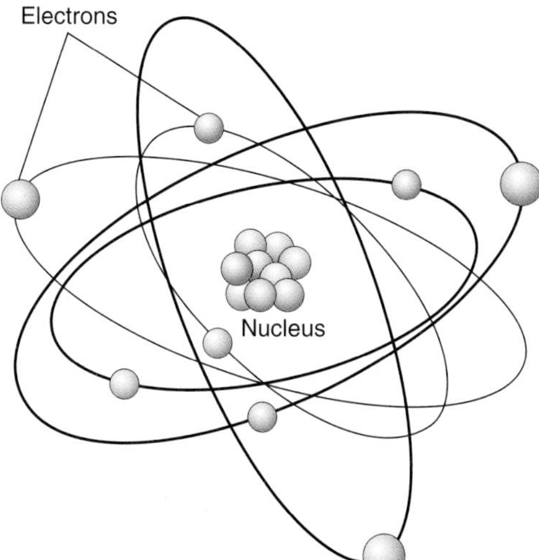

Figure 2.6 A Copper Wire (Conductor) Surrounded by Rubber (Insulator)

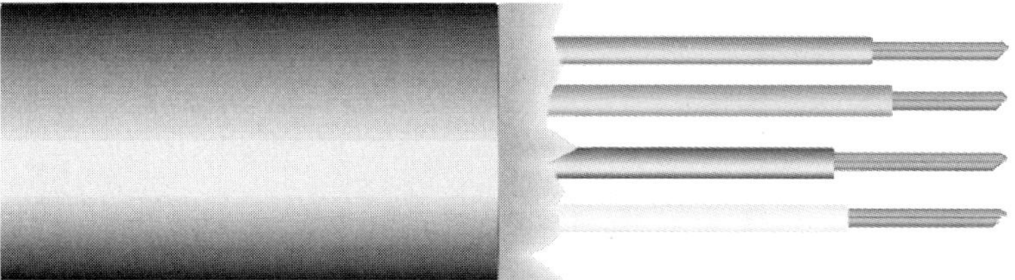

A **semiconductor** is a material that is neither a good conductor of electricity nor a good insulator. Computer chips, such as the microprocessor, RAM, and motherboard support chips are composed of semiconductor materials.

Resistance is the opposition to current. Components that are specifically designed to oppose current are known as resistors. Resistance is measured in ohm's (Ω) by an **ohmmeter.**

Electrons are provided by an electronic power supply or a battery. The force to move the electrons generated by the power supply or battery is called **voltage.** It is measured in volts (V).

Computers use many electrical circuits consisting of integrated chips, transistors, resistors, capacitors, and inductors. Each of these electrical components reacts in a predictable way when a certain voltage is applied. If the circuit has more resistance, the current will be less. If the circuit has less resistance, the current will be more. This can be shown by a common mathematical equation known as Ohm's law.

$$V = IR$$

V is the voltage supplied by the battery.
I is the current of the circuit.
R is the resistance of the circuit.

Power (P) is the rate of energy consumption or the amount of energy used in a certain length of time. In electronics, it is expressed in watts.

When a conductor such as a wire is moved through a magnetic field, a voltage is produced across the conductor. If the conductor is part of a circuit, current will be produced. In addition, when current is being sent through a wire, the current will produce an electromagnetic field.

The voltage source (power supply or battery) and electronic components are connected with a conductor such as a wire or metal trace to form a **circuit.** Electrons leave the voltage source through the path of least resistance to a common return known as *ground.* The **ground** is a reference point in electronic circuits.

A circuit can be broken down to its elementary blocks of a power source (such as battery or power supply), the path (wire or metal traces on a circuit board), and a load. The load will consist of resistors, capacitors, inductors, diodes, transistors, and other electronic components.

If the conductor has a break in it (known as an **open**) and there is no other pathway for the electrons, the current will not flow. A **short** is when a circuit has no or an abnormally low resistance path between two points, resulting in excessive current. See figure 2.7.

If a wire is made into a coil (**inductor**), the magnetic field is intensified causing a greater voltage across the conductor. The inductance of an inductor is measured in Henrys (H). An inductor is a device coil, which generates an electromagnetic field to resist change in current.

A **capacitor** is a device that stores an electric charge. The amount of charge per unit of voltage that can be stored is known as capacitance. The capacitance of a capacitor is measured in Farads (F). A capacitor can hold its charge for long periods. Therefore, before working with any circuit containing capacitors, the capacitors should be discharged.

A **switch** is an electrical or electronic device that opens and closes a current path. While the switch is open (off), the resistance across the switch would be infinite, not allowing current to flow. While the switch is closed (on), the resistance across the switch would be 0 ohms, allowing current to flow.

Figure 2.7 A Circuit

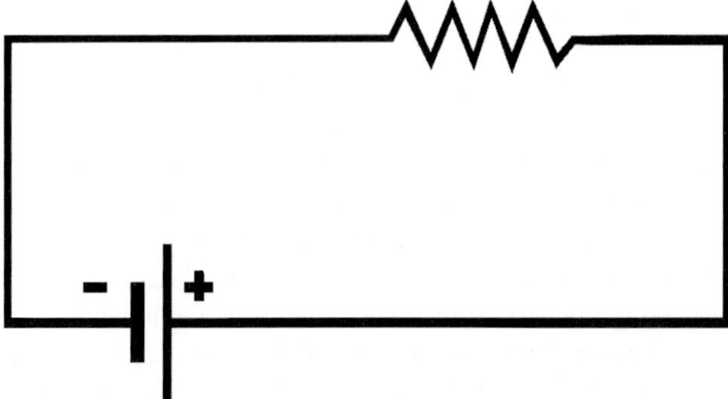

Figure 2.8 A Fuse

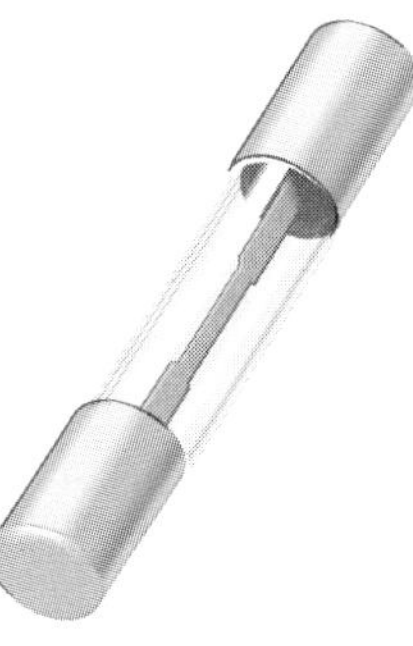

Figure 2.9 A Transistor

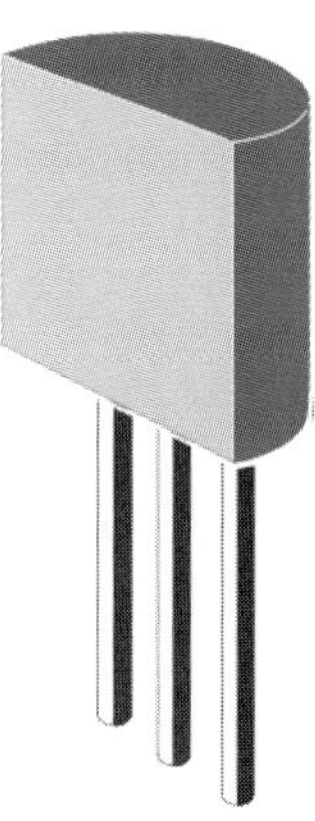

A **fuse** is a protective device that burns open when there is an excessive current in a circuit. Therefore, when the fuse is good, the fuse completes the circuit. When the fuse is open, the fuse opens the circuit, not allowing current to flow. See figure 2.8.

A **transistor** is a small electronic component that is found in virtually every electronic device. See figure 2.9. It has two basic applications. First, it can amplify an electric signal. The second application is fast switching. Switching is important to computers, which are based on millions of lightning-fast on-off decisions. Table 2.5 lists directions for testing common electronic devices.

An **integrated circuit (IC),** sometimes referred to as a chip, is a small electronic device made of semiconductor material (usually silicon) consisting of transistors, resistors, and capacitors. See figure 2.10. The transistors on integrated chips are small, fast, reliable, and use relatively little power compared to a transistor component.

There are two types of integrated circuits. The first type is the **transistor-transistor logic (TTL) chips,** which are based on two transistors. TTL chips run on + 5 V DC power.

The second type is **complementary metal-oxide semiconductor (CMOS).** CMOS chips are widely used in both NMOS (negative polarity) and PMOS (positive polarity) circuits. Because only one of the circuit types is on at any given time, CMOS chips require less power than the TTL chips. Therefore, you will find CMOS chips running on 5.0 V DC or less.

Computers use **direct current (DC).** Its current flows in only one direction and has a fixed polarity (positive or negative). If the voltage is steady, the graph of the voltage represents a straight horizontal line in relation with time without change. See figure 2.11.

The opposite of the direct current voltage source is the **alternating current (AC)** voltage source, which uses AC power. Its current reverses directions in cycles. Unlike the dc voltage, its polarity changes from positive to negative to positive again. See figure 2.12. The frequency of an AC source is the number of complete cycles per second measured in Hertz (Hz).

Although most electronic devices use DC power, AC power is sent to your house or workplace through the power lines to the AC power outlets. The reason is that the AC power can be sent over long distances much more efficiently than dc power. In the United States and Canada, the voltage sent is between 115 and 125 V at a frequency of 60 Hz. Again, the 60 Hz means that there are 60 complete cycles per second. Most countries outside North America use 220 V electricity at a frequency of 50 Hz.

Table 2.5 Common Electronic Devices

Electronic Device	Description	How to Test the Electronic Device
Battery	A device that supplies DC power. Example: The CMOS battery powers the CMOS RAM and real-time clock to function when the computer is off.	Voltmeter (or multimeter) must be set to dc. One lead is connected to the positive end of the battery and the other lead to the negative end.
Power supply	A device that converts ac into clean dc power. Example: The power supply converts AC power to +5 V dc, −5 V dc, +12 V dc, −12 V dc.	Voltmeter (or multimeter) must be set to dc. One lead is connected to a voltage output (such as +5 V or +12 V wire) while the other lead is connected to ground.
Resistor	A device that resists current. Example: Used in most electronic devices.	To properly test a resistor, it must be removed from the circuit. *NOTE:* If an ohmmeter is used to test a resistor, it could damage some electronic devices because the voltmeter uses voltage to determine the resistance.
Wire (including metal traces)	A conductor that connects other electronic devices. Through the electrical pathway, current can flow. Example: It is contained in every circuit including the power supply, motherboard, and expansion cards.	Use an ohmmeter (or multimeter). A wire, for all intents and purposes, has zero resistance indicating continuity. If the wire has infinity resistance, the wire has an open in it and is considered bad.
Fuse	A protective device that melts when the circuit has too much current, causing an open in the circuit pathway. Example: Some are contained within power supplies and motherboards.	Use an ohmmeter (or multimeter). A good fuse should have no resistance. A bad fuse with an open should measure infinity.
Capacitor	A device that stores electric charge (electrons). Example: Used in RAM IC chips and power supplies.	To properly test a capacitor, it must be removed from the circuit. To remove a capacitor from a computer takes special skills and tools.
Inductor	A coil of wire that can transfer voltage or current using magnetic fields (without physical contact). It resists the change of current. Example: Used in power supplies and power protection devices.	To properly test an inductor, it must be removed from the circuit. To remove an inductor from a computer takes special skills and tools.
Transformer	A device that has two or more coil windings used to step up or step down voltage. Example: Used in power supplies and power protection devices.	To properly test a transformer, it must be removed from the circuit. To remove a transformer from a computer takes special skills and tools.
Diode	A device that allows current to flow in only one direction. Example: Used in power supplies and power protection devices. ***NOTE:*** An LED light is a special diode.	To properly test a diode, it must be removed from the circuit. To remove a diode from a computer takes special skills and tools.

Continued

Table 2.5 Continued

Electronic Device	Description	How to Test the Electronic Device
Transistor	A device that can amplify signals or be used as an electronic on/off switch. Example: Used within power supplies and IC chips such as the microprocessor and RAM chips.	To properly test a transistor, it must be removed from the circuit. To remove a transistor from a computer takes special skills and tools.
Integrated circuit (IC)	A device containing transistors, diodes, resistors, and capacitors in one miniaturized package. Example: Microprocessors, RAM chips, and motherboard support chips, to name a few.	To properly test an integrated circuit, it must be removed from the circuit. To remove an integrated circuit from a computer takes special skills and tools.

Figure 2.10 Integrated Chip

Figure 2.11 DC Voltage

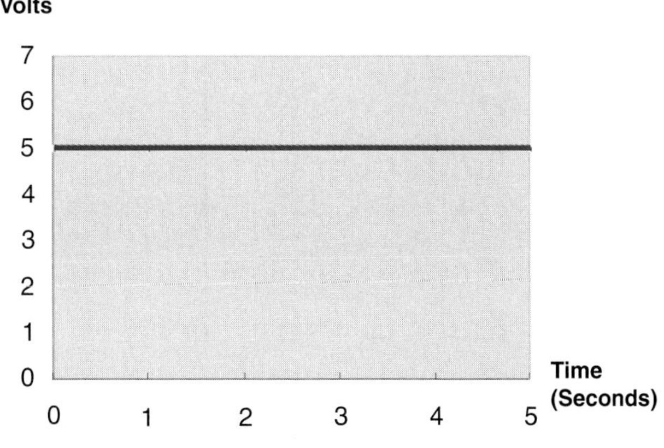

Figure 2.12 Alternating Current Voltage

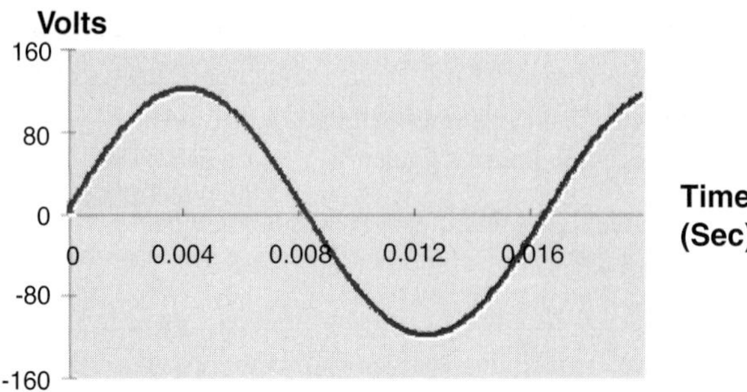

Figure 2.13 Alternating Current Outlet

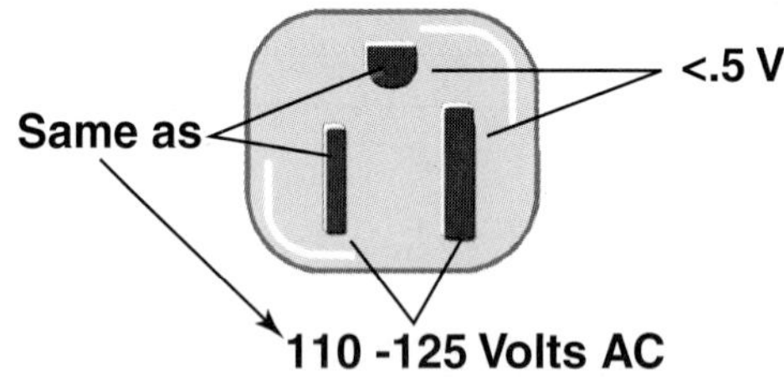

Figure 2.14 Outlet Wire Tester

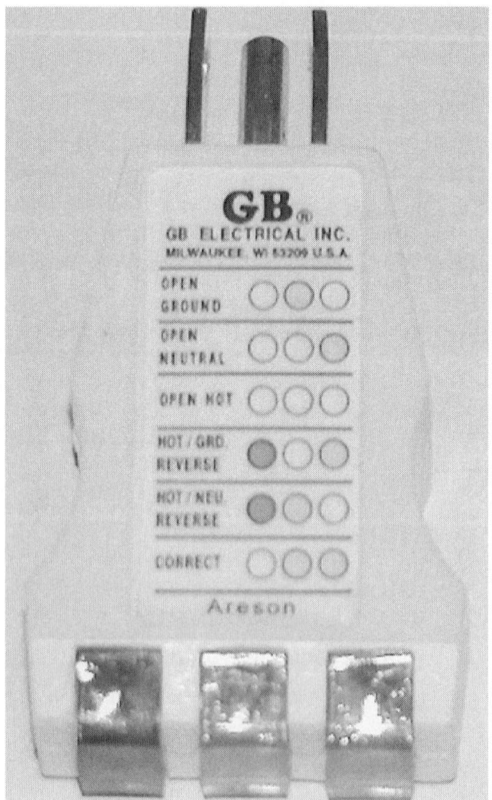

The AC power outlet in the United States has three wires leading to three connectors. A power plug connects to the AC power outlet and will have two blades and a ground. The smaller blade is the hot wire whereas the other blade is the return. The wire leading to the slot used for the small blade is usually black; the wire leading to the slot used by the large blade is usually white. The ground is typically green.

To test a power outlet, the voltage between the two slots should be between 110 and 125 V ac. The voltage between the smaller slot and ground should be the same voltage as measured between the two slots. Lastly, the voltage between the larger blade and the ground should be 0.5 V ac or less. See figure 2.13.

NOTE: A $5–10 outlet wire tester can be bought at any hardware store. See figure 2.14.

It is important to have and use the ground connector. It makes electronic equipment (including computers) safer to work with, prevents continuous electrical shock, and will minimize errors on the PC.

If your appliance supports dual voltage, you can switch it between 120 V and 220 V. You should note that you may need a different power cord that connects to the ac outlet. If your appliance or power supply does not support dual voltage, you will need a converter or transformer to change the voltage and frequency from one to the other.

IMPORTANT NOTE: If you connect a 220-volt appliance into a 120-volt outlet, the device will not function properly or not at all. If you connect a 120-volt appliance into a 220-volt outlet, the device will most likely be damaged or destroyed and may cause fire.

The electrical outlets outside the United States and Canada are usually different from those in North America. The plug on the appliance you use in the United States won't fit into the outlet in most foreign countries. Therefore, you will need a plug adapter to plug your appliance into foreign outlets. See table 2.6.

For more information, about the various voltages and outlet types, see the following websites:

World-Wide Electricity Guide

http://www.travelproducts.com/store/electricity_guide.htm

Table 2.6 Country Voltages and Adapters

Country	Voltage (V)	Frequency (Hz)	Type of Grounded Adapter
Australia	240 V	50 Hz	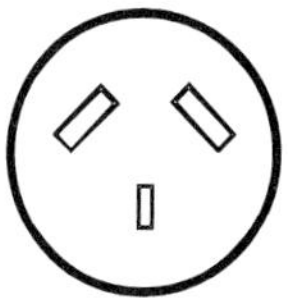
Brazil	110 V	60 Hz	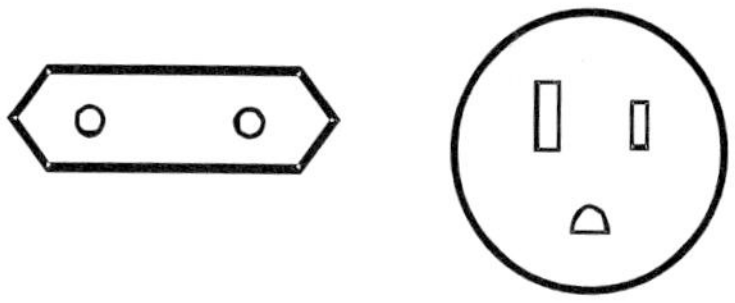
Canada	110 V	60 Hz	
China	220–240 V	50 Hz	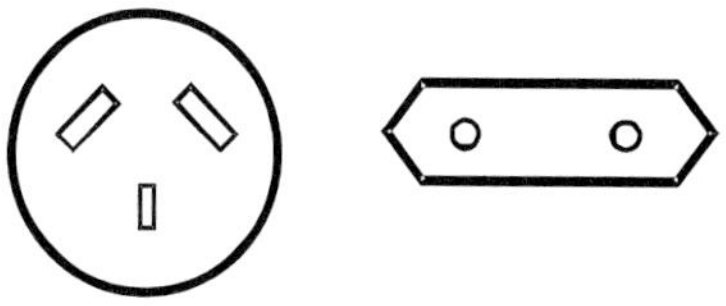
England	230 V	50 Hz	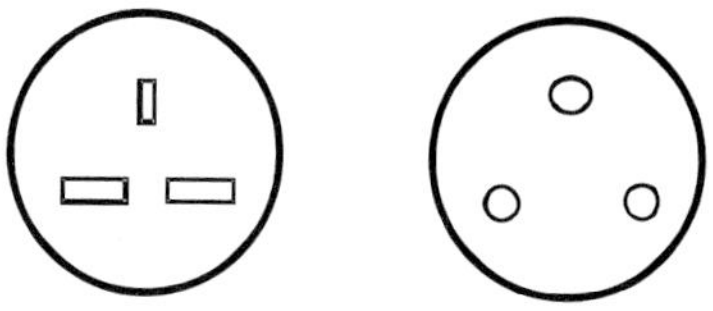

Continued

Table 2.6 Continued

Country	Voltage (V)	Frequency (Hz)	Type of Grounded Adapter
France	230 V	50 Hz	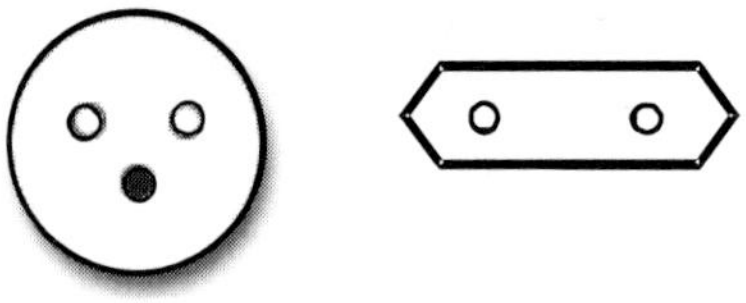
Germany	230 V	50 Hz	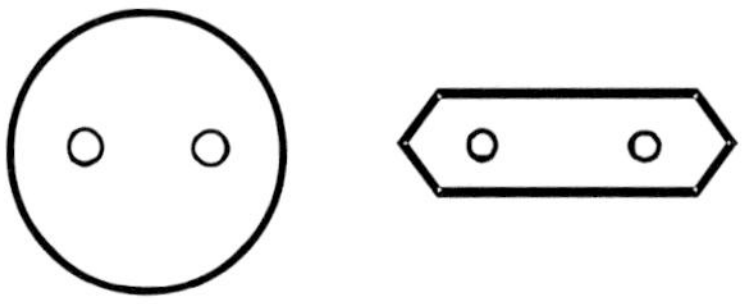
India	220 (and 250) V	50 Hz	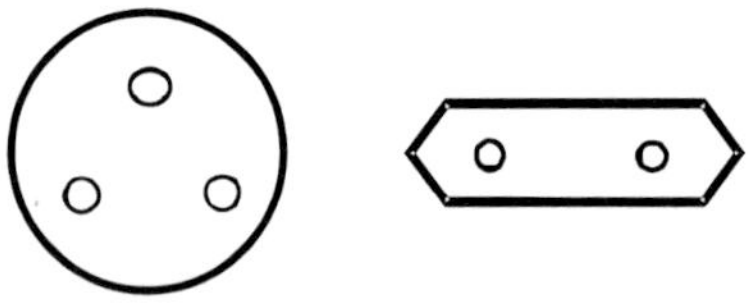
Italy	230 V	50 Hz	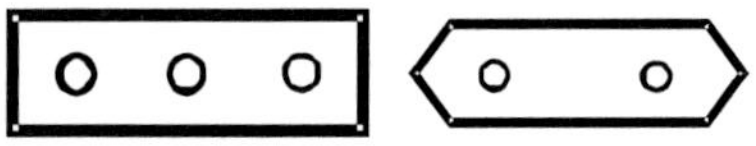
Japan	100 V	50 and 60 Hz	
Mexico	110 V	50 and 60 Hz	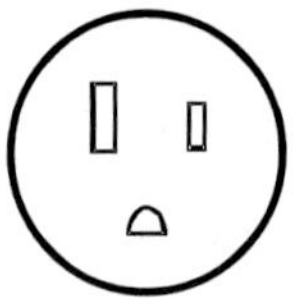
Russia and former USSR	220 V	50 Hz	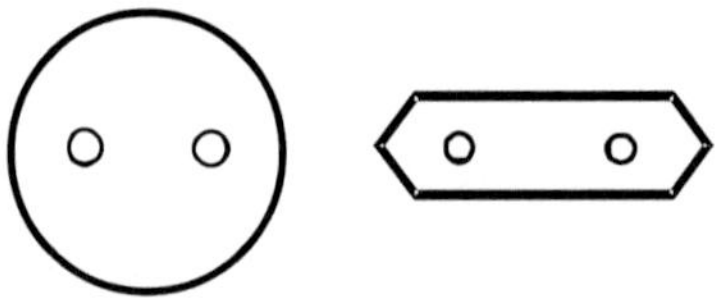
Spain	230 V	50 Hz	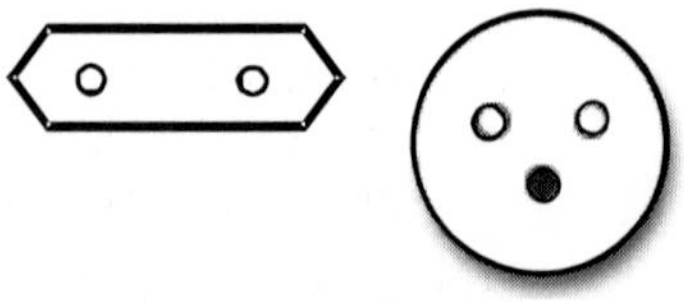

Continued

Table 2.6 Continued

Country	Voltage (V)	Frequency (Hz)	Type of Grounded Adapter
Taiwan	110 V	60 Hz	
USA	110 V	60 Hz	

Voltage Specifications by Country

http://www.currentsolutions.com/knowledge/country_spec_a-g.htm

Country Voltages and Plug Styles

http://www.powerstream.com/cv.htm

2.8 TROUBLESHOOTING TOOLS

When a component fails to work, identifying what causes the failure is not always an easy task. However, several troubleshooting tools will help you isolate computer-related problems. They are:

1. POST error codes
2. POST cards
3. Software diagnostic packages
4. Measurements and inspection

2.8.1 POST Error Codes

During boot-up, the system ROM BIOS controls the power-on self-test (POST) during boot-up to perform a series of brief tests on major components. The purpose of the tests is to make sure the PC is functional before opening any files. If a test fails, an audio code consisting of a series of beeps will be heard or a video code consisting of a number or message will be displayed to identify the problem. This is known as a POST error code.

NOTE: A single beep indicates a normal operation of the PC or speaker test.

Question:

You have turned on your computer, but you don't hear a beep upon a successful boot-up. What does this tell you?

Answer:

A single beep during boot-up usually indicates a successful boot, so there may be something wrong with the speakers or their connections. Check that the the speaker is connected properly and that the internal speaker is working properly. A good speaker should measure approximately 8 ohms.

When deciphering the meaning of a POST error code, you must first determine which system ROM BIOS manufacturer the computer has. Common manufacturers are IBM, AMI, Award, and Phoenix.

To identify which system ROM BIOS the machine has, you can:

1. Open the machine and look at the system ROM BIOS chip.
2. Look at the screen during boot-up. The manufacturer will be the second item listed on the screen. (The first item is the video ROM BIOS that activated the monitor.)
3. Use a software diagnostic package (assuming the computer can boot).

Example 2.4:

You have an IBM PC with a Pentium processor 16 MB of RAM, 3 1/2-in. floppy drives, and a 512 MB hard drive running DOS 6.22. You boot up the computer and you see *301* on the screen, and the computer seems to stop booting. What is the problem?

The problem is identified by the *301* error code. Because it is displayed on the screen, it is a video code. The first thing you need to know is which type of system BIOS your computer has. Because it is an IBM machine, it will, of course, have an IBM BIOS (this can also be verified by locating the ROM chips on the motherboard). Next, look in appendix B, table B.8 (IBM POST Error Codes), and look up the *301* code. The *301* error code means *stuck key or improper response.* By doing a quick inspection and checking the obvious, you may find that you left your keyboard unplugged.

Example 2.5:

You are using an ACME PC (PC clone) that contains a Pentium III microprocessor, 128 MB of RAM, a 3 1/2-in. floppy drives, a CD-ROM drive, and a 12 GB hard drive running Windows 2000. When the computer is booted up, you hear three short beeps and nothing appears on the screen. What is the problem?

Again, the first thing you need to know is which BIOS the Acme computer is using. After a quick inspection, you find that the BIOS is made by AMI. In this particular case, you have to locate the ROM chips on the motherboard because nothing showed up on the screen. Next, go to appendix B, table B.2 (AMI BIOS Beep Codes), and look up the three short beeps. The three short beeps mean it is *base 64 KB memory failure.* We will talk about what this means in following chapters.

Another tool to help diagnose problems with the PC during boot up is the **I/O POST card.** See figure 2.15. The POST card was originally designed to *burn in* systems (test new systems to find

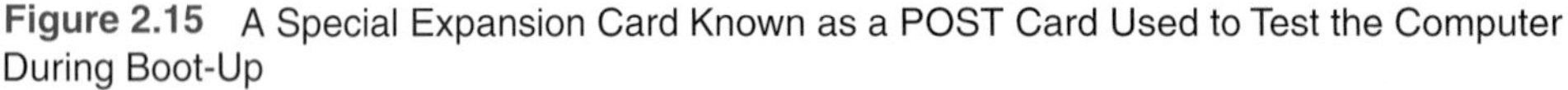

Figure 2.15 A Special Expansion Card Known as a POST Card Used to Test the Computer During Boot-Up

problems that would usually occur during the first few days of operation) on an assembly line. The POST card can also be used to diagnose a computer that does not boot and does not generate an audio or video error code.

During boot-up, the BIOS sends a test code to a special I/O (input/output) port address at the beginning of each test. These codes can be read and displayed (two or three numeric displays or a series of LEDs) with a special expansion card that is plugged into one of the expansion slots. If a test fails and the computer no longer boots, the code shown on the POST card will indicate what test failed.

Example 2.6:

We are using the same computer as in example 2.3. When you boot up the computer, it freezes. Nothing is displayed on the screen, and no beeps occurred. How can you isolate the problem?

The first thing to check is if there are any lights on and if the fan is running. If there are no lights on and the fan is not running, it is probably a power-related problem. For now, we will assume that power checks out and is not the source of the problem. Shut down the machine and insert an I/O POST card that will work with AMI BIOS into one of the expansion slots. Next, turn on the computer. When the computer boots, the POST card displays two characters, *52.* Look in appendix B, table B.3 (AMI POST Error Codes), and find that it says *Memory test above 1 M complete. Going to prepare to go back to real mode.* Because the computer froze at this point and this code is showing, the system could not switch back to real mode, for whatever reason. Therefore, it is probably a CPU or motherboard problem. If you don't understand what the microprocessor's real mode is, don't worry. It will be discussed in chapter 4.

NOTE: POST error messages occur during boot-up, before the operating system is loaded into RAM. Error messages can also be generated by the operating system and software applications.

2.8.2 Troubleshooting Disks

A valuable tool for the computer technician is a good set of troubleshooting disks. They can be used to gather information about a system or a computer problem, help to isolate a problem, and correct some of the problems. The troubleshooting disks can be divided into three categories:

1. Boot disk
2. Diagnostic package
3. Antivirus software

The **boot disk** is a disk that can load the operating system using the A drive. Therefore, if the hard drive is no longer bootable, you can boot using the A drive and then change over to the C drive to further investigate the problem and to perform repairs. You should have a boot disk for every operating system that you typically deal with, and it should contain common operating system files that will help you isolate or fix problems. (See exercise 1 at the end of this chapter.)

A software diagnostic package can report resources (I/O addresses, IRQs, DMAs, and memory addresses) used by devices, hardware diagnostics, software troubleshooting, and software optimization. I/O addresses, IRQs, DMAs and memory addresses allow hardware devices to be accessed by other devices and software. (The hardware resources are explained in chapter 7.) The most common software diagnostic packages are shown in table 2.7. Note that DOS and Windows provide some utilities (MSD, Device Manager, and Microsoft Diagnostic) to report and analyze the hardware. See figure. 2.16.

While some of the software packages can do a lot, they are really only tools that allow you to gather information. Software packages that test hardware components and try to troubleshoot software problems are far from foolproof. For example, when testing a hardware component, the software sends a predetermined code, signal, or pattern to the component being tested. If the component replies back with the correct response, it is considered a good component. However, if the problem is intermittent, you may run every test that the software has, but unless the problem occurs during the test, you will never know that the problem exists. In addition, even when a component test fails, it may not be

Table 2.7 Common Software Diagnostic Packages

Software Title	Company and Website	Comments
Checkit	TouchStone Software Corp. http://www.touchstonesoftware.com	Good reporting and hardware diagnostic package.
Norton Utilities	Symantec Corp. http://www.symantec.com	Excellent software troubleshooting and optimization package with hardware diagnostic and reporting. Well known for Norton Disk Doctor (enhanced version of SCANDISK).
AMI Diag	American Megatrends http://www.ami.com	Good hardware diagnostic package.
Dr. Hardware	http://www.drhardware.de	Excellent system information and reporting package.

Figure 2.16 MSD Utility

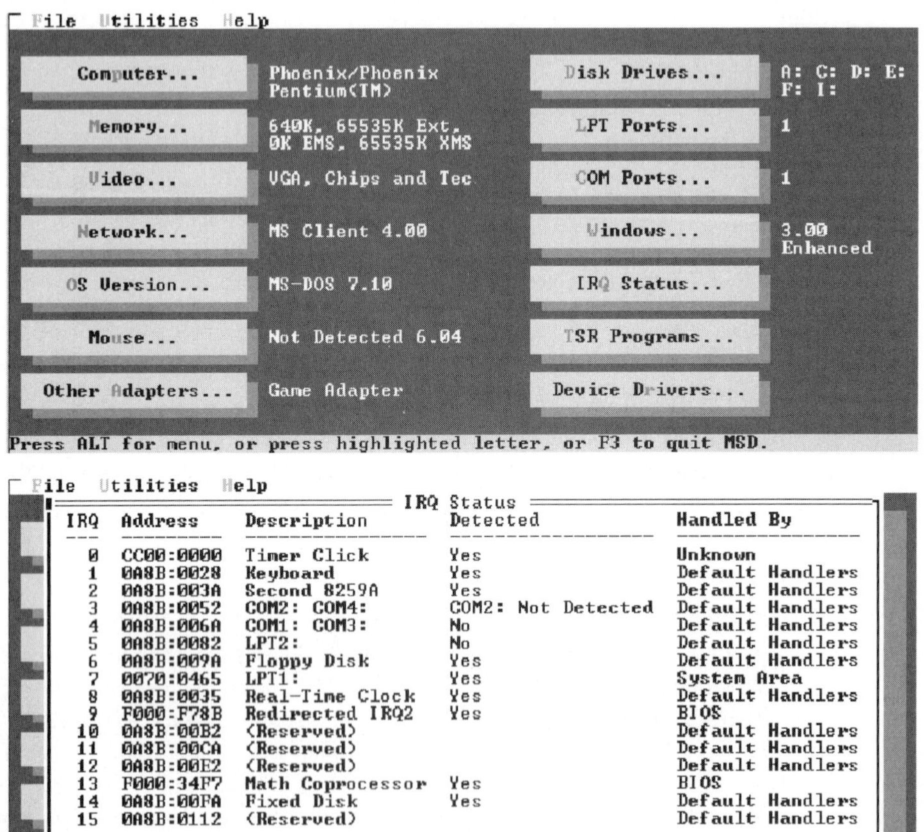

bad—the problem could be caused indirectly by another bad component. Note that if the computer fails to boot, you can't run any software, including software diagnostic packages.

Finally, you should have an up-to-date copy of **antivirus software** on floppy disks. **Viruses** are small programs that can damage data on hard drives and floppy disks. Much like a virus attacking the human body and spreading from one person to another, these programs spread from computer to computer as they transfer themselves from disk to disk. When a virus is suspected, you need to boot with a clean (noninfected) disk and start the antivirus program to check and clean the disk. The most popular antivirus software packages are shown in table 2.8.

Table 2.8 Popular Antivirus Software Packages

Software Title	Company and Website
Integrity Master	Stiller Research http://www.stiller.com
Norton AntiVirus (NAV)	Symantec Corporation http://www.symantec.com
McAfee VirusScan	Network Associates http://www.networkassociate.com

2.8.3 Measurements and Inspection

The last method in troubleshooting a computer involves measurements and inspection. Voltmeters and ohmmeters are used to take certain electronic measurements of the computer. A voltmeter can be used to see if a device is generating the correct voltage output or signal. An ohmmeter can be used to check wires and connectors and measure the resistance of an electronic device. A digital multimeter (DMM) combines several measuring devices, including a voltmeter and an ohmmeter. Some DMMs also measure capacitance, check diodes and transistors, and act as frequency counters, but these features are usually not needed to repair individual computers.

To make proper measurements and to complete a thorough inspection, you will need to have a working knowledge of how the computer operates. You will also need to know what the measurements are supposed to read. When measuring voltage, three things must be set on the DMM before making the measurement. They are:

1. Voltage.
2. Voltage type (DC or AC).
3. The expected range. If you don't know the expected range, set the DMM to the highest voltage range before taking the first measurement. This will prevent damage to the voltmeter. Note: Some voltmeters have an autorange feature.

After the DMM is configured, you then attach the red lead to the high-voltage, or positive, connector, and the black lead to the ground, or negative, connector. See figure 2.17. To measure the resistance of an electronic component, first switch the DMM to the ohms setting. Because the ohmmeter

Figure 2.17 Measuring Voltage with a Voltmeter or DMM

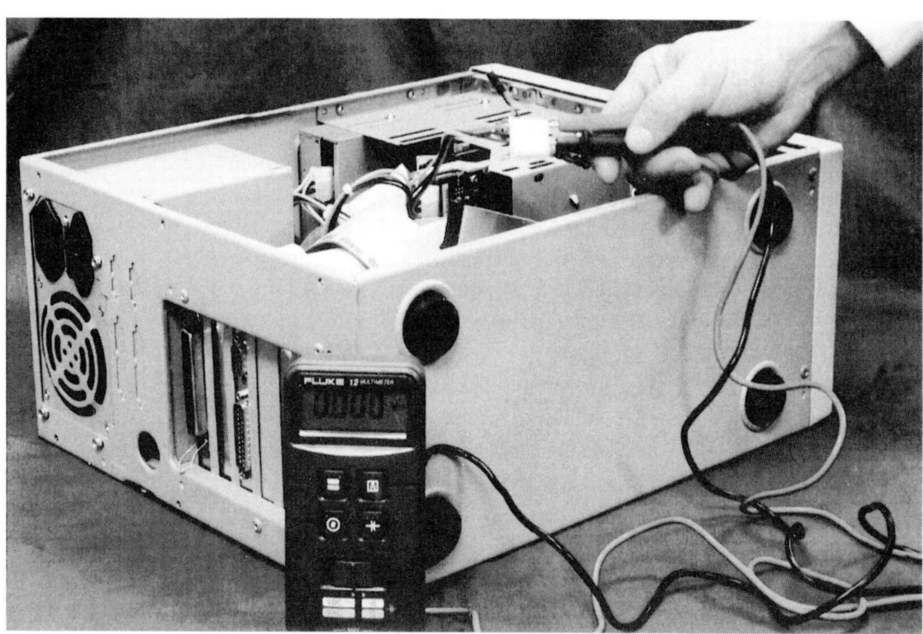

generates its own current to measure resistance, you must remove the electronic component from the circuit before taking a measurement—the comparatively large amount of current in the circuit could damage the ohmmeter or electronic component. Removing an electronic component requires special equipment and skills, and damage to the electronic device might result if done by an inexperienced electronics technician. *Therefore the resistance of an electronic device is not usually measured.*

The ohmmeter can be used to a fuse or wire. Because a fuse or wire is a conductor, it should measure no resistance (0Ω). This is known as a continuity check, a test to see whether the circuit is continuous—without breaks.

2.9 ELECTROSTATIC DISCHARGE

Electrostatic electricity is a potential electrical charge created by friction and separation. You experience **electrostatic discharge (ESD)** when you get a shock from touching a doorknob after walking across a carpet on a dry day or when your clothes cling to each other when you remove them from the dryer. If the proper steps are not taken to avoid ESD, it could damage the electronic components of a PC or cause the PC to lose data and programs.

ESD is caused by what is known as the *triboelectric effect.* Friction produces heat that excites molecular particles. When two materials are separated, electrons transfer from one material to the other, and the resulting imbalance of electrons generates a charge. The amount of static electricity generated depends upon the materials subjected to friction or separation, the amount of friction or separation, and the relative humidity of the environment. Common items that easily generate electrostatic discharge are waxed, painted, or varnished surfaces; plastics, including trays, bags, and wrap; common clothing items, including clean room smocks (especially if they are made of wool, cotton, or nylon); paper, including documentation; and Styrofoam and wood.

The electrostatic charge remains static until it comes into contact with a conductor. Most electronic components within a PC, for example, are integrated chips with metal pins and wires that carry electrical signals into and out of the chip. If material holding an electrical charge touches an electronic device, a small arc is formed, causing the circuit's semiconductor material to break down and its metal parts to short together.

PCs use two types of chips, transistor-transistor logic (TTL) and metal-oxide semiconductor (MOS) chips. The TTL chips run at 5 V, and the CMOS chips run at 3.3 V or less. Although both are susceptible to ESD, MOS chips are more susceptible since they have a thin film of silicon dioxide that can easily break down.

When an ESD-damaged component is dissected and photographed with an electron microscope, the inside of the component looks much like metal that has been welded. Unfortunately, not all ESD damage is obvious from the outside. It may not show up for days, weeks, or even months, which may lead you to think that you did not cause the problem.

To give you an idea of how much charge can be generated from ESD, your body can generate up to 35,000 V on a dry day. The shock from touching a doorknob is at least 3,000 V. Lifting a foot or moving a chair can easily generate 1,000 V. Computer components can be destroyed or degraded by a charge as low as 20 to 30 V, depending on the type of chip. These voltages are not lethal because the discharge occurs within a fraction of a second. Table 2.9 shows charges generated from some everyday actions and that electrostatic discharge occurs more often at low humidity (less than 50 percent) than at high humidity. If you are working on open computers, keep the humidity between 70 and 90 percent.

It is imperative for a technician to avoid electrostatic discharge. This will allow you to keep fewer repair parts in stock, and the computer you work on will have less downtime. You will have fewer difficult-to-trace intermittent problems and fewer unnecessary service visits to make, which will lead to fewer disgruntled customers and therefore more job security and future business.

The best way to avoid electrostatic discharge is to wear a properly grounded wrist strap. The strap can be grounded by attaching it to the metal frame of a PC (preferably an area free of paint). The metal part within the strap must make good contact with the skin, since it is you who is being grounded, not your clothing. The strap should be kept clean and in good condition, and it should be tested daily to verify that there is continuity (a good connection) between you and the ground. In addition, you should roll up your sleeves and secure your necktie so that they do not make contact with the electronic device. See figure 2.18.

Table 2.9 Electrostatic Charges

Electrostatic Charges Generated by Technical Personnel		
Action	**High Humidity**	**Low Humidity**
Walking across carpet	1,500 V	35,000 V
Removing item from plastic bag	1,200 V	20,000 V
Sliding off of or onto plastic chair	1,500 V	18,000 V
Opening a vinyl envelope containing work instructions	600 V	7,000 V
Walking across vinyl floor	250 V	12,000 V
Sliding sleeve across laminated bench	100 V	6,000 V

Figure 2.18 You should wear an ESD wrist strap when handling any electrostatically sensitive components.

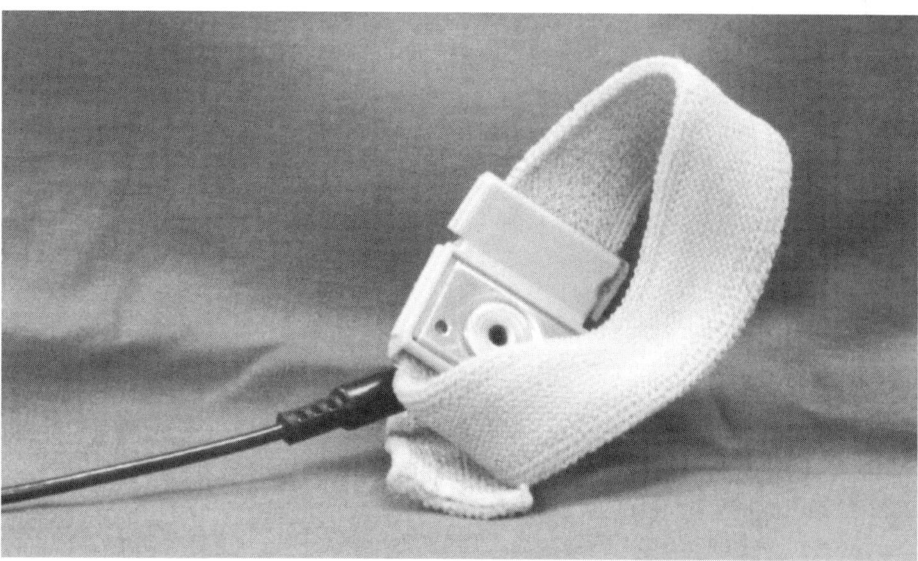

WARNING

When working on high-voltage devices such as monitors or power supplies, a wrist strap should *not* be used since the voltage stored in these devices can kill a person. Monitors and power supplies should be serviced only by trained, experienced electronic technicians.

Some books recommend an alternative method if you do not have a wrist strap. You can touch the power supply or metal case before working within the computer. You should then touch the power supply or metal case often while you are handling computer components to reduce any charge buildup. This method is not as effective as using a wrist strap, however, and is therefore not recommended.

Wrist bands are commonly made of an elastic nylon fabric that has conductive fibers on the inside surface. These conductive fibers connect to the skin with a coiled cord. The coil cord snaps to the wrist band and plugs into a ground point. A 1 megohm (1,000,000) resistor is included in the cord to prevent accidental shock to the wearer. The wrist band can also be made of metal, similar to a watch band, or hook and loop (Velcro) material. Features include size adjustment, color, cord length, snaps, clips, and buckles. The key items to look for are a comfortable fit on employees, good strain relief at the cord's bending points, and that the wrist strap and cord set meets EOS/ESD Standard 1.

Another device that you can use to avoid ESD is an **electrostatic mat.** The computer that you are repairing sits on top of the mat, which absorbs static electricity. Of course, the mat is grounded much like the electrostatic wrist strap.

When transporting and storing electronic devices, electrostatic bags should be used. See figure 2.19. An electrostatic-shielded bag is usually either silver-colored or smoke-gray and is grid-lined. The static-shielded bag must be securely closed to be effective and should not have holes. Always keep spare static-shielded bags.

NOTE: An antistatic bag, usually tinted pink or blue, doesn't shield its contents from external static fields and should be avoided in storing and transporting boards and integrated circuits.

When handling integrated chips, you should avoid touching any of the metal parts. When handling circuit boards, you should avoid touching any of the chips, electronic components, metal traces, or edge connectors. When inserting or removing any integrated chips or expansion cards, you should make sure that the computer is turned off and unplugged.

For more information about electrostatic discharge, visit the following websites:

Electrostatic Discharge Association
http://www.esda.org/

ANSI/ESD S20.20 Electrostatic Discharge Control Program Standard
http://www.esda.org/S2020.html

Basic of Static Electricity: Sources, Damage, Prevention
http://www.staticcontrol.com/pdfs/G1%20Basics%20of%20Static%20Electricity.pdf

ESD SYSTEMS.COM Installation and Maintenance of ESD Protective Surfaces
http://esdstore.esdsystems.com/pdf/ps-2013.pdf

Figure 2.19 Electrostatic-shielded bag used to prevent electrostatic electricity from damaging the device inside the bag. Electrostatic-shielded bags should be used to transport and store electrostatic-sensitive devices.

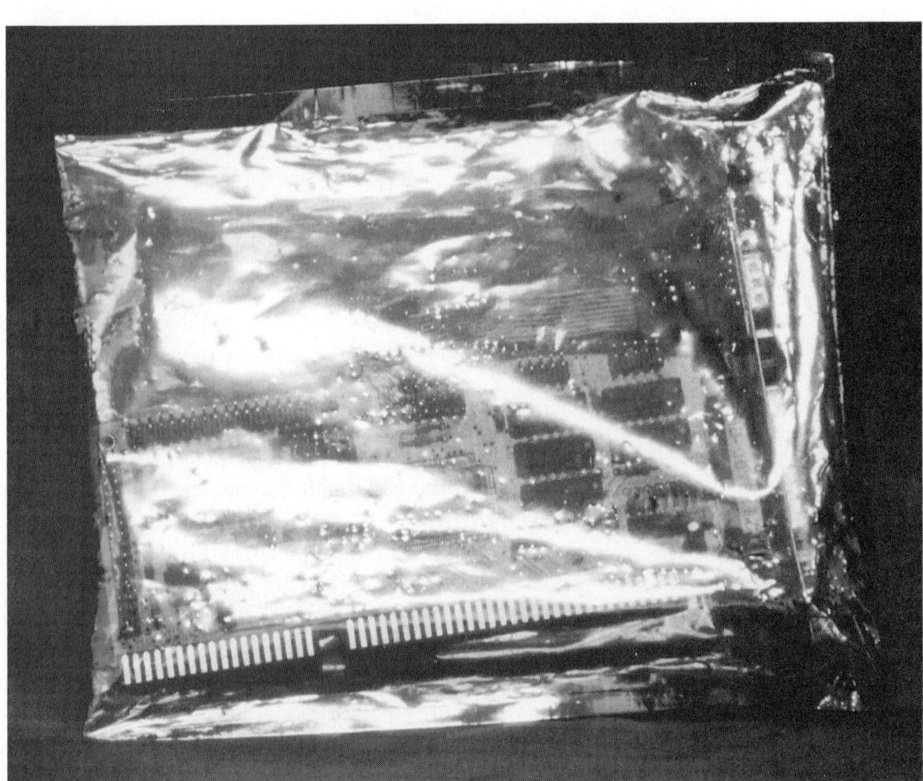

2.10 ELECTRICAL SAFETY

There is always the chance of electric shock when working on computers. A device that uses high voltage will usually have a bright yellow-and-black sticker warning of the high voltage. See figure 2.20. If you don't follow safety recommendations when working on a PC, the electricity from a device can cause shock, burns, blindness, or death as well as catastrophic equipment damage.

Safety Guidelines—Electricity

- Never use both hands to handle an electronic device.
- Wear rubber-soled shoes.
- Do not wear jewelry or any other articles that could accidentally contact circuitry and conduct current or get caught in moving parts.
- Connect or disconnect any test leads or connections with the equipment turned off and unplugged.
- Never assume anything without checking it out for yourself.
- Don't take shortcuts.

2.11 IN CASE OF FIRE

Although fires don't usually occur around computers, you should still know how to put out a fire correctly. The three major classes of fire extinguishers are: Class A, used for wood and paper; Class B, used for flammable liquids; and Class C, used for electrical fires. Because computers are electrical devices, you should use a Class C or an ABC-rated fire extinguisher. See figure 2.21.

Figure 2.20 Warning of Electric Shock

Figure 2.21 A Fire Extinguisher

SUMMARY

1. CompTIA uses a general troubleshooting strategy that consists of the following steps:
   a. Establish the symptoms
   b. Identify the affected area
   c. Establish what has changed
   d. Select the most probable cause
   e. Implement a solution
   f. Test the result
   g. Recognize the potential effects of the solution
   h. Document the solution
2. During boot-up, the system ROM controls the power-on self-test (POST) to perform a series of brief tests on major components.
3. If a test fails, an audio code consisting of a series of beeps will be heard or a video code consisting of a number or message will be displayed to identify the problem. This is known as a POST error code.
4. Concentration is key to troubleshooting.
5. When troubleshooting computer problems, you must keep an open mind as to the cause of the problem. The problem could be hardware failure, a compatibility problem, an improper configuration, a software glitch, an environmental factor, or a user error.
6. Before trying to fix the problem, gather information.
7. After you have gathered as much information as you can, you are ready to make the repair or fix. Sometimes you will know exactly what to change or replace. At other times you will have to isolate the problem.
8. You are expected to understand computers well enough to investigate and isolate problems, know when you need to find more information, and know how to get the information in a timely manner so that you can fix the problem.
9. You can use mild detergent and a damp cloth to clean the outside of the computer.
10. To clean the monitor screen, use a damp cloth or special antistatic wipes.
11. To reduce the risk of component failure and to provide better system cooling, you can use a brush, vacuum cleaner, or a can of compressed air to clean the inside of the computer.
12. The brush, can of compressed air, and vacuum cleaner must be designed not to generate electrostatic discharge.
13. To clean the electrical contacts inside the computer, use metal contact cleaner or isopropyl alcohol with a cotton swab.
14. Electrostatic discharge, or ESD (electricity caused from friction), is easily generated by the technician and can damage electronic components.
15. The best way to minimize electrostatic discharge is to wear a grounded wrist strap and to use electrostatic-shielded bags when transporting and storing electronic components.
16. If you don't follow safety recommendations when working on a PC, the electricity from a device can cause shock, burns, blindness, or death as well as catastrophic equipment damage.
17. When using special cleaners or other chemicals, you should be aware of the proper usage, storage, and disposal of the chemicals and their impact on the environment.
18. This information is usually found on the cleaner's container or on the Material Safety Directions Sheet (MSDS) that comes with the container or from the vendor.
19. The position of computer technician is a job that requires dealing with people.
20. Because computers are electrical devices, you should use a Class C or an ABC-rated fire extinguisher.

QUESTIONS

1. Before troubleshooting a problem, you must be able to (choose two answers)
   a. duplicate the problem.
   b. replace the faulty component.
   c. reformat the hard drive.
   d. gather information.
   e. run the CMOS setup program and change the number of wait states.
2. Which of the following would be a logical first step in troubleshooting a PC?
   a. Check the computer CMOS.
   b. Call the vendor.
   c. Define what applications are being used.
   d. Fire the user.
   e. Find the circumstances of the problem.
3. The most important part of the computer to the user is the
   a. microprocessor.
   b. RAM.
   c. keyboard.
   d. data.
   e. monitor.
4. What is the most frequent cause of computer problems?
   a. hardware failure
   b. software glitches
   c. compatibility problems
   d. user errors
5. A customer complains because she has been on hold for a long time and has been transferred several times. What should you do?

a. Apologize for the inconvenience and offer to help her now.
b. Give her your home phone number or cellular phone number.
c. Tell her the best time to call back.
d. Explain how busy you are.

6. A customer calls and tells you that the hard drive you just sold him was defective. What should you do?
a. Tell the customer to call the manufacturer.
b. Call the manufacturer for the customer.
c. Tell him you will replace it if he can prove that it is defective.
d. Replace the drive.

7. A customer calls and complains that the computer you just repaired is still not working properly. What should you do?
a. Apologize and explain that it is a different problem than the one you repaired.
b. Explain that the customer did something wrong.
c. Refer the customer to another repair facility.
d. Offer to replace any new components you installed or reservice the computer.

8. A customer on the telephone can't understand your directions. What is the one thing that you should *not* do?
a. Ask if there is someone else you can speak to.
b. Hang up on him because he can't follow directions.
c. Refer him to a customer center.
d. Tell him someone will call him back.

9. What is the last thing you should do to complete a service call?
a. Hand the customer a bill.
b. Thank the customer for his or her business.
c. Explain why the repair took so long.
d. Tell the customer how he or she could have repaired the problem.

10. Why do we want a backup of the system?
a. It is the best way to overcome data loss.
b. Data may be erased during the fixing of computers.
c. Data is the most important thing in the computer.
d. All the above.
e. None of the above.

11. *True or false*—Before isolating a computer problem, you must be able to duplicate the problem.

12. You conclude that three components could be causing a particular problem. Which of the following is the best course of action?
a. Replace the one that you think is failing and return the system to the customer.
b. Replace them one at a time to verify the failing part and then return the system to the customer.
c. Replace the least expensive part and return the system to the customer.
d. Replace all three and return the system to the customer.

13. One of the first things to do when repairing a PC is
a. confirm that the 120 V ac power supply is filtered for noise.
b. confirm that the user is not part of the problem.
c. check the hard drive for correct format information in the CMOS setup program.
d. replace all components that can cause the problem.

14. During boot-up, what does a single beep indicate?
a. a hardware problem with the PC
b. an operating system or application program problem
c. an incompatible expansion card
d. normal operation of the PC or speaker test

15. Which of the following could be a valuable source of information during troubleshooting?
a. the customer
b. hardware and software documentation
c. the Internet
d. all of the above

16. You have a computer that generates six beeps during boot-up. What is the first thing you must find out when determining the meaning of the beeps?
a. the type of microprocessor
b. the manufacturer of the system ROM BIOS
c. the manufacturer of the video ROM BIOS
d. the type of operating system on the hard drive

17. You have a computer that has a Pentium II microprocessor, an AMI system ROM BIOS, 64 MB of RAM, a 6 GB hard drive, and an All-Tech monitor. During boot-up, it generates six beeps. What is the problem?
a. the read/write memory on the video card
b. the A20 line
c. the base 64 KB RAM
d. a bad hard drive
e. corrupt boot files
f. a virus

18. You have a computer problem. What is the best method to determine if the problem is a hardware problem or a software problem?
a. Upgrade the operating system.
b. Format the C drive and reload the operating system.
c. Replace the motherboard.
d. Move the hard drive to another computer.
e. Boot the computer with a clean boot disk.

19. What is the simplest and most efficient method of testing a component?
a. Run a software diagnostic test on the component.
b. Make measurements with a multimeter or oscilloscope.
c. Run the CMOS setup program.
d. Boot the computer.
e. Observe the component and see if it operates properly.

20. A computer will not boot properly. The computer never begins the load of the OS and the technician suspects a POST error. What is the proper way to use a POST diagnostics hardware adapter?
    a. Insert the card into an open bus slot, boot the computer, and the error codes will display on the adapter.
    b. Insert the card into an open bus slot, boot the computer, and the error codes will output on the default printer.
    c. Insert the card into an open bus slot, boot the computer using the supplied floppy disk, and the error codes will be stored on disk.
    d. Connect the adapter to a serial or parallel port, boot the computer, and the error codes will be stored in a memory buffer created by the adapter.
21. Before opening a computer, removing a component or installing a component, you should make sure that
    a. the computer is off.
    b. the monitor is unplugged.
    c. the keyboard is unplugged.
    d. the modem is unplugged.
22. Static electricity is generated
    a. by the "triboelectric effect."
    b. easily on dry days (low relative humidity).
    c. by rubbing certain materials together.
    d. all of the above.
23. Wrist straps will be useful only if
    a. they are plugged into the wrist strap jack.
    b. they are clean and make good skin contact.
    c. the cord has not been damaged.
    d. all of the above.
24. Before opening a static-shielding container you should
    a. look inside to see if it really is sensitive.
    b. check for paperwork inside the container.
    c. ground yourself in an ESD-protected area.
    d. none of the above.
25. If a ground strap fails the daily test, you should
    a. get a new one from your supervisor.
    b. use it the rest of that day.
    c. take the rest of the day off.
    d. try to fix the test box.
26. Before transporting an ESD-sensitive device, it must be
    a. enclosed in a static shielding container or bag.
    b. put into a cardboard box.
    c. thoroughly cleaned.
    d. wrapped in newspaper.
27. Which of the following could generate electrostatic voltages high enough to cause ESD damage?
    a. combing your hair
    b. walking across a carpeted floor
    c. taking off your coat
    d. all of the above
28. To avoid ESD when working on a PC
    a. ensure that you and the PC are at the same electrical charge level.
    b. connect your grounding wire from the PC to a nonconductor.
    c. connect your grounding wrist strap to the PC's motherboard.
    d. connect your grounding wrist strap to your shoes.
29. An ESD wrist strap contains which of the following to protect you from an electrical shock?
    a. a transistor
    b. a capacitor
    c. a resistor
    d. a fuse
30. To prevent ESD, humidity should be kept at least at ______________ when working on computers.
    a. 10%
    b. 50%
    c. 25%
    d. 75%
31. *True or false*—When working with high voltages such as in monitors or power supply, you should always use a wrist strap with at least a 1 megaohm resistor.
32. What type of fire extinguisher can you use on a computer fire (choose all that apply)?
    a. Class A
    b. Class C
    c. Class B
    d. Class ABC

HANDS-ON EXERCISES

Exercise 1: Making a Windows 95/Windows 98 Troubleshooting Boot Disk

These exercises assume that you have a Windows 95 or Windows 98 machine.

1. Label the outside of the disk "Windows Boot Disks."
2. From the Control Panel, open the Add/Remove Programs applet/icon.
3. From the Startup Disk tab, click on the Create Disk button.

   NOTE: You may need a Windows 95 or Windows 98 CD-ROM disk or another source of the Windows installation files.

4. Write-protect the disk.
5. Boot from the floppy disk to make sure that it boots properly.

Exercise 2: Identifying PC Hardware Configuration I

1. Perform a cold boot (use the reset switch or on/off switch). If the computer displays information about the type of CPU, amount of RAM, the number and types of drives, and other useful information, press the Pause key.
2. Identify the following:

   type of microprocessor
   size of all hard drives and CD drives
   amount of extended memory

Exercise 3: Identifying PC Hardware Configuration II

1. Right-click My Computer and select Properties. If you are using Windows XP, click the Start button, then right-click My Computer and select Properties.
2. Identify the OS and service pack (if any) listed under the System section.
3. Identify the processor and amount of RAM that the OS recognizes.
4. Select the Hardware tab and click the Device Manager button.
5. Under Processors, identify the processor.
6. Under ports, identify the number of parallel and serial ports.
7. Under disk drives, identify the number of disk drives.
8. Under Display adapter, identify the video card.
9. Start the System Information program located under Accessories and then System Tools.
10. Identify the OS, OS version, and service pack (if any).
11. Identify the processor and processor speed.
12. Identify the mother manufacturer and model.
13. Identify the BIOS version.
14. Identify the amount of RAM.
15. Identify the directory used to hold Windows.
16. Under components, determine the number of parallel ports and serial ports.
17. Under Storage, determine the size of all drives.
18. Under Internet Settings, determine the version of Internet Explorer.
19. Close System Information.

Exercise 4: Identifying PC Hardware Configuration and Diagnostic Programs

1. Start Internet Explorer.
2. Download SiSoftware Sandra (Standard shareware version). It can be found at http://www.sisoftware.net/ or http://www.cnet.com (you will need to perform a search).
3. Execute the Sandra executable file and install Sandra.
4. Launch Sandra.
5. Double-click System Summary.
6. Identify the processor and speed of the processor. Identify the L2 cache size of the processor.
7. Identify the Front Side Bus Speed of the processor.
8. Identify the memory bus speed.
9. Identify the video card and monitor.
10. Identify the hard drives and their size.
11. Identify if your system is using a sound card and network card.
12. Close the System Information window.
13. Access some of the Information modules.
14. Close the Sandra program.
15. Go to the http://www.dr-hardware.com website and download Dr. Hardware SysInfo.
16. If you don't have WinZip, download and install WinZip (found at http://winzip.com).
17. Open the Dr. Hardware zip file.
18. Create a c:\drhard directory and copy all of the files from the c:\drhard directory.
19. Close WinZip.
20. Open a Command prompt window. It can be found under Accessories.
21. Change to the drhard directory by executing the `cd c:\drhard` command.
22. Insert a new floppy disk in drive A. Don't use the boot disk that you created in exercise 1.
23. Execute the `install a:` command. Press Enter to copy the files to the floppy disk.

24. Remove the floppy disk and label it Dr. Hardware.
25. Shut down Windows and boot the computer with the boot disk that you created in exercise 1.
26. Remove the boot disk and insert the Dr. Hardware floppy disk.
27. Execute the `cd drhard` command.
28. Execute the `drhard` command.
29. Press the S key to start the quick start test. Read the notice about registering the software and press the Enter key. This step may take a few minutes.
30. Using the http://www.download.com.website, search for tufftest. Download the tufftest program.
31. Execute the tufftest program and create a tufftest floppy disk. Label the disk "Tufftest."
32. Shut down Windows and boot the system with the tufftest disk.
33. Using the tufftest program, view system information and perform some diagnostic tests.
34. Reboot the computer and restart Windows.
35. From the http://www.download.com website, search for diagnostic and view the various diagnostic programs available.

Exercise 5: Using a Digital Multimeter

1. Take a digital multimeter and set it to measure ohms (2 megaohms or greater).
2. Take a wire and measure the resistance across the wire by connecting the clips that connect to the multimeter to the two ends of the wire. Turn on the digital multimeter and measure the resistance. Record what you measured.
3. Unplug the power cable from the ac outlet and remove it from the PC.
4. Measure the resistance of the power cable.
5. Take an electrostatic wrist strap and exam it.
6. Measure the resistance from one of the electrostatic straps to the other end. Record what you measured.
7. Change the settings of the digital multimeter to measure dc volts and set it to measure 15 volts or greater.
8. Measure the voltage across the wire. You should measure 0 volts.
9. Get a battery (AA, AAA, or 9 volt) from your instructor and measure the voltage across the battery.
10. Change the settings of the digital multimeter to measure ac volts and set it to measure 250 volts or greater.
11. Measure the voltage across the two plugs used on your ac socket.

Exercise 6: Learning About ESD

1. Go to the following website and read the document about static electricity:

   http://www.staticcontrol.com/pdfs/G1%20Basics%20of%20Static%20Electricity.pdf

2. Go to the following website and read the document about ESD protective surfaces:

   http://esdstore.esdsystems.com/pdf/ps-2013.pdf

3. Go to the following websites and look at the various products available to control ESD.

   http://www.staticcontrol.com/
   http://esdsystems.com/
   http://esdstore.esdsystems.com/

4. Attach your ESD strap to one end to the outside of the power supply of your computer. Then put the wrist strap around your wrist. Make sure that the metal contact makes contact with your skin. Show this to your instructor to verify its proper use.

Exercise 7: Creating a Flowchart for Troubleshooting

Create a generic troubleshooting plan in the form of a flowchart.

Exercise 8: Reading About Software Piracy

1. Go to the http://www.spa.org/piracy website.
2. Record the antipiracy phone number. View the online report form.
3. Read at least three articles on software piracy.
4. Go to the http://www.microsoft.com/piracy website.
5. In the left pane, click on Piracy Basics.
6. Read What is Piracy, How Piracy Impacts You, and Worldwide Piracy.
7. Read about Microsoft Product Activation.
8. In the left pane, click on How to tell. Read about how you can tell if you have a counterfeit copy of Microsoft Windows or Microsoft Office.
9. In the left pane, select Reporting Piracy and determine how you can contact Microsoft about piracy.

CHAPTER 3

The Disassembly and Assembly of the PC

Topics Covered in This Chapter

Introduction

To become a better technician and better understand how the computer works, you must learn how to identify its major components and how to disassemble and reassemble it in a timely manner while following ESD and safety guidelines. In addition, you must be able to determine which devices are field-replaceable units (FRUs) so that you can determine whether to fix the device or to replace it.

Objectives

1. Identify common ports and explain their primary function.
2. Identify standard PC components.
3. When handling PC components, demonstrate proper ESD procedures.
4. Given a PC, disassemble the PC to its basic FRU components and reassemble it.
5. Given a list of PC components, identify which items are FRUs.

3.1 THE PC CASE

The PC **case,** which contains most of the computer components, comes in many sizes and two orientations (desktop and tower). It is sometimes referred to as the chassis. The **desktop case** lies flat; the **tower case** stands erect. See figure 3.1. Today's PC cases usually have a reset switch, and a lock. An LED is a small light that usually indicates if a component is on or active. The reset switch provides an easy way to reboot the computer. The lock is used to secure the system by disabling the keyboard or preventing entry into the case. (Caution: Many system locks can be opened with commonly used keys.)

Before opening the PC, identify the **ports** that are located at the back of the case. See figure 3.2. Ports are plug sockets that enable an external device, such as a printer, to be attached to the computer. These ports are usually identified by the shape of the plug socket, the number of pins, the number of rows in which the pins are aligned, and the orientation of the pins (male or female). The most common ports are shown in table 3.1

Figure 3.1 The Desktop PC and Tower PC

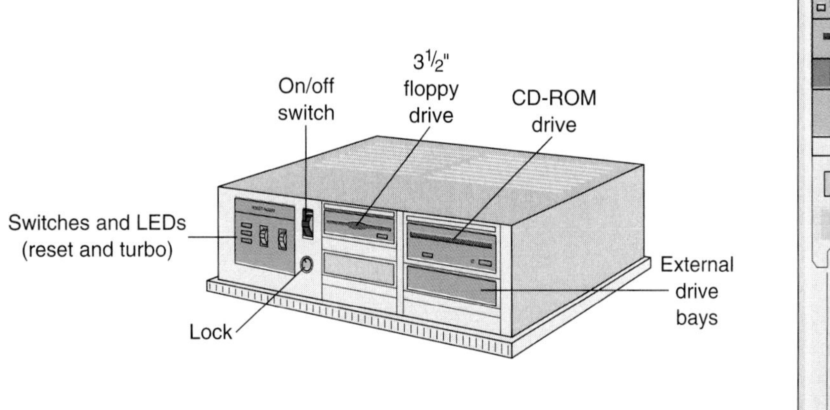

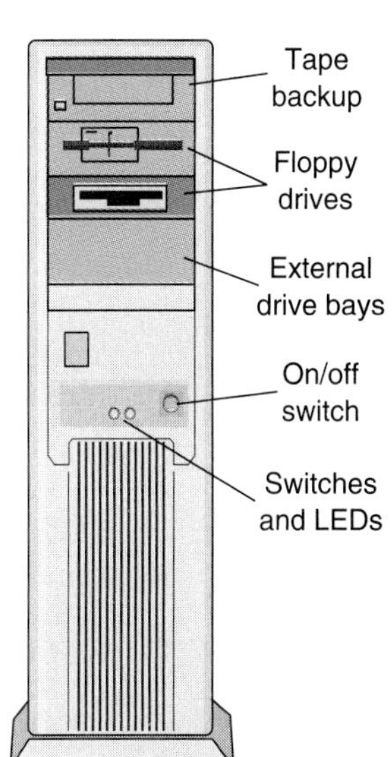

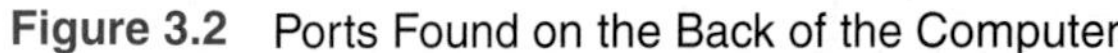

Figure 3.2 Ports Found on the Back of the Computer

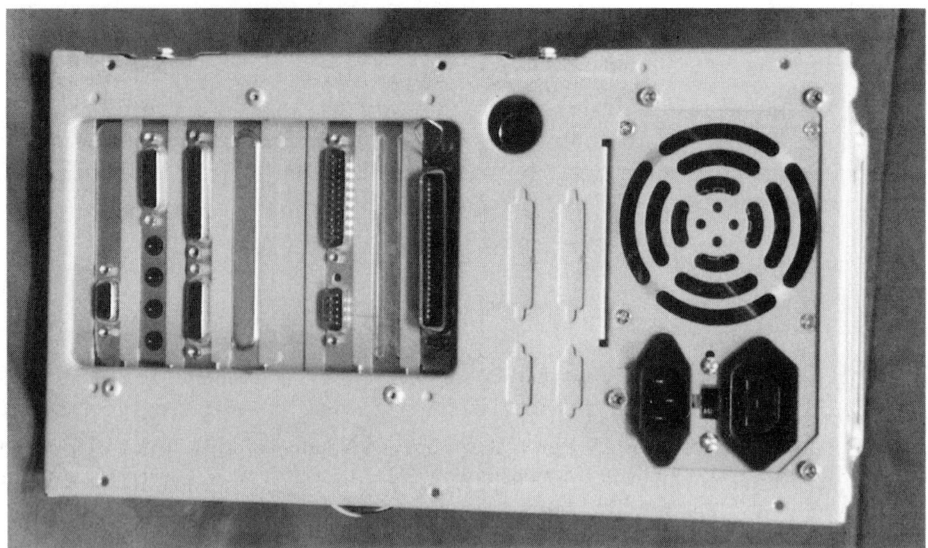

3.2 DISASSEMBLING THE COMPUTER

Before you disassemble or assemble a computer, you should always do the following:

- Back up everything important (if possible).
- Have a clean workspace with all the necessary tools and equipment.
- Take ESD precautions.
- Document everything.
- Power-off all devices and disconnect the power from them.
- Take your time.

To disassemble a computer, you would typically follow these generic steps:

1. Detach the keyboard and mouse from the back of the computer.
2. Detach the monitor.
3. Detach the serial and parallel devices.
4. Detach network cables, speaker cables, joystick, modem, phone lines, and any other data cables.
5. Detach the power cable.
6. Remove the system case lid.
7. Detach internal power cables from the drives.
8. Remove the drives.
9. Remove the expansion cards.
10. Remove power cables from the motherboard. Note: You typically don't have to remove the power supply from the case.
11. Remove the RAM.
12. Remove the processor.
13. Remove the cables from the motherboard.
14. Remove screws and clips that hold the motherboard in place.
15. Remove the system board.

To reassemble the system, you would perform these steps in reverse order.

To open the PC, you must remove the screws that hold the cover on. They are usually found on the back of the PC, near the edge of the case. Make sure not to remove the screws that hold the power supply in place. Some desktop cases have screws located at each corner, while other cases may include a fifth screw located at the top center. Other desktop cases have screws located near the bottom of the

Table 3.1 Common PC Ports

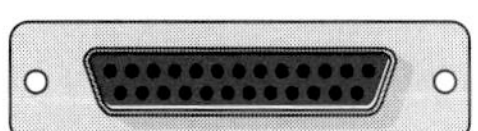 **Parallel Port**	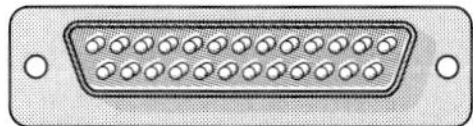 **Serial Port**	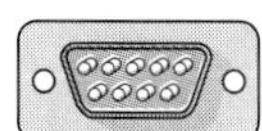 **Serial Port**
2-row, 25-pin female D connector The parallel port (also known as LPT1, LPT2, or LPT3) is used primarily to connect printers to the computer.	2-row, 25-pin male D connector The serial port (also known as COM1, COM2, COM3, or COM4) is used primarily to connect external modems, mice, and miscellaneous devices. Note that there are two types of serial ports.	2-row, 9-pin male D connector The serial port (also known as COM1, COM2, COM3, or COM4) is used primarily to connect external modems, mice, and miscellaneous devices. Note that there are two types of serial ports.
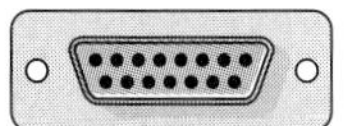 **Game Port**	 **VGA or Super VGA Port**	 **Monochrome, CGA, or EGA Port**
2-row, 15-pin female D connector The game port is used to connect joysticks to the computer. If the 2-row, 15-pin female D connector is on a sound card, it is probably a MIDI port or game port.	3-row, 15-pin female D connector The VGA or Super VGA port is used to connect the VGA and Super VGA monitors to the computer.	2-row, 9-pin female D connector The DB-9F connector is used to connect the older monochrome, CGA, or EGA monitors.
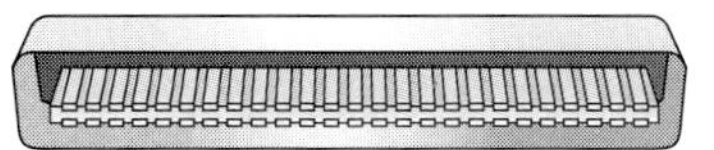 **SCSI Port**	 **SCSI Port**	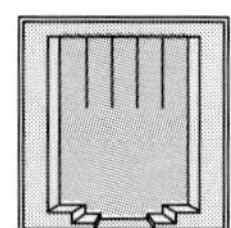 **Phone Jack Modem Port**
50-pin centronics port The SCSI port is used to connect SCSI printers, CD-ROMs, scanners, and hard drives. The SCSI-1 and SCSI-2 interfaces can connect up to 7 peripherals, while the SCSI-3 interface can connect up to 127 devices.	50-pin and 68-pin miniport The SCSI port is used to connect SCSI printers, CD-ROMs, scanners, and hard drives. The SCSI-1 and SCSI-2 interfaces can connect up to 7 peripherals, while the SCSI-3 interface can connect up to 127 devices.	RJ-11 connector These two connectors are used to connect to the telephone wall jack and the telephone.
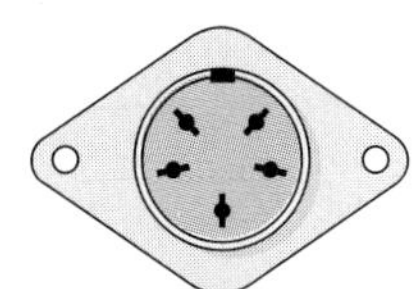 **Keyboard**	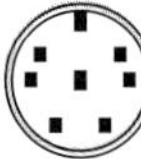 **PS/2 Mouse Port or PS/2 Keyboard Port**	 **Universal Serial Bus (USB)**
5-pin DIN This port is used to connect a keyboard to the PC. The keyboard port is always connected directly to the motherboard.	6-pin mini-DIN This port is used to connect a mouse without using a serial port or to connect a PS/2 keyboard.	This external port allows you to connect up to 127 external PC peripherals, including mice, keyboards, printers, modems, and external disk drives.
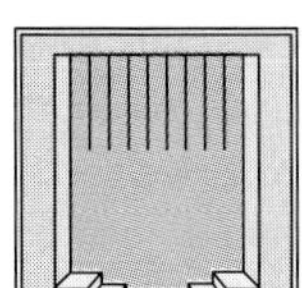 **10BaseT/100BaseT Network Port**	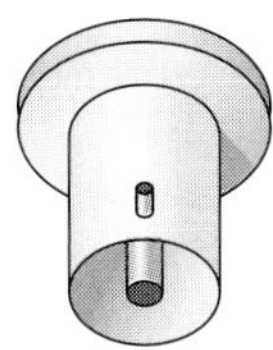 **BNC Connector**	
RJ-45 connector These connectors are used to connect to a network using a 10BaseT cable.	Coaxial connector These connectors are used to connect to a network using a coaxial cable.	

Figure 3.3 Screws Used to Open Case

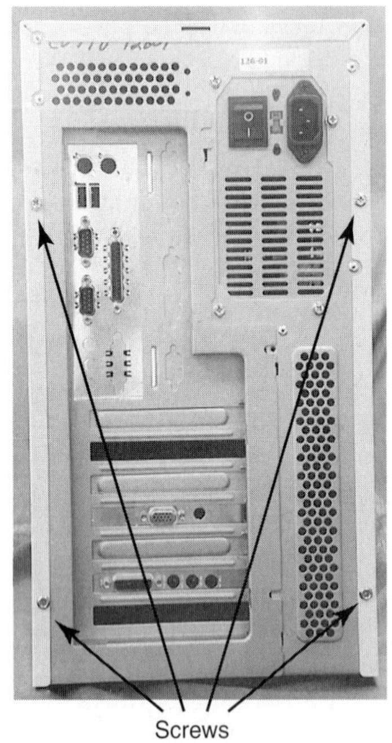

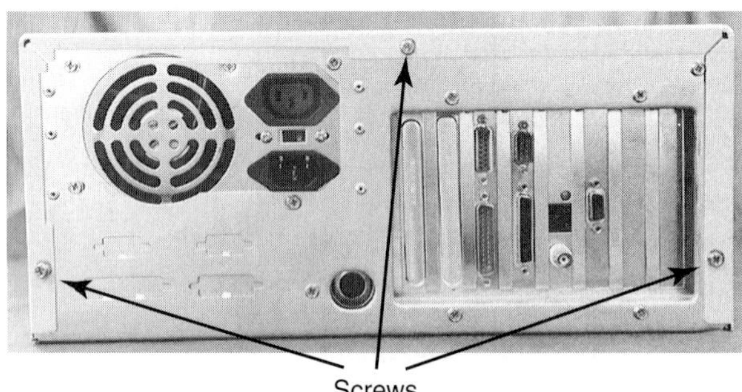

sides. Tower cases usually have their screws in the back, along the outer edge. Depending on how big the case is, it will have three to eight screws. See figure 3.3. After the screws are removed, slide the cover off as you are lifting it up.

IMPORTANT NOTES

1. Before opening the computer and removing or installing components, make sure that the power is off and that the power cable is unplugged.
2. When removing the cover, do it with care. Sometimes parts of the case may snag some of the cables within the PC. As a computer technician, you should not introduce new problems.
3. Follow the ESD procedures discussed in chapter 2.

3.2.1 Expansion Cards and Slots

After opening the case, the major components are easily identified. They are the motherboard, the power supply, the drive bays (drives), and the expansion cards. See figure 3.4.

The **motherboard,** the largest circuit board in the PC, contains the essential electronic components, including the microprocessor, the RAM, the system ROM BIOS, and support circuitry. To make the PC more configurable and expandable, the PC uses **expansion cards** (circuit boards), which are inserted into expansion slots on the motherboard. Expansion cards can be used to connect drives, I/O ports (parallel ports, serial ports, and game ports), mice, speakers, and monitors. Of course, they are usually identified by the type of ports and cable connectors they use.

Several types of **expansion slots** have been used over the years. The IBM PC used an 8-bit PC slot, and the IBM AT used a 16-bit ISA slot. Later, the Micro Channel Architecture (MCA) and the Extended Industry Standard Architecture (EISA), both having a 32-bit bus (a set of wires used to carry data and power), were introduced for use with the 386 machine. Today's desktop computers use a combination of ISA slots and local bus slots, mostly PCI (Peripheral Component Interconnect) and AGP (Accelerated Graphics Port), whereas notebooks use a PC/CardBus slot.

To remove an expansion card, you must first disconnect any cables that may be attached to it. Next, remove the card's mounting screw. Grasp the board firmly along its top edge and rock it gently up and out. Avoid touching any of the chips, electronic components, or metal traces. Once the card is out of its slot, avoid touching the edge connector.

Figure 3.4 Picture of Desktop and Tower Computers (Courtesy of International Business Machines Corporation; unauthorized use not permitted)

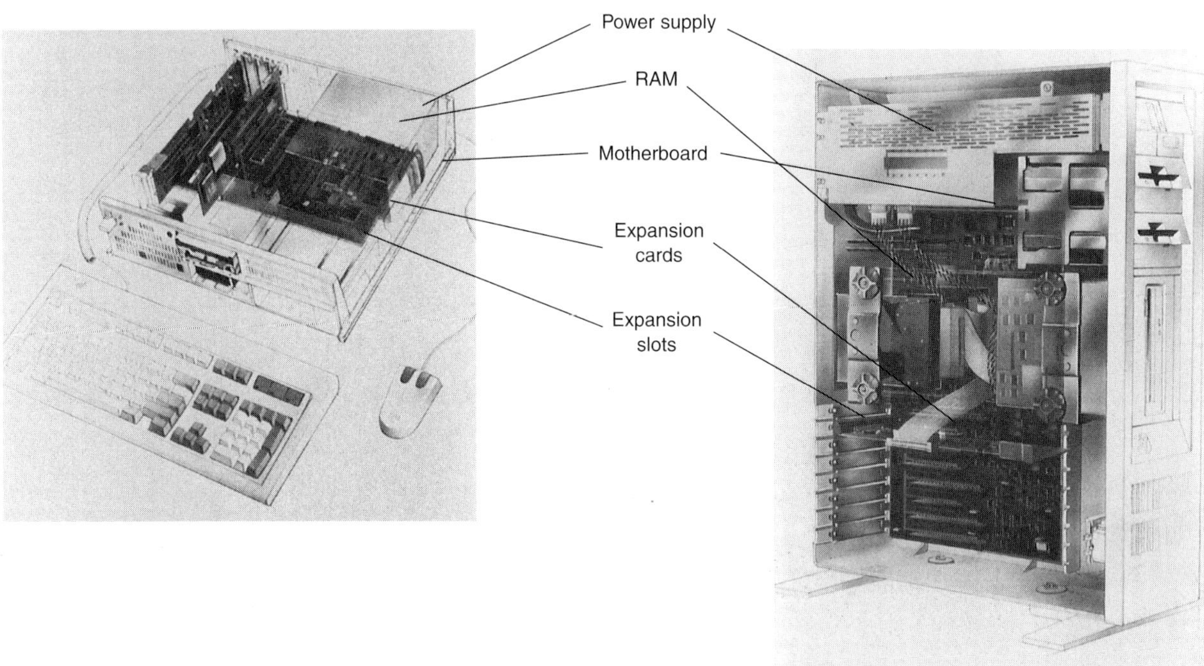

NOTE: Make sure that the computer is off and unplugged before removing or inserting expansion cards.

To insert a card into an expansion slot, find an empty slot that matches the expansion card that you are inserting. If you have several matching slots to choose from, it should not matter which slot you use; they should all be the same. It is recommended that the cards be spaced out so that they can be accessed more easily in the future. (If there is a metal cover over the slot hole of the case, remove the screw that holds it in place to remove the slot hole cover.) Slide the card into the slot and insert the mounting screw.

NOTE: Installing an expansion card is usually not this easy. Often, the cards need to be configured with jumpers or software. For more information on configuring expansion cards, see chapter 7.

3.2.2 RAM

RAM is packaged as DIPs, SIPPs, SIMMs, DIMMs, and RIMMs. A **DIP (dual in-line package),** which resembles a bug with many legs, lies horizontally on the motherboard with metal leads extending down from its two long sides. The metal leads are inserted directly into the motherboard's DIP sockets. Note: Some older RAM cache chips are DIPs.

To remove a DIP, you could use a special chip puller designed to grab and firmly hold the chip so that it can be pulled out of the IC socket. The chip puller that comes with most $10 to $50 tool kits does not work well, however, since it doesn't hold the chip firmly as it is pulled from the socket. Another way to remove a DIP is to use a small, flat-edge screwdriver blade. By gently sliding the screwdriver under one end of the chip and prying just a little, then going to the other end and prying that end up, you can prevent the legs from bending while you continue to alternate prying both ends until the chip can be easily removed.

To insert a DIP into an IC socket, you must first position the DIP so that pin 1 is in the proper orientation. Pin 1 of the chip and the socket is usually identified by a notch on one end of the DIP. (See fig. 3.5.) Next, align the pins with the socket and gently push the chip into its socket without bending any of its pins in the process. If a pin is bent by accident, the chip could be ruined.

A **SIPP (single in-line pin package)** is a small circuit board onto which several DIPs are soldered. The circuit board has a single row of pins for insertion into the motherboard. To remove a SIPP, you firmly grasp the small circuit board and pull straight up. To insert a SIPP, you must align the pins with the SIPP socket and gently press down on the SIPP so that the pins go into the pin holes without bending. If the pins are bent by accident, the SIPP could be ruined.

Figure 3.5 IC chip. Notice the notch to indicate which end has pin 1.

Figure 3.6 To install a SIMM chip, insert the SIMM into the socket at a 45° angle and snap it into place.

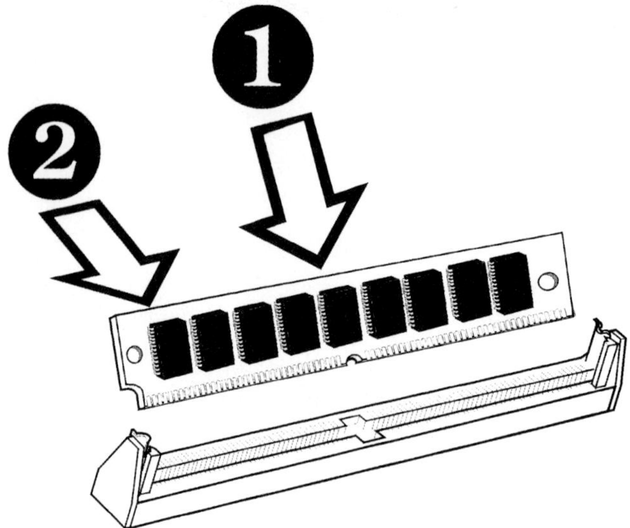

Figure 3.7 Remove a SIMM by pulling apart the two clips that keep the SIMM in place.

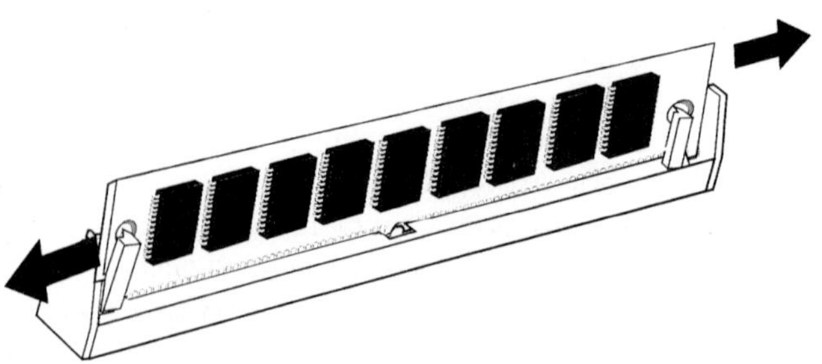

SIMMs (single in-line memory modules) consist of integrated chips soldered onto a small circuit board. A row of tin or gold metal plates (contacts) along the bottom of the module connects it to the motherboard. Metal pins on the motherboard make contact with the metal plates.

To install a SIMM chip, insert it into the slot at a 45° angle. Make sure the SIMM is seated properly in the slot. Push the SIMM until it clicks into place. See figure 3.6. To remove a SIMM, pull apart the two clips located at the ends, tilt the SIMM back to a 45° angle, and pull it out. See figure 3.7. Be careful not to bend, mangle, or break the clips. Turn the SIMM back to a 45° angle and lift it away from the slot.

DIMMs (dual in-line memory modules) and RIMMs (Rambus in-line memory modules) are the most common forms of RAM. To install a DIMM (or a RIMM), line up the notches on the DIMM with

Figure 3.8 To insert a DIMM or RIMM, put it into the socket and press down.

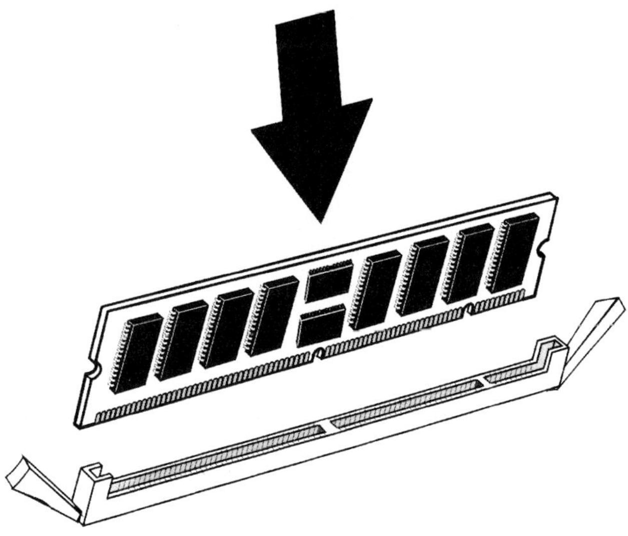

Figure 3.9 To remove a DIMM or RIMM, pull apart the two ejector tabs.

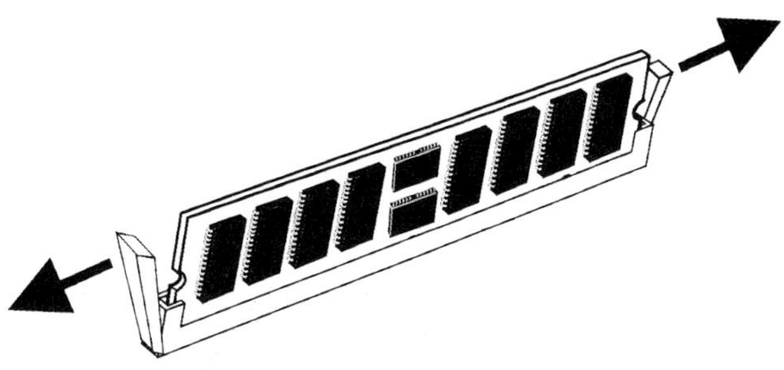

the plastic tabs located in the DIMM socket. Once the notches are lined up, apply pressure to the module by pushing it into the socket until it is firmly seated. See figure 3.8. To remove a DIMM (or a RIMM), push down the ejector tabs gently and pull the DIMM or RIMM out of the socket. See figure 3.9. (For more information on RAM chips, see chapter 5.)

3.2.3 Drives

The hard drives, CD-ROM drives, and floppy drives are connected to an expansion card or directly to the motherboard with a long, flat, gray cable known as a **ribbon cable.** The **floppy drive cable** has 34 pins, the **IDE cable** (used with IDE hard drives and IDE CD-ROM drives) has 40 pins, and the **SCSI cable** (used with SCSI hard drives, SCSI CD-ROM drives, and tape backup drives) has 50 or 68 pins. Note: The Ultra DMA-66 and Ultra DMA-100 use a 40-pin, 80-conductor ribbon cable. The ribbon cables use two-row connectors.

When connecting a ribbon cable, you must make sure the cable is correctly oriented. See figure 3.10. Pin 1 of the cable (marked with a red or blue stripe along one edge) must be connected to pin 1 of the drive and pin 1 of the cable connector on the motherboard or expansion card. Pin 1 of the drive is designated by a small 1 or 2 printed on the drive's circuit board. Pin 1 of the expansion card or motherboard connector can be identified by a small 1 or 2 printed on the circuit board or by a square solder (other pins have a round solder). Some drives and cables are notched to prevent the cable from being inserted incorrectly. If the cable is connected incorrectly, the hard drive or compact disk may cause a short, preventing the computer from booting. If the floppy drive is connected backward, the floppy drive light will remain on and any floppy disk inserted onto the drive will usually be unreadable.

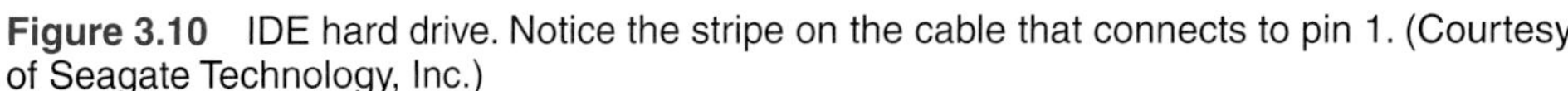

Figure 3.10 IDE hard drive. Notice the stripe on the cable that connects to pin 1. (Courtesy of Seagate Technology, Inc.)

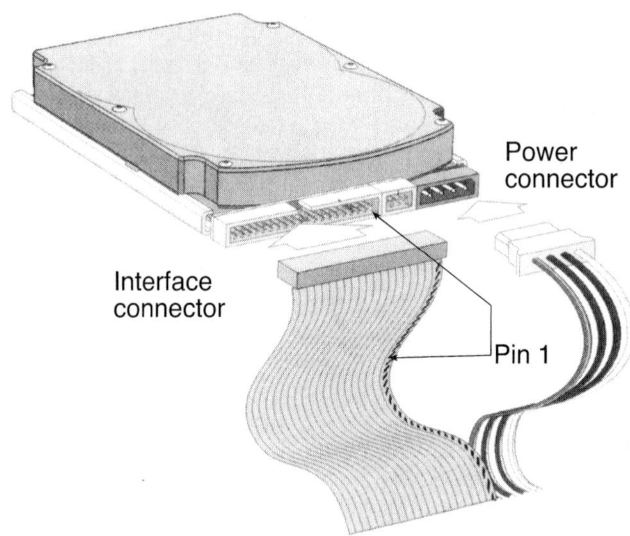

Figure 3.11 34-Pin Floppy Drive Ribbon Cable

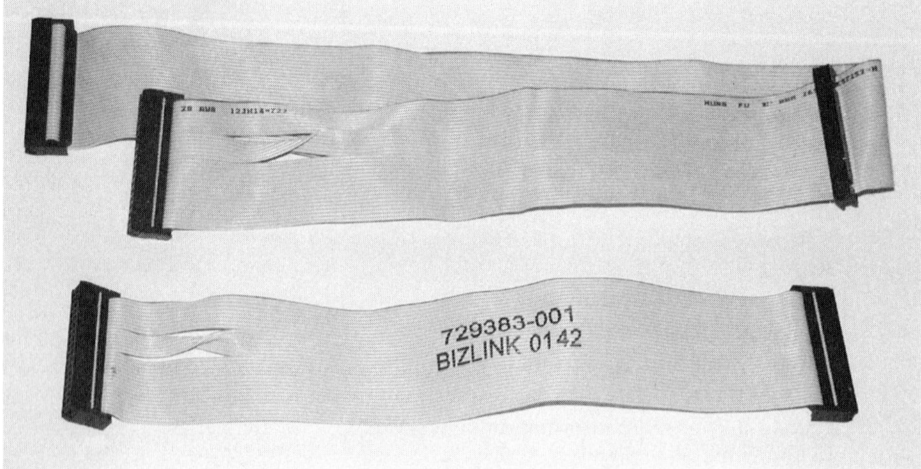

When connecting **IDE (integrated drive electronics)** devices, it does not matter where the IDE device is or where the IDE controller is connected to the ribbon cable. When connecting **SCSI (small computer system interface)** devices, including the SCSI expansion card, the two devices with terminated resistors must be on the two ends of the chain. (For more information on hard drives and terminating resistors, see chapter 9.) The floppy drive controller goes on the long end of the ribbon cable, drive B goes in the middle, and drive A goes on the other end. See figure 3.11. For more information on floppy disk drives, see chapter 10.

Many motherboards include a floppy drive cable that has only two connectors. One connector connects to the motherboard and the other end goes to the floppy drive. The cable has only two connectors because most computers have only one floppy drive, so the other connector or connectors are not really needed. What is important to notice is that on one connector, pin 6 is filled in. Therefore, if you are connecting the cable to the floppy drive and the cable appears not to go on, try reversing the cable.

A drive is placed in a drive bay and is held in place by four screws. Openings in the front of the computer case allow disks and tapes to be inserted and removed from the floppy, compact disk, and tape drives. When the opening is not needed, it is usually covered with a removable plate.

3.2.4 Processors

Desktop processors come in two main types of packages. The first package, a pin grid array (PGA), lays flat on the motherboard that plugs into a zero insertion force (ZIF) socket. To install the processor, you raise the handle on the socket, align pin A1 on the processor to pin A1 on the socket, and carefully insert the processor into the socket. Be sure not to bend the pins. You then close the lever and apply the thermal solution, usually consisting of a heat sink and fan. If necessary, connect the fan cable to the fan and motherboard. To remove the processor, remove the thermal solution, open the handle on the socket, and remove the processor.

The second type, a single-edge cartridge (SEC), stands up on the motherboard that plugs into a slot. To install the processor, apply the thermal solution to the processor, align the processor to the slot, making sure that the key is aligned properly, and insert the processor into the slot. The key is used to make sure that the processor is not inserted incorrectly. If necessary, connect the fan cable to the fan and motherboard.

3.2.5 Motherboards

To remove the motherboard, you must first disconnect all external connectors (including those for power, the keyboard, mouse, printer, and speakers). Next, disconnect the internal connectors (including those for the battery, keylock, power light, and the reset button). If you don't know which cable is connected to which plug, it is a good idea to record how they are connected on a piece of paper or to label them with a piece of tape.

Most motherboards are attached with one to eight screws. In addition, most use white plastic **standoffs** or brass mounting sockets, as shown in figure 3.12, to prevent the motherboard from shorting against the computer case. After removing the screws, slide the motherboard away from the power supply about 1/2 in., until the standoffs have disengaged from their mounting slots. Lift the motherboard up and out of the case. Some motherboards are mounted on a metal plate that swings open, whereas others have a removable bottom plate that allows the motherboard to slide out through the bottom of the case.

To install a motherboard, you perform the same actions but in reverse order. First, mount the motherboard onto the back plate of the case. To do this, lay the board down on top of the plate to see which of the holes in the board are above the mounting holes in the plate. Make sure the board is oriented correctly. Press the white plastic standoffs into the holes in the motherboard that correspond to the openings on the plate. Align the motherboard above the plate so that the spaces engage with the plate. You should be able to see the brass mounting sockets exposed through the holes in the motherboard. Place small insulating washers on top of these holes and screw finely threaded screws into the brass sockets.

NOTE: Don't tighten the screws too much. If you tighten them too much, it may cause a short in the motherboard, and the system won't boot. Lastly, install the expansion cards and connect all cables.

> **IMPORTANT NOTE**
>
> If you have an AT power supply (typically used in older systems), it will have two connectors (known as P8 and P9), each with six colored wires. When connecting the two power cables, make sure that the ground wires (black wires) are in the middle.

Figure 3.12 White Plastic Standoffs

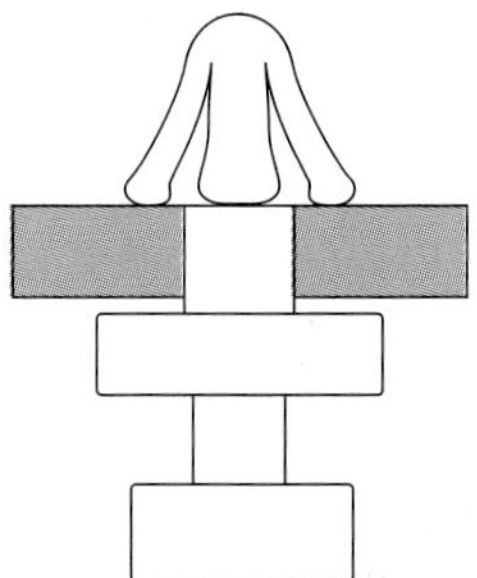

3.3 ASSEMBLING AND DISASSEMBLING NOTEBOOK COMPUTERS

While installing or removing a component in a notebook computer, it is recommended that you use a set of precision screwdrivers and pliers. Because the components and screws are smaller than those found in the desktop computer, you will find that the precision tools are a better fit than typical screwdrivers.

Because each notebook computer seems to be more proprietary than desktop computers in general and the instructions for taking a notebook apart differ greatly from notebook to notebook, it is recommended that you follow the directions in the service guide for the specific notebook. Unfortunately, these service guides may be difficult to obtain.

Finally, when disassembling and assembling a notebook, you should not have any leftover screws. It is important for the reliability of the notebook computer that you use all the screws that come with the notebook. In addition, if you lose a screw, you should make an extra effort to find that screw before continuing. These small screws have a tendency to find their way inside the notebook, causing other problems. Be sure to use the correct screw. A screw of the wrong length can cause malfunction or failure.

The main screws that hold a notebook computer are located underneath the notebook. In addition, some screws are located on the top part of the computer or around the edges of the LCD panel. These screws would typically be visible but are covered up with a small plastic covering that is the same color and texture as the rest of the notebook. Because the plastic coverings are stuck over the screws with a mild adhesive, they can be easily removed by prying them with a small, precision flat-edge screwdriver. See figure 3.13.

Before working on a notebook computer, you should first unplug the ac power and then remove the battery. The battery is released by a sliding latch, which then allows the battery to slide out from the side or the bottom.

Today, notebook computers will have RAM that is soldered onto the motherboard or use small circuit boards called SO-DIMMs, which are usually accessed from a panel located on the bottom of the notebook (see figure 3.14) or underneath the keyboard. The small circuit boards that lay flat are inserted into a socket via a connector that is embedded on the circuit board. SO-DIMMs, short for small outline DIMM, are basically mini-DIMMs, except instead of standing erect on the motherboard, they lay flat. Therefore, to install them, you insert them into a SO-DIMM socket at a 45° angle and press down to click them into place. See figure 3.15. To remove them, you gently pull apart the two clamps, and the SO-DIMM will pop back up to a 45° angle so that you can pull them from their socket.

For notebooks, some hard drives are removable, much like a battery. You pull a latch or remove a screw, and the hard drive slides out from the side. Other hard drives are internal devices that you have to open the notebook to access. You will always find that it is enclosed in a plastic container or a set of brackets.

The keyboard used in a notebook computer is smaller than a standard desktop keyboard. Notebook keyboards contain approximately 90 keys. The keyboard is connected to the rest of the computer with a small sturdy ribbon cable. See figure 3.16. The keyboard can be removed by removing the screws that hold it in place or by sliding small latches or clips. Underneath the keyboard, you will often find access to the processor, RAM, and other components that make up the computer.

Figure 3.13 Exposing the Outside Screws of a Notebook Computer

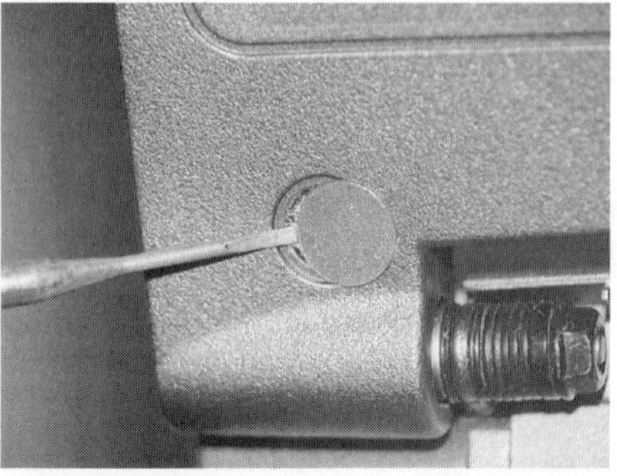

Figure 3.14 Panel Found on the Bottom of the Notebook Computer

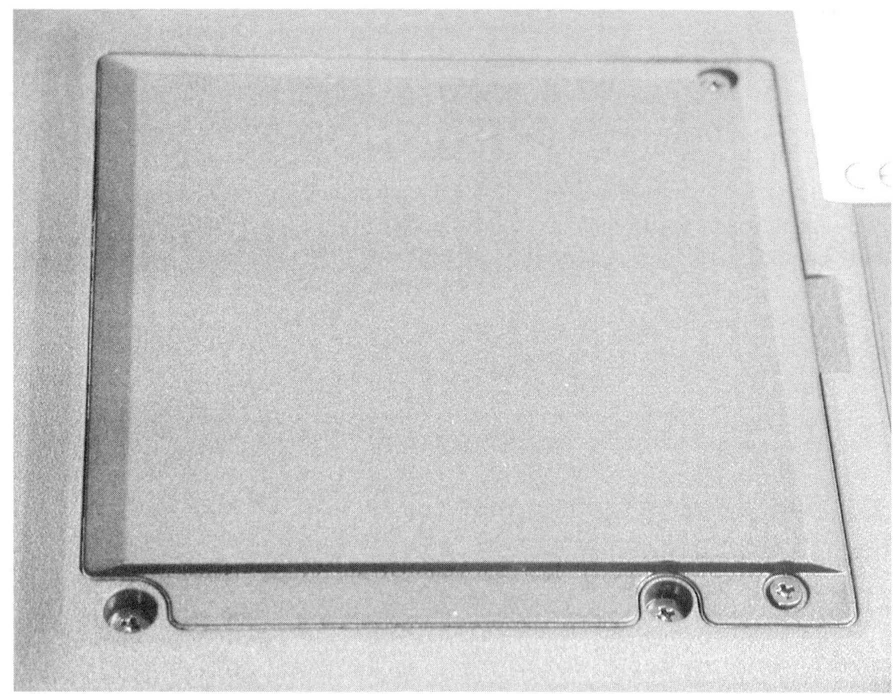

Figure 3.15 Installing an SO-DIMM

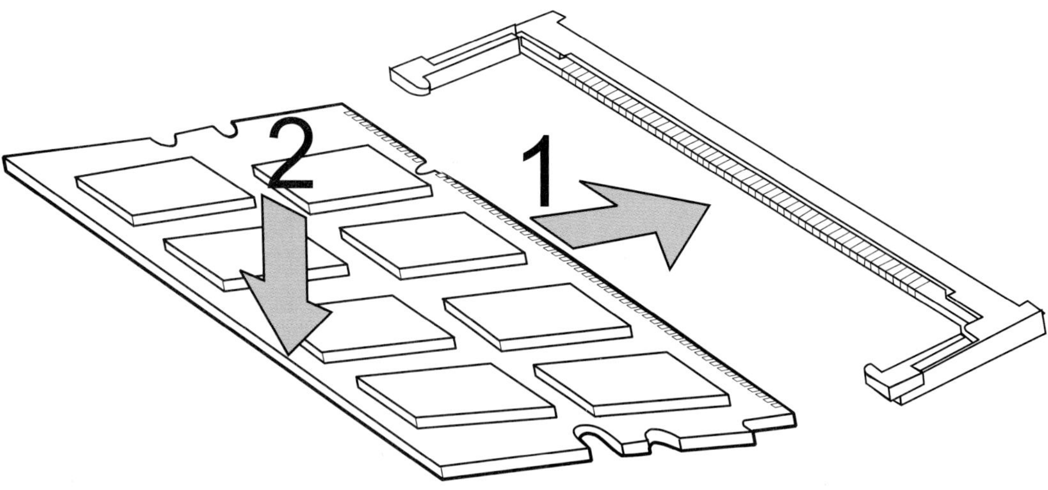

Figure 3.16 Ribbon Cables Used in Notebook Computers with Clasp Locked and Unlocked

Mobile processors look very similar to desktop processors, yet they have been customized for the mobile environment. The differences include extra power-saving features, higher maximum operating temperatures, less heat dissipation, and smaller package/footprint size. Today, processors come in several types of packages. The most common two are micro-PGAs, which is inserted into a socket, and micro-BGA, which is soldered onto the motherboard. Micro-PGAs can be removed by first removing the heat sink and fan and releasing the processor by turning a screw or pulling a lever.

To expand the capability of notebook computers, notebooks can use PC cards, Mini-PCI cards, and/or a docking station. PC cards are expansion cards created specifically for portable systems. Different from expansion cards installed internally, PC cards slide into sockets located on the side of the computer. To remove them, you press a button to eject the card. Mini-PCI cards are small cards that are located inside the notebook. Since the entire notebook must be opened to access the Mini-PCI cards, only the manufacturer or trained technician can access them. The docking station, also known as a port replicator is a device that remains on a desk, and the notebook computer connects to it by sliding into place. The docking station allows you to connect a full-size monitor and keyboard, and it will provide additional ports. Some will even allow full-size expansion cards to be used.

3.4 FIELD-REPLACEABLE UNITS (FRUs)

A **field-replaceable unit (FRU)** is any device that can be easily replaced in the field on a service call. No soldering or special equipment is needed to replace the component. FRUs include monitors, keyboards, most microprocessors, most RAM, motherboards, and expansion cards.

When a device is found to be faulty, the entire component (FRU) is replaced. Some computer technicians can do electronic repair, but there are several reasons why isolating and fixing a faulty electronic component (such as an integrated chip, capacitor, transistor, or resistor) on a circuit board is not cost effective. First, most electronic components require special skills or equipment to measure or replace. In addition, electronic documentation is not available for most circuit boards, and replacement components are not always obtainable. Finally, the labor to make such a repair costs more than a replacement device. Therefore, if you find a faulty power supply or video card, it is best to replace the failed item.

Before replacing any FRU, you should do the following:

- Confirm that all cables and connections are connected properly and securely.
- Verify BIOS setup settings.
- Verify that all drivers are installed properly.
- Check for an updated BIOS image and drivers.

When an older machine fails and you need to repair the PC and replace parts, it may be better to replace the machine. In addition, when the operating system or applications become damaged or corrupted, it may be easier and quicker to reload the entire software on the machine.

SUMMARY

1. A port is a plug-in socket that enables an external device, such as a printer, to be attached to the computer.
2. To make the PC more configurable and expandable, it has expansion cards (circuit boards) that are inserted into expansion slots on the motherboard.
3. Expansion cards, identified by type of port and cable connector, can be used to connect drivers, I/O ports (parallel ports, serial ports, and game ports), mice, speakers, and monitors.
4. SIMMS and DIMMs, consisting of DIPs soldered onto a small circuit board, are the most common forms of RAM.
5. Pin 1 of a DIP chip and socket is usually identified with a notch on one end.
6. To remove a SIMM, pull apart the two clips located at the ends, tilt the SIMM backward to a 45° angle, and pull it out.
7. To install a RAM chip, insert the SIMM into a slot at a 45° angle. Make sure that the SIMM is seated properly in the slot. Push the SIMM until it clicks into place.
8. To install a DIMM or RIMM, line up the notches on the module with the plastic tabs located in the socket. Once the notches are lined up, apply pressure to the module by pushing it into the socket until it is firmly seated.

9. When connecting ribbon cables, the cable must be correctly oriented.
10. Pin 1 of the cable (marked with a red or blue stripe along one edge) must be connected to pin 1 of the drive and pin 1 of the cable connector on the motherboard or expansion card.
11. Pin 1 of the drive is designated by a small 1 or 2 printed on the drive's circuit board, and pin 1 of the expansion card or motherboard connector can be identified by a small 1 or 2 printed on the circuit board or by a square solder (other pins have a round solder).
12. Motherboards are held in place by screws and white plastic or brass standoffs.
13. When connecting the two power connectors known as P8 and P9, make sure that the ground wires (black wires) are in the middle.
14. A field-replaceable unit (FRU) is any device that can be easily replaced in the field on a service call.
15. When a device is found faulty, the entire component (FRU) is replaced.
16. Before working on a notebook computer, you should first unplug the ac power and then remove the battery.
17. Today, notebook computers will have RAM that is soldered onto the motherboard or use small circuit boards called SO-DIMMs, which are usually accessed from a panel located on the bottom of the notebook or underneath the keyboard.
18. Mobile processors look very similar to desktop processors, yet they have been customized for the mobile environment. The differences include extra power-saving features, higher maximum operating temperatures, less heat dissipation, and smaller package/footprint size.
19. To expand the capability of notebook computers, notebooks can use PC cards, Mini-PCI cards, and/or docking stations.
20. The parallel port (two-row, 25-pin female D connector) is used primarily to connect printers to the computer.
21. The serial port (two-row, 25-pin D connector or two-row, 9-pin male D connector) is used primarily to connect external modems, mice, and miscellaneous devices.
22. The game port (two-row, 15-pin female D connector) is used to connect joysticks to the computer.
23. The VGA or Super VGA port (three-row female D connector) is used to connect VGA and Super VGA monitors to the computer.

QUESTIONS

1. A 25-pin female D connector on a computer is used to connect a
   a. digitizer. b. modem.
   c. scanner. d. printer.
2. The parallel printer port on a PC is usually what type of connector?
   a. 9-pin male D b. 15-pin female D
   c. 25-pin male D d. 25-pin female D
3. Which port is usually used to connect printers?
   a. parallel b. serial
   c. game d. video
4. Which of the following ports would you use to connect a mouse?
   a. parallel b. serial
   c. game d. video
5. Before opening a computer, removing a component, or installing a component, you should make sure that
   a. the computer is off.
   b. the keyboard is unplugged.
   c. the monitor is unplugged.
   d. the modem is unplugged.
6. Which of the following describes an IC chip that resembles a bug with many legs on the two long sides?
   a. SIPP b. SIMM
   c. DIMM d. DIP
   e. ESD
7. Pin 1 of the DIP is designated by
   a. a notch on one end.
   b. a red or blue stripe.
   c. a square solder.
   d. a small 1 printed on the DIP.
8. When inserting SIMMs, which of the following statements is *false?*
   a. When inserting SIMMs, gently slide the SIMM into the SIMM socket at a 45° angle. Then tilt it up gently until it clicks into place.
   b. When inserting SIMMs, make sure *not* to bend or mangle the plastic or metal clips that hold the SIMM in place.
   c. When inserting SIMMs, make sure *not* to break the plastic or metal braces that hold the SIMM in place.
   d. When inserting a SIMM, you do not have to worry about ESD since SIMMs are on a circuit board.
9. When pulling a DIP or other chip from its socket, you should
   a. pull the chip with a chip puller.
   b. use a small screwdriver and gently pry on one side, then gently pry on the other side, and repeat this process until the chip is free.
   c. press first, then pull gently.
   d. have the computer on.

10. An IDE hard drive ribbon cable has __________ pins.
    a. 34 b. 40
    c. 50 d. 68
11. A ribbon cable has a red stripe along one edge. What does this mean?
    a. This is the positive lead.
    b. This is the negative lead.
    c. The cable carries hazardous voltage.
    d. The conductor with the stripe connects to pin 1 of the connector.
12. When connecting the power connectors to the motherboard, the connectors should
    a. have the black cables together.
    b. have the black cables on the outside.
    c. have the black cables on the right.
    d. have the red cables on the right.
13. When inserting an expansion card into an expansion bus, you should
    a. force it into the slot.
    b. have the PC turned on.
    c. wear an ESD wrist strap.
    d. carry it down the hallway in your hand.
14. Which of the following is *not* a FRU?
    a. math coprocessor b. video card
    c. hard drive d. resistor
15. Which of the following is a FRU (choose all that apply)?
    a. power supply
    b. keyboard
    c. a SIMM
    d. a DIP on a SIMM
16. Suppose that you have a failure caused by one of several possible field-replaceable units (FRUs). What should you do after turning off the power?
    a. Replace the indicated parts one at a time until the problem is resolved and return the unused FRUs to stock.
    b. Replace all of the indicated FRUs at once and return the machine to the customer if the problem is resolved.
    c. Replace the indicated parts one at a time until the problem is resolved; if the motherboard is one of the FRUs, replace it first.
    d. If multiple FRUs are indicated, then software is the most likely source of the problem.
17. Look at the accompanying figure and identify the following:
    a. PCI slots
    b. AGP slot
    c. DIMM slots
    d. CPU socket
    e. ports
    f. IDE connectors
    g. floppy disk drive connector
    h. ATX power supply connector
    i. CMOS battery

18. Look at the accompanying figure and identify the following:
    a. parallel port b. serial port c. game port d. audio ports
    e. USB ports f. keyboard port g. mouse port

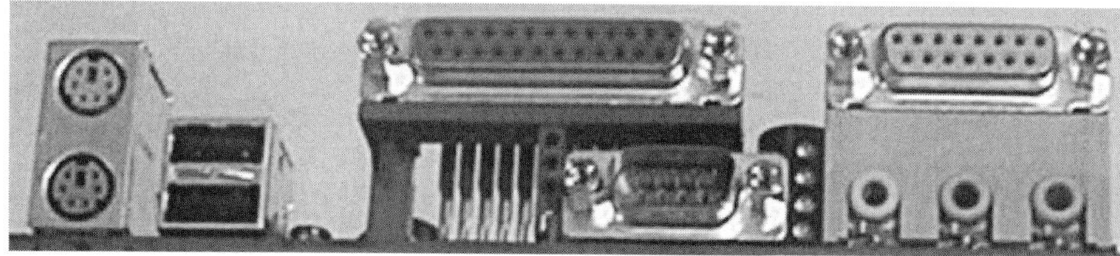

HANDS-ON EXERCISES

Exercise 1: Disassembling and Reassembling the PC

Be sure to follow ESD preventative measures.

1. If your PC has a manual, read it.
2. If your PC does not have a manual, find it on the Internet and download it. Note: Not all PCs have manuals. If a PC is assembled by a company or vendor and is without a name brand, it will not have a manual.
3. If you have a manual for your motherboard, find and read your motherboard manual.
4. If you do not have a manual for your motherboard, find it on the Internet and download it.
5. Look to see if you have any manuals for your expansion cards. If you do, browse through them.
6. Identify all the ports on the back of the computer. If any device is connected to the port, identify the device.
7. Open the PC.
8. Identify the type of hard drives used in your system (IDE or SCSI).
9. Identify pin 1 of the ribbon cables and the drives. Disconnect and remove all ribbon cables from the PC. Notice the number of pins each connector has.
10. Disconnect the power connectors to the drive and remove the drives. Notice how the connectors connect to the drive.
11. Remove all expansion cards from the expansion slots. As you take each one out, identify each card (this can be done by looking at the connectors and ports on the card) and the type of expansion card.
12. Remove the SIMMs, DIMMs, or RIMMs from the motherboard.
13. Notice how the power connectors to the motherboard are connected. If you have an AT power supply with two power connectors that stand next to each other, notice that the black or ground cables are next to each other. If you have an ATX power supply, you should have only one primary cable. Some ATX power supplies may have some smaller secondary power cables. Disconnect the power connector or connectors from the motherboard.
14. Most systems will have small cables from the chassis or case that connect to the motherboard. These connectors include the power on/off switch, power LED, and HDD LED. Find them and record on a piece of paper how they are connected. As you disconnect them, notice that pin 1 of these cables is usually designated with a small embossed triangle.
15. Look for the screws that hold the motherboard in place. Remove the screws. Remove the motherboard. Notice the plastic spacers on the motherboard or the brass or plastic spacers on the case that prevent the motherboard from shorting against the case.
16. Find and identify the processor (you may need to remove the thermal solution) and system ROM BIOS chip. Identify CMOS battery.
17. If it is a socketed processor, determine the orientation of the processor. Remove the processor. Look at the pins of the processor. Notice if any of the corner pins are missing and then compare the missing pins to the socket. If it is a slotted processor, remove the processor and notice how the processor is keyed so that it will go in only one way.
18. Reinstall the processor. If you are using a Zif socket, it should fall into the socket without you pressing on it. If you have to press on it, make sure that the processor is oriented correctly. If you removed the thermal solution, replace the thermal solution.
19. Reinstall the motherboard in the PC and reinsert the memory chips onto the motherboard. Be careful not to mangle the clips or plastic backstops.

20. Reattach the small cables that come from the chassis.

    NOTE: If you don't connect the power on/off switch cable, you will not be able to boot your system using the on/off switch.

21. Reconnect the power connectors to the motherboard. Make sure that the cables are oriented correctly. If you are using an AT power supply, make sure the cables are black to black.
22. Insert all the expansion cards.
23. Reinstall the drives and reconnect the ribbon cables and power connectors.
24. Close and test the PC.

Exercise 2: Identifying Parts of the PC

Get various expansion cards from your instructor and identify them.

Exercise 3: Identifying Error Codes and Messages

1. Make sure the computer is off. Insert a POST card (if available) into one of the empty expansion slots.
2. Unplug the keyboard. Turn on the system and record what happens. If a series of beeps occurs or a message appears on the screen, look up the meaning of the beeps or message. If a POST code is shown on the POST card, look up the meaning of the code.
3. Turn off the computer and reconnect the keyboard.
4. Remove the video card. If the video card is built in, enter the CMOS setup program and disable the video. Turn on the system and record what happens. If a series of beeps occurs or a message appears on the screen, look up the meaning of the beeps or message. If a POST code is shown on the POST card, look up the meaning of the code.
5. Turn off the computer and reinsert the video card.
6. Remove the SIMM, DIMM, or RIMM, turn on the system, and record what happens. If a series of beeps occurs or a message appears on the screen, look up the meaning of the beeps or message. If a POST code is shown on the POST card, look up the meaning of the code.
7. Turn off the computer and reinsert the SIMM, DIMM, or RIMM.
8. Disconnect the hard drive cable from the hard drive. Turn on the system and record what happens. If a series of beeps occurs or a message appears on the screen, look up the meaning of the beeps or message. If a POST code is shown on the POST card, look up the meaning of the code.
9. Turn off the computer and connect the hard drive cable to the hard drive backward. Turn on the system and record what happens. If a series of beeps occurs or a message appears on the screen, look up the meaning of the beeps or message. If a POST code is shown on the POST card, look up the meaning of the code.
10. Turn off the computer and reconnect the hard drive cable to the hard drive correctly.
11. Disconnect the floppy drive cable from the 3 1/2-in. floppy disk drive. Turn on the system and record what happens. If a series of beeps occurs or a message appears on the screen, look up the meaning of the beeps or message. If a POST code is shown on the POST card, look up the meaning of the code.
12. Turn off the computer and connect the floppy drive cable to the 3 1/2-in. floppy drive backward. Turn on the system and record what happens. If a series of beeps occurs or a message appears on the screen, look up the meaning of the beeps or message. If a POST code is shown on the POST card, look up the meaning of the code.
13. Turn off the computer and reconnect the floppy drive cable to the floppy drive correctly.

Exercise 4: Reading Motherboard Documentation

1. Go to http://www.intel.com and search for and download the Quick Reference Guide for the Intel D845BG desktop board.
2. Determine the processors that the D845BG desktop board supports.
3. Determine the type of power supply that is needed for the D845BG desktop board.
4. The D845BG desktop board supports several fans. Determine which fan connector is used for the processor fan.
5. Read the instructions on how to install the desktop board.
6. Read the instructions on how to install the processor.
7. Go to http://www.intel.com and search for and download the Technical Product Specification for the Intel D845BG desktop board.

8. Determine the type of processor, the type of processor socket, and the speed of the system bus for the D845BG desktop board.
9. Determine the number and type of RAM sockets.
10. Determine the maximum amount of RAM and the largest DIMM that the D845BG desktop board will support.
11. Determine the speed of the SDRAM that the D845GB desktop board will support.
12. Determine the chipsets used on the D845BG desktop board.
13. Determine the number of add-in card PCI connectors used on the D845BG desktop board.
14. The D845BG has audio ports on the back of the motherboard. What color is the audio line out port?

CHAPTER 4

Microprocessors

Topics Covered in This Chapter

Introduction

A **microprocessor,** also known as the CPU (central processing unit) or processor, is an integrated circuit that acts as the brain of the computer. Unlike most integrated chips, the processor is programmable, so it can be made to perform many tasks. Through the years, the CPU has gone through many changes. Today's processors are far more complicated compared to the chips used in the 1981 IBM PC and are at least a few thousand times faster.

Objectives

1. Explain what the processor is and how it works.
2. Describe how the processor interfaces with the rest of the computer.
3. List and explain the characteristics that determine the speed and performance of the processor.
4. Differentiate between RISC and CISC chips.
5. State the characteristics of a processor.
6. List the characteristics of today's common processors from Intel, AMD, and VIA.
7. Describe each processor's operating mode.
8. Explain what a math coprocessor is and how it aids the processor.
9. Describe the various multimedia instruction sets used by the processor including MMX, SSE, SSE2, and SSE3, 3DNow!
10. Identify the different ways to cool a processor.
11. Install and remove a processor.
12. Describe and troubleshoot problems caused by a faulty processor.
13. List the requirements of setting up a dual- or multiprocessor system.

4.1 PROCESSORS

A **processor,** also known as a **microprocessor** or **CPU (central processing unit),** is an integrated circuit that acts as the brain of a computer. It is made from a silicon wafer (see figure 4.1) consisting of many transistors that act like tiny on/off switches. See figures 4.2 and 4.3. Unlike most integrated chips, a microprocessor is programmable, so it can be made to perform many tasks. The older 8088 and 8086 processors had 29,000 transistors; the newer Pentium 4 processor has 42 million or more transistors.

The processor has three major areas, including the input/output unit (or I/O unit), the control unit, and the arithmetic/logic unit (or ALU). The ALU does the actual processing of data, whereas the I/O unit links the processor to the rest of the computer. Its purpose is to carry software instructions and data into and out of the processor. The control unit controls the operation of the entire chip. See figure 4.4.

Figure 4.1 Silicon Wafer

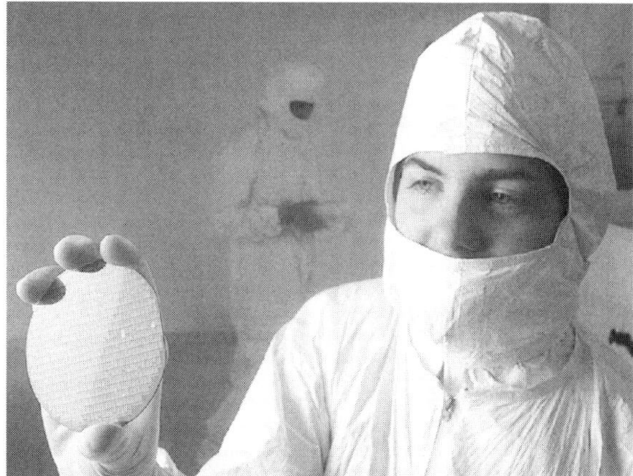

Figure 4.2 Pentium Processor with MMX Technology Without the Package

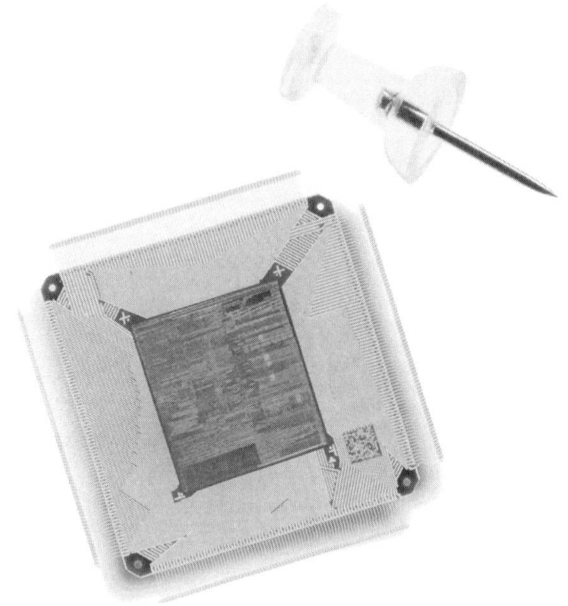

Figure 4.3 Intel Pentium Processor with MMX Technology Processor with Packaging

Figure 4.4 Inside the Processor

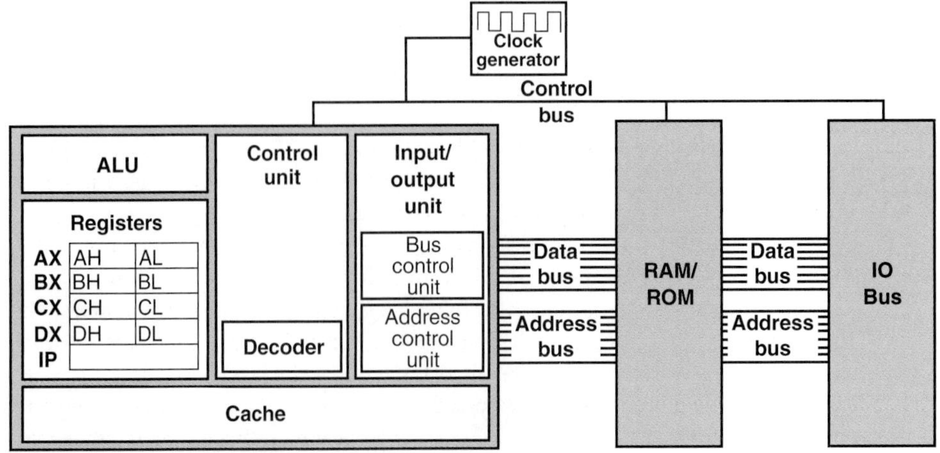

Table 4.1 The process technology determines the size of the transistors used in the processor.

Processor	Process Technology (μm)
8088	3
80286	1.5
80386	1
80486	0.8
Pentium	0.6 and 0.35
Pentium Pro	0.35
Pentium II	0.25
Pentium III	0.25, 0.18, and 0.13
Pentium 4	0.18, 0.13, and 0.09
Athlon	0.25, 0.18, and 0.13
Duron	0.18
Opteron	0.13 and 0.09
Athlon 64	0.13 and 0.09

4.1.1 Transistor Technology and Moore's Law

The size and spacing of the processor's transistors (silicon etchings) partially determine the switching speed. The diameter of transistors is measured in microns/micrometers; one micrometer (μm) is one-millionth of a meter. A human hair is, on average, 30 μm in diameter. Smaller transistors can be packed more tightly in a given area. If they are closer together, there is less distance for the electrical signals to travel, creating a faster processor that runs cooler. For example, a mobile Pentium II processor using 0.25 μm technology running at 366 MHz dissipated 13.10 W. Yet a mobile Pentium II processor using 0.18 μm technology running at 400 MHz dissipated 9.8 W of power. Early processors, such as the 8088 processor, used transistors that were 3 μm in size. Today, the Pentium III and Pentium 4 processors use transistors that are only 0.18 and 0.13 μm (or smaller) in size. See table table 4.1.

Moore's law gives a better understanding of how the IC chip (including the microprocessor) has progressed over the years. In 1965 Gordon Moore, cofounder of Intel, stated that the number of transistors per square inch on integrated circuits had doubled and would continue to double every year since the integrated chip was invented. Since his prediction, the number of transistors per square inch has doubled every 12 to 18 months. In the 26 years since the invention, the number of transistors on a processor chip has increased more than 18,200 times—from 2,300 on the 4004 in 1971 to 29,000 for the 8086/8088 in 1978 to 42 million on the Pentium 4 processor in 2001. Between 1978 and 2001, the performance speed has increased more than 2,000 times. Moore and other experts expect Moore's law to hold for approximately two more decades, until technology restrictions prevent transistors from becoming any smaller.

4.1.2 Clock Speed

Clock speed is the speed at which the processor executes instructions; every computer contains an internal clock. More importantly, the clock synchronizes all the various components. If the components were not synchronized, they would get confused.

A computer works by using many on/off switches made up of transistors. A bit is transferred by an on/off switch. When a switch switches from on to off or off to on, it takes a small amount of time for the change to occur. If a circuit tries to read a signal when the switch is in transition, the circuit is confused, because it is not on or off. The clock cycle (tick) indicates when a circuit is supposed to do its next task, such as reading a signal or performing a calculation. See figure 4.5.

Clock speed frequency is expressed in **megahertz (MHz),** 1 MHz being equal to 1 million cycles per second, or **gigahertz (GHz),** 1 GHz being equal to 1 billion cycles per second. The faster the clock

Figure 4.5 A clock signal is used by the processor to indicate when it is to perform a task.

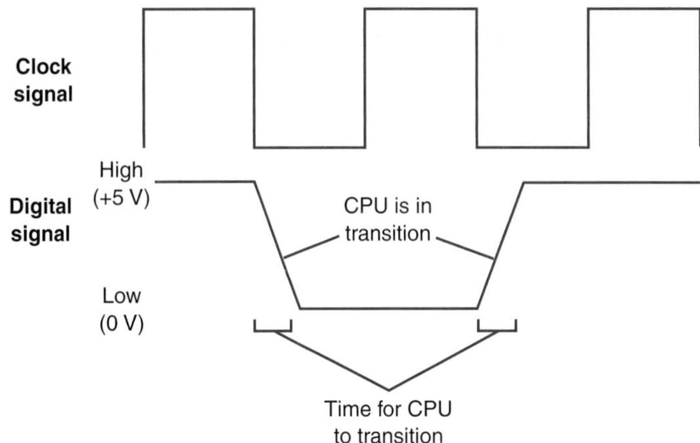

speed, the more instructions the microprocessor can execute per second. The IBM PC had a clock speed of 4.77 MHz; machines now exceed 3.4 GHz. The frequency of the clock and the time required for the transistors to switch from low to high or from high to low are related as follows:

$$f = \frac{1}{t} \text{ or } t = \frac{1}{f}$$

where t is time and f is frequency.

In a 4.77 MHz processor, the transistor has to transition within 1/4.77 MHz = 209.6 nanosecond (ns). In a 200 MHz processor, the transistor must transition within 1/200 MHz = 5 ns, and a 2 GHz processor must transition within 1/2 GHz = 0.5 ns. The maximum clock speed of the processor is determined primarily by the speed of the switching transistor.

Overclocking is the process of running the processor at a clock speed faster than specified. A clock signal that is too fast does not allow the transistors enough time to change states, so the processor will experience errors.

IMPORTANT NOTE

Some motherboards can accommodate several different processor speeds, which can be changed by using jumpers or DIP switches on the motherboard or by using the BIOS setup program. If you choose a speed that is too fast, the microprocessor may be damaged or produce errors, and its life span will usually be shortened. It may also void your warranty.

Intel provides a program called the Processor Frequency ID program for its processors. Besides identifying your processor, it can also determine if certain Intel processors are being overlocked (Pentium III, Pentium 4, and newer Intel Celeron processors). This program can also determine if you purchased a remarked processor, where the processor was manufactured at one speed, but it was intentionally modified to run at another. Because these processors are running out of specification, the processor could be unreliable or its life could be shortened. For more information and to download the Processor Frequency ID program, visit the following website:

http://support.intel.com/support/processors/tools/frequencyid/index.htm

4.1.3 Registers

A **register,** located inside the processor, is a high-speed internal storage area that acts as the processor's short-term memory and work area. Data must first be put in a register before it is processed by the ALU. For example, if two numbers are to be added, they are put into two different registers and then added together by the ALU. The result is stored in one of the two registers. It can then be used for something else or stored in the RAM through the I/O unit for later use. In addition, the register can contain the address of a memory location where data is stored rather than the actual data itself.

Figure 4.6 This illegal operation in Windows shows the registers at the time the illegal operation occurred.

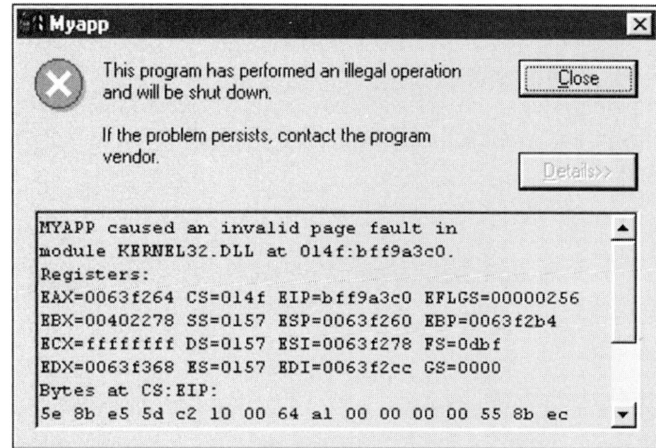

The number of registers and their sizes (word size, or number of bits) help determine the power and speed of the processor. For example, a 32-bit processor, such as the 386DX and 486, has 32-bit registers, which can manipulate 32-bit data. Of course, if software is not written to make use of the entire register or the extra registers, the processor will not perform at its peak.

The 8086 processor has fourteen 16-bit registers designed to store integers (whole numbers). The general-purpose registers include the AX, BX, CX, and DX registers. Although these registers can serve any purpose, they have designated uses. For example, the AX (accumulator) register is used for most arithmetic and logical computations, and the CX (count) register is used to count things.

A 16-bit register can be addressed as two independent 8-bit registers. For example, the AX register can be accessed as the AL and AH register. The H indicates the high byte (bits 8 through 15) and the L is the low byte (bits 0 through 7). Beginning with the 386, processors contain 32-bit registers (EAX, EBX, ECX, and EDX), which can also be used as 16-bit registers (AX, BX, CX, and DX) and 8-bit registers (AL, AH, BL, BH, CL, CH, DL, and DH).

NOTE: On occasion, you will see error messages that list the registers (AX, BX, CX, and DX or EAX, EBX, ECX, and EDX) and their contents (four hexadecimal digits or eight hexadecimal digits) at the time that error occurred. Although these values are not much use to a normal computer technician, they can be very helpful for programmers in tracing the cause of the problem. See figure 4.6.

Processors now also include registers specifically made to store floating-point values. A **floating-point number** is a number with a decimal point or a number that includes an exponent.

A floating-point number has three parts: the sign, the significant, and the exponent. A sign indicates if the number is positive or negative. A significant (sometimes called a mantissa) refers to the bits used to hold the fractional part. The more bits used for the mantissa, the more exactly or precisely it can represent fractional quantities. The exponent determines the order of magnitude of the significant. In other words, the exponent tells you how large it is. If the entire 80 bits are used to store a floating-point value, 64 bits store the mantissa value, 15 bits store the exponent, and 1 bit is used to designate if the value is positive or negative.

Besides holding data to be worked on, the instruction pointer contains the address of the next instruction to be executed. This way, the computer can keep track of what to do next.

4.1.4 The ALU

The **arithmetic/logic unit (ALU),** sometimes referred to as the execution unit, follows the instructions of the control unit and is the calculator part of the processor. It takes the instructions (i.e., performing mathematical operations such as adding, subtracting, multiplying, and dividing and logical comparisons) decoded by the control unit and executes those instructions. The results are eventually passed back out of the processor through the I/O unit.

Processors have multiple ALUs so that several instructions can be executed at the same time. Processors that can execute more than one instruction per clock cycle are said to be **superscalar.** There are two types of ALUs, integer units and floating-point units. The integer unit is a basic ALU, which carries out only the simplest mathematical operations on integers.

Floating-point units (FPU) are chips that specialize in floating-point mathematical calculations, typically at greater precision. Such units can also be referred to as numeric processing units. Although the floating-point unit can be at least 200 times faster than the ALU when performing calculations on floating-point values, the software has been written to take advantage of the FPUs. CAD programs, spreadsheets, and graphic manipulation programs written to make use of the FPU significantly increase performance.

Question:

If a computer does not have a math coprocessor or floating-point unit, can it still multiply two numbers with decimal points and exponents?

Answer:

Yes. Remember that a processor's ALU unit performs mathematical operations (including numbers with decimal points and exponents) and logical comparisons. Unfortunately, the processor is designed to work exclusively with integers. Because processors' ALUs do not have commands that work on floating-point numbers, the floating-point numbers have to be broken down into integers before an operation can be performed. This, of course, takes much longer than operations involving just integer calculations.

4.1.5 The Control Unit

The control unit is a clocked logic circuit that controls the entire chip, including the ALU. It translates and follows the instructions contained in an external program (such as the ROM BIOS, the operating system, or application software) and keeps track of which step of the program is being executed.

Every task that is done by the processor is completed simultaneously by the different parts of the processor. Some of the earlier microprocessors were not very efficient because they would bring in an instruction, decode it, process it, and output any results using the different parts of the microprocessor. Therefore, most of the microprocessor was idle while the different parts waited for the next instruction. For example, the 8088 or 8086 processor used 12 clock cycles to execute a single instruction, such as adding two numbers together.

Later processors used pipelines. **Pipelines** execute an instruction much like an assembly line. When one part of the processor is done with the instruction, it hands it off to the next part of the processor and starts on the next instruction. Today, all processors can perform multiple instructions per clock cycle. Pentium processors can add two numbers together in one clock cycle, whereas the Pentium Pro processor can add three numbers.

The processor's pipeline generally determines the clock speed its architecture can successfully support. The more states that are in a pipeline, the less each stage has to do, and the faster you can push data through. However, a long pipeline is beneficial only if you can run it at high speeds. If you cannot increase the speed of the assembly line, a long pipeline can actually hurt performance. In addition, if a pipeline is too long, your performance decreases with branch misprediction. To minimize the impact of branch misprediction, run at a faster speed.

With newer processors, the control unit has become more sophisticated. It will decide how to route signals between multiple processing units and coordinate the out-of-order execution and branch prediction.

Breaking up instruction execution into several smaller steps helps maintain the best performance by keeping the pipelines full and always moving. In programs, branches occur when decisions have to be made. Depending on the results of calculations and decisions made within a program, different pathways could be taken. Instead of waiting to see which pathway to take, the processor uses branch prediction to speculate which branch to use before it is actually needed in an attempt to keep the pipelines full. If it guesses correctly there is a significant performance increase, because it has already executed some of the needed instructions. If it is incorrect, it must discard the results executed from the speculated branch and execute the correct instruction.

Out-of-order execution means exactly what it sounds like—instructions are sometimes performed out of sequence. This also helps keep the pipelines full when an instruction cannot be performed until another instruction is completed or when the processor has to wait for the system to access RAM. Therefore, while the processor is waiting for the results, it will start on another instruction that does not depend on those results.

Performing out-of-order execution takes a lot of coordination. Sometimes two different instructions may refer to the same time. When this happens, the processor will produce confusing results and errors. To avoid this problem, the processor can rename registers dynamically. If it needs two registers with the same name, it just renames two registers with the same name.

4.1.6 CISC and RISC

The commands recognized by the processor are either **complex instruction set computer (CISC)** commands or **reduced instruction set computer (RISC)** commands. CISC commands are used in many earlier Intel processors; RISC commands are used in DEC Alpha, Power PC, and, to some extent, in recent Intel processors.

CISC commands are considered complex commands because they consist of several small commands (microcode) grouped together. As they are sent to the processor, the processor figures out how many bytes of processing room the commands require and then determines the correct way to load and store them. The final step is sending the commands to the decode unit, which translates them into the hard-wired microcode consisting of 1s and 0s. By grouping the commands together, CISC processors do not have to access the slower RAM as much.

RISC commands consist of smaller commands of the same size that are not grouped together. These can be performed in one clock cycle or less, and so the microprocessor does not have to determine the correct way to load and store the RISC commands and they do not have to go through a decode unit. Consequently, when the RISC and CISC processors perform the same tasks, the RISC processor can execute the several smaller commands faster than the CISC can perform one complex command. Because the decode unit is not required by the RISC microprocessor, it also consumes less power and generates less heat.

There is still considerable controversy among experts about the ultimate value of RISC architectures. Skeptics note that by making the hardware simpler, RISC architectures put a greater burden on the software. They argue that this is not worth the trouble because conventional processors are becoming increasingly fast and cheap anyway. In addition, to some extent, the argument is becoming moot because CISC and RISC implementations are becoming more and more alike. Many of today's RISC chips support as many instructions as yesterday's CISC chips. CISC chips now use many techniques formerly associated with RISC chips.

Because Intel introduced the P6 architecture with the Pentium Pro processor, instead of hard-coding the computer's CISC instructions set, Intel built a RISC processor to implement the entire ×86 instruction. Each CISC instruction is rebuilt out of the smaller and faster RISC instructions (micro-operations, or microops). To still provide backward compatibility, Intel added a decode unit that will translate the CISC instructions into RISC instructions.

4.1.7 Multimedia Instruction Sets

With the growth in graphics and presentation software, processor throughput often bogged down with the intensive calculations that were required. It became necessary to speed up certain computer-intensive processing and calculation procedures related to multimedia and communications applications. Although those processes typically occupy 10 percent or less of the overall application code, they can account for up to 90 percent of the program's execution time.

Most people think that MMX technology stands for multimedia extension or matrix math extensions. However, Intel claims that it doesn't really stand for anything. **MMX technology** consists of 57 multimedia instructions designed to improve video compression/decompression, image manipulation, encryption, and the I/O processor. In addition, it introduces **single instruction, multiple data (SIMD).** If you have several values sitting in a register (for example, four 16-bit values sitting in a 64-bit register), you can then have one instruction to perform the same function on multiple pieces of data at the same time. Therefore, SIMD helps reduce processor-intensive loops common with video, audio, graphics, and animation. Unfortunately, MMX had several drawbacks. First, it works only on integer values. Second, because it uses floating-point registers, time is lost if it has to process floating-point values and it has to change modes to do that. Lastly, only software especially written to call MMX instructions, so-called MMX-enabled software, can take advantage of the MMX instruction set.

By 1999, Intel had updated its multimedia extensions by introducing **SSE (streaming SIMD extensions)** for the Pentium III processor. SSE is an extension to MMX consisting of 70 new instructions to enhance advanced imaging, powerful 3D graphics (floating-point) processing, streaming video and audio, speech recognition, and added Internet features. One of the main benefits of SSE over MMX is that it supports single-precision (32-bit values), floating-point SIMD operations, which have posed a bottleneck in the 3D graphics processing. Much like MMX, SSE can operate on four floating-point values simultaneously. Like MMX, the SSE uses the floating-point registers. Therefore, SSE floating-point instructions can be mixed with MMX instructions with no performance penalties. In addition, SSE supports data prefetching, which is a mechanism for reading data into the cache before it is actually called for.

As with MMX, you must use SSE-aware applications to benefit from the SSE instructions. Most software companies writing graphics and sound-related software have updated those applications to be SSE-aware.

Streaming SIMD extensions 2, or SSE2, encompasses 144 new instructions, which include instructions for memory and cacheability management. The registers used with the SIMD and SSE commands extend from 64-bit to 128-bit registers, which doubles the amount of data that can be executed at once. In addition, it allows two double-precision, floating-point operations to be executed at the same time. Note: Double-precision, floating-point (64-bit floating-point values) helps accelerate financial, engineering, and scientific applications. SSE2 instructions allow software developers to have maximum flexibility to implement algorithms and provide performance enhancements when running software such as MPEG-2, MP3, 3D graphics, and so on.

In 2004 and 2005, Intel will extend its instruction sets with the streaming SIMD extensions 3 (SSE3) and the Tejas New Instructions (TNI). SSE3 will include 13 instructions for video encoding and thread synchronization and the rest for complex arithmetic operations, floating-point-to-integer conversions and SIMD floating-point operations. TNI includes new high-performance audio standards that support Dolby Digital, multistreaming, and improved speech recognition.

As with Intel, AMD also saw the need to optimize a processor's multimedia capability. AMD licensed MMX from Intel and then added 3DNow! technology to its processors. 3DNow! consists of 21 new instructions that use SIMD techniques to operate on multiple values at the same time. This allows greater performance for 3D graphics images, MPEG decoding, and other floating-point-intensive PC applications. Because 3DNow! offered enhanced 3D processing 9 months ahead of Intel's SSE, 3DNow! appealed to some people for 3D games and visualization programs.

Enhanced 3DNow! (3DNow+) adds 24 more instructions to the original 21 3DNow! instructions for a total of 45 new instructions. Although similar in capability, they are not compatible at the instruction levels; hence, that software written to support SSE will not support 3DNow!, and vice versa. 3DNow! professional technology incorporates 52 new instructions, which further extend the capability of 3DNow! technology and include Intel's SSE.

4.1.8 Input/Output Unit

The input/output unit manages three external connections: the data bus, the address bus, and the control bus. The **data bus,** which is managed by the bus control unit, actually carries the instruction and data into and out of the processor. The size of the data bus is measured in bits. Each wire allows 1 bit of information to flow into or out of the processor. A processor with a data bus size of 32 bits has 32 wires connected to it for data transfer. If a processor has more wires, it can transfer more data at the same time, making the processor faster. The Pentium, Pentium Pro, Pentium II, Pentium III, and Pentium 4 processors have a 64-bit data bus.

The signals of the address bus, controlled by the address control unit, determine where the data bus signals are going to or coming from. Like the data bus, it is also measured in bits. For every wire or bit added to it, the amount of RAM that is addressable by the microprocessor is doubled. The amount of RAM the address bus can access is determined by the following equation:

$$\text{Amount of RAM} = 2^{\text{size of address bus}}$$

Using this equation, a 32-bit address bus can address up to 4 GB of RAM, and a 36-bit address bus can address up to 64 GB of RAM.

Example 4.1:

If you have a 20-bit address bus, the largest binary number that you can access is 1111111111 1111111111. If this is converted to a decimal, it is equivalent to 1,048,575 bytes (1 MB) of RAM. Note: The highest address that can be accessed in a 20-bit address bus is 1,048,575, not 1,048,576. This is because the byte numbers begins at 0, not 1.

The **control bus** coordinates the data transfer between the microprocessor and another device. It contains the address status lines, the data control lines, power lines, interrupt control lines, and operating control lines, including the clock signal input.

4.1.9 System Bus and Wait States

Bus speed is the speed at which data moves on a bus. The only bus that connects directly to the processor is called the *system bus,* which is also referred to as the frontside bus. It connects the processor to the RAM and is actually the fastest bus within the system. Today, common bus speeds are 66, 100, 133, 200, 266, 400, and 533 MHz.

If a processor operates at 500 MHz but has a system bus speed of 100 MHz, the processor is operating at five times the speed of the bus. This factor is called the multiplier. If you multiply the system bus speed by the multiplier, you get the processor speed.

$$\text{Processor speed} = \text{memory bus speed} \times \text{multiplier}$$

Using jumpers, DIP switches, or the BIOS setup program, you set the system bus speed or bus clock and use other jumpers, DIP switches, or the BIOS setup program to set the multiplier (also known as the bus ratio). With some motherboards and some newer processors, when you insert the processor into the processor socket or slot, it will automatically set the correct bus speed and multiplier, which in turn will set the correct processor speed. It is also worth mentioning that many processors have a locked multiplier, meaning they cannot be changed.

As processors have become faster and faster, the system bus has become one of the chief bottlenecks in a modern PC, and it greatly affects the overall performance of the system. For example, the Pentium II processor started out at 233 MHz, yet the system bus communicated only at 66 MHz. Therefore, the processor ran 3.5 times faster than the RAM. With the Pentium III processor running at 1 GHz and having a 133 MHz system bus, the processor is running 7.5 times faster than the memory.

The evolution from the 8-bit bus to the 64-bit bus and the increase in bus speeds have been for the purpose of increasing bandwidth. Intel's dual independent bus design on the P6 architecture was implemented to "free up" some bandwidth by moving the L2 cache onto its own bus. This bus is called the backside bus.

Memory bandwidth may be a major consideration for system performance because the processor can theoretically handle the total amount of data equal to the clock speed times the bus width. This means that a 233 MHz processor with a 64-bit memory bus has the ability to handle 1.8 gigabytes per second (GBps) of data under ideal conditions, but a 66 MHz system bus limits the bandwidth to 533 megabytes per second (MBps).

Because the processor is the fastest component in the computer, the processor occasionally has to wait for other components to catch up. The catch-up period is called a *wait state,* during which the processor lies idle. If the processor is set to zero wait states, it is running at maximum speed without any timeouts to compensate for slow components such as memory. If the processor is set to two wait states, it will wait two clock cycles when it has to communicate with the memory.

The only way to provide data at the rate at which it can be accepted by the processor is to increase the memory bus speed to be equal to the processor speed. In actual practice, however, only heavily loaded multitasking, multiuser systems would be able to utilize the full bandwidth. In fact, most desktop systems will rarely utilize even 50 percent of the available bandwidth.

4.1.10 Cache

Cache memory is a special ultrafast memory that acts as a buffer between the microprocessor and the slower RAM. The data stored in the cache is based on an old computer science principle stating that if the processor recently referred to a location in memory, it is likely that it will refer to it again in the near future. Using a cache to hold recently used memory values saves the processor from going to memory each time to reload the values.

A special circuit called a cache controller attempts to keep the cache filled with the data or instructions that the processor is most likely to need next. If the information the processor requests next is held within the static RAM of the cache, it can be retrieved without wait states. When information is found in the RAM cache, it is called a cache hit. When information is found not in the RAM cache but in the RAM, it is called a cache miss.

In general, there are two levels of cache memory; in some cases there are three levels. The primary cache is known as the L1 cache. It is usually the smallest cache, ranging from 16 to 64 KB, and is the one electrically closest to the processor's core logic, built into the processor itself.

Since the 486DX processor, all Intel processors have had an L1 internal cache built into the processor. In the Pentium processor, the data path between the internal cache and the rest of the processor is 16 bytes (256 bits) wide, allowing for extremely fast retrieval of data. If the processor finds data in the L1 cache, it can retrieve the data with no wait states.

Although the L1 cache is faster, the L2 cache is typically much larger than the L1 cache, ranging from 64 KB to 4 MB. It is used when the data does not fit in the L1 cache. On earlier systems, the L2 cache was on the motherboard. Therefore, the L1 cache was referred to as internal cache and the L2 cache was referred to as the external cache. Today, the L2 cache is internal to the processor, which takes about three or four processor cycles to access. Besides the amount of cache and the speed, the only difference between the two caches is the caching protocols and technology that specifies how the data will be stored and retrieved.

As more and more processors begin to include L2 cache into their architectures, L3 cache is the name for the extra cache built into motherboards between the processor and the main memory. Quite simply, what was once L2 cache on motherboards now becomes L3 cache when used with processors containing built-in L2 caches. You should note that some processors such as the Intel Itanium and some Intel Xeon processors do include their L3 cache on the processor.

Most systems offer 256 KB or to 1 MB of RAM cache. Tests done by ZD Labs found that by adding 256 KB of pipelined-burst L2 cache to a Pentium system with 16 MB of EDO DRAM, performance increased 36 percent. Although increasing the RAM cache to 512 KB does increase PC performance, the increase is not as dramatic for the second 256 KB as for the first 256 KB.

Question:

How much cache should you have?

Answer:

On processors with 256 KB of cache, studies have shown that the cache will receive a cache hit rate of at least 90 percent. Unfortunately, as processors continue to increase in speed and the working set size of mainstream applications grows larger, cache implementations must be constantly modified and tuned. At some point, simply adding more cache (or more cache levels) reaches a point of diminishing returns and may even begin to reduce performance.

Question:

When should you have a bigger cache?

Answer:

Significant improvement can be seen with larger caches on workstations and servers that are working with large data sets such as large databases and heavy graphics applications. For example, moving from a 512 KB L2 cache to a 1 MB L2 cache also increases the performance from 10 to 25 percent, depending on the application and load.

Different RAM caches use different methods for copying instructions and data into the cache. The method used depends on the amount of RAM cache, how it is arranged and addressed, and how information is found and accessed in the cache. Today, most PCs use set associative.

In a multitasking environment, such as Windows, you are running multiple programs at the same time. If you cache one program or memory area and you switch to another program (which is what occurs in Windows many times per second), all the information that was previously cached is useless, and the system must go to the slower RAM to find all information.

To overcome this limitation, set associative cache maps the RAM into several smaller cache areas. Each cache area can cache a memory area or program. Therefore, when a processor has eight-way cache associativity, it can cache up to eight programs at the same time. Therefore, in a multitasking environment, as you switch between programs, there is still a good chance that you can find the needed information in the cache. In addition, this form of RAM cache is even faster because each cache can be checked simultaneously by the cache controller.

4.1.11 Voltage Regulators

A voltage regulator is a small device or circuit that regulates the voltage fed to the processor. Most PCs generate power at 5 V, but most processors require a voltage below 3.5 V. The voltage regulator's job is to reduce the 5 V signal to the lower voltage required by the processor. Typically, voltage regulators are surrounded by head sinks because they generate significant heat.

Pentium processors with MMX actually require two voltage regulators because the processors use two different voltages, one for the internal (core) voltage and one for the I/O drivers at 3.3 V. Today, some voltage regulators, particularly those packaged as voltage regulator modules (VRM), are voltage ID (VID) programmable, which means that the processor can program the voltage regulator to provide the correct voltage during power-up.

When choosing a motherboard for a processor, specifically for processors designed for workstation or server applications, you must pay attention to which version of the VRM that the motherboard uses. For example, to use the newer Pentium III processors based on .13 μm process technology, you must use VRM 8.5. In addition, when installing a single processor into a dual- or multiprocessor motherboard, the empty processor slot or socket may require a VRM.

4.1.12 Processor Operating Modes

The IA-32 architecture (including the Intel Pentium, Pentium II, Pentium II Xeon, Pentium III, Pentium III Xeon, Pentium 4, Xeon, and Celeron processors) supports four operating modes:

- Real-address mode
- Protected mode
- Virtual 8086 mode
- System-management mode (SMM)

Real-address mode, introduced with the 80286 processor, is a mode that provides backward compatibility for those programs written for the 8088 and 8086 processors. It provides the programming environment of the Intel 8086 processor, with a few extensions or commands to change to the other modes. In other words, it pretends to be a 8086 processor. Unfortunately, it also inherited the limitations of the 8086 in that it recognizes only 1 MB of RAM and it can execute only 16-bit instructions using 16-bit registers. When you first turn on your computer or you perform a power reset, the processor starts in real-address mode.

Protected mode is the native operating mode of the processor. Although DOS is not designed to take advantage of these features, later versions of DOS can run in protected mode using special drivers (such as HIMEM.SYS). More sophisticated operating systems, such as Windows 95, Windows 98, Windows Me, Windows NT, Windows 2000, Windows XP, and UNIX (including Linux), have built-in support for protected mode.

In protected mode all instructions and architectural features, including the 32-bit instructions, provide the highest performance and capability. In addition, this mode can recognize RAM above 1 MB (extended memory). This is the recommended mode for all new applications and operating systems. In protected mode, the processor can run multiple programs in RAM and isolate them so that one program does not interfere with another. As the computer runs, the processor switches from one program to another so that computer can execute several programs at once (multitasking).

Lastly, protected mode allows for virtual memory. Virtual memory is hard drive space pretending to be RAM. Even though the hard drive is much slower than RAM, allocating part of it to virtual memory does permit the running of programs that could not be run before because of memory constraints. Intel processors use demand paging, which swaps data between the RAM and disk only on the demand of the processor. It does not try to anticipate the needs of the processor.

The **virtual 8086 mode,** sometimes considered a quasi-operating mode of the protected mode, allows the processor to execute 8086 software in a protected, multitasking environment. It does this by dividing the RAM into several "pretend" 8086 machines, each consisting of 1 MB of RAM. The processor then switches rapidly between the different virtual (pretend) machines so it appears that all the machines are working at the same time (multitasking). The advantage of a virtual machine is that if one of the machine goes down, the processor can terminate that machine without affecting the other virtual machines.

As Intel has put faster and more powerful processors in laptop computers, it has created power-management circuitry. This circuitry enables processors to conserve energy and lengthen battery life. **System-management mode (SMM)** provides an operating system with a transparent mechanism for implementing power management. It allows the user to specify time intervals after which the processor will be partially or fully powered down. It also supports the suspend/resume features that allows for instant power on and power off, used mostly with laptop computers. These settings are normally controlled using the system's CMOS setup program or through the operating system (for example, the power manager applet in the Window's Control Panel).

With the introduction of the Intel 64-bit extension technology and AMD's x64 technology, new operating mode we also introduced. Intel refers to its operating mode as IA-32e, which includes two submodes:

- **Compatibility mode**—Enables a 64-bit operating system to run most existing legacy 32-bit software.
- **64-bit mode**—Enables a 64-bit operating system to run applications written specifically to access 64-bit address space. In the 64-bit submode of 64-bit extension technology, applications can access a 64-bit flat linear addressing, additional general-purpose registers, new streaming SIMD registers, and a 64-bit-wide general-purpose register and instruction pointer.

Before moving on, we need to discuss the 386 protection mechanism. Processors since the time of the 386 processor have the **386 protection mechanism,** whereby it assigns data and instructions to a privilege ring or level. See figure 4.7. The four privilege levels are 0, 1, 2, and 3. The privilege level 0 is the highest and level 3 is the lowest. Programs in ring 0 can access programs in all rings, but programs in ring 3 cannot access the programs in rings 0, 1, and 2. Today, some operating systems, such as Windows and Linux, assign the operating system kernel to level 0 and other programs to level 3. If a program becomes corrupted in ring 3, then the program will not affect the operating system.

Figure 4.7 386 Protection Mechanism

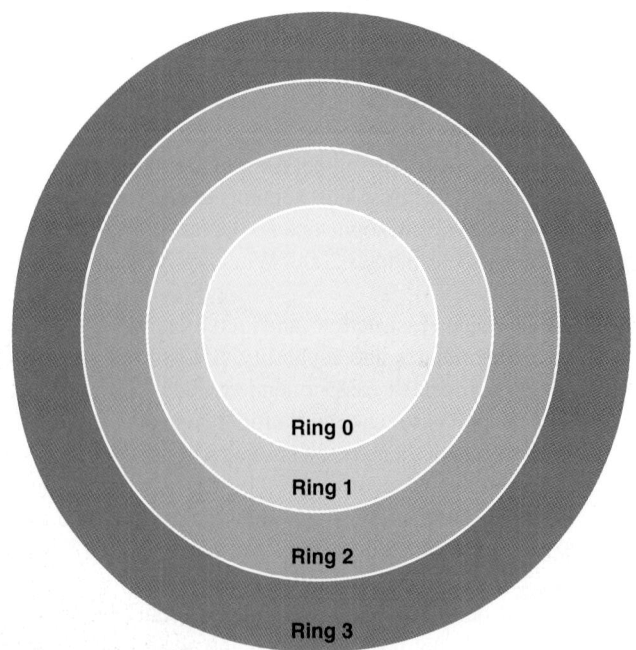

4.1.13 Future Processors

Although shrinking the transistors will get more difficult as time goes by, and as it becomes harder to increase the frequency because of transistor speed and thermal constraints, Intel and AMD are rethinking their strategies in making faster processors. Instead of increased clock speed, they are trying to get the processors to do more per clock cycle. Instead of increasing the number of control ALUs, future processors will have multiple processor cores in the same package, each with its own ALUs, control units, and input/output units.

4.2 INTEL PROCESSORS

Due to the quick success in 1981 of the IBM PC, which used an Intel processor, Intel became the manufacturer of choice for PC processors. Since the introduction of the 8086 processor in 1978, Intel has created many distinct versions of its processors.

4.2.1 The Pentium Processor

Intel introduced the Pentium processor in 1993. See figure 4.8. The Pentium processor uses two linked execution units. The first execution unit, similar to a 486DX with floating-point unit, has a single 32-bit pathway known as the U pipeline. The second execution unit, similar to a 486SX without floating-point unit, has a second 32-bit pathway known as the V pipeline. Because the processor has more than one pipeline, it can perform two tasks at the same time. Of course, to utilize this superscalar technology, software had to be recompiled for the Pentium processor.

The bus interface unit sends and receives data and code along two separate paths, each of which handles 64 bits at a time. One path leads to an 8 KB storage unit, or cache, used for data. The other path leads to an identical cache used only for code that tells the processor what to do with the data. The data and code stay in the caches until other parts of the processor need them. Other improvements included a floating-point unit that can process floating-point calculations three to five times faster than the 486DX and five levels of pipelining. Lastly, some of the internal links inside the processor are as wide as 256 bits.

The original Pentium processors running at 60 and 66 used a larger PGA-type package called socket 5. All other Pentiums used a staggered pin grid array (SPGA). The SPGA, as its name indicates, staggers the pins, enabling a higher pin density and a smaller case. Later, advancements in processor technology enabled manufacturers to redesign the classic ceramic SPGA package, using high-thermal plastics under the new name of plastic pin grid array (PPGA).

The second wave of Pentium chips used 3.3 V chips and 0.6 μm silicon traces. The third version of the Pentium chips ran at 2.9 V and eventually 2.5 V. In addition, it had 0.35 μm silicon traces, which

Figure 4.8 Intel® Pentium® Processor

allowed the chip to be smaller. The two standard sockets for the lower powered Pentium's were known as sockets 5 and 7. The socket 7 SPGA package continues to be the most popular package for most Pentium-class processors.

The 75 MHz Pentium processor became faster than the fastest motherboard. Pentium chips running at 75 to 100 MHz run at 1.5 times the speed of the motherboard's system bus, and Pentium processors running at 120 to 133 MHz run at 2.0 times the speed of the system bus. Pentium chips running at 150 to 166 MHz are running at 2.5 times the speed of the system bus, and faster processors run 3 times faster. All this demonstrates that the processor has improved much more than any other PC component. Today, the processor continues to run at a multiple of the speed of the system bus.

Although Pentium-class processors ran at voltages lower than 3.3 V, the processor still needed 3.3 V in order to communicate with other chips on the motherboard. To fulfill both needs, all later Pentium-class processors have split voltage. If you used a processor with split voltage in early socket 7 Pentium motherboards, the Pentium processor would not operate correctly because these boards fail to provide the proper voltage.

MMX technology was first introduced in the Pentium processor with MMX technology. It included four 64-bit MMX registers. In addition, it has a larger memory cache (32 KB), requiring fewer accesses to memory that is outside the processor. A Pentium processor with MMX technology can run a multimedia application that is written for MMX technology up to 60 percent faster than a Pentium processor without MMX. In addition, an MMX processor can run other applications 10 percent faster.

The Pentium OverDrive processor installed in a 486-based computer was known as the P24T. The Pentium OverDrive was a Pentium processor with a 32-bit external data bus and two 16 KB caches. Although the OverDrive chip is faster than a 486 processor, it is not as fast as a Pentium chip in a Pentium computer.

4.2.2 The P6 Architecture

The P6 architecture uses a longer pipeline than the Pentium processor. The pipeline is divided into three units: the in-order front unit, the out-of-order execution unit, and the in-order retirement unit. The in-order front unit brings and decodes the instructions in the correct program sequence. The execution unit determines the optimal order and executes the instructions. The retirement unit then saves the results of the instructions in the correct order.

Although the Pentium was a dual-pipelined processor, the P6 could handle four separate pipelines simultaneously. On average, this enabled the equivalent of three simultaneous processes. This is the reason that the processor can add three numbers during the time that Pentium processor can add two numbers.

To make the processor work more efficiently than previous processors, P6 architecture uses advanced algorithms (multiple-branch prediction, data flow analysis, and speculative execution) and a dual independent bus (DIB) architecture. The advanced algorithms are designed to keep the assembly lines working while they wait for certain parts of the processor to catch up. The DIB uses two buses (one from the processor to the RAM and one from the processor to the L2 cache) that can be accessed simultaneously.

With these features, the P6 architecture has approximately 50 percent higher performance than a Pentium processor of the same clock speed when running 32-bit programs (Windows 95, Windows 98, Windows Me, Windows NT, and Windows 2000). Unfortunately, the Pentium Pro ran slower than a Pentium processor when running 16-bit code (DOS and Windows 3.X). The Pentium Pro, Pentium II, Pentium III, and Intel Celeron processors are based on the P6 architecture.

Intel took a somewhat different approach in making the Pentium Pro chip compatible with the previous x86 processors. Instead of hard-coding the computer's CISC instruction set, Intel built a RISC processor to implement each x86 instruction. Therefore, each CISC instruction is rebuilt out of the smaller and faster RISC instructions. Consequently, each x86 instruction is called a RISC86 instruction.

The Pentium Pro processor is constructed with a dual-cavity pin grid array (PGA) package, which includes an internal 256 or 512 KB L2 RAM cache running at the full speed of the processor core. The connection from the processor to the memory controller and RAM is called the frontside bus (also referred to as the system bus). See figure 4.9, and tables 4.2 and 4.3.

Figure 4.9 Intel Pentium Pro Processor

Figure 4.10 Intel® Pentium® II Processor

The 0.25 μm Pentium II OverDrive is a chip-for-chip processor upgrade designed for Pentium Pro–based systems. The Pentium II OverDrive uses a socket 8 PGA and adds MMX functionality. Higher performance over the original Pentium Pro is achieved through a higher clock speed and double the amount of L1 and L2 cache. Unlike the Pentium II, the Pentium II OverDrive follows the tradition set by the Pentium Pro and operates its level 2 cache at the full frequency of the processor core.

The Pentium II processor uses the same P6 architecture as the Pentium Pro processor and includes MMX technology. It includes 512 KB of cache that runs at half the speed of the processor core. Instead of using a PGA package, it uses a single-edge contact (SEC) package, which has a single-edge connector that is inserted into slot 1 on the motherboard. The SEC cartridge uses a retention bracket or retention mechanism to hold the processor in place. See figure 4.10.

The SEC cartridge is covered with a metal shell that covers the top of the entire cartridge assembly. The back of the cartridge is called the thermal plate. It acts as a heat sink, although for most processors, it does not offer sufficient cooling by itself. Instead, it acts as a channel to route heat from the circuit elements of the processor to the outside, which can be more effectively removed with heatsinks and fans. Inside the SEC is a printed circuit board called the *substrate* that links together processor, the L2 cache, and the bus termination circuits.

Table 4.2 Intel Pentium Processors

Processor	Year Introduced	Package Types (Connector)	Frequency	Architecture	No. of Transistors (Process Technology)	Data Bus Size	Memory Bus Speed	Address Bus (Addressable Memory)	L1 Cache	L2 Cache	Comments
Pentium[1]	3/93	PGA (socket 4)	60 or 66 MHz	Super-scalar	3.1 mil (0.8 μ)	64-bit	Same as frequency	32-bit (4 GB)	16 KB	None	
Pentium[1]	3/94	SPGA (socket 5 or 7)	75, 90, 100, 120 MHz	Super-scalar	3.3 mil (0.6 μ)	64-bit	50, 60, 66 MHz	32-bit (4 GB)	16 KB	None	
Pentium[1]	3/95	SPGA (socket 7)	133, 150, 166, 200 MHz	Super-scalar	3.3 mil (0.35 μ)	64-bit	60 or 66 MHz	32-bit (4 GB)	16 KB	None	
Pentium[1] with MMX (P55C)	1/97	SPGA (socket 7)	133, 150, 166, 200, 233 MHz	Super-scalar	4.5 mil (0.35 μ)	64-bit	66 MHz	32-bit (4 GB)	32 KB	None	MMX

[1]Designed for a uniprocessor and dual-processing server system.

Table 4.3 Intel Processors Based on the P6 Architecture

Processor	Year Intro	Package Types	Frequency	Architecture	No. of Transistors (Process Technology)	Data Bus Size	Memory Bus Speed	Address Bus (Addressable Memory)	L1 Cache	L2 Cache	Additional Instruction Sets
Pentium Pro[2] (P6)	11/95	Dual-Cavity PGA (socket 8)	150, 166, 180, 200 MHz	P6	5.5 mil (0.35 μ)	64-bit	60 or 66 MHz	36-bit (64 GB)	16 KB	256 or 512 KB on die	
Pentium II[2] (Klammath)	5/97	SECC (slot 1)	233, 266, 300 MHz	P6	7.5 mil (0.35 μ)	64-bit	66 MHz	36-bit (64 GB)	16 KB data cache/16 KB instruction cache	512 KB half-speed 4-way discrete	MMX
Pentium II[2] (Deschutes)	1/98	SECC/ SECC2 (slot 1)	266, 300, 333, 350, 400, 450 MHz	P6	7.5 mil (0.25 μ)	64-bit	66 or 100 MHz	36-bit (64 GB)	16 KB data cache/16 KB instruction cache	512 KB half-speed 4-way discrete	MMX
Celeron (Covington)	4/98	SEPP (slot 1)	266, 300 MHz	P6	7.5 mil (0.25 μ)	64-bit	66 MHz	32-bit (4 GB)	16 KB data cache/16 KB instruction cache	None	MMX
Celeron (Mendocino)	8/98	SEPP (slot 1) or PPGA (PGA370)	300A, 333, 366, 400, 433, 466, 500, 533 MHz	P6	19 mil (0.25 μ)	64-bit	66 MHz	32-bit (4 GB)	16 KB data cache/16 KB instruction cache	128 KB on-die full-speed 4-way discrete	MMX
Celeron (Coppermine-128)	3/00	FC-PGA2 (PGA370)	566, 600, 633, 667, 700, 733, 766, 800, 850, 900, 950 MHz, 1.0, 1.1 GHz	P6	28.1 mil (0.18 μ)	64-bit	66 or 100 MHz	32-bit (4 GB)	16 KB data cache/16 KB instruction cache	128 KB on-die full-speed 4-way ATC	MMX SSE
Celeron (Tualatin)	10/01	FC-PGA and FC-PGA2 (PGA370)	1.2, 1.3, 1.4 GHz	P6	28.1 mil (0.13 μ)	64-bit	100 MHz	36-bit (4 GB)	16 KB data cache/16 KB instruction cache	256 KB on-die full-speed 8-way ATC	MMX SSE

Continued

Table 4.3 Continued

Processor	Year Intro	Package Types	Frequency	Architecture	No. of Transistors (Process Technology)	Data Bus Size	Memory Bus Speed	Address Bus (Addressable Memory)	L1 Cache	L2 Cache	Additional Instruction Sets
Pentium III[2] (Katmai)	2/99	SECC2 (slot 1)	450, 500, 550, 600 MHz	P6	9.5 mil ($0.25\ \mu$)	64-bit	100 or 133 MHz	36-bit (64 GB)	16 KB data cache/16 KB instruction cache	512 KB on-package half-speed 4-way discrete	MMX SSE
Pentium III[2] (Coppermine)	10/99	SECC2 (slot 1), FC-PGA and FC-PGA2 (PGA370)	500, 533, 550, 600, 650, 667, 700, 733, 750, 850, 866, 933 MHz, 1.0, 1.1 GHz	P6	28.1 mil ($0.18\ \mu$)	64-bit	100 or 133 MHz	36-bit (64 GB)	16 KB data cache/16 KB instruction cache	256 KB on-die full-speed 8-way ATC	MMX SSE
Pentium III (Tualatin)	10/01	FC-PGA2 (PGA370)	1.13, 1.2 GHz	P6	28.1 mil ($0.13\ \mu$)	64-bit	133 MHz	36-bit (64 GB)	16 KB data cache/16 KB instruction cache	256 KB on-die full-speed 8-way ATC	MMX SSE

Table 4.3 Continued

Processor	Year Intro	Package Types	Frequency	Architecture	No. of Transistors (Process Technology)	Data Bus Size	Memory Bus Speed	Address Bus (Addressable Memory)	L1 Cache	L2 Cache	Additional Instruction Sets
Pentium III-S[2] (Tualatin)	6/01	FC-PGA2 (PGA370)	1.13, 1.26, 1.4 GHz	P6	46 mil (0.13 μ)	64-bit	133 MHz	36-bit (64 GB)	16 KB data cache/16 KB instruction cache	512 KB on-die full-speed 8-way ATC	MMX SSE
Pentium II Xeon[1,2] (Drake)	6/98	SC-320 (slot 2)	400, 450 MHz	P6	7.5 mil (0.25 μ)	64-bit	100 MHz	36-bit (64 GB)	16 KB data cache/16 KB instruction cache	512/ KB/ 1 MB/2 MB on-package full-speed 4-way discrete	MMX
Pentium III Xeon[1,2] (Tanner)	3/99	SC-320 (slot 2)	500, 550 MHz	P6	9.5 mil (0.25 μ)	64-bit	100 MHz	36-bit (64 GB)	16 KB data cache/16 KB instruction cache	512 KB/ 1 MB/2 MB on-package full-speed 4-way discrete	MMX SSE
Pentium III Xeon[1,2] (Cascades)	10/99	SC-320 (slot 2)	600, 667, 700, 733, 800, 866, 900, 933 MHz, 1.0 GHz	P6	28 mil (0.18 μ)	64-bit	100 or 133 MHz	36-bit (64 GB)	16 KB data cache/16 KB instruction cache	512 KB/ 1 MB/2 MB on-die full-speed 8-way ATC	MMX SSE

[1]Includes Advanced Management Features designed for the server platform to monitor and protect the processor and its environment.
[2]Designed for a uniprocessor and dual-processing server system.

Figure 4.11 Intel® Pentium® III Processor in the SECC2 and FC-PGA Packages

The Pentium III, which starts at 450 MHz and goes above 1 GHz, supports 100 and 133 MHz bus speeds. The biggest performance increase comes from the Internet streaming SIMD extensions to improve performance for three-dimensional graphics, video performance, audio performance, and speech recognition.

Early Pentium III processors are based on the 0.25 μm technology, which used the discrete 512 KB L2 cache running at half the speed of the processor. The second version of the Pentium III processors is based on the 0.18 μm technology (sometimes referred to as Coppermine), which used a 256 KB L2 advanced transfer cache running at full speed. Because the advanced transfer cache is more efficient than discrete cache and it runs at full speed, the 256 KB L2 advanced transfer cache runs faster than the 512 KB L2 discrete cache. The newest version of the Pentium III is based on the 0.13 μm technology (sometimes referred to as Tualatin), which used a 256 KB L2 advanced transfer or the 512 KB L2 advanced transfer cache. Note: Because these use different voltages to run, you must have a motherboard that supports a specific processor.

The Pentium III processor can be found in the SECC2 package and flip-chip (FC-PGA) package. The SECC2 uses less casing and does not include the thermal plate. The FC-PGA looks very similar to the PPGA, except the die is on the top of the chip for better heat dissipation. The FC-PGA has 370 pins and therefore fits in a socket 370. See figure 4.11.

Intel also introduced the Pentium III processor in the FC-PGA2 package. The FC-PGA2 package is very similar to the FC-PGA package except the die is covered by an integrated heat spreader (IHS). With the use of the integrated heat spreader, the processor has a larger surface area to dissipate the heat, which allows the processor to use a smaller heat sink than required by the processor without the IHS.

The Pentium III processors include the Intel processor serial number. The processor serial number can serve as a means of identifying a system. Because the serial number has generated some concerns about consumer privacy and newer technology has become available, Intel has been chosen to remove the serial number in future processors.

The flagship of the Pentium II and III processor families includes the Pentium II Xeon and Pentium III Xeon processors. Physically, the Pentium II Xeon and Pentium III Xeon processors are about twice as tall as the standard Pentium II processor. They incorporate an L2 cache ranging from 256 KB to 2 MB, which operates at the same speed as the processor core. In addition, they have a 36-bit address that allows the processors to address up to 64 GB of RAM. Different from the Pentium II and III processors, the Xeon processors connect to the motherboard via slot 2 (also referred to as a 330-contact slot connector). Today's Pentium II Xeon and Pentium III Xeon processors are typically found in high-power workstations or servers and so contain additional management features that make it easier to monitor performance and reliability of the processor. See figure 4.12.

The Intel Celeron processor is Intel's value processor. Early Intel Celeron processors used the SEPP and PPGA packages, no cache, and a 66 MHz system bus. The SEPP package is similar to a SECC or SECC2 package, but it has no covering. The second version of the Intel Celeron processor is very similar to the Pentium II processor, except it has 128 KB of L2 cache running at full speed and a 66 MHz

Figure 4.12 Intel® Pentium® III Xeon Processor

Figure 4.13 Intel® Pentium® 4 and Intel Xeon Processors

system bus. The third version is similar to the Pentium III processor in the FC-PGA package, except it has 128 KB of L2 cache running at a full speed and a 66 or 100 MHz system bus.

4.2.3 Intel NetBurst Microarchitecture

Intel's first all-new chip architecture since the Pentium Pro is called NetBurst microarchitecture and is used by the Pentium 4 and Intel Xeon processors. The Pentium 4 processor started out at 1.3, 1.4, and 1.5 GHz, but it has the ability to scale much higher in the future. See figure 4.13. The Intel Xeon processor is similar to a Pentium 4 processor but is multiprocessor-capable and may support larger cache. See table 4.4 on pp. 102–105.

The NetBurst microarchitecture refers to a technology that rearranges the way data is processed within the chip.

- Hyperpipelined technology, which uses a 20-stage pipeline (double that of the Pentium III), increases processor frequency and hence performance.
- A rapid-execution engine can execute arithmetic instructions in half a clock cycle, effectively doubling the core frequency and reducing latency for those functions.
- The 400 MHz system bus gives the processor a transfer rate of 3.2 Gbps. Newer processors have greater speeds.
- An execution trace cache is an intelligent caching system that stores decoded microoperations in the order of program execution. As a result, it makes more efficient use of cache memory and reduces latency.
- Advanced dynamic execution processes data more efficiently by choosing from 126 instructions in the execution buffer (triple the Pentium III processor) and predicting program flow more accurately.

Table 4.4 Intel Processors Based on Intel NetBurst Microarchitecture

Processor	Year Introduced	Package Types	Frequency (Model Number)	Architecture	No. of Transistors (Process Technology)	Data Bus Size	Memory Bus Speed	Address Bus (Addressable Memory)	L1 Cache	L2 Cache	Additional Instruction Sets
Pentium 4 (Williamette)	11/00	OOI (PGA423) and micro-FCPGA (socket 478)	1.3, 1.4, 1.5, 1.6, 1.7, 1.8, 1.9, 2.0 GHz	Intel NetBurst	42 mil (0.18 μ)	64-bit	400 MHz	36-bit (64 GB)	8 KB data cache/ 12 KB execution trace cache	256 KB on-die full-speed 8-way ATC	MMX SSE SSE2
Pentium 4 (Northwood)	1/02	Micro-FCPGA (socket 478)	1.6, 1.8, 2.0, 2.2, 2.4, 2.5, 2.6 GHz	Intel NetBurst	55 mil (0.13 μ)	64-bit	400 MHz	36-bit (64 GB)	8 KB data cache/ 12 KB execution trace cache	512 KB on-die full-speed 8-way ATC	MMX SSE SSE2
Pentium 4 (Northwood-B)	5/02	Micro-FCPGA (socket 478)	2.26, 2.4, 2.53, 2.67, 2.8 GHz	Intel NetBurst	55 mil (0.13 μ)	64-bit	533 MHz	36-bit (64 GB)	8 KB data cache/ 12 KB execution trace cache	512 KB on-die full-speed 8-way ATC	MMX SSE SSE2
Pentium 4 (Northwood-HT)[3]	11/02	Micro-FCPGA (socket 478)	2.4, 2.6, 2.8, 3.0, 3.2, 3.4 GHz	Intel NetBurst	55 mil (0.13 μ)	64-bit	533 or 800 MHz	36-bit (64 GB)	8 KB data cache/ 12 KB execution trace cache	512 KB on-die full-speed 8-way ATC	MMX SSE SSE2
Pentium 4 (Prescott)[4]	5/04	Micro-FCPGA (socket 478)	4.0 GHz (580), 3.80 GHz (570), 3.60 GHz (560), 3.40 GHz (550), 3.20 GHz (540), 3.00 GHz (530), 2.80 GHz (520)	Intel NetBurst	125 mil (0.09 μ)	64-bit	800 MHz	36-bit (64 GB)	8 KB/L1 data cache/ 12 KB execution trace cache	1 MB on-die full-speed 8-way ATC	MMX SSE SSE2 SSE3

Pentium 4 (Tejas)[5]	TBD (2005)	LGA 775 Package (socket T)	4.4 GHz	Intel NetBurst	TBD (0.09 μ)	64-bit	800 or 1066 MHz	36-bit (64 GB)	24 KB data cache/ 16 KB execution trace cache	1 MB on-die full-speed 8-way ATC	MMX SSE SSE2 SSE3 TNI
Celeron (Willamette)	5/02	FC-PGA2 (socket 478)	1.7, 1.8 GHz	NetBurst	42 mil (0.18 μ)	64-bit	400 MHz	36-bit (64 GB)	8 KB L1 data cache/ 12 KB execution trace cache	128 KB on-die full-speed 8-way ATC	MMX SSE SSE2
Celeron (Northwood)	9/02	FC-PGA2 (socket 478)	2.0, 2.1, 2.2, 2.3, 2.4, 2.7, 2.8 GHz	NetBurst	55 mil (0.13 μ)	64-bit	400 MHz	36-bit (64 GB)	8 KB L1 data cache/ 12 KB execution trace cache	128 KB on-die full-speed 8-way ATC	MMX SSE SSE2
Celeron D (Prescott)	5/04	Micro-FCPGA (socket 478)	2.40 GHz (320), 2.53 GHz (325), 2.66 GHz (330), 2.80 GHz (335), 2.93 GHz (340), 3.06 GHz (345), 3.20 GHz (350)	NetBurst	125 mil (0.09 μ)	64-bit	533 MHz	32-bit (4 GB)	8 KB L1 data cache/ 12 KB execution trace cache	256 KB on-die full-speed 8-way ATC	MMX SSE SSE2 SSE3
Xeon[1,2] (Foster)	5/01	PGA603 (socket 603)	1.4, 1.5, 1.7, 2.0 GHz	Intel NetBurst	42 mil (0.18 μ)	64-bit	400 MHz	36-bit (64 GB)	8 KB data cache/ 12 KB execution trace cache	256 KB on-die full-speed 8-way ATC	MMX SSE SSE2
Xeon MP[1,2,3] (Foster)	1/02	PGA603 (socket 603)	1.4, 1.5, 1.6 GHz	Intel NetBurst	108 mil (0.18 μ)	64-bit	400 MHz	36-bit (64 GB)	8 KB data cache/ 12 KB execution trace cache	256 KB on-die full-speed 8-way ATC and 512 KB or 1 MB L3 cache	MMX SSE SSE2

Continued

Table 4.4 Continued

Processor	Year Introduced	Package Types	Frequency	Architecture	No. of Transistors (Process Technology)	Data Bus Size	Memory Bus Speed	Address Bus (Addressable Memory)	L1 Cache	L2 Cache	Additional Instruction Sets
Xeon[1,2,3] (Prestonia)	2/02	PGA603 (socket 603)	1.8, 2.0, 2.2, 2.4, 2.6, 2.8 GHz	Intel NetBurst	55 mil (0.13 μ)	64-bit	400 MHz	36-bit (64 GB)	8 KB data cache/ 12 KB execution trace cache	512 KB on-die full-speed 8-way ATC	MMX SSE SSE2
Xeon[1,2,3] (Prestonia)	2/02	PGA604 (socket 604)	2.0, 2.4, 2.66, 2.8, 3.06 GHz	Intel NetBurst	108 mil (0.13 μ)	64-bit	533 MHz	36-bit (64 GB)	8 KB data cache/ 12 KB execution trace cache	512 KB on-die full-speed 8-way ATC	MMX SSE SSE2
Xeon[1,2,3] (Prestonia)	7/03	PGA604 (socket 604)	3.06, 3.2 GHz	NetBurst	108 mil (0.18 μ)	64-bit	533 MHz	36-bit (64 GB)	8 KB L1 data cache/ 12 KB execution trace cache	256 KB on-die full-speed 8-way ATC	MMX SSE SSE2
Xeon MP[1,3] (Gallatin)	6/02	PGA604 (socket 604)	2.2, 2.7, 2.8 GHz	NetBurst	169 mil (0.13 μ)	64-bit	400 MHz	36-bit (64 GB)	8 KB L1 data cache/ 12 KB execution trace cache	512 KB on-die full-speed 8-way ATC and 2 MB L3 cache	MMX SSE SSE2
Xeon MP[1,3] (Gallatin)	3/04	PGA604 (socket 604)	3.0 GHz	NetBurst	169 mil (0.13 μ)	64-bit	400 MHz	36-bit (64 GB)	8 KB L1 data cache/ 12 KB execution trace cache	512 KB on-die full-speed 8-way ATC and 4 MB L3 cache	MMX SSE SSE2
Xeon (Nocona)[1,2,3]	2004	PGA604 (socket 604)	2.8, 3.0, 3.2, 3.4[6], 3.6[6] GHz	NetBurst	169 mil (0.13 μ)	64-bit	800 MHz	36-bit (64 GB)	8 KB L1 data cache/ 12 KB execution trace cache	512 KB on-die full-speed 8-way ATC and 2 MB L3 cache	MMX SSE SSE2 SSE3 64-bit ext

Xeon MP[1,3] (Gallatin)	11/02	PGA604 (socket 604)	1.5, 1.9, 2.0 GHz	NetBurst	108 mil (0.13 μ)	64-bit	400 MHz	36-bit (64 GB)	8 KB data cache/ 12 KB execution trace cache	512 KB on-die full-speed 8-way ATC and 1 MB or 2 MB on-die full-speed 8-way L3 cache	MMX SSE SSE2
Pentium 4 Extreme edition (Northwood-HT)[3]	11/03	Micro-FCPGA (socket 478)	3.2. 3.4 GHz	NetBurst	178 mil (0.13 μ)	64-bit	800 MHz	36-bit (64 GB)	8 KB data cache/ 12 KB execution trace cache	512 KB on-die full-speed 8-way ATC and 2 MB L3 cache	MMX SSE SSE2
Pentium 4 Extreme[3] (Prescott)	2004	Micro-FCPGA (socket 478)	3.73 GHz (720)	NetBurst	178 mil (0.09 μ)	64-bit	1066 MHz	36-bit (64 GB)	8 KB L1 data cache/ 12 KB execution trace cache	512 KB on-die full-speed 8-way ATC and 2 MB L3 cache	MMX SSE SSE2 SSE3

[1]Includes Advanced Management Features designed for the server platform to monitor and protect the processor and its environment.
[2]Designed for a uniprocessor and dual-processing server system.
[3]Supports Hyper-Threading.
[4]Supports Enhanced Hyper-Threading.
[5]Supports Extended Enhanced Hyper-Threading.
[6]Includes SpeedStop technology.

- An advanced transfer cache optimizes data transfer to the processor core. The advanced transfer cache consists of a 256-bit (32-byte) interface that transfers data on each core clock. As a result, the Pentium 4 processor at 1.50 GHz can deliver a data transfer rate of 48 GBps. This compares to a transfer rate of 16 GBps on the Pentium III processor at 1 GHz.
- An enhanced floating-point and multimedia unit accelerates processor-intensive tasks such as streaming video, voice recognition, video and audio encoding, and image processing.
- The SSE2 consisting of 144 new instructions to accelerate video and encryption/decryption and support the next generation of Internet applications; it also supports newer, more computationally intensive graphics.

Currently, the Pentium 4 processors support 400, 533, and 800 MHz system bus speeds. This is accomplished through a physical signaling scheme of quad pumping the data transfer. Therefore, while a bus may actually run at 200 MHz clocked system, a buffering scheme that reacts four times every clock allows for a sustained 800 MHz data transfer rate. Of course, the 533 and 400 MHz system bus is actually running at 133 and 100 MHz. As a result, the 800 MHz bus can deliver 6.4 GBps into and out of the processor, the 533 MHz can deliver 4.2 GBps, and the 400 MHz can deliver 3.2 GBps. This compares to 1.06 GBps delivered on the Pentium III processor's 133 MHz system bus.

Similar to when the Pentium Pro processor was introduced with the P6 architecture, software has to be optimized for the Intel NetBurst microarchitecture. Therefore, if you are using older software that is not optimized for the Pentium 4 family, the programs, including software that measure performance, may actually run slower than the Pentium III processor, but when it is optimized, it is very fast.

Early Pentium 4 processors are packaged in the 423-pin OLGA On Interposer (OOI) package. The Organic Land Grid Array (OLGA) core is covered by an Integrated Heat Spreader (IHS) that helps heat sink dissipation to a properly attached fan heat sink. Newer Pentium 4 processors use the 478-pin Flip-Chip Pin Grid Array (FC-PGA2) package with an Integrated Heat Spreader.

The newest Pentium 4 processor (Prescott), based on 0.09 μm technology, has an increased cache, 24 KB L1 data cache, 16 KB execution trace cache, and 1 MB L2 cache. In addition, the pipeline was increased from 20 to 31 stages and a dedicated integer multiplier was added to the ALU so that it would not have to send such calculations to the floating-point side. Lastly, streaming SIMD extensions 3 was added.

Intel will be adding **data execution prevention** technology to its processor starting with Intel Prescott processors. This new technology, used with software such as Windows XP Service Pack 2 and newer Linux operating systems, is designed to prevent buffer overrun exploits that occur when a malicious piece of code (such as a virus or worm) accesses system memory and uses it to execute its payload. This is accomplished by using a register bit that marks vulnerable memory as data only, with no executables allowed to run.

The Intel Xeon processor with a 400 MHz Front Side Bus is packaged in the 603-pin OLGA On Interposer (OOI) package. The Intel Xeon Processor with a 533 MHz Front Side Bus is packaged in the 604-pin Flip Chip-Micro Pin Grid Array 2 (FC-μPGA2) package. Both the Organic Land Grid Array (OLGA) core and Flip Chip-Micro Pin Grid Array 2 (FC-μPGA2) package are covered by an Integrated Heat Spreader.

Systems based on the Pentium 4 processor must use chassis that comply with the ATX specification (revision 2.01 or later) and have the Pentium 4 processor-specific mounting support. Power supplies must comply with the ATX12V or SFX12V design guidelines and supply additional current on the 12 V power rail. Some power supplies may use a new 2×2 connector to supply the additional 12 V power and a 1×6 connector to supply additional 3.3 and 5 V current.

The more recent enhancement to the Pentium 4 and Intel Xeon processors (and upcoming mobile Pentium 4 processors) is the addition of **Hyper-Threading Technology (HT).** Hyper-Threading Technology is **simultaneously multithreading (SMT),** which allows the processor to act like two processors (logical processors) so that it can utilize the processor resources more efficiently and improve performance. Of course, these programs would have to support multiple threads to take advantage of Hyper-Threading. To carry the Intel Processor with HT Technology logo, systems must have:

- An Intel Pentium 4 family processor that supports HT Technology.
- An Intel chipset that supports HT Technology.
- A system BIOS that supports HT Technology and has it enabled.
- An operating system that includes optimizations for HT Technology. Currently, Windows XP, Windows Server 2003 and some versions of Linux support HT.

Enhanced Hyper-Threading Technology and Extended Enhanced Hyper-Threading Technology are improved versions of the Hyper-Threading Technology used in the newest Intel Pentium 4 processor family introduced in 2004.

For more information about Hyper-Threading Technology, visit the following website:

http://www.intel.com/labs/htt/index.htm

In 2004, Intel will use a 775-contact pinless Land Grid Array inserted into a socket T, which is much cheaper than PGA or BGA, is upgradeable, and offers a high-contact density. The additional contacts/pins were required for the additional I/O and power requirements. The LGA 775 will use a direct socket loading technique that traps the LGA package inside a socket body stiffener much like a waffle iron. This will prevent it from breaking contact with the motherboard and insulate the processor from potential damage from the heat sink.

4.2.4 IA-64 Architecture and 64-Bit Extensions

The next class of processors will be 64-bit processors. What most people don't realize is that 64-bit processing is not new, since government research labs that run complex computational and scientific programs have been using 64-bit UNIX machines for quite some time. Because 64-bit processors have been getting more attention lately, and many IT managers are keeping an eye on the new technology, they say 32-bit computing at the desktop and server levels is sufficient to handle most of the applications they run—at least for now. It remains to be seen if and when this will change, particularly as the 64-bit architecture incorporates a broader range of hardware and software products in the market.

A 64-bit processor is a processor with a word size of 64 bits and 64-bit external data bus, a requirement for memory- and data-intensive applications, such as computer-aided design (CAD) applications, database management systems, technical and scientific applications, and high-performance servers. Sixty-four-bit computer architecture provides higher performance than 32-bit architecture by handling twice as many bits of information in the same clock cycle.

Most people don't realize that today's processors can already handle 64-bit calculations, particularly the floating-point units. But one of the main benefits of 64-bit processors is that they can process significantly more memory than 32-bit processors. Although 32-bit can manage 4 GB of memory, 64-bit can manage up to 2^{64} or 18 billion gigabytes of memory. With more data in memory, a 64-bit processor can work faster because it doesn't have to swap large sets of information in and out of memory the way a 32-bit processor does.

Intel has introduced its first 64-bit processor based on the IA-64 processor based on the IA-64 architecture. While we already have processors with a 64-bit external data bus and registers, the IA-64 processors also have a 64-bit address bus that will allow the processor to access 2^{64} = 18,466,744,073,709,551,616 bytes of RAM.

The Itanium, based on the IA-64 architecture, is a new processor family and architecture, designed by Intel and Hewlett-Packard, with the future of high-end server and workstation computing. It is designed for fast parallel instruction execution. See figure 4.14.

Figure 4.14 Intel® Itanium 2 Processor

The Itanium uses four-way associative, 16 KB L1 on-die instruction cache and a four-way associative 16 KB integer-only L1 on-die data cache. It also has a six-way associative, 96 KB L2 on-die cache with a 256-bit bus. Lastly, the Itanium processor has a 2 or 4 MB four-way set-associative off-die L3 cache.

The IA-64 architecture differs from IA-32 in several ways. Rather than using variable-length instructions, it uses fixed-length, 4-byte instructions bundled in sets of three "long instruction words." It uses 256 registers for integer and floating-point operations compared to 16 in the IA-32. The IA-64 employs a technique known as predication, where both sides of a branch instruction are executed in parallel. When the correct branch is determined, the results for the incorrect side are discarded. With IA-64, compilers have to be more intelligent, placing codes into the instruction bundles that tell the CPU how to execute instructions in parallel. They also have to place instructions in interleaved order for predication.

If predication is not set up, the CPU will perform traditional branch prediction, whereby it attempts to guess the outcome of a branch and executes those instructions in parallel. The IA-64 also supports speculative loading, which loads data into its registers before the instructions actually need to process it. Explicitly Parallel Instruction Computing (EPIC) is Intel's brand name for its new parallel architecture. Therefore, although x86-based software (IA-32 software) will run intact on IA-64 machines, programs have to be recompiled in order to take full advantage of the new architecture.

Later, Intel introduced the Itanium 2 processor. With a greater clock speed (900 MHz and 1 GHz), increased level 2 cache, increased data bus speed and small tweaks in the architecture, the Itanium 2 processor performs significantly better than the Itanium processor. Unfortunately, because of the poor performance of the Itanium family, and the lack of backward compatibility of 32-bit software, the Itanium processor is off to a rocky start. Note: The 32-bit software can be executed with software emulation. Unfortunately, the performance is slow.

In 2005, Intel is expected to release a new line of Itanium chips that contain two processor cores and a 24 MB level 3 cache. The new Itanium chips will contain enhanced power management and include the ability to correct data errors in the cache.

When AMD successfully introduced its 64-bit processors and extended the 32-bit architecture to include 64-bit memory access and commands, it prompted Intel to follow suit. Beginning with Intel Xeon processors designed for servers and workstations, Intel added 64-bit operating mode and additional 64-bit extensions to the existing x86 architecture, allowing the processor to directly support more than 4 GB of memory. Eventually, Intel will extend the 64-bit extensions to its mainstream desktop processors. Intel has already stated that the new processors will be broadly compatible with the AMD64 family.

Although the 64-bit extensions do allow the processor to run newly written 64-bit code and access larger amounts of memory, the processor does not run code written for the Intel Itanium processor. Intel will offer both the IA-64 architecture and 64-bit extensions, but is positioning the 64-bit processors for general usage and the IA-64 Itanium processor family to provide the highest performing and most reliable product family for high-end, multiprocessor systems. Table 4.5 lists Intel's processors based on IA-64 architecture.

4.2.5 Mobile Processors

The mobile processors produced by Intel are similar to their desktop counterparts, but they are designed to consume less power for longer battery life and to produce less heat. For example, a mobile Pentium II processor running at 266 MHz consumes almost half the power of a Pentium II processor running at 33 MHz, yet it provides a 35 percent increase in performance over the Pentium processor with MMX technology running at the same speed. In addition, mobile processors include self-testing circuitry and thermal sensors that provide valuable data for managing software. See table 4.6 on pp. 111–113.

The mobile Intel Pentium III processors run up to 1.33 GHz and higher and have a 133 MHz system bus and 256 KB advanced transfer cache. The mobile Pentium III processors starting at 600 MHz include Intel SpeedStep technology, which allows you to customize high-performance computing on your mobile PC. When the notebook computer is connected to the ac outlet, the new mobile PC runs the most complex business and Internet applications with speed virtually identical to a desktop system. When powered by a battery, the processor drops to a lower frequency (by changing the bus ratios)

Table 4.5 Intel Processors Based on IA-64 Architecture

Processor	Year Introduced	Package Types	Frequency	Architecture	No. of Transistors (Process Technology)	Data Bus Size	Memory Bus Speed	Address Bus (Addressable Memory)	L1 Cache	L2 Cache	Additional Instruction Sets
Itanium^2 (Merced)	5/01	PAC418 cartridge (PAC418 VLIF socket)	733, 800 MHz	IA-64	25.4 mil (0.18 μ) 300 mil cache	64-bit	266 MHz	64-bit (16 TB)	16 KB data cache/16 KB instruction cache dual-ported	96 KB on-die full-speed 6-way dual-ported and 2, or 4 MB L3 cache on-package 4-way	MMX SSE
Itanium^2 2 (McKinley)	11/02	PAC611 cartridge (PAC611 VLIF socket)	900 MHz and 1.0 GHz	IA-64	221 mil (0.18 μ)	228-bit	400 MHz	64-bit (16 TB)	16 KB data cache/16 KB instruction cache dual-ported	256 KB on-die full-speed 8-way dual-ported and 1.5 or 3 MB L3 cache on-die 4-way	MMX SSE
Itanium^2 2 (Madison)	6/03	PAC611 cartridge (PAC611 VLIF socket)	1.2–1.6 GHz	IA-64	410 mil (0.13 μ)	128-bit	400 MHz	64-bit (16 TB)	16 KB data cache/16 KB instruction cache dual-ported	256 KB on-die full-speed 8-way dual-ported and 3, 4, or 6 MB L3 cache on-die 4-way	MMX SSE

Continued

Table 4.5 Continued

Processor	Year Introduced	Package Types	Frequency	Architecture	No. of Transistors (Process Technology)	Data Bus Size	Memory Bus Speed	Address Bus (Addressable Memory)	L1 Cache	L2 Cache	Additional Instruction Sets
Itanium[2] 2 (Low voltage) (Deerfield)	9/03	PAC611 cartridge (PAC611 VLIF socket)	1 GHz	IA-64	410 mil (0.13 μ)	128-bit	400 MHz	64-bit (16 TB)	16 KB data cache/16 KB instruction cache dual-ported	256 KBon-die full-speed 6-way dual-ported and 1.5 L3 cache on-die 4-way	MMX SSE
Itanium 2 (Madison)	2004	PAC611 cartridge (PAC611 VLIF socket)	1.7 GHz	IA-64	410 mil (0.13 μ)	128-bit	400 MHz	64-bit (16 TB)	16 KB data cache/16 KB instruction cache dual-ported	256 KB on-die full-speed 6-way dual-ported and 9 MB L3 cache on-die 4-way	MMX SSE
Itanium 2 (Fanwood)	2004	PAC611 cartridge (PAC611 VLIF socket)	1.4, 1.6 GHz	IA-64	410 mil (0.13 μ)	128-bit	400 MHz	64-bit (16 TB)	16 KB data cache/16 KB instruction cache dual-ported	256 KB on-die full-speed 6-way dual-ported and 3 MB L3 cache on-die 4-way	MMX SSE
Itanium 2 (Montecito)	2005	PAC611 cartridge (PAC611 VLIF socket)	1.4, 1.6 GHz	IA-64 (dual processor cores	410 mil (0.13 μ)	128-bit	400 MHz	64-bit (16 TB)	16 KB data cache/16 KB instruction cache dual-ported	256 KB on-die full-speed 6-way dual-ported and 24 MB L3 cache on-die 4-way	MMX SSE

Table 4.6 Inter Mobile Processors

Processor	Year Introduced	Package Types	Frequency	Architecture	No. of Transistors (Process Technology)	Data Bus Size	Memory Bus Speed	Address bus (Addressable Memory)	L1 Cache	L2 Cache	Additional Instruction Sets
Mobile Pentium with MMX Technology (Tillamook)	9/97	Tape carrier package	200, 233, 266, 300 MHz	Super-scalar	4.5 mil (0.25 μ)	64-bit	66 MHz	32-bit (4 GB)	16 KB data cache/16 KB instruction cache	None	MMX
Mobile Pentium II (Deschutes)	4/98	Minicartridge MMC-1, MMC-2 BGA	233, 266, 300, 333, 366, 400 MHz	P6	7.5 mil (0.25 μ)	64-bit	66 MHz	32-bit (4 GB)	16 KB data cache/16 KB instruction cache	512 KB on-package half-speed 4-way discrete	MMX
Mobile Pentium III (Coppermine)	10/99	BGA, micro-PGA, MMC-2	400, 450, 500 MHz	P6	28 mil (0.18 μ)	64-bit	100 MHz	36-bit (64 GB)	16 KB data cache/16 KB instruction cache	256 KB on-die full-speed 4-way ATC	MMX, SIMD
Mobile Pentium III[2] (Coppermine)	1/00	BGA2, micro-PGA2, MMC-2	600, 650, 700, 750, 800, 850, 900 MHz, 1 GHz	P6	28 mil (0.18 μ)	64-bit	100 MHz	36-bit (64 GB)	16 KB data cache/16 KB instruction cache	256 KB on-die full-speed 4-way ATC	MMX SIMD
Mobile Pentium III[2] (Tualatin)	10/01	Micro-FCBGA, micro-FCPGA	866, 933 MHz, 1.0, 1.06, 1.13, 1.2, 1.3 GHz	P6	44 mil (0.13 μ)	64-bit	133 MHz	36-bit (64 GB)	16 KB data cache/16 KB instruction cache	512 KB on-die full-speed 8-way ATC	MMX SIMD
Mobile Intel Celeron	1/99	Ball grid array	266, 300, 333, 366, 433, 466 MHz	P6	18.9 mil (0.25 μ)	64-bit	66 MHz	32-bit (4 GB)	16 KB data cache/16 KB instruction cache	128 KB on-die full-speed 4-way ATC	MMX

Continued

Table 4.6 Continued

Processor	Year Introduced	Package Types	Frequency (Model Number)	Architecture	No. of Transistors (Process Technology)	Data Bus Size	Memory Bus Speed	Address bus (Addressable Memory)	L1 Cache	L2 Cache	Additional Instruction Sets
Mobile Intel Celeron (Coppermine)	5/01	BGA2, PGA2, MMC2	450, 500, 550, 600, 650, 700, 750, 800, 850 MHz	P6	18.9 mil (0.18 μ)	64-bit	100 MHz	32-bit (4 GB)	16 KB data cache/16 KB instruction cache	128 KB on-die full-speed 4-way ATC	MMX SIMD
Mobile Intel Celeron (Coppermine-T)	10/01	Micro-FCPGA, micro-FCBGA	800, 866, 900, 933 MHz	P6	18.9 mil (0.18 μ)	64-bit	100 MHz	32-bit (4 GB)	16 KB data cache/16 KB instruction cache	128 KB on-die full-speed 4-way ATC	MMX SIMD
Mobile Pentium 4^2 (Northwood-M)	6/03	Micro-FCPGA2, (478-pin socket)	2.4, 2.66, 2.8, 3.06 GHz	NetBurst	55 mil (0.13 μ)	64-bit	533 MHz	32-bit (4 GB)	8 KB data cache/12 KB execution trace cache	512 KB on-die full-speed 8-way ATC	MMX SSE SSE2
Mobile Pentium 4^2-M^2 (Northwood-M)	3/02	Micro-FCPGA2, (478-pin socket)	1.4, 1.5, 1.6, 1.7, 1.8, 1.9, 2.0, 2.2, 2.4, 2.5 GHz	NetBurst	55 mil (0.13 μ)	64-bit	400 MHz	32-bit (4 GB)	8 KB data cache/12 KB execution trace cache	512 KB on-die full-speed 8-way ATC	MMX SSE SSE2
Mobile Pentium M^2 (Banias)	3/03	Micro-FCPGA2, (478-pin socket)	1.3, 1.4, 1.5, 1.6, 1.7 GHz	Intel Architecture	77 mil (0.13 μ)	64-bit	400 MHz	32-bit (4 GB)	32 KB data cache/32 KB instruction cache	1 MB on-die full-speed 8-way ATC	MMX SSE SSE2

Mobile Pentium 4[2,3]	6/04	Micro-FCPGA (socket 478)	3.60 GHz (558), 3.46 GHz (552), 3.20 GHz (538), 3.06 GHz (532), 2.80 GHz (518)	NetBurst	125 mil (0.09 μ)	64-bit	533 MHz	32-bit (4 GB)	8 KB L1 data cache/12 KB execution trace cache	1 MB on-die full-speed 8-way ATC	MMX SSE SSE2 SSE3
Mobile Pentium M[2,3]	5/04	Micro-FCPGA (socket 478)	2.10 GHz (765), 2.00 GHz (755), 1.80 GHz (745), 1.70 GHz (735), 1.60 GHz (725), 1.50 GHz (715)	NetBurst	77 mil (0.09 μ)	64-bit	400 MHz	32-bit (4 GB)	8 KB L1 data cache/12 KB execution trace cache	2 MB on-die full-speed 8-way ATC	MMX SSE SSE2 SSE3
Mobile Pentium M[2]	TBA	Micro-FCPGA (socket 478)	2.13 GHz (770), 2.00 GHz (760), 1.86 GHz (750), 1.73 GHz (740), 1.60 GHz (730)	NetBurst	77 mil (0.09 μ)	64-bit	533 MHz	32-bit (4 GB)	8 KB L1 data cache/12 KB execution trace cache	2 MB on-die full-speed 8-way ATC	MMX SSE SSE2 SSE3
Mobile Celeron D	TBA	Micro-FCPGA (socket 478)	3.20 GHz (350), 3.06 GHz (345), 2.93 GHz (340), 2.80 GHz (335), 2.66 GHz (330), 2.53 GHz (325), 2.40 GHz (320)	NetBurst	125 mil (0.09 μ)	64-bit	533 MHz	32-bit (4 GB)	8 KB L1 data cache/12 KB execution trace cache	256 MB on-die full-speed 8-way ATC	MMX SSE SSE2 SSE3

[1] Includes Intel SpeedStep technology.
[2] Includes Enhanced Intel SpeedStep technology.
[3] Includes Hyper-Threading Technology.

and voltage, conserving battery life while maintaining a high level of performance. Manual override lets you boost the frequency back to the high frequency when on battery, allowing you to customize performance.

NOTE: For SpeedStep technology to function, you must load the SpeedStep driver (built into Windows XP).

Newer mobile Pentium III processors, labeled as Mobile Pentium III Processors-M, are based on the 0.13 μm technology have a 512 KB cache and Intel Enhanced SpeedStep technology. Intel Enhanced SpeedStep technology changes the bus ratio and voltage based on the processor's load. If you don't need the extra processing power, the processor will conserve power.

The mobile Intel Pentium 4 Processor-M and mobile Intel Pentium 4 processors are Intel's mobile processors based on the Intel NetBurst architecture, the same architecture used in the Pentium 4 processor. Like the Pentium III processor-M, the mobile Pentium 4 Processor-M features Intel's Enhanced SpeedStep technology, which enables real-time dynamic switching of the voltage and frequency between two performance modes based on CPU demand. The processor also features a new ultra-low power-alert state called Deeper Sleep, which enables the processor to retain critical data at very low voltages and minimizes power dissipation when the processor is not active. These low-power features extend battery life, increasing the efficiency and productivity of mobile PC users.

The Intel Pentium M processor is a high-performance, low-power mobile processor with several micro-architectural enhancements over existing Intel mobile processors. The Intel Pentium M processor uses the Intel Architecture (a new architecture that is not P6 or Intel NetBurst architecture), which is designed as a high-performance core with features like Micro-op Fusion and Advanced Stack Management to reduce the number of operations handled by the processor. This results in more efficient scheduling and better performance at lower power. The on-die 32 KB level 1 instruction and data caches and the 1 MB level 2 cache with Advanced Transfer Cache Architecture enable significant performance improvement over existing mobile processors. The processor also features a very advanced branch prediction architecture that significantly reduces the number of mispredicted branches. The processor's Data Prefetch Logic speculatively fetches data to the L2 cache before an L1 cache requests occurs, resulting in reduced bus cycle penalties and improved performance.

Because the Pentium M processor has greater performance with a lower clock speed, many customers do not understand the true performance of the processor. Therefore in 2004, Intel introduced a model number system that will describe their performance. Similar to what AMD processors use today, the model number system is designed to take away some emphasis from clock speed. Instead, the performance number is based on the processor clock speed, cache size, and bus speed. Intel intends the ratings to be used only to compare chips within a line, but not to compare different families of processors.

The Intel Processor-M features Enhanced Intel SpeedStep technology, which enables real-time dynamic switching between multiple voltage and frequency points instead of two points supported on previous versions of Intel SpeedStep technology. This results in optimal performance without compromising low power.

For a notebook computer to use Intel SpeedStep technology, the notebook must have the following:

- A processor with Intel SpeedStep technology.
- A chipset, BIOS, voltage regulator, and operating system that supports Intel SpeedStep technology.
- An Intel SpeedStep technology driver.

While Windows XP has the Intel SpeedStep technology driver, you must load the Intel SpeedStep technology driver if you are using older versions of Windows.

Mobile Intel Celeron processors are similar to the mobile Pentium II, mobile Pentium III, and mobile Pentium 4 processors, except that they have a lower clock speed, lower bus speed, and a smaller cache. In addition, they do not use Intel SpeedStep technology.

Before moving on, it should be mentioned that not all processors used in notebook computers are mobile processors. Since mobile processors are much more expensive than desktop processors, some vendors offer notebook computers with desktop processors. Of course, these notebooks must be designed with a little bit better cooling systems since desktop processors dissipate more heat. In addition, these processors consume more power, which gives the system a lower battery life.

Mobile processors use the minicartridge, BGA, BGA2, micro-PGA, micro-PGA2, MMC-1 cartridge, MMC-2 cartridge, and microflip chip. The BGA packages, which are soldered onto the mother-

Figure 4.15 Intel® Mobile Processors in Micro-PGA, Micro-BGA, and MMC-2 Cartridge

board, use small balls, which act instead of pins as contacts for the processor. The advantage of using balls instead of pins is that there are no pins that bend, allowing for a low profile.

The micro-PGA and micro-PGA2 consist of a BGA package mounted to an interposer with small pins. The pins are 1.25 mm long and 0.30 mm in diameter. There are several micro-PGA2 socket designs available, which are designed to allow zero-insertion-force removal and insertion of the mobile Pentium III processor. See figure 4.15.

The mobile module cartridge 2 (MMC-2) package has a mobile Pentium III processor and the host bridge system controller (consisting of the processor bus controller, memory controller and PCI bus controller) on a small circuit. It connects to the system via a 400-pin connector. On the MMC-2 package, the thermal transfer plate (TTP) provides heat dissipation from the processor and host bridge system controller.

The newest version used in mobile processors is the micro-flip chip used with the mobile Intel Pentium III processors. It is based on 0.13-μm process technology and will be used in upcoming desktop processors, including the new version of the Pentium 4 processor. The microflip chip resembles the pins on the micro-PGA2, yet it doesn't use an interposer to connect to the balls of a ball grid array processor and it has capacitors on the processor. Note: Mobile Pentium III, mobile Pentium 4, and desktop Pentium 4 processors use the 478-pin package. However, they are not electrically compatible, so they are not interchangeable.

4.3 AMD AND VIA/CYRIX PROCESSORS

Although Intel processors are considered the de facto standard, Intel is not the only company that produces PC processors. Two other manufacturers are Advanced Micro Devices (AMD) and Cyrix. Both companies offer similar processors that cost less.

4.3.1 Early AMD Processors

The AMD 5K86, once called the K5, has a design similar to that of the Pentium Pro. It converts x86 code to RISC-like operations, which AMD calls Risc ops (ROPs). It also has other features, including superscalar design, out-of-order speculative execution, dynamic cache, and line-oriented branch prediction. In addition, it has a 16 KB instruction cache and an 8 KB data cache.

AMD-K6 and AMD-K6-2 are AMD's sixth-generation processors. They are packaged in a ceramic pin grid array (CPGA) using C4 (controlled collapse chip connection) flip-chip interconnection technology that can be inserted in a standard Pentium socket. This technology permits a smaller chip, which helps performance because the signals have smaller distance to travel. Unlike the Pentium Pro

Table 4.7 Recent AMD Desktop Processors

Processor	MHz Maximum Clock Speed[2]	MHz Bus Speed	Connector	Cache (Speed)	Die Size	No. of Transistors	Additional Instruction Sets
K6	300	100	Super 7	L1: 64 KB	0.25μ	8.8 million	MMX
K6-2	550	100	Super 7	L1: 64 KB (L2: 1024 KB) (Bus)	0.25μ	9.3 million	3DNow!
K6-III	450	100	Super 7	L1: 64 KB L2: 256 KB (Full Speed) (L3: 1 MB) (Bus Speed)	0.25μ	21.3 million	3DNow!
Athlon (Thunderbird/K7)	1400	266	Socket A	L1: 64 KB L2: 256 KB (Newer processors run at Full Speed)	0.18μ	37 million	3DNow!+
Athlon MP (Palomino)	1600	266	Super A	L1: 128 KB L2: 256 KB (Full Speed)	0.18μ	37.5 million	3DNow! Pro[1]
Athlon XP (Palomino)	1733 (2100+/1733, 2000+/1733, 1900+/1600, 1800+/1533, 1700+/1467, 1600+/1400, 1500+/1333)	266	Super A	L1: 128 KB L2: 256 KB (Full Speed)	0.18μ	37.5 million	3DNow! Pro[1]
Athlon XP (Thoroughbred)	1733 (2100+/1733, 2000+/1667, 1900+/1600, 1800+/1533, 1700+/1467)	266	Super A	L1: 128 KB L2: 256 KB (Full Speed)	0.13μ	37.5 million	3DNow! Pro[1]
Athlon XP (Thoroughbred-B)	2250 (2800+/2250, 2700+/2166, 2600+/2083, 2600+[3]/2133, 2400+[3]/2000, 2200+[3]/1800)	266 or 333	Super A	L1: 128 KB L2: 256 KB (Full Speed)	0.13μ	37.6 million	3DNow! Pro[1]
Athlon XP (Barton)	2167 (3000+/2167, 2800+/2086, 2500+/1833)	333	Super A	L1: 128 KB L2: 512 KB (Full Speed)	0.13μ	54.3 million	3DNow! Pro[1]
Duron (Spitfire)	950	200	Super A	L1: 128 KB L2: 64 KB (Full Speed)	0.18μ	25 million	3DNow!+ SSE
Duron (Morgan)	1300	200	Super A	L1: 128 KB L2: 64 KB (Full Speed)	0.18μ	25 million	3DNow! Pro[1]

Table 4.7 Continued

Processor	MHz Maximum Clock Speed[2]	MHz Bus Speed	Connector	Cache (Speed)	Die Size	No. of Transistors	Additional Instruction Sets
Opteron (Sledgehammer)	2.4 GHz	Speed of processor	Socket 940	L1: 128 L2: 1 MB (Full Speed)	0.13μ	106 million	3DNow! Pro[1] SSE2 AMD64
Athlon 64 (Clawhammer)	2.4 GHz (3500+/2.2 GHz, 3800+/2.4 GHz)	2.0 GHz[4]	Socket 939	L1: 128 L2: 512 KB (Full Speed)	0.13μ	68.5 million	3DNow! Pro[1] SSE2 AMD64
Athlon 64 (Clawhammer)	2.4 GHz (3000+2.0 GHz, 3200+/2.2 GHz, 3400+/2.4 GHz)	1.6 GHz[4]	Socket 754	L1: 128 L2: 512 KB (Full Speed)	0.13μ	68.5 million	3DNow! Pro[1] SSE2 AMD64
Athlon 64 (Clawhammer)	2.4 GHz (3700+/2.4 GHz)	1.6 GHz[4]	Socket 754	L1: 128 L2: 1 KB (Full Speed)	0.13μ	106 million	3DNow! Pro[1] SSE2 AMD64
Athlon 64 FX (Clawhammer)	2.4 GHz (FX-51/2.2 GHz, FX-53/2.4 GHz)	1.6 GHz[4]	Socket 940	L1: 128 L2: 1 MB (Full Speed)	0.13μ	106 million	3DNow! Pro[1] SSE2 AMD64
Athlon 64 FX (Clawhammer)	2.4 GHz (FX-53/2.4 GHz)	2 GHz[4]	Socket 939	L1: 128 L2: 1 MB (Full Speed)	0.13μ	106 million	3DNow! Pro[1] SSE2 AMD64

[1]Includes Intel's SSE.
[2]The numbers in parentheses represent the model number and the actual speed.
[3]Have 266 Bus speed.
[4]The front-side bus has been replaced by a dedicated memory bus and a HyperTransport link. The HyperTransport link operates at this speed.

processor, the K6 is optimized for both 16- and 32-bit code. It contains two 32 KB RAM caches, one for data and one for code, and contains the MMX extensions. The AMD-K6-2 processor includes 3DNow! technology, which significantly enhances 3D graphics, multimedia, and other floating-point intensive PC applications. See table 4.7.

The speeds of the AMD 5K86 and K6 are not rated in megahertz. Instead, the chips have a P rating system, which reflects performance relative to similar Intel Pentium processors. A 5K86 runs at 133 MHz with a P166 speed rating, because it can perform similar to a Pentium chip running at 166 MHz.

4.3.2 AMD Athlon and Duron

With the release of the Athlon (codename K7), AMD has become a major player in the processor market. The early AMD Athlon was manufactured in 0.25 μm technology and consisted of no less than 22 million transistors. Currently, the newer Athlon processor is manufactured on an 0.18 μm process and uses approximately 37 million transistors on 120 mm^2 die. In addition, the newer Athlon processors use copper metal technology, a first in the PC processor business. Eventually all other processors will follow because copper interconnects allow for lower power consumption and faster operation.

The AMD Athlon has a nine-issue superpipelined, superscalar x86 processor microarchitecture designed for high clock frequencies. It includes multiple parallel x86 instruction decoders; three out-of-order, superscalar, fully pipelined floating-point execution units that execute x87 (floating point); MMX, and 3DNow! instructions; three out-of-order, superscalar, pipelined integer units; and three out-of-order, superscalar, pipelined address calculation units. Therefore, it can start up to nine instructions on each tick of the clock.

The chip's floating-point unit can add and multiply at the same time, just like many digital signal processors. In addition to the 3DNow! and Enhanced 3DNow! instructions, AMD has added some instructions, specifically designed for signal processing, hoping that they will be used in software modems, speech recognition, and similar applications.

Athlon processors have 128 KB of L1 cache. Early Athlon processors had 512 KB of L2 cache on the package running at ½, ⅖, or ⅓ the clock speed of the processor. The newer versions have 256 KB of integrated, on-chip L2 cache running at full speed.

The Athlon processor was AMD's first product to drop any attempt at pin compatibility with Intel chips. The first Athlon processor used an SEC package called Slot A that was mechanically compatible but not pin-compatible with slot 1. Later versions of the Athlon were built for socket A, which can access 200 and 266 MHz system buses based on Alpha EV6 bus protocol. See figure 4.16.

The biggest disadvantage for AMD processors is that they consume more power and dissipate much more heat than their Intel counterparts. Therefore, they need to have a higher level cooling solution. In addition, if the cooling solution fails, it may end up burning up the processor.

In October 2001, AMD released a new version of the Athlon, the Athlon XP. While AMD does not admit it, XP was most likely chosen to ride on the fanfare of the Windows XP release. In addition to the normal features of the Athlon, AMD uses QuantiSpeed Architecture that includes adding a data prefetch and translation look-aside buffers for faster performance. In addition, it includes Intel's SSE instructions and 52 new 3DNow! instructions. It also has lower power consumption, similar to the Athlon 4, and has an on-die thermal diode. Note: For the on-die thermal diode, you need to have a motherboard that can read the thermal diode and force the computer to shut down when it exceeds its maximum temperature.

The Athlon MP processor, made for dual-processing systems, requires a large-capacity power supply. In addition, AMD chose to use a proprietary power supply that many power supply manufacturers may not build and may cost more than one of the ATX or ATX 12 V power supplies.

To compete more against the success of the Pentium 4 processor, AMD introduced a new metric, which AMD executives called the "True Performance Initiative." It is used by the Athlon XP and MP processors. Based on what AMD considers to be equivalent performance as compared to the Intel Pentium 4 processor (similar to the PR system used by Cyrix), Model 1500, Model 1600, Model 1700, Model 1800, and Model 1900 processors actually run at 1.33, 1.40, 1.47, 1.53, and 1.60 GHz, respectively.

A debate exists about which processors (Intel Pentium 4 and AMD Athlon) are faster. Both processors are good products. People like to compare both processors of like speed, for example an Intel Pentium processor and an AMD Athlon processor, both running at 1.60 GHz. While this may seem like a fair comparison, since they have different architectures and handle clock speed differently, you should compare the fastest processors from both companies. Another consideration is price.

Figure 4.16 AMD Athlon Processor

For the value market, AMD manufactures the Duron processor. The Duron processor is similar to the Athlon processor, but it has only a 64 KB full-speed 16-way set-associative L2 cache. The Duron uses the same 100 MHz double-pumped (equivalent to 200 MHz) front-side bus that the Athlon has used since it began production.

To compete in the mobile market against Intel mobile Pentium III processor, AMD introduced the Athlon 4 processor. The Athlon 4 and Athlon 64 processors include AMD's PowerNow! technology, which dynamically adjusts the clock speed based on the tasks you are performing to stretch battery life. AMD claims PowerNow! can deliver 30 percent more battery life. Unfortunately, the power consumption of the Athlon 4 processor is still greater than Intel's processors running at the same speed. See table 4.8.

Table 4.8 Recent AMD Mobile Processors

Processor	MHz Maximum Clock Speed[3]	MHz Bus Speed	Connector	Cache (Speed)	Die Size	No. of Transistors	Additional Instruction Sets
Mobile K6	300	100	PGA/BGA	L1: 64 KB	0.25μ	8.8 million	MMX
Mobile K6-2	475	100	Socket 7 Super 7	L1: 64 KB L2: 512 KB (Bus Speed)	0.25μ	9.3 million	3DNow!
Mobile Only K6-2+	550	100	Super 7	L1: 64 KB L2: 128 KB (Full Speed)	0.18μ	21.3 million	3DNow!+
Mobile K6-III	450	100	Super 7	L1: 64 KB L2: 256 KB (Full Speed) (L3: 1 MB) (Bus Speed)	0.25μm	21.3 million	3DNow!
Mobile Only K6-III+	550	100	Super 7	L1: 64 KB L2: 256 KB (Full Speed) L3: 1024 KB (Bus Speed)	0.18μ	21.3 million	3DNow!+
Mobile Duron	850	200	Super A	L1: 128 KB L2: 64 KB (Full Speed)	0.18μ	25 million	3DNow!+ or 3DNow! Pro[1]
Athlon 4[2] (Palomino)	400 (1600+/1400, 1500+/1300)	200	Socket A	L1: 128 KB L2: 256 KB (Full Speed)	0.18μ	37.5 million	3DNow! Pro[1]
Athlon XP[2] (Thoroughbred)	1533 (1800+/1533, 1700+/1467, 1600+/1400, 1500+/1333, 1400+/1200)	200	Socket A	L1: 128 KB L2: 256 KB (Full Speed)	0.13μ	37.5 million	3DNow! Pro[1]
Athlon 64[2] (Clawhammer)	2000 (3200+/2000, 3000+/1800, 2800+/1600)	1600	Socket 754	L1: 128 KB L2: 1 MB (Full Speed)	0.13μ	106 million	3DNow! Pro[1] SS2 AMD64

[1]Includes Intel's SSE.
[2]Includes PowerNow!
[3]The numbers in parentheses represent the model number and the actual speed.
[4]The front-side bus has been replaced by a dedicated memory bus and a HyperTransport link. The HyperTransport link operates at this speed.

4.3.3 AMD Opteron and Athlon 64

In 2003, AMD entered the 64-bit arena with the AMD Opteron, made for workstations and servers, and the AMD Athlon 64. Both of these are based on a new technology AMD calls ×86-64, which extends the current architecture to address 64 bits of data, yet remains backward-compatible for 32-bit software. Opteron executes both software types natively and thus at full speed. This gives users the opportunity to stick with 32-bit software for the time being, saving the costs of a complete software revamp and still leaving the chance for a future "upgrade" to 64-bit software without having to buy a new platform. In addition, it includes a 40-bit address bus, which allows it to recognize up to 1024 GB of RAM, but that may be extended in the future. In 2004 Microsoft will release a Windows and Office version optimized for the x86-64 architecture, and there are already Linux versions that support the x86-64 architecture.

The Opteron processor can be used in single-processor systems through eight-way multiprocessor systems. The Athlon 64 processor does not support dual- or multiprocessing. See figure 4.17. The Athlon 64 processor family includes the Athlon 64 and Athlon 64 FX. The sockets or form factors for these processors are as follows:

- The Athlon 64 will use socket 754 and 939
- The Athlon FX will use socket 939 and 940
- The Opteron will use socket 940

The AMD Opteron and Athlon 64 FX have different electrical specifications. Therefore, you will not be able to use an Opteron processor in an Athlon 64 FX motherboard and vice versa. In addition, the Athlon 64 FX will move over to the 939-pin socket to restore the physical product differentiation between the Athlon 64 FX and the Opteron.

The Opteron has a three-digit part number scheme for the Opteron. The first Opteron models were 240, 242, 244, 840, 842, and 844. The first digit indicates the intended symmetric multiprocessing scalability (SMP will be discussed later in this chapter). Therefore, the 240 will support up to two processors in a system and the 840 will support up to eight processors. AMD will also manufacture a one-way Opteron (Model 144) for high-performance, lower cost systems. The second and third digits indicate its clock speed:

40	1.4 GHz
42	1.6 GHz
44	1.8 GHz
46	2.0 GHz
48	2.2 GHz
50	2.4 GHz

Figure 4.17 AMD Opteron Processor

The Athlon 64 FX starts with the Athlon 64 FX-51 model for desktops, which runs at 2.2 GHz, and FX-53, which runs at 2.4 GHz.

The different pin count of the two processors is due to the additional memory channels and HyperTransport ports. The current Opterons use nearly 106 million transistors in a 130 nanometer (nm) Silicon on Insulator (SOI) process and use the ceramic micro-PGA package. SOI refers to placing a thin layer of silicon on top of an insulator such as silicon oxide or glass so that the SOI layer will reduce the capacitance of the switch, which allows the switch to operate faster.

The L1 cache has 128 KB capacity, split into a 64 KB instruction cache and a 64 KB data cache. The Opteron and Athlon FX will have a 1 MB L2 cache, and the Athlon 64 processors will have a 512 KB or 1 MB L2 cache. AMD will later release Athlon 64 processor models with 256 KB of L2 cache.

These processors will have built-in memory controllers with increased performance over the traditional memory controllers that are found on the motherboard. The Opteron, Athlon FX, and the Athlon 64 processors with socket 939 or 940 will have 128-bit memory controllers, whereas the Athlon 64 processors with socket 754 will have a 64-bit memory controller. The Athlon 64 FX uses registered DIMMs (socket 940) or unbuffered memory (socket 939), whereas the Athlon 64 connects to a single-channel 64-bit memory bus that uses unbuffered memory. The Opteron processors use registered double data rate (DDR) memory.

The HyperTransport is the interface for processor-to-processor and processor-to-chipset, providing a bandwidth of up to 6.4 Gbps (3.2 Gbps in each direction) and thus about 50 percent more than what the Pentium 4 or Xeon processors with 533 MHz processor bus clock are able to provide. Similar to newer forms of memory, the earlier interface is clocked at 800 MHz, but transports data at double data rate. The bandwidth for the various AMD 64-bit processors are:

- The AMD Athlon has one HyperTransport link (running at 1.6 GHz) which allows 6.4 GBps to the system and 64-bit 3.2 GBps to the memory, giving a total of 9.6 GBps. Newer processors will have a 2.0 GHz system bus with up to 14.4 GBps total processor-to-system bandwidth.
- Early AMD Athlon FX processors have one HyperTransport that allows 128-bit 6.4 GBps (running at 1.6 GHz) to the system and 6.4 GBps to the memory, giving a total of 12.8 GBps. Later AMD Athlon FX models have one HyperTransport that allows 128-bit 8.0 Gbps (running at 2.0 GHz) to the system and 6.4 GBps to the memory, for a total of 14.4 GBps. The 754-pin processors run at 1.6 GHz and the 939-pin processors run at 2.0 GHz.
- The Opteron has three coherent HyperTransport links that provide 19.2 GBps peak bandwidth per processor.

With the 64-bit AMD processors, AMD added its **Enhanced Virus Protection security technology** into its processors that will work with Microsoft's Data Execution Prevention System that is released with Windows XP Service Pack 2 and is available with 64-bit-enabled Linux operating systems. As mentioned earlier, this technology is designed to prevent buffer overrun exploits that occur when a malicious piece of code is executed.

For 64-bit mobile processors, you can use the Athlon 64 processors as desktop replacement notebooks or you can use low-power mobile AMD Athlon 64 processors. In the past, increased processor performance meant increased power consumption and increased noise level. AMD's Cool'n' Quiet technology lowers the power consumption and fan noise while delivering performance on demand. It controls your system's level of processor performance automatically by adjusting the operating frequency and voltage up to 30 times per second, according to the task at hand. As a result, the system will run cooler and quieter. Performance is designed to still be responsive, with maximum processor performance being delivered when required, and automatic power savings when possible.

To be able to use the Cool'n' Quiet technology, you will need the following:

1. AMD Athlon 64 processor that includes Cool'n' Quiet technology. At this time, only the AMD Athlon 64 processors supports Cool'n' Quiet technology.
2. Motherboard with BIOS support for Cool'n' Quiet technology
3. Processor driver/Cool'n' Quiet software, which can be downloaded from http://www.amd.com.
4. Required for noise reduction, you will need a heat sink/fan that can be thermally controlled (speed control).

Figure 4.18 Cyrix Media GX Processor

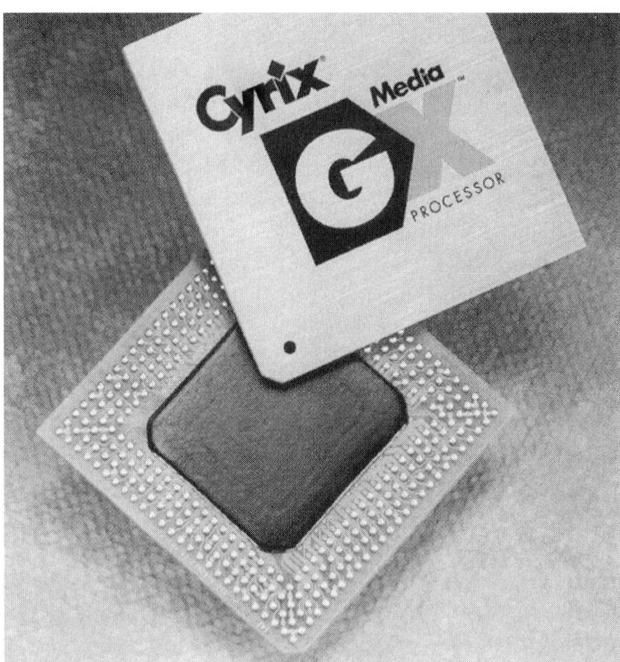

4.3.4 VIA/Cyrix Processors

The Cyrix MediaGX, introduced in February 1997, was created to be a low-cost multimedia chip that would run like a Pentium chip. See figure 4.18. To make it faster, Cyrix used six pipeline stages and included a 16 KB cache. Like Intel's Pentium chips, the MediaGX has two 32-bit internal registers and a 64-bit external data bus. The chip's main boost comes from its built-in graphics system with its own pipeline and built-in support for SoundBlaster-compatible audio, an MIDI interface, and digital audio processing. In addition, the Cyrix processor handles functions usually found on other support chips on the motherboard. These include a bridge logic to the ISA bus, four ATA ports to be used with the enhanced IDE drives, an AT-compatible timer, an interrupt controller, a DMA controller, and a PCI interface.

The newest version of the MediaGX family is the MMX-Enhanced MediaGX processor (desktop version and mobile version). In addition to the main features of the MediaGX processor, the MMX-Enhanced MediaGX processor features support for MPEG1 and two USB ports, includes an integrated game port control, and supports MMX technology. The Cyrix 6x86, formerly codenamed M1, does not convert the CISC instructions into RISC-like instructions. Instead, the 6x86 operates on a nonuniform-size x86 code more efficiently than other processors do. It has a superpipelined architecture with seven stages (instead of the Pentium chip's five stages). This allows the Cyrix processor to start an instruction before the previous one is finished. Other features include multibranch prediction, speculative execution, out-of-order completion, and register renaming.

For a while, Cyrix and AMD used a P rating system (short for "performance rating") to describe the performance of their processors. This extra label suggests that their processors have better code execution and execute faster (at a given frequency) than Intel's Pentium or Pentium II processors. They use the Winstone97 benchmark for comparisons. For example, a processor with Pentium processor running at 75 MHz performance is labeled PR75, yet an AMD or Cyrix processor, which ran at 60 MHz but had a PR75 label, would run the same as a Pentium processor running at 75 MHz. Unfortunately, this system caused a lot of confusion and was not widely accepted.

The 6×86 MX processor was formerly referred to as the M2. See figure 4.19. It runs at a lesser voltage, can use the same slot as the corresponding Pentium chip and is optimized for both 16- and 32-bit applications. Its pipeline has 9 or 10 stages, more than the 7 stages used in the M1, and it includes a 64 KB, four-way associative L1 cache. Unlike AMD, which licensed the MMX instruction set from Intel, Cyrix developed its own MMX-compatible instructions.

Figure 4.19 Cyrix 6x86 MX Processor

The VIA Cyrix III processor (codename Samuel) uses the industry standard socket 370 interface and is currently available at speeds of 500 to 700 MHz. The VIA Cyrix^{Reg} III processor comes with a host of enhanced features, such as a 128 KB full-speed level 1 cache and a 100/133 MHz front-side bus. It includes MMX technology and 3DNow! instructions.

The first processor on the market to be built using the 0.15 μm manufacturing process and later with the 0.13 μm manufacturing process, the new VIA C3 processor (codename Samuel 2) is a low-power, low-cost x86 processor. It uses the industry standard socket 370 interface and has a 128 KB full-speed level 1 cache and 64 KB full-speed level 2 cache. It supports a 133 MHz front-side bus as well as MMX and 3DNOW! multimedia instruction.

VIA has also released two other processors. The VIA Antaur processor, aimed at slim and light notebook PC systems, uses the CoolStream architecture designed to increase performance while decreasing power consumption. It has clock speeds of at least 1 GHz and uses a 16-stage pipeline while consuming only 11 W at 1 GHz. It uses an enhanced 64 KB full-speed exclusive L2 cache with 16-way associativity and includes SSE instructions. It also includes the PadLock Data Encryption Engine Power efficient on-die Hardware Random Number Generator (RNG).

The other processor is the Eden-N processor, based on the streamlined Nehemiah core architecture. VIA considers this processor to be the most advanced embedded hardware security technologies in a tiny nanoBGA package designal to deliver enhanced digital media performance features. With only a 15 mm × 15 mm die, it is the world's smallest, low-power, most secure native ×86 processor. Compared to other processors, it consumes only 7 W of power at 1 GHz.

4.3.5 Transmeta Processors

In January 2000, Transmeta Corporation introduced Crusoe, a new processor marketed as a high-performance processor that consumes little power and has little heat dissipation. Currently, the Crusoe processors are used in thin-and-light notebooks and ultra-dense servers. The Crusoe processor Model TM5900, which can range from 800 MHz to 1 GHz, has 128 KB L1 cache and 512 KB L2 cache. Based on 0.13 μm technology, it consumes between 9.5 W (including Northbridge power) at 1 GHz. It includes on-chip SDRAM and DDR SDRAM memory interfaces and on-chip 32-bit, 33 MHz PCI bus controller. Unfortunately the Crusoe has had limited success (mostly in Japan) because of low performance in early models.

4.4 THERMAL SOLUTIONS

Most of today's faster processors produce a lot of heat, and this heat has to be dissipated or the system will operate only intermittently or even fail completely. Heat is dissipated inseveral ways. The IBM PC and XT were cooled by adding holes in the side of the case, which allowed the heat to escape by convection.

Figure 4.20 Heat Sink

When the 286 was introduced, it produced more heat, which could not be released fast enough. To alleviate this problem, fans were added to the power supply to suck the hot air out instead of letting it build up. If the power supply fan fails in a computer with a 386 processor or better, the case of the computer will be warm to the touch.

By the time the 486 processors were being introduced, a fan could not handle the load; it needed help. To overcome this problem, a heat sink was placed on top of the processor. A **heat sink** is a finned piece of metal that is clipped or glued to the top of the processor. See figure 4.20. The finned piece of metal has more surface area than a flat piece, so it will pull the heat away from the processor faster. Note: For a heat sink to cool a processor efficiently, a thermal transfer material should be used between the heat sink and fan. The thermal transfer compound is either a thermal conductive adhesive tape or a thermal grease.

Thermally conductive adhesive tapes are double-sided pressure-sensitive adhesive films filled with sufficient ceramic powder to balance their thermal and adhesive properties. Adhesive tapes provide convenience in attaching a heat sink to a semiconductor package because no cure time is required. The film is applied to one of the surfaces, usually to the heat sink, and it is then forced into contact with the semiconductor package to complete the thermal joint. The application pressure is typically 10 to 50 pounds per square inch (lb/in^2) for a few seconds' duration. Note: If you remove the heat sink with the thermal interface adhesive, you should inspect the thermal interface adhesive. If you remove it more than twice or change it to another processor, you should replace the adhesive.

Thermal greases are made by dispersing thermally conductive ceramic fillers in silicone or hydrocarbon oils to form a paste. Sufficient grease is applied to one of the mating surfaces so that when it is pressed against the other surface, the grease flows into all voids to eliminate gaps. Excess grease flows out past the edges and the thinnest possible thermal joint is formed as the two surfaces come into contact at their high points. Joint integrity has to be maintained with spring clips or mounting hardware. Excess grease that flows from the joint should be cleaned up to prevent contamination problems. Greased joints can also dry out with time, resulting in increased thermal resistance. Note: If you apply thermal grease and break the seal after it is applied, you should clean off the old thermal grease and apply fresh thermal grease.

When the faster 486 processors and the Pentium processors were introduced, a small fan had to be added to the top of the heat sink to suck the heat away from the processor. See figure 4.21. Some newer motherboards, cases, and power supplies are designed to eliminate the need for a fan by blowing air into the computer. To improve the efficiency of the system, the fan is positioned to blow directly over the processor.

The fan power cable must be connected to a motherboard power header or a power cable from the power supply. The fans connected to the motherboard use a three-wire cable, two pins supply +12 V and GND. The third wire can be used to transmit fan-speed information to motherboards that support fan-speed detection, which can be monitored in the BIOS setup program or monitoring software.

Figure 4.21 Processor Fan with Heat Sink

While the shrinking of transistors have allowed each transistor to dissipate less heat, the increase in the number of transistors packed in a smaller area means that the processors needed bigger cooling systems. This means larger heat sinks and fans and more efficient thermal compounds or liquid cooling.

Liquid cooling is essentially a radiator for the processor inside of the computer. Just like a radiator for a car, a liquid cooling system circulates a liquid through a heat sink attached to the processor inside of the computer. As the liquid passes through the heat sink, heat is transferred from the hot processor to the cooler liquid. The hot liquid then moves out to a radiator at the back of the case and transfers the heat to the ambient air outside of the case. The cooled liquid then travels back through the system to the processor to continue the process.

Liquid cooling is a much more efficient system at drawing heat away from the processor and outside of the system. This benefits the system by allowing for higher clock speeds in the processor as the ambient temperatures of the processor core are still within the manufacturer's specifications.

The other benefit of liquid cooling is the reduction of noise within the computer. Most current heat sink and fan combinations tend to generate a lot of noise for the fans that need to circulate air over the CPU and through the system. Many high-performance CPUs require fan speeds in excess of 7000 revolutions per minute (rpm) that generate noise of 60+ decibels of noise. Over clocking a CPU requires even more airflow over the CPU, but when a liquid cooling solution, there is much less noise.

Generally there are two moving parts to a liquid cooling system. The first is the impeller which is a fan immersed in the liquid to circulate the liquid through the system. These are generally fairly low in noise because the liquid acts as a noise insulator. The second is a fan at the exterior of the case to help pull air over the cooling tubes of the radiator. Both of these do not need to run at very high speeds which reduces the amount of noise by the system.

A disadvantage to liquid cooling in computer systems is that there may be some technical skill required to install the kit to make sure it is installed properly and does not leak.

Another cooling method commonly used by overclockers is Peltier coolers. **Peltier coolers,** also known as thermoelectric coolers, are solid state heat pumps that, with the application of electrical current, transfer heat from one side of the device to the other. While the amount of heat reduction they can achieve varies with the quality of Peltier, a temperature differential between the two sides of 130°F (55°C) for a very high-end model. While Peltier coolers cost more than other cooling devices and they consume much more power than the other cooling devices, there are certain precautions that you must take. First, you must make sure that the hot side is connected to the heat sink and the cold side is connected to the processor. Second, you will have worry about condensation, especially in humid regions.

If a motherboard or processor has a thermal sensor, the temperature of the processor can be monitored. If the motherboard thinks that the processor is running too hot, it will throttle the processor in attempt to cool it or it could shut down the entire system. These motherboards may allow you to view the temperature using the CMOS/BIOS setup program or by running a software package such as the Intel Active Monitor that comes with Intel boxed motherboards.

Sometimes, in particular when a new family or stepping of a processor is released, the motherboard may misread the temperature of the processor. If this occurs with different processors on the same motherboard, you should question whether it is the processor or the motherboard. If you feel little heat coming from the processor and/or heat sink, it is most likely the motherboard misreading the temperature.

NOTE: A heat sink can get very hot, so you should be careful not to burn yourself. To get an accurate reading, you will have to use a thermal measuring device that you put on top of the processor die. If the motherboard misreads the temperature, it can usually be corrected with a BIOS update.

4.5 STEPPINGS AND ERRATAS

Many people think all versions of the same processor are the same. However, there may be several versions of a Pentium III processor running at 933 MHz. Much like software, hardware often contains errata (bugs) due to its tremendous complexity, and so it is revised and new versions are put out. In addition, sometimes the processor goes through some form of enhancement, such as a die shrink or a voltage change. These changes are not widely publicized, and often people don't realize that there are many different versions of popular processors on the market, with newer ones often fixing problems occurring with older ones.

Some companies (Cyrix for example) use an explicit version number with their chips. Intel instead uses a term called a *stepping*. Essentially, a stepping number is the same as a revision number. The word itself comes from the name of the machine that is used to make the chip, which is called a stepper. The stepping can be identified by the CPUID number, accessing the support website, the specification update guide, and the Frequency ID Utility.

Processors can be identified by their S-Spec number (a five-character string starting with *SL*), which is printed on the box of a boxed processor or on the processor itself. See figure 4.22. By looking up the S-Spec number at the processor support website or by using the specification update guide, the characteristics of the processor can be identified, including the stepping, CPUID, bus speed, and cache speed.

When viewing the specification update guide, each specification is assigned a CPUID string, which is four characters in length. The first character is typically a 0, and the second and third characters represent the family and model number. The fourth character represents the processor stepping. For example, if you find one processor with a CPUID of 0672 and a second processor with a CPUID of 0673, both processors have the same family and model number (67) but have different steppings.

Figure 4.22 Sample Processor Specification Guide

Pentium® III Processor Identification and Package Information

S-Spec	Core Steppings	CPUID	Speed (MHz) Core/Bus[11]	L2 Size (Kbytes)	Tag RAM/ Steppings	ECC/ Non-ECC	Processor Substrate Revision	Package and Revision	Notes
SL5LT	tA1	06B1h	1.13GHz/133	256	N/A	ECC		FC-PGA2 (370 pin)	7
SL5VX	tA1	06B1h	1.333GHz /133	256	N/A	ECC		FC-PGA2 (370 pin)	
SL5GR	tA1	06B1h	1GHz-S /133	256	N/A	ECC		FC-PGA2 (370 pin)	
SL5PU	tA1	06B1h	1.13GHz-S /133	512	N/A	ECC		FC-PGA2 (370 pin)	20
SL5LV	tA1	06B1h	1.13GHz-S /133	512	N/A	ECC		FC-PGA2 (370 pin)	7, 20
SL5QL	tA1	06B1h	1.26 GHz-S /133	512	N/A	ECC		FC-PGA2 (370 pin)	20
SL5LW	tA1	06B1h	1.26 GHz-S /133	512	N/A	ECC		FC-PGA2 (370 pin)	7, 20

† Unless otherwise noted, all Pentium III processors in S.E.C.C.2 package have an OLGA package core.

NOTES:

1. These parts will only operate at the specified core to bus frequency ratio at which they were manufactured and tested. It is not necessary to configure the core frequency ratios by using the A20M#, IGNEE#, LINT[1]/NMI and LINT[0]/INTR pins during RESET.
2. These processors will not shut down automatically upon assertion of THERMTRIP#.
3. This is a boxed processor with an attached heatsink.
4. Performance-monitoring event counters do not reflect MOVD and MOVQ stores to memory on these processors.
5. These parts will not assert THERMTRIP#, nor will they shut down in the event of an over-temperature condition (e.g., Tj = ~135° C).
6. Pin AJ3 is removed from these parts.
7. This is a boxed processor with an unattached fan heatsink.
8. This is a boxed processor with an attached fan heatsink.
9. These processors will not be validated in Dual Processor (DP) applications.
10. The "E" and "B" designators distinguish between Pentium® III processors with the same core frequency but different system bus frequencies and/or cache implementations.
    B = 133 MHz System Bus
    E = Processors with "Advanced Transfer Cache" (CPUID 068x and greater only if a frequency overlap exists)
    If, for a given core frequency, Pentium III processors are only available with one system bus frequency and one cache

It can be difficult to determine the stepping number of a processor, because this isn't something most retailers even understand, but getting the wrong version of a processor can lead to system problems later on. Some early versions of certain processors can have extreme problems, and it can be very hard to tell what version you are getting because different versions can exist for the same chip running at the same speed.

4.6 INSTALLING A PROCESSOR

Before installing a processor, make sure that the motherboard will accommodate the new processor. You should verify that the motherboard was designed to handle the specific processor (based on the type of processor, its frequency, its voltage, its cache size, and its stepping) that you want to install. This may include contacting the motherboard manufacturer or visiting its website. In addition, for the motherboard to be identified correctly and to operate properly, you may need to make sure that the motherboard has the newest BIOS available for that motherboard.

First, when installing a processor, avoid electrostatic discharge (ESD). This is even more important today than in the past because newer chips run at a lower voltage, which makes them more susceptible to ESD than were the older processors. Second, keep in mind that not all processors use the same sockets or slots. The older processors, of course, had fewer pins or contacts because of their smaller address and data buses and 5 V operation. The newer processors have well over 300 pins and use lower voltages. Finally, avoid breaking or cracking the processor and the motherboard, and avoid bending or mangling the chip pins.

Many motherboard manufacturers began using low-insertion-force (LIF) sockets, which typically require only 60 lb of insertion force for a 169-pin chip. Inserting a processor using a LIF socket takes a bit more work and care because you must be sure to have the pins lined up properly with the holes of the socket. If they are not lined up and you press down with 60 to 100 lb of force, the pins will bend. It will then take a pair of needle-nose pliers to straighten the pins, which may cause further ESD damage as you are working on the chip. Removing a processor inserted into a LIF socket also takes a bit of care. The best technique is to insert a small flat-edge screwdriver between the chip and the socket and gently pry the processor away from the socket. Each of the sides of the chip must be pried up until the chip can be easily pulled away from the socket.

Today, nearly all motherboard manufacturers that use sockets are using zero-insertion-force (ZIF) sockets. These sockets almost eliminate the risk involved in upgrading because no insertion force is necessary to install the chip. Most ZIF sockets are handle-actuated; you simply lift the handle, drop the chip into the socket, and then close the handle. This design makes replacing the original processor with the upgraded processor an easy task.

When installing a processor, the chip must be oriented properly on the motherboard. If a processor is off by 90° or inserted backward, it may damage the processor or the motherboard. Today, most processors are keyed so that they will go in only one way. For the PGA processors, pin A1 on the chip is designated by a slightly clipped corner, a small dot or triangle on one corner, or a missing pin on one or two of its corners. See table 4.9 and figure 4.23.

Slotted processors are inserted into a slot. The slot and processor are keyed so that they can be inserted only one way. To hold the processors in place, most motherboards use a retention mechanism.

After the processor is installed, you will need to apply the thermal solution, usually consisting of heat sinks and fans. The fan power cable must be connected to the fan power connector and the motherboard power header. The motherboard three-pin power header uses two pins to supply +12 V and GND. The fan uses the third pin to transmit fan-speed information to motherboards that support fan-speed detection. Your motherboard must have a three-pin fan power header located close to the slot or socket. Refer to your motherboard manual for the location of the power header.

Mobile processors in the MMC-2 cartridge or micro-PGA2 package are not difficult. The hardest part is disassembling the notebook to get to the processor socket. Then, you insert the processor connector into a wide slot. The micro-PGA2 and micro-flip chip processors are similar to a ZIF socket, except instead of using a handle, it uses a screw that you turn to tighten down or loosen the processor. Micro-BGA processors are soldered to the notebook and so require special skills and tools to replace them.

Table 4.9 Various Sockets and Slots Used with Processors

Designator	Number of Pins or Contacts	Voltage	Supported Processors
Socket 1	169 pins	5 V	486DX, 486SX, 486DX2, 486DX4, Pentium OverDrive
Socket 2	238 pins	5 V	486DX, 486SX, 486DX2, 486DX OverDrive, Pentium OverDrive 63 and 83
Socket 3	237 pins	5 V/3.3 V	486DX, 486SX, 486DX2, 486DX4, AMD 5x85, Cyrix 5x86, Pentium OverDrive 63 and 83
Socket 4	273 pins	5 V	Pentium 60–66, Pentium OverDrive 120, 133
Socket 5	320 pins	3.3 V	Pentium 75–133, Pentium OverDrive 125–166, Pentium with MMX OverDrive 125–166
Socket 7	321 pins	2.5 V–3.3 V	Pentium 75–200, Pentium OverDrive, Pentium with MMX, Pentium with MMX OverDrive, 6x86, K5, K6, 6x86 MX
Socket 8	387 pins	3.1 V, 3.3 V	Pentium Pro
Socket 370	370 pins	N/A	Pentium III, Celeron
Socket 423	423 pins	N/A	Pentium 4
Socket 478	478 pins	N/A	Pentium 4
Socket 603	603 pins	N/A	Intel Xeon
Socket 604	604 pins	N/A	Intel Xeon
Socket 754	754 pins	N/A	Athlon 64
Socket 939	939 pins	N/A	Athlon 64, Athlon 64 FX
Socket 940	940 pins	N/A	Opteron, Athlon 64 FX
Socket A	462 pins	1.75 V	Athlon, Duron
Slot 1	242 contacts	2.8 V, 3.3 V	Pentium II, Pentium Pro with socket 8 on daughtercard, Intel Celeron
Slot 2	330 contacts	N/A	Pentium II Xeon, Pentium III Xeon
Slot A	242 contacts	N/A	Athlon, Duron
Socket T	775 contacts	N/A	Pentium 4
PAC418 Socket	418 contacts	N/A	Itanium
PAC611	611 contacts	N/A	Itanium 2

After the processor is inserted into the motherboard, the motherboard may need to be configured. Today's motherboards are designed to take various processors. They may need to be configured using jumpers, DIP switches, or the CMOS setup program to set them to the proper processor, speed, bus ratio, system bus speed, and voltage. Note: Newer motherboards will autoconfigure. For some systems to work properly, the CMOS setup program may have to be run to configure the wait states if the motherboard cannot keep up with the processor.

Intel's move from slot 1 to socket 370 FC-PGA packages created a demand for special converters called socket-to-slot adapters, or slockets, to enable an Intel socket 370 processor to be run in a

Figure 4.23 Socket 7 or ZIF socket. Pin 1 is located on the top left corner.

slot 1 motherboard. Although Intel does not recommend these devices, if you do use them, make sure that the adapter is recommended by the motherboard manufacturer for the specific processor. By using these adapters, you are increasing the pathway for signals and may throw the processor out of specification, which may cause erratic errors, not work at all, or damage the processor and/or motherboard.

4.7 SYMMETRIC MULTIPROCESSING (SMP)

Symmetric multiprocessing (SMP) involves a computer that uses two or more microprocessors that share the same memory. If software is written to use the multiple microprocessors, several programs can be executed at the same time, or multithreaded applications can be executed faster. A multithreaded application is an application that is broken into several smaller parts and executed simultaneously. For example, Microsoft Word uses a thread to respond to keys typed on the keyboard by the user to place characters in a document. Other threads are used to check spelling, paginate the document as you type, and spool a document to the printer in the background. The ability for an OS to use additional microprocessors is known as *multiprocessing scalability.*

When verifying if processors will work for your multiprocessing system, you must first determine if the processors will support multiprocessing and if the processors will work with each other. Therefore, you must check the following:

1. The only processors that are multiprocessing-capable are Intel Pentium II, Intel Pentium III, Intel Pentium II Xeon, Pentium III Xeon, and Intel Xeon processors. Note: Not all these processors support multiprocessing. The Intel Celeron, Pentium 4, and mobile processors do not support multiprocessing. For AMD, the only processor that supports multiprocessing is the Athlon MP and Opteron.
2. Make sure the processor supports multiprocessing. This can be determined by using the respective specification update guide. To determine if the processor supports multiprocessing, find your S-Spec in the processor identification and package information tables and read the notes for the particular processor to determine if the processor is multiprocessing capable.

Figure 4.24 The DP platform matrix used in the specification update guides can determine if steppings are compatible. In this example, a Pentium® III processor running at 600 MHz with a 133 MHz bus and 256 KB cache have no issues between processors using the cBO stepping and the cCO stepping.

DP Platform Population Matrix for the Pentium® III Processor with 133-MHz System Bus in the FC-PGA370 Package from 866 MHz to 1 GHz

Pentium® III Processor Stepping	866 MHz cB0	933 MHz cB0	866 MHz cC0	933 MHz cC0	1B GHz cC0	866 MHz cD0	933 MHz cD0	1B GHz cD0
866-MHz cB0	NI	X	NI	X	X	NI	X	X
933-MHz cB0	X	NI	X	NI	X	X	NI	X
866-MHz cC0	NI	X	NI	X	X	NI	X	X
933-MHz cC0	X	NI	X	NI	X	X	NI	X
1B-GHz cC0	X	X	X	X	NI	X	X	NI
866-MHz cD0	NI	X	NI	X	X	NI	X	X
933-MHz cD0	X	NI	X	NI	X	X	NI	X
1B-GHz cD0	X	X	X	X	NI	X	X	NI

NOTES:

X= Mixing processors at different frequencies is not supported.

NI= Currently no known issues associated with mixing these steppings.

TBD= No issues are expected, however further investigation is required to fully validate this DP solution.

3. The processors must have identical frequency, bus speed, and cache size. Processors used in a multiprocessing system must share the same family and model number. This will ensure that processors used in a multiprocessing system will have the same speed, same cache size, and same bus speed. In many cases, you may mix processor steppings in a multiprocessor system.
4. Processors must have compatible steppings. By using the specification update guide, you can determine the stepping by referring to the S-Spec in the processor identification and package information tables. Then you need to cross-reference both steppings, processor speed, and bus speed with the DP platform population matrix tables to see if there are any issues and, if there are any issues, what they are. NI indicates no issues. See figure 4.24. Note: Identical silicon steppings may sometimes be shipped with different test specification numbers, depending on whether they are for OEMs (tray processors) or for system integrators (boxed processors).

Even though Intel recommends using identical processor steppings in multiprocessor systems whenever possible (as this is the only configuration that receives Intel's full testing), Intel supports mixing processor steppings and does not actively prevent various steppings of the Pentium III processor from working together in dual-processor systems. However, because Intel cannot test every possible combination of devices, each new stepping of a device is fully tested only against the latest steppings of other processors and chipset components. In addition, when partially populated systems are shipped, a customer returning for additional processors may have difficulty locating a processor with the same stepping. If this occurs, the customer may have to replace the original processor to obtain a system with two processors of the same stepping.

To ensure that the processors will work in a multiprocessing system, you must make sure that the motherboard will fully support multiprocessing and that it will support the specific processors you want to use. Therefore, you should check the following:

1. Due to the variety of motherboard vendors in the market and the number of system BIOS revisions, some system-level issues may occur that lie outside the realm of any mixed stepping evaluation performed by Intel. Intel recommends the following:
   - Choose a motherboard vendor with a history of dual-processor experience.
   - Contact your motherboard vendor for information on mixed stepping validation performed on your particular dual-processor motherboard.

   NOTE: Although Intel includes a multiprocessing "known issues" table, only the motherboard vendor can say definitively if a particular pair of mixed steppings has been validated in that particular board.

2. The power supply must be able to provide sufficient power to the motherboard with multiprocessors and all peripherals connected to the motherboard.
3. If you use two processors that have different voltages, the motherboard must have two voltage regulators to operate both processors properly.

In dual-processor systems, the processor with the lowest feature set, as determined by the CPUID feature bytes, must be the bootstrap processor (BSP). The BSP is the processor that starts the booting process. In the event of a tie in feature-set values, the tie should be resolved by selecting the BSP to be the processor with the lowest stepping, as determined by the CPUID instruction. For example, if you have two Pentium III processors with the same core frequency, same cache, and same bus speed, yet one is a b0 stepping and the second is the c0, you should designate the processor with the b0 stepping as the bootstrap processor.

Be sure to use an operating system that supports multiprocessing. Currently, Microsoft Windows NT, Windows 2000, Windows XP, and Windows Server 2003 support multiprocessor and most versions of Linux. Microsoft Windows 95, Windows 98, and Windows Me do not. If you have only one processor installed when you install Windows NT, Windows 2000, or Windows XP, you will need to change the HAL to a multiprocessing HAL when you start using more than one processor. For Linux to support multiple processors, you may have to recompile the kernel. Check with the documentation that comes with the OS. Note: For a program to use multiple processors, the program must be multithreaded.

If you use a multiprocessing motherboard and you don't use all the processors, some motherboards require having a special terminator or VRM in the empty processor slot. If the motherboard is self-terminating and you are having problems booting, you may try inserting a special terminator or a matched processor in the empty slot or socket to verify that the self-termination is actually working properly. Lastly, check the BIOS settings. Some boards may have options to retest or enable/disable processors.

Eventually, you will see processors that include simultaneously multithreading (SMT), which will present two "virtual" processors to software applications. As a result, the processor will allow multiple program paths (threads) to be run concurrently. In other words, SMT allows a single processor to appear to the OS as two or more logical processors, thus giving dual processing or better performance without having to spend the money for a dual processor or better platform.

4.8 MEASURING PROCESSOR PERFORMANCE

When trying to figure out which processor you want to purchase, you want to know which processor is the fastest. Because the various processors made by the different manufacturers are a little different in how they execute instructions, you would have to look at benchmarks to get an idea how well a processor performs.

4.8.1 MIPS and FLOPS

MIPS (millions of instructions per second) is an old measurement of microprocessor speed and performance. MIPS roughly measures the number of arithmetic machine instructions that a microprocessor executes in one second. However, different instructions require more or less time than others, and no standard method exists for measuring MIPS effectively. MIPS refers only to microprocessor speed, whereas applications are generally limited by other factors, components, and computer subsystem (such as I/O speed).

FLOPS (floating-point operations per second) is a measurement for rating the speed of a microprocessor's floating-point unit. Floating-point operations include any operations that involve fractional numbers. Such operations, which take much longer to compute than integer operations, occur often in some applications.

Most modern microprocessors include a floating-point unit (FPU), which is a specialized part of the microprocessor responsible for executing floating-point operations. FLOPS actually measures the speed of the FPU. Many experts feel that FLOPS is not a relevant measurement because it fails to take into account factors such as the condition under which the microprocessor is running (e.g., heavy or light loads) and which exact operations are included as floating-point operations.

4.8.2 Standard Performance Evaluation (SPEC)

A consortium of PC hardware, software, and component makers created the Standard Performance Evaluation Corporation (SPEC), which provides more meaningful benchmark values that are more easily understood and used for comparison purposes. SPEC is a nonprofit corporation that creates a standard suite of benchmark tests. For more information, visit the http://open.specbench.org/ website.

As the successor to CPU95, SPEC CPU2000 is the next-generation industry-standardized CPU-intensive benchmark suite. SPEC designed CPU2000 to provide a comparative measure of computer-intensive performance across the widest practical range of hardware. The implementation resulted in source code benchmarks developed from real user applications. These benchmarks measure the performance of the processor, memory, and compiler on the tested system. Note: As time goes on, it is very possible that the SPEC CPU2000 test may be replaced by a newer test. Therefore, to find out the newest test offered by SPEC, visit the website.

4.8.3 Composite Theoretical Performance (CTP)

Intel does publish the Composite Theoretical Performance (CTP) values for Intel's processors. The CTP calculations are based upon a modified formula and stated in millions of theoretical operations per second (MTOPS), which are used as export control of processors to foreign countries. To view the CTP values for Intel processors, visit the following website:

http://support.intel.com/support/processors/CTP.HTM

4.8.4 Other Performance Indicators

In 1992, Intel introduced the iCOMP Index to provide PC consumers with an easy-to-use tool to understand and compare the relative performance differences among Intel processors. The index comprised four industry-standard benchmarks weighted to reflect the mix of 16- and 32-bit software applications in use at that time and those expected to be in use for the next three to four years.

In 1996, Intel updated the Index to iCOMP Index 2.0 to reflect the trend toward 32-bit software and the proliferation of multimedia applications. The index comprised four industry-standard 32-bit benchmarks and a multimedia benchmark that reflected software applications in use at that time and those expected to be in use for the next few years.

To reflect the rapid adoption of new technology and software that is commonly used on PCs with increased use of 3D, multimedia, and Internet, Intel has updated the iCOMP Index with six industry-standard benchmarks. The updated index is called iCOMP Index 3.0. The iCOMP Index 3.0 measures Intel's families of Performance PC processors across the Spectrum of Performance LINK TO SoP Site. Performance measurements based on a single benchmark or application will focus primarily on a single aspect of processor performance. The iCOMP Index 3.0 measures performance based on a broader, more comprehensive spectrum of processor benchmarks to provide a more complete performance perspective. The iCOMP Index 3.0 measures the Spectrum of Performance through incorporating benchmarks in productivity, multimedia, 3D, and the Internet.

These categories are based on the usage patterns of today's PC user as well as anticipated future software trends. By examining performance metrics in each of these four categories, PC users will obtain a better understanding of how their processor will perform on the wide variety of applications they will be using. The iCOMP Index 3.0 is based on the Spectrum of Performance and is intended to reflect native Intel processor performance for the application mix that a typical end user will be using today and over the next several years. Multimedia, 3D, and Internet application use has increased sharply over the past few years, and this trend is anticipated to continue in the future. For this reason, a wide range of benchmarks should be considered when evaluating processor and system performance. PC users and buyers should consider the entire Spectrum of Performance, which includes productivity, multimedia, 3D, and Internet performance.

Unfortunately, the iCOMP Index 3.0 is outdated as newer processors, such as the Pentium 4, have been introduced. The older tested models that make up the composite score have not been updated yet to take advantage of the advanced features of the processor.

4.9 TROUBLESHOOTING PROCESSORS

Because the processor is the brain of the computer, the processor is a critical part of the computer. Therefore, if it fails, it greatly affects the computer. The computer may not boot at all, it may cause an error with the software, or it may lock up (the computer remains on and the image remains on the screen, but the mouse and keyboard do not respond and all program activity stops).

If you suspect problems with the processor, you should check the following:

- Make sure that the motherboard supports the specific processor.
- Make sure the processor is installed correctly.
- Make sure that the voltage and frequency are correctly configured for the processor.
- Make sure that the system and processor have an adequate thermal solution.
- Try a BIOS update.

Make sure that the motherboard supports the specific processor, as explained in section 4.6. You need to find out if the processor is completely inserted in the socket or slot and oriented correctly. If the voltage and frequency are not configured correctly, the processor may not boot at all, may act erratically, or may be damaged after several months of use. If the system or the processor does not have an adequate thermal solution, the processor may burn itself out, which may result in smoke and flame or internal damage.

Make sure that the thermal solution is applied correctly; if you are using a heat sink, make sure that the heat sink has the appropriate thermal interface material or thermal grease. With the thermal solution, make sure that the power supply fan, processor fan, and any external fans are operating well and that you have enough room around the case to provide a good airflow.

Many people will not think of doing a BIOS update to correct processor problems. But today, the BIOS upgrade may add bits of code so that the system can properly identify the processor (especially if the processor came out after the motherboard), it may tell the system some of the operational parameters of the processor, including the frequency and voltage, and it may overcome some errata with the processor. BIOS upgrades can correct Windows stop errors and a wide range of other problems.

When troubleshooting the computer, you should consider that because the processor is the heart of the computer, problems with the processor and those with the overall system could sometimes be considered to be interchangeable. For example, when the system locks up, the processor is locking up (and vice versa).

Example 4.2:

The processor appears to be dead and the computer does not boot. You get no beep codes and nothing appears on the monitor.

There are many possible reasons why a processor can appear to have failed. In the real world, processor failures are rare if the processor has worked for more than a month, hasn't been affected by ESD, and hasn't been abused (including not being overclocked) and if it has the proper working thermal solution. Problems with processors are far more likely to be misconfigurations, overheating problems, or misdiagnoses of other failed components.

When troubleshooting any PC problem, you should always first check the obvious. Because you have no fan and no lights, you should make sure that you have power to the system. Therefore, make sure that the system is plugged in and that you have power to the AC outlet. If you are using a surge protector, make sure that the surge protector is on. A common problem is that the input voltage selection on the back of the power supply is not set to the correct 115 or 230 V.

Next, you should do a quick inspection of the system. Make sure that the power connectors are connected to the motherboard; if you are using an ATX power supply, make sure that the power on/off switch cable is connected properly to the motherboard. Lastly, make sure that the ribbon cables are oriented properly, especially the IDE cables.

If you have recently built the system or recently installed the processor, make sure that the processor is tightly inserted into its socket and that is has been inserted correctly and not rotated in the socket somehow. Double-check the jumpers and/or BIOS settings for the frequency and voltage settings. You should also make sure the motherboard does support the processor that you are trying to install. If the motherboard was made before the processor that you want to use, you may need to do a BIOS upgrade, even though the manual and website says that it supports the processor.

To determine if you have a faulty processor, you need to try a working processor of the same type into the system and try the suspected faulty processor in another system. If the good processor works in the system and the suspected faulty processor does not work in the other system, it probably means that the processor is bad.

If both processors fail in the system and the suspected processor works in another system, the processors are probably good and you have some other problem with the system. The motherboard may not be correctly installed, you may have incorrect or too aggressive CMOS settings, the RAM may be bad or installed incorrectly, or the power supply may be faulty. To test the RAM or motherboard, you can try swapping these components with known good components. If the CMOS settings are too aggressive, you may need to remove or discharge the CMOS battery to put the CMOS settings back to default. If there is a power problem, you should measure the power supply to see if it is supplying the proper voltage and check to see if any of the components are causing a short or overload. The motherboard, RAM, CMOS settings, and power-related problems are discussed in later chapters.

Example 4.3:

You receive an audio or POST code indicating a processor failure.

These codes can be caused by a faulty power supply, a bad motherboard, or a bad processor. Again, check to see if the processor is installed properly. Next, isolate the bad motherboard and processor by swapping them for others one by one. Don't forget to try the suspected component in a working system.

Example 4.4:

The PC crashes or freezes when certain applications are run.

Crashing can be caused by the processor, motherboard, RAM chips, or corrupt files. First, check for viruses. Then try to run a diagnostic program to test the processor, the motherboard, and the RAM. If Windows itself is crashing or freezing, try Windows in safe mode. If the problem doesn't occur in safe mode, most likely you have a corrupt or incompatible driver or some other program that starts up when Windows starts. If it is another application, try reinstalling the software that is giving you the error message. If the problem still persists, try reformatting the hard drive and then reinstall the operating system and application software. If the problem still persists, make sure that you have the newest BIOS and double-check the jumpers and/or CMOS settings for the frequency and voltage settings for the processor. You also may have incorrect or too aggressive CMOS settings. Therefore, you should try to enter the CMOS setup program and adjust the settings, especially those that deal with the processor and memory. Lastly, try isolating the RAM chips, processor, and motherboard.

Example 4.5:

The PC crashes or reboots after several minutes of operations.

The most likely cause is overheating. First, make sure that the PC has enough room around it so that it gets adequate ventilation. Next, feel the PC case to see if it is warmer than normal. If it is very warm to the touch, it probably means the power supply fan is faulty. If it is not, check to see if the processor itself is overheating, including checking that the heat sink is in place and the processor fan is running.

If the problem occurs only when you use a specific peripheral, such as a mouse or modem, there are three typical possible causes specific to this situation. First, there may be a problem with the particular peripheral you are trying to use. Second, you may have a resource conflict such as IRQ or

DMA that is causing the system to lock up when you try to have two devices access the same resources. Finally, there may be a driver problem with the device, if it is something that uses a driver in the operating system you are using. To help isolate this, try loading Windows in the safe mode to see if the problem still persists.

Next, you should scan for viruses and scan the hard disk for file system corruption; check for bad sectors as well. If you experience the problem when running a specific application program, suspect that the application is the problem. Drivers can cause seemingly random glitches and lockups if they are poorly written, especially the video driver. Try running the system with a "slow but sure" default driver or a different version obtained from the manufacturer. In Windows, make sure you have a large-enough swap or paging file (virtual memory) and that you have enough free disk space.

In the CMOS setup program, you should disable all power-management options. If you have recently changed any settings using the CMOS setup program, especially with system timing or memory, try changing the CMOS setting back to the previous value or resetting the CMOS settings to conservative defaults to see if the problem goes away.

If you have unreliable power, it can cause all sorts of strange problems including causing your computer to reboot and lock up. If you notice the lights dim briefly at around the time that this problem occurs, it is a power problem. In these cases, try a line conditioner or UPS and make sure that you don't have devices that consume a lot of power on the same circuit as the computer. If practical, try swapping in a new power supply.

Lastly, if the problem still persists, you will need to swap out the processor, RAM, and motherboard with known good components, one at a time. You should also try the suspicious components in a working system.

Example 4.6:

The system is reporting the wrong processor or wrong processor speed.

During boot-up, the BIOS usually reports the current speed of the processor, but remember that this speed is controlled by how the motherboard is set up. Therefore, check the frequency, system bus speed, or bus ratio setup with jumpers or the CMOS setup program. In addition, make sure that the system has the newest BIOS, especially if the motherboard came out before the processor. Note: If the reported speed of the processor is off slightly, such as a Pentium II processor running at 300 MHz and reporting at 299 or 301 MHz, this is probably just a quirk.

If you have an Intel Pentium III, Intel Celeron (FC-PGA or micro-FC), or Pentium 4 processor, use the Intel frequency ID program to verify that the processor installed is that actually processor that you think you have in the system.

First, if the speed is misreported incorrectly on an LED speed readout on the front of your case, this display does not have anything to do with the processor at all and is determined with jumpers on the case.

If the system software is misreporting, including the operating system, the most likely problem is that the software came out before the processor existed. For example, Microsoft Windows 95 and 98 were released prior to the introduction of the Pentium III processor, so they may not identify the processor correctly. This is cosmetic and does not affect the operation or functionality of the system. When this does happen, you should check to see if there is a patch or update that you can download from the software manufacturer. For example, Microsoft updated Windows so that it can recognize the Pentium III processor with the release of Windows 98 SE.

Some software will identify the processor so that it knows what features the processor has. This way, the software can use those features to get the best performance out of the processor. Unfortunately, depending on how well the software was written to identify the processor, some software cannot identify when new processor types come out. Therefore, one of the two things will happen. First, the processor will assume the processor with the least features. In this case, the software will not run as fast as it would if it could take advantage of the more advanced features of the processor. Second, it will not know what the processor is and will refuse to run on that processor. In either case, the only thing that can be done to correct this is to see if there is a software update from the software manufacturer.

Example 4.7:

Your system is running slow.

There are two generic causes for this problem: either something has changed gradually over time to cause performance to degrade, or there has been an abrupt hardware or software change that is responsible for reduced performance. There are a number of different situations that can be responsible for the system performance changing.

First, scan the system for viruses and make sure that your disk is defragmented. If the hard disk light flickers a lot when you load programs into Windows and your system, does your machine have enough memory? The PC is probably thrashing as it accesses virtual memory (disk pretending to be RAM). You should also see if you have lots of free disk space on your hard drive.

Try updating your Windows drivers and looking at your computer load. Your computer might be so busy because it is running a lot of programs, including those small programs that might be running in the background, such as when you upgrade the operating system.

Double-check all CMOS parameters to make sure nothing has been changed and that they are correct, particularly the frequency settings for the processor, the cache settings, memory timings, and hard disk modes.

Check the processor to make sure it is not overheating, and make sure the CPU fan is still running. Some processors will intentionally slow the processor when the processor begins to overheat in an attempt to cool it.

If you have an older system and you recently added more memory to your system (more than 64 MB of system RAM), your motherboard may not support caching of more than 64 MB of system memory. This will cause performance to be degraded when accessing the uncached memory.

Lastly, refer to chapters 21 and 22 to see other tips for optimizing Windows and using the system or performance monitor to analyze the load of the processor, RAM, and disk system.

SUMMARY

1. A microprocessor, also known as the processor and CPU (central processing unit), is an integrated circuit that acts as the brain of the computer.
2. The microprocessor has three major areas including the input/output (I/O) unit, the control unit, and the arithmetic/logic unit (ALU).
3. The ALU does the actual processing of data, whereas the I/O unit links the microprocessor to the rest of the computer.
4. The size and spacing of the microprocessor's transistors (silicon etchings) partially determine the switching speed. The diameter of transistors is measured in microns; (micrometer) one micron is one-millionth of a meter.
5. In 1965, Moore's law stated that the number of transistors per square inch on integrated circuits had doubled and would double every year since the time the integrated chip was invented.
6. The clock speed (measured in MHz and GHz) is the speed at which the processor executes instructions; every computer contains an internal clock.
7. Overclocking is the process of running the microprocessor at a clock speed faster than specified.
8. A register is a high-speed internal storage area that acts as the microprocessor's short-term memory and work area.
9. A floating-point number is a number with a decimal point or a number that includes an exponent.
10. The arithmetic/logic unit (ALU), sometimes referred to as execution unit, follows the instructions of the control unit and is the calculator part of the microprocessor.
11. Processors that can execute more than one instruction per clock cycle are known to be superscalar.
12. Floating-point units (FPUs) are chips that specialize in floating-point mathematical calculations typically at greater precision.
13. The control unit is a clocked logic circuit that controls the entire chip, including the ALU. It translates and follows the instructions contained in an external program (such as the ROM BIOS, the operating system, or application software) and keeps track of which step of the program is being executed.
14. Pipelines execute an instruction much like an assembly line.
15. CISC commands are considered complex commands because they consist of several small commands (microcode) grouped together.
16. RISC commands consist of smaller commands of the same size that are not grouped together. These can be performed in one clock cycle or fewer.

17. MMX technology consists of 57 multimedia instructions designed to improve video compression and decompression, image manipulation, encryption, and I/O processor.
18. Single instruction, multiple data (SIMD) uses one instruction to perform the same function on multiple pieces of data at the same time.
19. The data bus, which is managed by the bus control unit, is what actually carries the instruction and data into and out of the microprocessor.
20. The signals of the address bus, controlled by the address control unit, determine where the data bus signals are going to or coming from.
21. The control bus coordinates the data transfer between the microprocessor and another device.
22. Bus speed is the speed at which data moves on a bus.
23. Cache memory is a special ultrafast memory that acts as a buffer between the microprocessor and the slower RAM.
24. Although L1 cache is faster, the L2 cache is typically much larger than the L1 cache, ranging from 64 KB to 4 MB.
25. Real-address mode provides backward compatibility for those programs written for the 8088 and 8086 processors. The processor pretends to be an 8086 processor.
26. Protected mode is the native operating mode of the processor that allows it to use more than 1 MB of RAM. It protects two programs that are running simultaneously.
27. The 386 protection mechanism assigns data and instructions to a privilege ring or level.
28. Before installing a processor, make sure that the motherboard will accommodate the new processor. You should verify that the motherboard was designed to handle the specific processor (based on the type of processor, its frequency, its voltage, its cache size, and its stepping) that you want to install.
29. After the processor is installed, you will need to apply the thermal solution, usually consisting of heat sinks and fans.
30. Today, socketed processors use low-insertion-force (LIF) or zero-insertion-force (ZIF) sockets.
31. When installing a socketed processor, the chip must be oriented properly on the motherboard. Today, most processors are keyed so that they will go in only one way.
32. On PGA processors, pin A1 on the chip is designated by a slightly clipped corner, a small dot or triangle on one corner, or a missing pin on one or two of its corners.
33. Slotted processors are inserted into a slot. The slot and processor are keyed so that they can be inserted only one way.
34. Most of today's faster processors produce a lot of heat. This heat has to be dissipated or the system will operate only intermittently or even fail completely.
35. To dissipate this heat, processors use heat sinks and active cooling systems (fans or liquid cooling systems).
36. A heat sink is a finned piece of metal that has more surface area than a flat piece, so it will pull the heat away from the processor faster.
37. To make a sufficient thermal connection between the heat sink and the processor, you will most likely use thermal conductive adhesive tape or thermal grease.
38. Symmetric multiprocessing (SMP) involves a computer that uses two or more processors that share the same memory.
39. If software is written to use the multiple processors, several programs can be executed at the same time, or multithreaded applications can be executed faster.
40. When using processors in a multiprocessing system, the processor must support multiprocessing and each processor must be the same type of processor, the same speed, the same cache size, and have compatible steppings.
41. The Pentium processor used socket 4, socket 5, or socket 5.
42. The Pentium with MM technology used socket 7.
43. The Pentium II processor used slot 1.
44. Pentium III processors used slot 1 or socket 370.
45. The Pentium 4 processor used socket 423, socket 478, or socket T (775 contacts).
46. AMD Athlon and Duron processors used slot A or socket A.
47. The Athlon 64 uses socket 754 and the Opteron uses socket 940.
48. Cache memory is a special ultrafast memory that acts as a buffer between the processor and the slower RAM.
49. Although the L1 cache is faster, the L2 cache is typically much larger, ranging from 64 KB to 6 MB.

QUESTIONS

1. Another term for *microprocessor* is
   a. motherboard. b. system unit.
   c. CPU. d. RAM.
2. The main integrated chip around which the PC is built is the
   a. UART.
   b. CPU.
   c. RAM.
   d. real-time clock.
   e. System ROM BIOS

3. Which of the following describes a processor (choose two answers)?
   a. executes software instructions
   b. performs arithmetic functions
   c. stores system configuration
   d. controls the hard drive
4. Data that is processed in a processor is placed in small storage areas and manipulated. The small storage areas are called
   a. RAM.
   b. registers.
   c. clipboards.
   d. accumulators.
   e. scratchpads.
5. Computer clock speeds are expressed in (choose two answers)
   a. gigahertz.
   b. megahertz.
   c. hertz.
   d. kilohertz.
6. What determines the location of RAM that data is coming from and going to?
   a. data bus
   b. address bus
   c. registers
   d. control unit
7. What part of the CPU actually completes the mathematical calculations and logical comparisons?
   a. ALU
   b. instruction queue
   c. control unit
   d. registers
8. Which of the following is *not* an advantage of the RISC commands over the CISC commands?
   a. RISC commands are smaller.
   b. RISC commands can be executed in one cycle.
   c. RISC commands have to be translated by the CPU before execution.
   d. RISC commands can be executed out of order.
9. What is the maximum amount of RAM that the 8086 processor can access?
   a. 640 KB
   b. 1 MB
   c. 4 MB
   d. 16 MB
10. What size are the data path and the address bus for the Intel Pentium III processor?
    a. 32-bit and 32-bit
    b. 3-bit and 36-bit
    c. 64-bit and 32-bit
    d. 64-bit and 36-bit
11. Which of the following processors include MMX technology (choose all that apply)?
    a. 486DX
    b. Pentium
    c. Pentium with MMX
    d. Pentium Pro
    e. Pentium II
    f. Pentium III
12. Which of the following processors include SSE2 (choose all that apply)?
    a. Pentium II
    b. Pentium III
    c. Pentium 4
    d. Pentium III Xeon
    e. Intel Xeon
    f. Athlon
13. Which of the following uses the superscalar architecture?
    a. 386DX
    b. 486SX
    c. 486DX
    d. Pentium
14. Which of the following have a built-in L2 RAM cache (choose all that apply)?
    a. Pentium with MMX
    b. Athlon
    c. Pentium Pro
    d. Pentium II
    e. Duron
15. If a processor has a 32-bit address bus, how much RAM can the processor work with?
    a. 1 MB
    b. 4 MB
    c. 16 MB
    d. 256 MB
    e. 4 GB
    f. 64 GB
16. When the processor starts in real mode, how much RAM can the processor work with?
    a. 1 MB
    b. 4 MB
    c. 16 MB
    d. 256 MB
    e. 1024 MB
    f. 4 GB
17. Protected mode refers to the processor's ability to
    a. run two or more programs at the same time, with each program protected from the actions of the other.
    b. protect the processor from power surges and spikes.
    c. protect the data generated by the processor.
    d. protect the processor from external damage.
18. What type of socket does the Pentium with MMX use?
    a. socket 5
    b. socket 7
    c. socket 8
    d. socket A
    e. socket M
    f. socket MX
19. Which of the following uses a single-edge connector?
    a. Pentium
    b. Pentium with MMX
    c. Pentium Pro
    d. Pentium II
20. Which of the following enhances a computer's ability to process arithmetic operations quickly, particularly floating-point calculations?
    a. video controller
    b. SCSI controller
    c. math coprocessor
    d. DMA
21. Which of the following should be done when replacing a processor?
    a. wearing an ESD wrist strap
    b. aligning the notch on the chip with the socket
    c. cleaning the pins before inserting
    d. all of the above
22. Which of the following affects the reliability of a processor?
    a. ESD
    b. high temperature
    c. too much voltage
    d. all of the above
23. Which component may be failing if the fan and hard drive run, yet the system appears dead?
    a. on/off switch
    b. power supply
    c. power cord
    d. processor
    e. keyboard

24. Microprocessors since the 386 use the Intel Protection model. Which ring allows the greatest access to the processor?
    a. 0
    b. 1
    c. 2
    d. 3
    e. 7
25. *True or false*—A computer with an AMD K5 processor can run MS-DOS and Windows 98.
26. You are troubleshooting a problem with a computer and you suspect that the problem is the processor. What is the best way to make sure that processor works properly?
    a. Return it to the manufacturer.
    b. Swap it out with a known good spare.
    c. Run system diagnostics in the system BIOS.
    d. Check the continuity between the first and last pins on the processor.
27. You are troubleshooting a problem with a Windows 98 computer. Sometimes it fails during POST and locks up just after POST. Other times it will successfully load Windows and work properly for a short time before locking up. Which hardware component is the most likely source of this problem?
    a. processor
    b. system board
    c. graphics adapter
    d. power supply
    e. disk controller
28. What is the area of memory called that is reserved for storing data that the processor will soon need again?
    a. BIOS
    b. sector
    c. ROM
    d. cache
    e. virtual drive
29. You are troubleshooting a problem with a computer that you are assembling with parts from several older systems. The motherboard you are using originally had a Pentium 166 processor installed. You replaced the original processor with a Pentium 233 processor, but POST identifies the processor as a Pentium 166. Which action is required to fix this problem?
    a. Reseat the processor.
    b. Temporarily remove the CMOS battery.
    c. Configure jumpers on the motherboard.
    d. Short out the reset pins on the motherboard.
30. Which processor is also known by the codename K7?
    a. Cyrix III
    b. AMD Athlon
    c. Intel Pentium II
    d. AMD Duron
    e. Cyrix/VIA M3
    f. Intel Pentium III Xeon
31. Intel reduced the voltage requirements of its second-generation Pentium processors to what voltage?
    a. 5 V DC
    b. 3.3 V DC
    c. 12 V DC
    d. 15 V DC
32. The Pentium II processor is housed in an SEC cartridge. What does the cartridge use to hold the processor in place?
    a. solder
    b. retention mechanism
    c. integrated peripheral controller
    d. heat sink
    e. plastic quad flat package
33. A Pentium 4 uses which package type (choose two answers)?
    a. SECC
    b. 423-pin PPGA
    c. FC-PGA
    d. FC-PGA2
34. The Pentium 4 processor uses which architecture?
    a. superscalar architecture
    b. P6 architecture
    c. NetBurst microarchitecture
    d. x86-64 architecture
35. The Athlon 64 chip uses which architecture?
    a. superscalar architecture
    b. P6 architecture
    c. NetBurst microarchitecture
    d. x86-64 architecture
36. The Opteron processor uses which socket?
    a. socket 370
    b. socket 754
    c. socket 423
    d. socket 940

HANDS-ON EXERCISES

Exercise 1: Identifing the Processor

1. What kind of processor does your system have?
2. What is the actual speed of the processor and what is the bus speed for the processor?
3. Calculate the bus multiplier by dividing the actual speed of the processor by the bus speed. Round off to the nearest 0.5.
4. If it is a slotted processor, see how the processor is keyed. If it is a socketed processor, look to see how pin A1 is designated on the motherboard and how pin A1 is designated on the processor.
5. If the processor has a fan, disconnect the power cable that powers the fan from the motherboard.
6. If the processor has a heat sink, carefully remove the heat sink from the processor (if possible). Look at the thermal compound used.

7. Remove the fan from the heat sink.
8. If the processor is not soldered on to the motherboard, carefully remove the processor from the motherboard. Do not bend or mangle the pins of the processor.
9. Reinstall the processor, heat sink, and fan and test the system.
10. Look at your motherboard documentation for jumpers on how to configure the processor. If there are any, find them on the motherboard and record how they are configured.
11. Look at the BIOS setup program for options in the BIOS setup program used to configure the processor. Also look in the motherboard documentation for these settings. If there are any, find them on the motherboard and record how they are configured.
12. Start Task Manager by pressing the Ctrl+Alt+Del buttons. If necessary, click on the Task Manager button.
13. Click the Performance tab. Notice the CPU Usage and CPU Usage History.
14. While task manager is still running, start Adobe Acrobat Reader and note what the CPU usage is.
15. Click the Processes tab and look at the CPU usage that each program uses.
16. Close the Task Manager.

Exercise 2: Researching Processors

Intel Processors

1. Go to the http://www.intel.com/support/processors website.
2. Click on the Pentium 4 processor link.
3. Click and read the product overview link.
4. Click on the Back button.
5. In the Identifying Your Processor section, select the Processor Spec Finder tool link. Then click on the Go to Processor Spec Finder now link.
6. Identify the fastest Pentium 4 processor. Identify its bus speed and package type.
7. Click on the S-Spec number. Determine core stepping, L2 cache size, core voltage, heat dissipation (thermal guideline), maximum temperature (thermal spec), and manufacturing technology.
8. Click on the Back button.
9. Using the Processor Spec Finder, if you have an Intel processor with an SL6SM, determine the package type, speed of the processor, bus speed, core stepping, L2 cache size, core voltage, and manufacturing technology.
10. Using the Processor Spec Finder, if you have an Intel processor with an SL4X5, determine the package type, speed of the processor, bus speed, core stepping, L2 cache size, core voltage, and manufacturing technology.
11. Go back to the http://www.intel.com/support/processors/pentium4/ website.
12. Click and read the Advanced integration notes for Pentium 4 processors in the 478-pin package.
13. Go back to the http://www.intel.com/support/processors/ website.
14. Click and read the Processor Package Type Guide and view the different package types.
15. Click the Specification Update link.
16. Go back to the http://www.intel.com/support/processors/pentium4/ website and click the specification update in the left pane. Click the Intel Pentium 4 Processor Specification Update link and open the Intel Pentium 4 Processor Specification Update guide.
17. Scroll down to the General Information section and look at how to identify the frequency, cache size, bus speed, and voltage of a Pentium 4 processor.
18. Scroll further until you get to the Intel Pentium 4 Processor Identification Information.
19. Find the SL684 S-Spec and determine the core stepping, the L2 cache size, the CPUID, the core speed, and the bus speed. In addition, read the notes associated with the SL684 processor.
20. Go back to the http://www.intel.com/support/processors/ website and click the Intel Xeon Processor link.
21. Click and read the Differences between Intel Xeon Processors and Intel Xeon Processors MP.
22. Click on the Back button.
23. Open the Specification Update Guide for the Intel Xeon processors.
24. Scroll down to table 1: Intel Xeon Processor Identification and Package Information.
25. Find the SL56H S-Spec and identify the core stepping, processor signature, core and bus speed, and L2 cache.
26. Find the SL5TD S-Spec and identify the core stepping, processor signature, core and bus speed, and L2 cache.
27. Find the SL5U6 S-Spec and identify the core stepping, processor signature, core and bus speed, and L2 cache.
28. Find the SL5TE S-Spec and identify the core stepping, processor signature, core and bus speed, and L2 cache.
29. Scroll down to table 2 and determine which of these four processors can be used together in a dual-processing system.

AMD Processors

1. Go to the http://www.amd.com website.
2. Click on the Processors link located at the top of the page.
3. Select the AMD Athlon XP Desktop link.
4. Find and click the Product Brief link and read about the AMD Athlon XP Desktop processor.
5. Find and click the Architectural Features and read about the AMD Athlon PX Desktop processor.
6. Open and read the Socket A AMD Processor and Heatsink Installation Guide.
7. Click on the Back button.
8. Select the Processor & Heatsink Installation Videos. Watch all five videos.
9. Go back to the AMD processor home page and access the information for the AMD Athlon MP Workstations processors.
10. Find and read information on the AMD Athlon, Opteron, and Opteron FX processors.

Exercise 3: Testing Your Processor

1. If you have an Intel processor, go to the http://www.intel.com/support/processors/index.htm website and download the Intel Processor Frequency ID Utility.
2. Run the program and identify your processor. Determine if your processor is being overclocked.
3. Go to the http://download.com website. Find and download the Hot CPU Tester Pro program and use it to test your processor.

Exercise 4: Looking at Processor Speeds, Bus Speeds, and Ratios

1. If you have an Intel Pentium III processor running at 1.0 GHz that has a system bus of 133 MHz, what is the bus ratio? Round to the nearest 0.5.
2. If the system bus was set to 100 MHz, what would the processor run at?
3. If you have an Intel Pentium III processor running at 800 MHz that has a system bus of 100 MHz, what is the bus ratio? Round to the nearest 0.5.
4. If the system bus was set to 133 MHz, what would the processor run at? Note: Of course, this is not recommended since this is overclocking the processor.
5. If you have an Intel Pentium 4 processor running with a 533 MHz system bus speed, what is the actual system bus speed?
6. If you take the actual system bus speed and use a multiplier of 23, what is the speed of the processor?

CHAPTER 5

RAM

Topics Covered in This Chapter

Introduction

Random access memory (RAM) is the computer's primary memory. This means that the programs are executed and data is created and manipulated in the RAM by the microprocessor. The amount of RAM determines how many programs you can run, how big each program can be, and how many documents you can have open at the same time. In addition, the amount of RAM is a big factor in your PC's performance.

Objectives

1. Define *RAM* and list the characteristics of RAM.
2. Compare and differentiate DRAM and SRAM.
3. Explain how RAM is addressed.
4. Explain why DRAM needs to be refreshed.
5. Compare and differentiate FPM RAM, EDO RAM, BEDO RAM, SDRAM, DDR SDRAM, and DDR2 SDRAM.
6. List and describe the memory areas.
7. Explain how RAM can increase PC performance.
8. Define *virtual memory* and explain how it interacts with RAM.
9. Compare and differentiate the different packages of RAM including DIP, SIPP, SIMM, DIMM, SO-DIMM, Micro-DIMM, and RIMM.
10. Install and remove RAM from a system.
11. List and explain the different forms of error control used in RAM.
12. Describe what a bank of RAM is and explain how a bank relates to the data bus and size of the RAM chip.
13. Given a RAM chip, determine its speed and capacity.
14. List and describe the different symptoms caused by faulty RAM.
15. Explain how to isolate faulty RAM.

5.1 RANDOM ACCESS MEMORY (RAM)

Random access memory, more commonly referred to as **RAM,** consists of electronic memory chips that store information inside the computer. It is called *random access* memory because the information is accessed nonsequentially. Unlike a reel of data storage tape, which is accessed starting at one end until the location of the data is reached, information in the RAM can be accessed directly without going through preceding information.

RAM is known as *volatile* memory because it loses its content when the power is turned off. This is the reason that the user must save the contents of RAM to a disk. Much like a blackboard, information on RAM can be taken away from it and overwritten.

RAM is considered the main memory or the *primary memory* because it is the memory that the microprocessor accesses directly. This means the program instruction that the CPU is executing must first be copied to the RAM from a device such as a disk. In addition, the data, such as letters, reports, and charts, generated by programs must be in the RAM to be manipulated. Therefore, it is the amount of RAM that determines how many programs can be executed at one time and how much data can be available to a program. In addition, the amount of memory is a major factor in determining how fast your computer will operate.

5.2 RAM ARCHITECTURE

RAM chips are based on two types of technology. The most common is dynamic RAM **(DRAM),** which is normally used for the primary memory; the other type is static RAM **(SRAM),** which is usually used for RAM cache.

5.2.1 DRAM

To store information, DRAM uses a storage cell consisting of a tiny solid-state capacitor and a transistor. A **capacitor** is a simple electrical device, similar to a battery, that is capable of storing a charge of electrons. The charge or lack of charge represents a single bit of data. If the capacitor is charged, it has a logic state of 1. If it is discharged, it has a logic state of 0. A **transistor** is a tiny electronic switch that can be turned on or shut off by the flow of input voltage. When the input voltage is off, the switch is open and no current flows through the circuit. When the input voltage is turned on, the switch closes and current is permitted to flow.

The memory storage cells are organized into a large two-dimensional array or table made up of rows and columns. Similar to cells in a spreadsheet, each memory cell is identified by a row and column address, known as the **physical address.** Each row is activated with its own word line. After the row is activated, a pair of bit lines specifies which memory cell (column) to access within the activated row. Both the word lines and bit lines are controlled by the memory controller.

After the read or write operations are completed, the column deactivates to get ready for the next read/write cycle. Unfortunately, during the time needed for deactivation, the microprocessor is waiting. The period during which the CPU is waiting is called a **wait state.**

A DRAM chip can contain millions of storage cells. That many capacitors in a small space requires that the capacitors be extremely small. Since they are extremely small, charges can be added or withdrawn from them in just a few nanoseconds, but unfortunately, their small size also means they can hold their charge only for a few milliseconds. Therefore, the DRAM must be refreshed (recharged) often to maintain its information. To recharge the DRAM storage cells, the computer uses a special circuit to run a **refresh routine.** The routine takes control of the data and address buses from the microprocessor and recharges all of the cells in each row by reading and rewriting each storage cell, row by row. While older computers use the DMA controller to run the refresh routine, newer computers use a special circuit within the chipset.

5.2.2 SRAM

Static RAM consists of storage cells, each having four transistors and two resistors that act as an electronic switch (flip-flop latch). If the switch is on, it allows electricity to flow, representing the binary value of one (1). If the switch is off, electricity stops flowing, and the circuit represents a binary value of zero (0). The advantage of SRAM over DRAM is that SRAM chips are faster and do not require refreshing. Unfortunately, SRAM storage cells (six components) are larger, more complicated, and cost more than DRAM storage cells (two components). SRAM also consumes more power because current is always flowing through the cells.

5.2.3 Access Time and Bandwidth

Bandwidth is the maximum amount of data that can be delivered in a given period of time, and it can be computed by multiplying the bus speed by the bus width. Bus width is the number of bits that can be transferred simultaneously. Doubling the bus width will allow twice as much data to be transferred without increasing the bus speed.

For a 1 GHz processor with a 133 MHz system bus that has a 64-bit data bus, the maximum bandwidth for the processor is 133 million × 64 bits/8 bits/byte = 1.064 GB/s. However, it is virtually impossible to achieve this kind of throughput.

The speed and performance of memory is sometimes confusing because the memory speed is usually expressed in nanoseconds and processor speed has always been expressed in megahertz. Note: A nanosecond is defined as one billionth of a second. Recently, some newer and faster types of memory have speeds expressed in MHz, adding to the confusion. Typically, frequency = 1/time. However, system memory timing is a little more involved than simply converting nanoseconds to megahertz.

As described before, the system memory is arranged in a grid consisting of rows and columns. All memory accesses involve selecting a row address, selecting a column address, and transferring the data. The initial setup for a memory transfer or the time before data begins to flow is called *latency.* The access time is the delay from the time data in memory are successfully addressed to the point at which the data are successfully delivered to the data bus.

As mentioned in chapter 4, if a processor is trying to read multiple bytes of data from slower memory, wait states have to be added. The wait state is a catch-up period during which the processor lies idle. To reduce the number of wait states required, several types of faster memory and cache are available, and newer ones are currently under development.

A typical memory cycle, also called access speed (also known as cycle time), for a DRAM chip in the early PCs was 120 ns or slower. Later, the access speed was dropped to 70 or 80 ns. Today, the memory cycle might be as low as 8 or 10 ns. Of course, a lower number indicates a faster speed.

With the original DRAM used in the IBM PC, the DRAM was rated with a memory access rate of 120 ns. To access data, it took 5 clock cycles to activate the row and column, send the data, and deactivate the row and column. Therefore, it would take 5 clock cycles × 120 ns/clock cycle = 600 ns to access memory. To access the second piece of memory, even if it was next to the last piece of memory, it would take another 600 ns. Therefore, the burst cycle timing is expressed as 5-5-5-5 which means that it would take 5 clock cycles to access the first piece of data and 5 clock cycles to access sequential data. Therefore, with a 16-bit data bus, it would take 20 clock cycles or 2400 ns to access 8 bytes of data.

With SDRAM, a typical memory cycle might be 8 ns. But with pipelining techniques, newer RAM uses a burst cycle timing of 5-1-1-1. To access the first piece of data, it still takes 5 clock cycles. Therefore, to access the first piece of memory, it would take 8 ns/clock cycles × 5 clock cycles = 40 ns to access the first piece of memory. It would then take only 1 clock cycle or 8 ns to access the next few memory spaces. Therefore, with a 64-bit data bus, it would take 8 clock cycles or 64 ns to access 32 bytes of data.

Assuming that no other factors slow down the data transfer, with 64 ns to transfer 32 bytes of data, the actual throughput is only 32 bytes/64 ns = 500 MB/s. In other words, due to the limitations of the SDRAM itself, only half of the bandwidth can be utilized.

Of course, the burst length may be longer than 4 cycles, which would provide better utilization of the bandwidth, but the example also did not take into account certain propagation delays. The chipset itself needs to perform a few operations, which also takes up a few cycles. As a result, the typical SDRAM timings from system perspective is more likely 7-1-1-1 or even 8-1-1-1, thereby causing the effective bandwidth utilization to drop even lower.

When RAM is addressed by the memory controller, each row is activated. The memory addresses, representing by a row/column value, are read from or written to. The row is then deactivated, and the next row is processed. Memory timings control how quickly the memory controller processes each row of memory. The faster the controller processes the data in memory, the faster your PC moves.

Today, the memory timing may be expressed in the following format:

CAS-tRCD-RAS Precharge-tRAS-tRP-Command Rate

An example of the memory timing would be:

2-3-3-7-1T

See table 5.1. For the best performance, you want the smallest value possible for each parameter that allows the system to run without crashing or becoming unstable.

Table 5.1 System Training for SDRAM/DDR RAM

Memory Parameter	Common Abbreviation	What It Does	Range of Typical Values (in Clock Cycles)
RAS to CAS delay	tRCD	Activates row	2 or 3
CAS latency	CAS or CL	Causes delay between activation of row and reading of row	2, 2.5, or 3 for DDR 2 or 3 for SDRAM
RAS precharge	tRP	Deactivates row	2 or 3
Command rate		Causes delay between chip select and command	1 or 2
Active or precharge delay	tRAS	Specifies the number of clock cycles between activation and deactivates row	3, 4, 5, 6, or 7

Table 5.2 Types of RAM Chips

Type of RAM Chip	Typical Access Time	Burst Cycle Timing	Time of First Access	Time of Sequential Access
DRAM	150 ns	5-5-5-5	750 ns	750 ns
FPM RAM	70 ns	5-3-3-3	350 ns	210 ns
EDO RAM	60 ns	5-2-2-2	300 ns	120 ns
BEDO RAM	50 ns	5-1-1-1	250 ns	50 ns
SDRAM	10 ns	5-1-1-1	50 ns	10 ns

5.2.4 Fast Page Mode RAM (FPM RAM)

Newer machines, up through 1995, used **fast page mode RAM (FPM RAM),** which had typical speeds of 70 or 80 ns. The fast page mode RAM works like the DRAM chip except that it tries to reduce the number of wait states. If data are accessed in the same row (sometimes referred to as a *page*) as the preceding data, the chip saves time by not deactivating and reactivating the row for the second piece of data. Ideally, a read from a 70 ns FPM memory can achieve a burst cycle timing of 5-3-3-3, quicker than the 5-5-5-5 of DRAM. (See table 5.2.)

5.2.5 Extended Data Output RAM (EDO RAM)

Extended data output RAM, usually referred to as **EDO RAM,** takes the fast page mode RAM technology one step further. The two-stage pipeline of the EDO RAM chip lets the memory controller read data off the chip while it is being reset for the next operation. Instead of deactivating the column and turning off the output buffer, EDO RAM keeps the output data buffer on. If the data that needs to be transferred is sequential to the data just sent, it will be sent more efficiently. As a result of this design, the burst cycle timing of the EDO RAM chip is reduced to 5-2-2-2, giving it approximately 10–15 percent better performance than FPM RAM. The speed of an EDO RAM chip is therefore either 50 or 60 ns.

A faster form of EDO RAM is burst extended data output RAM **(BEDO RAM).** It is faster because it allows the page-access cycle to be divided into two components. To achieve faster access time, data is read from the memory array at the same time data is transferred through the data bus. In addition, a counter on the chip is used to keep track of the next address so that sequential data can be accessed faster. As a result, BEDO RAM offers an average of 15–25 percent increase in efficiency over FPM RAM and reduces the transfer of sequential data to 1 clock cycle (5-1-1-1). Although EDO RAM and BEDO RAM are faster than FPM RAM, their popularity is already decreasing because they do not work well with the bus speeds higher than 66 MHz that some motherboards are already using.

5.2.6 Synchronous Dynamic RAM (SDRAM)

Synchronous DRAM (SDRAM) runs in synchronization with the memory bus. SDRAM delivers information in very high speed bursts using a high-speed, clocked interface. SDRAM removes most of the latency involved in asynchronous DRAM because the signals are already in synchronization with the motherboard clock.

SDRAM works with bus speeds up to 133 MHz. SDRAM is usually expressed in 2-2-2 or 1-1-1. With the exception of using the external clock speed, it is still similar to the other forms of DRAM and therefore still has latency. The fast 12, 10, and 8 ns numbers that everyone talks about refer only to the second, third, and fourth accesses in a four-access burst. The first access is still a relatively slow 5 cycles. Therefore, SDRAM has a burst cycle timing of 5-2-2-2 or 5-1-1-1.

The SDRAMs also have a MHz rating, such as 100 or 133 MHz. Because SDRAMs are synchronous, they must be fast enough for the system in which they are being used. With SDRAM, however, the whole point of the technology is to be able to run with zero wait states. In order to do this, the memory must be fast enough for the bus speed of the system. One place where you might run into trouble in this regard is if you take the reciprocal of the nanosecond rating of the module and conclude that the module can run at that speed.

Table 5.3 SDRAM Timing, Actual Speed, and Rated Speed

Timing	Actual Speed	Rated Speed
15 ns	66 MHz	PC66
10 ns	100 MHz	PC66
8 ns	125 MHz	PC100
7.5 ns	133 MHz	PC133

For example, the reciprocal of 10 ns is 100 MHz, so you might assume that 10 ns modules will definitely be able to run on a 100 MHz system. The problem is that this allows absolutely no room for slack. In practice, you really want memory rated slightly higher than what is required, so 10 ns modules are really intended for 83 MHz operation. The 100 MHz systems require faster memory, which is why the Joint Electron Device Engineering Council (JEDEC) developed the PC100 specification. Of course, PC66 is designed to run on a 66 MHz bus, PC100 SDRAM is designed to run on a 100 MHz bus, and PC133 SDRAM is designed to run on a 133 MHz bus. SDRAM PC133 has a peak bandwidth of 1066 MB/s. But because SDRAM is approximately 70 percent efficient, its effective bandwidth is more like 750 MB/s. See table 5.3.

To keep SDRAM working at full capacity at all times, SDRAM uses internal pipelining and interleaving. Internal pipelining brings in additional data while the previous data is being processed to improve throughput.

Banks of SDRAM operate in parallel performing the same sequence of commands required for reading and writing data. Some DIMMs may actually have two banks on a single DIMM. One bank populates each face of the module, but only one bank can transmit or receive data at a time.

Interleaving occurs when two banks of memory chips work together to service a bus. (See section 5.6.2.) When one bank is getting ready for access, the other bank is being accessed. DIMMs can have up to four banks, regardless of their size. It makes sense that two 512 MB DIMMs of SDRAM will outperform a single 1 GB DIMM because of the increased number of banks.

Most motherboards now being created require the use of special SDRAM modules that include a **serial presence detect (SPD)** chip. This is an EEPROM that contains speed and design information about the module. The motherboard queries the chip for information about the module and makes adjustments to system operation based on what it finds.

5.2.7 Double Data Rate Synchronous DRAM (DDR SDRAM)

DDR SDRAM is similar in function to regular SDRAM, but it doubles the bandwidth of the memory by transferring data twice per cycle—on both the rising and falling edges of the clock signal. The clock signal transitions from 0 to 1 and back to 0 each cycle; the first is called the *rising edge* and the second, the *falling edge*.

There are three current forms of DDR system memory, each with a variety of interesting names. The first is DDR-200 (PC1600), DDR-266 (PC2100), DDR-333 (PC2700) DDR-400 (PC3200), DDR-433 (PC3500) and DDR-500 (PC4000). The DDR-200 runs at a 100 MHz DDR for an equivalent of 200 MHz of bandwidth. On a 64-bit-wide memory bus, the memory bandwidth is 1600 MB/s, hence the name PC1600. Note: While the 1600 MB/s is the peak bandwidth, the DDR DRAM is about 65 percent efficient. The DDR-266 (PC2100) runs on a 133 MHz bus, giving an equivalent of 266 MHz bandwidth on a 64-bit-wide memory, the theoretical peak is 2100 MB/s of memory bandwidth, hence the name PC2100. The DDR-333 gives a peak bandwidth of 2666 MB/s. Note: The latency for DDR-266 is typically 2-2-2 (JEDEC 1.0 addendum compliant) while other DDR memory may be 2-2-2, 2.5-3-3, 2-3-3, 3-3-3, or 3-4-4. At the time of this writing DDR-333 and DDR-400 are the most common.

The long-term successor of DDR memory will be DDR2. The specifications of DDR2 use new memory technologies to increase bandwidth in order to keep DDR competitive. The first DDR2 modules run at 200 and 266 MHz, which is equivalent to 400 and 533 MHz when they use the rise and fall of the clock signal. However, they can double their bandwidth again by having a DRAM core that can prefetch 4 data bits instead of DDR's 2.

Table 5.4 DDR-II Memory

Memory Speed	Memory Chip Classification	Module Classification	Module Bandwidth	Dual-Channel System Bandwidth
400 MHz	DDR2-400	PC2-3200	3.2 GB/sec	6.4 GB/sec
533 MHz	DDR2-533	PC2-4300	4.3 GB/sec	8.6 GB/sec
667 MHz	DDR2-667	PC2-5300	5.4 GB/sec	10.8 GB/sec

Using a standard 64-bit bus would give a bandwidth of 3.2 and 4.3 Gbps. With the 333 MHz module (667 MHz DDR), the bandwidth will be 5.4 Gbps. See table 5.4. There are some graphic applications that have already used DDR2 that run up to 1.6 GHz. With its current design and increased bandwidth, DDR2 will excel when dealing with streaming data such as found in video cards. However, when dealing with random requests typically found in database servers it will experience a higher latency; in particular, the Column Address Strobe will increase from 2 cycles as seen on current low-latency modules and 3 cycles as used by very high bus speed DDR, to a minimum of 4 or 5 cycles for DDR2. Similarly, tRAS is likely to increase to 8 cycles whereas some high-speed DDR will run only 5 cycles.

Unlike DDR memory that runs at 2.5 V and is terminated on the motherboard, the DDR-2 runs at 1.8 V and is terminated on the memory chip. The termination of the memory chip results in a cleaner signal as it prevents reflected signal transmission errors.

Because the speed of the DRAM cores themselves are the same as DDR of half the bandwidth, costs should be reduced; however, in order to use DDR2, a new motherboard will be required because DDR2 is incompatible with DDR memory due to the increased pin count—240 pins instead of 184 pins for DDR—and the lower DIMM voltage. SO-DIMMs will have 200 pins, Mini-DIMMs would have 244 pins, and Micro-DIMMs would have 214 pins.

As processor speeds have increased significantly over the last few years, so has the speed of graphics (or video) cards. The speed of a graphics card is determined by its graphical processing unit (GPU) and the RAM on the card. Since the video card is often a bottleneck, the card needs to use ultra-high-performance memory. Therefore, graphics card manufacturers often use new technology even before it becomes standardized or widely used. Before DDR2 became standardized and widely used on motherboards, video card manufacturers had been using it on their video cards. Although DDR2 RAM on the motherboard may reach speeds of only 333 to 667 MHz, DDR2 modules running up to 1.6 GHz have been used on video cards.

DDR2 is the predecessor to DDR3, which is already starting to be used in graphics cards even before DDR2 is widely used on motherboards. DDR3 will be able to achieve faster operating speeds by using on-die termination and open drain to absorb reflected noise caused by the movement of the data signal through a chip. DDR3 chips also use a dynamic controller that manages the flow of data between the memory and the chipset. The controller examines the signals as they leave the memory chips and adjusts those signals to maximize signal quality.

DDR2 includes a memory array that is addressable by even and odd word addresses. The logic circuitry with a burst increment mode accesses the array starting at an even word address, and a burst decrement mode accesses the array starting at an odd word address. DDR3 will abandon the sequential output mode and support only the interleaved mode, which allows simplifying the memory controller.

5.2.8 FB-DIMMs

For servers, Intel will be introducing the fully buffered DIMM (**FB-DIMM**). Well beyond the registered ECC modules in use by today's servers, FB-DIMM is Intel's answer to the shrinking number of slots per memory channel, the bridge from DDR2 to DDR3, and a solution to those memory types' latency problems.

One of the problems with DDR RAM is that when you have additional capacity by increasing the chip density, by ramping speed, and by using additional DIMMs, you have to increase latency for it to operate properly. Because SDRAM and DDR RAM uses a stub-bus configuration where a controller communicates with multiple DRAM chips using the same pathway, unfortunately, with each DRAM chip you get a slight signal degradation. This is one of the reasons that many motherboards have only two DIMM slots per channel. Although DIMMs may reach 4 GB or higher per DIMM, which is adequate for desktop computer, this is not adequate for servers.

The FB-DIMMs resemble the current DDR DIMMs except they have a square chip—the buffer chip—in the center where the two chips for Registered DDR belong. There is also a lack of pins at the bottom.

Instead of using the stub-bus configuration, the FB-DIMM memory system is point-to-point. There are no stubs; the memory controller talks to the buffer directly. Each buffer then in turn can pass the signal on to the next buffer in the chain, and so on and so on. The signals are sent from the buffer to the memory controller in a differential serial fashion, like PCI Express or RDRAM, at basically higher speed and lower width, which means lower pin count. Whereas the buffer chip used with low-cost DDR2 chips adds cost, it is far less expensive than making a whole new type of RAM chip.

Different from RDRAM, the memory controller and buffer can make up for unequal length traces, which simplifies board design. Upon initialization, the controller will measure the signal timings on each pin, and delay the fastest to match the slowest. In practice, this delay does not cause any real-world performance degradation. It allows you to put in three channels of FB for the same pin cost as a single DDR2 channel, which will make dual channels, the standard. In addition, although there will be some latency, especially on systems with high capacity, the buffers will minimize the latency by not storing the signals but retransmitting them.

FB-DIMMs are ideal for servers because of their increased reliability. The goal of the manufacturers was to have only one silent data error per 100 years or fewer. A silent data error is an error that is not caught, which causes bad things to happen in the future. Instead of using ECC, a robust CRC scheme protecting the commands and the data is used. In addition, FB-DIMMs use a Bit Lane Fail Over Correction, which has the ability to shut down a data path/RAM chip that is known to be bad. This is sometimes referred to as chip-kill.

5.2.9 Rambus DRAM (RDRAM)

Rambus DRAM (RDRAM), also known as direct Rambus DRAM (DRDRAM), rethinks DRAM technology from the ground up on how it should be integrated into a system. It's a new memory design with changes to the bus structure and how signals are carried. RDRAM was developed by Rambus, Incorporated.

Rambus DRAM (RDRAM) is based on the Rambus channel, a high-speed 16-bit bus running at a clock rate up to 400 MHz. The Rambus channel is routed through the RIMM modules and is terminated on the motherboard after the last RIMM module. The Rambus channel requires that all sockets be populated with either a RIMM module or a continuity RIMM so that the channel remains continuous to the termination resistors.

Like DDR SDRAM, transfers are accomplished on the rising and falling edges of the clock, yielding an effective theoretical bandwidth of approximately 1.6 GB/s for a single Rambus channel and 3.2 GB/s for dual Rambus channels. RDRAM efficiency is about 80 percent. It may seem counterproductive to narrow the channel because that reduces bandwidth; however, the channel is then capable of running at much higher speeds than would be possible if the bus were wide.

To get the bus speed up that high, the board has to be manufactured to a very high standard of quality in order to reduce noise, stray capacitance, variations in line impedance, and other problems associated with rising bus speeds. In some cases, you may even have to add more layers to the motherboard just to be able to provide a clean enough signal.

In an SDRAM system, each module is only a few inches from the memory controller, so commands and data don't have to travel very far to reach their destination. The Rambus channel gets longer as more RDRAM devices are added to it, which means that the amount of time that commands and data must travel to reach the outermost device can get pretty high. What makes this even worse is that the system-read latency of the entire system can be only as fast as that farthest (and, by extension, slowest) RDRAM.

To reduce the latency for RDRAM, Rambus uses a high number of banks. Each individual RDRAM chip can hold up to 32 banks of memory. In an ideal world, you could keep a row in each of those 32 banks active in order to maximize the odds that you're going to be able to get data from an active row. In reality, though, you can have only 16 banks open at once, or half the number of banks on the chip.

Because the RDRAM devices farther out on the bus need more time to send a signal, the RDRAM devices closer to the memory controller need to have a longer amount of delay so that all the memory sent arrives at the memory controller at the same time. Therefore, during boot-up, the Rambus system has to go through an elaborate initialization ritual to determine the amount of delay for each device. Note: As with SDRAM, DRDRAM makes use of a serial presence detect (SPD) chip to tell the motherboard certain characteristics of the RDRAM module when the system is booted.

As you add more devices to a Rambus system, the entire system has higher and higher read latency. So, although individual RDRAM chips might have a read latency (access time) of 20 ns, which is about the same read latency as some SDRAMs, once you put them in a system with three full RIMMs, the overall system latency can be significantly worse than the system latency for an SDRAM system.

Memory requests are typically bursty in nature, tending to appear in groups, followed by quiet periods with no requests. So although the average memory bandwidth required by a program may be low, during periods of bursty activity, the bandwidth requested can be much higher. The high bank count and separate row and column address buses make RDRAMs much better suited to bursty communication than other memory technologies.

Question:

Which RAM is the best RAM to use, DDR SDRAM or RDRAM?

Answer:

This is one of the huge debates in today's PC markets. Although Rambus modules have the ability to transfer data faster, they appear to have higher latency than that of DDR SDRAM. In other words, the first data item transfer in a Rambus transaction takes longer to initiate than the first data item moved in a DDR SDRAM system. In an environment where data transactions involve lengthy streams of data, such as gaming or in workstation-type environments, Rambus has outstanding performance. If a computer does many small transactions regularly, such as a server, DDR SDRAM is a better choice. Note: Unfortunately, because companies have to pay a royalty to Rambus Incorporated and RDRAM is more expensive than SDRAM or DDR RAM, RDRAM is becoming less popular than DDR RAM.

5.2.10 Video RAM

Today, video cards will have a minimum of 8 to 16 MB (or more) of video RAM. Another type of RAM chip is called video RAM **(VRAM).** Video RAM, usually used on video cards, is a special form of DRAM that has two separate data ports. One port is dedicated to updating the image on the screen while the other one is used for changing the image data stored in the RAM on the video card. This "dual-ported design" gives higher performance (up to 40 percent) than DRAM, which cannot read and write simultaneously.

A newer version of VRAM is windows RAM **(WRAM),** which was developed by Samsung. The chip uses a dual-color block write to perform very rapid pattern and text fills, and it can perform fast buffer-to-buffer transfers for video and double-buffered 3D animation. As a result, WRAM offers a 40–50 percent increase in performance over the VRAM chips.

SGRAM is a video-specific extension of SDRAM that includes graphics-specific read/write features. SGRAM also allows data to be retrieved and modified in blocks, instead of individually. This reduces the number of reads and writes that memory must perform and increases the performance of the graphics controller by making the process more efficient.

As mentioned earlier in the chapter, since video cards must process and transfer a lot of data, the video card often becomes a bottleneck. To help alleviate some of the bottlenecks, video card manufacturers have been using faster forms of memory, even before they have become standardized or widely used. Today's video card will contain SDRAM, DDR2 or DDR3 RAM and they will often run at faster speeds than you will find with motherboard RAM. As mentioned earlier, while DDR-II RAM on the motherboard may reach speeds of 333 or 400 MHZ, DDR-II can be found running at 1.6 GHz. DDR3 RAM will most likely be higher.

Whereas DDR2 is designed to run at 1.8 V, high-end graphical DDR2 (GDDR2) used an increased voltage swing of 0 to 2.5 V so that it can achieve the much faster operating speeds. Unfortunately, there is an increased power drain through the center tap termination, which also produces an increase in heat dissipation. As a result, DDR2 has already reached its end of life for the graphics market.

GDDR3 uses on-die termination and open drain to absorb reflected noise caused by the movement of the data signal through a chip. It also uses a dynamic controller that manages the flow of data between the memory and the chipset. The controller examines the signals as they leave the memory chips and adjusts those signals to maximize signal quality. Different from GDDR2, GDDR3 will run at 1.8 V, which reduces power usage and heat dissipation. Because manufacturers have agreed on the GDDR3 specifications, GDDR3 should get a much faster approval than GDDR2, and it should consume half the power of GDDR2 while operating up to 50 percent faster.

5.3 MEMORY AREAS

When the IBM PC was first introduced, the RAM was divided into conventional and reserve memory. PC architecture changed through the years, and new techniques were developed to divide and address RAM. Today, the RAM in a PC is broken down into several memory areas: conventional memory, reserve memory, upper memory, expanded memory, and extended memory.

The early IBM PC was built around the Intel 8088 microprocessor. Because of the limitations of the microprocessor, the most RAM that the IBM PC could recognize was 1 MB. Therefore, when the PC was being developed, IBM, Intel, and Microsoft took that 1 MB of RAM and broke it into two memory areas: conventional memory and reserve memory. See figure 5.1. Conventional memory was used to hold the operating system, application programs, and data, while the reserve memory was reserved for the hardware.

5.3.1 Conventional Memory

Conventional memory is the first 640 KB of RAM. It is also known as *lower memory* and *base memory.* Although DOS could read and write to the entire first megabyte, it could only load application programs in conventional memory. Conventional memory, therefore, was used to store DOS itself, device drivers, TSRs (small programs that control hardware or perform a useful function), and application programs.

The first kilobyte of conventional memory stores the interrupt vector table, which is used to directly control hardware by accessing special low-level routines. When the routine needs to be accessed, its location is found in the interrupt vector table. The routine itself is part of either the BIOS or the operating system. The next 256 bytes are used for the BIOS data area, which is the work area for the ROM BIOS chips and includes the I/O address of the COM and LPT ports and a keyboard buffer area.

Figure 5.1 First 1 MB of RAM

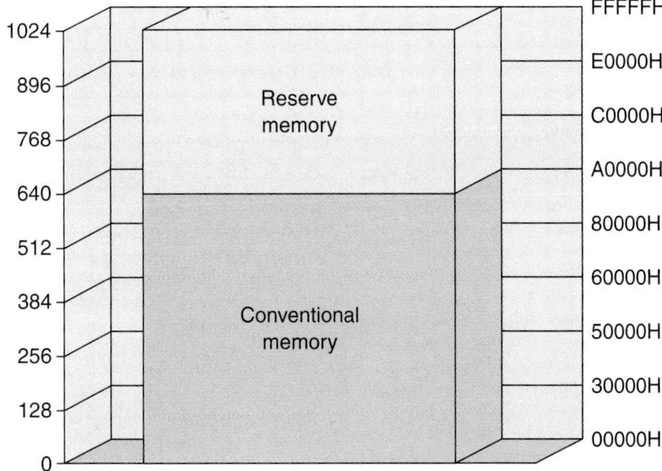

5.3.2 Reserve Memory

Reserve memory, between 640 KB and 1 MB, is reserved for hardware. The reserve memory can be used as a working area for the expansion cards or can be used by the ROM BIOS chips, such as the system ROM BIOS, video ROM BIOS, and other ROM chips found on expansion cards.

The first 128 KB (A0000H to BFFFFH) of reserve memory is for the video RAM (this is not to be confused with the memory on the video card) and holds character and graphics information for display. The video ROM BIOS uses up to 32 KB of memory, starting at C0000H. Generally, if a video expansion card has a higher resolution and more colors, the card will use more reserve memory than is available. Since DOS could use only available contiguous (continuous) memory in the first megabyte as conventional memory, it is the memory location of the EGA, VGA, and super VGA cards that restrict the conventional memory to 640 KB.

The second 128 KB (C0000H to DFFFFH) is reserved for the BIOS chips found on expansion cards. During boot-up, the system ROM BIOS looks for additional ROM BIOS chips and uses them to expand its own instruction set. The more common cards that contain ROM BIOS chips include the hard drive controller (including SCSI controller cards), network cards, and sound cards. The memory areas used by ROM chips on the expansion cards are configured using jumpers, DIP switches, or a software configuration program, or the cards are plug-and-play. If ROM BIOS chips from two different expansion cards try to use the same memory area, the devices will usually fail.

The last 128 KB (E0000H to FFFFFH) is reserved for the system ROM BIOS, which controls the boot-up procedure and contains instructions for controlling basic hardware. (Note: Some system ROM BIOS chips use only 64 KB, located between F0000 and FFFFFH, even though 128 KB is reserved for the system ROM BIOS.) If the computer is accessing the memory between 640 KB and 1 MB, which is occupied by a ROM chip, it is accessing the ROM memory, not RAM memory. Since the ROM chips occupy the same memory address as RAM, the RAM is sometimes readdressed as extended memory. In other instances, since ROM chips are slower than RAM chips, the instructions within the ROM chips can be copied to the corresponding RAM address and accessed from the RAM. Since RAM is faster and usually has a bigger data path, performance can thus be greatly increased. This method of speeding up the computer is called **RAM shadowing.**

5.3.3 Upper Memory

After the conventional memory and reserve memory were divided up, engineers eventually discovered that not all of the 384 KB of reserve memory were actually being used. Therefore, the memory between A0000H to FFFFFH not used by hardware is commonly referred to as the **upper memory.** It is divided into **upper memory blocks** or **UMBs.** See figure 5.2. In the later versions of DOS and Windows 95, **TSRs** (small programs that control hardware or perform a useful function) and **device drivers** (instructions that control hardware) were moved from conventional memory to the upper memory, freeing up conventional memory.

5.3.4 Expanded Memory

Expanded memory was the first memory configuration that allowed computers to break the 1 MB boundary. In the early 1980s, many applications programs, such as spreadsheets, needed more RAM. Lotus and Intel, later joined by Microsoft, proposed EMS (expanded memory specification), which be-

Figure 5.2 Memory Areas

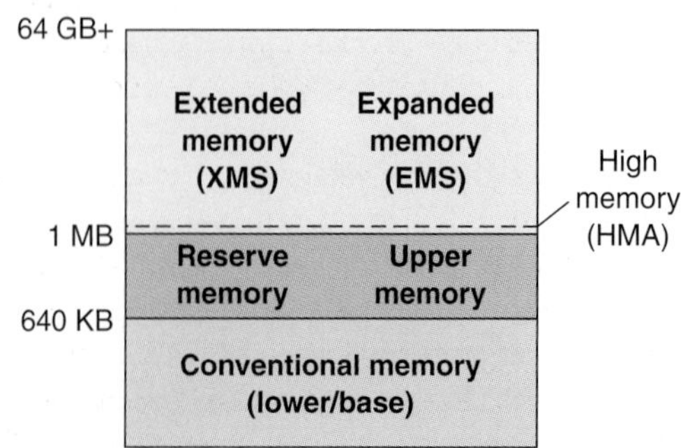

came known as the LIM (Lotus/Intel/Microsoft) EMS. The LIM expanded memory specification (EMS version 3.0) used 64 KB of contiguous memory in the upper memory area as a window of up to 8 MB of expanded memory. The 64 KB window was further divided into four 16 KB page frames. Data is kept in expanded memory and is accessed using bank switching.

Because DOS could access only the first megabyte of RAM, the data had to be stored in the first 1 MB of RAM. So, instead of shuffling data back and forth between the page frame in upper memory and the expanded memory, bank switching was used to change the addresses of the storage cells so that a cell's address was between 640 KB and 1 MB. As far as the programs were concerned, the same memory areas were addressed—only the contents of each memory area were changed. Therefore, expanded memory involved mapping addresses of logical pages to physical pages.

Eventually, EMS version 4.0 was introduced. It increased the expanded memory from 8 to 32 MB, and it allowed any contiguous spaces located within upper memory that were 16 KB to be used as page frames. In addition, the expanded memory was enhanced so that it could contain both code (instructions) and data.

As with any new technology that is introduced, software had to be created or rewritten in order to use EMS 4.0. Software was written to request the expanded memory from a piece of internal software called an expanded memory manager (EMM). The 8088/8086 and 286-based machines contain an expanded memory board with an EMM manager. Today's computers (386 and above) use software like DOS's EMM386.EXE, which allows extended memory to emulate (pretend to be) expanded memory.

5.3.5 Extended Memory

The memory above 1 MB (FFFFFH) found on today's newer machines (386 and above) is known as **extended memory.** When the extended memory configuration was introduced, DOS could not normally use it except to provide a RAM disk (RAM pretending to be a disk) or to create a disk cache (buffer area between RAM and the slower hard drive). This was because DOS could run only in real mode, which can recognize only 1 MB of RAM. Some later programs, such as games, were able to switch the microprocessor from real mode to protected mode by means of the DOS protected mode interface (DPMI).

When Windows 3.XX was introduced, it would switch the microprocessor from real mode to protected mode by loading the HIMEM.SYS file during boot-up. Windows could then use the extended memory to hold data and code. (Note: Windows 3.1X will not run unless HIMEM.SYS is loaded.) Windows 95 and 98 operate mostly in protected mode but still make calls in real mode to access certain hardware components to keep the amount of RAM required to run Windows 95 smaller. Windows NT is a true protected mode operating system and does not use real mode.

The extended memory specification (XMS) was developed in 1987 by Microsoft, Intel, AST, and Lotus to specify how programs would use extended memory. Although the XMS can function on a 286 chip or higher, it wasn't fully utilized until the 386. This was because the 286 could switch to protected mode but could not switch back to real mode (needed for the older programs not written for protected mode) without rebooting the computer. To ensure cooperation between programs using extended memory, HIMEM.SYS grabbed all of the extended memory for itself and distributed it to the programs that followed the XMS standard. It was the job of the HIMEM.SYS to make sure that no two programs overwrote each other's designated memory areas, and it allowed the microprocessor to switch back and forth between real mode and protected mode.

5.3.6 High Memory Area

The **high memory area (HMA),** often referred to as high memory, is an area of 64 KB minus 16 bytes starting at the 1 MB boundary. The distinguishing feature of high memory is that it can be used to access a small part of extended memory while the microprocessor is in real mode, which can see only up to 1 MB of RAM.

The memory address of a computer running in real mode is 20 bits long (numbers 0 to 19). Unfortunately, early microprocessors had registers that were only 16 bits wide. Therefore, they had to use two registers and add them together to access the entire 20-bit line. When an 8088/8086 added the registers together and the value was larger than 1 MB, the carry (excess above 1 MB) was dropped. Newer microprocessors have 24-bit or larger address lines, which allow the carry to extend to the 21st address line (A20). This allows the CPU to access another 64 KB of RAM (HMA) while in real mode. To fully utilize the A20 line, special circuitry was built into the keyboard ROM BIOS chip, which controls the A20 line.

5.3.7 Real and Protected Mode

DOS uses what is known as real-mode memory management, which allows only one 16-bit program to run at one time. Originally, real-mode processing allowed for the use of 1024 KB of memory to be used. A special device driver is required (HIMEM.SYS) to access memory over 1024 KB.

Windows 9X allowed for protected-mode memory management, which allows for more than one 32-bit program to run at one time. It also allowed the use of over 1024 KB of memory and for the operating system to manage access of memory by the programs that are running. DOS programs (which are 16-bit) and all 16-bit Windows programs require the OS to run in real mode. To run 16-bit real mode programs in a protected mode operating system, the OS can create a virtual DOS machine or VDM. The VDM "looks" like DOS to the running program—conventional, upper, extended memory, and so on. If a VDM cannot be used, then Windows has to run in 16-bit real mode (running one program at a time, etc.).

The Windows NT family operating systems are true 32-bit protected mode operating systems. They can only run 32-bit programs natively since these operating systems cannot switch to real mode. To run a 16-bit program, a VDM has to be used. If the 16-bit program does not work correctly in the VDM then it cannot be run. A true 32-bit OS has linear address space that allows each program and driver access to any part of memory.

5.4 RAM LIMITATIONS

The Pentium processor had only a 32-bit address bus, which allowed the processor to address 4 GB of memory. Note: Often the motherboard and the number and capacity of the RAM chips will further limit this number. Most OS reserve 2 GB for the use of the kernel and 2 GB for applications. But you can change its use by using 4 GB RAM Tuning (4GT), which reserves 1 GB for the kernel and 3 GB for applications. To activate the 4GT in Windows 2000 or Windows XP, you would add a /3GB switch to the Advanced RISC Computing (ARC) path in the BOOT.INI file.

Processors using the P6 or Intel NetBurst architecture (including the Pentium Pro, Pentium II, Pentium III, and Pentium 4 processors) have a 36-bit address bus, which allows the processor address 64 GB of memory. Intel Celevon's are cut-down versions of the Pentium III and Pentium 4 processors. Therefore, they only have a 32-bit address bus.

NOTE: Like Pentium motherboards, often the motherboard and the number and capacity of the RAM chips will further limit this number. In addition, unless you are running a server operating system, Windows will not see more than 4 GB of memory.

However, even though the processor can now address these large amounts of RAM, most motherboards are designed to recognize much less. For example, if a motherboard can recognize 256 MB DIMMs and it includes only four DIMM slots, the most RAM that the motherboard can use is 1 GB. Of course, as time goes on, SIMMs and DIMMs with larger capacities will be created. Eventually, the PC will reach the maximum amount of RAM a CPU can recognize.

Question:

How much RAM is enough?

Answer:

The listed minimum values of RAM for the various operating systems are:

Windows 95	4 MB
Windows 98	16 MB
Windows Me	32 MB
Windows NT 4.0	12 MB
Windows 2000 Professional	64 MB
Windows XP	64 MB

Unfortunately, these minimum requirements are grossly understated. For usable performance, you should double these requirements. You should not load Windows 95 in less than 32 MB, Windows 98 and Windows NT in less than 64 MB, and Windows Me, Windows 2000, and Windows XP in 128 MB. If you are running heavy graphical packages or other packages requiring a lot of RAM, you should add even more RAM. As a general rule, the more, the better.

RAM can be used for more than just programs. You can use it to enlarge a disk cache, which helps reduce the time it takes to access a disk. More RAM will also reduce the need for virtual memory. For example, programs such as Adobe Photo Paint need more memory, and working several programs at the same time (such as Microsoft Word and Microsoft Excel) to create a single report requires more memory.

Kingston (one of the leading memory manufacturers) has done studies showing that by increasing RAM on a Windows 98 machine from 32 to 64 MB, you can see a performance increase of 45 to 65 percent. Of course, additional RAM would improve performance even more, although it won't be as significant.

5.5 VIRTUAL MEMORY

Another major feature of the 386 chip was its ability to use up to 64 terabytes of virtual memory. **Virtual memory** is disk space that acts like RAM, which allows the operating system to load more programs and data. Parts of all the programs and data to be accessed are constantly swapped back and forth between RAM and disk so the virtual memory looks and acts like regular RAM. This is beneficial to the user because disk memory is far cheaper than RAM. Unfortunately, a disk is a thousand times slower than RAM, and since the disk consists of mechanical parts and pieces, it has a higher failure rate than RAM. Intel microprocessors use a technology called **demand paging,** which swaps data between the RAM and disk only on the demand of the processor rather than trying to anticipate the needs of the processor.

The RAM and virtual memory are broken down into chunks of information called **pages,** which are monitored by the operating system. When the RAM becomes full, the virtual memory system copies the least recently used programs and data to the virtual memory. Since this frees part of the RAM, it then has room to copy something else from virtual memory, load another program, or load more data. Windows 95, Windows 98, and Windows Me virtual memory takes the form of an ordinary file called a *swap file,* whereas Windows NT, Windows 2000, and Windows XP call their virtual memory a *paging file.*

5.6 RAM PACKAGING

As RAM technology improved, so did its packaging. When the IBM PC was introduced, it used ICs (DIPs), which were inserted into the motherboard. Since then, SIPPs, SIMMs, and DIMMs have been developed. Table 5.5 describes the various types of chip packaging.

Table 5.5 Types of RAM Packages

Type of RAM Package	Description
Dual in-line package (DIP)	DIP chips, resembling a bug with many legs, lie horizontally with metal leads extending down from the two long sides. The metal leads are inserted directly into the motherboard's DIP sockets. Note: Some RAM cache chips are packaged as DIP chips.
Single in-line pin package (SIPP)	SIPP is a small circuit board that has several DIPs soldered onto it. The circuit board has a single row of pins that are inserted into the motherboard.
Single in-line memory module (SIMM)	A SIMM is a small circuit board consisting of several DIP chips soldered together. The SIMM connects to the motherboard by means of a row of tin or gold metal plates (contacts) along the bottom of the module. As they are inserted into the motherboard, the metal pins make contact with its metal plates.
Dual in-line memory module (DIMM)	DIMMs closely resemble SIMMs.
Rambus in-line memory module (RIMM)	RIMMs closely resemble DIMMs.

5.6.1 Dual In-Line Package (DIP)

The form of RAM known as the **dual in-line package (DIP),** used on the original IBM PC and continued in the IBM XT and IBM AT, was inserted directly into the motherboard. Resembling a bug with many legs, these IC chips lie horizontally with metal leads extending down from the two long sides. See figure 5.3.

DIPs can be inserted into IC sockets very easily. First, position the IC so that pin 1 is in the proper orientation. (Pin 1 of the chip and the motherboard will usually have a notch on one end.) Next, align the pins with the socket, and then gently push the chip into the socket. Avoid bending the pins in the process; a bent pin could easily ruin the IC. (Note: When handling RAM chips, remember to take precautions against ESD.) Removing a DIP is best done with a small, flat-edge screwdriver blade. Gently slide the screwdriver under the chip and pry just a little. Then alternately pry up the ends of the chip, which prevents the legs from bending, until the chip can be removed easily.

Some of the early PCs had problems with something called *chip creep.* This was caused by the constant expansion and contraction of the motherboard due to the temperature fluctuations associated with turning on and off the computer. Eventually, the chips would work themselves out of the sockets just enough so that they would not make a good connection. When a memory problem occurred, a common solution was to gently press the DIP chips into the motherboard. Another solution to the chip creep problem was to solder the DIPs onto the motherboard. Although this did correct the initial problem, it often caused other problems later when a technician tried to desolder a bad RAM chip.

5.6.2 Single In-Line Memory Module (SIMM)

Today, the majority of modern PCs use a **single in-line memory module,** usually referred to as a **SIMM.** Like the SIPP, the SIMM is a small circuit board consisting of several soldered DIP chips. Its connection to the motherboard is made by a row of tin or gold metal plates (contacts) along the bottom of the module. As the module is inserted into the motherboard, metal pins make contact with the metal plates. See figures 5.4 and 5.5.

Figure 5.3 DIPS

Figure 5.4 SIMM Sockets

Figure 5.5 72-pin and 30-pin SIMMs

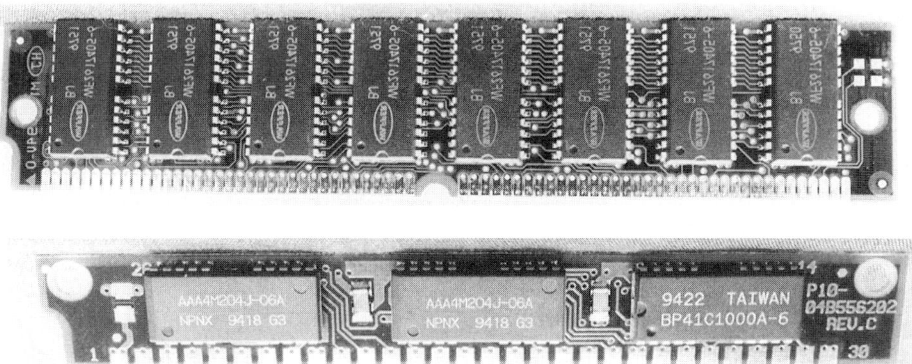

Figure 5.6 DIMM

SIMMs are available in a wide range of capacities (from 256 K to 64 MB and higher) and in two pin configurations: 30-pin (8 or 9 bits) and 72-pin (32 or 36 bits). If a 30-pin uses parity for error control (see section 6.6), it will have 9 bits; if it does not use parity, it will have 8 bits. If a 72-pin uses parity, it will have 36 bits; if it does not, it will have 32 bits. The 72-pin SIMM is approximately 25 percent larger in size than the 30-pin SIMM and includes a notch in the center to identify it and so prevent the insertion of a 30-pin SIMM into a 72-pin socket. Both SIMMs also have notches that prevent them from being connected backward. Four of the pins in the 72-pin SIMM are used to indicate the speed rating of the chip.

5.6.3 Dual In-Line Memory Module (DIMM)

The **dual in-line memory module,** or **DIMM,** closely resembles a SIMM. See figure 5.6. Like SIMMs, DIMMS are installed into a memory expansion socket vertically. But the opposing pins on both sides of the SIMM circuit board are connected as one, whereas the pins of DIMMs are electrically isolated to form two separate contacts. Another difference between the two is that DIMMs support 64-bit pathways (72 bits with parity).

SDRAMs use the 168-pin DIMM, which—like the 72-pin SIMM—has electrical provisions (serial presence detect, or SPD) for telling the PC the speed rating of the module. The module connector has 8 pins for signaling this information. The DDR SDRAM use the 184-pin DIMM. Both DIMMs have the same physical dimensions (5 1/4 in. across), yet they differ in the number and location of the notches. The SDRAM has two notches and the DDR SDRAM has one notch. DDR SDRAM is not backward-compatible with SDRAM and requires motherboards designed for DDR.

DIMMs can come in several different varieties, including unbuffered, buffered or registered, and 3.3 or 5 V. While buffered memory is used with FPM or EDO memory, which are often used with SIMMs, registered memory is used on DIMMs with high-end workstations and high-end servers. Since buffer chips slow down the DIMM, they are not effective at high speeds. Registered memory also enacts a deliberate pause of one clock cycle in the module to ensure that all communication from the chipset arrives properly. For this reason, all desktop PC systems use unbuffered DIMMs. Today, modern systems use only unbuffered 3.3 V DIMMs. However, buffered and registered memories are used on high-end workstations and servers to redrive or amplify the signal entering the module and assist the chipset in handling the larger electrical load when the system has a full load of installed memory. Fortunately, key notches at the bottom of the DIMM are spaced differently so that only the correct DIMM can be inserted into the motherboard. See figure 5.7.

5.6.4 Notebook Memory

A smaller version of the DIMM, called the **small-outline DIMM (SO-DIMM),** which is narrowing and thinner than the full-size DIMM, is usually found in notebook computers and some video cards. A small-outline DIMM comes in two forms. The 72-pin model is 2.35 in. across and only supports 32-bit transfers. The 144-pin model is 2.66 inches across and supports 64-bit transfers. See figure 5.8.

A **micro dual in-line memory module (Micro-DIMM)** consists of a number of memory components (usually black) that are attached to a printed circuit board (usually green). Micro-DIMMs get their name because they are smaller than both regular DIMMs and SO-DIMMs. The 144-pin Micro-DIMMs are commonly found in subnotebook computers. Each 144-pin Micro-DIMM provides a 64-bit data path, and is installed singly in 64-bit systems. The number of black components on a 144-pin Micro-DIMM may vary, but they always have 72 pins on the front and 72 pins on the back for a total of 144. The 144-pin Micro-DIMMs are approximately 1.545 in. long and 1 in. high, though the heights may vary. Unlike SO-DIMMs, Micro-DIMMs do not have any notches along the bottom edge.

5.6.5 Rambus In-Line Memory Module (RIMM)

The **Rambus in-line memory module (RIMM)** conforms to the standard DIMM form factor. See figure 5.9. However, because it has 184 pins, it is not pin-compatible. Because the RAM runs at a faster speed than the DIMMs, RIMMs typically include a heat spreader to help dissipate heat faster. The motherboards that support RIMMs will support two or more RIMMs. Because the RIMMs fit into a channel, low-cost continuity modules must be used on the empty memory slots to maintain channel integrity. See figure 5.10.

Although not as common, Rambus memory also comes in SO-RIMM packages. The SO-RIMM looks similar to the SO-DIMM and has 160 pins.

Even though it is true that an individual RDRAM can consume more power than an individual SDRAM, at the module level (DIMM versus RIMM), RIMM modules can consume much less power while providing higher bandwidth than equivalent-capacity SDRAM DIMM modules. On a DIMM,

Figure 5.7 Notches Found on DIMMs

Figure 5.8 SO-DIMMs

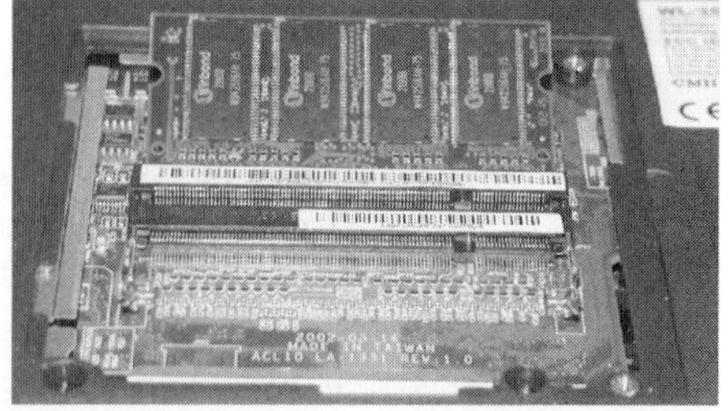

Figure 5.9 RIMM

Figure 5.10 Continuity Modules

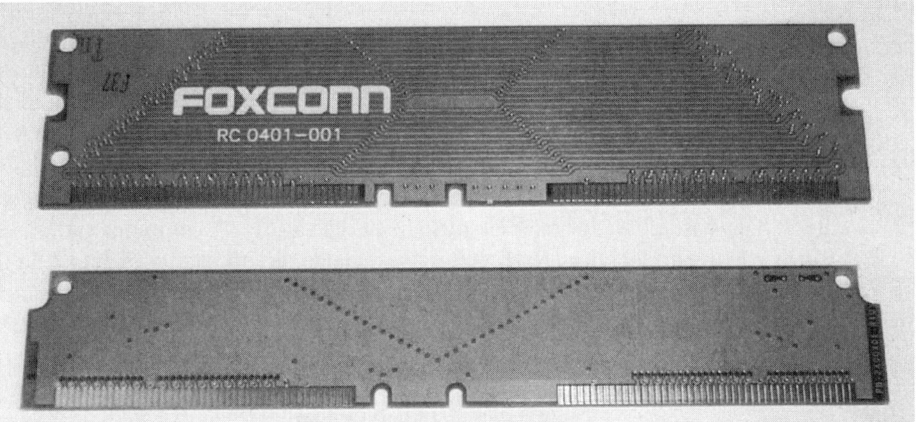

eight SDRAMs respond to each request to provide the data requested by the CPU, so eight devices in the same rank are all dissipating the same amount of power. On an equivalent RIMM module with eight devices, only one RDRAM is providing data; the other seven devices are in lower-power states. On DIMM modules, power is thus evenly spread among all devices in the same rank. On RIMM modules, power can be localized in one RDRAM, with others at much lower power levels. At maximum module bandwidth, the power dissipated by the eight SDRAMs exceeds the total power dissipated by the one active RDRAM and seven other RDRAMs in lower-power states.

5.7 RAM CHARACTERISTICS

RAM chips are arranged on the motherboard or within a SIPP, SIMM, or DIMM module in a special way. Some chips have parity while others don't; in addition, RAM is divided into banks, and RAM is arranged in many arrays of rows and columns. Depending on the microprocessor and the type of RAM, the system determines the size of the data and address bus.

5.7.1 Parity Versus Nonparity

RAM chips are arranged in sets of either 8 or 9 bits. In the 9-bit arrangement, 8 of the 9 bits are used for data and the ninth one is used to provide an error check on the other eight. The DIPs used in the IBM PC, IBM XT, and IBM AT were arranged in neat little rows of nine chips; some of the later SIMMs and DIMMs used a ninth bit for parity. **Parity** chips ensure accurate reading and writing of data, particularly on systems released prior to the introduction of Pentium motherboards. A PC using parity checking is using *odd* parity checking. As the 8 individual bits in a byte are stored in memory, a parity generator/checker, which is either part of the microprocessor or is located in a special chip on the motherboard, evaluates the data bits by counting the number of 1s in a byte. If an even number of 1s is in the byte, the parity generator/checker creates a 1 and stores it in the ninth (parity) bit. This makes the total sum of all 9 bits an odd number. If the sum of the 8 data bits is an odd created is 0, again keeping the 9-bit sum an odd number. The value of the ninth parity bit is always chosen so that the sum of all 9 bits is an odd number.

When the system reads memory, it checks the parity information. If the stored 9 bits equal an even number, that byte must have an error. When a parity-check error is detected, the motherboard parity-checking circuits generate a **nonmaskable interrupt (NMI),** which halts processing and diverts the system's attention to the error. The NMI causes a routine in the system ROM BIOS chip to be executed. The routine clears the screen and then displays a message such as "Parity Error" or "Parity Check 1" in the upper-left corner of the screen.

There are two disadvantages of using parity for error control. First, RAM will discover errors only when 1, 3, 5, or 7 bits have changed. It will not discover a problem if 2 bits have been changed since the 2 bits cancel each other out. Second, it only detects the error but does not correct it.

Most systems do not halt the CPU when a parity error is detected; instead, they offer you a choice of either rebooting the system or continuing as though nothing happened. If you can, you should shut off the NMI (parity checking) and save your work. When saving your work, save it to a different name in case the file you are working on has become corrupted. This gives you the opportunity to first use the file you are currently working on. If it is too corrupted to use, you can then go back to the original file. (Note: You should save your work approximately every 5 to 10 minutes to prevent loss of work from a technical difficulty.)

A computer system that checks for errors using parity must use RAM chips that contain the extra bit. An 8-bit chip may cause the computer not to boot and not to recognize all the RAM and can cause memory errors almost immediately during boot. The parity chip makes the computer more reliable, but it does cost a little bit more because of the extra chip. A computer system that does not check for parity can use a 9-bit chip, but it will not, of course, use the parity chip to hold information. One type of RAM offers fake parity. A computer system set up for parity checking can use RAM that sends a fake "parity good" signal. This saves money because you don't have to pay for the extra memory chip.

Other systems, such as most Pentium systems, use **error checking and correcting (ECC) memory** rather than parity checking. Every time data is stored in memory, this code is responsible for the generation of check bits, which are stored along with the data. When the content of a memory location is referenced, the ECC memory logic uses the check bit information and the data itself to generate a series of "syndrome bits." If these syndrome bits are all zeros, then the data is valid and operation continues. If any bits are 1s, then the data has an error and the ECC memory logic isolates the error and reports it to the operating system. In the case of a correctable error, the ECC memory scheme can detect single- and double-bit errors and correct single-bit errors. Of course, if you use ECC for parity, 1 bit of RAM is needed for every 8 bits, and 7 bits are needed to check 32 bits.

On many of today's machines, parity and ECC can be enabled or disabled in the CMOS setup program. Therefore, if parity is enabled in the CMOS setup program and a parity error occurs, make sure you are using RAM that uses parity.

5.7.2 Memory Banks

When working with PCs and their RAM, it is common to hear the phrases *banks of memory* or *banks of RAM*. A bank is a collection of memory chips that make up a block of memory readable by the processor in a single bus cycle. The block must, therefore, be as large as the data bus of the particular processor. In today's PC systems, the processor data bus is either 64 bits plus any parity bits that may be needed. Parity is discussed later.

Example 5.1:

Consider a Pentium III processor. A Pentium III has an external data bus of 64 bits. If a memory module has a 64-bit pathway, only one memory module would be needed to make a bank.

Double-sided chips is combining two sets of chips into one package. For example, if you have DIMMs that are double-sided, it is like having two single-sided DIMMs in one package. However, if a motherboard has two DIMM slots and was made to handle three banks of RAM chips, you can insert two single-sided DIMMs (two banks) or one single-sided DIMM and one double-sided DIMM (three banks). If you insert two double-sided DIMMs, the motherboard will not boot—it will not recognize the last DIMM, or it will not recognize the last bank of memory.

5.7.3 Chip Speed

One of the last things to look for when matching RAM chips is the access time (which indicates the speed) of the chips. The lower the number, the faster the chip. Therefore, if a PC requires a 100 ns DRAM, then a 150 ns DRAM may be cheaper but most likely will not work. Generally, you can use DRAM chips with faster access times than those called for. A PC that requires 100 ns DRAM will work fine with 80 ns chips, but the faster chips will not deliver a speed boost. The PC will still operate as if you had installed 100 ns DRAM. (Note: Sometimes compatibility problems occur when using RAM chips with different speeds.)

5.7.4 Reading the Chip Label

Determining how much RAM a system has is more of an art than a science. Some RAM chips can be identified with little difficulty, and others are impossible to decipher. The method is to determine the manufacturer of the RAM chip and use the Internet to access the manufacturer's home page to look up the part number.

In the top left corner is the logo of the company that made the RAM chip. In the first line of numbers and letters is the part number and the speed; the second line usually states the date (year and month or Julian date) when the RAM chip was created. The first digit of the part number acts as a placeholder. The second digit indicates if the chip is set up to contain a 1-bit (one data bus) word or a 4-bit word (four data buses). The rest of the part number indicates the number of words that the chip holds. To find out how much a RAM chip holds, you must look at the code of each DIP and add them together. The number after the dash indicates the speed of the RAM chip, either as the number stands or after adding a 0 to the end of it.

Let's look at two examples. A DIP labeled −70 means that the chip runs at 70 ns. But another DIP labeled −7 might run at 70 ns or 7 ns. Unless you contact the manufacturer (or use the Internet), you must use good judgment to determine which speed it is. If the chip is used for regular RAM, probably consisting of DRAM chips, the label must mean 70 ns because DRAM runs only between 50 and 70 ns. If the DIP is used for SRAM in RAM cache, the label could very well mean 7 ns. (Note: Some of the DIPs used in the XT and AT were labeled −3 and ran at 150 ns.)

5.8 INSTALLING RAM

When installing RAM, the first thing you need to determine is how many empty memory slots you have. You will then need to determine which memory is compatible with the motherboard and which is compatible with any existing memory. This includes the following:

- Package type
- Type of RAM technology
- RAM capacity
- Bus/clock speed
- Voltage
- Type of error control
- Buffered, nonbuffered, or registered memory
- The number of banks (including single- and double-sided RAM chips)

Before you actually install the memory, you should check the system or motherboard documentation. Some servers require the installation of two memory chips at a time. Some support the installation of one memory chip at a time. If you are using RIMMs, you may need to use continuity modules. The final step is to physically install the memory.

Generally, memory manufacturers are very conservative in their memory timings. According to the *Maximum PC* magazine, you can use the BIOS setup program to disable SPD settings in the BIOS setup program and then to tweak the RAM settings to improve memory performance. By changing the memory's default CAS latency from 2.5 to 2, lowering the RAS to CAS delay from 3 to 2, lowering the RAS precharge from 3 to 2, lowering the Active to precharge from 6 to 5 and, lowering the command rate from 2T to 1T, you may gain approximately a 3 percent faster memory performance. However, if you decide to change your settings, you need to make sure that your machine is still stable.

5.9 TROUBLESHOOTING RAM

Memory problems can occur in many forms. Some error messages will be obvious (audio or video code), but others will not be so obvious. Some symptoms that may indicate a memory problem are as follows:

The following are common ways for the computer to tell you it is having problems with memory:

1. The computer won't boot but merely beeps.
2. The computer boots but doesn't recognize all the installed memory.
3. The computer doesn't boot, nothing appears on the screen, and there are no audio beeps.
4. The computer reports a memory error.
5. There is a memory mismatch error.
6. There is a memory parity interrupt at xxxxx.
7. There is a memory address error at xxxxx.
8. There is a memory failure at xxxxx, read xxxxx, expecting xxxxx.
9. There is a memory verify error at xxxxx.
10. The computer intermittently reports errors, crashes frequently, or spontaneously reboots.
11. Registry errors occur.
12. General-protection faults, page faults, and exception errors occur.
13. The server system manager reports a memory error.
14. Serial presence detect (SPD) is not detected.
15. Random errors in programs or software problems occur.
16. Unrecoverable application errors, general protection faults, stop errors, or equivalent errors occur.
17. The computer locks up periodically often without any noticeable pattern or obvious explanation.
18. Nonmaskable interrupt error occur.

When you have a problem with memory, the cause is usually one of three things:

- Improper configuration, including having the wrong part for your computer or not following the configuration rules
- Incompatibilities with memory modules from different manufacturers, different part numbers, or different speeds
- Improper installation, including the memory not being seated correctly or needing cleaning
- Defective hardware, including a faulty motherboard or memory module
- For RDRAM systems, memory slots or sockets for a channel do not contain a RIMM or a continuity RIMMs or the RIMM or continuity RIMM is not installed properly. Note: You will have to check the motherboard documentation to determine which memory slots or sockets are assigned to which channels.
- Motherboard problem
- Power-related problem

The fact that many computer problems manifest themselves as memory problems makes troubleshooting difficult. For example, a problem with the motherboard or software may produce a memory error message.

The following basic steps apply to almost all situations:

- Make sure you have the right memory part for your computer. At the manufacturer's website you can look up the part number. Many memory manufacturers have configurators, which indicate the compatibilities of your module. If not, phone the memory manufacturer, consult your computer manual, or phone the computer manufacturer.
- Confirm that you configured the memory correctly. Many computers require module installation in banks of equal-capacity modules. Some computers require the highest-capacity module to be in the lowest-labeled bank. Other computers require that all sockets be filled; still others require single-banked memory.
- Reinstall the module. Push the module firmly into the socket. In most cases you will hear a click when the module is in position. To make sure you have a module all the way in the socket, compare the height of the module to the height of other modules in neighboring sockets.

- Swap modules. Remove the new memory and see whether the problem disappears. Remove the old memory, reinstall the new, and see whether the problem persists. Try the memory in different sockets. Swapping reveals whether the problem is a particular memory module or socket or whether two types of memory aren't compatible.
- Clean the socket and pins on the memory module. Use a soft cloth to wipe the pins on the module. Use a PC vacuum or compressed air to blow dust off the socket. Do *not* use solvent, which may corrode the metal or prevent the leads from making full contact. Flux Off is a cleaner used specifically for contacts. You can purchase it at electronics or computer equipment stores.
- Update the BIOS. Computer manufacturers update BIOS information frequently and post revisions on their websites. Make sure you have the most recent BIOS for your computer. This especially applies when you have recently installed new software or you are significantly upgrading memory.
- Check the BIOS settings. See section 6.11.2 for more information.
- Verify the power output of the power supply.
- Replace the power supply.
- Replace the motherboard.
- Make sure that the computer is on its own ac circuit.
- Verify the ac power outlet.

Memory problems are caused by one of three things, the most obvious being the RAM itself and the other being the motherboard (to which the RAM directly connects) and power-related problems (bad power supply or power fluctuations). You will need to isolate each of these components, one at a time, until you find the cause.

One way to test the RAM is to use a software diagnostic, and it is best to use it after booting the computer without loading a memory-management program, such as HIMEM.SYS. If you load a memory manager, the memory goes into protected mode, and in that mode, memory above 1 MB cannot be tested. The other way to test the RAM is to run the comprehensive test (long test). By default, most of the software diagnostic packages perform the quick test. The comprehensive test takes longer, but it will do a much more thorough job. In addition, you should disable the system caches so that you test the RAM and not the cache. If a memory error is discovered during testing, it will usually be caused by a faulty RAM chip or a faulty motherboard.

Example 5.2:

A computer produces three beeps (AMI BIOS) during boot-up and nothing appears on the screen.

If you look up the error code, you will find that it means "Base 64 KB Error," which is a very common error message. It indicates that the first bank of chips (DIP, SIPP, SIMM, or DIMM) is faulty. To isolate the actual cause of the problem, you should first check to see if all the RAM chips are seated properly. If one of the chips is not connected or seated properly, the entire bank may not be recognized. After you check this, you should swap the suspected RAM chip with one that you know is good. If the problem still exists, it is most likely a motherboard problem.

Example 5.3:

All the RAM doesn't show up during the POST.

This is usually caused by either a faulty RAM chip or module or a faulty motherboard. Check the obvious first by making sure that the RAM is seated properly in the RAM slots. If the RAM is seated properly, replace each of the banks of RAM one at time until the problem goes away. After you find out which bank is causing the problem, you can then swap one RAM chip back into the system until you find out which individual chip is causing the problem.

Example 5.4:

You get an "Incorrect Memory Size" message during boot after you either increased or decreased the amount of RAM in the system.

This is usually not a major problem. During boot, the system instructs the ROM BIOS, which controls the boot procedure, to look in the CMOS RAM to see how much RAM the computer is supposed to have. It then tests the specified amount of RAM. When you change the amount of RAM, therefore, the information within the CMOS RAM does not match the actual amount of RAM. To fix this problem, go into the CMOS setup program and enter the standard CMOS settings. The new amount of RAM will automatically be written to the CMOS RAM when you save the changes and exit the program. The computer should then boot properly. (Note: Newer systems will automatically update the CMOS values when the amount of RAM is changed.)

If the *incorrect memory* message appears but you did not change the amount of RAM, then the CMOS value changed (because of bad CMOS battery or bad CMOS chip), the RAM became bad, or the motherboard became faulty.

Example 5.5:

You turn on the computer and the system indicates a "Gate A20 Failure."

This error message indicates in a 286 or higher machine that the computer must change to protected mode to utilize more than 1 MB of RAM. The first 1 MB of RAM is indicated with 20 address lines, identified A0 to A19; therefore, A20 is the 21st address line, which is the beginning of the extended memory. The gate A20 failure error indicates that the system, for whatever reason, could not activate the A20 line and change to protected mode. Since the A20 line is controlled by the keyboard controller, the gate A20 failure may be caused by either a faulty keyboard or a faulty motherboard.

To isolate the problem, check to see if the keyboard is configured correctly (XT versus AT). Next, replace the keyboard with a known good one. If the problem still exists, replace the motherboard.

SUMMARY

1. Random access memory, more commonly referred to as RAM, consists of electronic memory chips that store information inside the computer.
2. RAM is known as volatile (loses its content when the power is turned off) memory.
3. The RAM is considered the main memory or the primary memory because it is the memory that the microprocessor accesses directly.
4. Dynamic RAM (DRAM) needs to be constantly recharged (refreshed).
5. RAM cache consists of static RAM (SRAM) chips, which are faster than DRAM.
6. Synchronous dynamic RAM (SDRAM) runs in synchronization with the memory bus.
7. DDR SDRAM (double data rate SDRAM) is similar in function to regular SDRAM, but doubles the bandwidth of the memory by transferring data twice per cycle.
8. Rambus DRAM (RDRAM) is based on the Rambus channel, a high-speed 16-bit bus running at a clock rate up to 400 MHz.
9. Rambus channel requires that all sockets be populated with either a RIMM module or a continuity RIMM so that the channel remains continuous to the termination resistors.
10. When installing RAM, the first thing that you need to determine is how many empty memory slots you have. You will then need to determine which memory is compatible with the motherboard and which is compatible with any existing memory.
11. This includes the package type; type of RAM technology; RAM capacity; voltage; bus/clock speed; type of error control; buffered, nonbuffered, or registered memory; and single-sided or double-sided RAM.
12. The amount of RAM determines how many programs can be run at the same time, how large each program can be, and how many documents can be open at the same time. In addition, the amount of RAM is a big factor in the speed of the PC.
13. Virtual memory is space reserved on the hard drive to act like RAM.
14. When upgrading RAM in a system, you need to see if your motherboard supports the RAM's package type; type of RAM technology; RAM capacity; voltage; bus/clock speed; type of error control; buffered, nonbuffered, or registered memory; and number of banks.
15. Memory problems are caused by faulty RAM chips, a faulty motherboard, or power-related problems (bad power supply or power fluctuations).
16. VRAM, usually used in video cards, is a special form of DRAM that can read and write at the same time.

17. Compared to DDR SDRAM, DDR2 doubles performance by doubling the prefetch. In addition, it has on-die termination for cleaner signals and runs at 1.8 V compared to SDRAM which runs at 2.5 V.
18. Dual in-line package (DIP) chips, found on the original IBM PC, are inserted directly into a motherboard designed for them.
19. SIMMs and DIMMs are small circuit boards with several DIP chips soldered onto them.
20. SIMMs have 30 pins (8 or 9 bits) and 72 pins (32 or 36 bits).
21. SDRAM DIMMs have 168 pins, DDR DIMMs have 184 pins, and DDR2 DIMMs have 240 pins.
22. RIMMs are the form-factor or physical package for RDRAMs, which resemble DIMMs.
23. RIMMs have 184 pins.
24. A smaller version of the DIMM, called the small-outline DIMM (SO-DIMM), is narrower and thinner than the full-size DIMM. The SO-DIMM is usually found in notebook computers and some video cards.
25. A small-outline DIMM has only 72 pins (32-bit transfers) or 144 pins (64-bit transfers).
26. A micro dual in-line memory module (Micro-DIMM) consists of a number of memory components that are attached to a printer circuit board.
27. Micro-DIMMs have 144 pins.
28. RAM is divided into 8- or 9-bit patterns. The 8- bits represent a byte of data; the 9th bit is a parity bit used for error control.
29. Error checking and correcting (ECC) memory will detect 1-bit and 2-bit errors and correct 1-bit errors.
30. A bank is a collection of memory chips (data bus size) that make up a block of memory readable by the processor in a single bus cycle.
31. Double-sided chips result from combining two sets of chips into one package.
32. If a motherboard has two DIMM slots and was made to handle three banks of RAM chips, you can insert two single-sided DIMMs (two banks) or one single-sided DIMM and one double-sided DIMM (three banks), but it will not support two double-sided DIMMs.

QUESTIONS

1. RAM is considered volatile memory. Which of the following best describes volatile memory?
   a. UV light is used to erase the contents of the chip.
   b. Data in RAM is permanent and can't be erased.
   c. Data in RAM can be changed and is not permanent.
   d. The data is maintained by a small battery when the power is shut off.
2. Which type of memory involves mapping addresses of logical pages to physical pages?
   a. extended
   b. expanded
   c. conventional
   d. reserve
   e. high
3. Which of the following is the fastest form of RAM?
   a. FPM RAM
   b. EDO RAM
   c. Burst EDO RAM
   d. SDRAM
4. Which of the following does *not* require the RAM to be refreshed?
   a. FPM RAM
   b. EDO RAM
   c. Burst EDO RAM
   d. SDRAM
   e. SRAM
5. Which of the following best describe DRAM (choose two)?
   a. Chips that use tiny capacitors to represent bits of information.
   b. Chips that use tiny electronic switches to represent bits of information.
   c. Chips that need to be constantly recharged.
   d. Chips that do not need recharging.
   e. DRAM is faster than SRAM.
6. Which type of RAM is used for RAM cache?
   a. DRAM
   b. VRAM
   c. SRAM
   d. EDO RAM
7. Which of the following best describes burst mode?
   a. One memory address is sent, followed by several sequential pieces of data.
   b. The memory and data addresses are sent simultaneously.
   c. Data is sent at a faster speed.
   d. Memory reads and writes at the same time.
8. VRAM is faster than DRAM because
   a. VRAM supports burst mode.
   b. VRAM can read and write at the same time.
   c. VRAM does not need recharging.
   d. VRAM runs at a higher speed than DRAM.
9. The first 640 KB of memory is known as
   a. conventional memory.
   b. CMOS memory.
   c. extended memory.
   d. reserve memory.
10. Memory between 640 KB and 1 MB used by hardware is known as
    a. conventional memory.
    b. upper memory.
    c. reserve memory.
    d. expanded memory.
    e. extended memory.

11. Which of the following was developed to work around some of the limitations of DOS and early microcomputers?
    a. upper memory area (UMA)
    b. expanded memory (EMS)
    c. high memory area (HMA)
    d. extended memory (XMS)
12. Which memory area is above 1 MB and is found on any new IBM PC or compatible?
    a. upper memory
    c. reserve memory
    c. extended memory
    d. expanded memory
13. What is the hexadecimal range for conventional memory?
    a. A0000 to 7FFFF b. 00000 to A0000
    c. 00000 to 9FFFF d. 00000 to A0000
14. The video ROM BIOS memory address is commonly located between
    a. A0000 and AFFFFH.
    b. B0000 and BFFFFH.
    c. C0000 and CFFFFH.
    d. D0000 and DFFFFH.
    e. F0000 and FFFFFH.
15. Virtual memory is
    a. extended memory pretending to be expanded memory.
    b. ROM chips pretending to be memory.
    c. extended memory being used for video RAM.
    d. hard disk space pretending to be RAM.
16. A small circuit board consisting of several DRAM chips and small metal plates that is inserted into the motherboard is known as a
    a. DIPP. b. SIPP.
    c. SIMM. d. SRAM.
    e. none of the above.
17. Which of the following has a 64-bit data path?
    a. DIPP b. SIPP
    c. SIMM d. DIMM
18. Which of the following has a 32-bit data path (choose two)?
    a. 30-pin SIMM b. 72-pin SIMM
    c. DIMM d. SO-DIMM
19. Generally, how many 72-pin SIMMs are needed to make a bank in a Pentium microprocessor?
    a. 1 b. 2
    c. 4 d. 8
20. RAM is often divided into a 9-bit pattern. Eight of the bits represent 1 byte of data. What is the ninth bit used for?
    a. a spare bit
    b. error control
    c. data storage
    d. the address of the data
21. Some IC chips mounted in sockets can work loose over time because of
    a. thermal cycling of the chip and the socket.
    b. metal stresses from the leads of the chip.
    c. vertical mounting of chips on circuit boards.
    d. vibration caused by disk drive and cooling fan motors.
22. Which of the following will *not* cause a memory error?
    a. faulty hard drive
    b. faulty RAM chip
    c. power fluctuations
    d. faulty power supply
    e. faulty motherboard
23. Which component may be failing if the fan and hard drive run, yet the system appears dead?
    a. the on/off switch
    b. the power supply
    c. the power cord
    d. the RAM
    e. the floppy drive
24. How many bits of data do nonparity DIMMs transfer at a time?
    a. 8 b. 32
    c. 72 d. 16
    e. 64 f. 128
25. How many bits of data do 168-pin parity DIMMs transfer at a time?
    a. 16 b. 32
    c. 36 d. 64
    e. 72
26. Which type of RAM enables a memory address to hold data for multiple reads?
    a. EDO b. VRAM
    c. WRAM d. DRAM
    e. RDRAM
27. How can you tell the difference between the DDR DRAM and SDRAM (choose all that apply)?
    a. SDRAM DIMMs have a 168-pin connector while DDR DRAM DIMMs have a 184-pin connector.
    b. SDRAM DIMMs have a 168-pin connector while SDRAM have a 200-pin connector.
    c. SDRAM DIMMs have one key while DDR RAM DIMMs have two keys
    d. SDRAM DIMMs have two keys while DDR RAM DIMMs have one key.

HANDS-ON EXERCISES

Exercise 1: Analyzing Memory in Windows

1. Start Windows.
2. Within the Control Panel, start the System applet. Determine the actual amount of memory.
3. If you are using Windows 9X, click the Virtual Memory button under the Performance tab. If you are using Windows 2000 or Windows XP, select the Advanced tab and click the Settings button under the Performance section.
4. Depending on your Windows version, click on the Virtual Memory button or the Change button under the Virtual Memory section. Determine what drive the virtual memory is stored on and how big the virtual memory is.
5. Close the Virtual Memory window and System Properties window.
6. Start the System Information program.
7. Click to highlight System Summary. In the right pane, view your total memory, total physical memory, available physical memory, total virtual memory, available virtual memory, page file space, and the page file.
8. Open the Components section, the Storage area, and select Drives. View the size of the hard drives and how much free space is available on each one. Remember that running out of disk space can lead to "out of memory" errors.
9. Close the System Information program.
10. Start Task Manager by pressing the Ctrl+Alt+Del buttons. If necessary, click on the Task Manager button.
11. Click the Performance tab. Notice the Physical Memory section and the Page File Usage section.
12. Click the Processes tab and look at the programs and the amount that each program uses.
13. Close the Task Manager.

Exercise 2: Testing the RAM Using a Software Diagnostic Package

1. Using a software diagnostic package, determine the amount of RAM your system has.
2. Using a software diagnostic package, test the RAM. Note: If the software has a short/quick test and a long/comprehensive test, run both.

Exercise 3: Troubleshooting

1. Shut off the computer and remove all the RAM chips.
2. Turn on the computer. What kind of error, if any, occurred?
3. Shut off the computer and reinsert all the RAM chips.
4. Remove the first RAM chip.
5. Turn on the computer. What kind of error, if any, occurred?
6. Shut off the computer and reinsert the first RAM chip.
7. Turn on the computer and test to make sure everything is running properly.
8. Look at your motherboard documentation to see how much RAM your motherboard supports and what RAM chips your motherboard supports. Also look to see how the RAM needs to be installed such as if the RAM needs to be loaded in the first RAM slot or if it can use any slot. If you are using RDRAM, determine what makes up a bank.
9. Look at your motherboard documentation for jumpers or BIOS in your BIOS setup program used to configure the RAM.
10. For your system, determine how many RAM chips make up a bank.

CHAPTER 6

Motherboards

Topics Covered in This Chapter

Introduction

The motherboard acts as the central nervous system of the computer and allows the microprocessor to connect to other components. The motherboard holds the microprocessor, the RAM, expansion slots, and a wide array of chips known as the motherboard chipset. These support chips allow all the different components to work together.

Two important motherboard support chips are the system ROM BIOS chip and the CMOS RAM chip. The system ROM BIOS chip might be said to represent the "instincts" of the computer; it works very closely with the CMOS RAM chip, which holds valuable hardware configuration information.

Objectives

1. Identify and describe the motherboard.
2. Explain the advantages of a printed circuit board.
3. List and describe motherboard form factors.
4. State the different forms of memory and explain their advantages and disadvantages.
5. List the different BIOS chips used in a PC and describe their functions.
6. Describe the boot-up procedure of the PC.
7. Explain how the system ROM BIOS is supplemented.
8. Given a motherboard and the motherboard documentation, configure the DIP switches and jumpers.
9. Describe the function of the CMOS RAM and how it relates to the system BIOS.
10. Describe the function of the real-time clock (RTC) and the CMOS battery.
11. Describe the chipset/PC support chips.
12. Differentiate among the system clock, the crystal oscillator, and the timer chip.
13. Enter and configure the CMOS setup program.
14. State some common problems caused by a faulty motherboard.
15. Describe how to determine if the motherboard is faulty.

6.1 INTRODUCTION TO MOTHERBOARDS

Examples of concepts and modules are:

- Motherboard

The **motherboard,** also referred to as the *main board* or the *system board,* is the primary printed circuit board located within the PC. It includes connectors for attaching additional boards (expansion slots) and additional devices (ports). In addition, it contains the microprocessor, the RAM chips, the RAM cache, several ROM BIOS chips, CMOS RAM, the real-time clock, and several support chips.

Printed circuit boards have thin metal traces embedded within their glass-epoxy construction that connect the different electronic components. Since the microprocessor talks to the other components by sending signals through the metal traces, the motherboard can be thought of as the PC's nervous system. Since so many electronic devices require many connections, modern motherboards will usually contain several layers of metal traces.

Question:

Why don't PC designers use wires instead of metal traces?

Answer:

The motherboard as well as other printed circuit boards actually simplifies the insides of a computer. Without the printed circuit board, the PC would have hundreds of wires, which must be connected and soldered, making the computer cost more. Wires are also more fragile, and it would be difficult to troubleshoot hundreds of wires. See figure 6.1.

Figure 6.1 This is an original IBM PC prototype motherboard before it was made into a printed circuit board. (Courtesy of International Business Machines Corporation; unauthorized use not permitted)

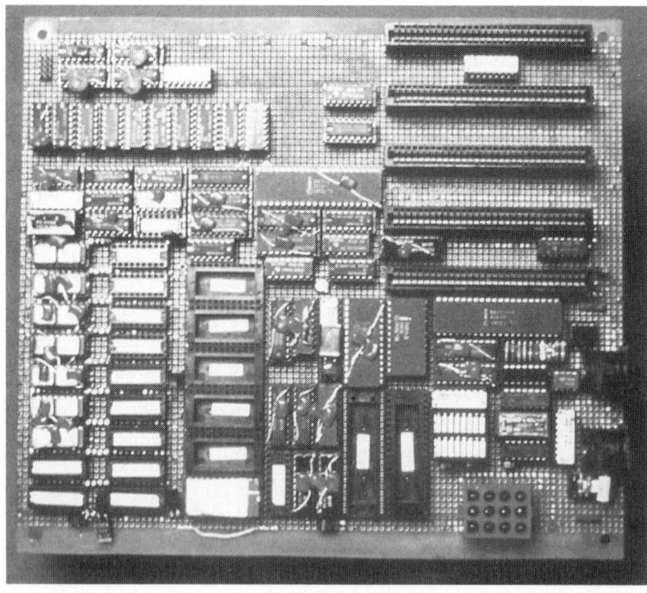

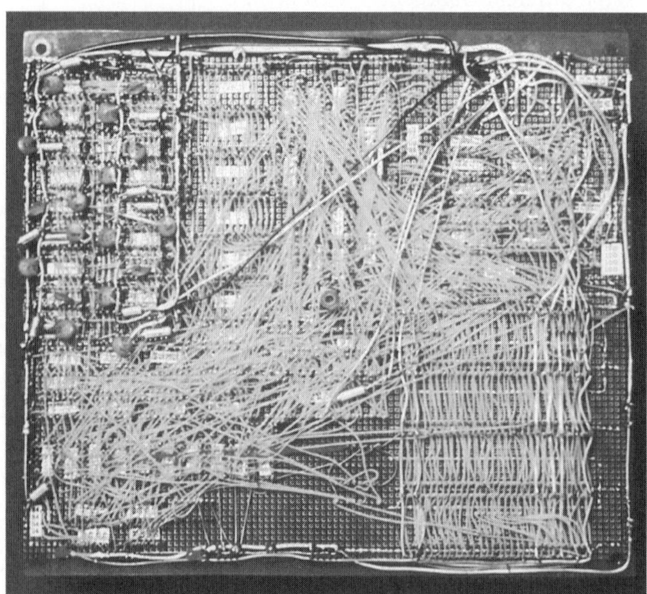

6.2 MOTHERBOARD FORM FACTORS

Motherboards are often described by their form factors (physical dimensions and sizes). The main form factors are shown in table 6.1. Up until 1996, the AT and Baby AT form factors were the most common motherboard form factor. Both of them are very similar, including their use of the standard 5-pin DIN type connector. The Baby AT is essentially the same as the original IBM XT motherboard, whereas the full-size AT motherboard matches the original IBM AT motherboard design. Because the full-size AT motherboard is 12 in. wide, they don't typically fit into minidesktop or minitower cases. These motherboard designs are considered obsolete, so they have mostly been replaced by newer form factors, such as the ATX or NLX designs.

Table 6.1 Motherboard Form Factors

Style	Dimensions	Comments
Full AT	12″ × 11–13″	Used in older PCs
Baby AT	8.5″ × 11–13″	Used in older PCs
ATX	12.0″ × 9.6″	Common in today's systems; allows better cooling of processor
Mini-ATX	11.2″ × 8.2″	Smaller version of the ATX
Micro-ATX	9.6″ × 9.6″	Popular in today's systems
Flex-ATX	9.0″ × 7.5″	Popular in today's systems
LPX	9″ × 11–13″	Uses riser card
Mini-LPX	8.9″ × 10–11″	Uses riser card
NLX	9.0″ × 13.6″	Provides better access to motherboard components
BTX Board	Up to 12.8″ × 10.5″	Upcoming popular standard
MicroBTX	Up to 10.4″ × 10.5″	Upcoming popular standard
PicoBTX	8.0″ × 10.5″	Upcoming popular standard

For more information on current form factors, visit the following website:

http://www.formfactors.org/formfactors/form_factors.htm

The most common form factors used today are the ATX motherboard and its derivatives, mini-ATX, micro-ATX, and Flex-ATX. The ATX motherboard is similar to the Baby AT. It uses the same width of the full AT board, allowing many existing AT form-factor chassis or cases to accept Baby AT, full AT, ATX or mini-ATX form-factor boards with a minimum number of changes. The main difference is the components are placed differently. The expansion slots are parallel to the short side of the board, which allows more space for other components. The processor and RAM are next to the power supply so that the airflow generated by the power supply runs over the processor to help keep it cooler. In addition, the processor and memory modules can be replaced or upgraded without removing any of the expansion cards. The ATX motherboard contains integrated I/O port connectors, an integrated PS/2 mouse connector, and a single-keyed 20-pin power supply connector (which also includes 3.3 V). The internal I/O connectors for the floppy and hard disk drives (two IDE channels) are relocated to be near the drive bays. Lastly, ATX motherboards allow you to turn off the computer via software (known as soft power switch).

The mini-ATX, micro-ATX and flex-ATX are smaller than the ATX motherboard, reducing the number of expansion slots and reducing the cost. The mini-ATX allows a manufacturer to cut four printed circuit boards per 24 × 18-in. panel, reducing the cost of the printed circuit board by approximately 30 percent. The flex-ATX form factor is smallest of these, designed to support current-socketed processor technology and to include the ATX 2.03 I/O panel specification.

Expansion cards for **LPX motherboards** are inserted into a *riser card* that protrudes from the motherboard. Consequently, the expansion boards are parallel to the motherboard rather than at right angles to it, allowing for smaller cases. Some motherboards that have a planar design also use a riser card to hold the expansion slots. The **NLX motherboard,** though similar to the LPX, contains several improvements. It supports larger memory modules and newer microprocessors and provides better access to motherboard components. See figure 6.2.

Most likely, the next popular form factor will be the **balanced technology extended (BTX) form factor.** This form factor is similar to that of ATX, but is designed to balance size, performance, features, and cost. To improve heat dissipation and acoustics, the board has been redesigned to improve airflow through the system; moving the CPU to the "front" of the case allows it to be right next to the intake

Figure 6.2 NLX Motherboard (Courtesy of Intel Corporation)

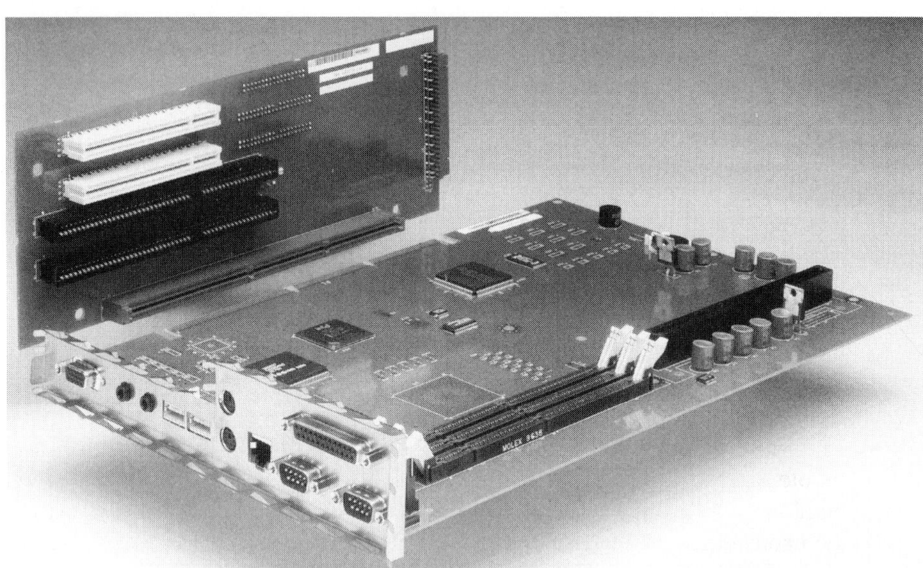

fan, giving it the coolest air out of any component in the system. The airflow is also channeled over the chipset, graphics card, and memory chips. The BTX emphasizes phasing out legacy I/O ports such as the serial, parallel, and PS/2 ports and AGP graphics. Instead, BTX will be optimized for PCI Express and Serial ATA and will include additional USB ports. When it comes to power supplies, the BTX form factor does not stray from ATX power supplies. The BTX standard supports ATX12V, SFX12V, CFX12V, and LFX12V.

Some computers, including most name-brand computers, use proprietary motherboards. The motherboards therefore will not normally fit into another case, and cases will not accommodate most non-brand motherboards. The same is true for motherboards for notebook computers. If you need to replace a motherboard for a notebook computer, you must make sure that it is from the same manufacturer and that they are interchangeable.

6.3 FORMS OF MEMORY

6.3.1 RAM and Disks

RAM, which stands for **random access memory,** is the computer's short-term or temporary memory. It stores instructions and data that the microprocessor accesses directly. If power is discontinued to the RAM, such as when you shut off your PC, the contents of the RAM disappear. This is the reason we use disks (floppy disks and hard disks) for long-term storage.

Disks (hard drives and floppy drives) are the PC's long-term memory. They consist of mechanical parts that use magnetic patterns to store information on specially coated platters. Although they can hold large amounts of information, they are slow and have a high failure rate as compared to other nonmechanical components.

6.3.2 ROM Chips

Read-only memory (ROM) chips contain instructions and data that the microprocessor accesses directly. Unlike the contents of the RAM, the contents of the ROM are permanent. They can't be changed or erased by normal means and are maintained when power is off. Although they are much faster than any disk, ROM chips are slower than RAM chips. There are several types of ROM chips, including:

1. Mask ROM
2. Programmable read-only memory (PROM)
3. Erasable programmable read-only memory (EPROM)

4. Electrically erasable programmable read-only memory (EEPROM)
5. Flash memory

Mask ROM chips are programmed during manufacturing; PROM chips are manufactured as a blank chip and are programmed later by using a PROM burner. Both chips are permanent and nonchangeable after programming and are therefore unsuited to today's fast-changing PC.

Erasable programmable read-only memory (EPROM) is a special type of PROM that can be erased by shining ultraviolet light through a clear window on top of the chip. To prevent inadvertent erasure of the contents of the chip, a label or tape covers the window. Once the chip is erased, it can be reprogrammed. Because the EPROM chip holds instructions that allow a device to run properly, erasing the chip will cause the device to not function properly, so the chip has to be reprogrammed with an EPROM burner or replaced. **Electrically erasable programmable read-only memory (EEPROM)** chips (pronounced "double-E PROM") can also be reprogrammed. The chips are erased using higher-than-normal voltage instead of ultraviolet light. Unfortunately, EPROM chips can be erased only a set number of times.

Flash memory chips are similar to EEPROM chips except they can be erased and reprogrammed in blocks instead of 1 byte at a time. In addition, they can be reprogrammed with the normal voltage used in the PC. Many modern PCs have their BIOS stored on a flash memory chip so that it can easily be updated if necessary. Such a BIOS is sometimes called flash BIOS. The first generation of flash memory chips were limited to a finite number of changes but were eventually improved to act more like normal RAM. Other uses of flash memory include plug-and-play systems that store the expansion card configuration information and modems that support new protocols as they become standardized.

6.4 ROM BIOS CHIPS

As mentioned earlier, ROM chips (including flash memory) are used within the PC to provide instructions and data to the processor. The chips and the software (programs and data) that have been written onto these chips are called **firmware.**

The basic input/output system (BIOS) contains ROM chips that provide instructions and data to the processor. BIOS is the built-in software that determines what a computer can do without accessing programs from a disk. Therefore, you can think of these ROM chips as the instincts of the computer. They contain all the code required to control the boot process and control many hardware devices, including the keyboard, display screen, disk drives, serial communications, and others.

Every PC has several BIOS chips, including the system ROM BIOS, the keyboard ROM BIOS, and the video ROM BIOS. The **system ROM BIOS,** which is located on the motherboard, directs the boot-up and allows basic control of the majority of the hardware. The **keyboard ROM BIOS** (see figure 6.3), which is also found on the motherboard, controls the keyboard. The **video ROM BIOS,** which is located on the video card, or on the motherboard if the video card is built into the motherboard, controls the video systems.

Other ROM chips, which are often found on expansion cards, supplement the instructions of the system ROM BIOS. They provide instructions used to control new or nonstandard hardware not included in the original system ROM BIOS and include SCSI controller cards, enhanced IDE controller cards, sound cards, proprietary CD-ROM drive controller cards, and network cards.

The ROM chips, which are mapped with the RAM, occupy the reserve memory between 640 KB and 1 MB. The reserve memory got its name because it was reserved for the BIOS. The system ROM

Figure 6.3 Keyboard ROM BIOS

BIOS uses up to 128 KB of reserved RAM; it may use as little as 64 KB (F0000-FFFFF). The video BIOS has 128 KB of reserved memory (C0000-C7FFF), and other expansion cards use the last 128 KB. Therefore, when these memory locations within reserve memory are accessed, it may be the ROM chip that is accessed instead of the RAM chip.

6.5 SYSTEM ROM BIOS

The primary ROM BIOS chip is the system ROM BIOS. See figure 6.4. On today's PCs, there is only one system ROM BIOS chip; older systems may have up to four ROM BIOS chips. The system ROM BIOS has the following functions:

1. Controlling the boot-up procedure
2. Performing a series of diagnostic tests known as the power-on self-test (POST) during boot-up
3. Generating hardware error codes (audio and video) if a problem is found during boot-up
4. Finding other ROM BIOS chips on the expansion cards
5. Finding a boot sector or boot files to boot an operating system
6. Providing the most basic commands to control hardware
7. Providing compatibility between the operating system and the hardware
8. Containing the CMOS setup program

6.5.1 Boot-Up Sequence

The computer performs a quick power check when it is first turned on. When the processor receives a power-good signal, it starts reading and executing the instructions in the system ROM BIOS on how to boot the computer. The processor will then initialize and test the essential PC components (RAM and motherboards) and perform an inventory of the hardware devices installed in the computer. When a component does not respond correctly to the test, the failure will be identified as a series of beeps (audio codes) or a number code or message (video code), as described in chapter 2.

NOTE: To complete POST, a system needs only a motherboard, processor, RAM, and a video card.

During this time, the system ROM BIOS has instructions to search for additional ROM BIOS chips. Since the system ROM BIOS cannot possibly hold instructions for every piece of hardware or include instructions for all the new pieces of hardware that are introduced every day, a way to store additional instructions to control hardware was needed. These additional hardware instructions are located in the other ROM BIOS chips found on the expansion cards.

The last thing that the system ROM BIOS chip does during boot-up is to find a boot device to load the operating system. If all goes well, the system will finish with a prompt waiting for a command input (DOS or UNIX, including Linux) or will display a GUI interface (Windows 95, Windows 98, Windows Millennium, Windows NT, Windows 2000, Windows XP, or X Window).

Figure 6.4 AMI System ROM BIOS (Courtesy of American Megatrends Inc.)

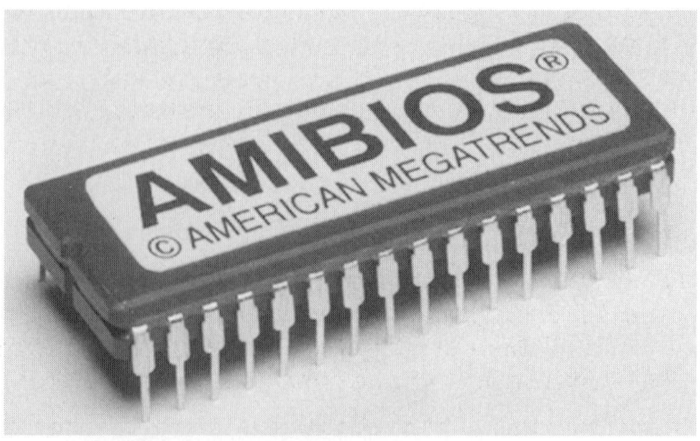

BOOT PROCEDURE

Hardware Initialization

Step 1. After the PC is turned on, the microprocessor timer chip generates a reset signal.

Step 2. The power supply performs a self-test to make sure that all voltages and current levels are acceptable. The power supply indicates that the power is stable by sending the power-good signal to the microprocessor timer chip.

Step 3. The microprocessor timer chip stops generating a reset signal to the microprocessor and starts executing the instructions at address FFFF:0000H.

Step 4. The microprocessor begins executing instructions located within the system ROM BIOS. These instructions perform tests of the central hardware to verify basic system functionality. Any errors that occur are indicated by audio codes because the video system has not yet been initialized.

Step 5. The system ROM BIOS performs a search for the video ROM BIOS, which is located on the video card. If it does not find the video ROM BIOS, it uses the system ROM BIOS to initialize the monitor. A cursor will appear on the screen.

Step 6. The system ROM BIOS searches for other ROM chips (C0000H to EFFFFH) located on other adapter cards. A checksum test is done on the ROM modules. If the test fails, it will give a message (XXXX ROM Error), the XXXX being the segment address of the failed ROM module.

Step 7. The system ROM BIOS reads the information stored in the CMOS RAM. The CMOS RAM stores hardware information, such as the number and size of the drives and the amount of RAM in the system. If the information in the CMOS does not match the actual hardware found during testing, an error message will be generated stating what hardware could not be found.

Step 8. The ROM BIOS checks to see if the start is cold or warm. If a cold start, it will do the memory (RAM) test. If it is a warm start, it will skip the memory test. The test can be seen on the screen as the memory counts up from zero.

Step 9. If it is a cold start, the POST (power-on self-test) executes. The POST performs additional tests on the system. If an error occurs, it will be identified by a combination of audio and video codes. A successful POST is indicated by a single beep.

Booting from Disk

Step 10. The ROM BIOS searches for a volume boot sector at cylinder 0, head 0, sector 1 (the very first sector) on the A drive. This sector is loaded into the RAM and tested. If a disk is in the drive but the sector cannot be read or no disk is present, the BIOS continues to the next step. If the PC cannot boot from the floppy disk, a disk boot failure occurs or a "Nonsystem Disk or Disk Error" message is generated. Note: The boot order can be changed in some systems (the A drive followed by the C drive, the C drive followed by the A drive, or another combination of boot devices); the A drive followed by the C drive is the default order.

Step 11. If no volume boot sector can be read from the A drive, the BIOS looks for a master boot record (MBR), located at cylinder 0, head 0, sector 1, to find out which partition to boot from. If an active partition cannot be found, it will generate a "Missing Operating System" error message.

Step 12. If there is a problem at this point, a message will appear. Depending on the BIOS manufacturer, the message will say that there is no boot device available, no ROM BASIC, or an invalid partition. If the system does boot from this drive, it will go to step 14.

Step 13. The system then goes to the active partition and tries to boot from it. If it can't boot from the partition, a loading operating system or a missing operating system error message will be generated.

Loading DOS

Step 14. After finding the drive or partition to boot from, the system then goes to the root directory and finds the boot files for the operating system. For DOS, it is IO.SYS (or IBMBIO.COM for PC DOS) and MSDOS.SYS (or IBMDOS for PC DOS). If a problem occurs, a "Nonsystem Disk or Disk Error" message is generated.

Loading DOS—*continued*

Step 15. The IO.SYS file will read the CONFIG.SYS and then load the COMMAND.COM followed by the AUTOEXEC.BAT file. If the CONFIG.SYS file or AUTOEXEC.BAT file is missing, it will continue to boot. If the COMMAND.COM file is missing, a "Bad or Missing Command Interpreter" message appears.

Step 16. When the computer is finished booting, a prompt will appear on the screen (usually C:\> if DOS) or a GUI environment will appear (if Windows 3.XX is loading from within the AUTOEXEC.BAT file).

Loading Windows 95, Windows 98, and Windows Millennium

Step 14. After finding the drive or partition to boot from, the system then goes to the root directory and finds the boot files for the operating system. For Windows 95, Windows 98, and Windows Millennium, it is IO.SYS. If a problem occurs, a "Nonsystem Disk or Disk Error" message is generated.

Step 15. IO.SYS then reads the MSDOS.SYS, CONFIG.SYS (if it exists), COMMAND.COM, and AUTOEXEC.BAT (if it exists) files. Note: Windows loads certain CONFIG.SYS entries automatically, including HIMEM.SYS, IFSHELP.SYS, and SETVER.EXE.

Step 16. The IO.SYS loads WIN.COM, which then loads the VMM32.VXD file. The VMM32 loads virtual drivers, switches the computer's processor from real mode to protected mode, and loads the KRNL32.DLL, GDI.EXE, and USER.EXE.

Step 17. Lastly, VMM32.VXD loads the EXPLORER.EXE, the default Windows GUI shell. When the computer is finished booting, a GUI environment (default) or a prompt will appear on the screen.

Loading Windows NT, Windows 2000, and Windows XP

Step 14. After finding the drive or partition to boot from, the system then goes to the root directory and finds the boot file called NTLDR.

Step 15. The NTLDR reads the BOOT.INI file and displays the boot menu.

Step 16. When Windows NT, Windows 2000, or Windows XP is selected from the boot menu, NTDETECT.COM, NTOSKERNL.EXE, and the hardware abstraction layer (HAL.DLL) are loaded.

Step 17. When the computer is finished booting, a GUI environment appears on the screen.

Loading Linux

Step 14. The boot manager, such as Linux Loader (LILO) and GRUB, is located which gives the user the ability to boot between multiple operatings systems.

Step 15. If Linux is chosen, it will first load the kernel (vmlinuz located in the /boot directory).

Step 16. The kernel runs the init program, which then starts a complicated startup sequence.

Step 17. If your X Window loads automatically, you will log in at a command login prompt, which, in turn, will load a user shell (the default shell is bash). If X Window loads automatically, the display manager (xdm), an X server, and a desktop manager are loaded. The xdm will then provide a graphical login screen.

6.5.2 Hardware Control

The system ROM BIOS and the other ROM chips found during boot-up contain many small individual programs called **system routines** or BIOS services. They are low-level programs that directly manipulate the PC hardware. See table 6.2.

The system routines located within the system ROM BIOS provide a level of compatibility between hardware and the system software. With so many different PCs of many different designs, you would expect that there would have to be several different versions of the operating system and software applications, one for each PC design. Yet when you buy a copy of DOS 6.22 or Windows 95, it operates on any PC as long as the PC has the minimum CPU, RAM capacity, and hard disk space. The reason only one version is needed is that the system ROM BIOS provides a translation between the operating system and the many different types of hardware. Even today's latest and most powerful PCs still duplicate everything the old AT did, so older software that ran on the AT also runs on the newer PCs.

Table 6.2 System Routines (BIOS Services)

Interrupt	Type of Interrupt	Event
00H	Processor	Divided by zero
01H	Processor	Single-step interrupt handler
02H	Processor	Nonmaskable interrupt (NMI)
03H	Processor	Breakpoint
04H	Processor	Arithmetic overflow handler
05H	Software	Print screen
06H	Processor	Invalid op-code
07H	Processor	Coprocessor not available
08H	Hardware	System timer service routine
09H	Hardware	Keyboard device service routine
0AH	Hardware	Cascade from 2nd programmable interrupt controller (IRQ2)
0BH	Hardware	Serial port service (COM2-IRQ3)
0CH	Hardware	Serial port service (COM1-IRQ4)
0DH	Hardware	Parallel printer service (LPT2-IRQ5)
0EH	Hardware	Floppy disk drive service (IRQ6)
DFH	Hardware	Parallel printer service (LPT1-IRQ7)
10H	Software	Video service routine
11H	Software	Equipment list service routine
12H	Software	Memory size service routine
13H	Software	Hard disk drive service
14H	Software	Serial communication service routines
15H	Software	System services support routines
16H	Software	Keyboard support service routines
17H	Software	Parallel printer support services
18H	Software	Load and run ROM BASIC
19H	Software	DOS loading routine
1AH	Software	Real-time clock service routines
1BH	Software	<Ctrl><Break> service routine
1CH	Software	User timer service routines
1DH	Software	Video control parameter table
1EH	Software	Floppy disk parameter table
1FH	Software	Video graphics character table
20H–3FH	Software	DOS interrupt points
40H	Software	Floppy disk revector routine
41H	Software	Hard disk drive C parameter table
42H	Software	EGA default video driver
43H	Software	Video graphic characters
44H	Software	Novell NetWare API
46H	Software	Hard disk drive D parameter table
4AH	Software	User alarm
64H	Software	Novell NetWare IPX
67H	Software	EMS support routines

Continued

Table 6.2 Continued

Interrupt	Type of Interrupt	Event
70H	Hardware	Real-time clock (IRQ8)
71H	Hardware	Redirect interrupt cascade (IRQ9)
72H–73H	Hardware	Reserved (IRQ10-11)
74H	Hardware	Bus mouse (IRQ12)
75H	Hardware	Math coprocessor exception (IRQ13)
76H	Hardware	Hard disk support (IRQ14)
77H	Hardware	Suspend request (IRQ15)
7AH	Software	Novell NetWare API

Table 6.3 Popular BIOS Manufacturers

BIOS Manufacturer	Description
IBM	IBM represents today's personal computer standard. All other ROM BIOS chips need to be compatible with the IBM BIOS if they wish to be truly IBM compatible.
AMI	AMI became a popular BIOS because of its many features and enhancements. **Home:** http://www.ami.com/ **Document Library:** http://www.ami.com/support/doclib.cfm **Motherboard ID Utility:** http://www.ami.com/support/mbid.html
Award	Award is unique among BIOS developers because it sells its BIOS code to other vendors and allows those vendors to customize the BIOS for their particular systems. Note: Award software became part of Phoenix Technology. **AwardBIOS Setup Information:** http://www.phoenix.com/pcuser/phoenixbios/setup_information.html **Index of CMOS Setup Program Options:** http://www.phoenix.com/pcuser/phoenixbios/setup_index.html **Motherboard Manufacturers:** http://www.phoenix.com/pcuser/phoenixbios/motherboard.html **Award Error Messages:** http://www.phoenix.com/pcuser/awardbios/award_error_codes.html
Phoenix	Phoenix was one of the first BIOS developers to design its own IBM-compatable BIOS and has become the standard for IBM-compatible BIOS. Phoenix ROM BIOS is efficient and very reliable. **Home:** http://www.phoenix.com/index.html **PhoenixBIOS User's Manual:** http://www.phoenix.com/pcuser/PDF-Files/userman.pdf

NOTE: AMI, Award, and Phoenix are by far the most popular. You should note that there are many other companies that sell their own BIOS. These BIOS are proprietary or compatible with common ROM BIOS. Some of the more popular are DTK, Epson, Hewlett-Packard, NCR, Compaq, Wang, and Zenith.

Several companies specialize in developing compatible IBM system ROM BIOS chips. The most popular are American Megatrends Incorporated (AMI), Phoenix, and Award. See table 6.3. After a system ROM BIOS is developed, these companies license their ROM BIOS chips to a motherboard manufacturer. The motherboard manufacturer matches the hardware to a chosen system ROM BIOS or has one developed specifically for its motherboard.

NOTE: To identify the system ROM BIOS manufacturer and the date and version ID of the system BIOS, you would either look at the initial POST screen during boot or look at the BIOS setup screen. It would also be helpful to know the motherboard make, model, and version, especially when you have to update the BIOS.

The system routines of the ROM BIOS are executed using interrupts. An **interrupt** is something that causes the processor to stop its current task so that it can do another task. When the second task is completed, it will go back to the original task to continue where it left off.

The PC supports 256 types of software interrupts and 15 hardware interrupts. Each type of software interrupt is associated with an interrupt handler, a routine that takes control when the interrupt occurs. When a device or a program needs some action on the part of the processor, it signals by sending an interrupt signal. It then examines the interrupt vector table located in the first 1 KB of RAM to determine where the code is that can handle the interrupt. The code may be stored in the ROM BIOS or in the RAM. If multiple interrupts exist, the interrupt assigned a lower number would be handled first.

The terms *interrupt* and *exception* are very close in meaning. Both can be used to refer to either hardware or software. The only real difference is that an exception usually indicates an error condition.

An interrupt can be generated by one of three sources. When a processor detects that a program does something wrong, it generates an interrupt to deal with the problem. The most common problems are divide errors (divide by zero), stack faults, invalid instructions, and general protection faults. See table 6.4 for a list of processor interrupts. Some of the main processor interrupts are:

- **Divide Error (Int 00)**—If a program tries to divide a number by zero, the processor will generate INT 00H. Software should provide a divide error handler in order to avoid killing the current application or hanging the system. Memory corruption, other hardware problems, corrupt software, or poor programming can cause this error.

Table 6.4 Processor Interrupts

Interrupt	Event
00	Divide error
01	Single-step debugging exceptions
02	Nonmaskable interrupt
03	Breakpoint
04	Info detected overflow
05	Bound range exceeded
06	Invalid instruction
07	Coprocessor not available
08	Double exception detected
09	Coprocessor
0A	Invalid task state segment
0B	Segment not present
0C	Stack fault
0D	Protection fault
0E	Page fault
10	Coprocessor error
11	Alignment check
12	Machine check

- **NMI Interrupt (Int 02)**—*NMI* stands for *nonmaskable interrupt.* All the regular interrupts that we normally use and refer to by number are called maskable interrupts. The processor is able to mask, or temporarily ignore, any interrupt, if it needs to, in order to finish something else that it is doing. In addition, however, the PC has a nonmaskable interrupt (NMI) that can be used for serious conditions that demand the processor's immediate attention. The NMI cannot be ignored by the system and is normally used only for critical problem situations, such as serious hardware errors. The most common use of NMI is to signal a memory parity error.
- **Invalid Opcode (Int 06)**—If the processor attempts to run an invalid instruction, it will generate an INT 06H, memory corruption. The most common cause of this is hardware memory corruption.
- **Double Fault (Int 08)**—A double fault occurs when an exception happens while trying to call the handler for a prior exception. Normally, the two exceptions can be handled one after the other. However, there are several exceptions that cannot be handled serially, and in this situation the processor signals a double fault. This is almost always caused by hardware problems.
- **General Protection Fault (Int 0D)**—Any condition that is not covered by any of the other processor exceptions will result in a general protection fault. The exception indicates that this program has been corrupted in memory, usually resulting in immediate termination of the application.
- **Page Fault (Int 0E)**—A page fault occurs when the PC needs to access information that is stored in virtual memory or a program requests data that is not currently in RAM or virtual memory. A page fault also occurs when a paging protection rule is violated. In these cases the operating system takes over for the appropriate action.
- **Machine Check (Int 12)**—It flags parity errors on data reads and unsuccessful completions of a bus cycle.

Errors that show processor interrupts include *A fatal exception XY has occurred at xxxx:xxxxxxxx* in Windows 95, Windows 98, or Windows Millennium, and Stop 7F Errors in Windows NT, Windows 2000, or Windows XP. Note: When errors occur that indicate one of these interrupts, the errors were detected only by the processor and do not necessarily indicate a bad processor. Because the error can be caused by hardware compatibility, faulty hardware (typically motherboard, RAM or processor), faulty software, faulty ROM BIOS instructions, or old ROM BIOS instructions, the problems still need to be isolated.

Software interrupts are generated when a hardware device must be checked or manipulated by the PC. Each type of software is associated with a routine that takes control when the interrupt occurs. Hardware interrupts are used when a device needs the attention of the processor. These are discussed in more detail in chapter 7.

6.5.3 ROM BIOS Shortcomings

All PCs are compatible to the ROM BIOS level, but ROM BIOS chips have two shortcomings. First, the BIOS cannot hold every instruction for every hardware device, nor can it handle devices based on newer technology. To overcome this problem, PC designers use several techniques to supplement the standard ROM BIOS:

1. Additional ROM BIOS chips located on expansion cards to supplement the instructions of the system ROM BIOS
2. Software written to access and control the hardware directly
3. Device drivers that enhance the BIOS instructions and TSRs that modify the interrupt vector table

To see examples of these techniques, let's examine IDE hard drives and enhanced IDE (EIDE) hard drives. Older computer systems, specifically the system ROM BIOS, were designed to see IDE hard drives only up to 504 MB of capacity. This is considered an extremely small size today but was considered large when it was introduced. Enhanced IDE drives were developed to extend the size of IDE hard drives and to make them faster. If you had a computer with an IDE controller card (expansion card) and tried to connect a 1 GB EIDE hard drive, the hard drive would not work properly. To overcome this problem, you would have to do one of the following:

1. Obtain a system with a newer system ROM chip or purchase a replacement system ROM BIOS chip, which includes instructions for handling EIDE hard drives
2. Update the ROM chip using special software if the system ROM BIOS is flash RAM

3. Purchase an EIDE controller card, which includes a ROM BIOS chip, to supplement the system ROM BIOS chip
4. Set the computer to recognize a 10 MB hard drive and to use a device driver that includes instructions for handling EIDE hard drives

As you can see, the ROM BIOS chips are vitally important to the operation of the computers and are in continuous use. Unfortunately, ROM BIOS chips are slow for performing these essential tasks, which causes the performance of the PC to be slow. ROM BIOS chips run as slowly as 200 ns and are accessed 8 bits at a time. To increase the speed of the ROM BIOS chips, the contents of the chips can be copied to the faster RAM during boot-up and accessed directly from RAM. RAM runs much faster than ROM (50 ns versus 80 ns) and can be accessed up to 32 bits at a time. This process of copying the ROM instructions to the RAM is called **ROM shadowing,** which can be activated or deactivated within the CMOS setup program.

A second way to increase PC performance is to have the applications (usually the operating system) work directly with the PC hardware rather than go through the ROM BIOS chips. Of course, this causes more work for software programmers, especially considering the number of hardware components available.

Question:

Are all system ROM BIOSes the same?

Answer:

No, they are not. First, when a company makes an IBM-compatible ROM BIOS chip, it must do so from scratch since the IBM ROM BIOS program code is copyrighted. Second, the ROM BIOS codes have been designed for specific hardware. Next, some BIOS chips are better optimized for hardware than other BIOS chips, and therefore allow the PC to operate faster. Lastly, some ROM BIOS chips may include instructions for handling newer hardware, while others do not.

Occasionally, you may need to upgrade or replace the system ROM BIOS. Reasons to upgrade the system BIOS are:

1. New hardware is introduced and the system ROM BIOS does not know how to work with the new hardware
2. There are programming glitches
3. The newer system ROM BIOS runs more efficiently than the older system BIOS

When replacing system ROM BIOS, you must use one that is compatible with the motherboard. The system ROM BIOS can be identified by the manufacturer, serial numbers, and dates, which are printed on the label. Typically, the only time you have to physically replace the BIOS chip is if it is a nonflash ROM chip or if it is corrupted; the system will fail to boot and it cannot be recovered.

6.5.4 Updating the System ROM BIOS

As mentioned several times throughout the book, updating the system ROM BIOS (also known as flashing the BIOS) can correct a wide range of problems and will allow the system to work with components that did not exist at the time the motherboard was manufactured.

Before upgrading to the latest BIOS, it is very important that you enter the *BIOS Setup Utility* and write down all your current CMOS settings. For Intel boards, you can also go to the Exit menu and choose the Save Custom Defaults options. Choosing Yes will cause the current BIOS settings to be saved as a custom default setting. When the CMOS memory is cleared during the BIOS upgrade, the BIOS will default to these custom default settings. If you do not choose to save the defaults as custom defaults, you will need to manually reenter these settings after you have upgraded to the latest BIOS.

There are three ways that motherboard system ROM BIOS can be updated. The first method is to download an image of the ROM BIOS chip programs and a flash program (an executable program such as FLASH.EXE or IFLASH.EXE), which can be downloaded from the motherboard manufacturer. When you upgrade your BIOS and you download the image of the BIOS chip, you need to know the make, model, and version of the motherboard so that you can download the correct image. Before you update the BIOS, you should read the instructions on how to do it. If you make a mistake, it could make your motherboard inoperable. Second, be sure to use the correct flash program and image. Most of these programs must be placed on a bootable floppy disk. Typically, when you download the image and flash program, you will create a bootable floppy disk when you unzip or uncompress the files. You then reboot the computer with the disk in drive A, and the BIOS will be updated automatically. When this occurs, be sure that the computer does not get shut off while the BIOS is being updated. If you accidentally shut it off or the power goes off, the motherboard will again most likely be inoperable.

The other two methods are used today on Intel motherboards and may be used by other manufacturers. The easiest way to update the BIOS is to use the Intel Express BIOS Update program specific to your motherboard. By executing the downloaded file within Windows 98, Windows ME, Windows NT, Windows 2000, or Windows XP, the executable file will run a Windows InstallShield program, which automatically updates the BIOS.

Most Intel motherboards have a single jumper block. When the jumper specifies configure mode, the BIOS/CMOS setup program will run, which also includes a maintenance menu that is not available during normal access of the program. **CAUTION:** Do not move the jumper with the power on. Always turn off the power and unplug the power cord from the computer before changing the jumper.

The other method is to use the BIOS Recovery option. If you are sure that you have integrated the PC components correctly, but the system is not booting properly and you cannot enter the BIOS/CMOS setup program or reflash the BIOS, then you may need to perform a BIOS recovery. Place the latest BIOS revision on a bootable floppy disk and place it into the floppy disk when the system is off. For Intel motherboards, remove the BIOS configuration jumper and turn on the PC. Wait several minutes while the BIOS is reinstalled into the desktop board flash memory. There will not be any video during the BIOS recovery. After you hear two beeps and the floppy disk drive light turns off, remove the BIOS disk. Turn off the PC and replace the BIOS configuration jumper on the motherboard.

Other motherboards might have a redundant system ROM BIOS in case the primary system ROM BIOS has been corrupted or you accidentally loaded the wrong image onto the motherboard. If you move a jumper on the motherboard, the system will copy the ROM BIOS image from the secondary ROM BIOS chip to the first.

6.5.5 ROM BASIC Chips

When the IBM PC was introduced in 1981, the BASIC language could be used to create simple programs for the PC. The BASIC language interpreter was stored on a ROM chip located on the motherboard. Instead of saving the programs to a disk, the user would save them to a cassette tape. The use of the cassette tape is why ROM BASIC was also called Cassette BASIC. If an IBM PC did not have a system disk in any of the bootable drives, the machine would start executing the BASIC language from the ROM BASIC chip. Compatible computers (PCs using AMI, Award, or Phoenix BIOS) and newer IBM computers do not include the ROM BASIC chip. AMI BIOS strives to be as compatible as possible to the IBM ROM BIOS, including looking for a BASIC ROM chip if a bootable device (drive A or drive C) can't be found. If a computer with AMI BIOS boots and can't find a bootable device, it will display the following error message:

```
NO ROM BASIC - SYSTEM HALTED
```

To fix this problem, check the CMOS settings. In addition, check to see if the partition that contains the operating system is set to "active." See section 6.12 and chapter 9 for more information.

6.6 CHIPSETS AND OTHER MOTHERBOARD COMPONENTS

One essential yet inexpensive part of the PC is the motherboard chipset. See figure 6.5. A **chipset** consists of the chips and other components on the motherboard that allow different PC components, including the microprocessor, to communicate with each other. It consists of the bus controllers, peripheral controllers, memory controllers, cache controllers, clocks, and timers. Although the chipset consists of several components, they may all be contained on several integrated chips or combined into one or two VLSI integrated chips (chips with over 20,000 circuits). The combining of dozens of related

Figure 6.5 Intel 430 VX Chipset (Courtesy of Intel Corporation; Intel is a Registered Trademark of Intel Corporation)

Table 6.5 Common Chipset Manufacturers

Manufacturer	Website
Acer Labs	**Home:** http://www.ali.com.tw **Driver Downloads:** http://www.ali.com.tw/es.htm
Advanced More Devices Inc.	**Home:** http://www.amd.com/
Broadcom ServerWorks	**Home:** http://www.broadcom.com **Product:** http://www.broadcom.com/serversproducts.html and http://www. serverworks.com/frames/ products_frame.html
Intel	**Home:** http://www.intel.com **Chipset Products:** http://www.intel.com/design/chipsets
OPTI	**Home:** http://www.opti.com/
Silicon Integrated Systems Corp. (SIS)	**Home:** http://www.sis.com.tw
VIA Technologies	**Home:** http://www.viatech.com/ **Product:** http://www.viatech.com/products/index.htm

computer functions into a few packages individually is called application-specific integrated circuits, or ASICs. The chipset used in a motherboard design greatly influences the performance and limitations of the PC. It defines how much RAM a motherboard can use and what type of RAM chips it will accommodate, cache size and speed, processor types and speed, and types of expansion slots.

Chipsets are constantly being introduced and improved and enhanced over time to allow for new technology. Since the chipsets are constantly changing, the older chipsets become harder to find. Therefore, if a component of a chipset is faulty, the difficulty of finding a replacement, not to mention the work and skill of replacing the component, will most likely lead to the replacement of the entire motherboard. Table 6.5 lists a number of chipset manufacturers and how to locate their products.

6.6.1 Oscillators and Timers

The **system clock** acts as the heartbeat of the computer. The system clock allows the many circuits of the PC to work in harmony with each other. Every time it beats, they react.

PCs mostly consist of digital electronics made up of switching circuits. Each switch in the circuit usually represents bits that are either being processed, stored, or transported. When a switch turns on or off, it takes a miniscule amount of time for it to change from one state to the other. If a circuit tries to read the voltage of the switch during this transition, a mistake could occur because the voltage of the switch is not high or low but somewhere in between. The *clock signal* prevents this problem by telling the circuits when to react. The clock signal is generated by a **quartz crystal (oscillator)** and a *timer* chip. The quartz crystal is made of piezoelectric material, which vibrates in the presence of electricity. The frequency of this vibration is controlled by varying the size and shape of the piezoelectric material. The signal from the quartz crystal is fed into the timer chip, which is connected to the various PC components. See figure 6.6.

Beginning with the 486 processors, the motherboard or external bus runs at a fraction of the speed of the processor. This means that the data moving between the microprocessor and the other parts of the computer, such as the RAM and peripherals, is running at a slower speed than the processor. For example, the Pentium processor runs between 2 and 4.5 times faster than the motherboard; newer processors may run up to 10 times faster. Common motherboard speeds used today (known as the *bus speed*) are 66, 100, 133, 200, 266, 400, 533, and 800 MHz.

6.6.2 Bus Controllers and Peripheral Controllers

Expansion cards are inserted into expansion slots (also known as the *expansion bus*) on the motherboard to extend the reach of the processor. There are several types of expansion slots: ISA, MCA, EISA, VLB, PCI, AGP, and PC Bus.

The speed and frequency of the signals on the motherboard and the signals on the expansion bus usually do not match. Therefore, when a signal on the expansion card needs to be read by the processor, it is translated by the bus controller. For example, the PCI bridge handles all the functions of the PCI bus, which communicates at 33 MHz. The ISA expansion bus runs at 8.33 MHz. It therefore uses a fraction of the signal from the clock generator chip. If the clock generator chip is running at 33 MHz, the ISA bus runs at CLKIN/4, which is equivalent to 33 MHz/4 = 8.33 MHz.

The expansion card uses hardware interrupts and DMAs to communicate with the rest of the system. **Hardware interrupts,** known as **IRQ,** consist of wires that connect the CPU, RAM, and expansion slots. When the expansion cards need the CPU to do something, a signal is sent through one of the hardware interrupt wires to get the CPU's attention. The purpose of the hardware interrupt controller is to manage the interrupts and keep track of which one has the highest priority.

Another way the expansion card moves data from one location to another is by using a **direct memory address (DMA),** which consists of wires leading from the expansion slot to the RAM. The DMA controller moves the data from an expansion card to the RAM without any direction from the CPU. The performance of the PC improves because the CPU can use the time saved to do something else.

The peripheral controller creates the interfaces needed for other devices to link to your processor. The primary functions of the peripheral controller include the floppy disk interface, the hard disk interface, the keyboard controller, and the I/O port controller.

Figure 6.6 Three Common Crystal Oscillators

6.6.3 Memory Controller and Cache Controllers

Compared to the other devices, the microprocessor is the fastest component of the PC. When signals are sent between the microprocessor and the slower RAM, it is the job of the **memory controller** to translate the signals between the two. The RAM is connected to the CPU and expansion slots or ports via a data bus and address bus. The data bus carries the data while the address bus carries a signal defining the location of the data on the RAM. The memory controller translates the needed memory address and controls the address lines. In addition, the memory controller defines what capacity and type of RAM chips (standard, EDO, burst EDO, SDRAM, or other) the motherboard can use.

A second purpose of the memory controller is to provide a refresh signal every few milliseconds to the DRAM chips (RAM). DRAM chips use small capacitors within the chips to store information. A charged capacitor represents an *on* bit (switch) and a discharged capacitor represents an *off* bit (switch). Capacitors cannot hold their charge permanently. Therefore, they need to be constantly recharged so that they do not forget their content.

The **RAM cache** is ultrafast RAM that buffers the CPU and the RAM by keeping copies of instructions and data. When the CPU needs some information, it will first look in the RAM cache before searching the slower RAM. Finding the needed information in the RAM cache is much faster than searching the RAM for it, and little time is wasted if the information is not in the RAM cache. The purpose of the cache controller is to anticipate what information is needed by the CPU and to place it into the RAM cache.

6.6.4 North Bridge and South Bridge

Most of Intel's earlier chipsets, including the 440BX and 440GX, and many non-Intel chipsets are broken into a multitiered architecture incorporating North and South Bridge components (also called a super I/O chip). The North Bridge holds the memory controller, AGP controller, and PCI controller. The South Bridge, which sits on the North Bridge's PCI bus, handles most other forms of I/O, including the PCI peripherals, the ISA bus, floppy drives, hard drives, USB, and keyboard and motherboard I/O devices (parallel ports, serial ports, and PS/2 ports). Because the IDE and USB interfaces connect to the North Bridge via the South Bridge and PCI, the disk and USB data transfers are subject to PCI bus contention and arbitration. The memory bus (100 MHz) communicates up to 2 GB, the AGP bus (66 MHz) has a 533 MB/s transfer rate, and the PCI bus (33 MHz) communicates at 132 MB/s. See figure 6.7.

Figure 6.7 North Bridge/South Bridge Chipset Diagram

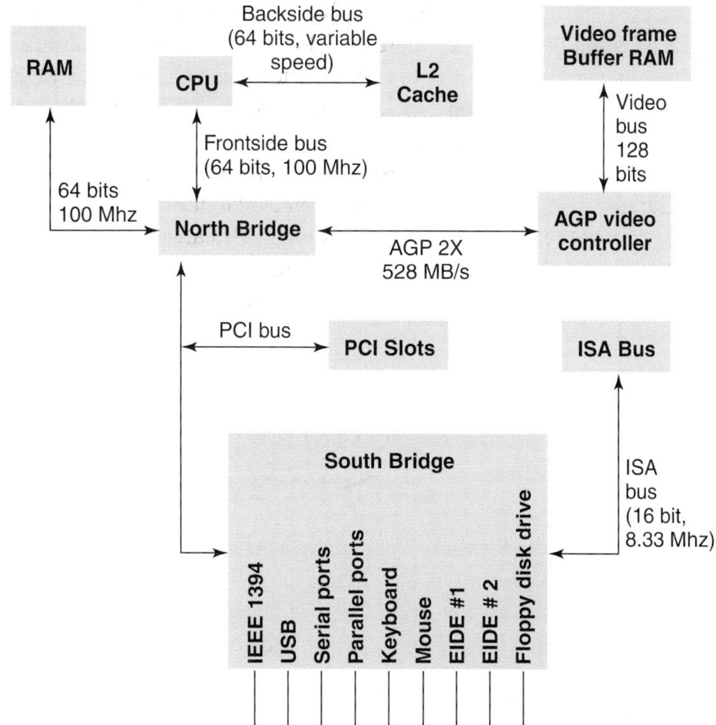

Figure 6.8 MCH/ICH Chipset Diagram

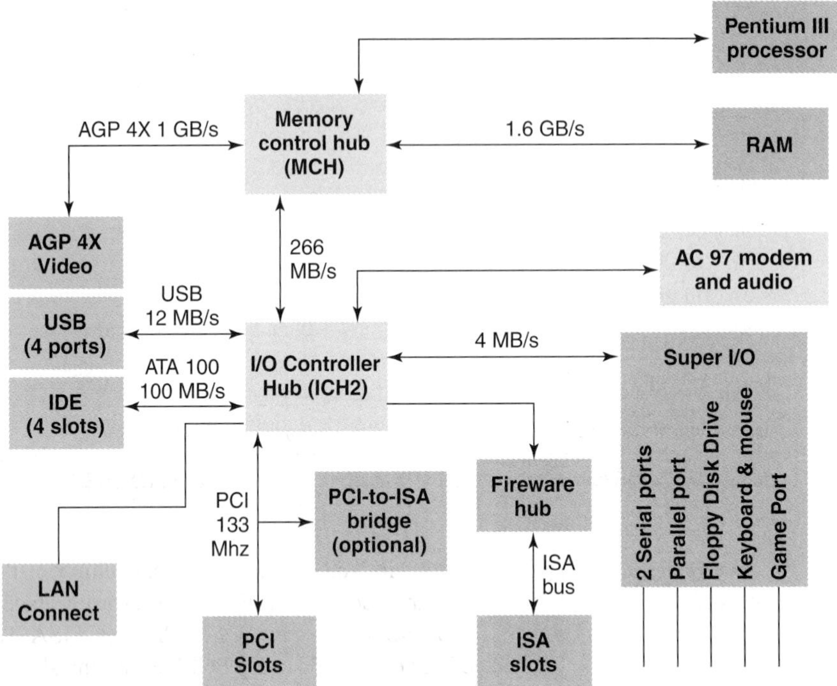

6.6.5 Intel Hub Architecture

Instead of the normal North Bridge/South Bridge setup, newer Intel boards, including the 810, 815, 820, 840, and 850 chipsets, use the Intel Hub Architecture (IHA). Like the old system, IHA has two parts, the graphics and AGP memory controller hub (GMCH) and the I/O controller hub (ICH). See figure 6.8.

The GMCH, like the North Bridge, communicates with the CPU over the system bus and acts as a controller for memory and AGP. Like the North Bridge, the GMCH sometimes comes with integrated video. Unlike a North Bridge, the GMCH does not come with a PCI controller.

The I/O controller hub (ICH) is connected via a high-speed, 266 MB/s interface to the GMCH, which is twice the bandwidth of the normal North Bridge/South Bridge connection. It provides a connection to a PCI bus, an Ultra ATA/66 disk interface, a USB controller, and the firmware hub (FWH). The 815E and 820E include the newer ICH2, which integrates 1 MB/s HomePNA and 10/100MB/s Ethernet network ports, full six-channel AC97 audio controller, two USB controllers for two separate USB buses, and support for Ultra ATA/100 disk drives. Even more importantly, this new bus can detect different kinds of data, such as streamed audio or hard drive accesses, and optimize the flow of data for those types of audio.

The firmware hub stores system and video BIOS and includes a hardware-based random number generator (RNG). The Intel RNG provides truly random numbers through the use of thermal noise, thereby enabling stronger encryption, digital signing, and security protocols.

Both the ICH and ICH2 provide an optional low-pin count (LPC) interface to a super I/O device supporting legacy devices such as keyboards, mice, and floppy disk drives, as well as parallel and serial ports. System vendors might also want to include an optional ISA bridge chip that connects an ISA bus to the PCI bus. However, attaching ISA cards is now frowned upon for reliability and compatibility reasons.

6.6.6 Intel Chipsets

With the release of the Pentium processor in March 1993, Intel also introduced its first Pentium chipset, the 430LX chipset. See table 6.6. Because other manufacturers took months to get their Pentium chipsets ready for the market, Intel has dominated the chipset market. A year later, Intel released the 430NX chipset, which was designed to run the new 3.3 V second-generation Pentium processors.

The 430FX (Triton) chipset rapidly became the most popular chipset for the Pentium processor. It was the first to support extended data out (EDO) RAM, which also became popular at the time. Unfortunately, the chipset did not support parity checking for memory and it would support only a single processor.

Table 6.6 Older Intel Chipsets

Chipset	PIIXn Device	IDE h/w Interface
Intel 430FX PCIset	82371FB (PIIX)	ATA/16
Intel 430VX PCIset	82371SB (PIIX3)	ATA/16
Intel 430HX PCIset	82371SB (PIIX3)	ATA/16
Intel 430TX PCIset	82371AB (PIIX4)	Ultra DMA/33
Intel 440FX PCIset	82371SB (PIIX3)	ATA/16
Intel 440LX AGPset	82371AB/EB (PIIX4/4E)	Ultra DMA/33
Intel 440EX AGPset	82371EB (PIIX4E)	Ultra DMA/33
Intel 440BX AGPset	82371AB/EB (PIIX4/4E)	Ultra DMA/33
Intel 440GX AGPset	82371EB (PIIX4E)	Ultra DMA/33

The 430FX consisted of a three-chip North Bridge. The main chip was the 82437FX system controller, which included the memory and cache controllers, processor interface, and PCI bus controller. The South Bridge was the 82371FB chip, which was the first PIIX (PCI ISA IDE Xcelerator) chip. This chip acted not only as the bridge between the 33 MHz PCI bus and the slower 8 MHz ISA bus, but it also incorporated for the first time a dual-channel IDE interface, which allowed for faster bus master IDE transfers.

The 430HX (Triton II) chipset used a one-chip North Bridge. It added some of the high-speed memory features, including support for EDO memory and pipeline burst L2 cache. It also had dual-processor support, and it supported parity checking to detect memory errors and error-correcting code (ECC) to detect memory errors and correct single-bit errors.

The 430VX (Triton III) designed to be a replacement for the low-end 430FX chipset. It supported the 66 MHz SDRAM, had no parity or ECC memory support, supported only a single processor, supported 128 MB of RAM, and supported only 64 MB of cache RAM.

The 440BX chipset was the last and most powerful X-series chipset. It consists of the 82443BX AGP host bridge controller (North Bridge) and the 82371EB (PIIX4E) PCI-ISA peripheral bus controller (South Bridge). The chipset supports both 66 and 100 MHz processor speeds, which support a wide range of Pentium II, Pentium III, and Intel Celeron processors. Memory support is provided through an integrated DRAM controller, allowing up to four SDRAM DIMMs, for a total of 1 GM of memory. It also supports AGP 2X. The PIIX4E controller provides PC98 ACPI power-management support that allows use of the 440BX in mobile systems. The chip is PCI version 2.1– compliant to support PCI-to-ISA bridges in both 3.3 V and 5 V, 33 MHz configurations. It includes the enhanced DMA controller, interrupt controller, and timer functions. The USB host interface has support for two USB ports, and the integrated IDE controller supports up to UDMA/33.

The Intel 440GX AGP set is the first chipset optimized for high-volume midrange workstations and lower cost servers. The 440GX is essentially a version of the 440BX that has been upgraded to support the Slot 2 processor slot for the Pentium II and III Xeon processors. It supports up to 2 GB of memory.

The Intel 820 chipset was designed to support mainstream and performance systems and was the first to use the IHA. See tables 6.7 and 6.8. It supports the AGP 4X technology and allows graphics controllers to access main memory at more than 1 GB/s. The 820 chipset employs the accelerated hub architecture to support a bandwidth of 266 MB/s, and with it is optimized arbitration rules, allowing more functions to run concurrently, it delivers significantly improved audio and video handling. The memory controller hub provides a high-performance interface for the processor, memory, and AGP and supports up to 1 GB of memory via a single channel of RDRAM using 64, 128, and 256 Mbit technology. With an internal bus running at 1.6 GB/s and an advanced buffering and queuing structure, the memory hub controller balances system resources and enables concurrent processing in single or dual processors. To capitalize further on this faster path to main memory, the 820 chipset features an integrated AC97 audio controller, an ATA-66 drive controller, dual USB ports, and PCI add-in cards.

Table 6.7 Recent Intel Chipsets with Integrated Graphics

Chipset	I/O Controller Hub (ICH)	Graphics Memory Controller Hub (GMCH)	Firmware Hub (FWH)
Intel 810	82801AA or 82801AB	FW82810 or FW82810DC100	82802AB or 82802AC
Intel 810E	82801AA or 82801AB	FW82810E or FW82810DC100	82802AB or 82802AC
Intel 810E2	82801AA or 82801AB	FW82810E or FW82810DC100	82802AB or 82802AC
Intel 815	82801AA or 82801AB	FW82815	82802AB or 82802AC
Intel 815E	82801BA	FW82815E	82802AB or 82802AC
Intel 815EM	82801BA	FW82815EM	82802AB or 82802AC
Intel 815 (B-Step)	82801BA	FW82815B	82802AB or 82802AC
Intel 815G	82801AA or 82801AB	FW82815	82802AB or 82802AC
Intel 815EG	82801BA	FW82815	82802AB or 82802AC
Intel 830M	82801CAM	FW82830M	82802AB or 82802AC
Intel 830MG	82801CAM	FW82830MG	82802AB or 82802AC
Intel 845G	828101DB	FW82845G	82802AB or 82802AC
Intel 845GE	828101DB	FW82845GE	82802AB or 82802AC
Intel 845GL	828101DB	FW82845GL	82802AB or 82802AC
Intel 845GV	828101DB	FW82845GV	82802AB or 82802AC
Intel 852/855 GM/GME	82801DBM	FW82852GM	82802AB or 82802AC

Table 6.8 Recent Intel Chipsets Without Integrated Graphics

Chipset	I/O Controller Hub (ICH)	Graphics Memory Controller Hub (GMCH)	Firmware Hub (FWH)
Intel 815EP	82801BA	82815EP	82802AB or 82802AC
Intel 815P	82801AA or 82801AB	82815P	82802AB or 82802AC
Intel 820	82801AA or 82801AB	82820	82802AB or 82802AC
Intel 820E	82801BA	82820	82802AB or 82802AC
Intel 840	82801AA or 82801AB	82840	82802AB or 82802AC
Intel 845	82801BA	82845	82802AB or 82802AC
Intel 850	82801BA	82850	82802AB or 82802AC
Intel 860	82801BA	82860	82802AB or 82802AC
Intel 875P	82801EB/82801ER	FW82875P	82802AB or 82802AC
Intel E7205	82801DB	E7205	82802AB or 82802AC
Intel E7500	82801CA	E7500	82802AB or 82802AC
Intel E7501	82801CA	E7501	82802AB or 82802AC
Intel E7505	82801DB	E7505	82802AB or 82802AC

The 820E chipset is an updated version that uses the 82801BA I/O controller hub (ICH2). It supports ATA-100 and incorporates dual USB controllers with two ports each, for a total of four USB ports.

In the summer of 1999 Intel released the 810 chipset to compete in the low-cost integrated market. It consisted of the 82810 graphics memory controller hub (GMCH), 82801 I/O controller hub (ICH), and 82802 firmware hub (FWH). The FWH was used to store the system and video BIOS. The SDRAM memory interface is also unusual because it runs at 100 MHz, although the system bus runs at 66 or 100 MHz. The 810E chipset was extended to support processors with a 133 MHz system bus.

The Intel 840 chipset was designed to be a high-performance workstation member of the 800-series chipset family. This chip provides 2X and 4X AGP support, dual RDRAM memory channels, and multiple PCI segments for high-performance I/O. This chipset supports processors using a 133 MHz system bus and hard drives using UDMA/66 technology.

The Intel 815 and 815E provide support for PC133 memory and 133 MHz FSB and are optimized for use with Intel Celeron and Pentium III using a flip-chip 370-pin grid array (FC-PGA) package. It was designed with integrated graphics and 4X AGP. It can also use the communication and network riser (CNR) card option, which allows audio, modem, and/or LAN configurations. It uses the 82815 graphics and AGP memory controller hub (GMCH) and the 82801AA I/O controller hub (ICH), which makes a direct connection from the graphics and memory to the integrated AC97 audio controller, IDE controllers, dual USB ports, and PCI add-in cards.

Another interesting chipset limitation is that the memory controller supports six rows of SDRAM (three banks) only when PC100 SDRAM is used. Intel supports only four rows of SDRAM (two banks) when PC133 SDRAM is used. What this means is that you are supposed to be able to use only two double-sided DIMMs when running at 133 MHz, and if you insert three double-sided DIMMs, the motherboard is supposed to default back down to the 100 MHz memory bus setting.

The i815E chipset, just like the i820, features the new 802BA ICH2 that adds Ultra ATA/100 support as well as an additional USB 1.1 controller, which supports up to four USB ports. One of the biggest features ICH2 supports is its integrated 82559 network core, which allows for 10/100 Ethernet or HomePNA ports to be placed on the motherboard at a relatively low cost because the core is integrated into the ICH2. If motherboard manufacturers don't want to place the ports on the motherboard itself, they can still use the CNR.

The 850 chipset is based on Intel Hub Architecture and was made to support the Intel Pentium 4 processor. The 82850 memory controller hub (MCH) delivers dual RDRAM memory channels, providing 3.2 GB/s bandwidth and a 400 MHz system bus, providing the latest graphics support through 4X AGP technology. The ICH2 makes a direct connection from the graphics and memory for faster access to peripherals and provides the features and bandwidth required for the extended PC. Two USB controllers double the bandwidth available for USB peripherals to 24 Mbps over four ports. The latest AC97 audio delivers six channels of audio for enhanced sound quality and full surround-sound capability for live broadcast and other digital dashboard programming. It supports dual Ultra ATA/100 IDE controllers. The LAN connect interface (LCI) provides flexible network solutions, such as home phone line, 10/100 Mbps Ethernet, and 10/100 Mbps Ethernet with LAN manageability. All three network options utilize Intel SingleDriver technology, which supports multiple products to simplify network connectivity and increase ease of deployment.

Early versions of the Intel 845 chipset were designed, validated, and optimized for the Pentium 4 processor using PC133 SDRAM memory technology. The Intel 845 chipset consists of two controller hubs connected to each other through Intel's high-bandwidth hub architecture. The 82845 memory controller hub (MCH) supports a 400 MHz system bus delivering a high-bandwidth connection between the Pentium 4 processor and the rest of the platform, providing three times the system bus bandwidth over platforms based on Intel Pentium III processors. Also included in the MCH, which has a wider data path, a write cache, and flexible memory refresh technology to enable optimum PC133 SDRAM performance, are the latest graphics devices through the 1.5 V AGP 4X interface enabling 1 GB/s of graphics bandwidth. Later versions of the Intel 845 chipset support DDR RAM and a 533 MHz and/or 800 MHz bus.

In 2003, Intel introduced the 865 and 875 chipset. The 865 chipset improves upon Intel's 845 chipset for mainstream PCs and corporate desktop systems. To serve this broad segment of the PC market, the 865 family comes in three distinct flavors: 865G, 865PE, and 865P. The *G* in the 865G chipset stands for *graphics* because it includes integrated graphics in the form of Intel's Extreme Graphics 2—a vastly improved version of Intel's previous integrated graphics solution. Like the 865P and the 865PE.

the 865G supports AGP 8X, should home users want to add a discrete graphics card for better 3D graphics performance. The 865P and 865PE chipsets, however, require a third-party graphics card because they do not integrate graphics on the motherboard. The 865P serves the low end of the mainstream market and supports only 533 or 400 MHz front-side bus (FSB) speeds; it does not offer support for the new 800 MHz FSB found on both the 865G and 865PE chipsets.

The 865 chipset family offers support for Serial ATA, integrated RAID, AGP 8X, Gigabit Ethernet, and Intel's own Hyper-Threading technology. The real differentiator between the 865 chipset family and the 875P chipset is something Intel calls Performance Acceleration Technology (PAT), found only on the high-end 875P. PAT gives you a slight performance gain by reducing memory latencies.

Intel's newest chipsets are the 915 and 925 Express. The 900-series chipsets will include new features designed to increase desktop performance. Those features include using DDR2 memory and PCI Express. The 915G will also include the Intel Graphics Media Accelerator 900, an improved graphics engine Intel says can handle video games. Later, these PCs will also serve as wireless access points, eliminating the need for a wireless router. The optional feature will start to appear in PCs later this year and in greater volume in 2005. Finally, the release of the 900 family of chipsets will also coincide with the launch of a new 775-pin socket for attaching Intel's processors to the motherboard, or main circuit board of a PC.

For more information on Intel chipsets, see the following websites:

Intel Chipset Comparison Chart
http://www.intel.com/design/chipsets/linecard.htm

Intel Chipset Identification Utility
http://support.intel.com/support/chipsets/inf/chipsetid.htm

6.6.7 VIA Chipsets

VIA is the greatest threat to Intel's dominance of the chipset market. Its line of Apollo chipsets provided an effective alternative for the Intel processors and the most common chipset for the AMD processors. See table 6.9

The Apollo Pro was designed to be a high-performance chipset for slot 1, mobile, and desktop PC systems. The Apollo Pro includes support for advanced system power-management capabilities, PC-100 SDRAM, 2X AGP, and multiple CPU/DRAM timing configurations. The Apollo Pro chipset is comparable in features to the 440BX and PIIX4e chipset from Intel and represents one of the first non-Intel chipsets to support the socket 1 architecture. It consists of two devices: the VT82C691 North Bridge and VT82C596 South Bridge.

The Apollo Pro133 was the first chipset on the market designed to support PC133 SDRAM memory. This chipset supports slot 1 and socket processors such as the Intel Pentium III, Intel Celeron, and VIA Cyrix III processors. It supports 2X AGP graphics, an ATA-66 interface, four USB ports, a AC97 link for audio and modem, hardware monitoring, and power management. An improved version of the Apollo Pro133 was the VIA Apollo Pro133A chipset, which supports 4X AGP bus.

The Apollo Pro266 combines high-bandwidth DDR-266 SDRAM (up to 4.0 GB running at 2.1 GB/s), a 133 MHz front-side bus and a new high-speed V-link memory link controller to the Intel Pentium III, Intel Celeron, and VIA Cyrix processors. DDR-266 SDRAM lowers memory power consumption to 2.5 V, providing the ideal solution for small-form-factor desktops and notebooks. It also has a 4X AGP and ATA-100. Additional key features include support for six USB ports, an AC-97 link for audio and modem, hardware monitoring, and ACPI/OnNow power management. The VIA Apollo Pro266 chipset is a two-chip set consisting of the VT8633 North Bridge controller and the VT8233 South Bridge controller.

The VIA Apollo KX133 chipset brings AGP 4X, PC133 SDRAM, a 200 MHz front-side bus, and ATA-66 technologies to the AMD Athlon processor. It supports 4X AGP, four USB ports, AC97 link for audio and modem, hardware monitoring, and power management. The VIA Apollo KX133 is a two-chip set consisting of the VT8371 North Bridge controller and the VT82C686A South Bridge controller.

VIA Apollo KT266 brings high-bandwidth DDR-266 SDRAM with a 266 MHz front-side bus to the AMD Athlon processor. It supports up to 4.0 GB of DDR-266 SDRAM at a peak bandwidth of 2.1 Gbit/s. Like the VIA Apollo KX133, it supports 4X AGP and ATA-100 and lowers memory power con-

Table 6.9 VIA Chipsets

Platform	Chipset	North Bridge	South Bridge	Integrated Graphics	Supported Processors
Intel/Cyrix	Apollo Pro266	VT8633	VT8233	NA	Supports Intel Pentium III, Intel Celeron, and VIA C3
	Apollo Pro133A	VT82C694X	VT8231 or VT82C686A/B	NA	Supports Intel Pentium III, Intel Celeron, and VIA C3
	Apollo Pro133	VT82C693A	VT8231 or VT82C686A/B	NA	Supports Intel Pentium III, Intel Celeron, and VIA C3
	ProSavage PM133	VT8605	VT8231 or VT82C686A/B	Savage4 Graphics Core	Supports Intel Pentium III, Intel Celeron, and VIA C3
	Apollo PLE133	VT8601	VT8231 or VT82C686A/B	NA	Supports Intel Pentium III, Intel Celeron, and VIA C3
	Apollo P4X266A	VT8753A	VT8233	NA	Supports Intel Pentium 4
	Apollo P4X266	VT8753	VT8233	NA	Supports Intel Pentium 4
	Apollo Pro266T	VT8653	VT8233C	NA	Supports Intel Pentium III, Intel Celeron, and VIA C3
AMD	Apollo KT266	VT8366	VT8233	NA	AMD Duron and Athlon
	Apollo KT133A	VT8363A	VT82C686A/B	NA	AMD Duron and Athlon
	ProSavage KM133	VT8365	VT8231 or VT82C686A/B	Savage4 Graphics Core	AMD Duron and Athlon
	Apollo KT133	VT8363	VT82C686A/B	NA	AMD Duron and Athlon
	Apollo KX133	VT8371	VT82C686A/B	NA	
	Apollo KT333	VT8367	VT8233	NA	Supports AMD Athlon XP
	Apollo K8T400M	K8T400M	VT8237	NA	Supports AMD Opteron and Athlon 64
Socket 7	Apollo MVP4	VT8501	VT82C686A/B	NA	AMD-K6, AMD-K6-2, AMD-K6-III, and VIA Cyrix MII
	Apollo MVP3	VT82C598	VT82C686A or VT82C596A/B	NA	AMD-K6, AMD-K6-2, AMD-K6-III, and VIA Cyrix MII

sumption for the SDRAM to 2.5 V. Additional key features include support for six USB ports, an AC-97 link for audio and modem, hardware monitoring, and ACPI/OnNow power management. The VIA Apollo KT266 chipset is a two-chip set consisting of the VT8366 North Bridge controller and the VT8233 South Bridge controller.

6.7 CHIPSET DRIVERS

Installing BIOS on a ROM is extremely inflexible and is rarely done for most devices. Far more popular is adding special programs called *device drivers* to the system. A device driver is nothing more than a file stored on the PC's hard drive that contains all the BIOS commands necessary to talk to whatever device they were written to support. All operating systems employ a method of loading these device drivers into RAM every time the system boots. They know which device drivers to install because of some form of editable file or files that contain a "list" of which device drivers the system needs to load at boot time. All operating systems are designed to look at this list early on in the boot process and employ some method of copying this list of files into RAM, thereby giving the processor the ability to communicate with the hardware supported by the device driver.

Because many of the devices are on the motherboard that used to be on expansion cards and other devices have been created to increase the performance of the PC, you will need to load drivers to control these devices on the motherboard. Immediately loading the operating system and any service packs for that operating system, you should load the chipset drivers before loading any other driver, including the video driver and network driver.

For example, for Intel motherboards, the Intel Chipset Software Installation Utility was developed to update Windows operating systems with the plug-and-play feature on the Intel chipset. This utility allows the operating system to correctly identify the Intel chipset components and properly configure the system. The Intel Chipset Software Installation Utility installs specific Windows INF files. The INF files inform the operating system how to properly configure the chipset for specific functionality, such as AGP, USB, core PCI, and ISA PnP services. Because these components are necessary for optimum stability and performance, the Intel Chipset Software Installation Utility should be the first driver loaded after the operating system and its service packs are installed. Note: Newer versions of Windows will sometimes have these built in, but it will not hurt if you load them again.

The chipset software can be found on the CD that comes with the motherboard or it can be downloaded from the Internet. The Intel Chipset Software Installation chipsets can be downloaded from the following website:

http://support.intel.com/support/chipsets/driver.htm

NOTE: To determine if you need to install a specific INF file to a specific version of Windows, refer to the following website:

http://support.intel.com/support/chipsets/chip_man.htm

The drivers for the VIA chipset can be found at:

http://www.viatech.com/jsp/en/driver/driver.jsp

6.8 MOTHERBOARD FRONT PANEL

When looking at the front panel of a computer, you will notice that you have an on/off button, power-on LED, reset switch, hard drive LED, and PC speaker. For these to operate properly, you must connect the front panel to the motherboard. Virtually all desktop motherboards will have a single or double row of connectors. See figure 6.9. To know which pins connect to which front panel connectors, you must refer to the motherboard documentation.

Since the on-off capability in ATX motherboard is controlled through software, you must connect the on/off switch to the motherboard. When you press the on/off button on the front panel, it shorts or connects the two pins on the front panel connectors on the motherboard. This tells the motherboard to start the computer. If you don't connect the front panel on/off power connector, the on/off switch will not work. The only other way to start the motherboard is by taking a screwdriver and touching the two pins together.

6.9 MOTHERBOARD JUMPERS AND DIP SWITCHES

IBM wanted to design the IBM PC (Model 5150) and IBM XT (Model 5160) to be flexible and allow for growth. Consequently, IBM used expansion slots and cards to expand the system as needed. In addition, these computers could have different amounts of RAM and up to two floppy disk drives. DIP switches were used to specify the amount of RAM or the number of floppy disk drives within a system. See figure 6.10.

DIP switches are small devices consisting of 4 to 12 on/off switches. The IBM PC used two banks of DIP switches (designated as switch block 1 and switch block 2); the IBM XT used one bank. Each

Figure 6.9 Motherboard Front Panel Connector

Figure 6.10 DIP Switches

Figure 6.11 Motherboard Jumpers

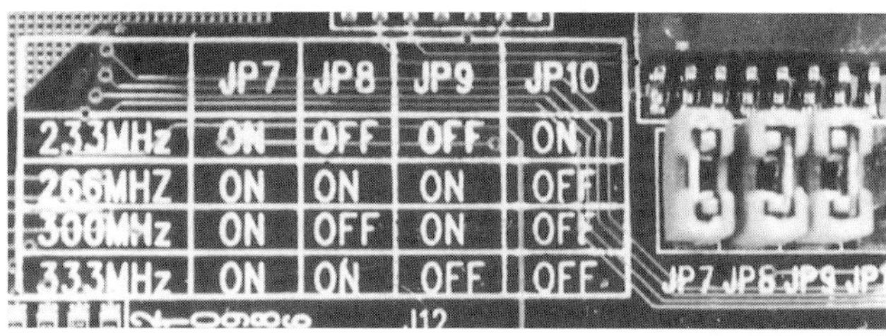

bank consisted of 8 on/off switches. DIP switches come in two forms: sliding switches and rocker switches. To indicate which direction is on and which direction is off, the bank will be labeled on, off, open, or closed. When a switch is on, the circuit is closed, allowing current to flow. When a switch is off, the circuit is open, allowing no current to flow.

DIP switches are no longer used on today's motherboards to specify the number of floppy drives or the amount of RAM a PC has. Instead, this is done electronically by running a BIOS setup program from a floppy disk (AT and early 386 computers) or from the system ROM BIOS. To configure these motherboards; **jumpers** (sometimes called *shunts*) are used. A jumper is a small, plastic-covered metal clip that is used to connect two pins protruding from the motherboard. The jumper (which is the same as an on switch) closes the circuit, allowing current to flow. See figure 6.11. Some motherboards now use the BIOS setup program in place of the jumpers to specify the CPU speed, the amount of RAM cache, port settings (COMX and LPTX), and drive controller settings.

6.10 CMOS RAM

The PC tests the major components of the PC during boot-up. In order to properly test a computer, the PC needs to know what there is to test (the amount of RAM, the number of floppy drives, the presence of a math coprocessor, the type of monitor, and so forth). Therefore, the PC must have this information available during boot-up.

As mentioned, when the IBM PC was released in 1981, the computer had two sets of eight DIP switches that defined the system configuration information. When the IBM XT was introduced, only one set of eight DIP switches was needed. As new technology became available, newer systems had more options available. A system with more options required more DIP switches, which meant the motherboards had more complicated designs and configurations. To make things worse, DIP switches would occasionally fail simply because they are small mechanical devices.

Starting with the IBM AT, IBM replaced the DIP switches with a special chip that combined 64 bytes of **CMOS RAM** with a **real-time clock (RTC).** CMOS chips (such as MC146818) operate at 3.3 volts, which consumes less power than the older TTL chips. The real-time clock keeps track of the time and date. See figure 6.12.

Question:

Why does the computer care what time it is?

Answer:

The computer does not actually care; it has no understanding of date or time. However, date and time can be used by the operating systems and application programs. Operating systems use the date and time to time-stamp each file to indicate when it was created and last edited. In addition, some programs can use the date and time within a document, keep track of appointments, or automatically time-stamp activities involving a database.

The RAM portion of the chip holds the basic system configuration. As motherboards have become more complicated by the addition of more configuration options, the size of the CMOS RAM chip has had to be increased. See figure 6.13.

To change the configuration options contained in the CMOS RAM, you must run a *BIOS/CMOS setup program.* At the time the IBM AT was introduced, the BIOS setup program was kept on a floppy disk. Unfortunately, if the floppy disk configuration was incorrect, accessing the disk to run the setup

Figure 6.12 Dallas CMOS with Real-Time Clock next to the Award System ROM BIOS

Figure 6.13 The processor communicates with different forms of memory, including the system ROM BIOS. The CMOS RAM (powered by a CMOS battery) stores the hardware configuration information.

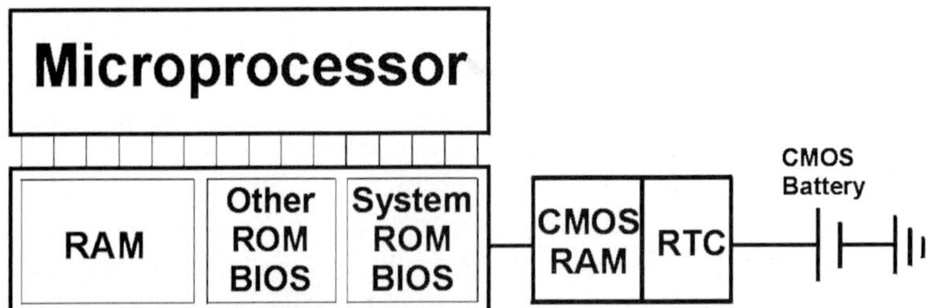

program might not be possible. The BIOS setup program could not be kept in the RAM (including the CMOS RAM) because if power is discontinued to RAM, the contents will disappear, losing the setup program. Therefore, the CMOS setup program was placed in the system ROM BIOS.

Question:

If the CMOS setup program is stored in the system ROM BIOS, why can't the configuration information be stored in the system ROM BIOS?

Answer:

The configuration information can't be stored in the system ROM BIOS because the system ROM BIOS is a permanent form of memory. Therefore, if a second floppy drive is added or a hard drive replaced, the configuration information could not be changed.

6.11 CMOS BATTERY

The configuration information is stored in CMOS, a special form of RAM. When you disconnect the power from the RAM, it will forget its content. Yet, when you turn on the system later, the PC still remembers the configuration information and the clock still has the correct date and time. This is because the CMOS chip is connected to a battery, which keeps the CMOS circuit powered while the PC is off. This battery is often referred to as the **CMOS battery.**

NOTE: When your CMOS battery starts losing its power, symptoms include CMOS checksum or mismatch errors and the date and time of your computer starts to drift or is incorrect.

The most common batteries used in the PC are lithium and nickel-cadmium (NiCad). See figure 6.14. Lithium batteries are small and light and offer a high-energy density. When used as a CMOS battery, they last up to 5 years. NiCad batteries don't last as long as lithium batteries but can be recharged every time you turn on your computer. Both types of batteries usually do not leak, which could damage other PC components.

Three types of CMOS batteries are available: the coin cell, the battery pack, and the soldered battery. Coin cells are disc-like batteries that resemble a coin. The external battery pack is connected to the motherboard via a four-prong connector. See figure 6.15. The soldered battery is permanently soldered

Figure 6.14 Common CMOS Batteries

Figure 6.15 External Battery Pack

onto the motherboard. When replacing a battery, you must match not only the battery type but also the voltage. The batteries used in PCs are normally either 3.6, 4.5, or 6 V. Another important issue when replacing the batteries is to make sure that the polarity is correct. If the battery is connected backward, it will damage the CMOS RAM chip. Since the CMOS RAM chip is soldered onto the motherboard, this could be an expensive mistake.

When the CMOS battery is replaced or when the motherboard is removed, the information in the CMOS RAM will usually be lost. Therefore, *it is recommended that all the CMOS configuration information stored in the CMOS RAM be recorded by using the BIOS setup program.*

A few newer systems don't require a CMOS battery. Some of these systems have a special capacitor that automatically recharges anytime the system is plugged in. If the system is unplugged, the capacitor will power the CMOS RAM chip for up to a week or more. If the system remains unplugged for a long time, the CMOS RAM information will be lost. Fortunately, the contents of the CMOS RAM can be restored from a backup copy kept in a flash ROM chip. Other systems contain a CMOS chip (such as those produced by Dallas Semiconductor Corporation) that includes nonvolatile SRAM technology (low-power SRAM and a tiny lithium battery) that does not require an external battery.

6.12 CMOS SETUP PROGRAM

The BIOS setup program (sometimes called the CMOS setup program) is stored in the system ROM BIOS. It varies greatly from computer to computer. Even PCs from the same manufacturer containing a processor and a system ROM BIOS made by the same supplier may have major differences.

To access the BIOS setup program, you need to know which keys to press and when to press them. During boot-up most systems will show how to enter the BIOS setup program on the screen. AMI BIOS and other systems will display a "Hit <DEL> if you want to run SETUP" message. See figure 6.16. Therefore, when this message is displayed, you will press the Delete key. Often, these systems include the option of enabling or disabling the message. If the message is not displayed, the best time to press the Delete key is when the memory is counting.

- **AMI BIOS**—Press Delete during POST.
- **Phoenix BIOS**—Press F2 during POST.
- **Older Phoenix BIOS**—Boot to safe mode DOS command prompt, and then press Ctrl+Alt+Esc or Ctrl+Alt+S.
- **Award BIOS**—Press Delete or Ctrl+Alt+Esc during POST.

Figure 6.16 During POST, most systems display the key to press to enter the CMOS setup program.

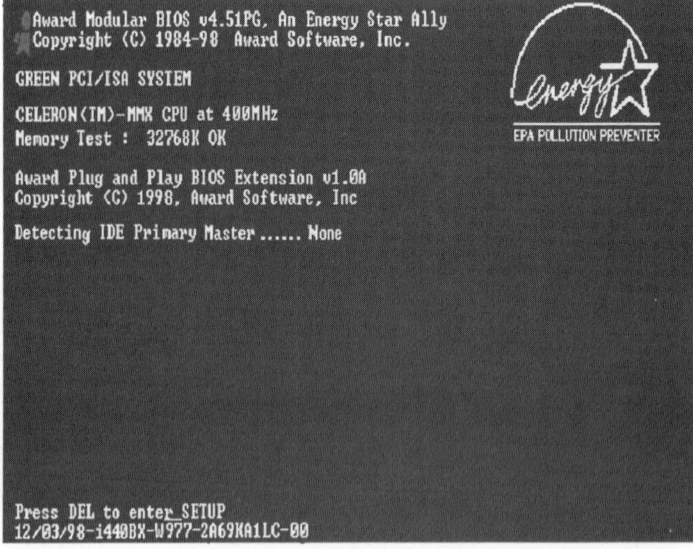

- **Microid Research BIOS**—Press Esc during POST.
- **IBM Aptiva/Valuepoint**—Press F1 during POST.
- **Compaq**—Press F10 during POST.
- **Gateway 2000 PC**—Press F1 during POST.
- **Sony PC**—Press F3 during POST (Sony logo) and then press F1.
- **PS/2**—Press Ctrl+Alt+Ins after Ctrl+Alt+Del or use a reference diskette to access the CMOS setup program.
- **Intel motherboards**—Press F2 during POST.

The best way to find out how to enter the BIOS setup program is to look either at the screen or in the motherboard documentation. For Intel motherboards, you use the F2 key to enter the BIOS setup program. The important thing to note is that to access maintenance options by changing a jumper on the motherboard, you would configure the processor speed and clear all passwords.

For more information on the BIOS setup program options, refer to the manual that comes with the motherboard or system and visit the following websites:

> **THE BIOS OPTIMIZATION GUIDE**
>
> http://www.rojakpot.com/Speed_Demonz/BIOS_Guide/BIOS_Guide_Index.htm
>
> **Award CMOS Setup Program Options**
>
> http://www.phoenix.com/pcuser/phoenixbios/setup_index.html

> **WARNING**
>
> Because incorrect CMOS settings can cause the computer to run properly, record the CMOS settings before making any changes. In addition, if you don't know what a CMOS setting does, it is usually best to leave it at its default settings.

Today's setup programs include many options. To organize them, they are often grouped together. Most CMOS setup programs are menu-based. See figure 6.17. A couple of years ago, AMI did introduce a newer GUI interface similar to Windows, yet it has gone back to the menu interface. Modern PCs include a standard CMOS setup and an advanced BIOS setup. Other commonly used options include advanced chipset setup, power management, PCI configuration, and peripherals.

Figure 6.17 An Example CMOS Setup Program Main Menu

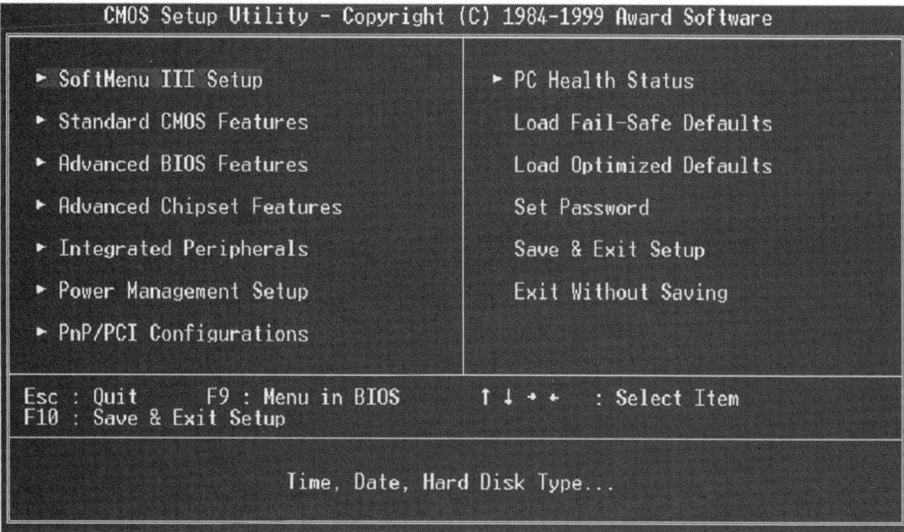

Figure 6.18 Standard Setup Options of the CMOS Setup Program

```
CMOS Setup Utility - Copyright (C) 1984-1999 Award Software
                 Standard CMOS Features

  Date (mm:dd:yy)            Tue, Sep  7 1999     Item Help
  Time (hh:mm:ss)            16 : 27 : 15
                                                  Menu Level  ►
► IDE Primary Master         Press Enter None
► IDE Primary Slave          Press Enter None     Change the day, month,
► IDE Secondary Master       Press Enter None     year and century
► IDE Secondary Slave        Press Enter None

  Drive A                    1.44M, 3.5 in.
  Drive B                    None
  Floppy 3 Mode Support      Disabled

  Video                      EGA/VGA
  Halt On                    All,But Keyboard

  Base Memory                  640K
  Extended Memory            64512K
  Total Memory               65536K

↑↓→←:Move  Enter:Select  +/-/PU/PD:Value  F10:Save  ESC:Exit  F1:General Help
   F5:Previous Values     F6:Fail-Safe Defaults     F7:Optimized Defaults
```

6.12.1 Standard CMOS Setup

The standard CMOS setup has not changed much through the years. It includes the information for the date, time, floppy drives, hard drives, keyboard, and video card. See figure 6.18.

Date and Time

The time and date appear at the top of the standard CMOS setup screen. The date and time displayed in the setup program are the date and time in the real-clock chip. They can be changed with the setup program, with commands (DOS's DATE and TIME commands), or with a GUI interface (Windows' Control Panel). Note: Most modern system ROM BIOSes account for daylight savings time.

Hard Drive

The next set of options are the hard disk settings, which must define the parameters of the hard drive. The options are hard drive type, number of cylinders, number of read/write heads, number of sectors per track, write precompensation, and landing zone. Note: The standard CMOS setup screen shows only two hard drives. Newer system ROM BIOSes may show four types because enhanced IDE can have up to four hard drives.

The hard drives are disk parameters predefined in the system ROM BIOS. The type, number of cylinders, number of read/write heads, number of sectors per track, and other parameters are automatically set. For example, if you select a type 1, you will get the following information:

Type	Cylinders	Heads	Write PreComp	LZ	Capacity (MB)
1	306	4	128	305	10

There are a limited number of drive types, but there are literally an unlimited number of drives with different CMOS parameters. Instead of making more drives, companies created a user-definable type. By selecting type 47 or type 48, you can then input the rest of the hard drive parameters. The number of cylinders, number of read/write heads, and number of sectors per track, multiplied together, define the number of sectors. The computer then takes the number of sectors times 512 bytes per sector to determine the capacity.

Newer systems also allow you to select the addressing mode: auto, normal, large, or LBA. In auto, the BIOS automatically determines the optimal mode. The normal mode uses cylinders, heads, and sectors to address a specific sector. To overcome drives that have more than 1,024 cylinders, the large and LBA modes use different parameters for the cylinders, heads, and sectors that calculated to the same capacity and translate them into the actual parameters.

SCSI hard drives are a little different. When installing an SCSI hard drive, the CMOS is set to No Hard Drive Defined. The BIOS on the SCSI controller card and the firmware on the hard drive run the hard drive.

If you do not enter the correct hard disk information in the CMOS setup program, the hard drive may fail to boot and the information may be inaccessible. Common error messages include "Missing Operating System" and "Drive C Error." In addition, you could permanently damage the hard drive. When working inside a system, it is a very good idea to record the CMOS parameters before opening the system. Most newer computers feature a hard drive autodetect feature. This feature will automatically look in the firmware of the hard drive and set the CMOS accordingly.

Floppy Disk Drives

The floppy drives define the type of floppy disks to be used. The choices include 1.44 MB, 720 KB, 1.2 MB, and 360 KB; newer systems include 2.88 MB. If the wrong type of drive is selected, the drive may not function and you may get an "FDD Controller Failure" or similar message.

Video and Keyboard

The monitor type is always set to EGA/VGA. Other choices include monochrome and CGA, which are extremely outdated. Keyboard options are "installed" or "not installed," which determines whether a keyboard is looked for during boot-up.

6.12.2 Advanced CMOS Setup Options

The advanced CMOS setup (see figure 6.19) and advanced chipset (see figure 6.20) are used to fine-tune the hardware setup of the system. Hardware differs from computer to computer, so these options also are different. Most of the settings are used to enable or fine-tune the cache system, memory system, or I/O system. See table 6.10 through table 6.19 and figure 6.21 through figure 6.25.

The peripherals setup options include onboard floppy disk drives, parallel ports, and serial ports that can be disabled or configured using the CMOS setup program. This process includes defining the IRQ and I/O addresses. In addition, parallel ports can be configured to be normal, bidirectional, EPP, or ECP.

The PCI control, plug-and-play options enable the plug-and-play features and will enable or disable PCI expansion slots. In addition, they define the IRQ and DMA, which the PCI slots use. Other options may enable or disable built-in IDE controllers.

Figure 6.19 Advanced Setup Options for the CMOS Setup Program

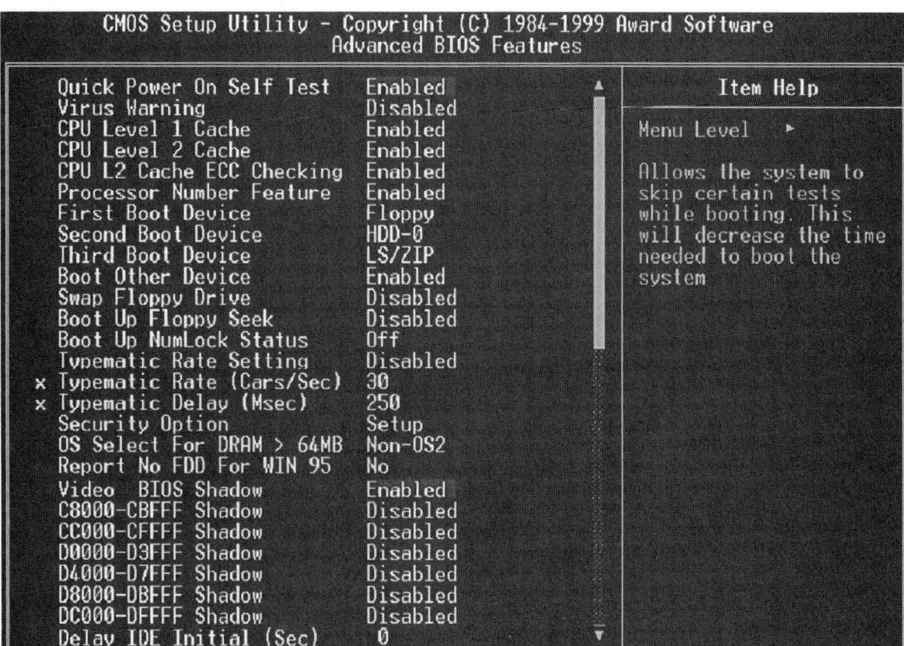

Figure 6.20 Advanced Chipset Features Option for the CMOS Setup Program

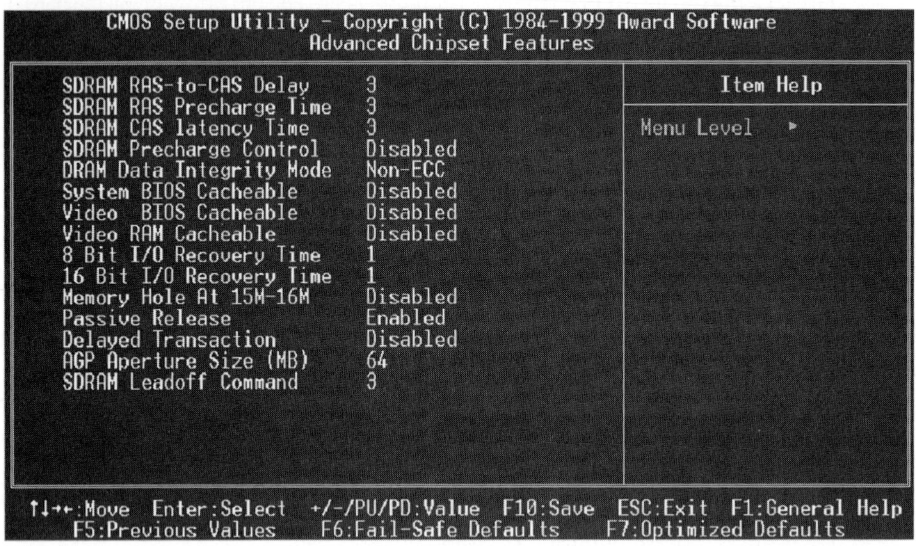

Table 6.10 Boot Options

Setting	Description
System Boot-up Num Lock	When this option is set to off, the Num Lock key will be off automatically during boot. Therefore, you can use the arrow keys on both the numeric keypad and the keyboard. When the option is on, the keypad can be used for quick number input.
Typematic Rate Setting	This feature enables you to control the keystroke repeat rate when you depress a key continuously. When enabled, you can manually adjust the settings using the two typematic controls (Typematic Rate and Typematic Rate Delay). If disabled, the BIOS will use the default setting. Note: Windows will typically overwrite this setting.
Boot-up Sequence	This option sets the sequence of boot drives. The standard boot sequence is the A drive followed by the C drive. With this option, you change the sequence to the C drive followed by the A drive. Note: Newer programs allow booting from CD-ROM drives, LS-120 drives, and Zip drives.
Password Checking Option	These options are Disabled, Always, and Setup. When set to the always option, the system will prompt for a password during POST. The setup password option means the system will prompt for a password when the user accesses the CMOS setup program.
Boot-up Floppy Seek	This feature controls whether the BIOS checks for a floppy drive while booting up. If it cannot detect one (either due to improper configuration or physical unavailability), it will flash an error message. This feature should be set as Disabled for a faster booting process.
Quick Power On Self Test/Intel Rapid BIOS Boot	When enabled, this feature will shorten some tests and skip others that are performed during the booting-up process. Disable this option when you are experiencing problems with your system. You should enable this feature for full testing so that you can see all messages during POST. If not, you should enable this option so that the system boots quicker.
Quiet Boot	When this option is disabled, it displays normal POST messages. When the option is enabled, it displays the OEM graphics instead of POST messages.

Table 6.11 Video Options

Setting	Description
PCI/VGA Palette Snoop/Palette Snooping	The VGA "palette" is the set of colors that are in use by the video card when it is in 256-color mode. Since there are thousands of colors and only 256 can be used in that mode, a palette containing the current colors is used. Some MPEG and add-on cards need to look at the video card's VGA palette to determine what colors are currently in use. This option is rarely needed. It should be left at Disabled unless a video device specifically requires the setting enabled upon installation.
Assign IRQ for VGA	Many high-end graphics accelerator cards require an IRQ to function properly. It is also needed for cards that need bus mastering. If this feature is enabled, it will give you a faster transfer between the processor and the video card. Check your graphics card's documentation. If it states that the card does not require an IRQ, you can disable it. But when in doubt, it is best to leave it enabled unless you really need to free up the IRQ.
AGP Aperture Size (MB)	AGP cards can access system memory to store texture maps and offers a higher-speed bus. The AGP aperture setting specifies to the AGP chipset how much of a PC's system memory, including virtual memory, is addressable by an AGP video card. Since the system needs AGP uncached memory, an equal amount of write combined memory, and 12 MB for virtual addressing, AGP aperture size is set by maximum usable AGP memory size × 2 plus 12 MB. If your graphics card has very little graphics memory, you should set an AGP aperture size up to half the system RAM. For cards with more graphics memory, you shouldn't set the aperture size to half the system RAM since the size of the aperture does not correspond to performance.
AGP 2X Mode, AGP 4X Mode, or AGP 8X Mode	This BIOS feature enables or disables the AGP 2X, AGP 4X, or AGP 8X transfer protocol. If your motherboard and video card support 2X, 4X and/or 8X, you should enable this feature for the best performance for your video system. You should disable this feature only to select 1X if you are suspecting stability issues.
AGP Master 1WS Read and AGP Master 1WS Write	With these disabled, the AGP waits two cycles before reading or writing. Enable them, and AGP waits only one cycle. If your card does not support these settings, you can have display problems in the form of corrupted graphics, incorrect texture mapping, missing polygons, and pixel popping.
Video BIOS Shadowing	When this feature is enabled, the Video BIOS is copied to the system RAM for quicker access. Shadowing improves the BIOS's performance because the BIOS can now be read by the CPU through the 64-bit DRAM bus as opposed to the 8-bit XT bus. This seems quite attractive since that's at least a 100X increase in transfer rate, and the only price is the loss of some system RAM, which is used to mirror the ROM contents. However, modern operating systems bypass the BIOS completely and access the graphics card's hardware directly. So, no BIOS calls are made, and no benefit from BIOS shadowing is realized. In light of this, there's no use in wasting RAM just to shadow the Video BIOS when it's not used at all.

Table 6.12 Processor Options

Setting	Description
CPU Operating Frequency	This sets or displays the processor speed (front-side bus clock speed × multiplier factor). Of course, the wrong settings of the multiplier, the front-side bus clock, or the CPU operating frequency would cause the processor to be overclocked. When a processor is overclocked, the processor or motherboard can be physically damaged or the system could have memory errors, system hands, data loss, and other problems.
CPU Hyper-Threading	Assuming that you have a processor and motherboard that support Hyper-Threading, you can enable or disable the feature using the BIOS setup program. As a result, the processor will pretend to be two logical processors so that it can utilize its resources more efficiently. Note: You will also need an operating system that supports Hyper-Threading.
Processor Number Feature	This feature allows you to enable or disable the Pentium III processor serial number.
MPS Control Version for OS	The multi-processor specification (MPS) is a specification by which the PC manufacturers design and build Intel systems with two or more processors. MPS 1.1 was the original specification, while MPS 1.4 added extended configuration tables for improved support of multiple PCI bus configurations and greater expandability in the future. In addition, MPS 1.4 introduces support for a secondary PCI bus without requiring a PCI bridge. For Windows NT, Windows 2000, and Windows XP, you should use MPS 1.4.
Spread Spectrum	To reduce the EMI generated by the processor and motherboard, the Spread Spectrum feature modulates the pulse (you would choose 0.25% or 0.5% modulation). You typically need to use this feature only if your system affects other electronics in your area including those devices in your system. Since your computer case should already minimize the amount of EMI that your system generates, you should not have to use this feature often. Some systems also offer a Smart Clock option that turns off the AGP, PCI, and SDRAM clock signals that are not in use. In addition to reducing the EMI generated by these signals, it also reduces power consumption.

Table 6.13 Cache Memory Settings

Setting	Description
Cache Memory	Some motherboards will give you the option to enable or disable the L1 or L2 cache. When you enable the cache, you should expect a significant decrease in performance. Typically, you want to have the cache memory enabled unless you suspect that you have bad cache memory and you disable it to see if the problem goes away. If the problem goes away, then you will have to replace the cache. Of course, since most cache is in the processor, this means replacing the processor. Note: Some processors do not allow you to disable the cache.
Cache Timing	If you have external L2 cache, you need to specify its timing in the form of *x-y-y-y* (for example 4-1-1-1). The *x* represents the number of clock cycles it takes to read the first 64-bit value from the RAM cache. The *y* is the number of clock cycles to read the next three sequential values in the RAM cache. In general, the lower these numbers, the faster your system will be. If the values are too fast, your system may experience problems since your cache cannot respond fast enough.
Level 2 Cacheable DRAM Size/ Cache Over 64 MB of DRAM	For older systems, this setting determines how much of the RAM is cache by the size of the level 2 cache. For best performance, the value should be set to the total amount of RAM in the system.
CPU L2 Cache ECC Checking	Today, processors use error checking and correction (ECC) to verify and protect the content of the L2 cache in the processor. Some people prefer to disable this feature because the ECC actions reduce the processor performance. With most processors, although this feature may be available in the BIOS setup program, the ECC of the cache cannot be disabled. In either case, it is always recommended to have the ECC enabled.

Table 6.14 RAM Options

Setting	Description
RAM access time or DRAM read timing/DRAM burst read timing/ DRAM read wait states or DRAM writing timing/DRAM burst write timing/DRAM write wait states	These settings determine how many clock cycles in the form of *x-y-y-y* (for example 4-1-1-1) it takes to access RAM. The *x* represents the number of clock cycles it takes to read the first 64-bit value from the RAM. The *y* is the number of clock cycles to read the next three sequential values in the RAM cache. In general, the lower these numbers, the faster your system will be. If the values are too fast, your system may experience problems since your cache cannot respond fast enough.
SDRAM CAS Latency Time	This specifies the time delay (in clock cycles) that passes before the SDRAM starts to carry out a read command after receiving it. You should use 3 if you are using 67 or 83 MHz SDRAM DIMM module or 2 if you are using 100 MHz SDRAM DIMM module. You can also use Auto if your DIMMs have SPD. While 2 does offer you better performance, you should use 3 if your system becomes unreliable.
SDRAM Bank Interleave	This feature enables you to set the interleave mode of the SDRAM interface. Interleaving allows banks of SDRAM to alternate their refresh and access cycles. One bank will undergo its refresh cycle while another is being accessed. Each SDRAM DIMM consists of either 2 banks or 4 banks. Two-bank SDRAM DIMMs use 16 Mbit SDRAM chips and are usually 32 MB or less in size. Four-bank SDRAM DIMMs, on the other hand, usually use 64 Mbit SDRAM chips though the SDRAM density may be up to 256 Mbit per chip. All SDRAM DIMMs of at least 64 MB in size or greater are 4-banked in nature. If you are using a single 2-bank SDRAM DIMM, set this feature to 2-bank. But if you have two 2-bank SDRAM DIMMs, you can use 4-bank as well. If you are using 4-bank SDRAM DIMMs, you can set either 2-bank or 4-bank interleave. Naturally, 4-bank interleave is better than 2-bank interleave, so if possible, set it to 4-bank. Use 2-bank only if you are using a single 2-bank SDRAM DIMM.
DRAM Data Integrity Mode	If enabled, your memory will use error checking and correction (ECC) to detect and correct single-bit errors and detect double-bit errors. This provides increased data integrity and system stability, but it does reduce performance. Note: For this option to work, you must be using ECC RAM.
Parity Checking	Some systems have RAM with 9 bits per byte, while others have 8 bits per byte. Eight bits represent a byte of data. If the ninth (parity) bit is used, it is for error control. Note: If the RAM does not have parity capability and the parity option is turned on, the system will experience parity error.
Wait States	Each wait state slows the processor one clock cycle so that slower RAM can function properly. The fastest setting would be no wait states.

Table 6.15 Bus Options

Setting	Description
PCI Clock/CPU FSB Clock or Bus clock	Three options are typically available: ½, ⅓, and ¼. This item lets you set the PCI bus clock as a fraction (½, ⅓, or ¼) of the processor front-side bus clock. For example, if you set the processor FSB clock to 100 MHz and choose ⅓ here, the PCI bus clock will be 33.3 MHz.
AGP Clock/CPU FSB Clock	Similar to the PCI Clock/CPU FSB, this sets the AGP as a fraction of the front-side bus clock. The default setting is 1/1. If your CPU front-side bus clock is 100 MHz higher, you should select ⅔. For a 100 MHz, this would give you a 66 MHz AGP clock signal.
Shadowing Address Ranges (xxxxx-xxxxx Shadow)	This option allows you to decide if the memory block of an add-on card in the address range of xxxxx-xxxxx will be shadowed or not. Leave it as Disabled if you don't have an add-on card using that memory range. Also, like Video BIOS Shadowing, there's no benefit in enabling this option if you run Win 9X and have the proper drivers for your add-on card.
PCI Slot 1 IRQ Priority	This option specifies the IRQ priority for PCI devices installed in the computer. The settings are Auto, 3, 4, 5, 7, 9, 10, 11, 12, and 14, in priority order. If Auto is selected, AMI BIOS automatically determines the optimal IRQ priority order. The Optimal and Fail-Safe default settings are Auto.
Slot X using INT#	This entry selects an interrupt (INT#) channel for a PCI slot, and there are four (A, B, C, and D) for each one. INT #A is allocated automatically, and you would only use #B, #C, and #D if the PCI card needs to use more than one (PCI) interrupt service. For example, select #D if your PCI cards needs four interrupts. Often, it is simplest to use the Auto mode.
PCI Slot x INTx	Use this entry to assign PCI interrupts (INT#s) to specify PCI slots. Once an interrupt is assigned with PCI Slot x INTx, this option programs PCI IRQs to single-edge or logic-level triggering modes. Most PCI cards use level triggering, while most ISA cards use edge triggering. However, try selecting edge triggering for PCI IDE.

Table 6.16 Disk Options

Setting	Description
IDE HDD Block Mode	This option speeds up hard disk access by transferring data from multiple sectors at once instead of using the single-sector transfer mode. Assuming that your drive supports block transfers, it can transfer up to 64 KB of data per interrupt. Today, virtually all hard disks now support block transfers, there is normally no reason why IDE HDD Block Mode should not be enabled.
32-bit Disk Access	This option when enabled combines two 16-bit reads from the hard disk into a single 32-bit double word transfer to the processor. Note: For Windows NT systems, Microsoft recommends that you disable 32-bit Disk Access.
Onboard IDE-1/IDE-2 Controller	These options allow you to enable or disable your IDE channels on your motherboard. As a result, you can use the IRQ for other devices, and you will have a faster boot-up time since the system will not have to autodetect the devices connected to the channel.
Master/Slave Drive PIO Mode, Master/Slave DMA Mode or Ultra/Slave UltraDMA	These options allow you to specify the PIO, DMA, or UltraDMA mode of the drive. Normally, you should leave these options to Auto and let the BIOS auto-detect the fastest mode available. You should set these manually only if the BIOS cannot detect the correct mode.

Table 6.17 Peripherals Options

Setting	Description
USB Controller	This option allows you to assign an IRQ for USB or to disable IRQ allocation for the USB. If you don't use any USB devices, set the option to Disabled if you need to free up an IRQ for other devices to use.
Legacy USB Support	Enables or disables USB legacy support, which includes USB keyboards and mice, even through no operating system has been loaded.
Onboard FDD Controller	This function allows you to enable or disable the onboard floppy drive controller.
Onboard Serial Port ½	This feature allows you to disable the onboard serial port or to manually select the I/O address and IRQ for it.
Onboard Parallel Port	This function allows you to select the I/O address and IRQ for the onboard parallel port. The default I/O address of 378h and IRQ of 7. Normally, you should leave it as Auto so that the BIOS can select the best settings unless you have a reason to manually select an alternate IRQ.
Parallel Port Mode	This allows select standard parallel port (SPP), extended capabilities port (ECP), and enhanced parallel port (EPP) for your parallel port. While SPP will work with all devices, it is the slowest. Generally, ECP is good for large data transfers (useful for scanners and printers), and EPP is better with links that switch directions frequently (like parallel port drives). Of course, you should check with the manufacturer of your parallel port peripheral for the preferred parallel port mode. Some motherboards will offer an ECP+EPP mode that allows a device to use either one of these modes.
Audio	Enables or disables the onboard audio subsystem.

Table 6.18 Miscellaneous Options

Setting	Description
Plug & Play O/S	If your operating systems support Plug & Play (PnP), select Yes so that they can take over the management of device resources. Windows 9X, Windows 2000, and Windows XP are PnP operating systems, while Windows NT is not. Note: For Windows 2000 and Windows XP, Microsoft recommends that you set this to No or Disabled in the computer's BIOS.
Force Update ESCD/Reset Configuration Data	Extended System Configuration Data (ESCD) is a feature of the Plug & Play BIOS that stores the IRQ, DMA, I/O, and memory configurations of all the ISA, PCI, and AGP cards in the system (PnP or otherwise). Normally, you should leave the setting as Disabled. But if you have installed a new expansion card and that card causes conflict problems, you should enable it so that the BIOS will reset and reconfigure the settings for all PnP cards in the system during boot up. The BIOS will automatically reset the setting to Disabled the next time you boot.
Antivirus	When this option is enabled, it will issue a warning when anything attempts to write to the boot sector to the hard disk drive attached to the build-in IDE controllers. When a warning appears, you must determine if you were writing to the boot sector or whether it is a virus. Note: Having this option enabled will cause problems with some applications, including installing Windows 9X. Also, many disk diagnostic utilities that access the boot sector can trigger the error message as well. Therefore, you may need to disable this feature when installing or using these applications. You should first disable this option before using such utilities.

Continued

Table 6.18 Continued

Setting	Description
Gate A20 Option	This option determines how Gate A20 is used to address memory above 1 MB. When this option is set to Fast, the motherboard chipset controls the operation of Gate A20. But when set to Normal, a pin in the keyboard controller controls Gate A20. Setting Gate A20 to Fast improves memory access speed and thus, overall system speed, especially with OS/2 and Windows.
BIOS Update/Microcode Update	When newer BIOS versions are introduced, they may contain parts of microcode that would not be included in the original BIOS version. If this feature is disabled, the microcode will not load into RAM during POST.
BIOS Flash Protection	This function protects the BIOS from accidental corruption by unauthorized users or computer viruses. When enabled, the BIOS's data cannot be changed when attempting to update the BIOS with a flash utility. To successfully update the BIOS, you'll need to disable this flash BIOS Protection function. You should enable this function at all times. The only time when you need to disable it is when you want to update the BIOS. After updating the BIOS, you should immediately reenable it to protect it against viruses.
Hardware Reset Protect	This function is useful for file-servers, routers, an so on that need to be running 24 hours a day. When enabled, the system's hardware reset button will not function. This prevents the possibility of any accidental resets. When set as Disabled, the Reset button will function as normal. It is recommended that you leave it disabled unless you are running a server and you have kids running around who just love to press that little red button.

Table 6.19 Power-Saving Options

Setting	Description
APM	Sets the APM power management options.
ACPI	Sets the ACPI power management options.
After Power Failure	Specifies the mode of operation if an AC power loss occurs. *Stays Off* keeps the power off until the power button is pressed. *Last State* restores the previous power state before power loss occurred. *Power On* restores power to the computer.
Wake on LAN	In APM soft-off mode only, determines how the system responds to a LAN wake-up event.
Wake on PME	In APM soft-off mode only, determines how the system responds to a PCI-PME wake-up event.
Wake on Modem Ring	In APM soft-off mode only, specifies how the computer responds to a Modem Ring wake-up event on an installed modem.
ACPI Suspend State	Specifies the ACPI sleep state.

Clock Speeds

Figure 6.21 Clock Speed Options for the CMOS Setup Program

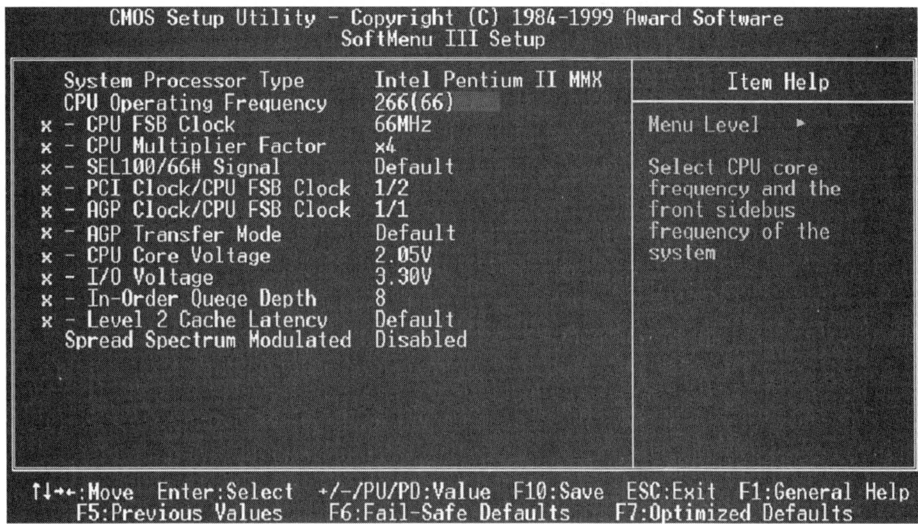

PCI Options

Figure 6.22 PnP/PCI Configuration Options on the CMOS Setup Program

```
CMOS Setup Utility - Copyright (C) 1984-1999 Award Software
PnP/PCI Configurations

   PNP OS Installed             No                  Item Help
   Force Update ESCD            Disabled
                                                    Menu Level  ►
   Resources Controlled By      Auto(ESCD)
 x IRQ Resources                Press Enter         Select Yes if you are
 x DMA Resources                Press Enter         using a Plug and Play
 x Memory Resources             Press Enter         capable operating
                                                    system Select No if
   PCI/VGA Palette Snoop        Disabled            you need the BIOS to
   Assign IRQ For VGA           Disabled            configure non-boot
   Assign IRQ For USB           Enabled             devices
   PIRQ_0 Use IRQ No.           Auto
   PIRQ_1 Use IRQ No.           Auto
   PIRQ_2 Use IRQ No.           Auto
   PIRQ_3 Use IRQ No.           Auto

↑↓→←:Move  Enter:Select  +/-/PU/PD:Value  F10:Save  ESC:Exit  F1:General Help
    F5:Previous Values    F6:Fail-Safe Defaults    F7:Optimized Defaults
```

Figure 6.23 PCI/ISA IRQ Resources Configuration Screen on the CMOS Setup Program

```
CMOS Setup Utility - Copyright (C) 1984-1999 Award Software
IRQ Resources

   IRQ-3  assigned to           PCI/ISA PnP         Item Help
   IRQ-4  assigned to           PCI/ISA PnP
   IRQ-5  assigned to           PCI/ISA PnP         Menu Level  ►►
   IRQ-7  assigned to           PCI/ISA PnP
   IRQ-9  assigned to           PCI/ISA PnP         Legacy ISA for devices
   IRQ-10 assigned to           PCI/ISA PnP         compliant with the
   IRQ-11 assigned to           PCI/ISA PnP         original PC AT bus
   IRQ-12 assigned to           PCI/ISA PnP         specification, PCI/ISA
   IRQ-14 assigned to           PCI/ISA PnP         PnP for devices
   IRQ-15 assigned to           PCI/ISA PnP         compliant with the
                                                    Plug and Play standard
                                                    whether designed for
                                                    PCI or ISA bus
                                                    architecture

↑↓→←:Move  Enter:Select  +/-/PU/PD:Value  F10:Save  ESC:Exit  F1:General Help
    F5:Previous Values    F6:Fail-Safe Defaults    F7:Optimized Defaults
```

Peripherals Options

Figure 6.24 Integrated Peripherals for the CMOS Setup Program

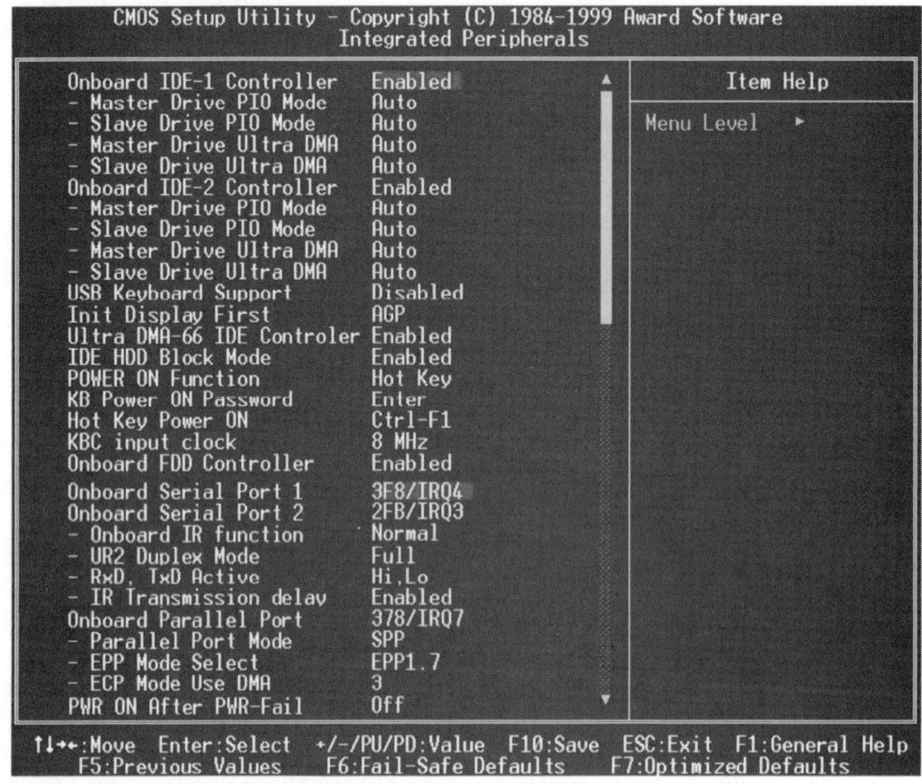

Figure 6.25 CMOS Setup Program Power Management

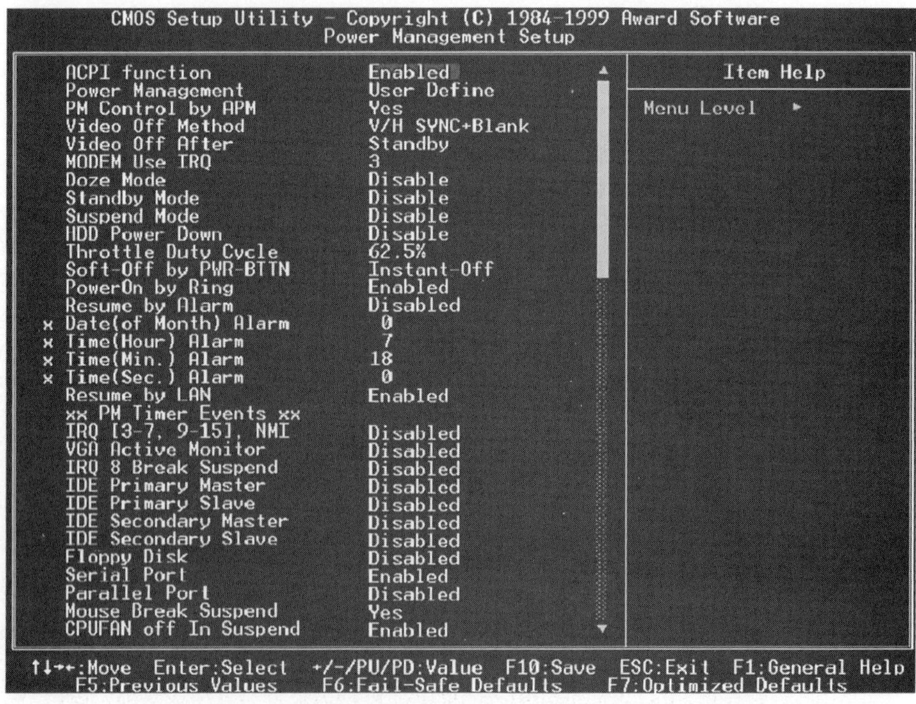

Power management includes several options to extend the battery life of notebook computers and to conserve power on desktop computers. Some options control how many minutes of nonuse occur before the monitor shuts off and the hard drive spins down. Where these features are enabled, they may slow the PC.

Most motherboards also include password options to help secure your system. You can enable a password to start up the computer and to enter the CMOS/BIOS setup program. In addition, some systems will allow you to place passwords on the hard drive, which is required to be entered during boot.

6.12.3 BIOS Defaults and Power-On Defaults

The BIOS defaults and power-on defaults are used to automatically set the CMOS settings. When the BIOS defaults are chosen, the CMOS settings will be optimized for the quickest speed possible. When the power-on defaults are selected, the CMOS will be set to the most conservative settings. Although the conservative settings are slower, this may allow some hardware to function that did not function under the BIOS defaults. Systems with the CMOS setup program that have the GUI interface call these optimal and fail-safe BIOS setup settings. They are designated by a rabbit and a turtle icon.

Question:

A user sets the password option to Always so that whenever the computer is turned on, it will ask for the password. Unfortunately, the user forgot the password. What can you do?

Answer:

To remove the password, you need to remove or short out the battery while the computer is off. Unfortunately, this will remove all the contents of the CMOS RAM, so they will have to be reentered. To erase the contents of the CMOS RAM, you would do one of the following:

1. If there is a coin package battery, remove it and let the computer sit without the battery for 15 to 30 minutes.
2. If you have access to the motherboard documentation, look for a password or CMOS jumper. Remove the jumper, then put the jumper back in place.
3. If there is a soldered-in battery, there should be a four-prong jumper connecting to an external battery pack. Remove the jumper for 15 to 30 minutes.
4. If you cannot find a jumper next to the soldered-in battery, use a wire to short both ends of the battery for 30 seconds.

6.13 EXTENSIBLE FIRMWARE INTERFACE

The **Extensible Firmware Interface (EFI)** platform is a new firmware architecture that replaces the legacy BIOS. By providing a standard application programming interface to access hardware devices, it adds an interface between the operating system and the computer firmware (BIOS). It initializes chipset, buses, and drivers and locates OS loaders. Once the EFI boots up the system, it hands over the system operation to the OS, where it runs in the background of the operating system to provide the system with simple runtime services such as monitoring firmware settings and system reset. It also provides interfaces with other industry standards such as ACPI and System Management BIOS (SMBIOS). See figure 6.26.

6.13.1 EFI File System

EFI was first implemented in Intel Itanium-based platforms, but will also be implemented in Intel IA-32-based platforms. The EFI file system resides in its own EFI System Partition on the boot drive and contains all EFI images, including drivers, applications, and vendor-developed tools for the EFI pre-OS environment. EFI executables use the .efi extension, which must be used to name all EFI applications and commands. Several tools allow you to partition and format hard drives for use with EFI. The partition tools create and check the Globally Unique Identifier (GUID) partition table GUID Partition Table (GPT) on the disk and format the disk as a FAT32 (File Allocation Table, 32 bits) partition. These

Figure 6.26 EFI Model

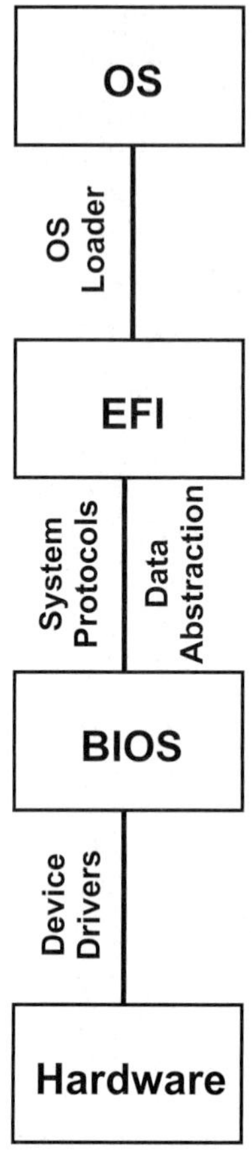

tools are provided on the system's operating system setup disk. The following EFI disk tools are also downloadable from the http://www.intel.com/technology/efi/diskutil_overview.htm website:

- DISKPART.EFI creates an EFI GPT (GUID partition table) system partition
- EFICHK.EFI checks an EFI GPT partition for correctness
- EFIFMT.EFI formats a GPT system partition or standard FAT formats on other partitions

When formatted with the EFI disk tools, each EFI-formatted partition is assigned a GUID. Many logical and physical resources, except legacy and removable media devices, in the system are assigned a GUID for unique identification.

EFI allows a hard drive to have multiple partitions and to have more than one system partition to allow multiple operating systems to exist. EFI reads only FAT-formatted partitions. Non-FAT partitions are recognized as other block devices, but EFI cannot read them. EFI can read a drive's Master Boot Record (MBR) and recognizes FAT32 partitions that do not have a GUID because they were not partitioned with EFI disk tools. With the new EFI partition scheme, you can create an unlimited number of disk partitions with multiple system partitions on the same disk.

EFI provides two partition headers: a primary header and a backup header to allow hard drive restoration applications developed for EFI to easily restore a hard drive. Whereas GUIDs can be assigned to uniquely identify a particular installation of a bootable disk partition, the device path uniquely describes to the system the physical location of that device. In EFI, this device path is shown in device path notation. If a device is assigned a GUID, it appears in the path.

A GUID is generally expressed as a series of 32 hexadecimal digits, as follows:

AF6AC311-84C3-11D2-8E3C-00A0C969723B

An example of a device path notation for a SCSI hard drive containing the EFI system partition is:

Acpi(PNP0A03,1)/Pci(0|0)/Scsi(Pun6,Lun0)/HD(Part1,SigAF6AC311-84C3-11D2-8E3C-00A0C969723B))

The slash (/) separates device path nodes, which are descriptions of a boot path for a particular device.

6.13.2 EFI Boot Manager

The Boot Manager application, which resides in the EFI firmware, controls how the system is booted. After the hardware is powered on and initialized, the Boot Manager reads global variables from Non-volatile RAM (NVRAM) containing the list of drivers to load (driver options list) and the list of bootable applications (boot order list). The lists contain the device paths for each loadable device, whether a driver or application, such as OS loaders. The drivers are automatically loaded, and the targets of the boot order list appear in the Boot menu. The Boot Manager can be written to automatically try each bootable device in the boot order list, such as an OS loader, until it successfully loads one. When an OS loader is successfully loaded, control of the system is transferred to the OS loader.

Normally, the end user of a workstation will see only the Boot Manager's Boot menu. The Boot menu allows users to select from predefined boot-up choices. A time-out period can be set to automatically boot if a choice is not made. To make changes to the boot code, administrators and developers can access the Boot Maintenance Manager. This menu allows administrators to define the boot options, change boot order, and set input, output, and error devices. See figure 6.27.

From the Boot Maintenance Manager menu, you can boot from a file and change boot options as follows:

- Using Boot from a File, you can select any available bootable file to boot.
- The add, delete, and change boot functions let you modify the Boot menu.
- Manage BootNext setting lets you bypass the Boot menu on the next boot-up and execute a fixed boot location once before returning to the normal boot options list.
- Set Auto Boot TimeOut changes the automatic boot-up delay period.
- The Select functions let you activate and deactivate input and output devices (displays and keyboards).
- Cold Reset reboots the system.
- Exit returns you to the Boot menu.

See figure 6.28.

Figure 6.27 EFI Boot Manager Menu

```
EFI Boot Manager ver 1.02[12.38]

Please select a boot option

    Microsoft Windows XP 64-Bit
    Microsoft Windows XP Professional
    EFI Shell
    CDROM
    LS120
    Legacy C:Drive
    Legacy Floppy
    Boot option maintenance menu

Use ▲ and ▼ to change option(s). Use Enter to select an option.
```

Figure 6.28 EFI Boot Maintenance Manager Menu

```
EFI Boot Maintenance Manager ver 1.02[12.38]

Main Menu. Select an Operation

    Boot from a File
    Add a Boot Option
    Delete Boot Option(s)
    Change Boot Order

    Manage BootNext setting
    Set Auto Boot TimeOut

    Select Active Console Output Devices
    Select Active Console Input Devices
    Select Active Standard Error Devices

    Cold Reset
    Exit

Timeout → [30] sec
```

Table 6.20 List of EFI Shell Commands

Command	Description
alias	Displays, creates, or deletes aliases in the EFI shell
attrib	Displays or changes the attributes of files or directories
bcfg	Displays or modifies the driver/boot configuration
break	Executes a debugger break point
cd	Displays or changes the current directory
child	Displays the device tree starting at a handle
cls	Clears the standard output with an optional background color
comp	Compares the contents of two files
connect	Binds an EFI driver to a device and starts the driver
cp	Copies one or more files or directories to another location
date	Displays the current date or sets the date in the system
dblk	Displays the contents of blocks from a block device
dh	Displays the handles in the EFI environment
disconnect	Disconnects one or more drivers from a device
dmem	Displays the contents of memory
dmpstore	Displays all NVRAM variables
echo	Displays messages or turns command echoing on or off
edit	Edits an ASCII or UNICODE file in full screen
efiCompress	Compresses a file
efiDecompress	Decompresses a file
err	Displays or changes the error level
exit	Exits the EFI Shell
for/endfor	Executes commands for each item in a set of items
getmtc	Displays the current monotonic counter value
goto	Makes batch file execution jump to another location

6.13.3 EFI Shell

The EFI Shell is an EFI application that allows you to interface with the EFI environment using a command line interface prior to the time the OS is loaded. Once the OS starts loading, the EFI environment is no longer accessible through the Shell. The EFI Shell can be accessed locally and remotely.

The EFI Shell allows you to load drivers, set environment variables, manipulate memory, create batch script files and run them, execute EFI commands, and run other EFI applications. You can use the Shell to load and test drivers and pre-OS applications. When each EFI Shell is invoked, it first runs a script file, STARTUP.NSH, and executes any commands in it. If you want particular variables defined and set in your Shell environment, you would customize the STARTUP.NSH file. After running this file, the Shell waits for input from the console. The EFI Shell commands are listed in table 6.20.

Table 6.20 Continued

Command	Description
guid	Displays all the GUIDs in the EFI environment
help	Displays commands list or verbose help of a command
hexedit	Edits with hex mode in full screen
if/endif	Executes commands in specified conditions
load	Loads EFI drivers
loadPciRom	Loads a PCI Option ROM image from a file
ls	Displays a list of files and subdirectories in a directory
map	Displays or defines mappings
memmap	Displays the memory map
mkdir	Creates one or more directories
mm	Displays or modifies MEM/IO/PCI
mode	Displays or changes the mode of the console output device
mount	Mounts a file system on a block device
mv	Moves one or more files or directories to destination
openinfo	Displays the protocols on a handle and the agents
pause	Prints a message and suspends for keyboard input
pci	Displays PCI devices or PCI function configuration space
reset	Resets the system
rm	Deletes one or more files or directories
set	Displays, creates, changes, or deletes EFI environment variables
setsize	Sets the size of a file
stall	Stalls the processor for some microseconds
time	Displays the current time or sets the time of the system
touch	Sets the time and date of a file to the current time and date
type	Displays the contents of a file
unload	Unloads the protocol image
ver	Displays the version information

NOTE: The startup file is not necessary to run the Shell.

A handle is a hexadecimal value given to a device. This DH command shows you the handles for all devices detected in the system, along with the EFI protocols used to access the device, plus the device notation showing the device path. See figure 6.29. To examine the details of a device, use the DH HANDLE command, where the *handle* identifies the devices. See figure 6.30.

The MAP command shows you which logical names are mapped to which storage devices. See figure 6.31. Whenever you need a driver loaded or reloaded, use the LOAD command followed by the location of the driver file. The system will return the memory location the image is loaded to. See figure 6.32.

Figure 6.29 Use the DH command to list devices and their handle.

```
Shell> dh
Handle dump
  1: varstore
  2: DevIo DevPath()
  3: varstore
  4: unicode
  5: Image(Serial16550)
  6: serialio DevPath(..NP0500,3F8)/Uart(115384 N81))
  7: Image(BiosKeyboard)
  8: txtin DevPath(Acpi(PNP0303,0))
  9: Image(VgaClass)
  A: VgaClass
  B: Image(VgaBiosMini)
  C: txtout DevPath(Acpi(PNP0A03,0)/Pci(1|0))
  D: Image(PcAnsi)
  E: txtout DevPath(..t(115384 N81)/VenMsg(PcAnsi))
```

Figure 6.30 Use the DH HANDLE command to give details on the device.

```
Shell> dh 46
Handle 46 (3F1ABD88)
   diskio
   blkio Fixed MId:0 bsize 200, lblock 63FFF (209,715,200), partition rw cached
   fs
   dpath
      PNP Device Path for PnP
       HID A0341D0, UID 1
      Hardware Device Path for PCI
      Messaging Device Path for SCSI
      Media Device Path for Hard Drive
       Partition (1) Start (0000000000000022) Size (0000000000064000)
   AsStr: 'Acpi(PNP0A03,1)/Pci(0|0)/Scsi(Pun6,Lun0)/HD(Part1,Sig
   AF6AC311-84C3-11D2-8E3C-00A0C969723B '
   ESP
```

Figure 6.31 The MAP command shows which logical names are mapped to which storage devices.

```
Shell> map
Device mapping table
  fs0  : Acpi(PNP0A03,1)/Pci(0|0)/Scsi(Pun6,Lun0)/HD(Part1,Sig19772100-1DD2-100)
  fs1  : Acpi(PNP0A03,1)/Pci(0|0)/Scsi(Pun6,Lun0)/HD(Part2,Sig2562E300-1DD2-100)
  fs2  : Acpi(PNP0A03,0)/Pci(3|1)/Ata(Primary,Master)
  blk0 : Acpi(PNP0A03,1)/Pci(0|0)/Scsi(Pun6,Lun0)
  blk1 : Acpi(PNP0A03,1)/Pci(0|0)/Scsi(Pun6,Lun0)/HD(Part1,Sig19772100-1DD2-100)
  blk2 : Acpi(PNP0A03,1)/Pci(0|0)/Scsi(Pun6,Lun0)/HD(Part2,Sig2562E300-1DD2-100)
  blk3 : Acpi(PNP0A03,0)/Pci(3|1)/Ata(Primary,Master)
```

Figure 6.32 The LOAD command is used to load drivers.

```
Shell> load fs0:\mydrivers\isabus.efi
load: Image 'fs0:\mydrivers\isabus.efi' loaded at 18FE000. returned Success
```

6.14 TROUBLESHOOTING THE MOTHERBOARD AND MOTHERBOARD SUPPORT CHIPS

Because the motherboard contains the majority of the system components and acts as the central point of connection, it is a suspect in every problem that you encounter. To help eliminate the motherboard as a suspect, the system ROM BIOS is written to test each major component on the motherboard during boot-up. The testing doesn't eliminate the motherboard as the source of a problem, but it does help to identify obvious problems with the motherboard. When an error code or message indicates that the motherboard is faulty or that one of the support chips on the motherboard is faulty, it means only that a specific response to a code sent out to test the component was expected back. The problem may be in the device actually tested or in some other, related device.

Table 6.21 Common Motherboard Manufacturers

Manufacturer	Website
Abit	**Home:** http://www.abit.com.tw
American Megatrends	**Home:** http://www.megatrends.com **Technical Support:** http://www.megatrends.com/
ASUS	**Home:** http://www.asus.com **Product Information:** http://www.asus.com/products.asp
First International Computer	**Home:** http://www.fica.com
Giga-Byte Technology	**Home:** http://www.giga-byte.com **Technical Support:** http://www.giga-byte.com/support.html
Intel Corporation	**Home:** http://www.intel.com **Motherboards:** http://developers.intel.com/design/motherbd/index.htm **Motherboard Manuals:** http://www.x86.org/intel.doc/IntelMotherBoards.html
Micronics Computers	**Home:** http://www.micronics.com **Product:** http://www.micronics.com/micronics/products/index.asp **Support:** http://www.micronics.com/micronic/support/index.html
Supermicro Computer, Inc.	**Home:** http://www.supermicro.com **Technical Support:** http://www.supermicro.com/TechSupport.htm
Tyan Computer	**Home:** http://www.tyan.com

NOTE: For other motherboard manufacturers, Intel and ASUS manuals, and identifying motherboards using the Award and AMI BIOS ID number, consult the following website: http://www.sysopt.com/mboard.html.

Troubleshooting individual components on the motherboard is usually quite difficult and can be done only by an experienced electronics technician. Motherboards contain several layers of metal traces (metal trails acting as electrical wires to connect to the different components), and it is impossible to peel apart the layers to get to the metal traces. In addition, most of the time you do not have electronic diagrams of the motherboard, nor do you usually have replacement parts. Also, the majority of the components on the motherboard are soldered to it using surface mount technology. Special equipment and skill are required to desolder and solder surface mount chips. For all these reasons, it is not worth the time and effort to find the problem and fix it; the motherboard should just be replaced.

Of course, before throwing away the motherboard, you should still check for the obvious things. First, make sure that everything is connected properly, particularly the ribbon cables and the power connectors (especially if you have an AT power supply, you should have the P8 and P9 grounds next to each other, black to black). In addition, check the voltage levels of the power supply and make sure that none of the expansion cards is causing a short or overload. Next, make sure the processor is inserted properly and that the proper speed and voltage have been selected for it by checking the settings for the DIP switches and the positions of the jumpers on the motherboard or by using the CMOS setup program.

Problems may also have been caused by inserting the motherboard without properly using the white or brass spacers. The spacers prevent the motherboard from shorting out against the metal case. A foreign object, such as a screw or paper clip, may have fallen into the case. Loosen the motherboard mounting screw that holds the motherboard in place. If, after loosening it, the problem goes away, the overtight screw was causing some part of the motherboard to short against something. For more information about motherboards, their replacements, drivers, BIOS updates and troubleshooting, refer to table 6.21 for a list of common motherboard manufacturers.

Many problems can be corrected or overcome by upgrading the system ROM BIOS to the newest version. In chapter 4, it was mentioned that newer versions of the ROM BIOS may allow the system to recognize and to be able to use newer processors that came out after the motherboard was developed and overcome certain errata. Second, it could allow devices that were introduced after the motherboard was manufactured and may correct timing issues and other problems. It may also correct problems found in Windows, including general protection fault (GPF) errors and stop errors.

Lastly, settings in your CMOS setup program can also cause problems. Some devices and motherboard modules are enabled and configured using the CMOS setup program. Therefore, if these devices are having problems, you should check the CMOS setup program. In addition, incorrect settings in the CMOS setup program for the processor, RAM, and buses can make your system not boot, may cause a wide range of problems, and may make your system unreliable.

Example 6.1:

You get an error code or message indicating a BIOS ROM checksum error.

During boot-up and when using a software diagnostic package, a checksum (a mathematical computation) is performed on the ROM contents and compared with a number stored within the ROM chip. If the two numbers are equal, then the ROM is considered good. If the two numbers are not equal, the error message appears. To fix the problem, the ROM chip will have to be replaced with one that matches the motherboard, or the entire motherboard will have to be replaced.

Example 6.2:

You get an error message that says your CMOS battery is low, the date and time are off, or you have invalid settings in the CMOS setup program.

This indicates that the CMOS battery, for some reason, lost its charge. If you were working within the computer, it is very possible that you shorted out the CMOS battery. This usually happens when you remove and replace motherboards. All that you have to do is reset the settings in the CMOS setup program.

If the computer uses a NiCd battery, which requires recharging, and it has not been turned on for several weeks, the battery ran out of power. Again, reset the settings in the CMOS setup program and leave the computer on for several hours so that the battery can be fully recharged.

If the problem still exists or occurs often, either the battery or the motherboard is the source. A lithium battery (coin or battery pack) is easily replaced. If the battery is a NiCd battery soldered unto the motherboard, it is best to purchase an external battery pack. If the problem still exists after replacing the battery, replace the motherboard.

Example 6.3:

The CMOS information has been erased and you do not know the correct settings for the hard drive. Trying settings that are not the same as the original ones gives a "Drive C Failure" error message and the hard drive will not boot.

The hard drive was originally prepared (partitioned and formatted) with certain parameters in the CMOS. Therefore, if the CMOS parameters are later changed for some reason, the drive may not boot and may not be accessible. The only way to fix this and access the information is to enter the same parameters as before. If you don't know what those parameters were, you will probably need to reprep the drive. This means you will have to repartition and reformat the drive. Unfortunately, this will erase all of the existing data.

Example 6.4:

After having some jumpers and DIP switches on the motherboard adjusted or some of the CMOS settings changed, the computer does not boot.

This problem is usually caused by trying to improve performance by adjusting the wait states, bus speed, clock speed, or RAM settings. If you were working on the motherboard, put the jumpers back to where they were originally. If you don't know what the original positions were, consult the motherboard manual to figure out the correct settings. If you were making changes in the CMOS setup program, restore the original settings. If you don't know what the original settings were, the best approach would be to set the BIOS defaults or the power-on defaults. Try the BIOS defaults first since they will give the quickest speed. If this doesn't work, then try the power-on defaults. If this works, then you can proceed to change the settings one at a time to achieve the most speed possible for the system.

SUMMARY

1. Motherboards are large printed circuit boards made of a glass-epoxy layer. They contain metal traces instead of wires to connect a large array of electronic circuits and devices.
2. Read-only memory (ROM), also known as firmware, is considered a permanent form of memory that contains software (instructions).
3. Erasable programmable ROM (EPROM) can be erased with ultraviolet light so that it can be reused.
4. Flash ROM, rewritable ROM that retains its contents even without power, is used within plug-and-play systems and as ROM BIOS chips.
5. Basic input/output system (BIOS) chips include special instructions that control the hardware.
6. The primary ROM BIOS chip is the system ROM BIOS, which controls the boot-up procedure and hardware, provides compatibility between the operating systems and the hardware, finds the sector/boot files to boot an operating system, and stores the CMOS setup program.
7. Every system has a minimum of two other ROM chips: the video ROM BIOS, which controls the video system, and the keyboard ROM BIOS, which controls the keyboard.
8. The system ROM BIOS uses other ROM BIOS chips found on expansion cards to supplement itself.
9. Updating the system ROM BIOS (also known as flashing your BIOS) can correct a wide range of problems and will allow the system to work with components that did not exist at the time the motherboard was manufactured.
10. Because many of the devices on the motherboard used to be on expansion cards and other devices have been created to increase the performance of the PC, you will need to load drivers to control these devices on the motherboard.
11. Immediately after loading the operating system and any service packs for that operating system, you should load the chipset drivers before loading any other driver, including the video driver and network driver.
12. Because the motherboard contains the majority of the system components and acts as the central point of connection, it is a suspect in every problem that you encounter.
13. Before throwing away a motherboard, you should check for the obvious such as making sure that everything is connected properly. Also check the voltage levels of the power supply to ensure that none of the expansion cards are causing a short or overload.
14. Problems may also have been caused by inserting the motherboard without properly using the white or brass spacers.
15. Many problems can be corrected or overcome by upgrading the system ROM BIOS to the newest version.
16. Some devices and motherboard modules are enabled and configured using the CMOS setup program. Therefore, if these devices are having problems, you should enter the CMOS setup program.
17. Incorrect settings in the CMOS setup program for the processor, RAM, and buses can make your system not boot, may cause a wide range of problems, and may make your system unreliable.
18. Motherboards come in several different physical dimensions and sizes known as form factors. The common form factors include full-size AT, Baby AT, ATX, mini-ATX, LPX, and mini-LPX.
19. The AT motherboard uses the 5-pin DIN type connector.
20. The most common form factors used today are the ATX motherboard and its derivatives, mini-ATX, micro-ATX, and flex-ATX.
21. The AXT motherboard is similar to the Baby AT. The main difference is that the components are placed differently. The expansion slots are parallel to the short side of the board, which allows more space for other components. The processor and RAM are next to the power supply so that the airflow generated by the power supply runs over the processor to help keep it cooler. The ATX motherboard contains integrated I/O port connects, an integrated PS/2 mouse connector, and a single-keyed 20-pin power supply connector (which also includes 3.3 V). Lastly, the ATX motherboard allows you

to turn off the computer via software (known as a soft-power switch).

22. LPX and NLX motherboards are inserted into a riser card that protrudes from the motherboard.
23. Motherboard chipsets consist of the additional chips on the motherboard that allow the CPU to communicate with the rest of the system.
24. The system clock acts as the heartbeat of the computer, keeping the chips in sync with each other.
25. Most of Intel's earlier chipsets, including the 440BX and 440GX, and many non-Intel chipsets are broken into a multitiered architecture incorporating what are referred to as North and South Bridge components as well as a super I/O chip.
26. The North Bridge holds the memory controller, AGP controller, and PCI controller.
27. The South Bridge, which sits on the North Bridge's PCI bus, handles most other forms of I/O, including the PCI peripherals, the ISA bus, floppy drives, hard drives, USB, keyboard, and motherboard I/O devices (parallel ports, serial ports, and PS/2 ports).
28. Instead of the normal North Bridge/South Bridge setup, newer Intel boards, including the 810, 815, 820, 840, 845, 850, 865, and 875 chipsets, use the Intel Hub Architecture (IHA).
29. Like the old system, IHA has two parts, the graphics and AGP memory controller hub (GMCH) and the I/O controller hub (ICH).
30. CMOS RAM is used to store hardware configuration information. The contents are changed using a CMOS setup program.
31. Because CMOS RAM is RAM, it uses a battery to keep the chip powered while the PC is off.
32. The CMOS setup program is used to configure the hardware.
33. Because many of the devices on the motherboard used to be on expansion cards and other devices have been created to increase the performance of the PC, you will need to load drivers to control these devices on the motherboard.
34. Before loading the operating system and any service packs for that system, you should load the chipset drivers and any other drivers, including the video driver and the network driver.

QUESTIONS

1. Most AT-type motherboards configure the size of the hard drives by
   a. setting jumpers.
   b. running the CMOS setup program.
   c. setting DIP switches.
   d. reading a text file on the floppy drive.
2. After replacing a faulty motherboard to repair a computer, what is the first thing you do before returning the computer to the customer?
   a. edit the CONFIG.SYS and AUTOEXEC.BAT files
   b. repartition and reformat the hard drive
   c. run the CMOS setup program
   d. record the serial number of the motherboard
3. What type of memory is usually maintained by a battery?
   a. dynamic RAM (DRAM)
   b. ROM
   c. CMOS
   d. cache RAM (SRAM)
4. Flash ROM chips can be
   a. erased when power is discontinued.
   b. changed or reprogrammed as needed.
   c. programmed once using quick jolts of electricity.
   d. moved from one computer to any other computer.
5. What does *BIOS* stand for?
   a. beginning instruction operating system
   b. basic input/output system
   c. basic interpreter output system
   d. beginning interpreter operating system
6. Which of the following functions is performed by the system ROM BIOS (choose all that apply)?
   a. containing application programs
   b. controlling the POST
   c. containing the CMOS setup program
   d. containing the operating system
   e. containing the microprocessor
7. The system ROM BIOS contains which of the following?
   a. the PC's real-time clock
   b. the file allocation table for the boot device
   c. device drivers and TSRs
   d. instructions for communicating with I/O devices
8. Which of the following is *not* a manufacturer of system ROM BIOS?
   a. Microsoft
   b. Phoenix
   c. AMI
   d. IBM
   e. HP
9. Where is the system ROM BIOS chip located?
   a. on the motherboard
   b. within the microprocessor
   c. on the video card
   d. on an expansion card
10. What type of memory stores the BIOS?
    a. dynamic RAM (DRAM)
    b. ROM
    c. CMOS
    d. cache RAM (SRAM)

11. How can you disable the CMOS password in a computer that has a coin-cell CMOS battery?
    a. Call the company that makes the system ROM BIOS and ask for the secret password.
    b. Shut off the computer.
    c. Disconnect the battery.
    d. Remove the battery.
12. When shadowing is enabled in the computer's CMOS setup program
    a. the conventional memory is moved to the top of extended memory.
    b. everything in RAM is stored twice.
    c. the contents of the system ROM BIOS or other ROM chips are copied into the extended memory.
    d. the contents of the system ROM BIOS or other ROM chips are copied into reserve memory.
13. Which component may be failing if the fan and hard drive run, yet the system appears dead (choose two)?
    a. the on/off switch
    b. the power supply
    c. the power cord
    d. the motherboard
    e. the RAM
14. When the computer is powered up, POST (power-on self-test) does what first?
    a. resets the CMOS RAM
    b. finds and reads the boot device
    c. resets the microprocessor and sets the program counter to F000
    d. finds and initializes the video controller
    e. resets the RTC
15. The CMOS holds only
    a. BIOS.
    b. drivers.
    c. hardware commands.
    d. configuration data.
16. The following process determines the amount of memory present, the date/time, and which communications ports and display adapters are installed in a PC:
    a. start-up utility test
    b. power-on self-test
    c. power-up boot process
    d. power-on start-up process
17. If the date and time clock have stopped even though the battery has been replaced, which of the following may be causing the problem?
    a. hard drive
    b. motherboard
    c. video controller
    d. keyboard controller
    e. RAM
    f. corrupted CMOS data
18. You activated the CMOS password but don't know or remember it. How can you disable the password?
    a. boot from a floppy disk and format the hard drive
    b. press Ctrl+Alt+Del to reboot the computer and enter the CMOS setup program to disable the password
    c. discharge the CMOS battery by removing the battery or by shorting the CMOS jumper
    d. enter the default password used by the manufacturer of the system ROM BIOS
19. After you upgrade the hard disk drive from 540 MB to 4 GB, you get a "Drive Mismatch Error" message during boot-up. What happened?
    a. The information stored with the CMOS setup program does not match the new hard drive.
    b. The new hard drive is incompatible with the hard disk controller.
    c. The system ROM BIOS does not accommodate drives over 540 MB.
    d. The controller cable on the hard drive is damaged, missing, or not connected.
20. What keeps the chips on the motherboard in sync with each other?
    a. the CMOS battery
    b. the clock crystal/oscillator
    c. the microprocessor
    d. the system ROM BIOS
    e. the RTC
21. The bulk of the chips on the motherboard that allow the microprocessor to communicate with the rest of the computer and determine what technology can be used are known as
    a. the CMOS RAM.
    b. the system chipset.
    c. the clock crystal.
    d. the RTC.
22. What is most likely the problem if the system date and time seem to be off every time you turn on your computer?
    a. faulty CMOS RAM
    b. faulty CMOS battery
    c. faulty clock crystal
    d. faulty power cable
23. The motherboard contains which of the following (choose all that apply)?
    a. the microprocessor
    b. expansion slots
    c. the hard drive
    d. the clock oscillator
24. Hardware error codes are generated by
    a. the crystal oscillator.
    b. RAM.
    c. the system ROM BIOS.
    d. video ROM BIOS.
    e. CMOS.
25. Which are the most common motherboard form factors (choose two)?
    a. ATX
    b. LPX
    c. NLX
    d. Baby AT
26. When should you upgrade the flash BIOS on a computer's mainboard?
    a. whenever an update is issued
    b. only when a bug is corrected

c. whenever a new feature is added
d. only when an update affecting operation of your machine is issued

27. Which are valid motherboard form factors (choose all that apply)?

a. FTX
b. STX
c. Baby AT
d. NLX
e. LPX
f. WTX

HANDS-ON EXERCISES

Exercise 1: Identifying the System ROM BIOS and CMOS Battery

1. Open the computer case and identify the system ROM BIOS.
2. Identify the chipsets in the computer.
3. Determine if the motherboard has any jumpers or DIP switches. By using the motherboard manual, find out what the settings are.
4. Boot the computer and identify the system ROM BIOS during boot-up.

Exercise 2: Testing the Motherboard Components with Software Diagnostics

Test the system components.

Exercise 3: Using the CMOS Setup Program

1. Start the computer and enter the CMOS setup program.
2. If the option is available, enter the standard CMOS setup.
3. Record the hard drive and floppy drive settings. For hard drives, include the hard drive type, the number of cylinders, the number of read/write heads, and the number of sectors per track.
4. Change the A drive to a 1.44 MB disk drive and the B drive to a 1.2 MB disk drive.
5. Change the A drive and B drive back to their original settings.
6. Change drive C or the primary master to type 1.
7. Exit the CMOS setup program and save the changes. Reboot the computer. Notice the error message, if any, and check whether the hard drive boots.
8. Reboot the computer and enter the CMOS setup program. Set the hard drive parameters to a user-definable type/type 47 and set the following parameters:

   Number of cylinders: 2,700
   Number of read/write heads: 32
   Number of sectors per track: 63

9. Exit the CMOS setup program and save the changes. Reboot the computer. Notice the error message, if any, and check whether the hard drive boots.
10. Reboot the computer and enter the CMOS setup program. Reset the hard drive to its original settings. Notice the size of the drive.
11. Divide the number of cylinders by 2 and enter this number for the C drive.
12. Multiply the number of read/write heads by 2 and enter this number for the C drive. Notice the size of the drive.
13. Exit the CMOS setup program and save the changes. Reboot the computer. Notice the error message, if any, and check whether the hard drive boots.
14. Determine whether your hard drive has different addressing modes, such as normal, large, and LBA mode.
15. Find and run the HD autodetect within the CMOS setup program.
16. Exit the CMOS setup program and save the changes. Reboot the computer. Notice the error message, if any, and check whether the hard drive boots.
17. Reboot the computer and enter the CMOS setup program. Reset the hard drive to its original settings.
18. Set drive D or primary slave to a type 10.
19. Exit the CMOS setup program and save the changes. Reboot the computer. Notice the error messages, if any, and check whether the hard drive boots.

20. Reboot the computer and enter the CMOS setup program. Reset the hard drive to its original settings. Save the changes and reboot the computer.
21. Boot the computer from a floppy disk.
22. Enter the CMOS setup program. Set the boot sequence to C followed by A, which is probably under the advanced CMOS setup screen (or equivalent). Save the changes and reboot the computer with the bootable floppy disk in drive A.
23. Enter the CMOS setup program and change the boot sequence back to A followed by C.
24. Determine if your system has shadow ROM/RAM options. If the option is available and either system or video ROM chips are not shadowed, enable them.
25. If the options are available, record the settings for wait states and memory speeds.
26. If the motherboard has built-in serial ports, find and reconfigure the first serial port to COM3 with IRQ 3.
27. Change the first serial port back to COM3 and IRQ 4.
28. If the motherboard has built-in parallel ports, change the parallel port to LPT2 and reboot the computer.
29. Change the parallel port from bidirectional or normal mode to ECP mode.
30. Change the parallel port back to its original configuration.
31. Find where to disable the parallel port.
32. Exit the BIOS setup program and save the changes. Try to reboot from the floppy disk.
33. Reboot the computer and enter the BIOS setup program. Enable the parallel port.
34. Activate the LOAD BIOS DEFAULT or equivalent. View the advanced CMOS setup and the CMOS chipset setup. Save the changes in the CMOS setup program and reboot the computer and see how long it takes to boot.
35. Enter the BIOS setup program and activate the LOAD SETUP DEFAULTS or equivalent option. Try to find at least four different options that were changed between the two defaults.
36. Save the changes in the BIOS setup program, reboot the computer, and time how long it takes to boot.
37. Activate the LOAD BIOS DEFAULT or equivalent.
38. Make sure the computer boots. If it doesn't boot, use the LOAD SETUP DEFAULTS and see if the problem goes away. If it does, make adjustments until you find out which parameter or parameters stopped the system from booting.

Exercise 4: Discharging the CMOS Battery

1. Enter the BIOS setup program and record the hard drive and floppy drive settings. For hard drives, include the hard drive type, the number of cylinders, the number of read/write heads, and the number of sectors per track.
2. Enter the BIOS setup program and change the BIOS setup program to PC.
3. Reboot the computer and notice what happens during boot-up.
4. Shut off the computer. Using a voltmeter, measure the voltage of the CMOS battery.
5. If it is a removable battery, remove the battery. After a couple of minutes, reinstall the battery. If the battery is soldered onto the motherboard, discharge the battery.
6. Start the computer and record any messages that may appear.
7. Enter the BIOS setup program and reenter the BIOS information.

Exercise 5: Updating the System ROM BIOS

1. Open the System Information program and determine the BIOS version and date.
2. Identify the make and model of the motherboard.
3. Enter the BIOS setup program and record any important settings.
4. Go to the manufacturer website and download the system ROM BIOS for the motherboard. Show your instructor which BIOS image you downloaded to make sure you downloaded the correct one.
5. Read the instructions on how to upgrade the BIOS.
6. Update the BIOS according to the instructions. Make sure that you do not shut off the computer until the BIOS is complete.

Exercise 6: Loading the Chipset Drivers

1. Find and download the chipset drivers for your motherboard.
2. Load the chipset drivers for your system.

CHAPTER 7

The Expansion Slots and Cards

Topics Covered in This Chapter

Introduction

The expansion slot, also known as the I/O bus, extends the reach of the microprocessor so that it can communicate with peripheral devices. They are called expansion slots because they allow the system to be expanded by the insertion of circuit boards, called expansion cards, into the motherboard. When an I/O device (including expansion cards) is installed into a system, it must not use the same resources allocated to another device. If it does, the two cards will most likely not work properly or at all. Therefore, when installing an expansion card, you must be familiar with the different types of expansion slots and be able to configure the expansion card using jumpers, DIP switches, and software. Consequently, you must be able to interpret the documentation that comes with the PC and expansion card.

Objectives

1. Explain the purpose of the expansion slot and card.
2. List and describe the resources used by an expansion card.
3. Describe the different methods to configure an expansion card.
4. Given an expansion card and its documentation, configure the expansion card for use within a PC.
5. Using software diagnostic packages, determine which resources are free.
6. Given an expansion slot, identify which expansion slot it is.
7. List the different types of expansion slots and describe their characteristics.
8. Describe how plug-and-play systems work.
9. If documentation is not available for an expansion card, state the different methods for locating the documentation.
10. Given a failed expansion card within a system, determine and correct the problem.

7.1 MOTHERBOARD DESIGN

When the IBM PC was being designed in 1981, two major motherboard designs were being used: the single-board design and the bus-oriented design.

The single-board motherboard included all of the electronic devices on a single circuit board. The advantage of a single-board design was that it required less labor and fewer materials and so was cheaper to produce. In addition, since connections and slots are more prone to failure and the single-board design had fewer of them, it was considered more reliable. But that usually meant that upgrades to the system or partial failures in the board required that the entire board be replaced.

The bus-oriented design had a different approach. Instead of having one circuit board containing everything, it used one primary circuit board to connect several smaller circuit boards. The main advantage to this design was expandability, since an individual circuit board could be added or a faulty board could be replaced with a new one without affecting the rest of the boards. The disadvantage of the bus-oriented design was that it had a higher failure rate than the single-board design because it relied on connections and slots, which are more prone to failure. The bus-oriented design also cost more because it required more material and more labor to produce.

The design that IBM chose had the best features from both designs. The central part of the computer was the motherboard, which contained the essential circuitry. Expansion slots were added to it to expand the system (video cards, disk drive connectors, and other devices).

7.2 EXPANSION SLOT OPERATION

The **expansion slot,** also known as the **I/O bus,** extends the reach of the microprocessor so it can communicate with peripheral devices. Expansion slots are so named because they allow the system to be expanded by the insertion of circuits boards, called **expansion cards.** These are essential to the computer because a basic system cannot satisfy everyone's needs, and they allow the system to use new technology as it becomes available. Expansion slots consist of connectors and metal traces that carry signals from the expansion card to the rest of the computer, specifically the RAM and CPU. These connections are used for power, data, addressing, and control lines.

7.2.1 Data Bus and Address Bus

The primary purpose of the data and address bus slots is to carry data between the expansion cards and the CPU and RAM. The **data bus** carries the actual data between the expansion card, the RAM, and the CPU, and the **address bus** determines the memory location of the data—where the data is going to or coming from. Ideally, the size of the expansion slot's data bus should match the size of the CPU's data bus.

Much like the other digital electronic components of the PC, the expansion buses coordinate their actions with an oscillator. It requires at least two clock cycles to transfer a piece of data. The first clock cycle is used for the address bus to signify the memory address where the data is going to or coming from. After the address is sent, the data is sent along the data bus into the RAM. The data and address buses can carry only one set of signals at a time. If two signals were sent at the same time, they would collide and both would be corrupted. To prevent two devices from using the address and data buses at the same time, certain steps must be taken.

7.2.2 Hardware Interrupts

The first method of preventing two devices from communicating at the same time is the **hardware interrupt (IRQ).** When a device needs the attention of the microprocessor, it sends a special signal to the CPU. The microprocessor recognizes only two types of interrupt. The first is microprocessor interrupts, such as divide error (when it tries to divide by zero) or a nonmaskable interrupt (used to identify RAM parity errors). The second type of interrupt understood by the CPU is connected to the interrupt controller, which branches to several other devices.

When a device (such as a modem, mouse, keyboard, hard drive controller, floppy drive controller, or sound card) needs the attention of the microprocessor, the device sends a signal through an interrupt line to the **interrupt controller.** When this happens, the CPU saves all the data located in the CPU register (small storage areas within the CPU) to a stack (area in RAM used to store the contents of the CPU). It then goes to the interrupt vector table to determine the location of the routine (stored in either a device driver or a ROM BIOS chip) that controls the device and then interacts with the device. When the CPU has completed interacting with the device, it will restore to the register the information that had been moved to the stack. The CPU can then continue with its previous task. In short, the interrupt is used to interrupt the CPU in order to complete another task.

The first two device interrupts are reserved for the system timer and the keyboard controller. IRQ 0 is controlled by the system timer, which generates a periodic interrupt at a rate of 18.2 times per second. The processor uses it to keep track of the date and time and to check the status of a device, such as an alarm. IRQ 1 is used every time a key is pressed on the keyboard. The other device IRQs are wired by metal traces to the expansion bus, specifically each of the expansion slots. A single expansion card is set to use a single interrupt. When the device needs to interrupt the CPU, it sends a signal through the selected interrupt. If two devices are set to use the same interrupt, at the same time the cards will function improperly because the processor will not know which device needs its attention.

The first IBM PC had eight interrupts (IRQ 0–7), which were managed by the Intel 8259 interrupt controller. Since two devices may need the CPU at the same time, interrupts are prioritized. Generally, the interrupt with a lower number has a higher priority than one with a higher number.

Question:

The CPU is performing a task. A device using IRQ 5 sends an interrupt signal to the CPU. As a result, the CPU saves its registers to the stacks and begins interacting with the device using IRQ 5. What happens if a device using IRQ 3 sends an interrupt signal?

Answer:

When an interrupt of higher priority interrupts another interrupt, the CPU must stop what it is doing to divert its attention to the second device. This is called a *nested interrupt.* The CPU then saves its registers again onto the stack. The reason they are called *stacks* is that sets of information are stacked on top of each other much like a stack of plates. If a second set of information is stacked on top of a first set of information, the second set of information must first be removed before the first set of information can be accessed.

In this example, the CPU has already put information into the stack and is working on a second task. It will stop doing the second task (device using IRQ 5) and store its information to the stack. The CPU will then interact with the device using IRQ 3. When it is done interacting with the device using IRQ 3, it will restore the information for the device using IRQ 5 and finish interacting with that device. Lastly, it will restore the last of the information kept in the stack to the CPU registers to continue working on its original task.

If too many devices are generating interrupts, the stacks can't hold all of the CPU information. As a result, operating systems such as DOS will generate an "Internal Stack Overflow" error message.

When the IBM AT with its 16-bit ISA slots was introduced, the computer had to have more interrupts. These machines (and machines since the IBM AT) has 16 interrupts (IRQ 0–15). To increase the number of interrupts without redesigning the entire motherboard, a second Intel 8259 interrupt controller (IRQ 8–15) was added by wiring IRQ 2 and IRQ 9 together. Unfortunately, this reduced the number of interrupts available by one. Because the last eight interrupts are accessed through IRQ 2, the order of priority is modified. IRQ 0 and 1 have the highest priority, followed by IRQ 8 through 15, since these all go through IRQ 2. IRQ 3–7 have the lowest priority. See table 7.1 for a description of which devices are assigned to the interrupts.

With the wide assortment of devices available, it is possible to run out of interrupts. Therefore, some bus designs such as PCI allowed for interrupt sharing. Interrupt sharing allows two different devices to use the same interrupt. The interrupt-handling software or firmware distinguishes for the processor which device is making the request. (Note: Unless sharing interrupts is unavoidable and only if two devices are made to be shared with each other, it is best not to have two devices use the same interrupt.)

When a system assigns IRQs, the first ones assigned are to the expansion cards that are hardware configured, followed by the CMOS configured IRQs. Lastly, the IRQs are assigned to plug-and-play expansion cards and devices.

Table 7.1 AT Default Interrupt Assignments

IRQ	Default Use	Bus Slot
0	System timer	No
1	Keyboard controller	No
2	2nd IRQ controller (cascade)	No
3	Serial port 2 (COM2)	Yes (8-bit)
4	Serial port 1 (COM1)	Yes (8-bit)
5	Parallel port 2 (LPT2)	Yes (8-bit)
6	Floppy disk controller	Yes (8-bit)
7	Parallel port 1 (LPT1)	Yes (8-bit)
8	Real-time clock	No
9	Available	Yes (8/16-bit)
10	Available	Yes (8/16-bit)
11	Available	Yes (8/16-bit)
12	Bus mouse (or available)	Yes (8/16-bit)
13	Math coprocessor	No
14	Primary IDE	Yes (8/16-bit)
15	Secondary IDE (or available)	Yes (8/16-bit)

> **NOTE:**
> Instead of using interrupts, data may be transferred by the microprocessor by polling. Polling is the microprocessor going to each device in turn and asking if it has anything for the microprocessor to do. Of course, this is very wasteful of clock cycles since the microprocessor is occupied with asking each device instead of doing something useful. Joysticks use polling.

Table 7.2 AT Default Interrupt Assignments

DMA	Default Use	Bus Slot
0	Unused	Yes (8-bit)
1	Unused	Yes (8-bit)
2	Floppy disk controller	Yes (8-bit)
3	Unused	Yes (8-bit)
4	First DMA controller	No
5	Unused	Yes (16-bit)
6	Unused	Yes (16-bit)
7	Unused	Yes (16-bit)

7.2.3 Direct Memory Address

Direct memory address (DMA) channels are used by high-speed communication devices that must send and receive large amounts of information at high speed (sound cards, some network cards, and some SCSI cards). The DMA controller takes over the data bus and address lines to bring data from an I/O device to the RAM without any assistance or direction from the CPU. Since the CPU can perform other tasks while the data transfer is taking place, the PC performs better.

A device using a DMA address channel is very similar to a device using an IRQ. DMA lines link the DMA controller to each of the expansion slots. When a device uses DMA to transfer data using a DMA channel, it will first send a signal along a single DMA channel to the DMA controller. The DMA controller will then send a request to the CPU. When the CPU acknowledges the request, the DMA controller takes control of the data bus and the address bus. The DMA controller then sends another signal to the device, telling the device to start sending information (up to 64 KB of data). After the transfer is done, the DMA controller will release the data bus and address bus back to the CPU.

As with IRQs, devices that want to make a DMA transfer are assigned a priority level. If its DMA has a low number, it has a higher priority than a device that has a higher number. The IBM PC and IBM XT had four DMA channels when they used an 8237A DMA controller. When the AT needed more DMA channels, IBM cascaded (connected) two DMA controllers together through the DMA 4 channel, giving the IBM AT eight DMA channels, of which seven were available for use. See tables 7.2.

Today, the only standard DMA channel used in all systems is DMA 2, which is used by the floppy controller. DMA 4 is not used because it connects the two DMA controllers. DMA channels 1 and 5 are most commonly used by ISA sound cards such as the Sound Blaster 16. These cards use both an 8- and 16-bit DMA channel for high-speed transfers. PCI adapters don't use DMA channels.

7.2.4 Bus Mastering

Bus mastering is the taking of temporary control of the data and address bus by an expansion card with its own processor to move information from one device to another. This makes the PC faster. This is not the same as the DMA controller taking control of the buses. If several devices try to use the data and address bus at the same time, the data being transferred would, of course, become corrupted, so the bus is managed by the integrated system peripheral (ISP) chips. As with IRQs and DMAs, the devices using the bus are assigned priorities. These are as follows:

1. RAM refresh
2. DMA transfers

3. CPU
4. Bus master expansion cards

EISA, MCA, and PCI support bus mastering.

7.2.5 I/O Addresses

As the processor communicates with a device, it will use either an OUT command or an IN command. The OUT command is an assembly language command used to send data or a command to an I/O device. The IN command is used to read data from the device or to check the status of a device. In either case, the IN and OUT commands must include the **I/O address,** which identifies the device. To make sure that the PC doesn't confuse an I/O address with a RAM address, a special signal is sent with the I/O address.

Each device is configured to respond to a range of addresses known as **ports.** Generally, a device will respond to a range of addresses. For example, the COM1 port responds to addresses 03F8 to 03FF, with 03F8 handling all of the data. Four of the remaining addresses are used to configure the line (speed and parity), to control the telephone (hang up and begin), to check modem status, and to perform other housekeeping tasks. (Note that the addresses are expressed in hexadecimal form.) The I/O address, therefore, is a memory address used to identify the input/output (I/O) device much like a street address identifies a house or building. Of course, no two devices can be set to use the same I/O address or range of addresses. See table 7.3 for examples of I/O addresses for various devices. Intel designed 65,536 I/O ports, each address being 16 bits long, into its microprocessors. The engineers didn't think all those ports would be needed, so they limited the usable addresses to 1,024.

7.2.6 Memory Addresses

Many expansion cards need to use a range of **memory addresses** in the reserve memory between 640 KB and 1 MB of RAM. The reserve memory will either be used as a working area for the expansion card or it will used by the ROM BIOS chips. Again, no two devices can be set to use the same memory areas.

7.2.7 Power Connections and Control Signals

Connections essential to the expansion slots are the power connections that provide the cards with the power to operate. The power supply provides +5, +12, −5, −12, and 3.3 dc voltage. Most expansion cards have either TTL chips, which use 5 V, or CMOS chips, which use 3.3 V. The TTL chips can use the +5 V directly, but the 3.3 V chips must use an on-board voltage regulator. A handful of devices, such as the hard drive card (expansion card with a hard drive mounted on it), use the +12 V to power

Table 7.3 Common IBM PC AT I/O Addresses

Hex 000-0FF for System I/O Board		Common Expansion Cards and Ports	
000-01F	DMA controller #1	170-177	Secondary IDE controller
020-03F	Interrupt controller #1	1F0-1FF	Primary IDE controller
040-05F	Timer	200-207	Game port
060-06F	Keyboard	278-27F	Parallel port 2 (LPT2)
		02F8-2FF	Serial port 2 (COM2)
070-07F	Real-time clock, NMI mask	330-333	SCSI controller
		378-37F	Parallel printer port #1 (LPT1)
0A0-0BF	Interrupt controller #2	3B0-3BF	Monochrome display and printer adapter
0C0-0DF	DMA controller #2	3C0-3CF	Enhanced graphics adapter
0F8-0FF	Math coprocessor	3D0-3DF	CGA monitor adapter
		3F0-3F7	Diskette controller
		3F8-3FF	Serial port 1 (COM1)
		FF80-FF9F	USB

the drive's motor. Very few devices actually use the −5 and −12 V power. (Note: There are several more +5 voltage lines than there are for the other voltage levels.)

For electricity to flow, a circuit must be a complete loop. Therefore, two wires are needed, one to send the power to the card and one to send it back (ground). Although all circuits inside the PC share a common system ground, which appears in several places, the additional ground wires are needed to allow more current to flow and reduce signal interference like crosstalk. Less interference means that engineers can design faster bus speeds.

Expansion slots also carry control signals. These can range from the system clock signal to the read/write signals that indicate if data is going from the device or to the device.

7.3 TYPES OF EXPANSION SLOTS

Through the years, several types of expansion slots have been developed. The original IBM PC used the 8-bit PC slot, and the IBM AT used the 16-bit ISA slot. Later, the micro channel architecture (MCA) and the EISA were introduced for 386 machines. Today's desktop computers use a combination of ISA slots and local bus slots (VESA and PCI); notebooks use a PC slot/CardBus slot. See table 7.4 for some common types of expansion slots.

7.3.1 PC Bus

Most technology used for personal computers in the early 1980s was based on 8-bit technology. Therefore, IBM chose the 8088 microprocessor, which had an external 8-bit data bus. This became known as the **PC slot** or the 8-bit ISA bus. See figures 7.1 and 7.2. Since the bus was controlled directly by the processor, both ran at 4.77 MHz. To move information back and forth between the bus and the RAM or the bus and the CPU, the bus used 62 contacts, which included connections for the various data lines, address lines, power lines, IRQs, DMAs, and the various control lines. Instead of making its PC a proprietary machine, IBM opened up the PC's architecture, which means it licensed the technology for a small fee. This strengthened the architecture because other companies could then produce IBM-compatible computers and develop add-on devices.

Table 7.4 Common Expansion Slots

Name	Date	Bus Width	Operating Speed	Maximum Bandwidth	Addressing	Comments
PC Bus	1981	8	4.77 MHz	2.385 MB/s	1 MB	Used in IBM PC and XT
ISA	1984	16	8.33 MHz	8.33 MB/s	16 MB	Used in IBM AT
MCA	1987	32	10 MHz	20 MB/s	4 GB	Used in PS/2
EISA	1988	32	8.33 MHz	16.6 MB/s	4 GB	Created to compete against MCA
VL Bus	1992	32	33 MHz	105.6 MB/s	4 GB	Used mostly in 486 computers
PCI	1992	32	33 MHz	66.6 MB/s or higher (nonburst mode) 133 MB/s (burst mode)	4 GB	Used in 486 and some Pentium machines
PCI	1992	64	66 MHz (or higher)	264 MB/s or higher (nonburst mode) 528 MB/s (burst mode)	4 GB	Used in Pentium machines
AGP	1996	32	66 MHz (or higher)	1X - 266 MB/s 2X - 533 MB/s 4X - 1.07 GB/s 8X - 2.1 GB/s	4 GB	Used in newer Pentium systems
PC Card	1990	16	8 MHz	16 MB/s	64 MB	Used in notebook computers
CardBus	1994	32	33 MHz	133 MB/s	4 GB	Used in notebook computers
PCI-X	1998	64	133 MHz	1,066 MB/s	4 GB	Update to the PCI

Figure 7.1 PC Slot (Top), Sometimes Known as the 8-Bit ISA Slot, and the 16-Bit ISA Slot (Bottom)

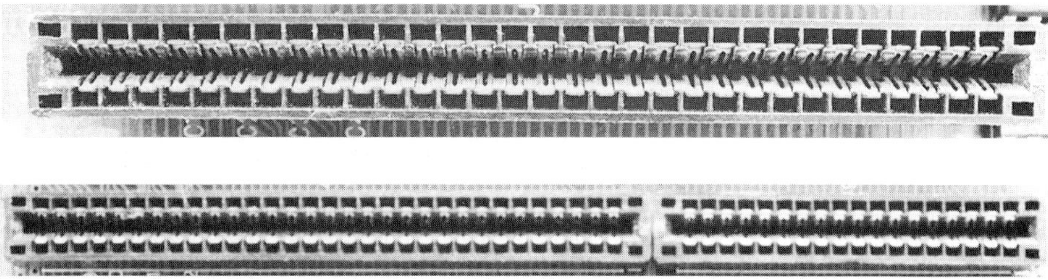

Figure 7.2 Expansion Card Used in the 8-Bit PC Slot

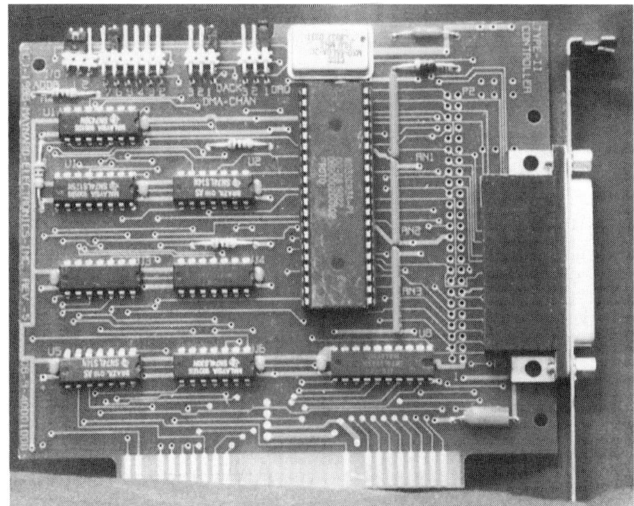

7.3.2 Industry Standard Architecture (ISA) Bus

In 1984, Intel released the 286 processor. The 286 used an external 16-bit data bus and a 24-bit address bus, which allowed the processor to see up to 16 MB of RAM. This gave IBM two choices. First, it could choose to develop a new motherboard from scratch to take advantage of the new technology. Unfortunately, this would have meant that the large base of 8-bit cards could not be used. The second choice was to somehow modify the older design to use both the 8-bit cards and the new 16-bit cards.

IBM's solution was the IBM AT. The AT motherboard still used the older 8-bit connector to accommodate the 8-bit cards. To accommodate 16-bit cards, the 8-bit slots were extended by adding a second 36-pin connector. The second connector contained the additional data and address lines. In addition, there were five more interrupt lines and four additional DMA channels. At this time, processors were getting faster. Therefore, IBM tried to increase the speed of the expansion bus to match the speed of the processor but quickly discovered that some expansion boards failed at 10 MHz and most of them failed at 12 MHz. Since the expansion cards did not use chips that could transition from high to low or low to high, the new 16-bit slot stayed at the 8.33 MHz speed. Even today, computers that run at 300 MHz or faster have ISA slots that still can run only at 8.33 MHz. Because of the difference in speed between the processor and the expansion bus, IBM had to use several oscillators in the AT. One oscillator was used to control the CPU speed and the other oscillator controlled the bus speed. By 1987, a committee of the Institute of Electrical and Electronic Engineers (IEEE) approved the AT bus as the **industry standard architecture (ISA).** Even though the ISA slot is considered old technology, even the most advanced motherboards contain some of them. Other names for it include the *classic bus,* the *AT bus,* or the *legacy bus.* See figure 7.3.

As has been discussed, the data bus carries data back and forth between the processor, RAM, and the input/output devices. The ISA slot has a total of 16 bits to match the data bus of the processor. Eight data bus lines are in the first connector and eight are in the second connector. Each 16-bit line is

Figure 7.3 ISA Card and Bus

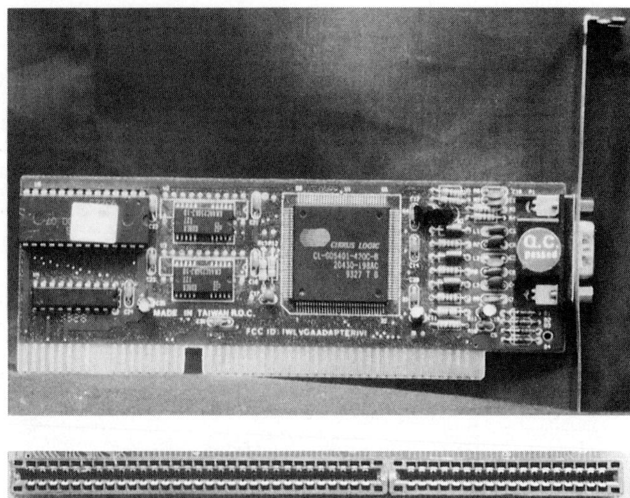

numbered from 0 to 15. The zero indicates the least significant bit in each data transfer. To specify the location where data is going to or coming from, the connector uses the address bus. The original connector has 20 address lines and the extension connector has an additional 4 address lines. The 24 total lines are identified with the numbers 0 through 23, again with line zero being the least significant.

Another signal, the Refresh signal, is used to indicate the RAM is being refreshed using the data and address buses. This will prevent interruptions so that the RAM doesn't lose its contents.

Finally, the ISA bus has 11 Interrupt Request lines out of a total of 16 interrupts that run through each expansion slot. Numbers 0, 1, 2, 8, and 13 are reserved for the motherboard. These lines are used by devices to signal the processor to stop what it is doing and to perform a different process with the device.

When a device needs to cause an interrupt, it will use edge-triggering, in which the device sends a signal that shifts the voltage on the interrupt request line from high to low or low to high. The high or low level of the signal is maintained throughout the processing of the interrupt. It is not whether the signal is on or off, but whether it has changed that triggers the interrupt-handling software or firmware. As a result, the software or firmware directs the processor to take action to service the device making the interrupt and to run the proper interrupt routine.

The ISA design allows **interrupt sharing** so that one interrupt can be used by several devices. Because the motherboard cannot recognize which slot contains the card that used an interrupt line to generate the interrupt, confusion would result if more than one card were set to use a particular interrupt because the system may lose track of the interrupt it is serving. Therefore, two devices sharing the same interrupt is typically possible only if the two devices are not being used at the same time. Thus, on the ISA bus each interrupt is usually designated for a single hardware device.

Because the processor is faster than the bus, it can easily generate or demand more data than the bus and devices can handle. Therefore, when the I/O Channel Ready line is shut off, that tells the processor to pause for one or more clock cycles. It will wait as long as the ready signal is not present. IBM specifications do not allow these delays to extend for longer than 10 clock cycles. In addition to this slow-down signal, there is a speed-up signal. The Zero Wait State signal indicates that the current bus cycle can be completed without wait states.

The ISA bus did not change significantly until 1993 when Intel and Microsoft introduced the **plug-and-play (PnP) ISA.** The PnP ISA bus allows a PnP ISA card to be inserted and its resources automatically assigned without any need to use jumpers or DIP switches to configure the card. (Note: ISA cards that are not plug-and-play are referred to as **legacy cards.**) A plug-and-play manager (software) identifies the card and assigns the resources it needs. This is possible because the PnP cards have a ROM chip that contains a number. The number identifies the type of card, not the model number, so several cards can be used within the same system, such as two network cards or two hard drive controllers. After the card is identified, the plug-and-play manager assigns the required I/O and memory addresses, IRQs, and DMAs to the card. The ISA slot, therefore, does not need to be changed physically.

7.3.3 PCI

When you hear the term *local bus* today, it probably refers to the **peripheral component interconnect (PCI) local bus.** The PCI slot was developed by Intel to eventually replace the older bus designs. Unlike the VESA, the PCI local bus is not an extension of any other slot; it is offset from the normal ISA, MCA, or EISA connector. In addition, the PCI design provides between three and five slots. See figures 7.4 and 7.5. Unlike the VESA bus, the PCI is not a true local bus. Instead, it occupies an intermediate level between the CPU local bus (processor/memory/cache subsystem) and the standard expansion bus (ISA), which is why it is sometimes called the *mezzanine* bus. The different versions of PCI are shown in table 7.5.

Figure 7.4 PCI Slot

Figure 7.5 PCI Video Card

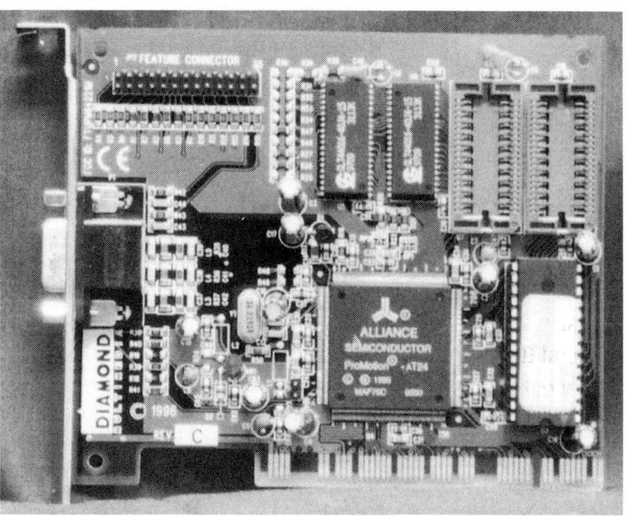

Table 7.5 PCI Standards

PCI Standard	Date	Specification
PCI 1.0	June 1992	• Developed by Intel • 33 MHz, 32-bit, 5 V • IRQ sharing to prevent all the IRQs from being used up • True bus mastering with effective bus arbitration to reduce latency • 0–5 connector availability, with expansion available through addition of a bridge chip
PCI 2.0	April 1993	• Confirmed by PCI Special Interest Group (PCI SIG) • Added connector and add-in card specification
PCI 2.1	June 1995	• Added expandability from 32- to 64-bit and 33 to 66 MHz. • Introduced variable voltage capability, in order to accommodate the expected migration from 5 to 3.3 V systems
PCI 2.2	December 1998	• Added PCI Power Management (PCI-PM) and Hot Plug features • Incorporated riser and lower profile specifications
PCI 2.3	March 2002	• Supports only the 3.3 V and Universal keyed add-in cards
PCI 3.0	August 2002	• Removed support for 5 V keyed system board connectors

Figure 7.6 Type of PCI Cards

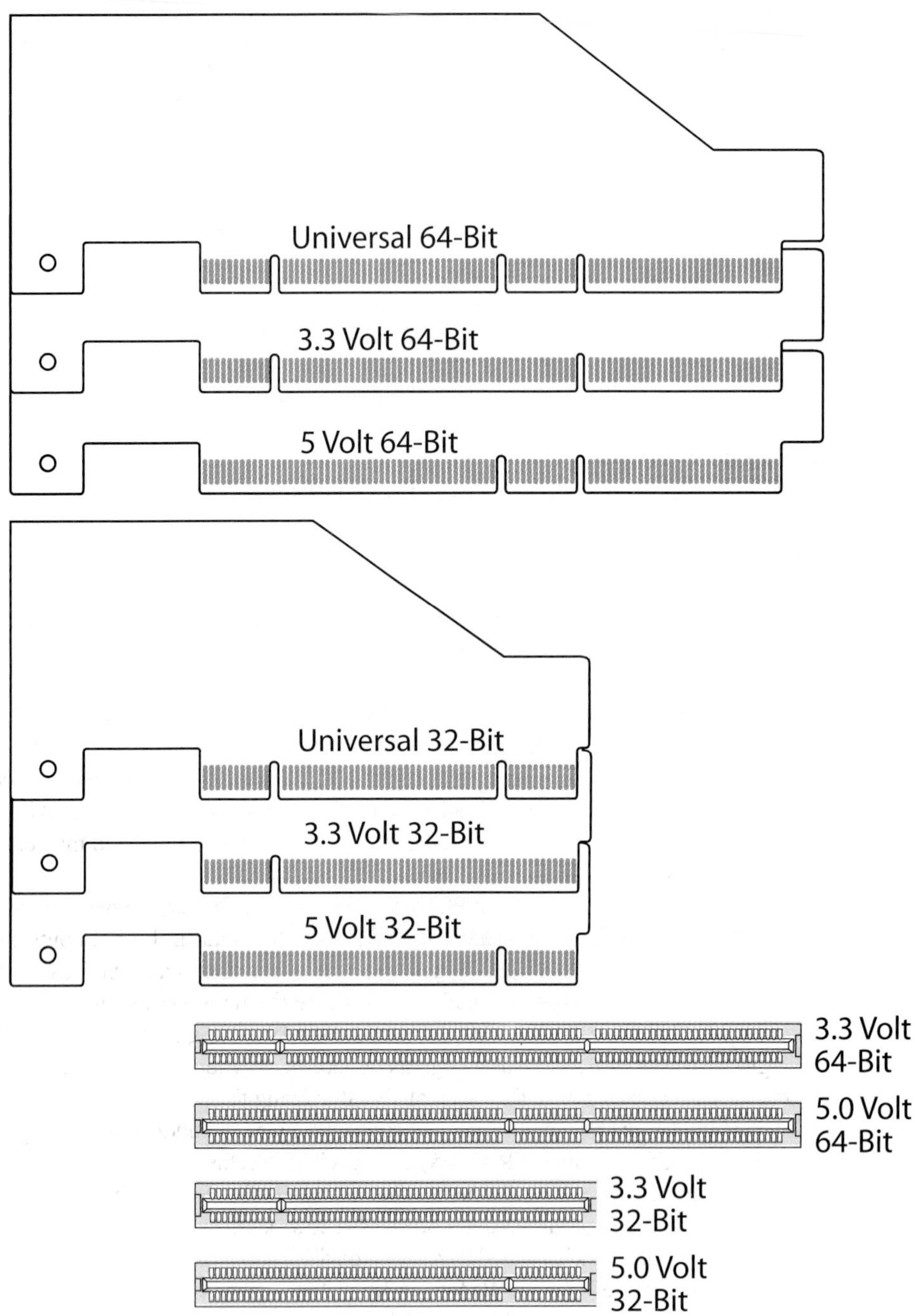

While the PCI interface matured, it eventually transitioned from 5 V to 3.3 V. The transition was accomplished with three add-in board types:

- 5 V expansion card that would operate exclusively in a 5 V signaling environment
- 3.3 V boards that would operate exclusively in a 3.3 V signaling environment
- The universal board that would operate in either the 3.3 or 5 V signaling environment.

PCI 2.1 and 2.2 both define six add-in card configurations, with support for 5.0, 3.3, and Universal (3.3/5 V) signaling in both 32- and 64-bit variants. Each card type is designed with notches, and each connector type is designed with ridges, so that cards can be inserted with compatible connectors only. See figure 7.6.

After 10 years, the traditional 32-bit PCI connector is just now starting to be replaced with 64-bit connectors, especially on servers and high-end systems. A 32-bit card will fit into a 64-bit connector and work properly. In addition, a 64-bit connector will fit into a 32-bit connector, and configure itself for 32-bit transfers. In this case, a portion of the 64-bit card simply hands off the end of the 32-bit connector.

Although the PCI bus is an excellent bus with strong features, a saturated PCI bus (one with many high-speed devices on it) can cause a bottleneck to occur on the PCI bus. This is common on high-end server systems using high-speed network cards and hardware RAID adapters, especially when more than one of these adapter types is installed. To alleviate this bottleneck, some systems use a "bridged" or "dual-peer" PCI design, where two separate PCI buses exist and are connected either to each other (bridged) or to the system bus (dual-peer).

Electrical limitations keep the number of slots that a PCI bus can support to four or fewer. To increase the number of PCI adapter slots, system designers are adding PCI bridges, circuits that connect distinct buses. Using a bridge, a second PCI bus can be added to the system. Although it creates the ability to have additional PCI slots, it isn't as good as the previously discussed dual-peer arrangement because it doesn't really provide a separate bus. This ends up being slower because all of the devices are sharing the bandwidth of the existing PCI bus (i.e., 132 MBps for a 33 MHz 32-bit PCI bus) and so must contend for the limited bandwidth. This arrangement also increases PCI bus latency because more devices are competing for the same PCI bus.

With dual-peer PCI, the two buses run concurrently, each providing the full 132 MBps of bus bandwidth (assumes 32-bit 33 MHz, the typical configuration for most PCI buses). This can have the combined benefit of increasing the number of available PCI slots to eight (as with bridged PCI) and also increasing the maximum theoretical aggregate throughput for PCI devices to 264 MBps (2 × 132 MBps). However, a more real-world performance figure for these designs is closer to around 200 MBps. This arrangement also reduces PCI bus latency because the total load is shared between two separate PCI buses.

If your system has dual-peer PCI buses, it is a good idea to place the video adapter on a different PCI bus than the disk and network controllers because these are typically the three most highly taxed adapters on an NT system. Also, this creates a better balance across the PCI buses because the nature of the data transfers used by these devices is also different: Disk and network controllers tend to use long data bursts, while the video adapter tends to perform short bursts. Also, some video adapter chipsets are not fully compatible with the peer PCI bus arrangement and may cause problems if shared with these other devices on the same bus.

The PCI bus is controlled by a PCI bridge/controller. To increase performance, the microprocessor writes data to a PCI device by immediately storing the data in the bus controller's buffer. While the processor goes on to its next operation, the stored data is then fed to the PCI device. Since the bus was made to run at incredible speeds, Intel chose reflected signaling rather than direct signaling for the PCI. Therefore, a card that would run at 5 V dc under the ISA design would send a 2.5 V signal instead of a 5 V signal in the PCI design. These signals bounce back when they get to the end of a wire, and the reflected signal combines with the original signal to bring the value up to 5 V.

To reduce the number of pins needed for the PCI slot, the address bus and the data bus use the same pins. When the Cycle Frame (FRAME#) signal is inactive, the address/data pins carry the address. When the address is valid, the Cycle Frame becomes active, indicating that the address/data pins will be carrying data. The PCI bus's built-in burst mode will keep sending data as long as the Cycle Frame is active and until the address/data bus is needed by another device, such as RAM refresh. Consequently, while in burst mode, the transfer rate is 132 MB/s for the 32-bit PCI design and 264 MB/s for the 64-bit PCI design.

Like the other newer slot designs, PCI supports bus mastering. The DMA controller and each device gets its own dedicated Request and Grant lines. When a device needs to use the data/address bus, it sends a signal to the central resource (the PCI bus-mastering arbitrator), which grants the device permission. Several flow control signals ensure that the PCI bus speed does not exceed the speed of the expansion card. A Target Ready (TRDY#) signal indicates that the device is ready to read or write data. An Initiator Ready (IRDY#) signal indicates information will be sent over the address/data bus. When the device has completed its data transfer, a Stop (STOP#) signal is sent.

Unlike most of the other bus designs, the PCI specification uses parity checking to ensure the integrity of the data being sent. For 32-bit transfers, it uses a single parity bit (PAR) signal; for 64-bit transfers it uses two parity bits. If a parity error is detected, it will then send a Parity Error signal (PERR#), which prompts other actions, depending on the system.

PCI supports interrupts and interrupt sharing. PCI also supports plug-and-play technology. Unlike other expansion bus designs, PCI expansion cards store their own configuration information. Therefore, most are not configured using jumpers or DIP switches but by software or a true plug-and-play system.

PCI uses level-sensitive interrupts. A level-sensitive interrupt signals the interrupt condition by shifting the voltage on the interrupt request line, for example, from low to high. It then maintains that shifted condition throughout the processing of the interrupt. It effectively ties up the interrupt line during the processing of the interrupt so no other device can get attention through that interrupt line. Although it would seem that one device would hog the interrupt line and not share with anything, the presence of the signal on the line effectively warns other devices to wait before sending out their own interrupt requests. Interrupts are less likely to be confused.

The PCI bus does not use the old AT-compatible interrupt controller; instead it integrates its own control circuitry in its host bridge in the PCI chipset. The PCI system uses four interrupt lines (INTA#, INTB#, INTC#, and INTD#). In fact, all single devices or single-function PCI chips or cards only use one interrupt, INTA#. If there are additional devices within a chip or on board a card, the additional devices can use INTB# through INTD#. Because there are very few multifunction PCI chips or boards, this means that practically all the devices on a given PCI bus will be sharing INTA#. In order for the PCI bus to function in a PC, the PCI interrupt must be mapped to ISA interrupts.

To find a unique IRQ for each device on both the ISA and PCI buses has always been a problem because there aren't enough free ones to go around. But because the PCI uses level-sensitive signaling combined with using newer system BIOS and plug-and-play operating systems, such as Windows 95B (OSR 2) or later, Windows 98, Windows Me, Windows 2000, and Windows XP, interrupt sharing is possible because of PCI IRQ Steering.

Normally, the BIOS assigns unique IRQs to PCI devices. If your system supports PCI IRQ Steering and it is enabled, the BIOS will assign the IRQs to the PCI devices and Windows will typically change only the IRQ settings if it detects a conflict. If there are free IRQs to go around, IRQ Steering allows Windows to assign multiple PCI devices to a single IRQ, thus enabling all the devices in the system to function properly. Without IRQ Steering, Windows will begin to disable devices once it runs out of free IRQs to assign.

In Windows 95 (OSR2), Windows 98, and Windows Me, to determine if your system is using IRQ Steering, you can access the Windows' Device Manager, double-click the PCI Bus, click the IRQ Steering tab, and look at the check box for IRQ Steering. See figure 7.7.

Figure 7.7 IRQ Steering Configuration for the PCI Bus

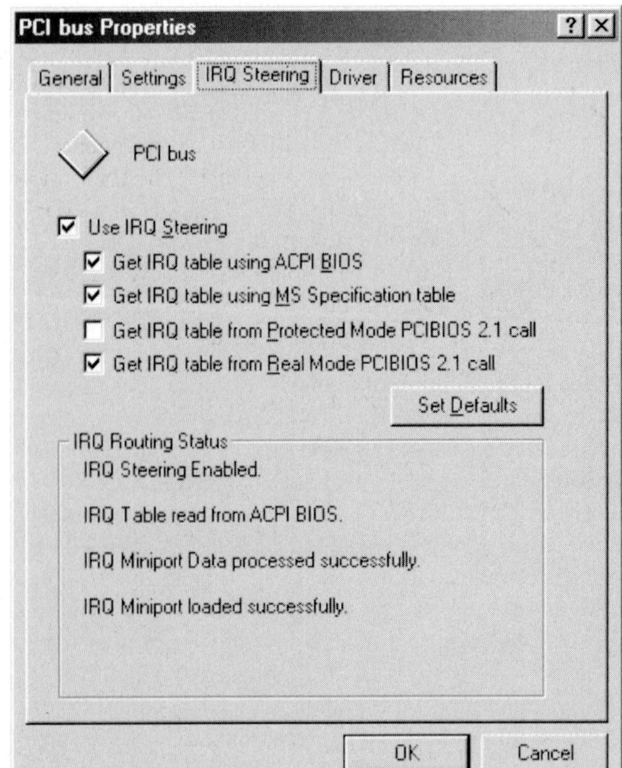

In Windows 2000 and Windows XP, some or all of the devices on your ACPI motherboard may be listed on the Resources tab in Device Manager as using the same IRQ (IRQ 9). You cannot change the IRQ setting because the setting is unavailable. This occurs because Windows takes advantage of the ACPI features of the motherboard, including advanced PCI sharing. IRQ 9 is used by the PCI bus for IRQ steering. This feature lets you add more devices without generating IRQ conflicts.

The plug-and-play operating system settings in the computer's BIOS should not affect how Windows 2000 and Windows XP handle the hardware in general. However, Microsoft recommends that you set this setting to No or Disabled in the computer's BIOS. In addition, manually assigning IRQs to PCI slots in the system BIOS as a troubleshooting method may work on some non-ACPI systems when using a standard PC HAL, but these settings are ignored by plug-and-play in Windows if ACPI support is enabled. If you need to manually assign IRQ addresses through the BIOS to a device on an ACPI motherboard, you will have to disable ACPI support by installing the standard PC HAL, which usually means you will have to reinstall the operating system.

The PCI specification identifies three board configurations. The 5 V specification is for stationary computer systems, the 3.3 V specification is for portable machines, and the universal specification is for motherboards and cards that work in either type of system. For pins for which the voltage is different, the universal specification labels the pin simply V I/P. This type of pin represents a special power pin for defining and driving the PCI signaling rail.

7.3.4 PCI-X

In 1998, Compaq, Hewlett-Packard, and IBM announced their intention to expand on the PCI design to increase I/O bandwidth. The bandwidth can be used in industry standard servers running enterprise applications, such as Gigabit Ethernet, Fibre Channel, Ultra3 SCSI, and Cluster Interconnects.

The PCI-X specification defines two frequency design points for PCI-X adapters: PCI-X 66 MHz and PCI-X 133 MHz. When operating in PCI-X mode, PCI-X 66 MHz adapters have actual clock frequencies ranging from 50 to 66 MHz, and PCI-X 133 MHz adapters have clock frequencies ranging from 50 to 133 MHz. To support more adapter slots on the PCI-X bus, system designers can lower the bus frequency to a minimum of 50 MHz. For example, a PCI-X bus segment with two expansion slots would typically operate at 100 MHz rather than at the full 133 MHz. A PCI-X bus segment with four expansion slots would typically operate at 66 MHz. Like conventional PCI adapters, PCI-X adapters can implement a 64-bit interface or a 32-bit interface. A 64-bit adapter running at 133 MHz gives a bandwidth of 1066 MB/s.

A PCI-X adapter can operate in a conventional PCI system, and vice versa. If the adapter and system both support PCI-X, the new PCI-X adapter can immediately take advantage of the higher operating frequencies of a PCI-X system. When the PCI-X adapter is put in a conventional 33 MHz PCI system, the adapter will function at 33 MHz. If a conventional PCI device is installed on a PCI-X bus, the bus clock remains at a frequency acceptable to the conventional adapter, and the other adapters on that bus segment will run at the same speed. PCI-X systems don't require OS or device-driver updates to work, but you'll need new device drivers if you want to take advantage of the new PCI-X features.

If a PCI-X bus segment includes only PCI-X devices, the bus operates in PCI-X mode. A PCI-X system automatically adjusts the bus frequency to match the frequency of the slowest adapter on that bus segment. For example, if the bus includes a 66 MHz PCI-X adapter, the maximum clock frequency of the bus segment is 66 MHz. PCI-X supports up to 256 bus segments, and each segment is initialized separately so that different operating frequencies can be used.

In addition to the faster bus speed, design improvements (e.g., eliminating wasted clock cycles that PCI uses as wait states, supporting split transactions that eliminate polling across the bus, transferring predetermined transaction byte counts) permit PCI-X devices to perform up to 10 times as fast as 32-bit 33 MHz PCI devices. Realtime audio and video applications benefit from relaxed ordering, which lets PCI bridges handle transactions from multiple PCI-X devices in the most efficient order rather than the first in/first out (FIFO) order that earlier PCI protocols enforce. Non-cache-coherent transaction support lets the PCI device driver tell the system cache controllers not to snoop the processors, thus reducing processor-bus utilization and increasing system efficiency.

PCI cards and slots are keyed by voltage (i.e., 5 or 3.3 V). Although universal PCI cards are notched for both 5 and 3.3 V, PCI slot connectors can be keyed for only one voltage. PCI 2.1 and 2.0 specifications permitted both 5 and 3.3 V signaling; PCI 2.2 favored 3.3 V signaling but also supported 5 V signaling. (PCI 2.2 cards can be 5 V, 3.3 V, or universal; vendors have designed most PCI 2.2 cards as universal cards.) When PCI cards and slots use 5 V signaling, they operate at a maximum speed of 33 MHz; only 3.3 V PCI slots can support higher bandwidths. Therefore, all PCI-X slots are 3.3 V slots. PCI-X slots work with universal PCI cards and 3.3 V cards but don't work with 5 V only cards. Universal PCI-X cards operate at 33 MHz in a 5 V slot, at speeds as fast as 66 MHz in a 3.3 V PCI 2.2 slot, and at speeds as fast as 133 MHz in a 3.3 V PCI-X slot. As when you mix SCSI devices of different speeds, mixing PCI and PCI-X cards on the same bus causes the speed of the PCI-X bus and all other cards on the bus to operate at the slowest card's speed.

7.3.5 Accelerated Graphics Port (AGP)

The **accelerated graphics port (AGP)** is a spinoff of the PCI slot (based on the PCI 2.1 specification). It is called a *port,* not a bus, because a bus can support multiple devices and the AGP cannot—it is made exclusively for video cards. It is similar to the PCI slot in shape and size but is offset further from the edge of the motherboard than PCI slots are. See figures 7.8 and 7.9.

Current PCI cards are still able to run up to 66 MHz; the AGP uses a 32-bit path running at 66 MHz (with the capability of increasing to 100 MHz). It can handle 266 MB/s, and this flow can be doubled by sending information on both the rising and falling edges of the clock signal. A 4X mode performs four transfers per clock cycle, allowing a bandwidth of 1.07 GB/s and an 8X mode performs eight transfers per clock cycle, allowing a bandwidth of 2 GB/s. By comparison, the Pentium microprocessor, which uses a 64-bit bus running at 66 MHz, supports only 533 MB/s, and a 64-bit bus running at 100 MHz supports only 807 MB/s. Because the video card is removed from the PCI bus, in addition to the faster speed for the video system, other PCI devices also benefit from the improved bandwidth. To increase performance still further, the AGP uses video pipelining. Video pipelining

Figure 7.8 AGP Port Next to a PCI Slot

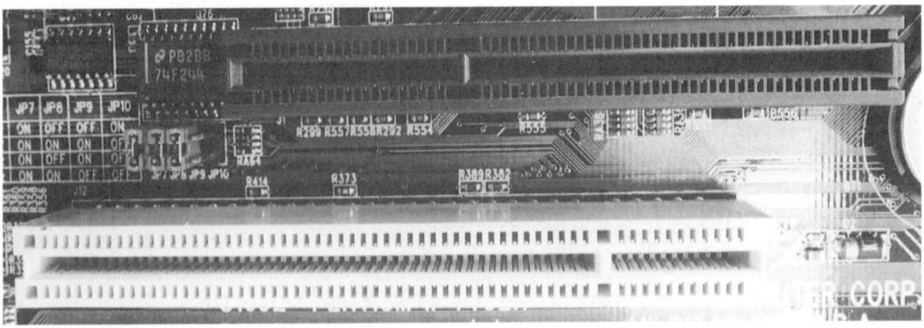

Figure 7.9 AGP cards are keyed based on their speed and voltage.

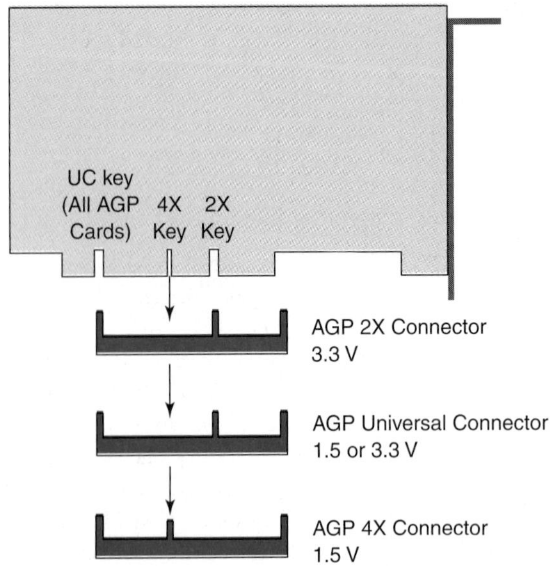

means that while the video card works on one task, it will start on a second task. Therefore, pipelining allows sequential parts of tasks to overlap.

AGP has the ability to allow the video chipset to share the system RAM, allowing the video system access to larger amounts of RAM for 3D and other processing without requiring large amounts of special video memory. For example, textures, which can be as large as 128 KB, previously had to be loaded into the video card's RAM and processed by the graphic processor. With AGP, textures can be loaded into the main memory without impacting performance. Since the main memory is faster than the memory being accessed on a video card through the PCI slot, the processing of graphical data is faster. Note: The main memory provided by the AGP doesn't replace the screen buffer of the graphic accelerator; it is additional memory specifically used for processing.

7.3.6 PCI Express

PCI Express, formerly called third-generation I/O (3GIO), is both a hardware interface and a transmission protocol. Like other emerging PC technologies, the PCI Express architecture does not use a wide parallel bus that requires complex and expensive electrical paths. Instead, it uses an individually clocked lane, each consisting of two pairs of data lines to carry data upstream and downstream.

Because these lanes are serial in design, they can scale to higher speeds with fewer wires. As the technology goes to market, each of these lanes should be capable of a 2.5 Gb/s data rate in each direction, with speeds expected to increase with advances in silicon technology up to possibly around 10Gb/s in each direction. Although PCI-X 2.0 adds bandwidth by increasing the clock speed to double data rate (DDR) or quad data rate (QDR), system designers increase the bandwidth of a PCI Express slot by adding lanes. Desktop expansion slots are expected to range from 1X to 4X; servers will likely range from 4X to 8X; and graphic cards will run off 16X slots and provide at least 4GB/s in each direction, allowing double the bandwidth offered by AGP 8X. As the PCI Express standard matures, you can expect even greater bandwidth with increased speed and possibly a 32X slot.

PCI Express connectors are similar in appearance and connection method as current 32-bit PCI slots. PCI Express 1X slots will be about the size of current modem riser slots (about 1 in. long), whereas the X16 interface (164 pins) for graphics will be very similar in appearance to the standard AGP port. PCI Express is fully hot-pluggable.

Currently PCI Express X16 is being designed to provide up to 75 W of power for video cards, as opposed to the current 25–42 W allowed by AGP 8X. Most modern cards already consume more than this amount, as evidenced by the extra power connectors that appear on today's high-end video cards.

The PCI Express bus will be completely software compatible with PCI 2.2–compliant devices. Intel has already stated that all current operating systems will support PCI 2.2–compatible interface cards in the new PCI Express system using the existing PCI drivers.

7.3.7 PC Card

Users buy laptop and notebook computers because they are small and portable. Unfortunately, their size does not permit use of any of the traditional expansion cards (ISA, MCA, EISA, and local bus). Therefore, a new type of expansion slot had to be created specifically for portable systems.

The Personal Computer Memory Card International Association (PCMCIA) established several standards for a laptop expansion system that was later developed and implemented by over 300 manufacturers, including IBM, Toshiba, and Apple. Consequently, there are four types of **PC cards** (formerly known as **PCMCIA cards**): Type I, II, III, and IV. See figure 7.10. All PC cards are about the size of a credit card (3.4 × 2.1 in.) and use a 68-pin (two rows) connector and a 16-bit data bus. The Type I cards, which are 3.3 mm thick, are memory expansion cards. Unlike a SIMM or DIMM, which expand a system's RAM, the Type I card acts more like a RAM drive. Type II cards, which are 5 mm thick, are the most common and are the standard expansion card. They are the cards used for modems, fax/modems, SCSI, networks, and sound. See figure 7.11. Some cards include two functions in one package (fax/modem and network or sound and SCSI). Because the Type I and Type II cards have the same type of connector, the Type II slot can accommodate Type I cards. The Type III and Type IV cards are small hard drives. Type III cards are up to 10.5 mm thick; Type IV cards are thicker than 10.5 mm. Most machines will accommodate two Type II cards or one Type III card. Because the Type III cards are much larger than the Type II cards, one Type III card takes up the space of two Type II cards. Type III slots can accommodate Type I and Type II cards, and Type IV slots can accommodate Type I, II, and III cards. (Note: The Type IV cards are not described in the PC card specification.)

Figure 7.10 PCMCIA/PC Card

Figure 7.11 Inside a Fax/Modem PC (PCMCIA) Card

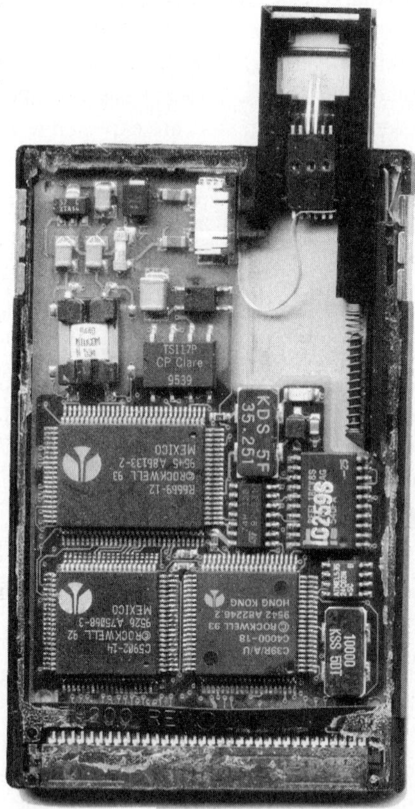

PC cards have power-saving capabilities to increase battery life. The cards operate at 3.3 V and support APM (advanced power management). The PC cards are **hot-swappable,** which means they can be inserted and removed while the power is on. Hot-swappable technology is possible because the pins used to connect the PC card vary in length. The power and ground connectors are longer and the two activation pins are shorter, ensuring that the power is connected before anything else is.

The original PC cards were 16-bit, and there soon was a need to create a 32-bit version, which would operate at a faster speed. By 1995, the **CardBus** had been introduced with speeds up to 33 MHz (133 MB/s). To make it backward compatible with the 16-bit PC cards, the address pins and data pins were multiplexed. To increase MPEG (Motion Picture Experts Group) and video performance, the CardBus uses **zoomed video (ZV),** which is a direct connection to the system's VGA controller. The zoomed video is used for videoconferencing applications and MPEG decoders.

With the release of PCI Express, the PCMCIA group created the **ExpressCard,** which is meant to bridge the gap between current notebook designs and future PCI Express–enabled cards. The interface and form factor are similar in appearance to the current PC card form factor and supports both USB 2.0 and PCI Express. The PCI ExpressCard will support the same 200 MB/s point-to-point connections, which could be extended over cable outside the box to a distance of approximately 5 meters (m). Unfortunately, it is not designed to handle graphics, so the possibilities of video upgrades on a laptop are still virtually nonexistent. ExpressCard/34 modules and ExpressCard/54 modules both use the same connector interface. The card connector has just 26 pins.

The ExpressCard comes in two sizes, both of which are smaller than today's CardBus cards. The smallest card, the ExpressCard/34 module, which is 34 mm across, is almost half the size of a CardBus card. The standard also specifies a wider card called an ExpressCard/54 module, which is 54 mm across. This is to support those technologies that require a physically larger module such as smartcard readers, CompactFlash adapters, and 1.8-in. hard drives. Both module formats are 5 mm thick, the same as the Type II PC card. The standard module length is 75 mm, which is 10.6 mm shorter than a standard PC card.

To enable the PC card and to allow it to be recognized by the operating system, two programs need to be loaded. The first one is a socket services program that activates the PC socket itself. The program can be implemented within a ROM BIOS chip, a device driver, a TSR, or a service running on an operating system (such as Windows 95 or 98). The second program is card services. Card services are responsible for assigning the appropriate hardware resources to the PC cards by means of a configuration file/software driver, by typing a command at the prompt, or by using plug-and-play.

7.3.8 Mini-PCI Cards

Mobile systems have different requirements for expansion capability than those of desktops. Although mobile systems have the electrical equivalent of a desktop PCI bus, desktop PCI cards are too large and require too much power to be used on a portable computer. Therefore, the Mini-PCI card was developed.

There are three types of Mini-PCI cards. All three have different form factors and all are intended to be installed by manufacturers or service technicians rather than users. These different form factors allow portable computer makers considerable design flexibility. See table 7.6.

Type I cards use a cable to connect to the phone (RJ-11) or network (RJ-45) connectors located at the edge of the portable computer chassis or docking station. This approach allows designers to place the card away from the edge of the chassis. In contrast, Type II cards include built-in RJ-11 and/or RJ-45 I/O connectors. These cards must be located at the edge of the computer or docking station so that the RJ-11 and RJ-45 ports can be mounted for external access. Both Type I and Type II cards connect to the system board via a miniature 100-pin stacking connector with a 4 mm minimum stacking height.

Table 7.6 Summary of Mini-PCI Card Types

Mini-PCI Card Types	Size in mm (width × length × depth)	I/O Connection	System Connector
Type IA Type IB	45 × 70 × 7.5 45 × 70 × 5.5	Link via cable to external I/O connectors	100-pin stacking connector with a 4 mm minimum stacking height
Type IIA Type IIB	45 × 78 × 14.5 Same as Type IIA*	Built-in I/O connectors	Same as Type I
Type IIIA Type IIIB	50.8 × 59.6 × 4.9 44.45 × 59.6 × 4.9	Link via cable to external I/O connectors or route I/O through card-edge connector	124-pin card-edge connector; 3 mm in height

*Types IIA and IIB have the same dimensions, but each has a different cavity space to accommodate RJ-11 and/or RJ-45 jacks that are recessed into the system board.

Figure 7.12 Mini-PCI Card

Instead of the stacking connector used on Type I and Type II cards, Type III cards have a card-edge connector similar to that used by small-outline dual in-line memory modules (SO-DIMMs). See figure 7.12. Type III cards can use a cable to connect to I/O connectors at the edge of the chassis (like Type II cards) or they can route the I/O through the card-edge connector, in which case the signals are routed through the system board to the I/O jacks.

The Type III card-edge connector has 124 pins and is 3 mm in height. The additional 24 pins provide the extra signals required to route I/O back through the system connector. Type III cards have a lower profile than Types I and II, allowing portable computer makers to design a smaller chassis. As a result, Type III cards are expected to be the most commonly implemented.

The system connectors for all three Mini-PCI card types provide electrical signals that form a PCI bus identical to that formed by desktop PCI cards. Additional sideband signals accommodate communications signals such as audio and AC97 AC-Link. The audio signals allow a modem to be connected to the sound system of the computer. The AC-Link signals allow the modem to be implemented as either an AC97 Host Signal Processing (HSP) modem or as a modem on the PCI bus. The I/O connections such as modem "tip and ring" (transmit and receive wires) and local area network (LAN) I/O are routed to the RJ-11 or RJ-45 connectors depending on the Mini-PCI card type. In addition to these sideband signals, an area is defined to allow for connecting cellular and integrated services digital network (ISDN) modems. Although the Mini-PCI specification initially addresses only modem and network communications, it is designed to be extensible to accommodate new portable computer capabilities.

7.3.9 Universal Serial Bus (USB)

The universal serial bus (USB) is an external port allowing connection of external PC peripherals in series. The USB connector will accept any USB peripheral, including mice, keyboards, printers, modems, and external disk drives. Seven devices can be connected directly using the standard 4-pin connector. These seven devices can then be connected to a total of 127 other devices by connecting external hubs

Figure 7.13 (A) USB Type A Ports; (B) USB Type B Port; (C) USB Type A and B Connectors

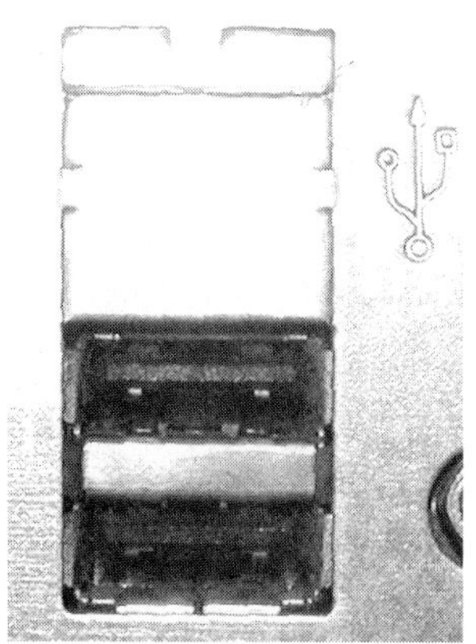

(each hub accommodates another seven devices) in a chain (hence, the term *daisy chain* for this type of serial connection). See figure 7.13. One of the biggest advantages of the USB interface is that it requires only a single interrupt from the PC for all 127 devices. Note: Although USB can support up to 127 devices, it is usually limited by bus speed and power limitations.

NOTE: If you have do not have enough USB ports for all of your USB devices, you can buy either a hub to increase the number of ports, install another expansion card with USB ports, or obtain a USB-to-PS/2 adapter to connect a USB mouse or keyboard to the PS/2 ports.

A USB port or hub can provide power to the attached peripherals. A hub recognizes the dynamic attachment of a peripheral and provides at least 0.5 W per peripheral during initialization. Under control of the host PC driver software, the hub may provide more device power, up to a maximum of 2.5 W, for peripheral operations. Typically, if you have a device providing more than 0.5 W, the device must have an external power source, such as an ac adapter.

When you attach a universal serial bus (USB) device on a Windows system that supports USB, you may receive a "USB Hub Power Exceeded" error message containing the following text:

> The hub does not have enough power available to operate the device driver name. Would you like assistance in solving this problem? If you click No, the device may not function properly.

When this happens, the USB device mentioned in the error message does not work properly and the device listing (in the system properties of the Device Manager properties window for the device) appears with the following error message:

> A USB device has requested more power than the hub can provide. Windows cannot enable the device. Remove the device and restart your computer.

To resolve this issue, replace the passive USB hub with an active (powered) hub, disconnect the affected device from the passive hub and connect it directly to the USB host controller's hub (in the back of the computer), or attach an AC adapter if one is available.

USB 1.1 offers a data transfer rate of up to 12 Mbit/s. For low-speed peripherals such as pointing devices and keyboards, the USB also has a slower 1.5 Mbit/s subchannel. Maximum cable length between two full-speed (12 Mbit/s) devices or a device and a hub is 5 m using twisted-pair shielded cable with 20-gauge wire. Maximum cable length for low-speed (1.5 Mbit/s) devices using non-twisted-pair wire is 3 m. These distance limits are shorter if smaller gauge wire is used.

Two different connectors are specified for USB, called Series A and Series B. The Series A connector is designed for devices where the cable remains permanently attached, such as hubs, keyboards, and mice. The USB ports on most motherboards are also normally Series A connectors. Series B connectors are designed for devices that require detachable cables, such as printers, scanners, modems, telephones, and speakers. The physical USB plugs are smaller than the Series A connector.

Although USB was supported in many PCs many years ago, it has only recently started to gain widespread acceptance. All new PCs are now equipped with USB support, and USB ports can also be added to many older systems as well. USB is already supported by specific chipsets of Pentium and Pentium Pro processor–equipped host PCs. The original release of Windows 95 and Windows NT does not support USB. Windows 95 OSR-2 will require that you add or install the USB drivers, whereas Windows 95C, Windows 98, Windows Me, Windows 2000, and Windows XP include the USB drivers. With the proper chipset and drivers, a USB device will work without rebooting or reconfiguring every time a peripheral is added or removed. USB devices can also be hot-swapped.

A new version of USB, USB 2.0, is similar to USB 1.1 except it runs up to 480 Mbit/s, yet it remains backward compatible. It uses the same cables, connectors, and software interfaces. The support of higher speed USB 2.0 peripherals requires a USB 2.0 hub. You can still use older USB 1.1 hubs on a 2.0 bus, but any peripherals or additional hubs connected downstream from a 1.1 hub will operate at the slower 1.5 MB/s.

However, to take advantage of the USB 2.0 hardware, users must also upgrade their current USB 1.1 systems with USB 2.0—compliant PCI cards or purchase motherboards with built-in USB 2.0 support. On the software side, operating systems with full USB 2.0 support will continue to work with USB 1.1 peripherals but will also able to recognize USB 2.0 hardware. The system software will be able to optimize the performance on a mixed environment where USB 1.1 and USB 2.0 hardware is connected concurrently to a USB 2.0 bus. If the system detects a USB 2.0 peripheral attached to a USB 1.1 system, then it will notify the user of the detection of a suboptimal configuration and recommend a better configuration for attaching the device.

7.3.10 IEEE 1394

Another external bus standard is **IEEE 1394,** sometimes called **FireWire.** IEEE 1394 supports data transfer rates of up to 400 Mbit/s. A single 1394 port can connect up to six external devices. It can deliver data at a guaranteed rate, which makes it ideal for devices that need to transfer large amounts of data in real-time, such as video cameras and other video devices. Like USB, 1394 supports plug-and-play and hot-swapping and provides power to IEEE 1394 port using a tree topology (physical layout), whereby any device can be connected to any other device as long as there are no loops. The IEEE 1394 port B shown in figure 7.14.

IEEE 1394 is defined part of the SCSI-3 family of related standards and was at one point sometimes called *serial SCSI.* It is, in fact, a type of SCSI, based on the broad converage of SCSI-3, which goes beyond regular SCSI to cover several similar SCSI-like technologies. In terms of signaling and some aspects of operation, IEEE 1394 really can be thought of as serial SCSI. Yet IEEE 1394 is better thought of as USB.

In reality, though, IEEE 1394 still has not taken off as a storage interface within the PC. There could be any number of reasons for this, but as of 2000, IEEE 1394 is not a major player in the storage industry. Some systems are now equipped with this interface, and a variety of storage devices are made

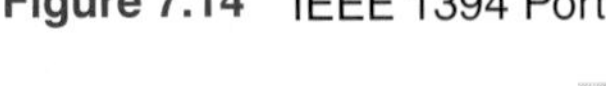
Figure 7.14 IEEE 1394 Port

for it, so it is a viable option if your system supports it or if you wish to add support for it. IEEE 1394 does continue to grow in popularity in a variety of specialty markets, especially digital video, where it has established quite a following. It may well become the next big interfacing standard for consumer electronics devices like camcorders and VCRs.

7.3.11 AMRs and CNRs

Audio/Modem Riser (AMR) is a specification developed by Intel for packaging the analog I/O audio functions of modem circuitry together with a codec chip (which converts back and forth from analog to digital) on a small board that plugs directly into a computer's motherboard. The small board is called a riser because it rises above the motherboard rather than lying flatly on it.

Since the circuitry is on the riser, it doesn't have to be part of the motherboard. Because getting certifications for the manufacture of a new motherboard design is a lengthy process, removing this function from the motherboard provides more flexibility for manufacturers and allows advances in audio modem design to be implemented more easily. Another specification, MDC (Mobile Daughter Card) is the equivalent of AMR but for use in mobile computers.

Since the AMR provides a connection to the motherboard, other circuitry can be connected to the AMR slot. For example, the AMR card can also provide the foundation for higher-quality audio solutions such as 3D positional audio and better MIDI music production.

Communication and Networking Riser (CNR), which was developed by Intel, is an open industry standard for a scalable riser card, which is a hardware device that plugs into a motherboard and holds chips for functions like modems and audio devices. The CNR architecture, and electrical, mechanical, and thermal requirements of the riser interface are defined in the specification. See figure 7.15.

The specification was developed for products used to implement low-cost local area network (LAN), modem, and audio subsystems, and it supports broadband, multichannel audio, V.90 analog modem, Home PNA, and Ethernet-based networking; it can be expanded upon to meet the requirements of developing technologies, such as DSL. In addition to cost benefits, CNR has the capacity to minimize electrical noise interference through physical separation of noise-sensitive elements from the motherboard's own communication systems.

For more information about CRN, see the following website:

http://www.intel.com/technology/cnr

Figure 7.15 A CNR Adapter and Slot

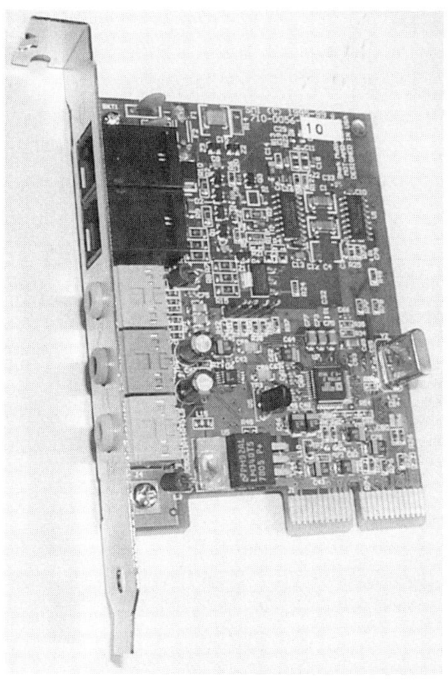

7.4 EXPANSION CARDS

When an expansion card is inserted into a system, it must be configured to use the proper resources. The resources include I/O addresses (including COMX/LTPX), IRQs, DMAs, and memory addresses. One general rule applies when configuring a card: No two devices can use the same resource. Therefore, two expansion cards should not be set to use the same DMA channel or the same I/O address. If two devices are using the same setting, they will not work properly or will not work at all. The available resources can be determined by using diagnostic software, such as QA Plus or Checkit Pro, or utilities that come with the operating system, such as Microsoft Software Diagnostic (MSD) or the Windows System icon located within the control panel. The card itself can be configured in one of several ways:

1. With DIP switches and/or jumpers
2. With a software setup program
3. Using plug-and-play (PnP)

Determining which resources the card can use and how to select them most likely will require the expansion board documentation. Most documentation is included in a manual; some will be silk-screened on the card itself or placed within a file on a disk. Without the documentation, a lot of trial and error is usually required to figure out the correct settings. (Note: Many expansion cards require software drivers to function. Windows drivers are typically loaded by running the Add New Hardware Driver icon or by using the installation disks that come with the expansion card.)

If you, your customers, or your clients lose the documentation or drivers, you can look for information on the Internet, contact the manufacturer of the device, or consult the Microhouse Technical Library/On-line Service. Many companies post their documentation on the Internet for quick-and-easy access. Microhouse Incorporated publishes a technical library (book/CD-ROM) and has an online service for motherboard, expansion card, and hard drive documentation.

7.4.1 DIP Switches

DIP switches, found on the motherboard or on the expansion card of many older computers, consist of a bank of tiny on/off switches.

Example 7.1:

When installing a fax/modem card, you must specify which COM port and IRQ the modem will use.

Figure 7.16 shows a Zoltrix fax/modem card. As you can see, in this case the DIP switches are with the ports at the end of the card (although they could have been on the circuit board surface). The IRQ and the COM port the modem uses must be configured. According to the documentation that comes with the modem, when the COM port is selected, the I/O address is also chosen. Therefore, if the card is set to COM2, the modem will use the I/O address of 2F8 to 2FF. Modems can use COM1, COM2, COM3, or COM4. Whichever port you choose, including the 9-pin and 25-pin ports, make sure it is not being used by another device and that the software that will be running the modem will support it. (Note: If the serial port is not being used but is still active, it is still assigned a COM port and an IRQ.)

To select the COM port, you must look at the accompanying documentation. In our example, to set the modem to COM2, you must find switches 5 and 6. Switch 5 must be off (up) and switch 6 must be on (down). The on position of a DIP switch is indicated by the word *on* stamped on the DIP switch bank. When changing these two switches, remember not to change any of the others since they are used to configure other parameters. The standard IRQ for COM2 is IRQ 3. Unless there is a good reason for not using the standard assignments (such as to get all of the expansion devices to work), you should always use the standard. To configure the modem as IRQ 3, again look at the documentation. The IRQ requires setting switches 1, 2, 3, 4, and 7. The settings for COM2 are:

Switch 1	Switch 2	Switch 3	Switch 4	Switch 7
Off (Up)	Off (Up)	Off (Up)	On (Down)	Off (Up)

Most documentation will indicate what the default settings for the DIP switches are. These should be the settings when you first open the box, but even though the switches are supposed to be preset correctly, check the settings before inserting the card.

Figure 7.16 A Fax/Modem with Documentation

COM PORT ADDRESSES

Each COM port in your computer uses a specific computer addresses. The addresses for each COM port are:

COM1 3F8–3FF
COM2 2F8–2FF
COM3 3F8–3FF
COM4 2F8–2FF

IRQ	SW1	SW2	SW3	SW4	SW7	COMPORT	SW5	SW6
2	Off	Off	Off	Off	On	COM1	On	On
3*	Off	Off	Off	On	Off	COM2*	Off	On
4	Off	Off	On	Off	Off	COM3	On	Off
5	Off	On	Off	Off	Off	COM4	Off	Off
7	On	Off	Off	Off	Off			

*Indicates the factor (default) setting.

7.4.2 Jumpers

A **jumper,** sometimes called a *shunt,* is a small, plastic-covered metal clip used to connect two pins protruding from an expansion card. See figure 7.17. The jumper (which operates the same as an on switch) connects the pins closing the circuit and allowing current to flow. Two-pin configurations that need to be jumped are the two-pin configuration and the three-pin configuration.

The two-pin configuration will either be connected with a jumper or will not be connected. If the jumper is to be used, the documentation will either indicate on or closed or include a small diagram showing where the jumper should be placed. If a jumper is not to be placed over the two pins, the documentation will indicate off or open or include a small diagram showing that a jumper should not be used. (Note: To avoid losing jumpers that are not being used, they can be placed over one pin.) The three-pin connection has a high/low configuration. If the documentation indicates high, you will jumper the two pins on the side indicated with an *H.* If the documentation indicates low, you will jumper the two pins on the side indicated with a *L.* In either case the center pin is used.

Example 7.2:

The expansion card shown in figures 7.18, 7.19, 7.20, and 7.21 (on pp. 246–249) is an example of a standard I/O card found in many systems. It holds an IDE hard disk controller, a floppy disk controller, two serial ports, one parallel port, and a game port. Since the card houses so many devices on one circuit board, it also includes many jumpers.

Figure 7.17 Jumpers on an Expansion Card

Figure 7.18 Common Multifunction I/O Card

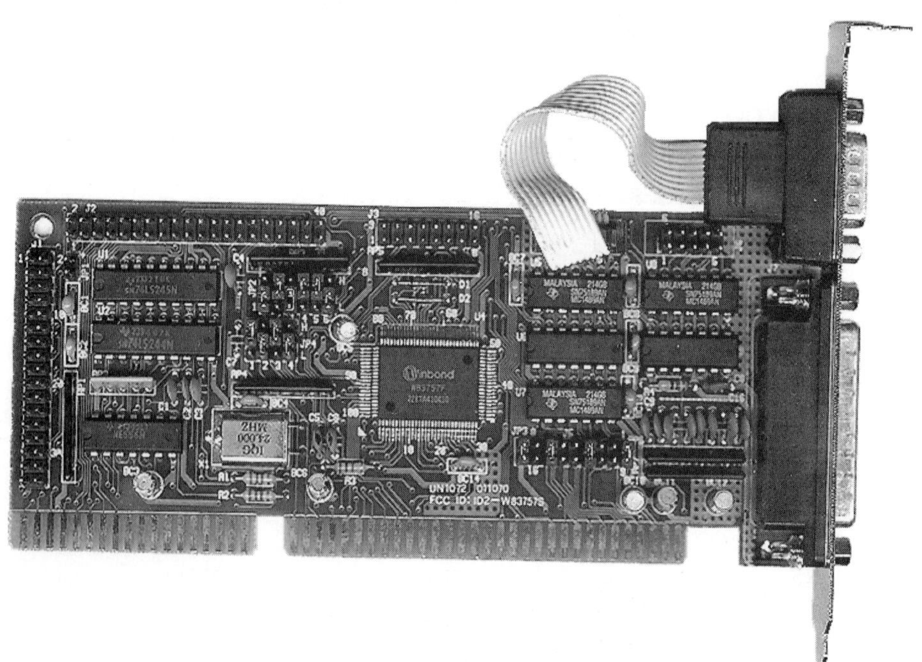

Let's take a look at the serial ports and the parallel ports that also require an IRQ. As already mentioned, the card has two serial ports, designated as Serial Port I/RS-232 I and Serial Port II/ RS-232 II. Note that these names do not designate the COM ports. The COM ports are set with jumpers. The ports (9-pin male and 25-pin male) connect to a 10-pin connector on the card. The 9-pin port is usually connected to the Serial Port I connector and is usually configured as COM1. The 25-pin port is usually connected to the Serial Port II and is usually configured as COM2. If you wish the 25-pin connector to be connected to Serial Port I and the 9-pin connector to Serial Port II, you just have to change the connection.

Figure 7.19 Multifunction Card Documentation—Part A

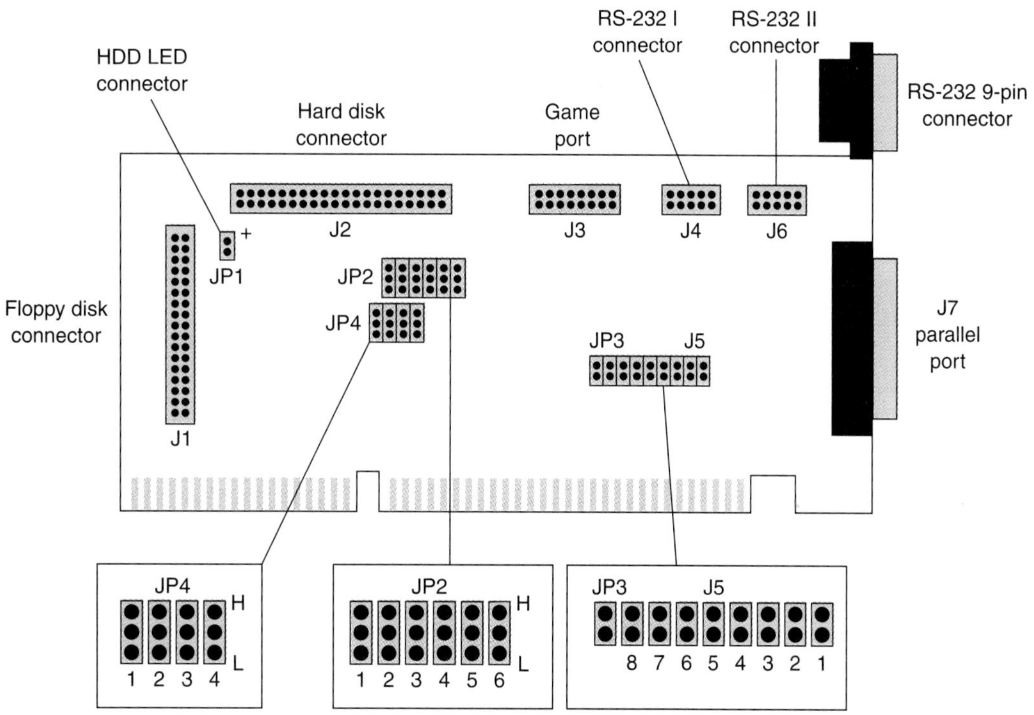

JP2 (5-6)	Parallel Port
JP2-5: Low JP2-6: Low	LPT3 (3BCh)
JP2-5: Low JP2-6: High	LPT2 (278h)
JP2-5: High JP2-6: Low	LPT1 (378h) (Default)
JP2-5: High JP2-6: High	Disable

J5 (7-8)	Parallel Port
JP5-7: On JP5-8: Off	IRQ7 (Default)
JP5-7: Off JP5-8: On	IRQ5 (2F8h)

Figure 7.20 Multifunction Card Documentation—Part B

JP3		Parallel Port Function
	On	Output (Default)
	Off	Input

JP2 (1-2)		Serial Port I
1 2 H L	JP2-1: Low JP2-2: Low	COM4 (2E8h)
1 2 H L	JP2-1: Low JP2-2: High	COM1 (3F8h) (Default)
1 2 H L	JP2-1: High JP2-2: Low	COM3 (3E8h)
1 2 H L	JP2-1: High JP2-2: High	Disable

JP2 (3-4)		Serial Port II
3 4 H L	JP2-3: Low JP2-4: Low	COM3 (3E8h)
3 4 H L	JP2-3: Low JP2-4: High	COM2 (2F8h) (Default)
3 4 H L	JP2-3: High JP2-4: Low	COM4 (2E8h)
3 4 H L	JP2-3: High JP2-4: High	Disable

To configure Serial Port I as COM1 using IRQ4, the documentation indicates the jumpers used to do this are the set of jumpers designated JP2, specifically, jumpers 1 and 2. As you can see, to set Serial Port I to COM1, jumper 1 must be set to low and jumper 2 must be set to high. If you wanted to truly disable Serial Port I, you would set both jumpers to high. Again, the other jumpers should be left alone since they are used to control other items. To set the IRQ, the documentation indicates you must use jumper set J5, jumpers 1, 2, and 3. To set the port to use IRQ 4, you must have a jumper on 1 and no jumpers on 2 and 3. (Note: The jumpers are numbered from the left, not the right. Jumper 1 is designated by a small number 1.)

7.4.3 Software Configuration and Plug-and-Play

To simplify the configuration of expansion cards, new technology was developed that allowed the cards to be configured electronically. This is done by running a software setup program from a disk that comes with the expansion card. These cards are not to be confused with preset plug-and-play cards since the settings for the resources they use must be physically activated. Today, many motherboards contain built-in serial ports, parallel ports, and video cards. Some motherboards even have a sound card. Since the serial ports, parallel ports, and sound cards use hardware resources, they are usually configured using the CMOS setup program.

Another way to configure an expansion card is to let the computer do it by using plug-and-play (PnP). However, the system has to support plug-and-play, which means that the computer must have a system ROM BIOS/plug-and-play BIOS, the expansion card must have a plug-and-play ISA and PCI and PC Cards/PCMCIA, and the operating system (or the appropriate drivers) must support plug-and-play. If all this is in place, then during boot-up, the plug-and-play BIOS will track the insertion and removal of plug-and-play devices. If the device can identify itself and its system requirements to the

Figure 7.21 Multifunction Card Documentation—Part C

J5 (1-3)		Serial Port I
3 2 1	J5-1: On J5-2: Off J5-3: Off	IRQ4 (Default)
3 2 1	J5-1: Off J5-2: On J5-3: Off	IRQ3
3 2 1	J5-1: Off J5-2: Off J5-3: On	IRQ5

J5 (4-6)		Serial Port II
6 5 4	J5-4: On J5-5: Off J5-6: Off	IRQ3 (Default)
6 5 4	J5-4: Off J5-5: On J5-6: Off	IRQ4
6 5 4	J5-4: Off J5-5: Off J5-6: On	IRQ5

JP4-1	Hard Disk Address Selection
H L High	3F6-3F7 1F0-1F7
H L Low	376-377 170-177

JP4-2	IDE Hard Disk
H L Low	Enabled (Default)
H L High	Disabled

JP4-3	Hard Disk Address Selection
H L High	3F0-3F7 (Default)
H L Low	370-377

JP4-4	IDE Hard Disk
H L Low	Enabled (Default)
H L High	Disabled

system, the plug-and-play BIOS will assign the needed resources and avoid conflicts with the known legacy cards. Operating systems such as Windows 95, 98, Me, 2000, and XP that support plug-and-play will allow you to overcome the resources assigned to the plug-and-play device if there is a conflict.

To make sure that the resource assignments and device placements are the same each time the computer is powered on, the system uses the **extended system configuration data (ESCD)** method, which stores the legacy information and the last working configuration (LWC) of configurable devices in a nonvolatile CMOS memory area. This is important when using device drivers that get their resource allocation information from a static source, such as the command line parameters in the CONFIG.SYS file.

ESCD is also used as a communications link between the BIOS and the operating system. Both use the ESCD area to read the current status of the hardware and to record changes. Windows reads the ESCD to see if hardware has been changed and react accordingly. Windows also allows users to override plug-and-play resource assignments by manually changing resources in the Device Manager. This information is recorded in the ESCD area so the BIOS knows about the change at the next boot and doesn't try to change the assignment back again.

Many motherboards have a Force Update ESCD option or a Reset Configuration Data option in the CMOS setup program. Normally, you should leave the setting disabled. But if you have installed a new add-on card and the consequent system reconfiguration causes a serious conflict of resources, such as the OS not booting, then you should enable it so that the BIOS will reset and reconfigure the settings for all PnP cards in the system during boot-up. The BIOS will automatically reset the setting to Disabled the next time you boot.

7.5 TROUBLESHOOTING EXPANSION CARDS AND SLOTS

When an expansion card fails to work, it is because of the card itself or the motherboard. The card could be physically damaged, or it could be in conflict (I/O address, IRQ, DMA, memory usage) with another card. Or it may not function because the proper software drivers (built into the operating system or as drivers or TSRs) are not installed to activate the card.

Depending on the Windows version that you are using, you can use the Device Manager to the System Information program to view the use of resources for an expansion card or the status of the drivers for a particular device. See chapters 21 and 22 for more information.

Example 7.3:

You just inserted an expansion card and the card does not work.

The first thing to do is to check the obvious: Is the card inserted properly? Are the cables connected properly? Does the card require any drivers or TSRs, which must be loaded for the card to function? Wipe off any oxides or dust that may have accumulated on the metal connectors of the expansion card. You can use contact cleaning solution. Then try the card again.

Try inserting the card into another expansion slot. If the card starts working, then the first expansion slot is most likely bad. The metal fingers within the slot, which provide the contact with the expansion card, eventually wear out if expansion cards are frequently inserted and removed or if an expansion card is inserted with excessive force, which would break the connector or even the motherboard. If the expansion slot is bad, you should label it and be sure to tell your customer. If you choose to repair it, the best course of action would be to replace the motherboard. Replacing the expansion slot would require some special knowledge, skill, and equipment as well as time. It is quicker and more cost effective to replace the motherboard.

After trying the obvious, look elsewhere. Since you just inserted the card, check the resources used by the expansion card. If the card uses jumpers or DIP switches, remove the card and verify that they are configured properly. If the card is software configurable, rerun the configuration software and verify the card's resources. If the card is plug-and-play, use the plug-and-play manager (DOS) or use the Windows 95 or 98 System icon to verify the settings of the card. Make sure that the plug-and-play software chooses nonconflicting resources. In either case, remove the card and run diagnostic software, run the System icon within the Control Panel (Windows 95 and 98), use Microsoft Diagnostic (Windows NT) or use System Information, to verify that the resources chosen are not being used by another device. If there is no conflict, then the card must be physically bad. Try to install another card.

Example 7.4:

After you inserted a card, the computer does not boot.

First, remove the card to see if the computer boots properly. If it does, try reinserting the card. If the same problem occurs, the card is most likely causing the problem or the card is causing the motherboard to short against some part of the case. Look at the card carefully for bad solder and burn marks. If you find bad solder, the card is probably being shorted out by the solder as it bridges two circuits that shouldn't be connected (referred to as a *bridge*). If you find burn marks, the card probably heated up, which usually indicates the card is bad.

If the visual inspection of the card is fine, the next thing to do is to verify the resource configuration (IRQ, DMA, I/O address, and memory address) used by the card. If the card appears to be good, try it in another system. If the same problem occurs, the card is probably bad. If the system has been booting properly, this would indicate that when the card is inserted into the slot, it is somehow causing the motherboard to short against the case. Check the motherboard to see whether there are any loose screws or paper clips within the computer; then check to see whether the motherboard is positioned correctly against the spacers.

SUMMARY

1. The expansion slot, also known as the I/O bus, extends the reach of the processor so that it can communicate with peripheral devices.
2. The data bus carries the actual data between the expansion card, the RAM, and the CPU; the address bus determines the memory location for the data.
3. Both USB and IEEE 1394/FireWire are hot-swappable and plug-and-play. Therefore, you connect the device and the device is recognized. Of course, depending on the device, you may need to load an additional driver.
4. PCMCIA and Mini-PCI adapters are plug-and-play devices.
5. The PCMCIA/PC cards are hot-swappable.
6. Generally no two devices can share the same resources (IRQ, DMA, I/O address, and memory address).
7. A hardware interrupt (IRQ) is a signal sent to the processor to redirect its attention to another task.
8. The AT design and above had 16 interrupts.
9. Direct memory address (DMA) channels are used to take over the data bus and address lines to bring data from an I/O device to the RAM without any assistance or direction from the CPU.
10. The AT has eight DMA channels.
11. Bus mastering is a process by which an expansion card with its own processor takes temporary control of the data and address bus to move information from one point to another.
12. The I/O address is a memory address used to identify the input/output (I/O) device.
13. Many expansion cards need to use a range of memory addresses in the reserve memory between 640 KB and 1 MB of RAM.
14. Expansion cards can be configured with DIP switches, jumpers, or special software. Today, most are automatically configured with plug-and-play (PnP) technology.
15. Because the PCI uses level-sensitive signaling and also uses newer BIOS and plug-and-play operating systems—such as Windows 95B (OSR2) or later, Windows 98, Windows Me, Windows 2000, and Windows XP—interrupt sharing is possible due to PCI IRQ Steering.
16. One of the biggest advantages of the USB interface is that it requires only a single interrupt from the PC for all 127 devices.
17. With the proper chipset and drivers, a USB device will work without rebooting or reconfiguring every time a peripheral is added or removed. USB devices can also be hot-swapped.
18. Two different connectors are specified for USB, called Series A and Series B.
19. The series A connector is designed for devices where the cable remains permanently attached, such as hubs, keyboards, and mice.
20. The USB ports on most motherboards are also normally Series A connectors.
21. Series B connectors are designed for devices that require detachable cables, such as printers, scanners, modems, telephones, and speakers.
22. USB 1.1 offers a data transfer rate of up to 12 Mbit/s. Maximum cable length between two full-speed (12 Mbit/s) devices or a device and a hub is 5 m using twisted-pair shielded cable with 20-gauge wire.
23. For low-speed peripherals such as pointing devices and keyboards, the USB also has a slower 1.5 Mbit/s subchannel. Maximum cable length of low-speed (1.5 Mbit/s) devices using non-twisted-pair wire is 3 m.
24. USB 2.0 is similar to USB 1.1, except it runs up to 480 Mbit/s, yet it remains backward compatible.
25. Most external storage devices are either USB or IEEE 1394/Firewire. Therefore, you connect them to your system that supports USB or IEEE 1394, and the device should be recognized.
26. Legacy devices are not plug-and-play. Therefore, if you upgrade or change a legacy device, you many need to reconfigure the driver.
27. When an expansion card fails to work, it is because of the card itself or the motherboard. The card could be physically damaged or it could be in conflict (I/O address, IRQ, DMA, memory usage) with another card. It may fail to function because the proper software drivers are not installed to activate the card.
28. The IBM PC and IBM XT use an 8-bit expansion bus called the PC slot or the 8-bit ISA bus.
29. The IBM AT introduced a 16-bit expansion bus called the industry standard architecture (ISA) bus.
30. The local bus, such as VESA local bus and PCI local bus, was originally designed to run at or near the speed of the processor.
31. PCI slots come with either a 32-bit bus or a 64-bit bus operating up to 66 MHz. It can support up to 264 MB/s in nonburst mode or 528 MB/s in burst mode.
32. PCI Express is both a hardware interface and a transmission protocol that uses an individual clocked lane, consisting of two pairs of data lines to carry data upstream and downstream.
33. Because PCI Express is based on a single pathway rather than having multiple pathways placed next to each other, it can be clocked up to higher speeds.
34. The accelerated graphics port (AGP) is a spinoff of the PCI slot.
35. The AGP port is called a port, not a bus, because a bus can support multiple devices and the AGP cannot.

36. AGP is used exclusively for video cards.
37. The AGP port is similar to the PCI slot in shape and size but is offset further from the edge of the motherboard than PCI slots are.
38. AGP uses a 32-bit path running at 66 MHz, giving it the capability to handle 266 Mbit/s.
39. Currently, there are also the AGP 2X, 4X, and 8X, which can transfer 2, 4 and 8 transfers per clock cycle, which multiples the data transfer.
40. Notebook and laptop computers use PC (formerly PCMCIA) cards and CardBus cards.
41. The Personal Computer Memory Card International Association (PCMCIA) established several standards for laptop expansion system PC Cards: Type I, II, III, and IV.
42. PC Cards have power-saving capability to increase battery life. The cards operate at 3.3 V, support APM, and are hot-swappable.
43. The original PC cards were 16-bit.
44. The successor to PC cards is the CardBus, which provides speeds up to 33 MHz at 32 bits.
45. To expand the notebook computer similar to the PCI card, the mini-PCI card was developed which is smaller and consumes less power.
46. The universal serial bus (USB) is an external port allowing connection of external PC peripherals in series.
47. The USB connector will accept any USB peripheral, including mice, keyboards, printers, modems, and external disk drivers.
48. Seven USB devices can be connected directly using the standard four-pin connector. These seven devices can then be connected to a total of 127 other devices by connecting external hubs in a chain.
49. Although USB can support up to 127 devices, it is usually limited by bus speed and power limitations.
50. Another external bus standard is IEEE 1394, sometimes called FireWire.
51. IEEE supports data transfer rates up to 400 Mbit/s.
52. A single 1394 port can connect up to six external devices.

QUESTIONS

1. COM1 is usually assigned which interrupt?
   a. IRQ 1　　b. IRQ 2
   c. IRQ 3　　d. IRQ 4
   e. IRQ 9
2. The DMA channel used for the floppy controller is
   a. DMA 1.　　b. DMA 2.
   c. DMA 3.　　d. DMA 5.
3. The Type II PC bus card
   a. fits in a Type 1 slot.
   b. is 3 mm thick.
   c. is 5 mm thick.
   d. is 10.5 mm thick.
4. After installing a new sound card, the system fails to boot. Which of the following could be causing the problem?
   a. The operating system does not support the sound card.
   b. The cables to the sound card are connected wrong.
   c. There is an IRQ conflict
   d. The device driver is not loaded.
   e. None of the above.
5. PC (PCMCIA) cards were designed for use in
   a. notebook and subnotebook computers.
   b. desktop computers.
   c. tower computers.
   d. palmtop computers.
   e. none of the above.
6. Which type of slot is the fastest?
   a. ISA　　b. EISA
   c. MCA　　d. PCI local bus
   e. PCMCIA
7. Which of the following are *not* possible conflicts when installing an expansion card?
   a. port conflict
   b. I/O address conflict
   c. IRQ conflict
   d. power conflict
   e. memory conflict
8. You suspect an IRQ conflict when installing a sound card. How would you check to see which IRQs are free?
   a. reboot the computer
   b. install the operating system
   c. run a software diagnostic program
   d. enter the CMOS setup program
9. Which of the following describes an IRQ?
   a. an address that points to an input or output device
   b. a line that allows access to memory without using the CPU
   c. a line that temporarily stops the CPU from doing something so that it can give its attention to something else
   d. a line that supplies power to an interface card
10. Which of the following describes a DMA?
   a. an address that points to an input or output device
   b. a line that allows access to memory without using the CPU
   c. a line that temporarily stops the CPU from doing something so that it can give its attention to something else
   d. a line that supplies power to an interface card

11. The device I/O address
   a. must be unique and correspond to a port or device.
   b. must be the same for each device.
   c. is not needed for some devices.
   d. is needed only for devices that do not require or use a DMA.
12. Expansion boards are configured in which of the following ways (choose all that apply)?
   a. with jumpers that need to be set
   b. with DIP switches that need to be set
   c. with a special preprogrammed ROM chip
   d. with software
13. When installing an expansion board, what is the best method of determining the current settings?
   a. Run MSD to view the IRQs after the board is installed.
   b. Consult the documentation for the board.
   c. Systematically change the DIP switch settings on the board.
   d. Remove all the jumpers on the expansion card and reinstall them one by one until the board functions.
14. Which of the following statements are *true* about IRQs (choose two answers)?
   a. Under the correct conditions, several devices on a PC can share the same interrupt.
   b. IRQ settings are stored in the system ROM BIOS.
   c. After processing an IRQ, the CPU must find where it left off with processing other tasks.
   d. Each device on a PC must have a unique IRQ number.
15. How many DMA channels does a Pentium computer have?
   a. 2 b. 4
   c. 8 d. 16
16. What is the standard I/O address for LPT1?
   a. 3F8-3FF b. 2F8-2FF
   c. 3F0-3F7 d. 278-27F
   e. 378-37F
17. What is the standard I/O address for COM1?
   a. 3F8-3FF b. 2F8-2FF
   c. 3F0-3F7 d. 278-27F
   e. 378-37F
18. What is meant by the term *memory address* in relation to expansion boards?
   a. an area above 640 KB that a device can use exclusively for its operations
   b. an address in RAM that alerts the CPU to an expansion board's presence
   c. a unique number assigned to a device to identify the expansion card to the computer
   d. ROM that specifies what drivers are needed
19. After installing and configuring an expansion card, such as the sound card or fax/modem, to activate the card you will need to
   a. run the CMOS setup program.
   b. turn on the expansion card's power switch.
   c. load the appropriate drivers.
   d. insert a ROM chip into the expansion card.
   e. insert a ROM chip into the motherboard.
20. Which of the following statements about PC cards are *true* (choose all that apply)?
   a. Type 1 cards are memory cards and are accepted by Type 1, Type 2, and Type 3 slots.
   b. Type 2 cards are normally expansion cards, such as fax/modems and sound cards, and are accepted by Type 2 and Type 3 slots.
   c. Type 3 cards often support small hard drives and are not accepted by Type 1 and 2 slots.
   d. All three types of cards have the same physical dimensions and plug into a 68-pin connector.
21. PCMCIA/PC cards are characterized by their
   a. small size, low power, and hot-swap capability.
   b. portability and bus-mastering capabilities.
   c. ability to fit both ISA and EISA buses.
   d. small size and 32-bit data bus.
22. Which of the following is made for and is only used by video cards?
   a. AGP b. PCI
   c. ISA d. VLB
   e. none of the above
23. Which of the following support data paths of 64-bits?
   a. MCA b. EISA
   c. VLB d. PCI
   e. CardBus
24. Which of the following will automatically choose card resources such as IRQ and DMA?
   a. plug-and-play systems
   b. IRQ and DMA controllers
   c. I/O manager
   d. device driver
25. How do you configure a PC card?
   a. set jumpers or DIP switches
   b. run the CMOS setup program
   c. install software drivers
   d. write a program and transfer it to the PC card using the parallel or serial port
26. You just installed a sound card that causes the computer to lock up when a parallel port Zip drive is used. What is most likely the problem?
   a. an I/O addresses conflict
   b. an IRQ conflict
   c. a DMA conflict
   d. a defective sound card
   e. a defective parallel port
   f. a defective Zip drive
27. Which of the following is used to connect up to 127 external devices such as mice, keyboards, printers, hard drives, tape drives, and removable drives?
   a. AGP b. PCI
   c. PC d. USB
   e. none of the above

28. Which of the following is used to connect devices that transfer large amounts of data in real-time?
    a. AGP
    b. PCI
    c. PC
    d. USB
    e. FireWire
    f. none of the above
29. Which statement about IRQ 2 is true?
    a. It is the default setting for COM4.
    b. It is the default resource setting for LPT2.
    c. It is unavailable for assignment on most newer computers.
    d. It links the first bank of eight IRQs to the second bank.
    e. It is the preferred IRQ to use with NE2000 compatible boards.
    f. It is generally reserved for the LPT2 port but can be used for the real-time clock.
30. Which component is *not* tested during the POST?
    a. system RAM
    b. motherboard
    c. video card
    d. Sound Blaster card
31. You are checking a jumper on a network adapter card, and you find that it has shunt that is occupying only one of the two pins. Which term correctly describe this circuit?
    a. open
    b. closed
    c. shorted
    d. grounded
32. A user in your company is attempting to connect a new USB keyboard to his computer. The computer has two USB ports, and both ports are being used by other devices. The user reports that he cannot connect the USB keyboard to his computer. You verify that the computer's available ports are a parallel port, a serial port, and two PS/2 ports. You need to ensure that the user can use the new keyboard and the two existing USB devices. Your solution must minimize additional hardware expense. What should you instruct the user to do?
    a. Obtain a USB-to-PS/2 adapter. Then attach the keyboard to an open PS/2 port by using the adapter.
    b. Obtain a serial port version of one of the two existing USB devices. Then connect that device to the open serial port to free up a USB port for the keyboard.
    c. Obtain a self-powered USB hub. Connect all three USB devices to the hub. Then connect the hub to the computer.
    d. Obtain a bus-powered USB hub. Connect all three USB devices to the hub. Then connect the hub to the computer.

HANDS-ON EXERCISES

Exercise 1: Using the Operating System Internal Software

1. Boot the computer to Windows.
2. Click on the Start button, select the Settings option, and select the Control Panel. Double-click on the System applet. Click on the Device Manager tab. To show the IRQ and other resources, double-click on the computer on top of the tree structure or select the computer and click on the Properties button. Determine the free IRQs. Record the IRQs for COM1 and COM2.
3. Open the System Tools option and select the System Information program. Click on the plus sign (+) next to the Hardware Resources option from the System Information tree and select IRQs. Determine the free IRQs. Record the IRQs for COM1 and COM2.
4. Using these programs, what device is actually using IRQ 4?
5. What device is actually using IRQ 5?
6. What device is actually using IRQ 7?
7. What device is actually using IRQ 11?
8. What device is actually using DMA 2?
9. What device is actually using DMA 3?

Exercise 2: Using Diagnostic Software

Using diagnostic software, answer the following questions.

1. What device is actually using IRQ 4?
2. What device is actually using IRQ 5?
3. What device is actually using IRQ 7?
4. What device is actually using IRQ 11?
5. What device is actually using DMA 2?
6. What device is actually using DMA 3?

Exercise 3: Configuring an I/O Card

1. Make sure the computer is off.
2. Identify all expansion cards in your system.
3. Find and read all manuals that come with those expansion cards.
4. Look for any expansion card that has jumpers or dip switches. Look at the documentation and identify what each jumper or dip switch does.
5. If your instructor has an expansion card, retrieve the expansion card, manual, and drivers. Read the manual.
6. If the card has jumpers or dip switches, configure the card for your system.
7. Insert the expansion card into the appropriate expansion slot.
8. Start Windows.
9. If necessary, load the appropriate drivers.
10. Go the manufacturer of the expansion card and look for and download any updated drivers for the expansion card.
11. If available, install the updated drivers.
12. In the Control Panel, open the System applet.
13. Open the Device Manager.
14. Find and double-click the newly installed device. View the General tab, driver information, and Resources tab.
15. Shut off the computer.
16. Remove the newly installed expansion card.

Exercise 4: Installing and Configuring a USB Device

1. Obtain a USB device and manual such as keyboard, mouse, storage, printer, or any other type of device.
2. Read the manual.
3. With the system on and Windows loaded, install the USB device and any appropriate drivers (if needed).
4. In the Notification area (right part of the taskbar), find and double-click the safely remove hard device icon. Find and click the USB device, and click the Stop button.
5. Remove the USB device.

CHAPTER 8

The Case and Power Supply

Topics Covered in This Chapter

Introduction

The computer consists of three obvious parts: the case, the keyboard, and the monitor. The case (sometimes known as the CPU) is the box that most of the computer components rest in. It will usually contain the power supply, the motherboard, the floppy drives, the hard drive, and the RAM.

The power supply is the "blood" of the computer. It takes AC power from an outlet and converts it into clean (without fluctuation) DC power to run the computer chips. In addition, the power supply helps keep the computer cool so that heat will not prematurely destroy any of the electronic circuitry.

Objectives

1. Identify the two main functions of the case.
2. State the major characteristics to consider when choosing a case.
3. Describe the function of the power supply.
4. List the common voltages supplied by a PC power supply and describe their use.
5. Describe the major characteristics for the switching power supply.
6. Differentiate between the various power supply form factors.
7. Properly connect and disconnect the power connectors.
8. Given a power supply, be able to install and remove it from a PC.
9. Given a PC with a power-related problem, determine and correct the problem.
10. List and describe the different types of power fluctuations.
11. List and describe the power protection devices.

8.1 THE CASE

The **case** of the PC is a large metal or plastic box designed to hold and protect the motherboard, the drives, and the power supply. Like motherboards and microprocessors, cases come in many different configurations, which are characterized by the orientation of the box, the number of drives and expansion slots it can hold, and the size of the expansion cards it can take. See figure 8.1.

8.1.1 Choosing the Right Case

Cases come in two orientations. A PC that lies flat is known as a **desktop case** (much like the IBM PC); a case that stands erect is known as a **tower case.** The desktop case comes in two sizes, the slimline and regular, whereas the tower comes in three sizes—the minitower, the medium tower, and the full-size tower. It stands to reason the larger the case, the more room for expansion. Before choosing a case, you must be sure that the case will fulfill all of your needs.

When looking for a case, you should ask the following questions:

1. Does the case have enough drive bays (including open drive bays)?
2. Does your motherboard fit into the new case?
3. How many expansion slots does the case have and how are the expansion slots oriented?
4. What type of power supply does the case have and what is the wattage rating of the power supply?
5. If the case doesn't come with a power supply, what kind of power supply and on/off switch will it accommodate?

The case must have enough closed and open drive bays to accommodate all of the hard drives, floppy drives, and miscellaneous peripherals. A drive bay is an empty space where a drive or other peripherals sit. An open drive bay has an opening in the front of the case. The opening is used to insert a floppy disk or CD into the drive. The closed drive bay is completely enclosed by the case. Drive bays come in two

Figure 8.1 Case (Courtesy of PC Power & Cooling, Inc.)

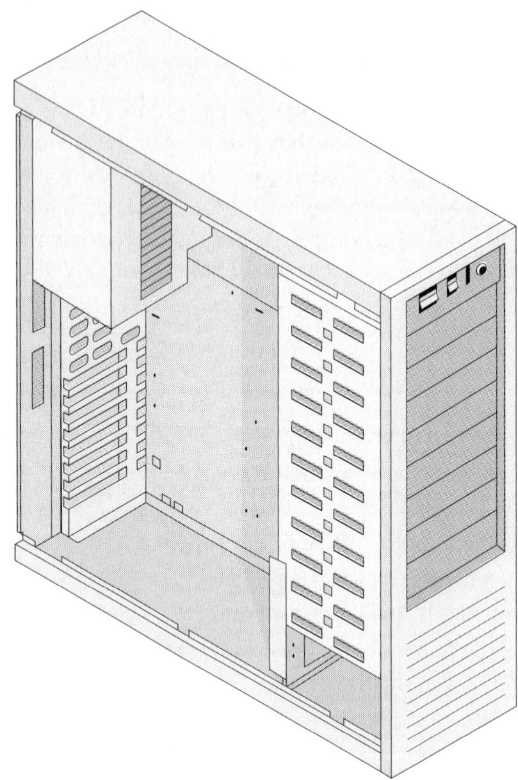

sizes, 5¼ in. and 3½ in. The 5¼-in. drive bay will hold 5¼-in. floppy disk drives, internal stereo speakers, CD-ROM drives, and some hard drives. The 3½-in. drive bays hold 3½-in. floppy disk drives and some hard drives.

You should choose a case that has at least three drive bays, including an open 5¼-in. drive bay (for a CD-ROM drive), an open 3½-in. drive bay (for a 3½-in. disk drive), and a closed drive bay (for the hard drive). Be sure to pick a case that has extra drive bays. This will allow you to add other peripherals to your system, such as additional drives (hard drives, tape backups, or removable drives such as Zip drives) or some internal speakers.

A second criterion in choosing the case is how well it accommodates the motherboard. The motherboard is mounted to the bottom of the case by standoffs and screws. **Standoffs** are small plastic or metal pieces that keep the motherboard from touching the case. If the motherboard touches the case, it will short itself out and could damage the electronic chips. Make sure that the screws and standoffs line up with the holes drilled in the motherboard. (Note: Some proprietary cases will accommodate only proprietary motherboards.) Another factor in matching a case with a motherboard is how many expansion slots the case will accommodate. More importantly, if the motherboard is inserted properly into the case, do the expansion slots line up with the expansion gaps located at the back of the computer, which allows you to access your expansion cards from the outside?

The last criterion for choosing the case concerns the power supply. Most cases today come with power supplies. If you are installing a power supply into a case, make sure it has the same type of on/off switch and is located in the same place. Some systems may use a toggle switch or a push-button switch. The switches may be located on the side, front, or back of the system.

Cases will usually have other options. One option is a reset switch, which allows you to reset the computer without actually using the on/off switch. Using the reset switch is a little easier on the system's power supply. Another option cases can have is a locking device that can lock the case so that no one can open it. It can also prevent anyone from typing on the keyboard. The locking devices can be locked and unlocked with a key. Unfortunately, most keys are generic keys, which are mass-produced.

8.1.2 Case Form Factors

Like motherboards and power supplies, cases come in different form factors. The **form factor** describes the general layout of the case, the positioning of the slots in the back of the case, and the type of motherboard it accommodates.

The most popular case form factors today are the Baby AT, ATX, and NLX, with the newer micro-ATX/SFX form factor becoming more popular on lower-end systems. Obsolete form factors include PC/XT and AT form factors. These cases are not interchangeable because they are shaped differently and require motherboards with a different form factor. If you are building your own system, you must ensure your motherboard and case/power supply form factors match. There are cases that can handle both Baby AT and ATX motherboards.

As AT-style machines became popular, manufacturers quickly developed a preference for the Baby AT form factor over the AT form factor, because it provided the same capabilities at reduced size and cost. Until the rise of ATX, the Baby AT form factor dominated the industry. Baby AT cases are found in both desktop and tower configurations, like AT, and in a large variety of styles, shapes, and sizes. Baby AT cases are used with Baby AT form factor power supplies and Baby AT–style motherboards, which can be recognized by their dimensions and placement of components. Many Baby AT cases are also supplied with slimline LPX power supplies.

The ATX form factor was invented by Intel in 1995. Since then, ATX and its variants—mini-ATX, micro-ATX, flex-ATX, and extended ATX—have become the industry standard in most segments of the market. The ATX design has several significant advantages over the older designs. The ATX case is similar to a Baby AT case except that the holes in the back are altered to fit the changed design of the ATX form factor motherboard, in particular the integrated I/O ports. In most cases a user-replaceable I/O template is used to allow different configurations of I/O ports installed directly on the motherboard. The ATX case also uses a different ATX power supply, which is also used for NLX form factor cases.

The extended ATX form factor, also sometimes called *EATX,* is essentially the same as ATX except that the board can be up to 12 × 13 in. in size. These boards are uncommon, and the extended ATX form factor is likely to receive significant competition from the new WTX form factor, which was designed especially for workstations that can accommodate motherboards up to 14 × 16.75 in.

Without knowing it, retail PC customers have made LPX a very popular form factor during the last decade. Most PCs sold in slimline, or low-profile, cases in the late 1980s and early 1990s use the LPX form factor or a variant of it. The goal of the LPX design was to reduce the size and cost of the PC system box.

NLX is similar to LPX, with a riser-card arrangement and a low-profile, slimline case. However, it has been updated and modernized to allow support for the latest technologies while keeping costs down. Many slimline systems that were formerly designed to fit the LPX form factor are now moving over to NLX. Note: The NLX specification does not define a new, specific NLX power supply form factor. NLX systems are intended to use ATX form factor power supplies.

The next popular family of case form factors will most likely be the BTX cases:

- The regular-size BTX supports up to a full seven expansion slots and amounts to the case using 10 mounting screws. Regular BTX cases will most likely support three or more 3.5-in. drive bays and three or more 5.25-in. bays.
- The picoBTX standard can support either one or two expansion slots and has four mounting holes. PicoBTX cases will probably have one 3.5-in. and one 5.25-in. drive bay.
- The microBTX standard, which is expected to be the most popular of the three, has support for four expansion slots and has seven mounting holes. MicroBTX cases will feature one 3.5-in. bay and up to two 5.25-in. bays.

The BTX standard allows for two case heights—Type I and Type II. Type I cases are 3.98-in. in height and can use normal expansion cards, whereas Type II cases are for small form-factor designs and are 3.0 in. in height. Expansion cards would use either risers or be low profile in a Type II case.

8.1.3 RFI Radiation

Protecting the PC components is not the only function of the case. It also limits the flow of **RFI radiation** (radio frequency interference) from the computer. Since some of the radiation is broadcast as radio and television signals, an electronic component can interrupt a radio, a television set, or the navigation equipment used in aircraft.

The amount of RFI generated by an electronic device is monitored by the Federal Communications Commission (FCC). The FCC divides electronic devices into two classifications. Class A digital devices are those suited only for business, commercial, and industrial applications. They include mainframes and minicomputers. For a device to be accepted as a class A device, it must not cause interference to radio or television reception when separated from the television set or radio by one wall and 300 ft or more. These standards are considered to describe the average business or industrial site. Class B devices are those likely to be used in the home. Personal computers are class B devices. Class B equipment cannot produce interference with a radio or television reception when separated from the television set or radio by one wall and 30 ft. The 30 ft and the one wall are considered to describe the average household. Naturally, for a device to achieve a class B certification, it must be better designed and have better quality control than a class A device. (Note: The FCC does not classify motherboards, processors, cases, and power supplies by themselves but all of them together.)

Computer manufacturers use several techniques to minimize the RFI radiation. A steel case does a fair job of limiting RFI. A plastic case is treated with conductive paint made with silver to minimize radiation. The chassis is grounded to the case, and the cables are shielded. As the frequencies of the PC increase, so does the radiation. Radio signals can leak out through any cracks in the case or if parts of the chassis are not electrically connected to the case. Cables attached to the computer can act as an antenna, sending out radio signals. To reduce the emissions, special metal fingers on the edge of the case and its lid ensure that the two pieces have good electrical contact and that the cables are shielded.

8.2 THE POWER SUPPLY

Since the power outlet supplies AC power and the computer needs DC power, something is needed to convert the AC power to DC. The primary function of the PC power supply is to convert AC power to clean DC power (±5 V and ±12 V). Clean power has very little voltage variation, or *noise*. The +5 V is used by most of the integrated chips that make up the PC. Therefore, power supplies are designed to produce large amounts of 5 V current (20 or more amperes).

As stated in chapter 1, computers transfer information by means of binary code–based on/off switches. An *on* switch represents a 1, which is a high logic state; an *off* switch represents a 0, which is a low logic state. The most common type of digital integrated chip (IC) used in the computer is the transistor-transistor logic (TTL) chip, which is characterized by its fast switching speed. All TTL ICs use a +5 V power supply. The high logic state is indicated by a signal measuring between 2 and 5 V, whereas the low logic state signal uses 0 to 0.8 V. The voltage between 0.8 and 2 V is the undefined region. This voltage range is used as the signal changes from high to low or low to high.

The +12 V are used by the hard drives and floppy drives. The higher voltage is needed to operate the motors, which spin the drives, and is used to generate the output voltages of older serial ports. The −12 V is also used to generate the output voltages for older serial ports, while −5 V was used in older floppy disk drive controller cards. Most modern PCs do not usually use −5 V and −12 V signals, even though you will find −5 V within the ISA expansion slot because it is part of the ISA standard. The Micro Channel Architecture and the local bus slots do not include a connection for −5 V.

Some chips that include the newest microprocessors use 3.3 V to operate. The motherboard has to convert the 5 V of older power supplies to 3.3 V. Newer power supplies, such as the ATX power supply, include a 3.3 V power line.

Most personal computers use a **switching power supply,** also known as a *self-resetting, foldback power supply.* These power supplies are smaller yet more efficient than the linear power supply.

In a switching power supply, the AC voltage is sent through a rectifier and a filter, which convert the AC voltage into high-voltage DC power. The rectifier usually consists of a diode bridge or a voltage doubler. The voltage leaving the rectifier is between 150 and 300 V. The power is sent through an oscillator, which switches on and off at high rates of speed (20 to 40 kHz). The oscillation will vary depending on the DC output required. If the output voltage needs to increase, the oscillator will remain on longer, supplying more power. If the output voltage needs to decrease, the oscillator will not stay on as long. The resulting voltage is then bridged to form DC power by means of capacitors and a second set of filters, which are both used to even out current flow. See figure 8.3. In PCs, this output is then sent across a second transformer, which breaks down the output voltage into the needed voltages (+/−5 V and +/−12 V).

Figure 8.2 XT (left) and AT (right) Power Supplies (Courtesy of PC Power & Cooling, Inc.)

Figure 8.3 Picture of Inside Power Supply

The switching power supply gets its name from the switching action of the oscillator. The oscillator is not an ideal switch for this system, but it does produce little heat, so efficiency can be as high as 85 percent. The switching power supply is ideal for personal computers because of another, unique characteristic—overload protection. If a power supply is either shorted or overloaded, it kicks into idle mode and does not supply power to the computer. The idle mode helps protect the computer circuitry from damaging power fluctuations. See figure 8.2.

8.2.1 Power Supply Form Factor

Like cases and motherboards, power supplies come in many different sizes and shapes. The traditional ones are the XT, AT, Baby AT, tower, baby tower, and ministyle power supplies; the most common is the Baby AT power supply. See figure 8.3 and table 8.1. The Baby AT form factor is so named because it is a smaller version of the original AT form factor. It has the same height and depth but is about 2-in. narrower. Because it is similar but smaller, the Baby AT power supply will fit both in Baby AT form factor cases and in full-size AT cases as well, in both tower and desktop styles. It has the same output motherboard and drive connectors as the AT.

The *LP* in **LPX** stands for *low profile* and was used in the slimline cases, which were also used in IBM's PS/2 computers. Compared to the Baby AT power supply, the LPX power supply is significantly reduced.

The newer type of power supply is the **ATX power supply.** Instead of blowing air out of the system, it blows air into the system directly over the processor. This helps cool the processor and pressurizes the inside of the case, keeping it cleaner. The ATX form factor includes a new 20-pin connector that also supplies 3.3 V, reducing the need for voltage regulators on the motherboard to power the processor

Table 8.1 Power Supply Form Factors

Form Factor	Typical Dimensions (*W* × *D* × *H*, mm)	Usual Style(s)	Motherboard Connectors	Match to Case Form Factor	Match to Motherboard Form Factor
PC/XT	222 × 142 × 120	Desktop	AT style	PC/XT	PC/XT
AT	213 × 150 × 150	Desktop or tower	AT style	AT	AT, Baby AT
Baby AT	165 × 150 × 150	Desktop or tower	AT style	Baby AT, AT, AT/ATX Combo	AT, Baby AT, AT/ATX Combo
LPX	150 × 140 × 86	Desktop	AT style	LPX, some Baby AT, AT/ATX Combo	LPX, AT, Baby AT, AT/ATX Combo
ATX/NLX	150 × 140 × 86	Desktop or tower	ATX style	ATX, mini-ATX, extended ATX, NLX, micro-ATX, AT/ATX Combo	ATX, mini-ATX, extended ATX, NLX, micro-ATX, flex-ATX
SFX	100 × 125 × 63.5	Desktop or tower	ATX style	Micro-ATX, flex-ATX, ATX, mini-ATX, NLX	Micro-ATX, flex-ATX, ATX, mini-ATX, NLX
CFX	150 × 86 × 96	Desktop or tower	BTX style	BTX, microBTX, picoBTX	BTX, microBTX, picoBTX
TFX	175 × 65 × 70	Desktop or tower	BTX style	BTX, microBTX, picoBTX	BTX, microBTX, picoBTX

NOTE: For more information on case and power supply form factors, refer to http://www.formfactors.org.

and other +3.3 V circuits. In addition, it includes a Power_On (PS_ON) and 5V_Standby (5VSB) signals, known collectively as Soft Power. Power_On is a motherboard signal that operating systems such as Windows use to power the system on or off via software. This is the reason that with Windows, you can shut off the system by clicking on the Start button and selecting shutdown. In addition, this allows features to be implemented such as Wake on Ring or Wake on LAN, in which a signal from a modem or network adapter can actually cause a PC to wake up and power on. The 5 V Standby signal is always active, giving the motherboard a limited source of power even when off and enabling these features. Note: The ATX power supply is also used on NLX systems.

Recently, a new superset of the original ATX power supply is the **ATX12V.** One difference between the ATX and the ATX12V is that the ATX12V has an increase of +12 V DC power supply output and +5 V output. The increase in +12 V DC is primarily due to the higher power conversions and transmission efficiencies of +12 V DC compared to +5 V DC or +3.3 V DC and to accommodate an increase in +12 V DC current requirements, all of which addresses issues of cross-regulation, capacitive loading, transient surge tolerance, cable voltage drop, and cooling. To enable the delivery of more +12 V DC current to the motherboard, a new four-pin receptacle/header combination has been added.

NOTE: It is highly recommended that Pentium 4 systems use an ATX12 power supply.

The **SFX** power supply form factor was created for the smaller systems such as the micro-ATX and flex-ATX. The *S* in SFX is for *small.* Micro-ATX and flex-ATX systems can also use the ATX power supply, although because miniaturization is the key with these systems, the SFX power supply makes much more sense. The "regular" SFX power supply is nominally 100 mm wide, 125 mm deep, and 63.5 mm in height. It includes a 60 mm power supply fan for cooling. An optional configuration calls for the placement of a larger fan on the top of the power supply. This fan option is 80 mm and is very often selected by manufacturers because it provides for improved system cooling. It increases the height of the supply by about 10 mm. Another option is for an extra-small power supply with dimensions of only 100 × 125 × 50 and a 40 mm power supply fan. However, this configuration requires an additional fan for system cooling, because the small 40 mm fan is only sufficient to cool the power supply itself. The SFX power supply specification does not call for providing the −5 V compatibility voltage and therefore is not compatible with the ISA bus. The SFX power supply specification calls for the power supply fan to be internally thermally speed-controlled, but an additional Fan On/Off signal is included on the SFX optional motherboard connector. Lastly, the specified output rating of the SFX power supply is 90 W. This is sufficient to run rather small systems with low-powered CPUs and few peripherals, but it makes things a bit tight and leaves little room for expansion. Fortunately, some manufacturers are producing SFX power supplies with much higher output ratings.

Some BTX motherboards will use an ATX12V power supply. Because the BTX design includes PCI Express and Serial ATA devices, many of these motherboards require a 2 mm × 12 mm connector, instead of a 2 mm × 10 mm connector, to accommodate the PCI Express X16 connector.

To accommodate smaller PC designs, several smaller power supply designs were introduced, including the TFX, CFX, and LFX power supplies. The TFX, short for *thin form factor*, is designed for small systems while supporting the next generation of high-performance processors and the PCI Express and Serial ATA devices. The CFX is the power supply that you will see in the current BTX reference system designs. The power supply is odd shaped, being elongated to the width of an optical media drive in the upper portion and the width of a hard drive disk in the lower portion, allowing for a very compact design. The smallest of these designs is the LFX, which is created for ultra-compact systems such as the small form factor PCs and the upcoming reference system which is only 6.9 liters.

8.2.2 The Power-Good Signal and the Reset Switch

In addition to supplying power to the PC components, the power supply also provides the **power-good signal.** You may recall from chapter 6 that the microprocessor timer chip tells the computer to reset constantly. As soon as the power supply performs a self-test, testing whether all voltage and current levels are acceptable, it will send a power-good signal (+5 V) to the microprocessor timer chip. When the power-good signal is sent, the computer will finish the boot process.

If the power supply experiences a short or overload, the switching power supply will go into idle mode by stopping the power-good signal. The purpose of the power-good signal is to prevent the computer from running on intolerable voltages. If the power-good signal is grounded with a wire and the power supply goes into idle mode, the PC will shut down. If the same ground wire has a switch (for example, a push button) added to it, the switch will reboot the computer. This push button, called a **reset button,** is found on most cases. This is useful when the computer "freezes up" and a soft boot (Ctrl + Alt + Del) does not work.

Another voltage line found on newer power supplies that is worth mentioning is the 5VSB. The 5VSB is the standby voltage that may be used to power circuits that require power input during the power down. In addition, this power may be used to operate circuits such as soft power control and Wake on LAN technology.

8.2.3 Power Supplies Overseas

As already stated, most power supplies designed to be used in the United States operate at 120 V with a frequency of 60 Hz. In other nations, the supply voltage and frequency may be different. In Europe, 230 V with a 50 Hz frequency is the standard. Most modern switching power supplies are willing to operate at either voltage. Some can automatically switch over to the proper voltage, while most are adjusted by a small switch on the rear of the power supply. Make sure when plugging in your PC and before turning it on that the correct voltage is selected. If the power supply is switched to 230 V and the voltage is 120 V, there will be no problem, except the PC will not boot. If, however, the power supply is set to 120 V and it is connected to a 230 V outlet, the power supply and other important components will be seriously damaged.

Inexpensive voltage converters should not be used to convert a PC's power supply. Even though the voltage levels will be correct, the frequency usually will not be adjusted, which may damage the PC.

8.2.4 Power Supply Connections

The IBM PC had four connectors coming from the power supply; newer power supplies usually have more. Two of these connectors attach to the motherboard and the others connect to the floppy drives, hard drives, CD drives, and other devices.

Figure 8.4 Power supply connectors (P8 and P9) that connect to the motherboard. Note that the black cables are together.

Table 8.2 AT Motherboard Power Connectors

	Connector	AT Voltages*	Typical Colors
P8 (motherboard connector 1)	P8-1	+5 V (power-good signal)	Orange
	P8-2	+5 V	Red
	P8-3	+12 V	Yellow
	P8-4	−12 V	Blue
	P8-5	0 V (ground)	Black
	P8-6	0 V (ground)	Black
P9 (motherboard connector 2)	P9-1	0 V (ground)	Black
	P9-2	0 V (ground)	Black
	P9-3	−5 V	White
	P9-4	+5 V	Red
	P9-5	+5 V	Red
	P9-6	+5 V	Red

*Acceptable voltage ranges are 4.5 to 5.4 for 5 V, and 10.8 to 12.9 for 12 V.

Older motherboards have two motherboard connectors, identified as P8 and P9, that use **Burndy connectors.** See figure 8.4 and table 8.2. These connectors are supposed to be keyed—that is, they have small tabs sticking out—so that you cannot put one in the wrong place. Unfortunately, some replacement power supplies are shipped without the proper keying. Therefore, a good rule to follow is to place the black wires of each connector together. If you fail to do this, you will destroy the motherboard or the microprocessor, or both. ATX motherboards have a single 20-pin or 24-pin connector. The 24-pin connector has additional connectors to support PCI-Express. See figures 8.5 and 8.6 and table 8.3. It supplies all the standard voltages that older previous power supplies do, but it also supplies 3.3 V, so the motherboard does not have to convert 5 to 3.3 V.

As mentioned earlier, the new BTX design calls for a 2 mm × 12 mm connector to accommodate PCI Express. See figure 8.7.

Figure 8.5 ATX Power Supply Connector

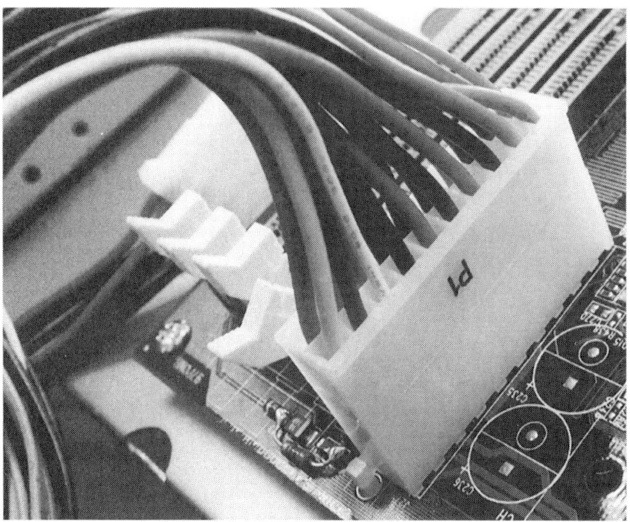

Figure 8.6 ATX Power Connectors

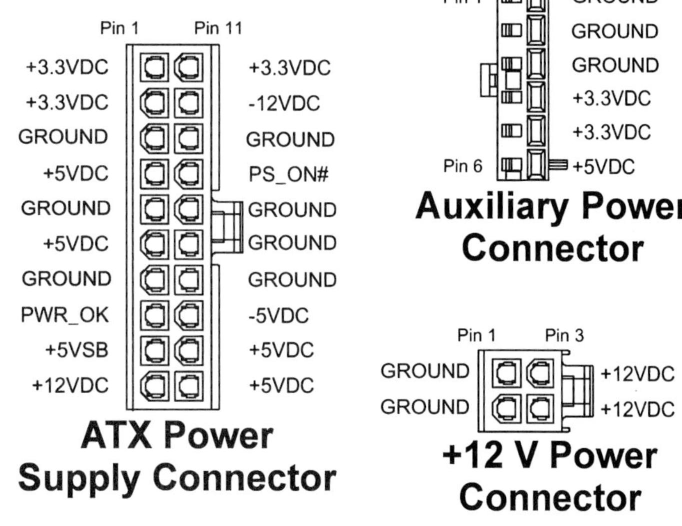

Note: +3.3 V, +5 V, +12 V output lines should be within –5% tolerance.
–5 V and –12 V output lines should be within –10% tolerance.

Not all motherboards use the two Burndy connectors or the ATX connector. Some use a Molex connector, which is slightly different from a Burndy, while others use a connector that combines the two Burndy connectors into one large connection. The Molex connectors use smaller, square pins; the combined Burndy connection has rectangular pins. The only way that you can plug in the wrong connector is by forcing it.

NOTE: Pin 9 of the ATX connector has the 15 V standby signal, which is always receiving power from the power supply when connected to an AC outlet, even when the computer is shut off. Therefore, it is more important to unplug an ATX system from the AC outlet before working inside the case.

For power supplies of 250 W or more, an auxiliary power connector is recommended to supply the additional 5 and 3.3 V the motherboard might need. This is a six-pin Molex-type connector, similar to

Table 8.3 ATX Power Supply Motherboard Power Connectors

Pin	ATX Voltage	Color	Pin	ATX Voltage	Color
1	+3.3 V	Orange	11	+3.3 V	Orange
2	+3.3 V	Orange	12	−12 V	Blue
3	0 V (ground)	Black	13	0 V (ground)	Black
4	+5 V	Red	14	+5 V (power supply on)	Green
5	0 V (ground)	Black	15	0 V (ground)	Black
6	+5 V	Red	16	0 V (ground)	Black
7	0 V (ground)	Black	17	0 V (ground)	Black
8	+5 V (power-good signal)	Gray	18	−5 V	White
9	+5 V (standby signal)	Purple	19	+5 V	Red
10	+12 V	Yellow	20	+5 V	Red

Figure 8.7 Newer ATX and BTX Main Power Supply Connector

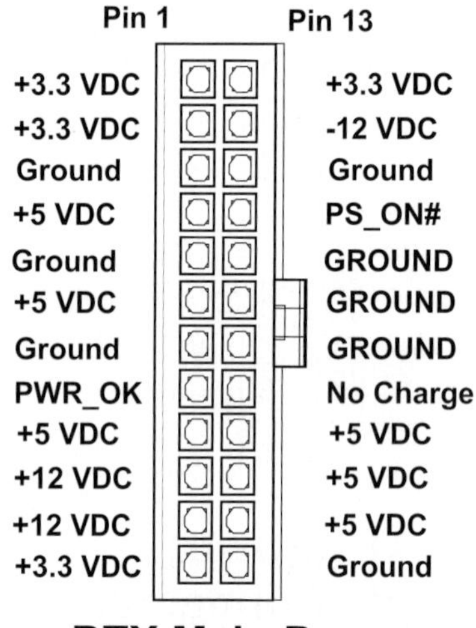

the one of the motherboard power connectors used on LPX supplies. See table 8.4. In addition, the ATX12 power supply includes a four-pin Molex connector to supply the additional 12 V power for the processor voltage regulator. See table 8.5.

Some ATX power supplies may also have an auxiliary power connector. The original ATX specification defines an optional six-pin connector (two rows of three pins each) to provide signals to monitor and control the cooling fan, monitor the voltage of the +3.3 V signal to the motherboard, and provide power and grounding to devices compliant with the IEEE 1394 (FireWire) standard. See table 8.6.

Table 8.4 ATX Auxiliary Power Connectors

Pin	ATX Voltage	Color
1	Ground	Black
2	Ground	Black
3	Ground	Black
4	+3.3 V	Orange
5	+3.3 V	Orange
6	+5 V	Red

Table 8.5 +12 V Power Connectors Used in ATX12

Pin	ATX Voltage	Color
1	Ground	Black
2	Ground	Black
3	+12 V	Yellow
4	+12 V	Yellow

Table 8.6 ATX Optional Power Supply Connectors

Pin	ATX Voltage	Color	Pin	ATX Voltage	Color
1	FanM	White	4	1394R	White with black stripe
2	FanC	White with blue stripe	5	1394V	White with red stripe
3	+3.3 V sense	White with brown stripe	6	Reserved	

Figure 8.8 5¼-in. and 3½-in. Power Connectors

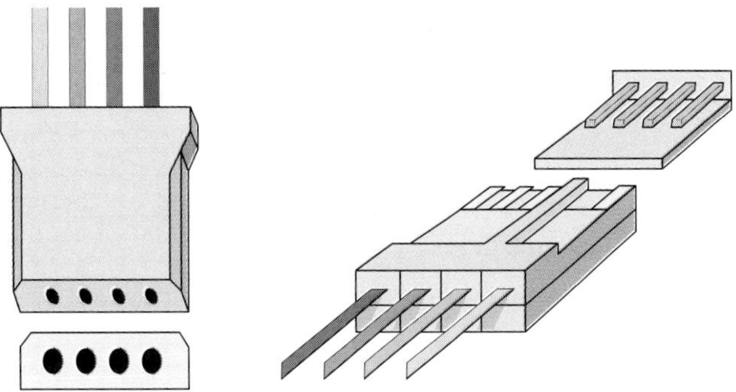

The remaining connectors are used for floppy drives, hard drives, tape drives, and other peripherals and come in two sizes. The 5¼-in. connector was part of the IBM PC. It has a rectangular shape with two corners clipped off. When the connector is plugged into the drive, the two clipped corners prevent it from being connected upside down. The other connector is smaller and is used to connect 3½-in. drives. This connector has a ridge that allows the plug to be inserted in only one way. See figure 8.8 and table 8.7.

Table 8.7 Disk Drive Power Connectors

Connector	Voltage*	Color
P10-1	+12 V	Yellow
P10-2	0 V (ground)	Black
P10-3	0 V (ground)	Black
P10-4	+5 V	Red

*Acceptable voltage ranges are 4.5 to 5.4 for 5 V, and 10.8 to 12.9 for 12 V.

WARNING:

Be careful to insert the plug correctly and not force it. If it is improperly connected, 12 V will enter components that are made for 5 V. This will result in damaged or blown chips, and the cable may catch on fire.

8.2.5 Power Supply Capacity

The power supply capacity is measured in watts (W). The wattage rating of a power supply is the maximum amount of electric power a device can safely handle continuously. If the amount of power exceeds the wattage rating of the power supply, the power supply detects an overload and shuts down into idle mode.

When the IBM PC was introduced, it had a small (63.5 W) power supply. This power supply could handle two floppy drives, a video card, and the XT motherboard. If a hard drive and a memory expansion card were added, the power supply would sometimes kick into idle mode because the power supply was overloaded.

The IBM XT and IBM AT had larger power supplies (130 W), which allowed expandability. Most power supplies today have ratings between 200 and 300 W. The more devices connected to the computer, the more wattage the PC will need.

The power supply capacity is measured in watts (W). The wattage rating of a power supply is the maximum amount of electric power a device can safely handle continuously. In other words, because $W = I \times V$, the power supply can supply a current at a set voltage continuously. If the amount of power exceeds the wattage rating of the power supply, the power supply detects an overload and shuts down into idle mode.

When the IBM PC was introduced, it had a small (63.5 W) power supply. This power supply could handle two floppy drives, a video card, and the XT motherboard. If a hard drive and a memory expansion card were added, the power supply would sometimes kick into idle mode because the power supply was overloaded. The IBM XT and IBM AT had larger power supplies (130 W), which allowed expandability. Most power supplies today have ratings between 200 and 300 W. The more devices connected to the computer, the more wattage the PC will need.

When looking at the power supply specifications, the most important specifications that you will find listed are probably those that relate to its output signals. Some manufacturers will list the values separately for each of the specifications shown here. Other manufacturers may provide a table that shows all the relevant output statistics (and, sometimes, some of the electrical characteristics of each voltage level at the same time).

Output Specifications

- **Output Rating (watts)**—The nominal, total, maximum output of the power supply in watts. This is sometimes not supplied in the specification sheet; the name of the power supply will usually have a number in it that is supposed to represent this value, and sometimes it even does.
- **Output Current Ratings (Maximum Load by Voltage)**—The maximum amount of current provided by the power supply at each voltage level.
- **Minimum Current Ratings (Minimum Load Requirement by Voltage)**—The minimum amount of current that must be drawn by loads within the PC, for each voltage level it provides, in order for it to function properly. See the discussion of output power loading for more.

- **+ 3.3 V/+5 V Combination Maximum—**The maximum amount of total power, in watts, that the power supply can provide simultaneously for the combination of the +3.3 and +5 V signals. This is an upper limit that constrains any maximum load levels for either of the +3.3 or +5 V signals individually.
- **Peak Output—**The amount of current that the voltage specified can supply for a limited amount of time. Usually this is specified only for the +12 V signal. Ideally, the manufacturer will specify not only the peak output current but also the amount of time the supply is rated to sustain that peak. For example, the continuous maximum for +12 V may be 10 A (amps) and the peak level may be 14 A, and the peak level may be sustainable for 10s.
- **Output Voltage Range—**For each output voltage, the range or tolerance that the power supply guarantees its output to be within. For example, the power supply might be +4.8 to +5.2 V or be a percentage such as 4%.
- **Efficiency—**The percentage of the total energy supplied to the power supply that is converted to usable form by the power supply and conveyed to the PC's components. Typical numbers for PC power supplies are 60 to 85 percent; the other 15 to 40 percent is wasted as heat. Clearly, the more efficient the power supply, the better! Not only will you save electricity, you will ensure that the power supply runs cooler at the same time, making the supply's components last longer and the system work better overall. At the same time, don't give too much credence to this parameter, especially if you are comparing two units that have similar numbers (and many do). Seventy-one percent efficiency versus 73 percent efficiency doesn't really translate to much difference in the real world. Efficiency is probably more important for supplies that provide a lot of power, because the percentages equate to larger numbers.
- **Power-Good Delay—**The typical time from when the power is applied to the supply until the power-good signal is asserted.

Input Specifications

- **Input Voltage Range—**Acceptable range of input voltages. Because most power supplies can function on nominal 115 or 230 V electricity, you will usually see two sets of numbers, such as 85 to 135 V AC or 170 to 270 V AC. The input range is not usually that critical in determining the suitability of a power supply, because most utility power stays fairly close to the nominal level under normal circumstances. However, the minimum voltage level can have some impact on how well the power supply rides through brownouts.
- **Voltage Selection—**If the power supply supports both 115 and 230 V nominal voltage and it automatically selects between them or is there a manual switch.
- **Frequency—**Acceptable frequency of input power (50 Hz, 60 Hz, or 50 and 60 Hz). Alternatively, a range of acceptable frequencies (for example, 48–62 Hz). Most power supplies can handle both nominal 50 and 60 Hz input.
- **Power Factor—**A measure of how efficiently a piece of equipment uses its electricity supply. PCs are notorious for having low power factors. The switching power supplies used in PCs tend to draw power only at the peak of the main cycle. Traditional power supplies have a power factor of about 0.6 to 0.7. A power factor of 0.6 means that the current drawn by the PC is 1.67 times that necessary to supply the amount of power it really needs. For instance, a PC server might need around 300 W during standard use, yet the current it draws might be 3 A. Multiplying voltage (115 V AC power in the United States) by the current gives you 115 V × 4 A = 460 VA, so the power factor is 300/460 = 0.65.

NOTE: Some newer power supplies, especially larger ones for servers, have additional circuitry added to correct the power factor of the supply. These are, unsurprisingly, called power-factor-corrected supplies and have a power factor of (or near) 1.0.

If you check the output specifications for the power supply, you will normally see listed all the different voltages that the power supply provides and the amount of current it can supply for each. You can also use the power distribution to calculate the actual total output rating of the supply. Multiplying each voltage and maximum current value and adding them together should yield the approximate total output power of the supply. Note that the negative sign is ignored.

Example 8.1:

Let's look at a 300 W power supply. For DC electricity, the computation of power is as simple as multiplying its current in amperes by its voltage in volts. Of course, power supplies produce several different voltages. That's the first reason why just knowing the total number of watts is insufficient.

Output Voltage Level	Maximum Current (Amperes)	Maximum Power at the Output Voltage Level (Watts)
+12 V	8	$12 \times 8 = 96$
+5 V	30	$5 \times 30 = 150$
+3.3 V	14	$3.3 \times 14 = 46.2$
−5 V	0.5	$5 \times 0.5 = 2.5$
−12 V	0.5	$12 \times 0.5 = 6$
+5 V Standby	1.5	$5 \times 1.5 = 7.5$
Total		**96 + 150 + 2.5 + 6 + 7.5 = 262**

As you can see, the actual wattage available is only 262 W instead of 300 W. In addition, the power supply specification might specify a +3.3 V/+5 V limit. For example, if this power supply has a +3.3 V/+5 V limit of 150 W, it can provide 30 A of +5 V and 0 A of +3.3 V, 20.8 A of +5 V and 14 A of +3.3 V, or any combination in between.

8.2.6 On/Off Power Switch

If you buy a case with a power supply, the power supply is already connected to the on/off switch. The on/off switch is either a push-button or a paddle/rocker switch. If you have to add a power supply to the case or replace a power supply, you must connect four cables to the on/off switch. The colors of the connectors used in AT cases in the switch are brown, blue, white, and black. See figure 8.9. If the cables are connected 90° off (such as the brown cable connected where blue is supposed to be, black connected where brown is supposed to be, white connected where black is supposed to be, and blue connected where white is supposed to be), you will blow a fuse in the fuse box and knock out all power to the AC outlet as well as any other power outlets on the same circuit. (Note: Because some on/off switches use nonstandard color schemes, it is important to record how the wires are connected before disconnecting them.)

NOTE: The cables that connect to the on/off power switch carry 110 V AC at all times. You could be electrocuted if you touch the end of these wires with the power supply plugged in. Therefore, always make sure that the power supply is unplugged before connecting or disconnecting the power switch.

Figure 8.9 On/Off Switches

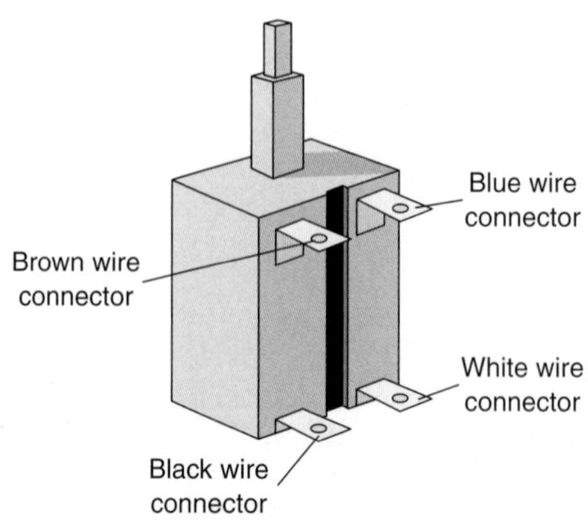

Different from the AT power supply, the ATX power supply uses the PS_ON signal to power up the system. A +5 V signal is constantly sent through pin 14 (PS_ON) of the ATX power connector. When the PS_ON is shorted, the power supply is told to turn on and start the boot process. A push-button contact switch is connected to two pins on the motherboard that link to the PS_ON signal to ground. When the push button is pushed, it connects the PS_ON signal with ground, shorting it out. Therefore, when you are installing an ATX motherboard, you need to connect the push-button wires (usually labeled PWR SW) to the motherboard. If you decide to test a motherboard without physically installing it in an ATX case, you can start the system by either connecting a push-button switch to the motherboard and pressing the button or by taking a small screwdriver and making contact with the two pins that make up the power switch connector. Because the switch toggles only the on/off status, the switch carries only +5 V of DC power rather than the full 110 V AC current used in the AT power supplies.

Because the ATX power supply uses the PS_ON signal to turn off the computer, you can typically configure how the ATX soft power options function. For example, most systems will be configured so that if you press the on/off button and keep it pressed for 4 or 5 s, the system will shut off. This can come in handy if your system appears to have locked up. Yet you can typically set the soft power options in the CMOS setup program. For example, you can configure the power switch to act like an AT switch (instant off) or you configure it to go into sleep mode. Note: Most ATX power supplies also provide a real on/off switch on the back of the power supply. Therefore, if nothing else works, you can use the on/off switch on the back of the power supply or you can unplug it.

8.2.7 Power Equipment Certification

To make sure that power supplies are safe to use, several testing and certification organizations have set up standards for their design and manufature. One of the most well known of these organizations is **Underwriters Laboratories Inc. (UL),** an independent, nonprofit organization. The purpose of UL is to act as a safety engineering consultant and provide certification. Owing to UL's strict standards and solid reputation, companies pay UL to detect flaws and defects in their products before the products hit the market.

Underwriters Laboratories deals with all electronic devices. Computers and other related equipment, including desktop PCs, disk drives, printers, main frame computers, desktop calculators, and electric typewriters, come under the UL 1950 standard. UL gives a product a UL Listing or UL Recognition. A UL Listing applies to a complete product, such as a desktop PC, a monitor, or a power supply. UL Recognition applies to a component used to make up products such as the power supply.

In Canada, the CSE International is equivalent to the Underwriters Laboratories. NEMKO in Norway and TUV and VDE in Germany do most of the electrical component certifications for Europe. The **CE Declaration of Conformity** is the official marking required by the European Community for all electric and electronic equipment that will be sold or put into service for the first time anywhere in the European community. It proves to the buyer or user that this product fulfills all essential safety and environmental requirements for machinery, low voltage, and electromagnetic compatibility as they are defined in the European Directives.

8.2.8 Keeping the PC Cool

One of the biggest enemies of the PC, and particularly of its semiconductor circuits, is heat buildup. Heat is generated when a current flows against electrical resistance and whenever an element of a computer circuit changes logical states. Inside the case, heat cannot escape, so it builds up, driving up the temperature. Heat shortens the life span of the circuits, which will lead to computer failure. Therefore, keeping a system cool means prolonging its life.

Ventilation holes were added to the case of the IBM PC to keep the PC cooler by letting the heat out. When setting up a PC, remember to allow good ventilation and to not block or restrict the ventilation holes. The ventilation slots in the case should have at least three feet of free space. Additionally, if the power supply is run close to its full capacity or exceeds it, it tends to overheat.

Most PCs produce heat faster than heat can escape through the ventilation holes. Therefore, they need some active cooling to force the heat away from the circuits. A fan has been added to the power supply to circulate the air around the case.To ensure adequate cooling of a computer system, the case

Figure 8.10 Microprocessor Cooling Fan (Courtesy of PC Power & Cooling, Inc.)

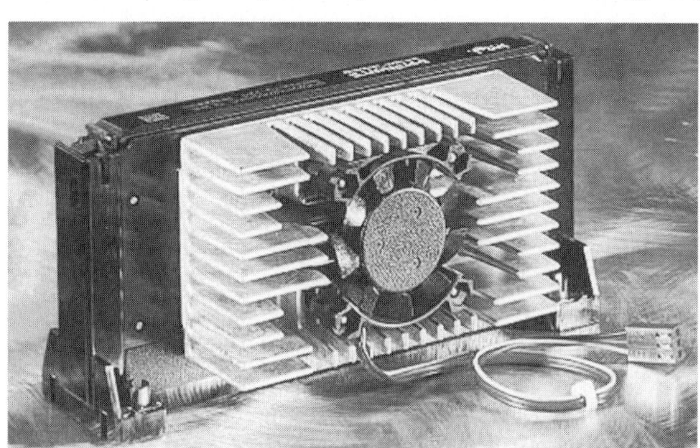

should always be kept closed. In addition the following must be in place so that the airflow within the case will be maintained:

- **The Front Cover—**In many systems, the front cover can be removed.
- **Front Cover Plates—**The plates that go in front of drive bays that are not being used.
- **The Slot Covers—**The plates that cover an expansion card hole in the back of the computer when an expansion slot is not being used.

See figure 8.10. One fan is not enough, however, for the newer microprocessors. Some power supplies use two fans; others use a heat sink and/or fan on the microprocessor. The **heat sink** is a piece of metal with a large surface area. It takes heat away from the microprocessor and dissipates it faster than a fan system.

Question:

Should you shut off your computer when you leave your desk or should you keep it on all day?

Answer:

If you are coming and going from your desk, leave the computer on all the time. Studies show that computers will last longer if you leave them on. It is not the sudden electrical surge that does the damage when the system is turned on, but the sudden heating and cooling. Of course, at the end of the day, you can shut off your computer.

8.3 TROUBLESHOOTING POWER SUPPLIES

Because the power supply is a half-electronic and half-mechanical component, it is considered a high-failure item compared to other items within the PC that do not have any mechanical parts. The mechanical part of the power supply is the fan. If the fan fails, the PC will heat to a level that can damage other components. In addition, if the power supply is supplying the proper power and the fan has failed, the PC may have boot-up failures, boot-up errors, memory errors, and device failures and may give off electrical shock when the case or connections are touched.

As a general rule, when a power supply fails, it is easier, quicker, and usually cheaper to replace it than to repair it. Replacement is usually cheaper because it takes more time to diagnose and repair a power supply. It is the time spent that drives the cost up. In addition, you need to have some skills as an electronic technician to be able to successfully repair a power supply.

When checking a system that has no power, the first thing to do is to see if the power supply is plugged into the AC outlet and the PC is on. Remember that the power should be 120 V AC at 60 Hz. Next, check the AC power cord to see if it is good.

Before opening the power supply, check that the fan is running and that the power supply is generating the proper DC voltages. The best way to check for proper voltages is to use a voltmeter or a digital multimeter (DMM). To check the voltage level, the power supply must have a load. This can be done by connecting an inexpensive peripheral or using a dummy load. Floppy drives should not be used because they are devices that come on only when they are being accessed. A dummy load may be a 2 or

3Ω 15 W resistor on the +5 output (red wire). If there is no load on the power supply, the power supply will falsely detect a short, which causes it to go into idle mode. (Note: Power supplies that fail to go into idle mode without a load are not well designed and fail to offer as much protection against power problems.) Next, set the voltmeter to the proper DC scale and measure the voltage. Be sure to check multiple connections. If the power is bad on one connection but is good on the others, that indicates a power cable and/or connector is bad.

The large-filter capacitors are second only to the fan as a common source of failure within the power supply. To test the capacitors, you would set a voltmeter to the AC scale to measure ripple (AC fluctuations). The AC scale will show how clean the output voltage is. The AC voltage should be 200 millivolt (mV) or less (zero or almost zero). If the capacitors are dried up or have an open in them, this will cause a pulsing at 60 or 120 Hz and all kinds of regulation problems.

If you choose to repair the power supply rather than replace it, there are certain things that you must consider.

> **WARNING:**
>
> The filter capacitors used in switching power supplies can store an amount of energy that can kill. What makes things more dangerous is that these capacitors can store the energy for months after nonuse of the power supply. In addition, if the capacitors are discharged into other components of the power supply, there is a good chance that those components will be damaged. Always discharge the capacitors before working within the power supply.

Many books recommend using a screwdriver to short out the two connecting wires to discharge the capacitor. A better method is to use a high-wattage resistor. This resistor will prevent an electrical arc yet allow the capacitor to be discharged within a few seconds. After discharging the capacitor, check to see if there is a fuse within the power supply that may have been blown. The fuse protects against an overload resulting from a short circuit. If there is excessive current, the heat generated by the excessive current will melt the fuse, which will, of course, shut down the power supply and, in turn, protect the computer. A blown fuse is easy to diagnose and repair. What you need to be concerned with is why there was an overload that caused the fuse to blow in the first place. After checking the fuse, inspect the other components (resistors, capacitors, and diodes) and visually check the solder joints and traces for damage. Lastly, remember that damage that cannot be seen can occur inside the chip or component.

8.4 POWER FLUCTUATIONS

When you turn on a PC, you expect the power to be there. Unfortunately, the power that you get from the power company is not always 120 V AC. The voltage level may drop or increase. While the power supply can handle many of these power fluctuations, other power fluctuations may shut down or damage the computer, corrupt the data, and lose unsaved work. See figure 8.11.

Studies done by IBM show that a typical computer is subject to more than 120 power problems per month. The most common of these are voltage sags. Obvious power problems such as blackouts and

Figure 8.11 Power Irregularities

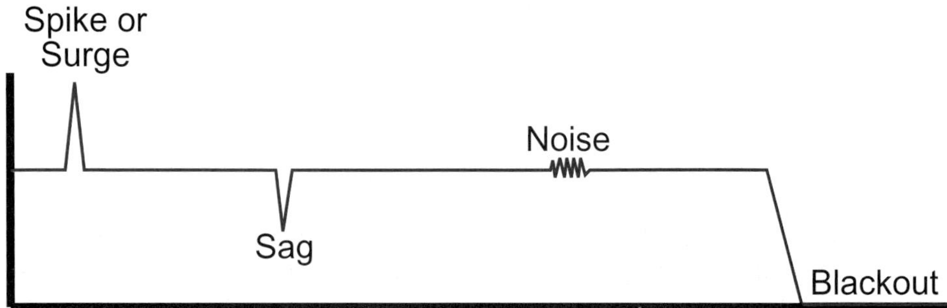

lightning make up only 12 percent of power problems. American Power Conversion states that power problems cause 45.3 percent of data losses.

Symptoms of bad power are frozen computers or keyboards, errors in data transmissions, corrupted or lost data, frequently aborted modem transfers, and total failure of a computer or computer component.

8.4.1 Overvoltages and Undervoltages

Power line irregularities can be classified into two categories: overvoltages and undervoltages. The more dangerous is overvoltage, which is defined as voltage in excess of 10 percent of the power supply rating. The worst of these is a spike, which lasts only a nanosecond but can measure as high as 25,000 V (normally caused by lightning). A **spike** is sometimes defined as transient overvoltage. A **surge,** which can stretch into milliseconds, is overvoltage of longer duration. Spikes and surges can visibly damage the electronic components or can cause microdamage, which cannot be seen. Other causes of overvoltage besides lightning include when overburdened power grids switch from one source to another and when a high-powered electrical motor tries to grab power.

Undervoltages (including total power failure) make up 87 percent of all power problems and occur when the computer gets less voltage than is needed to run properly. Most PCs are designed to withstand prolonged voltage dips of about 20 percent without shutting down. Power outages and short drops in power typically do not physically damage the computer. Unfortunately, they do result in lost and corrupted data.

Undervoltage takes the form of sags, brownouts, and blackouts. **Sags,** which usually are not a problem, are very short drops lasting only a few milliseconds. **Brownouts** last longer than sags and can force the computer to shut down, introduce memory errors, and cause unsaved work to be lost. (Note: Brownouts or power failures of 200 ms are sufficient to cause power problems with the PC. These problems can be caused by damaged power lines and by equipment that draws massive amounts of power, such as air conditioners, copy machines, laser printers, space heaters, and coffee makers. To help reduce the effect of brownouts, PC should be on their own power circuit (if possible.) **Blackouts** are total power failures.

8.4.2 Noise

In addition to power line overvoltages and undervoltages, the computer may experience electrical **noise,** radio frequency interference (RFI), caused by telephones, motors, fluorescent lights, and radio transmitters. Noise can introduce errors into executable programs and files. (Note: To limit the chance of AC line noise, a computer should be installed on its own power circuit.)

8.4.3 Power Protection

Most voltage fluctuations can be prevented from doing any damage. There are several devices that can protect the computer from overvoltages and undervoltages: surge protectors, line conditioners, standby power supplies, and uninterruptible power supplies.

The most common of the power protection devices is the **surge protector.** Surge suppressors are similar to surge protectors except they contain filters to smooth out variations (although these filters are not as good as those used in line conditioners). A surge protector is designed to prevent most short-duration, high-intensity spikes and surges from reaching the PC by absorbing excess voltages. See figure 8.12. The most common surge protector uses a metal oxide varistor (MOV). A MOV looks like a brightly colored plastic-coated disk capacitor and works by siphoning electricity to ground when the

Figure 8.12 Surge Protector

voltage exceeds 200 V. Consequently, the voltage spike is "clipped" and the excess electricity is then converted into heat. Other devices used to suppress overvoltages are gas discharge tubes, pellet arrestors, and coaxial arrestors. The better surge protectors use a combination of these.

When purchasing a surge protector, you should consider the following:

- **Energy Absorption**—Surge protectors are rated by the amount of energy that can be absorbed (measured in joules): 200 J is basic, 400 J is good, and 600+ J is excellent.
- **UL Standards for Voltage Let-Through**—Underwriters Laboratories has established the UL 1449 standard for surge suppressors. It rates suppressors by the amount of voltage they allow to pass through to the protected equipment. There are three levels of rated protection: 330 V, 400 V, and 500 V. The lower the number, the better the protection.
- **Protection Indicator**—An LED indicating if the MOVs are working or not.
- **Circuit Breaker or Fuse**—Most suppressors have either a fuse or a resettable circuit breaker, which will blow or trip if there is a short circuit or severe surge that causes excessive current to flow. Breakers are better because fuses, once blown, have to be replaced.
- **Protection Guarantee**—This is usually an equipment protection guarantee, which says if your equipment is damaged when plugged into the suppressor, the manufacturer will pay to have it repaired or replaced.

Phone-line surge protectors are also available. If a modem, fax/modem, or fax is connected to the PC, consider getting one. It will prevent surges and spikes that travel through the telephone lines.

Surge protectors have several drawbacks. First, they protect only against overvoltages, not undervoltages. In addition, the life expectancy of a MOV is limited. With every spike, the MOV gets weaker and weaker until it can't protect the PC anymore. When buying a surge protector, make sure it has some kind of indicator (LED light or a beep) to indicate when it can no longer protect. In addition, be extremely careful that the device is not one that just provides extra power connections, like an extension cord.

The next level of protection is the **line conditioner.** It uses the inductance of transformers to filter out noise, and capacitors (and other circuits) to "fill in" brownouts. In addition, most line conditioners include surge protection.

The last two forms of protection are the standby power supply (SPS) and the uninterruptible power supply (UPS). Both of these are based on a large battery. The **standby power supply (SPS)** consists of a battery connected in parallel to the PC. When the SPS detects a power fluctuation, the system switches over to the battery. Of course, the SPS requires a small but measurable amount of time to switch over (usually one-half of one cycle of the AC current, or less than 10 milliseconds). Most built-in surge protection devices are SPSs. The **uninterruptible power supply (UPS)** differs from the SPS in that the battery is connected in series with the PC. The AC power is connected directly to the battery. Since the battery always provides clean DC power, the PC is protected against overvoltages and undervoltages. See figure 8.13. When the SPS and UPS send DC power from the battery, it has to be converted back to AC power before reaching the PC's power supply. Most SPSs

Figure 8.13 UPS

and UPSs will generate a sine wave. (Note: Poorer quality SPSs and UPSs generate a square wave instead of a sine wave and should be avoided.) Uninterruptible power supplies are usually not designed to keep the PC running for hours without power. Instead, they are usually intended to give the user or users enough time to save all files and to properly shut down the PC. Laser printers should not be connected to a UPS since they have large current demands and can generate line noise.

NOTE: If a UPS or SPS has not been used for a long period of time, do not discharge the battery. If you do, the battery may lose some of its capacity to store power or may be unable to accept a charge at all. Of course, always check the manufacturer's documentation.

When deciding on the UPS to use, the most important factor is its load. You must be sure that the UPS will support the equipment connected to it. The volt-amp capacity of the UPS should be slightly more than the peak power demands of the equipment connected to it. So, before buying a UPS, add up the peak power requirement for each device and buy an appropriate UPS. A useful way to determine the best UPS is to use an online calculator such as the one from the following website:

http://www.apcc.com/sizing/selectors.cfm

As you can imagine, a UPS is ideal for servers. By connecting a serial cable between the UPS and the server and by using UPS software, you can configure the server to automatically send messages to the network for the users to log off, save all information, and properly shut down the server when there is no longer AC power available. This will help prevent data from being corrupted. It can also send email messages or alerts to the administrator and perform backups.

If the server does not properly shut down during a power outage, you should make sure that the serial cable is connected, there are no conflicts with the serial port, and that the UPS software is configured properly. If the UPS starts beeping immediately when you start the server, make sure that you connected power from the UPS to a working AC outlet. This usually indicates that no AC power is being received.

8.5 TROUBLESHOOTING POWER-RELATED PROBLEMS

When troubleshooting the PC, you should always be concerned with power-related problems. As you have seen, the power problems may be caused by a power supply, bad power provided by the AC power outlet, or a PC component that causes a short or overload. Power problems can cause errors and may cause failure in RAM chips, microprocessors, and hard drives. Power-related problems may be harder to diagnose because they are sometimes not obvious and are often intermittent.

Example 8.2:

You turn on the PC and it does not boot, nor do the lights on the front panel light up. After a quick inspection, you notice that the fan is not spinning.

The first thing to check is the obvious. Is the power cord plugged into the AC power outlet and into the back of the computer? You will be amazed how many times this is the problem. Next, make sure that the AC outlet power is on and not shut off with an on/off light switch somewhere within the room.

If the machine is properly connected, make a list of what can cause total failure:

1. A bad power supply
2. The AC outlet
3. The power cable connecting the PC to the AC outlet
4. The power plugs that connect the power supply to the motherboard and drives
5. A short or open in the computer
6. Overloading the power supply

Remember that this is only a list and may not represent the order in which you want to check everything.

Make sure you have AC power from the power outlet. Use a voltmeter or connect another device to the outlet. If the other device works properly, the power is probably good. It may be a good idea to check the voltage at the other end of the power cable or use the same power cable when connecting the other device. This will verify the presence of AC power and verify that the power cord is good.

After checking everything outside of the computer, it is time to open the computer and take a look inside. After opening the case, check the power connectors leading to the motherboard to see if they are connected properly (at the power supply, they should be black to black) and that the drives are connected properly. Remember, to run most switching power supplies, you must have a load. In addition, inspect the floppy drive and hard drive ribbon cables for proper connection.

If the computer is connected properly, you should test the power supply. Disconnect everything connected to the power supply and put a load (inexpensive device or a dummy load) on the power supply. If the power supply does not operate, it is bad. If the power comes on, then there is a short or overload, which is causing the power supply to go into idle mode.

To check for shorts and overloads, you need to use isolation. First take out all of the expansion cards except the video card and the floppy drive/hard drive controller card and disconnect all drives except the floppy disk drive and primary hard drive. If the machine powers on with the minimum devices, one of the components that was removed or disconnected is causing a short or overload, or all of the components together are too much for the power supply. To find out the cause of the problem, insert one expansion card or connect one drive at a time and turn on the machine to find out if that device is the one causing the power supply to go into idle mode.

If the computer still does not work after removing all of the extra devices, the motherboard/RAM, video card, floppy drive/hard drive controller card, floppy drive, or hard drive must be causing the problem. In this case, you must use isolation and replace one device at a time until you find out which one is causing the problem.

8.6 AC ADAPTERS AND PORTABLE BATTERIES

Since the power outlet supplies AC power and computer needs DC power, something is needed to convert AC power to DC. On desktop computers, an AC adapter supply converts AC power to clean DC power. On notebook computers, an AC adapter does the converting, which is typically part of the notebook power cord. Therefore, power that goes into the notebook is DC power. When the computer is not using AC power, power is supplied from the battery, which is already supplying DC power. When connecting an AC adapter to a notebook, you must make sure that you use the AC adapter that is made for the specific notebook.

The power requirements of portable computers (laptops and notebooks) differ from those of a desktop computer because portable computers are designed to decrease power consumption to provide a longer battery life. Therefore, portable computers use a +5 V motor for their hard disk, which eliminates the need for a plug for +12 V. Most newer microprocessors are designed to operate at 3.3 V or less. Finally, portable computers need little power protection because the battery within the portable computer always provides clean low-voltage DC power. See figure 8.14.

To stretch the power of the battery, most notebook and laptop computers have their own power-management functions to conserve power. Some may dim the screen down, much like a screen saver, or stop the hard drive from spinning if a certain time of nonuse has passed. If the computer does not have built-in power management features, many of the operating systems have software that helps prolong the life of the battery. For example, you can enable Windows power management feature by using the Power Management applet in the Control Panel.

Figure 8.14 Notebook Battery

Table 8.8 Common Types of Portable Batteries

Nickel-Cadmium (NiCad)	NiCad batteries provide considerable power but last only 2 to 4 hours. Older NiCad batteries can take as much as 12 hours to recharge; newer batteries take only a few hours. NiCads also suffer from memory effects, where if they are partially drained and then recharged, they lose about 40 percent of their charge. Lastly, NiCad batteries can only be recharged about 1,000 times.
Nickle-Metal Hydride (NiMH)	NiMH batteries store up to 50 percent more power than NiCad batteries, and they do not suffer from memory effects. In addition, they do not use the dangerous substances found in NiCads. They can be recharged as many as 500 times; they take nearly twice as long to recharge as NiCads.
Lithium-Ion (Li-ion)	Lithium is the lightest metal and has the highest electrochemical potential. Since lithium itself is unstable, lithium-ion batteries are made from lithium ions produced from chemicals. These batteries do not use poisonous metals. *Note:* Do not insert a Li-ion battery into a system designed for a NiCad or NiMH battery; it can result in fire.
Lithium-Ion Polymer (LIP or Li-Poly)	The LIP, or Pi-Poly, is the newest battery type that uses lithium ion and cobalt oxide cell that can be formed into flat, thin sheets, allowing for a smaller battery. Although the battery has a slightly lower energy density, it is usually found in cell phones, PDAs, and other small devices.

The most common types of portable batteries are described in table 8.8. Since many of these batteries contain harmful or poisonous chemicals and improper handling and disposal can result in fire or explosion, you should always check the battery label for information on special disposal procedures.

Most notebook batteries are charged by a DC board or charge board that attaches to the system motherboard. When a battery does not charge, the problem is with the battery or the DC/charge board (or its fuse, if it has one). Often, technicians replace the battery and the system appears to be running fine and the battery is charging, only to have the same problem recur later.

To dissipate a collective charge on the outside of the battery, you should attempt to fully charge the battery, remove the battery from the notebook computer, let the battery sit for 1 hour, and then replace it in the unit until it is totally discharged. If the battery is not holding its charge as well as it should or the battery is not charging, you should try to fully charge the battery, remove it from the notebook computer, let it sit for 1 hour, and then replace it in the unit until it is totally discharged.

A new type of portable power for notebooks is fuel cells. Current fuel cells produce energy by creating a chemical reaction between methanol and oxygen. Electrodes draw those substances toward a plastic membrane, and when they come in contact with the membrane, the methanol breaks down and releases electrons, which are then funneled to power the host device. The by-products of the reaction eventually recombine with the electrons to form water and carbon dioxide.

However, the amount of electrons produced is directly related to the surface area of the membrane. Increasing the power means expanding the physical size of the fuel system. Polymer membranes can also tear and leak.

8.7 POWER MANAGEMENT

For notebook computers, power consumption is reduced to extend the time a machine can operate between battery charges. Recently, because of rising power costs, there has also been a push to reduce the power consumption of desktop computers. To reduce power, engineers can design circuits and components to use less power and they can manage the power used by the devices. Managing power usually means switching off whatever system components aren't being actively used.

Processors were among the first devices to have built-in power management. System Management Mode gave processors the ability to slow down and shut off unnecessary circuits when they were idle.

PC makers made it possible to put the hard drives into sleep mode, whereas the platters spin down when the system isn't being used. And, of course, most PCs have timers that darken the screen to further conserve power. Advanced Power Management (APM) and Advanced Configuration and Power Interface (ACPI) were developed subsequently to conserve power. The APM and ACPI can be controlled using the CMOS setup program and Windows Control Panel.

8.7.1 Advanced Power Management (APM)

The Advanced Power Management interface specification was jointly developed by Intel and Microsoft to integrate the control of hardware power-saving features with software control. Although nominally a BIOS interface, the APM controls PC devices to reduce power consumption using both BIOS and API interfaces. To be fully functional, APM requires a compatible BIOS and hardware devices that recognize APM commands.

Although it has the ability to individually control the features of each device it manages, the basic-design APM controls all devices together to control power use. It manages system power consumption by shifting the overall operating mode of the PC to APM states.

- **Full-On State—**The system is operating at full power without any management at all. The APM software is not in control, and no power savings can be achieved. A system without APM or with its APM features disabled operates in full-on state.
- **APM Standby State—**The processor may stop and many of the system devices are turned off or operate at reduced power. The system usually cannot process data, but its memory is kept alive and the status of all devices is preserved. When activity or an event such as key press or mouse move occurs, the PC can rapidly shift from standby to enabled states.
- **APM Suspend State—**The system shifts to its maximum power-saving mode, where most devices are switched off and processor is in its lowest power state with its clock turned off.
- **Hibernation—**This is special implementation of suspend mode that allows the system to be switched entirely off and still be restored to the point at which it entered the suspended state. When entering the suspended state, the system saves all its operating parameters as content in memory, and other status data is stored to the hard disk, allowing it to switch off memory power. A system event can shift back to the enabled state from suspend to hibernation, but changing modes from suspend to enabled takes substantially longer than from standby to enabled.
- **Off State—**Power to the system is entirely off. No status information or memory is saved. The system must run through the entire boot-up process.

8.7.2 Advanced Configuration and Power Interface

Advanced Configuration and Power Interface (ACPI), the next generation of power management, integrates PC hardware and operating systems into a cooperative power-saving machine. It was developed jointly by Intel, Microsoft, and Toshiba. It was built on the foundation of APM but with the goal of putting the operating system in control of the PC power system. To be functional, ACPI requires an ACPI BIOS, an operating system that supports ACPI and devices that support ACPI.

Using the Smart Battery specification, under ACPI the operating system takes command of battery charging and monitoring. It also monitors the thermal operation of the system, reducing speed or shutting down a PC that overheats.

The fundamental and most noticeable change made by ACPI is the power button on the front of new PCs. In systems equipped to handle APCI, the power switch does not actually switch the power to the system on and off. Rather, it sends a command to the system to put itself into soft-off mode. In soft-off mode, the PC acts as if you have shut it off and requires rebooting to restart it. But it doesn't remove all power from the system. A slight bit of power continues to be supplied to the motherboard and expansion boards, enabling them to monitor external events. For example, a network board will still listen to network traffic for packets targeted at it. A modem or fax board may lie in wait for a telephone call. Or, you can set a time to start the tape-backup system. When one of these designated external events occurs, the PC automatically switches itself back on to deal with it.

As with APM, the ACPI design works by shifting modes called ACPI states. Under ACPI, there are a great variety of states, which are classified into four basic types—global, special sleep, microprocessor, and device.

Global States

- **G0**—Working state in which the PC is operating normally. Programs execute actively. Even in G0 state, some devices that are inactive may automatically power down, but they will quickly resume normal operations when they are called upon.
- **G1**—Sleeping state, during which it may appear your PC has shut down. Although there are active circuits, there is no evidence of operation on the monitor screen. The active circuits constantly monitor internal and external events and can switch your PC back to its working state when necessary. Various system events can cause the PC to return to working state.
- **G2**—The new soft-off state
- **G3**—Complete power off

The ACPI device mode varies with the device type. The states differ in four chief characteristics: the amount of power that the state saves over normal operating; how long is required to restore the device from the state to normal operation; how much of the operating context of the device is saved in entering the states; and what must be done to return the device back to normal operation.

Device States

- **D0**—designates the fully on state, in which the device operates at top speed, is fully responsive, and consumes the most power.
- **D1**—saves power over the D0 state. How it achieves that goal depends on the type of device. In general, the device can quickly shift back to the D0 state without needing to rest or losing data.
- **D2**—further saves power over the D1 state and is device-specific. In general, the device becomes less responsible. It may need to reset itself or go through its power-on sequence to return to the D0 state.
- **D3**—corresponds to the power-off state. Electrical power is removed from the device, and the device does not function. It must go through its power-on sequence to begin operations again. Upon entering D3, none of its operating context gets saved. This achieves the greatest power saving but requires the longest restoration time.

Processor States

- **C0**—It designates the state in which the processor executes at full speed.
- **C1**—It puts the processor in its halt state under command of the ACPI driver without affecting other aspects of its operation.
- **C2**—It shifts the processor to low-power state and maintains the integrity of the system's memory cache. In a fully implemented ACPI system, the processor will shift to this state if a bus master takes control of the system.
- **C3**—It pushes the processor down to low-power state and does not maintain cache memory.

Sleeping States

Sleeping, defined as a global mode of the system (G1), is not a single defined state under ACPI but has several variations. PCs may implement one or more of these sleeping states to provide progressively greater power savings.

- **S0**—It is not sleeping at all but is a fully awake and operating PC.
- **S1**—It shuts down the processor but maintains full system integrity, including the memory cache. Most PCs can emerge from the S1 state instantly with virtually no delay.
- **S2**—It maintains the processor state as well as that of the rest of the PC except the memory cache. The PC can wake up quickly with only the loss of a few wasted processor cycles as the cache fills and regains operation.
- **S3**—It saves the processor registers and system device data to memory, shuts down most of the circuitry of the system, and then shifts the memory to its low-power mode. The low-power mode allows the memory to be refreshed but cannot be read or written to. Only enough circuitry stays away to revive the system, including the real-time clock, which may wake up the system at a preset time. Because all data is held in solid-state memory, waking up is quite quick, typically taking only a few seconds.

- S4—It powers down all devices in the PC. The system hardware no longer maintains memory integrity or device context. The ACPI-compliant operating system is responsible for saving this information, typically spooling the contents of memory and devices states to disk. Memory support circuits shut down to save power. Waking up requires shifting all data saved on disk back into memory. With today's systems with 128 MB or more of memory, this process can range from a few seconds to a minute.
- S5—This mode is not G2 sleeping but is the G3 soft-off condition.

8.7.3 Troubleshooting Power Management

Typically, when you are having problems with power management, the problem is caused by an old driver or a driver that fails to support power management, or else the BIOS does not support power management. In either case, you should look for newer versions of these.

To determine whether the problem is due to standby mode, hibernate mode, the shutdown of the monitor, or the shutdown of the disk drive, on the Power Schemes tab in the Power Options Properties page, set three of the four options to Never and the fourth to its original setting. Allow the time-out to occur, and determine whether the system appears to stop responding. Isolate the failure by trying each of the four combinations: First test the monitor timer, then the disk drive timer, then the system standby timer, and then the system hibernate timer.

To determine which device is causing the problem, disable all devices in Device Manager except the display adapter(s), the mouse, anything under the USB Devices category (if you have either a USB keyboard or a USB mouse), and anything under the System Devices category. Restart the computer. If the system goes on standby successfully, reenable one-half of the currently disabled devices. Restart again. If the system continues to go on standby successfully, reenable half of the remaining disabled devices. Otherwise, disable the devices you just reenabled, and reenable the devices that were disabled. Continue in this manner until the offending device is pinpointed.

SUMMARY

1. The PC power supply converts AC power in to clean DC power. Clean power has very little voltage variation, or noise. The power supply produces +3.3 V, ±5 V, and ±12 V power.
2. The secondary function of the power supply is to cool the system.
3. Most PCs have switching power supplies. Switching power supplies are small, efficient, and go into idle mode when a short or overload is detected.
4. Two Burndy connectors connect many older motherboards to the power supply. When you connect a Burndy connector, the ground wires (black) need to be together.
5. The power supply capacity is measured in watts (W).
6. Older systems use AT power supply whereas today's systems use the ATX or BTX power supply.
7. The wattage rating of a power supply is a maximum amount of electric power a device can safely handle continuously.
8. If the amount of power exceeds the wattage rating of the power supply, the power supply detects an overload and shuts down into idle mode.
9. The power requirements of portable computers differ from those of desktop computers because portable computers are designed to decrease power consumption to provide a long battery life.
10. NiMH batteries store up to 50 percent more power than older NiCad batteries, and they do not suffer from memory effects. They can be recharged as many as 500 times.
11. Lithium is the lightest metal and has the high electrochemical potential. Because lithium itself is unstable, lithium-ion batteries are made from lithium ion produced from chemicals.
12. Current fuel cells produce energy by creating a chemical reaction between methanol and oxygen.
13. Heat shortens the life span of a circuit, which leads to computer failure.
14. If the fan fails, the PC will heat to a level that can damage other components.
15. If the power supply is supplying the proper power and the fan failed, the PC may have boot-up failures, boot-up errors, memory errors, and device failures and may give off electrical shock when the case or connections are touched.
16. As a general rule, when a power supply fails, it is easier, quicker, and usually cheaper to replace it than to repair it.
17. When checking a system that has no power, the first thing to do is to see if the power supply is plugged into the AC outlet and the PC is on.
18. When the power supply can handle many of these power fluctuations, other power fluctuations may shut down or damage the computer, corrupt the data, and lose unsaved work.

19. Symptoms of bad power are frozen computers or keyboards, errors in data transmissions, corrupted or lost data, frequently aborted modem transfers, and total failure of a computer or computer component.
20. Most notebook batteries are charged by a DC board or charge board that attaches to the system motherboard. When a battery does not charge, the problem is with the battery or the DC/charge board (or its fuse, if it has one).
21. If the battery is not holding its charge as well as it should or the battery is not charging, you should try to fully charge the battery, remove it from the notebook, let it sit for 1 hour, and then replace it in the unit until it is totally discharged.
22. Surge protectors protect against overvoltages; line conditioners protect against undervoltages.
23. Standby power supplies (SPSs) and uninterruptible power supplies (UPSs) use a battery to power the PC during power irregularities.
24. To limit the chance of AC line noise, a computer should be installed on its own power circuit.
25. Because many of these batteries contain harmful or poisonous chemicals and improper handling and disposal can result in fire or explosion, you should always check the battery label for information on special disposal procedure.

QUESTIONS

1. Which of the following is *not* true about cases?
   a. They protect the components inside the PC.
   b. They reduce RFI emanating from the PC.
   c. They are not important for computer operations.
   d. They include the power supply, motherboard, RAM, and expansion cards.
2. What should you do to ensure adequate cooling in a computer system?
   a. turn off the system when not in use
   b. keep the system fan well lubricated
   c. always keep the case closed
   d. remove an empty slot cover
3. The primary function of the power supply is to
   a. produce clean DC power.
   b. convert AC power into clean DC power.
   c. act as a large battery.
   d. cool the PC.
4. The type of power supply most computers use is
   a. standby power supply.
   b. turn-down power supply.
   c. linear power supply.
   d. switching power supply.
5. When the switching power supply detects a short or overload, the power supply
   a. displays a message on the monitor.
   b. goes into idle mode.
   c. compensates by providing more power.
   d. keeps working without change.
6. To check the output of the power supply, you would set the meter to
   a. DC voltage.
   b. AC voltage.
   c. resistance.
   d. capacitance.
7. A switching power supply steps down voltage by means of
   a. a transformer.
   b. a network of resistor conduits.
   c. turning off and back on in rapid cycles.
   d. a network of capacitors.
8. When you purchase a replacement power supply for a PC, you should pay particular attention to
   a. how P8 and P9 are connected.
   b. the form factor, including shape, size, mounting holes, and power switch location and its capacity.
   c. its voltage rating.
   d. the type of regulation used.
9. Which of the following voltages is *not* normally present at the output of a personal computer power supply?
   a. +5 V
   b. −5 V
   c. +12 V
   d. −12 V
   e. 120 V
10. The wires coming from the power supply in a personal computer are color coded. What color is used for the ground (or common) wires?
    a. red
    b. black
    c. yellow
    d. blue
11. The wires coming from the power supply in a personal computer are color coded. What color is used for the +5 V wires?
    a. red
    b. black
    c. yellow
    d. blue
12. You have a Windows 2000 workstation. When you insert a CD-ROM disk and boot up the computer, the computer starts to spin the CD but then reboots. What is the most likely cause of the problem?
    a. a bad CD
    b. a bad power supply
    c. an improperly loaded driver
    d. a bad drive
    e. a bad motherboard
13. Which of the following is the smallest power interruption that can cause memory errors or cause the computer to lock up?
    a. 1 s
    b. 1/5 s
    c. 10 s
    d. 1 min

14. What is the best way to protect a PC during an electrical storm?
    a. back up the hard drive
    b. use a surge protector
    c. power off the system
    d. unplug the power cord
15. To test for ripple on a PC power supply, you should set the multimeter for
    a. DC voltage.   b. AC voltage.
    c. ohms.   d. farads.
16. Which of the following can be caused by power fluctuations (choose all that apply)?
    a. random memory errors
    b. damaged components inside the computer
    c. hard disk read/write errors
    d. computer lock-up
17. After turning on the computer, it does not boot. You notice that no LEDs are lit on the computer and the fan is not spinning. What is the most likely cause of the problem?
    a. The hard drive has been reformatted.
    b. The CMOS battery failed.
    c. The LED lights are not connected.
    d. The hard drive partition has been deleted.
    e. The power supply is bad or the power supply is not receiving any power.
18. What is the difference between a sag and a brownout?
    a. A sag typically lasts a few seconds, while a brownout lasts a few hours.
    b. A sag typically lasts less than a few milliseconds, while a brownout lasts for a prolonged period.
    c. Sags are measured in nanoseconds, while brownouts are measured in milliseconds.
    d. *Sag* and *brownout* are terms that describe the same condition.
19. What is the difference between a spike and a surge?
    a. A spike is a very short overvoltage condition measured in nanoseconds, while a surge is measured in microseconds or minutes.
    b. A spike is a very short overvoltage condition measured in nanoseconds, while a surge is measured in milliseconds
    c. A surge occurs when the power first drops and then overcorrects within 5 milliseconds, while a spike drops and overcorrects in less than 10 milliseconds.
    d. *Spike* and *surge* are terms that describe the same condition.
20. Which of the following contains a battery that is connected between the AC line and the computer and provides constant surge protection?
    a. a power conditioner
    b. a surge suppressor
    c. an uninterruptible power supply (UPS)
    d. a standby power supply (SPS)
21. The output of a UPS should be
    a. DC voltage.   b. sine wave.
    c. square wave.   d. saw wave.
22. To limit AC line noise, you should
    a. use extension cords and surge protectors
    b. install the computer system on its own power circuit.
    c. install the computer system on a circuit with other high-wattage units.
    d. avoid using a ground connection.
23. Which of the following items would require you to comply with EPA disposal guidelines?
    a. keyboard   b. system board
    c. power supply   d. battery
24. PCs are
    a. FCC class A devices.
    b. FCC class B devices.
    c. FCC class C devices.
    d. FCC class D devices.
    e. not rated by the FCC.
25. Which motherboard form factors use the 20-pin Molex connector to connect the power supply unit to the motherboard (choose three)?
    a. ATX   b. NLX
    c. LPX   d. Baby AT
    e. FTX   f. SFX
    g. PC/TX
26. What are the most important elements to consider when choosing a surge suppressor?
    a. clamping speed and line conditioning
    b. switching speed and protection indicator
    c. energy absorption and voltage let-through
    d. protection guarantee and switching voltage

HANDS-ON EXERCISES

Exercise 1: Checking the Alternating Current Power Outlet

Use a voltmeter to measure the following voltages:

hot slot and neutral slot
hot slot and ground
neutral slot and ground

Exercise 2: Checking the Power Supply

1. Make sure the computer is off.
2. Disconnect the connectors that lead to the motherboard.
3. Turn on the computer and measure the following voltages from the motherboard power connector: red wire and black wire; yellow wire and black wire.
4. Turn off the computer and reconnect the motherboard connectors.
5. Turn on the computer and measure the following voltages from one of the drive power connectors: red wire and black wire; yellow wire and black wire.
6. Using the drive power connectors, measure the AC voltage between the yellow wire and black wire.
7. Turn off the computer.
8. If your power supply has a voltage selector switch, change the switch to 220 V. (Note: If your computer is designed to use 220 V, do not switch it to 110 V.)
9. Turn on the computer.
10. Shut off the computer and change the voltage selection switch back to 110 V.

Exercise 3: Removing and Installing a Power Supply

1. Disconnect the AC power cable from the computer.
2. First see if there is any documentation on the power supply indicating how the on/off switch is connected.
3. Find the power cables connected to the on/off switch and motherboard and study how they are connected. Compare this connection to the documentation for the power supply. (Note: You may choose to draw a sketch of how the connectors are connected.)
4. Remove the power supply from the computer, including all cables.
5. Reinstall the power supply from the computer. Make sure that the on/off switch is connected properly and that the connectors leading to the motherboard are connected properly.

CHAPTER 9

The Hard Drive

Topics Covered in This Chapter

Introduction

Hard drives are half-electronic, half-mechanical devices that store information on rotating platters. They are considered long-term storage and are the primary mass storage system. Of course, since the hard drive contains the bulk of the data files used within the PC, its failure could be disastrous unless the data files have been backed up.

Objectives

1. Describe the function of the hard drive.
2. Define *track, sectors,* and *cylinders.*
3. Given the number of read/write heads, the number of sectors and track, and the number of cylinders, calculate the capacity of a hard drive.
4. Explain zone recordings and sector translation.
5. Compare and contrast CHS addressing, translation addressing, and LBA.
6. List the factors that contribute to the hard drive performance.
7. Describe the basic steps in installing a hard drive.
8. Given an IDE or SCSI hard drive, configure and install it in a system.
9. Differentiate between parallel IDE and serial IDE.
10. Perform a low-level format, partitioning, and high-level format on a hard drive.
11. Explain the need for terminating resistors and describe where they are needed in a daisy chain.
12. Given a hard drive problem, determine and correct the problem.

9.1 WHAT IS A HARD DRIVE?

Hard drives are half-electronic and half-mechanical devices that use magnetic patterns to store information on rotating platters. They are considered long-term storage devices because they do not "forget" their information when power is disconnected. They are also considered the primary mass storage system because they hold all the programs and data files that are fed into RAM. The first hard drive used in a PC had a capacity of only 5 MB. Today, hard drives can be 160 GB or larger. Hard drives are sometimes referred to as *fixed disks* because they usually cannot be removed from the PC easily like a floppy disk. This term does not describe all hard drives because there are external hard drives (disks that rest outside the case) and removable hard drives.

Hard drives communicate with the rest of the computer by means of a cable connected to a controller card, which is either an expansion card or built into the motherboard. All hard drives consist of the following components: rotating platters, read/write heads, and head actuators. See figure 9.1. Another type of hard drive is the hard card. A **hard card,** made for systems that do not have available drive bays, is a hard disk drive and controller on a single expansion card. The capacity of a hard card is usually limited.

9.1.1 Platters

The name *hard drive* is derived from the fact that the platters are solid. The **platters** rotate around a spindle with speeds as low as 3,600 revolutions per minute (rpm) and as fast as 10,000 rpm or more. A typical speed is 7,200 rpm. A faster speed usually means that the access time (the time it takes to find the data) and throughput time (the time needed for data transfer) are greater.

Figure 9.1 Inside a Hard Drive

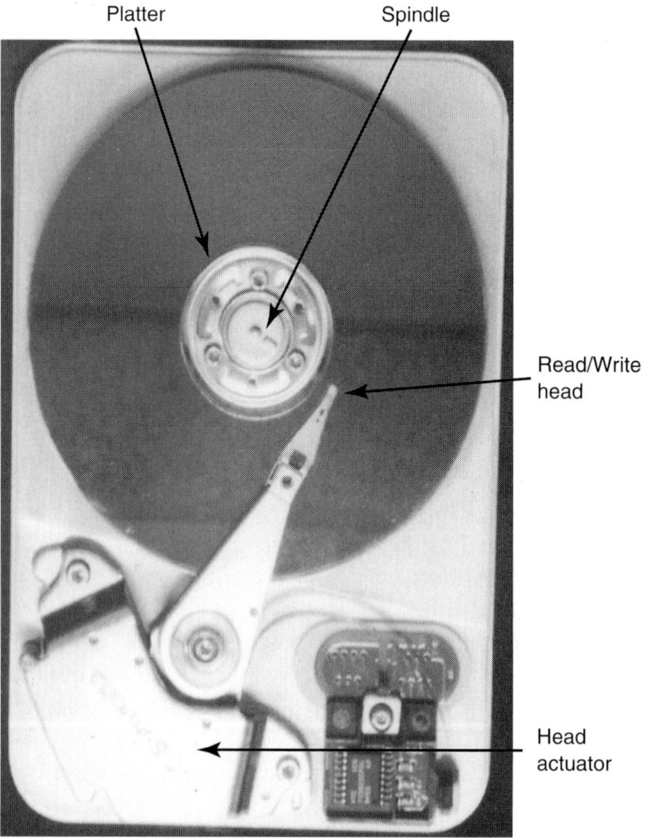

The platters do not store the actual data. Instead, they store patterns of 0s and 1s. The platters are coated with a magnetic material (iron oxide or a thin-film material) that can hold many tiny magnetic fields. When these fields are placed in certain patterns, they represent 0s and 1s. The bits of information are written and read using a read/write head.

The size of the drive is partially determined by the size of each platter and the number of platters stacked on top of each other. When drives were first used in the IBM PC, the platters were 5¼-in. in diameter. Later drives were reduced to 3.5-in. Today, there are 2½-in. and 1.8-in. drives that hold more information than the older models.

The platters are made of aluminum, glass, or ceramic material, chosen because they are light, inexpensive, inherently flat, nonmagnetic, and rugged and have a low thermal coefficient. The platters must be light to minimize the power required to spin them. Their low thermal coefficient means that temperature changes do not have much effect on the size and shape of the platters. If they are inherently flat, the read/write heads can get closer to the surface without touching it. If a read/write head is closer to the platter, it can generate a denser magnetic field, which allows more information to be stored in a smaller area. The platters need to be nonmagnetic because it is the coating that needs to be magnetized, not the platter. Lastly, the platters must be rugged enough to withstand the high rotational speeds without changing size or shape. Some drives use aluminum platters and others use a newer glass-ceramic composite. These glass platters resist cracking better than normal glass and are more rigid than aluminum platters, permitting the platters to be half as thick as aluminum platters or less. In addition, they resist expanding and contracting with temperature changes better than aluminum.

Newer hard drives use a thin-film medium that appears as a smooth, shiny silver surface. The thin-film medium is thinner and smoother than the older iron oxide coating and is much harder. This allows for read/write heads to be closer to the platters, and the platter is more resistant to surface damage if the read/write head makes contact with the surface.

Do not take a hard drive or any other type of medium that uses magnetism to store data through a metal detector. Since metal detectors use strong magnetic fields to find metal objects, the magnetic media could easily be destroyed.

9.1.2 Read/Write Heads

A read/write head reads the data from a platter and writes the data to a platter. See figure 9.2. A hard disk drive usually has one read/write head for each side of a platter. If, therefore, a drive has three platters, it could have up to six read/write heads. The read/write heads are connected by a head rack, which resembles a "multifingered" arm. The arm is moved back and forth by the head actuator.

The basic read/write head is a wire shaped like a coil winding (inductor). When electricity is applied to the coil, it acts as an electromagnet. To write to a disk, current is sent through the wire and an electromagnetic field forms around the wire. As it passes through the coil, the electromagnetic field is intensified. When this electromagnetic field crosses the magnetic material on the platters, the magnetic material also becomes magnetized. To read from the platter, the process is reversed. The read/write head approaches the magnetized material, and when the coil detects a magnetic charge, it causes a small amount of current to flow in the coil. After this signal is amplified and filtered, the current is translated into 0s and 1s.

When the computer is shut off, the heads, which are spring-loaded, touch the platter. When the computer is turned on, air pressure caused by the spinning of the platters within the sealed drive causes the read/write head to rise off the platter. Therefore, the read/write head does not actually touch the platter while it spins. The distance between the read/write head and the platter is between 3 to 20 millionths of an inch. Since the gap is so small, the smallest particle of dust or cigarette smoke would act like a boulder placed between the read/write head and platter. These tiny boulders could cause the heads to read improperly and could cause physical damage to the read/write head and the platter. A grinding noise might be heard. This damage is called **head-to-disk interference (HDI).** See figure 9.3. A hard drive should therefore not be opened except in a clean-room environment (a specially designed room or area from which most of the particles in the air have been filtered out). For hard drives, the clean room cannot contain more than 100 particles larger than 19.7 millionths of an inch per cubic foot. A typical person just breathing puts out approximately 500 of these particles in a single minute. Therefore, when working in a clean room, a technician must wear special clothing and a mask to reduce the number of particles in the air.

Figure 9.2 Read/Write Head

Figure 9.3 Objects That Can Cause Head-to-Disk Interference (HDI)

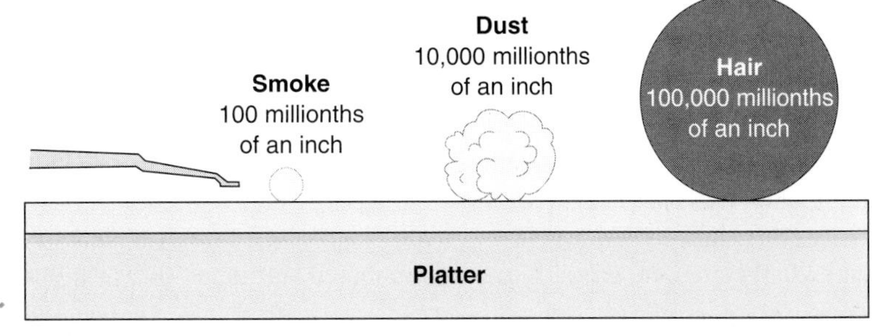

Areal density is the term for the physical amount of data that can be held on an area of a platter; it is expressed in bits per square inch. It is calculated by multiplying the bit density (bits per inch, or BPI) by the track density (tracks per inch, or TPI). Hard drives are capable of areal densities of 500 to 1,000 megabits per square inch. **Coercitivity** measures the strength of the magnetic field used to store data on the platters. The coercitivity of hard drive media usually exceeds 1,400 oersteds compared with 600 oersteds for floppy media. If the coercitivity of a magnetic platter is high, it will take a stronger magnetic field to change it. The coercitivity is influenced by the type of platter, the magnetic material on the platter, the type of read/write head, the amount of current through the head, and the distance between the head and the platter.

9.1.3 Head Actuator

The **head actuator** is the component that moves the read/write heads back and forth. There are two types: the stepper motor actuator and the voice coil actuator.

Most newer hard drives, including the IDE and SCSI hard drives, use voice coil actuators. Instead of using a physical motor to move the read/write heads, voice coil actuators use electromagnetic force. An electromagnetic coil is attached to the end of the head rack and placed near a stationary magnet. As current is sent through the coil, a magnetic field is created that attracts or repels the stationary magnet and moves the head rack.

Voice coil actuators are quicker, more efficient, and quieter than stepper motors. Instead of moving in steps, the voice coil actuator moves directly to the needed location because it gets constant feedback of its location from a closed loop, allowing the read/write heads to adjust their position. The feedback comes from servo information—magnetic markings written on the platters—placed there during manufacturing. These markings are unaffected by temperature changes.

9.1.4 Logic Boards and Connectors

The drive contains several connectors to the rest of the computer. Newer hard drives (IDE and SCSI) require one gray ribbon cable for direct connections with the computer. The hard drive also uses a 5½-in. power connector for power. The power connector has a +12 V line to power the motor and a +5 V line to power the chips on the drive.

Commands and instructions are issued by the operating system and sent through an expansion card (sometimes referred to as the *controller card* or *I/O card*) through the gray ribbon cable to the hard drive—specifically, to the hard drive's logic board. The logic board is the printed circuit board located under the drive. It makes sure that the platters are rotating at a constant speed, and it translates the commands received from the controller card into voltage fluctuations that control the head actuator and read/write heads.

As mentioned at the beginning of the chapter, the hard drive is a half-mechanical, half-electronic device. Because it is half-mechanical, the device has a high failure rate compared to nonmechanical devices. This is because mechanical parts and pieces eventually wear out. Although most failures are mechanical in nature, some hard drive problems occur in the logic board. If this is the case, the drive can easily be repaired by removing and replacing the logic board, not the entire drive. Although this is not the most cost-effective solution (since drives are so inexpensive), it may be the only choice if the data stored on the disk is irreplaceable and the drive was not backed up as it should have been. Of course, the new logic board must match the drive.

A few older drives include a grounding tab that connects to a grounding wire. Grounding is important because it provides a positive ground connection between the drive and the system's chassis. Improper grounding of the drive may result in improper operation, intermittent failure, or general read/write errors. Most drives do not need a grounding tab because they are grounded when screwed into a metal case. If a drive has plastic or fiberglass rails, which do not provide proper grounding, the grounding wire must be attached to the grounding tab.

9.1.5 Tracks, Cylinders, and Sectors

Information is stored on the platters according to a system of tracks and sectors forming a circular grid. See figure 9.4. The platters are first divided into concentric circles called **tracks.** (*Concentric* means circles that share the same center—much like rings in a tree.) A platter can have anywhere between 312 and 3,000 or more tracks. Tracks are numbered starting at 0 for the outside track. The tracks are then

Figure 9.4 Track and Sector

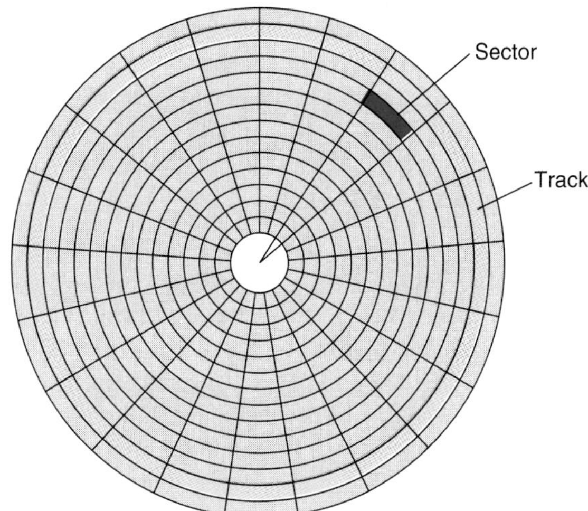

divided into **sectors;** each sector contains 512 bytes of usable data. A hard drive track can have as few as 17 sectors per track or may have more than 100 sectors per track. Sectors on a track are numbered starting with 1.

So far, tracks and sectors have been described as the division of one side of a platter into a circular grid. But actually, each side of a platter has a track 0, a track 1, a track 2, and so on. As the platters are stacked on top of each other, the track 0s are also stacked on top of each other, and these start to form a cylinder (much like a can). Therefore, the number of tracks equals the number of cylinders. Of course, tracks are two-dimensional and cylinders are three-dimensional—a cylinder would be able to hold more data because it has the third dimension, height.

Since the AT computer, computers have included a BIOS setup program to specify the number and size of hard drives and floppy drives, the amount of RAM, and other important hardware configuration information. The hard drive option in the program includes the type of hard drive, the number of cylinders, the number of read/write heads, and the number of sectors and tracks. By selecting the type of hard drive, the other parameters are automatically chosen. Today, most computers have the Type 47/48 or User-Definable Type option, which allows (and requires) the other parameters to be selected.

Example 9.1:

How much data can a hard drive that has 4,092 tracks, 16 read/write heads, and 63 sectors per track hold?

Multipling the three numbers together gives the total number of sectors used by the hard drive. (Note: The number of read/write heads indicates that there are 8 platters since each side of the platter has a read/write head.)

4,092 tracks × 16 read/write heads × 63 sectors per track = 4,124,736 sectors

Because each sector contains 512 bytes of data, multiply the number of sectors by 512 to find the number of bytes:

4,124,736 sectors × 512 bytes per sector = 2,111,864,832 bytes

Most people think *mega-* means 1 million and *giga-* means 1 billion, so the companies selling hard drives will state that this hard drive is a 2.1 GB drive. But the computer is based on the binary numbering system, in which 2^{10} = 1,024 and so

1024 bytes = 1 KB
1024 KB = 1 MB
1024 MB = 1 GB

Therefore,

2,111,864,832 ÷ 1,024 bytes per kilobyte = 2,062,368 KB
2,062,368 KB ÷ 1,024 KB per megabyte = 2,014.03 MB
2,014.03 MB ÷ 1,024 MB per gigabyte = 1.97 GB

The companies are not lying; they are just using numbers based on 1,000 (the decimal system), but computers use numbers based on 1,024.

On older hard drives, all the tracks have the same number of sectors even though the tracks are much larger toward the outside of the platter than the inside. This is known as a *fixed-sector-per-track system.* Although this simplifies the organization of the sectors on the drive, it does waste a lot of usable disk space. If the sectors were the same distance apart on all the tracks, the outer tracks would hold more sectors. Today's hard drives divide the tracks into zones. The tracks within the outer zones have more sectors per track than the tracks within the inner zones. Consequently, the capacity of the hard drive is increased by 20 to 50 percent. Today, most IDE and SCSI drives use **zoned recordings.** See figure 9.5.

Several sector-addressing schemes are used in hard drives. The simplest addressing scheme identifies each sector by its exact physical address. It is known as *cylinder-head-sector* addressing or **CHS addressing.** When using the CHS addressing mode, the CHS parameters must be specified at some point during the installation of the hard drive. On modern systems, this will be done with the CMOS setup program; in older systems the parameters will be entered during low-level formatting (see section 9.3.2). The CHS addressing mode can't be used in many situations. First, it can't be used in systems with ROM BIOS because these do not recognize more than 1,024 cylinders. Second, it can't be used with drives using zoned recording because in that system the number of sectors varies with different tracks. To accommodate these two situations, hard drive manufacturers developed sector translation, which makes CHS addresses usable by these other two systems.

Example 9.2:

A drive has 1,600 cylinders, 4 read/write heads, and 49 sectors per track. How much data can it hold?

Multipling the three numbers together gives the number of sectors per track:

1,600 cylinders × 4 heads × 49 sectors per track = 311,600 sectors

Since each sector is 512 bytes, the total disk capacity is

313,600 sectors × 512 bytes per sector = 160,563,200 bytes

Figure 9.5 Zoned Recordings

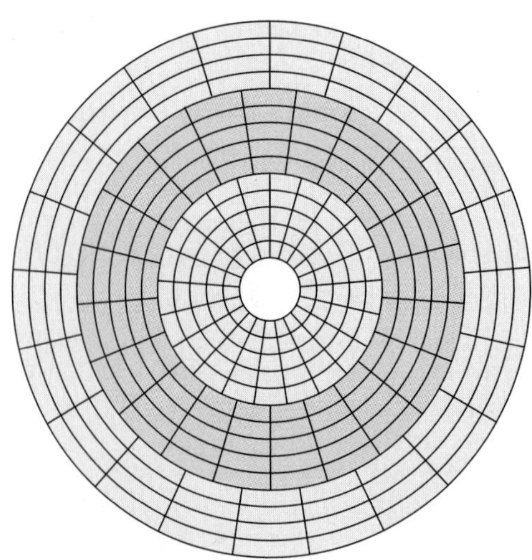

Unfortunately, when you format the disk with some systems, it will format only to 102,760,448 bytes because older system ROM BIOSes can recognize only up to 1,024 cylinders. To fix this problem, you would use **large addressing** (also known as **extended CHS**), where you "lie" to the system and say that you have 800 cylinders and 8 read/write heads. These values still give you the same number of sectors and the same number of bytes:

800 cylinders × 8 heads × 49 sectors per track = 313,600 sectors
313,600 sectors × 512 bytes per sector = 160,563,200 bytes

Of course, because the drive has translating electronics, the entire capacity can be seen when it is partitioned and formatted.

The newest addressing scheme is **logical block addressing (LBA).** LBA uses a 28-bit number to indicate the total number of sectors on a hard drive. The 28-bit number used to indicate the number of sectors is equivalent to the number of bits used to list the number of cylinders, the number of read/write heads, and the number of sectors per track in CHS. It allows up to 268,435,456 sectors, or 128 GB. Instead of using the cylinder number, read/write number, and sector number to identify the sector, LBA numbers each sector sequentially starting at 1. Unfortunately, some software can access the hard drive only by using the CHS addressing scheme. In these systems, the system ROM BIOS has to translate the CHS address to the LBA address and the ROM BIOS recognizes only up to 7.9 GB.

NOTE: A newer version of LBA, 48-bit LBA, was introduced that accommodates drives up to 144 petabytes (144,000,000 gigabytes).

Each track is identified with a track identifier. Each sector of the track contains a sector header, 512 bytes of data, and some form of error control. The sector header, which identifies the sector, contains the cylinder, head, and sector number of the sector. The **cyclical redundancy check (CRC)** is used to verify the address, while **error correction code (ECC)** is used to verify the actual data.

There is a small gap within each track that allows the read/write heads time to move from the end of one track to the next. If the gap didn't exist and the read/write head just missed the first sector in the next track, it would have to wait until the first sector came around again. If the read/write heads cannot move fast enough, some hard drives can be formatted to use head skewing. Head skewing offsets the first logical sector on each track from the first sector on the next track. See figure 9.6.

9.2 HARD DRIVE CHARACTERISTICS

The worth of a hard drive can be determined by several criteria. Most of these are concerned with the speed of the hard drive.

Figure 9.6 Sector Skewing

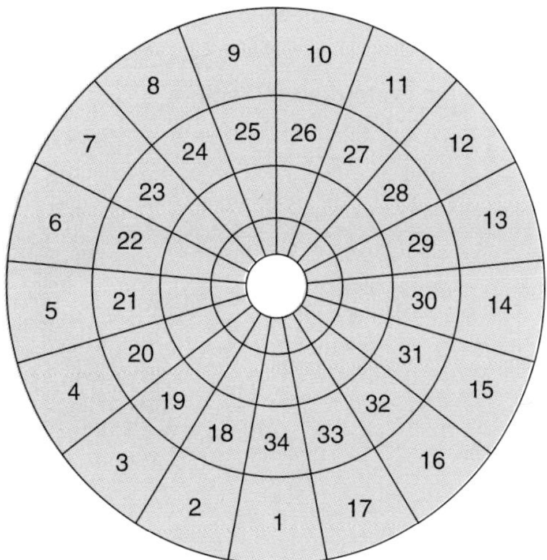

9.2.1 Hard Drive Performance

Because programs and data files are larger than ever, more and more information has to be stored on hard drives. Therefore, the overall performance of the PC is partially dependent on how long it takes to get the information from the hard drive into the RAM so that it can be processed by the microprocessor. Hard drive performance can be measured by the access time (consisting of seek time and latency period), the data transfer rate, the drive rpms, and PC data handling, as shown in figure 9.7.

The **access time** is the average amount of time it takes for the read/write head to move to the requested sector. It is the sum of the seek time and latency period. The **seek time** is the average time it takes the read/write head to move to the requested track—usually the time it takes the read/write head to move one-third of the way across the platter. The **latency period** is the time it takes for the requested sector to spin underneath the read/write head after the read/write head moves to the requested track. The latency period is usually one-half the time it takes for a single revolution of the disk platter. All of these intervals are measured in milliseconds (ms).

The disk transfer rate is the speed at which data is transferred to and from the platters. This is usually measured in bits per second or bytes per second and is dependent on the speed of the disk (rpm) and the density of the data on the disk (bits per inch). Since most modern drives use zoned recording, the outer zones have a faster disk transfer rate because they have more bytes per track. The maximum disk transfer rate can be calculated by the following equation:

$$\text{Disk transfer rate in MB/s} = \frac{(\text{sectors per track})(512\ \text{bytes})(\text{rpm})}{(60\ \text{s})(1{,}000{,}000\ \text{bits/megabits})}$$

The host transfer rate is determined according to the method by which data are transferred through the hard drive interface (IDE, EIDE, SCSI, etc). IDE hard drives use either a processor input/output mode or a direct memory access (DMA) mode; SCSI drives use either SCSII, SCSI II, or SCSI III. These topics will be discussed later in the chapter.

Data handling occurs after the data has been transferred to the controller card. The time it takes for the data to be transferred to the RAM is not necessarily a factor of the hard drive but of the PC itself. It depends on the type and speed of the microprocessor, the speed and amount of the RAM, the speed and amount of RAM cache, and the speed of the hard drive controller card (expansion card).

The speed of the hard drive can be enhanced by using a software cache or buffer area, or both. A buffer area, a software disk cache, and a 32-bit disk access operating system must be set up.

The buffer area, usually set up with the BUFFERS command, is a block of memory (RAM) used to store data temporarily. It collects large amounts of data as it is being moved between the microprocessor and the controller card. The data transfer rate is increased since the data is accessed in larger chunks from the RAM, and since the data is being accessed in larger chunks, which helps to fill up the data transfer pathways, the buffer area moves data more efficiently.

Like the buffer area, the software disk cache (set up with SMARTDRV.EXE, VCACHE, or equivalent program) sets aside a cache area to store both data and instructions. But the software controlling the disk cache tries to anticipate what the microprocessor needs next. One method it uses is to keep a copy of information that has been recently accessed on the assumption that if it has already been ac-

Figure 9.7 Hard Drive Performance Factors

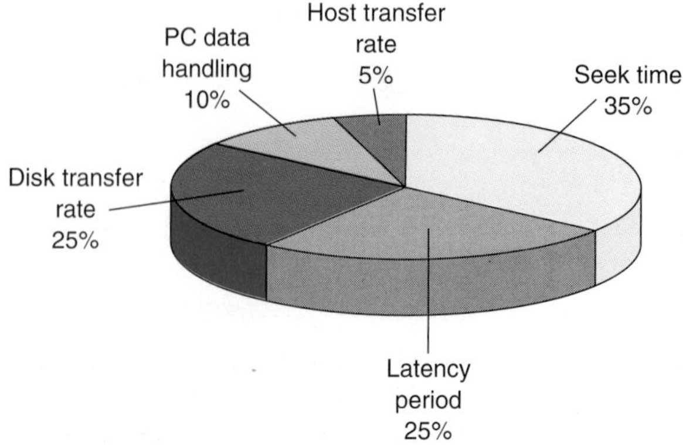

cessed, there is a good chance that it will be accessed again. Another method is to read ahead to the next sector after one has been accessed. Whatever the method used, when data needs to be accessed, the cache area will be searched first before the slower hard drive. The time it takes to search the cache area (RAM) is almost negligible compared to the time required to access the hard drive. Therefore, finding the needed information in the RAM greatly increases PC performance. Another form of cache is the hardware cache located on the hard drive controller card or the hard drive logic board. This cache is not to be confused with the hardware cache located on the motherboard or within the microprocessor. The hardware cache on the controller card or logic board fulfills the same functions as the software disk cache—that is, it speeds up the processing of data. Instead of sending a hard drive software interrupt to the microprocessor, the controller card physically completes the task.

Another way to increase performance is to use 32-bit access. (This is not to be confused with Windows 3.XX 32-bit disk access and 32-bit file access.) Some drives typically transfer only 16 bits at a time, a legacy from the original IBM AT design, which used the 16-bit ISA bus. If a system is designed to enable 32-bit disk access (through the CMOS setup program or some other method), it allows a PCI hard disk controller card to transfer two 16-bit chunks at the same time.

9.2.2 Hard Drive Reliability

MTBF is Mean Time Between Failure and is typically expressed in hours. The hours are calculated by dividing the total number of failures into the total number of operating hours observed. MTBF represents the average number of hours a field population of drives will work before a failure occurs. If a drive has an MTBF specification of 300,000 hours and if it is operated for 24 hours a day, 365 days a year, it would take an average of 34 years before this disk drive will fail. Typically, the higher the MTBF, the more reliable the product. In other words, if a drive has a 300,000 hours MTFB period and you have 1,000 of these drives, half would fail in 34 years.

MTBF is calculated using Highly Accelerated Life Testing where the drives are placed under environmental stresses such as thermal cycling and random vibration. A typical sequence might start with low temperature, then high temperature, and then multi-axis vibration. Therefore, some people take it with a grain of salt since the drives were not actually tested for years.

Instead, these people use a drive's warranty length and stated service life. Hard disks (as well as most computer components) follow the so-called bathtub curve model of failures: They have a relatively high rate of "infant mortality" (or early failure), a period of very low failures for several years, and then a gradual reduction in reliability as they reach the end of their useful life. To ensure that those who rely on hard drives do not continue to use them as they enter the period of increased failure that results from component wear-out, every hard disk has defined as one of its specifications the manufacturer's intended service life for the product.

The service life of a modern hard disk is usually about 3 to 5 years. This is stating that the drive is expected to give you good service for this length of time without any trouble. If reliability is important to you, you should consider getting a new drive at the end of the service life because the chances of failure increase significantly the longer you use it past the service length.

9.3 INSTALLATION OF HARD DRIVES

When installing a hard drive, there are some basic steps to take when configuring it:

1. Physically install and configure the hard drive system
2. Low-level format the drive
3. Partition the drive
4. High-level format the drive (and make bootable if needed)
5. Install and configure the operating system and application programs

9.3.1 Installing and Configuring the Hard Drive System

After physically installing the hard drive and its related components, they must be configured to work with the rest of the computer. The hard drive is connected to one or two gray ribbon cables that are connected to a hard drive controller, which is either an expansion card or is built into the motherboard. The hard drive is held in the drive bay with screws. Try to use the shortest screws possible since some hard drive logic boards or circuit boards are placed directly behind the screw holes. Therefore, if the screw is too long, it will short the hard drive.

NOTE: Because some hard drives have gotten faster, so has the speed of the platters. Unfortunately, these drives also dissipate a lot more heat than older drives with slower platters. Therefore, you must make sure that the system has sufficient air flow to keep the drives under their maximum operating temperature. Therefore, systems may need additional chassis fans. In addition, if you get a special kit that converts the fixed hard drive into a removable drive, make sure that the kit also includes small fans so that the heat can be pulled from the computer with the kit.

To configure the hard drive controller (expansion card), you must select its resources, such as IRQs, DMAs, I/O addresses, and memory usage, which you will do with the appropriate arrangement of jumpers and DIP switches or with a software configuration program or a plug-and-play card. Many controller cards also include a floppy disk drive controller and an I/O controller (serial, parallel, and game ports), which also need to be configured. Extra steps may be required by some controller cards to prepare the hard drive for use. Many controller cards have ROM BIOS chips, and some of the ROM BIOS chips include low-level format programs; also, drive-activation programs must be run. If the hard drive controller is part of the motherboard, it will be configured with either jumpers and DIP switches or the CMOS setup program. The hard drive also needs to be configured to work with the other devices connected to the controller card. The drive and devices must have proper designation numbers and terminating resistors.

The ribbon cable must be connected properly. To indicate the correct way to connect the cable, pin 1 of the cable is designated with a red or blue stripe. The expansion card/motherboard connectors will either have a small 1 or 2 to designate which end has pin 1 or will use a square solder (other pins will use a round solder). Pin 1 of the drive is also designated by a small 1 or 2. If one of the cable ends is connected backward, the hard drive will not function and the computer may not boot.

Today, the IDE interface cable is keyed to prevent the possibility of installing it backward. To create a keyed connector, pin 20 on the drive and controller male connector is removed and the hole for pin 20 of the female connector on the cable is filled in or blocked. Some cables also incorporate a protrusion on the top, which fits into a notch on the drive or controller. Note: Some lower-cost board and cable manufactures leave out the keying. Therefore, if you have one of the systems and you have a connector with pin 20 not blocked, you need to either get a cable with pin 20 not blocked or break off pin 20 from the board.

In addition to the ribbon cable, a hard drive also uses a power connector. Most hard drives use a 5¼-in. connector, which supplies +5 and +12 V. The +5 V is used to power the chips, whereas the +12 V power the motors.

The final step in installation is to enter the proper CMOS parameters for the hard drive or drives. For IDE drives, the number of cylinders, the number of read/write heads, and the number of sectors per track must be defined. For SCSI hard drives, Hard Drive Not Installed or SCSI would be selected. See table 9.1. Most newer CMOS setup programs have an autodetect option that will automatically detect the CMOS parameters for any IDE drive connected. If the drive is using this option, it is installed properly. If the drive is not, it is installed incorrectly or there is a faulty component, such as the driver, controller card, or cable.

9.3.2 Low-Level Formatting

Low-level formatting (LLF) is the process that defines the tracks and sectors on the platters of the hard drive. Any information already on the platters will be completely replaced with new tracks and sectors. See figure 9.8.

When a disk drive is manufactured, it is thoroughly tested by special equipment for any areas that might have errors. The sectors with errors are called *bad sectors* or *bad blocks.* The bad sectors are considered unreliable and are listed in a special table called the defect mapping. On older hard disks, these bad sectors were actually listed on a label located on the top of the drive. When a low-level format is performed, the program will ask the user to enter the location of the bad sectors. If any other bad sectors are discovered at a later time, they should be written on the label. On newer hard drives, the bad sectors are listed within the hard drive. When formatting these hard drives, the proper low-level format program must be used, one that is made for that specific drive. If the right program is not used, it may erase the table listing the bad sectors and may damage the drive.

Table 9.1 CMOS Parameters

CMOS

Older computers will recognize two hard drives (drive C and drive D). Newer computers will recognize four hard drives (drive C/Primary Master, drive D/Primary Slave, drive E/Secondary Master, drive F/Secondary Slave).

Hard Drive Parameter

Type number—Most CMOS programs have type numbers 1 through 46. By selecting a type number, common CMOS parameters are selected (number of tracks for each platter, number of read/write heads, and the number of sectors per track). Today, most computers will use Type 47/User Definable, which allows the common CMOS parameters to be entered by the user.

Cylinders—Number of tracks for each platter

Heads—Number of read/write heads

Sectors—Number of sectors per track

LZ (landing zone)—The cylinder used as a safe area for read/write heads when the computer is shut off. It is needed for nonautoparking hard drives.

Wpcom (write precompensation)—The write precompensation is used only in older hard drives. Since the bits are stored much closer together, the magnetic fields start to run together. Therefore, when writing, the current in the read/write heads is increased to strengthen the magnetic fields. The Wpcom specifies which cylinder starts the increased current. Note: In modern hard drives (IDE and SCSI) this entry is useless. Set it to either 21 or 65535. The IDE HDD will ignore it because it has its own built-in parameters.

Mode—Auto, normal, large, or LBA

Auto—The BIOS automatically determines the optimal mode.

Normal—Maximum number of cylinders, heads, and sectors supported are 1,024, 16, and 63.

Large—This mode is for drives that do not support LBA and have more than 1,024 cylinders. Applicable to only a few drives.

LBA (Logical Block Addressing)—During drive accesses, the IDE controller transforms the data address described by sector, head, and cylinder number into a physical block address, significantly improving data transfer rates for drives with greater than 1,024 cylinders.

Type of Hard Drive

IDE—Select the correct hard drive type. If the drive is set to Type 47/User Definable, enter the appropriate number of cylinders, heads, and sectors. LZ should be set to 0 and Wpcom should be set to either −1 or 65535. Some drives will use CHS (normal), translated (large), or LBA mode.

SCSI—Select SCSI (if available) or No Hard Drive Installed.

Figure 9.8 Low-Level Formatting (Before and After)

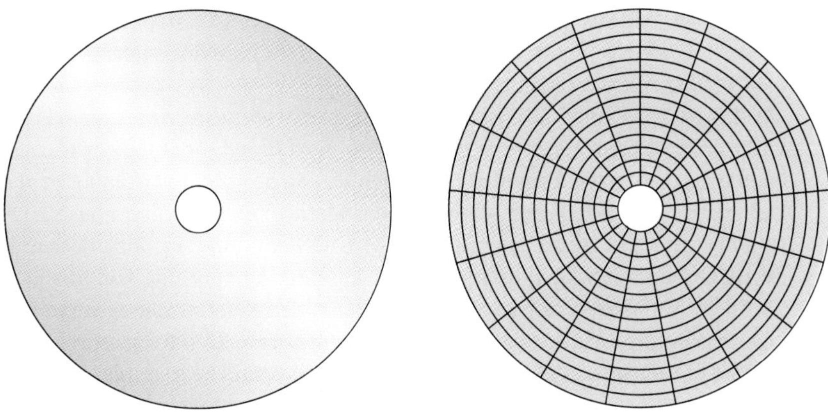

Table 9.2 Useful Websites for Hard Drives and Hard Drive Controllers

Company	Websites	
Adaptec	Home:	http://www.adaptec.com
	Support:	http://www.adaptec.com/support/index.html
	Drivers:	http://www.adaptec.com/worldwide/support/supportindex.html
Maxtor	Home:	http://www.maxtor.com
	Support:	http://www.maxtor.com/product.support/default.htm
	Download Library:	http://www.maxtor.com/Softwaredownload/default.htm
Seagate	Home:	http://www.seagate.com
	Support:	http://www.seagate.com/support/index.html
	Disk Utilities:	http://www.seagate.com/support/disc/drivers/discwiz.html
	Disc Diagnostic:	http://www.seagate.com/support/seatools/
Western Digital	Home:	http://www.westerndigital.com
	Support:	http://www.westerndigital.com/service/
	Soft Library:	http://www.westerndigital.com/service/ftp/drives.html

Most people don't like the idea of having a hard drive with bad sectors. Therefore, modern drives use spare sectoring. **Spare sectoring** is the setting aside of extra sectors on a drive. When the drive finds an unreliable sector, it will mark the sector as bad and then move the data to one of the spare sectors. Therefore, when the drive is analyzed by the user, it still has the same capacity with no visible errors. If a drive is using spare sectoring, bad sectors should not show up during normal operations. If they do, this means that all of the spare sectors have been used, which indicates a far greater problem. It is highly recommended to perform an immediate backup of the hard drive and to start looking for a replacement drive.

A critical area of the hard drive is Track 00, which stores the hard drive's master boot record and other vital disk information. If a bad sector occurs on Track 00, the hard drive will usually become unusable. If this happens, try a low-level format to correct the problem. If it doesn't, the entire hard drive will have to be replaced. See table 9.2.

NOTE: Track 00 can always be checked with diagnostic software.

The low-level format process also sets the interleaving of the hard drive. Interleaving establishes the interleave ratio, or the number of sectors that pass beneath the read/write heads before the next numbered sector arrives. Today's hard drives have a 1:1 ratio, meaning that each sector is read in sequence. Many older drives, such as the ST-506, used 3:1 interleaving. This means that a sector was read, then two sectors were skipped, and then the 3rd sector was read as the next numbered sector. The fastest interface is 1:1, assuming that the read/write heads are fast enough to read each sector in sequence. If they cannot, the read/write heads will read the first sector but have to wait an entire revolution before they can read the next sector. See figure 9.9. (Note: IDE and SCSI hard drive interleaves cannot be changed since they are established electronically.)

Low-level formats are completed with special software. Since there is no one software package that will low-level format every hard drive, you must be sure that the software package used will correctly handle the drive to be formatted. The software can be executed from disk (manufacturer's own software, On-Track's Disk Manager, MicroScope's Micro 2000, or Microhouse's Drive Pro), with the CMOS setup program, or by means of the ROM BIOS chip on the controller card (accessed through DOS's DEBUG program or by pressing specific keys during boot-up). But unless you are formatting an older ST-506 or ESDI drive as part of maintenance, there is not much reason to low-level format a hard drive. One reason for doing it would be to completely erase all information from a drive so that it could not be used or seen by someone else. Another reason would be to remove a corrupted or non-DOS partition or operating system or to remove a virus that could not be removed by normal means.

Figure 9.9 Disk interleaving: The left image shows 1:1 interleaving; the right image shows 3:1 interleaving.

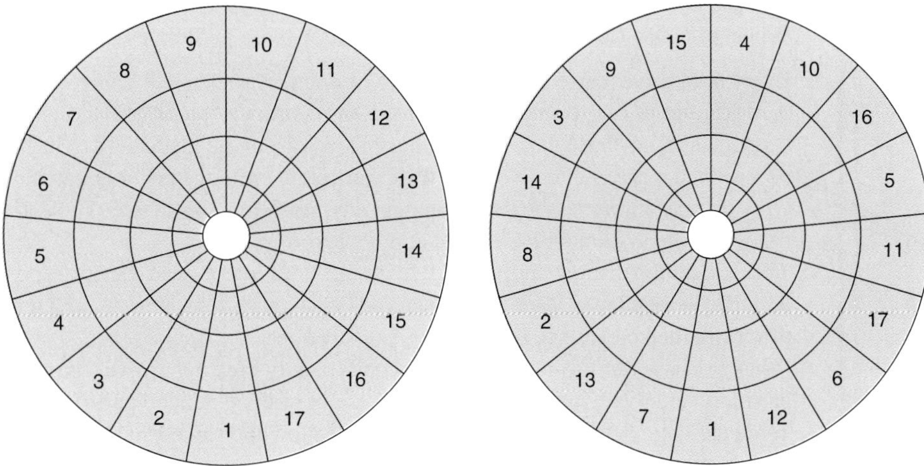

Figure 9.10 Partitioning (Before and After)

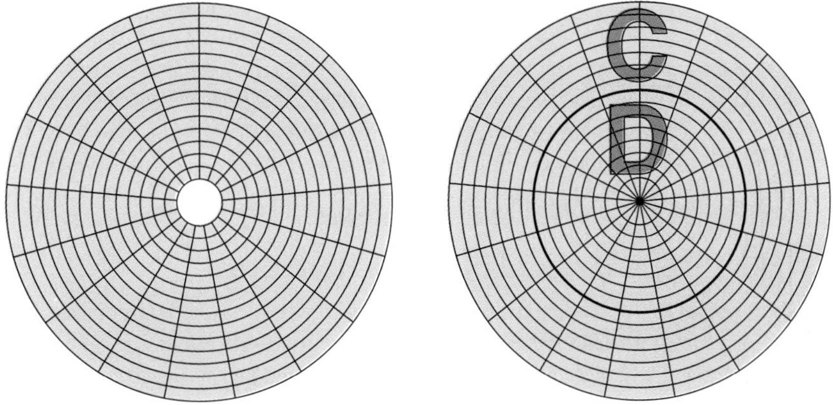

9.3.3 Partitioning the Hard Drive

Partitioning is defining and dividing the physical drive into logical volumes called *partitions*. Each partition functions as if it were a separate hard disk. See figure 9.10. It is the physical drive that is installed and configured, but the logical drive (the partitions) is what the system "thinks" it has. Every drive must include at least one partition. The reason for partitioning hard drives is to overcome operating system size limits, to use a drive more efficiently, to have multiple operating systems, and to isolate data areas.

Example 9.3:

The first step in installing and configuring a 4 GB hard drive would be to install the controller card, connect the cable, configure the hard drive, and run the CMOS setup program. If the drive requires a low-level format, it must be done with the proper software. The drive is then partitioned into two hard drives, drive C and drive D. Although only one hard drive was installed, the operating system, including File Manager/Explorer, recognizes drives C and D.

The information about how a hard drive is partitioned is stored in the master boot record (MBR), which is located in the first sector of the disk. The MBR contains a small program that reads the partition table, checks which partition is active (marked as bootable), and reads the first sector of the bootable partition. A common utility used to partition a hard drive is the FDISK utility, which is found in DOS and Windows 9X (see exercise 1 for more information about using the FDISK program). Windows NT uses

Disk Administrator to partition the drive while Windows 2000 or Windows XP use the Disk Management console (which is part of Computer Management console). Disk Administrator and Disk Management console are described more in chapter 21.

When you partition your drive, you must follow these guidelines:

- Every hard drive has to have a minimum of one partition.
- A maximum of four primary partitions or three primary partitions and one extended partition can be placed on any hard disk. The primary partition can be made active. Each primary partition can be assigned a drive letter. Note: FDISK can create only one primary partition.
- Only one partition may be designated, at any given time, as active. The active partition is the partition that the system will read first and boot from.
- The extended partition can be subdivided into multiple logical partitions, each of which could be assigned a drive letter. Therefore, to create logical partitions, you must first create an extended partition and then create one or more logical partitions.
- When you want to use logical drives, you typically create a primary partition, create an extended partition, and then you create logical drives out of the extended partition.
- To delete the extended partition, you would follow the same steps in creating the partition except you do them in reverse order. This means that you would first delete the logical drives and then delete the extended partition.

In DOS and Windows, the primary partition on the hard drive is assigned to be drive C. Any other primary partitions are assigned drive letters before any logical partitions. The drive letters are not permanent. If you install another hard drive and define a primary partition on the drive, it will grab the next drive letter after the first primary partition. The logical drives are reassigned new drive letters as well. Unfortunately, programs configured to look under a certain drive letter to find a particular directory or file will not find them causing all kinds of software execution errors. Note: Windows 2000 and Windows XP do have the capability to assign drive letters to partitions when you create them.

NOTE: For more information about partitions and file systems, see chapter 12.

9.3.4 Final Steps for Preparing the Hard Drive

High-level formatting is the process of writing the file system structure on the disk so that it can be used to store programs and data. This includes creating a file allocation table (an index listing all directories and files and where they are located on the disk) and a root directory to start with. In addition, high-level formatting creates a volume boot sector, which is used to store the boot files of an operating system. (Note: If you high-level format a disk that already has files and a directory, you will usually recreate the file allocation tables. Of course, without the index used to find the files, the previous information becomes inaccessible.) During high-level formatting, the partition can be made bootable by copying the operating system's boot files, such as DOS's IO.SYS, MSDOS.SYS, and COMMAND.COM. High-level formatting is usually performed with the FORMAT.COM command. If the disk was not made bootable during formatting, it will have to be reformatted, which of course will erase all data on the partition, or it will have to be done with a special operating system utility or command, such as the SYS command.

Much of the installation can be simplified by using the operating system's installation disks (or CD-ROM). If there are no partitions, the installation program will usually partition the drive. If there are partitions but they have not been formatted, the installation disks will format the individual partitions. They will also transfer the boot files to the disk, making it bootable, and copy the operating system files to the hard drive.

If you try to access a drive and you receive an "Invalid Media Type" error message, the drive has not been high-level formatted. If the drive was high-level formatted and is no longer, you need to check the hard drive for viruses and other problems.

9.4 DATA PROTECTION OF HARD DRIVES

The best method of protecting the data on the hard drive is to do a complete backup on a regular basis. Therefore, if the hard drive physically fails or the data become corrupt, the drive can be repaired or replaced and the data can be restored to the hard drive.

Table 9.3 Levels of RAID

Level 0—Disk striping	Data striping is the spreading out of blocks of each file across multiple disks. It offers no fault tolerance, but it increases performance. Level 0 is the fastest and most efficient form of RAID.
Level 1—Disk mirroring/ disk duplexing	Disk mirroring duplicates a partition onto two hard drives. When information is written, it is written to both hard drives simultaneously. It increases performance and provides fault tolerance. Disk duplexing is a form of disk mirroring. Disk mirroring uses two hard drives connected to the same card; disk duplexing uses two controller cards, two cables, and two hard drives.
Level 2—Disk striping with ECC	Level 2 uses data striping plus ECC to detect errors. It is rarely used today since ECC is embedded in almost all modern disk drives.
Level 3—ECC stored as parity	Level 3 dedicates one disk to error correction data. It provides good performance and some level of fault tolerance.
Level 4—Disk striping with large blocks	Level 4 offers no advantages over RAID 5 and does not support multiple simultaneous write operations.
Level 5—Striping with parity	RAID 5 uses disk striping and includes byte error correction on one of the disks. If one disk goes bad, the system will continue to function. After the faulty disk is replaced, the information on the replaced disk can be rebuilt. This system requires at least three drives. It offers excellent performance and good fault tolerance.

To help with data protection, there is **RAID (redundant arrays of inexpensive disks)**—two or more drives used in combination to create a fault tolerance system to protect against physical hard drive failure and to increase hard drive performance. A RAID can be accomplished with either hardware or software and is usually used in network servers. (Note: RAID does not replace a good backup since it does not protect against data corruption or viruses.)

There are several levels of RAID. See table 9.3. A common one used in networked PCs is RAID level 1, known as disk mirroring. **Disk mirroring** copies a partition onto a second hard drive. As information is written, it is written to both hard drives simultaneously. If one of the hard drives fails, the PC will still function because it can access the other hard drive. Another kind of disk mirroring is disk duplexing. **Disk duplexing** duplicates not only the hard drive but also the controller card and cable. Therefore, if the hard drive, controller card, or cable fails, the computer will still function.

RAID 0 is the base of RAID technology. RAID 0 stripes data across all drives. With striping, all available hard drives are combined into a single large virtual file system, with the file system's blocks arrayed so they are spread evenly across all the drives. For example, if you have three 500 MB hard drives, RAID 0 provides for a 1.5 GB virtual hard drive (sometimes referred to as a volume). When you store files, they are written across all three drives. When a large file, such as a 100 MB multimedia presentation, is saved to the virtual drive, a part of it may be written to the first drive, the next chunk to the second, more to the third, and perhaps more wrapping back to the first drive to start the sequence again. The exact manner in which the chunks of data move from physical drive to physical drive depends on the way the virtual drive has been set up, which includes considering drive capacity and the way in which blocks are allocated on each drive. No parity control or fault tolerance is provided with RAID 0, therefore, it really is not a true form of RAID. RAID 0 does have several advantages, though. Most important is that striping provides some increase in performance through load-balancing.

RAID 5 is very similar to RAID 0, but one of the hard drives is used for parity (error-correction) to provide fault tolerance. To increase performance, spreads the error-correction drive across all hard drives in the array to avoid the one drive of doing all of the work in calculating the parity bits. RAID 5 is supported by NT 4.0 and most RAID vendors because it is a good compromise between data integrity, speed, and cost. RAID 5 has better performance than RAID 1 (mirroring). RAID 5 usually requires at least three drives, with more drives preferable.

When using software RAID, RAID provided by the OS or other software, the overhead RAID 5 imposes on RAM can be significant, too, so Microsoft recommends at least an additional 16 MB RAM when RAID 5 is used. As with RAID 1, though, drives of disparate capacities may result in a lot of unused disk space because most RAID 5 systems use the smallest drive capacity in the array for all RAID 5 drives. Extra disk space can be used for unstriped partitions, but these are not protected by the RAID system.

9.5 IDE HARD DRIVES

IDE (integrated drive electronics) was developed in 1988 as a fast, low-cost hard drive interface. Three modifications were developed to connect the new IDE hard drives to the existing architecture: the AT attachment (ATA), made for the 16-bit ISA slot; the XT IDE interface, made for the 8-bit PC slot; and the MCAIDE for the IBM Micro Channel architecture. Today, most IDE controllers are built into the motherboard with a few available through a PCI card.

9.5.1 ATA IDE Hard Drives

All of the controlling electronics of the IDE drive are located on the drive itself, not the controller card as in older drives. The BIOS instructions that control the IDE drives are contained in the system ROM BIOS. Therefore, the controller card is only a paddleboard used to connect the cable to the rest of the computer. The hard drive is connected to the controller card with a 40-pin cable, which should not exceed 61 cm (24 in.). (Note: Some older IBM computers use a 44-pin and a 76-pin cable. The Ultra DMA/66 mode, and Ultra DMA/100 require a special 40-pin cable that has 80 wires, 40 pins for the signal, and 40 ground pins to reduce noise.) See figure 9.11.

The IDE drive is considered an intelligent drive because it can support drive translation. While in translation mode, any combination of cylinders, heads, and sectors can be used in the CMOS setup program as long as the total number of sectors is equal to or less than the actual number of sectors on the drive. The controller electronics on the drive translate the CHS sector to the actual sector on the drive and support zoned recordings since each track uses a different number of sectors. If a drive with translating electronics is installed, configured, partitioned, and formatted with one set of CMOS parameters and then changed to another, the drive may not boot (a "Drive C: Error" message may appear) or be accessible. Therefore, it is important to record the CMOS information and store it in a safe place. To find the correct CMOS parameter to use for a hard drive, it is best to use the documentation (some documentation is listed on the drive) that comes with the drive or to check the manufacturer's website or bul-

Figure 9.11 Connector Ribbon Cable and Power Connector (Courtesy of Seagate Corporation, Inc.)

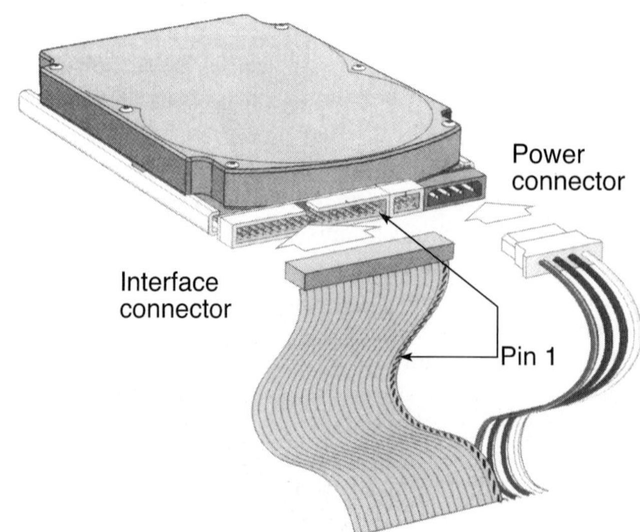

letin board. Newer CMOS setup programs can do an excellent job of automatically detecting the correct CMOS parameters.

The ATA IDE interface was modeled after the WD1003 controller used in the IBM AT. In addition to supporting the WD1003 commands, the ATA specification added other commands to increase performance and enhance capabilities. One important command is the IDENTIFY DRIVE command, which displays important identification information stored within the firmware of the drive. This information includes the drive manufacturer, the model number, and the operating parameters (number of cylinders, number of read/write heads, and number of tracks) of the drive. This is the reason that most modern CMOS setup programs and other hard drive-configuring software can automatically detect the drive and set the CMOS parameters. The primary IDE controller uses interrupt 14 and I/O address assignments of 1F0–1FF. The secondary IDE controller uses interrupt 15 and I/O address assignments of 0170–0177.

The BIOS-based driver for IDE hard disks is accessed using software interrupt 13h, which offers functions for reading and writing drives at the sector level. INT13h requires that the particular sector be addressed using CHS addressing. This interface is used by the operating system and low-level disk utilities to access the drive.

When working with ATA IDE hard drives, you will often encounter two limitations. First, because of the limitation of their older ROM BIOS chips (some dating back to 1996), the system cannot see more than 1,024 cylinders. This can be overcome with translating electronics (extended CHS), however. Second, due to the ROM BIOS and the limitations of the IDE hard drive itself, IDE hard drives cannot be bigger than 504 MB (528 MB if you define MB as 1 million bytes). See table 9.4.

Up to two hard drives can be connected with the IDE cable. If one drive is installed, it is known as a *stand-alone drive.* If two hard drives are installed, the physical drive C is known as the *master drive* while the physical drive D is known as the *slave drive.* The master drive got its name because its controlling electronics on the logic board control both the master drive and the slave drive. The stand-alone, master, and slave drives are determined by jumper connections on the hard drive. It makes no difference where the drive and controller card are connected to the cable. See figure 9.12. The jumpers most

Table 9.4 Limitations of IDE Hard Drives

	BIOS Limitation	ATA IDE Limitation	Combined Limitation
Number of cylinders	1,024	65,536	1,024
Number of read/write heads	256	16	16
Maximum sectors per track	63	255	63
Maximum capacity	7.9 GB	127.5 GB	504 MB

Figure 9.12 IDE Hard Drive Connected to Controller Card (Courtesy of Seagate Corporation, Inc.)

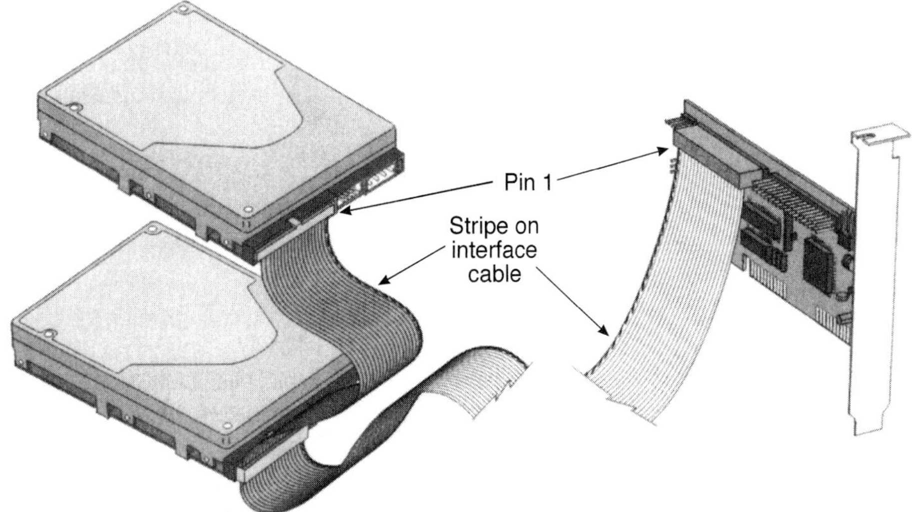

Figure 9.13 Typical Jumper Setting of an IDE Hard Drive (Courtesy of Seagate Corporation, Inc.)

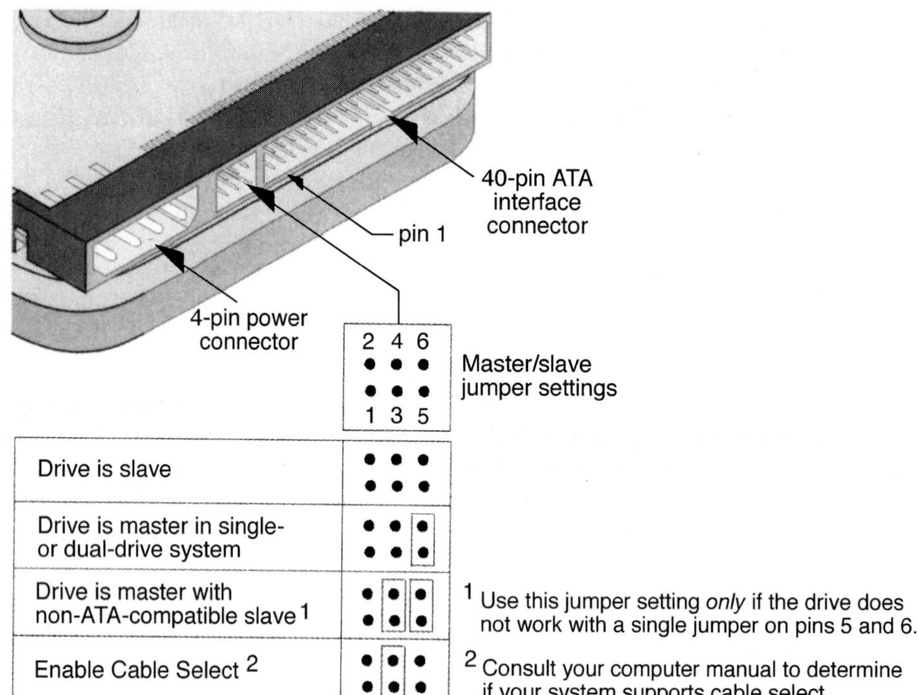

Table 9.5 Typical Jumper Settings for an ATA IDE Hard Drive

	Master (M/S)	Slave Present (SP)
Stand-alone (master with no slave drive)	On	Off
Master	On	On
Slave	Off	Off

commonly used to determine a drive as a stand-alone, master, or slave are the master (M/S) jumper and the slave present (SP). See figure 9.13 and table 9.5.

The ATA interface connector is normally a 40-pin header-type connector with pins. Newer IDE connectors are keyed to prevent the possibility of installing it upside. Pin 20 is removed from the male connector, and pin 20 is blocked on the female connector. Some cables also use a protrusion on the top of the female cable connector that fits into a notch in the shroud surrounding the mating male connector on the device. To maximize signal integrity and eliminate potential timing and noise problems, IDE cables should not be longer than 18 in. (0.46 m).

Hard drives used in notebook computers are 2½-in. IDE hard drives. When placed in a notebook, the IDE hard drives are often encased in a set of brackets, which are used to hold the drive into place. To connect the hard drive to the notebook computers, you would use a smaller 50-pin connector (40 pins for data and 10 for power and jumpering). Normally, the cable plugs into a connector that has 44 pins. Pin 31 provides +V power to the drive logic board, pin 43 provides +5 V power to the motor, and pin 43 provides a power ground.

After the hard drive, controller card, and system are configured, the IDE drive must then be partitioned and high-level formatted. Since the drive is already low-level formatted by the manufacturer, that does not have to be done during installation.

Many people say never low-level format any hard drive. In reality, an IDE hard drive can be low-level formatted if it is done properly and with the correct software. The correct software will not erase the servo information or the defect-map information, and it will set the optimal head and sector-skew factor. To prevent improper formatting, some IDE hard drives require special codes to unlock the format routines. In addition, while the drive is in translation mode, which always occurs in zone recordings, the skew factors cannot be changed and the defect map cannot be overwritten.

NOTE: If a low-level format is done while the drive is under warranty, it may void the warranty.

The best place to get the proper low-level format software is the manufacturer's website (such as Seagate, Western Digital, or Maxtor) or bulletin board. Conner hard drives (owned by Seagate) are different from the others in that a special device must be connected to the serial port to unlock the low-level format capabilities. If the proper low-level format program cannot be found on the Internet or manufacturer's bulletin board, a commercial package like Ontrack's Disk Manager, Microscope's Micro 2000, or Microhouse's Drive Pro can be used.

Some compatibility issues may prevent IDE drives from working properly (and may prevent the system from booting). Some IDE hard drives are incompatible with IDE hard drives made by other manufacturers. This is usually true of older IDE drives, which did not adhere to the ATA IDE specification. Also, only PCs made since 1990 are fully compatible with ATA IDE drives. Therefore, if working on a machine made before 1990, you should consider upgrading the system ROM BIOS.

9.5.2 Enhanced IDE (EIDE) Hard Drives

Today, when you hear the term *IDE,* it refers to the Enhanced IDE hard drive. To compete against SCSI drives and to overcome some of the limitations of the IDE, **enhanced IDE (EIDE)/AT attachment interface with extensions (ATA-2)** was developed. The EIDE interface supports up to four IDE devices using two IDE cables (primary and secondary). Each cable is its own channel, consisting of its own master and slave device. Instead of supporting only hard drives, EIDE supports nondisk peripherals that follow the ATAPI (ATA packet interface) protocol. ATAPI is the protocol used on the enhanced IDE devices (IDE CD-ROM drives, IDE tape backup drives, and other IDE storage devices).

NOTE: The bootable drive should be connected to the first or second connector from the primary IDE controller.

The parallel ATA interface has evolved into several successive standard versions. See table 9.6. Each version of ATA is backward compatible with the previous versions.

The 504 MB capacity limitation of the IDE was broken by the introduction of **large addressing/ extended CHS addressing** and **logical block addressing (LBA).** Large addressing uses different parameters for the cylinders, heads, and sectors that calculate to the same capacity and translate them into the actual parameters. LBA uses the 28 bits of the CHS address as a binary number. LBA numbers each sector starting at 0 and continuing to the last physical sector. Its binary number base allows up to 268,435,456 sectors, or 128 GB.

NOTE: Starting with ATA-6, IDE drives LBA mode uses 48 bits which allows up to 144 petabytes (a quadrillion bytes).

To maintain compatibility with older operating systems like DOS, the system ROM BIOS must translate the CHS addresses generated by software into the LBA address. However, since the older operating systems communicate with the BIOS and the BIOS recognizes only up to 7.9 GB, a drive must be ATA-2 compatible and the BIOS must understand LBA to access the increased capacity. If the system ROM BIOS does not support EIDE/ATA-2 drives, the system ROM BIOS needs to be either updated or modified, which can be done by:

1. Adding a newer system ROM chip that includes instructions for handling EIDE/ATA-2 hard drives
2. Updating the ROM chip (if the system ROM BIOS is flash ROM) by using special software
3. Inserting an EIDE controller card that includes a ROM BIOS chip to supplement the system ROM BIOS chip
4. Configuring the computer to recognize the drive and using software or a device driver (sometimes called a *dynamic drive overlay*) that includes instructions for handling EIDE hard drives

Table 9.6 ATA Standards

Standard	Timeframe	Modes	Speed	Features
ATA-1	1986–1994	PIO modes 0–2 DMA mode 0	8.33 MB/s	Drives support up to 136.9 GB. Unfortunately, BIOS issues were not addressed.
ATA-2	1995–1996	PIO modes 0–4 DMA modes 0–2	16.67 MB/s	CHS/LBA BIOS translation defined up to 8.4 GB.
ATA-3	1996–1997	PIO modes 0–4 DMA modes 0–2	16.67 MB/s	Added S.M.A.R.T., LBA support mandatory, eliminated single-word DMA modes.
ATA-4	1997–1998	PIO modes 0–4 DMA modes 0–2 UDMA modes 0–2	33.33 MB/s	Ultra DMA modes, BIOS support up to 136.9 GB.
ATA-5	1998–2000	PIO modes 0–4 DMA modes 0–2 UDMA modes 0–4	66.67 MB/s	Faster UDMA modes; 40-pin/80-conductor cable with autodetection.
ATA-6	2000–2001	PIO modes 0–4 DMA modes 0–2 UDMA modes 0–5	100 MB/s	100 MB/s UDMA mode, extend drive and BIOS support up to 144 petabyte (a quadrillion bytes).
ATA-7	2001–present	PIO modes 0–4 DMA modes 0–2 UDMA modes 0–6	133 MB/s	133 MB/s UDMA mode.

Modern CMOS setup programs include several hard drive options or modes: normal, large, or LBA mode. The normal mode, for older IDE drives, uses CHS translation mode for drives that do not exceed 1,024 cylinders. The large mode uses CHS mode under translation mode, making it possible for drives to exceed 1,024 cylinders. The LBA mode allows the sectors to be numbered in sequence.

Unfortunately, translating the parameters pushed the 504 MB barrier to 7.9 GB (8.4 billion bytes), limited by the BIOS maximum. Over the last 5 years, drives have doubled every year. Therefore, it was not long before drives approached the 7.9 GB boundary. In 1998 newer BIOS included the BIOS Enhanced Disk Drive Specification that no longer used the CHS numbers and used only LBA. The BIOS with the new specification could handle 2^{64} sectors or 9.4 giga-tera (billion trillion) bytes, but the ATA specification currently limits this to 136.9 GB. Note: If you are using software including utilities, applications, and operating systems that rely exclusively on CHS parameters, they will see all drives over 7.9 GB as 7.9 GB only.

The limited data transfer rate of the IDE also had to be overcome. Enhanced IDE, depending on the transfer mode, allows a transfer rate up to 33.3 MB/s. The two methods of transferring data are **processor input/output (PIO)** and **direct memory access (DMA).**

PIO is the transfer method used on most IDE drives, with the microprocessor using in and out instructions to handle data transfers. There are currently five PIO modes in use: PIO modes 0, 1, and 2 use the old ATA specification; PIO modes 3 and 4 use the ATA-2 specification. See table 9.7. Modes 3 and 4 run at such high speeds that the EIDE interface can experience some errors. Therefore, the higher modes have an IORDY hardware flow control signal to slow the interface when necessary. (Note: PIO modes 3 and 4 require local bus access because the ISA bus cannot handle transfer rates of over 10 MB/s.) ATA-2 also allows block mode PIO, sometimes referred to as *multisector data transfer.* Rather than generating one interrupt for each sector being transferred, block mode PIO will process up to 32 multiple sectors using one interrupt. This greatly reduces the number of interrupts sent to the microprocessor, which reduces the traffic. (Note: Block mode PIO requires a local bus connection, a compatible drive and controller, and software that supports multisector data transfers.)

The other mode of data transfer is DMA, specifically bus mastering. Bus mastering transfers the information through the address and data bus without any direction from the microprocessor. In older DMA, transfers were performed by the DMA controller on the motherboard; the bus mastering trans-

Table 9.7 PIO Modes Used with EIDE Services

PIO Mode	Average Transfer Rate	Cycle Time	Flow Controlled	Specification
0	3.3 MB/s	600 ns	No	ATA
1	5.2 MB/s	383 ns	No	ATA
2	8.3 MB/s	240 ns	No	ATA
3	11.1 MB/s	180 ns	Yes	ATA-2
4	16.6 MB/s	120 ns	Yes	ATA-2

Table 9.8 DMA Mode Used with EIDE Devices

DMA Mode	Cycle Time	Average Transfer Rate	Requirements	Standard
0—Single Word	960	2.08 MB/s		ATA
1—Single Word	480	4.16 MB/s		ATA
2—Single Word	240	8.33 MB/s		ATA
0—Multiword	480	4.16 MB/s	Local-bus controller	ATA
1—Multiword	150	13.33 MB/s	Local-bus controller	ATA-2
2—Multiword	120	16.6 MB/s	Local-bus controller	ATA-3
3—Multiword	90	33.3 MB/s	Local-bus controller	Ultra DMA/33
4—Multiword	60	66.6 MB/s	Local-bus controller and 40-pin/80-conductor cable	Ultra DMA/66
5—Multiword	40	100.0 MB/s	Local-bus controller and 40-pin/80-conductor cable	Ultra DMA/100

fer is controlled by the controller card. Because the microprocessor can perform other tasks during the data transfer, DMA transfers are ideal for multitasking operating systems. Single-word DMA transfer uses DMA "handshaking," consisting of requests and acknowledgements for each transfer. Multiword DMA transfer reduces the traffic by handling several DMA transfers at the same time without using the DMA requests and acknowledgments. See table 9.8.

ATA specification (ATA-4) is the Ultra DMA/33 mode. It supports a burst mode data transfer rate of 33.3 MB/s, which is twice as fast as previous modes. In addition to increasing through-put, Ultra DMA/33 improves data integrity by using a **cyclic redundancy check (CRC)** to flag any data transfer errors that may have been made over the ATA bus. Systems on which the master and slave devices are running at different speeds may be limited to the speed of the slower device. Therefore, it is best to isolate the slower device by putting it on a different channel.

DMA began to rise in popularity at around the time the first version of Windows 95 was released but the original version of Windows 95 did not have native support for bus-mastering DMA, so drivers had to be added to support DMA. These frequently caused compatibility and stability problems. Starting with the Windows 95 OSR2, DMA support was provided by the operating system and did not suffer from the earlier problems.

On modern systems, unless you have installed the Intel Ultra ATA Storage Driver, DMA support should be enabled by default. You can check for DMA support by looking in the Device Manager. From the Control Panel, open System; then click the Device Manager tab. Open the icon for Disk drives and then highlight the drive you are interested in. Click Properties and then the Settings tab. If it is not enabled, try checking it to enable DMA support. If you then reboot and the check box does not stay checked, this probably means your system does not support Ultra DMA.

The ATA interface is designed for the AT's 16-bit ISA bus, which, of course, transfers data 16 bits at a time, but the local bus can transfer at a 32-bit rate. Therefore, if the system includes a 32-bit Access option in the CMOS setup program and it is enabled, it will allow two 16-bit chunks of data to be transferred at the same time. (Note: This is not to be confused with Windows 3.XX 32-bit disk and file access.)

9.5.3 Ultra DMA/66 and Ultra DMA/100

Ultra DMA/66 has a transfer rate of 66 MB/s and Ultra DMA/100 has a transfer rate of 100 MB/s. Unfortunately, the original 40-conductor IDE cable could not handle the faster data rate. Therefore, starting with DMA/66, a 40-pin conductor, 80-conductor IDE/ATA cable was introduced. Forty conductors or wires carried the data and 40 ground conductors or wires reduced cross talk between adjacent wires. Ultra DMA/133 has also been introduced, but has not received wide acceptance. Instead, most vendors will most likely adopt the serial ATA interface.

Because no changes have been made to the connector, the new cable is pin compatible with older IDE drives. Therefore, the 80-conductor cable can be used in systems up to 33.3 MB/s is optional, but it is required for Ultra DMA/66 and higher.

On the standard 40-pin/40-conductor IDE interfaces, pin 34 was not grounded, and on the newer 40-pin/80-conductor IDE interface, pin 34 is grounded. By sending a signal on pin 34, it can tell if the system is using the older cable or the newer cable. Therefore, on systems that can use Ultra DMA/66 or Ultra DMA/100, if you connect an Ultra DMA/100 drive, it will detect the drive, detect the type of cable, and automatically configure for the appropriate data transfer rate.

Different from older IDE drives, the connectors on the cable define which connector goes with which device. The blue connector attaches to the controller. The gray connector is in the middle of the cable and goes to any slave drive (if present). The black connector is at the opposite end from the controller connector and goes to the master drive or to a single drive if only one is used. This was done because if you connect a single drive to the middle connector of the ribbon cable, the unconnected cable can cause signaling problems.

An alternative to the standard master/slave jumpering system used in most IDE systems is the cable-select system. By connecting the drives to a specific connector on the cable, the system will determine which device is master and which is slave. Because pin 28 is grounded at the host's connector, which is connected to the master, it detects the end drive as the master and the middle drive—which is not connected with pin 28—becomes the slave drive.

Therefore, instead of setting the master and slave jumpers, the jumpers are set to Cable Select (CS); connected to the appropriate connector, the drives will be assigned the appropriate master or slave designation. Unfortunately, most people do not know of this option, and it was never accepted in the industry, so most drives come already jumpered as a master or single drive by default. Therefore, you still have to change the jumper to enable this feature.

9.5.4 Serial ATA Interface

The current IDE/ATA standard is a parallel interface (this is the reason it is sometimes referred to as Parallel ATA [PATA]) this means that multiple bits of data are transmitted at one time. In the case of ATA, 16 bits are moved across the interface simultaneously during each transfer. The advantage of the parallel interface is that it allows for high throughput, the disadvantage is that as the frequency of the interface is increased, signaling problems, (crosstalk adds noise which causes signal error) and interface between signals become common.

The Serial ATA interface, often abbreviated SATA or S-ATA, is based on one signal. Therefore, serial interface will enable much higher speeds than would be possible from a parallel implementation, because the signaling problems are largely eliminated. In fact, this is the same reasoning that led to the creation of other high-speed serial interface, such as IEEE 1394. Serial ATA 1 has a bandwidth of 150 MB/s. When Serial ATA II and III are introduced, it is envisioned to have a bandwidth of 300 or 600 MB/s. See figures 9.14 and 9.15.

The IDE ribbon cables are bulky, inflexible, fragile, and too short. The width of those cables blocks airflow and generally creates a clumsy setup. The SATA drives require two cable connectors, the data cable and power cable. Since the data cables are smaller and contain only seven wires, the connectors are more compact. It should also be noted that serial ATA is a serial technology. Therefore, it can only talk to one device per channel. Since the cable and connectors are smaller, they can be easily fit in even if you have one of each per device. While IDE cables could only be up to 18 in. (0.46 m), Serial ATA cables can be up to 1 m.

The interface cable consists of a transmit signal differential pair, a receive signal differential pair, and three ground connections. The use of differential signals improves tolerance to electrical noise. Differential signaling is explained with Differential SCSI drives.

Figure 9.14 Serial IDE drive with data cable. The power connector is to the right of the data connector.

Figure 9.15 Serial IDE Data and Power Connector Next to a Parallel IDE Power and Data Cables

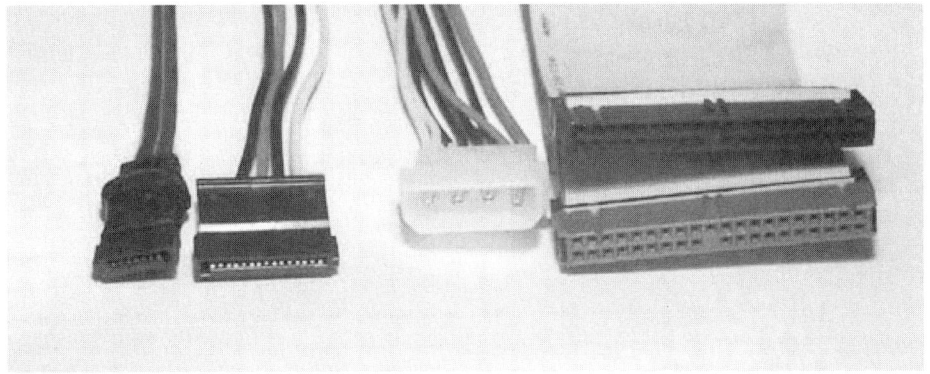

Serial ATA is extremely easy to set up. It is software compatible with Parallel ATA, and although it won't officially be supported until Microsoft's Longhorn OS (the next version of Windows after Windows XP and Windows Server 2003), Serial ATA devices will work with all versions of Windows. Since there is only one device per channel, there is no need to worry about master and slave configurations any longer.

One of the most important features contributing to the success of Serial ATA is its backward compatibility with Ultra ATA. It is particularly interesting that current Serial ATA controllers work fine with conventional Ultra ATA/133 hard disks (or older). Not only are there motherboards available with Serial ATA and Ultra ATA/133 connectors, there are also stand-alone Serial ATA controllers on the market that use adapters to work with conventional ATA drives. The downside of the conversion is reduced performance when you convert from parallel to serial transmission.

9.5.5 Intel Ultra ATA Storage Driver and Intel Application Accelerator

The Intel Ultra ATA storage driver is a driver that is designed to take advantage of devices supporting ATA DMA/Ultra DMA technologies and improve system performance. It is not a requirement for your operating system to work properly. Currently, the Intel Ultra ATA Storage Driver supports Intel 810, 815, 820, 840, and 850 chipsets. In addition, you must have either Windows 98, Windows 98 Second Edition (SE), Windows Millennium Edition (Me), Windows NT 4.0, Windows 2000, or Windows XP. To install the Intel Ultra ATA Storage Driver.

1. Install the Intel Chipset Software Installation Utility before installing the Intel Ultra ATA Storage Driver so that the Intel chipset is properly recognized by the operating system.
2. Download the Intel Ultra ATA Storage Driver from the Intel website (http://support.intel.com/support/chipsets/storagedrivers/ultra/ATA/incon.htm). Save the file to a known location on your computer's hard drive.
3. The installation program will automatically launch from this location.
4. Click Next at the Welcome screen.
5. Read the license agreement and click Yes to continue.
6. Click Next to install the driver in the default folder location.
7. Click Next to create the default Program Folder.
8. The driver files will now be installed. When finished installing, choose Yes to the reboot option and click Finish to restart your computer. The driver should now be loaded.

An approved version of the Intel Ultra ATA Storage Driver is the Intel Application Accelerator (located at http://support.intel.com/support/chipsets/iaa/). It provides faster boot time via Accelerated Operating System Load Time; accelerated disk I/O for games, graphics applications, disk utilities, and media authoring applications; performance-enhancing data prefetcher for Intel Pentium 4 processor-based systems; and support for 137 GB and larger hard drives.

9.6 SCSI HARD DRIVES

Another very popular hard drive and system interface is the small computer system interface (SCSI, pronounced "skuzzy"), which evolved from Shugart Associates standard interface (SASI). SCSI is a much more advanced interface than the ATA/ATA-2 IDE drives and is ideal for high-end computers, including network servers. Its cable supports multiple devices in and out of the computer. See figure 9.16.

SCSI interfaces that have an 8-bit data bus, referred to as narrow interfaces, allow up to seven devices (hard drives, tape drives, CD-ROM drives, removable drives/disks and scanners) connected to one SCSI adapter/controller. It is eight devices if you count the controller card. SCSI interfaces with a 16-bit data bus, referred to as wide interfaces, allow up to 15 devices (16 devices including the controller card). See table 9.9.

Like any other expansion card, you may need to configure the card's resources. The standard SCSI I/O address range is 0330–0333. The IRQs are typically assigned to the unused IRQs, such as IRQ 11, or they will be plug-and-play. Today, the cards typically do not use DMAs.

With a SCSI host adapter, the BIOS on the adapter is used to control SCSI hard disk drives and perform the boot function. The BIOS also intercepts all hardware interrupt 13 calls (read and write to disk) and passes the non-SCSI interrupt to the system ROM BIOS. The SCSI host adapter then translates these interrupt 13 commands into SCSI commands for the SCSI disk drives.

Figure 9.16 Older SCSI Adapter

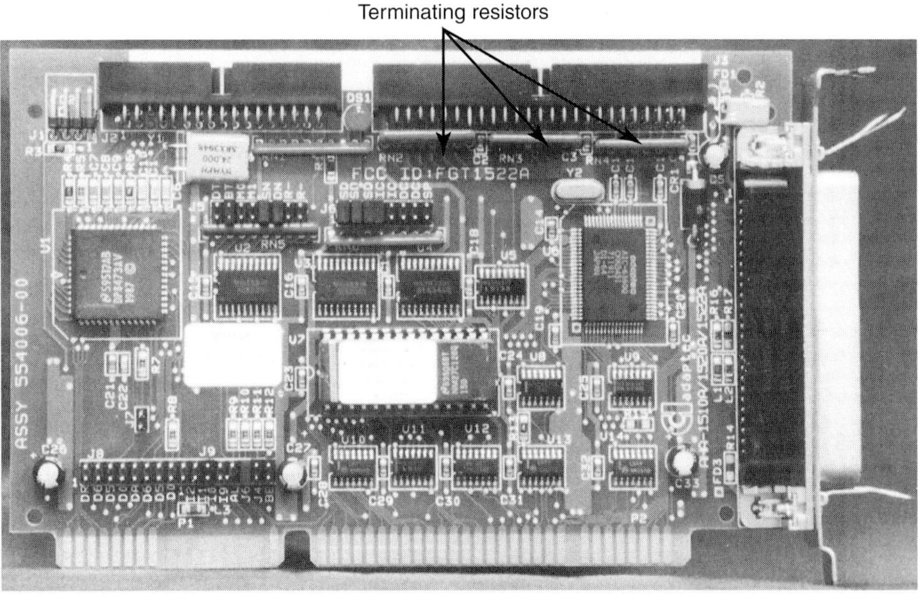

9.6.1 SCSI-1

The SCSI standard (SCSI-1) was approved in 1986 by the American National Standards Institute (ANSI). SCSI-1 defines the basics of the first SCSI buses, including cable length, signaling characteristics, commands, and transfer modes. It specified an 8-bit bus with a 5 MB/s transfer rate. It supports only single-ended transmission with passive termination. (Don't worry, these terms will be explained a little later.) Unfortunately, the standard included only the hardware connection and did not specify the driver specification/Common Command Set required to communicate with the SCSI hard drive. Therefore, manufacturers used their own communication standard, which led to many compatibility problems between different devices, drivers, and adapters.

SCSI-1 is now obsolete, and the standard has, in fact, been withdrawn by ANSI. Devices that adhere to the SCSI-1 standard can in most cases be used with host adapters and other devices that use the higher transfer rates of the more advanced SCSI-2 protocols, but they will still function at their original slow speed. Note: Because all SCSI-1 devices are single-ended, they may cause performance degradation if they are placed onto a multimode LVD SCSI bus. If you want to run LVD devices to their full potential, you will want to avoid mixing them with single-ended devices.

9.6.2 SCSI-2

To overcome some of the shortcomings of the SCSI-1 interface, ANSI approved the SCSI-2 standard in 1992. It included a set of 18 basic SCSI commands called the Common Command Set (CCS) used to support different peripherals, including CD-ROM drives, tape drives, removable drives/disks, and scanners.

In addition, SCSI-2 used command queuing. **Command queuing** allows a device to accept multiple commands and execute them in an order that is more efficient rather than in the order received. You can think of command queuing as similar to having a busload of people. You can travel to each person's stop in the order that he or she entered the bus or you can try to figure out the best way to drop these people off. Therefore, if two people live in a nearby area, you would drop them off one after the other. For SCSI hard drives, this increases the performance of computers running multitasking operating systems and makes it ideal for servers.

In addition, SCSI-2 established faster SCSI variations, such as Fast SCSI and Fast Wide SCSI, which increased the data path from 8 bits to 16 bits and improved data transfer up to 20 MB/s. On buses that that are running with Wide SCSI, 16 devices are supported (as opposed to 8 with regular SCSI).

Table 9.9 Types of SCSI Devices and Interfaces

Transfer Mode	SCSI Spec	Bus Width[1] (bits)	Throughput (MB/s)	Cabling	Signaling Method	Maximum Devices per Bus	Maximum Cable Length (m)
"Regular" SCSI (SCSI-1)	SCSI-1/ SCSI-2	8	5	50-pin	SE	8	6
					HVD	8	25
Wide SCSI	SCSI-2	16	10	50-pin	SE	16	6
					HVD	16	25
Fast SCSI (also known as Fast Narrow)	SCSI-2	8	10	50-pin	SE	8	3
					HVD	8	25
Fast Wide SCSI (also known as Fast SCSI)	SCSI-2	16	20	68-pin	SE	16	3
					HVD	16	25
Ultra SCSI (also known as Ultra Narrow or Fast-20 SCSI)	SCSI-3/ SPI[2]	8	20	50-pin	SE	8	1.5
						4	3
					HVD	8	25
Wide Ultra SCSI (also known as Fast Wide 20)	SCSI-3/ SPI	16	40	68-pin	SE	8	1.5
						4	3
					HVD	16	25
Ultra2 SCSI	SCSI-3/ SPI-2	8	40	50-pin	LVD	8	12
						2	25
					HVD	8	25
Wide Ultra2 SCSI	SCSI-3/ SPI-2	16	80	68-pin	LVD	16	12
						2	25
					HVD	16	25
Ultra3 SCSI (also known as Ultra160 SCSI)	SCSI-3/ SPI-3	16	160	68-pin	LVD	16	12
						2	25
Ultra 320 SCSI	SCSI-3	16	320	68-pin	LVD	16	12
						2	25
Serial SCSI (Fiber Channel SCSI I)	SCSI-3	Serial	100 MB/s	126-pin	NA	10,000	NA
Serial SCSI (Fiber Channel SCSI II)	SCSI-3	Serial	200 MB/s	126-pin	NA	10,000	NA

[1]Narrow = 8 bits and wide = 16 bits.
[2]SPI = SCSI Parallel Interface.

To have improved bandwidth, SCSI-2 uses a large number of different cable and connectors. For example, SCSI-2 defined new higher density connections, extending the basic 50-pin connectors defined in SCSI-1. It also defined the use of active termination, which provides more reliable termination of the bus and differential signaling to allow longer cable lengths. Note: The differential signaling was later renamed high-voltage differential (HVD) to distinguish it from low-voltage differential (LVD) signaling.

9.6.3 SCSI-3

As SCSI-3 was being developed, it became a huge specification with a large number of different technologies, command sets, and features. Because such a huge specification would have required too many people to work on it and the development of hardware would have been slow, the SCSI-3 specification was broken into subspecifications so that impatient companies would not start developing their own proprietary extensions. The most implemented form of SCSI, which was known as just SCSI in the earlier standards, became the SCSI-3 Parallel Interface (SPI) under SCSI-3. There are now several versions of SPI, each defining new features and transfer speeds for conventional, parallel SCSI devices.

SCSI-3 specifies a high-speed synchronous transfer called ultra SCSI and Ultra Wide SCSI using a type A cable (8-bit data bus) and P cable (16-bit data bus). SCSI-3 allows a data transfer rate up to 320 MB/s and up to 16 devices using the same cable.

9.6.4 Fiber Channel SCSI

A miscellaneous SCSI interface is the Serial SCSI/Fiber Channel SCSI. The Fiber Channel SCSI is a serial connection made of fiber or coaxial cable using lengths up to 10,000 m, and it supports up to 126 devices. It can support 100 MB/s and a 200 MB/s data transfer rate. Although serial SCSI was not used in mainstream SCSI, it has found a niche in storage area networks (SANs), where the hard drives are shared among several systems that act as redundancy for each other. Therefore, if one computer goes down, the other computers will fill in for the down computer. The hard drives are centrally located so that they can access the same data.

9.6.5 Serial Attached SCSI

Because serial technology can communicate faster than parallel technology with fewer errors, many forms of technology are shifting from parallel technology to serial technology. Like Parallel ATA IDE is shifting to Serial ATA IDE, Parallel SCSI will eventually shift to **Serial Attached SCSI (SAS).**

Parallel SCSI is based on shared-access topologies that allow only two devices to communicate at once. Unfortunately, as throughput needs increase, the shared-access medium can become a bottleneck and slow down communication. In addition, shared-access topologies also are typically more complex and have arbitration schemes that are more time consuming than point-to-point architectures.

Serial Attached SCSI is a point-to-point architecture that establishes a link directly from the controller to a disk drive or through an expander switching matrix. The point-to-point architectures can connect multiple devices simultaneously, have simplified cabling requirements, and provide greater scalability and performance than with shared-access topologies. The first versions of SAS will support at 3 Gbit/s, but will be extended in the future. See table 9.10.

To improve drive addressability and connectivity, SAS uses an expander that enables one or more SAS host controllers to connect to a large number of drives. Each expander allows connectivity to 128 physical links, which may include other host connections, other SAS expanders, or hard disks. In addition, these drivers can easily support multinode clustering for automatic failover availability or load balancing.

Because the SAS interface does not require many wires to carry data, the SAS interface can use a thinner cable and smaller connectors, all of which improve routing, airflow, and controlling; reduce

Table 9.10 Comparing Serial ATA, Fiber Channel SCSI, and Serial Attached SCSI

	Serial ATA	Fiber Channel SCSI	Serial Attached SCSI
Transfer mode	Half-duplex	Full-duplex	Full-duplex with wide links
Performance	1.5 Gbit/s	2.0 Gbit/s	3.0 Gbit/s
Number of devices	One device	127 devices using a loop or loop switch	128 devices using an expander
Type of devices	SATA devices	FC devices only	SAS and SATA devices

crosstalk and signal error; and simplify electrical design. SAS technology permits universal connection between SATA and SAS drives to ease configuration and improve hot-swap capability. The future designs for the smaller 2.5-in. dual-port SAS drivers should also provide additional space savings. Finally, due to its small connector, SAS offers full dual-ported connections on 3.5-in. and smaller 2.5-in. hard disk drives, a feature previously found only on larger 3.5-in. Fiber Channel disk drives. This is an essential feature in applications requiring redundant drive spindles in a dense server form factor such as blade servers.

Serial Attached SCSI technology will support three main protocols. By adding support for Serial ATA Tunneling Protocol, Serial Attached SCSI controllers will be able to communicate with both SAS and SATA drive devices. The subsystem will use SATA Tunneling Protocol for SATA devices and serial SCSI Protocol for SAS drive devices. As well, drives will be able to be hot-swapped and may be physically inserted on the same back plane connector.

9.6.6 Signaling Methods

Traditional SCSI uses single-ended signaling (SE), which is very similar to that used for most other interfaces and buses within the PC. A positive voltage is a 1 and a zero voltage is a 0. It was relatively simple compared to today's more advanced methods and inexpensive to implement. As SCSI became faster, problems arose with bouncing signals, interference, degradation over distance, and crosstalk from adjacent signals. In addition, the length of a single-ended SCSI cable is rather limited.

To get around these problems, differential signaling was used. For a logical zero, zero voltage is sent on both wires. For a logical 1, the first wire of each signal pair contains a positive voltage, similar to the signal on an SE bus, but not necessarily at the same voltage. The second wire contains the electrical opposite of the first wire. The circuitry at the receiving device takes the difference between the two signals sent and thus sees a relatively high voltage for a 1, and a zero voltage for a 0. Unfortunately, because differential signals are more expensive and use more power than those for single-ended SCSI and single-ended SCSI was good enough for most users, differential signaling never became popular.

Because SE could not handle the faster speeds and the cost of differential signaling was considered too high, another form of differential signaling was created. Low-voltage differential (LVD), which was defined in SPI-2, took the best attributes of both SE and HVD signaling. It used a lower voltage, which reduced cost and power requirements. It also allowed LVD devices to function on a single-ended SCSI bus. LVD signaling is required for Ultra2 or Wide Ultra2 SCSI (unless HVD) is used) and is required for any SCSI method faster than Ultra2. As you might imagine, LVD has become very popular.

NOTE: Because single-ended and HVD SCSI use very different voltage levels, they are incompatible at the electrical level. You should not mix single-ended or low-voltage differential devices with high-voltage differential SCSI devices on the same bus. If you do, you may damage the single-ended or LVD devices.

Some LVD devices can automatically switch between LVD and single-ended operation by detecting whether the other devices on the chain are running in SE or LVD mode. These devices are called multimode LVD devices and are abbreviated LVD/SE or LVD/MSE (the *M* is for *multimode*). Note: As soon as multimode LVD devices begin running as single-ended, all the rules and restrictions of single-ended operations apply, including cable length.

In addition, to the usual SCSI rules, LVD operation requires the following:

- All devices on the chain must be LVD-capable; if even one device is only SE, all devices "drop down" and run as single-ended.
- All devices must not be set to run in SE mode; some multimode devices have a jumper to force SE operation, which will cause the entire SCSI chain not to work in LVD.
- LVD (or multimode LVD/SE) terminators must be used.
- Because single-ended singling does not support bus speeds greater than 20 MHz, if you use a faster LVD/MSE device on a single-ended chain, it will run at a maximum of only 40 MB/s.

Because devices using the SE, LVD, and HVD can be easily connected together, icons are often imprinted on SCSI hardware devices that indicate the signaling method used by each device. See figure 9.17.

Figure 9.17 Icons Representing SE, HVD, LVD, and LVD/SE Signaling Cable

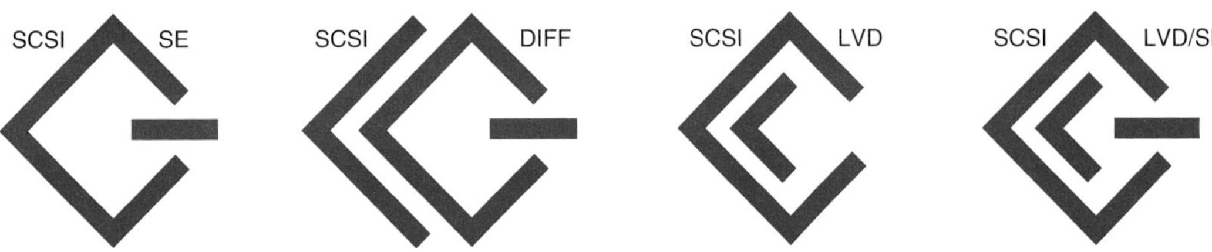

9.6.7 SCSI Cables and Connectors

Currently, there are many types of SCSI cables available. Because each SCSI cable must meet the specific electrical requirements associated with the SCSI signaling speeds and signaling methods, the design of any SCSI cable is based on a combination of different attributes chosen to implement a particular kind of SCSI bus. Some characteristics of the cable include the number of pins, the type of cable (internal or external), the connector type, the length of the cable, the number of connectors, spacing of the connectors on the cable, and the overall quality of the cable. In addition, some cables have a built-in terminator at the end of the cable, whereas others require the addition of a separate terminator.

Narrow cables, officially called *A cables,* are used for all narrow (8-bit) SCSI transfer modes. These are also sometimes called 50-conductor or 50-pin cables after the number of wires in the cable and pins in its connectors. They are organized into 25 pairs of two wires each. Traditionally, each pair generally consists of a signal and a signal return, which is the same as a ground line. *Wide cables,* officially called *P cables,* are used for 16-bit SCSI transfer modes. These are also sometimes called 68-conductor or 68-pin cables after the number of wires in the cable or pins in its connectors. Similar to the narrow cable, the wide cables are also organized into 34 pairs.

Lastly, cables are classified as single-ended or low-voltage differential. LVD narrow cables are similar to SE cables, except each pair consists of a positive and negative complement of the signal. There is also a change in the function of one cable conductor, which is used to control the differential signaling. Although the SE and LVD cables use the same connectors, the LVE are typically a much higher quality to accommodate the faster speeds used in LVD signaling. Therefore, it is not wise to use an SE cable for an LVD implementation. Of course, to determine if a cable is an SE cable or an LVD cable, you would have to look at the connectors for the appropriate icons or text stating the type of cable or to look on the cable itself.

For external cables, you want to use cabling that is specifically rated for LVD use; these cables have been designed and tested for LVD applications, even if they look the same as their single-ended cousins. As with regular wide cables, they may be found with either high density or very high-density connectors. Internal LVD cables are actually very different from SE cables. The reason is that to improve signal integrity, internal LVD cables typically don't use regular flat ribbon cabling. Instead, they use *twist-n-flat* cabling, where adjacent pairs of wires are twisted between the connectors, and the wires "flatten out" where the connectors attach.

SCSI cables come in two distinct varieties, external and internal. External cables are used to connect SCSI devices that do not reside inside the PC but rather have their own enclosures and power supplies.

NOTE: If you have external hard drives, you should make sure that the hard drives are powered on first before you start the computer so that the computer can detect them during the OS boot.

Internal cables connect SCSI devices installed within the PC case. Internal cables are flat ribbon cables like IDE or floppy disk drive cables.

Because external cases are more affected by external environment factors such as electromagnetic interfaces, the external cables are shielded to protect the data from being corrupted. First, they use twisted-pair wiring, where the two wires are twisted around each other to reduce the affects of cross talk. Crosstalk occurs when you have two copper wires next to each other and the signal inducts (law of induction) or transfers from one wire to the other. Therefore, by twisting the wires around each other, the electromagnetic fields cancel each other, greatly reducing the crosstalk. So, an external narrow cable with 50 wires actually contains 25 pairs and a 68-wire cable has 34 pairs. Second, to reduce the noise and interference, the wires are shielded, or wrapped with a metallic shield such as aluminum, copper foil, or braid. Because these cables are not simple to manufacture, external SCSI cables quite expensive compared to the internal cables.

Even with internal cables, there are differences in construction such as the thickness of the wire and the insulation that goes over the wires. Better cables generally use Teflon as a wire-insulation material, whereas cheaper ones may use polyvinyl chloride or vinyl. Regular flat cables are typically used for single-ended SCSI applications up to Ultra speeds (20 MHz). For Ultra2 or faster internal cables using LVD signaling, newer wires also use twisted pairs but overall still keep the shape of a flat ribbon, which gives connectors that can be connected easily.

Connectors are the physical devices that are used to attach an SCSI cable to an SCSI device. Different from IDE, there are several different types of SCSI connectors.

Internal Connectors

- **Regular Density**—A SCSI-1 standard–defined connector for internal narrow (8-bit) devices. The regular density cable is similar to an IDE cable connector except it is a 2-row, 50-pin connector. It is most often seen in older devices and also some newer, slower drives. See figure 9.18.
- **High Density**—A SCSI-2 standard–defined cable that comes in 50-pin and 68-pin versions. The pins are spaced half the distance between the bins as the regular-density cable, making them much smaller. These are the most common internal SCSI connectors used today.
- **Single Connector Attachment (SCA)**—An 80-contact connector typically used in RAID systems or hot-swappable drives where the drive is slid into a drive bay. Different from all of the other connectors, it also includes the power for the device.

External Connectors

- **D-Shell (D-Sub, DD)**—The earliest SCSI standard, SCSI-1, defined a 3-row, 50-pin D-shell (similar to a parallel port except for the number of rows and number of pins) connector for narrow SCSI implementations. This connector type was very large and cumbersome, never really became popular.
- **Centronics**—For early external connections, Centronics was defined by the SCSI-1 standard as a 50-pin connector, similar to what you would connect to the printer from the parallel port. In Centronics connectors, instead of thin pins, two rows of flat contacts are used. Two latches on either side are used to hold the connector in place. See figure 9.18.

Figure 9.18 This single-ended 50-pin SCSI ribbon cable has regular-density internal connectors (in front) and 68-pin low-voltage differential with high-density internal connectors and built-in termination.

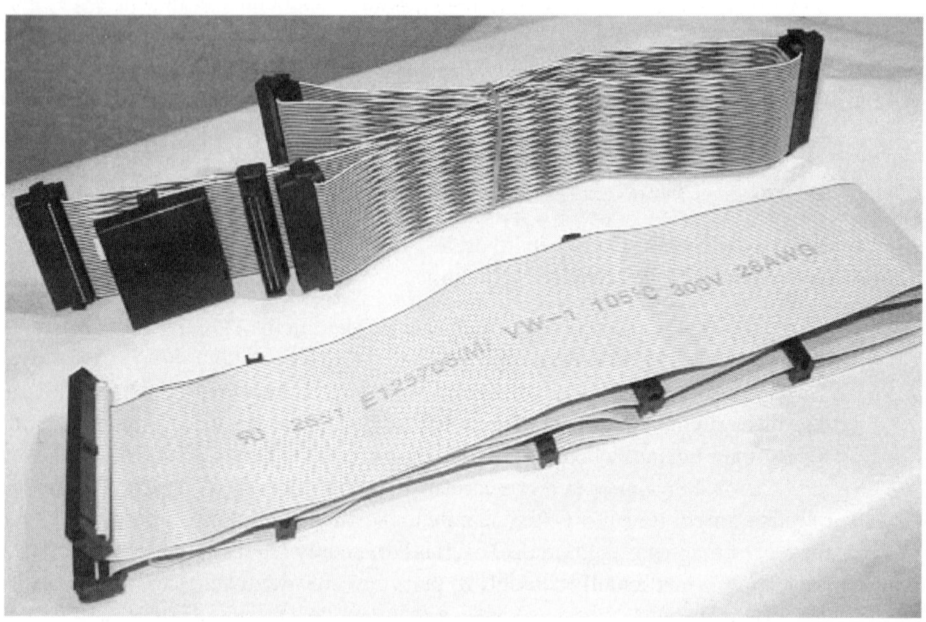

Figure 9.19 Typical SCSI Connectors (Centronics and Mini-SCSI [VHDCI] Port)

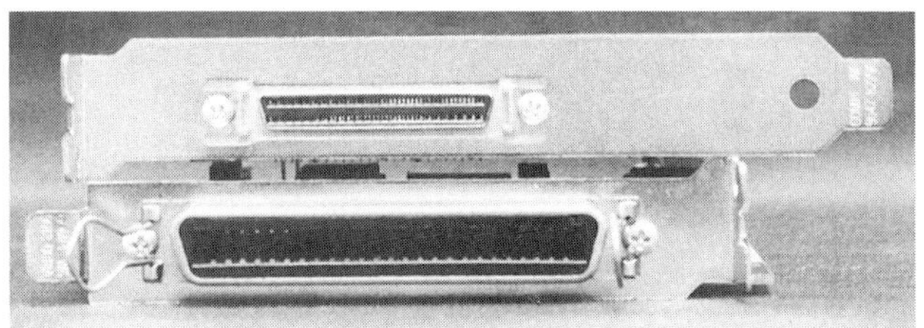

- **High-Density (HD)**—SCSI-2 replaced the D-shell connectors with newer, high-density shielded connectors. These are really not all that different from the older D-shell connectors, but the space between pins was reduced, making the connectors smaller, cheaper to make, and easier to use. These connectors use a "squeeze-to-release" latching mechanism.
- **Very High Density Cable Interconnect (VHDCI)**—These 68-pin external connectors are similar to Centronics connectors but the contacts are smaller and closer together. Since these connectors are much smaller than the standard Centronics connector, you can squeeze two SCSI connectors within the width of a single SCSI host adapter's back edge (expansion slot insert). See figure 9.19.

9.6.8 SCSI ID Numbers

As mentioned before, the standard SCSI interface allows up to 7 devices connected to one SCSI adapter/controller (8 devices if you count the controller card). Newer SCSI interfaces allow up to 15 devices (16 devices including the controller card).

Each device, including the adapter/controller card, is numbered with a SCSI ID number from 0 to 7. The numbers are selected with jumpers, DIP switches, or a thumb wheel. The SCSI adapter is usually set to ID #7. The primary SCSI hard drive or any other boot device is set to #0. The SCSI ID numbers do not have to be in order, nor do they have to be sequential. Of course, no two devices within the same chain can use the same SCSI ID number.

The priority that a device has on the SCSI bus is based on its ID number. For the first 8 IDs, higher numbers have higher priority, so 7 is the highest and 0 is the lowest. Therefore, if two devices need to communicate on the SCSI bus, the device with the highest priority will go first and the lower-priority device will have to wait. For wide SCSI, the additional IDs from 8 to 15 again give the highest number the highest priority, but the entire sequence is of lower priority than the numbers from 0 to 7. So the overall priority sequence for wide SCSI is 7, 6, 5, 4, 3, 2, 1, 0, 15, 14, 13, 12, 11, 10, 9, 8.

In high-traffic settings, you typically want to set the slower devices (scanners, tape drives) to the higher priority IDs to ensure that they are not crowded off the bus by the faster devices, such as hard disks. For best performance, you might consider moving the slow devices to their own SCSI controller card because they may significantly degrade the performance of the bus. Lastly, if you have devices that absolutely cannot tolerate delays in receiving their stream of data, such as CD recording drives or video encoders, you should also give these devices top priority on the bus.

For older host adapters, the highest priority device is the bus, which is why host adapters will stay at the default SCSI ID of 7. In addition, some older host adapters insist on having the boot device on device ID 0. In addition, these older adapters would recognize only SCSI hard drives configured as SCSI ID #0 and SCSI ID #1 without loading some drivers. Typically, these have been done away with in newer hardware.

Today, most SCSI devices use jumpers to configure the SCSI ID numbers. For a narrow bus, three jumpers are required to set the SCSI ID. The SCSI ID number is actually derived from the binary representation of the jumpers. For example, setting all three ID jumpers off yields a binary number of 0 0 0, which translates to an ID of 0. A binary setting of 0 0 1 equals ID 1, 0 1 0 equals 2, 0 1 1 equals 3, and so on. Of course, 1 1 1 is 7. Unfortunately, the jumper can appear either forward or backward, depending on how the manufacturer sets it up. See figures. 9.20 and 9.21 and tables 9.11 and 9.12.

Each SCSI device can have a number of subdevices contained within itself. The most common example is one of the new SCSI CD-ROMs that handle more than one disk at a time. Each CD is addressed as a Logical Unit Number (LUN) of that particular device. But most devices, such as hard disks, tape drives and such are only one device, and will be assigned to LUN zero.

Figure 9.20 Terminating Resistors and Jumpers Found on an Older SCSI Hard Drive

Figure 9.21 An old SCSI terminating resistor. Pin 1 is indicated by the square block on the left.

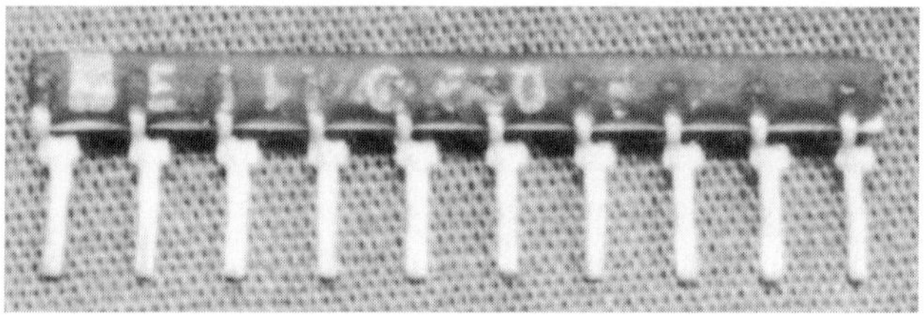

Table 9.11 SCSI ID Jumper Setting with the Most Significant Bit to the Left for Narrow SCSI

SCSI ID	Jumper Settings		
	4	2	1
0	0 (Off)	0 (Off)	0 (Off)
1	0 (Off)	0 (Off)	1 (On)
2	0 (Off)	1 (On)	0 (Off)
3	0 (Off)	1 (On)	1 (On)
4	1 (On)	0 (Off)	0 (Off)
5	1 (On)	0 (Off)	1 (On)
6	1 (On)	1 (On)	0 (Off)
7	1 (On)	1 (On)	1 (On)

Table 9.12 SCSI ID Jumper Setting with the Most Significant Bit to the Right for Narrow SCSI

SCSI ID	Jumper Settings		
	1	2	4
0	0 (Off)	0 (Off)	0 (Off)
1	1 (On)	0 (Off)	0 (Off)
2	0 (Off)	1 (On)	0 (Off)
3	1 (On	1 (On)	0 (Off)
4	0 (Off)	0 (Off)	1 (On)
5	1 (On)	0 (Off)	1 (On)
6	0 (Off)	1 (On)	1 (On)
7	1 (On)	1 (On)	1 (On)

Figure 9.22 Internal Daisy Chain

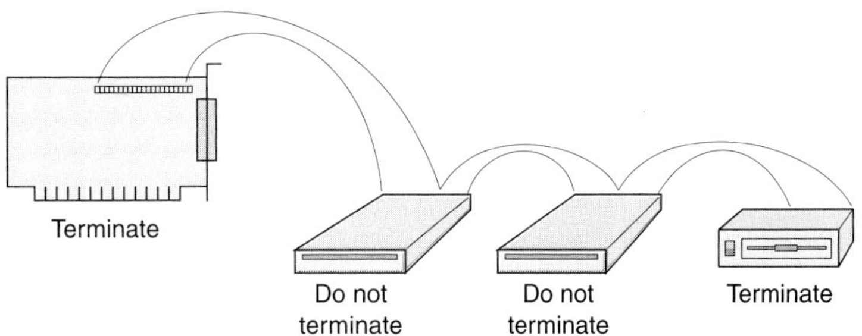

9.6.9 Termination

The two SCSI devices at either end of the chain must be terminated; the other devices should not be terminated. If only an internal cable is used, the adapter card and the device at the end of the cable need to be terminated, but the other devices in between should not be terminated. If you are using an internal cable and an external cable, the two devices located at the end of each cable should be terminated. To terminate/not terminate a device, the terminators are inserted/removed or enabled/disabled with jumpers or DIP switches. Some SCSI devices can be automatically terminated as needed. See figures 9.22, 9.23, and 9.24.

Question:

What is a terminating resistor?

Answer:

Terminating resistors are used to control the signal in the SCSI pathway. Termination is needed because when signals get to the end of a cable segment, they have a tendency to bounce back, colliding with new data packets. Termination dampens these signals. It also reduces noise on the lines.

Figure 9.23 External Daisy Chain

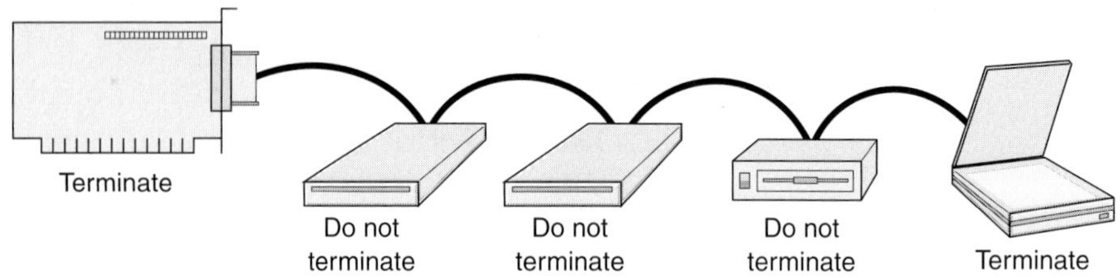

Figure 9.24 Internal and External Daisy Chain

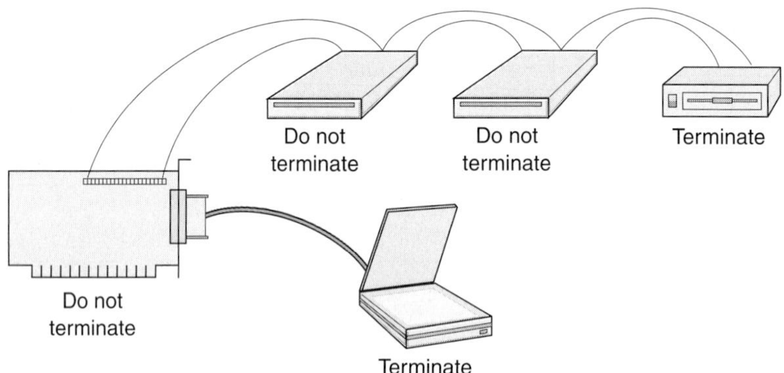

There are several different kinds of termination used on SCSI buses. They differ in the electrical circuitry that is used to terminate the bus. Better forms of termination give more reliable SCSI chains; the better the termination, the fewer problems (all else being equal) with the bus, although cost is generally higher as well. In general terms, slower buses are less particular about the kind of termination used, whereas faster ones have more demanding requirements. In addition, buses using differential signaling (either HVD or LVD) require special termination.

- **Passive Terminator—**The classic/standard terminator is the passive terminator. The passive terminator uses special electrical resistors (220 and 330 resistors for each bus line) to act as voltage dividers. Because they help ensure that the chain has the correct impedance load, they prevent signals from reflecting or echoing when the signal reaches the end of the chain. Passive terminating resistors work well for chains of short distances (2–3 ft) and slower speeds (SCSI-1 specification). The chain should never exceed 6 m. It is only for single-ended SCSI buses, which should be used only in narrow (8-bit) SCSI buses running at 5 MHz.
- **Active Termination—**Active termination acts as voltage regulator (using 110 V resistors) to maintain a stable voltage through the chain by utilizing the termination power lines to compensate for voltage drops. Because active termination helps reduce noise, it allows for longer cable lengths and faster speeds. In fact, active termination is the minimum required for any of the faster-speed single-ended SCSI buses. The chain should never exceed 18 m. It is for single-ended SCSI buses only.
- **Forced Perfect Terminator (FPT)—**The forced perfect terminator diode clamps are added to the circuitry to automatically match the line impedance by forcing the termination to the correct voltage, thus allowing "perfect" termination. It is for single-ended SCSI buses only and should be used for single-ended applications that experience high levels of electrical noise.
- **High-Voltage Differential (HVD)—**Buses using high-voltage differential signaling require the use of special HVD terminators.
- **Low-Voltage Differential (LVD)—**Newer buses using low-voltage differential signaling also require their own special type of terminators. In addition, there are special LVD/SE terminators designed for use with multimode LVD devices that can function in either LVD or SE modes; when the bus is running single-ended, these behave like active terminators. Note: Many internal cables have a built-in LVD terminator at the end of the cable.

NOTE: LVD/SE multimode terminators are available. They will function as LVD types on an LVD bus and as active types on a SE bus. If there are any SE devices on the bus, it will function in SE mode and never use LVD mode, severely limiting bus length and performance. If any SE-only terminators or SE devices are on the bus, the bus will default into SE mode.

9.6.10 SCSI BIOS Program

Although IDE drives are controlled by the system ROM BIOS, SCSI devices are controlled by a SCSI ROM chip that is on the SCSI controller card or the motherboard if the SCSI is built into the motherboard. During boot-up, the SCSI BIOS will search and activate the individual SCSI devices, which is shown during boot-up before the operating system is loaded.

As the SCSI BIOS activates the individual SCSI devices, the SCSI BIOS will usually display a message to press a key or key combination to enter a SCSI setup program. Most of these setup programs allow you to configure the SCSI card (set the host adapters SCSI ID and enable/disable SCSI parity checking and host adapter SCSI termination), configure the SCSI devices (set up sync negotiation and maximum sync transfer rate, enable disconnection, and so on), and configure SCSI disk utilities (low-level format SCSI hard drives and verify disk media).

Adaptec is probably the de facto standard for SCSI adapters. It makes an adapter that works well and comes with all the necessary formatting and operating software. In addition, Windows 9X and Windows 2000 have built-in support for the Adaptec SCSI adapters. For Adaptec SCSI controllers, you would press Ctrl + A when instructed to do so during the POST to enter the SCSI BIOS program called SCSISelect. Note: The Adaptec host adapters are often abbreviated *AHA*.

Software Interrupt 19 handles the boot function. The boot code is typically handled by the motherboards BIOS, but for some host adapters, optionally it can be handled by the host adapter BIOS. If a host adapter does not have a BIOS or does not have the BIOS enabled, then hard disk drives controlled by that host adapter cannot be used to boot the system. Instead, you will have to boot from floppy, IDE, or another SCSI host adapter.

As mentioned in chapter 8, the hard drive can consume three or four times more power during the first few seconds after power-on than during normal operations. If several drives are drawing all this power at the same time, the power supply may be overloaded, which can cause the system to hang, have intermittent start problems, or constantly reboot. Therefore, nearly all SCSI drives provide a way to delay drive spinning so that this problem does not occur. When enabled, the SCSI drive will wait until it gets a command from the SCSI host adapter before spinning. It actually does this in order from highest to lowest priority. Note: This is not necessary for external hard drives because they get their power from an external power source.

SCSI parity is a limited form of error checking that helps ensure that all data transfers are reliable. Virtually all host adapters support SCSI parity checking, so this option should be enabled on every device. The only reason that you disable this feature is if some older host adapter or SCSI does not work with SCSI parity or does not have SCSI parity.

Much like in RAM, SCSI parity is useful, but it is limited in its effectiveness, especially for very high transfer rates. It cannot detect if 2 bits changed. Therefore, starting in SPI-3, cyclic redundancy checking (CRC) was introduced to SCSI. Different from parity checking, which checks each byte, CRC checks an entire block of data by performing a mathematical calculation on the data to be sent before and after the data.

The terminators at each end of the SCSI bus require power from at least one device on the bus. In most cases, the host adapter supplies this terminator power. If no device supplies terminator power, the bus will not be terminated correctly and will not function properly. To ensure that this is not a problem, some people configure all devices to supply terminator power.

Many of these adapters have a setting for the sync transfer rate or synchronous transfer rate. This determines the maximum synchronous data transfer rate that the SCSI card supports. It is usually recommended to leave the maximum (default value) of the card.

The SCSI bus can run in two modes: asynchronous (default) and synchronous. The bus actually switches modes during transfers through a protocol called synchronous negotiation. Before data is transferred across the SCSI bus, the sending device and the receiving device negotiate how the transfer will take place. If both devices support synchronous transfers, they will discover this fact through the negotiation, and the transfer will take place at the faster synchronous rate. By default, all devices today should support synchronous mode so it can work with older devices. Unfortunately, some older devices do not respond to a request for synchronous transfers, and this request can actually disable such devices. Therefore, both the host adapter and devices that support synchronous negotiation usually have a jumper that can disable this feature so that it can work with older devices.

Some cards have an Initiate Wide Negotiation setting. By default, it is set to Yes, where it will attempt 16-bit data transfers. When set to No, the SCSI card uses 8-bit data transfers unless the SCSI device requests wide negotiation. Although you would typically want this feature enabled, you should disable it if one of your 8-bit SCSI devices causes the system to hand or exhibit other performance problems with a 16-bit data transfer rate.

The Enable Disconnection option, when set to Yes, allows the SCSI device to disconnect from the SCSI bus. Typically, you want to leave the setting at Yes if two or more SCSI devices are connected to the SCSI card. If only one SCSI device is connected, changing the setting to No results in slightly better performance.

Lastly, some adapters can support devices identified with their Logical Unit Number (LUN). If the adapter has the BIOS multiple LUN support, the default will be set to No. If the device does have multiple logical unit numbers, then you can set this option to Yes and the SCSI card BIOS provides boot support for an SCSI device with multiple LUNs (for example a CD jukebox which would contain multiple CDs that can be accessed simultaneously). You can then define which device to boot from using the boot LUN number option. Note: If the SCSI device is old or poorly designed, it might not handle being probed, resulting in the SCSI device locking up or taking down the entire SCSI bus.

9.6.11 Hot-Swappable Hard Drives

A newer type of drive is the hot-swappable drive, which can be removed or installed while the computer is running. The ability to hot-swap a disk drive is beneficial in those situations where computers cannot be shut off for even a few minutes, such as network servers. Typically, hot-swappable drives are SCSI drives.

Hot-swappable drives do not use the standard drive connectors. Instead, they use a two-piece unit that mounts into a drive bay and a removable drawer or caddy that encases the hard drive. The drawer connects to the bay via a connector such as the single connector attachment (SCA), which includes connection pins for the power cables as well as the data wires. The current version of SCA, called SCA-2, uses 80 pins and is frequently used for high-end SCSI devices.

These special connectors on the drives are designed to ensure that the ground connections between the drive and the bus are maintained whenever the device has power. This means that when removing a device, the power connection has to be broken before the ground connection, and when reinserting a device, the ground connection has to be made before the power connection is reestablished. Typically, a locking mechanism controls power to the drive to prevent it from being removed while operating. A handle-activated drawer release mechanism allows the drive to be inserted or removed with minimal force.

True hot-swapping requires support from all of the components in the system: the RAID controller, the bus (usually SCSI), the enclosure (which must have open bays for the drives so they can be accessed from the front of the case), and the interface. Other hot-swappable drives require drivers and software that allows you to properly shut down the drive only before removing it.

9.7 S.M.A.R.T.

As mentioned several times throughout this book, the most important thing on your computer is data. Although data is mostly contained on hard drives, people expect hard drives to be reliable and they don't expect their hard drives to fail. Therefore, several manufacturers have taken steps to predict if a hard drive will fail in the near future. Self-monitoring, analysis, and reporting technology (S.M.A.R.T.) is an open standard for developing disk drives and software systems that automatically monitor a disk drive's health and report potential problems. Ideally, this should allow you to be proactive in preventing impending disk crashes.

9.8 TROUBLESHOOTING HARD DRIVES

Because hard drives are half-mechanical, half-electronic devices, they have a high failure rate compared to nonmechanical devices. They include most of the data created by the computer, so it is essential to keep them operating properly and to keep a timely backup of all data on the hard drive. The hard drive can fail because of its own internal problems or because of problems in the cable, the card, the motherboard, or the power connector. Failures can also be caused by power fluctuations or improper configuration of the drive, controller card, BIOS setup program, or motherboard. Data can also be lost by other means, such as viruses or badly written software.

Example 9.4:

The computer is turned on. During boot-up, you get one of the following error messages (or an equivalent message):

HDD Controller Failure
Hard Disk 0 Failure
No fixed Disk Present while running FDISK
1701
Hard drive appearing dead
Hard drive not recognized

These error messages and symptoms indicate that either the hard drive or hard drive controller card has failed. In either case, the error message can be caused by many things.

First check the obvious: Before opening the system, check the CMOS values to see if they are correct. Today, most systems have an auto detect feature to detect the correct CMOS parameters. Remember that SCSI drives should have the BIOS setup to SCSI (if available) or No Hard Drive Available. Check this first because it does not require the system to be opened. If the CMOS values keep disappearing, check the CMOS battery.

The next step is to see if the cables (ribbon cables and power connectors) are connected properly. In addition, make sure that you are using the correct cables. For example, if you have Ultra DMA/66 or Ultra DMA/100 drives, make sure to use the 40-pin, 80-conductor IDE cable. If you have SCSI drives and you are using single-ended devices, make sure that they are attached to a single-ended cable and controller card; if you have low-differential devices, make sure that they are attached to a low-differential cable and controller card.

Next, verify the configuration, including the controller card resources (I/O address, IRQ, DMA, and memory usage) and the hard drive configuration (master/slave settings, the SCSI ID number and terminating resistors). If there is no resource conflict, replace the cable to see if the problem goes away. If not, replace the controller card. If the problem persists, the next step would be to measure the voltage level of the power connector to make sure that the cable is supplying the correct +5 and +12 V. If it is, the next thing to do would be to replace the hard drive. Lastly, replace the motherboard.

Example 9.5:

During boot-up, you get one of the following error messages:

- Nonsystem disk or disk error, Replace and strike any key when ready
- No ROM Basic-System Halted
- Missing Operating System
- Disk Boot Error, Replace and Strike Key to Retry
- Disk Boot Failure
- DISK BOOT FAILURE, INSERT SYSTEM DISK AND PRESS ENTER
- BOOT: Couldn't find NTLDR, Please insert another disk

All these error messages indicate that the system could not find an operating system to boot from. If you are trying to boot from the floppy disk drive, you need to make sure that the floppy disk drive has the proper boot files and that the files are not corrupt. If you are trying to boot from the floppy disk drive, try to boot from a known working bootable floppy disk. If it still doesn't boot, suspect it is a floppy disk drive problem. See chapter 10.

If you are trying to boot from the hard drive, make sure that there is no floppy disk in drive A. Next, check the BIOS settings to make sure that the hard drives are enabled, that the proper hard drive parameters are being used, and that the correct boot order is set. If the BIOS setup program has an autodetect feature for the motherboard, use to see if it can detect and communicate with the hard drive. Next, boot using the A drive and make sure that the hard drive boot files are in place and intact. If the boot files are missing or corrupted, restore the boot files.

- For DOS and Windows 9X, try to reinstall the necessary boot files by using the SYS or FORMAT commands. To rebuild the master boot record, use FDISK /MBR.
- For Windows NT, use the Windows NT Setup Disk, and at the first screen, press R for Repair. Then select the Inspect Boot Sector and Verify Windows NT system files. If you have mass storage devices that require drives, select S to specify additional drivers.
- For Windows 2000 or Windows XP, start the Windows installation program and choose R to repair. To automatically fix these files, select F for fast repair.

If you cannot correct the bootable files, you should consider reformatting. Unfortunately, this will cause all your work to be lost. You also need to verify that your primary partition is active. Finally, you should also check for viruses. You may also consider doing a low-level format. You will, of course, partition, format, and reinstall the operating system.

If you cannot switch over to the hard drive, make sure that the hard drive power connector is connected and that the ribbon cables are connected properly. In addition, make sure that you are using the correct cables. For example, if you have Ultra DMA/66 or Ultra DMA/100 drives, make sure to use the 40-pin 80-conductor IDE cable. If you have SCSI drives and you are using single-ended devices, make sure that they are attached to a single-ended cable and controller card; if you have low-differential devices, make sure that they are attached to a low-differential cable and controller card.

Next, verify the configuration, including the controller card resources (I/O address, IRQ, DMA, and memory usage) and the hard drive configuration (master/slave settings, the SCSI ID number, and terminating resistors). If there is no resource conflict, replace the cable to see if the problem goes away. The next step is to measure the voltage level of the power connector to make sure that the cable is supplying the correct +5 and +12 V. The last thing to try is to swap the controller card, cable, hard drive, and motherboard, one at a time.

Example 9.6:

You get an "Error reading drive C:" error message during boot-up.

This error typically indicates a problem with the disk media but may also indicate viruses, incorrect configurations, or signaling problems. First, make sure that the ribbon is connected properly. Then enter the BIOS setup program and make sure that the correct BIOS settings are chosen for the drive.

NOTE: On most systems, you can use the autodetect feature to determine the correct BIOS parameters.

Next check for viruses and run Scandisk or some other similar utility. Try to reformat the drive and make the drive bootable again. If the format does not work, try a low-level format. Then partition, format, and add the system files to the hard drive. Check the drive's power, including the +5 and +12 V connectors. If the power is OK, swap the controller card, cable, hard drive, and motherboard, one at a time.

Example 9.7:

You get a "Track 0 bad, disk unusable" error message.

If track 00 of the drive becomes disabled or damaged, the entire drive can be damaged. Most of the time, this indicates a bad drive. But before throwing away the drive, check the CMOS settings to make sure that you have the correct hard drive parameters. If the BIOS setup program has an autodetect feature for the motherboard, use to see if it can detect and communicate with the hard drive.

Next, boot using the A drive and make sure that the hard drive boot files are in place and intact. If the boot files are missing or corrupted, restore the boot files.

- For DOS and Windows 9X, try to reinstall the necessary boot files by using the SYS or FORMAT commands. To rebuild the master boot record, use FDISK/MBR.
- For Windows NT, use the Windows NT Setup Disk; at the first screen, press R for repair. Then select the Inspect Boot Sector and Verify Windows NT systcm files. If you have mass storage device that require drives, select S to specify additional drivers.
- For Windows 2000 or Windows XP, start the Windows installation program and choose R to repair. To automatically fix these files, select F for fast repair.

If you cannot correct the problem, you should consider reformatting. Unfortunately, this will cause all your work to be lost. You also need to verify that your primary partition is active. Lastly, you should also check for viruses. You may also consider during a low-level format. You will, of course, partition, format, and reinstall the operating system.

Make sure that the ribbon cable and power connector are connected properly. Next, try replacing the ribbon cable. Check the drive's power, including the +5 and +12 V connectors. Swap the controller card (or motherboard), cable, and hard drive, one at a time. Swap the motherboard.

Example 9.8:

The master boot record is corrupted, FDISK causes the computer to lock up, or changes to the partition cannot be saved.

The first thing to check is the BIOS settings for the hard drive. If the master boot record is corrupted in DOS or Windows 9X, it can be recreated with the following command:

- For DOS and Windows 9X, to rebuild the master boot record, use FDISK/MBR.
- For Windows NT, use the Windows NT Setup Disk; at the first screen, press R for repair. Then select the Inspect Boot Sector and Verify Windows NT system files. If you have mass storage device that require drives, select S to specify additional drivers.
- For Windows 2000 or Windows XP, start the Windows installation program and choose R to repair. To automatically fix these files, select F for fast repair.

If you cannot correct the problem, you should consider a low-level format. You will, of course, partition, format, and reinstall the operating system.

If this corrects the problem, you should be concerned with what caused the corruption of the master boot record. It could have been caused by a virus, power fluctuations when the drive was being accessed, or a failing hard drive. If you have problems with a SCSI drive, verify that you are using the correct cable and that your SCSI termination is correct. If the problem still exists, expect more of a hardware problem. Therefore, check the drive's power, including the +5 and +12 V connectors.

Example 9.9:

The hard drive seems to be running slow.

Most of the time, if your drive is running fine and then it appears to run slowly, you should check for viruses and defrag your hard drive. If it is a new installation, check to see if you have a slow device on the cable. For example, if you have an Ultra DMA/100 hard drive connected on the same cable has a slow CD-ROM, the two will communicate at the slower speed. For SCSI drives, check termination and check that you are using the correct cable. If it is an IDE drive, enter the BIOS setup program and check to see if it is set to Ultra DMA or PIO mode. For SCSI drives, enter the SCSI BIOS and check the settings. Check to see if anyone did a low-level format on the drive. If the proper low-level format program is not used, essential tracking information can be erased. Lastly, try a clean boot and maybe a fresh installation.

Example 9.10:

During boot-up, one of the IDE devices is not recognized.

First check the obvious: Before opening the system, check the CMOS values to see if they are correct and that the drive is enabled in the BIOS setup program. Today, most systems have an auto detect feature to detect the correct BIOS parameters. Check this first because it does not require the system to be opened. If the BIOS values keep disappearing, check the CMOS battery.

The next step is to see if the cables (ribbon cables and power connectors) are connected properly. In addition, make sure that you are using the correct cables. For example, if you have Ultra DMA/66 or Ultra DMA/100 drives, make sure to use the 40-pin 80-conductor IDE cable. Make sure that the proper drivers (if any) are loaded correctly.

Next, check the jumpers on the hard drive (master/slave settings). If the problem persists, the next step would be to measure the voltage level of the power connector to make sure that the cable is supplying the correct +5 and +12 V. Then try to swap the cables, controller card, drive and motherboard, one at a time with known working replacements.

Example 9.11:

During boot-up, a SCSI device is not recognized. First, make sure that the cables (ribbon cables and power connectors) are connected properly. In addition, make sure that you are using the correct cables. If you have SCSI drives and you are using single-ended devices, make sure that they are attached to a single-ended cable and controller card; if you have low-differential devices, make sure that they are attached to a low-differential cable and controller card. Next, verify the configuration, including the controller card resources (I/O address, IRQ, DMA, and memory usage) and the hard drive configuration (SCSI ID number and terminating resistors). Make sure that the proper drivers (if any) are loaded correctly. The next step is to measure the voltage level of the power connector to make sure that the cable is supplying the correct +5 and +12 V. Then try to swap the cables, controller card, drive, and motherboard, one at a time, with known working replacements.

Notebook computers almost always use IDE hard drives. Typically, the only difference is that notebooks use the 2.5-in. drives instead of the 3.5-in. drives. Therefore, troubleshooting hard drives in notebook computers is no different from troubleshooting hard drives in desktop systems. To determine if a drive is good or bad, you can connect the hard drive into another notebook computer and try a good drive in the notebook computer. You can also use a 2½- to 3½-in. IDE cable adapter so that you can try a 3½-in. IDE hard drive on the notebook's IDE interface and use a 2½- to 3½-in. IDE cable adapter to try a 2½-in. IDE hard drive on a desktop PC's IDE interface. You would also check CMOS settings and jumper settings.

To end this chapter, it should be mentioned that there are hard drive recovery programs and hard drive recovery services. Assuming that the hard drive is able to power up, the hard drive recovery programs can recover recently deleted files, corrupted partitions, recently deleted partitions, and corrupt master boot records. Hard drive recovery services can recover everything that hard drive recovery programs can recover and they can often recover information from hard drives that cannot power up, boot, or is extremely damaged. Unfortunately, these services are usually very expensive, but if the data is important enough and is irreplaceable, the price may be well worth it. Of course, performing backups on a regular basis will help you avoid these situations.

SUMMARY

1. Hard drives are half-electronic, half-mechanical devices that use magnetic patterns to store information onto rotating platters.
2. Hard drives are considered long-term storage devices because they do not "forget" their information when power is disconnected. They are considered the primary mass storage system because they hold all the programs and data files that are fed into RAM.
3. Hard drives communicate with the rest of the computer by means of a cable connected to a controller card (either an expansion card or card built into motherboard).
4. A head-to-disk interference (HDI) occurs when particles cause the read/write head or platters to read improperly.
5. A platter is divided into a circular grid consisting of tracks (concentric circles) and sectors (512 bytes).
6. Hard drive performance is often measured in access time (average seek time + latency period) and data transfer rate.
7. The basic steps for installing and configuring a hard drive are physical installation of the hard drive system, low-level formatting, partitioning, high-level formatting (and making bootable if necessary), and installing and configuring the operating system and application programs.
8. Low-level formatting (LLF) is the process that defines the tracks and sectors of the hard drive. It must be done with special software.
9. Partitioning is defining and dividing the physical driver into logical volumes called partitions. Each partition functions as if it were a separate hard disk.
10. High-level formatting is the process of writing the file system structure on the disk so that it can be used to store programs and data.
11. Hard drives used in notebook computers are 2½-in. IDE hard drives.
12. To connect the hard drive to the notebook computers, you would use a smaller 50-pin connector (40 pins for data and 10 pins for power and jumpering).
13. The primary IDE controller uses interrupt 14 and I/O address assignments of 1F0–1FF. The second IDE controller uses interrupt 15 and I/O address assignments of 0170–0177.
14. The standard SCSI I/O address range is 0330–0333. The IRQs are typically assigned to the unused IRQs such as IRQ/11, or they will be plug-and-play.
15. The IDE hard drive is connected to the controller using a 40-pin cable.
16. Ultra DMA/66 and Ultra DMA/100 require a special 40-pin cable that has 80 wires, 40 pins for the signal, and 40 ground pins to reduce noise.
17. The IDE drive is considered an intelligent drive because it can support drive translation.
18. IDE hard drives can connect one drive (standalone) or two hard drives (master and slave).
19. The EIDE interface supports up to four IDE devices (IDE hard drives, IDE CD-ROM drives, IDE tape backup drives, and other IDE storage devices) using two IDE cables. It is faster than the IDE interface and can use LBA mode.
20. The two methods of transferring data are processor input/output (PIO) and direct memory access (DMA).
21. The Serial ATA (SATA) interface is based on one signal instead of 16 parallel signals, allowing much higher speeds than would be possible from a parallel implementation.
22. Serial ATA is based on serial technology; therefore, it can talk to only one device per channel.
23. The SATA drives require two connectors, the data cable and power cable. Because the data cables are smaller and contain only seven wires, the connectors are more compact.
24. The traditional SCSI interface with an 8-bit data bus allows up to seven devices (hard drives, tape drives, CD-ROM drives, removable drives or disks, and scanners) to be connected to one SCSI adapter/controller.
25. SCSI interfaces with a 16-bit data bus, referred to as wide interface, allow up to 15 devices (16 devices including the controller card).
26. With a SCSI host adapter, the BIOS on the adapter is used to control SCSI hard disk drives and perform the boot function.
27. There are several types of signaling methods used in SCSI interfaces including single-ended signaling, low-voltage differential, and high-voltage differential.
28. Traditional SCSI devices use single-ended signaling (SE).
29. Newer SCSI devices use low-voltage differential signaling.
30. Narrow cables, refused to as A cables, are used for 8-bit transfers and have 50 pins.
31. Wide cables, officially called P cables, are used for 16-bit SCSI transfer modes. They are also sometimes called 68-conductor.
32. Each device, including the adapter/controller card, is numbered with a SCSI ID number (0–7 or 0–15), which must be unique on the chain.
33. The host adapter has the default SCSI ID of 7.
34. With SCSI devices, the two devices at both ends of the chain must be terminated; the other devices are not.
35. There are several different kinds of termination including passive termination, active termination, forced perfect termination, high-voltage differential termination, and low-voltage differential termination.

36. Data protection is improved by RAID (redundant arrays of inexpensive disk) by using two or more drives in combination as a fault tolerance system to protect against physical hard drive failure and to increase hard drive performance.
37. RAID 1, known as disk mirroring, copies a partition onto a second hard drive. As information is written, it is written to both hard drives simultaneously. If one of the hard drives fails, the PC will still function because it can access the other hard drive.
38. Disk duplexing duplicates not only the hard drive but also the controller card and cable.
39. RAID 0 stripes data across all drives. Striping provides some increase in performance through load-balancing.
40. RAID 5 is very similar to RAID 0, but one of the hard drives is used for parity (error-correction) to provide fault tolerance. RAID 5 is a good compromise among data integrity, speed, and cost.
41. SCSI is a much more advanced interface than ATA/ATA-2 IDE drives and is ideal for high-end computers, including network servers.
42. The capacity of the hard drive is the product of the number of cylinders, number of read/write heads, number of sectors per track, and 512 bytes per sector.
43. Hard drive sectors are addressed in CHS (cylinder-head-sector), translation mode, or LBA mode.
44. If the system ROM BIOS does not support EIDE/ATA-2 drives, it needs to be either updated or modified.
45. Early versions of IDE had limitations of 504 MB and 7.9 GB.
46. Since hard drives are half-mechanical, half-electronic devices, they have a high failure rate compared to nonmechanical devices.
47. Hard drive failure can be caused by failure of the hard drive itself, the cable, the card, the motherboard, or the power connector. It can also be caused by power fluctuations or improper configuration (drive, controller card, CMOS setup program, or motherboard). In addition, data can be lost through other means, such as viruses or badly written software.
48. Virtually all motherboards have IDE interfaces built into the motherboard.
49. For IDE drives, you need to select the correct hard drive type. Today, just about all drives are set to Type 47/User Definable type where you enter the appropriate number of cylinders, heads, and sectors. Most systems have an autodetect feature.
50. For SCSI drives, you would select SCSI (if available) or No Hard Drive installed.
51. When using LBA (logical block addressing), the IDE controller transforms the data address described by sector, head, and cylinder number into a physical block address.
52. To rebuild master boot records, you can use FDISK/MBR.

QUESTIONS

1. Magnetic fields can
   a. distort the circuitry within the microprocessor.
   b. shut down the PC.
   c. cause a RAM error message.
   d. cause problems with data integrity on magnetic media.
2. A hard drive HDI means
   a. hard drive interference.
   b. hard drive interface.
   c. head-to-disk interference.
   d. head distortion inside.
   e. none of the above.
3. The hard drive makes a grinding noise. The cause is probably
   a. HDI.
   b. resource conflict.
   c. a corrupted file.
   d. a SCSI ID number conflict.
   e. incorrect CMOS configuration.
4. A ribbon cable has a red stripe along one edge. What does this mean?
   a. It is the positive lead.
   b. It is the negative lead.
   c. The cable carries hazardous voltage.
   d. The conductor with the stripe connects to pin 1 of the connector.
5. How many bytes are in a sector?
   a. 256 bytes
   b. 512 bytes
   c. 1,024 bytes
   d. 4 KB
6. If a hard drive has three platters, 5,600 cylinders, and 63 sectors per track, what is the capacity of the hard drive?
   a. 1,058,400 bytes
   b. 1.033.6 MB
   c. 516.8 MB
   d. 2,116,800 bytes
7. Which of the following pertain to the speed with which data can be transferred to the PC from a hard drive?
   a. disk seek time
   b. rotational latency period
   c. interleaving
   d. data transfer rate
8. The time it takes for the hard drive to find data is called
   a. rotational latency period.
   b. access time.
   c. data transfer rate.
   d. seek time.

9. What is the latency period?
   a. the time it takes the head to be positioned over the proper track
   b. the time it takes the desired sector to move under the head
   c. the time it takes the data to be sent to the PC
   d. the time required for the disk to make one rotation
10. The time required for positioning the head over the proper track is
   a. seek time. b. access time.
   c. latency period. d. data transfer rate.
11. Which of the following should be done before replacing a hard drive?
   a. back up the hard drive
   b. run the CMOS setup program
   c. run CHKDSK
   d. erase the hard drive
12. What does *RAID* stand for?
   a. random access interrupt driver
   b. redundant array of interchangeable disks
   c. redundant array of inexpensive disks
   d. redundant access information data
13. Which program partitions a hard drive?
   a. SCANDISK b. DISKCOPY
   c. FORMAT d. FDISK
   e. SETUP
14. When configuring a system with preloaded software, formatting the primary hard disk will
   a. improve system performance.
   b. erase the partitions.
   c. compress preloaded programs.
   d. provide additional partition and format options.
15. CHS mode is
   a. physical CMOS parameters for cylinders, heads, and sectors.
   b. physical CMOS parameters using translating electronics.
   c. a fast method of data transfer.
   d. a 28-bit binary number indicating the physical number of sectors on a drive.
16. What is the first step in configuring the hard disk drive?
   a. partition the drive
   b. format DOS
   c. format the drive physically
   d. set the jumpers on the drive
17. What is it called when a hard drive writes a sector, skips one or more sectors, and then writes another sector?
   a. sectoring b. interweaving
   c. interleaving d. sector skipping
18. When you replace an IDE hard drive, you must
   a. set the ID jumper on the drive.
   b. set the master/slave jumper on the drive.
   c. set the speed jumper on the drive.
   d. set the speed jumper on the motherboard.
19. When you have two IDE drives on a cable, the boot IDE hard drive is known as
   a. stand-alone. b. master.
   c. slave. d. active.
20. Which of the following would be the correct configuration for a dual IDE drive system?
   a. The primary drive would have the M/S jumper and the SP jumper on, while the secondary drive would have the M/S jumper and the SP jumper on.
   b. The primary drive would have the M/S jumper and the SP jumper on, while the secondary drive would have the M/S jumper and the SP jumper off.
   c. The primary drive would have the M/S jumper on and the SP jumper off, while the secondary drive would have the M/S jumper off and the SP jumper on.
   d. The primary drive would have the M/S jumper off and the SP jumper on, while the secondary drive would have the M/S jumper on and the SP jumper off.
   e. The primary drive would have the M/S jumper and the SP jumper off, while the secondary drive would have the M/S jumper and the SP jumper off.
21. How many devices do EIDE controllers support?
   a. 2 b. 4
   c. 7 d. 8
22. What is the maximum number of devices that can be connected to a standard SCSI-2 adapter?
   a. 2 b. 4
   c. 7 d. 8
23. When installing a system with four SCSI drives on one cable, where should the terminator be installed? (Assume the controller card is already terminated.)
   a. on the last drive on the cable
   b. on the first drive on the cable
   c. on the first and last drive
   d. none of the above
24. When you replace a SCSI hard drive, you must (choose all that apply)
   a. set the ID jumper on the drive.
   b. set the master/slave jumper on the drive.
   c. set the speed jumper on the drive.
   d. set the terminating resistors on the SCSI devices.
25. What is the SCSI ID number commonly assigned to the boot device in a PC?
   a. 0 b. 15
   c. 7 d. 8
26. What is the jumper setting on a SCSI device to configure it to use the SCSI ID 5? Remember, SCSI IDs start with 0.
   a. 010 b. 110
   c. 011 d. 101
   e. 001
27. The total length of your standard SCSI cables with passive termination should not exceed
   a. 3 ft. b. 6 ft.
   c. 20 ft. d. 100 ft.

28. You are installing a SCSI hard drive as your boot drive. How should you configure the hard drive?
    a. set the SCSI ID number to 0
    b. set the SCSI ID number to 1
    c. set the SCSI ID number to 7
    d. set the SCSI ID number to any number that is free.
    e. enable the boot jumper
29. Which of the following IRQ's would probably be free so that it could be used by a SCSI card if the system has a standard IDE controller card (choose two answers)?
    a. IRQ 7
    b. IRQ 6
    c. IRQ 10
    d. IRQ 14
    e. IRQ 15
30. What is the highest binary number that can be referred to on a three-position jumper block?
    a. 4
    b. 6
    c. 5
    d. 7
31. An internal SCSI device uses which type of cabling?
    a. 34-pin ribbon cable
    b. 40-pin ribbon cable
    c. 50-pin ribbon cable
    d. 50-pin Centronics cabling
    e. 25-pin shielded cable
32. Which implementation of SCSI has a transfer rate of 20 MB/s?
    a. Fast SCSI-2
    b. Fast-Wide SCSI-2
    c. SCSI-3
    d. Ultra SCSI
33. Which of the following will *not* cause an HDD controller failure?
    a. ribbon cable not on properly
    b. bad ribbon cable
    c. bad hard drive
    d. bad controller card
    e. power cable not connected
    f. bad RAM chip
34. Which of the following are the most likely failing components if the hard drive activity light is on solid and the system fails to boot (choose two answers)?
    a. hard drive
    b. motherboard
    c. hard drive controller
    d. power supply
35. After upgrading a hard disk drive from 540 MB to 2.1 GB, a "Drive Mismatch Error" message appears when you power up the system. What has happened?
    a. The information stored in the CMOS setup program does not match the new hard drive.
    b. The new hard drive is incompatible with the hard disk controller.
    c. The new hard drive requires a local bus.
    d. The controller cable on the hard drive is damaged or missing from the new installation.
    e. The driver needs to be loaded.
36. Suppose you had an incurable computer virus and decided to wipe out all the data and partitions on your hard drive and reformat. What is the order in which you must delete the partitions?
    a. extended, logical, primary
    b. primary, extended, logical
    c. logical, extended, primary
    d. logical, primary, extended
37. A single hard drive has a primary hard drive (drive C) and two logical drives (drives D and E). You add a second hard drive and create a primary partition. Which of the following is correct?
    a. The second drive becomes drive D and the logical drives become E and F.
    b. The second drive becomes F and the logical drives are unchanged.
    c. The second drive becomes D and the logical drive D is deleted.
    d. The second drive becomes E and the logical drive E is deleted.
    e. The second drive becomes C and the first primary partition is deleted.
38. During boot-up, you get an "HDD Controller Failure" error message. Upon further investigation, you cannot hear the hard drive. Therefore, you should
    a. check to make sure that the power cable is connected.
    b. replace the hard drive.
    c. replace the hard drive controller.
    d. replace the hard drive cable.
    e. use the CMOS setup program.
39. Which ID number is normally assigned to the SCSI controller?
    a. 0
    b. 1
    c. 7
    d. 8
40. How many conductors are there in an ATA 66 ribbon cable?
    a. 34
    b. 40
    c. 50
    d. 68
    e. 80
41. What is the default I/O address for the SCSI controller?
    a. 02E8–02EF
    b. 03E8–03EF
    c. 0330–0333
    d. 0378–037F
    e. FF80–FF9F
42. Which statements about SCSI are *true?*
    a. Each SCSI controller can accommodate 9 SCSI devices.
    b. Normally, the SCSI Host Bus Adapter uses ID number 0.
    c. Normally, the SCSI Host Bus Adapter uses ID number 7.
    d. When installing a SCSI controller, set the CMOS to 47, or "User Defined."
    e. When installing a SCSI controller, you should set the CMOS to 0, or "Not Installed."

HANDS-ON EXERCISES

Exercise 1: Installing an IDE Hard Drive

1. Make sure that the computer can boot to drive C.
2. With the CMOS setup program, record the drive type, number of tracks, number of read/write heads, number of sectors per track, and hard drive mode (if any).
3. Using the FDISK utility, view the partitions (option 4; see figure below and figure at top of next page). Look for the number and type of partitions.

NOTE: If it asked to support large disks, say yes.

```
Microsoft Windows 98
Fixed Disk Setup Program
(C)Copyright Microsoft Corp. 1983 - 1998

FDISK Options

Current fixed disk drive: 1

Choose one of the following:

1. Create DOS partition or Logical DOS Drive
2. Set active partition
3. Delete partition or Logical DOS Drive
4. Display partition information

Enter choice: [4]

Press Esc to exit FDISK
```

```
Display Partition Information

Current fixed disk drive: 1

Partition  Status  Type     Volume Label  Mbytes  System  Usage
C: 1       A       PRI DOS                1039    FAT16   50%
   2               EXT DOS                1024    FAT32   50%

Total disk space is 2067 Mbytes (1 Mbyte = 1048576 bytes)

The Extended DOS Partition contains Logical DOS Drives.
Do you want to display the logical drive information (Y/N)......?[Y]

Press Esc to return to FDISK Options.
```

```
Delete DOS Partition or Logical DOS Drive

Current fixed disk drive: 1

Choose one of the following:

1. Delete Primary DOS Partition
2. Delete Extended DOS Partition
3. Delete Logical DOS Drive(s) in the Extended DOS Partition
4. Delete Non-DOS Partition

Enter choice: [ ]

Press Esc to return to FDISK Options
```

4. Using the FDISK utility, delete all partitions (option 3; see second figure on this page).

   NOTE: This is done by deleting any logical partitions, then deleting the extended partition and the primary partition.

5. After the partitions are deleted, press the Esc key several times until a request is made to insert a system disk.
6. Shut off the computer. Disconnect the power cable and remove the hard drive, cable, and controller card from the system. Observe how the cable, particularly pin 1, is connected to the card and the drive.
7. Reinstall the hard drive, cable, and controller into the system and connect the power to the hard drive.
8. Set the proper CMOS settings for the hard drive.
9. Try to boot the computer with the C drive. Record the error message.
10. Boot the computer with the A drive.
11. Run FDISK to create (option 1; see figure below) a primary DOS partition. Do not maximize the partition and do not make it active. Specify the size of the primary DOS partition to be 75%.

    NOTE: You must include the % sign. If you don't, it will create a partition of 75 MB instead of 75%.

```
Delete DOS Partition or Logical DOS Drive

Current fixed disk drive: 1

Choose one of the following:

1. Create Primary DOS Partition
2. Create Extended DOS Partition
3. Create Logical DOS Drive(s) in the Extended DOS Partition

Enter choice: [1]

Press Esc to return to FDISK Options
```

12. Go back to the main menu. Notice the warning at the bottom of the screen.
13. Use the rest of the free disk space to create an extended DOS partition. Assign one logical drive (drive D).
14. Press the Esc key until a request is made to insert a system disk.
15. Boot the computer using drive C. Record the error message.
16. Using FDISK, make the primary DOS partition active (option 2).
17. Boot the computer using drive C. Record the error message.
18. Boot the computer using drive A. Switch over to the C drive. Perform a DIR command. Record the error message.
19. Use the Abort/Fail options to move back to the A drive.
20. Boot the computer using drive A. Format the hard drive, but do not make it bootable.
21. Boot the computer using drive C and record the error message.
22. Boot the computer using drive A. Make the hard drive bootable with either a FORMAT command or a SYS command.
23. Format the D drive.
24. Boot the computer using drive C.
25. Using the CMOS setup program, reduce the number of cylinders by 50% and double the number of read/write heads.

    NOTE: You may need to use a user-definable type if you are not already using one. Save the changes.

26. Boot the computer using drive C. Record any error messages or if it doesn't boot.
27. Using the CMOS setup program, put the original settings back.
28. Boot the computer to drive C.
29. Shut off the computer. Remove the cable connector from the hard drive and place it on backward.
30. Boot the computer using drive C. Record any error messages or if it doesn't boot.
31. Shut off the computer. Reconnect the cable properly.
32. Disconnect the gray ribbon cable.
33. Boot the computer to drive C. Record any error messages or if it doesn't boot.
34. Shut off the computer. Reconnect the gray ribbon cable and disconnect the power connector.
35. Boot the computer to drive C. Record any error messages or if it doesn't boot.
36. Shut off the computer. Reconnect the power cable.
37. Go into the CMOS setup program and set drive D to be a type I drive.
38. Boot the computer to drive C. Record any error messages or if it doesn't boot.
39. Go into the CMOS setup program and disable drive D.
40. Make sure that the computer boots properly.

Exercise 2: Installing a Second IDE Hard Drive

1. Make sure that the computer can boot to drive C.
2. With the CMOS setup program, record the drive type, number of tracks, number of read/write heads, and number of sectors per track.

3. Shut off the computer. Remove the hard drive that is already in the computer. Examine the jumpers on the hard drive. They should be set to be a stand-alone hard drive.
4. Set the jumpers on the original hard drive to master and set the jumpers on the second hard drive to slave.
5. Connect both hard drives to the cable and connect the power cables.
6. Set the CMOS parameters for drives C and D.
7. Boot the computer using drive C.
8. Using FDISK, switch to the second hard drive (option 5). Create a primary DOS partition (option 1).
9. Press the Esc key until a request is made to insert a system disk.
10. Boot the computer using drive C. Change over to the D drive. Remember that all primary partitions are given drive letters first.
11. Use the Abort/Fail options to move back to the A drive. Format the D drive.
12. Change to the E drive, which should be the extended DOS partition on the first hard drive.
13. Remove the second hard drive.
14. Change the first drive back to a stand-alone drive.
15. Disable drive D in the CMOS setup program.
16. Make sure that the computer boots properly.

Exercise 3: Low-Level Formatting the IDE Hard Drive

1. Access the Internet and download the proper low-level format program for your hard drive.
2. Low-level format the hard drive.
3. Boot the computer using the A drive.
4. Run FDISK to create a primary DOS partition (2 GB) and an extended DOS partition (remaining amount). In addition, make the primary DOS partition active.
5. Boot the computer to the A drive.
6. Format the C drive.
7. Make sure that the computer boots properly.

Exercise 4: Installing a SCSI Hard Drive

1. Remove any IDE drives from your system.
2. Disable drive C in the CMOS setup program.
3. Set the resources of the SCSI expansion card. Use the card's documentation and a software diagnostic to determine the I/O addresses, IRQs, and DMA.
4. Locate the terminating resistors on the SCSI expansion card. Make sure that they are installed and enabled.
5. If the SCSI controller card has a floppy disk drive controller and one already exists in the computer, disable the one on the SCSI controller card.
6. Install the SCSI controller card.
7. Using the drive's documentation, set the boot drive to SCSI ID 0. Make sure that the terminating resistor is installed and enabled.
8. Install the boot drive to the end of the chain (cable) and connect the power.
9. Using the drive's documentation, set a second SCSI hard drive or a SCSI CD-ROM to SCSI ID 5.
10. Disable or remove the terminating resistor on the second drive.
11. Connect the second drive to the middle of the chain and connect the power.
12. Boot the computer using drive A.
13. Create a primary DOS partition. Use the entire drive for the partition and make it active.
14. Format the hard drive and make it bootable.
15. Using the correct software or using the SCSI BIOS, low-level format the first SCSI hard drive.
16. Remove all SCSI drives, including the controller card.
17. Reinstall the IDE hard drive.
18. Enter the correct parameters in the CMOS setup program.
19. Make sure that the computer boots properly.

Exercise 5: Researching on the Internet

1. Find the CMOS parameters for the Western Digital Caviar AC33200 (3.2 GB EIDE) hard drive.
2. Find the jumper settings to make the Western Digital Caviar AC33200 (3.2 GB EIDE) a master drive.
3. Find the jumper settings to make the Western Digital Caviar AC33200 (3.2 GB EIDE) a slave drive.
4. Find and download the low-level format program for the Western Digital Caviar AC33200 (3.2 GB EIDE).
5. Find the jumper settings to make a Seagate ST-11900N (1.7 GB SCSI hard drive) SCSI ID 0.
6. Find the jumper settings to make a Seagate ST-11900 N (1.7 GB SCSI hard drive) SCSI ID 5.
7. Find how to terminate the resistance on a Seagate ST-11900N (1.7 GB SCSI hard drive).
8. Find and download the software to make a Seagate Medallist Pro hard drive overcome certain system BIOS and operating system limitations.
9. Find and download the Windows NT driver for the AHA-2940 SCSI card.
10. Find and download the installation guide for the Adaptec 2940 Ultra SCSI card.

CHAPTER 10

The Floppy Disk Drive and Other Removable Media

Topics Covered in This Chapter

Introduction

Floppy drives are half-electronic, half-mechanical devices that use magnetic patterns to store information on a removable disk consisting of a single rotating platter.

Floppy drives are essential to a computer technician because they are needed to prepare the hard drive for first-time use (partitioning and formatting), to load essential device drivers, and to analyze a system that has failed.

Objectives

1. Explain the function of the floppy drive.
2. List and describe the characteristics of a floppy drive platter.
3. Describe the read/write head and explain how it reads and writes to the platter.
4. Identify the head actuator's function.
5. List and describe the basic steps in installing a hard drive.
6. Define *track* and *sectors.*
7. Giving a floppy drive problem, determine and correct the problem.
8. Describe at least three different removable media drives.
9. Given a removable media problem, determine and correct the problem.

10.1 WHAT IS A FLOPPY DRIVE?

A **floppy disk drive** is a half-electronic, half-mechanical device that uses magnetic patterns to store information on a removable disk consisting of a single rotating platter. It is considered a long-term storage device because it does not lose information when power is disconnected. Today, floppy drives are considered secondary storage systems because of their size limitations and slow speeds.

NOTE: Since floppy disks are slow and with limited capacity, floppy disk drives are now considered a legacy device. Over the next couple of years, the floppy disk drive will be fazed out and replaced with other types of drives or removable media.

Although floppy drives do not play as important a role as they did when the IBM PC was introduced, they can be a useful component of the PC. They can be used to prepare the hard drive for first-time use (partitioning and formatting) and to load essential device drivers. The floppy disk is a valuable tool for the PC technician in analyzing a hard drive that isn't booting or is not accessible. Lastly, the floppy drive can be used for storing and backing up small files and is still a common way to transfer files from one computer to another.

Floppy disk drives communicate with the rest of the computer by means of a 34-pin ribbon cable connected to a controller card. The controller card could be an expansion card or could be built onto the motherboard. All floppy drives consist of the following components: floppy disks, read/write heads, and head actuators.

10.1.1 Floppy Disks

Unlike hard drives, floppy disk drives use **floppy disks,** which are removable from the system, to store data. The reason they are called *floppy disks* is because they are flexible platters made of Mylar. Some people wrongly call the 3½-in. floppy disk a *hard disk* because of its sturdy protective casing. Of course, the terms *floppy* and *hard* are based on the platter, not the casing for the platter. The Mylar platters don't actually store data. Instead, it is their coating of magnetic material, such as iron oxide, that stores data. The magnetic coating is made up of tiny particles that can hold magnetic fields. When these fields are placed in certain patterns, they represent 0s and 1s. The bits of information are written (stored) and read (retrieved) using a **read/write head.**

Table 10.1 Different Floppy Disk Drives

Disks	Capacity	Sectors per Track	Tracks per Inch	Bits per Inch	Coercivity
DS/DD 3½"	720 KB	9	135	8,717	650 oersteds
DS/HD 3½"	1.44 MB	18	135	17,434	720 oersteds

NOTE: There are also double-sided, *extra-density* (DS/ED) 3½-in. disks and drives, which have a 2.88 MB capacity. Although these disks can hold twice as much as other floppy disks, they aren't widely used.

Figure 10.1 3½-in. Floppy Disk

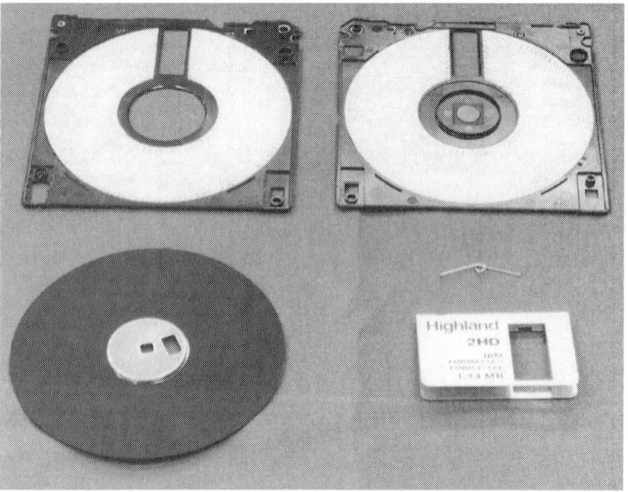

All 3½-in. floppy disk platters rotate around a **spindle** at 300 revolutions per minute (rpm). The faster the drive spins, the less time it takes to access data. The spindle motor, which spins the platter, uses very little power and generates very little heat.

The standard floppy disk today is the 3½-in. disk. See figure 10.1 and table 10.1. The platter is enclosed in a sturdy protective casing. Rather than part of the platter being exposed so that the read/write head can access it, the 3½-in. platter includes a metal shutter that opens as it slides into the drive. When the disk is removed from the computer, a small metal spring automatically closes the shutter. The disk is made so that it can't be inserted upside down or backwards. The 3½-in. disk is write-protected by a small hole with a sliding plastic cover. When the cover is open, the disk is write-protected; when the cover is closed, it is not write-protected.

The *density* of a disk refers to the amount of data that can be stored in a given amount of space, which depends on how many tracks can fit on the disk and how many bits can fit on each track. A density hole on 3½-in. disks identifies the disk as a DD disk or a HD disk. If a density key or hole is present, the disk is a 1.44 MB disk; if the density key is not present, the disk is a 720 KB disk.

To store information on a platter, it is divided into a circular grid consisting of tracks and sectors. The platter is first divided into concentric circles called **tracks.** (*Concentric* means circles that share the same center, much like rings of a tree.) A floppy disk platter will have either 40 or 80 tracks. Tracks are numbered starting with the outside track as track 0. The tracks are then further divided into **sectors;** each sector contains 512 bytes of usable data. A floppy disk has 9 to 18 sectors per track. Sectors are numbered on a track starting with 1. Information written to the platter is represented by tiny magnetic fields (flux) whose polarity flows from north to south or south to north. The read/write heads do not measure the polarity of the magnetic fields, but instead the flux reversals.

Encoding the data on the platter is the method or pattern used to represent the bits. The first encoding method, used before the IBM PC, was frequency modulation (FM). In FM encoding, the value of 1 is represented with two flux reversals, the first for the clock and the second for the 1. A 0 is represented by a flux reversal (clock) followed by a no reversal. Unfortunately, FM encoding is wasteful since each bit requires two flux-reversal positions. Modern floppy disks use MFM encoding. Instead of inserting a clock reversal before each bit, one is inserted only between consecutive zeroes. This means far fewer reversals are needed on average per bit and allows approximately double the storage capacity of FM encoding. This is why the early floppy disks were called *double-density* disks.

Although desktop floppy drives are quite reliable, the same can't be said about floppy disks. Since the magnetic fields used to represent data are not very strong and the platter, the magnetic coating, and the protective case are not as sturdy as a hard drive, the floppy disk will often develop unreadable areas. These errors may appear as read/write errors during disk reading and writing or can appear as bad blocks when using software to analyze the disk. These types of problems are usually caused by stray magnetic fields or certain areas of the platter losing their magnetic properties. In addition, the surface of the platter is exposed to the open air, which can contaminate the surface and damage the magnetic material on the platter. (Note: Since floppy disks are so inexpensive and not very reliable, a disk should be thrown away if it develops any read/write errors.)

10.1.2 Read/Write Heads

The read/write head is an iron core with wire (a coil) wrapped around it. When electricity is applied to the coil, it acts as an electromagnet. To write to a disk, current is sent through the wire, which causes an electromagnetic field to form around the wire. The coil intensifies the electromagnetic field. As the electromagnetic field crosses the platter, the magnetic material on the platter becomes magnetized. To read from the disk, the process is reversed. The read/write head passes over the magnetized material, and as the coil detects the changes (flux) in the magnetic charge, a small amount of current is caused to flow in the head. After this signal is amplified and filtered, it is translated into 0s and 1s.

Compared to the read/write head of a hard drive, the read/write head of a floppy drive is larger and much less precise. This is because they are generic so that they can work on disks made by different manufacturers. As a result, the density of the floppy disk is much lower. Since the floppy read/write heads are not as precise, floppy disk drives must use tunnel erasing to keep the tracks well defined. See figure 10.2. The floppy read/write assembly consists of a single read/write head and two erase heads (placed on each side of the read/write head). The erase heads erase any stray magnetic information that the read/write head might have recorded outside the designated track. If tunnel erasing were not done, interference might result between the tracks.

Since data can be stored on both sides of a platter, a read/write head is used for each side. The bottom head is the first read/write head while the top head is the second. Because the operations of the read/write heads may affect one another, the top read/write head is offset by four or eight tracks (depending on the type of drive) inward from the bottom head. Unlike those in most hard drives, the floppy drive heads make contact with the platter. The platters do not spin at high speeds and are flexible, so the read/write heads and the platter are not damaged when the two make contact. Unfortunately, since the read/write heads are exposed to the air and make contact with the platters, magnetic oxide and dirt build up on the heads. This is the reason that the floppy drive read/write heads have to be cleaned with a special cleaning disk made of a soft cloth platter that uses a special cleaning solution.

Figure 10.2 Tunnel Erasing Used in Floppy Disk Drive

10.1.3 Head Actuator

The **head actuator** is the component that moves the read/write heads back and forth. Floppy drives use the **stepper motor** head actuator. Stepper motors are electrical motors that move from one position to another in steps. Unfortunately, the stepper motor cannot take half steps. If the stepper motor is to move the read/write heads to a particular location, it counts the appropriate number of steps, but unfortunately, it has no way of determining whether it has arrived at the correct location. If, for instance, the platters have been left overnight in a cold building, they would contract (shrink). Consequently, when the stepper motor moves the read/write heads the appropriate number of steps, the data would have shifted inward. When the read/write heads try to read the data, they are actually reading between tracks, resulting in read/write errors. But since floppy disks have a lower track density, this is usually not a problem.

The head actuators on a floppy disk drive are very slow compared to those on hard disk drives. It takes the read/write heads about 200 ms to move from the outer track to the inner track, a distance of approximately 1 in. This is one reason why floppy disks are much slower than hard disks.

10.1.4 Floppy Drive Characteristics

The 3½-in. drive is much smaller and is considered a one-third-height device measuring 1 in. As disks are inserted into the disk drive, a spindle clamp clamps around the spindle hub. This is done automatically in the 3½-in. disk drive. The button on the 3½-in. disk drive is used to release the disk. Because floppy drives use a clamping mechanism to hold the disk in place, the drive can be placed horizontally or vertically.

On the underside of each floppy drive, there is an integrated logic board. It controls the read/write heads, the spindle motor, and head actuator and communicates with the floppy disk controller.

10.1.5 Floppy Disk Controller

The floppy disk controller electronically interfaces the floppy disk drives to the rest of the PC. It manages the flow and transfer of information from the floppy disk drives to the microprocessor and RAM. The controller card will be either an expansion card (usually part of a multifunction expansion card) or built into the motherboard.

Today a floppy disk controller will run every type of standard floppy disk drive. Older controllers will not always work on newer drives since some cannot run at the faster speeds required by the newer drives. The speed required of the controller is directly related to the density of the floppy disk media being used, in particular the bit density per track. The closer the information is, the faster the controller must work to read and write information within the same time frame. The newer controllers perform at 500 kilobits per second (Kbit/s) and support the 360 KB, 1.2 MB, 720 KB, and 1.44 MB drives. The most modern floppy disk controller performs at 1 Mbit/s. It supports all standard floppy drives, including the 2.88 MB floppy and proprietary floppy drive devices such as tape backups.

As with any other disk, the files on a floppy disk are located by reading the FAT (file allocation table) and directory information. Every time a disk is inserted in the drive, a change-disk signal is sent to the controller through pin 34 of the floppy drive cable. The controller then copies the FAT and directory information to the RAM. Every time the disk is accessed, the location of the file is read from the RAM. Consequently, the performance of the disk is increased.

10.2 INSTALLING A FLOPPY DISK DRIVE

The first step to installing any floppy drive is to physically install the controller card and floppy drive. The floppy drive is usually held in an external drive bay with screws. The disk controller could be an expansion card (possibly the same card as the hard drive controller) or it could be already incorporated on the motherboard. The resources used by the floppy disk drive controller are quite standard and universal. The floppy disk drive controller uses IRQ 6, DMA channel 2, and I/O address 3F0–3F7H. Most of the time, these resources can't be changed, and most computer component manufacturers avoid using these resources since they know that these are used for the floppy disk drive controller.

The drive and controller are connected with a gray 34-pin ribbon cable, which must be connected properly. See figure 10.3.

Figure 10.3 34-Pin Floppy Drive Ribbon Cables

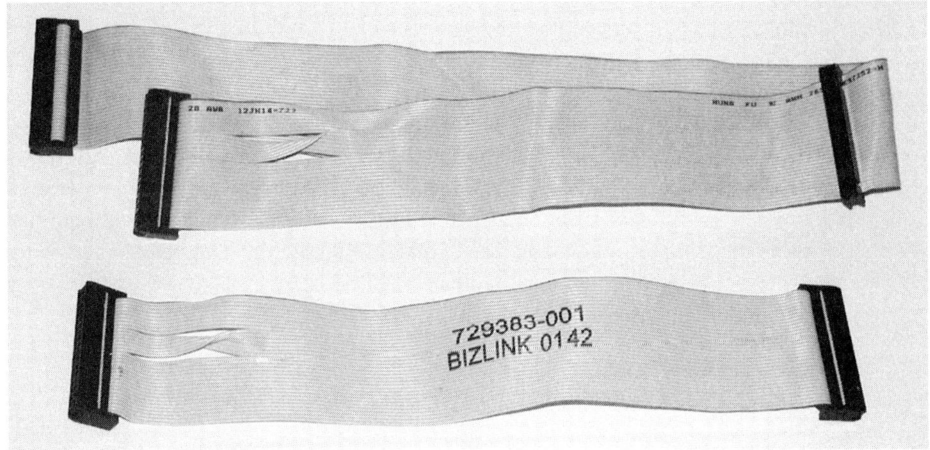

Figure 10.4 3½-in. Floppy Drive Connector

Newer controller cards and 3½-in. floppy disk drives use a 34-pin connector. See figure 10.4. Pin 1 of the cable is designated with a red or blue stripe. The controller card and drive are marked with either a small number 1 or 2 to designate which end has pin 1, or they use a square solder (other pins use a round solder). If one of the cable ends is connected backward, the floppy drive light or lights remain on. If a 3½-in. disk is inserted, the drive will not make any unnecessary noise yet will still destroy the disk.

NOTE: The drive itself is rarely damaged if the ribbon cable is connected backward.

In addition to the gray ribbon cable, the floppy drive also uses a power connector. A 3½-in. floppy drive will use a 3½-in. power connector. The drive requires +5 V to power the chips and +12 V to power the motors. Floppy disk drives in notebook computers use +5 V for the motor. The power cable must be connected properly. To ensure proper orientation, the 5¼-in. power cable connector has a rectangular shape with two corners clipped off; the 3½-in. power connector has a ridge on the bottom. If the cable is improperly connected, 12 V will enter components that are designed for 5 V, which will result in damaged or blown chips and a possible fire in the cable.

Today, the gray floppy ribbon cable will have two or three connectors. The connector on the long end will connect to the controller card or motherboard and the other end is for drive A. If the cable has three connectors, the middle connector is for drive B.

Most current motherboards include a floppy drive cable that has only two connectors. One connector connects to the motherboard and the other end goes to the floppy drive. The reason that the cable has only two connectors is that the other connector is not really needed because most computers have only one floppy drive. What is important to notice is that on one connector, pin 6 is filled in. Therefore, if you are connecting the cable to the floppy drive and the cable appears not to connect, try reversing the cable. Connect the other connector to the motherboard and use the previous connector for the floppy disk drive. It is also important to know that a lot of these motherboards do not support a second floppy disk drive, even if you are using a connector that will accommodate two floppy disk drives.

The last step in installing the floppy disk drive is to set the floppy drive parameters using the CMOS setup program. The possible options are Not Installed, 360 KB, 720 KB, 1.2 MB, 1.44 MB, and 2.88 MB. On newer systems, the advanced CMOS setup screen has other parameters that will affect the floppy disk drives. The Boot Sequence controls which drive it will boot from first. By default, the boot order is the A drive followed by the C drive, although this can be changed to the C drive followed by the A drive. Newer systems will include other boot drives such as SCSI drives and CD-ROMs. (Note: You cannot boot with the B drive.)

10.3 PREPARING THE FLOPPY DISK

Before a floppy disk can store files, it must be properly prepared. This includes low-level and high-level formatting. Low-level formatting defines the tracks and sectors on the disk. High-level formatting is the process of writing the file system structure on the disk so that it can be used to store programs and data, including a root directory to start with and a file allocation table (an index listing all directories and files and where they are located on the disk).

Both types of formats can be done with the FORMAT command or equivalent. If the drive has never been formatted, the FORMAT command will low-level format the disk and follow it by a high-level format. Normally, if a floppy disk has already been formatted, only a high-level format will be completed. If you wish to redraw the tracks and sectors, you must specify the unconditional format. Of course, whichever type of formatting is done, all information on the disk will be lost. Today, virtually all disks are preformatted.

10.4 TROUBLESHOOTING FLOPPY DISK DRIVES

A floppy disk drive problem is most likely caused by a faulty disk, drive, cable, or controller card. Incorrect power and incorrect CMOS values can also cause problems. Since the drive and controller card are inexpensive, it is best to replace the faulty components rather than repair them.

Example 10.1:

The computer is turned on. During boot-up, an "FDD Controller Failure" error message or equivalent appears on the screen.

The "FDD Controller Failure" error message (or *601* error message) indicates that the controller card tried to control the floppy drive during boot-up and could not. The reason that it could not needs to be determined.

Check the obvious first: Before opening the system, check the CMOS values to see if they are correct. This should be checked first because it does not require opening the system. If the CMOS values keep disappearing, check the CMOS battery. The next step would be to see if the cables (ribbon cables and power connectors) are connected properly. Make sure that the A drive is located at the end of the cable and that the B drive is located in the middle.

If nothing has been recently changed or added, replace the cable. If the problem does not go away, replace the controller card. The next step would be to measure the voltage level of the power connector to make sure that the cable is supplying +5 and +12 V. If the voltage level is correct, replace the floppy drive.

If the installation is new or changes have been made to the hard drive system, verify the configuration, including the controller card resources (I/O address, IRQ, DMA, and memory usage), and that no other devices are using the same resources. If there are no conflicts, replace the cable. If the problem does not go away, replace the controller card. The next step would be to measure the voltage level of the power connector to make sure that the cable is supplying +5 and +12 V. If the voltage is correct, replace the drive.

Example 10.2:

The system can't read the floppy disk and the drive lights will not shut off.

The most common cause for this problem is the cable not being connected properly (a connector is backward or the cable is not connected to all of the pins). If the cable is connected properly, then the problem is a bad cable, controller card, or floppy disk drive. To isolate these, you would swap them one by one until the problem is fixed.

Example 10.3:

First Scenario: You place a disk in drive A and perform a DIR command. You then remove the first disk and place a second disk in drive A. When you perform the DIR command again, the same directory listing as the one for the first disk appears. *Second Scenario:* When installing a program, you insert disk 1 and start the installation program. When it asks for disk 2, you put the second disk in drive A and press the Enter key, but the installation program still asks you to place disk 2 in the A drive.

This problem is called a *phantom directory,* and it occurs when the change-disk signal through pin 34 is not being received when a new disk is inserted, which should indicate to read the second disk's FAT and directory areas into RAM for faster access. The cause will be a bad cable, controller card, or floppy drive. A temporary solution when using DOS would be to press Ctrl + Break or Ctrl + C to force the system to reread the FAT and directory areas. It is important not to save to the disk when the second disk is in the drive.

Example 10.4:

You get a read/write error when accessing a floppy disk.

Because floppy disks are not very sturdy, floppy read/write errors are common. To determine whether the disk is bad or the computer itself is bad, take the floppy to another machine and try to access the disk in the same way. If the same error occurs, then the disk is bad. If the disk works with no problems, then the floppy drive system must be at fault. The first thing to do would be to clean the read/write heads with a special cleaning disk that uses denatured alcohol pads. If the problem still occurs, it is caused by the floppy disk drive, the controller card, or the cable.

NOTE: If the disk starts showing bad sectors, it is recommended that it be thrown away.

Example 10.5:

A disk works fine on one system. When the disk is taken to another computer, read/write errors occur. Yet, when it is taken back to the first system, the disk again works fine.

The problem is that the disk drive system of the second computer is bad or that the floppy disk read/write heads in the first computer are misaligned. To determine which problem it is, try the disk in a third machine. If the problem does not occur, the second computer has a floppy drive problem. If the same problem occurs, the read/write heads in the first computer are misaligned.

A head alignment problem occurs when the floppy disk head actuator drifts. To fix the alignment problem, you could realign the read/write heads by adjusting the drive with the aid of a special disk and software, but it is easier and cheaper to replace the floppy disk drive. Of course, this does not fix the floppy disks themselves, which were prepared with the faulty disk drive. To fix this problem, copy the contents of all floppy drives prepared with the faulty drive to another drive. Then replace the drive.

Example 10.6:

You try to boot the computer using the A drive. Instead, the computer boots from the C drive.

The first thing to check is the CMOS setup program, specifically the boot order. Although the default boot order is the A drive followed by the C drive, it could have been changed to the C drive followed by the A drive. If the CMOS setup program is fine, check the disk on another machine to make sure that it is readable. (If the disk can't be read, the system goes to the C drive.) If the problem still exists, it has to be due to the floppy disk drive, the cable, or the controller card.

Example 10.7:

A disk is stuck in the drive and will not eject.

This is usually caused by the label, which has peeled and stuck to the inside of the drive, or the metal slider on the disk which has come loose and has snagged on something inside the drive. Using a small flat-edge screwdriver or knife, carefully pry the disk out of the drive. After the disk is removed, test the drive with another disk to make sure that the drive itself was not damaged. (Note: If the metal slider is loose, you can remove it from the disk and can then make a copy of the disk.)

Occasionally, the metal slider will come completely off and become stuck in the drive. Again, use a small flat-edge screwdriver or knife to carefully pry the disk out of the drive. You can also use a small hook made out of a large paperclip to grab the metal slider. After the disk is removed, test the drive with another disk to make sure that the drive itself was not damaged.

10.5 REMOVABLE MEDIA DRIVES

Today, it is very easy to create a large document or picture that is several megabytes in size. Floppy disks are obviously too small to store these large files. Currently, several companies make high-capacity removable magneto-optical disk drives. See table 10.2. Some of these are designed to replace the floppy disk drive.

10.5.1 Magneto-Optical Media Drives

Magneto-optical media drives have read/write heads that are similar to the read/write heads of a floppy disk drive. Since the magneto-optical disk contains many more tracks than a floppy disk, its capacity is considerably greater. To guide the read/write heads to the correct track, the platters include servo information, which is read by a laser beam. The servo information, placed there during manufacturing, consists of magnetic markings used to identify the track.

The first magneto-optical drive was the floptical, developed by Insite. The floptical disk held 20 MB, rotated at 720 rpm, and offered a 10 megabit per minute (Mbit/m) transfer rate. The drive used a SCSI interface. Therefore, when connecting this drive, a SCSI ID number that was not being used had to be selected and the terminating resistors had to be checked. (For more information on SCSI devices, see chapter 9.) Unfortunately, this drive was not supported by any major companies, including Microsoft and IBM, so, the drive was not widely used.

Table 10.2 Websites for Manufacturers of Removable Media

Company	Website
Iomega	**Home:** http://www.iomega.com/ **Support:** http://www.iomega.com/support/index.html **Software:** http://www.iomega.com/support/software/index.html
SyQuest Technology	**Home:** http://www.syquest.com/index.html **Support:** http://www.syquest.com/support/index.html
Imation (LS-120/Super disk)	**Information:** http://www.imation.com/dsp/ls120/index.html

10.5.2 LS-120 Drives

One of the newest magneto-optical drives is the LS-120, a drive developed by 3M and Matsushita-Kotobuki Electronics Industries, Ltd. and currently controlled by Imation (*LS* stands for *laser servo*). The LS-120 disk is the same size and shape as a 1.44 MB 3½-in. floppy disk yet has a track density of 2,490 tracks per inch and a 120 MB capacity. The LS-120 drive is an IDE device that can also read and write 720 KB and 1.44 MB floppy disks at three times the speed and access the 120 MB disk at five times the speed of a standard floppy drive.

The LS-120 is bootable in both 120 and 1.44 MB modes, so you can boot from either size disk. However, you will need a motherboard or drive controller BIOS that is designed to accommodate the LS-120. Typically, you will see LS-120 as a boot option in the CMOS setup "Boot Order" entry. If your BIOS does not recognize the LS-120, you may need to upgrade the BIOS. The following three BIOS versions support LS-120 technology:

Award BIOS version 4.51PG or later
AMI BIOS version 6.26.02 or later
Phoenix BIOS version 6.0 or later

Although the LS-120 drive will work in DOS with the appropriate drivers and in all versions of Windows, only Windows 95 (OSR2) and later will treat the LS-120 as bootable. All older versions of Windows support the drive only as a removable and nonbootable disk, which will not be assigned to drive letter A or B.

NOTE: For Windows NT to recognize the LS-120 drive, you must install service pack 5 or greater.
NOTE: Macintosh computers can also use the USB-based LS-120 drives, so data (and the drive itself) can be shared between PCs and Macs.

10.5.3 Bernoulli Drives

Another popular type of drive is the Bernoulli removable media drive, which was developed by Iomega. The Bernoulli drive is connected to the computer as an IDE device or as an external SCSI card. The original Bernoulli drive is approximately the same size as the older 5¼-in. disk drive, although it includes a large shutter, similar to the shutter on a 3½-in. floppy disk. The disks come in several capacities, up to 230 MB. Unlike floppy disk drives, air pressure is used to pull the disk toward the drive heads. The air-flow is controlled by a Bernoulli plate. The disk spins at approximately 3,600 rpm and has an average seek time of 18 ms.

10.5.4 Zip Drives

One of the more popular removable drive systems is the Iomega **Zip drive.** See figure 10.5. The Zip disk is about twice as thick as a standard 3½-in. floppy disk, can hold 100, 250 or 750 MB of data, has an access time of 29 ms, rotates at 2,968 rpm, and has a transfer rate of 1 MB/s. The Zip drive comes with a SCSI, IDE, parallel port or USB interface. Iomega also produces the 1 and 2 GB Jaz drive.

When installing Zip and Jaz drives, you usually have to install drivers to activate the devices. Today, some system ROM BIOS chips support and activate the Zip drives during boot-up. When you

Figure 10.5 Iomega Zip Drive

insert a Zip disk into your Zip drive, the drive heads will click to acquire the Zip disk media. However, if a disk is inserted into the drive and the heads make a continual clicking noise, this sound usually indicates a problem. You should then try another disk in the drive. If the second disk works, then the problem is most likely a disk that has become defective. If both disks make a continuous clicking noise, the drive should not be used. To help avoid this problem, it is recommended that when transporting Zip drives, eject disks so that the drive heads can park in their natural position.

10.5.5 USB Storage Devices

Since floppy drives are too slow and are limited in capacity and no other forms of removable media have dominated the removable media market, the USB interface has provided a new class of removable media. First, you can connect a wide range of portable drives including CD drives, DVD drives, hard drives, Zip drives, Jaz drives, and so forth using the USB connector. See figure 10.6. As long as your system has a USB device and the operating system supports USB, you just connect the device to your system and load any drivers if needed. Note: For some hard drives, you may need to use Windows Disk Management console to activate the drive.

Recently, a new class of USB devices have been introduced called flash drives on sticks. Flash drives are storages devices that contain flash chips on a stick, which are no bigger than a house or car key. The capacity of these devices range from 128 MB to 2 GB, and it is safe to say that larger sizes will be introduced in the future. When you connect most of these flash devices to your system, they are automatically detected and no drivers are needed for them to operate. In Windows, when you open My Computer window, the drive will be recognized. Some of these devices can also be used to boot the computer and some include encryption and password security to help secure the contents of the device. See figure 10.7. Note: Drives made of flash RAM do have a limited number of writes. Therefore, if you are saving often to the drives, you should estimate the life of these devices.

Similar to inserting a bootable disk in drive A, many flash drives allow you to boot from them. Unfortunately, if you have USB flash drive inserted into the USB slot and you reboot the computer, some computers will try to boot from the USB device. If you have the bootable files properly installed on the flash device, it will boot. If you do not have the bootable files, you will get the boot failure. Sometimes these errors may be misleading because it indicates diskette boot error when it is the flash device. Therefore, if you get a diskette error, check the A drive for a bootable floppy disk followed by checking to see if you have any USB flash drives.

Figure 10.6 USB Hard Drives

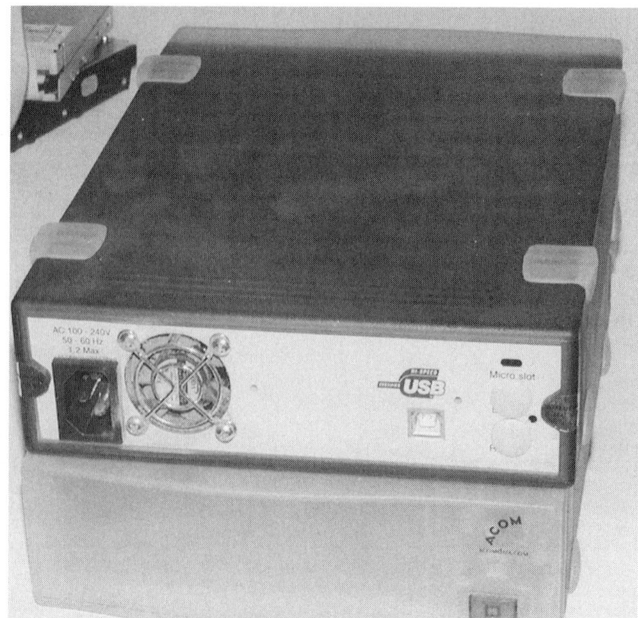

Figure 10.7 USB Flash Sticks

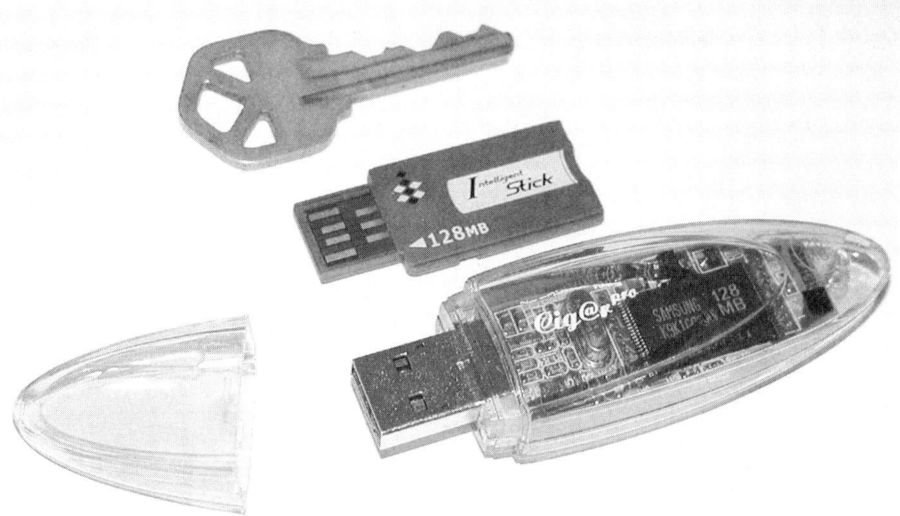

SUMMARY

1. Floppy drives are half-electronic, half-mechanical devices that use magnetic patterns to store information on a removable disk consisting of a single rotating platter.
2. Although they are considered long-term storage devices, floppy disks are classified as secondary storage systems because of their size limitations and slow speeds.
3. Floppy disk drives are used to load essential device drivers, to analyze a hard drive that isn't booting or is not accessible, to back up small files, and to transfer files from one computer to another.
4. A floppy disk is a flexible platter made of Mylar and coated with a magnetic material such as iron oxide.
5. Today, floppy drives are considered legacy devices. Therefore, they are being replaced by other forms of removable media.
6. Floppy disk drives communicate with the rest of the computer by means of a 34-pin cable connected to a controller card.
7. The connector or connector set located on the *long* end of the connector cable will connect to the controller card; the set of connectors on the other end is for drive A, and the set in the middle (if available) is for drive B.
8. The resources used by the floppy disk drive controller (IRQ 6, DMA channel 2, and I/O address 3F0–3F7H) are quite standard and universal.
9. External storage devices can be a SCSI, IDE, parallel port, or USB interface.
10. USB flash drives are storage devices that contain flash chips on a stick, which are no bigger than a house or car key. The capacity of these devices ranges from 128 MB to 1 GB.
11. When you connect most of the flash devices to your system, they are automatically detected and no drivers are needed to operate them.
12. Because floppy drive read/write heads are exposed to the air and make contact with the platter, magnetic oxide and dirt build up on the heads, making it necessary to clean the heads occasionally.
13. If one of the cable ends is connected backward, the floppy drive light or lights remain on.
14. An "FDD Controller Failure" error can be caused by a faulty floppy drive, cable, controller card, power cable, or motherboard, or an incorrect CMOS settings.
15. A phantom directory (the second disk showing the same FAT listing as the first) is caused by a faulty ribbon cable, controller card, or floppy drive.
16. Floppy drive read/write heads have to be cleaned with a special cleaning disk made of a soft cloth platter and a special cleaning solution.

QUESTIONS

1. The DMA channel used for the floppy controller is
   a. 1. b. 2.
   c. 3. d. 5.
   e. 6.
2. The IRQ used for the floppy controller is
   a. IRQ 2. b. IRQ 3.
   c. IRQ 4. d. IRQ 6.
   e. IRQ 11. f. IRQ 14.
3. The storage capacity of a 3½-in. high-density diskette is
   a. 360 KB. b. 720 KB.
   c. 1.2 MB. d. 1.44 MB.
   e. 2.88 MB.
4. A red stripe on one of the edges of the ribbon cable indicates
   a. the positive/hot lead.
   b. the ground lead.
   c. pin 1.
   d. the cable is made for the hard drive.
5. What moves the read/write heads in and out on a floppy disk drive?
   a. stepper motor b. voice coil
   c. spindle d. hub
   e. head springs
6. How do you write-protect a 3½-in. disk?
   a. by covering the write-protect notch
   b. by uncovering the write-protect notch
   c. by closing the write-protect hole
   d. by opening the write-protect hole
   e. with special software
7. How does the PC identify a high-density 3½-in. floppy disk?
   a. by a label with a magnetic strip
   b. by a metallic label
   c. by an extra hole in the case
   d. by a small arrow along one side
8. A customer says that she cannot slide her hard disk into the drive. Which component is she probably talking about?
   a. hard drive
   b. 5¼-in. floppy disk
   c. 3½-in. floppy disk
   d. Zip disk
   e. CD-ROM disk
9. During boot-up, you get a "Non-System Disk or Disk Error. Replace and Strike any Key When Ready" error message. What is the first thing you should check or do?
   a. check the operation of the hard drive
   b. reinstall DOS
   c. check if a disk is in drive A
   d. check to see if the proper drivers are loaded
10. What is the most likely problem when you connect two floppy drives in the computer and both drive lights are on at the same time?
    a. bad cable
    b. cable is on backward
    c. bad power connection
    d. CMOS parameters are reversed
    e. none of the above
11. You insert a disk in drive A, perform a DIR, and find out that it is not the disk you wanted. Therefore, you insert a second disk and perform another DIR command, yet you get the same listing as for the first disk. Which of the following could *not* cause this problem?
    a. the RAM
    b. the floppy disk drive
    c. the floppy ribbon cable
    d. the floppy drive controller
12. Which of the following should be used to clean floppy drive heads?
    a. sandpaper
    b. water and mild soap
    c. a general-purpose cleaner such as Windex or 409
    d. denatured alcohol
    e. a paper clip

HANDS-ON EXERCISES

Exercise 1: Reinstalling a Floppy Disk Drive

1. Enter the CMOS setup program and set the floppy disk drives to Disabled/Not installed.
2. Shut off the computer.
3. Disconnect the floppy disk drive ribbon cable.
4. Disconnect the floppy disk drive power connectors.
5. Remove the floppy disk drives from the PC.
6. Remove the floppy disk drive controller card.
7. Reinstall the floppy disk drive controller card.
8. Reinstall the floppy disk drives.
9. Reinstall the floppy disk drive ribbon cable and the drive power connectors.
10. Turn on the PC. Enter the CMOS setup program and set the floppy disk drives to the correct CMOS settings.

Exercise 2: Troubleshooting the Floppy Disk Drive

1. Shut off the computer and disconnect the power connector from the A drive.
2. Turn on the PC and record the error message.
3. Shut off the computer and reconnect the power connector.
4. Disconnect the floppy ribbon cable from the A drive.
5. Turn on the PC and record the error message.
6. Turn off the PC and reconnect the ribbon cable, but connect it backwards.
7. Turn on the PC and notice the drive lights.
8. Turn off the PC and reconnect the ribbon cable properly.

Exercise 3: Troubleshooting the Phantom Directory

1. Format one floppy disk and give it "Disk 1" as its volume label; format a second floppy disk and give it "Disk 2" as its volume label.
2. Shut off the computer and remove the ribbon cable.
3. Get a special floppy drive ribbon cable (pin 34 is clipped) and install it in the computer.
4. Turn on the computer and boot from the C drive.
5. Insert the first disk in drive A. Switch over to drive A and perform a DIR command. Notice the volume label of the disk.
6. Remove the first disk and insert the second disk. Perform a DIR command. Notice the volume label of the disk.
7. Press Ctrl + Break on the keyboard. Perform a DIR command. Notice the volume label of the disk.

CHAPTER 11

The Compact Disk Drive

Topics Covered in This Chapter

Introduction

The compact disk (CD) is a 4.72-in. encoded platter that is read by laser. Because the CD can hold a combination of data tracks, audio tracks, and video tracks, it can store large amounts of information. CDs are commonly used to distribute programs (operating systems, application software, device drivers, and multimedia libraries), so knowing how to install and troubleshoot a CD drive is essential.

Objectives

1. Define *compact disk* and explain how it stores information on the platter.
2. List and describe the different compact disk standards.
3. Install an IDE and SCSI CD-ROM drive.
4. Given a CD-ROM problem, identify and correct the problem.

11.1 WHAT IS A COMPACT DISK?

A **compact disk (CD)** is a 4.72-in. encoded platter that is read by laser. A CD drive is needed to read a CD. Since they can hold large amounts of information and are very inexpensive, CDs are used to distribute programs, including:

1. Operating systems (such as Windows 95 and 98 and Windows NT)
2. Application software (Microsoft Office 97, Adobe Photoshop, various encyclopedias, and most games)
3. Device drivers
4. Multimedia libraries (pictures, sound clips, and video clips)

Several different kinds of compact disks have been developed. The more common ones include the audio CD, CD-ROM, CD-R and CD-W, and DVD. See table 11.1.

11.1.1 CD-Digital Audio (CD-DA)

The **CD-Digital Audio (CD-DA)** was jointly developed by Philips and Sony Corporation and was introduced in the United States in 1983. The CD-DA, also known as the audio CD and the Red Book (its specifications were originally put into a red binder), is the standard for the compact disk used in a stereo system. Even though the compact disk measures only 4.72-in. across, it can hold up to 74–80 minutes of high-fidelity audio. (Note: Most CD-ROM drives can play an audio CD.)

The compact disks, or platters, are made of a polycarbonate wafer coated with an aluminum alloy. The data is stored as lands (similar to ridges) and pits, which are etched into the aluminum coating. Each pit is about 0.12 μm deep and about 0.6 μm wide. A pit and land together are 1.6 μm long, allowing 16,000 tracks per inch. To protect the data, the aluminum alloy is coated with a plastic polycarbonate coating. Currently, audio CDs are single sided, storing data only on the bottom side. Once an audio compact disk is recorded, the data cannot be changed.

Similar to hard disks, the pits and lands do not translate directly into 0s and 1s. Instead, the CD-ROM disk uses eight-to-fourteen modulation (EFM) encoding. An EFM binary 1 is represented by a transition (pit-to-land or land-to-pit). When 14 lands and pits are put together, the EFM pattern will represent 8 bits (1 byte) of information. See table 11.2.

CD-ROM drives use laser light (class 1 laser) to read the disks, so the disks are not affected by magnetic fields. In addition, they are subject to less wear and tear since the read assembly does not actually make contact with the disk. However, dirt on the surface of the platter or dirt on the read assembly can cause errors. And even though CDs are sturdier than floppy disks, the platters must be handled with care. Scratching the surface, specifically the bottom half, should be avoided, and the disks should not be left in direct sunlight on a hot day or bent or otherwise handled carelessly.

Table 11.1 Compact Disk Standards

Technology Type	Drive and CD Type	Description
CD	CD-DA	Compact disk used in stereo systems. It can hold up to 74–80 minutes of high-fidelity audio.
	CD-ROM	A compact disk that cannot be changed or written to and which can store 650–703 MB of data.
	CD-R	A recordable CD that can be written once and read many times.
	CD-E	A CD that can be written and read many times.
DVD	DVD-ROM	A DVD disk that is a read-only disk. A DVD-ROM drive can also read CD-ROMs. The standard DVD-5 can hold 4.7 GB on a single-sided, single layer and 17.0 GB on a double-sided double layer disk.
	DVD-R	DVD recordable that can be written only once and read many times. Holds about 4.7 GB of data. DVD-ROM disk drives can read DVD-ROM disks.
	DVD-R/RW or DVD-ER	Rewritable (also known as erasable) recordable DVD device that can be rewritten about 1,000 times. Media can be read by most DVD-ROM drives. DVD-RW media comes in only 4.7 and 9.4 GB. The DVD-R/RW is a competing standard against the DVD+R/RW.
	DVD+R/RW	Rewritable (also known as erasable), recordable DVD device that can be rewritten about 1,000 times. Media can be read by most DVD-ROM drives. The DVD+R/RW drive can read DVD-ROM and CD-ROM disks, but may not be compatible with DVD-RAM disks. The DVD+R/RW is a competing standard against the DVD-R/RW.
	DVD-RAM	Disks that can be recorded and erased repeatedly but are compatible only with devices manufactured by the companies that support the DVD-RAM format. DVD-RAM is rewritable as many 100,000 times.

Table 11.2 Partial Listing of EFM Encoding

Number	Binary Pattern	EFM Pattern
0	00000000	01001000100000
1	00000001	10000100000000
2	00000010	10010000100000
3	00000011	10001000100000
4	00000100	01000100000000
5	00000101	00000100010000
6	00000110	00010000100000
7	00000111	00100100000000
8	00001000	01001001000000
9	00001001	10000001000000
10	00001010	10010001000000

Much like the old vinyl records, CDs store data in a single, long spiral track. There are a maximum of 99 tracks on a CD. Part of each track has a pause area, which separates each of the audio selections. Each track is divided into large frames consisting of 2,352 bytes of information. It takes 75 large frames to make one second of recorded sound. Each frame includes a synchronization field (12 bytes), sector address tag field (12 bytes), and auxiliary field (288 bytes) and has at least 2,048 bytes of data. The auxiliary field is used for additional data and error detection and correction. The large frames are further divided into 98 small frames containing 24 bytes of information. This is enough data to store about 136 microseconds of music containing six samples (layers of sounds) for each stereophonic channel. Each sample is 16 bits of data, so there is a total of 65,536 different levels, giving the audio CD the quality of FM radio.

Since audio compact disks are time-sensitive, they use **constant linear velocity (CLV)** to access data. The outer tracks hold more information than the inner tracks, so the platter spins faster on the inner tracks than the outer tracks to keep a constant data rate. If it didn't, parts of the compact disk would play too slow or too fast. No matter which track is being read, the drive reads 75 blocks of data per second, giving the drive a transfer rate of 150 KB/s. Some compact disk drives use **constant angular velocity (CAV);** that is, they rotate at a constant speed and have different data transfer rates depending on which location on the CD is being read.

Since errors on a CD can cause significant problems for the PC and the compact disk is considered permanent, several techniques are used to find and correct errors. The primary error detection and correction method is error checking and correction (ECC). ECC is a special data encoding protocol that uses extra bits to provide a redundancy of information. If a bit is missing or is bad within a byte, special algorithms can correct it while the data is being accessed. (Note: Because the CD-ROM is read-only, an ECC correction is only a soft fix.) For audio CDs, another technique used in error correction is called *linear interpolation.* When data is missing, the drive estimates the missing value. Because thousands of values are being read each second and the interpolated value is probably close to the missing value, it is impossible to tell when the drive is making the substitution.

11.1.2 The CD-ROM

The **CD-ROM (compact disk–read-only memory)** is the standard compact disk used in the PC. It follows the CD-DA (digital audio) standard, also known as the Yellow Book. CD-ROMs are used to install operating systems, application software, device drivers, and large amounts of data. Each disk can store 650–703 MB of data, or up to 333,000 pages of text, and can hold sound, video, and digital data (in separate tracks). CD-ROMs must follow a standard so that they can be read by all CD-ROM drives. Two standards are used today. The standard known as the "High Sierra" standard became, after some modifications, the official adopted standard, known as the ISO 9660 standard. When someone refers to the High Sierra standard, he or she usually means ISO 9660.

Another format worth mentioning is the Joliet file system. The Joliet specification is an extension to the ISO 9660 specifications. In addition it overcame some of the limitations of the original ISO 9660 file system and provided long filename support for Windows.

Since video and digital data used by the PC is not based on time like audio data is, the compact disk drive can spin the disk at a higher linear velocity. Drives that spin twice as fast as the single-speed drive are known as *double speed* (2X); drives that spin at four times the speed of the single-speed are known as *quad speed* (4X). See table 11.3.

Table 11.3 Drive Speeds

Drive Speed	Transfer Rate (KB/s)	Access Time (ms)
Single-speed (1X)	150	400
Double-speed (2X)	300	300
Triple-speed (3X)	450	200
Quad-speed (4X)	600	150
Six-speed (6X)	900	150
Eight-speed (8X)	1,200	100
Ten-speed (10X)	1,500	100
Twelve-speed (12X)	1,800	100
Sixteen-speed (16X)	2,400	90
Twenty-four speed (24X)	3,600	90
Thirty-two speed (32X)	4,800	80

Figure 11.1 Inside the CD-ROM Drive

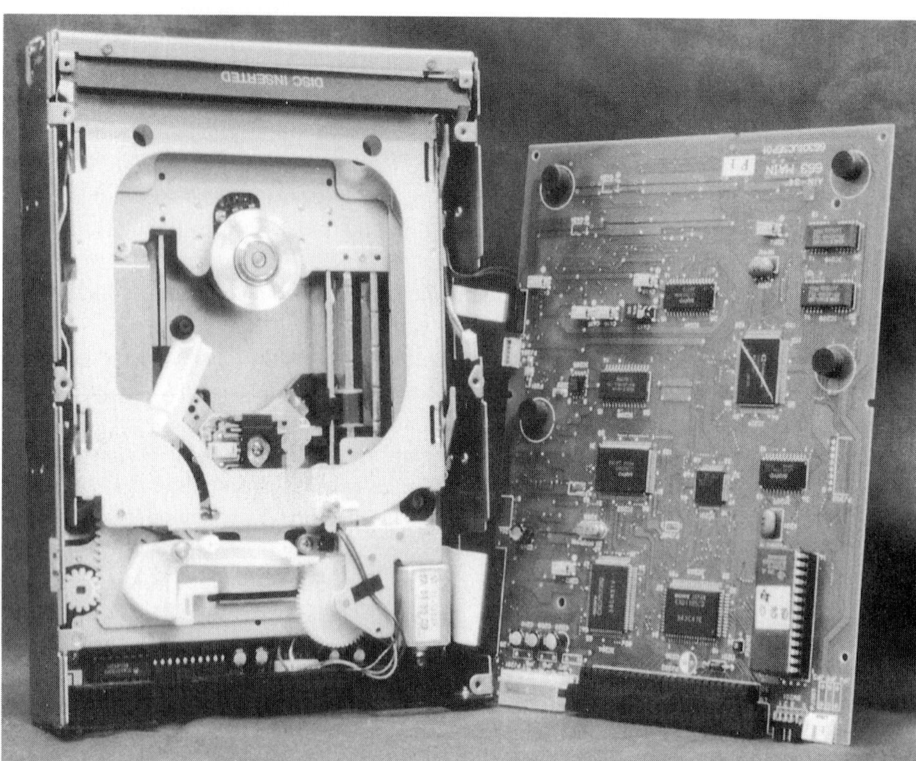

As mentioned, the data is stored on the CD as lands and pits. To read the data, a low-powered laser is emitted from an infrared laser diode and aimed at a reflecting mirror that is part of the head assembly moving linearly along the surface of the disk. The read assembly is moved back and forth by a microcontroller, which uses a servo system to determine its location. Written on the platter is servo data, consisting of markings used to guide the read assembly to the right location. See figure 11.1. The laser beam reflects off the mirror and is sent through a lens that focuses it onto a specific point on the disk. The light is reflected back from this area of the disk into a series of collectors, mirrors, and lenses, which focus it on a photodetector, an electronic device that is sensitive to light. When light hits a land and is reflected back to the detector, its signal is strong and the photodetector produces a strong output signal. When a light strikes a pit, it is diffused and scattered in all directions, causing the photodetector to produce a very weak output signal. See figure 11.2. The electrical signals are finally decoded by the processor into a binary code.

Many people don't realize that the data surface of the CD is actually the top of the disk. The media layer is directly under the CD label, and the player reads the CD from the bottom by focusing the laser through the 1.2 mm thickness of the CD's substrate. This is one reason that the bottom of the disk can have small scratches, yet operate correctly. Of course, you should avoid damaging both sides, including from scratching, overly flexing them, and exposing them to excess heat.

The loading mechanism is the mechanical component that loads the CDs into the CD-ROM drive. The most popular type is the tray. When the user presses the eject button, the tray slides out, and after the CD is placed in the tray, the tray is retracted into the drive when the user presses the eject button a second time or gently presses against the tray. (Note: While the tray is out, it can be easily broken if it is bumped with enough force or if enough weight is placed on it.) Older systems and some high-end drives use a caddy, a small plastic cartridge. A CD is placed inside the caddy, which is inserted into the CD-ROM drive. The advantage of a caddy is that it protects the disk. See figure 11.3.

CD-ROM drives will also play audio CDs and most drives come with a headphone jack so that you can listen to audio disks. Unfortunately, the sound quality through the headphone jack is poor, so it is best to connect to the sound card. Note: To play audio disks, you need to connect the audio cable from the CD drive to the sound card. See figure 11.4.

Figure 11.2 Lands and Pits

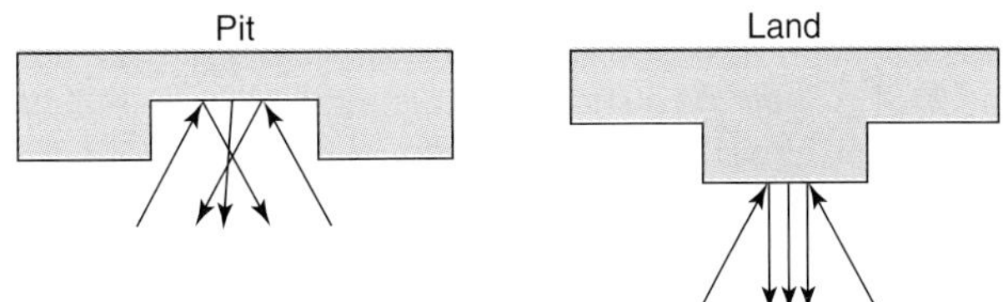

Figure 11.3 CD Tray and Caddy

Figure 11.4 Audio cable connected to CD drive

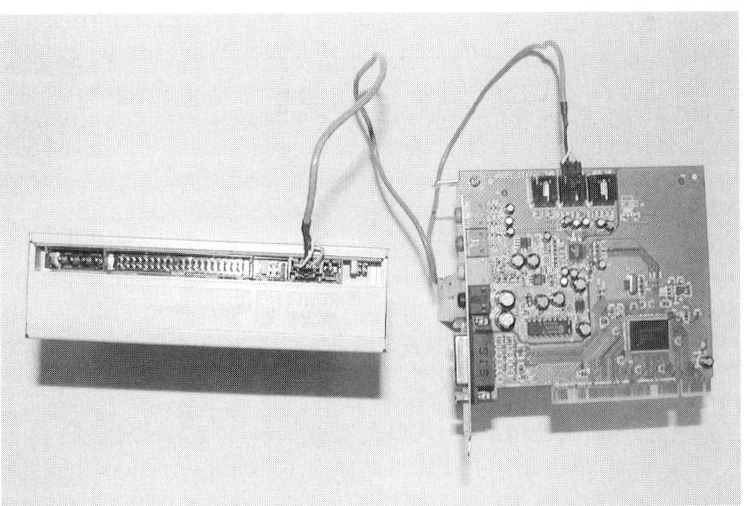

11.1.3 Recordable CD (CD-R)

In 1990, Philips introduced the **recordable CD,** also known as CD-WORM (write once, read many) and CD-WO (write once). As the *write once* name implies, the disks can be recorded only once and cannot be changed after that. The standard for the recordable CD is also known as the Orange Book.

CD-R disks have a polycarbonate substrate, much like a regular CD, but the spiral is already stamped on the surface. The disk is then coated with a special photosensitive dye followed by a metal reflective layer, usually made of gold or silver alloy. Finally, a plastic protective layer to help protect the disk is applied.

The process that writes data to the CD-R is called *burning the disk.* The data is written to disk by an intense laser beam (contained within a CD-R drive), which heats the surface rapidly. The burned areas reflect less light (pit) than the unburned areas (land). (Note: Some older CD-ROM drives cannot read the CD-R.) Some drives record in a single session; others allow multisession recording. Multisession recording allows additional information to be recorded on the unused portions of the disk at a later time.

Since most drives are faster than single speed, CD-R disks can be read faster than they can be written to. A 4X drive, for example, might be 4X when reading but only 2X when writing to a disk. A CD-R moves at a constant speed as the laser writes the data, and the data flow can't be interrupted. This means that the disk can't be stopped and it can't wait for data. Therefore, the faster the disk spins, the more data flow it will require. To generate the required amount of data flow, most CD-R drives use the SCSI interface, and a few use the faster ATAPI (IDE) interface.

11.1.4 Erasable CD (CD-E)

The **CD-E** is a CD that can be written to more than once. It is sometimes referred to as the *rewriteable* CD or CD-RW. Much like the CD-R, the CD-E is a polycarbonate disk with a molded pregrooved spiral. The disk is then covered with a special phase-change recording layer. When the surface is heated to a certain temperature and is then cooled, the special layer crystallizes. In its crystalline form, it reflects more light, much as a land does. If it is heated to a higher temperature and then cooled, it forms a noncystalline structure. The noncrystalline form does not reflect light very well and therefore acts as a pit. However, the media doesn't emulate the pits and lands as well as the CD-R disk does, so CD-Es do not work on all CD-ROM drives. The CD-E is not a perfect storage medium. Although the disk is being improved, it can be written to only a set number of times before the special layer does not change states anymore. The speed at which the CD-E is read is slow compared to the speed of a hard drive, and the writing of a CD-E disk is usually limited to 12X speed.

11.1.5 Digital Versatile or Video Disk (DVD)

The **digital video disk,** also called the digital versatile disc, is the newest type of compact disk, and it has the capability to store massive computer applications, such as a full multimedia encyclopedia, or a feature-length movie on one disk. The standard DVD-5 can hold up to 4.7 GB on a single-sided disk, and the DVD-10 can hold up to 9.4 GB on a double-sided disk. The increased capacity is the result of reduced track pitch and pit size and reduced error correction overhead. To increase the storage capacity even further, DVD technology allows a single side to be double layered. Distinguishing the individual layers requires focusing the laser on the desired layer, which increases the capacity of the disk to 8.5 GB on a side, or 17.0 GB total for a two-sided disk.

There are two basic types of DVD devices currently available: DVD-ROM drives and DVD-Video players. DVD-ROM drives attach to a computer and function like CD-ROM drives; DVD-Video players attach to a TV and function like a VCR. Depending on whether a disk is single or double sided and single or dual layered, the DVD disk can store up to 17.0 GB (enough for a 480-minute movie at 60 frames per second and 1,280 × 720 resolution) using MPEG-2 compression. See table 11.4. DVD standards are under development for DVD-Recordable drives (write once) DVD-RAM drives (rewritable). To get the full benefit of a DVD system, a DVD-Video board and an MPEG-2 decoder board are required, and in order to get Dolby AC-3 Digital Surround Sound, Dolby Pro Logic speakers or an AC-3-capable stereo receiver have to be added to the system. A single-speed (1X) DVD has a transfer

Table 11.4 DVD Drive Standards

Standard	Sides	Layers	Capacity	Playing Time
DVD-5	1	1	4.7 GB	133 min
DVD-9	1	2	8.5 GB	240 min
DVD-10	2	1	9.4 GB	266 min
DVD-18	2	2	17.0 GB	480 min

rate of 1,250 KB/s, which is almost nine times faster than the 1X CD-ROM. Therefore, a 2X DVD drive could have a transfer rate of 2,500 KB/s, but when playing back video, the 2X DVD drive still performs at the 1,250 KB/s because, like the audio CD, the video CD is time-sensitive.

DVD-Recordable (DVD-R) and DVD+Recordable (DVD+R) are recordable DVD formats similar to CD-R. A DVD-R can only record data once, and then the data becomes permanent on the disk. The disk cannot be recorded onto a second time. Two additional standards for DVD-R disks are DVD-RG for general use, and DVD-RA for authoring, which is used for mastering DVD video or data and is not typically available to the general public.

DVD-ReWritable (DVD-RW) and DVD+ReWritable (DVD+RW) are re-recordable DVD formats. The data on a DVD-RW disk can be erased and recorded over numerous times without damaging the medium. DVD-RW and DVD+RW are rewritable as many as 1,000 times. DVD-RW media come in only 4.7 and 9.4 GB.

DVD-RAM disks can be recorded and erased repeatedly but are only compatible with devices manufactured by the companies that support the DVD-RAM format. DVD-RAM disks are typically housed in cartridges. DVD-RAM is rewritable as many as 100,000 times.

DVD-R, DVD-RW, and DVD-RAM are supported by Panasonic, Toshiba, Apple Computer, Hitachi, NEC, Pioneer, Samsung, and Sharp as well as the DVD Forum. These formats are also supported by the DVD Forum. DVD+R and DVD+RW formats are supported by Philips, Sony, Hewlett-Packard, Dell, Ricoh, Yamaha, and others. DVDs can last more than 100 years except for DVD-RAM, which has a lifespan of more than 30 years.

Some systems will include a DVD decoder, which is used to decode MPEG-2 video and sound data before it is output. Although most DVD players include a DVD decoder card, it is possible to decode MPEG data using software, but requires a powerful processor so that it does not bog down the machine. Typically, the DVD decoder card will have connections for audio in, audio out, and video in, video out. In addition, there may be external ports for TV out and Dolby digital sound out.

11.1.6 Raw DAO-96

A sector on an audio CD holds 2,352 bytes, enough for 1/75 of a second of stereo sound. A sector on a MODE-1 CD-ROM holds 2,048 bytes of data. The 304 bytes are used for sector addressing, synchronization, and error correction. If you read a MODE-1 CD-ROM sector in "cooked" mode, you get 2,048 bytes of data. When you write that to a CD-R or CD-RW, the error correction bytes are reconstructed. If you read that sector in "raw" mode, you get all 2,352 bytes of data with the original error correction bytes.

One method to help protect disks (often used in games and in Windows XP) from being copied is to deliberately distort the error correction bytes. Therefore, when you perform a normal copy, the error corrections are recalculated and burned to the CD. As a result, the CD fails because it expected the original error correction bytes.

To make a copy of the original CD including the original 304 bytes used for sector addressing, synchronization, and error correction, you must copy in RAW DAO-96 mode. DAO is short for Disk At Once.

11.2 PERFORMANCE

Since hard drives can attain transfer rates of 16 MB/s and have access times as low as 9 ms, the fastest CD drives are significantly slower than even the slowest hard drives. Most CD drives use constant linear velocity (CLV), but some newer drives are using constant angular velocity (CAV). While CLV varies the rotational speed of the disk depending on the track being read, CAV does not. Therefore, when reading the outside of the disk, where there is more data, the CLV drive will have a higher transfer rate than when it is reading the inside of the disk. A CLV drive is faster than a CAV drive—a 12X CLV drive, for example, is faster than a 16X CAV drive because the 16X CAV is equivalent to a 6X to 16X CLV drive, depending on which track is being read.

Another factor in defining the performance of the CD drive is its access time. Access time is the average amount of time it takes to find a piece of data, and it is based on the speed change time, access time, and latency period. The speed change time is the time it takes for the spindle motor to change to the correct speed, depending on which track it is reading. The seek time is the time it takes for the drive to move the heads to the right location on the disk. The latency period is the amount of time it takes for the correct block of data to spin under the read assembly. The access time tends to be faster on the higher-speed drives.

Although the CD drive is slower than a hard drive, its performance can be significantly increased if parts of the RAM are used to cache the CD. As with the hard drive, the microprocessor's controller software controls the RAM cache area, which tries to anticipate what the microprocessor needs next. One method it uses is storing a copy of information that has been recently accessed. Information that has already been accessed may well be accessed again. Another method it uses is to read ahead an additional sector after the one being accessed. Whatever the method or methods used, when the disk needs to be accessed, the microprocessor will look in the cache area first. If it can't find the information, it will access the slower CD drive. The time it takes to search the cache area (RAM) is almost negligible compared to the time it takes to access the CD drive. If the needed information is found in the RAM, therefore, PC performance is greatly increased. Another form of cache is the hardware cache located on the CD controller card or the CD drive logic board. (This cache is not to be confused with the hardware cache located on the motherboard or within the microprocessor.) Much like its software counterparts, it fulfills the same functions as the RAM cache.

11.3 INSTALLATION

Internal CD drives are half-height devices designed to fit into a standard 5.25-in. open drive bay. Like other drives, it is typically held in place with four screws. External drive bays, of course, sit outside the computer. Much like hard drives, every CD drive contains a logic board. The logic board controls the drive and allows it to connect to the rest of the PC. Most drives today are either IDE/ATAPI, SCSI, or USB devices; some older systems connected through the parallel port or had a proprietary interface. Because compact disk drives are much slower than hard drives, connecting a compact disk drive and a hard drive on the same cable is not recommended.

11.3.1 IDE/ATAPI CD Drives

The most common interface used in the CD drive is the AT attachment packet interface (ATAPI) protocol associated with the enhanced IDE standard. The enhanced IDE is an improvement over the standard IDE interface and allows for CD drives, tape drives, and other storage devices.

When connecting IDE devices using a 40-pin IDE cable, the drives must be configured as stand-alone, master, or slave. (Note: An older sound card may have a 40-pin connector that is usually not an IDE connector but a proprietary CD-ROM connector.) If one drive is installed on a cable, that drive is a stand-alone drive. If two drives (hard drive, CD-ROM, or any other IDE device) are installed on the same cable, the primary drive is the master drive and the secondary drive is the slave drive. The master drive is so called because the controlling electronics on the logic board of the master drive control both the master drive and the slave drive. The stand-alone, master, and slave drives are determined by setting the jumpers on the hard drive. (Note: It does not matter where the drive and controller card are connected to the cable.) The enhanced IDE standard supports up to four IDE devices and two IDE cables. Each cable is its own channel with its own master and slave device. (Note: Performance may be improved if the IDE hard drive and the CD drive are installed on separate channels.)

In order to use an enhanced IDE device such as a CD-ROM drive, the BIOS must use the ATAPI protocol. If the system ROM BIOS does not support ATAPI, it needs to be either updated or modified, which can be done the following ways:

1. Install a newer system ROM chip that includes instructions in handling EIDE/ATA-2 hard drives
2. If the system ROM BIOS is flash ROM, update the ROM chip using special software
3. Supplement the system ROM BIOS chip with an EIDE controller card, which includes a ROM BIOS chip
4. Set the computer to recognize the drive and use software or a device driver (sometimes called a dynamic drive overlay) that includes instructions for handling EIDE hard drives

The most popular interface for the CD-ROM drive is IDE. The general steps to install a CD-ROM drive include:

1. Configure the jumpers (master, slave, or stand-alone). You should also check the jumpers on any other devices that are connected to the same IDE cable.
2. Slide the drive into the drive bay and secure it with screws.
3. Connect a power and IDE cable to the drive. Of course, pin 1 of the IDE cable (red or blue stripe) must be connected to pin 1 of the connector on the drive and controller card or motherboard.
4. Attach the audio cable from the CD drive to the sound card. Be sure *not* to connect the 3½-inch power connector to this connector.
5. Turn on the PC. Windows should automatically load the appropriate driver. If not, you will have to use the Add New Hardware applet. Windows will then assign the next available drive letter to the drive. With Windows 2000 and Windows XP, you can change the drivc letter by using the Device Manager or Disk Manager.

To install a DVD drive, perform the following steps:

1. Configure the jumpers (master, slave, or stand-alone). You should also check the jumpers on any other devices that are connected to the same IDE cable.
2. Slide the drive into the drive bay and secure it with screws.
3. Connect a power and IDE cable to the drive. Of course, pin 1 of the IDE cable (red or blue stripe) must be connected to pin 1 of the connector on the drive and controller card or motherboard.
4. Insert the DVD decoder card in an expansion slot and secure it with a screw.
5. Attach the audio cable from the DVD drive to the DVD decoder card. Be sure *not* to connect the 3½-inch power connector to this connector.
6. Connect the second audio cable to the audio out connect on the DVD decoder card and then to the audio in connection on the sound card.
7. Install the video loopback cable, which presents video data to the DVD decoder for decoding before the decoder sends the video data on to the monitor.
8. Turn on the PC. Windows should automatically load the appropriate driver. If not, you will have to use the Add New Hardware applet. Windows will then assign the next available drive letter to the drive. With Windows 2000 and Windows XP, you can change the drive letter by using the Device Manager or Disk Manager.

11.3.2 Small Computer System Interface (SCSI)

The standard SCSI interface allows up to seven devices (hard drives, tape drives, CD drives, removable drives and disks, and scanners) to be connected to one SCSI adapter/controller. It is most commonly used in higher-end systems and tends to provide better performance, though at a higher cost, than ATAPI drives. (Note: The SCSI-3 standard still under development has a single controller that can connect 16 or 128 devices, depending on its specification.) The SCSI devices are connected in series, forming a chain (daisy chain). The cables are characterized by the number of pins (50, 68, or 80 pins) and whether they are intended for internal or external use. The 50-pin connector (type A) has an 8-bit data path; the 68-pin (type P) and 80-pin cables have a 16-bit (wide) data path.

The SCSI devices, including the SCSI controller card and CD drive, are identified with a SCSI ID number ranging from 0 to 7, which are selected with jumpers, DIP switches, or a thumb wheel. The SCSI adapter is usually set to ID 7, and the primary SCSI hard drive (or any other boot device) is set to ID 0. The SCSI ID numbers do not have to be in order, nor do they have to be sequential. Of course, no two devices within the same chain can use the same SCSI ID number.

The SCSI devices at each end of the chain must be terminated; the other devices are not. On an internal cable, the adapter card and the device at the end of the cable need to be terminated but all the other devices in between are not. On an internal cable and an external cable, the two devices located at the end of each cable will be terminated, while other devices, including the adapter/controller card, will not be terminated. Terminating and not terminating a device is accomplished by either inserting or removing the terminators or enabling or disabling them with jumpers or DIP switches. Some SCSI devices have automatic termination.

11.3.3 Proprietary Interfaces

Some of the early CD-ROM drives were sold as part of a multimedia kit. These kits included a sound card that had a 40-pin proprietary interface for the CD-ROM drive, a cable, and a set of speakers. The three main proprietary interfaces are those developed by Panasonic, Sony, and Mitsumi. The biggest disadvantage of the proprietary interface is that it works only with a specific drive. Therefore, if the original drive is replaced, the interface probably will not work with the new drive. It's also difficult to tell the different proprietary interfaces apart, causing a lot of confusion for the service technician.

Another type of CD drive is the CD-ROM connected to the parallel port, specifically bidirectional parallel ports. Although these drives are portable and easily moved from computer to computer, they are much slower than the IDE and SCSI drives.

11.3.4 Software Drivers

After the CD drive is physically installed and configured, the final step to activating it is to load the device drivers and configure the operating system so that it recognizes the CD drive. This is usually done with an installation disk that comes with the CD drive or the controller card. Some operating systems will install the proper drivers automatically during installation. Some newer systems do not require drivers and will even boot from the CD-ROM drive.

In DOS and Windows 9X machines, EIDE CD drives require a device driver, which allows the operating system to control the CD-ROM drive, to be loaded in the CONFIG.SYS; SCSI drives usually require a device driver for the controller card and a device driver for the CD-ROM drive. Since there are many drives on the market, make sure that the driver matches the CD-ROM drive. Another driver needed to activate the CD drive is a file system extension, which enables the operating system to identify and use data from CDs attached to the system. For DOS, the file system extension is the Microsoft compact disk extension (MSCDEX.EXE), which is loaded in the AUTOEXEC.BAT. The file system extension is built into Windows 9X. (Note: If you boot a Windows 9X machine to Windows 95 DOS mode, the CONFIG.SYS will have the necessary device drivers but will not have the file system extension, MSCDEX.EXE, loaded. Therefore, it needs to be executed at the command prompt.)

11.3.5 Bootable CD Drives

Some system ROM BIOS chips support a bootable IDE-CD drive (El Torito standard) without any CD drivers being loaded. A bootable compact disk can be inserted in the drive; if the CMOS setup program is set to search the CD drive for a bootable disk, it will boot just like the A drive or the C drive. Note: Most systems will need to have their compact disk drive configured as the primary master drive. In addition, some SCSI interfaces with SCSI BIOS that permits bootable CDs can also be used. SCSI bootable CDs require INT13h.

For a CD disk to be bootable, it must contain a special version of the boot files found on any disk or hard drive to start a system. To create a bootable CD, you will need the following:

- A system in which the CD-ROM can be designated as a boot drive. Note: Check your BIOS to see if it supports bootable CDs.
- Mastering software, such as Adaptec Easy CD Creator, that allows creation of a bootable CD.
- A floppy disk containing your operating system boot files. Note: You can use the emergency recover disk created in Windows 95 or Windows 98. In addition, you will need to make sure that the CD-ROM drivers to the disk or verify that the Windows 98 startup disk will work with your CD-ROM drive.

The basic procedure for creating a bootable CD is as follows:

1. Create a bootable floppy for the operating system you want to install on the CD.
2. Get a blank CD-R and place it into your CD-R/CDRW drive.
3. Start your mastering software.
4. Under Disc layout, make sure that ISO 9660 is selected. See figure 11.5. Note: The ISO 9660 does not support long file names, so make sure your other files don't use long file names.
5. Make sure that the bootable option is enabled in the disk layout.
6. When prompted, insert the disk containing boot files into the A drive.

Figure 11.5 Software Used to Make a CD-R Bootable

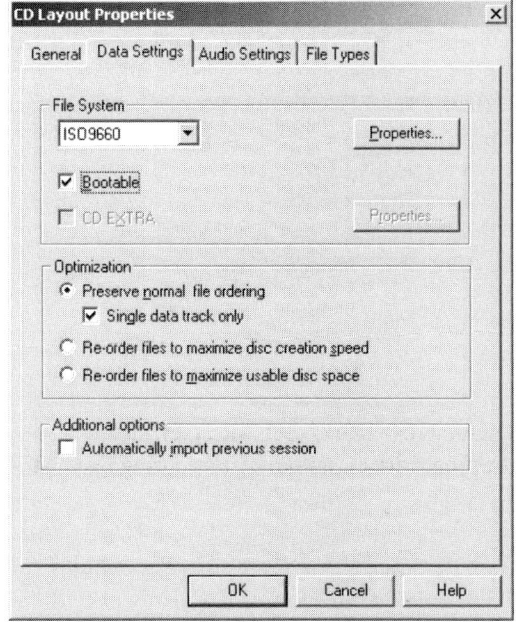

7. These files are copied to your CD layout. Note that the names of files are not the same as the normal operating system boot files. The files are called BOOTCAT.BIN and BOOTIMG.BIN.
8. Add additional files (image files, operating system install files, diagnostic files, etc.) to your layout.
9. Start the CD creation process.
10. When the process is completed, view the contents of the finished CD-R.
11. Close your mastering program, saving the layout if desired.
12. Insert the bootable CD you just created into your CD-ROM drive and restart the computer to see if your system boots from the CD.

Even through the bootable CD is able to start the computer, you will still need to add and load the appropriate software driver loaded in the CONFIG.SYS (device=*driver.sys*/d:mscd001) and the AUTOEXEC.BAT (mscdex/d:mscd001) on the CD.

11.4 ISO FILES

The ISO image is a single file containing an image of compact disk, which can be transferred to a CD-ROM disk. This file is typically obtained from the Internet. To transfer the ISO image to a CD, refer to the software and hardware documentation that comes with your writable CD drive. For example, if you have Adaptec/Roxio CD Creation loaded on your system, when you double-click the ISO file, it automatically starts CD Creation to create the disk.

11.5 TROUBLESHOOTING CD DRIVES

Problems with a CD drive or compact disk can be caused by the drive, compact disk, cable, power supply, drive configuration, or software configuration.

Example 11.1:

The computer cannot read the CD.

Most problems with the CD drive are caused by compact disks, such as dirty or scratched disks. Determine if the problem is with the drive or the disk by trying the disk in another computer. If the disk works, then the problem is with the drive. If the disk does not work, the problem is with the disk.

Many disk problems can be corrected by cleaning the disk with a special compact disk cleaning kit or by using a soft cloth. Compact disk cleaning solutions are also available. When cleaning the disk with a cloth, it is best to wipe the disk in a radial pattern beginning with the center and working toward the edge. Remember that the data on a standard compact disk is on the bottom of the disk, not the top. Deep scratches can sometimes be buffed out with a commercial plastic polish or cleaner that has a very mild abrasive.

A read problem caused by the drive could be corrected by cleaning the read lens. This is best done with a CD drive cleaner or with a can of compressed air. If the problem still exists, the drive, cable, or controller board should be replaced.

NOTE: CD drives use a laser beam, and you should never make eye contact with the beam. Always turn off the power before working inside a CD drive.

Example 11.2:

The computer does not recognize the CD-ROM drive.

This problem is caused by incorrect drive configuration, controller configuration, software configuration, a cable problem, or a power problem.

The easiest thing to check is the software configuration since that doesn't require opening the computer. For DOS and Windows 95 and 98, a device driver (a SYS file loaded in the CONFIG.SYS file) is needed for the IDE CD drive; a SCSI or proprietary drive needs a device driver for the SCSI controller card (if any). In addition, DOS needs the MSCDEX.EXE file loaded in the AUTOEXEC.BAT file, which should have the same drive signature as the device driver for the CD drive.

If the software configuration does not show a problem, the problem must be with the hardware. After opening the PC, the first thing to do is make sure the data and control cables are connected properly and that the drive has power. If everything is fine, the next item to check is the drive and controller card configuration. If the problem still exists, the drive, the controller card, or the cable must be bad. Therefore, each needs to be replaced, one at a time, until the bad component is discovered.

Example 11.3:

The CD drive will not accept or reject the compact disk.

When the drive will not accept or reject a disk, it usually has a mechanical problem. Of course, before replacing the drive, make sure that the power cable is connected to the drive and that nothing is jammed in the drive. If it appears the problem is with the drive, the drive would have to be replaced or repaired. Although you could try to repair the drive, it is easier to replace it.

NOTE: Some CD-ROM trays and caddies can be manually opened by inserting the end of a paper clip in a tiny hole located in the front of the drive.

SUMMARY

1. The compact disk (CD) is a 4.72-in. encoded platter, which is read by laser.
2. The CD-DA, also known as the audio CD, is the standard for the compact disk used in a stereo system. It can hold 74–80 minutes of high-fidelity audio.
3. The data is stored as lands and pits, which are etched in the aluminum coating.
4. Since the CD drive uses light to read the surface of the platter, dirt on the surface of the platter or dirt on the read assembly can cause errors.
5. Most CD drives use constant linear velocity (CLV) to access data, which allows for a constant data rate.
6. The CD-ROM (compact disk–read-only memory) is the standard compact disk used in the PC. It can hold 650–703 MB of data.

7. The standard for CD is known as the ISO 9660 standard.
8. The CD-R, also known as CD-WORM (write once, read many) and CD-WO (write once), can be written only once and cannot be changed after that.
9. The CD-E allows the CD to be written more than once.
10. Digital video disk (DVD) is the newest type compact disk, which has the capability to store 4.7 GB on a single-sided single layer and 17 GB of information on a double-sided double layer disk.
11. DVD-Recordable (DVD-R) and DVD+Recordable (DVD+R) are recordable DVD formats similar to CD-R.
12. DVD-ReWritable (DVD-RW) and DVD+ReWritable (DVD+RW) are re-recordable DVD formats.
13. DVD-RAM disks can be recorded and erased repeatedly but are compatible only with devices manufactured by the companies that support the DVD-RAM format.
14. CD disk drives will either use an EIDE (most common), a SCSI, a USB, or a proprietary interface.
15. When installing an IDE CD drive, the drive must be configured as a master, slave, or stand-alone drive.
16. When installing a SCSI CD drive, the SCSI ID number and the terminating resistors must be configured on the drive.
17. Most CD drives will require software drivers before they will function.
18. Some systems with ROM BIOS chips support a bootable IDE CD drive without any CD drivers being loaded.
19. Problems with a CD drive or compact disk can be caused by the drive, compact disk, cable, power supply, drive configuration, or software configuration.
20. Some systems will include a DVD decoder, which is used to decode MPEG-2 video and sound data before it is output.
21. Typically, the DVD decoder card will have connections for audio in, audio out, and video in, video out.
22. Many disk problems can be corrected by cleaning the disk with a special compact disk cleaning kit or by using a soft cloth. Compact disk cleaning solutions are also available.
23. When cleaning the disk with a cloth, it is best to wipe the disk in a radial pattern beginning with the center and working toward the edge.

QUESTIONS

1. Which type of compact disk is most commonly used to install applications and device drivers or to access multimedia libraries?
   a. CD-DA b. CD-ROM
   c. CD-R d. CD-E
   e. DVD
2. Which of the following is sometimes referred to as a WORM (write once, read many)?
   a. CD-DA b. CD-ROM
   c. CD-R d. CD-E
   e. DVD
3. Which of the following has the greatest capacity?
   a. CD-DA b. CD-ROM
   c. CD-R d. CD-E
   e. DVD
4. Which of the following will you *not* find as a CD drive interface?
   a. EIDE b. SCSI
   c. floppy drive d. proprietary
5. To make sure that all drives can read a CD, the CD must follow the
   a. Amiga standard.
   b. High Sierra standard.
   c. ISO 9660.
   d. DOS standard.
6. Which speed should the CD be playing at when playing an audio track?
   a. single speed b. double speed
   c. 12X speed d. 24X speed
7. A single-speed CD-ROM drive transfers data at
   a. 1 KB/s. b. 100 KB/s.
   c. 150 KB/s. d. 1 MB/s.
   e. 1.5 MB/s.
8. When installing an EIDE CD-ROM drive, you must configure the drive's (choose all that apply)
   a. terminating resistors.
   b. SCSI ID number.
   c. type (stand-alone, master, or slave).
   d. frequency modulation.
9. When installing a SCSI CD-ROM drive, you must configure the drive's (choose all that apply)
   a. terminating resistors.
   b. SCSI ID number.
   c. type (stand-alone, master, or slave).
   d. frequency modulation.
10. If the CD has a read/write error, you should
   a. throw away the disk.
   b. clean the disk.
   c. throw away the CD drive.
   d. replace the RAM.
11. When the CD drive is not being recognized by the system, the first thing you should check is the
   a. power connector. b. ribbon cable.
   c. drive. d. drivers.
12. You insert a Microsoft Office installation CD in your computer running DOS. The computer does not recognize the CD drive, although you can play audio compact disks by using the headphone jack

in the front of the drive. During boot-up, you notice that the driver is loaded. What is the problem?

a. the installation CD is not compatible with the drive
b. the installation CD is bad
c. the CD drive is bad
d. although the device driver is loaded, MSCDEX.EXE is not loaded

13. You recently created an emergency recovery CD for your Windows 98 computer. You did so by writing a compressed image of the system to a CD-RW using the ISO 9660 format and making the disk bootable. You now want to use the emergency recovery CD to restore your crashed system, but the system does not boot from the CD when you place the CD in the CD-ROM drive and reboot. What should you do first to solve this problem?
    a. replace the CD-ROM drive
    b. configure BIOS to boot from the CD-ROM
    c. make sure the CD-ROM drive is set to master
    d. change the disk format from ISO 9660 to Joliet
14. You are unable to access a CD-ROM loaded into the CD-ROM drive. Upon inspecting the CD-ROM disk, you find fingerprints and a smear of something resembling grape jam on the bottom surface of the CD. How should you clean the CD?
    a. send the CD back to the manufacturer for cleaning
    b. spray a lens cleaner or glass cleaner on a soft cloth and wipe in circles
    c. soak the CD in a lens cleaner or glass cleaner for several minutes and air dry
    d. spray a lens cleaner or glass cleaner on a soft cloth and wipe from the inside of the disk to the outer edge
15. Which specification must a computer system support to boot from the Windows 9X or Windows 2000 CD-ROM?
    a. El Torito
    b. ISO 2997
    c. IEEE 1394
    d. El Segundo

HANDS-ON EXERCISES

Exercise 1: Installing an IDE CD-ROM Drive

1. Configure the IDE CD-ROM drive as either a master, slave, or stand-alone, as appropriate.
2. If the system already has an IDE device, configure the device as either a master, slave, or stand-alone, as appropriate.
3. Connect the CD to the appropriate IDE channel.
4. Boot the system and install the appropriate drivers for the CD drive.
5. Insert a CD into the drive and test it.
6. Remove the CD-ROM drive and reconfigure the system.

Exercise 2: Installing a SCSI CD-ROM Drive

1. Configure the SCSI drive's SCSI ID number and terminating resistors.
2. Connect the CD to the appropriate SCSI connector.
3. Boot the system and install the appropriate drivers for the CD drive.
4. Insert a CD into the drive and test it.
5. Remove the CD-ROM drive and reconfigure the system.

CHAPTER 12

The Disk Structure

Topics Covered in This Chapter

Introduction

Because the data on the disk is the most important part of the computer, it is necessary to protect the integrity of the disk. Disk problems and errors can occur without warning and may easily result in data loss. To recognize and correct problems with the disk structure, you must have a good understanding of the general layout of the disk.

Objectives

1. Describe the disk boot sequence.
2. Define *master boot record* and describe how it relates to the partition table.
3. Partition a hard drive to one or more partitions as needed.
4. Describe the file allocation table.
5. Explain how the file allocation table relates to clusters or allocation units.
6. Describe how a file is retrieved using a file allocation table and directory.
7. List and describe the common file systems used in Windows and Linux.
8. Explain how disk compression works.
9. Given a disk problem, identify and correct the problem.
10. Run the SCANDISK and DEFRAG programs on a volume.

12.1 WHAT IS DISK STRUCTURE?

The disk structure does not describe how a hard drive or floppy disk physically works but how it stores files on the disk. In other words, it describes the formatting of the disk (file system, partitions, the root directory, and the directories). Since the data on the disk is the most important part of the computer, it is necessary to protect the integrity of the disk. Disk problems and errors can occur without warning and may easily result in data loss.

12.2 BOOT SEQUENCE

To boot the computer is to make it operational and to load the operating system into RAM. The process begins with turning on the on/off switch, and, if everything goes well, it usually ends with a command prompt or a GUI interface. During this time, the system ROM BIOS is looking for an operating system to boot.

By default, the system ROM BIOS will begin searching the volume boot sector of drive A, which is the first sector on the A drive (cylinder 0, head 0, sector 1), for the operating system boot files. If a disk is in the drive but the sector cannot be read or there is no disk in the drive, the system ROM BIOS continues to the hard drive. The system ROM BIOS looks for the master partition boot sector at cylinder 0, head 0, sector 1 of the first physical drive (drive C) and then reads the partition table to see which partition is active (marked as bootable).

It then searches the volume boot sector of the active partition and looks at the first sector for the operating system boot files. Depending on the operating system, some of the boot files are:

DOS	IO.SYS and MSDOS.SYS
Windows 9X	IO.SYS
Windows NT, Windows 2000, and Windows XP	NTLDR
Linux	LILO or GRUB boot manager

12.3 BOOT SECTORS AND PARTITIONS

The **master boot record (MBR)** is always found on the first sector of a hard drive (master boot sector). It tells the system ROM BIOS how the hard drive is divided and which part to boot from. The first 466 bytes consist of a special program code called the **bootstrap loader,** which locates the first active or bootable partition on the disk. The next 2 bytes of this 512-byte sector are an identification header, and the last 44 bytes contain the **master partition table,** which lists all partitions on the hard drive.

Partitioning is the defining and dividing of the physical drive into logical volumes called *partitions*. Each partition functions as if it were a separate hard disk. Therefore, although it is the physical drive that is installed and configured, the logical drive is the drive the system "thinks" it has. All hard drives must have at least one partition. (Note: Because floppy disks are small, they do not have partitions; the entire disk is considered a volume.)

The partition table is defined with the FDISK utility or an equivalent program. (See section 12.10.) Each entry in the partition table is 16 bytes of data and contains the following:

1. Start of the partition in CHS coordinates
2. End of the partition in CHS coordinates
3. Start of the partition in LBA coordinates
4. Number of sectors for the partition
5. Partition type
6. Active flag

CHS coordinates express a location in cylinder-head-sector terms; the LBA (logical block addressing) coordinate defines the actual number of the sector. The boot sector is in the first sector. Where the partition expressed in LBA mode ends can be calculated by adding the start of the partition in LBA coordinates and the number of sectors in the partition. The partition type (see table 12.1.) defines the type of file system being used; for example, 12-bit FAT, 16-bit FAT, NTFS, and extended partitions. (See section 12.6.) Three kinds of partitions are found in PCs: primary, extended, and logical. Only four primary partitions (the partition table has only four entries) can exist on one drive, one of which can be an extended partition (a BIOS limitation). The extended partition can contain many logical partitions. Every hard disk drive must have at least one partition. IDE disks can have up to 16 partitions and SCSI disks can have up to 15. Of the primary partitions, only one can be marked active because the computer can boot from only one partition. If the MBR cannot locate a bootable partition, it will issue the "Missing Operating System" error message.

In most versions of FDISK, the first sector of a partition, the volume boot sector, will be aligned so that it is at head 0, sector 1 of a cylinder. This means that there may be unused sectors on the track prior to the first sector of a partition and unused sectors following a partition table sector. Some software packages and drivers will use these spaces to "lock down," or secure, the system or to overcome limitations of the hard drive or system ROM BIOS. Unfortunately, these unused spaces are also good places for boot sector virus programs to hide.

The **volume boot sector (VBS),** the first sector of any partition or the first sector of a floppy disk, is created by a high-level format program (DOS's FORMAT program or equivalent). Within the VBS, the media parameter block or disk parameter block contains information used by the operating system to verify the capacity of the disk volume as well as to determine the location of the file allocation table. The VBS also contains the partition's boot program, which checks and executes the necessary boot files (IO.SYS or MSDOS.SYS, WINBOOT.SYS, or NTLDR).

12.4 FILE ALLOCATION TABLES

When you save a file, the file can be stored at the beginning, the middle, or the end of the disk. When you retrieve a file, you do not worry about its physical location. Instead, you specify a name (and sometimes the path) and the operating system finds the file. The directory structure, methods for organizing a volume (a partition or floppy disk), and how the system stores and retrieves a file is called the *file system*.

Table 12.1 Common Partition Types and Their Values

Partition Type	Value	Partition Type	Value
No allocated partition in this entry	00	Hidden FAT16	16
DOS 12-bit FAT	01	Hidden HPFS/NTFS	17
XENIX root	02	PartitionMagic	3C
XENIX usr	03	Dynamic disk volume	42
DOS 16-bit ≤32M	04	Novell	51
Extended	05	IBM 386/ix, UNIX System V/386 or GNU HURD	63
DOS 16-bit ≥32	06	Novell Netware 286	64
OS/2 HPFS/NTFS	07	Novell Netware 386	65
AIX	08	Old MINIX	80
AIX bootable	09	Linux/MINUX	81
OS/2 Boot Manager	0A	Linux swap	82
Win95 FAT32	0B	Linux native	83
Win95 FAT32 (LBA)	0C	Linux extended	85
Win95 FAT16 (LBA)	0E	BSD/386	A5
Win95 Extended (LBA)	0F	OpenBSD	A6
Hidden FAT12	11	CP/M	DB
Compaq Diagnostic	12	UNIX Bad Block Table	FF
Hidden FAT16 ≤32M	14		

Disks are divided into a circular grid consisting of tracks and sectors. **Tracks** are concentric circles; that is, the circles share the same center, much like rings in a tree. Tracks are numbered sequentially, starting with the outside track as track 0, and are further divided into **sectors,** 512-byte chunks of usable data. Sectors on a track are numbered starting with 1. For operating systems, the most basic storage unit is not a sector but a **cluster** (also called an *allocation unit*). It consists of one or more sectors (usually more than one), the size of the cluster depending on the operating system, the version of the operating system, the file system the operating system is using, and the size of the volume (partition or floppy disk).

The **file allocation table (FAT)** is an index used to "remember" which file is located in which cluster. It lists each cluster in a partition (or floppy disk), whether the cluster is being used by a file, the name of the file in the cluster, and all the clusters the file takes up.

Question:

Why doesn't the file allocation table list each sector?

Answer:

Grouping sectors into clusters reduces the number of entries in the file allocation table, making the table smaller and thus enabling it to be searched faster. This allows the operating system to retrieve a file more quickly.

Unfortunately, because an entry in the file allocation table can be only one file, the space remaining is unused and wasted if a file doesn't use the entire cluster.

Example 12.1:

A partition is using clusters consisting of eight sectors (4,096 bytes). A file that is 2,048 bytes will have an entry for the cluster and file belonging to the cluster in the file allocation table. Although the file is only half the size of the cluster, the file allocation table can list only one file for that allocation unit. Therefore, the entire 4,096-byte sector will be used for the 2,048-byte file.

Example 12.2:

A partition is using clusters consisting of eight sectors (4,096 bytes). A file of 8,193 bytes would therefore be listed as three entries in the file allocation table. The first part of the file is stored in one cluster. After the first cluster is filled, there are still 4,097 bytes left over. Therefore, the entry for the first cluster will list the location of the second cluster occupied by the file. (Note: The cluster may or may not be the next one.) The second cluster would then be filled up, but 1 byte would be left over. Again, the second cluster would list the third cluster, where this last byte of the file resides. Since the file allocation table can list only one file per cluster, the single byte would take up the entire 4,096 bytes of disk space in the third cluster.

The larger the cluster, the more disk space the system tends to waste. Therefore, some people divide their hard drives into smaller partitions to use space more efficiently.

The file allocation table is created during the high-level format process—when using the FORMAT.COM command or equivalent program, for example. The table is stored in the space immediately following the volume boot sector. Each volume actually has two file allocation tables, the second being a duplicate of the first one. When an entry is changed in one file allocation table, both allocation tables are changed. The second table is read only when the first one can't be read. Unfortunately, most operating systems place the two file allocation tables next to each other, and so if one becomes physically damaged, there is a good chance the other table would also be damaged. Of course, if the file allocation table is lost, there is no index of where the files are located, resulting in a loss of data.

12.5 DIRECTORIES, FILES, AND ATTRIBUTES

The model for storage in the PC is based on an inverted directory tree structure. Every volume has a starting point called the **root directory,** located at the top of the tree structure. The root directory holds files and directories. The **directories** under the root directory are also referred to **subdirectories.** (Note: Newer operating systems may refer to a directory as a *folder*.) Each directory can also hold files and more subdirectories.

12.5.1 The Root Directory

The root directory is typically located directly after the two copies of the file allocation tables. It is not like the other directories within a volume. First, there can be only one root directory for any disk volume. In addition, the root directory is usually limited to a certain size and therefore can have only a certain number of entries. See table 12.2. When the maximum number of files and subdirectories in the root directory is reached, no more can be added even though plenty of disk space may be left. Subdirectories and root directories in newer operating systems such as FAT32 do not have to follow the file allocation table and so have no limits on the number of entries in the root directory.

NOTE: Long file names in the older file systems use multiple directory entries.

12.5.2 Directories and Files

Every file on the system is stored in a directory. The directory, a specially marked file, is a table that contains information about the files and subdirectories stored within it.

Table 12.2 The Maximum Number of Root Directory Entries Under FAT

Volume Type	Maximum Number of Root Directory Entries
360 KB 5¼-in. floppy disk	112
720 KB 3½-in. floppy disk	112
1.2 MB 5¼-in. floppy disk	224
1.44 MB 3½-in. floppy disk	224
2.88 MB 3½-in. floppy disk	448
Hard disk	512

Table 12.3 DOS Directory Format

Content	Size
File name	8 bytes
File extension	3 bytes
File attributes	1 byte
Reserved	10 bytes
Time of creation	2 bytes
Date of creation	2 bytes
Starting cluster	2 bytes
Size in bytes	4 bytes

For DOS systems, every directory, including the root directory, consists of a small database. Each entry in the database contains 32 bytes of information. See table 12.3. Although in most operating systems the number of entries in the root directory is fixed, the number of entries in directories is not fixed. If a directory needs more space for more entries, it will expand to another cluster. A directory entry in DOS will use 11 bytes for the entire file name, 8 bytes for the file name, and 3 bytes for the extension. The file name is meant to identify the file, so the name should represent the contents of the file. The extension is used to identify the type of file. For example, files that have a DOC extension are usually Microsoft Word documents, and files that have EXE or COM extension are executable files. See table 12.4. (Note: To indicate that a file is deleted, the operating system changes the first character of the file name to a lowercase sigma (σ). This way, assuming that all of the clusters are intact and have not been used by other files, a file can be undeleted by substituting another character for the sigma). If all eight characters (bytes) available for the file name are not used and the three characters for the file extension are not used, the leftover bytes become spaces. (Note: The dot separating the file name and the extension is not stored as part of the file allocation table or the directory. It is shown by the operating system to indicate a separation between the two.)

After the bytes reserved for the file name and extension, 1 byte is used for file attributes. The **file attribute** field stores a number of characteristics about each file, the most common attributes being read-only, hidden, system, and archive. See table 12.5. Attributes can be either on or off. If the file has the particular characteristic, the file attribute is on; if it doesn't, the file attribute is off. (Note: One of these attributes indicates whether the file is a real file or a directory.) Since DOS reserves 1 byte for attributes, it can keep track of up to eight attributes (remember, 1 byte equals 8 bits). The ATTRIB command or Explorer is used to change file attributes.

Next, DOS and other operating systems also record the date and time that the file or directory was created or modified and the size of the file in bytes. The files are stamped with the date and time from the real-time clock (RTC) on the motherboard. If, of course, the RTC clock is not set to the correct date and time, the file will also have the incorrect date and time.

Table 12.4 Common File Name Extensions

Ext.	Description	Ext.	Description
.avi	Audio/Video Interleaved—movie clip—open with *mplayer,* IE, or Navigator with plugin	.mov	QuickTime movie file
.bak	backup file, which is used by many applications—often created automatically	.mp3	audio file in MP3 format—CD-quality sound, with 10x compression
.bat	DOS batch file	.mpg	Video movie in MPEG format (Motion Picture Experts Group)
.bmp	Microsoft bitmap graphic file	msi	Windows Installer File
.cab	Microsoft installation archive (cabinet file)—similar to .zip archive	.old	backup file (generic)
.csv	Comma Separated Variable file—a way of presenting tabular data in a text file—usually viewed in MS Excel	.pdf	Portable Document Format, which is opened using Adobe Acrobat reader
.com	executable file	.png	graphic in Portable Network Graphics format
.dat	data file, which is used by several applications	.ppt	Microsoft PowerPoint file, which is used for creating slides and overhead presentations
.dll	dynamic link library, software used by Windows to provide services to applications	.ram	Real Audio file
.doc	Microsoft Word file	rar	compressed file
.dot	Microsoft Word template	.rtf	Rich Text Format, a generic word-processor file with formatting codes
.drv	older device driver	.scr	screen saver
.exe	self-extracting or executable file—run by double-clicking in Win95	.sys	DOS system file, a device driver, or hardware configuration info
.fnt	font file	.tif	Tagged Image File graphic format
.gif	graphic in GIF format	.tmp	temporary file used by many programs
.htm	hypertext document, which is opened in a web browser	.ttf	True Type Font file
.ico	Windows icon	.txt	text file that contains only ASCII code
.ini	initialization file, which is a configuration used by Windows and many applications	.wav	sound file in Waveform format
.jpg	graphic in JPEG format (Joint Photographic Experts Group) program	.xls	Microsoft Excel worksheet file
.log	data file created by many applications, usually a text file	.xml	extensible markup language used in web pages
.mid	audio file in MIDI format	.zip	compressed file created and opened with WinZip or PKZip.

Table 12.5 DOS File Attributes

Attribute	Abbreviation	Description
Read-only	R or RO	When a file is marked as read-only, it cannot be deleted or modified. (Note: The opposite of read-only is read-write.)
Hidden	H	When a file is marked as hidden, it cannot be seen during normal directory listings.
System	S or Sy	When a file is marked as system, it should not be moved. In addition, it usually can't be seen during normal directory listings.
Volume label		The name of the volume.
Subdirectory		A table that contains information about files and subdirectories.
Archive	A	When a file is marked as archive, it has not been backed up. Anytime a file is new or has been changed, the operating system automatically turns on the archive attribute, indicating that the file needs to be backed up. When the archive attribute is off, the file is not new or changed and does not have to be backed up.

The last part of the entry is the number of the cluster that starts the file or subdirectory. When a file is retrieved from a subdirectory, the system reads the directory first to find the starting point of the file and, since files are often bigger than one cluster, it then goes to the file allocation table to find the location of the second cluster, the third cluster, and so on until the file has been retrieved into RAM.

Every directory, excluding the root directory, has two additional entries. The first one is the "." (single dot), which indicates the current directory and its location. The second one is the ".." (double dot), which indicates the parent directory and its location. When performing the CD.. command at the prompt or by clicking on the .. within Windows dialog boxes, the double-dot entry tells the operating system to jump to the location of the parent directory.

Each file, a collection of related information that is referenced by name, or directory on a volume can be uniquely identified by using the file name (including the file extension, if any) and the path (or location on the tree). Files are stored in clusters. Since files are often larger than a cluster, a file will be spread among many clusters. On the last cluster, to indicate the end of a file, a special end-of-file (EOF) character is used so the operating system knows to ignore the rest of the cluster since it does not have any valid data. The file allocation table and the directory work very closely together. The file name is entered to open a file. The system looks in the specified directory. If no directory is specified, it looks in the current directory. After the system finds the file name, it looks at the starting cluster and reads the data. The operating system then jumps to the file allocation table, specifically the starting cluster, to read the next cluster where the file is located. It then jumps to the next cluster and retrieves that data. It will continue jumping between the file allocation table to find the next cluster and the clusters to retrieve the data until it gets to the EOF.

12.6 MICROSOFT FILE SYSTEMS

Different file systems have been used for the PC. The most common file systems are shown in table 12.6. DOS and Windows support the following file systems:

- DOS and Windows 95A support FAT (up to 2 GB).
- Windows 95B, Windows 98, and Windows Millennium support FAT (up to 2 GB) and FAT32.
- Windows NT supports FAT and NTFS4 (NTFS5 with Service Pack 4 or higher).
- Windows 2000 and Windows XP support FAT, FAT32, and NTFS5.

When using FDISK with Windows 95B or later, you can create either FAT or FAT32 partitions. When you first start FDISK with hard drives larger than 512 MB, it will ask if you want to support large disks.

Table 12.6 Common Microsoft File Systems

System Type	FAT	FAT32	NTFS
Operating systems	Used by DOS and all Microsoft Windows versions	Used by Windows versions since 95B/OSR2	Used by the Windows NT family
Long filenames	VFAT supports up to 255 characters	Up to 255 characters	Up to 255 characters
Maximum path length	FAT supports up to 255 characters VFAT supports up to 260 characters	Up to 260 characters	Up to 255 characters
Volume size	Floppy disk to 4 GB	512 MB to 32 GB	10 MB to 2 TB
Maximum file size	2 GB	4 GB	Limited by size of volume
Limit on entries in root directory	Yes	No	No
File and directory security	No	No	Yes
Directory and file compression	No	No	Yes
Cluster remapping	No	No	Yes

NOTES:

* While FAT16 can be up to 4 GB, FAT16 volumes larger than 2 GB are not accessible from computers running MS-DOS or Windows 9X and many other operating systems. This limitation occurs because these operating systems do not support cluster sizes larger than 32 KB, which results in the 2 GB limit.

** In theory, FAT32 volumes can be up to about 8 terabytes; however, the maximum FAT32 volume size that Windows XP Professional can format is 32 GB. Therefore, you must use NTFS to format volumes larger than 32 GB. However, Windows XP Professional can read and write to larger FAT32 volumes formatted by other operating systems.

If you want to create a FAT partition, you would say No. If you want to create a FAT32 partition, you would say Yes.

While Windows 2000 and Windows XP do support NTFS5, they do not support earlier versions of NTFS (NTFS4). When you use Windows 2000 or Windows XP to access an NTFS4 volume, Windows will automatically convert an NTFS volume to NTFS5 format when Windows mounts the volume.

12.6.1 FAT

The most common file system is the **file allocation table (FAT).** It is the standard file system used by DOS, Windows 95. FAT is a simple and reliable file system and uses minimal memory. Because of its cluster sizes, it is not as efficient for partitions larger than 32 MB. It supports file names of 11 characters, which include 8 characters for the file name and 3 characters for the file extension.

Older DOS systems used FAT12. In FAT12, a 12-bit binary number is used to number each cluster. The biggest cluster number that FAT12 could see, therefore, was 4,086, which would have been 4,096 except that some clusters are reserved. FAT12 is still used on floppy disks and hard disk partitions smaller than 16 MB. See table 12.7. Most current DOS systems use FAT16, which, instead of a 12-bit number uses a 16-bit number to number the clusters, giving 65,526 clusters. References to FAT probably mean FAT16. It is used for volumes up to 2 GB. See table 12.8.

VFAT is an enhanced version of the FAT structure that allows Windows to support long file names (LFN) of up to 255 characters. If someone refers to a FAT partition in a Windows operating system, they are probably talking about VFAT. Because it is built on ordinary FAT, each file has to have an 8-character name and 3-character extension to be backward compatible to DOS and Windows 3.XX applications. Programs running in DOS and Windows 3.XX will not see the longer file names. WIN32 programs (programs made for Windows IX or Windows NT family) can see and make use of the longer names. To accommodate both the DOS file names and the long file names, VFAT uses additional directory entries to store the long file names. When a long file name is saved, the first entry will be a trun-

Table 12.7 Cluster Size for Floppy Disks

Disk Type	Number of Sectors	Number of Bytes
3½-in. DS/DD disk (720 KB)	2	1,024
3½-in. DS/HD disk (1.44 MB)	1	512

Table 12.8 Cluster Size for Hard Drives

Volume Size	Number of Sectors	Number of Bytes	FAT Type
0 MB to 16 MB	8	4,096	12-bit
More than 16 MB to 128 MB	4	2,048	16-bit
More than 128 MB to 256 MB	8	4,096	16-bit
More than 256 MB to 512 MB	16	8,192	16-bit
More than 512 MB to 1,024 MB	32	16,384	16-bit
More than 1,024 MB to 2,048 MB	64	32,768	16-bit

cated name (known as the *alias*) for the file. Additional directory entries will hold the rest of the long file name. Each entry is 32 bytes in length. A single long file name can use many directory entries (since each entry is only 32 bytes in length), and for this reason it is recommended that long file names not be placed in the root directory, where the total number of directory entries is limited.

Example 12.3:

The first entry for a file called *The Budget for 1999 and 2000.DOC* saved in Windows 95 or 98 will use the first six characters, ignoring the spaces and adding a tilde (~) followed by a number, and appear in the directory as *THEBUD ~ 1.DOC*. A DOS or Windows 3.XX program would see *THEBUD ~ 1.DOC*; Windows 95 and 98 and Windows NT programs would see *The Budget for 1999 and 2000.DOC*. Of course, it would take several directory entries to store the alias and a couple more to save the long file name. A second file saved with the name *The Budget for 2000 and 2001.DOC* would have the alias *THEBUD ~ 2.DOC*.

To make sure that DOS and Windows 3.XX do not use the directory entries that hold the long file names, the entries have the read-only, hidden, system, and volume attributes enabled. With all of these labels active, older software basically ignores the extra directory entries being used by VFAT. Disk problems can be caused by older utilities in an operating system that does not know how to handle VFAT because they will usually truncate the long file names or cause other problems. Make sure that Windows 95 or 98 SCANDISK, DEFRAG, or similar utilities made specifically for Windows 95 and 98 or VFAT are installed.

12.6.2 FAT32

FAT32, with 32-bit FAT entries, was introduced with the second major release of Windows 95 (OSR2/Windows 95B) and is an enhancement of the FAT file system. It supports hard drives up to 2 terabytes (TB) and uses space more efficiently. It has, for example, 4 KB clusters for drives up to 8 GB, which results in a 15 percent more efficient use of disk space in large FAT drives. Unlike VFAT, all of Microsoft's disk utilities (DEFRAG and SCANDISK) have been revised to work with FAT32. FAT32 supports long file names up to 255 characters.

FAT32's root directory is an ordinary cluster chain and can, therefore, be located anywhere in the drive. In addition, the system allows dynamic resizing of FAT32 partitions (without losing data) and the disabling of FAT mirroring, which allows a copy of the FAT other than the first to be active. Consequently, FAT32 drives are less prone to the failure of critical data areas such as the FAT. In addition FAT32 is faster than FAT.

The FDISK utility from Windows 95 OSR2/Windows 95B must be used to install FAT32 on a volume on a hard drive over 512 MB. The utility will ask whether to enable large disk support. If the answer is yes, any partition that is greater than 512 MB will be marked as a FAT32 partition. At this time, Windows 95 (OSR2/Windows 95B), Windows 98, Windows Me, Windows 2000, and Windows XP are the only operating systems capable of accessing FAT32 volumes. Windows 3.1, MS-DOS, the original version of Windows 95, and Windows NT do not recognize FAT32 partitions and are not able to boot from a FAT32 volume.

Windows 98 and Windows Me have a Drive Converter (FAT32) program that will convert FAT/VAT program to FAT32. To start the program, click the Start button, select the Programs option, select the Accessories option, select the System Tools option, and select the Drive Convert (FAT32) program.

NOTE: The Drive Converter (FAT32) program is CVT1.EXE, which is located in the Windows folder.

12.6.3 NTFS

NTFS (NT file system) is a new file system for Windows NT. Because it was designed for both the server and workstation, it has many enhancements and features built into it. It supports long file names (up to 255 characters), yet maintains an 8.3 name for DOS and Windows 3.XX programs. The NTFS is a 64-bit architecture and is designed to support drive sizes up to 2^{64} bytes (18,446,744,073,709,551,616 bytes = 16 exabytes).

When you create (format) an NTFS volume, the high-level format program creates a set of files that contain the metadata used to implement the file system structure. The NTFS file system uses approximately 1 MB for the metadata files. (See table 12.9.)

Windows NT includes enhanced security and supports a variety of multiuser security models. It allows computers running other operating systems, including DOS, Windows 3.XX, Windows 95, Windows NT Workstation, UNIX, POSIX, and even Macintosh computers, to save files to the NTFS volume on an NT server. It does not allow DOS to access an NTFS volume directory directly but only through the network (assuming the operator has the proper permissions or rights to access the volume). It can compress individual files or directories, including infrequently used files or directories. To make an NTFS volume more resistant to failure, NTFS writes updates to a log area. If a system crash occurs, the log area can be used to quickly clean up problems.

Table 12.9 NTFS File System

System File	File Name	Description
Master File Table	$Mft	The file allocation table for the NTFS volume that lists all contents of the NTFS volume
Master File Table2	$MftMirr	A mirror or copy of the Master File Table, used when a Master File Table becomes unreadable
Log File	$LogFile	A list of transaction steps, used by the Log File System for recoverability
Volume	$Volume	The name, version, and other information about the volume
Attribute Definitions	$AttrDef	A table of attribute names, numbers, and descriptions
Root Filename Index	$.	Root directory
Cluster Bitmap	$Bitmap	A representation of the volume showing which allocation units are in use
Partition Boot Sector	$Boot	Includes the bootstrap for the volume, if this is a bootable volume
Bad Cluster File	$BadClus	A location where all the bad clusters in the volume are located
Quota Table	$Quota	Disk quota usage for each user on a volume
Uppercase Table	$Upcase	Used for converting lowercase characters to the matching Unicode uppercase characters

Although FAT is simpler and smaller than NTFS. NTFS is generally faster because it minimizes the number of disk accesses required to find a file, which makes access to the file faster, especially if it is a large folder. In addition, it tries to keep the hard drive unfragmented. Unlike the other file systems. NTFS supports a "volume set," the combination of several hard drives (or parts of hard drives) into a single volume. If the volume needs to be expanded, another hard drive is added.

The NTFS file system used on Windows NT 4.0 was known as NTFS4, and the NTFS file system used on Windows 2000 and Windows XP was NTFS5. The changes required to update NTFS4 to NTFS5 were implemented in Windows NT 4.0 Service Pack 4. Upgrading a system from Windows NT 4.0 to Windows 2000 will also update the NTFS4 volumes to NTFS5 volumes. Unfortunately, if a Windows NT computer does not have Service Pack 4 or higher, it will not be able to directly use the NTFS5 volume.

Some of the updates included with NTFS5 volume included the ability to encrypt files or folders to protect them. It had the ability to mount NTFS volumes onto an NTFS folder without assigning additional drive letters. It also had the ability to retain shortcuts and other file information when files were transferred between volumes. In addition, NTFS5 had disk quotas to monitor and control disk usage and had full text and property indexing to allow fast retrieval of documents.

(Note: You can set up a computer to dual-boot between Windows 95 and Windows NT 4.0 and have both operating systems access the same files if they are both running VFAT. Remember that Windows 95 cannot read or access NTFS and Windows NT 3.51 or 4.0 cannot read or access FAT32. In addition, drive compression for Windows 95 and Windows NT are not compatible.)

In Windows NT, Windows 2000, or Windows XP, one way to convert a partition or volume to NTFS is reformat it. Of course, all information on the volume will then be lost. Another way to convert a FAT/VFAT or FAT32 partition or volume to NTFS volume or partition would be to use the convert command:

```
CONVERT x: /FS:NTFS
```

where *x*: is the drive letter that you want to convert.

12.7 LINUX FILE SYSTEMS

On a Linux machine, the file system structure is quite different. First, Linux treats all devices as files and has actual files that represent each device. In Linux, these device files are located in the /dev directory. Linux file names are similar to MS-DOS file names except that they do not use drive letters such as A and C and they substitute the slash (/) for the MS-DOS backslash as the separator between directory names.

Because Linux treats a device as a file in the /dev directory, the hard disk names start with /dev. Table 12.10 lists the hard disk and floppy drive names that you may have to use. Of course, when you use the Red Hat Disk Druid or Linux fdisk program to prepare the Linux partitions, you have to identify the disk drive by its name such as /dev/hda.

Table 12.10 Hard Disk and Floppy Drive Names

Device Type	Name	Description
IDE hard drives	/dev/hda	First IDE hard drive (typically the C drive)
	/dev/hdb	Second IDE hard drive
SCSI hard drives	/dev/sda	First SCSI hard drive
	/dev/sdb	Second SCSI hard drive
Floppy disks	/dev/fd60	First floppy drive (A drive)
	/dev/fd1	Second floppy drive (B drive)

Figure 12.1 Sample Linux File System Using Mounted Points

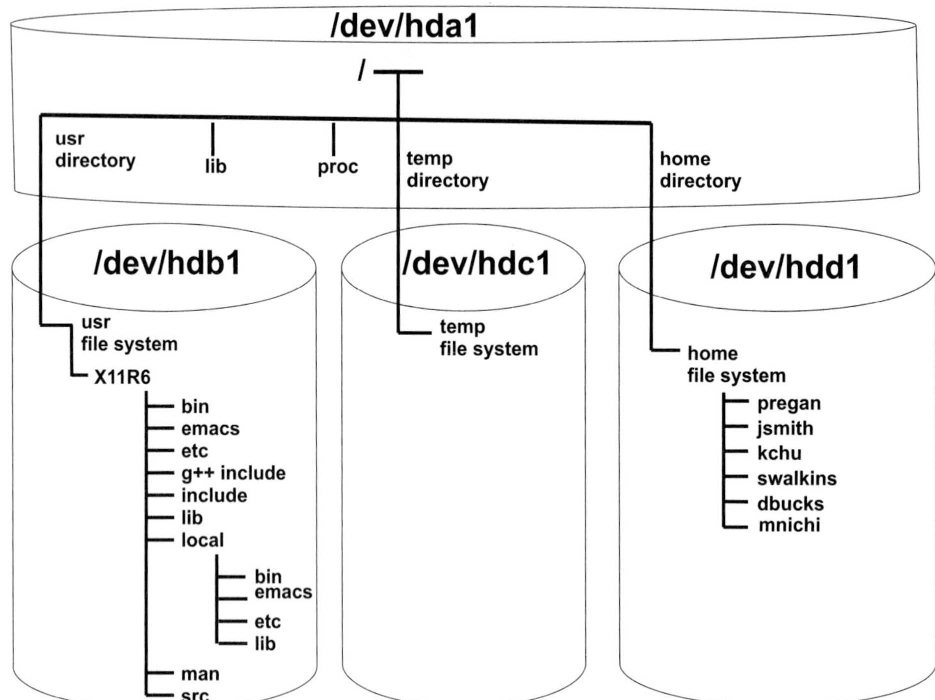

When Disk Druid or fdisk displays the list of partitions, the partition names are /dev/hda1, /dev/hda2, and so on. Linux constructs each partition name by appending the partition number (1 through 4 for the four primary partitions on a hard disk) to the disk name. Therefore, if your PC's single IDE hard drive has two partitions, the installation program uses /dev/hda1 and /dev/hda2 as the names of these partitions.

DOS and Windows use drive letters to identify logical drives or partitions that may be on the one hard drive or several hard drives. Each drive has a root directory and its hierarchical file system.

In Linux, all of the drives and their partitions make up a single directory file system. If you have more than one physical disk partition, it is associated with a specific part of the file system. All you have to do is decide which part of the Linux directory tree should be located on each partition. This process is known in Linux as mounting a file system on a device (the disk partition). The term **mount point** refers to the directory you associate with a disk partition or any other device. In other words, each mount point is a disk partition, and that disk partition is mounted on the directory of the limb above it.

Although you can get by with a single large partition for the entire Linux file system and another for the swap space, you can better manage the disk space if you create separate partitions for the key parts of the Linux file system. See figure 12.1. Some of the recommended partitions are:

- /bin
- /boot
- /home
- /lib
- /root
- /tmp
- /var

At the very minimum, you will need two partitions for your system, root (/) and swap. For performance reasons, Linux likes to have swap on its own partition. For most other installations, I would recommend three partitions: swap, root, and home. If you require complicated system requirements and decide to use multiple partitions, you should refer to table 12.11.

Table 12.11 Directory Guidelines for a Complicated Disk Structure for Linux

Name	Minimum Size	Usage
Swap	128 MB	Virtual memory, which is used to store inactive memory to disk until it is later used
/	250 MB	Root file system including basic libraries, programs, and configuration
/var	250 MB	For files that change frequently including logs, spool files, and lock files
/usr	500 MB	Used by most applications
/boot	16 MB	Used to store the kernel
/home	500 MB	Home directory of users including user-specific configurations and data

The size of the swap file usually varies between the amount of physical memory (RAM) and twice the amount of physical memory. There are situations where an increased swap partition is desired. But if the swap file is too big, you will most likely see a degradation in performance because the disk is much slower than RAM.

Files are identified by their file names. These names usually identify the file and its contents in some form that is meaningful to you. There is no standard format for file names as there is under MS-DOS and some other operating systems; in general, a file name can contain any character (except the / character) and is limited to 256 characters in length. Although DOS and Windows applications use the COM, EXE, and BAT extensions to identify executable files, Linux uses file permissions.

Like other operating systems, Linux requires you to partition and prepare a hard disk before you can install Linux. The Disk Druid is a Red Hat utility program that uses text dialogs to enable you to partition the disk and, at the same time, specify which parts of the Linux file system are to be loaded on which partition.

The fdisk program is a Linux disk partitioning program, similar to the FDISK utility that comes with DOS, but with many more capabilities. When you use the Linux fdisk program, you have to type cryptic one-letter commands to manipulate disk partitions. Once you learn the commands, however, you may find fdisk more powerful than Disk Druid. For example, Disk Druid does not let you change the partition type, which indicates the type of file system to be stored on the partition; but you can easily change the partition type with fdisk.

FOR MORE INFORMATION ON FILE SYSTEMS, SEE THE FOLLOWING WEBSITE:

File systems-HOWTO

http://www.linux.org/docs/ldp/howto/File systems-HOWTO.html

12.7.1 Second Extended File System (Ext2)

When you partition each drive and mount the partition or volume into the Linux file system, you may have various file systems attached to one large tree structure. Traditionally, the most common file system used in Linux systems was ext2, but today, you will find that the ext2 file system is being replaced by ext3 and reiserfs.

The second extended file system, referred to as ext2, is considered the native Linux file system. It is very similar to other modern UNIX file systems but most closely resembles the Berkeley Fast File system used by BSD systems. The maximum size of an ext2 file system is 4 TB, whereas the maximum file size is currently limited to 2 GB by the Linux kernel.

The ext2 file system, like a lot of the file systems, is built on the premise that the data held in files is kept in data blocks. You can think of data blocks as being similar to clusters or allocation units. These data blocks are all of the same length and, although that length can vary between different ext2 systems, the block size of a particular ext2 file system is set when it is created (during formatting with the mke2fs program).

Figure 12.2 The Ext2 File System Structure

Super Block	Group Descriptors	Block Bitmap	Inode Bitmap	Inode Table	Data Blocks

Every file's size is rounded up to an integral number of blocks. If the block size is 1024 bytes, then a file of 1025 bytes will occupy two 1024-byte blocks. Unfortunately, this means that on average you waste half a block per file. Along with most operating systems, the ext2 trades off a relatively inefficient disk usage in order to reduce the workload on the processor.

So far as each file system is concerned, block devices are just a series of blocks that can be read and written. A file system does not need to concern itself with where on the physical media a block should be put; that is the job of the device driver. Whenever a file system needs to read information or data from the block device containing it, it requests that its supporting device driver reads an integral number of blocks.

As you can see from figure 12.2, not all of the blocks in the file system hold data; some must be used to contain the information that describes the structure of the file system. The ext2 file system divides the logical partition that it occupies into block groups. Because the block groups are essential to access the data blocks, each group duplicates information critical to the integrity. This duplication is necessary should a disaster occur and the file system need recovering.

NOTE: Only the first copies of these groups are actually used by the ext2 file system. The other copies are typically accessed only when the primary copies become corrupted or unreadable.

The ext2 defines file system topology by describing each file in the system with an inode data structure. An *inode* describes which blocks of data belong to which files, the access rights of the file, the file's modification times, and the type of file. Every file in the ext2 file system is described by a single inode. Each inode has a single unique number identifying it and it is listed in the inode table. You can think of the inode table as being similar to the file allocation table. An inode contains the following fields:

- **Mode**—Contains data block information as described by the inode, and the permissions that users have to it. For ext2, an inode can describe a file, directory, symbolic link, block device, character device, or FIFO.
- **Owner Information**—The user and group identifiers of the owners of this file or directory.
- **Size**—The size of the file in bytes.
- **Timestamps**—The time that the inode was created and the last time that it was modified.
- **Datablocks**—Pointers to the blocks that contain the data that this inode is describing.

In the ext2 file system, a directory is a special file that lists its contents (such as files and other directories) and the access paths to access the item. Each one of these entries contains the following information:

- **Inode**—The inode for this directory entry. This is an index into the array of inodes held in the inode table of the block group.
- **Name length**—The length of this directory entry in bytes.
- **Name**—The name of this directory entry.

The first two entries for every directory are always the standard "." and ".." entries meaning "this current directory" and "the parent directory," respectively.

You should note that ext2 inodes can describe special device files. These are not real files but handles that programs can use to access devices. All of the device files in/dev are there to allow programs to access Linux's devices. For example, the mount program takes the device file that it wishes to mount as an argument.

The **superblock,** found at the beginning of the disk system, contains a description of the basic size and shape of this file system. The information within it allows the file system manager to use and maintain the file system. Usually only the superblock in block group 0 is read when the file system is mounted. It holds the following information:

- **Magic Number**—This allows the mounting software to check that this is indeed the superblock for an ext2 file system. For the current version of ext2 this is 0xEF53.

- **Revision Level**—The major and minor revision levels allow the mounting code to determine whether or not this file system supports features that are available only in particular revisions of the file system. There are also feature compatibility fields that help the mounting code to determine which new features can safely be used on this file system.
- **Mount Count and Maximum Mount Count**—Together these allow the system to determine if the file system should be fully checked. The mount count is incremented each time the file system is mounted and when it equals the maximum mount count, the warning message "maximal mount count reached, running e2fsck is recommended" is displayed
- **Block Group Number**—The block group number that holds this copy of the superblock.
- **Block Size**—The size of the block for this file system in bytes, for example 1024 bytes.
- **Blocks per Group**—The number of blocks in a group. Like the block size, this is fixed when the file system is created.
- **Free Blocks**—The number of free blocks in the file system.
- **Free Inodes**—The number of free inodes in the file system.
- **First Inode**—The number of the first inode in the file system. The first inode in an ext2 root file system would be the directory entry for the '/' directory.

The group descriptor table contains information on the other block groups including:

- **Blocks Bitmap**—The block number of the block allocation bitmap for this block group. This is used during block allocation and deallocation.
- **Inode Bitmap**—The block number of the inode allocation bitmap for this block group. This is used during inode allocation and deallocation.
- **Inode Table**—The block number of the starting block for the inode table for this block group.
- **Free Blocks Count**—The number of blocks not used.
- **Free Inodes Count**—The number of inodes not used.
- **Used Directory Count**—The number of directories used.

When you access a file on the disk system, the file is kept in a directory. If the file is several directories deep, each directory name is separated by forward slashes (/) and the path name ends with the file's name. One example file name would be */home/pregan/file1.txt* where */home* and */pregan* are directory names and the file's name is *file1.txt*. Like all other UNIX systems, Linux does not care about the format of the file name itself; it can be any length and consist of any of the printable characters. To find the inode representing this file within an ext2 file system the system must parse the file name a directory at a time until getting to the file itself.

If you were to access the file1.txt file, the first inode that you need is the inode for the root of the file system. Its number is found in the file system's superblock. After finding the location of the root inode (which is marked as a directory), it will go through the root inode to find the location of the directory listing for the /home directory. You have to read this /home directory (by first reading its inode and then reading the directory entries from the data blocks described by its inode) to find the pregan entry which gives us the number of the inode describing the /home/pregan directory. Finally, it reads the directory entries pointed at by the inode describing the /home/pregan directory to find the inode number of the file 1.txt file so that it can determine which data blocks contain the file 1.txt file.

When a new file or directory is created, the ext2 file system must decide where to store the data. If the disk is mostly empty, then data can be stored almost anywhere. However, performance is maximized if the data is clustered together with other related data to minimize seek times.

The ext2 file system attempts to allocate each new directory in the group containing its parent directory, on the theory that accesses to parent and children directories are likely to be closely related. The ext2 file system also attempts to place files in the same group as their directory entries, because directory accesses often lead to file accesses. However, if the group is full, then the new file or new directory is placed in some other non-full group.

The data blocks needed to store directories and files can be found by looking in the block bitmap. Any needed space in the inode table can be found by looking in the inode allocation bitmap.

12.7.2 Journaling File Systems

The ext2 system is not perfect. It is a static file system, which does not guarantee that all updates to your hard drive are performed safely. If the computer is shut down improperly, for example because of a power outage or a system crash, it can take several minutes for Linux to verify the integrity of the partition when the computer reboots. In addition, to make things worse, ext2 is not fault tolerant. To overcome such situations, journaling file systems were created, which becomes more important with mission-critical servers and maintaining large datasets.

Journaling file systems are superior to static file systems when it comes to guaranteeing data integrity and increasing overall file system performance. Journaling and logging file systems can either keep track of the changes to a file's "metadata" (information such as ownership, creation dates, etc.), to the data blocks associated with a file, or to both, rather than maintaining a single static snapshot of the state of a file.

When modifying the blocks in the middle of a file and then adding new blocks to the end, a journaling file system would first store the pending changes (modified and new blocks) in a special section of the disk known as the "log." The file system would then update the actual file and directory inodes using the data from the log, and would mark that log operation as having been completed ("committed," in logging terms).

Whenever a file is accessed, the last snapshot of the file is retrieved from the disk and the log is consulted to see if any uncommitted changes have been made to the file since the snapshot was taken. Every so often, the file system will update file snapshots and record the changes in the log, thereby "trimming" the log and reducing access time. Committing operations from the log and synchronizing the log and its associated file system is called a "checkpoint."

Journaling and logging file systems get around the problem of inconsistencies introduced during a system crash by using the log. Before any on-disk structures are changed, an "intent-to-commit" record is written to the log. The directory structure is then updated and the log entry is marked as committed. Because every change to the file system structure is recorded in the log, file system consistency can be checked by looking in the log without the need for verifying the entire file system. When disks are mounted, if an intent-to-commit entry is found but not marked as committed, then the file structure for that block is checked and fixed if necessary.

After a crash, file systems can come online almost immediately because only the log entries after the last checkpoint need to be examined. Any changes in the log can be quickly "replayed," and the corrupted part of the disk will always correspond to the last change added to the log. The log can then be truncated because it will be invalid, and no data is lost except for any changes that were being logged when the system went down. Mounting a heavily populated directory that requires subsequent validation for database partitions might take 10 to 20 minutes to fsck with a standard static file system. A journaled file system can reduce that time to a few seconds.

The disadvantage of logging generally requires more disk writes because you have to first append log records to the log, then replay them against the file system. However, in practice, the system can operate more efficiently by using its "free time" to commit entries from the log and checkpoint the file system records. Also, because logs are stored separately on the disk from file system data and are only appended to, logging changes happen much faster than actually making those changes.

There are multiple offerings from commercial software vendors who have released journaled file systems for Linux, and there are a few contenders from the open source community. The most popular two are ext3 and reiser.

The ext3 file system is designed to make the migration from static ext2 file systems to ext3 as easy as possible. The initial proposal of ext3 was to simply add logging capabilities to ext2 through a log file in that file system. Although it is slow, it is extremely reliable.

The reiser file system is a new, general-purpose system for Linux that is designed for flexibility and efficiency. In some cases, it still extracts a slight performance penalty in the interest of increased reliability and faster restart times. Reiserfs is more space efficient than most files as it can pack many small files into a single block. In addition, reiser supports file system plug-ins that make it easy to create your own types of directories and files. This guarantees reiserfs a place in the Linux file systems of the future by making it easy to extend reiserfs to support the requirements for protocols that are still being finalized, such as streaming audio and video. For example, a system administrator can create a special file system object for streaming audio or video files, and then create his or her own special item and search handlers for the new object types. The content of such files can already be stored in TCP/IP packet format, reducing processing latency during subsequent transmission of the actual file.

12.7.3 Virtual File System (VFS)

The virtual file system (VFS) is a kernel software layer that handles all system calls related to the Linux file system. It must manage all of the different file systems that are mounted at any given time. It provides a common interface to several kinds of file systems including disk-based file systems, network-based file systems, and special file systems including the /proc file system and /dev file systems. To do this it maintains data structures that describe the whole (virtual) file system and the real mounted file systems. VFS describes the system's files in terms of superblocks and inodes in much the same way as the ext2 file system.

As each file system is initialized, it registers itself with the VFS. This happens as the operating system initializes itself at system boot time. The file system drivers are either built into the kernel itself or are built as loadable modules. File system modules are loaded as the system needs them, so, for example, if the VFAT file system is implemented as a kernel module, then it is loaded only when a VFAT file system is mounted. When a block-device-based file system is mounted, and this includes the root file system, the VFS must read its superblock. Each file system type's superblock read routine must work out the file system's topology and map that information onto a VFS superblock data structure. The VFS keeps a list of the mounted file systems in the system together with their VFS superblocks. Each VFS superblock contains information and pointers to routines that perform particular functions.

For example, the superblock representing a mounted ext2 file system contains a pointer to the ext2 specific inode reading routine. This ext2 inode read routine, like all of the file system specific inode read routines, fills out the fields in a VFS inode. Each VFS superblock contains a pointer to the first VFS inode on the file system. For the root file system, this is the inode that represents the "/" directory. This mapping of information is very efficient for the ext2 file system, but moderately less so for other file systems.

The flexibility of the virtual file system is shown in the /proc and /dev file systems. The file systems and their file and directories do not actually exist, yet they act like real file systems for quick and easy access.

In Linux, you can find out a great deal about your computer by consulting the contents of a special file system known as the /proc file system. The /proc file system is not a real directory on the disk, but a collection of data structures in memory, registered with the virtual file system and managed by the Linux kernel so that it appears to the user to be a set of directories and files. The /proc file system does not store data; rather, its contents are computed on demand according to user file I/O requests. When the VFS makes calls to it requesting inodes as its files and directories are opened, the /proc file system collects the appropriate information, formats it into text form, and places it into the requesting process's read buffer.

The purpose of /proc (also called the process file system) is to allow users to access information about the Linux kernel and the processes that are currently running on your system. See figure 10.1. Table 12.12 lists some of the entries found in the /proc file system.

To view these files, you can use any text editor or command that views text files. For example, if you are the command prompt, you can type the following command to view the interrupts:

```
cat /proc/interrupts
```

In addition, the KDE Desktop that provides a configurable graphics interface provides a GUI interface to view many of these files. (See figure 12.3.)

As mentioned before, Linux represents its hardware devices as special files. So, for example, /dev/null is the null device. A device file does not use any data space in the file system; it is only an access point to the device driver. The ext2 file system and the Linux VFS both implement device files as special types of inode. There are two types of device file—character and block special files. Within the kernel itself, the device drivers implement file semantics: you can open them, close them, and so on. Character devices allow I/O operations in character mode and block devices require that all I/O is via the buffer cache. When an I/O request is made to a device file, it is forwarded to the appropriate device driver within the system. Often this is not a real device driver but a pseudo-device driver for some subsystem such as the SCSI device driver layer. Device files are referenced by a major number that identifies the device type, and a minor type, which identifies the unit, or instance of that major type. For example, the IDE disks on the first IDE controller in the system have a major number of 3 and the first partition of an IDE disk would have a minor number of 1.

Table 12.12 Entries in the /proc File System

File	Description
/proc/apm	Lists information about the battery
/proc/cpuinfo	Lists the key characteristics of your system, such as processor type and floating-point processor information
/proc/devices	Shows information about the various devices on your system
/proc/dma	Lists the DMA channels that are being used
/proc/file systems	Shows the file system types that are used on your system
/proc/interrupts	Lists information about the IRQs that are being used
/proc/ioports	Lists the I/O port address ranges that are being used
/proc/meminfo	Lists how the memory is being used
/proc/modules	A text list of the modules that have been loaded by the system
/proc/pci	Lists information about the PCI devices on your system
/proc/scsi	Lists all SCSI devices known to the kernel
/proc/sound	Displays sound driver status

Figure 12.3 KDE System Information Program

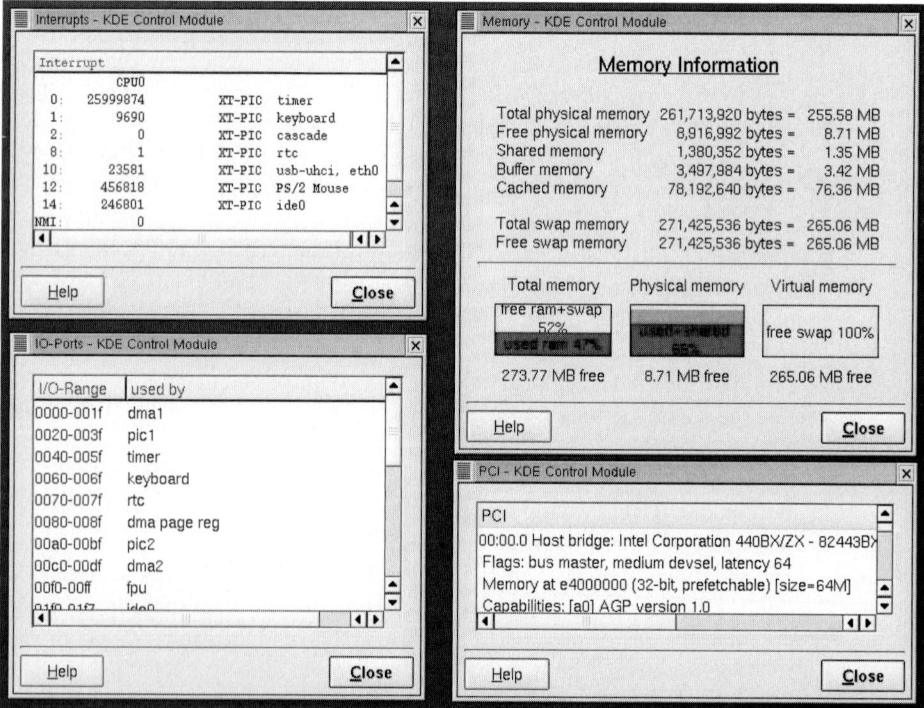

12.7.4 VFS Cache

Most file systems rely heavily on caching. A cache is a part of RAM dedicated to holding file system data. The cache holds directory information, inode information, and actual file contents. Whenever an application (like a text editor or a compiler) tries to look up a file name or requests file data, the file system first checks the cache. If the answer can be found in the cache, then the request can be answered very quickly without using the disk.

The cache is filled with data from old requests. Therefore, if you request data that you have never requested before, the data will not be in the cache, and must be retrieved from disk. Luckily, most of the time people ask for data they have used before. These repeat requests are answered quickly from the cache, saving the disk drive much effort while providing the user quick access.

All Linux file systems use a common buffer cache to cache data buffers from the underlying devices to help speed up access by the file systems to the physical devices holding the systems.

Of course, each computer has a limited amount of RAM available. Most of that RAM is used for other things like running applications, leaving perhaps 10 to 30 percent of total RAM available for the cache. When the cache becomes full, the oldest unused data (least recently used data) is thrown out. Only recently used data remains in the cache. Because larger caches can hold more data, they can also satisfy a larger number of requests. Using more RAM for caching increases the number of requests answered from the cache, and therefore increases the apparent speed of the file system.

The VFS also keeps a cache of directory lookups so that the inodes for frequently used directories can be found quickly. As an experiment, try listing a directory that you have not listed recently. The first time you list it, you may notice a slight pause; the second time you list its contents, the result is immediate. The directory cache does not store the inodes for the directories—these should be in the inode cache. However, it does store the mapping between the full directory names and their inode numbers.

12.8 DISK AND FILE COMPRESSION

Disk compression, used by Windows 9X, expands the amount of space on a disk and is accomplished in two ways: first, by reducing the amount of wasted and unused space created by large clusters; second, by squeezing the files on the disk so that they will take up less space.

When a volume is compressed, a compression interface (DBLSPACE, DRVSPACE, or Stacker, among others) simulates a file allocation table for the compressed drive. The normal file allocation table allocates a fixed number of clusters to a file. The simulated file allocation table allocates a variable number of sectors to a cluster. Therefore, if a small file fits within one sector, it will use only one sector, not an entire cluster.

When a drive is compressed, the compression software changes the drive letter. The compression software might change the drive letter of the existing C drive to H, for example. The drive with the new drive letter is known as the *host drive* for the compressed volume. A large hidden file created on the host drive, which usually uses most of the volume space, is called the **compressed volume file (CVF).** It is at the beginning of the hidden file that the simulated file allocation table is created and stored. The rest of the hidden file is used to store files in compressed format. The reason that the CVF does not include the entire volume is because some files, such as certain boot files and swap files, need to be uncompressed.

File compression works by substitution. It starts by locating repetitive patterns and replacing the repetitive data with another, shorter pattern. Most operating systems and disk compression software packages will compress files as they are written to disk. When a compressed file is accessed, it has to be uncompressed in RAM before it can be used. If a file stored on a compressed drive is copied to another drive that is not compressed, the file is uncompressed in RAM and stored on the target drive uncompressed. As far as the user is concerned, the compressed drive is drive that works just like any other drive. But although the amount of space for a volume is expanded through file compression, the performance of the PC will be slower since it has to process the compression and decompression of files. In addition, the disk compression software must remain in RAM to handle the compression and decompression, which uses up resources that could have been used for something else.

NTFS compression (available in Windows 2000 or Windows XP, which uses NTFS5) is the ability to selectively compress the contents of individual files, entire directories, or entire drives on an NTFS volume. NTFS compression uses file compression that works by substitution. It starts by locating repetitive patterns and replaces the repetitive data with another pattern, which is shorter. Windows keeps track of which files and folders are compressed by using a file attribute. As far as the user is concerned, the compressed drive, folder, or file is another drive folder or file that works just like any other. I should point out at this time, although you expand the amount of space for a volume, the performance of the PC will be slower since it has to process the compression and decompression of files. Therefore, I would not recommend compression unless you are compressing files that are rarely used or when disk space is critical. Of course, if disk space is critical, I would use this as a temporary solution until you can delete or move files from the drive or extend the volume. Note: Drives, directories and files cannot be compressed with NTFS compression and be encrypted with the Encrypting File System (EFS).

To compress a file or folder on an NTFS drive:

1. Open Windows Explorer.
2. Right-click the file or folder that you want to compress and select the Properties option.
3. Select the Advanced button.
4. Select the Compress contents to save disk space check box.
5. Click on the OK or Apply button.
6. If you select to compress a folder, select Apply changes to this folder only or Apply changes to the folder, subfolder and files and click on the OK button.

To compress an NTFS drive:

1. Open My Computer.
2. Right-click the drive that you want to compress.
3. Select the Compress drive to save disk space.

NOTE: To uncompress a drive, folder, or file, unselect the option.

To display compressed files and folders in a different color:

1. Open the Control Panel.
2. Double-click the Folder Options applet.
3. Click the View tab.
4. Select the Display compressed files and folders with alternate color check box.
5. Click on the OK or Apply button.

When you copy and move files and folders from one location to another, you need to understand how the NTFS folder and file compression are affected. If you copy a file or folder to another NTFS volume, the new folder and file will automatically acquire the compression attribute of the drive or folder that the folder and file is being copied to.

If the folder or file is moved within the same volume, the folder or file will retain the same compression attribute that was already assigned. This means that if it was compressed, it will remain compressed at the new location, and if it was uncompressed, it will remain uncompressed at the new location. When the folder or file is moved from one volume to another NTFS volume, the folder or file will automatically acquire the compression attribute of the drive or folder that file is being copied to. An easy way to remember the difference is when you move a folder or file from within the same volume, the folder and file is not physically moved, but the Master File Table is adjusted to indicate a different folder. When you move a folder or file from one volume to another, it copies the folder or file to the new location and then deletes the old location. Therefore, the moved folder and files are new to the volume and acquire the new compression attribute.

12.9 FILE ENCRYPTION

Encryption is the process of converting data into a format that cannot be read by another user. Once a user has encrypted a file, the file automatically remains encrypted whenever the file is stored on disk. Decryption is the process of converting data from encrypted format back to its original format. Once a user has decrypted a file, the file remains decrypted whenever the file is stored on disk.

Windows 2000 and Windows XP includes the **Encrypting File System (EFS)** which allows a user to encrypt and decrypt files that are stored on a NTFS volume. By using EFS, folders and files are still kept secure against those intruders who might gain unauthorized physical access to the drive such as stealing a notebook computer or a removable drive. EFS is not intended to support accessing an encrypted file by multiple users, and EFS does not decrypt or encrypt files that are transmitted over the network. Instead, another protocol would have to be used to secure the data sent over the network.

When EFS is enabled, the encrypting and decrypting of a file is transparent to the user. As a file is encrypted, each file has a unique file encryption key, which is later used to decrypt the file's data. The file encryption key is also encrypted by the user's public key. When decrypting a file, the file encryption key must first be decrypted. The file encryption is decrypted when the user has a private key that matches the public key. If a user who doesn't have the right private key tries to open, copy, move, or rename an encrypted file, the user will get an access denied message.

There are certain guidelines that you should follow when using EFS:

- You cannot encrypt files or folders that are compressed.
- Encrypted files can become decrypted if you copy or move the file to a volume that is not an NTFS volume.
- Use cutting and pasting to move files into an encrypted folder. If you use a drag-and-drop operation to move the files, they will not automatically be encrypted in the new folder.
- System files cannot be encrypted.
- Encrypting a folder or file does not protect against deletion. Anyone with delete permission can delete encrypted folders or files.
- Temporary files, which are created by some programs when documents are edited, are also encrypted as long as all the files are on an NTFS volume and in an encrypted folder. It is recommended that you encrypt the Temp folder on your hard disk for this reason.
- Encrypt the My Documents folder if this is the place where you save most of your documents. This ensures that your personal documents are encrypted by default.

12.9.1 Encrypt Attribute

To encrypt a folder or file:

1. Right-click the folder or file and select the Properties option.
2. Click on the Advanced button.
3. Select the Encrypt contents to secure data option.

When a folder is encrypted, the folder itself is not encrypted, but all of the files in the folder are encrypted. To decrypt the folder or file, unselect the Encrypt contents to secure data option.

You can also encrypt or decrypt a file or folder by using the CIPHER command. For more information on the CIPHER command, type `CIPHER/?` at the command prompt. See figure 12.4.

12.9.2 Recovering Encrypted Files

If a person leaves the company and his or her data is encrypted, the data will have to be encrypted before someone else can use it. A recovery agent is an administrator authorized to decrypt data that was encrypted by another user. Before you can add a recovery agent for a domain, you must ensure that each recovery agent has been issued an X.509 Version 3 certificate.

The recovery agent has a special certificate and associated private key that allow data recovery for the scope of influence of the recovery policy. If you are the recovery agent, you should be sure to use the **Export** command from Certificates in Microsoft Management Console (MMC) to back up the recovery certificate and associated private key to a secure location. After backing them up, you should use Certificates in MMC to delete the recovery certificate. Then, when you need to perform a recovery operation for a user, you should first restore the recovery certificate and associated private key using the **Import** command from Certificates in MMC. After recovering the data, you should again delete the recovery certificate. You do not have to repeat the export process.

Figure 12.4 CIPHER Command

```
Displays or alters the encryption of directories [files] on NTFS partitions.

  CIPHER [/E | /D] [/S:dir] [/A] [/I] [/F] [/Q] [/H] [/K] [pathname [...]]

    /E  Encrypts the specified directories. Directories will be marked
        so that files added afterward will be encrypted.
    /D  Decrypts the specified directories. Directories will be marked
        so that files added afterward will not be encrypted.
    /S  Performs the specified operation on directories in the given
        directory and all subdirectories.
    /A  Operation for files as well as directories. The encrypted file
        could become decrypted when it is modified if the parent directory
        is not encrypted. It is recommended that you encrypt the file and
        the parent directory.
    /I  Continues performing the specified operation even after errors have
        occurred. By default, CIPHER stops when an error is encountered.
    /F  Forces the encryption operation on all specified objects, even
        those which are already encrypted. Already-encrypted objects are
        skipped by default.
    /Q  Reports only the most essential information.
    /H  Displays files with the hidden or system attributes. These files
        are omitted by default.
    /K  Create new file encryption key for the user running CIPHER. If this
        option is chosen, all the other options will be ignored, pathname
        specifies a pattern, file or directory.

    Used without parameters, CIPHER displays the encryption state of the
    current directory and any files it contains. You may use multiple
    directory names and wildcards. You must put spaces between multiple
    parameters.
```

12.10 DISK PROBLEMS

Since the data on the disk is the most important part of the computer, it is necessary to protect the integrity of the disk. Disk problems and errors can occur without warning and may easily result in a data loss. Some causes include power fluctuations, viruses, parts of the hard drive wearing out, badly written software, user wear and tear, and user errors. Some of the errors these problems can cause include:

Invalid entries in the file allocation table
Invalid directory entries
Bad sectors (unreadable areas on the disk)
Corrupt MBR or corrupt volume boot sector
Corrupt compressed header, compressed file structure, compression structure, and signatures
Lost clusters
Cross-linked files

The file allocation table and directory entries are databases. Therefore, if part of these databases becomes corrupted, part or all of the databases may be unusable. Without these two databases, the operating system would not be able to find the clusters belonging to a file. Consequently, the data would be lost.

Bad sectors are areas on the disk that cannot reliably store the magnetic patterns that make up data. If an area of the disk becomes unreliable, the operating system marks as bad those sectors on the file allocation table and will not use these areas in the future to avoid data loss.

If the master boot record, which consists of the startup program to boot from the disk, becomes unreadable, the volume boot sector will not be found during boot-up. Of course, if the volume boot sector becomes corrupt, the computer cannot load the operating system's boot files. In either case, the computer does not boot.

If the compressed header, compressed file structure, compression structure, or signatures become corrupt, the files within a compressed volume may not be accessed and could be permanently damaged.

Lost clusters are clusters that get "lost" or detached from a file when a program unexpectedly stops running or isn't shut down properly, when there are power fluctuations, or when disk system problems occur. Unfortunately, the lost clusters may be a very important part of the file (an executable file or a data file). When the cluster is no longer part of the file, it may cause the computer to "lock up" or act erratic when the system tries to execute the missing instructions or it may make a data file inaccessible. If the disk system is going bad or the system is experiencing power problems, the system may generate lost clusters. When lost clusters are found on a system, the most likely cause is that the user may be shutting off the computer without closing all programs and performing the proper shutdown procedure (Start, Shutdown in Windows). Some utilities that search for and retrieve lost clusters will make them available as a file on the disk. Unfortunately, since most files are in machine code, you cannot reattach them to the file they came from, you would have to figure out not only which files they came from but exactly which part of the files they are. Therefore, it is best to delete the file. If the lost cluster was vital to the proper running of a program, the program would have to be reinstalled or the data file would have to be restored from a backup.

A **cross-link file** is the opposite of a lost cluster. Instead of the cluster being separated from a file, cross-linked errors occur when two or more files use the same cluster. Usually, the cluster belongs to only one of the files, so repairing cross-linked files usually results in only one file remaining usable.

12.11 DISK UTILITIES

There are several utilities that can help fix disk errors. Some of these utilities are FDISK, CHKDSK, SCANDISK, and DEFRAG.

12.11.1 Fixing the Master Boot Record

The FDISK is the standard utility used to partition a hard drive. When the hard drive does not boot, FDISK causes the computer to lock up, or the changes to the partition table cannot be saved; this may indicate that the master boot record (MBR) may be bad. What most people who use FDISK don't know is that it can also be used to recreate the master boot record for DOS and Windows 9X machines without changing the partition table. To recreate the MBR, boot with a bootable floppy containing the FDISK EXE program, change to the drive with the corrupt MBR, and perform the command FDISK/MBR. If this corrects the problem, you should be concerned with what caused the corruption of the master boot record. Perhaps the cause is a boot sector virus, power fluctuations when the drive is being accessed, or a failing hard drive. If the problem still exists, try a low-level format. It can also be used to replace a Windows NT family (NTLDR) or Linux MBR with a DOS/Windows 9X MBR.

For Windows NT machines, you can correct the master boot record by using the Windows NT Setup Disk and at the first screen, press R for repair. Then select the Inspect Boot Sector and Verify Windows NT system files. If you have mass storage device that require drives, select S to specify additional drivers. For Windows 2000 or Windows XP, start the Windows installation program and choose R to repair. To automatically fix these files, select F for fast repair.

12.11.2 CHKDSK Utility

CHKDSK has been around since DOS 1.0. It is probably the first utility that was developed to analyze a disk. It shows the disk statistics, including the amount of space being used, the amount of free space, the number of files and directories, and the size of the clusters. It also inspects directories and FATs to see if there are any discrepancies and will check if a file is contiguous or fragmented. CHKDSK can identify and recover (if the /F is used) lost clusters, cross-linked files, FAT allocation errors, and invalid directories. Since CHKDSK is an old utility, it is recommended for DOS 6.00 and higher to run SCANDISK to fix disk problems.

Figure 12.5 Windows 95's SCANDISK Utility

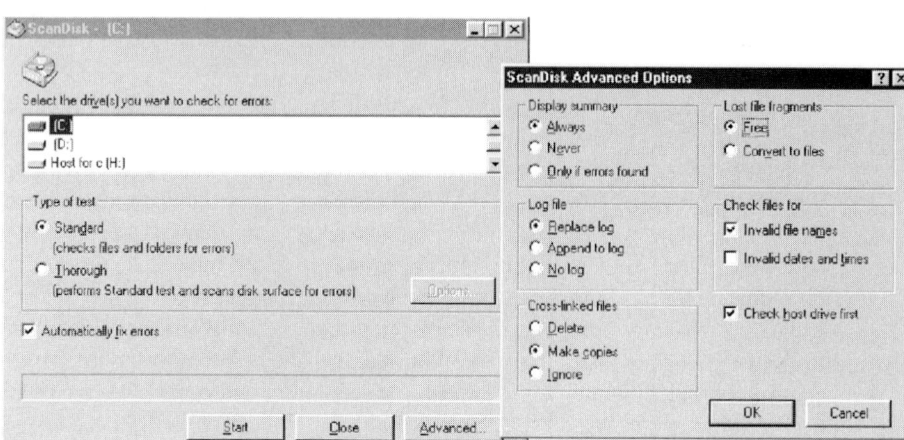

12.11.3 SCANDISK Utility

SCANDISK, Norton Disk Doctor, and similar utilities are intended to fix disk errors, including invalid entries in the file allocation table, invalid directory entries, lost clusters, cross-linked files, problems with the compressed volume, files left in an open status, and bad sectors. Unlike FDISK and CHKDSK, SCANDISK is a menu-based utility. See figure 12.5. As SCANDISK checks a hard drive, it first checks disk structure and then completes a surface scan.

With SCANDISK, you can choose to save the lost clusters to files or to delete them to free up disk space. If you choose to save them, they will be saved with a CHK extension (for example, FILE0000.CHK, FILE0001.CHK, FILE0002.CHK) in the root directory. If you find that you do not need the converted files, they can be deleted at any time. The surface scan test identifies any sector that may be failing. It accomplishes this by reading the data of a sector, writing a predetermined pattern to the sector, and rereading the sector to make sure that the pattern is the same. If the data is the same, the original information is placed back in the sector. If the sector is unreliable, SCANDISK marks the sector as bad and moves the data to another sector.

Whichever disk utility is used, it must be made for the operating system and file system. If not, the long file names may be truncated or corrupted, the file allocation table and directories may be corrupted, or files may become inaccessible. (Note: You should not run SCANDISK while running Windows 3.XX.)

In Linux, the fsck program can locate and fix structural problems with file systems such as disk blocks marked as free that are actually in use (and vice versa), incorrect link counts in inodes (indicating missing or extra directory entries for the corresponding file), and inconsistencies between the inode total size value and the actual amount of data blocks contained in the lists. As such, fsck can ensure the consistency of the file system's defining data structures. However, keep in mind that its scope is limited to the file system structure; it can do nothing for missing or corrupted data within structurally sound files. Note that like mkfs, fsck is actually a front end to other tools, such as e2fsck (also known as fsck.ext2).

The syntax for fsck is as follows:

```
fsck -ACVRTNP [-t fstype] [--] [fsck-options] filesystems
```

Options are shown in table 12.13.

Normally, you run fsck with only the file system name. For example, to check the third partition on the first SCSI drive, you would run the following command:

```
fsck /dev/sda3
```

> **IMPORTANT NOTE:**
>
> You should run fsck only on file systems that are not currently mounted, or are mounted as read-only. Changes written to disk during normal read/write operations can confuse fsck and result in file system corruption.

Table 12.13 The Fsck Options

Option	Description
–A	This option causes fsck to check all the file systems marked to be checked in /etc/fstab. This option is normally used in system startup scripts.
–C	This option displays a text-mode progress indicator of the check process. Most file systems don't support this feature, but ext2fs does.
–V	This option produces verbose output of the check process.
–N	This option tells fsck to display what it would normally do, without actually doing it.
–t fstype	Normally, fsck determines the file system type automatically. You can force the type with this flag, though. It used in conjunction with –A; this causes the system to check only the specified file system types, even if others are marked to be checked. If fstype is prefixed with *no*, then all file systems except the specified type are checked.
– –fsck-options	File system check programs for specific file systems often have their own options. The fsck passes options it doesn't understand, or those that follow a double dash (– –), to the underlying check program. Common options include –a or –p (perform an automatic check), –r (perform an interactive check), and –f (force a full file system check if it appears to be clean).
filesystems	The name of the file system or systems being checked such as /dev/sda3.

Figure 12.6 Windows 95's Disk Defragmenter Utility

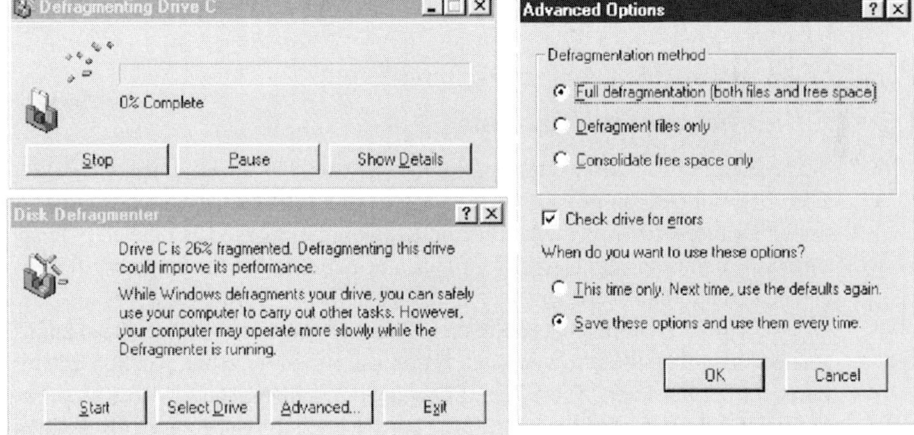

12.11.4 DEFRAG Utility

When a file is created, it is assigned the number of clusters needed to hold the amount of data. After the file is saved to the disk, other information is usually saved to the clusters following those assigned to the saved file. Therefore, if the original file is changed or more information is added to it, the bigger file doesn't fit within the allocated clusters when it is saved back to the disk. Part of the file will be saved in the original clusters and the remaining amount will be placed elsewhere on the disk. Over time, files become fragmented as they are spread across the disk. The fragmented files are still complete when they are opened, but it takes longer for the computer to read them, and opening them causes more wear and tear on the hard disk. DEFRAG fixes this fragmentation problem by bringing these scattered segments of a file back into a more efficient order on the storage medium. See figure 12.6.

DEFRAG and other similar utilities reorganize the files on the hard drive to optimize disk performance. It does this by gathering all parts of a file and placing them in continuous sectors. If the drive is badly fragmented, the program may take several hours to finish. DEFRAG cannot move files that are marked as system (system file attribute) or hidden (hidden file attribute) because some of these files are placed in a particular position on the disk.

NOTE: DEFRAG and related utilities will take an excess amount of time to complete if files are being modified on the drive, antivirus software, or screen savers.

When you execute the DEFRAG command at the command prompt, the syntax is:

```
defrag volume
defrag volume [/a]
defrag volume [/a] [/v]
defrag volume [/v]
defrag volume [/f]
```

Parameters

- volume—The drive letter or a mount point of the volume to be defragmented.
- /a—Analyzes the volume and displays a summary of the analysis report.
- /v—Displays the complete analysis and defragmentation reports. When used in combination with /a, displays only the analysis report. When used alone, displays both the analysis and defragmentation reports.
- /f—Forces defragmentation of the volume regardless of whether it needs to be defragmented.
- /?—Displays help at the command prompt.

Therefore, if you want to defrag the C drive, you would execute the following command:

```
DEFRAG C:
```

To force a defrag of the C drive, you would execute the following command:

```
DEFRAG C: /F
```

12.11.5 Other Microsoft Utilities

The remaining utilities worth mentioning are the UNDELETE and UNFORMAT utilities. The UNDELETE utilities can be used to recover files (not subdirectories) that were deleted with the DEL command because a file is not actually deleted but rather marked as deleted by changing the first character of the file name to a sigma (σ). The file can be undeleted as long the entire file is intact and has not been replaced with another file.

Windows environments like to create a lot of temporary files so the chances of undeleting a file are reduced significantly. But Window's systems have a recycle bin, which is actually a subdirectory where deleted files are stored. Therefore, if you need to undelete the file, look in the recycle bin and restore it back to the drive. See figure 12.7. If the hard drive starts to become full, it will start to delete the oldest files first.

Most of the time when the FORMAT command is used to format a disk, it performs a safe format. A safe format copies the file allocation table to an unused portion of the disk and then erases the original file allocation table. The UNFORMAT utility can recover a disk that has been accidentally formatted with a safe format by copying the copy of the file allocation table back to the file allocation table position on the disk.

12.12 TROUBLESHOOTING DISK PROBLEMS

When troubleshooting any kind of disk problem, keep in mind that it could be either a hardware problem or a formatting problem, such as a corrupt file allocation table, corrupt partition table, or corrupt file. If the problem is a formatting problem, then you need to investigate to determine how the disk acquired its problems. This may lead back to a hardware problem or to a virus or user error.

Figure 12.7 Windows 95's Recycle Bin

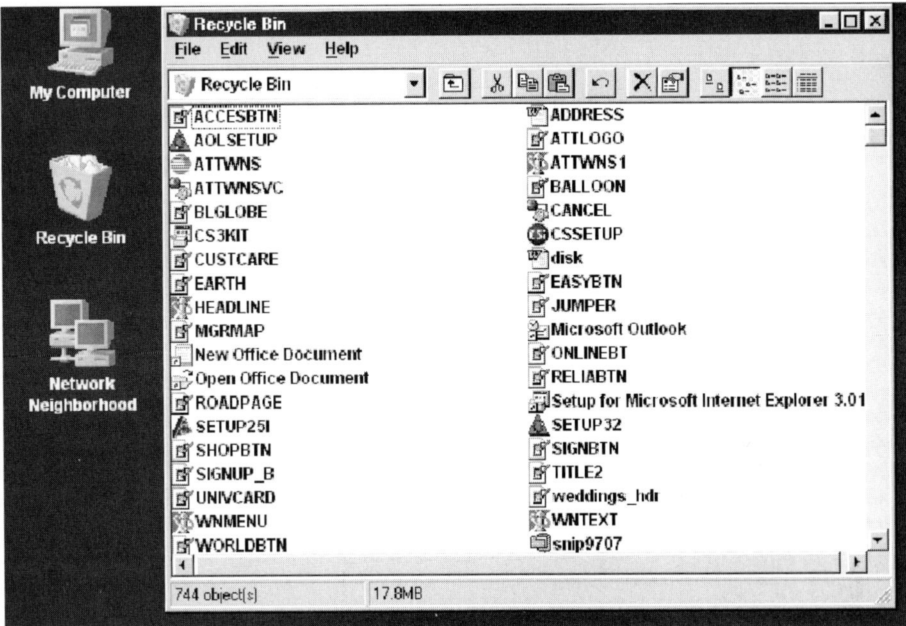

Example 12.4:

A client is using Windows 95 or 98 on the computer. While Microsoft Word for Windows is running, it locks up often, and occasionally an exception error occurs.

This is most likely a software problem, probably with Word. Check for viruses and run SCANDISK on the hard drive. If there are lost clusters, most likely they are clusters from important Word files. Therefore, the best thing to do would be to reinstall Word. If the problem still exists, try to reinstall Windows. If this clears up the problem, make sure that the user knows how to properly shut down Windows. If SCANDISK detects a lot of bad sectors on the hard drive, that indicates the hard drive is going bad. Therefore, it is best to back up the hard drive immediately and start looking for a replacement drive. If the problem still exists after replacing the drive, it is probably caused by the the RAM, microprocessor, or motherboard.

Example 12.5:

A file name consists of strange ASCII characters. It cannot be deleted with DEL, DELTREE, File Manager, or Explorer.

To correct this problem, run SCANDISK on the drive. In addition, it is probably not a bad idea to check for viruses.

SUMMARY

1. By default, the system ROM BIOS will begin searching the volume boot sector of drive A followed by the volume boot sector of drive C for the operating system boot files.
2. The master boot record (MBR), always found on the first sector of a hard drive, tells the system ROM BIOS how the hard drive is divided (master partition table) and which partition to boot from.
3. Partitioning is the process of defining and dividing the physical drive into logical volumes called partitions. Each partition functions as if it were a separate hard disk.
4. Three kinds of partitions are found in PCs: primary, extended, and logical.
5. Only four primary partitions (the partition table has only four entries) can exist on one drive, one of which can be an extended partition.

6. The extended partition can contain many logical partitions.
7. Every hard drive must have at least one partition.
8. IDE disks can have up to 16 partitions and SCSI disks can have up to 15.
9. Of the primary partitions, only one can be marked active because the computer can boot from only one partition.
10. The file system consists of the directory structure, methods for organizing a volume (partition or floppy disk), and methods of storing and retrieving files.
11. Disks are divided into circular grids consisting of tracks (concentric circles) and sectors (512-byte chunks of usable data).
12. The most basic storage unit for an operating system is a cluster or allocation unit. A cluster is one or more sectors that make up one entry in the file allocation table (FAT).
13. The FAT is an index used to "remember" which file is located in which cluster.
14. The FAT is created during a high-level format, such as when using the FORMAT.COM command or an equivalent program.
15. Every volume has a starting point called the root directory, which is located at the top of the tree structure.
16. The directories under the root directory are also referred to as subdirectories.
17. Every directory, including the root directory, consists of a small database. The database stores the file name, file attributes, starting cluster, size of the file, and the date and time that the file was created or last modified.
18. The file attribute field stores a number of characteristics about each file, such as read-only, hidden, system, and archive.
19. The file allocation table is the most common file system (used by DOS, Windows 9X, and Windows NT).
20. VFAT is an enhanced version of the FAT structure that allows Windows 9X and Windows NT to support long file names (up to 255 characters).
21. FAT32 is an enhancement of the FAT file system. It supports hard drives up to 2 TB and uses space more efficiently on large hard drives.
22. NTFS (NT file system) is a new file system for Windows NT. Because it was made for a server and workstation, it offers many enhancements and features.
23. File names in DOS use the 8.3 format which allows up to 8 characters for the file name and 0–3 characters for the file name extension.
24. Long file names can be up to 255 characters.
25. FAT and NTFS have a maximum path length of 255 characters and VFAT and FAT32 can be up to 260 characters.
26. Windows 2000 and Windows XP support NTFS5.
27. Different from DOS and Windows, all volumes are combined or mounted to create one large tree structure for all drives and file systems.
28. In Linux, the traditional file system used is ext2.
29. Journaling file systems used by Linux are ext3 and reiser.
30. Disk compression is expanding the amount of space on a disk.
31. Disk compression works by reducing the amount of wasted and unused space created by large clusters and by squeezing the files on the disk so that they will take up less space.
32. Encryption is the process of converting data into a format that cannot be read by another user.
33. Windows 2000 and Windows XP support Encrypting File System (EFS), which allows users to encrypt and decrypt files that are stored on an NTFS volume.
34. FDISK (or an equivalent program) can create the master boot record and define the partition table.
35. Because the data on the disk is the most important part of the computer, it is necessary to protect the integrity of the disk.
36. Disk problems and errors can occur without warning and may easily result in data loss.
37. Lost clusters are clusters that get "lost," or detached, from a file.
38. A cross-link is two or more files using the same cluster.
39. In DOS and Windows, CHKDKSK, SCANDISK, and similar utilities are made to fix disk errors.
40. DEFRAG and other similar utilities reorganize the files on the hard drive to optimize disk performance.
41. In Linux, fsck is used to check and fix disk errors.

QUESTIONS

1. By default, the BIOS will boot from
   a. the A drive followed by the C drive.
   b. the A drive followed by the B drive followed by the C drive.
   c. the C drive followed by the A drive.
   d. the C drive followed by the B drive followed by the A drive.
   e. the CD-ROM drive.
2. A cluster is a collection of
   a. heads.
   b. tracks.
   c. sectors.
   d. cylinders.
3. The small unit of storage for an operating system is a
   a. sector.
   b. cluster.
   c. cylinder.
   d. track.

4. The master boot record holds the
   a. partition table.
   b. volume boot sector.
   c. file allocation table.
   d. root directory.
5. What utility is used to partition the drive?
   a. FORMAT b. FDISK
   c. SCANDISK d. CHKDSK
   e. DEFRAG
6. The index of the disk is the
   a. partition table.
   b. file allocation table.
   c. directory.
   d. root directory.
7. The file allocation table is created during the
   a. low-level formatting.
   b. partitioning.
   c. high-level formatting.
   d. CMOS setup.
8. The top of a file structure tree is the
   a. partition table. b. root directory.
   c. subdirectory. d. MBR.
9. Which of the following is *not* listed in the directory?
   a. starting cluster
   b. file name and extension
   c. attributes
   d. date and time that the file was created or edited
   e. ending cluster
10. What kind of file cannot be deleted or changed?
    a. read-only b. system
    c. hidden d. archive
11. Which file attribute is used by backup programs?
    a. R b. S
    c. H d. A
12. The most common file system used in DOS, Windows 95 and 98, and Windows NT is
    a. FAT. b. HPFS.
    c. VFAT. d. NTFS.
13. Which of the following does *not* support long file names?
    a. FAT b. VFAT
    c. FAT32 d. NTFS
    e. HPFS
14. What is the maximum number of files and directories in the root directory supported by Windows 95 using the FAT file system?
    a. 128 b. 256
    c. 512 d. 1,024
15. What is the maximum partition size used in DOS or Windows 95 running FAT?
    a. 512 MB b. 1 GB
    c. 2 GB d. 4 GB
    e. 8 GB
16. The compressed volume file is located on
    a. drive C.
    b. CD-ROM.
    c. the host drive.
    d. a floppy disk.
    e. the first partition of the first hard drive.
17. When a cluster becomes detached from its file, it is called a
    a. lost cluster.
    b. cross-linked file.
    c. bad sector.
    d. corrupt volume boot sector.
18. Which utility identifies and corrects files that are not contiguous?
    a. SCANDISK b. DEFRAG
    c. MEMMAKER d. BACKUP
19. Which best describes a fragmented hard drive?
    a. the platters are bad or cracked
    b. the platters are slipping on the spindle
    c. data files are corrupted
    d. files are not stored in consecutive clusters
20. SCANDISK can be used to
    a. locate lost clusters and provide the option to save or delete them.
    b. look for viruses.
    c. reconfigure and optimize the programs in RAM.
    d. locate a specific program on a disk or drive.
21. A hard drive has slowed down considerably over time. What should be done to improve the performance of the hard drive?
    a. use DriveSpace or DoubleSpace
    b. use Fast Disk
    c. use Disk Defragmenter
    d. use CHKDSK
    e. increase the maximum amount of virtual memory
22. What are some advantages of using SCANDISK rather than CHKDSK (choose two answers)?
    a. SCANDISK can perform a surface scan.
    b. SCANDISK can repair CD-ROM disks.
    c. SCANDISK can repair physical damage to a disk.
    d. SCANDISK can repair lost clusters on a compressed drive.
    e. SCANDISK can repair a corrupt partition table.
23. How does DriveSpace 3 in Windows 98 store compressed files?
    a. .ZIP b. .RAR
    c. .CVF d. .TAR
24. Which Windows versions support the FAT32 file system (choose four)?
    a. Windows 3.1 b. Windows 95B
    c. Windows NT 3.51 d. Windows 2000
    e. Windows 95A f. Windows 98
    g. Windows NT 4.0 h. Windows XP
25. You have two computers. One is running a default installation of Windows NT 4.0 on a single NTFS partition, and the other is running a default installation of Windows 2000 on a single NTFS partition. What must you do to make the file system compatible?
    a. Install Service Pack 1 or later on the Windows 2000 machine.
    b. Install Service Pack 4 or later on Windows NT 4.0 machine.

c. Use the NTFS4TO5 conversion utility on the Windows NT 4.0 file system.
d. Do nothing; the NTFS file system running on Windows NT 4.0 and Windows 2000 is the same.

26. What does the Windows 2000 master boot record do?
   a. loads and initiates the MSGINA.DLL file
   b. checks the basic memory and other hardware functions
   c. puts the processor into Windows 2000's 32-bit flat memory mode
   d. starts the file system corresponding to the Windows 2000 boot partition
   e. searches for an active partition on the boot device and loads the boot sector
   f. reads the BOOT.INI file to locate the Windows 2000 operating system and builds the boot-loader menu
27. Which file system supports standard UNIX file types and is the most widely used Linux system?
   a. ext2
   b. ext3
   c. FAT16
   d. reiser
28. Which file systems provide journaling capabilities (choose all that apply)?
   a. NTFS
   b. ext3
   c. ext2
   d. reiser

HANDS-ON EXERCISES

Exercise 1: Running SCANDISK and DEFRAG

1. Using DOS or Windows, run SCANDISK on the hard drive.
2. Using DOS or Windows, run DEFRAG on the hard drive.

Exercise 2: Using the CHKDSK Command

Use the CHKDSK utility with the Fix option.

Exercise 3: Using the FDISK Command

Use the FDISK utility to create a new master boot record.

Exercise 4: Looking at Clusters and Long File Names

1. Insert a formatted DS/HD 3 1/2-in. disk in drive A. Use the CHKDSK command to find the size of the clusters on the A drive.
2. Create and format a 10 MB FAT partition on the hard drive.
3. Boot with a DOS bootable disk. Using the FDISK command, find the type of file system being used on the C drive.
4. Using the CHKDSK command, find the size of the clusters on the D drive.
5. Delete the 10 MB partition on the hard drive.
6. Create and format a 600 MB FAT32 primary partition on the hard drive.
7. Using the FDISK command, find the type of file system being used on the D drive.
8. Using the CHKDSK command, find the size of the cluster on the D drive.
9. Record the number of bytes on the D drive.
10. Using the COPY command or EDIT utility, create a file consisting of the word "SCHOOL."
11. Use the DIR command to view the file size and record it.
12. Using the CHKDSK command, record the number of bytes free on the C drive.
13. Determine the difference between the bytes of free space before the file was added and the bytes of free space after the file was added. Compare the result with the size of the cluster. Since the file should have taken approximately 7 bytes (5 bytes for the 5 characters of school) and 2 bytes for an end-of-file character. Yet, the file consumes the entire cluster because only one file can be assigned to a cluster.
14. Start Windows.

15. On the D drive, create the following text files using a text editor with your name in them.

    This is a long file name generated today 1.txt
    This is a long file name generated today 2.txt
    This is a long file name generated today 3.txt
    This is a long file name generated today 4.txt
    This is a long file name generated today 5.txt

16. Boot with the DOS bootable disk and list the files with a DIR command. Look at the short 8.3 file names generated.

CHAPTER 13

Tape Drives and Data Protection

Topics Covered in This Chapter

Introduction

Data is the most important thing on the computer. It represents hours of work, and the information is sometimes irreplaceable. The best way to protect data is to back up, back up, back up. Because the data can be lost due to hardware failure, software glitches, viruses, and user error, as a technician, consultant, or support person, you need to emphasize to the customer or client the importance of a good backup. Backups can be performed with floppy disks, hard disks, compact disks, removable disks, and tapes. One of the best, easiest, and most inexpensive ways to back up a system is with a tape drive.

Objectives

1. Given a scenario, recommend the best device for backup.
2. Install an antivirus software package.
3. Look for, detect, and remove a virus.
4. List and describe the various recording methods used with tapes.
5. Install a tape drive and back up the hard drive.
6. Given a tape drive problem, identify and correct the problem.

13.1 DATA

Data is the raw facts, numbers, letters, or symbols that the computer processes into meaningful information. Examples of data include a letter to a company or a client, a report for your boss, a budget proposal for a large project, and an address book of your friends and business associates. Whatever the data, it can be saved (or written to disk) so that it can be retrieved at any time, printed on paper, or sent to someone else over the telephone line.

As mentioned throughout this book, data is the most important part of the computer. Your data usually represents hours of work and is sometimes irreplaceable. Since data is the most important part of the computer, it is essential that you protect data. Data loss can be caused by many things. Previous chapters have discussed how hardware failure, especially drive failure, disk failure, or power fluctuations, can cause data loss. Data loss can also be caused by software problems, viruses, and user error.

13.2 VIRUSES

A virus is a program designed to replicate and spread, generally without the knowledge or permission of the user. Computer viruses spread by attaching themselves to other programs or to the boot sector of a disk. When an infected file is executed or accessed or the computer is started with an infected disk, the virus spreads into the computer. Some viruses are cute, some are annoying, and others are disastrous. See figure 13.1. Some of the disastrous symptoms of a virus include the following:

The computer fails to boot.
Disks have been formatted.
The partitions are deleted or the partition table is corrupt.
A disk can't be read.
Data or entire files are corrupt or are disappearing.
Programs don't run anymore.
Files become larger.
The system is slower than normal.
The system has less memory available than it should.
Information being sent to and from a device is intercepted.

Figure 13.1 Viruses can cause a wide range of problems.

Question:

How does a virus spread?

Answer:

Viruses are small programs that are made to replicate themselves, so they spread very easily. For example, you are handed an infected disk or you download a file from the Internet or a bulletin board. When the disk or file is accessed, the virus replicates itself to RAM. When you access any files on your hard drive, the virus again replicates itself to your hard drive. If you shut off your computer, the virus in the RAM will disappear, but unfortunately, because your hard drive is infected, the RAM becomes infected every time you boot from the hard drive. When you insert and access another disk, that disk also becomes infected. You then hand the disk or send an infected file to someone else and the cycle repeats itself.

Symantec, developer of Norton Antivirus, says that most current infections are caused by viruses that are at least 3 years old. Stiller Research, developer of Integrity Master, states that viruses are very widespread but only a relatively small number (about 100) account for 90 percent of all infections. Table 13.1 lists a number of facts about viruses.

Table 13.1 Virus Facts

Viruses can't infect write-protected disks.	Viruses can infect read-only, hidden, and system files.
Viruses don't typically infect a document (except macro viruses).	Viruses typically infect boot sectors and executable files.
Viruses do not infect compressed files.	A file within a compressed file could have been infected before being compressed.
Viruses don't infect computer hardware, such as monitors or chips.	Viruses can change your CMOS values, causing your computer not to boot.
You cannot get a virus just by being on the Internet or a bulletin board.	You can download an infected file.
Viruses cannot be activated by reading an email message (except macro viruses).	Viruses can be part of a file attached to email.

13.2.1 Types of Viruses

Computer viruses can be categorized into five types:

1. Boot sector
2. File
3. Multipartite
4. Macro
5. Trojan horse

Every logical drive (hard drive partition and floppy disk) has a boot sector with both bootable and non-bootable components. The boot sector contains specific information relating to the formatting of the disk and a small program called the *boot program,* which loads the operating system files. On hard drives, the first physical sector (side 0, track 0, sector 1) contains the master boot record (MBR) and partition table. The master boot program uses the partition table to find the starting location of the bootable partition (active partition). It then tells the computer to go to the boot sector of the partition and load the boot program. A **boot sector virus** is transmitted by rebooting the machine from an infected diskette. When the boot sector program on the diskette is read and executed, the virus goes into memory and infects the hard drive, specifically the boot sector or the master boot program.

File infector viruses attach themselves to or replace executable files (usually files with the COM or EXE file name extension), but they can also infect SYS, DRV, BIN, OVL, and OVY files. Uninfected programs become infected when files are executed with the virus in memory; in other cases, programs are infected when they are opened, including from the DOS DIR command. Or the virus simply infects all of the files in the directory from which it was run.

A **multipartite virus** has the characteristics of both boot sector viruses and file viruses. It may start as a boot sector virus and spread to executable files, or start from an infected file and spread to the boot sector.

A macro, or formula language, used in word processing, spreadsheets, and other application programs, is a set of instructions that a program executes on command. Macros group several keystrokes into one command or perform complex menu selections. They therefore simplify redundant or complex tasks. The **macro viruses** are the newest strain and are currently the most common type of virus. Unlike previous viruses, macro viruses are stored in a data document and spread when the infected documents are accessed or transferred. Currently, the most vulnerable applications are Microsoft Word and Microsoft Excel. Some macro viruses modify the contents of the document and can even cause documents to be sent out via email.

The fifth type of virus is the **Trojan horse virus,** which, by definition, is not really a virus since it does not replicate itself. Nonetheless, the Trojan horse virus is a program that appears to be legitimate software, such as a game or useful utility. Unfortunately, when you run the Trojan horse and the trigger event occurs, the program will do its damage, such as formatting your hard drive.

Some viruses can be characterized as polymorphic viruses or stealth viruses. A **polymorphic virus** mutates, or changes its code, so that it cannot be as easily detected. **Stealth viruses** try to hide themselves by monitoring and intercepting a system's call. For example, when the system seeks to open an infected file, the stealth virus uninfects the file and allows the operating system to open it. When the operating system closes the file, the virus reinfects the file.

For more information on viruses, how they work, and how they affect your computer and for descriptions of particular viruses, check out the websites in table 13.2.

Table 13.2 General Information About Viruses

Virus Information Library	http://vil.mcafee.com/default.asp
Virus Encyclopedia	http://www.symantec.com/avcenter/vinfodb.html
Virus Hoaxes	http://vil.mcafee.com/hoax.asp
	http://www.symantec.com/avcenter/hoax.html
Virus Reference Area	http://www.symantec.com/avcenter/refa.html
Virus Screenshot Archive	http://www.datafellows.com/virus-info/v-pics

13.2.2 Worms

A worm is a program or algorithm that replicates itself over a computer network (without file or disk) and usually performs malicious actions, such as using up the computer's resources and possibly shutting down the system. Typically, a worm enters the computer because of vulnerabilities available in the computer's operating system.

The Computer Emergency Response Team (CERT) Coordination Center was started in December 1988 by the Defense Advanced Research Projects Agency, which was part of the U.S. Department of Defense, after the Morris Worm disabled about 10 percent of all computers connected to the Internet. CERT studies Internet security vulnerabilities, provides services to websites that have been attacked, and publishes security alerts. CERT/CC's research activities include the area of WAN computing and developing improved Internet security. The organization also provides training to incident response professionals.

CERT website:

http://www.cert.org/

Microsoft Personal Security Advisor

http://www.microsoft.com/technet/mpsa/start.asp

Symantec Security Advisory List

http://securityresponse.symantec.com/avcenter/security/Advisories.html

13.2.3 Virus Hoaxes

A virus hoax is a letter or email message warning you about a virus that does not exist. For example, the letter or warning may tell you that certain email messages may harm your computer if you open them. In addition, the letter or message usually tells you to forward the letter or email message to your friends, which creates more network traffic. Some hoaxes will tell you to search for and delete certain files in which it says is a virus. But the file ends up being an important operating system or application file that is needed for the computer to function properly.

13.2.4 Antivirus Software

Antivirus software will detect and remove viruses and help protect the computer against viruses. Whichever software package is chosen, it should include a scanner-disinfector and an interceptor-resident monitor. The scanner-disinfector software will look for known virus patterns in the RAM, the boot sector, and the disk files. If a virus is detected, the software will typically attempt to remove the virus. The interceptor-resident monitor is a piece of software that is loaded and remains in the RAM. Every time a disk is accessed or file is read, the interceptor-resident monitor software will check the disk or file for the same virus patterns that the scanner-disinfector software does. In addition, some interceptor- resident monitor software will detect files as you download them from the Internet or bulletin board.

Unfortunately, scanner-disinfector software has three disadvantages. First, it can detect only viruses that it knows about. Therefore, the antivirus software package must be continually updated. The easiest way to do this is through the Internet. Second, it cannot always remove the virus. Therefore, the file may need to be deleted or a low-level format may need to be performed on the hard drive. Lastly, if it succeeds in removing the virus, the file or boot sector may still have been damaged. Therefore, the infected file still needs to be deleted or replaced, the boot sector needs to be recreated, or a low-level format needs to be performed on the disk.

If you think a virus is present even though interceptor software is installed, boot from a clean write-protected disk. This will ensure that the RAM does not contain a virus. Without changing to or accessing the hard drive, run an updated virus scanner-disinfector from the floppy disk. If a virus is detected and removed, it is then best to reboot the computer when the scanner-disinfector has finished checking the hard drive. (Note: Also boot from a bootable floppy and check the hard drive before installing any antivirus software.)

13.2.5 Protecting Against Viruses and Worms

To avoid viruses and worms, do the following:

1. Do not use pirated software because there is more of a chance that such software will have a virus.
2. Treat files downloaded from the Internet and bulletin boards with suspicion.
3. Do not boot from or access a floppy disk of unknown origin.
4. Educate fellow users.
5. Use an updated antivirus software package that constantly detects viruses. If possible configure the antivirus software to automatically update itself.
6. Back up your files on a regular basis.
7. You should not use the Administrative accounts for general use.
8. You should not give more rights than what is needed.
9. Keep your operating system up-to-date with patches.

13.2.6 Removing a Virus

If you suspect a virus, immediately check the hard drive and disk with a current antivirus software package. If you think that the hard drive is infected, use a noninfected, write-protected bootable floppy disk that contains the antivirus software to boot the computer without accessing the hard drive. Next, run the software to check the hard drive and remove the virus. If you think that there is a virus on a floppy disk, boot the computer using the hard drive. If you have been using the possibly infected disk, first check the hard drive for viruses. Then execute the antivirus program to check the floppy disk.

To remove a worm, you will follow many of the same steps as cleaning a virus including using an antivirus software package and booting with a clean disk. In addition, Microsoft and many of the antivirus companies will provide detectors and cleaners for specific worms. You may also need to apply the necessary service packs and security patches.

13.2.7 Spyware

A new threat to computers that can cause problems similar to a virus is spyware. Spyware (including adware) programs are more like Trojan horse viruses. For your machine to become infected with adware, it is usually bundled with other software without the user's knowledge or is slipped into the fine print of an End User License Agreement (EULA). Spyware applications are typically bundled as a hidden component of freeware or shareware programs that can be downloaded from the Internet such as loading certain peer-to-peer file-swapping products such as Kazaa. Spyware can also be picked up by simply visiting various websites since they are often hidden as ActiveX controls. Some of the companies that have been associated with spyware and adware include Gator, GAIN, C2, Comet Systems, Cydoor, and Marketscore.

Once installed, the spyware can monitor user activity on the Internet and transmits that information such as email addresses, passwords, and credit card numbers without the user's knowledge. This information could be used for advertising or marketing purposes, to sell the information to other parties, or to use the information for illegal purposes. Spyware can do the following:

- Generates annoying popups. Note that not all popups are generated by spyware, however. Some are generated when you visit certain websites.
- Monitors keystrokes.
- Scans files on the hard drive.
- Snoops other applications such as chat programs or word processors.
- Installs other spyware programs.
- Reads cookies.
- Changes the default home page on the web browsers or other links or default pages.
- Opens your computer to be accessed by others.

Spyware can also use network bandwidth and computer memory and can lead to system crashes or general system instability.

NOTE: There are commercial spyware programs that can be used by employers to monitor employee systems and for parents to monitor their children's computers.

To reduce your chance of being affected by spyware, you still should:

- Use a good antivirus package like Norton AntiVirus or McAfee VirusScan.
- Be sure that your machine has all security patches and fixes loaded.
- Install software only from websites you trust.
- Be careful about what software you install on your system. Be sure to read the EULA for any piece of shareware or file sharing package you plan on installing.
- Keep your web browser security settings to medium or higher.
- Install a personal firewall on your system such as ZoneAlarm so that it can alert you to both inbound and outbound activity on your network and allow you to control exactly what type of traffic is allowed to pass through.
- Use popup blockers that come with personal firewalls and Internet browser add-on toolbars such as Google and Yahoo.
- Use spyware detecting and removal programs.

Even some antivirus packages and personal firewalls are being enhanced to protect against certain non-virus threats such as spyware and keystroke-logging programs and detect when spyware is installed.

Web browser security settings determine how much or little information you are willing to accept from a website. The higher the security level, the lower the risk. The downside: using the highest security levels may make websites less usable. By default, Internet Explorer classifies all websites into a single zone (the Internet zone) and assigns everything medium-level security. When you are using this level of security, Internet Explorer should ask you to confirm that you want to download a file, unless you have previously indicated that the website or publisher is trusted. If you have to change the security level to "low," to access a website or to download software, try to change the settings back to medium or higher as soon as possible.

Spyware detecting and removal programs that you can use include:

LavaSoft's Ad-Ware
http://www.lavasoftusa.com/

PestPatrol
http://www.pestpatrol.com/pestinfo/#search

Spybot Search and Destroy
http://www.safer-networking.org/index.php?page=download

Spy's Spychecker and SpywareStopper
http://www.spychecker.com/

SwatIt Anti Trojan and Bot Scanner and Remover
http://swatit.org/download.html.

Of course, while using these utilities, you still need to use a little common sense.

For more information about spyware, visit the following sites:

Spyware Guide Database
http://www.spywareguide.com/

PestPatrol Pest Information
http://www.pestpatrol.com/pestinfo/#search

13.3 WHAT IS A TAPE DRIVE?

The main storage device within a PC is the hard drive. It contains the operating system, applications, and data generated by the applications. Because the data represents hours of work and the information is sometimes irreplaceable, data is the most important part of the computer. The best way to protect data is to perform a **backup,** which is an extra copy of data. Unfortunately; most people fail to do this and do not think about it until it is too late. As a technician, consultant, or support person, you need to emphasize to the customer or client the importance of "backup, backup, backup." You may have to select and install the backup equipment, perform the backup, or train other people to perform the backup. Whichever method and equipment are chosen and whichever person is selected to perform the backup, make sure that backup is completed on a regular basis. Remember that even with the best equipment and software, if no one completes the backup, the equipment and software are wasted.

Backups can be performed with floppy disks, hard disks, compact disks, removable disks, and tapes. Although floppy disks can be easily moved from computer to computer, it would take hundreds, maybe thousands, of them to back up today's computer. This method would also be slow and require a lot of work, as each disk would have to be inserted one at a time. Hard drives have large capacities but are usually permanently installed within the system. Compact disks also have large capacities for storage but are slow and are limited in terms of the number of times they can be written to. In either case, both devices are relatively expensive compared to others that can be used for backup. In some situations, hard drives configured in a RAID system can enhance data protection. **RAID,** which stands for **redundant arrays of inexpensive disks,** uses two or more drives in combination to create a fault tolerance system. But because this system simply duplicates information with the extra hard drives, it protects only against physical hard drive failure. If a file gets infected with a virus or becomes corrupt, the duplicated information becomes infected and corrupt on all hard drives within the RAID system.

A newer way to back up a system is with removable disks like Zip disks, Jaz disks, and LS-120 disks. These disks have a large capacity, great speed, and are relatively inexpensive, so they are an excellent choice for some systems. Unfortunately, they are not yet widely accepted and their capacity, though large, is still limited.

Tape drives are ideal for backing up hard drives on a regular basis. See figure 13.2. They read and write to a long magnetic tape and so offer large storage capacities. They are also relatively inexpensive. To back up a hard drive with tape, insert a tape into the tape drive, start a backup software package, and select the drive or files you want to back up and it will be done. If a drive or file is lost, the backup software can be used to restore the data from the tape to the hard drive. Some tape drives and backup software automatically back up the hard drive at night, when it is being used least. The only thing to remember is to replace the tape each day. (Note: Tapes have been known to fail, and there have been times when people think they have selected a drive or file to be backed up only to find that they have a blank tape when disaster occurs. Therefore, it is important to occasionally test the tapes by choosing a nonimportant file and restoring it to the hard drive.)

13.3.1 The Tape Medium

Magnetic tapes were used on older mainframes as a primary storage device and as a backup storage device. Eventually, magnetic tape evolved into the floppy disk and then the hard drive. When the IBM PC was introduced, it included a drive port for a cassette tape storage device.

Floppy disks as a medium are the most similar to a tape. They are made of a Mylar platter coated with a magnetic substance to hold magnetic fields. Floppy disks are random-access devices, which means that no matter where the data is located on the disk, the read/write heads can move directly to the proper sector and start to read or write. Instead of being a Mylar platter, **tapes** are a long polyester substrate coated with a layer of magnetic material. Unlike a floppy disk, a tape stores and retrieves data

Figure 13.2 Tape Drive

Figure 13.3 A Quarter-Inch Cartridge (QIC) and Digital Audio Tape (DAT)

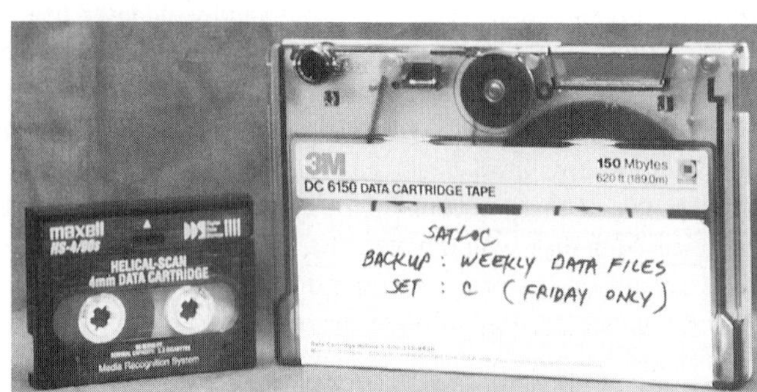

sequentially. Therefore, when a file needs to be retrieved, the read/write head has to start at the beginning of the tape and read each area to get to the correct file. Because it takes so much time to find the appropriate file, tapes are completely inappropriate as a PC's primary storage device.

Tapes come in different sizes and shapes and offer different speeds and capacities. As a result, several standards have been developed, including the quarter-inch cartridge (QIC) and the digital audio tape (DAT). See figure 13.3.

13.3.2 Recording Methods

A tape is divided into parallel tracks across its width. The number of tracks varies with the drive and the standard it follows. The data is recorded either in a parallel, serpentine, or helical scan fashion.

Parallel recording spreads the data throughout the different tracks. For example, if a tape is divided into 9 tracks, a byte of information with parity could be spread throughout all 9 tracks (1 bit per track). Newer tape systems may lay 18 or 36 tracks across the tape, totalling 2 or 4 bytes of information over the tracks. Although such a tape offers high transfer rates, data retrieval time is slow because the drive might have to fast-forward across the entire tape before retrieving all of the data required. The read/write assembly for these tapes is also quite complicated because it has to consist of several poles and gaps, one for each track. This complexity increases the cost of the drive.

Most PC tape systems use **serpentine recording.** The tape is still divided into several tracks, but the data is first written onto one track, and when the end of the track is reached, the drive moves to the next track and writes to it. It repeats this process until it runs out of tracks. A serpentine tape drive can access data quickly by moving its head among the different tracks. The read/write assembly requires only one pole and gap, so the drives are cheaper.

The newest method of recording is **helical scan.** Much like a VCR read/write head, tape backup drives with helical scan use heads mounted at an angle on a cylindrical drum. The tape is partially wrapped around the drum, and as the tape slides across the drum, the read/write heads rotate. As each head approaches the tape, it takes swipes at the tape to read or write the data. The tape is moved only slightly between swipes, allowing data to be packed very tightly. In addition, since each head is skewed slightly from the others, they respond well to signals written in the same orientation but not to other signals. Blank spaces are therefore not needed. And if two more heads are added to the drum, data can be read immediately after it is written. Therefore, if any errors are detected, the data can be rewritten immediately on the next piece of tape.

13.3.3 Quarter-Inch Cartridge (QIC)

The first tape drives, used before the PC, were reel-to-reel systems. A tape mounted on one spool was threaded through an open disk drive and fed onto another spool. Later, the tape was enclosed in a cassette and inserted into a capstan drive system. The cassette consisted of two spools (a supply and a takeup spool) and a rubber drive wheel, all connected with a small belt. When the drive wheel turned, the belt caused the spools to move, moving the tape across a linear read/write head.

In 1972, 3M company introduced the first quarter-inch tape cartridge (QIC) designed for data storage. The cartridge measured $6 \times 4 \times \frac{5}{8}$ in. Although the cartridge became the standard, each tape drive manufacturer used different encoding methods, varied the number of tracks, and varied the data density on the tape, causing all kinds of compatibility problems. As a result, in 1982 a group of manufacturers formed the QIC Committee to standardize tape drive construction and application. The full-size quarter-inch cartridge standardized by the QIC Committee is the DC 6000 cartridge (the *DC* stands for data cartridge). The first tape that the QIC committee approved was the QIC-24, which used serpentine recording. It had nine tracks and a density of 8,000 bits per inch (BPI), giving it the total storage capacity of 60 MB. It achieved a read/write speed of 90 in./s and, with the QIC-02 interface, offered a data transfer rate of 720 Kbit/s.

The data density and number of tracks have increased over the years. The QIC-1000-DC packed 30 tracks across the tape at 36,000 BPI, allowing up to 1.2 GB per tape cartridge. Its speed was also increased to 2.8 Mbit/s. Yet the QIC-1000-DC drives could read earlier QIC tapes. By 1989, the QIC committee had revamped the original QIC standard by approving 1,7 RRL encoding and higher coercivity, which allowed higher bit density, a higher number of tracks, and faster transfer rates. By 1995, the QIC standard became the QIC-5210-DC, which had 144 tracks and 76,200 BPI, producing 25 GB storage space. (See table 13.3 for a description of QIC data tapes and cartridges.)

The full-size QIC is too large to fit into a drive bay, so the QIC committee created the minicartridge, which measured 3.25 × 2.50 × 1.59 in. Minicartridges are also referred to as DC 2000 cartridges. The QIC-40-MC was the first cartridge standard adopted. It fit into the 5¼-in. drive bay and connected to the computer by using the floppy drive controller. Since floppy disk drives use MFM encoding, so did the QIC-40-MC. Unlike earlier tapes, QIC-40 specified the format for the data recorded on the tape, including how sectors were assigned to files and FAT for listing bad sectors. Thus the tapes had to be formatted, but they could be bought formatted or unformatted. These tapes could also be accessed randomly. The tape had to be moved to the proper sector, but each file did not have to be read sequentially. To increase storage capacity even further, the Sony Corporation introduced the 8 mm (0.315-in.) tape. It used the same size cartridge, but the extra width allowed for more tracks. It became known as the QIC-Wide minicartridge. (See table 13.4 for a description of QIC minicartridges.)

In 1995, a number of tape and drive manufacturers, including Conner, Iomega, HP, 3M, and Sony, introduced Travan technology, which, unlike the standard QIC cartridge, measured 0.5 × 3.6 × 2.8 in. The smaller front was inserted into the drive; the larger back contained the tape spools. The larger size allowed longer tapes and more data capacity. In addition, the Travan drive accepts standard DC 2000 cartridges and QIC-Wide cartridges.

Table 13.3 QIC Data Cartridges

QIC Standard Number	Capacity Without Compression	Tracks	Interface	Original Adoption Date
QIC-24-DC	45 MB or 60 MB[1]	9	SCSI or QIC-02	4/83
QIC-120-DC	125 MB	15	SCSI or QIC-02	10/85
QIC-150-DC	150 MB or 250 MB[1]	18	SCSI or QIC-02	2/87
QIC-525-DC	320 MB or 525 MB[1]	26	SCSI or SCSI-2	5/89
QIC-1350-DC	1.35 GB	30	SCSI-2	5/89
QIC-1000-DC	1.0 GB	30	SCSI or SCSI-2	10/90
QIC-6000C	6 GB	96	SCSI-2	2/91
QIC-2100-DC	2.1 GB	30	SCSI-2	6/91
QIC-5010-DC	13 GB	144	SCSI-2	2/92
QIC-2GB-DC	2.0 GB	42	SCSI-2	6/92
QIC-5GB-DC	5 GB	44	SCSI-2	12/92
QIC-4GB-DC	4 GB	45	SCSI-2	3/93
QIC-5210-DC	25 GB	144	SCSI-2	8/95

[1]Depending on length of tape.

Table 13.4 QIC Minicartridges

Type of Cartridge	Capacity Without Compression	Tracks	Interface	Original Adoption Date
QIC-40-MC	40 MB or 60 MB[1]	20	Floppy or optional card	6/86
QIC-80-MC	80 MB or 120 MB[1]	28	Floppy or optional card	2/88
QIC-128-MC	86 MB or 128 MB	32	SCSI or QIC	5/89
QIC-3030-MC	555 MB	40	SCSI-2 or QIC	4/91
QIC-3020-MC	500 MB	40	Floppy or IDE	6/91
QIC-3070-MC	4 GB	144	SCSI-2 or QIC	2/92
QIC-3010-MC	255 MB	40	Floppy or IDE	6/93
QIC-3040-MC	840 MB	42/52	SCSI-2 or QIC	12/93
QIC-3080-MC	1.6 GB	60	SCSI-2 or QIC	1/94
QIC-3110-MC	2 GB	48	SCSI-2 or QIC	1/94
QIC-3230-MC	15.5 GB	180	SCSI-2 or QIC	6/95
QIC-3095-MC	4 GB	72	SCSI-2 or QIC	12/95

[1]Depending on length of tape.

13.3.4 Digital Audio Tapes (DAT)

The newest type of audio tape is the 8 mm **digital audio tape (DAT),** which uses the same helical scan technology as VCR tapes and has a storage capacity of up to 72 GB. The DAT standard has been developed and marketed primarily by Hewlett-Packard, which chairs the DDS (Digital Data Storage) Manufacturers Group that developed the DDS standards. Data is not recorded on the DAT tape in the MFM or RLL format; instead, bits of data received by the tape drive are assigned numerical values, or digits. These digits are then translated into a stream of electronic pulses that are placed on the tape. Later, when information is being restored to a computer system from the tape, the DAT tape drive translates these digits back into binary bits that can be stored on the computer.

Digital Data Storage (DDS) tapes are the newest standard for the digital audio tape. DDS-3 can hold 24 GB (the equivalent of over 40 CD-ROMs) and supports data transfer rates of 2 Mbit/s, and it is only slightly larger than a credit card. In a DDS drive, the tape barely creeps along—it requires about 3 s to move 1 in. The head drum spins at 2,000 rpm, putting down 1,869 tracks across a linear inch of tape, which can store 61 Kbit/in. The main advantage of the DAT is its access speed and capacity.

One of the newest tapes is the *DLT (digital linear tape).* Designed for high capacity, high speed, and highly reliable backup, DLTs are ½-in. wide, have capacities of 35–160 GB compressed, and support data transfer rates of 5–10 Mbit/s or more. Unfortunately, the drives are quite expensive and so are used primarily for network server backup. See figure 13.4.

13.3.5 Installing Tape Drives

Installing tape drives is not much different from installing other drives. They fit into an open drive bay or will be connected externally though the back of an expansion card. The power connected to the drive will be either a 3½- or 5¼-in. power connector for internal devices and an ac adapter for external devices. (Note: A few proprietary external tape drives are powered through the interface cable.)

Tape drives will usually use one of four interfaces: (1) QIC-standard (external), (2) floppy (internal), (3) SCSI adapter (internal and external), or (4) EIDE (internal). The floppy disk interface either connects to the unused connector on the floppy drive ribbon cable or will be attached with a special cable link-splitter. SCSI tape drives will need their termination and SCSI ID numbers configured; EIDE tape drives will have to be configured for either stand-alone, master, or slave. (See chapter 10.) Some drives will also require a SCSI-to-parallel port converter.

Figure 13.4 DLT Tape

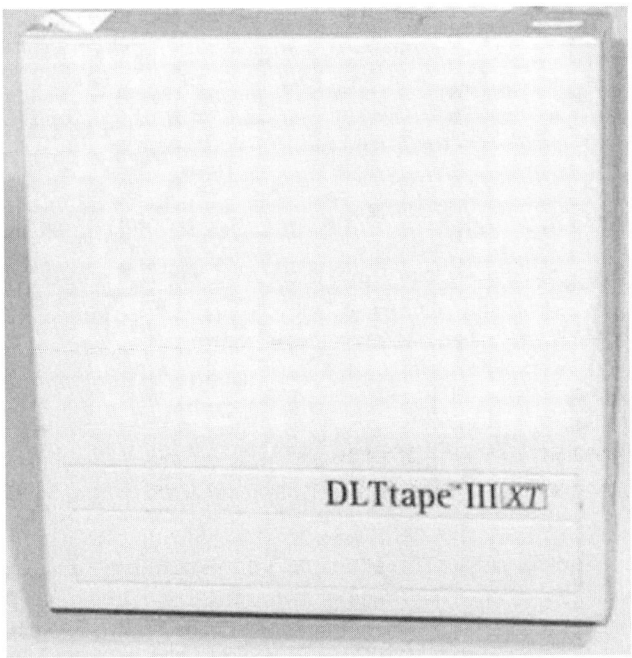

The next step in installing and configuring a tape drive is to install any drivers. This may involve running a setup program, adding lines to the AUTOEXEC.BAT/CONFIG.SYS file, and using the Control panel (Add New Hardware or SCSI Devices). Lastly, backup software that will recognize the tape drive must be installed. Most drives include a backup software package, but you may choose to purchase a commercial package, which may offer more "bells and whistles."

13.3.6 Troubleshooting Tape Drives

All tape drives are half-mechanical, half-electronic devices. Therefore, like any other drive, they can be a high-failure item. Also, the tapes and tape cartridges do not last forever. If a problem does occur, check the drive and drive interface documentation and the backup software documentation for help in diagnosing the problem and interpreting error symptoms and messages.

Since tape drives and tape cartridges go bad, sometimes without warning, it is important to test the drive system from time to time. First, make sure that the files are actually on the tape. Many times, people have thought they were backing up the files only to find out when the computer fails that the tape is blank. Test the system by choosing a file that is not important and try to restore it to the hard drive. Lastly, since tapes do go bad, keep several backups.

Example 13.1: The system does not recognize the drive.

First check the obvious. Make sure that the correct drivers are installed and the correct drive is selected. Next, make sure the power cable is connected properly and is supplying power. Lastly, check to see if the data or control cable is attached properly.

If the problem still exists and the drive had been working before and no hardware changes have been made to the computer, it is probably a hardware failure (the interface card or port, the power cable, the data or control cable, or the drive itself). To determine which one is causing the problem, swap one component at a time until the problem is discovered.

If the tape drive is being installed for the first time, it could be hardware failure or it could be a resource or drive conflict. The resource conflicts include I/O addresses, IRQs, DMAs, or memory addresses. The drive conflicts include terminating resistors (SCSI), SCSI ID numbers, and standalone, master, or slave (EIDE) configurations.

Example 13.2: The tape does not load or eject.

When the drive will not accept or reject a tape, there is usually a mechanical problem with the drive. Of course, before replacing the drive make sure that the power cable is connected to the drive and that nothing is jammed in the drive. If the problem appears to be the drive, it is easier to replace the drive than to repair it.

Example 13.3: The drive writes to a write-protected tape.

To check the obvious, make sure that the tape *is* write-protected. If it is, the problem must be with the drive, specifically the sensor that detects the write-protect lever or the drive's logic board. In either case, it would be best to replace the drive.

Example 13.4: You get read/write errors on the tape.

A read/write error is caused by the drive or the tape. As with floppy disk drives, the read/write heads become covered with magnetic oxide (caused by the contact of the read/write heads with the tape), dust particles, or smoke contamination. To remove these contaminations, you need to use a prepackaged cleaning cartridge. If the problem still exists, the tape must be bad or the drive must be bad. If the tape works in another tape drive, then you know the tape drive is bad. If not, the tape is bad.

13.4 BACK UP, BACK UP, BACK UP

The best method of recovering lost or corrupted data is to back up, back up, back up. When the system does not have a backup of its important files, it is often too late to recover them when disaster occurs. A backup of a system is an extra copy of data and programs. As a technician, consultant, or support person, you need to emphasize at every moment the importance of backing up a system. There are three important parts of a backup system:

1. Developing a backup plan
2. Sticking to the backup plan
3. Testing the backup system

When developing a backup plan, consider the following:

1. What equipment will be used?
2. How much data needs to be backed up?
3. How long will it take to do the backup?
4. How often must the data be backed up?
5. When will the backup take place?
6. Who will do that backup?

Whatever equipment, person, or method is chosen, make sure that the backup will be done. If the backup is not done for whatever reason, the best equipment, the best software, and the brightest person are wasted resources and the data is put at risk.

Backups can be done with floppy disks, extra hard drives (including network drives), compact disk drives, tape drives, and other forms of removable media. Due to the size of floppy disks, they are used to copy only a few files. Extra hard drives, compact disks, tape drives, and other forms of removable media are ideal for the storage of large or many files. If the entire hard drive is backed up on a regular basis, a backup software package can be used. A basic software package comes with Windows 95 and 98 and Windows NT, and one usually comes with the tape drives. There are also other commercial packages with more bells and whistles.

Table 13.5 Types of Backup

Type	Description
Full (normal)	The full backup will back up all files selected and shut off the archive file attribute, indicating the file has been backed up.
Incremental	An incremental backup will back up the files selected if the archive file attribute is on (files changed since the last full or incremental backup). After the file has been backed up, it will shut off the file attribute, indicating that the file has been backed up.
Differential	A differential backup will back up the files selected if the archive file attribute is on (files changed since the last full backup). Unlike the incremental backup, it does not shut off the archive attribute.
Copy	A copy backup will back up the files selected regardless of the archive attribute and it will not shut off the archive attribute after the file has been copied. The copy backup is not typically used as part of a backup procedure. Instead, it would be used as an interim backup in case something goes wrong during major changes or upgrades.
Daily	A daily backup copies all selected files that have been modified on the day the daily backup is performed. During the backup, files are not marked as having been backed up (archive attribute is not cleared).

Question:

How often should the backup be done?

Answer:

How often the backup is done depends on the importance of the data. If many customers are loaded into a database that is constantly changed or the files represent the livelihood of a business, they should be backed up every day. If only a few letters are sent out during the week and none are vitally important, backing up once a week is enough.

Table 13.5 describes the five types of backup.

Example 13.5:

You decide to back up the entire hard drive once a week on Friday, and you decide to use the full backup method. If the hard drive goes bad, you use the most recent backup to restore the hard drive.

Example 13.6:

You decide to back up the entire hard drive once a week on Friday, and you decide to use the incremental method. Therefore, you perform a full backup on week 1. This will shut off all of the archive attributes, indicating that all of the files have been backed up. On week 2, week 3, and week 4, you perform incremental backups using a different tape or disk. Since the incremental backup turns off the archive attribute, only new files and changed files are backed up. Therefore, all four backups make up the entire backup. It is much quicker to back up a drive using an incremental backup than a full one. Of course, if the hard drive fails, you must use backups 1, 2, 3, and 4 to restore the entire hard drive.

Example 13.7:

You decide to back up the entire hard drive once a week on Friday, and you decide to use the differential method. Therefore, you perform a full backup on week 1. This will shut off all the archive attributes, indicating that all the files have been backed up. On week 2, week 3, and week 4, you perform differential backups using a different tape or disk. Since the differential backup does not turn off the archive attribute, it backs up the new files and the files changed since the last full backup. Therefore, the full backup and the last differential backup make up the entire backup. It is much quicker to back up a drive using a differential backup than a full backup but slower than using an incremental backup. If the hard drive fails, you must restore backup 1 and the last differential backup to restore the entire hard drive.

After the backups are complete, check to see that they actually worked by selecting a nonessential file and restoring it to the hard drive. This will reveal empty backups or a faulty backup/restore device. Keep more than one backup. Tapes and disks do fail. One technique is to rotate through three sets of backups. If you perform a full backup once a week, you would then use three sets of backup tapes or disks. During week 1, you would use tape or disk 1. During week 2, you would use tape or disk 2, and during week 3, you would use tape or disk 3. On week 4, you start over and use tape or disk 1. If you have to restore a hard drive and the tape or disk fails, you can always go to the tape or disk from the week before. If the data is important enough, consider keeping a backup set in a fireproof safe off-site.

SUMMARY

1. A virus is a program designed to replicate and spread, generally without the knowledge or permission of the user.
2. Some viruses are cute, some are annoying, and others are disastrous.
3. A boot sector virus infects the computer by rebooting from an infected diskette.
4. File infector viruses attach themselves to or replace executable files.
5. A multipartite virus has the characteristics of both boot sector viruses and file viruses.
6. The macro viruses are the newest strain of viruses and currently are the most common type of virus. Unlike previous viruses, macro viruses are stored in a data document and spread when the infected documents are transferred.
7. A Trojan horse virus hoax is a letter or email message warning you about a virus that does exist. It will generate additional network traffic as people forward them to other people and can cause problems if people follow instructions in the hoax and delete needed files.
8. Antivirus software will detect and remove viruses and help protect the computer against viruses.
9. Antivirus software must be continually updated.
10. Spyware programs, like Trojan horse viruses, are usually bundled with other software without the user's knowledge. It monitors user activity on the Internet and transmits confidential information or generates popup windows.
11. Tapes are ideal for backing up hard drives on a regular basis because they are relatively inexpensive, easy to use, and offer large storage capacities.
12. Tape drives read and write to a long magnetic tape.
13. Several standards have been developed for tapes and tape drives, including the quarter-inch cartridge (QIC) and the digital audio tape (DAT).
14. Tapes are divided into parallel tracks across the width of the tape. The number of tracks varies with the drive and the standard (parallel, serpentine, or helical scan) it follows.
15. Digital audio tape (DAT) uses the same technology as a VCR tape (helical scan).
16. A tape backup will use a QIC, floppy, SCSI, or EIDE interface.
17. When troubleshooting tape drives, follow the normal troubleshooting procedures for IDE or SCSI devices.
18. Restore user data files (if applicable).
19. Because data represents hours of work and the information is sometimes irreplaceable, data is the most important part of the computer.
20. Backing up a system is making an extra copy of data and programs.
21. The best way to protect data is to perform a backup.
22. Backups can be performed with floppy disks, hard disks, compact disks, removable disks, and tapes.
23. After backups are completed, you should check that the backups actually work.

QUESTIONS

1. What is the most important part of the computer?
   a. the microprocessor   b. the hard drive
   c. the RAM   d. the data
2. The best method for protecting the data is
   a. RAID.
   b. back up, back up, back up.
   c. a surge protector.
   d. antivirus software.
3. A small program that replicates itself and sometimes has destructive tendencies is a
   a. macro.   b. TSR.
   c. device driver.   d. virus.

4. Which of the following is *not* a symptom of a virus?
   a. the computer fails to boot
   b. files are corrupted
   c. the system is slower than normal
   d. a disk cannot be read
   e. The monitor bursts into flames
5. Which of the following statements is *not* true?
   a. A virus cannot infect a write-protected disk.
   b. A virus can hide in the CMOS RAM.
   c. Opening an email message cannot infect a system with a virus.
   d. A virus cannot infect a compressed file.
6. Which statement best describes a boot sector virus?
   a. Boot sector viruses are spawned from a bad sector in the boot sector.
   b. A boot sector virus replaces the volume's boot sector program with its own and is loaded into RAM upon boot-up.
   c. Unlike file infector viruses, the boot sector virus does not replicate.
   d. Boot sector viruses cause the volume not to boot but are harmless to data.
   e. Boot sector viruses cause the volume not to be a volume but are harmless to data.
7. A virus that infects both the boot sector and a file is known as a
   a. multipartite virus.
   b. macro virus.
   c. stealth virus.
   d. polymorphic virus.
   e. Trojan horse virus.
8. A Trojan horse virus is
   a. a virus that uses the term *Trojan* or shows a wooden Trojan horse before doing damage.
   b. the first recorded virus.
   c. a virus that appears as a legitimate program but harms the computer when it is executed.
   d. a virus that replicates when it is executed.
9. To protect yourself from a virus, you should do the following *except*
   a. use pirated software.
   b. not boot from or access a floppy disk of unknown origin.
   c. use an antivirus software package.
   d. educate your fellow users.
10. You suspect a virus has entered your computer. Where can the virus *not* reside?
    a. ROM BIOS b. boot sector
    c. floppy disks d. program files
11. Which is ideal for backing up an entire hard drive?
    a. Zip drive
    b. second hard drive
    c. RAID
    d. tape drive
12. Which of the following records using one track and then gets to the end of the tape and proceeds to the next track?
    a. parallel b. serpentine
    c. helical scan d. none of the above
13. Which of the following records data much like a VCR does?
    a. parallel b. serpentine
    c. helical scan d. none of the above
14. The full-size quarter-inch cartridge is known as
    a. DC 2000. b. DC 6000.
    c. Travan. d. DAT.
15. A newer type of tape, which offers large capacities within a small cartridge, is
    a. DAT. b. quarter-inch.
    c. CD. d. open-face.
16. When installing an EIDE tape drive, you must configure the drive as a
    a. master.
    b. slave.
    c. stand-alone.
    d. depends on the system.
17. *True or false*—When troubleshooting a tape drive, never suspect the tapes because they rarely go bad.
18. You have tried several tapes and the tape drive does not read any of them. What is the first thing you should do?
    a. buy a new pack of tapes and try them
    b. format the tape
    c. replace the tape drive
    d. clean the tape drive
19. After backing up a drive, you should occasionally
    a. restore a nonessential file to the hard drive.
    b. reformat the hard drive.
    c. shut down the system.
    d. reformat the tape.
20. The archive attribute is the attribute that indicates whether a file is backed up. Which of the following backups does *not* shut off the archive attribute?
    a. full b. incremental
    c. differential d. none of the above
21. Which Windows 2000 backup mode provides the fastest complete restore in case of a hard drive crash?
    a. normal (full)
    b. increment with differential
    c. normal with incremental (full with incremental)
    d. normal with differential (full with differential)
22. Which five specific backup types are provided by Windows 2000 (choose five)?
    a. copy b. normal
    c. incremental d. daily
    e. weekly f. referential
23. A customer running Windows XP Home Edition with an antivirus application installed reports that he downloaded a program from the Internet and installed it on his computer. After installing the program, he began to receive email messages from people whom he does not know. These email messages state that he sent an email message to them. The user removed the program but is still receiving the email messages with the

same message content from people whom he does not know. You need to identify the cause of these email messages. What should you instruct the user to do?

a. connect to the Microsoft Windows Update website and scan his computer.
b. download the most recent virus signature files and scan his computer for viruses.
c. run the Microsoft Baseline Security Analyzer (MBSA) tool and scan for security updates.
d. run the Security Configuration and Analysis tool and analyze his computer by using the HISECWS.INF security template.

HANDS-ON EXERCISES

Exercise 1: Installing an Antivirus Software Package

1. Install an antivirus software package.
2. Find and download the update for the package.
3. Install the update.

Exercise 2: Finding and Removing Viruses

1. Use the antivirus software package to check your hard drives for viruses.
2. Insert a formatted floppy disk in drive A and use the antivirus software package to check the disk for viruses.
3. Get an infected disk from your instructor and remove the virus from the disk.

Exercise 3: Finding and Removing Adware and Spyware

1. Go to the http://www.lavasoftusa.com website and download an adware program.
2. Install the adware program.
3. Scan your system for spyware programs and remove them if found.

Exercise 4: Installing a Backup Tape Drive

1. Configure and physically install the tape backup drive using a floppy, EIDE, SCSI, or proprietary interface.
2. Install any drivers needed to activate the tape backup drive.
3. Install a backup software package that supports the tape drive.
4. Back up the entire hard drive using the backup software package (full backup).
5. Choose several nonessential files from the hard drive and delete them.
6. Using the tape drive, restore the deleted files.
7. Create or add three files and change at least two others.
8. Select all files on the hard drives, but choose an incremental backup to back up only the new or changed files.
9. Remove the tape drive from the system.

Exercise 5: Backing Up the Hard Drive

This exercise requires Windows 9X loaded on drive C.

1. Create a DATA directory on the C drive.
2. In the DATA directory, create a PICTURE directory and a TEXT directory.
3. Copy all files that have a BMP file name extension from the C:\WINDOWS directory to the PICTURE directory.
4. Copy all of the files that have a TXT file name extension from the C:\WINDOWS directory to the TEXT directory.
5. Create a CHANGE.TXT file in the TEXT directory. Include your name in the text file.
6. Start the backup software that comes with tape drive or the Windows Backup program.
7. Select the entire hard drive so that it can be backed up. Determine the total number of bytes. (Do not back up the drive.)
8. Deselect the hard drive.
9. Select the PICTURE and DATA directories, including the files within the PICTURE and DATA directories. Determine the total number of bytes.

10. Back up the selected files to a tape or to floppy disks.
11. Determine the status of the archive attribute of the CHANGE.TXT file.
12. Edit the CHANGE.TXT file, add today's date into the file, and save the file.
13. Determine the status of the archive attribute of the CHANGE.TXT file.
14. Create a file called NEW.TXT in the TEXT directory.
15. Determine the status of the archive attribute of the NEW.TXT file.
16. Back up the first name directory using an incremental backup.
17. Delete the TEXT directory.
18. Restore the TEXT directory from the tape or disks.

Exercise 6: Performing a Backup and Restore with Windows 2000 or Windows XP

Using the Backup Wizard

1. Log in as the administrator.
2. On your D drive, create a DATA directory.
3. From the C:\WINNT\WEB\WALLPAPER or C:\WINDOWS\WEB\WALLPAPER folder, copy all the files to the D:\DATA folder.
4. To start the Microsoft Backup program, click on the Start button, select the Programs option, select the Accessories option, select the System Tools option, and select the Backup option.
5. At the Welcome to Windows 2000 Backup and Recovery Tools page, click on the Backup Wizard button. Click on the Next button.
6. Select the Backup Selected Files, Drives, Network Data option and click on the Next button.
7. In the Items Backup page, find the DATA folder in the C drive. Click on the DATA folder to show its contents in the box to the right. To select the DATA folder to be backed up, put a checkmark in the box next to the DATA folder. Click on the Next button.
8. In a real-world network, you would typically back up to a tape drive. Because many schools do not have tape drives for every student nor do typical users at home have a tape drive, back up to the floppy drive. Therefore, for the Backup media or file name text box, keep the A:\BACKUP.BKT and click on the Next button.
9. Before clicking on the Finish button, click on the Advanced button.
10. Open the Select the Type of Backup Operation to Perform text box and look at the options. When done, choose the Normal option and click on the Next button.
11. Select the Verify data after backup option and click on the Next button.
12. If the archive media already contains a backup, replace the data on media with this backup. Therefore, select this option and click on the Next button.
13. Accept the default labels and click on the Next button.
14. Keep the default of doing the backup now and click the Next button.
15. Insert the blank floppy disk in drive A.
16. Click on the Finish button.
17. When the backup is complete, click on the Close button.
18. Remove the tape (or disk) and label the name of the backup. In addition, log the backup either in a table or notebook or on the disk label. Write "Backup—Data folder" and today's date on the label of the disk.

Using the Restore Wizard

1. Delete the DATA folder on the C drive.
2. Back at the Welcome to the Windows 2000 Backup and Recovery Tools page, click on the Restore Wizard button. Click on the Next button.
3. Notice that because of the catalogs, Windows 2000 remembers the backups that were done. Therefore, click on the plus(+) sign next to File, click on the next plus sign, and put a checkmark for the C drive. Click on the Next button.
4. Before clicking on the Finish button, click on the Advanced button. If you want to specify the files to be restored to a different location, there is where it is done. Click on the Next button.
5. In this case, because there is no longer a DATA folder, it doesn't matter which option you choose. Therefore, keep the default option and click on the Next button.
6. Since there is no system or security information to restore, click on the Next button.
7. Click the Finish button.
8. Click on the OK button to restore from the default file.
9. Click on the Close button.

CHAPTER 14

The Video System

Topics Covered in This Chapter

Introduction

The video system, consisting of the monitor and video card, displays the results of computing. The monitor, a device similar to a television, is the computer's primary output device and the user's direct link to the computer. The video card is the component that connects the monitor to the rest of the computer. The quality of the monitor greatly affects the productivity of the user.

Objectives

1. Compare and contrast the two types of displays.
2. Using the controls of the monitor, adjust the contrast, brightness, horizontal and vertical positioning, horizontal and vertical size, and pin cushioning.
3. Compare and contrast passive LCD screens and active LCD screens.
4. Define *pixels, aspect ratio, resolution, dot pitch,* and *convergence.*
5. List the advantages and disadvantages of text mode and graphics mode.
6. Define *refresh rate* and explain how it relates to flicker.
7. Enable and adjust the power management features within the CMOS setup program and Windows Control Panel.
8. Given a bit depth, calculate the total number of colors that can be used by the system.
9. Given the resolution and bit depth of a video system, calculate the required amount of video RAM needed.
10. Explain the difference between a standard VGA card and a video accelerator.
11. List and compare the different forms of RAM used on video cards.
12. List the different buses used with video cards and explain which is the best one to use.
13. Compare and contrast the different forms of video interfaces.
14. Install a video card and monitor.
15. Given a video system problem, determine and correct the problem.

14.1 THE MONITOR

The video system, which displays the results of computing, consists of the monitor and video card. The **monitor,** which connects to the video card, is the computer's primary output device. It is sometimes referred to as a *display* or *video.* Since the user must use the monitor to see results, the monitor is the user's direct link to the computer.

Like televisions, the size of the monitor is measured diagonally across the screen. See figure 14.1. The most popular sizes for monitors are 14 in., 15 in., 17 in., and 21 in. Because some monitors become significantly distorted near the edges of the screen, they have a black border around the edges, reducing the size of the actual picture.

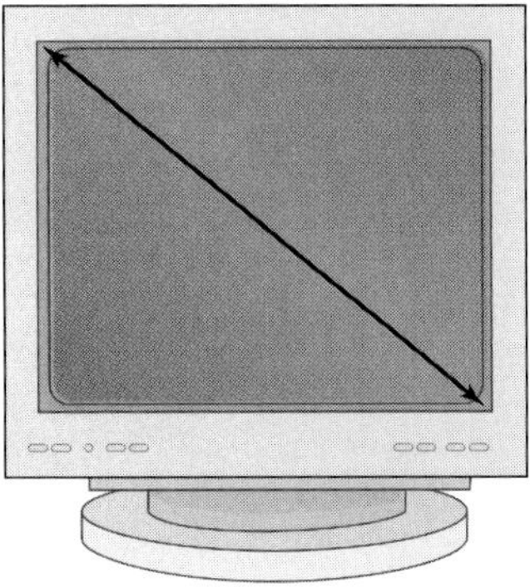

Figure 14.1 Monitor size is determined by measuring diagonally across the screen.

Monitors are of two types, cathode-ray tube (CRT) and liquid-crystal display (LCD). CRTs are the displays that resemble a television. They are usually found on desktop and tower computers. LCD displays are usually found on laptop and notebook computers and are the most expensive component of a portable computer.

14.1.1 The CRT Monitor

The **cathode-ray tube (CRT)** inside the monitor consists of an electronic screen that is lined with a phosphorescent material. See figure 14.2. An electron gun shoots electrons at the phosphorescent material and the material glows as it is struck. The intensity of the electron beam determines the intensity of the color produced. Since the phosphorescent material will glow for only a fraction of a second, it has to be constantly recharged.

To aim and focus the beams of electrons, the CRT uses a magnetic deflection yoke to bend the path of the electrons with electromagnetic fields. See figure 14.3. To keep the electron beams from affecting nearby pixels on the screen, the CRT uses a shadow mask or an aperture grill to focus the beams. The most commonly used is the **shadow mask,** a fine metal mesh with openings that line up with the pix-

Figure 14.2 Inside the CRT Monitor

Figure 14.3 A CRT uses an electron gun to shoot electrons at a phosphorescent screen.

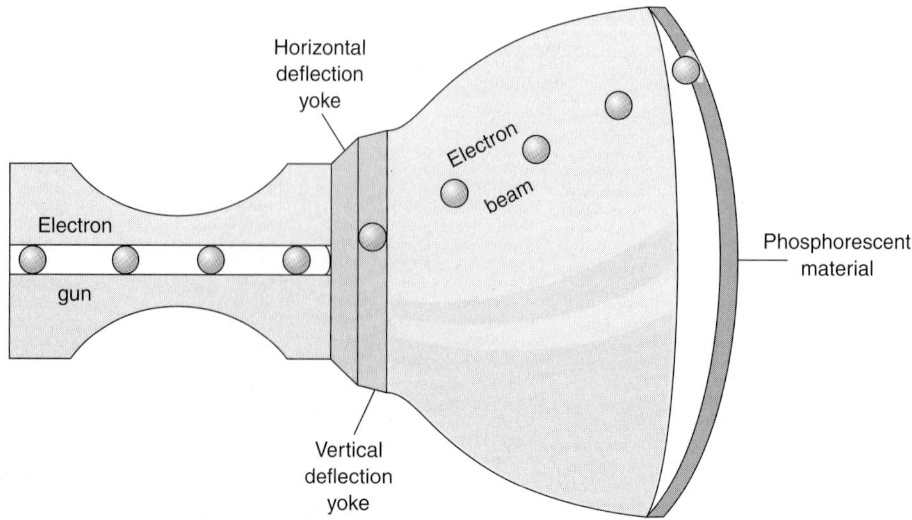

els. The **aperture grill** is made up of hundreds of fine metal strips that run vertically from the top of the screen to the bottom. The aperture grill allows for a brighter monitor and less glare from a flat vertical screen, but it requires one or more stabilizing wires, which run horizontally across the screen, to prevent the grill from vibrating. The stabilizing wires may show as extremely faint lines on the screen, although they usually are noticeable only on a full white screen.

Some monitors have a curved screen; some newer monitors are flat. The curved screens are less expensive, but they tend to have more glare from overhead lights than flat screens do. The glare makes it harder to see the image on the screen and eventually leads to eyestrain and fatigue. To reduce the surface glare, most monitor screens have a special film or coating. (Note: The screen should be cleaned only with a water-dampened cloth or a cloth with a special cleaning solution made for monitors that will not remove the coating. Do not use Windex glass cleaner or 409 multipurpose cleaner.)

The CRT monitor can generate a lot of heat, so every monitor case has special ventilation holes to allow for the cooling of the system components. If the holes are covered or blocked, the monitor will overheat, causing damage to the monitor. CRT monitors also produce large amounts of electromagnetic radiation. To someone who spends a lot of time around a monitor that is on, the electromagnetic radiation can be harmful over a period of time. Today, monitors are being designed to reduce the amount of electromagnetic radiation.

As on a television, the sharpness, brightness, contrast, vertical and horizontal position (sometimes known as vertical and horizontal center), vertical and horizontal size, and pin cushioning (straightness of the vertical and horizontal lines) of a monitor can be adjusted with analog or digital controls. Most of these controls are located at the front of the monitor, but they may also be found at the back or the side of the monitor or inside the monitor. Analog controls are usually knobs; a digital control is a single menu button that selects the feature to change with up and down arrows for adjusting the feature. The digital controls are not always intuitive, but they do reduce the number of analog controls on the monitor.

14.1.2 The LCD Panel

LCD stands for **liquid-crystal display,** which uses **liquid crystal (LC),** an organic material that has the characteristics of both a liquid and a solid. Liquid crystal consists of a large array of rod-shaped molecules. It appears to be a liquid but has a crystalline molecular structure usually found in solid objects. In an LCD display, the liquid-crystal material is pressed between two pieces of clear plastic, which are polarized. The polarized plastic allows light to vibrate in only one way. Tiny grooves in the plastic sheets align the molecules. When electricity is sent through the LC material, the molecules twist, which will bend any light shown through them. When the electricity is stopped, the molecules go back to their normal orientation.

As a light (**backlit light**) is shone through the first layer of polarized plastic, it passes through a filter (allowing the light to shine in only one direction) and into the LC material. The second polarized sheet bends the light to a different angle from that of the first sheet. Normally, when electricity is not being applied to the LC material, the light passes through the first sheet and LC material but cannot pass through the second polarized sheet. When electricity is applied, the LC molecules twist, bending the light to the proper angle so that it can pass through the second sheet. The amount of electricity controls the amount of the twist and the intensity of the light. See figure 14.4. If the backlit light goes out, the image on the screen will be very faint. This is most likely caused by a blown fuse on the inverter board (if there is one), the inverter board or the phosphorus light. The function of the inverter board is to distribute low-voltage dc electricity through the LCD panel. See figure 14.5.

Passive matrix displays use row and column electrodes to send electricity through the LC material. An electrode is a conductor used to establish electrical contact with a nonmetallic part of a circuit. Much like CRT monitors, each cell in the matrix has to be constantly refreshed and in sequence. Unfortunately, the electrical charges fade quickly, causing colors to look faded. To increase the brightness, some passive matrix displays use double-scan, a technique that splits the screen into a top half and a bottom half and allows both halves to be refreshed at the same time. Since the cells can be refreshed quicker, the screen is brighter and has a quicker response time.

Active matrix displays, known as *thin-film transistor (TFT) displays,* have a rear glass screen to hold the electrodes for each cell and a front glass screen that contains a single, large common electrode for every screen element. To control the flow of electricity, each cell uses a transistor, which acts as an

Figure 14.4 In the left-hand picture, light is not allowed through because the polarizing filters let light in at two different angles. In the picture on the right, liquid crystal bends the light to the angle of the second filter.

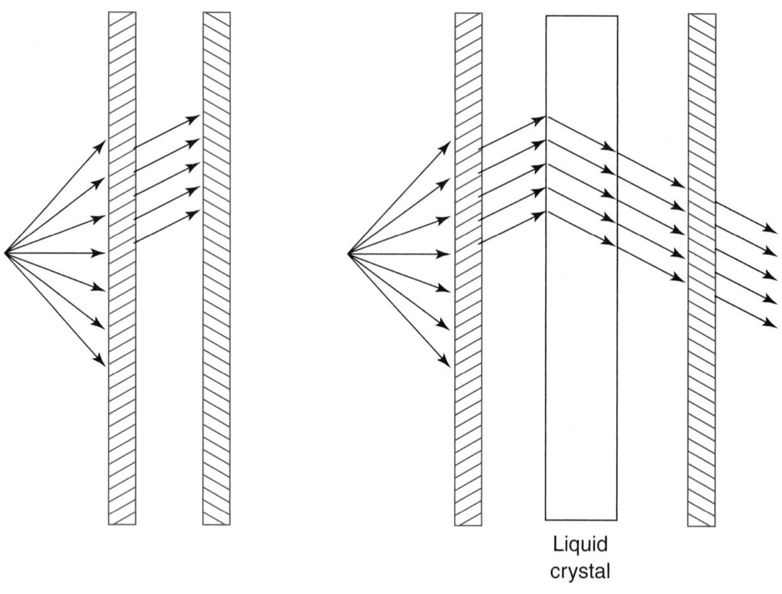

Figure 14.5 An LCD Panel with Inverter Board

on/off switch. Since the transistor can provide a constant charge that does not need refreshing, colors are brighter. As a result, the screen can be viewed at an angle of up to 45° and has a contrast of 40:1. This means that the brightness of an "on" pixel is 40 times greater than that of an "off" pixel. The disadvantage of active matrix displays is cost and, because the TFTs block a fraction of the light, the need for a more intense backlighting system.

When handling an LCD display, be careful not to scratch the surface and make sure that you do not expose the screen to high amounts of force or pressure, since this may crack the LCD panel. Lastly, to clean the LCD screen, you should use a water-dampened lint-free cloth or a lint-free cloth with isopropyl alcohol or ethyl alcohol.

Occasionally, an LCD panel will have dead pixels. (Note: The LCD specifications for bad pixels is an industry standard and is available from the notebook manufacturer.) The manufacturer will supply these specifications when supplying LCDs, and they will not exchange them if they are within the specs. Therefore, if you have a single dead pixel (the pixel is always black), the manufacturer will most likely not replace the LCD panel. Instead, you must have either several dead pixels on the screen or a couple of pixels grouped together before the manufacturer will replace the LCD screen. Check with the distributor or notebook manufacturer for the criteria used in deciding whether or not to replace the LCD screen. Of course, as LCD screens have matured and manufacturers have gotten more efficient, the occurence of dead pixels have decreased.

NOTE: Another problem that may occur is that a pixel, or subpixel (red, green or blue), may actually stay on and not turn off. While the manufacturer treats this similar to a dead pixel, you may be able fix your monitor by gently tapping the area of the pixel.

14.1.3 Pixels and the Monitor Resolution

The image (text, lines, boxes, and pictures) on the monitor is made up of many dots called **picture elements** or **pixels.** See figure 14.6. The number of pixels that can be displayed on the screen at one time is called the **resolution** of the screen. The resolution consists of two numbers, the number of pixels going from left to right and the number of pixels going from top to bottom. The **aspect ratio** of most monitors is 4:3. This means that for every four pixels going across the screen, there are three pixels going down. The horizontal number of pixels divided by the vertical number of pixels is 1.33; therefore, if there are 480 pixels vertically, the number of pixels going across would be $480 \times 1.33 = 640$ pixels. See table 14.1.

Another term relating to the resolution of the monitor is the monitor's **dot pitch.** Dot pitch is the distance between the pixels. See figure 14.6. Typical values range from .25 to .41 mm. If the dot pitch is too large, the picture may be "grainy." If the dot pitch is too small, the monitor tends to have decreased brightness and contrast. A good dot pitch is between .28 and .31 mm. **Convergence** describes the clarity and sharpness of each pixel. It is the capability of the color monitor to focus the three colored electron beams into a single point. If a monitor has poor convergence, the picture will be fuzzy and blurry.

Figure 14.6 Picture Elements (Pixels) Make Up Images on the Screen

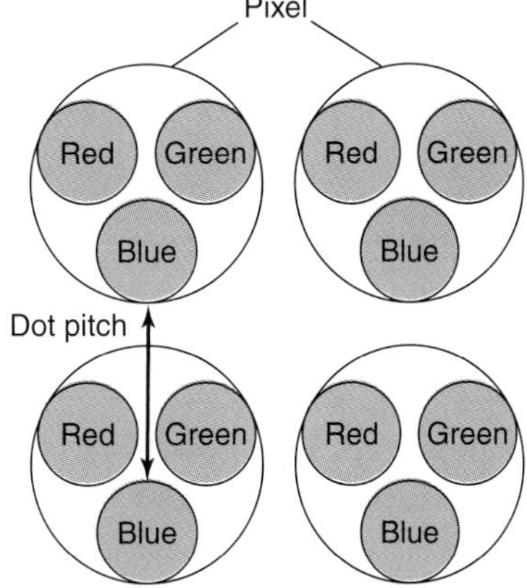

Table 14.1 Typical Resolution and Aspect Ratios

Resolution	Number of Pixels	Aspect Ratio
320 × 200	64,000	8:5
640 × 480	307,200	4:3
800 × 600	480,000	4:3
1024 × 768	786,432	4:3
1280 × 1024	1,310,720	5:4
1600 × 1200	1,920,000	4:3

Question:

If a VGA monitor has a resolution of 640 × 480, how many pixels does it have?

Answer:

A screen with a resolution of 640 × 480 has 640 pixels going across and 480 pixels going down. Multiplying these two numbers gives a total of 307,200 pixels on the screen.

Question:

Is a monitor with a higher resolution better than a monitor with a lower resolution?

Answer:

Typically, a monitor with a higher resolution is a better monitor, although the higher resolution may not always be the best resolution to use. Most programs are made to work with a certain resolution and will not adjust for a different one. For example, a Windows application that takes up the entire 640 pixels going across and 480 pixels going down would fill the entire screen. At a higher resolution, such as 1024 × 768, the program still displays the box using 640 pixels going across and 480 pixels going down. The problem is that the box would be 38 percent smaller. If software is made for a monitor with a higher resolution and can adjust to the higher resolution proportionately, the picture tends to be sharper and more detailed than it is on a monitor with a lower resolution.

As the computer is operating, the video system runs in either text mode or graphics mode. When the computer is first turned on or when it is running a command-driven operating system (such as DOS), the video system uses text mode, typically displaying 25 rows of 80 characters (80 × 25). Most monitors can also support other modes, such as 43 rows of 80 characters (80 × 43). The instructions (ROM BIOS, operating system, or software programs) specify what characters are to be shown on the screen by sending the ASCII character and its location (row and column) to the video card. The pixel information, defined in the video ROM BIOS, is then sent from the video card to the monitor. Text mode is simple and fast, but its simplicity limits it to the set of predefined ASCII characters.

Question:

How much information is used by a video system that runs in 80 × 25 text mode?

Answer:

In this mode, there can be a total of 80 × 25 = 2,000 characters at any one time. Because each character (ASCII character) uses 1 byte to define it, the entire screen can display 2,000 bytes of data.

The GUI operating system or environments (Windows) and most programs run in graphics mode. In graphics mode, the information that is to be displayed is broken down into pixels and the pixel information is sent to the video card. The video card will then send the proper signals to the monitor. Graphics mode is more complicated than text mode and can use the pixels to make any form of text or picture.

All video systems support the text and graphics modes at different resolutions. This allows one program to use one resolution while another program uses another resolution. The maximum resolution that a monitor can display is determined by its technology, its size (larger monitors can contain more pixels), the capabilities of the video card (including the amount of video memory), and the software being used. (Note: The resolution supported by the monitor must match the resolution supported by the video card.)

14.1.4 Refresh Rate

In order to draw the entire screen before the phosphorescent material fades, the electron guns must be fast. The number of times that the screen is redrawn in a second is referred to as the **refresh rate,** which is measured in Hertz (Hz). If the refresh rate is too low, the electron guns do not recharge the phosphorescent material before it fades, which causes the monitor to flicker. Although the flicker is hardly noticeable, it can lead to eyestrain. To avoid flickering, a refresh rate with at least 70 Hz is required. The Video Electronics Standards Association (VESA) has established an 85 Hz refresh rate as the standard for flicker-free monitors.

High-quality monitors that support high resolutions refresh the screen one line at a time, from top to bottom. This is called **noninterlacing** or conventional mode. Some monitors use **interlacing** to refresh the screen, which redraws the screen in two sweeps, refreshing every other line. During the first sweep, the monitor refreshes the odd-numbered lines; during the second sweep, it refreshes the even-numbered lines. The refresh rate is lower as a result, allowing for a cheaper monitor. Unfortunately, the monitor's reaction speed is reduced, which may introduce flicker.

14.1.5 Monitor Burn-In and Screen Savers

Older monitors, particularly monochrome monitors, were susceptible to burn-in when a particular image was displayed on a screen for a long time, which burned out the phosphorescent material and left behind a ghost image. To prevent this problem, **screen savers** were used to blank the screen or to provide a constant moving pattern. Although screens savers are not needed today, hundreds are available and with every conceivable theme. The screen saver has therefore progressed to a form of entertainment.

NOTE: LCD panels can be affected from burn-in.

14.1.6 DPMS

The monitor, like the computer case, uses a power supply. To help reduce power consumption, the Environmental Protection Agency (EPA) began a program called Energy Star to certify PCs and monitors that reduce power consumption. These PCs are sometimes called **green PCs,** and the Energy Star logo appears on the screen when the monitor is initialized by the computer.

In an effort to conserve power, Intel and Microsoft created the **advanced power management (APM)** standard that allows the system ROM BIOS (enabled in the CMOS setup program) or software to manage the power consumption of the system. Part of the APM standard is the **display power management system (DPMS)** standard, which was introduced by the Video Electronics Standards Association (VESA). DPMS allows the monitor to go into stand-by mode (which uses less power than the normal operational state) and suspend or shut-down mode (which turns off the monitor) during periods of inactivity.

14.2 THE VIDEO CARD

The **video card** is the component that takes the visual output of the computer and sends it to the monitor. It tells the monitor which pixels to light up, what color the pixels should be, and what intensity they should have. The video card is an expansion card (see figure 14.7) or is built into the motherboard. It is identified with its 3-row, 15-pin female port (VGA or SVGA) or a DVI connector.

14.2.1 Number of Colors

All monitors can be classified as either monochrome or color. **Monochrome** monitors display two colors, one for the background and one for the foreground. The background color is black, and the foreground color is white, green, or amber. A gray-scale monitor, a special kind of monochrome monitor, can display different shades of white. Depending on the type of video system, it can support either up to 64 or up to 256 different shades.

Figure 14.7 PCI Video Card

Table 14.2 Color Depth

Common Name	Color Depth	Number of Displayed Colors	Bytes of Storage per Pixel
Monochrome	1 bit	2	⅛ byte
16 colors (VGA mode)	4 bits	16	½ byte
256 colors	8 bits	256	1 byte
High color	16 bits	65,536	2 bytes
True color	24 bits	16,777,216	3 bytes

The most common type of monitor is the color monitor. Depending on the monitor and video card, the monitor can display from 4 to 16 million colors. The pixel of a color monitor is actually made of a red, a green, and a blue dot. As the three colors are mixed at various intensities, they can produce virtually any color. When all three colors are at the highest intensity, the color displayed is white. If all colors are at the lowest intensity, the color displayed is black.

Color depth, or bit depth, is the amount of information that determines the color of a pixel. The more colors each pixel can show, the more colors the screen can show and the more shades of the same color, which can produce a more realistic, detailed picture. However, the higher number of bits required to give each pixel a higher color depth requires more video memory for the video system to store the pixel's information and more processing by the computer. See table 14.2.

Question:

How much memory is required for a monochrome monitor with a resolution of 640 × 480?

Answer:

A monochrome monitor displays a single color, which represents either *on* or *off.* The data to describe the status of the pixel is stored as 1 bit of information (the 0 indicates the pixel is off and the 1 indicates the pixel is on). A 640 × 480 screen resolution with 307,200 dots will require 307,200 dots, or 38,400 bytes (8 bits per byte).

Early color monitors were digital devices that could show only a set number of predetermined colors. The color of the pixel was specified by a binary code. VGA monitors and Super VGA monitors are analog devices capable of showing an unlimited number of colors. The VGA system can display 16 colors at a resolution of 640 × 480 or 256 colors at a resolution of 320 × 200. As an image is drawn on the screen, a binary code is sent to the video card. The video card then looks up the color in a palette (preselected colors) to define the intensities of the red, green, and blue colors of the pixel and sends that information to the monitor. If a picture has more than 256 unique colors, it can still be displayed on a 256 color video system. The other colors are created by choosing the 256 closest colors and using dithering. Dithering is the process of creating more colors and shades by intermixing colors. Unfortunately, these pictures often look grainy or patchy.

Question:

How much information is required for a monitor with a resolution of 640 × 480 that displays up to 256 colors?

Answer:

A binary number of eight 0s and 1s has 256 different combinations (each combination representing a particular color), so each pixel uses 1 byte of information. The monitor has 307,200 pixels, so it requires 307,200 pixels × 1 byte per pixel, or 307,200 bytes.

For high-quality pictures, the computer would use high color or true color. **High color** uses 16 bits to define the color of the pixel, and the 16 bits allow 65,536 different combinations of 0s and 1s, or 65,536 different colors. Blue and red use 5 bits each to specify 32 different intensities or shades, while green uses 6 bits to define 64 intensities. (Note: Some systems may use a 15-bit model, which allows only 32,768 different colors.)

High color gives you a very slight loss of visible image quality but with the advantages of a lower memory requirement and faster performance.

True color uses three bytes to define each pixel, which allows up to 16,777,216 colors. Because each pixel uses 3 bytes of data, each color (blue, red, and green) is defined with a 1-byte binary code that specifies 256 different intensities.

However, some graphics cards actually require 32 bits for each pixel to display true color because of the way in which they use the video memory. The extra 8 bits generally are used for an alpha channel (transparencies). The darkest areas of an alpha channel are most transparent, white areas are opaque, and shades of gray represent varying levels of transparency.

14.2.2 Video Memory

The amount of information sent to the monitor in the early PCs was extremely small. A monitor in text mode (25 rows of 80 characters) had only 2,000 characters, which required only 2,000 bytes of data. On these older systems, the video data was generated by the microprocessor and stored in the reserve memory (RAM between 640 MB and 1 MB). The data was then constantly read by the video card and sent to the monitor to be displayed.

As computers shifted from text mode to graphics, and systems with higher resolutions and more colors were developed, the reserve memory was not big enough to hold the increased video data. Therefore, the modern video card contains **video memory** (also called **frame buffer**). For example, a VGA video system with a maximum resolution of 640 × 480 (307,200 pixels) can show 16 colors (4 bits), requiring a minimum of 153,600 bytes of video memory. Because video cards do not come with exactly 153,600 bytes, a card with 256 KB (or higher) would be used. If the monitor is set at 1024 × 768 (786,432 pixels) and displays 16 million colors (24 bits), the video card requires a minimum of 2,359,296 bytes. Therefore, a 3 or 4 MB (or more) video card would have to be used. (Note: Modern video cards perform some of the video processing, so some higher-end video cards also use the video memory for processing.)

The **RAMDAC** (RAM digital–analog converter), located on the video card, translates the digital information into the analog information used by the monitor. It uses a lookup table located within the video ROM BIOS to determine the voltage intensities for each of the primary colors (red, green, and blue). The speed of the video card, or video card bandwidth, is the amount of data that can be generated by the video card and sent to the monitor. It depends mainly on the speed of the RAMDAC, the speed of the RAM, and the speed of the PC interface.

Question:

A monitor has a resolution of 640 × 480 and a bit depth of 4 bits (16 colors). How much bandwidth is required if the picture is being redrawn at a rate of 10 updates per second?

Answer:

There are 307,200 pixels on the screen using 307,200 pixels × 0.5 bytes = 153,600 bytes of data at one time. The screen must be redrawn 10 times per second, so there is required bus *bandwidth* of 153,600 bytes × 10 = 1.54 MB/s.

Question:

A monitor is using a resolution of 1,024 × 768 with a bit depth of 24 bits (16 million colors). How much bandwidth is required if a real-time video is being shown at 30 frames per second?

Answer:

There are 786,432 pixels on the screen using 786,432 pixels × 3 bytes = 2,359,296 bytes of data at one time. The screen must be redrawn 30 times per second, so there is a required bandwidth of 2,359,296 bytes × 30 = 70.8 MB/s.

3D adapters need additional memory for special operations. Double buffering doubles the memory needs by using two separate frame buffers to work. In addition, these types of cards need additional memory for z-buffering and to perform certain calculations and for holding textures. Therefore, some of these cards may have 64 MB, 128 MB, or 256 MB of memory and more could be used in the future.

In recent years as the video was integrated on the motherboard, some systems use the **unified memory architecture (UMA),** which is when the motherboard uses part of the computer's main memory for video memory. Because both the processor and video controller have access to this memory, it is sometimes called shared memory architecture. While the advantage of UMA is a lower cost of the computer since a video RAM is not needed, the disadvantage is that the entire RAM is not available to your applications. In addition, these systems will be slower than a system with a dedicated graphics adapter with video RAM.

Dynamic video memory technology (DVMT) is an enhancement of the UMA concept, wherein the optimum amount of memory is allocated for balanced graphics and system performance, through direct AGP (known as non-local video memory, or NLVM), and a highly efficient memory utilization scheme. DVMT ensures the most efficient use of available memory—regardless of frame buffer or main memory sizing—for maximum 2D/3D graphics performance. DVMT dynamically responds to system requirements, and application demands, by allocating the proper amount of display, texturing and buffer memory after the operating system has booted. For example, a 3D application when launched may require more vertex buffer memory to enhance the complexity of objects, or more texture memory to enhance the richness of the 3D environment. The operating system views the integrated graphics driver as an application, which uses direct AGP to request allocation of additional memory for 3D applications, and returns the memory to the operating system when no longer required.

14.2.3 Video RAM

Video RAM, much like regular RAM, can be described by the memory technology used and its access time. The older and slower video cards use the standard **dynamic RAM (DRAM)** chip, specifically **fast page mode DRAM (FPM DRAM)** and **extended data out (EDO) RAM.** It is single ported (it can do only one access at a time) and has a low speed and small access width. Another type of RAM chip is **video RAM (VRAM).** Video RAM, usually used on video cards, is a special form of DRAM that has two separate data ports. One port is dedicated to updating the image on the screen while the other one is used for changing the image data stored in the RAM on the video card. This dual-ported design gives higher performance (up to 40 percent) than DRAM. (Note: Don't confuse VRAM, a type of memory used in video cards, and the generic term *video memory,* which refers to memory in the video system.)

Table 14.3 Types of Memory Used for Video Cards

Technology	Access Ports	Approximate Bandwidth	Speed (Typical)	Usage
Standard (FPM) DRAM	Single	Low	70–80 ns	Low-end ISA cards, obsolete
EDO DRAM	Single	Low	50–60 ns	Low-end PCI bus
SDRAM	Single	Fast	10–15 ns	Low-end PCI bus
VRAM	Dual	High	50–60 ns	Obsolete
WRAM	Dual	High	50–60 ns	Obsolete
SGRAM	Single	Very high	8–10 ns	High-end PCI/AGP; replaced by DDR SDRAM
MDRAM	Single	High	50–60 ns	Obsolete
DDR SDRAM	Single	Very high	3–6 ns	High-end AGP

A newer version of VRAM is **Windows RAM (WRAM)** developed by Samsung and used on high-end video cards. It has a dual-color block write to perform very fast pattern and text fills and can perform fast buffer-to-buffer transfers for video and double-buffered 3D animation. As a result, WRAM offers 25 percent more bandwidth than VRAM and up to a 40–50 percent increase in performance when doing text drawing and block fills. In addition, WRAM is cheaper than VRAM.

Rather than using a single block of video memory, MDRAM, **multibank DRAM (MDRAM),** breaks its memory into multiple 32 KB banks that can be accessed independently. This allows interleaving of the RAM. (Interleaving is two banks working together.) When one bank is getting ready for access, the other bank is being accessed. MDRAM also allows video cards to have customized memory sizes, so there is no wasted RAM, which reduces the cost of the video card.

SGRAM, SDRAM, and DDR SDRAM have replaced VRAM, WRAM, and MDRAM as high-speed video RAM solutions. **Synchronous DRAM (SDRAM)** is the same type of RAM used on many types of systems. This memory is designed to work with bus speeds up to 200 MHz and provides performance just slightly slower than SGRAM.

Synchronous graphics RAM (SGRAM) is similar to SDRAM in its capability to be synchronized to high-speed buses up to 200 MHz. Different from SDRAM, it can perform block writes to increase the speed of graphics fill or 3D Z-buffer operations. It also incorporates performance-enhancing features like the acceleration features built into a video card. Although it is single ported, it offers performance close to VRAM because it can open two memory pages at the same time, simulating a dual-port design. Matrox Graphics is probably the company best known for making extensive use of SGRAM.

Double data rate SDRAM (DDR SDRAM) is similar to SDRAM, but it transfers data at speeds twice that of SDRAM by transferring data on both the rising and falling parts of the processing clock cycle. See table 14.3. Today's high-end cards use graphical DDR, DDR2, or DDR3, which are clocked at much higher rates compared to desktop RAM, and before being standardized.

Much like normal RAM used on the motherboard, the video RAM chips are available in different access speeds. The lower the access speed, the faster the RAM. Although the access speed is a factor in video card performance, it is not as important as the type of technology used in the RAM chip.

NOTE: As new forms of memory are created, they are often used in video cards before they are used in motherboards.

14.2.4 Video Card Interface

The video card interface is *the* interface to the rest of the computer. Initially, the PC used the PC bus or 8-bit ISA and 16-bit ISA bus to transfer data between the system and the video card. The 16-bit ISA bus had a 16-bit data path, ran at 8 MHz, and had a maximum bandwidth of 8.33 MB per second. As higher resolutions were introduced and the number of colors was increased, the ISA bus quickly became a bottleneck in the transferring of data between the microprocessor and the video card. To overcome the video bottleneck, the Micro Channel Architecture (MCA) and the EISA buses were introduced. Although these cards had 32-bit access and could transfer data more quickly than the ISA bus, the performance increase was not great enough to justify the increased cost.

Newer machines use a local bus video card. Since the local bus was initially designed to run at or near the speed of the microprocessor and had at least a 32-bit data bus, it was far faster than anything previously used in the PC. The first widely accepted local bus was the **VESA local bus (VL bus)** created by the **Video Electronics Standards Association (VESA),** which was originally formed to standardize Super VGA monitors. Its interest in developing a local bus was to improve video performance. The VESA local bus was built around the 486 microprocessor and was intended to supplement the existing slots (ISA, EISA, or MCA). When coupled with the ISA slot, the VESA slot was directly in line with it. Because it was built to accommodate the 486, the VESA used a 32-bit data bus to match the microprocessor and ran at the same speed. In addition to its faster speed and larger data bus, the VESA also offered burst mode and bus mastering. While in burst mode, sequential data was transferred faster by accessing one memory address to transfer up to four pieces of data. In burst mode at 33 MHz, the VESA bus could transfer up to 105.6 MB per second. In nonburst mode it could transfer only up to 66 MB per second. Both speeds were far greater than the ISA's 8.33 MB per second. Bus mastering is an advanced form of DMA that allows a data transfer to occur without aid from the microprocessor. As a result, the microprocessor can do something as the data transfer takes place, increasing the overall performance of the system.

Today, the term *local bus* usually refers to the **peripheral component interconnect (PCI)** local bus, which is usually found on Pentium machines. The PCI slot was developed by Intel and designed to eventually replace the older bus designs. Unlike the VESA, the PCI local bus is not an extension of any other slot; it is offset from the normal ISA, MCA, or EISA connector. The PCI bus is available in 32 bits (486 machines and some early Pentium machines) and 64 bits. The PCI bus is controlled by a PCI bridge or controller. To increase performance, the microprocessor writes data to a PCI device by immediately storing the data in the controller buffer of the bus. While the microprocessor goes on to its next operation, the stored data is then fed to the PCI device. Much like the VLB, the PCI bus also supports burst mode and bus mastering.

A popular bus or interface is the **accelerated graphics port (AGP).** AGP is based on the PCI 2.1 64-bit extension, which has a 64-bit interface that will run at 66 MHz. It multiplies the theoretical bandwidth of current PCI buses and has the potential to go even higher. (See chapter 7 for more information.) In the future, AGP will be replaced by PCI Express.

14.2.5 Video Accelerators and Coprocessors

In early ISA video cards, the display image was stored in the frame buffer. All processing for the images were done by the computer's processors. Graphics coprocessors are cards that have their own processor to perform this work. Graphics coprocessors are typically used in CAD and engineering workstations.

As previous sections have pointed out, modern video systems with their high resolution and number of colors require massive amounts of information that must be processed by the microprocessor and transferred to the video card and monitor. Video cards are now graphics accelerators, which help process the video data. Instead of the microprocessor processing each individual pixel and then sending the information to the video card, these cards perform the same processing with instructions consisting of only a few bytes. For example, let's say you need to draw a line 100 pixels long on the computer screen. Instead of the microprocessor calculating all 100 pixels one by one, the microprocessor would send an instruction to the coprocessor on the video card. The instruction would include the starting point and ending point of the line. The accelerator would then process each pixel. Because the processor has much less to do, it can do something else and the bus traffic is greatly reduced.

The video chipset, which includes the video coprocessor, is the logic circuit that controls the video card. More advanced chipsets are more efficient, include more acceleration features, and may also include 3D acceleration or MPEG decoding. The chipset is a major factor in determining overall video performance.

14.2.6 3D Video Chipsets and Adapters

Up to now, this chapter has been mostly discussing a video card that is generating 2D images such as the Windows desktop, a word processor, or a picture. If you are into interactive computer games or special applications that use 3D modeling, your computer must be able to simulate depth to the flat images on the monitor and give 3D motion to your images. The motion part is actually the toughest part because it has to make them fast enough (at least 30 frames per second) so that you think the objects on the screen are moving rather than being flashed one frame at a time. Therefore, for acceptable performance (and sometimes necessary to run certain programs), you should use a 3D video card (or a video card that is a combo 2D/3D video card). Like the 2D graphics accelerator that was discussed before, a 3D video card will do most of the processing so that the processor does not have to.

In the real world, objects are not isolated, but they interact with other objects. They overlap one another, cast shadows, reflect light, and they appear dimmer when in the distance. There are very complex mathematical equations that are used to determine when an object is visible in a scene based on a given angle, what color it should be, etc. If you are playing a 3D game and want smooth animation, these calculations must be redone at least 30 times per second! This is why 3D accelerators are used—they are customized to performing these resource-intensive computations. Each time the screen is recalculated (because of movement in a game, for example), it is necessary to recalculate the color and intensity of each pixel on the 2D screen.

To display a 3D object in real-time, an object is first represented as a set of points (or vertices) in a 3D coordinates consisting of *x, y,* and *z* coordinates. If you are looking at a piece of graph paper, the graph paper will be divided into *x*-scale going across the paper and the *y* is going up and down. If you take several sheets of graph paper and stack them, you are adding a third dimension, the *y* dimension. So a two-dimensional square becomes a three-dimensional box. The vertices of each object stored in system RAM and completely define the object(s). To display the objects on a flat 2D monitor screen, the object must be rendered or drawn.

Rendering is the act of calculating, on a per pixel basis, the different color and position information that tracks the viewer into perceiving depth on the 2D screen. For example, if you are looking down a street, the buildings farther away appear smaller and slightly darker to establish a 3D effect.

Since a computer works only with numbers, objects must be represented mathematically. Instead of finding a set of equations to describe a complex object, complex objects are broken down into small pieces and the pieces are manipulated. The process of breaking the image into these pieces, specifically polygons or triangles, is called *tessellation.* A complex object may require 20,000 or more polygons. If you rotate these polygons at 15 updates per second, your video system has to render 300,000 polygons per second.

Because of the sequential nature of 3D graphics rendering, and because there are so many calculations to be done and volumes of data to be handled, the entire process is broken down into component steps, sometimes called stages. These stages are serialized into the 3D graphics pipeline. The steps in generating a 3D image, the following steps occur:

- **Triangularize**—Breaks down a 3D object into triangles based on three vertices.
- **Transformation—**Translates, rotates, and zooms the object as necessary on the basis of the camera angle.
- **Clipping**—Eliminates any portion that is outside the window representing the viewer's line of sight.
- **Lighting—**Calculates shadow, light, or fog information depending on where the light sources in the 3D world are positioned.
- **Map triangles to screen—**Calculates the depth of each object and maps the object to a 2D screen. If a triangle is farther away, that triangle will be smaller than those triangles that are closer so that you can give an appearance of depth.
- **Drawn the triangle—**Draws triangles using a variety of shading and texture.

The huge amount of work involved in creating a scene has led 3D rendering system designers (both hardware and software) to look for all possible ways to avoid doing unnecessary work. In other words, to reduce visual detail in a scene so as to gain better performance, but do it in such a way that the viewer doesn't notice the loss of quality. Processor and memory bandwidth are precious commodities, so anything designers can do to conserve them benefits performance greatly.

When the 3D engine draws the pixels, the bottleneck is the memory access or how fast the pixels read and write to the frame buffer. There are thousands of polygons for each frame of a scene, and these must be updated and transmitted through the memory at least 30 times a second, to give the illusion of movement. This transfer to the frame buffer is known as frame rate and is measured in frames per second (fps). From there, the frames are transmitted to the RAMDAC and converted into an analogue signal for the monitor where, after much mathematical manipulation, the action takes place.

The speed of a 3D graphics engine is typically rated in either millions of textured pixels (called **texels**) or polygons/triangles per second. Current 3D graphics accelerators can provide hundreds of millions of texels per second. For example, a graphics chipset can render 4.6 billion texels or 125 million triangles per second.

Because 3D graphics adapters are optimized for video processor, they can carry out most image-oriented operations faster than a processor, even if the processor was able to devote its full time to image processing. In addition, the coprocessor and accelerators are connected to the frame buffer, and they can move bytes *to and from the buffer much faster without going* through a slower bus such as the ISA, PCI, or AGP bus. In addition, the graphics adapter can access the buffer using a wide bus. The processor only needs to send high-level drawing commands across the expansion bus.

Many factors affect the performance of a graphics adapter. Like a processor, the graphics chips have a clock speed. If a graphics chip has a faster clock speed, it will perform faster. In addition, if you have faster video memory, the information can be accessed faster.

Since the basic data for modern graphics operations is 32 bits (24-bit True Color with an alpha channel), many graphics adapters are 64- or 128-bit adapters that can process 2 or 4 pixels at once. This allows the graphics adapter to process more data during each clock cycle.

Several different types of computations are performed in 3D processing. Some cards support more of them than others, and some are more efficient at certain ones than others are. Here are some of the more common 3D operations:

- **Gourad shading**—This is an algorithm that is used to give 3D surfaces realistic shading. The effect helps the object appear to have depth and helps to define the shape better. It is a popular computation used in many 3D games.
- **Clipping**—This operation determines what part of an object is visible on the screen and "clips out" any part that the user cannot see. This saves time since the parts of objects that are off-screen are ignored.
- **Lighting**—Objects in the real world have their appearance shaped by the light sources in the scene. Lighting effects cause color shading, light reflection, shadows, and other effects to be added to objects based on their position and the position of light sources in the room. Light sources can be anything from an overhead light or lights, the sun, the moon, the stars or a spot light.
- **Transparency**—Some objects in the real world are transparent or semitransparent. Special calculations can be done to determine what objects are visible through glass.
- **Texture mapping**—For realistic objects, it is necessary to overlay pictures on them to give them texture. For example, instead of having a solid, flat color and substance, most walls are made of a material such as brick, wood, plaster or metal, and they may have pictures, tapestry, or signs on them.
- **Dithering**—Dithering is the process of mixing a small number of colors together in specific patterns to create the illusion of there being a larger number of colors.
- **Fogging**—An effect used in outdoor scenes, fogging serves two purposes by blurring objects that are in the distance. First, it helps make the scene appear more realistic. If you've ever looked at a mountain scene, you know that in the distance, objects to appear fuzzy due to atmospheric moisture. Second, fogging allows the 3D process to be performed more quickly because those objects in the distance that are "fogged out" can be computed more quickly since they are shown in less detail.
- **Filtering**—Filters are used to "clean up" the image and smooth out textures and shapes. In particular, bilinear filtering is used when showing textures up close to remove the "blocky" look that results from magnifying an object when showing it at the front of a scene.
- **Buffering**—Advanced 3D cards include memory buffers that are used for various tasks during these complex calculations. The more buffers the card has available, the more flexibility it has when doing advanced operations. This is why 3D cards usually need more memory than would strictly be necessary just to hold the screen image. Newer AGP systems can use the system memory for this.

Double-buffering requires having two areas reserved on the frame buffer of the 3D graphics card. One buffer is used to render the next frame of the animation while the other displays the previously rendered animation frame on the monitor. Under Windows, double-buffering requires the use of bit-blitting to copy the animation from buffer to buffer.

To create the illusion of motion, 3D cards use a kind of "flip-book" animation technique involving two, three, or sometimes more screens' worth of data. So while the current image is being displayed, the 3D chip is already at work on the next several frames of animation. Called "page flipping," this technique can take several configurations.

The result of double-buffering is that subsequent frames can be displayed more smoothly. Page flips typically are synchronized with the CRT's vertical blanking interval (VBI), also called "Vsync" or "vertical sync." During the VBI, the CRT's electron beams are turned off and repositioned from bottom-right to top-left and turned back on for the next scan pass. When flipping the back buffer to the front during this Vsync interval, users will not perceive any abnormal flickering of the image.

Triple-buffering is a process that adds a second back buffer to give the 3D chip a place to write the next two frames of animation. Triple-buffering is also useful for benchmarking graphics boards as it partially alleviates the problem of Vsync interference with measuring 3D performance. The graphics chip can keep working and rendering information into the second back buffer—even when the first back buffer is rendered, and ready to be swapped to the front, but waiting for the Vsync interval. Without a triple buffer, with Vsync enabled, the graphics chip would have to wait for the single back buffer to flip to the front. Only then could it start rendering to the "new" back buffer (which was just previously the front buffer). A triple-buffer allows the graphics chip rendering to not stall as frequently as with a double-buffer, thus improving overall performance.

On a whole, memory serves as storage for a variety of items including pixel color data and z-buffer information. Additionally, a stencil buffer can be available for use as a scratch pad for rendering effects such as shadows. Any additional memory is used for command (typically a few MB), geometry, and texture storage.

A crude **z-buffering** technique system is called the Painter's Algorithm (a back-to-front method), which begins from the back of the scene and draws everything in the scene, including full rendering of objects that might be covered by objects nearer to the camera. In most cases, this algorithm achieves correct depth sorting, but it's inefficient and can cause some drawing errors where triangles overlap one another. Further, it is costly in terms of how many times a given pixel might be rendered. Therefore, this method is not used anymore.

Remember that although screen space is pretty much a "2D" mapping to the screen coordinates, say 1600×1200, the z-values have been carried through all of the previous operations in the pipeline. As the scene is rendered, the z-value (depth information) for new pixels are compared to the values stored in the z-buffer to determine which pixels are in front of others and should be rendered. Pixels that are "behind" other pixels are not rendered, increasing the speed. To set up the z-buffer for depth tests for the next frame of animation (generally at the end of the previous scene being drawn), the z-buffer is cleared, meaning that the value of zmax gets written to all pixel positions in preparation for the next frame of animation's depth testing.

Earlier in the chapter, we discussed higher resolution and a higher number of colors, which allow images to be more realistic. Instead of painting a 3D object as one color, the object can be covered by a texture. A **texture** is the digital representation of the surface of an object. In addition to two-dimensional qualities, such as color and brightness, a texture is also encoded with three-dimensional properties, such as how transparent and reflective the object is. A texture can resemble wood, stone, marble, metal, felt, and any other surface that you can imagine. Once a texture has been defined, it can be wrapped around any three-dimensional object. This is called texture mapping. Well-defined textures are very important for rendering realistic 3D images. However, they also require a lot of memory, so they're not used as often as they might be.

Mip mapping can be viewed as a cut-down form of texture mapping in which more texels are created without performing the equivalent number of calculations. If a mip-map is one-fourth the size of the original texture, reading a single texel from this mip-map is the same as reading four texels from the original texture. If applied using proper filters, the image quality is actually higher, as it smoothes out jagged edges.

To make an image sharper, some 3D adapters may use filtering and/or anti-aliasing. Bilinear filtering reads four texels, calculates their average—that is, the average of their relative positions—color and so on, and displays the result as a single-screen texel. This results in blurring at close quarters, which in turn reduces an otherwise blocky, pixelated appearance. Bilinear filtering is now standard on most PC graphics cards.

Anti-aliasing is a technique for disguising the jagged edges of a curved line or a line with very low or very high slope. These jagged edges were especially visible at lower resolutions with each pixel appearing as a stair step rather than a smooth line. Anti-aliasing is a way to use color information to make up for a lack of screen resolution. It simulates higher resolution by using color information to trick our eyes into seeing a smoother line or edge than the screen can physically allow. By adding pixels of a slightly different color next to the line or curve at the transition points the edge is blurred. The eye sees this as a smooth edge rather than a different color.

Full Scene Anti-Aliasing (FSAA) is the current high-performance implementation of this feature. FSAA smoothes the jagged lines and eliminates the scintillating of very thin objects by taking many samples of the scene and blending them together. The result is a much smoother, far more realistic and pleasing image. Of course, FSAA requires a lot of resources and may slow 3D rendering to an unacceptable level in some PC configurations. The video adapter's adjustment/configuration utility will usually allow you to toggle this feature on and off.

14.2.7 Driver Software

A modern graphics card's driver software is vitally important when it comes to performance and features. For most applications, the drivers translate what the application wants to display on the screen into instructions that the graphics processor can use. The way the drivers translate these instructions is of paramount importance. Modern graphics processors do more than change single pixels at a time; they have sophisticated line- and shape-drawing capabilities, and they can move around large blocks of information. It is the driver's job to decide on the most efficient way to use these graphics processor features, depending on what the application requires to be displayed.

In most cases, a separate driver is used for each resolution or color depth. This means that, even taking into account the different overheads associated with different resolutions and colors, a graphics card can have markedly different performance at different resolutions, depending on how well a particular driver has been written and optimized.

If you are having video problems, you should always make sure that you have the correct video driver loaded (and monitor selected) and that you have selected a resolution, color depth, and frequency that is supported by both the monitor and video card. In addition, you should check for updated video drivers and Windows service packs, fixes, and patches.

14.2.8 Adapter Heat Sink and Fan

Similar to processors, graphics adapters have gotten faster and faster over the last few years. Because of this, the graphics adapters generate a lot of heat. Therefore, today there are many graphics adapters that require heat sinks and fans to keep them cool. Of course, you must make sure that your system has sufficient ventilation, and that you do not overclock the graphics adapter.

14.3 INSTALLING A VIDEO CARD

A video card is probably one of the easiest devices to install into a computer. The video card is physically installed into an empty expansion slot, the holding screw for the expansion card is secured, and the monitor is connected. Because every computer must have a monitor and most monitors are VGA or SVGA, the VGA/SVGA card resources (I/O addresses 3B0–3BBH and 3C0–3DFH) are well established.

As with many other hardware devices, after the card is installed the correct driver usually needs to be loaded to take full advantage of the card's capabilities. If the correct driver is not loaded, the higher resolutions, higher number of colors, higher refresh rates, and coprocessing capabilities of the video card may not be available.

14.4 TYPES OF VIDEO SYSTEMS

Like other computer components, the video system has gone through significant changes since the IBM PC was introduced in 1981. Table 14.4 describes a number of common video systems and their characteristics used by PCs through the years.

Today most machines use Super VGA monitors. Super VGA, which was derived from the video graphics array (VGA) monitor, IBM developed **video graphics array (VGA)** as part of the PS/2 line. It supports a resolution of 640 × 480 at 16 colors or a resolution of 320 × 200 at 256 colors (chosen from a palette of 262,144 colors). It was also the first analog monitor used for the PC (all previous monitors had been digital). Standard VGA did not, however, include any kind of coprocessor or acceleration feature on the card. Table 14.5 lists the VGA pins and their function. The VGA standard became widely accepted but it was the last standard developed by IBM.

Table 14.4 Common Video Systems

Name	Year Introduced	Resolution	Colors
Monochrome display adapter (MDA)	1981	720 × 350 (25 × 80 characters)	Mono
Hercules graphics card	1982	720 × 350	Mono
Color graphics adapter (CGA)	1982	320 × 200	4
		640 × 200	2
Enhanced graphics adapter (EGA)	1984	640 × 350	16
Variable graphics array (VGA)	1989	640 × 480	16
		320 × 200	256
Super VGA (SVGA)	1990	800 × 600	256
		1024 × 768	16
Extended VGA (XVGA)	1992	800 × 600	65,536
		1024 × 768	256

Table 14.5 VGA Pinout

Pin	Function	Direction
1	Red	Out
2	Green	Out
3	Blue	Out
4	Monitor ID2	In
5	Digital ground (monitor self-test)	NA
6	Red analog ground	NA
7	Green analog ground	NA
8	Blue analog ground	NA
9	Key (plugged hole)	NA
10	Sync ground	NA
11	Monitor ID 0	In
12	Monitor ID1	In
13	Horizontal sync	Out
14	Vertical sync	Out
15	Monitor ID 3	In

Computer users wanted still higher resolutions and more colors. Since IBM was no longer the computer leader as it had once been, and no company replaced it as the leader, so many companies made VGA video cards with higher resolution and more colors. But a video card made by one company and a monitor made by another company had all sorts of compatibility problems. To overcome these compatibility problems, the Video Electronics Standards Association (VESA) was formed by major computer, monitor, and video card manufacturers. VESA developed a Super VGA (SVGA) standard, called the *VESA BIOS extension (VBE)*. If a system has a resolution higher than 640 × 480 or can display more than 16 colors at the 640 × 480 resolution, the video system is probably Super VGA (SVGA), not VGA. Today, video systems support much higher resolutions.

14.5 VIDEO CONNECTORS

The most common connector on computer monitors and video cards is the 15-pin (3 rows of 5 pins each) high-density D-shell connector. It is used to attach the display device you are using (the monitor, flat panel, or even TV) to your graphics card. See table 14.5.

Some high-resolution systems use a separate coaxial cable for every signal they receive. The 15-pin high-density D-shell connector can limit bandwidth, especially as signal frequencies climb above 30 MHz. Instead, these systems use BNC connectors, which are designed for frequencies into the gigahertz range. See figure 14.8. The connections are red, green, blue, horizontal sync, and vertical sync.

When LCD panels first emerged, they connected to a graphics card via its VGA connector. This, of course, required that the graphics card first convert the signal to analog via its RAMDAC. Since LCDs are—unlike CRT monitors—fundamentally digital in nature, the analog signal is immediately reconverted to digital. The internal circuitry needed to do this increases the cost of LCD displays, impinges on image quality, particularly in the area of color accuracy, and presents synchronization issues that can be difficult to adjust on some graphics adapters. While digital LCD displays promise a better, more reliable image, they also required a new connector and internal circuitry on the graphics card.

Although a couple of connectors were introduced, they were not widely accepted. The matter was finally resolved by the Digital Display Working Group (DDWG)—formed for the express purpose of developing a universal standard for attaching a flat-panel display to a PC. Its specification of the Digital Visual Interface (DVI) standard was published in the spring of 1999, and it was not long before graphics cards and flat-panel displays with DVI connectors began to emerge.

Once a widely accepted standard had been established, both graphics card and LCD manufacturers began producing compliant products, with many adapters and displays supporting both the new DVI connector and the traditional VGA interface, for maximum versatility. DVI-I—a subset of the DVI stan-

Figure 14.8 BNC Connectors Found on the Back of a Monitor

Figure 14.9 An ATI card with a video capture port (coaxial connector), the DVI-I connector (notice the plus symbol [+]), connector for an input/output adapter (for TV, VCR, laserdisc player, camcorder, DV camcorder), and an IEEE 1394/FireWire port.

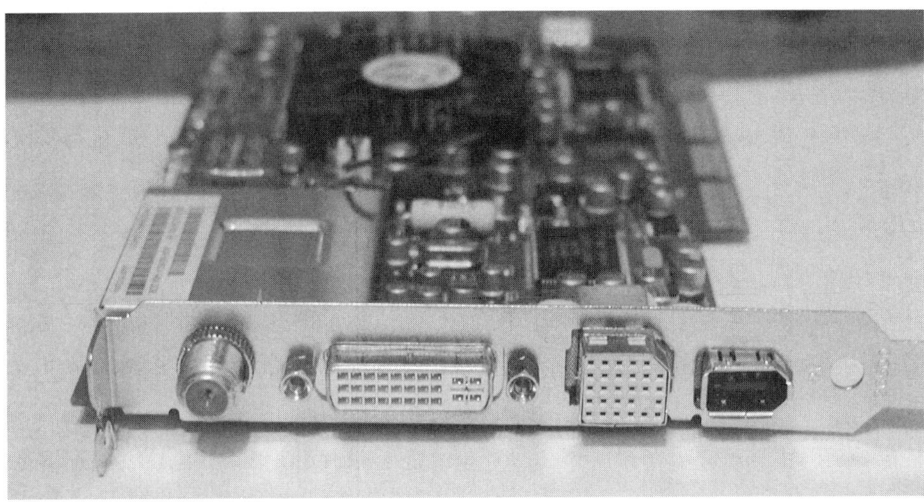

dard which stands for DVI Integrated—includes both digital and analog display signals on the DVI connector so that both analog CRTs/LCDs as well as wholly digital LCDs can be supported. Because DVI-I allows for both digital and analog support on graphics cards, users can maintain their analog compatibility and take advantage of the benefits of digital by using a combination of analog and digital displays until a complete digital upgrade becomes feasible. Note: To tell the difference between a DVI connector and a DVI-I connector, note that part of the DVI-I connector forms a plus sign (+), while the DVI (DVI-D for digital signal only) forms a dash symbol only (−). See figure 14.9.

One of the most common socket connectors found on graphics cards is the "feature connector." The feature connector allows you to add video-related peripherals, like TV tuners and video capture devices, to your card. Some video cards will even include IEEE 1394 connectors.

14.6 TROUBLESHOOTING A VIDEO SYSTEM

Many video system problems are caused by incorrect monitor control settings (the brightness and the contrast controls), incorrect video drivers, a failed video card, or a failed monitor. The obvious solutions to a failed video system should be checked first:

1. Are the computer and monitor on?
2. Is the monitor plugged into the power outlet and the computer?
3. Is the power outlet supplying sufficient power?
4. Are the brightness and contrast controls set properly?
5. Is the screen saver on or is the monitor in a power-saving mode, such as DPMS?
6. Do you have the proper resolution, number of colors and refresh rate?

Probably, the number one cause of video problems is an incorrect, faulty, or old video driver. If the monitor is on but the display is acting very erratically, the wrong video driver may have been selected. This is probably the case if the monitor comes on during boot-up (text mode) but starts to act erratic when a GUI operating system (Windows) is being loaded. The correct driver must be loaded to take full advantage of the card's capabilities, and a well-written driver will allow the video card to be faster and more reliable. If the wrong video driver has been selected, or an "Unable to initialize display adapter" message is displayed, Windows will allow you to go into standard VGA mode (640 × 480 with 16 colors), which will then allow you to choose the correct video driver and settings such as refresh rate, resolution or number of colors.

NOTE: If you upgrade your processor, you may need to update your video driver.

Windows 95, 98, and Me	To start safe mode, press the F5 key when the "Starting Windows 95/98" message appears on the screen during boot-up. The display settings can then be changed by using the Display icon/applet within the Control Panel.
Windows NT	If you have made a change in the Windows NT system and the machine does not boot properly, you can choose Last Known Good Configuration during boot-up. This will restore the previous driver setup and configuration. If you have not made a change, you must choose the Windows NT Server or Windows NT Workstation VGA mode. The display settings can then be changed from within the Display icon/applet within the Control Panel.
Windows 2000 and XP	If you press F8 while the Windows Boot menu is listed, it will display the Advanced Boot menu. You can then select Enable VGA mode, which starts Windows with basic VGA drivers. The display settings can then be changed from within the Display icon/applet in the Control Panel.
Linux	If you are booting to the GUI prompt using the LILO boot manager, you will have to press the Ctrl-X to enter text mode to start the LILO boot prompt. If you are booting to the GUI interface using the GRUB boot manager, you will need to press the E key for edit, add 2 to the kernel command line to specify the second run level, and press the B key to boot.

Besides having the incorrect driver, there are other things that can cause an erratic or blank screen. First be sure that the refresh rate, resolution, or number of colors are not too high and that they are supported by the monitor and video card. Lastly, you can adjust the levels of hardware acceleration controlled by device drivers. If you open the Display applet in the Windows Control Panel and access the Advanced options, you can find hardware acceleration, which can be adjusted by dragging the slider from Full to None. The slider gradually disables portions of hardware acceleration and enables you to detect which areas might be causing you to have problems with your graphics hardware.

If the card is bad and is still under warranty, you can get a replacement card. If it is not under warranty, it is probably best to throw away the card and get a new one because you will most likely not have its schematic diagram, replacement parts, or surface mount soldering and desoldering equipment. Having the video card repaired usually costs more than purchasing a new one.

Monitors, on the other hand, cost more than a video card, and so it may be best to try to have a bad monitor repaired. You won't usually have the schematic or replacement parts, so it is best to have the manufacturer or its representatives fix the monitor or to send it to a monitor repair depot. A monitor should be opened and repaired only by an experienced technician—the monitor can hold a lethal charge (enough to kill a person) for long periods, even after it has been unplugged. If you do choose to open a CRT monitor, certain guidelines must be followed. First, make sure that the monitor is unplugged, and allow at least 15 minutes for it to discharge before disassembling it. Second, do not wear an ESD wrist strap—the monitor can contain high charges that can flow through the ESD strap into you. You should also not wear any jewelry. Do not operate the monitor without its X-ray and RF shields in place. Lastly, have a second person nearby in case the unexpected happens.

The case of the monitor is usually held together by several screws located in the back. To disassemble the monitor, remove the screws and carefully remove the rear enclosure. Make sure that you have removed all the screws; if you don't you may break the neck of the CRT when you pull on the rear enclosure. Because the CRT can store up to a 50,000 V dc charge, it is important to discharge the monitor before touching any wiring (especially the red wire that connects to the top of the CRT) or boards. Use a regular flat-blade screwdriver or a high-voltage logic probe with a heavy-duty alligator clip that is connected to a 1 MΩ resistor, which is connected to ground. The resistor will prevent damage to some of the monitor components from a sudden surge of electricity. While grasping the insulated handle of the screw driver only, gently insert the screwdriver blade or a high-voltage logic probe under the anode

Figure 14.10 Discharging a CRT Monitor

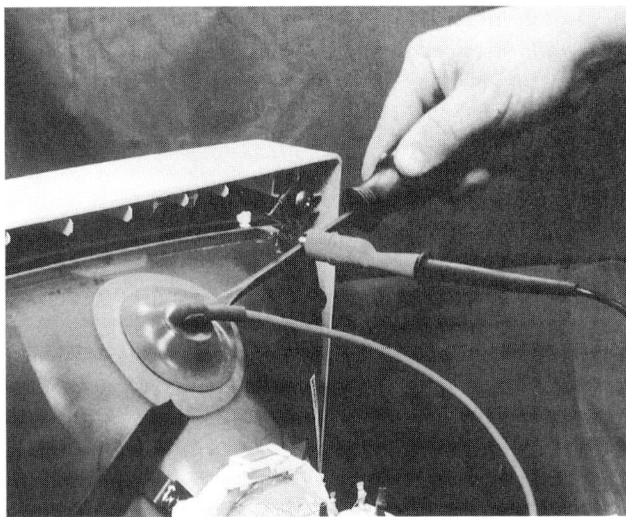

cap until it touches the metal contacts. The **anode cap** is a flat, circular object resembling a suction cup located on the top of the CRT. Do not rotate the screwdriver or force it into the CRT. You will usually hear a mild crackle as the CRT is being discharged. Once the crackle stops (a couple of seconds), remove the screwdriver. After the monitor is discharged, it is a good idea to connect a grounded alligator clip to the anode cap to avoid any charge that may rebuild inside the monitor. See figure 14.10. If the anode lead needs to be removed, such as when replacing the CRT, squeeze the lead while rocking it back and forth. Note: If you are adjusting some of the monitor controls, you shouldn't have to discharge the monitor, although you should make sure not to touch anything else.

NOTE: CRT monitors are considered hazardous waste and are not allowed in landfills in most states. The frit, which joins the front and back panels of the monitor, is made of almost pure lead. Therefore, when disposing of a CRT monitor, ship it to a computer or electronics recycler or donate it to a needy organization.

Magnetic fields, such as those generated by stereo speakers, can distort images and cause discoloration of isolated areas on the screen. Strong magnetic fields can also cause the internal components of the monitor to become magnetized. The process of eliminating magnetization on a CRT is called *degaussing.* Some monitors have a built-in degaussing circuit, which can be activated automatically or by pressing a button or switch. If the degaussing circuit does not work, a **degausser,** which is a special demagnetizing device that is moved over the outside surface of the CRT to eliminate magnetic fields, should be used.

If an LCD display is cracked or broken and liquid-crystal material leaks out, use rubber gloves to wipe up the spill with soap and water. Immediately wash off any LC material that makes contact with your skin.

For notebook computers, if the brightness or contrast adjustments are malfunctioning, you can try to replace the adjustment switch. If the backlit light is not functioning, you should make sure everything is connected properly. Then you can try to replace the inverter board and the backlit light. If that doesn't work, you would then replace the entire LCD panel. Of course, you must have access to the adjustment switch, backlit light, inverter boards, and LCD panel from the manufacturer.

One way to test a video system is to use a software diagnostic package. These packages contain several tests that will display a grid to test pincushioning and several color blocks to test the purity of the colors. Unlike most tests, many of the video tests are interactive in that you have to determine if the system passed or failed.

Example 14.1:

You turn on the computer and during boot-up, you get an audio beep code (such as AMI's eight beeps) indicating "Display Memory Read/Write Test Failure."

The first thing to check is whether the system has a video card. If there is a video card, then the error message indicates that the RAM on the video card failed. The video card will have to be replaced. If the problem persists, check the motherboard.

Example 14.2:

The sides of the images on the screen bulge inward or outward.

Check the monitor controls first, specifically the pincushioning controls. If the problem still exists, plug the monitor into another computer to see if the problem is with the monitor. If the problem does not appear on the other system, replace the video card in the original system.

Example 14.3:

The image is shifted over, or the image is shifted over and part of it looks distorted.

Check the monitor controls first, specifically the horizontal and vertical size and horizontal and vertical positioning. If the problem still exists, plug the monitor into another computer to see if the problem goes away. If the problem still exists, it must be the monitor. If the problem does not appear on the other system, replace the video card in the original system.

Example 14.4:

The image is wavy.

This can be caused by outside electromagnetic interference (EMI) or a monitor power supply problem. EMI problems can be caused by equipment or machinery (such as fluorescent lights and space heaters) on the same electrical circuit as the monitor or in the same proximity of these devices. To solve EMI problems, you should move the computer component experiencing the problem away from the EMI source or eliminate the EMI source.

The other cause of waves on the monitor is a faulty monitor power supply. To isolate this problem, plug the monitor into another computer to see if the monitor is causing it. Also, try another monitor with the computer to see if the computer is causing the problem. If the monitor appears to be the problem, then the power supply will have to be replaced. Again, only experienced electronic technicians who have the proper training on monitors should attempt this.

Example 14.5:

The image is red, cyan (greenish blue), blue, yellow, green, or magenta (bluish red).

First, check the cable, especially if the monitor uses a coaxial cable that has connections for the red, green, and blue. After the cable has been checked, plug the monitor into another computer to see if the monitor is the problem. Also try another monitor with the computer to see if the computer is causing the problem. If the monitor appears to be the problem, it will have to be opened and the specific problem diagnosed. Most likely, one of the color video circuits is faulty. Again, to fix the problem requires an experienced technician who has access to schematics and parts.

Example 14.6:

A high-pitched noise comes from the computer when it is turned on.

The noise is most likely caused by the video system (monitor or video card), although it can also be caused by the hard drive or power supply. Before taking the machine apart, try to determine if the sound is coming from the monitor or the computer case. This will help you isolate it. To determine which component is causing the problem, swap each component one at a time.

14.7 VIDEO SYSTEM ERGONOMICS

If you use the computer for long stretches of time, you need to develop some good habits to reduce eyestrain, muscle stiffness, back problems, and headaches. When viewing the monitor, you should sit high enough so that your eyes are slightly higher than the screen. To reduce eyestrain, your eyes should be between 24 and 30 in. away from the screen (compared to the 16-in. distance recommended for reading books). In addition, if you are typing from hard copy, such as a report or a book, try to keep them the same distance from you as the computer screen.

Another key to being comfortable is controlling glare. Although glare itself won't lead to permanent eye damage, it can cause eyestrain and headaches. To control sources of glare on your screen, adjust the colors on your monitor to differentiate foreground from background. Position your monitor so that the bright light from a lamp or the sun is neither directly in front of you nor behind you (causing glare to be reflected in the screen). If your monitor doesn't have a built-in antiglare feature, consider buying an antiglare device.

Lastly, control the refresh rate of the monitor. It should be 70 Hz or higher.

14.8 VIDEO AND TELEVISION

Television signals are analog because analog signals can carry a lot of information using a low bandwidth. In the United States and Japan, the color TV signal is the **NTSC (National Television System Committee).** In many parts of Europe, the color TV signal is **PAL (phase alternate line).** As computers become more powerful, more and more software applications are using animation and video, and people want to display computer images on a large television screen and incorporate television images or television clips in the computer. These interactions require some form of signal conversion.

To display a computer image on a television, a VGA-to-NTSC adapter is needed. In addition, if you are recording to a VCR tape, the VGA-to-NTSC adapter must include genlocking. Genlocking enables the board to synchronize signals from multiple video sources or video with PC graphics and provides signal stability. Some VGA-to-NTSC converters are expansion cards; others are external boxes that are connected to the VGA or SVGA port. Many of these adapters have an S-Video and composite video interface, and some may include an antiflicker circuit to help stabilize the picture.

To capture a still image from a television, camcorder, or VCR, a still-image **video capture card** (NTSC-to-VGA converter) is used. Although image quality is limited by the input signal, the results are good enough for presentations and desktop publishing applications. These devices usually accept video input from VHS, Super VHS, and Hi-8 devices.

A video digitizer or video grabber is used to capture an entire video clip from the NTSC television signal. The video images within an NTSC television signal allows for approximately 32,000 colors and requires 30 frames per second (fps). As a result, to display full-motion video requires a fast microprocessor, large amounts of RAM, huge amounts of disk space, and a local bus connection. Without these resources, images are often jerky or less than full screen.

Because full-motion video consumes huge amounts of disk space, most full-motion video systems use **compression and decompression (codec).** By using compression and decompression, files take up less space and perform better because there is less data to process. There are two forms of codecs: hardware codecs and software codecs. Hardware codecs require additional hardware but offer high-quality images and a high-compression ratio. Software codecs don't require special hardware but usually do not offer the same high-quality images, compression ratio, and performance as the hardware codec. Two common forms of compression are the **Joint Photographic Experts Group (JPEG)** and the **Motion Picture Experts Group (MPEG).** JPEG, originally developed for pictures, compresses each frame by eliminating redundant data for each individual image. JPEG offers rates acceptable for nearly full-motion video (30 fps), a compression ratio of 30:1, and easy editing. MPEG can compress up to 200:1 at high quality levels yet is faster than JPEG. It compresses movies by storing only incremental changes. Unfortunately, because it does not include full information for every frame, it does not allow for easy editing.

There are three major MPEG standards: MPEG-1, MPEG-2, and MPEG-4. The most common implementations of the MPEG-1 standard provide a video resolution of 352 × 240 at 30 fps. This produces video quality slightly below the quality of conventional VCR videos. MPEG-2 offers resolutions of 720 × 480 and 1280 × 720 at 60 fps, with full CD-quality audio. This is sufficient for all the major TV standards, including NTSC, and even HDTV. MPEG-2 is used by DVD-ROMs. MPEG-2 can compress a 2-hour video into a few gigabytes. While decompressing an MPEG-2 data stream requires only modest computing power, encoding video in MPEG-2 format requires significantly more processing power. MPEG-4 is a graphics and video compression algorithm standard that is based on MPEG-1 and MPEG-2 and Apple QuickTime technology. Wavelet-based MPEG-4 files are smaller than JPEG or QuickTime files, so they are designed to transmit video and images over a narrower bandwidth and can mix video with text, graphics and 2D and 3D animation layers.

DivX, a trademark of DivXNetworks, Inc., is a digital video compression format based on the MPEG-4 technology. DivX files can be downloaded over high-speed lines in a relatively short time without sacrificing the quality of the digital video. To view the compressed version of the video, you need a media player designed to play DivX-encoded content. In other words, it needs the DivX codec. One DivX player can downloaded from http://www.divx.com.

There are several other video file formats. A common format on the PC is Video for Windows (developed by Microsoft), which uses **audio video interleave (AVI)** files. Just as the name implies, it interleaves video and audio data. This means that it has a segment of video data followed by a segment of audio data. AVI files are limited to 320 × 240 resolution and 30 fps, neither of which is adequate for full-screen, full-motion video. However, Video for Windows does not require any special hardware, making it a popular format. Another popular format is **QuickTime,** developed by Apple Computers, which uses an MOV file name extension. It can be played with the software on most common platforms and supports a variety of encoding types, including JPEG, Indeo, Cinepak, Animation, and so on. In February 1998, the ISO standards body gave QuickTime a boost by deciding to use it as the basis for the new MPEG-4 standard being defined. Two of the newer popular formats are the **Real video** and **Real audio** formats developed by Real Networks. Unlike the other formats, the Real video and audio format supports streaming, so the files can be played over the Internet. The Real video and Real audio files have an RA file name extension and are played with RealPlayer. Finally, Microsoft created the Advanced Systems Format (ASF), which is used by Windows Media. Audio and video content is compressed with a wide variety of codecs. In addition, ASF supports streaming with Windows Media Services or is optionally packaged with Windows Media Rights Manager.

SUMMARY

1. The monitor, a device similar to a television, is the computer's primary output device.
2. Like televisions, the size of the monitor is usually measured diagonally across the screen.
3. Monitors are of two types, cathode-ray tube (CRT) and liquid-crystal display (LCD), which is mostly used on notebook and laptop computers.
4. The cathode-ray tube (CRT) consists of an electronic screen that is lined with a phosphorescent material that glows when struck by electrons.
5. Liquid crystal (LC) is an organic material made up of rod-shaped molecules that can bend light under the proper conditions.
6. The image (text, lines, boxes, and pictures) on the monitor is made up of many dots called picture elements or pixels.
7. The number of pixels that can be displayed on the screen at one time is called the resolution of the screen. It is expressed by two numbers.
8. While in text mode (the simplest operating mode), the system will usually display 25 rows of 80 characters (80 × 25).
9. Dot pitch is the distance between the pixels.
10. The number of times that the screen is redrawn in a second is referred to as refresh rate. It is measured in hertz (Hz).
11. The Video Electronics Standards Association (VESA) has established an 85 MHz refresh rate as the standard for flicker-free monitors.
12. Interlacing monitors will redraw the screen in two sweeps, refreshing every other line in each sweep.
13. To prevent screen burn-in on older monitors, screen savers were used to blank the screen or to provide a constant moving pattern. Today they are more of a form of entertainment.
14. The video card can be identified by its 3-row, 15-pin female port (VGA or SVGA) and the DVI connector (used for digital LCD panels).

15. The amount of information that determines the color of pixel is known as color depth or bit depth. The more bits used to define the number of colors for each pixel, the greater the number of colors the screen can show.
16. The amount of video memory determines the resolution and number of colors available and may enhance performance for 3D video cards.
17. Video cards can use DRAM, EDO RAM, VRAM, SGRAM, SDRAM, WRAM, MDRAM, and DDR RAM.
18. Modern video cards include coprocessors to help process video data. These are known as video accelerators.
19. 3D accelerator cards calculate an object's relative position, size, light levels, shadowing, relative motion, and sharpness.
20. The video graphics array (VGA) system supports a resolution of 640 × 480 at 16 colors or a resolution of 320 × 200 at 256 colors (chosen from a palette of 262,144 colors).
21. When viewing the monitor, your eyes should be slightly higher than your computer screen and be between 24 and 30 in. away from the screen.
22. A video card is probably one of the easiest devices to install into a computer.
23. Because every computer and most monitors are SVGA, the VGA/SVGA card resources (I/O addresses 3B0–3BBH and 3C0–3DFH) are well established.
24. As with many other hardware devices, after the card is installed the correct driver usually needs to be loaded to take full advantage of the card's capabilities.
25. When handling an LCD display, be careful not to scratch the surface and make sure that you do not expose the screen to high amounts of force or pressure because this may crack the LCD panel.
26. In the United States and Japan, the color TV signal is the NTSC (National Television System Committee signal.)
27. Most video system problems are caused by incorrect monitor control settings (the brightness and the contrast controls), incorrect video drivers, a failed video card, or a failed monitor.
28. Today, there are many graphics adapters that require heat sinks and fans to keep them cool. Of course, you must make sure that your system has sufficient ventilation.
29. If the monitor is on but the display is acting erratically, the wrong driver may have been selected.
30. If the backlit light of an LCD panel goes out, the image on the screen will be very faint. This is most likely caused by a blown fuse on the inverter board (if there is one), the inverter board, or the phosphorus light. The function of the inverter board is to distribute the electricity through the LCD panel.
31. To clean the screen, you should use a water-dampened cloth or a cloth with a special cleaning solution made for monitors.
32. Before touching any wiring (especially the red wire that connects to the top of the CRT) or boards in the monitor, it is important to make sure that the CRT is fully discharged.
33. To discharge a monitor, use a regular flat-blade screwdriver or a high-voltage logic probe with a heavy-duty alligator clip grounded with a 1 MΩ resistor. Gently insert the screwdriver blade under the high-voltage anode cap and keep it there for a few seconds.
34. Do not wear an ESD wrist strap when working within a monitor.
35. Today, video cards will use the PCI, AGP, or PCI Express interfaces.
36. Windows will allow you to go into standard VGA mode (640 × 480 with 16 colors), which will then allow you to chose the correct video driver.
37. To enable VGA mode for Windows 9X, press the F5 key when the "Starting Windows 95/98" message appears on the screen.
38. To enable VGA mode for Windows NT, choose Last Known Good Configuration during boot-up.
39. To enable VGA mode for Windows 2000 and Windows XP, press F8 while the Windows Boot menu is listed to display the Advanced Boot menu. Then select Enable VGA mode.

REVIEW QUESTIONS

1. Which of the following is the primary output device of the computer?
   a. keyboard
   b. monitor
   c. printer
   d. mouse
2. The size of the monitor is measured in
   a. inches diagonally across the screen.
   b. square inches of the screen.
   c. dots going across and dots going down.
   d. pounds.
3. Which of the following uses electrons to energize a phosphorescent material to display images on the screen?
   a. VGA
   b. LCD
   c. MDA
   d. CRT
4. Dots on the screen are known as (choose two)
   a. pixels.
   b. dot pitch.
   c. resolution.
   d. picture elements.
   e. lights.

5. Which of the following statements are correct if a monitor has a 0.28 dot pitch?
   a. Each dot is 0.28 cm wide.
   b. Each dot is 0.28 mm wide.
   c. Each dot is 0.28 cm apart.
   d. Each dot is 0.28 mm apart.
6. A monitor has a refresh rate of 72 Hz. Which of the following statements are true (choose all that apply)?
   a. The refresh rate is 72 times per second.
   b. The number of vertical lines is 72 per inch.
   c. The monitor probably produces more flicker than a 60 Hz monitor.
   d. The monitor probably produces less flicker than a 60 Hz monitor.
7. Which of the following describes a noninterlaced monitor?
   a. The pixels on the screen are illuminated from left to right and from top to bottom.
   b. Three electron guns shoot electrons beams that are not in sync with one another.
   c. Three electron guns shoot electron beams that are not interlaced with one another.
   d. The lines on the screen are scanned in two or more passes.
   e. All the lines on the screen are scanned in one pass.
8. If characters on a monitor are squashed to one side, which adjustment will correct this problem?
   a. vertical size
   b. horizontal centering
   c. horizontal hold
   d. vertical linearity
   e. pincushioning
9. Which of the following will prevent screen burn-in?
   a. increasing the refresh rate
   b. decreasing the refresh rate
   c. reducing the screen resolution
   d. using a screen saver
   e. increasing the number of colors used
10. Which of the following best describes the VGA connector on the PC?
    a. 25-pin male connector
    b. female connector with 3 rows of 5 pins each
    c. 9-pin female connector
    d. 25-pin female connector
11. Which of the following best describes the EGA connector on the PC?
    a. 25-pin male connector
    b. female connector with 3 rows of 5 pins each
    c. 9-pin female connector
    d. 25-pin female connector
12. How many different colors can a video system show with a 16-bit color depth?
    a. 256 b. 65,536
    c. 16,777,216 d. 4,294,967,296
13. You want to display high color with a resolution of 800 × 600 on a 15-in. monitor. (The monitor has a refresh rate of 72 Hz.) How much video RAM would you need?
    a. 937.5 KB b. 7.4 MB
    c. 13.8 MB d. 66.0 MB
14. Which of the following types of RAM used in video cards is dual-ported?
    a. VRAM b. SGRAM
    c. EDO d. MDRAM
15. Which is the best bus to use when choosing a video card?
    a. ISA b. MCA
    c. EISA d. PCI
16. Which of the following best describes a video accelerator?
    a. The video accelerator uses a faster bus speed.
    b. The video accelerator does all of the video processing.
    c. The video accelerator has a microprocessor that does a lot of the video processing.
    d. The video accelerator bypasses the microprocessor.
17. Which of the following best describes 3D accelerator cards?
    a. The 3D video accelerator is three cards in one.
    b. The 3D video accelerator compresses the data sent to the monitor by a ratio of 1:3.
    c. The 3D video accelerator performs many of the complicated video calculations that relate to size, relative position, and relative motion.
    d. The 3D video accelerator uses a clock crystal that is three times faster than the motherboard clock crystal.
18. What are the number of characters per line and the number of lines that may be displayed in text mode?
    a. 64 characters by 28 lines
    b. 120 characters by 40 lines
    c. 75 characters by 30 lines
    d. 80 characters by 25 lines
19. Which mode is a video resolution of 800 × 600?
    a. CGA b. EGA
    c. VGA d. SVGA
20. Which of the following produces an image that has a resolution of 640 × 480 and 16 colors?
    a. CGA b. EGA
    c. MCGA d. VGA
21. Which of the following is best to use when cleaning a CRT monitor?
    a. hot water
    b. a damp cloth
    c. WD-40
    d. denatured alcohol
    e. Windex
22. Why do windows located near the PC need curtains?
    a. The sunlight can cause the phosphorous within the CRT to glow.

b. They prevent or reduce glare caused by the sunlight shining through the window.
c. They protect the video display from UV damage.
d. Sunlight can cause problems with fiber-optic cables connected to the back of the PC.

23. The grid voltages of a color monitor are in the range of

a. 15,000 V. b. 2,500 V.
c. 35,000 V. d. 50,000 V.

24. Which of the following procedures must be observed while working on a monitor (choose all that apply)?

a. discharging the CRT anode
b. removing all jewelry
c. leaving the monitor plugged in to provide a ground
d. wearing an ESD wrist strap

25. Which of the following may cause the monitor to emit a high-pitched sound?

a. the video controller
b. the hard drive controller
c. the monitor power cable
d. none of the above

26. When should you *not* wear an ESD wrist strap?

a. when working on a disk drive
b. when working on a CPU
c. when working on memory
d. when working on an exposed cathode-ray tube (CRT)

27. The presence of electromagnetic fields can result in which of the following problems (choose all that apply)?

a. distortion of the video display
b. shutdown of the PC
c. RAM errors
d. read/write errors on the disk

28. What is the first thing you should do when you discharge a CRT monitor?

a. With the power turned off, disconnect all of the cables and let the monitor discharge for at least 15 minutes.
b. With the power turned off, disconnect all of the cables and let the monitor discharge for at least 5 seconds.
c. Remove the outside cover.
d. Remove the monitor's power supply.

29. Which of the following components *cannot* cause a video problem?

a. the microprocessor
b. the video card
c. the video signal cable between the monitor and the video card
d. the monitor
e. the video driver

30. Which would you do first when troubleshooting a faulty monitor?

a. check its connections to the computer and power source
b. use a meter to check the CRT and internal circuitry for continuity
c. power down the monitor, then turn it on again to see if that corrects the problem
d. power down the computer, then turn it on again to see if that corrects the problem

31. To reduce eyestrain and headaches, which of the following should you do (choose all that apply)?

a. enable your screen saver
b. keep your eyes level with the monitor or slightly above the monitor
c. use a refresh rate of 60 Hz or more
d. shut off all lights in the room

32. Which of the following standards are used in the United States to send television signals?

a. NTSC b. PAL
c. VHS d. Super VHS
e. Beta

33. What should you do if a customer calls and complains that his monitor has waves going across it?

a. Ask the customer to reboot the computer.
b. Make an appointment to go out and replace the video card.
c. Ask the customer what electrical equipment is near the computer.
d. Ask the customer to change out his monitor with another monitor to see if the problem is fixed.

34. You are troubleshooting a problem with a Windows 98 computer. When you boot up the computer, you hear the hard disk start, the computer beeps once, and everything appears normal except the display, which is blank. You confirm that the monitor's power switch is on and the monitor is plugged in. What should you do next to troubleshoot the problem?

a. swap out the monitor
b. replace the power supply
c. replace the video card
d. install new video display drivers

35. Why should an old CRT be disposed of as hazardous waste?

a. lead content
b. silver emulsion
c. residual electronic charge
d. copper wiring
e. phosphorus screens

36. What are the primary sources of video problems (choose four)?

a. monitor
b. data cable
c. video signal cable
d. video controller card
e. processor
f. power supply
g. video driver software

37. Which component emits the highest level of electromagnetic radiation?
    a. modem
    b. monitor
    c. hard drives
    d. mouse
    e. processor
    f. CD/DVD-ROM drive
38. What are common symptoms associated with display failures (choose two)?
    a. blank screen
    b. pale green screen
    c. excessive power consumption
    d. diagonal lines across the screen (no horizontal control)
39. A customer calls and says that she has no display on her monitor. She wants to avoid the cost of a service call and asks you to help her find the source of the problem over the phone. To do so, you will need to ask her a series of questions to determine the source of the problem. Which question should you ask first?
    a. Is the monitor plugged in?
    b. Is your mouse operating properly?
    c. How much video RAM is installed in your video card?
    d. When was the last time you updated the video drivers?
40. You are troubleshooting a problem with a computer running Windows 98. The computer starts and displays the POST messages, but when it starts Windows it does not display properly. What should you do first?
    a. replace the monitor
    b. replace the video cable
    c. replace the video card
    d. install new video drivers

HANDS-ON EXERCISES

Exercise 1: Using the Monitor Controls

1. Find the controls for brightness. Adjust the brightness all the way up.
2. Find the controls for contrast. Adjust the contrast all the way up.
3. Adjust the brightness all the way down.
4. Adjust the contrast all the way down.
5. Adjust the brightness approximately halfway.
6. Adjust the contrast and brightness controls to their proper settings.
7. Find the controls for horizontal centering. Adjust the horizontal centering all the way to the right.
8. Adjust the horizontal centering to its proper setting.
9. Find the controls for vertical centering. Adjust the vertical centering all the way to the top.
10. Adjust the vertical centering to its proper setting.
11. Find the controls for horizontal size. Reduce the picture to its smallest setting.
12. Using the horizontal size controls, change the picture to its largest setting.
13. Adjust the horizontal size to its proper setting.
14. Find the controls for pincushioning. Adjust the pincushioning all the way in.
15. Adjust the pincushioning all the way out.
16. Adjust the pincushioning to its proper setting.
17. Using the CMOS setup program, enable the power management feature within the program. Set the monitor so that it will power down after 5 to 10 minutes of nonuse.
18. Disable the power management feature.

Exercise 2: Testing the Video Card Using Software Diagnostics

Run a software diagnostic package to test the video card and monitor. Note: When you are running most of these tests, you must determine if the monitor and card passed or failed. Therefore, look for normal colors (pure white, red, blue, and yellow) and straight lines.

Exercise 3: Loading and Configuring Video Drivers

1. Using Windows (Display icon or applet in the Control Panel), determine the video driver currently being used.
2. Change the video driver to standard VGA.
3. After restarting Windows, select a Video 7 video card (or another one specified by your instructor).

4. If the computer did not boot properly, restart Windows in VGA mode.
5. Load the proper video drivers.
6. Using the Display icon or applet in the Control Panel, try to find out the maximum resolution and maximum number of colors your system can use.
7. If you have the video card setup disk or if the option is available in the Display icon, try to change the refresh rate to a higher value.
8. If your monitor is using an 800 × 600 or higher resolution, try to use large fonts (if available).
9. If your monitor is using an 800 × 600 or higher resolution, adjust it to 640 × 480 and to the most colors that resolution will support. Note how the picture changes.
10. Activate a screen saver.

Exercise 4: Analyzing the Video Card and Connector

1. Shut off the computer.
2. If the video card is an expansion card, remove it. If the video card is on the motherboard, disable it using the motherboard documentation.
3. Turn on the computer. Note the error message, if any.
4. Turn off the computer.
5. Find the video RAM on the video card or motherboard. Try to determine the amount of RAM.
6. Replace the video card back in the system.
7. Test the system to make sure that it still works.
8. Look at the number of pins on the video card connector that plug into the VGA/SVGA port. Don't be alarmed if some pins are missing.

Exercise 5: Loading Video Drivers from the Internet

1. Find and download the drivers for the following video cards using the Internet:
   - ATI Technologies—Graphics Ultra Pro (Windows 95)
   - Diamond Multimedia Systems, Inc.—Steal 3D 4000 (Windows 98)
   - Nvidia-Quadro FX 2000 (Windows XP)
   - The driver for your system
2. Find and install the driver for your system.

Exercise 6: Researching Graphics Adapters and Monitors

1. Go to the following two sites and determine the faster adapter from each company:

   http://www.ati.com
   http://www.nvidia.com

2. Go to the following site and read about Intel's integrated graphics chip and its features:

   http://www.intel.com/design/graphics/

3. Go to Tom's Hardware Guide's website located at the following URLs and read the reviews of some video cards and monitors:

   http://www6.tomshardware.com/graphic/index.html
   http://www6.tomshardware.com/display/index.html

CHAPTER 15

Input Devices

Topics Covered in This Chapter

Introduction

Input devices move information into the computer. The keyboard (the primary input device) and the mouse (including trackballs and other pointing devices) are the two most common input devices, but there are also others. For the game enthusiast, the game port connects paddles, joysticks, flight sticks, and other types of game-related peripherals. For notebook and laptop computers, there are IrDA ports, which allow two devices to communicate without wires. Lastly, there is the scanner that can convert pictures into data that the computer can read.

Objectives

1. Given a list of computer devices, determine which ones are input devices.
2. Clean a keyboard.
3. Given a keyboard problem, determine and correct the problem.
4. Describe proper use of keyboards to minimize repetitive stress injuries.
5. Explain how the pointing device works and how it interfaces with your operating system.
6. List and describe the different pointing devices.
7. Given a pointing device, physically install and configure the device and load the appropriate software and drivers.
8. Given a pointing device problem, determine and correct the problem.
9. Install and configure a joystick using a game port.
10. List examples or uses of IrDA ports.
11. Describe how a scanner works.
12. Install a scanner and any necessary scanner software, and scan a picture with text.
13. Explain the purpose of OCR software.
14. Explain how TWAIN relates to graphics software packages.
15. Install and operate a scanner.
16. Given a scanner problem, determine and correct the problem.

15.1 THE KEYBOARD

The computer **keyboard** is used to input, or enter, letters, numbers, symbols, punctuation, and commands into the computer. It includes the same keys as a typewriter and it also has a numeric keypad, cursor controls, and 10 or more function keys. The standard typewriter layout is called the **QWERTY layout** and is by far the most common. Over the years, there have been attempts to change the standard keyboard layout to improve typing speed and ergonomics. The other standard is the **Dvorak layout,** which has vowels in the home row under the left hand and the most commonly used consonants in the home row under the right hand. Although most tests of this layout show it produces a moderate speed increase, the public is resistant to the change.

15.1.1 Types of Keyboards

Many different keyboards are available and they offer many different features.

All keyboards today are the **101-key/102-key** or the **104-key enhanced keyboards**. In addition to the standard typewriter keys, they include separate cursor controls, a numeric keyboard, and 12 function keys. The 104-key Windows keyboard has a Windows key and an application key. The Windows key opens the Start menu without using the mouse, and the application key simulates the right mouse button to access Windows quick menus. Some keyboards also include built-in pointing devices.

15.1.2 How a Keyboard Works

The keyboard is a mechanical device consisting of many small mechanical parts (the keys). There are many different kinds of keys used within the keyboard; some are quiet, and others click. Most of the keys can be categorized as a mechanical, membrane, or capacitive key switch.

The mechanical key switch has two bronze contacts separated by a plastic actuator bar. The key is kept in the up position with a spring. When the key is pressed, the bar slides down, allowing the contacts to touch two gold-plated contacts. When the key is released, the spring pushes the key back into its normal position.

The membrane key switch is a plastic actuator that rests on top of a soft rubber boot coated with a conductive silver-carbon compound. When the key is pressed, the plastic actuator collapses the rubber boot, allowing the conductive material to make contact with two open PC board contacts. When the key is released, the compressed rubber boot returns to its original shape.

The capacitive key is different from the other keys because it is not a mechanical device. Instead of making contact between conductors, the capacitive key uses two plates to store electric changes in a switch matrix that is designed to detect changes in the capacitance of the circuit. When the key is pressed, the top plate moves toward the bottom plate. As a result, a change in capacitance occurs that is detected by a comparator circuit in the keyboard. While these keys are more durable and are almost immune to dirt and corrosion, they are more expensive.

The keys are arranged in rows and columns. When a key is pressed, a unique row-and-column signal is generated and sent to the keyboard interface IC on the keyboard. The keyboard interface then converts the row-and-column signal into a single-byte code called a *key code* or *scan code*. See tables 15.1 and 15.2. When the key is released, a second signal is sent to the keyboard interface IC, which generates a break code. This allows you to press several keys at the same time, such as Alt + Tab, Alt + Enter, or Ctrl + F. The keyboard interface IC then sends the scan codes by means of a serial connection through the keyboard interface to the computer. Unlike transfers from other serial devices, which send data asynchronously, the transfer from the keyboard occurs synchronously with a clock signal. The **keyboard controller,** located on the motherboard, converts the signals to parallel data and generates an interrupt so that the input can be serviced by the microprocessor.

A keyboard can be connected through an AT keyboard port, a PS/2 keyboard port, or a USB port. The AT keyboard port, which will be found only on older systems, uses a 5-pin DIN connector, while the PS/2 keyboard port uses a smaller 6-pin mini-DIN port. Today, most motherboards offer a PS/2 keyboard and PS/2 mouse port, which look identical. While many of these ports may be labeled, you will find that the keyboard port will be located below the mouse port. The pinouts for the AT keyboard port and the PS/2 keyboard port are shown in table 15.3.

The newest type of keyboard is the USB keyboard, which is considered a USB Human Interface Device (HID). The USB keyboard is becoming more popular and may replace the other types of keyboards since they are starting to be considered as legacy devices. Of course, for these types of keyboards to operate, your system and OS must support USB, USB must be enabled, and the appropriate drivers loaded. Note: A USB mouse may show up as a USB Human Interface Device in Windows Device Manager.

15.1.3 Troubleshooting the Keyboard

Keyboard problems are among the more common problems that occur with the PC because there are so many small mechanical components and keyboards sometimes are abused by users. Typically, the problem will be caused by a faulty keyboard, faulty keyboard connector, or faulty motherboard. In addition, if a different type of keyboard is added to a system, some operating systems may require a change in the keyboard driver.

The easiest way to verify a keyboard is faulty is to replace it with a known good keyboard. If the problem goes away, the original keyboard must be bad. If the keyboard is bad, check the cords. Some keyboard cords can be easily disconnected and replaced, which might make replacing the entire keyboard unnecessary. If the problem does not go away, check the motherboard.

To test the keyboard connector on the motherboard, measure the voltages of several pins of the keyboard connector. The keyboard clock pin should measure between +2.0 and +5.5 V, the keyboard data pin should be between +4.8 and +5.5 V, and the power pin should be between +2.0 and +5.5 V. Some

Table 15.1 Scan Codes for Alphanumeric Keys on PC Keyboards

Key	Make Code	Break Code	Key	Make Code	Break Code
A	1E	9E	] or }	1B	9B
B	30	B0	; or :	27	A7
C	2E	AE	' or "	28	A8
D	20	A0	, or <	33	B3
E	12	92	/ or ?	35	B5
F	21	A1	Left Shift	2A	AA
G	22	A2	Left Control	1D	9D
H	23	A3	Left Alt	38	B8
I	17	97	Right Shift	36	B6
J	24	A4	Right Control	E0 1D	E0 9D
K	25	A5	Right Alt	E0 38	E0 B8
L	26	A6	Caps	3A	BA
M	32	B2	Backspace	0E	8E
N	31	B1	Tab	0F	8F
O	18	98	Space Bar	39	B9
P	19	99	Enter	1C	9C
Q	10	90	Escape	01	81
R	13	93	F1	3B	BB
S	1F	9F	F2	3C	BC
T	14	94	F3	3D	BD
U	16	96	F4	3E	BE
V	2F	AF	F5	3F	BF
W	11	91	F6	40	C0
X	2D	AD	F7	41	C1
Y	15	95	F8	42	C2
Z	2C	AC	F9	43	C3
0 or /	0B	8B	F10	44	C4
1 or !	02	82	F11	57	D7
2 or @	03	83	F12	58	D8
3 or #	04	84	Up Arrow	E0 48	E0 C8
4 or $	05	85	Down Arrow	E0 50	E0 D0
5 or %	06	86	Left Arrow	E0 4B	EO CB
6 or	07	87	Right Arrow	E0 4D	E0 CD
7 or &	08	88	Insert	E0 52	E0 D2
8 or *	09	89	Delete	E0 53	E0 D3
9 or (	0A	8A	Home	E0 47	E0 C7
. or >	29	A9	End	E0 4F	E0 CF
- or	0C	8C	Page Up	E0 49	E0 C9
= or +	0D	8D	Page Down	E0 51	E0 D1
[or {	1A	9A	Scroll Lock	46	C6

Table 15.2 Numeric and Cursor Keypad Scan Codes

Key	Make Code	Break Code	Key	Make Code	Break Code
Num Lock	76	F0 76	**5**	73	F0 73
*	7E	F0 7E	**6**	74	F0 74
–	84	F0 84	**7**	6C	F0 C6
+	7C	F0 7C	**8**	75	F0 75
Enter	79	F0 79	**9**	7D	F0 7D
0	70	F0 70	**Home**	6C	F0 6C
1	69	F0 69	**End**	69	F0 69
2	72	F0 72	**Page Up**	7D	F0 7D
3	7A	F0 7A	**Page Down**	7A	F0 7A
4	6B	F0 6B	**Insert**	70	F0 70

Table 15.3 Typical Keyboard Ports

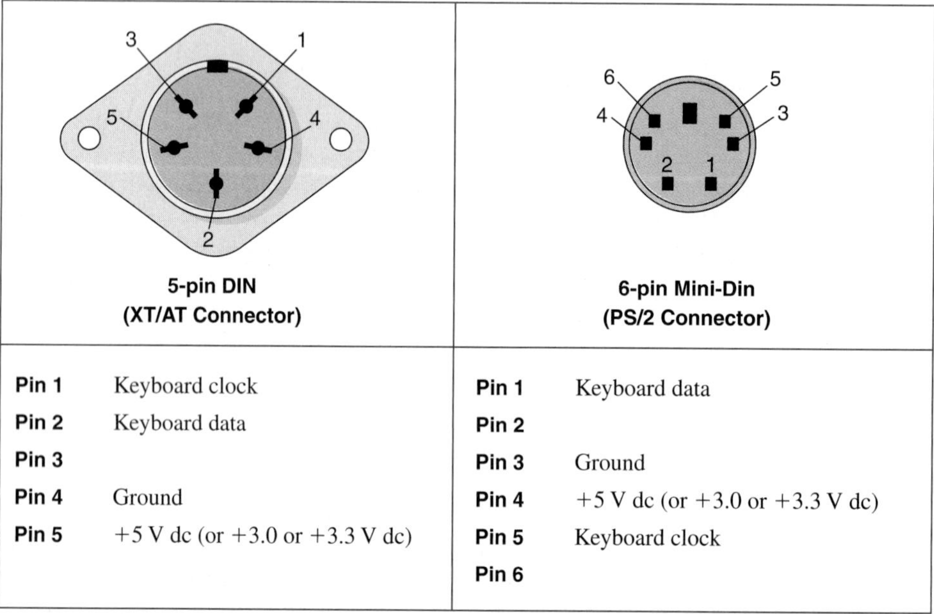

5-pin DIN (XT/AT Connector)		6-pin Mini-Din (PS/2 Connector)	
Pin 1	Keyboard clock	**Pin 1**	Keyboard data
Pin 2	Keyboard data	**Pin 2**	
Pin 3		**Pin 3**	Ground
Pin 4	Ground	**Pin 4**	+5 V dc (or +3.0 or +3.3 V dc)
Pin 5	+5 V dc (or +3.0 or +3.3 V dc)	**Pin 5**	Keyboard clock
		Pin 6	

motherboards have a fuse to protect them from electrical surges that may come through the keyboard. If a sufficient surge causes the fuse to open, the keyboard will not function and the fuse will have to be replaced.

One of the best ways to keep a keyboard in good condition is to clean it periodically. This includes vacuuming between the keys or using a can of compressed air while the keyboard is upside down. This will remove dust and dirt before they cause a key to stick or not to function. If a key sticks, the keycap can be removed and cleaned. An excellent tool for removing keycaps on most keyboards is the U-shaped chip-puller tool found in most PC repair kits. After the keycap is removed, use a can of compressed air to remove dust and dirt. If this doesn't work, the best course of action is to replace the keyboard. Besides dust and dirt, a stuck key or keys can be caused by something spilled on the keyboard, such as coffee or soda. If this occurs, it is best to immediately flush out the keyboard with distilled water. Distilled water is best because it doesn't have any minerals that may corrode the contacts used in the keys. In addition, you can partially disassemble a keyboard and wash the components with water. If the spilled liquid has dried, soak the keyboard in water and then rinse it. Make sure the keyboard is dry before trying to use it. Lastly, silicon lubricant can be used to increase keyboard performance.

If one or more keys wear out, keyboards can be taken apart and individual components replaced. However, some keyboards are made up of hundreds of little pieces and are sometimes impossible to reassemble if you go too far in taking them apart. It is sometimes easier and more cost efficient to replace the keyboard rather than spend a lot of time on it.

Example 15.1:

You turn on the computer and a "301" error message or "keyboard error" appears on the screen.

One of the most common error messages encountered on a PC is the "301" or "keyboard error" message. This usually happens when the keyboard is not connected to the computer, a common mistake for anyone, including experienced technicians. Of course, the experienced technician will check that the keyboard is connected before going any further. If the keyboard is plugged in and the system is still giving this error, there could be a stuck key on the keyboard. To unstick a key, try pressing each key on the keyboard. Also try cleaning under the keycaps. If the error still appears, the keyboard, keyboard cable, or motherboard will have to be replaced. The faulty component can be isolated by swapping one part at a time. The keyboard can be tested by trying it on another system. The motherboard can be tested by measuring the voltages of the keyboard connector.

Example 15.2:

You turn on the computer and the system indicates a "Gate A20 Failure."

This error message indicates that a 286 or higher machine must change to protected mode to utilize more than 1 MB of RAM. The first 1 MB of RAM is indicated with 20 address lines, identified as A0 to A19. Therefore, A20 is the 21st address line, which is the beginning of the extended memory. The gate A20 failure error indicates that the system, for some reason, could not activate the A20 line and change to protected mode. Since the A20 line is controlled by the keyboard controller, the gate A20 failure may be caused by either a faulty keyboard or a faulty motherboard.

To isolate the problem, replace the keyboard with a known good one. If the problem still exists, replace the motherboard.

Example 15.3:

The computer starts making a continuous beep noise that will not stop.

This error is almost always caused by a key on the keyboard when it is stuck in the down position. First, check to see if anything is resting on the keyboard. Then check for stuck keys by visual inspection and by pressing each key to see if it will free the key. If the problem still persists, clean the keyboard or replace the keyboard.

15.1.4 Keyboard Ergonomics

People who use the computer for long hours should be concerned with keyboard **ergonomics.** It is important that the wrists rest comfortably on the table in front of the keyboard and that the shoulders be relaxed. The wrists should not have to be bent to reach the keyboard. If they are, place a wrist pad in front of the keyboard to straighten them out. In addition, the chair should be adjusted so that elbows are at a 90° angle when the hands are on the keyboard. If these basic guidelines are not followed, the user may develop carpal tunnel syndrome. **Carpal tunnel syndrome** is a wrist and hand injury caused by holding the wrists stiff for long periods. This repetitive stress injury makes the nerves in the wrist swell, causing great pain.

To reduce the tension on the wrist, some companies have introduced ergonomically designed keyboards. Some are wedge shaped, allowing the shoulders to be straighter and the arms to be in a more relaxed position. Others have a built-in palm rest and a wrist-leveling device that allows the height of the front of the keyboard to be adjusted to help maintain a straight wrist.

15.2 POINTING DEVICES

The classic first pointing device is the **mouse,** which was invented in 1964 by Douglas Englebart. At that time, the mouse was called the X-Y Position Indicator for a Display System. Xerox later used the mouse with its experimental Alto computer in 1973. By 1979, Apple was using the mouse for the Lisa and later for the Macintosh computer. Today, the mouse and other pointing devices (trackballs, glide-pads, and pointing sticks) are used to navigate most modern operating systems and environments, including Windows.

15.2.1 How the Mouse Works

The traditional mouse is a simple device consisting of a housing, a mouse ball, roller sensors, and a logic board. The mouse ball is a hard rubber ball located inside the mouse. When it is placed on a flat surface, the mouse ball protrudes from the bottom of the housing and makes contact with the surface. Inside the mouse, the mouse ball also makes contact with two rollers. One roller is for the *X*-direction (left and right) and the other is for the *Y*-direction (up and down). As the rollers are moved, sensors detect the motion and generate a series of electrical pulses. The pulses from both directions are amplified by the logic board contained within the mouse and sent to the computer. The signals are then interpreted by a software driver. The driver, which interacts with the operating system, generates the mouse pointer, reports its position, and moves the cursor on the screen.

Mice are mechanical, optomechanical, or optical. Early mice were mechanical. As the *X* and *Y* rollers were moved, they would move a shaft containing copper contacts. As the copper contacts moved and made contact with other metal contacts on the logic board, this would generate pulses of electricity. By counting the number of pulses in each direction, the computer could calculate the movement of the mouse. Unfortunately, the friction of metal on metal would cause the contacts to wear out, and the mouse was affected by dust, dirt, and hair interfering with the two contacts, causing the mouse to skip or not move. The mouse pad provided a clean surface for the mouse.

The optomechanical mice use light to detect motion. See figure 15.1. As the mouse ball is rotated, the two *X-Y* rollers move and rotate slotted wheels. As the slotted wheels turn, light (generated by an LED) shines through the slots. A photodiode or phototransistor located on the other side of the wheel detects the alternating light signals and converts them to an electrical signal. As with the mechanical mouse, the electrical signal is then sent to the computer, causing the mouse pointer to move.

An optical mouse is a mouse that does not have a ball like the mechanical or optomechanical mouse does. By using optical sensors that use light to detect motion, it can be used on virtually any surface, and since it does not have a ball or any moving parts, you don't have to worry about the mouse getting dirty and malfunctioning. In addition, optical mice tend to be more precise than other mice. While some mice may have no ball and no buttons, instead the whole mouse is a super-sensitive button.

A special kind of mouse is the **trackball,** which is nothing more than an inverted mouse. Instead of physically moving the entire mouse, the hand or fingers move the ball, which protrudes from the top.

Figure 15.1 Optomechanical Mouse

The advantage of the trackball over the mouse is that the trackball is stationary and doesn't require moving space, which is why some keyboards include trackballs.

No matter what the type of mouse (or trackball), they all have one, two, or three buttons. The primary button is used to perform a click (to select an option, such as a button or a menu) or double-click (to start a process, such as starting a program icon). For Windows, the secondary mouse button is used to access context or quick-access menus.

15.2.2 Trackpoint and Glidepad

In an attempt to keep the fingers on the home keys on the keyboard, IBM introduced the trackpoint. The **trackpoint** is a small rubber cap above the B key between the G and H keys that moves the mouse pointer by means of pressure transducers. The pressure transducers measure the amount of force being applied and the direction of the force. The more force, the faster the pointer moves. Consequently, a signal is sent to the rest of the computer and the mouse pointer moves.

The last pointing device is the **glidepad,** a flat, square pad usually located below the keyboard. See figure 15.2. As a finger touches the glidepad, transducers under the pad sense the body capacitance. As the finger moves, the pad generates electrical signals, which move the mouse pointer. The glidepad is a small, stationary device, but its location allows it to be bumped easily, which can move the cursor to a different location.

15.2.3 Installing a Mouse

The first step in installing a mouse is physically connecting the mouse to the computer through a serial port, PS/2 mouse port, bus port, or USB port. Today, the PS/2 and USB ports are the most common. The serial port is a 9- or 25-pin, two-row male connector. Most systems today come with two serial ports (COM1 and COM2). COM1 usually uses IRQ 4 and I/O addresses 3F8H–3FFH; COM2 usually uses IRQ 3 and I/O addresses 2F8H–2FFH.

Figure 15.2 Glidepad and Trackpoint

The **PS/2 mouse port,** first introduced with the IBM PS/2, looks exactly like a PS/2 keyboard port. But even though they look alike, the PS/2 mouse can't be used in a PS/2 keyboard port and vice versa. The advantage of the PS/2 mouse is that it doesn't take up a COM port. The standard resources for the PS/2 mouse port are IRQ 12 and I/O addresses 60H–64H. Because the mouse is controlled by the 8042-type keyboard controller chip located on the motherboard, it uses the same I/O address as the keyboard controller.

A third type of mouse connection is the bus port. A **bus mouse** connects to a special expansion card usually used when there are no serial ports available and the system does not have a PS/2 mouse port. A bus mouse should not be connected to a PS/2 mouse port. Since the bus mouse interface expansion card is an 8-bit card, which is extremely limited in its choice of IRQs, the bus mouse is not used very much. Today, the bus mouse is hard to find.

The last type of mouse, the USB mouse, considered a USB Human Interface Device (HID), has become very popular over the last couple of years. It has become so popular that all other mice types are considered legacy devices. For a USB mouse to operate, your system and OS must support USB, USB must be enabled, and the appropriate drivers loaded. Note: A USB mouse may show up as a USB Human Interface Device in Windows Device Manager.

After connecting the mouse, the correct software drivers must be loaded. DOS requires a file with a COM or EXE extension loaded in the AUTOEXEC.BAT file or a file with a SYS extension loaded in the CONFIG.SYS file with the DEVICE or DEVICEHIGH command. Windows have their own drivers built into the operating system and environment. If one manufacturer's mouse is replaced by one made by another manufacturer, the mouse may not work properly until the driver is changed to match the mouse. The mouse drivers in Windows can be changed using the Mouse icon or applet in the Control Panel. Lastly, the software being used must be written to accept a mouse. While all Windows programs use the mouse, many DOS programs do not. Some programs will automatically accept a mouse and others have to be configured to do so.

15.2.4 Troubleshooting Pointing Devices

One of the most common problems with mice is that dirt, dust, and hair get inside the housing and cause the mouse to skip or not move. To check for and remove any foreign substance, mice and trackballs have a panel that opens so that the mouse ball can be removed. For mice, the panel is located on the bottom; on trackball housings, the panel is located on the top. These panels usually rotate in order to release, but some may have to be pushed in one direction to release. The mouse ball falls out when the housing is then tipped. The ball should be washed thoroughly in warm, soapy water or in an ammonia–water mix. After the ball is washed, it should be completely dried with a lint-free cloth or paper towel. Next, use a can of compressed air to blow out loose accumulations of dust and other foreign substances from the housing. Wipe each roller carefully with a cotton swab with isopropyl alcohol. Finally, check the LED and photodiode or phototransistor for dust and dirt to make sure that nothing is blocking the light pathway. (Note: Do not use harsh solvents or other cleaners unless they are specifically made to clean the mouse because some of these can melt the plastic or mouse ball and others may make surfaces too slippery.) Then reassemble the mouse or trackball.

Example 15.4:

The mouse is not recognized during boot-up.

Before disassembling the mouse and computer, check the obvious causes first. Make sure that the mouse is connected to the computer, and check under the mouse to see if there is an MS-PC configuration switch. If the mouse is connected and configured properly, the problem could be no software driver, an incorrect software driver, a faulty mouse, a resource conflict, or a faulty port.

The first thing to check is the driver. Make sure that the mouse was connected when the DOS driver was loaded or when Windows was starting. For DOS, the mouse driver can be verified with the MEM command and the TYPE or EDIT command (used to view the AUTOEXEC.BAT and CONFIG.SYS files). For Windows, the mouse driver can be loaded or changed using the SETUP.EXE located in the Windows directory or the Setup icon located in the MAIN group. For Windows, use the Mouse icon or applet in the Control Panel.

If the driver appears to be loaded properly, swap the mouse with a known good mouse. You can also try the mouse in another system. If the mouse is bad, replace it. If there is no problem with the mouse, then the problem must be with the port. The port may be disabled or not working properly because of an IRQ or I/O address conflict or a COM conflict (two devices configured to the same COM port). To verify that the port is enabled, look at jumpers on the expansion card or motherboard or use the BIOS setup program. To look for resource conflicts, use a software diagnostic package (QAPlus, Checkit Pro, Micro 2000, Windows Device Manager, or Windows NT WINMSD). You can also verify the positioning of jumpers on the expansion card or motherboard or use the BIOS setup program. If no conflict is found, the port will have to be replaced or the mouse will have to be assigned to another port.

When the mouse malfunctions, there are times when you need to navigate in Windows with the keyboard.

- To toggle between programs, you would use Alt+Tab or Alt+Esc keys.
- To open the main menu, you would press the menu key on the keyboard or press the Ctrl+Esc key.
- When you open a window with files and folders or the Control Panel, you will use the arrow keys to move from one file or applet to another.
- When you want to open the file, folder, or applet, you move to it and press the Enter key.
- When you are in Device Manager, you would use the arrow keys to move from one device to another.
- To open a menu in your current window, you would press the Alt key.
- To open the shortcut menu, highlight the object that you want the shortcut menu to show and press the shortcut menu key.
- Help will be opened typically with the F1 key.
- Press Ctrl+C to copy, Ctrl+X to cut, and Ctrl+Ins or Ctrl+V to paste.

15.3 JOYSTICKS

The **game port** is a 2-row, 15-pin female port that allows up to four paddles or two joysticks to be attached to a PC. The paddle is a knob that can be rotated clockwise or counterclockwise to move an object on the screen. The joystick (including flight sticks and anything similar to a joystick) has a central stick that controls two variable resistors. See figure 15.3. Much like the mouse, one resistor is for the *X*-axis and the other is for the *Y*-axis. As the stick is moved, the value of the variable resistor changes, causing a different analog electrical signal to go into the computer. The software then interprets the electrical signals.

The game port does not use an IRQ, DMA channel, or memory address. It needs only the single I/O address 201H. Because it doesn't use an interrupt, it has to be constantly scanned (polling) and requires a calibration program in most applications to interpret the variations in its variable resistance.

Figure 15.3 Joystick

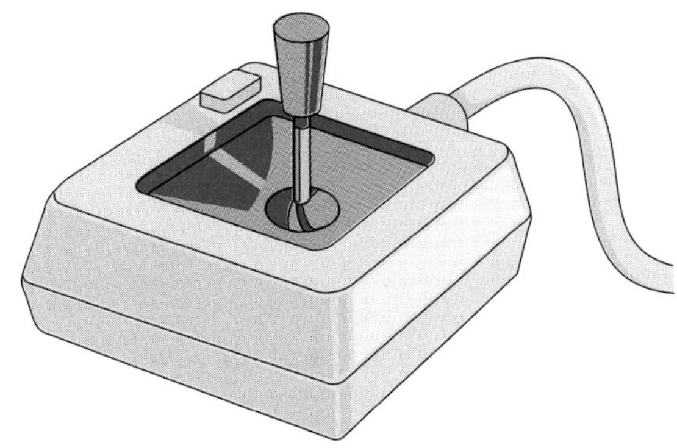

Example 15.5:

The joystick does not function.

A program must be able to use a joystick. Second, the software package must be configured to use the joystick. If there are two game ports (one on the I/O card and one on the sound card), there may be an I/O port address that must be set. If the joystick still does not function, either the joystick is faulty, the game port is faulty, or the game port is disabled (by jumpers or by software).

15.4 TOUCH SCREENS

A **touch screen** is a touch-sensitive transparent panel that covers a monitor screen. Instead of using a pointing device to select options, they can be selected by touching the screen. As the screen is touched, sensors detect a voltage change that is passed to the touch screen controller. The controller then processes the signal from the touch screen sensor and passes the data to the computer. Although touch screens seem like a neat concept, they are not widely used because the finger is a relatively large object compared to the objects displayed on the screen, which produces errors. Most people find that using touch screens causes the arms to tire after long periods.

If you want to use touch screen input with your PC, you have two options: Buy a touch screen monitor or convert an existing monitor by installing a touch screen to the front of the monitor. Besides a power cord to provide ac power, you will typically need to attach an RS-232 or USB cable from the touch screen to a serial port or USB port. Next, you will have to install software and possibly run a calibration program.

One of the newest upcoming PCs is known as the tablet PC. A **tablet PC** is a type of notebook computer that has an LCD screen on which the user can write using a special-purpose pen, or stylus. The handwriting is digitized and can be converted to standard text through handwriting recognition, or it can remain as handwritten text. Tablet PCs also typically have a keyboard and/or a mouse for input. Different from conventional touch screens, tablet PCs use special digitizing pens or styli instead of working with any penpoint or fingertip the way conventional (and slower-responding) touch screens do. On many of these systems, you must be careful not to lose the special digitizing pen or styli.

15.5 IrDA

The **IrDA** port, sometimes known as the **Infrared Ir** port, was developed by the Infrared Developers Association (IrDA) to make use of wireless technology for the notebook and laptop computer. Some keyboards, serial port devices (mice and other pointing devices), and parallel port devices use IrDA. As the name indicates, IrDA ports use infrared light (like TV or VCR remote controls) to send data. Infrared light is an invisible electromagnetic radiation that has a wavelength longer than that of visible light. So far, the IrDA data rate is 4 Mbit/s. Unlike other wireless technology, infrared does not use any radio waves. Therefore, it is not regulated by the FCC and will not cause interference on other electronic devices such as navigation and communication equipment, televisions, and radios.

Infrared signals are generated by a tiny light-emitting diode (LED) that focuses its beam into a 30° cone. To avoid interfering with other infrared devices, IrDA devices don't use much power. Consequently, the two communicating devices must be within a few feet of each other and must have a clear line of sight between them. In addition, bright sunlight may drown out the signal.

To install an infrared interface, you configure and install the expansion card or connect it to a USB port. See figure 15.4. You then load the appropriate drivers. Infrared comes standard with many notebook computers. In these cases, you just need to make sure it is enabled in the BIOS program and load the appropriate drivers. In desktop systems, you will need to make sure that the IrDA device is connected properly and the appropriate driver is loaded.

Because the IrDA port communicates by sending and receiving a serial stream of light pulses, it is normally configured to work with the UART of the system's second serial port. This arrangement must be established in the Peripherals screen of the CMOS Setup utility. In this manner, the infrared port is assigned the same system resources normally reserved for the COM2/COM4 serial ports (IRQ 3 and I/O address 2F8–2FFh or 2E8–2Efh).

Figure 15.4 Infrared Port Found on a Notebook Computer

To enable the IrDA port, the mode for the COM2 UART must be set to automatic, and one of the infrared protocol settings (HPSIR or ASKIR) must be selected. In addition, the transmission duplex mode must be selected (normally half-duplex). The operation of the infrared port and the second serial port are mutually exclusive. When the infrared option is enabled in CMOS, the second serial port will be disabled.

15.6 BLUETOOTH TECHNOLOGY

BlueTooth is a radio frequency (RF) specification for short-range, point-to-multipoint voice and data transfer. An advantage of BlueTooth is its similarity to many other specifications already deployed and its borrowing of many a feature from these specifications. The 2.4 GHz band is used by IEEE 802.11 to enable wireless LAN connectivity. BlueTooth borrows specifications to enable file sharing and data transfers between devices from IrDA (a wireless specification that uses infrared light to connect devices). HomeRF SWAP, a specification aimed at a small network of devices for the home environment, is another source for BlueTooth.

BlueTooth is omnidirectional and has a present nominal link range of 10 cm to 10 m, which can be extended to 100 m, with increased transmitting power. BlueTooth operates in the 2.4 GHz Industrial-Scientific-Medical (ISM) band and uses a frequency hop (FH) spread spectrum technology in which packets are transmitted in defined time slots on defined frequencies. A full-duplex information interchange rate of up to 1 Mbit/s may be achieved in which a time-division duplex (TDD) scheme is used.

Work on the BlueTooth specification is progressing and is primarily the responsibility of the BlueTooth Special Group (SIG). This is an industry group consisting of leaders in telecommunications and computing industries. The promoter group within the SIG currently consists of 3 Com, Ericsson, IBM, Intel, Lucent Technologies, Microsoft, Motorola, Nokia, and Toshiba.

A BlueTooth system essentially comprises the following four major components:

- **A Radio Unit**—A radio transceiver, which provides the radio link between the BlueTooth devices.
- **A Baseband Unit**—Flash memory and a CPU that interface with the radio unit and the host device electronics.
- **Link Management Software**—A driver software or firmware that enables the application software to interface with the baseband unit.
- **Application Software**—Software that implements the user interface and is the application that can run on wireless. For example, this could be a chat software that allows two laptop users in a conference hall to talk to each other wirelessly.

15.7 SCANNERS

A scanner (sometimes known as an optical scanner) is a device that can scan or digitize images on paper (much like a copy machine does) and convert them to data that the computer can use. They can then be stored in a file, displayed on the screen, added to documents, or manipulated.

15.7.1 Characteristics of Scanners

A scanner uses a series of charge-coupled devices (CCDs) mounted in a row. When a light source illuminates a piece of paper, the white spaces on the paper reflect more light than the dark areas. Some of the CCDs detect the presence or absence of light (black and white) while others detect the intensity of light (grayscale). Each CCD, at any moment, transmits its reading as a dot on the document being scanned. As the CCDs are moved from one edge to the other, the entire page is digitized row by row. Consequently, the document is made into a **bitmap.**

There are two types of scanners: flatbed and handheld. The **flatbed scanner** has a flat bed of glass on which the paper to be scanned is put face down. The CCDs are mounted on a moving arm, which moves from top to bottom. See figure 15.5. A special type of flatbed scanner is the sheetfed scanner, which can be fed loose sheets of paper continuously, much like a copy machine.

The **handheld scanner** is much smaller than the flatbed scanner. See figure 15.6. Instead of the CCDs being moved by the scanner, the handheld scanner is physically moved by the operator from one end to the other of a page. Although the handheld scanner is very portable, it can scan pictures and text only from 2 to 5 in. at a time. To keep the scanner moving straight and to help it differentiate among the rows to be scanned, the handheld scanner has small wheels.

The resolution of the scanner is the result of the number of CCDs and therefore the number of dots generated by the scanner. The denser the bitmap, the higher the resolution. Of course, higher resolution

Figure 15.5 Flatbed Scanner

Figure 15.6 Handheld Scanner

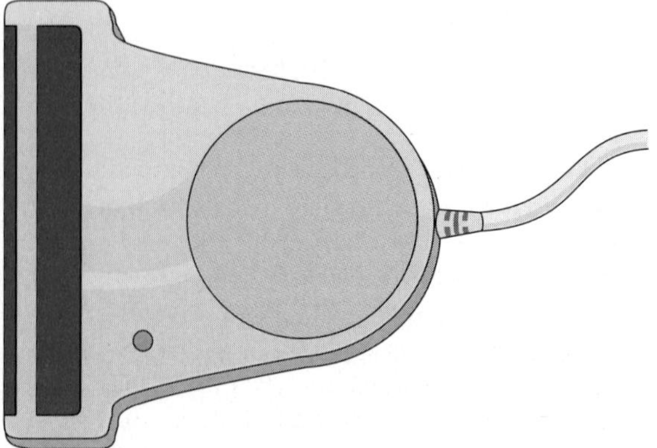

means that there is a lot more data to process and save. The number of CCDs and their density determine the horizontal resolution. The speed of the moving CCD and the focusing mirror determine the vertical resolution. Typical scanners support between 72 and 1200 dots per inch (dpi). Most flatbed scanners are typically 600 × 1200 dpi.

Color scanners are enhanced grayscale scanners. Instead of scanning for one color, they scan for the three basic colors (red, green, and blue) by making multiple scans. Some scanners perform all three scans in one pass. The software then recombines the three colors to create a full-color image.

Much like monitors, scanners have a bit depth, which is the number of bits used to represent each dot. If more bits are used to describe the color of the dot, the document scanned can be represented by more colors or grayscales. For example, a pure black-and-white image requires only 1 bit for each dot, while a 24-bit color scanner can represent 16.7 million colors.

15.7.2 Installing and Using the Scanner

Scanners can be connected to the computer using a SCSI interface, parallel port, USB interface, FireWire interface, or proprietary interface. Therefore, you might have to check for resource conflicts (I/O addresses, IRQ, DMA, and memory usage) when installing a scanner and install the appropriate drivers.

After the scanner is installed and configured, the scanner software that controls the scanner must be installed. This software allows you to choose when to scan, which areas to scan, brightness and other control settings, and to save the data into a bitmap (picture made of dots) graphics file, such as BMP or PCX. (Note: There are two types of graphics files, bitmap files and vector graphics files. **Vector graphics** files can save information as lines or circles instead of as individual dots. Bitmap graphics files can be modified with a paint program like Adobe Photoshop or Corel Photo-Paint, and vector graphics files can be modified with a draw program like Adobe Illustrator or Corel Draw. See table 15.4.) After the image is saved to file, it can then be modified with a paint program or other graphics package. Some of

Table 15.4 Common Bitmap Picture File Formats

Bitmap Picture Format	Description
Paintbrush file format (PCX)	PCX files were originally developed in the early 1980s by ZSOFT for its PC Paintbrush program. It can support up to 24-bit color and uses run-length encoding (RLE) to compress the image data. Since it was one of the first graphics formats, it is supported by most optical scanners, desktop publishing systems, and most graphics software packages.
Bitmap (BMP)	The standard bitmapped graphics format used in Windows 3.XX, Windows 95 and 98, and Windows NT (such as wallpapers and boot-up screens). Windows bitmap files are stored in a device-independent bitmap format that allows Windows to display the bitmap on any type of display. BMP is the default file name extension, but it may have others. The LOGO.SYS file (hidden file in the root directory of the C drive) in Windows 95 contains the bitmap image of the clouds and the Windows 95 logo shown during boot-up. Bitmap files can be stored in black-and-white, 4-bit, 8-bit, and 24-bit formats. In addition, bitmap files can be compressed by using run-length encoding (RLE). Another type of bitmap file is OS/2 BMP files. They are similar to Windows BMP files except for the way data is defined in the file.
Tagged image file format (TIFF)	TIFF files are one of the most widely supported file formats for storing bitmapped images for both the PC and Macintosh computers. TIFF files can be any resolution and any color level. They normally have a TIF file name extension.
Graphics interchange format (GIF)	A popular bitmap graphics file format used on the Internet because of its file compression. Although it does not compress as well as JPEG files, it does retain all of its detail. Animated GIF files are several individual GIF files combined into a single file. As each image is cycled through, the image is animated. Animated GIF files are also popular on the Internet because of their size as compared to Java applets and video formats (AVI or QuickTime files).
Joint Photographic Experts Group (JPEG) format	A popular bitmap graphics file format used on the Internet because of its file compression. Although it can reduce files to about 5% of their size, some detail is lost in the compression. JPEG files will usually have a JPG file name extension.

the changes possible are resizing, cropping (cutting off the sides of an image to make it the proper size or to remove unwanted parts), cutting, pasting, and recoloring. Most graphics software can also save the file in a different format.

The de facto standard for scanners is **TWAIN,** which some claim stands for "technology without an interesting name." TWAIN-compatible scanners include a TWAIN driver, which works with TWAIN-supported software like the common graphics programs (Adobe Photoshop and Corel Photo-Paint). Therefore, the scanner can be controlled with the normal graphics editing program and the image can be scanned into the program for immediate editing.

A scanned page of text is treated as an image made of dots. **Optical character recognition (OCR)** software converts the image of the text to actual text by analyzing the shape of each character and comparing its features against a set of rules that distinguishes each character and font. Most OCR software packages will then save the text into a Word, WordPerfect, RTF (rich text format), or ASCII text file.

15.8 DIGITAL CAMERAS

A digital camera stores images digitally rather than recording them on film. Once a picture has been taken, it can be downloaded to a computer system via a serial port or USB and then manipulated with a graphics program and printed. Unlike film photographs, which have an almost infinite resolution, digital photos are limited by the amount of memory in the camera, the optical resolution of the digitizing mechanism, and, finally, by the resolution of the final output device. Even the best digital cameras connected to the best printers cannot produce film-quality photos. However, if the final output device is a laser printer, it doesn't really matter whether you take a real photo and then scan it or take a digital photo. In both cases, the image must eventually be reduced to the resolution of the printer.

The big advantage of digital cameras is that making photos is both inexpensive and fast because there is no film processing. Interestingly, one of the biggest boosters of digital photography is Kodak, the largest producer of film. Kodak developed the Kodak PhotoCD format, which has become the de facto standard for storing digital photographs.

15.8.1 The Workings of a Digital Camera

In principal, a digital camera is similar to a traditional film-based camera. It consists of a viewfinder to aim it, a lens to focus the image onto a light-sensitive device, some means by which several images can be stored and removed for later use, and a box into which it all fits. In a conventional camera, light-sensitive film captures images and is used to store them after chemical development. Digital photography uses a combination of advanced image sensor technology and memory storage, which allows images to be captured in a digital format that is available instantly with no need for a "development" process.

Although the principle may be the same as for a film camera, the inner workings of a digital camera are quite different, the imaging being performed either by a charge-coupled device (CCD) or CMOS (complementary metal-oxide semiconductor) sensors. Each sensor element converts light into a voltage proportional to the brightness, which is passed into an analog-to-digital converter (ADC) that translates the fluctuations of the CCD into discrete binary code. The digital output of the ADC is sent to a digital signal processor (DSP), which adjusts contrast and detail, and compresses the image before sending it to the storage medium. The brighter the light, the higher the voltage and the brighter the resulting computer pixel. The more elements, the higher the resolution and the greater the detail that can be captured.

CCD works like an electronic version of a human eye. Each CCD consists of millions of cells, known as photosites or photodiodes. These are essentially light-collecting wells that convert optical information into an electric charge. When light particles known as photons enter the silicon body of the photosite, they provide enough energy for negatively charged electrons to be released. The more light that enters the photosite, the more free electrons that are available. Each photosite has an electrical contact attached to it, and when a voltage is applied to this, the silicon below each photosite becomes receptive to the freed electrons and acts as a container for them. Thus, each photosite has a particular charge associated with it; the greater the charge, the brighter the intensity of the associated pixel.

The next stage in the process passes this current to what is known as a *read-out register.* As the charges enter and then exit the read-out register, they're deleted and, because the charge in each row is "coupled" to the next, this has the effect of dragging the next charge in behind the first one. The signals are then passed—as free of signal noise as possible—to an amplifier and on to the ADC.

The photosites on a CCD actually respond only to light, not to color. Color is added to the image by means of red, green, and blue filters placed over each pixel. Because the CCD mimics the human eye, the ratio of green filters to red and blue is 2:1, because the human eye is most sensitive to yellow-green light. A pixel can represent only one color, so the true color is made by averaging the light intensity of the pixels around it, a process known as *color interpolation.*

In 1998 CMOS sensors emerged as an alternative image-capture technology to CCDs. The CMOS manufacturing processes are the same as those used to produce millions of processors and memory chips worldwide. Because these are established high-yield techniques with an existing infrastructure already in place, CMOS chips are significantly less expensive to fabricate than specialist CCDs. Another advantage is that they have significantly lower power requirements than CCDs. Furthermore, although CCDs have the single function of registering where light falls on each of the hundreds of thousands of sampling points, CMOS can be loaded with a host of other tasks, such as analog-to-digital conversion, load signal processing, handling white balance and camera controls, and more. It's also possible to increase CMOS density and bit depth without bumping up the cost.

15.8.2 The Picture

The picture quality of a digital camera depends on several factors, including the optical quality of the lens and image-capture chip, compression algorithms, and other components. However, the most important determinant of image quality is the resolution of the CCD. The more elements, the higher the resolution and thus the greater the detail that can be captured.

The resolution is measured in dpi, or dots per inch. Like a monitor, a picture is broken down into pixels or a dot of color. For example, 640 × 480 has 480 lines from top to bottom and 640 pixels that make up each of those lines. A typical inexpensive camera will be 640 × 480, which is suitable for the web or emailing, but if you want to print pictures, anything below 1280 × 1024 is basically considered unacceptable.

The horizontal sensor count multiplied by the vertical sensor count and then divided by one million is the camera's megapixel rating. The greater the number of individual sensors a camera has, the greater the potential detail in an image that it creates. Most digital cameras have sensors ranging from 2 to 5 megapixels but can go as high as 9 megapixels.

Another limiting factor is the image-compression routines used by many digital cameras to enable more images to be stored in a given amount of memory. Some digital cameras store images in a proprietary format, requiring the manufacturer's supplied software for access, but most digital cameras compress and save their images in the industry-standard JPEG or FlashPIX formats, readable on almost every graphics package. Both use slightly lossy compression, leading to some loss of image quality. However, many cameras have several different compression settings, allowing the user a trade-off between resolution quality and image capacity, including the option to store images in with no compression at all (*CCD raw mode*) for the very best quality.

15.8.3 Camera Features

A color LCD panel is a feature that is present on virtually all modern digital cameras. It acts as a mini-GUI, allowing the user to adjust the full range of settings offered by the camera, and is an invaluable aid to previewing and arranging photos without needing to connect to a PC to do so. Typically, it can be used to display a number of thumbnails of the stored images simultaneously, or provide the option to view a particular image full-screen, zoom in close and, if required, delete it from memory.

Digital cameras are often described as having lenses with equivalent focal lengths to popular 35 mm camera lenses. In fact, most digital cameras feature autofocus lenses with focal lengths around 8 mm; these provide equivalent coverage to a standard film camera because the imaging CCDs are so much smaller than a frame of 35 mm film. Aperture and shutter speed control are also fully automated with some cameras, also allowing manual adjustment. Although optical resolution is not an aspect that features greatly in the way digital cameras are marketed, it can play a very important role in image quality. Digital camera lenses typically have an effective range of up to 20 ft, an ISO equivalency of between 100 and 160, and support shutter speeds in the 1/4 s to 1/500 s range.

Zoom capability—motorized zoom lenses with a focal length range equivalent to anything between a 36 mm (moderate wide angle) and 114 mm (moderate telephoto) lens on a 35 mm format camera—is becoming an ever-more-popular feature. Some cameras have a gradual zoom action across the total focal range; others provide two or three predefined settings. Digital zoom doesn't increase the image quality but merely takes a portion of an image and uses the camera's software to automatically resize it to a full-screen image by interpolation. Some digital cameras provide a digital zoom feature as an alternative to a true optical zoom, and others provide it as an additional feature, effectively doubling the range of the camera's zoom capability.

For close-up work, a macro function is often provided, allowing photos to be taken at a distance as close as 3 cm but more typically supporting a focal range of around 10 to 50 cm. Some digital cameras even have swiveling lens units, capable of rotating through 270° and allowing a view of the LCD viewfinder panel regardless of the angle of the lens itself.

Some cameras offer a number of image exposure options. One of the most popular is a burst mode that allows a number of exposures to be taken with a single press of the shutter—as many as 15 shots in a burst at rates of between 1 and 3 shots per second. Also common is time lapse, which delays multipicture capture over a preselected interval. Other examples are the capability to have four consecutive shots each use only a quarter of the available CCD array, resulting in a single frame with four separate images stored on it, and to take multiple exposures at a preset delay interval, tiling the resulting images in a single frame.

A self-timer is a common feature, typically providing a 10 s delay between the time the shutter is activated and when the picture is taken. Also, digital cameras now have a built-in automatic flash, with a manual override option. The best have a working range of up to 12 ft and provide a number of different modes, such as auto-lowlight and backlight flash, fill flash for bright lighting shadow reduction, force-off for indoor and mood photography, and red-eye reduction. Red-eye is caused by light reflected back from the retina, which is covered in blood vessels. One system works by shining an amber light at the subject for a second before the main burst of light, causing the pupil to shrink so that the amount of red light reflected back is reduced.

Most digital cameras use rechargeable nickel cadmium or nickel hydride batteries as well as regular alkaline batteries (generally four AA batteries). Battery lifetimes vary greatly from camera to camera. As a general rule, however, the rechargeables are typically good for between 45 min to 2 h of shooting, depending on how much the LCD and flash are used, whereas a set of four alkaline AA cells have a typical lifetime of 1 h.

15.8.4 Memory Storage

Many first-generation digital cameras contained 1 or 2 MB of internal memory suitable for storing about 30 standard-quality images at a size of 640 × 480 pixels. Unfortunately, once the memory had been filled, no more pictures could be taken until they had been transferred to a PC and deleted from the camera.

Modern digital cameras use removable storage. This offers two main advantages: first, once a memory card is full, it can simply be removed and replaced by another; second, given the necessary PC hardware, memory cards can be inserted directly into a PC, and the photos can be read as if from a hard disk. By early 1999 two rival formats were battling for domination of the digital camera arena:

- **CompactFlash**—First introduced in 1994 by SanDisk corporation and based on flash memory technology, CompactFlash provides nonvolatile storage that doesn't require a battery to retain data. It's essentially a PC card flash card that's been reduced to about one-quarter of its original size and uses a 50-pin connection that fits into a standard 68-pin Type II PC card adapter. This makes it easily compatible with devices designed to use PC card flash RAM. CompactFlash cards measure 43 mm by 36 mm. They are available in both Type I and Type II cards, although predominately the former. A Type I card is 3.3 mm thick and will operate in both a Type I and a Type II slot. A Type II card 5 mm and will operate in a Type II slot only. By late 2000, maximum capacities were 192 MB for Type I cards and 300 MB for Type II.
- **SmartMedia**—Originally known by the awkward acronym SSFDC (solid-state floppy disk card) when it first appeared in 1996, the Toshiba-developed SmartMedia cards are significantly smaller and lighter than CompactFlash cards, weighing 0.48 g with a form factor of 45 mm by 37 mm and a thickness of only 0.78 mm. It uses its own proprietary 22-pin connection, but like its rival format it is PCMCIA-ATA-compatible and can therefore be adapted for use in notebook PC card slots. Capacities are less than for CompactFlash—128 MB was the maximum capacity in late 2000, capable of storing 560 high-resolution (1200 × 1024) still photographs—but at a lower cost per megabyte. See figure 15.7.

Figure 15.7 The SmartMedia Memory Storage

15.8.5 Accessing the Pictures

Since cameras store the images on the flash memory cards, you then need a way to move them to your computer so that you store them, use them in documents, or manipulate them. For this purpose, these cameras typically have a serial interface or a USB interface so that you can connect the computer and the camera together. The USB interface will often require you to load a driver that comes with the camera. Then by using software that typically comes with the cameras, you can access and copy the images to your computer. Another option available is that some cameras will include or you can purchase memory card readers. The memory card readers will connect to your PC through a USB port or expansion card. You then remove the memory card from your camera and insert them into the memory card reader.

15.9 PERSONAL DIGITAL ASSISTANT

A personal digital assistant (PDA), also known as palmtop, handheld computer and pocket computer, is a handheld device that combines computing, telephone/fax, Internet, and networking features. A typical PDA can function as a cellular phone, fax sender, web browser, and personal organizer. Unlike portable computers, most PDAs began as a pen-based stylus to make selections on the screen rather than a keyboard for input. See figure 15.8. In addition, the pen can also incorporate handwriting recognition features. Some PDAs can also react to voice input by using voice recognition technologies.

These PDAs can be connected to your computer. For example, you can use Microsoft Outlook to keep track of your appointments for the day. Then when you are traveling or going to meetings, you can connect your PDA to your computer to copy your schedule to the PDA. At the end of the day, you can reconnect your PDA and any new appointments that you have made will be copied back to your computer. This is typically done through a USB port or through an IrDA interface.

One of the more popular operating systems used in PDAs is Windows CE, which is based on the Microsoft Windows operating system but is designed for including or embedding in mobile and other space-constrained devices. Although Microsoft does not explain the "CE," it is reported to have originally stood for "Consumer Electronics." Like the full-scale Windows systems, Windows CE is a 32-bit multitasking, multithreading operating system.

Figure 15.8 A Personal Digital Assistant

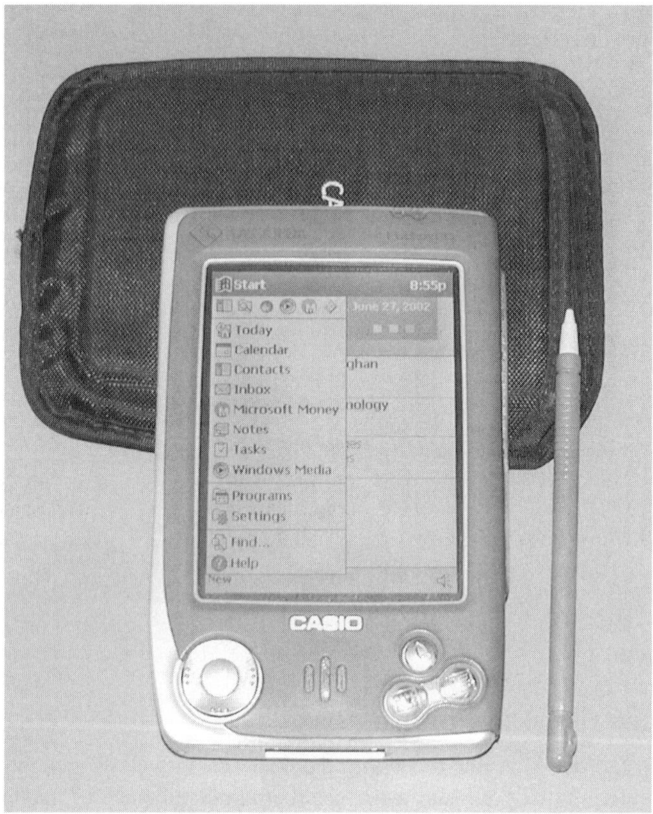

SUMMARY

1. To install a keyboard, just connect it in the appropriate port (AT 5-pin DIN, PS/2 mini-DIN, or USB).
2. For some keyboards, you may need to load the appropriate driver so that you can use all keys on the keyboard.
3. To test the keyboard connector on the motherboard, measure the voltage of several pins of the keyboard connector. Also try running a software diagnostic program that allows you to test every key.
4. The first step in installing a pointing device such as a mouse is physically connecting it through a serial port, PS/2 mouse port, bus port, or USB port.
5. After connecting the pointing device (mouse), the next step is to load the correct software drivers.
6. One of the most common problems with mice is that dirt, dust, and hair get inside the housing and cause the mouse to skip or not move.
7. If the pointing device is connected properly, the port is activated in the CMOS setup program. Make sure that the correct mouse pointer is loaded. If the pointing device does not operate properly, suspect the mouse and port (most likely the motherboard) that the pointing device is connected to.
8. Keyboards and pointing devices can use the PS/2 mini-DIN connector.
9. To troubleshoot a touch screen, make sure that you connect all cables including the power cable correctly. Then load the appropriate drivers and run the calibration program.
10. The infrared port (also known as the IrDA and the Infrared Ir port) uses infrared light to send data.
11. To install infrared devices, load the appropriate drivers for the infrared port and the infrared device.
12. To enable the IrDA port, the mode for the COM2 UART must be set to automatic and one of the infrared protocol settings (HPSIR or ASKIR) must be selected.
13. *To use a digital camera,* you connect the digital camera, load the appropriate drivers, and load the appropriate software.
14. To connect a PDA to a computer, load the appropriate drivers and software.

QUESTIONS

1. Which of the following are *not* input devices (choose two)?
   a. mouse
   b. keyboard
   c. printer
   d. monitor
2. Which of the following is the primary input device for the PC?
   a. keyboard
   b. mouse
   c. trackball
   d. scanner
3. Which of the following should be used to clean a keyboard?
   a. acetone
   b. Clorox
   c. 409
   d. a wet cloth with a mild detergent
4. Which keyboard layout is most common?
   a. QWERTY
   b. Dvorak
   c. layman
   d. optomechanical
5. Which of the following statements is *true?*
   a. The AT keyboard is backward compatible with the XT system.
   b. The AT system is backward compatible; therefore, an AT keyboard will work with an XT.
   c. The XT keyboard will work only on an XT machine, and the AT keyboard will work only on a 286 machine.
   d. The XT keyboard will work only on an XT machine, and the AT keyboard will work with a 286 or later machine.
6. Which of the following technologies are used in keyboard keys (choose three)?
   a. mechanical
   b. capacitors
   c. analog
   d. transistors
   e. membrane
7. A scan code is
   a. a code use to control the scanner.
   b. a code used to check for viruses.
   c. a code that indentifies a key being pressed on the keyboard.
   d. a code telling the computer to start polling the game port.
8. Which of the following are types of keyboard connectors in use today (choose Two)?
   a. mini-DIN-5
   b. mini-DIN-6
   c. DIN-5
   d. DIN-6
   e. DB-15
9. In which of the following ways can you check the AT keyboard connector on the motherboard?
   a. putting one lead of an ohmmeter in socket 4 and checking the remaining socket for 2.5 to 5Ω readings
   b. putting one lead of an ammeter in socket 4 and checking for a current of 250 to 500 mA
   c. putting one lead of a voltmeter in socket 4 and checking the remaining sockets for 2.5 to 5 V
   d. putting one lead of a voltmeter in socket 1 and the other in socket 5 and looking for 3.5 V
10. A *301* error code appears on an IBM Aptiva computer on boot-up. What is the problem?
    a. the keyboard
    b. the RAM
    c. the floppy disk drive
    d. the hard drive
    e. none of the above
11. When a key is no longer functioning, you should
    a. throw away the keyboard immediately.
    b. clean under the key (which may require removing the keycap); if this does not correct the problem, throw away the keyboard.
    c. wash the keyboard in a sink of hot, soapy water; if this does not correct the problem, throw away the keyboard.
    d. desolder the bad key and solder a new one.
12. What is the correct way to use a keyboard?
    a. bend the wrist up
    b. bend the wrist down
    c. use the mouse instead of the keyboard
    d. keep the wrist straight
13. An optomechanical mouse works on which of the following principles?
    a. Mechanical-driven plastic slotted wheels break beams of light, generating pulses that may be counted.
    b. Data is transmitted using an infrared beam.
    c. Infrared light bounces off a reflective mouse pad.
    d. Location is calculated using simple trigonometry theories to calculate the position of two infrared light sources placed at 90° to each other.
14. Which of the following is *not* a pointing device?
    a. touch screen
    b. trackball
    c. mouse
    d. glidepoint
    e. trackpoint
15. The mouse can be connected using all of the following ports except the
    a. Ir.
    b. PS/2.
    c. bus.
    d. serial.
    e. parallel.
16. The mouse works in MS-DOS but not in Windows 95. What do you do?
    a. Check for the proper mouse driver in the Mouse icon or applet in the Control Panel.
    b. Check jumpers on the motherboard.
    c. Check for the proper mouse driver in the AUTOEXEC.BAT and CONFIG.SYS files.
    d. Check the mouse cable and connector.
17. The mouse pointer moves erratically on the screen. What is the most likely problem?
    a. ESD damage
    b. incompatible mouse
    c. dirty mouse
    d. bad cable

18. Which of the following describes a game port?
    a. female 2-row, 15-pin D connector
    b. female 3-row, 15-pin D connector
    c. male 2-row, 9-pin D connector
    d. male 2-row, 25-pin D connector
    e. female 2-row, 9-pin D connector
19. Which device allows the user to digitize information on a piece of paper?
    a. an optical mouse b. a glidepad
    c. a scanner d. a screen
20. The de facto standard for scanners is
    a. HP. b. Epson.
    c. OCR. d. TWAIN.
21. Which of the following interfaces is best suited for receiving input from a scanner?
    a. the serial port b. the parallel port
    c. the IDE port d. the SCSI port
22. What software converts images of text to actual text?
    a. OCR
    b. drivers for the scanner
    c. computer reader
    d. glidepad
23. Which of the following is *not* a bitmap graphic format?
    a. BMP b. PCX
    c. GIF d. JPG
    e. DOC
24. A customer calls you and says, "My monitor and keyboard have stopped working all of a sudden, but the power light on the panel is still lit." You arrive on site and notice that the monitor is displaying "Keyboard Error." What is the most likely repair scenario?
    a. Change out the system board.
    b. Replace the on-board power supply.
    c. Swap out the keyboard and monitor with known working parts.
    d. Unplug the mouse because it is interfering with the keyboard.
    e. Verify that the keyboard is connected properly and replace it necessary.

HANDS-ON EXERCISES

Exercise 1: Taking Apart a Keyboard

1. Turn the keyboard over, and remove the screws that hold the keyboard together.
2. For each tab that holds the keyboard together, slide the blade of a flat-edge screwdriver between the cover (top part of the keyboard) and the base (bottom of the keyboard). Then pry them apart by twisting the screwdriver.
3. Hold the keyboard together and turn right side up. Then lift the cover free of the base and set the cover aside.
4. See how the cable is connected.
5. Identify the interface circuit board.
6. Hold the keyboard upside down and spray it with a can of compressed air.
7. Reassemble the keyboard.
8. Using a chip puller or similar tool, pull a keycap off.
9. Hold the keyboard upside down and spray it with a can of compressed air.
10. Put the keycap back on.

Exercise 2: Testing a Keyboard

1. Enter the CMOS setup program and make sure that the keyboard is enabled.
2. Shut off the computer, unplug the keyboard, and boot the computer. Notice any error messages.
3. Shut off the computer and plug in the keyboard. Next, enter the CMOS setup program and disable the keyboard. Save the changes.
4. Shut off the computer, unplug the keyboard, and boot the computer. Notice any error messages.
5. Shut off the computer and reconnect the keyboard. Enable the keyboard in the CMOS setup program.
6. Using the CMOS setup program, enable the Num Lock setting and save the changes to CMOS.
7. After boot-up, observe whether the Num Lock is on or off.
8. Using the CMOS setup program, disable the Num Lock setting and save the changes to CMOS.
9. After boot-up, look to see if the Num Lock is on or off.
10. Turn on the computer. During boot-up, press the Z key and keep it down. Notice the error message that appears on the screen.
11. Turn off the computer.
12. Determine whether there is an XT/AT switch underneath the keyboard. If there is, set the keyboard to XT and turn on the machine. Notice what happens.
13. Shut off the keyboard and set the keyboard back to AT.

Exercise 3: Disassembling and Cleaning the Mouse

1. Shut off the computer and disconnect the mouse or trackball.
2. Remove the mouse ball. This can be done by rotating the holding panel or by pushing the panel in one direction. Then tip the mouse so that the mouse ball falls out.
3. Find the *X*-axis and the *Y*-axis rollers. Use a cotton swab to clean any debris that is on the rollers.
4. Remove the screws on the bottom of the housing that hold the mouse together.
5. Gently separate the top and bottom halves and identify the buttons.
6. Look for the light source (LED), sensor, and slotted wheel on one end of the *x*-axis or *y*-axis roller. Spin the roller.
7. Reassemble the mouse and test the mouse to make sure it is working properly.

Exercise 4: Testing the Input Devices

1. Make sure that the correct driver is loaded for the mouse.
2. Run the software diagnostic package for the keyboard, mouse, and game port.

Exercise 5: Installing a Mouse Driver in Windows

1. In Windows 95 or 98, change the mouse to a Genius mouse (or another one assigned by your instructor). Restart Windows.
2. Without using the mouse, install the correct mouse driver. For Windows 95 or 98, use the Mouse icon or applet in the Control Panel. Restart Windows.
3. Shut down Windows and unplug the mouse.
4. Start Windows and let it boot.

Exercise 6: Configuring the Mouse and Keyboard in Windows

1. Using the Keyboard icon or applet in the Control Panel, set the repeat delay to long and the repeat rate to slow.
2. Start Microsoft Word, WordPad, or Write. Press the H key and hold it down. Notice how long it takes before it starts repeating and how fast the letters are repeating.
3. Using the Keyboard icon or applet in the Control Panel, set the repeat delay to short and the repeat rate to fast.
4. From Microsoft Word, WordPad, or Write, press the F key and hold it down. Notice how long it takes before it starts repeating and how fast the letters are repeating.
5. Change the repeat delay and repeat rate to settings that feel comfortable to you.
6. Using the Mouse icon or applet in the Control Panel, set the double-click speed to fast.
7. Go to the test area and try to perform a double-click.
8. Set the double-click speed to slow.
9. Go to the test area and try to perform a double-click.
10. Change the double-click speed to a setting that feels comfortable to you.
11. Adjust the pointer speed to fast. Move the mouse across the screen. Notice how far you have to move the mouse to move the mouse pointer across the screen.
12. Adjust the pointer speed to slow. Move the mouse across the screen. Notice how far you have to move the mouse to move the mouse pointer across the screen.
13. Change the pointer speed to a setting that feels comfortable to you.

Exercise 7: Installing a Scanner

1. If an expansion card is needed to connect the scanner, configure the resources (I/O addresses; IRQ, DMA, or memory addresses) and physically install the card.
2. Configure the scanner (if necessary).
3. Install any drivers (if necessary).
4. Install the scanner software.
5. Scan a picture.

Exercise 8: Using a Digital Camera

1. Get a digital camera and take a couple of pictures of your class.
2. By reading the user manual that comes with the camera, connect the camera to your PC.
3. Load any software and drivers needed to access the camera.
4. Access the pictures and transfer them to your PC.

CHAPTER **16**

Sound Cards

Topics Covered in This Chapter

Introduction

Although sound cards were not used in early personal computers, they are considered standard in today's multimedia computer. They allow the computer to record sound from a microphone, manipulate sound files, and output sound through a set of speakers. This allows presentations to have music and special sound effects and moves games to a new level. Sound cards also allow the user to play audio compact disks, compose music, create special sound effects, and use voice recognition programs.

Objectives

1. Describe sound and its characteristics.
2. Explain how sound is converted to a sound file.
3. Explain how a sound is played through the sound card.
4. Describe Nyquist's sampling theorem.
5. Explain bit resolution as it relates to sound cards.
6. Define *MIDI.*
7. List the difference between FM synthesis and wavetable MIDI cards.
8. List and describe what is needed to produce 3D sound.
9. Install, configure, and connect to a sound card.
10. Given a sound problem, determine and correct the problem.

16.1 SOUND

To understand how sound cards work, you need to understand what sound is. **Sound** is produced by vibrations of compressed air. Sound travels in all directions away from the source. When the sound reaches the human ear, it causes the eardrum to vibrate, allowing you to hear the sound.

Sound is characterized by its amplitude and its frequency. The amplitude (loudness or intensity) is measured in **decibels (dB),** a unit of measurement based on a logarithmic curve. For example, a sound that is 100 times as intense as another is only 20 dB larger. A whisper measures 10 dB, normal conversation measures 65 dB, and a rock band with amplifiers can measure 110 dB of intensity. **Frequency** (pitch) is the rate of the vibration. It is measured in **hertz (Hz),** or cycles per second. Very few people can hear frequencies lower than 16 Hz or higher than 20 kHz (kilohertz). The lowest note on the piano has a frequency of 27 Hz, while the highest note has a frequency of approximately 4 kHz.

16.2 THE SOUND CARD

Sound cards, which were not used in early personal computers, are considered standard in today's computer. See figure 16.1. They allow the computer to record sound from a microphone, manipulate sound files, and output sound through a set of speakers. Sound can be saved to a file, so it can be used to improve presentations and make games more exciting. The de facto standard for sound cards are those developed by Creative Labs, such as their Sound Blaster cards.

16.2.1 Recording Sound

The vibrations in the air that make up sound must be converted into electrical signals in order for them to be manipulated by the computer. A **microphone** is used to convert sound into analog electrical signals. *Analog* means that the signal varies continuously without any discrete, or incremental, values. See figure 16.2.

Figure 16.1 Sound Card

Figure 16.2 Original Signal

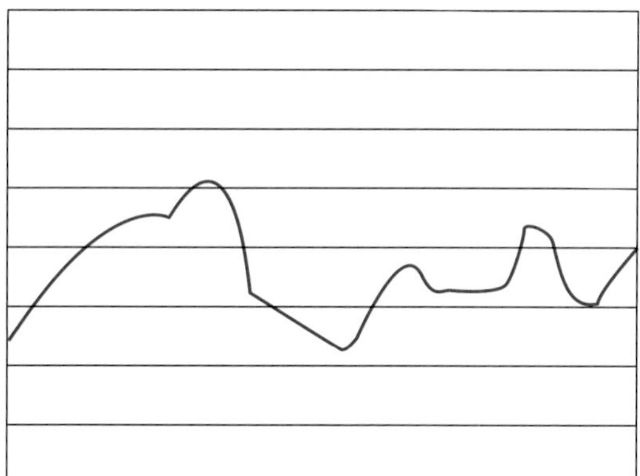

Most microphones used with the computer are either dynamic microphones or condenser microphones. Dynamic microphones have a diaphragm connected to a coil of wire (voice coil) that is wrapped around a permanent magnet. The diaphragm is usually a cone made of plastic. Sound causes the diaphragm to vibrate, which causes the voice coil to move. The voice coil thus generates a signal, which is sent into the sound card. Another type of microphone is the condenser microphone. The condenser microphone works by sending voltages through a capacitor. Instead of the diaphragm being wired in series with a magnet, it acts as one plate of a capacitor. As the diaphragm vibrates, the distance between the two plates changes, capacitance changes, and consequently the voltage is changed, causing different signals to be sent to the sound card.

The sound card amplifies and **digitizes** the signals; that is, it converts the signals into data that the computer can understand. The device that performs the analog-to-digital conversion is known as an analog-to-digital converter (ADC). Digitizing involves sampling the electrical signal and assigning a binary value to its amplitude. The larger the number of samples, the closer the recorded sound will be to

Figure 16.3 Two examples of sampling. The second one has more samples; therefore, the reconstructed signal is much closer to the original signal than the first one.

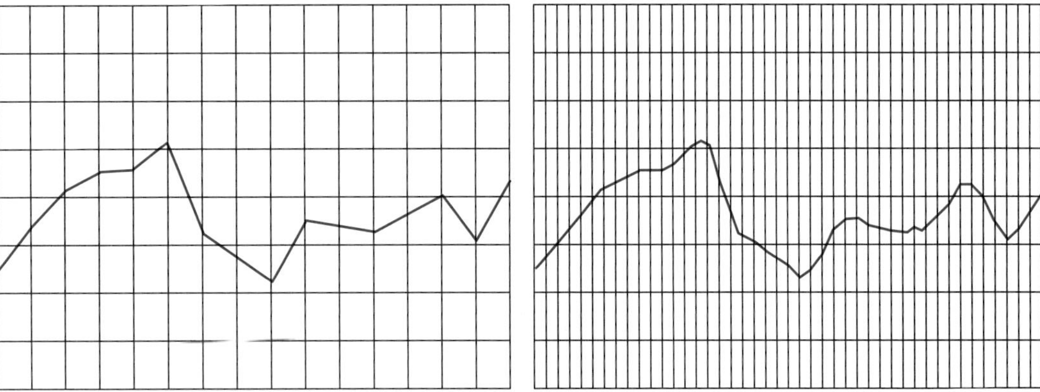

Table 16.1 Common Sample Rate and Bit Resolution Comparisons

Sample Rate	Bits per Sample	Stereo/Mono	Size per Second
11,025 Hz[1]	8 bits	Mono	11 KB
11,025 Hz	8 bits	Stereo	22 KB
11,025 Hz	16 bits	Mono	22 KB
11,025 Hz	16 bits	Stereo	43 KB
22,050 Hz[2]	8 bits	Mono	22 KB
22,050 Hz	8 bits	Stereo	43 KB
22,050 Hz	16 bits	Mono	43 KB
22,050 Hz	16 bits	Stereo	86 KB
44,100 Hz	8 bits	Mono	43 KB
44,100 Hz	8 bits	Stereo	86 KB
44,100 Hz	16 bits	Mono	86 KB
44,100 Hz[3]	16 bits	Stereo	172 KB
48,000 Hz[4]	16 bits	Stereo	187 KB

[1]Telephone quality.
[2]Radio quality.
[3]CD quality.
[4]DVD quality.

the real sound. Unfortunately, sound files with a large number of samples are larger in size. See figure 17.3. Recording should be done according to Nyquist's sampling theorem, which states that the sampling rate should be at least twice as fast as the highest frequency in the signal. The lowest standard sampling rate is 11 kHz, which is fine for normal speech. Since the human range of hearing does not go above about 22 kHz, audio compact disks use a 44 kHz sampling rate, which is often referred to as *CD-quality* sampling.

The number of bits that represent the binary number assigned to the signal sample is known as bit resolution. An 8-bit sound card (a card with a bit resolution of 8 bits, or 1 byte) can store one of 256 combinations of eight 0s and 1s. When amplitude is measured during a sample, it is assigned one of these specific binary values to indicate how loud the signal is. A 16-bit card allows greater accuracy because it can store one of 65,536 combinations of 16 0s and 1s. Most sound cards today are 16-bit cards. See table 16.1

The core of the sound card is the **digital signal processor (DSP),** which is specifically designed to manipulate large volumes of digital data offloading some of the work done by the processor. The processor follows instructions provided by a ROM chip on the sound card that operate the DSP and direct the board's major operations. In addition to the ROM, the sound card has a small amount of RAM for calculations and for buffering information being sent to and from the expansion bus.

Table 16.2 Common Sound File Formats

WAV	*Short for waveform audio.* It was developed jointly by Microsoft and IBM. Since WAV support was built into Windows 95, WAV became the de facto standard for sound on the PC. Unfortunately, WAV files tend to be large. For example, a single minute of audio can require more than 1 MB of storage.
AU	*Short for audio.* A common format for sound files found on UNIX machines, on the Internet, and in the Java programming language.
AIF or IEF	*Short for audio interchange file format.* A common format for storing and transmitting sampled sound. The format was developed by Apple Computer and is the standard format for Macintosh computers. The format encodes audio data in 8-bit mono or stereo waveforms. AIF format does not support data compression, so AIF and IEF files tend to be large.
MP3	*Short for MPEG layer 3.* MP3 is a type of audio data compression that can reduce digital sound files by a 12:1 ratio with virtually no loss in quality.
RA	*Short for RealAudio.* RealAudio format was developed by RealNetworks and supports FM-stereo-quality sound. It is the de facto standard for streaming audio data over the Internet. Streaming allows the sound files to start playing while being transferred. To hear a web page that includes a RealAudio sound file, you need a RealAudio player or plug-in.

16.2.2 Playing Back Sound

The analog signals coming from the microphone are greatly amplified, sampled, and converted to a binary value by the analog-to-digital converter. (Note: Signals from a CD player or a stereo system don't require as much amplification.) Eventually the data is organized and stored in a file. (See table 16.2 for other common sound file formats.)

To play back sound, a software program reads the sound file and passes the data to the sound card. The sound card combines or mixes signals from the DSP, audio CD, and synthesizer into a single analog signal. If a sound card operates in stereo mode, it will have two mixers and amplifiers (one for the left side and one for the right side). The signal is then amplified and sent to a voice coil in the speaker. As the voltages change, the magnetic field changes, causing the voice coil to move. Sound is then generated by a diaphragm in the speaker connected to the voice coil.

Of course, anytime analog signals are converted to digital signals and then back to analog signals, the sound is distorted. This is because samples are taken only at intervals, so changes in between samples are not taken into account. The sample is assigned a binary number based on increments—it can't be assigned a fraction of an increment. Therefore, the amount of distortion depends on the rate of sampling and the bit resolution. The distortion is called **aliasing.**

To produce high-quality sound, you need to purchase a high-quality sound card and speakers. Any sound system should produce sound that is realistic and accurate and should not add unwanted background noise during playback. Manufacturers measure sound system quality in these ways:

- **Signal-to-noise ratio (SNR or S/N ratio)**—The signal is the sound you are playing and the noise is the humming, hissing, and crackling that you don't want to play and that you can hear when nothing is playing. A high SNR (measured in decibels) means more signal and less noise. Very high-quality audio components will have an SNR of 100 dB or more; lower-quality consumer audio products will usually have SNRs between 75 and 90 dB.
- **Total harmonic distortion (THD)**—Distortion is the amount of unwanted noise that is picked up through the CD, hard drive, sound card, and speakers. The lower the percentage, the lower the noise. The sound card or speakers should have 0.5 percent or less THD. At reasonable volumes, distortion this low is undetectable and painless for the human ear.
- **Frequency response**—The frequencies or levels of sound that measure how loudly your equipment can play each frequency is referred to as frequency response. The perfect frequency response

would be one with no deviation (no gain or loss) at any frequency and across the broadest range of frequencies. Many cards support 30 Hz to 20 kHz. The wider the spread, the better the sound card and speaker.

- **Watts per channel**—Watts per channel refers to the amount of amplification available to drive speakers. Many audio adapters have built-in amplifiers providing from 4 to 8 W.

Sound cards have little or no power to drive a high-quality external speaker. Therefore, to get the best sound from a sound card, power must be supplied to the speakers, either through batteries or an ac outlet.

Unfortunately, some companies may interpret these calculations differently, which sometimes make the sound cards seem better than they really are. Therefore, when shopping or choosing audio equipment (sound card and speakers), you also need to listen to the output to verify their quality.

A good basic sound card will have several connections to attach speakers and microphones and will usually include ports for other external devices. If you watch a lot of DVD movies on your computer or play a lot of 3D games with 3D audio, you should look for additional speaker output connectors or digital connectors that allow five or more speakers and make sure that the sound card supports surround sound and 3D sound.

Speakers can generate a magnetic field. If they are placed near the monitor, they may distort the display; if they are placed near a disk or other magnetic media, the data could be corrupted.

In sound systems, channels have dual meaning. Audio channels refer to how many sets of speakers and headphones you can connect to the sound card. A sound card with only one stereo output jack would support two channels (left and right). Sound cards that support surround sound will have multiple jacks—each jack supports a pair of speakers. Channels can also mean the number of simultaneous sounds the sound card can handle at once on its DSP. If the sound card has a DSP, it should support at least 32 channels. Today's higher-quality cards support 64 and 128 channels.

When purchasing a sound card, you need to look at its API support. APIs, short for application programming interfaces, are little libraries of special functions a game or application will use to speak to a sound card. For example, your sound card should support Microsoft's DirectSound, a widely used API for games and Creative Labs' EAX, a widely used API used for 3-D action games.

High-quality cards will include a digital signal processor and use a PCI bus, which allows for increased system performance. The DSP does much of the processing for sound so that the processor can do other things, and the PCI bus allows for faster transfer.

Finally, when selecting a sound card, you should select a card that has a good track record of delivering quality hardware and drivers that have been tested. For example, if you are using a sound card with Microsoft Windows, you should make sure the card comes with drivers that have been tested by Microsoft's Windows Hardware Quality Labs (WHQL).

16.2.3 MIDI

Today, most sound cards have a **musical instrument digital interface (MIDI)** port (2-row, 15-pin female D connector). MIDI is an interface and protocol for connecting musical instruments to a PC and storing musical instrument data. Through the MIDI interface, several musical instruments can be daisy-chained together and played simultaneously. In addition, with sequencer software, the music can be captured, saved, edited, and played back.

A MIDI file and a sound file are quite different from each other. A sound file is made by sampling an analog signal; a MIDI file acts more like an enhanced music sheet. It contains information on each note, including its timing, volume, pitch, and instrument type (such as piano, guitar, drum, or flute). The MIDI file is processed by the DSP, but the sounds are actually generated by one of two types of synthesizer IC, FM, or wavetable. FM synthesis mimics different musical instruments according to built-in mathematical formulas. Wavetable synthesis relies on recordings of actual instruments to produce sound, so it produces a more accurate sound than FM synthesis. Synthesizers have multiple channels, and several instruments can be played at the same time. In addition, the sounds from one instrument can be captured and played back as another instrument.

If people do not have musical instruments or do not want to connect them to the MIDI interface, most MIDI interfaces can be converted to a game port by changing a jumper on the sound card. Of course, if there is an existing game port, that may create an I/O address conflict.

16.2.4 Compression

When sound cards sample at 44 kHz using 16-bit resolution, the sound files can consume as much as 11 MB for every minute of recording. To reduce the disk space required, many sound cards have built-in data compression. File compression can also be done with software. The most efficient compression methods focus on compressing what a human can hear and ignore what a human can't hear.

16.2.5 Sound Card Connectors

Sound cards typically have several 1/8-in. minijack connectors. The audio-out connector is used to send sound signals from the sound card to a device (speakers, headphones, or a stereo system) outside of the computer. If the sound card supports stereo output, it may have two output connectors, one for the left channel and one for the right channel. An additional connector may be used specifically for a set of speakers or headphones. The line-in connector is used to record or mix sound signals on the computer's hard disks. There is also the microphone connector. (Note: The microphone connector records only in mono, not in stereo.) Lastly, most sound cards have a MIDI/joystick connector (2-row, 15-pin female).

The microphone and speaker jacks on a sound card can be difficult to distinguish. The jacks are the same size, and it is easy to mistakenly plug the speakers into the microphone jack and vice versa. Most sound cards have symbols or text stamped under the jacks to label each connector, but these can be difficult to read because of their small size. Most sound cards also use a color code, which makes it easier to determine the purpose of each jack.

The most commonly used color code, as specified in the PC99 design guide, is:

- **Lime green**—stereo line or audio-out connector. The line-out connector is used to send sound signals from the audio adapter to a device outside the computer. This connector can be used to connect speakers, headsets, and your stereo system.
- **Light blue**—stereo line or audio-in connector. With the line-in connector, you can record or mix sound signals from an external source such as a stereo system or VCR.
- **Pink**—microphone. The microphone connector allows you to connect a microphone to record voice or other sounds to disk.
- **No standard color**—rear-out or speaker/headphone connector. This jack is used for rear speakers in four-speaker setups. Note: Often, the rear-out jack is disabled by default.

See figure 16.4.

In addition to the external connections, most sound cards feature at least one internal CD-audio connector. Most audio adapters have an internal 4-pin connector to plug an internal CD-ROM drive directly into the audio adapter, using a small round cable. If you do not connect this cable, you will not be able to play audio CDs from your CD-ROM through your speakers. Other connectors might be a joystick or midi connector which are 15-pin, D-shaped connectors.

Figure 16.4 Sound Card Connectors

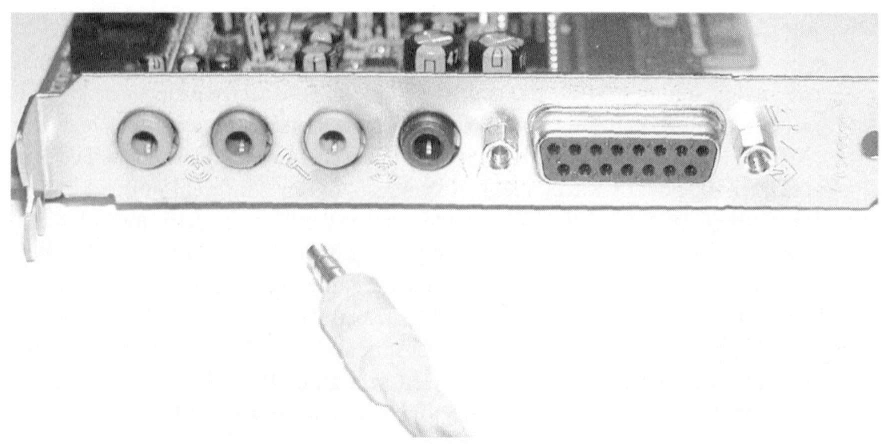

16.2.6 3D Audio

3D audio means that you will be able to hear sounds that appear to move toward you, away from you, and at various angles. Similar to a video accelerator, some sound cards act as 3D sound acceleration cards because the cards do much of the processing of sound instead of the processor, which speeds up game play.

3D sound can be experienced with headphones or with two speakers, but it sounds better on four or more speakers set up all around you. This way, if something is supposed to sneak up behind you or come in at an angle in a game or a movie, that's exactly what it will sound like. Look for a sound card that supports DirectSound3D, EAX, or Dolby Digital.

DirectX is set of APIs developed by Microsoft that enables programmers to write programs that access hardware features of a computer without knowing exactly what hardware will be installed on the machine where the program eventually runs. DirectX achieves this by creating an intermediate layer that translates generic hardware commands into specific commands for particular pieces of hardware. In particular, DirectX lets multimedia applications take advantage of hardware acceleration features supported by graphics accelerators. DirectSound supports sound input and output, including DirectSound3D for advanced spatial effects like 3D sound placement and real-time echoes.

EAX (short for Environmental Audio Extensions), developed by Creative Labs, is one of the most popular 3D standards. It encompasses sophisticated audio technologies, both hardware and software based, that work together or independently to deliver a truly amazing audio experience across Creative Lab's products.

Dolby Surround encodes four sound channels (left, center, right, and surround) onto the two tracks of any conventional stereo program source, either analog or digital. Dolby Digital soundtracks, on the other hand, can be carried only by digital formats such as DVD and DTV. Dolby Surround-encoded programs can be played back in mono, stereo, or with a Dolby Surround Pro Logic decoder that recovers the four original channels. Although Dolby Surround supports four channels, only the dominant signal can be decoded at one time.

At the option of their producers, Dolby Digital 5.1 programs can deliver surround sound with five discrete full-range channels—left, center, right, left surround, and right surround—plus a sixth channel for those powerful low-frequency effects (LFE) that are felt more than heard in movie theaters. Because it covers only about one-tenth the audible bandwidth of the other channels, LFE is referred to as a ".1" channel. In addition, Dolby Digital's multiple discrete channels enable more sharply delineated spatial effects, and its .1 LFE track makes it possible to reproduce low bass effects with stunning impact (twice as loud as the other channels). Although the surround channels cover the entire audible range (20–20,000 Hz), the range of Dolby Surround's single surround channel is limited (100–7,000 Hz). Last, Dolby supports six discrete signals, each channel able to carry a different signal simultaneously.

16.3 INSTALLING A SOUND CARD

Sound cards are one of the more difficult expansion cards to install because they usually use one IRQ, two DMA channels, and up to four I/O addresses. These are set with jumpers, DIP switches, software, or by plug-and-play. Table 16.3 lists the default resources for a Sound Blaster card, which can, of course, be changed as needed.

Table 16.3 Default Resources for a Legacy Sound Blaster Sound Card

Device	Interrupt	I/O Port	16-Bit DMA Channel	8-Bit DMA Channel
Audio	IRQ 5	220H–233H	DMA 5	DMA 1
MIDI port		330H–331H		
FM synthesizer		388H–38BH		
Game port		200H–207H		

Physically insert the sound card into an empty expansion slot and secure it with the holding screw. Next, attach speakers, the microphone, and other connectors to the appropriate jacks. After the card is physically installed and configured, load the proper software drivers. For DOS, drivers are loaded in the AUTOEXEC.BAT and CONFIG.SYS files. For Windows 95 and 98 and Windows NT, the drivers are loaded directly into the operating system. If they don't load automatically, the drivers can be loaded using the Add New Hardware icon or applet in the Control Panel.

After the installation is complete, you will usually notice an environmental variable in the AUTOEXEC.BAT file, for example:

```
SET BLASTER=A220 I5 D1
```

The A220 means the card is using I/O port address A220, the I5 indicates the card is using IRQ 5, and the D1 indicates the card is using DMA 1. The last step before using the sound card is installing an application that uses the sound card. Most sound cards come with bundled software, which includes a multimedia player, a sound recorder, sound control panel, and a mixer. Some sound card applications need to be configured with the I/O addresses, IRQ, and DMAs of the sound card. Of course, today's modern sound cards are plug-and-play.

Last, you will need to load the appropriate drivers. These drivers can be provided with the sound card or motherboard or downloaded from the Internet. The more popular sound card and sound card chip manufacturers are:

Creative Labs
http://www.creative.com

Analog Devices
http://www.soundmax.com

ESS Technology, Inc.
http://www.esstech.com

Cirrus Logic
http://www.cirrus.com

C-Media
http://www.cmedia.com.tw

RealTek
http://www.realtek.com.tw

16.4 TROUBLESHOOTING SOUND PROBLEMS

Most sound problems are often caused by a disconnected or improperly connected cable or a resource conflict (IRQ, DMA, or I/O address). Other problems could be caused by faulty speakers or a faulty sound card. They can also be caused by having the wrong driver installed, the driver is not configured with the proper parameters such as which resources the card is using, or an old driver is being used.

NOTE: If you upgrade your processor, you may need to update the sound driver.

Example 16.1:

No sound is coming from new speakers or headphones.

Check the obvious first. Make sure that the speakers are turned on and that they have power. Check the volume control on the sound card, software mixer, and the speakers. In addition, make sure that the cables are connected properly to the speakers or headphones.

Before opening the computer, make sure that the drivers are installed properly, the environment is present (if needed), and the application software is configured for the sound card's resources. If the problem still exists, swap the cables, speakers or headphones, or sound card one at a time until you discover the problem.

Figure 16.5 An Audio Connector with Two Bands

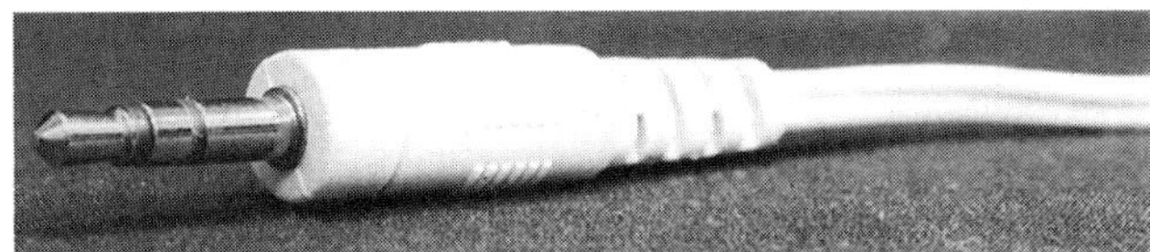

Example 16.2:

One speaker or both produces a noticeable buzz or hum.

This problem is usually caused by a cable that isn't completely connected or by unshielded cables experiencing interference from an outside source. If the cable is experiencing interference, move the path of the cables or use better-shielded cables. If the problem still exists, swap the speakers and sound card one at a time until you discover the problem.

Example 16.3:

The volume is low.

First, check the volume control on the sound card, software mixers, and the speakers. In addition, make sure that the cables are connected properly. Next, make sure that the speakers are adequate and that they have enough power (from an ac outlet or batteries). Lastly, try using a stereo amplifier between the sound card and speakers.

Example 16.4:

Sound is coming from only one speaker.

First, make sure that cables are connected properly and that a mono plug is not inserted in the stereo jack. (Note: A mono connector has only one stripe, while a stereo connector has two stripes. See figure 16.5.) Next, make sure that the correct driver is loaded and that the software mixer's balance control is set properly.

Example 16.5:

Scratchy sounds are coming from the speakers.

Scratchy sound is usually caused by either the speakers or the sound card picking up electrical interference. You can usually solve this problem by moving the speakers or the audio card away from the source of the electrical interference. Scratchy sound can also be caused by less expensive sound cards that use an FM synthesizer instead of wavetable sound generation. If the audio adapter drivers were not loaded, you would either get no sound or you might get sound out of one side of the speaker, depending upon the audio adapter card. Lastly, if the speakers needed more power than the sound card can produce, then the sound volume would be too low.

SUMMARY

1. Sound that you hear is produced by vibrations of compressed air.
2. Sound is characterized by its amplitude or loudness (measured in decibels) and its frequency, measured in hertz.
3. Sound cards are considered standard in today's computer. They allow the computer to record sound from a microphone, manipulate sound files, and output sound through a set of speakers.
4. The de facto standard for sound cards is the sound card developed by Creative Labs (Sound Blaster).
5. A microphone is used to convert sound into analog electrical signals.

6. The sound card then amplifies and digitizes the sound.
7. Digitizing (also known as sampling) is done by taking samples of the electrical signal and assigning a binary value to the amplitude of the signal.
8. The core of the sound card is the digital signal processor (DSP), which is specifically designed to manipulate large volumes of digital data.
9. The amplitude is assigned a binary number depending on the resolution of the sound card (usually 8- or 16-bit).
10. To play back sound, a software program reads the sound file and passes the data to the sound card. The sound card combines or mixes signals from the DSP, audio CD, and synthesizer into a single analog signal, which it then amplifies and sends to a set of speakers.
11. MIDI is an interface or protocol for connecting musical instruments to a microcomputer and storing musical instrument data.
12. Whereas a sound file makes samples of an analog signal, a MIDI file has instructions for playing specific notes.
13. FM synthesis mimics different musical instruments according to built-in mathematical formulas.
14. Wavetable synthesis relies on recordings of actual instruments to produce sound.
15. 3D audio means that you are able to hear sounds that appear to move toward you, away from you, and at various angles.
16. Sounds cards are one of the more difficult expansion cards to install because they usually use one IRQ, two DMA channels, and up to four I/O addresses.
17. Sound card resources are set with jumpers, DIP switches, software, or by plug-and-play.
18. The default resources for a Sound Blaster card are IRQ 5, DMA 5, DMA 1, and I/O addresses 220H–233H, 330H–331H, 388H–38BH, and 200H–207H.
19. Most sound cards are often caused by a disconnected or improperly connected cable or a resource conflict (IRQ, DMA, or I/O address).
20. Other problems could be caused by faulty speakers or a faulty sound card, by having the wrong driver installed, by using a driver that is not configured with the proper parameters, or by using an old driver that needs upgrading.

QUESTIONS

1. Sound is measured in (choose two)
   a. amplitude.
   b. frequency.
   c. phase.
   d. distortion.
   e. distance.
2. Which device allows you to record sounds?
   a. speaker
   b. keyboard
   c. capacitor
   d. microphone
3. Taking measurements at intervals of time is called
   a. bit resolution.
   b. amplifying.
   c. sampling.
   d. gain.
4. How many tones can an 8-bit sound card produce?
   a. 16
   b. 256
   c. 512
   d. 1,024
   e. 4,096
   f. 65,536
5. Which of the following is a sound file?
   a. WAV
   b. MOV
   c. JPG
   d. AVI
6. The distortion caused by converting an analog signal to a digital signal and back to an analog signal is called
   a. amplifying.
   b. aliasing.
   c. sensitivity.
   d. harmonic.
   e. modulation.
7. An electromagnetic field caused by a set of speakers can result in which of the following problems (choose all that apply)?
   a. distortion of the video display
   b. total shutdown of the PC
   c. RAM errors
   d. read/write problem on magnetic disks and tapes
8. A MIDI interface is described as a
   a. 2-row, 25-pin female D connector.
   b. 3-row, 15-pin female D connector.
   c. 2-row, 15-pin female D connector.
   d. 2-row, 15-pin male D connector.
   e. 2-row, 9-pin female D connector.
9. Which form of synthesizer uses recordings of actual sounds?
   a. condenser
   b. FM synthesis
   c. wavetable
   d. amplifying
   e. dynamic
10. Which of the following is *least* likely to cause a sound problem?
    a. magnetic distortion
    b. IRQ conflict
    c. incorrect drivers
    d. improperly connected cable
11. A customer calls you and says that he cannot get any sound out of the new computer speakers he installed on his Windows 98 desktop computer. Even though the old speakers still work, he is trying to replace the small external set of speakers with a much nicer surround-sound set. The new surround-sound speakers work fine when he plugs them into his notebook computer, but he cannot get them to work on his desktop computer. He has made no software configuration changes to the Windows 98 desktop computer since removing the older speakers. What should you do first?
    a. replace the speaker power supply
    b. install the drivers for the speakers

c. make sure the Windows mute setting is not on
d. make sure that he connected the speaker in the speaker jack and not the microphone jack

12. A customer calls you and says her computer speakers suddenly stopped working. She remembers hearing sound come out of the speakers in the morning but by afternoon, the speakers were silent. She did not restart the system during that time. She says that it is a minor annoyance and does not want to pay for you to come to her site to repair the problem, but she is willing to pay your fee if you could help her solve the problem over the phone. Which question should you ask her first?
    a. Are the speakers powered?
    b. Do you have a screwdriver handy?
    c. Are the speakers close to the monitor?
    d. Did you recently update the audio drivers?
13. Which three conditions are most likely to cause scratchy sound (choose three)?
    a. the audio adapter drivers are not loaded
    b. the speakers are placed next to the monitor
    c. the audio adapter is installed next to an internal modem
    d. the audio adapter uses an FM synthesizer instead of wavetables
    e. the speakers need more power than the audio adapter can produce

HANDS-ON EXERCISES

Exercise 1: Installing a Sound Card

1. Using a sound card's documentation, configure it to use free resources (IRQ, I/O addresses, DMA, and memory addresses).
2. Install the sound card drivers. (Install the drivers using the Add New Hardware icon or applet in the Control Panel. Note that you may still need to use the disks or CD-ROM that came with the sound card.)
3. Connect speakers or headphones to the sound card.

Exercise 2: Using a Sound Card

1. Install software that will use the sound card. (If you have Windows 95 or 98 or Windows NT, make sure that the Media Player, Sound Recorder, Volume Control, CD-ROM Player, and Multimedia Sound Schemes are loaded. They are usually executed by using the Start button and Programs, Accessories, Multimedia menu. If they are not loaded, they can be loaded by using the Add or Remove Software icon or applet in the Control Panel. Note: If the sound card has bundled software, you may also want to install it so that you can compare it to programs that come with Windows 95 and 98 or Windows NT.)
2. Using Media Player or equivalent software, find, load, and play a file with a WAV file name extension. Windows will usually have WAV files in the WINDOWS\MEDIA directory.
3. Adjust the volume controls on the speaker and sound card. Play the WAV file.
4. Using the volume control or equivalent software, mute the volume. Play the WAV file.
5. Using the volume control, activate the sound and close the WAV file.
6. Connect a microphone to your sound card. Using the Sound Recorder or equivalent software, record a 5 to 10 s message using 8-bit resolution at 22,000 Hz mono settings. Save the file on the hard drive. (For Sound Recorder, the bit resolution, sample rate, and mono and stereo settings can be configured by using Properties under the File menu, and clicking on the Convert Now button.)
7. Using the Sound Recorder or equivalent software, record the same message using 16-bit resolution at 44,000-Hz stereo settings. Save the file to the hard drive under a different name from the first file.
8. Look at the size of the two files.
9. Using Media Player, play one of your recordings.
10. If you have a CD-ROM drive and an audio CD, perform the following:
    a. Insert the audio CD in the CD-ROM drive.
    b. Using the Volume Control or equivalent software, mute the microphone recording. (When you first start Volume Control, it usually shows the controls for playback. To switch to the Volume Control for recording, select Properties under the Options menu.)
    c. Load the CD Player and select the track that you want to record.
    d. Start the Sound Recorder and then the CD Player.
    e. Stop the recording after 30 s.
    f. Play the recorded sound using Sound Recorder.
    g. Save the file as a WAV file.
    h. Load and play the WAV file using Media Player.
11. If you have Windows, open the Sounds icon or applet from the Control Panel. Change the Close a Program event to CHIMES.WAV.
12. Start a program and exit the program.
13. Change the Close a Program event back to the way it was.

CHAPTER 17

Serial Ports and Modems

Topics Covered in This Chapter

Introduction

The serial port interface is a general-purpose interface that can be used for almost any type of device. It is used mostly for mice and modems, but it can also be used for serial printers, plotters, label makers, bar code readers, scales, and device control circuits. In addition, the serial port can be used to talk to other computers. Today, all of the popular operating systems, including DOS with Windows 3.XX, Windows 95 and 98, and Windows NT, use a mouse to navigate. In addition, the Internet has made the modem (modulator-demodulator) more common than ever. Unfortunately, installing and configuring a modem can cause all kinds of headaches.

Objectives

1. By looking at the back of a computer or an expansion card, identify the serial port.
2. List the characteristics of a serial port.
3. Explain how the RS-232C and RS-422/RS-423 standards relate to the serial port.
4. State how many serial ports a system can have.
5. Define *data frame* and describe each of its components.
6. Compare and contrast baud and bits per second.
7. Explain how the serial port communicates.
8. State the purpose of a null modem cable and explain how it differs from a normal serial cable.
9. Install and configure a serial port.
10. Given a serial port problem, determine and correct the problem.
11. Explain how a modem communicates with another computer using a typical phone line.
12. List the different methods by which data can be encoded in telephone transmissions.
13. Transfer a file using your modem.
14. Explain the AT command set.
15. Explain the process in using a fax/modem to send and receive documents.
16. Compare and contrast normal modems and ISDN modems.
17. Install and configure a modem.
18. Given a modem problem, determine and correct the problem.

17.1 SERIAL PORTS

The **serial port interface** is a general-purpose interface that can be used for almost any type of device. It can be identified by its two-row male D port that has either 9 or 25 pins. See figure 17.1. Serial ports are bidirectional asynchronous devices. They send data over a single wire as bits lined up single-file in series. The advantage of serial communications is that they are simple and are able to go long distances. As the name implies, the serial port is a **full-duplex** device, which means that data can travel in both directions at the same time and without synchronization or a timer (**asynchronous**).

The serial port on the PC conforms to the Electronics Industries Association (EIA) RS-232C standard (Recommended Standard Number 232; C is the latest revision of the standard). The full RS-232C standard specifies a 25-pin D connector, of which 22 pins are used; serial ports use only a few pins, so they follow a subset of the RS-232C standard. The RS-422 and RS-423 standards have since replaced the RS-232 standard because they support higher data rates and greater immunity to electrical interference. RS-422 supports multipoint connections; the RS-423 supports only point-to-point connections.

The typical computer can support up to 4 serial ports with an ISA bus or later standard. The IBM PS/2 supports 8 serial ports. If more serial ports are needed, a multiport board, which has up to 128 serial ports, can be purchased. Of course, the operating system and application software must be able to recognize all of the ports. DOS 3.3 or higher supports only 4 serial ports; Windows 95 and 98 and Windows NT support up to 128 serial ports. Serial ports use reserved computer names such as COM1, COM2, COM3, and COM4 (COM stands for communication).

Figure 17.1 Serial Port Signal

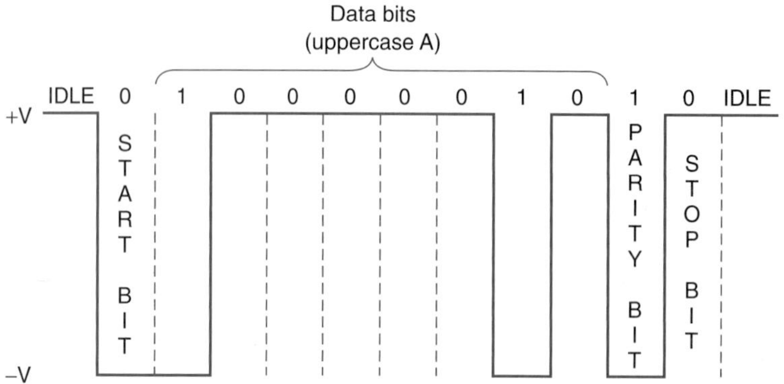

17.1.1 Characteristics of a Serial Port

As a full-duplex device, the serial port uses separate lines for sending and receiving data and has a common signal ground wire. Not all of the devices that can be attached to a serial port require two-way communications, so these devices require only a transmit line and signal ground. The signals used by the serial ports are bipolar, which means they consist of positive and negative voltages. A value of 0 (space state) is represented with a positive value between +3 and +15 V dc and a value of 1 (mark state) is represented by a negative voltage between −3 and −15 V dc. These voltages differ, of course, from the voltages most commonly used by PCs, which are +5 V dc, −5 V dc, +12 V dc, and −12 V dc produced by the power supply. The advantage of a bipolar signal is that it supports very long cabling with minimum noise. In addition, the sending and receiving devices can distinguish between an idle state and a disconnected line.

Information sent through a serial port is sent as *data frame.* The data frame consists of a start bit, a number of data bits, one to two stop bits, and possibly some parity bits. Because the serial ports are asynchronous (no timer), they need some way to coordinate with each other. Therefore, whenever data is sent, a start bit is sent to notify the other end that data is coming. Since the serial line is kept positive when idle, the start bit (logical 1) drops the line to a negative voltage. After the start bit has been sent, the transmitting device sends the actual data bits. Most computers and computer devices use 5, 6, 7, or 8 bits to represent the data being sent, and both the receiving and transmitting devices must agree on the number of data bits transmitted. Seven data bits allow up to 128 different characters, and 8 data bits allow up to 256 different characters (such as the ASCII characters). After the data has been transmitted, a stop bit is sent to indicate the end of the data frame. It can consist of 1, 1, 1½, or 2 bits with a logical value of 1. Again, the sending and transmitting device must count the same number of stop bits.

To check for errors, serial devices will use parity checking or CRC checking. **Parity** error control could be odd parity, even parity, mark parity, or space parity. Mark parity will always have the parity bit set to a 1 and the space parity set to a 0. During parity checking, the 1s of the data bits are counted. If the data bits have an odd number, the parity bit is assigned a 0, keeping the data bits and parity bit an odd number. If the data bits have an even number, the parity is assigned a 1, keeping the data bits and parity bit an odd number. Therefore, when the data is sent to a receiving device, the receiving device counts the data bits and parity bit to make sure that the number is still odd. If the bit count is even, an error has occurred. Even parity is the opposite of odd parity. When the data bits and parity bit are counted, the total number should be even. Consequently, when the data is sent to a receiving device, the receiving device counts the data bits and parity bit to make sure that the number is still even. If the bit count is odd, an error has occurred. Unfortunately, if two or any even number of errors occur, the odd parity remains odd and the even parity remains even. Therefore, no error is detected. Of course, both the sending and the receiving device must use the same parity-checking scheme.

Another form of error checking is **CRC (cyclical redundancy check).** Although parity checking monitors a group of 7 or 8 bits, CRC checks an entire block of data, such as 1,024 bytes. CRC performs a mathematical calculation (CRC value) on the data to be sent, and when the block of data is sent, this value is also sent. When the data reaches its destination, the same mathematical calculation is done and the result is compared to the CRC value sent. If the values are not the same, an error occurred during transmission.

17.1.2 Universal Asynchronous Receiver/Transmitter (UART)

The central part of the serial port is the **universal asynchronous receiver/transmitter (UART),** which is a single IC chip located on the motherboard or on an I/O expansion card. It is the translator between the serial port and the system bus and is the component that processes, transmits, and receives data. For flexibility, the UART includes several registers that allow it to be programmed or configured. By using communications software, the number of data bits, the length of the stop bit, and the baud rate can be specified and modified as needed for each serial port.

Inside the computer, data is generated by the microprocessor and moved around in parallel format (system bus). This means that several bits are being moved from one place to another simultaneously using several wires. Of course, the more wires there are, the more data can be transported. As the data comes from the system bus, the UART converts it to a serial signal (bits in a single file), adds the start and stop bits, and adds any error control (such as parity). Then the UART converts the digital signals (+5 V dc TTL) to a bipolar signal. The data is then sent through the serial port out to the serial cable. As data comes in from the serial port, the UART must reverse the process. First, the UART converts the bipolar signal to a +5 V dc TTL digital signal. It then strips the start and stop bits, checks for errors, and strips the error-control information. Finally, it converts the data back into parallel format through the system bus so that it can be processed by the computer.

Early UARTS (8250 and 16450) used a FIFO (first in, first out) buffer. If the computer did not retrieve the data fast enough, the data would be overwritten by new data coming in through the serial port. Newer systems use a 16-byte FIFO-buffered UART, like the 16550. Because the buffer is larger, the microprocessor only has to process the data every 16 bytes before any data is overwritten. Consequently, the serial communication is faster.

17.1.3 Serial Port Signals

Two terms are often used with reference to serial ports, **data terminal equipment (DTE)** and **data carrier equipment (DCE).** These terms indicate the pinouts for the connector on the device and the direction of the signals on the pins. See tables 17.1 and 17.2. Typically, the computer is the DTE device, and the serial device connected to the computer is the DCE device. All of the signals sent through the

Table 17.1 25-pin Serial Port

Pin	Signal	Direction
1	Protective ground	
2	Transmit data (TD)	Output
3	Receive data (RD)	Input
4	Request to send (RTS)	Output
5	Clear to send (CTS)	Input
6	Data set ready (DSR)	Input
7	Signal ground (GND)	
8	Data carrier detect (DCD)	Input
9	+Transmit current loop	Output
11	−Transmit current loop	Output
18	+Receive current loop	Input
20	Data terminal ready (DTR)	Output
22	Ring indicator (RI)	Input
23	Data signal rate indicator (DSRD)	I/O
25	−Receive current loop	Input

Table 17.2 9-pin Serial Port

Pin	Signal	Direction
1	Data carrier detect (DCD)	Input
2	Receive data (RD)	Input
3	Transmit data (TD)	Output
4	Data terminal ready (DTR)	Output
5	Signal ground (GND)	
6	Data set ready (DSR)	Input
7	Request to send (RTS)	Output
8	Clear to send (CTS)	Input
9	Ring indicator (RI)	Input

serial port can be categorized as data lines, **handshaking** (flow control) lines, and ground lines. The data and handshaking signals are swapped at the DCE end.

When the computer (DTE) is turned on or initialized, it must initialize a serial device (DCE) and make a connection with it. This process begins when the computer sends a data terminal ready (DTR) signal to the serial device, telling it that the computer is ready to establish a connection. When the device is initialized and is ready for a connection, it will send a data set ready (DSR) signal back to the computer, establishing a connection. To maintain the connection, the DTR and DSR signals must remain on. If either stops, the connection is terminated. Before the two devices are ready to communicate, the request to send (RTS) signal is generated by the computer to tell the device that the computer wants to send data. When the device is ready, the device sends a clear to send (CTS) signal to the computer, telling it that it is ready to receive data. Together, these make up RTS/CTS, which is also known as hardware flow control. The data is then sent from the computer to the serial device using the transmit data (TD) wire, and data is sent from the serial device to the computer using the receive data (RD) wire.

Not all data sent by the serial port is controlled by hardware flow control (hardware handshaking); some is under software flow control (software handshaking), known as **Xon/Xoff,** which transmits special control characters from one device to another to tell it to stop or start sending data. To start sending data (Xon), the computer or device will send a Control-Q (ASCII value 17); to stop sending data (Xoff), the computer or device will send a Control-S (ASCII value 19). The last two signals are available only when communicating with a modem. The carrier detect (CD) signal is used by a modem to signal that it has made a connection with another modem or has detected a carrier tone. The ring indicator (RI) is used to tell the computer when a telephone ring is detected, such as when a remote user is trying to call in and access the computer.

17.1.4 Serial Connectors and Cables

The first serial port used on the PC was the 25-pin male D connector, as specified by the RS-232 standard. The most basic full-duplex communication requires three lines (the transmit line, the receive line, and the signal ground), but other forms of serial communications use up to 10 different wires.

NOTE: Included in these 10 are the chassis ground and the signal ground. These two wires have different functions and should not be connected together. See figure 17.2.

When multi-I/O cards were being developed, manufacturers found that they could not have a 25-pin parallel port and a 25-pin serial port on the same retaining bracket of an expansion card. To overcome the size restrictions, the 9-pin serial port (the 10 signals used in the 25-pin serial port minus the chassis ground) was introduced and has since become the standard serial port. A computer today usually has two serial ports. COM1 is usually a 9-pin serial port (most often used by mice and newer devices), and COM2 is usually a 25-pin serial port (most often used by serial plotters, printers, and modems). Of course, there may be times when two serial devices, both of which require the 9-pin connector or the 25-pin connector, are being used. To accommodate both devices, one is connected to the 25-pin connector using a 9-pin connector to a 25-pin port adapter. Table 17.3 shows the connections used by the standard 9-pin to 25-pin adapter.

Figure 17.2 Serial Ports

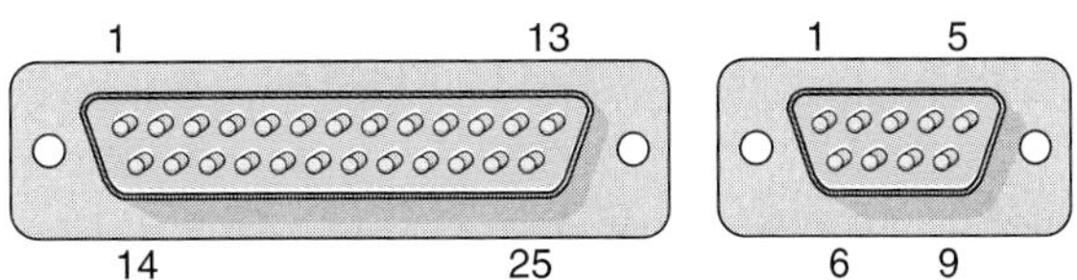

Table 17.3 9-pin to 25-pin Adapter

9-Pin Connector	25-Pin Connector
Pin 1 DCD	Pin 8 DCD
Pin 2 RD	Pin 3 RD
Pin 3 TD	Pin 2 TD
Pin 4 DTR	Pin 20 DTR
Pin 5 GND	Pin 7 GND
Pin 6 DSR	Pin 6 DSR
Pin 7 RTS	Pin 4 RTS
Pin 8 CTS	Pin 5 CTS
Pin 9 RI	Pin 22 RI

The RS-232C standard imposed a cable length limit of 50 ft. If a cable is in an electrically noisy environment, even very short cables can pick up stray signals. If the cable is well made and well shielded, the length can be increased significantly. A shielded cable has a wire braid or aluminum-coated plastic film wrapped around the wires to prevent signals from leaking in or out. In addition, the shielding of the cable is connected to the signal ground.

17.1.5 Null Modem Cable

A normal serial cable, known as a straight-through cable, is made to connect one computer (DTE) and one serial device (DCE). Therefore, if two computers (to transfer data or to play a game against an opponent) or other DTE devices were connected with a serial cable, the transmit line and receive line of one computer would be connected to the transmit and receive lines on the other computer, and the DTE devices would not be able to communicate with each other. Therefore, to make two computers communicate with each other, a **null modem cable** (sometimes known as a *crossover* cable) is used. The null modem cable crosses the receive and transmit wires—the DTR and RTS wires and the DSR and CTS wires. The reason that the cable is called a *null modem* cable is because it allows two computers to communicate with each other without a modem. Tables 17.4 and 17.5 illustrate how the null modem cable works and when it is used.

Table 17.4 Null Modem Cable

DCE #1				DCE #2		
Signal	DB-9	DB-25	↔	DB-25	DB-9	Signal
TD	3	2	↔	3	2	**RD**
RD	2	3	↔	2	3	**TD**
RTS	7	4	↔	5	8	**CTS**
CTS	8	5	↔	4	7	**RTS**
DSR	6	6	↔	20	4	**DTR**
DTR	4	20	↔	6	6	**DSR**

Table 17.5 Null Modem or Crossover Cable

Peripheral	Device Type	Cable Needed to Connect to PC
PC	DTE	Null modem cable
Modem	DCE	Straight-through cable
Mouse or trackball	DCE	Straight-through cable
Digitizer or scanner	DCE	Straight-through cable
Serial printer	DTE	Null modem cable
Serial plotter	DTE	Null modem cable

Table 17.6 Typical Serial Port Resources

Bus Architecture	Port	Address	Alternative Addresses	IRQ
All systems	COM1	03F8H		IRQ 4
All systems	COM2	02F8H		IRQ 3
ISA	COM3	03E8H	03E0H, 0338H	IRQ 4
ISA	COM4	02E8H	02E0H, 0238H	IRQ 3

17.1.6 High-Speed Serial Ports

Enhanced serial ports (ESP), or super high-speed serial ports, are ports that can communicate up to 921,600 bit/s using a 28,800 baud modem. The main reason for the speed increase is a faster UART (such as the 16550AF or 16550AFN) that has a 1,024 byte buffer and onboard data flow control. Of course, to use the faster speed, both the computer and the serial device must be able to communicate at that speed.

17.1.7 Installing a Serial Port

Installing a serial port requires choosing an available IRQ and a free COM designation or I/O address. Again, no two devices can use the same IRQ and no two devices can use the same I/O address.

As the computer is initializing, the following I/O addresses are checked in order for serial ports: 03F8H, 02F8H, 03E8H, 02E8H, 03E0H, 02E0H, 0338H, and 0238H. When a serial port is found, a COM designation is assigned. Typically, COM1 is set to 03F8H and COM2 is set to 02F8H. See table 17.6. The actual I/O addresses for each COM port are kept in the BIOS data area of RAM starting at 0400H. (Note: DOS recognizes only COM1 and COM2.) As table 17.6 indicates, COM1 typically uses IRQ 4 and COM2 uses IRQ 3. When the IBM AT computer was introduced, the BIOS was expanded to support up to four serial ports (COM1–COM4) but unfortunately there were no extra IRQ lines available. Therefore, COM1 and COM3 shared the same interrupt and COM2 and COM4 shared the same interrupt. This was possible as long as COM1 and COM3 were not being used at the same time and COM2 and COM4 were not being used at the same time. Today, with GUI interfaces requiring a mouse or some other pointing device, COM3 and COM4 can usually be assigned to other IRQs, such as IRQ 5 (usually used by LTP2, which most people do not have). Of course, a PS/2 or bus mouse can free up one of the COM ports, and if more than four serial ports are needed, a multiport adapter can be purchased that can support up to 128 serial ports using one IRQ.

The serial port I/O address (which is assigned a COM designation) and IRQ can be configured in many ways. If the serial port is part of an expansion card, it can be configured with jumpers, DIP switches, or special software, or the card can automatically configure itself as a plug-and-play device. If the serial port is on the motherboard, it can be configured with jumpers or DIP switches, or it can be configured by using the BIOS setup program.

NOTE: Disconnecting the serial port cables will not disable the port, even if the cables are disconnected inside the computer.

Question:

Most expansion cards specify a COM designation instead of the I/O address. Therefore, what happens if you install a COM1, a COM2, and a COM4 in your system?

Answer:

If you install a COM1, a COM2, and a COM4, you are really selecting the I/O address. During boot-up, the system checks the I/O addresses for serial ports and assigns the COM designation. Therefore, the three COM ports are assigned to be COM1, COM2, and COM3.

The last step before using the serial port is installing software drivers. You will rarely install software for the serial port (COM1, COM2, COM3, and COM4). However, many of the devices that connect to the serial port (such as the mouse or a label maker) may require drivers. Some of the drivers will automatically search for the appropriate serial port, while other drivers must be told which I/O address and COM port or IRQ the device is using.

17.1.8 Troubleshooting Serial Ports

A serial port problem can be caused by a disconnected cable, bad cable, resource conflict, invalid software configuration, bad or incorrect drivers, or the serial port itself. Check the cable that goes from the male D connector to the I/O expansion card or motherboard. For those serial devices that also have a power cable, make sure it is connected correctly as well. Much like hard drive and floppy drive cables, pin 1 is indicated with a red or blue stripe on the cable to match the small number 1 or 2 on the expansion card or motherboard.

Check that the resources used by the serial port, including the IRQ and I/O address and COM designation, are correct. Again, these are set with jumpers, DIP switches, the BIOS setup program, or configuration software, or by using plug-and-play. In addition, make sure that the software that is using the serial device is configured with the proper COM designation, I/O address, or IRQ. Also make sure that both the computer's serial port and the serial device are set to use the same baud rate, same number of data bits, same number of stop bits, and same parity method. If not, the data will be garbled at the end.

The device connected to the serial port will most likely need a driver. For example, if a mouse is running in DOS, a device driver (file with a SYS extension) is loaded in the CONFIG.SYS file or a TSR (file with a COM or EXE extension) is loaded in the AUTOEXEC.BAT file. In Windows the driver will be loaded during installation of Windows, by using the Add New Hardware applet in the Control Panel or by using a program that comes with the device.

A serial port can be tested by using a **serial port loopback plug.** The loopback plug is a special device that attaches to the serial port D connector and is nothing more than a cable that takes data being sent from the serial port and reroutes it back into the serial port. Therefore, the data received should be the same data that was sent out. A 25-pin serial loopback connector has the following pins connected together:

1 and 7
2 and 3
4, 5, and 8
6, 11, 20, and 22
15, 17, and 23
18 and 25

For a 9-pin serial loopback connector, the following pins are connected together:

1, 7, and 8
2 and 3
4, 6, and 9

Most software diagnostic packages also have serial port tests. Because of the variety of devices that can connect to the serial port, most software diagnostic packages offer a selection of device-specific tests (mouse, modem, loopback plug, or nothing). Of course, if you run a test for the wrong device, the test will most likely fail.

If the serial port is bad, it will have to be replaced. If the serial port is on the expansion card, replace the expansion card. If the serial port is on the motherboard, either replace the motherboard (sometimes a costly repair) or disable the serial port on the motherboard and install an expansion card that has a serial port.

Example 17.1:

Data is lost or corrupted.

Before opening the computer, make sure the cable is connected properly and that it is in good condition. Next, make sure that no devices are around that may generate large amounts of electromagnetic interference. If there are, either reroute the cable (or the device generating the electromagnetic interference) or try a well-shielded cable.

If the cable seems fine, check the software and hardware configurations to make sure that the serial port and device are set to the same baud rate, number of data bits, number of stop bits, and parity method. In addition, make sure that the correct driver is loaded and that the device is using the correct handshaking (software or hardware).

If all of these items are correct, then the problem has to be with the serial port or the device. To figure out which, try the serial device on another computer. If it works there, the problem must be the serial port; if it doesn't work, the problem must be the serial device.

17.2 PUBLIC SWITCHED TELEPHONE NETWORK (PSTN)

Public Switched Telephone Network (PSTN) is the international telephone system based on copper wires (UTP cabling) carrying analog voice data. The PSTN, also known as the plain old telephone service (POTS), is the standard telephone service that most homes use. PSTN is a huge network with multiple paths that link source and destination devices. PSTN uses circuit switching when you make a call. Therefore, the data is switched to a dedicated path throughout the conversation.

The original concept of the Bell system was a series of PSTN trunks connecting the major U.S. cities. The PSTN network originally began with human operators sitting at a switchboard manually routing calls. Today, PSTN systems still use analog signals from the end node (phone) to the first switch. The switch then converts the analog signal to a digital signal and routes the call on to its destination. Because the digital signal travels on fiber-optic cabling, the signals are switched at high speeds. Once the call is received on the other end, the last switch in the loop converts the signal back to analog, and the call is initiated. The connection will stay active until the call is terminated (user hangs up). The active circuit enables you to hear the other person almost instantaneously.

The **subscriber loop,** or **local loop,** is the telephone line that runs from your home or office to the telephone company's central office (CO) or neighborhood switching station (often a small building with no windows). Although its cable length can be as long as 20 miles, it is referred to as the **last mile,** not because of its length, but because it is the slow link in the telecommunications infrastructure as it carries analog signals on a twisted-pair cable. The point where the local loop ends at the customer's premises is called the **demarcation point (demarc).** Note: Unless you have an agreement with the phone company, the phone company is responsible only from the central office to the demarc. See figure 17.3.

The standard home phone communicates over the local loop using analog signals. Therefore, when a PC needs to communicate over the local loop, it must use a modem to convert the PC's digital data to analog signals. Unfortunately, the analog lines can reach a maximum speed of only 53 Kbit/s due to FCC regulations that restrict the power output. Unfortunately, the speed is not guaranteed and often is not reached.

17.3 MODEMS

A **modem (modulator-demodulator)** is a device that enables a computer to transmit data over telephone lines. Since computer information is stored and processed digitally and telephone lines transmit data using analog waves, the modem converts digital signals to analog signals (modulates) and analog signals to digital signals (demodulates).

Figure 17.3 Public Switched Telephone Network

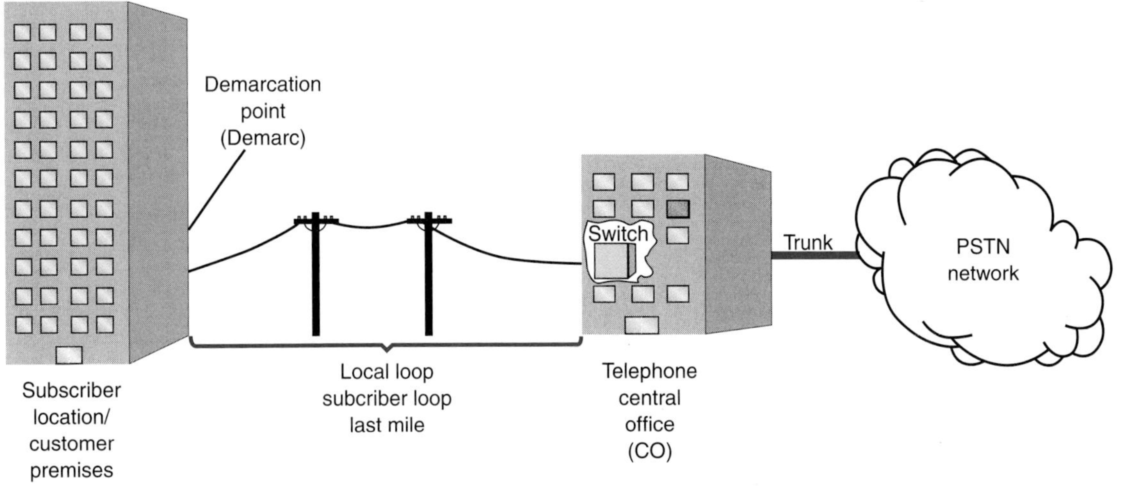

Figure 17.4 A Modem

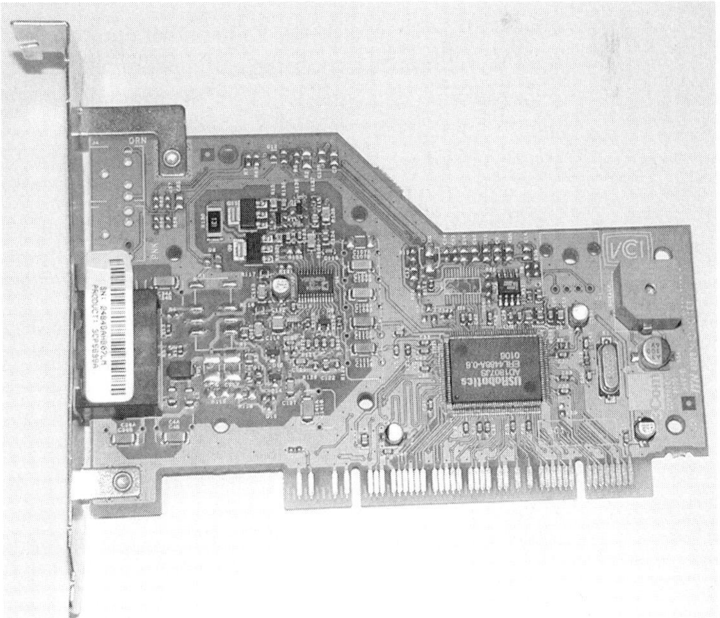

Modems can be either internal or external. See figure 17.4. Today, most modems are internal. The internal modem is an expansion card that is plugged into an expansion slot; the external modem can be attached to the computer using a serial port. In either case, the modem has at least one RJ-11 connector for the twisted-pair cable that connects the modem and the wall telephone jack. Some include a second RJ-11 jack to connect a phone. See figure 17.5.

Figure 17.5 RJ-11 Connector

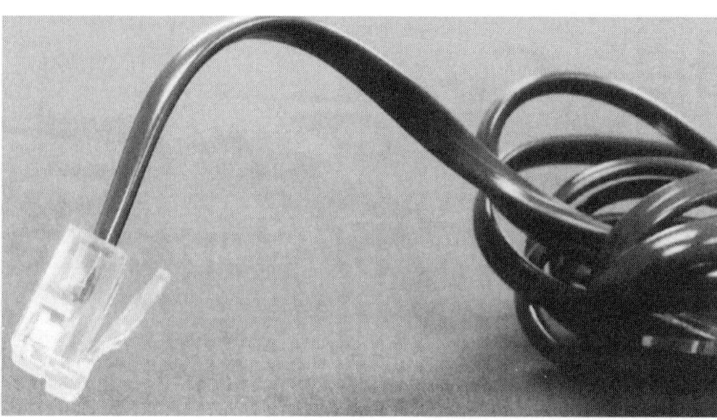

AMR (Audio/Modem Riser) is a specification developed by Intel for packaging the analog I/O audio functions of modem circuitry together with a codec chip (which converts back and forth from analog to digital) on a small board that plugs directly into a computer's motherboard. The small board is called a riser because it rises above the motherboard rather than laying flatly on it.

Since the circuitry is on the riser, it doesn't have to be part of the motherboard. Because getting certification for the manufacture of a new motherboard design is a lengthy process, removing this function from the motherboard provides more flexibility for manufacturers and allows advances in audio modem design to be implemented more easily. Another specification, MDC (Mobile Daughter Card), is the equivalent of AMR but is used in mobile computers.

Since the AMR provides a connection to the motherboard, other circuitry can be connected to the AMR slot. For example, the AMR card can also provide the foundation for higher-quality audio solutions such as 3D positional audio and better MIDI music production.

17.3.1 How a Modem Works

When a computer wishes to call another computer, such as one used by an Internet provider or a bulletin board service (BBS), the calling computer activates the modem and dials the telephone number. The receiving computer will hear the ring and answer the call. As the receiving modem answers the call, it immediately puts out a guard tone, which is a certain frequency used to identify the device on the other end as a modem. This way, different tones can be used to distinguish among faxes, modems, and voice (no tone). Next, the receiving modem sends an unmodulated carrier tone, which is used to inquire about the sending modem's capabilities, such as speed. The two modems also send several signals to measure the quality of the line. When both modems agree on a speed, they then determine the appropriate error control and compression. Finally, the modems turn on the carrier detect signal, which remains on throughout the modem connection. If the carrier signal stops, the connection is broken.

NOTE: The carrier signals use different frequencies so that they can exist at the same time.

Sending data through the modem begins with the receipt of digital data from the computer. The modem then converts the digital signals into analog signals. The UART of the modem then adds the start and stop bits and any error control bits, such as parity. When the data reaches the other modem, the UART strips the start and stop bits, checks for errors, and converts the analog signal to a digital signal, which is then processed by the computer. As the modem is communicating, it is continuously monitoring the status of the line, the quality of the signals, and the number of errors encountered. When the modems register excessive problems, they interrupt the carries and reevaluate the line, thus reducing the speed of transmission. If the reduced speed decreases the number of errors, the line will be reevaluated again to see if the speed can then be increased. Of course, the two communicating computers must be set to the same number of bits used for data, the length of the stop bit, and the type of error control. If they are not, the receiving computer would misinterpret the data, resulting in errors or garbage. Usually, it is the calling computer that will be configured to the settings of the receiving computer.

Example 17.2:

You need to download some technical information that is not available on the Internet but is available on a BBS computer. You are given the phone number to the BBS computer and the following information: 9,600 baud at 7E1. The 9,600 baud is the speed of the modem on the other end, the 7 indicates 7 bits are used for data, and the E indicates that it uses even parity checking (a 0 would indicate odd parity). Lastly, the 1 indicates that the computer uses one stop bit.

17.3.2 Baud Rate Versus Bits per Second

Baud rate refers to the modulation rate, or the number of times per second that a line changes state. This is not always the same as bits per second (bit/s often labeled as bps). When two serial devices are connected with direct cables, then the baud rate and the bit/s are the same. If the computer is running at 19,200-bit/s, then the line is also changing states 19,200 times per second to represent 19,200 logical 1s and 0s. As with the data and stop bits, the sending and receiving devices must agree on the baud rate. The speed of a normal serial port is 115.2 Kbit/s.

But when computers are communicating over telephone lines, the baud and bits per second rates differ. Telephone lines are limited to a maximum of 2,400 baud, but because they use analog and not digital signals, encoding can increase the bits per second by incorporating more bits into each signal change. The 9,600 bit/s rate is based on encoding 4 bits at the same time, the 14,400 rate encodes 6 bits, and the 28.8 rate encodes 12 bits. The bits per second can also be increased by using data compression. Although the speed of modems is usually expressed in bauds, the actual speed depends on how many bits per second they can transmit.

17.3.3 Modulation Schemes

The analog signals used to send data over telephone lines have sinusoidal waveforms. The sinusoidal waveform is characterized by its amplitude and frequency. See figure 17.6. The **amplitude** represents the peak voltage of the sine wave; the **frequency** indicates the number of times that a single wave will repeat over specific period of time and is measured in hertz (Hz), or cycles per second. Another aspect of modulation is its time reference, or phase, which is measured in degrees as 0°, 90°, 180°, and 270° or 0°, 45°, 90°, 135°, 180°, 225°, 270°, 315°, and 360°.

Data is sent over the telephone lines by varying the amplitude, frequency, and phase of the signal. Frequency shift keying (FSK) was the earliest form of **encoding** data over telephone lines and is very similar to the frequency modulation used for FM radio signals. FSK sends a logical 1 at one particular frequency (usually 1,750 Hz) and a logical 0 at another frequency (often 1,080 Hz). FSK was usually used with 300 baud modems. Modulation also involves phase shift keying (PSK), which is the varying of the phase angle to represent data. Because a phase has four different values, it can represent 2 bits of

Figure 17.6 Characteristics of a Sine Wave

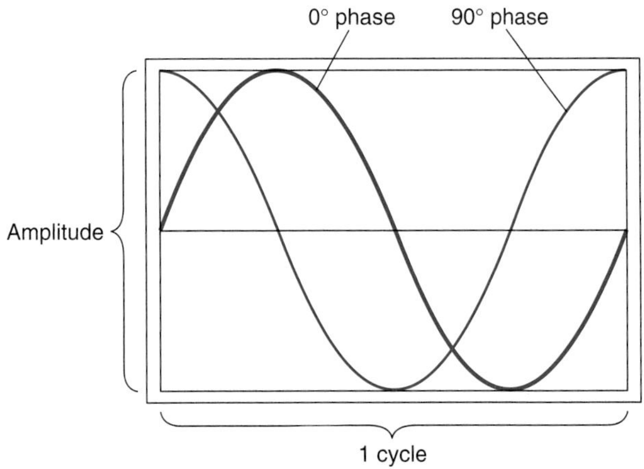

data. Therefore, a 1,200 baud modem using PSK can transmit data at 2,400 bit/s. Quadrature amplitude modulation (QAM) combines phase and amplitude modulation to encode up to 6 bits for every baud (usually 4 bits). Therefore, a 2,400 baud signal can carry up to 9,600 bit/s. Trellis coded quadrature amplitude modulation (TCQAM or TCM) encodes 6 bits for every baud, so, a 2,400 baud signal can carry 14,000 bit/s.

17.3.4 Communication Standards

While the modem interface is standardized, a number of standards and protocols specify how formatted data is to be transmitted over telephones lines. International Telecommunications Union (ITU), formerly known as the Comité Consultatif International Téléphonique et Télégraphique (CCITT), has defined many important standards for data communications. Most modems have built-in support for the more common standards. V.22bis, V.32, and V.32bis were early standards specifying speeds of 2.4, 9.6, and 14.4 Kbit/s, respectively. See table 17.7.

The V.34 standard was introduced toward the end of 1994, supporting 28.8 Kbit/s, and it is now considered the minimum acceptable standard. V.34 modems are able to drop their speed to communicate with slower modems and interrogate the line, adjusting their speed up or down according to the prevailing line conditions. In 1996, the V.34 standard was upgraded to V.34+, which allows for data transfer speeds of up to 33.6 Kbit/s, is backward compatible with all previous standards, and adapts to line conditions to eke out the greatest usable amount of bandwidth.

Error correction is the capability of some modems to identify errors during transmission by embedding some error checking scheme into the data being sent. If the data seems to be corrupt, it is automatically resent. Of course, since the error correction information is sent by one modem and interpreted by another modem, both modems must agree on the same error-correction method.

Table 17.7 Communications Protocols

Protocol	Maximum Transmission Rate (Bits per Second)	Duplex Mode	Comments
Bell 103	300	Full	Used FSK. Bell 103 is the only standard in which the baud rate is equal to the data rate.
CCITT V.21	300	Full	
Bell 212A	1,200	Full	Uses quadrature modulation.
ITU V.22	1,200	Half	
ITU V.22bis	2,400	Full	Uses QAM (4 bits per baud) at 600 baud.
ITU V.29	9,600	Half	Data transmission standard for Group III facsimile (fax) transmission.
ITU V.32	9,600	Full	Uses TCQAM (4 bits per baud) at 2,400 baud.
ITU V.32bis	14,400	Full	Uses TCQAM (6 bits per baud) at 2,400.
ITU V.34	28,800	Full	Most reliable standard for 28,800 bit/s communication.
ITU V.34bis	33,600	Full	Enhanced V.34 standard.
ITU V.42	33,600	Full	An error-detection standard for high-speed modems.
ITU V.42bis	38,400	Full	Uses data compression protocol.
ITU V.90	56,600	Full	The fastest transmissions standard available for analog transmission, it is capable of 56,000 bit/s.
ITU V.92	56,600	Full	Transmits at the same speed as V.90 but offers a reduced handshake time and an on-hold feature.

The most successful proprietary protocols are the **Microcom Networking Protocols (MNP).** The MNP standards go from MNP Class 1 to MNP Class 10. They do not stand alone, but operate in conjunction with other modem standards. MNP 1 is half-duplex. MNP Classes 2 to 4 deal with error control and can transmit data error-free by resending blocks of data that become corrupted in transmission. Today, when the modems are negotiating on operation parameters during initialization, the modems will try to agree on V.42 standard. If one of the modems cannot use the V.42 standard, it will try MNP 4, followed by MNP 3, MNP 2, and MNP 1. If the modems can't use any of the error-control methods, then they will use none. Note: While the error-detection technique is effective, it is still possible to experience data loss or corruption due to buffer overflow, interrupt conflicts, loose connectors, faulty cables, and faulty modems.

MNP Class 5 and the V.42bis standards support data compression. Data compression refers to the modem's ability to compress data as it is being sent. Because the data can be compressed to one-fourth its original size, the effective speed of the modem is quadrupled. A 28,000 modem, for example, can yield a transfer rate up to 115,200 Kbit/s. Some of the newer protocols, such as V.42 and MNP 4, use synchronization bits on the line to act as clock pulses. The data is then sent between the clock pulses, which enhances error control and leads to faster speeds. Of course, the modem on the other end must have a UART chip that can translate from synchronous to asynchronous. The 56K standard allows the fastest data transmission. When possible, 56K modems do not translate information from a digital to an analog form, making maximum use of the digital circuits available in most of the Public Switched Telephone Network (PSTN).

MNP Classes 5 to 10 address various modem operating parameters. Class 5 was already discussed. Class 10 is Microcom's proprietary error-control protocol. It provides a set of "adverse channel enhancements," which help modems cope with bad phone connections by making multiple attempts to make a connection, and adjust both the size of the data packets and the speed of the transfer according to the condition of the line. The most common MNP protocols are numbers 2 to 5, with 10 also often included.

The year 1997 saw the arrival of the 56 Kbit/s modem, despite the absence of any international standard for this speed. The K56Flex group of companies, including 3Com, Ascend, Hayes, Motorola, Lucent, and Rockwell, used Rockwell chipsets to achieve the faster speed, while companies like US Robotics used its own x2 technology. The two systems were not compatible, forcing users and Internet service providers (ISPs) to opt for one or the other. Moreover, there are basic limitations to 56K technology. It uses asymmetric data rates and thus can achieve high speeds only when downloading data from such as an ISP's server.

Most telephone central offices (CO), or exchanges, in this and almost every other country around the world are digital, and so are the connections between COs. All ISPs have digital lines linking them to the telephone network (in Europe, either E1 or ISDN lines). But the lines to most homes and offices are still analog, which limits bandwidth and suffers from line noise (mostly static). They were designed to transfer telephone conversations rather than digital data, so even after compression there is only so much data that can be squeezed onto them.

The 56K speed makes the most of the much faster part of the connection—the digital lines. Data can be sent from the ISP over an entirely digital network until it reaches the final part of the journey from a local CO to the home or office. It then uses pulse code modulation (PCM) to overlay the analog signal and squeeze as much as possible out of the analog line side of the connection. However, there is a catch: 56K technology allows for one conversion from digital to analog, so if, by chance, there is a section in the connection which runs over analog and then returns to digital, it will only be possible to connect at 33.6 Kbit/s (maximum). Note: Analog lines can reach a maximum speed of only 53 Kbit/s because of FCC regulations that restrict the power output.

The reason it's not possible to upload at 56 Kbit/s is simply because the analog lines are not good enough. There are innumerable possible obstacles to prevent a clear signal getting through, such as in-house wiring anomalies, varying wiring distances (between 1 to 6 Km), and splices. It is still theoretically possible to achieve a 33.6 Kbit/s data transfer rate upstream, and work is being carried out to perfect a standard that will increase this by a further 20 to 30 percent. Another problem created by sending a signal from an analog line to a digital line is the quantization noise produced by the analog-to-digital (ADC) conversion.

The digital-to-analog conversion (DAC) can be thought of as representing each 8 bits, as one of 256 voltages—a translation done 8,000 times a second. By sampling this signal at the same rate, the 56 Kbit/s modem can in theory pass 64 Kbit/s (8,000 $\times$ 8) without loss. This simplified description omits other losses which limit the speed to 56 Kbit/s.

There is also some confusion as to the possible need to upgrade the PC serial port to cope with 56 Kbit/s operation. These days this usually uses the 16550 UART chip, itself once an upgrade to cope with faster modems. It is rated at 115 Kbit/s, but 56 Kbit/s modems can overload it because they compress and decompress data on the fly. In normal Internet use, data is mostly compressed before being sent, so compression by the modem is minimal.

On February 4, 1998, the ITU finally brought the year-long standards battle to an end by agreeing to a 56 Kbit/s standard, known as V.90. The V.90 standard uses techniques similar to both and the expectation was that manufacturers would be able to ship the compliant product within weeks rather than months. The new standard was formally ratified in the summer of 1998, following a several month's approval process.

The V.90 standard is neither x2 nor K56Flex, although it does use techniques from both. It is actually two standards in one, the specification defining a digital modem and analog modem pair capable of transmitting data at up to 56 Kbit/s downstream and up to 33.6 Kbit/s upstream. In this case, downstream means from the digital to the analog modem. The former is connected to the PSTN via an ISDN line and will usually be part of a bank of modems connected to a multiple-line ISDN at an ISP. The analog modem plugs into the PSTN at the subscriber's end.

The key to V.90's 56 Kbit/s capability is the PCM coding scheme introduced by the standard's proprietary forerunners. PCM codes are digital representations of audio signals and are the telephone system's native language. The exchange generates these on receipt of analog signals from the subscriber's handset. They're 8 bits long and are transferred at a rate of 8,000 per second—a total throughput of 64 Kbit/s. A V.90 digital modem uses a large subset of these codes to encode data and delivers them to the telephone system via an ISDN link. At the subscriber's end, the codes are converted to an analog signal by the exchange—as if they had been created in the usual way—and these tones are sent to the subscriber's modem.

Most of the work in creating V.90 went into the line-probing and signal-generation schemes. When a V.90 connection is first established, the two modems send each other a list of their capabilities. If V.90 communication is possible, the analog and digital modems send test signals to each other to check the quality of their connection and establish whether there are any digital impairments in the telephone system that might prevent the PCM codes from arriving correctly. For example, on some long distance or international calls, the 64 Kbit/s signal is compressed to 32 Kbit/s (or more) for reasons of economics, which ruins V.90.

If there are no impairments, the analog modem analyzes the signals from the digital modem and informs it how best to encode its data. The two modems also sort out what the round-trip delay is and work out what equalization to apply to the line to get the best possible frequency response.

Coding the information into PCM is a complex business. The telephone system doesn't treat PCM codes linearly. Instead, it allocates more PCM codes to lower signal levels and fewer codes to higher levels. This corresponds with the way the human ear responds to sound, but it also means that the receiving modem might not be able to distinguish between some of the adjacent codes accurately. Also, the signal synthesized by the digital modem must be able to be accurately converted to analog and sent through the analog parts of the telephone exchange.

Error connection and detection systems also limit the sequential permutations possible. In short, there are sequences of codes that can't be sent and others that must be sent, but these depend on the data being transmitted. A final complication is that the American and European telephone systems use different sets of PCM codes.

The V.90 standard was formally ratified on September, 15 1998, following a several months' approval process. Beyond V.90, an ITU study group is looking into the next generation of PCM modems, with the intention of achieving a 40 to 45 Kbit/s transmission speed from the analog modem.

Announced in 2000, the ITU's V.92 analog modem standard has the same download speed as the V.90 standard (56 Kbit/s) but increases the maximum upload speed from 33.6 to 48 Kbit/s. As well as this performance improvement, the new standard also introduces a couple of user convenience features:

- QuickConnect shortens the time it takes to make a connection by reducing up to 30 seconds modem handshake procedure by up to 50 percent. The reduction is accomplished by having the modem "remember" the phone line characteristics, which are then stored for future use.
- Modem-on-Hold allows users—provided they subscribe to their phone company's Call-Waiting service—to be connected to the Internet via a given phone line while concurrently using it to receive or initiate a voice call.

Table 17.8 Data Transfer Protocols

Protocol	Description
XMODEM	A widely used file transfer protocol that uses 128 byte packets and a simple "checksum" method of error detection.
XMODEM-CRC	An XMODEM version that uses cyclic redundancy check (CRC) for error detection.
XMODEM-1K	XMODEM CRC with 1,024 byte packets.
YMODEM	Similar to XMODEM-1K but has a batch mode that allows multiple files to be transferred with a single command. It is sometimes called YMODEM Batch.
YMODEM-G	Designed for modems that already have error correction. It is similar to YMODEM except it does not provide software error correction. It is a streaming protocol that sends and receives a 1 KB continuous stream until instructed to stop. If any block is unsuccessful, the entire transfer is canceled.
ZMODEM	Like YMODEM-G, ZMODEM can restart a transfer from where it left off.
Kermit	Uses blocks (or packets) and checksum error detection but adjusts its packet size to accommodate the fixed packet sizes used by some computer systems and the condition of the lines. Like ZMODEM, it can recover from major line errors by resynchronizing the transmissions of modems after interruption.

17.3.5 Data Transfer Protocols

Transferring files from one computer to another through a modem requires the use of a protocol, which establishes rules for uploading and downloading files. Several years ago, the most common transfer protocols were XMODEM, YMODEM, ZMODEM, and Kermit. See table 17.8. Note that these protocols are not needed when connecting to the Internet, which is the main reason most people buy a modem. To connect to the Internet using a modem, arrangements must be made with an **Internet service provider (ISP)**, which provides either a **Serial Line Internet Protocol (SLIP)** or **Point-to-Point Protocol (PPP)** software package to make the connection. The **TCP/IP protocol**—in reality, a complete set of protocols—is used for communicating with the Internet. The **Terminal Emulation (Telnet)** protocol allows using another computer as a terminal, the **File Transfer Protocol (FTP)** allows the transfer of files, and the **Simple Mail Transfer Protocol (SMTP)** allows the sending of electronic mail messages.

17.3.6 Command Set

When the computer sends data using the modem, it sends a command to control the modem. The instructions the modem understands are referred to as the **Hayes command set** or the **AT commands.** Today, virtually all modems are Hayes compatible and follow the same set of basic commands. Most of the time, the user does not have to know these commands because most communications software packages know them. Some programs, however, require the user to enter these commands.

The AT commands that must sometimes be entered by the user can be divided into the basic command set, an extended command set, and register commands. See table 17.9. The basic commands begin with a capital character followed by a digit. The extended commands begin with an ampersand (&) and a capital letter followed by a digit. The register commands access small memory locations (registers) located within the modem. The order in which the commands are issued is important, and every command must begin with *AT.* In addition, there are no spaces between any of the commands or the numbers specified.

Example 17.3:

To make sure that the cables are connected properly and that the baud rate is set correctly, you would type in the AT command and press the Enter key. If everything is fine, an OK will be given.

To dial a number using a touch-tone telephone, you would type in the ATDT2633077 command and press the Enter key.

To dial a number using a pulse telephone, you would type in the ATDP2633077 command and press the Enter key.

Table 17.9 Common AT Command Parameters

Parameter	Description
AT	The AT command tells the modem that it is going to receive a command. *AT* must be typed before any other command. AT as a command all by itself will elicit OK as a response from the modem. This indicates that the cables are connected correctly and the baud rate is set properly.
D	D tells the modem to dial the numbers following the *D*.
H	Hangs up the telephone.
P	P is a subcommand of the D command that tells the modem to dial in pulse mode. It is used if the phone line is not touch-tone.
Z	Resets the modem to default state.
~	Makes the software pause for half a second. More than one ~ can be used.
ˆM	Sends the terminating carriage return character to the modem.
AT$	Command quick reference.
&$	Help for ampersand commands.
D$	Help for dial commands.
S$	Help for S registers.

To hang up the phone, you would type in the ATH command and press the Enter key.

To show all of the ampersand commands, you would type in the AT&$ command and press the Enter key.

To perform a hardware reset for the modem, you would type in the ATZ command and press the Enter key.

17.3.7 Fax/Modems

Fax is short for *facsimile transmission.* A fax machine scans a message written on a piece of paper, digitizes the text and pictures, and sends the data over a telephone line. A fax machine on the other end reassembles the text and images and prints them out on paper. Many computers today have a fax/modem, which can send a word-processed document (such as from Microsoft Word) directly to another computer. If the other machine has a fax/modem, the document can be displayed on the screen or printed to paper.

17.3.8 Installing a Modem

The first step in installing a modem is to configure the resources. If it is an internal modem, you would usually choose a free IRQ, COM port, and I/O address. If it is an external modem, you must then configure the serial port. Even though the serial port is already assigned an IRQ, COM port, and I/O address, its speed usually has to be configured.

Question:

A computer running Windows 98 has two serial ports (COM1 and COM2). COM1 is being used by the mouse and COM2 is not being used at all. A proprietary communications software package needed for your business will use only COM1 and COM2. Therefore, you purchase an internal modem. How should you configure the modem?

Answer:

If you configure the modem to use COM3, the communications software package will not recognize the modem. If you configure the modem as COM1 or COM2, you have a resource conflict.

Since you need the mouse (COM1) for Windows 98, you should configure the modem as COM2 and IRQ 3. Of course, for this to work, you will need to disable COM2 using either jumpers, DIP switches, configuration software, or the CMOS setup program.

The next step is to physically install and connect the modem. The modem is connected to the telephone wall jack with a twisted-pair cable with RJ-11 connectors. You must then load the modem software drivers and install and configure the communications software. If you are using DOS, the driver is loaded when the modem is selected in the communications software. (Note: When selecting the modem, you will have to specify its COM port and IRQ.) If you have Windows, the driver is loaded by using the Add New Hardware icon or applet from the Control Panel.

NOTE: Not having an updated driver can cause unreliable connections and/or slow speeds.

The communications software package usually allows you to choose the baud rate (up to the speed of the modem), the number of data bits, the number of stop bits, and the parity method. In addition, many of these packages allow you to establish different parameters for different telephone numbers. When you call a particular telephone number, the software will automatically use the same parameters that were used for that number before. In Windows, this is accessed from the Modem (or Phone and Modem) applet in the control panel.

When the driver is loaded, it will specify an **initialization string** for the chosen modem. The initialization string is the list of AT commands that the communications software will use to initialize and prepare the modem for connection. The string typically sets the speed, error correction, compression, various timeout values, and how the results will be displayed on the screen. Of course, if the modem is not listed in the software, you will have to choose a generic modem and specify the initialization string manually. The following are a few examples:

Generic 28.8 modem	AT&F&C1&D1&K3
Hayes Accura 144	AT&F
Hayes Optima 14400 V.32bis	AT&F&D0
Hayes V-Series/Ultra	AT&Q5S36=7&C1&D0&K3
US Robotics Courier HST Dual	AT&F&C1&D0
US Robotics Courier V.32bis/as	AT&F&D0&H1&K2
US Robotics Sportster 14.4	AT&F&H1&C1&D0
US Robotics Sportster 9600	AT&F&H1

Extra commands can be added to the setup string so that these commands are executed every time the modem is started. For example, an AT command can be added to the dial-up string that will deactivate call waiting (such as *70). Changing the command for a number dialed with the AT command ATDT9224225 to ATDT*70,92244225 will deactivate call waiting. Today, the initialization string is rarely used.

17.3.9 Troubleshooting a Modem

Modem problems can be caused by bad or unconnected cable, bad or incorrect drivers, incorrectly configured software, a resource conflict, an incorrect setup string, a faulty serial port, or a faulty modem.

Cables to check are the serial port cable that goes from the D connector to the motherboard or I/O card and the twisted-pair cable that goes from the phone jack to the modem. In addition, if it is an external modem, the power cable and the cable that connects the serial port to the modem must be checked.

Make sure that the modem is not experiencing a resource conflict (I/O address or COM designation and IRQ). The modem resources are usually set with jumpers or DIP switches or the modem is plug-and-play. If it is an external modem, make sure that the serial port is not experiencing a conflict and that the serial port is not disabled.

If there are no resource conflicts, make sure that correct modem has been selected in the operating system or communications software package and that the software is pointed to the correct resources. In DOS, the modem is selected in the communications software. In Windows the driver can be loaded using the Add New Hardware icon or applet located in the Control Panel. Lastly, make sure that the modem and software are set to use the correct baud rate, number of data bits, number of stop bits, and parity method. If not, the data will end up garbled.

If you are dealing with an external modem connected to a serial port, the serial port can be tested with a loopback plug. If it is an internal modem, it can be tested with a software diagnostic package. If the serial port is bad, it will have to be replaced: If the serial port is on the expansion card, replace the expansion card; if the serial port is on the motherboard, replace the motherboard (sometimes a costly repair) or disable the serial port on the motherboard and install an expansion card that has a serial port. If the modem is bad, replace the modem.

Example 17.4:

There is no response from the modem.

When the modem does not respond, first make sure that it is connected properly. If it is an external modem, make sure that the modem has power and it is turned on. Next, make sure the operating system or communications software has the right driver installed and that the correct parameters (baud, data bits, stop bits, and parity) are set properly. In addition, if a setup string had to be entered, make sure that it is the correct one for the modem being used. If the modem is still not working, check it for resource conflicts. If the problem still exists, swap the modem with a known good modem. If the second modem works, then the problem is with the first modem. If the second modem doesn't work, the serial port or the motherboard is probably causing the problem.

Example 17.5:

The modem does not detect a dial tone.

If the modem does not detect a dial tone, make sure that the telephone cable is connected. Next, make sure that the telephone line is active. This can be done with a telephone line tester or by plugging a telephone into the jack and making sure that there is a dial tone. (Note: Most businesses have a switching telephone system. If this is the case, you may need to add a dial-out prefix to the telephone number.) Check for resource conflicts, operating parameters (baud, data bits, stop bits, and parity method), drivers, and setup strings. Lastly, swap the modem with a known good modem. If the second modem works, then the problem is with the first modem. If the second modem doesn't work, the serial port or the motherboard is probably causing the problem.

Example 17.6:

The modem outputs garbage.

Before opening the computer, make sure the cables are connected properly and are in good condition. Next, make sure that no devices are around that may generate large amounts of electromagnetic interference. If there are, either reroute the cable (or the device generating the electromagnetic interference) or try a well-shielded cable.

If the cable seems fine, check the software and hardware configurations to make sure that the serial port and device are set to the same baud rate, number of data bits, number of stop bits, and parity method. In addition, make sure that the correct driver is loaded and that the correct handshaking (hardware or software) has been used.

If all of these items are correct, then the problem has to be with the serial port, the modem, or the modem on the other end. To determine which you can try swapping out the modem and serial port. In addition, you can try calling another number or use another computer to call the same number.

Example 17.7:

The modem keeps hanging up.

Hanging up is caused by a bad telephone connection, a bad cable, interruption by call waiting, someone picking up the telephone at another extension, a bad modem, or a bad serial port. To determine whether it is a bad telephone connection, try another phone number; also try the same phone number from a different site. If the telephone connection is bad, the telephone company will probably have to be called in to repair it. To check the cable, replace it to see if the problem goes away. If the problem is call waiting, that can usually be disabled. Contact the telephone company (or look in the telephone book) to find out how to do this. To check the modem, swap it with a known good modem or try the modem in another system. Lastly, the serial port could be bad.

Example 17.8:

The modem is not running at its full speed.

Rarely, will the modem run at full speed. As explained in section 17.3.4, because of noise on the analog lines, the best speed that you can attain is 33.6 Kbit/s, even if the sending and receiving modems are both 56K modems. Of course, you would like to run at the fastest speed possible. First, the sending and receiving modems need to run at the fastest speed possible. If a 56K modem dials into a 19.2K modem, the fastest connection will only be 19.2 Kbit/s. If both modems do run at faster speeds that you cannot obtain, you need to check for the most up-to-date modem drivers. You should also try to replace the modem and phone cables and look for sources of EMI, such as lights and electrical motors. Also make sure that the phone cables are not too long. Lastly, have the phone lines checked (source and destination lines). Of course, you will often not have control of the destination lines.

Failure in a point-to-point communications link can be very expensive and can be attributed to a fault in the local DTE, the local modem, the telephone network, the remote modem, or the remote DTE. Similar to the serial loop back test, the modem's diagnostic and test facilities are provided to enable you to efficiently locate the faults through looping procedures. See figure 17.7. Loops 2 and 3 directly relate to the modem's operation.

To perform these tests, you will use the AT commands, specifically the &T commands, which are available only when the modem is set for non-error corrected operation, that is, the \N0 command has been issued. The remote and local digital loopback tests are available only after a successful connection has been established. In this instance, the test command is issued after returning to command mode by using the escape sequence.

All the tests are initiated using the following &T commands:

&T0 Terminating a test
&T1 Local analog loopback (loop 3)
&T3 Local digital loopback
&T4 Grant request digital loopback request from remote modem
&T5 Deny request digital loopback request from remote modem

Figure 17.7 Using Loopback Tests to Test Modems

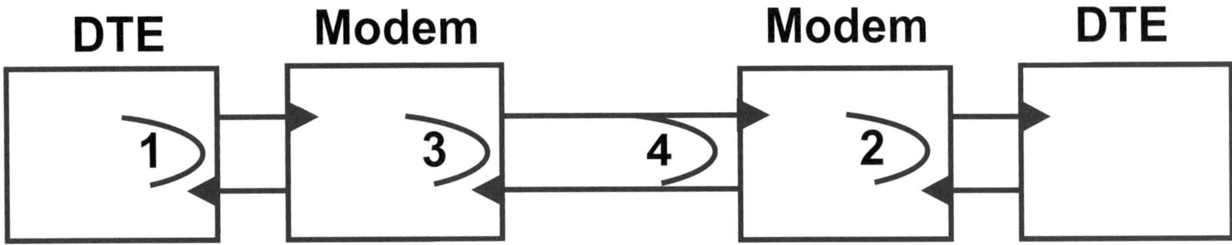

&T6 Remote digital loopback (loop 2)
&T7 Remote digital loopback (loop 2) with self-test
&T8 Local analog loopback (loop 3) with self-test

Start performing a local analog loopback test with both the local and remote modem and their respective DTEs. If they pass this test, perform a remote digital loopback with or without self-test to verify the complete communications link from one modem to the other. The success of the local analog loopback test and the failure of the remote digital loopback test may indicate a fault in the telephone network, especially if many attempts for a satisfactory connection failed.

17.4 DIGITAL MODEMS

Recall that when you make a phone call, voices or data are sent as an analog signal and converted into a digital signal when they reach the first switch at the telephone company. The only reason that the "last mile" still exists is because of the huge cost of rewiring every house and business. Unfortunately, this is the bottleneck when using an analog modem. If you want to connect to the Internet, you have to somehow bypass the last mile.

17.4.1 Integrated Services Digital Network (ISDN) Modems

Integrated services digital network (ISDN) lines allow voice, video, and data to be sent over digital telephone lines with an ISDN modem. Of course, an ISDN modem isn't really a modem because it does not modulate (convert digital signals to analog signals) or demodulate (convert analog signals to digital signals). Nevertheless, it acts very much like a modem. It responds to the AT commands, generates the same set of responses as a modem, and uses the same control signals (DTR, TRS, and CTS).

Basic ISDN (BRI) divides the telephone line into three digital channels: two B channels and one D channel. The B channels can transmit up to 64 Kbit/s of uncompressed data. The D channel, which can transmit 16 Kbit/s, does the administrative work, such as connecting and disconnecting the call and communicating with the telephone network, and it can also be used to carry data. Because there are three channels, the ISDN line can have three connections, such as a voice conversation, Internet access, and a credit card authorization line. In addition, the two B channels can be used together to deliver performance of up to 128 Kbit/s. This high bandwidth makes ISDN lines ideal for audio and video applications and any application that needs to move large amounts of data from one location to another.

The ISDN line can be set up by the phone company and can be installed and hooked up to the normal home or office phone cable. It uses the same four-wire (two pairs) twisted-pair cable. If analog signals (such as voice, group 3 fax, and standard modem data) are also to be carried over ISDN lines, an ISDN terminator adapter (TA) must be used. In addition, if the ISDN line is to be used to communicate with an analog device, such as a standard modem or fax machine, special software or firmware, which emulates the analog-modulated waveforms of modems and fax machines, must be installed.

17.4.2 Digital Subscriber Line (DSL)

The digital subscriber line (DSL) is a special communication line that uses sophisticated modulation technology to maximize the amount of data that can be sent over plain twisted-pair copper wiring that is already carrying phone service to subscribers homes. It was originally intended to transmit video signals to compete against the cable companies, but it soon found use as a high-speed data connection with the explosion of the Internet. DSL is sometimes expressed as xDSL, because there are various kinds of digital subscriber line technologies, including ADSL, R-DSL, HDSL, SDSL, and VDSL.

The best thing about DSL technologies is their ability to transport large amounts of information across existing copper telephone lines. This is possible because DSL modems leverage signal-processing techniques that insert and extract more digital data onto analog lines. The key is modulation, a process in which one signal modifies the property of another.

As its name implies, asymmetrical DSL (ADSL) transmits an asymmetric data stream, with much more going downstream to the subscriber and much less coming back. The reason for this has less to do with transmission technology than with the cable plant itself. Twisted-pair telephone wires are bundled together in large cables. Fifty pairs to a cable is a typical configuration toward the subscriber, but cables coming out of a central office (CO) may have hundreds or even thousands of pairs bundled together. An individual line from a CO to a subscriber is spliced together from many cable sections as they fan out from the central office (Bellcore claims that the average U.S. subscriber line has 22 splices). Alexander Bell invented twisted-pair wiring to minimize crosstalk. Because a small amount of crosstalk does occur, the amount of crosstalk increases as the frequencies and the length of line increase. Therefore, if symmetric signals occur in many pairs within the same cable, the crosstalk significantly limits the data rate and the length of the line.

Because most people download information as they view web pages and download files, the amount of information downloaded is far greater than the amount of information that a user uploads, or transfers to the other computers. This asymmetry, combined with "always-on" access (which eliminates call setup), makes ADSL ideal for Internet/intranet surfing, video on demand, and remote LAN access.

ADSL modems usually include a POTS (plain old telephone service) splitter, which enables simultaneous access to voice telephony and high-speed data. Some vendors provide active POTS splitters, which enable simultaneous telephone and data access. However, if the power fails or the modem fails with an active POTS splitter, then the telephone fails. A passive POTS splitter, on the other hand, maintains lifeline telephone access even if the modem fails (due to a power outage, for example), because the telephone is not powered by external electricity. Telephone access in the case of a passive POTS splitter is a regular analog voice channel, the same as customers currently receive to their homes.

Downstream, ADSL supports speeds between 1.5 and 8 Mbit/s, whereas upstream, the rate is between 640 Kbit/s and 1.544 Mbit/s. ADSL can provide 1.544 Mbit/s transmission rates at distances of up to 18,000 ft over one wire pair. Optimal speeds of 6 to 8 Mbit/s can be achieved at distances of 10,000 to 12,000 ft using standard 24-gauge wire.

Currently, the ADSL Lite specification, also known as Lite, is a low-cost, easy-to-install version of ADSL specifically designed for the consumer marketplace. ADSL Lite is a lower-speed version of ADSL that will eliminate the need for the telephone company to install and maintain a premises-based POTS splitter. ADSL Lite is also supposed to work over longer distances than full-rate ADSL, making it more widely available to mass-market consumers. It will support both data and voice and provide an evolution path to full-rate ADSL.

17.4.3 Cable Modems

Cable systems were originally designed to deliver broadcast television signals efficiently to subscribers' homes. To ensure that consumers could obtain cable service with the same TV sets they use to receive over-the-air broadcast TV signals, cable operators recreate a portion of the over-the-air radio frequency (RF) spectrum within a sealed coaxial cable line.

Traditional coaxial cable systems typically operate with 330 or 450 MHz of capacity, whereas modern hybrid fiber/coax (HFC) systems are expanded to 750 MHz or more. Logically, downstream video programming signals begin around 50 MHz, the equivalent of channel 2 for over-the-air television signals. Each standard television channel occupies 6 MHz of the RF spectrum. Thus a traditional cable system with 400 MHz of downstream bandwidth can carry the equivalent of 60 analog TV channels and a modern HFC system with 700 MHz of downstream bandwidth has the capacity for about 110 channels.

Although regular cable is analog, digital cable uses digital signals. Digital signals can be compressed much more than analog signals. Digital cable can give 200 to 300 channels of the same bandwidth as analog cable.

To deliver data services over a cable network, one television channel in the 50 to 750 MHz range is typically allocated for downstream traffic to homes and another channel in the 5 to 42 MHz band is used to carry upstream signals. A cable modem termination system (CMTS) communicates through these channels with cable modems located in subscriber homes to create a virtual local area network (LAN) connection. Most cable modems are external devices that connect to a personal computer (PC) through a standard 10Base T Ethernet card and twisted-pair wiring, external universal serial bus (USB) modems, and internal PCI modem cards.

A single downstream 6 MHz television channel may support up to 27 Mbit/s of downstream data throughput from the cable using 64 QAM (quadrature amplitude modulation) transmission technology. Speeds can be boosted to 36 Mbit/s using 256 QAM. Upstream channels may deliver 500 Kbit/s to 10 Mbit/s from homes using 16 QAM or QPSK (quadrature phase-shift key) modulation techniques, depending on the amount of spectrum allocated for service. This upstream and downstream bandwidth is shared by the active data subscribers connected to a given cable network segment, typically 500 to 2,000 homes on a modern HFC network.

An individual cable modem subscriber may experience access speeds from 500 Kbit/s to 1.5 Mbit/s or more, depending on the network architecture and traffic load, blazing performance compared to dial-up alternatives. However, when surfing the Web, performance can be affected by Internet backbone congestion. In addition to speed, cable modems offer another key benefit: constant connectivity. Because cable modems use connectionless technology, much as in an office LAN, a subscriber's PC is always online with the network. That means there's no need to dial-in to begin a session, so users do not have to worry about receiving busy signals. Additionally, going online does not tie up the telephone line.

17.4.4 Installing a Digital Modem

These modems are not installed much differently than a normal modem. If you have an ISDN, DSL, or cable modem on an expansion card, you insert them into the slot. Most of these will be plug-and-play, so there are no resources that you should have to assign. You then go into Windows and load the appropriate drivers for the card. The second kind will have a box that connects to a USB port or a network card. For the USB port, you would also have to load the appropriate drivers. For the box that connects to the network card, you would load the drivers for the network card. You then configure the Internet Protocol (IP), where you assign the IP address, subnet mask, default gateway, and the DNS server to the ISDN modem, the USB box, or the network card.

SUMMARY

1. The first step in installing a modem is to configure the resources. If it is an internal modem, you would usually choose a free IRQ, COM port, and I/O address.
2. The next step is to physically install and connect the modem.
3. The communications software package usually allows you to choose the baud rate (up to the speed of the modem), the number of data bits, the number of stop bits, and the parity method.
4. PCMCIA/mini-PCI adapters are plug-and-play devices.
5. The installation of a serial port requires choosing an available IRQ, a free COM designation, and an I/O address.
6. The default resources for the first serial device (COM1) are I/O address 03F8H and IRQ 4.
7. The default resources for the second serial device (COM2) are I/O address 02F8H and IRQ 3.
8. If the serial port is not part of the motherboard, it will most likely be configured using DIP switches or jumpers.
9. To configure a modem's resources, the modems will use jumpers, DIP switches, configuration software, or be plug-and-play.
10. The serial port interface (9- or 25-pin two-row D connector) is a general-purpose interface that can be used for almost any type of device (mice, external modems, serial printers, plotters, label makers, bar code readers, device control circuits, and other computers).
11. Information is sent through a serial port as a data frame. The data frame consists of a start bit, number of data bits, one to two stop bits, and possibly some parity bits.
12. The baud rate is the modulation rate, or the number of times per second that a signal changes start, which is not necessarily the number of bits being sent per second.
13. The central part of the serial port is the universal asynchronous receiver/transmitter (UART), which acts as translator between the serial and system bus.
14. The RS-232C standard imposed a cable length limit of 50 ft.
15. A normal serial cable, known as a straight-through cable, is made to connect one computer (DTE) and one serial device (DCE), such as a modem.
16. The null modem cable, also known as a crossover cable, is a special cable that crosses the receive and transmit wires. It allows two DTEs (such as computers) to communicate with each other.
17. A modem (modulator-demodulator) is a device that enables a computer to transmit data over telephone lines.
18. Modems encode bits by varying the signal amplitude, frequency, and phase of data sent over telephone lines.
19. The instructions the modem understands are referred to as the Hayes command set or the modem AT commands. Any modem that understands the Hayes modem commands is said to be Hayes compatible.
20. The modem is connected to the telephone wall jack with a twisted-pair cable with RJ-11 connectors.
21. Internal ISDN modems, cable modems, and DSL modems are installed much like a normal modem. You configure the expansion card's resources and connect the card.

22. Some ISDN modems, cable modems, and DSL modems are connected through a USB connection.
23. Other ISDN modems, cable modems, and DSL modems are connected to a network card, which is assigned resources such as an I/O address and IRQ.
24. A serial port problem can be caused by a disconnected cable, bad cable, resource conflict, invalid software configuration, bad or incorrect drivers, or the serial port itself.
25. A serial port can be tested by using a serial port loopback plug.
26. Modem problems can be caused by bad or unconnected cables, bad or incorrect drivers, incorrectly configuration software, resource conflicts, an incorrect setup string, a faulty serial port, or a faulty modem.
27. Internal modems can be tested with a software diagnostic package.
28. If your modem is hanging up, it can be caused by a bad telephone connection, a bad cable, interruption by call waiting, someone picking up the telephone at another extension, a bad modem, or a bad serial port.
29. Serial ports are bidirectional asynchronous devices that send data over a single wire, each bit lined up single-file in series.
30. The serial port is a full-duplex device that uses separate lines for sending and receiving data and a line for a signal ground.
31. AMR (Audio/Modem Riser) is a specification for packaging the analog I/O audio functions of modem circuitry together with a codec chip on a small board that plugs directly into a computer's motherboard.
32. Today, most serial ports' resources are configured using the CMOS setup program. The port can also be disabled with the CMOS setup program.
33. If there are no resource conflicts, make sure that the correct modem has been selected in the operating system or communications software package and that the software is pointed to the correct resources.
34. A modem will rarely run at full speed.
35. Usually caused by noise on the analog lines, the best speed that you can attain is 33.6 Kbit/s, even if the sending and receiving modems are both 56K modems.

QUESTIONS

1. Which of the following has a 2-row, 9-pin male D connector?
   a. serial port b. parallel port
   c. game port d. VGA port
   e. EGA port
2. Which of the following devices are usually found connected to a serial port (choose two)?
   a. joystick b. modem
   c. printer d. mouse
3. How many bits of data can a serial port receive or transmit at a time?
   a. 1 b. 8
   c. 16 d. 32
4. What port takes 8 bits as they come off the eight wires of the data bus and turns them on end so that they are on one wire in single file?
   a. serial
   b. parallel
   c. LPT1, LPT2, and LPT3
   d. SCSI
   e. IDE
5. In serial asynchronous transmissions, what bit is used to signal the beginning of a new data frame?
   a. start b. stop
   c. parity d. data
6. Which IRQ is usually assigned to COM1?
   a. IRQ 3 b. IRQ 4
   c. IRQ 5 d. IRQ 7
7. When installing an internal modem set to COM2, what should the interrupt be set to?
   a. IRQ 3 b. IRQ 4
   c. IRQ 5 d. IRQ 7
8. How many serial ports are supported by the PC?
   a. 2 b. 4
   c. 8 d. 32
9. Which of the following is the term for the number of signal changes per second?
   a. baud b. bits per second
   c. raw transfer speed d. bit speed
10. The central part of the serial port is the
    a. microprocessor. b. ADC.
    c. DAC. d. UART.
11. Which hardware component controls serial port communications?
    a. ROM BIOS b. CPU
    c. DMA 8223 d. UART 16550
12. What should the length limit (in feet) be for a serial cable?
    a. 6 b. 10
    c. 12 d. 50
    e. 100
13. A cable has a female DB-25 connector on each end. Pin 2 is crossed with pin 3, and pin 4 is crossed with pin 5. What is the most likely explanation?
    a. The cable was incorrectly made.
    b. It is a proprietary cable.
    c. It is a null modem cable.
    d. The cable is a printer cable used to connect a parallel port to a switch box.
14. When is a null modem cable used?
    a. to exchange data between two DCE devices
    b. to exchange data between two DTE devices

c. to send data from a DTE device to a DCE device
d. to send data from a DCE device to a DTE device

15. A loopback plug tests which of the following?
a. IDE hard drive cable
b. serial port
c. modem
d. game port

16. Which of the following devices converts digital signals from the computer to analog signals to be used on the phone lines and converts analog signals back to digital signals?
a. parallel port
b. serial port
c. modem
d. ADC/DAC converter

17. A full-duplex device allows which of the following?
a. transmitting and receiving data simultaneously
b. transmitting or receiving data only at a specific time
c. transmitting only
d. receiving only

18. If you are transmitting the 8-bit binary number 11011000 and are using even parity, what would the parity bit be?
a. 0 b. 1

19. Which of the following can be used to connect two computers together?
a. null modem cable b. modem
c. VGA cable d. SCSI connector

20. Which of the following signals must be present for a modem to receive data?
a. high speed (HS)
b. carrier detect (CD)
c. transmit data (TD)
d. receive data (RD)

21. In modem technology, *CD* stands for
a. change directory. b. call data.
c. change dial. d. carrier detect.
e. comm detect. f. cease deliver.

22. What is the term used to refer to the process of two modems establishing communications with each other?
a. interacting b. connecting
c. handshaking d. linking
e. pinging

23. Which of the following asynchronous lines does the terminal activate when it wants to send data to a modem?
a. CTS b. DSR
c. RTS d. DTR

24. Modems use what kind of transmission?
a. synchronous b. asynchronous
c. linking d. pinging

25. Which of the following is *not* a method of encoding data?
a. PSK b. FSK
c. QAM d. WRE

26. A modem that follows the AT command set is known as a(n)
a. AT follower.
b. Hayes-compatible modem.
c. modem that can only work on a 286.
d. modem that can only work on a 286 and higher.

27. Which AT command defines a hardware reset for a modem?
a. ATF b. ATZ
c. ATE0 d. AT1

28. Which AT command is used for hang-up or disconnect?
a. ATF b. ATZ
c. ATH d. ATD
e. AT

29. If a cable has two pairs of twisted wires inside a single jacket connected to a phone, what is it called?
a. unshielded twisted pair (UTP)
b. coaxial
c. power cable
d. fiber-optic cable

30. Which of the following parameters does not have to be specified when installing and configuring a modem?
a. number of data bits
b. number of stop bits
c. baud rate
d. type of parity
e. number of start bits

31. If a customer reports that he is unable to make a connection with his modem, which of the following should you check (choose all that apply)?
a. the jumpers or DIP switches on the modem
b. the telephone cable
c. the hard drive
d. the configuration of the communications software
e. the keyboard

32. What is the small plastic connector called that is on the end of an unshielded twisted-pair wire such as the ones used on a telephone?
a. RJ-5 b. RJ-11
c. RJ-45 d. RJ-62

33. A new external modem does not work properly. Which of the following should be checked (choose all that apply)?
a. the modem cable and connector
b. the serial port settings
c. the communications parameters, such as speed, parity, data bits, and stop bits
d. the modem selected with the communications software

34. A modem cannot connect to another computer. The other computer indicates "no carrier detected." The problem is most likely
  a. the modem in the original computer.
  b. the phone lines computer.
  c. the original computer.
  d. the modem on the second.
  e. the second computer.
35. If a high-speed internal modem is consistently not working at its full advertised speed, you may want to check (choose all that apply)
  a. the other modem's maximum throughput speed.
  b. the maximum bus speed in the CMOS setup program.
  c. the version of the UART chip used by the serial port or modem.
  d. the version of the UART chip used by the parallel port.
36. A customer complains that a modem is bad. It connects to another computer, but it transmits and receives garbage. What do you do (choose two answers)?
  a. Check the version of the software that it is using.
  b. Check the version of the operating system that it is using.
  c. Check the settings for the data bits, parity, and stop bits in both modems.
  d. Check the driver.
37. You are having trouble establishing a connection to the Internet. You suspect the external 56 Kbit/s modem connected to your Windows 98 workstation is failing. What is the best way to determine whether the modem's transmission and receiving hardware is working properly?
  a. Test the modem by performing a loopback test.
  b. Use Tracert to determine where the connection is failing.
  c. Use a multimeter to determine whether any signals are being transmitted or received.
  d. Test the modem using the Windows 98 diagnostics in the Modems applet of the Control Panel.

HANDS-ON EXERCISES

Exercise 1: Installing a Modem

1. Configure and install the modem. For an internal modem,
   a. If your system has a COM2, disable it.
   b. Configure your modem as a COM2 using IRQ 3 and I/O address 2F8H.
   b. Connect the twisted-pair phone cable from the phone jack to the modem.

   For an external modem,

   a. Make sure that COM2 is active.
   b. Connect the twisted-pair phone cable from the phone jack to the modem.
2. If you have an external modem, tell the operating system/environment the operating parameters of the serial port. Use the Device Manager (System icon or applet in the Control Panel) to configure the operating parameters (baud rate, data bits, parity, stop, and flow control) of COM2.
3. If you have Windows 95 or 98, load the drivers for the modem. (This can be done with Add New Hardware applet from the Control Panel.)
4. Install the communications software package provided by an ISP to connect to the Internet.
5. Connect to the Internet.
6. Start Internet Explorer.
7. Find the web page for your school or business.
8. Disconnect from the Internet and close all programs.
9. Shut off the computer and remove the modem.

CHAPTER 18

Parallel Ports and Printers

Topics Covered in This Chapter

Introduction

The parallel port can be used to connect printers (common output devices that print text or pictures on paper) and other external devices, including external hard drives, tape drives, removable disk drives, scanners, and network cards. In addition, the parrallel port can be used with device control circuits and to transfer data between two computers.

Objectives

1. Given several ports, identify the parallel port.
2. List the characteristics and uses of a parallel port.
3. Install and configure a parallel port.
4. Describe how a parallel port communicates with a printer.
5. Given a parallel port problem, determine and correct the problem.
6. List the advantages and disadvantages of the main type of printers.
7. Describe the printing process.
8. Explain how page description languages speed up printing.
9. Describe the characteristics of paper and how they affect the reliability and quality of a printer.
10. Load paper and change the ribbon, ink, or toner cartridges on a typical printer.
11. Remove the print head from the dot-matrix printer, clean it, and reassemble it.
12. Given a printer problem, determine and correct the problem.
13. List and describe the steps of the EP process.
14. Perform preventive maintenance on a printer.
15. Install and configure a printer.

18.1 PARALLEL PORTS

The **parallel port,** sometimes referred to as the *printer port,* is a female, 2-row, 25-pin D connector. When the IBM PC was introduced, the parallel port was part of the monochrome display adapter (MDA) video card. Later, it was placed on its own expansion card or became part of a multifunction I/O expansion card. Today, many parallel ports are built into the motherboard. The typical PC can recognize up to three parallel ports (some computers can recognize four). The parallel ports are designated with the reserve names LPT1, LPT2, and LPT3 (*LPT* stands for *line printer*). In addition, the LPT1 has an alias, PRN. This means that if you copy a text file to PRN, it will be sent to the device connected to LPT1.

The parallel port is much faster than the serial port. While the serial port can transfer only 1 bit at a time, the parallel port can transfer 8 bits of data using eight different wires. In addition, parallel ports are synchronous devices that use a strobe signal as a clock signal. The maximum data transfer rate of a standard parallel port is 150 kilobytes per second (KB/s).

18.1.1 Standard Mode

The standard for the parallel port interface is specified in the IEEE 1284 standard ("Standard Signaling Method for a Bidirectional Parallel Peripheral Interface for Personal Computers"), which was approved for final release in March of 1994. The first parallel port, standard parallel port (SPP), was designed by the Centronics Corporation and adapted for the PC by the Epson Corporation.

The parallel port consists of 17 signal lines (8 data lines, 4 control lines, and 5 status lines) and 8 ground lines. The data lines carry data from the computer to the parallel device (printer). The control lines are used for interface handshaking (control) signals from the PC to the printer. The status lines, which carry signals from the parallel device to the computer, are used for handshake signals and as status indicators (paper empty, busy, or peripheral error). See table 18.1

Table 18.1 SPP Signal Definitions

Parallel Port (Type A)	Printer Port (Type B)	Printer Port (Type C)	Designation	Direction
1	1	15	-Strobe (-STR)	Port to printer
2	2	6	Data bit 0 (D0)	Port to printer
3	3	7	Data bit 1 (D1)	Port to printer
4	4	8	Data bit 2 (D2)	Port to printer
5	5	9	Data bit 3 (D3)	Port to printer
6	6	10	Data bit 4 (D4)	Port to printer
7	7	11	Data bit 5 (D5)	Port to printer
8	8	12	Data bit 6 (D6)	Port to printer
9	9	13	Data bit 7 (D7)	Port to printer
10	10	3	-Acknowledge (-ACK)	Printer to port
11	11	1	Busy (BSY)	Printer to port
12	12	5	Paper out (PAPER)	Printer to port
13	13	2	Select input (SEL)	Printer to port
14	14	17	-Auto feed (-AUTO)	Port to printer
15	32	4	-Error (-ERROR)	Printer to port
16	31	14	-Initialize (-INI)	Port to printer
17	36	16	-Device select (-DSL)	Port to printer
18		33	Strobe ground	Printer to port
19	20 and 21	24 and 25	Data 0 and 1 ground	Printer to port
20	22 and 23	26 and 27	Data 2 and 3 ground	Printer to port
21	24 and 25	28 and 29	Data 4 and 5 ground	Printer to port
22	26 and 27	30 and 31	Data 6 and 7 ground	Printer to port
23	29	19 and 22	Busy and faulty ground	Printer to port
24	28	20, 21, and 23	Paper out, select input, and acknowledge ground	Printer to port
25	30	32, 34, and 35	Auto feed, device select, and initialize ground	Printer to port
	16		Logic ground (0 V)	
	17		Chassis ground	
	18		Not used	
	34		Not used	
	35		Not used	

Like a serial port, the parallel port has a unique base I/O address. The I/O address is kept in the BIOS data area between 00408H and 0040FH. The data port, which includes the eight data lines, is accessed using the base address. The status port is accessed using the base address +1, and the control port is accessed using the base address +2. See table 18.2.

Before data can be sent to the printer, the printer has to be initialized. During normal operations, the computer puts out a constant +5 V dc charge on the initialize signal. If the voltage is removed, the printer resets. Therefore, every time the computer reboots or software switches the initialize signal to a low voltage, the printer resets. After the printer is initialized, it must be online to accept data. The device select signal is sent when the printer is online and is discontinued when it is offline. The select input signal indicates that the printer has been selected.

Data can be sent to the parallel port by using polling or interrupts. In **polling,** the most popular method, the BIOS polls, or checks, to see if the parallel port device is ready to accept another character.

Table 18.2 Typical I/O Addresses Used by Parallel Ports

Parallel Port	Typical Data Port Address	Typical Status Port Address	Typical Control Port Address
LPT1	0378H	0379H	037AH
LPT2	0278H	0279H	027AH
LPT3	03BCH	03BDH	027AH

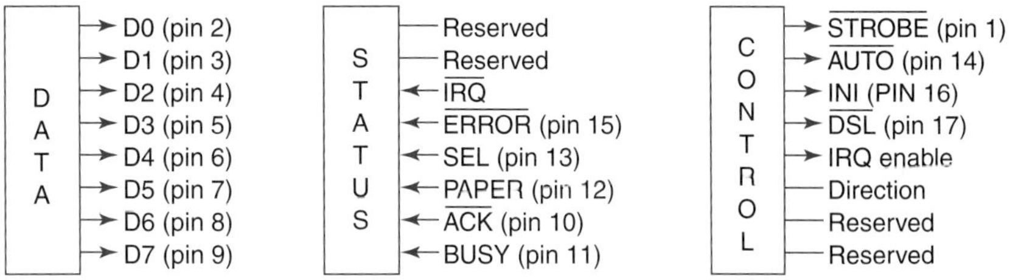

DATA	STATUS	CONTROL
→ D0 (pin 2)	Reserved	→ $\overline{\text{STROBE}}$ (pin 1)
→ D1 (pin 3)	Reserved	→ $\overline{\text{AUTO}}$ (pin 14)
→ D2 (pin 4)	← $\overline{\text{IRQ}}$	→ INI (PIN 16)
→ D3 (pin 5)	← $\overline{\text{ERROR}}$ (pin 15)	→ $\overline{\text{DSL}}$ (pin 17)
→ D4 (pin 6)	← SEL (pin 13)	→ IRQ enable
→ D5 (pin 7)	← PAPER (pin 12)	Direction
→ D6 (pin 8)	← $\overline{\text{ACK}}$ (pin 10)	Reserved
→ D7 (pin 9)	← BUSY (pin 11)	Reserved

Interrupts are more efficient but can significantly slow down the computer while printing. To move data from the parallel port to the printer, the microprocessor writes it to the data register of the parallel port, which puts data on the data lines. Next, software reads the status register to make sure that the printer is not busy and that the printer is not signalling errors. If the printer is ready to accept data, the microprocessor activates the strobe signal, which is connected through the control register. When the strobe signal is sent, the voltage of the strobe line, normally +5 V dc, is dropped to near zero for at least a half of a microsecond. The printer then activates the busy line so that no more information is sent until the current data is read and processed. It is the busy signal that is read during polling. After the character is processed, the printer then stops the busy signal and sends an acknowledge signal by dropping its normally high voltage to a low voltage.

The last control signal is the auto feed signal, which activates a line feed when the printer receives a carriage return signal. The status port also has an error signal and paper-out signal. The error signal tells the computer that there is some sort of problem with the printer. The paper out signal tells the computer when the printer is out of paper.

18.1.2 Bidirectional Modes

In older PCs, the data register was designed only to send data, not receive it. Therefore, the port was unidirectional. However, most 386 machines and all machines since the 386 are bidirectional and half-duplex. *Half-duplex* means that data can travel in both directions, but only in one direction at a time.

Either the status signals (nibble mode) or the data signals (byte mode) can send data to the parallel port. The status signals, however, can send only four signals (bits) at a time. The byte mode requires the newer bidirectional port, which includes a direction bit. Many parallel ports can be reconfigured as bidirectional by setting jumpers or DIP switches, configuring the BIOS setup program, or running a software configuration program. In both modes interrupts are used to transfer data from the parallel device to the computer.

18.1.3 Enhanced Parallel Port Mode and Extended Capabilities Port Mode

Although parallel ports were much faster than serial ports, some parallel devices eventually required faster data tansfers than the standard parallel port could provide. Eventually, two standards for a faster parallel port emerged, the **enhanced parallel port (EPP)** and **extended capabilities port (ECP).** Both standards increased data transferral rates tenfold.

EPP achieves higher transfer speeds by moving the handshaking signals from the software to the hardware circuitry on the parallel port. In addition, the EPP standard uses additional registers beyond the status and control registers. ECP is similar to EPP but it can also use DMAs and data compression. Ports may need to be configured for EPP or ECP by setting jumpers or DIP switches or by using the BIOS setup program or a configuration program.

18.1.4 Installing Parallel Ports

When installing and configuring a parallel port, you must set the parallel port's resources, specifically I/O addresses and IRQs, with jumpers, DIP switches, setup software, or the BIOS setup program. LPT1 usually uses IRQ 7 and I/O address 378H; LPT2 (if any) usually uses IRQ 5 and 278H. If the parallel port is using polling (that is, it is not interrupt driven), it can share interrupts with other parallel ports.

18.1.5 Connectors and Cables

The parallel port on the computer (type A) is a 2-row, 25-pin female D connector. The port on the printer (type B) is a 36-pin Centronics connector. A newer parallel port connector, introduced as part of the 1284 standard, is the type C connector, a high-density connector that uses all of the signals of the type B connector. The standard printer cable acts as an adapter between the connectors. (Note: parallel cables are more susceptible to noise and crosstalk, so they should be only between 6 and 10 ft long. If the cable is too long or is faulty, the data sent between the parallel port and the parallel device could become corrupted.)

There are two ways of connecting one computer to another computer using the parallel ports. The first way is with a **lap link cable** (sometimes referred to as an *interlink cable*), which, unfortunately, transfers data only 4 bits at a time. The second way is with a universal connection module (UCM) cable made by Parallel Technologies, a cable that includes a special circuit on one of the wires that permits connecting PCs through two ECP ports.

> For more information on Parallel Technologies and its universal connection module, see the following website:
>
> **http://www.lpt.com/**

18.1.6 Troubleshooting Parallel Ports

A parallel port that is not functioning or being recognized by the system can have one of the following problems:

1. A resource conflict (IRQ or I/O address-LPT designation)
2. Jumpers or DIP switches not set correctly or configuration software or CMOS setup program that has not been run, such as ECP/EPP settings
3. An unconnected cable (connecting the female 25-pin D connector to the I/O expansion card or motherboard)
4. A fault in the parallel port itself

These problems can also cause a device, such as a printer or a Zip drive, using the parallel port to not work. The device malfunction could also be caused by:

1. No driver loaded
2. Corrupt or improperly loaded driver
3. Faulty device

In either case, first check the obvious and then isolate. In addition, if the data is garbled, that is usually caused either by the cable being too long or by electromagnetic interference or an incorrect driver.

One tool that can be used to test the parallel port is the parallel loopback plug, similar to the serial loopback plug. The plug sends data out through the data port using a software diagnostic package and loops it back into the status port. Unfortunately, only a few bits can be tested in this way and therefore the test isn't a thorough one. Table 18.3 illustrates how the loopback plug is connected to the parallel port.

Table 18.3 Parallel Loopback Plug Connection

Pin 1	*connects to*	Pin 13
Pin 2	*connects to*	Pin 15
Pin 16	*connects to*	Pin 10
Pin 17	*connects to*	Pin 11

18.2 PRINTERS

A **printer** is a commonly used output device that prints text or pictures on paper. Today, most printers are connected through the USB or parallel port; a few older printers are connected through the serial port. Some printers can also be connected directly to the network and accessed through a network card. Printers can also be connected through SCSI, IEEE 1394, infrared, or wireless. As the computer age dawned, it was thought that computers would lead to a paperless office. However, the opposite has occurred and paper consumption has increased because it is so easy to print a document, proofread it and make changes, and print it again. More sophisticated software packages have also made it easy to produce stunning, professional-looking documents.

There are two major categories of printers: **impact printers,** which transfer ink onto the paper by pressing or striking against a ribbon, and **nonimpact printers,** which do not press or strike against a ribbon. The most common types of printers today are the dot-matrix printer, the ink-jet printer (also known as ink dispersion printers), and the laser printer.

Other, less common printers are:

- **Daisy-wheel printers**—Impact printers that use a ball or wheel imprinted with characters. They can produce a clear image but are limited to the characters on the ball or wheel and cannot reproduce pictures or change fonts and styles or print unusual characters. Today, daisy-wheel printers are considered old technology and are rarely found.
- **Thermal printers**—Inexpensive printers that print by pressing heated pins onto a special heat-sensitive paper.
- **Thermal wax printers**—Used mostly for business presentation transparencies and for color proofing (creating test documents and images for close quality inspection before sending off master documents to be pressed on industrial four-color offset printers). Thermal wax printers use sheet-sized, belt driven CMYK ribbons and specially coated paper or transparencies. The printhead contains heating contacts that melt each colored wax onto the paper as it is rolled through the printer.
- **Dye-sublimation printers**—A printer with a high cost-per-page that can provide high detail and print quality. The concepts behind dye-sub printers are similar to thermal wax printers except for the use of diffusive plastic dye film instead of colored wax as the ink element. The printhead heats the colored film and vaporizes the image onto specially coated paper.
- **Solid ink printers**—Used mostly in the packaging and industrial design industries, solid ink printers are prized for their ability to print on several paper stocks. Solid ink printers, as the name implies, use hardened ink sticks that are melted and sprayed through small nozzles on the printhead. The ink is then sent through a fuser roller which further absorbs the ink onto the paper. The solid ink printer is ideal for prototyping and proofing new designs for product packages; as such, most service-oriented businesses would not find a need for such a niche printer type.

18.2.1 The Printing Process

In order to print, a software interface is needed to communicate the text and images to the printer. The simplest print systems use a few bitmapped fonts that are stored in ROM chips inside the printer or other fonts added by using font cartridges. When a print command is issued by the operating system or application software, a series of command codes are sent to the printer. Some of the commands define which bitmap font and style to use, and other codes indicate which characters are to be printed. The codes are matched against a font table in the printer ROM chips and the appropriate letters are printed to paper. Additional codes are paper movement commands, such as tabs and carriage returns. Another system specifies each dot that makes up a character, but this method takes a lot of PC processing. To alleviate some of the work done by the computer and to speed up the print process, most modern printers use a page description language. A **page description language** describes to the printer the whole page to be printed by using draw and position commands and mathematical formulas. The two most common page description languages, which are usually used in laser printers, are Adobe's **Postscript** and Hewlett-Packard's **Printer Control Language (PCL).**

Normally, the user does not specify these printer codes and commands. Instead, the user creates the document and issues the print command. The print driver then translates the document into commands that the printer understands and sends them to the printer. Therefore, it is important to select the correct print driver. Otherwise, the incorrect codes would be sent and the printer would usually print garbage.

Many printers today are able to produce color, including some dot-matrix printers, many ink-jet printers, and some laser printers. The colors are usually based on the **CMYK color model,** which prints in four basic colors—cyan (greenish blue), magenta (deep purplish red), yellow, and black. By combining these colors, other colors can be produced. Some lower-quality printers use only three of these colors (cyan, magenta, and yellow) without the black. Although these printers cost less, they cannot print true black and their colors tend to be faded.

18.2.2 Paper

Paper is usually characterized by its weight, thickness, texture, and finish. The type of paper used can affect the quality of a print job. The **weight** is the total weight of a **ream** (500 sheets) of 17 × 22½-in. paper. The **caliper** is the thickness of the paper, which is usually expressed in thousandths of an inch. Generally, the greater the caliper, the greater the weight of the paper. The weight determines how well the paper will feed through the printer and how well the paper will accept the toner. Lightweight paper is not suitable for most printers and will usually cause frequent paper jams. Paper can be described by its **finish,** or the texture on the top surface of the paper. The smoothness or grain of the paper will affect how clearly the characters are formed. Depending on the type of printer being used, the smoothness will affect how well the image adheres to the surface. If the paper is not smooth, the rollers can't grab it as well, causing paper jams. In addition, rough paper can put excess wear on paper-path components.

Paper must be kept dry. Damp paper does not feed well—the printer will grab multiple sheets, causing a paper jam—and may give the printed image a patchy appearance. In addition, paper being fed into the printer should be free of dust and dirt, which could contaminate the printer mechanism.

18.2.3 Dot-Matrix Printers

The **dot-matrix printer** is an impact printer that creates characters and images by striking tiny pins against an ink ribbon, paper, and platen. These printers are inexpensive, relatively fast (depending on their print mode), and very reliable. Unfortunately, they are also noisy and do not produce high-quality output. One advantage of any kind of impact printer is that they can be used to print out multilayered forms (by using carbon or NCR paper) that require the same image on all layers. The two early standards for dot-matrix printers were Epson and IBM. Today, the most common dot-matrix printers are made by Epson and Panasonic.

The pins, or print wires, are part of the printhead. See figure 18.1. Behind the pins there is a permanent magnet that holds the pins back. When a pin is to strike the paper, electricity is sent through a coil wrapped around the pin. The electricity causes the coil to create an intense magnetic field that pushes the

Figure 18.1 Parts of a Dot-Matrix Printer

Figure 18.2 Dot-Matrix Printhead

pin against the ribbon. After the current stops, the magnetic field collapses and the pin is pulled back to its resting position by the permanent magnet. The coils are not very efficient electrical devices and so they dissipate a lot of heat. The printheads therefore become hot, which can cause print wire jamming and coil burnout. The housing of the printhead is shaped into a heat sink to dissipate heat faster.

Most printheads contain 9 or 24 pins. A 9-pin head that prints text and images with one pass is known as *draft mode.* In draft mode, the individual dots are very visible. For better quality, the 9-pin head could print in near-letter-quality mode, in which the printhead prints an individual line twice (making it equivalent to 18 pins). The best quality from a dot-matrix printer is produced by the 24-pin printhead. The 24-pin head has more than one column of pins and more pins, so it does a much better job of filling in the tiny gaps than a 9-pin printhead. See figure 18.2.

Most modern dot-matrix printers are bidirectional; that is, they can print right to left and left to right. Because the printhead does not have to return to the beginning to print the next line, the printer is faster. The printhead is moved back and forth on the paper by the carriage transport unit (sometimes called the printhead carriage assembly), which rides on one or two bars placed in front of the platen. The unit is moved back and forth with a timing belt (toothed belt), which is moved by the printhead positioning motor. The printhead must be stopped each time the print wires strike the paper. If it isn't, the dot could be smeared or the paper could be damaged. The printhead is connected to a control board (the main circuit board, which acts almost like a motherboard) with a flexible cable. As the printhead moves back and forth, the cable unfolds when it gets to the far end and folds up when it gets to the near end. Small optical sensors detect the current position of the printhead.

The ribbon used in the dot-matrix printer is very similar to a typewriter ribbon. It is usually made of a continuous loop of nylon fabric contained in a cartridge. See figure 18.3. Depending on the cartridge and the dot-matrix printer, the cartridge may remain stationary or move with the printhead. To make sure that the printhead does not use the same spot repeatedly, the ribbon is forwarded as the printer prints. If the ribbon did not forward, the spot on the ribbon that the printer is using would quickly run out of ink. If the ribbon moves forward erratically, the print image would be faded at certain places. Most ribbon cartridges have a tension knob used to keep the ribbon taut.

The paper is inserted into the printer as single sheets or as fanfold paper (also known as continuous form). Most printers can handle both types. The single sheets can be fed individually or by a paper feeder (the paper feeder can hold a stack of paper). Friction rollers or a tractor feed feeds the paper into the printer. Friction rollers wrap the paper halfway around the platen. To make sure that the paper does not slip, a set of rollers presses the paper against the platen. Since paper comes in different thicknesses, the distance between the printhead and the platen is adjustable, usually by means of a level on the top of the printer. If the printhead is too far away from the paper, the text and images print lightly, and if it is too close, the text and images can become smudged. Fanfold paper, which is continuous paper divided by perforations into 8½ × 11-in. sheets and has small holes on the left and right sides, is fed into the printer by **tractor feed** (also known as pin-feed). Sprockets on a wheel or belt are placed in the holes

Figure 18.3 Common Ribbons Used in Dot-Matrix Printers

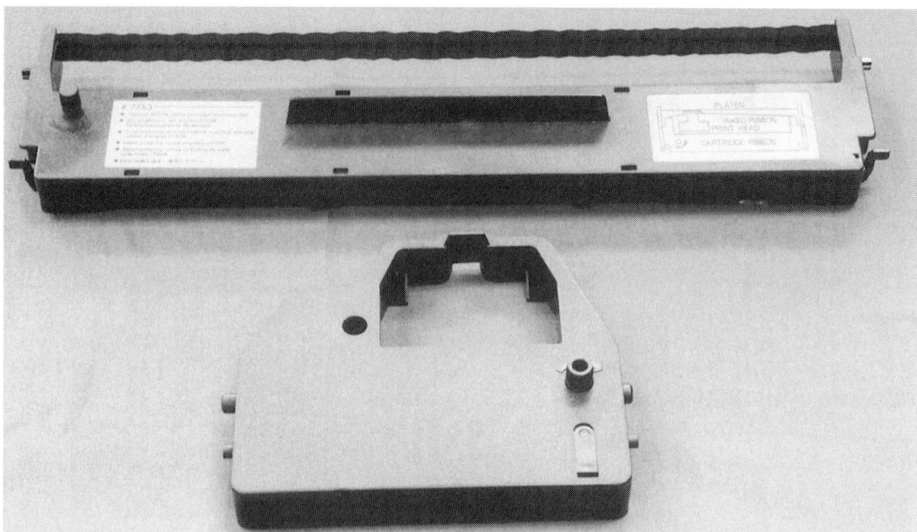

of the fanfold paper. As the sprockets rotate around a wheel, the paper is pushed or pulled past the printhead. The friction-feed rollers must be released when the tractor feed is used so that they don't interfere with the movement of the paper. It is best to remove paper from a dot-matrix printer by using the page feed or line feed controls on the printer. The paper should not be pulled out unless the friction-feed rollers are released and the paper is free of the tractor feed. In addition, the knobs on the side of the printer should be turned only when the printer is off. Turning the knobs when the printer is on will strip some of the gears inside the printer.

Most people don't realize that the printer has a microcontroller (microprocessor). As data is sent from the computer to the printer, the microcontroller receives it and the control signals and processes the information. It will then control the printhead, the printhead carriage unit, the paper-feed motors, and the ribbon. In addition, it monitors several optical sensors, including the paper-out sensor, printhead position, and the home position sensor (so the sensor knows where to begin), and the control panel (form feed, line feed, online, and offline).

Some dot-matrix printers can print in color. Most of these use a multicolored ribbon with three or four bands corresponding to the primary colors (usually black, red, green, and blue). To print different colors, the ribbon is moved up and down so that the printhead pin prints with the correct color. Other colors are formed by combining the primary colors on the ribbon. Because this requires printing the color images more than once in order to mix the colors, color printing is slower than printing in black and white.

The speed of the dot-matrix printer is usually expressed in characters per second (cps); a few line printers are measured in lines per minute. The speed, of course, will vary according to the print mode (draft mode or near-letter quality), whether it is printing color, and the complexity of the document.

18.2.4 Ink-Jet Printers

The **ink-jet printer** works by spraying small droplets of ionized ink onto a sheet of paper. Modern ink-jet printers produce high-quality print (including color) that approaches the quality produced by laser printers, yet cost much less. And, because ink-jet printers are much smaller than laser printers, their portability has added to their popularity. The best-selling ink-jet printers are made by Hewlett-Packard and, to a lesser extent, Canon. See figure 18.4.

A typical ink-jet printer prints with a resolution of 300 dots per inch, although some newer models have higher resolutions. Since the droplets are smaller than the dot-matrix pins, the printer can achieve a better image. The ink comes from an ink reservoir stored in a removable ink cartridge and is sprayed through tiny nozzles located on the printhead. See figure 18.5. Each nozzle ejects ink droplets as they are formed by a piezoelectric pump or a bubble pump. The piezoelectric pump is a ring of piezoelectric ceramic material (a crystal that changes shape when subjected to electricity) placed in front of the print

Figure 18.4 Epson Stylus Color 850 Ink-Jet Printer (Courtesy of Epson America, Inc.)

Figure 18.5 Ink-Jet Cartridge

nozzle. As electricity flows through the ring, the piezoelectric material vibrates at approximately 100 kHz and constricts, squeezing the ink out through the nozzle. When the flow of current stops, the ring returns to its original size, forming a vacuum. The pressure of the vacuum causes fresh ink to replace the ink that was sprayed out. The bubble pump creates the droplets by heating a resistor at the bottom of the ink-jet nozzle. The ink boils and forms a bubble, pushing ink through the nozzle. When the droplet is large enough, it breaks away from the printhead and attaches to the paper. As the resistor cools, the bubble collapses, causing a vacuum. The pressure of the vacuum causes fresh ink to replace the ink that was sprayed out. While the ink-jet is sitting idle, the close nozzle gate keeps the ink from leaking out of the ink cartridge.

The ink-jet cartridge can be easily replaced when it runs out of ink. It is important not to touch the printhead when replacing the cartridge because the ink-jet holes are about half the diameter of a human hair and can clog easily with dirt or grease from fingers. Most ink-jet printers have a self-cleaning function that can unclog a nozzle, but the process does use a large amount of ink. Most ink-jet printers are also self-sealing so that air will not cause the ink to dry in the nozzle. The ink cartridge is designed to be used until the ink runs out and then thrown away. Unfortunately, there is no warning when the cartridges are running low. The page simply starts to fade as it is being printed. Today, many ink-jets can print in color. Like the dot-matrix printer, the ink-jet printer has three colors (cyan, magenta, and yellow), four colors (black, cyan, magenta, and yellow), or seven colors, which are mixed together to form other colors.

Question:

Should an ink cartridge be refilled?

Answer:

There are kits for refilling ink cartridges, which of course save money, but it is not usually a good idea. As ink passes through the nozzle, the nozzle wears down, and the nozzles are easily clogged with grease and dirt. Therefore, to improve poor print quality, first try a new ink cartridge.

As with a dot-matrix printer, the cartridge for an ink-jet printer is inserted into the printhead assembly, which rides on one or two bars placed in front of the platen. The assembly is moved back and forth with a timing belt, which is moved by a printhead positioning motor. The printhead assembly is connected to a control board by a flexible cable. As the printhead moves back and forth, the cable unfolds as it moves to the far end and folds up when it moves to the near end. Small optical sensors detect the current position of the printhead.

Paper is inserted into the printer as single sheets. The single sheets are usually fed by friction rollers that pin the paper against the platen. The paper is usually stored in a bin, often located at the bottom of the printer. When the ink hits the paper, it must dry before the paper can be handled. How well it dries depends on the type of paper and ink being used. If the paper absorbs too much of the ink, the image will be faded because there is not much ink on the surface. If the paper has a finish that causes the ink to bleed, the image will look blurry. If the paper doesn't absorb enough ink, such as with a glossy surface or plastic transparencies, for example, the ink will easily smear. The moisture of the ink may cause low-quality paper to become warped. Therefore, although the cost is a little more than regular copy paper, it is best to use special ink-jet paper.

18.2.5 Laser Printers

Laser printers, like copy machines, use an **electrophoto (EP)** process to form images on paper with toner instead of ink. Consequently, laser printers produce very high-quality print and are capable of printing almost any text or image. They are also relatively fast—a typical laser printer is rated between 4 and 8 pages per minute (ppm), and some network printers can print up to 20 pages per minute. Of course, this speed does not include the time needed for the processing done by the computer and the printer.

Operation

The central part of the laser printer is a **photosensitive drum,** an aluminum cylinder coated with a nontoxic organic material that reacts to light. In darkness, the material can hold an electrical charge. As light is exposed to the drum, the drum discharges electricity. **Toner** is the material that is transferred onto the paper. It is an extremely fine powder made of plastic resin bonded to iron particles. The iron particles react to electrical charges and the plastic resin has a low melting temperature.

NOTE: With these characteristics, toner spills cannot be cleaned up by normal means. The best way to clean a toner spill is to use a vacuum cleaner with special filter bags, required because the toner is so fine that it would be sucked through a normal vacuum bag back into the air. A moist cloth can be used to wipe up some toner, but a dry cloth should be used to wipe toner off clothing. Toner has a low melting point, so only cold water should be used to wash hands, clothing, and carpets. Lastly, toner is toxic. Therefore, you should minimize contact with it.

There are six basic steps to transferring the image onto the paper. See figure 18.6.

1. Cleaning
2. Conditioning
3. Writing
4. Developing
5. Transferring
6. Fusing

Figure 18.6 The six stages of laser printing. During the cleaning stage, a photosensitive drum is cleaned to remove any residual toner (rubber scraper) and residual charge (eraser lamp). During the conditioning stage, the main corona wire charges the drum with a negative voltage. During the writing stage, the image is formed on the drum by the laser. The developing stage transfers toner to the drum, where it sticks on the areas that are still charged. The transferring stage transfers the toner to the positively charged paper, and the fusing stage melts the toner into the paper.

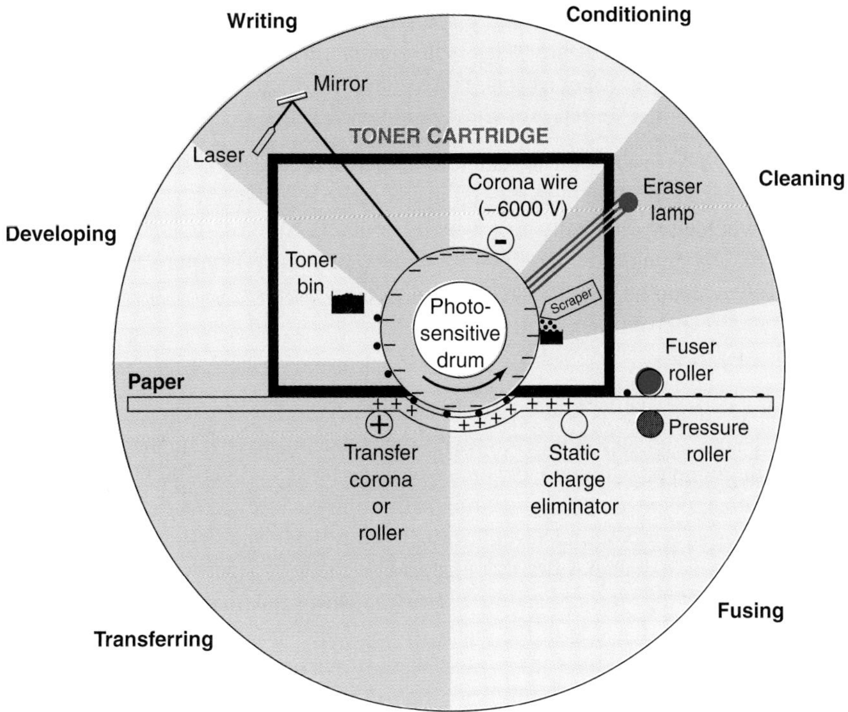

During the cleaning stage, the photosensitive drum is cleaned to remove any residual toner and residual electrical charge. The toner is removed with a soft rubber scraper so that it won't transfer to subsequent pages and appear as random black speckles. The rubber scraper is used to avoid scratching the delicate photosensitive material on the drum; any scratch would appear on every image printed. The residual electrical charge is removed by an eraser lamp, leaving the drum's surface with a neutral charge. If ghost images of previously printed documents appear on new printouts, the toner or electrical charge is not being completed during the cleaning phase. Most likely, you will have to replace the toner cartridge.

During the conditioning stage, the main **corona wire,** which has a charge of −6,000 V dc, is located near the drum's surface. Since the drum and corona wire share the same ground, an electrical field is established between the two that transfers between −600 V dc and −1,000 V dc. The voltage transfer is regulated by the primary grid. At this point, the drum is ready to receive the image to be printed. If there is any dirt or debris on the corona wire, it will generate an uneven charge on the drum, resulting in lines or streaks.

During the writing stage, the laser light (a class 1 laser), aimed by mirrors, sweeps along the drum line by line, selectively hitting parts of it. As the light touches areas of the drum, the photosensitive material it strikes grounds itself to the aluminum cylinder, reducing the charge to −100 V dc. Consequently, an electrostatic image is formed on the drum. Some faster laser printers have several laser beams working simultaneously.

In the developing stage, the toner, which has a negative charge, is applied to the drum by a developer roller (toner roller). The areas of the drum that were not hit by the light still have a strong negative charge, so the toner is repelled from them. The toner adheres to those areas of the drum that were struck by the light. The printer is now ready for the transferring stage. During this stage, paper is positively charged by a transfer roller (a black sponge-rubber roller) or a transfer corona wire. Because the paper is positively charged and the toner is negatively charged, the toner is attracted to the paper (opposites attract). (Note: Toner does not adhere to a rough surface as well, and a wrinkled or creased sheet of paper cannot be charged uniformly. If the print media is too thick, its attraction to a negative charge will not be as strong, and the toner may not adhere to the surface as well as it should.) To make sure that the paper is not attracted to the drum and does not wrap around it, it is discharged by a static charge eliminator (or eliminator comb) after the toner has been transferred. (Note: Transfer rollers should never be touched with the fingers. Skin oils on the roller can cause print quality problems.)

The last stage in the printing process is the fusing stage, in which the paper and fresh toner are pressed against each other and fused with two rollers, a fuser roller made of a Teflon-coated aluminum and a rubberized pressure roller. When paper emerges from the printer, the toner is permanently bonded to it. As the fuser roller rotates, excess toner is wiped off and silicon oil is added by a cleaning pad. The EP process then starts again with the cleaning stage.

NOTE: The fuser roller is heated to approximately 180°C by a high-intensity quartz lamp. To prevent the toner from sticking to the roller, the roller is made of a nonstick substance such as Teflon. If work anywhere near the fusing area is being done, it is best to unplug the printer and wait at least 10 minutes so the fusing unit and lamp have a chance to cool. When performing periodic maintenance on a laser printer, clean the fuser assembly with a damp cloth.

Print Media

Because parts of the laser printer are extremely hot, it can accommodate only print media (paper, transparencies, and self-adhesive labels) designed for laser printers. Otherwise, transparencies may melt while in the printer and labels may become loose and get stuck in the printer or wrap around a roller. The component that moves the media through the laser printer is the **paper transport assembly,** which consists of a motor and several rubberized rollers. The first roller, known as the *feed* or *paper pickup* roller, is a D-shaped roller that pushes one sheet of paper into the printer. Then the registration rollers move the rollers through the EP cartridge. Most printers are **simplex** printers. This means that they can print on only one side of the paper. A few larger laser printers are duplex printers, which means they have a duplex tray that turns each sheet of paper over so that it can be printed on the other side. Of course, when duplex printing, the printer's output speed will be halved. Unfortunately, the duplex unit or paper swapping unit is mechanically complicated and the printer is more likely to jam.

The print media is usually fed through a tray or trays. Laser printers that are designed for heavy use may have large trays that can accommodate an entire ream of paper. Other printers may actually have multiple trays, for different types of paper such as letterheads, envelopes, or different sizes of paper. In addition to the trays, many laser printers have a door that you can open on the printer so that you can manually feed paper into the printer. This is typically used for special paper that is not loaded in the tray such as letterheads or transparencies.

Some copy machines can act as print servers/printers, while other machines are a combined printer, scanner, and fax. The only thing needed to connect to these printers is to load the proper protocol on the client system and load the appropriate driver. The copy machines that can be used for printing typically have large trays of paper and a wide range of print options. Since they are connected to a network, any user can connect to these printers and use it to print documents. Lastly, the deluxe printers will have more finishing options such as automatically stapling and various ways of sorting. Of course, as you add more of these options to a printer, you also add more items that may fail in the future.

Control

The large circuit board that converts signals from the computer into signals understood by the different components of the laser printer is the **printer controller circuitry.** It sends a signal through a cable to the printer controller assembly. The controller assembly formats a page of information into a series of commands for the different components and sends the signal through the appropriate cables to the appropriate components.

The power for the laser printer is supplied by the high-voltage power supply (HVPS) and the dc power supply (DCPS). The HVPS provides high-voltage electricity to energize the corona wire and transfer corona wire. The DCPS powers the logic circuitry with +5 V and −5 V and with +24 V for the paper transport motors. Because a laser printer consumes large amounts of power, it can cause power fluctuations, especially when warming up, which may affect the reliability of a computer on the same circuit. The corona wire (or wires) produces ozone as a result of the ionization of the surrounding air.

Ozone is a corrosive gas that in large quantities can cause respiratory ailments, nausea, headaches, and premature aging of the skin. To reduce the amount of ozone released into the air, a laser printer will often have an ozone filter. If the filter becomes clogged, the ozone seeps undetected into a room in its pure form. Most **ozone filters** should, therefore, be replaced every 20,000 to 30,000 pages printed. The filter is usually accessible when the printer is opened for cleaning or it may be part of the toner cartridge.

Since printers have gotten more complex over the years, many printers have built-in operating systems that guide the actions of the printers. These operating systems are stored as firmware. Occasionally, the firmware may need to be upgraded to fix bugs in the operating system or to close security holes when the printer is used as a network printer.

Toner Cartridges

Most laser printers use replaceable **toner cartridges,** which simplify the adding of toner and help prevent many problems. A typical cartridge contains the toner, photosensitive drum, cleaning scraper blade, primary corona wire, developing roller, and a debris cavity that catches excess toner. See figure 18.7. The photosensitive drum is very sensitive to light and so should not be exposed to any source of bright light, including sunlight, or to extremes of temperature and humidity. (Note: When installing or replacing the toner cartridge, it is best to shake the toner cartridge so that the toner will be distributed evenly.) Because parts of the toner cartridge wear out, it is best to use a new toner cartridge instead of a refilled toner cartridge. If refilled toner cartridges are used (because they are cheaper), make sure that the company that refills the toner refills the cartridge only once, since the drum will eventually wear out.

Dry toner and empty toner cartridges are not regulated as a hazardous waste and may be disposed as trash. However, these items should be sealed in heavy plastic bags before being placed in trash to protect custodial workers from fine dust. It is highly encouraged to participate in a toner cartridge recycling program in which empty cartridges are returned to the vendor for refilling.

Resolution

A typical laser printer will have a resolution of between 300 and 600 dots per inch (dpi); some high-end printers can achieve 1,200 dpi. Some laser printers can achieve an even higher resolution by using resolution enhancement and "microfine" toner. Hewlett-Packard's **Resolution Enhancement**

Figure 18.7 Laser Toner Cartridge and the Photosensitive Drum

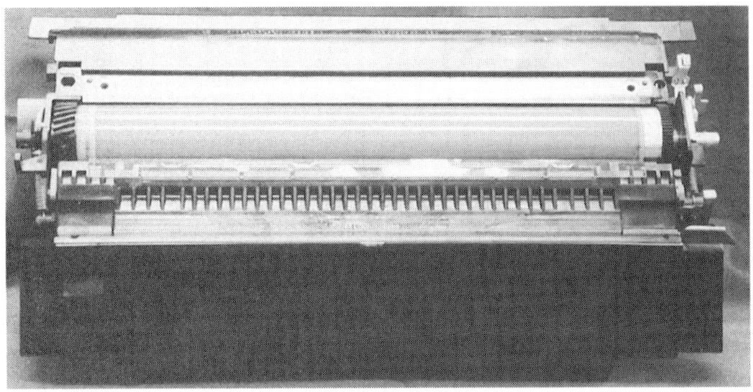

Technology (RET) prints like any other laser printer except it produces smaller dots. The smaller dots fill some of the gaps between two normal-size dots so that a line or curve appears smoother. Another advantage of RET is its ability to reproduce more shades of gray. Laser printers can't print a true gray color. Instead, they use **halftones,** which simulate shades of gray by assembling patterns of black and white dots. Printers that have Resolution Enhancement Technology or the equivalent can generate more shades of gray because the dots are smaller than normal. Color laser printers are also available, and they work much like other printers in that they use four colors to create all of the other colors. Unfortunately, color laser printers tend to be about five to ten times as expensive as black-and-white printers.

Graphics are a particular challenge for all printers. Graphics are either bitmap graphic images or vector images. **Bitmap graphics** are sent to the printer as an array of dots. Because an image can contain many dots (a 300 dpi printer uses 90,000 dots per square inch), a bitmap graphic contains lots of information. The printer requires a great deal of memory to store this information, and it also needs to do a lot of processing. **Vector graphics** use lines and curves to define an image. A line or curve is defined by mathematical equations, so they require a lot less printer RAM and processing and can be printed faster than bitmap images. Certain images, however, such as photographs (images made of dots), can be printed only as bitmap images. Laser printers were designed to print graphics. As with a PC, the complexity of the graphics that can be printed is partially determined by the amount of RAM the printer has. To print a full-page complex graphics document at 300 dpi, at least 1 MB of RAM (probably more) is needed. For a 600 dpi graphics document, at least 4 MB of RAM (probably more) is needed. Adding more RAM to some printers can increase performance, specifically the processing speed.

If a printer outputs a page and the printer only prints a portion of the page or if the printer gets an overflow error, it is possible that you have to increase the memory for your printer or decrease the resolution of your printer. Note: In Windows, you typically have to specify the amount of RAM a printer has using the printer properties window.

Network Interfaces

Today, many printers have network interfaces or cards built into the printer. This allows the printer to connect directly to the network, allowing many people to connect to the printer and print. In these cases, you will have to configure the network interface, usually by using buttons on the panel of the printer. Since TCP/IP is the most popular network traffic, you will have to configure the IP address and subnet mask, and you might also have to configure the default gateway. Then, depending on the capabilities of the printer, users can connect much like a Windows printer that uses SMB or CIFS protocol or a UNIX printer that uses the LPR protocol. Users will also need to use the appropriate driver.

Maintenance

A good preventive maintenance and cleaning program will stop most laser-printer problems before they occur and will help ensure that the printer has the highest quality output possible. The program should include:

1. Cleaning the main and transfer corona wires with denatured alcohol
2. Cleaning the transfer guide and paper-feed guide with a lint-free cloth dampened with cold, demineralized water
3. Using the soft end of the corona cleaning brush to sweep away any paper dust or debris on the static eliminator
4. Cleaning the fuser separation pawls (claws) with a lint-free cloth dampened with cold, demineralized water
5. Replacing the ozone filter

18.2.6 Physically Installing a Printer

A printer is one of the easiest peripheral devices to install. Traditionally, the printer cable is connected from the PC's parallel port to the printer's Centronics connector, and then the printer's power cable is plugged in. Today, printers may connect using a USB cable, an IEEE 1394 cable, infrared connection, or some other cable. (Note: New printers will usually have packing inside to prevent the printhead and other internal devices from moving around during shipping. These must be removed from the system, of course, before the printer can be used.) The next step is installing the driver for the software that is using the printer. For Windows, only one driver has to be loaded for all Windows applications. When Windows detects a USB, IEEE 1394, or infrared printer, it automatically starts the Found New Hardware wizard. The driver is used to convert data from a document to commands that the printer understands. Although most of the alphanumeric data is standard for most printers, the control codes are not. Therefore, attempting to print a document using the wrong device driver will result in the wrong control codes being sent to the printer and it will print garbage (strange characters or many pages of programming code). A system may contain several print drivers for several different printers, so the correct one must be activated before printing. If it is not, the printer will usually output garbage.

Depending on the work environment, several people may share the same printer. This can be accomplished by installing a network or by means of a switch box. Most switch boxes have one port that connects to the printer using a normal printer cable and other connectors, anywhere from 2 to 16, that use 25-pin male to 25-pin male straight-through cables. Some switch boxes are manual and others are autoswitching. Manual switch boxes need to be manually set to the port (computer) before the printer can print. The autoswitching boxes automatically detect which printer is sending a print signal and switch to that port as needed. Autoswitching boxes should be used when connecting laser printers to a switch box because laser printers need a constant signal. If they don't get one, a printer error message will probably appear on the printer display.

18.2.7 Windows Printing

Windows 9X systems divide the print mechanism into three parts, the printer, the print driver, and the print spooler. When you send out a print job, as when you click on the Print button (usually found under the File menu and often found on a toolbar at the top of the screen), the application sends the print job to the print spooler, sometimes referred to as the print queue. The word *spool* is an acronym for *simultaneous peripheral operations on line.*

By default, the Windows 9X spooling files are stored in the C:\WINDOWS\SPOOL\PRINTERS directory and Windows NT family systems spooler files are stored in the %SYSTEMROOT%\ SYSTEM32\ SPOOL\PRINTERS folder. Note: %SYSTEMROOT% is usually the C:\WINNT or the C:\WINDOWS folder. Because the documents are temporarily stored on the disk waiting to be sent to the printer, you can perform other tasks on the computer while the printing takes place in the background. The spooler also lets you place a number of print jobs in a queue so you don't have to wait for completion of one print job before specifying another one.

The print spooler, working with the print driver, formats the print job in a language that the printer can understand and stores it as a temporary file on the hard drive. Once the print job has been "spooled" to the hard drive, the print job is then sent to the printer. Most printing from Windows 9X and Windows NT family systems use the enhanced metafiles (EMF) data type.

Because Windows NT, Windows 2000, and Windows XP are designed for network environment, the printing is a bit more complex. First, to Windows, a printer is not a physical device. It is a program that controls one or more physical printers. The physical printer is called a print device. Printing drivers and a spooler are still present, but in Windows, they are integrated into the printer itself. With this arrangement, one printer (remember, it is the program) can support multiple print devices, enabling a system to act as a print server. If one print device is down, the printer automatically redirects the output to a working printer. Windows 2000 also provides support for nonstandard ports, enabling extra functions for networked printers.

Although these printer systems vary between the Windows 9X and Windows NT family, the installation, configuration, and troubleshooting are basically the same. Today, most printers are plug-and-play, so installing a printer is automatically done when you plug the printer to the computer and load the driver. If the system does not detect the printer or if the printer is not PnP, click the Start button, select the Settings option, and Select Printers to open the Printers window. You can also open the Printers window by double-clicking on the Printers applet in the Control Panel.

To actually start the printer installation, double-click the Add Printer applet to start the Add Printer Wizard. You may then choose to install a printer plugged directly into your system or a network printer. Network printers are discussed in chapter 25. Some of the newer versions of Windows have added the Automatically Detect and Install My PnP Printer option. When a printer is not included in the list of printers, you need to use manual mode to install the printer. If you choose a local printer, Windows will

Figure 18.8 Selecting the Printer Port and Printer Type When Installing a Printer

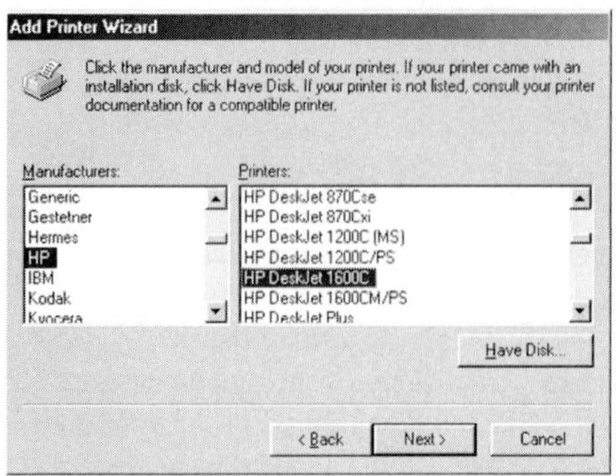

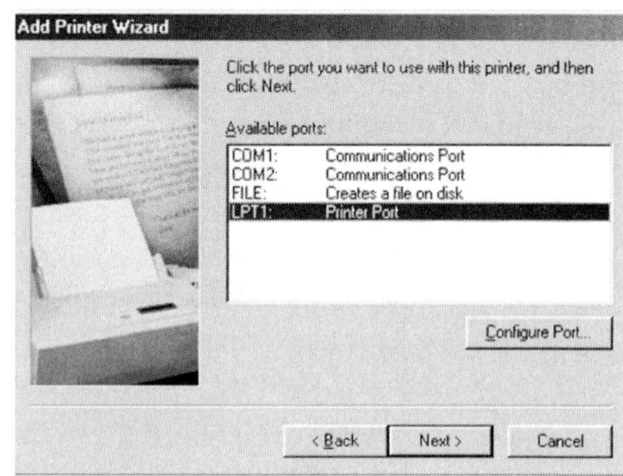

Figure 18.9 Managing the Print Queue

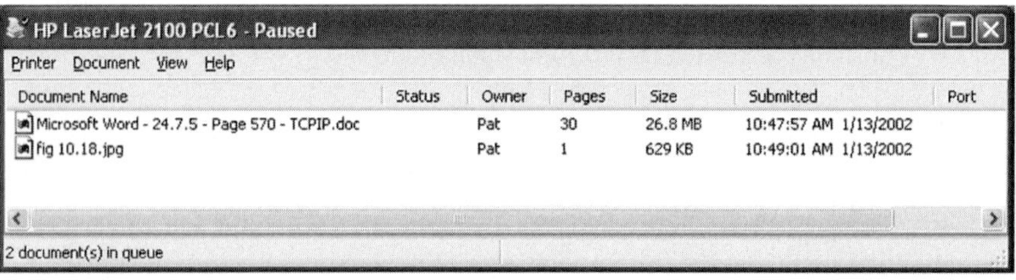

then give you options to select a port (LPT1, LPT2, LPT3, COM1, COM2, etc.) and the type of printer. See figure 18.8. You can select the type from the list or use the Have Disk option, just as you would for any other device.

When the printer or printers are installed, the default printer or the printer that you print to by default has a small checkmark in the corner. If you have multiple printers, you can change the default printer by selecting the printer's properties and checking Make Default Printer. If you delete a printer that was configured as the default printer, Windows will choose one of the other printers as the default printer.

When you print in Windows and the print job is still in the spooler, you can manage the individual print jobs. To pause a document, open the PRINTERS folder and double-click the printer you are using to open the print queue. See figure 18.9. When you right-click a document, you can typically pause the printer job or delete the print job.

NOTE: You can also access the printer queue by double-clicking the tiny printer icon in the system tray (if it is present). In addition, if you don't want to spool the print jobs, you can select the Print directly to the printer option in the Spool Settings dialog box.

Print spoolers can easily overflow or become corrupt due to a lack of disk space or too many print jobs, disk errors, power fluctuations, and so on. If the parallel port, the printer cable, and the printer all support bidirectional communication, communication from the printer to Windows is possible. For example, Windows can ask the printer how much printer memory is available and what fonts are installed. The printer can send messages to Windows, such as an out-of-paper or paper-jam message. If print jobs become stalled in Windows, you can try to restart the spooler.

18.2.8 Troubleshooting Printers

Although printers are easy to install, they can cause all sorts of headaches. Any problem that occurs with a printer has one of four sources:

1. The printer (including cartridges and ribbons)
2. The print cable
3. The parallel or USB port (or other interface)
4. The software (including drivers)

Most printers can perform a self-test that can be initiated by pressing one or more buttons (such as the online, form-feed, or line-feed buttons) while turning on the printer or by using the printer's control panel. Instructions on how to activate the print test are included in the printer documentation. The test will usually print all of the alphanumeric characters, and many of them will print the configuration for the printer, different types of fonts, or a graphic image.

NOTE: Windows also has a print test page option.

A common problem that occurs is the paper jam—a sheet of paper catching or refusing to pass through the printer mechanism. A paper jam may be caused by using incorrect paper (the paper is too heavy or too light), damp paper, a wornout roller, or the buildup of paper fragments, toner, or other debris. Sometimes the printer may jam for no apparent reason. Of course, if the printer has regular maintenance performed on it, the jams will occur less frequently. Single-feed paper should be fanned before loading it into a holding tray with the paper curling downward. An important clue to what part of the printer is causing the jam is where the first part of the paper stopped. When removing the jam, be careful not to snatch the paper from the printer or pull fiercely, which is likely to rip the paper and leave a small piece behind, which may cause more paper jams. Many gears can turn only one way, so when turning knobs and pulling paper, make sure the knobs are being turned or the paper is being pulled in the right direction. If the rollers do not turn in the direction in which you are pulling, the paper will most likely tear. Lastly, make sure the printer is off and unplugged, that the dot-matrix printhead and fuser assembly has had a chance to cool, and that the corona wire is not carrying an electrical charge. If you remove a paper jam from a laser printer and it says that there still is a jam, open and close the lid. Always refer to the printer manual for the proper way to remove a paper jam.

If the printer does not come on at all, that is probably a power supply problem. Make sure the power cord is plugged into both the ac wall jack and the printer, that the ac wall jack has power, and that the printer is turned on. If the printer still does not come on, open the housing and locate the printer's power supply. Before replacing the power supply, check the power supply fuse. If the fuse is blown, replace it. Of course, you should then be concerned with what blew the fuse to begin with. If the fuse is not blown, you will probably need to replace the power supply.

On a few occasions, we have seen preprinted forms where the paper is not actually rectangular, or the printing on the paper is skewed. Particularly in the case of skewed printing, this may not be true for the entire batch of forms. If close examination reveals that the first form in a package is slightly skewed, check another form near the end of the batch to determine if the problem is still present. If it is, you may need to adjust the printer slightly so that the printing lines up precisely in the boxes on preprinted forms. To accomplish this, you have to use the software that comes with the printer or printer properties or options in Windows to adjust the Print Position vertically or horizontally. If it is not clear how to do this, you should check with your printer documentation. After you have completed and tested the adjustment, it is important that you document the adjustment so that you know how to make the same adjustment in the future.

Example 18.1:

You give the print command and nothing happens.

As with any other problem, check the obvious first:

Check to see if the printer is plugged in.
Check to see if the printer is on.
Check to see if the printer is online.
Check to see if the printer cable is connected properly.
If a switch box is being used, make sure that all of the cables are connected properly and that the switch box is switched to the computer you are trying to print from.
Make sure you have enough free disk space.

If the problem still exists, you need to isolate it. The printer, the printer cable, the parallel port, or the software could be at fault. The easiest of these to check and one of the most common sources of problems is the software. Make sure that the correct driver is loaded and selected and that the software points to the correct printer port (LPT1, LPT2, or other).

If the computer is using Windows, print using another program. If the other program prints fine, then the first program has become corrupt and will probably have to be reinstalled. If the problem occurs in both applications, check the print manager to see if a particular print job is causing the problem or if the print manager or print spooler is stalled or having problems. If the print manager or print spooler is having problems, these can usually be corrected by rebooting the computer or restarting the print manager or spooler.

If the problem still exists, isolate it further as a hardware problem or software problem by booting the system to DOS or the command prompt (Windows) and sending something to the printer. This can be done by sending a text file (such as AUTOEXEC.BAT) to the printer:

```
TYPE AUTOEXEC.BAT > LPT1
```

or

```
COPY AUTOEXEC.BAT LPT1
```

Of course, for these two commands to work, the printer must be connected to LPT1. (Note: Text files sent to a laser printer do not have a form-feed code. Therefore, you will usually have to perform a form-feed code manually using the control panel on the printer.) If the document prints, then you know that the hardware is working properly and that there is a software problem.

If the document does not print, then there is a hardware problem. The next step is having the printer perform a self-test. If the self-test fails, the problem is most likely caused by the printer. If the self-test works properly, the problem must be with the printer interface, the printer configuration, the parallel port, or the cable. If the self-test fails, the problem is most likely caused by the printer. To determine which component is causing the problem, start swapping them. The easiest one to swap is the printer cable. If there is a switch box, two cables and the switch box will have to be swapped. Swap one component at a time until you find which component is bad.

Next, try the printer on a different computer or try a different printer on the same computer. If the printer prints on another computer, the parallel port (or other interface) must be at fault. Make sure there is no resource conflict (IRQ or I/O address or LPT designation) and that the port is active (the jumpers, DIP switches, software, or CMOS setup program are correctly configured). If the parallel port uses a ribbon cable to connect the 25-pin D connector to the motherboard or expansion card, make sure that it is connected properly. If the printer is a serial printer, a null modem cable must be used and the serial port must be configured properly (baud rate, data bits, stop bits, and parity). If a different printer prints on the same computer, the problem must be with the printer configuration (DIP switches or Control Panel) or the printer interface. The printer configuration is the easiest and quickest to check, so this should be checked first. If the configuration seems fine, replace the printer or take apart the printer and diagnose the problem.

Example 18.2:

A document prints as garbage.

The most common cause of garbage (strange characters or many pages of what appears to be programming code) is the wrong driver being loaded or selected, but it could also be a software problem. Try printing from another application. If the printer prints in one application and not the other, the first application is causing the problem. Next, reboot the computer or restart the print manager or spooler so that the print manager or spooler has a chance to refresh itself. Finally, try reinstalling the driver, since the driver could have become corrupt.

If the problem still exists, make sure that the cable is connected properly and that it is no longer than 10 ft. A long cable is much more susceptible to electromagnetic interference. Also make sure the cable does not go near any device that generates a lot of electromagnetic interference (EMI). Before swapping any components, perform the printer's self-test. If the self-test fails, the problem is most likely being caused by the printer.

A faulty print cable, a faulty parallel port, or a faulty printer are the next likely causes of the problem. Swap the cable (or switch box and cables) first; then try the printer on a different computer or try a different printer on the same computer. If the same printer prints on another computer with no problems, the problem must lie with the parallel port (or other interface). If a different printer works on the same computer, the problem must be with the printer. The printer must be disassembled and fixed or it will have to be replaced. If the printer is a serial printer, make sure a null modem cable is being used and the serial port is configured properly (baud rate, data bits, stop bits, and parity).

Troubleshooting Dot-Matrix Printers

On occasion, the dot-matrix printhead will have to be cleaned (pins become clogged with residual ink and dust) or replaced when some of the pins are not firing or they fire erratically. First, make sure that the printer is shut off and unplugged. Remove the printhead (usually done by unsnapping plastic holding clips or removing some screws) and disconnect the ribbon cable leading to the printhead, noting how the cable is oriented so that you can reconnect it properly. After the printhead is removed, pour a small amount of denatured alcohol into a cup or other container and insert the nose of the printhead in the alcohol. Next, insert the part of the printhead that contains the pins for 2 or 3 minutes. Do not submerse the printhead. After the printhead has had a chance to soak, dry it off, reinstall it, and reconnect the ribbon cable leading to the printhead. Remove the ribbon, load the paper into the printer, and run the self-test a few times without the ribbon so that any ink inside the pins will be transferred to the paper. Depending on how dirty the printhead was, this process may have to be repeated several times. When the printhead is clean, apply one or two drops of light oil to the pins to lubricate them.

When performing periodic maintenance on a printer, make sure that you do not use harsh solvents, such as 409 all-purpose cleaner, since these will usually either soften parts of the printer or cause them to melt. Use a damp cloth or denatured alcohol instead. In addition, do not lubricate the gear trains or platen assembly of a dot-matrix printer.

Example 18.3:

Documents have light or uneven print.

The first thing to check on a dot-matrix printer is the distance between the printhead and platen. If the distance is correct, replace the ribbon—it is most likely running out of ink. If the problem occurs again, make sure that the ribbon is advancing. If it is not, the problem is probably caused by a bad gear, the belt on the ribbon feed assembly, a bad ribbon, or incorrect insertion of the ribbon.

Example 18.4:

The printhead does not print.

The first thing to check on a dot-matrix printer is the distance between the printhead and platen. If the distance is correct, replace the ribbon—it is most likely running out of ink. If the problem occurs again, make sure that the ribbon is advancing. If it is not, the problem is probably caused by a bad gear, the belt on the ribbon feed assembly, a bad ribbon, or incorrect insertion of the ribbon. If the ribbon is advancing, the ribbon cable to the printhead is not connected properly, the printhead needs to be replaced, or the control board inside the printer needs to be replaced.

Example 18.5:

The printhead does not move.

Make sure that nothing is jammed in the printer that may prevent the printhead from moving back and forth. The problem could also be caused by the home position sensor, the printhead position motor, the timing belt, or the control board.

Example 18.6:

The paper is not advancing.

First, check the paper-feed selector level to make sure that the correct type of paper feed (tractor feed or friction feed) is selected. Next, check for paper jams. If the problem still occurs, check the paper-feed motor.

Troubleshooting the Ink-Jet Printer

Most problems with an ink-jet printer occur because either the cartridge is empty (or low) or the nozzles on the print cartridge are clogged. In either case, it is usually best to replace the print cartridge. (Note: If you install a print cartridge and later remove it, it should not be reinstalled in the printer.) Most of the other problems encountered are very similar to those encountered with dot-matrix printers.

Troubleshooting the Laser Printer

Troubleshooting a laser printer is quite different from troubleshooting a dot-matrix or an ink-jet printer. Fortunately, many of the laser printer components are modular (such as the toner cartridge) and can therefore be replaced without too much difficulty.

NOTE: Consumers usually dispose of a toner cartridge by throwing it into the trash. Businesses, on the other hand, need to follow state and federal laws on the proper method of disposal. Recycling the print cartridge is always recommended.

Example 18.7:

Documents are light or have uneven print.

If the print image becomes faint or uneven, first attempt to change the printer contrast or density control. If this does not help, remove the toner cartridge and shake it so that the toner is distributed more evenly. If this does not correct the problem, replace the toner cartridge. If the cartridge is older than 6 months (the normal shelf life of a typical toner cartridge), it should be replaced. If replacing the toner cartridge does not fix the problem, then check the transfer corona wire and transfer roller, the high-voltage power supply assembly, and the drum ground contacts.

Example 18.8:

The printed documents are completely black.

If the pages coming from the laser printer are completely black, the problem is probably caused by a faulty main corona wire. If the corona wire cannot charge the entire drum, the drum will not hold a negative charge and no matter what image is drawn with the laser light, the toner will be attracted to the entire drum. Consequently, all of the toner will be transferred to the paper, making it completely black. Therefore, examine the corona wire. If it is broken, it will have to be replaced or the toner cartridge will have to be replaced. If the corona wire is dirty, a cleaning with alcohol should correct the problem. (Note: A dirty main corona wire can cause black streaks.)

Example 18.9:

The documents are completely white.

Try replacing the toner cartridge. If this doesn't fix the problem, look at the transfer corona wire. If it is broken or dirty, it will not attract the negatively charged toner from the drum. (Note: A dirty transfer corona wire may cause white streaks.)

Example 18.10:

The image smears on the paper.

If the image on the paper smears or the toner is not permanently fused to the paper, the fusing roller was not hot enough. If the problem occurs randomly—on one page the toner is fused properly, and on another the image smears—first clean the thermistor temperature sensor. If the problem still occurs, replace the thermistor temperature sensor and test it again. If the problem still exists, replace the fusing unit and cleaning pads.

Example 18.11:

Speckles appear on printed documents.

Speckles may be caused by loose toner caught inside the printer. Most of the time these speckles may be removed by running several pages through the printer. If the problem still occurs, try cleaning the corona wire or replacing the toner cartridge.

Example 18.12:

The paper in a laser printer is continuously jamming.

Determine first how far the paper gets before jamming. This will help you isolate the location of the jam. Although the most common area for paper jams is the pickup area, jams may also occur in the fusing area and registration area. Also make sure that the paper is dry. If the problem still occurs, check for worn rollers or for broken or missing teeth on the drive gear of the pickup roller.

Example 18.13:

Your print jobs are not printing or the spooler is overloaded.

If the printer does appear to be printing, make sure that the printer is on and online, connected properly, and that the correct driver is loaded. You also need to make sure that you have sufficient free disk space since this is where the print jobs are being stored on the disk until they are printed.

You can also try to clear the print queue. Besides rebooting the computer for Windows 9X, you can double-click the Printer icon on the Taskbar and, under the Printer menu item, and click *Cancel.* In Windows NT, Windows 2000, or Windows XP, you can achieve the same thing by selecting *Cancel All Documents.*

For a server or XP machine, you will not always be allowed to delete the print job. Locate the Services icon in the Control Panel or Administrative Tools, stop the print spooler, and then delete the print jobs. You can also try restarting the print spooler.

If you find that you keep running out of disk space on Windows NT, Windows 2000, and Windows XP, you can move the print spooler to another drive. This is done as follows:

- Click Start, point to Settings, and then click Printers.
- On the File menu, click Server Properties, and then click the Advanced tab.
- In the Spool folder box, type the path and the name of the new default spool folder for this print server, and then click Close.
- Either restart the spooler service or restart the server.

SUMMARY

1. LPT1 usually uses IRQ 7 and the I/O address 378H; LPT2 (if any) generally uses IRQ 5 and 278H.
2. Most parallel ports are built into the motherboard. Therefore, they are configured using the CMOS setup program.
3. Other parallel ports are usually configured using DIP switches, jumpers, a software configuration program, or they are plug-and-play.
4. The parallel port, sometimes referred to as the printer port, is a female, 2-row, 25-pin D connector. Its primary function is to connect printers.
5. The PC can usually recognize up to three parallel ports.
6. The standard for the parallel port interface is specified in the IEEE 1284 standard.
7. Polling is the most popular method of sending data. The BIOS polls, or checks, to see if the parallel port device is ready to accept another character. Polling allows printer ports to share interrupts.
8. The interrupt method of sending data to the parallel port is efficient but can significantly slow the printing process.
9. Most parallel ports since the 386 processor are bidirectional.
10. The port on the printer (type B) is a 36-pin Centronics connector.

11. A printer is one of the easiest peripheral devices to install. Just connect the printer and load the appropriate drivers.
12. When a parallel port does not function or is unrecognized by the system, the problem can be caused by a resource conflict, a disabled parallel port, an unconnected cable, or a faulty port.
13. If the device is connected to the parallel port, you should also check to see if the proper driver is loaded for the device, the driver is not corrupt, and that the device is not faulty.
14. One tool that can be used to test the parallel port is the parallel loopback plug, similar to a serial loopback plug.
15. The serial port can transfer only 1 bit at a time, whereas the parallel port can transfer 8 bits of data using eight different wires.
16. The first parallel port is the standard parallel port (SPP).
17. Two standards for a faster parallel port are the enhanced parallel port (EPP) and extended capabilities port (ECP), which increase data transfer rates tenfold.
18. EPP achieves higher transfer speeds by moving the handshaking signals from the software to the hardware circuitry on the parallel port.
19. ECP is similar to EPP, but it can also use DMAs and data compression.
20. Ports may need to be configured for EPP or ECP by setting jumpers or DIP switches or by using the BIOS setup program or a configuration program.
21. A printer, the most commonly used output device, prints text or pictures on paper.
22. A page description language describes the whole page to be printed with draw and position commands and mathematical formulas.
23. Paper is usually characterized by its weight, thickness, texture, and finish.
24. Most printheads on dot-matrix printers contain 9 or 24 pins.
25. The ink-jet printer (also known as an ink dispersion printer) works by spraying small droplets of ionized ink onto a sheet of paper. Modern ink-jet printers produce high-quality print (including color printing) that approaches the quality produced by laser printers, yet cost much less.
26. Laser printers, like copy machines, use an electrophoto (EP) process to form images with toner on paper.
27. The EP process has six basic stages: cleaning, conditioning, writing, developing, transferring, and fusing.
28. Thermal printers are inexpensive printers that print by pressing heated pins onto a special heat-sensitive paper.
29. Dye-sublimation printers are printers that use diffusive plastic dye film as the ink element. The printhead heats the colored film and vaporizes the image onto specially coated paper.
30. Today, most printers are connected through the USB or parallel port. Printers can also be connected through SCSI, IEEE 1394, infrared, or wireless. In addition, they can be connected through a network.
31. Solid ink printers are used mostly in the packaging and industrial design industries. They use hardened ink sticks that are melted and sprayed through small nozzles on the printhead.
32. Most printers are simplex printers, which means that they can print on only one side of the paper.
33. A few larger laser printers are duplex printers, which means they have a duplex tray that turns over each sheet of paper so that it can be printed on the other side.
34. Some copy machines can act as print servers and printers, whereas other machines are a combined printer, scanner, and fax.
35. More deluxe printers will have finishing options such as automatic stapling and various sorting methods.
36. As with a PC, the complexity of the graphics that can be printed is partially determined by the amount of RAM the printer has.
37. In Windows, you typically have to specify the amount of RAM a printer has using the printer properties window.
38. Any problem that occurs with printers has one of four sources: the printer (including cartridges and ribbons), the print cable, the parallel or USB (or other interface), and the software (including the drivers).
39. Most printers can perform a self-test that can be initiated by pressing one or more buttons while turning on the printer or by using the printer's control panel. Windows also has a print test.
40. Replacing the ribbon or ink cartridge on a dot-matrix or ink-jet printer may solve a light print problem.
41. If the correct print driver is not loaded, the printed document will usually be garbage.
42. Toner is toxic. Therefore, you should minimize contact with it.
43. Dry toner and empty toner cartridges are not regulated as a hazardous waste and may be disposed as trash.
44. Because the fuser roller is heated to approximately 180°C, it is best to unplug the printer and wait at least 10 minutes so the fusing unit has a chance to cool.
45. The duplex unit, or paper swapping unit, is mechanically complicated and the printer is more likely to jam.
46. As printers have gotten more complex, printers have built-in operating systems stored as firmware to guide the actions of the printers. Occasionally, the firmware may need to be upgraded to fix bugs in the operating system or to close security holes when the printer is used as a network printer.

47. A common problem that occurs in laser printers is the paper jam—a sheet of paper catching or refusing to pass through the printer mechanism. A paper jam may be caused by incorrect paper or damp paper; a wornout roller; or the buildup of paper fragments, toner, or other debris.
48. If a document has light or uneven print, the first two things to check in the dot-matrix printer is the distance between the printhead and platen and the ribbon.
49. Most problems with an ink-jet printer occur because either the cartridge is empty (or low) or the nozzles on the print cartridge are clogged.
50. If the print image is faint or uneven on a laser printer, first adjust the printer contrast or density control. If this does not help, remove the toner cartridge and shake it so that the toner is distributed more evenly. If the printer still does not work, replace the toner cartridge.
51. If the pages coming from the laser printer are completely black, the problem is probably caused by a faulty main corona wire. Most likely you will need to change the toner cartridge.
52. If the image on the paper in a laser printer smears or the toner is not permanently fused to the paper, the fusing roller was not hot enough. First, clean the thermistor temperature sensor. If the problem still occurs, replace the thermistor temperature sensor and test it again. If the problem still exists, replace the fusing unit and cleaning pads.
53. A good preventive maintenance and cleaning program will stop most laser printer problems before they occur and will help ensure that the printer has the highest quality output possible.
54. Print spoolers can easily overflow or become corrupt due to a lack of disk space or too many print jobs, disk errors, power fluctuations, and so on.
55. If the correct print driver is not loaded, the printed document will usually be garbage.
56. If a printer outputs a page and the printer prints only a portion of the page or if the printer gets an overflow error, it is possible to have to increase the memory for your printer or decrease the resolution of your printer.

QUESTIONS

1. The parallel port is described as a
   a. 2-row, 25-pin male D connector.
   b. 2-row, 25-pin female D connector.
   c. 2-row, 9-pin male D connector.
   d. 2-row, 9-pin female D connector.
   e. 2-row, 15-pin female D connector.
2. Which of the following is a printer most likely connected to?
   a. serial port b. parallel port
   c. SCSI port d. keyboard port
   e. video port
3. How many bits does a parallel port send at one time?
   a. 1 b. 4
   c. 8 d. 16
   e. 32
4. Parallel cables use
   a. one wire to transmit data with start and stop bits.
   b. eight wires to transmit data.
   c. eight wires to transmit data with start and stop bits.
   d. two wires to send data.
   e. two wires to send data with start and stop bits.
5. What should the maximum length of a parallel cable be?
   a. 3 ft b. 6–10 ft
   c. 50 ft d. 100 ft
6. What happens if a parallel port is configured as LPT2 but there is no LPT1?
   a. It is used as LPT2.
   b. It is converted to LPT1 during boot-up.
   c. The port will not work.
   d. It is converted to a serial port.
7. What is the standard IRQ for LPT1?
   a. IRQ 2 b. IRQ 3
   c. IRQ 4 d. IRQ 5
   e. IRQ 7
8. What is the standard IRQ for LPT2?
   a. IRQ 2 b. IRQ 3
   c. IRQ 4 d. IRQ 5
   e. IRQ 7
9. If information is to be transferred between two computers using the parallel ports and a lap link (interlink) cable, which type of parallel port(s) does the computer need to have (choose all that apply)?
   a. standard b. bidirectional
   c. EPP d. ECP
10. The connector found on a printer is usually the
    a. female 25-pin, 2-row D connector.
    b. male 25-pin, 2-row D connector.
    c. male 36-pin, 2-row D connector.
    d. 36-pin Centronics connector.
11. Which of the following is an output device?
    a. printer b. modem
    c. mouse d. touch screen
12. Two popular page description languages are
    a. Raster. b. PostScript.
    c. Vector. d. PCL.
    e. QBASIC.

13. When printing with a paper that has a surface other than that specified by the laser printer manufacturer, what is likely to happen?
    a. broken or missing parts of letters
    b. the top of each letter missing
    c. a faded appearance on the characters
    d. an outlined appearance of the uppercase letters
14. How is paper weight determined?
    a. the weight in pounds of an 8½ × 11-in. single sheet of paper.
    b. the weight in pounds of 1,000 sheets of 8½ × 11-in. paper.
    c. the weight in pounds of 500 sheets of 8½ × 11-in. paper.
    d. the weight in pounds of 500 sheets of 17 × 22½-in. paper.
    e. the weight in pounds of 1,000 sheets of 17 × 22½-in. paper.
15. Using paper with a surface roughness greater than the specifications of a laser printer manufacturer will
    a. result in excess wear of paper path components.
    b. void the printer's warranty.
    c. cause the laser to concentrate, decreasing the image size.
    d. cause paper jams at the start of each print cycle.
16. In reference to types of paper, the term *finish* means
    a. the texture or smoothness of both surfaces of the paper.
    b. the quality of the edges of the paper.
    c. the texture or smoothness of the front surface of the paper.
    d. the distortion properties of the material used to make the paper.
17. What product must be used to clean rubber rollers on a printer?
    a. denatured alcohol
    b. 409 all-purpose cleaner
    c. soap and water
    d. glass cleaner
18. Dot-matrix printers have how many pins in their printhead (select two)?
    a. 5
    b. 9
    c. 16
    d. 24
    e. 32
19. What activates the print wire in a dot-matrix printer?
    a. power is applied to an electromagnet, forcing the print wire away from a permanent magnet in the printhead
    b. a spring is released
    c. power is removed from an electromagnet, forcing the print wire forward by means of a spring
    d. the polarity of an electromagnet in the printhead is reversed, moving the print wire forward
    e. a motor pushes the print wire forward
20. Which of the following should *not* be lubricated on a dot-matrix printer (choose two answers)?
    a. printhead guide rail
    b. platen assembly
    c. paper-feed gears
    d. paper advance motor
    e. printhead pins
21. When a dot-matrix printer produces light or uneven print, what are the first two things that should be checked?
    a. the distance between the printthead and platen
    b. the ribbon
    c. the printer cable
    d. power fluctuations
    e. the carriage assembly
22. Which of the following solutions should be tried first to fix light or uneven print on an ink-jet printer?
    a. adjusting the paper-feed assembly
    b. using a paper that will absorb more ink
    c. replacing the print cartridge
    d. adjusting the printhead closer to the paper
23. Which type(s) of printers can be used with multipart forms (choose all that apply)?
    a. dot-matrix printers
    b. ink-jet printers
    c. laser printers
    d. thermal printers
24. Why should ink cartridges in an ink-jet printer be replaced rather than refilled?
    a. The new nozzles on the ink cartridge print a sharper image
    b. Refilling cartridges may void the warranty
    c. The ink may not be compatible with the paper
    d. The ink may not be compatible with the printer
    e. The nozzles may become corroded.
25. What happens if the paper is too absorbent when printing with an ink-jet printer?
    a. The ink has a tendency to smear.
    b. The ink will fade.
    c. The ink will bleed, causing a blurry image.
    d. The ink will dry too quickly.
26. In laser printing, what occurs after the conditioning phase?
    a. the writing phase
    b. the fusing phase
    c. the cleaning phase
    e. the transferring phase
27. In laser printing, what occurs after the fusing phase?
    a. the writing phase
    b. the conditioning phase
    c. the developing phase
    d. the cleaning phase
    e. the transferring phase
28. In laser printing, what occurs after the developing phase?

a. the writing phase
b. the fusing phase
c. the conditioning phase
d. the cleaning phase
e. the transferring phase

29. In laser printing, what occurs during the developing phase?
a. light is used to discharge an image on the drum
b. toner is attracted to the drum
c. toner is attracted to the paper
d. toner is fixed to the paper

30. In laser printing, what occurs during the cleaning phase (choose two)?
a. leftover toner is removed from the drum
b. a uniform negative charge is applied to the drum
c. light is used to discharge an image on the drum
d. toner is attracted to the drum
e. the drum is reheated

31. The function of the corona wire in a laser printer is to
a. apply a strong negative charge on the print media to attract toner.
b. apply a strong positive charge on the print media to attract toner.
c. apply a uniform negative charge to the photosensitive drum.
d. apply a uniform positive charge to the photosensitive drum.
e. negate the charge on the photosensitive drum.

32. Which of the following charges the paper with a uniform positive charge?
a. primary corona
b. laser
c. fuser
d. pressure roller
e. transfer corona or transfer roller

33. The fuser assembly in a laser printer performs which of the following functions?
a. presses toner particles into the print media using high-pitched sounds
b. eliminates static electricity from the photosensitive drum
c. places a positive charge on the print media to attract the toner
d. presses toner particles into the print media while melting them

34. Which of the following is found in most laser toner cartridges?
a. a drum, developing roller, corona wire, and scraper blade
b. a drum, transfer roller, fusing roller, and transfer corona wire
c. a main corona wire, transfer corona wire, drum, and pressure roller
d. a fusing roller, drum, charging roller, and wiper blade

35. Which of the following should be part of any preventive maintenance routine for laser printers (choose two)?
a. vacuuming the ozone filter
b. adjusting the paper tray
c. cleaning the fuser
d. replacing the feed assembly

36. After cleaning a laser printer, the pages are speckled. How can this be corrected?
a. by running several blank pages through the printer
b. by installing another toner cartridge
c. by cleaning the printhead
d. by resetting the printer

37. If, after a paper jam is cleared from the tray in a laser printer, the printer still indicates a jam, what should be done?
a. Run the self-test.
b. Turn off the printer to let it cool and then turn it on after approximately 10 minutes.
c. Look for another jam in the paper tray.
d. Open and close the top cover.

38. Which of the following may cause light print from a laser printer (choose two)?
a. rotating mirrors
b. the control board
c. the transfer corona
d. the fuser unit
e. the toner cartridge

39. Which of the following is the best way to remove toner?
a. hot water
b. denatured alcohol
c. compressed air
d. vacuuming

40. Which part of the laser printer should *not* be exposed to sunlight?
a. the transfer corona assembly
b. the toner cartridge
c. the PC drum
d. the transfer corona wire

41. To prevent toner from sticking to a laser printer's heat rollers, the cleaning pads apply which of the following?
a. alcohol
b. oil
c. ammonia
d. water

42. You are trying to determine why a printer cannot print. After checking the cable connections and making sure the printer is on and online, you decide to perform the printer's self-test. If the self-test works, which of the following is most likely the problem (choose two answers)?
a. a bad toner cartridge
b. an incorrectly inserted toner cartridge
c. the cable
d. the printer interface

43. The laser printer is on and the fan is running, but it won't print. What is the first thing to check?
a. that the printer is online
b. that all the cables are connected properly
c. that the correct print driver is loaded
d. that the printer has paper
e. that the printer is not jammed

44. When trying to fix a paper jam, you should
    a. note where in the paper path the paper stops.
    b. check all voltages.
    c. turn the printer off, then on again.
    d. run a test page.
    e. remove the paper jam.
45. Which part of the printer is hot and can cause burns?
    a. the fuser
    b. the platen
    c. the ribbon carriage
    d. the dot-matrix printhead
    e. the ink-jet cartridge
46. An HP LaserJet IV printer isn't printing at all. The computer indicates that the "device on LPT1 isn't ready." Therefore, you decide to do a printer self-test. The front panel test is unsuccessful, but the test print is successful. Which component do you suspect is causing the problem?
    a. the printer is not online
    b. the fuser
    c. the power supply
    d. the coronoa wire
    e. the formatter
47. After using a new laser printer for only 2 months, ghost images of previously printed documents appear on the new printouts. What will usually solve this problem?
    a. changing the transfer roller
    b. replacing the toner cartridge
    c. changing the fuser
    d. refilling the toner cartridge
48. What is the standard for a bidirectional parallel cable?
    a. RJ-45
    b. RS-232C
    c. LTP1
    d. IEEE 1284
49. A user has noticed faint and fuzzy white lines running vertically down the printed pages of a laser printer. You inspect the laser printer and find clumps of toner and paper fragments on the corona. What should you use to clean the corona's surface?
    a. vacuum
    b. lint-free swab
    c. hard coarse brush
    d. pencil eraser
    e. damp, soapy cloth
    f. knife or flat screwdriver
50. Which component is responsible for controlling the laser printer functions?
    a. laser
    b. fuser roller
    c. formatter board
    d. transfer corona wire
    e. primary grid
    f. toner cartridge
    g. primary corona wire

HANDS-ON EXERCISES

Exercise 1: Configuring and Testing a Parallel Port

1. Disable the parallel port using jumpers, DIP switches, configuring software, or the BIOS setup program.
2. Configure the parallel port as LPT1 (IRQ 7 and I/O address 378H).
3. Boot the computer and perform the MODE command at the prompt.
4. Using the MSD program, find the I/O address and IRQ of LPT1.
5. Connect a loopback plug to a parallel port.
6. Using a software diagnostic package, test the parallel port. (Note: You may need to tell the software diagnostic package that you have a loopback plug.)
7. Determine whether your printer supports ECP or EPP using jumpers, DIP switches, configuring software, or the BIOS setup program.

Exercise 2: Installing a Printer

1. Plug the power cable into the printer and the ac wall outlet.
2. Connect a printer cable from the parallel port to the printer.
3. Turn on the printer.
4. Turn on the computer and boot Windows.
5. Load the appropriate print driver and make it the default printer. For Windows use the Add Printer icon (in the PRINTERS folder in My Computer).
6. Using Microsoft Word, WordPad, or Microsoft Write, create a document that uses at least three different fonts at two different sizes and includes at least one boldface word and one italic word.
7. Print the document to the printer using the Print option under the File menu. Make sure that the proper driver has been selected.
8. Install a second driver as designated by your instructor.
9. Using Microsoft Word, WordPad, or Microsoft Write, print the same document but use the second driver.
10. By using the printer's control panel, take the printer offline.
11. Print the document at least three more times with the correct driver.

12. Switch over to the print manager or print spooler to see the print jobs waiting for the printer to come back online. (For Windows the print manager or print spooler can be accessed by double-clicking on the small printer icon in the taskbar or by double-clicking on the printer driver in the PRINTERS folder.)
13. Delete the last two print jobs.
14. By using the printer's control panel, put the printer back online and let the print job print.
15. Reboot the computer to DOS or another command prompt.
16. Send the AUTOEXEC.BAT (or another text file) to the printer. (Note: For laser printers, you usually need to perform a form feed after the text file has been sent to the printer.)
17. Delete the print driver and disconnect the printer.

Exercise 3: Taking Apart a Dot-Matrix Printer

1. Remove the ribbon cartridge and paper.
2. Identify the printhead, tension knob on the ribbon cartridge, guide rails, platen, and timing belt.
3. Reinstall the ribbon cartridge and the paper.
4. Turn on the dot-matrix printer and perform a self-test.
5. Using the control panel, take the printer offline.
6. Using the control panel, put the printer online.
7. Perform a line feed and a form feed.
8. Increase the distance between the platen and the printhead and perform another self-test.
9. Change the distance between the platen and the printhead back to the way it was.
10. Remove the ribbon cartridge and paper.
11. Remove the printhead.
12. Take off the top part of the printer so that you can see inside.
13. Identify the power supply, power supply fuse, printhead positioning motor, paper-feed motor, and the main control board.
14. Reassemble the printer.
15. Perform another self-test.

Exercise 4: Taking Apart an Ink-Jet Printer

1. Turn on the ink-jet printer and perform a self-test.
2. Perform a self-cleaning on the ink-jet printer.
3. Identify the print cartridge or print cartridges, guide rails, platen, timing belt, and drive assembly.
4. Take off the top part of the printer so that you can see inside. Don't remove the ink cartridge unless the ink cartridge is out of ink.
5. Identify the power supply, power supply fuse, printhead positioning motor, paper-feed motor, and the main control board.
6. Reassemble the printer.
7. Perform another self-test.

Exercise 5: Taking Apart a Laser Printer

1. Remove the toner cartridge and the paper.
2. Reinstall the toner cartridge and the paper.
3. Turn on the laser printer and perform a self-test.
4. Using the control panel, take the printer offline.
5. Using the control panel, put the printer online.
6. Using the control panel, perform a form feed.
7. Remove the toner cartridge and the paper tray.
8. Locate and open the compartment that has the RAM for the printer.
9. Identify the corona wires, the fuser assembly, and the cleaning pads. (Note: These are usually found in the toner cartridge.)
10. Locate and identify the ozone filter (some ozone filters are part of the toner cartridge), the power supply and power supply fuse (if any), and the fuser and pressure roller.
11. Reassemble the printer and install the toner cartridge and the paper.
12. Perform a self-test. During the self-test, turn off the printer while it is printing but before the paper comes out of the printer.
13. Remove the paper jam.
14. Perform another self-test.

CHAPTER 19

The DOS Interface

Topics Covered in This Chapter

Introduction

MS-DOS stands for Microsoft Disk Operating System. It was the first operating system used on the original IBM PC. Because the IBM PC became the de facto standard for personal computers, DOS became the de facto standard for operating systems. The introduction of new operating systems (Windows 95 and 98 and Windows NT) has replaced DOS. But DOS and the DOS interface are still used to troubleshoot and fix many problems in Windows.

Objectives

1. List the DOS boot files in order of boot-up and define their function.
2. Differentiate between internal DOS commands and external DOS commands.
3. Determine which command to use under a given situation and to perform the common DOS commands (CD, CLS, COPY, DATE, DEL, DIR, MD, PATH, PROMPT, RD, REN, SET, TIME, TYPE, VER, VOL, ATTRIB, CHKDSK, DELTREE, DISKCOPY, EDIT, FDISK, HELP, FORMAT, LABEL, MEM, MOVE, MORE, SYS, TREE, UNDELETE, UNFORMAT, and XCOPY).
4. Given a file or subdirectory and its location, state the path of the file or directory.
5. Define *batch file* and then list and define the commands used in a batch file.
6. Create a batch file.
7. Create an AUTOEXEC.BAT file with the appropriate commands including the PATH, PROMPT, and SET commands.
8. Create a CONFIG.SYS file.
9. List and define the commands used in the CONFIG.SYS file.
10. Load the appropriate commands to enable the necessary memory areas.
11. Given a problem during boot-up, determine and correct the problem.

19.1 ACCESSING THE COMMAND PROMPT

DOS was a command-driven operating system, which means that all of the commands must be typed in the correct way (spelling and syntax). Compared to other operating systems, DOS was small and very simple—so small, in fact, that it can be booted from a floppy disk.

While DOS is considered a dead operating system, you can perform certain troubleshooting and administrative tasks by either booting using a Windows boot disk or boot Windows to a command prompt interface. In addition, you can open a command window while running Windows by clicking the Start button, selecting Accessories, and selecting Command Prompt. You can also open the same command prompt window by clicking on the Start button, selecting the Run option, and executing the CMD command in Windows NT, Windows 2000, or Windows XP, or by executing the `COMMAND.COM` command in Windows 9X or Windows XP. CMD.EXE is a 32-bit command prompt that supports long file names natively and a host of other tricks such as typing a partial file name in Windows XP and hitting the Tab key to auto complete. COMMAND.COM is a 16-bit shell that can overcome some problems running DOS programs.

To make a Windows boot disk, you would start Windows 9X, open the Control Panel, double-click the Add/Remove Software applet, and select the Startup Disk tab. The Windows 9X disks includes basic DOS commands and drivers to activate standard IDE or SCSI CD-ROM drivers, which can come in handy when you have a system that does not contain a bootable CD drive. Note: When you are booting from the Windows 9X boot disk, a startup menu will appear, which gives you the option to boot with and without CD support.

Windows XP does have an option to create a bootable disk, but the disk does not contain any DOS files or drivers. To create this disk, you would open My Computer, right-click the A drive, and select the Format option. Note: You must have a floppy in the disk drive. You then select the Create an MS-DOS startup disk option and perform a format on the A drive.

When you use these disks, you simply place the disk in the A drive and turn on the system. This is assuming that the BIOS program has been configured to boot first from the floppy drive. After booting the system, you should note that you will only be able to access FAT and FAT32 drives. If your system has NTFS or any other type of partition, those drives are ignored and are not assigned drive letters. Of course, the exception for this is when you use the FDISK to partition drives where you can delete the partition.

19.2 THE BOOT PROCESS

No matter which operating system is installed on a computer, when the computer is first turned on, the processor starts in real mode (pretends to be an 8086 processor). After the system does its POST, it searches for a disk from which to boot. If it is booting from a DOS boot disk, it finds, reads, and loads the following files:

1. IO.SYS
2. MSDOS.SYS
3. CONFIG.SYS
4. COMMAND.COM
5. AUTOEXEC.BAT

To be read during boot-up, these files must be in the root directory of the disk from which the computer is being booted. Of these five files, only IO.SYS, MSDOS.SYS, and COMMAND.COM are needed for boot-up. The CONFIG.SYS and AUTOEXEC.BAT files are important configuration files that are usually needed to run most common applications.

Both IO.SYS and MSDOS.SYS are hidden (normally cannot be seen), read-only (normally cannot be deleted or changed) system files (files used by the operating system). For the disk to boot, IO.SYS must be the first directory entry in the root directory and MSDOS must be the second entry. In addition, IO.SYS must be the first physical file on the volume boot sector.

The IO.SYS file is the real-mode configuration manager and operating system. The file contains enough information to start the computer, read the file system (FAT or FAT32), and automatically load several files and commands that are specified in the CONFIG.SYS and AUTOEXEC.BAT files.

The first configuration file processed by the IO.SYS file is the MSDOS.SYS file. Unlike the DOS MSDOS.SYS file, this is a text file that specifies the location of the necessary boot files, the location of the Registry (configuration database), and several startup options. In addition to holding important configuration information, the MSDOS.SYS file is needed to provide backward compatibility with older software programs, as are the CONFIG.SYS, COMMAND.COM, and AUTOEXEC.BAT files, which provide backward compatibility for DOS drivers and applications. These files are used to load a DOS device driver (a file with a SYS file name extension loaded in the CONFIG.SYS) and a TSR (an executable file loaded in the AUTOEXEC.BAT). Note: TSR is short for Terminate and Stay Resident.

If IO.SYS is corrupt or missing, a "Nonsystem Disk or Disk Error" or similar error message will usually appear. A "No Room for System on Destination Disk" error message appearing when attempting to create a bootable disk using the SYS command (or some other method) means there is not enough disk space to hold IO.SYS or MSDOS.SYS or that IO.SYS or MSDOS.SYS can't be placed properly in the root directory or the volume boot sector.

COMMAND.COM, the command interpreter and command processor, is the user's interface to the command prompt interface. It reads commands that are executed at the keyboard and determines whether to execute them or to find the additional files to execute. It also contains many of the internal commands, like DIR, CD, VER, and COPY. Unlike the other boot files, COMMAND.COM is partly permanent and partly transient, which means that part of it can be removed from RAM to make room for something else and reloaded when needed. If COMMAND.COM is missing or corrupted, a "Bad or Missing Command Interpreter" error message usually appears.

The CONFIG.SYS and AUTOEXEC.BAT files are text files that can be changed with a text editor, like EDIT or Windows Notepad, or with a word processor if the file is first saved as a pure text file with no format codes. The CONFIG.SYS file is read three times during boot-up, executing certain commands each time that activate or manage the different memory areas and load device drivers. The AUTOEXEC.BAT file is a special batch file that can execute any command entered at the prompt. It typically loads TSRs and configures the command prompt environment.

19.3 DOS COMMANDS AND FILE NAMES

All DOS commands can be divided into two categories, internal DOS commands and external DOS commands. The instructions for the **internal DOS commands** are kept in the COMMAND.COM file loaded in the RAM. See table 19.1. Therefore, if booting to a prompt, any of the internal DOS commands can be executed. **External DOS commands** are commands for which instructions are not kept in the COMMAND.COM file. See table 19.2. Therefore, when executing these commands, DOS must search for a file with either a COM or EXE extension that contains the additional instructions. If the computer cannot find the file that has the instructions for the external DOS command, a "Bad Command or Filename" error message will appear.

Using most DOS commands requires an understanding of how to specify the path or location of a file or directory, a necessary skill because DOS assumes very little and must be told exactly what to do. To identify the location of a particular file or directory on a disk, start by designating the drive, followed by the root directory. Then each directory that leads to the file must be listed, followed by the file name and extension.

Example 19.1:

In figure 19.1, the path of the COMMAND.COM file is C:\COMMAND.COM. The path of the README.TXT file is C:\DOS\README.TXT. The path of the DOS directory is C:\DOS.

Table 19.1 Common Internal DOS Commands

Command	Description
CD (or CHDIR)	Displays the name of the current directory or changes the current directory.
CLS	Clears the screen, leaving the command prompt and cursor at the top left corner of the screen.
COPY	Copies one or more files to the location the user specifies. The COPY command will not copy hidden or system files.
DATE	Displays the date and prompts the user to change the date.
DEL (or ERASE)	Deletes the files specified.
DIR	Displays a list of the files and subdirectories that are in the directory specified. DIR is probably the most commonly used DOS command.
MD (or MKDIR)	Creates a directory.
PATH	Indicates which directories MS-DOS should search to execute executable files (files with a COM, EXE, or BAT file name extension).
PROMPT	Changes the appearance of the command prompt.
RD (or RMDIR)	Deletes an empty directory.
REN (or RENAME)	Changes the name of the file or files specified.
SET	Displays, sets, or removes MS-DOS environment variables.
TIME	Displays the system time or sets the computer's internal clock.
TYPE	Displays the contents of a text file.
VER	Displays the MS-DOS version number.
VOL	Displays the disk volume label and serial number (if the disk has them).

Table 19.2 Common External DOS Commands

Command	Description
ATTRIB	Displays or changes file and directory attributes.
CHKDSK	Checks the status of a disk and displays a status report. It can also fix disk errors.
DELTREE	Deletes a directory and all files and subdirectories that are in it. This command is available in DOS 6.0 and later.
DISKCOPY	Copies the entire contents of one floppy disk to another floppy disk. Since DISKCOPY performs a sector-by-sector copy, it overwrites the existing contents of the destination disk.
EDIT	Starts MS-DOS Editor, a text editor that can create and edit ASCII text files.
FDISK	Starts the Fix Disk program, which creates and deletes partitions on a hard drive.
HELP	Starts MS-DOS Help.
FORMAT	Creates a new root directory and file allocation table for the disk. It can also check for bad areas on the disk, delete all data on the disk, and make a disk bootable. All disks must be formatted to be used.
LABEL	Creates, changes, or deletes the volume label of a disk.
MEM	Displays the amount of used and free memory (RAM) on the computer.
MOVE	Moves one or more files to the location specified. The MOVE command can also be used to rename directories.
MORE	Displays one screen of output at a time. It is often used with the TREE and MEM commands.
SYS	Makes a disk bootable by copying IO.SYS, MSDOS.SYS, and COMMAND.COM to the disk without reformatting it.
TREE	Graphically displays the structure of a directory.
UNDELETE	Restores files that were previously deleted by using the DEL or ERASE command.
UNFORMAT	Restores a disk that was erased by using the FORMAT command as long as it wasn't unconditionally formatted.
XCOPY	Copies directories, their subdirectories, and files (except hidden and system files).

Unlike today's newer operating systems, DOS can use only eight characters for a file name and three characters for a file name extension. The file name extension usually identifies the type of file. For example, files with a COM, EXE, or BAT extension are executable files, while files with the DOC extension are Microsoft Word files and files with the GIF extension are graphics files. In DOS, certain characters are reserved and can't be used for file names and file name extensions. For example, the period (.) is used to divide the file name and file name extension, the backward slash (\) is used for dividing directories and file names, and the * is a wild-card character. The characters that can't be used in DOS file names are: + = / [ ] “ : ; , ? * \ < > ¦. In addition, spaces and ASCII control characters cannot be used.

Wild-card characters (* and ?) are used to specify groups of files. The asterisk (*) means any string of characters and the question mark (?) means any single character. For example, to specify all files that have a COM file name extension, you would use *.COM. To specify all files whose file name begins with MS, you would use MS*.*. To specify a file name that is four characters in length and ends in DOS, you would use ?DOS.*.

19.4 COMMANDS THAT EVERY PC TECHNICIAN SHOULD KNOW

No matter which operating system you are working on (DOS or Windows), there are certain DOS commands that you should know. If the GUI cannot boot for some reason, you will often need to fix the problem by booting with a bootable floppy disk and performing commands at the prompt.

When performing DOS commands, there is always confusion about when to use the backslash (\) and the forward slash (/). The backslash is always used to designate a location while the forward slash is used to designate a switch (nothing to do with location). Note that the backward slash is always the

Figure 19.1 Sample of a Disk Structure

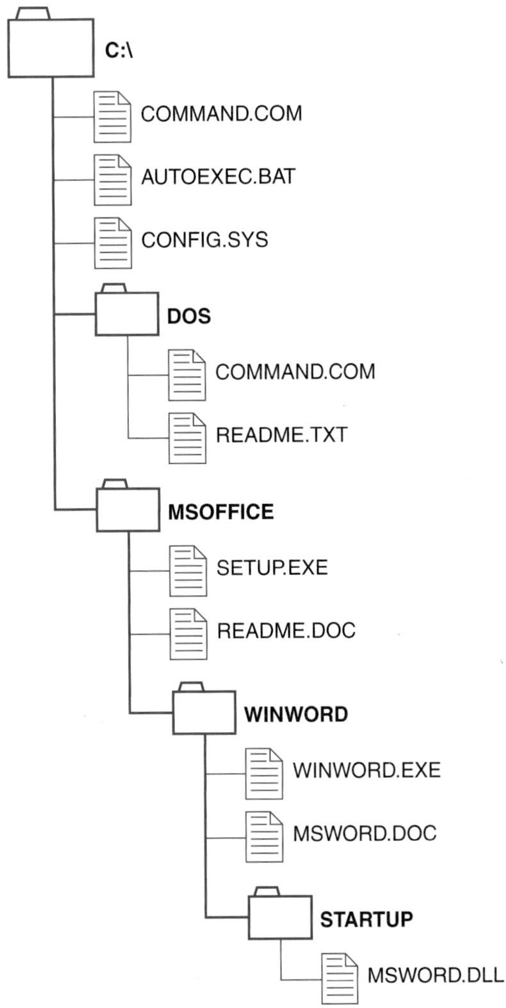

same as the backslash in the prompt shown on the screen. This is because the prompt is showing the current drive and directory (location). For example:

FORMAT A: /S	Makes a disk bootable (switch)
CD\DOS	Changes the current directory (location)
COPY C:\DOS\FORMAT.COM A:\DOS	Copy files from one location to another
XCOPY C:\DATA*.* C:\DOS /S	Copy files from one location to another, but also include subdirectories (switch)

NOTE: While DOS does not need a space before the forward slash, some programs that are executed at the command prompt do. Therefore, it is best to use the space.

Another point that should be made is that most commands have a help feature explaining what the command does and what parameters are available for the command. This can be accessed by typing the following:

```
command /?
```

19.4.1 The VER Command

To see the version of the OS that you are running, you would use the VER command. See figure 19.2. By knowing the version of the OS, you can determine its capabilities.

Figure 19.2 The VER Command

```
C:\>ver

Windows 98[Version 4.10.2222]
```

Figure 19.3 The DIR Command

```
C:\>dir

Volume in drive D has no label
Volume Serial Number is 1CE8-1C7A
Directory of C:\

DOS                 <DIR>                 06-10-98    7:32p
WINDOWS             <DIR>                 06-10-98    7:32p
COMMAND    COM               93,812       08-24-96   11:11a
CONFIG     SYS                   91       06-06-98   11:03a
AUTOEXEC   BAT                  183       06-06-98   10:44a
DATA                <DIR>                 06-10-98    7:33p
3 file(s)                    94,086 bytes
3 dir(s)               179,634, 176 bytes free
```

19.4.2 The DIR and CD Commands

The DIR command, which displays a list of the files and subdirectories, is probably the most commonly used DOS command. See figure 19.3. When the DIR command is used without any parameters or switches, it displays the following:

1. The disk's volume label and serial number
2. The file name or directory name and the extension
3. The date and time the file was created or last modified and the data and time when a directory was made
4. The file size in bytes
5. The total number of files listed, their cumulative size, and the free space in bytes remaining on the disk

The DIR command has many switches. Some of the more common ones used by a technician are shown in table 19.3. Many of the DIR command switches can be combined.

Example 19.2:

To show all files one screen at a time, perform the following command:

```
DIR /P
```

To show all files in alphabetical order, one screen at a time, perform the following command:

```
DIR /ON/P
```

To show the hidden files in the current directory, perform the following command:

```
DIR /AH
```

To show all files that have a GIF file name extension, perform the following command:

```
DIR *.GIF
```

To change the current drive, you would type in the drive letter followed by a colon (:) and press the Enter key. To change the current directory, you would use the CD command. To go up to the root directory you would specify the backslash (\); to go up to the parent directory (up one directory) you would specify the double dot (..).

Table 19.3 Helpful DIR Command Switches

Switch	Description
/P	Displays one screen of the DIR listing at a time. This comes in handy when there are too many files to be shown on the screen at once.
/W	Displays the listing in wide format (five columns). This comes in handy when there are too many files to be shown on the screen at once. It does not show the dates, times, and byte size of the files. Note: Directories are indicated with brackets [ ].
/ON	O stands for order; N stands for name.Therefore, when this switch is used with the DIR command, the files will be listed in alphabetical order by file name. This comes in handy when looking for a certain file.
/AH	A stands for attribute; H stands for hidden. Therefore, when this switch is used with the DIR command, it will show all hidden files. This comes in handy when verifying the boot files on a disk.
/AD	A stands for attribute; D stands for directories. This command shows directories only.
/S	S stands for subdirectory. Therefore, when used, it will list every occurrence in the specified directory and all subdirectories. It comes in handy when looking for the location of a certain file or when trying to get the total byte size of a directory (including all subdirectories and files within the directory).

Example 19.3:

To change to the TEST directory, which is located under the directory that you are currently in, perform the following command:

```
CD TEST
```

To change to the root directory no matter how many directories deep you are, perform the following command:

```
CD\
```

To change to the parent directory (one directory up), perform the following command:

```
CD..
```

To change to the SYSTEM directory under the WINDOWS directory (located off the root directory) no matter what directory you are in, use the following command:

```
CD\WINDOWS\SYSTEM
```

The TREE command graphically displays the structure of a directory.

Example 19.4:

If you are in the root directory of the disk and perform the TREE command, it will show every directory on the disk:

```
TREE
```

If you also wish to show the files in the directory, add a /F (files) switch:

```
TREE /F ¦MORE
```

The ¦MORE pauses the TREE command one screen at a time. (Note: The ¦ is called a *pipe.*)

19.4.3 The MD, RD, and DEL/ERASE Commands

The MD command is used to create directories, the RD command is used to delete empty subdirectories. DELTREE can delete files and directories (including those that have files and subdirectories) and files and directories that are hidden, system, and read-only. (Note: DELTREE is available only in DOS 6.0 and above.)

Example 19.5:

To create a TEST directory, type in the following command:

```
MD TEST
```

If the TEST directory is empty (no files or subdirectories), you would then use the following command to delete it:

```
RD TEST
```

To delete a file called TEST.TXT, you would use the following command:

```
DEL TEST.TXT
```

To delete all files in the current directory, you would use the following command:

```
DEL *.*
```

To delete a TEST directory that has files or other subdirectories in it, you would perform the following command at the prompt:

```
DELTREE TEST
```

19.4.4 The Copy Commands (COPY, DISKCOPY, and XCOPY)

The three primary copy commands used in DOS are COPY, DISKCOPY, and XCOPY. All of these commands have the same three parts: command, source, and target. The source is what is being copied and the target is the location where the copy is going.

The COPY command makes an exact duplicate of the file or files specified. It will not copy hidden or system files.

Example 19.6:

To make a copy of the RESUME.DOC file and call the copy JOB.DOC, use:

```
COPY RESUME.DOC JOB.DOC
```

To copy the AUTOEXEC.BAT file (located in the current directory) to the A drive, you would perform the following command at the prompt:

```
COPY AUTOEXEC.BAT A:
```

To copy the README.TXT file located in the C:\DOS directory to the A:\DOS directory while you are in another directory, you would type:

```
COPY C:\DOS\README.TXT A:\DOS
```

The command is COPY, the source is C:\DOS\README.TXT, and the target is A:\DOS. To copy the README.TXT file located in the C:\DOS directory to the A:\DOS directory while you are in another directory and to name the copy INFO.TXT, you would type:

```
COPY C:\README.TXT A:\DOS\INFO.TXT
```

Notice that all the examples have three parts divided by single spaces.

The XCOPY command, like the COPY command, copies only the files specified and will not copy hidden or system files. The main difference between the commands is that if a /S is used with XCOPY, the command will also copy all the subdirectories that have files in them. If /E is used with the /S, it will copy the empty subdirectories.

Example 19.7:

To copy the data directory from the current directory to the F drive and all files and subdirectories (including empty subdirectories) in the current directory, you would use:

```
XCOPY *.* F: /S /E
```

To make an exact duplicate of a floppy disk, you would use the DISKCOPY command. Since the DISKCOPY command performs a sector-by-sector copy, the source disk and the target disk must be the same size and density. For example, to make a copy of DOS installation disk #1 (on a DS/HD 3½-in. 1.44 MB disk), you would need another DS/HD 3½-in. 1.44 MB disk. Because the DISKCOPY command does a sector-by-sector copy to the destination disk, any previous information on the destination disk will be lost. (Note: DISKCOPY is the only copy command that gives you the opportunity to switch disks back and forth when the same drive is the source and the target.) But because it does a sector-by-sector copy, it will copy directories, system files, and read-only files.

Example 19.8:

To make an exact duplicate of a disk using the A drive, you would perform the following command at the prompt:

```
DISKCOPY A: A:
```

The REN and MOVE commands are similar to the COPY command, yet they are not copy commands. The REN command allows you to rename a file, and the MOVE command allows you to move a file from one location to another or to rename a directory. Unlike the COPY command, which produces two files (the source and the target), the REN and MOVE commands leave only one.

Example 19.9:

To rename the README.TXT file to the INFO.TXT file, you would perform the following command:

```
REN README.TXT INFO.TXT
```

To move the README.TXT file (located in the C:\DOS directory) to the root directory of the C drive, you would perform the following command:

```
MOVE C:\DOS\README.TXT C:\
```

To rename the TEST directory to JOB directory:

```
MOVE TEST JOB
```

19.4.5 The FORMAT and SYS Commands

The FORMAT command is used to prepare a disk for use or to erase everything on a disk. It creates the root directory (starting point on the disk) and the file allocation table (an index of files and directories on the disk and their location). In addition, if the /S parameter is used, it also makes the disk bootable. To perform an unconditional format when the disk can't be unformatted or if there have been read and write errors, you would use the /U switch.

Example 19.10:

To format the D drive, perform the following command:

```
FORMAT D:
```

To make a bootable floppy disk using drive A (Windows 9X only) perform the following command:

```
FORMAT A: /S
```

To perform an unconditional format (Windows 9X only) on the floppy and make the disk bootable using drive A, perform the following command:

```
FORMAT A: /S /U
```

To format a DS/DD 3½-in. floppy disk in a DS/HD 3½-in. floppy drive using drive B, perform either of the following commands:

```
FORMAT B: /F:720
```

When looking at the FORMAT command used in Windows NT, Windows 2000, and Windows XP, the FORMAT command has many of the same options that were available in the FORMAT command in Windows 9X, yet it also has many other options where you can specify the file system used and the size of the allocation unit. For example, if you are formatting the E drive and you are formatting the drive as an NTFS file system and you want to specify 2,048 byte allocation units, you would use the following command:

```
format e: /fs:NTFS /a:2048
```

For other options that are available in Windows NT, Windows 2000, and Windows XP, you should use:

```
format /?
```

To make a disk bootable without reformatting it, use the SYS command in Windows 9X. This will copy the IO.SYS, MSDOS.SYS, and COMMAND.COM files and place them in the correct place, assuming that there is enough room for them to fit on the disk.

Example 19.11:

To make an important software diagnostic disk bootable using drive A, you would perform the following command (assuming you are not in the A drive):

```
SYS A:
```

Example 19.12:

When you try to format your hard disk, you may receive the following error message:

```
Insufficient memory to load system files.
Format terminated.
```

This problem can occur if either of the following conditions exists:

1. You attempt to format your hard disk using the FORMAT C: /Q/U/S/V command at a command prompt, and there is not enough free conventional memory to use the /S parameter (switch).
2. You start your computer using the Windows Startup disk and then attempt to format your hard disk.

To work around this, format the disk without the /S option. After the format is complete, transfer the system files to the hard disk using the SYS C: command.

19.4.6 The ATTRIB Command

The ATTRIB command displays, sets, or removes the read-only (R), archive (A), system (S), and hidden (H) attributes assigned to a file or directory. (For more information on attributes, see chapter 12.) The archive attribute indicates whether a file has been backed up or not. To turn on an attribute, you use a plus sign (+), and to turn off an attribute, you use a minus sign (−).

Example 19.13:

To show all files and their attributes, you would perform the following command:

```
ATTRIB
```

To make the AUTOEXEC.BAT file read-only, you would perform either of the following commands:

```
ATTRIB +R AUTOEXEC.BAT or ATTRIB AUTOEXEC.BAT +R (only on
recent versions of DOS)
```

To turn off the read-only, system, and hidden attributes of the BOOT.INI file, you would perform the following command at the prompt. Note that you must include spaces between each of the attributes.

```
ATTRIB -R -S -H BOOT.INI.
```

Question:

What happens if you try to delete a file that is read-only?

Answer:

If you try to delete a file that is read-only with the DEL command, DOS will respond with the "Access Denied" error message. DELTREE, on the other hand, can delete read-only files. In addition, if you are using File Manager (Windows 3.XX) or Explorer (Windows 95 and 98 or Windows NT), Windows will ask if you are sure that you want to delete a read-only file. If you say yes, the file is deleted. If you use DOS EDIT to modify a read-only file, EDIT will respond with a "Path/File Access Error" error message when you try to save it.

19.4.7 The MEM Command

The MEM command is a useful command prompt that displays information about allocated memory areas (conventional memory, extended memory, and expanded memory), free memory areas, and programs that are currently loaded into memory in the MS-DOS subsystem. The syntax for the MEM command is:

```
MEM[{/program|/debug|/classify}]
```

- **/program**—Displays the status of programs that are currently loaded into memory.
- **/debug**—Displays the status of currently loaded programs and internal drivers, and other programming information.
- **/classify**—Displays the status of programs loaded into conventional memory and the upper memory area (UMA).
- **/?**—Displays help at the command prompt.

Used without parameters, MEM displays the status of the MS-DOS subsystem's used and free memory. See figure 19.4.

Figure 19.4 The MEM Command

```
C:\>MEM

   655360 bytes total conventional memory
   655360 bytes available to MS-DOS
   633776 largest executable program size

  1048576 bytes total contiguous extended memory
        0 bytes available contiguous extended memory
   941056 bytes available XMS memory
          MS-DOS resident in High Memory Area
```

19.4.8 The EDIT and TYPE Commands

Text files are files that contain only ASCII characters with no formatting codes. Common text files include batch files, the AUTOEXEC.BAT file, the CONFIG.SYS file, and Windows initialization files (files with an INI file name extension). To create a text file, you could use either the COPY command or the EDIT command.

To create a text file, you can use the COPY command with CON as the source. CON is short for Console, which indicates the keyboard when it is used as the source. Since the COPY command is an internal DOS command, you only have to boot the computer to a prompt to use the COPY CON command.

Example 19.14:

To create a text file called GO.TXT, perform the following command at the prompt:

```
COPY CON GO.TXT
```

Notice that the COPY command has three parts.

After starting the COPY CON command, you can then enter the content of the file. Unfortunately, if you press the Enter key to go to the next line, you can't go back to make changes. To save the file and return to the prompt, press the Ctrl + Z keys or the F6 key.

To display a text file, you would use the TYPE command. If the text file is too large to show on one screen, you can show it one screen at a time by adding the MORE command.

Example 19.15:

To display the contents of the GO.BAT file, you would perform the following command at the prompt:

```
TYPE GO.BAT
```

To display the contents of the README.TXT file one screen at a time, you would perform the following command at the prompt:

```
TYPE README.BAT ¦MORE
```

To create long or complicated text files, it is best to use the DOS text editor, called EDIT. See figure 19.5. EDIT, like many other text editors, is similar to a word processor. Of course, it does not support any formatting (fonts, font size, or styles) and it doesn't have word wrap. Therefore, to go

Figure 19.5 The MS-DOS Editor Program (EDIT)

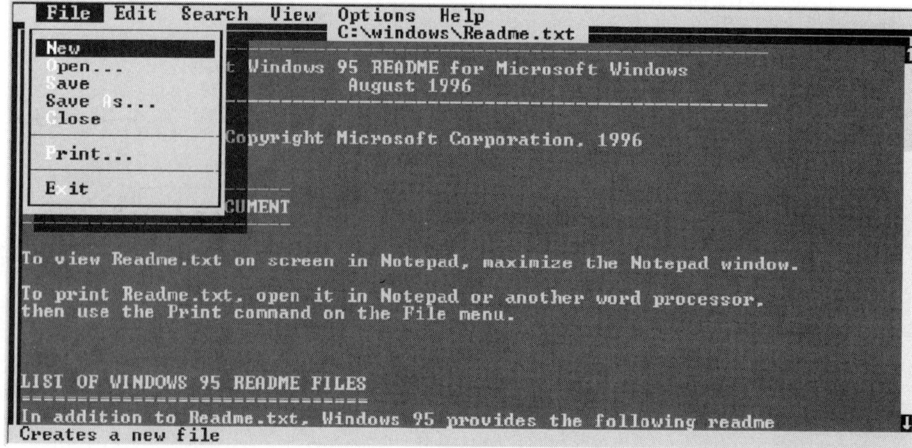

to the next line, you must insert a hard return by pressing the Enter key. (Note: If you wish to copy EDIT to a floppy disk so that you can use it on any computer, you need to copy EDIT.COM and QBASIC.EXE.)

19.5 BATCH FILES

Batch files are text files that have a BAT file name extension. They contain commands that can be executed at the prompt. Therefore, a batch file can be used to group several commands into one command or to simplify the execution of complicated commands.

Example 19.16:

Let's take a look at an example of a simple batch file, called M.BAT, which contains the following:

```
CD\DOS
MSD.EXE
CD\
```

As you can see, it contains simple commands that can be executed at the prompt. Therefore, if you type *M* followed by the Enter key or *M.BAT* followed by the Enter key, the batch file will change to the DOS directory (which is off the root directory) and execute the MSD.EXE file. When you exit from MSD, the batch file will continue by returning to the root directory.

Example 19.17:

Let's take a look at another example of a batch file, called GO.BAT, which contains the following:

```
FORMAT A: /S
COPY C:\C:\DOS\MSD.EXE A:
COPY C:\DOS\EDIT.COM A:
COPY C:\DOS\QBASIC.EXE A:
COPY C:\DOS\FORMAT.COM A:
COPY C:\DOS\FDISK.EXE A:
COPY C:\DOS\ATTRIB.EXE A:
```

Again, the batch file contains commands exactly as they would be typed at the prompt. Notice that the prompt is not included in the batch file.

There are certain internal commands made specifically for batch files. They are the CALL, ECHO, PAUSE, and REM commands. See table 19.4.

Table 19.4 Common Commands Used in Batch Files

Command	Description
CALL	Calls one batch program from another without causing the first batch program to stop.
ECHO	Displays messages for the user running the batch file or turns off the DOS prompt temporarily to give the batch file a cleaner appearance.
PAUSE	Suspends processing of a batch program and displays a message that prompts the user to press a key to continue.
REM	Enables the user to include comments in a batch or in the CONFIG.SYS file. The REM command is also useful for disabling commands without deleting the line.

Example 19.18:

Let's take a look at a more complicated batch file called C.BAT:

```
@ECHO OFF
REM THE FOLLOWING COMMAND MAKES A COPY OF REM DOS'S TEXT FILES
CLS
ECHO INSERT A DISK IN DRIVE A
PAUSE
COPY C:\DOS\*.TXT A:
REM COPY A:\REDME.TXT A:\INFO.TXT
ECHO .
ECHO COPY IS DONE
ECHO .
ECHO YOU CAN NOW REMOVE THE DISK
PAUSE
```

The @ECHO OFF command, which should be placed on the first line, shuts off the prompt while the batch file is running. When the batch file is done, the prompt automatically comes back on. Although this is not necessary for the batch file to run, it can enhance its appearance. The ECHO INSERT A DISK IN DRIVE A, ECHO COPY IS DONE, and ECHO YOU CAN NOW REMOVE THE DISK commands leave messages telling the user what to do. The ECHO . skips a blank line. Much like the @ECHO OFF command, the ECHO . command is not needed for the program to run, but it does enhance the appearance as the batch file executes.

The PAUSE command is used to temporarily stop the batch file so that the user has a chance to read a message or to perform some action, such as insert a disk in a drive. The PAUSE command automatically generates a "Press Any Key to Continue" message.

Any text that is listed after the REM command is ignored by the batch file. The REM command is used to add comments or to disable a command within the batch file. If the batch file begins with an @ECHO OFF, the user will not see the REM statements on the screen. However, if the EDIT or TYPE command is used to view the text file, the REM statements can be seen. The first REM command is used to comment on what the batch file does. It should be used to comment on an uncommon command or to give warnings about the batch file that the user does not have to know about. A second REM statement disables the COPY command. If REM is inserted before a command, the command will be ignored when the batch file is executed.

The CALL command is used to run a batch file from within another batch file. If the command is not used when the first batch file is being executed, it will reach and execute the second batch file. Unfortunately, when it reaches the end of the second batch file, the system will not return to execute the rest of the first batch file.

Example 19.19:

To run the DOITNOW.BAT program from another batch program, you would include the following command:

```
CALL DOITNOW.BAT
```

19.6 AUTOEXEC.BAT

The AUTOEXEC.BAT file is a special batch file that automatically executes during boot-up. It has a BAT file extension and contains commands that you would normally perform at the prompt. In the AUTOEXEC.BAT files, you will usually find the PATH, PROMPT, and SET commands. An example of the AUTOEXEC.BAT file might be:

```
@ECHO OFF
PATH=C:\DOS;C:\WINDOWS
```

```
PROMPT $P$G
SET TEMP=C:\DOS
DEL C:\DOS\*.TMP
```

19.6.1 The PATH Command

When any command is performed at the prompt, COMMAND.COM looks for instructions to perform those commands. The order in which DOS looks for instructions for commands is:

1. Look in COMMAND.COM in RAM to see if the command is an internal DOS command
2. Look in the current directory for a file that has a COM file name extension, followed by the EXE file name extension, followed by the BAT file name extension
3. Look in each directory in the order listed with the PATH statement in RAM. For each directory, look for the files with a COM, EXE, or BAT file name extension before going on to the next directory

If COMMAND.COM determines the command is an internal command or it finds an executable file, it will stop searching and execute those instructions. If COMMAND.COM finishes the search and has not found the instructions to execute, it will generate a "Bad Command or Filename" message.

Example 19.20:

To display the directories that DOS will search for executables files, you would perform the following command at the prompt:

```
PATH
```

To configure DOS to search the C:\WINDOWS and C:\WINDOWS\COMMAND directories for executable files, you would perform one of the following commands at the prompt:

```
PATH=C:\WINDOWS;C:\WINDOWS\COMMAND
PATH=C:\WINDOWS;C:\WINDOWS\COMMAND;
PATH C:\WINDOWS;C:\WINDOWS\COMMAND
PATH C:\WINDOWS;C:\WINDOWS\COMMAND;
```

The PATH command must use an equal sign (=) or a space and can end with a semicolon, though it doesn't have to. Semicolons are used to separate each directory to be searched. When listing each directory, be sure to include the entire path (location) of the directory, starting with the drive letter.

Example 19.21:

The following PATH command has been executed:

```
PATH=C:\DOS;C:\WINDOWS
```

Your current directory is the C:\DATA directory. You type in *GO* and press the Enter key. COMMAND.COM will first check in the RAM for an internal DOS command called GO. Because GO is not an internal DOS command, it will then look in the current directory, which is C:\DATA. It will first look for GO.COM in the directory. If it doesn't find it, it will then look for GO.EXE. If it doesn't find GO.EXE, it will then look for GO.BAT. (Note: If there were a GO.EXE listed before the GO.COM, it would still execute the GO.COM, not the GO.EXE.)

If COMMAND.COM still has not found the instructions for GO, it will then look at the PATH statement loaded in RAM. The PATH statement specifies two subdirectories, the C:\DOS directory and C:\WINDOWS directory. (Note: It will search only the directories that are specified. It will not search the subdirectories of the directories specified.) Therefore, COMMAND.COM will first look in the C:\DOS directory for GO.COM, GO.EXE, and GO.BAT. If it has still not found the file, it will then go to the C:\WINDOWS directory for GO.COM, GO.EXE, and GO.BAT. Lastly, if the file was not found after all of this, it will generate a "Bad Command or Filename" error message.

Note that because the root directory was not the current directory and is not listed specifically in the PATH statement, COMMAND.COM did not search the root directory. The C:\ in C:\DOS and C:\WINDOWS is telling only where these directories are located. If you want to specify the root directory of the C drive, you would use PATH=C:\;C:\DOS;C:\WINDOWS.

If you execute a command at the prompt and get a "Bad Command or Filename" error message, one of the following has happened:

1. The command was typed wrong
2. You are not in the directory of the executable file
3. You did not list the directory of the executable file in the PATH statement or there is an error in the PATH statement
4. The executable file is missing

Question:

Which directories should you specify with the PATH statement?

Answer:

You should specify only directories that have files with the COM, EXE, or BAT file name extensions that you use a lot. This should include DOS, so that you can always format or copy a disk no matter what the current drive and directory. (Note: Windows 95 DOS commands are located in the C:\WINDOWS command directory.) In addition, since most DOS computers have Windows, you would usually include the C:\WINDOWS directory. You would not include directories that you rarely use. (Note: When running Windows, the path is not needed for programs that you start by double-clicking on an icon.)

Question:

At the C:\> prompt, you perform the following command:

```
COPY REDME.TXT A:
```

What error message would you get if the computer can find COPY but cannot find REDME.TXT?

Answer:

COPY is an internal DOS command; therefore, when COMMAND.COM performs a search for the instruction on how to COPY, it will quickly find those instructions in RAM. Since COMMAND.COM knows now how to copy, it then looks to see what it was supposed to copy. Therefore, by looking at the command entered at the prompt, it knows it is supposed to find REDME.TXT. Because no path (location) was specified for REDME.TXT, COMMAND.COM assumes the REDME.TXT is in the current directory (C:\). It then searches the root directory of the C drive and does not find the file. Therefore, the error message that you get is "File Not Found."

NOTE: The PATH command is used only to find instructions to execute, not data.

Question:

During boot-up, you notice that you get several "Bad Command or Filename" error messages. When the computer has finished booting, you type in *EDIT AUTOEXEC.BAT* and press the Enter key at the C:\> command prompt. DOS responds back with a "Bad Command or Filename" error message. What is the problem?

Answer:

The first thing to do is make sure that you typed the command correctly at the prompt. Next, check your PATH statement (by typing *PATH* and pressing the Enter key) and make sure that it includes the DOS directory. Check for spelling and semicolon placement. If there is an error in the PATH command, you must first provide a temporary solution and then a permanent one. To get access to the editor so that you can change the AUTOEXEC.BAT file, you must type the following command at the prompt:

```
PATH=C:\DOS
```

You can now execute the EDIT command to access the AUTOEXEC.BAT file. Of course, if you reboot the computer now, you will still have the same problem. Therefore, after correcting the PATH statement in the AUTOEXEC.BAT file, you would save the changes and then reboot the computer.

19.6.2 The PROMPT Command

The standard command prompt tells the user the location (current drive and directory) and prompts you for the next command. Examples of the prompt are C:\>, A:\>, C:\DOS, C:\DATA\LETTERS>, and F:\>. The PROMPT command changes the appearance of the command prompt. To help customize the prompt, the PROMPT command uses metastrings. A metastring is a group of characters that is transformed into another character or group of characters. The most common metastrings are the $P and $G. The $P shows the current drive and directory; the $G shows the greater-than sign (>). See table 19.5.

Example 19.22:

The following PROMPT command displays the standard prompt, including the current drive and directory and the greater-than sign (>).

```
PROMPT $P$G
```

The following PROMPT command makes the command prompt a little more user-friendly:

```
PROMPT I am located at $P$_How may I help you?
```

19.6.3 The SET Command

The SET command is used to display, set, or remove MS-DOS environment variables, which are used to control the behavior of some batch files and programs and to control the way MS-DOS appears and works. A variable works much like variables in math. If you declare the value of *X* with the following command:

```
SET X=3
```

Table 19.5 Metastrings Used by the PROMPT Command

Metastring	Display
$Q	Equal sign (=)
$$	Dollar sign ($)
$T	Current time
$D	Current date
$P	Current drive and directory
$V	MS-DOS version number
$N	Current drive
$G	Greater-than sign (>)
$L	Less-than sign (<)
$B	Pipe (¦)
$	Carriage return and line feed
$E	ASCII escape code (code 27)
$H	Backspace to delete a character that has been written to the PROMPT command line

and you are given the following equation:

$$Y = X + 2$$

you know to substitute the 3 wherever you see X. Therefore, $Y = X + 2$ becomes $Y = 3 + 2$, which makes $Y = 5$. MS-DOS environment variables work the same way. When a program is running and it comes across an environment variable, it then looks in the RAM to find what the value is for the variable. When it finds it, it substitutes it into the program.

The most important environment variable is the TEMP variable, which defines where any temporary files (files whose file names begin with a tilde (~) and have a TMP file name extension) are to be kept when they are created. Setting the TEMP variable does not create any temporary files; it only states a location. Some DOS commands (such as DISKCOPY), Windows, and most Windows applications need to create temporary files to function. For example, if DISKCOPY could not make temporary files, you would have to insert the source disk and the target disk four times to copy a 1.44-MB floppy disk. In addition, many of the programs would generate errors and not function properly. (Note: For the TEMP variable to work, the directory specified must exist and there must be enough free disk space to create the temporary files.) The files so created are temporary; therefore, when the program that made the temporary files is exited, the temporary files are automatically deleted. DOS 6.22 will automatically add the SET TEMP=C:\DOS line. If there is no SET TEMP line in the AUTOEXEC.BAT file, Windows 3.XX will add the SET TEMP=C:\WINDOWS\TEMP line.

If your computer locks up to the point where you are forced to reboot or the computer reboots for whatever reason and you have not exited the program that created the temporary files, when you try to start the program again it may try to use the temporary files, which in turn will create other problems. Therefore, it is beneficial to have the temporary files automatically deleted during boot-up. Set the SET variable to the C:\DOS directory, then use DEL C:\DOS*.TMP to delete the files. (Note: If you get a "File Not Found" when DOS tries to delete these files, it is not a bad thing—it just means that the DEL command tried to delete the temporary files but there were none to delete.)

If you find hundreds of temporary files in the temporary directory of a computer when no programs are running, it often indicates that the user has been shutting off the computer without properly exiting Windows. (Note: Another clue the computer has been shut off without exiting Windows is that the hard drive contains lost clusters—see chapter 12.)

Certain programs will add SET commands to the AUTOEXEC.BAT file on installation. The best advice to give you is that if you don't know what a command means, leave it alone. If you think that you have to delete a line, put a REM in front of the statement to disable it. Then, if you find that you need that line, you only have to remove REM.

Example 19.23:

To show the environment variables, perform the following command at the prompt:

```
SET
```

To set the TEMP variable to the C:\DOS directory, perform the following command at the prompt or list the following command in the AUTOEXEC.BAT file:

```
SET TEMP=C:\DOS
```

The next command is a common environment variable for the Sound Blaster sound card made by Creative Labs. It tells certain programs that the sound card is using the following resources: I/O address 220, IRQ 5, and DMA 1.

```
SET BLASTER=A220 I5 D1
```

A useful environment variable is the DIRCMD. To make the default DIR listing alphabetical, one screen at a time, you would use the following command:

```
SET DIRCMD=/ON/P
```

19.7 CONFIG.SYS

The CONFIG.SYS file is a special text file that executes special configuration commands that cannot be executed at the prompt. These commands configure your computer's hardware components so that MS-DOS and applications can use them and activate and manage the various memory areas.

Example 19.24:

A simple CONFIG.SYS might look like the following:

```
FILES=60
LASTDRIVE=Z
STACKS=9,256
```

19.7.1 The FILES Command

The FILES command defines the maximum number of file handles or files open in RAM. Each file handle uses a small amount of RAM to keep track of what files are in the RAM. If you have FILES=60, DOS can keep track of 60 files open at the same time. The maximum number of files allowed is 255. Although you could set the command to 255, the memory used to keep track of what files are in the RAM is kept in conventional memory (the first 640 KB of RAM), and because DOS has so little conventional memory (by today's standard), you don't want to waste it on something that you don't need. Windows 9X uses Files=60.

19.7.2 The LASTDRIVE Command

The LASTDRIVE command specifies the maximum number of drives that can be accessed. If the LASTDRIVE command is not used, the default value is the letter following the last one in use. Therefore, if drives A and C are used, the default value is D. If the command is set to LASTDRIVE=Z, DOS reserves memory to keep track of all 26 drive letters. Using a command such as LASTDRIVE=Z does not mean that you have 26 drives; it only means that DOS will recognize all 26 logical drives (floppy drives, hard drives, logical drives or partitions, CD drives, network drives, and RAM drives). Windows 9X uses LASTDRIVE=Z.

19.7.3 The STACKS Command

The STACKS command creates stacks (an area of RAM to be used for hardware interrupts). When a hardware interrupt occurs, all current information in the microprocessor is stored into a stack. When the interrupt is done, the information is copied back into the microprocessor so that it can continue where it left off. An example of a STACKS command is:

```
STACKS=9,256
```

which indicates 9 stacks of 256 bytes, not 9,256 stacks. Usually STACKS=9,256 is sufficient for most computers. If the number of stacks or the size of the stacks is not large enough, an "Internal Stack Overflow" error message will appear. To overcome the error, the number of stacks and the size of the stacks will have to be increased. For example, you could use STACKS=12,512. Windows 9X uses STACKS=9,256.

19.7.4 The SHELL Command

During boot-up, DOS tries to load COMMAND.COM from the root directory of the boot device. The SHELL command specifies the name and location of the command interpreter (COMMAND.COM in another directory or another command interpreter from a third-party company such as 4DOS) that you want DOS to use. Since you must tell DOS which command interpreter to use before COMMAND.COM is loaded, the SHELL command is loaded in the CONFIG.SYS file.

To load COMMAND.COM in the DOS directory, you could add the following command in the CONFIG.SYS file:

```
SHELL=C:\DOS\COMMAND.COM
```

In addition, COMMAND.COM specified with the SHELL command can also be used to increase the size of the environment space used by the environment variables. By default, the environment is 256 bytes. This means that if you add all the characters established as environment variables (PATH, PROMPT, SET, and SHELL), the environment space cannot hold more than 256 characters. If the amount of environment space is exceeded, an "Out of Environment Space" error message will appear. To increase the environment space to 512 bytes and to make it permanent, you would use the following command in CONFIG.SYS:

```
SHELL=C:\COMMAND.COM /E:512 /P
```

19.8 MEMORY MANAGEMENT

When a computer is booted from a disk that has no CONFIG.SYS and AUTOEXEC.BAT files, DOS will recognize only the conventional memory (first 640 KB of RAM), and the hardware will use the reserve memory between 640 KB and 1 MB of RAM. To activate and manage the other memory areas, certain lines must be loaded in the CONFIG.SYS file.

Example 19.25:

A typical CONFIG.SYS file might contain the following:

```
FILES=60
LASTDRIVE=Z
STACKS=9,256
DEVICE=C:\DOS\HIMEM.SYS
DEVICE=C:\DOS\EMM386.EXE NOEMS
DOS=HIGH,UMB
```

To show how much memory is available and how it is being used, you would use the MEM command. To see what is loaded in the conventional memory and upper memory, you would perform the MEM /C ¦ MORE or MEM /C /P. The /P for the MEM command is available only in DOS 6.0 and higher.

19.8.1 HIMEM.SYS

The HIMEM.SYS is the DOS extended memory manager (RAM above 1 MB found on any newer machine), which makes the extended memory available to DOS programs. It also prevents two programs from using the same memory area in the extended memory. The DEVICE command in the CONFIG.SYS file is used to load the HIMEM.SYS. Anytime the DEVICE command is used to load a driver, you should include the entire path (location) of the file specified and its file name extension. (Note: Because Windows 3.XX requires extended memory to run, it requires HIMEM.SYS to be loaded.) In addition, if /TESTMEM:OFF is added to the end of the HIMEM.SYS line, DOS will activate the extended memory but will skip the memory test.

Question:

HIMEM.SYS exists in DOS 4.0 and higher and all Windows 3.XX. Therefore, if the hard drive has two HIMEM.SYS files, which one should you use?

Answer:

You should use the one that is more recent. You can find out which is the more recent driver by using the DIR command and looking at the date of the file. Therefore, if you decide to use the file in Windows, the line in the CONFIG.SYS file would be DEVICE=C:\WINDOWS\ HIMEM.SYS.

19.8.2 EMM386.EXE

The EMM386.EXE file uses extended memory to simulate expanded memory and to provide access to the upper memory area (unused portion of memory between 640 KB and 1 MB not being used by hardware). Like the HIMEM.SYS file, the EMM386.EXE file is loaded in CONFIG.SYS with the DEVICE command, although it has an EXE file name extension. The parameters used will determine if it simulates expanded memory or provides access to upper memory. (Note: EMM386.EXE requires HIMEM.SYS to be loaded and will work only on a 386 machine or higher.)

Example 19.26:

To specify that EMM386.EXE use extended memory to simulate expanded memory without enabling the upper memory, you would use:

```
DEVICE=C:\DOS\EMM386.EXE
```

To allow the EMM386.EXE to enable the upper memory without simulating expanded memory, you would use:

```
DEVICE=C:\DOS\EMM386.EXE NOEMS
```

(NOEMS means no expanded memory [EMS].) To allow EMM386.EXE to use extended memory to simulate expanded memory and to enable the upper memory, you would use:

```
DEVICE=C:\DOS\EMM386.EXE RAM
```

To make the best use of the system's memory, you should use the NOEMS option unless a program requires expanded memory. (Note: To fully enable the upper memory, you also need DOS=UMB.)

Example 19.27:

To specify that EMM386.EXE allocate a maximum of only 4,096 KB to simulate expanded memory, you would use:

```
DEVICE=C:\DOS\EMM386.EXE 4096
```

If there is a possible conflict between a device driver or TSR and hardware using the memory between 640 KB and 1 MB of RAM, you can exclude a memory range so that it will be used by only hardware devices. The following command will prevent EMM386 from using the memory between A000-BFFF of RAM for upper or expanded memory:

```
DEVICE=C:\DOS\EMM386.EXE RAM X=A000-BFFF
```

To find out if a device driver or TSR is conflicting with hardware using reserve memory, you can exclude all of the memory between 640 KB and 1 MB by using X=A000-FFFF. If the problem goes away, then you know it was a memory conflict. You would then use the hardware manual to determine the memory address that the hardware device is using so that you can exclude only the area being used.

19.8.3 DOS=HIGH and DOS=UMB

When the DOS=HIGH command is used, DOS tries to load a large portion of itself in the high memory area (HMA) between 1 MB and 1 MB 64 KB, freeing conventional memory. Of course, this command requires HIMEM.SYS to be loaded first. When the DOS=UMB command is loaded in CONFIG.SYS, it does *not* try to load DOS into upper memory. Instead, DOS=UMB specifies that DOS should manage the upper memory blocks (UMB) created by the EMM386.EXE. Therefore, if you want to enable the upper memory, you must have HIMEM.SYS, EMM386 with the NOEMS or RAM option, and DOS=UMB loaded. (Note: The DOS=HIGH and DOS=UMB commands are often combined into one line: DOS=HIGH,UMB or DOS=UMB,HIGH.)

19.9 DEVICE DRIVERS AND TSRS

To enable hardware and to load useful utilities, you need to know how to load device drivers and TSRs. A **device driver** controls how DOS and applications interact with specific items of hardware. They can be identified with a SYS file name extension, which is loaded in the CONFIG.SYS file.

A **TSR,** which stands for Terminate and Stay Resident, loads instructions into the RAM to control some hardware device or to provide some useful function while giving control back to the operating system. The TSR then performs its function quietly in the background while other programs are loaded. A program that is not a TSR (for example, EDIT or a word processing program) is loaded in the RAM but typically does not allow any other commands to be performed at the prompt until you exit the program. Since TSRs have a COM or EXE file name extension, they are loaded in AUTOEXEC.BAT. Remember that the AUTOEXEC.BAT file is a batch file that can contain commands that can be executed at the prompt.

Example 19.28:

CONFIG.SYS:

```
FILES=60
LASTDRIVE=Z
STACKS=9,256
DEVICE=C:\DOS\HIMEM.SYS
DEVICE=C:\EMM386.EXE NOEMS
DOS=HIGH,UMB
DEVICE=c:\CDROM\ATAPI_CD.sys /D:CD0001
```

AUTOEXEC.BAT:

```
@ECHO OFF
PATH=C:\DOS;C:\WINDOWS
PROMPT $P$G
SET TEMP=C:\DOS
DEL C:\DOS\*.TMP
SET BLASTER=A220 I5 D1
C:\DOS\MSCDEX /D:CD0001 /m:12 /L:E
```

Most of the time when loading CD-ROM drivers, the floppy disk is inserted into a floppy drive and the SETUP.EXE, INSTALL.EXE, or similar file is executed to automatically install and configure the drivers. For DOS, the EIDE CD drives require a device driver to be loaded in the CONFIG.SYS; SCSI drives usually require a device driver for the controller card and a device driver for the CD-ROM drive. The driver for the Mitsumi IDE CD-ROM drive appears as:

```
DEVICE=c:\CDROM\ ATAPI_CD.sys /D:CD0001
```

The /D: is the drive signature to identify the drive. In addition to the driver, DOS requires the Microsoft compact disk extension (MSCDEX.EXE) file to be loaded in AUTOEXEC.BAT so that DOS can read the CD file system:

```
C:\DOS\MSCDEX /d:CD0001 /m:12 /L:E
```

The /D: indicates the drive signature, which must be the same as the one specified in the device driver loaded in CONFIG.SYS. The /M: specifies the number of sector buffers and the /L: specifies the drive letter assigned to the CD-ROM drive.

As mentioned, a device driver that has a SYS file name extension is always loaded in the CONFIG. SYS file with the DEVICE command, and TSRs that have a COM or EXE file name extension are usually loaded in the AUTOEXEC.BAT file. There are no exceptions to this system for file names with the SYS extension, but some EXE files are loaded in the CONFIG.SYS file, not the AUTOEXEC.BAT file. The most common examples are EMM386.EXE and SETVER.EXE. The EMM386.EXE file has already been discussed.

Example 19.29:

CONFIG.SYS:

```
FILES=60
LASTDRIVE=Z
STACKS=9,256
DEVICE=C:\DOS\HIMEM.SYS
DEVICE=C:\EMM386.EXE NOEMS
DOS=HIGH,UMB
DEVICE=C:\SB16\SB16.SYS
DEVICE=c:\CDROM\ATAPI_CD.SYS /D:CD0001
DEVICE=C:\DOS\SETVER.EXE
```

AUTOEXEC.BAT:

```
@ECHO
OFF
PATH=C:\DOS;C:\WINDOWS
PROMPT $P$G
SET TEMP=C:\DOS
DEL C:\DOS*.TMP
SET BLASTER=A220 I5 D1
C:\DOS\MSCDEX /D:CD0001 /M:12 /L:E
```

The loading of SETVER.EXE in the CONFIG.SYS file with the DEVICE command loads the MS-DOS version table into RAM. The MS-DOS version table lists names of programs and the versions of DOS they require that are supposed to be reported to the program when the program asks for the DOS version. For example, an old Novell utility used to connect to a File Server, called NETX.COM, was written to work with DOS 3.0 to 5.0. When NETX.COM is executed, it asks DOS what version it is to make sure that it can work with the version of DOS loaded into the RAM. If DOS 6.22 is running on a system, for example, NETX.COM asks what version is running. Of course, DOS replies with DOS 6.22. NETX.COM checks the DOS versions that it can work with and finds that it does not work with DOS 6.22. Therefore, an "Incorrect DOS Version" error message appears. To fix this problem, a command similar to the following one can be executed:

```
SETVER NETX.COM 5.00
```

Executing SETVER.EXE at the DOS prompt changes a table in the SETVER.EXE file. (Note: The DOS version number must have two decimal places.) After the SETVER command is executed at the prompt, the SETVER will display a lengthy message telling you to reboot the changes so that the changes to the table can be reloaded into RAM. When NETX.COM is executed, NETX.COM asks DOS what version is running. Instead of giving NETX.COM a straight answer, DOS searches the MS-DOS version table and finds that it is supposed to lie to NETX.COM and report DOS 5.00. Therefore, NETX.COM assumes it is working with DOS 5.00 and loads itself into RAM.

Question:

What happens if you boot from a DOS 6.22 floppy disk on a machine that has Windows 95 and you try to execute FORMAT.COM in the C:\WINDOWS\COMMAND directory?

Answer:

Many DOS files verify the DOS version before they execute. Because you have booted with a DOS 6.22 floppy disk, DOS 6.22 is loaded in the computer's RAM. Therefore, when you try to use the

FORMAT.COM from Windows 95, FORMAT.COM checks to see what DOS version is running and of course generates an "Incorrect DOS Version" message. To get around this problem, don't use the SETVER command to change the DOS version reported to FORMAT.COM. Instead, boot with a Windows 95 bootable disk.

19.10 LOADING DEVICE DRIVERS AND TSRS INTO UPPER MEMORY

By loading HIMEM.SYS, EMM386.EXE, and DOS=HIGH,UMB, all the memory areas are active. But, although the upper memory has been created, it has not yet been used. To load a device driver into upper memory, you would use the DEVICEHIGH command. To load a TSR into upper memory, you would use the LH (or LOADHIGH) command. (Note: DEVICEHIGH and LH command loads the program into the upper memory, not the high memory area.)

Example 19.30:

CONFIG.SYS:

```
FILES=60
LASTDRIVE=Z
STACKS=9,256
DEVICE=C:\DOS\HIMEM.SYS
DEVICE=C:\EMM386.EXE NOEMS
DOS-HIGH,UMB
DEVICEHIGH=C:\SB16\SB16.SYS
DEVICEHIGH=C:\CDROM\ATAPI_CD.SYS /D:CD0001
DEVICEHIGH=C:\ANSI.SYS
DEVICEHIGH=C:\DOS\SETVER.EXE
DEVICEHIGH=C:\DOS\POWER.EXE
```

AUTOEXEC.BAT:

```
@ECHO OFF
PATH=C:\DOS;C:\WINDOWS
PROMPT $P$G
SET TEMP=C:\DOS
DEL C:\DOS\*.TMP
SET BLASTER=A220 _I5 D1
LH C:\MOUSE\MOUSE.COM
LH C:\DOS\MSCDEX /D:CD0001 /M:12 /L:E
LH DOSKEY.COM
```

19.11 SMARTDRV AND BUFFERS

Today's GUI and Windows applications require more memory and more disk space than ever before. Because the hard disk is a mechanical device, it is slow compared to the microprocessor and RAM. The BUFFERS and SMARTDRV commands can be used to increase the disk performance.

Example 19.31:

CONFIG.SYS:

```
FILES=60
BUFFERS=10, 0
```

```
LASTDRIVE=Z
STACKS=9,256
DEVICE=C:\DOS\HIMEM.SYS
DEVICE=C:\EMM386.EXE NOEMS
DOS=HIGH,UMB
DEVICEHIGH=C:\CDROM\ATAPI_CD.SYS /D:CD0001
DEVICEHIGH=C:\DOS\SETVER.EXE
```

AUTOEXEC.BAT:

```
@ECHO OFF
PATH=C:\DOS;C:\WINDOWS
PROMPT $P$G
SET TEMP=C:\DOS
DEL C:\DOS\*.TMP
LH C:\DOS\MSCDEX /D:CD0001 /M:12 /L:E
SMARTDRV 4096 128
WIN
```

The BUFFERS command, loaded in the CONFIG.SYS file, specifies the amount of memory for a disk buffer or buffer area. The buffer area is a block of memory used to collect data as it is being moved between the microprocessor and the controller card. Each buffer is 512 bytes. After the data is collected, the buffer tries to group data into larger chunks and move them all at once. Since the larger chunks fill the data transfer pathways more efficiently, the PC runs more efficiently. The buffer keeps the most recent information read to and from the disk. When it needs to make more room, it moves the oldest accessed information and copies it to disk.

The BUFFERS command can also specify the number of additional sectors DOS reads each time it is instructed to read a file. If the next sector needed on the disk is sequential to the one just read, it will already be loaded in the RAM. The maximum number of buffers is 99, and the maximum number of read-ahead buffers is 8. If a BUFFERS command is not loaded, DOS will assign 15 buffers and 1 look-ahead buffer for computers that have 640 KB of RAM. The syntax for the BUFFERS command is:

```
BUFFERS=nn or BUFFERS=nn,mm
```

where *nn* is the number of buffers and *mm* is the number of look-ahead buffers.

SMARTDRV.EXE, a software disk cache that caches, or buffers, between the hard drive and the RAM, creates a much larger buffer area, called a *cache area,* in the extended memory. See table 19.6. In contrast to the way the buffer area operates, the software controlling the cache area tries to anticipate what the microprocessor needs next. One way it does this is to keep a copy of information that has been recently accessed. If the information has already been accessed, there is a good chance that it will be accessed again. Another way is to read ahead an additional sector after the one that has been accessed. Whatever method or methods are used, when the disk needs to be accessed, the system will look in the

Table 19.6 SMARTDRV Default Values

Extended Memory	Default Cache Size	Default Windows Cache Size
Up to 1 MB	All the extended memory	0 KB
Up to 2 MB	1 MB	256 KB
Up to 4 MB	1 MB	512 KB
Up to 6 MB	2 MB	1 MB
6 MB or more	2 MB	2 MB

cache area first. If it can't find what is needed, it will access the slower hard drive. The time it takes to search the cache area (RAM) is almost negligible compared to the time needed to access the hard drive. Therefore, if the needed information is in the RAM, the overall performance of the PC is increased. Another advantage that SMARTDRV.EXE has over BUFFERS is that when BUFFERS needs to make more room, it removes the oldest information accessed, while SMARTDRV removes the information that has been least accessed.

SMARTDRV.EXE has an EXE file name extension, so it is loaded in the AUTOEXEC.BAT file. SMARTDRV.EXE automatically loads into upper memory if available. (Note: For DOS versions 4.0 and 5.0, a disk cache is created by loading SMARTDRV.SYS in the CONFIG.SYS file using the DEVICE or DEVICEHIGH command.)

Example 19.32:

To create a disk cache with the default values, you would use the following command in the AUTOEXEC.BAT file:

```
SMARTDRV
```

To create a 4,096 KB cache area (overriding the default values), you would use the following command in the AUTOEXEC.BAT file:

```
SMARTDRV 4096
```

Because Windows for Workgroups 3.11 has its own built-in disk cache, you may want to reduce the disk cache when Windows is running. Therefore, to create a 4,096 KB cache area but reduce it to 128 KB when running Windows, you would use the following command in the AUTOEXEC.BAT:

```
SMARTDRV 4096 128
```

Some programs are written to access the disk, bypassing the cache area. If the disk has not been updated from the cache area, the program could encounter some problems. If you have such a program, you then need to disable the write-behind caching. This would be done with the following command:

```
SMARTDRV /X
```

If you are not loading SMARTDRV, you should use between 30 and 50 buffers. If you are using SMARTDRV, you should reduce the number of buffers to 10 or 15 and you should not use look-ahead buffers. To cache a CD-ROM, SMARTDRV must be loaded after MSCDEX.EXE. SMARTDRV does not cache network drives or compressed drives.

Some ESDI and SCSI hard drives need double-buffering so that they can work with memory provided by EMM386 or Windows running in 386 enhanced mode. To fix this problem, you can enable double-buffering using the SMARTDRV.EXE in the CONFIG.SYS file:

```
DEVICE=C:\DOS\SMARTDRV.EXE /DOUBLE_BUFFER
```

To determine if you need double-buffering, add SMARTDRV.EXE to the CONFIG.SYS file. After rebooting the computer, execute SMARTDRV.EXE at the command prompt. If there is a "Yes" under the buffering column, double-buffering is needed.

19.12 TROUBLESHOOTING CONFIG.SYS AND AUTOEXEC.BAT

Since the CONFIG.SYS and AUTOEXEC.BAT files are necessary to run Windows and other popular applications and to activate hardware, it is necessary to know how to troubleshoot them. Anytime you see "Bad Command or Filename" or "File Not Found" error messages during boot-up, the error is in the AUTOEXEC.BAT file. (Note: Files loaded with the LH [or LOADHIGH] command that can't be found will give a "File Not Found" error message.) There is not, however, a problem if a "File Not Found" error message appears when the system is deleting temporary files during boot-up.

If a file can't be executed in CONFIG.SYS, it will generate an error message similar to:

```
Unrecognized Command in CONFIG.SYS
Error in CONFIG.SYS line 6
```

If the machine is locking up during boot-up or a message is being displayed on the screen so fast that you can't see it, you need to isolate the problem. With Windows 9X boot disks, you can use the F5 or F8 key during boot-up. If the F5 key (or the Shift key) is pressed right before it says "Starting Windows 9X," the AUTOEXEC.BAT and CONFIG.SYS files will be skipped. If the F8 key is pressed instead of the F5 key, a Windows startup menu will appear where you can choose safe mode (bypassing the AUTOEXEC.BAT and CONFIG.SYS files) or you can choose step-by-step configuration. Therefore, if a problem causes the computer to lock up, first use the F8 key so that you can select the step-by-step configuration to find out which line is causing the problem. Then reboot the computer and use the F5 to bypass the AUTOEXEC.BAT and CONFIG.SYS files so that you can fix the problem.

If the HIMEM.SYS gets deleted or corrupted, you will get the "Missing or Corrupt Himem.sys" or "Himem.sys Not Loaded" error message. When this occurs, go to a command prompt and check to see if the HIMEM.SYS is loaded correctly within the CONFIG.SYS file and the HIMEM.SYS file exists in the correct directory. If the HIMEM.SYS file is specified correctly and the HIMEM.SYS file exists, verify the integrity of the HIMEM.SYS file.

If the COMMAND.COM file is deleted or corrupted, you will get the "Bad or Missing Command Interpreter" error message. First, you should check to see if the file exists. If it does exist, check the CONFIG.SYS command and look to see if there is a SHELL command that is specifying a different location. If there is, you will have to make sure that there is a command interpreter file located at the specified location or you will have to correct the CONFIG.SYS file. Lastly, you will have to verify the integrity of the COMMAND.COM file.

SUMMARY

1. DOS (Disk Operating System) was the first operating system used on the IBM PC created by Microsoft.
2. The DOS interface can be used to troubleshoot many types of problems in Windows.
3. When you boot DOS, DOS loads the IO.SYS, MSDOS.SYS, CONFIG.SYS, COMMAND.COM, and AUTOEXEC.BAT files.
4. The instructions for the internal DOS commands are kept in the COMMAND.COM file loaded in the RAM.
5. External DOS commands are commands for which instructions are kept in files that have a COM or EXE file name extension.
6. The DIR command, which displays a list of the files and subdirectories, is probably the most commonly used DOS command.
7. To change the current directory, you would use the CD command.
8. Copy commands (COPY, DISKCOPY, and XCOPY) always have three parts, the command, the source, and the target.
9. The FORMAT command is used to prepare a disk for the first time.
10. To make a disk bootable without reformatting the disk, you would use the SYS command.
11. The ATTRIB command displays, sets, or removes the read-only (R), archive (A), system (S), and hidden (H) attributes assigned to a file or directory.
12. Batch files are text files with a BAT file name extension that contain commands that can be executed at the prompt.
13. The AUTOEXEC.BAT file is a special batch file that automatically executes during boot-up.
14. When you perform any command at the prompt, COMMAND.COM looks for instructions to perform the command in the RAM (internal command), the current directory, and the PATH statement.
15. If COMMAND.COM can't find the instructions for a command, it replies with a "Bad Command or Filename" error message.
16. The PROMPT command changes the appearance of the command prompt.
17. The SET command is used to display, set, or remove MS-DOS environment variables.
18. The TEMP variable defines where any temporary files (files that begin with a tilde (~) and have a TMP file name extension) are to be kept when they are created.
19. The CONFIG.SYS is a special text file that executes special configuration commands (commands that cannot be executed at the prompt).
20. The FILES command defines the maximum number of file handles or files open in RAM.
21. The LASTDRIVE command specifies the maximum number of drives you can access.
22. The STACKS command creates stacks, an area of RAM to be used for hardware interrupts.

23. The HIMEM.SYS is the DOS extended memory manager so programs don't use the same memory areas. It is needed to load any other memory command.
24. The EMM386.EXE file loaded in the CONFIG.SYS uses extended memory to simulate expanded memory and provide access to the upper memory area.
25. When the DOS=HIGH command is used, DOS tries to load a large portion of itself in the high memory area (HMA).
26. The DOS=UMB specifies that DOS should manage the upper memory blocks (UMB) created by the EMM386.EXE file.
27. To enable hardware and to load useful utilities, you need to know how to load device drivers and TSRs.
28. To load a device driver into upper memory, you would use the DEVICEHIGH command. To load a TSR into upper memory, you would use the LH (or LOADHIGH) command.
29. The BUFFERS command, loaded in the CONFIG.SYS, specifies the amount of memory for a disk buffer (each buffer is 512 bytes) or buffer area.
30. SMARTDRV.EXE is a software disk cache that creates a cache area in the extended memory.

QUESTIONS

1. Which of the following files interprets the input entered at the DOS prompt?
   a. COMMAND.COM
   b. MSDOS.SYS
   c. IO.SYS
   d. AUTOEXEC.BAT
2. Which of the following files is the DOS kernel?
   a. COMMAND.COM
   b. MSDOS.SYS
   c. IO.SYS
   d. AUTOEXEC.BAT
3. What is the maximum allowable length of a DOS file name, including the extension (don't count the period)?
   a. 9 characters b. 10 characters
   c. 11 characters d. 13 characters
4. What is the correct boot sequence for DOS files?
   a. IO.SYS, MSDOS.SYS, COMMAND.COM, CONFIG.SYS, AUTOEXEC.BAT
   b. IO.SYS, MSDOS.SYS, CONFIG.SYS, COMMAND.COM, AUTOEXEC.BAT
   c. MSDOS.SYS, IO.SYS, COMMAND.COM, CONFIG.SYS, AUTOEXEC.BAT
   d. MSDOS.SYS, IO.SYS, CONFIG.SYS, COMMAND.COM, AUTOEXEC.BAT
5. The CD\ command has what effect?
   a. clears the disk
   b. changes to a new directory below the current one
   c. returns to the root directory
   d. goes to the parent directory
   e. goes to the child directory
6. What command shows all hidden files one screen at a time?
   a. DIR b. DIR /ON /W
   c. DIR /ON /P d. DIR /AH /W
   e. DIR /AH /P
7. Which of the following are external DOS commands (choose two?)
   a. FORMAT b. CLS
   c. VER d. COPY
   e. DISKCOPY
8. Identify the *incorrect* use of the COPY command.
   a. COPY A:RESUME.DOC A:
   b. COPY A:DATA.DAT A:DATA.TXT
   c. COPY A:*.* C:\DATA
   d. COPY A:??DOS.*
   e. none of the above
9. When using the XCOPY command, /S means
   a. subdirectories. b. search.
   c. bootable. d. system.
   e. none of the above.
10. You have a valuable disk that contains the QA Plus Diagnostic program, a diagnostic program used to test computer hardware. You need to make the diskette bootable using the A drive. What command would you use to make it bootable? Assume you are at the C:\ directory.
    a. SYS A:
    b. DISKCOPY A: A::
    c. FORMAT A: /S
    d. FORMAT A: /S /Q
    e. COPY SYS A:
11. How do you format a DS/HD 3½-in. disk in a 1.44 MB floppy disk drive using the A drive?
    a. FORMAT A:
    b. FORMAT A: /F:360
    c. FORMAT A: /F:720
    d. FORMAT A: /4
12. How do you format the C drive and make it bootable?
    a. FORMAT C: b. FORMAT C: /S
    c. FORMAT C: /Q d. FORMAT C: /U
    e. none of the above
13. To make the README.TXT file read-only, you would enter
    a. ATTRIB +H README.TXT.
    b. ATTRIB README.TXT -H.
    c. ATTRIB -R README.TXT.
    d. ATTRIB +R README.TXT.
    e. EDIT README.TXT.
    f. DIR /AR.
14. A user is in the A:\DATA directory, types *C:*, and is in the C:\ directory. Without changing directo-

ries, what is the shortest command to copy the entire contents of the A:\DATA directory to B:\?
   a. COPY A:\DATA B:\
   b. COPY A:\DATA*.* B:\
   c. COPY A:\DATA*.* B:*.*
   d. COPY A:*.* B:\
   e. none of the commands will copy the files to the B drive
15. Which command is *not* the proper use of switches?
   a. DEL C:\DATA*.*\P
   b. FORMAT A: /S/U
   c. DIR /AH /ON
   d. COPY C:*.DAT D:\DATA
16. Which statement about batch files is true?
   a. Batch files are executed only at system boot-up.
   b. Batch files can execute only COM and EXE files.
   c. Batch files can execute any combination of commands except those requiring parameter passing or variables.
   d. Batch files can execute any combination of commands performed at the command-line prompt.
17. What is the effect of the DOS PAUSE command?
   a. The CPU is locked until CTRL-C is true.
   b. The CPU is locked until the CONTINUE command is entered.
   c. Program execution is suspended waiting for action by the user.
   d. Program execution is suspended waiting for action by the user after a specified amount of time.
18. Which of the following correctly identifies the DOS search order?
   a. floppy disk, hard disk
   b. search path
   c. internal command, current directory, search path
   d. current directory, search path
   e. internal command, current directory, root directory, search path
19. When the file name GO is typed at the DOS prompt, COMMAND.COM looks in the current directory for a file name in what order?
   a. GO.EXE, then GO.COM, then GO.BAT
   b. GO.BAT, then GO.COM, then GO.EXE
   c. GO.COM, then GO.EXE, then GO.BAT
   d. GO.EXE, then GO.BAT, then GO.COM
20. A user has the directory C:\LEDGER in the path. What would the shortest command be at the end of the AUTOEXEC.BAT file in order to execute the LG.EXE command found in the C:\LEDGER directory?
   a. LG.EXE
   b. C:\LG.EXE
   c. C:\LEDGER\LG
   d. LG
   e. C:\LG
21. What happens when DOS can't find instructions to follow?
   a. a "File Not Found" message appears
   b. a "Bad Command or Filename" message appears
   c. an "Invalid Command" message appears
   d. DOS will then go directly to the root directory and search all other directories not searched
22. The $P used with the PROMPT command means
   a. prompt.
   b. paste.
   c. path (current drive and location).
   d. pink.
   e. pin.
23. Which of the following statements about where temporary files will be created is true?
   a. The SET TEMP line in the AUTOEXEC.BAT file determines where temporary files are stored.
   b. By default, TEMP files are stored in the DOS directory.
   c. By default, TEMP files are stored in the root directory.
   d. By default, TEMP files are stored in the C:\TEMP directory.
   e. By default, TEMP files are stored in a RAM drive.
   f. Temporary files must always be stored in the TEMP subdirectory under Windows.
24. The utility SMARTDRV.EXE found in MS-DOS
   a. utilizes expanded memory to create a disk cache.
   b. utilizes extended memory to create a disk cache.
   c. creates a disk from RAM.
   d. copies the ROM BIOS instructions into RAM.
   e. is a hard drive utility that translates CMOS parameters
25. The upper memory manager provided by DOS is called
   a. MEMMAKER.
   b. UMM386.EXE.
   c. EMM386.EXE.
   d. HIMEM.SYS.
   e. UMB386.EXE.
26. By default, DOS is loaded into and runs in conventional memory. However, this can be changed with which command in the CONFIG.SYS?
   a. DOS=HIGH,UMB
   b. HIMEM.SYS
   c. RUNDOS, HIGH
   d. DOS=XMS
27. Which parameter used with EMM386.EXE allows upper memory but no expanded memory?
   a. EXPAND
   b. RAM
   c. NOEMS
   d. DEVICEHIGH
   e. EMS
   f. no parameter is used
28. The extended memory manager for DOS is called
   a. MEMMAKER.
   b. UMM386.EXE.
   c. EMM386.EXE.
   d. HIMEM.SYS.
   e. UMB386.EXE.

29. Which DOS driver is used to emulate expanded memory?
   a. HIMEM.SYS
   b. EMM386.EXE
   c. RAMDRIVE.SYS
   d. SMARTDRV.EXE
30. Which of the following commands would be used to load programs (TSRs) into upper memory?
   a. DEVICEHIGH= in the CONFIG.SYS
   b. DEVICEHIGH= in the AUTOEXEC.BAT file
   c. LH in the CONFIG.SYS file
   d. LH in the AUTOEXEC.BAT file
31. Two common mouse drivers are
   a. MOUSE.COM, which is normally loaded with a line in the AUTOEXEC.BAT file, and MOUSE.SYS, which is normally loaded with a line in the CONFIG.SYS file.
   b. MOUSE.COM, which is normally loaded with a line in the CONFIG.SYS file, and MOUSE.SYS, which is normally loaded with a line in the AUTOEXEC.BAT file.
   c. MOUSE.COM and MOUSE.SYS, both of which are normally loaded with lines in the AUTOEXEC.BAT file.
   d. MOUSE.COM and MOUSE.SYS, both of which are normally loaded with lines in the CONFIG.SYS file.
   e. MOUSE.COM, MOUSE.SYS, and MOUSE.DRV, which are normally loaded with lines in the CONFIG.SYS file.
32. For PC-DOS, what utility automatically optimizes the use of RAM?
   a. MEMMAKER b. RAMBOOST
   c. E.EXE d. MEM /D
   e. MEMCONFIG
33. Pressing the F8 key when the "Starting MS-DOS . . . " message appears
   a. allows you to single-step through CONFIG.SYS and AUTOEXEC.BAT.
   b. skips the loading of DoubleSpace.
   c. causes DOS to skip CONFIG.SYS and AUTOEXEC.BAT.
   d. allows you to choose among different boot sequences.
34. What is wrong if a "Non-System Disk or Disk Error" message appears?
   a. COMMAND.COM has been deleted or corrupted.
   b. IO.SYS and/or MSDOS.SYS are missing or corrupted.
   c. CONFIG.SYS has an invalid command.
   d. AUTOEXEC.BAT has an invalid command.
35. What is wrong if a "Bad or Missing Command Interpreter" error message appears?
   a. COMMAND.COM has been deleted or corrupted
   b. IO.SYS and/or MSDOS.SYS are missing or corrupted.
   c. CONFIG.SYS has an invalid command.
   d. AUTOEXEC.BAT has an invalid command.
36. Which of the following commands will prevent a TSR or device drive from using upper memory?
   a. DEVICE=C:\DOS\EMM386.EXE RAM
   b. DEVICE=C:\DOS\EMM386.EXE X=A000-AFFF
   c. DEVICE=C:\DOS\EMM386.EXE X=A000-EFFF
   d. DEVICE=C:\DOS\EMM386.EXE X=0000-FFFF
37. After upgrading to a new DOS version, an older application displays the error message "Incorrect DOS Version." What should be done to run this application?
   a. use the SETVER command
   b. restore the old DOS version
   c. contact the application's vendor support line
   d. run the SYS command on the drive with the correct DOS version
38. Which DOS command will send print jobs normally sent to the parallel port to the serial port (you may need to research this question)?
   a. PARALLEL>SERIAL
   b. MODE LPT1=COM1
   c. DIRECT LPT1=COM1
   d. MODE PRINTER ()-SERIAL()
39. SMARTDRV.EXE can cache which of the following (select all that apply)?
   a. hard drives b. floppy drives
   c. CD-ROM drives d. network drives
   e. tape drives
40. Internal DOS commands are part of
   a. IO.SYS.
   b. MSDOS.SYS.
   c. CONFIG.SYS.
   d. COMMAND.COM.
   e. AUTOEXEC.BAT.

HANDS-ON EXERCISES

Exercise 1: Understanding Paths of Files and Directories

1. Using the accompanying figure, determine the path of the following files and directories:
   a. DOS b. MSOFFICE
   c. WINWORD d. STARTUP
   e. SETUP.EXE f. WINWORD.EXE
   g. MSWORD.DOC h. AUTOEXEC.BAT
   i. MSWORD.DLL

2. If you wanted to execute the SETUP.EXE file in the MSOFFICE directory, what would you type at the C:\> command prompt?
3. If you wanted to execute the SETUP.EXE file in the MSOFFICE directory, what would you type at the D:\> command prompt?
4. If you wanted to copy the CONFIG.SYS to the DOS directory, what would you type at the C:\> command prompt?
5. If you wanted to delete the MSWORD.DOC file, what would you type at the C:\> command prompt?

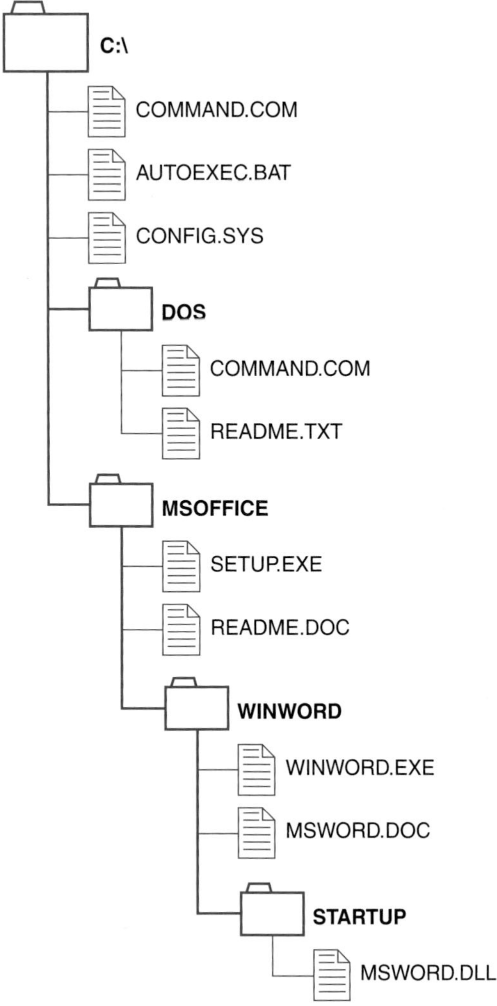

Exercise 2: Using Common DOS Commands

1. Format a floppy disk using drive A and make it bootable.
2. Create the directory structure shown in the accompanying figure on the A drive.
3. From the A:\ directory, show a graphical representation of the directory structure on the A drive.
4. From the C:\DOS directory, copy COUNTRY.TXT, EDIT.COM, FORMAT.COM, and LABEL.EXE to the DOS directory on the A drive.
5. Make the current directory A:\.
6. Without changing drives or directories, copy XCOPY.EXE from the C:\DOS directory to the A:\DOS directory.
7. Without changing drives or directories, copy COUNTRY.TXT to the JOB directory.
8. Change to the JOB directory.
9. Rename the COUNTRY.TXT file to TEXT.TXT.
10. Make a copy of the TEXT.TXT file and call it C.TXT.
11. Without changing directories, copy EDIT.COM from the A:\DOS directory to the JOB directory.
12. Move the EDIT.COM file from the JOB directory to the BACKUP directory.
13. Change to the DATA directory.
14. Change to the HOME directory.

15. Change back to the DATA directory.
16. Delete the HOME directory.
17. Delete the SCHOOL directory.
18. Change to the A:\DOS directory.
19. Using wild cards, delete the files that have an EXE file name extension.
20. Using wild cards, delete the files that have COM file name extension.
21. From the A:\ directory, show a graphical representation of the directory structure and its files on the A drive.
22. Perform a DIR /S.
23. Remove the first disk from drive A and insert a second floppy disk.
24. Format the disk using an unconditional format without making it bootable.
25. Copy the contents of the first disk to the second disk.
26. Format the second disk without making the disk bootable.
27. Without formatting the second disk, make the second disk bootable.
28. Create a TEST directory off of the C:\ directory.
29. Insert the first disk into drive A.
30. Copy the entire directory structure of the A drive, including the empty subdirectories, to the C:\TEST directory.
31. Delete the C:\TEST directory on the hard drive.
32. Change to the A:\ directory.
33. Perform a DIR command.
34. Show the hidden files using the DIR command.
35. Show the attributes of the files in the A:\ directory.
36. Using the COPY command, make a simple text file called NAME.TXT. In the text file, type your first name.

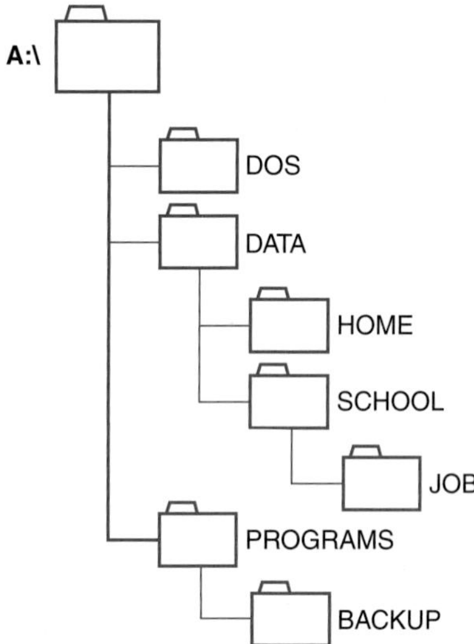

37. Display the contents of NAME.TXT without using EDIT.
38. Make the NAME.TXT file read-only.
39. Try to delete the NAME.TXT file using the DEL command.
40. Make the NAME.TXT file read/write (shut off the read-only attribute).
41. Make the NAME.TXT file hidden.
42. Use the DIR command to verify that the NAME.TXT file can't be seen.
43. Use the DIR command to display the NAME.TXT file.
44. Unhide the NAME.TXT file.
45. Make the NAME.TXT file read-only, hidden, and system.
46. Shut off the read-only, hidden, and system attributes of the NAME.TXT file.
47. Using EDIT, change the contents of the NAME.TXT file so that it contains your first name and your last name.
48. Load the README.TXT file that is located in the C:\DOS directory using EDIT.
49. Move to Section 5.1 of the README.TXT file, "Microsoft Antivirus." (Note: The beginning of the document is a chapter contents section followed by a table of contents and the information sections.) Read Section 5.1 to find out what you should do before cleaning a program with Microsoft Antivirus.
50. Reformat both disks.

Exercise 3: Creating a Batch File

1. On the A drive, create an M.BAT batch file that does the following:

```
CD\ DOS
MSD.EXE
CD\
```

2. Test it by running the M.BAT file.
3. Create a batch file called C.BAT that will copy MSD.EXE, EDIT.COM, QBASIC.EXE, FORMAT.COM, FDISK.EXE, and ATTRIB.EXE to the A drive.
4. Test it by running the C.BAT file.
5. Create a batch file called GO.BAT with the following content:

```
@ECHO OFF
REM THE FOLLOWING COMMAND MAKES A COPY OF DOS'S TEXT FILES
CLS
ECHO INSERT A DISK IN DRIVE A
PAUSE
COPY C:\DOS\*.TXT A:
COPY A:\README.TXT A:\INFO.TXT
ECHO .
ECHO COPY IS DONE
ECHO .
ECHO YOU CAN NOW REMOVE THE DISK
PAUSE
```

6. Test the GO.BAT batch file.
7. Put a REM in front of the @ECHO OFF and save the changes.
8. Test GO.BAT. Notice the difference.
9. Edit GO.BAT and remove REM from the @ECHO OFF line.

Exercise 4: Using the PATH Command

1. Change to the C:\ directory.
2. Use the PATH command to display the current path.
3. To erase the path, perform the following command at the prompt:

```
PATH;
```

4. Perform the VER, DIR, DATE, TIME, and VOL commands.
5. Insert a formatted disk in drive A.
6. Perform the VER, DIR, DATE, TIME, and VOL commands. Try to figure out why these commands worked on the C drive and the A drive with no path.
7. Change back to the C:\ directory.
8. Try to run the LABEL.EXE and EDIT.COM files.
9. Change to the C:\DOS directory.
10. Try to run the LABEL.EXE and EDIT.COM files. Try to figure out why these commands did not work the first time but worked the second time.
11. Change back to the C:\ directory.
12. Use the PATH command to include the C:\DOS directory.
13. Try to run the LABEL.EXE and EDIT.COM files.
14. If your computer has Windows 3.XX, try to run Windows. (Hint: It is a WIN.COM file in the C:\WINDOWS directory.)
15. Use the PATH command to include the C:\DOS and the C:\WINDOWS directories.
16. If your computer has Windows 3.XX, try to run Windows. Start Windows.

Exercise 5: Creating AUTOEXEC.BAT and CONFIG.SYS Files

1. Format a disk using the A drive and make it bootable.
2. Create an AUTOEXEC.BAT file on the A drive that does the following:

   Gives the standard DOS prompt (path and greater-than sign)
   Has a search path including the DOS and Windows directories

Stores the temporary files in the C:\DOS directory
Deletes the temporary files stored in the C:\DOS directory
Executes the SMARTDRV.EXE file in the C:\DOS directory

If your computer has Windows 3.XX, start Windows.

3. Create a CONFIG.SYS file on the A drive that does the following:

   Has a maximum of 50 files open at the same time
   Sets 30 buffers
   Establishes 9 stacks, each stack being 256 bytes
   Sets the last drive to Z
   Loads the HIMEM.SYS (Hint: DEVICE=C:\DOS\HIMEM.SYS)

4. Reboot the computer to make sure there are no problems.

Exercise 6: Managing Memory

1. Format a disk using the A drive and make it bootable.
2. Create an AUTOEXEC.BAT file on the A drive that does the following:

   Gives the standard DOS prompt (path and greater-than sign)
   Has a search path including the DOS and Windows directories
   Stores the temporary files in the C:\DOS directory
   Deletes the temporary files stored in the C:\DOS directory

3. Create a CONFIG.SYS file that allows 40 files to be open at the same time. Reboot the computer using the A drive.
4. Determine to see how much extended memory there is and how much is free using the MEM command.
5. Load the HIMEM.SYS in the CONFIG.SYS. Reboot the computer.
6. Determine how much extended memory there is and how much is free using the MEM command.
7. Load the EMM386.EXE with the RAM option in the CONFIG.SYS. Reboot the computer.
8. Determine how much expanded memory and how much upper memory there is and how much is free.
9. Have the EMM386.EXE use the NOEMS option instead. Reboot the computer.
10. Determine how much expanded memory and how much upper memory there is and how much is free.
11. Load DOS=UMB.
12. Determine how much upper memory there is and how much is free.
13. Put a REM in front of the EMM386.EXE line. Reboot the computer.
14. Determine how much upper memory there is and how much is free.
15. Remove the REM from the EMM386.EXE line. Reboot the computer.
16. Determine how much conventional memory there is and how much is free.
17. Add DOS=HIGH to the CONFIG.SYS file. Reboot the computer.
18. Determine how much conventional memory there is and how much is free.
19. Combine the DOS=HIGH and DOS=UMB into one line.
20. Put a REM in front of the HIMEM.SYS line. Reboot the computer.
21. Determine how much extended memory, upper memory, and conventional memory there is and how much is free.
22. Remove the REM from the HIMEM.SYS line. Reboot the computer.

Exercise 7: Loading Device Drivers and TSRs

1. Using the same disk from exercise 6, find and load a mouse driver in the appropriate file.
2. Load DOSKEY.COM and ANSI.SYS in the appropriate file.
3. Create a 2,048 KB disk cache that reduces to 128 KB when running Windows.
4. Load SETVER.EXE in the appropriate file.
5. Reboot the computer.
6. Check to see how much conventional memory there is and how much is free.
7. Use the MEM/C command to see what is loaded in conventional memory and what is loaded in upper memory.
8. Load the mouse driver, DOSKEY.COM, ANSI.SYS, and SETVER.EXE into upper memory.

Exercise 8: Fixing Boot Errors

1. Format a disk using the A drive and make it bootable.
2. Delete COMMAND.COM from the A drive.
3. Reboot the computer using the A drive. Notice the error message.
4. Reboot the computer using the C drive.
5. Copy the COMMAND.COM file from the C drive to the A drive.
6. Delete the IO.SYS file from the A drive.
7. Reboot the computer using the A drive. Notice the error message.
8. Reboot the computer using the C drive.
9. Make the disk in the A drive bootable without reformatting the disk.
10. Reboot the computer using the bootable disk.
11. Remove the bootable disk and insert a formatted nonbootable disk in the A drive.
12. Execute MSD.EXE from the C:\DOS directory.
13. Exit MSD.EXE. Notice the error message.
14. Remove the nonbootable disk and insert the boot disk into the A drive.

Exercise 9: Troubleshooting the AUTOEXEC.BAT and CONFIG.SYS Files

1. Format the disk from exercise 8 using drive A and make it bootable.
2. Create the following CONFIG.SYS file:

```
FILE=60
LASTDRIVE=Z
STACKS=9,256
DEVICE=C:\HIMEM.SYS
DEVICE=C:\EMM386.EXE NOEMS
DOS-HIGH
DEVICEHIGH=C:\ANSI.SYS
DEVICEHIGH=C:\DOS\SETVER.EXE
DEVICEHIGH=C:\DOS\DOSKEY.COM
```

3. Create the following AUTOEXEC.BAT file:

```
@ECHO OFF
PATH=C:\DOSC:\WINDOWS
PROMPT $P$G
SET TEMP=C:\DOS
DEL C:\DOS*.TMP
```

4. Find and correct all of the errors.

Exercise 10: Installing DOS

1. Reformat the hard drive.
2. Install DOS using the DOS installation disks.
3. Install the mouse driver.
4. Install the CD-ROM drivers and sound card drivers.
5. Modify the AUTOEXEC.BAT and CONFIG.SYS files to do the following:
   Load DOSKEY.COM in upper memory
   Set the standard DOS prompt (path and greater-than sign)
   Set the search path to include the DOS and Windows directories
   Store the temporary files in the C:\DOS directory
   Delete the temporary files stored in the C:\DOS directory
   If your computer has Windows 3.XX, start Windows
   Create a 2,048 KB disk cache that reduces to 128 KB when running Windows
   Load all device drivers needed for the mouse, CD-ROM, and sound card into upper memory

CHAPTER 20

Windows 9X

Topics Covered in This Chapter

Introduction

Windows 95, an innovative operating system for the PC, was designed to replace DOS and Windows 3.XX. It has a better, more intuitive user interface and it supports long file names (LFNs). Behind the interface, Windows 9X is a preemptive, multithreading, multitasking environment. A mostly 32-bit operating system that is not limited by the conventional memory restrictions, it provides compatibility for most DOS and Windows 3.XX device drivers and applications. It supports plug-and-play technology and has built-in multimedia and network capability. While the Windows 9X is becoming an outdated OS, it can still be found on 1 in every 4 computers that surf the Internet.

Objectives

1. List the minimum hardware and software requirements to run Windows 9X.
2. Describe the Windows 9X boot process.
3. Perform common file and disk management tasks.
4. Compare and contrast FAT, VFAT, and FAT32 file systems.
5. Install and execute Win32-based, Win16-based, and DOS applications.
6. Explain how Win32-based, Win16-based, and DOS applications run in the Windows 9X environment.
7. Terminate a nonresponding application.
8. Share data between documents.
9. Remove a Windows application from Windows 9X.
10. Print a document in Windows 9X and manage the print job.
11. Load the appropriate print driver.
12. Configure Windows using the Control Panel.
13. Use the Device Manager to find available resources, resource conflicts, and driver problems.
14. Create a startup disk.
15. Configure the desktop and Taskbar.
16. Make changes to the MSDOS.INI file when appropriate.
17. List and describe the six different keys found in the Windows 9X registry.
18. Back up the Windows 9X registry.
19. Use REGEDIT to make changes to the registry when appropriate.
20. Install and configure Windows 9X.
21. Given a problem in Windows 9X, determine and correct the problem.

20.1 WINDOWS 9X VERSIONS

Windows 95 is a complete operating system that was designed to replace DOS and Windows 3.XX. The most obvious differences between Windows 95 and Windows 3.XX is that Windows 95 has a better, more intuitive user interface that supports long file names. Yet, underneath, while DOS and Windows 3.XX was a 16-bit operating system and Windows NT was a 32-bit operating system, Windows 95 consisted of part 16-bit code and part 32-bit code. This had a lot more power than DOS and Windows 3.XX and it allowed a lot more flexibility than Windows NT. This way you could still run a lot of your DOS and Window 3.XX programs. Windows 95 introduced a 32-bit program, dynamically loaded device drivers, memory paging, networking, and many other features available that were available only in Windows NT. In addition, it brought plug-and-play to Windows.

At the same time that Windows 95 was released, Microsoft also sold Microsoft Plus! Companion for Windows 95. This was an add-on software package that included several utilities and desktop enhancements left out of Windows 95 that we would see in later versions of Windows. It included System Agent, DriveSpace 3, Internet Explorer, the Dial-up Networking system, and a 3D pinball game. System Agent schedules applications to automatically start at predefined times. DriveSpace 3 is an enhanced version of the disk compression software that comes with Windows 95. Internet Explorer 3.0 is a World Wide Web browser, and the Dial-up Networking server allows others to dial into a computer using a modem.

20.1.1 Windows 95 Updates

Since the Windows 95 release, the Windows 9X family has still gone through a lot of changes. Several months after the retail version of Windows 95 (version 4.00.950) was introduced, Microsoft issued Service Pack 1 (version 4.00.950A after installation). See table 20.1. Some of the fixes done by Service Pack 1 included:

1. An OLE32 update
2. A Microsoft Windows 95 shell update that permitted browsing NetWare Directory Service printers from the Add Printer Wizard
3. Windows 95 Common Dialog update for Windows 3.1 Legacy printer drivers
4. The Windows 95 Password List update to protect the password file against potential security violations
5. An update of LTP.VXD to support ECP (enhanced communications parallel) port bidirectional communications
6. Several network updates

OEM Service Release 2 (OSR2), released at the end of 1996, is an updated version of the retail version of Windows 95 and is sometimes referred to as Windows 95b. Unlike the retail version of Windows 95, OSR2 is available only to PC vendors and can be purchased only with a new computer, motherboard, or hard drive. Whereas the original version of Windows 95 was made to upgrade Windows 3.XX or to be installed on a new system, the OSR2 was made for new systems only. Therefore, the retail Windows 95 (version 950) cannot be upgraded with Windows 95 OSR2. The OSR2 provided a number of new features and bug fixes, including the fixes done with Service Pack 1. Some of the new features included:

- FAT32 file system
- DriveSpace 3 (disk compression)
- Internet Explorer 3.0
- Microsoft Internet Mail and News, Internet Connect Wizard, and Peer Web Server
- Control Panel display tool enhancements
- OpenGL support and screen savers
- DirectX 2.0
- ActiveMovie
- Online service software, including AOL, CompuServe, and MSN

Table 20.1 The Various Windows Versions

Version	Version Number	Comments
Windows 95 Retail	4.00.950	Original version.
Windows 95 Service Pack 1	4.00.950A	Major bug fix.
Windows 95 OSR2 Service Release 2 (OSR2)	4.00.1111	Added FAT32, IE 3.0, NetMeeting 1.0, DirectX 2.0, bug fixes, and other updates.
Windows 95 OSR2 Service Release 2.1 (OSR2.1)	4.03.1212	Added USB support.
Windows 95 OSR2 Service Release 2.5 (OSR2.5)	4.03.1214	Added IE 4.01, Outlook Express, Internet Connection Wizard, DirectX 5.0, NetMeeting 2.1, Java VM, bug fixes.
Windows 98	4.10.1998	Original version.
Windows 98 Second Edition (SE)	4.10.2222A	Added IE 5.0, DirectX 6.1, NetMeeting 3.0, Media Player 6.2, bug fixes, and other updates.
Windows Millennium	4.90.3000	Original version.

- Support for 32-bit PC cards
- Additional power management features
- Support for IrDA wireless communications
- Daylight Savings Time and time zone updates
- Updates user interface to include hardware profiles

Microsoft OpenGL is a 3D graphics language designed to improve performance on hardware that supports the OpenGL standard. To demonstrate OpenGL, OSR2 includes 3D screen savers. (Note: When the OpenGL screen savers are active, they consume a large amount of processing.) DirectX is an application programming interface (API) developed by Microsoft that enables programs to access hardware features of a computer without knowing exactly what hardware is installed on the machine. DirectX was originally designed to allow Windows 95 to become a gaming platform but has grown into a multimedia platform. DirectX achieves this by translating generic hardware commands into specific commands for particular pieces of hardware. In particular, DirectX lets multimedia applications take advantage of hardware acceleration features supported by graphics accelerators. DirectX 2, released in 1996, supports the Direct3D architecture.

In February 1998, Microsoft released OEM Service Release 2.5 (OSR2.5). Much like OSR2, OSR2.5 can be sold only with a new computer, new motherboard, or hard drive. The new features include Microsoft Internet Explorer 4.01, updated online services, universal serial bus (USB) support, IEEE 1394 buses, and a few minor fixes. In addition, it includes DirectX 5, which includes DirectDraw, DirectSound, DirectShow, and DirectAnimation to allow programs to manipulate multimedia objects and streams and supports accelerated graphics port (AGP) and multimedia extensions (MMX). The newest version of DirectX can be downloaded from the Microsoft website.

20.1.2 Windows 98

Windows 98 was released in June of 1998. The most obvious difference between Windows 95 and Windows 98 is the Active Desktop interface, which allows the operating system to use the same interface as Internet Explorer.

NOTE: The Active Desktop interface has been available with Internet Explorer 4.0.

In addition to the interface changes, Windows 98 offers the following:

- More stability—Microsoft fixed over 3,000 bugs
- Faster speed, particularly during boot-up and shutdown
- Advanced Power Management (APM) 1.2, allowing for a longer battery life on portable computers
- Automatic performance of maintenance tasks, such as defragmenting the hard disk
- Better protection for the registry by tracking changes to it with the last five copies of the registry
- Improved system diagnostics, including a Registry checker, a version conflict manager, the Microsoft System Information program, and several troubleshooting wizards to help isolate programs
- Automatic downloading and updating of the operating system and drivers
- The ability to connect several monitors to a computer
- Integration of a multimedia architecture, including broadcast architecture that allows you to watch TV on your computer
- Support for a number of new technologies, including FAT32, accelerated graphics port (AGP), multimedia extensions (MMX), universal serial bus (USB), and digital video disk (DVD)
- A new unified driver model for Windows 98 and Windows NT called the Win32 Driver Model (WDM)

When Windows 98 shipped, Microsoft also offered Microsoft Plus! 98, which contained several other utilities, including McAfee Viruscan, file cleaners, compressed folders, Deluxe CD Player (which can search the web for artists and songs), several new games, and online shopping.

Windows 98 second edition, also known as Windows 98 SE, included the normal bug fixes and driver updates and included better support for the Pentium III processors and new devices for USB and IEEE 1394 (FireWire). It included Internet Explorer 5.0, DirectX 6.1, NetMeeting 3.0, and Media Player 6.2. It also introduced Internet Connection Sharing (ICS), which lets you share a single Internet connection among a small group of home or small business computers.

20.1.3 Windows Millennium

The features of Windows Millennium (Windows Me) were originally planned to be released with Windows XP. But because of delays, the changes were incorporated on top of Windows 98 and Microsoft released Windows Millennium.

Windows Millennium includes novice-friendly add-ons. It has more multimedia support, including the new MovieMaker and Windows Media Player and an easy-to-use networking guide called the Home Networking Wizard. In addition, Windows Me includes home-friendly tools such as System Restore, which returns your system to a precrash state if you have a problem; System File Protection, which warns you against accidentally deleting essential Windows files; and AutoUpdate, which checks for OS updates, downloads, and fixes, and installs them automatically while you work.

Unlike previous versions of Windows 95 and Windows 98, Millennium doesn't let you boot into DOS at startup. Microsoft dropped the code that lets Windows 95/98 work with older DOS apps, largely so that Windows Me would boot faster. You can still run older games that require DOS, but it is not easy. To access a DOS prompt on a Millennium system, you must start up using a Windows Me boot disk that retains the DOS boot option.

20.2 WINDOWS INTERFACE

The Windows 9X interface is based on the desktop, where all of the work is done. On the desktop are the My Computer icon, the Recycle Bin, and the Taskbar (with the Start button). In addition, there may be a Network Neighborhood icon to access network resources (files, applications, and printers), an Inbox to receive electronic mail, and various folders (directories) and shortcuts to programs and documents. See figure 20.1. If a customer calls, complaining that the icons look different and the problem clears up after the system is rebooted, the user can refresh the screen and restore the icons by pressing Shift + F8.

Figure 20.1 Windows 95 Interface

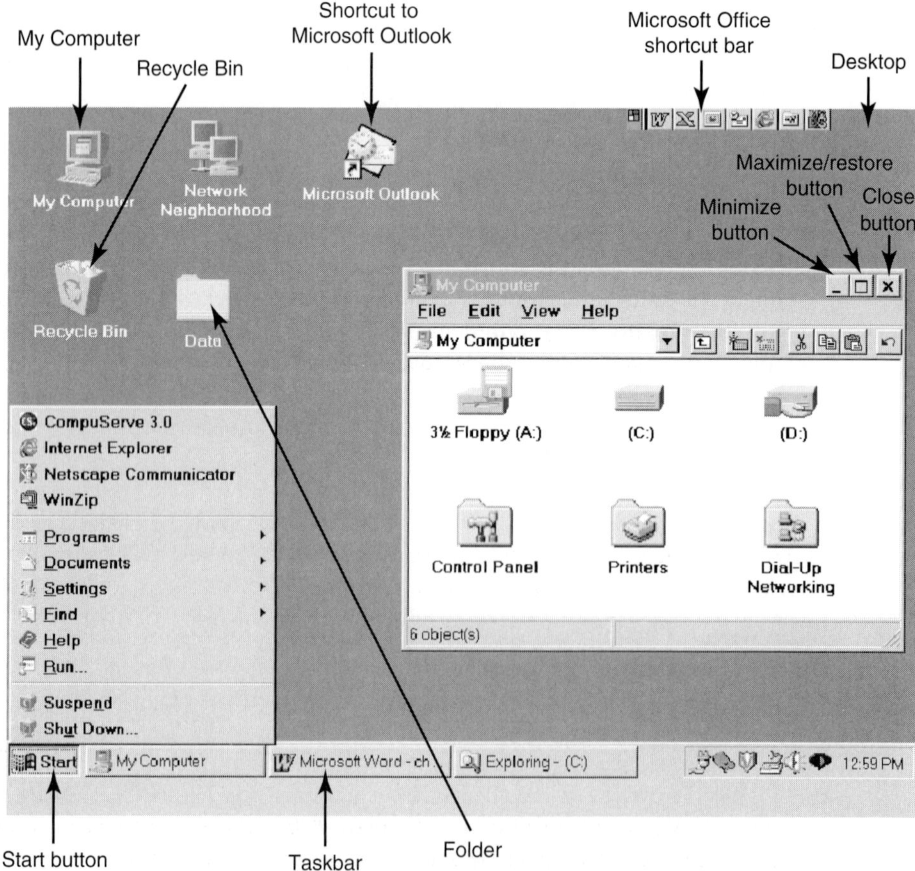

Figure 20.2 The Taskbar

20.2.1 Parts of Windows

The My Computer icon includes all disk drives, the Control Panel, and the PRINTERS folder. From within the My Computer icon, all files on the drives can be accessed and managed.

The Recycle Bin is used as a safe delete. When a file is deleted using the GUI interface, Windows will store the file in the Recycle Bin, and it will remain there until the Recycle Bin is emptied or until the computer is running out of disk space (at which point Windows 9X will delete the oldest files first). If a file is deleted and the user later decides to undelete the file, he or she can open the Recycle Bin and drag the file to any location or choose the Restore option from the File menu. Note: If you want your files to be automatically deleted instead of moved to the RECYCLE BIN folder, you can right-click the Recycle Bin, select Properties, and then select the "Do not move files to the Recycle Bin" option.

The Taskbar is located at the bottom of the screen. Some taskbars are always visible; others are configured to auto-hide and reappear only when the mouse pointer is moved to the bottom of the screen. These taskbars are configured to auto-hide so that there is more free area on the desktop. The Taskbar is divided into three areas: the Start button, the systray, and the active program buttons. See figure 20.2. The Start button is used to start programs. In addition, it can open recently accessed documents and access the Control Panel and PRINTERS folder, find files, and get Help for Windows 95. (Note: The Start button is actually a series of shortcuts to programs.) The systray (also known as the notificaton area), located on the right side of the Taskbar, is used for the clock and for any programs running in the background, such as printers and modems. The rest of the Taskbar is blank or holds the active program buttons, which can be used to switch between open programs.

When a window is open, the window will usually contain a minimize button, a maximize or restore button, and a close button in the top right corner and a control menu icon in the top left corner. In addition, most program windows will include a menu and many will include one or more toolbars.

20.2.2 Shortcut Menus

Shortcut menus have been added to Windows 9X. They are accessed by clicking the secondary mouse button (usually the right mouse button) and contain common commands for the item selected. For example, if a file is clicked with the right mouse button, the user can choose to open the file, copy the file, delete the file, or show the properties of the file. If the disk drive in My Computer is clicked with the right mouse button, the user can open the disk, format the disk, or show the properties of the disk. If the user highlights some text in a word processing program such as Microsoft Word and clicks on the text with the right mouse button, the Cut, Copy, and Paste options can be chosen or the formatting of the text can be changed.

20.3 DISK AND FILE MANAGEMENT

Disk and file management is usually done with My Computer or Windows Explorer (see figure 20.3), which can be started by using the Programs option under the Start button. The most common disk and file management commands are shown in table 20.2. If several files or folders are to be moved, deleted, or copied at the same time, the Ctrl and Shift keys can be used to select multiple files. For example, pressing the Ctrl key and holding it down will select any file or folder within the same drive or folder. Pressing the Shift key and holding it down and selecting two files or folders will select everything listed between the two. After the file or directories have been selected, they can be copied, deleted, or moved as one.

Other ways to manage programs, disks, directories, and files are to use:

- Program Manager (PROGMAN.EXE in the WINDOWS folder, which can be executed using Windows Explorer or by using the Run option under the Start button)

Figure 20.3 Windows Explorer

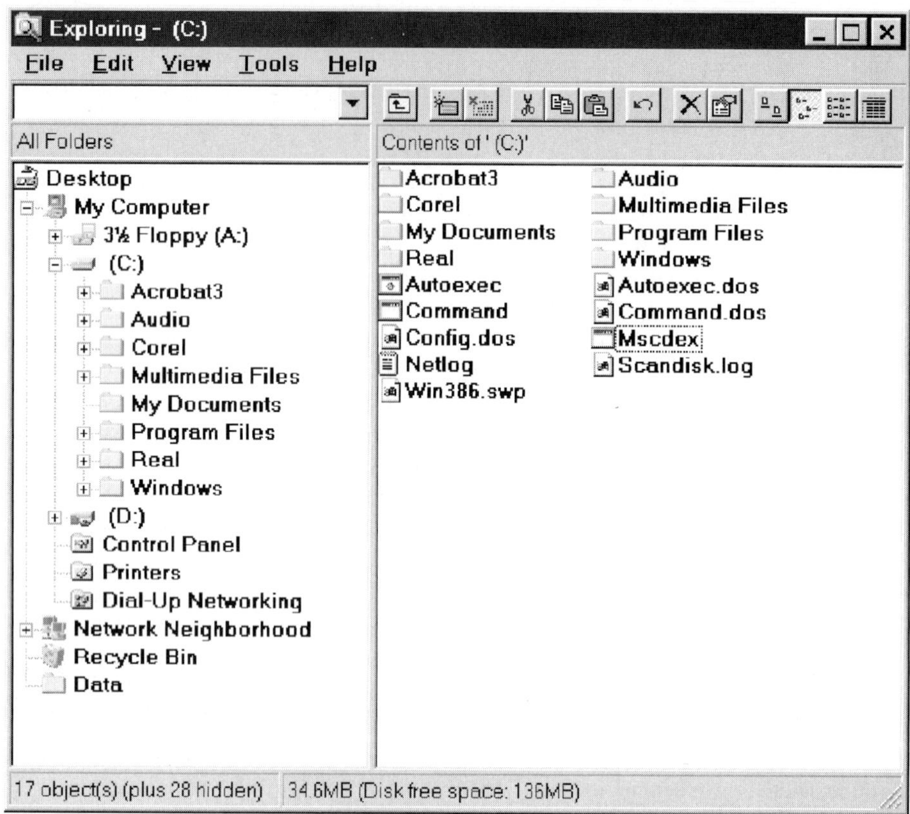

Table 20.2 Common Disk and File Management Commands

To create a folder (directory) on the desktop, in the root directory, or in another folder	Select New from the File menu or New from the shortcut menu (right mouse button) and select the Folder option.
To delete a file or directory	Select the file or folder by clicking on it and dragging it to the Recycle Bin, pick the Delete option from the shortcut or File menu, or press the Delete key on the keyboard.
To format a disk	Select the Format option from the drive's shortcut menu or select the Format option from the My Computer File menu.
To copy a floppy disk	Select the Copy Disk option from the drive's shortcut menu or from the My Computer File menu.
To copy a file or directory from one drive to another	Drag the file (click on the file and keep the left mouse button clicked while moving the mouse) to its new destination. Another way is to first select the file or directory and the Copy option from the shortcut or Edit menu (Explorer or any disk or folder window). Then select the destination and the Paste option from the shortcut or Edit menu.
To move a file or directory to a different folder within the same drive	Press the Ctrl key while dragging the file to its new destination. Note: If the Ctrl key is not pressed, dragging will make a shortcut to the file or directory instead of moving the file. Another way is to first select the file or directory and select the Cut option from the shortcut or Edit menu (Explorer or any disk or folder window). Then select the destination and the Paste option from the shortcut or Edit menu.
To rename a file	Select the file and choose the Rename option in the File menu or in the shortcut menu. Another way is to click once on the file name.
To view or change the directory or file attributes (read-only, hidden, or system)	Select the folder or file and select the Properties option from the File menu or shortcut menu. You can also show hidden files in Windows by opening any Windows Explorer window, opening the View menu, selecting options, and enabling the Show all files option.

NOTE: Many 32-bit Windows applications also allow Cut, Copy, Delete, and Rename by using the shortcut menu from within some dialog boxes, including the Open and Save As dialog boxes.

- File Manager (WINFILE.EXE in the WINDOWS folder, which can be executed using Windows Explorer or by using the Run option under the Start button)

NOTE: File Manager uses only the 8.3 file names and will truncate long file names.

- MS-DOS Prompt (to start a DOS session to perform DOS commands, select the MS-DOS Prompt from the Programs option under the Start button; or use the Run option, type *COMMAND,* and press the Enter key)

NOTE: The standard external DOS commands are located in the WINDOWS\COMMAND directory.

20.4 INSTALLING WINDOWS 9X

Windows can be installed from CD-ROM or over a network. To start the Windows installation, go to the CD-ROM and execute the SETUP.EXE file from within Windows 3.1 or later or at the DOS prompt (DOS 3.2 or later). Table 20.3 shows the requirements for installing and running Windows 9X. Although the requirements listed in the table for Windows come from its documentation, they offer slow and sometimes unreliable operation. For acceptable performance and reliability, I would recommend a Pentium II processor with 64 MB of RAM or better. Of course, with a faster processor and additional RAM, Windows will perform even better.

20.4.1 Installation Overview

There are several ways to start the installation process. If your system supports a bootable CD, the easiest way is to insert the Windows CD and turn on the computer. (Note: Windows 95 OEM Installation CD is not bootable.) If you have a Windows startup disk or any other disk with the CD drive drivers, insert the disk in drive A and turn on the computer. Then insert the CD, change over to the CD and execute the SETUP.EXE file. If you decide to do an upgrade so that you can keep your settings and

Table 20.3 Windows Requirements

Requirements	Windows 95	Windows 98	Windows Me
Processor	• Minimum—386DX processor (or higher) • Recommended—Pentium (or higher)	• Minimum—486DX/66 MHz or higher • Recommended—Pentium processor (or higher)	• Pentium 150 MHz processor or better
RAM	• Minimum—4 MB • Recommended minimum—16–32 MB	• Minimum—16 MB of memory (RAM) • Recommended minimum—32–64 MB recommended	• 32 MB of RAM or better
Drives	• A high-density floppy disk drive • CD-ROM drive • Hard drive with a minimum of 55 MB of free disk space	• 120 MB of free hard disk space. (Typical installation requires 195 MB. Depending on your system configuration and the options you choose to install, you may need between 120 and 355 MB.) • CD-ROM or DVD-ROM drive	• Hard drive with a minimum of 480 to 645 MB of free disk space • A high-density floppy disk drive or CD-ROM drive (recommended)
Video System	• Minimum—VGA or better • Recommended—Super VGA (16- or 24-bit color)	• Minimum—VGA or better • Recommended—Super VGA (16- or 24-bit color)	• Minimum—VGA or better • Recommended—Super VGA (16- or 24-bit color)
Pointing Devices	• Not required, but highly recommended	• Microsoft mouse or compatible pointing device	• Microsoft mouse or compatible pointing device

Table 20.4 Windows Setup Switches

Switch	Function
SETUP /IS	Disables SCANDISK
SETUP /ID	Does not check for disk space
SETUP /IM	Ignores the conventional memory check
SETUP /IL	Installs the Logitech mouse driver, which is available only when installing from DOS
SETUP /IQ	Disables the crosslink hard disk check if /IS is used
SETUP /C	Does not load SMARTDRV; available only when installing from DOS
SETUP /IN	Does not run Network Setup; available only when installing from DOS
SETUP /T:<path>	Defines the location of temporary setup files; the directory specified must already exist and will be deleted when the setup is done
SETUP /<batchfilename>	Specifies the batch file that contains setup options so Windows can be installed as an unattended installation
SETUP /?	Displays the Help screen

applications, you execute the SETUP.EXE file from within Windows by clicking on the Start button and selecting the Run option, or by using Explorer. Table 20.4 lists the switches for the Setup program.

A message informs you that Setup is going to perform a check. When you press Enter, Microsoft ScanDisk checks your disk drives for errors. When ScanDisk finishes, press the X key.

Next, it will initialize your system and copies the necessary files for installing Windows 98. When done, it will display Windows 98 Setup screen. This screen has an information bar on the left-hand side that displays the five steps that Setup will perform and a timer that shows the estimated time remaining to complete the installation. To begin the Setup process, click Continue. The five-step basic installation steps are:

1. Preparing to run Windows Setup
2. Collecting information about your computer
3. Copying Windows files to your computer
4. Restarting your computer
5. Setting up hardware and finalizing settings

During the first step, Setup prepares the Windows 98 Setup Wizard, which guides you through the installation process. During this time, it will:

- Create the SETUPLOG.TXT file in the root directory (C:\)
- Identify the drive where Windows 98 is being installed and the source drive where the Windows 98 installation files are located (drive assignment)
- Create the C:\WININST0.400 temporary directory and copy MINI.CAB to it. MINI.CAB contains the mini-Windows program files required by Setup.
- Extracts all files in PRECOPY1.CAB and PRECOPY2.CAB to C:\WININST0.400. These are the files necessary to run Setup Wizard.

Next, the computer will collect information about your computer and prepare it for copying the Windows 98 files through the following phases, where Setup Wizard:

- Presents the (License Agreement screen in figure 20.4)
- Prompts you to enter the Product Key (Product Key screen in figure 20.4)
- Prompts you to select a directory for installing Windows (Select Directory screen in figure 20.5)
- Informs you that it is preparing the directory where it will install Windows and verifying that there is enough space to install it (Preparing Directory screen)

Figure 20.4 License Agreement and Product Keys That Appear During the Installation Screen

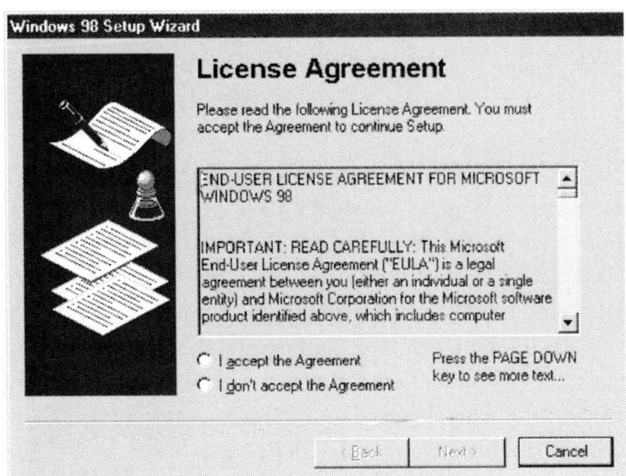

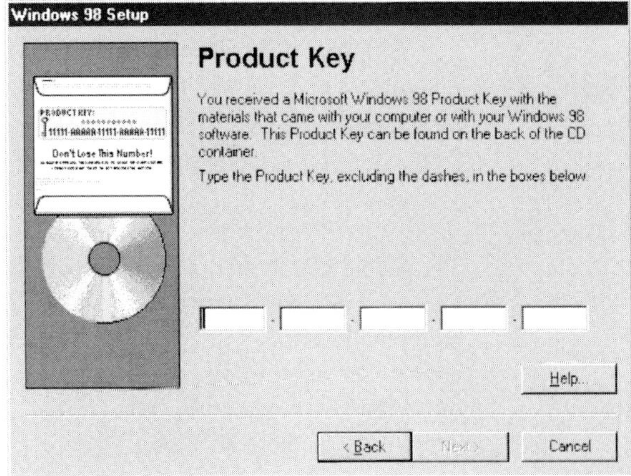

Figure 20.5 The Select Directory Screen of the Windows 98 Setup Wizard

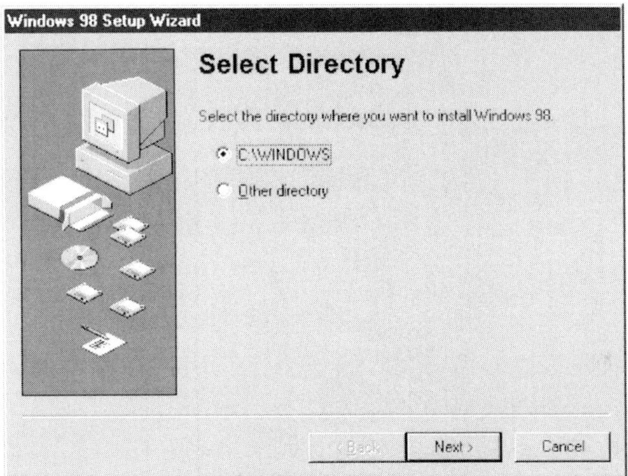

- Lets you choose the type of setup you want—Typical, Portable, Compact, or Custom (Setup Options screen in figure 20.6)
- Prompts you to enter your name and company name (User Information screen)
- Lets you install the most common components or customize your selection (Windows Components screen in figure 20.7)
- Lets you add or remove components (Select Components screen in figure 20.7)
- Prompts you to identify your computer on the network (Identification screen)
- Lets you select the location for getting region-specific information from the Internet (Establishing Your Location screen)
- Prompts you to create the startup disk (Startup Disk screen)
- Starts copying files (Start Copying Files screen)

The default directory is C:\WINDOWS. If you want to install Windows in a directory other than C:\WINDOWS, follow these steps. To install Windows 98 in a new directory, click Other directory in the Select Directory dialog box and then click the Next button. When the Change Directory dialog box appears, type a new directory name, and then click the Next button. If you specify a directory that does not exist, Setup creates one for you. See figure 20.5.

Once Setup finishes setting up the directory structure, it prompts you to select the type of setup you want through the Setup Options dialog box. Each Setup option contains a specific set of components to install. When you choose a Setup option, Setup selects by default a set of appropriate components based on your choice. Later, through the Select Components dialog box, Setup gives you the choice to either accept the default selection or select your own components. To choose a Setup option, in the Setup Options dialog box, click the Setup option you want, then click Next. The Typical Setup option is selected as the default. See figure 20.6 and table 20.5.

After the Setup Options phase, Windows Setup asks you to type your name and company name, which Windows uses to identify you for various operations. You must enter this information for Setup to continue.

After you provide the user information, Setup displays the Windows Components dialog box. If you select "Install the most common components," Setup continues the installation. If you select "Show me the list of components so I can choose," the Select Components dialog box appears. See figure 20.7. The Select Components dialog box lets you customize your installation by choosing the components you want to install. In the Components list, click a component set (for example, Communications), and then click Details. A shaded box means that only part of the component will be installed. A dialog box appears, listing the components in the category. Select or deselect the component you want to add or remove, and then click OK. Note: You can install or remove any of these components after Windows is installed by using Add/Remove Programs in the Control Panel.

After you have selected which components you want to install, Setup prompts you to identify how you want your computer to be identified on your network by displaying the Identification dialog box. The computer name must be unique on the network, and can be up to 15 characters long with no spaces (no blank characters). The name can contain only alphanumeric characters and the following special characters:

! @ # $ % ^ & ( ) - _ ' { } . ~

Figure 20.6 The Setup Options Screen of the Windows 98 Setup Wizard

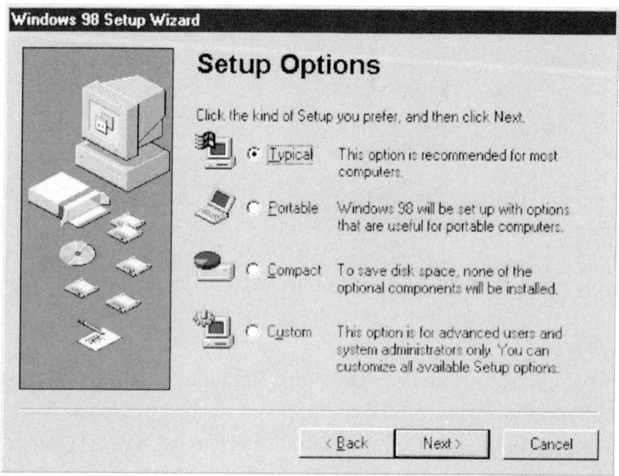

Table 20.5 Types of Windows Setups

Setup Option	Description
Typical	All of the components that are usually installed with Windows 9X. Most users should select this Setup option.
Portable	To install the options generally required for portable computers.
Compact	The smallest possible installation of Windows 9X. For example, you may want to perform a Compact installation if your hard disk does not have much free space. Setup then installs no optional components. If you later want to use an optional component, such as Games or WebTV for Windows, you have to install it. To install an optional component after Setup is completed, use Add/Remove Programs in the Control Panel.
Custom	To choose which optional components are installed. If you do not select a Custom installation, then Setup installs only the optional components that are selected by default. If you know you are going to need certain Windows components, you may want to select a Custom installation and ensure that those components are included during Setup.

Figure 20.7 Selecting the Windows Components During the Windows 9X Installation

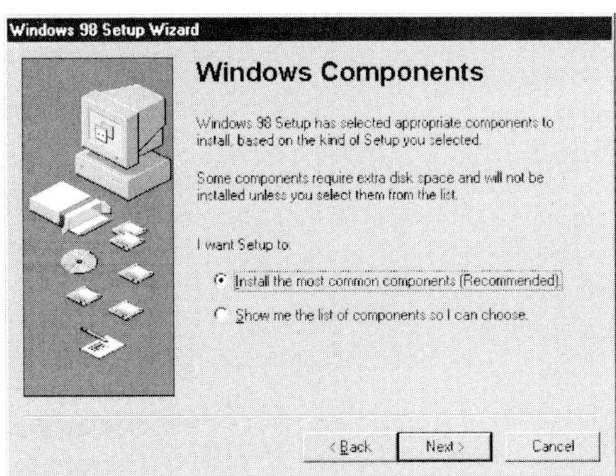

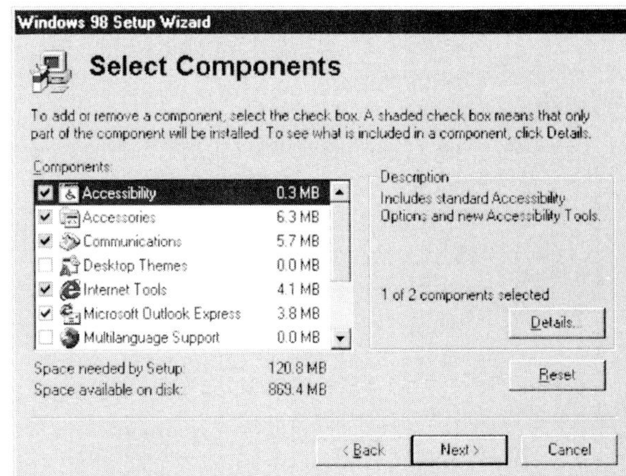

The workgroup name can be up to 15 characters long and uses the same naming convention as the computer name. The workgroup is used to associate groups of computers together for more efficient browsing.

Next, Setup prompts you to establish your location by displaying the Establishing Your Location dialog box. Select the location for getting region-specific news and other information through media such as channels (websites designed to deliver content from the Internet to your computer). Channels become available on your Windows desktop Channel Bar after you install Windows successfully.

After establishing your location, Setup prompts you to create a Windows startup disk by displaying the Startup Disk dialog box. You can create a startup disk during Setup or by using Add/Remove Programs in the Control Panel.

After Setup finishes creating the startup disk, the Start Copying Files dialog box appears. Click Next to start copying files. Note: Do not interrupt file copying. If Setup is interrupted during the file-copying phase, Windows may fail to run when you restart your computer because Windows 98 will not have all of the necessary files to start. If you interrupt Setup during this phase, you must run Setup again.

After Setup finishes copying the Windows files to your computer, you are prompted to restart your computer. You can click the Restart Now button to restart your computer immediately; if you do not click the button or wait more than 15 seconds to click it, Setup restarts your computer automatically. After Setup restarts your computer, the following message appears on your screen:

Getting ready to start Windows 98 for the first time.

During this phase, Setup configures the:

- Control Panel
- Programs on the Start menu
- Windows Help
- MS-DOS program settings
- Tuning Up Application Start
- Time zone
- System Configuration

When Setup finishes setting up hardware and configuring settings, Setup restarts your computer and asks you to log on. After you log on, Setup:

- Builds a driver information database
- Updates system settings
- Sets up personalized settings such as settings for the Internet Explorer 4 browsing software, Start menu, Online services, Volume Control, and Channels
- Then, Setup displays the Welcome to Windows 98 dialog box

20.4.2 Troubleshooting Installation Problems

When Setup experiences a problem, it attempts to automatically correct or work around the problem. To keep track of these, Setup relies on two log files that it creates during installation to determine the cause of the failure and overcome the problem. These log files are SETUPLOG.TXT and DETLOG. TXT.

If the failure occurs prior to the hardware detection phase, Setup reads the file SETUPLOG.TXT to determine the point at which the problem occurred. SETUPLOG.TXT is a text file to which Setup writes status information during the installation process. When a failure occurs and you restart Setup, it scans SETUPLOG.TXT to identify processes that started but did not complete. The processes that failed are skipped. Although it is possible that Setup could fail multiple times, the fact that Setup skips failed processes on subsequent tries ensures that the installation process always progresses, even though some items might not be installed completely. The end result is that Windows 98 often can install basic support and run, enabling you to incorporate the skipped items manually. Unfortunately, Setup does not inform you of which items it has skipped.

If you experience a problem with Setup, check your system for a copy of SETUPLOG.TXT and scan the file to determine if you can identify the point or points at which Setup failed. If you were able to install a minimal Windows 98 configuration and boot without support for certain devices, you can open Notepad or WordPad in Windows 98 to read SETUPLOG.TXT. If Setup was unable to install a minimal working copy of Windows 98, you should be able to boot your system to DOS and use the EDIT command to read the file. If you are unable to boot the system from the hard disk, you can boot using a DOS system disk. The following list explains the majority of sections you might find in a SETUPLOG.TXT file:

- [Choose Directory]. This section specifies the installation directory, information about the Windows 98 source files and directories, the type of installation you selected (typical, custom, and so on), and other general information about the Setup prior to the detection phase.
- [FileCopy]. This section provides a lengthy list of the files that were copied to your system during Setup.
- [OptionalComponents]. This section lists the optional components and which ones were installed. A value of 1 for a component, such as "Calculator"=1, indicates that the component was installed. A value of zero indicates that the component was not installed.
- [Restart]. This section lists processes that Setup performed after it restarted the system.
- [System]. This section lists your system hardware configuration, such as display type, keyboard type, and so forth.
- [NameAndOrg]. This section contains the user and organization names that were entered during Setup.
- [Destination]. This section lists paths that Setup uses to track file destinations.
- [Setup]. This section contains a variety of settings that specify options selected during Setup.
- [Network]. This section contains settings that indicate network setup options that were specified.
- [Started]. This section contains messages and options generated during the initial startup phase of Setup.
- [Detection]. This section contains status information and messages regarding the initial detection phase.

In addition to the sections described in the previous list, the SETUPLOG.TXT file also can contain additional sections and settings. If you scan through SETLOG.TXT, you will notice that the entries in the file follow the logical progression of the Setup process, with initial Setup actions appearing near the top of the file and actions that occur near the end of the Setup process appearing near the end of the file.

During the hardware detection phase, Setup creates and writes to a hidden file named DETLOG.TXT, which stores the hardware that was detected and the parameters for each device. The DETLOG.TXT file also is modified when you use the Device Manager or Add New Hardware Wizard from the Control Panel. DETLOG.TXT, therefore, serves as a common hardware detection log for each of the functions that adds hardware support for Windows 98. If a DETLOG.TXT file already exists, it is renamed DETLOG.OLD, and a new DETLOG.TXT file is created. Setup creates the DETLOG.TXT file in the root directory of the boot disk.

Although Setup can track and overcome hardware detection errors, it doesn't use DETLOG.TXT for that purpose. Instead, DETLOG.TXT serves only as a log that you can use to identify hardware detection problems. If a detection error occurs, Setup creates a binary file named DETCRASH.LOG and reads DETCRASH.LOG in subsequent installation attempts to overcome the hardware detection problem.

Table 20.6 DETLOG.TXT Settings

Setting	Function
Parameters	Lists command-line switches that were used to start Setup
WinVer	Lists DOS and Windows versions detected by Setup
AvoidMem	Specifies upper memory blocks that Setup avoids during detection
LogCrash	Specifies whether or not a valid DETCRASH.LOG file was found
DetectClass: Skip	Indicates that Setup Class found no hints for a class of devices and is skipping the class
Detected	Lists a component that was detected
UserOverride	Records classes that you directed Setup to skip during installation

If your system locks up during the hardware detection phase, Setup will bypass the failed device during the next installation attempt. If you want to track down the source of the problem, you can boot the system to DOS and scan DETLOG.TXT for possible problems. Table 20.6 describes settings you will find in a typical DETLOG.TXT file.

Another log file that is worth mentioning is the NETLOG.TXT file. This text file contains a record of all detected network components found during installation. The network detection phase consists of four parts. These correspond with the four class types of network configuration: network clients, network protocols, network adapters, and network services (such as file and print sharing). It is stored as a nonhidden file on the computer's root directory. Information is added to this file in the same order as the network detection phase. If you need to determine what caused the Windows Setup program's failure to communicate across the network, refer to the entries in this file. You will see where Windows found the network adapter and identified which protocols, clients, and services to bind to the card. At the end of each line, you should see OK. If you see a line such as "Couldn't determine . . . ," or some other failure notice, you have found your problem.

When installation fails early in the Setup process, it is often related to one or more of the following issues and you should:

- Double-check to make sure that your hardware is on the Microsoft Hardware Compatibility List.
- If you have any disk management utilities that may interfere with the installations, see if you can remove them. This may require a BIOS update or repartitioning your drive.
- If your disk is compressed, uncompress it.
- Disable your virus protection in the CMOS setup program and any software that might be loaded on the system. It can be reenabled when the installation is done.
- Check for viruses.
- Turn off any power management in the CMOS setup program and any software that might be loaded.
- If you are installing onto a SCSI drive, SmartDrive can cause a problem with double-buffering turned off. To work around this, use the C switch with the setup command.
- Check your CONFIG.SYS and AUTOEXEC.BAT for any device drivers or TSRs that might interfere with the installation. Typically use only what is necessary to boot the system and start the CD.

See Tables 20.7 and 20.8 for specific problems during Setup.

20.4.3 Service Packs, Patches, and Windows Update

After installing Windows, check if Microsoft has released any fixes or patches, and apply them to the Windows system. Sometimes, Microsoft will group the patches together and call them a service pack.

For your convenience, Microsoft produced the http://windowsupdate.microsoft.com website that is a catalog of fixes, updates, and enhancements to Windows and many programs that work with Windows. If you have a newer version of Internet Explorer, the easiest way to get there is open the Tools menu and select Windows Update. When you go to this website, Windows will scan your system to see what you have installed and gives you a list of suggested components. This system check ensures that you

Table 20.7 DOS Level Errors

Error	Description
"No boot device present" when booting off the startup disk	Either the startup disk is bad or the CMOS is not set to boot from the floppy disk first.
Windows has detected that drive C does not contain a valid FAT partition	Either the drive is not partitioned or you are trying to install on a partition type that Windows fails to understand. Delete all partitions and repartition the drive.
Windows setup requires XXXX amount of available drive space	Either you forgot to format the C drive or you need to delete some files from the C drive.
MSCDEX error "No CD-ROM detected"	The CD-ROM settings in your CONFIG.SYS or AUTOEXEC.BAT files are not valid. Be sure to check that the /D:XXXX parameter in the device driver in the CONFIG.SYS and the MSCDEX in the AUTOEXEC.BAT are the same.
"Not ready error" on CD-ROM	You either need to give the CD-ROM to catch up (press R for retry a few times) or you may have a dirty CD, the read heads in the CD drive are dirty, or the CD is bad. Try to clean the CD and the read heads in the CD drive. Try to replace the CD. Also look to see if your drive is too slow. Then try replacing the CD and replace the drive.

Table 20.8 Errors During Install (Graphical Interface)

Error	Description
Cannot read CAB files	You may have a dirty CD, the read heads in the CD drive are dirty, or the CD is bad. Try to clean the CD and the read heads in the CD drive. Try to replace the CD. Then try replacing the CD and replace the drive.
The system already has an OS	This is a common error when upgrading from 95 to 98. You are using a full-install CD-ROM for an upgrade. To work around this, exit the setup, change to the C:\WINDOWS\SYSTEM directory, and rename the SETUPX.DLL to SETUPX.OL1 and SETUPXW95 to SETUPX.OL2. Then start the setup again.

will get the most up-to-date and accurate versions of anything you choose to download from the site. Additionally, you won't waste time downloading components you have already installed. When the list of components appears on the page, you can browse it, decide which components you want, and download them right to your computer. Be sure to download any Critical Updates recommended for your system. Critical Updates will fix known problems (such as security issues) specific to your computer. Lastly, you can now download device drivers from the Product Updates catalog. A device driver is a program that controls a piece of hardware (such as a printer, monitor, disk drive, or video card) that is attached to your computer. Many device drivers come installed with Windows, but in some cases (for example, when you buy a new piece of hardware) you may need a driver that was not available when you installed Windows. To keep up with the newest hardware, Microsoft is constantly adding new drivers to the Product Updates site.

20.4.4 Dual Booting DOS and Windows 95

If the retail version (or the retail version with Service Pack A) of Windows 95 or Windows 98 is being installed on a system that already has DOS and Windows 3.XX, Windows can be made to dual boot between DOS and Windows by using the Custom Installation option. When prompted, install Windows 95 or 98 into a directory other than the one that is holding Windows 3.XX—Win95, for example. Before upgrading Windows 3.XX, make a copy of the necessary boot files, the CONFIG. SYS and AUTOEXEC.BAT files, Windows initialization (*.INI) and group files (*.GRP), dynamic link library files

(*.DLL), and any other critical files, such as necessary drivers. Keep in mind also that since both operating systems and environments are being loaded, additional disk space will be required.

To start Windows 95, let the system boot normally. To start DOS (and Windows 3.XX), press the F4 key as soon as "Starting Windows 95" appears during boot-up. Because Windows 95 does not have the initialization files for the Win16-based applications, they will have to be installed a second time. Fortunately, the same installation directories used in Windows 3.XX can be specified. When Windows 95 is booted, the DOS boot files are renamed IO.DOS, MSDOS.DOS, CONFIG.DOS, COMMAND.DOS, and AUTOEXEC.DOS. When booting to DOS, the DOS boot files are renamed with their original names and the Windows 95 boot files are renamed WINBOOT.SYS (formerly IO.SYS), MSDOS.W40, CONFIG.W40, COMMAND.W40, and AUTOEXEC.W40.

20.5 WINDOWS 9X CHARACTERISTICS

Before moving on to configuring and troubleshooting Windows, let's take a look at what makes Windows do what it does. Having a better understanding of what Windows does and what it is not supposed to do will give you a better understanding on how to troubleshoot Windows problems.

20.5.1 Windows 9X Boot Process

No matter which operating system is installed on a computer, when the computer is first turned on, the processor starts in real mode (pretends to be an 8086). After the system does its POST, it searches for and loads the IO.SYS file, the real-mode configuration manager, and the operating system. The file contains enough information to start the computer, read the file system, and automatically load several files and commands that in DOS are loaded by the CONFIG.SYS and AUTOEXEC.BAT files. See table 20.9. (Note: The GUI includes its own software disk cache and a mouse driver for DOS programs, so loading a disk cache or a mouse driver is not necessary nor should it be done.)

Table 20.9 Commands and Files Already Loaded by IO.SYS

Command/File	Function
HIMEM.SYS	Enables access to the extended memory and loads the real mode memory manager
DOS=HIGH,AUTO	Loads most of DOS into the high memory area (HMA)
IFSHLP.SYS	The Installable File System Helper loads device drivers that allow the system to make real file system calls
SETVER.EXE	Allows files that were made for an older version of DOS to work in Windows 95
FILES=60	Specifies the number of files that can be open at the same time. Unlike DOS, this command is not needed for Windows 95 and is included only for compatibility with older applications
LASTDRIVE=Z	Specifies the last drive letter available for assignment. Unlike DOS, this command is not needed for Windows 95 and is included only for compatibility with older applications
BUFFERS=30	Specifies the number of file buffers to create. Unlike DOS, this command is not needed for Windows 95 and is included only for compatibility with older applications
STACKS=9,256	Specifies 9 stacks of 256 bytes each to store information when interrupts occur. Unlike DOS, this command is not needed for Windows 95 and is included only for compatibility with older applications
SHELL=COMMAND.COM /P	Indicates which command interpreter should be used and that it cannot be unloaded
SET TEMP=C:\WINDOWS and SET TMP=C:\WINDOWS	Determines location of temporary files
PROMPT PG	Establishes standard DOS prompt at the command prompt
PATH=C:\WINDOWS; C:\WINDOWS\COMMAND	Sets the search path for executing files in the WINDOWS and COMMAND directories
COMSPEC=C:\WINDOWS\COMMAND.COM	Specifies the command interpreter used
NET START	Starts the network connection

The first configuration file processed by the IO.SYS file is the MSDOS.SYS file. Unlike the DOS MSDOS.SYS file, this is a text file that specifies the location of the necessary boot files, the location of the Registry (configuration database), and several startup options. In addition to holding important configuration information, the MSDOS.SYS file is needed to provide backward compatibility with older software programs, as are the CONFIG.SYS, COMMAND.COM, and AUTOEXEC.BAT files, which provide backward compatibility for DOS drivers and applications. These files are used to load a DOS device driver (a file with a SYS file name extension loaded in the CONFIG.SYS) and a TSR (an executable file loaded in the AUTOEXEC.BAT) if there is no equivalent driver in Windows 95.

Another file worth mentioning is the WINSTART.BAT file, which is also executed during boot-up. Like the AUTOEXEC.BAT file, the WINSTART.BAT file is used to load TSRs, but these TSRs are required for Windows-based programs that are not needed in MS-DOS sessions.

Next, WIN.COM is automatically executed and control is taken from the IO.SYS and given to the virtual memory manager (VMM32.VXD). The virtual memory manager then loads the Windows 3.XX device drivers, which have a DRV or a 386 (virtual mode driver) file name extension specified in the [ENH386] section of the SYSTEM.INI file. It then switches the microprocessor to protected mode and loads the protected mode operating system. The protected mode configuration manager is initialized and loads the 32-bit protected mode drivers (files with VxD), which are sometimes referred to as *virtual mode drivers*. As Windows 9X boots, it will scan the system for new devices. If one is found, the Hardware Configuration Wizard is executed. Sometimes, it will prompt the user to identify the hardware component so that it can load the appropriate drivers; otherwise, it will attempt to use the Add Hardware Wizard to automatically identify the hardware device and load the appropriate drivers.

After the device drivers are loaded, the Windows 95 core components are loaded, including the **kernel** (KERNL386.EXE and KERNEL32.DLL), GDI.EXE, GDI32.EXE, USER.EXE, and USER32.EXE files. The kernel file controls and allocates the machine resources, such as memory, and runs and coordinates software applications, including loading the appropriate EXE and DLL files. In addition, it performs file I/O services and virtual memory management. Finally, Windows 9X loads the Windows environment and the fonts, checks for values in the WIN.INI file, and loads the Windows 9X shell (normally EXPLORER.EXE) and the appropriate desktop components. The User component (USER.EXE and USER32.DLL) manages input (from the keyboard and mouse) and output to the user interface (windows, icons, menus, and so on). It also interfaces with the sound driver, timer, and communication ports. The GDI (GDI.EXE and GDI32.DLL) controls the graphics device interface, which creates images on the video system, including windows, icons, and buttons, and interacts with the video drivers. The USER.EXE file interprets a double-click on an icon and tells the GDI.EXE to draw a window on the screen. The GDI also provides graphics support for printers and other output devices.

Dynamic link library (DLL) files are sets of instructions and/or data that can be accessed at any time and that are used to modularize Windows 9X. This means that instead of there being one huge file containing all of the instructions needed for Windows, the instructions are broken down into smaller executable and DLL files. This allows executable files to share code and the division of applications into separate components that can be easily upgraded.

20.5.2 16-Bit and 32-Bit Programming

The IBM PC, which had the 8088 microprocessor, was a 16-bit computer because it could handle and process 16 bits of information at a time. Unfortunately, the 8088 data bus could bring in only 8 bits at a time. The later IBM AT, which included the 286 microprocessor, was a true 16-bit computer because it could process 16 bits of data at a time and had a 16-bit data bus. DOS, DOS programs, Windows 3.XX, and Windows 3.XX applications (Win16 applications) are 16-bit programs designed to work on 16-bit computers. When, a few years later, the 32-bit microprocessors (386 and 486) were introduced, DOS and Windows 3.XX could run on them and run faster because the microprocessor was faster, but the speed was not the fastest possible because the software was not written to use the entire microprocessor.

Windows 9X is mostly a 32-bit operating system so that it can take full advantage of 32-bit processing. Parts of it, however, are 16-bit so that it remains compatible with 16-bit applications, and also, since 32-bit code requires more memory, it reduces memory requirements. For example, the kernel is implemented as a 32-bit code to ensure high performance but runs older Windows applications

(16-bit applications) by **thunking,** a process by which a 16-bit instruction is paired with the next instruction to make it a 32-bit instruction during execution. And while most of the GDI file consists of 32-bit code to improve performance, most of the User component remains 16-bit for application compatibility.

20.5.3 Drivers

As mentioned, Windows 9X can use DOS drivers and Windows 3.XX drivers as well as Windows 9X drivers. These drivers can be divided into two categories, real mode and virtual mode.

The real mode drivers are 16-bit drivers stored in conventional or upper memory. As the name implies, real mode drivers can be accessed only in the microprocessor's real mode. Therefore, when Windows 9X is running in protected mode, it must switch the microprocessor back to real mode, access the driver, and switch back to protected mode, which significantly slows the PC's performance. In addition, while in real mode, only one application or process can be run at a time. Note: If the device manager does not list the CD-ROM properties and the CD-ROM is running without any problems, the driver is most likely a real mode driver loaded in the CONFIG.SYS.

The virtual mode drivers are 32-bit drivers stored in extended memory. When the microprocessor is running in protected mode, it allows more than one application or process to run at a time, which means that more than one application can use the resource that the driver controls at the same time (multitasking). The virtual device driver keeps track of the state of the device for each application and ensures that the device is in the correct state whenever an application continues.

VxD files support all of the hardware devices for a typical computer, including disk controllers, serial and parallel ports, keyboard and display devices, and so on. The *x* in the VxD extension name represents the type of virtual device driver. For example, a virtual device driver for a display device is known as a VDD, a driver for a timer device is a VTD, a driver for a printer device is a VPD, and so forth. Windows 3.XX drivers were statically loaded (loaded at the beginning and remained in RAM the entire time) and took up a lot of memory. Windows 9X dynamically loads VxDs or loads them when they are needed. In addition, VxDs under Windows 9X don't require all of their memory to be page locked, thereby further increasing the available memory in the system. Some examples of virtual mode drivers are VFAT, VCACHE, and CDFS. VFAT, which is short for virtual file allocation table, is the virtual installable files system driver and acts as an interface between the applications and the file allocation table (FAT). The VCACHE is the disk cache system that replaces the SmartDrive system used in DOS and Windows 3.XX. VCACHE can dynamically change the size of the disk cache depending on available disk space, application requirements, and amount of RAM available. CDFS, short for CD-ROM file system, replaces MSCDEX.EXE used in DOS and Windows 3.XX. The CDFS uses the VCACHE driver to control the CD-ROM disk cache, allowing much smoother playback.

During boot-up, Windows 9X automatically unloads any real mode drivers for which it has protected mode drivers that provide the same functionality. For example, the real mode DBLSPACE.BIN driver is unloaded and the protected mode DBLSPACE.VDX driver takes over. Real mode drivers that can be replaced safely are identified in the safe driver list (IOS.INI).

Windows Driver Model (WDM) allows program developers to write device drivers that are source-code compatible across all Microsoft Windows operating systems (such as Windows 98 and Windows 2000). The WDM is based on a modular architecture where Microsoft writes function class universal drivers and the device driver programmer writes a much easier function minidriver based on the universal drivers. There are three types of WDM drivers:

- **Bus drivers**—A bus driver services a bus controller, adapter, or bridge. Microsoft provides bus drivers for most common buses, such as PCI, PnP ISA, SCSI, and USB. Other bus drivers can be provided by manufacturers.
- **Function drivers**—Provide device functionality, and are composed of the class driver from Microsoft and the minidriver written by the device manufacturer. It is typically written by the device vendor and is required (unless the device is being used in raw mode). The PnP Manager loads, at most, one function driver for a device. A function driver can service one or more devices. Typically the function driver handles reads and writes to the device and manages device power policy.
- **Filter drivers**—Monitors, and may change, the output of a device.

20.6 VFAT, FAT32, AND CDFS

By default, Windows 9X uses **VFAT,** an enhanced version of the FAT structure. VFAT is backward compatible to DOS's FAT file structure but supports long file names (up to 255 characters). Of course, in DOS or Windows 3.XX applications, only the eight-character file name and three-character extension will appear. (Note: Windows 9X can still access and use disks that have only a FAT file structure.) Unfortunately, VFAT partitions cannot be larger than 2 GB.

FAT32 was introduced in the second major release of Windows 95 (OSR2/Windows 95B). An enhancement to the DOS FAT file system, FAT32 supported long file names and used 32-bit FAT entries that supported hard drives up to 2 TB. In addition, it used disk space more efficiently because it had smaller clusters. The FDISK utility (from the Windows 95 OSR2/Windows 95B) must be used to install FAT32 on a volume on a hard drive over 512 MB. Unlike earlier versions of FDISK, FDISK will ask if you want to enable large disk support. If you answer yes, any partition you create that is greater than 512 MB will be marked as a FAT32 partition. DOS 6.21, the retail version of Windows 95 (including Windows 95a) and Windows NT cannot access any files on a FAT32 volume. In addition, a drive with FAT32 cannot be compressed using Microsoft DriveSpace or DriveSpace 3.

Windows 98 and Windows Me has a Drive Converter (FAT32) program that will convert a FAT/VFAT program to FAT32. To start the program, click the Start button, select the Programs option, select the Accessories option, select the System Tools option, and select the Drive Converter (FAT32) program. Note: The Drive Converter (FAT32) program is CVT1.EXE, which is located in the WINDOWS folder. The Drive Converter (FAT32) program does the following:

- Launches the Drive Converter (FAT32)
- Scans your system for applications that may be incompatible with FAT32
- The list of programs that the Drive Converter (FAT32) will search for are kept in the registry at HKEY_LOCAL_MACHINE\SYSTEM\CurrentControlSet\Control\SessionManager\CheckBadApps400
- Warns you that the system will be restarted and prompts you to save your work
- Prompts you to specify which drive to convert; note that only one drive at a time can be converted
- Prompts you to back up your files

CDFS is the virtual CD-ROM file system. It has the same responsibilities for a CD-ROM device as VFAT has for a standard hard disk. The CDFS driver is loaded dynamically as needed and is a protected mode driver.

20.7 RUNNING PROGRAMS

Windows 9X will run Win16-based (Windows 3.XX) applications, Win32-based (Windows 9X and Windows NT) applications, and DOS applications. The program is selected by using the Programs option in the Start button. An executable file can also be started by:

1. Clicking on the file (or data document) using Windows 9X Explorer or My Computer
2. Creating a shortcut on the desktop or in any folder
3. Using the Run option in the Start button (see figure 20.8)
4. Typing the name of the executable file in an MS-DOS session

Figure 20.8 Run Option Under the Start Button

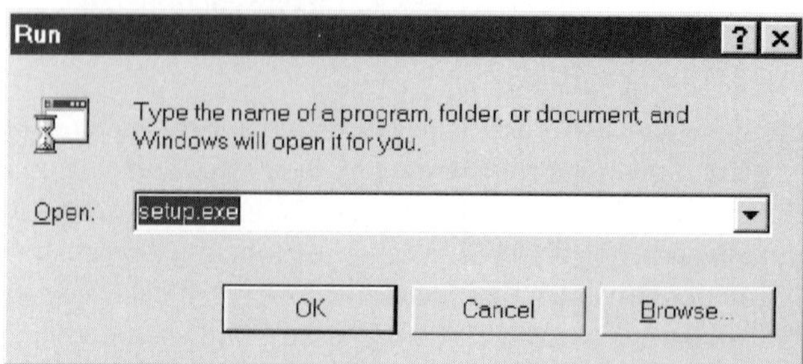

Windows 9X is a multitasking environment, so several programs can be run at the same time. The user can then change between different programs by:

- Pressing and holding down the Alt key and repeatedly pressing the Tab key until the desired application is reached
- Using the Alt+Esc keys to move to the next application
- Selecting the application button on the Taskbar

Windows 9X uses the Intel 386 microprocessor protection model. Processes (subprograms) running in ring 0 are protected by the microprocessor, while processes running in ring 3 are protected by the operating system. Because programs running in ring 0 have full privileges over programs running in ring 3, and programs in ring 3 have very little privilege over programs running in ring 0, the programs in ring 3 should not be able to cause problems for components in ring 0. Therefore, Windows 9X runs the file management subsystem and the virtual machine manager (VMM) subsystem in ring 0 and the system VM (including the system virtual machine, or VM, and virtual DOS machines, or VDM, in ring 3. The VM is used to run Win16-based and Win32-based applications, and the VDM runs DOS applications.

When running programs, Windows 9X uses dynamic memory allocation so that it can use the RAM more efficiently. Dynamic memory allocation gives a program memory when it needs it and takes it away when the program is not using it.

20.7.1 Windows Applications

For Win32-based applications, Windows 9X uses preemptive multitasking. **Preemptive multitasking** is the process by which the operating system assigns time slices to tasks and applications. Tasks and applications with a higher priority get a larger time slice. In addition, Win32-based applications can take advantage of multithreading. Multithreading is the ability of an operating system to execute different parts of a program, called *threads,* simultaneously. This can enhance a program by improving throughput, responsiveness, and background processing. For example, Microsoft Word uses a thread to respond to keys typed on the keyboard by the user to place characters in a document. Other threads are used to check spelling and to paginate the document as the user types. If the user prints, another thread spools, or feeds, a document to the printer in the background. Of course, the programmer must carefully design the program in such a way that all the threads can run at the same time without interfering with each other.

Win16-based applications use cooperative multitasking, so in Windows 9X these applications cannot take advantage of preemptive multitasking. Instead, the Win16-based applications share the same memory area or **virtual machine (VM)** and are all assigned a single time slice. Unfortunately, if a program causes problems, all of the Win16-based applications can crash. All of the Win16-based applications are, however, run preemptive with Win32-based applications and other Windows 9X processes, which improves the performance of Win16-based applications. See figure 20.9.

Figure 20.9 Programs Under Windows 95

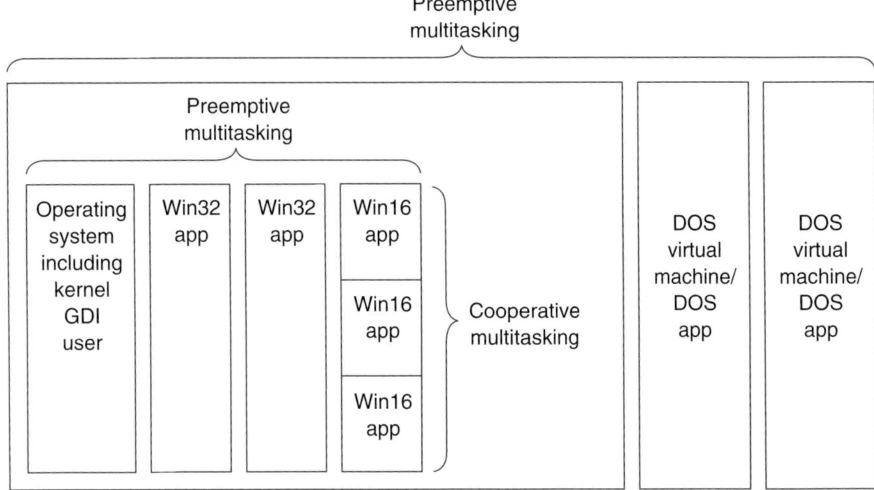

20.7.2 DOS Programs

As mentioned, each MS-DOS application executed is assigned its own virtual DOS machine (MS-DOS VM) with separate virtualized device access and addressable memory. The memory space created for an MS-DOS application mirrors that of a stand-alone DOS environment with 640 KB of conventional memory, 384 KB of upper memory, and whatever extended or expanded memory is specified.

DOS applications can be executed in an MS-DOS VM or in MS-DOS mode. When running in an MS-DOS VM, the operating parameters for the DOS program can be specified by choosing the Properties option from the shortcut menu or from the File menu. This creates a program information file (PIF), which has a PIF file name extension in the directory of the executable file or in the WINDOWS\ PIF file. Some of the available options include:

1. Running the program full screen or in a DOS window
2. The font used for text if it is running in a DOS window
3. The amount of memory for the program
4. Miscellaneous parameters, including interaction with screen savers and the mouse

Switching between full screen and a DOS window can be done by pressing the Alt + Enter keys. If an application cannot run in a DOS VM—for example, the application requires full access to the computer's resources or the application has video problems—the application would be run in DOS mode. To free up lots of lower memory for a DOS program, specify different AUTOEXEC.BAT and CONFIG.SYS commands for each application by using the Advanced button in the Program tab. See figure 20.10.

As mentioned, DOS programs do not require a mouse driver to be loaded in the CONFIG.SYS or AUTOEXEC.BAT files because Windows has its own built-in driver. Some programs, however, may lose synchronization with the mouse when it leaves the application window. To correct this problem, select the Exclusive mode on the Misc tab in the Properties option (see figure 20.11, which will lock the mouse inside the MS-DOS window.

20.7.3 Terminating a Program

To close a program, do one of the following:

1. Choose the Exit option under the File menu
2. Click on the Close button on the top right corner of the program window

Figure 20.10 Memory settings for a DOS program. The picture on the left is the memory tab within a DOS properties option. The picture on the right is the advanced button on the DOS properties option.

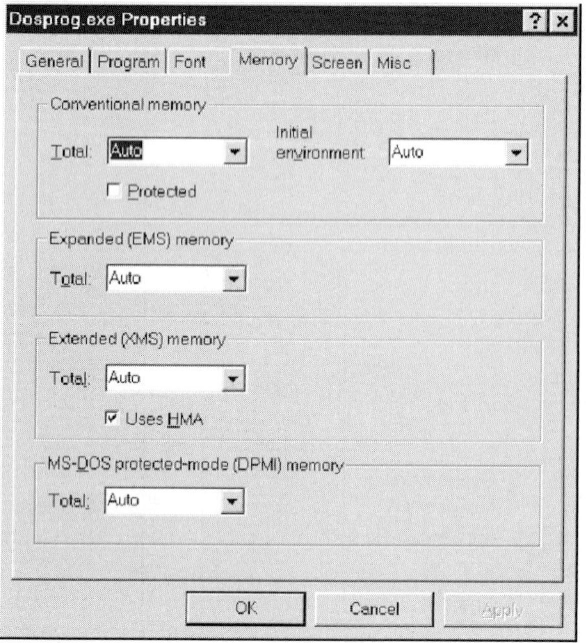

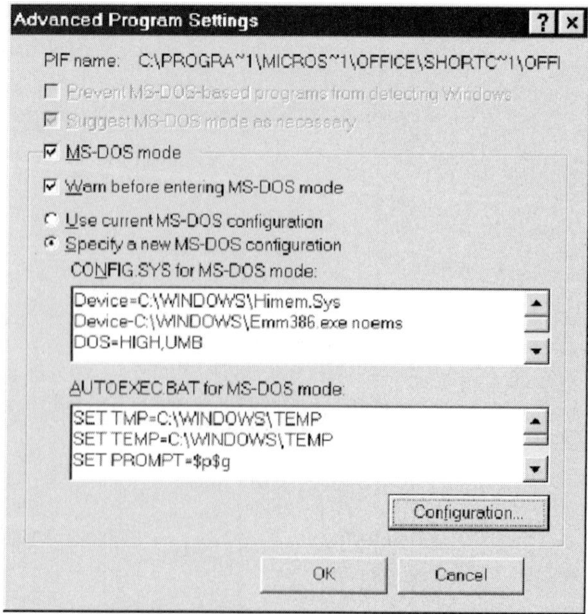

Figure 20.11 Screen and Misc Tabs Within the Properties Option of a DOS Program in Windows 95

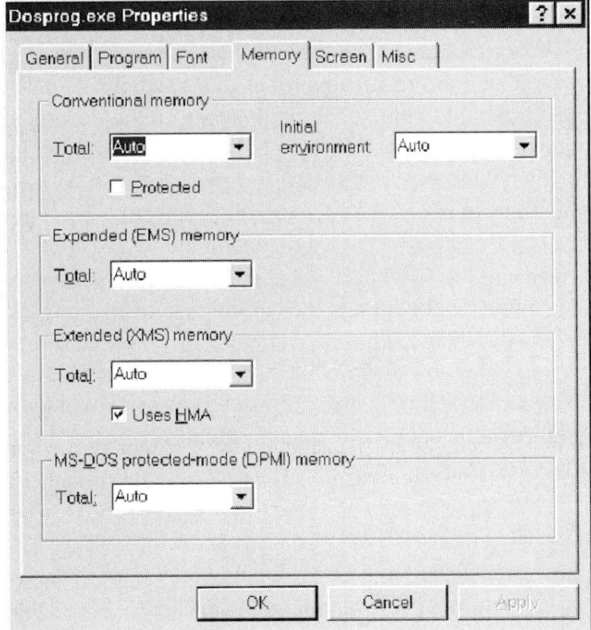

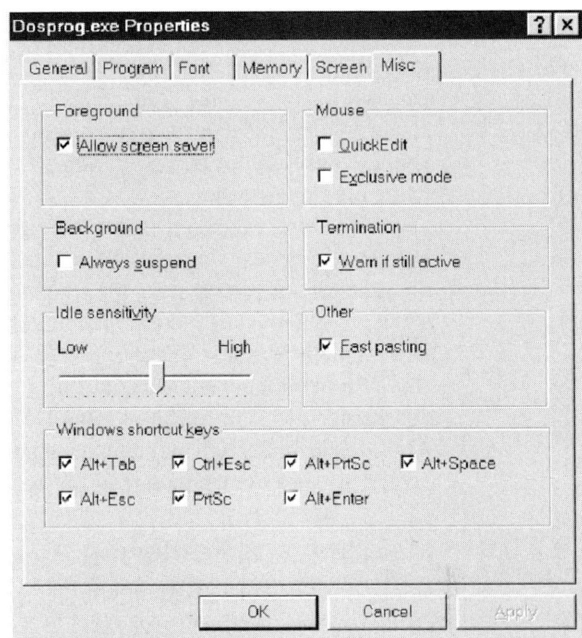

Figure 20.12 Close Program Dialog Box.

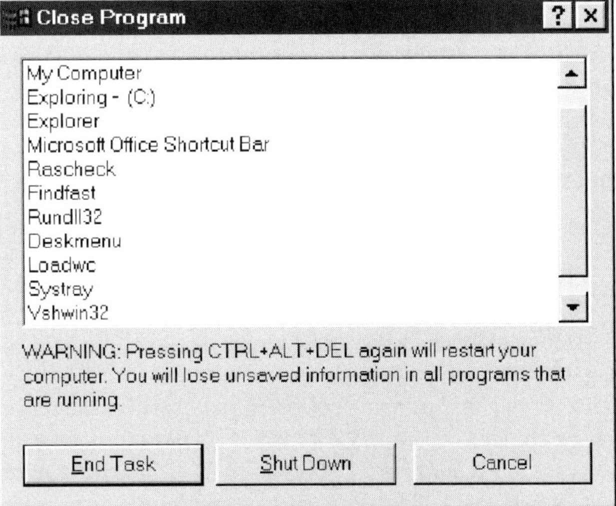

3. Select Close from the Control menu icon
4. Use the shortcut menu on the application button running in the Taskbar and click on the Close button
5. Press the Ctrl + Alt + Del keys to display the Close Program dialog box and close the application. See figure 20.12.

When a program locks up and does not respond, it can often be closed without affecting other programs by using the Close Program dialog box.

20.7.4 Sharing Data

To share data between documents, Windows applications can use dynamic data exchange (DDE) or object linking and embedding (OLE).

DDE was introduced with Windows 3.0 and allows users to copy data between applications while maintaining a link. Whenever data is changed at the source, it is also changed at the target. For example, an Excel chart in a Word document would change as the spreadsheet data changes. Although DDE is still used by many applications, it is slowly being replaced by OLE.

OLE (enhanced version of DDE) is a compound document standard developed by Microsoft. It allows objects created in one application to be linked or embedded in another application. Embedded objects keep their original format and links to the application that created them. For example, to make changes to an Excel chart in a Word document, you would double-click on the chart in the document and Excel would run from within the Word document. This allows changes to be made without going to the Program Manager and starting Excel in its own window.

A common way to move data between applications or documents is to use the Clipboard. By highlighting text or selecting a picture and using the Copy or Cut from the Edit menu in the source application, the text or picture goes into RAM, specifically to the Clipboard. Choosing Paste from the Edit menu when in the target document copies the data in the Clipboard into the current document using the first available format. If Paste Special is selected, the dialog box appears, listing the formats that can be chosen for pasting the data. With Paste Link, the application tries to make an OLE link to the source document. If the ObjectLink format isn't available, a DDE link is created instead. As with Windows 3.XX, the Print Screen option places a bitmap picture of the entire screen on the Clipboard. Alt + Print Screen places a bitmap picture of the active window on the Clipboard.

20.7.5 Installing and Removing Applications

To install a Windows program, start the executable program that starts the installation process. The executable file is usually named INSTALL.EXE or SETUP.EXE. To find out the name of the executable file, it is best to look in the program documentation or at the first installation disk. Of course, anytime that you install or upgrade applications, you should always confirm OS compatibility and determine minimum memory requirements. You should also perform a backup of the system. To start the executable file, click on the file using Windows 95 Explorer or My Computer, use the Run option in the Start button, or type the name of the executable file in an MS-DOS session.

When installed, a Windows program often adds information or modifies information in the registry. To remove these entries and the program files on the hard drive, many programs include an Uninstall program or have an Uninstall option within the installation program. In addition, if the program follows the API (application programming interface) standard, it can be removed by using the Add/ Remove Programs applet in the Control Panel.

NOTE: Although programs are uninstalled, some may still leave some files on the hard drive.

20.7.6 Windows Association

When a document in Windows 9X is double-clicked, Windows 9X will recognize the file name extension and start the appropriate program to open the file. This is known as *registering* a file. The information identifying the file name extensions is located in the registry and can be accessed and modified by selecting Options under the View menu in the My Computer, disk, or folder window and clicking on the File Types tab. See figure 20.13. If a file has a generic windows icon next to it and it will not open or execute when you double-click on it, either the file does not have an association or the application that opened the file was deleted or moved.

Parts of the registry can be stored in REG files. When you double-click a REG file, its content is merged with the registry. This may be used to configure options for a program or hardware device or to add a Windows association to your system. You should only double-click on a REG file that comes from a reliable source.

20.8 PRINTING IN WINDOWS 9X

After the printer is physically installed and configured, the appropriate printer driver must be loaded and the printer's location (LPT1, LPT2, LPT3, COM1, or COM2) specified. The driver is used to convert data from a document to commands that the printer understands. If the wrong driver is used when printing a document, the wrong control codes are sent to the printer and the printer will produce garbage (strange characters or many pages of programming code).

Figure 20.13 Windows 95 File Association

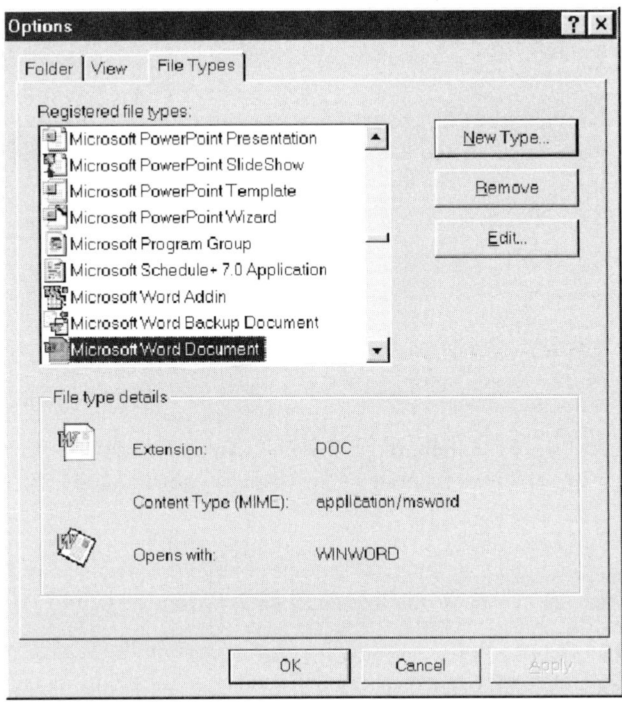

Figure 20.14 The Add Printer Wizard

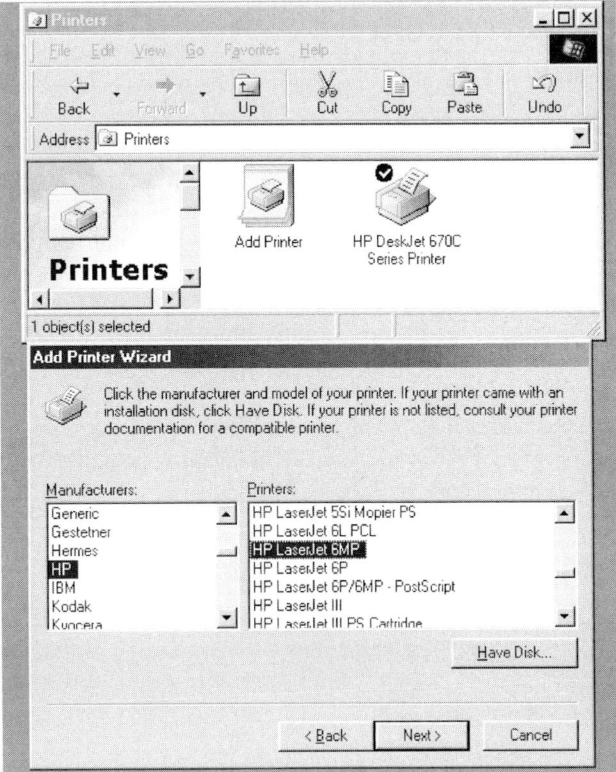

The printer driver can be loaded in one of two ways. One way is to start the Add Printer Wizard by double-clicking on the Add Printer icon in the PRINTERS folder. See figure 20.14. The PRINTERS folder can be accessed using My Computer, the Control Panel, Explorer, or the Settings option in the Start button. The second way is by using the setup disks that come with the printer.

Figure 20.15 Print manager. Notice the small printer icon located on the right side of the Taskbar.

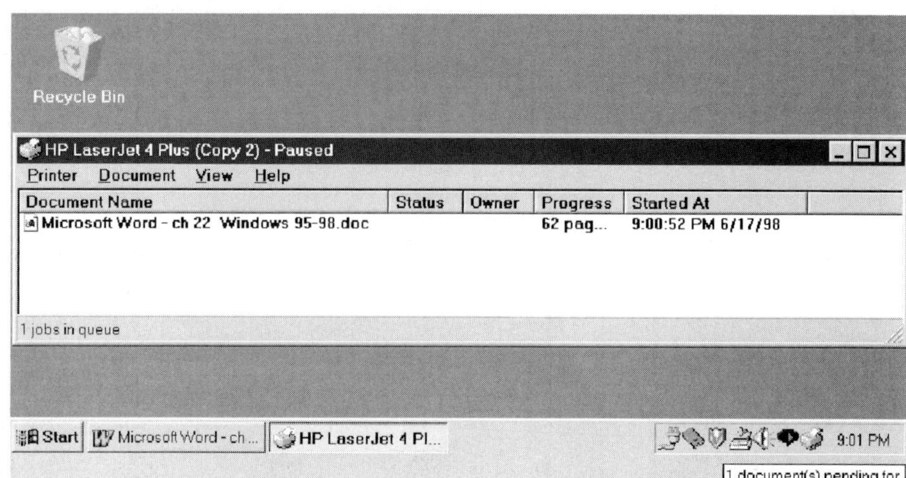

NOTE: Some printers, such as some newer Hewlett-Packard printers, are automatically detected and the drivers are automatically loaded from the Windows CD-ROM.

Printing is usually done by using the Print option on the File menu or a Print button on a toolbar. The application then creates a print file and sends it to the Print Manager, which holds the print job until the printer becomes available. As the Print Manager holds the print job, a small printer icon will appear on the right side of the Taskbar (in the systray). The status of a print job can be checked or changed by double-clicking on the printer icon in the systray or by double-clicking on the printer icon in the PRINTERS folder. See figure 20.15.

NOTE: The Print Manager works in the background, so other tasks can be performed while printing.

Question:

A user decides to print, but the document does not print. Therefore, the user decides to print again. After several attempts, the user figures that there must be a problem with the printer and after the printer problem is fixed, all of the print jobs sent to the printer start printing one by one. What can you do?

Answer:

Switch to the Print Manager, which will list all of the printers and all of the print jobs. The unneeded print jobs can be highlighted and deleted with a click on the Delete button.

NOTE: If the printer icon is grayed out, Windows cannot access the printer. This is usually caused by the printer being offline or the network connection not being up. For more information about printing in Windows, see sections 18.2.7 and 18.2.8.

20.9 CONFIGURING WINDOWS 9X

Windows 9X is a complex operating system consisting of many small programs. Because of its complexity, configuring Windows 9X can be done in several different ways. The most common is by using the Control Panel.

20.9.1 The Control Panel

The **Control Panel** is a graphical tool used to configure the Windows environment and hardware devices. See figure 20.16. It can be accessed from the Settings option in the Start button under My Computer. There are also various shortcuts to directly access certain Control Panel **applets** (icons). The default Control Panel applets are shown in table 20.10. The most commonly used applets are the System applet, the Display applet, the Add/Remove Programs applet, and the Add New Hardware applet.

Figure 20.16 The Control Panel

Table 20.10 Default Control Panel Applets

Applet	Function
32-bit ODBC	Configures the programming interface that enables applications to access data in a database management system that uses SQL as a data access standard
Accessibility Options	Used for people who have physical disabilities
Add New Hardware	Starts the Add New Hardware Wizard, which can automatically detect new hardware devices and load the appropriate drivers or allow you to select the hardware component
Add/Remove Programs	Used to install and remove programs, add Windows 95 components, and create a startup disk
Color	Used to select color schemes or customize the colors used for the desktop, the area of the screen in which windows, icons, and dialog boxes appear
Date/Time	Changes the system date and time
Display	Used to change the Windows environment, including menus, windows, and icons; controls the screen saver and allows you to install, change, or configure video drivers
Fonts	Used to manage the fonts on the system, including adding and deleting fonts
Joystick	Configures and calibrates joysticks and game paddles
Keyboard	Adjusts how the keyboard responds under Windows
Modems	Installs and configures modems
Mouse	Adjusts how the mouse responds under Windows
Multimedia	Used to configure audio, video, audio CD, and MIDI settings
Network	Installs and configures network cards and protocols
Passwords	Configures remote passwords and user profiles
PC Card (PCMCIA)	Installs and configures PC cards
Power	Enables and configures power-saving features so batteries used in notebook and laptop computers will last longer
Printers	Opens PRINTERS folder
Regional Settings	Configures international settings
Sounds	Assigns different sounds to system and application events or specifies MIDI settings
System	Shows version and OEM number and has the Device Manager, which allows you to configure all hardware devices and to resolve resource conflicts, set hardware profiles, and configure virtual memory

The System applet can be accessed through the Control Panel or through the Properties option in the shortcut menu of My Computer. The General tab shows the version of Windows 9X, the amount of physical RAM, and the OEM number of Windows 9X. See figure 20.17.

In the Device Manager tab, double-clicking on the computer on top of the tree structure or selecting the computer and clicking on the Properties button will reveal all the IRQ, DMA, I/O address, and memory areas used by the different hardware components. See figure 20.18. The rest of Device Manager shows all hardware devices organized in a tree structure. A red *X* through an icon means the hardware device has been disabled. A yellow circled exclamation point through the icon means that the hardware device has a problem. The problem could be a resource conflict (IRQ, DMA, I/O address, or memory address) or the drivers may not be loaded properly. See figures 20.19 and 20.20.

Figure 20.17 System Applet Within the Control Panel

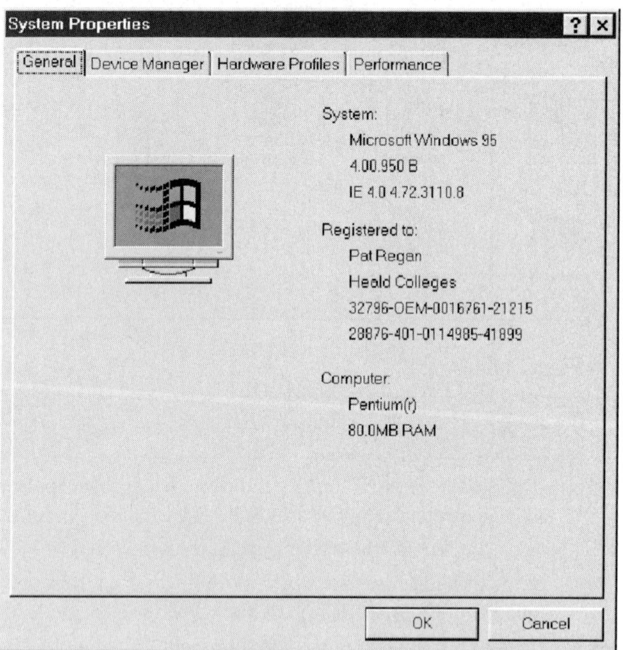

Figure 20.18 Device Manager Showing the Hardware Resources

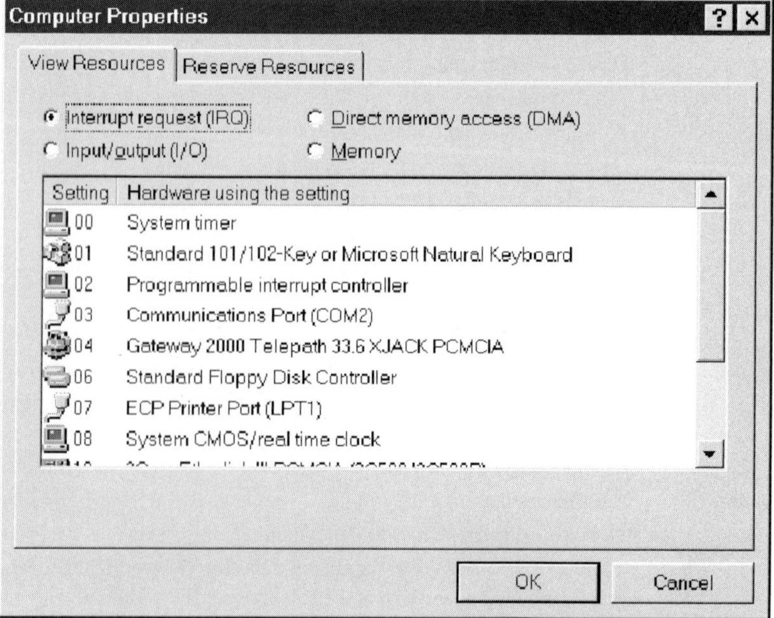

Figure 20.19 Windows 9X Device Manager. Notice that the 3Com Etherlink III card has a problem and that the Generic Ir Serial Port (COM1) is disabled.

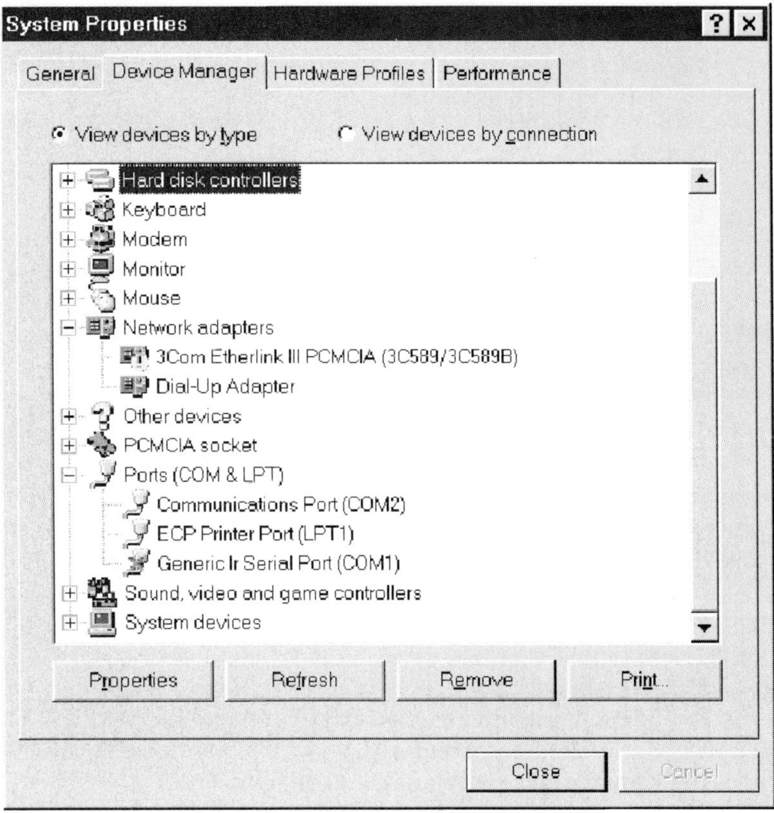

Figure 20.20 Properties of a device in Device Manager. Notice the resource conflict.

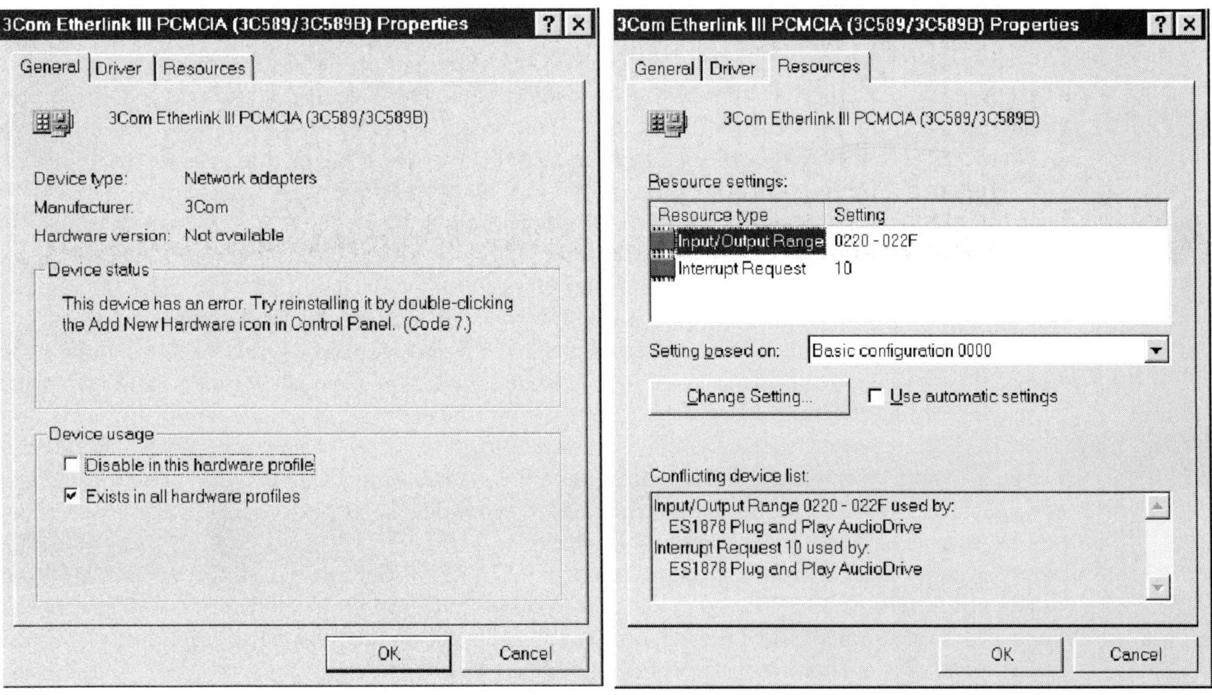

NOTE: To get a printout of the system configuration, you can click on the Print button from the Device Manager.

When viewing device information on your Windows 9X-based computer using Device Manager, you may see an unknown device listed next to a yellow question mark. Determining the cause of this unknown device can be difficult, because there are few indications of what could be creating it. The unknown device may also cause a conflict when trying to install a driver for another device.

The most common reasons Device Manager may list a device as unknown are as follows:

- The Device Manager does not have a device driver.
- Windows does not recognize the device ID.
- The device is created by software.
- The system has faulty hardware or firmware.

When a device driver for a device is not available, Device Manager displays the device as unknown and places it in the OTHER DEVICES folder. This commonly occurs with universal serial bus (USB) and IEEE 1394 composite devices. A status of *Error Code 1* or *Error Code 10* also may be displayed when you view the properties of the device in Device Manager.

Don't forget that most motherboards today need to have their chipset drivers loaded to recognize all of the drivers. For example, for Intel motherboards, the Intel Chipset Software Installation Utility was developed for updated Windows operating systems with the plug-and-play feature on Intel chipset. This utility allows the operating system to correctly identify the Intel chipset components and properly configure the system. The Intel Chipset Software Installation Utility installs specific Windows INF files. The INF files inform the operating system how to properly configure the chipset for specific functionality, such as AGP, USB, Core PCI, and ISA PnP services. Since these components are necessary for optimum stability and performance, the Intel Chipset Software Installation Utility should be the first driver loaded after the operating system and its service packs are installed.

Every hardware device has a special identifier used by plug-and-play (PnP). This identifier can consist of several different types, such as vendor ID, device ID, subsystem ID, subsystem vendor ID, or revision ID. If a device ID is not present, or your Windows-based computer does not recognize the device ID, Device Manager may list the device as unknown.

Virtual devices that are created with software also would be considered unknown when a driver tries to use the InstallShield installation program or a similar method and the device was removed in Device Manager, but still may have entries left over in the registry. To determine if an unknown device is being created by software, try starting Windows in safe mode. In addition, look at the COMPONENTS folder in the SYSTEM INFORMATION folder. The SYSTEM INFORMATION utility will be discussed in section 20.12. The COMPONENTS folder will list the common name for the device and the name of the device driver associated with it. In the PnP Device ID column, it will list the device IDs such as the PCI ID, ISA ID, and ID for some other bus type or unknown type. The Error Code column lists the error associated with a specific problem such as a bad or incompatible device driver.

The unknown device can also be caused by faulty hardware or firmware. To isolate the correct hardware device, remove the hardware devices from the Windows computer one at a time until the unknown device is no longer listed in Device Manager.

To see hardware in a category, click on the plus sign next to the hardware type. To see information about a piece of hardware, double-click on the Hardware device icon or select the hardware device and click on the Properties button. The properties menu will usually contain several tabs that indicate if the device is working properly and what drivers are loaded, and options for updating them and viewing and changing the device resources.

The Performance tab of the System Properties dialog box shows the amount of physical RAM, percentage of free system resources, and the type of file system, virtual memory, disk compression, and PC cards. See figure 20.21. All of the settings displayed should be 32 bit; if one or more of them is not 32 bit, then an old DOS driver is probably loaded.

Virtual memory is disk space pretending to be RAM. For Windows 9X, virtual memory is known as a swap file (WIN386.SWP). By default, the Windows 9X swap file is temporary and changeable. If hard disk space is running low, the size of the swap file is decreased. If hard disk space is available and more memory is required, the size of the swap file is increased. Note: When a program request memory that the memory manager cannot provide in Windows 9X is thrown as a page fault. (See section 20.14.1 for more information.)

The Display applet configures the Windows environment, including menus, windows, icons, the desktop, and the screen saver. It also configures the video system, installs or upgrades video drivers, and

Figure 20.21 Performance Tab of the System Applet of the Control Panel

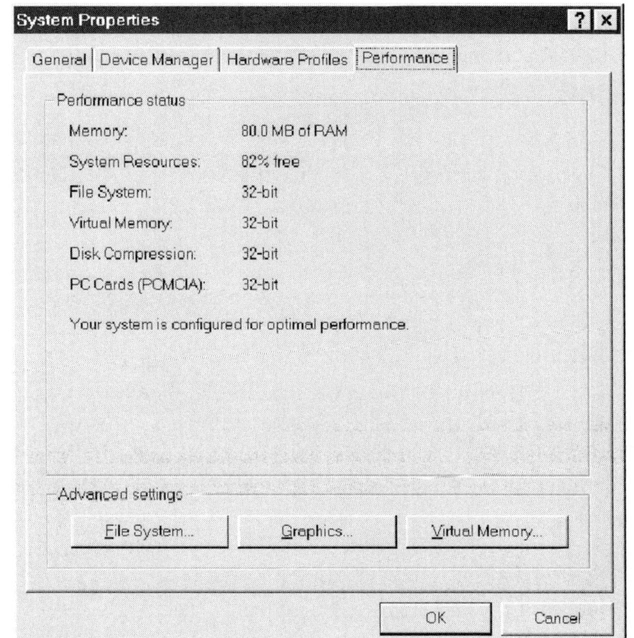

sets the video resolution and number of colors. It can be accessed through the Control Panel or by choosing the Properties option on the shortcut menu of the desktop. See figure 20.22. The Add/Remove Programs applet installs and uninstalls programs, adds or removes Windows 9X components, and creates a startup disk. The startup disk is used to start the computer to a command prompt to restart software programs that will not run and to fix boot problems. When creating a startup disk, you may be asked to insert the Windows installation disk or Windows installation CD so that a clean copy of all necessary files can be made. If you are working with systems that have different versions, you will have to create a startup disk for each version. See figure 20.23.

20.9.2 The Desktop and the Taskbar

As already stated, the desktop contains the My Computer and Recycle Bin icons. In addition, it can hold folders, files, and shortcuts. A folder or a shortcut is created with the desktop's shortcut menu and the New option. The desktop folders, files, and shortcuts are stored in the WINDOWS\DESKTOP folder.

The Taskbar can be configured by using the Properties button (Taskbar Options) on the Taskbar's shortcut menu or by using the Taskbar . . . option in the Settings option in the Start button menu. In the Taskbar Options tab, you can specify:

1. Whether the Taskbar auto-hides when it is not being used
2. Whether the Taskbar will show the time
3. Whether the Start menu will use small icons or large icons

From the Start Menu Programs tab, programs listed under the Start button can be added, removed, or reorganized or the documents menu can be cleared. See figure 20.24.

20.9.3 Fonts

A **font,** or **typeface,** is a collection of characters (letters, numerals, symbols, and punctuation marks) that have common characteristics. Font size is usually expressed in points, whereas a point is 1/72 of an inch. In addition, fonts can have different styles,—**bold,** *italics,* and <u>underline.</u> The font, the size of the font, and the style greatly affect the overall effect of the document.

The font can be described by its pitch, spacing, weight, and width. In a fixed font such as `Courier`, every character occupies the same amount of space. In a proportional font, such as Arial or Times New Roman, the character width varies. The letter *W* is much wider than the letter *i.* The pitch, usually used for fixed-width fonts, is specified in characters per inch (cpi): 10 cpi = 12 points and

Figure 20.22 Display Applet Within the Control Panel

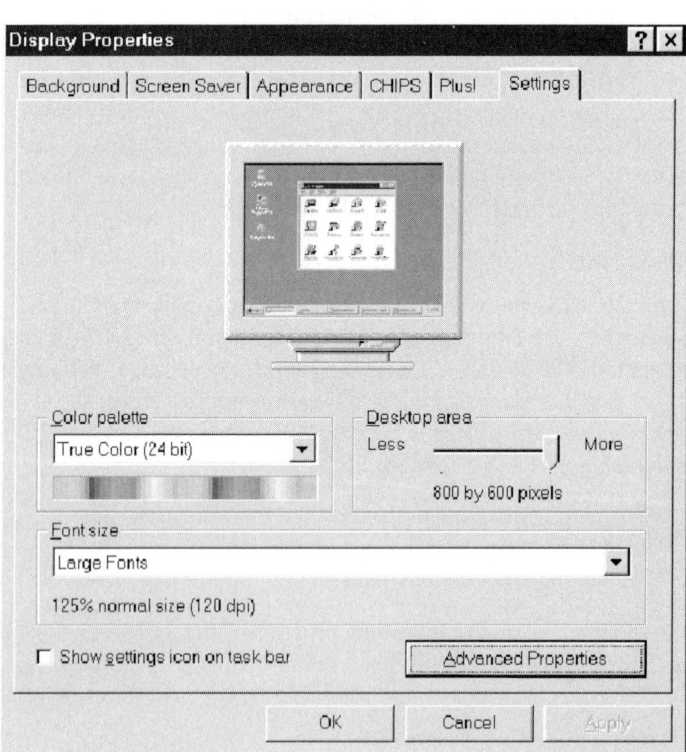

12 cpi = 10 points. The weight refers to the heaviness of the stroke for a specific font. They can be light, regular, book, demi, heavy, black, and extra bold. The width refers to whether the standard font has been expanded or compressed horizontally.

Fonts can be described as serif and sans serif fonts. A serif font, such as Times New Roman and `Courier`, have projections that extend from the upper and lower strokes of the letters. Sans serif fonts such as Arial do not have serifs.

Figure 20.23 Add/Remove Programs Applet Within the Control Panel

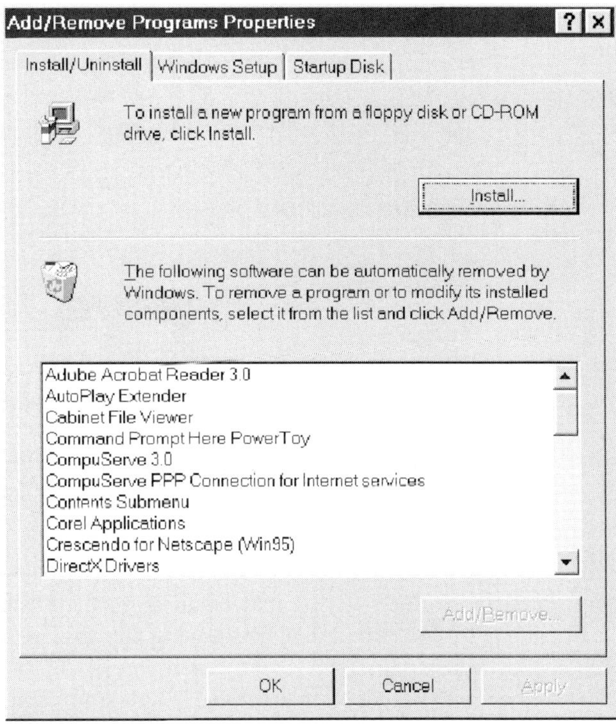

Figure 20.24 Taskbar Properties

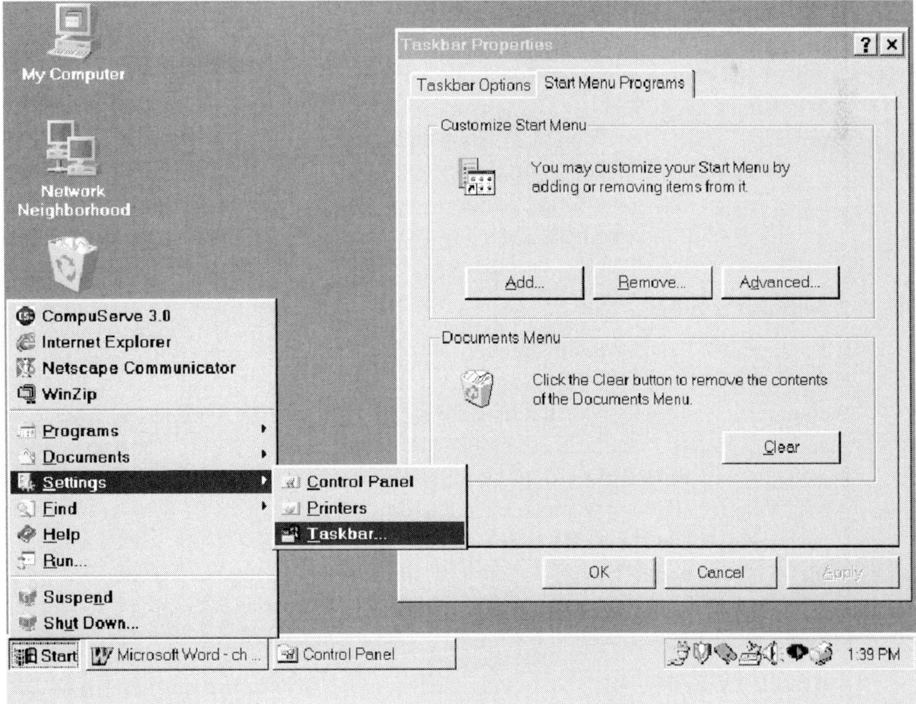

In Windows (Windows 9X, Windows NT, Windows 2000, and Windows XP), all fonts are broken into three categories. They are raster fonts, vector fonts, and TrueType fonts.

Raster fonts are bitmap pictures made of dots in different sizes for specific video display resolutions. For example, MS Serif comes in 8-, 10-, 12-, and 14-point size for CGA, EGA, VGA, and 8514 video systems. They have a FON file name extension. Raster fonts typically cannot be scaled or rotated.

Figure 20.25 Raster Fonts

10 12 24 48 72

Figure 20.26 Symbol Indicating a TrueType Font

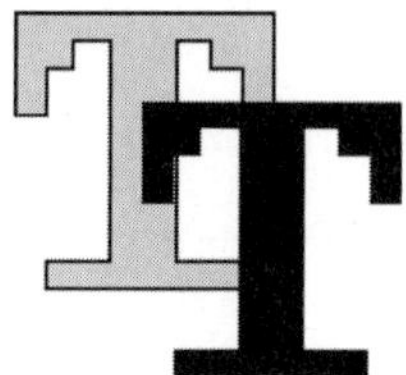

However, Windows can scale raster fonts to even multiples of their supplied size. For example, MS Serif can be scaled to 16-, 20-, 24-, and 28-point size. If you make the font too large, it becomes jagged. The jagged effect is what can be referred to as the "bitmap effect" (see figure 20.25).

Vector fonts are rendered using a mathematical model. Each character is defined as a set of lines drawn between points. Vector fonts can be scaled to any size, but cannot be rotated. Since the font has to be mathematically generated, the vector font requires more processing than the raster font. Examples of Windows vector fonts include Roman, Modern, and Script. **Outline fonts** are vector fonts that define the outline of each character geometrically. The most commonly used outline fonts are TrueType and PostScript fonts.

The most common fonts used in Windows are **TrueType fonts.** TrueType fonts, introduced in 1991 by Microsoft and Apple, are used for both the screen and the printer. Therefore, they allow Windows to be a ***What You See Is What You Get (WYSIWYG) interface.*** In addition, the TrueType fonts can be scaled and rotated without distortion. Each TrueType font requires only a file with an FOT file name extension and one with a TTF file name extension. The more popular TrueType fonts installed with Windows are Arial, Courier New, Times New Roman, and Symbol. See figure 20.26.

Managing fonts, including adding and deleting fonts, is done with the Font icon in the Control Panel. Note: If you load more fonts, Windows will use more resources to keep track of the fonts. If you load too many fonts, especially when using Windows 9X, it could lead to "Out of Memory" error messages.

20.9.4 MSDOS.SYS File

As mentioned earlier in the chapter, the MSDOS.SYS file is an important configuration text file used during boot-up. MSDOS.SYS is located in the root directory and is a hidden, system, read-only file. It contains a [Paths] section that lists the locations for other Windows 9X files (such as the Registry file) and an [Options] section that can be used to personalize the boot process. Some of the file's contents are shown in table 20.11. To make MSDOS.SYS backward compatible to some older programs, it contains a large section of *X*'s to keep it at a minimum size of 1,024 bytes. For example, if an antivirus program detects that the MSDOS.SYS file is less than 1,024 bytes, it may assume that the MSDOS.SYS file is infected with a virus. Therefore, the *X*'s should not be deleted. See figure 20.27. A text editor (such as EDIT or Notepad) or TWEAK UI, which provides a graphical interface, can be used to change the contents of the MSDOS.SYS file.

NOTE: TWEAK UI can be downloaded from the Microsoft website.

20.9.5 Information Files (INF)

Device information files provide information used by Windows to install software that supports a given hardware device or to install a program. When hardware manufacturers introduce new products, they must create INF files to explicitly define the resources and files required for each class of device. INF files can also be used to install and to uninstall programs.

Table 20.11 MS.DOS.SYS Contents

[Paths] Section	
HostWinBootDrv=⟨Root of Boot Drive⟩ Default: C	Specifies the location for the root of the boot drive.
WinBootDir=⟨Windows Directory⟩ Default: Directory specified during setup (for example, C:\WINDOWS)	Lists the location of the necessary files for booting.
WinDir=⟨Windows Directory⟩ Default: Directory specified during setup (for example, C:\WINDOWS)	Lists the location of the WINDOWS directory specified during setup.
[Options] Section	
AutoScan=⟨Boolean⟩ Default: 1	A setting of 1 will have SCANDISK run during boot when Windows is not shut down properly.
BootDelay=⟨Seconds⟩ Default: 2	Sets the amount of time the "Starting Windows" message remains on the screen before Windows 95 continues to boot.
Purpose: BootFailSafe=⟨Boolean⟩ Default: 0	A setting of 1 forces the computer to boot in safe mode.
BootGUI=⟨Boolean⟩ Default: 1	A setting of 1 forces the loading of the GUI interface. A setting of 0 disables the loading of the GUI interface.
BootKeys=⟨Boolean⟩ Default: 1	A setting of 1 enables the use of the function key boot options (that is, F4, F5, F6, and F8). A setting of 0 disables the use of these function keys during the boot process. A setting of BootKeys = 0 overrides the use of BootDelay = n.
BootMenu=⟨Boolean⟩ Default: 0	A setting of 1 enables the startup menu. A setting of 0 requires pressing the F8 key when "Starting Windows" appears to invoke the startup menu.
BootMenuDefault=⟨Number⟩ Default: 1 if the system is running correctly; 4 if the system hung in the previous instance	Sets the default menu item for startup.
BootMenuDelay=⟨Number⟩ Default: 30	This setting is used to set the number of seconds the system will pause on the startup menu. If the number of seconds counts down to 0 without intervention, the BootMenuDefault is activated.
BootMulti=⟨Boolean⟩ Default: 0	A setting of 0 disables the multiboot option. (for example, a setting of 0 prevents booting the previous operating system). A setting of 1 enables the F4 and F8 keys to boot the previous operating system. This setting is set to 0 by default to avoid the corruption of data by inadvertently booting MS-DOS and running a disk utility that does not recognize long file names.
BootWarn=⟨Boolean⟩ Default: 1	A setting of 0 disables the safe mode boot warning message and the startup menu.
BootWin=⟨Boolean⟩ Default: 1	A setting of 1 forces Windows 95 to load at startup. A setting of 0 disables Windows 95 as the default operating system (this is useful only if MS-DOS version 5.X or 6.X is on the computer). Note: Pressing F4 inverts the default only if BootMulti=1. (For example, pressing the F4 key with a setting of 0 forces Windows 95 to load.)
DRVSpace=⟨Boolean⟩ Default: 1	A setting of 1 allows the automatic loading of the DRVSPACE.BIN file. A setting of 0 prevents the automatic loading of this file.
LoadTop=⟨Boolean⟩ Default: 1	A setting of 0 does not let Windows 95 load COMMAND.COM, DRVSPACE.BIN, or DBLSPACE.BIN at the top of the 640 KB memory. If compatibility problems occur with software that makes assumptions about the available memory, try setting this to 0.
Logo=⟨Boolean⟩ Default: 1	A setting of 1 forces the default Windows 95 logo to appear. A setting of 0 prevents the animated logo from being displayed. A setting of 0 also avoids hooking a variety of interrupts that can create incompatibilities with certain third-party memory managers.

Figure 20.27 Windows 9X MSDOS.SYS File

```
[Paths]
WinDir=C: \WINDOWS
WinBootDir=C: \WINDOWS
HostWinBootDrv=C

[Options]
BootMulti=1
BootGUI=1
Network=1
;
;The following lines are required for compatibility with other programs.
;Do not remove them (MSDOS.SYS needs to be >1024 bytes).
;xxxxxxxxxxxxxxxxxxxxxxxxxxxxxxxxxxxxxxxxxxa
;xxxxxxxxxxxxxxxxxxxxxxxxxxxxxxxxxxxxxxxxxxb
;xxxxxxxxxxxxxxxxxxxxxxxxxxxxxxxxxxxxxxxxxxc
;xxxxxxxxxxxxxxxxxxxxxxxxxxxxxxxxxxxxxxxxxxd
;xxxxxxxxxxxxxxxxxxxxxxxxxxxxxxxxxxxxxxxxxxe
;xxxxxxxxxxxxxxxxxxxxxxxxxxxxxxxxxxxxxxxxxxf
;xxxxxxxxxxxxxxxxxxxxxxxxxxxxxxxxxxxxxxxxxxg
;xxxxxxxxxxxxxxxxxxxxxxxxxxxxxxxxxxxxxxxxxxh
;xxxxxxxxxxxxxxxxxxxxxxxxxxxxxxxxxxxxxxxxxxi
;xxxxxxxxxxxxxxxxxxxxxxxxxxxxxxxxxxxxxxxxxxj
;xxxxxxxxxxxxxxxxxxxxxxxxxxxxxxxxxxxxxxxxxxk
;xxxxxxxxxxxxxxxxxxxxxxxxxxxxxxxxxxxxxxxxxxl
;xxxxxxxxxxxxxxxxxxxxxxxxxxxxxxxxxxxxxxxxxxm
;xxxxxxxxxxxxxxxxxxxxxxxxxxxxxxxxxxxxxxxxxxn
;xxxxxxxxxxxxxxxxxxxxxxxxxxxxxxxxxxxxxxxxxxo
;xxxxxxxxxxxxxxxxxxxxxxxxxxxxxxxxxxxxxxxxxxp
;xxxxxxxxxxxxxxxxxxxxxxxxxxxxxxxxxxxxxxxxxxq
;xxxxxxxxxxxxxxxxxxxxxxxxxxxxxxxxxxxxxxxxxxr
;xxxxxxxxxxxxxxxxxxxxxxxxxxxxxxxxxxxxxxxxxxs
```

An INF file is a text file organized in several sections that define information that Setup and the hardware detection process used to determine the resource needs of the hardware device, and to install software for that device. An INF file is organized by hardware, with each class of device described in its own section. Within each device section, the following general organization applies: The [Install] section identifies the additional sections in the INF file that contain descriptions of the device and instructions for installing files and information needed by the device drivers. The install-section-name must be defined in a [Manufacturer Name] section and consist of printable characters.

20.9.6 Initialization Files

To hold configuration information, Windows uses **initialization files** (text files with an INI file name extension), which typically are used to hold configuration information about programs. While initialization files are not used as much as they once were, they are still used.

The initialization files are broken into logical groups called *sections.* The section names are denoted by a set of brackets ([ ]). The left bracket must be in the leftmost column on the screen. Each section consists of key names followed by an equal sign and its value. The value can be an integer or a string (group of characters). Initialization files are not case sensitive. For many entries, the value is shown as a Boolean expression. Therefore, the entry is enabled by entering *True, Yes, On,* or *1.* The entry is disabled by entering *False, No, Off,* or *0.* Commands, much like the REM statement in DOS, are lines that begin with a semicolon (;). A comment, ignored by Windows, is used to explain a line, provide a warning, or disable a command without removing the entire line. If a line is disabled by adding a semicolon or enabled by removing a semicolon, the changes will not be recognized until Windows restarts.

As mentioned before, there are two initialization files that are accessed during boot-up. They are WIN.INI and SYSTEM.INI. The only reason that they are still used in the Windows 9X environment is to provide backward compatibility with older programs, and in some cases, older devices.

The WIN.INI file is used to alter the Windows environment according to preference. For example, the LOAD= and the RUN= commands will automatically load the program specified when Windows starts. This line is modified when a program is added to the StartUp group. The LOAD command will run the program as a minimized icon, while the RUN command will not. (Note: Each of these lines can list several programs.)

The [386Enh] section of the SYSTEM.INI stores all the drivers for 386 enhanced mode, Microsoft's term for the OS accessing the processors 386 protected mode. Most of the problems associated with SYSTEM.INI on Windows 9X can be attributed directly to drivers within this section.

To edit an initialization file, you can use any text editor including the EDIT program from the command prompt or the Notepad program. In addition, Windows 9X includes the system editor program which allows you to modify the WIN.INI, SYSTEM.INI, AUTOEXEC.BAT, and CONFIG.SYS files. In addition, you can use the MSCONFIG.SYS command, which is explained later.

20.9.7 DOSSTART.BAT File

If you have CONFIG.SYS and AUTOEXEC.BAT files in your root directory, they are read by Windows during boot-up. If you shut down or restart the computer in MS-DOS mode, whatever was loaded in those files remains loaded, plus the DOSSTART.BAT file in the C:\WINDOWS directory gets executed.

The main purpose of the DOSSTART.BAT file is to load your DOS MOUSE.EXE and MSCDEX.EXE. Those programs are not otherwise needed in Windows 9X, but are needed in MS-DOS mode if you want to use your mouse or CD drive. In addition, for the MSCDEX.EXE to work, you need to have your DOS CD driver loaded, which is commonly done from your CONFIG.SYS file (for example, DEVICEHIGH=C:\CDROM\CDROM.SYS /D:MSC001). Depending on your system's requirements, you may wish to include entries for your sound card, joystick, and so on.

20.10 WINDOWS 9X REGISTRY

The Windows 9X **registry** is the central information database for Windows 9X and is organized into a tree-structured hierarchy. It replaces the DOS AUTOEXEC.BAT, CONFIG.SYS, and initialization files (files with an INI file name extension, such as the SYSTEM.INI and WIN.INI) and includes hundreds of additional system settings. If you were able to print out the entire registry, it would fill several thousand pages. Initialization files, which are limited to 64 KB of text and support only two levels of information (section name and values), still exist in Windows 9X but only to provide backward compatibility to older Windows applications. Changes made using the Control Panel, such as installing or removing a program or adding or removing a printer, are automatically made in the registry during boot-up. Changing the registry manually (such as changing a value that cannot be modified by using the Control Panel, Device Manager, or similar utility) requires using a program called Registry Editor (REGEDIT.EXE), located in the C:\WINDOWS directory. See figure 20.28.

The registry is divided into six HKEYs, as shown in table 20.12. If any key is highlighted in REGEDIT.EXE, its contents appear in the Contents pane. An HKEY is divided into keys (similar to folders). *H* stands for *handle,* which contains thousands of text strings that can be configured. A boxed plus sign to the left of the Registry key indicates it contains one or more subkeys (similar to subfolders). Each subkey may contain its own subkey, and so on for several levels. In addition to the keys and subkeys, the Contents pane shows the Windows 9X configuration settings broken down into values. REGEDIT.EXE shows the data type icon (which represents the type of data that the value can store), the name of the value, and the value in the Contents pane. The data types are shown in table 20.13. The master HKEYs are the HKEY_LOCAL_MACHINE and HKEY_USERS, which contain 90 percent of the registry's information. The master HKEYS are derived from registry files (USER.DAT, which contains the user-specific settings, and SYSTEM.DAT, which contains the computer hardware configuration) hidden in the WINDOWS directory. The other HKEYs, sometimes referred to as the *virtual registry,* are a host of files created by Windows 9X at startup.

The only time you should go into the registry is at the direction of an article, book, product documentation, or support person. If you ever decide to change the values in the registry, you should follow certain guidelines. First, back up the registry (SYSTEM.DAT and USER.DAT) to a safe location,

Figure 20.28 REGEDIT.EXE Showing the Windows 95 Registry

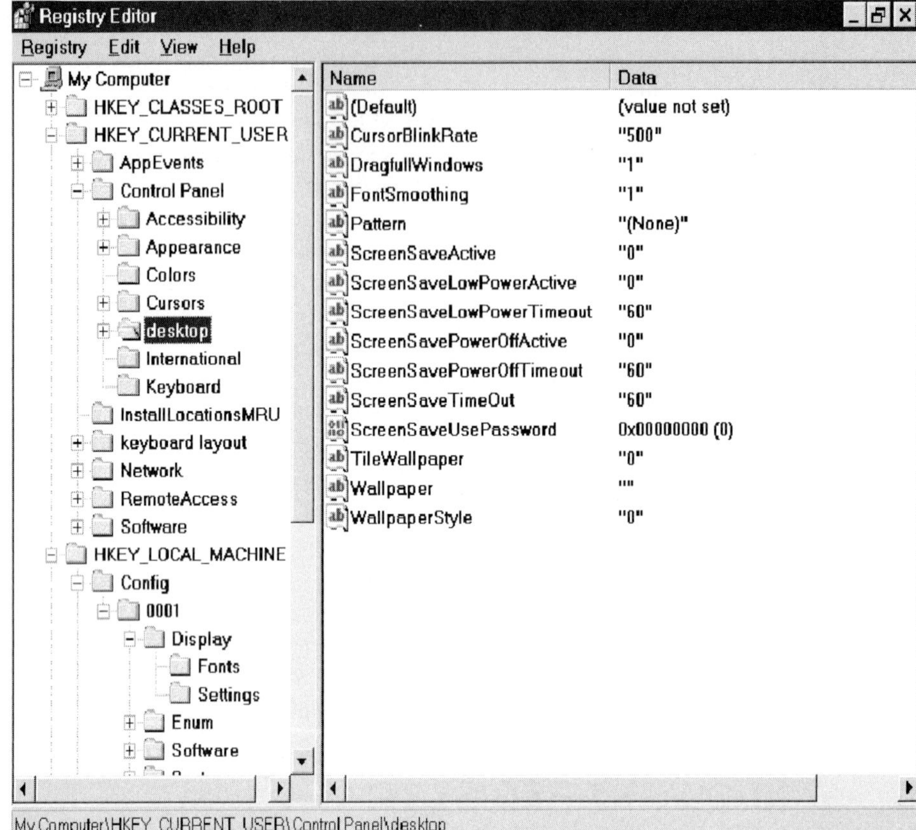

preferably to a floppy disk (if it fits on a floppy disk). If anything goes terribly wrong, you can restore the registry. Next, make only one change at a time so that if there is a problem, you know which value is causing the problem. See sections 20.12.4 and 20.12.5.

Two files that existed in Windows 95, but are not part of Windows 98, are SYSTEM.DA0 and USER.DA0. These files are backup copies of the registry that Windows 95 made every time the operating system started successfully. Since Windows 98 uses Registry Checker to make backup copies in CAB files, these files are no longer necessary.

20.11 DIRECTX

DirectX is an application programming interface (API) developed by Microsoft that enables programs to write programs that access hardware features of a computer without knowing exactly what hardware is installed on the machine. DirectX was originally designed to allow Windows 95 to become a gaming platform, but has grown into a multimedia platform. DirectX achieves this by creating an intermediate layer that translates generic hardware commands into specific commands for particular pieces of hardware.

With Windows 98 a version of DirectX 5 has already been included, and you can check for a proper DirectX setup by doing the following:

1. Click on the Start button and select the Run option.
2. In the Open field, type *DXINFO* and click on the OK button. See figure 20.29.

The screen that appears is a split window. On the left-hand side, at the bottom, you will find a section titled *DirectX Drivers.* It lists the drivers being utilized by the DirectX subsystem. At the end of each of the lines it should show *CERTIFIED.* If one or more of the items does not say *CERTIFIED,* this is most likely causing the problem you are having. Most often, the driver that is not certified is either the

Table 20.12 Root Keys of the Windows 95 Registry

Root Key	Description
HKEY_CLASSES_ROOT	Contains software settings for file associations and OLE information. This key points to a branch of HKEY_LOCAL_MACHINE.
HKEY_CURRENT_USER	Contains settings for applications, desktop configurations, and user preferences for the user currently logged on. It points to a branch of HKEY_USERS for the user who is currently logged on. **AppEvents:** Contains the settings for which sounds to play for system sound events. **Control Panel:** Stores Control Panel settings. **InstallLocationsMRU:** MRU stands for "most recently used." It contains paths for STARTUP folder programs. **Keyboard layout:** Specifies current keyboard layout. **Network:** Contains network connection information. **RemoteAccess:** Contains information about the current logon location if using Dial-up Networking. **Software:** Software configuration for the user currently logged on.
HKEY_LOCAL_MACHINE	Contains information about the type of hardware installed, drivers, and other system settings. **Config:** Configuration information. **Enum:** Hardware device information, such as monitor settings. **Hardware:** Serial communication port information and settings. **Network:** Information about networks for the user who is currently logged on. **Security:** Network security settings. **Software:** Software-specific information and settings. **System:** System startup and device driver information and operating system settings.
HKEY_USERS	Contains information (such as desktop settings) about all users who log on to the computer (each user has a subkey) including the DEFAULT generic user settings. The DEFAULT user is used as a template for any new users.
HKEY_CURRENT_CONFIG	Contains information about the current running hardware configuration. The HKEY_CURRENT_CONFIG points to a branch of the HKEY_LOCAL_MACHINE\CONFIG, which usually contains duplicate references to the same data. The duplicate references help prevent corruption in the Registry.
HKEY_DYN_DATA	Contains dynamic (continuously changing) status information for various devices as part of the plug-and-play configuration. It points to a branch of HKEY_LOCAL_MACHINE.

Table 20.13 Types of Data Found in the Registry

Type of Data	Definition and Examples
String data	One or more alphanumeric values enclosed in quotation marks (except when a value is not set). Examples: "0" (Value not set) " " "vxdfile"
Binary data	A hexadecimal number. Examples: D8 08 00 00 60 0d 00 a0 01 04 ff ff ff 00
DWORD	A 4-byte hexadecimal number. Examples: 0 × 00000240 0 × 00000300 *NOTE:* Because the DWORD (double-word) format uses the same data-type icon as binary data, it is identified by 0 × followed by an unspaced 4-byte (8-digit) hexadecimal number.

Figure 20.29 DirectX 5 Diagnostic Tool

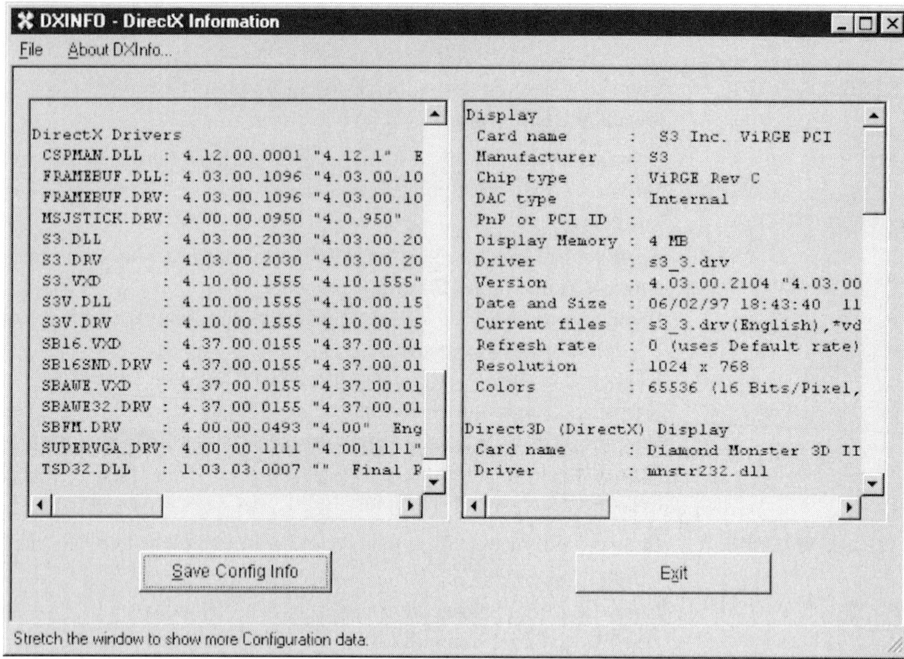

primary display driver and/or the audio driver. Most manufacturers of video cards and sound cards are releasing updated drivers for Windows to meet the DirectX standard. You will want to contact the manufacturer of any component that is not supported to ask about obtaining drivers that support DirectX.

If you experience trouble finding CERTIFIED drivers for a device, please be sure to download the newest end-user version of DirectX from Microsoft's website. Often the newer versions have support for hardware that was previously unsupported by DirectX. They should have a copy of DirectX at the following URL:

http://www.microsoft.com/directx

You may also want to check with Microsoft's Hardware Compatibility Labs to see if your device is listed as having drivers that are compatible.

With DirectX 6 or higher, you can check for a proper DirectX setup by doing the following:

1. Click on the Start button and select the Run option.
2. In the Open field type *DXDIAG,* and click on the OK button. See figure 20.30.

20.12 SYSTEM INFORMATION UTILITY AND OTHER RELATED UTILITIES

Starting with Windows 98, Microsoft includes the System Information utility (MSINFO32.EXE), which can analyze your system for problems. System Information collects and displays your system configuration information. For example, you can view:

- Operating system information, such as the version number and system boot options, plus process, system, and user environment variables
- Hardware details such as BIOS information, video resolution, CPU type, and CPU steppings
- Physical memory, paging file information, and direct memory access (DMA) usage
- The current state of each driver and service on the computer
- Drives and devices installed on the computer, plus related interrupt (IRQ) and port information
- Network information, including transports, configuration settings, and statistics
- Printer settings, font settings, and system processes that are running

Figure 20.30 DirectX 6 Diagnostic Tool

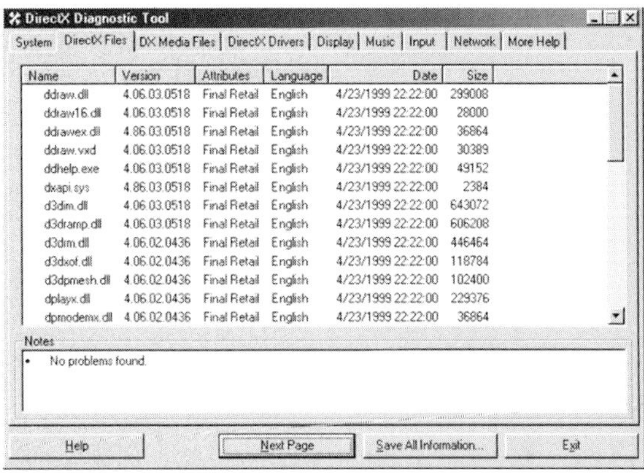

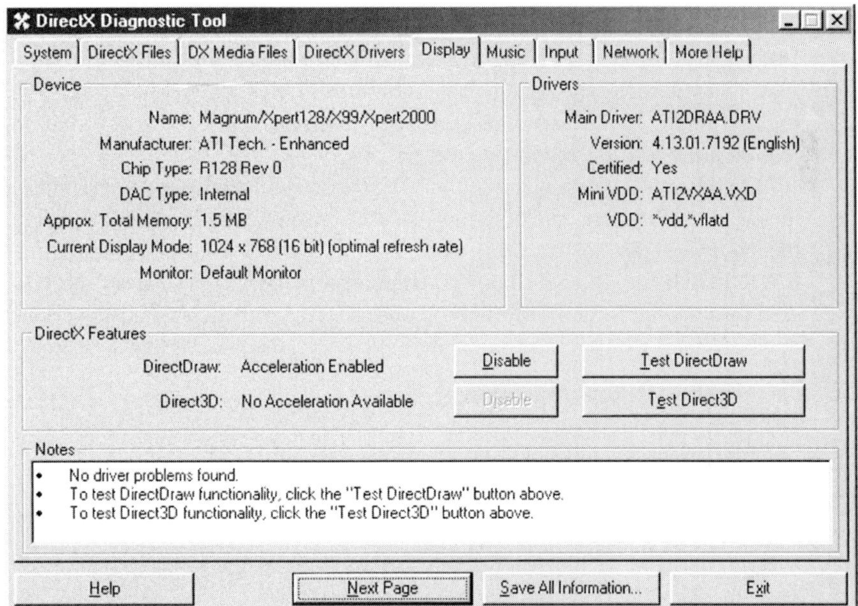

You can access the System Information utility by going to the Start menu and clicking Programs, clicking Accessories, clicking System Tools, and then selecting System Information.

System Information displays a comprehensive view of your hardware, system components, and software environment. The displayed system information is organized into three top-level categories that correspond to the resources, components, and software environment nodes:

- The resources node displays hardware-specific settings, namely DMA, IRQs, I/O addresses, and memory addresses. The Conflicts/Sharing node identifies devices that are sharing resources or are in conflict. This can help identify problems with a device.
- The components node displays information about your Windows configuration and is used to determine the status of your device drivers, networking, and multimedia software. In addition, there is a comprehensive driver history, which shows changes made to your components over time.
- The software environment node displays a snapshot of the software loaded in computer memory. This information can be used to see if a process is still running or to check version information.

Other applications may add nodes to System Information that display information specific to the application. See figure. 20.31

You can use the View menu to switch between the display of Basic and Advanced information. The Advanced view shows all of the information in the Basic view plus additional information that may be of interest to the more advanced user or to Microsoft Product Support Services.

Figure 20.31 System Information Utility

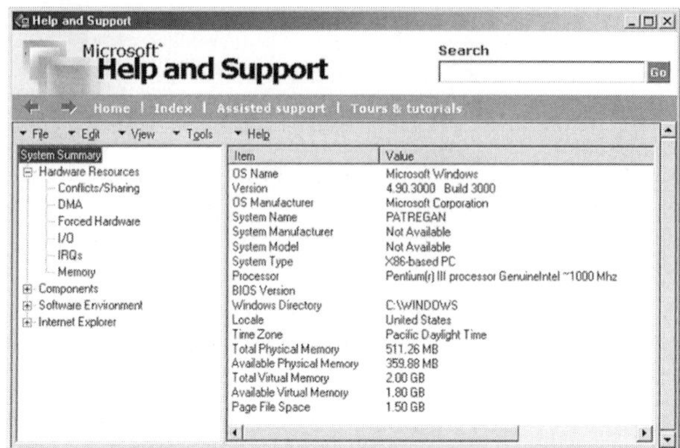

While the first step to solving complex problems is to get more information about the problem, information alone doesn't fix what's wrong. For this reason, the System Information utility includes 10 tools that you can use to fix a malfunctioning system. In the following sections, we'll cover each of these tools in detail. To access any of these tools, simply choose the appropriate tool from the System Information utility's Tools menu. See table 20.14.

Another tool worth mentioning is the hardware diagnostics tool (HWDIAG.EXE), which was first included in Windows 95 OSR2 and which is also included in Windows 98 and Windows Me. To start the hardware diagnostics tool, click on the Start button, select the Run option, and execute the HWINFO/UI file. Microsoft doesn't support this tool because all of the information can also be gathered through the System Information utility. The hardware diagnostics tool lists every key in the Windows Registry that refers to hardware in your system. The entries are color coded:

- **Green**—All keys from the registry
- **Pink**—File attributes information
- **Dark Red**—Configuration Manager information
- **Bold Red**—Error information
- **Bold Blue**—Warning information

Table 20.14 Tools Accessed Through the System Information Utility

Tool	Description
Windows Report Tool (WINREP.EXE and DOSREP.EXE)	The Windows Report tool will help solve problems that you just can't seem to figure out yourself. This tool asks you to describe your problem, what you're trying to accomplish, and the steps you've taken to reproduce the problem. When you've answered these questions, simply click Next and enter a file name. Windows 9X will build a CAB file containing answers to your questions and a summary of your system's configuration. You can now send this file to Microsoft's technical support staff for assistance with your problem.
Update Wizard Uninstall (UPWIZUN.EXE)	As you're aware, Windows 98 contains a Windows Update utility you can use to install software patches from the Internet. Unfortunately, sometimes a patch can do more harm than good. If you install a patch and it causes problems, you can use the Update Wizard Uninstall utility to remove the patch quickly and easily.
System File Checker (SFC.EXE)	Corrupted system files cause many of the most serious Windows problems. Until now, the easiest way to correct such problems was to reinstall Windows and replace all files. Unfortunately, since files get overwritten, you're forced to reload software (such as Exchange Client) that updates system files. Windows 98's System File Checker utility can examine Windows for changed or corrupted files and restore the original Windows 9X version if necessary. To do so, click Scan For Altered Files and click the Start button.

Table 20.14 Continued

Tool	Description
Signature VerificationTool (SIGVERIF.EXE)	Every piece of hardware in your computer requires a driver. Unfortunately, although several drivers come with Windows, many drivers are supplied by third parties—and aren't tested by Microsoft. A poorly written driver can affect more than just the device it controls: It can cause other devices to malfunction or result in general protection faults. With the release of Windows 98, Microsoft began digitally signing device drivers. The digital signature means that the driver has been tested by Microsoft and is certified to work with Windows 9X. The digital signature also proves that the driver hasn't been tampered with. Third-party vendors can now submit their drivers to Microsoft for testing and application of a digital signature. The Signature Verification tool will check your system for files that don't contain a digital signature. It's important to point out that Microsoft doesn't sign every file—only driver files contain digital signatures.
Registry Checker (SCANREG.EXE and SCANREGW.EXE)	If a registry gets corrupted, it is very difficult to fix it. Many times, you end up losing Windows completely and have to reinstall it from scratch. However, Windows 9X is much more forgiving when it comes to registry problems. Each time Windows 9X successfully boots, it creates a backup copy of the registry. Windows 9X stores several backup registries in a compressed format. When Windows 9X starts, the Registry Checker utility runs in the background. It scans for corruption and, if no corruption is detected, creates a backup copy of your registry. If a problem is detected, the utility reboots your computer and launches an MS-DOS version of the utility, which automatically restores the most recent backup of your registry. If no backup is available, the utility will attempt to correct the error it has detected. Since the utility runs automatically, you may wonder why it's included in the System Information tool. Keep in mind that the utility runs automatically at boot up. Since many people don't shut down their computers at night, you may want to manually run the utility if you suspect a problem.
Automatic Skip Driver Agent (ASD.EXE)	If you have the boot fail because of a malfunctioning driver or hardware components, you would typically boot to safe mode and guess about which device may be causing the problem. Then you would disable the device, reboot, and hope that you guessed right. Unfortunately, this can be a time-consuming activity. Windows 9X solves this problem with the Automatic Skip Driver Agent. This utility monitors the boot process. If a boot fails because of a driver or hardware problem, the agent makes a note of it. If a boot failure occurs twice in a row as a result of the same problem, the agent will disable the driver on the third attempt. You can then boot successfully and use the Automatic Skip Driver Agent to determine which driver is causing your problem.
Dr. Watson (DRWATSON.EXE)	At one time or another, you've probably seen a cryptic application fault screen. If this error occurs on a regular basis, use Dr. Watson. When you launch Dr. Watson, it runs minimized on your toolbar. Dr. Watson captures information about the error when it occurs. It can then be analyzed by Microsoft technical support.
System Configuration Utility (MSCONFIG.EXE)	The System Configuration utility allows you to perform a selective startup.
ScanDisk (SCANDSKW.EXE and SCANDISK.EXE)	ScanDisk utility repairs hard disk errors and corrects problems such as cross-linked files or damaged file allocation tables. It can also flag bad hard disk sectors to prevent Windows from writing information to them.
Version Conflict Manager (VCMUI.EXE)	The Version Conflict Manager will back up all altered files before switching to the Windows 98 version so that you can revert to the previous version if you have problems.

20.12.1 Version Conflict Manager

You can run the Version Conflict Manager by selecting it from the Tools pull-down menu in the System Information utility. This tool tracks certain files that were updated when you installed Windows 98 and provides a means by which you can restore the old version to your computer. To restore a file that was backed up by Windows 9X, simply select it from the list of available files and click on the Restore Selected Files button. As with many other Windows applications, you can select multiple files by holding down the Control (Ctrl) key on your keyboard as you select each file. After you have restored files, you might need to reboot your computer before the changes can take effect.

20.12.2 Extract and System File Checker

On the Windows CD, you will find cabinet files (files with a CAB extension). A cabinet file contains two or more compressed files. Occasionally, there may be a need to extract and expand one of these files to replace a deleted or corrupt file without reinstalling everything. This will be done with the EXTRACT.EXE command, which you will find in your \WINDOWS\COMMAND folder. If it isn't there, you can copy it from the \WIN9X folder on your Windows CD or on your startup disk. Because EXTRACT.EXE is a command-prompt utility, you'll need to launch a DOS session in order to use it. Once you've done so, you will be able to run the utility by typing commands at the prompt.

EXTRACT.EXE is particularly easy to use if you happen to know which cabinet the required file is stored in. In this case, you need to give the program only two items of information: the name and path of the cabinet file, and the name of the file you wish to extract. For example, suppose you need to retrieve a copy of the Windows default sound driver (SOUND.DRV) from the Windows CD, and you've been told that the file is stored in a cabinet file called MINI.CAB. To extract the file from the cabinet, you first insert your Windows CD into the drive, open an MS-DOS prompt window by selecting Programs, MS-DOS Prompt from the Start menu, and type the following command:

```
EXTRACT D:\WIN95\MINI.CAB SOUND.DRV
```

Here, D:\WIN95\MINI.CAB is the path and file name of the cabinet file (we're assuming that the drive letter of the CD-ROM drive is D). All cabinet files have the extension CAB, and, in the case of the Windows 95 CD, they are stored in a folder called WIN95. When used in this way, EXTRACT.EXE extracts the specified file to the current folder.

Alternatively, you can instruct EXTRACT.EXE to place the extracted file in a specific folder. To do so, add the /1 switch, followed by the folder name, to the command line. For example, the following command will extract SOUND.DRV from MINI.CAB and place it in the C:\WINDOWS\SYSTEM folder:

```
Extract D:\Win95\Mini.cab Sound.drv/1 C:\Windows\System
```

By using DOS wild-card characters, it's possible to instruct the EXTRACT.EXE utility to extract more than one file at a time. For example, to extract all 16 wallpaper files (which have the extension BMP) from the WIN95_03.CAB cabinet, you could type the following command:

```
Extract D:\Win95\Win95\_03.cab *.bmp
```

In the examples shown so far, we've assumed that you already know which cabinet the required file is stored in. More typically, you won't know which cabinet file contains the file you need to extract. Fortunately, EXTRACT.EXE can help in these cases by letting you see exactly which files are held in a given cabinet. To use EXTRACT.EXE in this way, add /d, followed by a cabinet name, to the command that runs the program. For example, the following command displays the contents of the PRECOPY1.CAB cabinet:

```
Extract /d D:\Win95\Precopy1.cab
```

NOTE: You can also use System File Checker, Winzip, or similar programs to view and extract files from the cabinet files.

You can use the System File Checker to periodically scan the system files on your computer to make sure they have not become corrupted and that the wrong version of a file hasn't been copied over the previously existing file. You can also use this tool to extract a system file from your Windows 98 CD-ROM.

If you want to have System File Checker check your system files for errors, choose that option and click on the Start button located in that window. It will then scan your files and, in all likelihood, simply bring up a dialog box telling you how many files were examined and providing you with some other related information. However, depending on the tool's settings that you have selected using the Settings button, if the System File Checker notifies you that one or more of the files has some type of error, you can use it to extract a copy of that file from the installation disk.

Although a system file can be corrupted sometime after installation, it is also possible that either you or some application might accidentally delete one or more system files from your computer. System File Checker can notify you of any such potential problems and prompt you to extract the file to reinstall it on your system.

Before examining the file extraction capabilities of this tool, click on the Settings button found in the main window of this tool. This will bring up a separate tabbed window containing a number of different options. Here you can specifically tell the tool to check for changed and deleted files. You can also expand or limit the scope of files the utility checks, and you can create a custom verification data file that the tool will use to check system files for errors.

The System File Checker can also be used to extract files from your cabinet files. You don't need to know which cabinet file the file you need is located in. All you have to know is the name of the file for which you are looking. Windows 9X should even recall the CD-ROM drive letter and the subdirectory on the Windows 9X CD-ROM on which the file is located. To extract a file, simply choose the option from the installation disk and enter the file's name into the text box. Click on the Start button and System File Checker will walk you through the steps needed to extract the file. The corrupted file will be backed up in case you want to reinstall it, and the extracted file will be placed in the appropriate location within your Windows 9X directory.

Although the System File Checker is a handy tool for detecting and fixing corrupted or missing system files, it has at least one limitation. Because some Windows 98 system files will be updated over time, the version of some of the system files on your installation disk will eventually become outdated. Therefore, unless you know that the system file you are extracting is the latest version, you might inadvertently extract an older version of that file in place of the newer file that has been deleted or corrupted in some way.

This is a significant limitation because some applications will probably require the newer version of that system file to function properly (or to function at all). If you encounter such a problem with a file you have extracted, you should try using the Update Wizard found within the Windows Update tool to check and see whether a newer version of that file is available from Microsoft. If so, you should download and install that update; this should then put your system back in proper working order.

One of the common problems associated with personal computers is hardware conflicts. These conflicts can have any number of causes, such as corrupted or poorly written device drivers, more than one hardware device set to the same IRQ setting, or other such problems. Unfortunately, when these conflicts arise they can prevent all or part of your operating system from functioning properly.

20.12.3 Automatic Skip Driver Agent

To help provide a short-term fix for such problems, Microsoft has included a new utility in Windows 9X known as Automatic Skip Driver Agent. As the name might imply, this utility acts as a system agent that monitors the loading of hardware drivers on your system and looks for problems associated with such drivers. If a hardware device fails to respond during the installation or loading of Windows 9X, this agent will display a dialog box informing you that there is a problem with the hardware device that could cause your system to stop responding. It will then ask you whether you want to automatically skip the loading of this driver from now on when you boot your computer. If you agree to this, Windows 9X will disable that driver and it will not be loaded until you attempt to fix the problem, such as by checking the System settings in the Control Panel.

Like some of the other tools discussed in this chapter, one way to load this utility is from the Tools pull-down menu in System Information. You can also load this program by clicking on the Start button and choosing Run. Enter *asd* in the text box that appears and click the OK button. Unless you have previously been notified of a problem, when you run this utility you will likely get nothing more than a simple dialog box stating that there are no current ASD critical operation failures on your computer, meaning everything appears to be running fine.

20.12.4 Registry Checker

Registry Checker is a system maintenance program that finds and resolves some registry problems and regularly backs up the registry. Windows 9X provides an MS-DOS-based version for scanning the registry, backing up, and restoring the registry and system configuration files, and a Windows-based version for scanning and backing up the registry.

Registry Checker backs up the registry each day following a successful Windows 98 system startup, maintaining one compressed backup for each day. If a serious problem is found in the registry, Registry Checker will restore the most recent registry from a backup copy. Note: If you want to restore an earlier version of the registry, you must use the MS-DOS-based utility outside of Windows. Registry Checker will attempt to fix the registry only if a valid backup cannot be found. You would use the Registry Checker if Windows cannot boot to safe mode or the Taskbar is missing.

ScanRegW is the Windows-based version. This program scans the registry for corruption and determines if it requires optimization, and then backs up the following system configuration files, registry (USER.DAT and SYSTEM.DAT), WIN.INI, and SYSTEM.INI. This scan occurs automatically when the system is started. You can run SCANREGW.EXE to force a scan and backup of these files. ScanRegW backs up the registry and configuration files using a compressed CAB file in the \WINDOWS\SYSBCKUP directory.

ScanReg is the MS-DOS-based version. If ScanRegW detects a problem with the registry, it prompts you to restart the computer to fix the problem, and ScanReg will run automatically. It either restores a known good backup or, if no backups are available, attempts to repair the current registry by removing the corruption. If ScanRegW detects that optimization is required, ScanReg will optimize the registry on the subsequent startup.

You can also manually make periodic backups of the registry using ScanRegW. There are several reasons to back up the registry, for example, before editing the registry using Registry Editor, or before installing an application. ScanRegW stores the backup as a RB0##.CAB file in \WINDOWS\SYSBCKUP, which is a hidden folder. The symbols ## represent backups using digits from 01 to 99 (05 is the default for the number of backups). The files are compressed CAB files (like the files on the Windows 98 compact disc). If you run ScanRegW and your system already has the maximum RB0##.CAB files as indicated in SCANREG.INI, the oldest one is deleted.

To back up your registry:

1. On the Start menu, click Run.
2. Type *ScanRegW,* and then click OK.
3. After scanning the system registry, ScanRegW displays a dialog box asking if you would like to back up the registry. Click Yes.
4. Click OK when backup is complete.

If you want to replace the current copy of the registry with an older copy, you can use the SCANREG/RESTORE command. If you want to check the registry for errors, you can use the SCANREG/RESTORE command. You can type *ScanRegW/autoscan* to automatically back up the registry without a dialog box.

20.12.5 Backing Up the Registry

One way to back up your registry files is to do it using the DOS prompt. At the command prompt, type the following lines:

```
cd windows
attrib -r -h -s system.dat
attrib -r -h -s user.dat
copy system.dat *.bu
copy user.dat *.bu
```

To restore your registry files, type the following lines at the command prompt:

```
cd windows
attrib -r -h -s system.dat
attrib -r -h -s system.da0
attrib -r -h -s user.dat
```

```
attrib -r -h -s user.da0
ren system.dat system.daa
ren system.da0 system.da1
ren user.dat user.daa
ren user.da0 user.da1
copy system.bu system.dat
copy user.bu user.dat
```

20.12.6 Emergency Recovery Utility

You can use the Windows 95 Emergency Recovery utility (ERU.EXE) to create a backup of your system configuration and registry files in case a problem should occur. This utility is located on the Windows 9X CD-ROM in the OTHER\MISC\ERU folder. You will need to choose a location for storing the backup information. By default, the information is stored on a floppy disk in drive A. However, it cannot back up all the configuration files if space is limited on the destination disk. Instead, it will back up as many files as it can, skipping the largest files first. For example, the Emergency Recovery utility usually cannot back up the registry files (SYSTEM. DAT and USER. DAT) if you try to back up the configuration files to your Windows 95 startup disk. While the default location to store the files is the A drive, you can choose to store the backup information in another location, such as a local hard disk or a mapped network drive.

The files are that backed up by default are:

CONFIG.SYS
AUTOEXEC.BAT
WIN.INI
SYSTEM.INI
PROTOCOL.INI
EXPLORER.EXE
USER.DAT
SYSTEM.DAT
IO.SYS
COMMAND.COM
MSDOS.SYS

It is recommended that you use the Emergency Recovery utility to create a new backup each time you make significant changes to your system, such as adding new hardware or software.

To restore the backup information, start your computer at a command prompt and then run ERD.EXE. If you do not want to restore all the files, press the Spacebar to select or deselect files. Note that you cannot run ERD.EXE within Windows. You must run this utility at a command prompt. If you saved your backup information to a network drive, you must be able to access the network drive at the DOS level.

20.12.7 Exporting and Importing the Registry

The easiest way to fix a damaged registry is to boot Windows into safe mode and run REGEDIT to make the corrections. Many times this technique will work even when registry problems prevent Windows from booting in normal mode, because safe mode uses a minimal set of drivers and registry instructions. Of course, for this technique to truly work, you must know where you made the initial mistake in the registry and what needs to be changed to make the correction.

The Registry Editor has the ability to import and export the registry to and from a text file. You can do this by using the Import Registry File and Export Registry File commands on the Registry Editor's Registry menu. If you plan on making modifications to your registry, you can export the registry to a text file. If something were to go wrong, you could later import your original registry back in. Note: To import a registry file, it must have the REG file name extension and it can contain only ASCII characters in a predefined format. It must contain the word REGEDIT4 in the first line. The second line must be blank.

The Microsoft Backup tool has the ability to back up and restore the registry. In Windows 9X, using the full system backup option automatically backs up the registry. Restoring a single file from such a backup set will restore the registry. The Windows Backup tool handles the registry differently. When preparing the backup, you can select the Options command from the Job menu. When you see the Backup Job Options dialog box, click the Advanced tab and select the Backup Windows Registry check box. Likewise, you can restore only the registry through a similar process.

Table 20.15 REGEDIT Command Switches

REGEDIT Command Switch	Purpose
/L:system	Location of SYSTEM.DAT
/R:USER	Location of USER.DAT
filename1	File to import into the registry
/C filename2	File to create registry from
/E filename3	File to export registry to
regpath1	Starting registry key to export from (defaults to exporting the entire registry)
/D regpath2	Specifies registry key to delete

The downside to using the backup program to restore the registry is that the registry will be restored to the exact state it was in at the time of the last backup. Therefore, if it's been awhile since your last backup and you restore the registry, you'll lose any information relating to programs you've installed since the backup as well as changes you've made to the operating system.

If you suspect that your registry problems are fairly simple, there are a couple of tools you can run that automatically repair registry errors. If you're using Windows 98 or Windows Me, you can use the Registry Checker program to revert to an older version of the registry. In some situations, Windows 98 is smart enough to detect a severely corrupted registry and revert to an older registry automatically. If you're not using Windows 95, the latest version of the Norton Utilities by Symantec offers a tool capable of repairing all but the most difficult registry problems.

If Windows won't boot at all, you have two options. You could delete your existing copy of Windows and either install a fresh copy or restore from a backup. Or you could export the registry to a text file, making the necessary changes, and import the changes back into Windows while in DOS mode. As you can see in table 20.15, the REGEDIT command, located on the Windows 98 or Windows ME startup disk or in the \WINDOWS directory, contains several MS-DOS mode switches.

```
REGEDIT [/L:system] [/R:user] filename1
REGEDIT [/L:system] [/R:user] /C filename2
REGEDIT [/L:system] [/R:user] /E filename3 [regpath1]
REGEDIT [/L:system] [/R:user] /D regpath2
```

To create the text file, you must export the registry. Assuming that your registry files are stored in the usual locations, you could do so with the following command:

```
REGEDIT /E REGTEXT.TXT
```

Therefore, you must have an MS-DOS-based text editor with an unlimited file size capability. The MS-DOS Editor won't work, since the registry export file can be a couple of megabytes.

Once you've made the necessary changes to the text file, you must import it. If you want to import the entire registry, you must use this command:

```
REGEDIT REGTEXT.TXT
```

Different from important and exporting using the Register Editor in Windows, the file does not have to have a REG file name extension.

20.12.8 Various Restore Methods

The first option that you may use is if you perform regular backups, you can restore Windows to a previous backup. When you are having problems with Windows, there are additional tools that may come in handy.

Many OEMs provide recovery CDs with their computers. If you are having problems with your computer, you can boot with the recovery CD and it will restore the computer back to the original software and configuration that the computer was shipped with. If you don't have your data files backed up, when you use the recovery CDs, it will also overwrite the data files and any programs that you have installed since you got the computer.

You can use disk image software, such as Drive Image, to take a snapshot of a partition or hard drive and save it in one large compressed file, which is best to do after all applications are installed. Since some Windows problems may take some time to figure out and fix, it may be easier and much faster to restore Windows to the saved image. Unfortunately, if you don't have your data files backed up or on a separate drive, when you restore the image, it will overwrite the data files.

Lastly, similar to System Restore available in Windows XP, all Windows versions can use a program called ConfigSafe. ConfigSafe protects Windows-based PCs from crashes and configuration problems by tracking changes to a system's configuration over time. It works by taking a "picture," or snapshot of a system's configuration. The snapshot stores information about the system's configuration at that exact point in time. Some examples of information tracked are as follows:

- Configuration files (WIN.INI, SYSTEM.INI, AUTOEXEC.BAT, CONFIG.SYS)
- System changes (memory, processor, Windows version)
- Drives (hard drives, CD-ROMs, network connections)
- Directories
- Windows registry
- System assets (for example, the Windows desktop)

As you can see, ConfigSafe tracks critically important system information. It is essential to have a stored record of this system information because these files and settings are often modified when new hardware and software is installed. Sometimes faulty installations or software conflicts cause a system to malfunction or completely stop working, not allowing the user to even boot into Windows. ConfigSafe lets you see what changes have been made to the system, which can help pinpoint the source of a problem. But more importantly, it lets you restore a system to a working state if you experience problems that result in an improperly working system. Using its unique SOS feature, ConfigSafe can even restore systems that won't boot into Windows.

20.13 TROUBLESHOOTING WINDOWS 9X

When you get a specific error message that you have never seen before, you should also do a search on Microsoft.com and possibly the rest of the Internet. If the exact match does not come up with anything useful, pick keywords from the message and do a search on those keywords. For a list of additional troubleshooting resources, visit the following websites:

Home:
http://www.microsoft.com

Microsoft Windows Update
http://windowsupdate.microsoft.com/

Windows Download Center
http://www.microsoft.com/downloads/search.asp?

Microsoft Technet
http://www.microsoft.com/technet/

Microsoft Knowledgebase
http://search.support.microsoft.com/kb/

Microsoft Windows 98 and Windows Me Error Message Resource Center
http://support.microsoft.com/support/windows/topics/errormsg/emresctr.asp

Microsoft Windows Tweak UI

http://www.microsoft.com/NTWorkstation/downloads/PowerToys/Networking/NTTweakUI.asp

Microsoft Office Resource Kit

http://www.microsoft.com/office/ork

WinDrivers.com

http://www.windrivers.com/

The Driver's Zone

http://www.driverzone.com/

20.13.1 Boot Problems

A large majority of the technical problems that arise under Windows 9X can be traced back to the configuration files and how these files control the boot process. Isolating which of these settings are incompatible with Windows 9X can be difficult. Windows 9X includes a number of features that will help you restart your system after a boot failure and find the source of the problem:

1. The Startup menu
2. The startup disk
3. Win.com switches
4. System Configuration utility (MSCONFIG.EXE)

Pressing the F8 for Windows 95 or Windows Millennium or the Ctrl key as soon as "Starting Windows 9X" appears on the screen during the startup of the operating system invokes the Windows Startup menu (see figure 20.32), which provides a number of different modes in which Windows can be booted. If the system fails to start normally, you may still be able to reboot into one of these alternative modes in order to troubleshoot the problem. The Startup menu options depend in part on the parameters specified in the MSDOS.SYS file, but generally consist of the options shown in table 20.16.

Safe mode bypasses the startup files and uses only basic system drivers. The safe boot-up also occurs when pressing the F5 key as soon as the "Starting Windows 9X" message appears on the screen during boot-up or by typing *WIN /D:M* at the command prompt. The Step-By-Step Confirmations option starts Windows but asks Yes or No for each line in the startup files. The command prompt starts the operating system with startup files and registry but does not start the GUI. The safe mode command prompt option starts the system in safe mode but bypasses the startup files and does not load the GUI.

Some systems will also have a Previous Version of MS-DOS option. This will start the version of MS-DOS previously installed on the computer. The previous DOS version can also be loaded by pressing the F4 key as soon as the "Starting Windows 95" message appears. This option is available only if BootMulti = 1

Figure 20.32 Windows Startup Menu

```
Microsoft Windows 95 Startup Menu
===========================

   1. Normal
   2. Logged (\BOOTLOG.TXT)
   3. Safe mode
   4. Safe mode with network support
   5. Step-by-step confirmation
   6. Command prompt only
   7. Safe mode command prompt only
   8. Previous version of MS-DOS
Enter a choice: 1

F5-Safe mode  Shift + F5=Command prompt  Shift + F8=Step-by-step Confirmation  [N]
```

Table 20.16 Windows 9X Startup Menu

Startup Menu Option	Description
Normal mode	This is the normal operation mode of Windows 9X. If you boot to the Startup menu but then decide to complete the boot process and start Windows 9X under normal conditions, select this mode.
Logged mode	When you select Logged mode, the entire boot process is logged to a file called BOOTLOG.TXT, which catalogs VxD initializations, driver loads, and various other boot-related events. BOOTLOG.TXT was described earlier in this chapter. You can use the boot log to determine where the boot failure occurs and what the system is doing at the time. Aside from the logging, the logged mode performs a normal boot procedure (of course it will be a bit slower because it writes to the BOOTLOG.TXT file). BOOTLOG.TXT will normally be found in the root directory. You can load BOOTLOG.TXT into a text editor such as Notepad to examine the contents.
Safe mode	Safe mode is likely the single most important troubleshooting tool available in Windows 98. In this mode, a number of key Windows 98 components and settings are disabled, including the following: • CONFIG.SYS and AUTOEXEC.BAT • The [Boot] and [386Enh] sections of SYSTEM.INI • The Load= and Run= parameters of WIN.INI • The Startup program group • The registry • All device drivers except the keyboard, mouse, and standard VGA video drivers Disabling these items allows the separation of fundamental operating system problems from those caused by a combination of software factors. In a situation in which the display is not functioning properly in normal mode, for example, if the problem does not appear in safe mode, the problem probably is video driver-related and is not due to a defective video card. Similarly, you can use safe mode to troubleshoot scenarios such as the following: • GPFs (general protection faults) • Application hangs • A hang during the boot process • A blank screen at boot time
Step-by-Step Confirmation mode	This boot mode is similar to the F8 function of previous versions of MS-DOS; it permits the user to step through the various stages of the boot process and specify whether each should or should not be completed. This mode can be very useful when you are trying to isolate boot stages to determine which may be causing a given problem. You can also use it to view system responses to various parameters in CONFIG.SYS and AUTOEXEC.BAT, which otherwise are displayed far too quickly to read.
Command-Prompt-Only mode	The Command-Prompt-Only mode option is similar to a normal boot of MS-DOS. Only CONFIG.SYS, AUTOEXEC.BAT, COMMAND.COM, and the registry are processed (along with any necessary disk compression drivers). This mode is useful in troubleshooting problems running MS-DOS applications in a VM under Windows 9X. If the application functions in this mode but not inside. Windows 9X, the problem is likely due to a compatibility issue. If the application does not function in command-prompt-only mode, the problem is likely a configuration problem in CONFIG.SYS or AUTOEXEC.BAT, or the application may be corrupt.
Safe Mode Command-Prompt-Only mode	The Safe Mode Command-Prompt-Only mode option is similar to a safe mode, except that COMMAND.COM is processed. Also, Startup does not load HIMEM.SYS or IFSHLP.SYS and does not execute WIN.COM to start theWindows interface. This mode is useful if your computer fails to boot properly in safe mode. Safe mode command-prompt-only mode offers slightly different options from safe mode, so you can use it for slightly different situations. For instance, you can use this mode if you don't want Windows to process WIN.COM or HIMEM.SYS.
Previous Version of MS-DOS	Although the Previous Version of MS-DOS boot mode option is not intended for troubleshooting, it can be used in situations in which particular MS-DOS–related functions worked in previous versions of MS-DOS but do not seem to function properly under Windows 98. Of course, you can boot to a previous version only if you upgraded the computer from a previous version and the partition is still FAT and not FAT32.

is in the MSDOS.SYS file. If, however, this option appears on Windows 95 OSR2 versions or later, you do not want to choose it; if you do, you will go to DOS once but the system will not boot after that.

You can create the startup disk at installation time or later at the Startup Disk tab of the Add/Remove Programs in the Control Panel. The disk serves as an emergency boot disk should the operating system fail to load. In addition to the boot files necessary to start Window 9X in command-prompt-only mode, the startup disk contains several tools you can use to troubleshoot boot problems.

For example, if you can boot to the Windows 9X startup disk, you can navigate through your hard drive to find a file that is interfering with the boot process. You can also troubleshoot your hard drive using SCANDISK, or even reformat and repartition your hard drive (start over) using FORMAT and FDISK. The CD-ROM drivers on the startup disk will provide you with access to the Windows 9X installation CD, in case you need to reinstall Windows 9X or copy files that are located on the CD.

WIN.COM includes support for a number of error-isolation switches. Although some are available from within Windows 9X, you may have to specify them from the command prompt in situations in which Windows 9X fails to load. These switches are specified in the following format:

win/d:[f] [m] [n] [s] [v] [x]

Switch	Function
F	Disables 32-bit file system drivers
M	Starts Windows 98 in safe mode
N	Starts safe mode with networking
S	Excludes the ROM address space between FOOO and 1 MB from use by Windows 98
V	Tells Windows 98 that the ROM routine should handle disk interrupts
X	Excludes the adapter area from the area that Windows 98 scans when looking for unused disk space

You can use these switches independently or together as part of a single command. If Windows won't start normally, you may be able to boot to a system disk and run WIN.COM using one or more of these switches to isolate the problem.

Boot failures are often caused by drivers or settings invoked through one of the Windows Startup configuration files. Therefore, starting with Windows 98, Windows included the System Configuration utility (MSCONFIG.EXE). The System Configuration utility lets you turn off or turn on specific entries in the Startup files AUTOEXEC.BAT, CONFIG.SYS, SYSTEM.INI, or WIN.INI. You can also make other changes to the startup process that may help with diagnosing startup problems. The System Configuration utility General tab is shown in figure 20.33.

Note that, in addition to a normal startup, you can choose Diagnostic startup, or you can choose to selectively disable files. The tabs named for the Startup files (AUTOEXEC.BAT, CONFIG.SYS, SYSTEM.INI, and WIN.INI) let you enable or disable specific statements within the file. You can also change the order of the statements within the file by using the Move Up and Move Down buttons. Or, you can add a new statement to the file or edit a statement by using the New and Edit buttons. The Startup tab lets you decide whether to load certain items at startup.

Windows system problems often occur at startup. These problems are, of course, impossible to troubleshoot if you can't start your system. Windows includes several methods for starting Windows that may help you diagnose a problem, or at least, start the system so you can pursue other troubleshooting remedies. The preceding sections discussed some of these options. The first step is usually to boot your system using the option boot modes of the Startup menu such as Safe mode or Step-by-Step Confirmation mode. The WIN.COM switches are usually for subtler problems. System Configuration utility is often useful for troubleshooting startup problems related to older devices and applications.

If Windows does not start in safe mode, any of the following conditions can be the cause of the problem:

- Your computer is infected with a virus.

Figure 20.33 System Configuration Utility

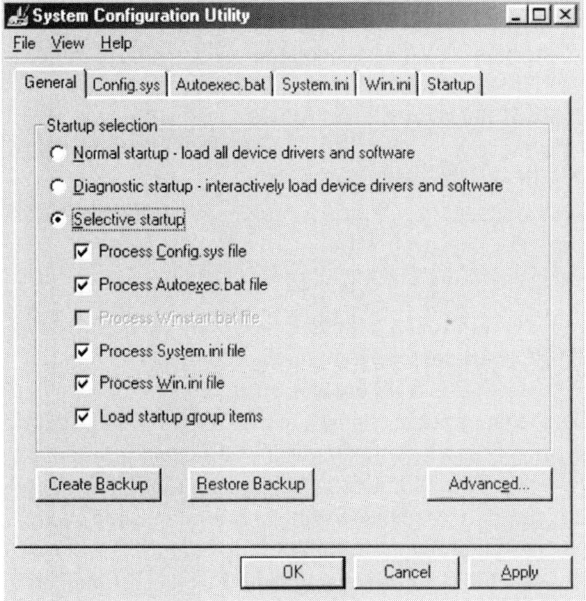

- Your computer's CMOS settings are not correct. Check to make sure they are correct. You may need to contact the computer manufacturer to verify these settings.
- There is a hardware conflict. These conflicts can include, but are not limited to, PCI BIOS settings, IRQ conflicts, redundant COM ports (for example, two COM1 ports, or an internal modem set to use the same COM port as an existing serial port), and defective RAM chips.
- A setting in the MSDOS.SYS file needs to be changed (for example, the Logo setting should be set to zero).
- You have a compressed drive that is unable to mount a compressed volume file (CVF).
- The registry could be corrupted. If you are still unable to start Windows in safe mode, run the Windows Registry Checker (SCANREG.EXE) tool as there may be a problem with the system registry. To start Windows Registry Checker, restart your computer, press and hold Ctrl, choose Command-Prompt-Only mode, type *scanreg,* and then press Enter.
- If you are still unable to start Windows 98 in safe mode after you use Windows Registry Checker, install Windows 98 into a new, empty folder. This step helps establish whether the problem is related to a remnant of the previous operating system (such as a configuration setting) or a hardware problem.

Example 20.1:

During boot-up, the following message appears on the screen:

```
Missing or Corrupt HIMEM.SYS
```

When this problem occurs, make sure that the HIMEM.SYS file is in the WINDOWS folder and that it is the right version. If the correct HIMEM.SYS file is in the correct directory, make sure the CONFIG.SYS file does not have a line that specifies a different HIMEM.SYS file.

Example 20.2:

During boot-up, you receive the following message:

```
VFAT Device Initialization Failed. A device or resource
required by VFAT is not present or is unavailable. VFAT cannot
continue loading. System halted . . .
```

This error message occurs for one of the following reason:

- The IFSHLP.SYS file is missing from the WINDOWS folder.
- The CONFIG.SYS file contains a line (such as DEVICE=C:\WINDOWS=IFSHELP.SYS) pointing to a previous version of the IFSHLP.SYS file.
- The command to load the IFSHLP.SYS was deleted from the CONFIG.SYS file after reinstalling Windows.
- The [Paths] section in the MSDOS.SYS file is incorrect.
- A WINBOOT.INI file from a previous incomplete installation is present in the root folder of the boot disk.
- If a "maxfile cache=9096" line is present in the SYSTEM.INI file.

If the IFSHLP.SYS file is missing from the WINDOWS folder, extract a new copy of the file from the original Windows installation disks or CD-ROM or copy it from another computer that is running the same version of Windows 95 or 98. If the CONFIG.SYS file is in error, reboot the computer to the command prompt and use EDIT to make the appropriate changes to the CONFIG.SYS file. If the MSDOS.SYS file contains the incorrect path, reboot the computer to the command prompt and shut off the system, hidden, and read-only attributes of the MSDOS.SYS file using EDIT. After saving the changes, turn on the system hidden and read-only attributes for the MSDOS.SYS file and reboot the computer. If the WINBOOT.INI file is present in the root folder of the boot drive, start the Windows 9X command prompt and delete the WINBOOT.INI file using the DELTREE command.

20.13.2 DLL Problems

Because Windows 9X is a complicated multitasking environment with a shared interface, it has more application problems than there were with DOS. Some of these problems have an error message, such as "Missing DLL File, Illegal Operation," while others will not, such as when the computer locks up.

As a Windows application is installed, Windows will often do the following:

- Create a folder for the new program
- Copy the necessary files into the program folder
- Create shortcuts in the Start menu
- Make additions to the registry or INI files
- Modify the AUTOEXEC.BAT or CONFIG.SYS files
- Copy DLL files into the WINDOWS or WINDOWS\SYSTEM directory

Many programs have an Uninstaller option (usually accessed through the Add/Remove Programs applet in the Control Panel) that can keep or remove these changes or additions.

As mentioned earlier in this chapter, DLL files (files with a DLL file name extension) are dynamic link libraries—libraries of program code sometimes shared by different programs. DLL files are used to modularize Windows and to allow other programs to share their resources. The DLL files for an application may be installed in the WINDOWS or WINDOWS\SYSTEM folder or stored in the individual program folder. Because several programs can use the DLL files with the same name and location, there can be version problems or missing DLL problems. For example, application A uses the shared DLL file called ABC.DLL. Application B uses the same ABC.DLL file but a later version. Because application B uses a newer version, it overwrites the existing ABC.DLL file. Depending on application A and the new ABC.DLL, application A may run with no problem, or problems such as locking up or general protection faults may occur. Unfortunately, you may not realize that the ABC.DLL file was changed, so you don't realize that the installation of application B caused the problem. To overcome this, check with the manufacturer for any updates for program A and reinstall application A and apply the updates.

Another problem occurs with DLL files when applications are removed using the Windows 9X Add/Remove Programs applet in the Control Panel. At some point during the uninstall, the program might ask if it is OK to remove any of the shared DLL files that are not being used by other applications. Unfortunately, if application B, which needs the shared DLL file, is started and the file isn't on the system, you will then get a missing DLL file error message. To fix this problem, you would reinstall application B to restore the DLL files.

20.13.3 Windows 9X Is Not Responding

Sometimes in Windows 9X and applications loaded on Windows 9X, a computer will stop responding. When this occurs, first try pressing the Ctrl + Alt + Del keys to bring up the Close Program dialog box. If the box appears, you can then see if one of the programs is not responding, select it, and click on the End Task button. If the problem still exists, press the Ctl + Alt + Del keys again and click on the Shut Down option. If problem still exists or if the Close Program dialog box does not appear, you will then be forced to reboot the computer by using the on/off switch or the reset button.

After rebooting the computer, you should check for viruses, run SCANDISK to clean up any lost clusters, and delete any temporary files that may be lingering from the previous Windows 9X session. The temporary files will usually have to be deleted using the DOS mode. If the problem occurs again after loading the same application, reload the application and check with the manufacturer for any updates, patches, or fixes and to see if there are any known conflicts with other software applications. If after reloading the application the problem still exists, try reloading Windows. Lastly, check for power fluctuations and faulty hardware (RAM cache, RAM chips, processor, motherboard, or any other device being accessed at the time that the problem occurs).

20.13.4 Windows 9X Does Not Shut Down

When you click on the Start button and select the Shut Down option, Windows 9X sends a software command to shut down Windows. Unfortunately, sometimes Windows does not shut down properly:

- It may appear to stop responding for several minutes while the "Please wait while your computer shuts down" is displayed on the screen.
- You may see only a blank screen and a blinking cursor.
- Your computer may restart instead of shutting down.

Windows 9X tries to perform many functions during the shutdown process, including completion of all disk write functions, flushing the disk cache, running the Close Window code to close all currently running programs, and transitioning all protected-mode drivers to real mode.

Shutdown problems can be caused by any of the following issues:

- The Fast Shutdown registry key is enabled.
- There is a damaged Exit Windows sound file.
- A program or Terminate and Stay Resident (TSR) program may not close correctly.
- An incompatible, damaged, or conflicting device driver is loaded.
- Shutdown problems may be caused by a virtual device driver (VXD file).
- There is an incompatible Advanced Power Management (APM) or Advanced Configuration and Power Interface (ACPI) setting.
- There is an incompatible basic input/output system (BIOS) configuration setting.
- The computer contains incorrectly configured or damaged hardware.
- There is a video adapter that is not assigned an IRQ in real mode.

The Microsoft System Configuration utility includes an option to Disable Fast Shutdown. If this option is not set in Windows, your computer may reboot instead of shutting down. To resolve this issue, change the FastReboot data value from 1 to 0 in the following registry key:

HKEY_LOCAL_MACHINES\System\CurrentControlSet\Control\Shutdown

NOTE: After you apply the Windows 98 Second Edition Shutdown Supplement (available from Microsoft), the Disable Fast Shutdown option is no longer listed on the Advanced tab in MSCONFIG.EXE.

To determine if a damaged Exit Windows sound file stops Windows from shutting down:

1. Click Start, point to Settings, click Control Panel, and then double-click Sounds and Multimedia.
2. Record the name and location of the Exit Windows sound, click Exit Windows in the Sound Events box, and then click None in the Name box.
3. Click OK, and then restart your computer.

If the issue is resolved, your Exit Windows sound file is damaged and must be replaced. To replace the sound file, restore the file from a backup, or reinstall the program that provided the sound file.

To determine if the shutdown problem is caused by a TSR or driver that is loaded automatically from the WIN.INI or SYSTEM.INI files:

1. Click Start, click Run, type *MSCONFIG,* and then click OK.
2. Click Selective Startup, and then click to clear WIN.INI and SYSTEM.INI file.

   NOTE: If any of these items is unavailable, that particular file does not contain any items to load.
3. Click OK, and then click Yes to restart the computer. Determine if the issue is resolved by restarting your computer.
4. If the problem still exists, reenable the processing of the WIN.INI and SYSTEM.INI files. Then to determine if the problem is with a TSR or drivers loaded in the CONFIG.SYS and AUTOEXEC.BAT files, click Start, click Run, type *MSCONFIG,* and then click OK.
5. Click Selective Startup, and then click to clear check boxes for the CONFIG.SYS and AUTOEXEC.BAT files.
6. Click OK, and then click Yes to restart the computer. Test to determine if the issue is resolved by restarting your computer.

To determine whether a program in the STARTUP folder conflicts with the startup process:

1. Click Start, click Run, type *MSCONFIG* in the Open box, and then click OK.
2. Click Selective Startup, click to clear the Load Startup Group Items check box, click Apply, click OK, and then click Yes to restart your computer.
3. Test to determine if the issue is resolved by restarting your computer.
4. If your computer shuts down correctly, one of your startup programs is probably causing this issue. To determine which startup program is at fault, click Start, click Run, type *MSCONFIG* in the Open box, and then click OK.
5. On the Startup tab, click to select a check box, click OK, and then click Yes to restart your computer. Test to determine if the startup program you disabled caused the issue. If not, repeat these steps but enable a different program. When your computer does not start correctly, you have determined that the last startup program you enabled is the cause of the issue.
6. If disabling startup programs does not resolve the problem, reenable the startup programs.

To determine if the problem is listed in the startup log file, you can look in your startup log file (BOOTLOG.PRV) to find information about problems that occur during shutdown. The BOOTLOG.PRV file is a hidden file in the root folder of drive C. If Windows is configured to hide system files, use these steps to display hidden files:

1. On the Windows desktop, double-click My Computer.
2. On the Tools menu, click Folder Options.
3. Click the View tab.
4. Click to clear the Hide protected operating system files check box, and then click Yes when you are prompted to confirm this action.
5. Click OK, and then look for the BOOTLOG.PRV file again.
6. Click Start, click Shut Down, and then click OK.

If your computer does not automatically shut off, press the power button on your computer to turn it off. Leave your computer off for approximately 15 seconds, and then turn it back on. While your computer is starting, press and hold the Ctrl key. When the Startup menu is displayed, use the Up Arrow and Down Arrow keys to choose Logged (\BOOTLOG.TXT), and then press Enter.

After Windows starts, click Start, click Shut Down, click Restart, and then click OK. To review your startup log file:

1. Double-click My Computer, double-click drive C, and then look for the BOOTLOG.PRV file.
2. Double-click the BOOTLOG.PRV file. If you are prompted to select a program to use to open the file, click WordPad, Notepad, or any text editor in the list.
3. Look for "Terminate=" entries. These entries, located at the bottom of the file, might provide clues about the cause of the problem. If a process that is started by a "Terminate=" entry is completed successfully, the file contains a matching "EndTerminate=" entry.

4. Check the last line in the BOOTLOG.PRV file to see if it is one of these items:
   - Terminate=Query Drivers: This is a memory manager problem. Your computer might have defective memory chips or damaged files. You might need to reinstall Windows.
   - Terminate=Reset Display: Try installing an updated video adapter driver.
   - Terminate=RIT: There may be timer-related problems with the sound card or an older mouse driver. Try installing updated drivers for these devices.
   - Terminate=Win32: A program is not shutting down properly. Try quitting all programs before you shut down Windows.

Some of the most common device drivers that may cause problems are sound card drivers, video adapter drivers, and network adapter drivers. To disable device drivers:

1. Right-click My Computer, click Properties, and then click the Device Manager tab.
2. Double-click a device type (for example, Sound, Video, and Game Controllers) to expand it.
3. Click one of the listed devices, and then click Properties.
4. Click to select the Disable In This Hardware Profile check box.
   IMPORTANT: Record all of the devices you disable in this manner so that you can enable them again later.
5. Click OK, and then restart your computer.

Test to determine if the issue is resolved by restarting your computer. If your computer does not shut down correctly, repeat the steps but with a different component.

To test your video adapter, click Start, click Run, type *MSCONFIG,* click OK, click Advanced, click to select the VGA 640 × 480 × 16 check box, and then click OK. If you disable your sound card, video adapter, and network adapter, but the issue is still not resolved, reenable these devices by clicking to clear the Disable In This Hardware Profile check box.

If you are unable to change the video adapter by using the preceding steps, change your video adapter driver to the Standard VGA driver by using these steps:

1. Click Start, point to Settings, click Control Panel, and then double-click Display.
2. Click the Settings tab, click Advanced, click the Adapter tab, and then click Change.
3. Click Next, click Display a list of all the drivers in a specific location, so you can select the driver you want, and then click Next.
4. Click Show All Hardware, click Standard Display Types in the Manufacturer box, click Standard Display Adapter (VGA) in the Models box, and then click Next.
5. Click Yes, click Next, and then click Finish.
6. Click Close, and then click Yes when you are prompted to restart your computer.
7. If changing your video adapter to the Standard VGA driver resolves the issue, contact your video adapter manufacturer to inquire about the availability of an updated Windows Me video adapter driver.

To determine if shutdown problems are being caused by a virtual device driver (VXD file):

1. Click Start, click Run, type *MSCONFIG,* and then click OK.
2. Click Selective Startup, and then click to clear the Load Static VxDs check box.
3. Click OK, and then click YES to restart the computer. Test to determine if the issue is resolved by restarting your computer. If your computer does not shut down correctly, click to select the Load Static VxDs check box, and then continue with the next step. If the problem is fixed, suspect one of the following files (this is a partial list):
   VNETSUP.VXD Microsoft networking
   NDIS.VXD Microsoft networking
   NDIS2SUP.VXD Microsoft networking
   JAVASUP.VXD Java support
   VRTWD.386 Clock
   VFIXD.VXD Video Phone helper
   VNETBIOS.VXD Microsoft networking
   VSERVER.VXD Microsoft networking
   VREDIR.VXD Microsoft networking

DFS.VXD Microsoft networking
NDISWAN.VXD Microsoft networking
MSMOUSE.VXD Microsoft mouse

Check the properties of the incompatible STATIC.VXD file to determine which program it is associated with. Uninstall and then reinstall the program to replace the VXD file with a new copy. To check the properties of a file, click Start, click Search, type the name of the file in the For Files or Folders box, and then click Search Now. After the file you are looking for is displayed in the list, right-click the file, and then click Properties.

To determine if Advanced Power Management (APM) is causing the shutdown problem by disabling it (assuming that your system has APM):

1. Click Start, point to Settings, click Control Panel, double-click System, and then click the Device Manager tab.
2. Double-click the System Devices branch to expand it.
3. Double-click Advanced Power Management in the device list, click the Settings tab, and then click to select the Force APM 1.0 Mode and Disable Power Status Polling check boxes.
4. Click OK until you return to Control Panel, and then restart your computer.
5. Test to determine if the issue is resolved by restarting your computer. If your computer does not shut down correctly, repeat the steps, but click to clear the Force APM 1.0 Mode and Disable Power Status Polling check boxes.

To determine if there is an incompatible basic input/output system (BIOS) configuration setting—PCI Bus IRQ Steering:

1. Click Start, point to Settings, click Control Panel, and then double-click System.
2. On the Device Manager tab, click System Devices.
3. Double-click PCI Bus, and then click to clear the Use IRQ Steering check box on the IRQ Steering tab.
4. Click OK, and then restart your computer.
5. After you restart the computer, attempt to shut down your computer again.

If your computer shuts down successfully, you may need to change the BIOS configuration or you may need a BIOS update.

To determine if there is an incompatible basic input/output system (BIOS) configuration setting—Resume on Ring and LAN disabling the "Resume on Ring and LAN" feature in the computer's BIOS.

To determine if there is an incompatible basic input/output system (BIOS) configuration setting—NVRAM/ESCD, do the following:

1. Click Start, point to Settings, click Control Panel, and then double-click System.
2. On the Device Manager tab, double-click System Devices.
3. Click Plug and Play BIOS, and then click to select the Disable NVRAM/ESCD updates check box on the Settings tab.
4. Click OK, and then restart your computer.
5. After you restart the computer, attempt to shut down your computer again.

To determine if there is an incompatible basic input/output system (BIOS) configuration setting—Plug-and-Play BIOS, you can configure Windows to ignore the presence of a Plug-and-Play BIOS and communicate directly with the hardware. Note: Use this method for testing purposes only. Leaving the Plug-and-Play BIOS disabled may cause some hardware to stop working. To configure Windows not to use the Plug-and-Play BIOS:

1. Restart your computer, and press and hold Ctrl until you see the Windows Start menu.
2. Rename the BIOS.VXD to BIOS.OLD in the WINDOWS\SYSTEM directory.
3. Restart your computer. After the computer restarts, attempt to shut down Windows. If the computer shuts down correctly, the system BIOS is likely to be contributing to the shutdown problems. Contact the motherboard or BIOS manufacturer for a possible update.

Lastly, if you have an antivirus program that is configured to scan your floppy disk drive when you shut down your computer, your computer may stop responding.

20.13.5 General Protection Faults and Exception Errors

Windows 9X may encounter a general protection fault (GPF). See figure 20.34. It signifies that something unexpected has happened within the Windows environment—usually, a program has tried to access a memory that belongs to another program or an application has tried to pass invalid parameters to another program. An exception error is a condition that causes the program to branch to a different routine. An illegal error occurs when an instruction is sent to the processor that it cannot perform. See figure 20.35.

Although applications should normally run without interruption, situations do arise when, due to either programming errors or incompatibilites, applications cease to function properly. Knowing how to handle application problems is important in being able to administer the operating system properly. The two main problems that occur with applications are general protection faults (GPFs) and application hangs.

A general protection fault typically is caused by an application that attempts to violate system integrity in one of a number of ways:

1. By making a request to read or write to a memory address space owned by another application
2. By attempting to access the system hardware directly
3. By attempting to interact with a failing hardware driver (drivers operate at ring 0, and so can seriously impact the operating system)

Figure 20.34 A general protection fault (GPF) is sometimes referred to as the "Blue Screen of Death."

Windows

An Illegal Operation 0E has occured at the address 000000EEEF:98EE8F1 in module VMM32.VXD:USER.DLL. Your program has stopped responding.

* Hit CTRL+ALT+DEL to restart the computer. Your program will be closed and you will loose any unsaved information.
* You can hit Enter to try continue with the program

Press Any Key to Continue_

Figure 20.35 An illegal operation is a form of general protection fault (GPF).

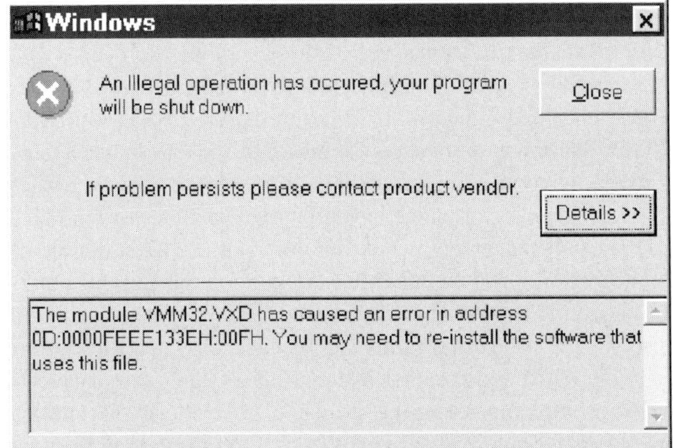

The GPF is generated when the operating system shuts down an offending application to prevent a system integrity violation. How the offending application is specifically handled depends on its application type. Because MS-DOS applications reside in their own virtual memory and have their own message queue, if they cause a GPF, a message is displayed and the application is terminated without impacting the rest of the operating system.

In the case of Win16 (Windows 3.XX) applications, the procedure is somewhat more complex. Because Win16 applications share both a common address space and a common message queue, when one application creates a GPF, all others are suspended until the offending application is terminated. After this is done, the remaining applications resume processing.

Finally, with 32-bit applications, the procedure is quite straightforward. Because 32-bit applications exist in their own separate address space, and each has a separate message queue, a GPF in one 32-bit application in no way affects any other 16- or 32-bit programs. Only the offending program is terminated.

Dr. Watson is a utility that tabulates information about the system at the time of an application fault. In order to tabulate this system information, Dr. Watson must be running at the time of the fault. If you know how to trigger the fault (for instance, if the fault always occurs when you open a specific application), start the Dr. Watson application, then trigger the fault. Dr. Watson will record the state of the software environment at the time of the failure. After the fault, the Details button in the error message dialog box will provide the information collected by Dr. Watson.

To start Dr. Watson, do the following:

1. Click on the Start menu and choose Programs, Accessories, System Tools.
2. Choose System Information from the System Tools menu.
3. In Microsoft System Information Utility, pull down the Tools menu and choose Dr. Watson.

Dr. Watson will start minimized in the systray (next to the clock). When you click on the Dr. Watson icon, it will generate a snapshot of your system. After Dr. Watson records the system information, the Dr. Watson main window appears on your screen. The default view is the standard view showing the Diagnosis tab, which provides relevant diagnostic information based on the state of the system at the time the snapshot was recorded.

Note that the Diagnosis tab includes a space for the user to write a note to the support technician describing what was happening at the time of the failure. For additional information on the state of the system at the time of the snapshot, choose Advanced View in the View menu. Dr. Watson's Advanced view provides several tabs describing different aspects of the system at the time of the snapshot. See figure 20.36.

When an application fault occurs, Dr. Watson saves the logged information to a file called WATSONXX.WLG in the \WINDOWS\DRWATSON directory. The XX (in WATSONXX.WLG) is an incremented number. You can also save a snapshot to a file using the Save and Save As options in the Dr. Watson File menu. You can view the contents of a Dr. Watson log file by opening it using the Open Log File option in the Dr. Watson File menu. You can also open a Dr. Watson in Microsoft System Information utility.

If you know an application fault will occur again but you don't know how to reproduce it, Microsoft suggests that you add a shortcut to Dr. Watson to the Start, Programs, STARTUP folder for your computer or user profile. Putting a shortcut to Dr. Watson in the STARTUP folder will cause Dr. Watson to start automatically when the system starts.

If a general protection fault occurs repeatedly, isolating a GPF can be a long and lengthy process. If the GPF message indicates a GPF with the GDI.EXE, USER.EXE, or video driver, the problem is most likely caused by the video system and driver. Try to use a new video driver from the manufacturer or try to use Windows 95 generic video drivers (the generic SVGA or VGA drivers). In addition, you can use the Video Performance tab and move the slide bar a notch or two to the left. The Video Performance tab can be accessed by starting the Control Panel, double-clicking on the System applet, clicking on the Performance tab, and then clicking on the Graphics button.

If you don't know what is causing the GFP, you are going to have to use the process of elimination. Because general protection faults can be caused by software or hardware, first, check to see that you have enough RAM and free disk space. If the virtual memory has become corrupted, you can boot to a command prompt and delete the swap file (WIN386.SWP) and let it rebuild itself during reboot. You also need to make sure that Windows 9X has the most recent service pack. If the problem persists, then

Figure 20.36 Dr. Watson allows a snapshot of the system when the problem occurred.

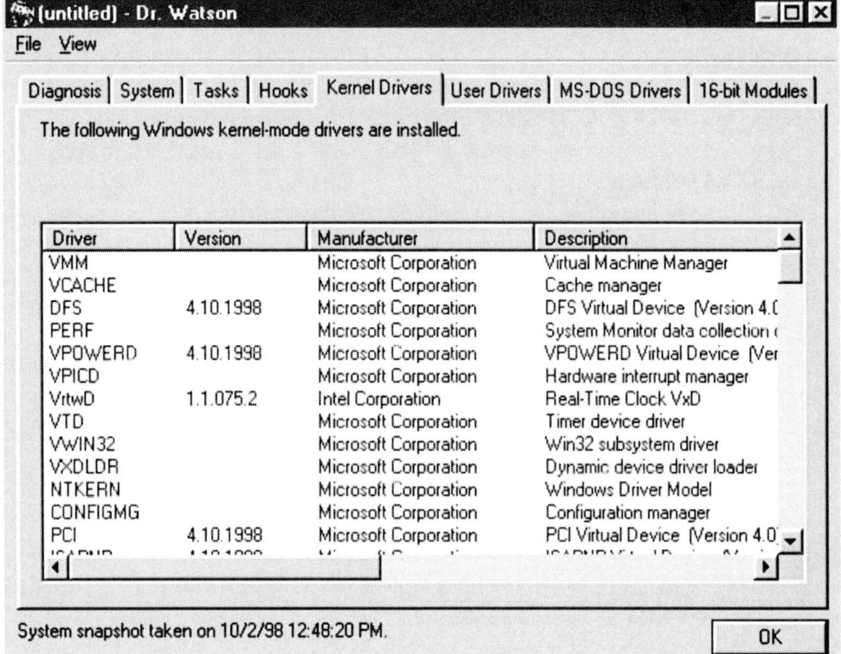

restart your computer in safe mode. Restarting in safe mode allows you to test your computer in a state in which only essential components of Windows are loaded. If you restart your computer in safe mode and the error message does not occur, the origin is more likely to be a driver or program. In which case, you use the System Configuration utility tool to isolate the offended driver or program. If you restart in safe mode and then test your computer and the error message does occur, the issue is more likely to be hardware or damaged Windows core files.

If the general protection fault occurs with the same application, check for lost clusters with SCANDISK, check for viruses, and delete any temporary files from the temporary directory (defined with the SET TEMP line in the AUTOEXEC.BAT file). Remember that both lost clusters and many temporary files in the temporary directory often indicate that a computer has been shutting down without properly exiting Windows. After checking for lost clusters, viruses, and temporary files, try to reinstall the program so that any incomplete files will be restored. You should also check to see if the software that you are using has a history of causing general protection faults and to see if there is a patch or fix that would correct the problem.

One cause of a general protection fault is an invalid page fault (IPF) or page fault error (PFE). An invalid page fault occurs when the operating system cannot find specific data that is stored in the RAM or virtual memory. It occurs more often when the system has little RAM or the hard drive is badly fragmented. Therefore, systems with more RAM and lots of free disk space on an unfragmented hard drive are more resistant against general protection faults. You can also delete the swap file (WIN386.SWP) so that it can be rebuilt.

To see if you have a corrupt registry, you should run the Registry Checker. You can also try to replace with a backup copy of the registry. If you don't have a backup copy of the registry, you could try installing a clean copy of Windows in an empty folder. This will also help you determine if the core files are not corrupt.

Lastly, GPFs can be caused by faulty RAM cache, faulty RAM chips, the processor, or the motherboard. To determine if you have faulty RAM cache, you can disable it usually using the CMOS setup program or by using jumpers/DIP switches on the motherboard. If the problem goes away, you know it is the RAM cache. If the problem still exists, you can enable the RAM cache and check elsewhere. To isolate the RAM, remove a bank of RAM chips, one at a time (if you have a lot of RAM), or swap a bank with known good RAM chips. For the processor and motherboard, replace one at a time and try the suspected component in another machine.

The KERNEL32.DLL file is a 32-bit dynamic link library file that is found in Windows 95, Windows 98, or Windows Millennium. The KERNEL32.DLL file handles memory management, input/output operations, and interrupts. When you start Windows, KERNEL32.DLL is loaded into a protected memory space so that other programs do not take over that memory space.

On occasion, you may receive an invalid page fault error message. This error message occurs when a program tries to access the KERNEL32.DLL protected memory space. Occasionally, the error message is caused by one particular program, and other times the error message is provoked by multiple files and programs.

If the problem results from running one program, the program needs to be replaced. If the problem occurs when you access multiple files and programs, the damage is likely caused by damaged hardware.

You may want to clean boot the computer to help you identify the particular third-party memory-resident software. Note that programs that are not memory-resident can also cause IPF error messages.

The following conditions can cause KERNEL32.DLL error messages:

- Damaged swap file
- File allocation damage
- Damaged password list (*PWL)
- Damaged or incorrect version of the KERNEL32.DLL file
- Damaged registry
- Hardware, hot CPU, overclocking, broken power supply, RF noise, ground bounce, or bad hard disk controller
- BIOS settings for wait states, RAM timing, or other BIOS settings
- Third-party software that is damaged or incorrectly installed
- DLL files that are saved to the desktop
- Nonexistent or broken TEMP folder
- A control panel (CPL) file is damaged
- Incorrect or damaged hardware driver
- Incorrectly installed printer drivers or HP Jetadmin drivers
- Damaged Java Machine
- Damaged LOG files
- Damaged entries in the HISTORY folder
- Incompatible or damaged dynamic link library files
- Viruses
- Damaged or incorrect MSINFO32.EXE file
- Low disk space
- Other problems that depend on the Kernel file

20.13.6 Windows Protection Errors

Sometimes Windows may refuse to boot and displays the message "Windows Protection Error. You need to restart your computer." This can occur when your computer is loading or unloading a virtual device driver (VxD). Usually the VxD that did not load or unload is mentioned in the error message.

Windows protection error messages can occur under any of the following conditions:

1. If a real mode driver and a protected mode driver are in conflict
2. If the registry is damaged
3. If either the WIN.COM file or the COMMAND.COM file are infected with a virus, or if either of the files is damaged
4. If a protected mode driver is loaded from the SYSTEM.INI file and the driver is already initialized
5. If there is a physical input/output (I/O) address conflict or a random access memory (RAM) address conflict
6. If there are incorrect CMOS settings for a built-in peripheral device (such as cache settings, CPU timing, hard disks, and so on)
7. If the plug-and-play feature of the computer's BIOS is not working correctly
8. If the computer contains a malfunctioning cache or malfunctioning memory
9. If the computer's motherboard is not working properly

The VxD that is generating the error message can be any VxD, either a default VxD that is installed or a third-party .386 driver that is loaded from the SYSTEM.INI file. If you do not know which driver is causing the error message, view the BOOTLOG.TXT file, and then check to see which driver is the last driver that is initialized. This is typically the driver that is causing the problem. You can also use the System Configuration utility to help isolate the driver that is causing the problem.

After that, start your computer in safe mode and make sure that you have the newest driver loaded. You should also verify that the computer's CMOS settings are correct. In addition, you can try to install a clean copy of Windows in an empty folder.

20.14 PERFORMANCE AND SYSTEM MONITOR

When trying to improve Windows performance or investigating why a machine is running slow, you should always make sure the machine has sufficient RAM and free disk space. This will also make the machine more reliable.

Wherever possible, Windows 9X is self-tuning, adjusting cache sizes or other elements of the system environment to provide the best performance for the current configuration. Windows 9X can also detect when the loaded drivers or other performance-related components are not providing the optimal performance. In the Control Panel, double-click System, and then click the Performance tab. Windows 9X reports the current performance status, including whether 32-bit, protected mode components are being used.

20.14.1 Optimizing the Swap File

Virtual memory is disk pretending to be RAM. For Windows 9X virtual memory is known as a swap file. By default, the Windows 9X swap file is dynamic. If hard disk space is running low, the size of the swap is decreased. If hard disk space is available and more memory is required, the size of the swap file is increased. See figure 20.37.

The single best way you can ensure high swap file performance is to make sure that the disk containing the swap file has ample free space so that the swap file size can shrink and grow as needed. If you completely disable virtual memory, it might cause the computer to stop operating properly. You might not be able to restart the computer, or system performance might be degraded. Having less than 10 MB of free disk space on the drive where the swap file is contained may cause numerous read/write errors, general protection faults, and drastically slow performance.

The most common reason for changing the default swap file is to move it to some drive other than the C drive. Many systems tend to fill up the C drive, so little or no room is left for the swap file. The swap file can use only the free space on a drive. When the space is filled, the swap file cannot get any

Figure 20.37 Virtual Memory Settings from Within the System Applet of the Control Panel

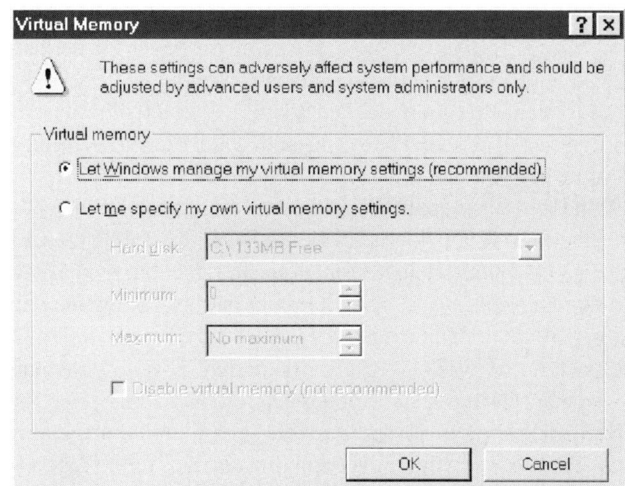

larger, resulting in the "Not Enough Memory" error. The solution is to move the swap file to another drive. To move the file in Windows 9X, click on the Let me specify my own virtual memory settings option and select another drive.

Although the system defaults usually provide the best performance, you can adjust the parameters used to define the swap file. For example, to optimize swap file performance on a computer with multiple hard disk drives, you might want to override the default location of the Windows swap file. The swap file should be placed on the drive with the fastest performance, unless that disk is overused. If a user usually loads all software from the same drive in a computer that has multiple drives, placing the swap file on one of the drives that is not as busy might boost performance.

You can manually set the minimum and maximum file sizes by selecting the Let me specify my own virtual memory settings option in the Virtual Memory dialog box. Entering the same number for Minimum and Maximum will fix the file's size. This may improve system performance because Windows no longer has to adjust the file size. However, you risk a memory shortage if the file size isn't large enough.

To adjust the virtual memory swap file:

1. In the Control Panel, double-click System, click the Performance tab, and then click Virtual Memory.
2. To specify a different hard disk, click the Let me specify my own virtual memory settings option. Then specify the new disk in the Hard disk box, or type values (in kilobytes) in the Minimum or Maximum box. Then click OK.

Windows 9X allows the swap file to become fragmented on the disk—that is, not stored in a single, contiguous block. In systems that make heavy use of virtual memory, this fragmentation can take a steep toll on performance. The easiest way to defragment the swap file is to use Norton Utilities' Speed Disk utility. You can also try Windows' Disk Defragmenter utility (under the System Tools menu). But since Disk Defragmenter treats the swap file as immovable, you'll first have to move the swap file to a second disk or partition—using the swap file "Hard disk" setting—then defragment the disk and finally move the file back. If you have just one disk, check Disable virtual memory, reboot, defrag the disk, enable virtual memory, and reboot again. But beware: If your system doesn't have enough RAM to run without virtual memory, it may not boot.

20.14.2 Optimizing File System Performance

In Windows, the disk cache is dynamic. You do not need to configure its size as part of system configuration. Changing the cache size is not a good method of limiting paging. Paging through the cache would quickly overwhelm it and make it useless for other file I/O. Although swap file I/O operations do not go through the cache, memory-mapped files and executable files do. The cache, however, is designed to make sure it cannot be overwhelmed by such I/O operations.

Changing the cache size (even if you could) probably would not have much effect on paging. The cache grows and shrinks as needed. If the system begins to page a lot, the cache shrinks automatically. People often think they are seeing a lot of paging, but they are really seeing other disk activity.

A common reason for excessive paging is that the working set of the applications you are running is greater than the amount of physical RAM available. If the amount of paging is extreme, to the point where system performance is poor, a real mode driver for the hard disk may be the cause, and should be replaced with a protected mode driver. If Windows 9X needs to use real mode for its disk I/O operations, a lot of code has to be locked down that would otherwise be pageable, and your working set increases significantly. Note: Paging through a real mode driver increases paging, and on a computer with 16 MB of memory, it can cause unacceptable performance.

In Windows, file system and disk performance can be controlled based on how the computer is used in most situations. If you double-click the System applet in the Control Panel, click on the Performance tab and click the File System button, you can select the typical role of the computer. This setting determines how much space is set aside in main memory to handle path and file name caching. The default is Desktop Computer, which allocates space for 32 paths and 677 file names. The Network Server allocates space for 64 paths and 2,729 file names. Even if the computer is not a network server, if there is more than 24 MB of RAM, it should be set to Network Server for better performance. See table 20.17. Note: Network Server is not an available option on the original release of Windows 95. To make this option available to the original version, the changes to the registry shown in table 20.18 would have to be made. See figure 20.38.

Table 20.17 Computer Role Descriptions

Role	Description
Desktop computer	A normal computer acting primarily as a network client, or an individual computer with no networking. This configuration assumes that there is more than the minimum required RAM, and that the computer is running on power (rather than battery).
Mobile or docking system	Any computer with limited memory. This configuration assumes that RAM is limited and that the computer is running on battery, so the disk cache should be flushed frequently.
Network server	A computer used primarily as a peer server for file or printer sharing. This configuration assumes that the computer has adequate RAM and frequent disk activity, so the system is optimized for a high amount of disk access.

Table 20.18 Changes Needed in the Registry to Make the Network Server Option Available in Windows 95

Registry Setting	Value
HKEY_LOCAL_MACHINE\SOFTWARE\Microsoft\Windows\Current\Version\FSTemplates\Server\NameCache	A9 0a 00 00
HKEY_LOCAL_MACHINE\SOFTWARE\Microsoft\Windows\Current\Version\FSTemplates\Server\PathCache	40 00 00 00

Figure 20.38 File System Properties

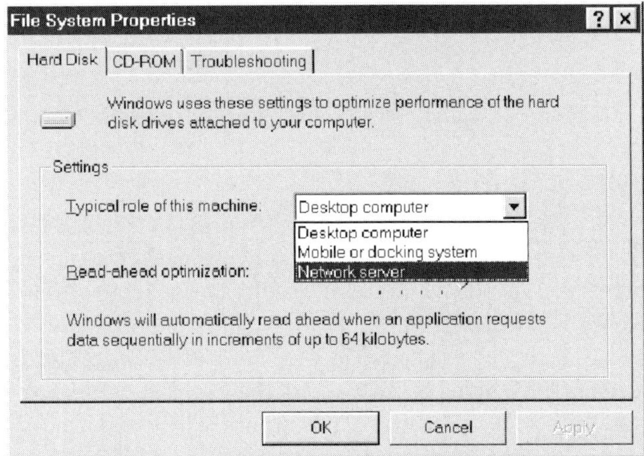

The 32-bit disk access feature is always turned on in Windows 98 unless Windows 98 detects a real mode disk driver that does not have a protected mode replacement. This could be, for example, an older Stacker driver or a hard disk security or encryption driver for a disk drive. To prevent the performance loss that occurs when Windows 98 is forced to use a real mode disk driver, upgrade to a protected mode replacement for that driver. If you need to determine why a Windows 98 real mode disk driver was installed, check the IOS.LOG file. The IOS.LOG file in the Windows directory is created when a protected mode driver is not available or the operating system detects that an unknown device driver is controlling a device. In most cases, the first line in IOS.LOG states why the protected mode driver was not loaded. If the first line mentions MBRINT13.SYS, the problem likely is a virus (unless you are using a driver that replaces the master boot record).

20.14.3 Optimizing CD-ROM File System Performance

The CD-ROM cache is separate from the cache used for disk file and network access because the performance characteristics of the CD-ROM are different. This cache can be paged to disk (the file and network cache cannot), reducing the working set for Windows 9X but still allowing for better CD-ROM performance. When Windows 9X is retrieving data from a compact disc, it is still faster to read a record from the cache even if it has been paged to disk, because the disk access time is much faster than the compact disc access time. Note: A small CD-ROM cache makes a big difference in streaming performance, but a much larger cache does not pay off as significantly, unless the cache is large enough to contain entire multimedia streams. In addition, many multimedia programs perform better with a smaller cache, because they tend not to reuse data.

To set the supplemental cache size for the **CD-ROM file system (CDFS)**:

1. In the Control Panel, double-click System, click the Performance tab, and then click File System.
2. Click the CD-ROM tab, and drag the slider to set the Supplemental cache size. Move the Supplemental Cache Size slider to the right to allocate more RAM for caching data from the CD-ROM drive or to the left to allocate less RAM for caching data.
3. In the Optimize access pattern for box, select a setting based on your computer's CD-ROM drive speed. Table 20.19 shows the size of the cache created for each CD-ROM drive speed setting.
4. Click OK, and then shut down and restart the computer.

20.14.4 Using File System Troubleshooting Options

The System option in the Control Panel presents a set of options for changing file system performance. You can use these options when you experience rare hardware or software compatibility problems. It is important to note that enabling any of the file system troubleshooting options will seriously degrade system performance. Typically, you want to enable these options if instructed to do so by a product support representative. Otherwise, these options should rarely, if ever, be used.

To display the file system troubleshooting options:

1. In the Control Panel, double-click System, and then click the Performance tab.
2. Click File System, and then click the Troubleshooting tab.

Table 20.20 summarizes the setting in Troubleshooting properties. Each option sets a value in the following registry key.

HKEY_LOCAL_MACHINE \System \Current ControlSet \Control \FileSystem

20.14.5 Graphics Compatibility Options

In Windows 9X, graphics hardware acceleration features can be turned off when system performance indicates incompatibility problems. Specifically, problems can occur when Windows 9X assumes a display adapter can support certain functionality that it cannot. In such cases, the side effects might be anything from small irregularities on the screen to system failure. You can disable hardware acceleration features of the display adapter so that the computer can still be used if there is a problem with the display adapter. If changing these settings fixes otherwise unexplained system crashes or performance problems, the source of the problem is probably the computer's display adapter.

Table 20.19 Optimizing Cache Size

CD-ROM Drive Speed	Cache Size
No read-ahead	1088 KB
Single-speed drives	1088 KB
Double-speed drives	1138 KB
Triple-speed drives	1188 KB
Quad-speed or higher	1238 KB

Table 20.20 File System Troubleshooting Options

File System Option	Description
Disable new file sharing and locking semantics	This option alters the internal rules for file sharing and locking on hard disks, governing whether certain processes can have access to open files in certain share modes that guarantee a file will not be modified. This option should be checked only in the rare case that an MS-DOS–based application has problems with sharing under Windows 98. This sets SoftCompactMode=0 in the registry.
Disable long name preservation for old programs	This option turns off the tunneling feature, which preserves long file names when files are opened and saved by applications that do not recognize long file names. This option should be checked in the rare case that an important legacy application is not compatible with long file names. This sets PreserveLong Names=0 in thc registry.
Disable protected mode hard disk interrupt handling	This option prevents Windows 98 from terminating interrupts from the hard disk controller and bypassing the read-only memory (ROM) routine that handles these interrupts. Some hard disk drives might require this option to be checked in order for interrupts to be processed correctly. If this option is checked, the ROM routine handles the interrupts, slowing system performance. This sets VirtualHDIRQ=1 in the registry. This setting is off by default in Windows 98.
Disable synchronous buffer commits	The file commit API is used to guarantee integrity of user data that is being written by an application to a disk. Normally, the file commit API is used by applications to ensure that critical data that the application is writing is written to the disk before returning from a call made to the file commit API. Choosing this option disables this feature. Data is still written to disk, but it is written to disk in the background at the discretion of the file system. Choosing this option can compromise data written to disk by an application should the system crash before the data is actually written. This option was added to allow adequate performance of a defective database application that used the file commit API incorrectly and excessively.
Disable all 32-bit protected mode disk drivers	This option ensures that no 32-bit disk drivers are loaded in the system, except the floppy driver. Typically, you would check this option if the computer does not start because of disk peripheral I/O problems. If this option is enabled, all I/O will go through real mode drivers or the BIOS. Notice that in this case, all disk drives that are visible only in protected mode will no longer be visible. This sets ForceRMIO=1 in the registry.
Disable write-behind caching for all drives	This option ensures that all data is flushed continually to the hard disk, removing any performance benefits grained from disk caching. This option should be checked only in the rare case that you are performing risky operations and must ensure prevention of data loss. For example, a software developer who is debugging data at ring 0 while creating a VxD would check this option. This sets Drive WriteBehind=0 in the registry.

To change graphics performance settings, double-click the System applet in the Control Panel, click the Performance tab, and then click Graphics. Drag the slider to change the Hardware acceleration setting, as summarized in the following list. Then click OK.

The default setting is Full, which turns on all graphics hardware acceleration features available in the display driver. The first notch from the right can be set to correct mouse pointer display problems. This setting disables hardware cursor support in the display driver by adding SwCursor=1 to the [Display] section of SYSTEM.INI. The second notch from the right can be set to correct certain display errors. This setting prevents some bit block transfers from being performed on the display card and disables memory-mapped I/O for some display drivers. This setting adds SwCursor=1 and Mmio=0 to the [Display] section of SYSTEM.INI, and SafeMode=1 to the [Windows] section of WIN.INI. The last notch from the right (None) can be set to correct problems if your computer frequently stops responding to input, or has other severe problems. This setting adds SafeMode=2 to the [Windows] section of WIN.INI, which removes all driver acceleration support and causes Windows 9X to use only the device-independent bitmap (DIB) engine rather than bit block transfers for displaying images.

20.14.6 Optimizing Printing

The way printing to a printer attached to a file or print server occurs depends on your server's operating system. If you print to a server running Windows 9X, the rendering from the EMF format to the printer-specific language happens on the server. This means that less work is performed on the client computer, giving the user better performance.

When you print to NetWare or Windows NT servers, the rendering from EMF to the printer-specific format happens on the client computer. Although this happens in the background, it still means more work is performed on the client computer. Printing to a printer attached locally causes both the EMF rendering and the device-specific rendering to happen on the computer.

To define spool settings for print performance, double-click Printers in the Control Panel, right-click a printer icon, and then click Properties. Then click the Details tab, and click Spool Settings. Select Spool print jobs so the program finishes printing faster, and then click one of the following options:

- Click Start printing after last page is spooled if you want the return-to-application time to be faster. This requires more disk space and increases the total print time. The second rendering does not start until the entire file is written to the EMF file, decreasing the amount of work performed on the computer as you print, but increasing the disk space because the entire file has to be written before the second rendering starts.
- Click Start printing after first page is spooled if you want the second rendering to take place simultaneously with the writing of the EMF file. This reduces the total print time and disk space required, but it increases the return-to-application time.

20.14.7 Windows 9X Resources

The kernel, GDI.EXE and USER.EXE, files were discussed earlier in the chapter. The kernel loads and runs Windows applications and handles their memory management, the GDI manages graphics and printing, and USER controls user input and output devices, including the keyboard and the mouse.

The GDI and USER use storage areas known as the *local heap*. The GDI heap contains information about graphical objects, such as pens, brushes, cursors, fonts, icons, buttons, scroll bars, and so on. The USER heap contains information about windows, icons, menus, and dialog boxes. Windows 9X has larger heaps than Windows 3.XX applications, including a larger 32-bit GDI heap, but it retains the same 16-bit GDI heap as Windows 3.XX so that it can support older programs. If any heap drops too low, the system can become unstable and cause problems even though there is a lot of free RAM. To view the amount of free system resources (the percentage of the heap, that has the lowest amount of free memory), use the Performance tab in the System applet in the Control Panel. To see the amount of free system resources for the System, USER, and GDI, use a utility called Resource Meter. See figure 20.39.

Some of the symptoms of running low on resources include:

- An out-of-memory error message appears
- Your screen takes a long time to redraw
- Parts of the dialog boxes are missing
- Warning messages and graphics do not appear

If you get these symptoms or you suspect that you are low on resources, you should make sure that you have a lot of RAM and free disk space. You can also try the following:

- Close any applications or documents that you are not using.
- Eliminate fonts that are not needed.
- Try to keep open an application that uses system resources every time it runs, instead of closing and reopening it many times.
- Clear the Clipboard.
- Disable the screen saver.
- Restart Windows to reclaim any resources that programs have not given back.
- If you are using Windows 95, you should consider upgrading to Windows 98, Windows Millennium, Windows 2000, or Windows XP. If you are using Windows 98 or Windows Millennium, you should consider upgrading to Windows 2000 or Windows XP.

Figure 20.39 Windows 95 Resource Meter

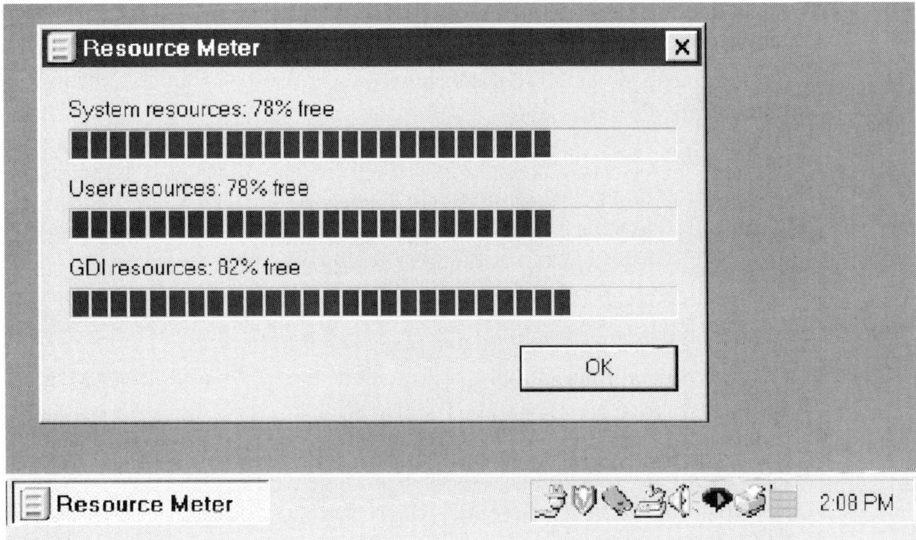

Figure 20.40 Windows 95 System Monitor

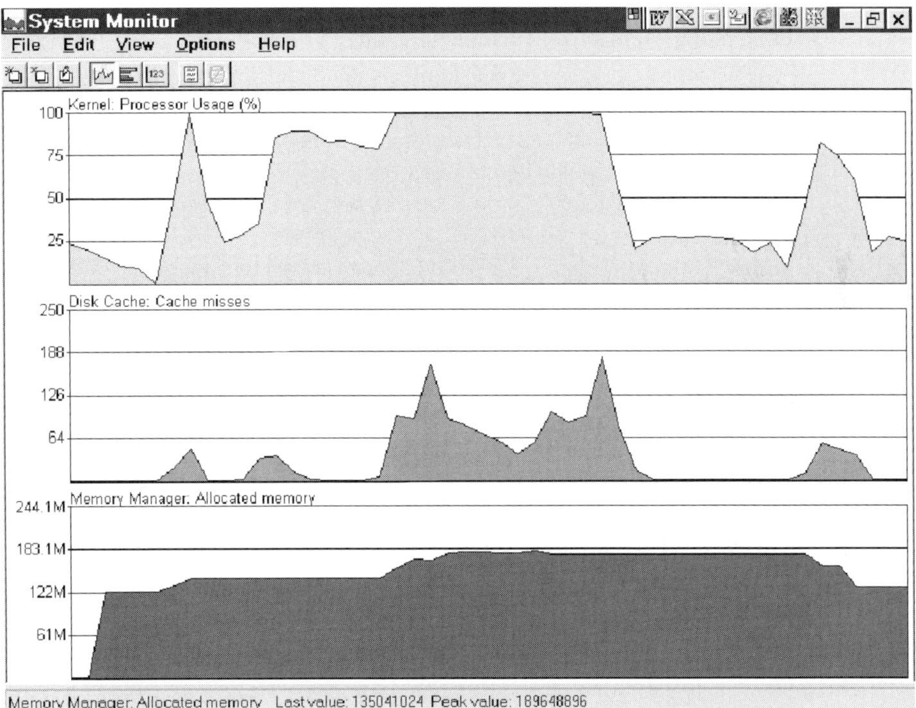

20.14.8 Using System Monitor

System Monitor is a useful tool to help measure the performance of hardware, software, services, and applications to determine what is acting as a bottleneck and slowing the system. By using real-time graphs, it can provide a snapshot of key performance statistics on memory CPU and other settings. Running System Monitor before making a change to the system and then running it after making a change shows how much the change has affected performance. See figure 20.40.

To install System Monitor:

1. In the Control Panel, double-click Add/Remove Programs.
2. Click the Windows Setup tab.

3. Click System Tools, and then click Details.
4. Click System Monitor, and then click OK.

To run System Monitor:

On the Start menu, point to Programs, point to Accessories, point to System Tools, and then click System Monitor.

To start logging:

1. In System Monitor, click File, and then click Start Logging.
2. Type a file name for the log file, and then click Save.
3. On the File menu, click Stop Logging to stop logging.

To edit an item in a chart:

1. In System Monitor, click Edit, and then click Edit Item.
2. Click Add Item, Remove Item, or Edit Item, and then make the changes you want.

NOTE: To view a definition of an item in the Item list, click the item, and then click Explain.

3. Click OK.

NOTE: You can edit only a chart that you are currently viewing.

To change the look of a chart:

In System Monitor, click View, and then click Line Charts, Bar Charts, or Numeric Charts.

NOTE: You can edit only a chart that you are currently viewing.

To use System Monitor to track performance problems:

1. In System Monitor, click the Edit menu, and then click Add Item.
2. In the Category list, click the resource that you want to monitor.
3. In the Item list, select one or more resources that you want to monitor.
   To select more than one item, press Ctrl while clicking the items that you want to select.
   To select several items in a row, click the first item, and then press and hold down Shift while clicking the last item.
4. Click Explain for more information about a selected resource.
5. Click OK. A performance chart of the resource is added to System Monitor.
6. To change the view of the data from a line chart to a bar chart or a numeric listing, click the related button on the toolbar.

System Monitor offers menu commands for configuring the charts:

- To change the update interval, click the Options menu, and then click Chart.
- To configure the color and scaling for a selected item, click the Edit menu, and then click Edit Item.
- To control the display of the toolbar, status bar, and title bar, click the View menu, and then click Toolbar, Status Bar, or Hide Title Bar, respectively.

If you browse System Monitor, you will find that there are far more statistics available than you would ever want to put on a single screen. Most of them are too technical for the average user. But a handful of statistics are useful to just about every PC user. See table 20.21.

Table 20.21 Useful Statistics for System Monitor

Statistic	Description	Statistic Usage
Kernel: Processor Usage (%)	Specifies the percentage of the time that the processor is doing work.	If your CPU usage consistently runs at over 80%, you're overtaxing your PC. The underlying cause may be insufficient memory, too many programs running at once, or a corrupt program that won't release the processor. In some cases, adding memory will fix the problem. In others, you need to get a more powerful system.

Continued

Table 20.21 Continued

Statistic	Description	Statistic Usage
Kernel: Threads	Specifies the active threads, small pieces of software that occupy RAM.	The right number of threads for your PC depends on the software you happen to be running. For this to be useful, you need to perform a baseline, a measurement of normal use. A non-networked Windows 98 machine desktop system usually has 50 to 70 active threads with no other applications open. A program that increases the number of threads when open but does not release those threads is known as a memory leak. In Windows 9X, you can usually release stranded threads by closing the offending application. If a newer 32-bit program (one written for Windows 9X) is causing a memory leak, the source of trouble may very well be a corrupted file. If this is the case, you need to reinstall the application.
Memory Manager: Unused physical memory	Specifies the amount of physical RAM that is still free for use.	You may be surprised at how little RAM remains available under Windows, even when only a few applications are running. This is because Windows constantly moves data in and out of the swap file on the hard disk. The Unused physical memory setting is most useful when viewed in conjunction with the following six memory statistics.
Memory Manager: Swapfile size	Windows uses a swap file (also called virtual memory) as a temporary holding area for RAM data not currently being used.	If your system has a limited amount of hard disk space, you can use this statistic to balance your hard disk storage needs against Windows' memory needs.
Memory Manager: Swapfile in use	This statistic indicates the amount of RAM data that is actually stored in the swap file at any given moment.	
Memory Manager: Page faults **Memory Manager: Page-outs**		For this to be useful, you need to perform a baseline, a measurement of normal use. If either of these two statistics jumps to higher-than-normal levels, Windows may be relying to heavily on the swap file. If the increase coincides with sluggish performance, you need to add more physical RAM to your system.
Memory Manager: Allocated memory	This identifies the total amount of data that Windows is manipulating in memory.	To determine exactly how much RAM a given program requires, subtract the "Memory Manager: Disk cache size" value from the amount of "Allocated memory," with and without the program running. The difference is the amount of RAM used by that program.
Memory Manager: Locked Memory	Locked memory refers to the amount of data that must remain in physical RAM and can't be swapped to the hard disk.	If an application forces a high percentage of data to be locked in physical RAM, other applications'performance can slow because a large amount of data must be shuttled on and off the hard disk.
Memory Manager: Disk cache size	This statistic reports the amount of RAM allocated to caching hard disk data.	On systems running the original version of Windows 95 with the FAT16 file system, you may be able to rescue a few megabytes of RAM by lowering this setting. Watch your disk cache values to determine your system's maximum cache needs. If you see more than a megabyte of difference between what your disk cache uses and its fixed maximum value—which is determined by the MaxFile Cache= setting listed under [vcache] in your SYSTEM.INI file—you can recover some of the wasted RAM by lowering the MaxFileCache= setting. Of course, the memory you save may not be worth the effort if your system has more than 32 MB of RAM. But if you're working with 32 MB of memory or less, your applications will benefit from the extra RAM.

SUMMARY

1. The Windows 9X interface is based on the desktop, where all the work is done.
2. The My Computer icon includes all disk drives, the Control Panel, and the PRINTERS folder.
3. The Recycle Bin is used as a safe delete.
4. The systray, located at the right side of the Taskbar, is used for the clock and for any programs running in the background, such as printers and modems.
5. Windows 95 (original version) supports FAT/VFAT file systems; Windows 95 OSR2, Windows 98, and Windows Millennium support FAT/VFAT and FAT32.
6. Shortcut menus, also known as context menus, have been added to Windows 9X and can be accessed by clicking the right mouse button. It contains common commands for the item selected.
7. The Control Panel is a graphical tool used to configure the Windows environment and hardware devices. It can be accessed from the Settings option in the Start button under My Computer.
8. The first configuration file processed during boot-up is IO.SYS. The IO.SYS file will then read the MSDOS.SYS file, which is a text file that specifies the location of the necessary boot files.
9. The Windows 9X registry is the central information database for Windows 9X, which includes thousands of system settings.
10. Disk and file management is usually done with My Computer and Windows Explorer, which can be started by using the Programs option under the Start button.
11. Starting with Windows 98, Microsoft includes the System Information utility (MSINFO32.EXE) that you can use to analyze your system to solve problems. System Information collects and displays your system configuration information.
12. Windows can be installed from CD-ROM or over the network. To start the Windows installation, go to the CD-ROM and execute the SETUP.EXE file.
13. Setup relies on two log files (SETUPLOG.TXT and DETLOG.TXT) that it creates during installation to determine the cause of the failure and overcome installation problems.
14. After installing Windows, check if Microsoft has released any fixes or patches and apply them to the Windows system.
15. Sometimes, Microsoft will group the patches together and call them a service pack.
16. For your convenience, Microsoft produced the http://windowsupdate.microsoft.com website that is a catalog of fixes, updates, and enhancements to Windows and many programs that work with Windows.
17. If the Windows 95 retail version or Windows 98 is being installed on a system that already has DOS and Windows 3.XX, Windows can be made to dual boot between DOS and Windows by using the Custom Installation option.
18. For a dual boot system, let the system boot normally. To start DOS (and Windows 3.XX), press the F4 key as soon as the "Starting Windows" message appears during boot-up.
19. For Windows 9X, virtual memory is known as a swap file. By default, the Windows 9X swap file is temporary and changeable.
20. When a program requests memory that the memory manager cannot provide in Windows 9X, it is known as a page fault.
21. In Windows 9X, the disk cache is dynamic. You do not need to configure its size as part of system configuration.
22. Registry Checker is a system maintenance program that finds and resolves some registry problems, and regularly backs up the registry.
23. A large majority of the technical problems that arise under Windows can be traced back to the configuration files and how these files control the boot process.
24. The red *X* through an icon in the Device Manager means that the hardware device has been disabled. A yellow circled exclamation point through the icon means the hardware device has a problem.
25. You can use the System File Checker to periodically scan the system files on your computer to make sure they have not been corrupted and that the wrong version of a file hasn't been copied over the previously existing file.
26. Pressing F8 for Windows 95 or Windows Millennium or the Ctrl key as soon as "Starting Windows 9X" appears on the screen during startup of the operating system invokes the Windows Startup menu, which provides a number of different modes in which Windows can be booted.
27. Safe mode bypasses the startup files and uses only basic system drivers.
28. A general protection fault (GPF) typically is caused by an application that attempts to violate system integrity. The GPF is generated when the operating system shuts down an offending application to prevent a system integrity violation. How the offending application is specifically handled depends on its application type.

QUESTIONS

1. You just installed a Windows application in Windows 95. Typically, to start the program, you would
   a. find the executable file using My Computer and double-click on it.
   b. find the executable file using Windows Explorer and double-click on it.
   c. click on the Start button, click on the Programs option, and then click on the program in the appropriate folder.
   d. click with the right mouse button on the desktop and select the program from the shortcut menu.
2. When you delete a file by mistake, the file can be undeleted using the
   a. Recycle Bin.
   b. trash can.
   c. swap file.
   d. paging file.
   e. C drive.
3. Which of the following will you *not* find in the My Computer icon?
   a. A drive
   b. C drive
   c. Control Panel
   d. Recycle Bin
   e. PRINTERS folder
4. What section of the SYSTEM.INI file is always read by Windows 95 when it boots?
   a. [386Enh]
   b. [Standard]
   c. [boot]
   d. [Drivers32]
5. What is the minimum amount of RAM needed to install and run Windows 95?
   a. 2 MB
   b. 4 MB
   c. 8 MB
   d. 16 MB
6. A collection of files is grouped and stored in
   a. folders.
   b. icons.
   c. applets.
   d. windows.
7. The three buttons on the right side of a window titlebar in Windows 95 are
   a. Minimize, Maximize, Close.
   b. Minimize, Restore, Close.
   c. Minimize, Maximize/Restore, Close.
   d. Minimize, Maximize, Restore.
8. How do you know whether an icon on the desktop of Windows 95 is a shortcut icon?
   a. It uses a special icon designated for shortcuts.
   b. The icon is a different color.
   c. The icon is smaller.
   d. The icon has a little arrow in one corner.
9. The F5 key does what (choose two answer)?
   a. If it is pressed during boot-up, it will start Windows 95 in safe mode.
   b. If it is pressed during boot-up, it will start the Windows 95 boot menu.
   c. If it is pressed during boot-up it will start the previous operating system.
   d. It is used to refresh a window.
   e. It opens the context/shortcut menu.
10. What are the programs found in the Control Panel of Windows 95 called?
    a. applications
    b. applets
    c. subprograms
    d. subicons
11. What Windows 95 Control Panel applet is used for removing the drivers for a hardware device?
    a. System applet
    b. Add/Remove Programs applet
    c. Add New Hardware applet
    d. Internet applet
12. You want to create a startup disk (a bootable disk used for troubleshooting Windows 95). Which applet would you use to create the disk?
    a. System applet
    b. Add/Remove Programs applet
    c. Add New Hardware applet
    d. Internet applet
13. You have a program that follows the API specification. While removing the program, you want to make sure that the registry settings and program files are removed. Which applet would you use?
    a. System applet
    b. Add/Remove Programs applet
    c. Add New Hardware applet
    d. Internet applet
14. How do you modify the appearance of the Windows 95 desktop (choose all that apply)?
    a. Double-click on the Display applet in the Control Panel.
    b. Double-click on the System applet in the Control Panel.
    c. Double-click on the Accessibility applet in the Control Panel.
    d. Right-click on the System applet and choose the Desktop option.
    e. Right-click on the desktop and choose the Properties option.
15. To change the video card driver, you would
    a. use the Add/Remove Programs applet in the Control Panel and select the Video tab.
    b. use the Display applet in the Control Panel and select the Settings tab.
    c. use the System applet in the Control Panel and select the video card in the Device Manager.
    d. modify the SYSTEM.INI file using a text editor.
16. Where do you find the Add a Printer applet in Windows 98?
    a. Double-click on the Add/Remove Programs applet in the Control Panel.
    b. Double-click on the System applet in the Control Panel and select the Device Manager tab.
    c. Click on the Start button, select the Settings option, and click on the Printers option.
    d. Click on the Add New Hardware applet in the Control Panel.

17. Which tool(s) can be used to install an updated driver for a Windows 95 device?
   a. the Registry Editor
   b. the SETUP.EXE program
   c. the Add/Remove Programs applet
   d. the Add New Hardware applet
   e. the Device Manager
18. What happens when you use your mouse to right-click on an object in Windows 95?
   a. The properties sheet for that object will open.
   b. A special Windows 95 properties sheet will open that allows you to configure the Windows 95 environment.
   c. A shortcut menu pertaining to that object will open.
   d. You copy the object onto the Clipboard.
   e. You open the Explorer for that object.
19. Which file systems does Windows 95 (OSR2) support?
   a. FAT, VFAT, and FAT32
   b. FAT, VFAT, and NTFS
   c. VFAT, FAT32, and NTFS
   d. FAT, NTFS, and HPFS
20. What does it mean when one of the devices shown in the Device Manager has a circled exclamation point?
   a. The hardware has a problem.
   b. The hardware is disabled.
   c. The device is a high-priority device.
   d. The device is currently being used and cannot be removed at this time.
   e. The hardware was never installed.
21. What is the easiest way to get information about a document being printed on the printer?
   a. Open the File menu and select the Properties option.
   b. Double-click on the small printer icon in the Taskbar.
   c. Double-click on the Print Manager icon in the Printers applet in the Control Panel.
   d. Double-click on the Print Manager icon in the Control Panel.
22. You have an MS-DOS–based game that has to be run in a full screen. What do you need to do to make sure the program will always start in a full screen?
   a. Use the PIF editor to create a PIF file for the game.
   b. Using the shortcut menu of the DOS program, select the Properties shortcut.
   c. Press the Alt + Enter keys.
   d. Right-click the icon for the program and choose Full Screen.
23. You have an email program installed on your computer. How can you start the program automatically when Windows 95 starts?
   a. by dragging the program file to the desktop
   b. by dragging the program file to the Start menu
   c. by creating a STARTUP folder on the desktop and dragging the program file to the folder
   d. by choosing Settings from the Start menu, clicking Taskbar, clicking the Start menu Programs tab, and dragging the program file to the STARTUP folder
   e. by dragging the program to the Recycle Bin
24. Which registry subkey stores hardware-related information?
   a. HKEY_SYSTEM
   b. HKEY_HARDWARE_DATA
   c. HKEY_USERS
   d. HKEY_LOCAL_MACHINE
25. You want to make sure deleted items are removed from the Recycle Bin immediately. What do you need to do to configure the Recycle Bin?
   a. Select the Display applet in the Control Panel.
   b. Select the System applet in the Control Panel.
   c. Right-click the Recycle Bin and select the Properties option.
   d. Delete the Recycle Bin from the desktop.
26. You have just purchased a new HP LaserJet printer. What do you need to do to install the printer (choose two)?
   a. Double-click on the Add New Hardware applet in the Control Panel.
   b. Reexecute the SETUP.EXE file on the Windows 95 installation CD and install the Add Printer button.
   c. Double-click on the System applet in the Control Panel and select the Add Printer button.
   d. Insert the disk containing the HP printer drivers in the disk drive and start the installation executable file.
   e. Double-click the Add Printer icon in the PRINTERS folder (Control Panel or My Computer).
   f. Double-click on the Add New Hardware applet in the Control Panel.
27. What files make up the registry (choose all that apply)?
   a. USER.DAT
   b. REGISTRY.DAT
   c. BOOT.INI
   d. SYSTEM.DAT
   e. SYSTEM.INI
   f. WIN.INI
   g. MSDOS.SYS
   h. IO.SYS
28. How can you copy a file to a floppy disk from Windows Explorer (select two answers)?
   a. by right-clicking the file name and choosing Send To
   b. by dragging the file to the floppy disk drive icon on the Taskbar
   c. by dragging the file to the desktop
   d. by right-clicking the file name and choosing Copy To
   e. by dragging the file to the A drive icon within My Computer

29. You are installing Windows 95 on your computer. Your computer locks up during the hardware detection phase. Which file will provide you with information on the possible causes of the problem?
   a. SETUP.LOG
   b. DETECT.LOG
   c. DETLOG.TXT
   d. DETCRASH.LOG
30. You installed a modem on your computer but the system does not recognize the modem. What do you do next?
   a. run the Add New Hardware applet in the Control Panel and ask Windows to search for new hardware
   b. run the Add/Remove Programs applet in the Control Panel
   c. reinstall Windows and let Setup automatically install all necessary drivers
   d. copy the required driver from the installation CD to the hard drive
31. Which mode would you use to start Windows 95 with the default settings to fix problems?
   a. standard mode b. enhanced mode
   c. safe mode d. real mode
   e. protected mode f. default mode
32. How can the Device Manager be found?
   a. by double-clicking the System applet in the Control Panel
   b. by clicking on the Start button and selecting the Settings option
   c. by double-clicking on the DEVMAN.EXE file
   d. by double-clicking on the Device Manager icon on the Taskbar
33. What command is used to install Windows 95?
   a. INSTALL b. SETUP
   c. SETVER d. START
   e. GO
34. What utility is used to perform common file and disk management functions?
   a. Explorer b. File Manager
   c. System Editor d. PIF Editor
35. Most of the Windows 98 configuration information is kept in
   a. initialization files (*.INI).
   b. system files (*.SYS).
   c. the Windows registry.
   d. configuration files (*.CFG).
   e. dynamic link files (*.DLL).
36. What does it mean when one of the devices shown in the Device Manager has a red *X?*
   a. The hardware has a problem.
   b. The hardware is disabled.
   c. The device is currently being used and cannot be removed at this time.
   d. The hardware was never installed.
   e. The device is not on or does not have power.
37. What program allows objects from one program to be inserted into another program?
   a. OLE b. Multitasking
   c. Networks d. IFSHLP.SYS
38. While running Windows 95, the performance of the computer declines drastically. What is the most likely problem?
   a. insufficient free disk space
   b. choosing the nonturbo option during boot-up
   c. a corrupted registry
   d. a faulty microprocessor or RAM chip
   e. a deactivated RAM cache
39. What would you use to track the performance of key system components?
   a. the system monitor
   b. the resource monitor
   c. the System applet within the Control Panel
   d. the network monitor
   e. Microsoft diagnostic
40. What would you do to install a program in Windows 98?
   a. Click on the Start button, choose the Run option, and specify the location and name of the executable file.
   b. From the Start button, select the Find option.
   c. From the desktop, select the Install option from the shortcut menu.
   d. From any window, select the View menu and select the Options option.
   e. Open the File menu, select the Run option, and specify the location and name of the executable file.
41. When upgrading from Windows 3.XX to Windows 95, which of the following must you do to allow dual booting between DOS and Windows 95?
   a. Install Windows 95 in a different directory from the directory used for Windows 3.XX.
   b. Install programs only on Windows 3.XX or Windows 95, but not both.
   c. Boot to safe mode.
   d. Boot to the command prompt.
   e. Purchase the Windows 95 Plus! package and install it on your system.
42. Which of the following files are *not* used in Windows 95 to provide backward compatibility for older programs?
   a. SYSTEM.INI
   b. WIN.INI
   c. MSDOS.SYS
   d. COMMAND.COM
   e. EXPLORER.EXE
43. HIMEM.SYS and other common commands loaded in the CONFIG.SYS file are automatically loaded by
   a. IO.SYS.
   b. MSDOS.SYS.
   c. COMMAND.COM.
   d. VMM32.VXD.
   e. the Device Manager.
   f. DOS.INI.

44. Which of the following describes an illegal operation?
   a. An instruction was sent to the microprocessor that the microprocessor could not do.
   b. There is a sharing violation as two programs try to use the same file at the same time.
   c. Software piracy has been detected.
   d. While connected to the Internet, it has been determined that you broke a federal, state, or local law.
45. Which Windows 9X system file manages all requests to create, move, size, and delete a window or icon?
   a. GDI.EXE b. HEAP.EXE
   c. KRNL386.EXE d. USER.EXE
   e. SYSTEM.INI
46. What should you do first if a Windows system experiences frequent page faults?
   a. Flash the BIOS.
   b. Scan the physical memory and all disks for viruses.
   c. Check to see if the system has adequate free disk space.
   d. Check to make sure all critical file updates have been installed on the system.
47. Which Windows 98 tool can you use to download the latest drivers to your computer?
   a. Windows Update
   b. Device Manager
   c. Signature Verification Tool
   d. Task Scheduler
   e. System Information
48. Which key should you press during the boot sequence to display the Windows 95 startup menu?
   a. F8 b. Alt
   c. F1 d. Del
49. Which system tool should you use to validate the integrity of your Windows 98 system files?
   a. ScanDisk
   b. Disk Defragmenter
   c. Drive Converter
   d. System File Checker
50. You have the following lines in your MS-DOS:SYS file
   [Paths]
   WinDir=C:\WINDOWS
   WinBootDir=C:\WINDOWS
   HostWinBootDrv=C
   [Options]
   AutoScan=1
   BootGUI=1
   BootMulti=1
   Which two conditions result from using this MSDOS.SYS file (choose two)?
   a. The boot drive root directory is C:\.
   b. The Windows directory is C:\WINDOWS.
   c. The startup files are located in C:\WIN.
   d. The user cannot boot to the previous operating system.
   e. SCANDISK will run when Windows is not shut down correctly.
51. Your Windows 98 system has suffered a boot failure and will not start normally. You suspect a problem or inconsistency with the registry that is preventing the system from starting. Which file should you use to evaluate your Windows 98 system and recover from the boot failure?
   a. Restore
   b. MSDOS.SYS
   c. CFGBACK.EXE
   d. MSD_EXE
   e. SCANREG.EXE
   f. MSCONFIG.EXE
52. What is the best way to recover from a corrupt registry?
   a. Use REGEDIT to connect subkeys.
   b. Use REGEDIT to correct affected parent keys.
   c. Use a backup disk to restore the registry data.
   d. Use the REGEDIT switch /L system to find the location of the corrupt key.
53. What is the default location for a Windows 9X printer spool file?
   a. C:\SPOOL\PRINTERS
   b. C:\WINDOWS\PRINTERS
   c. C:\WINDOWS\SPOOL\PRINTERS
   d. C:\WINDOWS\SYSTEM\SPOOL\PRINTERS
54. Which key should you press during startup to display the Windows 98 Startup menu?
   a. F7 b. Alt
   c. F1 d. Ctrl
55. What does the Automatic Skip Driver (ASD.EXE) do in Windows 98?
   a. loads previously defined alternate drivers for malfunctioning devices during boot-up
   b. allows IDE hard disks to take advantage of track-by-track interleave (skip) for faster disk access
   c. identifies and disables malfunction devices so that they are skipped when the computer is next booted
   d. provides automatic error correct when a CD-ROM drive malfunctions and skips one or more tracks of data
56. Which conditions can cause general protection faults (choose three)?
   a. bad video drivers
   b. network connections
   c. lack of hard drive space
   d. corrupted programs
   e. memory management errors
57. A user complains of errors with her system and that during Windows 98 shutdown the system hangs. What is the most likely cause of this problem?
   a. not enough RAM
   b. corrupt registry
   c. damaged device driver
   d. stack overflow
   e. not enough disk space

58. A user reports that he got the following message when he started Windows:

    Windows protection error. You need to restart your computer.

    What should you do to solve this problem?
    a. Add more system RAM.
    b. Make sure the username and password are entered correctly.
    c. Start the system in safe mode and verify the system settings.
    d. Edit the OSDETECT.COM to point to the operating system files.
59. You get an error message whenever you try to start a particular application in Windows 98. You contact the software manufacturer's technical support to resolve the problem, and they ask you to email a screen capture of the error message to them. How can you capture an image of the error message?
    a. Press F12 and paste the image into Paint.
    b. Drag the email message onto the My Briefcase icon.
    c. Press Alt + Print Screen and paste the image into a document.
    d. Right-click the error message, select Send To, and then click the Mail Recipient option.

HANDS-ON EXERCISES

Exercise 1: Installing Windows 9X

1. Boot the computer and install Windows 9X.
2. Install the appropriate chipset drivers for the motherboard. See section 6.7.

Exercise 2: Becoming Familiar with the Windows 9X Interface

1. If any windows are open, close them.
2. Open the System applet in the Control Panel. The Control Panel can be opened from within My Computer or the Settings option under the Start button.
3. Select the Performance tab and record the amount of free system resources.
4. Close the System Properties window.
5. Click with the right mouse button (secondary mouse button) on My Computer to access the shortcut menu. Select the Properties option. Again click on the Performance tab.
6. Start the Resource Meter. It can be started by clicking on the Start button, clicking on Programs, clicking on Accessories, clicking on System Tools, and clicking on Resource Meter. If the Resource Meter is not loaded, it can be loaded by opening the Control Panel, double-clicking on the Add/Remove Programs applet, clicking on the Windows Setup tab, clicking on Accessories, clicking on Details, and putting a checkmark next to Resource Meter.
7. The Resource Meter is currently running and is currently minimized as a small icon with green strips on the right side of the Taskbar. Move the mouse pointer to the Resource Meter without clicking. Notice the message that appears.
8. Double-click on the Resource Meter.
9. Start the Calculator by clicking on the Start button, clicking on Programs, clicking on Accessories, and selecting the Calculator. Close the Calculator by clicking on the Close button at the top right corner of the Calculator.
10. Start the calculator by double-clicking on My Computer, double-clicking on the WINDOWS folder, and double-clicking on the CALC file.
11. Start the Calculator by using Windows Explorer. Close the Calculator by double-clicking on the small calculator icon at the top left of the calculator.
12. Start the Calculator by using the run option under the Start button and specifying the path of C:\WINDOWS\CALC.EXE. Close the Calculator.
13. Start the Calculator by using the Run option under the Start button and using the Browse button to find CALC.EXE. Close the Calculator.
14. Open a window for the C:\WINDOWS\DESKTOP directory and notice the contents of the DESKTOP directory.
15. Create a shortcut for the Windows 95 Calculator (C:\WINDOWS\CALC.EXE). You can do this by using the shortcut menu and select the New option followed by the Shortcut option. Try to determine what distinguishes a shortcut.
16. Test the Calculator shortcut. Close the Calculator.
17. Use Notepad to create a text file called NAME.TXT located in the C:\ folder. Include your first and last name in the file. Close Notepad.

18. Double-click on the NAME file under the C drive. Notice that Notepad automatically started. Close Notepad.
19. On the desktop, make a shortcut to the NAME file. This can be done by accessing the shortcut menu (clicking on the desktop with the right mouse button—secondary mouse button), clicking on the New option, and clicking on the Shortcut option.
20. Test the shortcut to the NAME.TXT file. Close Notepad.
21. Create a new folder called COMMON APPS.
22. In the COMMON APPS group, create icons for the Calculator (CALC.EXE), Notepad (NOTEPAD.EXE), and Paintbrush (PBRUSH.EXE) files. (Hint: They are all located in the WINDOWS directory.)
23. Test the newly created shortcuts.
24. Open a window for the C:\WINDOWS\DESKTOP directory. Notice the contents of the DESKTOP folder. Try to figure out what the purpose of the DESKTOP folder is.
25. Open windows for the C:\, C:\WINDOWS, C:\WINDOWS\COMMAND, and C:\WINDOWS\SYSTEM folders.
26. Check and record the amount of free system resources.
27. Close all the windows.
28. Close all the programs that you just started.
29. Start Microsoft Write and Microsoft Paintbrush.
30. If you have Microsoft Word and Microsoft Excel, start them.
31. If you have a browser installed, such as Microsoft Internet Explorer or Netscape Navigator, start your browser.
32. Check and record the free system resources.
33. Close all of the programs.
34. Check and record the free system resources.
35. Delete the COMMON APPS folder, the Calculator shortcut, and the Names shortcut.
36. Open a window for the C:\WINDOWS directory.
37. Select the Large Icons option under the View menu.
38. Select the Small Icons option under the View menu.
39. Select the List option under the View menu.
40. Select the Details option under the View menu.
41. Select the Toolbars option in the View menu.
42. Find and click on the Large Icons button. You may need to increase the window size to show all the buttons of the toolbar.
43. Open the View menu and click on the Arrange Icons option under the By Type option. By Type means that the icons will be sorted by file name extension.
44. In the Windows window, without clicking on an icon, open the shortcut menu (click the right mouse button), click on the Arrange Icons option, and click on the By Name option.
45. Make sure the Windows window does not auto-arrange its icons. This can be done by opening the View menu and clicking on the Arrange Option menu. If there is a check mark on the Auto Arrange option, click on it to shut it off. If there is no check mark on the Auto Arrange option, click somewhere on the desktop to close the menu.
46. Move some of the icons around without putting one on top of another.
47. Enable the auto-arrange feature for the Windows window.
48. Close all windows.
49. Double-click on the My Computer icon.
50. Double-click on the C drive.
51. Open windows for the C:\WINDOWS, C:\WINDOWS\COMMAND, and C:\WINDOWS\SYSTEM folders.
52. Close all windows.
53. Double-click on the My Computer icon.
54. Select Options under the View menu.
55. Under the Folder tab, select Browse Folders by Using the Single Window That Changes as You Open Each Folder option and click on the OK button.
56. Double-click on the C drive, double-click on the WINDOWS folder, and double-click on the SYSTEM folder. Notice how many windows are open.
57. Activate the toolbar for the SYSTEM folder.
58. Click on the Up One Level button. Keep clicking on the Up One Level button until you get back to the My Computer windows.
59. Select Options under the View menu. Under the Folder tab, select Browse Folders Using a Separate Window for Each Folder and click on the OK button.
60. Close all the windows.
61. Start Microsoft WordPad.
62. Type your name.
63. Highlight your name and change the font to Arial using the Font option under the Format menu.

64. Increase the font size to 18 points and make the text bold.
65. While the name is highlighted, use the shortcut menu to change the font to Times Roman and change the color to blue.
66. Activate the PrintScreen key on the keyboard. On most keyboards, you will need to press Shift + PrintScreen.
67. Paste into the WordPad document.
68. Shrink the WordPad to half the screen.
69. Press the Alt key with the PrintScreen key. On most keyboards, you will need to press the Alt + Shift + PrintScreen.
70. Paste into the WordPad document.
71. Close WordPad without saving the file.

Exercise 3: Understanding File Management

1. Insert a disk in drive A. Under My Computer, use the shortcut menu of the A drive and format the disk. Do not make it bootable.
2. Open a window for the A drive.
3. Create a folder called COMMAND on the A drive using the shortcut menu.
4. Open the A:\COMMAND folder.
5. Open a window for C:\WINDOWS\COMMAND.
6. Close all windows except for the two COMMAND windows.
7. Copy the FORMAT.COM, FDISK.EXE,ATTRIB.EXE, and DISKCOPY.COM files from the C:\WINDOWS\COMMAND folder to the A:\COMMAND folder.
8. Create a DATA folder in the A:\ folder.
9. Move the FORMAT.COM file from the A:\COMMAND folder to the A:\DATA folder.
10. Copy the FORMAT.COM file from the A:\DATA folder to the A:\COMMAND directory.
11. Using the shortcut menu of the A drive, perform a disk copy to another disk.
12. Keep the second disk in drive A and format the disk as a bootable disk.
13. Insert the first disk into drive A.
14. Rename the FORMAT.COM file to DESTROY.COM in the A:\ folder.
15. Make the DESTROY.COM file hidden by using the shortcut menu of the DESTROY.COM file and selecting Properties.
16. If you can't see the hidden files, select Options under the View menu, click on the View tab, select Show All Files, and click on the OK button. (Note: If you are using Windows 98, select the Folder options, click on the View tab, and select Show All files under the Hidden Files section.)
17. Use the COPY option from the shortcut menu of DELTREE.EXE file in the C:\WINDOWS\COMMAND directory.
18. Make the A:\ window active. On the A:\ windows, select the Paste option from the shortcut menu.
19. Delete the DESTROY.COM file.
20. Using the A:\ window, highlight both folders at the same time and delete them.
21. Start Windows Explorer.
22. Using the shortcut menu of the A drive shown in Windows Explorer, format the first disk without making it bootable.
23. Using the Format option, make the disk bootable without reformatting it. (Hint: Do not do a Full or Quick format.)
24. Create a folder called DOS COMMAND on the C drive using the shortcut menu of the C drive window.
25. Click on the DOS COMMAND folder. The right side of the window should show no files.
26. Click on the plus (+) next to the C:\WINDOWS folder in Explorer to show the subdirectories under Windows.
27. Click on the COMMAND folder under the WINDOWS directory.
28. Copy the FORMAT.COM, FDISK.EXE,ATTRIB.EXE, and DISKCOPY.COM files from the C:\WINDOWS\COMMAND folder to the C:\DOS COMMAND folder.
29. Delete the FORMAT.COM and ATTRIB.EXE files from the C drive.
30. Double-click on the Recycle Bin. These are the files that you deleted in the GUI.
31. Drag the FORMAT.COM file to the desktop.
32. Highlight the ATTRIB.EXE file and select Restore from the shortcut menu.
33. Look in the DOS COMMAND folder and notice that the ATTRIB.EXE file is back.
34. Select the Empty Recycle Bin option from the File menu.
35. Close the Recycle Bin window.
36. Access the shortcut menu of the Recycle Bin and select Properties. Notice the maximum size of the Recycle Bin.
37. Click on the OK button.

Exercise 4: Using OLE

1. Start Microsoft WordPad. Type your name and a couple of lines of text.
2. Without closing Microsoft Write, start Microsoft Paintbrush.
3. Draw some circles and squares.
4. Highlight the area with the circles and squares and copy them onto the Clipboard using the Copy option in the Edit menu.
5. Change back to Microsoft WordPad. You can use the Taskbar or the Alt + Tab keys.
6. Paste the image into Microsoft Write using the Paste option under the Edit menu.
7. Switch over to Paintbrush and close the program without saving the image.
8. Save the current document in Microsoft WordPad with the TESTOLE.DOC file name.
9. Double-click on the picture in Microsoft WordPad.
10. Draw a line through the picture.
11. Close the Paintbrush program by double-clicking on the WordPad document.
12. Save the Microsoft WordPad document.
13. Close the TESTOLE.DOC document.
14. Open a new document in Microsoft WordPad.
15. Using the Paste Special option under the Edit menu, paste the picture as a bitmap.
16. Close the Microsoft WordPad document.
17. Change the text to 36-point Arial bold.
18. Highlight the text and copy the text onto the Clipboard.
19. Paste the text.
20. Using the Paste Special option under the Edit menu, paste the text as a picture.
21. Using the Paste Special option under the Edit menu, paste the text as unformatted text.
22. Start the DOS prompt.
23. If the DOS prompt is not running in Windows, press the Alt + Enter keys.
24. Perform the following command at the prompt:

    ```
    C:\WINDOWS>EDIT C:\WINDOWS\FAQ.TXT
    ```

25. Using the Mark button on the toolbar, highlight some text. If the toolbar for the DOS window is not showing, use the shortcut menu of the title bar to activate the toolbar.
26. Using the Copy button on the toolbar, not the Copy option under the Edit menu of EDIT, copy the text onto the Clipboard.
27. Switch to Microsoft WordPad and paste the text into the document.
28. Exit WordPad.
29. Delete the TESTOLE.DOC file.

Exercise 5: Using DOS Applications

1. Using Notepad, create a batch file called GO.BAT with the following content:

    ```
    MEM
    PAUSE
    ```

2. Save the batch file with the name GO.BAT in the C:\WINDOWS\COMMAND directory.
3. From the command prompt, test the GO.BAT batch file.
4. From the Run option under the Start button, execute the GO.BAT batch file.
5. Using Microsoft Explorer, execute the GO.BAT batch file.
6. Make a shortcut called SHOW MEMORY that points to the GO.BAT batch file.
7. Test the shortcut and record the amount of free extended memory. In addition, notice the prompt shown while the batch file is being executed.
8. Select the Properties option in the shortcut menu of the SHOW MEMORY shortcut. Notice the extra tabs for a DOS program compared to a Windows program.
9. Change the properties so that you have 4,096 KB of extended memory and change the working directory to C:\WINDOWS\SYSTEM. In addition, configure the shortcut to run in Windows.
10. Test the shortcut and record the amount of extended memory. In addition, notice the prompt shown while the batch file is being executed.
11. Delete the SHOW MEMORY shortcut and the GO.BAT file.

Exercise 6: Using the Control Panel

1. Start the Control Panel.
2. Double-click on the System applet. Record the Windows 95 version, OEM number, and the amount of physical RAM.

3. Click on the Device Manager.
4. Double-click on the computer at the top of the device tree.

   Find what device is using IRQ 5.
   Find which IRQ is being used for COM2 and the hard drive.
   Find which IRQs are free.
   Find what device is using I/O address 300.
   Find what device is using DMA 2.
   Find what DMAs are being used by the sound card.

5. Click on the OK button.
6. On the device tree, find and double-click on COM2.

   Find and record the device status.
   Find and record the bits per second, the number of data bits and stop bits, the type of parity, and the type of flow control.
   Find and record the resources used by COM2.
   Find and record the entries in the Conflicting Device List.

7. Disable COM2.
8. If you have a sound card loaded, find it and delete the sound card from the device tree.
9. Click on the Performance tab.
10. Record the amount of physical RAM and the percentage of free system resources.
11. Record the performance status of the file system, virtual memory, disk compression, and PC cards.
12. Click the File System button.
13. Change the Typical Role of This Machine to Network Server.
14. Click on the CD-ROM tab.
15. Click on the Troubleshooting tab.
16. It is recommended that only advanced users and system administrators change the settings in the Troubleshooting tab. Try to figure out when you would change these settings.
17. Click on the OK button.
18. Click on the Graphics button.
19. Try to figure out when you would move the Hardware Acceleration slidebar to the left.
20. Click on the OK button.
21. Click on the Virtual Memory button.
22. Click on the OK button to exit the Virtual Memory settings and click OK to exit the System Properties dialog box.
23. In the Control Panel, double-click on the Add New Hardware applet. Run the Add New Hardware applet to automatically detect any hardware that your computer may have, including the sound card. If the system doesn't find the sound card, you will have to manually choose the sound card.
24. In the Control Panel, double-click on the Add/Remove Programs applet.
25. Within the Install/Uninstall tab, count the number of programs that are registered.
26. Ask your instructor if there is a program that he or she wants you to remove.
27. Using Windows Setup, make sure the following Windows components are installed:

   Accessibility Options
   Character Map
   Backup

28. Create a startup disk using the Startup Disk tab.
29. Close the Add/Remove Programs Properties dialog box.
30. Using the Date/Time applet, change the date of the computer to March 17, 2001. Record the day of the week of March 17, 2001.
31. Change the time to 2:00 A.M.
32. Change the time zone to Greenwich Mean Time.
33. Change the date, time, and time zone back to their correct settings.
34. Using the Display applet, change the background pattern to brick.
35. Enable the Flying Windows screen saver and have it activate after 2 minutes of inactivity.
36. Load the High Contrast Black (Large) appearance schemes.
37. Load the Lilac appearance scheme.
38. Increase the horizontal icon spacing to 75 pixels.
39. Change the icon text to 15-point Arial bold.
40. Load the Windows default appearance scheme.
41. Click on the Settings tab.
42. Record the current resolution and number of colors.
43. Change the screen resolution to 640 × 480 and number of colors to 16. Click on the OK button.

44. Change the screen resolution to 800 × 600, number of colors to 256, and choose small fonts. Click on the OK button.
45. Change the screen resolution to 800 × 600, number of colors to high color, and choose large fonts. Click on the OK button.
46. Change the display back to the recorded resolution and number of colors.
47. Click on the Advanced Properties button.
48. Record the manufacturer and type of the video card and monitor.
49. Change the video card driver to Video 7 VRAM/VRAMII/1024i.
50. If the computer does not boot properly, press the F5 key as soon as the "Starting Windows 95__" message appears during boot-up.
51. Change the video driver back to the recorded video driver.
52. Using the Mouse applet, maximize the Mouse Tracking Speed. Test the mouse by moving it across the screen.
53. Minimize the Mouse Tracking Speed. Test the mouse by moving it across the screen.
54. Maximize the mouse double-clicking speed. Test the mouse by double-clicking in the test area.
55. Adjust the mouse double-clicking speed to your own preference.
56. Activate the Mouse Pointer Trails and move the mouse. The Mouse Pointer Trails are used on notebook and laptop computers with screens that cannot update fast enough to keep up with the movements of the mouse.
57. Deactivate the Mouse Pointer Trails.
58. Start Microsoft WordPad.
59. Press the T key and hold it down. Notice how long it takes before the key starts repeating and how fast it repeats after it starts.
60. Using the Keyboard applet in the Control Panel, set the Repeat Delay to Short and the Repeat Rate to Fast.
61. Go back to Microsoft WordPad. Press the Y key and hold it down. Notice how long the key takes before it starts repeating and how fast it repeats after it starts.
62. Using the Keyboard icon in the Control Panel, set the Repeat Delay to Long and the Repeat Rate to Slow.
63. Go back to Microsoft WordPad. Press the Q key and hold it down. Notice how long the key takes before it starts repeating and how fast it repeats after it starts.
64. Place the Repeat Delay and the Repeat Rate to somewhere near the middle.

Exercise 7: Configuring the Taskbar

1. Start WordPad and then Microsoft Paint.
2. Using the Taskbar, switch back to WordPad.
3. Using the shortcut menu of the WordPad button, close WordPad.
4. Select the Start button, select the Settings option, and select the Taskbar option.
5. Enable the Always on Top and the Auto Hide options and click the OK button.
6. Move the mouse pointer to the bottom of the screen to unhide the Taskbar and move the mouse pointer away from the Taskbar to make it hide.
7. Using the shortcut menu of the Taskbar, select the Properties option.
8. Click on the Start Menu Programs tab. Click on the Advanced button.
9. Expand the PROGRAMS folder. Compare that to the Programs option under the Start button.
10. Go back to the Explorer showing the Start menu programs. Expand the STARTUP folder. These are the programs that automatically start during boot-up.
11. From the ACCESSORIES folder, copy the calculator into the STARTUP folder.
12. Close all windows and the Taskbar Properties dialog box and restart Windows. Notice the calculator automatically started.
13. Go back into the Taskbar Properties option and remove the calculator from the STARTUP folder.
14. From the Start button, look at the files listed in the Documents option.
15. In the Taskbar Properties dialog box, click on the Clear button.
16. From the Start button, look at the files listed in the Documents option.
17. Close the Taskbar Properties dialog box.

Exercise 8: Printing

1. In the PRINTERS folder, delete all print drivers that already exist.
2. Install the Hewlett-Packard LaserJet III printer driver. Assume that the printer will use LPT1.
3. If a printer is connected to the computer, unplug the printer cable.
4. Using the shortcut menu of the HP LaserJet III icon in the PRINTERS folder, pause the printer.
5. Start Microsoft WordPad and load the README.TXT file located in the C:\WINDOWS directory.

6. Use the Print option in the File menu. Make sure that the LaserJet III printer is selected.
7. Print the document three times.
8. Switch over to Print Manager by double-clicking on the minimized printer icon in the Taskbar.
9. Delete the three print jobs.
10. Close Print Manager for the Laser Jet III.
11. Install the driver for the NEC Silentwriter 2 Model 90.
12. Install the correct print driver for your printer and make it the default printer.
13. Connect the printer cable to the printer.
14. Using the Print option in the File menu, print the first page of the document using the NEC Silentwriter 2 Model 90 printer. Notice what happens if you select the wrong driver.
15. If necessary, delete the print job from the Program Manager.
16. Install the correct printer driver.
17. Print the first page of the document again, but select the correct printer driver.
18. Using the shortcut menu of the LaserJet III Printer in the PRINTERS folder, select the Properties option.
19. Print by selecting Test Print Page.
20. Click on the Details tab.
21. Click on the Graphics tab. Record the resolution, form of dithering, and current intensity.
22. Close the Laser Jet III Properties dialog box.
23. Delete the NEC and the HP LaserJet III printer drivers.

Exercise 9: Booting Windows 9X

1. Reboot Windows. When the "Starting Windows 9X__" message appears, immediately press the F8 key to bring up a boot menu.
2. Choose Safe Mode.
3. Shut down Windows and reboot it by selecting Command Prompt from the Boot menu.
4. Reboot the computer and select the Boot Log option from the Boot menu. (Note: If you have Windows 95b or Windows 95c, do not choose the Previous Operating System option in the Boot menu.)
5. Boot using a floppy disk and access the boot log file using a text editor.

Exercise 10: Backing Up and Restoring the Windows 9X Registry

1. Press F8 when the "Starting Windows 9X" message appears on the screen.
2. Choose the Command Prompt Only option.
3. Create a folder under the WINDOWS directory called REGISTRY.
4. Perform the following two commands at the C:\WINDOWS prompt:

```
DIR SYSTEM.* /AH
DIR USER.* /AH
```

5. In the WINDOWS directory, shut off the hidden, system, and read-only attributes for the SYSTEM.DAT file by executing the following command:

```
ATTRIB -H -S -R SYSTEM.DAT
```

6. Shut off the hidden, system, and read-only attributes for the USER.DAT file.
7. Copy the SYSTEM.DAT file to the REGISTRY directory by performing the following command at the C:\WINDOWS prompt:

```
COPY SYSTEM.DAT C:\WINDOWS\REGISTRY
```

8. Copy the USER.DAT file to the REGISTRY directory.
9. Turn on the hidden, system, and read-only attributes for the SYSTEM.DAT and USER.DAT files.
10. Typically, Windows 9X keeps an extra copy of the registry (registry files with a DA0 file name extension). Restore the backup registry files that have a DA file name extension.
11. Start and test Windows 9X. If Windows 95 is not working properly, restore the copy of the Windows 9X registry kept in the REGISTRY directory.

Exercise 11: Working with REGEDIT.EXE

1. Start the Display applet in the Control Panel.
2. Set the Wallpaper to Bubbles and tile it.
3. Set the screen saver to Flying Windows and set the wait time to 3 minutes.

4. Record the resolution.
5. Set the number of colors to 65,536 (16-bit). If necessary, reboot the computer.
6. Start REGEDIT.EXE.
7. Find the following value:

   `HKEY_CURRENT_USER\Control Panel\Desktop\ScreenSaveTimeOut`

   Notice the value and compare it to the wait time of the screen saver. Remember that 1 minute equals 60 seconds.
8. Change the ScreenSaveTimeOut value to 120 seconds.
9. Find the following value:

   `HKEY_CURRENT_USER\Control Panel\Desktop\TileWallPaper`

   Although the TileWallPaper value is a string, the TileWallPaper uses only a 1 or a 0 value. A 1 indicates to tile the wallpaper; a 0 indicates not to tile the wallpaper.
10. Find the following value:

    `HKEY_CURRENT_USER\Control Panel\Desktop\WallPaper`
11. Find the following value:

    `HKEY_LOCAL_MACHINE\Config\0001\Display\Settings\Resolution`
12. Find the following value:

    `HKEY_LOCAL_MACHINE\Config\0001\Display\Settings\BitsPerPixel`
13. Change the BitsPerPixel to 8.
14. Exit REGEDIT.EXE and reboot the computer.
15. Open the Display applet from the Control Panel and notice the number of colors.
16. Start the REGEDIT.EXE program.
17. Open the HKEY_USERS root key. Notice the number of users, including the Default User.
18. Open the Default key. Notice the similarity between the HKEY_USERS\DEFAULT key and the HKEY_CURRENT_USERS key.
19. Open a window to show the large icons of the C:\WINDOWS directory.
20. Find the BUBBLES.BMP file and notice the icon.
21. Find the HKEY_CLASSES_ ROOT\PaintPicture\DefaultIcon value and change it to %1.
22. Go back to the C:\WINDOWS window and notice the appearance of the BUBBLES.BMP icon.
23. Exit REGEDIT.EXE.

Exercise 12: Installing and Configuring Microsoft Office 97 or Office 2000

1. Insert the MS Office 97 CD-ROM into the compact disk drive and start the installation program (unless told otherwise). Install all of Office using the Custom installation except the Microsoft Photo Editor (selected within Office Tools).
2. After the installation is complete, double-click on the Microsoft Office Setup icon (located in the C:\PROGRAM FILES\Microsoft Office directory). This will allow you to install or remove Office components.
3. Install the Microsoft Photo Editor.
4. When Microsoft Photo Editor is installed, start Microsoft Word.
5. Type in your first name followed by your last name. On the next line, type in your address.
6. Select Options located within the Tools menu. Click on the View tab.
7. To show the hardware returns, select the spaces and paragraph marks within the Nonprinting Characters section and click on the OK button.
8. Select Options located within the Tools menu and shut off the space and paragraph marks.
9. Click on the General tab. In addition, notice the number of recently used files and the measurement units.
10. Select the Save tab. Make sure that the Save AutoRecover Info option is selected and notice the time of Autosave. In addition, notice the default format that documents are saved as (Save Word Files As option).
11. Click on the Spelling and Grammar tab. Make sure that the Check Spelling as you type and Check Grammar as you type options are selected.
12. Select the File Location tab. Notice the default directory for Word documents.
13. Click on the OK button.
14. Go to any toolbar and click using the right (secondary) mouse button. Notice which toolbars are open. Select the WordArt toolbar.
15. Grab the title bar of the WordArt toolbar and drag it to the right of the screen until it becomes embedded.

16. Grab the top of the WordArt toolbar and drag it back to the center of Microsoft Word window.
17. Close the WordArt toolbar.
18. Click on the Customize option located within the Tools menu.
19. Click on the Commands tab.
20. On the Standard toolbar, drag the New button off the toolbar.
21. Within the File category, find the New command and drag it to the beginning of the Standard toolbar. Click on the Close button.
22. Select the AutoCorrect option within the Tools menu. Click on the Options button.
23. If you don't want automatic bullets and numbering, deselect the Automatic Bulleted Lists and Automatic Numbered Lists options located in the Apply As You Type section.
24. Click on the OK button.
25. Close the current document and don't save the changes.
26. Open a new document. Notice the default font and font size.
27. Close the document.
28. Open the C:\PROGRAM FILES\MICROSOFT OFFICE\TEMPLATES\NORMAL.DOT template.
29. Change the font to 12-point Arial.
30. Save the changes and close the NORMAL.DOT template.
31. Open a new document. Notice the default font and font size.
32. Close Microsoft Word.

Exercise 13: Using the System Information Utilities

1. Click on the Start button, select the Programs option, select the Accessories option, select the System Tools option, and select the System Information program.
2. Determine the processor speed.
3. Determine the amount of physical memory and virtual memory available to the system.
4. Determine how big the page file is.
5. Under Hardware Resources, determine the following:
   What is using IRQ 3 and IRQ 4. Determine what is using IRQ 9. Determine which IRQs are free.
   What devices use the 0378H IO address.
   Which IRQs are being shared?
6. Under the Tools menu, start the DirectX Diagnostic program.
7. Under the DirectX Files tab, determine the version of the DDRAW.DLL that the system is using.
8. In the Display tab, run the DirectDraw and Direct3D tests.
9. Back in the System Information program, open the Tools menu and select the Registry Checker program. If it asks if you want to back up your registry, say yes.
10. Open the Tools menu and select the System Configuration utility.
11. Select the Diagnostic Startup-Interactively load device drivers and software and click the OK button.
12. Reboot the computer and perform the interactive login.
13. Start the System Configuration utility again. In the WIN.INI tab, see if anything is loaded in the Run= or Load= parameters.
14. Go to the Startup tab and disable the LoadPowerProfile option(s). Reboot the computer.

CHAPTER 21

Windows NT Family

Topics Covered in This Chapter

Introduction

Today, the best designed and most powerful version of Windows is based on the Windows NT family, which consists of Windows NT, Windows 2000, and Windows XP. It starts by discussing the various methods of installing Windows NT, Windows 2000, and Windows XP and gives an overview of the OS architecture. Since the previous chapter discussed Windows 9X, you find that the Windows NT family is quite different from Windows 9X. This is because the Windows NT family was designed as a desktop operating system and a network operating system.

Objectives

1. Install Windows NT, 2000, and XP from the installation CD or a network drive.
2. List the system requirements for the Windows NT, 2000, and XP operating systems.
3. Given a scenario, recommend which Windows operating system would be needed.
4. Upgrade from a previous version of Windows to Windows 2000 or Windows XP.
5. Apply service packs, patches, and fixes.
6. Implement, manage, and troubleshoot input and output (I/O) devices.
7. Update drivers.
8. Compare the two major layers of Windows 2000, the user mode and the kernel mode.
9. Describe threads and processes and how they relate to each other.
10. Given an application, explain how Windows 2000 runs the program.
11. Describe real memory and virtual memory and how they relate to each other.
12. Explain the boot sequence.
13. Open and modify the BOOT.INI file.
14. Troubleshoot and fix common boot errors.
15. Demonstrate how to use the Windows 2000 Security dialog box and Task Manager.
16. Set priorities and start and stop processes.
17. Troubleshoot common Windows problems including Windows stop errors.

21.1 WHAT IS THE WINDOWS NT FAMILY?

Windows NT 4.0 Workstation, Windows 2000 Professional, and Windows XP are client operating systems for Windows NT 4.0 Server, Windows 2000 Server, and Windows Server 2003.

The biggest differences between Windows XP Professional and Windows 2000 Professional relate to the user interface, desktop management, and minor system architecture changes. They include:

- **Different file locations**—Windows 2000 uses the C:\WINNT directory whereas Windows XP uses C:\WINDOWS.
- **Dependability and security features**—Windows XP includes system restore, device driver rollback, Internet connection firewall, and smart card support.
- **Management and deployment features**—Windows XP has increased application compatibility, dynamic updates, Internet Explorer 6 administration kit, remote assistance, resultant set of policy (RSoP), improved help and support services, Windows update improvements, adaptive user environment, improved handling of file associations, context-sensitive task menus, and integrated compact disc (CD) burning.
- **Mobile and remote user functionality**—Windows XP has Microsoft ClearType, enhanced online conferencing, improved power management, wireless networking, network location awareness, Network Setup Wizard, network bridge, and peer-to-peer networking support.

Different from Windows NT Workstation and Windows 2000 Professional, Windows XP was introduced with two versions: Windows XP Home Edition and Windows XP Professional Edition. The Professional Edition allows you to connect to a large network (Windows domain), use the Encrypting File System (EFS), and it includes the Internet Information Services (IIS) Web server. In addition, it provides more robust options for backing up and restoring data than the Home Edition, supports up to two processors, and supports multiple languages. Lastly, it provides Remote Assistance that lets you invite someone to connect to your computer and help you with problems, and it provides Remote Desktop Connection that allows you to connect to a computer's desktop from a remote location, and run applications as if you were sitting at its console. Both versions include a personal firewall to protect your computer while you access the Internet; Windows XP includes a personal firewall.

Windows NT 4.0 uses the Windows 95 interface; Windows 2000 uses the Windows 98 active desktop interface (merging of the desktop interface) that lets you put active content from web pages on your desktop. The Windows XP provides a cleaner default desktop and more intuitive interface.

Under these popular interfaces, Windows NT family operating systems use a different architecture (32-bit kernel and driver set) that offers higher performance, greater reliability, and provides better security than DOS/Windows 3.XX and Windows 9X. Unfortunately, to achieve these benefits, Windows NT, Windows 2000, and Windows XP are not 100 percent backward compatible with all hardware and software. Note: In this chapter, Windows NT family will refer to Windows NT 4.0, Windows 2000, and Windows XP.

Windows NT supports FAT/VFAT and NTFS, while Windows 2000 and Windows XP support FAT/VFAT, FAT32, NTFS, and CDFS. The **file allocation table (FAT)** is a simple and reliable file system, which uses minimal memory. It supports file names of 11 characters, which include the 8 characters for the file name and 3 characters for the file extension.

VFAT is an enhanced version of the FAT structure, which allows Windows to support long file names (LFN) up to 255 characters. If someone refers to FAT, he or she probably means VFAT. Since it is built on ordinary FAT, each file has to have an 8-character name and 3-character extension to be backward compatible for DOS and Windows 3.XX applications. Therefore, programs running in DOS and Windows 3.XX will not see the longer file names. When running a Win32 program (programs made for Windows 9X and the Windows NT family), Win32 programs can see and make use of the longer names.

FAT32, which uses 32-bit FAT entries, was introduced in the second major release of Windows 95 (OSR2/Windows 95b), and it is an enhancement of the FAT/VFAT file system. It supports hard drives up to 2 TB. It uses space more efficiently, such as 4 KB clusters for drives up to 8 GB, which results in 15 percent more efficient use of disk space relative to large FAT drives.

The root directory is an ordinary cluster chain. Therefore, it can be located anywhere in the drive. In addition, it allows dynamic resizing of FAT32 partitions (without losing data) and allows the FAT mirroring to be disabled, which allows a copy of the FAT other than the first to be active. Consequently, FAT32 drives are less prone to failure of critical data areas such as the FAT.

NTFS is a file system for the Windows NT family operating systems designed for both the server and workstation. It provides a combination of performance, reliability, security, and compatibility. It supports long file names, yet it maintains an 8.3 name for DOS and Windows 3.XX programs. Since the NTFS is a 64-bit architecture, NTFS is designed to support up to 2^{64} bytes=18,446,744,073, 709,551,616 bytes = 16 exabytes.

Since Windows NT family operating systems include enhanced security, they support a variety of multiuser security models and allow computers running other operating systems to save files to the NTFS volume on a server. This includes DOS, Microsoft Windows, UNIX, Linux, and even Macintosh computers. It does not allow DOS to access an NTFS volume directly, only through the network (assuming you have the proper permissions or rights to access the volume).

To make an NTFS volume more resistant to failure, NTFS write updates to a log area (making NTFS a journaled file system) and supports remapped clusters. If a system crash occurs, the log area can be used to quickly clean up problems. If a cluster is found to be bad, it can move the data to another cluster and mark the cluster as bad so that the operating system doesn't use it.

FAT is simpler and smaller than NTFS and uses an unsorted directory structure. NTFS is generally faster because it uses a B-tree directory structure, which minimizes the number of disk accesses required to find a file, making access to the file faster, especially if it is a larger folder.

NTFS 4.0 supports volume set and directory/file compression. A volume set combines several hard drives (or parts of hard drives) to be combined into a single volume. If the volume needs to be expanded again, you just add another hard drive and expand the volume. NTFS allows an individual file or directory to be compressed without compressing the entire drive. NTFS 5.0, which comes with Windows XP, supports everything that NTFS 4.0 supports, but it also supports directory and file encryption.

The CDFS (CD-ROM file system) is the read-only file system used to access resources on a CD-ROM disk. Windows supports CDFS to allow CD-ROM file sharing. Because a CD-ROM is read-only, you cannot assign specific permissions to files through CDFS.

21.2 WINDOWS NT FAMILY INTERFACE

The Windows NT family interface is based on the desktop, which is the graphical space on the screen where all control and display presentations start. On the desktop, you will find the My Computer icon, the Recycle Bin, My Documents shortcut, and the Taskbar (with the Start button). In addition, you may have a My Network Place icon to access network resources (files, applications, and printing) and an Inbox to receive electronic mail and various folders (directory) and shortcuts to programs and documents. See figure 21.1.

The **My Computer** icon represents your computer. It includes all disk drives and the Control Panel. From within the My Computer icon you can access and manage all files on your drives.

Figure 21.1 Windows 2000 Interface

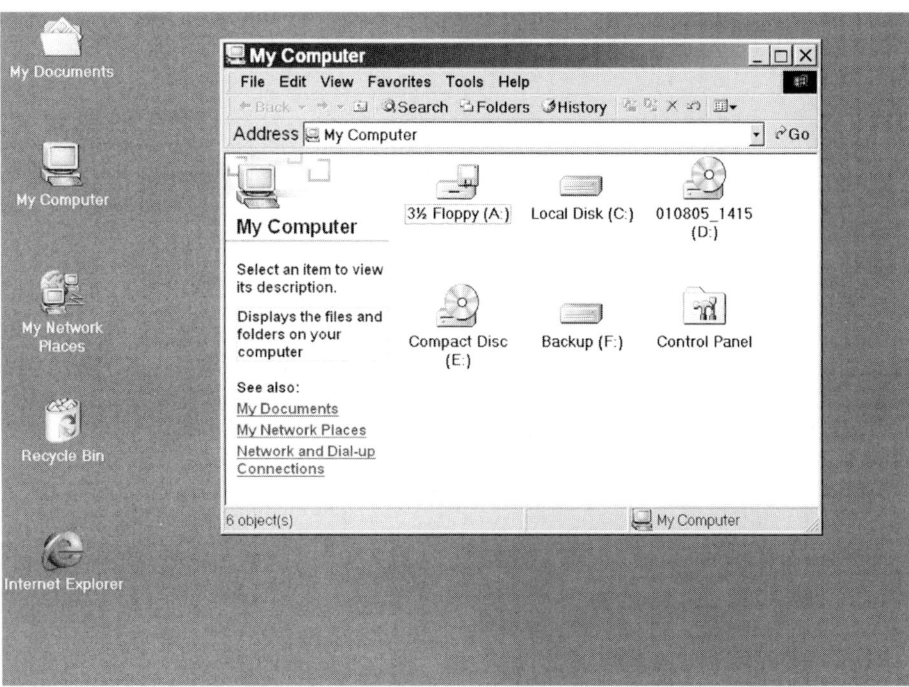

The **Recycle Bin** is used as a safe delete. Therefore, when you delete a file using the GUI interface, Windows will store the file in the Recycle Bin. It will remain there until you empty the Recycle Bin or when you start running out of disk space (at which time Windows will recycle the oldest files first). If you delete a file and decide that you want to undelete the file, open the Recycle Bin and drag it to any location, or choose the Restore option from the File menu.

The **My Documents** shortcut points to a MY DOCUMENTS folder. By default, the MY DOCUMENTS folder is stored in the C:\DOCUMENTS AND SETTINGS*USER_LOGIN_NAME* folder. The user can change the target folder location of his or her MY DOCUMENTS folder by right-clicking the My Documents icon on the desktop, selecting the Properties option, and specifying a new location on the Target tab. See figure 21.2.

The **Taskbar** is located at the bottom of the screen. You can configure the Taskbar to be always visible or to auto hide, so that it appears only when you move the mouse pointer to the bottom of the screen. Auto Hide can be used to give you more free area on the desktop. See figure 21.3.

NOTE: You can move the taskbar to the top, left, or right sides.

The Taskbar is divided into four areas: the Start button, the notification area, the active program buttons, and quick launch programs. The **Start button** is used to start programs. In addition, you can open recently accessed documents and access the Control Panel and PRINTERS folder, find files, and get help for Windows. Note: The Start button is a series of shortcuts to programs.

The systray, located on the right side of the Taskbar, is used for the clock and for any programs running in the background such as printers and modems. The rest of the Taskbar is blank or holds the active program buttons, which can be used to switch between open programs.

When a window is open, the window will usually contain a Minimize button, a Maximize/Restore button, and a Close button in the top right corner and a control menu icon in the top left corner. In addition, most program windows will include a menu, and many will include one or more toolbars.

Most of the Windows XP interface is the same as in Windows 2000. Yet, Windows XP is modified enough to give Windows a bright, fresh new look with a simple-to-use design. Besides an updated

Figure 21.2 Properties of My Documents

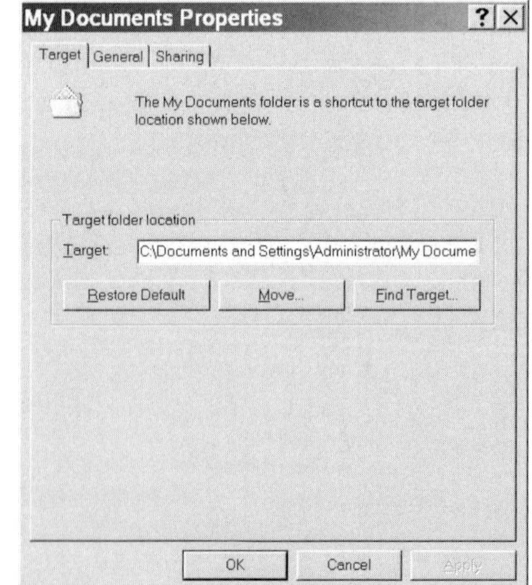

Figure 21.3 The Taskbar

Figure 21.4 Windows XP Interface and Start Menu

graphical look, the new interface is designed for the desktop and Taskbar to be less cluttered. By default, many of the icons such as My Computer and My Documents are accessed through the Start menu instead of the desktop. See figure 21.4.

The new Start menu is smarter and provides you with more customization options. It shows you who is logged on. It automatically adds the most frequently used programs to the top-level menu. It enables you to move any programs you want to the Start menu. Items such as the MY PICTURES and MY DOCUMENTS folders and Control Panel are also available from the Start menu.

When many document and program windows are open, Taskbar grouping creates more available space on the Taskbar. For example, if you have 10 windows open and 3 of them are WordPad documents, the three WordPad document Taskbar buttons will group together into one button named "WordPad." Click this button and then click one of the documents to view it.

To reduce Taskbar clutter, icons in the notification area (next to the clock) are hidden from view when they haven't been used in a while. If an icon becomes hidden, click the arrow (<) to temporarily display the hidden icons. If you click one of these icons, it is displayed again.

NOTE: Windows XP can be reconfigured to be the same as Windows 2000.

Windows NT family uses **shortcut menus** that are accessed by clicking the secondary mouse button (usually the right mouse button). It contains common commands that you can use on the item you clicked. For example, if you click a file with the right mouse button, you can choose to open the file, copy the file, delete the file, or show the properties of the file. If you click the disk drive in My Computer with the right mouse button, you can open the disk, format the disk, or show the properties of the disk. If you highlight some text in a word processor such as Microsoft Word and click on the text with the right mouse button, you can choose the Cut, Copy, or Paste options or change the formatting of the text.

As already stated, the desktop contains the My Computer and Recycle Bin icons. In addition, it can hold folders, files, and shortcuts. To create a folder or a shortcut, you just use the desktop's shortcut menu and select the New option. Note: Content that you see on the desktop is kept in C:\DOCUMENTS and SETTINGS*user_login_name*\DESKTOP folders.

The Taskbar can be configured by using the properties button (Taskbar Options) on the Taskbar's shortcut menu or by using Taskbar option in the Settings option in the Start button. In the Taskbar Options tab, you can specify:

1. If the Taskbar auto hides when it is not being used
2. If the Taskbar will show the time
3. If the Start menu will use small icons or large icons

From the Start Menu Programs tab, you can add, remove, or reorganize the programs listed under the Start button or you can clear the Documents menu. See figure 21.5.

Figure 21.5 Taskbar Properties

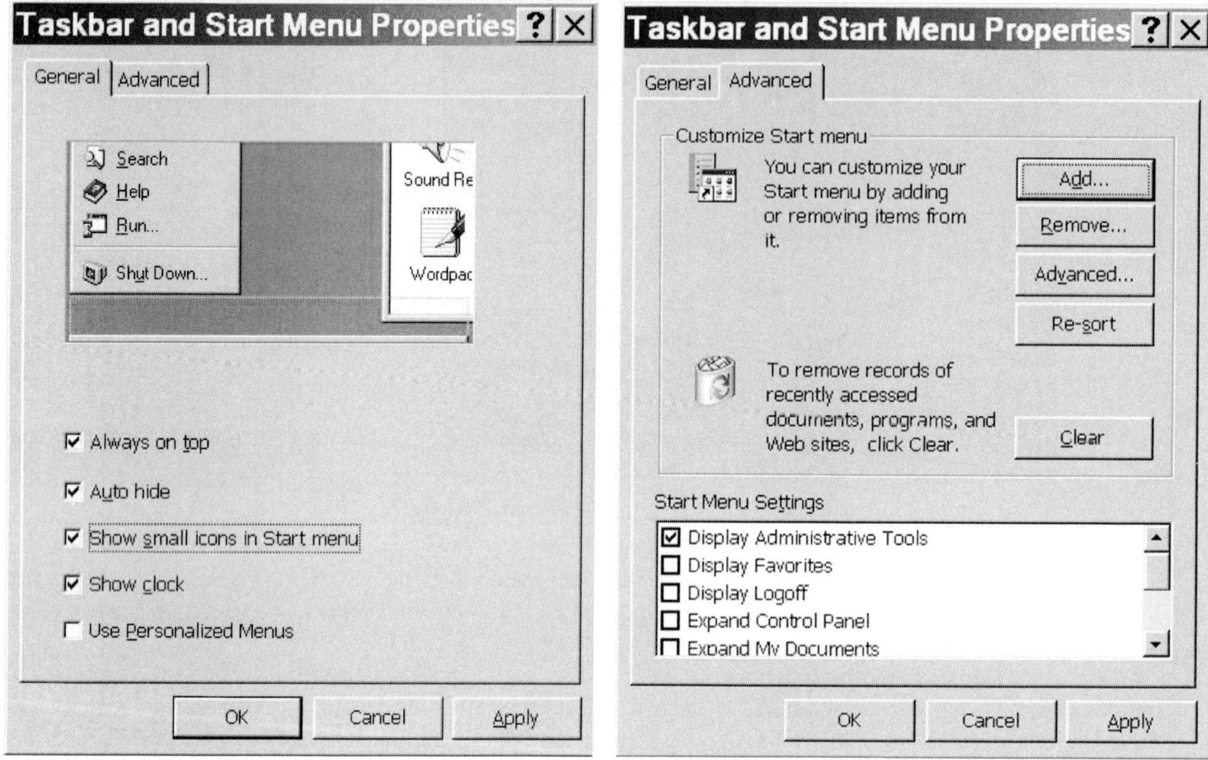

Figure 21.6 Windows Explorer

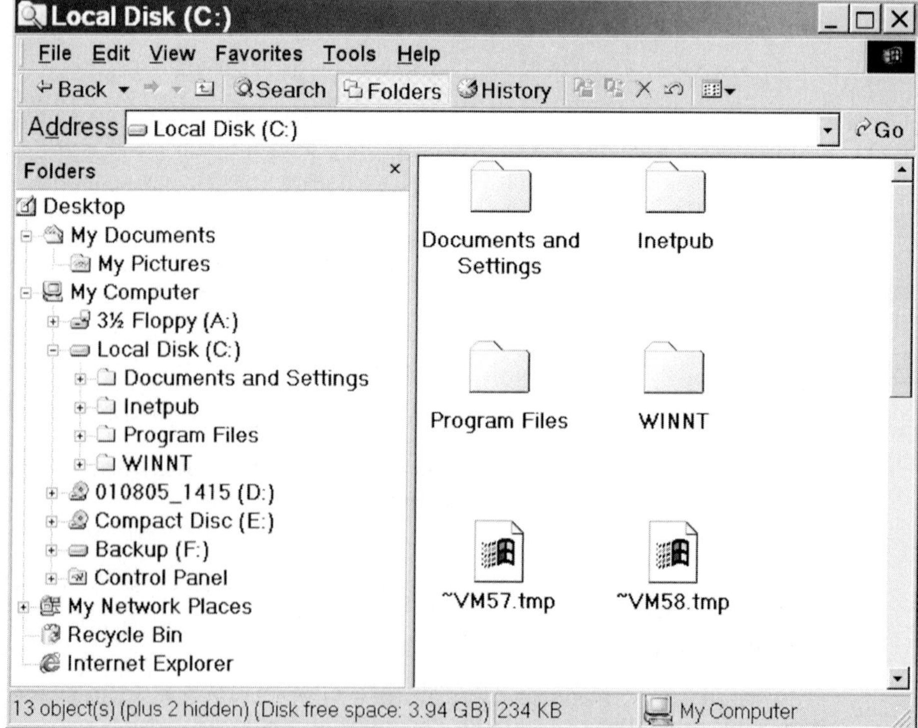

By default, the Taskbar is configured to be on top of all applications and is visible even when you are working in a maximized program. If you select the Keep the Taskbar on Top of Other Windows option in the Taskbar options, you will be able to see the Taskbar at all times except when the window is maximized or placed over the Taskbar. If the Taskbar disappears from the screen, you can make it visible at any time by pressing the Windows logo key or Ctrl + Esc. Because you move the Taskbar to another screen edge by dragging the Taskbar, you should try moving the mouse pointer to each edge of the screen to see if it will appear.

21.3 FILE MANAGEMENT

Since Windows is an operating system, you need to become familiar with how to accomplish common tasks. This includes file and disk management, running programs, and configuring the Windows environment.

Disk and file management is usually done with My Computer or **Windows Explorer.** See figure 21.6. You can start Windows Explorer by clicking on the Start button, selecting the Programs option, selecting the Accessories option, and then selecting Windows Explorer. The most common actions are shown in table 21.1

Table 21.1 Common Disk and File Management Commands

To create a folder (directory) on the desktop, in the root directory, or in another folder	Select New from the File menu or New from the shortcut menu (right mouse button) and select the Folder option.
To delete a file or directory	Select the file or folder by clicking on it and drag it to the Recycle Bin, pick the Delete option from the shortcut or File menu, or press the Del key on the keyboard.
To format a disk	Select the Format option from the drive's shortcut menu or select the Format option from the My Computer File menu.
To copy a floppy disk	Select the Copy Disk option from the drive's shortcut menu or from the My Computer File menu.
To copy a file or directory from one drive to another	Drag the file (click on the file and hold down the left mouse button while moving the mouse) to its new destination. Another way is to first select the file or directory and select the Copy option from the shortcut menu or the Edit menu (Explorer or any disk or folder window). You then go to your destination and select the Paste option from the shortcut or Edit menu.
To move a file or directory to a different folder within the same drive	Press the Ctrl key while dragging the file to its new destination. Note: If you don't press the Ctrl key, it will make a shortcut to the file or directory instead of moving the file. Another way is to first select the file or directory and select the Cut option from the shortcut or Edit menu (Explorer or any disk or folder window). You then go to your destination and select the Paste option from the shortcut or Edit menu.
To rename a file	Select the file and choose the Rename option in the File menu or in the shortcut menu. Another way is to click once on the file name.
To view or change the directory or file attributes (read-only, hidden, or system)	Select the folder or file and select the properties from the File or shortcut menu.

NOTE: Many 32-bit Windows applications also allow you to cut, copy, delete, and rename by using the shortcut menu from within some dialog boxes including the Open, Save, and Save As dialog boxes.

If you want to move, delete, or copy several files or folders at the same time, you can use the Ctrl Shift keys to select multiple files. For example, if you press the Ctrl key and hold it down, you can select any file or folder within the same drive or folder. If you press the Shift key and hold it down, you can select two files or folders and everything listed between the two will be selected. After the file or directories have been selected, you can then copy, delete, or move them as one. Note: Folders are sometimes referred to as directories.

To start a DOS session to perform DOS commands at a prompt, you would click on the Start button, select the Programs option, select the Accessories option, and then select the Command Prompt option.

21.4 INSTALLING WINDOWS NT, WINDOWS 2000, AND WINDOWS XP

You need the items listed in table 21.2 to install and run Windows NT family operating systems.

For acceptable performance and reliability, Windows NT family should have a Pentium III processor or better with a minimum of 128 MB of RAM.

To make sure that you know what hardware is compatible with Windows, Microsoft offers a **hardware compatibility list (HCL)** of devices that have been tested with and approved to work with Windows. The list is available on the Windows compact disk (\SUPPORT\CHL.TXT) and at http://www.microsoft.com/hcl/default.asp. Therefore, you should look at this list before installing Windows or before purchasing a system. Note: In addition to making sure that you have compatible hardware, you should also update to the newest system ROM BIOS for your motherboard.

21.4.1 Installing Windows NT 4.0

To install Windows NT Workstation, go to the installation CD, change to the I386 directory, and use the WINNT.EXE file to start the installation process. If you are upgrading a computer that is already using Windows NT, use WINNT32.EXE.

The WINNT.EXE will perform the following steps:

1. Create a set of setup boot disks for drive A on the computer.
2. It will create a WIN_NT.~LS temporary folder and then copy the Windows NT files.
3. Prompt the user to restart the computer with the first setup disk in drive A.

If you have a formatted partition, you can use the WINNT /B command to perform a floppyless installation. This way, it will not create the setup boot disks and it will copy everything it needs to the hard drive. If you already have setup disks and you want to perform an installation without creating additional setup boot disk, use WINNT /X. If you need to create the boot disks, use WINNT /OX.

21.4.2 Installing Windows 2000 and Windows XP

Windows 2000 and Windows XP can be installed from the installation CD or from a network server. While most Microsoft programs use SETUP.EXE to install their software, Windows uses the WINNT.EXE or WINNT32.EXE file (both of which are located in the I386 directory on the Windows installation CD). It differs from the Windows NT 4.0 in that you don't have to create the boot disk to perform the installation. Therefore, you do not have to use the /B parameter to perform a floppyless installation.

WINNT.EXE should be used for a clean installation on a computer running Microsoft MS-DOS or Microsoft Windows 3X (upgrades of these operating systems are not supported). **WINNT32.EXE** should be used on a clean installation or upgrade on a computer running Microsoft Windows NT version 4.0, or Microsoft Windows 9X. WINNT32.EXE can be executed from within the Windows command prompt or run option. You can upgrade Windows 9X and Windows NT Workstation to Windows 2000 Professional: and Windows 9X, Windows NT (service Pack 6 or greater), and Windows XP to Windows XP.

Switches are customization options added to WINNT.EXE or WINNT32.EXE commands to modify the network installation. To use a switch, type the command, followed by a space, followed by the switch. Some switches require additional information after the command. For example, to force Win-

Table 21.2 System Requirements for Windows NT, Windows 2000, and Windows XP

	Windows NT 4.0 Workstation (Windows NT Kernel 4.0)	Windows 2000 Professional (Windows NT Kernel 5.0)	Windows XP Home Edition (Windows NT Kernel 5.1)	Windows XP Professional (Windows NT Kernel 5.1)
Processor	• Minimum: Intel 486DX/33 or higher • Recommended: Pentium • Supports up to two processors	• Minimum: Pentium 133 MHz or higher • Recommended: Pentium II-350 MHz or higher • Supports up to two processors	• Minimum: 233 MHz or higher • Recommended: 300 MHz or higher • Supports one processor	• Minimum: 233 MHz or higher • Recommended: 300 MHz or higher • Supports up to two processors
RAM	• Minimum: 12 MB RAM • Recommended: 16 MB • Maximum: 4 GB	• Minimum: 64 MB RAM • Recommended: 128 MB or higher • Maximum: 4 GB	• Minimum: 64 MB RAM • Recommended: 128 MB RAM or higher • Maximum: 4 GB	• Minimum: 64 MB RAM • Recommended: 128 MB RAM or higher • Maximum: 4 GB
Disk Space	• Minimum: 110 MB free disk space	• 2 GB hard disk with a minimum of 650 MB free space. (Additional free hard disk space is required if you are installing over a network)	• Minimum: 1.5 GB available hard disk space	• Minimum: 1.5 GB available hard disk space
Display	• VGA or higher	• VGA or higher	• Minimum: VGA resolution • Recommended: SVGA (800 × 600) or higher video adapter and monitor	• Minimum: VGA resolution • Recommended: SVGA (800 × 600) or higher video adapter and monitor
Input Devices	• Keyboard and pointing device (such as mouse, trackball, or glidepad)	• Keyboard and pointing device (such as mouse, trackball, or glidepad)	• Keyboard and pointing device (such as mouse, trackball, or glidepad)	• Keyboard and pointing device (such as mouse, trackball, or glidepad)
Networking	• Network card if you need network connectivity	• Network card if you need network connectivity	• Network card if you need network connectivity	• Network card if you need network connectivity
Other	• CD-ROM (or network card for installation over the network)	• CD-ROM (or network card for installation over the network)	• CD-ROM (or network card for installation over the network) • Sound card and speakers or headphones recommended	• CD-ROM (or network card for installation over the network) • Sound card and speakers or headphones recommended

dows to install on drive D instead of drive C, type the *WINNT /T:D* command at the command prompt. If you execute WINNT /? at the prompt, it will show all of the parameters that can be used with the WINNT command. The /CHECKUPGRADEONLY switch used with the WINNT32.EXE command will check your system for incompatibilities that will prevent a successful upgrade and the /SYSPART: *drive_letter* specifies that you copy the Setup startup files to a hard disk, mark the disk as active, which can then be installed from the disk onto another computer and will automatically start the next phase of the setup.

If you are unfortunate to have a machine that does not support bootable CDs, you will need to use Windows setup floppy disks to do the installation. For Windows 2000 installations, you can create these boot disks by doing the following:

If you boot to DOS using a Windows Startup floppy disk with the appropriate CD-ROM drivers loaded, you can run the MAKEBOOT.EXE boot from the BOOTDISK folder located on the Windows 2000 installation CD. If you are running windows, you can run MAKEBT32.EXE.

NOTE: Disks created from the Windows 2000 Professional CD cannot be used with Windows 2000 Server; the reverse combination also does not work.

To create the setup disks for Windows XP, you will have to download an executable file and execute the executable file. Various versions are located at the following location:

Windows XP Home Edition Utility: Setup Disks for Floppy Boot Install

http://www.microsoft.com/downloads/details.aspx?displaylang=en&FamilyID=E8FE6868-6E4F-471C-B455-BD5AFEE126D8

Windows XP Home Edition with Service Pack 1 Utility: Setup Disks for Floppy Boot Install

http://www.microsoft.com/downloads/details.aspx?displaylang=en&FamilyID=FBE5E4FC-695F-43E5-AF05-719F45C382A4

Windows XP Professional Utility: Setup Disks for Floppy Boot Install

http://www.microsoft.com/downloads/details.aspx?displaylang=en&FamilyID=55820EDB-5039-4955-BCB7-4FED408EA73F

Windows XP Professional with Service Pack 1 Utility: Setup Disks for Floppy Boot Install

http://www.microsoft.com/downloads/details.aspx?displaylang=en&FamilyID=83F53BE9-28FA-40E8-8EC2-631504EF5E26

Windows XP Home Edition startup disks will not work for Windows XP Professional installations, and vice versa. They will also not work for Windows Server 2003 installations.

NOTE: Microsoft also has a Windows 2000 Readiness Analyzer tool (CHKUPGRD.EXE) that can be used to verify the upgradeability of a system to Windows 2000. In addition, to verify hardware for windows XP, insert the Windows XP CD in the drive while running windows, then choose Check System Compatibility and click Check My System Automatically.

Before running the installation program or during the installation process, you should create and size only the partition on which you will install Windows. After you install Windows 2000 or Windows XP, you can then use Disk Management to partition and format the remaining hard drive space. While Windows requires a minimum of 685 MB of disk space, Microsoft recommends that you install Windows on a 1 GB partition or larger, but a 2 GB partition is better so that you have a little growth if you need it. Then when you install other applications and setup data file storage, you should create them on other partitions.

Windows NT family supports FAT, FAT32, and NTFS. If you need file and folder security, disk compression, disk quotas (disk space limits for users), or encryption you should use NTFS. If you need to dual boot between the first version of Windows 95, you should use FAT. If you need to dual boot between the later versions of Windows 95 and Windows 98, you should use FAT or FAT32.

When executing the WINNT.EXE, the WINNT.EXE programs will copy the installation files from the installation CD or the network drive to a temporary directory ($WIN _NT$.~LS) on the destination hard drive. The system will then reboot and continue with the installation from the installation files in the temporary directory.

The Windows installation process is broken into four parts—running the Setup Program, running the Windows Setup Wizard, installing Windows Networking Components, and completing the installation. The WINNT will allow you to select the partition on which to install Windows, select the file system for the new partition, and give you the option to format the new partition.

Windows Setup can use various function keys to activate certain features and commands. The following list details the current function keys, what they do, and when you can use them. You will be prompted to press the following keys:

- **F2**—Automatically start the Automated System Recovery (Windows XP only)
- **F5**—For computer type or hardware abstraction layer
- **F6**—To install third-party SCSI or host controller drivers

You will have to press other keys when the "Welcome to Setup" screen is displayed:

- **F7**—To run Setup without Advanced Configuration and Power Interface
- **F10**—To bypass the menu screen and load the Recovery Console

When the computer reboots, the Setup Wizard (GUI-based program) runs. The Setup Wizard will set the regional settings, licensing mode, computer name, password, and optional Windows components.

During installation, you need to specify the type of network security group to join—a workgroup or a domain. If you want a computer to join an existing workgroup, you assign the name of an existing workgroup. Adding the computer doesn't give it access to any domain. To join a domain during setup, you must have a computer account in the domain you want to join. If you're upgrading from Windows NT, Setup uses your existing computer account. Otherwise, you'll be asked to provide a new computer account. You would then ask your network administrator to create a computer account during Setup and join the domain. To join a domain during Setup, you would need to provide the user name and password. If you do not have a computer account created and you don't have the rights to add a computer to the domain, finish the installation and add the computer to the domain later by starting the Network and Dial-up Connections applet in the Control Panel and selecting the Network Identification hypertext. Then click the properties button. For more information about workstations and domains, see chapter 25.

During the Installing Windows Networking Components operation, you will load the Client for Microsoft Networks, detect and load the network card driver, install protocols, and load the file and printer sharing for Microsoft networks. Of course, the Setup Wizard program will copy the necessary files to the hard disk and configure Windows. During the last phase of installation, it will save the configuration, remove any temporary files, and restart the computer.

21.4.3 Unattended Installations

If you have several computers that will be running Windows 2000 or Windows XP and they all have to be installed, you can use the Windows Setup Manager. The **Windows Setup Manager Wizard** allows you to create an **answer file** and a **uniqueness database file (UDF),** which can be used as scripts when using the WINNT command. The answer file is used as a generic script for many installations, whereas the UDF is used to supply unique information for an installation.

Example 21.1:

You plan to install Windows 2000 Server on 25 new computers on your company's network. The computers have identical hardware and software configuration. To simplify the process, you would use the Windows 2000 Setup Manager to create an UNATTEND.TXT file. You would then create a UDF file that identifies the names of the new computers. Finally, you would begin the installation by running the WINNT command with the /S, /U, and /UDF switches.

To automatically create the answer files, you can use the Setup Manager Wizard. The Setup Manager wizard (SETUPMGR.EXE) is one of the files found in the DEPLOY.CAB file located in the \SUPPORT\TOOLS folder on the Windows 2000 and XP installation CDs. It can be accessed directly from the Windows installation disk, or it can be extracted to your hard drive. To extract the SETUPMGR.EXE file and additional deployment files from the DEPLOY.CAB file, perform the following steps:

1. Create a folder at the root of C.
2. Select all files in the DEPLOY.CAB file, right-click any selected file, and then click Extract. The Setup Manager Wizard extracts all the selected files.
3. In the Browse for Folder dialog box, select the folder you created, and then click OK.

To start the Setup Manager Wizard, double-click SETUPMGR.EXE. When it starts, the wizard presents you with three options:

- Create a new answer file.
- Create an answer file that duplicates the current computer's configuration.
- Modify an existing answer file.

If you create a new answer file, you need to choose the type of answer file to create. The Setup Manager Wizard can create an answer file for:

- A Windows unattended installation
- A SYSPREP install
- Remote Installation Services

If you choose to create an answer file for a Windows 2000 unattended installation, you can select either Windows 2000 Professional or Windows 2000 Server. If you use the Windows XP unattended installation, you can select either Windows XP Home Edition, Windows XP Professional, or Windows 2002/2003 Server. Then the Setup Manager Wizard asks you to specify a level of user interaction. You can set the level of user interaction to one of five levels:

- **Provide Defaults**—The answers that you supply in the answer file are the default answers and Windows Setup prompts the user to review them. The user may change any answers that you supply.
- **Fully Automated**—Windows Setup does not prompt the user for any answers. You supply all required answers in the answer file.
- **Hide Pages**—If you supplied all of the answers on a Windows Setup Manager Wizard page, Setup hides the page from the user.
- **Read Only**—If a Windows Setup Manager Wizard page is not hidden from the user, the user may not change any answers that you supplied in the answer file.
- **GUI Attended**—Only the text mode portion of Windows Setup is automated.

If you are installing Windows from a compact disk, you can create an answer file that is designed to automatically provide answers for the installation. In the Setup Manager Wizard, specify the installation folder, select No, this answer file will be used to install from a CD on the Distribution Folder page, and then save the file to disk as WINNT.SIF.

If your system supports bootable CDs, you can use unattended installations to perform a clean installation. This is quite useful for computers at remote sites with slow links and no local IT department. To use a bootable CD, the following criteria must be met:

- Your computer must have El Torito No Emulation support for bootable CDs.
- The answer file must contain a [Data] section with the required keys:
  - UnattendedInstall=Yes
  - MSDosInitiated=0
  - AutoPartition=1
- The answer file must be called WINNT.SIF and be located on a floppy disk.

To install Windows by using a bootable compact disk:

1. Start the system from the Windows CD.
2. When the blue text mode screen with "Windows 2000 Setup" appears, place the floppy disk containing the WINNT.SIF file into the floppy disk drive.
3. Once the computer reads from the floppy disk drive, remove the floppy disk. Setup searches for the WINNT.SIF file when you start the computer from the CD-ROM drive and performs the installation as specified in the file.

You can use the advanced options to store additional applications, drivers, and utilities in the OEM subfolder so that they can be copied to the temporary folder on each new computer's hard disk. If you don't use the wizard, you must add the OEMPreinstall=Yes parameter in the [Unattended] section of the answer file.

As helpful as the wizard is in simplifying the installation process, the wizard does not contain every option that is available. Instead, you will have to manually create or modify the answer file. All of the options that are available in the answer file are listed in the document titled Microsoft Windows 2000 Guide to Unattended Setup, which is the UNATTEND.DOC file located in the DEPLOY.CAB file mentioned earlier. Some of the more useful options are described in the next few paragraphs.

For a fully unattended installation to complete, the Product ID (or product registration key) must be specified in the UserData section of the answer file. The syntax of this key is ProductID = "XXXXX-XXXXXXXXXX-XXXXX-XXXXX". If this key is missing and your system requires one, you will get a message saying "Unattended setup is unable to continue because a setup parameter specified by your system administrator or computer manufacturer is missing or invalid."

NOTE: This parameter is not required for customers who are using select CDs (special manufacturer. CD's that contain the Product key already). Also be aware that this parameter assigns the same Product ID to all computers; this may cause some difficulty when you try to receive support on multiple computers with the same Product ID.

The OemSkipEula=Yes option in the [Unattended] section will automatically accept the Microsoft license agreement (previously known as the End User License Agreement, or EULA) included with Windows. Of course, setting this parameter to Yes implies that the person performing the installation has read and agreed to the contents of the license agreement included with the product. It also implies that the end user on whose behalf Windows is being installed has agreed to the license agreement.

NOTE: OEMs must not use this key to bypass the Microsoft license agreement because end users are required to see and accept it.

The Repartition=yes option in the [Unattended] section specifies whether or not all partitions on the first drive on the client computer should be deleted and the drive reformatted with the NTFS file system. Note that repartition is valid only when performing an unattended installation by booting the computer from the Windows CD.

The ExtendOemPartition option in the [Unattended] section is used to extend the partition on which you are installing Windows. ExtendOemPartition=1 extends the partition to fill out the hard disk, and ExtendOemPartition=*extra_size_in_MB* has Setup increase the current partition size by the amount specified.

NOTE: Only NTFS partitions can be extended. If the destination partition you plan to extend is FAT or FAT32, set FileSystem = ConvertNTFS to convert the partition during text mode Setup.

Of course, after you create the answer files, you should test the unattended installation, especially if you have set it up for other people to use. Sometimes, there may be an additional parameter that you might need to require, or you will have to correct certain parameters. For example, as you run the Setup Manager Wizard, you can establish your parameters for your display. When the Setup file is created, these settings will be in the [Display] section and will include the following settings:

Number of bits per pixel (BitsPerPel=BB)
Valid refresh rate (Vrefresh=VV)
Valid X resolution (Xresolution=XXX)
Valid Y resolution (Yresolution=YYY)

Of course, if you select parameters that your video system cannot handle, your screen will be unreadable.

21.4.4 Mass Storage Drivers and HALs

If you have a mass storage controller such as a SCSI or RAID controller for your hard disk, in which the driver does not come with Windows, you must tell Windows where it can locate the third-party driver. Shortly after the first reboot, during the early part of Setup, a line at the bottom of the screen will prompt you to press F6 if you need to install a third-party SCSI or RAID driver. When you press the F6 key at this time, it will further prompt you to specify the location of the driver. If you don't, the installation will say that no hard drives are installed on your system. Of course, before using such a controller, you should check to see if the controller is on the hardware compatibility list. If the controller is not supported and you proceed with the installation, an error message will indicate a problem as *inaccessible boot device.*

If you use a newer version of an OEM device driver with the same name or Plug-and-Play identifier as a device driver that is included with Windows, Setup ignores the new OEM driver and uses the one included with Windows. If you require an updated OEM driver to support an existing controller that is natively supported by Windows but is not detected during Setup, you must replace the driver contained in the Windows Setup disks or located in the temporary installation folder (WIN_NT.~BT) with the new OEM driver. This allows Windows to use the updated OEM driver during text mode Setup, but you must copy the same updated OEM driver to the SYSTEM32\DRIVERS folder of the final Windows installation before the installation continues into graphics mode Setup.

The **hardware abstraction layer (HAL)** is a library of hardware manipulating routines that hides the hardware interface details. It contains the hardware-specific code that handles I/O interfaces, interrupt controllers, and multiprocessor operations so that it can act as the translator between specific hardware architectures and rest of the Windows software. As a result, programs written for Windows can work on other architectures, making those programs portable. Therefore, when you load Windows, you need to load the appropriate HAL. See table 21.3.

During Setup, typically the correct HAL is loaded. If it isn't, you can specify which HAL gets installed by pressing the F5 key at the same time that you would press the F6 key that was mentioned in the previous paragraph. Note: If you select the wrong HAL, unexpected results may occur, including an inability to boot the computer.

If you originally installed Windows on a computer with a single processor and you change your system to use multiple processors, the HAL on your computer must be updated so that it will recognize and use the multiple processors. To change the HAL:

1. Click on the Start button, select the Control Panel, and then select System.
2. Click the Hardware tab and click on the Device Manager button. See figure 21.7.
3. Double-click the Computer branch to expand it. You should note the type of support you currently have.

Table 21.3 Various HALs Available in Windows 2000/XP

HAL	Description
ACPI MultiProc	Use for multiprocessor ACPI systems.
ACPI UniProc	Use for ACPI multiprocessor board but with a single processor installed.
Advanced Configuration Power Interface PC	Use for single processor motherboard with single processor ACPI system.
Compaq Systempro	Use for Compaq Systempro computers.
MPS Uniprocessor PC	Use on non-ACPI systems dual processor motherboard with a single processor installed.
MPS Multiproc PC	Non-ACPI systems with a dual processor running.
Standard PC	Any Standard PC, non-ACPI, or non-MPS.

Figure 21.7 Changing the HAL in Device Manager

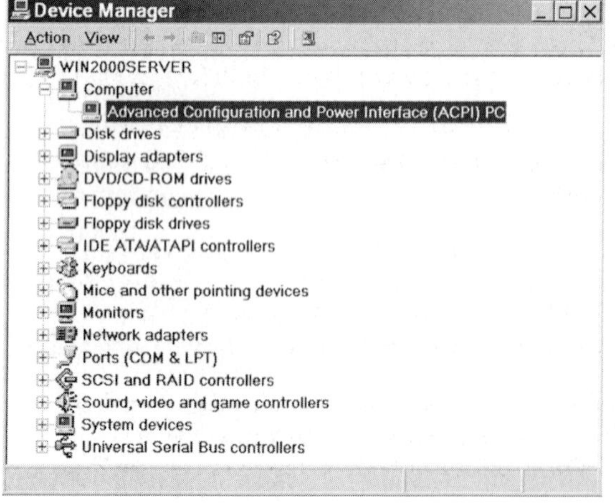

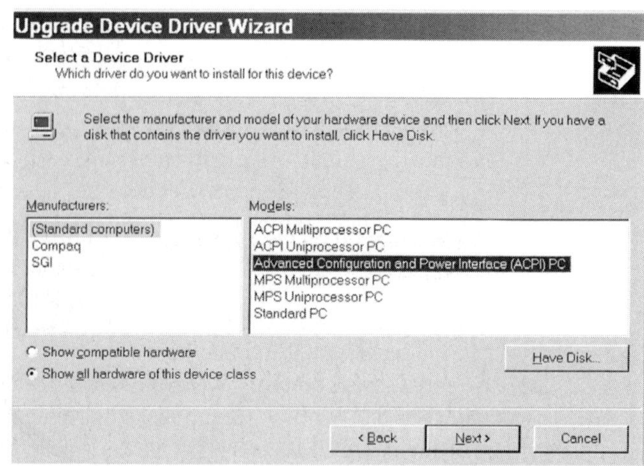

4. Double-click the computer type listed under the Computer branch, click the Drivers tab, click Update Driver, and then click Next.
5. Click Display a list of known drivers for this device, and then click Show all hardware of this device class.
6. Click the appropriate computer type (one that matches your current type, except for multiple processors), click Next, and then click Finish.

NOTE: You can use this procedure only to upgrade from a single-processor HAL to a multiple-processor HAL. If you use this procedure to change from a standard HAL to an ACPI HAL (for example, after a BIOS upgrade) or vice versa, unexpected results may occur, including an inability to boot the computer.

21.4.5 Troubleshooting Installation Problems

Some of the common troubleshooting problems that occur during installation are listed in table 21.4. For more information, refer to Windows Help files and the Microsoft Knowledge Base.

When troubleshooting installation problems, you can check the following:

- Make sure any new hardware or software is properly installed. Unplug each new hardware device, one at a time, to see if this resolves the error. Replace any hardware that proves faulty by this test. Also, try running any hardware diagnostic software supplied by your computer manufacturer. If this is a new installation of hardware or software, contact the manufacturer for any Windows updates or drivers you might need.
- Check the Microsoft hardware compatibility list (HCL) to verify that all the hardware and drivers are compatible with Windows. Disable or remove any newly installed hardware (RAM, adapters, hard disks, modems, etc.), drivers, or software. You can also use the Upgrade Advisor if available.
- If you have access to the Internet, visit the Microsoft Support site at http://support.microsoft.com.
- Using a current version of your antivirus software, check for viruses on your computer. If you find a virus, perform the steps required to eliminate it from your computer.
- Verify that your hardware device drivers and your system BIOS are the latest available versions.
- Disable BIOS memory options such as caching or shadowing.
- Run any system diagnostic software supplied by your computer manufacturer, especially the memory check.
- Verify that your computer has the latest service pack installed (if possible).

Table 21.4 Common Installation Errors

Media Errors	There is an error reading the installation files. If it is a CD, try cleaning the CD and CD drive. If this doesn't work, try a replacement CD. If you are installing over the network, check the integrity of the disk and files.
Nonsupported CD-ROM drive	The CD drive is not compatible. Replace the CD-ROM with one that is supported or try installing over the network.
Insufficient disk space	The destination does not have enough space to install Windows NT. Delete some files from the destination drive, reformat the destination drive, or delete and recreate the partitions so that they are bigger.
Failure of dependency service to start	The network services could not start. In the Windows 2000 Setup Wizard, return to the Network Settings dialog box and verify the protocol and network card settings.
Inability to connect to the domain controller	The computer can't connect to the domain controller. Verify the domain name is correct and check your protocol and network card settings. If you cannot locate a domain controller, install the computer into a workgroup and join the domain after the installation.
Failure of Windows 2000 to install or start	A hardware device on the computer has failed, which prevented Windows from installing or starting. Verify that Windows is detecting all of the hardware and that the hardware is on the HCL.

If you still cannot figure out the problem, you can look at the log files generated during Setup to help you determine the cause of the failed installation. You will find the following files in the directory in which you installed Windows:

- SETUPLOG.TXT
- SETUPAPI.LOG

These files can be copied to a floppy disk, taken to another computer, and then opened with Notepad or any other text editor. The files may contain clues about the installation problems that are occurring. For example, examine SETUPAPI.LOG for the last device that was installed. This may indicate a problem with that particular hardware device or driver. If the Setup log files indicate that a hardware device or driver may be causing the problem, verify that the hardware is supported by that version of Windows.

After the Setup program enters the GUI mode Setup, you will have extensive logging in these files:

- **SETUPERR.LOG**—This file is created if errors occur during Setup.
- **SETUPAPT.LOG**—This file records actions that are taken during Setup.
- **SETUPLOG.TXT**—This file describes tasks performed during Setup.
- **SETUPAPI.LOG and PNPLOG.TXT**—These files list hardware and driver detection and installation issues.

The easiest way to repair an installation is to perform an in-place upgrade (reinstallation) of the operating system. You may need to repair your installation for any of the following reasons:

- You cannot start Windows 2000 or Windows XP in safe mode.
- The problem is caused by a recently installed system update (Windows Update, hotfix, Windows service pack, or Microsoft Internet Explorer update), and you cannot solve the problem in any other way.
- There is a registry problem that cannot be solved by using other tools, such as System Restore.
- You must apply default file and registry permissions to your Windows installation.
- You must register Component Object Model (COM) components and Windows File Protection (WFP) files.
- You need Windows Setup to enumerate Plug-and-Play devices again, including the hardware abstraction layer (HAL).

There are two ways to reinstall Windows 2000 or Windows XP:

- Reinstall Windows from within the operating system. Start the computer and insert the Windows CD into the CD-ROM or DVD-ROM drive. At the "Welcome to Microsoft Windows" screen, click Install Windows. Click Upgrade (Recommended) in the Installation Type box, and follow the remaining setup instructions to reinstall the operating system.
- Reinstall Windows by starting your computer from the startup CD. Insert the Windows CD into the CD-ROM or DVD-ROM drive, and then restart your computer. When the "Press any key to boot from CD" message appears on the screen, press a key to start your computer from the Windows CD. Press Enter on the "Welcome to Setup" screen to set up Windows, and follow the remaining setup instructions.

21.4.6 Installing Additional Drivers, Service Packs, and Hot Fixes

After installing Windows, make sure that all drivers have loaded properly. This means going into the Control Panel, double-clicking the System applet, and starting the Device Manager. If any drivers have yellow exclamation points, there is a problem with the driver. Check to see if you have the drivers on disk or if you need to download any from the Internet, specifically the chipset drivers. You can follow the directions that come with drivers, use the Device Manager, or use the Add Hardware applet in the Control Panel.

After all drivers have been loaded or updated, check to see if Microsoft has released any fixes or patches and apply them to the Windows system. By adding these fixes and patches, you will keep Windows stable and secure. For Microsoft Windows, if there are many fixes or patches, Microsoft will release them together as a **service pack.** You should therefore look for the most recent service pack and install that before continuing. In addition, if you make any major changes including adding services to the computer, you should also reinstall the service pack. To see if there is a service pack or what the newest service pack is, refer to the http://support.microsoft.com/support/downloads website.

In earlier versions of Windows, each time you changed the system state by adding or removing components, you had to reapply any service packs. Windows now automatically recognizes that a service pack has been applied to the system and which files have been replaced or updated. Whenever you add or remove components from a computer running Windows, the system copies the required files from either the Windows installation files or from the service pack install location, so you don't have to reapply the service pack.

Although service packs group many fixes and security patches, Service Pack 2 for Windows XP offers much more. Service Pack 1 (SP1) for Windows XP was about 130 MB (compressed) in size and fixed 324 errors in the operating system; Service Pack 2 (SP2) is approximately 360 MB and will fix many errors. However, SP2 is designed to improve Windows security by offering improvement in the following four areas:

- Improved network protection
- Protection from memory overflow
- Safer email handling
- More secure Internet browsing

Some of the features of SP2 include:

- The Internet Connection Firewall is now enabled by default. Although this should improve security for home office and home users, it may cause problems when used within a corporation.
- The Messenger service is now disabled by default.
- A popup ad blocker has been turned on by default in Internet Explorer.
- A unified security application called the Windows Security Center has been added that brings the most basic security configuration information into one easy-to-manage place that will show whether your firewall is enabled, if your antivirus software is working, and if you have the latest software updates installed.
- NX, short for no execute, support is added to Windows XP that will allow NX-enabled CPUs to mark certain areas of memory as nonexecutable; that is, any code pushed into those areas (perhaps by malware such as Blaster or other viruses) will just sit there, unable to run and therefore will be rendered harmless. This will harden the OS against the notorious buffer overrun threats.
- DCOM (the Distributed Component Object Model) gets a new set of restrictions in the form of an access control list for nearly every action of any COM server.
- The improved port management will not rely on the application to close ports after it is finished. In addition, applications can be run as regular user rather than needing local administrator privileges to open ports in Internet Connection Firewall.
- New RPC (Remote Procedure Call) restrictions help tighten communications between applications and require an RPC caller to perform authentication.

For your convenience, Microsoft produced the http://windowsupdate.microsoft.com website that is a catalog of fixes, updates, and enhancements to Windows and many programs that work with Windows. The easiest way to get there is to use a newer version of Internet Explorer. Open the Tools menu and select Windows Update. When you go to this website, Windows will scan your system to see what you have installed and give you a list of suggested components. This system check ensures that you get the most up-to-date and accurate versions of anything you choose to download from the site. Additionally, you won't waste time downloading components you have already installed. When the list of components appears on the page, you can browse it, decide which components you want, and download them right to your computer. It is important to download any Critical Updates recommended for your system. Critical Updates will fix known problems (such as security issues) specific to your computer. Last, you can download drivers from the Product Updates catalog.

Microsoft has created two different updating features for its website for Windows XP—Dynamic Update and AutoUpdate. **Dynamic Update** is a new feature built into Windows Setup that automatically checks for new drivers, compatibility updates, and security fixes while Windows is being installed. All that is required is that you have a working connection to the Internet. During installation you can choose to have Dynamic Update check for updates; then it automatically downloads any device or application update and uses these replacement files instead of the files on the installation CD, ensuring that you've got the latest updates available. By updating your installation files on the fly, Windows can quickly integrate new, certified device drivers, critical security fixes, and compatibility updates, which ensures that the system you install doesn't immediately need to be patched and that your brand-new video card is recognized and supported just as soon as there are certified drivers available for it.

After you install Windows, you can then use **AutoUpdate** to ensure that critical security and compatibility updates are made available for installation automatically, without significantly impacting your regular Internet use. AutoUpdate works in the background when you are connected to the Internet to identify when new updates are available and download them to your computer. The download is managed so that it doesn't impact your web surfing, and will pick up where it left off if the download is interrupted. When you install Windows, you'll be prompted to set up AutoUpdate, and you can choose your options:

- Automatically download the updates and then be prompted to install them. This is the default, and is recommended for most users.
- Notify you before downloading, and then notify again after they're downloaded before installing. This option makes sense for users who travel and want to control when they perform the download.
- Disable AutoUpdate.

When the download has completed, you'll be notified that it's available and be prompted to install the update. You can install it then, get more details about what is included in the update, or let Windows remind you about it later. Some installations may require you to reboot, but some will not. Click the Details button to see what's in the update, and if a reboot is required. Even if a reboot is required for the update to be activated, you will control when the reboot happens.

Starting with Windows 2000, you can perform **slipstreaming,** which allows you to add service packs directly to the operating system's distribution share. When you install Windows from the modified distribution share, the service pack will already be included in the installation. You can also create new installation CDs that include the service packs by capturing the boot sector from a Windows installation CD through a program such as WinISO and then burning the boot sector and distribution share files (including any additional drivers and HALs that you might have applied) to a CD.

To apply a new service pack, you would download and extract the service pack (usually by using the –X parameter). You would then execute the UPDATE.EXE –S:FOLDER_NAME command to copy over the existing Windows files with the updated service pack files.

Besides doing a manual installation of the service pack or using http://windowsupdate.microsoft.com, there are other ways to automatically install and deploy service packs and other patches and fixes. They include:

- **Microsoft Systems Management Server (SMS)**—SMS provides a variety of tools to help you deploy the service pack in your organization. With the SMS version 2.0 software distribution feature, you can simultaneously upgrade all of the SMS client computers at your site with the new service pack. You can allow your users to run the service pack installation whenever they like, or you can schedule the service pack installation to run at a specific time. You can also schedule it to run on SMS client computers at a time when no users are logged on to the network.
- **Microsoft Windows Installer Service**—Windows Installer Service is a Windows component that standardizes the way you install software programs, such as the service pack, on multiple computers. This system-resident installation service enables you to manage the program installation, modification, repair, and removal. It provides consistent deployment, enabling you to manage shared resources, customize installation processes, make decisions about application usage, and resolve configuration problems.
- **UNATTEND.TXT**—The UNATTEND.TXT answer file identifies how Windows 2000 Setup should interact with the distribution folders and files you create, and supplies information about your preinstallation requirements. You can create or modify the UNATTEND.TXT answer file by using a text editor or through Setup Manager.
- **CMDLINES.TXT**—The CMDLINES.TXT file contains a list of the commands that run during Windows graphical user interface (GUI) mode Setup. These commands can, for example, run an application setup command, SYSDIFF.EXE, or another executable file. You can create the CMDLINES.TXT file by using a text editor or through Setup Manager.
- **Microsoft System Preparation Tool (SYSPREP.EXE)**—A utility that enables you to perform legal imaging, disk duplication, automation of mini-setup, and auditing.

- **SYSDIFF.EXE**—A utility that enables you to distribute and install applications automatically during or after Windows Setup and to distribute files or make application configuration changes during the setup process.

  For more information on deploying service packs, see the following website:

  Microsoft Windows 2000 Service Pack Installation and Deployment Guide

  http://www.microsoft.com/technet/treeview/default.asp?url=/technet/prodtechnol/windows2000serv/support/spdeploy.asp

When trying to keep your computers up-to-date, there are a few more programs or services that you should be aware of. The first one is the **Microsoft Software Update Services** or **SUS,** which is designed to greatly simplify the process of keeping IT systems up-to-date with the latest critical updates (Windows Critical Updates, Windows Critical Security Updates, and Windows Security Roll-ups, but not service packs). SUS enables administrators to quickly and reliably deploy critical updates to Windows 2000 with Service Pack 2, Windows XP, and the Windows Server 2003 family computers. In addition, it works inside your corporate firewall so that the users don't have to use the Internet to download the updates.

SUS functions as follows:

- The SUS server component regularly polls the Windows Update Service site and downloads all new updates.
- SUS notifies the administrator of the new updates.
- The administrator tests the new updates and, once approved, adds them to the distribution set.
- The SUS clients are configured to poll the SUS server for new updates. If an update is available, the SUS clients download it, and the Windows Update icon appears in the notification area.
- If a user is present, he or she can open the Windows Update Notification dialog box and initiate the installation.
- If no user is present or the user fails to manually initiate the installation at the defined installation time, the system will display a 5-minute warning. At the end of the 5-minute countdown, the update is installed and the system is rebooted.

For more information about Software Update Services and to download the SUS server and client components, see the following website:

Microsoft Software Update Services (SUS)

http://www.microsoft.com/windows2000/windowsupdate/sus/

Software Update Services Deployment White Paper

http://www.microsoft.com/windows2000/windowsupdate/sus/susdeployment.asp

21.4.7 Windows Licenses and Product Activation for Windows XP

Before purchasing Windows XP, you need to understand that Microsoft has different licensing available for Windows. The types of licenses include:

- **Original Equipment Manufacturer (OEM)**—These products, such as Windows operating systems, come installed when you purchase a new computer.
- **Full Packaged Product (FPP), Retail**—Physical, shrink-wrapped boxes of licensed product that can be purchased in a local retail store or any local software retailer.
- **Volume Licensing for Organizations**—You may enjoy potentially significant savings by acquiring multiple product licenses. Microsoft offers several volume licensing options.

Recently, Microsoft implemented a change in its volume licensing called Software Assurance (SA), which is meant to simplify how volume license customers acquire and administer licenses for Microsoft products, and streamlines how volume license customers obtain the newest releases. Software Assurance replaces the array of upgrade licenses previously offered. Under the SA program, customers acquire the right to install any new release of products covered in the agreement during the term of their coverage.

Microsoft claims that the benefits of the SA program include:

- **Comprehensive technology protection**—You can install any new release for licensed products enrolled in Software Assurance that become available during the covered period on your own schedule.

- **Predictable budgeting**—Software Assurance enables you to spread your license payments over 3 years when purchased through the Select License or Enterprise Agreement programs. In addition, you will avoid the financial spikes associated with varying product release schedules.
- **Better license management**—With Software Assurance, you can standardize software versions throughout your organization and maintain competitiveness through the latest products and technologies.
- **Cost savings**—Software Assurance coverage is priced at 29 percent of the license price per year for eligible application products and at 25 percent for eligible Microsoft server products.

For more information on Microsoft licensing, see the following websites:

Microsoft Licensing
http://www.microsoft.com/licensing/default.asp

Volume Licensing 101
http://www.microsoft.com/licensing/resources/overview.asp

Volume Licensing Overview
http://www.microsoft.com/licensing/programs/

Software Assurance and Volume Licensing 6.0 Programs
http://www.microsoft.com/licensing/programs/sa/

Software Assurance Overview
http://www.microsoft.com/licensing/programs/sa/sadefined.asp

Unless you are using volume licensing, you will need to activate your copy of Windows XP. Product activation is an antipiracy measure that will be included in all future Microsoft software applications. The first time that a user logs on to a computer running Windows, the Activate Windows dialog box appears, and the user is prompted to activate the installed copy of Windows. A user can choose not to activate the software, in which case reminders to activate will periodically appear until the user activates the software.

The easiest way to activate the software is to select the Yes, let's activate Windows over the Internet now option, and then click Next. If the computer is not connected to the Internet, the user can instead select the Telephone option, and then follow the directions for activating Windows over the telephone.

Users must activate Windows within 30 days of installation. If not activated within 30 days, users are prevented from gaining access to Windows until activation occurs.

NOTE: The clock for Windows Product Activation for OEM installations begins its countdown the first time Windows starts.

There is one final factor that you must be aware of. If you change enough hardware on your PC, you may need to reactivate Windows. In that case, users may need to contact a Microsoft customer service representative by telephone to reactivate.

For more information on the Microsoft product activation, you can visit the following websites:

Description of Microsoft Product Activation
http://support.microsoft.com/default.aspx?scid=KB;EN-US;Q302806&

Microsoft Product Activation: Frequently Asked Questions
http://www.microsoft.com/piracy/basics/activation/mpafaq.asp

Microsoft Product Activation: Volume Licensing FAQ
http://www.microsoft.com/piracy/basics/activation/mpavlfaq.asp

How to Activate Windows XP Using an UNATTEND.TXT File
http://support.microsoft.com/default.aspx?scid=KB;EN-US;Q291997&

21.5 WINDOWS NT FAMILY ARCHITECTURE

Windows NT family is a modular operating system that has many small self-contained software components that work together to perform the various operating system tasks. Each component provides a set of functions that acts as an interface to the rest of the system. See figure 21.8.

Figure 21.8 Windows 2000 XP Architecture

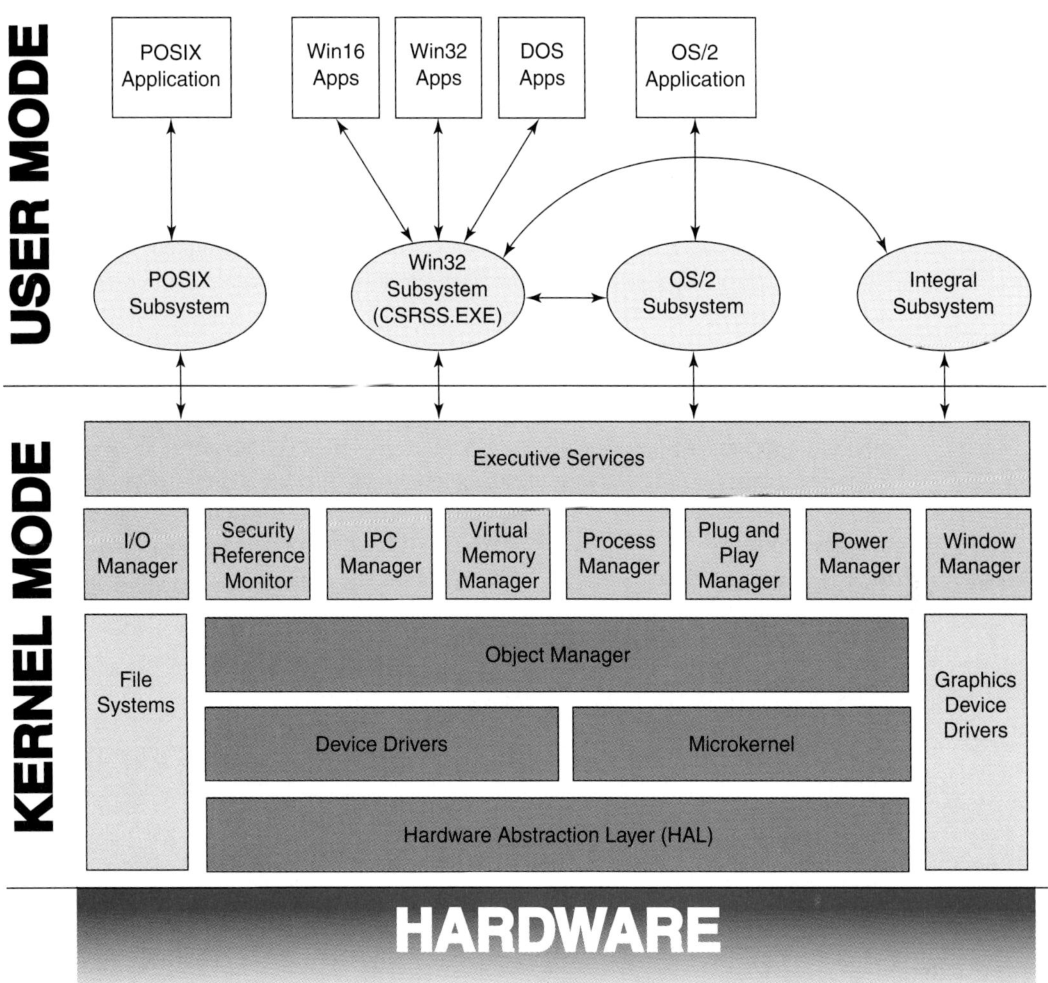

21.5.1 User Mode

The Windows NT family architecture can be divided into two major layers, user mode and kernel mode (also referred to as privileged mode). The **user mode** programs run in ring 3 of the **Intel 386 microprocessor protection model** are protected by the operating system. It is a less privileged processor mode that has no direct access to hardware and can only access its own address space. Since programs running in ring 3 have very little privilege to programs running in ring 0 (kernel mode), the programs in user mode should not be able to cause problems with components in kernel mode. Since most of the user's applications run in ring 3, an application can be terminated without causing problems with the other applications running on the computer. In addition, programs executed in user mode do not have direct access to hardware. If a program tries to access the hardware directly, the program will be terminated so the system can maintain reliability and security.

The user mode layer contains the environment subsystems and the integral subsystems. The **environment subsystem** provides the application programming interfaces (APIs) for the programs and converts them to the proper calls for Windows. APIs are a set of routines, protocols, and tools for building software applications. In the Windows environment, they provide building blocks that a program can use and a common interface. For example, when a Win32-based application such as Microsoft Word 97 asks the operating system to do something, the Win32 subsystem captures that request and converts to commands that Windows understands. The environment subsystems include:

- **32-bit Windows-based system (Client Server Runtime Subsystem—CSRSS.EXE)**—handles windows and graphics functions for all subsystems. It provides a working environment for Win32, Win16, and DOS–based applications.

- **OS/2 subsystem**—provides APIs for 16-bit character mode (DOS mode or bounded) OS/2 applications.
- **POSIX subsystem**—provides API for POSIX-compatible UNIX applications.

NOTE: The Windows 32-bit Windows-based subsystem controls the input/output (I/O) between subsystems so that all applications have a consistent user interface.

The **integral subsystem** performs essential operating system functions such as the security subsystem, the Workstation service, and the Server service. The security subsystem tracks rights and permissions associated with user accounts, tracks which system resources are audited, and performs login authentication. The Workstation services allow access to the network while the Server service provides API to access the network server.

21.5.2 Kernel Mode

The **kernel mode components** run in ring 0 of the Intel 386 processor protection model. While User mode components are protected by the OS, the kernel mode components are protected by the processor. It has direct access to all hardware and all memory including the address space of all user mode processes. It includes the Windows NT family Executive, hardware abstraction layer (HAL), and the Microkernel.

The **Windows NT Family Executive Service** consist of managers and device drivers. They include the I/O Manager, Object Manager, Security Reference Manager, Local Procedure Call Facility, Virtual Memory Manager (VMM), Win32K Window Manager & GDI, Hardware Device drivers, and Graphics Device Drivers. See table 21.5.

Table 21.5 Windows 2000 and XP Executive

Component	Function
I/O Manager	Manages input from and delivers output to the file systems, device drivers and software cache.
Security Reference Monitor	Enforces security policies on the local computer.
Interprocess Communication (IPC) Manager	Manages communications between clients and servers. It includes: Local Procedure Call (LPC)—Manages communication when clients and servers exist on the same computer. Remote Procedure Call (RPC)—Manages communications when clients and servers exist on separate computers.
Virtual Memory Manager (VMM)	Implements and controls memory (physical and virtual).
Process Manager	Creates and terminates processes and threads.
Plug-and-Play Manager	Maintains central control of the plug-and-play process. It communicates with device drivers so that drivers can be directed to add and start devices.
Power Manager	Controls power management APIs, coordinates power events, and generates power management requests.
Window Manager and Graphical Device Interface (GDI)	A device driver (WIN32K.SYS) that manages the display system and contains the Window Manager and GDI. The Window Manager will control window displays and manage screen output, and receives input from devices such as the keyboard and mouse. The GDI contains the functions that are required for drawing and manipulating graphics.
Object Manager	Creates, manages, and deletes objects that represent OS system resources such as processes, threads, and data structures.

A **kernel** is the central module of an operating system. It is the part of the operating system that loads first and it remains in RAM. Because it stays in memory, it is important for the kernel to be as small as possible while still providing all the essential services required by other parts of the operating system and applications. Typically, the kernel is responsible for memory management, process and task management and disk management.

The **Microkernel** is the central part of Windows NT family, which coordinates all I/O functions and synchronizes the activities of the Executive Services. Much like the other kernels in Windows 3.XX and Windows 9X, the Microkernel determines what is to be performed and when it is to be performed, while handling interrupts and exceptions. Lastly, it is designed to keep the microprocessor/microprocessors busy at all times.

21.5.3 Device Drivers and DLLs

Device drivers are programs that control a device. They act like a translator between the device and programs that use the device. Each device has its own set of specialized commands that only its driver knows. Although most programs access devices by using generic commands, the driver accepts the generic commands from the program and translates them into specialized commands for the device. Device drivers are installed into the Executive Services section of Windows. A device driver is a portion of kernel mode code that implements the Windows NT Driver Model specification. Many drivers used by Windows use the **Windows Driver Model (WDM),** which is also compatible for Windows 98 and Windows Millennium.

Microsoft Windows includes a large library of drivers for keyboards, pointing devices, printers, scanners, digital cameras, and other devices in a single compressed file called DRIVER.CAB. This file is located in the *SYSTEMROOT*\DRIVER CACHE\I386 folder. The folder location can be found and changed by using the following registry key:

HKEY_LOCAL_MACHINE\Software\Microsoft\Winodws\CurrentVersion\Setup\DriverCache

All the drivers in this file are certified to be fully compatible with Windows and are digitally signed by Microsoft. Digitally signed files are files that have been tested and approved by Microsoft and include an identifier saying so.

When you install a new Plug-and-Play–compatible device, Windows checks this file first. If Windows finds a suitable driver, the installation proceeds automatically. When a suitable driver is not located in DRIVER.CAB, you must obtain a driver from another source, such as the hardware device manufacturer.

A common method of updating a device driver is for the device manufacturer to provide a CD-ROM or downloadable executable file that installs the device driver automatically. To install these device drivers, close all open programs and run either the CD-ROM or the executable file that installs the device driver. In addition, some manufacturers post updated drivers on the Windows Update website.

Occasionally, manufacturers will release drivers that do not include their own setup program. This type of setup uses a setup information file (with the extension INF). This is a text file that contains detailed information about the device to be installed, including the names of its driver files, the locations where they are to be installed, any required registry settings, and version information.

In general, this type of driver will be available as a downloadable ZIP file. A ZIP file is a compressed archive file that contains all the files needed to install the device driver. Windows XP include a program that will uncompress a ZIP file, but Windows 2000 Professional does not. You will need to use a third-party program such as WinZip to uncompress a ZIP file on computers running Windows 2000. Once the file is uncompressed, you can install the driver by using the Update Driver Wizard in Device Manager. If it is a new device, you can also use the Add/Remove Hardware applet in the Control Panel.

Dynamic link library (DLL) files are sets of instructions and data that can be accessed at any time and that are used to modularize Windows. That means instead of one huge file containing all of the instructions for Windows, the instructions are broken down into small executable and DLL files. This allows executable files to share code and the division of applications into separate components that can be easily upgraded. Often, these DLL files are placed in the *SYSTEMROOT*\SYSTEM32 folder during an application's installation.

21.5.4 Services

A service is a program, routine, or process that performs a specific system function to support other programs. Different from a device driver, a service is a user mode process that implements the Service Controller specification. Different from application, services can still function when logged off. The Service Controller is the component of the system that controls starting, pausing, stopping, and continuing services in the system. It also starts and stops (loads and unloads) device drivers. In other words, the Service Controller provides a common user interface and application programming interface (API) for services and device drivers.

21.6 WINDOWS NT FAMILY BOOT SEQUENCE

During boot-up, the first Windows NT family file read is **NTLDR** (NT Loader), which switches the processor from real mode to protected mode and starts the appropriate minifile system drivers (built into NTLDR) so that it can read the VFAT/FAT16, FAT32, or NTFS file systems.

Next, NTLDR reads the **BOOT.INI** (if one is available) and displays the Boot Loader Operating System Selection menu. See figure 21.9. NTLDR then loads the operating system (such as Windows 2000 Server, Windows 2000 Professional, Windows 9X, or DOS) selected from the menu. If you do not select an entry before the timer reaches zero, NTLDR loads the default operating system specified in the BOOT.INI file. Note: If the BOOT.INI file is not present NTLDR tries to load Windows from the Windows directory (typically C:\WINNT). In addition, the menu will not be displayed if you have only one operating system or if you have an operating system that cannot read the NTFS partition and Windows 2000 XP.

NTLDR runs **NTDETECT.COM,** which attempts to detect the bus/adapter type, serial ports, floating-point coprocessor, floppy disks, keyboard, mouse/pointing device, parallel ports, SCSI adapters, and video adapters. If you have a system that has a SCSI hard disk for which the BIOS on the SCSI adapter is disabled, NTLDR will load NTBOOTDD.SYS to access the SCSI devices during boot-up.

After NTLDR collects the hardware information, it then gives you an option to press the spacebar to invoke the Hardware Profile/Configuration Recovery menu. This menu will list the hardware profiles that you have saved on your drive and list the Last Known Good Configuration option.

The NTLDR finally loads the NTOSKRNL (identified by the "Starting Windows" progress bar) followed by the hardware abstraction layer (HAL.DLL). When the NTOSKRNL is initialized, the NTOSKRNL will take control of the system, switching the system into graphical mode and displaying the animated "Starting Up" progress bar. It will then load the HKEY_LOCAL_MACHINE\SYSTEM registry key from the *systemroot*\SYSTEM32\CONFIG\SYSTEM directory. The SYSTEM hive specifies which device drivers to load during boot-up. When the device drivers are loaded, a hardware list is made and stored in the registry. Lastly, the Session Manager (SMSS.EXE) is loaded, which loads the

Figure 21.9 Windows 2000 Boot Loader Operating System Selection Menu

```
Please select the operating system to start:

Microsoft Windows 2000 Advanced Server
Microsoft Windows 2000 Professional
Windows 98

Use ↑ and ↓ and to move the highlight to your choice.
Press Enter to choose
Seconds until highlighted choice will be started automatically: 30



For troubleshooting and advanced startup options for Windows 2000, press F8.
```

appropriate services needed for Windows NT family to function such as the logon service. During this time, it will display the "Please wait" in the title bar.

The active partition that contains the NTLDR and BOOT.INI file is known as the **system partition.** The partition that contains the Windows NT family operating system files is called the **boot partition.** If a system has only one partition, which contains the initial boot files and the Windows family directory, the partition is both the system partition and the boot partition.

NOTE: The *%sytemroot%* or *systemroot* means the folder that Windows family is installed into, which is located on the boot partition. By default, the Windows family system root directory is C:\WINNT.

DOS or Windows 9X uses a different volume boot sector. In addition, the Windows family starts with NTLDR while DOS and Windows XP start with IO.SYS. If you already have DOS or Windows 9X boot files on a partition when you install Windows NT family, the old boot sector gets copied into a file called **BOOTSECT.DOS.** Therefore, when you select the old operating system from the Boot menu, NTLDR loads BOOTSECT.DOS and passes control to it. The operating system then starts up as normal. Note: If you are dual booting between Windows 2000/XP and DOS or Windows 9X, DOS and Windows 9X cannot read NTFS partitions. See figure 21.10.

21.6.1 BOOT.INI Files

During boot-up, the BOOT.INI file provides a Boot Loader Operating System Selection menu, which allows the selection between multiple operating systems. The BOOT.INI file is a read-only, hidden system text file located in the root directory of the system partition. See figure 21.11.

The BOOT.INI file is divided into two sections, [boot loader] (see table 21.6) and [operating system]. The entries in the [boot loader] section configure the number the seconds that the Boot Loader Operating System Selection menu appears on the screen and the default operating system loaded.

Figure 21.10 The BOOT.INI/Boot Menu Allows Two Pathways During Boot-Up

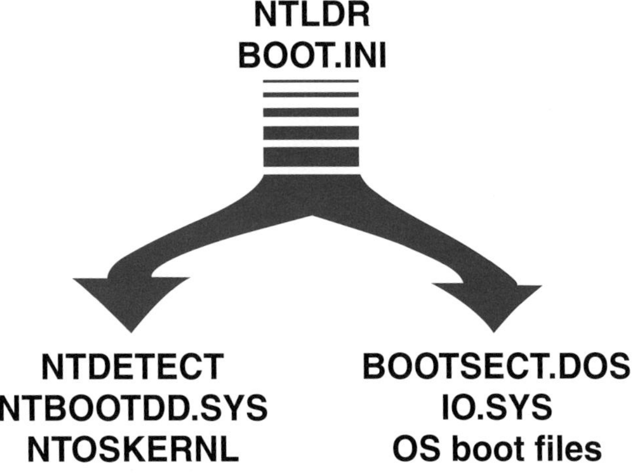

Figure 21.11 Typical BOOT.INI File

```
[boot loader]
timeout=30
default=multi(0)disk(0)rdisk(0)partition(1)\WINNT
[operating systems]
multi(0)disk(0)rdisk(0)parition(1)\WINNT="Microsoft Windows 2000 Advanced Server"/fastdetect
multi(0)disk(0)rdisk(1)partition(1)\WINNT="Microsoft Windows 2000 Professional"/fastdetect
C:\="Windows 98"
```

Table 21.6 The Settings in the [boot loader] Section of the BOOT.INI File

Timeout=*XX*	Specifies the number of seconds the user has to select an operating system from the boot loader screen before NTLDR loads the default operating system. If the value is 0, NTLDR immediately starts the default operating system without displaying the boot loader screen.
Default=	The ARC path to the default operating system

Table 21.7 Optional Parameters Found in the BOOT.INI File

/3GB	Changes the standard of allocating 2 GB for each process and 2 GB for the system to 3 GB for each process and 1 GB for the system.
/BASEVIDEO	Specifies that Windows NT uses the standard VGA video driver.
/fastdetect=[comx| comx,y,z]	Disables serial mouse detection. Without a port specification, this switch disables peripherals detection on all COM ports.
/maxmem:n	Specifies the amount of RAM that Windows 2000 uses. Use this switch if you suspect bad memory.
/noguiboot	Boots the computer without displaying the graphical boot status screen.
/SOS	Displays the device driver names while they are being loaded.

The [operating systems] section contains the list of available operating systems. Each entry includes an ARC path to the boot partition for the operating system, the string to display in the boot loader screen, and optional parameters. The optional parameters are shown in table 21.7.

There are also switches that you can use to make any of the safe modes available in the BOOT.INI file. You may want to do this if you frequently use one of these boot modes or you need to automate a process.

- **Mode**—Safe Mode
  Switch—/safeboot:minimal /sos /bootlog /noguiboot
- **Mode**—Safe Mode with Networking
  Switch—/safeboot:network /sos /bootlog /noguiboot
- **Mode**—Safe Mode with Command Prompt
  Switch—/safeboot:minimal(alternateshell) /sos /bootlog /noguiboot
- **Mode**—Enable Boot Logging
  Switch—/bootlog
- **Mode**—Enable VGA Mode
  Switch—/basevideo
- **Mode**—Directory Services Restore Mode (Domain Controllers Only)
  Switch—/safeboot:dsrepair /sos
- **Mode**—Debugging Mode
  Switch—/debug

An **ARC (Advanced RISC Computing) path** is used to specify the location (partition) of an operating system. It follows the format:

multi(x)disk(y)rdisk(z)partition(a)

or

scsi(x)disk(y)rdisk(x)partition(a)

SCSI is used for a SCSI disk with its BIOS disabled. MULTI is used for disks other than SCSI or a SCSI disk with its BIOS enabled. The number after MULTI is the ordinal number of the hardware adapter card starting from 0. The number after DISK is the SCSI bus number and will always be 0 for a non-SCSI disk or for a SCSI disk with its BIOS enabled. The number after RDISK is the ordinal number of the disk starting from 0. The number after PARTITION is the ordinal number of the partition. Unlike the other values, it starts at 1. Note: If you boot from a computer that does not use the correct ARC path, you could get one of the following error messages:

```
BOOT: Couldn't find NTLDR. Please insert another disk
NT could not start because the following file is missing or
  corrupt: \winntroot\ system32\ntoskrnl.exe
NTDETECT V1.0 Checking Hardware. . .
NTDETECT failed/missing
```

21.6.2 Advanced Boot Options

For the Windows NT family, there are two options during boot-up that can help troubleshoot and fix recently installed device drivers that are causing problems. The first one is used when, after installing a new device driver in Windows, the system does not boot properly. When this happens, you can then invoke the Last Known Good configuration when prompted before logging on to Windows NT, which will restore the previous configuration settings at the last login. The second option is used if the wrong video driver has been selected and you cannot see anything on the screen. When this happens, you can reboot the computer and select Windows [VGA mode], which will select the VGA driver (640 × 480 resolution with 16 colors). The 16 colors will not make for as attractive a screen as one with more colors, but the VGA mode will allow you to select the correct driver.

If you press F8 while the Windows Boot menu is listed, it will display the Advanced boot menu. The Advanced boot menu options are listed in table 21.8 and displayed in figure 21.12.

Table 21.8 Advanced Boot Menu Options

Option	Function	Use
Safe Mode	Starts the computer by using only the basic drivers and files needed (including the mouse, VGA monitor, keyboard, hard drive, and default system services). No network components are loaded.	To isolate if drivers or application startup files are the problem during a normal boot.
Safe Mode with Networking	Starts the computer by using only the basic files and drivers, plus network connections.	To isolate if drivers or application startup files are the problem during a normal boot.
Safe Mode with Command Prompt	Starts the computer by using only basic files and drivers. After logging on, the command prompt is displayed instead of the Windows desktop, Start menu, and Taskbar.	Use to isolate if drivers or application startup files are the problem during a normal boot.
Enable Boot Logging	Logs all of the drivers and services that are loaded at startup to a file named NTBTLOG.TXT that resides in the %WINDIR% directory. All of the safe mode options automatically log information to this file.	To determine the exact cause of system problems by determining which services and files did or did not load.
Enable VGA Mode	Loads the basic VGA driver, instead of any other video driver. All of the safe mode options automatically use VGA mode (resolution of 640 × 480 at 16 colors).	To start the computer when you have installed a new video driver that is causing Windows to not function properly.
Last Known Good Configuration	Starts the computer by using the configuration that was saved the last time the computer started properly.	To start the computer when there is a configuration problem that needs to be corrected. All configuration changes that were made since the last successful startup will be lost.
Debugging Mode	Sends debugging information through a serial cable to another computer.	To gather debugging information about the startup process when you cannot read debugging information on the damaged computer.

NOTE: In Windows 2000 and Windows XP, all options except the Last Known Good Configuration create the NTBTLOG.TXT file and use the VGA driver (resolution of 640 × 480 at 16 colors).

Figure 21.12 Windows Advanced Options Boot Menu

```
Windows 2000 Advanced Options Menu
Please Select an option:

Safe Mode
Safe Mode with Networking
Safe Mode with Command Prompt

Enable Boot Logging
Enable VGA Mode
Last Known Good Configuration
Directory Services Restore Mode (Windows 2000 domain controllers only)
Debugging Mode

Boot Normally
Return to OS Choices Menu

Use ↑ and ↓ and to move the highlight to your choice.
Press Enter to choose
```

After you reboot the computer and log on, the kernel copies the configuration information to the Last Known Good control set in the registry. If you install a driver and the driver causes problems during boot, you can then activate the Last Known Good Configuration. This can be executed by pressing F8 during the Boot menu or by pressing the spacebar when it says to open the OS Loader Recovery menu.

Safe mode lets you start your system with a minimal set of device drivers and services (PS/2 mouse, monitor, keyboard, mass storage, base video, default system services) with no network connection. Typically, you would use safe mode if you installed a device driver or software that prevents the computer from starting. You might be able to start the computer in safe mode in the hopes of removing the software or device drivers from your system. Two useful tools that are available are the System Configuration utility (MSCONFIG) and System Information tool (MSINFO32). See section 21.15 for more information. Networking-enabled safe mode adds network drivers and services to that of standard safe mode. Safe mode with the command prompt is identical to standard safe mode, except that Windows runs the command prompt application (CMD.EXE) instead of the Windows Explorer as the shell when the system switches into GUI mode. To keep track of which device drivers and services are part of the standard and networking enabled safe boots, the system uses HKEY_ LOCAL_MACHINES\SYSTEM\CurrentControl\Set\Control\SafeBoot Registry key. When any of the safe modes are selected, the NT Loader (NTLDR) passes the /SAFEBOOT parameter to the NTOSKRNL.EXE so that the kernel can specify to load only these drivers and services.

So, when should you start in safe mode? You should boot up in safe mode:

- When you have a startup or shutdown issue. Safe mode will eliminate all but the most basic components needed to start the operating system and which can affect the shutdown process as well.
- When the computer experiences errors, poor performance, or any other negative behavior during normal operations. The minimal configuration of safe mode may remove processes that are causing the problem in normal mode.

If the computer starts in safe mode successfully, use MSCONFIG to disable all startup options, and then restart the computer in normal mode. After a successful restart, use MSCONFIG to activate the various startup options in groups, restarting after each modification. If the problem reoccurs, return to safe mode and identify the specific component within the group last activated to determine the cause of the problem.

Microsoft recommends the following steps to troubleshoot Windows boot problems (as well as other system issues):

1. Attempt to boot into safe mode.
   a. If you can boot into safe mode, proceed to step 2.
   b. If you cannot boot into safe mode, proceed to step 7.

2. Attempt to uninstall or remove the component (or roll back the driver) that is suspected of causing the trouble, if applicable (Windows XP only).
3. If the user has been systematically creating System Restore points, attempt to restore the system to a previous configuration (Windows XP only).
4. Use MSCONFIG to troubleshoot startup options.
5. Use the Recovery Console to temporarily disable suspect services that might be interfering with the boot process, if applicable. If the problem persists, more complex measures might be necessary and this can be a good time to escalate the issue.
6. Attempt to invoke the Last Known Good Configuration.
7. Use the Recovery Console to replace corrupted files or to perform other manual recovery operations.
8. Examine and correct the following:
   a. BOOT.INI settings on x86–based systems
   b. BIOS settings
   c. Nonvolatile random access memory (NVRAM) startup settings on Itanium-based systems
9. Install *an additional instance* (a second installation) of the operating system into a different folder, and use the Backup utility to restore operating system files from backup media, if available.
10. Use Automated System Recovery, or ASR (XP Professional only) to reformat the system partition and restore operating system files from backup media.

21.7 WINDOWS NT FAMILY LOGON AND USER SETTINGS

To log on to a computer running Windows NT family, a user provides a user name and password. Windows NT family authenticates the user during the logon process to verify the identity of the user. Windows then controls access to system resources based on the permissions and rights that are associated with each user account. Only valid users can gain access to resources and data on a computer or the network. In addition, depending on the situation, you can specify the domain name or computer name in the Log on to text box. See figure 21.13.

NOTE: Although the user name is not case sensitive, the password is case sensitive. Therefore, when a user cannot log on, first check to see if Caps Lock is on and that the user is typing the same case-sensitive characters for the password.

A **domain** is a group of computers and devices on a network that is administered as a unit with common rules and procedures. A Windows 2000 Server or Windows Server 2003 computer acts as a **domain controller** and maintains a centralized security database for the domain and network resources within the domain. When you log on to a domain, authentication is performed by a domain controller. The user accounts are stored in the Active Directory database.

All Windows 2000 and XP computers have local accounts in a database called a **Security Account Manager (SAM).** When you log on to a computer and you are not logging in to a domain, you are logging on locally to the Windows computer. The SAM is the database that holds the users' credentials for the local machine. The SAM is stored in the Windows registry.

A **workgroup** is a group of computers connected together within network browsing services. For users to log on to any computer in a workgroup, they must create a separate user account on every

Figure 21.13 The Logon Dialog Box

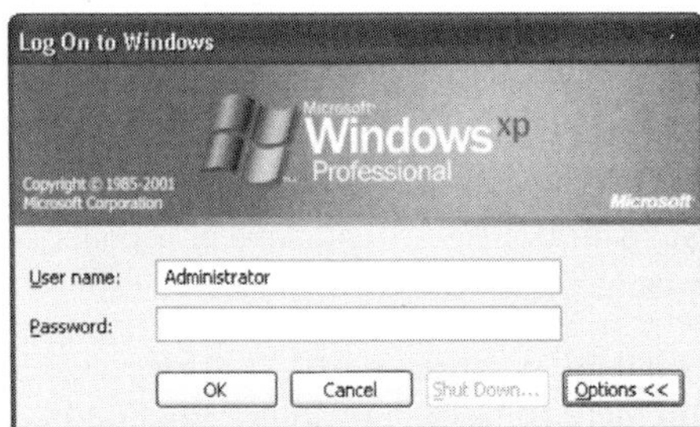

computer in the workgroup. Although you can create a large workgroup, it becomes impractical because you have to create separate accounts on each computer. Instead, you would use a domain that uses the single security database.

Each user account on the system is given a security identifier (SID), which is uniquely identified with a specific account. It is the SID that allows or denies access to resources between user accounts and system resources. Also, if the user account is deleted, the SID is discarded and never used again. If the account is recreated, a new SID is generated.

There are two forms of logging on—logging on locally to a computer (sometimes known as interactively) and logging on remotely to another computer. A user can log on locally to a computer that is a member of a workgroup or a computer that is a member of a domain but is not a domain controller. The user must select the computer name in the Log on to text box.

NOTE: A domain controller does not maintain a local security database. Local user accounts are unavailable on domain controllers, thus a user cannot log on locally to a domain controller.

21.7.1 User Accounts and Groups

The primary user account on a Windows machine is the administrator. Other user accounts are created by the administrator. Windows has the ability to make security settings different for each user. There are several types of user accounts in Windows:

- **Administrator account—**Allows the user to log on as an administrator. Installed on every computer running Microsoft Windows XP and Windows 2000 Professional.
- **System account—**Allows the operating system to access resources.
- **Guest account—**Allows the user to temporarily log on to the computer in an extremely limited capacity.
- **Local account—**Allows the user to log on to the computer rather than the domain. Each computer running Windows 2000 Professional and Windows XP maintains its own set of local accounts. Default local accounts include a local administrator account, a local guest account, and the system account.
- **Domain account—**Allows the user to log on to the domain where account management can be centrally administered. In an Active Directory domain, user accounts are centrally located and stored within the Microsoft Active Directory directory service, and they are considered domain accounts. These accounts should not be confused with each computer's local accounts.

On Windows XP computers, there are two types of local user accounts available: computer administrator and limited. The guest account is available for users with no assigned account on the computer.

The computer administrator account is intended for someone who can make systemwide changes to the computer, install programs, and access all files on the computer. Only a user with a computer administrator account has full access to other user accounts on the computer. This user:

- Can create and delete user accounts on the computer.
- Can create account passwords for other user accounts on the computer.
- Can change other people's account names, pictures, passwords, and account types.
- Cannot change his or her own account type to a limited account type unless there is at least one other user with a computer administrator account type on the computer. This ensures that there is always at least one user with a computer administrator account on the computer.

The limited account is intended for someone who should be prohibited from changing most computer settings and deleting important files. A user with a limited account:

- Cannot install software or hardware, but can access programs that have already been installed on the computer.
- Can change his or her account picture and can also create, change, or delete the password.
- Cannot change his or her account name or account type. A user with a computer administrator account must make these kinds of changes.

Some programs might not work properly for users with limited accounts. If so, change the user's account type to computer administrator, either temporarily or permanently.

Groups are used to connect users together so that you can assign rights and permissions more easily. By having the users listed in a group, when you assign rights and permissions to the group, all users listed in the group also get those rights and permissions.

Some of the built-in groups included in Windows 2000 and Windows XP include:

- **Administrators**—Have the largest amount of default permissions and the ability to change their own permissions.
- **Backup Operators**—Can back up and restore files on the computer, regardless of any permissions that protect those files. They can also log on to and shut down the computer, but they cannot change security settings.
- **Power Users**—Can create user accounts, but can modify and delete only those accounts they create. They can create local groups and remove users from local groups they have created. They can also remove users from the power users, users, and guests groups. They can also install programs that do not modify operating system files or install system services; customize system-wide resources including printers, date, time, power options, and other Control Panel resources; and stop and start system resources that are not started by default. They can also provide backward compatibility for running non-certified windows 2000/XP programs, such as windows NT applications. They cannot modify the administrators or backup operators groups, nor can they take ownership of files, back up or restore directories, load or unload device drivers, or manage the security and auditing logs.
- **Users**—Can perform most common tasks, such as running applications, using local and network printers, and shutting down and locking the workstation. Users can create local groups, but can modify only the local groups that they created. Users cannot share directories or create local printers.
- **Guests**—Granted limited abilities. Members of the guests group can also shut down the system on a workstation.

For Windows 2000 and Windows XP machines, you can use the Computer Management console to create and manage users and groups.

21.7.2 Permissions and Rights

Another problem may occur when a user logs in to a domain but does not have local administrative rights or permissions. These users are unable to perform advanced management tasks on their own computers, such as installing software or updating drivers or accessing files or printers. In addition, as a technician trying to fix problems, you would also need local administrative rights and permissions to troubleshoot and correct many types of problems.

Administrators can also assign rights to user accounts by creating custom user groups for specific tasks or logical organization. Because user groups provide or restrict additional rights to the user accounts contained within them, user accounts will inherit these additional rights and restrictions. When a user logs on, Windows distinguishes between two types of access, permissions and rights:

- **Permissions**—A permission is the ability to access a particular object. The owner of a resource, or an administrator, grants permissions to the resource, thereby defining who is allowed to access that resource.
- **Rights**—A right is the ability to perform an action. Administrators grant users rights, thereby defining what actions users are allowed to perform.

A **permission** defines the type of access that is granted to an object or object attribute. The permissions that are available for an object depend on the type of object. For example, a user has different permissions than a printer. When a user or service tries to access an object, its access will be granted or denied by an object manager. Common object types include files and folders; shares; Active Directory objects (domain) such as users, groups, and printers; registry keys; and services and printers.

A **right** authorizes a user to perform certain actions on a computer, such as logging on to a system interactively or backing up files and directories. Administrators can assign specific rights to individual user accounts or group accounts (a list of user accounts). Rights are managed with the User Rights policy, opening the Computer Configuration, opening Windows Settings, opening Security Settings, opening Local Policies, and then opening User Rights Assignments. The User Rights can also be assigned by site or domain if they are part of the domain.

Rights and permissions can be given to users or groups. You can create local users or groups on Windows NT, Windows 2000, and Windows XP computers.

Because the administrator (or anyone who is the member of the administrators group) has full control of the system, you should use the administrator account to do everyday tasks. For example, if the administrator receives a virus, the virus could potentially infect all files that the administrator has access to. Therefore, you should log on as a normal use and use the RUN AS command that allows a user to run specific tools and programs with different permissions than the user's current logon provides.

To start a program as an administrator:

1. In Windows Explorer, click the program executable file that you want to open.
2. Press and hold down the Shift key, right-click the program icon, and then click Run as.
3. To log on using an administrator account, click the option called the following user.
4. In User name and Password, type the administrator account name and password that you want to use.

You can also execute this program at the command prompt:

```
/runas /user: UserAccountName
```

For more information about the RUN AS command and for a list of its parameters, execute the RUNAS /? command.

NOTE: If the run as command fails, the secondary login service may not be running.

21.7.3 Profiles

A **user profile** is a collection of folders and data that store the user's current desktop environment and application settings including the personal registry settings and files that are specific to the user such as cookies, documents in the MY DOCUMENTS folder, web browser favorites, shortcuts to network places, and mapped drives to shared folders on a network server. When users log on to a system, they will get the same desktop environment that they had previously on the computer. On computers running Windows 2000 or Windows XP, user profiles are automatically created and maintained on the local computer when users log on to a computer for the first time.

The three main types of user profiles are as follows:

- **Local user profile**—Created the first time you log on to a computer and stored on a computer's local hard disk (C:\DOCUMENTS AND SETTINGS*USER_LOGON_NAME* folder). Any changes made to your local user profile are specific to the computer on which you made the changes.
- **Roaming user profile**—Created and stored on a server. Because the profile is on a server, it can be accessed from any computer. Therefore, this profile is available every time you log on to any computer on the network.
- **Mandatory user profile**—Used as a roaming profile to specify particular settings for individuals or an entire group of users. When the user logs off, Windows does not save any changes that the user made during the session. Mandatory user profile can be changed only by the administrator.

Another important user profile is the default user profile. It serves as the basis for all user profiles. Every user profile begins as a copy of the default user profile, which is stored on each computer running Windows 2000 or Windows XP.

NOTE: If a user's profile is damaged, the computer will experience problems after restarting, including not being able to access the Windows desktop.

Profile-related issues usually appear in the logon process. Some of these issues can be resolved by starting the computer in safe mode. For example, if an application that is set to launch at startup in HKEY_CURRENT_USER becomes a problem, standard safe mode troubleshooting procedures can detect and correct this issue.

If starting in safe mode does not resolve the issue, or if you are unable to locate the cause of the issue using standard safe mode troubleshooting procedures, you should consider troubleshooting the user profile. The first step in troubleshooting the user profile is to determine whether the user profile is the issue. This can be accomplished in several ways.

For local profiles:

- Can another user log on to the same computer with a different user account? Does the other user experience the issue? If not, the problem is definitely a user profile issue.

- If no other user accounts can access the computer, try to create a new user account. Then log off the computer, and log on again as the new user account. This forces the creation of a new local profile from the default user profile. Does the issue go away? If so, this is a user profile issue.
- If either of the preceding steps fails to solve the issue, troubleshoot the All Users profile.

For roaming profiles:

- If the user attempts to log on to another computer, does the issue go away? If so, the issue is most likely with the All Users profile on the afflicted computer.
- If the user is unable to log on to another computer, see if another user can log on to the afflicted computer. Does the issue still occur? If so, the issue is most likely with the All Users profile.

If you isolate a profile as the problem, try some or all of the following:

- Examine the amount of space that is available on the volume. If it is extremely low, instruct the user to create some free space.
- If you suspect the problem is within a certain profile subfolder, back up the contents of that folder and then delete its contents.
- Ensure that the user's account has sufficient permissions to access the profile folder.
- Restore the profile to previous settings using System Restore.
- If the preceding efforts fail, the user profile is probably corrupt and you must create a new profile. To create a new profile, you must log on to the computer as a user with administrative rights. Once logged on, delete the old profile and then log on to the computer with the user's account. A new profile will be created.

When you create a new profile for a user, all of the user's local configuration settings are lost. This includes desktop settings, favorites, access to the MY DOCUMENTS folder, and so on. Therefore, you should tell the user that some information may be irretrievable.

Other common profile-related logon issues include:

- **Changed desktop environment**—The probable cause is that the user has logged on with a new user account or has switched from logging on as a local user to logging on as a domain user. Copy the user's old profile into the new profile using the User Profiles copy tool.
- **Missing files**—The user may have created references in the roaming profile to files that are stored on the local drive of a different computer. Instruct the user either to place these files in the roaming profile or copy them to each computer on which he or she plans to access these files.

21.7.4 Windows Security Dialog Box and Task Manager

The Security dialog box provides information such as the user account currently logged on and the domain or computer to which the user is logged on. To access the Windows Security dialog box, you would press the Ctrl + Alt + Del keys. See figure 21.14. As you can see in the figure, it tells you who you are logged on as and when you logged on.

Figure 21.14 The Security Dialog Box

Figure 21.15 The Task Manager Showing Applications and Processes Running in Memory

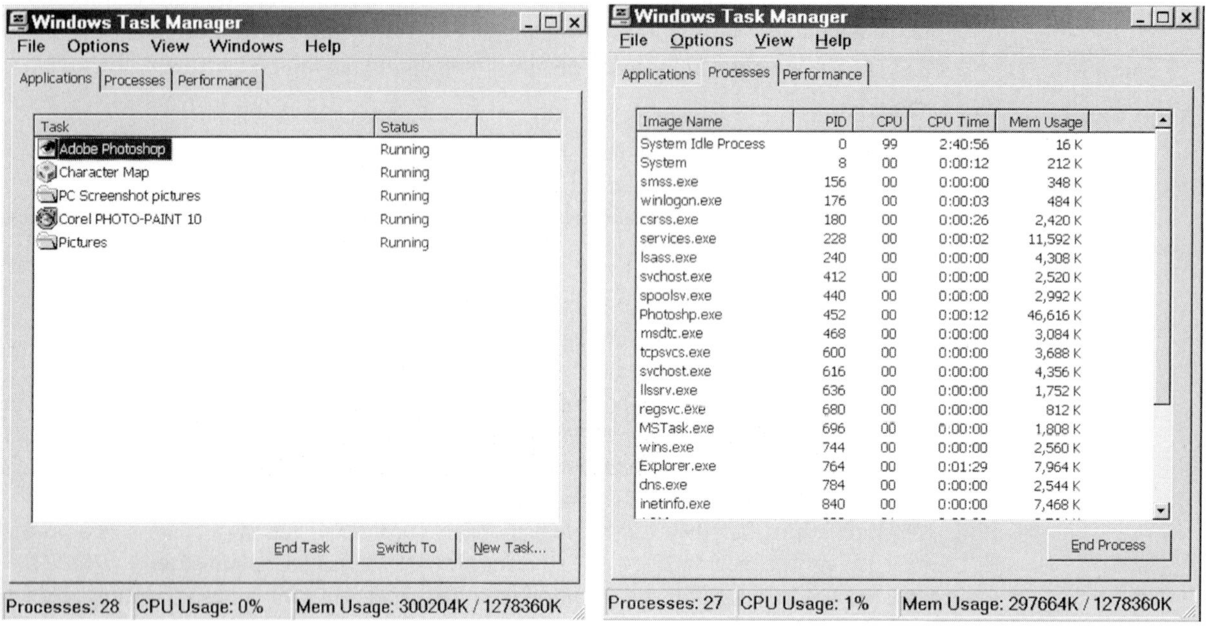

Windows Task Manager
File Options View Windows Help
Applications | Processes | Performance

Task	Status
Adobe Photoshop	Running
Character Map	Running
PC Screenshot pictures	Running
Corel PHOTO-PAINT 10	Running
Pictures	Running

End Task | Switch To | New Task...

Processes: 28 CPU Usage: 0% Mem Usage: 300204K / 1278360K

Windows Task Manager
File Options View Help
Applications | Processes | Performance

Image Name	PID	CPU	CPU Time	Mem Usage
System Idle Process	0	99	2:40:56	16 K
System	8	00	0:00:12	212 K
smss.exe	156	00	0:00:00	348 K
winlogon.exe	176	00	0:00:03	484 K
csrss.exe	180	00	0:00:26	2,420 K
services.exe	228	00	0:00:02	11,592 K
lsass.exe	240	00	0:00:00	4,308 K
svchost.exe	412	00	0:00:00	2,520 K
spoolsv.exe	440	00	0:00:00	2,992 K
Photoshp.exe	452	00	0:00:12	46,616 K
msdtc.exe	468	00	0:00:00	3,084 K
tcpsvcs.exe	600	00	0:00:00	3,688 K
svchost.exe	616	00	0:00:00	4,356 K
llssrv.exe	636	00	0:00:00	1,752 K
regsvc.exe	680	00	0:00:00	812 K
MSTask.exe	696	00	0:00:00	1,808 K
wins.exe	744	00	0:00:00	2,560 K
Explorer.exe	764	00	0:01:29	7,964 K
dns.exe	784	00	0:00:00	2,544 K
inetinfo.exe	840	00	0:00:00	7,468 K

End Process

Processes: 27 CPU Usage: 1% Mem Usage: 297664K / 1278360K

NOTE: The windows security dialog box is not available if you have Windows XP home or using Fast user switching mode.

In the dialog box, there are six buttons. The Log Off button allows you to log off the system without restarting or shutting down the computer. The Shutdown button allows you to shut down or reboot the computer. The Log Off button and the Shutdown button close all running programs. The Lock Workstation button allows you to secure the computer without logging off. All programs remain running. For security reasons, if you are leaving your computer alone, you should either lock your workstation or log off.

The Task Manager button opens the Task Manager dialog box. See figures 21.15 and 21.16. The Task Manager provides a list of the current programs that are running and the overall CPU (including the number of threads and processes) and memory usage (including the amount of physical memory, size of the file cache, paged memory, and nonpaged memory). You can also use the Task Manager to switch between programs and to stop a program that is not responding.

21.7.5 Resetting Passwords

Sometimes users forget the passwords to their local user accounts. To assist them, you can manually reset a user's password. However, the following information is lost:

- Email that is encrypted with the user's public key
- Internet passwords that are saved on the computer
- Files that the user has encrypted

There are two types of password resets: local password resets and domain password resets. To reset a local user account password, the user must log on to the computer with a different account, such as a local administrator account. To reset a local user account password:

1. Click Start, and then click on the Control Panel.
2. In the Control Panel, click Performance and Maintenance, click Administrative Tools, and then double-click Computer Management.
3. In the console tree, double-click Local Users and Groups.
4. In the console tree, click Users.
5. In the Details pane, right-click the user name, and then click Set Password.
6. Read the warning message, and then click Proceed.
7. In the New password and Confirm password boxes, type the new password, and then click OK.

Figure 21.16 The Performance tab of the Task Manager shows the processor utilization and memory utilization.

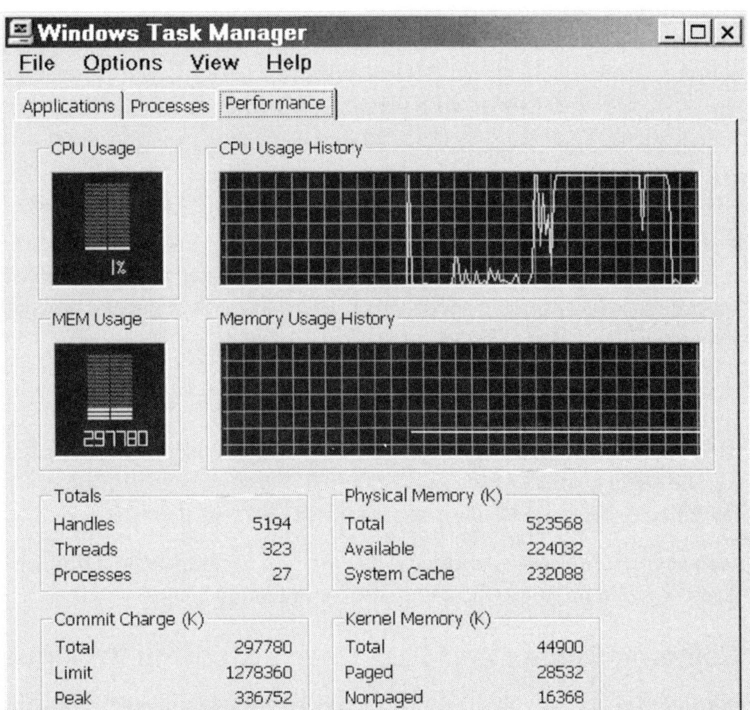

Of course, to reset a local uses account password you must be a member of the administrator group on the local computer or you must have the appropriate permissions.

Users do not normally have access to the Active Directory Users and Computers utility to reset their passwords. To reset a domain user account password, you will need to connect to an Active Directory domain controller. Use the following procedure to reset a domain user account password:

1. In the Control Panel, click Performance and Maintenance.
2. Click Administrative Tools, and then double-click Computer Management.
3. In the console tree, double-click Active Directory Users and Computers.
4. In the console tree, click Users.
5. In the Details pane, right-click the user name, and then click Reset Password.
6. In the New password and Confirm password boxes, type the new password, check the User must change password at next logon check box, and then click OK.

To reset domain passwords from a workstation, the domain administrative tools (ADMINPAK.MSI) must be installed on a Windows XP client.

In Windows XP, the password reset disk, which contains encrypted password information, allows users to change their password without knowing the old password. To create a password reset disk:

1. Press Ctrl + Alt + Del, and then click Change Password.
2. In the User name box, type the user name of the account for which you want to create a password reset disk.
3. In the Log on to box, click ComputerName, where ComputerName is your assigned computer name, and then click Backup.
4. Follow the steps in the Forgotten Password Wizard until the procedure is complete. Store the password reset disk in a secure place. When the wizard prompts a user for his current user account password, he must type the old password.

NOTE: Password reset disks can be used only for local computer accounts, not for domain accounts.

Users can change their password anytime after they create a password reset disk. They do not have to create a new password reset disk if they change their password or if the password is reset manually. When logging on, if a user forgets her password and she has previously created a password reset disk, she will be presented with an option to reset her password by using the password reset disk. Select the option to launch the Password Reset Wizard. The Password Reset Wizard asks users to create a new password and hint. Log on with the new password, and then return the password reset disk to its safe storage place. The user does not need to make a new password reset disk.

21.7.6 Automatic Login with Windows 2000 Professional

If you have a Windows 2000 Professional computer, you can configure Windows to automatically log in during boot-up. Typically, you would do this only if your computer is in a secure location and it is not being used by multiple people. To enable automatic login and prevent the password prompt in a non-domain system:

1. In the Control Panel, double-click Users and Passwords. This option does not appear on a system that is a member of a domain.
2. Click to clear the Users must enter a user name and password to use this computer check box. Click the Advanced tab.
3. Click to clear the Require users to press Ctrl + Alt + Del before logging on check box.

Automatic login is not supported when you are logging on to a domain. You will need to join a workgroup if you want to use the automatic login feature.

21.7.7 Welcome Screen and Fast User Switching in Windows XP

In Windows XP, there are two ways to log on to the computer. The Welcome screen is the fastest and easiest way to log on. You log on simply by clicking your account name and typing your password (if you have one). The classic logon prompt is the most secure way to log on because it requires you to type a user name and password.

To enable or disable the Welcome screen, you would:

1. Open User Accounts in the Control Panel.
2. Click Change the way users log on or off.
3. Enable or disable the Welcome screen option.

A user logs on to the computer by clicking his user account name on the Welcome screen. If a password is assigned to the account, the user is prompted to type it. Of course, you must be a computer administrator account to turn on or turn off the Welcome screen. In addition, logging on at the Welcome screen is not available on computers that are members of a network domain. If you disable the Welcome screen option, the Welcome screen will no longer appear when you start the computer.

When the Welcome screen is disabled, you will get the standard Log On to Windows dialog box, where you would specify the user name and password.

NOTE: You will have to press Ctrl + Alt + Del to open the Log On to Windows dialog box before logging on to Windows. Because the Log On to Windows dialog box is a more secure way to log on, it helps thwart certain Trojan horse programs and keyboard loggers while inputting your user name and password.

If you enabled the Windows XP Welcome screen, you can also enable fast user switching. Fast user switching allows multiple user accounts to be logged on to a computer simultaneously. With fast user switching, users can switch sessions without closing any windows or programs. For example, if a user is using the computer and another user wants to browse the Internet or check her email, she can.

For example, user A is logged on and is browsing the Internet, and user B wants to log on to her user account to check her email. User A can leave his programs running while user B logs on and checks her email. The first user can then return to his session where his programs are still running.

To enable fast user switching:

1. Log on to the computer as administrator.
2. In the Control Panel, click User Accounts.

3. Click Change the way users log on or off.
4. If it is not already selected, select Use the Welcome screen, select Use Fast User Switching, and then click Apply Options. To enable fast user switching, you must also enable the Use the Welcome screen option; otherwise, the fast user switching check box is unavailable.
5. To disable fast user switching, clear the Use Fast User Switching check box, and then click Apply Options.
6. Exit the User Accounts tool.

To initiate the Switch User option so that you can return to the Welcome screen and choose which user to log on to, you can use one of the following options:

- Click Start, click Log Off, and then click Switch User.
- Press Ctrl + Alt + Del to open Task Manager, and then on the Shut Down menu, click Switch User.
- Hold down the Windows key, and then press the L key.

21.7.8 Troubleshooting Logon Problems

When someone is having problems logging in, as already mentioned, check to see if the person is typing the correct user name and password. Remember that the password is case sensitive and that you should check to see if Caps Lock is on. If the user is using the correct user name and password, you should next determine if the problem is a local problem or with the network or server. If it is a problem with the network, you may have to contact the IT department for further assistance.

When a computer (and user) is part of a domain, the computer tries to contact the domain controller to validate the user name and password. When a computer cannot contact a domain controller, the user can usually log on to his or her computer by using cached credentials. Cached credentials are a copy of the security credentials that were last used to access the domain.

When using cached credentials, it is recommended that the computer has Service Pack 1 (SP1) or greater installed. In addition, if he or she tries to connect to a network resource such as a mapped drive, the user will need to recreate a new map to the network resource. Of course, if the domain controller cannot be contacted, it could be because there is a connection problem with the network. In secure network environments, computers are often configured to prohibit logon if a user incorrectly enters the password too many times. This is designed to prevent someone from repeatedly guessing the password. Usually, you must contact the IT department to reset the password.

Finally, when using the Windows Log On dialog box, the network may be able to communicate with more than one domain. Therefore, make sure that the user is logged on to the appropriate domain. The user can click the Options button in the Windows Log On dialog box and select the correct domain name from the Log on to list box.

It should be mentioned here that when you perform routine, nonadministrative tasks, you should not use an administrative account or an account with administrative rights because it may open viruses and Trojan horse programs to parts of your system that would not normally be exposed to them. Therefore, you should use two accounts, one with lesser rights for normal tasks, and administrative passwords for network or PC administrative tasks. In addition, when using the nonadministrative account, you can also use the RUN AS command to run tools as an administrator.

21.7.9 Group Policies

A security policy is a combination of security settings that affect the security on a computer. With security policies, you can control:

- Who accesses the computer
- Which resources users are authorized to use on the computer
- Which rights users have
- Whether a user's or group's actions are recorded in the Event Log (auditing)

A local security policy can be implemented on any computer to grant or deny rights to user accounts and groups that are local to that computer. Users should be aware that careless use of group policies can prevent them from performing certain tasks or may prevent them from logging on to the computer.

A local computer that is not part of a domain is only affected by the Local Security Policy. Group policies can come from multiple sources, the domain, site, or organizational unit. As a result, policies are applied in the following order:

- local computer policy
- site policy
- domain policy
- organizational unit policy

If a conflict occurs when applying policies, the last policy will override all previous policies unless a site, domain, or organizational unit has the no-override option. All group policies override local policies. The security settings are refreshed every 90 minutes on a workstation or server and every 5 minutes on a domain controller. The settings are also refreshed every 16 hours, whether or not there are changes.

To configure the local policy settings:

1. In the Control Panel, click Performance and Maintenance, click Administrative Tools, and then double-click Local Security Policy.
2. To edit Password Policy or Account Lockout Policy, click Account Policies in the console tree. To edit an Audit Policy, User Right Assignment, or Security Options, click Local Policies in the console tree.
3. In the Details pane, double-click the policy that you want to modify.
4. Make the appropriate changes, and then click OK.

Policy settings are cumulative, so all settings contribute to effective policy. The effective policy is called the Resultant Set of Policy (RSoP). In Windows XP, to see which settings are in effect for a particular user, you can use the command-line tool GPRESULT.EXE. To display RSoP, open a command prompt, and then type *GPRESULT.* For information about other options, type *GPRESULT /?* Of course, as a PC technician, you might not be able to affect policies on the user's local computer because of domain policy restrictions.

Another tool available to determine policies in effect for a user is the Group Policy tool accessed in Help and Support. To access the Group Policy tool:

1. Click Start, and then click Help and Support.
2. In the right pane, click Use Tools to view your computer information and diagnose problems.
3. In the left pane, click Advanced System Information.
4. In the right pane, click View Group Policy settings applied.

You can instruct the user to export the Help and Support information to a file. The user can then email the file to you for examination and troubleshooting.

Another tool that is more extensive in managing Group Policy settings is the Group Policy Management Console (GPMC). The GPMC allows administrators to manage Group Policy for multiple domains and sites within one or more forests (multiple trees linked together), all in a simplified user interface with drag-and-drop support. The functionality of this tool includes backup, restore, import, copy, and reporting of Group Policy Objects (GPOs). However, this tool must be downloaded and installed separately. For more information on the GPMC, see http://www.microsoft.com/windowsserver2003/gpmc/default.mspx.

21.7.10 Migrating Users and Settings

To help move your settings from one system to another, you can use the

- Files and Settings Transfer Wizard
- User State Migration tool (USMT)

The Files and Settings Transfer Wizard helps you move data files and personal settings from your old computer to your new one, without having to go through much of the same configuration you did with your old computer. For example, you can take your personal display properties, folder and Taskbar options, and Internet browser and mail settings from your old computer and place them on the new one. The wizard will also move specific files or entire folders, such as MY DOCUMENTS, MY PICTURES, and FAVORITES. To open the Files and Settings Transfer Wizard, click Start, point to All Programs, point to Accessories, point to System Tools, and then click Files and Settings Transfer Wizard.

The User State Migration tool (USMT) includes the same functionality as the Files and Settings Transfer Wizard, but also permits administrators to fully customize specific settings such as unique modifications to the registry. It supports the migration of individual user settings from Windows 95, Windows 98, Windows NT Workstation 4.0, and Windows 2000 Professional to a new installation of Windows XP Professional. The User State Migration tool is designed for administrators only and requires connection to a Microsoft Windows server-based domain controller. Note that the USMT supports only the migration of domain user profiles, not those profiles that are in a workgroup.

The User State Migration tool includes two program files that are named SCANSTATE.EXE and LOADSTATE.EXE, and four migration-rule information files that are named MIGAPP.INF, MIGSYS.INF, MIGUSER.INF, and SYSFILES.INF.

SCANSTATE.EXE collects user data and settings based on the information that is contained in the MIGAPP.INF, MIGSYS.INF, MIGUSER.INF, and SYSFILES.INF files. LOADSTATE.EXE deposits this user-state data on a computer that is running a "clean" (not upgraded) installation of Windows XP Professional. Both of these files are located on the Windows XP CD-ROM in the VALUEADD\MSFT\USMT folder.

You can create additional INF files for varied migration requirements. With no modification to the default settings, the User State Migration tool migrates:

- Microsoft Internet Explorer settings
- Microsoft Outlook Express settings and stores
- Microsoft Outlook settings and stores
- Dial-up connections
- Phone and modem options
- Accessibility options
- Classic desktop settings
- Screen saver selections
- Fonts
- Folder options
- Taskbar settings
- Mouse and keyboard settings
- Sound settings
- Regional options
- Microsoft Office settings
- Network drives and printers
- MY DOCUMENTS folder
- MY PICTURES folder
- COOKIES folder

You can modify the information that is included in the state that SCANSTATE.EXE collects. You can configure the tool to collect or leave specified files, folders, registry entries, or registry subtrees.

21.8 CONTROL PANEL

There are several utilities used to configure the Windows NT family. These main utilities are the Control Panel and the Registry Editor. The Windows NT family Control Panel is a graphical tool to configure the Windows environment and hardware devices. See figure 21.17. It can be accessed from the Settings option in the Start button under My Computer. Additionally, there are various shortcuts to directly access certain Control Panel applets (icons). The most commonly used applets are the System applet, the Display applet, the Add/Remove Programs applet, and the Add New Hardware applet.

Figure 21.17 The Control Panel

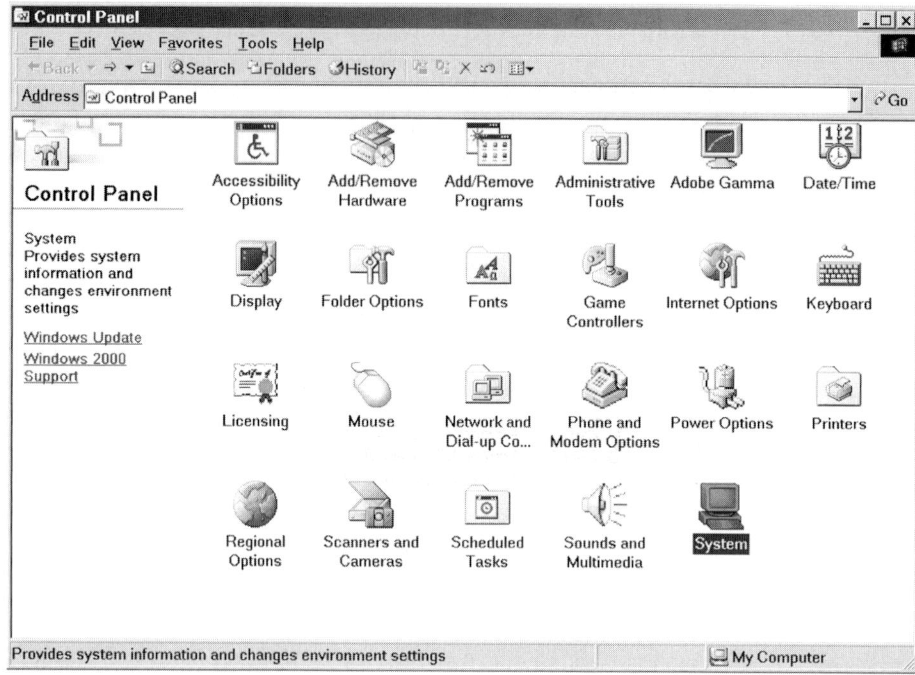

Figure 21.18 By opening the System applet in the Control Panel, it will display the System Properties dialog box. Within the dialog box, you will see five tabs: General, Network Identification, Hardware, User Profiles, and Advanced.

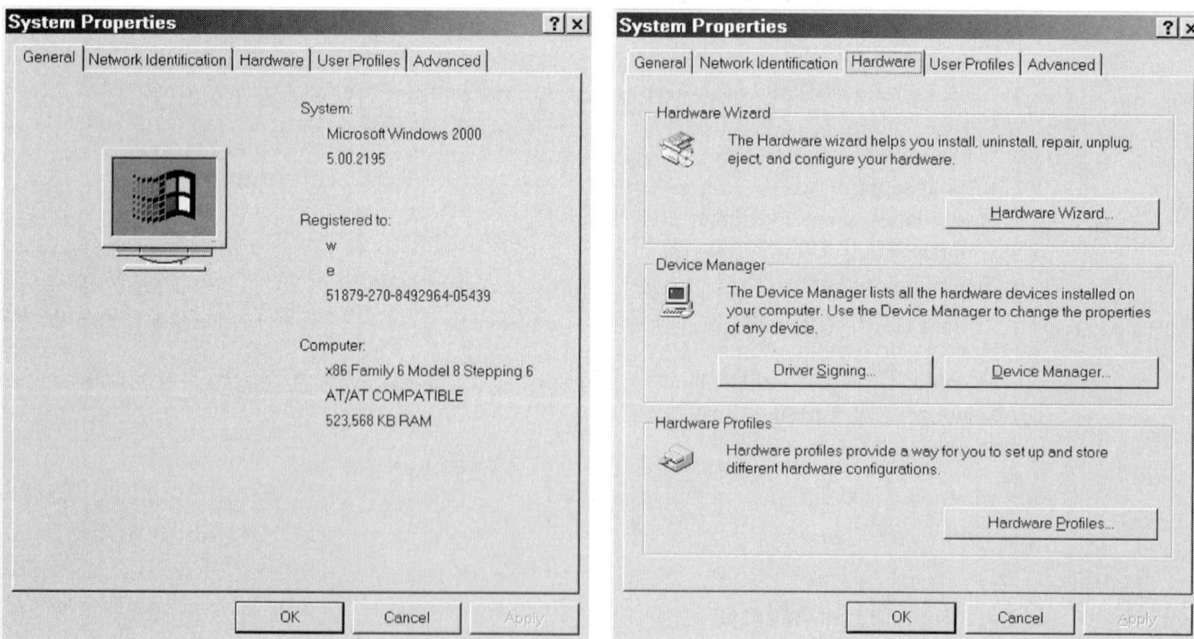

21.8.1 System Applet

The System applet has five tabs, including General, Network Identification, Hardware, User Profiles, and Advanced. The General tab shows the user name and company entered during installation, the type of processor, and the amount of RAM in the system. See figure 21.18. The Network Identification tab shows the full computer name.

The Hardware tab allows access to the Hardware Wizard, the Device Manager, and hardware profiles. The Hardware Wizard helps you install, uninstall, repair, eject, and configure your hardware.

Figure 21.19 Device Manager shows resources used by various devices within the computer.

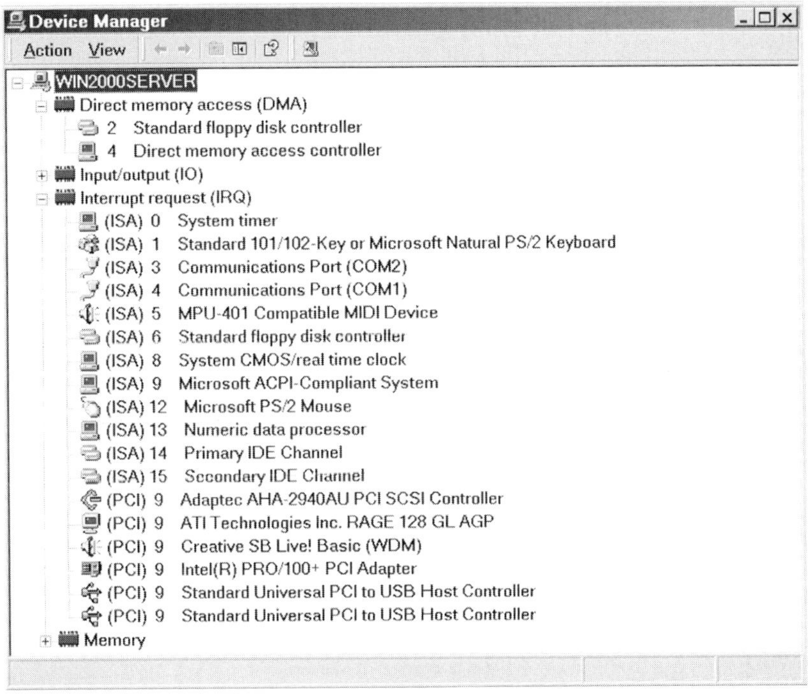

Device Manager
Action View
WIN2000SERVER
Direct memory access (DMA)
2 Standard floppy disk controller
4 Direct memory access controller
Input/output (IO)
Interrupt request (IRQ)
(ISA) 0 System timer
(ISA) 1 Standard 101/102-Key or Microsoft Natural PS/2 Keyboard
(ISA) 3 Communications Port (COM2)
(ISA) 4 Communications Port (COM1)
(ISA) 5 MPU-401 Compatible MIDI Device
(ISA) 6 Standard floppy disk controller
(ISA) 8 System CMOS/real time clock
(ISA) 9 Microsoft ACPI-Compliant System
(ISA) 12 Microsoft PS/2 Mouse
(ISA) 13 Numeric data processor
(ISA) 14 Primary IDE Channel
(ISA) 15 Secondary IDE Channel
(PCI) 9 Adaptec AHA-2940AU PCI SCSI Controller
(PCI) 9 ATI Technologies Inc. RAGE 128 GL AGP
(PCI) 9 Creative SB Live! Basic (WDM)
(PCI) 9 Intel(R) PRO/100+ PCI Adapter
(PCI) 9 Standard Universal PCI to USB Host Controller
(PCI) 9 Standard Universal PCI to USB Host Controller
Memory

Device Manager lists all of the hardware devices on your computer and allows you to change the properties of any device. If you open the View menu and select Resources by type, you will see the IRQ, DMA, I/O address, and memory areas used by the different hardware components. See figure 21.19.

If you open the View menu and select Devices by type or Devices by connection, you see all hardware devices organized in a tree structure. A red *X* appearing through an icon means the hardware device has been disabled. A yellow circled exclamation point through the icon means that the hardware device has a problem. The problem could be a resource conflict (IRQ, DMA, I/O address, or memory address) or the drivers are not loaded properly. See figures 21.20 through 21.24.

To see hardware in a category, click on the plus sign next to the hardware type. To see information about a piece of hardware, double-click on the hardware device icon or select the hardware device and click on the Properties button. The properties will usually contain several tabs indicating if the device is working properly, what drivers are loaded, and gives you an option to update them and to view and change the device resources (if it is a plug-and-play device).

With the **Roll Back Driver** feature, Windows XP has the ability to replace a device driver with a previously installed version. You can use this feature if you have installed a new device driver that causes your computer to be unstable. When you use the Roll Back Driver feature, you can restore the previous device driver version and continue to use the computer. To roll back a device driver, start Device Manager, double-click the device for which you want to restore the driver, click the Driver tab, and then click Roll Back Driver.

Windows NT does not support plug-and-play devices, but it can use them as long as the Windows NT device driver can activate the card and determine the card's resources. Unlike Windows 9X, Windows 2000, and Windows XP, Windows NT does not include a device manager or an Add Hardware applet. To view the use of I/O addresses, IRQs, DMAs, and memory address, you would use the Microsoft Windows NT Diagnostics program (discussed later in the chapter). Therefore, to load the various hardware device drivers, you have to use the other applets in the Control Panel. For example, to load the sound card drivers, you would use the Multimedia applet. Other device applets include the Keyboard, Mouse, Modem, Tape Devices, and SCSI Adapter applets.

Within the Advanced tab of the System Properties dialog box, you will find the Performance Options, the Environment Variables, and the Startup and Recovery buttons. See figure 21.25.

The Performance option allows you to adjust how the processor's resources are distributed among running programs. Selecting Applications in the Performance Options dialog box assigns more resources to the foreground applications, while selecting Background services assigns an equal amount of resources to all programs. You should select Background services if it is a server with network resources or services or Applications if you want the server to act more like a desktop machine. See figure 21.26.

The virtual memory area allows you to configure the paging file size (virtual memory) and the maximum size of the registry.

NOTE: The paging file is the PAGEFILE.SYS file.

Figure 21.20 Device Manager shows all of the devices on the computer.

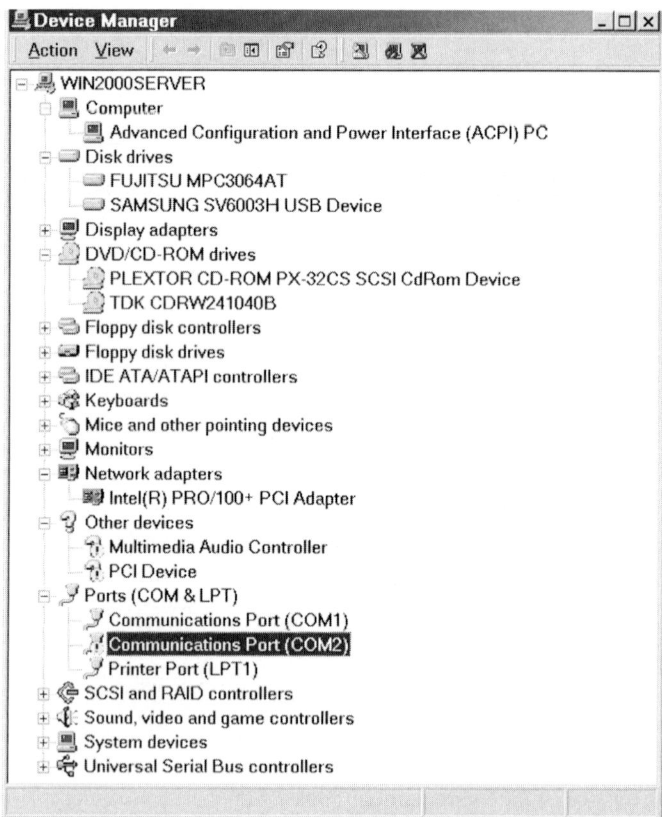

Figure 21.21 ECP Printer Port properties are accessed through Device Manager, including drivers and resources used.

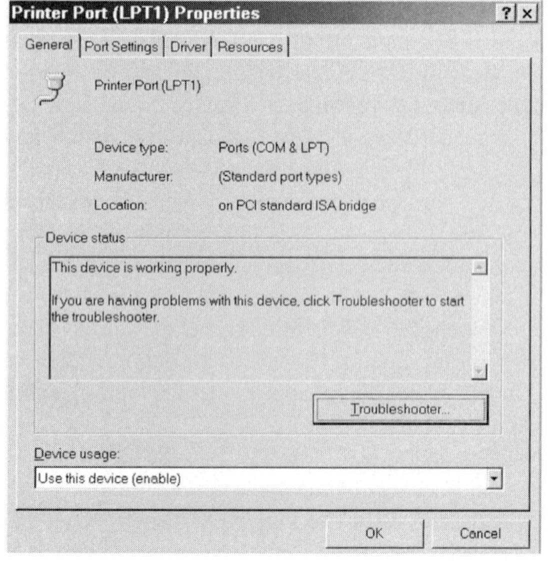

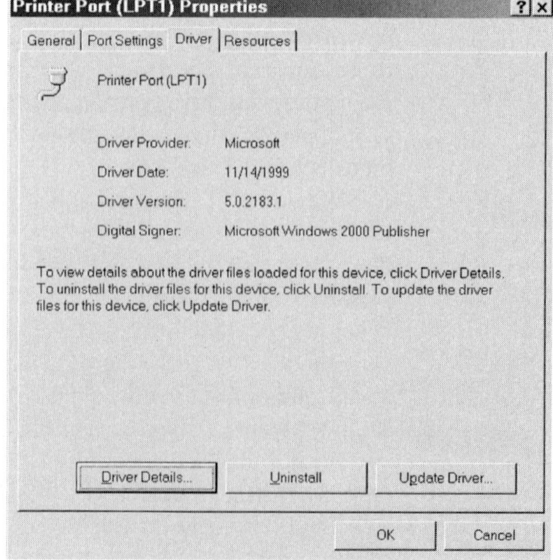

Figure 21.22 By using device manager, you can view the driver being used by a device and its resources.

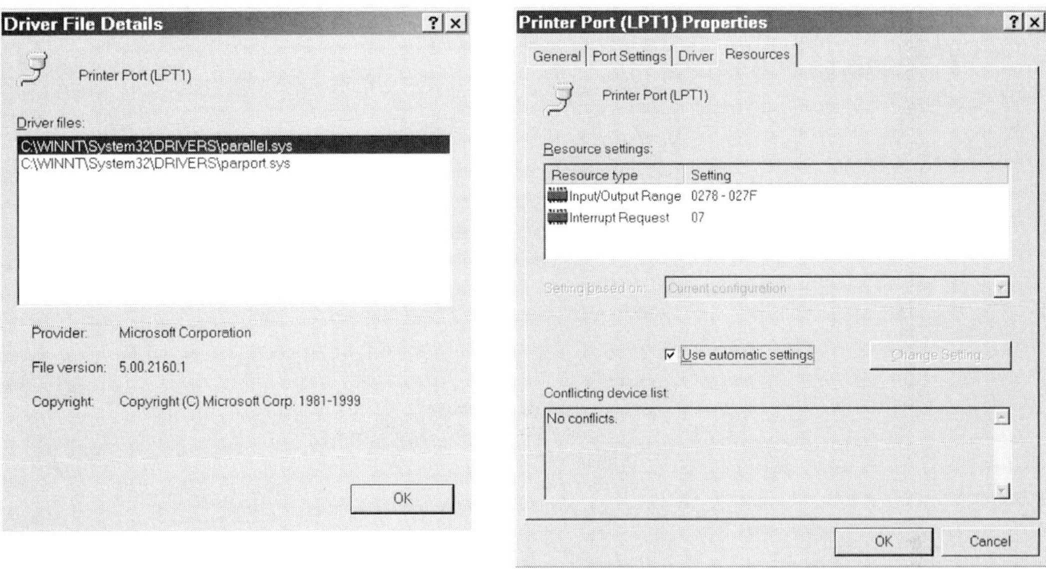

Figure 21.23 If a device is not working properly, you can find more information about the problem by showing the properties of the device in Device Manager.

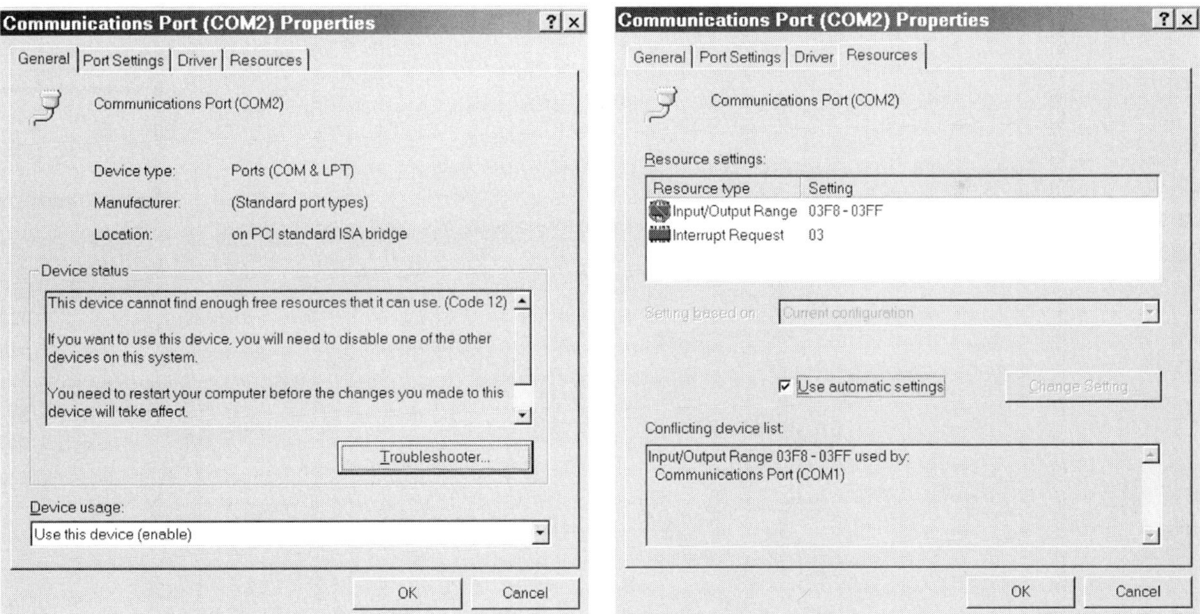

The minimum paging file is 2 MB. The default size of the file is equal to the total amount of RAM plus 12 MB, not to exceed the amount of available disk space. Usually the size of the paging file can stay at the default value assigned during installation, but the recommended size for the paging file should be 1.5 times the amount of RAM available on your system. Note: If you are changing the virtual memory settings, you must make sure to click on the OK button and not the Cancel button. See figure 21.27.

As mentioned in earlier chapters, virtual memory is much slower than physical RAM because the memory is on the hard drive, a mechanical device. If you want to enhance system performance and you have several physical hard drives (not necessary partitions/logical drives), you can create a paging file on each disk and by moving the paging file off the boot partition (the partition with the WINNT

Figure 21.24 You can enable or disable a device by using the properties device in Device Manager.

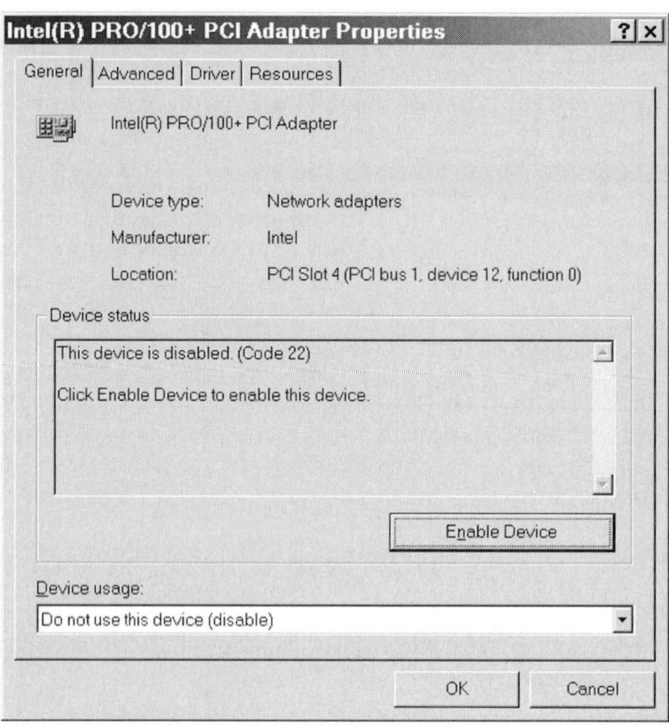

Figure 21.25 Advanced Tab in the System Properties Dialog Box

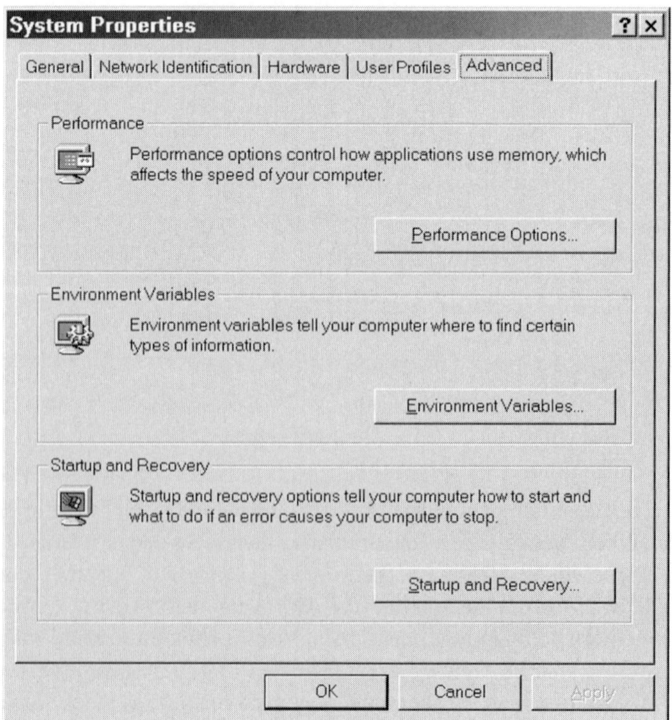

Figure 21.26 Performance Options Dialog Box

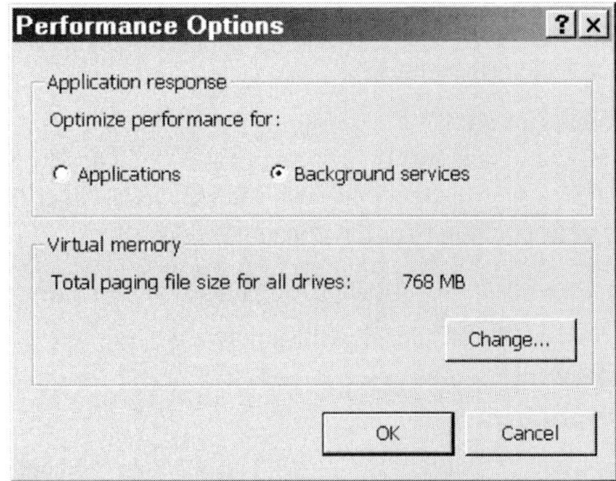

Figure 21.27 Changing the Virtual Memory Settings

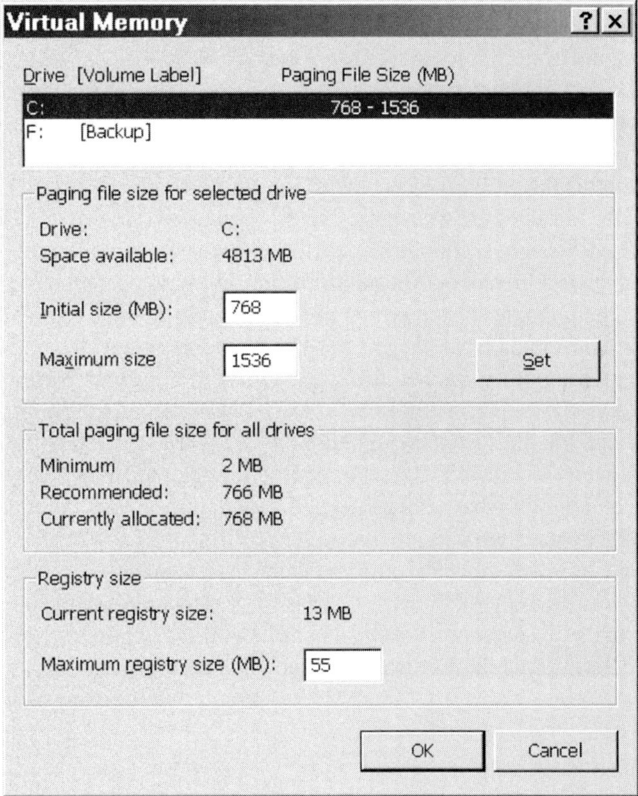

or WINDOWS directory). This is because the hard disk controller can read and write to multiple hard disks simultaneously and the virtual memory management (VMM) tries to write the page data to the paging file on the disk that is the least busy.

You can enhance system performance by setting the initial size of the paging file to the value displayed in the Maximum size box in the Virtual Memory dialog box. This is because when the system needs more RAM, it will increase the size of the paging file. If the file is already set to its maximum size, it eliminates the time required to enlarge the file from the initial size to the maximum size. Note: The maximum size of the file is determined the largest contiguous (continuous) space of disk space. The Disk Defragmenter utility under Accessories, System Tools is important because it ensures that a maximum amount of the drive is contiguous and available for page file use.

Some third-party programs may temporarily store unencrypted passwords and other sensitive information in memory. Because of Windows NT's virtual memory architecture, this information may be present in the paging file. You can increase the security of data by erasing this information during shutdown. Perform the following steps:

1. Start Registry Editor.
2. Change the data value of the HKEY_LOCAL_MACHINE\SYSTEM\CurrentControlSet\Control\Session Manager\Memory Management ClearPageFileAtShutdown value to a value of 1.
3. Restart your computer for the change to take effect.

If the value does not exist, add the following value:

Value Name: ClearPageFileAtShutdown
Value Type: REG_DWORD
Value: 1

The Environment Variables dialog box allows you to change system environment variables and user environment variables such as the TEMP and TMP variables. System environment variables are used for all users and user environment variables are different for each user. The environment variables are set by first using the AUTOEXEC.BAT file, then by using the system environment following by the user environment variables. Note: You can prevent Windows 2000 from searching the AUTOEXEC.BAT file by editing the \HKEY_CURRENT_USER\SOFTWARE\Microsoft\Windows NT\CurrentVersion\Winlogon\Parseutoexec and setting it to 0.

The last option in the System Properties dialog box is the Startup and Recovery Settings dialog box. It controls the startup and recovery settings for a computer. The System startup section allows you to determine the default operating system listed in the BOOT.INI file and the time in seconds that the Boot menu is displayed on the screen before automatically selecting the default operating system. Note: When these values are changed using this dialog box, the BOOT.INI file is changed.

The Recovery section provides options to assist in troubleshooting stop errors. Note: You must be logged on as a member of the administrator group to change these options. See table 21.9.

To help diagnose stop errors, create a memory dump containing debugging information. The debugging information can then be used by support engineers to resolve these errors. To write the debugging information, a paging file must be on the system partition (the partition with the WINNT directory), the paging file must be at least 1 MB larger than the amount of physical RAM in your computer, and you must have enough disk space to write the file in the location you specify.

A **hardware profile** is a set of instructions that tell Windows which devices to start when you start your computer or what settings to use for each device. For example, if you have a notebook computer, you might create two different hardware profiles, one for when the computer is docked in a docking station and one when it is not, or if you work from two locations.

To create or modify a hardware profile, you would use the System Properties dialog box (double-click on the System applet of the Control Panel, or right-click on My Computer and select the Properties applet). Select the Hardware tab and click on the Hardware Profile button.

Table 21.9 Recover Options

Option	Description
Write an Event to the System Log	If enabled, it writes an event to the system log when a system stops unexpectedly.
Send an Administrative Alert	If enabled, it sends an administrative alert to administrators when the system stops unexpectedly.
Write Debugging Information To	If enabled, it will write debugging information to the specified file name. This file can then be used by support engineers to diagnose problems.
Automatically Reboot	If enabled, it allows Windows 2000 to reboot whenever the system stops unexpectedly.

To create a new profile, you would select one of the profiles listed and click on the Copy button to create a copy of the selected profile. The first profile listed is the default. If you want to change the order of the profile, you can select a profile and use the arrows on the sides to move them up or down on the list.

One of the leading causes of instability in Windows NT is buggy device drivers. While you should only use hardware that is on the HCL, there is no guarantee that there are no bugs in the driver. Of course if they are on the HCL, there is a better chance that the device driver will not have any bugs.

To keep your system loaded exclusively with drivers from the compatibility list, Microsoft introduced **driver-signing** technology into Windows 2000 and Windows XP. To configure the device driver signature verification system, you would click on the Driver Signing button in the Hardware tab of the System applet. In the Driver Signing Options dialog box, you can disable this feature by selecting the Ignore option to display a warning if a driver is being loaded that does not have the signature or Block the driver with the signature all together.

21.8.2 Display Applet

The Display applet allows you to configure the Windows environment including menus, windows, icons, the desktop, and the screen saver. See figure 21.28. In addition, it allows you to configure your video system, install or upgrade video drivers, and choose the video resolution and number of colors. See figure 21.29. It can be accessed through the Control Panel or by choosing the Properties option on the shortcut menu of the desktop.

Screen savers were originally developed in order to prevent burn-in to a monitor. Burn-in occurred when a monitor displayed the same screen for such long periods of time that the screen image could still be seen even after that screen had changed. While screen savers are no longer needed to prevent burn-in, they have grown into a form of entertainment.

Assuming that most people who are using Windows 95 and Windows 98 are already familiar with screen savers, I would like to point out the password-protected feature. If you enable password protection, you add a level of security to your system in case you walk away from the system and forget to log off. When the screen saver activates and you press any key or move the mouse, you must specify the login password to be able to continue.

In addition, if you wish to use a screen saver, make sure that you select a simple screen saver and not a 3D screen saver, especially OpenGL screen savers. 3D screen savers have a tendency to take up too much processing.

If you have video problems, there are several tools available for troubleshooting. First, if you choose the wrong driver or you select the wrong resolution or refresh rate so that you can't see anything on the screen, you can reboot the computer, press F8 during the Boot menu, and select the VGA mode.

Figure 21.28 The Appearance and Effects tabs within the Display Properties dialog box allow you to change the appearance of Windows.

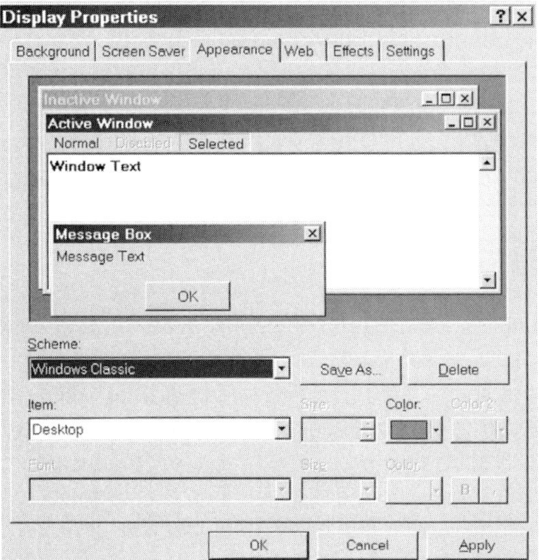

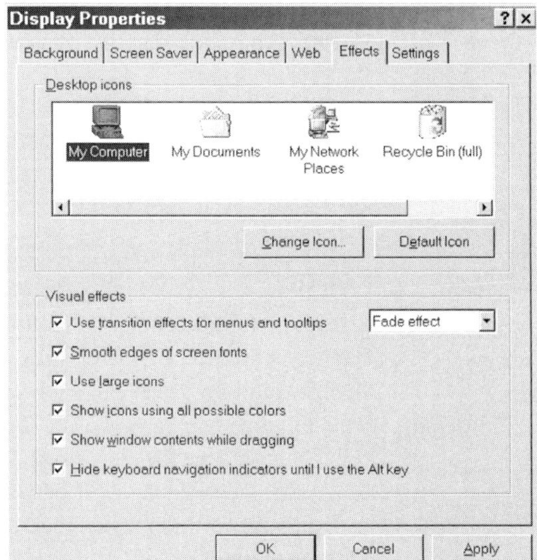

Figure 21.29 The Settings tab of the Display Properties dialog box can be used to adjust the number of colors and the resolution rate of the display system. By clicking on the Advanced button, you can adjust the monitor refresh rate.

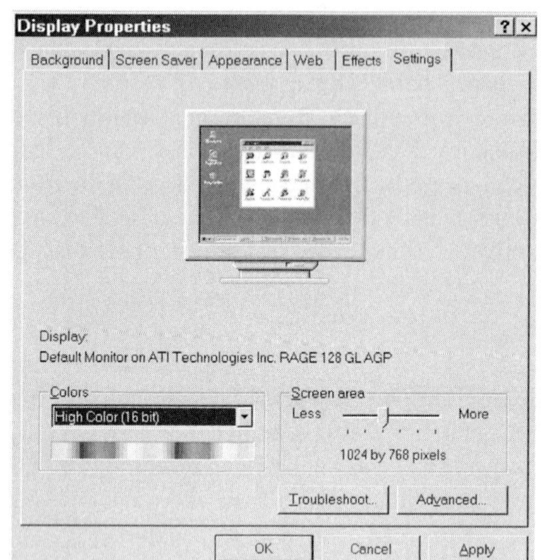

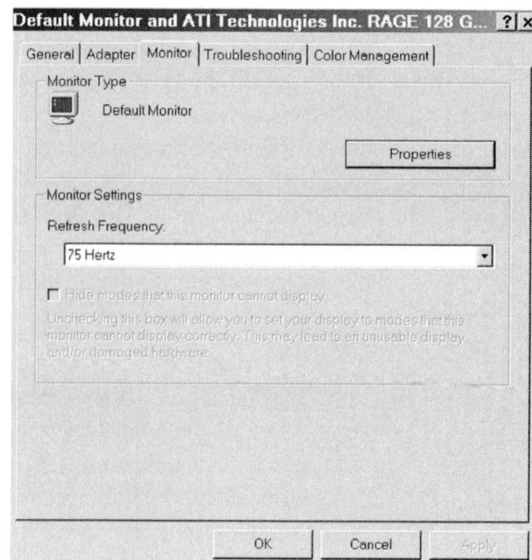

You might also use the troubleshooting tool tab (Display properties, settings tab, Advanced button) to reduce the hardware acceleration of the video card. If you suspect a video problem, reduce the hardware acceleration to see if the problem goes away.

21.8.3 Add/Remove Hardware and Add/Remove Software Applets

Differing from Windows NT 4.0, Windows 2000 and Windows XP support plug-and-play (PnP) hardware. This means that by physically installing or connecting a PnP device, Windows 2000 and XP will automatically configure the device (including the system resources such as I/O addresses, IRQs, and DMAs) and load the appropriate driver. Occasionally, you will need to use the Add/Remove Hardware Wizard to discover a PnP device. If the plug-and-play device causes a resource conflict, you can often use Device Manager to resolve these conflicts.

For non-plug-and-play devices, you will configure the device using jumpers or DIP switches, or by running a setup utility that comes with the device. To find out what the free resources are (I/O addresses, IRQ, DMA, and memory addresses), you can use Device Manager. After the card is configured and physically installed, Windows 2000/Windows XP can often identify the hardware and install the appropriate drivers to activate the driver. If not, you will have to use the Add/Remove Hardware Wizard. Note: You may need to provide configuration information such as the resources of the device. See figure 21.30.

The Add/Remove Programs applet helps you manage programs on your computer. It prompts you through the steps necessary to add a new program, change or remove an existing program, or add or remove Windows 2000/Windows XP components that were not installed during the original installation. See figures 21.31 and 21.32.

21.8.4 Fonts

A **font,** or **typeface,** is a collection of characters (letters, numerals, symbols, and punctuation marks) that have common characteristics. Font size is usually expressed in points, whereas a point is 1/72 of an inch. In addition, fonts can have different styles—**bold,** *italics,* and <u>underline.</u> The font, the size of the font, and the style greatly affect the overall effect of the document.

The font can be described by its pitch, spacing, weight, and width. In a fixed font such as `Courier,` every character occupies the same amount of space. In a proportional font, such as Arial or Times New Roman, the character width varies. The letter *W* is much wider than the letter *i.* The pitch, usually used for fixed-width fonts, is specified in characters per inch (cpi): 10 cpi = 12 points,

Figure 21.30 Using the Add/Remove Hardware Applet

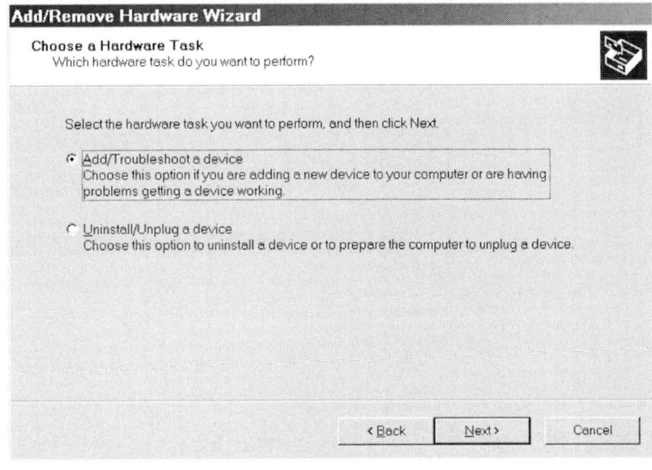

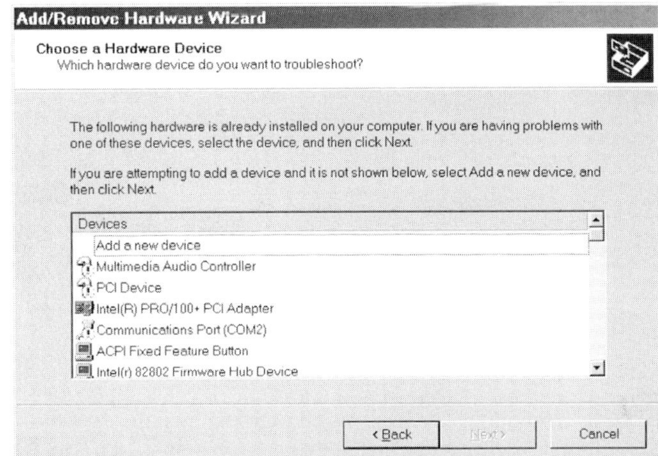

Figure 21.31 The Add/Remove Programs applet can be used to change or remove programs that are already installed on your system.

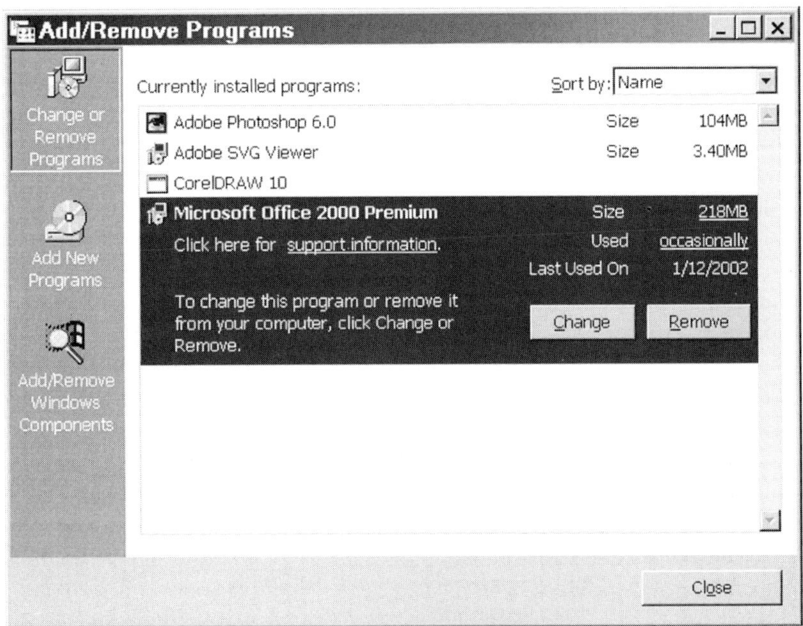

Figure 21.32 The Add/Remove applet can be used to add or remove Windows components without reinstalling Windows.

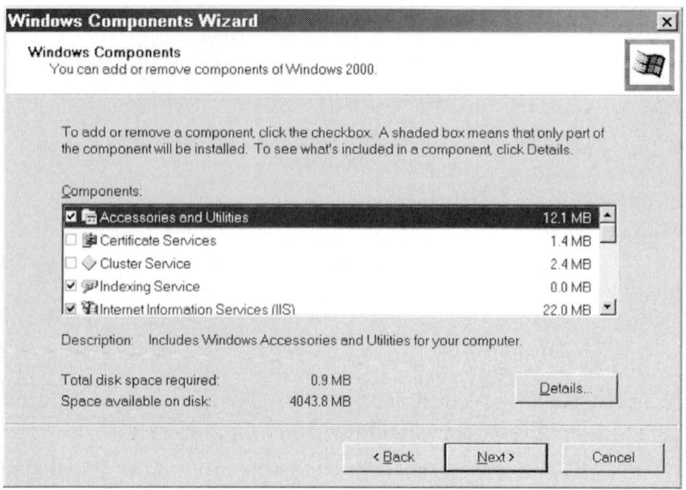

Figure 21.33 Raster Fonts

10 12 24 48 72

and 12 cpi = 10 points. The weight refers to the heaviness of the stroke for a specific font. Fonts can be light, regular, book, demi, heavy, black, and extra bold. The width refers to whether the standard font has been expanded or compressed horizontally.

Fonts can be described as serif and sans serif fonts. A serif font, such as Times New Roman and `Courier`, have projections that extend from the upper and lower strokes of the letters. Sans serif fonts such as Arial do not have serifs.

In Windows (Windows 9X, Windows NT, Windows 2000, and Windows XP), all fonts are broken into three categories. They are raster fonts, vector fonts, and TrueType fonts.

Raster fonts are bitmap pictures made of dots in different sizes for specific video display resolutions. For example, MS Serif comes in 8-, 10-, 12-, and 14-point size for CGA, EGA, VGA, and 8514 video systems. They have a FON file name extension. Raster fonts typically cannot be scaled or rotated. However, Windows can scale raster fonts to even multiples of their supplied size. For example, MS Serif can be scaled to 16-, 20-, 24-, and 28-point size. If you make the font too large, it becomes jagged. The jagged effect is what can be referred to as the "bitmap effect" (see figure 21.33).

Vector fonts are rendered using a mathematical model. Each character is defined as a set of lines drawn between points. Vector fonts can be scaled to any size, but cannot be rotated. Since the font has to be mathematically generated, the vector font requires more processing than the raster font. Examples of Windows vector fonts include Roman, Modern, and Script. **Outline fonts** are vector fonts that define the outline of each character geometrically. The most commonly used outline fonts are TrueType and PostScript fonts.

The most common fonts used in Windows are **TrueType fonts.** TrueType fonts, introduced in 1991 by Microsoft and Apple, are used for both the screen and the printer. Therefore, they allow Windows to be a ***What You See Is What You Get (WYSIWYG)*** **interface.** In addition, the TrueType fonts can be scaled and rotated without distortion. Each TrueType font requires only a file with an FOT file name extension and one with a TTF file name extension. The more popular TrueType fonts installed with Windows are Arial, Courier New, Times New Roman, and Symbol. See figure 21.34.

Figure 21.34 Symbol Indicating a TrueType Font

Managing fonts, including adding and deleting fonts, is done with the Font icon in the Control Panel. Note: If you load more fonts, Windows will use more resources to keep track of the fonts. In Windows 9X, loading too many fonts will lead to an "Out of Memory" error message. Windows 2000 and Windows XP have the ability to increase resources as needed.

21.8.5 Regional and Language Options

There are two levels of multilingual support provided for Windows XP and Windows 2000 Professional: localization and the Regional and Language Options feature. Localization refers to the language that is displayed by the operating system in the user interface. Regional and Language Options provide the ability to view, edit, and print Unicode-enabled documents for users within any localized version of Windows. The Unicode standard enables almost all the written languages of the world to be represented using a single character set.

To address worldwide language requirements, Windows XP and Windows 2000 Professional are offered in three distinct variations:

- **English version**—standard U.S version
- **Localized versions**—24 different varieties in Windows XP
- **Windows XP Multilanguage User Interface (MUI) and Windows 2000 Professional Multilanguage Version**

Users can change the language options only for Unicode-based applications. Users cannot change the localization of the operating system unless they are using a computer running Windows XP with MUI or Windows 2000 Professional, Multilanguage Version.

With the Regional and Language Options feature accessed in the Control Panel, you can change the format Windows uses to display dates, times, currency amounts, large numbers, and numbers with decimal fractions. You can also choose from a large number of input languages and text services, such as different keyboard layouts, Input Method Editors, and speech and handwriting recognition programs. When you switch to another input language, some programs offer special features, such as font characters or spelling checkers designed for different languages.

If you work in more than one language or communicate with speakers of other languages, you might want to install additional language groups. Each language group you install allows you to type and read documents composed in languages of that group, such as Western Europe, the United States, Central Europe, the Baltic region, and more.

Each language has a default keyboard layout, but many languages have alternate layouts. Even if you work mainly with one language, you may want to try other layouts. In English, for example, typing letters with accents might be simpler with the U.S.–International layout. To switch to another input locale, on the Taskbar click the indicator representing the current input locale, and then click the input locale you want to use.

You can switch to another input locale if you want to compose documents in a different language using the keyboard layout or Input Method Editor designed for that language. You can use a different input locale for each program you use. For example, you can use one input locale to create documents using WordPad and another input locale at the command prompt. To set this up, open the program you want, and then select the input locale to be used for that program. Each time you switch to that program while it is running, the input locale you selected is active. However, once you close the program, you will need to select the input locale again for that program the next time you start it. If the indicator does not appear on the Taskbar, click Start, point to Settings, and then click Control Panel. Double-click Regional Options, click the Input Locales tab, and then click Enable indicator on taskbar. This option is disabled if you have only one input locale installed.

You can increase the available input locales by installing additional language groups. Multiple input languages can be enabled on a Windows computer. An additional input language can be enabled by clicking on the Regional Options applet in the Control Panel, selecting the Input Locale tab, and then pressing the Add button and selecting the desired input language from the drop-down list.

To change the keyboard layout for an installed input locale:

- Open Regional Options in the Control Panel.
- On the Input Locales tab, under Input language, click the language whose keyboard layout or Input Method Editor you want to change, and then click Properties.
- In the Input Locale Properties dialog box, click the keyboard layout or Input Method Editor you want to use, and then click OK.

If you have the Windows Multilanguage Version, you can change the language used for menus and dialogs by opening the Regional Options in the Control Panel. On the General tab, under Menus and dialogs, select the language you want.

21.8.6 Using Power Schemes in Windows

Windows systems support ACPI only if all components are present and compatible during the installation including the motherboard, BIOS, and drivers. If you have legacy PC components, such as ISA expansion slots or out-of-date BIOS, Advanced Power Management (APM) may behave erratically or or can prevent ACPI from being installed.

A **power scheme** is a collection of power management settings that allow the user to conveniently configure power management options on a computer. When combined with ACPI–compliant hardware, an ACPI–enabled operating system such as Windows can provide a broad range of power management features. Although these options are used more with notebook computers to save power, they can also be used on desktop PCs to conserve electricity. For example, to maximize the life of your battery, select the Max Battery power scheme.

To change power settings that take advantage of ACPI, access Power Options in the Control Panel. See figure 21.35. The following capabilities are configured in the Power Options Properties dialog box:

Figure 21.35 Windows Power Options

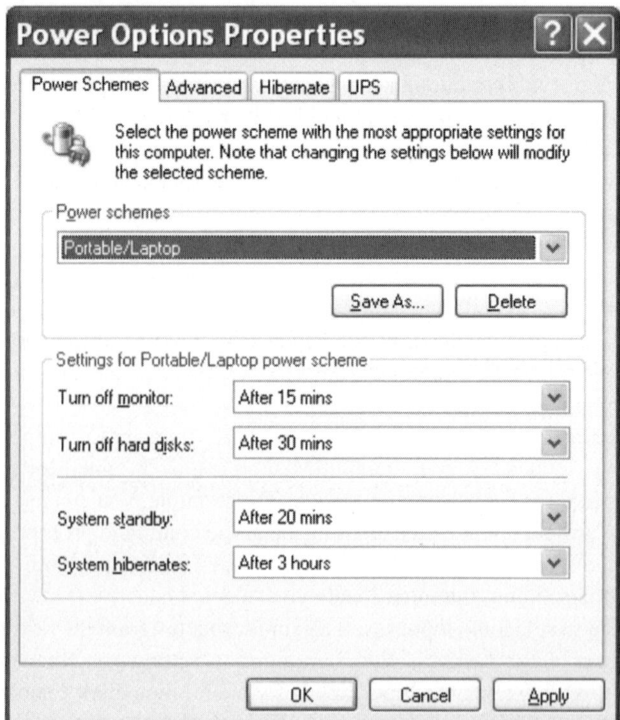

- **Turn off monitor**—This setting specifies the amount of time the computer can be idle before automatically shutting off the monitor.
- **Turn off hard disks**—This setting specifies the amount of time the computer can be idle before shutting off the hard disk.
- **System standby**—This setting specifies the amount of time the computer can be idle before going into standby mode.
- **Alarms**—This setting defines two alarms to warn the user when battery power is low.
- **Power meter**—This setting allows the power meter icon to be displayed in the notification area and displays the current power status.
- **Advanced**—This setting allows the user to set the default options for power buttons.
- **Hibernate**—This setting enables hibernation and allows the user to confirm that enough hard disk space is available.

ACPI can switch the computer into standby mode or hibernate mode. Standby mode switches the computer to a lower power state in which devices such as monitors and hard disks turn off so that the computer uses less power. When you use the computer again, the power comes out of standby quickly and the desktop is restored to its pre-idle state. Standby is particularly useful for conserving battery power in portable computers. However, standby does not save the desktop state to the hard disk, so a power failure during standby can result in a loss of any unsaved information. If you plan to be away from your computer for a while, set the power scheme on standby to put the entire system in a low-power state.

Hibernate goes one step further and saves everything in memory on hard disk, turns off the monitor and hard disk, and then turns off the computer. When you restart your computer, the desktop is restored exactly as you left it. It takes longer to bring the computer out of hibernation than out of standby mode. Put your computer in hibernation when you will be away from the computer for an extended time or overnight. When you restart the computer, the desktop is restored exactly as you left it.

When the system hibernates, Windows stores the contents of memory on your computer's boot partition in a file named HIBERFIL.SYS. As long as hibernation is enabled, you cannot delete it, rename it, or move it to another volume.

A computer goes into standby or hibernate mode when the idle timer reaches its preset time. When you perform an action on the computer, the idle timer is reset. Because Windows performs certain maintenance tasks to improve performance and reliability, Windows may also reset the idle timer, preventing or delaying the computer going into standby or hibernate mode. Some of these tasks includes scheduled tasks, event logging, network detection such as DHCP, loading of services or drivers, antivirus program, and Windows update checking the system state. To help eliminate the delay of entering standby or hibernate mode, manually put your computer in standby mode if it is going to be idle for more than a few minutes, turn off your wireless or LAN connection to prevent automated network tasks from occurring, and set up scheduled tasks to occur only if you are plugged into ac power.

The Power Options in properties dialog box contains default power schemes based on the specific configuration of each computer. Thus, it displays only the power settings that can be configured on that computer. At the dialog box you can create a new power scheme that is customized to your needs and work habits.

For ACPI to work in Windows, you must have correctly configured ACPI–compatible hardware and device drivers installed. Most ACPI–related issues occur during startup, shutdown, and standby and hibernation modes. Some of the common ACPI–related problems include:

- An inability to shut down the computer
- Standby and hibernate options not being available
- Problems with devices after resuming from standby or hibernation
- The computer not being able to resume after going into standby or hibernation
- The monitor not coming back on after being powered off by ACPI

If Windows did not correctly detect an ACPI–capable BIOS during setup, it will not install ACPI support. To determine whether the BIOS was detected as being ACPI capable, right-click My Computer, then click Properties. On the Hardware tab, click Device Manager and expand the entry called Computer. If the subentry is Advanced Configuration and Power Interface (ACPI) PC, ACPI is installed. If it says Standard PC, the computer BIOS was not detected as being ACPI capable.

Figure 21.36 Folder Options Dialog Box

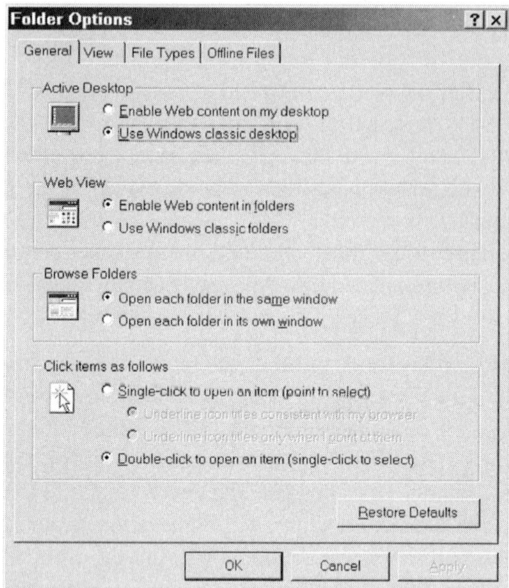

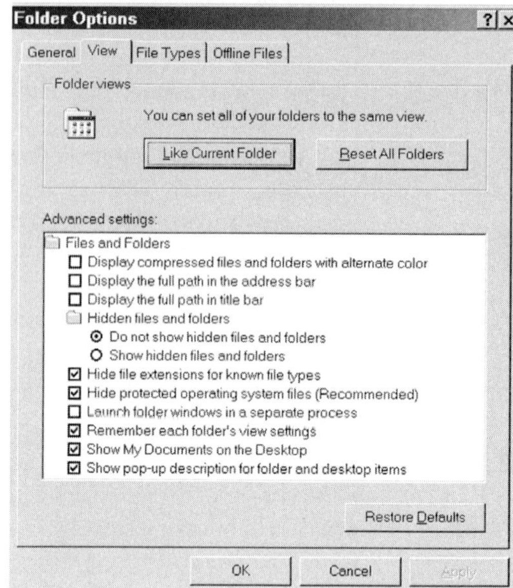

For an ACPI–capable BIOS to support ACPI features of Windows, the ACPI features of the BIOS needs to be enabled. This is usually done by going into the BIOS setup program, selecting the power menu, and ensuring that Power Manager or APM are enabled or configured as User Defined. However, you don't want the BIOS to control power management because problems will result if both the operating system (Windows) and the BIOS try to control the power. In addition, you need to make sure that the system ROM BIOS and device drivers are up-to-date.

21.8.7 Folder Options

The Folder Options dialog box is used to configure Windows to display hidden files in a window. The File Types tab shows the file name extensions for known file types and the View tab can be used to hide the protected operating system files. See figure 21.36.

21.9 SYSTEM AND ADMINISTRATIVE TOOLS

Utilities and tools may include the following:

- Diagnostic tools, utilities, and resources
  - Event Viewer

Besides the Control Panel, many of the utilities used to control and configure the system are located in System Tools located under Accessories. Many of the utilities used to control and configure network services are grouped into the ADMINISTRATIVE TOOLS folder, which can be accessed from within the Control Panel or by clicking on the Start button and selecting Programs.

21.9.1 System Tools and Accessories

Windows comes with various native system tools that were designed to perform every maintenance operation a computer requires. Windows includes the ScanDisk program to make sure your disks are error free by looking for a variety of problems including lost clusters and bad sectors. If you incorrectly shut down your computer (because of a crash, a power failure, or anything else), when you restart the system, a complete analysis of your hard disk(s) will be launched. In addition to getting optimal performance from your system, you can defragment your hard drive by using the Disk Defragmenter so that it can realign clusters to get the fastest disk access.

Included with Windows XP is the disk cleanup utility, which offers a few quick steps to retrieve some space on your disk like removing downloaded programs, removing temporary Internet files, removing offline synchronized pages, removing temporary files, emptying the Recycle Bin, deleting the System Restore archive sets, and so on. You just have to select what you want to remove and click the OK button so your hard disk will remain clean.

Windows XP comes with the System Restore utility. This application takes images or snapshots of your system at various times so you can revert to the state your system was in just before it totally crashed. To do so, the System Restore applet automatically creates in the background a backup of your system that'll be stored in a hidden folder of your hard disk. Each backup set is assigned to a checkpoint. You can also choose to create checkpoints yourself to make sure the installation of new drivers won't mess up the system. Restoring your PC to a previous state is easy: from the System Restore application you just have to choose a date where a checkpoint has been generated and let the computer work. However, the System Restore feature is far from perfect since, for example, you cannot recover erased files.

Microsoft Windows 2000 and Windows XP come with a small but efficient backup utility. You can program it through a wizard to save the MY DOCUMENTS folder and your settings, or the MY DOCUMENTS folders and settings of every user, or the contents of your hard disk to a backup unit. You can choose to schedule backup operations so they can be done at regular intervals without your intervention.

When connected to the Internet, Windows XP will regularly check in the background if any new updates are available for your system. This automatic process takes place with the user's permission to automatically download critical and security updates. If the computer is disconnected while an update is being retrieved, the update automatically resumes upon reconnection. Once the update has been downloaded, the user can choose to install it.

If you have certain tasks that you want to occur on a regular basis or a one-time job done in the middle of the night, you can use scheduled tasks. For example, you want to run a program once a week, you can start the scheduled task program, double-click the Add scheduled task icon and use the wizard to enable the task.

One tool that you should be familiar with is a communication tool called Hyperterminal. Hyperterminal starts a telnet connection in a window with a BBS, another computer or device connected on your network, or a device connected through one of your ports, such as a serial port.

The accessibility tools that ship with Windows are intended to provide a minimum level of functionality for users with special needs. You can adjust the appearance and behavior of Windows to enhance accessibility for users who have vision or hearing impairments or physical disabilities without requiring additional software or hardware. Windows includes the following programs to enhance accessibility, even if you choose not to install accessibility services:

- **Magnifier**—Enlarges a portion of the screen for ease of viewing
- **Narrator**—Uses text-to-speech technology to read the contents of the screen aloud. This is useful for people who are blind or who have impaired vision
- **On-screen keyboard**—Provides users with limited mobility the ability to type on-screen using a pointing device
- **Utility Manager**—Enables users with administrator-level access to check an accessibility program's status, start or stop an accessibility program, and designate to have the program start when Windows starts

The accessibility tools available in Accessibility Options in the Control Panel perform various functions:

- Sticky keys enable simultaneous keystrokes while pressing one key at a time.
- Filter keys adjust the response of your keyboard.
- Toggle keys emit sounds when certain locking keys are pressed.
- Sound sentry provides visual warnings for system sounds.
- Show sounds instructs programs to display captions for program speech and sounds.
- High contrast improves screen contrast with alternative colors and font sizes.
- Mouse keys enable the keyboard to perform mouse functions.
- Serial keys allow the use of alternative input devices instead of a keyboard and mouse.

A wide variety of hardware and software products are available to make personal computers easier to use for people with disabilities. The different types of products available for MS-DOS and Microsoft Windows operating systems include:

- Programs that enlarge or alter the color of information on the screen for people with visual impairments.
- Programs that describe information on the screen in Braille or synthesized speech for people who are blind or have difficulty reading.
- Hardware and software utilities that modify the behavior of the mouse and keyboard.
- Programs that enable the user to type using a mouse or his or her voice.
- Word or phrase prediction software that allows users to type more quickly and with fewer keystrokes.
- Alternate input devices, such as single switch or puff-and-sip devices, for people who cannot use a mouse or a keyboard.

Mouse users with disabilities need utility programs with higher functionality for daily use. For a list of Windows-based accessibility utilities, see Microsoft Accessibility on the Microsoft website.

21.9.2 Microsoft Management Console (MMC)

The **Microsoft Management Console (MMC)** was introduced with Internet Information Service (IIS) for Windows NT 4.0 and is one of the primary administrative tools used to manage Windows 2000 and Windows XP. It provides a standardized method to create, save, and open the various administrative tools provided by Windows 2000, BackOffice products, and third-party services. Some of the Windows 2000/Windows XP snap-ins include:

- System Tools—container for managing local users and groups
- System Information—container for managing hardware resources, monitoring the software environment and controlling system services
- Storage—container contains a disk defrag tool, a removable storage control panel, and an optional archive manager
- Server applications and services—DHCP, DNS, RAS, and IIS services
- Links to shared directories, web links, and resource kits

NOTE: Most snap-ins can be used on remote computers.

To start the Microsoft Management Console:

1. Click the Start button.
2. Click on the Programs option.
3. Click on the Administrative Tools option.
4. Select the Computer Management option.

To start an empty MMC, go to the command prompt and type *MMC.EXE.* Every MMC has a console tree that displays the hierarchical organization of snap-ins (plugable modules) and extensions (a snap-in that requires a parent snap-in). Adding and deleting of the snap-ins and extensions allows each user to customize the console. The console settings can then be saved to an MMC console file (file with a MSC extension) and can be used later, shared by others, or even emailed to other computers. By default, MMC stores snap-ins in the *%systemroot%*\SYSTEM32 folder. Note: The *%systemroot%* means the folder that Windows is installed into. By default, the Windows NT and Windows 2000 directory is C:\WINNT and Windows XP is C:\WINDOWS.

When building a custom console, you can assign various console modes (access options). They are listed in table 21.10. By default, all new MMC consoles are saved in author mode. To change the console mode, you open the Console menu, select the Option option, and click on the Console tab. See figure 21.37.

To add snap-ins:

1. Open MMC.
2. Select the Add/Remove Snap-in from the Console menu.
3. Click on the Add button from within the Add Standalone Snap-in dialog box.
4. Click the snap-in that you want and click on the Add button.
5. Repeat steps 3 and 4 as needed.

Table 21.10 MMC Console Modes

Console Mode	Description
Author mode	In author mode, you can add or remove snap-ins, create new windows, view all portions of the console tree, and save the MMC consoles.
User mode—full access	Usually used to distribute an MMC console to other administrators. Users can't add snap-ins, remove snap-ins, or save the MMC console.
User mode—limited access, multiple window	Users can't add snap-ins, remove snap-ins, or save the MMC console. While users can view the console in multiple windows, they can't open new windows or gain access to a portion of the console tree.
User mode—limited access, single window	Users can't add snap-ins, remove snap-ins, or save the MMC console. Users cannot view the console in multiple windows, and they can't open new windows or gain access to a portion of the console tree.

Figure 21.37 Changing the MMC Console Mode

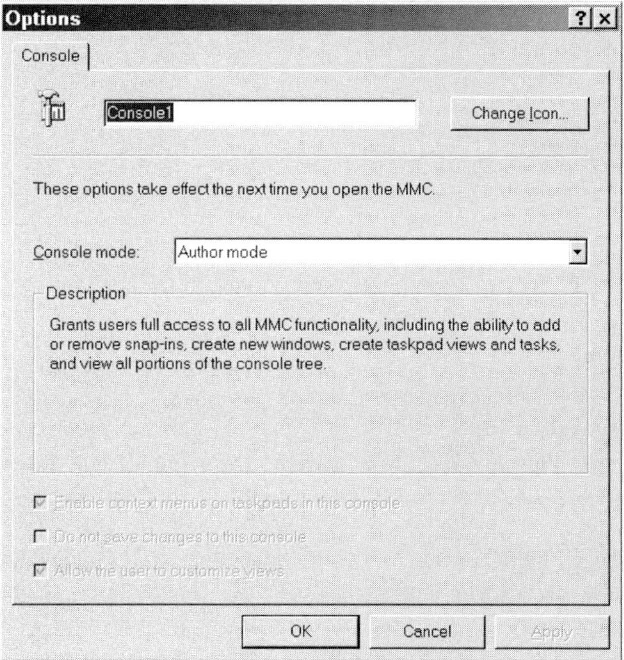

To remove a snap-in:

1. Open MMC.
2. Select the Add/Remove Snap-in from the Console menu.
3. Click on the snap-in that you want to remove.
4. Click on the Remove button.
5. Repeat steps 3 and 4 as needed.

21.9.3 Computer Management Console

Computer Management is a collection of Windows administrative tools that you can use to manage a local or remote computer. The tools are organized into a single console, which makes it easy to view administrative properties and to gain access to the tools that are necessary to perform your computer-management tasks.

Figure 21.38 The Computer Management Console

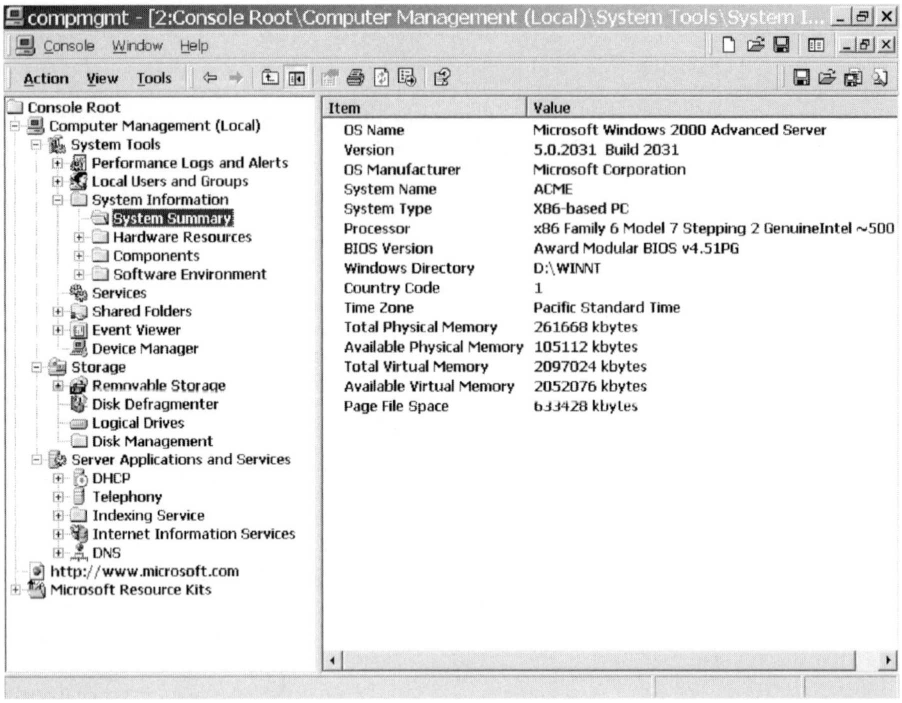

The Computer Management console consists of a window divided into two panes. The left pane contains the console tree; the right pane contains details. When you click an item in the console tree, information about that item is displayed in the details pane. The information that is displayed is specific to the item that you select. See figure 21.38.

The administrative tools in Computer Management are grouped into System Tools, Storage, and Server Applications and Services. Then each category includes several tools or services:

System Tools

- **Event Viewer**—Used to manage and view events that are recorded in the Application, Security, and System logs. You can monitor the logs to track security events and to identify possible software, hardware, and system problems.
- **Shared Folders**—Used to view connections and resource in use on the computer. You can create, view, and manage shares, view open files and sessions, and close files and disconnect sessions.
- **Local Users and Groups**—Used to create and manage your local user accounts and groups. Note: This is available only in Windows XP Professional.
- **Performance Logs and Alerts**—Use the Performance Logs and Alerts tool to configure performance logs and alerts to monitor and collect data about your computer's performance.
- **Device Manager**—Used to view the hardware devices installed in your computer, update device drivers, modify hardware settings, and troubleshoot device conflicts.

Storage

- **Removable Storage**—Used to track your removable storage media and manage the libraries, or data-storage systems, that contain them.
- **Disk Defragmenter**—Used to analyze and defragment volumes on your hard disks.
- **Disk Management**—Used to perform disk-related tasks such as converting disks or creating and formatting volumes. Disk Management helps you manage your hard disks, and the partitions or volumes that they contain.

Server Applications and Services

- **Services**—Used to manage services on local and remote computers. You can start, stop, pause, resume, or disable a service.

- **WMI Control**—Used to configure and manage the Windows Management Instrumentation (WMI) service.
- **Indexing Service**—Used to manage the Indexing service, and to create and configure additional catalogs to store index information.

NOTE: The actual set of tools and services that is listed in Computer Management depends on the services that are installed on the host computer.

21.9.4 Event Viewer

The **event viewer** is a very useful utility for viewing and managing logs of system, program, and security events on your computer. Event viewer gathers information about hardware and software problems, and monitors Windows NT family security events. The event viewer can be executed by clicking on the Start button, clicking on Programs, clicking on Administrative Tools and clicking on Event Viewer, or by adding it to the MMC console.

Windows NT family event viewer starts with three kinds of logs:

Application log—The application log contains events logged by programs. For example, a database program might record a file error in the programs log. Program developers decide which events to monitor. The application log can be viewed by all users.

Security log—The security log contains valid and invalid logon attempts as well as events related to resource use, such as creating, opening, or deleting files or other objects. For example, if you have enabled logon and logoff auditing, attempts to log on to the system are recorded in the security log. By default, security logging is turned off. To enable security logging, use Group Policy to set the audit policy or by changing the registry. To audit files and folders, you must be logged on as a member of the administrators group or have been granted the Manage auditing and security log right in Group Policy.

System log—The system log contains events logged by the Windows 2000/XP system components. For example, the failure of a driver or other system component to load during startup is recorded in the system log. The event types logged by system components are predetermined by Windows 2000/XP. The application log can be viewed by all users.

There are five types of event types—error, warning, information, success audit, and failure audit. They are shown table 21.11.

When you double-click on an event, the Event Properties window will appear. The event properties can be divided into two parts, event header and event description. The event header information is shown in table 21.12.

The description of the event is the most important information within the Event Properties window and will usually indicate what happened or the significance of the event.

Table 21.11 Event Viewer Event Types

Event Type	Description
Error	A significant problem, such as loss of data or loss of functionality (e.g., when a service fails during startup).
Warning	An event that is not necessarily significant, but may indicate a possible future problem. For example, when disk space is low, a warning will be logged.
Information	An event that describes the successful operation of an application, driver, or service. For example, when a network driver loads successfully, an information event will be logged.
Success audit	An audited security access attempt that succeeds. For example, a user's successful attempt to log on to the system will be logged as a success audit event.
Failure audit	An audited security access attempt that fails. For example, if a user tries to access a network drive and fails, the attempt will be logged as a failure audit event.

Table 21.12 Event Header Information

Information	Meaning
Date	The date the event occurred.
Time	The local time the event occurred.
User	The user name of the user on whose behalf the event occurred.
Computer	The name of the computer where the event occurred. The computer name is usually your own, unless you are viewing an event log on another Windows 2000 computer.
Event ID	A number identifying the particular event type. The first line of the description usually contains the name of the event type.
Source	The software that logged the event, which can be either a program name such as "SQL Server," or a component of the system or of a large program, such as a driver name.
Type	A classification of the event severity: error, information, or warning in the system and application logs; success audit or failure audit in the security log. In event viewer's normal list view, these are represented by a symbol.
Category	A classification of the event by the event source. This information is primarily used in the security log. For example, for security audits, this corresponds to one of the event types for which success or failure auditing can be enabled in Group Policy.

Figure 21.39 Services Console

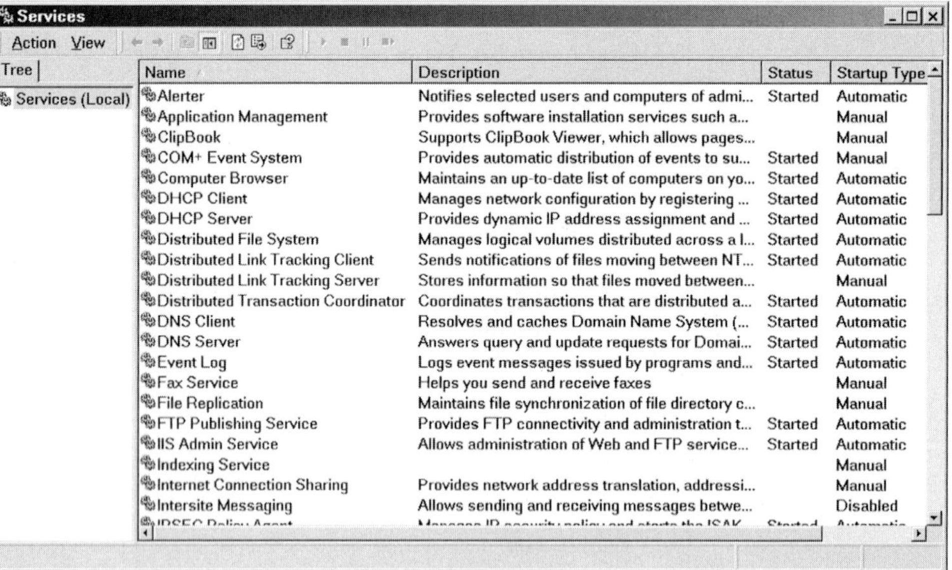

21.9.5 Services Console

A **service** is a program, routine, or process that performs a specific system function to support other programs. For Windows NT, you will use the Control Panel's Services applet to manage the services. To manage the services in Windows 2000 or Windows XP, you would use the Services console (located under Administrative Tools) or the MMC with the Services snap-in. To start, stop, pause, resume, or restart services, you would right-click on the service and click on the desired option. As you can see in figure 21.39 there are many services.

To configure a service, you would right-click the service and click on the Properties option. On the General tab, under the Startup type pull-down option, you can set the following options:

- Automatic—specifies that the service should start automatically when the system starts.
- Manual—specifies that a user or a dependent service can start the service. Services with manual startup do not start automatically when the system starts.
- Disable—prevents the service from being started by the system, a user, or any dependent service.

The workstation service allows a user sitting at the computer to access the network resources such as shared folders. The workstation is also known as the Redirector.

The server allows a computer to provide network resources. When you pause the Server service, only users in the computer's administrators and server operators groups will be able to make new connections to the computer. When you stop the Server service, all users who are connected over the network to the computer will be disconnected.

Of course, if you stop a Server service, the affected computer can no longer be administered remotely and you must start the Server service locally. It is a good idea to warn connected users before stopping the Server service.

21.10 DISK MANAGEMENT

For Windows 2000 and Windows XP, you would use the **Disk Management** console, or the Computer Management console (click on the Start button, click on the Programs option, click on the Administrative Tools, and select the Computer Management option) to configure and manage your disks. See figure 21.40. For Windows NT, you would use Disk Administrator. To use the Disk Management console to configure and manage your disks, you need to be a member of the administrator or server operator group.

> The data on the system is probably the most important thing on the network and server. Therefore, before making any changes to the disk systems you should back up all important data. In addition, you should be backing up important data on a regular basis.

Figure 21.40 Disk Management Console

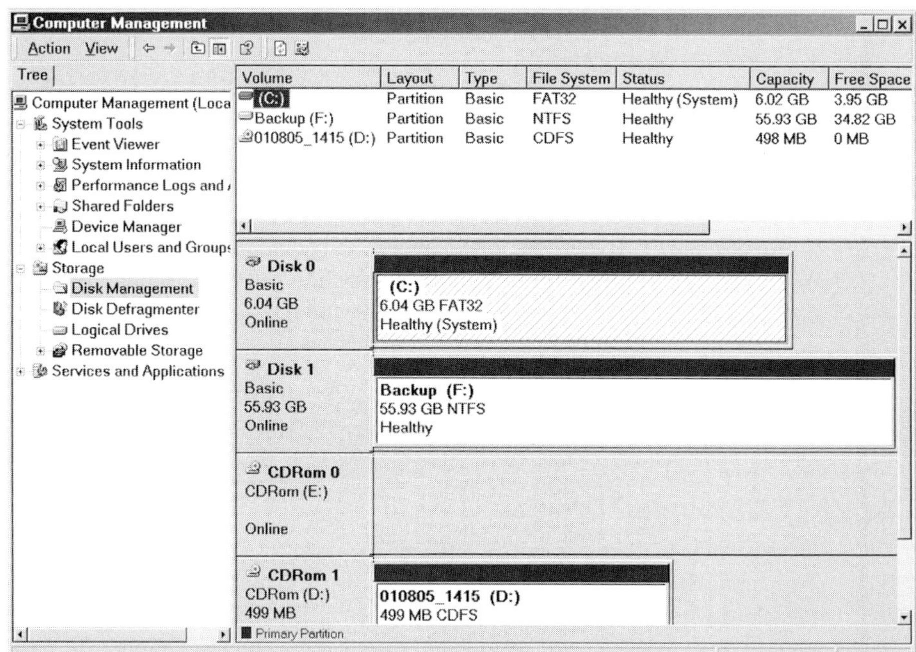

After you make changes to your disk configuration, right-click Disk Management, or open the Action menu, you can use the Refresh and Rescan Disks options. The Refresh option updates drive letters, file system information, volume information, and removable media information. The Rescan Disks option updates hardware information by scanning all attached disks for disk configuration changes. Note: Rescanning the disk may take several minutes, depending on the number of drives.

When you connect a hard drive from another computer, the disks are imported automatically. However, if the status of the disk appears as Foreign, you must right-click the new disk and use the Import Foreign Disk option. Note: If the status of an imported volume appears as "Failed: Incomplete Volume," you have imported one or more disks that have a spanned, striped volume or RAID-5 volumes, or you are missing one or more disks.

21.10.1 Drive Letters and Paths

Windows 2000 and Windows XP allow you to have as many volumes as you wish. Unfortunately, you cannot assign more than 26 drive letters (A–Z). Typically letters *A* and *B* are reserved for the floppy disk. If you do not have a floppy disk drive B, you can use the letter *B* as a network drive. These drive letters apply to only the local machine, not network machines that connect to a Windows server.

For many operating systems, drive letters are dynamic, meaning that every time you turn on the machine, a drive letter is assigned to each volume. Unfortunately, sometimes when you add a drive or create partitions, the drive letters are remapped. The problem occurs when a program is set to look for or access a particular drive letter only to find that the folder or files are not at the designated location because drive letters have been assigned differently.

Windows allows the static assignment of drive letters. This means that a drive letter can be permanently assigned to a specific hard disk and volume. Then when a hard disk is added to the existing computer system or partitions and volumes are created, it does not affect statically assigned drive letters.

Windows 2000 and Windows XP allow you to change drive letters. Of course, since many DOS and Windows programs refer to specific drive letters, you need to be careful when making drive-letter assignments. In addition, you cannot change a drive letter assigned to a boot volume or system volume.

To assign a drive letter to a volume that doesn't currently have a drive letter:

1. Open Disk Management.
2. Right-click the volume that you want to assign a drive letter to.
3. Select the Change Drive Letter and Paths option and click on the Add button.
4. Select a drive letter and click the OK button.

To remove a drive letter:

1. Open Disk Management.
2. Right-click the volume that you want to remove the drive letter from and click the Remove button.
3. Click on the Yes button to confirm your actions.

To change a drive letter:

1. Open Disk Management.
2. Right-click the volume that you want to change the assigned drive letter.
3. Select the Change Drive Letter and Paths option and click on the Edit button.
4. Select a new drive letter and click the OK button.
5. Click on the Yes button to confirm your actions.

NOTE: You can also assign a drive letter to a network drive by right-clicking My Computer or My Network Places and selecting Map Network Drive.

21.10.2 NTFS Mounted Drives

An NTFS mounted drive is a drive attached to an empty folder on an NTFS volume, which is assigned a path, not a drive letter. Of course, volumes created after the 26th drive letter have to be accessed as a mounted drive. When you open the drive or directory that holds the mounted drive and you open the mounted drive, you are automatically redirected to the mounted volume. To the user, the mounted drive acts just like a folder or directory at the assigned location.

Figure 21.41 Mounting a Drive

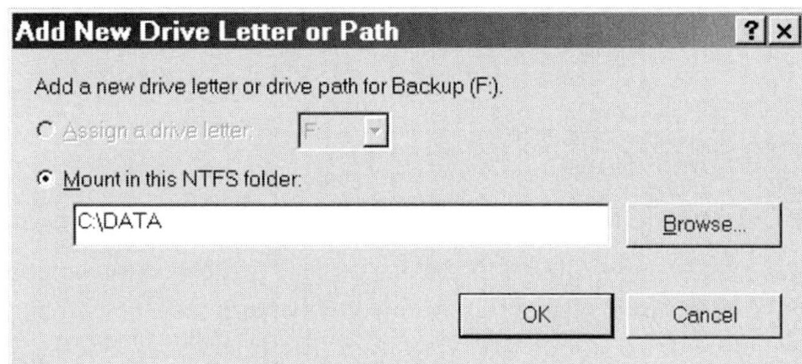

To create a mounted drive:

1. Create a folder where you want the drive mounted.
2. Open Disk Management.
3. Right-click the volume that you want to mount and select the Change Drive Letter and Paths option.
4. Click on the Add button if it is a volume without a drive letter or is not already mounted, or click on the Edit button if the volume already has a drive letter or is already mounted.
5. Select the Mount in this NTFS folder option and type or browse the path of the new folder. Click on the OK button. See figure 21.41.

21.10.3 Formatting Volumes

Before you can store files and directories on a volume or partition, you must perform a high-level format on it. A high-level format creates the file allocation table and root directory. It can be performed when creating a volume or partitions with Disk Management or can be formatted at a later time.

1. Open Disk Management.
2. Right-click on the partition or volume that you want to format, type the volume label if desired, select the file system, and select the allocation unit size. Click on the OK button.
3. If you get a warning that all information will be lost during a format, click on the OK button.

Instead of a normal format, you can perform a quick format. While a quick format removes the files from the disk, it does not scan the disk for bad sectors. Using a quick format is not recommended.

21.10.4 Deleting Volumes

Sometimes you may need to delete a volume so that you can reallocate the disk space. You cannot delete the boot volume, although you can delete the system volume. To delete the volume:

1. Open Disk Management.
2. Right-click the volume that you want to delete and select the Delete Volume option.
3. For the warning stating that all data will be lost, click on the Yes button.

21.10.5 Converting FAT or FAT32 to NTFS

One way to convert a partition or volume to NTFS is reformat it. Of course, all information on the volume will then be lost. Another way to convert it is to open a command prompt window and use the following command:

```
CONVERT x: /FS:NTFS
```

where *x:* is the drive letter that you want to convert. If the CONVERT command cannot lock the drive, it will offer to convert it the next time the computer restarts, such as the system volume. Note: You cannot convert an NTFS partition or volume to FAT or FAT32.

If you select to convert a system volume and you decide that you do not want to convert it during the next boot, access the following subkey:

HKEY_LOCAL_MACHINE\SYSTEM\CurrentControlSet\Control\Session Manager

Change the BootExecute entry from:

```
autoconv \DosDevices\x: /FS:NTFS
```

to:

```
autocheck autochk *
```

21.10.6 File Compression and EFS

Windows 2000 and Windows XP using an NTFS file system support file compression and encryption. NTFS compression is the ability to selectively compress the contents of individual files, entire directories, or entire drivers of an NTFS volume. The Encrypting File System (EFS) allows a user to encrypt files that are stored on an NTFS volume. By using EFS, folders and files are still kept secure against intruders who gain unauthorized physical access to the drive by stealing a notebook computer or a removable drive, for example. EFS is not intended to support accessing an encrypted file by multiple users, however, and does not decrypt or encrypt files that are transmitted over the network. Last, drives, directories, and files cannot be compressed with NTFS compression or be encrypted with EFS. See chapter 12 for more information.

21.10.7 Quotas

When working as a network administrator, you will find that the typical users consider the network drive as their own personal drive. Therefore, as users receive files from friends or find something they like on the Internet, they will save the files in the network drive. Unfortunately, after a period of time, a volume will become full.

To manage these types of situations, Windows 2000 and Windows XP offer **disk quotas,** which track and control disk space usage for an NTFS volume. When you enable disk quotas, you can set the disk quota limit and the disk quota warning level. The limit specifies the amount of disk space a user is allowed to use. The warning level specifies when it will log a system event if the warning level is met. Note that Disk quotas are based on file ownership and do not depend on where the file is located on the volume. In addition, file compression does not affect the quota statistics.

As soon as the disk quota feature is activated on a volume, it will begin tracking all disk usage by the users. When a user exceeds the disk quota, he or she could be denied the ability to save any more files to the volume. Enabling quotas but not limiting disk space is useful when you do not want to deny users access to a volume, but want to track disk space use on a per-user basis.

To administer quotas on an NTFS volume:

1. Double-click on My Computer.
2. Right-click the NTFS volume on which you want to enable disk quotas. See figure 21.42.
3. Click in the Enable quota management check box.
4. If you want users to be denied access when they have exceeded their disk quota, select the Deny disk space to users exceeding quota limit.
5. If you wish, under Select the default quota limit for new users on this volume, you can specify the default limit disk space and the warning level for the new users. Note that the default value is in KB.
6. Select the appropriate logging options.
7. Click on the OK or Apply button.

> *NOTE:* To administer quotas on a volume, you must be a member of the administrator group on the computer where the drive resides. The Quota tab will display only if you are a member of the administrator group or the volume is an NTFS volume. New members are those that write to a disk for the first time after the disk quotas has been enabled.

To manage the quota:

1. Double-click on My Computer.
2. Right-click the NTFS volume on which you want to enable disk quotas. See figure 21.43.
3. Select the Quotas Entries button.

Figure 21.42 Enabling Disk Quotas

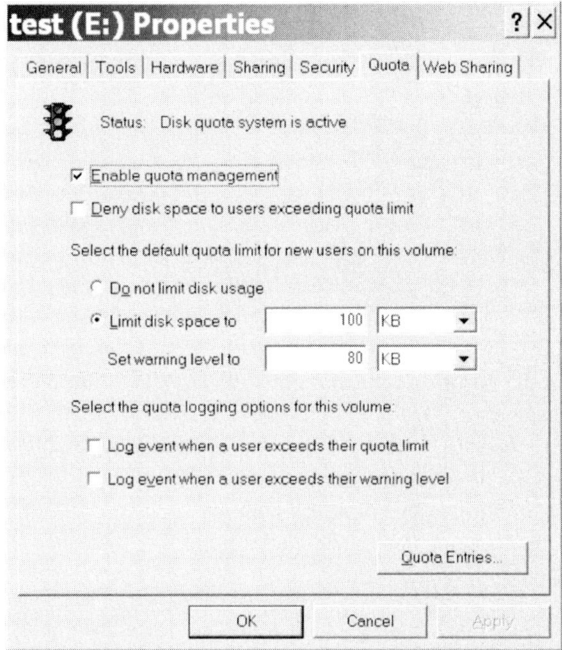

Figure 21.43 Managing Disk Quotas

Quota Entries for test (E:)

Quota Edit View Help

Status	Name	Logon Name	Amount Used	Quota Limit	Warning Level	Percent Used
OK	Frank J. Biggs	FJBiggs@acme01.com	0 bytes	100 KB	80 KB	0
OK	Charles L. Gee	CLGee@acme01.com	0 bytes	200 KB	200 KB	0
OK		BUILTIN\Administrators	0 bytes	No Limit	No Limit	N/A

3 total item(s), 0 selected.

To change a quota limit or warning level, double-click on the user name. To create a quota entry, open the Quota menu and select the New Quota entry. To delete an entry, right-click the entry and select the Delete option.

21.11 WINDOWS 2000/XP DISK STORAGE TYPES

Windows NT has only basic disk storage type, while Windows 2000 and Windows XP have two disk storage types—basic disks and dynamic disks. A **basic disk** is a physical disk that contains primary partitions, extended partitions, or logical drives that can be accessed directly using DOS, Windows 95, or Windows 98. Basic disks may contain volume sets, mirrored sets, striped sets, and striped sets with parity if they were created using Windows NT 4.0 or earlier and upgraded to Windows 2000. Windows 2000 offers limited support of striped sets and striped sets with parity. You can repair, regenerate, and delete striped sets and striped sets with parity, but you cannot create them. See table 21.13.

When you install Windows 2000/XP, your hard disks are automatically initialized as basic. Using Disk Manager in Windows 2000/XP, you can create, delete, and format partitions without having to restart your computer to make the changes effective.

To create a partition on a basic disk, you would:

1. Open Disk Management.
2. Right-click unallocated space on the basic disk where you want to create the partition, select the Create Volume option, and select the Next button.

Table 21.13 Types of Partitions and Volumes by the Windows NT Family

Windows NT	Windows 2000/Windows XP
Simple partition	Simple volume
Volume set	Spanned volume
Mirrored set	Mirrored volume
Striped set	Striped volume
Striped set with parity	RAID-5 volume

3. Select the partition type and click on the Next button. The default size is the amount of unallocated space.
4. Specify the size for the selected disk and click on the Next button.
5. Assign the drive letter or path and click on the Next button.
6. Select the Format this partition with the following settings; specify the file system, allocation unit sizes, and volume name; and click on the Next button.
7. Click on the Finish button.

A **dynamic storage** is a disk that is converted from basic to dynamic storage that contains simple volumes, spanned volumes, mirrored volumes, striped volumes, and RAID-5 volumes. Unlike basic disks, dynamic disks cannot contain partitions or logical drives and they cannot be accessed by DOS. The advantage of the dynamic storage is that they contain an unlimited number of volumes, and volumes can be extended to include noncontiguous space on available disks.

On a dynamic disk, the disk configuration information is stored on the disk and not in the registry. Therefore, to upgrade a drive from basic to dynamic, you must have at least 1 MB of free space at the end of the disk for the upgrade to succeed. To upgrade a basic disk to a dynamic disk, right-click the disk using Computer Manager, and select the Upgrade to Dynamic Disk option. When using the Computer Management program to create partitions or volumes on a disk, the Computer Management program will reserve the free space automatically. In addition, if you upgrade a boot disk or if a volume or partition is in use on the disk, the computer must be restarted for the upgrade to succeed. Note: Removable media devices can only contain primary partitions. Therefore, you cannot upgrade removable media devices. In addition, dynamic disks are not supported on portable computers.

After you upgrade a basic disk to a dynamic disk, you cannot change the dynamic volumes back to partitions. Instead, you must delete all dynamic volumes on the disk and then use the Revert to Basic Disk command.

You should be able to troubleshoot most issues with dynamic disks by using Disk Management. Disk Management will report the status of a disk, and, based on that status, you should be able to resolve the issue. The statuses that indicate a problem are the following:

- **Foreign**—This status occurs when you install a dynamic disk in the local computer. This usually occurs when the dynamic disk is from another system. Therefore, to overcome the problem, you must right-click the disk and then click Import Foreign Disks before you can access data on the disk.
- **Missing/Offline**—This status occurs when a dynamic disk is not accessible. The disk might be intermittently unavailable—that is, the disk was recently available on the system but can no longer be located or identified. The missing disk might be damaged, turned off, or disconnected. If the disk status remains offline or the disk name remains missing and you determine that the disk has a problem that cannot be repaired, you can remove the disk from the computer. To bring an offline or missing disk back online, repair the disk problem (hard disk, controller, or cable problem). Then, in Disk Management, right-click the disk, and then click Reactivate Disk.
- **Not Initialized**—This status indicates that the disk does not contain a valid disk signature in the MBR (master boot record) or a valid disk GUID (globally unique identifier) in the GUID partition table. You can initialize the disk by right-clicking the disk and then clicking Initialize Disk.

- **Online (errors)**—This status indicates that I/O errors have been detected on a region of the disk. A warning icon appears on the disk with errors. Only dynamic disks display the online (errors) status. You might be able to return the disk to online status by right-clicking the disk and then clicking Reactivate Disk.
- **Unreadable**—This status occurs when the disk is not accessible. The disk might not be available if it is spinning up; encountering hardware failure, corruption, or I/O errors; or the disk's copy of the dynamic disk database is corrupted. An error icon appears on disks that display the unreadable status. Try resolving this issue by rescanning the disks. In Disk Management, click Action, and then click Rescan Disks. You can also try restarting the computer to see if the status changes.

Because dynamic disks were new in Windows 2000 and do not use the traditional partition layout that was used by disks in Windows 9X or Windows NT 4.0, Microsoft provided DMDIAG.EXE, a command-line tool that displays the location and layout of dynamic disks and volumes. The DMDIAG.EXE tool can be used to decipher disk numbering, which may be useful for situations where your disk numbering is very complex.

NOTE: When running the utility, dynamic disks are indicated with dm Disk*X*.

DMDIAG can be loaded from the Resource Kit CD or downloaded from Microsoft.com:

http://www.microsoft.com/windows2000/techinfo/reskit/tools/existing/dmdiag-o.asp

21.11.1 Simple and Spanned Volumes

A simple volume is made up of disk space from a single physical disk (single region or multiple regions linked together. To create a simple volume:

1. Open Disk Management.
2. Right-click unallocated space on the dynamic disk where you want to create the simple volume, select the Create Volume option, and select the Next button.
3. Select Simple volume and click on the Next button.
4. Select the disk and the size for the selected disk and click on the Next button.
5. Assign the drive letter or path and click on the Next button.
6. Select the file system to use, select the allocation unit size, and enter the volume label. If you wish, you can also select quick format. Click on the Next button.
7. Click on the Finish button.

A spanned volume is having a volume across multiple disks. A spanned volume can free drive letters for other uses and allows the creation of extremely large volume for file system use. A spanned volume can be extended up to a maximum of 32 disks and can use FAT, FAT32, or NTFS. To create a spanned volume:

1. Open Disk Management.
2. Right-click unallocated space on the dynamic disk where you want to create the spanned volume, click the Create Volume option, and click on the Next button.
3. Select the Spanned Volume and click on the Next button.
4. Select the disks and the size for the selected disks and click on the Next button. Note: The selected disk size for the different drives can be different.
5. Assign the drive letter or path and click on the Next button.
6. Select the file system to use, select the allocation unit size, and enter the volume label. Click on the Next button.
7. Click on the Finish button.

To extend or expand an existing volume (simple or spanned), you would right-click the volume, select the Extend Volume option, and use the wizard to specify which unallocated space to use and the amount of unallocated space. Note: Only NTFS volumes can be extended; you cannot extend a system or boot volume. System and boot volumes are partitions that were contained in basic disks and upgraded to dynamic disks.

To delete a simple or spanned volume, right-click the volume and select the Delete option. The wizard will then ask you if you are sure. When you click on the Yes button, the volume is deleted.

21.12.2 Mirrored Volume

A mirrored volume (RAID-1) is two identical copies of a simple volume on separate hard disks. When data is written to one disk, the data is also written to the other disk. If one of the hard drives fails, the other hard drive will continue to function without loss of data or downtime. In addition, mirrored volumes have better overall read performance than simple volumes, spanned volumes, and RAID-5 volumes.

When a disk fails that contains a mirrored volume, you must break the mirrored volume to separate the working volume with its own drive letters. Note: Breaking the mirrored volume does not delete the information. You can recreate a new mirrored volume with unused free space of the same size or greater on another disk. If the second volume is larger, the remaining space becomes free space. Any existing volume, including the system and boot volumes, can be mirrored onto another volume of the size or greater on another disk. When creating mirrored volumes, it is best to use disks that are the same size, model, and manufacturer.

To create a mirrored set,

1. Open Disk Management.
2. Right-click unallocated space on the dynamic disk where you want to create the spanned volume, click the Create Volume option, and click on the Next button.
3. Select Mirrored Volume and click on the Next button.
4. Select the disks and the size for the selected disks and click on the Next button.
5. Assign the drive letter or path and click on the Next button.
6. Select the file system to use, select the allocation unit size, and enter the volume label. Click on the Next button.
7. Click on the Finish button.

If a basic disk that contains part of a mirrored set is disconnected or fails, the status of the mirrored set becomes Failed Redundancy and the status of the disk remains Online. To repair a basic mirrored set, open Disk Management, right-click the mirrored volume you want to repair, select the Repair Volume option, and follow the instructions on the screen. The mirrored volume's status should change to Regenerating, then Healthy. If the volume does not return to the Healthy status, right-click the volume and then click Resynchronize Mirror. If this does not work, you will have to right-click the volume and select the Remove Mirror option to delete one of the mirrors. Then rebuild the mirror by right-clicking the volume and selecting the Add Mirror option.

To delete a mirrored set, right-click the mirrored set and select the Delete the Volume option. To create two independent partitions or logical drives, right-click the mirrored set and select Break Mirror.

Note: The only way to make the system and boot volume fault tolerance is to mirror the volume. You should then create two different boot disks that point to both the boot partitions by using the appropriate Advanced RISC Computing (ARC) name. Of course, you should test each boot disk to make sure that they start Windows by booting the system with the boot disk.

21.11.3 Striped Volume

A striped set is similar to a volume set, as it is the combining of areas of free space on 2 to 32 disks onto one logical volume. The difference is that a striped volume has the data allocated alternately and evenly in 64 KB stripes through the various drives. Therefore, when data is read or written, it writes to all of the drives simultaneously. Striped volumes offer the best performance of all volumes available in Windows since the hard disks are working simultaneously. Like a volume set, if one of the disks in the striped volume fails, the entire volume is lost. Striped volumes cannot be mirrored or extended.

1. Open Disk Management.
2. Right-click unallocated space on the dynamic disk where you want to create the spanned volume, click the Create Volume option, and click on the Next button.
3. Select Striped Volume and click on the Next button.
4. Select the disks and the size for the selected disks and click on the Next button. Note: The selected disk size for the different drives can be different.
5. Assign the drive letter or path and click on the Next button.
6. Select the file system to use, select the allocation unit size, and enter the volume label. Click on the Next button.
7. Click on the Finish button.

Table 21.14 Comparing Mirrored Volumes and RAID-5 Volumes

Mirrored Volumes	RAID-5 Volumes
Support FAT and NTFS.	Support FAT and NTFS.
Can mirror system or boot volumes.	Cannot stripe system or boot volumes.
Require 2 hard disks.	Supports 3 to 32 hard disks.
Have higher cost per megabtye (50% utilization).	Have lower cost per megabyte.
Have good read and write performance.	Have moderate write performance and excellent read performance.
Use less system memory.	Require more system memory.

21.11.4 RAID-5 Volume

RAID-5 volumes are fault-tolerant striped volumes, except they use an extra drive to store parity information. In Windows NT, RAID-5 volume is very similar to Stripe Set with Parity. A RAID-5 volume can use between 3 and 32 drives. If a drive fails, Windows 2000 and Windows XP use the parity information in the stripe to reconstruct data, allowing the system to function. In addition, it still benefits from the performance offered by striping. See table 21.14.

When a hard disk fails in a RAID-5 volume, you repair or replace the failed hard drive, right-click the unallocated disk space that is the same size or larger than the other members of the RAID-5 volume, and select the Regenerate the Data. Note: Since the volume must be locked to regenerate, all network connections to the volume are lost and it may require a reboot.

21.12 NTFS PERMISSIONS

A primary advantage of NTFS over FAT and FAT32 is that NTFS volumes have the ability to apply NTFS permissions to secure folders and files. By setting the permissions, you specify the level of access for groups and users for accessing files or directories. For example, for one user or group of users, you can specify that they can only read the file; another user or group of users can read and write to the file while others have no access. No matter if you are logged on locally at the computer or accessing a computer through the network, NTFS permissions always apply.

The folder and file NTFS permissions (also known as special permissions) are listed in the following tables. To simplify the task of administration, the permissions have been logically grouped into the standard folder and file NTFS permissions as shown in tables 21.15 and 21.16. The standard folder permissions include Full Control, Modify, Read & Execute, List Folder Contents, and Read and Write. The standard file permissions include Full Control, Modify, Read & Execute, Read, and Write. The folder permissions are shown in tables 21.15 and table 21.16, while the file permissions are shown in tables 21.17 and 21.18.

The NTFS permissions that are granted are stored in an **access control list (ACL)** with every file and folder on an NTFS volume. The ACL contain an **access control entry (ACE)** for each user account and group that have been granted access for the file or folder as well as the permissions granted to each user and group.

To assign NTFS permissions you would right-click a drive, folder, and file (using My Computer or Windows Explorer), select the Properties option, and click on the Security tab. To assign the special permissions, click on the Advanced button within the Security tab and then click on the View Edit/ button. See figure 21.44.

Permissions are given to a folder or file as explicit permission and inherited permissions. **Explicit permissions** are those that are granted directly to the folder or file. Some of these permissions are granted automatically such as when a file or folder is created while others have to be assigned manually.

To explicitly grant a permission to a folder or file, you would select the permission by putting a check in the respective check box. To remove an explicit permission, deselect the permission to remove

Table 21.15 Standard NTFS Folder Permissions

NTFS Folder Permission	Type of Access
Read	Allows the user to display the file's data, attributes, owner, and permissions.
Write	Allows the user to create new files and subfolders within the folder, write to the file, append the file, read and change folder attributes, and view ownership.
List Folder Contents	Allows the user to see the names of folders and subfolders.
Read & Execute	Allows the user to display the folder's contents and display the data, attributes, owner, and permissions for files within the folder, and to execute files within the folder. In addition, it allows the user to navigate a folder to reach other files and folders, even if the user does not have permissions for these folders.
Modify	Allows the user to read files, execute files, write and modify files, create folders and subfolders, delete subfolders and files, and change attributes of subfolders and files.
Full Control	Allows the user to read files, execute files, write and modify files, create folders and subfolders, delete subfolders and files, change attributes of subfolders and files, change permissions, and take ownership of files.

NOTE: Groups or users granted Full Control for a folder can delete files and subfolders within that folder regardless of the permission protecting the files and subfolders.

Table 21.16 NTFS Folder Permissions

Special Permission	Full Control	Modify	Read & Execute	List Folder Contents	Read	Write
Traverse Folder/Execute File	x	x	x	x		
List Folder/Read Data	x	x	x	x	x	
Read Attributes	x	x	x	x	x	
Read Extended Attributes	x	x	x	x	x	
Create Files/Write Data	x	x				x
Create Folders/Append Data	x	x				x
Write Attributes	x	x				x
Write Extended Attributes	x	x				x
Delete Subfolders and Files	x					
Delete	x	x				
Read Permission	x	x	x	x	x	x
Change Permissions	x					
Take Ownership	x					
Synchronize	x	x	x	x	x	x

NOTE: Although List Folder Contents and Read & Execute appear to have the same permissions, these permissions are inherited differently. List Folder Contents is inherited by folders but not files, and it should appear only when you view folder permissions. Read & Execute is inherited by both files and folders and is always present when you view file or folder permissions.

Table 21.17 Standard NTFS File Permissions

NTFS File Permission	Type of Access
Read	Allows the user to display the file's data, attributes, owner, and permissions.
Write	Allows the user to write to the file, append to the file, overwrite the file, change file attributes, and view file ownership and permissions.
Read & Execute	Allows the user to display the data, attributes, owner, and permissions for the file and to execute the file.
Modify	Allows the user to read files, execute files, write and modify files, delete files, and change attributes of file.
Full Control	Allows the user to read files, execute files, write and modify and delete files, change attributes of files, change permissions, and take ownership of files.

NOTE: Groups or users granted Full Control for a folder can delete files and subfolders within that folder regardless of the permissions protecting the files and subfolders.

Table 21.18 NTFS File Permissions

Special Permission	Full Control	Modify	Read & Execute	Read	Write
Traverse Folder/Execute File	x	x	x		
List Folder/Read Data	x	x	x	x	
Read Attributes	x	x	x	x	
Read Extended Attributes	x	x	x	x	
Create Files/Write Data	x	x			x
Create Folders/Append Data	x	x			x
Write Attributes	x	x			x
Write Extended Attributes	x	x			x
Delete Subfolders and Files	x				
Delete	x	x			
Read Permissions	x	x	x	x	x
Change Permissions	x				
Take Ownership	x				
Synchronize	x	x	x	x	x

the check in the respective check box. To remove a user or group from being assigned explicit permissions, click to highlight the user, and click on the Remove button.

Since a user can be a member of several groups, it is possible for the user to have several sets of explicit permissions to a folder or file. When this happens, the permissions are added together to form the **effective permissions.** The effective permissions are the actual permissions when logging in and accessing a file or folder. They consist of explicit permissions plus any inherited permissions. Inherited permissions will be discussed later.

Figure 21.44 NTFS Permissions

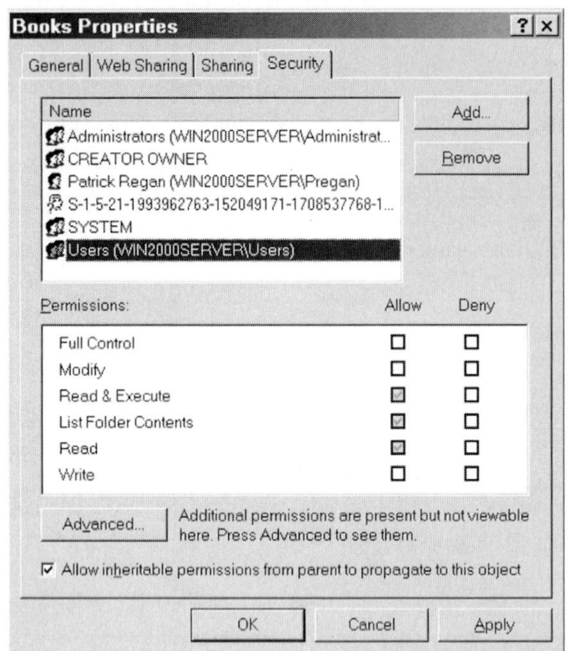

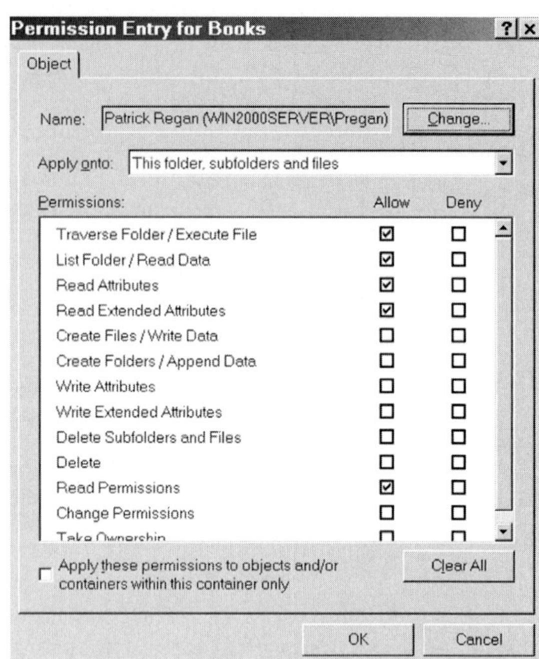

NTFS file permissions override folder permissions. Therefore, if a user has access to a file, the user will still be able to gain access to a file even if he or she does not have access to the folder containing the file. Of course, since the user doesn't have access to the folder, the user cannot navigate or browse through the folder to get to the file. Therefore, a user would have to use the universal naming convention (UNC) or local path to open the file.

When you set permissions to a folder (explicit permissions), the files and subfolders created in the folder inherit these permissions (**inherited permissions**). In other words, the permissions flow down from the folder into the subfolders and files, indirectly giving permissions to a user or group. Inherited permissions ease the task of managing permissions and ensure consistency of permissions among the subfolders and files within the folder.

When viewing the permissions, the permissions will be checked, cleared (unchecked), or shaded. If the permission is checked, the permission was explicitly assigned to the folder or file. If the permission is clear, the user or group does not have that permission explicitly granted to the folder or file. Note: A user may still obtain permission through a group permission or a group may still obtain permission through another group. If the check box is shaded, the permission was granted through inheritance from a parent folder.

The Effective Permissions tab contains information that is calculated from the existing permissions entries. Therefore, the information that appears on that page is read-only and does not support the change of a user's permissions if you select or clear permission check boxes. Manage shared files and folders by using Computer Management.

To view effective permissions on files and folders, follow these steps:

1. Click Start, select Programs, select Accessories, and then click Windows Explorer.
2. Locate the file or folder for which you want to view effective permissions.
3. Right-click the file or folder, click Properties, and then click the Security tab.
4. Click Advanced, and then click the Effective Permissions tab.
5. Click Select.
6. In the Name box, type the name of a user or group, and then click OK. The check boxes that are selected indicate the effective permissions of the user or group for that file or folder.

With the Computer Management tool, you can manage and view security settings for files and folders.

When you copy and move files and folders from one location to another, you need to understand how the NTFS folder and file permissions are affected. If you copy a file or folder, the new folder and file will automatically acquire the permissions of the drive or folder that the folder and file is being copied to.

If the folder or file is moved within the same volume, the folder or file will remain the same permissions that were already assigned. When the folder or file is moved from one volume to another volume, the folder or file will automatically acquire the permissions of the drive or folder and file is being copied to. An easy way to remember the difference is that when you move a folder or file from within the same volume, the folder and file is not physically moved but the master file table is adjusted to indicate a different folder. When you move a folder or file from one volume to another, it copies the folder or file to the new location and then deletes the old location. Therefore, the moved folder and files are new to the volume and acquire the new permissions.

21.13 PRINTING IN THE WINDOWS NT FAMILY

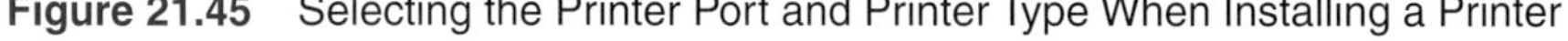

Because Windows NT, Windows 2000, and Windows XP are designed for a network environment, printing is more complex than with Windows 9X. First, to Windows NT family systems, a printer is not a physical device. It is a program that controls one or more physical printers. The physical printer is called a print device. Printing drivers and a spooler are still present, but in Windows, they are integrated into the "printer" itself. With this arrangement, one printer (remember, it is the program) can support multiple print devices, enabling a system to act as a print server. If one print device goes down, the printer automatically redirects the output to a working printer. The Windows NT family also provides support for nonstandard ports, enabling extra functions for networked printers.

21.13.1 Print Drivers

Today, most printers are plug-and-play, so installing a printer is automatically done when you plug the printer into the computer and load the driver. If the system does not detect the printer or if the printer is not PnP, click the Start button, select the Settings option, and select Printers to open the Printers window. You can also open the Printers window by double-clicking on the Printers applet in the Control Panel.

To actually start the printer installation, double-click the Add Printer applet to start the Add Printer Wizard. See figure 21.45. You may then choose to install a printer plugged directly into your system or a network printer. Network printers are discussed in chapter 25. Some of the newer versions of Windows have added the Automatically Detect and Install My PnP Printer option. If you choose a local printer, Windows will then give you options to select a port (LPT1, LPT2, LPT3, COM1, COM2 etc.) and the type of printer. You can select the type from the list or use the Have Disk option just as you would for any other device.

Figure 21.45 Selecting the Printer Port and Printer Type When Installing a Printer

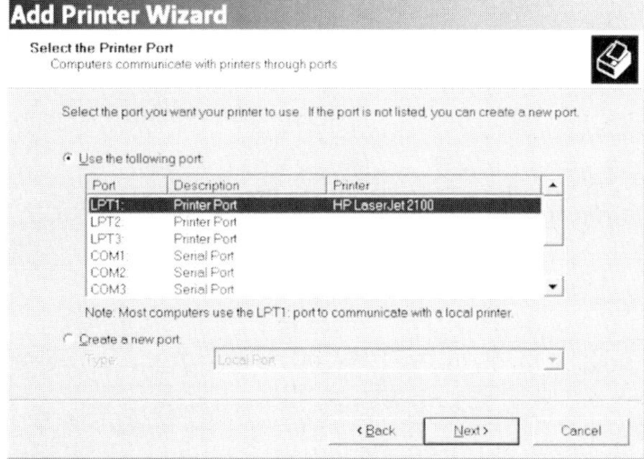

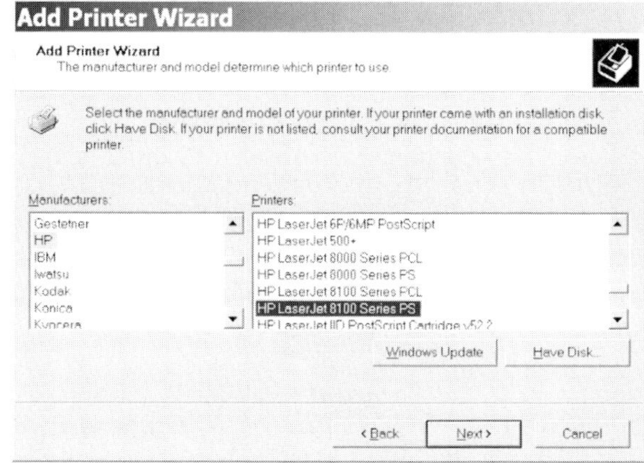

Most problems surrounding printer installations have to do with driver issues. The following are some of the more common problems and their solutions:

Problem:

The user prints a document and the printer prints garbage or strange symbols.

Solution:

You most likely have the wrong print driver, loose cable, faulty cable, or EMI.

Problem:

A user receives an error message and is unable to print because of a corrupted printer driver.

Solution:

Remove and then reinstall the driver. If, during the removal process, the user is prompted to remove extra files left on the system, instruct the user to click Yes.

Problem:

When a user clicks Finish in the Add Printer Wizard, she may receive the error message "Printer driver was not installed. Operation could not be completed."

Solution:

This message occurs if the user installed a Windows 95–based, Windows 98–based, or Windows Millennium Edition–based printer driver onto Windows XP. The Windows 95–based and Windows 98–based printer drivers are not compatible with Windows XP. Use a Windows XP–based printer driver that ships with Windows XP, or comes directly from the printer manufacturer. If a Windows XP–based printer driver is unavailable, try a Windows 2000 Professional–based printer driver.

Problem:

A user has a working printer driver installed and uses System Restore to create a checkpoint to preserve the current configuration. The user then upgrades the driver, or installs a new driver, with files that are in common with the currently installed driver. After the installation, the user cannot print because one of the printer driver files is incompatible with the other drivers that are installed on the computer. The user then restores the computer to the checkpoint that he created before using System Restore, but the printer still does not work.

Solution:

To resolve this problem, open the Printer Properties, and on the Advanced tab, select the last driver that the user installed from the driver list. When the printer or printers are installed, the default printer or the printer that you print to by default has a small checkmark in the corner. If you have multiple printers, you can change the default printer by select the printer's properties and checking Make Default Printer.

When you print in Windows and the print job is still in the spooler, you can manage the individual print jobs. To pause a document, open the PRINTERS folder and double-click the printer you are using to open the print queue. (See figure 21.46.) When you right-click a document you typically can pause the printer job or delete the print job.

Figure 21.46 Managing the Print Queue

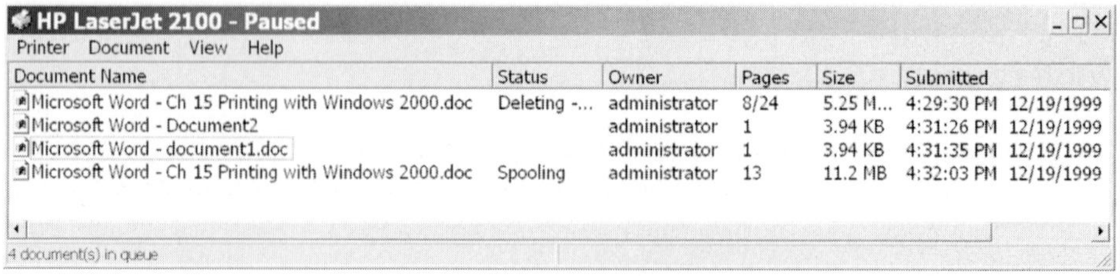

HP LaserJet 2100 - Paused

Printer Document View Help

Document Name	Status	Owner	Pages	Size	Submitted
Microsoft Word - Ch 15 Printing with Windows 2000.doc	Deleting -...	administrator	8/24	5.25 M...	4:29:30 PM 12/19/1999
Microsoft Word - Document2		administrator	1	3.94 KB	4:31:26 PM 12/19/1999
Microsoft Word - document1.doc		administrator	1	3.94 KB	4:31:35 PM 12/19/1999
Microsoft Word - Ch 15 Printing with Windows 2000.doc	Spooling	administrator	13	11.2 MB	4:32:03 PM 12/19/1999

4 document(s) in queue

Table 21.19 Printer Permissions

Printer Permission Capabilities	Print	Manage Documents	Manage Printer
Print documents	X	X	X
Pause, resume, restart, and cancel the user's own document	X	X	X
Connect to a printer	X	X	X
Control job settings for all documents		X	X
Pause, restart, and delete all documents		X	X
Share a printer			X
Change printer properties			X
Delete printers			X
Change printer permissions			X

NOTE: You can also access the printer queue by double-clicking the printer icon in the sytray (if it is present).

Print spoolers can easily overflow or become corrupt due to a lack of disk space, too many print jobs, disk errors, power fluctuations, and so on.

21.13.2 Printer Permissions

Printer permissions control who can use the printer and which print tasks a user can do. For example, if you have a very expensive color printer, you might want only a handful of people to have access to it. For all printers, you will need someone to be able to delete print jobs, change the printer properties, or change the printer permissions. Therefore, after you have added and shared a printer, you will need to assign the appropriate rights to the users.

There are three levels of printer permissions: Print, Manage Documents, and Manage Printer. By default, all users have the Print permission as members of the Everyone group. In addition, administrators, print operators, and server operators on a domain controller have Manage Printer permission. Last, the owner of the document has Manage Documents permission for that document only. Table 21.19 lists the capabilities of the different permission levels.

To set or remove permissions for a printer:

1. Open the PRINTERS folder.
2. Right-click the shared printer for which you want to set permissions and click the Properties option.
3. Select the Security tab.
4. To change permissions from an existing user or group, click the name of the user or group and select and deselect the appropriate rights. To add a user or group, click on the Add button, select the user or group, and click the OK button.

   NOTE: To remove an existing user or group, click the name of the user or group and then click the Remove button.

5. In the Permissions section, click Allow or Deny for each permission that you want to allow or deny. See figure 21.47.

21.13.3 Managing the Printer Spooler

While the print jobs are stored in the spooler, they are written to a spool (SPL) file. Administrative information, such as user name, document name, and data type, are stored in a shadow (SHD) file. This way, if a power failure or other disaster occurs before all jobs in the queue are printed, the print jobs are protected.

Figure 21.47 Printer Permissions

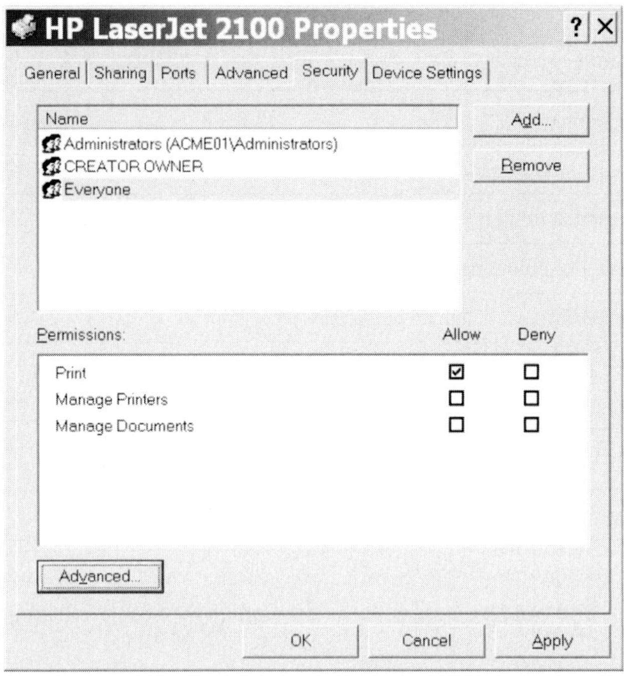

There may be instances, such as a lack of sufficient storage space on drive C, when it is desirable to move the spooler location. By default, the spooler files are written to the *%systemroot%*\SYSTEM32\SPOOL\PRINTERS folder. If the hard disk partition containing Windows 2000 does not have enough space for these files, you can change the location of the folder. To change the location of the default spool folder for all printers on a server:

1. In the Printers dialog box, on the File menu, click Server Properties.
2. In the Print Server Properties dialog box, click the Advanced tab.
3. Type the path and name for the new default spool folder, and then click OK.
4. The change is effective immediately. You do not need to restart your system.

NOTE: Do not attempt to spool to a root (such as C:\). This causes the files to revert to the old default.

At times, it may be necessary to reset the print spooler. For example, if documents become stuck in the queue and you are unable to remove or cancel them, you may need to clear them out by resetting the spooler. To reset the spooler:

1. Click Start, and then Run.
2. Type *SERVICES.MSC* and then click OK.
3. Right-click the Print Spooler service and select Restart.

The Windows registry entry for the default printer may become corrupted and cause print jobs to be unable to print. To reset the default printer entry in the registry, choose another printer as the default printer, and then choose the original printer again as the default printer.

21.14 THE REGISTRY AND REGISTRY EDITOR

The **registry** is a central, secure database in which the Windows NT family stores all hardware configuration information, software configuration information, and system security policy. Components that use the registry include the Windows NT kernel, device drivers, setup programs, NTDETECT.COM, hardware profiles, and user profiles.

The data kept in the registry is added and modified by a variety of system modules that start during boot-up and are modified by various configuration tools such as the Control Panel, Windows Setup

Figure 21.48 The Registry Editor for Windows 2000 (REGEDIT.EXE)

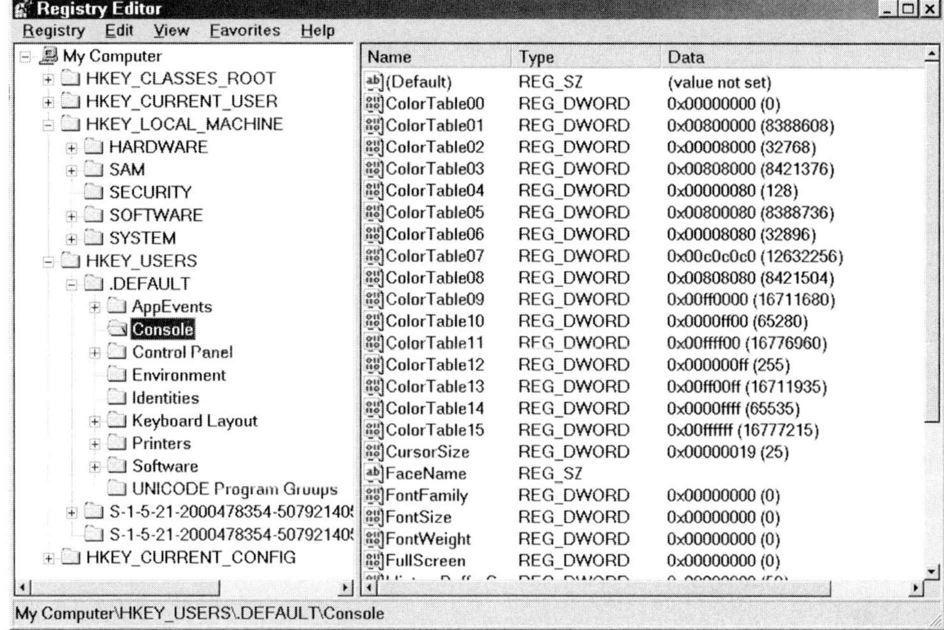

program, User Manager, adding or removing a hardware device, adding or removing a printer, and other administrative utilities.

In addition, data is added and modified when installing software that uses a single application programming interface (API). You can think of API as a set of standard commands that can be used by any software package to access the registry. For example, a software package can find out what type of hardware (including type of processor, resolution and number of colors of the video system, and the IRQ and DMA settings for a device), and the version of drivers and other software modules.

Since the Windows NT family is a multiuser system, it records and preserves security and graphical desktop information on an individual basis. Therefore, it contains a permanent record of per-user, per-application, per-machine configuration information. To keep the entire system secure, the key or setting within the registry is protected with an access control list (ACL), which allows selected users to modify the contents of the registry and grant to others read-only access to that data.

21.14.1 Registry Editor

If the need arises to view or change the registry, you can use the **Registry Editor (REGEDIT.EXE** or **REGEDT32.EXE)** utilities. REGEDT32.EXE is automatically installed in the WINNT\SYSTEM32 folder. REGEDIT.EXE is automatically installed in the WINNT folder. REGEDIT.EXE is easier to use because of its Explorer-style interface. See figure 21.48. REGEDT32.EXE is the Windows NT 4.0 version of the Registry Editor that provides access to Windows 2000/Windows XP security permissions and auditing.

Once in a while, you may have the need to view or edit the registry to add or change a value that cannot be changed in the Control Panel or other utility or to add, view, and change hardware settings that cannot be done with Device Manager. You should make changes only when following directions in a magazine article, a book, a manual, or from a support person. If you make the wrong changes, Windows 2000/Windows XP may not run properly or may not boot at all.

21.14.2 Structure of the Registry

The registry is organized in a hierarchical structure. The registry is first divided into five **subtrees.** See table 21.20. Subtrees have names that begin with the string HKEY, which stands for **"Handle to a Key."** A subtree is similar to a root directory of a disk.

Table 21.20 Windows NT Family Registry Subtrees

Subtree	Description
HKEY_CLASSES_ROOT	Contains file associations and OLE information.
HKEY_CURRENT_USER	Contains settings for applications, desktop configurations, and user preferences for the user currently logged on. The information retrieves a copy of each user account used to log on to the computer from the NTUSER.DAT file and stores it in the *systemroot*\PROFILES\username key. This subkey points to the same data contained in HKEY_USERS\SID_currently_logged_ on_user. Note: This subtree takes precedence over HKEY_LOCAL_ MACHINE for duplicated values.
HKEY_LOCAL_MACHINE	Contains information about the type of hardware installed, drivers, and other system settings. Information includes the bus type, system memory, device drivers, and startup control data. The data in this subtree remains constant regardless of the user.
HKEY_USERS	Contains information about all users who log on to the computer, including the DEFAULT generic user settings. The DEFAULT user is used as a template for any new users.
HKEY_CURRENT_CONFIG	Contains information about the current running hardware configuration. This information is used to configure settings such as which device drivers to load and the display resolution to use. This subtree is part of the HKEY_LOCAL_MACHINE subtree and maps to HKEY_LOCAL_ MACHINE\SYSTEM\CurrentControlSet\Hardware Profiles\Current.

Table 21.21 Windows NT Family Registry Data Types

Data Type	Description
REG_DWORD	Data represented by a number that is 4 bytes (double word) long. Many parameters for device drivers and services are this type and are displayed in Registry Editor in binary, hexadecimal, or decimal format.
REG_SZ	A fixed-length text string.
REG_EXPAND_SZ	A variable-length data string. This data type includes variables that are resolved when a program or service uses the data.
REG_BINARY	Raw binary data represented as a string of hexadecimal digits. Windows 2000 interprets every two hexadecimal digits as a byte value.
REG_MULTI_SZ	A multiple string. Values that contain lists or multiple values in a form that people can read are usually this type. Entries are separated by spaces, commas, or other marks.
REG_FUL_RESOURCE DESCRIPTOR	Stores a resource list for hardware components or drivers. You cannot add or modify any entries with this data type.

Of the different subtrees, the two main subtrees are the HKEY_LOCAL_MACHINE and the HKEY_USERS. The HKEY_LOCAL_MACHINE contains information about the type of hardware installed, drivers, and other system settings. The HKEY_USERS contains information about all users who log on to the computer including the DEFAULT generic user settings. The DEFAULT user is used as a template for any new users.

The root keys are then divided into **subkeys,** which may contain other subkeys. You can think of the subkeys as folders within the subtree.

Within the subkey, you will find a value entry that consists of three parts: the name of the value, the data type of the value, and the value itself. Data types describe the format of the data. The data types of the values are shown in table 21.21.

Table 21.22 HKEY_LOCAL_MACHINE Subkeys

Subkey	Description
HARDWARE	Contains type and state of physical devices attached to the computer. Much of this information is collected and built during boot-up. Therefore, it does not point to a specific file on a disk.
SAM	The directory database for the computer. The SAM subkey points to the SAM and SAM.LOG files in the systemroot\SYSTEM32\CONFIG directory.
SECURITY	The security information for the local computer. It maps to the SECURITY and SECURITY.LOG files in the systemroot\SYSTEM32\CONMFIG directory. Applications query information by using security APIs.
SOFTWARE	Information about the local computer software that covers all users. It points to the SOFTWARE and SOFTWARE.LOG files in the systemroot\SYSTEM32\CONFIG directory. It also contains file association and OLE information.
SYSTEM	Information about system devices and services. When you install or configure device drivers or services, they add or modify information under this hive. The SYSTEM hive maps to the SYSTEM and SYSTEM.LOG files in the systemroot\SYSTEM32\CONFIG directory. The registry keeps a backup of the data in the SYSTEM hive in the SYSTEM.ALT file.

21.14.3 HKEY_LOCAL_MACHINE Subtree

As mentioned earlier, the **HKEY_LOCAL_MACHINE** subtree is one of the two main trees that the other trees are made from. Its structure is similar to the others. It has five subkeys, which are shown in table 21.22. The HARDWARE key contains a detailed description of the installed hardware such as the type of the motherboard, video adapter, SCSI adapters, serial ports, parallel ports, sound cards, network adapters, and so on. Data in the HARDWARE key is volatile and computed at boot time. When your hardware configuration changes, the changes are reflected in the HARDWARE key at the next boot.

The next two keys—SAM, which stands for Security Account Manager, and SECURITY—have no visible information, as they point to security policies and user authentication information. The values in these two keys are created, modified, and removed with either the User Manager or the User Manager for Domains. To keep the Windows 2000/XP secure, the Registry Editor does not display this data.

The SOFTWARE key contains a list of file extensions and associated applications, one key for each application that follows the configuration database registration procedure, and one key for each loaded network driver. The SYSTEM key describes bootable and nonbootable configurations in a group of ControlSet, where each ControlSet represents a unique configuration. Within each ControlSet, two keys describe operating system components and service data for that configuration. This key also records the configuration used to boot the running system (CurrentControlSet), along with any failed configurations and the LastKnownGood configuration. Finally, the Setup key records the command used to install Windows 2000/XP and the boot disk and provides a list of the OEMSETUP files required to install hardware components.

As an example, let's look at the following value:

```
HKEY_LOCAL_MACHINE\HARDWARE\DESCRIPTION\System\
CentralProcessor\0\~MHz
```

See figure 21.49. Within the HKEY_LOCAL_MACHINE, you will find the HARDWARE subkey. By clicking on the + sign next to the HARDWARE subkey, you will open it up to show the DESCRIPTION subkey. In the System subkey, you will find the CentralProcessor subkey and under the CentralProcessor subkey you will find the 0 subkey. In the 0 subkey you will find the ~MHz value, which is shown on the left pane. Next to the ~MHz value, you will find the data type of REG_DWORD which means that we expected 8 hexadecimal digits (4 bytes of information). Lastly, the value is set to 0x000001F5 (hexadecimal), which is equivalent to 501 MHz (decimal).

Figure 21.49 HKEY_LOCAL_MACHINE Values

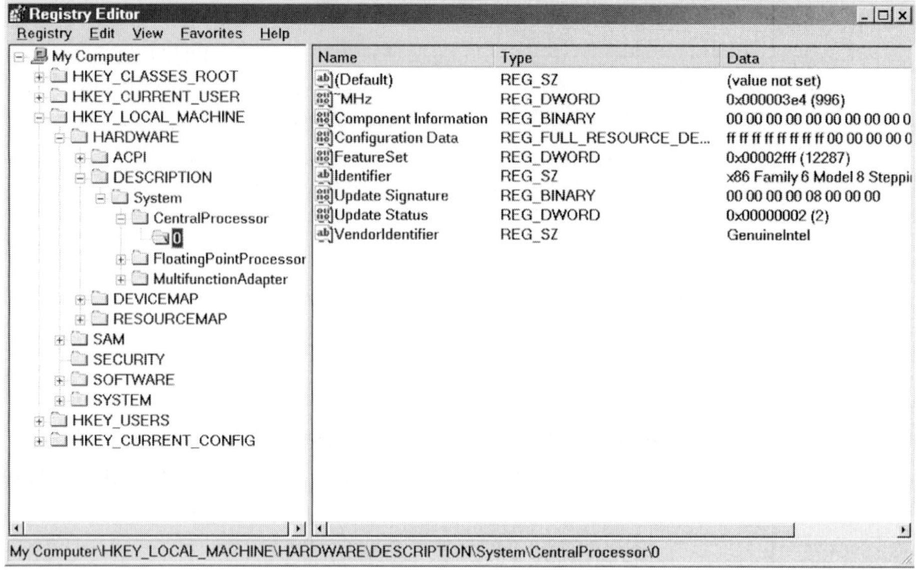

Table 21.23 Windows NT Family Hive

Hive	Hive Support Files
HKEY_LOCAL_MACHINE\SAM	SAM, SAM.LOG, SAM.SAV
HKEY_LOCAL_MACHINE\Security	SECURITY, SECURITY.LOG, SECURITY.SAV
HKEY_LOCAL_MACHINE\Software	SOFTWARE, SOFTWARE.LOG, SOFTWARE.SAV
HKEY_LOCAL_MACHINE\System	SYSTEM, SYSTEM.ALT, SYSTEM.LOG, SYSTEM.SAV
HKEY_CURRENT_CONFIG	SYSTEM, SYSTEM.ALT, SYSTEM.LOG, SYSTEM.SAV
HKEY_USERS\DEFAULT	DEFAULT, DEFAULT.LOG, DEFAULT.SAV
HKEY_CURRENT_USER	NTUSER.DAT, NTUSER.DAT.LOG

21.14.4 Hives

The registry stores most of its information in sets of files called hives. A **hive** is a discrete body of keys, subkeys, and values. Each hive has a corresponding registry file and LOG file located in the WINNT\SYSTEM32\CONFIG folder. Windows 2000/Windows XP uses the LOG file to record changes and ensure the integrity of the registry. While you work with the registry, you view and edit subtrees and their contents. When you back up and restore the registry, you are working with hives.

Files without extensions contain a copy of the hive. Files with the LOG extension contain a record of any changes to the hive. The files with the SAV extension contain copies of the hives at the end of Setup's text mode step. The ALT file contains the Last Known Good information, in case anything happens to the system hive. The DAT files contain user profile information. Table 21.23 lists the Windows NT family hives.

Under normal circumstances, your system will reference the files without extensions. When writing changes to a hive file, the system will note the changes in the hive's log, so that it can cancel any unfinished changes in case the hive's updating process is interrupted. If something happens to the critical system hive, the ALT version replaces it during the boot process. The ALT then makes itself the new system hive and creates another backup ALT file.

By default, most hive files are stored in the %systemroot%\SYSTEM32\CONFIG folder. The *%systemroot%* indicates the name of the directory that is holding the Windows files. By default, Windows NT family installs to the WINNT folder. The location of user profile information for each user of a computer, including the NTUSER.DAT and NTUSER.DAT.LOG, may depend on whether the installation of the operating system was a fresh installation or whether it was installed as an upgrade from Windows 9X, or Windows NT. In fresh installations and upgrades from Windows 9X, the NTUSER.DAT and NTUSER.DAT.LOG files are stored in the %systemdrive%:\DOCUMENT AND SETTINGS*Username* folder. In installations that are upgrades from Windows NT, the NTUSER.DAT and NTUSER.DAT.LOG files are stored in the *%systemroot%*\PROFILES*Username* folder.

21.14.5 Troubleshooting Registry Problems

A corrupt or damaged registry can manifest itself in a number of ways: You may notice that files are missing or that components are not behaving as expected, you may receive an error message or a stop error, or you may even be unable to start the operating system.

If you suspect a problem with the registry, you can try the following:

- If you have kept a record of the changes that you have made to the registry, try undoing the most recent change.
- If you know which components have been affected, determine what the correct registry settings are for those components.
- Try using the last known good configuration for your computer.
- If you have a backup copy of the registry (as part of your backup of System State data) and can open Windows Backup, try to restore your registry settings. If you cannot start Windows, try repairing the operating system with your Emergency Repair Disk (ERD).

Of course, in a worst-case scenario, you must then reinstall Windows and all of its applications. If you have backed up your entire system, this job will be much easier and quicker.

21.15 EMERGENCY REPAIR

If you have problems where Windows 2000/XP cannot load or start, there are several tools that you can use. They are the Advanced Boot menu, Windows Recovery Console, and Emergency Repair Disk (also available in Windows NT).

21.15.1 Windows Startup Floppy Disk

After installing and configuring Windows, you should make a Windows startup floppy disk. A startup floppy disk is used to access a drive with a faulty startup sequence, such as a corrupted boot sector, corrupted MBR, a virus infection, missing or corrupt NTLDR or NTDETECT.COM, or an incorrect NTBOOTDD.SYS file. In addition, the disk can be used to start a computer after the primary disk of a mirrored volume. Note: A mirrored volume is volumes or partitions located on two different hard drives with duplicate information. If one hard drive fails, the computer does not go down because the information can be read from the second disk. The startup disk cannot be used for incorrect or corrupted device drivers or startup problems that occur after NTLDR.

To create a boot disk, do the following:

1. Format a disk on a computer running Windows NT, 2000, or XP. Note that since DOS and Windows 9X use a different format and boot section, you must format with Windows NT, 2000, or XP.
2. For an Intel machine, save NTLDR, NTDETECT.COM, NTBOOTDD.SYS (if you have a SCSI controller without a SCSI BIOS), and BOOT.INI from the system partition to the floppy disk.
3. Test the boot files.

NOTE: If you are using a mirrored volume, you should have two startup floppy disks. One of the ARC paths points to the first disk and the second ARC path points to the second disk. Therefore, after creating the second disk, you will need to modify the BOOT.INI file manually using a text editor such as EDIT or Notepad.

21.15.2 Recovery Console

If your computer doesn't boot at all for Windows 2000 or Windows XP, even in safe mode, the best thing to use is the **Recovery Console.** The Recovery Console provides a command-line interface that will let you repair system problems using a limited set of command-line commands, including enabling or disabling services, repairing a corrupted master boot record, or read and write data on a local drive (FAT, FAT32, or NTFS). Note: Since the Recovery Console is a very powerful tool, it should only be used by advanced users who have a thorough knowledge of Windows 2000 or Windows XP. In addition, you must be an administrator to use the Recovery Console.

There are two ways to start the Recovery Console. You can run the Recovery Console from your Windows 2000/Windows XP Setup disks or from the Windows 2000/Windows XP Professional CD, or you can install the Recovery Console on your computer to make it available in case you are unable to restart Windows.

To start the computer and use the Recovery Console:

1. Insert the Windows Setup compact disk (CD), or the first floppy disk you created from the CD, in the appropriate drive. Of course, if you cannot boot from the CD drive, you must use a floppy disk. Restart the computer. If you are using floppy disks, you will be asked to switch disks.
2. When the text-based part of Setup begins, follow the prompts and choose the repair or recover option by pressing R. When prompted, choose the Recovery Console by pressing C. Again, if you are using floppy disks, you will be asked to switch disks.
3. If you have a dual-boot or multiple-boot system, choose the Windows 2000/XP installation that you need to access from the Recovery Console.
4. When prompted, type the Administrator password.
5. At the system prompt, type the Recovery Console commands.
6. To exit the Recovery Console and restart the computer, type *EXIT.*

To install the Recovery Console as a startup menu option:

1. Insert the Windows Setup CD into your CD-ROM drive.
2. Click No when prompted to upgrade to Windows.
3. At the command prompt, switch to your CD-ROM drive, and then type the following: *\I386\WINNT32.EXE /CMDCONS.*
4. When it asks if you want to install the Recovery Console, click on the Yes button.
5. Click OK when the Setup is complete.
6. To run the Recovery Console, restart your computer and select the Recovery Console option from the Boot menu.

To get a list of the commands that are available in the Recovery Console, you just have to type in help while in the Recovery Console. See table 21.24. For help about a specific command, type in HELP *commandname.*

For example, to restore a boot sector that may have been infected by a virus, use the FIXBOOT command. If Windows will not boot into the graphical user interface, you can use the Recovery Console to use copy, rename, or replace operating system files and folders, enable or disable services and devices, and add or remove partitions from starting when you next start your computer. You can also use the EXPAND command to retrieve files inside a compressed file such as a CAB file.

21.15.3 NTBackup

To start the backup program called NTBackup for Windows 2000 and Windows XP, click on the Start button, select the Programs option, select the Accessories option, select the System Tools option, and select Backup. The backup program can be used to back up and restore files and to create an emergency repair disk. The Welcome tab has buttons to start Backup, Restore, and Emergency Repair Disk Wizards. See figure 21.50

To back up or restore files, you must be an administrator or a member of the backup operator group. To back up files to a file or a tape:

1. Open the Backup program and click on the Backup tab.
2. Open the Job menu and click New.

Table 21.24 List of Commands Used in the Recovery Console

Command	Description
ATTRIB	Changes or displays attributes of files or directories
CD	Changes directory
CHKDSK	Executes a consistency check of the specified disk
CLS	Clears the screen
COPY	Copies a file
DEL	Deletes a file
DIR	Lists directory contents
DISKPART	Adds and deletes partitions
ENABLE	Starts or enables a system service or a device driver
DISABLE	Stops or disables a system service or device driver
EXTRACT	Extracts a file from a compressed file
FIXBOOT	Writes a new partition boot sector onto the system partition
FIXMRB	Repairs the master boot record of the partition boot sector
FORMAT	Formats a disk
LISTSVC	Lists the services and device drivers available on the computer
LOGON	Logs on to a Windows 2000 computer
MAP	Displays the drive letter mappings
MD	Creates a directory
TYPE	Displays a text file
RMDIR	Deletes a directory
REPAIR	Updates an installation with files with the Windows 2000 installation CD
REN	Renames a file
SYSTEMROOT	Changes to the installation system root directory (typically \WINNT)

3. Select the files and folders that you want to back up by clicking the box to the left of a file or folder. Note: You can back up files on other computers by using My Network Places located at the bottom of the tree. See figure 21.51.
4. In Backup destination, select a tape device if you want to back up to a tape drive, or the File option if you want to back up to a file. Note: If you do not have a tape device installed on your computer, File is selected by default.
5. In Backup media or file name, select the tape that you want to use or the path and file name. Note: Backup files have a BKF file name extension.
6. Open the Tools menu and select the Options menu to select the backup and type and log file type.
7. Click on the Start Backup button.
8. After making any changes to the Backup Job Information dialog box, click on the Start Backup button.
9. If you want to set data verification or hardware compression or change the backup type, you could click on the Advance button. Click on the OK button to close the Advanced Backup Options.
10. Click on the Start Backup button.

Figure 21.50 Windows 2000 Backup and Recovery Tools Welcome Screen

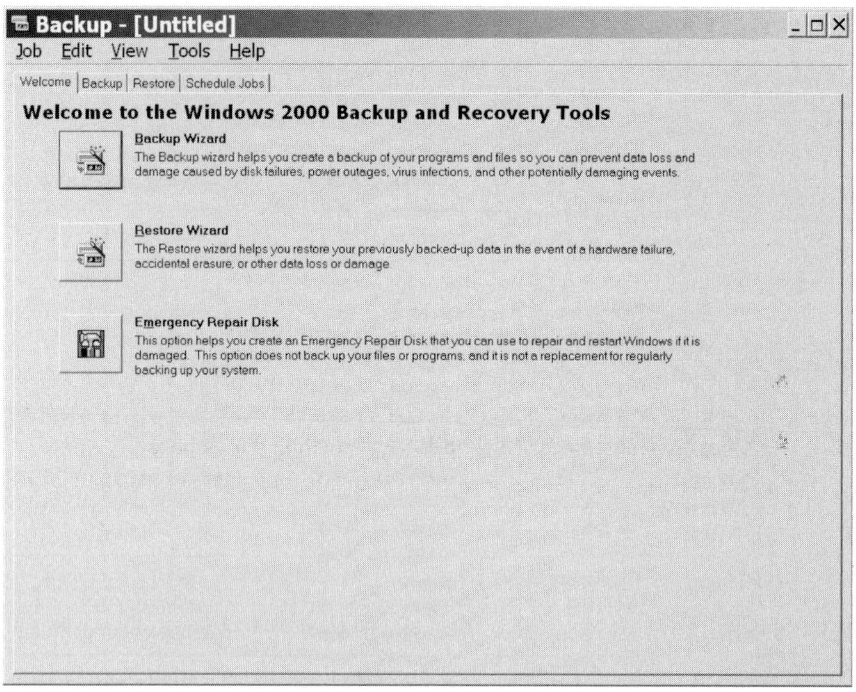

Figure 21.51 Using the Windows 2000 Backup Program

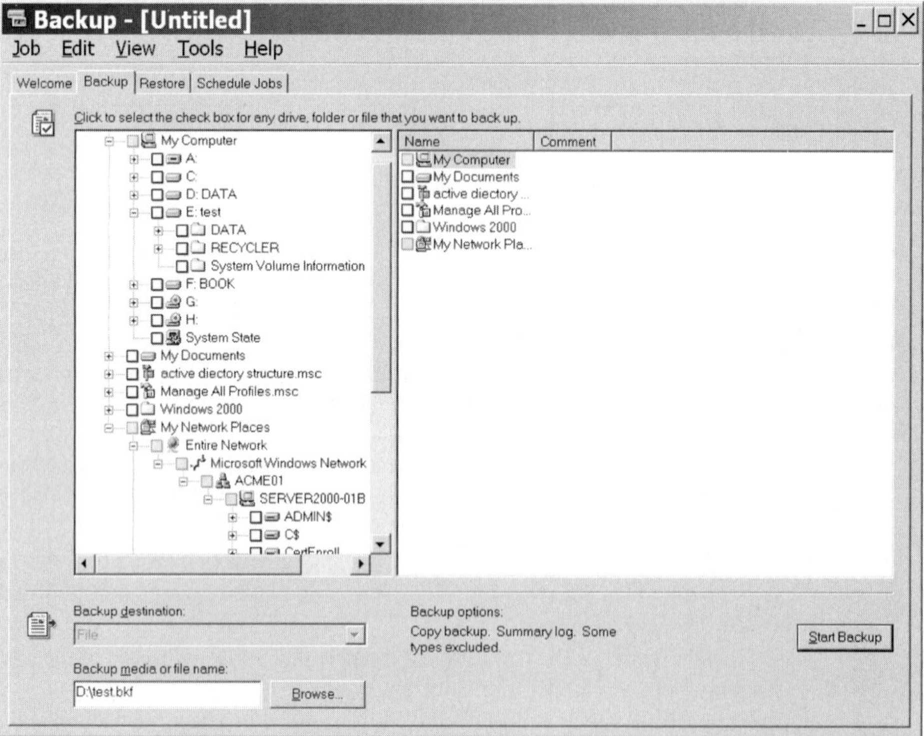

If you are attempting a backup and the Backup program indicates that there is no unused media available, you may have to use the Removable Storage console to add your tape to the Backup media pool. You can access the Removable Storage console by loading the Computer Management console located under Administrative Tools.

Since you need to do backup on a regular basis, and the best time to do a backup is when the network traffic is slow, you can schedule the backup to occur automatically. To schedule a backup:

1. Start the Backup program.
2. Using the Backup tab, open the Job menu and select the New option.
3. Select the files and folders that you want to back up by clicking the box to the left of a file or folder under Click to select the check box for any drive, folder or file that you want to back up.
4. In Backup destination, select File or a tape device and then save the file and folder selections by clicking the Job menu and then Save Selections.
5. In Backup media or file name, type a path and file name for the backup file or select tape.
6. If you want to select any backup options, open the Tools menu and select the Options menu. Click OK to close the Options dialog box.
7. Click Start Backup and make any changes you want to the Backup Job Information dialog box.
8. If you want to set advanced backup options such as data verification or hardware compression, click the Advanced button. To close the advanced backup options, click the OK button.
9. Click Schedule in the Backup Job Information dialog box.
10. In the Set Account Information dialog box, enter the user name and password that you want the schedule backup to run under.
11. In the Scheduled Job Options dialog box, in Job name, type a name for the scheduled backup job and then click Properties to set the data, time, and frequency parameters for the scheduled backup. When you have finished, click on the OK button twice.

NOTE: If you are scheduling a tape backup, you may have to use the removable storage option to make sure that your tape is available in the backup media pool. In addition, you must have the Task Scheduler service running before you can schedule a backup. You can change the settings of a scheduled backup job or delete the job after you schedule it by clicking on the Schedule Jobs tab and clicking on the job. See figure 21.52

Figure 21.52 Scheduling Backup Jobs

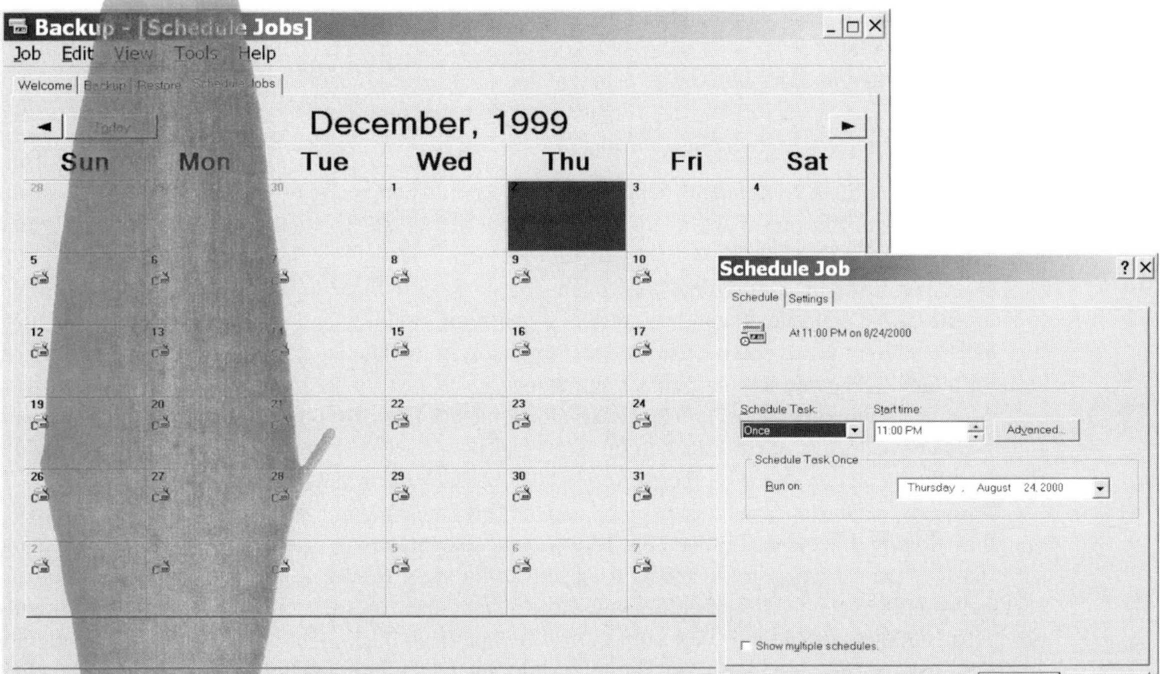

Figure 21.53 Backing Up the System State

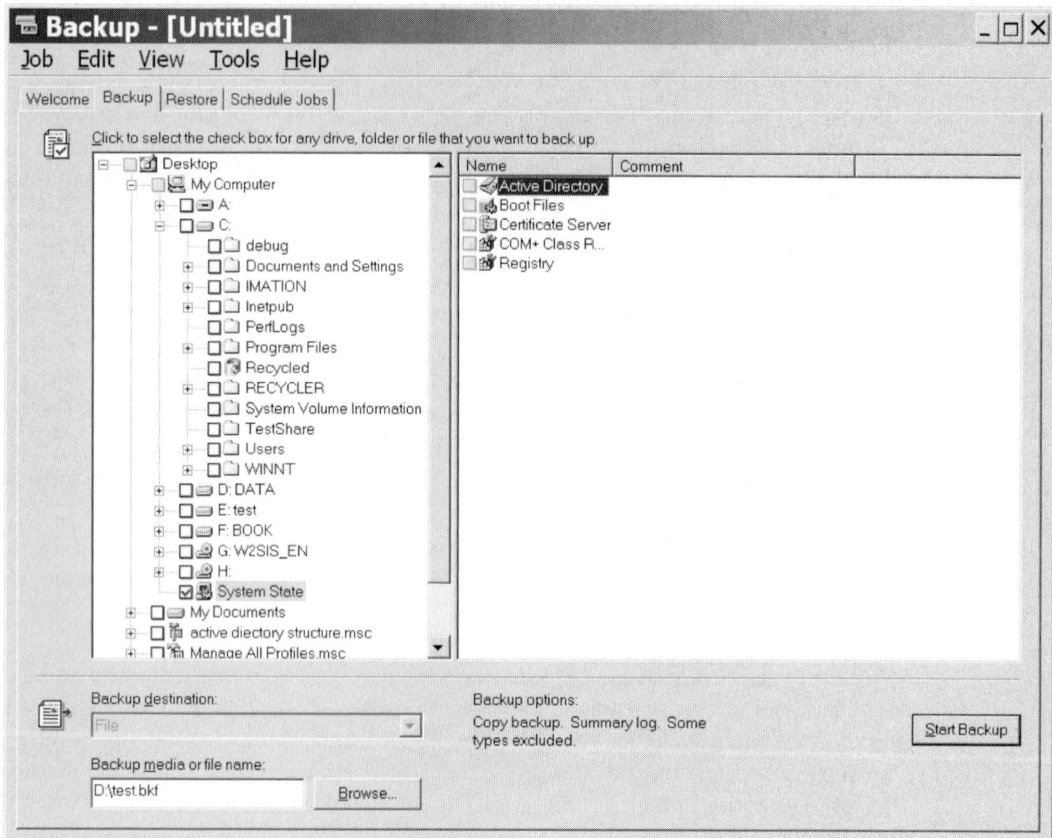

The **System State** data is a collection of system-specific data that can be backed up and restored. For Windows 2000 XP, it includes:

- Registry
- COM+ Class Registration database
- System boot files
- Certificate Services database on servers that operate as a certificate server
- Active Directory directory services database on domain controller
- SYSVOL directory on domain controllers

Since the System State components depend on each other, when you choose to back up or restore the System State data, you must back up all of the System State data. To back up the System State, put a check in the System State check box located after all local drive letters. See figure 21.53.

When you restore the individual components of the System State components, you can restore the registry files, SYSVOL directory files, cluster database information, and system boot files to an alternate location. Note: When you back up and restore the System State data, you can only back up and restore on a local computer, not on remote computers.

When performing backups, typically a catalog is made. The **catalog** is a summary of the files and folders that have been saved in a backup set. The on-disk catalog is stored on the local disk drive while the on-media catalog is stored on the backup storage media such as the backup tapes.

If you have all the tapes in the backup set and the tapes are not damaged or corrupted, you can speed up the cataloging process if you open the Tools menu, select Options, click the General tab, and make sure the Use the catalogs on the media to speed up building restore catalogs on disk check box is checked. See figure 21.54. However, if you want to restore data from several tapes and the tape with the on-media catalog is missing, or you want to restore data from media that is damaged, you should not select this option. Instead, the Backup program scans the backup set and builds an online disk catalog. Unfortunately, if your backup set is large enough, this could take several hours.

Figure 21.54 Windows 2000 Backup's General Options

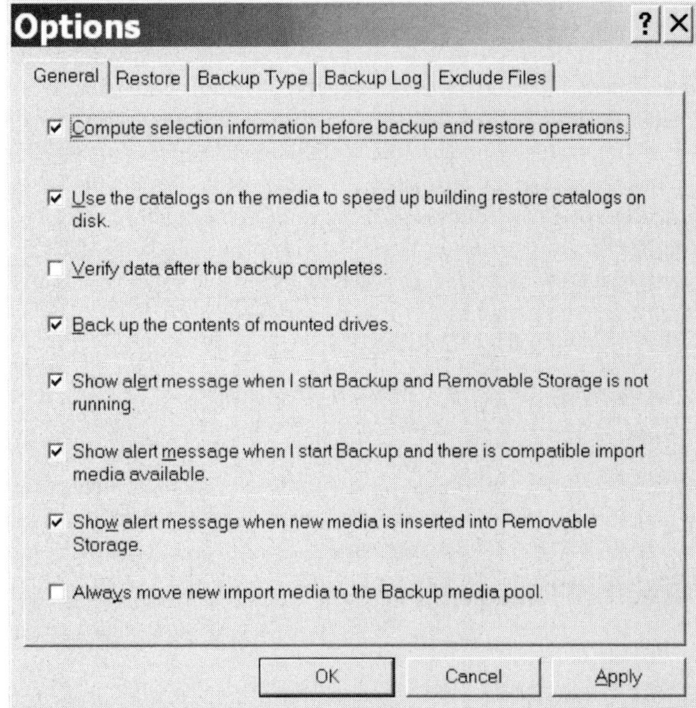

When a Windows computer fails and you lose all information, you must first correct any hardware problems and then reinstall Windows. Much like the backup, you can restore the computer using the Restore Wizard or the Restore tab, both of which are located in the Backup program. The restore process will reload the Windows operating system, the Active Directory, including database and registry settings, and any other services that you have loaded.

If you have other domain controllers, the domain controller would have replicas of the Active Directory, and if you had distributed directories (file replication), the Active Directory data and replicated directories would automatically get updated by the other servers.

One nice thing about using today's backup programs is that you can restore individual files or directories. For example, if someone accidentally deleted a file or a file has become corrupted, you can then restore that file without overwriting the other files.

To restore files:

1. Open the Backup program.
2. Click on the Restore tab.
3. Click to select the drive, folder, or file that you want to restore.
4. In the Restore Files to text box, select the location that the files will be restored:
   Original location
   Alternate location
   Single folder
   If you selected Alternate location or Single folder, type a path for the folder under Alternate location, or click the Browse button to find the folder.
5. Click on the Tools menu, click the Options option, click the Restore tab, and you can select:
   Do not replace the file on My Computer
   Replace the file on disk only if the file on disk is older
   Always replace the file on My Computer
6. Click on the Start Restore button.
7. If you want to change any of the advanced restore options, such as restoring security settings, click on the Advanced button. When done, click on the OK button.
8. Click OK to start the restore.

Let's say that you have a Windows 2000 Active Directory object that has been corrupted. Of course, you can choose to restore the System State data. If you have several domain controllers, the other domain controllers would automatically overwrite the newly restore Active Directory database. To overcome this problem, you will have to perform an authorative restore using NTDSUTIL utility so that the Active Directory objects will get replicated to the other domain servers even though the objects are older than the objects that are currently in the Active Directory database. The NTDSUTIL utility can be found on the Windows 2000 installation CD under the \SUPPORT\RESKIT\NETMGMT folder.

Another way to do a backup is by using batch files that uses the NTBACKUP command. The advantage of using batch files is that you can run the batch file quickly if you need to do a quick backup before making any major changes. Different from the NTBACKUP command, you can only back up folders, not individual files. In addition, you cannot use wild cards like you can with the command prompt commands such as the COPY command.

The syntax for the NTBACKUP command is:

```
ntbackup backup [systemstate] "bks file name" /J {"job name"} [/P
{"pool name"}] [/G {"guid name"}] [/T { "tape name"}] [/N {"media
name"}] [/F {"file name"}] [/D {"set description"}] [/DS {"server
name"}] [/IS {"server name"}] [/A] [/V:{yes|no}] [/R:{yes|no}]
[/L:{f|s|n}] [/M {backup type}] [/RS:{yes|no}] [/HC:{on|off}]
```

NTBACKUP Parameters:

systemstate

Specifies that you want to back up the System State data. Note: The backup type will be forced to normal or copy.

bks file name

Specifies the name of the backup selection file (BKS file) to be used for this backup operation. A backup selection file contains information on the files and folders you have selected for backup. You have to create the file using the graphical user interface (GUI) version of Backup.

/J {"*job name*"}

Specifies the job name to be used in the log file.

/P {"*pool name*"}

Specifies the media pool from which you want to use media. If you select this you must not use the following switches: **/A /G /F /T.**

/G {"*guid name*"}

Overwrites or appends to this tape. Do not use this switch in conjunction with **/P.**

/T {"*tape name*"}

Overwrites or appends to this tape. Do not use this switch in conjunction with **/P.**

/N {"*media name*"}

Specifies the new tape name. You must not use **/A** with this switch.

/F {"*file name*"}

Logical disk path and file name. You must not use the following switches with this switch: **/P /G /T.**

/D {"*set description*"}

Specifies a label for each backup set.

/DS {"*server name*"}

Backs up the directory service file for the specified Microsoft Exchange Server.

/IS {"*server name*"}

Backs up the Information Store file for the specified Microsoft Exchange Server.

/A

Performs an append operation. Either **/G** or **/T** must be used in conjunction with this switch. Do not use this switch in conjunction with **/P.**

/V:{yes|no}

Verifies the data after the backup is complete.

/R:{yes|no}
Restricts access to this tape to the owner or members of the administrator group.

/L:{f|s|n}
Specifies the type of log file: **f**=full, **s**=summary, **n**=none (no log file is created)

/M {*backup type*}
Specifies the backup type. It must be one of the following: normal, copy, differential, incremental, or daily.

/RS:{yes|no}
Backs up the Removable Storage database.

/HC:{on|off}
Uses hardware compression, if available, on the tape drive.

Example 21.1:

NTBACKUP BACKUP C:\ /J "JOB1" /A /T "Tape 1" /M COPY

This example will perform a copy backup type called JOB1 of the entire C drive (logical drive). The backup files and folders will be appended (/A) to the tape called TAPE1.

21.15.4 Emergency Repair Disks and Automated System Recovery

The **emergency repair disk (ERD)** is a disk that contains information about your current Windows system settings. You can use this disk to repair your computer if it will not start or if your system files are damaged or erased. See table 21.25.

To create an emergency repair disk for Windows NT, insert an empty, formatted disk in the A drive and execute RDISK.EXE in the SYSTEM32 folder (located in the WINNT folder). Click the Repair Disk button and select Update Repair Info. When the operating finishes, click on the Exit button. This disk will, of course, be good only for the computer that made it. (Note: To create an emergency repair disk that contains the most current Security Account Manager [SAM] database, you must use the /S option with the Repair Disk utility [RDISK].)

To use the emergency repair disk in Windows NT, start the computer from Windows NT Setup disk #1 (setup disks are made during installation or by using WINNT/OX). When requested, insert disk #2. When prompted, select the option to repair by pressing the R key. Setup will then display options to inspect the registry files, inspect the startup environment, verify Windows NT system files, and inspect

Table 21.25 Emergency Repair Disk Options

Inspect Registry Files	You will be prompted for the replacement of each registry file. Any changes to the security and SAM registry hives are lost, and these files will be restored to how they were at system installation. Changes to software and system are restored to the last updates of the emergency repair information.
Inspect Startup Environment	Verifies that Windows is an option in the Operating System Select menu. If it is not listed in the BOOT.INI file, then the emergency repair process adds a Windows option for the next boot image.
Verify Windows System Files	This option identifies and offers to replace files that have been altered from their original state on the Windows CD. This option verifies that the boot files, such as NTLDR and NTOSKRNL.EXE, are present and valid. If you have installed service packs on this machine, check Files on each service pack to see if they have to be reinstalled.
Inspect Boot Sector	Verifies that the primary boot sector still references NTLDR and updates the boot sector if it does not. This is useful if someone uses the MS-DOS SYS.COM utility or anything that destroys the NT boot sector.

the boot sector. You would then clear all sections that you do not want to use and click Continue to perform the selected tasks. After disk #3, you will be prompted for the emergency repair disk. You then remove the disk when prompted and reboot the computer.

To create an emergency repair disk in Windows 2000:

1. Open the Backup program.
2. On the Tools menu, click Create an Emergency Repair Disk. Note that you could also use the Emergency Repair Disk Wizard.
3. Insert a blank formatted floppy disk into the drive. Select the check box if you want a backup copy of the registry copied to the REPAIR folder (highly recommended) and click on the OK button.
4. Click on the OK button when the disk has been created.
5. Label the disk "Emergency Repair Disk" and put it in a safe place.

NOTE: When using the emergency repair disk, it relies on information that has been saved to the *systemroot*\REPAIR folder. Therefore, do not change or delete this folder. In addition, you should recreate the ERD after each service pack, system change, or updated driver.

To use an emergency repair disk for system repairs for Windows 2000:

1. Insert the Windows Setup compact disc (CD), or the first floppy disk you created from the CD, in the appropriate drive.
2. When the text-based part of Setup begins, follow the prompts; choose the repair or recover option by pressing R.
3. When prompted, insert the Windows Setup CD in the appropriate drive.
4. When prompted, choose the emergency repair process by pressing R.
5. When prompted, choose between the following:
   - Manual Repair (press M): This should be used only by advanced users or administrators. Use this option to choose whether you want to repair system files, partition-boot sector problems, or startup environment problems.
   - Fast Repair (press F): This is the easiest option, and does not require input. This option will attempt to repair problems related to system files, the partition boot sector on your system disk, and your startup environment (if you have a dual-boot or multiple-boot system).
6. Follow the instructions on the screen and, when prompted, insert the emergency repair disk in the appropriate drive.
7. During the repair process, missing or corrupted files are replaced with files from the Windows CD or from the SYSTEMROOT\REPAIR folder on the system partition. Note: Follow the instructions on the screen. You might want to write down the names of files that are detected as faulty or incorrect to help you diagnose how the system was damaged.
8. If the repair was successful, allow the process to complete; it will restart the computer. The restarting of the computer indicates that replacement files were successfully copied to the hard disk.

If you have performed the emergency repair process and the computer still does not operate normally, you can use the Windows Setup CD to perform an *in-place upgrade* over the existing installation. This is a last resort before reinstalling the operating system. The time required to complete the following procedure is equal to the time it takes to reinstall the operating system.

To perform an in-place upgrade of Windows 2000:

1. Mount the Windows Setup CD.
2. Press Enter to install a copy of Windows.
3. When you are prompted to repair the existing Windows installation, press R.

Instead of using ERD in Windows XP, you would use the **Automated System Recovery (ASR)** that allows you to recover from a system crash. Automated System Recovery is a two-part system recovery—ASR backup and ASR restore—that will back up essential information such as the System State, system services, and disk configuration. You should create ASR sets on a regular basis as part of an overall plan for system recovery in case of system failure. ASR should be a last resort for system recovery, however, used only after you have exhausted other options such as Safe Mode Boot and Last Known Good Configuration.

NOTE: ASR is not supported in Windows XP Home Edition unless the NTBackup program is installed from the value add folder on the Windows XP Home Edition CD.

The backup portion is accomplished through the ASR Wizard located in Backup. To create an Automated System Recovery set using Backup:

1. Open Backup. Click Start, point to All Programs, point to Accessories, point to System Tools, and then click Backup. The Backup Utility Wizard starts by default, unless it is disabled.
2. Click the Advanced Mode button in the Backup Utility Wizard.
3. On the Tools menu, click ASR Wizard.
4. Follow the instructions that appear on your screen. Note that only those system files necessary for starting up your system will be backed up by this procedure.

You can access the restore portion of ASR by pressing F2 when prompted in the text mode portion of Setup. ASR will read the disk configurations from the file that it creates and restore all of the disk signatures, volumes, and partitions on, at a minimum, the disks required to start the computer. It will attempt to restore all of the disk configurations, but under some circumstances, it might not be able to. ASR then installs a simple installation of Windows and automatically starts a restoration using the backup created by the ASR Wizard.

To recover from a system failure using Automated System Recovery, you will need the following items:

- Your previously created Automated System Recovery (ASR) floppy disk.
- Your previously created backup media.
- The original operating system installation CD.

If an ASR floppy disk is not available, both the ASR.SIF and ASRPNP.SIF files can be extracted from the ASR backup set, and then transferred to a floppy disk by completing the following steps:

1. Format a 1.44 MB floppy disk and insert the disk into the floppy disk drive.
2. In System Tools, start the Backup program.
3. When the Backup and Restore Wizard is displayed, click Next. Click Restore Files and Settings, and then click Next.
4. In the What to Restore dialog box, select the media that contains the ASR backup. Ensure that the media is inserted.
5. Expand the Automated System Recovery Backup Set that corresponds to the ASR floppy disk that you want to create.
6. Expand the second instance of the drive letter that contains the system folder.
7. Expand the WINDOWS_FOLDER/REPAIR folder.
8. Click the ASR.SIF and ASRPNP.SIF files and then click Next.
9. At the Completing Backup or Restore Wizard screen, click Advanced.
10. Set the Folder Name dialog box to the root of your floppy drive. Click Next.
11. When the wizard is finished, the files are copied to the floppy disk.

To perform the Automated System Recovery, do the following:

1. Insert the original operating system installation CD into your CD drive.
2. Restart your computer. If prompted to press a key in order to start the computer from CD, press the appropriate key.
3. Press F2 when prompted during the text only mode section of Setup. You will be prompted to insert the ASR floppy disk you have previously created.
4. Follow the directions on the screen.

You should note that the ASR will not restore your data files. For that you will need to have normal backup procedures.

21.15.5 System Configuration Utility

Similar to Windows 98 and Windows Millennium, Windows XP includes the System Configuration utility (MSCONFIG.EXE). The System Configuration utility lets you turn off or turn on specific entries in the BOOT.INI, SYSTEM.INI, or WIN.INI, and it allows you to turn off or on any programs

Figure 21.55 The System Configuration (MSCONFIG) Utility

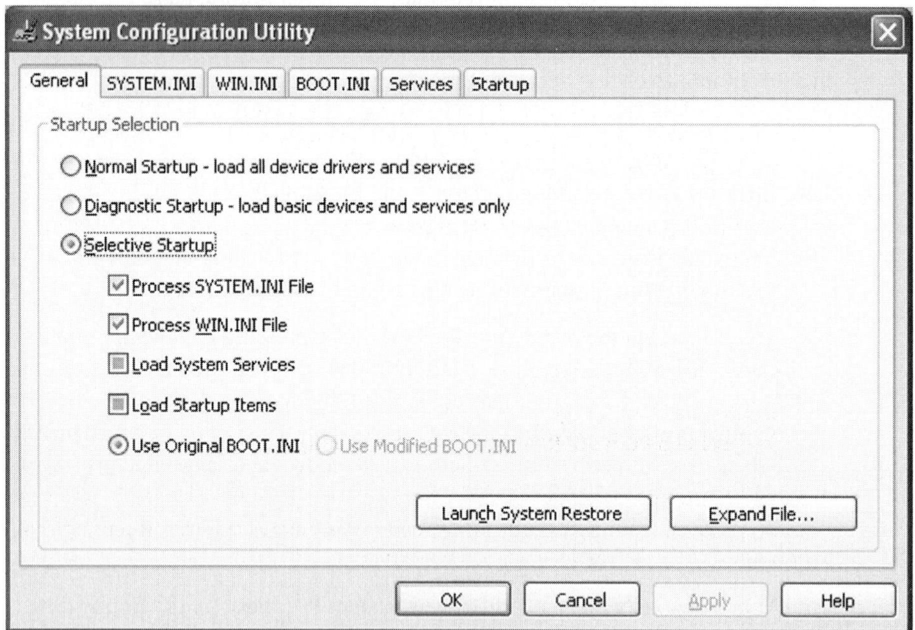

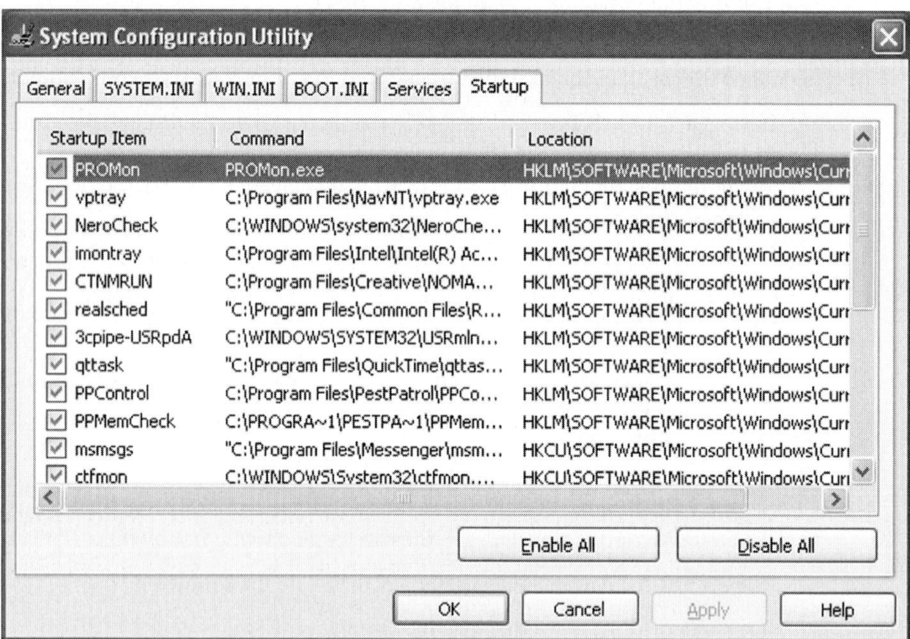

or services that are set to start during boot-up. From the General tab, besides the normal startup, you can choose Diagnostic startup, or you can choose to selectively disable files. You can also make other changes to the startup process that may help with diagnosing startup problems. In addition, you can change the order of the statements within the file by using the Move Up and Move Down buttons. Or, you can add a new statement to the file or edit a statement by using the New and Edit buttons. See figure 21.55.

Windows XP has a prefetcher component, which shortens the amount of time it takes to start Windows and programs. When troubleshooting either Windows or program startup issues, it might be helpful to disable the prefetcher because it runs as a background service while other applications are running or loading.

To disable the prefetcher:

1. Start the Registry Editor.
2. Go to HKEY_LOCAL_MACHINE\SYSTEM\CurrentControlSet\Control\SessionManager\Memory Management\PrefetchParameters.
3. Double-click the EnablePrefetcher value (remember the value that EnablePrefetcher is set to!).
4. Change the value data to 0 to disable the prefetcher.
5. Close the Registry Editor and reboot the computer for the changes to take effect.

When done troubleshooting, you can reenable the prefetcher by changing the Value data to its original value.

Values for EnablePrefetcher are:

0—no prefetch
1—prefetch applications only
2—prefetch boot only
3—prefetch both applications & boot (default)

It may also be useful to periodically clean up the prefetch folder, as it may contain obsolete links. The PREFETCH folder can be found in the WINDOWS folder on your system drive. Select all the files, and delete them. When done, reboot your computer.

21.15.6 Various Restore Methods

The first option that you may use if you perform regular backups is to restore Windows from a previous backup. When you are having problems with Windows, additional tools may come in handy.

Many OEMs provide recovery CDs with their computers. If you are having problems with your computer, you can boot with the recovery CD, and it will restore the computer back to the original software and configuration that the computer was shipped with. If you don't have your data files backed up, when you use the recovery CDs, it will also overwrite the data files and any programs that you have installed since you got the computer.

You can use disk image software, such as Drive Image, to take a snapshot of a partition or hard drive and save it in one large compressed file, which is best to do after all applications are installed. Since some Windows problems may take some time to figure out and fix, it may be easier and much faster to restore Windows to the saved image. Unfortunately, if you don't have your data files backed up or on a separate drive, when you restore the image, it will overwrite the data files.

Lastly, similar to System Restore available in Windows XP, all Windows versions can use a program called ConfigSafe. ConfigSafe protects Windows-based PCs from crashes and configuration problems by tracking changes to a system's configuration over time. It works by taking a "picture," or snapshot of a system's configuration. The snapshot stores information about the system's configuration at that exact point in time. Some examples of information tracked are as follows:

- Configuration files (WIN.INI, SYSTEM.INI, AUTOEXEC.BAT, CONFIG.SYS)
- System changes (memory, processor, Windows version)
- Drives (hard drives, CD-ROMs, network connections)
- Directories
- Windows registry
- System assets (for example, the Windows desktop)

As you can see, ConfigSafe tracks critically important system information. It is essential to have a stored record of this system information because these files and settings are often modified when new hardware and software is installed. Sometimes faulty installations or software conflicts cause a system to malfunction or completely stop working, not allowing the user to even boot into Windows. ConfigSafe lets you see what changes have been made to the system, which can help pinpoint the source of a problem. But more importantly, it lets you restore a system to a working state if you experience problems that result in an improperly working system. Using its unique SOS feature, ConfigSafe can even restore systems that won't boot into Windows.

21.16 WINDOWS NT FAMILY ERROR MESSAGES

Much like other graphical operating systems, Windows NT, Windows 2000, and Windows XP can have a wide range of problems. To help isolate these errors, Windows provides several programs and options.

21.16.1 Windows NT Microsoft Diagnostics

The Windows NT Diagnostics shows computer hardware and operating system data stored in the Windows NT registry. Like the System applet in the Windows 95 Control Panel, it includes the system resources (IRQ, I/O addresses, DMA, memory usage, and device drivers).

21.16.2 System Information Utility

Windows NT, Windows 2000, and Windows XP includes the System Information utility (WINMSD.EXE), which you can use to analyze your system for problems. System Information collects and displays your system configuration information. For example, you can view:

- Operating system information, such as the version number and system boot options, plus process, system, and user environment variables
- Hardware details such as BIOS information, video resolution, CPU type, and CPU steppings
- Physical memory, paging file information, and direct memory access (DMA) usage
- The current state of each driver and service on the computer
- Drives and devices installed on the computer, plus related interrupt (IRQ) and port information
- Network information, including transports, configuration settings, and statistics
- Printer settings, font settings, and system processes that are running

You can access the System Information utility by going to the Start menu and clicking Programs, Accessories, System Tools, and then selecting System Information.

System Information displays a comprehensive view of your hardware, system components, and software environment. The displayed system information is organized into three top-level categories that correspond to the resources, components, and software environment nodes.

- The resources node displays hardware-specific settings, namely DMA, IRQs, I/O addresses, and memory addresses. The conflicts/sharing node identifies devices that are sharing resources or are in conflict. This can help identify problems with a device.
- The components node displays information about your Windows configuration and is used to determine the status of your device drivers, networking, and multimedia software. In addition, there is a comprehensive driver history, which shows changes made to your components over time.
- The software environment node displays a snapshot of the software loaded in computer memory. This information can be used to see if a process is still running or to check version information.

Other applications may add nodes to System Information that display information specific to the application.

You can use the View menu to switch between the display of Basic and Advanced information. The Advanced view shows all of the information in the Basic view plus additional information that may be of interest to the more advanced user or to Microsoft Product Support Services.

While the first step to solving complex problems is to get more information about the problem, information alone doesn't fix what's wrong. For this reason, the System Information utility includes several tools that you can use to fix a malfunctioning system (see table 21.26). To access any of these tools, simply choose the appropriate tool from the System Information utility's Tools menu.

21.16.3 Invalid Page Faults and Exception Errors

A program error or stop error signifies that something unexpected has happened within the Windows environment. This is usually a program that tried to access a memory area that belongs to another program (**invalid page faults**) or that an application tried to pass an invalid parameter to another program (**exception error**).

Dr. Watson is a program that starts automatically when a program error occurs, detects information about the system and the program failure, and records the information into a log file. Dr. Watson

Table 21.26 Useful Troubleshooting Tools Used in Windows 2000 and Windows XP

Tools	Description
Windows Report Tool	The Windows Report tool will help solve problems that you just can't seem to figure out yourself. This tool asks you to describe your problem, what you're trying to accomplish, and the steps you've taken to reproduce the problem. When you've answered these questions, simply click Next and enter a file name. Windows will build a CAB file containing answers to your questions and a summary of your system's configuration. You can now send this file to Microsoft's technical support staff for assistance with your problem.
Update Wizard Uninstall	Windows 2000/XP contains a Windows Update utility you can use to install software patches from the Internet. Unfortunately, sometimes a patch can do more harm than good. If you install a patch and it causes problems, you can use the Update Wizard Uninstall utility to remove the patch quickly and easily.
Signature Verification Tool	Every piece of hardware in your computer requires a driver. Unfortunately, although several drivers come with Windows, many drivers are supplied by third parties—and aren't tested by Microsoft. A poorly written driver can affect more than just the device it controls: It can cause other devices to malfunction or result in general protection faults. With the release of Windows 98, Microsoft has begun digitally signing device drivers. The digital signature means that the driver has been tested by Microsoft and is certified to work with Windows. The digital signature also proves that the driver hasn't been tampered with. Third-party vendors can now submit their drivers to Microsoft for testing and application of a digital signature. The Signature Verification tool will check your system for files that don't contain a digital signature. It's important to point out that Microsoft doesn't sign every file—only driver files contain digital signatures.
Dr. Watson	At one time or another, you've probably seen a cryptic application fault screen. If this error occurs on a regular basis, use Dr. Watson. When you launch Dr. Watson, it runs minimized on your toolbar. Dr. Watson captures information about the error when it occurs. It can then be analyzed by Microsoft technical support.

will not prevent errors, but the log file can be used by technical support personnel to diagnose the problem. To open Dr. Watson, click the Start button, select the Run option, and execute the DRWTSN32 program. For more information about the Dr. Watson log file, see Dr. Watson Log File Overview using the Windows 2000 or XP Help program.

21.16.4 Stop Errors

Applications run in the user mode layer (Intel 386 protection model—ring 3). When an application causes an error, Windows NT family halts the process and generates an *Illegal Operation* error. Because every Win32 application has its own virtual protected memory space, this error condition doesn't affect any other Win32 program running. If the application tries to access the hardware without going through the correct methods, Windows notices this and generates an exception error. In these cases, if the application faults, you can close the offending program and resume work without affecting the other programs.

The Windows NT family kernel runs in the kernel mode layer (Intel 386 protection model—ring 0). When the kernel encounters a fatal error such as a hardware problem, inconsistencies within data necessary for its operation or similar error, Windows can displays a **stop error,** sometimes known as a "Blue Screen of Death." During this time, the system is stopped so that it will not corrupt any data. These errors can be caused by hardware errors, corrupted files, corrupted file system, or software glitch.

Even though a stop screen may look intimidating, only a small amount of data on the stop screen is important in determining the cause of the error. At the top of the screen, you will find the error code and parameters. In the middle of the screen you will find the list of modules that have successfully loaded and initialized and at the bottom of the screen you will find a list of modules that are currently on the stack. See figure 21.56.

Figure 21.56 A Typical Stop Error

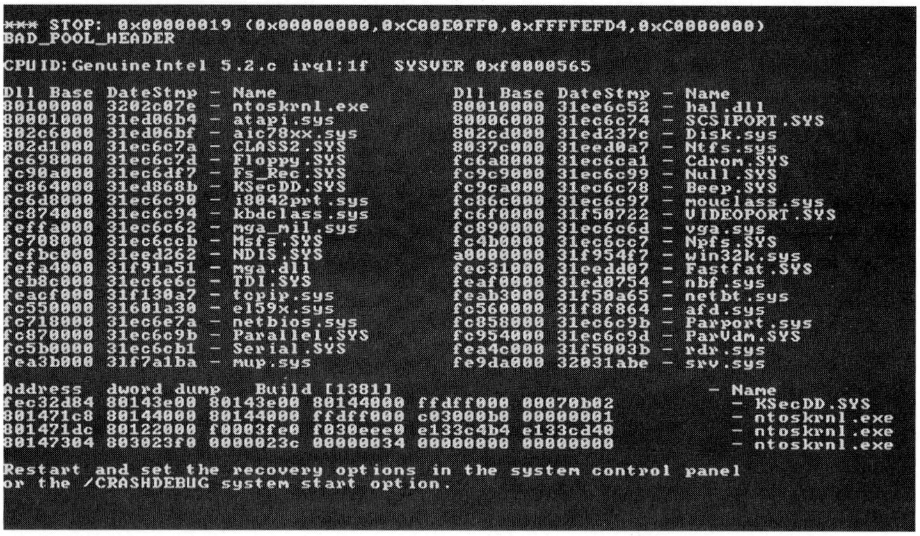

```
*** STOP: 0x00000019 (0x00000000,0xC00E0FF0,0xFFFFEFD4,0xC0000000)
BAD_POOL_HEADER

CPUID:GenuineIntel 5.2.c irql:1f   SYSVER 0xf0000565

Dll Base DateStmp - Name              Dll Base DateStmp - Name
80100000 3202c07e - ntoskrnl.exe      80010000 31ee6c52 - hal.dll
80001000 31ed06b4 - atapi.sys         80006000 31ec6c74 - SCSIPORT.SYS
802c6000 31ed06bf - aic78xx.sys       802cd000 31ed237c - Disk.sys
802d1000 31ec6c7a - CLASS2.SYS        8037c000 31eed0a7 - Ntfs.sys
fc698000 31ec6c7d - Floppy.SYS        fc6a8000 31ec6ca1 - Cdrom.SYS
fc90a000 31ec6df7 - Fs_Rec.SYS        fc9c9000 31ec6c99 - Null.SYS
fc864000 31ed868b - KSecDD.SYS        fc9ca000 31ec6c78 - Beep.SYS
fc6d8000 31ec6c90 - i8042prt.sys      fc86c000 31ec6c97 - mouclass.sys
fc874000 31ec6c94 - kbdclass.sys      fc6f0000 31f50722 - VIDEOPORT.SYS
feffa000 31ec6c62 - mga_mil.sys       fc890000 31ec6c6d - vga.sys
fc708000 31ec6ccb - Msfs.SYS          fc4b0000 31ec6cc7 - Npfs.SYS
fefbc000 31eed262 - NDIS.SYS          a0000000 31f954f7 - win32k.sys
fefa4000 31f91a51 - mga.dll           fec31000 31eedd07 - Fastfat.SYS
feb8c000 31ec6e6c - TDI.SYS           feaf0000 31ed0754 - nbf.sys
feacf000 31f130a7 - tcpip.sys         feab3000 31f50a65 - netbt.sys
fc550000 31601a30 - el59x.sys         fc560000 31f8f864 - afd.sys
fc718000 31ec6e7a - netbios.sys       fc858000 31ec6c9b - Parport.sys
fc870000 31ec6c9b - Parallel.SYS      fc954000 31ec6c9d - ParVdm.SYS
fc5b0000 31ec6cb1 - Serial.SYS        fea4c000 31f5003b - rdr.sys
fea3b000 31f7a1ba - mup.sys           fe9da000 32031abe - srv.sys

Address  dword dump   Build [1381]                          - Name
fec32d84 80143e00 80143e00 80144000 ffdff000 00070b02       - KSecDD.SYS
801471c8 80144000 80144000 ffdff000 c03000b0 00000001       - ntoskrnl.exe
801471dc 80122000 f0003fe0 f030eee0 e133c4b4 e133cd40       - ntoskrnl.exe
80147304 803023f0 0000023c 00000034 00000000 00000000       - ntoskrnl.exe

Restart and set the recovery options in the system control panel
or the /CRASHDEBUG system start option.
```

You can configure Windows NT family to write a memory dump file each time it generates a kernel stop error. To make a memory dump file, you must have sufficient space on a hard disk partition for the resulting memory dump file, which will be as large as your RAM memory. Therefore, if your system has 256 MB of RAM, you must have 256 MB of free disk space.

To configure the Windows NT family to save STOP information to a memory dump file, you would double-click on the System applet in the Control Panel, click on the Advanced tab, and click on the Startup and Recovery button. Within the Startup/Shutdown tab, you would put a checkmark in the Write debugging information under the Recovery section. You can then specify the file location and name. Note: If the Overwrite any existing file option does not have a check mark and there is a file with that name, Windows will not overwrite the file.

Since most of the data in the dump file is useless to most support technicians who examine the file to troubleshoot the cause of the crash (instead it is aimed at programmers), Windows 2000 introduces a new option where it saves only the Windows 2000 kernel information that contains the state of the system at the time of a crash, which applications were active, which device drivers were loaded, and what code was executing. A kernel-data-only crash dump is much smaller in size compared to the full dump. To choose the type of dump kernel memory dump, right-click My Computer and select Properties or double-click the System applet in the Control Panel. From the Advanced tab, click the Startup and Recovery button.

Many of the common stop errors are already listed and explained in Windows 2000 Server help files. Other places to look for information on stop error appears should include searching Microsoft's website and/or Microsoft Technet for possible solutions. In any case, make sure that the system has the most updated system BIOS and the newest Windows 2000 service pack. Also see Appendix E.

21.16.5 Troubleshooting a Missing Taskbar or Start Menu

When you start Windows XP, you may experience one or more of the following behaviors:

- When you log on normally, the Taskbar does not appear.
- If you press Ctrl + Esc, the Start menu does not appear.
- If you log on to Windows in safe mode, the Taskbar *does* appear.

This behavior can occur if the Windows settings for a particular user account has become corrupted or there is a damaged or incompatible driver or file. To determine whether a damaged or incompatible driver or file is causing the problem, reboot Windows in safe mode. If the problem goes away, then some program is causing the problem. Therefore, use MSCONFIG to help you isolate the program with the problem.

If user account settings have become corrupted, restart Windows in safe mode and create a new user account. Then reboot the computer (normal boot) and log on as the new user that you created. If the issue is resolved, reinstall the programs that you want, and then copy the documents that you want from the MY DOCUMENTS folder of the old user account. To copy the contents of the MY DOCUMENTS folder of the old user account, follow these steps:

1. Log off Windows.
2. Press Ctrl + Alt + Del twice. The Log On to Windows dialog box appears.
3. In the User name box, type *Administrator.* In the Password box, type the administrator password, and then click OK.
4. Right-click Start, and then click Explore on the shortcut menu that appears.
5. In the folders tree, expand the old user account under Documents and Settings.
6. Click [*user name's*] Documents (where *user name* is the name of the old user account with which you experience this issue).
7. On the Edit menu, click Select All, and then click Copy.
8. Under Documents and Settings, expand the new user account folder.
9. Click [*new user's*] Documents (where *new user* is the name of the new user account that you created).
10. On the Edit menu, click Paste.
11. If you are prompted to replace files or folders, click Yes to All to confirm the replacement.
12. On the File menu, click Close.
13. Log off Windows.

If the Taskbar or Start button still does not show, try to perform an in-place repair of Windows XP. Start the installation of Windows XP, but select the option to repair the existing installation. This will replace all of the Windows files, leaving the installed programs and data intact.

21.16.6 Driver and DLL Problems

When installing new software on your computer, system files (including DLL files) and device driver files are sometimes overwritten by unsigned or incompatible versions, causing system instability. To help overcome these problems, Windows device drivers and operating system files have been digitally signed by Microsoft to ensure their quality. A Microsoft digital signature is your assurance that a particular file has met a certain level of testing, and that the file has not been altered or overwritten by another program's installation process.

Microsoft offers a DLL Help website to assist developers, system administrators, and other IT professionals who face file version conflicts with Microsoft software. It can be found at:

http://support.microsoft.com/default.aspx?scid=/servicedesks/fileversion/dllinfo.asp&SD=msdn

Windows includes the following features to ensure that your device drivers and system files remain in their original, digitally signed state:

- File Signature Verification
- System File Checker
- Windows File Protection
- Driver Signing

Using **File Signature Verification,** you can identify unsigned files on your computer and view the following information about them:

- File name
- File location
- File modification date
- File type
- File version number
- Open File Signature Verification

To start File Signature Verification, click Start, click Run, type *SIGVERIF,* and then click OK.

The **System File Checker (SFC.EXE)** tool scans all the protected files to make sure they are not modified by programs that were installed by using an unattended installation at the end of GUI mode Setup. The System File Checker tool also checks all the catalog files that are used to track correct file versions. If any of the catalog files are missing or damaged, Windows File Protection (WFP) renames the affected catalog file and retrieves a cached version of that file from the cache folder. If a cached copy of the catalog file is not available in the cache folder, the WFP feature requests the appropriate media to retrieve a new copy of the catalog file.

The System File Checker tool gives an administrator the ability to scan all the protected files to verify their versions. The System File Checker also checks and repopulates the cache folder (by default, %SYSTEMROOT%\SYSTEM32\DLLCACHE). If the cache folder becomes damaged or unusable, you can use either the SFC/SCANONCE command or the SFC/SCANBOOT command at a command prompt to repair the contents of the folder.

Windows File Protection (WFP) prevents programs from replacing critical Windows system and DLL files. Programs must not overwrite these files because they are used by the operating system and by other programs. Protecting these files prevents problems with programs and the operating system.

WFP protects critical system files that are installed as part of Windows (for example, files with a DLL, EXE, OCX, and SYS extension and some TrueType fonts). By default, Windows File Protection is always enabled and allows Windows digitally signed files to replace existing files. WFP uses the file signatures and catalog files that are generated by code signing to verify if protected system files are the correct Microsoft versions.

- Windows service pack installation using UPDATE.EXE
- Hotfixes installed using HOTFIX.EXE or UPDATE.EXE
- Operating system upgrades using WINNT32.EXE
- Windows Update
- Windows Device Manager/Class Installer

If a program uses a different way to replace protected files, WFP restores the original files. The Windows Installer adheres to WFP when installing critical system files and calls WFP with a request to install or replace the protected file instead of trying to install or replace a protected file itself.

NOTE: Protected system files are backed up each time you perform a System State backup.

Finally, **driver signing** is used to make sure that only Microsoft signed drivers are used. Using the System applet in the Control Panel, you can configure Windows to block or ignore device drivers that are not digitally signed. The default setting is that it will warn you if it detects device drivers that are not digitally signed. See figure 21.57.

Figure 21.57 Configuring Driver Signing

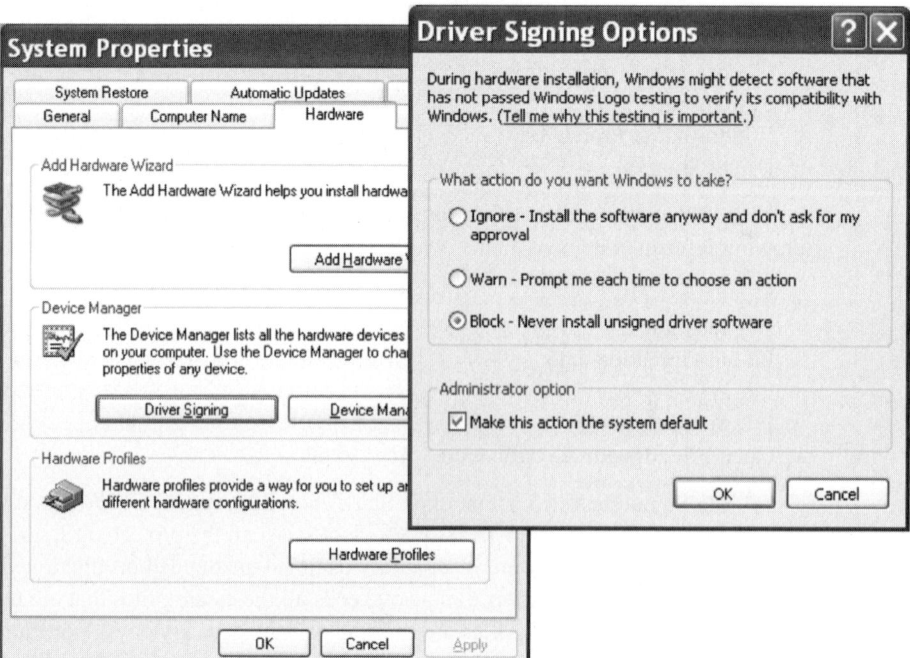

Figure 21.58 Using the Driver Verifier Manager to Show Its Settings

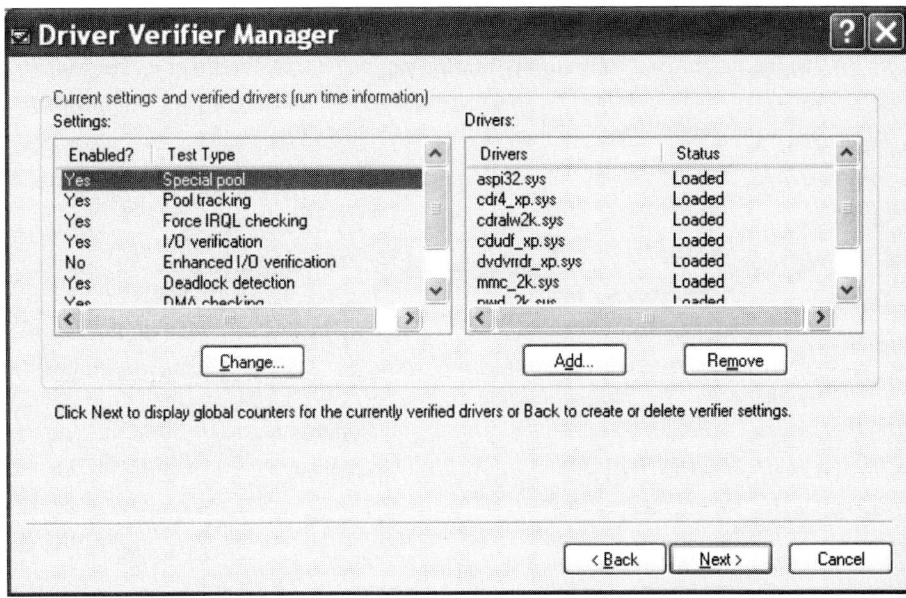

Figure 21.59 Using the Driver Verifier Manager to Show a Driver's Statistics

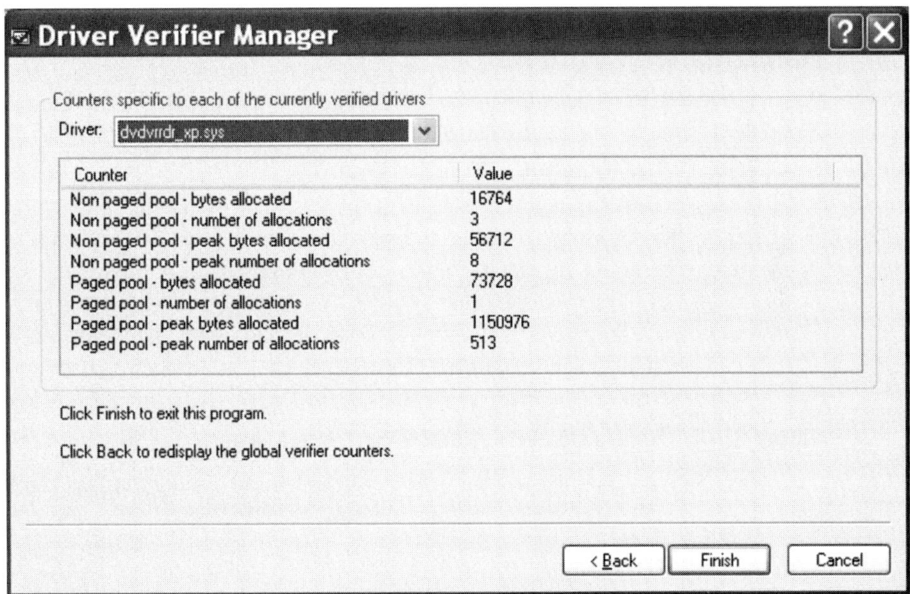

Driver Verifier (VERIFIER.EXE located in the SYSTEM32 folder), available in Windows 2000 and Windows XP, is a tool for monitoring Windows kernel mode drivers and graphics drivers. By running VERIFIER.COM, you will first establish which drivers that you want to verify and monitor. After the machine is rebooted, you can then use VERIFIER.COM to view the statistics in real-time, as shown in figures 21.58 and 21.59. You can also run VERIFIER.EXE from a command line. For more information, type this command at a command prompt:

```
verifier.exe /?
```

Driver Verifier can automatically track pool allocations and driver unload checking. At driver unload time, a bug check occurs if any of the allocations or resources are not freed. You can use this command to show all the allocations that are not freed:

```
verifier 3 kernel-debugger
```

You can also use the command before unloading to view the outstanding allocations the driver has at any point in time.

Driver unload checking is performed to catch drivers that unload and do not clean up resources used (which increases the possibility of a system bug check shortly after the driver unloads). Resources that the driver may not delete include look-aside lists, pending deferred procedure calls (DPCs), worker threads, queues, timers, and other resources.

NOTE: If Norton Antivirus is installed, do not enable Driver Verifier's Deadlock Detection.

21.17 WINDOWS NT FAMILY PERFORMANCE

Performance is the overall effectiveness of how data moves through the system. To be able to improve performance, you must determine the part of the system that is slowing down the throughput; it could be the speed of the processor, the amount of RAM on the machine, the speed of the disk system, the speed of your network adapter card, or some other factor. This limiting factor is referred to as the bottleneck of the system. With System monitor, you can measure the performance of your own computer or other computers on the network.

When you first start Performance Monitor, all you see is a blank screen. You must select the objects, instances, and counters that you want to monitor. An object is any Windows NT family system component that possesses a set of measurable property. It can be a physical part of the system such as the processor, RAM, disk subsystem and network interface, a logical component such as a disk volume, or software element such as a process or a thread. An instance shows how many occurrences of an object are available in the system. A counter represents one measurable characteristic of an object. See figure 21.60.

21.17.1 Performance Counters

As mentioned before, the computer is centered around the processor. Therefore, the performance of the computer is greatly affected by the performance of the processor.

Processor: % Processor Time

% Processor Time measures how busy the processor is. While the processor may jump up to 100 percent processor usage, you need to look at the overall average. If the processor is at 80 percent all the time, you should upgrade the processor (faster processor or adding the number of processors) or move some of the services to other systems. If you want to see what percentage of the processor utilization each process is using, use the Task Manager. Note: Do not use 3D screen savers since they can consume 90 percent of the processor utilization. Instead, use a blank screen saver.

Figure 21.60 Adding Counters to the Performance Monitor

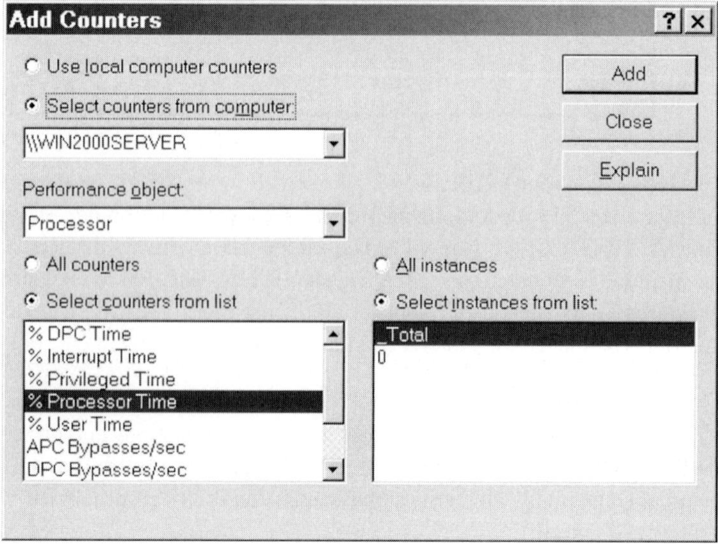

Processor: Interrupts/sec

Interrupts/sec measures how many hardware interrupts per second are occurring. A server running 100 interrupts/second can be normal. If the counter is increasing without a corresponding increase in the server load, it may be due to a hardware problem. You should always view this counter when you load a new device driver to make sure that it functions properly. A poorly written device driver can cause huge increases in interrupt activity.

System: Processor Queue Length

The number of threads indicated by the Processor Queue Length is a significant indicator of system performance, because each thread requires a certain number of processor cycles. If demand exceeds supply, long processor queues develop and system response suffers. Therefore, a sustained processor queue length greater than 2 on a single processor generally indicates that the processor is a bottleneck. This counter is always 0 unless you are monitoring a thread counter as well.

As mentioned before, RAM is one of the biggest factors in PC performance. You can typically increase the PC performance by adding more RAM. The best five RAM counters are:

Memory: Available Bytes

Available Bytes measures the amount of available virtual memory. It is calculated by summing space on the zeroed, free, and standby memory lists. Free memory is ready for use. Zeroed memory is pages of memory filled with zeros to prevent later processes from seeing data used by a previous process. Standby memory is memory removed from a process' working set (physical memory) on route to disk, but is still available to be recalled. If it is less than 4 MB, consider adding more RAM.

Memory: Page Faults/sec

A page fault occurs when a process attempts to access a virtual memory page that is not available in its working set in RAM. Hard page faults must be retrieved from disk, which greatly slows performance. Soft page faults are those that can be retrieved from the standby list, and therefore do not require disk I/O. If this value is high (20) or increasing, it is a sign that you need to add physical RAM to your server.

Memory: Cache Bytes

The Memory\Cache Bytes monitor the size of the File System Cache. When memory is scarce the system trims the cache, and when memory is ample the system enlarges the cache. Note: You should compare this to general memory availability. In addition, you should keep track of how small the cache gets, and how often that happens. This data is useful when associating the size of the cache with its performance.

Memory: Pages/sec

The pages/second indicates the number of requested pages that were not immediately available in RAM and had to be read from the disk or written to the disk to make room in RAM for other pages. If your system experiences a high rate of hard page faults, the value for Pages/sec can be high.

Paging File: % Usage

% Usage of the Paging File is the percentage of space allocated to the page file (virtual memory) that is actually in use. To calculate how much more RAM you would need to add to a server to minimize paging, you would multiple the percentage by the size of the page file.

Paging File: % Usage Peak

The % Usage Peak is the highest percentage usage of the page file. If this value frequently exceeds 90 percent, allocate more space to the page file and possibly more RAM. A 100 percent usage peak indicates that the server has, at least momentarily, run out of both physical and virtual memory.

Since one of the tasks of a server is to provide file access, a hard drive system is an important factor in server performance. The important hard drive counters include:

Physical Disk: % Disk Time

The % Disk Time measures the percentage of elapsed time that a disk drive is actually occupied in reading data from and writing data to the disk. A value greater than 90 percent indicates that the disk is the bottleneck.

Physical Disk: % Avg. Disk Queue Length

The % Avg. Disk Queue Length is the average number of read requests and write queued for the disk in question. A sustained average higher than 2 indicates that the disk is being overutilized.

LogicalDisk: % Free Disk Space

Free Disk Space reports the percentage of unallocated disk space to the total usable space on the logical volume.

LogicalDisk: Avg. Disk Bytes/Transfer and PhysicalDisk:Avg. Disk Bytes/Transfer

The Avg. Disk Bytes/Transfer measures the size of I/O operations. The disk is efficient if it transfers large amounts of data relatively quickly.

LogicalDisk: Avg. Disk sec/Transfer and PhysicalDisk:Avg. Disk sec/Transfer

Avg. Disk sec/Transfer indicates how fast data is being moved (in seconds). It measures the average time of each data transfer, regardless of the number of bytes read or written. A high value for this counter might mean that the system is retrying requests due to lengthy queuing or, less commonly, disk failures.

LogicalDisk: Disk Bytes/sec and PhysicalDisk:Disk Bytes/sec

Disk Bytes/sec indicates the rate at which bytes are transferred and is the primary measure of disk throughput.

LogicalDisk: Disk Transfer/sec and PhysicalDisk:Disk Transfers/sec

Disk Transfer/sec measures disk utilization by indicating the number of read and writes completed per second, regardless of how much data they involve. If value exceeds 50 (per physical disk in the case of a stripe set), then a bottleneck might be developing.

NOTE: For Windows NT, the system is set to collect physical drive data by default. Logical drive data is not collected by default; you must enable it specifically. To enable the disk counters, you would execute the DISKPERF–Y command at the command prompt and restart the computer. For Windows 2000 and Windows XP, DISKPERF–Y is already enabled.

21.17.2 System Monitor

There are several views in System Monitor including chart and report. A real-time activity chart displays the value of the counter over time in a graph. You want to use a chart to investigate why a computer or application is slow or inefficient, to continuously monitor the system to find intermittent performance problems, and to discover why the capacity of a subsystem needs to be increased. See figure 21.61. A report view allows you to display constantly changing counter and instance values for selected objects. See figure 21.62.

To add counters, right-click the chart or report pane (right-pane) and select the Add Counters option. After you have identified the counters you want to monitor, you can save the information and reuse it later. To save chart settings, right-click the chart or report pane and select the Save as option.

21.17.3 Logging Performance Data

The System Monitor supports three types of logs: counter logs, trace logs, and alert logs. **Counter logs** record data from local or remote computers about hardware usage and system service activity. **Trace logs** are event-driven, recording monitored data such as disk I/O or page faults. When a traced event occurs, it is recorded in the log. Alert logs take trace logs one step further. **Alert logs** are trace logs that monitor counters, wait for them to exceed user-defined tolerances, and log the event. You can even set up the alert log to send a message or run an application when a particular value is exceeded.

To create a log, click on the Performance Logs and Alert in the left pane of System Monitor, and open the folder for the type of log that you want. Right-click the empty space in the Details window and choose an option for creating a new log from the popup menu that appears. If you save the file as a binary file (*.BLG), you can use System Monitor to open the log and view it later. If you save the file as a comma-delimited file (*.CSV) or a tab-delimited file (*.TSV), you can open them with Excel to perform your own data analysis.

Figure 21.61 Chart View Using the Performance Monitor

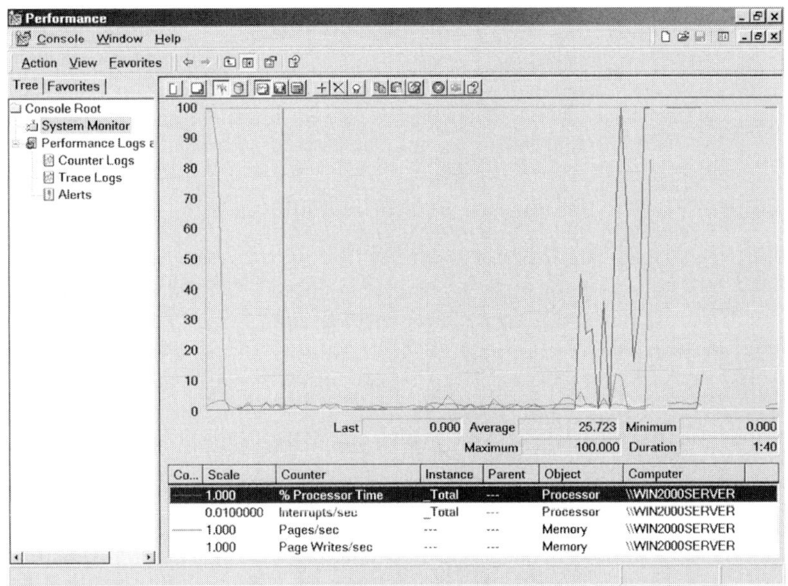

Figure 21.62 Report View Using the Performance Monitor

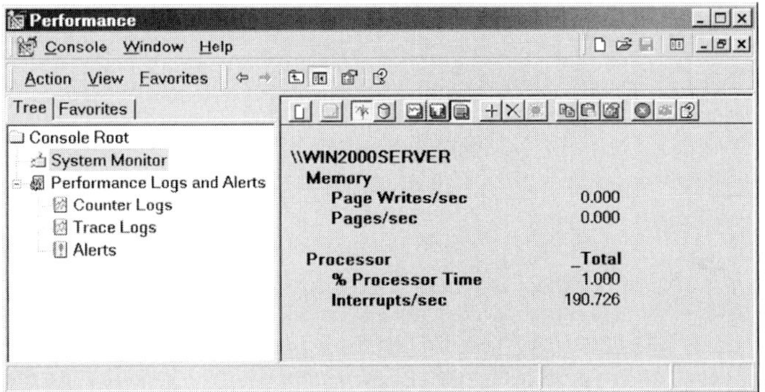

SUMMARY

1. Windows NT, Windows 2000, and Windows XP are operating systems that can function as desktop operating systems or as network file, print, or application servers.
2. Under these popular interfaces, Windows NT family operating systems use a different architecture, which offers higher performance and greater reliability and provides better security than DOS, Windows 3.XX, and Windows 9X. Unfortunately, to achieve these benefits, Windows NT, Windows 2000, and Windows XP are not 100 percent backward compatible with all hardware and software.
3. The Windows NT, Windows 2000, and Windows XP interface is based on the desktop, which is the graphical space on the screen where all control and display presentations start.
4. The hardware abstraction layer (HAL) is a library of hardware manipulating routines that hide the hardware interface details.
5. The Windows NT family architecture can be divided into two major layers—user mode and kernel mode (also referred to as privileged mode). The user mode programs run in ring 3 of the Intel 386 microprocessor protection model and are protected by the operating system. The kernel mode components run in ring 0 of the Intel 386 microprocessor protection model.
6. A kernel is the central module of an operating system. It is the part of the operating system that loads first and it remains in RAM.
7. The microkernel is the central part of the Windows NT family that coordinates all I/O functions and synchronizes the activities of the Execute Services.
8. A program, sometimes referred to as a process, is an executable program that follows a sequence of steps. A program consists of initializing code and data, a private memory address space, system

resources (such as files, communication ports, and Windows resources), and one or more threads.

9. A thread is part of a program that can execute independently of other parts.
10. Windows NT family is a preemptive multitasking operating system. Preemptive multitasking is when the operating system assigns time slices to threads, tasks, and applications.
11. There are several utilities used to configure the Windows NT family. The main utilities are the Control Panel and the Registry Editor.
12. The Device Manager lists all of the hardware devices on your computer and allows you to change the properties of any device.
13. The Microsoft Management Console (MMC) was introduced with Internet Information Service (IIS) for Windows NT 4.0 and is one of the primary administrative tools used to manage Windows 2000 and Windows XP.
14. The Computer Management console is a collection of Windows administrative tools that you can use to manage a local or remote computer. It includes Event Viewer, Shared Folders, Local Users and Groups, Performance Logs and Alerts, and Device Manager.
15. The registry is a central, secure database in which Windows stores all hardware configuration information, software configuration information, and system security policy.
16. During the boot-up, the first Windows NT family file read is NTLDR, which switches the processor from real mode to protected mode and starts the appropriate minifile system drivers (built into NTLDR) so that it can read the VFAT/FAT16, FAT32, or NTFS file systems.
17. Next, NTLDR reads the BOOT.INI (if one is available) and displays the Boot Loader Operating System Selection menu.
18. For Windows 2000 and Windows XP, you would use the Disk Management console or the Computer Management console (click on the Start button, click on the Programs option, click on Administrative Tools, and then select the Computer Management option) to configure and manage your disks.
19. A basic disk is a physical disk that contains primary partitions, extended partitions, or logical drivers that can be accessed directly using DOS or Windows 9X.
20. A dynamic storage is a disk that is converted from basic to dynamic storage that contains simple volumes, spanned volumes, mirrored volumes, striped volumes, and RAID-5 volumes.
21. A primary advantage of NTFS over FAT and FAT32 is that NTFS volumes have the ability to apply NTFS permissions to secure folders and files.
22. Disk and file management is usually done with My Computer or Windows Explorer.
23. If you want to move, delete, or copy several files or folders at the same time, you can use the Ctrl and Shift keys to select multiple files.
24. The event viewer is a very useful utility used to view and manage logs of system, program, and security events on your computer.
25. If the need arises to view or change the registry, you can use the Registry Editor (REGEDIT.EXE or REGEDT32.EXE) utilities.
26. The System Configuration utility (MSCONFIG.EXE) lets you turn off or turn on specific entries in the BOOT.INI, SYSTEM.INI, or WIN.INI files and allows you to turn off or on any programs or services that set up during boot-up.
27. To make sure that you know what hardware is compatible with Windows, Microsoft offers a hardware compatibility list (HCL) of devices that have been tested and approved to work with Windows.
28. To install Windows NT Workstation, go to the installation CD, change to the I386 directory, and use the WINNT.EXE file to start the installation process. If you have a formatted partition, you can use the WINNT/B command to perform a floppyless installation.
29. To install Windows 2000 or Windows XP, go to the installation CD, change to the I386 directory, and use the WINNT.EXE file to start the installation process.
30. WINNT32.EXE should be used on a clean installation or upgrade on a computer running Windows NT version 4.0, Windows 95, or Windows 98.
31. A service pack is many fixes or patches bundled together.
32. The active partition that contains the NTLDR and BOOT.INI files is known as the system partition. The partition that contains the Windows NT family operating system files is called the boot partition.
33. An ARC (Advanced RISC Computing) path is used to specify the location (partition) of an operating system.
34. For the Windows NT family, there are two options (Last Known Configuration and Advanced Options Menu) during boot-up that can help troubleshoot and fix recently installed device drivers causing problems.
35. Windows XP comes with the System Restore utility, which takes images or snapshots of your system at various times so you can revert to the state of your system before it crashed.
36. To log on to a computer running Windows NT family, a user provides a user name and password. Windows NT family authenticates the user during the logon process to verify the identity of the user.
37. If you have problems where Windows 2000 or Windows XP cannot load or start, there are several tools that you can use. They are the Advanced Boot menu, Windows 2000 Recovery Console, and emergency repair disk (also available in Windows NT).
38. Device drivers are programs that control a device. They act like a translator between the device and programs that use the device.

39. A service is a program, routine, or process that performs a specific system function to support other programs.
40. Windows NT does not support plug-and-play devices, but it can use them as long as the Windows NT device driver can activate the card and determine the card's resources.
41. The virtual memory area allows you to configure the paging file size (virtual memory) and the maximum size of the registry. The minimum paging file is 2 MB. For Windows 2000 and Windows XP, the default size of the file is equal to the total amount of RAM plus 12 MB, not to exceed the amount of available disk space.
42. The Task Manager provides a list of the current programs that are running and the overall CPU (including number of threads and processes) and memory usage (including the amount of physical memory, size of the file cache, paged memory, and nonpaged memory).
43. A program error or stop error signifies that something unexpected has happened within the Windows environment.

QUESTIONS

1. *True or false*—Because Windows NT 4.0 uses the Windows 95 interface, any programs that will work on Windows 95 will work on Windows NT.
2. Which of the following does *not* describe Windows NT?
   a. Windows NT uses preemptive multitasking.
   b. Windows NT uses cooperative multitasking.
   c. Windows NT is multithreaded.
   d. Windows NT supports multiple microprocessors.
3. How would you upgrade Windows 95 or 98 to Windows NT?
   a. You would use the WINNT32.EXE utility.
   b. You can install Windows NT into the same folder as Windows 95 if Windows 95 is using VFAT.
   c. You would use the CONVERT.EXE utility.
   d. You cannot upgrade Windows 95 or 98 to Windows NT.
4. The file that contains the Boot Loader Operating System Selection menu is known as the
   a. NTLDR.
   b. NTDETECT.COM.
   c. BOOT.INI.
   d. MSDOS.SYS.
   e. NTOSKRNL.
5. For additional security, what file system in Windows NT or Windows 2000 would you use?
   a. FAT
   b. VFAT
   c. HPFS
   d. NTFS
   e. CDFS
6. Which of the following provides faster access and fault tolerance (choose all that apply)?
   a. volume set
   b. striped set
   c. striped set with parity checking
   d. mirroring
7. The location of a partition in the BOOT.INI file is known as the
   a. search path.
   b. boot path.
   c. access path.
   d. ARC path.
   e. security path.
8. In Windows NT, the virtual memory is called a(n)
   a. temporary swap file.
   b. permanent swap file.
   c. expanded system file.
   d. paging file.
9. *True or false*—Like Windows 95, Windows NT 4.0 supports plug-and-play devices.
10. Which utility allows you to see the log of problems encountered on a Windows NT machine?
    a. Performance Monitor
    b. Network Monitor
    c. Event Viewer
    d. Boot Viewer
11. The registry is corrupted on a Windows NT machine. The best way to fix it is
    a. reformat the hard drive and reinstall everything.
    b. boot the computer using the NT Setup disks and use the ERD disk.
    c. back up the hard drive, reinstall Windows NT, and restore the backup.
    d. select Windows NT-VGA during boot-up.
12. You have installed a new hard disk in your Windows NT Workstation computer, and you want to format this disk with the NTFS file system. How should you proceed to partition and format this disk?
    a. Use FDISK at the command prompt.
    b. Use Windows NT Disk Administrator.
    c. Use CHKDSK/F at the command prompt.
    d. Select the Start button, open the Control Panel, and then double-click on Devices.
13. Which Windows 2000 file contains the code that enables the operating system to interact with the system hardware?
    a. HAL
    b. NTLDR
    c. NTOSKRNL
    d. NTDETECT
14. In which two situations will INT 13 BIOS calls *not* work on a Windows 2000 computer (choose two)?
    a. You have installed one or more IDE drives on the computer.
    b. The Windows 2000 boot partition ends before the 1,024 cylinder of the drive.

c. The BIOS is disabled on the SCSI controller connected to the disk where Windows 2000 is installed.
d. The Windows 2000 boot partition is not completely contained within the first 1,024 cylinders of the drive.

15. You are troubleshooting a Windows 2000 system. While loading Windows 2000 the system displays an "NTDETECT failed" error. Which action should you take to resolve the error?
    a. Restore from backup.
    b. Ensure there is no floppy in the floppy disk drive.
    c. Edit the BOOT.INI to point to the correct location.
    d. Make sure the user name and password are entered correctly.
    e. Copy the NTDETECT.COM file from the Windows 2000 CD-ROM or another Windows 2000 system.
16. You are upgrading a Windows NT 4.0 computer to Windows 2000. What should you do to gather information on hardware and software applications that are compatible with Windows 2000 (choose two)?
    a. Visit the Microsoft compatibility website before you begin your installation to make sure that your hardware and software will work with Windows 2000.
    b. It is not necessary to check further, because compatibility checks are performed automatically based on information included on the Windows 2000.
    c. Since you are upgrading from Windows NT 4.0, you should not be concerned. Any hardware and software that works with Windows NT 4.0 will also work with Windows 2000.
    d. Click on the button displayed during installation to visit a Microsoft site to discover the latest compatibility news about computers, hardware devices and software.
17. You have a Pentium III 550 MHz Windows 2000 computer with a 10 GB hard disk and 128 MB of RAM. There has never been a modem installed on this computer, and you must install a modem that is not on the hardware compatibility list (HCL). How can you install the modem on this Windows 2000 computer (choose two)?
    a. Set the driver signing option to Block.
    b. Set the driver signing option to Warn or Ignore.
    c. Install the driver from the Driver tab of the modem's Properties page in Device Manager.
    d. Use the Add/Remove Hardware Wizard and manually select the device type and location of the driver.
18. Which MS-DOS commands are no longer supported in Windows 2000 (choose three)?
    a. SYS b. ERASE
    c. PROMPT d. RESTORE
    e. SCANDISK f. DISKCOPY
19. What is one important difference between basic and dynamic storage in Windows 2000?
    a. Dynamic storage supports RAID-5.
    b. Dynamic storage supports striped sets.
    c. Dynamic storage supports mirrored sets.
    d. Dynamic storage allows disk management without restarting the operating system.
20. You make changes to the video refresh rate on your Windows 2000 computer and now the display does not work properly. What should you do?
    a. Run the SYSEDIT utility.
    b. Reinstall the Windows 2000 operating system.
    c. Reboot the system with an emergency repair disk.
    d. Press F8 during the boot-up sequence and select Last Known Good Configuration.
21. How much RAM will Windows 2000 Professional support?
    a. 256 MB b. 512 MB
    c. 1 GB d. 4 GB
22. Which installation and configuration features does Windows 2000 Professional share with Windows 98 (choose three)?
    a. USB support
    b. New Installer
    c. Dynamic partitions
    d. 1394/FireWire support
    e. multiprocessor support
    f. plug-and-play for most devices
    g. Safe mode boot and command console
23. When installing Windows NT 4.0, what do you accomplish by running the WINNT.EXT or WINNT32.EXE install program with the /b switch?
    a. You create the three setup floppy disks.
    b. You install Windows NT 4.0 without the setup floppy disks.
    c. You automatically back up the registry when the installation is complete.
    d. You automatically generate an emergency repair disk during installation.
24. You have added a new device to your Windows 2000 computer. The device is plug-and-play compliant, and Windows 2000 has the appropriate. What does a user need to do to install and configure the device?
    a. Install the device and restart the computer.
    b. Install the device, restart the computer, and then click on the Add New Hardware icon in the Control Panel.
    c. Windows 2000, like Windows NT 4.0, does not support plug-and-play. You will have to install the correct driver manually.
    d. Install the device, restart the computer, use Device Manager to identify the correct driver, and add a registry key to associate the driver with the correct device.

25. Where can you go to delete a default Windows NT spooler file?
   a. C:\WINNT\PRINTERS
   b. C:\WINNT\PRINTERS\QUE
   c. C:\WINNT\SPOOOL\PRINTERS
   d. C:\WINNT\SPOOL\PRINTERS
   e. C:\WINNT\SYSTEM32\SPOOL\PRINTERS
26. Which component loads and unloads device drivers in Windows NT and Windows 2000?
   a. MBR
   b. NTLDR
   c. Service Controller
   d. Control Panel Devices application
27. What does driver signing from Microsoft mean?
   a. The hardware manufacturer has paid Microsoft to develop a compatible driver with guaranteed functionality.
   b. The driver has passed a series of tests in the WHQL (Windows Hardware Quality Labs) that ensure driver quality.
   c. The driver has received either a plus sign (+) or a minus sign (−) rating from the Microsoft Windows 2000 development team.
   d. Microsoft provides a signed guarantee from Bill Gates that the driver will not crash your properly configured Windows 2000 computer.
28. What are the two sections of a Windows 2000 BOOT.INI file (choose two)?
   a. [mbr]
   b. [nt loader]
   c. [nt detect]
   d. [boot loader]
   e. [operating systems]
   f. [hardware abstractions]
29. How do you create a Windows 2000 ERD?
   a. Run RDISK from the command prompt.
   b. Click the Start button, select Settings, select the Control Panel, select System, then select ERD.
   c. At the Run option in the Start button, enter *<Drive>:\WINNT\ERD* and press OK.
   d. Click the Start button, select the Programs option, select the Accessories option, select System Tools, select Backup, select Tools, and create an emergency repair disk.
30. Which utility can you use to back up the complete Windows NT registry?
   a. REGEDIT   b. REGEDT32
   c. MSBACKUP   d. EXTRACT
31. Which command should you use if you want to install Windows 2000 on a computer running Windows NT 4.0?
   a. SETUP.EXE   b. WINNT.EXE
   c. WINNT32.EXE   d. WINNT16.EXE
32. Which Windows 2000 file queries the computer BIOS to retrieve device and configuration information?
   a. HAL   b. NTLDR
   c. NTOSKRNL   d. NTDETECT
33. Which container holds the most common Windows 2000 Professional MMC snap-ins, divided into the System Tools, Storage, and Server Applications and Services categories?
   a. My Computer
   b. System Information
   c. My System Manager
   d. Computer Manager
34. What is the absolute minimum amount of RAM needed to install Windows 2000 Professional?
   a. 16 MB   b. 32 Mb
   c. 64 MB   d. 128 MB
35. What happens when the Windows 2000 animated "Starting Up" progress bar is displayed?
   a. The operating system kernel (NTOSKRNL.EXE) is loaded.
   b. The Session Manager (SMSS.EXE) loads the high order services.
   c. The operating system kernel (NTOSKRNL.EXE) loads the Session Manager (SMSS.EXE).
   d. The operating system kernel (NTOSKRNL.EXE) is initialized and takes control of the system.
36. Your Windows XP Server has encountered a series of stop errors. How do you configure Windows 2000 to save stop error information to a memory dump file?
   a. Specify the recovery option in Dr. Watson.
   b. Specify the recovery option in Performance Monitor.
   c. Specify the proper recovery option on the Startup/Shutdown tab in System Properties.
   d. Specify the recovery option in Server Manager.
37. You are the administrator of a Windows 2000 Professional computer. You install a non-plug-and-play modem, and Windows 2000 Professional does not detect the modem. Which procedures can you use to install the modem and ensure that its manufacturer-specific features are available (choose two)?
   a. Use the Add/Remove Hardware Wizard to reinstall the modem.
   b. Install the modem as a standard modem using the Install New Modem Wizard.
   c. Download and install a Windows 2000 INF file from the modem manufacturer.
   d. Open Device Manager and choose the Scan for hardware changes option from the Action menu to reinstall the modem.

HANDS-ON EXERCISES

Exercise 1: Installing Windows XP

You will need an 8 GB hard drive or larger.

1. Boot with the Windows XP installation CD.
2. If you have an evaluation copy, it will give you a warning saying that the evaluation copy will expire. Press the Enter key.
3. When the "Welcome to Setup" screen appears, press the Enter key.
4. When the license agreement appears, press the F8 key to continue.
5. If you have any previous versions of Windows XP on your system and it asks you to repair, press Esc for don't repair.
6. If you have any partitions, delete them by highlighting each partition and pressing the D key to delete the partition. If it asks whether you are deleting the system partition, press the Enter key. Press the L key to delete the partition.
7. When you are back to the partition screen, press C to create a partition. Specify 6144 MB and press the Enter key.
8. Create another partition (D drive) as 1,024 MB. Leave the rest of the drive unpartitioned.
9. With the C drive highlighted, press the Enter key to install.
10. Format the partition as a FAT file system. When it states that it will format with the FAT32 file system, press the Enter key.
11. When the system reboots and start a graphical interface, it will then automatically detect and install the hardware devices. Next it will ask for the regional settings. Select the appropriate regional settings and click on the Next button.
12. To personalize your software, enter the name and the company that you work for. Click on the Next button.
13. Type in your product code and click on the Next button.
14. The next screen shows a random computer name. Change the computer name to ServerXP-*xxy* where *xx* represent your two-digit partner number in the class and *y* represents A if you are computer A or B if you are computer B. If you are not doing this in class, use 01. Therefore, if you are the first set of partners and you are using the computer on the left, you would use ServerXP-01A. If you are the first set of partners and you are using the computer on the right, you would use ServerXP-01B. Lastly, enter the password of *password* in the Administrator password and confirm password text boxes. Click on the Next button.
15. If your computer has a modem, a modem dialing information box will appear. Enter your area code and type in the appropriate options for your computer. Click on the Next button.
16. For the Date and Time Settings, enter the proper information and click on the Next button.
17. Windows XP will configure the Networking Settings. Select typical settings and click on the Next button.
18. The next window asks if you want to be a member of a workgroup or a computer domain. For now, select No and click on the Next button. It will then copy some files and perform final tasks.
19. When the Windows XP Setup Wizard is complete, click on the Finish button and the computer will reboot.
20. Windows will adjust your screen resolution. When it asks if you can read text in a dialog box, click on OK to continue.
21. When Windows XP thanks you for the purchase, click on the Next button.
22. Type your first name in the Your Name text box. Click on the Next button.
23. Click on the Finish button.
24. When it asks to take a tour of Windows XP, click on the *X* button in the top right corner of the dialog box.
25. Install the appropriate chipset drivers for the motherboard and any other drivers that are needed for your system (video, network, sound, etc.).
26. If you are connected to the Internet, start Internet Explorer, open the Tools menu, and select the Windows update option to go Microsoft's website to search for updates. Download and install any updates that are needed.

Exercise 2: Exploring the Windows XP Security Dialog Box and Windows Task Manager

1. Click on the Start button and select Log Off.
2. Log in as your user account.
3. Click on the Start button and select Shutdown. Click on Restart.
4. After Windows starts, press the Ctrl + Alt + Del keys, open the Shut Down menu, and select Switch users. If you had more than one user, this is where you can switch from one person to another. Click on your user account again.

5. Press Ctrl+Alt+Del to open the Task Manager. Open the Shut Down menu and select Restart. Notice that the system automatically logs in as your user account.
6. Open the Start button and select the Control Panel option. Select the User Accounts option.
7. Select the Change way users log on or off.
8. Read the text under the Use the Welcome Screen and the Use Fast User Switching options.
9. To make the system more secure, deselect the Use the Welcome Screen. Click on Apply Options.
10. Click the Change an Account button.
11. Click your account.
12. Click the Create a password and specify the password of *password.* Click the Create Password button.
13. Close the Control Panel.
14. Reboot the computer and log in as your computer account.
15. Press Ctrl+Alt+Del to open the Windows XP Security dialog box.
16. Click on the Lock Computer option.
17. Unlock the computer.
18. Open the Windows XP Security dialog box and click on the Change Password button. Change the password to *today.*
19. Change the password back to *password.*
20. Open the Windows XP Security dialog box and select Task Manager. Click on the Process tab. After you study the Process tab, click the Performance tab.
21. At the bottom of the Windows Task Manager window, notice the number of processors and the CPU usage. In addition, notice the amount of system cache, located beneath the graphs.
22. Go back to the Process tab and check briefly for a WORDPAD.EXE listing.
23. Open the WordPad program by clicking on the Start button, selecting the Accessories option, and selecting the WordPad option.
24. Notice the WORDPAD.EXE listing in the Processes tab and a Document-WordPad listed in the Application tab. In the Application tab, click on the Document-WordPad listing and click on the End Task button.
25. Click on the Start button and select the Run option. In the Open box, type CMD and click on the OK button. This is another way to open a command prompt window.
26. If you go back to the Windows Task Manager, you will find a *Command Prompt* entry under the Application tab and an *NTVDM.EXE* entry under the Process tab. Remember that the command prompt and DOS programs run under a NTVDM. You should also notice that the NTVDM.EXE entry has almost no CPU activity and the CPU is not very busy as shown by the System Idle Process entry and the CPU Usage shown at the bottom of the Task Manager window.
27. Be sure that you arrange the command prompt window and the Task Manager window so that you can see both at the same time.
28. Switch to the command prompt window and type *in edit.*
29. Again, look at the CPU usage for the NTVDM.EXE and System Idle Process and look at the CPU Usage at the bottom of the Task Manager window.
30. In the DOS command windows, press the Alt+F keys to open the File menu. To constantly scroll through the File menu, press the down arrow key and keep it pressed. Look at the CPU activity for the NTVDM.EXE and System Idle process and look at the CPU Usage.
31. After releasing the down arrow key, click on the Performance tab and look at the CPU Usage History graph.
32. Edit the Edit program and close the command prompt.
33. Close the Task Manager.

Exercise 3: Booting Windows XP

1. Click the Start button and select the Turn Off Computer button. Click the Restart button. During the reboot, notice that the Boot menu does not appear. This is because there is only one entry in the Boot menu.
2. Reboot the computer again. As soon as the POST screen ends and Windows is about to start loading, press the F8 key to show the Boot menu.
3. As you can see at the bottom of the screen, the "For Troubleshooting and advanced startup" options for Windows, press F8 message. Press the F8 key.
4. The Windows Advanced Options menu appears. Select the safe mode and press the Enter key. With Windows XP highlighted, press the Enter key.
5. Log in as administrator.
6. Click the Start button and select the Run option.
7. From the Run option, execute the MSCONFIG and MSINFO32 commands.
8. Close MSCONFIG and MSINFO32 utilites.
9. Shut down Windows and restart it again. Enter the Advanced Options menu and select safe mode with command prompt. Select the Windows XP and press the Enter key.

10. Log in as administrator. Reboot once more and perform a normal boot.
11. Start a command prompt window by clicking the Start button, clicking on All Programs, clicking on Accessories, and then selecting Command Prompt.
12. Change to the C:\WINDOWS directory and execute the edit NTBTLOG.TXT file. This is the text file that shows what was loaded and not loaded during the safe boots.
13. Close Edit and close the Command Prompt window.
14. Open the Start button and select the Run option. Execute the CMD command.
15. Execute the CD\ command.
16. The C:> prompt should be showing. Type in the *DIR* command and press the Enter key.
17. The directory shows the Windows, Document and Settings, and Program Files directories. Type *DIR/AH* and press the Enter key.
18. The directory listing shows the NTLDR, NTDETECT.COM, BOOT.INI, and PAGEFILE.SYS (virtual memory–paging file) files.
19. By default, Windows NT and Windows 2000 have the BOOT.INI file read-only, hidden, and system. Windows XP has it as a hidden file and system file. To shut off attributes, execute this command

    ```
    attrib -r-s-h boot.ini
    ```
20. Type *EDIT BOOT.INI* and press the Enter key.
21. At the end of the [operating system] section, add the following line:

    ```
    multi(0)disk(0)rdisk(0) partition(2)\Windows="2nd menu option"
    /fastdetect
    ```
22. Notice the default timeout. Save the file by pressing Alt+F key and selecting Save. Then exit edit and the command prompt.
23. Reboot the computer, let the 15 seconds run out, and let the default boot menu load.
24. Reboot the computer and select the second menu option. Notice the error. This was caused because it is looking for a \WINDOWS directory in the second partition, which does not exist.
25. Open the Start button, right-click My Computer, and select Properties. Click the Advanced tab. Click the Settings button in the Startup and Recovery section. Click the Edit button on the Boot menu option and change partition 2 to 1 from the second menu option. Save the changes.
26. Open the Start menu and open My Computer. Open the C drive. Right-click the BOOT.INI file and select Properties. Make the file hidden again. Click the OK button.
27. Reboot Windows and enter the Advanced Boot menu.
28. If you install a driver and the driver prevents you from starting Windows or logging on to Windows, you would select the Last Known Good Configuration option. Therefore, select the Last Known Good Configuration option. Then select the appropriate Windows that you want to boot, and boot Windows.
29. Click the Start button and select the Run option. Type in MSCONFIG and click on the OK button.
30. Using the System Configuration utility, you can select which drivers, services, and programs you want to automatically start up during the startup of Windows.
31. Click the SYSTEM.INI and WIN.INI tabs and view the contents. These options are used if you have an older program or driver that was created for the Windows 3.XX environment.
32. Click the BOOT.INI tab. This allows you to easily configure the BOOT.INI file.
33. Click the Services tab. This allows you to enable or disable services during boot-up. Of course, you can always use the Services console.
34. Click the Startup tab. These are all of the small programs that are loaded automatically during startup. Notice that they have the command and its location. The location will specify how it is being loaded using the registry settings or the Common Startup folder. Often when loading applications software such as Microsoft Office, WinZip, Real Player, and virus checkers, small programs will be loaded during boot-up so that they are activated during boot-up or to increase the startup of the application when you want to start it. Unfortunately, this slows down your boot time. Therefore, you can experiment by unchecking an option and seeing if it affects the boot-up of Windows.
35. Click the OK button.

Exercise 4: Learning the Windows XP Interface

1. Start Windows XP and log in.
2. If any windows are open, close them.
3. Open the Start menu and select My Computer.
4. Double-click on the C drive to open a C:\ window.
5. If you cannot see the BOOT.INI file and the other boot files (NTLDR and NTDETECT), open the Tools menu, click on Folder Options, and select the View tab. If the option is not already enabled, select the Show hidden

files and folders option. Also, deselect the Hide extensions for known file types and Hide protected operating system files (Recommended) options. If it asks if you are sure you want to display these files, click on the Yes button. Click on the OK button.

6. Start the Calculator by clicking on the Start button, clicking on All Programs, clicking on Accessories, and selecting the Calculator. Close the Calculator by clicking on the Close button on the top right corner of the Calculator.
7. Start the Calculator by double-clicking on My Computer, double-clicking on the C drive, double-clicking Windows, double-clicking the SYSTEM32 folder, and double-clicking on the CALC file.
8. Start the Calculator by using the Run option under the Start button and specifying the path of C:\WINDOWS\SYSTEM32\CALC.EXE. Close the Calculator.
9. Start the Calculator by using the Run option under the Start button and using the Browse button to find CALC.EXE. Close the Calculator.
10. Under Accessories, open Windows Explorer. Find the Calculator program and start it. Close the Calculator.
11. Click on the Start button and select My Documents. Click on the Folders button in the toolbar. Notice the similarities between this window and Windows Explorer. This is because Windows Explorer is providing the interface that we are using. Again, find the Calculator program and start it. Close the Calculator program.
12. Click on the Start button and select the Search option.
13. Click on the All files and folders option. Type *CALC* in the All or part of the file name text box. Click on the Search button.
14. When the CALC.EXE file is found, double-click the program to start it. Close the Calculator.
15. Right-click the CALC.EXE entry in the search results list and select Open Containing Folder. Notice the folder that it opened. Close the C:\WINDOWS\SYSTEM32 window and search window.
16. Open a window for the C:\DOCUMENTS AND SETTINGS*USER_LOGIN_NAME* folder (where *user_login_name* is the name used during the login) and notice the DESKTOP folder.
17. Double-click to open the DESKTOP folder and look at its contents.
18. Minimize the DESKTOP folder.
19. Create a shortcut for the Calculator (C:\WINDOWS\SYSTEM32\CALC.EXE) program. You can do this by using the shortcut menu (right-click the mouse button on the desktop) and selecting the New option followed by the Shortcut option. Notice the small arrow that indicates that this icon is a shortcut.
20. Test the Calculator shortcut. Close the Calculator.
21. Right-click the desktop, select the New option, and then select the Text Document option. Use Notepad to create a text file named NAME.TXT. Include your first and last name on the first line and Desktop on the second line. Save the changes and close Notepad.
22. Double-click the NAME (Desktop).TXT file. Notice that Notepad automatically opens. That is because this file has a TXT file name extension and files with a TXT extension are associated (file association) with Notepad.
23. Close Notepad.
24. If you remember, the DESKTOP folder is minimized. To switch to it, you can use either the Alt+Tab keys or you can find and click on the task from the Taskbar. Find it on the Taskbar and click on it. Notice the shortcuts that you have created on the desktop are located in the DESKTOP folder.
25. Open the Tools menu and select Folder Options. Click the File Types tab. Find the TXT file name extension and click on it. Notice that it shows that these files open with Notepad.
26. Close the Folders Options dialog box and the Desktop window.
27. Open the C:\WINDOWS directory.
28. Open the Tiles option under the View menu.
29. Select the Icons option under the View menu.
30. Select the List option under the View menu.
31. Select the Details option under the View menu.
32. Find and click on the View button on the toolbar and select the Icons option.
33. Select the Details view.
34. Open the View menu, point to Toolbars, and deselect Standard Toolbar. The toolbar should disappear.
35. Open the View menu, point to Toolbars, and select the Standard Toolbar.
36. Open the View menu, point to Arrange Icons by, and select Type (by type means that it will sort by file name extension).
37. Select the Icons view.
38. In the Windows window, without clicking on an icon, open the shortcut menu (by right-clicking), point to the Arrange Icons by option, and click on the Name option.
39. Make sure the Windows window does not auto-arrange its icons. This can be done by opening the View menu and pointing to the Arrange Icons by option. If there is a check mark on the Auto Arrange option, click on it to shut if off. If there is not a check mark on the Auto Arrange option, click somewhere on the desktop to close the menu.
40. Move around some of the files (not folders) and place some of them on top of other files.

41. Open the View menu and select Refresh.
42. Enable the Auto Arrange feature for the Windows window.
43. Close all windows.
44. Click on the Start button and open My Computer.
45. Double-click on the C drive.
46. Open the WINDOWS folder.
47. Open the SYSTEM32 folder.
48. Click on the Up One Level button. Keep clicking on the Up One Level button until you get back to the My Computer window.
49. When you have a window open and you double-click on a folder, the current window will change to the folder that you are opening. To change this, open the Tools menu, select Folder Options, and select the General tab. Then select the Open each folder in its own window option.
50. In the C drive window, double-click the WINDOWS folder.
51. In the C:\WINDOWS folder, double-click the FONTS folder.
52. Change back to the C:\WINDOWS folder by using the Alt+Tab keys.
53. In the C:\WINDOWS folder, double-click the SYSTEM32 folder.
54. Open the Tools menu, select Folder Options, and select the General tab. Then select the Open each folder in its same window option.
55. Close all windows.
56. Right-click My Documents and select Properties. Notice the Target Folder Location. If you had another location in which you want to make the default location for your data documents, you would change it here. Examples may be another drive specifically used to hold data or a network drive that gets backup on a regular basis.
57. Click the OK button.

Exercise 5: Understanding File Management

1. During the installation, you created a second partition but it has not been formatted. Double-click the D drive. When it asks if you want to format it, click the No button.
2. Right-click the D drive and select Format. Format the partition with the NTFS file system and enable compression. Click on the Start button and the OK button.
3. Insert a disk in drive A. Under My Computer, use the shortcut menu of the A drive and format the disk.
4. Under My Computer, use the shortcut menu of the D drive and format the disk as an NTFS partition.
5. Open a window for the A drive.
6. Create a folder called COMMAND on the A drive using the shortcut menu.
7. Open the A:\COMMAND folder
8. Open a window for the C:\WINDOWS\SYTEM32.
9. Close all windows except for the COMMAND and SYSTEM32 windows.
10. Copy the FORMAT.COM and ATTRIB.EXE files from the C:\WINDOWS\SYSTEM32 folder to the A:\COMMAND folder.
11. Right-click the DISKCOPY.COM file in the SYSTEM32 folder, select the Send to option, and select the A drive. This will copy the file to the A drive.
12. Switch to the A:\ folder. Right-click in the empty space of the A:\ window, select New, and select folder. Call the folder DATA.
13. Move the FORMAT.COM file from the A:\COMMAND folder to the A:\DATA folder.
14. Copy the FORMAT.COM file from the A:\DATA folder.
15. Using the shortcut menu of the A drive, perform a disk copy to another disk. Note: A disk has to be in the disk drive before the Copy disk option will appear.
16. Rename the FORMAT.COM file to DESTROY.COM in the A:\DATA folder.
17. Make the DESTROY.COM file hidden by using the shortcut menu of the DESTROY.COM file and selecting Properties.
18. If you cannot see hidden files, select Options under the View menu, click on the View menu, select Show All Files, and click on the OK button.
19. Use the Copy option from the shortcut menu of XCOPY.EXE file in the C:\WINDOWS\SYTEM32 folder to the C:\COMMAND folder.
20. Make the A:\ window active. On the A:\ window, select the Paste option from the shortcut menu.
21. Delete the DESTROY.COM file.
22. Using the A:\ window, highlight both folders at the same time and delete them.
23. Start Windows Explorer.
24. Using the shortcut menu of the A drive shown in Windows Explorer, format the disk.
25. Create a folder called COMMAND on the C drive using the shortcut menu of the C drive window.

26. Click on the COMMAND folder. Notice that the right side of the windows should show no files.
27. Click on the plus (+) next to the C:\WINDOWS folder in Explorer to show the subdirectories under WINDOWS.
28. Click on the SYSTEM32 folder under the WINDOWS directory.
29. Copy FORMAT.COM, ATTRIB.EXE, and DISKCOPY.COM files from the C:\WINDOWS\SYSTEM32 folder to the C:\COMMAND folder.
30. Delete the FORMAT.COM and ATTRIB.EXE files from the C:\COMMAND directory.
31. Double-click on the Recycle Bin. These are the files that you deleted in the GUI interface.
32. Drag the FORMAT.COM file to the desktop.
33. Highlight ATTRIB.EXE and select Restore from the shortcut menu or click on the Restore button on the left side of the Recycle Bin window.
34. Look in the COMMAND folder and notice that the ATTRIB.EXE file is back.
35. Select the Empty Recycle Bin option from the File menu.
36. Close the Recycle Bin window.
37. Access the shortcut menu of the Recycle Bin and select Properties. Notice the maximize size of the Recycle Bin.
38. Click on the OK button.
39. In the My Computer window, right-click the A drive and format it as a system disk.
40. View the contents of the drive and notice the files that it added.
41. Use the disk to boot the system.
42. Try to access the C drive and the D drive. Can you figure out why it can access the C drive and not the D drive?

Exercise 6: Using the Control Panel

System Applet

1. Open the Start button, right-click My Computers, and select Properties. This will open the System Properties.
2. Close the System Properties dialog box.
3. Open the Start button and select the Control Panel.
4. Select Performance and Maintenance. Click the System applet.
5. Close the System Properties dialog box.
6. Click on the Up button on the toolbar.
7. In the left pane, click the switch to Classic View.
8. Double-click the System applet. Record the Windows XP version, the processor ID listed under Computer, and the amount of physical memory.
9. Click on the Hardware tab followed by clicking on the Device Manager button.
10. Open the View menu and select the Resources By Type option.
    a. Find what device is using IRQ 5.
    b. Find which IRQ is being used for COM2 and the hard drive.
    c. Find which IRQs are free.
    d. Find what device is using I/O address 300.
    e. Find what device is using DMA 2.
    f. Find what DMAs are being used by the sound card.
11. Open the View menu and select the Devices By Type option.
12. On the device tree, find and double-click on COM2.
    a. Find and record the device status.
    b. Find and record the bits per second, the number of data bits and stop bits, the type of parity, and the type of flow control.
    c. Find and record the resources used by COM2.
    d. Find and record the entries in the Conflicting Device List
13. Disable the COM2 by using the Device usage option in the General tab.
14. If you have a sound card loaded, find it and delete the sound card from the device tree.
15. Close the Device Manager.
16. Click on the Add Hardware Wizard button. Note: You can also use the Add/Remove Hardware applet in the Control Panel. Click on the Next button.
17. Select the Add/Troubleshoot a device option and click the Next button. The sound card should automatically be detected and the drivers loaded. If not, you will have to manually load the drivers by either specifying the type of card or the location of the drivers. When done, click on the Finish button.
18. Click on the Driver Signing button. By default, it will warn or prompt you if a driver is being loaded that is not signed. Click the Cancel button.
19. Click on the Advanced tab followed by clicking on the Performance option. If the computer is going to be used as a production server used by many people, optimize for Background services. If it is used primarily by you to run applications, optimize for Applications.

20. Click on the Change button under Virtual memory.
21. Notice the initial size and maximize size. Add 20 MB to the initial size by typing the number and clicking on the Set button.
22. Select the D drive. Type in *384 MB* for the initial size and *768 MB* for the maximize size. Click on the Set button. Note: You should create two paging files on the same physical driver. Instead, it is better to put them on two or more physical drivers, not logical drives. In addition, it is best not to use the drive that has the boot volume (the drive with the WINDOWS directory).
23. Remove the entry for the D drive by putting in 0 for the initial size and maximize size. Click on the Set button. Click on the OK button to close the Virtual Memory dialog box and click on the OK button to close the Performance Options dialog box.
24. Click on the Startup and Recovery button. Change the time to display the operating systems to 20 seconds. Click on the OK button.
25. Open the BOOT.INI file. Look at the file and notice that the new time is 20 seconds.
26. Close the System applet.

Display Applet

27. Click the Start button, select the Control Panel, and select the Display applet.
28. Select the Desktop tab and change the background pattern to Windows XP. Click the Apply button.
29. Select the Screen Saver tab and enable the Starfield screen saver and have it activate after 2 minutes of inactivity. If the computer needs to be kept secure, you would enable On resume, password protect.
30. Select the Appearance tab. Under Windows and buttons, select Windows Classic Style.
31. Under the color scheme, load the High Contrast Black appearance schemes. Click the Apply button.
32. Load the Lilac appearance scheme.
33. Load the Windows Standard appearance scheme.
34. Under the Windows and buttons, select Windows XP style.
35. Under the Appearance tab, click the Advanced button. Increase the horizontal icon spacing to 75 pixels and change the icon text to bold, 15-point Arial. Click the Apply button.
36. Change the horizontal icon spacing to 43 and the icon text to 8-point Tahoma. Click the Apply button.
37. Under the Appearance tab, select the Font size, Normal option and click the Apply button.
38. Click the Desktop tab and click the Customize Desktop button.
39. If you want to add My Computer, My Documents, or Internet Explorer to the desktop, you would enable the corresponding option. Click the OK button.
40. Click on the Settings tab.
41. Record the current resolution and color quality.
42. If possible, change the screen resolution to 640 × 480 and number of colors to 16 (4-bit). Click on the OK button.
43. Change the screen resolution to 800 × 600, number of colors to 256 colors (8-bit), and small fonts. Click on the OK button.
44. Change the screen resolution to 800 × 600, number of colors to high color (16-bit), and large fonts. Click on the OK button.
45. Try to change the screen resolution to 1024 × 768 and number of colors to True color (32-bit).
46. Change the display back to the recorded resolution and number of colors.
47. Click on the Advanced Properties button.
48. Record the manufacturer and type of the video card and monitor.
49. Close the Display dialog box.

Add/Remove Programs

50. Go to the http://www.adobe.com and download the Adobe Acrobat Reader. Install Adobe Acrobat Reader.
51. Double-click the Add or Remove Programs applet in the Control Panel.
52. Under Change or Remove Programs, find Adobe Acrobat Reader and click on it. Then click on the Change/Remove button to remove the program.
53. Click on the Add/Remove Windows Components, click on the Other Network File and Print Services option, click on the Details button, and select the Print services for UNIX. Click on the OK button.
54. Click on the Next button. Use the wizard to finish the installation. You may need your Windows Installation CD.
55. Close the Add/Remove Programs dialog box.

Date and Time Applet

56. Using the Date/Time applet, change the date of the computer to March 17, 2005.
    Record the day of the week of March 17, 2005.
    Change the time to 2:00 A.M.

57. Change the time zone to Greenwich Mean Time.
58. Close the Date/Time dialog box.
59. On the Taskbar, double-click the time.
60. Change the date, time, and time zone back to the correct settings.

Mouse and Keyboard Applet

61. Using the Mouse applet, maximize the Mouse Tracking Speed. Test the mouse by moving it across the screen.
62. Minimize the Mouse Tracking Speed. Testing the mouse by moving it across the screen.
63. Maximize the mouse double-clicking speed. Test the mouse by double-clicking in the test area.
64. Adjust the mouse double-clicking speed. Test the mouse by double-clicking in the test area.
65. Adjust the mouse double-clicking speed to your own preference.
66. Activate the Mouse Pointer Trails and move the mouse. The Mouse Pointer Trails are used on notebook and laptop computers with screens that cannot update fast enough to keep up with the movement of the mouse.
67. Deactivate the Mouse Pointer Trail.
68. Start Microsoft WordPad.
69. Press the T key and hold it down. Notice how long it takes before the key starts repeating and how fast it repeats after it starts.
70. Using the Keyboard applet in the Control Panel, set the Repeat Delay to Short and the Repeat Rate to Fast.
71. Go back to the Microsoft WordPad. Press the Q key and hold it down. Notice how long the key takes before it starts repeating and how fast it repeats after it starts.
72. Place the Repeat Delay and the Repeat Rate to somewhere near the middle.

Power Options Applet

73. Open the Power Options applet.
74. Record the current power scheme and turning off monitor and hard disk settings.
75. Select the Portable/Laptop power scheme. View the turning off monitor and hard disk settings.
76. Select the Presentation power scheme. View the turning off monitor and hard disk settings.
77. Select the Max Battery power scheme. View the turning off monitor and hard disk settings.
78. Select the original power scheme and change the turning off monitor and hard disk settings back to their original settings.
79. Click the Hibernate tab. Read the use for hibernate mode.
80. Click the UPS tab. If you had a UPS, this is how you enable it to work with Windows.
81. Close the Power Options dialog box.

Exercise 7: Configuring the Taskbar

1. Right-click the Taskbar and select Properties. Select the Auto-hide the taskbar and show Quick Launch options. Click on the OK button.
2. When the mouse is not on the Taskbar, notice that it hides itself.
3. Move the mouse pointer so that the Taskbar shows.
4. Next to the Start button, you will find the Quick Launch icons, which consist of the Internet Explorer, Media Player, and Show Desktop quick start icons.
5. Open the MY DOCUMENTS window.
6. Click on the Show Desktop icon.
7. Click on it again.
8. Try to drag the Taskbar to the other three corners.
9. Right-click the Taskbar and unlock the Taskbar by deselecting the Lock the Taskbar option.
10. Drag the Taskbar to the other three corners.
11. Drag the Taskbar back down to the bottom of the screen.
12. Go to the C:\WINDOWS\SYSTEM32 folder. Right-click the CALCULATOR.EXE program and select the Create Shortcut option.
13. Take the new shortcut that you just created and drag it to the Quick Launch section.
14. Click on the calculator quick launch icon.
15. Close the Calculator.
16. Right-click the calculator quick launch icon and delete the icon.
17. Start WordPad and then Paint.
18. Using the Taskbar, switch back to WordPad.
19. Using the shortcut menu of the WordPad button, close WordPad.
20. Start WordPad several times.

21. Notice that all instances of the WordPad program are grouped together on the Taskbar. To move from one WordPad document to another, click on the WordPad button on the Taskbar and select the one you want to switch to.
22. Open the Taskbar properties and deselect the Group Similar taskbar buttons. Click on the OK button.
23. You can expand the Taskbar by dragging the top edge of the Taskbar up.
24. Select the Start button, select the Settings option, and select the Taskbar option.
25. Right-click the Taskbar and select Lock the Taskbar.
26. Using the shortcut menu of the Taskbar, select the Properties option. Select the Start Menu tab. Click on the Customize button. Look at the options that are available in the General and the Advanced tab.
27. Open My Computer and click on the Folders button on the toolbar.
28. Navigate to the C:\DOCUMENTS AND SETTINGS\ *USER_LOGIN_NAME*\ directory and notice the content of the Start menu folder.
29. Navigate to the C:\DOCUMENTS AND SETTINGS\ALL USERS\START MENU directory and notice the content of the Start menu folder.
30. Compare the contents of these two Start menu folders to the programs under the Start button.
31. Go back to the Explorer showing the Start menu programs. Expand the STARTUP folder. These are the programs that automatically start during boot-up.
32. Create a shortcut to the Calculator and copy it to your *USER_LOGIN_NAME*\START MENU folder.
33. Close all windows and the Taskbar Properties dialog box and restart Windows. Notice the calculator automatically started.
34. Go back into the Taskbar Properties option and remove the calculator from the STARTUP folder.

Exercise 8: Using the MMC Console

Administrative Tools

1. Click on the Start button and open the Control Panel.
2. Double-click Administrative Tools.
3. Use the Up arrow button to go back to the Control Panel.
4. Right-click the Taskbar and select Properties.
5. Click the Start Menu tab and click the Customize tab. Click the Advanced tab.
6. In the System Administrative section, enable Display on the All Programs menu and the Start Menu option.
7. Look at the other options that are available on this dialog box.
8. Click the OK button on the Customized Start Menu dialog box.
9. Click the OK button on the Taskbar and Start Menu Properties dialog box. You will now find Administrative Tools on the Start menu.

Computer Management Console

10. Click on the Start button, select the Programs option, select the Administrative Tools option, and select the Computer Management option.
11. Open the Event Viewer. Click on the System option under Event Viewer. Look for any errors. If you find one, double-click it to view it.
12. Go back to the Event Viewer and click on the Application option under the Event Viewer. Look for any errors. If you find one, double-click to view it.
13. Close the Event Viewer branch.
14. Click on the System Summary under System information. Record the amount of virtual memory currently being used.
15. Double-click on the Hardware resources and click on the IRQs to show which devices are using which devices.
16. Click on the Services option located under Services and Applications. This will display all of the services loaded on your system.
17. To get a better view of the services, open the View menu and select the Detail option. Record the status of the service, workstation, and print spooler service.
18. Right-click the Server option and select the Stop option.
19. Right-click the Server option and select the Start option.
20. Right-click the Server option and select the Properties option.
21. Record the Startup type.
22. Close the Computer Management console.

Adding and Removing Components to the MMC

23. Click on the Start button and select the Run option. Execute the MMC command.
24. Open the Console menu and select the Add/Remove Snap-in option. Click on the Add button.

25. Double-click on the Disk Defragmenter and the Event Viewer. If the Select Computer dialog box comes up, select local computer. Note: It is the Select Computer dialog box that allows you to remotely administer other computers. Click on the Close button. Click on the OK button.
26. Click on the Defragmenter. Double-click on Event Viewer.
27. Open the Console menu and select the Save option. Save the MMC console as MISC.MSC on the desktop. Close the console.
28. From the Desktop, double-click on the MISC.MSC file. Close the console.
29. Right-click the MISC.MSC file and select the Copy option.
30. Right-click the Taskbar and select the Properties option. Select the Advanced tab and follow by clicking on the Advanced button.
31. The Start menu should already be highlighted. In the right pane, right-click and select the Paste option.
32. Close the Start Menu dialog box. Close the Taskbar dialog box by clicking on the OK button.
33. Click on the Start button and run the MISC.MSC program.
34. Right-click on the System Event Viewer and select the New window from here option. Open the View menu and select the Tile Horizontally option.
35. Open the Console menu and select the Options option. Change the Console mode to User mode—Limited Access, Single window. Click on the OK button.
36. Close the Console and save the settings. When a warning appears asking if you are sure that you want to display a single window, click on the Yes button.
37. Start the MISC.MSC file. If you right-click any of the components, you will notice that there is New window from here option.
38. Close the Console.

Exercise 9: Working with the Registry

1. Start the Display applet in the Control Panel.
2. Set the Wallpaper to Water Color and Tile it.
3. Set the screen saver to flying windows and set the wait time to 3 minutes.
4. Start REGEDIT.EXE.
5. Find the following value:

   HKEY_CURRENT_USER\Control Panel\Desktop\ScreenSaveTimeOut
   Notice the value and compare it to the wait time of the screen saver. Remember, 1 minute equals 60 seconds.

6. Change the ScreenSaveTimeOut value to 120 seconds.
7. Find the following value:

   HKEY_CURRENT_USER\Control Panel\Desktop\TileWallPaper
   Although the TileWallPaper value is a string, the TileWallPaper uses only a 1 or a 0 value. 1 indicates to tile the wallpaper and a 0 indicates not to tile the wallpaper.

8. Find the following value:

   HKEY_CURRENT_USER\Control Panel\Desktop\WallPaper

9. Find the following value:

   HKEY_LOCAL_MACHINE\hardware\description\system.
   Record the BIOS and BIOS date.

10. Find the following value:

    HKEY_LOCAL_MACHINE\hardware\description\system\centralprocessing\0
    Record the processor identifier and the speed.

11. Click on My Computer listed at the top of the tree.
12. Open the Edit menu and select the Find option. Search for processor until you get to HKEY_LOCAL_MACHINE\hardware\description\system\centralprocessor\0 parameters.
13. Exit REGEDIT.EXE.

Exercise 10: Creating a Volume

1. Start Computer Management.
2. In the left pane, click on Disk Management.
3. Right-click on Disk 0 and select the Properties option. Don't click on the partitions or volumes.
4. Click on the OK button to close the Disk 0 Properties dialog box.

5. Right-click the C drive and select the Properties option.
6. Click OK to close the Local Disk (C) dialog box.
7. You should have free disk space at the end of the first disk.
8. Right-click the unallocated disk space and select Create partition.
9. Select the Extended partition and click on the Next button.
10. Use the entire disk space for the partition and click on the Next button.
11. Assign the M drive to the partition. Click on the Next button.
12. Select to use the FAT32 file system and click on the Next button. Do not select Perform a Quick Format. Instead, for a network environment, you would rather have the system perform a more thorough format to find problems with the drive.
13. Click on the Finish button.
14. Right-click the M drive and select to format the drive as an NTFS partition.
15. Right-click the M drive and select the Delete option.

Exercise 11: Converting a FAT or FAT32 Partition to an NTFS Partition

NOTE: It is always recommended to perform a backup of all important data before doing a conversion to NTFS.

1. Right-click the unallocated disk space and create a FAT32 partition. Assign the drive letter M to the drive.
2. Start a command prompt.
3. At the command prompt, execute the CONVERT M: /FS:NTFS.
4. At the command prompt, execute the CONVERT C: /FS:NTFS. After the CONVERT command displays a message saying that it has to reboot the computer to finish the conversion, complete a proper shutdown of Windows XP and reboot the computer.

Exercise 12: Creating a Local User Account

1. Open the Control Panel and click the User Accounts option.
2. Click on the Create a New Account option. Create a CBrown account as a limited account.

Exercise 13: Understanding NTFS Rights

1. Open My Computer.
2. Open the Tools menu and select Folder Options. Select the View tab.
3. Under the Advanced settings section, deselect Use Simple File Sharing (recommended) option. Click the OK button.
4. On your C drive (which should be NTFS volume) create a folder called DIRN1.
5. In the DIRN1 folder, create a DIR2 folder.
6. In the DIRN2 folder, create a DIR3 folder.
7. In the DIRN3 folder, create a text file called FILE1.TXT. To create a text file, open the DIRN3 folder and right-click the empty space and select New, Text File. In the FILE1.TXT file, put in your first name.
8. Right-click the DIRN1 folder and select the Properties option. Click on the Security tab.
9. Click on the Add button. Type *CBrown* and click the OK button. Note the default permissions.
10. Log out as your account and log in as Charlie Brown.
11. Try to open the FILE1.TXT file.
12. Try to add your last name to the FILE1.TXT file, save the changes, and exit the program.
13. Try to delete the FILE1.TXT file and try to delete the DIRN2 folder.
14. Try to create a new text file called FILE2.TXT in the DIR1 folder.
15. Log out as CBrown and log in as your account.
16. Right-click the C drive and select Properties. On the Security tab, click on the Advanced button. Notice the special create permissions that are assigned to users which CBrown is a member of. This is why CBrown was able to create FILE2.TXT file.
17. Right-click the DIRN1 folder and click the Properties option.
18. From the Security tab, click to highlight Charlie Brown. Give Charlie Brown the Full Control permission.
19. Log out as your account and log in as CBrown.
20. Try to open the FILE1.TXT file.
21. Try to add your last name to the FILE1.TXT file, save the changes, and exit the program.
22. Try to delete the FILE1.TXT file and try to delete the DIRN2 folder.

Exercise 14: Using Windows XP Recovery

1. Insert the Windows XP Setup CD into your CD-ROM drive and boot from the CD.
2. When you get to the "Welcome to Setup" screen, press R for repair.
3. When it gets to the Recovery Console, type *1* and press Enter.
4. Enter the administrator password.
5. Change to the drive that contains the CD.
6. Change into the I386 director.
7. Copy the NTLDR file to the C:\.
8. Remove the CD and reboot the system.
9. Log in as your account.
10. Insert the Windows XP Setup CD into your CD-ROM drive. Click No when prompted to upgrade to Windows XP.
11. At the command prompt, switch to your CD-ROM drive, and then type the following:

    ```
    \I386\WINNT32.EXE /CMDCONS
    ```

12. When it asks if you want to install the Recovery Console, click on the Yes button.
13. Click OK when the Setup is complete.
14. Restart your computer and select the Recovery Console option from the Boot menu.
15. When it ask which Windows XP installation you would like, select the number listed next to the C:\WINDOWS directory and press the Enter key. When it asks you to type the administrator password, type in the password and press the Enter key.
16. At the C:\WINDOWS> command prompt, execute the HELP command. Press the spacebar to go back to the prompt.
17. Type in the DIR command. Keep pressing the spacebar until you are back to the command prompt.
18. At the command prompt, execute the FIXBOOT command. When it ask if you are sure, type in a *Y* and press the Enter key.
19. At the command prompt, execute the LISTSVC command. Keep pressing the spacebar until you are back to the command prompt.
20. At the command prompt, execute the EXIT command to reboot the computer.

Exercise 15: Using Roll Back Driver

1. Log on with your account.
2. Click Start, right-click My Computer, and then click Properties.
3. In the System Properties dialog box, click the Hardware tab, and then click Device Manager.
4. In Device Manager, expand Display Adapters, select the name of your display adapter, and then press Enter.
5. In the property sheet for your display adapter, click the Driver tab, and then click the Update Driver button.
6. The Hardware Update Wizard starts. Notice that Install the software automatically is the default option, and is the recommended option.
7. In the Update Hardware Wizard, select the Install from a list or specific location (Advanced) option, and then click Next.
8. Select the Don't search. I will choose the driver to install option, and then click Next.
9. Clear the Show compatible hardware check box, and then select a driver option that is different from your display adapter.
10. After selecting a different display adapter, click Next. An Update Driver Warning message may appear, informing you that the device driver is not recommended and Windows XP cannot verify that it is compatible with your hardware.
11. If the Update Driver Warning message appears, click Yes. Windows XP will copy the appropriate driver files for the device driver that you specified. At this time, a message may prompt you for the location of the Windows XP source CD-ROM. If this happens, insert your Windows XP Professional CD-ROM into your CD-ROM drive.
12. When the installation is complete, click Finish, and then click Close.
13. You may be prompted to restart your computer. Close all open windows, and then, if you are not prompted to restart the computer, shut down the computer.
14. Turn on the computer. After POST has finished and the display goes blank, press F8 to access the Windows Advanced Options menu.
15. On the Advanced Options menu, select safe mode and press Enter. You may need to press Enter again to select Windows XP Professional as the operating system.
16. You will notice that safe mode is displayed at each of the four corners of the screen.

17. Press Ctrl+Alt+Del display the Log On dialog box, and then log on as administrator with a password of *password.* A Desktop Warning message appears; click Yes.
18. Click Start, right-click My Computer, and then click Properties.
19. In the System Properties dialog box, click the Hardware tab, and then click Device Manager.
20. In Device Manager, expand Display Adapters, select the display adapter that you chose, and then press Enter. If a yellow circle with a black exclamation point icon appears next to your display adapter name, this means that the display adapter device driver that you chose to install is not compatible with the actual device you have installed.
21. In the property sheet for your display adapter, click the Driver tab, and then click Roll Back Driver. A message displays, asking if you are sure you would like to roll back to the previous driver. Click Yes.
22. You will notice that the name of the display adapter will change back to the name of the original device driver. Click Close. There is no file copy process this time because the previous driver was already available in the Windows system folders.
23. If you are prompted to restart the computer, click Yes. If you are not prompted to restart the computer, close all open windows, and then log off.

Exercise 16: Using System Restore

1. Under Accessories, point to System Tools and click on System Restore.
2. If you are installing software or making changes to your system, it is recommended that you create a restore point. Note: Some restore points are made automatically. Click on the Next button.
3. Type *Test* for the Restore point description. Click on the Create button.
4. Click on the Home button.
5. If software is misbehaving because of corruption or misconfiguration or there is not an easy way to undo a configuration, you can use System Restore. Click Restore My Computer to an earlier time. Click the Next button.
6. Look at the restore points created on the calendar as shown by the dates in bold.
7. Select the restore point that you just created and click the Next button.
8. Read the warnings and click on the Next button.
9. Let the system reboot so the restore can take place. When the system reboots, log back in.
10. Click the OK button in the System Restore window.

Exercise 17: Using System Information

1. Click on the Start button, All Programs, Accessories, System Tools, and System Information.
2. In the System Information dialog box, determine what version OS you are using.
3. Identify the system model (motherboard), processor, and BIOS (including the BIOS version and date).
4. Determine the amount of RAM the system is using.
5. Under Hardware Resources, select the Conflicts and Sharing option.
6. Select and view the IRQs and I/O addresses.
7. Under Components, select Display. Determine the video card it is using.
8. Under Internet Settings, open Internet Explorer and select Summary. Determine the version of Internet Explorer.

Exercise 18: Printing

1. Click the Start button and select Printers and Fax.
2. Install the Hewlett-Packard 4 printer driver. Assume that the printer will use LTP1.
3. If a printer is connected to the computer, unplug the printer cable.
4. Using the shortcut menu of the HP LaserJet III icon in the PRINTERS folder, pause the printer. Start Microsoft WordPad and load the README.TXT file coated in the C:\WINDOWS directory.
5. Use the Print option in the File menu. Make sure that the LaserJet III printer is selected.
6. Print the document three times.
7. Switch over to Print Manager by double-clicking on the minimized printer icon in the Taskbar.
8. Delete the three print jobs.
9. Close Print Manager for the LaserJet 4.
10. Install the driver for the NEC SilentWriter 2 Model 90.
11. Install the correct print driver for your printer and make it the default printer.
12. Connect the printer cable to the printer.

13. Using the Print option in the File menu, print the first page of the document using the NEC SilentWriter 2 Model 90 printer. Notice what happens if you select the wrong driver.
14. If necessary, delete the print job from the Program Manager.
15. Install the correct printer driver.
16. Make the correct printer the default printer.
17. Print the first page of the document again with the correct printer driver.
18. Right-click the printer and select Properties. Under the General tab, click the Print Test Page button.
19. In the General tab, click the Printing Preferences button followed by clicking the Advanced button. Notice the print quality and dithering settings.
20. Close the Printer dialog boxes.
21. Delete the NEC SilentWriter 2 and HP LaserJet 4 printer drivers.
22. If your printer becomes stalled, you first need to make sure you have plenty of free disk space. You then may need to restart the printer service. Under Administrative Tools, open the Services console. In the right pane, right-click Print spooler and select Restart.
23. Close the Services console.

Exercise 19: Using Performance Monitor

1. Start the Performance console from Administrative Tools.
2. Right-click the right pane and select the Add Counters option.
3. The % Performance Time option is already selected; click on the Explain button.
4. Click on the Add button to add % Performance Time counter to Performance Monitor.
5. Select the Interrupts/sec and click on the Add button.
6. Select the Cache for the Performance Object. Select the Copy Read Hits % from the counters list and click on the Add button.
7. Select the Paging File for the Performance Object. Select the % Usage from the counters list and click on the Add button.
8. Click on the Close button.
9. Start the Pinball game and play for a minute. Observe the graph.
10. Right-click the graph and select the Histogram option. Click on the OK button.
11. Play the Pinball game for a minute. Observe the histograph.
    Right-click the graph and select the Report option. Click on the OK button.
12. Play the Pinball game for a minute. Observe the report.
13. Close the Pinball game.
14. In the left pane, right-click the Counter Logs. In the New Log Settings dialog box, type in LOG1 and click the OK button.
15. Click the Add button and Add the % Processor Time counter.
16. Click the Close button, then click the OK button.
17. Start the Pinball game and play for 1 minute.
18. Right-click the LOG1 option in the right pane, and select the Stop option.
19. Click the System Monitor option in the left pane.
20. Right-click the chart and select the Properties option.
21. In the Source tab, click the Browse button and open C:\PERFLOGS\LOG1_000001.BLG. Click the OK button.
22. Add the % Processor Time counter.
23. Right-click the LOG1 from the left-pane of the Performance console and select the Properties option.
24. In the Log Files tab, change the Log file type to Text file–CSV. Click on the OK button.
25. Right-click the LOG1 from the left pane of the Performance console and select the Start option.
26. Start the Pinball game and play for 1 minute.
27. Right-click the LOG1 from the left pane of the Performance console and select the Stop option.
28. If you have access to Microsoft Excel, view the LOG1_000001.CSV located in the C:\PERFLOGS folder.

CHAPTER 22

Supporting Windows and Windows Applications

Topics Covered in This Chapter

Introduction

Along with troubleshooting hardware and the operating system, you also need to be able to troubleshoot the applications that are being run. Sometimes, many of these problems can be overcome with configuration changes. Others may be a result of drivers. In either case, you need to understand how the application runs on the computer and what the application does so that you can properly troubleshoot it.

Objectives

1. Differentiate among the three types of applications that Windows can run and explain how they multitask with other programs.
2. Run the Windows XP Compatibility Wizard.
3. Uninstall applications.
4. Install and configure Microsoft Office.
5. Update Microsoft Office.
6. Using Outlook Express and Outlook, retrieve and send emails.
7. Troubleshoot common problems with Microsoft Outlook.
8. Start the DirectX Diagnostic tool to verify DirectX functionality.

22.1 RUNNING PROGRAMS

Although Windows 2000 and Windows XP are 32-bit operating systems designed to run Win32 applications (such as Microsoft Office 97, 2000, and 2003), they will also run Win16 applications (programs written for Windows 3.XX) and DOS applications. Of course, when running any of these applications, problems can occur at any time. Therefore, it is best to understand how they run and what you can do to make them run if a problem does occur.

A **program,** sometimes referred to as a **process,** is a sequence of instructions that can be executed by a computer. A program consists of initializing code and data, a private memory address space, system resources (such as files, communication ports, and Windows resources), and one or more threads.

A **thread** is part of a program that can execute independently of other parts. Operating systems that support multithreading enable programmers to design programs whose threaded parts can execute concurrently. This can enhance a program by allowing multitasking, improving throughput, enhancing responsiveness, and aiding background processing. For example, Microsoft Word uses a thread to respond to keys typed on the keyboard by the user to place characters in a document. Other threads are used to check spelling and to paginate the document as the user types. If the user prints, another thread spools or feeds a document to the printer in the background. Of course, when a program uses multithreading, the programmer must carefully design the program in such a way that all the threads can run at the same time without interfering with each other.

Threads, tasks, and applications with a higher priority get a larger time slice. At the end of the time slice, the kernel can take back control of the computer without permission from the thread or program. See figure 22.1.

Win16-based applications (used by Windows 3.XX applications) use cooperative multitasking. Cooperative multitasking depends on applications cooperating with each other. Because Windows 3.XX uses cooperative multitasking, the application uses the microprocessor and voluntarily gives control back for other programs. Poorly written software applications that do not give up control can cause problems for other applications.

Win16–based applications in Windows 2000 and XP cannot take advantage of preemptive multitasking. Instead, the Win16-based applications share the same memory area or **virtual machine (VM)** and will all be assigned a single time slice. Unfortunately, if a program causes problems, it can cause all Win16-based applications to crash. However, all of the Win16-based applications are run preemptive with Win32-based applications and other Windows processes, which improves the performance of Win16-based applications.

Figure 22.1 Programs Under Windows 2000

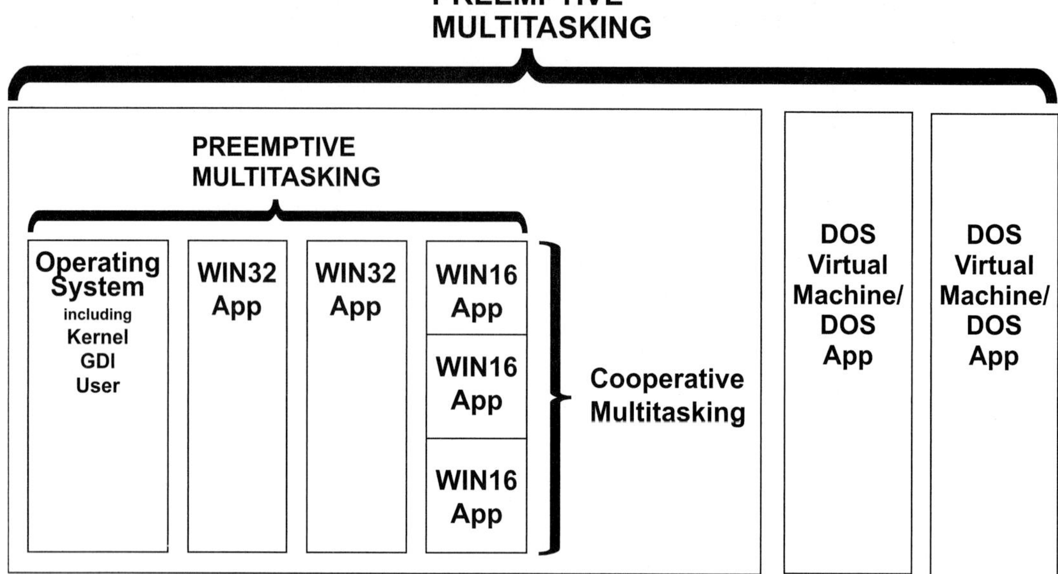

When the Windows kernel controls access to the processor, Windows assigns 32 different priorities to each process, numbered 0 to 31. The levels are divided as follows:

- Levels 0–15 are for user mode components
- Levels 16–31 are reserved for kernel mode components

The Windows kernel assigns each process a base priority level and a base priority level to each thread that executes within that process. The base priority for a thread can be adjusted by the kernel by two levels below to two levels above the level initially assigned. For example, if a thread were assigned a priority level of 8, the range would be from 6 to 10. If the thread is accepting user input, the kernel might raise the thread's priority level and if the thread requires computations, the kernel might assign it a lower priority.

22.1.1 Shortcuts and the Start Menu

When you need to start a program, you usually go to the Start menu and select the program that you want to start. You can also create and add shortcuts to the quick launch area on the Taskbar, on the desktop, or in a folder. Besides executable files to start a program, shortcuts can also point to data files, folders, printers, or computers.

To create and place a shortcut:

1. Open My Computer.
2. Double-click a drive or folder.
3. Click the item you want, such as a file, program, folder, printer, or computer.
4. On the File menu, click Create Shortcut.
5. Resize the window so you can see the desktop.
6. Drag the new shortcut to the desktop, a folder, quick launch area on the Taskbar, or the Start menu.

You can also drag an item to the desktop with the right mouse button, and then click Create Shortcut(s) Here. To change the shortcut's properties, right-click the shortcut, and then click Properties. When you delete a shortcut to an item, the original item is not deleted. It still exists on your computer in its original location.

When you right-click a file or folder, you display information such as size, location, and the date the file or folder was created. When you view the properties of a file or folder, you can also get information about the file or folder attributes, type of file, name of the program that opens the file, number of files and subfolders contained in the folder, and the last time the file was modified or accessed.

If you click on the Shortcut tab, it lists the shortcut name, target information, and shortcut key. It also allows you to choose the way the item is displayed when you open the shortcut: in a standard win-

Figure 22.2 Properties of a Shortcut

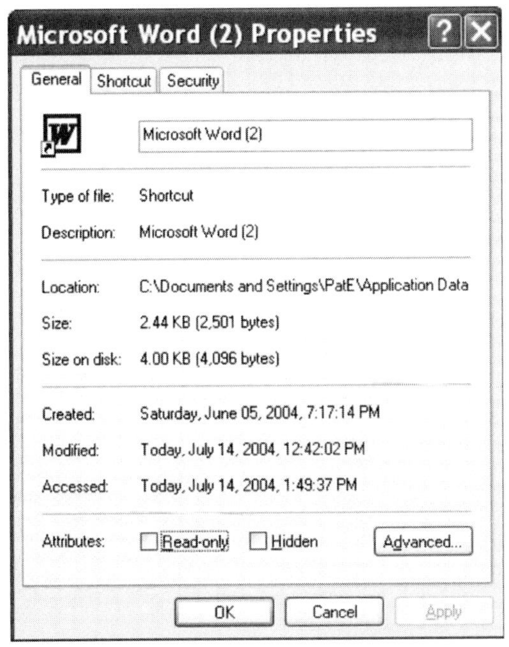

dow, a full screen (maximized), or as a button on the Taskbar (minimized). You can also view the shortcut's target, change the icon for the shortcut, and open a shortcut as a different user. See figure 22.2.

The Start menu is a collection of folders and shortcuts that are usually stored in the C:\DOCUMENT AND SETTINGS folder as part of a user profile. Because Windows 2000 and Windows XP are multiuser operating systems, they can keep track of start menus for each user. Therefore, you could modify one user's start menu by adding shortcuts that will not be seen by other users. For example, shortcuts found on the Start menu for all users are stored in the C:\DOCUMENTS AND SETTINGS\ALL USERS\START MENU folder.

To add a subfolder to the Start menu for all users in Windows XP, do the following:

1. Right-click the Start button, and then click Open All Users. In Windows 2000 or Windows XP, you can also navigate to the C:\DOCUMENTS AND SETTINGS\ALL USERS\START MENU folder using My Computer or Windows Explorer.
2. Double-click the folder in which you want to add a submenu, usually the PROGRAMS folder.
3. On the File menu, point to New, and then click Folder.
4. Type a name for the new submenu, and then press Enter.

Assuming that you are logged on as an administrator or member of the administrators group, to add programs to a submenu, in My Computer or Windows Explorer, click the icon for the program you want to add, drag it to the Start button, then to the submenu you added, and then to the list of programs in the submenu. You can either create new shortcuts or move existing shortcuts into the folder. Any shortcuts you add will appear on the Start menu for all users who log on to the computer.

NOTE: If your computer is connected to a network, network policy settings may also prevent you from completing this procedure.

To add or delete a shortcut from the Start menu for a single user, if you are logged in as that user, you can drag shortcuts on or off the Start menu or you can open the C:\DOCUMENTS AND SETTINGS*USER_NAME*\START MENU folder and add or delete shortcuts. If you are logged in as the administrator, you would have to open the C:\DOCUMENTS AND SETTINGS*USER_NAME*\START MENU folder and add or delete shortcuts. Again, if your computer is connected to a network, network policy settings may also prevent you from completing this procedure.

If you add or remove Start menu shortcuts for the default user profile, you will affect new users that you create afterward. However, these shortcuts will not affect any created users and their profiles.

22.1.2 Configuring DOS Applications

DOS programs run in a special Win32-based application called the NT virtual DOS machine (NTVDM). The NTVDM provides a simulated MS-DOS environment for MS-DOS–based applications. In addition, because each NTVDM has a single thread and its own address space, if one NTVDM fails, no other NTVDM is affected.

To customize an NTVDM for an MS-DOS–based application, go to the application file name and select Properties from the shortcut menu to create a **program information file (PIF)** for the MS-DOS application. The PIF describes how the DOS program will run under the Windows 2000 environment. These settings include specifying memory settings, screen settings, and customized CONFIG.NT and AUTOEXEC.NT files for the DOS application. See figures 22.3, 22.4, and 22.5.

Figure 22.3 Modifying the PIF Settings of a DOS Program

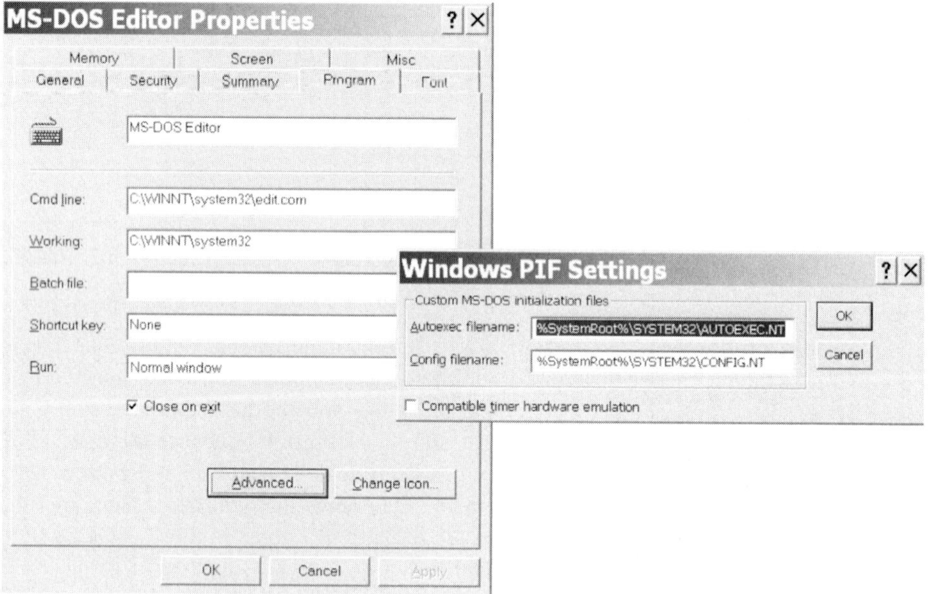

Figure 22.4 Screen and Misc Tabs within the Properties of a DOS Program in Windows 2000 and Windows XP

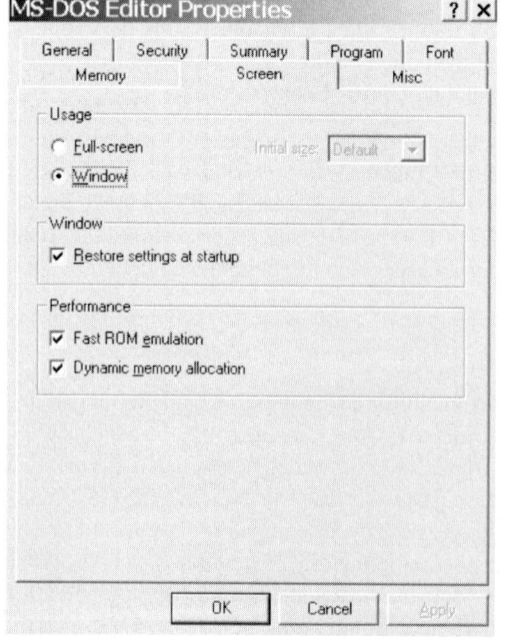

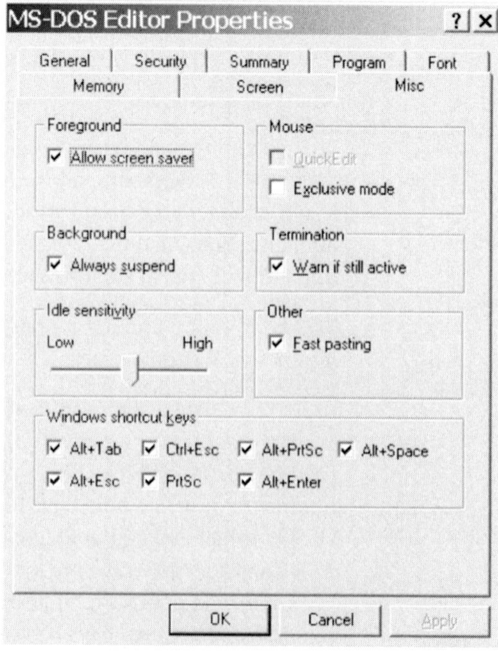

Figure 22.5 Memory Settings for a DOS Program

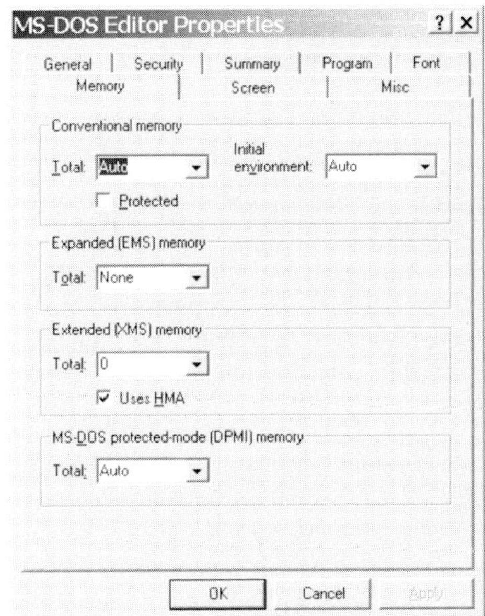

To create customized CONFIG.NT and AUTOEXEC.NT files, do the following:

1. Use a text editor such as Notepad or EDIT to edit the CONFIG.NT or AUTOEXEC.NT files located in the *SYSTEMROOT*\SYSTEM32 directory.
2. Save each file with a new name.
3. Right-click the MS-DOS–based program shortcut and select the Properties option.
4. Click on the Program tab and select the Advanced button.
5. Under Custom MS-DOS initialization files, type the new name for your custom start files in the textbox.

If Windows displays an error message concerning the CONFIG.NT or AUTOEXEC.NT files, or if you have problems running MS-DOS–based programs, check CONFIG.NT or AUTOEXEC.NT for the particular program that you are trying to run.

You can switch between a full screen or DOS window by pressing Alt + Enter. If an application cannot run in a DOS VM—for example, if the application requires full access to the computer's resources or has video problems—you would run the application in DOS mode.

If you're trying to free up lots of lower memory for a DOS program, you specify different AUTOEXEC.BAT and CONFIG.SYS commands for each application by using the Advanced button in the Program tab.

If the DOS application that you are running appears scrambled while running Windows, some legacy DOS applications can run in only 256 color mode. You should therefore set the video adapter to 256 colors. In addition, you can also try to run the DOS application in full-screen mode.

22.1.3 Win16-Based Applications

Win16-based applications are executed by **Win16 on Win32 (WOW)**, which translates or thunks 16-bit calls to 32-bit calls. With the introduction of 64-bit versions of Microsoft Windows, there is also **Windows on Windows 64 (WOW64)**, which is a 32-bit subsystem that allows you to run 32-bit applications on 64-bit operating systems. Because 32-bit applications run in an emulation mode, Microsoft recommends running 32-bit applications on 32-bit hardware for optimal performance.

To determine if any 16-bit applications are currently running:

1. Right-click a blank spot on the Taskbar, and click Task Manager.
2. On the Processes tab, note the contents of the Image Name column.
3. If any 16-bit programs are running, you will see an entry for NTVDM.EXE.

You will also see WOWEXEC.EXE and the executable name of each 16-bit program that is running in that WOW virtual machine. As a helpful visual aid, WOWEXEC.EXE and the 16-bit executable file names are indented.

To start a Win16-bit application in its one separate memory space, you can do one of the following:

- At the command prompt, type the following:

  ```
  START /SEPARATE filename
  ```

- On the Start menu, select the Open option from the Start button and select the Run in Separate Memory Space option.
- Create a shortcut and select the Run in Separate Memory Space option in the Properties shortcut tab.
- In Windows NT Explorer, click Options from the View menu, select the File Types tab, and click the Win16 applications to be edited. Click Edit, and then double-click Open. Edit the open line to include the /separate switch using the following syntax:

  ```
  cmd /c start /separate path\application_executable %1
  ```

To configure a Win16 application to automatically start in a separate NTVDM, create a shortcut for the application. Right-click the shortcut, and then click Properties. In the Properties dialog box, click the Shortcut tab, and then select the Run in Separate Memory Space check box. Each time the application is started by using the shortcut, it is automatically in a separate NTVDM.

While running multiple NTVDMs for 16-bit applications, there are some disadvantages. First, starting Win16 applications in their own memory spaces introduces additional overhead. In addition, if Win16-based applications do not follow the OLE and DDE specifications, they cannot communicate with other NTVDMs.

22.1.4 Sharing Data

To share data between documents, Windows applications can use **dynamic data exchange (DDE)** or **object linking and embedding (OLE).** DDE was introduced with Windows 3.0 by allowing users to copy data between applications while maintaining a link. Whenever data was changed at the source, it was also changed at the target. For example, you could insert an Excel chart into a Word document. As the spreadsheet data changes, the chart in the document changes. Although DDE is still used by many applications, it is slowly being replaced by OLE.

OLE (enhanced version of DDE) is a compound document standard developed by Microsoft. It allows you to create objects with one application and then link or embed objects into another application. Embedded objects keep their original format and links to the application that created them. To make changes to an Excel chart inserted in a Word document, for instance, you would double-click on the chart from within the Word document and Excel would run from within Word. This would allow you to make changes without going to the Program Manager and starting Excel in its own window.

A common way to move data between applications or documents is to use the Clipboard. When you highlight the text or select a picture and you use Copy or Cut from the Edit menu in the source application, the text and picture go into RAM, specifically to the Clipboard.

When you move to the target document and you choose Paste from the Edit menu, the source application copies the data in the Clipboard into the current document using the first available format. If you choose Paste Special, the dialog box appears listing the formats that you can choose for pasting the data. If you choose Paste Link, the application tries to make an OLE link to the source document. If the OLE format isn't available, a DDE link is created instead.

If you press the Print Screen button, you can place a bitmap picture of the entire screen to the Clipboard. By pressing Alt + Print Screen, a bitmap picture is placed onto the Clipboard of the active window.

22.1.5 Installing Applications

To install most programs, you will use an executable such as SETUP.EXE or INSTALL.EXE or an MSI file (Windows Installer). With many of these programs, you just insert the CD into the drive and the installation program will start. If you have to install software to several computers, you can also use Microsoft Active Directory (directory service on a domain controller) or System Management Server

(SMS). Before you start any installation, you should review the installation and configuration manual that comes with the application.

Installing applications involves much more than just creating a directory and copying files into the directory. An installation process begins with the user choosing installation parameters and components or reading installation parameters from a text file. The application will create or write entries to the registry, particularly the HKEY_LOCAL_MACHINE or the HKEY_CURRENT_USER keys, create temporary files, and copy DLL files to the default System32 directory (*SYSTEMROOT*\ SYSTEM32).

When installing applications, you should consider the following potential problems:

- Is the software compatible with the operating system?
- Does the computer have the minimum system requirements and the correct hardware? Check the processor, minimum RAM, video cards, and sound cards.
- Do you have sufficient disk space on the system drive and the drive on which you are installing the application? Many applications need space for program files, data files, and temporary files.
- Have you had problems installing the program before or have you installed earlier versions of the program? Both of these factors can cause problems with installations.
- Do you have sufficient rights and privileges to install and run the application?
- Is there a local policy, group policy, or security template that is being used that might stop the application from installing or running?
- For network applications or installations that occur over the network, is there a firewall (personal or network firewall) that may cause problems? Firewalls can block certain packets from reaching a host computer.
- If your operating system supports multiusers, such as in Windows XP Fast User Switching where multiple users are logged on to the same computer, resource problems can occur, especially if other users are trying to install the same application at the same time.

When installing applications, the newly installed application will not be available to other users unless the administrator assigns the application to be available to all users.

In addition to installation-related problems, you also need to be aware that the software itself can compromise the reliability and security of the Windows machine. Earlier in this book we discussed viruses (including worms and Trojan horses). Besides deleting or corrupting files, formatting hard drives, making your computer unusable, or slowing performance, programs could allow confidential information to be read by or sent to unknown parties. You also need to secure the use of ActiveX controls, JavaScripts, and document macros, and carefully monitor changes being made to the registry.

Buffer overruns can create problems as well, as discussed previously. A buffer is an area of memory that is set aside to hold values, keep track of components or data sets in memory, and to speed execution. A buffer temporarily stores data sets so that they can be processed together, making the system run more efficiently.

Most of these problems can be solved by using an up-to-date virus checker and by keeping the system up-to-date with service packs—security fixes and patches for the operating system and the applications and services running on the computer. In addition, the operating system and many of the applications have features and configuration options that will help make your system more secure. Finally, whenever possible you should use only software that comes from a reliable source or that has been thoroughly tested for compatibility, security, and reliability. Of course, you should consider testing all software before you deploy it to an entire organization.

22.1.6 Program Compatibility Problems

Most programs run properly on the Windows 2000 and Windows XP. The exceptions are some older games and other programs that were written specifically for an earlier version of Windows. Although there are a great number of problems that can occur and an equal number of possible solutions, there are some guidelines that could help:

- Check the Internet for updates and fixes, check the program manufacturer's website to see if an update or patch is available, and check the Microsoft Windows Update website to see if a fix is available for the program.

- Because many programs must be installed by an administrator account, use an administrator account to install programs.
- If the computer is using a secure (SECURE*.INF) or highly secure template (HISEC*.INF), which modify local and group policies including user rights, try the compatible (COMPAT*.INF) security template. Of course, this will reduce the security level of a system.
- Log off all users except the account that will install the program.
- If your program uses Java, use the most current version of the Sun or Microsoft virtual machine (VM) for Java. Java can be downloaded from the http://www.java.com website.
- If your program uses DirectX, use the most current version.
- If you upgraded to Windows from an earlier version of Windows, uninstall and reinstall the software. If the issue is not resolved, it is recommended that you contact the software manufacturer looking for workarounds, patches, or updates.

Starting with Windows XP, Windows has a Program Compatibility Wizard to configure Windows to run a program under an older Windows environment. For example, if you have a program that will run under only Windows 9X, but will not run under Windows 2000 or Windows XP, you can configure Windows to run that program under the Windows 95 environment. This means that when Windows XP is running this application, it will pretend to be a Windows 95 system. The wizard also allows you to try different settings, such as switching the display to 256 colors and the screen resolution to 640 × 480 pixels.

To start the Program Compatibility Wizard, right-click the executable file that you are using to start the program, select Properties, and select the Compatibility tab. Enable the Run this program in compatibility mode for option and select the appropriate operating system environment. See figure 22.6.

22.1.7 Removing a Windows Application

When you install a Windows program, the Windows program often adds information or modifies information to the registry. Therefore, to remove these entries and the programs files on the hard drive, many programs include an uninstall program or have an uninstall option within the installation program. In addition, if the program follows the API (application programming interface) standard, the program can be removed by using the Add/Remove Programs applet in the Control Panel.

NOTE: Although you uninstalled the program, some programs may still leave some files on your hard drive.

Figure 22.6 Windows Program Compatibility Wizard with Compatibility Mode Selected

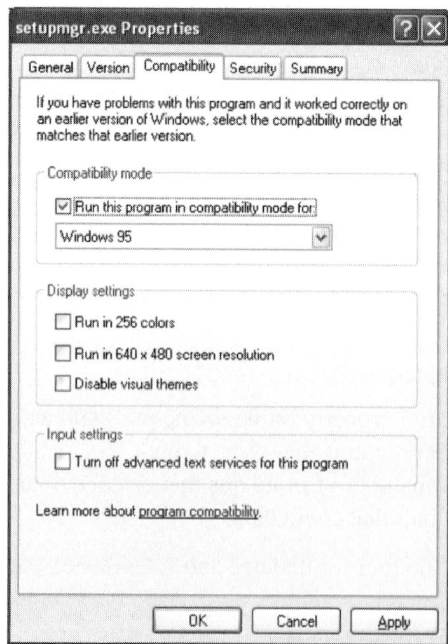

22.1.8 Windows Associations

In Windows 2000 and XP, when you double-click on a document, Windows will recognize the file name extension and start the appropriate program to open the file. Associating an extension with a program is known as registering a file. The information identifying the file name extension is located in the registry and can be accessed and modified by selecting the Options option under the View menu in the My Computer, disk, or folder window and clicking on the File Types tab, or by opening the Folder Options dialog box in the Control Panel. See figure 22.7.

22.1.9 Troubleshooting Windows Applications

Besides compatibility problems with hardware and other software applications, software problems may be also caused by viruses, corrupt program files, corrupt data files, and the amount of free disk space. Because viruses can corrupt or delete program and data files, you need to use up-to-date antivirus software. If your file system, files, or hard drives becomes corrupt, you may need to reinstall Windows and the program and restore backups of your data files. If you run out of free disk space on the system drive, the drive that contains the application and the drive that contains the data files may cause problems with some programs as they create temporary files. You also need to make sure that you have sufficient RAM for your system to handle the operating system and all running applications and services. You should also confirm your system requirements for the software that you are trying to run.

Of course, when preparing for an installation or dealing with application problems, you need to use a sound troubleshooting strategy that combines process, knowledge, and experience. In addition, you need to understand the capabilities of the application and know how to use the application.

To help you gather more information, you can use Dr. Watson (mentioned in chapter 21). You should also see if the application has any logs files and you should check the Window's system logs (event viewer). Log files often display errors and warnings.

After gathering information about the problem, you will have to isolate the problem. First, you should determine if the application was working properly at one time. If the program was working, try to determine what changed on the system. To further isolate the problem, check to see if the data file is corrupt. You can try to open and test the data file on another system with a working program to see if it is corrupt. To see if there is a problem with the program, try to open another data file or create another data file. Check the system requirements for the software and check disk space using disk properties and amount of free RAM using Task Manager. You should also check for configuration options that are available for the operating system and the application.

Figure 22.7 The Registered Files Shown in the Folder Options Dialog Box

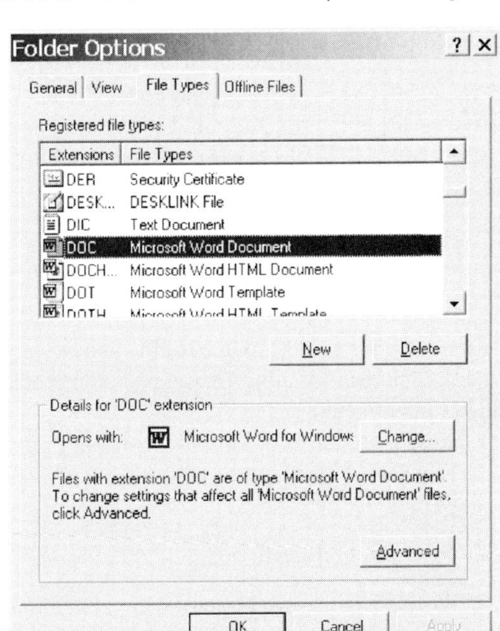

Last, always check the user manual and help files for any troubleshooting tips or wizards and to make sure that you did the installation properly and that the system is configured properly. You should also check the Microsoft website and the website of the application for the described problem and for any updates, patches, or fixes. In addition, check for permissions and rights that might affect running the application or accessing data files. Of course, you may try a clean installation. If the problem still occurs, you may try to contact Microsoft or the software vendor for more help.

22.2 CONFIGURING AND TROUBLESHOOTING MICROSOFT OFFICE

An **office suite** is a collection of productivity applications bundled together and sold as a single package. A suite typically consists of a word processor and spreadsheet program, and often contains other software packages such as database and presentation software. Applications bundled as a suite generally offer additional interoperability between the individual applications. Although office suites are among the most expensive products on the software market, they are cheaper than buying the individual applications.

Microsoft Office is a family of products designed to help users complete common business tasks. Microsoft Office applications are available in suites, or groups of programs bundled together to address different user requirements. For example, Microsoft Office Standard and Microsoft Office Professional are suites of Microsoft Office applications.

The core applications in the Microsoft Office family and the purpose of each application are as follows:

- **Microsoft Word**—Creating written documents
- **Microsoft Excel**—Creating spreadsheets
- **Microsoft Outlook**—Creating and managing email, calendars, and contacts
- **Microsoft PowerPoint**—Creating presentations and slide shows
- **Microsoft Access**—Creating and managing databases

Additional, stand-alone applications included in the Microsoft Office family are:

- **Microsoft Visio**—Creating diagrams
- **Microsoft FrontPage**—Building websites
- **Microsoft Publisher**—Desktop publishing
- **Microsoft Project**—Project management

Today, Microsoft offers several Office suites:

- **Standard**—Word, Excel, Outlook, and PowerPoint
- **Professional**—Word, Excel, Outlook, PowerPoint, and Access
- **Professional Special Edition**—Word, Excel, Outlook, PowerPoint, Access, FrontPage, and Publisher

Microsoft Office 2003 is available in seven different editions. Each edition is designed for a different type of user and categorized according to the way in which the user will acquire that edition. The four categories are:

- **Retail**—Retail editions are available online and in stores
- **Preinstalled**—Preinstalled editions are available preinstalled on a new computer from participating computer manufacturers
- **Volume License**—Office 2003 editions are available through Microsoft volume licensing programs
- **Academic License**—Office 2003 Editions are available through Microsoft academic volume licensing programs

The recent versions of Office include:

- **Office 95 (Word 95, etc.)**—Released 1995
- **Office 97 (Word 97, etc.)**—Released January 1997
- **Office 2000 (Word 2000, etc.)**—Released June 1999

- **Office XP (Word 2002, etc.)**—Released June 2001
- **Office 2003 (Word 2003, etc.)**—Released October 2003

Besides the user manual and help files that comes with Microsoft Office, a useful reference for installing, deploying, and maintaining Microsoft Office is the Microsoft Office Resource Kit, which can be found at:

http://www.microsoft.com/office/ork/xp/default.htm

22.2.1 Installing Office

There are three ways to install Microsoft Office in Windows 2000 and Windows XP:

1. **Manual Installation**—You begin the installation process and follow the on-screen prompts to complete the installation. You can specify the files that are installed and advanced settings for the Office applications.
2. **Automated Installation**—The installation proceeds according to an installation script that was created specifically for your computer or network. All installation options choices are preselected.
3. **Upgrade Installation**—You have a previous version of Microsoft Office installed and you want to install a new version, or you want to update a specific component of the current version.

Microsoft Office is available as a nonupgrade version (full version) and as an upgrade version. If you have an upgrade version of Office, you must have an older version of Office installed on your machine or must insert the installation CD of the older version of Office into the drive. If Setup cannot find an older version of Office, it will display an error message saying that if you do not have a valid qualifying product, return the Office 2003 Upgrade product, and purchase a full retail version of the Office product.

Because organizations have many users that need to use Microsoft Office, Microsoft offers several ways to perform multiple or automated installations. Two common ways would be to use group policies or the Microsoft System Management Server (SMS).

Before you start the installation, you should always do the following:

- Back up your C drive and any other drive on which you will install Office.
- Make sure that you have plenty of disk space available on the C drive and the drive on which you will install Office.
- Look at the box or system requirements to determine the processor, RAM, disk space, and operating system required.
- Make sure that Windows has the appropriate patches and fixes installed, most likely installed from the Microsoft Update website.

It is also recommended that users close other applications that they are currently running, especially Office applications if you are doing an upgrade and antivirus programs that are performing disk scans.

Office will usually come on a single CD, but some suites come on several CDs. To start the installation, insert Disk 1 into your CD-ROM drive and installation should start automatically. If installation doesn't start automatically, click Start, Run, and browse to find the setup executable file (SETUPPLS.EXE) on the CD-ROM disk. This file may be hidden.

After you enter the CD key, you will be asked to upgrade previous versions of Office or to install Office in its default location. You can also choose Customize to change the default location, choose which applications you want to install, and make other choices.

When installing Office 2000, Office XP, and Office 2003, you can choose one of the following options:

- **Run from My Computer**—The specified feature is stored on your hard drive.
- **Run all from My Computer**—The specified feature and all included subfeatures are stored on your hard drive.
- **Run from CD**—The specified feature is executed from the CD. The CD inserted in the drive will be required for this feature.
- **Run all from CD**—The specified feature and all included subfeatures are executed from the CD. The CD inserted in the drive will be required for this feature.
- **Run from Network**—The specified feature is executed from files located on the network.
- **Run all from Network**—The specified feature and all included subfeatures are executed from the network.

Figure 22.8 Microsoft Office Setup

- **Installed on First Use**—The first time you use this feature, it will be installed on your hard drive from either the network or CD-ROM source of the original installation.
- **Not Available**—The feature isn't installed, but can be installed later.

At the bottom of the screen, the amount of disk space used for the features selected displays. To select detail options in a category, click the + sign next to the category icon. This will let you select and deselect subfeatures of a program. After you select the options, you use the screen to customize your choices and then start the installation by clicking the Install Now button. See figure 22.8.

For Office XP or Office 2003, unless you have the corporate edition of Office, you will need to activate Office, either through the Internet or by using a toll-free activation number to obtain an activation code over the phone. If Office is not activated, it will usually tell you that it is not activated and it will tell you the steps to follow. However, sometimes if Office activation is not processed properly and you loaded individual Office applications at least 50 times for all Office applications combined, Office will go into reduced functionality mode, which means that although you can start Office applications to view documents, you will not be able to create or edit until you active or reactivate Office.

If you need to add or remove an Office application without affecting the other Office applications or if you want to repair your Office applications, you can open the Control Panel, and double-click the Add/Remove Programs applet. When you find the correct version of Office, highlight it and click the Add/Remove button or Change button. When the Maintenance Mode Options dialog box appears, select the Add or Remove features radio button if you want to remove an application or component or to add an application or component that you did not install before. Similar to the initial installation process, you can expand entries by clicking on the plus sign next to them to access subcomponents. When you find an entry that you want to add or remove, click the icon next to it and click Run from My Computer if you want to install the component or Not Available if you want to remove it. When you are finished, click Update to complete the installation or removal process. When prompted, insert your Office CD so that it can copy any additional files needed.

22.2.2 Updating Office

Like Windows, you should keep Microsoft Office updated so that it will run more reliably and securely. These updates are provided to help resolve known issues, and to protect your computer from known security vulnerabilities. You can access the Office Update website from the Windows Update website or from the following URL:

http://office.microsoft.com/officeupdate/default.aspx.

You should check the Office Update site regularly by performing the following steps:

1. When you enter the Office Update website, click Scan for updates.

2. As you browse through the available updates in each category, click Add to select the update of your choice and add it to the collection of updates you want to install. You can also read a full description of each item by clicking the Read more link.
3. When you have selected all the updates you want, click Review and install updates, and then click Install Now.

22.2.3 Repairing Office

Microsoft Office has some built-in self-repairing features through the Microsoft Windows Installer. If a resource that is required to start an Office program is missing, such as a file or registry key, the Windows Installer detects the missing resource and repairs the program. If you have a broken program, you can insert the Office Installation CD into your CD drive and choose the Reinstall or Repair radio button in the Maintenance Mode Options dialog box, and click the Next button. Choose the Detect and Repair Errors. In addition, Office 2003 offers a Detect and Repair command, accessed from the Help menu of any of the major Office applications. If the problem still exists, you need to check for viruses, corrupted template files, and corrupted data documents. In addition, verify that Windows is not corrupt, especially the registry.

22.2.4 Configuring Office

Microsoft Office applications can be configured and customized as needed. The first place to configure Office applications is to open the Tools menu and select Options. When the Options dialog box appears, you will have several tabs including the following:

- **View Tab**—You can configure what you want to show on the screen such as tab characters, spaces, and paragraph marks.
- **General Tab**—You can specify how many recently used files are listed at the bottom of the File menu.
- **Save Tab**—You can specify how often it will save autorecovery information so that if your machine freezes or your power goes out, when you restart the Office application, you can recover most, if not all, of the work. In addition, you can also specify the default format of the documents.
- **Spelling & Grammar Tab**—Gives you some options to configure the spelling and grammar checking features of the application.
- **File Locations Tab**—You can specify the locations of the files including where the documents are saved by default.
- **Security Tab**—You can secure your documents by establishing encryption and passwords and you can configure the Macro Security so that you will be more resistant against macro viruses.

See figure 22.9.

Figure 22.9 Microsoft Word Options

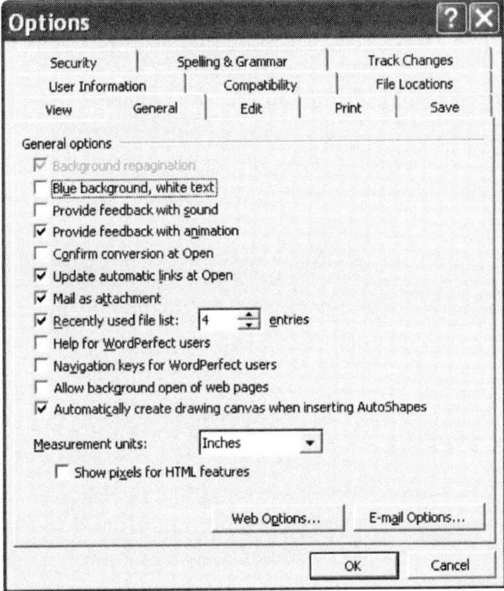

When you open the Tools menu and select the Customize option, you can use the Customize dialog box to configure the toolbar and menus. The tabs include:

- **Toolbars Tab**—Allows you to enable or disable toolbars. You can also right-click any toolbar to add or remove toolbars.
- **Commands Tab**—Allows you to drag different options into the toolbar. It also specifies which template the toolbar changes are saved to.
- **Options Tab**—Allows you to configure if you use full menus or personalized menus and other menu parameters.

Last, if you open the Tools menu and select the AutoCorrect Options, you can choose how the Office application corrects or changes items as you type. For example, by default, it will capitalize the first letter of a sentence and names of days. It will also allow you to enable or disable automatic bullets and number lists and correct common spelling mistakes.

22.2.5 AutoRecover and Application Recovery

You can configure Office applications to automatically save a backup copy whenever you save a document. Each time you save the document, a new backup copy replaces the existing backup copy. Word saves the backup copy (with a file name extension WBK) in the same folder as the original. This will help protect your work if you accidentally save changes you don't want to keep or you delete the original. It will also help if the working file becomes corrupt. When you select Always create backup copy, Word clears the Allow fast saves check box because Word can create backup copies only when it performs a full save.

You can further protect your work by using the AutoRecover feature to periodically save a temporary copy of the file you're working on. By default, AutoRecover saves documents every 10 minutes. If you set a more frequent interval, such as every 5 minutes, you will lose up to only 5 minutes of work instead of 10 minutes. However, if you set it to save frequently and you are working with big files, your system will slow down when working on these documents because it needs to use resources to save these large files often.

NOTE: Although AutoRecover is a handy tool in data recovery, you should manually save your files often and back up your files on a regular basis.

With AutoRecover on, if an Office program stops responding while you have files open, you can use the Microsoft Office Application Recovery dialog box. Recovered files will be displayed in the Document Recovery task pane. The data in the files reflects the last time AutoRecover saved the files. To use the Microsoft Office Application Recovery tool:

1. Click Start, point to All Programs, point to Microsoft Office, point to Microsoft Office Tools, and then click Microsoft Office Application Recovery. The Microsoft Office Application Recovery dialog box lists all of the Office applications that are currently running and displays status information for each.
2. Select the name of the application that you want to recover, and then click Recover Application.

Recovering the application will terminate the application and cause it to attempt to save any unsaved changes. Clicking End Application in the Microsoft Office Application Recovery tool will cause the specified application to terminate without attempting to save your data.

If you have a power failure or your machine shuts down unexpectedly, you can retrieve the document that was last saved through AutoRecover by starting the Office application. The AutoRecover files will be listed in the Document Recovery pane. You can then choose to open them or delete them.

NOTE: You should always save the AutoRecover files under a different name in case they have become corrupted. This way, you can still open the original uncorrupted document if you find out that it is corrupted.

22.2.6 File Formats

One advantage that Microsoft currently has with Microsoft Office is that the file formats have become defacto standards. This is one of the reasons why organizations find it difficult to use other applications; they would most likely not be able to access old documents and templates and have trouble accessing applications from outside the organization. Even when deploying newer versions of Office applications, users need to be able to work with documents from previous versions and need to share documents with users that have different versions. Therefore, it is important to understand the file formats for the various Office versions and know the capabilities of the new application or new version of Microsoft Office.

For Microsoft Word, Excel, and PowerPoint, the file formats are interchangeable between Office 97, Office 2000, Office XP, and Office 2003. Therefore, if users upgrade from Office 97 to Office 2000 to Office XP to Office 2003, users are able to open and share existing documents with no or little problem without having to convert them or use special readers.

You should note that the newer versions may have features that did not exist in the older versions of Office. Although you can still share documents with the various versions of Office, the document may view differently. For example, Microsoft Word 2002 allows for a nested table (table inside of a table). If you open a document with a nested table with a version of Office that does not support nested table, it will show as indented lines.

If you have clients or customers that are still using Office 95, the file formats of Office 95 are not the same as later versions of Office. In these cases, you will need to convert your documents or use a file viewer (available from http://www.Microsoft.com). You could also instruct the newer users of Office to save their files using a dual-file format. This is done by opening the File menu and selecting the Save As option. Then in the Save As Type text box, select the following:

Word 97-2002 & 6.0/95-RFT
Microsoft Excel 97-2002 & 5.0/95
PowerPoint 97-2002 & 95

When you save in dual-file format, you are creating two data streams, which means you are saving two files in one—one for the file format and features of Office XP/2000/97 and one for the Office 95 version. Of course, because you are saving two files in one, the file will be twice as large. After all users are upgraded to the newer version of Office, you can then instruct users to save their files in the newer format. When users of earlier versions open dual-file-saved format files, they are prompted to open the file as read-only. If you choose to say no, Office may remove some of the newer features.

NOTE: You can use group policies to set the file save type as the default after installation.

A **macro** is a symbol, name, or key that represents a list of commands, actions, or keystrokes. Many programs allow you to create macros so that you can enter a single character or word to perform a whole series of actions. By using macros, you can create sophisticated or automated documents.

Word 95 used WordBasic to create macros, whereas newer versions of Word and Excel use Microsoft Visual Basic. If you open a file with a newer version of Office, the macro will automatically be converted to Visual Basic. When the Word 95 tries to open the document after it has been converted, the macro will not function.

The various versions of Microsoft Access are not necessarily compatible with each other. In some of these examples, when you open an older file (Access 2000) with a newer version of Access (Access 2002), the newer version of Access will ask to convert the older file to the newer format. If you say no, you can still work with the file and save as normal under the old format. On the other hand, Access 97 must be converted to Access 2000 or Access 2002 if they are to be used in Access 2002. If a file needs to be sent back to a user who is using Access 97, you would have to convert the file back to the 97 format.

Starting with Microsoft Office 2003, Office also supports Extensible Markup Language (XML). XML is an open data description language standard that can be used by a computer network, operating system, and program. By using this universal format, it is hoped that documents will be opened and shared among different programs.

Last, Office has the ability to save in other formats so that they can be opened by other programs. In addition, you can search the Microsoft and other vendor websites for converters for other formats such as Microsoft Works.

Some of the generic formats (which may lose some or much of the formatting) include:

- **Rich Text Format (*.RTF)**—ASCII file with special commands to indicate formatting information, such as fonts, styles, colors, and margins.

- **Hypertext Markup Language, or HTML (*.HTM/*.HTML)**—Formatting used by webpages. Keeps most normal formatting including fonts, styles, and colors.
- **Plain Text (*.TXT) Formats**—Generic formats that consist of the text (ASCII) only with no formatting codes.

22.2.7 Proofing Tools

Microsoft Office provides proofing tools that allow you to edit the document in multiple languages including spelling and grammar checkers, AutoCorrect, and translation dictionary.

- **Spell Checker**—The component that checks for misspellings in a text file by comparing the contents of the file with a database or dictionary of accepted spellings. When used in Microsoft Word, it indicates a misspelling with a red wavy underline. To make the spell checker more flexible, it allows you to add terms to the dictionary or to temporarily disregard a word that is not listed in the dictionary.
- **Grammar and Style Checker**—The component that identifies potential problems with grammar and punctuation. Microsoft Word identifies potential grammar errors with a green wavy underline.
- **AutoCorrect**—The component that automatically detects and corrects typos, misspelled words, grammatical errors, and incorrect capitalization. For example, if you type "teh" followed by a space, AutoCorrect will replace "teh" with "the." You can also use AutoCorrect to quickly insert text, graphics, or symbols. For example, type *(c)* to insert ©, or type *ac* to insert "Acme Corporation."
- **Thesaurus**—The component that allows you to look up synonyms (words with the same meaning) for a particular word.
- **Hyphenation**—The component that enables a user to connect or divide words with a hyphen. This feature can be useful to eliminate large gaps of spacing when using justified text.
- **Translation Dictionary**—The component that looks up individual words in the dictionary of a different language. If you need to translate a longer piece of text, you may need a full translation program, service, or website.
- **Input Method Editor (IME)**—The component that allows you to enter double-byte characters, such as Asian text, in Windows and enabled applications by converting your keystrokes into the double-byte characters. Often the only visual indication that an IME is installed on a computer is a floating toolbar for controlling the conversions, and an indicator on the Windows Taskbar.

Besides the Translation Dictionary and the Input Method Editor, Office also includes the Multilingual User Interface (MUI), which provides translated text for the user interface, dialog boxes, Help, wizards, and templates for Office programs. Plug-in language capability in Microsoft Office 2003 is provided by the Office 2003 MUI Pack, which can be configured to be included with Office installation files. The MUI Pack works with Windows Installer to install the necessary files only when users run Office 2003 with a particular language configuration.

22.2.8 Templates

Office documents are based on templates. A template determines the basic structure for a document and contains document settings such as page layout (including paper size and margins), fonts, styles, toolbar buttons, menus, AutoText entries, macros, and special formatting. Templates can be divided into two categories, global templates and document templates.

Global templates contain settings that are available to all documents. When you work on a document, you can typically use only the settings and features that are available in the template attached to the document template. For example, the standard global template for Microsoft Word is NORMAL.DOT. Therefore, when you create a new document, it will read the NORMAL.DOT for the settings of the documents. If you want different default margins or fonts, open the NORMAL.DOT file, make the appropriate changes, and save the NORMAL.DOT file. Then any new documents that are created will have the new settings.

Document templates are templates that you open that are preformatted or includes wizards to configure the formatting and content of the document you are creating. Examples of document templates includes memo templates, fax templates, and resume templates.

When you open the File menu and select New, you can select New from General Templates. You will then be shown categories (tabs) of templates. If you want to create custom tabs for your templates in the Templates dialog box, create a new subfolder in the TEMPLATES folder and save your templates in that subfolder. The name you give that subfolder will appear on the new tab.

You can also create your own templates in Word. Click Open from the File menu. Find the document you want to set as a template and open it. Choose Save As from the File menu. For Word templates, when the Save As dialog box opens, select Document Template (*.DOT) from the Save As Type drop-down list. From the Save In drop-down list, select the folder where you want the template to be stored. In the File Name box, type the name of your template, making sure the file extension is DOT. Click Save. Of course, if you don't save a template in the TEMPLATES folder or its subfolders, it will not appear in the Templates dialog box. When the templates are stored in this format, they have DOT extensions, but when you open and save them in Microsoft Word, they have DOC extensions.

If you suspect that the NORMAL.DOT file has become inadvertently changed or corrupted, you just need to search for and delete the NORMAL.DOT (hidden file) document. The next time you start Microsoft Word, a new NORMAL.DOT file will be created.

22.2.9 Security and Macro Protection

Microsoft applications offer various forms of security. First, you can assign passwords to open or modify a document. You can also specify the file to be read-only, which forces the user to save the file under a different name. You can also assign digital signatures to help verify who created or sent the document and keep track of the changes that are made to a document. In addition, you also have privacy options such as removing personal information from the file when you save the document. See figure 22.10.

To make Microsoft applications more powerful and more flexible, Visual Basic capabilities are included through macros. As stated previously, a macro, or formula language, is a set of instructions that a program executes on command. Macros group several keystrokes into one command or perform complex menu selections such as changing colors on your desktop. Therefore, they simplify redundant or complex tasks. In fact, you can create macros by recording a series of mouse or keyboard actions and save them within the document. Unfortunately, this capability inadvertently opened the Windows data files to a new type of virus, the macro virus.

Macro viruses are stored in Office documents such as Word and Excel. When you open the document, the macro virus infects the global template of the program. Because macros are very powerful, they allow a large range of actions including modifying documents, deleting documents, formatting the hard drives, and causing documents to be sent out via email. Unfortunately, because macros are easy to create, it is easy to create macro viruses that can be transferred through data documents. As a result, macro viruses are the most widespread virus type.

For the best protection against macro viruses, you should purchase and install specialized antivirus software and make sure that you apply all security patches to Windows and Microsoft Office. If you are using a server that is running Microsoft Exchange, you can block Office file types in email messages

Figure 22.10 Security Tab in the Options Dialog Box

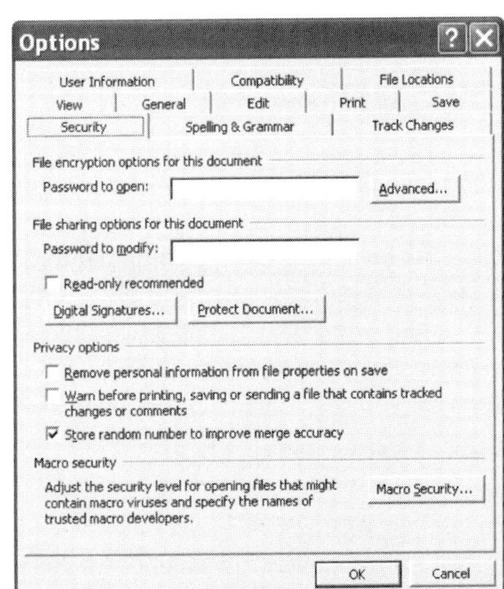

Figure 22.11 Macro Protection

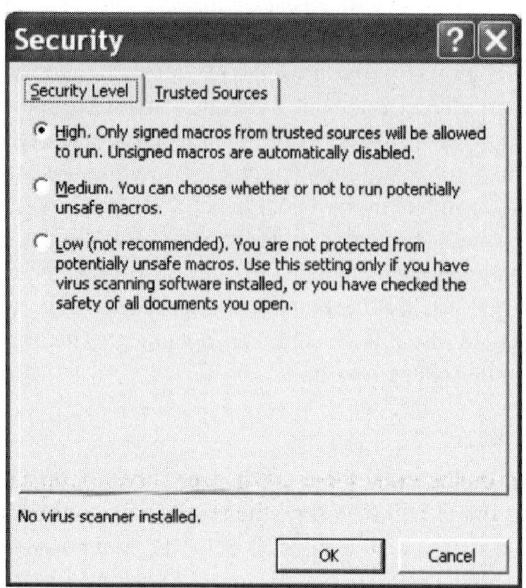

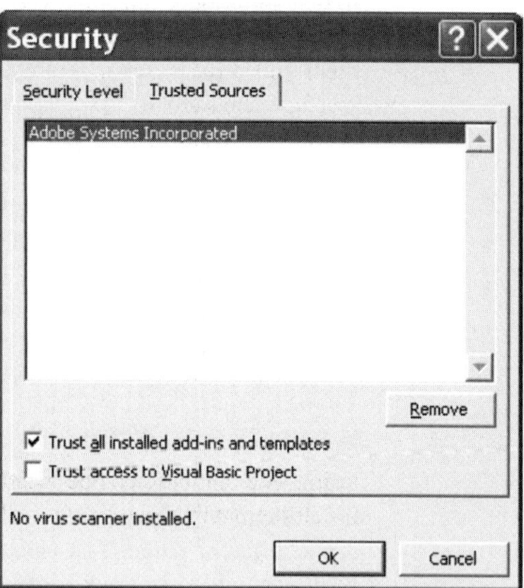

for computers running Office 97. This prevents users with unsecured programs from accidentally spreading viruses when they open attached files. Microsoft Outlook 2000 and later automatically block unsafe attachments.

Recent versions of Microsoft Office include macro security options to help protect your documents and your system. To further reduce the risk of macro infection in Office files, set the macro security level to High or Medium and use digital signatures. To do this, open the Tools menu, click Options, and choose the Security tab. Next, click the Macro Security button to see a list of available macro security levels. At the lowest setting (Low), your only protection against macro viruses comes from your antivirus software. At the Medium level, Word automatically asks whether you want to run potentially unsafe macros. At the High and Very High levels, Word accepts macros only from trusted locations and disables all others. See figure 22.11.

You can also use digital certificates to reduce the likelihood of malicious macros. A digital certificate is an electronic document that says who the macros comes from. Although this does not stop a macro virus, it should tell you if the macro is coming from a trusted source or not. Before you decide to do this, you should review the details of the digital certificate. For example, look at the Issued to and Issued by fields to determine whether you trust its source, and look at the Valid from field to determine if the certificate is current. The certificate may also include details such as the email name or website of the person who obtained the certificate for the macro. If you add a person or organization to your list of trusted sources, Office will automatically trust the macro from the trusted source without showing you a security warning.

22.3 WEB BROWSERS

The terms the *Internet* and the *World Wide Web* are often used interchangeably, but they have different meanings. As was pointed out earlier, the **Internet** refers to the huge global WAN (wide area network). Until the early 1990s, to be able to use the computer to communicate with another computer via the Internet required a good deal of knowledge and the ability to understand and use some fairly unfriendly commands. The **World Wide Web (WWW)** was created in 1992, and refers to the means of organizing, presenting, and accessing information over the Internet.

To access the web, you would use the following technologies:

1. Hypertext Markup Language (HTML)
2. Web server
3. Web browser
4. Hypertext Transfer Protocol (HTTP) and File Transfer Protocol (FTP)

Web pages are written using the **Hypertext Markup Language (HTML).** This language is pretty simple and is implemented as special ASCII tags or codes that you embed within your document to give the browser a general idea of how the information should be displayed. The browsers understand the standard HTML tags, although they may display the same document a little differently. If you want your documents to be accessible by people using different browsers, you should stick with the standard tags. The HTML standard is still actively evolving, so new tags are constantly becoming available to support new browser features.

A **web server** is a computer equipped with the server software that uses Internet protocols such as Hypertext Transfer Protocol (HTTP) and File Transfer Protocol (FTP) to respond to web client requests on a TCP/IP network via web browsers. One server can service a large number of clients. There are several free server programs available on the Internet. Most web browsers are built to process two basic types of requests: File Server and Database Server requests. New features are always being added to provide additional support for new technology. A web server acting as a file server simply accepts a request for a document, validates the request, and sends the requested files back to the browser. In addition, the browser can act as a front-end tool or interface to collect data and feed it in a database or script. The database can be located either on the same server as the web server or on a different server. When the database responds with the results, it will then send the results back to the browser.

The **web browser** is the client program or software that you run on your local machine to gain access to a web server. It receives the HTML commands, interprets the HTML, and displays the results. It is strictly a user-interface/document presentation tool. It knows nothing about the application it is attached to and only knows how to take the information from the server and present it to the user. It is also able to capture data entry made into a form and get the information back to the server for processing.

By far, Microsoft Internet Explorer (IE) is the most common browser available because it comes with every version of Windows. For Linux machines and as an alternative to Internet Explorer, you can use Netscape Navigator or Mozilla. Netscape, which has been around as long as Internet Explorer, can be downloaded from the following website:

http://home.netscape.com/download/index.html

Mozilla started on March 21, 1998, when Netscape released its browser source code under open source license and created a nonprofit organization, mozilla.org, to oversee this. The idea was to create a successor to the Netscape Communicator 4.XX series with a pool of outside talent. The name *Mozilla* was derived from the fact that the first Netscape was intended to be the "Mosiac killer." Mosaic was the first graphical web browser and quite popular during its time. Because Mozilla and Netscape use the same code, you will find that both browsers are very similar.

These browsers are used to search and access web pages on the Internet and can be used by an organization's website or provide an interface to a program. Thus, as a PC technician, you will need to understand how to configure, customize, and troubleshoot browser issues.

22.3.1 General and Advanced Settings

Most of the configuration options for Internet Explorer are accessed by opening the Tools menu and selecting Internet Options. It can also be accessed from the Internet Options applet in the Control Panel. The Internet Options dialog box has several tabs including General, Security, Privacy, Content, Connections, Programs, and Advanced.

At the top of the General tab (see figure 22.12), you can configure the home page or the default page that is loaded when you start Internet Explorer. This allows you to have your favorite search engine, news website, portal, or an organization's internal website load automatically when you start Internet Explorer. By going to a web page and then clicking the Use Current button, you will make the page that is currently being displayed your home page. You can also configure it to show a blank page. Of course, to make the change go in effect, you have to click on the Apply or OK button.

Some organizations may configure the organization's home page as the default home page so that users cannot make changes to Internet Explorer using group policies. Other times, if you experience an unexpected change in the home page, it was most likely caused by visiting a particular website (usually you have to click on Yes to change the website, but that is not always the case), installing a program that changes the Internet Explorer home page, or being infected by a virus.

Figure 22.12 Internet Options Dialog Box and the Settings Dialog Box

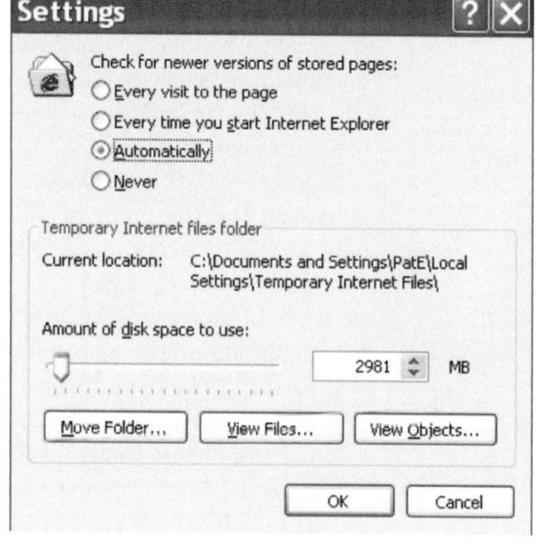

Below the home page, you will find the section to configure how Internet Explorer uses temporary Internet files, which is used as a disk cache for Internet browsing. When you visit a website, parts of the web page (such as pictures, sound, and video files) are copied on the system as a temporary Internet file so that on future visits to that site, it will load faster. If you click on the Settings button, you can configure the browser to check for newer versions of the saved page on every visit, every time you start Internet Explorer, automatically or never. If you need to force Internet Explorer to reload a fresh web page, you can hold down the Shift key while you click Refresh, or press Shift + F5. You can also click the View Files button to view the temporary Internet files.

You can determine how much disk space you want to use as a cache and where the folder is located that stores the temporary files. By default, Internet Explorer reserves 3 percent of the space on your system disk for the web cache. If you click on View Files, you will open the folder that stores the temporary files so that you can inspect them directly.

History specifies the number of days that Internet Explorer should keep track of your viewed pages in the History list. IE creates shortcuts to pages you viewed in this and previous browsing sessions. If you are low on disk space, you might want to decrease this number. You can also clear your history from here. If you need to look at what websites someone has viewed, the history is stored in C:\DOCUMENTS AND SETTINGS*USERNAME*\LOCAL SETTINGS\HISTORY. You can also access the history by clicking on the History button.

If you click on the Advanced options, you can configure a wide range of configuration options including disabling script debugging, enabling folder view for FTP sites, enabling personalized favorites menu, notifying when downloads are complete, enabling automatic image resizing, and playing sounds and videos in web pages. It also has several security features such as emptying temporary Internet files when the browser is closed, enabling Profile Assistant, using SSL 2.0 or 3.0 (needed to connect to secure web pages as indicated by https://), warning about invalid site certificates, and warning if form is being redirected. See figure 22.13.

22.3.2 Cookies and Privacy Settings

A **cookie** is a message given to a web browser by a web server, which is typically stored in a text file on the PC's hard drive. The message is then sent back to the server each time the browser requests a page from the server.

A command line in the HTML of a document tell the browser to set a cookie of a certain name or value. An example of using a cookie would be:

```
Set-Cookie: NAME=VALUE; expires=DATE; path=PATH; domain=DOMAIN_NAME;
```

Figure 22.13 Advanced Options in Internet Explorer

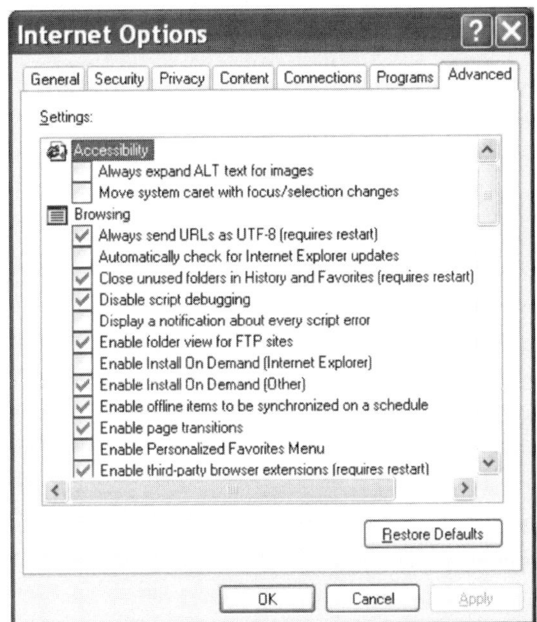

The main purpose of cookies is to identify users and possibly prepare customized web pages for them. When you enter a website using cookies, you may be asked to fill out a form providing such information as your name and interests. This information is packaged into a cookie and sent to your web browser, which stores it for later use. The next time you go to the same website, your browser will send the cookie to the web server. The server can use this information to present you with custom web pages. So, for example, instead of seeing just a generic welcome page you might see a welcome page with your name on it. Some uses of cookies include keeping track of what a person buys, using online ordering systems, personalizing a website, storing a person's profile, storing user IDs, and providing support to older web browsers that do not support host header names.

A cookie cannot be used to get data from your hard drive, get your email address, or steal sensitive information about you. Early implementations of Java and JavaScript could allow people to do this, but for the most part these security leaks have been plugged. Although using cookies typically makes accessing web pages easier for the user, they can be easily done without using cookies.

From the General tab, you can delete the cookies that are stored on your hard drive. By clicking on the Privacy tab, you can determine how much of your personal information can be accessed by websites and whether a website can save cookies on your computer by adjusting the tab slider on the privacy scale.

To view privacy settings, select the Privacy tab of the Internet Options dialog box. To adjust your privacy settings, adjust the tab slider to a new position on the privacy scale. A description of the privacy setting that you select displays on the right side of the tab slider. The default level is Medium; it is recommended to configure Medium or higher. You can also override the default for cookies in each security zone. In addition, you can override certain settings (automatic cookie handling and session cookies) by clicking on the Advanced button or allow or block cookies from individual websites by clicking on the Edit button. See figure 22.14.

Many websites provide privacy statements that you view. A site's privacy policy tells you what kind of information the site collects and stores and what it does with the information. Information that you should mostly be concerned with is how the website uses personally identifiable information such as your name, email address, address, and telephone number. Websites also might provide a Platform for Privacy Preferences (P3P) privacy policy, which can be used by browsers to filter cookie transactions on the basis of the cookie's content and purpose. To view the Privacy Report, open the View menu and click Privacy Report. To view a site's privacy statement, select the website and click on the Summary button.

Figure 22.14 Privacy Settings for Internet Explorer

22.3.3 Plug-Ins, Scripting Languages, and Content Zones

A **plug-in** is a software module that adds a specific feature or service to the browser to display or play different types of audio or video messages. The most common plug-ins are Shockwave and RealMedia (RealAudio and RealVideo). Of course, the number of plug-ins available are countless.

Shockwave is a technology developed by Macromedia, Inc. that enables web pages to include multimedia objects. To create a shockwave object, you use Macromedia's multimedia authoring tool called Macromedia Director, and then compress the object with a program called Afterburner. You then insert a reference to the "shocked" file in your web page. To see a Shockwave object, you need the Shockwave plug-in, a program that integrates seamlessly with your web browser. The plug-in is freely available from Macromedia's website. Shockwave supports audio, animation, video, and even processes user actions such as mouse clicks. It runs on all Windows platforms as well as Macintosh.

Streaming technology is a technique for transferring data such that it can be processed as a steady and continuous stream. Streaming technologies are becoming increasingly important with the growth of the Internet because most users do not have fast enough access to download large multimedia files quickly. With streaming, the client browser or plug-in can start displaying the data before the entire file has been transmitted.

For streaming to work, the client side receiving the data must be able to collect the data and send it as a steady stream to the application that is processing the data and converting it to sound or pictures. This means that if the streaming client receives the data more quickly than required, it needs to save the excess data in a buffer. If the data doesn't come quickly enough, however, the presentation of the data will not be smooth.

There are a number of competing streaming technologies emerging. One standard for audio data on the Internet is Progressive Network's RealAudio. RealAudio was developed by **RealNetworks** and supports FM-stereo-quality sound. To hear a web page that includes a RealAudio sound file, you need a RealAudio player or plug-in. RealVideo is a streaming technology developed by RealNetworks for transmitting live video over the Internet. It uses a variety of data compression techniques and works with both normal IP connections as well as IP Multicast connections. A competing standard is the Advanced Streaming Format (ASF), a streaming multimedia file format developed by Microsoft.

Adobe Acrobat is used to read and create **Portable Document Format (PDF)** files. PDF files are an open de facto standard for electronic document distribution worldwide. Adobe PDF is a universal file format that preserves all the fonts, formatting, graphics, and color of any source document, regardless of the application and platform used to create it. Adobe PDF files are compact and can be shared, viewed, navigated, and printed exactly as intended by anyone with free Adobe Acrobat Reader software (program and plug-in).

In an effort to make browsing more functional, web developers created and enabled active content. Active content is done by using small executables or script code that is executed and shown within the client's web browser. Unfortunately, like a Trojan horse virus, this feature is an added security risk where some scripts could be used to perform harmful actions on a client machine. Some of the most popular types of active content are VBScript, JavaScript, and ActiveX components.

VBScript, Short for Visual Basic Scripting Edition, is a scripting language developed by Microsoft and supported by Microsoft's Internet Explorer web browser. VBScript is based on the Visual Basic programming language, but is much simpler. It enables web authors to include interactive controls, (such as buttons and scroll bars) on their web pages.

An **applet** is a component in a distributed environment that is downloaded and executed by a web browser. Web browsers, which are designed to display text and graphics and also accept data input on forms, aren't very good at processing information locally on the client system, so applets were invented to solve this problem. Applets are also known as mobile code because they are downloaded from a server and run on a client.

Java is a programmable language developed by Sun Microsystems that has a number of features that make it well suited for use on the web. **Java applets** are self-contained Internet applications that are written in Java. Initially, Java applets are stored on a web server. When you first access a web page that contains HTML code to access the Java applet, the Java applet is downloaded onto the client computer. When the client subsequently accesses the server, the applet is already cache on the client's computer and is accessed with a download delay. The Java source code is run through a client-side engine or Java virtual machine (VM).

By default, and for security reasons, Java applets are contained within a **sandbox.** This means that the applets cannot do anything that might be construed as threatening to the user's machine (e.g., reading, writing, or deleting local files; putting up arbitrary message windows; communicating with arbitrary other machines; or querying various system parameters). Any attempt to access a resource outside the sandbox will result in a security violation and the program will terminate. Early browsers had no provisions for Java applets to reach outside the sandbox. Recent browsers, however, have provisions to give "trusted" applets the ability to work outside the sandbox. For this power to be granted to one of your applets, the applet's code must be digitally signed with your unforgeable digital ID, and then the user must state that he or she trusts applets signed with your ID.

Netscape Corporation created **JavaScript,** which is not Java nor is it a lightweight version of Java, although it does share many of the structure and features of Java. It is a scripting language that was originally called LiveScript. Most web browsers support JavaScript, which is typically embedded inside an HTML page and read by the client browser. A SCRIPT tag inside the HTML code is used to denote the JavaScript. JavaScript is commonly used to communicate with other components or to accept user input. JavaScript can be used to open Java applets.

Because JavaScript is a simple scripting language, it has no built-in means of accessing resources on the client machine and it doesn't have the means to subvert the security of a machine. If a web page that contains dynamic HTML written in JavaScript runs in a sandbox, it does not have access to the resources of the host machine and is safe to run. Like Java applets, if the JavaScript is digitally signed, you can grant it additional access to a JavaScript that is not digitally signed. An Active Server Page (ASP) containing JavaScript or a Windows Scripting Host (WSH) script containing JavaScript is potentially hazardous because these environments allow scripts unrestricted access to machine resources (file system, registry, etc.) and application objects (via COM).

In both cases of Java applets and JavaScripts, from time to time, there are vulnerabilities that are found. Therefore, you must keep checking for services packs, patches, and security fixes for your browsers. Another option to stop Java applets and JavaScripts from compromising your client system is to disable Java in the web browser.

An ActiveX control is similar to a Java applet. **ActiveX** is not a programming language, but rather a set of rules for how applications should share information. Programmers can develop ActiveX controls and plug-ins in a variety of languages, including C, C++, Visual Basic, and Java. Unlike Java applets, however, ActiveX controls are downloaded and executed by a web browser (Internet Explorer) and have full access to the Windows operating system. Since ActiveX has the full access to the Windows operating system, it constitutes the greatest potential threat. For example, ActiveX technology allows users to view Word and Excel documents directly from a browser interface. In addition, Microsoft

Office applications (Microsoft Word, Excel, Access, and PowerPoint) are examples of built-in ActiveX components. This gives them much more power than Java applets, but with this power comes a certain risk that the applet may damage software or data on your machine.

ActiveX uses code signing, specifically the Microsoft Authenticode technology. Authenticode allows you to verify the origin of a control and thus assess its reliability and safety. If a control destroys your system, at least you'll know whom to blame. Independent certificate authorities (CAs) like VeriSign issue the digital signatures to mark the code. Developers have to pay for the certificates, and in order to be considered for a certificate you must pass through a screening process. The digital signature is 1024 bits and thus essentially impossible to reverse engineer.

Authenticode is based on Microsoft's code-signing proposal now being evaluated by the World Wide Web Consortium. Authenticode uses X.509 v3 cryptography certificates as well as the PKCS #7 and #10 signature standards. The digital signature uses both a public key and a private key, known as a key pair. Only the private key owner knows the private key, whereas the public key is available to the world. The private key is used to generate the signature, and the public key is used to validate it.

To help manage Internet Explorer security when visiting sites, Internet Explorer divides the network connection into four content types. For each of the web content zones, there is a default security level. The security levels available in Internet Explorer are:

1. **High**—Excludes any content that could damage your computer.
2. **Medium**—Warns you before running potentially damaging content.
3. **Medium-Low**—Available only in Internet Explorer 5.0. Does not prompt you each time potentially damaging content appears. Most content will run without prompts, and unsigned ActiveX controls will not be downloaded.
4. **Low**—Does not warn you before running potentially damaging content.
5. **Custom**—A security setting of your own design. Use this level to customize the behavior of Active Data Objects (ADO) and Remote Data Services (RDS) objects in a specific zone.

The four content types are:

- **Internet Zone**—Anything that is not assigned to any other zone and anything that is not on your computer, or your organization's network (intranet). The default security level for the Internet zone is Medium.
- **Local Iintranet Zone**—Computers that are part of your organization's network (intranet) that do not require a proxy server, as defined by the system administrator. These include sites specified on the Connections tab, network paths, such as *\COMPUTERNAME\FOLDERNAME*, and local intranet sites, such as http:*//internal*. You can add sites to this zone. The default security level for the Local intranet zone is Medium-Low, which means Internet Explorer will allow all cookies from websites in this zone to be saved on your computer and read by the website that created them.
- **Trusted Sites Zone**—Contains trusted sites from which you believe you can download or run files without damaging your computer or data or that you consider is not a security risk. You can assign sites to this zone. The default security level for the Trusted sites zone is Low, which means Internet Explorer will allow all cookies from websites in this zone to be saved on your computer and read by the website that created them.
- **Restricted Sites Zone**—Contains sites you do not trust from which downloading or running files may damage your computer or data or that are considered a security risk. You can assign sites to this zone. The default security level for the Restricted sites zone is High, which means Internet Explorer will block all cookies from websites in this zone.

Whenever you access a website, Internet Explorer checks the security settings for zone of the website. To tell which zones the current web page falls into, you look at the right site of the Internet Explorer status bar. Besides adjusting the zones or assigning a website to a zone, you can also customize settings for a zone by importing a privacy settings file from a certificate authority.

To modify the security level for a web content zone:

1. In Internet Explorer, on the Tools menu, click Internet Options.
2. In the Internet Options dialog box, on the Security tab, click the zone on which you want to set the security level.

3. Drag the slider to set the security level to High, Medium, Medium-low, or Low. Internet Explorer describes each option to help you decide which level to choose. You are prompted to confirm any reduction in security level. You can also choose the Custom Level button for more detailed control. See figure 22.15.
4. Click OK to close the Internet Options dialog box.

As mentioned before, software publisher certificates (third-party digital certificates) are used to validate software code such as Java or ActiveX controls or plug-ins. Depending on the security settings for a zone, when software code is accessed from a website, you will automatically download the software code, disable the software code, or prompt to download the software code via a security warning. If you open the Tools menu and select Internet Options, select the Security tab, and click the Custom Level button, you can select enable, disable, or prompt to download ActiveX controls (signed and unsigned) and scripting of Java applets.

To view the certificates for Internet Explorer, click on the Content button and then click on the Certificates button. To see list of certificates, click on the appropriate certificates. From here, you can also import and export individual certificates. See figure 22.16.

Figure 22.15 The Security Settings for Zones

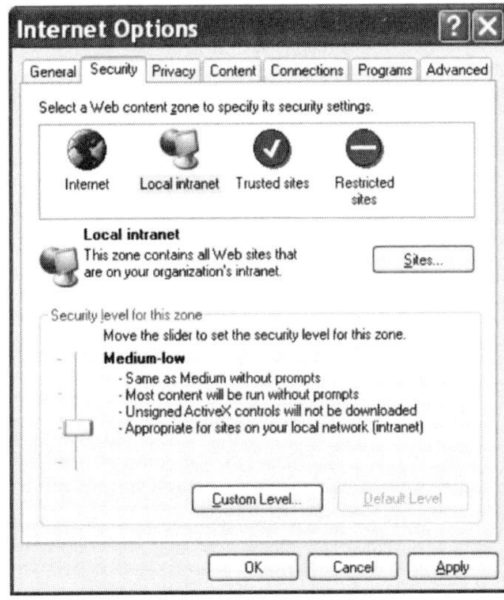

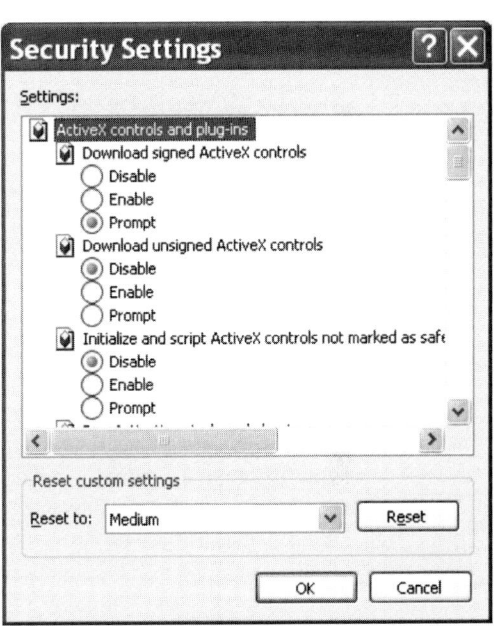

Figure 22.16 Certificates Shown in Internet Explorer

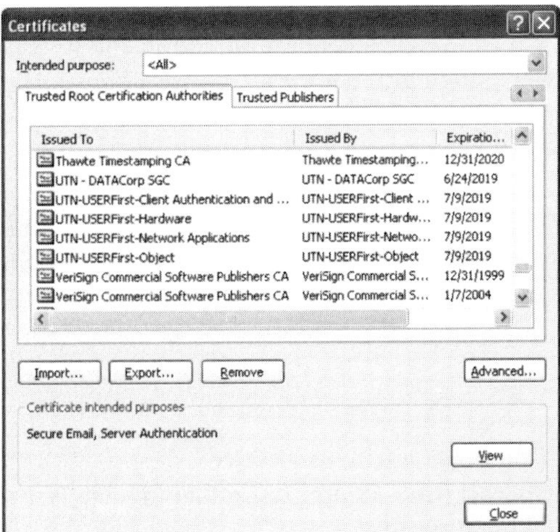

Figure 22.17 Content Advisor, AutoComplete, and My Profile are accessed from the Content tab.

22.3.4 Content Advisor

Of course, with the ability of the Internet to reach virtually any topic, it also allows for easy access to pornography websites and violent websites, which may not be suitable for some people and may be offensive. To help manage such content, you can use Content Advisor. If you are logged on with an administrative account, you can activate Content Advisor and assign a supervisor password. When Content Advisor is enabled, if a user tries to go to a web page that is beyond the limits you set, Internet Explorer won't show this page. Instead, it displays a warning message. Users who know the supervisor passwords can bypass the warning and view the page.

By default, Internet Explorer comes with one system, the Recreational Software Advisory Council's Internet rating system (RSACi) that uses four categories—language, nudity, sex, and violence—and five levels numbered 0 through 4. A higher number indicates more explicit or intense content. When you first enable Content Advisor, the settings that are least likely to offend are in effect by default. You can adjust these settings to meet your own preferences. You should note that not all Internet content is rated. If you choose to allow other people to view unrated sites on your computer, some of those sites could contain material some users will regard as inappropriate. See Figure 22.17.

NOTE: RSAC no longer exists. Instead, it has been "folded into" a new organization, the Internet Content Rating Association (ICRA).

22.3.5 Profile Assistant and AutoComplete

To help you manage your personal information and to make surfing the Internet a little bit easier by automatically entering information on web-based forms, Internet Explorer offers the Profile Assistant and AutoComplete.

The Profile Assistant stores your personal information, such as your address or email name, on your computer. When you visit a new website that requests such information, the Profile Assistant can enter it for you. This saves you from having to enter the same information every time you visit a new site. None of this information can be viewed on your computer, or shared with others, without your permission.

When a website requests information from Profile Assistant, the request includes:

- The URL of the site requesting the information.
- What information the site is requesting from Profile Assistant, so you can choose to exclude information.
- How this information will be used.
- Whether the site has a secure connection (Secure Sockets Layer, or SSL). If it does, you can verify the site's certificate.

You can encrypt your personally identifiable information both when it is transmitted and when it is stored on your computer. To view and edit the specific information used by Profile Assistant, in Internet Explorer, click Tools, and then click Internet Options. On the Content tab, click My Profile. You can create a new profile or modify an existing profile in the Properties dialog box.

The AutoComplete feature remembers previous entries you have made for web addresses, forms, and passwords. When you type information in one of these fields, AutoComplete suggests possible matches. These matches can include folder and program names you type into the Address bar, as well as search queries, stock quotes, or other information that you type in forms on web pages. To use AutoComplete, start typing the information in the Address bar, in a field on a web page, or in a box for a user name or password. If you have typed a similar entry before, AutoComplete lists possible matches as you type. If a suggestion in the list matches what you want to enter in that field, click the suggestion. If no suggestion matches what you are typing, continue typing.

To select AutoComplete settings, in Internet Explorer, click Tools, and then click Internet Options. On the Content tab, click AutoComplete. You can specify whether you want to use AutoComplete for web addresses, forms, user names, and passwords. You can also clear the history of previous AutoComplete entries. When typing information in web forms, and when typing passwords, you can remove an item from the list of suggestions by clicking the item and then pressing the Delete key. See figure 22.17.

22.3.6 Connection Configuration

For the browser to go through a proxy server, the browser must be configured. These configuration settings include automatic configuration, configuring through scripts, or by manually specifying the settings. The automatic configuration and configuring through scripts enable you to change settings after you deploy Internet Explorer. By providing a pointer to configuration files on a server, you can change the settings globally without having to change each user's computer. This can help reduce administrative overhead and potentially reduce help desk calls about browser settings.

To configure the proxy selection and proxy bypass settings in Internet Explorer:

1. Open the Tools menu, and then click Internet Options.
2. Click the Connections tab, and then click LAN Settings.
3. In the Proxy Server area, select the Use a proxy server check box.
4. Click Advanced, and then fill in the proxy location and port number for each Internet protocol that is supported. See figure 22.18.

NOTE: In most cases, only a single proxy server is used for all protocols. In those cases, enter the proxy location and port number for the HTTP setting, and then select the Use the same proxy server for all protocols check box. You can also manually set the addresses and then enable the Use a proxy server and specify the address and port number of the proxy server. If you need to specify different addresses or port numbers for the various Internet services, click on the Advanced button.

Figure 22.18 Configuring the Proxy Selection and Proxy Bypass Settings in Internet Explorer

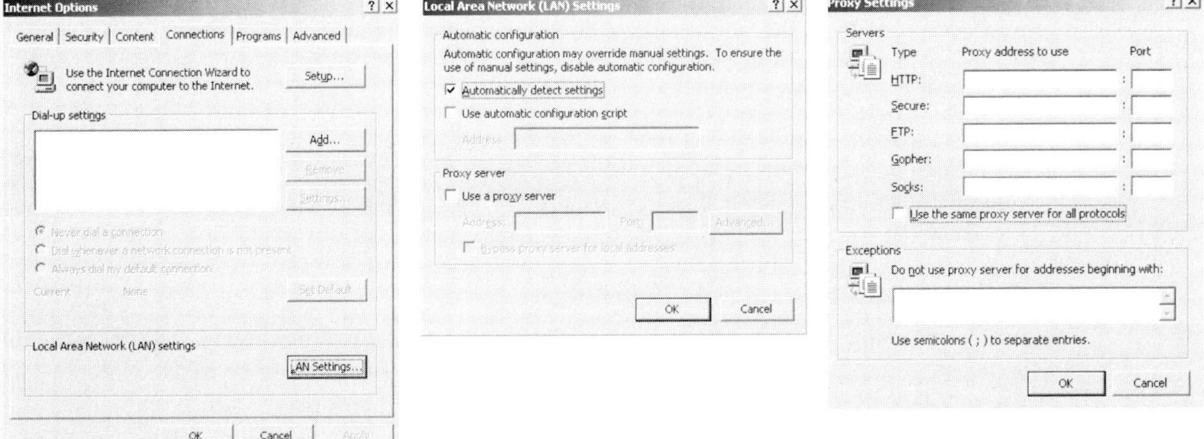

22.3.7 Configuring Toolbars

Similar to toolbars in Microsoft applications, Internet Explorer is designed to float. To prevent toolbars from being moved, you can lock the toolbar by opening the View menu, selecting Toolbars, and then clicking Lock the Toolbars to select or deselect the option. You can also right-click the toolbar and select Lock the Toolbar. You can select or deselect toolbars by using the same method.

NOTE: In full screen mode, you cannot lock or unlock toolbars.

22.3.8 Managing Favorites

Favorites are Internet shortcuts that point to websites that the user wants to visit frequently or access quickly. When you are visiting a site that you want to add to your Favorites, you can open the Favorites menu and select the Add to Favorites submenu. To view your favorites, you would open the Favorites menu and click the Favorites button on the Standard Buttons toolbar, or press Ctrl + I. If you want to create folders, rename folders or favorites, move favorites to folders or delete folders or favorites, you can open the Favorites menu and select the Organize button. If you have certain sites that you visit frequently and you want easy access to them, you can use the Links toolbar. Favorites that are in the LINKS folder show in the Links toolbar. In addition, since most users quickly accumulate so many favorites, you can press Ctrl + D to add the current page to the top level of your FAVORITES folder.

Like History, the Favorites are stored in a person's profile. The default location of the FAVORITES folder is C:\DOCUMENTS AND SETTINGS*USERNAME*\FAVORITES. If you want to back up your favorites or share them with another computer, you can copy them from the FAVORITES folder or you can open the File menu and use the Import and Export options. When you import or export favorites, by default, it will save the files in a BOOKMARK.HTM file.

22.3.9 Offline Web Pages

Offline web pages store copies of select websites so that you can use them when you are not connected to the Internet. You can also specify how much content you want available offline, such as just a page, or a page and all of its links, and you can choose how you want that content updated. Offline web page synchronization is the process of keeping offline web page content up-to-date. This topic looks at the procedure for setting up synchronization, and whether it is a system or a user setting.

To make the current web page available offline:

1. On the Favorites menu, click Add to Favorites.
2. Select the Make available offline check box.
3. To specify a schedule for updating that page, and how much content to download, click Customize.
4. Follow the instructions on your screen.

To customize an existing offline web page:

1. In Internet Explorer, on the Favorites menu, click Organize Favorites.
2. Select the offline web page you want to modify, select Make available offline, and then click Properties.

If you want to synchronize your offline websites or change when to synchronize the website, open the Tools menu and pick the Synchronize option. If you want to remove your synchronized web pages, you need to delete the files in TEMPORARY INTERNET FILES. To delete the files in the TEMPORARY INTERNET FILES folder:

1. In the Internet Options dialog box, on the General tab, under Temporary Internet files, click Delete Files.
2. In the Delete Files dialog box, select Delete all offline content if you want to delete all web page content that you have made available offline, and then click OK.

22.3.10 Troubleshooting Browser Problems

If you cannot connect to any website, it is most likely a connectivity problem or a TCP/IP configuration problem. Therefore, you will need to check your dial-up connections or network connection and check your TCP/IP properties. Some ISPs and many organizations use proxy servers or firewalls to protect their network. Therefore, you will need to verify the proxy settings configured in the Connection tab of the Internet Explorer Options dialog box. Also be sure to use a backslash (\) instead of a slash (/)

in the proxy server's address; the settings disappear from the Proxy Server field and Internet Explorer will not be able to find the proxy server. For more information about networking and troubleshooting of network problems, see chapter 25.

HTTP status codes are returned by web servers to indicate the status of a request. The status code is a three-digit code indicating the particular response. The first digit of this code identifies the class of the status code. The remaining two digits correspond to the specific condition within the response class. Table 22.1 outlines all status codes defined for the HTTP/1.1 draft specification outlined in IETF RFC 2068.

The 4XX errors indicate that the client has sent bad data or a malformed request to the server. Client errors are generally issued by the web server when a client tries to gain access to a protected area using a bad user name and password. For example, the *403* indicates that the requested resource is forbidden, which generally means you don't have the privileges needed to access that page. A *404* indicates that a host server responded to your browser but it cannot find the web page on the server. This usually means that the web page was moved or deleted or that you typed in the wrong URL. See Table 22.1.

Table 22.1 4XX Browser Errors

400	Bad Request
401	Unauthorized 401.1 Logon failed 401.2 Logon failed due to server configuration 401.3 Unauthorized due to ACL on resource 401.4 Authorization failed by filter 401.5 Authorization failed by ISAPI/CGI application
402	Payment Required
403	Forbidden 403.1 Execute access forbidden 403.2 Read access forbidden 403.3 Write access forbidden 403.4 SSL required 403.5 SSL 128 required 403.6 IP address rejected 403.7 Client certificate required 403.8 Site access denied 403.9 Too many users 403.10 Invalid configuration 403.11 Password change 403.12 Mapper denied access 403.13 Client certificate revoked 403.14 Directory listing denied 403.15 Client Access Licenses exceeded 403.16 Client certificate untrusted or invalid 403.17 Client certificate has expired or is not yet valid
404	Not Found
405	Method Not Allowed
406	Not Acceptable
407	Proxy Authentication Required
408	Request Timeout
409	Conflict
410	Gone
411	Length Required
412	Precondition Failed
413	Request Entity Too Long
414	Request-URI Too Long
415	Unsupported Media Type

Table 22.2 5XX Browser Errors

500	Internal Server Error—An internal server error has caused the server to abort your request. This is an error condition that may also indicate a misconfiguration with the web server. However, the most common reason for *500* server errors is when you try to execute a script that has syntax errors.
501	Not Implemented—This code is generated by a web server when the client requests a service that is not implemented on the server. Typically, codes not implemented are returned when a client attempts to POST data to a non-CGI (i.e., the form action tag refers to a nonexecutable file).
502	Bad Gateway—The server, when acting as a proxy, issues this response when it receives a bad response from an upstream or support server.
503	Service Unavailable—The web server is too busy processing current requests to listen to a new client. This error represents a serious problem with the web server (normally solved with a reboot).
504	Gateway Timeout—Gateway timeouts are normally issued by proxy servers when an upstream or support server doesn't respond to a request in a timely fashion.
505	HTTP Version Not Supported—The server issues this status code when a client tries to talk using an HTTP protocol that the server doesn't support or is configured to ignore.

Figure 22.19 Configuring the Proxy Settings for Netscape

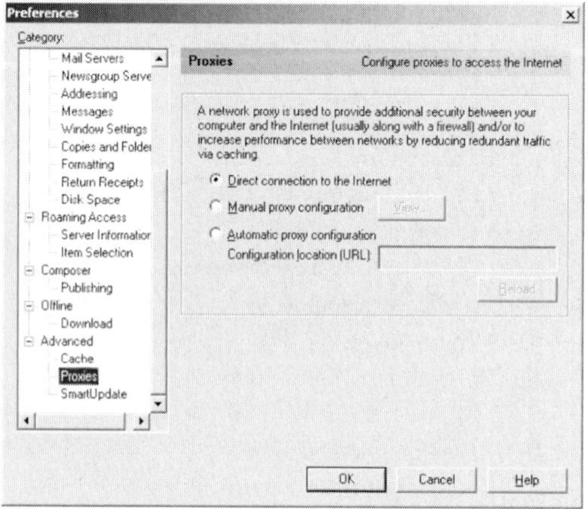

The 5XX errors indicate a server error, which means that the client's request couldn't be successfully processed due to some internal error in the web server. These error codes may indicate something is seriously wrong with the web server. See table 22.2.

22.3.11 Netscape and Mozilla

Many options that are available in Internet Explorer are also available in Netscape and Mozilla. Instead of opening the Tools menu and selecting Internet Options, you open the Edit menu and select the Preferences option. Instead of using tabs, Netscape and Mozilla use a tree structure. See figure 22.19.

22.4 MICROSOFT OUTLOOK EXPRESS

Electronic mail (email) is the transmission of messages over communication networks. The messages can be notes entered from the keyboard or electronic files stored on disk. Most mainframes, minicomputers, and computer networks have an email system. Some email systems are confined to a single computer system or network, but most allow the user to connect anywhere in the world. Companies that are

Figure 22.20 Outlook Express

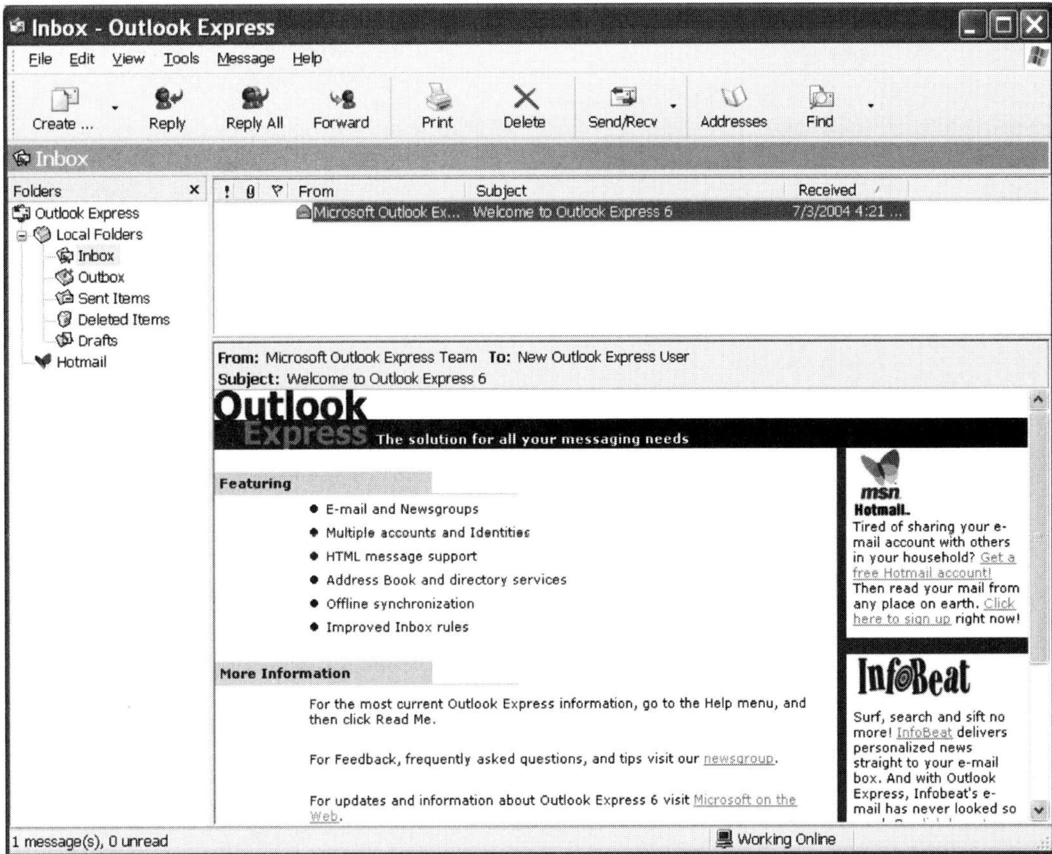

fully computerized make extensive use of email because it is fast, flexible, and reliable. Therefore, it is essential that you know how to configure and troubleshoot Microsoft Outlook and Outlook Express (OE) so that clients can send and receive emails. *By default, Outlook Express is installed with Windows 2000 or Windows XP*. See figure 22.20. Microsoft Outlook is included with Microsoft Office.

For you to be able to send emails using Outlook Express, you must be connected to a TCP/IP network and be able to communicate with an email server (or servers). Networking will be discussed more in chapter 25. Last, you will need to know the type of email server you use (POP3, IMAP, or HTTP), your account name and password, the name of the outcoming email server (SMTP servers), and the name of the POP3 or IMAP servers.

To send email, your system will be using the Simple Mail Transfer Protocol (SMTP). To receive email, you will be using the Post Office Protocol 3 (POP3) or the Internet Message Access Protocol 4 (IMAP-4). You can also send and receive email using HTTP, such as when you access a Hotmail or Yahoo! mail. Although all three allow you to retrieve email, POP3 downloads all emails to your local computer and allows you to manipulate them there. This is beneficial when you are not connected to the network or Internet all of the time. IMAP and HTTP have you work on the emails directly from the email boxes.

22.4.1 Managing Accounts

Before using Outlook Express, you need to add an account to Outlook Express. To add a user account to Outlook Express, you would do the following:

1. On the Tools menu, click Accounts.
2. In the Internet Accounts dialog box, click Add.
3. Select either Mail or News to open the Internet Connection Wizard, and then follow the instructions to establish a connection with an email or news server.

For example, if you create a POP3 account, you would do the following:

1. On the Tools menu, click Accounts.
2. In the Internet Accounts dialog box, click Add.
3. Select Mail to open the Internet Connection Wizard.
4. Enter UserName in the appropriate field, and then click Next.
5. Enter UserName@servername in the appropriate field, and then click Next.
6. Select POP3 in the drop-down list.
7. For Incoming Mail Server, enter *IncomingServerName*. If you don't know the Incoming Server Name, contact your IT department or Internet service provider (ISP).
8. For Outgoing Mail Server, enter *OutgoingServerName*, and then click Next. If you don't know the Outcoming Server Name, contact your IT department or Internet service provider (ISP).
9. Enter User_name's Password, and then click Next.
10. Click Finish.

After the account is added, you can click on the Send/Recv button or press the Ctrl + M keys to retrieve mail from you mail server. You can also open the Tools menu, select the Send and Receive options, and select the appropriate option. By default, Outlook checks every 30 minutes for new messages. If you want to create a message, click the Create button or press Ctrl + N. You can also open the Message menu and select New Message. When you are ready to send the new message, click on the Send button. See figure 22.21.

Outlook Express can store information from your email account and messages from Usenet (newsgroup) in the STORE root folder located at C:\DOCUMENTS AND SETTINGS*USER_NAME*\LOCAL SETTINGS\APPLICATION DATA\IDENTITIES*GUID*\MICROSOFT\OUTLOOK EXPRESS. The GUID is a unique personal identifier.

Because you can add several accounts, the STORE root folder consists of a series of files that represent folders in Outlook. They are:

- **FOLDERS.DBX**—The main index of the store root folder.
- **INBOX.DBX**—This is the default message delivery location.

Figure 22.21 Using Outlook Express to Send a Message

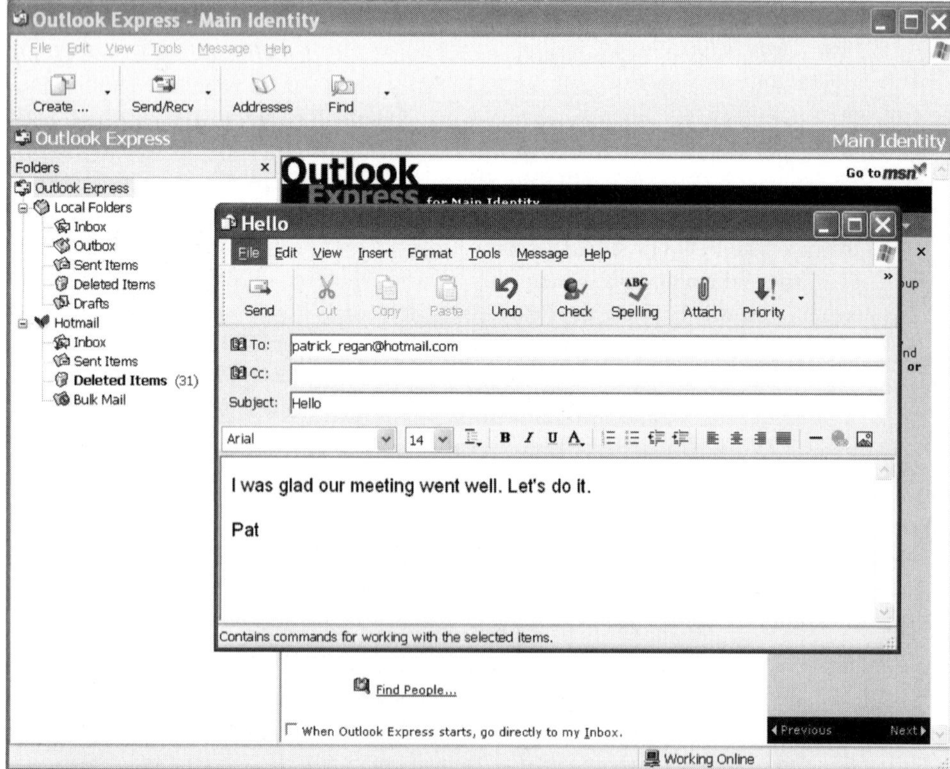

- **DRAFTS.DBX**—Draft messages are saved here prior to being sent.
- **SENT ITEMS.DBX**—All sent messages are stored here.
- **DELETED ITEMS.DBX**—Deleted items from any of the other folders are stored here.

All files in this directory will have a DBX extension and will be hidden by default. If any of these folders cannot be found, they will be automatically created. If they become damaged or corrupted, you will most likely need to delete them and recreate them. To back up your STORE root folder, copy the contents of the folder into a different folder of your choice. If you want to change the location of your Store Information, click Options on the Tools menu, select the Maintenance tab, and click the Store Folder button. See figure 22.22.

To help you organize your emails, you can create folders, which will be called *NAME_OF_FOLDER*.DBX. You can have as many of these folders as you desire, but if these folders exceed 1 MB in size, you may experience various problems including retrieving email to any other folder. Fortunately, when Outlook Express is idle, the folders and files are automatically compressed. If you want to disable this feature, you would do the following:

1. On the Tools menu, click Options.
2. On the Maintenance tab, deselect the Compact messages in the background check box.

If one of the default mail folders becomes damaged, you can recover it. To recover a damaged folder:

1. Copy all of the messages in the damaged folder to another location for safekeeping.
2. Delete the damaged folder.
3. Restart Outlook Express. Outlook Express will search for the default folder, find that it is not there, and create an empty folder of the same name in its place.
4. Copy or move the files that were in the deleted or damaged folder into the new folder.

Outlook Express has the ability to back up your information and settings, on an individual identity basis and restore it later if desired. To back up your settings, you would do the following:

1. On the Tools menu, click Accounts.
2. Select the account, and then click Export.
3. Select the destination, and then type the file name. Outlook Express creates an IAF file.
4. Click Save.

Then, to restore your settings:

1. On the Tools menu, click Accounts.
2. Click Import, select the IAF file that contains the settings for that account, and then click Open.
3. Click OK.

Figure 22.22 Outlook Express Options Maintenance Tab

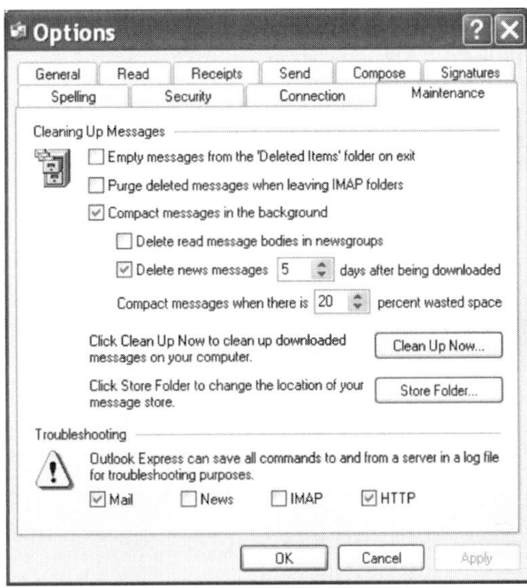

Finally, if you have multiple users who share a computer, you can create a new identity for each user. Outlook Express starts with one identity called the Main Identity. You can then switch over from one identity at any time. For security, you can assign passwords. To create a new identity:

1. On the File menu, point to Identities, and then click Add New Identity.
2. Type the name of the new user.
3. If you want to include a password for this identity, select the Require a password option, and then enter a password.

To switch identities, you just have to open the File menu and select Switch Identity.

22.4.2 Address Books and Electronic Business Cards

The Address Book is a separate application from Outlook Express that is used to store and organize contact information for easy retrieval by programs such as Microsoft Outlook Express. It also features access to Internet directory services, which you can use to look up people and businesses on the Internet. Some people would be lost without their address book because it stores email addresses, home and work addresses, phone and fax numbers, digital IDs, conferencing information, instant messaging addresses, and personal information such as birthdays or anniversaries. You can also store individual and business Internet addresses and link directly to them from your Address Book. For any additional information, you can use notes. See figure 22.23.

To open the Address book, click on the Tools menu and select Address Book, or you can press Ctrl + Shift + B. To create a new contact, click on the New button, select New Contact, and add the appropriate information. To create a new message to a contact in your address book, you can open the Address Book, right-click the contact, select Action, and the select Send Mail. Address Book normally shows only the current identity's contacts and the shared contacts. You can see the contacts of all the identities defined in Outlook Express by starting Address Book from a command line-using the following command:

```
wab /a
```

Under the Name tab, you can also specify whether to send messages only in plain text to this contact. Select this check box if you know that the contact has a program that cannot read HTML-formatted email. When you send an HTML-formatted message, the message is displayed as plain text with an HTML file attached. The recipient can view the attached file by opening it in any web browser.

You can create groups of contacts to make it easy to send emails to multiple people. To create a group, click on the New button and select group. Then name the group and click the Select Members button to select different people. After the group is created, anytime you want to send email to everyone in the group, just use the group name instead of entering each contact individually.

If you use identities, each user can organize contacts into his or her folder. In addition, each user can put contacts into a SHARED CONTACTS folder so that other identities can use them. To share contacts:

1. In the contacts list, select the contact you want to share.
2. Drag the contact to the SHARED CONTACTS folder or to one of its subfolders. This will allow other identities to see the contact.

Figure 22.23 Using the Address Book

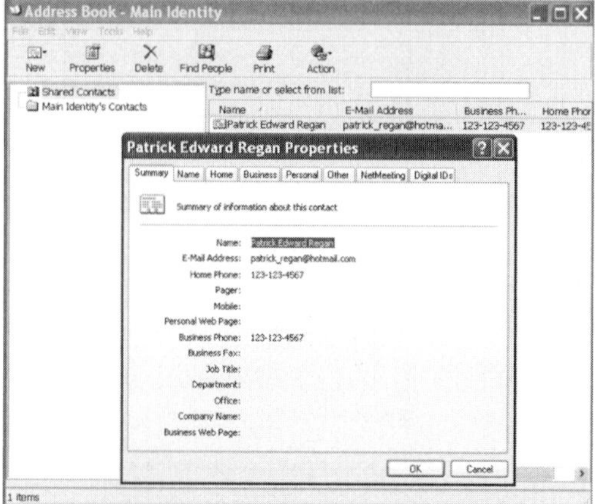

If you cannot see the SHARED CONTACTS folder on the left, on the View menu, select Folders and Groups.

You can keep contacts in your main folder, as well as organize them into subfolders. If you have contacts you would like to share with the other people with whom you share Outlook Express, you can move contacts into the SHARED CONTACTS folder, where other identities can view them when they use the Address Book. Subfolders are always in alphabetical order; you cannot reorganize them.

If you drag a contact to the SHARED CONTACTS folder, you have moved it, and it no longer exists in the original folder. You can make a copy of the contact information for your folder, but changes there will not be reflected in the SHARED CONTACTS folder, or vice versa. Last, you can print your Address Book to add to your personal planner. With three page styles to choose from, you can print all contact information, only business information, or only phone numbers, for any or all contacts.

In addition to the address book, you can also store, send, and receive electronic business cards. Business cards are the new way to send contact information electronically. When you create a business card in Address Book, your contact information is stored in vCard format (*.VCF), so it can be exchanged between different programs (such as email, address books, and personal planners) and between different digital devices (such as desktop computers, laptops or portable computers, personal digital assistants, and telephony equipment). To create a vCard file to send to another person as an attachment, open the File menu and select the Export option. To import a vCard into your Address Book, open the File menu and select the Import option.

Directory services are powerful search tools that enable you to look up names and addresses on the Internet. The Address Book supports Lightweight Directory Access Protocol (LDAP)—which is used by Microsoft's Active Directory and Novell NetWare Directory Service—for using Internet directory services, but it does not check addresses against entries in an LDAP server by default. To add a directory service to your Address Book, you will need the name of the computer server (available from the directory service provider).

1. In either the Address Book or Outlook Express, on the Tools menu, click Accounts.
2. In Outlook Express, select the Directory Service tab, click Add, click Directory Service, and then follow the instructions in the Internet Connection Wizard.
3. In the Address Book, click Add, and follow the instructions in the Internet Connection Wizard.

22.4.3 Configuring Outlook Express

Like most Microsoft applications, most of the configuration will be done by opening the Tools menu and selecting options. See figure 22.24. In the Options dialog box, you can change:

- How often it checks for new mail
- If it plays a sound when you receive email

Figure 22.24 General and Send Options in Outlook Express

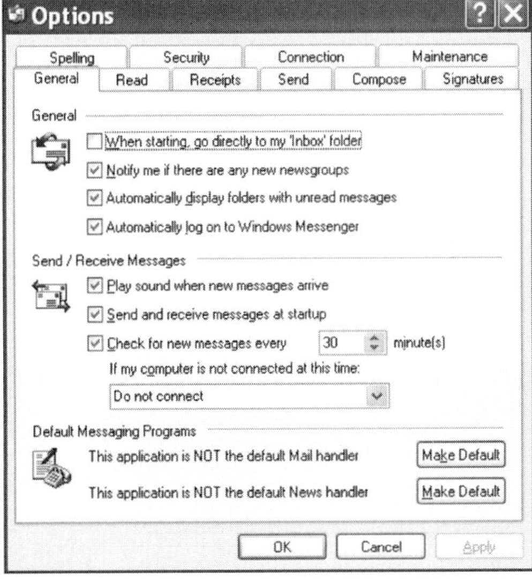

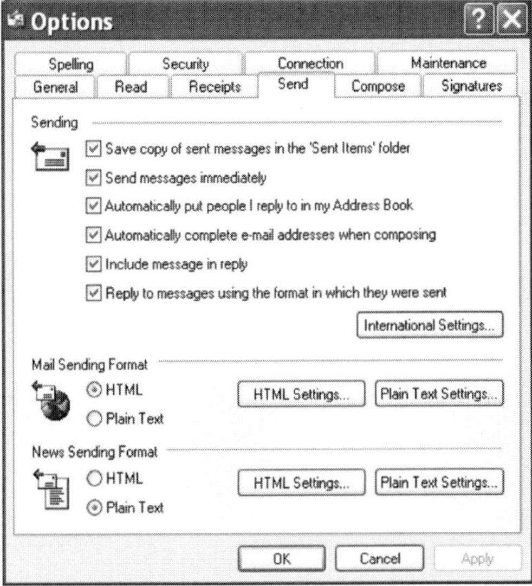

- What default format you want to send messages in such as plain text or HTML
- Default font
- Maintenance and log options
- Spell checking options
- Default mail or news handler program
- Security options

Of course, if you want more information about any of these options, you can click on the question mark button in the top right corner of the Options dialog box and click on the option you want more information about.

Because most email goes through the Internet, you will need to take additional steps to keep your system secure. Besides having a good virus checker and having all of the security patches loaded, you can specify which Internet zone Outlook Express can use and have it warn you if any other applications try to send email. In addition, you can choose whether or not to allow attachments to be saved or opened when they could potentially contain a virus. See figure 22.25.

22.4.4 Troubleshooting Outlook Express

Anytime that you have trouble sending or receiving email, you should first make sure that you are connected properly to the network or Internet. This would include checking TCP/IP settings, cables, and network connectivity.

If you cannot receive email, the most common causes are:

- You are working offline. You need to open the File menu and select Online.
- Your receiving/read options are not set to receive email messages immediately by using the correct connection. Open the Tools menu and select Options, then check the Read and Connections tab.
- Your mail folders or email messages within the folders are damaged.

When you try to send an email message and the message moves to your Outbox instead of being sent, some of common causes could be:

- You opened the email message in the Outbox before the message was sent. You need to resend the message.
- You are working offline. You need to open the File menu and select Online.
- Your sending options are not set to send email messages immediately by using the correct connection. Open the Tools menu and select Options, then check the Send and Connection tab.
- Your mail folders or email messages within the folders are damaged.

Figure 22.25 Security Options in Outlook Express

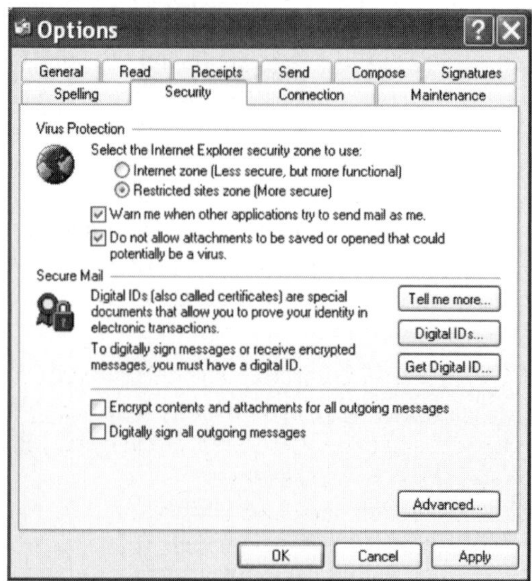

In any case, many issues can be resolved by doing the following:

- Create a new identity.
- Create a new account with the Internet Connection Wizard.
- Rename and repair damaged files.

You also can create logs to help you troubleshoot. This is done by opening the Tools menu, selecting Options, and then selecting the Maintenance tab. In the Troubleshooting section, you can check the types of logs that you want. The logs files will be in the same folder as your STORE root folder. You should note that these log files can get quite large. Therefore, when you finish troubleshooting, make sure you clear the log options.

22.4.5 Importing and Exporting Data

You can import and export the Address Book and emails so that you can move them from one email application to another or from one computer to another. Outlook Express can save individual email messages by opening the messages, opening the File menu, and selecting Save As. The formats in which the emails can saved as include:

- **Mail (*.EML)**—Default format
- **Text (*.TXT)**—Text files
- **HTML (*.HTM, *.HTML)**—web page format read by any web browser and other applications.

You can import or export a mailbox by opening the File menu and selecting either Import or Export. You will then be able to import or export from many formats including Outlook, various versions of Outlook Express, and other formats. In addition, you will be able to import your Address Book contacts (WAB files), Microsoft Exchange Personal Address Book, (PAB files) or any Comma Separated Value (CSV) file. CSV is a file that uses a comma (,) to separate the different fields such as first name and last name. Because it is a generic text file, it can be imported and exported to many different applications.

If you don't want to recreate accounts on other computers, you can import or export accounts by opening the Tools menu, selecting Accounts, selecting your account name, and then clicking Import or Export. Outlook Express will save your account settings in an Internet Account File (*.IAF).

If you have trouble importing or exporting, first verify that you are specifying the correct path. Then try to import or export a different file to determine if the problem is with the file or Outlook Express. Of course, if you get an error message, you can use the Knowledge Base or other websites to determine the meaning of the message.

22.4.6 Newsgroups in Outlook Express

Microsoft Outlook can also connect to a newsgroup on the Internet and act as a newsgroup reader to receive messages from the newsgroup. A newsgroup is a forum on the Internet for threaded discussions on a specified range of subjects. A newsgroup consists of articles and follow-up posts. An article with all of its follow-up posts, which are supposed to be related to the specific subject named in the original article's subject line, constitutes a thread.

To use newsgroups in Outlook Express, your ISP must offer links to one or more news servers. After you set up an account for each server you want, you can use Outlook Express to read and post messages in any of the newsgroups stored on that news server.

When you find a newsgroup you like, you can subscribe to it so that it is displayed in your Outlook Express Folders list. Subscribing provides easy access to your favorite newsgroups, eliminating the need to scroll through the long list on the server each time you want to visit a favorite newsgroup. Newsgroups can contain thousands of messages, and sorting through them can be a time-consuming process. Outlook Express has a variety of features that make it easier to find the information you want in newsgroups.

To subscribe to a private newsgroup:

1. In Outlook Express, on the Tools menu, click Accounts.
2. In the Internet Accounts dialog box, click Add, and then select either Mail or News.
3. In the Internet Connection Wizard, specify a display name (the name that you want to display in your messages), and then click Next.
4. Type your email address, and then click Next.
5. Type the name of the NNTP news server, select the My news server requires me to log on check box, and then click Next.

6. Enter your name and password, and then select the Secure password authentication check box, if appropriate.
7. Click Next, and then click Finish.

To set Outlook Express as your default newsreader:

1. On the Tools menu, click Options.
2. On the General tab, in the Default Messaging Programs area, next to This application is NOT the default News handler, click Make Default.
3. Click OK.

22.5 MICROSOFT OUTLOOK

Microsoft Outlook Express, which is included with Windows, is designed for the casual email user who occasionally saves email messages for future use or reference. Corporate and more serious email users should use an advanced email package such as Microsoft Outlook, which is included with Microsoft Office. Besides supporting much larger email folders, Outlook provides an integrated solution for managing and organizing email messages, schedules, tasks, notes, contacts, and other information, so that you can work more efficiently.

The primary components of Outlook are:

- **E-mail**—Enables users to receive and organize their email messages.
- **Contacts**—Enables users to store names, addresses, phone numbers, email addresses, and an assortment of other information about coworkers, friends, and family.
- **Calendar**—Enables users to organize meetings and appointments by storing and sharing appointments, and generating reminders of upcoming appointments.
- **Tasks**—Enables users to organize assignments, responsibilities, or errands. By using Tasks, you can track your progress and set up a recurring task.
- **Notes**—Enables users to write notes that they can display on the screen or list in the notes area of Outlook.
- **Journal**—Automatically creates records on actions, contacts, notes, and emails and can be used to keep track of phone conversations and handwritten letters.

See figure 22.26.

22.5.1 Accounts in Outlook

Before you start receiving email from Outlook, you must first create a profile followed by adding the email account. A profile is a group of email accounts, address books, and personal folders. A user can create any number of profiles. Similar to identities in Outlook Express, multiple profiles are useful if more than one person uses the computer. To create a new profile with an email account:

1. Click Start and then click the Control Panel.
2. Click Switch to Classic View, and then double-click Mail.
3. In the Mail Setup dialog box, click the Show Profiles button.
4. On the General tab, select the Prompt for a profile to be used check box.
5. Click Add.
6. In the Profile Name field, type a descriptive name for the new profile, and then click OK.
7. In the E-mail Accounts dialog box, click Add a new e-mail account, and then click Next.
8. Select the appropriate server type for your new email account, and then click Next.
9. Fill in the appropriate information as prompted, and then click Next and Finish as needed.
10. Click OK.

You can also create a profile by right-clicking the Microsoft Outlook icon on the desktop and selecting Properties.

Like Outlook Express, you have to add an account to Microsoft Outlook before you can send and receive email. To do this, open the Tools menu and select E-mail Accounts. Then click Add a new e-mail account and click Next. Choose the e-mail server type and click Next. After that, follow the

Figure 22.26 Microsoft Outlook

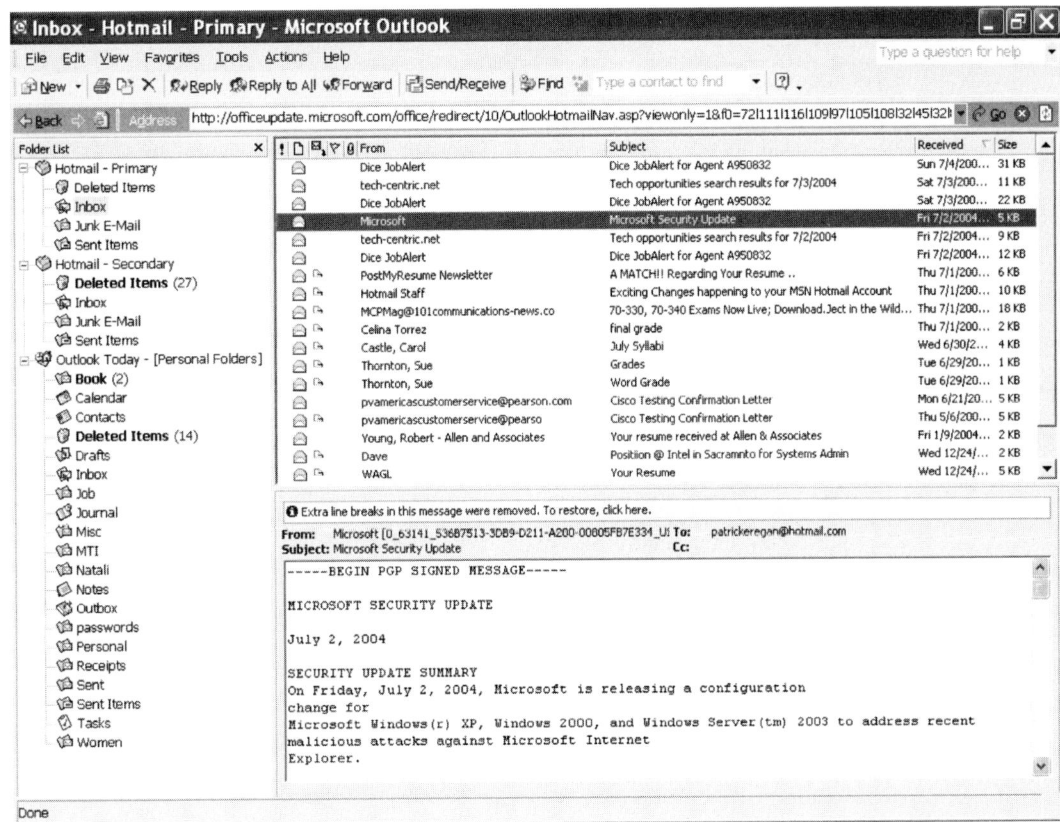

directions on the screen. For example, if you need to configure a POP3 email service, you would do the following:

1. Click Start, and then click Microsoft Office Outlook.
2. On the Tools menu, select E-mail Accounts.
3. In the E-mail Accounts dialog box, click Add a new e-mail account, and then click Next.
4. In the Server Type dialog box, click POP3, and then click Next.
5. In the E-mail Accounts dialog box, enter required information including user information, logon information, password and names of incoming e-mail server (POP3), and Outgoing e-mail server (SMTP). If you do not know the names of your email servers, contact your IT department or Internet service provider.
6. Click Test Account Settings so that it can verify the system is set correctly.
7. Click Next, and then Finish.

If a user cannot connect to an email server and receive or send their email messages, the most likely cause is that the user entered the wrong configuration information including incorrect user name or password, incorrect email server name, and network connectivity problems. You also need to see if your ISP requires Secure Password Authentication (SPA) or if the Outgoing email server requires authentication. Of course, you should also verify your TCP/IP settings and network connectivity.

If you access your email from several different locations, you can configure Outlook to leave copies of your email on the email servers so that you can access it from the other locations. To leave copies of email on the server:

1. In Microsoft Outlook, click the Tools menu, and then click E-mail Accounts.
2. In the E-mail Accounts dialog box, click View or change existing E-mail Accounts, and then click Next.
3. Select your POP3 email account and then click Change.
4. Click More Settings.

5. On the Advanced tab, select Leave a copy of messages on the server.
6. Click OK.
7. Click Next, and then click Finish.

If your deleted messages remain on the server, you may have set an option to keep a copy of your messages on the POP3 email server. If you delete a message that was delivered to a local file, the copy stored on the Internet email server is not affected. If copies of messages are not stored on the server, you may have set an option to delete copies of your messages from the POP3 email server after a specified number of days. When you set this option, messages left on the Internet email server are removed after 5 days unless you specify otherwise. In addition, you may be using a different computer than the one you used to set the option to keep a copy of messages on the server. If you didn't select the Leave a copy of messages on the server check box in the E-mail Accounts dialog box on this additional computer, your messages will be downloaded to it and deleted from the server.

Besides connecting to POP3, IMAP, and HTTP, you can use Outlook to connect to an Exchange email server. Exchange email server is Microsoft's email server, which is often used in corporations. To add an Exchange email account to an existing profile, you would do the following:

1. On the Start menu, click the Control Panel.
2. Click Switch to Classic View, and then double-click Mail.
3. In the Mail Setup dialog box, click Show Profiles.
4. On the General tab, click the profile that you want to use.
5. Click Properties.
6. In the Mail Setup dialog box, click E-mail Accounts.
7. In the E-mail Accounts dialog box, click Add a new e-mail account, and then click Next.
8. In the Server Type dialog box, click Microsoft Exchange Server, and then click Next.
9. In the E-mail Accounts dialog box, enter required information including the name of the Exchange server, user name, and cached exchange mode.
10. Click Next, and then click Finish.
11. In the Mail Setup dialog box, click Close, and then click OK.
12. Close the Control Panel.

Within a corporate network, Outlook communicates with Exchange servers using remote procedure call (RPC), which operates using TCP/IP. To access email from outside the corporate network, you will have to establish a virtual private network (VPN), which would allow users to connect to the corporate network via using the Internet, which would then allow access to the Exchange server.

Another method that is available is to directly connect to the Exchange server using RPC over HTTP, assuming that the corporate firewall allows such a connection. HTTP, short for Hypertext Transfer Protocol, is the protocol used in web pages. To connect to the Exchange server by using HTTP, you would do the following:

1. In Microsoft Outlook, click the Tools menu, and then click E-mail Accounts.
2. Click View or change existing e-mail accounts, click Next, select the Exchange e-mail account, and then click Change.
3. Click More Settings.
4. On the Connection tab, in the Exchange over the Internet area, select Connect to my Exchange mailbox using HTTP.
5. Click Exchange proxy settings.
6. Under Connection settings, in the Use this URL to connect to my proxy server for Exchange box, type the Internet address provided by your Exchange server administrator.
7. Set any additional options specified by your Exchange server administrator.

To view details about Exchange settings:

1. In the E-mail Accounts dialog box, click View or change existing e-mail accounts, click Next, select the Exchange e-mail account, and then click Change.
2. Click More Settings.
3. On the Connection tab, in the Exchange over the Internet area, select Connect to my Exchange mailbox using HTTP.
4. Click Exchange proxy settings.

Outlook includes its own address book. If you want to share the Windows address book used with Outlook Express, you need to open the Registry Edit to change the HKEY_CURRENT_USER\Software\Microsoft\WAB\WAB4\UseOutlook key to 1. If the value (DWORD) is not there, create it.

22.5.2 Offline, Public, and Private Files

If you do not have connection to your corporate network (such as when you are working at home or out in the field), you can work offline to access the local copy of your information. You can also create and respond to messages, which will sit in your Outbox. Then when you connect to the corporate network and you are online, the messages will be automatically sent. If you have a dial-up connection or a slow connection, they will also stay in the Outbox until you choose to send the messages at that time.

To allow for offline access and synchronization, you must first create an **offline folder** (OST) file and then specify which folders to synchronize with the Exchange server. The INBOX, OUTBOX, DELETED ITEMS, SENT ITEMS, CALENDAR, CONTACTS, TASKS, JOURNAL, NOTES, and DRAFTS folders are automatically made available offline when you set up offline folders. After you select the synchronization settings, the user must connect to the Exchange server to synchronize the data. To create an offline folder file:

1. In Microsoft Outlook, click the Tools menu, and then click E-Mail Accounts.
2. Click View or change existing e-mail accounts, and then click Next.
3. In the Outlook processes e-mail for these accounts in the following order list, click Microsoft Exchange Server, and then click Change.
4. Click More Settings.
5. Click the Advanced tab, and then click Offline Folder File Settings.
6. In the File box, type the path to the file you want to use as the offline folder file.

The default file name of the newly created offline folder file is OUTLOOK.OST. If this file already exists, you are prompted for a new name.

To specify which files and folders are available offline:

1. On the Tools menu, point to Send/Receive Settings, and then click Define Send/Receive Groups.
2. In the list, click a Send/Receive group containing an Exchange Server account, and then click Edit.
3. Under Accounts, select your Exchange Server account.
4. In the list, select the folders that you want to use offline in addition to your default folders.
5. If you want to apply a filter to a specific folder, click the folder, click Filter Selected Folder, and then select the options that you want.
6. If you want to limit the size of messages to download when you synchronize folders, click Limit Message Size, and then click the options that you want.
7. Click OK.

Outlook 2003 offers a cached exchange mode that allows you access files while offline. When using a Microsoft Exchange server, the default data store is typically stored on the server. If you have cached exchanged mode enabled, a local copy of the data is kept in the offline folder file. You can change the default delivery location, so that all email is sent to a Personal Folders File (PST) instead of the default data store.

Public folders in Microsoft Exchange allow you collect, organize, and share documents with other users in an organization. Public folders allow you to post information on an electronic bulletin board; share Outlook items in a calendar, contact list, or task list; and share files.

To create a public folder:

1. On the File menu, point to New, and then click Folder.
2. In the Name box, enter a name for the folder.
3. In the Folder Contains box, click the type of folder you want to create.
4. In the Select where to place the folder list, click the location for the folder.
5. In the Folder List, right-click the public folder you want to share, and then click Properties on the shortcut menu.
6. Click the Permissions tab.
7. Click Add.

8. In the Type name or select from list box, enter the name of the person you want to grant sharing permissions to.
9. Click Add, and then click OK.
10. In the Name box, click the name of the person you just added.
11. Under Permissions, choose the settings you want.

A **personal folder** is a data file (file with a PST file name extension) that stores personal information such as messages, appointments, tasks, and journal entries on your computer. You can also configure Outlook to automatically move your messages to the personal folder. You can then create folders within the personal folder to organize your messages. Of course, files stored in the personal folder are available at all times, whether you are working online or offline. The disadvantage would be that if you access your email from another computer that does not have the PST file, you will not be able to access the files stored in the PST file. Because a single file makes up your personal folder, it is also very easy to back up.

Personal folder files can grow very large in size and require a lot of hard disk space. Personal folder files in Outlook 97, Outlook 98, Outlook 2000, and Outlook 2002 are limited to a maximum of 2 GB. Personal folder files in Outlook 2003 can be as large as 20 GB by default, but may be increased to more than 1 TB. The personal folder files format used in Outlook 2003 also supports multilingual Unicode, which means the user can store data in a PST file in most languages.

Outlook 2003 does not support automatically upgrading older personal folders to the new format. Instead, you will have to create a personal folder in Outlook 2003 and then import items from the old data file to the new file. To create a new personal folder file:

1. In Microsoft Outlook, click the File menu, point to New, and then click Outlook Data File.
2. In the New Outlook Data File dialog box, click OK.
3. In the File name box, type a name for the file, and then click OK.
4. In the Name box, type a display name for the PST folder.
5. Select any other options you prefer, and then click OK. The name of the folder that is associated with the data file appears in the Folder List.

The default location for personal folders files is C:\DOCUMENTS AND SETTINGS*USER_NAME*\LOCAL SETTINGS\APPLICATION DATA\MICROSOFT\OUTLOOK.

If you get a message saying that the PST file is corrupt, you can use the Inbox Repair tool (SCANPST.EXE) to diagnose and repair errors in the file. SCANPST.EXE scans only the PST or OST file, making sure that the file structure is intact. It does not scan your mailbox on the Microsoft Exchange server.

Because the personal files can become quite large, you can archive older data that does not need to be accessed regularly. Microsoft Outlook includes a tool called AutoArchive that allows you to archive your data. AutoArchive is on by default and runs automatically at scheduled intervals, clearing out old and expired items from folders.

The AutoArchive option in Outlook enables you to specify which folder to archive, the age of data to be archived, and the interval between the times the archive happens. AutoArchive can either permanently delete expired items or archive (move) old items into an archive file. The first time that you run AutoArchive, Outlook creates the archive file automatically in the following location:

C:\DOCUMENTS AND SETTINGS*USER_NAME*\LOCAL SETTINGS\
APPLICATION DATA\ MICROSOFT\ OUTLOOK\ ARCHIVE.PST

After Outlook archives items for the first time, you can access these items in the file directly from archive folders in your Outlook Folder List.

To turn on AutoArchive:

1. In Microsoft Outlook, click the Tools menu, and then click Options.
2. On the Other tab, click AutoArchive.
3. Select the Run AutoArchive Every check box, and then specify how often the AutoArchive process will run by typing a number in the days box.
4. If you want to be notified before the items are archived, select the Prompt Before AutoArchive check box.
5. In the Move Old Items to box, type a file name for the archived items to be transferred to, or click Browse to select from a list.

Figure 22.27 Microsoft Outlook AutoArchive Options

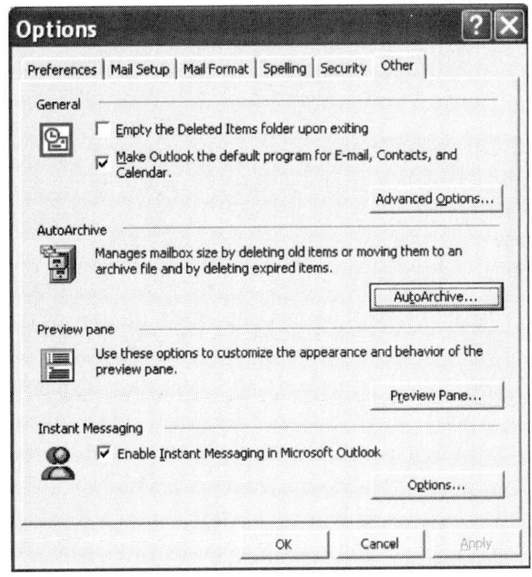

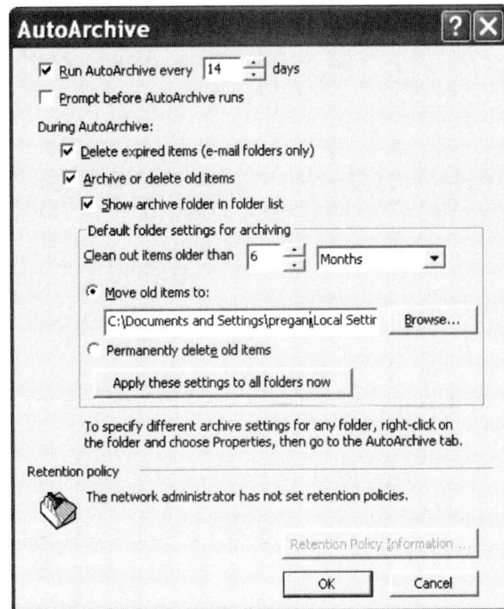

6. Click OK, and then click OK again to close Options. After you have turned on AutoArchive, you can set AutoArchive properties for each folder.

   To set AutoArchive properties:

1. In Microsoft Outlook, in the Folder List, right-click the folder that you want to AutoArchive, and then click Properties.
2. Click the AutoArchive tab.
3. To set AutoArchive for this folder, select Archive this folder using these settings.
4. To specify when items should be automatically transferred to your archive file, type a number in the Months box.
5. To specify a folder for the archived items to be transferred to, click Move old items to.
6. In the Move old items to box, type a file name for the archived items, or click Browse to select from a list, and then click OK.

To archive items manually, open the File menu and click Archive. To access an archive file, since it is a PST file you can import it back into a folder. See figure 22.27.

22.5.3 Junk Mail Filters and Rules

To help reduce the amount of junk mail or spam that you have to deal with, Outlook can automatically move it from your Inbox to your DELETE ITEMS folder or any other folder that you specify including a JUNK MAIL folder. If you use a JUNK MAIL folder, you can then view the junk mail when you are ready to verify that it is junk mail before deleting it. If you still wish for your email to be delivered to your Inbox, you can have it color coded so that you can easily identify it.

You can view the list of terms that Outlook uses to filter suspected junk email messages at C:\PROGRAM FILES\MICROSOFT OFFICE\OFFICE11\1033\FILTERS.TXT. To view your junk mail list, or to delete, move, or color-code all junk email messages in Office XP:

1. In Microsoft Outlook, on the toolbar, click the Organize icon.
2. Click Junk E-mail.
3. Select the options that you want, and then click Turn on for each set of options that you choose.

   To add someone to the junk senders list:

1. In Microsoft Outlook, in the Inbox, click a message from the sender whose messages you want to automatically delete.
2. Click the Actions menu, point to Junk E-mail, and then click Add to Junk Senders list.

Outlook 2003 includes a new feature called the Junk E-mail Filter tool, which replaces the rules functionality used in previous versions of Microsoft Outlook to filter email messages. In addition, in Outlook 2003, to use the Junk E-mail Filter with a Microsoft Exchange email account, you must enable cached exchange mode.

To change the level of junk mail filtering:

1. Click Start, and then click Microsoft Office Outlook.
2. On the Tools menu, click Options, and then click Junk E-mail.
3. On the Preferences tab, click Junk E-mail.
4. Select one of the following protection levels:
   a. **No Protection.** Although this turns off the Junk E-mail Filter tool, Outlook 2003 will continue to evaluate messages by using domain names and email addresses on your Blocked Senders list, and messages will continue to be moved to your JUNK MAIL folder.
   b. **Low.** If you do not receive many junk email messages and want to see all but the most obvious junk messages, you should select this option.
   c. **High.** If you receive a large volume of junk email messages, you should select this option. However, you should periodically review the messages moved to your JUNK MAIL folder because some wanted messages may be moved there as well.
   d. **Safe Lists Only.** Any email messages sent from someone not on your Safe Senders list or sent to a mailing list not on the Safe Recipients list will be treated as junk e-mail messages.
5. Click OK.
6. Click OK to close Options.
7. Close all windows.

To stop receiving email from a particular source you can add the sender's email address or the domain name to the Junk E-mail list:

1. Click Start, and then click Microsoft Office Outlook.
2. On the Tools menu, click Options, and then click Junk E-mail.
3. On the Blocked Senders tab, and then click Add.
4. In the Enter an e-mail address or Internet domain name to be added to the list box, enter the name or address you want added, and then click OK.
5. Repeat steps 3 and 4 for each name or address that you want to add.
6. Click OK to close Junk E-mail Options.
7. Click OK to close Options.
8. Close all Windows

If you want your contacts to be considered trusted senders, select the Also trust e-mail from my Contacts check box on the Safe Senders tab. All email addresses in your CONTACTS folder will then be used by the Junk E-mail Filter to evaluate messages.

In addition to the junk filters, Microsoft Outlook allows you to establish rules that automatically process and organize messages to your specifications. After you create a rule, Outlook applies the rule when a message arrives in your Inbox or when you send a message. For example, you can forward messages from a specific person to another person or a box. To make the rules more flexible, you can also apply exceptions to the primary rules.

To create a rule:

1. In Microsoft Outlook, in the Navigation pane, click Mail.
2. On the Tools menu, click Rules and Alerts.
3. If you have more than one email account, in the Apply changes to this folder list, click the Inbox you want.
4. Click New Rule.
5. You can now choose one of the following:
   - Click Start creating a rule from a template. Under Select the template, select the template you want to use.
   - Click Start from a blank rule. Under Select when messages should be checked, select Check messages when they arrive or Check messages after sending, and then click Next.
6. Follow the remaining instructions in the Rules Wizard.

To run a rule on an existing folder:

1. In Microsoft Outlook, in the Navigation pane, click Mail.
2. On the Tools menu, click Rules and Alerts.
3. Click Run Rule Now.
4. In the Run Rule Now dialog box, select the rules you want to run.
5. In the Run in folder section, click browse, select the folder you want to run the rule on, and then click OK.
6. Click the Include subfolders check box, if you want the rule to run on all the subfolders as well.
7. In the Apply rules to section, select which messages you want the rule applied to. You can select All Messages, Unread Messages, and Read Messages.
8. Click Run Now.
9. When the rule finishes running, click Close.

If you are using Microsoft Exchange servers, you can use Out of Office Assistance to automatically send return messages when you are out of the office such as when you are on a business trip or on vacation. To do this:

1. On the Tools menu, click Out of Office Assistant.
2. Click Add Rule.
3. Under When a message arrives that meets the following conditions section, specify the conditions of the rule that the message must meet for the action to occur.
4. To specify more conditions, click Advanced, select the options you want, and then click OK.
5. To specify that this rule must be the last one applied, select the Do not process subsequent rules check box.

To turn on or off the out-of-office rules, open the Tools menu and select Out of Office Assistant. Then in the Status box, select or clear the check box next to the rule you want to turn on or off.

22.5.4 Importing and Exporting for Outlook

Outlook allows you to copy data from and to many programs so that you can use that data in Outlook. For example, you might want to import existing information such as names and addresses from other programs, such as Microsoft Mail, or Microsoft Schedule+, so that you do not have to manually reenter the same data in Outlook. In addition, you can copy data to Microsoft Access and Microsoft Excel. Microsoft Outlook provides a tool called the Import/Export Wizard to help you import data from other programs into Outlook and export Outlook data to other programs.

To import a file by using the Import/Export Wizard:

1. In Microsoft Outlook, click the File menu, and then click Import and Export.
2. Click Import from another program or file, and then click Next.
3. Select the type of file to import, and then click Next.
4. Click Browse, and then select the file you want to import and choose one of the following:
   - Replace duplicates with items imported. Existing data will be overwritten with the information in the file being imported.
   - Allow duplicates to be created. Existing data will not be overwritten, and duplicates will be added to the current Outlook folder.
   - Do not import duplicate items. Existing data will be kept, and the duplicate information in the file will not be copied to the current Outlook folder.
5. Click Next.
6. Select the folder you want to import data into, and then click Next.
7. If necessary, map fields from the file you are importing to Outlook fields, and then click Next.
8. Click OK.

To use the Import/Export Wizard to export a file:

1. In Microsoft Outlook, click the File menu, and then click Import and Export.
2. Click Export to a file, and then click Next.
3. In the list, click the file type you want to export to, and then click Next.

4. If you want to export to a file for use in Word or PowerPoint, choose either Tab Separated Values or Comma Separated Values.
5. Follow the remaining instructions in the Import/Export Wizard.

Folder design properties, such as permissions, rules, description, forms, and views, are not preserved when you export to a personal folders file. Only the content itself is exported.

22.6 ADOBE ACROBAT READER

Adobe Reader is free software that lets you view and print Adobe Portable Document Format (PDF) files on a variety of devices and operating systems. PDF files are created using Adobe Acrobat. As PC technicians, you will find that most system, hardware, and software documentation will be available only in PDF format. In addition, you will find that many other types of documents are available only in PDF format. Therefore, you need to know how to install, use, and troubleshoot Acrobat Reader. Of course, most problems can be corrected by downloading a fresh copy of Adobe Acrobat Reader and re-installing the software. For further assistance, you can go to http://www.adobe.com to download the software and visit the support website.

22.7 DIRECTX

DirectX is an application programming interface (API) developed by Microsoft to *provide a common programming interface to write programs* that access hardware features of a computer without knowing exactly what hardware is installed on the machine. DirectX was originally designed to allow Windows to become a gaming platform, but has grown into a multimedia platform. DirectX achieves this by creating an intermediate layer that translates generic hardware commands into specific commands for particular pieces of hardware.

When you have a program that requires DirectX, verify that you have the required version or higher. You can verify the DirectX version on your machine and verify other DirectX parameters by using the DirectX Diagnostic Tool. To open the DirectX Diagnostic Tool, do the following:

1. Click on the Start button and select the Run option.
2. In the Open field, type *DXDIAG* and click on the OK button. See figure 22.28.

The newer versions of DXDIAG will ask you to verify that the drivers are all digitally signed. The biggest problem of DirectX is incompatible hardware and drivers, particularly the sound and video drivers. Therefore, you should make sure that the hardware is on the hardware compatibility list and that you download and install the newest drivers. You can also test the DirectDraw and Direct3D (video) and DirectSound and DirectMusic (sound card) by clicking on the Display, Sound, and Music tabs and selecting the appropriate Test buttons.

Figure 22.28 DirectX 6 Diagnostic Tool

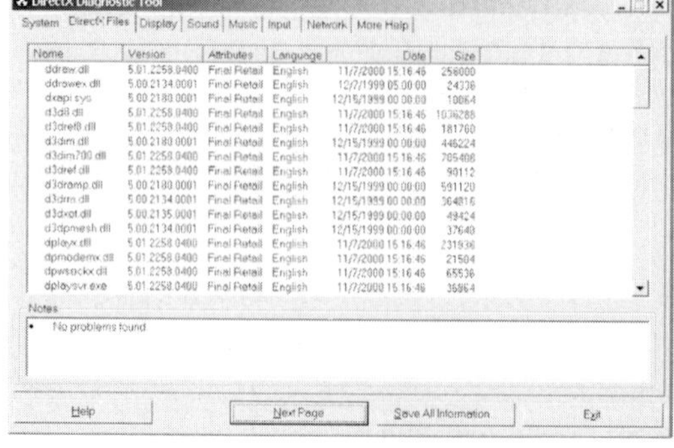

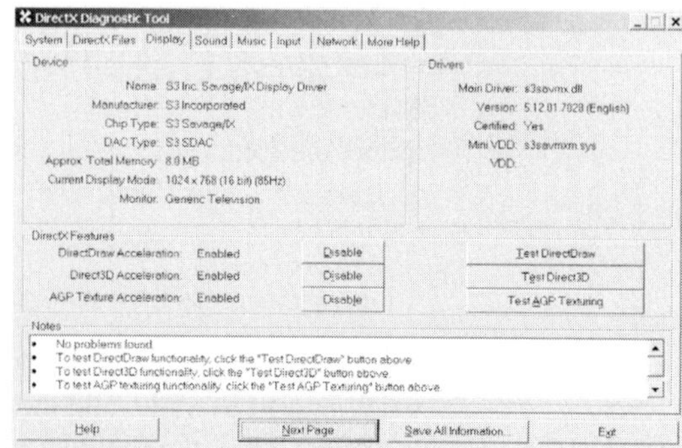

22.8 REMOTE DESKTOP AND REMOTE ASSISTANT

Starting with Windows XP, Microsoft introduced Remote Desktop and Remote Assistance. Similar to Terminal Services used in Windows 2000 servers, you can have access to a Windows session that is running on your computer when you are at another computer. This means, for example, that you can connect to your work computer from home and have access to all of your applications, files, and network resources as though you were in front of your computer at work. You can leave programs running at work and when you get home, you can see your desktop at work displayed on your home computer, with the same programs running.

NOTE: Many work environments may establish a proxy server or firewall that may block this capability.

When you connect to your computer at work, Remote Desktop automatically locks that computer so no one else can access your applications and files while you are gone. When you come back to your computer at work, you can unlock it by typing Ctrl + Alt + Del. Remote Desktop also allows more than one user to have active sessions on a single computer. This means that multiple users can leave their applications running and preserve the state of their Windows session even while others are logged on.

With Fast User Switching, you can easily switch from one user to another on the same computer. For example, suppose you are working at home and have logged on to the computer at your office to update an expense report. While you are working, a family member needs to use your home computer to check for an important email message. You can disconnect Remote Desktop, allow the other user to log on and check mail, and then reconnect to the computer at your office, where you see the expense report exactly as you left it. Fast User Switching works on stand-alone computers and computers that are members of workgroups.

To use Remote Desktop, you need the following:

- A computer running Windows XP Professional ("remote" computer) with a connection to a local area network or the Internet.
- A second computer ("home" computer) with access to the local area network via network connection, modem, or virtual private network (VPN) connection. This computer must have Remote Desktop Connection, formerly called the Terminal Services client, installed.
- Appropriate user accounts and permissions.

To set up this computer to use Remote Desktop:

1. Open System in the Control Panel.
2. On the Remote tab, select the Allow users to connect remotely to this computer check box. See figure 22.29.
3. Ensure that you have the proper permissions to connect to your computer remotely, and click OK. You must be an administrator or a member of the Remote Desktop Users group on your computer. For more information, see To allow other users to connect to your computer.

You must be logged on as an administrator or a member of the administrators group to enable the Remote Desktop feature.

To allow other users to connect to your computer:

1. Open System in the Control Panel.
2. Click the Remote tab.
3. In the Remote Desktop area, click the Select Remote Users button.
4. On the Remote Desktop Users dialog box, click the Add button.
5. On the Select Users dialog box, click the Locations button to specify the search location.
6. Click the Object Types button to specify the types of objects you want to search for.
7. In the Enter the object names to select (examples) box, type the names of the objects you want to search for.
8. Click Check Names.
9. When the name is located, click OK. The name now appears in the list of users on the Remote Desktop Users dialog box.

Again, you must be logged on as an administrator or a member of the administrators group to add a user to the Remote Users Group.

Figure 22.29 Configuring Remote Assistance and Remote Desktop

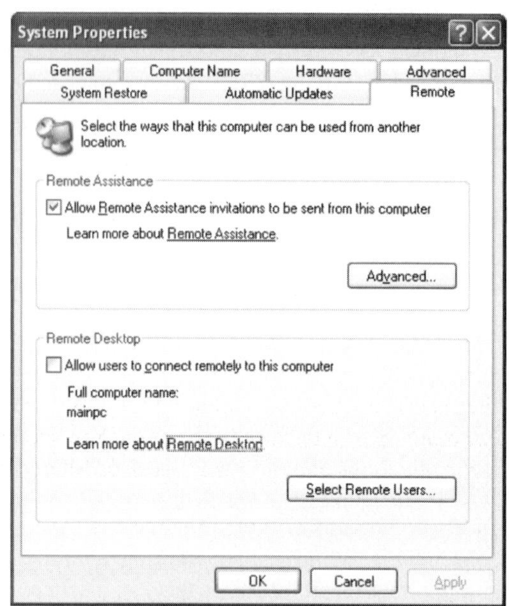

Sometimes the best way to fix a problem is to have someone show you how. Remote Assistance is a convenient way for a friend to connect to your computer from another computer running a compatible operating system, such as Microsoft Windows XP, and walk you through your solution. By following the easy steps in Remote Assistance, you can use Windows Messenger Service (MSN) or an email message to invite a friend to connect to your computer. After he or she is connected, your friend will be able to view your computer screen and chat with you in real-time about what you both see. With your permission, your assistant can even use his or her mouse and keyboard to work with you on your computer.

To start Remote Assistance:

1. Click Start, and then click Help and Support.
2. Click Get help from a friend by using Remote Assistance.

Both you and your helper must be using either Windows Messenger Service or a MAPI-compliant email account such as Microsoft Outlook or Outlook Express. You and your helper need to be connected to the Internet while using Remote Assistance.

If, for some reason, you are unable to send an invitation by using email or Windows Messenger Service, you can create and save an invitation. On the first page of Remote Assistance, click Invite someone to help you, and then click the Save option at the bottom of the next page. You can then send the saved invitation file to your helper in the manner you choose, such as copying it onto a floppy disk or a shared network location, sending it over another email service or an FTP connection, and so on.

22.9 WINDOWS SECURITY

As was mentioned earlier in this chapter, anytime that you deal with applications and anytime that you are connected to a network (including the Internet), you must take precautions to protect yourself. If you are a client that connects to an organization's network, you should coordinate with the organization's network administrators about security. Of course, there are certain steps that you can take or verify.

First, don't forget the obvious by making sure that your machine is physically secure. Keep your workstation in an office that locks or install a lock on the CPU case. Don't forget to securely store the keys away from the computer. If you have a notebook computer, you should even be more careful and buy a locking system that allows you to physically secure the system.

You should also consider using BIOS passwords or a hard drive password that will make it more difficult for a person to turn on the computer and access the information. You should also use Windows 2000 or Windows XP so that you can require a user name and password to log on to the computer. In addition, it's a good idea to enable password-protected screen savers so that if you temporarily leave your computer while still logged in, you will need to type in the password to unlock the computer after the screen saver has started.

NOTE: You should not use Fast User Switching with Windows XP since it can automatically log on as the default user.

Always use up-to-date antivirus software (preferably one that updates itself automatically) and make sure that your system (operating system and applications) have all of the necessary service packs, patches, and fixes. You may want to search for spyware on a regular basis and install only software from a reputable vendor. You should also consider using AutoUpdate to help keep up with Microsoft's patches; you can use Microsoft Baseline Security Analyzer (MBSA) to help check your machine for known vulnerabilities. MBSA can be found at

http://www.microsoft.com/technet/security/tools/mbsahome.mspx.

Assuming that you are using Windows 2000 or Windows XP, you should always use the NTFS file system with the NTFS permissions and encryption to secure your file and the NTFS fault tolerance features to make it more resistant against corruption. You should also consider using passwords on confidential files for applications that offer them such as Microsoft Word or Microsoft Excel.

If you have Windows XP Professional, you should disable Simple File sharing. You should also make sure that the Guess account is disabled. When using passwords, make sure that you always use passwords and that the passwords are *strong* passwords (passwords that are at least eight characters in length and contain a combination of uppercase, lowercase, digits, and special characters). Be sure not to use common words or numbers representing birthdays, children or pet names, or obvious passwords such as "God."

Avoid the temptation of using the local administrator account as your default login account. By always using the administrator account, you increase the odds that malicious code executed via an email attachment or a Trojan horse can do more damage because the administrator has access to more. In a workgroup, consider placing local users with a greater need for control in the local power users group, instead of the administrators group. You could also rename the administrator account and create a dummy administrator account that has no or little rights and permissions.

Consider using a firewall to help protect your computer on a network or the Internet, especially if you have full-time Internet connection. Windows XP comes with ICF, which is not enabled by default and filters only incoming traffic without attempting to manage or restrict outbound connections. It is highly recommended to use a third-party personal firewall such as BlackIce or Zone Lab's ZoneAlarm, or the new firewall that is available in Windows XP Service Pack 2 (SP2). See chapter 25 for more information.

If you need to share a network or Internet connection with several computers, use a router instead of Internet Connection Sharing (ICS). A router will give you better performance and will be more secure. For small home or office, the Linksys Cable/DSL Routers are strongly recommended, which are usually under $100.

When you make backups or use removable media including floppy disks, CDs, DVDs, USB flash drives, Zip disks, and so forth, be sure that you secure the media. Of course, be sure that you back up your system and important files on a regular basis. For Windows, you can also create emergency repair disks and have them locked up and stored away from the PC.

If you are using a wireless network, you should take extra steps to secure the transmissions that can be picked up by anyone with an antenna. Read Microsoft's Knowledge Base article 309369 titled "How to Make Your 802.11b Wireless Home Network More Secure" as a starting point.

You should also consider disabling any programs or services that you are not using. You may wish to consider disabling the following services:

- **Internet Information Server (IIS)**—If you don't need to host a website or FTP site, you should not install IIS. If it is installed, disable it or uninstall it. It is not installed by default in Windows XP. If you are using IIS on your workstation, you need to take extra precautions to lock it down and stay on top of security vulnerabilities specific to web services.
- **Messenger**—The messenger service is used to receive service messages between clients and servers but can also be used to spam your system. It has nothing to do with MSN messenger. If you are connected directly to the Internet and not behind a corporate firewall, you probably don't need it.
- **Netmeeting/Remote Desktop Sharing**—Enables an authorized user to access the computer remotely by using Netmeeting.

- **Remote Desktop Help Session Manager**—Manages and controls Remote Assistant.
- **Remote Registry**—Enables remote users to modify registry settings on this computer.
- **Routing & Remote Access**—offers routing services and remote access via VPN tunnels or dial-in services.
- **SSDP Discovery Service**—This collects and manages announcements of network devices. By disabling this also disables Universal Plug and Play Service used by network devices.
- **Universal Plug and Play Device Host**—This is designed to allow your computer to automatically connect to network-enabled appliances. Although there are no practical uses for this technology yet, several severe security flaws have already been discovered. Use the UnPlug and Play utility from Gibson Research to disable Universal Plug and Play.
- **Telnet**—Telnet is disabled by default. Be aware that telnet sends text unencrypted. Therefore, anyone can read the user name and passwords that you use to connect to a computer and that data being sent between the computers.

You should also consider disabling Remote Desktop.

Auditing is a feature of Windows 2000 and Windows XP that monitors various security-related events so that you can detect intruders and attempts to compromise data on the system. Some of the events that you can monitor include access to objects such as folders or files, management of user and group accounts, and logging on and off a system. The security events are then viewed in the Event Viewer. Therefore, the auditing is one way to find security holes in your network and to ensure accountability for people's actions including the administrators.

Events are not audited by default. If you have administrator permissions, you can specify what types of system events to audit using group policies (COMPUTER CONFIGURATION\WINDOWS SETTINGS\SECURITY SETTINGS\LOCAL POLICIES\AUDIT POLICY).

For files and folders, you can only audit files and folders that are volume formatted with NTFS. To set, view, or change auditing a file or folder:

1. Open Windows Explorer and locate the file or folder that you want to audit.
2. Right-click the file or folder and select the Properties option.

Figure 22.30 Auditing with Local Policies

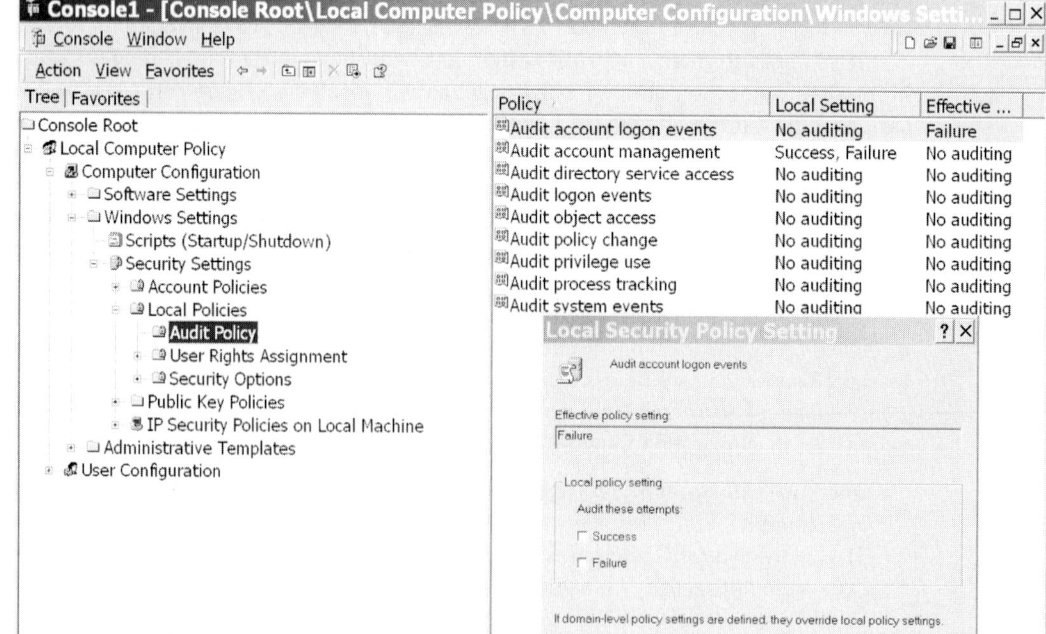

Table 22.3 Audit Best Practices

Potential Threat	Audit Event
To watch for uses trying random passwords to bypass security	Failure audit for logon/logoff.
To watch for stolen password usage	Success audit for logon/logoff.
To watch for misuse of privileges including those of administrators	Success audit for user rights, user and group management, security change policies, restart, shutdown, and system events
To watch the use of sensitive files	Success and failure audit for file-access and object-access events. File Manager success and failure audit of Read/Write access by suspect users or groups for the sensitive files.
To watch for the improper use of printers	Success and failure audit for file-access printers and object-access events. Print Manager success and failure audit of print access by suspect users or groups for the printers.
To watch for a virus outbreak	Success and failure write access auditing for program files (EXE and DLL extensions). Success and failure auditing for process tracking. Run suspect programs; examine security log for unexpected attempts to modify program files or create unexpected processes. You should do this when you actively monitor the system log.

3. Click the Security tab, click on the Advanced button, and then click on the Auditing tab.
   - To set up auditing for a new group or user, click Add, specify the name of the user you want, and click the OK button to open the Auditing Entry dialog box.
   - To view or change auditing for an existing group or user, click the name and click the View/Edit button.
   - To remove auditing for an existing group or user, click the name and click the Remove button.

   NOTE: To perform auditing, you must be logged on as a member of the administrator group or have been granted the Manage auditing and security log right in group policy.

Last, because the security log is limited in size, you should select only those objects that you need to audit and you should consider the amount of disk space that the security log will require. The maximum size of the security log is defined in Event Viewer by right-clicking Security log and selecting the Properties option.

To minimize the risk of security threats, there are a number of auditing steps you can take. Table 22.3 lists various events that you should audit, as well as the specific security threat that the audit event monitors.

SUMMARY

1. A program, sometimes referred to as a process, is a sequence of instructions that can be executed by a computer.
2. A program consists of initializing code and data, a private memory address space, system resources (such as files, communication ports, and Windows resources) and one or more threads.
3. A thread is part of a program that can execute independently of other parts.
4. Operating systems that support multithreading enable programmers to design programs whose threaded parts can execute concurrently.
5. Win16-based applications (used by Windows 3.XX applications) use cooperative multitasking.
6. Win16-based applications share the same memory area or virtual machine (VM) and will all be assigned a single time slice. Unfortunately, if a program causes problems, it can cause all Win16-based applications to crash.

7. When you need to start a program, you will usually go to the Start menu and select the program that you want. You can also create and add shortcuts to the quick launch area on the Taskbar, on the desktop, or in a folder.
8. The Start menu is a collection of folders and shortcuts that are usually stored in the C:\DOCUMENT AND SETTINGS folder as part of a user profile.
9. DOS programs run in a special Win32-based application called the NT virtual DOS machine (NTVDM). The NTVDM provides a simulated MS-DOS environment for MS-DOS–based applications.
10. To customize an NTVDM for an MS-DOS–based application, go to the application file name and select Properties from the shortcut menu to create a Program Information File (PIF) for the MS-DOS application.
11. Win16-based applications are executed by Win16 on Win32 (WOW) which translates or thunks 16-bit calls to 32-bit calls.
12. With the introduction of 64-bit versions of Microsoft Windows, there is also Windows on Windows 64 (WOW64), which is a 32-bit subsystem that allows you to run 32-bit applications on 64-bit operating systems.
13. To share data between documents, Windows applications can use dynamic data exchange (DDE) or object linking and embedding (OLE).
14. A common way to move data between applications or documents is to use the Clipboard. When you highlight the text or select a picture and you use Copy or Cut from the Edit menu in the source application, the text and picture go into RAM, specifically to the Clipboard.
15. To install most programs, you will use an executable such as SETUP.EXE or INSTALL.EXE or an MSI file (Windows Installer).
16. Installing applications involves much more than just creating a directory and copying some files into the directory. An installation process will begin with the user choosing installation parameters and components or reading installation parameters from a text file. During the installation, the application will create or write entries to the registry.
17. Most programs run properly on Windows 2000 and Windows XP. The exceptions are some older games and other programs that were written specifically for earlier versions of Windows.
18. Starting with Windows XP, Windows has a Program Compatibility Wizard to configure Windows to run a program under an older Windows environment.
19. When you install a Windows program, the program often adds information or modifies information to the registry. Therefore, to remove these entries and the program files on the hard drive, many programs include an uninstall program or have an uninstall option within the installation program.
20. In Windows 2000 and XP, when you double-click on a document, Windows will recognize the file name extension and start the appropriate program to open the file. Associating an extension with a program is known as registering a file.
21. Besides compatibility problems with hardware and other software applications, software problems also may be caused by viruses, corrupt program files, corrupt data files, and the amount of free disk space.
22. When preparing for an installation or dealing with application problems, you need to use a sound troubleshooting strategy that combines process, knowledge, and experience. In addition, you need to understand the capabilities of the application and know how to use the application.
23. An office suite is a collection of productivity applications bundled together and sold as a single package. A suite typically consists of a word processor and spreadsheet program, and often contains other software packages such as database and presentation software.
24. Microsoft Office is a family of products designed to help users complete common business tasks. Microsoft Office applications are available in suites, or groups of programs bundled together to address different user requirements.
25. Like Windows, you should keep Microsoft Office updated so that it will run more reliably and securely.
26. Microsoft Office has some built-in self-repairing features through the Microsoft Windows Installer. If a resource that is required to start an Office program is missing, such as a file or registry key, the Windows Installer detects the missing resource and repairs the program.
27. Microsoft Office applications can be configured and customized as needed. The first place to configure Office applications is to open the Tools menu and select Options.
28. One advantage that Microsoft currently has with Microsoft Office is that the file formats have become standards de facto. This is one of the reasons why organizations find it difficult to use other applications; they would most likely not be able to access old documents and templates or documents from other organizations.
29. Microsoft Office provides an add-in feature called Proofing Tools, which is a collection of editing technologies that enable users to proof Office documents in multiple languages.
30. Office documents are based on templates. A template determines the basic structure for a document and contains document settings such as AutoText entries, fonts, key assignments, macros, toolbar buttons, menus, page layout, special formatting, and styles.
31. Global templates contain settings that are available to all documents. When you work on a document, you can typically use only the settings and features that are available in the template at-

tached to the document (or Microsoft's Word Normal [(NORMAL.DOT)] template).

32. Microsoft applications offer various forms of security including password protection, use of digital signatures, and the removal of privacy information.
33. To make Microsoft applications more powerful and more flexible, they include Visual Basic capabilities through macros. A macro, or formula language, is a set of instructions that program executes on command. Macros group several keystrokes into one command or perform complex menu selections such as changing colors on your desktop. Therefore, they simplify redundant or complex tasks.
34. Unfortunately, macros inadvertently opened the Windows data files to a new type of virus, the macro virus.
35. Macro viruses are stored in Office documents such as Word and Excel. When you open the document, the macro virus infects the global template of the program. Because macros are a very power tool, they allow a large range of actions including modifying documents, deleting documents, formatting the hard drives, and causing documents to be sent out via email.
36. Unfortunately, since macros are easy to create, macro viruses are the most widespread virus type.
37. The web browser is the client program or software that you run on your local machine to gain access to a web server.
38. By far, Microsoft Internet Explorer (IE) is the most common browser available because it comes with every version of Windows. For Linux machines and as an alternative to Internet Explorer, you can use Netscape Navigator or Mozilla.
39. Most of the configuration options for Internet Explorer are accessed by opening the Tools menu and selecting Internet Options. It can also be accessed from the Internet Options applet in the Control Panel.
40. A cookie is a message given to a web browser by a web server, which is typically stored in a text file on the PC's hard drive.
41. From the General tab in Internet Explorer, you can delete the cookies that are stored on your hard drive. By clicking on the Privacy tab, you can determine how much of your personal information can be accessed by websites and whether a website can save cookies on your computer by adjusting the tab slider on the privacy scale.
42. A plug-in is a software module that adds a specific feature or service to the browser such as to display or play different types of audio or video messages. The most common two plug-ins are Shockwave and RealMedia.
43. Adobe Acrobat is used to read and create Portable Document Format (PDF) files. PDF files are an open de facto standard for electronic document distribution worldwide. Adobe PDF is a universal file format that preserves all the fonts, formatting, graphics, and color of any source document, regardless of the application and platform used to create it. Adobe PDF files are compact and can be shared, viewed, navigated, and printed exactly as intended by anyone with free Adobe Acrobat Reader software (program and plug-in).
44. VBScript, Short for Visual Basic Scripting Edition, is a scripting language developed by Microsoft and supported by Microsoft's Internet Explorer web browser.
45. An applet is a component in a distributed environment that is downloaded and executed by a web browser.
46. Java applets are self-contained Internet applications that are written in Java.
47. An ActiveX control is similar to a Java applet. ActiveX is not a programming language, but rather a set of rules for how applications should share information. Programmers can develop ActiveX controls and plug-ins in a variety of languages, including C, C++, Visual Basic, and Java.
48. Unlike Java applets, however, ActiveX controls are downloaded and executed by a web browser (Internet Explorer) and have full access to the Windows operating system. Because ActiveX has full access to the Windows operating system, it constitutes the greatest potential threat.
49. ActiveX uses code signing, specifically the Microsoft Authenticode technology. Authenticode allows you to verify the origin of a control and thus assess its reliability and safety.
50. For the browser to go through a proxy server, the browser must be configured. These configuration settings include automatic configuration, configuring through scripts, or by manually specifying the settings.
51. Favorites are Internet shortcuts that point to websites that the user wants to visit frequently or access quickly.
52. Like History, the Favorites are stored in a person's profile. The default location of the FAVORITES folder is C:\DOCUMENTS AND SETTINGS*USERNAME*\FAVORITES.
53. Offline web pages store copies of select websites so that you can use them when you are not connected to the Internet. You can also specify how much content you want available offline, such as just a page, or a page and all of its links, and you can choose how you want that content updated.
54. If you cannot connect to any website, it is most likely a connectivity problem or a TCP/IP configuration problem. Therefore, you will need to check your dial-up connections or network connection and check your TCP/IP properties.
55. Electronic mail (email) is the transmission of messages over communication networks. Popular applications through which to send and receive email are Outlook Express and Outlook.

56. The Address Book is a separate application from Outlook Express that is used to store and organize contact information for easy retrieval by programs such as Microsoft Outlook Express.
57. Since most email goes through the Internet, you will need to take additional steps to keep your system secure. Besides having a good virus checker and all of the security patches loaded, you can specify which Internet zone Outlook Express can use and have it warn you if any other applications try to send email.
58. DirectX is an application programming interface (API) developed by Microsoft that provides a common programming environment to write programs that access hardware features of a computer without knowing exactly what hardware is installed on the machine.
59. You can verify the DirectX version on your machine and verify other DirectX parameters by using the DirectX Diagnostic Tool (DXDIAG).
60. Starting with Windows XP, Microsoft introduced Remote Desktop and Remote Assistance. Similar to Terminal Services used in Windows 2000 servers, you can have access to a Windows session that is running on your computer when you are at another computer.
61. If you are a client that connects to an organization's network, you should coordinate with your network administrators about security. Of course, there are certain steps that you can take or verify.

QUESTIONS

1. All client computers run Windows XP Professional and an application named App1. A user reports that whenever she attempts to open a file for App1, she is directed to the C:\PROGRAM FILES folder, not to her home directory. You discover that the user runs App1 by clicking a shortcut on her desktop. You need to ensure that the user is directed to her home directory when she opens a file for App1. What should you do?
   a. Alter the target path for the MY DOCUMENTS folder.
   b. Alter the Target setting for the shortcut properties.
   c. Alter the Start in setting for the shortcut properties.
   d. Alter the PATH system variable to include the home directory.
2. All client computers run Windows XP Professional. A user in the company wants to be able to open all BMP files by using a custom application. The user reports that when he double-clicks BMP files, they open in Microsoft Paint, not in the custom application. You need to ensure that all BMP files are opened by using the custom application. What should you do?
   a. Create a software restriction policy for the custom application.
   b. Configure the file association for BMP files to open with the custom application.
   c. Instruct the user to right-click on the BMP file and select the Open with option.
   d. Instruct the user to move the BMP file to the same folder as the custom application.
3. All client computers run Windows XP Professional. All users use Microsoft Internet Explorer as their web browser. A user reports that the Address bar in Internet Explorer does not retain any frequently used URLs. The user states that the contents of the Address bar is always empty. The user wants to access frequently used websites from the Address bar, thus you need to ensure that the Address bar stores frequently used URLs. What should you instruct the user to do in Internet Options in the Control Panel?
   a. Configure the History settings to keep pages in history for 30 days.
   b. Configure the Temporary Internet Files settings to check for newer versions of stored pages automatically.
   c. Select the Enable Personalized Favorites Menu check box on the Advanced tab.
   d. Increase the amount of disk space available in the Temporary Internet Files settings.
4. All client computers run Windows XP Professional. All users use Microsoft Internet Explorer as their web browser. A user reports that she is trying to establish a connection to websites that have URLs starting with *https://*. However, Internet Explorer does not establish a connection, and the user receives the following error message: "The page cannot be displayed." You need to ensure that the user can establish a secure connection to websites that have URLs starting with *https://*. What should you instruct the user to do in Internet Options in the Control Panel?
   a. Select the Use SSL 2.0 and Use SSL 3.0 check boxes on the Advanced tab.
   b. Select the Do not save encrypted pages to disk check box on the Advanced tab.
   c. Click the Clear SSL State button.
   d. Click the Certificates button and import a user certificate to the personal certificate store.
5. All client computers run Windows XP Professional. A user reports that he wants to move a shortcut from his desktop to the Start menu. You need to ensure that the shortcut is moved to the Start menu. What should you instruct the user to do?
   a. Drag and drop the shortcut to the Start menu.
   b. Configure the Start menu to use the Classic Start menu.

c. Increase the number of programs available on the Start menu.
d. Ensure that the recently used programs list is disabled.

6. A user in the company upgrades her computer from Windows 98 to Windows XP Professional. The user reports that a mission-critical custom application no longer works on her computer. She states that the application will not start, but it does not display any error messages. You discover that the custom application is a 32-bit Windows application that does not use the Windows registry. You confirm that the application is compatible with Windows XP Professional. You need to ensure that the custom application can successfully run on the user's computer. What should you do?
   a. Instruct the user to start the application by using the Start command.
   b. Instruct the user to modify the properties of the application's EXE file so that the application runs in Windows 98 compatibility mode.
   c. Ask an administrator to reset the domain computer account for the user's computer.
   d. Remotely add the user's user account to the local administrators group on the user's computer.
7. A customer uses Microsoft Word on his home computer to produce proposals. The customer's computer runs Windows XP Professional and Microsoft Office XP. The customer reports that he frequently encounters problems with specific Word features. You discover that the problems have been addresses in an Office XP service release. You need to ensure that the customer installs the correct service release. What should you instruct the customer to do?
   a. Visit the Microsoft Windows Update website. Scan for and install all available updates.
   b. Visit the Microsoft Office Product Updates website. Scan for and install all available updates.
   c. Select the Detect and Repair Wizard from the Help menu in Word.
   d. Repair Word by using Add or Remove Programs in the Control Panel.
8. All client computers run Windows XP Professional and Microsoft XP. A user reports that Microsoft Excel will no longer open on her computer. When the user attempts to open Excel, she receives an error message indicating that a required file or DLL is missing. You need to ensure that the user can open Excel. You want to achieve this goal as quickly as possible. What should you instruct the user to do?
   a. Repair Office by using Add or Remove Programs in the Control Panel.
   b. Copy the DLL files from a network-based Office installation point to her local computer.
   c. Visit the Microsoft Update website. Scan for and install all available updates.
   d. Select Detect and Repair from the Help menu in an Office application other than Excel.
9. All client computers run Windows XP Professional and Microsoft Office 2003. A user reports that his Microsoft Excel spreadsheet is not working properly. You discover that he receives a message stating that his security settings prevent him from running macros when he opens the Excel file. You need to ensure that the user can open the Excel file and run the macros. What should you instruct the user to do?
   a. Add the user to the computer's power users group.
   b. Add the user to the computer's administrators group.
   c. In Excel, in the Macro option on the Tools menu, select Macros.
   d. In Excel, change the Macro security settings to Medium and enable macros if prompted.
10. A home user running Windows XP Home Edition and Microsoft Internet Explorer reports that her Favorites list is frequently altered. You discover that she shares her computer with other family members. You need to ensure that her Favorites list stays consistent when she logs on. What should you do for each family member?
    a. Create and use a user profile.
    b. Create and use a Microsoft Outlook Express identity.
    c. Create and use an Internet Explorer Address Book identity.
    d. Create a separate FAVORITES folder under the MY DOCUMENTS folder.
11. Windows XP is one of the mainstream operating systems deployed. Your major duty is to assist in the configuration and maintenance of desktop applications. You are deploying Internet Explorer's Content Advisor. By default, the content rating system that comes with IE has how many categories defined?
    a. 4
    b. 5
    c. 6
    d. 8
12. WinXP is one of the mainstream OS deployed. Your major duty is to assist in the configuration and maintenance of desktop applications. You are deploying IE's Content Advisor. By default, the content rating system that comes with IE has several categories defined. Which of the following are the valid categories (choose all that apply)?
    a. language
    b. nudity
    c. sex
    d. violence
13. All client computers run Windows XP Professional. All users use Microsoft Internet Explorer as their web browser. A user reports that his Address bar in Internet Explorer has disappeared. Now, he cannot type website URLs to connect to websites. You discover that the user has recently made some changes in Internet Explorer. You need to ensure that the user can type website

URLs in the appropriate toolbar. What should you instruct the user to do?
   a. Lock the toolbars.
   b. Enable the Address bar.
   c. Enable the Links toolbar.
   d. Enable the Standard Buttons toolbar.

14. All client computers run Windows XP Professional. All users use Microsoft Internet Explorer as their web browser. A user wants to have the highest degree of protection against cookies that still allows her to log on to websites and store personal data. She wants to prevent cookies from advertisers on third-party websites from being stored on her computer. You need to ensure that the user's Internet options are configured properly. What should you instruct the user to do in Internet Options in the Control Panel?
   a. Enable the Content Advisor.
   b. Configure the Privacy setting to Medium-High.
   c. Configure the custom security setting to High for the Internet security zone.
   d. Add all third-party websites to the Restricted sites security zone.
15. Windows XP is one of the mainstream operating systems deployed. Your major duty is to assist in the configuration and maintenance of desktop applications. Your user wants to display the IE Favorites Explorer bar. What shortcut keys should you tell him to press?
   a. Ctrl + I b. Ctrl + E
   c. Ctrl + A d. Ctrl + D
16. Windows XP is one of the mainstream operating systems deployed. Your major duty is to assist in the configuration and maintenance of desktop applications. Your user wants to quickly add the current web page to the top level of the IE FAVORITES folder. What shortcut keys should you tell him to press?
   a. Ctrl + I b. Ctrl + E
   c. Ctrl + A d. Ctrl + D
17. Windows XP is one of the mainstream operating systems deployed. Your major duty is to assist in the configuration and maintenance of desktop applications. You want to have Internet Explorer download a copy of the current page to your TEMPORARY INTERNET FILES folder. What should you do?
   a. Click on the Favorites menu and select Add to Favorites. Then select Make available offline.
   b. Choose Edit, Select All, Copy.
   c. Choose Edit, FrontPage.
   d. Press Ctrl + PrintScreen.
18. Windows XP is one of the mainstream operating systems deployed. Your major duty is to assist in the configuration and maintenance of desktop applications. Your user asks you what program can be used to open and read a cookie file. Which of the following programs can help?
   a. Notepad b. Photo Editor
   c. REGEDT32 d. NetDom
19. In Internet Explorer 6, by supporting which standard can cookie transactions be filtered on the basis of the cookie's content and purposes?
   a. P3P b. PGP
   c. RDP d. ASP
20. Windows XP is one of the mainstream operating systems deployed. Your major duty is to assist in the configuration and maintenance of desktop applications. You are configuring the privacy level of your IE. Which of the following are valid descriptions of a Medium-High privacy level (choose all that apply)?
   a. blocks cookies from third-party sites that do not have a compact privacy statement
   b. blocks third-party cookies that use personally identifiable information without your explicit consent
   c. Blocks first-party cookies that use personally identifiable information without your implicit consent
   d. accepts cookies from third-party sites that use personally identifiable information without your explicit consent, but deletes those cookies when you close Internet Explorer
   e. accepts all first-person cookies
21. Windows XP is one of the mainstream operating systems deployed. Your major duty is to assist in the configuration and maintenance of desktop applications. You are configuring the privacy level of your IE. Which of the following is the default privacy level?
   a. High b. Medium-High
   c. Medium d. Low
   e. Accept All Cookies
22. Windows XP is one of the mainstream operating systems deployed. Your major duty is to assist in the configuration and maintenance of desktop applications. You are concerned about web browsing safety. By default, for Internet Explorer 6 on Windows XP, which of the following active content types constitute the greatest potential threat?
   a. ActiveX controls
   b. Java applets
   c. Scripts
   d. none of the above
23. Windows XP is one of the mainstream operating systems deployed. Your major duty is to assist in the configuration and maintenance of desktop applications. You are concerned about web browsing safety. By default, Internet Explorer 6 on Windows XP can download which of the following kinds of active content (choose all that apply)?
   a. ActiveX controls
   b. Java applets
   c. Scripts
   d. none of the above

24. Windows XP is one of the mainstream operating systems deployed. Your major duty is to assist in the configuration and maintenance of desktop applications. You have set up Content Advisor on a user desktop. Your user wants to bypass the content advisor warning when viewing a page. What should you do?
   a. Give him the supervisor password.
   b. This is not possible.
   c. Tell him to refresh the browser and delete the existing cookies and then retry.
   d. Tell him to download the page for offline viewing.
25. Windows XP is one of the mainstream operating systems deployed. Your major duty is to assist in the configuration and maintenance of desktop applications. You are deploying IE's Content Advisor. By default, IE comes with which content rating system?
   a. RSACi b. RBAC
   c. RICS d. REDT
26. A customer running Windows XP Home Edition reports that she cannot find several of the buttons that usually appear on the Standard Buttons toolbar in Microsoft Internet Explorer. You need to ensure that the customer can return the standard buttons to the Standard Buttons toolbar. What should you instruct the customer to do?
   a. Click the Restore Defaults button on the Advanced tab in Internet Options in the Control Panel.
   b. Click the Reset Web Settings button on the Programs tab in Internet Options in the Control Panel.
   c. On the View menu in Internet Explorer, point to Toolbars and clear Lock the Toolbars.
   d. On the View menu in Internet Explorer, point to Toolbars, select Customize, and click the Reset button.
27. Windows XP is one of the mainstream operating systems deployed. Your major duty is to assist in the configuration and maintenance of desktop applications. You are configuring IE on an XP desktop. By default, IE maintains connections which of the following programs related to the use of the Internet (choose all that apply)?
   a. an HTML editor
   b. an email client
   c. a newsgroup reader
   d. an Internet conferencing program
   e. a calendar program
28. A customer running Windows XP Home Edition and Microsoft Outlook Express installs a new evaluation copy of a third-party email client on his computer. The customer reports that Outlook Express is not the email client that starts when he accesses saved email messages. You need to ensure that Outlook Express is the email client that starts when the customer accesses saved email messages. What should you do?
   a. Define a new view in Outlook Express that shows all messages.
   b. Customize the existing view in Outlook Express to show all messages.
   c. Configure Outlook Express to be the default email client.
   d. Configure Outlook Express to send and receive messages at startup.
29. Windows XP is one of the mainstream operating systems deployed. Your major duty is to assist in the configuration and maintenance of desktop applications. You need to set up OE as your email client. In OE you need to set up several different email accounts that have similar settings. What should you do to avoid typing the settings for every account?
   a. Copy and paste the accounts.
   b. Export and import the accounts.
   c. Run an account creation script.
   d. Create the accounts from the command line.
30. Windows XP is one of the mainstream operating systems deployed. Your major duty is to assist in the configuration and maintenance of desktop applications. You need to set up OE as your email client. If you export an existing account, what file format will OE use for this export?
   a. IAF b. IRC
   c. DBX d. IDX
31. Windows XP is one of the mainstream operating systems deployed. Your major duty is to assist in the configuration and maintenance of desktop applications. You need to set up OE as your email client. What are used by OE to organize messages (choose all that apply)?
   a. folders b. boxes
   c. units d. domains
32. Windows XP is one of the mainstream operating systems deployed. Your major duty is to assist in the configuration and maintenance of desktop applications. Your user is using OE as the email client. By default, OE checks every ________________ minutes to see whether a user has mail.
   a. 1 b. 5
   c. 15 d. 30
   e. 60
33. Windows XP is one of the mainstream operating systems deployed. Your major duty is to assist in the configuration and maintenance of desktop applications. Your user is using OE as the email client. What shortcut keys can your user press so that she can send and receive at any time?
   a. Ctrl + M b. Ctrl + E
   c. Ctrl + R d. Ctrl + S
34. Windows XP is one of the mainstream operating systems deployed. Your major duty is to assist in the configuration and maintenance of desktop applications. Your users need to use OE to send plain text emails. What should you do to ensure

that only plain text emails are sent to the intended recipients?

a. You need to make changes to the recipients' records in the Address Book.
b. You need to make changes to the sending options of OE.
c. You need to make changes to the server options of OE.
d. You need to make changes to the signature options of OE.
e. You do not need to do anything.

35. Windows XP is one of the mainstream operating systems deployed. Your major duty is to assist in the configuration and maintenance of desktop applications. You use OE as your mail client. You want to change the default identity used by OE. What should you do?
 a. select Main Identity - Properties in the Manage Identities dialog box
 b. select Default Identity - Advanced Properties in the Manage Identities dialog box
 c. select Identity - Settings in the Manage Identities dialog box
 d. the default one cannot be changed
 e. none of the above.
36. Windows XP is one of the mainstream operating systems deployed. Your major duty is to assist in the configuration and maintenance of desktop applications. Multiple identities have been created on your OE. Now you want to consolidate all messages into one identity. What should you do?
 a. Import and export the messages between identities.
 b. Copy and paste the messages folder by folder.
 c. Save all messages into a text file and then copy all content to the current identity.
 d. There is nothing you can do.
 e. None of the above.
37. All client computers run Windows XP Professional and Microsoft Outlook Express. A user reports that he wants to copy contacts from his mobile phone to Outlook Express. The mobile phone does not have a synchronization application that is compatible with Outlook Express. However, the phone does support saving the contacts to a comma-delimited file. You need to help the user select a file type that allows him to import the contacts from his phone to Outlook Express. Which file type should you instruct the user to use?
 a. an LDIF file
 b. a text file
 c. an Excel spreadsheet file
 d. a Windows Address Book file
38. Windows XP is one of the mainstream operating system deployed. Your major duty is to assist in the configuration and maintenance of desktop applications. You are using OE as your mail client. You want to exchange electronic business cards with other users via email. What electronic business card standard does OE support?
 a. vCard b. X700
 c. X600 d. eCard
 e. sCard
39. Windows XP is one of the mainstream operating system deployed. Your major duty is to assist in the configuration and maintenance of desktop applications. You are using OE as your mail client. You want to exchange electronic business cards with other users via email. What file format must you use for such exchange?
 a. VCF b. VDR
 c. VAC d. VRB
40. What feature of Outlook Express allows multiple users to send and receive mail, each using a separate account?
 a. Identities
 b. Group Sharing
 c. Fast User Switching
 d. Virtual Account
41. All client computers run Windows XP Professional and Microsoft Office XP. The company uses a Microsoft Exchange Server 2003 computer for all messaging. The Exchange server is configured to accept POP3, IMAP4, and SMTP connections from remote users. The server is configured to allow SMTP relaying from authenticated users only. A user reports that she has just received a new portable computer. The user states that she can receive email by using POP3, but she cannot send email. You confirm that the user can make SMTP connections to the Exchange server. You also confirm that Outlook is configured to have the proper SMTP server address. You need to ensure that the user can use Outlook to send email from her new computer. What should you instruct the user to do?
 a. Configure Outlook to act as an IMAP-4 client.
 b. Configure Outlook to work only with message headers.
 c. Configure Outlook to use encrypted SMTP connections.
 d. Configure Outlook to use her POP3 credentials to authenticate to the SMTP server.
42. When a folder has been archived, what default file name extension is assigned to the archived file?
 a. PTS b. STP
 c. PST d. SPT
43. All client computers run Windows XP Professional and Microsoft Office XP. The company uses a Microsoft Exchange Server 2003 computer for all messaging. All users access email by using Microsoft Outlook 2002. A user reports that he will be on vacation and wants Outlook to automatically reply to incoming email messages. The user states that his computer will be turned off while he is on vacation, but he wants Outlook's reply to tell senders that he will be on vacation for 2 weeks. You need to ensure that the user successfully configures the automatic reply to senders. What should you instruct the user to do?

a. Enable the Out of Office Assistant.
b. Create a new rule that replies to all incoming email.
c. Use the Scheduled Task Wizard to create a task that opens Outlook every morning.
d. Delegate permissions on his Inbox to a coworker. Instruct the coworker to open the vacationing user's Inbox in Outlook.

44. You are the help desk support staff for a houseware manufacturer that uses Windows XP as the mainstream desktop operating system. While you are on vacation, a user who has a problem with her XP computer calls you and asks for help. What should you ask her to do so that you can help her out remotely?
a. Use the Remote Assistance function.
b. Use the Remote Administration function.
c. Use the Remote Access function.
d. Use the Safe mode feature.
e. Use PC Anywhere.

45. You are the help desk support staff for a houseware manufacturer that uses Windows XP as the mainstream desktop operating system. You send a remote assistance email to your friend asking for help. He says yes after an hour, and by that time he can no longer connect to your computer because your computer's IP address has been changed. What should you do so that the problem can be resolved ASAP?
a. Maintain the ISP connection, then resend the request and wait for his reply.
b. Terminate the ISP connection, then resend the request and wait for his reply 12 hours later.
c. Request a fix IP address from the ISP and retry.
d. Request a fix IP address from your friend and retry.
e. Enable ICS and retry.

46. All client computers run Windows XP Professional. The network consists of a Windows 2000 Active Directory domain. A department manager reports that some of the files on drive D on her computer were deleted and other data was modified. You need to track when unauthorized users attempt to modify or delete data from drive D on the manager's computer. What should you do first?
a. Run the SECEDIT command on the client computer.
b. Run the GPUPDATE command on the client computer.
c. Configure the security access control list for drive D on the client computer to audit the Everyone group.
d. Configure the access control list for drive D on the client computer to assign the Deny Permission.

47. All client computers run Windows XP Professional and have an antivirus application installed. A user reports that files in a shared folder on his computer are being deleted. You verify that the user's computer has the most recent virus signature file and that no viruses are detected. You need to identify who is deleting files from the user's computer. What should you do?
a. View the system log in Event Viewer.
b. Enable successful object access for the shared folder.
c. Run the File Signature Verification tool and view the contents of the SIGVERIF.TXT file.
d. Run the Microsoft Baseline Security Analyzer (MBSA) tool and scan for Windows vulnerabilities.

HANDS-ON EXERCISES

Exercise 1: Checking Windows XP Application Compatibility

1. Log in as your account.
2. Go to the http://www.adobe.com website and download Adobe Reader.
3. If you have a program that was made for an older version of Windows and will not run in Windows XP you can try to use the Application Wizard. Right-click the file you have just downloaded and select Properties. Then click on the Compatibility tab.
4. Select the Run this program in compatibility mode and select Windows 95. Click on the OK button. Whenever you run this program, it will run under a Windows 95 environment.

Exercise 2: Installing Microsoft Office

1. Log in as your account.
2. Insert the Office XP CD. The installation program should automatically start. If it does not, open My Computer and double-click the CD drive.
3. Input the product key.
4. Read the End-user License Agreement and select I accept the terms in the License Agreement. Click the Next button.

5. Click the Install button.
6. When the installation is complete, click the OK button.
7. Start Microsoft Word.
8. Type in your first and last name. On the next line, type in your address.
9. Open the Tools menu and select Options.
10. Click the View tab. To show the hardware returns, select the spaces and paragraph marks within the Formatting Marks section and click on the OK button.
11. Open the Tools menu and select Options. Turn on the spaces and paragraph marks.
12. Click on the General tab. Notice the number of recently used files and measurement units.
13. Select the Save tab. Make sure that the Save AutoRecover Info option is selected and notice the time of Autosave. In addition, notice the default format that documents are saved as (Save Word Files as option).
14. Click on the Spelling and Grammar tab. Make sure that the Check Spelling as you type and Check Grammar as you type options are selected.
15. Select the File Location tab. Notice the default directory for Word documents.
16. Click on the OK button.
17. Go to any toolbar and click using the right (secondary) mouse button. Notice which toolbars are open. Select thc WordArt toolbar.
18. Grab the title bar of the WordArt toolbar and drag it to the right of the screen until it becomes embedded.
19. Grab the top of the WordArt toolbar and drag it back to the center of Microsoft Word window.
20. Close the WordArt toolbar.
21. Click on the Customize option located within the Tools menu.
22. Click on the Commands tab.
23. On the Standard toolbar, drag the New button off the toolbar.
24. Within the File category, find the New command drag it to the beginning of the Standard toolbar. Click on the Close button.
25. Select the AutoCorrect option within the Tools menu. Click on the Options button.
26. If you don't want automatic bullets and number, deselect the Automatic Bulleted Lists and Automatic Number Lists options located in the Apply As You Type section.
27. Click on the OK button.
28. Close the current document and don't save the changes.
29. Open a new document and notice the default font and font size.
30. Close Microsoft Word.
31. Click the Start button and select Search.
32. Select All files and folders option.
33. Select More advanced options.
34. Enable search hidden file and folders.
35. Search for the NORMAL.DOT file.
36. Record the location of the NORMAL.DOT file.
37. Start Microsoft Word.
38. Open the File menu and select Open.
39. For file type (Files of type), select Document Templates (*.DOT).
40. Change the font to Arial. Save the changes and Microsoft Word.
41. Start Microsoft Word again and notice the default font.
42. Click Start, click the Control Panel, and then click Add or Remove Programs.
43. From Add or Remove Programs, select Microsoft Office, and then click Change.
44. From Maintenance Mode Options, click Reinstall or Repair Office, and then click Next.
45. From Reinstall or Repair Office, click Reinstall Office, and then click Install.
46. In Reinstalling Office progress dialog box, click Cancel.
47. From the Microsoft Office Setup box, click Yes, and then click OK.
48. Close all windows.
49. From Microsoft Word, click Tools, click the double down arrows to expand the list, click Macro, and then click Security. Notice what the default macro security is set to.
50. Close the Security dialog box.
51. Visit the Microsoft Office Update website and update Microsoft Office.

Exercise 3: Working with Internet Explorer

1. Start Internet Explorer and open the http://www.microsoft.com website.
2. In Internet Explorer, on the Tools menu, click Internet Options.
3. In the Internet Options dialog box, on the General tab, click Use Current, and then click OK.
4. Close and restart Internet Explorer to verify that the new home page appears.

5. In Internet Explorer, click Tools and then click Internet Options.
6. In the Internet Options dialog box, on the General tab and click the Settings button.
7. In the Settings dialog box, click the View Files button.
8. From the Temporary Internet Files window, click the column heading Type to arrange the files in order of file type, and scroll through the list to see the various kinds of files.
9. Close the Temporary Internet Files window.
10. Click OK to close the Settings dialog box.
11. From the Internet Options dialog box, click Delete Files.
12. In the Delete Files warning box, select Delete all offline content, and then click OK.
13. From the Internet Options dialog box, click Settings.
14. From the Settings dialog box, click View Files.
15. Scroll through the Temporary Internet Files window, and notice that all the files, except cookies, were deleted.
16. Close the Temporary Internet Files window.
17. Click OK to close the Settings dialog box.
18. Click OK to close the Internet Options dialog box.
19. Click the History button on the Internet Explorer toolbar to view a list of the visited pages.
20. In the History pane, click Today to expand today's viewed websites.
21. From Internet Explorer, click Tools and then click Internet Options.
22. In the Internet Options dialog box, on the General tab click the Clear History button.
23. In the Internet Options information box, click Yes.
24. Click OK in the Internet Options dialog box. Notice that the History pane is now blank indicating that the contents of the HISTORY folder have been deleted.
25. In Internet Explorer, click Tools, and then click Internet Options.
26. From the Internet Options dialog box, on the General tab click Settings.
27. From the Settings dialog box, click the View Files button.
28. Locate a file in the list that begins with *Cookie,* and then double-click it.
29. In the Internet Explorer popup box, click Yes.
30. From Notepad, view the contents of the file. After viewing it, close Notepad.
31. Close the Temporary Internet Files window.
32. Click OK to close the Settings dialog box.
33. In the Internet Options dialog box, click the Security tab, click the Internet icon, and then click Custom Level.
34. In the Security Settings dialog box, under Download signed ActiveX controls select Disable, and then click OK.
35. From the Warning dialog box, click Yes.
36. Click OK to close the Internet Options dialog box.
37. To view the impact of changing this security setting type this in the Address bar of Internet Explorer and press Enter:

    http://moneycentral.msn.com/investor/charts/charting.asp?Symbol=msft

38. From MSN Money, click Upgrade now!
39. From Charts, click download MSN Money.
40. Click OK in the Microsoft Internet Explorer warning box.
41. Close all windows.
42. Start Internet Explorer again.
43. Open the Tools menu, and then click Internet Options.
44. In the Internet Options dialog box, click the Security tab, click the Internet icon, and then select Custom Level.
45. From the Security Settings dialog box, under Download signed ActiveX controls select Prompt, and then click OK.
46. Click Yes in the Warning dialog box.
47. Click OK to close the Internet Options dialog box.
48. To view the impact of changing the security setting type this in the Address bar of Internet Explorer and press Enter.

    moneycentral.msn.com/investor/charts/charting.asp?Symbol=msft

49. From MSN Money, click Upgrade now!
50. From Charts, click download MSN Money.
51. Now you will be able download the ActiveX control.
52. Click Yes in the Security Warning dialog box.
53. Once you see the chart, close Internet Explorer.
54. In Internet Explorer, on the Tools menu, click Internet Options.
55. To reset the web settings to their default state, on the Programs tab, click the Reset Web Settings.
56. When the reset web setting box appears, click the Yes button.
57. In the Internet options dialog box, select the Advanced tab.

58. Click the question mark (?) button at the top right of the dialog box and click Disable Script Debugging (Internet Explorer).
59. Select to enable the Disable Script Debugging (Internet Explorer).
60. Select to disable Enable Personalized Favorites Menu.
61. Scroll down to the security options and look at the various options.
62. Close Internet Explorer.

Exercise 4: Working with Outlook Express

1. Open Internet Explorer and open the http://www.msn.com website.
2. Click on the Hotmail link.
3. To create a new hotmail account, click New Account Sign Up.
4. Fill out the Profile Information and Account Information.
    a. Write down the email address?
    b. Write down your password?
5. Click the I Agree button.
6. You don't have to pay for a hotmail account. Therefore, click on the Free E-mail hyperlink.
7. On the newsletter page, scroll down to the bottom and click the Continue button. If an additional page appears listing newsletters, click the Continue button again.
8. Close Internet Explorer.
9. Click Start, point to All Programs, and then Click Outlook Express.
10. If the Internet Connection Wizard opens, click Cancel, and then click Yes to close the Internet Connection Wizard.
11. In Outlook Express, click Tools, and then click Accounts.
12. In the Internet Accounts dialog box, click Add, and then click Mail.
13. In the Your Name page, in the Display name box, enter your first and last name, and then click Next.
14. In the Internet E-mail Address page, in the E-mail address box, type the email address for the hotmail account that you created. Click Next.
15. In the E-mail Server Names page, select the HTTP type server and then select Hotmail for your HTTP service provider. Click the Next button.
16. Enter your password and click the Next button.
17. In the Congratulations page, click Finish.
18. Click Close to close the Internet Accounts dialog box.
19. When it ask you to download a folder from the mail server, click the Yes button.
20. In the left pane, under the Hotmail section, click the Inbox folder. All messages should show up in the right pane.
21. Click the Hotmail Staff message and see it appear in the preview window.
22. Double-click the Hotmail Staff message to open it.
23. Click the Delete button to delete the message from your box.
24. On the Outlook Express toolbar, click Create Mail.
25. From New Message in the To field, type in your email address.
26. In the Subject field, type *Test E-mail* and in the body of the email, type *Test Message*.
27. Click the Send button.
28. Click the Send and Receive (Send/Recv) button on the toolbar.
29. In the Folders list, click Inbox.
30. Double-click the e-mail message with *Test E-mail* in the Subject line to open the message.
31. In the Test E-mail window, click File, and then Close.
32. Click Tools and then click Options.
33. From the Options dialog box, click the Maintenance tab, and then click Store Folder.
34. In the Store Location dialog box, highlight the entire path given, and then right-click on the path and select Copy.
35. Click OK to close the Store Location dialog box.
36. Click OK to close the Options dialog box.
37. In Outlook Express, click File and then Exit.
38. Click Start, and then Run.
39. In the Run dialog box, right-click on the Open field and select Paste.
40. Click OK.
41. After reviewing the files, close the Outlook Express window.
42. Right-click on an empty space of the Desktop, point to New, click Folder, and type *Exported Mail.*
43. Click Start, point to All Programs, and then click Outlook Express.
44. If necessary, resize the Outlook Express window so that the portion of the desktop that shows the EXPORTED MAIL folder is still visible.
45. In Outlook Express, in the Folders list, click the Inbox folder.

46. Click the message with the subject *Test E-mail*.
47. Drag the selected messages from the Outlook Express window to the EXPORTED MAIL folder on your desktop.
48. From Windows desktop, double-click EXPORTED MAIL.
49. Select the *Test Email* message that you want to import.
50. Drag the messages from the Exported Mail window into the Inbox folder in the Local Folders section.
51. Click the Inbox under Local Folders.
52. Close Outlook Express.

Exercise 5: Working with Outlook

1. Start Microsoft Outlook.
2. On the Outlook Startup page, click Next.
3. On the E-mail Upgrade Options page, click Do not upgrade, and then click Next.
4. On the E-mail Accounts page, verify that Yes is selected, and then click Next.
5. On the Server Type page, select HTTP, and then click Next.
6. On the Internet E-mail Settings (HTTP) page, enter the following information:
   - Your Name: first and last name
   - E-mail Address: your Hotmail email account.
   - Password: your password
   - Service provider: Hotmail

   Notice the server URL.
7. On the E-mail Accounts page, click Finish.
8. Notice the messages automatically download into the hotmail inbox.
9. Close Outlook.
10. Click Start, and then click Run.
11. From the RUN command, type *C:\PROGRAM FILES\COMMON FILES\SYSTEM\MAPI\1033\SCANPST.EXE* and then click OK. Note that some versions of Outlook may use the C:\PROGRAM FILES\COMMON FILES\SYSTEM\MSMAPI\1033\SCANPST.EXE.
12. In the Inbox Repair Tool dialog box, click Browse.
13. In the Select File to Scan dialog box, browse to C:\DOCUMENTS AND SETTINGS*COMPUTER_LOGIN_ACCOUNT_NAME*\LOCAL SETTINGS\APPLICATION DATA\MICROSOFT\OUTLOOK\OUTLOOK.PST, and then click Open.
14. In the Inbox Repair Tool dialog box, click Start.
15. When the scanning is completed, and if errors were found, you will be prompted to start the repair process. Click Repair, and then click OK.
16. Click OK.
17. Start Outlook.
18. Open the File menu and click Import and Export. Select Export to a File and click the Next button.
19. Select the Personal Folder File (.pst) and click the Next button.
20. Select the hotmail inbox and click the Next button.
21. Keep the default export file of BACKUP.PST, then click the Finish button.
22. When it asks to create a Microsoft personal file, click the OK button.
23. Using Outlook, delete the messages from your inbox so that you have an empty hotmail inbox.
24. Open the File menu and select Import and Export. Select Import from another program or file and click the Next button.
25. Choose Personal Folder File (.pst) and click the Next button.
26. If necessary, browse to the C:\DOCUMENTS AND SETTINGS*ACCOUNT_LOGIN_NAME*\LOCAL SETTINGS\APPLICATION DATA\MICROSOFT\OUTLOOK\BACKUP.PST file and click the Next button.
27. Click the Finish button. When the exporting is done, all of your files should be back.
28. Close Outlook.

Exercise 6: Working with DirectX

1. Click the Start button, select the Run option, and execute the DXDIAG command.
2. Looking at the System Information, determine the version of DirectX that your system is using.
3. Click the Display tab and then click the Test DirectDraw button. Run through the tests and answer yes or no to the prompts that appear.
4. Select the Sound tab and click the Test DirectSound button. Run through the tests and answer yes or no to the prompts that appear.
5. Exit DirectX Diagnostic tool.

CHAPTER 23

Introduction to Linux

Topics Covered in This Chapter

Introduction

Linux is become a popular alternative operating system to Microsoft Windows. Therefore, this chapter will discuss installing Linux, executing commands at the Linux command prompt, and using and configuring X Window, the Linux GUI interface.

Objectives

1. Explain how Linux relates to UNIX.
2. Explain how the Linux kernel relates to a Linux distribution.
3. Define the purpose of the kernel.
4. Describe and use the available Linux documentation.
5. Identify where to obtain Linux.
6. Identify all system hardware required and validate that it is supported by Linux (e.g., CPUs, RAM, graphics cards, storage devices, network interface cards, modem).
7. Install Linux.
8. Determine how storage space will be allocated to file systems (e.g., partition scheme).
9. Partition according to your preinstallation plan using fdisk (e.g., /boot, /usr, /var,/home, and /swap).
10. Manage and navigate the Linux hierarchy (e.g., /etc, /usr, /bin, and /var).
11. Manage and navigate the standard Linux file system (e.g., mv, mkdir, ls, and rm).
12. Use common shell commands and expressions.
13. Create, edit, and save files using vi.
14. Reconfigure the X Window System with automated utilities (e.g., Xconfigurator, XF86Setup).
15. Install and configure monitors and video cards.
16. Manage and navigate the graphical user interface (e.g., menus, xterm).
17. Start and use X Window applications including text editors, terminals, and common applications.
18. Configure the KDE and GNOME environments.
19. Identify, execute, and kill processes (ps, kill, and killall).
20. Examine, start, and stop processes based on the signs and symptoms of a problem.
21. Send print jobs at the command prompt and within X Window.
22. Add and configure printers.
23. Manage print spools and queues.

23.1 WHAT IS LINUX?

In 1991, Linus Torvalds, a 21-year-old college student at the University of Helsinki in Finland, decided that he wasn't pleased with the Microsoft DOS that came with his computer. Therefore, he decided to write his own program modeled around Minux. A few months later, with a short announcement on comp.os.minux, the Linux kernel was born. The **kernel** is the central core of the operating system that interacts directly with the hardware. To complete the operating system, Torvalds and other team members used system components developed by members of the Free Software Foundation for the GNU project.

Linux (pronounced LIH-nuhks with a short "i") is a UNIX-like operating system that was designed to provide personal computer users a free or very low-cost operating system comparable to traditional and usually more expensive UNIX systems. Linux comes in versions for all the major microprocessor platforms including the Intel, PowerPC, Sparc, and Alpha platforms. Because it conforms to the POSIX (which stands for portable operating system interface for UNIX) standard user and programming interfaces, developers can write programs that can be ported to other platforms running Linux (or UNIX that also conforms to the POSIX standard).

23.1.1 GNU Licenses

Linux can be downloaded for free or purchased from many Linux distributors. So the question is, why would you purchase Linux from a company? The answer basically comes down to "you get what you pay for." Although Linux is an excellent operating system, when you download it from a website, you typically get a software package that is not supported. Therefore, if you have a problem, you must search the Internet for the solution. If the solution is not readily available, you have no one to contact to help you overcome your problem. In addition, you may not be eligible for upgrades and updates. Therefore, when you purchase a license for Linux, you are also purchasing the support from that company. Of course, you will most likely find that that cost of these licenses is cheaper than for other popular operating systems.

Another factor to help decide if you will download Linux or purchase a Linux package is that if you try to download a Linux from the Internet via a slow connection (for example, a 56 Kbit modem), it will take an extremely long time to download. Therefore, it may not always be feasible to download Linux.

Linux is distributed under the GNU license agreement. **GNU,** which is self-referential, is short for *GNUs not UNIX.* It was started in 1983 by Richard Stallman at the Massachusetts Institute of Technology. GNU refers to a UNIX-compatible software system developed by the Free Software Foundation. As GNU was started, hundreds of programmers created new, open source versions of all major UNIX utility programs with Linux providing the kernel. Many of the GNU utilities were so powerful that they have become the virtual standard on all UNIX systems. For example, gcc became the dominant C compiler, and GNU emacs became the dominant programmer's text editor.

The philosophy behind GNU is to produce software that is nonproprietary: Anyone can download, modify, and redistribute GNU software. The only restriction is that further redistribution cannot be limited. In other words, you can download it off the Internet at no charge, pass on copies to friends, and even modify its internals, as long as you make the source code available. In addition, the **General Public License (GPL)** form of using copyright to protect the software from being taken over and kept from free public use is referred to as "**copyleft.**"

The GPL software tends to create a community of programmers who all contribute to the development of a better program. Because the GPL software evolves around an entity that is not really controlled by any one person, organization, or company, it focuses on a collaborative effort. GPL software is unique because the needs of the users are what drives the development of the product. In addition, since you have access to the source code you can tailor the software to meet your needs, as well as fix any bugs yourself (assuming you know how to program). Companies tend to either bring in consultants to tailor their software or they might rely on the Internet community or internal employees.

GNU is considered software *free* software in the sense that users have the freedom to run, copy, distribute, study, change, and improve the software. It is not necessarily free of cost. Linux is distributed commercially by a number of companies. Most distributions are available to download for free, without support, purchased as an inexpensive CD or available as a boxed set with manuals and different level of support. Table 23.1 shows some of the websites where you can find Linux to download or purchase.

Table 23.1 Linux Download Sites

Website	Description
Debian http://www.debian.org/distrib/ftplist	Debian is an organization that seeks to both develop and keep it commercial free. Therefore, it does not sell Linux, although it has no problem with others selling its Linux. Debian GNU/Linux Debian 2.1, also known as "slink," is available on Intel, SPARC, Alpha, and Motorola 680×0 platforms. It's based on the Debian package format (.deb), which uses the dpkg package manager, dselect, and apt for package management interfaces.
Mandrake http://www.linux-mandrake.com **Mandrake Download Site** http://www.linux-mandrake.com/en/ftp.php3	The Mandrake Linux is built on top of Red Hat Linux. It stresses ease of use for both personal users and server installation, offering customer support with each purchase. It includes a host of add-on packages, including StarOffice 5.1, WordPerfect 8.0 word processor, IBM Lotus eSuite DevPack, Applixware 4.4.2 for Linux (limited version or demo), Applix Shelf scripting language, Adobe Acrobat Reader 4.0 PDF viewer, Arkeia back up, VMware (limited version), Blender Animation Studio, and more.
Red Hat http://www.redhat.com **Red Hat Download Site** http://www.redhat.com/apps/download/ **Red Hat Mirror Sites** http://www.redhat.com/download/mirror.html	Arguably the most popular Linux distribution, Red Hat Linux comes in three different editions (depending on whether it's used as a server or as a personal workstation) and stresses ease of installation. It includes a slew of personal productivity tools, as well as server essentials like Apache, samba, and sendmail. It ships with both KDE and GNOME interfaces, whereas advanced features like LDAP integration make Red Hat Linux an attractive tool for the enterprise.
Slackware Linux http://www.slackware.com/ **Slackware Download site** ftp://ftp.slackware.com/pub/slackware/slackware	Slackware Linux was the first commercial Linux distribution, designed specifically for the Intel platform. Slackware Linux includes kernel, XFree86, KDE, and October Gnome.
SuSE http://www.suse.com/ **SuSE Download Site** http://www.suse.com/us/support/download/index.html	SuSE works closely with the XFree86 Project, and its distribution has the most recent modifications to, and device drivers for, the X11R6 X Window System. Also, the SuSE CD-ROM distribution has the most bundled applications. It includes the YaST2 installation and configuration tool, KDE 1.1.2, October Gnome, VMWare (limited version), Hummingbird PC X-server for Windows, SuSE Proxy Suite, StarOffice, and more. SuSE Linux is particularly popular in Europe, although the U.S. release is growing in popularity. SuSE is now owned by Novell.
Turbolinux http://www.turbolinux.com/ **Turbolinux Download** http://www.turbolinux.com/downloads/	There are several products distributed under the Turbolinux name. Turbolinux Workstation is a product designed for single users that includes Netscape Navigator and WordPerfect. Turbolinux Server includes a mail server, DNS server, web server, news server, caching server, file/print server, FTP server, and more. TurboCluster Server is the world's first software Linux clustering solution. Turbolinux is based upon Red Hat. Turbolinux tends to be used more outside the United States than inside.

NOTE: For Linux retailers throughout the world, go to http://www.linux.org/dist/english.html, http://www.linux.org/dist/nonenglish.html, and http://www.linux.org/vendors/retailers.html. In addition, you can find sites to download the source code from http://www.linux.org/dist/kernel.html.

GENERAL LINUX RELATED SITES

Linux Online

http://www.linux.org/

Linux Kernel Archives

http://www.kernel.org

GNU Public License for Linux

http://www.linux.org/info/gnu.html

Linux WWW Resources

http://oak.ece.ul.ie/~griffini/linux.html

23.1.2 Linux Kernel

The Linux kernel acts as a mediator for your programs and your hardware. Like the UNIX kernel, the Linux kernel is designed to do one thing well: It handles low-level tasks like managing memory, files, programs that are running, networking, and various hardware devices. For example, it arranges for the memory management for all of the running programs (processes), and makes sure that they all get a fair share of the processor clock cycles. In addition, the Linux Kernel provides a nice, fairly portable interface for programs to talk to the hardware. Therefore, you can often think of the kernel as a cop directing traffic. Unlike Microsoft Windows, it does not include a windowing system or GUI. Instead, Linux users can choose among a number of X servers and window managers.

In 1996, the Linux 2.0 kernel was released. Version 2 saw the preliminary support for symmetric multiprocessor (SMP) machines. It also was fully functional on multiple platforms, including the x86, Alpha, SPARC, Motorola 68K, PowerPC, and MIPS platforms. In 1999, version 2.2 was released. The 2.2 kernel fully supports the SMP machines, and it more fully supports multiple platforms, including the 64-bit platforms. In addition, version 2.2 is significantly faster than previous versions.

In 2001, the Linux 2.4 kernel was released. To make it more suitable for enterprise-level applications, the new kernel allows for better symmetric multiprocessing scalability up to 32 processors on large x86 Intel servers. In addition, it supports up to 64 GB of physical memory. Other enhancements include new drivers for hardware including USB, IEEE 1394 (FireWire), and 3D-accelerated graphics cards, along with support for IBM's S/390 mainframe and Intel's IA-64 architecture.

As newer versions of the kernel are released, bugs are found and fixed, more device drivers are added so that they can talk to more types of hardware, and better process management is achieved so that they can run faster than the older versions. The kernel numbering system is relatively simple to follow. The versions are expressed in the following format:

major.minor.patch

such as version 2.4.2 or 2.4.7. Because Linux follows the "open development model," all new versions will be released to the public, whether or not they are considered production quality. To help people tell whether they are getting a stable version, the following scheme has been implemented:

- Versions n.x.y, where x (the minor version) is an even number, are stable versions, and only bug fixes will be applied as y is incremented. So from version 1.2.2 to 1.2.3, there were only bug fixes, and no new features.
- Versions n.x.y, where x is an odd number, are beta-quality releases for developers only, may be unstable and may crash, and are having new features added to them all the time.

From time to time, as the correct development kernel stabilizes, it will be frozen as the new "stable" kernel, and development will continue on a new development version of the kernel.

After the minor version number comes the build number, which is the number of patches added onto the major.minor kernel version thus far. Sometimes if there are minor changes or distribution-specific alterations to the kernel, there will be a dash on the end with another number listing how many changes were made there.

23.1.3 General Features

As described earlier in the textbook, a program, sometimes referred to as a **process,** is a sequence of instructions that can be executed by a computer. A program consists of initializing code and data, a private memory address space, system resources, and one or more threads.

A **thread** is part of a program that can execute independently of other parts. As an operating system, such as Linux, supports multithreading, it enables programmers to design programs whose threaded parts can execute concurrently. This can enhance a program by allowing multitasking, improving throughput, enhancing responsiveness, and aiding background processing. For example, a word processor uses a thread to respond to keys typed on the keyboard by the user to place characters in a document. Other threads are used to check spelling and to paginate the document as the user types. If the user prints, another thread spools or feeds a document to the printer in the background. Of course, when a program uses multithreading, the programmer must carefully design the program in such a way that all the threads can run at the same time without interfering with each other. In addition, since Linux also supports symmetrical multiprocessing (SMP), Linux, with a multiprocessing kernel, can perform better on a system with multiprocessors with programs that are multithreaded.

Linux for Intel machines were made to run on any Intel processor since the 386 processor. In addition, because it runs in the protected mode of the 386 processor, Linux provides memory protection between processes, so that one program cannot bring down the whole system.

In addition, as modern operating system supports virtual memory, so does Linux. Virtual memory uses paging (virtual memory) where the whole processes are swapped from memory to disk. This increases the amount of available memory so that you can run more programs at the same time and work with more data.

Linux supports various file systems for storing data including the ext2 file system (developed specifically for Linux), the Xenix and UNIX System V file systems, Microsoft's VFAT file systems (used in Windows 95/98), and ISO 9660 CD-ROM file system. File systems were discussed earlier in this textbook. In addition, the Linux computer acts as a server, thus various computer systems can store files on the server include DOS, Microsoft Windows, Apple Macintosh, UNIX, and Linux.

23.1.4 Linux Interfaces

Virtually every utility that you would expect to find on standard implementations of UNIX has been ported to Linux. This includes basic commands such as *ls, awk, tr, sed, bc, more,* and so on. Therefore, you can expect your familiar working environment on other UNIX systems to be duplicated on Linux.

The most important utility to many Linux users is the shell. The **shell** is a program that reads and executes commands from the user. In addition, many shells provide features such as job control (allowing the user to manage several running processes at once), input and output redirection, and a command language for writing shell scripts. A shell script is a file containing a program in the shell command language, analogous to a "batch file" under MS-DOS. By default, most Linux distributions use the GNU Bourne Again Shell (bash).

Because most computer users are accustomed to a graphical interface such as that provided by Microsoft Windows or Apple Macintosh OS, Linux uses X Window to provide a graphical interface to the Linux operating system. The version of X Window available for Linux is known as XFree86.

As for an intuitive graphical interface, Linux has at least a dozen different, highly configurable graphical interfaces (known as window managers), which run on top of XFree86. The most popular window managers at the moment are KDE (K Desktop Environment) and GNOME (GNU Network Object Model Environment).

GNOME is a powerful graphics-driven environment that includes a panel (for starting applications and displaying status), a desktop (where data and applications can be placed), multiple window managers (which control the look and feel of your desktop), and a standard set of desktop tools and applications. GNOME's session manager remembers settings and currently running programs, so once you've set things the way you like, they'll stay that way.

KDE provides a complete desktop environment, including a file manager, a window manager, an integrated help system, a configuration system, numerous tools and utilities, and an ever-increasing number of applications. It uses a contemporary desktop, a searchable help system with convenient access to help on the use of the KDE desktop and its applications, standardized menus and toolbars, keybindings, color schemes, and more.

23.1.5 Linux Documentation Project

Although many Linux distributors provide extensive documentation for their distribution of Linux, the Linux operating system is not owned by any one person or company. To provide free, high-quality documentation for the GNU/Linux operating system, the **Linux Documentation Project (LDP)** was created. The LDP is a loose team of writers, proofreaders, and editors who are working on a set of definitive Linux manuals.

Linux Documentation Project

http://www.linuxdoc.org/

http://www.ibiblio.org/mdw/index.html

http://www.linux.org/docs/index.html

23.2 INSTALLING LINUX

Linux works with many types of hardware, however, it does not work with every piece of hardware. Therefore, hardware compatibility is particularly important if you have an older system or a system that you may have to build yourself. To determine if your computer is compatible for Linux, you can use the hardware compatibility list provided by the Linux distributor.

Linux Hardware Compatibility HOWTO

http://users.bart.nl/~patrickr/hardware-howto/Hardware-HOWTO.html

http://www.linuxdoc.org/HOWTO/Hardware-HOWTO.html

Red Hat Linux Hardware Compatibility List

http://hardware.redhat.com/hcl/

SuSE Supported Hardware

http://hardwaredb.suse.de/index.php?LANG5en_UK

Mandrake Linux Hardware Database

http://www.linux-mandrake.com/en/hardware.php3

Because Linux requires task-switching and memory management facilities found on 80386 and later processors, it requires a 386 or greater. However, most Linux distributions require a Pentium processor (or equivalent) or better. Linux supports ISA, EISA, VESA local bus, and PCI. Even though Linux command interface will run on 2 MB with special installation procedure until the disk swap space is installed, you should run with at least 4 MB of memory. If you are planning on using X Window, 32 MB should be minimum, but it is recommended to have at least 64 MB. X11 components use approximately 30 MB. Again, most Linux distributions require more RAM. As a general rule, if you have more memory, Linux will run faster. Linux will run any standard graphics card. However, X Window does not run on all video card chipsets. Therefore, you should either run SuperProbe (a program included in the XFree86 distribution) or by looking on the hardware compatibility list (HCL).

To install a minimal copy of Linux, you will need at least 10 MB. Of course, you can try Linux and not much else. You can also fit an installation that includes X Window in 80 MB. Most Linux distributions will take between 500 MB and 1.7 GB, depending on which options you choose, including the kernel source code, some space for user files, and a spool area. To install a commercial distribution that has a desktop GUI environment, a commercial word processor, and a front-office productivity suite will take 2 GB of disk space or more.

As Linux has become more popular, many people have also tried to run on notebook computers. Although the notebooks are more than capable to run Linux, they are sometimes hindered by a lack of drivers. Refer to the websites shown on the next page for information on laptop hardware.

Linux Laptop—HOWTO

http://www.linuxdoc.org/HOWTO/Laptop-HOWTO.html

Linux on a Laptop

http://www.linux.org/hardware/laptop.html

Linux on Laptops

http://www.linux-laptop.net

As stated earlier Linux comes in a *distribution,* which means that an organization has packaged the software and bundled an install program with it. Install programs are miniature versions of Linux itself, which runs shell scripts to perform install operations. Linux can be installed using CD-ROM, MS-DOS partition, floppy disk, FTP, NFS and SAMBA.

All distribution installation programs must go through the following steps. The essential difference is whether the installation program displays these steps explicitly and which information user must input, or whether it performs the steps silently.

1. Select language, keyboard format, mouse type, and so on.
2. Plan hard disk allocation including:
   a. Choosing either a single OS Linux installation or a dual boot installation.
   b. If the dual boot option is selected, deciding whether to share the same hard disk or whether separate hard disks will be used.
   c. Deciding the number and size of Linux partitions. A minimum of two is usually required, one for swap space and one for a root file system. Generally, the swap partition should be twice the size of physical memory up to a maximum of 100 MB.
3. Boot from the installation media, including booting the install kernel and install program from the CD-ROM or from boot floppies. If the BIOS cannot boot directly from the CD-ROM, then boot floppies must be constructed by employing the DOS-based program rawrite or by using the Linux dd command.
4. Create Linux partitions using fdisk, Disk Druid, cfdisk, or some other program to write native file systems and swap partitions.
5. Select which packages to load.
6. Format file system and swap partitions using the mk32fs and mkswap commands.
7. Dearchive (uncompress) and copy files and create the default configuration files from the CD-ROM, network, or floppies onto the newly partitioned hard disk and reboot.
8. Configure a boot-up sequence mechanism.
   a. Have the LILO (Linux Loader) write itself to the primary master hard disk drive MBR. Use the LILO to boot Linux or the other OS (if any). The LILO can boot either OS as the default.
   b. Use a DOS program such as System Command or Partition Magic to boot Linux or Windows.
   c. Leave the old boot program intact so that it boots the other OS, and use a floppy disk to boot Linux.
9. If the network was not used as the installation media, then configure the network driver, network address, and routing table.
10. Set up the X Window System including selecting the correct X server for the video adapter and configuring the mouse type, monitor resolution, applicable video RAM, and pixel depth.

At the end of an installation, install program usually asks if you would like to create a boot floppy disk. Be sure to follow this procedure and keep the floppy in a well-known place for later reference.

Linux Installation and Getting Started

http://www.linuxdoc.org/LDP/gs/gs.html

The Linux Installation HOWTO

http://www.linux.org/docs/ldp/howto/Installation-HOWTO.html

Debian New Installations

http://www.debian.org/releases/stable/#new-inst

Red Hat Manuals

http://www.redhat.com/docs/manuals/linux/RHL-7.2-Manual/

http://www.redhat.com/support/resources/howto/rhl72.html

SuSE Linux 7.2 (Reference Guide)

ftp://ftp.suse.com/pub/suse/i386/7.2/docu/

Caldera OpenLinux Documentation

http://www.caldera.com/support/docs/openlinux/

Mandrake Linux Documentations

http://www.linux-mandrake.com/en/fdoc.php3

This boot floppy will be very important in effecting recovery in situations where the system fails to boot or fails to allow anyone access. If such a situation occurs, the user files become unreachable, and without the boot diskette a new version of Linux would have to be installed, erasing the root partition in the process.

Occasionally, you will need a driver disk so that Linux can support hardware that is not included within the Linux installation program. The driver disk could be produced by a distributor of Linux such as Red Hat, it could be a disk you make yourself, or it could be a disk that a hardware vendor includes with a piece of hardware.

There is really no need to use a driver disk unless you need a particular device in order to install Linux. You will most likely use a driver disk for SCSI adapters and NICs, as those are really the only devices that are used during the installation that might require driver disk support. If an unsupported device is not needed to install Linux on your system, continue with a regular installation and then add support for the new piece of hardware once the installation is complete. While the Linux installation program is loading, you may see a screen that asks you for a driver disk. The driver disk screen is most often seen in three scenarios:

- if you are running the installation program in expert mode
- if you run the installation program by entering *linux dd* at the boot prompt
- if you run the installation program on a computer that does not have any PCI devices

One place to find driver disk information is on Red Hat's website at http://www.redhat.com/support/errata/ under the section called Bug Fixes. If you find a driver disk that is appropriate for your device support needs, create a boot disk using that filename.img file.

23.3 PARTITIONS AND PARTITIONING

During the installation process of Linux, when the installation program reaches the partitioning phase, it will give you options to automatically partition your hard drive, to use Disk Druid, fdisk, cfdisk, or some other partitioning program.

Like other operating systems, Linux requires you to partition and prepare a hard disk before you can install Linux. The Disk Druid is a Red Hat utility program that uses text dialogs to enable you to partition the disk and, at the same time, specify which parts of the Linux file system are to be loaded on which partition.

The fdisk program is a Linux disk partitioning program, similar to the FDISK that comes with DOS, but with many more capabilities. When you use the Linux fdisk program, you have to type cryptic one-letter commands to manipulate disk partitions. Once you learn the commands, however, you may find fdisk more powerful than Disk Druid (Red Hat Linux graphical partitioning utility). For example, Disk Druid does not let you change the partition type, which indicates the type of file system to be stored on the partition; but you can easily change the partition type with fdisk.

> **FOR MORE INFORMATION ON PARTITIONS, REFER TO:**
>
> **Linux Partition mini-HOWTO**
>
> http://www.linux.org/docs/ldp/howto/mini/Partition.html

23.3.1 Partitioning Large Hard Drives

In the past, using large hard drives caused problems with Linux. Today there are no problems with the large hard disk, yet a number of problems are caused by users who *think* there might be a problem and install a disk manager, go into fdisk expert mode, or specify explicit disk parameters to LILO or on the kernel command line. Typical problem areas are caused by old hardware or several operating systems on the same disk, and sometimes booting.

Linux does not use the BIOS, but some other systems do. The BIOS, which predates LBA, uses INT13 disk I/O routines that have CHS input. Because 10 bits store the cylinder number, the cylinder number can range from 0 to 1,023, which means that no more than 1,024 cylinders are BIOS addressable.

When the system is booted, the BIOS reads the master boot record (MBR) from the first disk and jumps to the bootstrap loader. Since these small bootstrap programs use BIOS services instead of disk drivers the Linux kernel can be booted only when it is entirely located within the first 1,024 cylinders, unless both have a modern BIOS (a BIOS that supports the Extended INT13 functions) and a modern boot loader.

Because Linux supported SCSI early on in its development and the SCSI BIOS controls the SCSI devices, there are no problems with large hard drives. For large IDE hard drives over 8.4 GB, you will need recent stable kernel (2.0.34 or later) if you use large mode or LBA mode. Drives larger than 33.8 GB will not work with kernels, older than 2.3.21. If not, you must make that the kernel and other files used during boot-up (/boot) are entirely contained in the first 1,024 cylinders of a disk that the BIOS can access. This can be done by creating a small partition (for example, 10 MB) and mount it as /boot, which will hold the boot manager such as LILO or GRUB. Mounting and LILO will be explained in this chapter.

23.3.2 Disk Names in Linux

Before continuing on how to install Linux, there are some concepts that you should be familiar with. This includes having a basic understanding of how Linux uses disks, how Linux refers to disks, and of the directory structure used in Linux and how that relates to disks.

Linux treats all devices as files and has actual files that represent each device. In Linux, these device files are located in the /dev directory. Linux file names are similar to MS-DOS file names except that they do not use drive letters such as A and C and they substitute the slash (/) for the MS-DOS backslash as the separator between directory names.

Because Linux treats a device as a file in the /dev directory, the hard disk names start with /dev. Table 23.2 lists the hard disk and floppy drive names that you may have to use. Of course, when you use the Red Hat Disk Druid or Linux fdisk program to prepare the Linux partitions, you have to identify the disk drive by its name such as /dev/hda.

Table 23.2 Hard Disk and Floppy Drive Names

Device Type	Name	Description
IDE Hard Drive	/dev/hda	First IDE hard drive (typically the C drive)
	/dev/hdb	Second IDE hard drive
SCSI Hard Drive	/dev/sda	First SCSI hard drive
	/dev/sdb	Second SCSI hard drive
Floppy Disk	/dev/fd0	First floppy drive (A drive)
	/dev/fd1	Second floppy drive (B drive)

When Disk Druid or fdisk displays the list of partitions, the partition names take the form of /dev/hda1, /dev/hda2, and so on. Linux constructs each partition name by appending the partition number (1 through 4 for the four primary partitions on a hard disk) to the disk name. Therefore, if your PC's single IDE hard drive has two partitions, the installation program uses /dev/hda1 and /dev/hda2 as the names of these partitions.

23.3.3 Linux File System

Although you can get by with a single large partition for the entire Linux file system and another for the swap space, you can better manage the disk space if you create separate partitions for the key parts of the Linux file system.

Under most operating systems (including Linux), there is the concept of a file, which is just a bundle of information given a file name. Examples of files might be your paper or report, an email message, or an actual program that can be executed. Essentially, anything saved on disk is saved in an individual file.

Files are identified by their file names. These names usually identify the file and its contents in some form that is meaningful to you. There is no standard format for file names as there is under MS-DOS and some other operating systems; in general, a file name can contain any character (except the /character) and is limited to 256 characters in length.

With the concept of files comes the concept of directories. A directory is a collection of files. It can be thought of as a folder that contains many different files. Directories are given names, with which you can identify them. Furthermore, directories are maintained in a treelike structure, in which directories may contain other directories.

Most Linux systems use a standard layout for files so that system resources and programs can be easily located. This layout forms a directory tree, which starts at the root directory (designated as the /directory). Directly underneath / are important subdirectories: /bin, /etc, /dev, and /usr, among others.

Red Hat and other Linux distributors are committed to the file system hierarchy standard (FHS), a collaborative document that defines the names and locations of many files and directories. The current FHS document is the authoritative reference to any FHS compliant file system. The complete standard can be viewed at http://www.pathname.com/fhs/. Unfortunately, the standard leaves many areas undefined or extensible. See table 23.3 for a list of well-known directories used in Linux.

Table 23.3 Key Directories Used in the Red Hat Linux File System Hierarchy

Directory Name	Description
root (/)	In this setup, all files (except those stored in /boot) reside on the root partition. For Red Hat Linux, a 900 MB root partition will permit the equivalent of a workstation-class installation with very little free space. However, a 1.7 GB root partition will let you install every package in Red Hat Linux.
/bin	Contains the executable programs that are part of the Linux operating system that are available to all users. Many commands, such as cat, cp, ls, more, and tar, are located in /bin.
/boot	The /boot directory contains the operating system kernel (which allows your system to boot Linux), along with files used during the bootstrap process. Due to the limitations of older PC BIOSes, creating a small partition to hold these files is a good idea. This partition should be no larger than 16MB.
/dev	Contains all device files. The /dev directory contains files divided into subdirectories that contain files for a specific device. These directory names are based on type of device files they contain. Some examples are hda1 for the first IDE hard drive, fd0 for the floppy disk, and cdrom, which is the symbolic link created to the CD-ROM device that Linux was installed from.
/etc	The location for configuration files and for the system boot scripts. These boot scripts are located under the /etc/rc.d/ directory. The services that run at boot-up are located under /etc/rc.d/init.d/.
/home	The /home directory is where users store their own files. When planning the size of the /home partition, you must consider how many users you have and how much space you want to allocate for each user.

Continued

Table 23.3 Continued

Directory Name	Description
/lib	Contains library files for C and other programming languages.
/lost + found	The system's directory for placing lost files that are found or created by disk errors or improper system shutdowns. At boot, programs such as fsck find the inodes, which have no directory entries, and reattach them as files in this directory for lost files. Every disk partition has a lost+found directory.
/mnt	An empty directory, typically used to mount devices temporarily such as floppy disks and disk partitions. Also contains the /mnt/floppy directory for mounting floppy disks, and the /mnt/cdrom directory for mounting the CD-ROM drive. You also can mount the CD-ROM drive on another directory.
/opt	The location for optional packages.
/proc	A special directory that contains information about various aspects of the Linux system configuration information (interrupt usage, I/O port use, and CPU type) and the running processes (programs).
/root	The home directory for the root user.
/sbin	The location of some system configuration and system administrator executable files. Most of the general administration commands such as lilo, fdisk, fsck, and route are located here and are typically available only to root.
/swap	The /swap directory is where the swap files (virtual memory) are located. If you have more swap space, it will allow more programs to run simultaneously or larger programs to run with more data. If you have 16 MB or less, you must have a swap partition. Even if you have more memory, a swap partition is still recommended. The minimum size of your swap partition should be equal to the amount of RAM in your system or 16 MB, whichever is larger. Linux allows each up to 16 swap partitions.
/tmp	The /tmp directory is used to hold temporary files, and typically is needed in larger multiuser systems and network file servers.
/usr	The /usr directory is where most of the software on the Linux system resides. It should be about 150 to 600 MB, depending on which packages are installed. */usr/bin*—Contains executable files for many Linux commands, including utility programs commonly available in Linux, but is not part of the core Linux operating system. */usr/doc*—Contains the documentation files for the Linux operating system, as well as many utility programs such as the Bash shell, mtools, the xfm File Manager, and the xv image viewer. */usr/games*—Contains some old Linux games such as fortune, banner, and trojka. */usr/include*—Contains the header files (files with names ending in .h) for the C and C++ programming languages. */usr/lib* — Contains the libraries for C and C++ programming languages. */usr/local* — Used for storing programs that you want to separate from the rest of the Red Hat Linux software. */usr/man*—Contains the online manual, which can can be read by using the man command. */usr/sbin*—Contains many administrative commands, such as commands for electronic mail and networking. */usr/share*—Contains shared data such as default configuration files and images for many applications. */usr/src*—Contains much of the Linux source code. */usr/X11R6*—Contains the XFree86 (X Window System) software.
/var	Short for *various*. It is used to store files that change often such as for spooling, logging, and other data.

Figure 23.1 Sample Linux File System Using Mounted Points

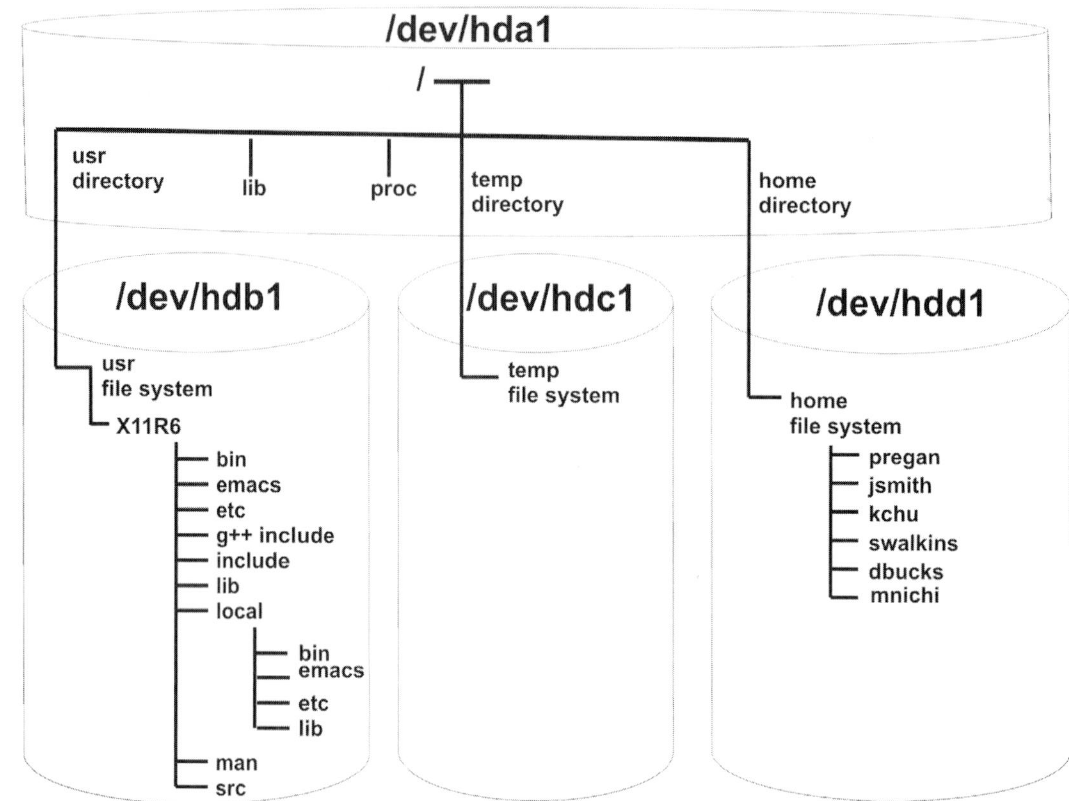

23.3.4 Mount Points

DOS and Microsoft Windows use drive letters to identify logical drives or partitions that may be on the one hard drive or several hard drives. Each drive has a root directory and its hierarchical file system.

In Linux, all of the drives and their partitions make up a single directory file system. If you have more than one physical disk partition, it is associated with a specific part of the file system. All you have to do is decide which part of the Linux directory tree should be located on each partition. This process is known in Linux as mounting a file system on a device (the disk partition). The term **mount point** refers to the directory you associate with a disk partition or any other device. In other words, each mount point is a disk partition, and that disk partition is mounted on the directory of the limb above it.

Although you can get by with a single large partition for the entire Linux file system and another for the swap space, you can better manage the disk space if you create separate partitions for the key parts of the Linux file system. See figure 23.1. Some of the recommended partitions are:

- /bin
- /boot
- /home
- /lib
- /root
- /tmp
- /var

At the very minimum, you will need two partitions for your system, root (/) and swap. For performance reasons, Linux likes to have swap on its own partition. For most other installations, three partitions are recommended: swap, root, and home. If you need complicated system requirements and decide to use multiple partitions, you should refer to table 23.4.

The size of the swap file usually varies between the amount of physical memory (RAM) and twice the amount of physical memory. There are situations, such as certain databases, where an increased

Table 23.4 Directory Guidelines for a Complicated Disk Structure for Linux

Name	Minimum Size	Usage
Swap	128 MB	Virtual memory, which is used to store inactive memory to disk until it is later used
/	250 MB	Root file system including basic libraries, programs, and configuration
/var	250 MB	For files that change frequently including logs, spool files, lock files
/usr	500 MB	Used by most applications
/boot	16 MB	Used to store the kernel
/home	500 MB	Home directory of users including user-specific configuration and data

Table 23.5 The fdisk Commands

Command	What It Does
b	Enters BSD disklabel command-line mode
m	Displays help
p	Displays the current partition table
d	Deletes a partition
n	Creates a new partition
w	Writes the partition table to disk
t	Sets the type of partition
l	Displays the list of partition types
q	Quits fdisk

swap partition is desired. But if the swap file is too big, you will most likely see a degradation in performance since disk is much slower than RAM.

Partitions like /usr and /home tend to fill up quickly, so if you have extra space, it should be put there. Depending on the function of the computer, extra space could go to other partitions. For example, if you are using it as a mail server, you would have little need for the /home partition, but you would want lots of space in /var to store all the mail. If you have a file server, you would not have many binary files in /bin, but its /home might need to be quite large.

23.3.5 FDISK

Fdisk is available in every distribution of Linux. If you have chosen to use fdisk, a screen will prompt you to select a drive to partition using fdisk. Once you have chosen which drive to partition, you will be presented with the fdisk command screen. If you are unsure as to what command you should use, type *m* at the prompt for help. See table 23.5.

You'll need to be aware of a few issues regarding partitioning with fdisk. First, Linux fdisk creates partitions of type unknown by default. When you create partitions, don't forget to change swap partitions to type Linux swap, and Linux partitions to type ext2 using the t command. The value for the Linux swap type is 1; ext2 partitions are 8. For other partition types, use the l command to see a list of partition types and values. See figure 23.2.

Figure 23.2 Using the P Command to Print Out the Partition Table

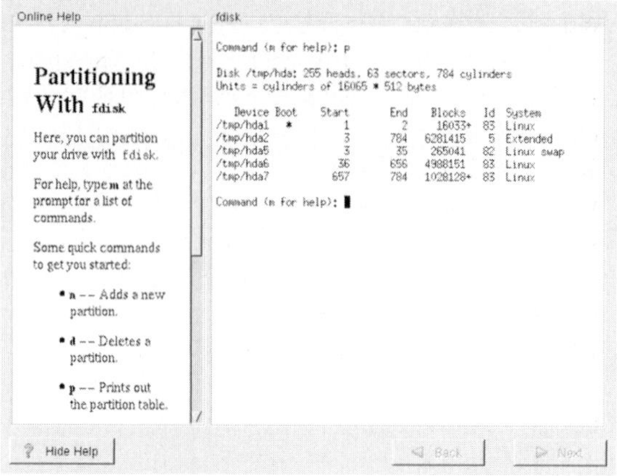

Linux allows up to four partitions on one disk. If you wish to create more than that, one (and only one) of the four can be made into an extended partition, which will act as a container for one or more logical partitions each of which will be mounted.

NOTE: Linux supports primary partitions and logical partitions.

When you've finished making partitions, type *w* to save your changes and quit. You will be taken back to the original fdisk screen where you can choose to partition another drive or continue with your installation. When you are finished partitioning your disks, press Done; you may see a message indicating that the installation program needs to reboot. This is a normal occurrence after changing a disk's partition data; it usually happens if you created, changed, or deleted any extended partitions. After you press OK, the machine will reboot and the installation will begin again. Repeat the same installation steps you performed earlier until you reach the Partition Disks dialog; then simply choose Done. You can quit fdisk at any time without saving changes using the q command.

23.3.6 Verifying Your Installation

After you complete your installation, the first thing you will do is restart the machine. When the machine successfully boots, log in as "root" with the root password you selected during installation. Before trying to use programs or services on the newly installed Linux machine, view the dmesg log file by entering *cat /var/log/dmesg* at the prompt. The output of dmesg is a log of the messages that you see during boot-time. Within the dmesg log, you can look for the messages stating that the kernel has initialized your partitions, your Ethernet card, and more.

After viewing the dmesg file, check to see that things are working properly. Then take a look at the /var/log messages file to see if any processes have any errors. In addition, examine the installation process in /temp/install.log.

When looking at the logs, if you notice that a specific piece of hardware isn't loading properly, you should check for compatibility issues or the driver for the hardware that was not available during installation. (You can check out the *Hardware Compatibility HOWTO* from the Linux Documentation Project and any hardware guides that your distribution might have.)

Finally, you must check for errata. Errata lists contain updates and bug fixes. You should download and install all necessary update packages.

23.3.7 Troubleshooting Linux Installation Problems

If you cannot boot from your Linux Installation CD, check your CMOS setup program to make sure that your CD-ROM is recognized first. If this does not work, you will have to boot from the boot disk that loads the CD driver. Next, make sure that the floppy disk and CD-ROM disk are readable by trying to access them in another machine. You should also check to see if the hardware is listed in the hardware compatibility list. If you are still having problems, check the manufacturer's website for an updated boot disk image and for any errata that might exist.

If the Automatic Partitioning screen does not appear during installation, you probably do not have enough free space in which to install Red Hat Linux. If you do not want to partition manually, you should exit out of the installation, which can be done by rebooting the system once you have removed any diskettes or CD-ROMs, and then you can reallocate space for installation.

If you are having trouble creating a partition, for instance a root (/) partition, there are a couple of things you should be aware of. Make sure you are setting it as a Linux Native partition type. On older machines where BIOS does not support drives that exceed 1,023 cylinders, you will not be able to create a /boot or a / partition.

One common installation problem occurs when inadequate space is allocated for installation of all packages. If you are using Disk Druid to create partitions, but cannot move to the next screen, you probably have not created all the partitions necessary for Disk Druid's dependencies to be satisfied. Make sure that you created the / (root) partition set as a Linux Native type and the <swap> partition set as a Linux swap type.

If you have other problems during installation such as read errors, files not found, or other problems as the files are being copied onto the hard drive, there may be corrupted files, bad blocks on the hard drive, or the partition may be too small. See table 23.6.

One of the most commonly encountered problems is hardware not recognized properly. This can happen to a CD-ROM, a network card, and hard disk. Most of the time this is caused by a conflict in the IRQ (interrupt), DMA (direct memory address), or I/O address settings. When two devices have the same settings on any one of the three characteristics, Linux and the BIOS may not be able to communicate with the device properly.

A symptom of this problem may be Linux hanging when it tries to find a specific device, as explained on the boot messages. When Linux boots up, it generates verbose messages on the console that explain what it is doing. If a card has failed, Linux typically ignores the device that it cannot access. If you see a message that it is trying to connect to the network card, for example, and it never gets past that point, chances are the network card has a conflict with another device. To check for conflicts, you can run a diagnostic utility under DOS such as MSD, Norton Info, or Dr. Hardware.

Table 23.6 Common Installation Problems

Problem	Description
`"Read Error"` or `"File Not Found"` error or the installation program stalls while reading a package when installing Linux	This is probably caused by poor quality media, wrong media format (such as a Macintosh floppy in a PC floppy drive), or missing files.
Archive errors when installing Linux such as tar, `"Read error"` or gzip, `"Not in gzip Format While Installing Linux."`	The media is OK but the archive contents have been corrupted. Downloaded a new copy (in binary mode) from a different site.
`"Device Full"` error message when installing Linux.	The disk partitions created at the beginning of the installation process are too small for the Linux distribution. You must start over and make new, larger partitions that will hold the software you want.
A Read Interrupt error message when installing Linux. For example: `Read_intr: 0x10 error`	If this occurs with general hard disk access, then the disk drive has bad blocks. Either use the badblocks command to search the device for bad blocks or reinstall Linux; regardless, be sure to check the scan-for-bad blocks option. Another possibility is that this error occurs while formatting a new volume with mkd2fs or mkswap. In these cases, the hard disk stated partition size in blocks is probably smaller than the real partition size. You may also want to run the badblocks program stand-alone to check the device.
`"File Not Found"` or `"Permission Denied"` Error during installation	It means that either there are missing files or the installation software has bugs that set the wrong permissions. Try a different version of the distribution or a different Linux distribution.

Table 23.7 Common SCSI Problems and Their Solutions

Problem	Probable Solution
SCSI device at all possible IDs	One or more devices are at the same SCSI ID as the controller. Check and change device IDs. Controllers should be ID 7.
Sense errors	Probably caused by bad termination. Check that both ends of the SCSI chain are terminated. If that is not the problem, the cable is likely at fault.
Timeout errors	Usually caused by a DMA, IRQ, or I/O address conflict. See the preceding section for more information.
SCSI adapter not detected	The BIOS is disabled or the SCSI adapter is not recognized by the kernel. Check the drivers.
Cylinders beyond 1,024	Your disk has more than 1,024 cylinders, which the PC BIOS can't handle. Linux can use more than 1,024 cylinders, but it can't boot from a partition that extends across that cylinder boundary.
CD-ROM drive not recognized	Some CD-ROMs require a CD in the drive to be recognized properly. Insert a CD and reboot.

Table 23.8 The Various Consoles Available During Installation

Console	Keystroke	Purpose
1	Ctrl + Alt + F1	Installation dialog box
2	Ctrl + Alt + F2	Shell prompt
3	Ctrl + Alt + F3	Install log (messages from the install program)
4	Ctrl + Alt + F4	System log (messages from the kernel and other system programs)
5	Ctrl + Alt + F5	Other messages
7	Ctrl + Alt + F7	X graphical display

SCSI is one of the most versatile interfaces, and it pays for that versatility in potential problems. Linux is usually good about reporting problems with SCSI devices. See table 23.7.

During the installation process, you can look at different diagnostic messages by switching among various virtual consoles. Table 23.8 shows the six consoles available in Red Hat Linux.

23.4 STARTING AND SHUTTING DOWN LINUX

When you boot Linux, you will typically start with a LILO boot prompt or a LILO GUI prompt. At the LILO boot prompt, you can do one of the following:

- Press the Enter key to cause LILO to boot its default boot entry.
- Type in the name of the boot label to specify which image to boot.
- If you wait until the LILO timeout period expires (default is 5 seconds), LILO will automatically boot the default boot entry.

However, if you forget the boot labels defined on your system, you can always press the Tab key at the LILO boot prompt to display a list of defined boot labels.

If the system boots with a LILO GUI prompt, you can do any of the following:

- Press Enter to cause LILO default boot entry to be booted.
- From the list of boot labels, select one with the arrow keys and press the Enter key. This causes LILO to boot the operating system corresponding to the boot label.
- If you wait until the LILO timeout period expires (default is 5 seconds), LILO will automatically boot the default boot entry.

Before you can start using Linux, you will need to log in. Like Windows NT or Windows 2000, Linux uses accounts to manage privileges, maintain security, and more. Not all accounts are created equal; some have fewer rights to access files or services than others. Earlier in this chapter, we mentioned the root account which is the all-powerful account to the Linux system. It is always recommended that you create a second account for yourself and use this account when you need to access the computer as a normal user. When you need to modify the configuration of Linux, you would then use the root account.

NOTE: Linux is case sensitive. Therefore, Linux account names and passwords are case sensitive. This means that typing *root* refers to a different account than when typing *Root.* Of course, the lowercase root is the name of the root login, or system administrator.

The login command prompt for Linux will include the name of the computer. The name of the computer will probably be called localhost unless you gave a machine a name in the network setting. You type in the account name, press the Enter key, type the account password, and press Enter again. See figure 23.3. The prompt will then change to something similar to [**accountname@localhost/root**].

If you are using the graphical login screen, type the account name in the Login text box and press Enter. See figure 23.4.

NOTE: If you still see a console screen instead of a graphical desktop, you can start the X Window System by typing *startx* and pressing Enter after logging in at the command prompt.

Logging out of the system depends on how the shell has been configured. By default, shell will accept the end-of-file (EOF) character Ctrl + D as the termination command and return the user to the Login prompt. Alternatively, some shells may be configured to prompt the user to use the built-in shell commands logout or exit.

Figure 23.3 Logging in to Linux Using the Text-Based Interface

```
Red Hat Linux release 7.0
Kernel 2.2.16 on an i686

localhost login:accountname↵

Password:accountpassword↵

[accountname@localhost/accountname]
```

Figure 23.4 The Graphical Login Screen

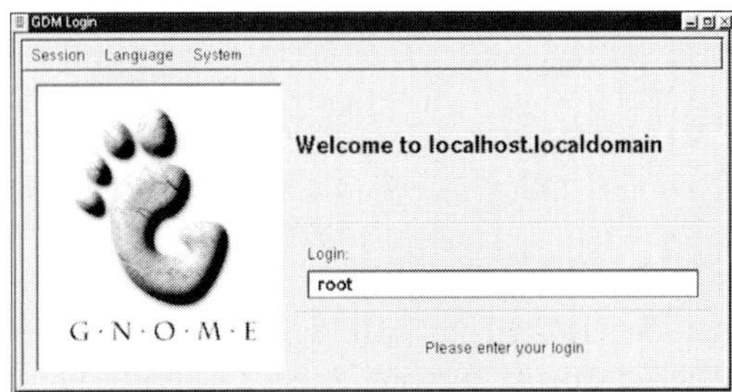

Figure 23.5 GNOME and KDE Main Menus

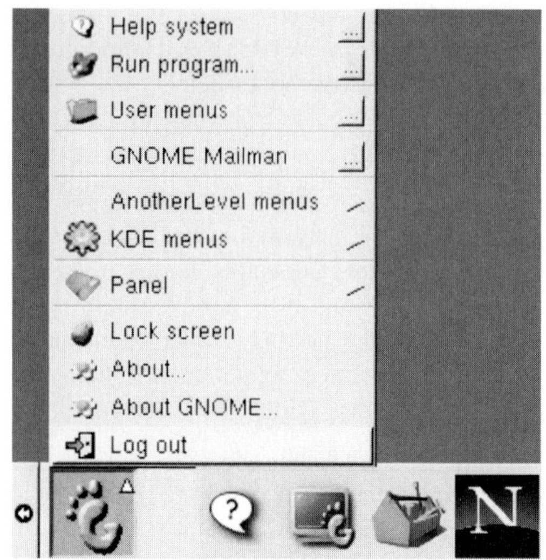

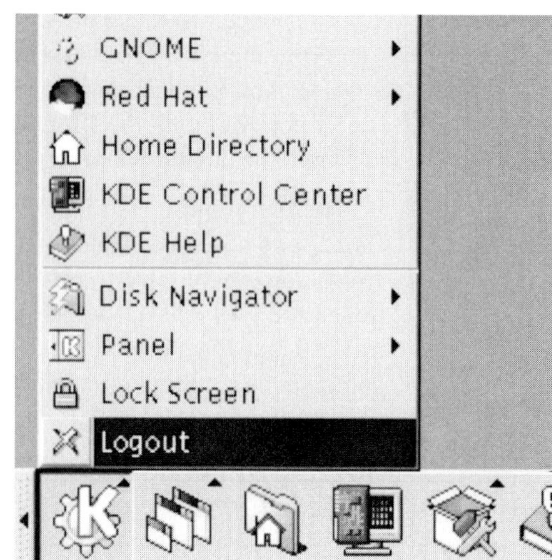

To log out from GNOME, click once on the Main Menu button on the Panel and drag the mouse cursor to the first item, labeled Logout. When the confirmation dialog appears, select the Logout option and click the Yes button. If you want to save the configuration of your Panel, as well as any programs that are running, check the Save current setup option, as well. To log out in KDE, you can log out from the Menu button on the Panel. It is located near the Taskbar, at the center of the Panel. You'll either return to the graphical login screen or the shell prompt, depending on how you chose to log in. See figure 23.5.

The fastest way to stop X Windows and go back to the command prompt is to press Ctrl + Alt + Backspace. If you press Ctrl + Alt + Del or select Log out from the Panel's Main Menu button, you will get a logout dialog box asking if you want to really log out. You then have three options to select:

- **Logout**—logs you out of your account and returns you to the login screen, leaving the system running.
- **Halt**—logs you out of your account and shuts down the system.
- **Reboot**—logs you out of your account and restarts the system.

Select any of the options and press the Yes button to continue. See figure 23.6. Also, select the Save current setup option if you want to save your session. Saving your session will preserve your current configuration of the Panel and save the programs you might have open. If you don't wish to proceed, choose the No button to continue with your session.

Like modern operating systems, Linux uses a data cache to reduce long disk I/O delays by saving previously accessed disk blocks in main memory so that they are quickly accessible when needed. The blocks are flushed to the hard disk when they are no longer needed. In Linux, the data cache grows and shrinks in size depending on the amount of memory not used by other programs. Approximately 1.5 MB of memory is left unallocated for new programs, and the remainder is given to the data cache. As a result, it not uncommon to see the data cache occupy one to two thirds of physical memory.

Although this system makes Linux one of the fastest operating systems used today, a problem may occur in the event of a power failure or improperly shutting down the computer. The disk blocks in main memory are lost, and the file system can be corrupted. Linux will minimize this problem by periodically saving any outstanding modified disk blocks. Therefore, to turn off Linux, you must first terminate the system programs that reset open files and flush the data cache.

There are three ways to shut down the Linux system properly. Shutting down using the Halt or Reboot options on the GNOME or KDE desktops was already discussed. On many Linux versions, this Ctrl + Alt + Del keyboard combination issues a shutdown command that closes all the processes prop-

Figure 23.6 Configuration Logout Dialog Box

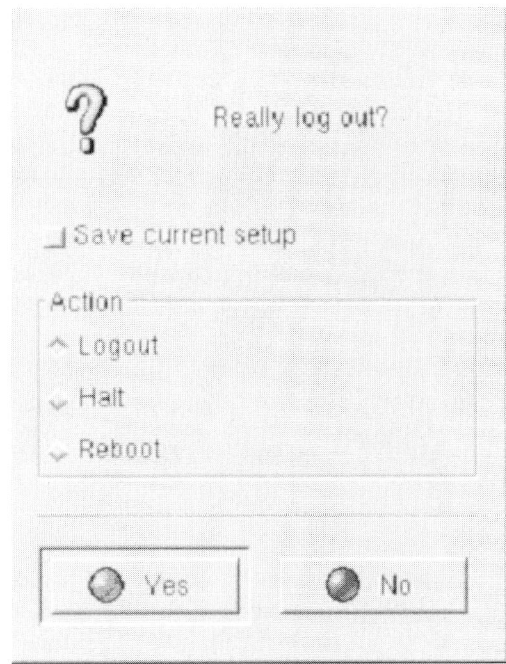

erly, and then reboots the machine. Not all versions of Linux support this sequence, though, so check your documentation carefully.

NOTE: If there are Windows NT or Windows 2000 users around, this option may be removed from the /etc/inittab file to prevent them from shutting down the Linux box inadvertently when using the NT login technique.

Another method of shutting down Linux is with the UNIX shutdown command. When you issue the shutdown command, Linux starts to terminate all processes and then shuts down the kernel. The shutdown command displays several different messages, depending on the version of Linux, but all inform you of the process or check that you really want to shut down the system. The shutdown command allows you to specify a time until shutdown, as well as an optional warning message to be displayed to all users logged in.

`shutdown -r now`	The -r means reboot, and will restart your machine.
`shutdown -r 5`	Reboots the system after 5 minutes.
`shutdown -h now`	The -h means halt, and will shut down the system.
`shutdown 15 'Backup Time!'`	Shuts down the system after 15 minutes and display the message "Backup Time!" to all users on the system, prompting them to log off. This command is handy when you enforce a policy of shutting down at specific intervals, either for maintenance or backups.
`shutdown -k now`	Does not perform a shutdown but sends the shutdown announcement to all users.
`shutdown -c now`	Cancels a running shutdown.

In most cases, using Ctrl + Alt + Del or the shutdown command results in the display of a number of status messages on the main console. When Linux has finished shutting down the system, you see the message "The system is halted." When this message appears on-screen, it is safe to shut off the system power or reboot the machine. You can also use init 0 to perform a shutdown, issue the halt command, which is the same as the issuing the shutdown -h now command, or the reboot command which is the same as issuing the shutdown -r now command.

23.5 REMOVING LINUX

To delete Linux, you need to delete the partitions that hold Linux. This can be done with any utility that deletes non-DOS partitions. Therefore, you can use FDISK with Windows 95 or Windows 98, Disk Administrator for Windows NT or Windows 2000, and Partition Magic. You cannot use FDISK that comes with DOS. In addition, you can start the install program again and select the Linux expert option. When it comes to partitioning the drive, choose fdisk. In fdisk, press the P key to display the partition numbers and remove the Linux partitions with the d command. When you're satisfied with the changes you have made, you can quit with a [w] and the changes will be saved to disk. If you accidentally delete the wrong partition, type *q* and the changes to the partition table will not be saved. Once you have removed the Linux partitions, you can reboot your computer by pressing Ctrl + Alt + Del instead of continuing with the install.

To finish the uninstall, you will also need to remove the LILO information from the master boot record. There are several methods to remove LILO from the master boot record including:

- In DOS, Windows 95, or Windows 98, you can use FDISK to create a new MBR by using the command at the prompt:

  ```
  fdisk /mbr
  ```

- Inside of Linux, you can replace the MBR with an earlier saved version of the MBR using the /sbin/lilo command:

  ```
  /sbin/lilo -u
  ```

23.6 INTRODUCTION TO THE SHELL

A **shell** is a program designed to accept commands that you type in at a prompt and execute them. You can think of a shell as a command interpreter, much like the COMMAND.COM does in DOS. A shell uses a command-driven interface. Because the shell serves as the primary interface between the operating system and the user, many users identify the shell with Linux. In reality, the shell is not part of the kernel; instead it is the interface.

As you type in a command at the keyboard, you must know the correct spelling, syntax, parameters, and punctuation for the command to work. If not, you will receive an error message or an incorrect response. Therefore, to be successful at using the shell, it will require a little memorization. Different from DOS, all commands in Linux are case sensitive. This means that you have to type in the same lowercase and uppercase letters. In addition, Linux uses the slash (/) rather than the backslash (\).

When you type in a command at the prompt, the shell will create a new environment for the command to be executed in and determine what should be standard input and standard output to the command. Standard input is normally the keyboard and standard output is normally the monitor.

Many commands can use wild cards. A wild-card character is a special symbol that stands for one or more characters. If you used partial names combined with wild cards, you can specify one or more files. If wild cards are used with the command, the shell will determine the files that match the wild cards. Wild cards will be explained in more detail later in this chapter.

When you execute a command in the shell, the instructions for that command must be found. If you type a command that isn't one of that shell's built-in commands, the shell has to locate an executable file whose name matches the command that you typed in. Therefore, the shell will search the current directory for the file with the same name. If it cannot find the file, it will then search the PATH environment variable, again looking in each directory specified for the file with the name of the command being executed. The PATH environment variable will be explained later in this chapter. Most of commands shown in this chapter are found in /bin, /sbin, and /usr/bin directories. When the file with the instructions is found, the shell will pass on any options or specifications typed in with the command to the instructions and performs the command. After the command is run, the shell returns to the current environment, throwing away all the side effects that occurred in the new environment.

When you log in, Linux places you in your home directory and runs the appropriate shell. The home directory is a directory designated for the user to store his or her files. You can think of it as a personal directory. The normal prompt uses this syntax:

```
[username@hostname dirname] $
```

The username is the name of the user and the hostname is the system's name. The dirname is the name of the current working directory. The $ indicates the end of the prompt. If you log in as the root, the prompt will end with the pound sign (#).

23.6.1 Files and Directories

Linux has a hierarchical, unified file system containing directories and files, which follows a standard layout for files. The standard layout allows for system resources and programs to be located easier. This layout forms a directory tree, which starts at the root (/) directory. Directly underneath the root directory are some important subdirectories: /bin, /etc, /dev, and /usr, among others, which contain system configuration files, programs, and so on.

A file is just a bundle of information that is identified with a file name. Examples of files would be your term paper or report, an email message, or an executable program. For example, the file containing your term paper might be saved with the file name class-term-paper. The file name can be up to 256 characters with no symbols and punctuations except for the dot (.), dash (-), and underscore (_). These names should identify the file and its contents in some form that is meaningful to you.

Directories are used to organize the files. They can be thought of as "folders" that contain many different files or other directories. The directories form a treelike structure. Like files, directories should be given names that describe their contents.

A file may be referred to by its path name, which is made up of the file name, preceded by the name of the directory that contains the file. For example, let's say that you have a directory called papers and in the papers directory, you have the class-term-paper file. The file path would be:

```
/papers/class-term-paper
```

because papers is at the top of the tree structure (except the root directory) and class-term-paper is directly in the papers directory. If you have a directory called history in the papers directory and the file class-term-paper is in the history directory, the path name would be:

```
/papers/history/class-term-paper
```

Again, papers is at the top of the tree structure. In the papers directory you will find the history directory, and in the history directory you will find the class-term-paper file. Because the history directory is located in the papers directory, the history directory is sometimes referred to as a subdirectory. You can also refer to the papers directory as the parent directory to the history directory.

One of the concepts that you must understand from this chapter is that the path name specifies the location of the file within the hierarchal tree structure. In addition, you should have noticed that the single slash (/) is used to separate directories and file names. For this reason, file names themselves cannot contain the forward slash character. This is similar to MS-DOS, except MS-DOS uses the backslash (\).

You may have noticed that the two path names above started with a forward slash. If you begin a file name with a forward slash, the system interprets this as a full path name—that is, a path name including the entire path to the file, starting from the root directory (/). This is known as an absolute path name. In other words, an absolute path name specifies a location of a file, no matter which working directory you are located at.

At any given time, commands that do not use absolute file names must be given in terms of your current working directory. The prompt shows the name of the working directory and the pwd command can be used to showing the path name for your working directory. When you first log in, your working directory is set to your home directory. Each user has a home directory, which is set aside for that user to store his or her files. Usually, user home directories are contained under /home, and are named for the user who owns that directory using the login name. Therefore, Pat's home directory could be called /home/Pat.

When you reference a file in relationship to your current working directory, instead of specifying the absolute path name, you are using a relative path name. For example, the Pat directory (located in the home directory) has a subdirectory (child directory) called papers, which the class-term-paper is in. The absolute path name of the file is:

```
/home/Pat/papers/class-term-paper
```

If your current directory were the Pat directory, the relative path to the class-term-paper would be:

```
papers/class-term-paper
```

If you begin a file name (such as papers/final) with a character other than "/", the system assumes that you are using a relative path name. Since you are in the Pat directory and you did not begin with a /, it assumes the file you want is in the working directory+relative pathname=/home/pat/ + papers/class-term-paper =/home/pat/papers/class-term-paper. Of course, these two path names listed above reference the same file as long as the working directory is the Pat directory. If you are using a different working directory, then the absolute path name will still work but the relative path name would not.

Under both tcsh and bash, your home directory can be referred to using the tilde character ("~"). For example, the command

```
~/papers/class-term-paper
```

is equivalent to

```
/home/Pat/papers/class-term-paper
```

The "~" character is simply replaced with the name of your home directory by the shell.

23.6.2 Wild-Card Characters

Wild-card characters (* and ?) are used to specify groups of files. The asterisk (*) means any string of characters and the question mark (?) means any single character. For example, to specify all files that begin with the letters *ra,* you would use ra*. To specify a file name that is four characters in length and ends in *TST,* you would use ?TST. To specify all files with the letter *o* in the file name, you can use *o*.

In addition to the * and the ?, you can also use brackets ([ ]) to list characters or to specify a range of characters. For example, to specify files that begin with *report* and end with numbers ranging from 1 to 5, you would use report[1-5]. To list all files that begin with either a lowercase *r* or a uppercase *R* and end with *eport,* you would specify [Rr]eport. To take this one step further, if you want to specify all files that begin with either *Report* or *report,* you would use [Rr]eport*.

23.7 COMMON COMMANDS

The common commands can be divided into categories. Navigating the Linux file structure and viewing the contents of a directory will be first. You will then make and create directories followed by working with files. This chapter will not cover every command in Linux, but it will cover the most commonly used ones.

You will find that executing the commands at a Linux prompt is similar to executing the commands at a DOS command prompt. Different from DOS, however, is the fact that Linux commands and files are case sensitive.

23.7.1 The Ls Command

To list the contents (files and subdirectories) of a directory, you would use the list (ls) command. In its simplest form, ls will list the names of any files and directories that do not begin with a period (.).

ls—lists directory contents

-a	Displays all files and directories (useful for seeing hidden files)
-s	Displays size in blocks
-F	Appends a character to indicate the type of file * executable / directory @ symbolic link ¦ FIFOs \ UNIX domain socket
-i	Shows the inode number
-l	Displays long listings (owner, permissions, etc.)
-r	Reverses the order
-R	Does a recursive order
-t	Sorts by modification date
-u	Sorts by access time

To see all of the names, use the all option (-a):

```
ls -a
```

Even if you have not yet created any files in your directory, you should see the names *login* and *cshrc* and two entries, one with a single period (.) and one with a double period (..). The . entry represents the current directory or the directory that you are working in. The .. entry is a link to its parent directory.

NOTE: -A acts the same as -a except that . and .. are not listed.

To see how big your files are, and to see their protection modes, use the -l (long) flag:

```
ls -l
```

The protection modes determine what actions you and others may perform on the files. The details about protection mode will be explained later in the book.

The -F flag is also useful. It marks the names of directories with a trailing slash (/) character and the names of executable files with a trailing asterisk (*). It can also be combined with the -a option or the -l option:

```
ls -a -l -F
```

or

```
ls -alF
```

The ls command can be used to list the contents of other directories instead of just the working directory. For this, you just have to specify either an absolute path name to the directory or a relative path name to the directory. For example, if you want to list the contents of the boot directory from my home directory, you could do

```
ls -a /boot
```

If my current directory is my home directory and I have a papers directory in my home directory, just specify the name of paper directory:

```
ls -a paper
```

This worked because paper was specified relative from my current directory. If you execute the following command

```
ls .. -a
```

it will specify the content of the parent directory.

The list command can also use wild cards. For example, to list all files that begin with the letter *s*, you would use:

```
ls s*
```

The file command will use tests to identify the type of file. The types of files are:

- **Text**—The file contains only ASCII characters and is probably safe to read on an ASCII terminal.
- **Executable**—The file contains the results of compiling a program in a form understandable to a Linux kernel.
- **Data**—Anything else not defined as a text file or executable file. It usually is considered a binary file or nonprintable file. Examples would include graphic files such as JPEG and GIF.

The file command can use the magic number test to check for files with data in a particular fixed format. These files have a "magic number" stored in a particular place near the beginning of the file that tells the Linux operating system that the file is a binary executable, of which there are several types. The information in these files is read from the magic file /usr/share/misc/magic.

If an argument appears to be an ASCII file, the file command attempts to guess its language. The language tests. Unfortunately, this test is not as reliable as the other functions.

23.7.2 Changing Directories

To move from one directory to another, you use the change directory (cd) command. The following command will look for the papers directory in your current directory:

```
cd papers
```

The following command will look for the papers directory located in the root directory:

```
cd /papers
```

NOTE: You must add a space after the cd command. To move to the history directory, which is located under the papers directory, you would use:

```
cd /papers/history
```

Of course, if you type the command

```
cd papers/history
```

it will change to the history folder located in the papers directory which is located under your current directory, not under the root directory.

If you wanted to go up a directory, you would use the following command:

```
cd ..
```

To change to the root directory, you would specify the root directory (/):

```
cd /
```

Last, if you want to move to the home directory, no matter where you are, you would use the following command:

```
cd
```

If you use cd very often to change working directories, you may need to be reminded where you are. To display the absolute path name of your working directory, use the print working directory (pwd) command:

```
pwd
```

23.7.3 Copying, Moving, Renaming, and Deleting Files

To make a copy or duplicate of a file's content, you would use the cp (copy) command. The syntax for the cp command is

```
cp from to.
```

cp—copies files

-f	Forces overwrite
-i	Interactively prompts before overwriting
-p	Preserves original file characteristics
-R	Recursively copies directories and files
-u	Overwrites if file is newer than destination
-v	Changes to verbose mode

For example, if you have a file called resume and you wanted to call it Pats-resume, you would use the following command:

```
cp resume Pats-resume
```

When this command was executed, you would be left with two identical files. If you wanted to copy a file from your current directory to another directory, while keeping the same name, you would specify the directory for its destination. For example, if you wanted to copy resume to the /home/data directory, you would perform the following command:

```
cp resume /home/data
```

You could also copy the file that is not located in the current directory to another directory. For example, if you are not in the data directory, to copy the resume directory to the backup directory, you would use:

```
cp /data/resume /backup
```

If you want to make a copy of the same file to the backup directory, but give it the name of Pats-resume, you would do the following command:

```
cp /data/resume /backup/Pats-resume
```

To move files from one directory to another, use the move (mv) command. Be sure to include the needed path information on the source and destination if is not your working directory.

mv—moves (and renames) files or directories

-f	Forces overwrite
-i	Interactive prompts move
-v	Changes to verbose mode

For example, suppose you want to move file source.a from your home directory to the next lower directory, Mysources. If Mysources is in your working directory, you would use the following command:

```
mv source.a Mysources/source.a
```

The mv command can also be used to rename files and directories. For example, to rename the xyz to the abc directory, you would use:

```
mv xyz abc
```

NOTE: This does not affect the contents of the directory.

To prevent destroying a file that already exists, include the -i flag. For example, if you type

```
mv -i source.a oldsource.a
```

and oldsource.a already exists, mv will ask if you really want to overwrite that old copy with the newer one. The copy and mv command can also use wild cards.

To delete files, you use the remove (rm) command. To delete a file you don't own, you need to read and write permission for that file.

rm—removes files or directories

- -r Recursively removes files in a directory structure
- -d Specifies that the target is a directory
- -i Changes to interactive mode
- -f Ignores all errors and never prompts user

To delete the source.a file, you would type the following command:

```
rm source.a
```

Of course, if you do not include a path name, the files are assumed to be in your working directory. If you use wild-card characters, it is a good precaution to add the -i flag, like this:

```
rm -i file*
```

This interactive option displays each file to be deleted one at a time. To remove the file, type *y* (for "yes") and press the Enter key. Any other response keeps the file. Once rm has removed a file, that file cannot be retrieved; there is no "undelete" command.

One way to quickly create an empty file without opening it to edit it is to use the touch command. For example, to create an empty file called test, you would execute the following command:

```
touch test
```

23.7.4 Creating and Removing Directories

If you have many projects, you want to create multiple directory to hold the files of the individual projects. To create a subdirectory, you would use the mkdir (short for "make directory") command.

mkdir—makes a directory

- -m Sets the permissions (mode) of directories being created
- -p Ensures each directory exists

For example, to create the directory called papers in your current directory, perform the following command:

```
mkdir paper
```

You can also use absolute and relative path names. For example, in your current directory, you must create the paper directory, and you can then create the english directory under the paper directory by using the following command:

```
mkdir paper/english
```

To remove a directory that you no longer need, use rmdir.

rmdir—removes directories

- -p Removes the directory specified and then tries to remove each parent directory that is included in the directory path name

To remove the empty papers directory, you can use this command:

```
rmdir papers
```

The rmdir command will not delete a directory while it is your working directory, nor will it delete a directory that contains any files or subdirectories (besides . and ..).

The -p option can be used with the rmdir command so that it will also attempt to remove the parent directories. For example, if you type in the following command

```
rmdir -p /dir1/dir2/dir3
```

and the path to dir3 is /dir1/dir2/dir3, it will first try to delete /dir1/dir2/dir3, then it will try to delete /dir1/dir2, and finally it will try to delete /dir1.

To remove a directory and any files and subdirectories it contains, as well as files in those subdirectories, use the recursive (-r) switch with the rm command. To delete the paper directory that may or may not contain files or subdirectories, perform the following command:

```
rm -r paper
```

Because it is possible to quickly delete entire directories, which may result in deleting something that you did not want to delete, you can use the -i switch. The -i switch will prompt you for confirmation before removing each subdirectory, and file. For example, use:

```
rm -ir paper
```

To delete files, you are going to use the remove (rm) command. To delete the source.a file, you would type:

```
rm source.a
```

Of course, if you do not include a path name, the files are assumed to be in your working directory. If you use wild-card characters, it is a good precaution to add the -i flag, like this:

```
rm -i filc*
```

This interactive option displays each file to be deleted one at a time. To remove the file, type *y* (for "yes") and press the Enter key. Any other response keeps the file.

NOTE: Once rm has removed a file, that file cannot be retrieved; there is no formal "undelete" command.

23.7.5 Finding Files

The find command locates files and directories that meet specified search criteria. The find command is one of the most useful Linux commands. Unfortunately, it is also one of the more difficult commands to use. The Linux version of the find command comes from GNU, and it has more extensive options than the standard UNIX version.

To locate a file in the file system, use the find command:

```
find pathname -name filename -print
```

As the path name defines the directory to start from, each subdirectory of this directory will be searched. If you use wild cards for the file name, you must put the file name in quotes. The -print option must be used to display results.

Limiting your search to one or more directories might be more efficient. For example, if you know that a file is probably in the /usr or /usr2 directory, you can use the following command instead:

```
find /usr /usr2 -name filename -print
```

If you want to find a selection of file names that can't be collectively represented with wild cards, you can use the or option (-o) to obtain a list. The syntax would be:

```
find /home (-name file1 -o -name file2) -print
```

Other options are located in table 23.9.

To find all files in the /tmp directory that have not been accessed in at least 7 days, use the following command:

```
find /tmp -atime 7 -print
```

To find all files in /home that end in .jpg and are over 100 KB in size, you would use:

```
find /home -name "*.jpg" -size 100k -print
```

One of the most useful parameters to find is -exec. It allows find to execute a command on any file it finds. To find all files in /usr/src whose names are core and to delete them:

```
find /usr/src -name core -exec rm
```

Two other commands worth mentioning are the locate and which commands. The locate command does find files and it is much faster than the find command since it searches a database of files. But the

Table 23.9 Find Command Options

Option for Find	Description
-mount	Do not search file systems other than the one from which search starts.
-atime *n*	File was accessed at least n^*24 hours ago.
-ctime *n*	File was changed at least n^*24 hours ago.
-inum *n*	File has I-node *n*.
-amin *n*	File as accessed *n* minutes ago.
-cmin *n*	File was changed *n* minutes ago.
-empty	File is empty.
-mmin *n*	File was modified *n* minutes ago.
-mtime *n*	File was modified n^*24 hours ago.
-nouser	File's UID does not correspond to a real user in /etc/passwd.
-nogroup	File's GID does not correspond to a real group in /etc/group.
-perm mode	File's permissions are exactly set to mode.
-size *n[bck]*	File is at least *n* *b*locks/*c*haracters/*k*ilobytes. One block equals 512 bytes.
print	Print the file names found.
exec *cmd*	On every file found, execute cmd. To avoid BASH from getting confused, you should follow every command with the \; characters.
-name *name*	File's name should be name. You use regular expressions here.

database may not include recent additions to the file system. To update the locate database, you would use the updatedb command. Note that most Linux installations are configured to run the updatedb program in the evening. To find a file name, you just have to type *locate filename.*

The which command (syntax which *filename*) searches your path and will return the first instance of the file specified. If there are other instances of the file, the which command will not tell you. Instead, you would need to use the locate or find command.

23.7.6 Getting Help

To get online help for the various commands, you can type *man.* Linux then displays any information it has on the command one screen at a time. If you aren't sure what command to use, you can try the -k parameter and enter a simple keyword that represents the topic of interest. Man then searches through its help files (called man, or manual pages) for a topic that contains the keyword. If you type the command *man ls,* Linux provides help on the ls command, including all its parameters. The command man -k ls provides a listing of help files that contain *ls.*

You can also use the info utility to display documention on the GNU utilities. To see the info for bash, at the command line, you would type:

```
info bash
```

If you execute the info command, it will show the main menu screen that contains a list of all the utilities for which the info command works, organized by sections (miscellaneous, GNU file utilities, programming languages, and so on).

Following each asterisk is the name of the item, and within each set of parentheses is the text you type to see the entry for it. You can also move the cursor to the asterisk or the text after the asterisk, press the Enter key, and info will jump to that page.

23.7.7 Setting the Date and Time

To view the date and time of the computer, you would type *date* at the prompt and press Enter. The output of this command would look something like this:

```
Sun May 5 18:56:36 BST 2002
```

If you are logged in as root, to set the time and date with date, you would do the following command:

```
date -s 'Sun May 5 19:00 BST 2002'
```

You can also do the following:

```
date MMDDhhmmYYYY.ss
```

MM	month
DD	day within month
hh	hour
mm	minute
YYYY	The year (optional)
ss	second (optional)

So, to configure the date, you could use the following command:

```
date 050519002002.00
```

Since seconds is option, you can simplify this command to:

```
date 050519002002
```

23.7.8 Dealing with DOS Files Under Linux

If a DOS partition is accessed through Linux and you want to copy these files to floppy disks, the cp command might cause problems because Linux treats text files a little differently than DOS, especially when dealing with carriage returns and linefeeds. To help you overcome this problem, developers created a group of programs to help deal with MS-DOS files under a UNIX environment. These programs are the m- commands, which include such commands as mcopy, mdel, and mrd. As you may have noticed, they resemble their DOS counterparts, except that they begin with the letter *m,* hence the name m- commands. The m- commands are part of the mtools package, which is a collection of public-domain programs that allow UNIX to interact with DOS files much more easily. See table 23.10.

Table 23.10 The mtools Command

Command	Description
mattrib	Displays the file attributes for the specified files(s)
mcd	Changes the directory to the specified path
mcopy	Copies the specified files to the new path
mdel	Deletes the specified files
mformat	Formats a floppy
mlabel	Labels the DOS file system
mmd	Makes a directory
mrd	Removes an empty directory
mren	Renames an existing DOS file
mtype	Displays the text contents of a DOS file

For example, if you have a Linux-based WordPerfect file, you can copy it to an MS-DOS–based disk by executing the following command:

```
mcopy document.wpd a:
```

The file transfer can then be confirmed with the command:

```
mdir a:
```

Occasionally, you may come across a partition such as used by Windows that contains directories or files with embedded blanks. To show a command for directories or files that contain blanks, you need to prefix every blank with a backslash or use double quotes. For example, to view the Program Files directory list, you would use the following command:

```
ls /cdrive/program\ files
```

or

```
ls "/cdrive/Program Files"
```

23.8 REDIRECTING AND FILTERS

While using Linux commands at the prompt, you can actually make these commands more powerful by redirection inputs and outputs and by using filters. Therefore, this section will explain how to use redirection and filters.

23.8.1 Using >, >>, and <

When using Linux, there are always three default "files" open, stdin (the keyboard), stdout (the screen), and stderr (error messages output to the screen). When you type something on the keyboard, it will be received by stdin. When something is sent to stdout, it will then be displayed on the screen.

Redirection means to make the shell change what it considers standard input or where the standard output is going. Since the monitor is the standard output device, you could use the > (greater than) symbol to redirect the output to the monitor into a file. In other words, what would normally have been displayed on the monitor could be redirected to a file. For example, if you would type in the date command, it would display the time and date of the system on the screen. If you want to store the current time and date in a file named date-file, for instance, you can enter the following command at the prompt:

```
date>now
```

If you want to append (add information to the end of) an existing file, you use two >> symbols. To append the current date to a file named report, for example, you can enter the following command:

```
date >>report
```

The < (less than) symbol is used to redirect input into a command or program so that it comes from a file instead of the keyboard. Suppose that you want to send a file named info by email to someone whose address is sarah. Rather than retype the contents of the file to the mail command, you can give this command to use the info file as the input (stdin) to the mail command:

```
mail sarah <info
```

Placing > after the cat command (or after any utility or application that writes to standard output) will direct its output to the file name following the symbol.

The sort command sorts the contents of a file. You can then type *sort file1>file2* which will sort file1 and save it as file2. If you wanted to append the sorted list to the end of file2, you would then use *sort file1>>file2.*

23.8.2 The Cat Command

The cat command is simple, easy to use, and one of the most useful Linux commands. *Cat* commands stands for *concatenate,* which means to add to the end of. The cat command takes all the input (typically from the keyboard) and outputs it to the screen. You can also use the cat command to display a text file to the screen just by typing:

```
cat filename
```

To redirect from the keyboard to the monitor, you type *cat* at the prompt. The cursor then moves to the next line and waits for you to start typing the contents of the text file. When you are done typing the contents of the text file, you press the Ctrl + D, which will put an end-of-file (EOF) character, ^D, at the end of the file.

NOTE: If you are not at the beginning of a line, press Ctrl + D twice.

To create a simple text file, you are redirecting from the keyboard to a file. Therefore, if you type

```
cat > filename
```

you are saving what you type at the keyboard to the file specified. If you use >>, you append the text to the end of the file. If you type *cat filename,* it will then display the text file to the screen. You could even use the >> to combine several files. For example, if you type

```
cat file1 file2 file3 file4 >fileout
```

you will combine the four files into one file called fileout. When you finish, be sure to end the session with ^D.

23.8.3 More and Less Commands

If you try to display large files by using cat, the file scrolls past your screen so fast as the screen can handle the character stream. Both the more command and less command display one screen of data at a time. If you type *more filename,* it will display the file, one screen at a time. If you want to go on to the next screen, press the spacebar. If you press Enter, only the next line is displayed. If you are looking through a series of files by using this command:

```
more file1 file2. . .
```

and you want to stop to edit one, you can do so by using the e or v command. Pressing e within more invokes whatever editor you have defined in your EDIT shell environment variable on the current file. Pressing v indicates using whatever editor has been defined in the VISUAL variable. If you have not defined those variables in your environment, the more command defaults to the ed editor for the e command and to the vi editor for the v command.

You can also use the more command in combination of other files. For example, if you use the ls command and the listing from the command displays more than what a screen can display, you can use the |more command to pause one screen at a time:

```
ls |more
```

In reality, the pipe (|) redirects the output of one program to the input of another program. In this case, instead of displaying the output on the screen, it redirects it to the more program. It is the more command that displays it one screen at a time.

Frequently, you need to use the output of one program or command as the input of another. Rather than enter each command separately and save results in intermediate files, you can connect a sequence of commands by using a pipe. In Linux, pipes connect the standard output of one command to the standard input of another command.

You can sort a file named file1 and then print it, you can enter the following:

```
sort file1 |lp
```

Again, the pipe was used to redirect the sorting of file1 and send it to the printer.

The less command is similar to the more command. It is different in that it does not allow you to use an editor on the file being displayed; however, it will allow you move forward and backward through the file. To advance to the next screen, press the spacebar as with the more command. To move backward in a file, press the *b* key. To go to a certain position expressed as a percentage of the file, press *p* and specify the percentage at the : prompt. To quit, just press Q.

23.8.4 Grep, Head, and Tail Commands

The grep tool is very popular for searching files for a specific term or string. The output of the grep command displays only the lines that contain the term or string that was "grepped." The grep tool can be used by itself, or it can be used to filter the output of another filter, such as cat. For example, both

```
cat filename |grep error
```

and

```
grep error filename
```

would search the contents of the specified file name for the word *error*.

The wc filter is helpful when you need to count the number of bytes (-c), words (-w), or lines (-l) from the output of a file. The following command takes the file name, pipes it or redirects it through grep, prints the lines that contain the term *error*, and counts the number of lines of output by piping or redirecting the output through wc -l:

```
cat filename |grep error |wc -l
```

The tail filter is commonly used to print logs and other large files. Simply running the following command

```
tail /var/log/messages
```

prints the last 10 lines of var/log/messages. However, to run a continuous output of a log, you use the -f option. For example, running

```
tail -f /var/log/messages
```

prints a running log of the /var/log/messages file.

The opposite of tail, called head, prints the first part of a message file. To print the first 10 lines of a log, for instance, type:

```
head -n 10 /var/log/messages
```

23.9 ENVIRONMENT VARIABLES

In Linux, the term *process* refers to a program executing in memory and its associated environment. The environment includes the input and output files that belong to the program and a collection of environment variables. Essentially, you create a process whenever you type a command at the shell prompt. Of course, the shell itself is just another process that creates new processes at your command.

An environment variable works much like variables in math. If you declare the value of X with the following command:

$$\text{SET } X = 3$$

and you are given the following equation:

$$Y = X + 2$$

you know to substitute the 3 wherever you see X. Therefore, $Y = X + 2$ becomes $Y = 3 + 2$, which makes $Y = 5$.

Linux maintains several dozen environment variables. An environment variable is simply a way to associate a name with a string. The shell has a standard set of environment variables. To display the environment variables, just execute the env command at the command prompt. The way you define an environment variable depends on the shell that you use. In bash, you set an environment variable by using the following syntax:

NAME=*VALUE;* export *NAME*

or

export *NAME*=*VALUE*

NAME is the name of the environment variable and VALUE is a string that denotes the value associated with NAME. A shorter way to define and use an export variable is to use the following syntax. The

Table 23.11 Common Shell Environment Variables

Variable Name	Description
HOME=	The HOME variable always specifies your home directory, which is the location from which you start. Login represents your login name.
LOGNAME=	The LOGNAME variable holds your login name, the name or string of characters that the system associates with you.
OLDPWD=	Old working directory ("OLD-print-working-directory," previous directory you were in).
PATH=	The PATH option represents the list of directories that the shell looks through for commands.
PS1=	PS1 is the primary shell prompt that defines what your prompt looks like. If you don't set it to anything specific, your prompt is the dollar sign ($). If you prefer, you can set it to something more creative.
PWD=	PWD is automatically set for you. It defines where you are in the file system. For example, if you checked PWD (by entering *echo SPID* at the command line) and Linux displays /usr/bin, you're in the /usr/bin directory. The pwd command also displays the current directory.
SHELL=	SHELL identifies the location of the program that serves as your shell. For example, you can set SHELL in your .profile or .login file as SHELL=/bin/ksh to make the Korn shell your login shell or SHELL=/bin/bash for the Bourne Again Shell.
TERM=	This variable sets the name of your terminal type, as specified by the terminal database. For example, you can set TERM in your .profile or .login file as TERM=vt100 or TERM=xterm.
MAIL=	This variable sets the full path name of your mailbox. Whenever mail comes into the system for you, it's put into the file specified by the MAIL variable. If you have a program that notifies you new mail arrived, it checks the file associated with the MAIL variable.
TZ=	The TZ variable holds a string that identifies your time zone. The date program and some other programs require this information. Your computer keeps track of time according to Greenwich Mean Time (GMT). If the TZ variable is set to PST8PDT, the time and date are determined as Pacific Standard Time (PST), 8 hours west of GMT, with support for Pacific Daylight Savings Time (PDT). Your computer system automatically changes between daylight savings time and standard time.

export command makes it the variables accessible by subroutines and child processes. To access the environment variable, you precede the environment variable with the dollar sign ($).

NOTE: Don't forget that when you are setting and using environment variables, they are case sensitive.

When an environment variable is created, it is stored in the RAM. Of course, when you shut down your computer, the environment variable goes away. When you restart your computer, you will need to reexecute the command to reestablish the variable. To avoid doing this every time you need to use your computer, if you are using the bash or Bourne shell, you could place the definition in your .profile file (located in your home directory). This way, every time you log in, the commands will automatically be executed. The common shell environment variables are shown in table 23.11 and figure 23.7.

A common environment variable that you use is the PATH variable. For example, if you type a command that isn't one of that shell's built-in commands, the shell has to locate an executable file (whose name matches the command that you type). The shell needs to know which directories to search for those files. The environment variable named PATH specifies which directory that will be searched. An example of the PATH environment variable would be:

PATH=/usr/local/bin:/bin:/usr/bin:.:/user/X11R6/bin

The string to the right of the equal sign is the value of the PATH environment variable. By convention, the PATH environment variable is a sequence of directory names, each name separated from the preceding one by a colon (:). The period in the list of directories also denotes a directory; it represents the current directory. If you type in the command PAT, since PAT is not an internal Linux command, Linux

Figure 23.7 Example Environment Variables

```
BASH=/bin/bash

COLORTERM=gnome-terminal

HISTFILE=/root/.bash_history

HISTFILESIZE=1000

HISTSIZE=1000

HOME=/root

HOSTNAME=Pat-home.pacbell.net

HOSTTYPE=i386

LANG=en_US

LOGNAME=root

MACHTYPE=i386-redhat-linux-gnu

MAIL=/var/spool/mail/root

OSTYPE=linux-gnu

PATH=/usr/local/sbin:/usr/sbin:/sbin:/usr/local/sbin:/usr/local/bin:/sbin:/bin:
/usr/sbin:/usr/bin:/usr/X11R6/bin:/root/bin

PROMPT_COMMAND='echo -ne "\033]0;${USER}@${HOSTNAME}: ${PWD}\007"'

PS1='[\u@\h \W]\$ '
PWD=/root

SHELL=/bin/bash

TERM=xterm

UID=0

USERNAME=root
```

will then search each of these directories for an executable file called PAT in order of their appearance. If there are two executable PAT files, the shell executes the one that it finds first.

To change the PATH, you would type the following commands:

```
PATH=/usr/local/bin:/bin:/usr/bin:.:/user/X11R6/bin:/etc/rc.d/
init.d; export path
```

To add a directory to the current path, you would then use the $PATH. Therefore, to add the /opt/bin, you would type the following command:

```
PATH=$PATH:/opt/bin;export path
```

Table 23.12 Prompt (PS1) Environment Variable

Code	What Appears in Prompt
\t	Current time in HH:MM:SS format
\d	Date in "Weekday Month Date" format such as Sat Mar 17
\n	Newline
\s	Name of the shell, such as bash
\w	Full name of the current working directory, such as /usr/src/linux
\W	Base name of the current working directory, such as linux for /usr/src/linux
\u	User name of the current user
\h	Host name
#	Command number of this command
\!	History number of this command
\$	$ if the effective user ID is 0 (indicating the user is root; otherwise a $)
\nnn	Character corresponding to the octal number nnn
\\	A backslash
\[	Begins a sequence of nonprinting characters, which could be used to embed a terminal control sequence into the prompt
\]	Ends a sequence of nonprinting characters

You can display the current directory in the shell prompt. The bash shell uses the value of the environment variable PS1 as the primary prompt. Another variable, PS2, functions as the secondary prompt when a command requires further input from the user. You can view these variables with the echo command. For example, type

```
echo $PS1
```

to view the setting of PS1. By default, the PS1 variable is defined in the Red Hat Linux as follows:

```
PS1=[\u@\h \W]\$
```

With this setting for PS1, the prompt looks like:

```
[username@hostname dirname]$
```

In this example, username is the name of the user; hostname is the system's name; and dirname is the last part of the current working directory. Thus, if the current directory is /usr/src/linux, the dirname is linux. You can use the following character sequences in the PS1 environment variable to customize your prompt. See table 23.12.

23.10 USING UNAME

The uname program can be used to show system details. For example, if you type *uname,* the -v command will display the Linux kernel version. The uname -s -r command will get the operating system's name and release. To get all information, use the -a argument. See table 23.13.

Table 23.13 Uname Options

Option for Uname	Description
-m	Prints the machine hardware type (such as i686 for Pentium Pro and better architecture)
-n	Prints the machine's host name
-r	Prints the operating system's release name
-s	Prints the operating system's name
-v	Prints the operating system's version
-a	Prints all of the above

23.11 TEXT EDITORS

A text file is a file that holds text. It is often used as a synonym for ASCII file, a file in which characters are represented by their ASCII codes. A text file does not include formatting such as margins, text styles (boldface, italics, and underline), fonts, pictures, and lines.

A text editor is a program that enables you to create and edit text files. It enables you to insert, delete, move, and search text. There are many different types of editors, but they all fall into two general categories:

- **Line Editor**—Primitive form of edit that requires you to specify a specific line of text before you can make changes to it.
- **Screen-Oriented Editors**—Also known as a full-screen editors, these editors enable you to modify any text that appears on the display screen by moving the cursor to the desired location.

Text editors are different from word processors because word processors add formatting and soft returns to documents. Soft returns are inserted automatically by the word processor when a word will not fit at the end of the line. In other words, soft returns allows word wrap to occur.

To be able to optimize, configure, and troubleshoot Linux, a text editor is one of the most important tools to learn. With an editor, you can create and modify text files that have a wide variety of applications:

- User configuration files such as .login
- System files
- Shell programs
- Documents
- Mail messages

Linux includes several editors and many others can be added to Linux. Vi is the most popular text-based text editor.

To start the vi editor, you would type the following command

```
vi filename
```

where *filename* is the name of the file that you want to edit. Vi automatically sets aside a temporary buffer as a working space for use during this editing session. If the file you specify when calling vi does not already exist in your current working directory, a new file will be created with the name that you have specified. For example, if you wanted to create a new file called testfile, you would type:

```
vi testfile
```

When the vi editor creates a new file, the cursor will be placed on the screen in the home position (upper left-hand corner). The cursor on most terminals is a rectangle that completely covers the character space it is situated upon and reflects your current position within the buffer. Below the cursor along the left side of the screen, is a tilde (~) character positioned in the first character space on each line. The

Figure 23.8 Starting Vi Editor to Create a New File

tilde is used to indicate a void area in the file where there are no characters, not even blank spaces. At the bottom of the screen, the editor displays a file information line that presents the name of the file being edited, in this case testfile, followed by "[New file]" to indicate that this is a new file and it has never been opened before. (See figure 23.8.)

The vi editor allows a user to modify and add material to an already existing file. This is done by using the name of a current file when calling vi. Vi will then fetch a copy of the contents of the specified file from disk storage, leaving the original undisturbed, and place the copy into the buffer. It is here, in the buffer, where vi permits you to do your editing. The idea of editing in the buffer is very beneficial, because if you really botch up your editing job (such as deleting a major section) the original file on the disk remains unaffected.

Upon opening a file, vi will display the first screenful of text starting at the top of the file, place the cursor in the home position, and print the file information line which displays the name of the file along with the number of lines and characters it contains on the last line of the screen. For example, to edit the file, named sample which has 7 lines and 169 characters, you would use the following command:

```
vi sample
```

See figure 23.9.

When you start vi, the cursor sits in the home position, overlaying the first character of the file. When the cursor is moved, this character will be exposed, unchanged. In general, most terminal screens will display only 20 to 24 lines of text. If a file has more text than will fit on one screen, the unviewed material remains in the buffer until needed.

Vi has two modes, an insert mode and a command mode. Insert mode is used when you want to insert text to the screen. When you are in insert mode, all you can do is to insert text, and to rewrite over text using the Backspace key. Command mode is used for issuing special commands to vi. When using command mode, you cannot insert text. However, you can search for a specific string, substitute certain words for other words, quit vi, save the text to a file, and so on.

As mentioned before, when the vi editor is invoked a temporary working area is created called a buffer. This buffer or work space is available for your use only while you are using the editor. It is into this buffer that vi either places a duplicate copy of the file as it exists on the disk or creates a new file. When you exit the editor, this work area is discarded. To avoid losing all of your work, you will have to save the file before exiting vi. Therefore, you should periodically save the file in case something unexpected happens.

To save the file, you need to execute the write command. This is done by typing:

```
:w
```

Figure 23.9 Opening a File with Vi

```
This is some sample text 1.

This is some sample text 2.

This is some sample text 3.

This is some sample text 4.

This is some sample text 5.

This is some sample text 6.


~

~

~

"sample" 7L, 169C
```

As soon as you type the colon (:), vi switches to command mode. The cursor jumps to the bottom of the screen where the :w command is echoed. Then a copy of all material in the buffer is transported to the disk, overwriting the previous contents of the disk file. When you have finished editing, you need to tell vi that you wish to quit the editor and return to the shell. This is done by typing:

```
:q
```

Vi will respond by updating the file information line with the name of your file in quotes followed by the current number of lines and characters. After exiting the editor, the Linux prompt will again appear on the screen.

Vi requires that the buffer be empty of newly edited material when you type *:q.* Thus if you have made any alterations to the file since the last time you typed *:w,* vi will not know how you want these changes handled. The editor will print the statement

```
No write since last change (:quit! overrides)
```

at the bottom of the screen. If you decide you want to retain these changes, you must type *:w* before issuing a new *:q* command. Most experienced users get in the habit of combining these two commands into a single command :wq (write and quit).

Sometimes when working on a file, it is desirable to leave the editor without saving the modifications. This is accomplished by typing:

```
:q!
```

Again, the colon (:) switches into command mode. The exclamation mark (!) means force. In short, you force vi to quit without saving the changes made to the file.

You might use this command if you started to edit a file and do not like the way the changes are shaping up. When you use this command, vi will immediately discard all alterations made to the file since the last :w. If you have not used a :w since opening the file, all changes since the beginning of the editing session will be abandoned.

NOTE: When you use the :quit! command, the editor believes you know what you are doing and will immediately follow your instructions. You will not have a second chance to retrieve your work once the buffer is closed, the file is discarded, and your changes are lost.

There may be a time when you are editing a file and cannot decide if you want to keep the original disk file and the new edited file that you are currently working on. You can then write the file to a different file name:

```
:w newfilename
```

Command mode is the initial state encountered when vi is started. It should be mentioned that when vi receives instructions on what action is required, the majority of the vi commands are not echoed on the screen. Instead, it simply executes the response the command requires. In general, the steps given below will be repeated again and again during each editing session while in command mode:

1. place text in terminal window
2. position the cursor
3. give editing command

After a short time of using the editor, these actions will become second nature to you and performance of them will be done without concentration.

To add or insert text into the text file, you must change to insert text mode. The easiest way to change to insert text mode is to press the Insert key or press the I key. When you do this, the bottom of the screen will display -- INSERT --. See figure 23.10. When -- INSERT -- is displayed, when you type the text will be inserted at the cursor that you are at. If you press the Insert key again, -- INSERT -- will be replaced with -- REPLACE -- and when you type it will overwrite the text. To go back to -- INSERT --, press the Insert key again. To leave insert mode, you would press the Esc key.

There are several ways to insert text other than the I command. The a (short for *append*) command inserts text beginning after the current cursor position, instead of at the current cursor position. The A command will insert the text at the end of the current line. To begin inserting text at the next line, use the o command (short for *open*).

The most obvious way to move around the file is by using the arrow key or by using the following commands:

h—move left one character
j—move down one character
k—move up one character
l—move right one character

Figure 23.10 Changing to Insert Text Mode

```
This is some sample text 1.

This is some sample text 2.

This is some sample text 3.

This is some sample text 4.

This is some sample text 5.

This is some sample text 6.

_

~

~

~

-- INSERT --
```

After using these three commands for a while, you may decide to become more precise in moving the cursor by adding a number to these command. For example, 3H would move the cursor to the third line from the top of the screen. The command 3L would likewise move the cursor to the third line from the bottom of the screen.

Yet, there are certain commands that you can issue to move around quicker. When giving the command Ctrl + d the terminal window moves downward toward the end of the file. The command Ctrl + u moves the terminal window upward toward the first line of the file. Thus, the window is pushed up or down revealing new text that either precedes or follows the current screen.

Scrolling through one screen after another in order to reach the portion of the text you want to look at can, at times, be laborious as well as boring. Sometimes it is easier to move the screen window directly to the location you are interested in viewing. If you know the line number or the general area you want to access, repositioning can be accomplished by using the G (for *goto*) command. The goto command, preceded by a line number, such as 250G, will position the cursor on the first character space of line number 250. If the requested line is not currently on the screen, the screen will be redrawn with the requested line situated in the window.

Typing *1G* will move the cursor to the first line of the file and redraw the screen if necessary. Not specifying a line number when typing *G* will move the cursor to the last line in the file. It is handy to be able to pop to the beginning or end of a file, so G and 1G are important commands to remember.

Discovering your current line number and overall file size information can be gotten by pressing Ctrl + g. The editor will then print the file name, the line number, the number of lines in the file, and the percentage of the way through the file all at the bottom of the screen. The line might look like this:

```
"filename" line 17 of 122 -- 13%
```

Generally, new users find the G command easier to use if all lines are numbered.

Another method to move within the file is by identifying a word, phrase, or string of characters for the editor to locate. To institute a search, you type a forward slash mark (/) followed by a string of characters, terminated by using the Enter key. The cursor will hop to the bottom of the screen where the search command will be echoed. For example, if you wanted to find the word *test* in your file, you would type:

```
/test
```

The editor will hunt downward from your current position in the file for this pattern and will then place the cursor on the first letter of next occurrence of *test*. If this is not the *test* you are seeking, type *n* (for *next*), and the editor will continue the search downward. The n command may be repeated as often as necessary to find the character string sought. If the pattern you have instructed vi to search for is not found throughout the entire file, the editor will respond at the bottom of the screen with:

```
Pattern not found
```

Remember, the editor will look per your instructions for an exact duplicate of the character string you have given it. If the editor does not locate your pattern, first check to see if you have mistyped the pattern you requested the editor to find. Note that spaces or absence of spaces can be important. If this is not the case, give thought to the possibility that the object in the file you are searching for is misspelled. In that case, try the pattern search again but using only a portion of the word.

To change a word in a document to another word (search and replace), use the following command:

```
%s/change_this_word/to_this_word/g
```

For example, to change the word *test* to *practice* through the entire document, type

```
%s/test/practice/g
```

Of course, the easiest way to delete characters is by using the Delete key or the Backspace key. You can also delete one character at a time by moving the cursor to a character and pressing the x key. To deleted a line, move the cursor to anywhere on the line and press *dd*. To delete several lines just specify the number before dd. For example, 4dd will delete four lines. To delete a word, place the cursor at the beginning of the word and use the dw (for *delete word*) command.

To copy an area of text and to paste it in another location, simply move the cursor over to the line you wish to copy and press yy to yank the line of text to the clipboard. Now there are two ways to paste text. After moving to the location that you want to paste the text, pressing p will paste the text right of the cursor, and pressing P will paste to the left of the cursor. To highlight the text that you want to cut or copy, press the v key to change it to — VISUAL — mode, move the cursor to highlight the text that you want, and use the x key to cut or the y key to copy. Then use the p or P key to paste.

The dot (.) operator repeats the last thing you did. If you just press the "." without specifying a number, it will repeat what you just did. To repeat a line, type in a line and press the Enter key to add a new line. Then type the following command:

```
#_of_lines.
```

Therefore, to repeat a line 50 times, type:

```
50.
```

See table 23.14 for commonly used vi commands.

Table 23.14 Vi Commands

Moving the Cursor		**Creating Text**	
Move to the left one character	h	Append text after cursor	a
Move down one line	j	Append text after end of line	A
Move up one line	k	Insert text before cursor	i
Move to the right one character	l	Insert text at beginning of line	I
Moving by Line		Open new line after current line	o
Beginning of current line	0 or ^	Open new line before current line	O
Beginning of first screen line	H	Read file in after specified line	:r *filename*
Beginning of last screen line	L	**Modifying Text**	
Beginning of middle screen line	M	Change current word	cw, cW
End of current line	$	Change current line (cursor to end)	C
Left to beginning of word	b, B	Delete character (cursor forward)	x
Right to end of word	e, E	Delete character (before cursor)	X
Right to beginning of word	w, W	Delete word	dw, dW
Beginning of next sentence	)	Delete line	dd
Beginning of previous sentence	(	Delete text to end of line	D
Paging Through Text		Join current line with next line	J
Back one screen	{ctrl-b}	Repeat last modification command	.
Down half a screen	{ctrl-d}	Replace current character	r
Down one screen	{ctrl-f}	Replace text to end of line	R
Forward to end of file	G	Substitute text for character	s
Move cursor to specified line	*line no.* G	Undo your previous command	u
Up half a screen	{ctrl-j}	Transpose characters	xp
Ending and Saving Your Editing Sessions		**Controlling the Screen Display of Your Session**	
Write changes to original file	:w	Repaint the current screen	{ctrl-l}
Write to specified file	:w *filename*	Display line #, # of lines, etc.	{ctrl-g}
Force write to a file	:w! *filename*	**Cut and Copy Commands**	
Quit (no changes made)	:q	Yank (copy) word into buffer	yw
Quit and save changes	ZZ, :wq	Yank (copy) current line into buffer	yy or Y
Quit and discard changes	:q!	Yank (copy) *n* lines	*n*yy or *n*Y
Searching Through Text		Put buffer text after cursor	p
Backward for pattern	?*pattern*	Put buffer text before cursor	P
Forward for pattern	/*pattern*	**Making Corrections During Text Insertions**	
Repeat previous search	n	Overwrite last character	delete
Reverse direction of previous search	N	Overwrite last word	ctrl-w

Continued

Table 23.14 Continued

Some Useful ex Commands for Use in vi	
:set all	Display all Set options
:set autoindent	Automatically indent following lines to the indentation of previous line
:set ignorecase	Ignore case during pattern matching
:set list	Show special characters in the file
:set number	Display line numbers
:set nonu	Disable display of line numbers
:set shiftwidth=n	Width for shifting operators <>
:set showmode	Display mode when in insert, append, or replace mode
:set wrapmargin=n	Set right margin 80-n for autowrapping lines (inserting new lines); 0 turns it off

23.12 INTRODUCTION TO THE X WINDOW SYSTEM

The X Window System, sometimes referred to as X, provides the graphical interface for Linux. It is a portable, network-transparent window system that runs on many different computers. A desktop environment sits on top of X, which provides the user interface and helps integrate applications. Most distributions of Linux include GNOME or KDE desktops. Combined, X Window and desktop environments provide a fully functional GUI interface.

There have been numerous versions of the X Window System, but it was not until the 11th version, known simply as "X11," that it was widely released and began to gain the popularity it enjoys today. Since then there have been many further releases, which added extra functionality while attempting to remain largely backward compatible. The current release is the sixth one, and is known as X11R6, or simply as R6.

The guiding philosophies of the X Window System (and also UNIX itself) is that its functionality is achieved through the cooperation of separate components, rather than everything being entwined in one huge mass (some people may refer to one huge mess). The advantage of this is that a particular part of the system can be changed simply by replacing the relevant component. The best example of this is the concept of a window manager, which is essentially the component that controls the appearance of windows and provides the means by which the user can interact with them. Virtually everything that appears on the screen in X is in a window, and a window manager simply manages them.

The X Window System can be divided into three main parts:

- X server
- Set of graphics libraries called widgets
- X clients that use the widgets

The **X server** is the component of the X Window System that you run on your desktop. It is responsible for drawing images on the screen, getting input from the keyboard and mouse, and controlling access to the display. The X Window applications, also referred to as clients or X clients, have a set of graphics libraries incorporated into the application. There are X clients for word processors, spreadsheets, games, and more. Most command-line utilities, including many system administration utilities, come in an X client version. When the application needs to send something to the display, it calls up a library routine and if necessary communicates with the X server using the X protocol.

A **window manager** is special type of X client. It is the piece of software responsible for managing the different windows that appear on the screen. The window manager controls the placement of windows, draws the borders and scroll bars, and is responsible for ensuring that the X Window programs get along. It receives commands indirectly from the user through mouse clicks and key presses. The window manager passes those commands to the set of graphics libraries. The graphics libraries then communicate with the server to manipulate windows on the graphics device, which is usually the screen, allowing you to launch applications. Because it is the main interface between the

X Window System and the user, it controls much of the look and feel of your X Window desktop. Window managers may also maintain an icon bar, which keeps icons easier to find and manage, as well as performs other functions. It even allows the user to customize the windows environment.

Since people use computers in different ways for different tasks, X Window allows you to vary the interface that you use by providing a large number of window managers that provide a large range of different appearances and behaviors. Furthermore, most of these window managers can be heavily customized. This means that when using X, you first have a choice of which window manager to use and then a choice of the precise configuration of the chosen window manager. Fvwm95 was used in early Red Hat Linux, which gave a look and feel similar to Windows 95. Sawfish is the default window manager for GNOME desktop and kwm, used in K Windows Manager. Enlightenment is another popular version, used primarily by the GNOME desktop.

At the following website, you will find descriptions, screenshots, configuration files, and links to several popular window managers:

http://xwinman.org/

The **display manager** configures an environment and sets up a graphical login screen. Examples of display manager are xdm (the original X display manager, gdm (the GNOME display manager), or kdm (the KDE display manager). Gdm is a reimplementation of xdm with some extra features. GNOME also provides a face browser if desired which allows you to select a picture of yourself from a list rather than type in your user name. The photo is stored in *~user/*.GNOME/photo, where *~user* is your home directory. The kdm display manager provides most of the same features as gdm. It has the added benefit of allowing you to choose what window manager you want to use at login time, which is nice if you switch window managers a lot.

The third component in the X11 system is the widgets. These library routines build and form the components within a window such as scroll bars, menu bars, taskbars, popup menus, requester boxes, and so on. Example widget libraries include LessTIF (an open source version of the commercial library called MoTif), GTK+ (a GPL library begun by the GNU image manipulation program), and the Qt library (free to individuals but proprietary to commercial users).

When people refer to GNOME programs, in reality, a GNOME program uses the GTK+ library. Likewise, KDE programs are written to use the Qt library. It is usually possible to use a Qt program within GNOME or a GTK+ program in KDE as long as you have the appropriate libraries installed. Because certain programs require additional parts of a competing environment to be installed, not all programs will work in environments other than what is intended.

On top of the windows manager, you have integrated **desktop environments,** which provide a consistent set of interface widgets (buttons, scroll bars, menus, etc.) and a set of interoperable clients for editing documents, reading email, web surfing, and other common tasks. Application developers work with a standardized **application programming interface (API).** As discussed in earlier chapters, an API is a set of consistent, reliable software libraries that interface their application with the user, the operating system, and other applications running on the desktop. Currently, the most common desktop environments are KDE (most widely used) and GNOME (pronounced "Gah-NOME"). GNOME is the default environment for Red Hat and Debian distributions, but is not quite as popular as KDE.

The desktop environments use a concept of a desktop, which is a screen that is organized much like your desk. You use icons to represent the documents and programs and folders to store your programs and documents. The root window, which really isn't a window, is the background of your screen or desktop.

Applications run within a window placed on top of the root window. A window is a frame in which any given application resides which is managed by the window manager. The **focused window,** or active window, is the window you are currently using, that will receive text when you type. (See figure 23.11.) Most of these windows have menus that behave much like any other windows system.

Figure 23.11 Focused window is the current active window, which in this case is the Kate text editor.

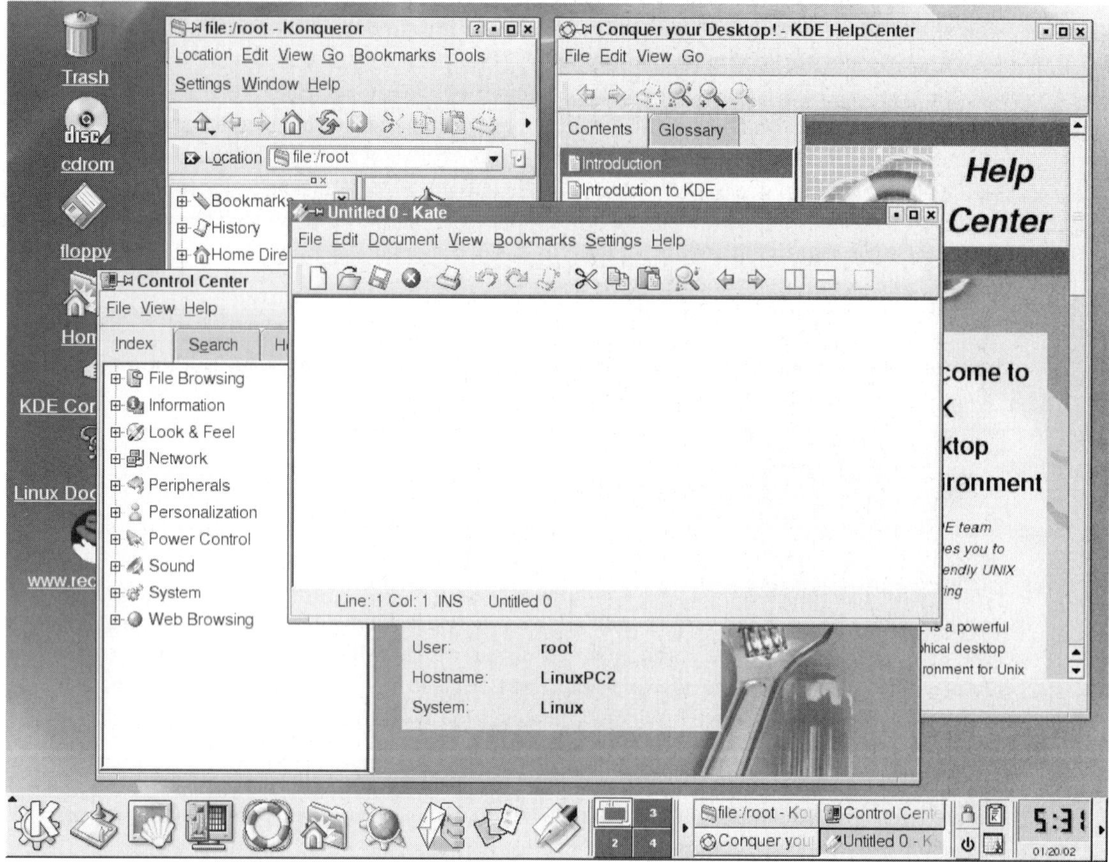

To effectively use any windows system, you need to use a pointing device such as a mouse or trackball. The mouse pointer represents the location your mouse corresponds to on the screen. Most systems will use an arrow, but the mouse can be changed. Depending on what the mouse is pointing to, when you move onto an object, it will give you contextual feedback (text that will appear when you click the mouse at that point on the screen).

As much as KDE and GNOME are different, there are many similarities between the two:

- **Desktop Panel**—The desktop panel provides quick access to applications by providing the main menu/application starter and panel buttons to start your favorite applications. You can also swallow applications, which means that what looks like a button can actually be a running application.
- **Taskbar**—The Taskbar shows all the currently available windows, which allows you to quickly switch between applications, even if they're minimized.
- **Pager**—A pager allows you to maintain several virtual desktops and easily switch between them. Each virtual desktop can have several programs running.
- **Files Directly on the Desktop**—You can drag files to the desktop and store them there as icons. Applications can be automatically launched by links placed on the desktop as well.
- **Session Management**—Session management means that applications can remember the state they were in when you logged out and restart the application in exactly the same state when you log back in. For example, you can log out and log in and continue in the same place that you were working on before.

Many modern window environments give you the options to select themes. A theme allows you to define the look and feel of the window manager in a central, consistent way. For example, if you like *Star Trek,* you could load the *Star Trek* theme which would change the background, colors, mouse pointer, and other facets of your GUI interface to something that describes or is part of *Star Trek.* As themes have become more popular, many themes are now available.

23.13 DESKTOP COMPONENTS

Of the common X Window environments (including GNOME and KDE) that are used with Linux, you will find that most of them have a lot in common. As mentioned before, the environment desktop includes:

- The desktop itself, on which shortcuts, frequently used files, and frequently used folders may be placed. This is the area in which the programs will run.
- A panel at the bottom of the screen, used to start applications and to switch between virtual desktops.
- The Taskbar displays a list of all programs currently running on the system in a window. It is used to quickly change from one window to another.

There are several ways to start a program. The easiest ways are to click on the Main Menu button and select the program from the menu or to click on a launcher (a shortcut button) on the Panel. If you have a folder to open, icon on the desktop or an icon in a folder that starts a program, you just have to click with the right mouse button if you are using KDE or double-click with the right mouse button if you are using GNOME on the associated icon and select the appropriate option.

The left mouse button is typically used to select an item to open or drag to another location. To drag the item, hold down the mouse button, and continue holding it down while dragging to the new location. Once at the desired location, release the mouse button to "drop" the item.

Using the right mouse button reveals a context menu, sometimes referred to as a shortcut menu (similar to Microsoft Windows). It is a context menu because the menu will vary depending on what item you right-click on. For example, if you right-click on the desktop, a menu will appear that allows you to create shortcuts on the desktop to an application, visit websites, or open documents. You can also rescan (redraw) or unclutter the desktop and to find a link to helpful documentation on using the desktop itself. If you right-click a file or folder, a different menu will appear that allows you to choose a program to open the file, to copy or delete the file, or to bring up the properties (including renaming) of the file or folder. If you are in a word processor, if you highlight some text and right-click the highlighted text, the menu will allow you to cut or copy the text or to format the text.

23.13.1 The Panel

The Panel, typically found at the bottom of the screen, is the heart of the user interface. It includes:

- The Main Menu button
- A tasklist of running applications
- Launchers that are buttons to launch frequently used applications or commands
- Virtual desktops

For the GNOME environment (see figures 23.12 and 23.14), the GNOME Main Menu button is the large button with a footprint on it. In the KDE environment (see figures 23.13 and 23.15), the KDE Main Menu button is the large button with a *K* on it. These menus provide access to almost all KDE or GNOME features including all the applications, configuration tools, command-line prompts, Logout Screens, Lock Screens, and much more. Both buttons are *located to the left of the Panel.* If you look at these buttons, you will notice a small arrow on the top to indicate that they will pop up a menu if you click on them. To start a program, you just have to click on the submenu item (see figure 23.16).

The primary component of the Main menu in each environment is the Programs submenu, which contains a list of preconfigured submenus and menu items including games, text editors, word processors, spreadsheets, Netscape Web Browser, File Manager, and a Help system.

On the Main menus, you will also find a Logout option, a Lock option, and a Run option. The Lock option begins the screen saver, which locks the screen. In order to remove the screen saver and access the GNOME session again, you must supply your password. The Logout button is used to exit the desktop environment. If you leave your computer in an insecure environment, you should lock the computer so that it cannot be used with your login credentials. In addition, you should have your screen saver

Figure 23.12 GNOME Desktop

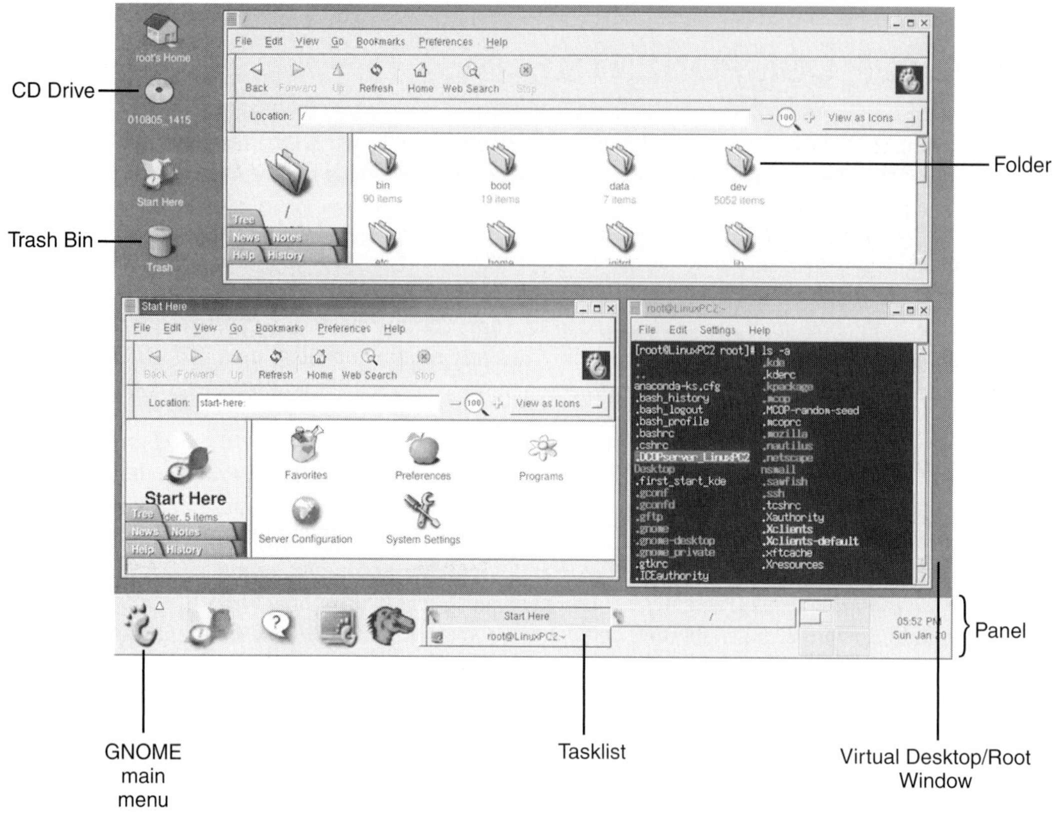

Figure 23.13 KDE Desktop

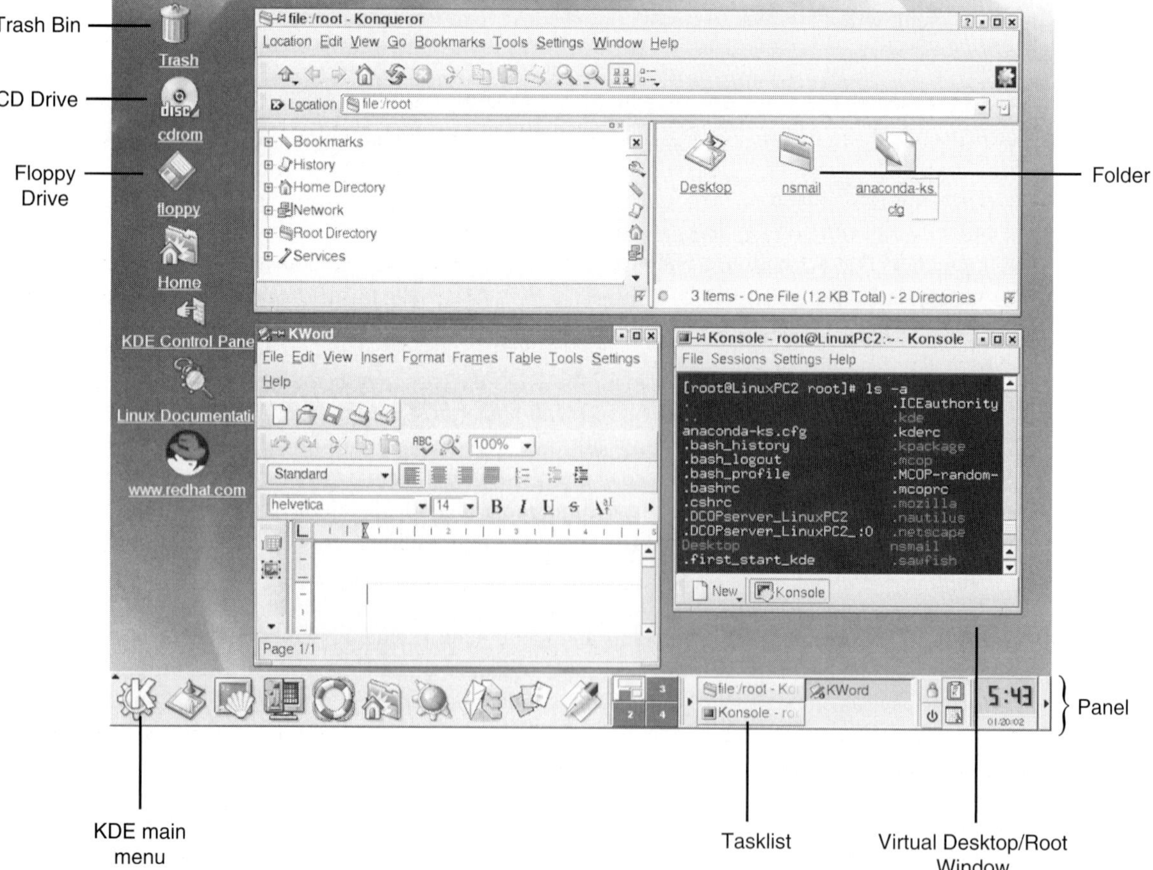

Figure 23.14 Sample GNOME Panel

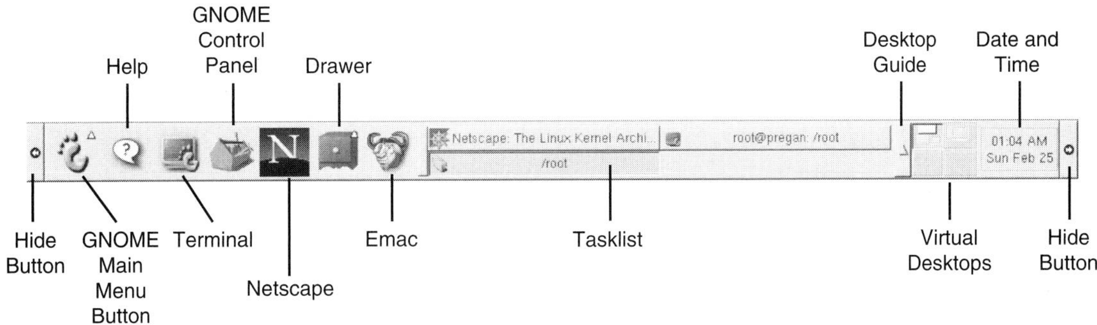

Figure 23.15 Sample KDE Panel

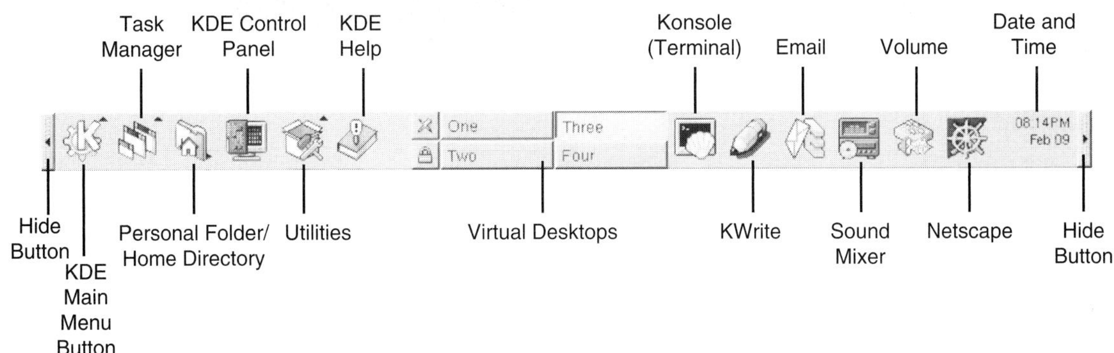

activate within 5 or 10 minutes with a required password so that if you leave your desk, the screen saver that requires a password will start so that it protects your computer.

The Run button opens the Run Program dialog box. This gives you access to the command-line prompt. It is only a partial shell, so it is not a replacement for GNOME terminal, but it is very convenient when you need to enter just one command quickly. You can also open the Run Program dialog box by using a keyboard short. (See figure 23.17.) The default keyboard shortcut is Alt + F2.

The command entry has a history buffer, which allows you to execute a previously entered command by pressing the down arrow button located at the right of the text field and selecting the command. It also has a Browse button, which allows you to choose a file; this file name will be appended to the end of your command. For example, you can enter *emacs* on the command line and then use the Browse button to select the file to be edited.

Launchers are essentially buttons that reside in your Panel and start an application or execute a command when clicked. A launcher can use any icon and has a customized **tooltip** to display a message indicating what the program does when the cursor is passed over the launcher.

You can change a launcher's properties, such as the icon it uses and its name, by right-clicking on the launcher and selecting Properties from the popup menu. In addition, GNOME and KDE do not make any distinction between menu items and launchers. These are just different presentations of the same thing. You can place any menu item on the panel, and it will show as a launcher.

To set the tooltip for a button, right-click the button and choose Properties from the menu. Click the Application tab, and type text for the tooltip in the Command field (KDE) or the Comment field (GNOME).

NOTE: In the KDE environment, you may need to restart the Panel for the changes to take effect. To restart the Panel, right-click the Panel and choose Restart.

The Panel was designed to be highly configurable. You can easily customize its behavior and appearance and add or remove objects to suit your personal needs and preferences. Both KDE and

Figure 23.16 GNOME and KDE Main Menus

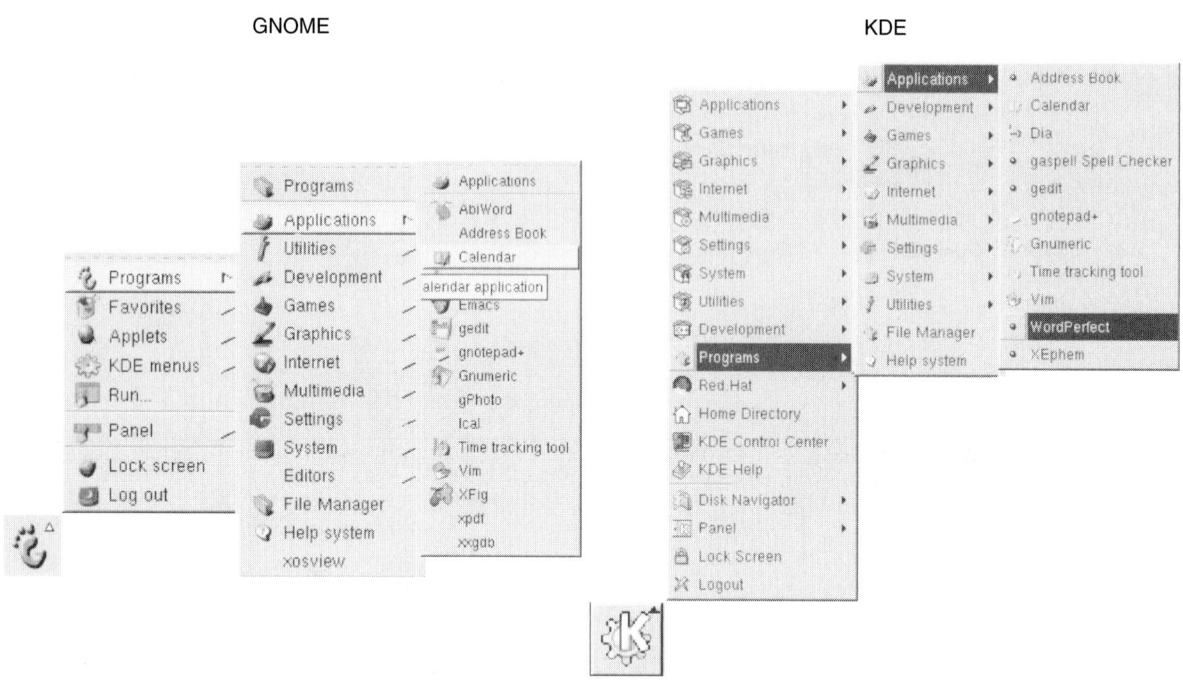

Figure 23.17 The Run Program Dialog Box

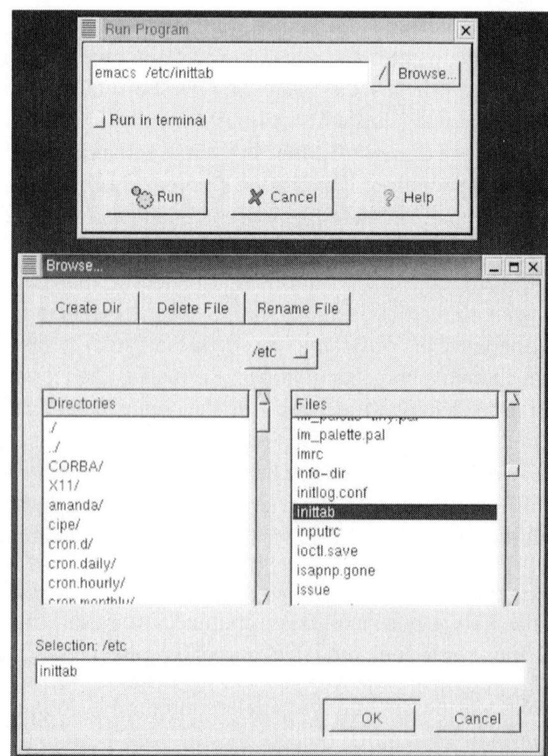

GNOME can be customized; you can add and remove applications and applets to the Panel by using one of the following methods:

- To place a Windowlist button (used to change between applications) in KDE, click on the application starter, point to? Panel, and select Add Windowlist. To place a Tasklist in GNOME, click on the Main Menu button, point to? Panel, select the Add to Panel option, select the Applet option, select the Utility option, and then select Tasklist.
- To place an application from the application starter onto the Panel, click on the application starter, select the Panel option, click the Add Application option, and continue through the menus to select the desired application. You can also place a submenu from the application starter directly on the panel using the same procedure.
- Drag-and-drop from the menu to the Panel.
- To place a .kdelnk file (a kde shortcut link file) or a folder containing a .kdelnk file onto the KDE Panel, drag it from a kfm window or the desktop to the Panel. Once you have placed an icon on the Panel, right-click the icon and choose Properties from the menu to set it up.

Note: When you place an icon on the Panel this way, be careful not to move or delete the original .kdelnk file or folder, or the Panel will be unable to display the icon.

The panel can also have applets. For example, the GNOME application may be represented by an applet to reveal the state of the applet or other information. Applets often have buttons, sliders, entries, or other methods to allow you to control their behavior. For example, you can have a Mixer applet that allows you to change the volume level and mute the sound.

GNOME also uses a Drawer, which is just a container to store things. Typically, you may use a Drawer to hold multiple launchers that are related to each other in some way, such as the various applications in GNOME Office. The Drawers in the GNOME Panel take this one step further by making a Drawer an actual extension of the Panel itself. Thus, a Drawer is a collapsible branch of an existing Panel. It can contain anything that a Panel can, including launchers, applets, and other Drawers.

To add a new empty Drawer, select the Add to Panel option, the select the Drawer option from the Panel menu. Once you have placed a Drawer on the Panel, you may click on it to "open" the Drawer, revealing its contents. You may then add items to the Drawer in the same way you would add items to the Panel, right-clicking on the end of the Drawer with the arrow. You can close the Drawer by clicking on its icon again or by clicking on the arrow at its end.

23.13.2 The Desktop

The desktop provides the functionality of any traditional operating system desktop. You can drag files, programs, and directory folders to the desktop. In addition, if a file type is associated with a program (Mime Type) and you double-click on the icon that represents the file, the application will automatically start and load that file. For example, if you have a JPEG graphics file and you double-click on it, it will either start a view program so that you can view the picture or start a paint program to edit the file. This would depend on which application is associated with JPEG files. You can also drag a file icon back into those applications, allowing quick access to those files.

If you right-click the desktop, the context menu will appear. If it is the GNOME desktop, you can create a new directory, file, or link; arrange or tidy icons (arrange icons to an invisible grid); rescan (redraw) the desktop directory; rescan (verify) devices; recreate default icons; configure background image; and view the desktop properties. If it is KDE, you can execute a command, display the desktop properties, refresh the desktop, unclutter (arrange icons to a grid) the windows, cascade windows, or arrange icons. You can also lock the screen and logout.

To access your home folder (usually /home/*user_name,* where *user_name* is the person's login name), both GNOME and KDE provide shortcuts. For GNOME, the shortcut is located on the desktop as an icon labeled Home directory. When you click on the icon, GNU Midnight Commander starts. For KDE, the shortcut is on the Panel identified with a house in front of a folder. When you open the home folder, the KDE file manager (KFM) starts. All items that are stored on the desktop are located in /home/*user_name*/.GNOME-desktop for GNOME desktops and /home/*user_name*/desktop for KDE.

When you access a floppy disk or CD-ROM, you must mount the disk to access these disks. Of course, you need permission to mount the device shown on your desktop before you can use these icons.

If you have a permission to mount a drive, you may right-click the drive icon on the desktop and select mount or unmount from the context menu. Once it is mounted you open the icon, and a file manager window will open, showing the contents of the disk.

NOTE: If you place a floppy diskette in the drive, then select the floppy drive on your desktop, you may receive an error message such as "wrong fs type, bad option, bad superblock on /dev/fd0 . . ." This is because the floppy you have placed in the drive is formatted with MS-DOS instead of the ext2 file system.

On the desktop, you will also find icons or shortcuts for removable disk drives including cdrom and floppy. GNOME uses symbolic links (symlinks) to represent the disk drives. If you right-click these shortcuts, you can mount and unmount disks; copy, move, or delete the symlink; edit the symlink; or view the properties. When you edit the symlink, you can change the location that the symlink points to. If you select Properties, on the Statistics tab you can see the file name of the symbolic link; the Options tab will allow you to change the icon. For the KDE desktop, KDE uses kdelnk shortcuts to link to the drives. If you right-click the shortcuts, you have options to copy, move to trash, or delete the shortcut; unmount the disk or eject the disk; or to bring up the properties of the shortcut. The General tab shows the name of the link, and the Device tab shows which device the icon is linked. It also shows which file system the disk is currently using and allows you to choose the icon to represent a mounted disk or an unmounted disk.

23.13.3 Virtual Desktops and Changing Between Programs

With the GNOME and KDE desktops, you can use multiple desktops so that you can keep a well-organized system when you have many tasks to perform at one time. Just like adding a new desk when you have too much material to fit on one, the desktop areas allow you to move to another area to launch more programs. The **Virtual Desktop** buttons represent completely different desktops, each displaying different windows.

If you have multiple windows running at the same time, there are several ways that you can use to change between these different programs. The easiest way is to click on the virtual desktop icon on the Panel window in the appropriate desktop. In addition, you can press the *middle mouse button* on the desktop and select the desktop that you want to move to.

There are several ways to change from one program to another. First, you can click on the program listed in the Taskbar or Tasklist, Windowlist, or Desktop Guide. Simply clicking with the left mouse button on the appropriate Taskbar button will bring you to the selected application immediately.

23.13.4 Working with Windows

When an application window is displayed, there will be some buttons in its borders for controlling the window. Their appearance can be configured and controlled by the window manager.

The title bar is the horizontal bar at the top of a window that contains the name of the window. Because you can have multiple windows open at the same time, you can toggle between these windows. The program that you are currently using is known as the focused window or active window, which is the window that will receive input from the keyboard at that time. If the window is not active, it is inactive. The inactive window continues to work in the background; it just does not get the input from the keyboard. Typically, the active window's title bar will be one color (the default is blue) and the inactive window's title bar will be another color (the default is gray).

In the upper left corner, you will see the Menu button. If you click on this button, you will open the window Operations menu. From this menu, you can maximize, iconify (minimize), move within the current desktop, move to another desktop, or close (delete) the window.

On the right side of the title bar, you will find the Iconify button, the Maximize button, and the Close button. The Iconify button is used to minimize the program. To open a minimized program, click on the program on the Taskbar or Tasklist or Windowlist or by pressing Alt + Tab to toggle to the program. To maximize the window to fill the entire screen, click the Maximize button. If a window is already maximized, you can shrink the window back to its original size by clicking on the Maximize button a second time.

Another way to manipulate the window size is to double-click the title bar. Although this solution may appear to be handy, be aware that it has its problems as well. For example, you may have made

Netscape full screen, but a requestor or dialog box pops up and is waiting for your input. If the window title bar has been double-clicked and is on top, the requestor or dialog box will be hidden under the Netscape window. Thus, the system will appear to be locked up; however, the real problem is simply that a hidden requestor or dialog box generated by the program is waiting for the OK button to be clicked. Double-clicking the title bar again will allow the other windows to appear.

Each window manager employs a widget set that provides common controls within a window, such as scrolling. Most X11 scroll bars work as expected. However, the default X Window scroll bar widget is found in older X11 applications, and it is unusual compared to other GUIs. Moving the mouse cursor along the scroll bar creates a double arrow cursor. Regardless of where the cursor is located in the scroll bar (top or bottom), clicking on the left mouse button scrolls the window down and clicking on the right mouse button scrolls the window up. Moving the cursor from the top toward the bottom of the scroll bar results in large "chunks" of scrolling either up or down with each mouse click.

One of the advantages of using windows is that a window can be resized and moved to accommodate a user's needs. (See figure 23.18.) To move a window, you can drag the window's title bar or hold down the Alt key and drag anywhere in the window. To resize a window, drag the window's border.

Using the Menu button (see figure 23.19), or a picture of a tack next to the Menu button in the KDE environment, you can make an application sticky or nonsticky. When you click on the button (sticky), you make that window appear in all virtual desktops. When you make a window unsticky, it will appear only in a single desktop. If you want to move an application to another desktop, you can make it sticky, move to the desired desktop that you want it to appear in, and then make it nonsticky.

Figure 23.18 GNOME and KDE Windows

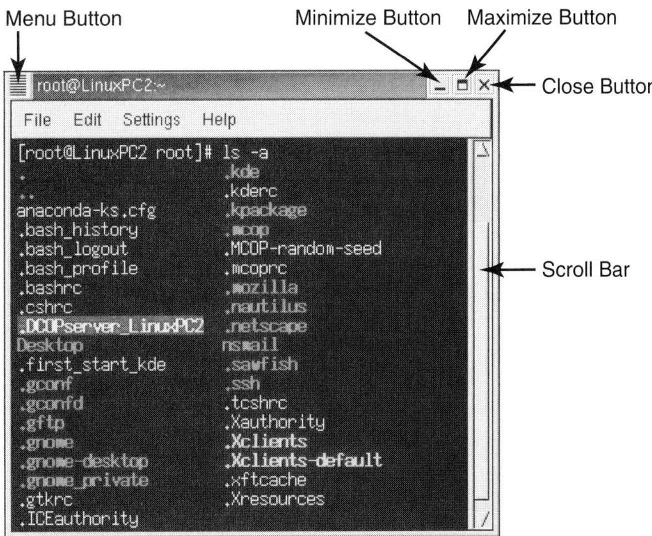

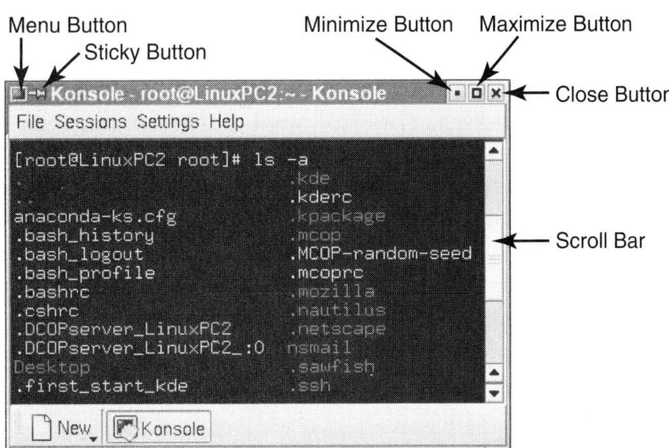

Figure 23.19 The KDE Menu Button

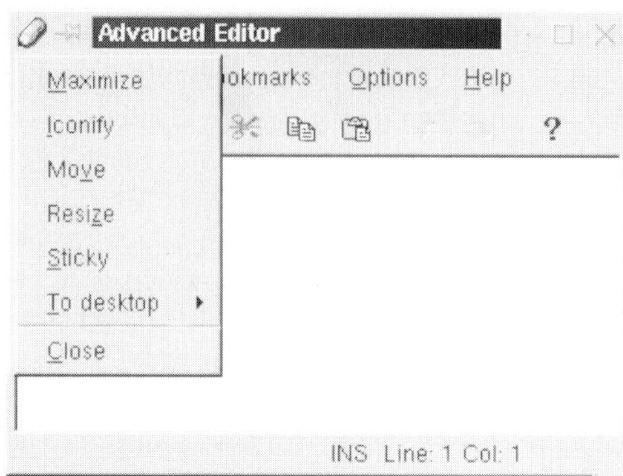

23.13.5 Cut, Copy, and Paste

Unlike Microsoft Windows, the X Window System does not have a fully evolved clipboard with edit commands such as Undo, Cut, Clear, and Select All. There is, however, a minimal copy and paste mechanism.

To copy, drag the cursor over the desired text. Move the focus to the destination window and position the program cursor (not the mouse cursor) to the desired position for insertion, and click the *middle mouse button* to paste the highlighted text.

NOTE: This only works between the highlight operation and the next paste mouse click. If the left mouse button is used to highlight other text, even in another window, then the previously highlighted text is forgotten.

If the mouse has only two buttons and three-button emulation has been enabled, then click both mouse buttons before releasing either one to emulate the third mouse button. The copy and paste operations generally work among X Window applications. However, large applications such as Star Office may not support the importing and exporting of the X Window copy and paste operations.

23.14 DIRECTORY AND FILE MANAGEMENT

The default home directory for users is located in the home directory. The name of the home directory is the same as the login name. If you are using the GNOME desktop, it will create a .GNOME-desktop directory in your home directory (see figure 23.20), which will contain the files, directories, and shortcuts that you see on the GNOME root window. If you are using the KDE desktop, it will create a Desktop directory in the home directory, which will contain the files, directories, and shortcuts that you see on the KDE root window.

To manage files in the X Window environment, GNOME comes with the GNU Midnight Commander file manager and KDE comes with the KDE file manager (kfm). Whereas the kfm offers a full web browser (although not as rich featured as Netscape Navigator), the Midnight Commander file manager does offer a number of additional benefits.

To access file and folders that are not on the desktop and that are not on the floppy disks or CDs, you can open the file manager in either environment. The file manager can be opened by using the Main menu or by opening the home directory using the launcher Panel or an icon on the desktop. Of course, the home directory will start you at the users home directory, but you can easily navigate to other directories.

No matter which file manager you use, you will find that doing most common directory and file management tasks are very similar. You can also use the arrows below the menu or double-click on the directories to navigate your file system. You can then drag files and folders from one folder to another folder on the tree, desktop, or another file manager window.

NOTE: If you drag a file or folder to the desktop, you may need to right-click the desktop and select to rescan the desktop.

Figure 23.20 The GNOME Home Directory

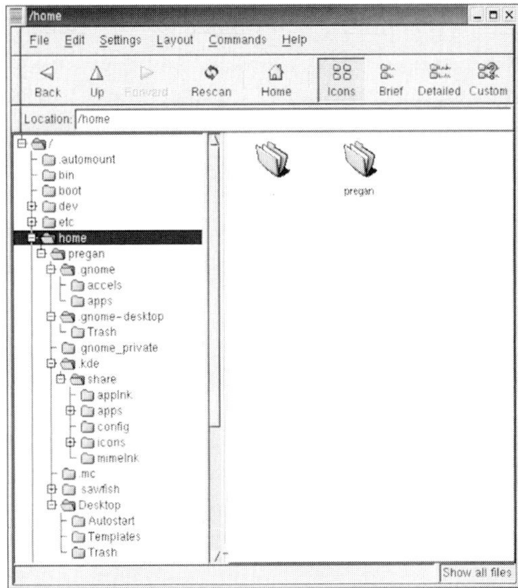

Figure 23.21 The GNU Midnight Command File Manager

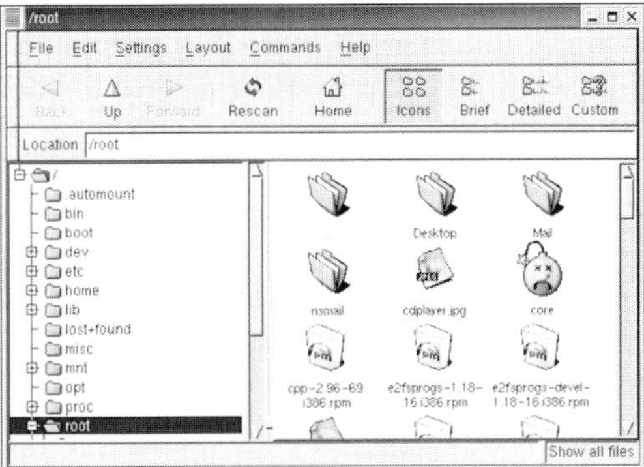

23.14.1 GNU Midnight Commander File Manager

Midnight Commander has buttons to display the contents as icons, brief view (file name and type), detailed view, and custom view (user-defined). You can quickly switch between different views of the files in your directory. You can also configure the Custom button by opening the Edit menu, selecting the Preferences option, and clicking on the Custom View tab. In the Preference dialog box, you can specify to show hidden files in the file display. See figure 23.21.

To open a file or folder, double-click the file or folder. If you right-click a file or folder, you can open, copy, delete, or move it or create a symlink for the file or folder. If you select Properties, you can rename the file or folder, view the size of the file, view the date and time that the file or folder was created, view when it was last modified or last accessed, or view the permissions for the file or folder.

To move a file or folder, drag the file or folder to another file manager window or to the desktop. If you want to create a shortcut or link to a file or folder, right-click the file or folder, select the Symlink option, and then provide the symbolic link file name and click OK. You can move the shortcut to anywhere it is convenient for you. A shortcut will be indicated by a small downward arrow on the bottom of the icon.

You can delete files in one of two ways. If you right-click a file and select the Delete option, it will ask if you want to delete the file. If you say yes, the file will be permanently deleted with no way to restore it. The second way is by using the Trash Bin, represented by a trashcan icon on the desktop. In reality, the icon is a shortcut to the /user/GNOME-desktop/Trash directory. To retrieve a deleted file from the Trash Bin, you just have to click on the trashcan icon and drag the file from the Trash folder. It will stay in the Trash directory until the Trash Bin is emptied (right-click Trash Bin and select the Empty Trash Bin option). Therefore, it is recommended to regularly empty the Trash Bin or you might run out of disk space.

If you have several files grouped together, you can select multiple files or folders by holding down the right mouse button when the pointer is not on a folder or file and drag the mouse pointer over the icons. Once you release the mouse button, each of the selected items will be highlighted. If you need to select multiple icons that are not together, you can highlight each item by holding down the Ctrl key and clicking once on each file or folder. After the files and folders are highlighted, you can then copy, move, or delete the files and folders as one.

23.14.2 KDE File Manager (kfm)

KDE's file manager is called kfm. At the same time it is a full-featured web browser, ftp client, and tar archive utility and it acts as a server for other KDE applications, since it offers its network service that make up KDE network transparent file access (see figure 23.22).

When you first start the KDE file manager, you cannot see the view option buttons or the tree structure. To vary the view, open the View menu and select either the Icon View, Text View, Long View, or Short View. To show the tree, open the View menu and select the Show Tree option. The kfm also has a Print option under the File menu to print the contents of the current directory.

To open a file or folder, click the file or folder. If you right-click a file or folder, you can copy, paste, move to trash, or delete the file or folder. If you move a file or folder to the trash, it will move to the */user/*Desktop/Trash directory. To retrieve a deleted file from the Trash Bin, you just have to click on the trashcan icon and drag the file from the Trash folder. It will stay in the Trash directory until the Trash Bin is emptied (right-click the trashcan icon and select the Empty Trash Bin option). Therefore, it is recommended to regularly empty the trashcan or you might run out of disk space. If you select Properties, you can rename the file or folder; view the size of the file; view the date and time that the file or folder was created, last modified, or last accessed; or view the permissions of the file or folder.

If you drag a file or folder to another file manager window or the desktop, a menu will appear to copy or move the file or folder or to create a shortcut link. Again, a shortcut will be indicated by a small downward arrow on the bottom of the icon.

If you have several files grouped together, you can select multiple files or folders by holding down the right mouse button when the pointer is not on a folder or file and drag the mouse pointer over the icons. Once you release the mouse button, each of the selected items will be highlighted. If you need to select multiple icons that are not together, you can highlight each item by holding down the Ctrl key and clicking once on each file or folder. After the files and folders are highlighted, you can then copy, move, or delete the files and folders as one.

Figure 23.22 KDE File Manager

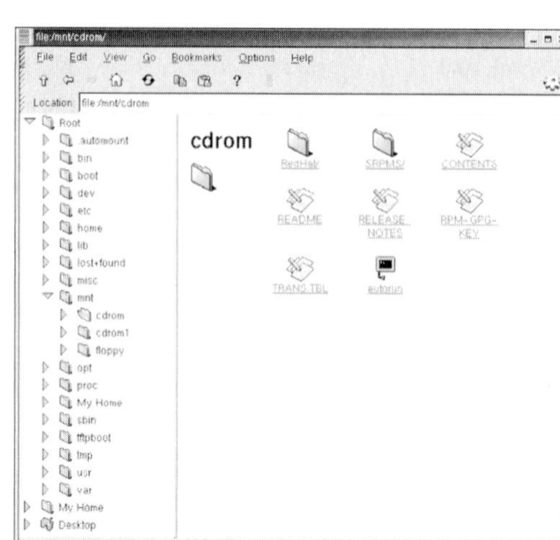

Figure 23.23 X Window Terminal Window

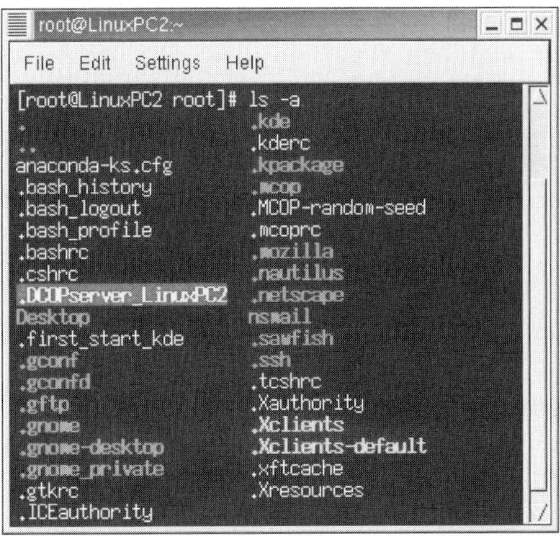

23.15 TERMINAL WINDOW

GNOME provides the terminal whereas KDE provides the Konsole. Both KDE and GNOME versions of the terminal emulator provide access to the Linux shell on the KDE and GNOME environment. These terminals start the default shell for the user and allow you to type in commands as if you were at a command prompt. In addition, since the terminal is being run in a window, the terminal provides a scroll bar so that you can scroll back and see previous commands and output. This is especially convenient when a command output does not fit in one screen (see figure 23.23).

Most terminals allow you to customize the terminal program including changing the terminal interface, changing the color scheme, and changing the fonts used in the terminal. In addition, many of the terminals used in X Window allow you to run multiple sessions at the same time.

When the virtual terminal window xterm is created, xterm lets you select text and copy it within the same or other windows. The left mouse button is used to save text into the cut buffer. You move the cursor to the beginning of the text and then press the button while moving the cursor to the end of the region; then you release the button. The selected text is highlighted and saved in the global cut buffer. This selected text is then made the primary selection when you release the button. Double-clicking selects entire words, triple-clicking selects lines, quadruple-clicking goes back to characters, and so on. If you have a middle button (check for right), it pastes the text from the cut buffer, inserting it as keyboard input.

23.16 CONFIGURATING X WINDOW

Like Microsoft Windows, configuring X Window can be very complicated. There are many things to configure using several different programs and modifying different files.

23.16.1 Starting X Window Automatically

If you boot to the command prompt and you log on, to start X Window you just have to execute the startx command. If you configured X Window to start automatically when the computer boots up, you don't have to worry about using the startx command because you will automatically get a graphical login screen and will be taken immediately into X Window when you log in. Of course, there are many reasons that you might want to start at the console prompt. For example, if you change your video card, you will have to configure X Window. Your new card probably will not be compatible with your old X Window configuration, so you might have to start up in a nongraphical mode to configure it.

If you have to execute the startx command to start X Window and you want to start automatically when you turn on your machine, you must edit the /etc/inittab file and change the following line

```
id:3:initdefault:
```

to

```
id:5:initdefault:
```

and then save the changes. To go back to booting to the command prompt instead of a GUI interface, just change the line back to

```
id:3:initdefault:
```

The 5 indicates run-level 5, which is multiuser capable with X Window; the 3 indicates run-level 3, which is multiuser capable in console mode.

If you have Linux automatically start with the GUI interface and the GUI interface does not start properly, you can start X Window in text mode by typing *telinit 3* (Suse Linux uses telinit 2).

23.16.2 Switching Desktop Environments

You can change desktops by using the Switchdesk utility. Whether you're using GNOME or KDE, you can select your new environment in Switchdesk, then log out of your session, or you can use a subprogram accessed from the Control Panel. When you restart your session, you will load the new environment. If you only want to switch to another desktop environment, yet you want to go back to the original desktop environment when you start X Window next time, you would select the Change only applies to current display option.

To start Switchdesk from the shell prompt of an Xterm window, perform the following tasks:

1. Open a terminal window.
2. Type *switchdesk* at the command prompt.
3. Select your new environment and click OK.
4. Close the terminal window.
5. Log out and log in again.

23.16.3 Configuring the XF86Config File

Unfortunately, there has not been a traditional home directory for the X Window System, and directory contents tend to change from installation to installation. Linux distributions have helped stabilize file positions, and the Linux effort at creating a file system hierarchy standard (FHS) has also helped. See table 23.15. To discover where other installation-specific X11-related files may be in the file system, use this command:

```
locate X11
```

Table 23.15 X Window Directory Structure

Directory	Description
/etc/X11	The FHS location for X Window configuration programs and symbolic link to the X server named "X."
/etc/X11/XF86Config	The X server configuration file. In older setups, this file is found at /sr/X11R6/lib/X11/XF86Config.
/usr/X11R6/bin/xdm	An X display manager for graphical logins.
/usr/X11R6/fvwm95	An X Window manager.
/usr/X11R6/bin/Afterstep	An X desktop manager.
/usr/X11R6/lib	X Window runtime libraries.
/usr/local/X11R6	Alternative window manager with configuration files.

The X servers read and interpret the XF86Config to find detailed information about your PC's monitor, video card, keyboard, and mouse. Additionally, the XF86Config file specifies the types of video modes that you want to use. The XF86Config file usually resides in the /usr/X11R6/etc/X11 or the /etc/X11 directory, but can also be found in /usr/X11R6/lib/X11. An example XF86Config file is provided as the XF86Config.eg file, which is configured for a standard VGA card and monitor with 640 × 480 resolution.

In the past, configuring XF86Config was a complex task. The easiest way to configure this file is to have it automatically configured when you initially install Linux, including installing X Window. If you need to change the XF86Config file or need to install X Window after Linux, there are several utilities used to make changes to this file without manually editing the file with a text editor. They are:

XF86Config—If you are running Red Hat or Debian Linux, you will use this program. XF86Config is similar to XF86Setup, but it does not use an X interface or the VGA16 server.

XF86Setup—This program will invoke a VGA16 server as it brings up X with a resolution of 640 × 480. As an interactive program, it walks through a series of five configuration panels, mouse, keyboard, (video) card, monitor, and other miscellaneous server options.

Xconfigurator—This program deals with setting up only the graphics card and monitor.

XFree86—The XFree86 server includes the capacity to query the hardware and produce an XF86Config file by typing the command *when no X server is running.* When this is done, it should create a file called /root/XF86Config.new. Note that this file may *not be optimized for optimal results,* but it is at least a starting point for manual modification.

xf86cfg—This utility works only with XFree86 4.0.x. It is a GUI interface program that lets you jump around to configure different elements in whatever order you like. Different from the other options, this program shows you a graphical interpretation of how the devices are connected together. In xf86cfg, you right-click an icon and select the resultant Configure option to configure an element, or you can select other options such as remove and disable the device.

NOTE: Not all distributions will include all of these options. Also, remember when executing these commands that they are case sensitive.

To start the Xconfigurator program, you just type in *Xconfigurator* at the command prompt. You maneuver through the Xconfigurator screens using the Tab key and the up and down arrow keys. To toggle a selection, use the spacebar. To click on OK or cancel, tab to the item and press the Enter key. When you start Xconfigurator, the first screen you see is a welcome screen with an OK button and a Cancel button at the bottom. The OK button is highlighted, which indicates that this is the default action that will happen when you press the Enter key.

If Xconfigurator is unable to determine what type of video card you are using, pressing Enter from the startup screen places you in the video card selection screen. Use the up and down arrow keys to select the video card from your system. If you do not see your card listed, your card may not be supported. If this is the case, there are several options you can try:

- Select a video card that is similar to your model and then edit /etc/X11/XF86Config.
- Check the web for others who are running the X Window System with the same type of hardware.
- Use either SVGA or VGA X Window servers.
- After you have selected your monitor, you can either press Tab to move or the OK button and then press the Enter key, or simply press Enter, to move on to the monitor selection screen. (See figure 23.24.)

After you have selected a monitor, Xconfigurator will ask whether it can probe your video card to determine the resolution it is capable of displaying. The default response is Don't Probe, but since this is generally a safe thing to allow, use the Tab key to highlight the Probe button and then press Enter. See figure 23.25.

During the probing process, the screen will blink several times and the monitor may click as different modes and resolutions are tried. After the probing process finishes, you may be asked to specify the amount of video RAM and type of clockchip you have. If you are not sure, consult the documentation for your video card. The recommended setting for the clockchip is No Clockchip Setting. See figure 23.26.

Figure 23.24 Selecting the Monitor Using the Xconfigurator Program

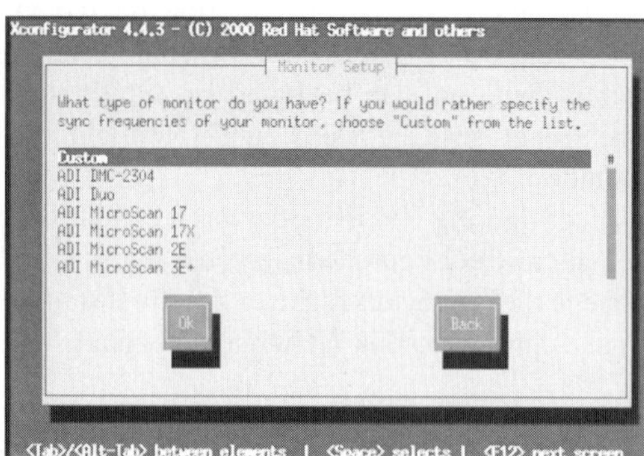

Figure 23.25 Selecting the Video Card Using the Xconfigurator Program

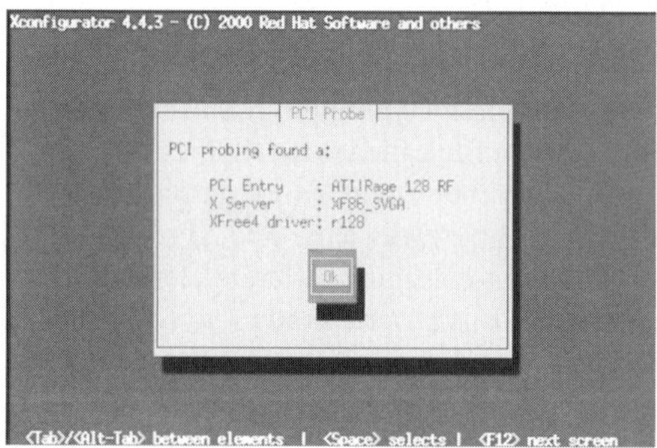

Figure 23.26 Configuring the Video Card Settings Using the Xconfigurator Program

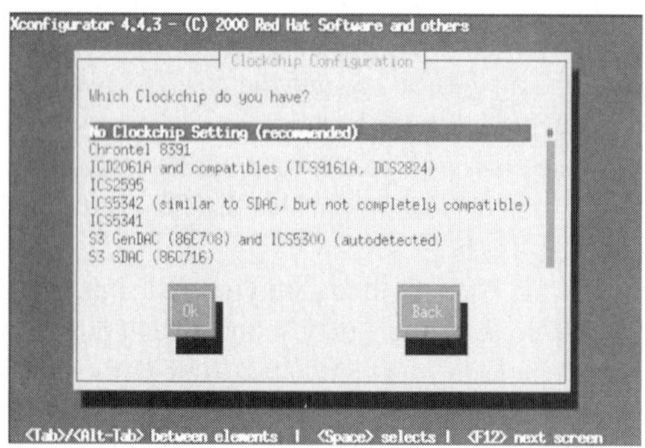

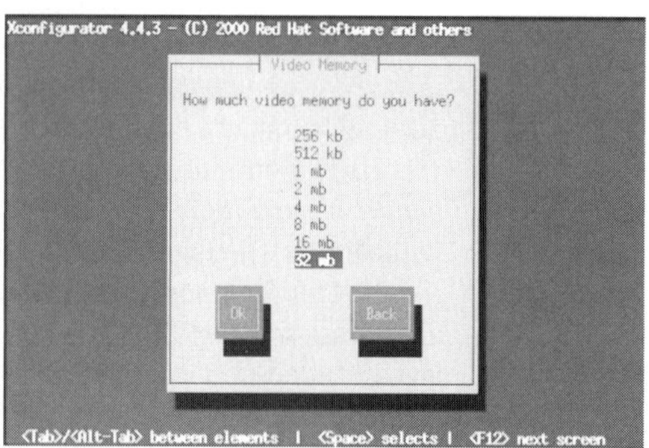

At this point, you are given a chance to select the video modes you wish to use. You probably want to select multiple video modes; you control the size and color depth of your display by switching video modes. Configuring multiple video modes is a good way to ensure that your X Window installation is successful. The video card may have difficulty displaying at a higher resolution video mode but may do fine at lower resolution. If you have configured the X server to support multiple video modes, you can switch between the different modes by pressing Ctrl, Alt, and the plus key from the numeric keypad at the same time until you find a mode that displays properly on your hardware. See figure 23.27.

After you have selected the video modes you want to use, Xconfigurator will ask whether it can start the X Window System to test your configuration. Select OK and the display will go blank while the X Window server starts. After a short interval, the X server should start and you should see a dialog box with a message asking whether you can read the display and with two buttons labeled Yes and No. If you can read the display and it looks like everything is working correctly, use the mouse to click Yes.

Figure 23.27 Selecting the Video Modes Using the Xconfigurator Program

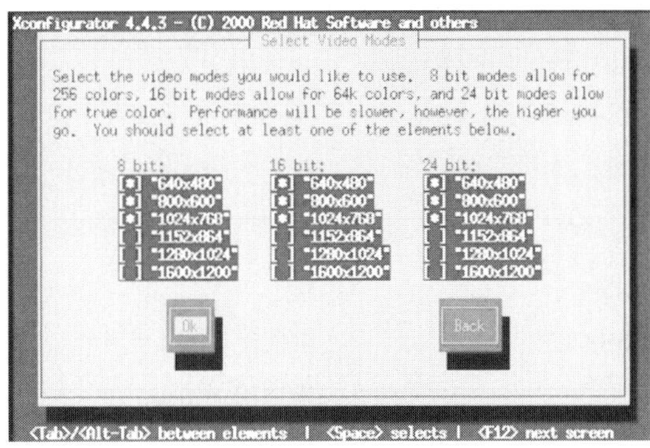

This will tell Xconfigurator that everything is working correctly. If the display isn't working properly or you cannot see the dialog box, don't worry. If you click the No button or wait 10 seconds, Xconfigurator switches back to the original video mode you are using and gives you the chance to retry the configuration or quit.

As the final step in configuring the X Window System, you are asked whether you want to automatically start the X server when the system boots. For most systems, the answer to this is Yes. If you decide not to configure the X Window System for automatic startup, it is very easy to change this setting later.

You run XF86Setup by typing *XF86Setup* at a command prompt. Unlike Xconfigurator, XF86Setup is an X Window program. You do not need X Window System running in order to use it. However, if you are trying to set up an initial X Window configuration, XF86Setup starts up a basic VGA X server so that you can run the program. Once you have finished configuring the X Window server, XF86Setup saves your configuration settings and starts up the X server for the hardware you have chosen. Of course, if you already have the X Window System running, you can run XF86Setup to make changes to your current X server configuration. Note that in order to run XF86Setup, you must install the XFree86 VGA16 server. XF86Setup is not available with Red Hat Linux 7.2.

23.17 FONTS

In Linux, the bitmap screen fonts typically have a bdf or pcf extension. Bitmap screen fonts are most useful for terminal windows, consoles, and text editors, where the lack of scalability and the fact that they are unprintable is not an issue. Today, the most common type of fonts are TrueType and PostScript fonts.

The standard X Window font server is xfs. This server supplies fonts to the X Window System display servers. Not only does xfs provide fonts for the local X server, but it can also provide large numbers of fonts to other hosts on the network.

Font servers are used to provide TrueType fonts to X applications. When an X client makes a request to the X server, the X server binds to the X font server to supply the requested TrueType font. The xfs server is run as a daemon from the /etc/rc.d/init.d/xfs init script. The configuration file for xfs is /etc/X11/fs/config. In the configuration file, you can specify the font servers, the font catalogs, and the font resolution to use.

There are a number of ways fonts can be added to X. First, XFree86 has a font path, which is just a list of several directories or font servers where it searches for fonts. To make fonts available, you need to set your font path. You can add a directory to your font path with this command:

```
xset fp+ directory
```

NOTE: Red Hat users can use this command:

```
use chkfontpath --add directory.
```

Once you have done this, you need to ask the X server to rescan for available fonts with the command:

```
xset fp rehash
```

Because you will want these commands to run automatically, you should put them in your .xinitrc file. Another way to have the commands set automatically is to edit XF86Config. For example, to add

```
/usr/share/fonts/myfonts
```

to the fontpath when X is started, edit XF86Config like this:

```
. . .
Section "Files"
. . .

FontPath /usr/share/fonts/myfonts
. . .
EndSection
. . .
```

The advantage of editing XF86Config is that the resulting changes are systemwide.

23.18 CONFIGURING THE KDE AND GNOME DESKTOPS

The tool used to configure KDE is known as the KDE Control Center, whereas the tool used to configure GNOME is the GNOME Control Center. Some distributions of Linux may have their own control center in addition to the KDE or GNOME Control Center such as those found in Mandrake Linux. You can think of these control centers as being similar to the Microsoft Windows Control Panel. The contents of the right-hand panel change to present you with the configuration choices for the selected option. See figure 23.28.

Although this book will not cover every option, you should become familiar with the System Information program found in the KDE Control Center. If your system has the KDE and GNOME desktops installed, you can usually run KDE programs in the GNOME desktop and vice versa. It is simply a place where system information is displayed for your reference. See figure 23.29. Most of the information can be found by looking at text files in the /proc subdirectories. See table 23.16.

Figure 23.28 The KDE Control Center

Figure 23.29 The KDE Control Center Information Options Showing Interrupts

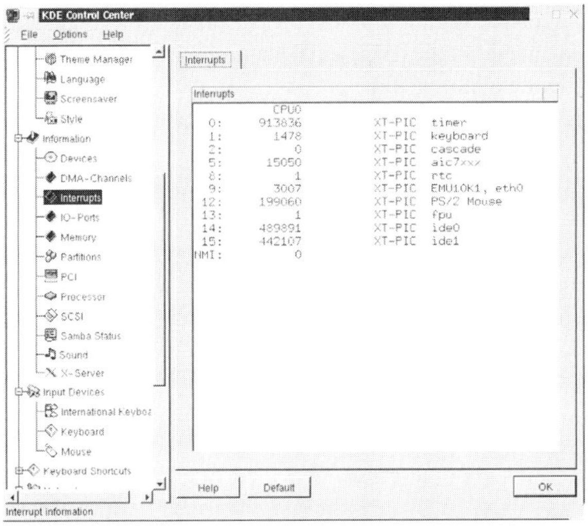

Table 23.16 System Information Available in Linux

Control Center Option	Command-Line Resource	Description
Devices	/proc/devices /proc/misc	UNIX character, block, miscellaneous devices
DMA–Channels	/proc/dma	Devices and which DMA channel they use
Interrupts	/proc/interrupts	Devices and which interrupts they use
IO–Ports	/proc/ioports	Device and which I/O range they use
Memory	/proc/meminfo	Memory totals and usage
Partitions	/proc/partitions	Partition type list
PCI	/proc/pci	Known PCI devices
Processor	/proc/cpuinfo	CPU type and information
SCSI	/proc/scsi	SCSI bus and devices
Samba Status	smbstatus	Samba server information
Sound	/proc/sound	Sound devices
X–Server	X–showconfig	X version and configuration

23.19 PACKAGES AND COMPRESSED FILES

A package is a compressed set of files, stored along with additional information, which can easily be unpacked and installed by the user. The additional information tells your system where the files need to be installed and which other files are required to make these files run. The easiest way to access and install a package is to use a package manager.

The most common package type is RPM (Red Hat Package Manager) files, the type used by Red Hat derivative distributions. RPM maintains a registrylike database of installed programs. By using this database, a package can be safely removed, much like an uninstall program, yet it will not remove the files needed by other packages. The packages can also be used to see if all of the files have been installed and placed correctly.

23.19.1 RPM Packages

RPM is an open packaging system that packages all the necessary files for a software product in a single file (referred to as an RPM file). Because RPM is a package manager, you can install, remove, build, rebuild, and view your packages.

The most basic syntax for installing an RPM package is

```
rpm -i package-1.2.3-4.i386.rpm
```

where *package-1.2.3-4.i386.rpm* is an example of RPM file names. Most RPM file names usually consist of the package name (*package*), the version (*1.2.3*), the build number or patch level by Red Hat (*4*), the architecture it was built to run on (*i386*), and the rpm extension. Instead of using just -i in the RPM command line to install RPMs, you probably want to use -ivh so you can see what is going on. See table 23.17. To view information about a package, you would use the -qi parameters. See figure 23.30.

Table 23.17 RPM Command

Command Syntax	Description
List RPM options `rpm --help ¦more`	To list the RPM options.
Install a package `rpm -i` *`package-1.2.3-4.i386.rpm`*	To install a package, use the -i parameter. You can see more of what is going on with the -ivh option instead.
Force an installation of an RPM package `rpm -i --force` *`package-1.2.3-4.i386.rpm`*	If you want to force a package to install in case some files got deleted and you want to have the complete package again, you can add *--force* to your RPM command line while installing a package. If you don't, you will probably get a message stating that the package is already installed.
Upgrade an RPM package `rpm -U` *`package-2.0.3-4.i386.rpm`*	When a new version of software comes out and new RPM packages are built for them, use the -U flag. Note that the *U* must be uppercase and not lowercase. Like installing, you can also see more of what is going on. Instead of just -U you can use -Uvh. Since many RPM packages depend on other RPM packages to run, when upgrading an RPM, it may complain about dependencies if you try to upgrade several packages. To avoid these messages, you can use the -nodeps flag.
Remove an RPM package `rpm -e` *`package-1.2.3`*	If you want to remove a RPM package, you would use the -e argument. Don't type the entire fine name, however; Many RPM packages depend on other RPM packages to run. Some are programs that need libraries to run, or programs that need other programs to run. It is generally a bad idea to remove packages without paying attention to what depends on those packages. RPM warns you about these dependencies unless you use the --nodeps flag.
Check if the package is installed `rpm -q somepackage`	To see if a package is installed, use the -q parameter.
View all packages `rpm -qa`	To get a simple printout of all the packages you have installed through RPM.
View package information `rpm -qi` *`package-1.2.3`*	To find out information about a package, use the -qi option. The *q* stands for *query* and the *i* stands for *information.*
List the files in a package file `rpm -qpl` *`package-1.2.3-4.i386.rpm`*	To list the files in a package that have not been installed.

Continued

Table 23.17 Continued

Command Syntax	Description
List the files in an installed package `rpm -ql` *`package-1.2.3`*	To list the files in a package that have been installed.
Find package owner `rpm -qf`*`/complete/path/to/file.ext`*	To find out which package is responsible for installing a given file anywhere on the hard disk, such as which package owns the file, use the -qf parameter.
Rebuild a package `rpm --rebuild` *`package-1.2.3-4.src.rpm`*	There are few situations where the typical user will need to rebuild RPM packages. If this comes up where you had to take the source RPM packages and use them to rebuild into an RPM package, you would use the rebuild option.
Verify an installed package `rpm -V` *`package-1.2.3-4.src.rpm`*	Besides verify that every file installed by a package actually exists on the system, it will check the owner, group, mode, MD5 Checksum, size, major number, minor number, symbolic link string, and modification time. If other packages are needed, it will also check to see if the other packages are installed.
Verify all packages `rpm -Va`	If you add -a to rpm -V, you can easily verify every installed package on your system. This may take awhile, however.

Figure 23.30 Using the RPM -qi Command to Display Package Information

```
rpm -qi package-1.2.3
Name        : perl                      Distribution: Manhattan
Version     : 5.004                          Vendor: Red Hat Software
Release     : 6                          Build Date: Fri May  8
12:08:09 1998 Install date: Tue Jun 16 10:36:49 1998   Build Host:
porky.redhat.com
Group       : Utilities/Text             Source RPM:
perl-5.004-6.src.rpm
Size        : 11696746
Packager    : Red Hat Software
Summary     : Practical Extraction and Report Language
Description :
Perl is an interpreted language optimized for scanning arbitrary text
files, extracting information from those text files, and printing reports
based on that information.  It's also a good language for many system
management tasks.  The language is intended to be practical (easy to
use,efficient, complete) rather than beautiful (tiny, elegant, minimal).
```

For documentation and more information about the RPM command, visit the following website:

http://www.rpm.org

23.19.2 GNOME RPM

GNOME RPM is a graphical GNOME tool that makes installing RPM programs quick and easy with just a few clicks. In addition, you can safely remove packages you don't like, upgrade existing software with the latest version, locate new packages to install, and display information about the software that you have already installed.

The GNOME RPM can be found in the Main System menu. If you want to install, upgrade, or uninstall software, you must be logged on as the root account of your Linux system. If all you want is to get information about a package, you can use any user account.

When you start GNOME RPM, it will resemble a file manager window. At the left side of the Package Panel, which resembles the tree view of the file manager, it displays a list of folders containing the packages you can install. The top folders represent broad categories of files, such as application, documentation, or utilities. Click a folder to open it. If a plus sign appears next to a folder name, you can click the plus sign to reveal the subfolders beneath. Click a minus sign next to a folder to collapse the display and hide its contents.

As you explore the folders, names and/or icons of packages installed or available for installation appear in the Display window to the right of the Package Panel. The folders appear as icons in the shape of an opening box. You may select one or more packages by clicking the package icon (to select the first package), and *Ctrl+clicking* to select subsequent packages.

If you want to view the package names as a list instead of icons, open the Operations menu and select the Preferences option. Then click the Interface tab and choose View As List.

You can install RPMs from the command line using the rpm command, but the various switches and options (such as *-replacepackages*) can be tricky to remember. GNOME RPM gives you graphical access to the same commands. See figure 23.31. To install a package:

1. Click the Install button on the toolbar to produce the dialog box.
2. Navigate to the location where the new packages are installed (usually a directory on your CD-ROM drive).
3. Double-click the name of the package you want to install, or click the Add button to place it in the Install window.
4. When you're ready to install, click the Install button. See figure 23.32.

GNOME RPM will follow the instructions in the RPM file to extract and install the elected program.

NOTE: A quick way to add packages to the Install window is to drag them from a File Manager window and drop them directly onto the Install pane.

If you want more information about a package before you install it, click the Query button in the Install window. You can read about the package and its developer, including the names of the directories in which it will install itself. If you decide to install the package as a new program, or update an existing version on your hard disk with the latest release, click the Install or Update buttons.

Figure 23.31 GNOME RPM Program

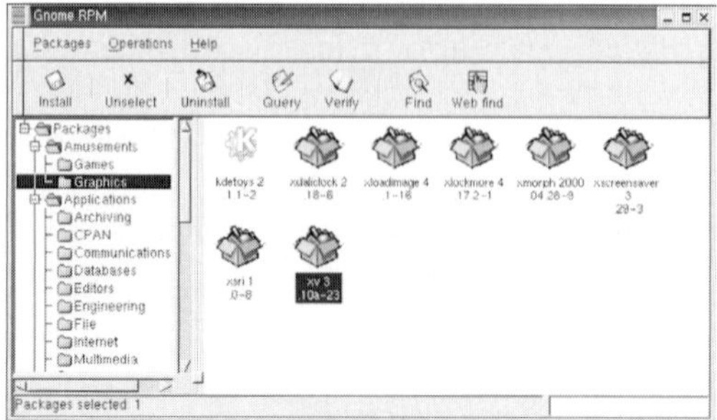

Figure 23.32 Installing an Application Using GNOME RPM

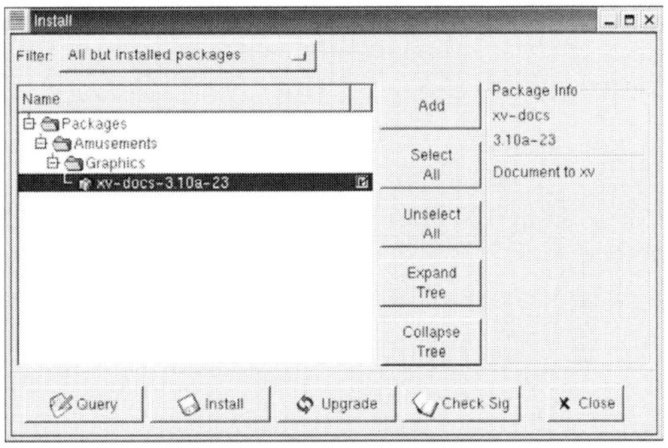

When you download or receive a new version of a program you already have installed, you can easily upgrade to the latest release. You should do this instead of just uninstalling the old version and then installing the new version because the upgrade method preserves any changes you might have made to the original program's settings. Just locate the RPM and click the Upgrade button. GNOME RPM installs the new version and removes any old versions, unless you tell it not to.

To uninstall an unwanted program, locate the name of the package you want to remove, highlight it, and click the Uninstall button in the GNOME RPM toolbar. A confirmation screen pops up so that you can verify the removal steps, and then the program's files are removed with the following exceptions:

- Any configuration files you may have created to control how the program operates are automatically saved. If you reinstall the program later, you have the option to use your old settings.
- Files that are used by other programs in addition to the one you are removing won't be deleted unless you tell GNOME RPM to go ahead when the confirmation dialog box appears. Note that the relationship of files to the programs that require them is called a dependency. If you remove a file that another program is dependent on, or if you try to install a package that is dependent on a file that you do not have (and must install first), Linux will let you know with a dependency error message.

GNOME RPM lets you compare a program on your hard disk with the files in the RPM that you used to install it. You might want to do this if a program has been acting erratically and you think one of its files may have been corrupted. Locate the file on your hard disk in the Package Display window and click the Verify button. GNOME RPM compares a number called a checksum (which verifies that your file is identified to the one in the original package) and checks other information such as the file size.

When you are using the RPM from the command line, there are several options, or switches, you can type to tell RPM how to act. Most of these are technical options that you'll rarely need such as allowing a package to be upgraded to an older version. GNOME RPM normally won't allow this to happen, yet these options are located in the Preferences dialog box.

23.19.3 Gzip

Compressed files use less disk space and download faster than large, uncompressed files. You can compress Linux files with the open-source compression tool Gzip, or with Zip, which is recognized by most operating systems. By convention, compressed files are given the extension .gz. The command Gzip creates a compressed file ending with .gz; Gunzip extracts the compressed files and removes the .gz file.

To compress a file, at a shell prompt, type the following command:

```
gzip filename.ext
```

The file will be compressed and saved as filename.ext.gz.

To expand a compressed file, type:

```
gunzip filename.ext.gz
```

The filename.ext.gz is deleted and replaced with filename.ext.

If you exchange files with non-Linux users, you may want to use zip to avoid compatibility problems. Red Hat Linux can easily open zip or gzip files, but non-Linux operating systems may have problems with gzip files.

To compress a file with zip, type the following:

```
zip -r filename.zip files
```

In this example, *filename* represents the file you are creating and *files* represents the files you want to put in the new file.

To extract the contents of a zip file, type:

```
unzip filename.zip
```

You can zip or gzip multiple files at the same time. List the files with a space between each one:

```
gzip filename.gz file1 file2 file3 /user/work/school
```

The above command will compress file1, file2, file3, and the contents of the /user/work/school directory and put them in filename.gz.

23.19.4 Tarballs

Tar files place several files or the contents of a directory or directories in one file. This is a good way to create backups and archives. Usually, tar files end with the .tar extension. See table 23.18.

To create a tar file, type:

```
tar -cvf filename.tar files/directories
```

In this example, *filename.tar* represents the file you are creating and *files/directories* represents the files or directories you want to put in the new file. You can use absolute or relative path names for these files and directories. Separate the names of files and directories with a space.

The following input would create a tar file using absolute path names:

```
tar -cvf foo.tar /home/mine/work /home/mine/school
```

The above command would place all the files in the /work subdirectory and the /school subdirectory in a new file called foo.tar in the current working directory. The command tar -cvf foo.tar file1.txt file2.txt file3.txt would place file1.txt, file2.txt and file3.txt in a new file called foo.tar.

To list the contents of a tar file, type:

```
tar -tvf foo.tar
```

Table 23.18 Common gzip and tar Extensions

Extension	Used By
.z	Compress/uncompress. Use uncompress fname foo.Z to uncompress the file, where fname is the name of the file that was uncompressed.
.z, .gz gzip.	Gzip is now used by many archive sites instead of compress. If you don't have gzip on your system, get it! To uncompress one of these files, use gzip -d fname.z. The new gzip extension is .gz.
.tar	Tar file. Use tar xvf fname.tar to unpack it. Or you can use tar tvf fname.tar to get an index listing of the tar file.
.taz	Compressed tar file. You can use zcat fname.taz | tar xvf or tar xvfz fname.taz to unpack it (some versions of tar don't have the z option).
.tpz, .tgz	Gzipped tar file. If you have gzip, zcat is linked to it, so you can use zcat foo.tpz | tar xvf to unpack it.
.tpz	The old extension. All gzipped tar files should now end in .tgz.

To extract the contents of a tar file, type:

```
tar -xvf foo.tar
```

This command does not remove the .tar file, but it places copies of the .tar contents in the current working directory.

The tar command does not compress files automatically. You can compress tar files with:

```
tar -czvf foo.tar
```

Compressed tar files are conventionally given the extension .tgz and are compressed with gzip. To expand a compressed tar file type:

```
tar -xzvf foo.tgz
```

If you are using the KDE desktop environment, and you can click on tarball files (compressed files that end with .tar.gz, .tar, or *.tgz) to access the contents of a tarball file. You can then delete files or drag files in or out of the tar file.

As mentioned earlier in the chapter, a programmer creates the source code and the program is then compiled or converted to an executable program. Many developers will first release their program source files as tarballs. It then takes several weeks for the executable program to be converted to RPM or some other packaging format. In addition, RPMs are not optimized for specific processors. This permit their RPM packages to be installed on all sorts of computers since compiling programs for an i386 machine can fit on all systems.

A tarball is many files archived into a single large file and then compressed, originally created for tape archives (back up and restore files in a Linux system). The tool used to create a tarball file is the tar and gzip utility; therefore, the tar files will end with .tar.gz. The tar utility combines the many files into a single large file and the gzip file is responsible for the compression.

NOTE: Do not confuse gzip with WinZip. They are two different programs that use two different (but similar) methods of compression. It should be noted that WinZip does know how to work with tarballs.

Typically, a single directory is selected in which to build and store tarballs. This allows the system administrator to keep the tarball of each package in a safe place in the event he or she needs to pull something out of it later. It also lets all the administrators know which packages are installed on the system in addition to the base system. A good directory for this is /usr/local/src, since software local to a site is generally installed in /usr/local.

When unpacked, most tarballs create a new directory for all files. For example, the foo tarball (foo-2.0.15.tar.gz) creates the subdirectory foo-2.0.15. Most packages follow this standard to define the name of the program and version. It also allows multiple builds to occur at the same time without the risk of the two builds conflicting.

To uncompress and install the tar files, you first download the tarball file and move the file into the /usr/local/src file. Then change into the src file and unpack the tarball with the following tar command:

```
tar -xvzf foo-2.0.15.tar.gz
```

The z parameter in the tar command invokes gzip to decompress the file before the untar process occurs. The v parameter tells tar to show the name of the file it is untarring as it goes through the process. This way, you will know the name of the directory where all the sources are being unpacked. For our example, you should then have a directory called /usr/local/src/foo-2.0.15 with the source files in the foo-2.0.15 directory. If you intend to compile the program into executable files, you should then look for the documentation in the directory on how to compile the program. Most distributions use gzipped tar files with the .tgz extension.

23.19.5 Working with Package Problems

Although the process in using the various forms of packages goes smoothly, there are times when it doesn't. The usual problems are caused by dependencies or conflicts between packages. The RPM and Debian package management systems are intended to help you locate and resolve such problems, but on occasion, particularly when mixing packages from different vendors, they can actually cause problems. In either event, you must be able to recognize these errors and knows how to resolve them.

When installing tarballs, you won't get any error messages during installation; you will see problems only when you try to run the program. These messages may relay an inability to locate a library or run a file, or they may simply cause the program to crash or otherwise misbehave. Occasionally, installing a package can break an existing one, and you might not notice the damage for some time.

Package dependencies and conflicts can arise for a variety of reasons, including the following:

- **Missing Libraries or Support Programs**—One of the most common dependency problems is caused by a missing support package.
- **Incompatible Libraries or Support Programs**—Even if a library or support program is installed on your system, it may be the wrong version.
- **Duplicate Files or Features**—Conflicts arise when one package includes files that are already installed and that belong to another package.
- **Mismatched Names**—RPM and Debian package management systems give names to their packages. The names don't always match across distributions. For this reason, if one package checks for another package by name, the first package may not install on another distribution, even if the appropriate package is installed, because the target package has a different name.

The proper way to overcome a package dependency problem is to install, upgrade, or replace the depended-upon package. If a program requires a newer version, you should upgrade an older version. To perform such an upgrade, you will need to track down and install the appropriate packages. This usually isn't too difficult if the new package you want comes from a Linux distribution; the appropriate depended-upon package should come with the same distribution.

One problem with this approach is that packages intended for different distributions sometimes have differing requirements. If you run Distribution A and install a package that was built for Distribution B, the package will express dependencies in terms of Distribution B's files and versions. The appropriate versions may be available in a form intended for Distribution A, and by installing Distribution B's versions, you can sometimes cause conflicts with other Distribution A packages. Even if you install the upgraded package and it works, you could run into problems in the future when it comes time to install some other program or upgrade the distribution as a whole—the upgrade installer might not recognize Distribution B's package or might not be able to upgrade to its own newer version.

Some dependencies result from the libraries and other support utilities installed on the computer that compiled the package, not from requirements in the underlying source code. If the software is recompiled on a system that has different packages, the dependencies will change. Therefore, rebuilding a package from source code can overcome at least some dependencies.

If you use an RPM-based system, the command to rebuild a package is to use the --rebuild option. Of course, to do this you must have the source RPM for the package.

23.20 USING THE MAKE PROGRAM

Since programs don't know the details of every user's configuration, and because most of them want their programs to work on several different hardware platforms and operating systems, you will find that many programs available for Linux are distributed as source code. So when you have source code, you must convert the source code into an executable program by using the make command.

The good thing is most programmers create installation scripts that do most of the work for you. But part of the process of creating the program to run on your Linux machine is running the make command, sometimes with some command-line options. You will usually find information on what those options are in the installation instructions that come with the program; they are usually found in a file named Readme or Install or something similar.

Although the installation process will vary from application to application, the most common first step involves some basic configuration. The software programs will usually select default options that work for most people, but there's so much variation that it is possible you will have to tweak some settings.

Sometimes the configuration step involves running a script such as configure. To find which file is the script, you should check the installation instructions. Running a script usually requires you to tell the shell where the file is located, even if you try to run it from the directory in which it is located. For example, if you are in the directory where the configure script is located, you might have to type the following command:

```
./configure
```

The ./ notation tells the shell that the configure file is located in the current directory. Once the script has been launched, a variety of system checks are performed, and several files are created.

Typically the next step would be to run the make command, but there are other methods to install the program including its own installation scripts. Again, to know what to do, refer to the installation instructions.

The make utility works by reading and interpreting a makefile, a text file that you have to prepare according to a specified syntax. The makefile describes which file constitutes a program and explains how to compile and link the files to build the program. Whenever you change one or more files, make determines which files should be recompiled and then issues the appropriate commands for compiling those files and rebuilding the program. Note that the make process can be time consuming.

By default, GNU make looks for a makefile with one of the following names, in the order shown:

1. GNUmakefile
2. makefile
3. Makefile

In UNIX systems, it is customary to use the name Makefile because it appears near the beginning of the directory listing since the uppercase names appear before the lowercase names. The Makefile is the key to the build process. In its simplest form, a Makefile is a script for compiling or building the "binaries," the executable portions of a package. The Makefile can also provide a means of updating a software package without having to recompile every source file in it, but that is a different story (or a different article).

If make finds one of these makefiles, it builds the first target specified in that makefile. However, if make does not find an appropriate makefile, it displays the following error message and exits:

```
make: *** No targets. Stop.
```

If your makefile happens to have a different name from the default ones, you have to use the -f option to specify the makefile. The syntax of this make option is

```
make -f filename
```

where *filename* is the name of the makefile.

Even when you have a makefile with a default name such as Makefile, you may want to build a specified target out of several targets defined in the makefile. In that case, you may have to run make with this syntax:

```
make target
```

If the makefile contains the target named clean, you can build that target with this command:

```
make clean
```

Only the simplest software uses a generic makefile. More complex installations require tailoring the makefile according to the location of libraries, files, and resources on your particular machine. This is especially the case when the build needs the X11 libraries to install. Imake and xmkmf accomplish this task.

Installing the freshly built binaries into the appropriate system directories is usually a matter of running make install as root or a superuser. The usual directories for systemwide binaries on modern Linux distributions are /usr/bin, /usr/X11R6/bin, and /usr/local/bin. The preferred directory for new packages is /usr/local/bin, as this will keep separate binaries not part of the original Linux installation.

23.21 APPLICATIONS

You can classify Linux X Window applications in two ways. Some X Window applications are very similar to programs you find on Microsoft Windows. Therefore, they share a common interface and they have a common look and feel to them. You will always find New, Open, Save, and Print on the File menu, and Cut, Copy, and Paste on the Edit menu. They often have a Window menu to toggle between various files using the same program, and a Help menu. Different from Windows, other programs use the right mouse button to pull up a menu or a dialog box.

23.21.1 OpenOffice

The OpenOffice.org suite is a set of office tools similar to those in Microsoft Office. OpenOffice.org is based on Sun's StarOffice code but is not tied to the proprietary Sun application in any way. The suite consists of a word processor (Writer), spreadsheet (Calc) application, presentation package (Impress), formula editor (Math), and drawing program (Draw). It also includes a data charting application and an HTML editor. Obviously, OpenOffice.org contains everything you'd expect in an office suite. The only thing that OpenOffice is missing is a database component.

One main advantage of OpenOffice is its ability to work with a wide range of file formats including Microsoft Office documents (Word, Excel, and PowerPoint) without the addition of any third-party add-ons. Its native format is the Extensible Markup Language (XML), which will seem to be the de facto standard for applications in the future.

OpenOffice is one of the easier applications to install. If OpenOffice is not included in your Linux distribution, you can download the tar.gz file and then perform the following steps:

1. Untar the package with this command:
   ```
   tar xvzf OOo_1.0.0_LinuxIntel_install.tar.gz
   ```
2. Change into the newly created install directory with the cd install command.
3. Run the setup command (as root) to begin the installation process.

After this, the installation is GUI based.

23.21.2 GNOME Office

GNOME Office is a metaproject with the mission to coordinate productivity applications for the GNOME desktop. It is intended to include a productivity suite composed of entirely free software.

The GNOME Office suite is not defined by an arbitrary, fixed number of applications. Rather, the suite is defined by underlying technologies, most notably the libraries these applications share and the component architecture, Bonobo. By permitting multiple applications in several categories, users can select the application most suited to their needs. Some of the GNOME Office applications include AbiWord, Gnumeric, and Gimp. For a more information about GNOME Office applications, visit the following website:

Gnome Office

http://www.gnome.org/gnome-office/index.shtml

23.21.3 AbiWord

AbiWord is the open-source word processor. It was originally developed by Abisource, Inc., but is now developed by an international team of free software volunteers. Extensive work has been done to integrate it into the GNOME Office environment, and it is included with most releases of Linux with the GNOME desktop. Ports are also available to Win32 and plain GTK+, among others.

AbiWord is a small and simple word processor that is fast and complete. It includes all the features that you expect from a word processor such as the ability to format pages and paragraphs, a spell checker, undo/redo, a find and replace function, and the image insertion. It is also able to import documents from Microsoft Word 97 and RTF (Rich Text Format) and to save documents using Internet HTML format or simple text. Several other features are planned for future releases; these include tables, lists, and a Microsoft Word exporter.

But the most significant difference between AbiWord and almost all the other word processors available is the format of its native files. A document saved under AbiWord has an extension by default of abw and is written in XML and thus in ASCII format. These files can then be read by any text editor. That does not mean that AbiWord is a XML editor. AbiWord is a word processor that uses XML like a practical syntax for representation of documents. It is totally new compared to the other traditional word processors and that ensures that when a document is written with AbiWord, it is tied to no particular word processor—word processors that will become obsolete in 5 years.

AbiWord should install and run properly on any Linux system with an Intel (or Intel-compatible) processor. It has been packaged in several different industry standard distribution formats to simplify the installation.

- **RPM**—Red Hat 5.2 or later, SuSE 6.1 or later
- **DEB**—Debian 2.1 (Slink) or later
- **Slp**—Stampede Linux
- **TAR**—works anywhere

You can start AbiWord in one of two ways:

1. Click on the AbiWord icon in your main menu or on the desktop.
2. Type *abiword* in a Terminal Emulation window.

AbiSource Home Page

http://www.abisource.com

AbiWord Downloads

http://www.abisource.com/free.phtml

AbiWord Documentation

http://www.abisource.com/help/index.html

23.21.4 Gnumeric

The Gnumeric spreadsheet is a highly versatile spreadsheet developed for the GNOME Office project, which is intended to be a complete replacement for a commercial spreadsheet. If you are familiar with Microsoft Excel, you will be familiar with Gnumeric because it includes 95 percent of the built-in Excel functions such as numbers, currency, accounting, date, time, percentage, fraction, scientific, and text and special formats.

NOTE: You can use the Gnumeric spreadsheet application in KDE, even though the application is part of the bundled GNOME applications.

The Gnumeric spreadsheet can import Excel (all summary information, all sheet text + formulae, styles, selection, embedded images, printer setups) files, XML (Gnumeric format), HTML, CSV (comma separated values), Lotus 1-2-3 .wk1 format, and GNU oleo (rudimentary). It can also export to Excel (summary information, all sheet text + formulae, names), XML (Gnumeric format—all data except embedded objects), HTML, LaTeX, Troff, PDF, EPS, DVI, and CSV. Last, you can install Graphtool that allows the user to create graphs from Gnumeric files.

GNOME Gnumeric

http://www.gnome.org/gnome-office/gnumeric.shtml

Gnumeric Manual

http://www.gnome.org/projects/gnumeric/doc/index.htm

Gnumeric Downloads

http://www.gnome.org/projects/gnumeric/download.shtml

23.21.5 KDE Applications

The most common applications made for the KDE desktop environment is KOffice. KOffice is an integrated office suite consisting of several applications including:

- KSpread is a spreadsheet application.
- KPresenter is a presentation application.
- Kontour is a vector drawing application.

- KWord is a FrameMaker-like word processor application.
- KChart draws charts and diagrams.
- KFormula is a formula editor.

Based on the KParts component model, KOffice offers a lot of interoperability between all its components. For example, you can embed every KOffice component into another component (e.g., a KSpread table into a KWord document) and a plug-in mechanism makes it possible to easily extend functionality.

KWord is the word processor of KOffice based on frames. Unlike Microsoft Word or StarWriter, text is not entered as one long stream. Instead, the text is always in a frameset consisting of several frames. Frames can be positioned anywhere on the page and they can be connected, so that text that doesn't fit into the first frame is continued in the connected frame. This may sound familiar to you if you've worked with desktop publishing programs like FrameMaker, QuarkXPress, and PageMaker

23.21.6 StarOffice

StarOffice, made by Sun Microsystems, is a very complete office suite: word processor, spreadsheet, presentation program, drawing program, HTML editor, all integrated with a monolithic "desktop." The full version of StarOffice is available for free for both Linux and Microsoft Windows; it can be downloaded over the Internet from the following website:

http://www.sun.com/star/staroffice/get.html

StarOffice looks and acts very much like MS Office. This includes richness of features, large size, and slow startup. You need to have at least 32 MB of memory; more is recommended. StarOffice has good file-level compatibility with MS Office: read and write MS Word, MS Excel, and MS PowerPoint file formats.

23.21.7 Netscape Navigator and Mozilla

Netscape Navigator is the most popular Internet browser for Linux and is a popular Internet browser for other platforms. Most Linux operating system distributions include a version of Netscape Navigator, or you download it for free from the following website:

http://home.netscape.com/download/index.html

Another common browser that is found on Linux machines is Mozilla. Mozilla started on March 31, 1998, when Netscape released its browser source code under an open-source license and created a nonprofit organization, mozilla.org, to oversee this. The idea was to create a successor to the Netscape Communicator 4.XX series with a pool of outside talent. The name of *Mozilla* was derived from the fact that the first Netscape Navigator was intended to be the "Mosaic killer." Mosaic was the first graphical web browser and quite popular during its time. Because Mozilla and Netscape Navigator use the same code, both browsers are very similar.

23.22 VIEWING POSTSCRIPT AND PDF FILES

Computer documentation will often be given using a Portable Document Format (PDF) or PostScript, both of which were developed by Adobe. A PDF file is an electronic image of a document that is usually read by Adobe Acrobat (which can be downloaded for free from http://www.adobe.com). You will often find the documentation of computers, computer components, and software in PDF files.

PostScript is a page description language (PDL), primarily a language for printing documents on laser printers, but it can be adapted to produce images on other types of devices. PostScript is the standard for desktop publishing because it is supported by imagesetters, the very high-resolution printers used by service bureaus to produce camera-ready copy. PostScript is an object-oriented language, meaning that it treats images, including fonts, as collections of geometrical objects rather than as bitmaps. PostScript fonts are called outline fonts because the outline of each character is defined. They are also called scalable fonts because their size can be changed with PostScript commands.

Ghostview is an open-source application that allows you to view and navigate both PostScript and PDF files. To start Ghostview, open the Main menu, select the Graphics option, and then select Ghostview.

Download Ghostview

http://www.cs.wisc.edu/~ghost/index.htm

Ghostview User Manual

http://wwwthep.physik.uni-mainz.de/~plass/gv/

A quick way to convert a PDF to PostScript is to open a shell prompt and type:

```
pdf2ps input.pdf output.ps
```

The *input.pdf* file is the file you want to convert and *output.ps* is the new PostScript file you want to create. The pdf2ps command is part of the Ghostscript tool, which is a PostScript interpreter, a PDF interpreter, and a conversion tool. To see the location of Ghostscript documentation on your system, type `gs -h` at a shell prompt:

Some Linux programs such as Red Hat Linux include an open-source application called xpdf. To access the list of menu options, right-click inside the screen. The toolbar at the bottom has navigational tools that let you move backward and forward through the document, as well as standard zoom, print, and find tools. The xpdf man page provides lots of useful information on xpdf options (open a shell prompt and type *man xpdf* at the command line). To start xpdf, open the Main menu, select the Applications option, and then select xpdf.

23.23 PRINTING IN LINUX

Linux supports several competing printing systems. The most popular are the original Berkeley Standard Distribution (BSD) printing system and the newer LPRng package. The Linux printing environment, which consists of several programs, also supports spooling. The spool directory contains the output files intended for the printer. The term *print job* refers to what you print with a single print command. The printing environment queues print jobs by storing them in the spool directory. A background process then can periodically send the print jobs from the spool directory to the printer.

In order to get printing working well, you need to understand how the spooling software works. All systems work in essentially the same way, although the exact order might vary a bit, and some systems skip a step or two:

1. The user submits a job along with his or her selection of options. The job data is usually, but not always, PostScript.
2. The spooling system copies the job into the spooling directory or print queue.
3. The spooling system waits for the printer to be available.
4. The spooling system applies the user's selected options to the job and translates the job data into the printer's native language, which is usually not PostScript. This step is called *filtering.*
5. When the job is done, the spooling system will usually do assorted cleanup tasks at this point. If there was an error along the way, the spooler typically will notify the user.

For Linux, the two parts of the printing process are:

1. The lpr command takes the data to be sent to the printer and puts it in a file in the spool directory.
2. The lpd command finds the file in the spool directory and sends the file to the printer.

Both the lpr and lpd programs access the /etc/printcap file for information about the printer.

NOTE: The print jobs in Linux printing (including printing to a local printer connected to the parallel port or USB port) are submitted via network protocols, although they don't have to use network hardware.

23.23.1 The Lpr Process

The lpr (short for line printer) program is the only program in Linux that queues print jobs. All other programs that need to print files do so by sending the data to lpr. When lpr runs, it gathers information about the print jobs from three sources:

- Command-line options used with the lpr command
- Environment variables, such as PRINTER, that identify the printer where the output is to appear
- System defaults that provide information that lpr needs, such as the default printer name (lp)

After lpr determines the destination printer's name, it looks up that printer in the system's printer database, /etc/printcap. Assuming that the printer has an entry in the /etc/printcap file, a field in that entry should tell lpr the name of the spool director for that printer. Typically, the spool directory is /usr/spool/printername, but the directory name can be something else (although it is always in /usr/spool).

23.23.2 The Lpd Process

LPD, short for Line Printer Daemon, was used in the original BSD UNIX and has been the standard on UNIX for years as a basic print spooler.

NOTE: The LPD is also the name given to the network printing protocol used in TCP/IP printing. It takes care of the actual printing—the act of sending a file to the printer. A copy of lpd is always running in the system

You can check for the existence of the lpd program with the following command:

```
ps ax |grep lpd
```

If you don't see the lpd process running, you cannot use the Linux printing environment. You have to log in as root and type *lpd* to start the printer daemon. Another characteristic of lpd is its capability to create copies of itself to handle print jobs in specific print queues.

After lpd receives a signal that there is a print job for specific printer, it checks the /etc/printcap files to determine whether the specified printer is on your system or on another system on the network (remote printer). If the printer is indeed connected to your system, lpd checks to see whether a copy of the printer daemon (also named lpd) is already running for that printer's queue. If not, lpd makes a copy of itself and sets up that copy to process print jobs in that printer's queue. The lpd for specific printer's queue sends all waiting print jobs to the printer, one at a time.

23.23.3 Spool Directory

The spool directory is where data destined for a printer accumulates in separate files before the lpd printer daemon sends those files to the printer. By default, the /var/spool directory queues for various UNIX/Linux programs. Mail and news programs, for example, have their spool directories here. The spool directories are named after the program that uses the directory. For example, the Mail program's spool directory is /var/spool/mail.

The printer spool directories are in /var/spool/lpd because lpd is the name of the program that spools print jobs. In /var/spool/lpd, each type of printer should have its own spool directory. You'll find it helpful to name each spool directory with the printer's name as it appears in the /etc/printcap file. Thus if you have an HP LaserJet printer named hplj, the spool directory will be /var/spool/lpd/hplj. The default printer name is lp and the corresponding spool directory is /var/spool/lpd/ld.

Incidentally, a single printer may go by two different names. An HP LaserJet 4M printer, for example, might be used as a printer that understands HP's printer control language (PCL) or PostScript. You might use printer names pcl and ps for the two ways in which you may access the LaserJet 4M printer. All these printer names appear in the /etc/printcap file.

Each printer's spool directory contains two files:

- The lock file, which contains information about the active job and ensures that only one lpd process prints the contents of this spool directory. The lpd process manipulates the permission settings of the lock file to enable or disable spooling for this printer.
- The status file, which contains a one-line message that describes the printer's state. The lpq command displays the message from the status file. You can change this message when you take down the printer with the lpc down command.

When you manually set up a new printer, you'll have to create a spool directory for the printer and set its permission appropriately.

23.23.4 LPRng

The LPRng software is an enhanced, extended, and portable implementation of the lpr print spooler. It was developed to a flexible and scalable approach to printing and has been used in demanding printing environments. LPRng provides a highly flexible configuration system that allows for optimal performance for a simple, single user system with a single or limited number of printers and it provides easy configuration and simple diagnostic procedures, this network-based printing system requires highly robust error logging, authentication, and failover support.

LPRng mimics many of the features of the Line Printer (LPR) package, which will print a document with little or no knowledge of the content or special processing required to print the document on a stand-alone machine or in a distributed printing environment. It also includes new advanced features such lightweight lpr, lpc, and lprm programs, along with dynamic redirection of print queues.

The companion ifhp print filter is used with the LPRng to provide hardware-level support for PostScript, PCL, text, and other printers. The ifhp filter also provides diagnostic and error information as well as accounting information.

23.23.5 The Printcap File

The /etc/printcap file is at the heart of Linux's printing environment. This text file describes the capabilities of various printers. The file must contain information about every printer that you can access from your system including printers that are on the same network as your PC. There is no harm done, however, if the /etc/printcap file contains descriptions of printers that you do not actually have. The lpr and lpd programs consult the /etc/printcap file only to look up information for a specified printer.

The guidelines for adding a printer to the printcap file are:

- An entry in printcap should fit on one line. The backslash at the end of the line tells lpd to ignore the newline character and treat the two entries as a single line. The use of the backslashes helps in making the entries more readable.
- The first field in each entry of the printcap file specifies the name of the printer. Multiple names are separated by the pipe symbol (¦).
- There should aways be an entry in printcap for lp. This becomes the default system printer and is used when no printer is specified with the lpr command.
- The rest of the entries relate to information such as the spool directory (sd), error log (lf), and the suppress header (sh).

NOTE: Each printer must have its own spool directory; printers cannot share spool directories. In addition, don't forget to create the spool directory.

To add a print queue to lpd, you must add an entry in /etc/printcap, and make the new spool directory under /var/spool/lpd. For a Hewlett-Packard 2100M laser printer that supports PostScript connected to the second parallel port, you could use:

```
laserjet2100M ¦LJ¦laser:
  :sd=/var/spool/lpd/lp:\
  :mx#0:\
  :lp=/dev/lp1:\
  :sh:
```

For a Hewlett-Packard 550C inkjet printer that does not support PostScript connected to the first parallel port, you could use

```
lp¦dj¦deskjet:\
  :sd=/var/spool/lpd/dj:\
  :mx#0:\
  :lp=/dev/lp0:\
  :ifhp=model=ghostscript,gs_device=cdj550
  :filter=/usr/libexec/filters/ifhp:\
  :sh:
```

If your printer does not understand PostScript, you will need a filter (sometimes referred to as a smart filter) that converts PostScript into your printer's format. The ifhlp filter (filters are available at http://www.astart.com/lprng/LPRng.html) should cover most cases. There are several smart filter packages available for Linux including rhs-printfilters (used in Red Hat and some of its derivatives), APS-Filter (used in several other distributions), and magicfilter.

The following sequence of commands is a typical example of a readable layout of an entry in the /etc/printcap file.

The follow command defines a spool called lp, dj, or deskjet:

```
lp¦dj¦deskjet:\
```

The pipes (¦) indicate an OR function. This line specifies the spool in the /var/spool/lpd/dj directory:

```
:sd=/var/spool/lpd/dj:\
```

This command indicates no per-job maximum size limit:

```
:mx#0:\
```

The line

```
:lp=/dev/lp0:\
```

indicates that it will print to /dev/lp0.

The command

```
:sh:
```

indicates that the print jobs will not have a banner page (with the name of the person who printed, etc.) added to the front of the print job.

The above example says the following:

- Send the print job to a printer device named /dev/lp1 (lp field)
- Store queue print jobs in the /var/spool/lpd/lp directory (sd field)
- Do not limit the size of the print jobs (mx field)
- Pass the print file through the filter (a command that reads from standard input and generates output on the standard output on the standard output named /var/spool/lpd/lp/hplj-if.pl (if field)
- Log errors in a file named /var/spool/lpd/lp/hplj-log, which must already exist for the error logging to work (lf field)
- Suppress heads—a separator page between print jobs (sh field)

Notice that you need a backslash (\) at the end of each line because the entire entry is supposed to be a single line. Make sure that you do not have any extra space after the backslash character at the end of the line. If a space or tab character appears after the backslash, the printing programs (lpr, lpd, and lpc) will not consider the following line to be a continuation. This error may cause printing to fail for a printer (even though the entry may look fine when you examine the /etc/printcap file). As true of most configuration files in Linux, the command lines in /etc/printcap start with a pound-sign character (#).

The first field of an entry (up to the first colon) lists the name of the printer and its aliases (other names that the printer responds to or is identified by). Typically, each printer has three names:

- A short name with at most four characters (such as hplj)
- A long name that indicates the printer's owner (such as LaserJet-IRM)
- A descriptive name that should fully identify the printer to the users on the system (for example, HP LaserJet 4M in IRM Division)

If you print automatically with lpr without specifying a printer, those print jobs automatically go to the system's default printer, named lp. Therefore, you should provide lp as the first name for the default printer.

After the names, the printer's entry has a sequence of fields. If you examine the sample entry, you notice that the fields are separated by colons (:). There are three types of fields:

- String fields, such as lp (which specify the printer's device name) are specified by the following syntax:

```
:field_name=string:
```

You can embed special characters in the string by using the backslash notation from the C program language. To specify the form-feed character (which might be used to eject a page on the printer), you would use \f.

- Number fields, such as mx (which specify the size of the print-job files), are specified as follows:

  ```
  :field_name#number
  ```

- Boolean fields, such as sh (which suppress printing of a header page separating consecutive print jobs), are true when they appear in the printer's entry; otherwise they are false.

Each field has a specific meaning. Through these fields, you control how output appears on the printer (for example, should the data file be processed by any intermediate program before output goes to the printer) and how errors are logged. See table 23.19 for descriptions of the fields in the /etc/printcap file.

The input filter is a shell script on an executable program that reads the print data from the standard input (stdin) and writes output to the standard output (stdout). The advantage of the input filter is that it enables you to process a text file and convert it to a format that your printer needs.

Table 23.19 Printcap File

Field	Type	Default	Description
Af	string	NULL	Name of accounting file
Br	number	none	Baud rate (applies only if the lp field specifies a serial port device)
cf	string	NULL	Name of ciplot data fiber
df	string	NULL	Name of TeX data filter (DVI format)
fc	number	0	Flag bits to clear (applies only if the lp field specifies a serial port device)
ff	string	\f (form feed)	String to send for a form feed
fo	Boolean	false	If specified, prints a form feed when device is opened
fs	number	0	Flag bits to set (applies only if the lp field specifies a serial port device)
gf	string	NULL	Name of graph data filter
hl	Boolean	false	If specified and if sh is not specified, prints the burst header page last (the burst header page separates one print job from another)
ic	Boolean	false	If specified, printer driver (identified by lp) supports control command to indent printout
if	string	NULL	Name of text filter, which is called once for each print job (you can use this to interpret the file and convert it to a format that is suitable for your printer)
lf	string	\dev\console	Name of file where errors are logged
lo	string	lock	Name of lock file
lp	string	\dev\lp	Device name to open to send output to printer
mx	number	1000	Maximum size of the print job file (in KB); a value of 0 means unlimited size
nf	string	NULL	Name of ditroff (device independent troff) data filter
of	string	NULL	Name of output-filtering program (called only if the if field is not specified, and called only once)
pc	number	200	Price per foot or page, in hundredths of cents
pl	number	66	Number of lines per page

Continued

Table 23.19 Continued

Field	Type	Default	Description
pw	number	132	Page width, in number of characters
px	number	0	Page width in pixels (horizontal)
py	number	0	Page length in pixels (vertical)
rf	string	NULL	Name of filter for printing FORTRAN-style text files
rg	string	NULL	Restricted group; only members of listed groups can access the printer
rm	string	NULL	Name of system for remote printer
rp	string	lp	Remote printer name
rs	Boolean	false	If true, print jobs submitted (from remote systems) by only those users with accounts on local system
rw	Boolean	false	If specified, opens the printer device for reading and writing
sb	Boolean	false	If specified, prints short banner (one line only)
sc	Boolean	false	If specified, does not print multiple copies
sd	string	/var/spool/lpd	Name of spool directory
sf	Boolean	false	If specified, does not print form feeds
sh	Boolean	false	If specified, does not print the burst page header
st	string	status	Name of status file
tr filter	string	NULL	Name of troff (typesetter) data
tr	string	NULL	Trailer string to print when the printer queue is emptied
vf	string	NULL	Name of raster image filter

23.24 USING PRINTTOOL

More advanced users can try to manually configure the /etc/printcap file, but it is much easier to automatically configure the file by using the printtool or printconf utility. The printconf utility is currently found on only Red Hat Linux 7.1. Others will use the printtool command.

NOTE: When you use these utilities, there should not be any need to edit the /etc/printcap file.

23.24.1 The PrintTool Program

When using the PrintTool program, you must be logged in as the root user. To start the utility, you can either type *printtool* at a terminal window or you can click the Main menu, select the System option, and then select the Printer Tool option.

To add a printer using PrintTool, click on the Add button. See figure 23.33. For parallel ports, serial ports, and USB ports, you would select the Local Printer in the Add a Printer Entry dialog box and click on the OK button. You will get an information dialog box that will tell what the system has autodetected. Click on the OK button.

When the Edit Local Printer Entry dialog box appears, you will specify the Names, Spool Directory, File Limit size, Printer Device, and the Input Filter. See figure 23.34. If you want aliases for the printer, type each name and separate it with a pipe (¦) symbol. It is advisable to have one printer with a name or alias of "lp" since this is the default printer name for the system.

Figure 23.33 Printtool utility

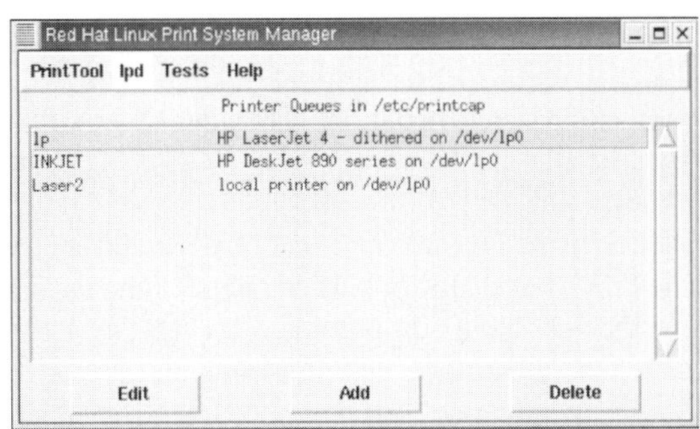

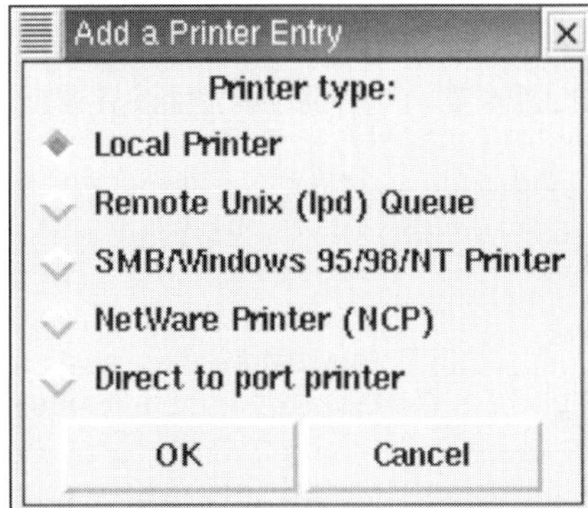

Figure 23.34 Printtool Local Printer Entry

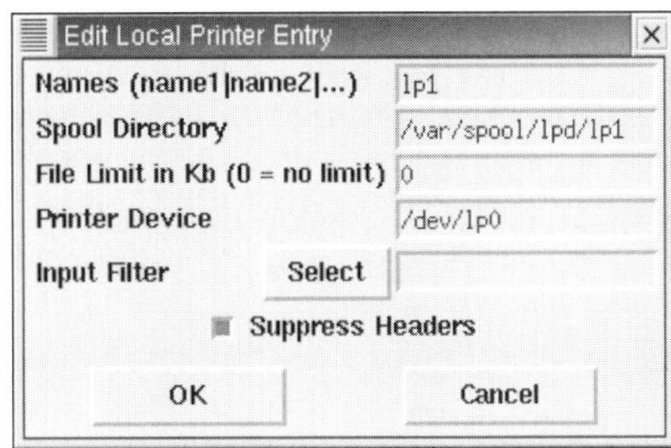

Figure 23.35 Printtool Printer Filter Selection

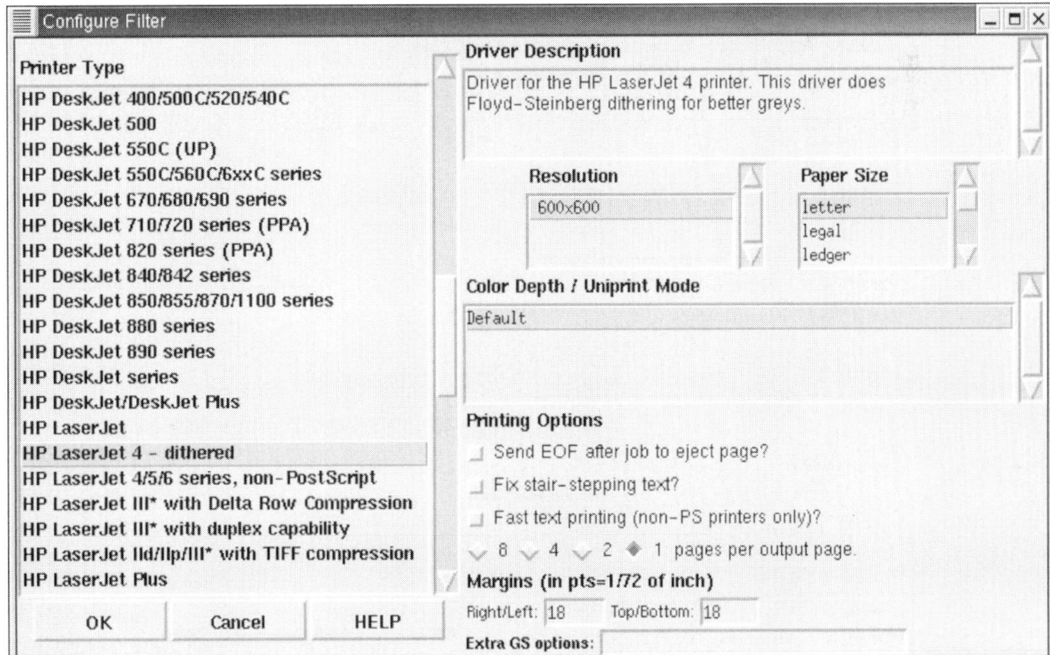

When you get to the Configure Filter dialog box, you select the printer that you are going to use. See figure 23.35. Of course, if it is a PostScript printer, you do not need to select a filter. You can also configure some of the printer options such as the default resolution and paper size. These options will vary from printer to printer. Then click the OK button to finalize your choices.

For these changes to go into effect, you must then open the lpd menu and select the Restart lpd option. To send print pages to the printer, open the Tests menu and select the appropriate test page.

23.24.2 The Printconf Program

To set up a new printer using printconf, click on the New button. When the Edit Queue dialog box appears, you must first specify the name and its aliases, the queue type, and then select the printer driver. See figure 23.36.

To specify the queue name, type a name in the Queue Name text box. For any aliases, Click on the Add button and type the alias name in the Edit Alias dialog box. If you need to change one of the aliases, just click to highlight the alias name and then click the Edit button.

To specify the queue type, click to select Queue Type and then click on the Local Printer button. Of course for a local printer connected to the parallel port, serial port, or USB port, select Local Printer. You will then select the printer device that the printer is connected to. For example, the default for printers that are connected to the first parallel port is /dev/lp0. See figure 23.37.

To select the print driver, click to highlight the Printer Driver option in the list on the left side of the Edit Queue dialog box. Then find the manufacturer under Printer on the right side of the dialog box. See figure 23.38. Again, if it is already a PostScript printer, you just have to select PostScript printer; you do not have to specify the specific printer or manufacturer. To configure any options that might be specific to the printer such as dot resolution and paper size, you would then select Driver Options.

NOTE: This screen will vary from printer to printer.

When done, click on the OK button.

Figure 23.36 Printconf Utility

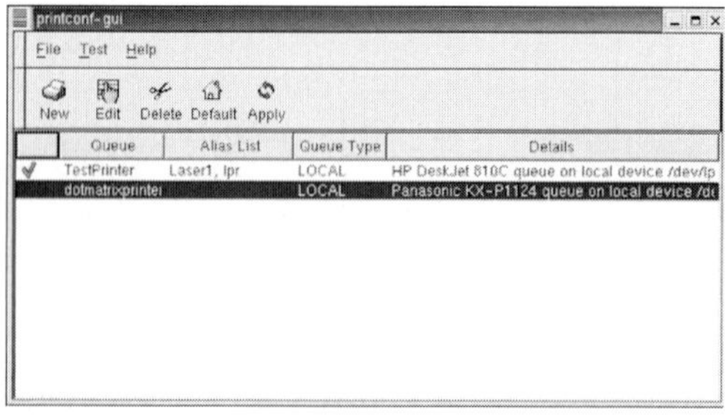

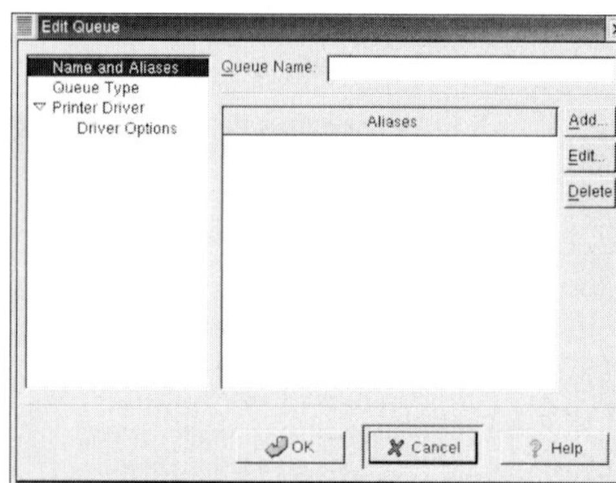

Figure 23.37 Adding a Queue Using the Printconf Utility

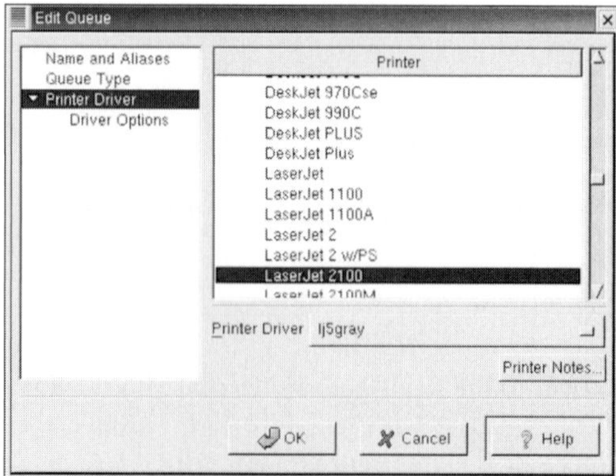

Figure 23.38 Configuring the Print Queue Using the Printconf Utility

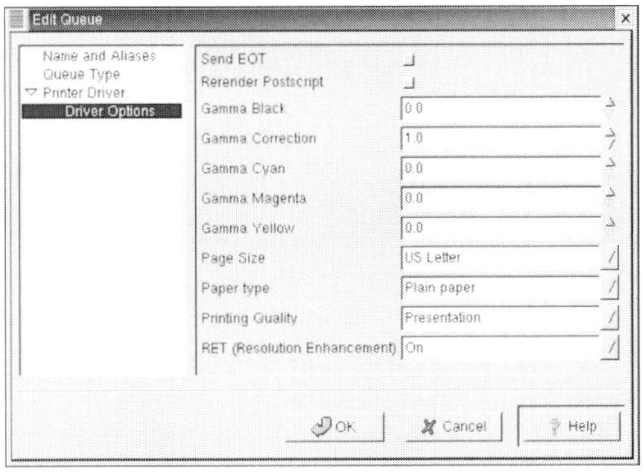

If you need to make any changes to a printer, just start the printconf utility, select the printer, and click on the Edit button. To delete the printer, highlight the printer and click the Delete button. If you have several printers, you can select which printer is the default printer by selecting the printer and clicking on the Default button. The default printer will then be signified with a checkmark. If your printer is connected, you can use the Test menu to print a PostScript test page, an A4 PostScript test page, or an ASCII text test page.

23.25 PRINTING DOCUMENTS AND MANAGING THE PRINT QUEUE

Once your printers have been set up, Linux provides a few tools that can be used to send print jobs to the printer and to manage them.

- Sending a print job to the printer can be done using the lpr command.
- Viewing a list of files currently in the print queue can be done with the lpq command.
- Running lpq with no options will return information about all files in the print queue.
- Deleting a file from the queue can be done with the command lprm followed by the job number of the print job you wish to delete.
- Job numbers can be obtained from the output of lpq.
- A tool named lpc is also used to manage printers. Lpc can be used by the system administrator to enable or disable a printer, change the order of jobs in the print queue, and perform a few other administrative functions.

23.25.1 Sending a File to the Printer at the Command Prompt

In Linux, you use the lpr command to queue a print job. To print the file1.txt file, you would type the following:

```
lpr file1.txt
```

The lpr command copies the file1.txt file to a spool directory (located in the /var/spool/lpd/lp directory). Periodically, a print spooling program known as lpd sends that file from the spool directory to the printer.

You can include the -P option to specify the printer. For example, if you have a Hewlett-Packard LaserJet printer named hplj (as specified in the/etc/printcap file), you would type:

```
lpr -Phplj file1.txt
```

If you have a printer connected to the /dev/lp1 parallel port, you can print a text file simply by sending the file to the printer with the following command:

```
cat file1.txt > /dev/lp0
```

This command would indeed produce a printout of the file1.txt file, provided that the following conditions are true:

- You have logged in as root. Linux allows only root and certain processes direct access to physical devices, such as printers.
- The print must be connected to the /dev/lp0 port, powered up, and online.

The problem with copying a file directly to the printer device is that the command will complete only when the copying is done. For a large file, this process could take awhile. If the printer is not turned on, the command will appear to hang. If this happens, just press Ctrl + C to abort the command.

23.25.2 Managing the Printer and Print Queue from the Command Prompt

All users can use the lpc status command to check the status of printers. If you log in as root, you can use lpc to perform many more printer control functions, such as starting and stopping spooling, enabling and disabling printers, and rearranging the order of print jobs. You can use the second argument to lpc to perform a specific task or run lpc in interactive mode.

To see the name of the default printer (lp0) that is connected to your system, use lpc status command. To see all printers, you would use lpc status all. As you can see from figure 23.39, the screen shows if the printing and spooling is enabled or disabled, the number of jobs, the server, and if the print jobs are being redirected. Note that if the printer names are too long, the columns may not line up with the column headers. See tables 23.20 and 23.21.)

Figure 23.39 Using the Lpc Command

```
[root@localhost /root]# lpc status

Printer            Printing Spooling  Jobs  Server Subserver Redirect Status/(Debug)

lp@localhost        enabled  enabled     0     none    none

[root@localhost /root]# lpc status all

Printer            Printing Spooling  Jobs  Server Subserver Redirect Status/(Debug)

lp@localhost        enabled  enabled     0     none    none

dotpr@localhost     enabled  enabled     0     none    none
```

Table 23.20 Lpc Commands That Anyone Can Use

Command	Description
`lpc restart` *`printer-name`*	Tries to restart the printer daemon (lpd). A user might try this command if the printer appears to be fine but nothing is printed, even though lpq shows jobs waiting in the spool area. Use *all* as the printer name if you want to restart all printers.
`lpc status` *`printer-name`*	Displays the status of the specified printer. If you do not provide a printer name, this command shows the status of the printer named lp, the default printer.
`lpc help`	Displays all options.
`lpc help command-name`	Provides help information on a specific lpc command.
`Exit`	Exits lpc (use in interactive mode only).
`Quit`	Exits lpc (use in interactive mode only).

Table 23.21 lpc Commands That Only Root Can Use

Command	Description
`lpc abort` *`printer-name`*	Behaves like stop, but does not allow the current job to complete. When printing is restarted, this current job prints again.
`lpc disable` *`printer-name`*	Disables spooling of print jobs to a specified printer. When spooling is disabled, users can no longer use lpr to print.
`lpc down` *`printer-name message`*	Disables spooling and stops the printer daemon from printing the spooled print jobs (combines the actions of disable and stop). The message will be displayed when users run the lpq command.
`lpc enable` *`printer-name`*	Enables spooling of print jobs to a specified printer.
`lpc hold` *`printer-name`* or `lpc hold` *`printer-name job-id`*	Holds the specified printer jobs (or jobs) in the queue. The job will not be printed even if spooling and printing is enabled. It must be released with the release command.
`lpc start` *`printer-name`*	Enables the printer daemon so that it can begin printing any jobs in that printer's spool directory.
`lpc stop` *`printer-name`*	Waits for the current print job to complete and then disables the printer daemon so that it stops printing the jobs in that printer's spool directory. When the printing is stopped, users can continue to issue lpr command to print, but the actual output does not appear until the printer daemon is started with the start command.
`lpc topq` *`printer-name job-id`*	Moves the specified print job to the beginning of the printer's queue. If you use a user name in place of job-id, all jobs that belong to that user are moved to the beginning of the queue.
`lpc up` *`printer-name`*	Reverses the action of the down command, enables spooling, and starts the printer daemon (combines the actions of enable and start).

NOTE: Printer-name can be the actual name of the printer or the all option to indicate all printers.

To stop the lpd print spooling daemon for the lj printer, you would use the following command:

```
lpc stop lj
```

To stop the lpd print spooling daemon for all printers, you would use this command:

```
lpc stop all
```

To start the lpd print spooling daemon for the lj printer, you would type:

```
lpc start lj
```

If the printer appears to be working properly, but nothing is printing although the lpq shows job waiting in the spool area for the lj printer, you could try to stop, then restart the print queue.

To run lpc in interactive mode, type *lpc* at the shell prompt. The system replies with this prompt:

```
lpc>
```

If you type *status* at the lpc prompt, you will get the status of the default printer. To exit the lpc program and go back to the command prompt, you can either use the exit or quit command.

To see the print jobs sitting in the print queue, you would use the lpq command. See figure 23.40. For example, to print the contents of the queue for lp, you would use:

```
lpq -P lp
```

To print out a long list of jobs in the queue, use the following command:

```
lpq -l
```

Figure 23.40 Using the Lpq Command

```
[root@PREGAN-DESK /root]# lpq
Printer: lp@localhost
 Queue: 3 printable jobs
 Server: pid 1359 active
 Unspooler: pid 1360 active
 Status: waiting for subserver to exit at 18:10:06.182
 Rank   Owner/ID                  Class Job Files                Size Time
active root@localhost+358           A    358 (stdin)          149614 18:09:23
2       root@localhost+387          A    387 (stdin)          159040 18:09:34
3       root@localhost+391          A    391 (stdin)          144611 18:10:06
[root@PREGAN-DESK /root]# lpq -l
Printer: lp@localhost
 Queue: 3 printable jobs
 Server: pid 1359 active
 Unspooler: pid 1360 active
 Status: waiting for subserver to exit at 18:09:34.746
 Status: waiting for subserver to exit at 18:10:06.182
 Rank   Owner/ID                  Class Job Files                Size Time
active root@localhost+358           A    358 (stdin)          149614 18:09:23
2       root@localhost+387          A    387 (stdin)          159040 18:09:34
3       root@localhost+391          A    391 (stdin)          144611 18:10:06
[root@PREGAN-DESK /root]# ▌
```

When lpr queues a print job, it does not print any messages. If you mistakenly print a large file and want to stop the print job before you waste too much paper, you have to use the lpq command to look at the current print jobs. The word *active* in the Rank column indicates the job that's currently printing. The rest of the entries show jobs in the order in which they'll be printed. If you do not see your print job listed, it has finished printing.

To remove the last print job that you submitted it if it is still in the queue, you would type the following command at the prompt:

```
lprm
```

To remove print job number 25 in spool queue lj4, you would type the following command at the prompt:

```
lprm -Plj4 25
```

To remove all of user pregan's jobs in spool queue lj4, you would type the following command at the prompt:

```
lprm -Plj4 pregan
```

To remove all jobs in the spool queue lj4, you would type in the following command at the prompt:

```
lprm -Plj4 all
```

To remove all jobs in the all spool queues, you would type this at the prompt:

```
lprm -a all
```

23.25.3 Printing in X Window

Like Microsoft applications, to print in X Window applications, you would click on the Print button located on a toolbar or select the Print option from the File menu.

On the KDE desktop, the printer icon represents your printer queue. You can drag and drop files onto the printer icon to send them to the printer. You can open the printer queue either by clicking on the printer icon on your desktop or by going to the Printer Queue item on the Utilities menu of the Panel. See figure 23.41. You can also open and manage the printer queue by typing *klpq* at the shell prompt.

GNOME offers a convenient way to drag and drop documents to the printer with the Printer applet, which can be placed on the Panel. To add the applet to the Panel, right-click on the Panel while selecting the Add Applet, Utility followed by the Printer Applet. When you release the mouse button

Figure 23.41 Viewing the Print Queue in the KDE Desktop

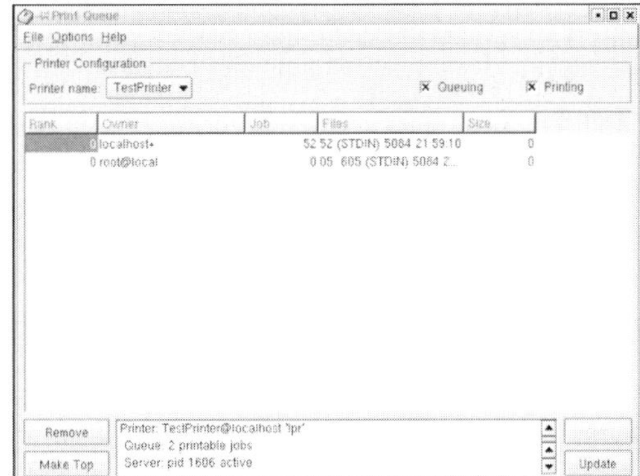

over Printer Applet, the applet will appear on your Panel. To use the applet, drag a document from a folder or from the file manager and "drop" it over the printer icon on the Panel. If you right-click the Printer Applet and select Properties, you can specify the name of the printer. In addition, your default print command will most likely be lpr, so you should leave the Print command entry to the default.

23.26 PROCESSES

A formal definition of a *process* is that it is a single program running in its own virtual address space. This means that everything running under Linux is a process. A *job,* in comparison, may involve several commands executing in series. Alternatively, a single command issued at the shell prompt may involve more than one process, especially when pipes or redirection are involved.

There are several types of processes involved with the Linux operating system. Each has its own special features and attributes. The processes involved with Linux are:

- **Interactive Processes—**Processes initiated from (and controlled by) a shell. Interactive processes may be in the foreground or background.
- **Batch Processes—**Processes that are not associated with a terminal but are submitted to a queue to be executed sequentially.
- **Daemon Processes—**Processes usually initiated when Linux boots and that run in the background until required.

23.26.1 The Ps Command

The easiest method of finding out what processes are running on your system is to use the ps command, which is short for *process status.* The ps command has a number of options and arguments, although most system administrators use only a couple of common command-line formats. The ps command is available to all system users, as well as root, although the output changes a little depending on whether you are logged in as root when you issue the command.

The output of the ps command is always organized in columns. Every process on the system has to have a unique identifier so Linux can tell which processes it is working with. Linux handles processes by assigning a unique number to each process, called the process ID number (or PID). PIDs start at zero when the system is booted and increment by one for each process run, up to some system-determined number (such as 65,564) at which point it starts numbering from zero again, ignoring those that are still active. Usually, the lowest number processes are the system kernel and daemons, which start when Linux boots, and remain active as long as Linux is running. When you are working with processes (such as terminating them), you must use the PID.

The TTY column in the ps command output shows you which terminal the process was started from. If you are logged in as a user, this will usually be your terminal or console window. If you are running on multiple console windows, you will see all the processes you started in every window displayed. A question mark (?) means that there is no terminal associated with the process.

The STAT column in the ps command output shows you the current status of the process. The two most common entries in the status column are S for sleeping and R for running. A running process is one that is currently executing on the CPU. A sleeping process is one that isn't currently active. Processes may switch between sleeping and running many times every second.

The TIME column shows the total amount of system (CPU) time used by the process so far. These numbers tend to be very small for most processes because they require only a short time to complete. The numbers under the TIME column are a total of the CPU time, not the amount of time the process has been alive.

Finally, the COMMAND column contains the name of the command line you are running. This is usually the command line you used, although some commands start up other processes. These are called "child" processes, and they show up in the ps output as if you had entered them as commands.

NOTE: Init (PID=1) and square brackets indicate kernel tasks that cannot be killed.

As a general convention, a login shell has a hyphen placed before its name (such as -bash) to help you distinguish the startup shell from any shells you may have started afterward. Any other shells that appear in the output do not have the hyphen in front of the name.

When normal users issue the ps command, they see only their own processes. If you issue the ps command when you are logged in as the superuser (usually root), you will see all the processes on the system because the root login owns everything running. This can produce very long outputs, especially on a system with several users, so you probably want to use the ps ¦ more command or redirect it to a file (ps >process.txt) for further examination. If you are looking for a specific entry with the output of the ps command, you can use the grep command combined with the ps command:

```
ps ax ¦ grep bash
```

If you are not logged in as the superuser, executing the ps command with no options will list only processes you own. The -A option shows all processes running on the system, including system processes. The -a option shows processes other users own. The -f option is "forest" mode, and shows process trees. The -l option is the long format; the -w option is the wide format; and the -ef shows you all processes with full information including the time of the processor. See figure 23.42. The ps -aux command displays user processes and processes owned by other users. It also shows processes that do not have a controlling terminal, such as system daemons.

23.26.2 The Top Command

The top command is an interactive version of the ps command. Instead of giving a static view of the processes, top refreshes the screen with a list of processes every 2 or 3 seconds. From this list, you can reprioritize processes or kill them. To exit top, press the q key. See figure 23.43 for a list of control keys.

The main disadvantage of using the top command is that it's a CPU hog. By default, top is shipped so that everyone can use. You may decide to restrict top to root only, so that several people don't run it at the same time and significantly slow the system. To do this, change the program's permissions with the following command:

```
chmod 0700 /usr/bin/top
```

23.26.3 To Kill a Process

Occasionally you will find a process that has locked up a terminal or isn't doing anything, which is generally referred to as a "hung" process. Sometimes a user will have a process that doesn't terminate properly, which is known as a "run-away" process. In both cases, the only way to get rid of the process and restore some normality to the system is to terminate the process entirely. This is done with the kill command.

To use kill, you need to have access to another window or console where you can issue commands. If your terminal is completely locked up, find another one to log in on. As a user (except the root user), you can kill only your own processes; you cannot affect any process another user or the system is running.

```
[root@LinuxPC2 root]# ps -ef
UID         PID  PPID  C STIME TTY          TIME CMD
root          1     0  0 Jan16 ?        00:00:03 init [3]
root          2     1  0 Jan16 ?        00:00:00 [keventd]
root          3     1  0 Jan16 ?        00:00:00 [kapm-idled]
root          4     0  0 Jan16 ?        00:00:00 [ksoftirqd_CPU
root          5     0  0 Jan16 ?        00:00:01 [kswapd]
root          6     0  0 Jan16 ?        00:00:00 [kreclaimd]
root          7     0  0 Jan16 ?        00:00:00 [bdflush]
root          8     0  0 Jan16 ?        00:00:00 [kupdated]
root          9     1  0 Jan16 ?        00:00:00 [mdrecoveryd]
root         80     1  0 Jan16 ?        00:00:00 [khubd]
root        174     1  0 Jan16 ?        00:00:00 [kjournald]
root        621     1  0 Jan16 ?        00:00:01 syslogd -m 0
root        626     1  0 Jan16 ?        00:00:00 klogd -2
rpc         646     1  0 Jan16 ?        00:00:00 portmap
rpcuser     674     1  0 Jan16 ?        00:00:00 rpc.statd
root        787     1  0 Jan16 ?        00:00:00 /usr/sbin/apmd
root        859     1  0 Jan16 ?        00:00:02 /usr/sbin/sshd
root        932     1  0 Jan16 ?        00:00:00 sendmail: acce
root        960     1  0 Jan16 ?        00:00:00 [scsi_eh_0]
root        979     1  0 Jan16 ?        00:00:00 gpm -t ps/2 -m
root        997     1  0 Jan16 ?        00:00:02 crond
xfs        1067     1  0 Jan16 ?        00:01:24 xfs -droppriv
daemon     1103     1  0 Jan16 ?        00:00:00 /usr/sbin/atd
root       1134     1  0 Jan16 tty2     00:00:00 /sbin/mingetty
root       1135     1  0 Jan16 tty3     00:00:00 /sbin/mingetty
root       1136     1  0 Jan16 tty4     00:00:00 /sbin/mingetty
root       1137     1  0 Jan16 tty5     00:00:00 /sbin/mingetty
root       1138     1  0 Jan16 tty6     00:00:00 /sbin/mingetty
named      2562     1  0 Jan16 ?        00:00:00 named -u named
named      2564  2562  0 Jan16 ?        00:00:00 named -u named
named      2565  2564  0 Jan16 ?        00:00:00 named -u named
named      2566  2564  0 Jan16 ?        00:00:00 named -u named
named      2567  2564  0 Jan16 ?        00:00:00 named -u named
root      12839     1  0 Jan18 tty1     00:00:00 login -- root
root      12840 12839  0 Jan18 tty1     00:00:00 -bash
root      18645     1  0 Jan19 ?        00:00:00 xinetd -stayal
root      18697     1  0 Jan19 ?        00:00:00 /usr/sbin/smbd
root      18703     1  0 Jan19 ?        00:00:00 /usr/sbin/nmbd
root      19065 18697  0 Jan19 ?        00:00:00 /usr/sbin/smbd
root       5939     1  0 22:50 ?        00:00:00 oafd --ac-acti
root       5944 12840  0 22:50 tty1     00:00:00 /bin/sh /usr/X
```

```
[root@LinuxPC2 root]# ps --help
********* simple selection *********  ********* selection by list *********
-A all processes                      -C by command name
-N negate selection                   -G by real group ID (supports names)
-a all w/ tty except session leaders  -U by real user ID (supports names)
-d all except session leaders         -g by session leader OR by group name
-e all processes                      -p by process ID
T  all processes on this terminal     -s processes in the sessions given
a  all w/ tty, including other users  -t by tty
g  all, even group leaders!           -u by effective user ID (supports names)
r  only running processes             U  processes for specified users
x  processes w/o controlling ttys     t  by tty
*********** output format **********  *********** long options ***********
-o,o user-defined  -f full            --Group --User --pid --cols
-j,j job control   s  signal          --group --user --sid --rows
-O,O preloaded -o  v  virtual memory  --cumulative --format --deselect
-l,l long          u  user-oriented   --sort --tty --forest --version
                   X  registers       --heading --no-heading
                    ********* misc options *********
-V,V show version      L  list format codes  f  ASCII art forest
-m,m show threads      S  children in sum    -y change -l format
-n,N set namelist file c  true command name  n  numeric WCHAN,UID
-w,w wide output       e  show environment   -H process heirarchy
```

Figure 23.42 The ps command can be used to show the running processes in Linux.

Figure 23.43 The Top Command

```
 11:16pm  up 4 days,  2:35,  5 users,  load average: 0.09, 0.13, 0.11
63 processes: 61 sleeping, 2 running, 0 zombie, 0 stopped
CPU states:  1.9% user,  0.9% system,  0.0% nice, 97.0% idle
Mem:   255580K av,  231984K used,   23596K free,      196K shrd,    5408K buff
Swap:  265064K av,       0K used,  265064K free                   172376K cached

  PID USER     PRI  NI  SIZE  RSS SHARE STAT %CPU %MEM   TIME COMMAND
 5954 root      18  -1 60164  10M  1996 S <   0.7  4.1   0:36 X
 6253 root      13   0  8732 8732  7856 R     0.5  3.4   0:03 kdeinit
 6287 root      14   0  1044 1044   836 R     0.5  0.4   0:02 top
 6064 root      12   0  9076 9076  7932 S     0.3  3.5   0:04 kdeinit
 6068 root      11   0 11892  11M  9736 S     0.3  4.6   0:07 kdeinit
    1 root       8   0   520  520   452 S     0.0  0.2   0:03 init
    2 root       9   0     0    0     0 SW    0.0  0.0   0:00 keventd
    3 root       9   0     0    0     0 SW    0.0  0.0   0:00 kapm-idled
    4 root      19  19     0    0     0 SWN   0.0  0.0   0:00 ksoftirqd_CPU0
    5 root       9   0     0    0     0 SW    0.0  0.0   0:01 kswapd
    6 root       9   0     0    0     0 SW    0.0  0.0   0:00 kreclaimd
    7 root       9   0     0    0     0 SW    0.0  0.0   0:00 bdflush
    8 root       9   0     0    0     0 SW    0.0  0.0   0:00 kupdated
    9 root      -1 -20     0    0     0 SW<   0.0  0.0   0:00 mdrecoveryd
   80 root       9   0     0    0     0 SW    0.0  0.0   0:00 khubd
  174 root       9   0     0    0     0 SW    0.0  0.0   0:00 kjournald
  621 root       9   0   620  620   524 S     0.0  0.2   0:01 syslogd
  626 root       9   0  1080 1080   448 S     0.0  0.4   0:00 klogd
  646 rpc        9   0   592  592   504 S     0.0  0.2   0:00 portmap
  674 rpcuser    9   0   760  760   664 S     0.0  0.2   0:00 rpc.statd
  787 root       8   0   524  524   464 S     0.0  0.2   0:00 apmd
  859 root       9   0  1272 1272  1080 S     0.0  0.4   0:02 sshd
  932 root       9   0  2064 2064  1496 S     0.0  0.8   0:00 sendmail
  960 root       9   0     0    0     0 SW    0.0  0.0   0:00 scsi_eh_0
  979 root       9   0   496  496   432 S     0.0  0.1   0:00 gpm
  997 root       8   0   660  660   576 S     0.0  0.2   0:02 crond
 1067 xfs        9   0  5104 5104  1092 S     0.0  1.9   1:24 xfs
 1103 daemon     9   0   568  568   500 S     0.0  0.2   0:00 atd
 1134 root       9   0   448  448   384 S     0.0  0.1   0:00 mingetty
 1135 root       9   0   448  448   384 S     0.0  0.1   0:00 mingetty
```

In order to use the kill command, you need the process ID number (PID) of the process to be terminated. Obtain the PID with the ps command and note the PID. Next, use the kill command with the PID as an argument:

```
kill 578
```

Killing a process actually sends a signal, which the program can trap and handle in its own way. Sometimes a process is hung, and will not respond to the kill, so a stronger kill must be used:

```
kill -9 478
```

This sends signal 9 (SIGKILL) to the process, which forces init to immediately destroy it. A normal kill sends signal 15 (SIGTERM), which gives the process a chance to clean itself up before closing. If that doesn't work, then the process may be unkillable. This does happen occasionally with Linux, and the only solution is to shut down and reboot the machine.

A variant on kill is killall. This command kills a process based on its name rather than its PID number. For instance, killall vi kills all the running processes called vi. You may specify a signal in the shortened form (-signal). As with kill, the default is 15 (SIGTERM). One potentially important option to killall is -i, which causes it to ask for confirmation before sending the signal to each process. Therefore, if you have multiple instances of the same program, you can say yes or no to each one and close only the ones that you say yes to.

23.26.4 Processes and X Window Utilities

Both KDE and GNOME desktops offer graphical utilities to view and manage processors. To start the GNOME System Monitor, open the GNOME Main menu, select Programs, select System, and then select the System Monitor or type *gtop* at the shell prompt. To start the KDE Process Management, you would select the KDE menu, select the System option, and then select the Process Management or type *kpm* at the shell prompt.

With these utilities, you click on the category header buttons to sort by that category. Therefore, if you click on the PID category header button, the processes will sort by the PID. If you then click on the CPU, it will sort by processor utilization.

23.26.5 Working Around Recurring Problems

If you find yourself regularly stopping or restarting processes because they hang or crash, the program is most likely buggy. Check for update versions of the program. Another possibility is a hardware problem, especially with processors, the motherboard, and RAM. These types of errors usually are accompanied by kernel problems or may cause the computer to crash entirely. Of course, if you are a system administrator who is responsible for many computers, it would be wise to first install untested software on a test computer before rolling it out to all of the computers.

If a software package is not working properly, you can view the software package's log files to troubleshoot the problem. If the software package produces a log file, the log files will be located in the /var/log directory.

SUMMARY

1. The kernel is the central core of the operating system that interacts directly with the hardware.
2. Linux (pronounced LIH-nuhks with a short "i") is a UNIX-like operating system that was designed to provide personal computer users a free or very low-cost operating system comparable to traditional and usually more expensive UNIX systems.
3. Linux is distributed under the GNU license agreement. GNU, which is self-referential, is short for *GNUs not UNIX.*
4. The philosophy behind GNU is to produce software that is nonproprietary. Anyone can download, modify, and redistribute GNU software.
5. The kernel versions n.x.y, where x (the minor version) is an even number, are stable versions, and only bug fixes will be applied as y is incremented.
6. A program, sometimes referred to as a process, is an executable program that follows a sequence of steps.
7. A thread is part of a program that can execute independently of other parts.
8. Virtually every utility that you would expect to find on standard implementations of UNIX has been ported to Linux. This includes basic commands such as ls, awk, tr, sed, bc, more, and so on. Therefore, you can expect your familiar working environment on other UNIX systems to be duplicated on Linux.
9. The shell is a program that reads and executes commands from the user.
10. Linux uses X Window to provide a graphical interface to the Linux operating system. The version of X Window available for Linux is known as XFree86.
11. As for an intuitive graphical interface, Linux has at least a dozen different, highly configurable graphical interfaces (known as window managers) that run on top of XFree86. The most popular window managers at the moment are KDE (K Desktop Environment) and GNOME (GNU Network Object Model Environment).
12. To provide free, high-quality documentation for the GNU/Linux operating system, the Linux Documentation Project (LDP) was created.
13. To determine if your computer is compatible with Linux, you can use the hardware compatibility list provided by the Linux distributor.
14. The fdisk program is a Linux disk partitioning program, similar to the FDISK utility that comes with DOS, but with many more capabilities.
15. Linux file names are similar to MS-DOS file names except that they do not use drive letters such as A and C and they substitute the slash (/) for the MS-DOS backslash as the separator between directory names.
16. The hard disk names start with /dev. You have to identify the disk drive by its name such as /dev/hda or /dev/sda.
17. Although you can get by with a single large partition for the entire Linux file system and another for the swap space, you can better manage the disk space if you create separate partitions for the key parts of the Linux file system.
18. A file name can contain any character (except the / character) and is limited to 256 characters in length.
19. Red Hat and other Linux distributors are committed to the file system hierarchy standard (FHS), a collaborative document that defines the names and locations of many files and directories.
20. In Linux, all of the drives and their partitions make up a single directory file system.
21. The term *mount point* refers to the directory you associate with a disk partition or any other device. In other words, each mount point is a disk partition, and that disk partition is mounted on the directory of the limb above it.
22. The size of the swap file usually varies between the amount of physical memory (RAM) and twice the amount of physical memory.

23. Like Windows NT or Windows 2000, Linux uses accounts to manage privileges, maintain security, and more.
24. The root account is the all-powerful account to the Linux system.
25. The fastest way to stop X Window and go back to the command prompt is to press Ctrl + Alt + Backspace.
26. As you type in a command at the keyboard, you must know the correct spelling, syntax, parameters, and punctuation for the command to work. In addition, all commands in Linux are case sensitive.
27. Wild-card characters (* and ?) are used to specify groups of files. The asterisk (*) means any string of characters and the question mark (?) means any single character.
28. To list the contents (files and subdirectories) of a directory, you would use the list (ls) command.
29. To move from one directory to another, use the change directory (cd) command.
30. To make a copy or duplicate of a file's content, you would use the cp (copy) command.
31. To move files from one directory to another, use the move (mv) command.
32. To create a subdirectory, you would use the mkdir (short for *make directory*) command.
33. To remove a directory that you no longer need, use the rmdir command.
34. The find command locates files and directories that meet specified search criteria.
35. To get online help for each of various commands, you can type *man*. Linux then displays any information it has on the command one screen at a time.
36. While using Linux commands at the prompt, you can actually make these commands more powerful by redirection inputs and outputs and by using filters.
37. The uname program can be used to show system details.
38. Vi is the most popular text-based text editor.
39. The Panel, typically found at the bottom of the screen, is the heart of the user interface. It includes the Main Menu button, a tasklist of running applications, launchers that are buttons to launch frequently used applications or commands, and virtual desktops.
40. The desktop provides the functionality of any traditional operating system desktop. You can drag files, programs, and directory folders to the desktop. In addition, if a file type is associated with a program (Mime Type) and you double-click on the icon that represents the file, the application will automatically start and load that file.
41. Unlike Microsoft Windows, the X Window System does not have a fully evolved clipboard with edit commands such as Undo, Cut, Clear, and Select All. There is, however, a minimal copy and paste mechanism.
42. Both KDE and GNOME versions of the terminal emulator provide access to the Linux shell on the KDE and GNOME environments.
43. If you boot to the command prompt and you log on, to start X Window, you just have to execute the startx command.
44. If you have to execute the startx command to start X Window and you want to start automatically when you turn on your machine, you must edit the /etc/inittab file.
45. If you need to change the XF86Config file or need to install X Window after Linux, there are several utilities used to make changes to this file without manually editing the file with a text editor.
46. The standard X Window font server is xfs. This server supplies fonts to the X Window System display servers.
47. The tool used to configure KDE is known as the KDE Control Center, whereas the tool used to configure GNOME is the GNOME Control Center. Some distributions of Linux may have their own control center in addition to the KDE or GNOME Control Centers such as those found in Mandrake Linux.
48. A package is a compressed set of files, stored along with additional information, that can easily be unpacked and installed by the user.
49. The most common package type is RPM files, which is the type used by Red Hat derivative distributions. RPM files maintain a registrylike database of installed programs.
50. Compressed files use less disk space and download faster than large, uncompressed files. You can compress Linux files with the open-source compression tool Gzip or with Zip, which is recognized by most operating systems.
51. By default, compressed files are given the extension .gz.
52. The command Gzip creates a compressed file ending with .gz; Gunzip extracts the compressed files and removes the .gz file.
53. Tar files place several files or the contents of a directory or directories in one file.
54. Linux supports several competing printing systems. The most popular are the original Berkeley Standard Distribution (BSD) printing system and the newer LPRng package.
55. Both the lpr and lpd programs access the /etc/printcap file for information about the printer.
56. The lpr (short for *line printer*) program is the only program in Linux that queues print jobs.
57. LPD, short for *line printer daemon,* was used in the original BSD UNIX and has been the standard on UNIX for years as a basic print spooler. Note that LPD is also the name given to the network printing protocol used in TCP/IP printing.
58. The spool directory is where data destined for a printer accumulates in separate files before the lpd printer daemon sends those files to the

printer. By default, the /var/spool directory queues for various UNIX/Linux programs.

59. More advanced users can try to manually configure the /etc/printcap file, but it is much easier to automatically configure the file by using the printtool or printconf utility.

60. The easiest method of finding out what processes are running on your system is to use the ps command, which is short for *process status.*

61. The top command is an interactive version of the ps command. Instead of giving a static view of the processes, top refreshes the screen with a list of processes every 2 or 3 seconds.

62. Occasionally you will find a process that has locked up a terminal or isn't doing anything, which is generally referred to as a "hung" process. Sometimes a user will have a process that doesn't terminate properly, which is known as a "run-away" process.

63. The only way to get rid of the process and restore some normality to the system is to terminate the process entirely with the kill command.

QUESTIONS

1. What is the central core of the operating system that interacts directly with the hardware?
 a. kernel b. program central
 c. worm d. shell

2. What component manages the computer's memory and allocates it to each process and schedules the work done by the processor?
 a. the kernel
 b. utility programs
 c. system configuration files
 d. the shell

3. In Linux, the command interpreter is known as the
 a. kernel.
 b. utility programs.
 c. system configuration files.
 d. shell.

4. Which of the following versions indicate a stable version of the Linux kernel (choose all that apply)?
 a. 2.4.2 b. 2.4.7
 c. 2.4.11 d. 2.5.4
 e. 2.5.9 f. 2.6.1

5. Which command sequence should you type if you want to delete the second disk partition using the Linux fdisk utility?
 a. fdisk, p, 2 b. fdisk, d, 1
 c. fdisk, d, 2 d. fdisk, p, 1

6. Which Linux fdisk command option is used to add a partition to a hard drive?
 a. a b. n
 c. p d. w

7. What is the difference between the /bin and /sbin directories?
 a. No difference. The /bin directory is a link to /sbin for backward compatibility.
 b. The /bin directory holds all binary files, and /sbin is not a valid directory.
 c. The /bin directory holds binary files, whereas /sbin holds the source code for those files.
 d. The /bin directory holds binary files necessary for all users, whereas /sbin holds binary files necessary only for root.

8. Suppose you have a single IDE hard drive, with three primary partitions. The first two are set aside for MS-DOS, and the third is an extended partition that contains two logical partitions, both used by Linux. Which one of these devices refers to the first Linux partition?
 a. /dev/hda1 b. /dev/hda2
 c. /dev/hda3 d. /dev/sda1
 e. /dev/hdc1 f. /dev/hda5

9. Which first-level segment of the file system contains a majority of system and server configuration files within its subdirectories?
 a. /var b. /etc
 c. /bin d. /sbin
 e. /lib

10. Where are all Linux system log files kept?
 a. /log b. /etc/log
 c. /var/log d. /usr/log

11. What is the default shell in most Linux distributions?
 a. bash b. tcsh
 c. Bourne Shell d. korn
 e. C shell

12. Pat, a Linux system user, needs to erase all the temporary files he has created for a software project. He has five files named test, test2, test3, test4, and test5. How can he erase these files?
 a. del test? b. rm test?
 c. del test* d. erase test?

13. Pat needs to create a new directory called newproj for testing a new software project. How can he do this?
 a. mkdir nowproj b. pico -d newproj
 c. md newproj d. newdir newproj

14. Pat is currently in the directory /var/spool/lpd/lpj and needs to change to the root directory. What is the fastest way to do this?
 a. chdir /root b. cd ..
 c. cd / d. cd /clb
 e. cd root

15. Which vi commands can be used to move you into insert mode (choose all that apply)?
 a. I, i, A b. O, a, I
 c. a, i, O d. I, A, O

16. Which mode in vi would you use to type text?
 a. ex mode b. type mode
 c. command mode d. edit mode

17. How would you remove two lines of text from a file using vi?
    a. In command mode, position the cursor on the first line and type *2dd.*
    b. In command mode, position the cursor on the last line and type *2yy.*
    c. In edit mode, position the cursor at the start of the first line, hold the Shift key down while pressing the down arrow key twice, and hit the Delete key on the keyboard.
    d. In edit mode, position the cursor at the start of the first line and press Ctrl + K twice.
18. What command is typically used to start X Window?
    a. xdm
    b. startx
    c. xstart
    d. go X
19. What is xterm?
    a. a terminal emulator for X Window
    b. a program used to configure X Window
    c. a program used in making remote X Window sessions
    d. a set of eyes in X Window that follows your mouse movements
20. Where do you find the Main Menu button?
    a. the Panel
    b. the tasklist
    c. right-clicking the desktop
    d. by pressing Ctrl + Alt + Del
21. Which packaging solution can be used for programs that will be distributed for Linux and UNIX platforms?
    a. RPM
    b. Debian
    c. tarball
    d. Winzip
22. Your Linux computer is running very slowly, and you suspect that one of the applications is using up all system resources. Which commands will show you if this is true (choose two answers)?
    a. top
    b. ps -aux
    c. taskmgr
    d. syscheck
23. What is usually the cause of a "core dump" message?
    a. A program just crashed.
    b. The kernel just crashed.
    c. Your processor just failed.
    d. All of your files were just erased.
24. Which command is used to cancel a Linux print job?
    a. lpr
    b. lpq
    c. lprm
    d. lpdel
25. What is the main printer configuration file?
    a. /etc/lp.conf
    b. /etc/printcap
    c. /etc/lpr.conf
    d. /etc/printers
26. Which Linux command displays what is currently in the print queue?
    a. lp
    b. lpr
    c. lpl
    d. lpq
27. Which of the following is generally true of Linux programs that print?
    a. They send data directory to the printer port.
    b. They produce PostScript output for printing.
    c. They include extensive collections of printer drivers.
    d. They can print only with the help of add-on commercial programs.

HANDS-ON EXERCISES

Exercise 1: Installing Mandrake Linux 9.1

1. Insert the Linux CD#1 in the CD drive and boot the computer. If your system does not have a bootable CD drive, you will have to use the bootable floppy disk instead.

   NOTE: You may need to enter the BIOS setup program to boot from the A drive or the CD drive.

2. On the first Mandrake screen, press Enter. You have the options <F1> for more options or <Enter> to install or upgrade Mandrake Linux. Press the Enter key.
3. Choose the appropriate language and click on the Next button.
4. When the license agreement appears, select the Accept option and click on the Next button.
5. Select the appropriate mouse and click on the Next button.
6. Read the security options. Select the standard security level and click the Next button.
7. When the DrakX partitioning wizard appears, select custom disk partitioning. Click the Next button.
8. If you have any volume or partitions already installed, select each one and click on the Delete button.
9. Click the white box under the hdd tab. Click the Create button.
10. Select the Journalized FS:ext3 filesystem type and specify approximately 6000 MB for the size. Keep the mount point as /. Click the OK button.
11. Click the white box again and click the Create button. Select the Linux Swap filesystem type. Specify the amount as twice your RAM. Click the OK button.
12. Click on the white box and click the Create button. Select the Linux native (ext2) filesystem type. Specify approximately 500 MB for the size and /home for the mount point. Click on the OK button.

13. Leave the rest of the drive free and click the Done button. When it warns that the partition table will be written to disk, click on the OK button.
14. When the package group selection appears, select all packages under Workstation and server. Click on the Next button.
15. Read the warning when it asks you if you are ready to install these servers. Select the Yes option and click on the Next button.
16. The installation program installs the system. This may take some time. When it asks you to insert Disk #2 or the International Disk (Disk #3), do so.
17. When it asks you to specify the root password, type *password* for the Password and Password (again) text boxes, and click on the Next button.
18. When it asks you to enter a user, enter the a user, specify user1 for the Real name and User name text boxes and specify *password* for the Password and Password (again) text boxes. Click on the Accept user button and click on the Next button.
19. When it asks if you want it to set up the computer to automatically log on as one user, deselect the "do you want to use this feature" and click on the Next button.
20. When it asks where you want to install the boot loader, select the first sector of drive (MBR) and click on the Next button.
21. Next, it shows you a summary of the system configuration. If the graphical interface is not configured, click the Configure button. Select the appropriate video card and click on the Next button. When it asks which configuration of XFree you want, select XFree 4.3 and click on the Next button. Select the desired resolution and number of colors and click on the OK button. When it asks you to test the configuration, select the Yes option and click on the Next button. If everything looks fine, click on the Yes button. When it asks you to start the graphical interface (XFree) upon booting, select the No option and click on the Next button.
22. Back on the system configuration summary, select the Network-LAN Configure button.
23. When the Network Configuration Wizard appears, be sure the Auto detection option is enabled and click the Next button. When it asks you to choose a connection to configure, enable LAN connection-Ethernet card detected and click on the Next button.
24. Deselect the Automatic IP option and use the wizard to provide the appropriate IP information for your system. If those settings are not available, use the following:

IP Address:	192.168.*XXX.YYY*, where *XXX* is your room number and *YYY* is your student number.
Netmask:	255.255.255.0
Gateway:	192.168.XXX.254
Hostname:	host*XX*, acme.cxm
DNS server:	192.168.XXX.255

    If you have the only computer, use 1.1 for *XXX.YYY*. If your network is connected to a router, enter the 192.168.*XXX*.254. Click on the Next button. At the end of the wizard, click on the Finish button to go back to the summary screen.
25. Configure the appropriate time zone and any other options that need to be configured. When finished, click on the Next button to continue with the installation.
26. Assuming that you are connected to the Internet, when it asks you to install any updates, select the Yes option and click on the Next button. Install any updates that are available.
27. When installation is complete, click on the Reboot button.

Exercise 2: Starting X Window

1. Log in as the root account.
2. Start X Window by using the startx command.
3. For root on Mandrake Linux, the graphical interface begins with the Mandrake Display Manager interface. If a warning appears stating that you are running a graphical interface as root, read the entire warning. Then uncheck the show this window again option and click on the Continue button.
4. Open the Main menu, select the Configuration option, then select the Mandrake Control Center. Click the Boot option in the left pane and click on DrakBoot.
5. Select the Launch the graphical environment when your system starts option. Do not use the Autologin option. Click on the OK button.
6. Exit X Window by opening the Main menu, selecting the Logout option, and clicking the Logout button.
7. Reboot the computer.
8. When the computer boots and X Window automatically starts, notice that root is not listed. Log in as user1 with the KDE session type. Click the Go button. Notice the longer boot time.
9. Log out from X Window by opening the Main menu. Select the Logout option and click on the OK button.

10. When the computer boots and X Window automatically starts, log in as user1 with the GNOME session type.
11. Log out of X Window by opening the Main menu and selecting Logout. Select the logout option and click the OK button.
12. Log in as user1 with the KDE session type.
13. Open the Main menu, select the Configuration option, and then select Mandrake Control Center.
14. Since you started the Mandrake Control Center and you are logged in as user1, the Mandrake Control Center asks you to log in with the root password. Type in the password and click on the OK button.
15. Select the Boot option in the left pane and select DrakBoot.
16. Deselect the Launch the graphical environment when your system starts option. Click on the OK button.
17. Log out and restart the computer.
18. Log in as root.
19. Change to the /etc directory.
20. Use vi and open the inittab file.
21. Find this line

    ```
    id:3:initdefault:
    ```

    and change it to

    ```
    id:5:initdefault:
    ```

    Save the file and exit vi.
22. Shut down Linux and reboot your system. X Window should start automatically.
23. Log in as user1 with the KDE session type.
24. To open a terminal window, open the Main menu, select the Terminals option, and select the Konsole command.
25. Since you are logged in as user1, you need to escalate yourself to root so that you can change the inittab file. You can do this by executing the su root command and providing the root password.
26. Change to the /etc directory, open the inittab file again and, using vi, change this line

    ```
    id:5:initdefault:
    ```

    to

    ```
    id:3:initdefault:
    ```

27. Shut down Linux and restart your computer. X Window should not boot automatically.

Exercise 3: Starting and Shutting Down Linux

1. At the login prompt, type *root* and press the Enter key.
2. When it asks for the password, type *password* and press the Enter key. Notice that since you logged in as the root, the prompt has a pound sign (#) and that your default directory is the root account: /root.
3. At the prompt, type *logout* and press the Enter key.
4. Log in as user1 and use *password* as the password. Notice the dollar sign ($) is used in the prompt and the default directory is your default name.
5. Log out again.
6. Log in as the root account.
7. To shut down Linux, press the Ctrl + Alt + Del keys.
8. Turn on the computer again and start Linux.
9. Log in as the root account.
10. At the prompt, type this command:

    ```
    shutdown -h now↵
    ```

11. Start Linux again and log in as the root account.
12. At the prompt, type:

    ```
    shutdown -r 1↵
    ```

13. Start Linux again and log in as the root account.
14. At the prompt, type:

    ```
    shutdown -r now↵
    ```

15. Start Linux again and log in as the root account.
16. At the prompt, type:

    ```
    startx↵
    ```

17. Click the Main Menu button on the Panel and select the Logout option. Select the Logout option and click the Yes button. You may need to press Enter one more time to get back to the prompt.
18. At the prompt, type:

    ```
    startx↵
    ```

19. Click the Main Menu button on the Panel and select the Logout option. Select the Shut Down option and click the Yes button.

Exercise 4: Navigating the Linux File System

1. Start Linux and log in as the root.
2. Your prompt shows that you are in the root directory. To go up one directory, type:

    ```
    cd ..↵
    ```

    Notice that now you are in the root directory (/) since the root directory is directly underneath the root directory.
3. To go back into the root directory, type:

    ```
    cd root↵
    ```

4. Currently the home directories for the other users are located under the home directory. To change to the home directory that is located in the root directory, type:

    ```
    cd /home↵
    ```

5. To list the contents of the home directory, type:

    ```
    ls -a↵
    ```

6. Change to the user1 home directory by typing:

    ```
    cd user1
    ```

7. To move up one directory, use the cd command.
8. Use the pwd command to show your current directory.
9. Change back to the user1 directory.
10. Use the pwd command to show your current directory.
11. To change to the root directory, no matter what directory that you are in, type:

    ```
    cd /↵
    ```

12. To go back to the user1 directory in one command, use this command:

    ```
    cd /home/user1
    ```

13. Change back to the root directory.
14. To list the contents of the home directory, type:

    ```
    ls -a↵
    ```

15. Change to the boot directory.
16. Execute the ls -a command to view the files in the boot directory. Notice the vmlinuz file, which is the kernel.
17. To change to the bin directory (located in the root directory) directly from the boot directory, type:

    ```
    cd /bin↵
    ```

18. Execute the ls -a command. You should be able to recognize the external Linux commands such as pwd, mov, sort, kill, cat, rm, rmdir, and others.
19. Using one command, change to the mnt directory.
20. Display the contents of the directory. This is where you would typically find the CD drive and the floppy disk drives.

Exercise 5: Working with Directories

1. Change to the user1 directories located under the home directory.
2. To make a docs directory, at the prompt type:

    ```
    mkdir docs↵
    ```

3. Change to the docs directory.
4. Execute the pwd command.
5. Make a reports directory and a letters directory in the docs directory.

6. Display a listing of the directory.
7. To delete the empty reports directory, type:

   ```
   rmdir reports↵
   ```

8. Display a listing of the directory.
9. Go up one directory to the test directory.
10. Try to delete the docs directory by typing:

    ```
    rmdir docs↵
    ```

11. To remove a directory with something in it, you have to use the rm command with the -r switch. Therefore, type:

    ```
    rm -r docs↵
    ```

    When it asks to descend into a directory or to remove a directory, type:

    ```
    y↵
    ```

Exercise 6: Working with Files

1. Change to the /tmp directory.
2. Display the contents of the directory.
3. To copy the install.log to the /home/user1 directory, type:

   ```
   cp install.log /home/user1↵
   ```

4. Change to the user1 directory.
5. To make a copy of the install.log file and call it file1.txt, type:

   ```
   cp install.log file1.txt↵
   ```

6. Display the contents of the directory.
7. Make three more copies of the install.log and call them file2.txt, file3.txt, and fileA.txt.
8. Display the contents of the directory.
9. To list all files using wild cards, type:

   ```
   ls -a *↵
   ```

10. To list all the files that begin with *file,* type:

    ```
    ls -a file*↵
    ```

11. To list all the files that begin with *file* that range from 0 through 3, type:

    ```
    ls -a file[1-3]*
    ```

12. To delete the fileA.txt file, type:

    ```
    rm fileA.txt↵
    ```

    When it asks to remove the file, type:

    ```
    y↵
    ```

13. To remove all files that start with *file,* type:

    ```
    rm -f file*↵
    ```

14. To look for a file, you will use the find command. Therefore, type:

    ```
    find / -name install.log -print↵
    ```

    Notice that it is listed twice, in the /home/user1 and the /tmp directories.

15. You should still be in the user1 directory. To move the install.log file to the home directory, you can type:

    ```
    mv install.log /home
    ```

    or

    ```
    mv install.log ..↵
    ```

    Therefore, type:

    ```
    mv install.log /home↵
    ```

16. Delete the install.log file from the home directory.

Exercise 7: Working with the Proc File System

1. Change to the /proc directory.
2. View the contents of the directory.
3. To view your IRQs, type:

   ```
   cat interrupts↵
   ```

   Look at which IRQ the mouse is using. Look to see which IRQs are free.
4. To view your IO addresses, type:

   ```
   cat ioports ¦more↵
   ```

5. To view the information about your processors, type:

   ```
   cat cpuinfo↵
   ```

6. View the information on your memory.
7. View the PCI devices.
8. View the information on your swap file.
9. View the version file to view the version of Linux.
10. To see the drivers that are loaded in memory, view the modules file.

Exercise 8: Using Help and the Alias command

1. At the command prompt, type:

   ```
   man cp↵
   ```

   Press Return to jump down one line at a time. Press the spacebar to jump down one screen at a time.
2. When you have read enough press the q key to return back to the prompt.
3. At the command prompt, type:

   ```
   man alias↵
   ```

   Press the q key to return back to the prompt.
4. To display all of the current aliases, type:

   ```
   alias↵
   ```

5. Try to execute the help cp command.
6. To set up an alias for help so that when you type in *help* it will call up the man command, type:

   ```
   alias help=man↵
   ```

7. Display the aliases again.
8. Type:

   ```
   help cp↵
   ```

   Go back to the command prompt.

Exercise 9: Using Virtual Terminals

1. At the command prompt, execute the following commands:

   uname -v
   uname -s -r
   uname -a

2. Press Alt + F2.
3. Log in as user1, not as the root account.
4. Use the env command to show the environment variables.
5. Record the directories listed in the search path.
6. Press Alt + F1.
7. Using the find command, search and record all instances of the telnet* file.
8. Using the which command, locate the first instance of the telnet command.
9. Change back to the second virtual terminal. Start X Window by executing the startx command.

10. Change back to the first terminal by using the Ctrl + Alt + F1 keys.
11. To show all the processes running in memory, execute the following command:

```
ps ax
```

12. To list only the process entries that have bash in them, use the following command:

```
ps ax | grep bash
```

13. Change back to X Window (Ctrl + Alt + F7) and exit X Window.
14. Log out as User1
15. Change to the first virtual terminal.

Exercise 10: Changing the Date and Time

1. Execute the date command at the command prompt.
2. Change the date and time of the computer to May 5, 2005 6:00 pm.
3. Change the date and time to the correct date and time.

Exercise 11: Exercise 10: Using Vi Text Editor

1. Change to the user1 directory located in the home directory.
2. To create file1.txt using vi, type:

```
vi file1.txt↵
```

3. To enter text, you will need to put vi in the input mode. Press a to append text after the cursor. This should appear at the bottom of the screen:

```
-- INSERT --
```

4. Type the following text:

```
This exercise is designed to familiarize the user↵
with the basic editing features of vi. We will go↵
over commands to move the cursor as well as↵
showing the user how to save the files he has created.↵
```

5. To put the vi back into command mode, press the Esc key.
6. To save the file and exit vi, type *:wq.*
7. Display the contents of the directory.
8. Use the cat command to display the contents of the file1.txt file.
9. To modify the text file, type:

```
vi file1.txt↵
```

10. Use the arrow keys to move the cursor around the screen.
11. Use the h, k, l, and j keys to move the cursor around the screen.
12. Move the cursor to the space after *he.*
13. Press the I key to change to insert mode. Press the spacebar and type:

```
or she↵
```

14. Move the cursor to the *h* in *has* and press the Enter key.
15. Press the Esc key to go back to command mode.
16. To save your work and remain in vi, type:

```
:w↵
```

17. Move the cursor to the third line.
18. To delete the entire line, type *dd.*
19. Delete the next line by typing *dd.*
20. To bring the last line back, type *P.*
21. Delete the word *user* in the fourth line.
22. To exit vi without saving changes, type:

```
:q!↵
```

23. Load the file1.txt file using vi.
24. Move the cursor to the last line and type *yy* to copy the line.

25. Press the Enter key to go to the next line.
26. Press the p key several times to paste the text.
27. To undo, type *u* several times.
28. Quit vi without saving the file.

Exercise 12: Starting X Window

1. Log in as the root account.
2. Start X Window.
3. Click the Main Menu button and select the Run option. Click the Advanced button. Execute the switchdesk program, select the KDE desktop, and click the OK button.
4. Exit X Window and restart it.
5. Start the switchdesk program and select the GNOME desktop.

   NOTE: Because GNOME is already selected, you may need to click on KDE and then click on GNOME for switchdesk to realize that you wanted to choose the GNOME desktop.

6. Restart X Window.
7. Exit X Window.
8. Change to the /etc directory.
9. Use vi and open the inittab file.
10. Change this line

    ```
    id:3:initdefault:
    ```

    to

    ```
    id:5:initdefault:
    ```

    Save the file and exit vi.

11. Shut down Linux and reboot your system. X Window should start automatically.
12. Start a terminal window by clicking on the terminal emulator window icon on the panel.
13. Change to the/etc directory, open the inittab file again and, using vi, change this line

    ```
    id:5:initdefault:
    ```

    to

    ```
    id:3:initdefault:
    ```

14. Shut down Linux and restart your computer. X Window should not boot automatically.

Exercise 13: Using the KDE Desktop

1. Log in as user1.
2. Start X Window.
3. Click on the Main Menu button, select Office, select Word Processors, and then select OpenOffice Writer. If the Address Data Source AutoPilot window opens, click the Cancel button.
4. Close OpenOffice Writer.
5. Click the Main Menu button to open the Main menu. Then select Applications, Editors, and KEdit.
6. In the text editor, type in your name.
7. Save the file in the user1 home directory (/home/user1/Documents) by opening the File menu and selecting the Save option. Type *name.txt* in the selection text box and click the OK button.
8. Save the file two more times with the names name2.txt and name3.txt by opening the File menu and using the Save As option.
9. Close KEdit.
10. Double-click the home icon on the desktop.
11. Double-click the name.txt file. Close KWrite.
12. Right-click the name2.txt file, select the Open with option and select GEdit. Close GEdit.
13. Right-click the name.txt file and select Delete from the shortcut menu.
14. Click the name2.txt file and select Move to Trash. Then click on the Trash button.
15. Double-click the Trash icon. Notice that name.txt is permanently deleted, whereas name2.txt file is in the trash folder.
16. Right-click the name2.txt file and select Cut from the shortcut menu.

17. Go back to the Konqueror window, which should be showing the /home/user1/Documents folder. Right-click the center of the home directory window and select Paste from the shortcut menu.
18. Highlight both name2.txt and name3.txt file by pressing the Ctrl button and clicking on the two files while holding down the Ctrl button. Release the Ctrl button, then right-click one of the files and select the Copy option.
19. Go to the desktop, right-click the desktop, and select Paste from the shortcut menu.
20. Right-click the desktop, select Icons, and select Line up Vertically.
21. Notice that the trash and /home/user1/Document folders are still open. Click on the second virtual desktop (located on the panel) button.
22. Open OpenOffice Writer.
23. Toggle back to the first virtual desktop.
24. Click on the terminal emulator window (Konsole) icon on the panel. If the tip of Day appears, close the window.
25. Type the ls –l command.
26. Click the show desktop icon on the panel.
27. Toggle back to the terminal window by selecting it from the tasklist located on the Panel.
28. Close the terminal window.
29. Open Main menu and select the Lock Screen option.
30. Move the mouse pointer. Enter the password to unlock the screen.
31. Close all windows.
32. Exit X Window. Log out and then log in as root. Restart X Window.
33. Open the Main menu, select Configuration, select KDE, select Information, and select IO-Ports.
34. Open the Main menu, select Configuration, select KDE, select Information, and select Interrupts.
35. Note what is using Interrupt 14.
36. Close the IO-Ports and interrupt windows.
37. Open the Main menu, select applications, select File Tools, and then select Find Files.
38. Under the Name text box, type *telnet.* Under the Look in text box, type /.Click on the Find button.
39. Note how many instances of telnet you found.
40. Right-click one of the telnet instances and select Open Directory.
41. Open the Main menu, select Documentation and then Help.
42. Maximize the Help window.
43. On the left pane, select KDE user's manual.
44. Scroll down and select a few links and read a few paragraphs.
45. Close all windows.

Exercise 14: Using the KDE Control Center

1. Click on the Main Menu button and select the Control Center.
2. Click on the + sign next to Look & Feel. Select the Background option.
3. Click on the wallpaper tab. Record the current wallpaper.
4. Select Single Wallpaper. Click on the Browse button. Select a wallpaper that you like. Because the automatic preview is enabled, when you click on a wallpaper, it will show you what the wallpaper looks like. When you find one that you like, click on the OK button. If it asks to apply the changes, click the Apply button.
5. Click the Desktop option in the left pane.
6. In the Desktop tab, note what the desktop path is set to. This is the directory that holds the documents and shortcuts that you have on your desktop.
7. Select the Panel option in the left pane.
8. Click on the Hiding tab. Enable the Enable Automatic Hide option. Click the Apply button.
9. Click on the desktop and watch the Taskbar disappear. Move the mouse pointer to the bottom of the screen and watch the Panel reappear.
10. Disable the Enable Automatic Hide option. Click on the Apply button.
11. Select the Screensaver option in the left pane.
12. Enable the Require Password option. Click the Apply button.
13. Click on the + sign next to Peripherals in the left pane. Select the Mouse option.
14. The default for KDE is that it takes a single click to open a file or folder. If you want to change this so that it takes a double-click, enable the Double-click to open files and folders option.
15. Click the + sign next to the Power Control option in the left pane.
16. If you are using a notebook computer, you could show the battery monitor by enabling the Show Battery Monitor option.
17. Click the + sign next to the System option in the left pane.
18. Select the Date and time option. Change the date and time if needed.
19. Close the Control Center.

Exercise 15: Using Mandrake Control Center

1. Log in as root.
2. Start X Window.
3. Open the Main menu, select Configuration, and select Mandrake Control Center.
4. Select the Hardware option in the left pane.
5. To reconfigure the monitor, click the Configure your monitor icon. Click the Cancel button.
6. Click the Change Your Screen Resolution icon.
7. If your video card and monitor support it, select 1024 × 768 resolution and 65,000 colors (16 bits). Click the OK button. When it asks you to relog into Kwin, click the OK button. Click the Logout button.
8. Restart X Window. Notice that if you had a window open when you logged out, it remembers that when you restart X Window.
9. Click on the System option in the left pane.
10. What program would you use to add a font to your system?
11. What program would you use to back up the system?
12. Click Software Management in the left pane and click on Mandrake Update.
13. When it asks to continue, click on the Yes button.
14. When it asks to check to see if your network is running, click the Yes button.
15. Pick a site and click the OK button.
16. If there are any updates to download, follow the instructions to load all updates.
17. Quit the Mandrake Update program.

Exercise 16: Running X Window Configuration Programs

1. At the command prompt, log in as the root account.
2. At the command prompt, execute the Xconfigurator command.
3. Read the welcome screen and press the Enter key.
4. The card should already be probed. Press the Enter key. If the system cannot detect the video card, select the video card from the video card select screen.
5. Select the appropriate monitor. If yours is not listed, select Custom and input the appropriate information.
6. Select the amount of video memory for your video card.
7. Select the appropriate clockchip. Notice the No Clockchip setting is the recommended option. Tab until the OK option is selected and press the Enter key.
8. Select the resolution and bit modes that you desire and make sure they are supported by both your monitor and video card. Tab until you get to the OK button and press the Enter key.
9. Xconfigurator will now start X Window to test your configuration. Press Enter.
10. If X Window loads correctly, click on the OK button.
11. If you want X Window to automatically start, you would click the Yes button. Click the No button. Read the notice and click OK.
12. Start X Window and make sure it is working properly.

Exercise 17: Working with Processes

1. Do not load X Window. Log in as the root account.
2. Type the following command:
   ```
   ps
   ```
3. Type the following command:
   ```
   ps -au
   ```
4. Type the following command:
   ```
   ps -aux
   ```
5. To show only the bash entires, type the following command:
   ```
   ps -aux | grep bash
   ```
6. To start the top program, type the following command:
   ```
   top
   ```
7. While top is running, press the P key to sort the list by processor utilization.
8. Press Ctrl + Alt + F2 to change to the second virtual terminal.

9. Log in as root and start X Window. As X Window is loading, quickly press Ctrl + Alt + F1 to change back to the first virtual terminal.
10. Watch for a minute as X Window loads since the top program will automatically update.
11. Press the q key to exit the top program.
12. Go back to X Window by pressing Ctrl + Alt + F7.
13. Start AbiWord and the calculator.
14. Toggle back to the first virtual terminal.
15. Type the ps -aux command and find the AbiWord and the Simple Calculator (under Utilities). They should be the last two entries next to the ps-aux command.
16. Record the PID for the AbiWord and Calculator programs.
17. To kill the calculator, type the following command

    ```
    kill PID
    ```

    where the *PID* is the PID for the calculator that you just recorded.
18. Type *ps -aux*. Notice that the calculator is no longer running.
19. Execute the *ps -x* command.
20. To kill AbiWord, type the following command:

    ```
    killall AbiWord_d
    ```

21. Toggle back to X Window.
22. Under the KDE menus, select System and then Process Management.
23. Maximize the screen.
24. Click the %CPU header to sort by processor utilization.
25. Exit X Window.
26. Toggle back to the first virtual terminal.

Exercise 18: Creating a Printer

1. Start X Window.
2. At the terminal window, execute the printtool command.
3. Click on the New button, then click on the Next button.
4. In the Queue Type text box, type *lp*. For the queue type, select Local Printer. Click on the Next button.
5. Select the /dev/lp0 device. Click on the Next button.
6. Select the appropriate printer. Click on the Next button.
7. Click on the Finish button.
8. Click to highlight the lp list and click the Edit button.
9. Click on the Add button to add an alias. Specify a short name that represents the printer. For example, HPLJ4 would represent a Hewlett-Packard LaserJet 4. Click on the OK button.
10. Click on the Driver Options tab to view the options that are available for your printer.
11. Click on the OK button.
12. Open the File menu and select Save Changes.
13. Open the File menu and select Restart lpd. Click on the OK button.
14. Open the Tests menu and select the appropriate test page to print. Click on the OK button.
15. Close the printconf-gui window.

Exercise 19: Using and Managing the Print Queue

1. Take the printer offline.
2. Create a text file called test.txt with your name in the file.
3. To send the file to the printer, type in the following command:

    ```
    lpr test.txt
    ```

4. At the command prompt, execute the following command to view the print job:

    ```
    lpq
    ```

5. Find the job number for the print job that you sent.
6. To delete the print job, use the following command:

    ```
    lprm printjob#
    ```

7. Take the printer online.

8. Type the following command to test your printer without going through the print queue:

```
cat test.txt > /dev/lp0
```

This can help you isolate the problem to see if the problem is with the print queue or the printer or printer connection.

9. Quickly execute the lpq command to show that there is no print job for the previous command.

NOTE: You may need to force the document to print since the text file did not have an end of page code. Refer to your printer documentation.

10. Take the printer offline.
11. Type the following command to get the status of your print queue:

```
lpc status lp
```

12. Type the following command to stop the print queue:

```
lpc stop lp
```

13. Type the following command to start the print queue:

```
lpc start lp
```

14. Start X Window.
15. Start AbiWord. Type in your name. Open the File menu and select the Print option. Click on the Print button.
16. Open a terminal window and execute the klpq command. If it asks the type of spooler system, select BSD.
17. Click on each print job and click on the Remove button. Click Yes to remove the print job.
18. Close the print queue.
19. Close AbiWord.

CHAPTER 24

Advanced Linux

Topics Covered in This Chapter

Introduction

Whereas chapter 23 introduced you to Linux as an alternative operating system to Microsoft Windows, this chapter continues with Linux but covers the more advanced topics in configuring, maintaining, and troubleshooting Linux.

Objectives

1. Identify core dumps and remove or forward as appropriate.
2. Reconfigure boot loaders such as LILO and GRUB.
3. Take appropriate action on boot errors (e.g., LILO and bootstrap).
4. Stop, start, and restart services (daemons) as needed.
5. Manage run levels using init and shutdown.
6. Inspect and determine the cause of errors from system log files.
7. Diagnose and fix kernel panic and oops errors.
8. Configure, compile, and install a Linux kernel.
9. Explain when and why the kernel will need to be recompiled.
10. Load and use the linuxconf utility.
11. Mount and manage file systems and devices (e.g., /mnt, /dev, du, df, mount, and umount).
12. Create and manage local storage devices and file systems (e.g., fsck, fdisk, mkfs).
13. Use disk utilities to solve file system problems (e.g., mount and umount).
14. Identify and change file permissions, modes, and types by using chmod, chown, and chgrp.

24.1 THE BOOT PROCESS

On the C drive, the BIOS will look in the master boot record on the hard drive and start executing the code found there. These instructions typically look at the partition table, determine which partition is active, and go to the volume boot sector of that partition to load the operating system.

The ROM BIOS will find the LILO or GRUB boot manager, which will then find and load the kernel (vmlinuz). With the kernel in memory, it can begin executing. It knows only whatever functionality is built into it, which means any parts of the kernel compiled as modules are useless at this point. During boot-up, the Linux kernel will print many messages describing the hardware that is attached to your computer and the configuration of the kernel. See figure 24.1. Some of the tasks completed by the kernel during boot-up include:

- Display the Linux version.
- Change to the processor to protected mode so that it can use memory above 1 MB.
- Detect the speed of the processor and measure the performance of the computer in BogoMIPS.
- Detect how much memory the system has.
- Set up the virtual memory subsystem.
- Detect what type of hardware it is running on (type of hard disks, type of mouse, if connected to a network, etc.).
- Activate hardware devices.
- Test different parts of the hardware and print messages about these tests.
- Activate network protocols.
- Throughout the boot-up procedure, Linux tests different parts of the hardware and prints messages about these tests.
- Mount the root partition, so that it can be made available to the users.

Figure 24.1 The Linux Boot Screen

```
Loading linux.....................
Uncompressing Linux... Ok, booting the kernel.
Linux version 2.2.16-22 (root@porky.devel.redhat.com) (gcc version egcs-2.91.66
19998314/Linux (egcs-1.1.2 release)) #1 Tue Aug 22 16:49:06 EDT 2000
Detected 501142 kHz processor.
Console: colour VGA+ 80x25
Calibrating delay loop... 999.42 BogoMIPS
Memory 257868k/262688k available (1048k kernel code, 412k reserved, 3828K data,
 64k init, 8k bigmem)
Dentry hash table entries: 262144 (order 9, 2048k)
Buffer cache hash table entries: 262144 (order 8, 1024k)
Page cache hash table entries: 65536 (order 6, 256k)
VFS: Diskquotas version dquot_6.4.0 initialized
Pentium-Pentium III serial number disabled.
CPU: Intel Pentium III (Katmai) stepping 02
Checking 386/387 coupling... OK, FPU using exception 16 error reporting.
Checking 'hit' instruction... OK.
POSIX conformance testing by UNIFIX
mtrr: v1.35a (1999B819) Richard Gooch (rgooch@atnf.csiro.au)
PCI: PCI BIOS revision 2.18 entry at 0xf0720
PCI: Using configuration type 1
PCI: Probing PCI hardware
Linux NET4.0 for Linux 2.2
Based upon Swansea University Computer Society NET3.039
NET4: Unix domain sockets 1.0 for Linux NET4.0.
```

Because the kernel merely manages other programs, when it considers that everything is OK, it will look in several places for the **init** program and run the first one it finds. The /sbin directory is the most common location. The init program is the first nonkernel process. As the init takes over control of the computer, the kernel will work in the background as a manager and will not start any other programs.

All further programs are either started directly by init or by one of its "child" processes. Since it is considered the father of all processes (a process is simply a running program) in the entire system, it is assigned a process ID (PID) of 1 and it is made to resist signal 9, which is used to kill a process.

The init program goes through a complicated startup sequence. The init program reads its configure file, /etc/inittab, and determines the run level where it should start. When it is told to enter a run level, init executes a script as specified in the /etc/inittab file. The default run level depends on whether you indicated the system should start with a text-based or X Window login during the installation phase.

Because of the number of services that need to be managed, rc scripts are used. The main one, etc/rc.d/rc, is responsible for calling the appropriate scripts in the correct order for each run level.

Figure 24.2 The Linux Boot Screen After Init Has Been Loaded

```
INIT: version 2.70 booting
                        Welcome to Red Hat Linux
                 Press 'I' to enter interactive startup.
Mounting proc filesystem:                                         [ OK ]
Configuring kernel parameters:                                    [ OK ]
Setting clock  (localtime): Sat Jan  6 13:09:58 PST 2001          [ OK ]
Loading default keymap (us):                                      [ OK ]
Activating swap partitions:                                       [ OK ]
Setting hostname localhost.localdomain:                           [ OK ]
Checking root filesystem
/1: clean, 61552/780288 files, 200707/1558297 blocks

.                                                                 [ OK ]
Remounting root filesystem in read-write mode:                    [ OK ]
Finding module dependencies:                                      [ OK ]
Loading sound module (emu10k1):                                   [ OK ]
Loading mixer settings:                                           [ OK ]
Checking filesystems                                              [ OK ]
/boot: clean, 26/6024 files, 3715/24066 blocks
.                                                                 [ OK ]
Mounting local filesystems:                                       [ OK ]
Turning on user and group quotas for local filesystems:           [ OK ]
Enabling swap space:                                              [ OK ]
INIT: Entering runlevel: 3
Entering non-interactive startup
Checking for new hardware
```

First, it runs /etc/rc.d/rc.sysinit, which sets your path, sets up networking if necessary, starts swapping, checks the file systems, and so on. See figure 24.2. Basically, rc.sysinit takes care of everything that your system needs to have done at system initialization by its own commands and by calling other shell scripts. For example, on a networked system rc.sysinit uses the information in the /etc/sysconfig/network and /etc/sysconfig/clock files to initialize network processes and the clock. Some of the other tasks that the system initialization file does include checking the file system on the various volumes and mounting them, enabling the swap space, deleting temporary files left by previous programs, and starting up a daemon to log system messages into the /var/log/message log file. As described in chapter 23, a daemon is a process or program that runs in the background and performs a specified operation at predefined times or in response to certain events. To keep track of the order of the different system startup folders, there is a master control file called /etc/inittab.

NOTE: The shell script is executed or interpreted by bash, the same program that gives you the command prompt.

The /etc/rc.d/rc.local file is used to configure local computers. All the commands and scripts that run with this file are executed after the computer boots but before anyone logs in to the system. The rc.local file is also executed after a system run level is changed. For instance, you may want to start up additional daemons, or initialize a printer. One of rc.local's job is to create the login banner that by default displays your kernel version and machine type. To change this you can edit the file with a text editor.

The /etc/rc.d/rc.serial file was used in older versions of Linux to configure the serial port during boot-up. It is rarely used on current systems and when it is, it is only for backward compatibility. Most of the functionality of the old rc.serial file can now be found in the rc.local file.

During the booting of Linux, the messages displayed on the screen often scroll by quickly. To see the messages that are displayed during boot, you can view them from a log by executing the dmesg command.

24.2 RUN LEVELS

A run level is an identifier that specifies the current system state such as single user mode, multiuser mode, multiuser mode with network modes, and others. By specifying a run level, you are specifying a software configuration that will permit only a select group of processes (programs) to run and what daemons to start or stop.

Although the exact run-level definitions vary between distributions, they all serve the same purpose, which is to boot the system to the desired state by using the /etc/inittab file. See figure 24.3. However, the Linux Standard Base Specification may standardize run levels across all Linux distributions.

Figure 24.3 Sample Inittab File

```
# inittab       This file describes how the INIT process should set up
#               the system in a certain run-level.
#
# Author:       Miquel van Smoorenburg, <miquels@drinkel.nl.mugnet.org>
#               Modified for RHS Linux by Marc Ewing and Donnie Barnes

# Default runlevel. The runlevels used by RHS are:
#   0 - halt (Do NOT set initdefault to this)
#   1 - Single user mode
#   2 - Multiuser, without NFS (The same as 3, if you do not have networking)
#   3 - Full multiuser mode
#   4 - unused
#   5 - X11
#   6 - reboot (Do NOT set initdefault to this)

id:3:initdefault:

# System initialization.
```

Figure 24.3 Continued

```
si::sysinit:/etc/rc.d/rc.sysinit

l0:0:wait:/etc/rc.d/rc 0
l1:1:wait:/etc/rc.d/rc 1
l2:2:wait:/etc/rc.d/rc 2
l3:3:wait:/etc/rc.d/rc 3
l4:4:wait:/etc/rc.d/rc 4
l5:5:wait:/etc/rc.d/rc 5
l6:6:wait:/etc/rc.d/rc 6

# Things to run in every runlevel.
ud::once:/sbin/update

# Trap CTRL-ALT-DELETE
ca::ctrlaltdel:/sbin/shutdown -t3 -r now# When our UPS tells us power has
failed, assume we have a few minutes
# of power left.  Schedule a shutdown for 2 minutes from now.
# This does, of course, assume you have powerd installed and your
# UPS connected and working correctly.
pf::powerfail:/sbin/shutdown -f -h +2 "Power Failure; System Shutting Down"

# If power was restored before the shutdown kicked in, cancel it.
pr::12345:powerokwait:/sbin/shutdown -c "Power Restored; Shutdown Cancelled"

# Run gettys in standard runlevels
1:2345:respawn:/sbin/mingetty tty1
2:2345:respawn:/sbin/mingetty tty2
3:2345:respawn:/sbin/mingetty tty3
4:2345:respawn:/sbin/mingetty tty4
5:2345:respawn:/sbin/mingetty tty5
6:2345:respawn:/sbin/mingetty tty6

# Run xdm in runlevel 5
# xdm is now a separate service
x:5:respawn:/etc/X11/prefdm -nodaemon
```

Table 24.1 Red Hat Linux Run Levels

Run Level	Red Hat Linux Run Level	Linux Standard Base Specification Run Level
0	Halt	Halt
1	Single user mode	Single user mode
2	Multiuser mode, without NFS	Multiuser mode, with no network services exported
3	Full multiuser mode	Normal or full multiuser mode
4	Not used	Reserved for local use; default is normal or full multiuser mode
5	Full multiuser mode (with an X-based login screen)	Multiuser mode with xdm or equivalent
6	Reboot	Reboot

Levels 0, 1, and 6 are reserved. Run level 0 is used to halt the system, run level 1 is used to place the system in single user mode (similar to a Windows safe command prompt mode), and run level 6 is used to reboot the system. Note that the default run level should never be 0 or 6. See table 24.1. Generally, Linux operates in full multiuser mode with network support.

You can discover what run level your computer is in with the run level command. The command displays the previous and current run levels as output. To change to run level 1, you would type the following command:

```
init 0
```

To change to run level 3, you would type the following command:

```
init 3
```

NOTE: You can also use the telinit program to alter the run level. Usually, the telinit program is a symbolic link to init.

24.2.1 The Inittab File

The /etc/inittab file contains the locations of all the scripts or programs that need to be run and the processes to kill or terminate to complete the change. There are scripts for each of the run levels (rc0.d, rc1.d, rc2.d, rc3.d, rc4.d, rc5.d, and rc6.d). The init.d file actually contains all of the scripts. The files in the rc#.d directories are really links to the scripts in the init.d directory. Whereas the directory names (for example, /etc/rc.d) may vary between Linux distributions, the init runs all the scripts during bootup for the default run level, which is determined in the /etc/inittab file.

If you remember back in chapter 4, whether or not Linux automatically starts X Window during boot is determined by the default level. You can change from text mode to a graphical login using the init 5 command or from graphical to text with the init 3 command.

The scripts pointed to in the /etc/rc.d/init.d directory perform the actual process of starting and stopping services. When /etc/rc.d/rc runs through a specific run level's directory, it invokes each script in numerical order. It first runs the scripts that begin with a *K,* and then the scripts that begin with an *S.* For the scripts that begin with a *K* a parameter of stop is passed, whereas in the scripts with *S,* a parameter start is passed.

24.2.2 Daemons

In Linux, a **daemon** is a background process or service that monitors and performs many critical system functions and services. Typically, a daemon is started when the system boots, and the daemon processes run as long as the system is running. Most daemons have the capability to restart copies of themselves to handle specific tasks. A number of daemons have names that end with *d.* Some of the common daemons are:

- **amd**—automount daemon; automatically mounts removable media.
- **anacron**—checks cron jobs that were left out due to downtime and executes them. Useful if you have cron jobs scheduled but don't run your machine all the time—anacron will detect that during boot-up.
- **apmd**—Advanced Power Management BIOS daemon; is used on machines, especially laptops, that support apm.
- **arpwatch**—keeps watch for Ethernet/Ip address pairings.
- **atd**—runs jobs queued by the at command.
- **autofs**—controls the operation of automount daemons (competition to amd).
- **crond**—automatic task scheduler; manages the execution of tasks that are executed at regular but infrequent intervals, such as rotating log files, cleaning up /tmp directories, and so on.
- **cupsd**—the Common UNIX Printing System (CUPS) daemon; functions as an advanced printer spooling system that allows setting of printer options and automatic availability of a printer configured on one server in the whole network. The default printing system of Linux Mandrake.
- **dhcpd**—implements the Dynamic Host Configuration Protocol (DHCP) and the Internet Bootstrap Protocol (BOOTP).
- **httpd**—functions as daemon for the Apache web server.
- **inetd**—listens for service requests on network connections, particularly dial-in services. This daemon can automatically load and unload other daemons (ftpd, telnetd, etc.), thereby economizing on system resources.
- **isdn**—controls ISDN services.
- **kerneld**—automatically loads and unloads kernel modules.
- **klogd**—intercepts and displays or logs the kernel messages depending on the priority level of the messages. The messages typically go to the appropriately named files in the directory /var/log/kernel.
- **kudzu**—detects and configures new or changed hardware during boot.
- **linuxconf**—the linuxconf configuration tool; the automated part runs if you want linuxconf to perform various tasks at boot time to maintain the system configuration.
- **lpd**—functions as printing daemon.
- **named**—serves as the Internet Domain Name System (DNS) daemon.
- **netfs**—network file system mounter; is used for mounting nfs, smb, and ncp shares on boot.
- **network**—activates all network interfaces at boot time by calling scripts in /etc/sysconfig/network-scripts.
- **nfsd**—used for exporting nfs shares when requested by remote systems.
- **nfslock**—starts and stops nfs file locking service.
- **numlock**—locks Numlock key at init run-level change.
- **pcmcia**—provides generic services for PCMCIA cards in laptops.
- **portmap**—needed for remote procedure calls.
- **routed**—manages routing tables.
- **rstatd**—functions as kernel statistics server.
- **sendmail**—serves as mail transfer agent; this is the agent that comes with Red Hat.
- **smbd**—the SAMBA (or smb) daemon; functions as a network connectivity service to Microsoft Windows computers on a network (hard drive sharing, printers, etc).
- **smtpd**—Simple Mail Transfer Protocol; exchanges electronic mail messages. Several daemons that support SMTP are available, including sendmail, smtpd, rsmtpd, qmail, zmail, and so forth.
- **squid**—an HTTP proxy with caching; relays requests from clients to the outside world, and returns the results. You would use this particular proxy if you wanted to use your Linux computer as a gateway to the Internet for other computers on the network. Another (and probably safer) way to do it is to set up masquarading.
- **syslogd**—manages system activity logging; the configuration file is /etc/syslog.conf.
- **usb**—used for devices on the universal serial bus.
- **xfs**—serves as the X font server.
- **xntpd**—finds the server for an NIS domain and stores the information about it in a binding file.
- **ypbind**—NIS binder; is needed if computer is part of Network Information Service domain.

A typical Linux configuration employs a minimum of 15 separate daemons running in the background and may run 50 or more daemons.

24.2.3 Starting, Stopping, and Restarting Daemons

To shut down a daemon under Linux, type the name of the daemon, followed by the stop. For example, to stop the smb daemon, type the following command:

```
smb stop
```

To start the daemon, you would use *start* instead of *stop*. To start the smb daemon, you would use the following command:

```
smb start
```

You can also use the restart parameter. Note that sometimes the daemons will include the path name. Therefore, the smb command might be:

```
/etc/rc.d/init.d/smb start
```

Before, moving on to the next section, we need to discuss the xinet daemon (xinetd). This daemon maintains quite a few network services including telnet, wu-ftp, swat, linuxconf-web, swat, and rsh commands to ensure system security. All of these services' configuration files are stored in the /etc/xinetd.d directory. To stop, start, or restart xinetd, which in turn will stop, start, or restart the services that it manages, you would use the following commands:

```
service xinetd stop
service xinetd start
service xinetd restart
```

24.2.4 Activating and Deactivating Daemons for Run Levels

There are several utilities that allow you to manage daemons. They include ntsysv, chkconfig, tksysv, and linuxconf. Linuxconf will be explained later in the chapter.

The ntsysv utility provides a simple interface for activating or deactivating services. You can use ntsysv to turn an xinetd-managed service on or off. You can also use ntsysv to start or stop a service in the /etc/rc.d hierarchy; in that case, the ntsysv command (without options) configures the current run level. If you want to configure a different run level, use something like ntsysv—levels 016. (In this example, you'd be setting the services for run levels 0, 1, and 6.)

NOTE: The GNOME desktop environment does offer a ksysv, a graphical interface version of the ntsysv.

The ntsysv interface works like the text mode installation program. Use the up and down arrows to navigate up and down the list. The spacebar selects and unselects services and is also used to "press" the OK and Cancel buttons. To move between the list of services and the OK and Cancel buttons, use the Tab key. An asterisk (*) signifies that a service is set to on. The F1 key will pop up a short description of each service. See figure 24.4.

The chkconfig command can also be used to activate and deactivate services. If you use the chkconfig--list command, you'll see a list of system services and whether they are started (on) or stopped (off) in run levels 0–6. See figure 24.5.

Figure 24.4 The Ntsysv Interface

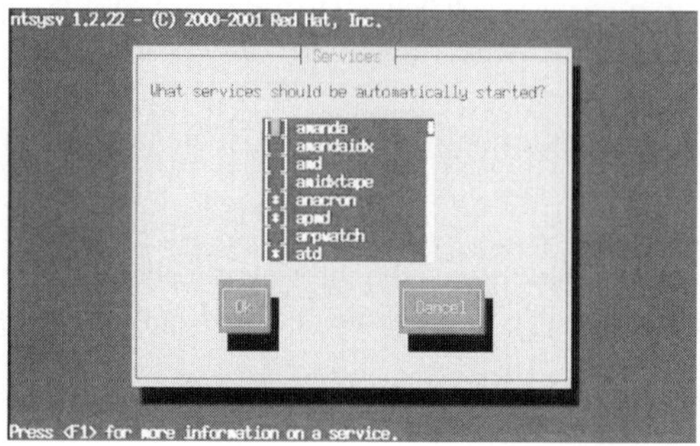

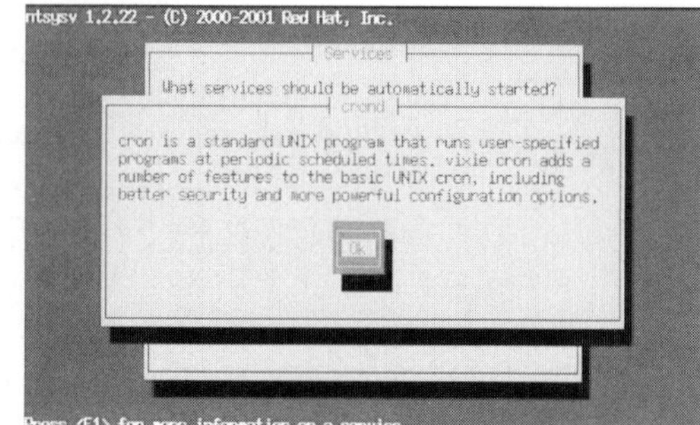

Figure 24.5 The Chkconfig --list Command

```
[root@LinuxPC root]# chkconfig --list
keytable        0:off   1:on    2:on    3:on    4:on    5:on    6:off
atd             0:off   1:off   2:off   3:on    4:on    5:on    6:off
kdcrotate       0:off   1:off   2:off   3:off   4:off   5:off   6:off
syslog          0:off   1:off   2:on    3:on    4:on    5:on    6:off
gpm             0:off   1:off   2:on    3:on    4:on    5:on    6:off
kudzu           0:off   1:off   2:off   3:on    4:on    5:on    6:off
sendmail        0:off   1:off   2:on    3:on    4:on    5:on    6:off
netfs           0:off   1:off   2:off   3:on    4:on    5:on    6:off
network         0:off   1:off   2:on    3:on    4:on    5:on    6:off
random          0:off   1:off   2:on    3:on    4:on    5:on    6:off
rawdevices      0:off   1:off   2:off   3:on    4:on    5:on    6:off
pcmcia          0:off   1:off   2:on    3:on    4:on    5:on    6:off
apmd            0:off   1:off   2:on    3:on    4:on    5:on    6:off
ipchains        0:off   1:off   2:on    3:on    4:on    5:on    6:off
iptables        0:off   1:off   2:on    3:on    4:on    5:on    6:off
crond           0:off   1:off   2:on    3:on    4:on    5:on    6:off
anacron         0:off   1:off   2:on    3:on    4:on    5:on    6:off
lpd             0:off   1:off   2:on    3:on    4:on    5:on    6:off
xfs             0:off   1:off   2:on    3:on    4:on    5:on    6:off
ntpd            0:off   1:off   2:off   3:off   4:off   5:off   6:off
irda            0:off   1:off   2:off   3:off   4:off   5:off   6:off
portmap         0:off   1:off   2:off   3:on    4:on    5:on    6:off
xinetd          0:off   1:off   2:off   3:on    4:on    5:on    6:off
autofs          0:off   1:off   2:off   3:on    4:on    5:on    6:off
nfs             0:off   1:off   2:off   3:off   4:off   5:off   6:off
nfslock         0:off   1:off   2:off   3:on    4:on    5:on    6:off
nscd            0:off   1:off   2:off   3:off   4:off   5:off   6:off
identd          0:off   1:off   2:off   3:off   4:off   5:off   6:off
radvd           0:off   1:off   2:off   3:off   4:off   5:off   6:off
rwhod           0:off   1:off   2:off   3:off   4:off   5:off   6:off
snmpd           0:off   1:off   2:off   3:off   4:off   5:off   6:off
rhnsd           0:off   1:off   2:off   3:off   4:off   5:off   6:off
ypbind          0:off   1:off   2:off   3:off   4:off   5:off   6:off
isdn            0:off   1:off   2:on    3:on    4:on    5:on    6:off
sshd            0:off   1:off   2:on    3:on    4:on    5:on    6:off
rstatd          0:off   1:off   2:off   3:off   4:off   5:off   6:off
rusersd         0:off   1:off   2:off   3:off   4:off   5:off   6:off
rwalld          0:off   1:off   2:off   3:off   4:off   5:off   6:off
vncserver       0:off   1:off   2:off   3:off   4:off   5:off   6:off
```

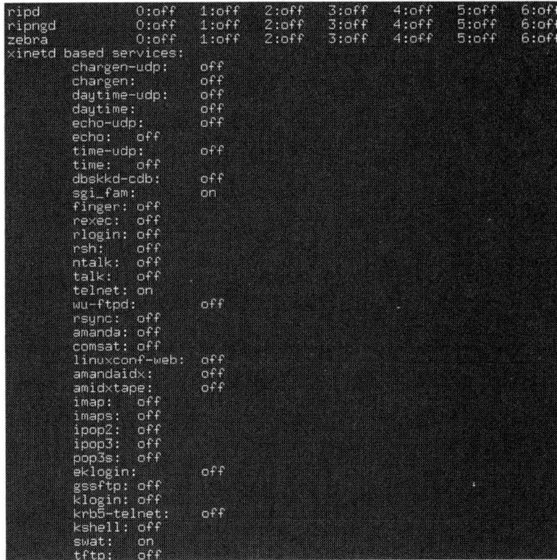

```
ripd            0:off   1:off   2:off   3:off   4:off   5:off   6:off
ripngd          0:off   1:off   2:off   3:off   4:off   5:off   6:off
zebra           0:off   1:off   2:off   3:off   4:off   5:off   6:off
xinetd based services:
        chargen-udp:    off
        chargen:        off
        daytime-udp:    off
        daytime:        off
        echo-udp:       off
        echo:   off
        time-udp:       off
        time:   off
        dbskkd-cdb:     off
        sgi_fam:        on
        finger: off
        rexec:  off
        rlogin: off
        rsh:    off
        ntalk:  off
        talk:   off
        telnet: on
        wu-ftpd:        off
        rsync:  off
        amanda: off
        comsat: off
        linuxconf-web:  off
        amandaidx:      off
        amidxtape:      off
        imap:   off
        imaps:  off
        ipop2:  off
        ipop3:  off
        pop3s:  off
        eklogin:        off
        gssftp: off
        klogin: off
        krb5-telnet:    off
        kshell: off
        swat:   on
        tftp:   off
```

You can also use chkconfig -list to query a service in /etc/rc.d; you will see the service's settings for each run level. For example, if you execute the following command

```
chkconfig --list anacron
```

it will return

```
anacron 0:off  1:off  2:on  3:on  4:on  5:on  6:off
```

More important, chkconfig can be used to set a service to be started (or not) in a specific run level. For example, if you want to turn off nscd in run levels 3, 4, and 5, you would use a command like this:

```
chkconfig --level 345 nscd off
```

A GUI utility to enable and disable services in any run level 2 through 5 is tksysv. Locate and select the service in the given run level, then click Remove. This removes its start and stop entry. Click the service in the Available list and then click Add. You will be prompted to enter a run level and whether to start or stop it. You may also need to enter a sequence number.

Changes do not take effect immediately after using ntsysv, chkconfig, and tksysv. You must stop or start the individual service manually, reboot the system, or change run levels.

24.3 LINUX LOADER (LILO)

Before Linux can start on your system, it must be told to boot by special instructions placed on a boot loader—code that exists on the primary hard drive that knows how to start the Linux kernel. If you are using an x86 system that boots only Linux, and if you use only one version of the Linux kernel, then the exact process used by the boot loader to start Linux is simplified.

If you want to have a choice of several versions of the kernel or several different operating systems, you will need to use a boot loader. Several boot loaders are available, some of which can boot a Linux kernel directly; others require help to do the job.

LILO is a boot manager that comes bundled as part of almost every Linux distribution, including Red Hat, Debian, Caldera, and SuSE Linux distributions. It can be installed in the master boot record or the volume boot sector and it allows you to boot MS-DOS, OS/2, Window 95 or Windows 98, or Windows Me. It is recommended to use the MBR, unless the MBR already starts another OS loader such as Norton's System Commander's or PowerQuest's Partition Maker's boot manager.

Using a boot manager such as LILO has its advantages and disadvantages. The advantage is that it gives you the opportunity to have multiple operating systems on a hard drive and it gives you the choice of which operating system to load. One disadvantage is a boot manager adds another level of complexity to the boot process. It must be modified or possibly reinstalled if you add, delete, or upgrade a version of any of the operating systems on your disk. Because it modifies the master boot record of your hard disk, so if something goes wrong, you might not be able to boot with anything other than a floppy disk until you reformat your hard drive, and possibly recreate the master boot record. Also, the boot manager that you choose might not be compatible with some operating systems.

24.3.1 Booting with LILO

If LILO is installed into the master boot record, after your system performs its default BIOS checks and detections, the LILO prompt or LILO GUI screen waits for the name of a boot image to load. If you do not respond within a specified period (this value is stored in the /etc/lilo.conf file), LILO loads the default boot image.

If you are at the LILO boot prompt and you press the Shift key, the boot loader will ask you which image to boot by displaying the "LILO" message. You then specify the name of the Linux boot image, followed by one or more options (command arguments). Note that the boot command-line options are case sensitive. LILO passes these boot command-line options directly to the Linux kernel. If you want to list your choices, press the Tab key or the ? if you have a United States keyboard. If LILO is not configured to be interactive, press and hold down the Alt or Shift key before the "LILO" message appears. If you are booting the GUI prompt, you will have to press Ctrl + X to enter text mode to start the LILO boot prompt. See figure 24.6.

24.3.2 Installing LILO

The easiest way to install LILO is to do it during the installation program. If it is not installed correctly, you can easily corrupt your hard disk. The only time you have to repeat LILO configuration and installation is when you update the kernel or add a new operating system that you want to boot through LILO.

Installing LILO involves two basic steps:

1. Prepare the LILO configuration file, which contains information that is necessary for installing LILO. The default LILO configuration file is /etc/lilo.conf.
2. Run the map installer (/sbin/lilo) program to update the boot sector and create the /boot/map file, which contains information that LILO uses during the boot process.

To prepare the LILO configuration file you have to log in as root and edit the /etc/lilo.conf file with a text editor. Essentially, you add or edit information about the operating systems that you want to boot with Linux and names of the disk partitions where those operating systems reside. When the LILO configuration file /etc/lilo.conf is ready, you can install LILO with the following command:

```
/sbin/lilo
```

Figure 24.6 Using the Tab key to display the Boot options/operating systems (DOS and Linux).

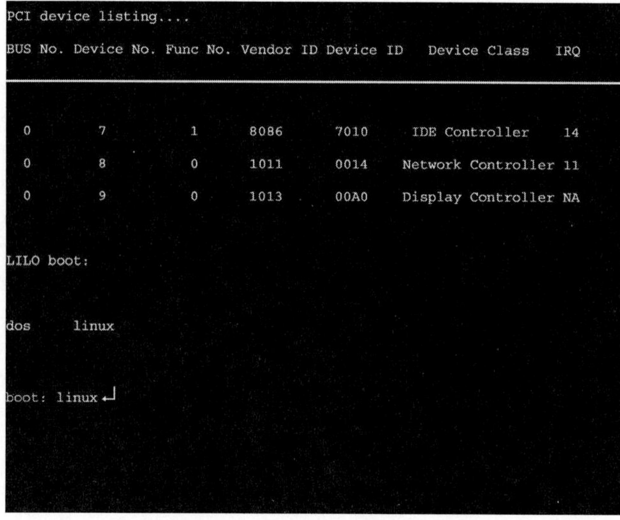

The LILO program looks for the lilo.conf file in the /etc directory, interprets its contents, prepares the necessary boot and map files, and initializes the boot record of the device specified by the boot line in the configuration line. If the boot device is specified as a hard disk partition, for example, LILO sets up the boot sector of that disk partition.

24.3.3 Lilo.conf File

The LILO configuration file (/etc/lilo.conf) is a simple text file used to figure out what operating systems are installed on your system and where their boot information is located. Each section lists the boot information specific to each operating system that LILO can boot. In figure 24.7, you will find an example of the lilo.conf file. The Linux section gives the boot information for Linux, whereas the other section, in this particular example, MS-DOS, indicates where the additional operating system is located.

Figure 24.7 Example of a Lilo.conf File

```
# LILO Configuration file
# Start LILO global Section
boot=/dev/had
backup=/boot/MBR.had.990428  # Backup file for the old MBR
map=/boot/map
install=/boot/boot.b
prompt
password = testpw    # Example LILO password
timeout=50           # wait at prompt for 5 s before default is booted
message=/boot/message
linear                # Generate linear section addresses
default=linux_71
# End LILO global section

# Linux bootable partition config begins
image=/boot/vmlinuz-2.4.2-2
        label=linux_71
        initrd=boot/initrd-2.4.2-2.img
        read-only
        root=/dev/hda2    # Root partition for kernel
# Linux bootable partition config ends

# DOS bootable partition config begins
other = /dev/hda1
    label = DOS
    loader = /boot/chain.b
    table = /dev/had
# DOS bootable partition config ends
```

Table 24.2 Lilo.conf Global Section

Parameter	Description
boot=<*bootdevice*>	The device on whose first sector LILO should be installed. The <bootdevice> may be a floppy disk drive (for example, /dev/fd0), a partition (for example /dev/hdb3), or a whole disk (for example, /dev/had). When it is installed on the whole disk, LILO is installed in the MBR. If the option is missing, LILO is installed on the current root partition.
prompt	Forces the LILO prompt to be displayed. The default is no prompt. It is recommend if LILO is managing more than one system.
timeout=<*tenth of seconds*>	Sets a timeout for the prompted option, thus enabling an automatic reboot if no entry occurs in a given time. The timeout parameter is recommend to guarantee an automatic boot if nothing is entered at the prompt.
message=<*messagefile*>	Specifies a file containing a message that is displayed before the boot prompt. No message is displayed while waiting for a shifting key after printing "LILO." In the message, the FF character ([Ctrl + L]) clears the local screen. The size of the message file is limited to 65535 bytes. The map file has to be rebuilt if the message file is changed or moved: If there are many systems installed, it is recommended that you list them in the special message file.
compact	Tries to merge read requests for adjacent sectors into a single read request. This drastically reduces load time and keeps the map smaller. Using *compact* is especially recommended when booting from a floppy disk.
default=*name*	Uses the specified image as the default boot image. If default is omitted, the image appearing first in the configuration file is used.
delay=*tsecs*	Specifies the number of tenths of a second the boot loader should wait before booting the first image. This is useful on systems that immediately boot from the hard disk after enabling the keyboard. The boot loader doesn't wait if *delay* is omitted or is set to zero.
map=*map-file*	Specifies the location of the map file. If *map* is omitted, the file */boot/map* is used.
password=*password*	The per-image option *password=* . . . (see below) applies to all images.
verbose=<*level*>	Using verbose mode turns on lots of progress reporting. Higher numbers give more verbose output. If -v is additionally specified on the LILO command line, the level is increased accordingly. The maximum verbosity level is 5.
lba32	This option enables the ability to boot kernels located past the 1,024th cylinder of the disk (about 8 MB on most modern hard drives).

The lilo.conf file can be divided into two or more sections. The first section is the global section, which establishes overall values for LILO. See tables 24.2, 24.3, and 24.4. Anything between a pound sign (#) and the end of line is regarded as a comment. The spaces and comments are ignored by LILO and can be used to improve readability by explaining what a line does. There can be up to 16 images mentioned in lilo.conf.

The first line, boot=/dev/hda, tells LILO where to write the boot sector. Usually, this is the first sector of the boot drive: /dev/hda for IDE-based disks, and /dev/sda for SCSI-based disks. When you want another program such as the NT OS loader to handle the master boot record (MBR), you can specify that the boot sector be written to another partition. The control can be passed to this partition from the code specified in the MBR.

The prompt instruction tells LILO to give the lilo prompt at boot time. The timeout=50 command tells LILO to wait for 50 deciseconds (5 seconds) before selecting the default boot image and starting the boot process (specified with the default=linux_7.1 line).

The next line begins a small block telling LILO which specific boot image to load:

```
image=/boot/vmlinuz-2.4.2-2
```

Table 24.3 Lilo.conf Linux Section

Parameter	Description
image=*<kernelimage>*	The name of the kernel image to be booted, including its directory location. With a new system, it will most likely be /boot/vmlinuz.
label=*<name>*	This name has to be unique in /etc/lilo.conf. Otherwise, you can freely choose a name for the system. Maximum length is 15 characters. You should use only letters, numbers, and underscore for names; no blanks or special characters including periods (.). The default is the file name of the kernel image such as /boot/vmlinuz. By entering this name at the LILO prompt, you select this system to boot.
root=*<rootdevice>*	This specifies the device that should be mounted as root (for example, /dev/hda2). If the special name current is used, the root device is set to the device on which the root file system is currently mounted. If the root has been changed with -r , the respective device is used. If the variable *root* is omitted, the root device setting contained in the kernel image is used.
read-only/read-write	Read-only specifies that the root file system should be mounted read-only. After the kernel loads and runs a check on it using the fsck tool, the root file system is remounted read/write.
vga=*mode*	This specifies the VGA text mode that should be selected when booting. The following values are recognized (case is ignored): normal: select normal 80×25 text mode. extended (or ext): select 80×50 text mode. ask: stop and ask for user input (at boot time). If this variable is omitted, the VGA mode setting contained in the kernel image is used. (That is set at compile time using the SVGA_MODE variable in the kernel Makefile, and can later be changed with the rdev[8]program.)
init=*<init program>*	Since Linux kernel version 1.3.43, the init option specifies which init= to execute another command instead of /sbin/init.
initrd=<image_file>	If the kernel does not include a needed driver for boot, the initrd can be used to load a RAM disk that will load the needed driver to complete the boot.
append	This optional line lets you pass parameters to the kernel. These parameters influence the way the kernel treats hardware and you can even load certain hardware drivers.

Table 24.4 Lilo.conf Other Systems Section

Parameter	Description
other=*<partition>*	Other tells LILO to start the partition of other systems such as DOS, for example /dev/hda1.
loader=*<Boot loader>*	To load boot sector that belongs to another operating system, LILO constructs a pseudo MBR in its map file. At boot time, LILO first starts this pseudo MBR, which in turn starts the other boot sector. This option specifies the file where the code for the pseudo MBR is to be found.
default:/boot/chain.b	Sometimes another OS that needs to be booted from the first hard drive is supposed to boot from another hard drive using LILO. There are additional options that cause the hard drives to swap according to their device numbers: map-drive=<Number> and to=<Number> The loader os2_d.b serves to load OS/2 from the second hard drive.

The image to boot is the file /boot/vmlinux-2.4.2-2, which is the Linux kernel. Inside the block is the line label=linux_71, which is the name that is displayed if the user asks for a list of available boot options at the lilo prompt.

The root=/dev/hda2 tells LILO the partition on which the /boot/vmlinuz-2.2.5-15 file is located. If you are not sure which partition holds your kernel, go to the kernel's directory and use the `df .` command.

The last option in the block is read-only, which tells LILO to mount the root file system with read-only permissions when starting the kernel. This is necessary so that the root file system can check itself for corruption during the boot process. Once this is done, the root file system is automatically re-mounted with read/write access.

24.3.4 Removing LILO

If you set up LILO on the hard disk's master boot record but later want to remove it, you can do so easily, provided that you have MS-DOS version 5.0 or later. All you have to do is boot from a DOS boot floppy and run FDISK with the /MBR option. The FDISK /MBR command will recreate the master boot record that MS-DOS uses. Another way to uninstall LILO is to use LILO itself as follows:

```
/sbin/lilo -u
```

LILO replaces the MBR from a saved copy of the old boot sector, which LILO saves when you first install it.

Use the /sbin/lilo -u command only if you have installed LILO on your hard disk's MBR. When you use the -u option, LILO simply copies a file named /boot/boot.nnnn where *nnnn* is the device numbers, such as 03000 for the /dev.hda and 0800 for /dev.sda to the disk's MBR. Of course, a bad MBR makes the disk unbootable. In such a case, boot from a DOS floppy disk and use the FDISK /MBR command to restore the MBR to boot DOS.

24.3.5 Updating LILO

When updating to a new version of LILO, the initial steps are the same as for a first-time installation: extract all files, configure the Makefile, run make to build the executables, and run make install to install the files.

If you want to update an existing version of LILO with a newer one, the process is the same as a first-time installation except that existing configuration files are renamed to .old automatically. For example, boot.b and chain.b are renamed to boot.old and chain.old. If the new version of LILO behaves properly, the .old files can be deleted. Because the locations of boot.b, chain.b, and so on have changed and because the map file format may be different too, you have to update the boot sector and the map file. Run /sbin/lilo to do this.

Normally, system upgrades such as installation or removal of packages and replacement installed binaries do not affect LILO. Of course, if a new kernel is installed in the process, the normal kernel update procedure has to be followed. This will be discussed later in the chapter. Also, if kernels are removed or added, it may be necessary to update the configuration file. If LILO is updated by this system upgrade, /sbin/lilo should be run before booting the upgraded system. It is generally a good idea not to rely on the upgrade procedure to perform this essential step automatically.

24.3.6 Adding a New Kernel to LILO

It is possible to configure LILO to boot either of two or more kernels using the same distribution. This can be very convenient when you want to test a new kernel. Rather than eliminate your old working configuration, you install a new kernel alongside the old one and create a new lilo.conf entry for the new kernel. You can then select either kernel at boot time. If the new kernel doesn't work as expected, you can reboot and select the old kernel.

To add a new kernel to LILO, do the following:

1. Install the new kernel file, typically in /boot. Ensure that you do not overwrite the existing kernel file just in case something goes wrong with the new one. If you compile your own kernel, remember to install the kernel modules with make modules_install.
2. Copy the section that represents the commands for the kernel for the existing kernel file in /etc/lilo.conf. The result is two identical sections.

3. Modify the name (label) of one of the sections that represents the kernels to reflect the new kernel name. You can use any arbitrary name you like, even a numeric one, such as 242 for the 2.4.2 kernel.
4. Adjust the image line in the new kernel's group to point to the new kernel file.
5. If you want to make the new kernel the default, change the default line to point to the new kernel.
6. Save your /etc/lilo.conf changes.
7. Type *lilo* to install LILO in the MBR or boot partition's boot sector.

24.3.7 Troubleshooting LILO

To help troubleshoot boot and other problems, you can force Linux to boot into single mode directly (run level 1), a sort of safe mode. In run level 1, you are booted into the most minimal environment possible. The root file system will be mounted read-only and almost nothing will be set up and you will have usable system maintenance shell (so all those prompt commands that you have been learning will come in handy).

To boot into single mode, type the following command at the LILO boot prompt

```
linux single
```

whereas *linux* is the boot label for the boot image that you want to start.

You can also start Linux in an emergency recovery mode by using the emergency parameter:

```
linux emergency
```

Again, *linux* is the boot label for the boot image that you want to start. Then if you press Ctrl + D, you can do a normal boot.

For example, if your system boots, but does not allow you to log in when it has completed booting, trying rebooting and specifying one of these options at the LILO boot prompt.

NOTE: If you use the emergency parameter, you will be required to provide the root password before performing any work on the system.

You can use the root= option at the prompt to tell the Linux kernel to mount as root of a different partition than the one appearing in /lilo.conf. This can come in handy if you accidently delete the root partition or the root partition has become corrupted. If you experience problems during the boot process, you can access the bare system by specifying init=/bin/sh. (When you are at the shell prompt you most likely will need to mount your disks. Try:

```
mount -w -n -o remount /
```

and

```
mount -a
```

The -a causes all file systems mentioned in fstab to be mounted as indicated (except for those whose line contains the *noauto* keyword).

NOTE: Don't forget to type the command *umount -a* before turning off the computer. If you specify a number on the kernel command line, you instruct init to enter a specific run level. The default is usually 2 or 3, depending on your Linux distribution.

One of the most common installation problems other than hardware relates to LILO. Occasionally, a disk sector is bad and LILO doesn't install properly. Other times, LILO doesn't work because it was configured incorrectly. One of the best ways to troubleshoot your LILO problems is to watch the output of LILO itself. If the BIOS signals an error when LILO is trying to load a boot image, the respective error code is displayed. See tables 24.5 and 24.6.

If your system repeats rebooting and never finishes booting, 9 of out of 10 times it is caused by someone making changes to the kernel file and forgetting to run the lilo command so that the new changes will take effect.

You can correct this problem by booting from the boot floppy and running the lilo command, or by using a rescue disk (see chapter 10 on making and using a rescue boot disk), mounting the boot partition under /mnt, and running LILO with the options to use a relative path:

```
lilo -r /mnt
```

Table 24.5 Lilo Output Showing an Error

Error	Description
Nothing appears on the screen	No part of LILO has been loaded. LILO either isn't installed or the partition on which its boot sector is located wasn't started. Use a boot floppy and check /etc/lilo.conf and run /sbin/lilo again. Check the boot line of /etc/lilo.conf, adjust it as necessary, and type *lilo* to reinstall LILO. If LILO is installed on a partition, you may have to make it the default boot partition using DOS's FDISK or Linux's fdisk.
L [error] . . .	The first-stage boot loader has been loaded and started, but it can't load the second-stage boot loader. The two-digit error codes indicate the type of problem; most indicate a hardware error. Some indicate a media failure or a geometry mismatch. The "geometry mismatch" error might occur if you've moved the kernel to a different location or changed the partition setup and forgot to run LILO afterward. Other geometry mismatch problems can often be overcome by changing disk geometry options in the BIOS or by adding or removing such options in /etc/lilo.conf.
LI	The first-stage boot loader was able to load the second-stage boot loader, but has failed to execute it. This can either be caused by a geometry mismatch, by moving /boot/boot.b without running the map installer, or because /boot/boot.b is missing or corrupt. These problems can often be overcome by changing disk geometry options in the BIOS or by adding or removing such options in /etc/lilo.conf. You may also need to go into your system's BIOS and make certain that LBA mode is enabled. If LBA was off, you will need to repartition and reinstall. Last, you may have installed LILO above the 1,024th cylinder on your hard drive. The kernel needs to reside entirely below the 1,023rd cylinder on the drive. If this is the case, you need to create a /boot partition that resides in these limits and reinstall LILO.
LIL	The second-stage boot loader can't load the descriptor table from the map file. This is typically caused by a media failure or by a geometry mismatch. Geometry mismatch problems can often be overcome by changing disk geometry options in the BIOS or by adding or removing such options in /etc/lilo.conf.
LIL?	Second-stage boot loader has been loaded at an incorrect address. See LI.
LIL-	Corrupt descriptor file table. See LI.
LI1010	LILO has booted, but it cannot locate the kernel image. This problem is usually caused by installing a new kernel over the old one and failing to rerun LILO.
LILO	The LILO program has loaded and run correctly. If Linux fails to boot at this point, the problem is most likely with the kernel, its drivers, or the system configuration files.

Table 24.6 LILO Fatal errors

Error	Description
Boot sector of *device_name* doesn't have a boot signature	The sector from which LILO should be uninstalled doesn't appear to be a LILO boot sector.
Boot sector of *device_name* doesn't have a LILO signature	The sector from which LILO should be uninstalled doesn't appear to be a LILO boot sector.
Can't put the boot sector on logical partition *number*	An attempt has been made to put LILO's boot sector on the current root file system partition which is on a logical partition. This usually doesn't have the desired effect, because common MBRs can only boot primary partitions. This check can be bypassed by explicitly specifying the boot partition with the -b option or by setting the configuration variable boot.
Checksum error	The descriptor table of the map file has an invalid checksum. Refresh the map file immediately.

Continued

Table 24.6 Continued

Error	Description
Device 0x *number:* Got bad geometry *sec/ hd/ cyl*	The device driver for the SCSI controller does not support geometry detection. You have to specify the geometry explicitly.
Device 0x *number:* Invalid partition table, entry *number*	The 3D and linear addresses of the first sector of the specified partition don't correspond. This is typically caused by partitioning a disk with a program that doesn't align partitions to tracks and later using PC/MS-DOS or OS/2 on that disk. LILO can attempt to correct the problem.
Device_name is not a valid partition device	The specified device is either not a device at all, a whole disk, or a partition on a different disk than the one in whose section its entry appears.
Device_name is not a whole disk device	Only the geometry of whole disks (e.g., /dev/hda, /dev/sdb, etc.) can be redefined when using disk sections.
DISKTAB and DISK are mutually exclusive	You cannot use a disktab file and disk geometry definitions in the configuration file at the same time. Maybe /etc/disktab was accidentally used, because that's the default for backward compatibility. You should delete /etc/disktab after completing the transition to disk sections.
Duplicate entry in partition table	A partition table entry appears twice. The partition table has to be fixed with fdisk.
Duplicate geometry definition for *device_name*	A disk or partition geometry definition entry for the same device appears twice in the configuration file. Note that you must not write a partition section for the whole disk—its start sector is always the first sector of the disk.
First sector of *device* doesn't have a valid boot signature	The first sector of the specified device does not appear to be a valid boot sector. You might have confused the device name.
Geo_comp_addr: Cylinder *number* is beyond end of media (*number*)	A file block appears to be located beyond the last cylinder of the disk. This probably indicates an error in the disk geometry specification or a file system corruption.
Geo_comp_addr: Cylinder number is too big (*number* > 1023)	Blocks of a file are located beyond the 1,024th cylinder of a hard disk. LILO can't access such files, because the BIOS limits cylinder numbers to the range 0–1,023. Try moving the file to a different place, preferably a partition that is entirely within the first 1,024 cylinders of the disk.
Hole found in map file (*location*)	The map installer is confused about the disk organization. Please report this error.
Item doesn't have a valid LILO signature	The specified item has been located, but is not part of LILO.
Item has an invalid stage code (*number*)	The specified item has probably been corrupted. Try rebuilding LILO.
Item is version *number.* Expecting version *number*	The specified entity is either too old or too new. Make sure all parts of LILO (map installer, boot loaders, and chain loaders) are from the same distribution.
Kernel *name* is too big	The kernel image (without the setup code) is bigger than 512 KB. LILO would overwrite itself when trying to load such a kernel. Try removing some unused drivers and compiling the kernel again. With recent (compressed) kernels, the reason for this error is most likely that the kernel image is damaged or that it contains trailing "junk" (e.g., as the result of copying an entire boot floppy to the hard disk).
Map *path* is not a regular file	This is probably the result of an attempt to omit writing a map file (e.g., with -m /dev/null). The -t option should be used to accomplish this.
Must specify LOADER for BIOS device *number*	When booting an operating system from any device than the first hard or floppy disk, specifying the chain loader (option loader in the image section) is now mandatory.
Must specify SECTORS and HEADS together	It is assumed that disks with a "strange" number of sectors will also have a "strange" number of heads. Therefore, it's all or nothing.

Continued

Table 24.6 Continued

Error	Description
Partition entry not found	The partition from which an other operating system should be booted isn't listed in the specified partition table. This either means that an incorrect partition table has been specified or that you're trying to boot from a logical partition. The latter usually doesn't work. You can bypass this check by omitting the partition table specification (e.g., omitting the variable table).
Sorry, don't know how to handle device *number*	LILO uses files that are located on a device for which there is no easy way to determine the disk geometry. Such devices have to be explicitly described.
Timestamp in boot sector of *device* differs from date of *file*	The backup copy of the boot sector does not appear to be an ancestor of the current boot sector. If you are absolutely sure that the boot sector is indeed correct, you can bypass this check by using -U instead of -u.
Trying to map files from your RAM disk. Please check -r option or ROOT environment variable.	Most likely, you or some installation script is trying to invoke LILO in a way that some of the files it has to access reside on the RAM disk. Normally, the ROOT environment variable should be set to the mount point of the effective root device if installing LILO with a different root directory.
Write *item: error_reason*	The disk is probably full or mounted read-only.

For more information on troubleshooting Lilo and other boot problems, refer to the following website:

LILO, Linux Crash Rescue HOW-TO

http://www.linux.org/docs/ldp/howto/LILO-crash-rescue-HOWTO.html

24.4 GRUB

Starting with Red Hat Linux 7.2, the default boot loader is GNU GRUB. GRUB (GRand Unified Bootloader) is a program that installs a boot loader to the MBR, which exists at the beginning sectors of a disk. It allows you to place specific instructions in the MBR that loads a GRUB menu or command environment, permitting you to start the operating system of your choice, pass special instructions to kernels when they boot, or discover system parameters (such as available RAM) before booting. Different from LILO, GRUB supports almost any operating system and most popular file systems.

To select the operating system that you want to load, use the arrow keys to highlight the operating system of your choice and press the Enter key. If you want to edit your selections, you can press the e key on the keyboard. To jump to the grub command line, you would press the c key on the keyboard.

GRUB's configuration file (/boot/grub/grub.conf) is read from the disk every time the system boots, preventing you from having to write over the MBR every time you change the boot options. Therefore, you do not have to change the configuration file, save the changes, and then execute a separate command to make the changes active.

Another advantage of GRUB over LILO is that if you make a mistake in the LILO configuration file and run a command that overwrites the system's MBR, your system could not be bootable. With GRUB, if you misconfigure the configuration file and reboot or the configuration file cannot be found, it will simply drop you to a command line and allow you to manually type commands that will launch the operating system.

NOTE: When changes are made to the GRUB configuration file, it is not necessary to restart GRUB. Any changes made are automatically detected. If you do restart GRUB, you will be dropped to the command-line GRUB shell.

In GRUB, it does not matter if your hard drives are IDE or SCSI. All hard drives start with *hd* and floppy disks start with *fd.* The first hard drive of a system is referred to as hd0. The first partition on that drive is called (hd0,0), whereas the fifth partition on the second hard drive is called (hd1,4). The parentheses and comma are very important in the name. Also note that GRUB's numbering system for devices starts at 0, and not 1. This is one of the most common mistakes made by new GRUB users. To specify an entire device without respect to its partitions, simply leave off the comma and the partition number. This is important when telling GRUB to configure the MBR for a particular disk. For example, (hd0) specifies the first device and (hd3) specifies the fourth device.

When typing commands to GRUB involving a file, such as a menu list to use when allowing the booting of multiple operating systems, you must include the file immediately after the specifying the device and partition. A sample file specification to an absolute file name is organized like this:

```
(<type-of-device><bios-device-number>,<partition-number>)/path/to/file
```

You can also specify files to GRUB that do not actually appear in the file system, such as a chain loader (used in Microsoft Windows) that appears in the first few blocks of a partition. To specify these files, you have to provide a blocklist, which tells GRUB, block by block, where the file is located in the partition. As a file can be comprised of several different sets of blocks, there is a specific way to write blocklists. Each file's section location is described by an offset number of blocks and then a number of blocks from that offset point, and the sections are put together in order, separated by commas.

This following blocklist tells GRUB to use a file that starts at the first block on the partition and uses blocks 0 through 49, 99 through 124, and 199.

```
0+50,100+25,200+1
```

You can leave off the offset number of blocks if you are starting at block 0. As an example, the chain loading file in the first partition of the first hard drive would have the following name:

```
(hd0,0)+1
```

You can also use the chainloader command with a similar blocklist designation at the GRUB command line after setting the correct device and partition as root:

```
chainloader +1
```

The GRUB root file system is the root partition for a particular device. GRUB uses this information to mount the device and load files from it, among other things.

NOTE: GRUB's root file system has nothing to do with the Linux root file system.

GRUB features three powerful interfaces that provide different levels of functionality. Each of these interfaces allows you to boot operating systems, and you can even move between interfaces within the GRUB environment.

If GRUB was automatically configured for you by the Linux installation program, this is the interface you already know. A menu of operating systems or kernels preconfigured with their own boot commands exists in this interface as a list, by name, after the system first starts. You can use the arrow keys to select an option other than the default selection and press the Enter key to boot it. Alternatively, a timeout period may have been set, so that GRUB will start loading the default option. From the menu interface, you can also press the e key to edit the highlighted menu entry's commands, or the c key to move to a command-line interface.

If you press the e key from the menu interface, the GRUB commands for that entry are displayed, and you can alter these command lines before booting the operating system by adding (o after the current line; O before it), editing (e), or deleting (d) them. After you have made your changes you can press the b key to execute them and boot the operating system. The Esc key deletes your changes and takes you to the standard menu interface.

The command-line interface is the most basic GRUB interface, but it is also the one that gives you the most control. You can type any relevant GRUB commands here followed by the Enter key to execute them. This interface features some advanced shell-like features, including Tab key completion, based on context, and Ctrl key combinations when typing commands such as Ctrl + a to move to the beginning of a line, and Ctrl + e to move to the end of a line. In addition, the arrow, Home, End, and Delete keys work as they do in the bash shell.

GRUB contains a number of different commands that may be executed interactively in the command-line interface. Some of the commands accept options after their name; these options should be separated from the command and other options on that line by space characters. The most useful commands are:

- **Boot**—Boots the operating system or chain loader that has been previously specified and loaded.
- **Chainloader <file-name>**—Loads the specified file as a chain loader. To grab the file at the first sector of the specified partition, you can use +1 as the file's name.
- **Displaymem**—Displays the current use of memory, based on information from the BIOS. This is useful if you are not sure how much RAM a system has and have yet to boot it.
- **Initrd <file-name>**—Allows you to specify an initial RAM disk to use when booting, necessary when the kernel needs certain modules in order to boot properly.
- **Install <stage-1> <install-disk> <stage-2> p <config-file>**—Installs GRUB to the MBR. This allows the GRUB interfaces to come up when the system is rebooted. The <stage-2> section tells the stage 1 boot loader where the stage 2 boot loader is located, such as (hd0,0)/grub/stage2. The p option tells the install command that a menu configuration file is being specified in the <config-file> section, such as (hd0,0)/grub/grub.conf.

  NOTE: This command will write over anything else in the MBR. If executed, anything you have been using to boot your operating system other than GRUB will be lost. Make sure you know what you are doing before you execute this command.

- **Kernel <kernel-file-name> <option-1> <option-N>**—Specifies the kernel file to load from GRUB's root file system when using direct loading to boot the operating system. Options can follow the kernel command that will be passed to the kernel when it is loaded. For Linux, you may have a line that looks like this:

  ```
  kernel /vmlinuz root=/dev/hda5
  ```

  This line specifies that the vmlinuz file is loaded from GRUB's root file system, such as (hd0,0). An option is also passed to the kernel specifying that the root file system for the Linux kernel when it loads should be on hda5, the fifth partition on the first IDE hard drive. Multiple options may be placed after this option, if you need them.
- **Root <device-and-partition>**—Configures GRUB's root partition to be the particular device and partition, such as (hd0,0), and mounts the partition so that files can be read.
- **Rootnoverify <device-and-partition>**—Does the same thing as the root command but does not mount the partition.

The menu configuration file, which is used to create the list in GRUB's menu interface of operating systems to boot, essentially allows the user to select a preset group of commands to execute. The commands given in the section called Commands can be used, as well as some special commands that may be used only in the configuration file.

The following commands can only be used in the GRUB menu configuration file:

- **Color <normal-color> <selected-color>**——Allows you to set up specific colors to be used in the menu, where two colors are configured as the foreground and background. You can just use the color names, such as red/black. An example line might look like this:

  ```
  color red/black green/blue
  ```

- **Default <title-name>**—The default entry title name that will be loaded if the menu interface times out.
- **Fallback <title-name>**—If used, the entry title name to try if first attempt failed.
- **Hiddenmenu**—If used, it prevents the GRUB menu interface from being displayed, loading the default entry when the timeout period expires. The user can see the standard GRUB menu by pressing the Esc key.
- **Password <password>**—If used, it prevents the user who does not know the password from editing the entries for this menu option. Optionally, you can specify an alternate menu configuration file after the <password>, so that, if the password is known, GRUB will restart the second stage of the boot loader and use this alternate configuration file to build the menu. If this alternate file is left out of the command, then a user who knows the password is able to edit the current configuration file.

Figure 24.8 Sample Grub.conf File

```
default linux
timeout 10
color green/black light-gray/blue

# section to load linux
title linux
root (hd0,1)
kernel /vmlinuz root=/dev/hda5
boot

# section to load Window 2000
title windows
rootnoverify (hd0,0)
chainloader +1
```

- **Splashimage**—Specifies the location of the splash screen image to be used when GRUB boots.
- **Timeout**—If used, sets the amount of time, in seconds, before GRUB loads the entry designated by the default command.
- **Title**—Sets a title to be used with a particular group of commands used to load an operating system.

The # character can be used to place comments in the menu configuration file.

The configuration file is actually divided into two main parts. The commands to set the global preferences for the GRUB menu interface are placed at the top of the file, followed by the different entries for each of the operating systems to boot. If you look at the example of the GRUB file in figure 24.8 you can see that this one is configured to boot either Linux or Microsoft Windows 2000. This file would tell GRUB to build a menu with Linux as the default operating system, set to autoboot it after 10 seconds.

24.5 LINUX LAYERS

Before getting into configuring Linux, we first need to discuss the components that make up Linux. Having a more thorough understanding of these components will also help you troubleshoot problems more efficiently.

To simplify the programming of Linux, Linux uses a layered structure. Each layer has a well-defined set of tasks, and uses the services provided by the underlying layer. This means that each layer provides services for the upper layer, and makes use of the ones exported by the lower layer. See figure 24.9. As a result, the operating system does the following:

- By reducing the architecture specific code to the minimum, with little effort the system ports or moves one program from one system to another with different hardware architectures. As a result, the operating system is more portable.
- As standard interfaces are defined to exchange information between the layers, the kernel components can be written without being aware of the details of the lower layers.
- The system becomes more reliable as problems inside upper layers cannot affect the lower layers.

Figure 24.9 The Linux Layers

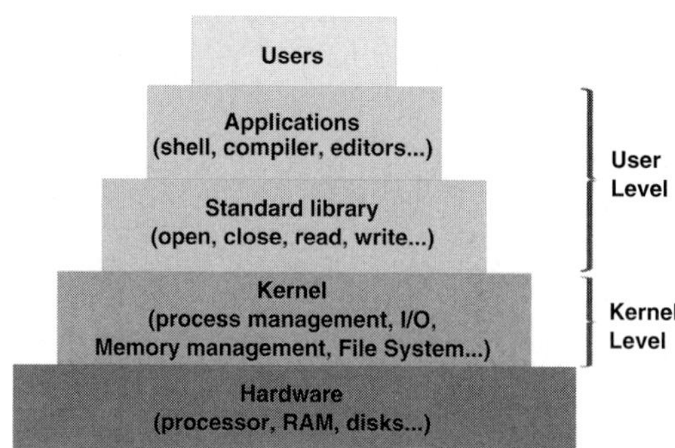

The kernel layer runs at a kernel level and the standard library and applications layers run on the user level. The kernel level is based on the ring 0 of the Intel 386 protection mechanism, whereas the user level uses ring 3. This means that the processes in the applications and standard layer cannot interfere with the processes in the kernel layer.

24.6 THE KERNEL

The Linux kernel provides critical low-level facilities. These include:

- Memory management, including handling swap space, if present
- Most low-level hardware drivers

  NOTE: X's video drivers and printer drivers are excluded.

- Process scheduling, which determines when specific programs get access to the processor
- Large chunks of the network stack that provide specific programs with network access
- File systems for access to files on the disk

For the most part, users don't interact directly with the kernel, except that the kernel handles the keyboard input and text-based video output.

All kernels can be divided into two types, monolithic and microkernel. A **monolithic kernel** is a very large and complex component. It carries out a large number of tasks, managing processes, file systems, memory, hardware, devices, and a lot more. See figure 24.10.

Microkernels, on the other hand, have a much simpler and lighter structure, as they generally just manage memory and processes, and provide a means of interprocess communication. All the other tasks are left to external modules communicating with the kernel through networklike protocols. A microkernel needs more careful design because all of its external components need to be developed together to make sure they work together in harmony.

Although the Linux kernel has grown to include some modular features such as the dynamically loadable modules, Linux is essentially a monolithic kernel. The advantage of a monolithic kernel is better performance since the microkernel spends time exchanging information between the various modules. In fact, the development model of Linux fits better with the monolithic structure because all the components, which may be developed by different programmers, must be integrated by Linus Torvalds. He controls the whole development process of the kernel, which could otherwise get fragmented into dozens of inconclusive and harmful subprojects.

On the other hand, the monolithic kernel has considerable drawbacks. First, the monolithic kernel has to deal with dozens of different file systems, four or five network protocols, simultaneously driving audio and video cards, modems, printers, and so on. As a result, the size of the kernel is much larger. Considering that these features are rarely all needed at once, Linux adapted to serve these needs by adopting a modular structure.

Figure 24.10 The Linux Architecture

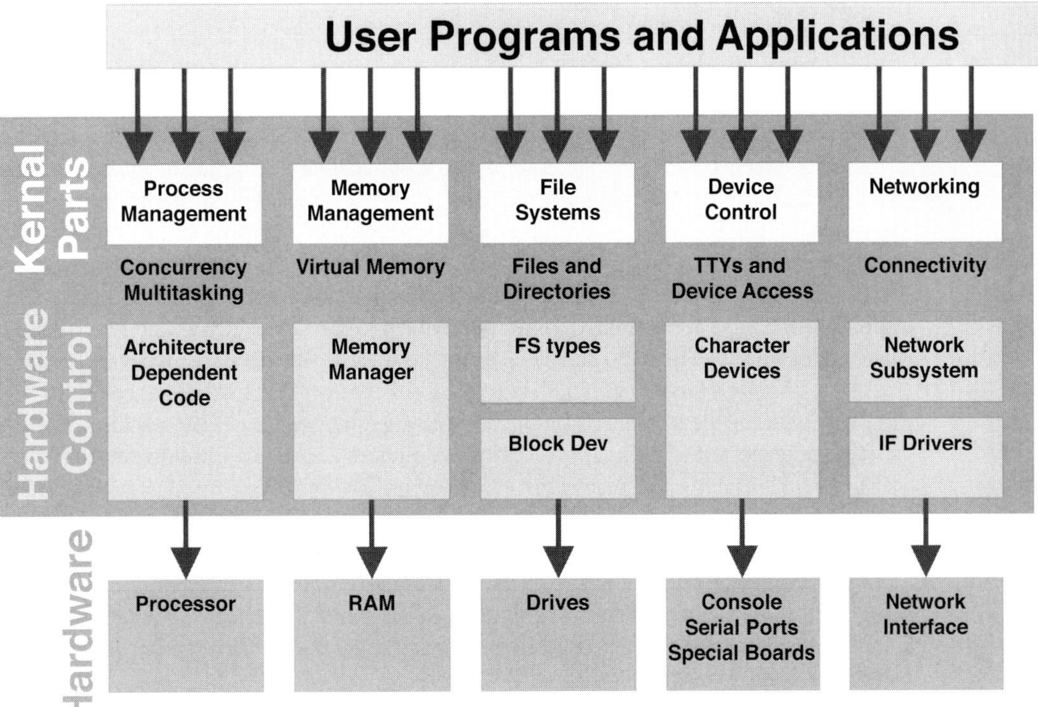

As mentioned in earlier chapters, the kernel is the central program of the operating system, which controls all other programs. First, the kernel is what makes Linux into a multitasking system. Traditionally, the processor can execute only one instruction at a time. The Linux system appears to be running lots of tasks simultaneously by switching from task to task quickly. It makes the best use of the processor by keeping track of which processes are ready to go, and which ones are waiting for something like a record from a hard disk file, or some keyboard input. This kernel task, called scheduling, makes sure that all processes get a fair share of the processor's cycles. The Linux scheduler tries to give the highest priority to "interactive" processes, that is, the ones that carry out some form of interaction with the user. This gives an impression of "promptness," even if the CPU power is always the same.

Processes are the active entities of Linux. When you run a program, a new process is started and the kernel assigns the process a memory space for it to use. The memory space is divided into pages. The kernel keeps track of which pages of which processes are being used the most. The pages that aren't used as much can be moved out to the swap partition (virtual memory). When they are needed again, another unused page can be paged out to make way for it.

The kernel also manages the file system. For example, when you access a file, it has to access the file no matter where it is on the disk and it must access every allocation unit in which the file is used. When the fragments are collected, it has to put them together and pass them on to the application that requested it. Therefore, the kernel takes care of hiding the file system complexity from the applications, and monitors the access to the resource. Applications just have to deal with the content of the file, identified by a file descriptor returned by the kernel. This descriptor is actually associated with a complex structure that contains all of the information related to that file—where its fragments are, who its owner is, its name, the creation and modification time, and so on.

The method used when writing to the hard disk has worked so well that when an application accesses physical devices such as modems or mice, it accesses their files and interacts with them through the same mechanism. For example, to use a modem, the modem must be opened, read, and closed just like a simple text file. It is the kernel that takes care of the translation.

24.7 DEVICE DRIVERS

Everything attached to the computer you are using to run Linux is treated as a device by the operating system. It doesn't matter whether the device is a terminal, a hard disk, a printer, a CD-ROM drive, or a modem. Everything that accepts or sends data to the operating system is a device.

Each device has a special section in the kernel, called a **device driver**, which includes all the instructions necessary for Linux to communicate with the device. When a new device is developed, it can be used with Linux by writing a device driver, which is usually a set of instructions that explains how to send and receive data.

Device drivers allow the Linux kernel to include only the operating system and support software. When an application instructs a device to perform an action, the Linux kernel doesn't have to worry about the mechanism. It simply passes the request to the device driver and lets it handle the communications. Similarly, when you're typing at the keyboard, your terminal's device driver accepts the keystrokes and passes them to the shell or application, filtering out any special codes that the kernel doesn't know how to handle by translating them into something the kernel can perform.

As a general rule, Linux makes hardware devices accessible through device file entries in the /dev file structure. The files all have ownership and permissions like other files, which will control who may access the device. See table 24.7. Note that it is permissible to keep device files anywhere on the file system, but keeping them all in /dev makes it obvious that they are device files.

In Linux, every device file is associated with two numbers: a major number and a minor number. Together, these numbers determine the device class and the specific device. For example, /dev/ttyS0 uses major number 4 and minor number 64, /dev/ttyS1 uses minor number 65 and /dev/ttyS2 uses minor number 66.

Table 24.7 Common Linux Device File Names

Device File Name	Major Numbers	Function
/dev/dsp*x*	14	Digital audio (sound cards)
/dev/fd*	2	Floppy disk access
/dev/hd*xy*	3, 22, 33, 34	EIDE hard disk access; *x* is a letter from *a* onward representing a disk drive; *y* is an optional number from 0 up representing a partition. Also used for EIDE CD-ROMs.
/dev/ht*x* and /dev/nht*x*	37	EIDE tape backup devices
/dev/lp*x*	6	Parallel ports
/dev/mixer*x*	14	Audio mixer (controls sound card volume)
/dev/psaux	10	PS/2-style mouse (note x is not a variable; there's only one) /dev/psaux device)
/dev/scd*x*	11	SCSI CD-ROM drives
/dev/sd*xy*	8, 65–71	SCSI hard disk access; *x* is a letter from *a* onward representing a disk drive; *y* is an optional number from 0 up representing a partition.
/dev/sequencers*x*	14	MIDI audio playback (sound cards)
/dev/sg*x*	21	"Generic" SCSI devices
/dev/st*x* and /dev/nst*x*	9	SCSI tape backup devices
/dev/ttyS*x*	4	RS-232 serial ports
/dev/usb/*	Variable	USB devices

Continued

To create device files in the /dev directory, you would use the make node (mknod) command (you will need the major and minor number). To remove device files from the /dev directory, you would use the standard rm command. Creating a device file with mknod is almost never necessary because Linux distributions typically ship device files for all common hardware. You will mostly need to create special device files if you are using a very new and experimental hardware driver. In these cases, you will need to consult your driver's documentation for details.

24.8 BUILDING THE KERNEL

Many Linux distribution kernels were compiled to install onto the largest range of systems. Therefore, they are compiled to run on the slowest processor of a particular architecture. For an Intel machine, the installation kernel is made for an Intel 386 and not a Pentium III or Pentium 4. To take advantage of the features available on the newer processors, you will need to rebuild at least the kernel, specifying the processor that you have. Other reasons to recompile or upgrade a Linux kernel are for better support of existing hardware, to fix a bug that may be in the kernel, or to fix security holes. In addition, if you install free VPN software for Linux, you will usually have to recompile the kernel.

NOTE: You must be logged in as root to perform these commands.

In the past, you would need to recompile the kernel if you added new hardware on your system because the monolithic kernel was static. Improvements in the Linux 2.0.x kernels allowed for much of the drivers for hardware to be modularized into components that could be inserted only on demand. However, there were major problems with having multiple kernels on a system that had been compiled for different advancements (for example, support for symmetrical multiprocessor and uniprocessor kernels). Further advancements with the modularization of the Linux 2.2.x kernel have allowed for multiple kernels to more easily coexist (though not share modules).

24.8.1 Downloading and Unpacking the Kernel Source Code

Your Linux distribution probably has the source code to a specific kernel. If you need to download a more updated version, you should go to the http://www.kernel.org website. The website listing of kernels available will contain folders for v1.0, v1.1, and so forth. Remember that the even-number kernels are considered ready-for-production systems. The first step would be to download the compressed tar files such as the tar.qz files.

NOTE: You can download the kernel RPM packages and then manually upgrade to the latest kernel from the Red Hat website.

Another option is that some Linux distributions will have some sort of automatic update feature. For example, Red Hat has the Red Hat Update Agent upgrade packages, which will upgrade the kernel on your system, create an initial RAM disk if needed, and configure the boot loader to boot the new kernel. All you have to do is reboot into the new kernel.

Before you upgrade your kernel, you need to take a few precautionary steps. The first step is to make sure you have a working boot diskette for your system in case a problem occurs. If the boot loader is not configured properly to boot the new kernel, you will be unable to boot your system unless you have a boot diskette.

To create a boot diskette for your system, you need to determine which version of the kernel you are currently running by running the uname –r command. Then, logged in as root, type the following command to create a boot disk on drive A (/dev/fd0):

```
/sbin/mkbootdisk kernelversion
```

If you want to actually specify the first floppy disk drive for the 2.4.2-2 kernel, you would use the following command:

```
mkbootdisk --device /dev/fd0 2.4.2-2
```

If you have an LS-120 drive that acts as a floppy disk drive but is connected as the second IDE drive, you would type this command:

```
mkbootdisk --device /dev/hdb 2.4.2-2
```

Of course, after making the disk, you should reboot your machine with the boot disk to verify it works. After it has been verified, put the disk in a safe place. There is also an X Window software utility that can make a boot disk. You can start the program by opening the KDE Main menu, selecting System, and selecting Create Boot Disk, or by executing mkbootdisk at a terminal window.

Now, to unpack the file, use the tar command introduced in the last chapter. For example, assuming the packed tar file is linux-2.4.tar.gz, you would use the following command:

```
tar -xzf linux-2.4.tar.gz.
```

You should note that this might take a couple of minutes.

24.8.2 Configuring the Kernel

The first step in building the kernel is configuring or choosing its features. Most of this will be based on the hardware that you have. Therefore, you should refer to a list of all of components. You can also look at the /proc/pci file to view hardware connected to the PCI bus.

The basic steps in configuring and compiling a kernel are:

- Configure the kernel (with make xconfig, make config, or make menuconfig).
- Compile the kernel and modules (with the make dep, make clean, make bzImage, and make modules commands).
- Copy the new kernel to the /boot directory.
- Copy the System.map to the /boot directory.
- Configure and update the boot loader to use the new kernel.
- Install the modules (with the make modules_install command).
- Test the new kernel.

To run the xconfig, start X Window with the startx command. Once X Window is running, open a terminal window and enter the following two commands

```
cd /usr/src/linux-kernelversion
make xconfig
```

whereas *kernelversion* is the version of the kernel such as 2.4.7-10.

The make xconfig command will compile and start the Linux Kernel Configuration tool. If you don't want to use X Window, you can execute make config or make menuconfig commands instead. The make menuconfig is a text mode, menu-driven program. Components are presented in a menu of categories; you select the desired components in the same manner used in the text mode Red Hat Linux installation program. Toggle the tag corresponding to the item you want included: [*] (built-in), [ ] (exclude), <M> (module), or < > (module capable).

The make config program is an interactive text program. Components are presented in a linear format and you answer them one at a time. Another command worth mentioning is the make oldconfig command, which works exactly like the make config command but it only asks questions that were not answered last time you configured. This is very useful when you upgrade to a newer kernel version and don't want to restate your answers to all the questions.

The make xconfig command displays in a window like that shown in figures 24.11 and 24.12. In the opening window, you will see all of the top-level configuration menus. See table 24.8. By clicking the buttons, you can open submenus listing all the specific features that you can enable. A default setting exists for most options, but it is recommended that you review all settings to make sure they are set as desired. When you have made your selections, click the Save and Exit button located in the last column of buttons.

Typically, when you open a submenu, the first three columns contain the option buttons Y (Yes), M (Module), and N (No). The forth column contains the name of the option, and the fifth column offers a Help button that will bring up a related window explaining the feature. Yes or No options will enable or

Figure 24.11 The xconfig program is used to configure the kernel before compiling it.

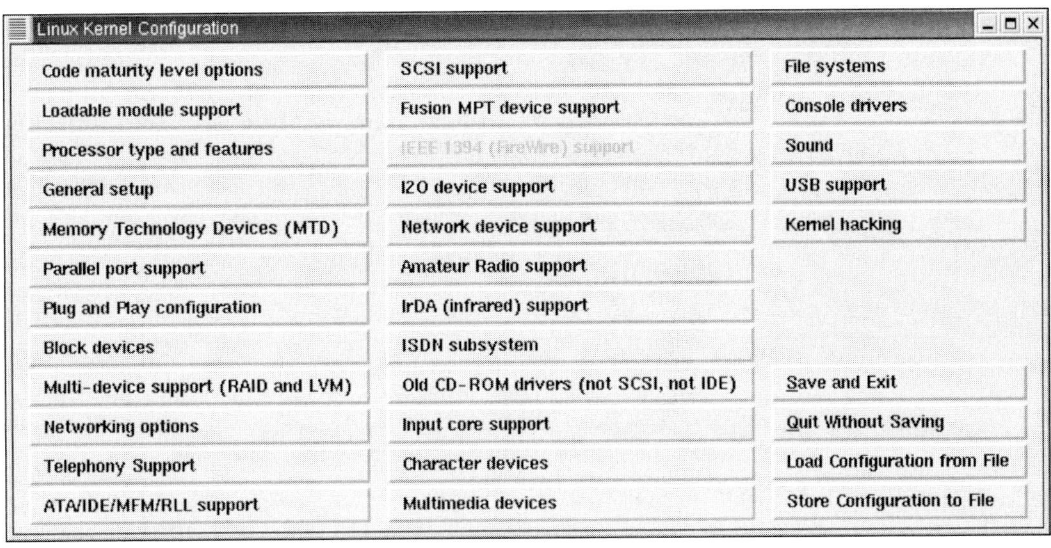

Figure 24.12 Processor Options in the Xconfig Program

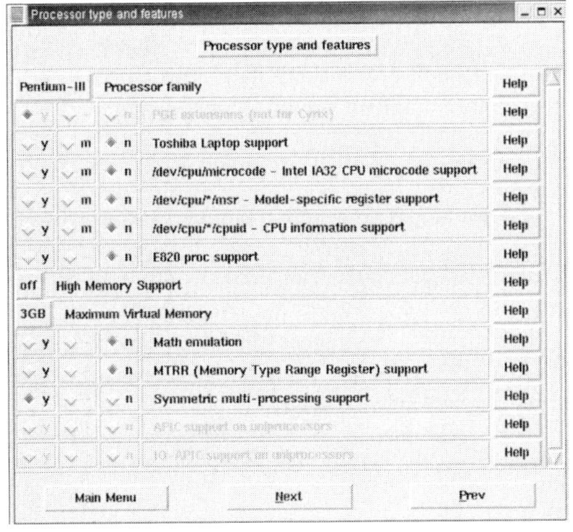

disable a kernel feature. If the Module option is available for an item, the Module option enables the item, but it makes it into a module rather than being part of the kernel. Therefore, the kernel can load and unload the module when that feature or component is being used. As a result, when the module is not loaded, you will have more memory for your other applications.

After choosing your components, click the Save and Exit button to create the configuration file /usr/src/linux-*kernelversion*/.config and exit the Linux Kernel Configuration program.

Table 24.8 Linux Kernel Configuration Options

Kernel Submenu	Description
Code Maturity Options	This submenu has only one option, Do you want access to the latest and greatest kernel developments? If you select Yes, you will have additional options available than if you would have selected No. Unfortunately, those options are basically experimental enhancements or features. Of course, if this is a production system, you should pick No, because you want to use options that have been reliable and thoroughly debugged.
Loadable Module Support	Loadable modules are pieces of the kernel that can be dynamically loaded and unloaded as needed. If you select No, options that could be made into loadable modules will not be available.
Processor Type and Features	This will allow you to select the type of processor that you are running, if you need math emulation (only necessary on 386-based processors and the 486SX processor), if you want to take advantages of memory registers, and if you need to support symmetrical multiprocessor (SMP) systems with multiple processors.
General Setup	Most of the options are self-explanatory except the item for binary file–type support. In the past, compiled programs, especially those used in UNIX systems, were stored in a file format known as a.out. Unfortunately, the file format had severe limitations when it came to shared libraries. The ELF format was created to address these limitations. Linux uses the ELF binary format for all of its programs. It is unlikely your system will need a.out support, so you can safely say no to this option.
Memory Technology Devices	This submenu is used to support special memory devices such as flash cards. Flash cards and other nonvolatile memory are common in embedded systems. Unless you have a specific need for such as device, you can ignore this menu.
Parallel Port Support	If you have a device that connects through the parallel port such as Zip drives, you would need to enable it in this menu. If you don't have any devices that need parallel port support, be sure to open this submenu and disable the features.
Plug and Play Support	This should be self-explanatory.
Block Devices	Configure type of IDE hard drives and other block I/O devices
Multi-Device Support (RAID and LVM)	If you want to configure a RAID system on your Linux server, you will need to enable the features in this menu. This includes support for software RAID as well as hardware-supported RAID. The Logical Volume Manager (LVM) configuration options are also set through these menus. The LVM allows you to group together several disks and treat them as one large disk. Note: LVM offers no redundancy.
Networking Options	At a minimum, you should enable the UNIX Domain Sockets and TCP/IP Networking options.
Telephony Support	This is used to configure IP telephony (VoIP).
ATA/IDE/MFM/RLL Support	Used to configure the IDE disks and optimize it for your chipset.
SCSI Support	Enables support for SCSI controllers
IEEE 1394 (FireWire Support)	This is used to configure IEEE1394 FireWire, a common protocol used by digital audio/video equipment such as digital cameras.
I20 Device Support	I2O is an intelligent interface for abstracting the devices from particular operating systems. Don't worry if it does not sound familiar. It has not become popular yet.
Network Device Support	Enables support for various network controllers and processes.
Amateur Radio Support	Used to connect to a network with a ham radio driver using TCP/IP.
IrDA Support	This option is used to configure infrared devices.

Continued

Table 24.8 Continued

Kernel Submenu	Description
ISDN Subsystem	Used to configure your ISDN modem.
Old CD-ROM Drivers	Used for older proprietary CD-ROM drives.
Input Core Support	The input core is the minimum amount of necessary code for Linux to communicate with the keyboard. Typically, you leave this to its default settings.
Character Devices	Provides support for various character and similar devices, such as system watchdogs.
Multimedia Devices	This is used to configure support for special use high-end video cards.
File Systems	Lets you configure support for various file systems.
Console Drivers	Provides support for various consoles (display devices).
USB Support	To configure your USB port and devices.
Kernel Hacking	Provides for profiling support in the kernel.

24.8.3 Compiling the Kernel

After you have configured the kernel, the next stage is to compile the kernel or convert the source code to machine code. Compiling the kernel occurs in three stages. The first stage (make dep) creates the dependency tree that determines which files need to be compiled and which can be ignored. The second stage is the cleanup. Any previous compiles in a particular tree get cleaned up and old files are removed. The last step is the actual compiling itself. Since this is a huge amount of code that needs to compiled, this may take a few minutes. Finally, you will use the make modules command to build any modules needed.

```
make dep
make clean
make bzImage
make modules
```

NOTE: Some documentation will show make zImage instead of make bzImage. You should use bzImage because if the kernel grows larger than 1 MB, it may overwrite part of the boot loader on older versions of LILO. Therefore, to make sure, you should specify bzImage, which will compress the kernel.

You can also perform all four commands as one command if you separate them with semicolons:

```
make dep;make clean;make bzImage;make modules
```

If you are having problems compiling the kernel, you can try performing the make mrproper command, which will do a more extensive cleaning. It is probably a good idea to do this at every patch.

NOTE: If you use the make mrproper command, it will delete your configuration file (.config), so you might want to make a backup of it or you will have to run the kernel configuration program again.

24.8.4 Installing the Kernel

Now that you have created a kernel, you have to install it. If you are working in the /usr/src/*linuxversion* directory, the compiled kernel will be called /usr/src/*linuxversion*/arch/i386/boot/bzImage. The map file for this will be /usr/src/*linuxversion*/System.map. You will need both files for the install phase.

Begin by copying the bzImage file into the /boot directory and renaming bzImage to vmlinuz-*x.x.xx,* where *x.x.xx* is the version number of the kernel. Therefore, if you have version 2.4.7-12, you would use the following command:

```
cp /usr/src/linuxversion/arch/i386/boot/bzImage
/boot/vmlinuz-2.4.7-12
```

NOTE: You can also tag extra components other than the version number to identify different options that you might have enabled. This comes in handy when you have several copies of the same kernel version, but with different options enabled.

The next step would be to copy the System.map. The System.map file is useful when the kernel is misbehaving and generating messages. These messages include a lot of detail about the current state of the system, including many hexadecimal numbers. System.map gives Linux a chance to turn those hexadecimal numbers into readable names, making debugging easier. Therefore, to copy the map file for our example, use the following command:

```
cp /usr/src/linuxversion/System.map /boot/System.map-2.4.7-12
```

If you get an error message like "System.map does not match current kernel," then probably System.map has not been copied.

After the kernel is installed, you need to install the modules by executing the following command:

```
make modules_install
```

Make sure that you type the underscore (_). This will install the kernel modules into the directory path /lib/modules/*kernelversion*/kernel/drivers, where *kernelversion* is the version specified in the Makefile.

Now some distributions will have a command that will automatically install the kernel and its associated files to the proper directories. For Red Hat Linux, they use the make install command. SuSe Linux uses the make bzlilo command that does the following:

```
cp /boot/vmlinuz /boot/vmlinuz.old
cp arch/i386/boot/bzImage /boot/vmlinuz
lilo
```

24.8.5 Updating LILO

Last, with the proper files in place, you are ready to edit the lilo.conf file so that the system recognizes these kernels as options when booting. Assuming that the kernel images are in /dev/hda1, you would insert the following lines in the /etc/lilo.conf file:

```
image=/boot/vmlinuz-2.4.7-12
   label=linux24712
   root=/dev/hda1
   read-only
```

NOTE: If you are just recompiling the kernel for better optimization or to support hardware that was not initially supported, yet it is the same kernel version, you may need to change the old lilo.conf entry and retain the old kernel in case there is a problem with the new kernel.

```
image=/boot/vmlinuz-2.4.7-12
   label=linux24712
   root=/dev/hda1
   read-only
image=/boot/vmlinuz-2.4.7-12old
   label=linux-24712old
   root=/dev/hda1
   read-only
```

Of course, for this to work, you have to rename the old kernel from vmlinuz-2.4.2-2 to vmlinuz-2.4.2-2old.

To make the new kernel boot by default, make sure to change the default line to:

```
default=linux24712
```

The last step is to run the lilo command at the prompt. The lilo output contains the boot option told to it by the /etc/lilo.conf file. The default kernel that will boot is the very first one (with the asterisks next to it). Then reboot to load the new kernel.

24.8.6 Patching the Kernel

Like any other operating system, Linux gets upgrades to fix bugs, improve performance, and add new features. These upgrades appears as entire kernel versions and a patch. Patches are small fixes for the kernel.

Patch files are located in the same directory from which the kernel is downloaded. This applies to each major release of Linux. So the patch to update 2.4.8-12 to 2.4.8.13 is located in the /pub/linux/kernel/v2.4/ directory of the Linux kernel FTP site. Each patch file name is prefixed with the term *patch* and suffixed with the Linux version number being installed by the patch.

NOTE: Each patch brings up Linux by only one version. This Linux 2.4.8-13 can be applied to only Linux 2.4.8-12. If you need to upgrade to Linux 2.4.8-14, you will have to apply the patch 2.4.8-13 before doing patch 2.4.8.14.

Patch files are stored on the FTP server in gzip-compressed format. Once you have downloaded the file, move it to the /usr/src directory (assuming that you unpacked the kernel from the preceding section into /usr/src/linux) and decompress the patch using the gzip command

```
gzip -d patch-2.4.8.13.gz
```

where patch-2.4.8.12.gz is the name of the patch. This leaves a file called patch.2.4.8.12 in the same directory; gzip automatically removes the gz file.

To apply the patch 2.4.8.13 to Linux 2.4.8.14, you need to change to the /usr/src/linux directory and issue the following command:

```
patch -p0 < patch-2.4.8.13
```

Several file names will then be printed on your screen. Next, recompile the kernel. While still in the /usr/src/linux directory, recompile the kernel using the same commands that you used before in making the kernel:

```
make dep;make clean;make bzImage;make modules
```

Then install the kernel just like you did before.

24.8.7 Troubleshooting a New Kernel

Rarely will you have problems when creating a new kernel. But when installing the new kernel and it doesn't seem to boot, the most common cause is that you did not run the lilo command or it is not configured correctly. It could be just as simple as the boot=/dev/hda1 in the lilo.conf command was accidentally typed as *boot=/dev/hda.* The best thing to do is boot with the rescue disk and mount the root (/) file system and the file system that contains the kernel. Then you will have to correct the lilo.conf file and run the lilo command or recreate the kernel. Before you reboot, however, make sure to unmount the normal file system. Mounting and unmounting file systems is discussed in chapter 10.

If the kernel halts during loading, it is typically caused by device probing or a resource conflict (IRQ, DMA, I/O address, or memory conflict) or the wrong driver is selected or loaded. Device probing is the most frequent cause of kernel halts while loading. For example, if you are configuring for a gateway/firewall machine with two network interfaces, the second probe may cause the kernel to halt. To avoid probing and resource conflicts, supply the correct configuration parameters in the /etc/lilo.conf append line. The exact parameters to use depend on your device, but you can find advice in the README files in /usr/src/linux-*kernel_version*/Documentation.

A kernel panic or oops message is a severe kernel error that often appears cryptic. The oops error displays what triggered the event and displays the contents of the processor registers. See figure 24.13. Although most of the time this does not mean much to a normal end user or a normal system administrator, it does tell a programmer what was its current task and what led up to the run. For the normal user and system administrator, knowing where the panic occurs is more useful than interpreting the message itself. The panic message does not have as much information as the oops message, but it sometimes give you a hint on how to correct the problem. See figure 24.14.

For more information on oops messages, refer to the /usr/src/linux-*kernel_version*/Documentation/oops-tracing.txt file.

Figure 24.13 Sample Oops Message

```
unable to handle kernel paging request at address C0000010
    oops: 0002
    EIP:   0010:XXXXXXXX
    eax: xxxxxxxx   ebx: xxxxxxxx   ecx: xxxxxxxx   edx: xxxxxxxx
    esi: xxxxxxxx   edi: xxxxxxxx   ebp: xxxxxxxx
    ds: xxxx  es: xxxx  fs: xxxx  gs: xxxx
    Pid: xx, process nr: xx
    xx xx xx xx xx xx xx xx xx xx
```

Figure 24.14 Sample Panic Message

```
vfs:cannot open root device "2105" or 21:05
please append a correct "root5" boot option
kernel panic: VFS: unable to mount root fs on 21:05
```

In production kernels, kernel panic and kernel oops messages are very rare and usually are due to faulty hardware, a configuration problem, missing modules, failure to load a module before using some essential feature, or using hardware that is not supported by the current kernel. With development kernels, kernel panics can become quite common.

If you do encounter an error, there are a couple things that you can do. Normally, the error message is read from the kernel buffers by klogd daemon and handed to the syslogd daemon, which writes it to the syslog file, typically the /var/log/messages. Sometimes klogd dies, in which case you can run dmesg > *file* to read the data from the kernel buffers and save it. You should also check /var/log/secure and /var/log/xdm-error.log (if loading X Window). Don't forget to check the workstation console (Ctrl + Alt + l). Often these may display an error message that triggered the panic or oops message.

For example, this line

```
NE*0000 ethercard probe at 0x300 failed to detect IRQ line
```

will cause the following panic error message:

```
IP-config NO network devices available
Root-NFS NO NFS server available  giving up
VFS: Unable to mount root fs via NFS, trying floppy
VFS: cannot open root device 02:00
PANIC VFS unable to mount root fs on 02:00
```

This usually indicates an IRQ conflict between the network card and another device in the system. Try removing the other cards, leaving only the network and video card.

If the machine has crashed so badly that you cannot enter commands or the disk is unavailable, then you have four options:

1. Hand copy the text from the screen and type it in after the machine has restarted. It is messy, but it is the only option if you have not planned for a crash.
2. Boot with a serial console (see Documentation/serial-console.txt), run a null modem to a second machine, and capture the output there using a communication program.
3. Make sure the kernel has the newest patches.

4. Patch the kernel with one of the crash dump patches. None of these are standard kernel patches so you have to find and apply them yourself. Search kernel archives for kmsgdump, lkcd, and oops+smram.

If you cannot resolve the panic or oops message on your own, you can search the Internet and newsgroups for the error message. Be sure to check the Linux distribution, software vendor, and hardware vendor websites. You can also look at the kernel developer's archive at the following website:

http://www.tux.org/lkml

If you choose to report this to your Linux distribution vendor, software vendors, or hardware vendor, be sure to include the entire error message, a detailed description of what you were doing that led up to the error message, a detailed list of your hardware, and a copy of the /proc/ksyms, /proc/modules, and /var/log/ksymoops files.

24.9 CORE DUMPS

When a program runs, or performs operations such as accessing areas of memory or writing data to disk, the kernel gives it authorization. If a program executes outside the bounds of what the kernel allows, the kernel will shut it down and perform a core dump. A core dump is an operation the kernel carries out when a program tries to perform a task that it is not allowed to do. Some types of crashes on Linux cause the system to create a special file called core. These files are often referred to as core dumps. You can then replace the software or, if you know how to program, you can fix the problem yourself.

NOTE: If the kernel crashes, the processor fails, or the files are erased, the core dump will not be completed.

A core dump is a copy of everything in RAM that the program was using at the time it crashed. A programmer can then look at the contents of the dump file, look at what instruction was being executed, and the data that the instruction was processing to see what the problem was. A short program that operates on little data will produce a small core file, but a large program that works on large data sets will produce a large core file.

Not all program crashes create core dumps. One common reason for this is that the user ran the program in a directory to which he or she did not have write access. Another reason is that the shell may have limited the size of core files. In bash, this can be done with the ulimit command, by passing it the c parameter and the maximum core size in kilobytes. For example, if you want to limit the core file to 100 KB, you would use the following command:

```
ulimit -c 100
```

To find all of the core files on your system, you would use the find command:

```
find / -name core
```

It is not always obvious what created the core files, but there some things that you can look at to help determine that. The core file will first have an owner of who executed the program. In addition, you can look at the creation date. Another tool is to use the following command to determine what program created the file:

```
gdb -c core
```

This will launch the GNU debugger, which will examine the core file and report the name of the program that generated the list. You will then need to type *quit* to exit from gdb.

After looking at the above information, you then have to decide what to do with the core file. You may move to a safe directory for later use, you may email it to someone who may be able to fix the problem, or you can delete the core file.

NOTE: Don't automatically delete files and directories called core. There are several files called core that are not core dumps.

24.10 LINUXCONF

Linuxconf is a graphical utility that gives you important configuration centralized in one location using a single interface. Linuxconf allows you to configure and control various aspects of your system including server configurations (DNS, Apache, mail, FTP, news), user accounts, password and account policies, Internet connections (modems, PPP, routing, NIS), LILO, system logs, shutdown options, date and time, and various services.

To run linuxconf, you need to be logged in as the root user. If you are using another user account, type *su* at a shell prompt to become root and then type the command *linuxconf.* If the directory /sbin is not in your path, type the command with the full path: */sbin/linuxconf.* If you want to run the GUI version of linuxconf, you need to have the X Window System installed as well as GNOME.

Linuxconf has four user interfaces:

- **Text-Based**—Using the same user interface style as the Red Hat Linux text mode installation program, the text-based interface makes it easy to navigate your way through linuxconf if you aren't running X. Use the Tab and arrow keys to navigate the text mode screens. A down arrow on a line indicates that a pull-down menu exists on that line. The Ctrl + X key combination will make pull-down menus appear.
- **Graphical User Interface (GUI)**—Linuxconf can take advantage of the X Window System. Red Hat Linux includes a GUI interface for linuxconf called gnome-linuxconf.
- **Web-Based**—A web-based interface makes remote system administration easy; it can also be displayed with the Lynx text mode browser. To use the linuxconf web interface, use your browser to connect to port 98 on the machine running linuxconf (i.e., http://your_machine:98). Before you use the web-based interface, you'll need to configure linuxconf to allow connections from the machine running the browser.
- **Command Line**—Linuxconf's command-line mode is handy for manipulating your system's configuration in scripts.

Linuxconf will start in either character-cell or X mode, depending on your DISPLAY environment variable. The first time you run linuxconf, an introductory message will be shown; although it is displayed only once, accessing Help from the main screen will give you the same basic information. See figure 24.15.

If you don't see the tree menu interface shown above, follow these instructions:

1. Click on the Control tab, select Control files and systems, and then select Configure Linuxconf modules.

Figure 24.15 The LinuxConf Program

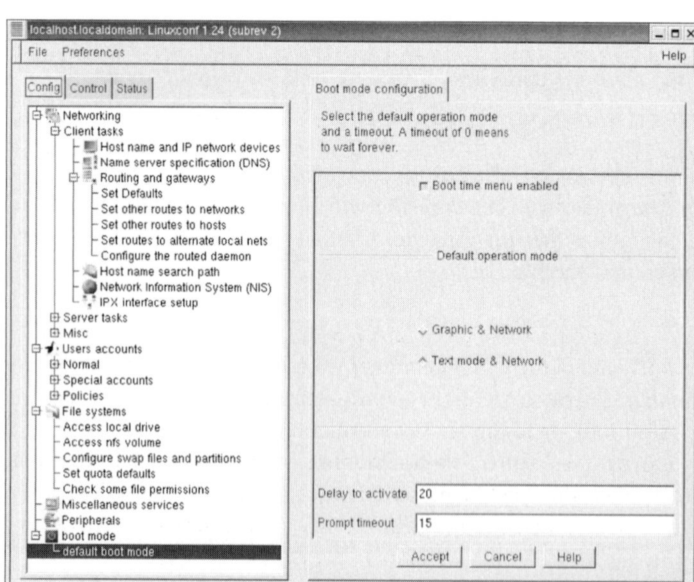

2. Select the Treemenu check box.
3. Click Accept.
4. Click Quit.
5. Restart linuxconf.

When you use the tree menu view, finding the appropriate panel should be simple and fast. Collapse and expand sections by clicking on the + or − signs next to the menu item.

Selected entries will appear as tabs in the panel on the right side and will remain there until closed. If you end up with more tabs open than you would like, just select Cancel on the bottom of each tab to close it without making any changes, or Accept to implement the changes you have made.

After configuring your system's settings through linuxconf, the changes are not activated immediately. You must activate the changes by choosing File and selecting the Act/Changes option from the pull-down menu in the GUI version of linuxconf, clicking on an Accept button in web-based linuxconf, or selecting the Accept button in text mode linuxconf.

As mentioned earlier, for security reasons, web-based access to linuxconf is disabled by default. Before attempting to access linuxconf with a web browser, you'll need to enable access.

- Click on the Config tab. Open the Networking option, select the Misc option, and then select the Linuxconf network access.
- In the Linuxconf html access control dialog box, enter the host name of any computers that should be allowed access to linuxconf. This includes your own system, if you wish to use the web-based interface locally. Web accesses related to linuxconf may be logged to your system's htmlaccess.log file by selecting the check box.
- Select the Accept button.
- You should also verify that the disable line in the /etc/xinetd.d/linuxconf-web file reads disable=no.
- Then run the command */sbin/service xinetd reload* from a shell prompt.

Web-based access should be enabled. To test it out, go to a system that you added to the access control list. Then, launch the web browser and enter the following URL

```
http://<host>:98/
```

whereas <host> is your system's host name. Note that you will need to enter your system's root password to gain access beyond the first page.

> **For more information about the linuxconf utility, visit the following website:**
>
> http://www.solucorp.qc.ca/linuxconf/

One example of using linuxconf is to specify which services are automatically loaded during boot. If you click on the Control tab and select the Control Service Activity under the Control Panel section, the services will be listed on the right side of the screen. If you highlight a service and press Enter, you can then place an *X* in Level 3 and Level 5 under the Run level tab so that it starts up in network/text mode and network/GUI mode. Then click on the Accept button. Before leaving linuxconf, be sure to activate the changes.

24.11 YAST AND YAST2

YaST (yet another setup tool) is used with SuSE Linux, can be used to configure and administer Linux including installing and removing system and user software and perform basic system administration tasks such as changing hardware, configuring networks, and adding users. YaST2 is just an improved version of YaST, with built-in intelligence.

You can start YaST from the prompt simply by typing the command *yast.* You navigate the menus and the screens in YaST with the arrow keys and the Tab key. You can move around in lists with the cursor keys and with up and down arrow keys, and you select items in the list with the spacebar. Normally you can use the Enter key to confirm your choices. To return to a previous menu, use the Esc key. If you want to save a particular choice (such as the selection of a package you wish to be installed) you would use the F10 key, which both saves the selection and returns to the previous menu. Where you are prompted for a yes or no response, you can use the Tab key to switch back and forth between the two options. If you use YaST in color mode, the active selection is always highlighted in blue.

When you first start YaST, you will be in the "main menu." To add or change hardware such as mice, modems, printers, CDs, scanners, and network devices, you would select the System administration option and then select Integrate hardware into system. In most cases, YaST will create a symbolic link (+Link) from the standard device to your particular hardware device. This will make it easier for you to access this device without having to remember the exact name of the device.

You can install one of the available precompiled kernels (from the SuSE-CD) with the menu option Select boot kernel, in the event that you want a different kernel than the one you chose during installation. In addition to installing the kernel that you select, YaST will also copy the kernel configuration file (.config) to the kernel source directory (/usr/src/linux).

Select the appropriate kernel for your computer, and then, as a rule, you should install LILO again, using YaST, if you have already booted successfully with LILO.

24.12 ADDING FILE SYSTEMS

Adding kernel support for any of these file systems is quite easy and may be done by selecting the corresponding configuration options when building a new kernel. For example, if you use make xconfig, then you can simply select the desired file system type within its File systems category. If you need support for a file system type because you want to move a disk from another environment onto a Linux system, be aware that you will also need to enable the appropriate partition type (via the Partition Types category) if the disk's original operating system environment uses a different partition table format from the one that Linux uses.

Adding a new disk or partition to the Linux file system is straightforward, and the steps for doing so are outlined below. (The corresponding commands are listed in parentheses.)

1. Configure the hard drive and physically attach the drive to the computer system if necessary.
2. Partition the new disk (fdisk or cfdisk).
3. Create a file system on the partition (mkfs).
4. Check the new file system for consistency errors (fsck).
5. Mount the new file system (mount).
6. Specifying the file system's boot-time behavior and other options in the file system configuration file (/etc/fstab).
7. Modify file system characteristics on ongoing basis as necessary (tune2fs).

24.12.1 Partitioning a New Disk

Before you can create a file system on the physical disk (or disk partition) you are adding, you first need to know which special device name to use when referring to that disk. If you recall from chapter 22, the first IDE hard drive is referred to as hda and the second IDE hard drive is referred to as hdb. Therefore, the first partition on the first IDE hard drive is /dev/hda1 and the second partition on the first IDE hard drive is /dev/hda2. The first SCSI drive is referred to as sda and the first partition on the first SCSI hard drive is referred to as /dev/sda1. An easy way to see what partition your system already has is to refer to the /proc/file system file, which will list all disk partitions that the system is currently recognizing.

To partition the drive, one partition utility that you should be familiar with is fdisk. Although fdisk is not always the easiest one to use, it is available in all Linux distributions. Of course, before you actually start creating and deleting partitions, you should look at the existing partitions to review the drive structures.

To start fdisk, type its name followed by the Linux device file name associated with your disk device, such as /dev/sda or /dev/hdb. For example, type:

```
fdisk /dev/hdb
```

To show the current partition layout, type *p* at the fdisk prompt to make sure that you are operating on the correct hard drive. With fdisk (or whatever utility you choose to use), you will need to specify the partition size.

Table 24.9 Mkfs Options

Option	Description
-V	Causes mkfs to generate verbose output, displaying additional information in the file system–creation process.
-t fstype	Specifies the file system type. Common file system types include ext2 (for EXT2fs) and msdos (for FAT). If you don't specify the file system type, it will default to EXT2.
options	You can pass file system–specific options to the utility. Most underlying file system creation tools support -c (to perform a low-level disk check to be sure the hardware is sound) and -v (to perform a verbose creation).
device	The name of the device on which you want to create the file system, such as /dev/hdb3, /dev/sda5, or /dev/fd0.
blocks	This is the size of the file system in blocks (usually 1,024 bytes in size). You don't normally need to specify this value, since mkfs can determine the file system size from the size of the partition.

24.12.2 Formatting the Partition

At this point the partition is blank. So next, you will need to create a file system on the partition by formatting the partition. Linux uses the mkfs program to do this. The mkfs syntax is:

```
mkfs [-V] [-t fstype] [options] device [blocks]
```

Options are shown in table 24.9.

Another program that you can use to format a new Linux native partition (EXT2FS) is the mke2fs program. If you were to format the third partition on the first IDE hard drive, you would type the following command:

```
mke2fs /dev/hda3
```

You should be warned that mkfs and mke2fs are destructive formats. Therefore, if you accidentally format the wrong drive, it will be extremely difficult to recover files from the old file system.

24.12.3 Checking the File System

The fsck program can locate and fix structural problems with file systems such as disk blocks marked as free that are actually in use and vice versa, incorrect link counts in inodes (indicating missing or extra directory entries for the corresponding file), and inconsistencies between the inode total size value and the actual amount of data blocks contained in the lists. As such, fsck can ensure the consistency of the file system's defining data structures. However, keep in mind that its scope is limited to the file system structure; it can do nothing for missing or corrupted data within structurally sound files.

NOTE: Like mkfs, fsck is actually a front-end to other tools, such as e2fsck (also known as fsck.ext2).

The syntax for fsck is as follows:

```
fsck -ACVRTNP [-t fstype] [—] [fsck-options] file systems
```

Options are shown in table 24.10.

Normally, you run fsck with only the file system name. For example, to check the third partition on the first SCSI drive, you would run the following command:

```
fsck /dev/sda3
```

IMPORTANT NOTE: You should run fsck only on file systems that are not currently mounted, or they are mounted as read-only. Changes written to disk during normal read/write operations can confuse fsck and result in file system corruption.

Table 24.10 The Fsck Options

Option	Description
-A	This option causes fsck to check all the file systems marked to be checked in /etc/fstab. The option is normally used in system startup scripts.
-C	This option displays a text mode progress indicator of the check process. Most file systems don't support this feature, but ext2fs does.
-V	This option produces verbose output of the check process.
-N	This option tells fsck to display what it would normally do, without actually doing it.
-t fstype	Normally, fsck determines the file system type automatically. You can force the type with this flag, though. If used in conjunction with -A, this causes the system to check only the specified file system types, even if others are marked to be checked. If fstype is prefixed with *no,* then all file systems except the specified type are checked.
--fsck-options	File system check programs for specific file systems often have their own options. Fsck passes options it doesn't understand, or those that follow a double dash (--), to the underlying check program. Common options include -a or -p (perform an automatic check), -r (perform an interactive check), and -f (force a full file system check if it appears to be clean).
file systems	The name of the file system or file systems being checked such as /dev/sda3.

24.12.4 Mounting and Unmounting Partitions

To add a partition to your Linux file system, you must first create a mount point for it. A mount point is the directory within the file system where the media's contents will reside. The /mnt directory exists as the base on which you add these items. Some administrators simply mount anything onto /mnt, but this approach works only if you mount one item at a time. Others prefer a more hierarchical approach.

If you prefer to create a mount hierarchy for each type of media, you need to create a directory for each media. A common set of directory choices would be /mnt/cdrom, /mnt/floppy, and /mnt/zip. Of course, you should use names that are easy to remember.

Once you have created the mount point, you need to know how Linux sees the device you want to mount. Some distributions create aliases and links, whereas others don't. The device files themselves are located in the /dev directory.

The syntax for the mount command is as follows:

```
mount [-alrsvw] [-t fstype] [-o options][device] [mountpoint]
```

Options are shown in tables 24.11 and 24.12.

To mount the /dev/sdb3 to the /mnt/shared directory, you would type the following command:

```
mount /dev/sdb3 /mnt/shared
```

To mount a data CD-ROM, you would type this command:

```
mount -t iso9660 /dev/cdrom /mnt/cdrom
```

NOTE: The Linux installation creates the /mnt directory specifically for temporary mounts (CDs, floppy disks, and other removable media). You do not have to use /mnt; you can mount them into any directory that you want.

If you need to remount a large number of file systems that are already listed in the fstab file, you can use the -a option in mount to remount all the entries in the fstab:

```
mount -a
```

Table 24.11 Mount Options

Option	Description
-a	Causes mount to mount all the files listed in the /etc/fstab file, which specifies the most-used partitions and devices.
-r	Causes Linux to mount the file system read-only, even if it's normally a read/write file system.
-v	As with many commands, -v produces verbose output.
-w	Causes Linux to attempt to mount the file system for both read and write options. This is the default for most file systems, but some experimental drivers default to read-only operation.
-t fstype	Specifies the file system type. Common file system types are ext2 (for ext2fs), vfat (for FAT with VFAT long file names and FAT32 partitions), msdos (for FAT using only short DOS file names), iso9660 (for CD-ROM file systems), ntfs (for NTFS partitions), and nfs (for NFS network exports). If this parameter is omitted, Linux will attempt to autodetect the file system type.
-o options	You can add many options using this parameter. Many of these are file system specific. See table 24.12.
Device	The device is the device file name associated with the partition or disk device, such as /dev/hda3. This parameter is usually required.
mountpoint	The directory to which the device's contents should be attached. As with device, it is usually required.

If it finds that the file system is already mounted, no action on the file system is performed. On the other hand, if it finds that an entry is not mounted, it will automatically mount it with the appropriate parameters.

Many Linux distributions ship with auto-mounter support, which causes the operating system to automatically mount removable media when it is inserted. For example, when you are running X Window and you insert a CD-ROM, it will mount the CD-ROM and open a file browser window.

To unmount a drive, you would use the umount command. The umount syntax is as follows:

```
umount [-anrv] [-t fstype] [device | mountpoint]
```

Most of these parameters have similar meanings to the mount command, but there are some differences that deserve mentioning. See table 24.13.

As with mount, normal users cannot ordinarily use umount. The exception is if the partition or device is listed in /etc/fstab and specifies the user or owner option, in which case normal users can unmount the device. In the case of owner, the user issuing the command must also own the device file, as with mount. This is most useful for removable-media devices.

To unmount a drive, you can either specify the device or mountpoint. To unmount a CD-ROM drive (with a mount point /mnt/cdrom), you would type the following command:

```
umount /mnt/cdrom
```

To unmount the device /dev/cdrom, you would type the following command:

```
umount /dev/cdrom
```

To unmount all file systems, you can use:

```
umount -a
```

NOTE: While a CD-ROM drive is mounted in Linux, the CD eject function is disabled. In order to manually eject a CD, you must first issue the umount (unmount) command.

Table 24.12 File System Options Used with the Mount Command

Option	Supported File System	Description
defaults	All	Uses the default options for this file system. It's used primarily in the /etc/fstab file to ensure that there's an option column in the file.
loop	All	Uses the loopback device for this mount. Allows you to mount a file as if it were a disk partition. For instance, mount -t vfat loop image.img /mnt/image mounts the file image.img as if it were a disk.
auto or noauto	All	Mounts or does not mount the file system at boot time or when root issues the mount -a command. Default is auto, but noauto is appropriate for removable media. It is typically used in /etc/fstab.
user or nouser	All	Allows or disallows ordinary users to mount the file system. Default is nouser, but user is often appropriate for removable media. Used in /etc/fstab. When included in this file, allows users to type *mount /mountpoint,* where */mountpoint* is the assigned mount point to mount a disk.
owner	All	Similar to user, except that the user must own the device file. Some distributions such as Red Hat assign ownership of certain device files (such as /dev/fd0 for the floppy disk) to the console user, so this can be a helpful option.
remount	All	Changes one or more mount options without explicitly unmounting a partition. To use this option, you issue a mount command on an already mounted file system, but with remount along with any options you want to change. Can be used to enable or disable write access to a partition, for example.
ro	All	Specifies a read-only mount of the file system. This is the default for file systems that include no write access and for some with particularly unreliable write support.
rw	All read/write read/write file systems	Specifies a read/write mount of the file system. This is the default for most read/write file systems.
uid=*value*	Most file systems that don'tsupport UNIX-system permissions such as vfat, hpfs, ntfs, and hfs	Sets the umask for the permission on files. Value is interpreted in binary as bits to be removed from permissions on files. For instance, umask=027 yields permissions or 750, or -rwxr-x–. Used in conjunction with uid=*value* and gid=*value,* this option lets you control files on FAT, HPFS, and many non-Linux file systems.
conv=code	Most file system used on Micro-soft and Apple operating sys-tems including msdos, umsdos, vfat, hpfs, ntfs, and hfs	If code is bo or binary, Linux doesn't modify the files' contents. If code is t or text, Linux automatically converts files between Linux-style and DOS- or Macintosh-style end-of-line characters. If code is an a or auto, Linux applies the convert unless the file is a known binary file format. It's usually best to leave this at its default value of binary because file conversions can cause serious problems for some applications and file types.
norock	iso9660	Disables Rock Ridge extensions for ISO 9660 CD-ROMs.
nojoliet	iso9660	Disables Joliet extentions for ISO 9660 CD-ROMs.

Table 24.13 Umount Options

Option	Description
-a	Rather than unmount partitions listed in /etc/fstab, this option causes the system to attempt to unmount all partitions listed in /etc/mtab. On a normally running system, this operation is likely to succeed only partly because it won't be able to unmount some key file systems, such as the root partition.
-r	This option tells umount that if it cannot unmount a file system, it should attempt to remount it in read-only mode.
-t fstype	This option tells the system to unmount only partitions of the specified type. You can list multiple file system types by separating them with commas.
device or mountpoint	You need to specify only the device or only the mount point, not both.

When working with floppy disks, you must make sure to unmount the floppy disk before removing it from the floppy disk drive. Linux caches access to floppy disks, which means that data may not be written to the disk until sometime after a write command. Therefore, if you remove the disk from the drive, it is possible to corrupt the floppy disk.

If you try to unmount a file system but get a "device is busy error" message, this means that some process has an open file on the device. However, it may not be obvious which process has the open file. One tool that can be helpful is the lsof, which lists all open files. You can pipe the output of lsof through grep, searching on the name of the mount point directory. For example, the following lsof command locates open files on /mnt/floppy:

```
lsof | grep /mnt/floppy
```

Once you have located the processes that are preventing you from unmounting the file system, you can shut them down manually, close whatever files are open in the target directory, or use the kill command to terminate the programs.

24.12.5 Installing Journaling File Systems

Ext 2 is not perfect since it is a stat file system that does not guarantee that all updates to your hard drive are performed safely. If the computer is shut down improperly, for example because of a power outage or a system crash, it can take several minutes for Linux to verify the integrity of the partition when the computer reboots. In addition, ext2 is not fault-tolerant. To overcome such situations, journaling file systems were created, which become more important with mission critical servers and the need to maintain large datasets.

Journaling file systems are superior to static file systems when it comes to guaranteeing data integrity and increasing overall file systems performance. Journaling and logging file systems can keep track of the changes to either a file's "metadata" (information such as ownership and creation date) or to the data blocks associated with a file, or to both, rather than maintaining a single static snapshot of the state of the file.

Ext3 comes as a patch of 2.2.19 kernel. Therefore, to install ext3, you will need to have Linux 2.2.19 kernel or later. You can create the ext3 partition during the Linux installation (such as Red Hat version 7.2 or greater), or you can use the mke2fs from the installed e2fsprogs, and use the -j option when running mke2fs

```
mke2fs -j /dev/xxx
```

where */dev/xxx* is the device in which you would create the ext3 file system. The -j flag tells mke2fs to create an ext3 file system with a hidden journal. You could control the size of the journal using the optional flag

```
-Jsize=<n>
```

where *n* is the preferred size of the journal in MB. To upgrade an existing ext2 file system to ext3, just use the following command:

```
tune2fs -j /dev/xxx
```

You can upgrade either a mounted or unmounted file system. If the file system is mounted, a file journal is created in the top-level directory of the file system; if it is unmounted, a hidden system inode is used for the journal. Either way, all the data in the file system is preserved.

You can mount the ext3 file system using the command:

```
mount -t ext3 /dev/xxx /mount_dir
```

Because ext3 is basically ext2 with journaling, a cleanly unmounted ext3 file system could be remounted as ext2 without any other commands.

Reiserfs has been in the official Linux kernel since 2.4.1-pre4. You always need to get the utils (e.g., mkreiserfs) to create reiserfs on an empty partition, the resizer, and so on. The up-to-date reiserfs version is available as a patch against either 2.2.x and 2.4.x kernels. Please note that if you choose to get the patch against 2.4.x kernel, you should get also the utils tarball reiserfsprogs-3.x.0j.tar.gz. Install the new kernel and reboot. Now you can create a new reiserfs file system with the command

```
mkreiserfs /dev/xxx
```

and mount it:

```
mount -t reiserfs /dev/xxx /mount_dir
```

24.12.6 The /etc/fstab File

The /etc/fstab file controls the mounting of devices. When you first install Linux, a default /etc/fstab file is created. This default file contains the mount points and partitions you created during the installation process. Some administrators may need to edit this file by hand. The format used in /etc/fstab is as follows:

```
Device Mount_Point File system_Type Mount_Options Dump Fsck_Order
```

See tables 24.14 and 24.15 for options used in the /etc/fstab file, and figure 24.16 for a sample /etc/fstab file.

Therefore, if you want to mount the file system as read-writeable, user-mountable but not automatically mounted, you would use the following string:

```
rw,suid,dev,exe,noauto,user,asynch
```

Table 24.14 Fstab Options

Option	Description
Device	Contains the name of the device to be mounted such as /dev/hda1.
Mount_Point	Contains the mount point within the file system that the kernel assigns to the device.
File system_Type	Contains the type of file system to be mounted such as ext2.
Mount_Options	Contains the controls and privileges to apply to the mounted partition.
Dump	Tells the kernel whether to dump the changes to disk immediately or cache them to memory until there's an idle moment to write the data or until the buffer is filled. You gain speed if dumping is used, but if there's a failure the data may be lost before it is written. A value of 0 in this field means dumping isn't used, whereas a value of 1 means dumping is used.
Fsck_Order	At boot time, Linux uses the fsck program to check file system integrity. This column specifies the order in which this check occurs. A 0 means that fsck should not check a file system. Higher numbers represent the check order. The root partition should have a value of 1 and all others that should be checked have a value of 2.

Table 24.15 Frequently Used Mount Options Within the Fstab File

Option	Description
Asynch	Handles file system input/output asynchronously
Auto	Mounts at boot time
Defaults	Shorthand for the following sets of options: rw, suid, dev, exec, auto, nouser, asynch
Dev	Accepts both character and block special devices
Exec	Allows binaries on the file system to be executed
Noauto	Does not mount at boot time
nodev	Does not accept either character or block special devices
noexec	Does not allow binaries on the file system to be executed
nosuid	Does not allow suid on the file system
nouser	Allows only the console or the superuser to mount
ro	Mounts as read-only
rw	Mounts as read/write
suid	Allows suid on the file system
user	Allows users to mount

Figure 24.16 A Sample /etc/fstab File

```
LABEL=/         /             ext2    defaults                 1 1
none            /dev/pts      devpts  gid=5,mode=620           0 0
LABEL=/home     /home         ext3    defaults                 1 2
none            /proc         proc    defaults                 0 0
none            /dev/shm      tmpfs   defaults                 0 0
/dev/hda3       swap          swap    defaults                 0 0
/dev/cdrom      /mnt/cdrom    iso9660 noauto,owner,kudzu,ro    0 0
/dev/fd0        /mnt/floppy   auto    noauto,owner,kudzu       0 0
```

One of the largest complaints on a single user or end user machine is that users cannot mount a floppy or CD-ROM on their own. In these cases, be sure to add the user item to the options list for that device.

24.13 CONFIGURING SWAP PARTITIONS

The swap partitions are used as swap space for virtual memory. Virtual memory is hard disk space pretending to be RAM. When your RAM fills with programs and data, Linux moves some of this information to its swap space, freeing physical RAM. Although this allows your system to run more programs and use more data, virtual memory is much slower than physical RAM since disks are slow mechanical devices. If your computer runs out of swap space, your program may behave erratically. In addition, if your system doesn't have enough RAM, it relies more on the swap space and your performance will significantly decrease.

Table 24.16 Free Command Options

Option	Description
-b or -k or -m	Specify output values to be displayed in bytes, kilobytes, or megabytes. If you don't include any of these parameters, free uses kilobytes by default.
-o	By default, free presents a correction for memory used by disk caches and buffers. Adding this parameter omits this correction.
-s *delay*	Causes free to display a memory-use report every *delay* second. The default shows a single report and quits.
-t	Adds a line to the output that includes total (RAM and swap space).
-V	Causes free to display its version number and then quit.

Figure 24.17 A Demonstration of the Free Command

```
[rootpregan-desk root]# free
             total      used      free    shared   buffers    cached
Mem:        513120    158544    354576      1220     29088     57480
-/+ buffers/cache:     71976    441144
Swap:       265064         0    265064
```

24.13.1 Evaluating Your Swap Partitions

To check your system's memory usage, you can use the free command. The free program displays information on your computer's total memory use. Its syntax is as follows:

```
free [-b|-k|-m] [-o] [-s delay] [-t] [-V]
```

Options are shown in table 24.16.

As shown in figure 24.17, there is 513,120 KB or 501 MB of memory (actually this system has 512 MB of memory). Of that, 158,544 KB is used and 354,576 KB is free. Yet if you take into account the memory used by buffers, shared memory, and caches, this system actually has 441,144 KB free. In addition, this system has a 265,064 KB of swap space that can be used. Currently, none of the swap file is needed.

If you use the -s portion and you redirect the content to a text file, you can then study the text file later. For example, you can use the following command:

```
free -s 600 > freemem.txt
```

Swap spaces should be between the amount of the physical RAM and twice the amount of the physical RAM. If your swap space use regularly exceeds twice your RAM, your overall system performance will be severely degraded. In addition, if the free column routinely approaches 0 when running the free command, then it's time to add RAM.

24.13.2 Adding a Swap Partition or File

If you determine that your swap file is too small or you add more RAM and you have to increase your swap files, you can create additional swap partitions. To do this, you would:

1. Clear space for the swap partition; this can be done by deleting existing partitions or by using a previously unused hard disk.
2. Create a new partition and give it a type code of 82, which indicates a Linux swap file.

3. To prepare the swap partition to be swap space, you would use the mkswap. For example, to prepare a swap partition on the third partition on the second SCSI hard drive, you would use this command:

```
mkswap /dev/sdb3
```

4. Once the swap space has been prepared, you must activate the swap space. This is done with the swap command. For example, to activate the sdb3 partition:

```
swapon /dev/sdb3
```

5. To use the swap partition permanently, you would then add an entry to the /etc/fstab.

What a lot of people don't realize is that you can also add a swap file, rather than an entire swap partition, assuming it is an ext2, vfat, and reiser file system. To add a swap file:

1. Create an empty file of the appropriate size by using the dd utility.

```
dd if=/dev/zero of=/swap.swp bs=1024 count 131072
```

2. The dd takes parameters of the block size in bytes (bs) and the number of blocks to copy (count) and multiplies them together to determine the file size of the swap file.
3. Use the mswap command to initialize the swap file for use by using the mkswap command. To initialize the swap.swp file, you would use the following command:

```
mkswap /swap.swp
```

4. Use the swapon command to initialize the swap space:

```
swapon /swap.swp
```

Typically, it is recommended to add a swap partition rather than a swap file. If the drive has been heavily used before adding the swap file, a large swap file will be scattered through the partition, decreasing performance. But, the swap file does give you a quick and easy way to add swap space.

24.14 USING DISK COMMANDS

The df command reports the system's disk space usage. If you type the command *df* at a shell prompt, the output looks similar to what is shown in figure 24.18. By default, this utility shows the partition size in 1 KB blocks and the amount of used and available disk space in kilobytes. To view the information in megabytes and gigabytes, use the command df -h. The -h argument stands for human-readable format.

Figure 24.18 A Sample of Using the Df Command

```
[root@pregan-desk root]# df
Filesystem          1k-blocks      Used Available Use% Mounted on
/dev/hda1             4127076   2805364   1112068  72% /
none                   256560         0    256560   0% /dev/shm
/dev/hda3              751076        20    712904   1% /home/m1
[root@pregan-desk root]# df -h
Filesystem             Size  used Avail Use% Mounted on
/dev/hda1              3.9G  2.7G  1.0G  72% /
none                   250M     0  250M   0% /dev/shm
/dev/hda3              733M   20k  686M   1% /home/m1
```

To view the system's disk space usage in a graphical format, you can use GDiskFree or KDiskFree. To start GDiskFree, open the GNOME Main menu, select Programs, click on System, and then select GNOME Disk Free; or type the command *gdiskfree* at a shell prompt. This utility displays all mounted file systems and their disk usage using a dial diagram. If you have the KDE desktop, you can execute the kdf file or you can click on the Main Menu button, select the System applet, and choose the Disk Free option.

You can also choose the File systems tab in the GNOME System Monitor. To start it, open the GNOME Main menu, click on Programs, select System, and then select System Monitor; or type *gtop* at a shell prompt. Then choose the File systems tab.

The du command displays the estimated amount of space being used by files in a directory. If you type *du* at a shell prompt, the disk usage for each of the subdirectories will be displayed in a list. The grand total for the current directory and subdirectories will also be shown, as the last line in the list. If you do not want to see all the subdirectories, type the command *du -hs* to see only the grand total for the directory in human-readable format.

24.15 TROUBLESHOOTING PROBLEMS WITH FILE SYSTEMS

When the Linux will not boot, it is time for emergency system rescue procedures. These steps involve taking out the custom boot disk and using it to boot the machine. Once booted, you can then mount partitions, check file systems, and make repairs where necessary. Once the system is installed, it is important to make a custom boot disk for that machine. This disk functions as the emergency rescue disk, or boot disk.

Some distributions have special ways to create this boot disk and special rescue disks to go along with it. Some even have rescue disk images on the distribution CD that you can place on a floppy using rewrite or dd.

To create a custom boot disk after installation, place an empty floppy disk into the floppy drive. Then use the mkbootdisk command to create the boot disk. The command in its most basic format is as follows:

```
mkbootdisk kernelversion
```

The boot disk is then written sector by sector with the kernel version installed on the machine.

To boot into a mode that allows system repairs, first try booting into run level 1. This is accomplished by typing *single* after the Linux label in the LILO prompt. For example, if the label was "linux" then you would type *linux single.*

If the system cannot boot into run level 1, then the rescue disk is necessary. Boot the system with the boot disk in the drive; it will come up in a raw form with only what was installed on the boot disk available to you until you mount partitions.

Once the machine is booted into Linux, the difficult task of tracking down the problem begins. You can get a listing of what partitions exist by typing *fdisk -l,* although this will not give you the mount point information. Often you can tell by size which is which, but if you cannot, it does not hurt to mount the wrong one intentionally. Once you get the root file system mounted, examine the boot message and logs. These items may or may not give you some hints as to where to start. Run file system checks using the fsck and scripts for potential problems. Make sure no important files have had their permissions or ownership inadvertently changed.

Common causes in boot failures are /etc/lilo.conf, /etc/inittab, and /etc/fstab. Another problem may be in the BIOS—the battery may have failed or some settings may have been reset accidentally.

Another thing to keep in mind is if you have to boot with boot or rescue disks and then mount a file system, you must type *sync* (sometimes more than once) before unmounting the drives to make sure that everything is handled properly. If you have to run LILO off a root partition that is mounted onto the /mnt hierarchy, which would be the case in this scenario, then you need to run /sbin/lilo with the -r flag and tell it the location of the root file system to install itself on. For example, if you mounted it as /mnt/root, then you would type

```
/mnt/root/sbin/lilo -r /mnt/root
```

For Red Hat systems, if you boot your system with an installation boot disk or the Red Hat Linux CD-ROM #1, you can boot your system into rescue mode by typing *linux rescue* at the boot prompt. Once you have your system in rescue mode, a shell prompt appears on VC2 (virtual console 2). To access the VC2, use the Ctrl + Alt + F2 keys.

Figure 24.19 Using the ls Command to Display Permissions

```
[root@host1-1 data]# ls -l
total 148
drwxr-xr-x   2 root    root       4096 Apr 15 17:38 archive
-rwxr-xr-x   1 user1   manager   33026 Apr 15 17:36 file1.txt
-rwxrwxrwx   1 user1   manager   35812 Apr 15 17:36 file2.txt
-rwxr-----   1 user1   user1     48738 Apr 15 17:36 file3.txt
-rwxrwx---   1 root    root      23196 Apr 15 17:36 file4.txt
```

24.16 FILE SECURITY

Besides login security, when you think of security, you think of file security where you determine who can access what directories and files and how they can access them. Therefore, it is obvious that if you are going to be setting up a network server or if you want to secure a Linux workstation, you will need to understand file security and how to configure it.

There are three components to Linux's file permission handling:

- **Username (or UID)**—A username (or UID) is associated with each file on the computer. This is frequently referred to as the file owner.
- **Group (or GID)**—Every file is associated with a particular GID, which links the file to a group. This is sometimes referred to as the group owner. Normally, the group of a file is one of the groups to which the file's owner belongs, but root may change the file's group to one unassociated with the file's owner.
- **File Access Permissions**—The file access permission is a code that represents who may access the file, relative to the file's owner, the file's group, and all others.

You can see all three elements by using the ls -l command on a file. See figure 24.19.

The ls command is one of the most useful commands. By using the ls command, you can view:

- **Permission String**—The output of this command has several different components, each with a specific meaning. The first component (for example, -rwxr-xr-x) is the permission string. Along with the user and group names, it's what determines who may access a file. As displayed by ls -l, the permission string is a series of codes. Sometimes the first character of this string is omitted, particularly when discussing ordinary files, but it's always present in an ls -l listing.
- **Number of Hard Links**—Linux supports hard links in its file systems. A hard link allows one file to be referred to by two or more different file names. Internally, Linux uses a data structure known as an inode to keep track of the file, and multiple file names point to the same inode. The number 1 in the preceding example ls -l means that just one file name points to this file; it has no hard links. Larger numbers indicate that hard links exist. For instance, 3 means that the file may be referred to by three different file names.
- **Owner**—The next field; in this example, root is the owner of the file. In the case of long user names, the user name may be truncated.
- **Group**—The kmem is the group to which the example file belongs. Many system files belong to the root owner and root group.
- **File Size**—In this example, 3302b is the size of the file in bytes.
- **Creation Time**—Contains the file creation time and date. If the file is older than a year, you'll see the year rather than the creation time, although the time is still stored with the file.
- **Filename**—The final field. When using the ls command, if the complete path to the file is used, the complete path appears in the output.

24.16.1 File Access Codes

The file access control string is 10 characters in length. The first character is the file type code, which determines how Linux will interpret the file; for example, it could be ordinary data, a directory, or a special file type (see table 24.17).

Table 24.17 File Type Codes

Code	Meaning
-	Normal data file—It may be text, an executable program, graphics, compressed data, or just about any other type of data.
d	Directory—Disk directories are files just like any other, but they are marked as a directory and they contain file names and pointers to disk inodes.
I	Symbolic link—The file contains the name of another file or directory. When Linux accesses the symbolic link, it tries to read the linked-to file.
p	Named pipe—A pipe allows two running Linux programs to communicate with each other. One opens the pipe for reading, and the other opens it for writing, allowing data to be transferred between the programs.
s	Socket—A socket is similar to a named pipe, but it permits network and bidirectional links.
b	Block device—A hardware device to and from which data is transferred in blocks of more than 1 byte. Disk devices (hard disks, floppies, CD-ROMs, and so on) are common block devices.
c	Character device—A hardware device to and from which data is transferred in units of 1 byte. Examples include parallel and serial port devices.

The remaining 9 characters represent the permissions (for example, rwxr-xr-x) broken into 3 groups of 3 characters. The first group controls the file owner's access to the file, the second controls the group's access to the file, and the third controls all other users' access to the file. This is often referred to as world permissions.

In each of the three groupings, the permission string determines the presence or absence of each of three types of access: read, write, and execute. The absence of the permission is denoted by a hyphen (-) in the permission string. The presence of the permission is indicated by a letter (*r* for read, *w* for write, and *x* for execute).

- **Read Permission (r)**—For a file, the read permission enables you to read the file. For a directory, read permission allows the ls command to list the names of the files in the directory. You must also have execute permission for the directory name to use the -l option of the ls command or to change to that directory. It has a value of 4.
- **Write Permission (w)**—For a file, the write permission means you can modify the file. For a directory, you can create or delete files inside that directory. It has a value of 2.
- **Execute Permission (x)**—For a file, the execute file means that you can type the name of the file and execute it. For a directory, execute permission means that you can change to that directory (with the cd command). It has a value of 1.

You cannot view or copy the file unless you also have read permission. This means that files containing executable Linux commands, called shell scripts, must be both executable and readable by the person executing them. Programs written in a compiled language such as C, however, can have only executable permissions, to protect them from being copied where they shouldn't be copied.

If you have the execute command and you do not have the read permission for the directory, you can change into the directory but ls -l will not work. You can list directories and files in that directory, but you cannot see additional information about the file or directory just by doing an ls -l command. This is a highly desirable characteristic for directories, so you'll almost never find a directory on which the execute bit is not set in conjunction with the read bit.

Directories can be confusing with respect to write permission. Recall that directories are files that are interpreted in a special way. As such, if a user can write to a directory, that user can create, delete, or rename files in the directory, even if the user isn't the owner of those files and does not have permission to write to those files.

Thus, the example of the permission string of rwxr-xr-x means that the file's owner members of the file's group, and all other users can read and execute the file. Only the file's owner has write permission to the file. You can easily exclude those who don't belong to the file's group, or even all but the file's owner, by changing the permission string.

Table 24.18 Example Permissions and Their Likely Uses

Permission String	Octal Code	Meaning
rwxrwxrwx	777	Read, write, and execute permissions for all users
rwxr-xr-x	755	Read and execute permissions for all users. The file's owner also has write permission.
rwxr-x---	750	Read and execute permissions for the owner and group. The file's owner also has write permission. Nongroup members have no access to the file.
rwx------	700	Read, write, and execute permissions for the file's owner only; all others have no access to the file.
rw-rw-rw-	666	Read and write permissions for all users. No execute permission to anybody.
rw-rw-r--	664	Read and write permissions for all users. No execute permission to anybody.
rw-rw----	660	Read and write permissions to the owner and group. No world permission.
rw-r--r--	644	Read and write permissions to the owner. Read-only permission to all others.
rw-r-----	640	Read and write permissions to the owner, and read-only permission to the group. No permission to others.
rw-------	600	Read and write permissions to the owner. No permission to anybody else.
r--------	400	Read permission to the owner. No permission to anybody else.

Individual permissions, such as execute access, for the file's owner are often referred to as permission bits. This is because Linux encodes this information in binary form. Because it is binary, the permission information can be expressed as a single 9-bit number. This number is usually expressed in octal (base 8 form because a base 8 number is 3 bits in length, which means that the base 8 representation of a permission string is three digits long, one digit for each of the owner, group, and world permissions. The read, write, and execute permissions each correspond to one of these bits. The result is that you can determine owner, group, and world permissions by adding base 8 numbers: 1 for execute permission, 2 for write permission, and 4 for read permission. See table 24.18 for more examples.

Permissions								
Owner			Group			World		
r	w	x	r	w	x	r	w	x
4	2	1	4	2	1	4	2	1

Example 24.1:

If you give the owner of the file all rights (read, write, and execute), you give the group read and execute, and you give everyone else no rights, the base 8 rights would be expressed as 750.

Permissions								
Owner			Group			World		
r	w	x	r	–	x	r	–	–
4	2	1	4	–	1	–	–	–
7			5			0		

Symbolic links are unusual with respect to permissions. This file type always has 777 (rwxrwxrwx) permissions, thus granting all users full access to the file. This access applies only to the link file itself, however, not to the linked-to file. In other words, all users can read the contents of the link to discover the name of the file to which it points, but the permissions on the linked-to file determine its file access. Attempting to change the permissions on a symbolic link affects the linked-to file.

Many of the permission rules do not apply to root. The superuser can read or write any file on the computer, even files that grant access to nobody (that is, those that have 000 permissions). The superuser still needs execute bits to be set to run a program file, but the superuser has the power to change the permissions on any file, so this limitation isn't very substantial.

There are a few special permissions options that are also supported, and they may be indicated by changes to the permission string:

- Set user ID (SUID)—The set user ID (SUID) option is used in conjunction with executable files, and it tells Linux to run the program with the type of permissions that run the program. For instance, if a file is owned by root and has its SUID bit set, the program runs with root privileges and can therefore read any file on the computer. Some servers and other system programs run in this way, which is often called SUID root.

Important Note: SUID programs represent a security risk if they are not carefully controlled. They are indicated by an *s* in the owner's execute bit position of the permission string, as in rw**s**r-xr-x.

- Set group ID (SGID)—The set group ID (SGID) option is similar to the SID option, but it sets the group of the running program to the group of the file. It's indicated by an *s* in the group execute bit position of the permission string, as in rwxr-**s**r-x.
- Sticky bit—In modern Linux implementations, it is used to protect files from being deleted by those who don't own the files. When this bit is present on a directory, the directory's files can be deleted only by the directory's owner or root. The sticky bit is indicated by a *t* in the world execute bit position, as in rwxr-xr-**t.**

24.16.2 Changing File Ownership and Permissions

Changing who can read, write, or execute a file can be done using several programs, depending upon the desired effect. Specifically, chown changes a file's owner, and optionally, its group; chgrp changes the file's group; and chmod changes the permissions string.

To begin, chown's syntax is as follows:

```
chown [-R] [newowner][.newgroup] filename...
```

Newowner and *newgroup* are, of course, the new owner and group of the file. One or both are required. If both are included, there must be no space between them, only a single period (.). For instance, the following command gives ownership of the file report.tex to Sally, and sets the file's group to project 2:

```
chown sally.project2 report.tex
```

The -R or --recursive option changes all the files within a directory and all its subdirectories.

The chgrp command is similar to chown, except that it doesn't change or alter the file's owner owner; it works on the group that it is assigned to. The group name is not preceded by a period. For example, to change the group of report.tex to project2, you could issue the following command:

```
chgrp project2 report.tex
```

Chgrp takes the same option as does chown.

NOTE: The owner may change the group of a file to any group to which the file's owner belongs but not to other groups.

You can modify a file's permissions using the chmod command. This command may be issued in many different ways to achieve the same effect. Its basic syntax is as follows:

```
chmod [options] [mod,mod...]] filename...
```

Table 24.19 Options Used with the Chmod Command

Permission Set Code	Meaning
u	Owner
g	Group
o	World
a	all
Change Type Code	**Meaning**
+	Add
–	Remove
=	Set equal to
Permission to Modify Code	**Meaning**
R	Read
W	Write
X	Execute
x	Execute only if file *is* a directory or already has the execute permission
s	SUID or SGID
t	Sticky bit
u	Existing owner's permissions
g	Existing group permissions
o	Existing world permissions

The chmod options are similar to those of chown and chgrp. In particular, --recursive (or -R) will change all the files within a directory tree. For the options for the chmod command, see table 24.19.

Most of the complexity of chmod comes in the specification of the file's mode—that is, its permissions. There are two basic forms in which you can specify the mode: as an octal number or as a symbolic mode, which is a set of codes related to the string representation of the permissions. For example, to change permissions on report.tex to rw-r--r--, you would issue the following command:

```
chmod 644 report.tex
```

A symbolic mode, by contrast, consists of three components: a code indicating the permission set you want to modify (the owner, the group, and so on); a symbol indicating whether to add, delete, or set the mode equal to the stated value; and a code specifying what the permission should be. Note that all these codes are all case sensitive.

NOTE: Sometimes you may use the chmod command with four digits instead of three. In this situation, the first digit selects the set user ID bit (4), the set group ID bit (2), and the save test image (1) attribute.

To use symbolic permission settings, you combine one or more of the codes from the first column with one symbol from the third column and one or more codes from the fifth column. You can combine multiple settings by separating them with commas. For examples, see table 24.20.

As a general rule, symbolic permissions are most useful when you want to make a simple change (such as adding execute or write permissions to one or more classes of users), or when you want to make similar changes to many files without affecting their other permissions—for instance, adding write

Table 24.20 Examples of Using the Chmod Command

Command	Initial Permission	Ending Permission
chmod a+x file1	rw-r--r--	rwxr-xr-x
chmod ug=rw file1	r--------	rw-rw----
chmod o-rwx file1	rwxrwxr-x	rwxrwx---
chmod g=u file1	rw-r--r--	rw-rw-r--
chmod g-w,o-rw file1	rw-rw-rw-	rw-r-----

permissions without affecting execute permissions. Octal permissions are most useful when you want to set some specific absolute permission, such as rw-r--r-- (644). A system administrator should be familiar with both methods of setting permissions.

A file's owner and root are the only users who may adjust a file's permissions. Even if other users have write access to a directory in which a file resides and write access to the file itself, they may not change the file's permission (but they may modify or even delete the file). To understand why this is so, you need to know that the file permissions are stored as part of the file's inode, which isn't part of the directory entry. Read/write access to the directory entry, or even the file itself, doesn't give a user the right to change the inode structures (except indirectly—for instance, if a write changes the file's size or a file directory eliminates the need for the inode).

24.16.3 Setting Default Permissions

When a user creates a file, that file has default ownership and permissions. The default owner is understandably the user who creates the file. The default group is the user's primary group. The default permissions, however, are configurable. These are defined by the usermask (umask), which is an octal file creation mask. The umask contains the bits that are off by default when a new file is created. This umask uses an octal value (0–7) that represents the bits to be removed from 777 permissions for directories, or from 666 permissions for files. You can not set the execute bit of a file with a usermask. The usermask is set by the umask command.

Example 24.2:

If you have a umask of 022 and you create a new file, the 022 will be subtracted from 666.

- Owner Permissions:
  - If you look at the first 6 of the 666, the 6 represents read and write (rw-=42-) permissions.
  - If you look at the 0 of the 022, you notice that 0 represents ---, which represents no permissions.
  - If you subtract the bit by bit, you get 4-0=4, 2-=2 and 0-0=0 gives you a 6 for the resultant group permission.
- Group Permissions:
  - If you look at the second 6 of the 666 represents 42-, which represents RW permissions.
  - If you look at the first 2 of the 022, you notice that 2 represents -2-, which represents the write permissions.
  - If you subtract the bit by bit, you get 4-0=4, 2-2=0 and 0-0=0 gives you a 4 for the resultant owner permission.
- World Permissions:
  - If you look at the last 6 of the 666 represents 42-, which represents RW permissions.
  - If you look at the second 2 of the 022, you notice that 2 represents -2-, which represents the write permissions.
  - If you subtract the bit by bit, you get 4-0=4, 2-2=0 and 0-0=0 gives you a 4 for the resultant owner permission.

Therefore, with a umask of 022 the owner of any file created will automatically have read and write permission. The group that the file is assigned to will have read permission and everyone else will have read permission as well.

If you have a umask of 002, the owner and the group will have read and write permission and everyone will have only read permission.

All Permissions								
Owner			**Group**			**World**		
r	w	x	r	w	x	r	w	x
4	2	–	4	2	–	4	2	–
6			6			6		
Unmask								
Owner			**Group**			**World**		
r	w	x	r	w	x	r	w	x
–	–	–	–	2	–	–	2	–
0			2			2		
Resulting Permissions								
Owner			**Group**			**World**		
r	w	x	r	w	x	r	w	x
4	2	–	4	–	–	4	–	–
6			4			4		

Example 24.3:

Let's say that you want the owner to have read and write permission, the group only to have read permission, and everyone to have no permission. You would do the following:

- The read and write permissions mean that you don't want to shut off any of the permissions for the owner. Therefore, it will be represented by ---=0.
- The read permission for the file means that you want to shut off the write permission for the group. Therefore, -W-, represented by -2-=2.
- The no permissions for the file means that you want to shut off read and write permission 42-=6.

Therefore, the umask should be 026. It would be set with the following command:

```
umask 026
```

To find what the current umask is, type *umask,* without any parameters. Typing *umask -S* produces the umask expressed symbolically, rather than in octal form. You may also specify a umask in this way when you want to change it, but in this case, you specify the bits that you do want set. For instance, umask u=rwx, g=rx, o=rx is equivalent to umask 022.

Ordinary users can enter the umask command to change the permissions on new files they create. The superuser can also modify the default setting for all users by modifying a system configuration file. Typically, /etc/profile contains one or more umask commands. Setting the umask in /etc/profile might or might not actually have an effect because it can be overridden at other points, such as user's own configuration files. Nonetheless, setting the umask in /etc/profile or other system files can be useful if you want to change the default system policy. Most Linux distributions use a default umask of 002 or 022.

24.17 GROUP STRATEGIES

The traditional way of creating user accounts is to create one or more groups in /etc/group and then assign one of these groups to be the primary group for each new user account that is added. For example, you may create one group for the accounting department, and a group for the information systems department in your organization. When you create accounts for new hires in the accounting department, each user receives a unique user account but the same group as the other accountants. Note that user accounts can belong to more than one group; the primary group for an account is simply the default group for that account.

The purpose of having groups is to allow users who are members of a particular group to share files. Typically, this is done by creating a directory and changing the group ownership of the directory so that the group can access all files in the directory. For example, suppose you have a group set up for the users in the accounting department called accgrp, and you would like to create a directory that will be shared by the group called accshared under /home. You would do the following:

```
mkdir /home/accshared
chown nobody.accgrp /home/accshared
chmod 775 /home/accshared
```

Any user who is a member of the accgrp group can now create files in the /home/accshared directory.

24.18 RECOVERING FROM A FORGOTTEN ROOT PASSWORD

If you forget the root password, you can follow these steps to set up up a new root password:

1. Power up your PC as usual. At the LILO boot prompt, type the name of the Linux boot partition followed by the word *single:*

   ```
   linux single
   ```

   This causes Linux to start up as usual, but run in a single user mode that does not require you to log in. After Linux starts, you will see the bash# command-line prompt.
2. Use the passwd command to change the root password and enter the new password. Note that the passwd command will ask you to verify the password. When complete, the passwd command changes the password and displays the message:

   ```
   passwd: all authentication tokens updated successfully
   ```

3. Reboot the PC by pressing Ctrl + Alt + Del. After Linux starts, it displays the familiar login screen. Log in as normal.

As you can see, it is not difficult to break into a Linux computer. Therefore, you will have to rely on BIOS passwords and physical security to help maintain your system security.

SUMMARY

1. On the C drive, the BIOS will look in the master boot record on the hard drive and start executing the code found there. These instructions typically look at the partition table, determine which partition is active and go to the volume boot sector of that partition to load the operating system.
2. The ROM BIOS will find the LILO or GRUB boot manager, which will then find and load the kernel (vmlinuz).
3. Since the kernel merely manages other programs, when it considers that everything is OK, it will look in several places for the init program and run the first one it finds.
4. All further programs are either started directly by init or by one of its "child" processes. Since it is considered the father of all processes (a process is simply a running program) in the entire system, it is assigned a process ID (PID) of 1.

5. The init program goes through a complicated startup sequence. init reads its configure file, /etc/inittab, and determines the run level where it should start. When it is told to enter a run level, init executes a script as specified in the /etc/inittab file.
6. A run level is an identifier that specifies the current system state such as single-user mode, multi-user mode, or multi-user mode with network modes and others. By specifying a run level, you are specifying a software configuration that will permit only a select group of processes (programs) to run and what daemons to start or stop.
7. While the exact run level definitions vary between distributions, they all serve the same purpose, which is to bring the system up to run in the desired state by using the /etc/inittab file.
8. In Linux, a daemon is a background process that monitors and performs many critical system functions and services. Most daemons have names that end with *d*.
9. Typically, a daemon is started when the system boots, and the daemon processes run as long as the system is running. Most daemons have the capability to restart copies of themselves to handle specific tasks.
10. To shut down a daemon under Linux, type the name of the daemon, followed by the *stop*. To start the daemon, you would use *start* instead of *stop*.
11. There are several utilities that allow you to manage your daemons. They include ntsysv, chkconfig, tksysv, and linuxconf.
12. If LILO is installed into the master boot record, after your system performs its default BIOS checks and detections, you will see the LILO: prompt or LILO GUI screen until a boot image is loaded.
13. To prepare the LILO configuration file, you have to log in as *root* and edit the /etc/lilo.conf file with a text editor. When the LILO configuration file /etc/lilo.conf is ready, you can install LILO with the /sbin/lilo command
14. Another popular boot manager is GRUB (GRand Unified Bootloader). GRUB's configuration file (/boot/grub/grub.conf) is read from the disk every time the system boots, preventing you from having to write over the MBR every time you change the boot options.
15. The Linux kernel provides critical low-level facilities. These include Memory management (including handling swap space most low-level hardware drivers), process scheduling, and file systems for access to files on the disk.
16. A device driver includes all the instructions necessary for Linux to communicate with a device.
17. As a general rule, Linux makes hardware devices accessible through device file entries in the /dev file structure. The files all have ownership and permissions like other files, which will control who may access the device.
18. Many Linux distribution kernels were compiled to install onto the largest range of systems. Therefore, they are compiled to run on the slowest processor of a particular architecture.
19. To take advantage of the features available on the newer processors, you will need to at least rebuild the kernel, specifying the processor that you have. Other reasons to recompile or upgrade a Linux kernel is for better support of existing hardware, to fix a bug that may be in the kernel, or to fix security holes.
20. After you have created a kernel, you have to install it and update your boot manager, such as LILO.
21. Adding a new disk or partition to the Linux file system is configure the hard drive, physically attach the drive to the computer system if necessary, partition the new disk (fdisk or cfdisk), create a file system on the partition (mkfs), check the new file system for consistency errors (fsck), and mount the new file system (mount).
22. Ext 2 is not perfect since it is a stat file system. It does not guarantee that all updates to your hard drive are performed safely.
23. Journaling file systems are superior to static file systems when it comes to guaranteeing data integrity and increasing overall file systems performance.
24. The swap partitions are used as swap space for virtual memory. Virtual memory is hard disk space pretending to be RAM.
25. To check your system's memory usage, you can use the free command.
26. The df command reports the system's disk space usage.
27. Besides login security, when you think of security, you think of file security where you determine who can access what directories and files and how they can access those directories and files.
28. The file access control string is ten characters in length. The first character is the file type code, which determines how Linux will interpret the file such as ordinary data, a directory, or a special file type.
29. The remaining nine characters represent the permissions (for example, rwxr-xr-x) that are broken into three groups of three characters. The first group controls the file owner's access to the file, the second controls the group's access to the file, and the third controls all other users' access to the file. This is often referred to as world permissions.
30. When a user creates a file, that file has default ownership and permissions. The default owner is the user who creates the file. The default group is the user's primary group.
31. The default permissions, however, are configurable. These are defined by the usermask (umask).

QUESTIONS

1. What is LILO?
   a. another name for the Linux kernel
   b. a program that Linux uses to replace the BIOS
   c. a file server used with the Linux operating system
   d. a bootstrap program that finds and loads an operating system
2. What is the main configuration file for LILO?
   a. /etc/lilo.conf
   b. /etc/conf.lilo
   c. /boot/lilo.conf
   d. /boot/conf.lilo
3. Where may LILO be installed?
   a. the MBR, a Linux partition's boot sector, or a floppy disk
   b. the MBR, a Linux partition's boot sector, or a Windows partition's boot sector
   c. a Linux partition's boot sector or a Windows partition's boot sector
   d. the MBR, a floppy disk, or a swap partition
4. Which of the following is an advantage of installing LILO in a primary Linux partition's boot sector?
   a. LILO can then boot a kernel from beyond the 1,024 cylinder mark.
   b. LILO can then redirect the boot process to other operating systems' boot sector.
   c. The DOS or Windows FDISK utility can be used to reset LILO as the boot loader if the MBR is overwritten.
   d. LILO can work in conjunction with LOADLIN to boot multiple kernels.
5. After changing the default operating system in /etc/lilo.conf, you reboot your computer to find that it still boots to the old default operating system. What did you forget to do that would cause this to happen?
   a. create a backup
   b. run /sbin/lilo
   c. copy the file to the /boot directory
   d. copy /etc/lilo.conf to /etc/liloconfig
6. Which two programs are considered Linux boot loaders (choose two answers)?
   a. boot
   b. grub
   c. lilo
   d. gnuboot
7. Which package is used to manage the kernel build process?
   a. make
   b. mk
   c. compile
   d. run
8. If you wanted to configure the kernel within the Linux GUI interface, which make option would you run?
   a. oldconfig
   b. xconfig
   c. menuconfig
   d. config
9. Which make option do you use to build the kernel itself?
   a. bzImage
   b. kernel
   c. vmlinuz
   d. version
10. What do you change the name of the kernel to once it is properly placed (not including the version number)?
    a. bzImage
    b. kernel
    c. vmlinuz
    d. initrd
11. What command moves the kernel's modules into place after they have been compiled?
    a. insmod
    b. make modules_move
    c. make modules
    d. make modules_install
12. Which file do you need to edit to ensure that the machine can boot with the new kernel?
    a. /boot
    b. /etc/lilo
    c. /etc/lilo.conf
    d. /sbin/lilo
13. What process lies at the root of the Linux process hierarchy?
    a. the BIOS
    b. LILO
    c. init
    d. ps
14. Which method is commonly provided with most new Linux distributions to start and stop a daemon?
    a. The only way is to reboot the machine.
    b. Type the name of the daemon followed by *load* or *kill.*
    c. Type the name of the daemon followed by *begin* or *end.*
    d. Type the name of the daemon followed by *start* or *stop.*
15. A user calls you and claims that he cannot mount the CD-ROM drive from the command line. When you ask which command he is using, he says mount /dev/cdrom /mnt/cdrom. Which command should he be using?
    a. mount /dev/cdrom /cdrom
    b. mount -t vfat /dev/cdrom /cdrom
    c. mount -t msdos /dev/cdrom /mnt/cdrom
    d. mount -t iso9660 /dev/cdrom /mnt/cdrom
16. Which command will show you how much disk space is available on each partition?
    a. du
    b. df
    c. ls
    d. dir
17. Which command is used to check and repair a Linux file system?
    a. fsck
    b. fdisk
    c. chkdsk
    d. diskfix
18. What should you always do before running fsck on a partition?
    a. Back up your data.
    b. Unmount the partition.
    c. Change your run level to single user mode.
    d. Make sure no one is saving anything to it.
19. What is the correct order in which to execute commands for installing a new hard drive?
    a. fdisk, mkfs, fsck, mount
    b. mount, fdisk, mkfs, fsck
    c. mkfs, fsck, mount, fdisk
    d. fdisk, mount, mkfs, fsck

20. Which command unmounts a CD-ROM drive?
    a. umount cdrom
    b. unmount cdrom
    c. umount /mnt/cdrom
    d. unmount /dev/cdrom
21. Whenever you restart a Linux system, you need to manually mount the /usr/local directory. What configuration file might you edit to automate this process?
    a. /etc/inittab
    b. /etc/mtab
    c. /usr/localtab
    d. /etc/fstab
22. Which command is used to add the read permission to the yourfile.txt file?
    a. chmod
    b. chgrp
    c. chown
    d. chedit
23. Which two commands perform the same task (choose two)?
    a. chmod 444 meeas.txt
    b. chmod meeas.txt 444
    c. chmod ugo=r meeas.txt
    d. chmod -rw-rw-rw- meeas.txt
24. As the user root, you created a new home directory for one of the users on your Linux computer with the command cp /etc/tests /home/pat. What would be the next step to allow the user Pat and users of the teacher group to use his home directory?
    a. chown pat /home/pat
    b. chown -R pat /home/pat
    c. chown pat.teacher /home/pat
    d. chown -R pat.teacher /home/pat
25. Which of the following umask values will result in files with rw-r----- permissions?
    a. 640
    b. 210
    c. 022
    d. 027
26. What is the octal representation of the permission rw-r--r--?
    a. 322
    b. 422
    c. 741
    d. 644
27. What is the umask of permission set rwxr--rw-?
    a. 746
    b. 031
    c. 022
    d. none of the above
28. Why are SUID and GUID dangerous to security?
    a. They are bits that can be set that grant users the ability to delete other users.
    b. They are bits that can be set on files that enable users to execute them in su mode.
    c. They are bits that can be set on a file to make it execute as its owner, usually root.
    d. They are bits that can be set on a file to allow you to grant access to more than one user.
29. What is a "sticky" bit?
    a. a bit that can be set on a file to make it execute as the file's owner
    b. a bit that can be set on a file that marks it as having been backed up
    c. a bit that can be set on a file to make it execute as the file's group owner
    d. a bit that can be set on a file that will allow only the file's owner to delete it

HANDS-ON EXERCISES

Exercise 1: Changing Run Levels

1. Boot to a command prompt. Do not load X Window.
2. Log in as root.
3. Run the following command at the command prompt:

   ```
   run level
   ```

4. Run the following command at the command prompt:

   ```
   init 5
   ```

5. Log in as root
6. Open a terminal window.
7. Run the following command at the command prompt:

   ```
   run level
   ```

8. Run the following command at the command prompt:

   ```
   init 3
   ```

9. If it seems to stop processing, press Enter to get to the command prompt.
10. Run the following command at the command prompt:

    ```
    run level
    ```

11. Configure the /etc/inittab file to automatically start X Window during boot.
12. Reboot the system and let X Window boot.
13. Configure the /etc/inittab file to boot to the command prompt.
14. Reboot the system to the command prompt.

Exercise 2: Starting and Stopping Daemons

1. Run the following command at the command prompt:

   ```
   chkconfig -list ¦ more
   ```

2. Keep pressing the spacebar until you get back to the command prompt.
3. Run the following command at the command prompt:

   ```
   chkconfig -list smb
   ```

4. Change to the /etc/rc.d/init.d directory, the directory that holds the system daemon scripts.
5. Run the following command at the command prompt:

   ```
   ls -l
   ```

6. Run the following command at the command prompt:

   ```
   ps -aux
   ```

7. Run the following command at the command prompt:

   ```
   /etc/rc.d/init.d/smb start
   ```

8. Run the following command at the command prompt:

   ```
   ps -aux
   ```

   See that the smbd and nmbd daemons are now loaded.

9. Run the following command at the command prompt:

   ```
   /etc/rc.d/init.d/smb restart
   ```

10. Run the following command at the command prompt:

    ```
    /etc/rc.d/init.d/smb stop
    ```

11. Run the following command at the command prompt:

    ```
    ps -aux
    ```

12. Run the following command at the command prompt:

    ```
    chkconfig --list smb
    ```

13. Run the following command at the command prompt:

    ```
    chkconfig --level 345 smb on
    ```

14. Run the following command at the command prompt:

    ```
    chkconfig --list smb
    ```

Exercise 3: Creating a Boot Disk

1. To get the kernel version, run the following command at the command prompt:

   ```
   uname -r
   ```

2. To make a boot disk, run the following command at the command prompt

   mkbootdisk *kernelversion*

   where *kernelversion* was retrieved with the uname command.

3. Insert a blank diskette and press the Enter key.
4. Boot the system with the boot disk to see if the system boots.

Exercise 4: Compiling and Installing a New Kernel

1. Log in as root.
2. Start X Window.
3. Start a terminal window.
4. Run the following command at the command prompt

   cd /usr/src/linux-*kernelversion*

   where *kernelversion* is actually the kernel version (example 2.4.7-10).

5. Run the following command at the command prompt:

```
make xconfig
```

6. Click on the Processor type and features button. Click on the button to the left of the processor family and select the appropriate processor for your machine. Click on the Main Menu button.
7. Click on the General Setup button and look at the available options. Click on the Main Menu button.
8. Click on the Parallel Port Support button. Then enable the following:

   - Parallel Port as a module
   - PC-Style hardware as a module
   - IEEE 1284 Transfer modes—Yes

   Return back to the Main menu.

9. If you expect to print to the printer, you will then need to click on the Character Devices and enable parallel port support as a module. In addition, select the Enhanced Real Time Clock support.
10. Scroll down to the bottom of the list. If your system is using one of the listed chipsets or video cards, be sure it is enabled.
11. Click on the Main Menu button.
12. Select Networking Options. Then enable the following:

   - Kernel/User Netlink Socket—Yes
   - Routing messages—Yes
   - Netlink device emulation—Yes

   Click on the Main Menu button.

13. Click on SCSI Support and choose the appropriate options for your system. Click on the Main Menu button.
14. Click on the File Systems button. Click on the Help button next to Quota Support. Close the Help dialog box by clicking on the OK button. Select Yes for Quota Support.
15. Select Ext3 Journaling File System Support. Note that although it says that it is experimental, it is not.
16. At the bottom of the screen, click on Network File Systems and enable SMB file system support. In addition, enable default NLS. Click OK.
17. Go back to the Main menu.
18. Click on the Save and Exit button. Click on the OK button.
19. Exit X Window.
20. Go to the /usr/src/linux-*kernelversion.*
21. Run the following commands at the command prompt. Note that some of these commands may take awhile.

```
make dep
make clean
make bzImage
make modules
```

22. Run the following command at the command prompt:

```
cd arch/i386/boot
```

   You are now in the /usr/src/linux*kernelversion*/arch/i386/boot directory.

23. Run the following command at the command prompt:

```
ls -l
```

   Look at the bzImage file and notice how big the bzImage file is.

24. Run the following command at the command prompt

```
cp bzImage /boot/vmlinuz-kernelversionnew
```

   where *kernelversion* is actually the kernel version (example 2.4.7-10).

25. Run the following command at the command prompt:

```
cd /usr/src/linux-kernelversion
```

26. Run the following command at the command prompt:

```
ls -l
```

27. Run the following command at the command prompt:

```
cp System.map /boot/System.map-kernelversion
```

   If it says to overwrite, type *y* (for yes).

28. Run the following command at the command prompt:

```
make modules_install
```

Exercise 5: Reconfiguring LILO

NOTE: Exercise 4 needs to be completed before doing this exercise.

1. Change to the /etc directory.
2. Open the /etc/lilo.conf file with a text editor.
3. Change the label=linux to label=linuxold.
4. Add the following lines at the end of the file:

```
image=/boot/vmlinuz-kernelversionnew
label=linuxnew
read-only
root=/dev/hda1
```

5. Change the default=linux to default=linuxnew.
6. Save the changes to the text file and exit the text editor.
7. Reboot the system. Notice that the changes did not show. This is because you did not run the lilo command to put the changes into effect.
8. At the command prompt, run the lilo command.
9. Reboot the system again and test both options.
10. Reboot the system again. When the LILO boot menu appears, press Ctrl + X for text mode.
11. At the boot prompt, press the Tab key to display the boot options.
12. Run the following command at the boot prompt:

```
linuxnew single
```

13. Reboot once more and press Ctrl + X again.
14. Run the following command at the boot prompt:

```
linuxnew emergency
```

15. Type the root password when it is requested.
16. Reboot the system one last time.

Exercise 6: Preparing a New Partition

1. At the command prompt, run the fdisk program by executing the following command:

```
fdisk /dev/hda
```

2. At the fdisk prompt, use the p option to show the partition table.
3. Notice the total number of cylinders and the last volume ending cylinder.
4. Type *m* at the fdisk prompt to show the Help screen.
5. To create a new partition, type *n* and press Enter. Then press *p* and press Enter to specify a primary partition, and 4 and Enter to specify the fourth partition. Press Enter to accept the first available cylinder and again to accept the last cylinder.
6. Display the partition table again. Notice that the partition default is type 83.
7. Use the l option to list the partition types. Look at the ext2, swap, and Win 95 FAT32 (LBA) partition types.
8. To change the partition to a Win95 FAT32 (LBA) partition, press the *t* key. Then press Enter, 4, and press Enter to specify the fourth partition. Press *c* and Enter to specify the FAT32 partition.
9. Display the partition table again.
10. Change the partition table for hda4 to an ext2 partition.
11. To write the partition table and exit fdisk, press the *w* key and press Enter. Reboot if told to do so.
12. To format the new partition as an ext2 partition, execute the following command:

```
mkfs /dev/hda4
```

13. Now you decide you want to reformat the partition as an ext3 partition. You did not have to format the partition as an ext2 partition first. To format it as an ext 3 partition, execute the following command:

```
mke2fs -j /dev/hda4
```

Notice that it took a little longer to format than previously.

14. To verify the integrity of the new partition, execute the following command:

```
fsck /dev/hda4
```

15. Execute the df command to view your file systems.
16. To create the mount point, you must first create the mount directory. Therefore, create a /share directory.
17. Next, to mount the hda4 partition, execute the following command:

```
mount /dev/hda4 /share
```

18. Execute the df command to view your file systems.
19. Try to run the fsck command on the hda4 partition. When it asks if you are sure, say no since it may corrupt the data on the partition.
20. Change to the /share directory.
21. Try to unmount the drive by executing the following command:

```
umount /dev/hda4
```

22. Because Linux sees the partition as busy, you need to figure out why. Therefore, use the following command to determine why the partition is busy:

```
lsof | grep share
```

Notice the bash entry. You cannot remove a drive when you are currently in the partition. Therefore, change to the / directory.

23. Now, unmount the drive.
24. Run the fsck command.
25. Reboot the system.
26. Execute the df command to view your file systems. Notice that the hda4 partition is not mounted.
27. To make the fourth partition automatically mount into the share mount point, open the /etc/fstab file with text edit and add the following line:

```
/dev/hda4  /share     ext3  defaults    0 2
```

28. Save the file and reboot the system.
29. Execute the df command.

Exercise 7: Mounting and Unmounting a CD

1. Insert the first installation CD-ROM disk in your system.
2. To mount it, try executing the following command:

```
mount -t iso9660 /dev/cdrom /mnt/cdrom
```

3. Change to the /mnt/cdrom directory and execute the ls command.
4. To unmount the CD, execute the following command:

```
umount /dev/cdrom
```

5. Mount the CD again.
6. To unmount the CD, execute the following command:

```
umount /mnt/cdrom
```

Exercise 8: Using Disk Commands

1. To view the file systems on your system, execute the df command.
2. To view the file systems on your system in human format, execute the df -h command.
3. Now, execute the du -hs command at the command prompt.
4. To see how much of your swap file is being accessed, execute the free command.
5. Start X Window.
6. Execute the kdf command.
7. Close the KDiskFree program and shut down X Window.

Exercise 9: Working with File Permissions

1. Create a user2 account.
2. Create a group2 group.

3. Assign user2 to group2.
4. If you don't already have one, create a /data directory.
5. Change to the /data directory.
6. Create three text files called file10.txt, file20.txt, and file30.txt with your name in them.
7. Use the ls -l command and record the permissions.
8. Change to the second virtual console.
9. Log in as user2.
10. Change to the data directory.
11. View the contents of file10.txt by using the cat command.
12. Try to add your age to the file10.txt file.
13. Try to delete the file10.txt file using the rm command.
14. Change back to the first virtual console.
15. Assuming that you are still in the /data directory, to change owner of the files to user2 and group2, type the following command:

    ```
    chown user2.group2 *
    ```

16. Change to the second virtual console.
17. View the contents of file10.txt by using the cat command.
18. Try to delete the file.
19. Change back to the first virtual console.
20. Change the permissions by typing the following command:

    ```
    chmod 660 file20.txt
    ```

21. Use the ls –l command to view the permissions.
22. Change back to the second virtual console.
23. Open the file20.txt file and add your age to the file. Save the file.
24. Try to delete the file. Remember that to delete a file, you must have the write permission for the directory that the file is in.
25. Change back to the first virtual console.
26. Change to the root directory. Execute the following command to directory permissions:

    ```
    chmod 660 data
    ```

27. Change back to the second virtual console.
28. Try to perform a listing of the data directory. Remember that for you to see a directory listing, you must have the execute permission for the directory.
29. Change back to the 1st virtual console.
30. Change the permissions for the data directory.

    ```
    chmod 770 data
    ```

31. Access the directory listing of the /data directory.
32. Delete file10.txt.
33. Change back to the first virtual console.
34. At the command prompt, type the following command to view the current umask:

    ```
    umask
    ```

35. To change the umask, type the following command:

    ```
    umask 007
    ```

36. To create an empty text file called file40.txt, type the following command:

    ```
    touch file40.txt
    ```

37. Use the ls -l command to view the permissions.

Exercise 10: Recovering a Lost Root Password

1. Reboot the computer and enter the text mode of LILO.
2. At the command prompt, boot into single mode.
3. At the command prompt, use the passwd command to change the password to *testpassword.*
4. Reboot the computer and test the new password.
5. Change the password back to *password.*

CHAPTER 25

Computers Connected to a Network

Topics Covered in This Chapter

Introduction

As networks have become more popular, it has become evident that a PC technician must also be familiar with how to connect a PC to a network and to the Internet. In addition, the technician must be able to differentiate between problems caused by the computer and problems caused by the network.

Objectives

1. Identify and describe the common types of network topologies.
2. Identify and describe the common types of network cables and connectors.
3. Identify common technologies available for establishing Internet connections and their characteristics.
4. Configure Windows and Linux to connect to a local area network and the Internet.
5. Share a folder and printer using Windows and Linux.
6. Troubleshoot common networking problems.
7. Identify and describe the common networking protocols.
8. Identify and describe the common TCP/IP protocols and services.

25.1 NETWORKS

A network is two or more computers connected together to share resources. See figure 25.1. Most computers communicate with the network by a cable attached to the computer's network interface card (NIC), while a few computers can use some form of wireless technology (infrared, microwaves, or radio waves). Computers are networked according to certain protocols (TCP/IP, IPX, and NetBEUI), which are the rules or standards that allow computers to connect to one another. Currently, the benefits of a network include:

1. Sharing data or access to a program loaded on the network (file sharing)
2. Sharing printers (print sharing)
3. Sending messages back and forth (electronic mail, or email)
4. Sending and receiving faxes
5. Accessing a modem or accessing the Internet directly
6. Accessing a centralized database
7. Scheduling appointments
8. Providing security for the network services and resources
9. Allowing for a central location of data files so that it is easier to perform a backup of essential files

Figure 25.1 Computers Networked Together

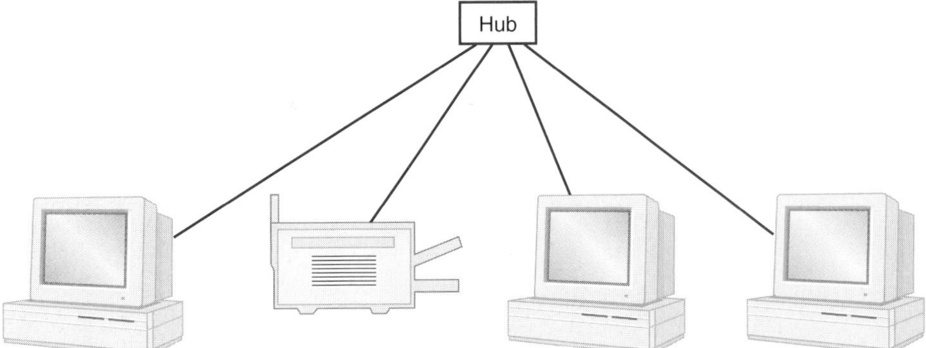

The two most common services provided by a network are file sharing and print sharing. File sharing allows files that are on another computer to be accessed without using a floppy disk or other form of removable media. To ensure that the file is secure, most networks can limit who has access to a directory or file and what kind of access (permission or rights) they have. For example, with full access to a home directory, the user can:

1. List, read, or execute the files in the home directory
2. Create files and directories within the home directory
3. Make changes to files in the home directory
4. Delete files or directories in the home directory

One group of people may be prevented from seeing or executing the files. A second group of people may be able to see or execute the files but cannot make any changes to the files and cannot delete them, while a third group can see, execute, and change the files.

Print sharing allows several people to send documents to a centrally located printer, eliminating the need for personal laser printers. As with files, networks can limit who has access to the printer. For example, if there are two laser printers, a standard laser printer and an expensive, high-resolution color laser printer, everyone can be assigned access to the standard laser printer, while only a handful of people can be allowed access to the expensive printer.

Two other popular network services include electronic mail (email) and Internet access. Electronic mail, or email, is a powerful, sophisticated tool that allows text messages and file attachments (documents, pictures, sound, and movies) to be sent to anyone with an email address. In 1997, it was estimated that there were over 25 million email users sending 15 billion messages per year. Much like mail handled by the post office, email is delivered to a mailbox (delivery location or holding area for messages). An Internet mail address includes the user name followed by the @ symbol and the name of the mail server. When the addressee connects to the network, the email message can be accessed. Other features of email may include a return receipt so that the sender knows the email was read or delivered, the ability to reply to the email message by clicking on a reply button or option, sending an email message to several people at the same time, or forwarding the message to someone else. See figure 25.2.

Figure 25.2 Email with Microsoft Outlook

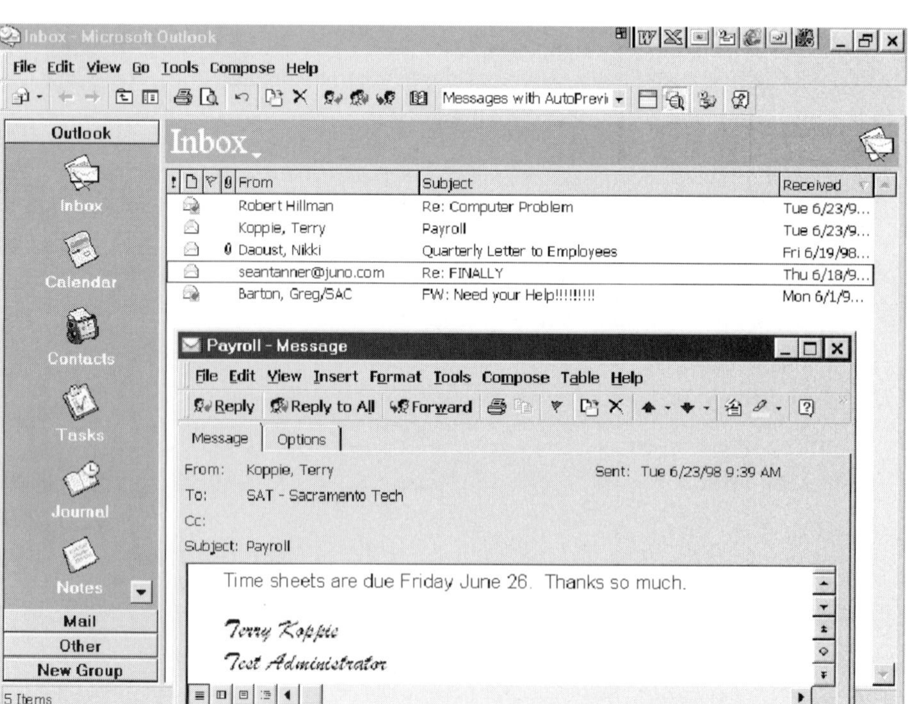

Networks can also become part of the Internet or can make a common connection to the Internet possible for many users. The Internet itself is essentially a huge network that many people and organizations have used to post their own web pages or to exchange information and perform research.

25.2 NETWORK CHARACTERISTICS

All networks can be characterized by (1) a client/server or peer-to-peer network, and (2) a LAN, MAN, or WAN configuration.

25.2.1 Servers, Clients, and Peers

Any computer on a network can provide services or request services depending on how the network is set up. A server is a computer that is a dedicated service provider, and a client is a computer that requests services. A network that is made up of dedicated servers and clients is known as a client/server network, a system designed for medium to large networks. Windows NT, Windows 2000, and Novell NetWare networks are primarily client/server networks. A peer-to-peer network has no dedicated servers. Instead, all computers can provide services and request services equally. Windows 95, Windows 98, and Windows Me can be used to form a peer-to-peer network.

25.2.2 LANs, MANs, and WANs

There are currently three main categories of networks: **local area networks (LANs), metropolitan area networks (MANs)**, and **wide area networks (WANs).** In a LAN, computers within a close geographical area, such as a building or a campus, are connected. A MAN is a network designed for a town or city, usually with high-speed connections such as fiber optics. A WAN network uses long-range telecommunication links to connect the network over long distances and often consist of two or more smaller LANs. Typically, these LANs are connected through public networks, such as the telephone system. See figure 25.3. A WAN can be either an enterprise WAN or a global WAN. An enterprise WAN is a WAN that is owned by one company or organization, while a global WAN is not owned by any one company and usually crosses national boundaries. The Internet is a global WAN that connects millions of computers. As of 1998, the Internet had more than 100 million users in over 100 countries, and the number is growing rapidly.

Another type of network is the intranet. An intranet is a network based on the TCP/IP, the same protocol the Internet uses, but unlike the Internet, the intranet belongs to a single organization and is accessible only by the organization's members. An intranet's websites look and act just like any other websites, but they are isolated by a firewall to stop illegal access. (Note: An intranet could have access to the Internet but does not require it.)

Figure 25.3 WAN

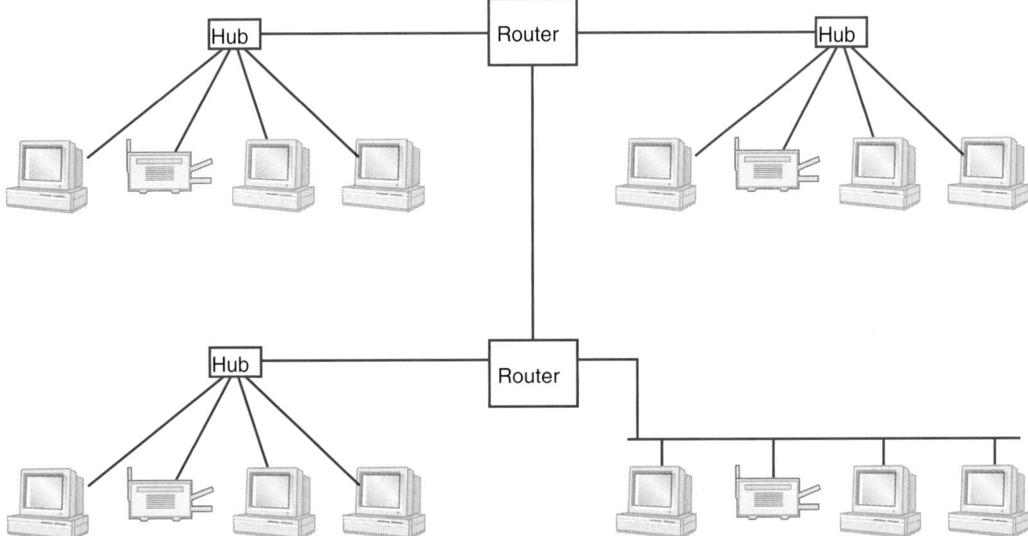

25.3 NETWORK INTERFACE CARDS (NICS)

The network interface card (NIC), sometimes referred to as the *network adapter card* or *network card,* is the physical interface, or connection, between the computer and the network cable. See figure 25.4. The role of the network card is to prepare and send data to another computer, receive data from another computer, and control the flow of data between the computer and the cabling system.

When selecting a network card, you need to first look at the type of network you are connecting to. For example, is the network Ethernet, token ring, or some other type? Next, you would have to look at the speed of the network. Are you going to be transmitting at 4, 10, 16, or 100 Mbit/s, 1 Gbit/s, or some other speeds. In addition, you must make sure that the network card has the proper network connector. If you are using unshielded twisted-pair (UTP), you would like to use an RJ-45 connector. If you are connecting to a 10Base2 coaxial cable, you will most likely use a BNC T-connector. Lastly, you should select a card based on the type of expansion bus (ISA, PCI, PCI-X, PC card, CardBus, or some other type). Today, the most popular cards are 10/100 UTP Ethernet cards. The 10/100 means that the cards can run at both 10 Mbit/s and 100 Mbit/s.

Like any other expansion card, the network card must be configured (IRQ, I/O address, DMA, and memory address) and inserted into an expansion slot. If the network card and another device share the same resources, the network card and/or the other device will act erratically or not work at all. Network cards are configured with jumpers, DIP switches, or a software configuration program. If the cards are plug-and-play, they will configure automatically. After the network card is installed, a software driver will have to be loaded to activate the card; in some cases, the software driver must be told the resources the card is using.

To identify itself to the network, each network card has a network address, known as the media access control (MAC) address. No two network cards can have the same network address on a single local area network. If two network cards are on separate local area networks, they may have the same address—much like two identical street addresses that are located in two separate cities. Most of the addresses (Ethernet and token ring cards) are burned into the ROM chips that come with the network card, while a few cards (such as ARCnet) use jumpers or DIP switches to determine the MAC address.

Today, most network cards will have up to two LEDs. One LED, the activation LED, will show that you are connected to the network. If you do not have a green light, it would mean that the cable is not connected to the card or the card is not activated (for example, not having a driver loaded or the driver or card is disabled). The other LED is a traffic LED, which shows if it is sending or receiving data packets. If this packet is always on, it might indicate that your network card is connected to a very busy network card. Of course, you should always check the network card documentation for the meaning and interpretation of the LEDs.

Figure 25.4 A Network Interface Card (NIC) with a BNC and RJ-45 Connectors

Table 25.1 Cable Types

Cable Type	Cable Cost	Ease of Installation	Installation Cost	EMI Sensitivity	Data Bandwidth	Comments
UTP	Lowest	Very simple	Lowest	Highest	Lowest to high	Used in more than 95% of LANs
STP	Medium	Simple to moderate	Moderate	Moderately low	Moderate	Usually found in older networks
Coaxial	Medium	Simple	Moderate	Moderate	High	Often used as a backbone cable
Fiber Optic	Highest	Difficult	Highest	None	Very high	Uses light instead of electrical signal

25.4 CABLE TYPES

The cabling system used in networks is the veins of the network that connects all of the computers together and allows them to communicate with each other. The common types of cabling include unshielded twisted-pair (UTP), shielded twisted-pair (STP), coaxial, and fiber optics. See table 25.1.

Frequency (bandwidth) is the number of cycles that are completed per unit of time and is generally expressed in hertz (cycles per second). Data cabling is typically rated in kilohertz (KHz) or megahertz (MHz). The more cycles per second, the more interference the cable generates and the more susceptible to data loss the cable is.

The data rate (or information) capacity is defined as the number of bits per second that move through a transmission medium. When you choose a cable, you must choose one that will handle your current network traffic and to allow for some growth.

With traditional cabling, there is a fundamental relationship between the number of cycles per second that a cable can support and the amount of data that can be pushed through the cable. For example, Category 5 and Category 5e cables are rated at 100 MHz. To implement a 100BaseTX network, you must be using Category 5 cabling since the cable must support a frequency of 100 MHz. During each digital cycle, a single bit is pushed through.

While this is a good way to think of the relationship between information rate and cable bandwidth, the IEEE recently approved the 803.3ab standard (1000BaseT), which covers running Gigabit Ethernet over Category 5 cabling. Category 5 does not operate at 1 GHz. Instead, the cable uses four data pairs to transmit the data and by using sophisticated encoding (multiplexing) techniques that are used to send more bits of data over the wire during each cycle.

In copper wiring, a signal loses energy during its travel because electrical properties at work in the cable. The opposition to the flow of current through a cable or circuit is expressed in impedance. Impedance is a combination of resistance, capacitance, and inductance and is expressed in ohms. A typical UTP cable is rated at between 100 and 120 ohms. All Category 3, 4, 5, and 5e cables are rated at 100 ohms.

Attenuation is when the strength of a signal falls off with distance over a transmission medium. This loss of signal strength is caused by several factors such as the signal converted to heat due to the resistance of the cable and as the energy is reflected as the signal encounters impedance changes throughout the cable. Low decibel values of attenuation are desirable since that means that less of the signal is lost on its way to the receiver.

Interference occurs when undesirable electromagnetic waves affect the desired signal. Interference can be caused by **electromagnetic interference (EMI)** due to large electromagnets used in industrial machinery, motors, fluorescent lighting, and power lines, and **radio frequency interference (RFI)** is caused by transmission sources such as a radio station. Another term used to describe instability in a signal wave is called **jitter;** jitter is caused by signal interference.

Besides looking at the capacity and electrical characteristics of the cable, you also need to look at two other factors when choosing a cable. First, you should look at cost. If you are installing a large network within a building, you will find that the cabling system can cost thousands of dollars. Note: The cost of installing the cable (planning and hourly wages) is many times the cost of the cable itself. Therefore, you must make sure that you have the financial resources available to install such a system.

Second, you should look at the ease of installation of the cabling system, since this affects your labor costs and can indirectly affect the reliability of the network. In addition you should look at the ease of troubleshooting, including how it is affected by media faults and if the cable system offers any fault tolerance.

25.4.1 Twisted-Pair Cable

Early networks that used UTP typically used Category 3, while today's newer high-speed networks typically use Category 5 or Enhanced Category 5 cabling. Category 3 has three to four twists per foot and could operate up to 16 MHz, while Category 5 uses three to four twists per inch, contains Teflon insulation, and can operate at 100 MHz. Enhanced Category 5 is a higher quality cable designed to reduce crosstalk even further.

A **twisted pair** consists of two insulated copper wires twisted around each other. While each pair acts as a single communication link, twisted pair is usually bundled together into a cable and wrapped in a protective sheath.

Question:

Why are the wires twisted around each other?

Answer:

Copper wire does not constrain electromagnetic signals well. This means that if you have two copper wires next to each other, the signal will induct (law of induction) or transfer from one wire to the other. This phenomenon is called **crosstalk.** By twisting the wires around each other, the electromagnetic fields cancel each other, greatly reducing the crosstalk.

Twisted pair comes in **unshielded twisted-pair (UTP)** and shielded twisted-pair (STP). Of these, unshielded twisted-pair is the type of cable used with telephones and is the most common cable used in networks. See figure 25.5. UTP cable consists of four pairs of wires in each cable. Each pair of wires is twisted about each other and used together to make a connection. Compared to other cable types (unshielded twisted-pair, shielded twisted-pair, coaxial cable, and fiber optics), UTP is inexpensive and is the easiest to install. The biggest disadvantages of UTP are its limited length of 100 meters (328 feet) and its susceptibility to interference and noise. Traditionally, UTP has had a limited network speed, but more recently UTP can be used in networks running between 4 Mbit/s and 1 Gbit/s. There are some companies, such as Hewlett-Packard, that are working on a 10 Gbit/s network standard. UTP cables use a RJ-45 connector.

Figure 25.5 Twisted-Pair Cable with RJ-45 Connector

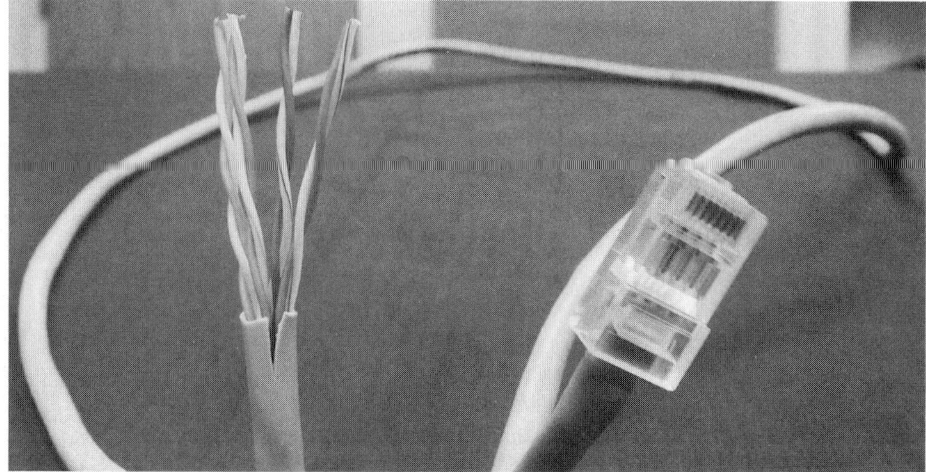

Table 25.2 Unshielded Twisted-Pair Cable Categories for Networks

Cable Type	Bandwidth (MHz)	Function	Attenuation (dB)	Impedance (Ω)	Network Usage
Category 3	16	Data	11.5	100	10BaseT (10 Mbit/s), token ring (4 Mbit/s), ARCnet, 100VG-ANYLAN (100 Mbit/s)
Category 4	20	Data	7.5	100	10BaseT (10 Mbit/s), token ring, ARCnet, 100VG-ANYLAN (100 Mbit/s)
Category 5	100	High-speed data	24.0	100	10BaseT (10 Mbit/s), token ring, Fast Ethernet (100 Mbit/s), Gigabit Ethernet (1000 Mbit/s), and ATM (155 Mbit/s)
Category 5E (enhanced)	100	High-speed data	24.0	100	10BaseT (10 Mbit/s), token ring, Fast Ethernet (100 Mbit/s), Gigabit Ethernet (1000 Mbit/s), and ATM (155 Mbit/s)
Category 6	250	High-speed data	19.8	100	10BaseT (10 Mbit/s), token ring, Fast Ethernet (100 Mbit/s), Gigabit Ethernet (1000 Mbit/s), and ATM (155 Mbit/s)
Category 6E (enhanced)	250	High-speed data	19.8	100	10BaseT (10 Mbit/s), token ring, Fast Ethernet (100 Mbit/s), Gigabit Ethernet (1000 Mbit/s), and ATM (155 Mbit/s)
Category 7 (not yet approved)	600	High-speed data	20.8	100	

Figure 25.6 IBM Shielded Twisted-Pair Cable

In 1995, UTP cable was categorized by the Electronic Industries Association (EIA) based on the quality and number of twists per unit. The UTP categories are published in EIA-568-A. See table 25.2.

Shielded twisted-pair (STP) cable is very similar to UTP cable except it uses a woven copper braid jacket and a foil wrap around both the individual wires and each pair of wires. The extra shielding makes the cable less susceptible to electrical interference and allows for higher transmission rates and longer distances. Shielded twisted-pair cable is used mostly by IBM and Apple networks. The connectors used with IBM networks is an IBM-type Data Connector (IDC), also known as universal data connector (UDC), which is a hermaphroditic connector (neither male nor female). See figure 25.6.

25.4.2 Coaxial Cable

Coaxial cable has a solid copper core surrounded by insulation, braided metal shielding, and an outer cover. See figure 25.7. It is called *coaxial* cable because the copper wire and the braided metal shielding share the same axis, or center. Because coaxial cable has more insulation, it can be used for longer distances than the twisted-pair cable. When coaxial cable is used in a network, it forms the backbone to

Figure 25.7 Coaxial Cable

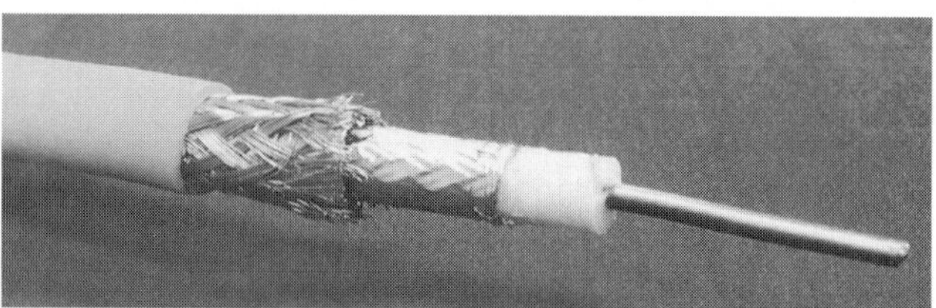

Figure 25.8 BNC Connector, T-connector, and Terminating Resistor

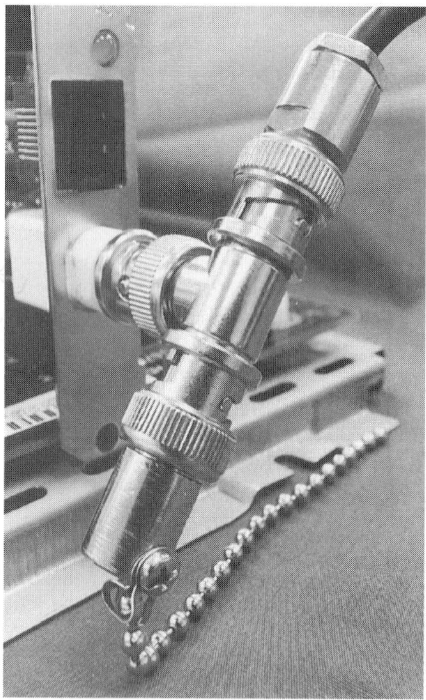

which all of the computers in the network connect. To prevent signals from bouncing back when they reach the end of the cable, coaxial cable has terminating resistors on both ends.

There are two types of coaxial cable: thin (referred to as *thinnet* or 10Base2) and thick (referred to as *thicknet* or 10Base5). Thinnet is a flexible cable resembling the type of cable used for cable TV. It connects to the network card by using BNC and T-connectors and can carry a signal up to approximately 185 meters (607 feet). See figure 25.8. Ethernet networks (10Base2) use an RG-58 coaxial cable with 50 ohm terminating resistors, while Ethernet networks (10Base5) use RG-6 or RG-8 with 50 ohm terminating resistors. Cable TV uses an RG-59 with a 75 ohm terminating resister. See table 25.3. A barrel connector is used to connect two cables. The thicknet type of cable is a bit more difficult to work with than thinnet. Instead of using T-connectors to connect computers directly into the cable "backbone," thicknet cable connects with T-connectors to a drop cable that then connects to the network card. Because thicknet cable is thicker, lengths of up to 500 meters (1,640 feet) can be used.

25.4.3 Fiber-Optic Cable

A **fiber-optic** cable consists of a bundle of glass or plastic threads, each which is capable of carrying data signals in the forms of modulated pulses of light. While glass can carry the light pulses (several kilometers) even further than plastic, plastic is easier to work with. Since each thread can carry a signal in only one direction, a cable consists of two threads in separate jackets, one to transmit and one to receive. The fiber-optics cable uses cladding that surrounds the optical fiber core, which helps reflect light

Table 25.3 Coaxial Cable Commonly Used Today

RG Rating	Popular Name	Ethernet Implementation	Type of Cable	Center Wire Gauge	Resistance Value
RG-6/U	Thicknet	10Base5	Solid copper	18 AWG	75 ohm
RG-8/U	Thicknet	10Base5	Solid copper	10 AWG	50 ohm
RG-58/U	NA	None	Solid copper	20 AWG	50 ohm
RG-58/AU	Thinnet	10Base2	Stranded copper	20 AWG	50 ohm
RG-59	Cable TV	None	Solid/stranded copper	20 AWG	75 ohm

Figure 25.9 Fiber-Optics Cable and Common Connectors (ST, SC, and MT-RJ)

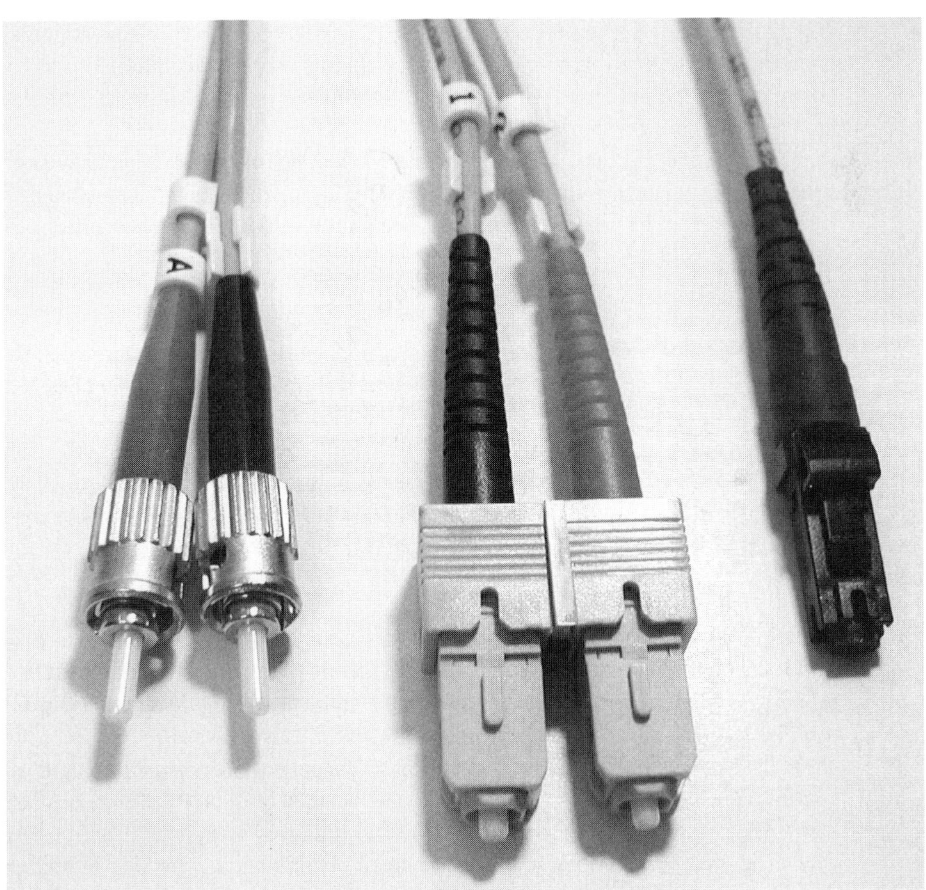

back to the core and to ensure that little of the light signal is lost. Lastly, the cable contains Kevlar strands to provide strength. See figure 25.9.

The light signal used in a fiber-optic cables is generated by light emitting diodes (LEDs) by injection laser diodes (ILDs). ILDs are similar to LEDs but produce laser light. Since laser light is purer than normal light, it can increase both the data rates and transmission distances. Signals are received by photodiodes, solid state devices that detect variations in light intensity.

Fiber-optic cables come in single-mode fiber and multimode fiber. **Multimode fiber (MMF)** is capable of transmitting multiple modes (independent light paths) at various wavelengths or phases. Unfortunately, the core's greater diameter makes light more likely to bounce off the sides of the core, resulting in dispersion and limiting the bandwidth to 2.5 Gbit/s and transmission distance between repeaters. MMF is usually the fiber-optic cable that is used with networking applications such as 10BaseFL, 10BaseF, FDDI, ATM, and other applications that require optical fiber cable for use as horizontal cable and backbone cable. Multimode cabling typically uses an orange sheath.

Single-mode fiber (SMF) can transmit light in only one mode, but the narrower diameter yields less dispersion, resulting in longer transmission distances. SMF is most commonly used by telephone companies and in data installations as backbone cable. Single-mode cabling typically uses a yellow sheath.

The types of fiber-optic cable are differentiated by mode, composition (glass or plastic), and core/cladding size. The size and purity of the core determines the amount of light that can be transmitted. Common types of fiber-optic cables include:

- 8.3 micron core/125 micron cladding single-mode
- 62.5 micron core/125 micron cladding multimode
- 50 micron core/125 micron cladding multimode
- 100 micron core/140 micron cladding multimode

The typical multimode fiber-optic cable consists of two strands of fiber (duplex). The core is 62.5 microns in diameter, and the cladding is 125 microns in diameter. This is often simply referred to as 62.5/125 micron. The newest version of the TIA/EIA568 standard also recognizes the use of 50/125 micron multimode fiber-optic cable. A typical indoor fiber-optic cable consists of a core/cladding surrounded by a 250 micron acrylate coating. A 900 micron buffer surrounds the cladding. Then this buffer is surrounded by Kevlar strands.

Over the past 5 years, optical fibers have found their way into cable television networks—increasing reliability, providing a greater bandwidth, and reducing costs. In the local area network, fiber cabling has been deployed as the primary media for campus and building backbones, offering high-speed connections between diverse LAN segments.

Fiber has the largest bandwidth (up to 10 GHz) of any media available. It can transmit signals over the longest distance (20 times farther than copper segments) at the lowest cost, with the fewest repeaters and the least amount of maintenance. In addition, since it has such a large bandwidth, it can support up to 1,000 stations, and it can support faster speeds introduced during the next 15 to 20 years.

Fiber optics is extremely difficult to tap, making it very secure and highly reliable. Since fiber does not use electrical signals running on copper wire, interference does not affect fiber traffic, and as a result the number of retransmissions is reduced and the network efficiency is increased.

To transmit data, two fibers are required. One strand of fiber is used to send and the other is used to receive. Fiber-optic cables can be divided into three categories based on the number of optical fibers:

- Simplex
- Duplex
- Multifiber

A simplex fiber-optic cable is a type of cable that has only one optical fiber inside the cable jacket. Since simplex cables only have one fiber inside them, there is usually a larger buffer and a thicker jacket to make the cable easier to handle. Duplex cables have two optical fibers inside a single jacket. The most popular use for duplex use for duplex fiber-optic cable is as a fiber-optic LAN backbone cable. Duplex cables are perfect because all LAN connections need a transmission fiber and a reception fiber. Multifiber cable has anywhere from three to several hundred optical fibers in them, typically in multiples of two.

The disadvantage of simplex connectors is that you have to keep careful track of polarity. In other words, you must make sure that the plug on the send fiber is always connected to the send jack and the receive plug is always connected to the receive jack. When using duplex plugs and jacks, color-coding and keying ensures that the plug will be inserted only one way in the jack and will always achieve correct polarity.

Fiber-optic cables use several connectors, but the two most popular and recognizable connectors are the straight tip (ST) and subscriber (SC) connectors. The ST fiber-optic connector, developed by AT&T, is probably the most widely used fiber-optic connector. It uses a BNC attachment mechanism similar to the thinnet connector mechanism.

The SC connector (sometimes known as the square connector) is typically a latched connector. This makes it impossible for the connector to be pulled out without releasing the connector's latch (usually by pressing some kind of button or release).

A new connector called the MT-RJ is similar to an RJ-45 connector. It offers a new small form-factor two-fiber connector that is lower in cost and smaller than the duplex SC interface.

The main disadvantage of fiber optics is that the cables are expensive to install and require special skills and equipment to split or splice cables. In addition, they are more fragile than wire. Fortunately, in recent years, while fiber-optics products are being mass produced, the cost gap between the high grades of UTP has narrowed significantly and there are many premade products available.

25.4.4 Plenum

PVC cable is the most common type of cable used today and consists of a chemical compound called poly vinyl chloride (thus the name PVC). If a fire occurs, burning PVC cable can emit large quantities of dense black toxic smoke. These fumes release acid gases that sear the eyes, nose, mouth, and throat while disorienting the victim, preventing escape from a fire, and causing severe respiratory damage. It can kill.

In buildings, the **plenum** is the space above the ceiling and below the floors used to circulate air throughout the workplace. It can also be found in some walls. If there is a fire, it becomes evident that the plenum will also circulate the toxic fumes generated by the burning cable.

While some international governments have already standardized zero-halogen cabling, the U.S. National Electrical Code (NEC) serves as the basis for local standards in most states to use halogen-sheathed cabling in the plenum spaces above ceilings and below floors in office buildings.

A **plenum cable** is a special cable that gives off little or no toxic fumes when burned. Depending on the building's fire code, the building's wiring will include plenum cabling unless it exists in a special sealed conduit that would prevent the toxic fumes from escaping into the open air. The major disadvantage of using plenum cable is that it is significantly more expensive.

25.5 TOPOLOGIES

Network **topology** refers to the arrangement, or physical layout, of connected computers and cables. These arrangements usually consist of the bus, star, or ring type.

25.5.1 Bus Topology

The bus topology, known as *linear bus,* is the simplest network arrangement, in which a single cable (called a *backbone* or a *trunk* or *segment*) connects all of the computers in series. See figure 25.10. Computers on the bus listen to the traffic on the network, and when a computer sees a message directed to it, it will then process the entire message. When a signal reaches the end of the cable on a bus network, the signal typically will bounce back if terminating resistors are not used on the two ends of the cable to drain the signal. If the backbone develops a break, the entire network will go down because the break would signify an end to the bus, which is not actually terminated. Typically, a bus network is connected by coaxial cable.

25.5.2 Ring Topology

A ring topology connects all of the computers in the network in a circle or loop with no ends. The signal travels around the loop in one direction. See figure 25.11. As it enters a computer, the computer regenerates the signal and sends it to the next computer. If a computer fails or there is a cable break, the entire network goes down.

Figure 25.10 Bus Topology

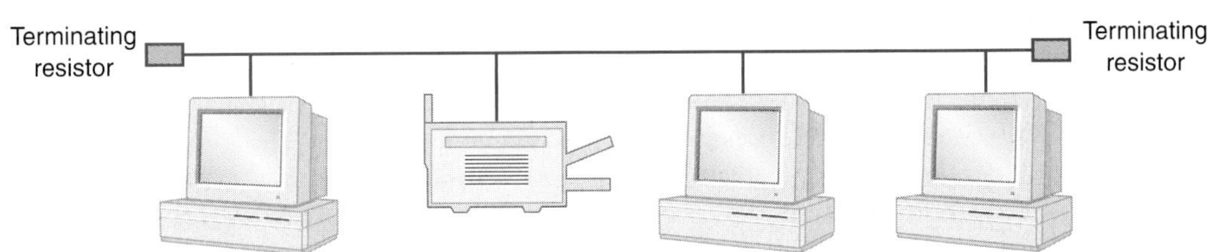

Figure 25.11 Ring Topology

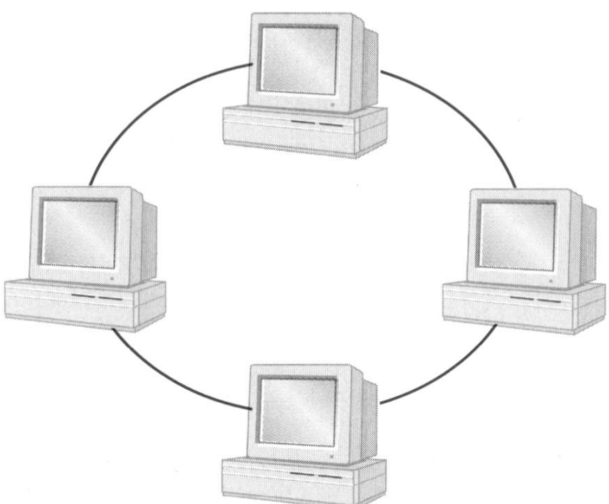

Figure 25.12 Star Topology

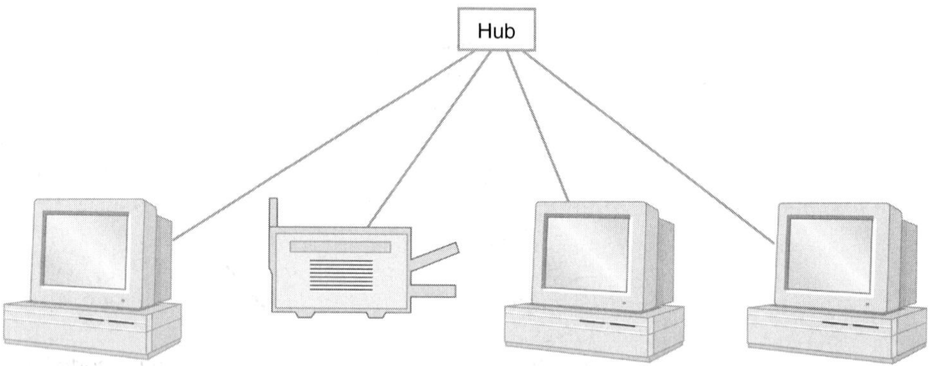

25.5.3 Star Topology

The star topology is probably the most common network configuration. All of the computers in the network are connected to a central device known as a *hub.* See figure 25.12. If a wire segment fails, the network is unaffected. Star networks usually use 10BaseT or 100BaseT twisted-pair cables.

25.5.4 Dialog Control

Data can flow in one of three ways—simplex, half-duplex, or full-duplex. Simplex dialog allows communications on the transmission channel to occur in only one direction. Essentially, one device is allowed to transmit and all of the other devices receive. This is often compared to a PA system where the speaker talks to an audience, yet the audience does not talk back to the speaker.

Half-duplex dialog allows each device to both transmit and receive, but not at the same time. Therefore, only one device can transmit at a time. This is often compared to a CB radio or walky-talkies. A full-duplex dialog allows every device to both transmit and receive simultaneously. For networks, the network media channels consist of two physical channels, one for receiving and one for transmitting.

25.6 CONNECTIVITY DEVICES

Several devices can be used to connect networks together. These include repeaters, hubs, bridges, routers, brouters, and gateways.

A **repeater,** which works at the physical OSI layer, is a network device used to regenerate or replicate a signal or to move packets from one physical media to another. Although a repeater cannot connect different network topologies or access methods, one can be used to regenerate analog or digital signals distorted by transmission loss, extended the length of a cable connection. Analog repeaters usually can amplify only the signal (including distortion), while digital repeaters can reconstruct a signal to near original quality.

A **hub,** which works at the physical OSI layer, is a multiported connection point used to connect network devices via a cable segment. When a PC needs to communicate with another computer, it sends a data packet to the port that the device is connected to. When the packet arrives at the port, it is forwarded or copied to the other ports so that all network devices can see the packet. In this way, all of the stations "see" every packet just as they do on a bus network. Of course, a standard hub is not very efficient on networks with heavy traffic since it causes a lot of collisions and retransmitted packets. See figure 25.13.

Hubs can be categorized as passive or active. A passive hub serves as a simple multiple connection point that does not act as a repeater for the signal. An active hub, which always requires a power source, acts as a multiported repeater for the signal. Note: When installing an active hub, make sure the fan (which provides cooling) is operating.

The most advanced hub is called the intelligent hub (also known as a manageable hub). An intelligent hub includes additional features that enable an administrator to monitor the traffic passing through the hub and to configure each port in the hub. For example, you can prevent certain computers from communicating with other computers, or you can stop certain types of packets from being forwarded. In addition, you can gather information on a variety of network parameters, such as the number of packets that pass through the hub and each of its ports, what type of packets they are, whether the packets contain errors, and how many collisions have occurred.

A **bridge,** which works at the data link OSI layer, is a device that connects two LANs and makes them appear as one, or that is used to connect two segments of the same LAN. The two LANs being connected can be alike or dissimilar, such as an Ethernet LAN connected to a token ring LAN. Differing from a repeater or hub, a bridge analyzes the incoming data packet and will forward the packet if its destination is on the other side of the bridge. Many bridges today filter and forward packets with very little delay, making them good for networks with high traffic.

Bridges that connect Ethernet networks are known as **spanning tree bridges.** Bridges that connect token ring networks are known as **source routing bridges.** Token ring bridges usually do not do any filtering like Ethernet bridges do.

A **switching hub** (sometimes referred to as a switch) is a fast, multiported bridge that actually reads the destination address of each packet and then forwards the packet to the correct port. A major advantage of a switching hub is that it allows one computer to open a connection to another computer (or LAN segment). While those two computers communicate, other connections between the other computers (or LAN segments) can be opened at the same time. Therefore, several computers can communicate at the same time through the switching hub. As a result, the switches are used to increase performance of a network by segmenting large networks into several smaller, less congested LANs, while providing necessary interconnectivity between them. Switches increase network performance by providing each port with dedicated bandwidth without requiring users to change any existing equipment, such as NICs, hubs, wiring, or any routers or bridges that are currently in place.

Figure 25.13 A Hub

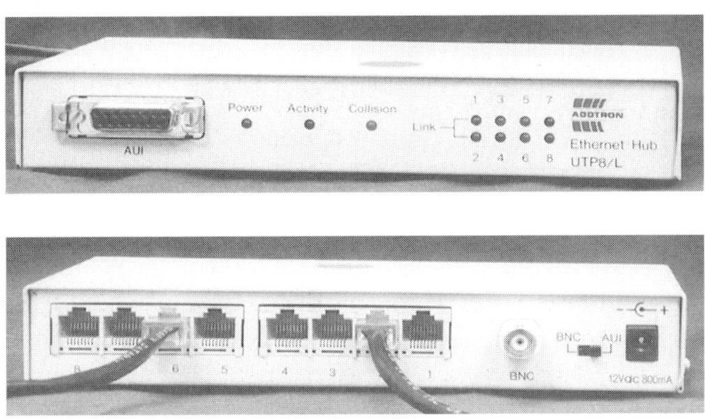

Many switching hubs also support load balancing, so that ports are dynamically reassigned to different LAN segments based on traffic patterns. In addition, some include fault tolerance, which can reroute traffic through other ports when a segment goes down.

A **router,** which works at the network OSI layer, is a device that connects two or more LANs. In addition, it can break a large network into smaller, more manageable subnets. As multiple LANs are connected together, multiple routes are created to get from one LAN to another. Routers then share status and routing information with other routers so that they can provide better traffic management and bypass slow connections. In addition, routers provide additional functionality, such as the ability to filter messages and forward them to different places based on various criteria. Most routers are multiprotocol routers because they can route data packets using many different protocols. Note: Routers cannot pass nonroutable protocols such as NetBEUI.

A **multihomed server** is a server that contains multiple network cards that acts as the router. Therefore, it can communicate with several networks at the same time and route data packets among them.

A **brouter** (short for bridge router) is a device that functions as both a router and a bridge. A brouter understands how to route specific types of packets (routable protocols), such as TCP/IP packets. For other specified packets (nonroutable protocols), it acts as a bridge, simply forwarding the packets to the other networks.

A **gateway** is hardware and/or software that links two different types of networks by repackaging and converting data from one network to another network, or from one network operating system to another. An example of a gateway would be a computer or device that connects a PC to a mainframe or minicomputer such as an AS400 midrange computer. This can be done by adding an Ethernet card or token ring card to the AS400 computer and adding software to the client computers, adding a special expansion card to the PC so that it can communicate with the AS400 directly, or by using a gateway computer to act as a translator between the AS400 network and client's network. Note: A gateway can be used at any layer of the OSI reference model but is usually identified with the application layer.

25.7 CONNECTION TECHNOLOGY

A **protocol** is a set of rules or standards designed to enable computers to connect with one another and peripheral devices to exchange information with as little error as possible. Common protocol suites are TCP/IP, IPX, and NetBEUI. (A suite is a set of protocols that work together.)

Protocols are usually designed to fit a seven-layer model called the **open system interconnection (OSI) reference model.** See table 25.4. The network services in the application layer hand off information to the layer below until it gets to the physical layer. The physical layer than sends the data through the network medium, such as a cable or wireless technology. When the information gets to the intended computer, it is then sent up to the application layer and is processed by the computer. Almost all networks include the functionality of the OSI model, although two or three of the OSI layers may be combined in a protocol.

Table 25.4 OSI Reference Model

Layer	Name	Function
7	Application layer	Covers network services, including program-to-program communication
6	Presentation layer	Manages data representation conversions; for example, the presentation layer would be responsible for converting from EBCDIC to ASCII
5	Session layer	Establishes and maintains communications channels
4	Transport layer	Ensures end-to-end integrity of data transmission; links the upper layers to the lower layers
3	Network layer	Routes data from one network to another
2	Data link layer	Physically passes data from one network connection to another
1	Physical layer	Manages putting data onto the network media (cable or wireless technology) and taking the data off

25.7.1 Ethernet

There are currently three LAN technologies being used. A LAN technology defines topologies, packet structures, and access methods that can be used together on a segment. This includes Ethernet, token ring, and ARCnet. Out of these, **Ethernet** is the most widely used LAN technology. It offers good balance between speed, price, reliability, and ease of installation. At least 95 percent of all LAN connections installed are Ethernet. All popular operating systems and applications are Ethernet compatible, as are upper layer protocol stacks such as TCP/IP, IPX, and NetBEUI.

Ethernet was traditionally used on light- to medium-traffic networks, and performs best when a network's data traffic is sent in short bursts. Recently, newer and faster Ethernet standards combined with switches have significantly increased the performance of the network.

Ethernet networks can be configured in either a star topology, using unshielded twisted-pair connected to a hub, or as a bus topology, using a coaxial cable acting as a backbone. Of these two, UTP cabling is by far the most commonly used. Ethernet cards can have one, two, or possibly all three of the following connectors:

- DIX (Digital Intel Xerox)/AUI connectors support 10Base5 external transceivers
- BNC (British Naval Connector) connectors support 10Base2 coax cabling
- RJ-45 connectors support 10BaseT/100BaseTX (UTP) cabling

When a network device wants to access the network, the access method used is *carrier sense multiple access with collision detection (CSMA/CD).* When a computer wants to send data over the network, it will listen to see if there is any traffic on the network. If the network is clear, it will then broadcast. Unfortunately, it is possible for two network devices to listen and try to send data at the same time. As a result, a collision occurs and both data packets are corrupted. While this is normal for an Ethernet network, both network devices will wait a different random amount of time and try again. Of course, if the network is heavily congested, the network will have more collisions, which results in more traffic, slowing the entire network even more.

Within an Ethernet network, you are limited to a 1,024 nodes identified by their MAC/physical addresses, which are burned into the ROM chip on the network card. IEEE assigns the first 3 bytes of the 6 byte address to the network card vendors. The vendor is then responsible for assigning the rest of the address to make sure that the MAC address is unique.

Ethernet_802.3 is an incomplete implementation of the IEEE 802.3 specification, sometimes called Ethernet-Raw. Novell implemented the 802.3 header but not the fields defined in the 802.2 specification. Instead, the IPX packet begins immediately after the 802.3 fields. The Novell frame type Ethernet_802.2 is a complete implementation (i.e., it includes the 802.3 and 802.2 fields). Ethernet_II is the standard frame type for TCP/IP networks. Ethernet_SNAP includes the 802.3, 802.2, and SNAP (subnetwork access protocol) fields.

The original Ethernet was called **10Base5** or **thicknet.** The name is derived because 10Base5 is 10 Mbit/s baseband network that can have a cable segments up to 500 meters (1,640 feet) long. It used a 50 ohm RG-8 and RG-11 as a backbone cable. 10Base5 uses physical and logical bus topology. Most network devices connected to the network use an external transceiver using a 4-pair AUI cable (sometimes referred to as a drop cable) via a DIX connector (2-row, 15-pin female connector). Other network devices can connect to the backbone cable by using a vampire tap, that uses teeth to make contact with the inner conductor, or by using a BNC barrel connector.

The **10Base2 (thinnet)** is a simplified version of the 10Base5 network. The name describes a 10 Mbit/s baseband network with a maximum cable segment length of approximately 200 meters (656 feet) (actually 185 meters (607 ft)). Instead of having external transceivers, the transceivers are on the network card, which attaches to the network using a BNC T-connector. The cable used is 50 ohm RG-58 A/U coaxial type cable. Different from the 10Base5 network, the 10Base2 does not use a drop cable.

Since 10Base5 and 10Base2 networks use coaxial cables, all unused ends must be terminated with 50 ohm terminating resistors. In addition, a grounded terminator must be used on only one end of the network segment.

Differing from 10Base2 and 10Base5, **10BaseT** uses UTP, which costs less, is smaller, and is easier to work with than coax cable. While Ethernet is a logical bus topology, 10BaseT is a physical star topology that has the network devices connected to a hub. It uses a Category 3 cable (or greater) with two pairs of wires (pins 1, 2, 3, & 6) connected with RJ-45 connectors.

When building a 10BaseT network, you must follow these rules:

- The maximum number of network segments or physical LAN is 1,024.
- The minimum unshielded cable segment length is 0.6 meter (2 feet).
- The maximum unshielded cable segment length is 100 meters (328 feet).
- To avoid EMI, you must route UTP cable no closer than 5 feet (1.5 meters) to any high-voltage (power) wiring or fluorescent lighting.

One advantage of using 10BaseT is that if you need to add another workstation, you just run an additional cable to the hub and plug it in. If there is a break in the cable, the hub has its own intelligence that will route traffic around the defective cable segment. As a result, the entire network is not effective.

NOTE: Since most networks are using Category 5 twisted-pair cabling (or enhanced Category 5 twisted pair) in a star topology, you should choose the same unless you have an overwhelming reason to choose differently.

There are two types of Ethernet cables: a straight-through cable and a crossover cable. The **straight-through cable,** which can be used to connect a network card to a hub or switch, has the same sequence of colored wires at both ends of the cable. A **crossover cable,** which can be used to connect one network card to another network card or a hub or switch to a hub or switch, reverses the transmit and receive wires. Note: Some hubs and switches will allow you to connect to another hub or switch using a straight-through cable connected to a crossover port. Sometimes, these hubs and switches have a port that can toggle between straight-through mode and crossover mode.

If the Ethernet connectors that connect to the switch are full duplex, a computer can send data to one computer and receive data from another computer at the same time. For this to be possible, the network card must be set to full-duplex Ethernet, and it must be connected to a switch port, not a hub.

Fast Ethernet is an extension of the 10BaseT Ethernet standard that transports data at 100 Mbit/s yet still keeps using the CSMA/CD protocol used by 10 Mbit/s Ethernet. The first type is 100BaseTX which uses two pairs of the standard Category 5 UTP. The second type is 100BaseT4, which runs over existing Category 3 UTP by using all 4 pairs; 3 pairs are to transmission simultaneously and the fourth pair is used for collision detect. Note: If Category 5 cable is used for backbone for Fast Ethernet, it should not exceed 5 meters (16.4 feet). The last one is 100BaseFX, which operates over multimode fiber-optic cabling.

The Gigabit Ethernet CSMA/CD method has been enhanced in order to maintain a 100 meter (328 foot) collision at gigabit speeds. Without this enhancement, minimum-sized Ethernet packets could complete transmission before the transmitting station sensed a collision, thereby violating the CSMA/CD method. To resolve this issue, both the minimum CSMA/CD carrier time and the Ethernet slot time have been extended from their present value of 64 bytes to a new value of 512 bytes. Note that the minimum packet length of 64 bytes has not been affected. Packets smaller than 512 bytes have an extra carrier extension. Packets longer than 512 bytes are not extended. These changes, which can impact small-packet performance, have been offset by incorporating a new feature, called packet bursting, into the CSMA/CD algorithm. Packet bursting will allow servers, switches, and other devices to send bursts of small packets in order to fully utilize available bandwidth.

25.7.2 Token Ring

While Ethernet networks make the majority of the LANs, Ethernet is not the only network technology available. There is also token ring, ARCnet, FDDI, and Appletalk.

Token ring rules are defined in the IEEE 802.5 specification. As mentioned earlier in the chapter, the physical topology of token ring is a star, but the logical topology is a ring. Therefore, it is actually implemented in what can best be described as a collapsed ring. In token ring LANs, each station is connected to a token ring wiring concentrator called a **multistation access unit (MAU),** using a shielded twisted-pair or unshielded twisted-pair. Like Ethernet hubs, MAUs are usually located in a wiring closet.

The access method used on token ring networks is called **token passing.** In token passing, a network device only communicates over the network when it has the token (a special data packet that is generated by the first computer that comes online in a token ring network). The token is passed from one station to another around a ring. When a station gets a free token and transmits a packet, it travels in one direction around the ring, passing all of the other stations along the way.

Each node acts as a repeater that receives token and data frames from its nearest active upstream neighbor (NAUN). After a frame is processed by the node, the frame is passed or rebroadcast downstream to the next attached node. Each token makes at least one trip around the entire ring and then returns to the originating node. Workstations that indicate problems send a beacon to identify an address of the potential failure.

If a station has not heard from its upstream neighbor in 7 seconds, it sends a packet down the ring that contains its address and the address of its NAUN. The token ring can then reconfigure itself to avoid the problem area.

Token ring network interface cards can run at 4 16 Mbit/s. The 4 Mbit/s cards can run only at that data rate. However, 16 Mbit/s cards can be configured to run at 4 or 16 Mbit/s. All cards on a given network ring must be running at the same rate. Of course, to run at 4 Mbit/s, you should use Category 3 UTP or better, while 16 Mbit/s requires Category 4 cable or higher, or Type 4 STP cable or higher.

Like Ethernet cards, the node address on each NIC is burned in at the manufacturer on a ROM chip and is unique to each card. For fault tolerance, a maximum of two token ring cards can be installed in any node, with each card being defined as the primary or alternate token ring card in the machine. The token ring card will use two types of connectors. One is equipped with a female (DB-9) 9-pin connector (of which only four pins are used), while the second is an RJ-45 connector. MAU's repeaters, and most other equipment, use a special IBM Type-1 unisex data connector. Note: To connect multiple MAU's, the Ring Out (RO) port of each MAU must be connected to the Ring In (RI) port of the next MAU so that it can complete a larger ring.

25.7.3 Serial Line Protocols

Serial line protocols are used for a computer to connect to a server—such as those used by an Internet service provider (ISP)—via a serial line, such as a modem, to become an actual node on the Internet. Serial line protocols include the **Serial Line Internet Protocol (SLIP),** Compressed Serial Line Internet Protocol (CSLIP), and the **Point-to-Point Protocol (PPP).** SLIP is an older and simpler protocol. Typically with the SLIP protocol, an automated script is used to make logging on more automatic.

The PPP protocol is an advanced version of the SLIP protocol. It is a full-duplex protocol that can be used on various physical media, including phone lines, twisted-pair, fiber-optic lines, or satellite transmission. It is usually preferred over the SLIP because it is more stable and can handle synchronous and asynchronous communication. In addition, it can share a line with other users and protocols such as TCP/IP, IPX, and AppleTalk, and has error detection that SLIP lacks.

PPP can negotiate configuration parameters at the start of the connection including automatic assigning of IP addresses, similar to Dynamic Host Configuration Protocol (DHCP). PPP provides two methods with which logins can be automated—**PAP (Password Authentication Protocol)** and **CHAP (Challenge-Handshake Authentication Protocol).** Both provide the means for your system to automatically send your login user ID and password information to the remote system.

25.8 WIRELESS NETWORKS

For decades, radio and television stations have used the atmosphere to transport information via analog signals. The atmosphere is also capable of carrying digital signals. Networks that transmit signals through the atmosphere are known as wireless networks.

25.8.1 Wireless Spectrum

All wireless signals are carried through the air along electromagnetic waves. Electromagnetic waves are waves of energy composed of both electric and magnetic components. Sound and light are both examples of electromagnetic waves. The waves that belong to the wireless spectrum (waves used for broadcasting, cellular phones, and satellite transmission) are not visible or audible, except by the receiver.

Table 25.5 Wireless Technology

Media	Frequency Range	Cost	Ease of Installation	Capacity Range	Attenuation	Immunity for Interference and Signal Capture
Low-power single frequency	Entire RF, high GHz is most common	Moderate (depends on equipment)	Simple	<1 to 10 Mbit/s	High	Extremely low
High-power single frequency	Entire RF, high GHz is most common	Moderately expensive	Difficult	<1 to 10 Mbit/s	Low	Extremely low
Spread spectrum radio	Entire RF, 902 to 928 MHz in US, 2.4 GHz band is most common	Moderate (depends on equipment)	Simple to moderate	2 to 6 Mbit/s	High	Moderate
Terrestrial microwave	Low GHz, 4 to 6 or 21 to 23 is most common	Moderate to high (depends on equipment)	Difficult	<1 to 10 Mbit/s	Variable	Low
Satellite microwave	Low GHz, 11 to 14 GHz most common	High	Extremely difficult	<1 to 10 Mbit/s	Variable	Low
Point-to-Point infrared	100 GHz to 1,000 THz	Low to moderate	Moderate to difficult	<1 to 16 Mbit/s	Variable	Moderate
Broadcast infrared	100 GHz to 1,000 THz	Low	Simple	≤1 Mbit/s	High	Low

The **wireless spectrum** is a continuum of electromagnetic waves, with varying frequencies and wavelengths that are used for telecommunications. See table 25.5. The wireless spectrum as defined by the FCC spans frequencies between 9 KHz and 300,000 GHz. Each type of wireless service is associated with one area of the wireless spectrum. AM broadcasting, for example, involves the low-frequency end of the wireless communication spectrum, using frequencies between 535 and 1605 KHz. Its wavelengths are between 560 (1,837 ft) and 190 m (623 ft) long. Note that the 535 KHz refers to the 560 m and the 160 5s KHz refers to the 190 m. Infrared waves make use of a wide band of frequencies at the high frequency end of the spectrum, between 300 and 300,000 GHz. Infrared wavelengths can be between 1 millimeter and 1 micrometer long.

Wireless networks typically use infrared or radio frequency signaling. By using a wireless network, these networks are suited to very specialized network environments that require mobility, long distances, or isolated locations. Note: Radio and Infrared are considered unbound media because they are not carried or bound with a physical cable.

When two senders use the same frequency for transmitting their information chaos will be the result. To prevent this chaos, there are national and international agreements about who can use which frequencies. Worldwide, an agency of the ITU (WARC) is supervising these agreements. In the United States, the FCC allocates spectrum. Unfortunately the FCC is not bound by WARC's recommendations, so some chaos does exist.

Radio frequency (RF) resides between 10 KHz to 1 GHz of the electromagnetic spectrum. It includes shortwave radio, very high frequency (VHF), and ultra-high frequency (UHF). Radio frequencies have been divided between regulated and unregulated bandwidths. Users of the regulated frequencies must get a license from the regulatory bodies that have jurisdiction over the desired operating area (the FCC in the United States and CDC in Canada). While the licensing process can be difficult, licensed frequencies typically guarantee clear transmission within a specific area.

The properties of radio waves strongly depend on the frequency used:

- Low frequencies: radio waves pass through obstacles easily, but the power declines sharply with the distance from the transmitter. The main problem with using these low frequencies for data communication is the relatively small bandwidth they offer.
- High frequencies: radio waves tend to travel in straight lines and bounce off obstacles like buildings. Transmitter and receiver need a direct line-of-sight connection. However, the waves that reach the ionosphere, a layer of charged particles circling the earth at a height of about 300 km (186 miles), are refracted by it and sent back to earth. Amateur radio operators (hams) use these bands to talk long distance.

At all frequencies, radio waves are subject to interference from other electrical equipment.

In radio network transmissions, a signal is transmitted in one or multiple directions, depending on the type of antenna that is used. The wave is very short in length with a low transmission strength (unless the transmission operator has a special license for a high-wattage transmission), which means it is best suited to short-range line-of-sight transmissions. A line-of-sight transmission is one in which the signal goes from point-to-point, rather than bouncing off the atmosphere over great distances. Of course, a limitation of line-of-sight transmissions is that they are interrupted by land masses such as mountains. Because of its ability to travel long distances, interference between users is a problem. Therefore all governments tightly license the user of radio transmitters.

When discussing wireless technology, many technologies that are wireless use a **cellular topology,** whereas an area is divided into cells. A broadcast device is located at the center and broadcasting in all directions to form an invisible circle (cell). All network devices located within the cell communicate with the network through the central station or hub, which are interconnected with the rest of the network infrastructure. If the cells are overlapped, devices may roam from cell to cell while maintaining connection to the network as the devices. The best-known example of cellular topology is cellular phones.

Since the bandwidth available increases in the higher frequency ranges, these higher frequencies will support higher data transfer rates. Therefore, many wireless bridge products being sold today operate in the 2.4 and 5.7 GHz frequencies. As throughput increases, computer networking becomes more of a real possibility. And, with more companies producing RF wireless networking products, prices are continuing to fall, making wireless networking a viable alternative to land-based lines in many local areas.

A **band** is a contiguous group of frequencies that are used for a single purpose. Commercial radio stations often refer to the band of frequencies they are using as a single frequency. However, typical radio transmissions actually cover a range of frequencies and wavelengths. Because most tuning equipment is designed to address the entire bandwidth at the kilohertz or megahertz level, the distinction between one frequency and a band is often overlooked.

A **narrowband radio system** transmits and receives user information on a specific radio frequency. Narrowband radio keeps the radio signal frequency as narrow as possible just to pass the information. Undesirable crosstalk between communications channels is avoided by carefully coordinating different users on different channel frequencies. In a radio system, privacy and noninterference are accomplished by the use of separate radio frequencies. The radio receiver filters out all radio signals except the ones on its designated frequency. Depending on the power and frequency of the radio signal, the range could be a room, an entire building, or long distances. A low-power (1–10 watts) single-frequency signals has a data capacity in the range of 1–10 Mbit/s.

Spread-spectrum signals are distributed over a wide range of frequencies and then collected onto their original frequency at the receiver. Different from narrowband signals, spread-spectrum signals use wider bands that transmit at a much lower spectral power density (measured in watts per hertz). Unless the receiver is not tuned to the right frequency or frequencies, a spread-spectrum signal resembles noise, making the signals harder to detect and harder to jam. As an additional bonus, spread-spectrum and narrowband signals can occupy the same band, with little or no interference. There are two types of spread-spectrum: direct sequence and frequency hopping. Spread-spectrum frequency ranges are very high, in the 902–928 MHz range and higher and typically send data at a rate of 2–6 Mbit/s.

Direct-sequence spread-spectrum (DSSS) generates a redundant bit pattern for each bit to be transmitted. This bit pattern is called a chip (or chipping code). The intended receiver knows which specific frequencies are valid and deciphers the signal by collecting valid signals and ignoring the spurious signals. The valid signals are then used to reassemble the data. Because multiple subsets can be used within any frequency range, direct-sequence signals can coexist with other signals. Although direct-sequence signals can be intercepted almost as easily as other RF signals, eavesdropping is ineffective because it is quite difficult to determine which specific frequencies to make up the bit pattern, retrieve the bit pattern, and interpret the signal. Because of modern error detection and correction methods, the longer the chip, the greater the probability that the original data can be recovered even if one or more bits in the chip are damaged during transmission.

Frequency hopping quickly switches between predetermined frequencies, many times each second. Both the transmitter and receiver must follow the same pattern and maintain complex timing intervals to be able to receive and interpret the data being sent. Similar to direct-sequence spread-spectrum, intercepting the data being sent is extremely difficult unless they know the signals to monitor and timing pattern. In addition, dummy signals can be added to increase security and confuse eavesdroppers. The length of time that the transmitter remains on a given frequency is known as the dwell time.

Before fiber optics came on the scene, for decades microwaves formed the heart of the long-distance telephone transmission system. Microwave communications is a form of electromagnetic energy that operates at a higher frequency (low GHz frequency range) than radio wave communications. These days, microwaves are widely used for long-distance telephone communication, cellular telephones, television distribution, and many other areas. Since it provides higher bandwidths than those available using radio waves and it can carry more bits on each eave, it is currently one of the most popular long-distance transmission technologies.

Above 10^8 Hz (or 100 MHz), waves travel in straight lines. Therefore the signals can be narrowly focused into a small beam using a parabolic antenna (like the familiar satellite TV dish). The transmitting and receiving antennas must be accurately aligned with each other. Since the microwaves travel in a straight line, repeaters placed in a tower are needed periodically. The higher the towers are, the further apart they can be. Using 100 m (328 ft) high towers, 80 km (50 miles) can be covered.

Microwave signals propagate in straight lines and are affected very little by the lower atmosphere. In addition, they are not refracted or reflected by ionized regions in the upper atmosphere. The attenuation of microwave systems is highly dependent on atmospheric conditions; for example, both rain and fog can reduce the maximum distance possible. Higher-frequency systems are usually affected most by such conditions. In addition, microwaves do not pass through buildings. The systems are not particularly resistant to EMI and protection for eavesdropping can only be achieved by encryption techniques.

Terrestrial systems are often used where cabling is difficult or the cost is prohibitively expensive. Relay towers are used to provide an unobstructed path over an extended distance. These line-of-sight systems use unidirectional parabolic dishes that must be aligned carefully.

The cost of these systems is relatively high and technical expertise is required to install them, as accurate alignment is required. But, putting up two towers with antennas is in many cases cheaper than getting 100 km (62 miles) of copper cable or fiber into the ground. Often, this service is leased from a service provider, which reduces installation costs and provides the required expertise.

Satellite transmission is much like line-of-sight microwave transmission in which one of the stations is a satellite orbiting the earth. This requires that the sending and receiving antennas be locked onto each other's location at all times. The satellite must move at the same speed as the earth so that it seems to remain fixed above a certain spot. These satellites must be in **geosynchronous (GEO) orbits** and are in positioned 35,800 km (22,300 mi) above the earth's equator. Satellite systems provide far bigger areas of coverage than can be achieved using other technologies because they can either relay signals between sites directly or via another satellite. The huge distances covered by the signal result in propagation delays of up to 5 seconds. The costs of launching and maintaining a satellite are enormous, and consequently customers usually lease the services from a provider.

Another form of wireless technology is the **infrared (IR) system,** which is based on infrared light (light that is just below the visible light in the electromagnetic spectrum). Similar to your TV or VCR remote controls, Infrared links use light emitting diodes (LEDs) or injection laser diodes (ILDs) to transmit signals and photodiodes to receive signals. It transmits in light frequency ranges of 100 GHz–1,000 THz. Unfortunately, IR only transmit up to 1 Mbit/s for omnidirectional communications and 16 Mbit/s for directional communications.

Since IR is essentially light, it cannot penetrate opaque objects. Infrared devices work as using either directed or diffused technology. **Directed IR** uses line-of-sight or point-to-point technology. **Diffused** (also known as **reflective** or **indirect**) IR technology spreads the light over an area to create a cell, limited to individual rooms. Since infrared light can bounce off walls, ceilings, and any other objects in the path, the indirect infrared is not confined to a specific pathway. Unfortunately, not being confined to a specific pathway means that the transmission of data is not very secure. Lastly, since infrared signals are not capable of penetrating walls or other opaque objects and are diluted by strong light sources, infrared is most useful in small or open indoor environments.

25.8.2 Wireless LAN (WLAN)

A wireless LAN (WLAN) is a local area network without wires. WLANs have been around for more than a decade, but are just beginning to gain momentum because of falling costs and improved standards. WLANs (152 m) transfer data through the air using radio frequencies instead of cables. They can reach a radius of 500 feet indoors and 1,000 feet (305 m) outdoors, but antennas, transmitters and other access devices can be used to widen that area. WLANs require a wired access point that plugs all the wireless devices into the wired network.

A wireless LAN system can provide LAN users with access to real-time information anywhere in their organization. Installing a wireless LAN system can be fast and easy and can eliminate the need to pull cable through walls and ceilings. In addition, wireless technology allows the network to go where wire cannot go. Thus, WLANs combined data connectivity with user mobility, and through simplified configuration, enable movable LANs.

WLAN configurations vary from simple, independent, peer-to-peer connections between a set of PCs, to more complex, intrabuilding infrastructure networks. There are also point-to-point and point-to-multipoint wireless solutions. A point-to-point solution is used to bridge between two local area networks, and to provide an alternative to cable between two geographically distant locations (up to 30 miles or 48 km). Point-to-multipoint solutions connect several, separate locations to one single location or building. Both point-to-point and point-to-multipoint can be based on the 802.11b standard or on more costly infrared-based solutions that can provide throughput rates up to 622 Mbit/s (OC-12 speed).

25.8.3 802.11 Wireless Standard

The 802.11 standards can be compared to the IEEE 802.3 standard for Ethernet for wired LANs. The 802.11 standard defines three physical layers for WLANs, two radio frequency specifications (RF—direct-sequence and frequency hopping spread-spectrum) and one infrared (IR). Most WLANs operate in the 2.4 GHz license-free frequency radio band and have throughput rates up to 2 Mbit/s. Note: The 2.4 GHz band is particularly attractive because it enjoys worldwide allocations for unlicensed operations. The most popular 802.11 types are:

- **802.11a**—Operates in the 5 GHz license-free frequency band and is expected to provide throughput rates up to 54 Mbit/s in normal mode or 75 Mbit/s in turbo mode but most commonly, communications takes place at 6 Mbit/s, 12 Mbit/s, or 24 Mbit/s. It uses a modulation scheme known as orthogonal frequency-division multiplexing (OFDM).
- **802.11b (Wi-Fi)**—Standard is direct-sequence only, and initially provided throughput rates up to 11 Mbit/s with the potential of three simultaneous channels, but has been recently increased to 22 Mbit/s. The modulation method selected for 802.11b is known as complementary code keying (CCK), which allows higher data speeds and is less susceptible to multipath-propagation interference. 802.11b is the clear leader in business and institutional wireless networking and is gaining share for home applications as well.
- **802.11g**—Has a nominal maximum throughput of 54 Mbit/s. But because it is using the 2.4 GHz frequency band, its products should be compatible with 802.11b products.

There are two operation modes defined in IEEE 802.11:

- Infrastructure mode
- Ad-hoc mode

The ad-hoc network, also referred to as the Independent Basic Service Set (IBSS), stands alone and is not connected to a base. The wireless stations communicate directly with each other without using an access point or any connection to a wired network. This basic topology is useful in order to quickly and easily set up a wireless network anywhere a wireless infrastructure does not exist such as a hotel room, a convention center, or an airport.

Figure 25.14 Wireless End Station and Wireless Access Point

In infrastructure mode, also known as Extended Service Set (ESS), the wireless network consists of at least one access point (AP) connected to the wired network infrastructure and a set of wireless end stations. See figure 25.14. An access point controls encryption on the network and may bridge or route the wireless traffic to a wired Ethernet network (or the Internet). Access points that act as routers can also assign an IP address to your PCs using DHCP services. APs can be compared with a base station used in cellular networks.

An Extended Service Set (ESS) consists of two or more BSSs forming a single subnetwork. Traffic is forwarded from one BSS to another to facilitate movement of wireless stations between BSSs using cellular topology. Almost always the distribution system which connects this network is an Ethernet LAN. Since most corporate WLANs require access to the wired LAN for services (file servers, printers, Internet links) they will operate in infrastructure mode.

One of the requirements of IEEE 802.11 is that it can be used with existing wired networks. 802.11 solved this challenge with the use of a portal. A **portal** is the logical integration between wired LANs and 802.11. It also can serve as the access point to the DS. All data going to an 802.11 LAN from an 802.X LAN must pass through a portal. It thus functions as a bridge between wired and wireless.

Today, 802.11a still has some issues to work out, particularly in the area of compatibility. Currently, products aren't backward compatible with 802.11b products, which clearly dominate the market. And although all 802.11a products use the same chipset, their implementation by each manufacturer differs enough to make them incompatible. Until an interoperability standard is established, 802.11a products from one company may not communicate with those of another.

The Wireless Ethernet Compatibility Alliance (WECA) is an industry consortium that tests for interoperability. Those 802.11b products tests that pass WECA's tests are given the wireless fidelity (Wi-Fi) seal of approval. WECA is working on an 802.11a certification called WiFi5.

The IEEE 802.1X standard is a relatively recent protocol enhancement that creates a standard for how authentication is performed over an 802 standards-based network. The 802.1X standard is designed to enhance the security of wireless local area networks (WLANs) that follow the IEEE 802.11 standard. 802.1X provides an authentication framework for wireless LANs, allowing a user to be authenticated by a central authority. The actual algorithm that is used to determine whether a user is authentic is left open and multiple algorithms are possible. 802.1X uses an existing protocol, the Extensible Authentication Protocol (EAP), specified in RFC 2284, that works on Ethernet, token ring, or wireless LANs, for message exchange during the authentication process.

25.8.4 BlueTooth

BlueTooth refers to a short-range radio technology aimed at simplifying communications among Net devices and between devices and the Internet. It also aims to simplify data synchronization between Net devices and other computers. An advantage of BlueTooth is its similarity to many other specifications already deployed and its borrowing of many features from these specifications. The BlueTooth standard is becoming more and more of a short time network between devices for a small amount of information.

BlueTooth has a present nominal link range of 10 cm (3.9 inches) to 10 m (32.8 ft) which can be extended to 100 m (328 ft), with increased transmitting power. BlueTooth operates in the 2.4 GHz Industrial-Scientific-Medical (ISM) Band and uses a frequency hop spread-spectrum technology in which packets are transmitted in defined time slots on defined frequencies. A full-duplex information interchange rate of up to 1 Mbit/s may be achieved in which a Time-Division Duplex (TDD) scheme is used. The second generation of BlueTooth supports up to 2 Mbit/s.

Work on the BlueTooth specification is progressing and is primarily the responsibility of the BlueTooth Special Group (SIG).This is an industry group consisting of leaders in telecommunications and computing industries. The promoter group within the SIG currently consists of 3Com, Ericsson, IBM, Intel, Lucent Technologies, Microsoft, Motorola, Nokia, and Toshiba.

A BlueTooth system essentially comprises of the following four major components:

- **Radio Unit**—Consisting of a radio transceiver, which provides the radio link between the BlueTooth devices.
- **Baseband Unit**—Hardware consisting of flash memory and a CPU. This interfaces with the radio unit and the host device electronics.
- **Link management Software**—Driver software or firmware that enables the application software to interface with the baseband unit and radio unit.
- **Application Software**—This implements the user interface and is the application that can run on wireless. For example, this could be chat software that allows two laptop users in a conference hall to talk to each other using wireless technology.

Each device has a unique 48-bit address from the IEEE 802 standard. In addition, a frequency hop scheme allows devices to communicate even in areas with a great deal of electromagnetic interference and it includes built-in encryption and verification.

One BlueTooth standard is **HomeRF SWAP** (SWAP is short for Shared Wireless Access Protocol). It is designed specifically for wireless networks in homes, which in contrast to 802.11 was created for use in businesses. HomeRF networks are designed to be more affordable to home users than other wireless technologies. It is based on frequency hopping and using radio frequency waves for the transmission of voice and data with a range of up to 150 feet (45.7 meters).

The Shared Wireless Access Protocol works together with the PSTN network and the Internet through existing cordless telephone and wireless LAN technologies to enable voice-activated home electronic systems, accessing the Internet from anywhere in the home and forwarding fax, voice, and email messages. SWAP uses Time Division Multiple Access for interactive data transfer and CSMA/CA for high-speed packet transfer. SWAP operates in the 2,400 MHz band at 50 hops per second to provide a data rate between 1 and 2 Mbit/s.

25.9 TCP/IP

TCP/IP (Transmission Control Protocol/Internet Protocol) is an industry suite of protocols on which the Internet is based. It is supported by Novell NetWare, Microsoft Windows NT, Microsoft Windows 2000, Windows XP, UNIX, and other network operating systems.

With the TCP/IP protocol suite, TCP/IP does not worry about how the hosts (computers or any other network connection) connect to the network. Instead, TCP/IP was designed to operate over nearly any underlying local or wide area network. See figure 25.15. This would include:

- LAN protocols: Ethernet, token ring, and ARCnet networks
- WAN protocols: ATM, Frame Relay, and X.25
- Serial line protocols: Serial Line Internet Protocol (SLIP) and Point-to-Point Protocol (PPP)

When you send or receive data, the data is divided into little chunks called packets. Each of these packets contains both the sender's TCP/IP address and the receiver's TCP/IP address. When the packet needs to go to another computer on another network, the packet is then sent to a gateway computer, usually a router. The gateway understands the networks that it is connected to directly. The gateway computer reads the destination address to determine in which direction the packet needs to be forwarded. It then forwards the packet to an adjacent gateway. The packet is forwarded from gateway to gateway until it

Figure 25.15 TCP/IP Protocol Suite

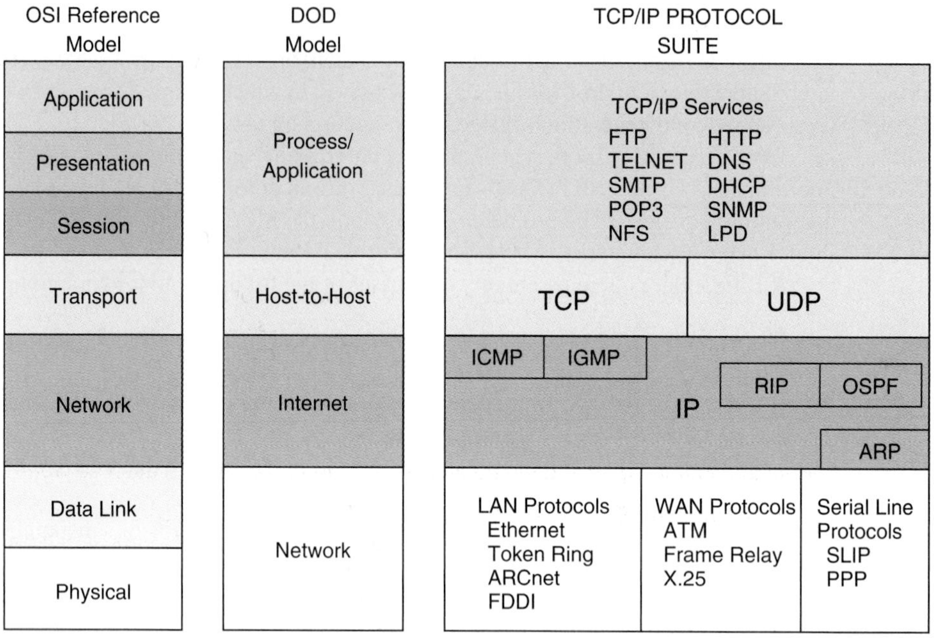

gets to the network to which the destination host belongs. The last gateway forwards the packet directly to the computer whose address is specified.

The lowest protocol within the TCP/IP suite is the **Internet Protocol (IP).** It specifies the format of the packets (also called datagrams) and worries about the delivery of the packets. IP is a connectionless protocol, which means that there is no established connection between the end points that are communicating. Each packet that travels through the Internet is treated as an independent unit of data. Therefore, it is not affected by other data packets. In addition, IP does not guarantee any deliveries. Therefore, packets can get lost, delivered out of sequence, or delayed.

The protocol that works on top of the IP protocol is the TCP and UDP protocol. The **Transport Control Protocol (TCP)** is a reliable, connection-oriented delivery service that breaks the data into manageable packets. It establishes a virtual connection between the two hosts or computers so that they can send messages back and forth for a period of time. A virtual connection appears to be always connected, but in reality it is made of many packets being sent back and forth independently.

The TCP protocol has two other important functions. First, TCP uses acknowledgments to verify that the data was received by the other host. If an acknowledgment is not sent, the data is resent. In addition, since the data packets can be delivered out of order, the TCP protocol must put the packets back in the correct order.

Another transport layer protocol is the **User Datagram Protocol (UDP).** Unlike the TCP protocol, UDP does not use acknowledgments to ensure data delivery. Therefore, the UDP is considered unreliable, "best effort" delivery. Since it is considered unreliable, UDP is used for protocols that transmit small amounts of data at one time or for broadcasts (packets sent to everyone). Note: "Unreliable" doesn't mean that the packets will not get delivered, just that there is no guarantee or check to make sure that they get to their destination.

25.9.1 TCP/IP Addressing

Each connection on a TCP/IP address is called a **host** (a computer or other network device that is connected to a TCP/IP network) and is assigned a unique **IP address.** A host is any network interface, including each network's interface cards or a network printer that connects directly onto the network. The format of the IP address is four 8-bit numbers divided by a period (.). Each number can be zero to 255. For example, a TCP/IP address could be 131.107.3.1 or 2.0.0.1. Since the address is used to identify the computer, no two connections can use the same IP address. If they do, one or both of the computers will not be able to communicate.

Internet Protocols

Route data packets between different hosts or networks.

- **Internet Protocol (IP)**—Connectionless protocol primarily responsible for addressing and routing packets between hosts (RFC 791).
- **Address Resolution Protocol (ARP)**—Used to obtain hardware addresses (MAC addresses) of hosts located on the same physical network (RFC 826).
- **Internet Control Message Protocol (ICMP)**—Sends messages and reports errors regarding the delivery of a packet (RFC 792).
- **Internet Group Management Protocol (IGMP)**—Used by IP hosts to report host group membership to local multicast routers (RFC 1112).
- **Router Information Protocol (RIP)**—Distance vector route discovery protocol where the entire routing table is periodically sent to the other routers (RFC 1723).
- **Open Shortest Path First (OSPF)**—Link State Route Discovery protocol where each router periodically advertises itself to other routers (RFC 1245, 1246, 1247, and 1253).

Host-to-Host Protocols

Maintain data integrity and set up reliable, end-to-end communication between hosts.

- **Transmission Control Protocol (TCP)**—Provides connection-oriented, reliable communications for applications that typically transfer large amounts of data at one time or that require an acknowledgment for data received (RFC 793).
- **User Datagram Protocol (UDP)**—Provides connectionless communications and does not guarantee that packets will be delivered. Applications that use UDP typically transfer small amounts of data as one. Reliable delivery is the responsibility of the application (RFC 768).

Process/Application Protocols

Act as the interface for the user. Provide applications that transfer data between hosts.

- **File Transfer Protocol (FTP)**—Allows a user to transfer files between local and remote host computers (RFC 959).
- **Telecommunication Network (TELNET)**—A virtual terminal protocol (terminal emulation) allowing a user to log on to another TCP/IP host to access network resources (RFC 854).
- **Simple Mail Transfer Protocol (SMTP)**—The standard protocol for the exchange of electronic mail over the Internet. It is used between email servers on the Internet or to allow an email client to send mail to a server (RFC 821 and 822).
- **Post Office Protocol (POP)**—Defines a simple interface between a user's mail client software and email server. It is used to download mail from the server to the client and allows the user to manage his or her mailboxes (RFC 1460).
- **Network File System (NFS)**—Provides transparent remote access to shared files across networks (RFC 1094).
- **Hypertext Transfer Protocol (HTTP)**—The basis for exchange over the World Wide Web (WWW). WWW pages are written in the Hypertext Markup Language (HTML), an ASCII-based, platform-independent formatting language (RFC 1945 and 1866).
- **Domain Name System (DNS)**—Defines the structure of Internet names and their association with IP addresses (RFC 1034 and 1035).
- **Dynamic Host Configuration Protocol (DHCP)**—Used to automatically assign TCP/IP addresses and other related information to clients (RFC 2131).
- **Simple Network Management Protocol (SNMP)**—Defines procedures and management information databases for managing TCP/IP-based network devices (RFC 1157 and 1441).
- **Line Printer Daemon (LPD)**—Provides printing on a TCP/IP network.

When connecting to the Internet, network numbers are assigned to a corporation or business. If the first number is between 1 and 126, the network is a class A. If the first number is between 128 and 191, the network is a class B. If the first number is between 192 and 223, the network is a class C. See table 25.6. Note: Every computer on a TCP/IP network must have the same network number.

The TCP/IP address is broken down into a network number and a host number. The network number identifies the entire network while the host number identifies the computer or connection on the specified network. If it is a class A network, the first octet describes the network number while the last

Table 25.6 Standard IP Classes for the IP Address of w.x.y.z

Class Type	First Octet	Network Number	Host Number	Default Subnet Mask	Comments
A	1–126	w	x.y.z	255.0.0.0	Supports 16 million hosts on each of 126 networks.
B	128–191	w.x	y.z	255.255.0.0	Supports 65,000 hosts on each of 16,000 networks.
C	192–223	w.x.y	z	255.255.255.0	Supports 254 hosts on each of 2 million networks.

three octets describe the host address. If it is a class B network, the first two octets describe the network number while the last two octets describe the host address. If it is a class C, the first three octets describe the network number while the last octet describes the host number.

Example 25.1:

You have the following network address:

131.107.20.4

The 131 is between 128 and 191, identifying the address as a class B network. Therefore, the 131.107 identifies the network and the 20.4 identifies the host or computer on the 131.107 network.

Example 25.2:

You have the following network address:

208.234.23.4

The 208 is between 192 and 223, identifying the address as a class C network. Therefore, the 208.234.23 identifies the network and the 4 identifies the host or computer on the 208.234.23 network.

NOTE: Several address values are reserved and/or have special meaning. The network number 127 is used for loopback testing and specific host address 127.0.0.1 refers to the **local host** or the actual host or computer that you are currently using.

Usually when defining the TCP/IP for a network connection, you would also specify a subnet mask. The **subnet mask** is used to define which bits describe the network number and which bits describe the host address. The default subnet mask for a class A network is 255.0.0.0. If you convert this to a binary equivalent, you would have 11111111.00000000.00000000.00000000, showing that the first 8 bits (first octet), marked with 1s, are used to define the network address, while the last 24 bits, marked with 0s, are used to define the host address. The default subnet mask for a class B network is 255.255.0.0 (11111111. 11111111.00000000.00000000) while the default subnet mask for a class C network is 255.255.255.0 (11111111.11111111.11111111.00000000).

NOTE: Like the network address, every computer on a network must have the same subnet mask.

If an individual network is connected to another network and you must communicate with any computers on the other network, you must also define the default gateway, which specifies the local address of a router. If the default gateway is not specified, you will be unable to communicate with computers on other networks. Note: If the local area network is connected to more than two or more networks, you only have to specify one gateway. This is because when a data packet is sent, it will first determine if the data packet needs to go to a local computer or a computer that is on another network. If it is meant to be sent to a computer on another network, the gateway will forward the data packet to the router. The router will then determine the best direction that the data packet must go to get to its destination. Occasionally, it will have to go back through the network to get to another gateway.

The subnet mask can be changed to take a large network and break it into small networks called subnets. This is the reason that the subnet mask must be defined so that the network can calculate which bits represent the network address and which bits represent the host address. Note: All subnets on a network must use the same network address. For a subnet, the subnet network number and the subnet mask must be the same for all computers.

25.9.2 Navigating a TCP/IP Network

Fully Qualified Domain Names (FQDNs), sometimes referred to as just domain names, are used to identify computers on a TCP/IP network. Examples include MICROSOFT.COM and EDUCATION.NOVELL.COM.

While IP addresses are 32 bits in length, most users do not memorize the numeric addresses of the hosts to which they attach. Instead, people are more comfortable with host names. Most IP hosts, then, have both a numeric IP address and a host name. While this is convenient for people, the name must be translated back to a numeric address for routing purposes. This is typically done with a DNS server.

One way to translate the Fully Qualified Domain Name to the IP address is to use a Domain Name System (DNS) server. DNS is a distributed database (database is contained in multiple servers) containing host name and IP address information for all domains on the Internet. For every domain, there is a single authoritative name server that contains all DNS-related information about the domain.

For example, type the web address *Microsoft.com* in your browser. Your computer will then communicate with your local area network's DNS server. If the DNS server does not know the address of Microsoft.com, another DNS server will be asked. This will continue until the computer finds the address of Microsoft.com or it determines that the host name is not listed and reply back with *No DNS Entry.*

NOTE: Besides the DNS server, a HOSTS file on each machine can also be used to translate domain/host names to IP addresses.

Another naming scheme used on TCP/IP networks is using the NetBIOS names (such that is used to identify share names for files and printers, *\\COMPUTERNAME\SHARENAME*). To translate NetBIOS names to IP addresses, you would use a WINS server or the LMHOSTS file.

If you try to access a network resource by name instead of IP address and the device cannot be found, it is most likely a problem with the DNS server/HOSTS file or the WINS server/LMHOSTS file. Either the servers cannot be contacted, or servers or files have the wrong address associated with the name. The failure of these servers or files can also affect network applications that need to access various network services or resources.

25.9.3 TCP/IP Ports and Sockets

Every time a TCP/IP host communicates with another TCP/IP host, it will use the IP address and port number to identify the host and service/program running on the host. A **TCP/IP port number** is a logical connection place by client programs to specify a particular server program running on a computer on the network defined at the transport layer. Port numbers are from 0 to 65536. Ports 0 to 1024 are reserved for use by certain privileged services and popular higher-level applications. These are known as "well-known ports," which have been assigned by the Internet Assigned Numbers Authority. Some of the well-known protocols are shown in table 25.7. For example, when using your browser to view a web page, the default port to indicate the HTTP service is identified as port 80 and the FTP service is identified as port 21. Other application processes are given port numbers dynamically for each connection so that a single computer can run several services. When a packet is delivered and processed, the TCP protocol (connection-based services) or UDP protocol (connectionless based services) will read the port number and forward the request to the appropriate program.

An application can create a socket and use it to send connectionless traffic to remote applications. An application creates a socket by specifying three items: the IP address of the host, the type of service, and the port the application is using. Note: For Windows, it is the **Windows socket (WinSock)** that provides the interface between the network program or service and the Windows environment.

Table 25.7 Popular TCP/IP Services and Their Default Assigned Port Numbers

Network Program/Service	Default Assigned Port Number
File Transfer Protocol (FTP)	Port 21
Telnet	Port 23
Simple Mail Transfer Protocol (SMTP)	Port 25
Domain Name Server (DNS)	Port 53
Hypertext Transfer Protocol (HTTP)	Port 80
Network News Transport Protocol (NNTP)	Port 119
NetBIOS Session Service	Port 139
Secure HTTP	Port 443

Table 25.8 Windows Troubleshooting TCP/IP Commands

Commands	Description
ARP	Displays and modifies the IP-to-MAC address translation tables used by the Address Resolution Protocol (ARP).
IPCONFIG/WINIPCFG	Display all current TCP/IP configuration, including the IP address. These commands are of particular use on systems running DHCP, allowing users to determine which TCP/IP configuration values have been configured by DHCP.
PING	Verifies connections to a remote computer or computers by verifying configurations and testing IP connectivity.
TRACERT	Traces the route that a packet takes to a destination and displays the series of IP routers used in delivering packets to the destination. If the packets are unable to be delivered to the destination, the TRACERT command displays the last router that successfully forwarded the packet.

25.9.4 Troubleshooting a TCP/IP Network

For a TCP/IP network, several utilities can be used to test and troubleshoot the network. To verify the TCP/IP configuration, you would use either the IP Configuration program (WINIPCFG.EXE) command (available in Windows 9X), the IPCONFIG.EXE (available in Windows 98, Windows NT, Windows 2000/XP) or ifconfig (Linur). In addition, you can also use the ARP, PING, and TRACERT commands.

1. WINIPCFG IPCONFIG, or ifconfig
2. PING 127.0.0.1 (Loopback address)
3. Ping IP Address of the Computer
4. Ping IP Address of Default Gateway (Router)
5. Ping IP Address of Remote Host

The IPCONFIG.EXE and WINIPCFG.EXE will display addressing and settings of the TCP/IP protocol. The PING utility can be used to verify a TCP/IP connection while the TRACERT will show all router addresses as it connects to another computer. The ARP protocol can be used to display the MAC address. See table 25.8 for TCP/IP commands available in Windows in troubleshooting TCP/IP networks.

To execute the Windows IP Configuration utility, you would type *WINIPCFG.EXE* from the Windows command prompt or from the Run option from the Start button. If you have more than one network interface, you can select the appropriate adapter from the pull-down menu. You can then view the

Figure 25.16 WINIPCFG utility. If there is more than one network adapter, the various cards can be selected at the pull-down box.

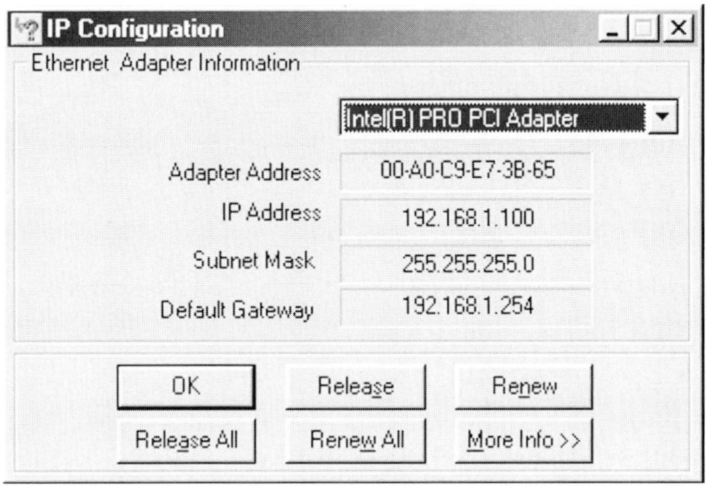

IP address, the subnet mask, and the default gateway/router for that interface. If you click on the More Info button, you also view other information such as addresses and configuration of the WINS, DNS, and DHCP server. See figure 25.16.

The IPCONFIG.EXE command can only be executed at the Command prompt. See figure 25.17. Much like the IP Configuration utility, it also shows the IP address, the subnet mask, and the default gateway/router address. To see additional information, you can type in *IPCONFIG/ALL.*

To make assigning the addresses easier, you can automatically assign the IP addresses to the computers using a DHCP server. To release the address assigned by the DHCP server, you would click on the IP Configurations Renew or Renew All buttons or you can type *IPCONFIG/ RELEASE.* To request new addresses from the DHCP server, you can click on the Renew or Renew All buttons. Note: The Release All and Renew All buttons apply to all settings including the WINS and DNS server addresses.

Anytime that you use the IP Configuration utility or the IPCONFIG.EXE command and are having trouble connecting to the network, you should verify the IP address (to make sure it is on the correct subnet), the subnet mask, and the router. If the address is not in the correct subnet, you would be unable to communicate with any other computer on the network. If the subnet mask is wrong, you may not be able to communicate with other computers. If the gateway address is wrong, you can communicate with computers on your subnet, but not on other subnets.

Another very useful command to verify a network connection is the PING.EXE command. It sends three packets to a host computer and receives a report on their round-trip time. If you ping the loopback address of 127.0.0.1 and the ping fails, you need to verify that the TCP/IP software is installed correctly. If you ping your own IP address and it is unsuccessful, you need to check the IP address. If you can't ping the IP address of the default gateway/router, you need to verify the IP address (make sure the address is in the correct subnet) and subnet mask. If you can't ping a remote computer on a different subnet or network, you need to verify the IP address of the default gateway/router, make sure the remote host/computer is functional, and verify the link between routers. See figure 25.18.

Examples are:

PING 127.0.01
PING 137.23.34.112

The PING command can also be used to ping a host/computer by NetBIOS (computer) name or host/DNS name. If you ping by address but not by name, it tells you that the TCP/IP is running fine but the name resolution is not working properly. Therefore, you must check the LMHOSTS file and the WINS server to resolve computer names and HOSTS file and the DNS server to resolve domain names.

Examples are:

PING FS1
PING WWW.MICROSOFT.COM

Figure 25.17 IPCONFIG Command

```
C:\>ipconfig

Windows 98 IP Configuration

0 Ethernet adapter :

      IP Address  . . . . . . . : 132.233.150.4
      Subnet Mask . . . . . . . : 255.255.255.0
      Default Gateway . . . . . : 132.233.150.1
```

```
C:\>IPCONFIG /ALL

Windows 98 IP Configuration

   Host Name  . . . . . : HOSTPC.DOMAIIN.COM
   DNS Servers  . . . . : 132.233.150.10
   Node Type  . . . . . : Hybrid
   NetBIOS Scope ID . . :
   IP Routing Enabled . : No
   WINS Proxy Enabled . . . . . : No
   NetBIOS Resolution Uses DNS  : Yes

0 Ethernet adapter :
   Description  . . . . . . . . : Intel (R) PRO PCI Adapter
   Physical Address . . . . . . : 00-A0-C9-E7-3B-65
   DHCP Enabled . . . . . . . . : No
   IP Address . . . . . . . . . : 132.233.150.4
   Subnet Mask  . . . . . . . . : 255.255.255.0
   Default Gateway  . . . . . . : 132.233.150.1
   Primary WINS Server  . . . . : 132.133.150.10
   Secondary WINS Server  . . . :
   Lease Obtained . . . . . . . :
   Lease Expires  . . . . . . . :
```

Figure 25.18 PING Command

```
C:\>ping 132.233.150.4

Pinging 132.233.150.4 with 32 bytes of data:

Reply from 132.233.150.4: bytes=32 time<10ms TTL=128
Reply from 132.233.150.4: bytes=32 time<10ms TTL=128
Reply from 132.233.150.4: bytes=32 time<10ms TTL=128
Reply from 132.233.150.4: bytes=32 time<10ms TTL=128

Ping statistics for 132.233.150.4:
    Packets: Sent = 4, Received = 4, Lost = 0 (0% loss),
Approximate round trip times in milli-seconds:
    Minimum = 0ms, Maximum = 0ms, Average = 0ms
```

Figure 25.19 PING Command Showing Total Failure

```
C:\>ping 132.233.150.2

Pinging 132.233.150.2 with 32 bytes of data:

Request timed out.
Request timed out.
Request timed out.
Request timed out.

Ping statistics for 132.233.150.2:
    Packets: Sent = 4, Received = 0, Lost = 4 (100% loss),
Approximate round trip times in milli-seconds:
    Minimum = 0ms, Maximum = 0ms, Average = 0ms
```

Figure 25.20 TRACERT Command

```
C:\>tracert www.novell.com

Tracing route to www.novell.com [137.65.2.11]
over a maximum of 30 hops:

  1    97 ms    92 ms   107 ms  tnt3-e1.scrm01.pbi.net [206.171.130.74]
  2    96 ms    98 ms   118 ms  core1-e3-3.scrm01.pbi.net [206.171.130.77]
  3    96 ms    95 ms   120 ms  edge1-fa0-0-0.scrm01.pbi.net [206.13.31.8]
  4    96 ms   102 ms    96 ms  sfralsr1-5-0.ca.us.ibm.net [165.87.225.10]
  5   105 ms   108 ms   114 ms  f1-0-0.sjc-bb1.cerf.net [134.24.88.55]
  6   107 ms   112 ms   106 ms  atm8-0-155M.sjc-bb3.cerf.net [134.24.29.38]
  7   106 ms   110 ms   120 ms  pos1-1-155M.sfo-bb3.cerf.net [134.24.32.89]
  8   109 ms   108 ms   110 ms  pos3-0-0-155M.sfo-bb1.cerf.net [134.24.29.202]
  9   122 ms   105 ms   115 ms  atm8-0.sac-bb1.cert.net [134.24.29.86]
 10   121 ms   120 ms   117 ms  atm3-0.slc-bb1.cerf.net [134.24.29.90]
 11   123 ms   131 ms   130 ms  novell-gw.slc-bb1.cerf.net [134.24.116.54]
 12     *        *        *     Request timed out.
 13   133 ms   139 ms   855 ms  www.novell.com [137.65.2.11]

Trace complete.
```

If the time takes up to 200 milliseconds, the time is considered very good. If the time is between 200 and 500 milliseconds, the time is considered marginal, and if the time is over 500 milliseconds, the time is unacceptable. A Request timed out indicates total failure as shown in figure 25.19.

The TRACERT.EXE command sends out a packet of information to each hop (gateway/router) individually, and does it three times. Therefore, the TRACERT command can help determine where the break is in a network. See figure 25.20. Another command that combines PING and TRACERT is PATHPING.

Viewing the current configuration (IPCONFIG), pinging the loopback address (PING 127.0.0.1), and pinging the IP address of your computer will verify that the TCP/IP protocol is properly functioning on your PC. By pinging the IP address of the default gateway or router, as well as other local IP computers, you determine if the computer is communicated on the local network. If it cannot connect to the gateway or any other local computer, either you are not connected properly or the IP protocol is misconfigured (IP address, IP subnet mask, or gateway address). If you cannot connect to the gateway but you can connect to other local computers, check your IP address, IP subnet mask, and gateway address; check to see if the gateway is functioning by using the PING command at the gateway to connect to your computer and other local computers on your network as well as pinging the other network connections on the gateway/router or pinging computers on other networks. If you cannot ping another local computer, but you can ping the gateway, most likely the other computer is having problems and you need to restart this procedure at that computer. If you can ping the gateway, but you cannot ping a computer on another gateway, you need to check the routers and pathways between the two computers by using the PING or TRACERT commands.

NSLOOKUP is a diagnostic tool that displays information from the DNS servers. It is only available if the TCP/IP protocol has been installed. NSLOOKUP has two modes—interactive and noninteractive. Use interactive mode when you require more than one piece of data. To run interactive mode, at the command prompt type *NSLOOKUP.* To exit interactive mode, type *EXIT.* Use noninteractive mode when you require a single piece of data. Type the *NSLOOKUP* command at the command prompt with the proper parameters, and the data is returned.

25.10 IPX PROTOCOL SUITE

IPX, which stands for Internetwork Packet Exchange, is a networking protocol suite used by the Novell NetWare, Windows NT, and Windows 2000. Note: Windows refers to the IPX protocol as NWLINK (NDIS-compliant version of the IPX protocol which is fully compatible with the Novell IPX/SPX protocol). IPX is the fastest routable network protocol suite available.

Similar to the TCP/IP network, you connect to an IPX network by using one of several interfaces including Ethernet, token ring, or ARCnet. For a Novell NetWare network, the software used to connect to an IPX network is first loading a **Multiple Link Interface Driver (MLID),** which is basically the driver to control the network card. Different previous software interfaces used by early versions of IPX and other protocols, the MLID complies with the **Novell Open Data-Link Interface (ODI) architecture** that allows a network driver to communicate with multiple protocols stacks such as TCP/IP and IPX.

Since the MLID supports multiple protocols, software is needed to identify the packets that come through the network card and routes to the proper protocol stack. This is known as the link support layer (LSL).

When you install IPX on Windows 95, Windows 98, Windows NT, or Windows 2000, you may have to consider setting the frame type. The frame type defines the way in which the network adapter formats data to be sent over a network. See table 25.9.

On Ethernet networks, the standard frame type for NetWare 2.2 and NetWare 3.11 is 802.3. Starting with NetWare 3.12, the default frame type was changed to 802.2. You can choose to automatically detect or manually configure the frame type. However, the frame type is automatically detected when NWLink is loaded. If multiple frame types are detected in addition to the 802.2 frame type, NWLink defaults to the 802.2 frame type. One of the biggest problems when connecting to an IPX network is using the wrong frame type. Therefore, if you need to have multiple frame types, you must manually configure the operating system to load multiple frame types simultaneously.

Table 25.9 Frame Types

Topology	Supported Frame Type
Ethernet	Ethernet II, 802.3, 802.2, and Sub Network Access Protocol (SNAP), which defaults to 802.2
Token Ring	802.5 and SNAP
Fiber Distributed Data Interface (FDDI)	802.2 and 802.3

25.11 NETBIOS AND NETBEUI

The **Network Basic Input/Output System (NetBIOS)** is a common program that runs on most Microsoft networks (Windows for Workgroups, Windows 9X, Windows NT, Windows 2000, and Windows XP). Originally created for IBM for its early PC networks, it was adopted by Microsoft and has since become a de facto industry standard.

NetBIOS is a session-level interface used by applications to communicate with NetBIOS-compliant transports such as NetBEUI, IPX, or TCP/IP. It is responsible for establishing logical names (computer names) on the network, establishing a logical connection between the two computers, and supporting reliable data transfer between computers that have established a session.

Once a logical connection is established, computers can then exchange data in the form of NetBIOS requests or in the form of a **Server Message Block (SMB).** The SMB protocol, which was jointly developed by Microsoft, Intel, and IBM, defines a series of commands used to pass information between networked computers. Clients connected to a network using NetBIOS over TCP/IP, NetBEUI, or IPX/SPX can send SMB commands. Note: Microsoft refers to NetBIOS over TCP/IP as NBT.

NetBEUI is short for **NetBIOS Enhanced User Interface,** which provides the transport and network layers for the NetBIOS protocol, usually found on Microsoft networks. NetBEUI is a protocol used to transport data packets between two nodes. While NetBEUI is smaller than TCP/IP or IPX and is extremely quick, it will only send packets within the same network. In other words, NetBEUI is not a routable protocol and cannot send a packet to computer on another network.

To navigate a Microsoft network, the computers are identified with computer names, no matter what protocol (TCP/IP, IPX, or NetBEUI) you are using. The NetBIOS/computer names are up to 15 characters long. To connect the TCP/IP address with the computer name (NetBIOS name), Microsoft networks can use an LMHOSTS file or a WINS server.

A WINS (Windows Internet Naming Service) server determines the IP address with computer's NetBIOS name. WINS uses a distributed database that is automatically updated with the names of computers available and the IP address assigned to each one. Note: UNIX machines do not use NetBIOS names. Therefore, if you want to use name resolution for these machines, you must use HOSTS files/DNS servers.

25.12 APPLETALK

The Apple network architecture is called **AppleTalk,** which has been included in Apple Macintosh computers for several years. By using the computer's built-in network interface, you would usually connect the computers and Apple printers using shielded twisted-pair, but could also use unshielded twisted-pair and fiber optics. **LocalTalk** is Apple's own network interface and cable system. Since LocalTalk can only operate at only 230 Kbit/s, it is not commonly used. Instead, Macintosh computers will usually use EtherTalk or TokenTalk to communicate with larger and faster networks.

LocalTalk uses a "bus topology" in which each device in the network is directly connected to the next device in a daisy chain. In addition, for its access method, it uses CSMA/CA. On a Macintosh or Apple IIgs, a small box with a pigtail connector is plugged into the printer port; the pigtail on LocalTalk boxes therefore comes in two variations to support computers with either DIN or 9-pin D printer ports. It is often assumed that the LocalTalk box is only used with a DIN-style printer port, so be careful to purchase the right one for your computer.

The Apple LocalTalk box is equipped with two further DIN sockets so that it can take its place in the daisy chain. The pigtail connector from the LocalTalk box plugs into the printer port and a length of cable connects the LocalTalk box to the next box on the daisy chain. For the LocalTalk boxes at each end of the chain, only one of the DIN sockets is used. The two ends of the chain should not be joined together. Apple LocalTalk boxes are self-terminating. Therefore, you do not have to provide external terminators.

In addition to the Apple cabling system, LocalTalk is often used with PhoneNet cabling. A PhoneNet box is used in place of the LocalTalk box, which is equipped with RJ-11 telephone-style jack connectors for connecting to the network. PhoneNet also normally uses a bus topology, although some vendors manufacture hubs to support a variety of star topologies. In bus topology, PhoneNet requires a terminator at each end of the chain and network performance is reduced without the terminators. The terminator is simply an RJ-11 connector with a suitable resistor across two of the pins.

The AppleTalk subprotocols that are significant for node-to-node communications are described as:

- **AppleShare—**Provides file-sharing services, print queuing services, password access to files or folders, and user-accounting information.
- **AppleTalk Filing Protocol (AFP)—**Provides transparent access to files on both local and remote systems.
- **AppleTalk Session Protocol (ASP)—**Establishes and maintains connections between nodes and servers.
- **AppleTalk Transaction Protocol (ATP)—**Ensures reliable delivery of data by checking connections between nodes, checking packet sequence, and retransmitting any data packets that become lost.
- **Name Binding Protocol (NBP)—**Translates human-readable node names into numeric AppleTalk addresses.
- **Routing Table Maintenance Protocol (RTMP)—**Maintains a routing table of AppleTalk zones and their networks, and uses ZIP to manage data in the routing table.
- **Zone Information Protocol (ZIP)—**Updates zone information maps that tie zones to their networks for routing purposes.
- **Datagram Delivery Protocol (DDP)—**Assigns an AppleTalk node's address upon startup and manages addressing for communications between AppleTalk nodes.

Traditional file sharing for Apple computers used the AppleTalk protocol to communicate with an AppleShare server. The AppleTalk protocol can be used over many network cabling systems, including LocalTalk, Ethernet, and token ring. Note: TCP/IP can run over LocalTalk networks but there are many limitations.

There are two types of routers—seed and nonseed routers. A seed router has the net numbers programmed into it and acts as a source of information for other routers connected to that wiring system. A nonseed router learns the net number for the wiring system to which it is attached by communicating with the other routers on the system. Normally you need to define the net number for only one side of the router; it finds out the other net number(s) from the seed router or other routers on the network.

Each station on an AppleTalk network uses an address that is 24 bits long. Sixteen of those bits are given to the network, and each network can support 254 nodes. Each network segment can be given either a single 16-bit network number or a range of 16-bit network numbers. If a network is assigned a range of numbers, that network is considered an Extended AppleTalk network because it can support more than 254 nodes. The node address is automatically assigned by the computer itself or can be dynamically assigned by a seed router. If more than 254 are needed, then multiple addresses can be assigned to a single network by using a Cable Range. The Cable Range is the network number or numbers used by the end nodes connected to the transmission media.

Larger networks can be divided into AppleTalk zones containing printers and computers. Zones are used to split a network into logical subdivisions; in a company, it might be convenient to create three zones called Accounting, Production, and Sales. A zone can be used to describe computers in a single physical location on a network or it can describe computers from the same department that are in entirely different locations. To manage zones, you will need a dedicated server or hardware router. Note: Although you can have multiple zones on an AppleTalk network, an AppleTalk node can belong to only one zone.

AppleTalk wasn't originally designed to be routed over a WAN, but with the release of AppleTalk version 2, Apple included routing functionality with the introduction of the Routing Table Maintenance Protocol (RTMP). RTMP is a distance vector routing protocol, like RIP for both IP and IPX.

AppleTalk uses the Name Binding Protocol (NBP) to associate the name of the computer with its network address as every station broadcast its name when it comes up on a network, the AppleTalk router on the network cache the names and respond to the NBP request. When a node requests a name resolution, the local router will answer with information it has obtained from this cache. If an AppleTalk network doesn't have a router, each node will perform both NBP requests and NBP responses.

The only computer that comes with AppleTalk installed by default is the Macintosh. Most Windows operating systems are able to use the AppleTalk protocol, but require that additional software be installed.

25.13 WORKGROUPS AND DOMAINS

A **workgroup** is a group of computers that can send email to one another, share data files, and schedule meetings. The computers in a workgroup keep track of their own user and group account information and do not share this information with other computers. A workgroup is a good network configuration for a small group of computers with a small number of user accounts or in an environment with a mix of Microsoft networks that does not include Windows servers.

A **domain** is a group of computers and devices on a network that is administered as a unit with common rules and procedures. For example, one Windows 2000 server computer acts as a domain controller and maintains the centralized security databases for the domain. Other Windows 2000 servers in the domain can act as backup domain controllers and can authenticate logon requests or act as standalone servers to provide network resources, but only after authenticating access through the centralized security databases. Internet domains are defined by the IP address. All devices sharing the network part of the IP address are typically in the same domain. To become a member of a domain, right-click My Computer, select Properties, and click on the network Identification button.

25.14 NETWORK SOFTWARE

A **network operating system (NOS)** includes special functions for connecting computers and devices into a local area network (LAN), managing the resources and services of the network, and providing network security for multiple users. The most common client/server network operating systems are Windows NT and Windows 2000 Server, Novell NetWare, and UNIX/Linux machines. (Note: Most modern operating systems including all Windows operating systems can provide such network resources as file and printer access even though they are not servers.)

25.15 LOADING AND CONFIGURING THE NETWORKING SOFTWARE

In Windows, the network components are installed and configured using the Network dialog box, which is accessed by clicking on the Network applet in the Control Panel or by accessing the shortcut menu of the Network Neighborhood icon and selecting the Properties option. See figure 25.21. Note: The Network Neighborhood icon does not show on the desktop unless you have some network components installed.

To get full access to the network, you would need the following network software, installed through the Configuration tab:

1. A client software choice such as Client for Microsoft Networks or Client for NetWare Networks
2. A network adapter driver or dial-adapter driver (such as a modem)
3. A protocol stack such as TCP/IP, IPX/NWLINK, or NetBEUI

25.15.1 Client Software

Client software often uses redirectors and designators. A **redirector** is a small section of code in the network operating system that intercepts requests in the computer and determines if they should be left alone to continue in the local computer's bus or be redirected out to the network to another server. For example, when a user requests a file from the server or sends a print job to a network printer, the request is intercepted by the redirector and forwarded out onto the network.

A **designator** keeps track of which drive designations are assigned to network resources. For example, when a user attaches or maps to a network drive, the user and the software applications may see a drive letter, such as Drive M or Drive P, just like any other local drive. When these drives are accessed, a redirector will route the request to the network.

The **Client for Microsoft Networks Component** provides the redirector (VREDIR.VXD) to support all Microsoft networking products that use the Server Message Block (SMB) protocol. This includes support for connecting computers to and accessing files and printers on Windows for Workgroups, Windows 95, Windows 98, Windows Me, Windows NT, Windows 2000, and Windows XP computers.

Figure 25.21 Windows 95 Network Dialog Box

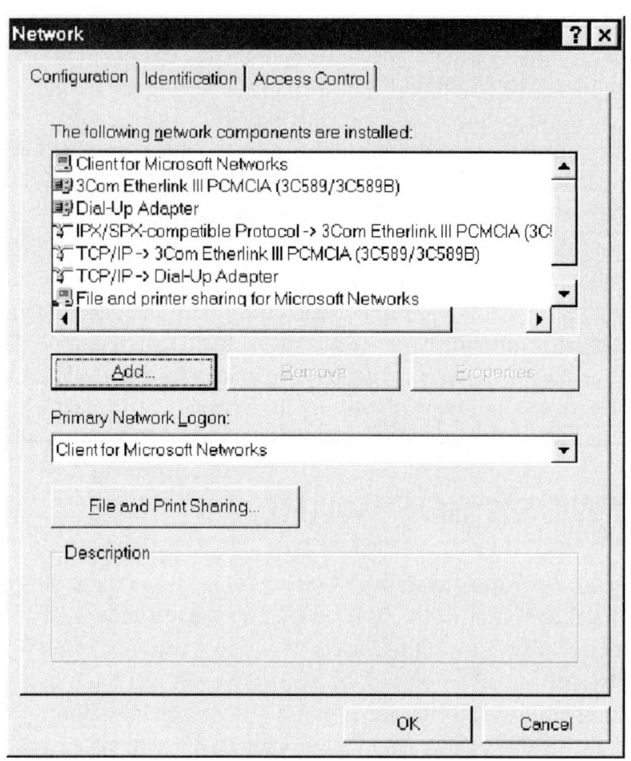

The Identification tab (or Network Identification tab) in the dialog box is used almost exclusively by Microsoft Networking to assign the NetBIOS computer name. Much like the MAC addresses, no two computers can have the same computer name on the same workgroup or domain. You can then use utilities such as the Network Neighborhood to access the computer and its network resources by using its computer name. Note: The computer name is up to 15 characters. See figure 25.22.

Under the properties of the Client for Microsoft Network, you can specify a domain name to log on to and you can specify the Network logon options. A **domain** is an organization unit consisting of computers that use one or more domain controllers to hold the centralized security account information. When a user logs on to a workstation/client computer on the network, the password is validated by one of the domain controllers and access is granted to the assigned network resources.

The Client for NetWare Networks Component run with the IPX protocol, is used to process login scripts, support all NetWare 3.XX command-line utilities and most 4.X command-line utilities, connect and browse to NetWare servers, access printers on the NetWare server, and process login scripts on the NetWare server. Note: If you decide to install Client for NetWare, you will need to load a network card driver that supports the ODI protocol. In addition, to get full access to all utilities, you should load the client software provided by Novell.

25.15.2 Protocol Stacks

Since Windows can use NDIS-and ODI-compatible network card drivers, it is possible to have one or more protocol stacks on your system. For example, you can load TCP/IP, IPX/SPX-compatible protocol, NetBEUI, and many others.

If you load the TCP/IP protocol, you must then configure it. If you highlight the TCP/IP protocol and click on the Properties button, you will be looking at several tabs. See figure 25.23. Within the IP Address tab, you assign the IP address or you can select to obtain an IP address automatically from a DHCP server. The gateway or address of the routers is set within the Gateway tab. The WINS Configuration and DNS Configuration are used to assign the addresses of the DNS and WINS servers, which are used for name resolution.

Figure 25.22 Network Dialog Box Showing the Windows 95 Identification Tab

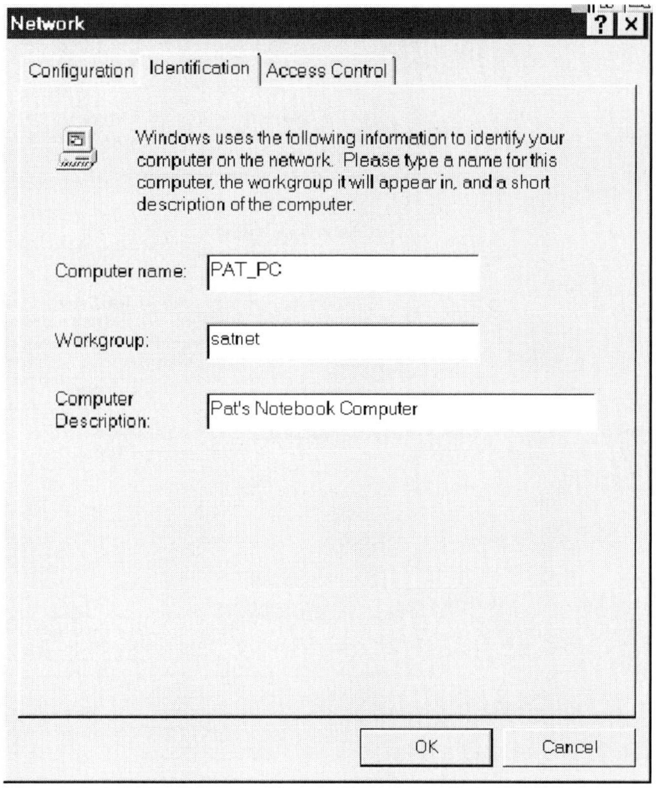

Network
Configuration
Identification
Access Control
Windows uses the following information to identify your computer on the network. Please type a name for this computer, the workgroup it will appear in, and a short description of the computer.
Computer name:
PAT_PC
Workgroup:
satnet
Computer Description:
Pat's Notebook Computer
OK
Cancel

Figure 25.23 TCP/IP Properties for Windows 95

TCP/IP Properties
Bindings
Advanced
NetBIOS
DNS Configuration
Gateway
WINS Configuration
IP Address
An IP address can be automatically assigned to this computer. If your network does not automatically assign IP addresses, ask your network administrator for an address, and then type it in the space below.
Obtain an IP address automatically
Specify an IP address:
IP Address:
Subnet Mask:
OK
Cancel

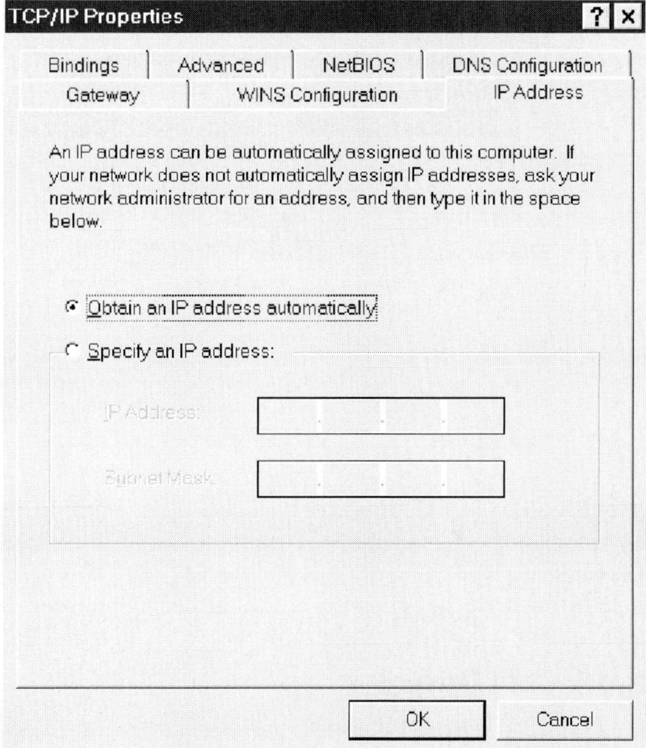

Figure 25.24 IPX/SPX Protocol Properties

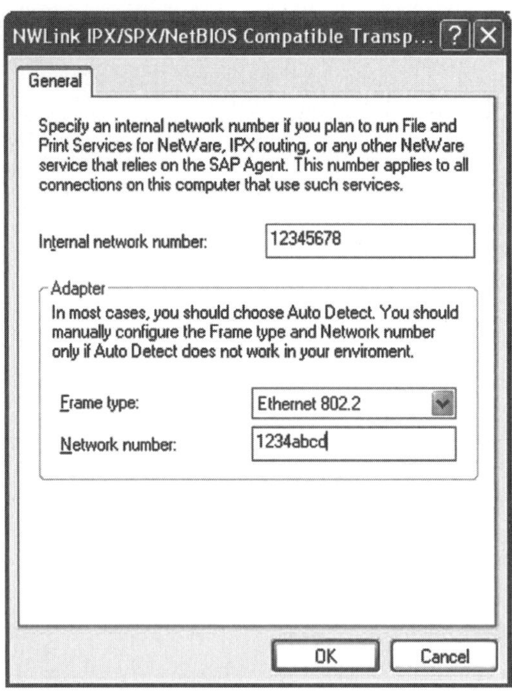

Figure 25.25 Adding a Network Card/Adapter Driver

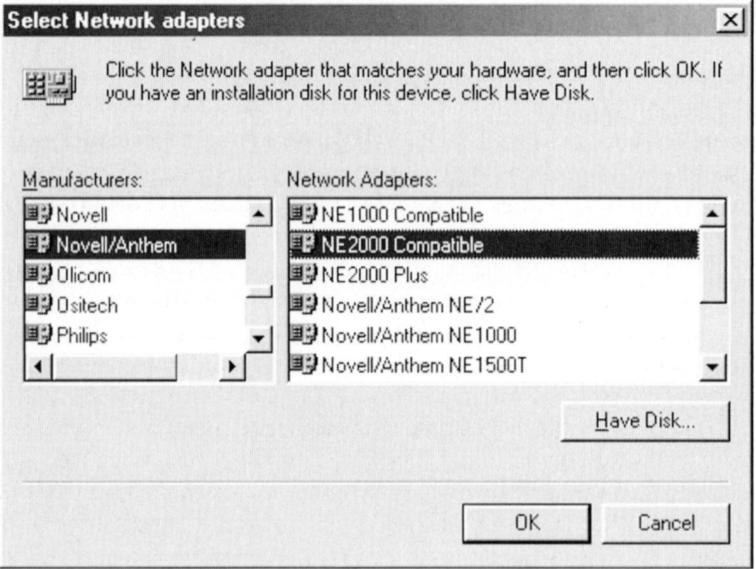

The IPX and NetBEUI protocols are not as complicated to configure as the TCP/IP protocol and usually require no configuration. See figures 25.24 and 25.25. Within the properties of the IPX protocol, you can select the IPX frame types and enable NetBIOS over IPX/SPX. In either case, TCP/IP, IPX, and NetBEUI all have the option to become the default protocol.

25.15.3 Network Card Drivers

While the network card or adapter is the hardware device that allows you to connect to the network, it requires a software driver before it can be used. If the driver that you need is not listed, press the Have Disk button and indicate where the installation files are for the driver that you want to install. See figure 25.26.

Figure 25.26 Network Card/Adapter Properties Dialog Box

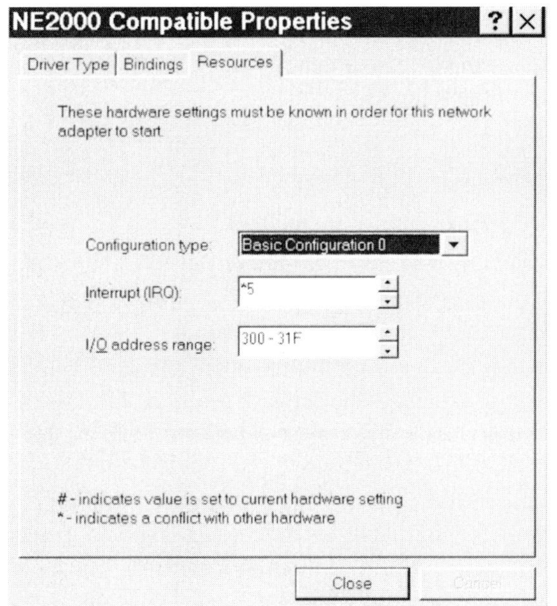

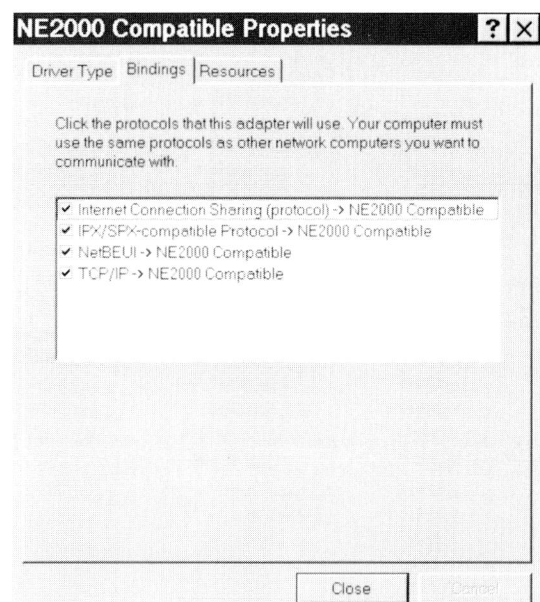

If the card is a legacy card, you will have to go into the properties of the network card and specify the network card's resources such as IO address and IRQ. While most protocols are automatically bonded to the network card, this can be configured in the network card's Properties dialog box under the Bindings tab. In addition, if a card has advanced features, it will usually be configured using the Adapter Properties dialog box.

25.15.4 Access Control

Depending on the version of Windows you are using and the options you choose, Windows can provide share-level or user-level security. Peer-to-peer networks normally incorporate share-level security, in which a network administrator assigns passwords to network resources. In a network that uses share-level security, users must remember many passwords. When users have to remember many passwords, network security can be violated because some users will write down their passwords and post the passwords near their computers. Share-level security is a decentralized network security method, which is only practical in small networks. You will find it in Windows 9X machines.

In the user-level security model, a user has a user account that includes a user name and password. The user account is provided with an access control list each time the user logs on to the network. A user can access a network resource only if that resource is on the ACL. The user-level security model allows the network administrator to manage network security from a central network location. An administrator would normally assign users to group accounts and then grant the group accounts permissions to resources on the network. Groups ease the administrative burden because the administrator must only change the permissions granted to a group account to change the permissions for the users in that group. Of course, servers would typically use the user-level security mode. User-level security models are found in the Windows NT family.

25.15.5 Linux Network Connectivity

To enable network connection, you must first activate the network device by loading the appropriate network driver and then loading and configuring the proper network protocols. The utilities used to do this will vary for Linux from distribution to distribution.

The ifconfig program is responsible for setting up network interface cards. Although ifconfig is natively accessed through the command prompt, many tools have been written to provide a menu-driven or graphical interface, which in turn accesses the ifconfig for you. For example, Caldera users can configure the network interface through COS, and Red Hat users can use the netcfg program. The ifconfig command is used to configure the IP address and netmask and it can also be used to display current settings.

The format of the ifconfig command is as follows

```
ifconfig device IP_address options
```

where *device* is the name of the Ethernet device (for example, eth0 or eth1), *address* is the IP address you wish to apply to the device, and *options* are one of the following:

up	Enables the device.
down	Disables the device.
arp	Enables this device to answer arp requests.
-arp	Disables the device from answering arp requests.
mtu *value*	Sets the maximum transmission unit (MTU) of the device to *value*. Under Ethernet, this defaults to 1500.
netmask *mask*	Sets the subnet mask to the interface to *mask*. If a value is not supplied, ifconfig calculates the netmask based on the class of the IP address. A class A address gets a netmask of 255.0.0.0, class B gets 255.255.0.0, and class C gets 255.255.255.0.
broadcast *bcast*	Sets the broadcast address to this interface to *bcast*. If a value is not supplied, ifconfig calculates the broadcast address based on the class of the IP address in a similar manner to netmask.
pointtopoint *ppp_address*	Sets up a point-to-point (PPP) connection where the remote address is *ppp_address*.

In its simplest usage, all you need to do is provide the name of the interface being configured and the static IP address. See figure 25.27. The ifconfig program will deduce the rest of the information based on the IP address. Thus, you could enter the following command at the command prompt to set the eth0 device to the IP address 192.168.1.65:

```
ifconfig eth0 192.168.1.65
```

Because 192.168.1.42 is a class C address, the calculated subnet mask will be 255.255.255.0, and the broadcast address will be 192.168.1.255.

If the IP address you are setting is a class A or class B address that is subnetted differently, you will need to explicitly set the broadcast and netmask address on the command line

```
ifconfig dev ip netmask mask broadcast bcast
```

where *dev* is the network device you are configuring, *ip* is the IP address you are setting it to, *nmask* is the netmask, and *bcast* is the broadcast address. For example:

```
ifconfig eth0 1.1.1.1 netmask 255.255.255.0 broadcast 1.1.1.255
```

Figure 25.27 Using the Ifconfig Command

```
[root@localhost /root]# ifconfig
eth0      Link encap:Ethernet  HWaddr 00:A0:C9:E7:3B:65
          inet addr:63.197.142.129  Bcast:63.197.142.255  Mask:255.255.255.0
          UP BROADCAST RUNNING MULTICAST  MTU:1500  Metric:1
          RX packets:696 errors:0 dropped:0 overruns:0 frame:0
          TX packets:826 errors:0 dropped:0 overruns:12 carrier:0
          collisions:0 txqueuelen:100
          Interrupt:10 Base address:0xcf80

lo        Link encap:Local Loopback
          inet addr:127.0.0.1  Mask:255.0.0.0
          UP LOOPBACK RUNNING  MTU:16436  Metric:1
          RX packets:10 errors:0 dropped:0 overruns:0 frame:0
          TX packets:10 errors:0 dropped:0 overruns:0 carrier:0
          collisions:0 txqueuelen:0

[root@localhost /root]#
```

You can list all of the active devices by running ifconfig with no parameters. You can list all devices, regardless of whether they are active, by running ifconfig -a.

If your host is connected to a network with multiple subnets, you need a router to communicate with the other networks. As your computer sends packets onto the network, your computer does not know the correct path to the destination computer. If it does not know the correct route, the packet will be sent out using its default route, which starts with the router connected to your network. When the router gets the packet, it will then determine which is the best path to use and forward it to the appropriate router. Then that router will do the same and the process will repeat itself until the packet gets to the destination network, which will then forward the packet to the host destination computer.

There are actually instances where you will need to change your routes manually. Typically, this is necessary when multiple network cards are installed into the same host where each NIC is connected to a different network. You should know how to add a route so that packets can be sent to the appropriate network based on the destination address.

A typical Linux host knows of three routes:

- The loopback route, which simply points toward the loopback device
- The route to the local area network so that packets destined to hosts within the same LAN are sent directly to them
- The default route or gateway

To change routes, you are going to use the route command. The typical route command is structured as follows:

```
route cmd type addy netmask mask gw gway dev dn
```

See table 25.10.

To set the default route on a sample host that has a single Ethernet device and a router of 192.168.1.1:

```
route add -net default gw 192.168.1.1 dev eth0
```

To delete the route destined to 192.168.1.42:

```
route del 192.168.1.42
```

To display the route table, simply run route without any parameters. See figure 25.28.

```
Route
```

Table 25.10 Route Command Parameters

Parameter	Description
Cmd	Either *add* or *del,* depending on whether you are adding or deleting a routing. If you are deleting a route, the only other parameter you need is *addy.*
Type	Either -net or -host, depending on whether *addy* represents a network address or a router address.
Addy	The destination network to which you want to offer a route.
netmask *mask*	Sets the netmask of the *addy* address to *mask.*
gw *gway*	Sets the router address for *addy* to *gway.* Typically used for the default route.
dev *dn*	Sends all packets destined to *addy* through the network device *dn* as set by ifconfig.

Figure 25.28 The Route Command Executed Without Any Parameters

```
Destination     Gateway         Genmask         Flags Metric Ref    Use Iface
192.168.1.0     *               255.255.255.0   U     0      0        0 eth0
127.0.0.0       *               255.0.0.0       U     0      0        0 lo
default         192.168.1.254   0.0.0.0         UG    0      0        0 eth0
```

Table 25.11 Information Display Using the Route Command

Entry	Description
The Flags are:	U The connection is up. H The destination is a host. G The destination is a gateway.
Metric	The cost of a route, usually measured in hops. This is meant for systems that have multiple paths to get to the same destination, but one path is preferred. The Linux kernel doesn't use this information, but certain advanced routing protocols do.
Ref	The number of references to this route. This is not used in the Linux kernel. It is here because the route tool itself is cross-platform. Thus it prints this value, since other operating systems do use it.
Use	The number of successful route cache lookups. To see this value, use the -F option when invoking route.

Table 25.11 explains the information the route command displays.

Note that the route command displays the host names to any IP address it can look up and resolve. If there are network difficulties, and DNS or NIS servers become unavailable, the route command will hang on, trying to resolve host names and waiting to see if the servers come back and resolve them. This wait will go on for several minutes until the request times out. To get around this, use the -n option with route so that the same information is shown. Route will make no attempt to perform host name resolution on the IP addresses.

Normally, the netstat program is used to display the status of all the network connections on a host. However, with the -r option, it can also display the routing table. Most UNIX-based operating systems require that you use this method of viewing routes. Like the route command, netstat can also take the -n parameter so that it does not perform host name resolution.

Red Hat Linux has a system setup that makes it easy to configure network cards at boot time. It is done through the creation of files in the /etc/sysconfig/network-scripts directory that are read at boot time. All of the graphical tools under Linux create these files.

For each network interface, there is an ifcfg file in /etc/sysconfig/network-scripts. This file name is suffixed by the name of the device, thus ifcfg-eth0 is for the eth0 device, ifcfg-eth1 is for the eth1 device, and so on. An example of these files are:

```
DEVICE= "eth0"
IPADDR= "192.168.1.1"
NETMASK= "255.255.255.0"
NETWORK=192.168.1.0
BROADCAST=192.168.1.255
ONBOOT="yes"
BOOTPROTO="none"
IPNETNUM_802_2=""
IPXPRIMARY_802_2="no"
IPXACTIVE_802_2="no"
IPXNETNUM_802_3=""
IPXPRIMARY_802_3="no"
IPXACTIVE_802.3="no"
IPXNETNUM_ETHERII=""
IPXPRIMARY_ETHERII="no"
IPXACTIVE_ETHERII= "no"
IPXNETNUM_SNAP=""
IPXPRIMARY_SNAP="no"
IPXACTIVE_SNAP="no"
```

If you want to make changes to the IP configuration, you just have to make the changes to the appropriate file and run the script. For example, if you make changes to the ifcfg-eth0 script, you would run the script by using the following commands:

```
[root@host1 /root] # cd /etc/sysconfig/network-scripts
[root@host network-scripts] # ./ifdown ifcfg-eth0
[root@ford network-scripts] # ./ifup ifcfg-eth0
```

The /etc/sysconfig/network file stores the host name and gateway for the computer. An example of this file is:

```
NETWORKING=yes
HOSTNAME="host1.acme01.cxm"
GATEWAY="192.168.254"
GATEWAYDEV="eth0"
FORWARD_IPV4="no"
```

In the/etc directory, you will find a text file called resolv.conf. This file specifies which server to use as the DNS server. To tell your machine to use the 10.10.10.10 as the DNS server, you just have to add the following line to the resolv.conf file:

```
nameserver 10.10.10.10
```

Another tool that can be used to configure network connectivity is the linuxconf utility. If you open the Network section on the Config tab, then open the Client tasks section, you can then select Host names and IP network devices. The Host Name tab will ask for a host name, which should be specified by default unless you did not set up your networking during the installation of Linux. If you don't have a host name and domain name, you should specify

```
localhost.localdomain
```

If you click on the Adaptor tabs on the right side of the utility, you can then configure the network device including its IP address and subnet mask. The first item on this screen is a check box to indicate whether this adaptor is enabled. If this is the one you intend to use, it should be checked. See figure 25.29.

Figure 25.29 Configuring Adaptor 1 Using the Linuxconf Program

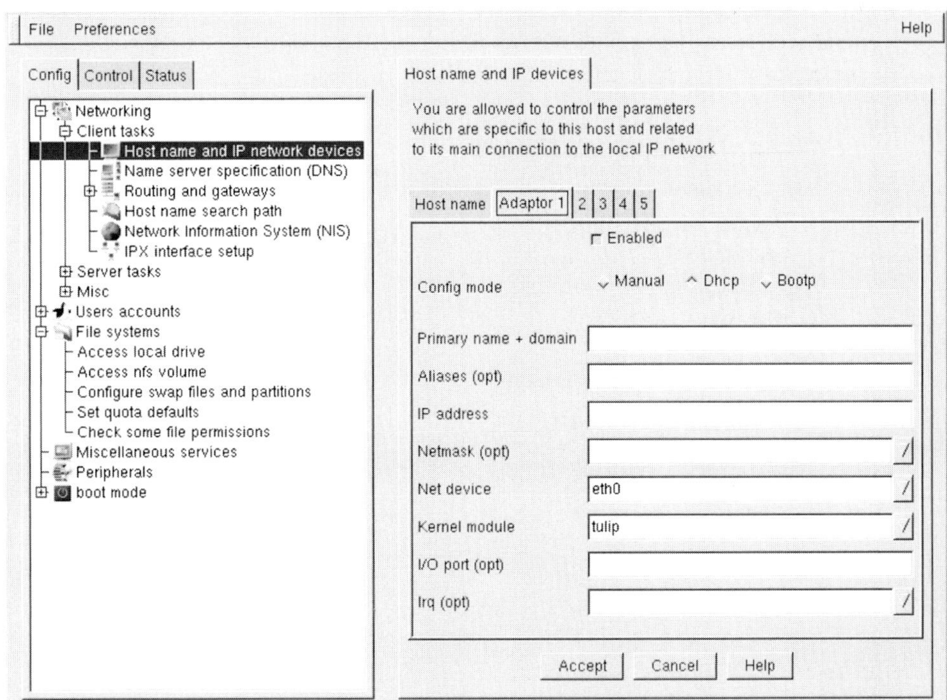

Below the Enabled option, you can choose if you want to provide a static IP address (Manual option) or if you want the machine to get its IP address from a DHCP or BOOTP server (Dhcp and Bootp options). When you configure the static IP addresses, you must include the following information:

- **Primary Name + Domain**—The primary name is the name of your computer (host name), whereas the domain is the name of the network you are on. For example, your computer could be called myhost and it could belong to the acme.com domain (myhost.acme.com).
- **IP Address**—The address of the machine will follow this pattern: *x.x.x.x*. For example, 192.168.0.13.
- **Net Device**—The type of network card you are using; eth0 would be the appropriate entry to use for the first Ethernet card.
- **Kernel Module**—The correct module based on your network card.

NOTE: The netmask information may already be set for you with the default mask. However, if your network is subnetted, you may need to change the default values.

When you are using a DHCP or BOOTP server to configure your network configuration, the required fields are:

- **Net Device**—The type of network card you are using; for example, eth0 would be the appropriate entry to use for the first Ethernet card.
- **Kernel Module**—The correct module based on your network card. An excellent reference for a list of kernel modules is Appendix A of the *Official Red Hat Linux Reference Guide.*

When computers connect to the Internet or a corporate network, they will typically use a DNS server to act as a name server, which will translate host names to IP addresses. To specify the DNS name server, select the Name server specification (DNS) option in the Config tab. The DNS server will translate from host names to IP addresses. As you can see from figure 25.30, you can specify several name servers. However, the second or third name server is accessed only when the first name server is inaccessible. Note: Each of these must be an IP address and not a name, since the computer has no way to resolve the name until it connects to a name server.

Figure 25.30 DNS Configuration Screen

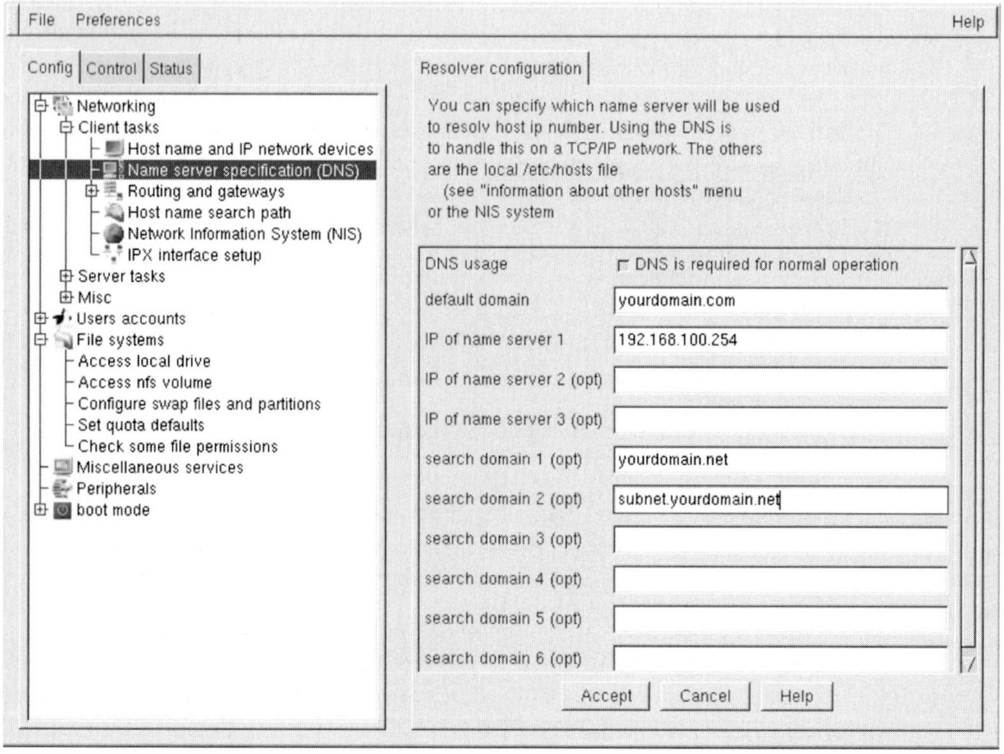

In addition to a default domain, you can also specify up to six search domains. Search domains are useful if you want to specify many host names with the same domain but do not want to type the domain name. For example, if you access a computer often in another domain, you can specify the domain of that computer. When you specify the host name, it will automatically resolve the host name to that domain. If you have to specify the acme.com domain, for instance, and you specify the daffy host, it will automatically search for daffy.acme.com. You can also add, modify, or delete entries from the /etc/hosts file by using the Config tab, selecting the Networking option, selecting the Misc option, and then selecting the Information about other hosts option.

Another way to provide name resolution for a host computer is to use the /etc/hosts files. Linuxconf provides a simple way to add entries to the hosts files. To modify or delete an entry, you must first select the entry. Then to delete the entry, click on the Dismissed button. To modify it, change the information as necessary.

To add a new entry, select Add at the bottom of the /etc/hosts screen. This will also open the host/network definition screen. You will then be required to provide the primary name + domain and the IP address. You also have the option to provide an alias or shortcut name for the fully qualified domain name. For example, if you have an entry for daffy.acme.com, you can create an alias for duck. Anytime you specify to communicate with duck, it will automatically resolve it to daffy.acme.com and the appropriate IP address.

After configuring your system settings through linuxconf, the changes are not activated immediately. You must activate the changes by choosing File and selecting the Act/Changes option from the pull-down menu in the GUI version of linuxconf, clicking on an Accept button in web-based linuxconf, or selecting the Accept button in text mode linuxconf.

NOTE: IP addresses and default routes will not change until you reboot the system.

Other tools used to configure network parameters is netconfig and network configurator. The simpler tool is the netconfig utility. It is a text-based tool that allows you to input the IP address, subnet mask, the default gateway, and the primary name server. Whereas it is much quicker than linuxconf, it also is much less flexible.

To start network configurator type *netcfg* from a shell prompt. Network devices can be added, removed, configured, activated, deactivated, and aliased. When using Network Configurator, click Save to write your changes to disk. To quit without making any changes, select Quit.

Network Configurator's Names panel serves two primary purposes: setting the host name and domain of the computer and determining which name server will be used to look up other hosts on the network. The Names panel cannot configure a machine to be a name server. To edit a field or add information to a field, simply click on the field with the left mouse button and type the new information.

In the Hosts management panel, you can add, edit, or remove hosts from the /etc/hosts file. Adding or editing an entry involves identical actions. An Edit dialog box will appear. Simply type the new information and click Done when you are finished.

If you have added a network interface to your machine since installing Red Hat Linux, or if you didn't configure your Ethernet card at install time, you can configure it here with a few clicks of a mouse.

NOTE: You may need to configure kmod to load a driver for the network interface you are adding (e.g., eth0). Begin adding an interface by clicking on Interfaces in the main panel. A list of configured devices and a row of available options will be displayed.

To add a device, first click the Add button. Then select the type of interface you want to configure from the box that appears.

NOTE: A Clone button is now available in Network Configurator. This button can be used to create a "clone" of an already existing interface. Using clone interfaces, a laptop can have one Ethernet interface defined for a work LAN, and a clone Ethernet device is defined for a home LAN.

To configure a SLIP interface, you must first supply a phone number, login name, and password. This information will provide the initial parameters for the chat script needed to establish a SLIP connection. When you choose Done, a dialog box titled Edit SLIP Interface appears that enables you to further customize the hardware, communication, and networking parameters for your SLIP interface.

To add a SLIP/PPP interface to your system, you only have to supply the IP address, the remote IP address, and the Netmask. You can also select whether you want to activate the interface at boot time.

If you are adding an Ethernet, ARCnet, token ring or pocket adapter to your computer, you will need to supply the following information:

- **Device**—This is determined by netconfig based on the devices already configured.
- **IP Address**—Enter an IP address for your network device.
- **Netmask**—Enter the network mask for your network device. The network and broadcast addresses are calculated automatically based on the IP address and netmask you enter.
- **Activate Interface at Boot Time**—If you want the device to be configured automatically when your machine boots, select this option.
- **Allow Any User to (de)activate Interface**—Check this if you want any user to be able to activate or deactivate the interface.
- **Interface Configuration Protocol**—If you have a BOOTP or DHCP server on your network and would like to use it to configure the interface, choose the appropriate option; otherwise, choose none.

After providing the configuration information for your new device, click Done. The device should appear in your Interfaces list as an inactive device. (The active column should have a label of "no.") To activate the new device, first select it with a mouse click and then choose the Activate button. If it does not come up properly, you may need to reconfigure it by choosing Edit.

In the Routing panel you have the ability to add, edit, or remove static networking routes. Adding or editing an entry involves identical actions, just like the Hosts panel. An Edit dialog box will appear; simply type the new information and click Done when you are finished.

25.16 SHARING DRIVES AND DIRECTORIES

Windows and Linux both have the ability to share their drives and printers so that they can be accessed through the network. Shared directories and printers are defined and accessed using Server Message Block (SMB)/Common Internet File System (CIFS) protocols that can be accessed through TCP/IP, IPX/SPX, or NetBEUI networks using universal naming convention based on NetBIOS names. Because the CIFS protocol has become a de facto standard in sharing drives, directories, and printers, it allows Microsoft computers, Linux computers, and Apple Macintosh computers to create and access these shares.

25.16.1 Microsoft Sharing

To create or access a NetBIOS/Microsoft share in Windows, you have to load the **File and Printer Sharing for Microsoft Networks** service. For Windows 2000 and Windows XP, it is already loaded by default. Windows 2000 and XP use user-based shares. See figure 25.31.

Windows 9X can use either user-based or password-based access to their shares. For Windows 9X, you need to verify that the File and Printer Sharing for Microsoft Networks utility is loaded. In addition, you will have to open the properties of File and Print Sharing and enable "I want to be able to give others access to my files," "I want to be able to allow others to print to my printer(s)," or both.

Even though you enable file and print sharing for an individual computer, you must still share a drive, directory, or printer before it can be accessed through the network. If you enabled file sharing on a Windows computer, you can share any drive or directory by right-clicking the drive or directory and selecting the Sharing option from the File menu or by selecting the Sharing option from the shortcut menu of the drive or directory. You would then provide a share name, the name seen by other clients, and type of access that users can have. A shared drive and directory will be indicated with a hand under the drive or directory (fobber)icon. See figure 25.32.

To view all the share drives and folders, you can start the Computer Management console, and perform the following steps:

1. Click Start, click Control Panel, and then click Administrative Tools.
2. Click Computer Management, and then click Shared Folders.
3. Double-click Shares to view a list of shared folders.

Figure 25.31 File and Printer Sharing for Microsoft Networks must be loaded to share drives, directories, and printers and to remotely access shared drives, directories, and printers.

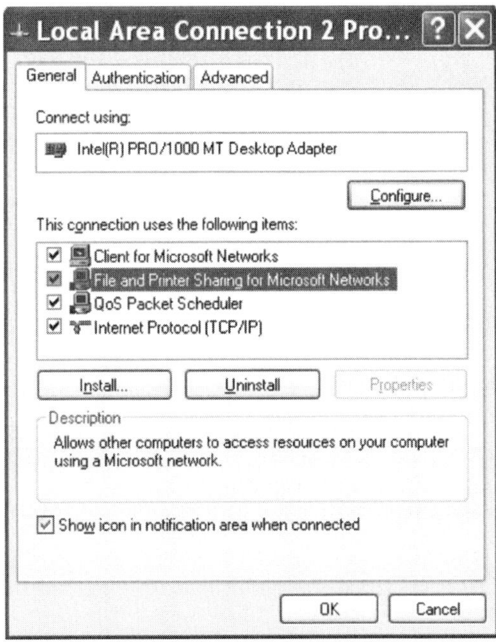

Figure 25.32 To share a drive or folder, you right-click the drive or folder and select sharing. When done, a shared drive or directory is indicated by a hand under the drive or directory folder icon.

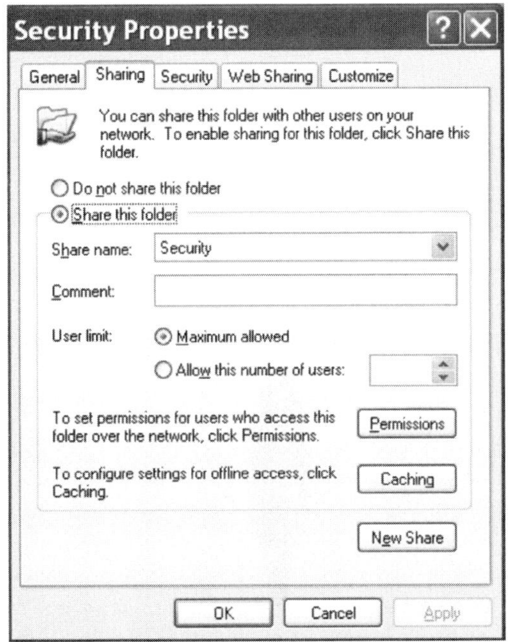

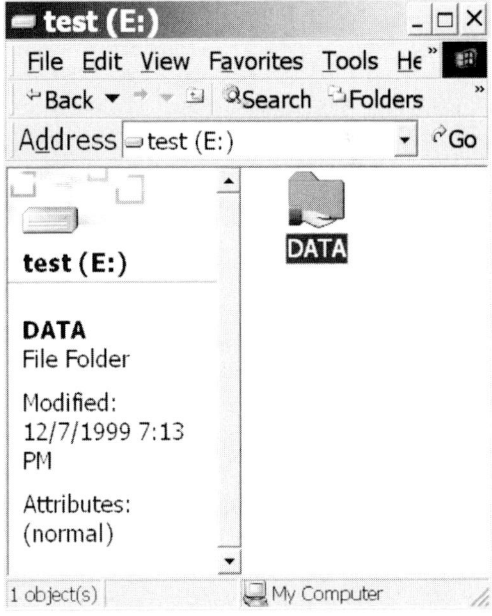

To control how users gain access to a shared folder, you assign shared folder permissions. Note that these permissions are not needed or used if the user is accessing the directory locally (logged on to the computer that has the shared drive or directory). The shared folder/drive permissions are shown in table 25.12.

To grant or change share permissions to a shared folder, you would right-click the shared folder or drive, select the Sharing option, and click on the Permissions button. To add a user or group, click on the Add button. To remove a user or group, click to highlight the user or group and then click on the

Table 25.12 Share Permissions

Share Permission	Description
Read	The Read permission allows the user to view folder names and file names, open and view subfolders files and their attributes, and navigate the tree structures.
Change	Allows all permissions granted by the Read permission and it also allows the user to create folders, add files to folders, change data in files, append data to files, change file attributes, and delete folders and files.
Full Control	The Full Control permission is granted by the Change permission and it also allows the user to change file permissions and take ownership of files.

Figure 25.33 Setting the Share Permissions

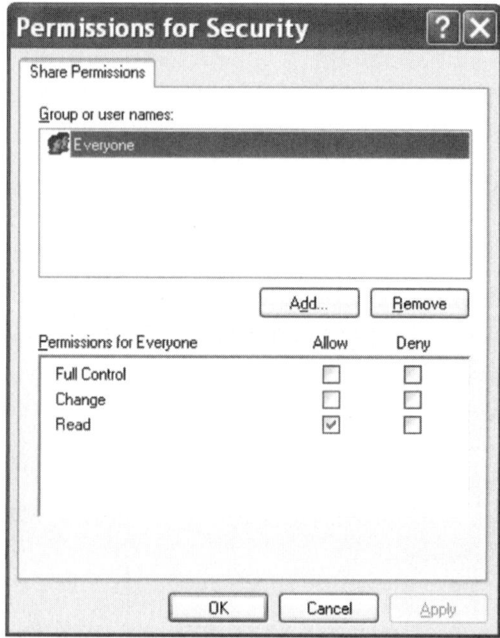

Remove button. To specify which permissions to grant, click to highlight the user or group and select or deselect the Allow and Deny options. See figure 25.33.

When accessing a shared folder on an NTFS volume, the effective permissions that a person can use in the share folder are calculated by combining the shared folder permissions and the NTFS permissions. When combining the two, you first determine the cumulative NTFS permissions and the cumulative shared permissions. Then you apply the more restrictive permission, or the permission that allows the least amount of access.

In Windows 2000 and Windows XP, several special shared folders are automatically created by Windows for administrative and system use. See table 25.13. Different from regular shares, these shares do not show when a user browses the computer resources using Network Neighborhood, My Network Place, or similar software. In most cases, special shared folders should not be deleted or modified. For Windows 2000 Professional and Windows XP Professional computers, only members of the administrators or backup operators groups can connect to these shares.

An **administrative share** is a shared folder typically used for administrative purposes. To make a shared folder or drive into an administrative share, the share name must have a dollar sign ($) at the end of it. Because the share folder or drive cannot be seen during browsing you would have to use a UNC name—the share name plus the $. It would have to be accessed using the Start button, selecting the Run

Table 25.13 Special Shares

Special Share	Description
Drive letter$	A shared folder that allows administrative personnel to connect to the root directory of a drive, also known as an administrative share. It is shown as A$, B$, C$, D$, and so on. For example, C$ is a shared folder name by which drive C might be accessed by an administrator over the network.
ADMIN$	A resource used by the system during remote administration of a computer. The path of this resource is always the path to the Windows 2000 system root (the directory in which Windows 2000 is installed: for example, C:\WINNT).
IPC$	A resource sharing the named pipes that are essential for communication between programs. It is used during remote administration of a computer and when viewing a computer's shared resources.
PRINT$	A resource used during remote administration of printers.
NETLOGON	A resource used by the Net Logon service of a Windows 2000 Server computer while processing domain logon requests. This resource is provided only for Windows 2000 Server computers. It is not provided for Windows 2000 Professional computers.
FAX$	A shared folder on a server used by fax clients in the process of sending a fax. The shared folder is used to temporarily cache files and access cover pages stored on the server.

Figure 25.34 Access a shared folder using Windows Explorer.

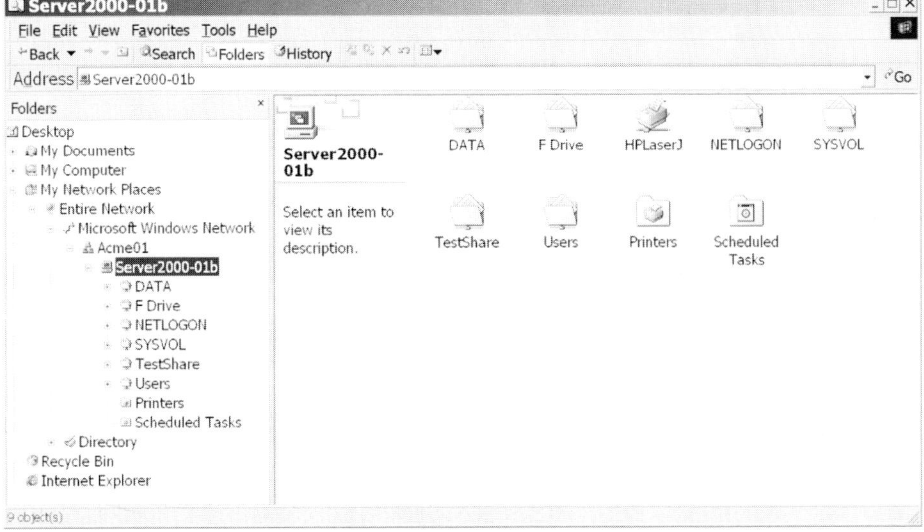

option, and typing the UNC name and then clicking the OK button. By default, all volumes with drive letters automatically have administrative shares (C$, D$, E$, etc). Other administrative shares can be created as needed for individual folders.

The shared drive or directory can then be accessed in one of three ways:

1. Using Network Neighborhood or My Network Places and accessing the resources under the server. See figure 25.34.
2. Specifying the universal naming convention (UNC) using the Run option under the Start button. The UNC format is specified as *\\COMPUTERNAME\SHARENAME.*
3. By selecting the Map Drive button on the toolbar of Network Neighborhood or Microsoft Explorer.

Mapped drives can also be created automatically by login scripts. In addition, newer versions of Windows will remember mapped drives using My Network Places via user profiles.

Anytime you access a share, you must be logged in. If you bypass the Windows 9X login by pressing the Esc key or clicking the Cancel button, you will not be able to access any network resources. In addition, it will use your user name and password by which you are currently logged on to access the shared resource. If the system that you are accessing does not have an account and matching password to access the resource, it will then prompt you for a user name and password.

25.16.2 Simple File Sharing on Windows XP

With Windows XP, Simple File Sharing simplifies share files and documents. You can access Simple File Sharing by opening a folder, selecting the Tools menu, and selecting Options. You can then configure both share and NTFS file system permissions at the folder level. Files and folders that are created in or copied to a folder inherit the permissions that are defined for their parent folder.

With Simple File Sharing, you can configure five levels of permissions. Level 1 is the most private and secure setting, and Level 5 is the most public and changeable (nonsecure) setting.

Access Level	Everyone (NTFS/File)	Owner	System	Administrators	Everyone (Share)
Level 1 My Documents (Private)	NA	Full Control	Full Control	NA	NA
Level 2 My Documents (Default)	NA	Full Control	Full Control	Full Control	NA
Level 3 Files in shared documents available to local users	Read	Full Control	Full Control	Full Control	NA
Level 4 Shared files on the network (readable by everyone)	Read	Full Control	Full Control	Full Control	Read
Level 5 Shared files on the network (readable and writable by everyone)	Change	Full Control	Full Control	Full Control	Full Control

By default, files that are stored in My Documents are at Level 2. To configure the levels, right-click the folder, and then click Sharing and Security to open the Simple File Sharing user interface. To configure Level 3, copy a file or folder into the SHARED DOCUMENTS folder under My Computer. Levels 1, 2, and 3 folders are available only to a user who is logging on locally. This includes users who log on to a Windows XP Professional–based computer from a remote desktop (RDP) session. Levels 4 and 5 folders are available to users who log on locally and to remote users from the network. See figure 25.35.

To configure a folder and all the files in it to Level 1, follow these steps:

1. Right-click the folder, and then click Sharing and Security.
2. Select the Make this folder private check box, and then click OK.

To configure a folder and all the files in it to Level 2, follow these steps:

1. Right-click the folder, and then click Sharing and Security.
2. Make sure that both the Make this folder private and the Share this folder on the network check boxes are cleared, and then click OK.

To configure a file or a folder and all the files in it to Level 3, start Microsoft Windows Explorer, and then copy or move the file or folder to the SHARED DOCUMENTS folder under My Computer.

To configure a folder and all the files in it to Level 4, follow these steps:

1. Right-click the folder, and then click Sharing and Security.
2. Click to select the Share this folder on the network check box.
3. Click to clear the Allow network users to change my files check box, and then click OK.

Figure 25.35 Simple File Sharing in Windows XP

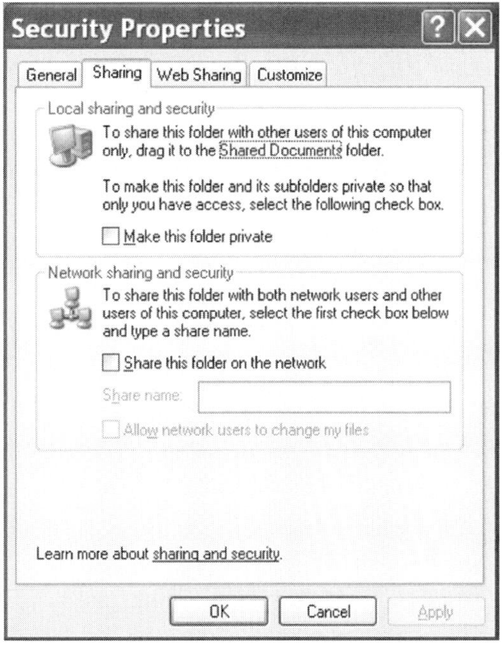

To configure a folder and all the files in it to Level 5, follow these steps:

1. Right-click the folder, and then click Sharing and Security
2. Click to select the Share this folder on the network check box, and then click OK.

Simple File Sharing is always turned on in Windows XP Home Edition–based computers. By default, the Simple File Sharing is turned on in Windows XP Professional–based computers that are joined to a workgroup. Windows XP Professional–based computers that are joined to a domain use only the classic file sharing and security interface. If you turn off Simple File Sharing, you have more control over the permissions to individual users.

When you access the properties of a folder or drive and the Security tab is not available on a Windows XP machine, either the drive is not an NTFS drive or Simple File Sharing is enabled. To turn off Simple File Sharing, follow these steps:

1. Double-click My Computer on the desktop.
2. On the Tools menu, click Folder Options.
3. Click the View tab, and then select the Use Simple File Sharing (Recommended) check box to turn on Simple File Sharing. (Clear this check box to turn off this feature.)

If you turn on and turn off Simple File Sharing, the permissions on files are not changed. The NTFS and share permissions do not change until you change the permissions in the interface.

25.16.3 Linux Sharing

For Linux to create and access NetBIOS shares, you will need to install Samba, which is installed by default in most Linux distributions. Samba supports both user-based and password shares.

In Linux, the easiest way to configure Samba is by using the Samba Web Administration tool (SWAT), which uses a browser interface. Different from other browser-based administration tools, SWAT does not rely on a web server like Apache. Typically, you will need to open the Main menu on the GNOME desktop, select Programs, select System, and then select Samba Configuration. A dialog box will appear asking for a user ID and password. You have to be root in order to configure Samba, so enter root as the user ID and the password for root. You will then click the Global button for universal configuration options and the Shares button to create the shares. See figure 25.36.

Samba shares can be accessed by SMB clients on Windows and Linux platforms. Linux access is via the smbclient and smbmount commands. The smbclient program allows Linux users to access SMB

Figure 25.36 Using SWAT to Create Shares

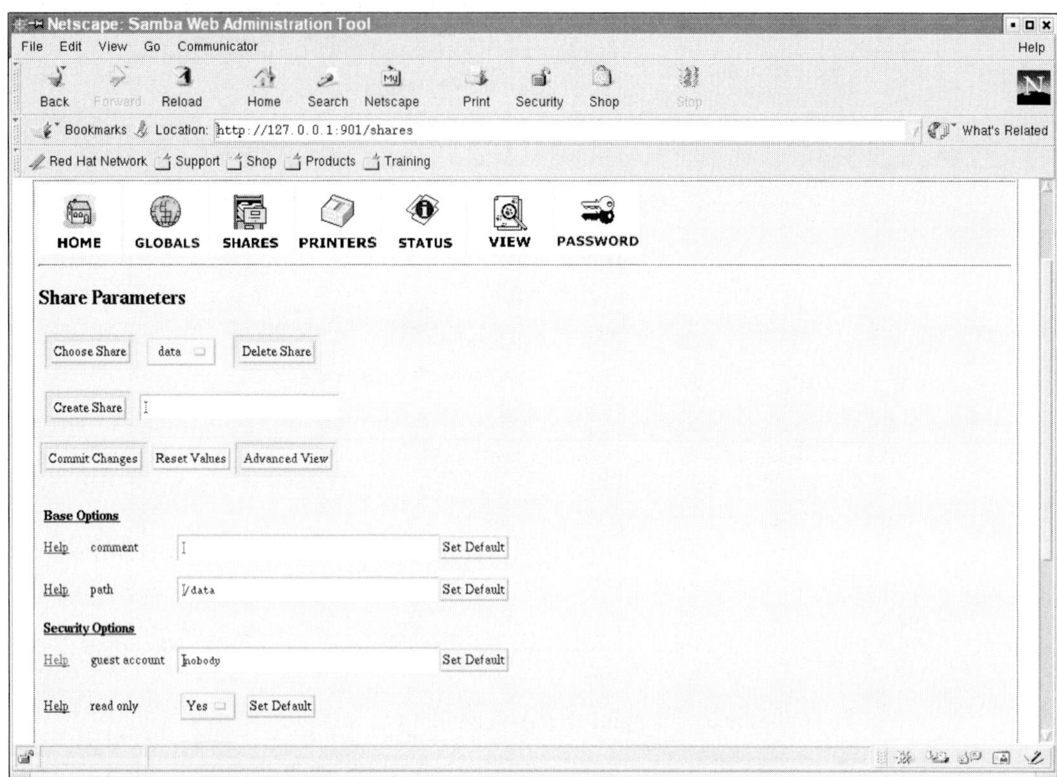

shares on other machines by providing an FTP-like interface that allows you to transfer files with a network share on another computer running an SMB server. Unlike NFS, smbclient does not allow you to mount another share as a local directory. Instead, you use smbmount to mount smb shares. Smbclient provides command-line options to query a server for the shared directories available or to exchange files. To list all of the available shares on the machine with an IP address of 192.168.100.1:

```
smbclient -NL 192.168.100.1
```

Any name resolving to the IP address can be substituted for the IP address. The -N parameter tells smbclient not to query for a password if one isn't needed, and the -L parameter requests the list.

To transfer a file, you must first connect to the Samba server using the following command:

```
smbclient //192.18.100.1/homes -U pregan
```

The *//192.168.100.1/homes* specifies the remote service on the other machine. The -U option enables you to specify the user name you want to connect with. In this case, the command is trying to log in as pregan.

You can specify the password on the command line by appending a percent sign to the user name followed the password:

```
smbclient //192.168.100.1/homes -U pregan%password
```

Although the preceding command is convenient, many versions of UNIX show the password portion of the command in clear text in a ps command. Red Hat Linux 7 installations show the password as a string of *X* characters, but in security-critical environments, it is better to let smbclient prompt for the password and accept it silently.

Most of the time, you will use the smbmount command which enables you to mount a Samba share to a local directory. To create a /mnt/test directory on your local workstation, you would run the following command:

```
mount -t smbfs //192.168.100.1/homes /mnt/test -o
username=pregan, dmask=777, fmask=777
```

This command is a smbmount command, even though it looks like an ordinary mount command. The *-t smbfs* tells the mount command to call smbmount to do the work. The preceding command grants all rights to anyone, via the directory mask (dmask) and the file mask (fmask) arguments.

Another way to use the same command is:

```
smbmount //192.168.100.1/homes /mnt/test -o username=pregan,
dmask=777, fmask=777
```

To unmount it, simply run the following command as user root:

```
umount /mnt/test
```

You can also use smbmount to mount shared Windows resources on a Linux computer. The following mounts Windows share called sharedirectory to the Linux directory/mnt/test directory:

```
mount -t smbfs //computername/sharedirectory /mnt/test
```

This must be done as root. You will be asked for a password. If Windows is in share mode, you would input the password of the share. If you mount a user share, use the –U option followed by a valid user name on the Windows computer. Of course, the user must have rights to the share and the /mnt/test directory must exist.

If you wish to have a smb partition automatically mount during boot, you can add a mount command to a script or you can add a line similar to the following in the fstab line:

```
//192.168.1.1/data /mnt/remote smb username=username,
password=password 1 2
```

Of course, this may not be the most secure method if users can view the fstab file.

25.16.4 Offline Folders

You can make network files available offline by storing shared files on your computer so they are accessible when you are not connected to the network. For example, if you have a notebook computer that you use at work and you wish to do some work at home, you can use offline files to access necessary files.

When you reconnect to the network, any changes that you made to files while working offline are updated to the network. This process is called synchronization. If you and someone else on the network made changes to the same file, you can save your version of the file to the network, keep the other version, or save both.

If you share folders on your computer with others on the network, they can work offline with those folders. To protect files in your shared folders, you can specify whether other users can change your documents or just view them. You can also control which shared files users can access offline.

Any shared files or folders on a Microsoft network can be made available offline. To change offline file access for shared folders:

1. Open My Computer.
2. Right-click a folder or drive that you have shared on the network, and then click Sharing.
3. Click the Caching button.
4. Make sure that the Allow caching of files in this shared folder check box is selected.
5. Select the setting you want.
    - Manual caching of documents—Provides offline access only to those files other users specifically identify. This caching option is ideal for a shared folder containing files that several people will access and modify. Manual caching is the default option when you make a shared folder available offline.
    - Automatic caching of documents—Makes every open file in a shared folder available offline. Older copies of files are automatically deleted to make way for newer versions.
    - Automatic caching of programs and documents—Provides offline access to shared folders containing files that cannot be changed. This caching option reduces network traffic because offline files are opened directly without accessing the network versions. The offline files generally start and run faster than the network versions. When you use automatic caching of programs and documents, be sure to restrict permissions on the files contained in the shared folder to read-only access.

The default cache size is set to 10 percent of available disk space, but you can change this setting. On the Offline Files tab, under Amount of disk space to use for temporary offline files, drag the slider to the right to increase the cache size or to the left to decrease the cache size. To see how much disk space the cache is using, open the OFFLINE FILES folder, and on the File menu, click Properties. You can also use the Shared Folders management console.

25.17 SHARING PRINTERS

Sharing a printer is very similar to sharing files. In windows, you would first install the print driver, using the Add Printer icon in the PRINTERS folder. You would then select the printer and choose the Sharing option. After assigning the printer share name and option password, click on the OK button and a hand will appear under the printer to indicate that it is shared. For Linux machines, select the Printer button in SWAT.

You would then go to the client's computers and run the Add Printer Wizard. Instead of choosing the local printer option, you will be choosing the network printer option. You will be prompted for the UNC name (//computername/sharename) of the printer. When you print to this printer, the print job will then be automatically redirected to the Windows machine and sent to the printer.

25.18 USING NETWORK NEIGHBORHOOD

Network Neighborhood or **My Network Places** is a **browser service** that shows the available network resources in a graphical environment and allows easy access to these resources. See figure 25.37.

After installing the appropriate network software (client software, network card driver, and protocol), the Network Neighborhood or my Network Places is automatically placed on the desktop. Note: For Windows XP, Network Neighborhood is located in the Start menu. When you double-click on the icon, it will open a window that displays computers that have network resources available. By double-clicking on one of the computers listed in the network neighborhood, a new window will open and display the network resources (mostly shared drives, directories, and printers) provided by that computer. See figure 25.38.

Figure 25.37 Network Neighborhood Showing a Computer with Network Services

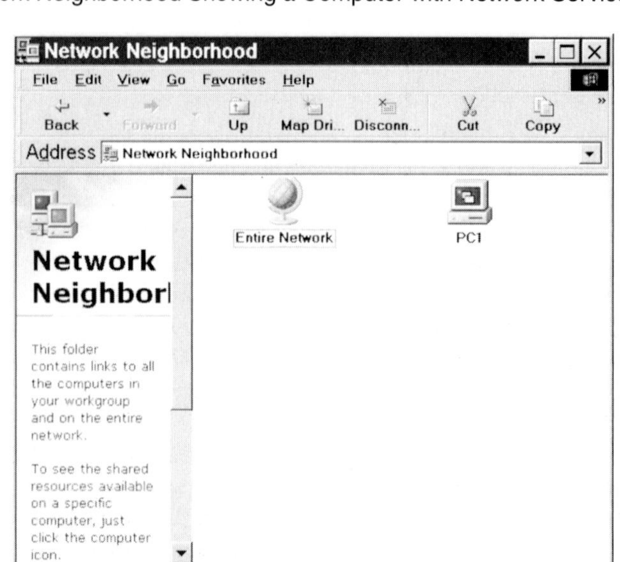

Figure 25.38 Network Resources

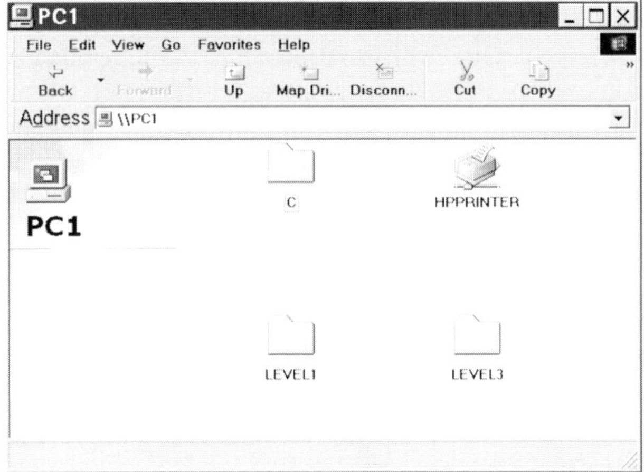

25.19 FIREWALLS

A firewall is a system designed to prevent unauthorized access to or from a private network. Firewalls can be implemented in both hardware and software, or a combination of both. Firewalls are frequently used to prevent unauthorized Internet users from accessing private networks connected to the Internet, especially intranets. All messages entering or leaving the intranet pass through the firewall, which examines each message and blocks those that do not meet the specified security criteria.

There are several types of firewall techniques:

- **Packet Filter**—Looks at each packet entering or leaving the network and accepts or rejects it based on user-defined rules. Packet filtering is fairly effective and transparent to users, but it is difficult to configure. In addition, it is susceptible to IP spoofing.
- **Application Gateway**—Applies security mechanisms to specific applications, such as FTP and Telnet servers. This is very effective, but can impose a performance degradation.
- **Circuit-Level Gateway**—Applies security mechanisms when a TCP or UDP connection is established. Once the connection has been made, packets can flow between the hosts without further checking.
- **Proxy Server**—Intercepts all messages entering and leaving the network. The proxy server effectively hides the true network addresses.

In practice, many firewalls use two or more of these techniques in concert. A firewall is considered a first line of defense in protecting private information.

25.19.1 Proxy Servers

A proxy server has the authority to act on behalf of other computers on the network. The proxy server acts as proxy by providing access to the TCP/IP networks such as the Internet while keeping the workstation address anonymous. The client workstation makes a TCP/IP-based protocol request, such as enter a URL into a web browser to pull up a web page. The client sends the request to the proxy server and waits for the reply. Then, the proxy server receives the request and sends it to the destination address, substituting its server address for the client address. This substitution maintains the anonymity of the client address. Next, the destination processes the request and sends the results back to the proxy server. Finally, the proxy returns the results to the client.

Since the workstation is kept anonymous, the proxy server gives the internal network two major advantages. First, it makes intruder attacks on a machine within the internal network much more difficult since the intruder will not know the address of the machine. Second, you can assign real Internet addresses to the proxy server and assign any addresses to the internal network. Therefore, if you are assigned a class C network, which allows up to 254 computers, and you have a network with 1,000 computers, you only have to assign the class C addresses to the proxy server and those computers connected directly to the Internet. The other computers can be assigned any network addressing scheme as long as they are configured to go through the proxy server to access the Internet.

Proxy servers can dramatically improve performance for groups of users because they save the results of all requests for a certain amount of time. Since certain files are constantly being accessed, these files will already be copied to the proxy server. Therefore, when those files are being accessed, the access will be quick. In addition, since these files don't have to be downloaded through the Internet connection, the connection will be a little bit less congested. Real proxy servers support hundreds or thousands of users. The major online services such as CompuServe and America Online, for example, employ an array of proxy servers.

Proxy servers can also be used to filter requests. For example, a company might use a proxy server to prevent its employees from accessing a specific set of websites.

Microsoft offers Microsoft Proxy Server 2.0 and Internet Security and Acceleration (ISA), which allows clients and servers to access the Internet while keeping your intranet free from intruders. The proxy packages do not ship with Windows.

25.19.2 Personal Firewalls

Today, many operating systems offer personal firewalls to protect an individual computer when connecting to the Internet. For example, Windows 98SE, Windows 2000, and Windows XP have the Internet Connection Firewall (ICF). Much like a full-blown firewall, a personal firewall restricts what information is communicated from your home or small office network to and from the Internet to your computer. See figure 25.39. Unfortunately, the ICF is only a packet filter that filters packets based on IP Addresses and ports. Packet filter is also known as a stateless filter.

Most of the personal firewalls, including the firewall that is included with Windows XP service pack 2, are considered "stateful" firewalls. A stateful firewall is one that monitors all aspects of the communications that cross its path and inspects the source and destination address of each message that it handles. To prevent unsolicited traffic from the public side of the connection from entering the private side, the private firewall keeps a table of all communications that have originated from the computer. Some of these firewalls can be used in conjunction with Internet sharing, which in turn will keep track of all traffic originated from the computers sharing the Internet link. All inbound traffic from the Internet is compared against the entries in the table. Inbound Internet traffic is only allowed to reach the computers in your network when there is a matching entry in the table that shows that the communication exchange began from within your computer or private network. Communications that originate from a *source on the Internet* are dropped by the firewall unless an entry is made using the configuration options of the personal firewall to allow passage.

Figure 25.39 Internet Connection Firewall (Personal Firewall) Used in Windows XP

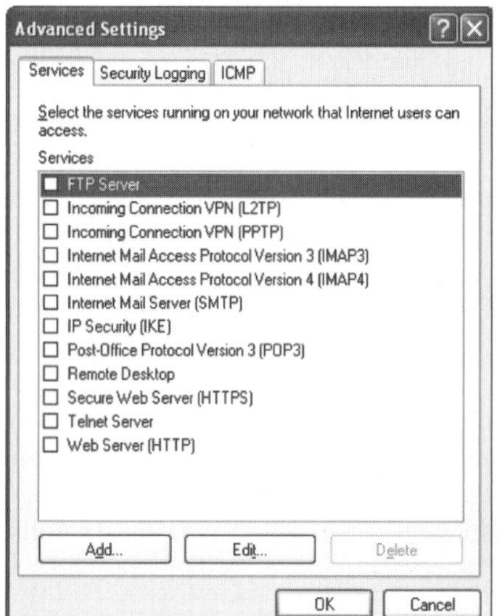

With these personal firewalls, the firewall can be configured to allow unsolicited traffic from the Internet to be forwarded by the computer to the private network. For example, if you are hosting an HTTP web server service and have enabled the HTTP service on your ICF computer, unsolicited HTTP traffic will be forwarded by the computer with the personal firewall to the HTTP web server.

25.20 INTRODUCTION TO WEB PAGES AND WEB SERVERS

The terms "the Internet" and "the World Wide Web" are often used interchangeably, but they have different meanings. The **Internet** refers to the huge global WAN. Until the early 1990s, for one to be able to use a computer to communicate with another computer via the Internet required a good deal of knowledge and the ability to understand and use some fairly unfriendly commands. The **World Wide Web (WWW)** was created in 1992, and refers to the means of organizing, presenting, and accessing information over the Internet.

To access the web, a user would be using these important technologies:

1. HTML
2. web server
3. web browser
4. HTTP and FTP

Web pages are written using the **Hypertext Markup Language (HTML)**. This language is pretty simple and is implemented as special ASCII tags or codes that you embed within your document to give the browser a general idea of how the information should be displayed. The browsers understand the standard HTML tags, although they may display the same document a little differently. If you want your documents to be accessible by people using different browsers, stick with the standard tags. The HTML standard is still actively evolving, so new tags are constantly becoming available to support new browser features. See figures 25.40 and 25.41.

A **web server** is a computer equipped with the server software that uses Internet protocols such as Hypertext Transfer Protocol (HTTP) and File Transfer Protocol (FTP) to respond to web client requests

Figure 25.40 Web Page

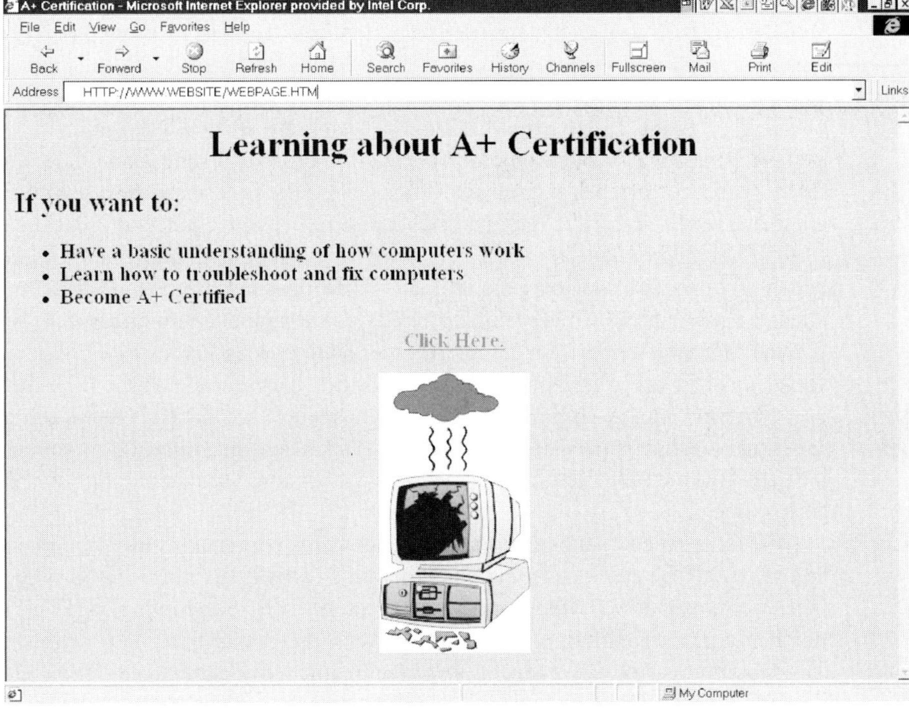

Figure 25.41 HTML Code for the Web Page Shown in Figure 25.40

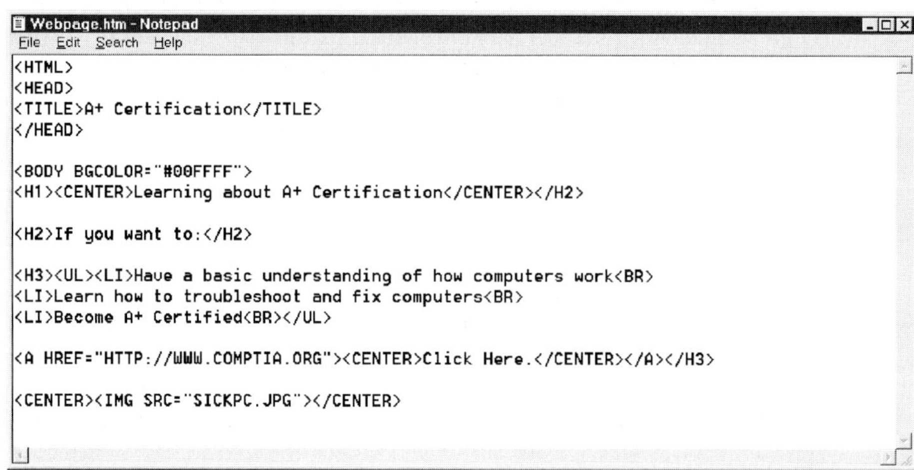


```
<HTML>
<HEAD>
<TITLE>A+ Certification</TITLE>
</HEAD>

<BODY BGCOLOR="#00FFFF">
<H1><CENTER>Learning about A+ Certification</CENTER></H2>

<H2>If you want to:</H2>

<H3><UL><LI>Have a basic understanding of how computers work<BR>
<LI>Learn how to troubleshoot and fix computers<BR>
<LI>Become A+ Certified<BR></UL>

<A HREF="HTTP://WWW.COMPTIA.ORG"><CENTER>Click Here.</CENTER></A></H3>

<CENTER><IMG SRC="SICKPC.JPG"></CENTER>
```

on a TCP/IP network via web browsers. One server can service a large number of clients. There are several free server programs available on the Internet. Most web browsers are built to process two basic types of requests—File Server and Database Server requests. New features are always being added to provide additional support for new technology. A web server acting as a file server simply accepts a request for a document, validates the request, and sends the requested files back to the browser. In addition, the browser can act as a front-end tool or interface to collect data and feed it in a database or script. The database can be located either on the same server as the web server or on a different server. When the database responds with the results, it will then send the results back to the browser.

The **web browser** is the client program/software that you run on your local machine to gain access to a web server. It receives the HTML commands, interprets the HTML, and displays the results. It is strictly a user-interface/document presentation tool. It knows nothing about the application it is attached to and only knows how to take the information from the server and present it to the user. It is also able to capture data entry made into a Form and get the information back to the server for processing. The most common browsers are Microsoft Internet Explorer and Netscape Communicator. Both of these tools are available for little or no charge on the Internet.

The application protocol that makes the web work is **Hypertext Transfer Protocol** or **HTTP.** While the HTML is the language used to write web pages, HTTP is the protocol that web browsers and web servers use to communicate with each other over the Internet. It is an application-level protocol because it sits on top of the TCP layer in the protocol stack and is used by specific applications to talk to one another. In this case the applications are web browsers and web servers.

HTTP is a text-based protocol. Clients (web browsers) send requests to web servers for web elements such as web pages and images. After the request is serviced by a server, the connection between client and server across the Internet is disconnected. A new connection must be made for each request. Most protocols are connection-oriented, meaning that the two computers communicating with each other keep the connection open over the Internet. HTTP does not. Before an HTTP request can be made by a client, a new connection must be made to the server. Another common protocol is the **File Transfer Protocol (FTP),** which is used on the Internet to send or download files. Note: When a user accesses an FTP server, most FTP servers anonymously authenticate the users so no user names or passwords are needed.

Currently, most web browsers and servers support **HTTP 1.1.** One of the main features of HTTP 1.1 is that it supports persistent connections. This means that once a browser connects to a web server, it can receive multiple files through the same connection. This should improve performance by as much as 20 percent.

HTTP is called a stateless protocol because each command is executed independently, without any knowledge of the commands that came before it. This is the main reason why it is difficult to implement websites that react intelligently to user input. This shortcoming of HTTP is being addressed in a number of new technologies, including ActiveX, Java, JavaScript, and cookies.

Most companies with connections to the Internet have implemented firewall solutions to protect the corporate network from unauthorized users coming in and unauthorized Internet sessions going out via the Internet. But while firewalls guard against intrusion or unauthorized use, they cannot guarantee the security of the link between a workstation and server on opposite sides of a firewall nor the security of the actual message being conveyed.

To create this level of security, two related Internet protocols, **Secure Sockets Layer (SSL),** ensure that sensitive information from passing through an Internet link is safe from prying eyes. SSL is designed to establish a secure connection between two computers. Secure Sockets Layer operates between the application and transport and layer and operates with application layer services such as at the HTTP, FTP, NNTP, and SMTP. When both a client (usually in the form of a web browser) and a server support SSL, any data transmitted between two becomes encrypted. It supports both server and client authentication and is designed to negotiate encryption keys as well as to authenticate the server before any data is exchanged.

When an SSL-client wants to communicate with an SSL-compliant server, an SSL handshake will occur, which starts when the client initiates a request to the server. After this handshake process, which results in the client and server agreeing on the security level, all data transfer between that client and that server for a particular session is encrypted using the session key. When a secure link has been created, the first part of the URL will change from http:// to https://. SSL supports several cryptographic algorithms to handle the authentication and encryption routines. Although SSL is optimized for use with HTTP, it can also be used with FTP or other relevant protocols. Note: While HTTP uses TCP port 80, HTTPS uses port 443.

The **Transport Layer Security (TLS)** protocol is based on and similar to SSL version 3 and is a draft standard of the IETF. TLS is essentially the latest version of SSL, but is not as widely available in browsers. Its primary goal is to provide privacy and data integrity between two communicating applications. While TLS protocol is based on Netscape's SSL 3.0 protocol, TLS and SSL are not interoperable. The TLS protocol does contain a mechanism that allows TLS implementation to back down to SSL 3.0. The most recent browser versions support TLS.

Common 40- or 56-bit web browsers are considered to have weak encryption because their keys can be cracked in a short time. The stronger browsers will use 128-bit ciphers, which would require more time and commitment of resources to break. Most SSL/TLS-enabled web servers allow the customization of types of encryption and what key sizes can and cannot be used while a connection is made.

Typically when accessing a web page, you will specify the web page location by using a **Uniform Resource Locator** or **URL.** The first part of the address indicates what protocol to use, and the second part specifies the IP address or the domain name where the resource is located. The last part indicates the folder and file name. See figure 25.42.

ftp://www.acme.com/files/run.exe
http://www.acme.com/index.html

When you type a URL into a web browser, this is what happens:

1. If the URL contains a domain name, the browser first connects to a DNS server and retrieves the corresponding IP address for the web server.
2. The web browser connects to the web server and sends an HTTP request (via the protocol stack) for the desired web page.
3. The web server receives the request and checks for the desired page. If the page exists, the web server sends it. If the server cannot find the requested page, it will send an HTTP *404* error message. (404 means "Page Not Found," as anyone who has surfed the web probably knows.)
4. The web browser receives the page back and the connection is closed.
5. The browser then parses through the page and looks for other page elements it needs to complete the web page. These usually include images, applets, and so on.

Figure 25.42 Typical URL

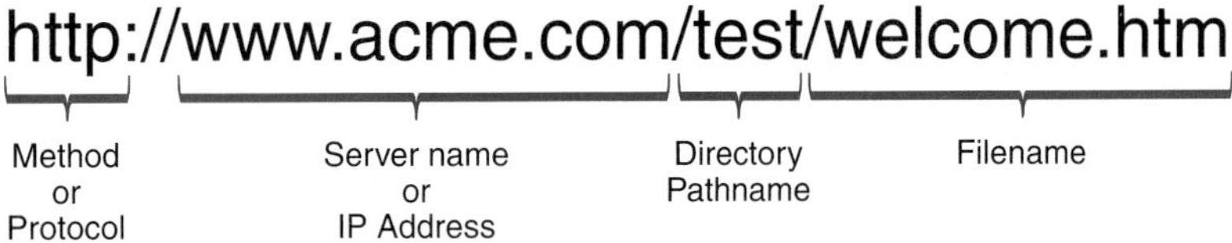

Table 25.14 Three-Letter Codes Indicating the Type of Organization

Code	Meaning
com	Commercial
edu	Educational
gov	Government
int	International organization
mil	Military
net	Network related
org	Miscellaneous organization

6. For each element needed, the browser makes additional connections and HTTP requests to the server for each element.
7. When the browser has finished loading all images, applets, and so forth, the page will be completely loaded in the browser window.

The COM extension is an example of a top-level domain. The top-level domain indicates a country, region, or type of organization. Three-letter codes indicate the type of organization. For example, COM indicates Commercial (business) and EDU stands for educational institution. They are listed in table 25.14.

Two-letter codes indicate countries, which follow the International Standard 3166. For example, CA stands for Canada, AU for Australia, FR for France, and UK for United Kingdom.

A **gopher** was a system predating the World Wide Web for organizing and displaying files on Internet servers. A gopher server presents its contents as a hierarchically structured list of files. Gophers have been basically replaced by search engines.

Since the Internet is so vast, consisting of countless web pages, it is often difficult to know the URL that a person wants. Therefore, the World Wide Web has several search engines that can be used to locate desired documents. A **search engine** is a program that searches documents for specified keywords and returns a list of the documents where the keywords were found. Typically, a search engine works by sending out a spider to fetch as many documents as possible. Another program, called an indexer, then reads these documents and creates an index based on the words contained in each document. Each search engine uses a proprietary algorithm to create its indices such that, ideally, only meaningful results are returned for each query.

25.21 CONNECTING TO THE INTERNET

The Internet is a global network connecting millions of computers. Today, the Internet has millions of users in countries throughout the world. Unlike online services such as AOL, Prodigy, and Compuserve, the Internet is decentralized by design. People can connect to the Internet through their employers who are part of the Internet or can gain access by using an online service, or **Internet service provider (ISP)**. For a monthly fee, the service provider gives you a software package, user name, password, and access phone number. Equipped with a modem, you can then log on to the Internet and browse the World Wide Web and USENET, and send and receive email.

Some computers can be connected using a dial-up connection via a modem. Other computers that need a faster connection can connect through a local area network that connects to the Internet by using a T-1 or E-1 (or faster) leased line or ISDN–PRI dial-up connection or connect using less expensive methods such as a cable modem, DSL line, or ISDN–BRI. See table 25.15. Other methods also include wireless technology (including satellite connection).

If you are using a dial-up connection, you would need a phone number to dial into. Many ISPs (remote access, cable, DSL, or ISDN) use CHAP or PAP authentication, which would require user names and passwords. Depending on your ISP and the options that you choose, you may need to specify a static IP address, subnet mask, default gateway, and DNS server while others will be assigned dynamically.

Table 25.15 WAN and Remote Access Technology

Carrier Technology	Speed	Physical Medium	Connection Type	Comment
Plain Old Telephone Service (POTS)	Up to 56 Kbit/s	Twisted-pair	Circuit switch	Used by home and small business
Asymmetrical Digital Subscriber Line Lite (ADSL Lite)	Up to 1.544 Mbit/s downstream Up to 512 Kbit/s upstream	2 twisted-pair	Circuit switch	Used by home and small business
Asymmetrical Digital Subscriber Line (ADSL)	1.5–8 Mbit/s downstream Up to 1.544 Mbit/s upstream	2 twisted-pair	Circuit switch	Used by small to medium business
High Bit-Rate Digital Subscriber Line (HDSL)	1.544 Mbit/s full duplex (T1) 2.048 Mbit/s full duplex (E1)	2 pair of twisted-pair	Circuit switch	Used by small to medium business
DS0 Leased Line	64 Kbit/s	1 or 2 pair of twisted-pair	Dedicated point-to-point	The base signal on a channel in the set of digital signal levels
Switched 56	56 Kbit/s	1 or 2 pair of UTP	Circuit switch	Used by home and small business
Switched 64	64 Kbit/s	1 or 2 pair of UTP	Circuit switch	Used by home and small business
Fractional T-1 Leased Line	64 Kbit/s to 1.536 Mbit/s in 64-Kbit/s increments	1 or 2 pair of twisted-pair	Dedicated point-to-point	Used by small to medium business
T-1 Leased Line (DS-1)	1.544 Mbit/s (24–64 Kbit/s channels)	2 pair UTP or UTP or optical fiber	Dedicated point-to-point	Used by medium to large business, ISP to connect to the Internet
T-3 Leased Line (DS-3)	44.736 Mbit/s	2 pair of UTP or optical fiber	Dedicated point-to-point	Used by large business, large ISP to connect to the Internet or as the backbone of the Internet
E-1	2.048 Mbit/s	Twisted-pair, coaxial cable, or optical fiber		32-channel European equivalent of T-1
ISDN–BRI	64–128 Kbit/s	1 or 2 pair of UTP	Circuit switch	Used by home and small business
ISDN–PRI	23–64 Kbit/s channels plus control channel up to 1.544 Mbit/s (T-1) or 2.048 (E1)	2 pair of UTP	Circuit switch	Used by medium to large business
FDDI/FDDI-2	100 Mbit/s/200 Mbit/s	Optical fiber	Packet switch	Large, wide-range LAN usually in a large company or a larger ISP
Cable Modems	500 Kbit/s to 1.5 Mbit/s or more	Coaxial cable	Leased point-to-point	Used by home and small business

To configure a client with Windows 95 and 98 to dial up a remote access server and connect using PPP and Windows 9X Dial-Up Networking (DUN), follow these steps:

1. Click on the Start button, select the Programs option, select the Accessories option, select Communications, and then select Dial-up Networking to open the Dial-up Networking dialog box.
2. Double-click Make New Connection and click the Next button.
3. Type the name of the system you will be dialing into in the Type a Name for the Computer You are Dialing text box. This field defaults to My Connection. Select the modem installed in your computer that you want to use for this connection from the Select a Device drop-down list. Click the Next button.
4. Enter the area code and phone numbers, and click the Next button.
5. The last screen informs you that you have successfully created the connection. Click the Finish button to return to the Dial-up Networking dialog box.
6. Right-click the connection you just made, and choose Properties from the shortcut menu.
7. Click the Server Types tab, and from the Type of Dial-Up Server drop-down list choose PPP: Windows 95, Windows NT 3.5, Internet. If you enable Require encrypted password, the client will use only Challenge Handshake Authentication Protocol and MS-CHAP encryption when generating a password. If this option is not selected, the client can also perform Password Authentication Protocol (PAP) if the server requests it. If you select the Require data encryption option, the client will refuse to connect with any server that does not use data encryption. Data encryption requires that the client and server share a common key, which is generated at connection time using Microsoft Challenge Handshake Authentication (MS-CHAP).
8. Clear the options you won't be using to connect to the server. For PPP connections, you can usually clear Log On to Network, NetBEUI, and IPX/SPX Compatibility.
9. Click OK to save the settings.

You can now double-click the connection you made, enter your user name and password, and click Connect to establish the connection.

To configure a client with Windows XP to dial up a remote access and connect using PPP, follow these steps:

1. Click on the Start button, select All Programs, Accessories, Communications, and New Connection Wizard. When the wizard starts, click on the Next button.
2. Select the Connect to the Network At My Workplace and click on the Next button.
3. Select the Dial-Up Connection and click the Next button.
4. Type in your company name and click the Next button.
5. Type in the phone number that you want to call and click the Next button.
6. Click on the Finish button.
7. To show all connections, click on the Start button, select the Connect to option and select Show all connections.
8. To connect to the computer, double-click the icon representing your new connection.
9. To configure the connection, click on the Properties button.
10. Select the Networking tab to select PPP or SLIP. PPP as the default.
11. Select the Security tab.
12. To enable secure passwords, select the required secure passwords or use smart cards.
13. To enable data encryption, select the Require data encryption. Data is encrypted only if MS-CHAP, MS-CHAP v2, or EAP/TLS authentication is negotiated since these are the only authentication protocols that generate their own initial encryption keys, which are required for encryption. Microsoft Point-to-Point Encryption (MPPE) encrypts data in PPP-based dial-up connections. Strong (128-bit key) and standard (40-bit key) MPPE encryption schemes are supported.
14. If you select the Advanced option and click on the Settings button, you can configure to require encryption and allow or disallow various authentication protocols (EAP, PAP, SPAP, CHAP, MS-CHAP, and MS-CHAP v2).
15. Click the OK button to close the Properties dialog box.
16. To make the connection, click the Dial button.

To connect to the Internet in Windows XP, do the following:

1. Click on the Start button, select All Programs, Accessories, Communications, and New Connection Wizard. When the wizard starts, click on the Next button.
2. Select the Connect to the Internet option and click on the Next button.
3. Select the Set Up My Connection manually. Click on the Next button.
4. Select the Connect using a dial-up modem. Click on the Next button.
5. Type in the ISP name and click on the Next button.
6. Type in the phone number to your ISP.
7. Enter your user name and password.
8. Click on the Next button.
9. To connect to the computer, double-click the icon representing your new connection.
10. To configure the connection, click on the Properties button.
11. To configure PPP, select the Networking tab.
12. To configure the security options (authentication and encryption), select the Security tab.
13. Click the OK button to close the Properties dialog box.
14. To make the connection, click the Dial button.

If you have a DSL or cable modem, you need to set up a connection to your ISP in Windows XP, do the following:

1. Click on the Start button, select All Programs, Accessories, Communications, and New Connection Wizard. When the wizard starts, click on the Next button.
2. Select the Connect to the Internet connection. Click the Next button.
3. Select the Set Up My Connection manually and click on the Next button.
4. Select the Connect using a broadband connection that requires a user name and password. If you want to always be connected through your broadband connection, use the Connect using a broadband connection that is always on.
5. Type in your ISP name and click on the Next button.
6. Type in your user name and password.
7. Click on the Properties button.
8. Click on the Networking tab and notice that the type of broadband connection is PPPOE.
9. Click on the Security options to configure authentication and encryption.
10. Click on the OK button to close the Properties dialog box.
11. To connect through your DSL, click on the OK button.

Often ISP providers provide email and newsgroup (NNTP) services. To send email, you will use the Simple Mail Transfer Protocol (SMTP) and to retrieve email, you would use Pop Office Protocol 3 (POP3) or the Internet Message Access Protocol 4 (IMAP4). If you are using email software, you will have to specify the name or addresses of the SMTP and POP3 or IMAP4 servers. You will also need to know the username and password for the email account. To communicate on newsgroups, you need to specify the IP address of your ISP's NNTP server.

The main lines of the Internet, called the *Internet backbone,* are the biggest networks in the system and are owned by major Internet service providers such as GTE, MCI, Sprint, UUNet, and AOL's ANS. By connecting to each other, these networks have created a superfast pipeline that crisscrosses the United States and extends throughout the world. Because the U.S. backbone has many intersecting points, if one part fails or slows down, data can be rerouted over another part. In the United States, there are also five points—located in San Francisco, San Jose (California), Chicago, Pennsauken (New Jersey), near New York, and Washington, DC—that form networks owned by smaller regional and local ISPs, which, in turn, lease access to companies and individuals in the areas they serve.

25.22 TROUBLESHOOTING NETWORKS

Much like any other computer problem, a network problem can be caused by hardware or software. Of these, cables cause about 50 percent of all network problems. Having an understanding of how the cables are connected together and how the signals travel through the cable system gives you a solid foundation for isolating and correcting cable problems.

When experiencing a network failure, you must first determine what is affected by the network failure. If only one computer is affected, it is most likely the cable that connects to the individual computer, a bad network card, or the driver and client software is installed or configured incorrectly. If multiple computers have failed, you will need to look for a network item that is common to all of the computers. If you are using a star topology, look for a hub or MAU, or a single cable that connects the hub or MAU to the rest of the network. If you are using a backbone cable such as a coaxial cable, look to see if there is a break anywhere within the backbone cable. Remember that a break will cause ends that are not terminated.

Example 25.3:

The computer cannot make a network connection after a network card has been connected.

First, make sure that the network cable is connected properly and that the network card connection light is on. If the problem still exists, make sure that the network driver, protocol, and network client software is installed and configured properly, including making sure that the proper protocol is loaded and the proper addresses are assigned. If all the software seems to be configured properly, check the card for resource conflicts (I/O address, IR, DMA, and memory addresses). Lastly, suspect a faulty cable or card.

Example 25.4:

A modem is not making a network connection.

First, make sure that the modem is connected properly. If the modem seems to be working, make sure that the modem is connected properly, including the dial-up network software, the software driver for the modem, the protocol, and the proper phone number. (Note: Some telephone connections within a company require a 9 to be dialed to get an outside line.) If the problem still exists, check the modem for resource conflicts (I/O address, IRQ, DMA, and memory addresses).

Example 25.5:

The computer cannot communicate with a TCP/IP computer.

First, make sure the network cable is connected properly and that the network card connection light is on. If the problem still exists, make sure that the network driver, protocol is loaded and the proper addresses, subnet mask, and gateway are assigned (using WINIPCFG, IPCONFIG, or IFCONFIG). If all the software seems to be configured properly, check the card for resource conflicts (I/O address, IRQ, DMA, and memory addresses). Try to ping yourself or ping the loopback address (127.0.0.1) to verify that TCP/IP is loaded. Then try to ping a computer on the same network as you to verify that you are connected to the network. If that does not work, suspect a faulty cable or card. Try to ping your router to see if your router is running. Then try to ping the far side of the router to see if the router is routing. Then ping the IP address of the remote host. If you ping both ports on the router and you cannot connect to the far computer, the computer that you are connecting to is having problems.

SUMMARY

1. A network is two or more computers connected together to share resources.
2. Most computers communicate with the network by a cable attached to the computer's network interface card (NIC); a few computers can use some form of wireless technology (infrared, microwaves, or radio waves).
3. A server is a computer that is a dedicated service provider, and a client is a computer that requests services.
4. A network that is made up of dedicated servers and clients is known as a client/server network.
5. A peer-to-peer network has no dedicated servers. Instead, all computers provide services and request services equally.

6. A LAN connects computers within a close geographical network, such as in a building or on a college campus.
7. The network interface card (NIC), sometimes referred to as the network adapter card or network card, is the physical interface, or connection, between the computer and the network cable.
8. A workgroup is a group of computers that can send email to one another, share data files, and schedule meetings.
9. A domain is a group of computers and devices on a network that are administrated as a unit with common rules and procedures.
10. A network operating system (NOS) includes special functions for connecting computers and devices to a local area network (LAN), to manage the resources and services of the network, and to provide network security for multiple users.
11. The common cable types used in networks include unshielded twisted pair, shielded twisted pair, coaxial, and fiber-optic.
12. Twisted pair cable use two insulated strands of copper wire twisted around each other. The twist in the cable helps reduce crosstalk.
13. The unshielded twisted pair (UTP) cable, which uses the 10BaseT specification, resembles telephone cable with an RJ-45 connector and is quickly becoming the most popular LAN cable.
14. Coaxial cable has a solid copper core surrounded by insulation, a braided metal shielding, and an outer cover.
15. To prevent signals from bouncing back when they reach the end of the cable, coaxial cables have terminating resistors on both ends.
16. The thinnest type of coaxial cable connects to the network card with BNC and T-connectors.
17. Fiber-optic cable is made of glass or fiberglass so that it can transmit light instead of electricity.
18. The three types of connectors used in fiber optic cables are the ST, SC, and MJ-45 connectors.
19. In buildings, the plenum is the space above the ceiling and below the floors used to circulate air throughout the workplace. If there is a fire, it becomes evident that the plenum will also circulate the toxic fumes generated by the burning of cabling.
20. A plenum cable is a special cable that gives off little or no toxic fumes when burned.
21. Network topology refers to the arrangement, or physical layout, of connected computers and cables.
22. The bus topology, known as linear bus, is the simplest network configuration in that a single cable (called a backbone, a trunk, or segment) connects all of the computers in series.
23. A ring topology connects computers in a circle or loop with no ends.
24. The star topology, the most common network configuration, connects computers to a central device known as a hub.
25. A bridge is a device that connects two local area networks or two segments of the same local area network.
26. A router connects two local area networks and also filters for certain protocols.
27. The Internet is a global network connecting millions of computers.
28. The two most common services provided by a network are file and print sharing.
29. A protocol is a set of rules or standards designed to enable computers and peripheral devices to connect to one another to exchange information with as little error as possible.
30. While local area networks can be Ethernet, Token Ring, or ARCnet, today, most local area networks are Ethernet networks.
31. The TCP/IP (transmission control protocol/ Internet protocol) is an industrial suite of protocols upon which the Internet is based.
32. IPX (Internetwork packet exchange) is the networking protocol used by the Novel NetWare operating system and Windows NT servers.
33. People can connect to the Internet through their employers who are part of the Internet, or can gain access by using an online service or Internet service provider (ISP).
34. The World Wide Web (WWW), a subset of the Internet, is a huge collection of interlinked documents called web pages written in hypertext markup language (HTML).
35. The Hypertext Transfer Protocol (HTTP) is the basis for exchange over the World Wide Web.
36. The HTTPS is an encrypted form of the HTTP so that the information sent over the Internet is secure.
37. To get email, you would use SMTP and the POP or IMAP protocol. The SMTP (short for simple mail transfer protocol), is the standard protocol for the exchange of electronic mail over the Internet. The POP (Short for Post Office Protocol (POP) and IMAP (short for Internet Message Access Protocol) are used to retrieve the email, and they define a simple interface between a user's mail client software and email server.
38. The file transfer protocol (FTP) allows users to transfer files between local and remote host computers.
39. A firewall is a system designed to prevent unauthorized access to or from a private network.
40. A proxy server has the authority to act on behalf of other computers on the network. The proxy server acts as the go-between or middleman by providing access to the TCP/IP networks such as the Internet while keeping the workstation's address anonymous.
41. Today, many operating systems offer personal firewalls to protect an individual computer when connecting to the Internet.
42. The personal firewall for Windows XP is the Internet Connection Firewall and Windows Firewall (Service Pack 2 only).

QUESTIONS

1. Which of the following is *not* a network resource?
   a. email
   b. file sharing
   c. print sharing
   d. IRQ sharing
2. Which of the following statements best describes a peer-to-peer network?
   a. A peer-to-peer network allows centralized administration of files and other network resources.
   b. A peer-to-peer network requires a centralized dedicated server.
   c. A peer-to-peer network provides the user the ability to manage his or her own shared resources.
   d. A peer-to-peer network requires at least one administrator to provide centralized resource administration.
3. Which of the following is a computer that handles requests from client computers for data and processing resources?
   a. a peer
   b. a client
   c. a server
   d. a LAN
4. Which type of network is a small network that is usually confined to a building or campus?
   a. LAN
   b. MAN
   c. enterprise WAN
   d. global WAN
5. A client machine cannot connect to the network but all the other computers in the network can. Which of the following is the most likely cause of the problem?
   a. a faulty coaxial cable on a bus topology
   b. a faulty network adapter card on the server
   c. a faulty network adapter card on the client computer
   d. too much traffic on the network
6. Pat has just installed a network adapter card in his computer, but the operating system is unable to detect the network adapter card. Which of the following is the most likely cause of the problem?
   a. the wrong protocol
   b. a resource conflict, such as an IRQ or DMA conflict
   c. a faulty cable
   d. a faulty terminating resistor
7. An NE2000-compatible card is configured to use IRQ 3 and I/O address 0x300. Which device is the card conflicting with?
   a. COM1
   b. COM2
   c. LPT1
   d. LPT2
8. You connect the leads from a digital multimeter (DMM) to each of the conductors in a twisted-pair cable. Which of the following settings should you use on the DMM to see if there is a short?
   a. resistance
   b. capacitance
   c. dc voltage
   d. ac voltage
   e. current
9. What is the minimum category of UTP cable required for an ethernet network running at 10 megabits?
   a. Category 1
   b. Category 2
   c. Category 3
   d. Category 4
   e. Category 5
10. Which of the following refers to signal overflow from an adjacent wire?
    a. attenuation
    b. crosstalk
    c. beaconing
    d. jitter
    e. chattering
    f. jabbering
11. A 10BaseT network uses what type of connector?
    a. RJ-11 connectors
    b. RJ-45 connectors
    c. UTP cabling
    d. BNC-T connectors
    e. 50 ohm terminating resistors
12. Which of the following refers to an element of an ethernet 10Base2 network (choose all that apply)?
    a. Category 3, 4, or 5 UTP cable
    b. RJ-11 connectors
    c. RJ-45 connectors
    d. BNC connectors
    e. 50 ohm terminating resistors
13. Which of the following access methods checks for network traffic before sending data?
    a. CSMA/CD
    b. testing
    c. token passing
    d. polling
14. Which of the following devices would you use to enable communications between dissimilar LANs that use different protocols?
    a. bridges
    b. routers
    c. gateways
    d. repeaters
15. The universal naming convention (UNC) provides a way for computers on the network to identify each other. Which of the following are included in a UNC string (select all that apply)?
    a. a domain name
    b. a computer name
    c. a workgroup name
    d. a share name
16. Which layer of the OSI model defines how cable is attached to a network adapter card?
    a. the cable layer
    b. the connection layer
    c. the hardware layer
    d. the physical layer
17. Which of the following uses 15-character names to identify computers on a network?
    a. TCP/IP
    b. IPX/SPX
    c. NetBIOS
    d. AppleTalk
18. Which of the following are dial-up communication protocols (choose two answers)?
    a. FTP
    b. PPP
    c. TCP
    d. SLIP

19. Pat is not able to access network resources from her computer. When she plugs her Ethernet cable into a coworker's machine, she is able to access the network without difficulty. Which of the following network components is causing the problem?
a. the server
b. the router or gateway
c. the cable
d. the network adapter

20. You have just installed a 28,800 bps fax modem on a Windows 95 computer. What else do you need to do to connect to an Internet access provider (select two answers)?
a. install TCP/IP
b. install dial-up networking
c. install remote access services
d. install the Microsoft Network

21. When configuring a new network interface card for installation, which of the following would be a valid I/O address?
a. 378 b. 2F8
c. 3F8 d. 360

22. The Internet uses which network protocol?
a. IPX b. TCP/IP
c. NetBEUI d. token passing

23. A standard naming scheme used to identify web pages on the Internet is
a. TCP/IP. b. NetBIOS.
c. URL. d. naming.

24. The language used to write web pages read by a browser is
a. HTML. b. URL.
c. HTTP. d. TCP/IP.
e. BASIC.

25. Which network type is contention based?
a. ATM b. ARCnet
c. token ring d. FDDI
e. Ethernet

26. What action should you take to troubleshoot a jabbering, chattering, or streaming network board or transceiver?
a. Check for improperly removed T-connectors.
b. Use a multimeter to check the resistance at a connection point.
c. Use a cable continuity-testing device to make sure the cable is intact.
d. Divide the network into smaller and smaller parts until the offending device is found.

27. Which network uses a logical ring topology (choose two answers)?
a. FDDI b. Ethernet
c. ARCnet d. token ring

28. Which statement describes the physical star network topology?
a. Every node must be properly terminated.
b. Every node is connected to a central device.
c. Every node has a direct connection to the backbone.
d. Every node has a separate cable connected it to every other node on the network.

29. Approximately what percentage of network failures are caused by cabling problems?
a. 10% b. 25%
c. 50% d. 85%

30. Which term describes your network connection if your computer can send and receive network data at the same time?
a. full-duplex b. half-duplex
c. simplex d. double-duplex
e. connected-oriented

31. Your 10 Mbit/s Ethernet network has 10/100 autoswitching hubs. Category 5 UTP cabling, and 10 Mbit/s network cards in all workstations and servers. What is the least expensive way to increase the bandwidth of your network?
a. Replace UTP cabling with coax.
b. Install 100 Mbit/s network cards in all computers.
c. Manually configure hubs for 100 Mbit/s operation.
d. Install fiber cabling and network cards for all workstations.

32. What are the characteristics of Ethernet using UTP cable (choose four)?
a. It is easy to install.
b. It is proven technology.
c. It performs well under high loads.
e. It is an inexpensive way to get high-speed transmission.
f. It works with numerous LAN and micro-to-mainframe applications.
g. It has built-in troubleshooting mechanisms, such as beaconing and auto-configuration.

33. Which statement about 10Base2 network segments is true?
a. You must terminate and ground both ends of every segment.
b. You must never terminate or ground either end of any segment.
c. You must terminate both ends of every segment and ground one end.
d. You must terminate both ends of every segment but do not ground either end.

34. Which wires would receive data on a 10BaseT network?
a. 1 and 2 b. 4 and 5
c. 3 and 6 d. 7 and 8

35. Which protocol is most closely associated with Windows networking?
a. DLC b. SPX/IPX
c. TCP/IP d. NetBEUI

36. How many wires does 100BaseTX uses to transmit and receive data?
a. 2 b. 6
c. 4 d. 8

37. You manually assigned a TCP/IP address to a computer connected to the company network.

The computer uses the same TCP/IP address every time it attaches to the network. Rebooting the computer does not change this fact. Where is the TCP/IP address for a computer workstation stored?
   a. BIOS
   b. boot Sector on the hard disk
   c. computer operating system
   d. ROM on the network interface card

38. Which protocol requires software to configure unique addresses for each host?
   a. DLC b. SPX/IPX
   c. TCP/IP d. NetBEUI

39. Which statements are true about IPX/SPX (choose two answers)?
   a. It is routable.
   b. It requires an administrator to configure addresses.
   c. It was originally developed for NetWare-based networks.
   d. It is the default networking protocol for Windows desktops.

40. When installing the network components in Windows 98, which of the following components are required to connect to the network (choose all that apply)?
   a. network client software
   b. network service
   c. network protocol
   d. network card driver

41. To connect to a Windows NT network, install
   a. Client Software for Microsoft.
   b. Client Software for NetWare.
   c. Client Software for UNIX.
   d. Client Software for Linux.

42. In Windows 98, to display the network resources that are available on the network, use
   a. Internet Explorer.
   b. Network Service Indexer.
   c. Network applet in the Control Panel.
   d. Network Neighborhood.

43. A hand under a drive or directory icon indicates the drive or directory is
   a. password protected.
   b. virus protected.
   c. shared.
   d. invisible to the public.

44. How can a user find a network printer on a Windows 9X workgroup?
   a. by protocol
   b. by cable name
   c. by manufacturer
   d. by NetBIOS name

45. To reach a secured Internet site named test.com, which of the following addresses must you type on the URL line of the browser?
   a. HTTP://TEST.COM
   b. HTTPS://TEST.COM
   c. TELLNET HTTP://TEST.COM
   d. HTTP://CURE.HTML/TEST.COM

46. What is a dynamic IP address?
   a. WINS assigned address
   b. DHCP assigned address
   c. manually entered address
   d. permanent assigned address

47. What is a static IP address?
   a. a DHCP client
   b. a permanently assigned address
   c. one that must be grounded before use
   d. one that was generated by a capacitor
   e. one that was generated for that session only

48. What is the first step you should take to connect to a shared printer over your network?
   a. From the Control Panel choose Connect to network printer.
   b. From Windows Explorer choose Connect to network printer.
   c. From the PRINTERS folder double-click Add printer and choose the network printer.
   d. From the Control Panel select Add new hardware and choose network printer.

49. What is the main function of a WINS server on the network?
   a. It assigns IP addresses.
   b. It assigns computer names.
   c. It resolves NetBIOS names to IP addresses.
   d. It allows dual booting between operating systems.

50. What is the proper convention for accessing network printer?
   a. \\PRINTERNAME\SYSTEMNAME
   b. \SYSTEMNAME\PRINTERNAME
   c. \\SYSTEMNAME\PRINTERNAME
   d. \PRINTERNAME\\SYSTEMNAME

51. What network protocol can you load to share the printers in Windows 9X? (choose three answers)?
   a. PPP b. PPTP
   c. TCP/IP d. NetBIOS
   e. NetBEUI f. IPX/SPX

52. Where can you change network identification in Windows 2000?
   a. Device Manager
   b. network properties
   c. system properties
   d. network and dial-up connections

53. Which command should be run in Windows NT 4.0 to get a computer's IP address?
   a. TRACERT b. NETSTAT
   c. IPCONFIG d. NBTSTAT

54. Which command should you use to test connectivity to every router between your system and the destination system?
   a. PING b. ROUTE
   c. TRACERT d. WINIPCFG

55. Which domain extension refers to universities and colleges?
   a. CC b. WS
   c. ORG d. EDU
   e. COM

56. Which of the following configuration settings are set in EEPROMS on a NIC (choose three answers)?
    a. IRQ
    b. protocol
    c. IP address
    d. I/O address
    e. MAC address
57. Which of the following operating systems come with ICS (Internet Connection Sharing) (choose two answers)?
    a. Windows 95
    b. Windows 95 OSR2
    c. Windows 98
    d. Windows 98 SE
    e. Windows 2000
    f. Windows NT 4.0
58. Which of the following protocols answers a request to an Internet site?
    a. HTTP
    b. SNMP
    c. SMTP
    d. Telnet
59. You have connected your Windows 2000 system to an Ethernet network and are using the TCP/IP protocol with DHCP. You verify that you have received an appropriate IP address, but you are unable to see any other computers in My Network Places. You have another system nearby configured similarly that is able to see other computers. Which command can you use to test connectivity between the two systems?
    a. PING
    b. NET TEST
    c. IPCONFIG
    d. WINIPCFG
60. You have just added a Windows 98 workstation to a TCP/IP network and you can't log in to the Windows NT server where your account has been set up. Which commands should you use to check for network connectivity (choose two answers)?
    a. WINIPCFG
    b. IPCONFIG
    c. REGEDT32
    d. NETCONFIG
    e. WINIPCONFIG
61. What command do you use to check the TCP/IP configuration?
    a. IPCONFIG
    b. WINIPCFG
    c. LIPCONFIG
    d. IFCONFIG
    d. NETCONFIG
62. What do you need to load on Linux to access shared directories on a Microsoft Windows computer?
    a. Ping
    b. Samba
    c. Loadshare
    d. Msshare
    e. Nfs
63. There are two groups of users in your network, one for accounting staffs and one for general users. They all need to use the network printer. When specifying the network printer *by name,* what format should be used?
    a. \\PRINT_SERVER\PRINTER_NAME
    b. //PRINT_SERVER/PRINTER_NAME
    c. \PRINT_SERVER:PRINTER_NAME
    d. \PRINT_SERVER,PRINTER_NAME
64. From the computer clientX you want to connect to a remote file server and fail by using the server's host name. Things work fine using IP address, though. What type of problem could it be?
    a. DNS problem
    b. DHCP problem
    c. Active Directory problem
    d. WINS problem
65. All client computers run Windows XP Professional and Microsoft Office XP. A user reports that she cannot access any network resources. You discover that the user can log on to the computer, but she cannot access her email messages or her mapped drives. You run the PING command on your client computer, but you cannot connect to the user's computer. You instruct the user to run the IPCONFIG command from her computer. You discover that the computer is using IP address 169.254.117.54. You need to ensure that the user can access network resources. What should you do first?
    a. Instruct the user to run the NETSTAT command.
    b. Instruct the user to run the IPCONFIG/RENEW command.
    c. Instruct the user to remove the user profile on the computer, restart the computer, and log on again.
    d. Ask a network administrator to remove the user's computer account from the domain and then add it to the domain.
66. All client computers run Windows XP Professional. A user reports that he cannot browse the network or access his email messages. You discover that the user's mapped network drives are not accessible. You look up the correct default gateway address for the user's subnet, but you are unable to ping to the gateway address from the user's computer. What is the most likely cause of the problem?
    a. The user's computer does not have a valid DNS server address.
    b. The user's computer does not have a hardware connection to the network.
    c. The user's computer does not have a valid computer account in the domain.
    d. The DHCP server is not renewing the client computer's IP address lease.
67. Windows XP is one of the mainstream operating systems deployed. Your major duty is to assist in the configuration and maintenance of desktop applications. Your user desktop is connected to the Internet through a DSL line directly. To protect this desktop, which of the following should you deploy?
    a. ICF
    b. ICS
    c. ARS
    d. ASR
68. All client computers run Windows XP Professional and Microsoft Office XP. The company

has a main office and a branch office. The user reports that he cannot use Remote Desktop to connect to his computer at the main office while he is on his computer at the branch office. You discover that the user has a computer at the main office and a computer at the branch office. The user runs Internet Connection Firewall (ICF) on both computers. You verify that Remote Desktop is enabled on the user's computer at the main office. You run the PING command between the user's two computers and find that they communicate with each other. You also ensure that the firewall between the main office and the branch office allows for Remote Desktop connections. You need to ensure that the user can connect to his computer at the main office by using a Remote Desktop connection while working at the branch office. What should you do?

a. Instruct the user to disable ICF on his computer located at the main office.
b. Instruct the user to disable ICF on his computer located at the branch office.
c. Enable Internet Connection Sharing (ICS) on the user's computer located at the main office.
d. Enable Internet Connection Sharing (ICS) on the user's computer located at the branch office.

HANDS-ON EXERCISES

Exercise 1: Using the TCP/IP Network

1. Start a DOS prompt by clicking on the Start button and then selecting Programs, Accessories, and Command Prompt.
2. Execute the IPCONFIG command and record the following settings:
   IP address
   Subnet mask
   Default gateway
3. Use the IPCONFIG/ALL command and record the following settings:
   MAC address
   WINS server (if any)
   DNS server (if any)
   If it is DHCP enabled or not
4. Ping the loopback address of 127.0.0.1.
5. Ping your IP address.
6. Ping your instructor's computer.
7. Ping your partner's computer.
8. Use the TRACERT command to your instructor's computer.
9. If you are connected to the Internet, use the TRACERT command to Novell.com.
10. If you have a router on your network, ping your gateway or local router connection.
11. If your network has a DHCP network, right-click My Network Places and select the Properties option.
12. Click on the Internet Protocol (TCP/IP) and then click on the Properties button.
13. In the Internet Protocol (TCP/IP) Properties dialog box, select Obtain an IP address automatically. Click on the OK button.
14. Execute the IPCONFIG command at the command prompt and record the following settings:
    IP address
    Subnet mask
    Default gateway
    WINS server (if any)
    DNS server (if any)
    If it is DHCP enabled or not
15. Ping the loopback address of 127.0.0.1.
16. Ping your IP address.
17. Ping your instructor's computer.
18. Ping your partner's computer.
19. If you have a router on your network, ping your gateway or local router connection.
20. At the command prompt execute the IPCONFIG/RELEASE command to remove your values specified by a DHCP server.
21. At the command prompt, execute the IPCONFIG command and compare the recorded values from number 2.

22. At the command prompt, execute the IPCONFIG/RENEW command.
23. At the command prompt, execute the IPCONFIG command and compare the recorded values from number 2.
24. Have your instructor stop the DHCP server (or DCHP service).
25. At the command prompt, execute the IPCONFIG/RELEASE command followed by the IPCONFIG/RENEW.

    NOTE: There will be a pause while Windows 2000 attempts to locate a DHCP server.

26. At the command prompt, execute the IPCONFIG prompt. Record the address and try to determine where this address came from.
27. Try to ping your instructor's computer and the local gateway. You should not be able to ping these IP addresses because they are on two different networks.
28. After your partner has acquired an Automatic Private IP address, try to ping each other. Since these addresses are on the same network (physically and logically), it should work.
29. Go back into the TCP/IP dialog box and enter the static addresses that you recorded in questions 2 and 3.
30. Test your network by pinging your partner's and instructor's computers and the gateway connection.
31. Disconnect the network cable from the back of the computer.
32. Look at the Taskbar in the notification area (near the clock) and notice the red *X*.
33. From the command prompt, type IPCONFIG.
34. Go into the Network and Dial-up Connection dialog box by right-clicking My Network Places and selecting Properties. Notice the red *X*.
35. Connect the cable back into the network card. Notice that the red *X* in both places goes away. In addition, notice that the icon disappears altogether from the notification area.
36. Right-click Local Area Connection and select Properties.
37. Select the Show icon in taskbar when connected. Click on the OK button. Close the Local Area Connection dialog box.
38. Go to the notification area and notice the new icon representing the network connection.
39. Without clicking on the new icon, move the mouse pointer over the icon. Without moving the mouse, notice the information given.
40. Double-click the icon to bring up the Local Area Connection dialog box.
41. From the command prompt, execute the ARP -A command.
42. Close all windows.

Exercise 2: File and Print Sharing

1. Share the C drive, the Windows directory, and the WINDOWS\SYSTEM directory.
2. Install a local print drive on the computer.
3. Install a network print drive pointing to your partner's printer.
4. Using Network Neighborhood or My Network Places, find your partner's computer to access the shared resources.
5. Using the Run option under the Start button, type the double backlash followed by the IP address of your partner's computer.
6. Using the Run option under the Start button, type the UNC name (*PARTNER'S_COMPUTER_NAME\SHARE_NAME*), specifying one of the shared drives or directories.

CHAPTER 26

Introduction to Apple Macintosh Computers

Topics Covered in This Chapter

Introduction

Although Apple Macintosh computers represent less than 5 percent of the total number of personal computers manufactured today, Macintosh computers have always had a loyal following, particularly in schools and for graphics, desktop publishing, and video editing applications. Therefore, you may need to support and troubleshoot these computers.

Objectives

1. Explain the differences between PCs and Apple Macintosh computers.
2. List and differentiate between the various models of Apple Macintosh computers.
3. List the common file systems used by Apple Macintosh computers and state their limitations.
4. Configure the network connection for an Apple Macintosh computer.

26.1 WHAT IS THE MACINTOSH OS?

The Apple Macintosh (often called "the Mac") was introduced in 1984. Before Windows 3.0, which brought the graphical interface to the IBM PC, Apple Macintosh was the first widely sold personal computer with a user-friendly, What-you-see-is-what-you-get (WYSIWYG) graphical user interface (GUI) that used a one-button mouse to perform point-and-click and click-and-drag.

Originally built on Motorola's 68000 series microprocessors, Mac versions today are powered by the PowerPC microprocessor, which was developed jointly by Apple, Motorola, and IBM. The Mac is actually a line of personal computers, configured for individual users and businesses with different needs. The iMac provides the Mac technology and interface in a low-cost package.

26.1.1 Mac OS

The Macintosh has its own operating system—the Mac OS—which, in its latest version is called the Mac OS X. The Mac OS has gone through several major revisions so far. The first OS, known as System 1, was released in 1984 in the original Macintosh. The Mac OS interface, which is called the Finder, was pretty bare. It contained the basic elements of the current Mac OS, but it had no color. It was one of the earliest GUI interfaces, even before Microsoft Windows 3.0.

System 6 was introduced in 1986, which added color to the OS. System 7 added multitasking with a program called Multifinder. In addition, it gave users support for TrueType fonts and the ability to share out a disk onto the network so that other Mac users could access it. It also gave users the ability to use virtual memory.

Mac OS 8 was released in 1997. Due to a partnership with Microsoft, Internet Explorer was installed as the default browser. Apple also increased its cross-platform connectivity with the introduction of an updated version of its PC Exchange product, which now had support for Windows 9X long file names. Finally, the OS contained its own Java virtual machine for running Java applications.

With Mac OS 9, Apple added multiuser features including the possibility to specify different settings and environments for multiple users of the same Macintosh. Along with that, Apple introduced the Keychain, which stored the various online passwords for a user so that only one password was required when a user went online. Finally, it included a network browser so that a user could browse the network easily for a network server.

The most recent version is the Mac OS X, introduced in 2001. It was the first major rewrite of the Mac OS in years. Whereas the basic interface still looked the same, the use of color, graphics, and moving graphics is much improved over previous versions. It is based on a Linux kernel, which makes it more stable, more scalable, and generally more powerful than previous versions. Windows "fly" open and get "squished" onto a bar called the Dock when minimized. Also, for the first time you can save directly to PDF format (format used by Adobe Acrobat).

The Mac OS can perform many functions on a network. In addition to being a client, a Macintosh can be a file and print server using AppleShare as well as an Internet server using various Apple and third-party software. The advantage of having a Macintosh as a server is that it is extremely easy to administrate. It is so easy, in fact, that many first-time users have no problems networking Macs and making them into file (or other) servers.

The Mac OS offers reliable security. Mac OS X has local user account security built in as part of the OS. Network security has also been taken into account. Many services that would be susceptible to a hacker are turned off by default, so a Mac is more secure than other operating systems right out of the box. Additionally, there are many third-party security products (including some that implement Kerberos security) that can make the Mac OS extremely secure over the network.

26.1.2 Macintosh Hardware

When looking at the Macintosh hardware, you will find many similarities to the PC. The Macintosh computer has a processor, RAM, ROM chips, hard drives, expansion slots, and ports. Instead of using Intel processors, today's Macs use the PowerPC processor, which is based primarily on reduced instruction set computing (RISC). Currently, the PowerPC processor used by Apple are the G4 and G5 processors.

The G4 processor, which can execute one billion floating-point instructions per second, contains a 1-square-inch wafer that is less than 0.1 inch thick. It connects to the motherboard via 360 pins. The G4 processor uses the Velocity Engine, which processes data in huge 128-bit chunks, instead of the smaller 32-bit or 64-bit chunks used in traditional processors, and it adds SIMD (Single Instruction, Multiple Data) abilities to the PPC family. Additionally, it employs an on-die L2 cache, running at processor speed, connecting the CPU core by a 256-bit-wide bus for superfast cache access. Last, the G4 has a bus speed of 167 MHz. The PowerPC G4 processor works with the PowerPC architecture to accelerate the data-intensive processing required by next-generation video, voice, and graphics applications. These processing advantages give the PowerPC G4 a significant edge when it comes to digital video, music, graphics, and 3D games.

The G5 processor is a 64-bit processor, which can address up to 8 GB of memory, but has the potential to scale up to 4 TB in the future. Each G5 model features a bus that runs at half the speed of the processor. So you'll get dual 900 MHz front-side buses on a dual 1.8 GHz Power Mac G5, dual 1 GHz front-side buses on a dual 2.0 GHz Power Mac G5, and dual 1.25 GHz front-side buses on a dual 2.5 GHz Power Mac G5 (which offers a 20 Gbit/s throughput).

Beginning with the original iBook introduced in July 1999, Apple started to integrate the Universal Motherboard Architecture (UMA) into its computers, making development and manufacturing new products less expensive. UMA added such features as FireWire Target Disk Mode and dual-channel USB to all motherboards. It also supports newer power management features (power manager 2.0). All Macintosh computers equipped with a UMA logic board are also equipped with a video card on an AGP bus.

To expand the system, most models have PCI slots. Typically, a desktop system has three or four 33 MHz slots that can take 32- or 64-bit cards. The maximum power consumption of all PCI cards on the bus should not exceed 50 watts.

Early Macintosh computers had an external SCSI port used for external hard drives. Today, the primary drive used by Apple computers is IDE. Of course, users can still install a SCSI card into an expansion bus at any time.

Depending on the model, the Macs will have CD-ROM drives, CD-RW drives, Combo drives (CD-RW/DVD), and Superdrives (CD-RW/DVD-R). In addition, all recent Macintosh computers come with built-in Ethernet ports. In addition, some models support BlueTooth, infrared, and modems connections.

26.1.3 Macintosh Models

The Mac is actually a line of personal computers configured for individual users and businesses with different needs. The iMac and eMac provides the Macintosh technology and interface in a low-cost package.

The iMac model is a low-cost version of the Macintosh computer, designed to attract people who have never owned a personal computer and also to win back former Mac users who have moved to the

Figure 26.1 The iMac (CRT) and eMac (LCD) Apple Macintosh Computers (Courtesy of Apple Computer, Inc.)

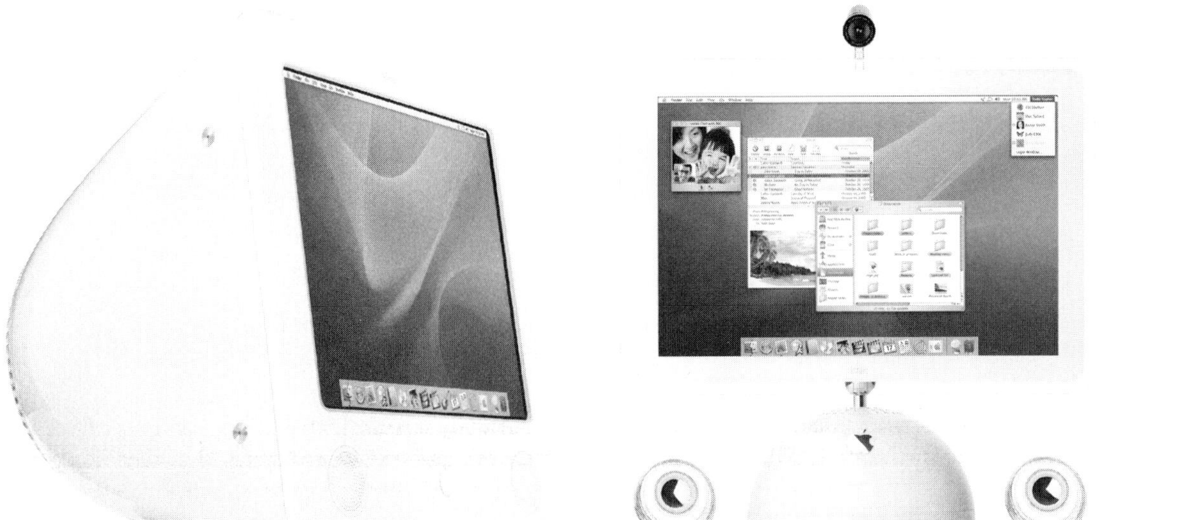

PC. Released in 1998, the initial version combined a PowerPC G3 (233 MHz) processor and a 15-inch CRT display in one unit enclosed in a sleekly molded designer-colored translucent case. The iMac did not include a floppy disk drive since it is considered a legacy device. When the iMac moved to the PowerPC G4 processor, the iMac's display changed to a flat-panel LCD rather than a CRT. The iMac models carry from each other in the type of memory modules used (SO-DIMM or DIMM), the cache, the size of the hard disk, the type of optical drive, the graphics card, the expansion possibilities, and whether or not connectors are available for external video. See figure 26.1.

In 2002, the eMac was introduced, which combined a PowerPC G4 processor and a 17-inch flat CRT display. Similar to the iMac, the eMac models varied from one another in their processor speed, the type of memory modules, the cache, the size of the hard disk, the kind of optical drive, the graphics card, the AirPort option (802.11 wireless technology), and the kind of video connectors. See figure 26.1.

The Power Mac G4 models were the workhorses of the Macintosh, offering top performance and maximum expandability from 1999 to 2003. The Power Mac G4 tower desktop used the PowerPC G4 processor and included PCI graphics, Gigibit Ethernet, Digital Audio, QuickSilver, and QuickSilver 2002. Later models include FireWire, AirPort Extreme, and Mac OS X. See figures 26.2 and 26.3.

The newest desktop model is the Power Mac G5 models. The PowerPC G5 processor brings 64-bit processing to the Mac platform. As with the AMD Athlon 64 processor, applications need to be optimized for 64-bit computing to take full advantage of the architecture. But the PowerPC G5 (like the Athlon 64) will continue to run 32-bit applications natively instead of in emulation mode, as with Intel's 64-bit Itanium processor. See figure 26.2.

The inside of the Power Mac G5 models have four discrete cooling zones. Each has its own fan (or fans), and each is self-contained when the air deflector is in place. The G5 draws air in through the holes in the front panel and passes it over the components. When any section runs hot, only the fan for that area runs faster. As a result, the G5 is a quiet machine, especially when compared to the G4 models.

For the notebook computer, Apple offers the iBook and the PowerBook G4. The iBook was designed for consumers, providing easy operation and connecting, long-running battery, a strong body, and easy portability. The first iBook was introduced in July 1999, with a 300 or 366 MHz G3 processor, 1 PC100, SO-DIMM slot, 3.3 or 6 GB hard drive, ATI RAGE video card, 12.1 TFT SVGA LCD, a USB 1.1 port, 10/100 BaseT Ethernet, 56K V.90 modem and AirPort, and used the Mac OS 8.6. The iBook G4, introduced in October 2003, used up to 1 GHz G4 processor, 1 PC 2100 SO-DIMM slot, up to 60 GB Ultra ATA drive, Combo drive, ATI Mobility Radeon 9200 with 32 MB and 4X AGP support, an LCD screen, 2 USB 2.0 ports, 1 FireWire port, 10/100 BaseT Ethernet, 56K V.90 modem, AirPort Extreme, and BlueTooth. See figure 26.4.

Figure 26.2 Power Mac G4 and Power Mac G5 Computers (Courtesy of Apple Computer, Inc.)

Figure 26.3 Inside the Power Mac G4 (Courtesy of Apple Computer, Inc.)

The PowerBook G4 notebook includes a PowerPC G4 processor, FireWire, USB, and support for AirPort wireless Internet connections and networking. Different from the iBook, it was designed for high performance.

Figure 26.4 Apple's iBook Portable Computer (Courtesy of Apple Computer, Inc.)

Table 26.1 Apple Macintosh Beep Codes

Beep Code	Problem Detected
1 beep	No RAM installed
2 beeps	Incompatible RAM types
3 beeps	No good banks
4 beeps	No good boot images in the boot ROM (and/or bad sys config block)
5 beeps	Processor is not usable

26.1.4 Apple Boot Process

When an Apple Macintosh computer boots, it follows these steps:

1. Self-test is controlled from ROM, similar to POST.
2. Parameter RAM (PRAM), similar to CMOS, settings are retrieved.
3. System folder is located.
4. Mac OS ROM file, which contains commands required for interaction with hardware and the lower levels of the OS, is loaded into RAM.
5. Smiling Mac icon and Welcome screen are displayed.
6. Enablers (similar to external drives) are loaded that allow new hardware to work that is not built into the operating system.
7. Disk First Aid (similar to Scandisk) runs if the Mac was not shut down properly.
8. Other system folder contents are located such as the Control Panels folder and the Exensions folder.
9. Mac desktop is displayed.
10. Finder and setup programs are located.

Similar to the PC, if your Macintosh computer finds a hardware problem during boot, it will notify you by playing a series of beeps or by displaying a code. Macs introduced after October 1999 use a revised set of power-on self-test beeps during startup. See table 26.1. In addition to the beeps, on some computers the power LED will flash a corresponding number of times plus one. The LED will repeat the sequence after approximately a 5-second pause. The tones are played only once.

26.1.5 Macintosh File Systems

The native file system used by newer Macintosh operating systems is the hierarchical file system (HFS) and HFS+, the Mac OS Extended file system. Like Windows (NTFS), HFS+ increases the number of allocation blocks per volume. In addition, HFS+ allows for smaller clusters, which allows for more efficient use of disk space. The first two sectors of the formatted disk are boot blocks in the volume information block. To keep track of the file name, logical locations, folder structure, and physical location, HFS+ uses a catalog b-tree to list all of its files.

The Mac file system allows file names to be up to 31 characters long, and it may use any character (including accented and other special characters) except for a colon (:). This restriction exists because the colon is used to separate subdirectories in the directory structure, like:

MACINTOSH HD:SYSTEM FOLDER:CONTROL PANELS:KEYBOARD

The previous line specifies the complete path of the Keyboard control panel; the colon serves the same purpose as a forward slash in Windows or a backslash in DOS.

Because Mac OS X is using a Linux core, Mac OS X uses the forward slash (/) to separate directories and files. For example, the same OS 9 directory above would be represented as follows:

MACINTOSHHD/SYSTEMFOLDER/CONTROLPANELS/KEYBOARD

Different from Windows and Linux, all Macintosh have two distinct parts: a resource fork and a data fork. For most applications, the resource fork contains most of the program code, associated icons, document encoding information, file identifiers, sounds, and other software necessary for running the program. For a document, such as a Word document or text file, the content is stored in the data fork. Some programs create documents that use both forks, so the data is stored in the data fork, and formatting, configuration, or preferences may be stored in the resource fork. When transporting a file from a Mac to another platform, the only part that is usually kept intact is the data fork; the other platform does not even know the resource fork exists. Macs use "file creator" and "file type" resources in the resource fork to keep track of the application to which a file belongs. A common Mac troubleshooting technique is Rebuilding the desktop, a procedure that forces the Mac to check all of the file types to make sure that the Finder knows to what applications the files belong.

Unfortunately, since the HFS is showing its age, it has some obvious limitations. First, it has a maximum of 65,536 blocks to use, per disk or partition. Therefore, you should not have partitions larger then 1 GB or you will be wasting valuable disk space, due to large block sizes. In addition, the maximum volume size under System 6 and System 7 is 2 GB, whereas System 7.5 increased that limit to 4 GB. System 7.5.2 (and later) increases that limit to 2 TB on some computers, including any system that shipped with System 7.5.2 or later, and any Macintosh system with PCI slots. The maximum number of volumes is theoretically limited to 173 due to the maximum number of open files in early Mac systems (from 7.0 to 8.0). Because there are other files open when the computer boots up, the actual maximum will vary depending upon how many files are opened by the operating system. Other limitations include:

- The maximum file size is 2 GB.
- The maximum number of files in a folder is 32,767.
- The maximum size of the data fork (in a file) is 2 GB.
- The maximum size of the resource fork (in a file) is 16 MB.

HFS+ (HFS Extended) was introduced to extend the filing system to accommodate larger hard drives including the number of files a volume can have and the large disks it can use. Under Mac OS 8.1, HPF+ has the following limitations:

- Maximum volume size is 2 TB (Mac OS 8–9.2).
- Maximum file size is 2 TB (Mac OS X). Mac OS 9 supports 2 GB files.
- Maximum data fork size is 2 TB (Mac OS X). Mac OS 9 supports 2 GB files.
- Maximum resource fork size is 16 MB.
- Maximum number of files is more than 2 billion.
- Maximum number of files/folders in a folder is 32,767.
- Long file names of up to 31 characters.

Under Mac OS X, HPF+ limitations include:

- Maximum number of files depends on the size of the volume (disk) size, although there is no set limit.
- Maximum volume and file size is 2 TB (Mac OS X 10.0–10.1), 8 TB (Mac OS X 10.2), and 16 TB (Mac OS X 10.3).

Figure 26.5 The Mac OS X top-level file system contains several permanent folders.

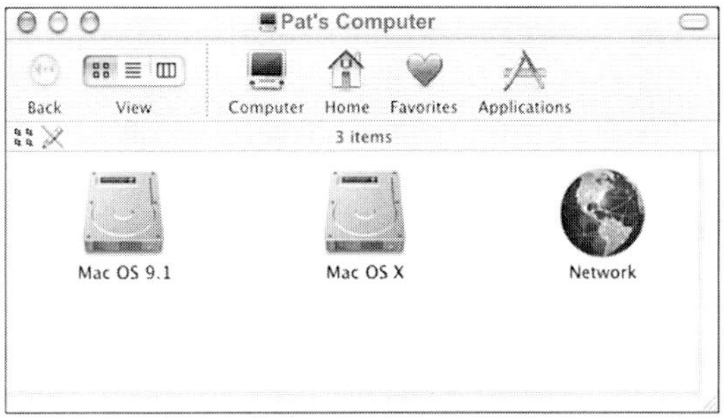

- Maximum number of files and folders in a folder is 4 billion.
- File system journaling (Mac OS X 10.3).
- Long file names of up to 256 characters.

Similar to Linux but different from Windows, HPF+/Mac OS X uses type codes and creator codes instead of using file name extensions such as DOC or TXT.

On the boot drive, Mac OS X has several permanent folders similar to those shown in figure 26.5. These directories contain all the preinstalled applications, utilities, and configuration files for your system. This will be the starting point of accessing most of the functions of your system. As a normal Mac OS X user, you cannot modify these folders by moving, renaming, or deleting them.

The APPLICATIONS folder contains all the preinstalled Mac OS X applications, such as TextEdit, Mail, QuickTime Player, and many others. Any application located within this folder will be accessible to any user on the system. If you're installing an application that should be accessed by only one person, it might make more sense to store the application within the user's home directory. The tools needed to set up your printer, calibrate your display, and specify other important tasks are located in the UTILITIES folder found in the APPLICATIONS folder.

The Library, new to the Mac OS file system, is used to the bring a modular approach to the OS X system by providing a storage location for systemwide application preferences, application libraries, and information that should be accessible to any user. Some of the default Library folders include application support (shared files used by several applications), audio, caches, ColorSync, Desktop pictures, Documentation, Fonts, Image capture, Internet plug-ins, Java, Logs, Modem scripts, Perl, Preferences, Printers, Receipts, Screen savers, Scripts, StartupItems, User Pictures, and Web Server (for CGIs and HTML files).

NOTE: When using the APPLICATIONS and LIBRARY directories, if you install or add a program or other files, the program or other files will be available to all users on the system. If you want the program or files available to a single account, you will have to install it directly into that home directory.

The Mac OS X SYSTEM folder contains the files that make up the Mac OS X operating system. It contains a single folder called LIBRARY, which includes the configuration software, fonts, sounds, and most preferences. The CORESERVICES folder, located within the LIBRARY folder, contains many of the key OS X services (including the Dock, help tool, Software Update application, and System and Finder files described later in the chapter).

Most items in the SYSTEM folder have a specific subfolder where they belong. The location of the subfolders determines the order in which they are loaded when booting up as well as if they will work at all. Therefore, it is imperative that these items are in their proper places. You can select Get Info from the File menu and get a file description for the selected item that would help determine where it should be. If you drag an extension or control panel onto the System folder icon, not the open window, the system will ask if you would like to place the item in the appropriate folder. Of course, this is if the system recognizes the file and knows where to place it.

The EXTENSIONS folder, used by OS 9 or earlier, contains Chooser extensions such as AppleShare (necessary for file sharing), System extensions such as QuickTime (for streaming video), and printer drivers. The files in this folder load before the control panels and usually offer no configuration options. It is not uncommon for a Macintosh to have an extension conflict. To troubleshoot such a problem, it may be necessary to disable extensions by removing them from the SYSTEM folder or using the Extensions Manager control panel. Not all extensions will appear in the Extensions Manager, so be aware of this fact when troubleshooting.

After all of the control panels and extensions have loaded, and after the Finder has established itself, the items inside the STARTUP ITEMS folder are launched. Like the EXTENSIONS and CONTROL PANELS folders, the STARTUP ITEMS folder is in the SYSTEM folder. The startup items are not loaded like system extensions (so placing any extensions into this folder will disable them and most likely give an error on startup); instead, these files are loaded as if you had double-clicked them.

The STARTUP ITEMS folder is a handy place to put items you use every time you launch the computer. Usually, instead of putting the original file or document into the STARTUP ITEMS folder, an alias of the item is used. You can disable a startup item by removing it from this folder.

Mac OS X does not use the STARTUP ITEMS folder the way previous versions of the Mac OS did. Instead of placing files directly into this folder, each individual user can determine what items are loaded on startup by customizing the Login Items tab of the Login System Preferences window.

The USERS folder holds the user home directories with personal settings and data files. Therefore, each home directory will have several default folders such as the DESKTOP, DOCUMENTS, LIBRARY, MOVIES, MUSIC, PICTURES, PUBLIC (meant for sharing over the network for the user), and SITES (personal website).

Since Mac OS X is based on a Linux operating system, each file and folder belongs to a specific user and group. Therefore, the permissions that can be assigned to any file and folder are the same as in Linux, which is owner permissions, group permissions, and world permissions.

26.2 MACINTOSH INTERFACE

Because the Mac OS X desktop is a GUI interface with many of the interface components used in Microsoft Windows, you will find many similarities between Windows and the Mac OS X. At the top of the screen is the Menu bar for the current active application. See figure 26.6.

Figure 26.6 Apple's Mac OS X Interface (Courtesy of Apple Computer, Inc.)

The dock that appears at the bottom of the desktop contains icons that provide access to frequently used applications. When you click the minus button to minimize a window, an icon representing that window appears in the dock. To open an application from its icon in the dock, just click it once. The icons in the dock that represent open application have a small triangle underneath them. The Mac OS X desktop also includes shortcut icons that are usually located on the right side of the screen and provide quick access to files, folders, and programs.

The Finder window functions similar to Explorer or My Computer in Windows, enabling the user to navigate and access the Mac's files and applications. The top level of the Finder is the computer, which shows hard drive and network icons to other workstations that you have recently connected to. At the top of the Finder windows and other windows, you will find buttons for the web browser.

If you want to create a folder, use the Finder to navigate to the location where you want to put the folder. Then open the File menu and select New Folder. Type in the new name and press the Enter key.

To find files, you will use the Sherlock utility. To start Sherlock, look for the Sherlock icon (looks like a hat and magnifying glass). Next, specify the name of the file, folder, or text that you want to find and click the check box next to the location you want to search. Click the green magnifying glass button to begin the search.

Of course, the idea of the Microsoft Windows Recycle Bin came from the Apple Macintosh. When you want to delete a file or folder, just drag its icon to the Trash Can until the Trash Can is highlighted and release the mouse button. Like the Recycle Bin, you can open the Trash Can, search through the trash, and recover the file or folder. If you want to empty the trash, open the File menu and select Empty Trash.

No matter what application you are running, you will always find an apple icon at the left side of the menu at the top of the screen. The Apple icon is similar to the Windows Start button. Clicking on it brings up a submenu with accessories and programs. To configure the Apple desktop and environment, you would open the Apple menu and select System Preferences, which is similar to the Windows Control Panel.

In Mac OS 9, you could customize the Apple menu to contain anything that you want by adding items to or removing items from the APPLE folder, which is located in the SYSTEM folder. Unfortunately, with OSX, the Apple menu is no longer customizable.

In Mac OS 9, you will find three submenus in the Apple menu: Recent Applications, Recent Documents, and Recent Servers. To customize these submenus from the Apple menu, select Control Panels, Apple Menu Options. From the control panel, you can select whether or not to use recent menus and how many items to include on them. In OS X, the Recent Items submenu gives you access to recently accessed documents and applications.

To start applications, double-click the icon for the application from the Finder window or another window or from the desktop. You can also choose the application from the Recent Application submenu on the Apple menu. Last, similar to Windows, you can double-click a data document and the associated application will open. When you have multiple applications running, you can access the application menu in the upper right corner of your screen (OS X 9) or use the dock.

26.3 NETWORKING WITH APPLE MACINTOSH COMPUTERS

The Mac OS can perform many functions on a network. In addition to being a client, a Macintosh computer can act as an integrated file, print, mail, and web server using AppleShare. In addition, newer versions of AppleShare (today known as AppleShare IP) allow you to share directories, files, and printers using the CIFS protocol so that Microsoft Windows and Linux computers running Samba can access those shared resources. The advantage of having a Macintosh as a server is that it is extremely easy to administrate. It is so easy, in fact, that many first-time users have no problems networking Macs and making them into file (or other) servers.

From the Apple menu, select Control Panels, then TCP/IP. If the machine does not have a TCP/IP control panel, then the machine is not using Open Transport networking; check for the existence of a MacTCP control panel instead.

With the advent of System 7.5.3, Apple released Open Transport (OT). OT changed the way the Mac OS looks at networking. In addition to increasing the performance of LocalTalk networks, Apple also simplified much software required for setting it up on any network. The easy way to tell whether you are using OT or Classic networking is to look at your control panels. If you have an AppleTalk control panel you are using Open Transport. If you have a Network control panel you are using Classic networking.

Open Transport/TCP works over Ethernet, token ring, AppleTalk (as MacIP), and serial lines such as MacPPP and InterSLIP. Open Transport/TCP is configured using the TCP/IP control panel. Configuration may be done manually, or through a BOOTP, DHCP, RARP, or MacIP server.

By default, the TCP/IP control panel comes up in basic mode. Advanced or administration mode may be entered via the Edit menu. These modes allow expert users additional choices as well as the ability to augment information returned from a configuration server or to fill in gaps in the returned information.

The TCP/IP control panel may be used at any time to reconfigure the system. However, TCP will not notice the new configuration until it has unloaded from the system. By default, this takes about 2 minutes after the last application using TCP or UDP has gone away.

To manually set up Open Transport/TCP, follow these steps:

1. Select the interface to use, or pick AppleTalk (MacIP) to run over AppleTalk on the interface selected in the AppleTalk control panel. See figure 26.7.
2. If an Ethernet interface is selected, a check box will appear offering the use of 802.3. By default, Open Transport/TCP uses Ethernet_II rather than 802.3.
3. Select Manually as the configuration method.
4. Fill in the IP address in dot notation (for example, 128.1.1.1).
5. Fill in the default domain extension to be used on name searches.
6. In Advanced User mode only, you may enter an Admin Domain. This is used to allow implicit searches.
7. Fill in the subnet mask in dot notation.
8. Fill in the IP address of the default IP router.
9. Fill in the IP address(es) of one or more DNS servers.
10. In Advanced User mode only, additional search domains may be entered. See the preceding description of the Domain Name Resolver operation for details.
11. If a Hosts file is required, select it using the Select Hosts File button. For details about the Hosts file, see the description that follows.

To use a DHCP server to set up Open Transport/TCP, follow these steps:

1. Select the interface to use in the AppleTalk control panel.
2. If an Ethernet interface is selected, a check box will appear offering the use of 802.3. By default, Open Transport/TCP uses Ethernet_II rather than 802.3.
3. Select Using DHCP as the configuration method.
4. In Advanced User mode only, you may enter an Admin Domain. This is used to allow implicit searches.
5. In Advanced User mode, a subnet mask may be entered but is not required. If a value is entered, it will be used if no subnet mask is returned from the DHCP server. Otherwise, any value entered is ignored.
6. In Advanced User mode, the manually entered IP addresses of routers are attached to the end of the (possibly empty) list of IP routers returned by the DHCP server.

Figure 26.7 TCP/IP Configuration for the Apple Macintosh Computer

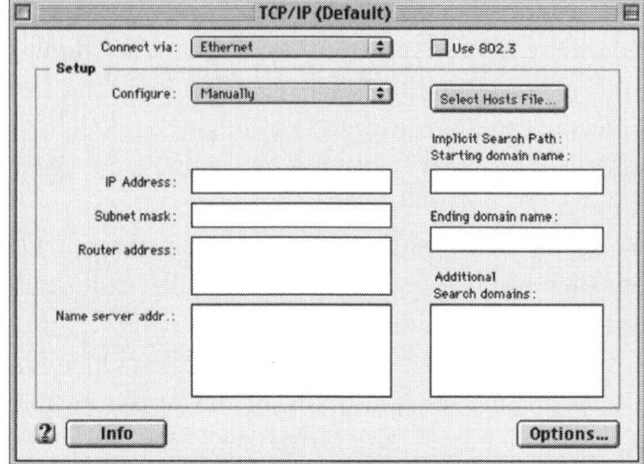

7. In Advanced User mode, the manually entered IP addresses of DNS servers are attached to the end of the (possibly empty) list of Name Servers returned by the DHCP server.
8. In Advanced User mode only, additional search domains may be entered. See the preceding description of the Domain Name Resolver operation for details.
9. If a Hosts file is required, select it using the Select Hosts File button. For details about the Hosts file, see the description that follows.

Once you have all the hardware connected, the next step is to try to see the other computers or printers on the network. Every Mac's window to the outside world is the **Chooser.** See figure 26.8. The Chooser is where you choose the items that your Mac is connected to like printers and other computers. Once you have chosen the type of networking in the AppleTalk or Network control panel you can open the Chooser and you should see the name of each computer that has been set up to share files on the network by simply selecting the AppleShare icon on the left side. If you are trying to access printers you will want to choose the printer type that you have; for many Apple laser printers you will be selecting LaserWriter 8.

When troubleshooting, note that Apple Macintosh computers do not have a PING command built into the operating system. Therefore, if you need to troubleshoot using the PING command, you will have to download a freeware or shareware software package.

To configure the network settings in the Mac OS X, do the following (see figure 26.9):

1. Pull down the Apple menu (top left) and select System Preferences.
2. Click on the Network icon.
3. Pull down the Location popup menu and select Automatic.
4. Pull down the Configure popup menu and select Built-in Ethernet.
5. If the lock icon (bottom left) is locked, make sure that you click it and enter your password to unlock it. This will allow you to save the changes you make in the following steps.
6. Click the TCP/IP tab.

Figure 26.8 Use the Chooser to access network resources.

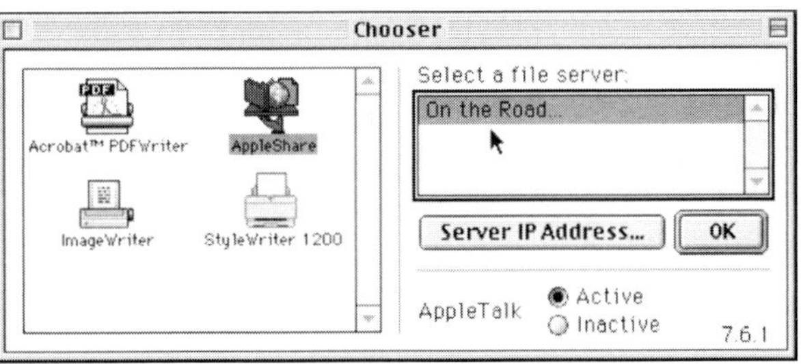

Figure 26.9 Configure networking settings using Mac OS X.

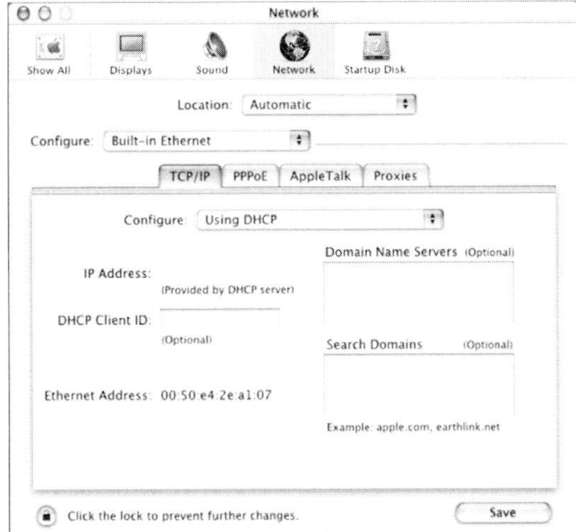

7. Pull down the Configure popup menu and select Using DHCP. If not, specify the IP address, subnet mask, gateway, DNS server, and the search domain field.
8. Click the Save button.

26.4 TROUBLESHOOTING MACINTOSH COMPUTERS

Troubleshooting Macintosh computers is very similar to troubleshooting any other PC. Of course, if you have a hardware problem, check the obvious such as trying to disconnect and reconnect cables (power, printer, monitor, etc.), check monitor controls, and shut down the Mac completely. Of course, since Mac OS X is a Linux-based operating system, you will most likely use the many Linux methods and tools to troubleshoot. In addition, like any other operating system, be sure that you have the latest updates loaded on your machine.

SUMMARY

1. The Apple Macintosh (often called "the Mac") was the first widely sold personal computer with a user-friendly, What-you-see-is-what-you-get (WYSIWYG) graphical user interface (GUI).
2. Mac versions today are powered by the PowerPC microprocessor, which was developed jointly by Apple, Motorola, and IBM.
3. The Mac is actually a line of personal computers configured for individual users and businesses with different needs. The iMac provides the Mac technology and interface in a low-cost package.
4. The Macintosh has its own operating system, Mac OS, which, in its latest version is called Mac OS X.
5. The Mac OS X is based on a Linux kernel, which makes it more stable, more scalable, and generally more powerful than previous versions.
6. The native file system used by newer Macintosh operating systems is the hierarchical file system (HFS) and HFS+, the Mac OS Extended file system.
7. HFS+ (HFS Extended) was introduced to extend the filing system to accommodate larger hard drives including the number of files a volume can have and the large disks it can use.
8. Because the Mac OS X desktop is a GUI interface and includes many interface components used in Microsoft Windows, you will find many similarities between Windows and the Mac OS X.
9. The Mac OS can perform many functions on a network. In addition to being a client, a Macintosh computer can act as an integrated file, print, mail, and web server using AppleShare.
10. Troubleshooting Macintosh computers is very similar to troubleshooting any other PC.

QUESTIONS

1. Which type of processors do today's Apple Macintosh computers use?
   a. Intel b. AMD
   c. Motorola d. PowerPC
2. The 64-bit processor used by the Power Mac G4 models is the
   a. G3. b. G4.
   c. G5. d. G6.
   e. Athlon 64.
3. The file system used by older Apple Macintosh operating systems is
   a. FAT. b. EXT2.
   c. HFS. d. HFS+.
4. Which operating system is a Linux-based operating system?
   a. Mac OS 8 b. Mac OS 9
   c. Mac OS 10 d. Mac OS X
5. Where are most of the Mac OS operating system files found?
   a. in the SYSTEM folder
   b. in the USERS folder
   c. in the APPLICATIONS folder
   d. in the WINDOWS folder
   e. in the DESKTOP folder
6. To access files on the hard drive, you use
   a. Internet Explorer. b. Finder.
   c. Chooser. d. Desktop.
   e. Sherlock.
7. What do Apple Macintosh computers use instead of the Recycle Bin?
   a. the Recycler
   b. the Trash Bin
   c. the Trash Can
   d. the Garbage Remover
8. What menu is generally used to start programs?
   a. Apple menu b. Chooser menu
   c. Finder menu d. Start menu

APPENDIX A

Useful Computer Tables

Table A.1 ASCII Character Set

DEC	BIN	HEX	ASCII	Ctrl	DEC	BIN	HEX	ASCII	DEC	BIN	HEX	ASCII
0	00000000	0	null	NUL	32	00100000	20	space	64	01000000	40	@
1	00000001	1	☺	SOH	33	00100001	21	!	65	01000001	41	A
2	00000010	2	☻	STX	34	00100010	22	“	66	01000010	42	B
3	00000011	3	♥	ETX	35	00100011	23	#	67	01000011	43	C
4	00000100	4	♦	EOT	36	00100100	24	$	68	01000100	44	D
5	00000101	5	♣	ENQ	37	00100101	25	%	69	01000101	45	E
6	00000110	6	♠	ACK	38	00100110	26	&	70	01000110	46	F
7	00000111	7	•	BEL	39	00100111	27	‘	71	01000111	47	G
8	00001000	8	◘	BS	40	00101000	28	(	72	01001000	48	H
9	00001001	9	°	HT	41	00101001	29	)	73	01001001	49	I
10	00001010	A	◙	LF	42	00101010	2A	*	74	01001010	4A	J
11	00001011	B	♂	VT	43	00101011	2B	+	75	01001011	4B	K
12	00001100	C	♀	FF	44	00101100	2C	,	76	01001100	4C	L
13	00001101	D	♪	CR	45	00101101	2D	-	77	01001101	4D	M
14	00001110	E	♫	SO	46	00101110	2E	.	78	01001110	4E	N
15	00001111	F	¤	SI	47	00101111	2F	/	79	01001111	4F	O
16	00010000	10	►	DLE	48	00110000	30	0	80	01010000	50	P
17	00010001	11	◄	DC1	49	00110001	31	1	81	01010001	51	Q
18	00010010	12	↕	DC2	50	00110010	32	2	82	01010010	52	R
19	00010011	13	!!	DC3	51	00110011	33	3	83	01010011	53	S
20	00010100	14	¶	DC4	52	00110100	34	4	84	01010100	54	T
21	00010101	15	§	NAK	53	00110101	35	5	85	01010101	55	U
22	00010110	16	-	SYN	54	00110110	36	6	86	01010110	56	V
23	00010111	17	↨	ETB	55	00110111	37	7	87	01010111	57	W
24	00011000	18	↑	CAN	56	00111000	38	8	88	01011000	58	X
25	00011001	19	↓	EM	57	00111001	39	9	89	01011001	59	Y
26	00011010	1A	→	SUB	58	00111010	3A	:	90	01011010	5A	Z
27	00011011	1B	←	ESC	59	00111011	3B	;	91	01011011	5B	[
28	00011100	1C	∟	FS	60	00111100	3C	<	92	01011100	5C	\
29	00011101	1D	↔	GS	61	00111101	3D	=	93	01011101	5D	]
30	00011110	1E	▲	RS	62	00111110	3E	>	94	01011110	5E	^
31	00011111	1F	▼	US	63	00111111	3F	?	95	01011111	5F	_

Table A.1 Continued

DEC	BIN	HEX	ASCII	DEC	BIN	HEX	ASCII	DEC	BIN	HEX	ASCII
96	01100000	60	`	140	10001100	8C	î	184	10111000	B8	╕
97	01100001	61	a	141	10001101	8D	ì	185	10111001	B9	╣
98	01100010	62	b	142	10001110	8E	Ä	186	10111010	BA	║
99	01100011	63	c	143	10001111	8F	Å	187	10111011	BB	╗
100	01100100	64	d	144	10010000	90	É	188	10111100	BC	╝
101	01100101	65	e	145	10010001	91	æ	189	10111101	BD	╜
102	01100110	66	f	146	10010010	92	Æ	190	10111110	BE	╛
103	01100111	67	g	147	10010011	93	ô	191	10111111	BF	┐
104	01101000	68	h	148	10010100	94	ö	192	11000000	C0	└
105	01101001	69	i	149	10010101	95	ò	193	11000001	C1	┴
106	01101010	6A	j	150	10010110	96	û	194	11000010	C2	┬
107	01101011	6B	k	151	10010111	97	ù	195	11000011	C3	├
108	01101100	6C	l	152	10011000	98	ÿ	196	11000100	C4	─
109	01101101	6D	m	153	10011001	99	Ö	197	11000101	C5	┼
110	01101110	6E	n	154	10011010	9A	Ü	198	11000110	C6	╞
111	01101111	6F	o	155	10011011	9B	¢	199	11000111	C7	╟
112	01110000	70	p	156	10011100	9C	£	200	11001000	C8	╚
113	01110001	71	q	157	10011101	9D	¥	201	11001001	C9	╔
114	01110010	72	r	158	10011110	9E	₧	202	11001010	CA	╩
115	01110011	73	s	159	10011111	9F	ƒ	203	11001011	CB	╦
116	01110100	74	t	160	10100000	A0	á	204	11001100	CC	╠
117	01110101	75	u	161	10100001	A1	í	205	11001101	CD	═
118	01110110	76	v	162	10100010	A2	ó	206	11001110	CE	╬
119	01110111	77	w	163	10100011	A3	ú	207	11001111	CF	╧
120	01111000	78	x	164	10100100	A4	ñ	208	11010000	D0	╨
121	01111001	79	y	165	10100101	A5	Ñ	209	11010001	D1	╤
122	01111010	7A	z	166	10100110	A6	ª	210	11010010	D2	╥
123	01111011	7B	{	167	10100111	A7	º	211	11010011	D3	╙
124	01111100	7C	¦	168	10101000	A8	¿	212	11010100	D4	╘
125	01111101	7D	}	169	10101001	A9	—	213	11010101	D5	╒
126	01111110	7E	~	170	10101010	AA	¬	214	11010110	D6	╓
127	01111111	7F	Δ	171	10101011	AB	½	215	11010111	D7	╫
128	10000000	80	Ç	172	10101100	AC	¼	216	11011000	D8	╪
129	10000001	81	ü	173	10101101	AD	¡	217	11011001	D9	┘
130	10000010	82	é	174	10101110	AE	«	218	11011010	DA	┌
131	10000011	83	â	175	10101111	AF	»	219	11011011	DB	█
132	10000100	84	ä	176	10110000	B0	░	220	11011100	DC	▄
133	10000101	85	à	177	10110001	B1	▒	221	11011101	DD	▌
134	10000110	86	å	178	10110010	B2	▓	222	11011110	DE	▐
135	10000111	87	ç	179	10110011	B3	│	223	11011111	DF	▀
136	10001000	88	ê	180	10110100	B4	┤	224	11100000	E0	α
137	10001001	89	ë	181	10110101	B5	╡	225	11100001	E1	β
138	10001010	8A	è	182	10110110	B6	╢	226	11100010	E2	Γ
139	10001011	8B	ï	183	10110111	B7	╖	227	11100011	E3	π

Table A.1 Continued

DEC	BIN	HEX	ASCII	DEC	BIN	HEX	ASCII	DEC	BIN	HEX	ASCII
228	11100100	E4	Σ	238	11101110	EE	ϵ	247	11110111	F7	≈
229	11100101	E5	σ	239	11101111	EF	∩	248	11111000	F8	°
230	11100110	E6	μ	240	11110000	F0	≡	249	11111001	F9	•
231	11100111	E7	τ	241	11110001	F1	±	250	11111010	FA	·
232	11101000	E8	Φ	242	11110010	F2	≥	251	11111011	FB	√
233	11101001	E9	Θ	243	11110011	F3	≤	252	11111100	FC	n
234	11101010	EA	Ω	244	11110100	F4	⌠	253	11111101	FD	²
235	11101011	EB	δ	245	11110101	F5	⌡	254	11111110	FE	■
236	11101100	EC	∞	246	11110110	F6	÷	255	11111111	FF	
237	11101101	ED	φ								

Table A.2 Metric System Prefixes

Multiplier	Exponent Form	Prefix	SI Symbol
1,000,000,000,000,000,000,000,000	10^{24}	yotta	Y
1,000,000,000,000,000,000,000	10^{21}	zetta	Z
1,000,000,000,000,000,000	10^{18}	exa	E
1,000,000,000,000,000	10^{15}	peta	P
1,000,000,000,000	10^{12}	tera	T
1,000,000,000	10^{9}	giga	G
1,000,000	10^{6}	mega	M
1,000	10^{3}	kilo	K
100	10^{2}	hecto	H
10	10^{1}	deca	Da
1	10^{0}		
.1	10^{-1}	deci	d
.01	10^{-2}	centi	c
.001	10^{-3}	milli	m
.000 001	10^{-6}	micro	μ
.000 000 001	10^{-9}	nano	n
.000 000 000 001	10^{-12}	pico	p
.000 000 000 000 001	10^{-15}	femto	f
.000 000 000 000 000 001	10^{-18}	atto	a
.000 000 000 000 000 000 001	10^{-21}	zepto	z
.000 000 000 000 000 000 000 001	10^{-24}	yocyo	y

Table A.3 Powers of Two

n	2^n	Hexadecimal	Binary Number
0	1	1	1
1	2	2	10
2	4	4	100
3	8	8	1000
4	16	10	1 0000
5	32	20	10 0000
6	64	40	100 0000
7	128	80	1000 0000
8	256	100	1 0000 0000
9	512	200	10 0000 0000
10	1,024	400	100 0000 0000
11	2,048	800	1000 0000 0000
12	4,096	1000	1 0000 0000 0000
13	8,192	2000	10 0000 0000 0000
14	16,384	4000	100 0000 0000 0000
15	32,768	8000	1000 0000 0000 0000
16	65,536	10000	1 0000 0000 0000 0000
17	131,072	20000	10 0000 0000 0000 0000
18	262,144	40000	100 0000 0000 0000 0000
19	524,288	80000	1000 0000 0000 0000 0000
20	1,048,576	100000	1 0000 0000 0000 0000 0000
21	2,097,152	200000	10 0000 0000 0000 0000 0000
22	4,194,304	400000	100 0000 0000 0000 0000 0000
23	8,388,608	800000	1000 0000 0000 0000 0000 0000
24	16,777,216	1000000	1 0000 0000 0000 0000 0000 0000
25	33,554,432	2000000	10 0000 0000 0000 0000 0000 0000
26	67,108,864	4000000	100 0000 0000 0000 0000 0000 0000
27	134,217,728	8000000	1000 0000 0000 0000 0000 0000 0000
28	268,435,456	10000000	1 0000 0000 0000 0000 0000 0000 0000
29	536,870,912	20000000	10 0000 0000 0000 0000 0000 0000 0000
30	1,073,741,824	40000000	100 0000 0000 0000 0000 0000 0000 0000
31	2,147,483,648	80000000	1000 0000 0000 0000 0000 0000 0000 0000
32	4,294,967,296	100000000	1 0000 0000 0000 0000 0000 0000 0000 0000

Table A.3 Continued

n	2^n	Hexadecimal	Binary Number
33	8,589,934,592	200000000	10 0000 0000 0000 0000 0000 0000 0000 0000
34	17,179,869,184	400000000	100 0000 0000 0000 0000 0000 0000 0000 0000
35	34,359,738,368	800000000	1000 0000 0000 0000 0000 0000 0000 0000 0000
36	68,719,476,736	1000000000	1 0000 0000 0000 0000 0000 0000 0000 0000 0000
37	137,438,953,472	2000000000	10 0000 0000 0000 0000 0000 0000 0000 0000 0000
38	274,877,906,944	4000000000	100 0000 0000 0000 0000 0000 0000 0000 0000 0000
39	549,755,813,888	8000000000	1000 0000 0000 0000 0000 0000 0000 0000 0000 0000
40	1,099,511,627,776	10000000000	1 0000 0000 0000 0000 0000 0000 0000 0000 0000 0000
41	2,199,023,255,552	20000000000	10 0000 0000 0000 0000 0000 0000 0000 0000 0000 0000
42	4,398,046,511,104	40000000000	100 0000 0000 0000 0000 0000 0000 0000 0000 0000 0000
43	8,796,093,022,208	80000000000	1000 0000 0000 0000 0000 0000 0000 0000 0000 0000 0000
44	17,592,186,044,416	100000000000	1 0000 0000 0000 0000 0000 0000 0000 0000 0000 0000 0000
45	35,184,372,088,832	200000000000	10 0000 0000 0000 0000 0000 0000 0000 0000 0000 0000 0000
46	70,368,744,177,664	400000000000	100 0000 0000 0000 0000 0000 0000 0000 0000 0000 0000 0000
47	140,737,488,355,328	800000000000	1000 0000 0000 0000 0000 0000 0000 0000 0000 0000 0000 0000
48	281,474,976,710,656	1000000000000	1 0000 0000 0000 0000 0000 0000 0000 0000 0000 0000 0000 0000
49	562,949,953,421,312	2000000000000	10 0000 0000 0000 0000 0000 0000 0000 0000 0000 0000 0000 0000
50	1,125,899,906,842,620	4000000000000	100 0000 0000 0000 0000 0000 0000 0000 0000 0000 0000 0000 0000
51	2,251,799,813,685,250	8000000000000	1000 0000 0000 0000 0000 0000 0000 0000 0000 0000 0000 0000 0000
52	4,503,599,627,370,500	10000000000000	1 0000 0000 0000 0000 0000 0000 0000 0000 0000 0000 0000 0000 0000
53	9,007,199,254,740,990	20000000000000	10 0000 0000 0000 0000 0000 0000 0000 0000 0000 0000 0000 0000 0000
54	18,014,398,509,482,000	40000000000000	100 0000 0000 0000 0000 0000 0000 0000 0000 0000 0000 0000 0000 0000
55	36,028,797,018,964,000	80000000000000	1000 0000 0000 0000 0000 0000 0000 0000 0000 0000 0000 0000 0000 0000
56	72,057,594,037,927,900	100000000000000	1 0000 0000 0000 0000 0000 0000 0000 0000 0000 0000 0000 0000 0000 0000
57	144,115,188,075,856,000	200000000000000	10 0000 0000 0000 0000 0000 0000 0000 0000 0000 0000 0000 0000 0000 0000
58	288,230,376,151,712,000	400000000000000	100 0000 0000 0000 0000 0000 0000 0000 0000 0000 0000 0000 0000 0000 0000
59	576,460,752,303,423,000	800000000000000	1000 0000 0000 0000 0000 0000 0000 0000 0000 0000 0000 0000 0000 0000 0000
60	1,152,921,504,606,850,000	1000000000000000	1 0000 0000 0000 0000 0000 0000 0000 0000 0000 0000 0000 0000 0000 0000 0000
61	2,305,843,009,213,690,000	2000000000000000	10 0000 0000 0000 0000 0000 0000 0000 0000 0000 0000 0000 0000 0000 0000 0000
62	4,611,686,018,427,390,000	4000000000000000	100 0000 0000 0000 0000 0000 0000 0000 0000 0000 0000 0000 0000 0000 0000 0000
63	9,223,372,036,854,780,000	8000000000000000	1000 0000 0000 0000 0000 0000 0000 0000 0000 0000 0000 0000 0000 0000 0000 0000
64	18,446,744,073,709,600,000	10000000000000000	1 0000 0000 0000 0000 0000 0000 0000 0000 0000 0000 0000 0000 0000 0000 0000 0000

APPENDIX B

POST Error Codes

Table B.1 AMI BIOS Beep Codes

You are getting beeps that indicate a memory failure: **1 Beep—Refresh error (with nothing on the screen and it is not a video problem)** **2 Beep—Parity error** **3 Beep—Base 64 K memory failure** • Reseat the memory. • Make sure that the contacts on the memory and the socket are clean. • Try removing one bank of memory modules at a time. Note: Some systems might need to have a memory module in Bank 0. • Try using RAM chips from the same manufacturer with the same part number and speed. • Check for a faulty memory module by trying the memory in a known good system. • Trying known good memory in the system. • Check the power supply and check for power fluctuations. • Swap the motherboard.
You are getting 4 beeps indicating a Timer not operational: • Check for foreign objects such as screws that may ground the motherboard. • Swap the motherboard.
You are getting 5 beeps indicating a Processor error: • Check for foreign objects such as screws that may ground the motherboard. • Make sure the processor is seated properly. • Swap the processor. • Remove the motherboard and reinstall it. • If the problem still persists, swap the motherboard.
You are getting 6 beeps indicating 8042 – gate A20 failure: • Check for foreign objects such as screws that may ground the motherboard. • Try reseating the keyboard controller chip (if possible). • Swap the keyboard. • Swap the processor.
You are getting 7 beeps indicating Processor exception interrupt error: • Make sure the processor is seated properly. • Swap the processor. • Swap the motherboard.

Table B.1 Continued

You are getting 8 beeps indicating Display memory read/write failure: • Make sure that you have a video card on your system. • If possible, swap the memory on the video card. • Swap the video car. • Swap the motherboard.
You are getting 11 beeps indicating Cache memory bad: • Make sure the system is configured properly (CMOS Setup Program and jumpers on the motherboard) for the RAM cache. • If possible, replace the RAM cache. • Swap the processor. • Swap the motherboard.

Table B.2 AMI POST Error Codes

POST Code	Description
01	Processor register test about to start, and NMI to be disabled.
02	NMI is disabled. Power on delay starting.
03	Power on delay complete. Any initialization before keyboard BAT is in progress.
04	Any initialization before keyboard BAT is complete. Reading keyboard SYS bit, to check soft reset/power-on.
05	Soft reset/power-on determined. Going to enable ROM, i.e., disable shadow RAM/cache if any.
06	ROM is enabled. Calculating ROM BIOS checksum and waiting for KB controller input buffer to be free.
07	ROM BIOS checksum passed, KB controller I/B free. Going to issue the BAT command to keyboard controller.
08	BAT command to keyboard controller is issued. Going to verify the BAT command.
09	Keyboard controller BAT result verified. Keyboard command byte to be written next.
0A	Keyboard command byte code is issued. Going to write command byte data.
0B	Keyboard controller command byte is written. Going to issue Pin-23, 24 blocking/unblocking command.
0C	Pin-23,24 of keyboard controller is blocked/unblocked. NOP command of keyboard controller to be issued next.
0D	NOP command processing is done. CMOS shutdown register test to be done next.
0E	CMOS shutdown register R/W test passed. Going to calculate CMOS checksum and update DIAG byte.
0F	CMOS checksum calculation is done; DIAG byte written. CMOS initialization to begin (if "INIT CMOS IN EVERY BOOT IS SET").
10	CMOS initialization done (if any). CMOS status register about to initialize for date and time.
11	CMOS status register initialized. Going to disable DMA and interrupt controllers.
12	DMA controller #1,#2, interrupt controller #1,#2 disabled. About to disable video display and initialize port-B.
13	Video display is disabled and port-B is initialized. Chipset initialization/auto memory detection about to begin.
14	Chipset initialization/auto memory detection over. 8254 timer test about to start.
15	CH-2 timer test halfway. 8254 CH-2 timer test to be complete.
16	Ch-2 timer test over. 8254 CH-1 timer test to be complete.
17	CH-1 timer test over. 8254 CH-0 timer test to be complete.
18	CH-0 timer test over. About to start memory refresh.
19	Memory refresh started. Memory refresh test to be done next.
1A	Memory refresh line is toggling. Going to check 15 microsecond on/off time.
1B	Memory refresh period 30 microsecond test complete. Base 64 K memory test about to start.
20	Base 64 K memory test started. Address line test to be done next.
21	Address line test passed. Going to do toggle parity.

Table B.2 Continued

POST Code	Description
22	Toggle parity over. Going for sequential data R/W test.
23	Base 64 K sequential data R/W test passed. Any setup before interrupt vector initialization about to start.
24	Setup required before vector initialization complete. Interrupt vector initialization about to begin.
25	Interrupt vector initialization done. Going to read I/O port of 8042 for turbo switch (if any).
26	I/O port of 8042 is read. Going to initialize global data for turbo switch.
27	Global data initialization is over. Any initialization after interrupt vector to be done next.
28	Initialization after interrupt vector is complete. Going for monochrome mode setting.
29	Monochrome mode setting is done. Going for color mode setting.
2A	Color mode setting is done. About to go for toggle parity before optional ROM test.
2B	Toggle parity over. About to give control for any setup required before optional video ROM check.
2C	Processing before video ROM control is done. About to look for optional video ROM and give control.
2D	Optional video ROM control is done. About to give control to do any processing after video ROM returns control.
2E	Return from processing after the video ROM control. If EGA/VGA not found, then do display memory R/W test.
2F	EGA/VGA not found. Display memory R/W test about to begin.
30	Display memory R/W test passed. About to look for the retrace checking.
31	Display memory R/W test or retrace checking failed. About to do alternate display memory R/W test.
32	Alternate display memory R/W test passed. About to look for the alternate display retrace checking.
33	Video display checking over. Verification of display type with switch setting and actual card to begin.
34	Verification of display adapter done. Display mode to be set next.
35	Display mode set complete. BIOS ROM data area about to be checked.
36	BIOS ROM data area check over. Going to set cursor for power-on message.
37	Cursor setting for power-on message is complete. Going to display the power-on message.
38	Power-on message display complete. Going to read new cursor positon.
39	New cursor position read and saved. Going to display the reference string.
3A	Reference string display is over. Going to display the Hit <ESC> message.
3B	Hit <ESC> message displayed. Virtual mode memory test about to start.
40	Preparation for virtual mode test started. Going to verify from video memory.
41	Returned after verifying from display memory. Going to prepare the descriptor tables.
42	Descriptor tables prepared. Going to enter in virtual mode for memory test.
43	Entered in the virtual mode. Going to enable interrupts for diagnostics mode.
44	Interrupts enabled (if diagnostics switch is on). Going to initialize data to check memory wraparound at 0:0.
45	Data initialized. Going to check for memory wraparound at 0:0 and find the total system memory size.
46	Memory wraparound test done. Memory size calculation over. About to go for writing patterns to test memory.
47	Pattern to be tested written in extended memory. Going to write patterns in Base 640 K memory.
48	Patterns written in base memory. Going to find out amount of memory below 1 M memory.
49	Amount of memory below 1 M found and verified. Going to find out amount of memory above 1 M memory.
4A	Amount of memory above 1 M found and verified. Going for BIOS ROM data area check.
4B	BIOS ROM data area check over. Going to check <ESC> and to clear memory below 1 M for soft reset.
4C	Memory below 1 M cleared (SOFT RESET). Going to clear memory above 1 M.
4D	Memory above 1 M cleared (SOFT RESET). Going to save the memory size.
4E	Memory test started (NO SOFT RESET). About to display the first 64 K memory test.
4F	Memory size display started. This will be updated during memory test. Going for sequential and random memory test.

Table B.2 Continued

POST Code	Description
50	Memory test below 1 M complete. Going to adjust memory size for relocation/shadow.
51	Memory size adjusted due to relocation/shadow. Memory test above 1 M to follow.
52	Memory test above 1 M complete. Going to prepare to go back to real mode.
53	CPU registers are saved, including memory size. Going to enter in real mode.
54	Shutdown successful; CPU in real mode. Going to restore registers saved during preparation for shutdown.
55	Registers restored. Going to disable gate A20 address line.
56	A20 address line disable successful. BIOS ROM data area about to be checked.
57	BIOS ROM data area check halfway. BIOS ROM data area check to be complete.
58	BIOS ROM data area check over. Going to clear Hit <ESC> message.
59	Hit <ESC> message cleared. <WAIT...> message displayed. About to start DMA and interrupt controller test.
60	DMA page register test passed. About to verify from display memory.
61	Display memory verification over. About to go for DMA #1 base register test.
62	DMA #1 base register test passed. About to go for DMA #2 base register test.
63	DMA #2 base register test passed. About to go for BIOS ROM data area check.
64	BIOS ROM data area check halfway. BIOS ROM data area check to be complete.
65	BIOS ROM data area check over. About to program DMA unit 1 and 2.
66	DMA unit 1 and 2 programming over. About to initialize 8259 interrupt controller.
67	8259 initialization over. About to start keyboard test.
80	Keyboard test started. Clearing output buffer, checking for stuck key, about to issue keyboard reset command.
81	Keyboard reset error/stuck key found. About to issue keyboard controller interface test command.
82	Keyboard controller interface test over. About to write command byte and initialize circular buffer.
83	Command byte written; global data initialization done. About to check for lock-key.
84	Lock-key checking over. About to check for memory size mismatch with CMOS.
85	Memory size check done. About to display soft error and check for password or bypass setup.
86	Password checked. About to do programming before setup.
87	Programming before setup complete. Going to CMOS setup program.
88	Returned from CMOS setup program and screen is cleared. About to do programming after setup.
89	Programming after setup complete. Going to display power-on screen message.
90	Floppy setup is over. Test for hard disk presence to be done.
91	Hard disk presence test over. Hard disk setup to follow.
92	Hard disk setup complete. About to go for BIOS ROM data area check.
93	BIOS ROM data area check halfway. BIOS ROM data area check to be complete.
94	BIOS ROM data area check over. Going to set base and extended memory size.
95	Memory size adjusted due to mouse support, hard disk type-47. Going to verify from display memory.
96	Returned after verifying from display memory. Going to do any initialization before C800 optional ROM control.
97	Any initialization before C800 optional ROM control is over. Optional ROM check and control will be done next.
98	Optional ROM control is done. About to give control to do any required processing after optional ROM returns control.
99	Any initialization required after optional ROM test over. Going to setup timer data area and printer base address.
9A	Return after setting timer and printer base address. Going to set the RS-232 base address.
9B	Returned after RS-232 base address. Going to do any initialization before coprocessor test.
9C	Required initialization before coprocessor is over. Going to initialize the coprocessor next.
9D	Coprocessor initialized. Going to do any initialization after coprocessor test.

Table B.2 Continued

POST Code	Description
9E	Initialization after coprocessor test is complete. Going to check extended keyboard, keyboard ID, and num-lock.
9F	Extended keyboard check is done, ID flag set, num-lock on/off. Keyboard ID command to be issued.
A0	Keyboard ID command issued. Keyboard ID flag to be reset.
A1	Keyboard ID flag reset. Cache memory test to follow.
A2	Cache memory test over. Going to display any soft errors.
A3	Soft error display complete. Going to set the keyboard typematic rate.
A4	Keyboard typematic rate set. Going to program memory wait states.
A5	Memory wait states programming over. Screen to be cleared next.
A6	Screen cleared. Going to enable parity and NMI.
A7	NMI and parity enabled. Going to do any initialization required before giving control to optional ROM at E000.
A8	Initialization before E000 ROM control over. E000 ROM to get control next.
A9	Returned from E000 ROM control. Going to do any initialization required.
AA	Initialization after E000 optional ROM control is over. Going to display the system configuration.
0	System configuration is displayed. Going to give control to INT 19h boot loader.

Table B.3 Award BIOS Beep Codes

You are getting 1 long and 2 short beeps indicating a video problem: • Make sure that you have a video card on your system. • If possible, swap the memory on the video card. • Swap the video card. • Swap the motherboard.
Any other beeps: • Determine if the system worked before. • Determine if there have been any recent changes. • Reseat the memory. • Try a different motherboard. • Make sure that the contacts on the memory and the socket are clean. • Try removing one bank of memory modules at a time. Note: Some systems might need to have a memory module in Bank 0. • Try using RAM chips from the same manufacturer with the same part number and speed. • Check for a faulty memory module by trying the memory in a known good system. • Swap RAM, motherboard, and processor one at a time. If you suspect one of these components, try it in another PC.

Table B.4 Award POST Codes

POST Code	Description
01H	Processor Test 1—Processor status (1FLAGS) verification. Tests the following processor status flags: carry, zero, sign, overflow. The BIOS sets each flag, verifies they are set, then turns each flag off and verifies it is off.
02H	Determine POST type. This test determines whether the status of the system is manufacturing or normal. The status can be set by a physical jumper on some motherboards. If the status is normal, the POST continues through and, assuming no errors, boot is attempted. If manufacturing POST is installed, POST is run in continuous loop, and boot is not attempted.
03H	8042 keyboard controller. Test controller by sending TEST_KBRD command (AAH) and verifying that controller reads commands.
04H	8042 keyboard controller. Verifies the keyboard controller returned AAH, sent in test 3.
05H	Get manufacturing status. The last test in the manufacturing cycle. If test 2 found the status to be manufacturing, this POST triggers a reset and POSTs 1 through 5 are repeated continuously.
06H	Initialize chips. POST 06H performs these functions: disables color and mono video, disables parity circuits, disables DMA (8237) chips, resets math coprocessor, initializes timer 1 (8255), clears DMA chip, clears all page registers, and clears CMOS shutdown byte.
07H	Processor test 2. Reads, writes, and verifies all CPU registers except SS, SP, and BP with data pattern FF and 00.
08H	Initialize CMOS timer. Updates timer cycle normally.
09H	EPROM checksum. Checksums EPROM; test failed if sum not equal to 0. Also checksums sign-on message.
0AH	Initialize video interface. Initializes video controller register 6845 to the following: 80 characters per row 25 rows per screen 8/14 scan lines per row for mono/color First scan line of cursor 6/11 Last scan line of cursor 7/12 Reset display offset to 0
0BH	Test timer (8254) channel 0. This and the next two timer tests verify that the 8254 timer chip is functioning properly.
0CH	Test timer (8254) channel 1.
0DH	Test timer (8254) channel 2.
0EH	Test CMOS shutdown byte. Uses a walking bit algorithm to check interface to CMOS circuit.
0FH	Test extended CMOS. On motherboards with chipsets that support extended information, this test is used to configure the chipset. These chipsets have an extended storage mechanism that enables the user to save a desired system configuration after the power is turned off. A checksum is used to verify the validity of the extended storage and, if valid, permit the information to be loaded into extended CMOS RAM.
10H	Test DMA channel 0. This and the next two functions initialize the DMA chip and then test the chip using an AA, 55, FF, 00 pattern. Part addresses are used to check the address circuit to DMA page registers.
11H	DMA channel 1.
12H	DMA page registers.
13H	Keyboard controller. Test keyboard controller interface.
14H	Test memory refresh. RAM must be refreshed periodically to keep the memory from decaying. This function ensures that the memory-refresh function is working properly.
15H	First 64 KB of system memory. An extensive parity test is performed on the first 64 KB of system memory. This memory is used by the BIOS.
16H	Interrupt vector table. Sets up and loads interrupt vector tables in memory for use by the 8259 PIC chip.
17H	Video I/O operations. This function initializes the video, either CGA, MDA, EGA, or VGA. If a CGA or MDA adapter is installed, the video is initialized by the system BIOS. If the system BIOS detects an EGA or VGA adapter, the option ROM BIOS installed on the video adapter is used to initialize and set up the video.
18H	Video memory. Tests memory for CGA and MDA video boards. This test is not performed by the system BIOS on EGA or VGA video adapters—the board's own EGA or VGA BIOS ensures that it is functioning properly.

Table B.4 Continued

POST Code	Description
19H	Test 8259 mask bits—channel 1. This and the next test verify 8259 masked interrupts by alternately turning the interrupt lines off and on. Unsuccessful completion generates a fatal error.
1AH	8259 mask bits—channel 2.
1BH	CMOS battery level. Verifies that the battery status bit is set to 1. A 0 value can indicate a bad battery or some other problem, such as bad CMOS.
1CH	CMOS checksum. This function tests the CMOS checksum data (located at 2EH and 2FH) and extended CMOS checksum, if present, to be sure that they are valid.
1DH	Configuration from CMOS. If the CMOS checksum is good, the values are used to configure the system.
1EH	System memory. The system memory size is determined by writing to addresses from 0 KB to 640 KB, starting at 0 and continuing until an address does not respond. Memory size value then is compared to the CMOS value to ensure that they are the same. If they are different, a flag is set and, at the end of POST, an error message is displayed.
1FH	Found system memory. Tests memory from 64 KB to the top of the memory found by writing the pattern FFAA and 5500 and then reading the pattern back, byte by byte, and verifying that it is correct.
20H	Stuck 8259 interrupt bits. This and the next two tests verify the functionality of the 8259 interrupt controller.
21H	Stuck NMI bits (parity or I/O channel check).
22H	8259 function.
23H	Protected mode. Verifies protected mode, 8086 virtual mode as well as 8086 page mode. Protected mode ensures that any data about to be written to extended memory (above 1 MB) is checked to ensure that it is suitable for storage.
24H	Extended memory. This function sizes memory above 1 MB by writing to addresses starting at 1 MB and continuing to 16 MB on 286 and 86SX systems, and to 64 MB on 386 systems until there is no response. This process determines the total extended memory, which is compared with CMOS to ensure that the values are the same. If the values are different, a flag is set and, at the end of POST, an error message is displayed.
25H	Found extended memory. This function tests extended memory using virtual 8086 paging mode and writing an FFFF, AA55, 0000 pattern.
26H	Protected mode exceptions. This function tests other aspects of protected mode operations.
27H	Cache control or shadow RAM. Tests for shadow RAM and cache controller (386 and 486 only) functionality. Systems with CGA and MDA adapters indicate that video shadow RAM is enabled, even though there is no BIOS ROM to shadow (this is normal).
28H	8242. Optional Intel 8242/8248 keyboard controller detection and support.
29H	Reserved.
2AH	Initialize keyboard. Initialize keyboard controller.
2BH	Floppy drive and controller. Initialize floppy disk drive controller and any drives present.
2CH	Detect and initialize serial ports. Initializes any serial ports present.
2DH	Detect and initialize parallel ports. Initializes any parallel ports present.
2FH	Detect and initialize math coprocessor. Initializes any option ROMs present from C800 to EFFFH.
30H	Reserved.
31H	Detect and initialize math coprocessor. Initializes math coprocessors.
3BH	Initialize secondary cache with OPTi chipset. Initializes secondary cache controller for systems based on the OPTi chipset (486 only).
CAH	Micronics cache initialization. Detects and initializes Micronics cache controller if present.
CCH	NMI handler shutdown. Detects untrapped nonmaskable interrupt during boot.
EEH	Unexpected processor exception.
FFH	Boot attempt. When the POST is complete, if all the system components and peripherals are initialized and if no error flags were set (such as memory size error), then the system attempts to boot.

Table B.5 IBM BIOS Beep Codes

Beeps	Description
1 short	Normal POST—system OK
2 short	Initialization error, DMA, ROM, floppy, serial, or parallel
1 long, 1 short	System board
1 long, 2 short	Display adapter (MDA, CGA)
1 long, 3 short	Enhanced graphics (EGA)
None	Power supply, RAM, or motherboard
Continuous	Power supply or motherboard
Repeating short	Power supply or motherboard

Table B.6 IBM POST Error Codes

100-Series	System Board Error	Recommended Solution
101	Interrupt failure; general system board failure	Replace the motherboard.
102	System timer failed	Replace the motherboard.
103	System timer interrupt failed	Replace the motherboard.
104	Protected mode (AT)	Replace the keyboard. If the error still exists, replace the motherboard.
105	8042 command not accepted; keyboard communication failure	Replace the keyboard, keyboard controller chip, or motherboard.
106	POST logic test problem	Replace the faulty expansion card or the motherboard.
107	NMI test failed	Replace the microprocessor or the motherboard.
108	Failed system timer test	Replace the motherboard.
109	Problem with first 64 KB RAM	Replace the memory. If the error still exists, replace the motherboard.
151	Real-time clock (or CMOS RAM)	Replace the CMOS battery. If the problem still exists, replace the motherboard.
152	System board circuitry	Replace the motherboard.
161	CMOS power failure	Replace the CMOS battery. If the problem still exists, replace the motherboard.
162	CMOS checksum error	Replace the CMOS battery. If the problem still exists, replace the motherboard.
163	Clock date error	
164	Memory size (POST finds value different from CMOS)	
165	Adapter added/removed (PS/2)	
200-Series	**Memory**	
201	Memory test failed	Replace the RAM. If the problem still exists, replace the motherboard. (Note: The address indicating which RAM chip is usually given.)
300-Series	**Keyboard**	
301	Stuck key or improper response	Make sure keyboard is plugged in and no keys are stuck. In addition, make sure nothing is resting on the keys.

Table B.6 Continued

300-Series	Keyboard	
302	Keyboard test error or keyboard is locked	The keyboard lock is on. If the keyboard lock is not on, you may have a faulty keylock switch or a keyboard key is stuck down.
303	Keyboard interface error (on system board)	Check the AT/XT switch on the keyboard. If the problem still exists, replace the keyboard cable or keyboard.
304 365 366	Nonspecific keyboard error Keyboard failure Keyboard cable failure	Check the AT/XT switch on the keyboard. If the problem still exists, replace the keyboard cable or keyboard.
400-Series	**Monochrome Display**	
401	Memory or sync test failure	Replace the monochrome video card.
432	Parallel port test failure	Replace the monochrome video card and/or parallel card.
500-Series	**Color Graphics Adapter**	
501	Memory or sync test failure	Replace the CGA card.
600-Series	**Floppy Disk System**	
601	Drive or adapter test failure	Check floppy drive CMOS settings. If the problem still exists, check the floppy drive cable, drive power connector, floppy drive card, and floppy drive.
602	Drive failure	Check floppy drive CMOS settings. If the problem still exists, check the floppy drive cable, drive power connector, floppy drive card, and floppy drive.
603	Wrong drive capacity	
606	Disk verify function error	
607	Write-protected diskette	
608	Bad command	
610	Disk initialization error	
611	Timeout error	
612	Bad controller chip	
613	DMA failure	
614	DMA boundary error	
621	Seek error	
622	CRC error	
623	Record not found	
624	Bad address mark	
625	Controller seek failure	
626	Data compare error	
627	Change line error	
628	Disk removed	
700-Series	**Floating-Point Unit**	
900-Series	**LPT1**	
1000-Series	**LPT2**	

Table B.6 Continued

1100-Series	**COM1**	
1200-Series	**COM2**	
1300-Series	**Game Control Adapter**	
1301	Adapter failure	
1302	Joystick failure	
1400-Series	**Printer**	
1500-Series	**SDLC Communications Adapter**	
1600-Series	**Display Station Emulation Adapter (DSEA)**	
1700-Series	**Hard Disk System**	
1701	Drive not ready; disk or adapter test failure	Check hard drive CMOS settings and hard drive configuration. If the problem still exists, check the hard drive cable, drive power connector, hard drive card, and hard drive.
1702	Time out; disk or adapter error	
1703	Drive error	
1704	Adapter or drive error	
1705	Record not found	
1706	Write fault	
1707	Track 0 error	
1708	Head select error	
1709	Bad error correction code	
1710	Read buffer overrun	
1711	Bad address mark	
1712	Nonspecific error	
1713	Data compare error	
1714	Drive not ready	
1730	Adapter error	
1731	Adapter error	
1732	Adapter error	
1780	Drive C boot failure	Check floppy drive CMOS settings and partitions. If the problem still exists, check the floppy drive cable, floppy drive card, and floppy drive.
1781	Drive D failure	Check floppy drive CMOS settings and partitions. If the problem still exists, check the floppy drive cable, floppy drive card, and floppy drive.
1782	Controller boot failure	Check hard drive controller configuration.
1790	Drive C error	Check floppy drive CMOS settings and partitions. If the problem still exists, check the floppy drive cable, floppy drive card, and floppy drive.
1791	Drive D error	
1800-Series	**PC or XT Expansion Chassis**	
2000-Series	**First Bisynchronous (BSC) Adapter**	
2100 Series	**Second Bisynchronous (BSC) Adapter**	

Table B.6 Continued

2200-Series	Cluster Adapter	
2400-Series	**Enhanced Graphics Adapter**	
2401	Adapter test failure	
2456	Light pen failure	
2500-Series	**Second Enhanced Graphics Adapter**	
2600-Series	**PC/370-M Adapter**	
2700-Series	**PC/3277 Emulation Adapter**	
2800-Series	**3278/79 Emulator Adapter**	
2900-Series	**Printer**	
3000-Series	**Network Adapter**	
3001	Adapter ROM test failure	
3002	Adapter RAM test failure	
3006	Interrupt conflict	
3100-Series	**Second Network Adapter**	
3300-Series	**Compact Printer**	
3600-Series	**IEEE-488 (GPIB) Adapter**	
3800-Series	**Data Acquisition Adapter**	
3900-Series	**Professional Graphics Controller Adapter**	
4400-Series	**5278 Display Attachment Unit and 5279 Display**	
4500-Series	**IEEE-488 (GPIB) Adapter**	
4600-Series	**Artic Interface Adapter**	
4800-Series	**Internal Modem**	
4900-Series	**Second Internal Modem**	
5600-Series	**Financial Communication System**	
7000-Series	**Phoenix BIOS Chipset**	
7000	CMOS failure	
7001	Shadow memory	
7002	CMOS configuration error	
7100-Series	**Voice Communication Adapter**	
7300-Series	**3.5-Inch Floppy Disk Drive**	
7301	Drive or adapter test failure	Check floppy drive CMOS settings. If the problem still exists, check the floppy drive cable, drive power connector, floppy drive card, and floppy drive.
7307	Write-protected diskette	
7308	Bad command	
7310	Track zero error	
7311	Timeout	

Table B.6 Continued

7300-Series	3.5-Inch Floppy Disk Drive
7312	Bad controller or DMA
7315	Bad index
7316	Speed error
7321	Bad seek
7322	Bad CRC
7323	Record not found
7324	Bad address mark
7325	Controller seek error
7400-Series	**8514/A Display Adapter**
7401	Test failure
7426	Monitor failure
7600-Series	**Page Printer**
8400-Series	**Speech Adapter**
8500-Series	**2 MB Memory Adapter**
8600-Series	**Pointing Device**
8900-Series	**MIDI Adapter**
10000-Series	**Multiprotocol Communications Adapter**
10100-Series	**Modem and Communications Adapter**
10400-Series	**ESDI Disk Controller**
10450	Write/read test error
10451	Read verify test error
10452	Seek test error
10453	Device type mismatch
10454	Controller buffer failure
10455	Controller failure
10400-Series	**ESDI Disk Controller**
10461	Format error
10463	Write/read sector error
10464	Drive map unreadable
10465	ECC error
10466	ECC error
10467	Soft seek error
10468	Hard seek error
10469	Soft seek error
10470	Controller diagnostic error
10499	Controller failure
10700-Series	**5.25-Inch External Floppy Disk Drive**
11200-Series	**SCSI Adapter**

Table B.6 Continued

12900-Series	Processor Platform
12901	Processor error
12902	Cache error
14900-Series	**PLASMA Display and Adapter**
16500-Series	**Streaming Tape Drive**
16520	Drive error
16540	Controller error
16600-Series	**First Token-Ring Network Adapter**
16700-Series	**Second Token-Ring Network Adapter**
19400-Series	**Adapter Memory Module**
21000-Series	**SCSI Hard Disk or Host Adapter**
21500-Series	**CD-ROM System**

Table B.7 Phoenix Beep Codes—Fatal System Board Errors

Beep Code	Description	Recommended Solution
None	CPU register test in progress	• Swap the processor. • Try reseating the motherboard. • Swap the motherboard.
1-1-3	CMOS write/read failure	• Try reseating the motherboard. • Swap the motherboard.
1-1-4	ROM BIOS checksum failure	• Try reflashing the BIOS. • Swap the motherboard.
1-2-1	Programmable interval timer failure	• Try reseating the motherboard. • Swap the motherboard.
1-2-2	DMA initialization failure	• Try reseating the motherboard. • Swap the motherboard.
1-2-3	DMA page register write/read failure	• Try reseating the motherboard. • Swap the motherboard.
1-3-1	RAM refresh verification failure	• Reseat the memory. • Make sure that the contacts on the memory and the sockets are clean. • Try removing one bank of memory modules at a time. Note: Some systems might need to have a memory module in Bank 0. • Try using RAM chips from the same manufacturer with the same part number and speed. • Check for a faulty memory module by trying the memory in a known good system. • Trying known good memory in the system. • Check the power supply and check for power fluctuations. • Swap the motherboard.
None	First 64K RAM test in progress	
1-3-3	First 64 KB RAM chip or data line failure, multibit	
1-3-4	First 64 KB RAM odd/even logic failure	
1-4-1	Address line failure fist 64 KB RAM	
1-4-2	Parity failure first 64 KB	
2-_-_	First 64 KB RAM Failure	
3-1-1	Slave DMA register failure	• Try reseating the motherboard. • Swap the motherboard.
3-1-2	Master DMA register failure	
3-1-3	Master interrupt mask register failure	
3-1-4	Slave interrupt mask register failure	
3-2-4	Keyboard controller test failure	Check keyboard XT/AT switch, keyboard cable, keyboard, or motherboard.
3-3-4	Screen initialization failure	• Make sure that you have a video card on your system. • If possible, swap the memory on the video card. • Swap the video card. • Swap the motherboard.
3-4-1	Screen retrace failure	
3-4-2	Search for video ROM in progress	

Table B.8 Phoenix Beep Codes—Nonfatal System Board Errors

Beep Code	Description	Recommended Solution
4-2-1	Timer tick interrupt test in progress or failure	• Try reseating the motherboard. • Swap the motherboard.
4-2-2	Shutdown test in progress or failure	• First check the keyboard for problems. If nothing, you have a bad motherboard.
4-2-3	Gate A20 failure	• Check for foreign objects such as screws that may ground the motherboard.
		• Try reseating the keyboard controller chip. • Swap the keyboard. • Swap the processor. • Try removing and reinstalling the motherboard. • If the problem still persists, swap the motherboard.
4-2-4	Unexpected interrupt in protected mode	• Check for a bad expansion card or bad motherboard.
4-3-1	RAM test in progress or address failure >FFFh	• Replace the motherboard.
4-3-3	Interval timer Channel 2 test or failure	• Try reseating the motherboard. • Swap the motherboard.
4-3-4	Time-of-day clock test or failure	• Try running the setup program that comes with the computer. Check the date and time. If that doesn't work, replace the battery or motherboard.
4-4-1	Serial port test or failure	• Reseat, or replace, the I/O card. If the serial port is on the motherboard, disable.
4-4-2	Parallel port test or failure	• Reseat, or replace, the I/O card. If the serial port is on the motherboard, disable.
4-4-3	Math coprocessor test or failure	• Run a test program to double-check it. If the problem does exist, replace the math coprocessor (or CPU).
Low 1-1-2	System board select failure	• Replace the motherboard.
Low 1-1-3	Extended CMOS RAM failure	• Replace the motherboard.

Table B.9 Phoenix POST Codes

POST Code	Description
02H	Verify real mode
03H	Disable nonmaskable interrupt (NMI)
04H	Get CPU type
06H	Initialize system hardware
08H	Initialize chipset with initial POST values
09H	Set IN POST flag
0AH	Initialize CPU registers

Table B.9 Continued

POST Code	Description
0BH	Enable CPU cache
0CH	Initialize caches to initial POST values
0EH	Initialize I/O component
0FH	Initialize the local bus IDE
10H	Initialize power management
11H	Load alternate registers with initial POST values
12H	Restore CPU control word during warm boot
13H	Initialize PCI bus mastering devices
14H	Initialize keyboard controller
16H	BIOS ROM checksum
17H	Initialize cache before memory autosize
18H	8254 timer initialization
1AH	8237 DMA controller initialization
1CH	Reset programmable interrupt controller
20H	Test DRAM refresh
22H	Test 8742 keyboard controller
24H	Set ES segment register to 4 GB
26H	Enable A20 line
28H	Autosize DRAM
29H	Initialize POST memory manager
2AH	Clear 512 KB base RAM
2CH	RAM failure on address line *xxxx**
2EH	1- 3- 4- 3 RAM failure on data bits *xxxx** of low byte of memory bus
2FH	Enable cache before system BIOS shadow
30H	RAM failure on data bits *xxxx** of high byte of memory bus
32H	Test CPU bus-clock frequency
33H	Initialize Phoenix dispatch manager
36H	Warm start shut down
38H	Shadow system BIOS ROM
3AH	Autosize cache
3CH	Advanced configuration of chipset registers
3DH	Load alternate registers with CMOS values
42H	Initialize interrupt vectors
45H	POST device initialization
46H	Check ROM copyright notice
48H	Check video configuration against CMOS
49H	Initialize PCI bus and devices
4AH	Initialize all video adapters in system
4BH	QuietBoot start (optional)
4CH	Shadow video BIOS ROM
4EH	Display BIOS copyright notice

*If BIOS detects 2CH, 2EH, or 30H, an additional word-bitmap (*xxxx*) is displayed indicating the address line or bits that failed.

Table B.9 Continued

POST Code	Description
50H	Display CPU type and speed
51H	Initialize EISA board
52H	Test keyboard
54H	Set key click if enabled
58H	Test for unexpected interrupts
59H	Initialize POST display service
5AH	Display prompt "Press F2 to enter SETUP"
5BH	Disable CPU cache
5CH	Test RAM between 512 and 640 KB
60H	Test extended memory
62H	Test extended memory address lines
64H	Jump to UserPatch1
66H	Configure advanced cache registers
67H	Initialize multiprocessor APIC
68H	Enable external and CPU caches
69H	Setup system management mode (SMM) area
6AH	Display external L2 cache size
6BH	Load custom defaults (optional)
6CH	Display shadow-area message
6EH	Display possible high address for UMB recovery
70H	Display error messages
72H	Check for configuration errors
76H	Check for keyboard errors
7CH	Setup hardware interrupt vectors
7EH	Initialize coprocessor if present
80H	Disable onboard super I/O ports and IRQs
81H	Late POST device initialization
82H	Detect and install external RS232 ports
83H	Configure non-MCD IDE controllers
84H	Detect and install external parallel ports
85H	Initialize PC-compatible PnP ISA devices
86H	Reinitialize onboard I/O ports
87H	Configure motherboard configurable devices (optional)
88H	Initialize BIOS data area
89H	Enable nonmaskable interrupts (NMIs)
8AH	Initialize extended BIOS data area
8BH	Test and initialize PS/2 mouse
8CH	Initialize floppy controller
8FH	Determine number of ATA drives (optional)
90H	Initialize hard disk controllers
91H	Initialize local bus hard disk controllers
92H	Jump to UserPatch2
93H	Build MPTABLE for multiprocessor boards

Table B.9 Continued

POST Code	Description
95H	Install CD ROM for boot
96H	Clear huge ES segment register
97H	Fix up multiprocessor table
98H	Search for option ROMs. One long, two short beeps on checksum failure.
99H	Check for SMART drive (optional)
9AH	Shadow option ROMs
9CH	Set up power management
9DH	Initialize security engine (optional)
9EH	Enable hardware interrupts
9FH	Determine number of ATA and SCSI drives
A0H	Set time of day
A2H	Check key lock
A4H	Initialize typematic rate
A8H	Erase F2 prompt
AAH	Scan for F2 keystroke
ACH	Enter SETUP
AEH	Clear boot flag
B0H	Check for errors
B2H	POST done—prepare to boot operating system
B4H	One short beep before boot
B5H	Terminate QuietBoot (optional)
B6H	Check password (optional)
B9H	Prepare boot
BAH	Initialize DMI parameters
BBH	Initialize PnP option ROMs
BCH	Clear parity checkers
BDH	Display MultiBoot menu
BEH	Clear screen (optional)
BFH	Check virus and backup reminders
C0H	Try to boot with INT 19
C1H	Initialize POST error manager (PEM)
C2H	Initialize error logging
C3H	Initialize error display function
C4H	Initialize system error handler
C5H	PnP and dual CMOS (optional)
C6H	Initialize notebook docking (optional)
C7H	Initialize notebook docking late
C8H	Force check (optional)
C9H	Extended checksum (optional)
D2H	Unknown interrupt

Table B.10 Phoenix POST Code Beeps for Boot Block in Flash ROM

POST Code	Description
E0H	Initialize the chipset
E1H	Initialize the bridge
E2H	Initialize the CPU
E3H	Initialize system timer
E4H	Initialize system I/O
E5H	Check force recovery boot
E6H	Checksum BIOS ROM
E7H	Go to BIOS
E8H	Set huge segment
E9H	Initialize multiprocessor
EAH	Initialize OEM special code
EBH	Initialize PIC and DMA
ECH	Initialize memory type
EDH	Initialize memory size
EEH	Shadow boot block
EFH	System memory test
F0H	Initialize interrupt vectors
F1H	Initialize run time clock
F2H	Initialize video
F3H	Initialize system management mode
F4H	Output one beep before boot
F5H	Boot to mini DOS
F6H	Clear huge segment
F7H	Boot to full DOS

Table B.11 POST Messages

128 KB Not OK, Parity Disabled	Replace the first bank of RAM or replace the motherboard.
8042 Gate-A20 Error	The Gate-A20 portion (21st address line used to access memory above 1 MB) of the keyboard controller has failed. Check XT/AT switch on keyboard and keyboard controller. Make sure the RAM chips are seated properly. Replace the keyboard controller or entire motherboard.
Address Line Short	There is a problem with the memory address decoding circuitry. Try rebooting (turn the system off and then on 10 seconds later). If the problem still exists, replace the motherboard.
Bad DMA Port=XX	Replace the motherboard.
Bad PnP Serial ID Checksum	The serial ID checksum of a plug-and-play card is invalid. Replace the expansion card.
BIOS ROM Checksum Error —System Halted	The checksum of the BIOS code in the BIOS chip is incorrect, indicating the BIOS code may have become corrupt. Replace the system ROM BIOS or the motherboard.
BUS Timeout NMI at Slot X	There was a bus timeout NMI at slot X.
C Drive Error	The system cannot get a response from drive C. Check the hard drive parameters in the CMOS parameter and make sure the disk is partitioned and formatted properly. Lastly, make sure that the hard drive is connected properly.

Table B.11 Continued

C: Drive Failure	The drive was detected but failed. Check hard drive CMOS settings and hard drive configuration. If the problem still exists, check the hard drive cable, drive power connector, hard drive card, and hard drive.
Cache Memory Bad	Make sure RAM cache is seated properly. Replace RAM cache or replace motherboard. (Note: You can also perform a temporary repair by disabling the RAM cache.)
CH-2 Timer Error	Could be caused by a peripheral or motherboard.
CMOS Battery Failed or **CMOS Battery Has Failed**	CMOS battery is no longer functional. Replace the battery.
CMOS Battery State Low	Record your CMOS settings as soon as possible and replace the CMOS battery.
CMOS Checksum Error	Checksum of CMOS is incorrect. This can indicate that CMOS has become corrupt. This error may have been caused by a weak battery. Check the CMOS battery.
CMOS Display Mismatch	The video type indicated in the CMOS RAM is not the one detected by the BIOS. Check the CMOS setup program to make sure that the correct video type is selected. (Note: Most computers have it set to VGA or EGA/VGA.)
CMOS Memory Size Mismatch	Run the CMOS setup program. If the CMOS setup program does not show the correct amount of RAM on the motherboard, make sure the RAM is seated properly. If the problem still exists, replace the RAM and motherboard.
CMOS Memory Size Mismatch	Usually caused when memory is added or removed from the system but could be caused by memory that has failed. Run CMOS setup program.
CMOS System Options Not Set	CMOS values are either corrupt or do not exist. Run CMOS setup program. If the problem reoccurs, check the CMOS battery. If the problem still exists, replace the motherboard.
CMOS Time and Date Not Set	Run the CMOS setup program. If the problem reoccurs, check the CMOS battery. If the problem still exists, replace the motherboard.
Disk Boot Error, Replace and Strike Key to Retry	If booting from the hard drive, take the disk out of the floppy drive and make sure that the hard drive is bootable. If booting from the floppy drive, make sure that the floppy disk is bootable.
Disk Boot Failure, Insert System Disk and Press Enter	No boot device was found. This could mean that either a boot drive was not detected or the drive does not contain proper system boot files. Insert a system disk into drive A and press Enter. If you assumed the system would boot from the hard drive, make sure the controller is inserted correctly and all cables are properly attached. Also be sure the disk is formatted as a boot device. Then reboot the system.
Diskette Boot Failure	The diskette in the specified boot-up drive is corrupt.
Diskette Drives or Types Mismatch Error—Run Setup	The type of diskette drive installed in the system is different from the CMOS definition. Run the CMOS setup program and enter the correct drive type.
Display Switch Is Set Incorrectly or **Display Switch Not Proper**	Many motherboards have a jumper or switch that specifies a monochrome or color video board. Check the jumper or switch and correct its position.
Display Type Has Changed Since Last Boot	Since the last system shutdown, the display has been changed. Run the CMOS setup program and reconfigure the display, if possible.
DMA Error or **DMA #1 Error** or **DMA #2 Error**	There is an error in the first DMA channel on the motherboard. This could be caused by a peripheral device. If the problem still exists, replace the motherboard.
DMA Bus Timeout	A device has driven the bus signal for more than 7.8 microseconds. Troubleshoot all expansion cards (remove them and try to isolate the failure).
DMA Error	There is an error within the DMA controller on the motherboard. Replace the motherboard.

Table B.11 Continued

EISA CMOS Checksum Failure	The checksum for EISA CMOS is bad, or the battery is bad.
EISA CMOS Inoperational	A read/write failure occurred in extended CMOS RAM. The battery may be bad.
EISA Configuration Checksum Error	The EISA nonvolatile RAM checksum is incorrect or cannot correctly read the EISA slot. Run the EISA Configuration utility. Either the EISA nonvolatile memory has become corrupt or the slot has been configured incorrectly. Also make sure the card is installed firmly in the slot. When this error appears, the system will boot in ISA mode, which allows you to run the EISA Configuration utility.
EISA Configuration Is Not Complete	The slot configuration information stored in the EISA nonvolatile memory is incomplete. When this error appears, the system will boot in ISA mode, which allows you to run the EISA Configuration utility. Run the EISA Configuration utility.
Error Encountered Initializing Hard Drive	The hard drive cannot be initialized. Be sure the adapter/controller is installed correctly and that all cables are correctly and firmly attached. Also make sure the correct hard drive type is selected in Setup.
Error Initializing Hard Drive Controller	Cannot initialize the controller card. Make sure the card is correctly and firmly seated in the system board. Be sure the correct hard drive type is selected in Setup. Also check to see if any jumpers need to be set on the hard drive.
Expansion Board Disabled at Slot X	The expansion board NMI was generated from slot X.
Expansion Board Not Ready at Slot X	AMI BIOS cannot find the expansion board in slot X. Verify that the board is in the correct slot and is seated properly.
Fail-Safe Timer NMI	A fail-safe timer NMI has been generated.
Fail-Safe Timer NMI Inoperational	Devices that depend on the fail-safe NMI timer are not operating correctly.
FDD Controller Failure	Check floppy drive CMOS settings. If the problem still exists, check the floppy drive cable, drive power connector, floppy drive card, and floppy drive.
Floppy Disk Controller Resource Conflict	The floppy disk controller has requested a resource (I/O address, IRQ, DMA, or memory address) that is already in use. Trying changing the resources used by the plug-and-play system.
Floppy Disk Cntrlr Error or No Cntrlr Present	Check floppy drive CMOS settings. If the problem still exists, check the floppy drive cable, drive power connector, floppy drive card, and floppy drive.
Floppy Disk(s) Fail	Check floppy drive CMOS settings. If the problem still exists, check the floppy drive cable, drive power connector, floppy drive card, and floppy drive.
Gate A20 Failure	The Gate-A20 portion (21st address line used to access memory above 1 MB) of the keyboard controller has failed. Check the XT/AT switch on the keyboard. Make sure the RAM chips are seated properly. Replace the keyboard controller or entire motherboard.
Hard Disk Install Failure	Check hard drive CMOS settings and the hard drive configuration. If the problem still exists, check the hard drive cable, drive power connector, hard drive controller, and hard drive.
Hard Disk(s) Diagnosis Fail	The system may run specific disk diagnostic routines. This message appears if one or more hard disks returns an error when the diagnostics run.
HDD Controller Failure	Check hard drive CMOS settings and the hard drive configuration. If the problem still exists, check the hard drive cable, drive power connector, and hard drive.
ID Information Mismatch for Slot X	The ID of the EISA expansion board in slot X does not match the ID in CMOS RAM.
INTR #1 Error	Interrupt channel 1 has failed the POST test. Check expansion cards for IRQs 0–7.
INTR #2 Error	Interrupt channel 2 has failed the POST test. Check expansion cards for IRQs 8–15.
Invalid Boot Diskette	The BIOS can read the disk in floppy drive A but it cannot boot from it. Try another bootable floppy disk or check the floppy drive, cable, or controller card.
Invalid Configuration Information for Slot X	The configuration information for EISA board X is not correct. Run the ECU.

Table B.11 Continued

Invalid EISA Configuration	The nonvolatile memory containing EISA configuration information was programmed incorrectly or has become corrupt. Rerun the EISA Configuration utility to correctly program the memory. When this error occurs, the system will boot in ISA mode, which allows you to run the EISA Configuration utility.
K/B Interface Error	The keyboard is not plugged in correctly, the keyboard cable is bad, the keyboard is bad, or the motherboard has to be replaced.
Keyboard Error	The keyboard is not plugged in correctly, the keyboard cable is bad, the keyboard is bad, or the motherboard has to be replaced.
Keyboard Error or no Keyboard Present	The keyboard is not plugged in correctly, the keyboard cable is bad, the keyboard is bad, or the motherboard has to be replaced.
Keyboard Is Locked...Unlock It	Unlock the keyboard. In addition, make sure there are no objects resting on the keyboard.
Memory Address Error at XXXX or **Memory Parity Error at XXXX**	Indicates a memory address error at XXXX location. Use the location along with the memory map for the system to find and replace the bad memory chips.
Memory Size Has Changed Since Last Boot	Memory has been added or removed since the last boot. In EISA mode, use the EISA Configuration utility to reconfigure the memory configuration. In ISA mode, enter Setup and enter the new memory size in the memory fields if possible.
Memory Test Fail	If POST detects an error during memory testing, additional information appears giving specifics about the type and location of the memory error.
Memory Verify Error at XXXX	Indicates an error verifying a value already written to memory. Use the location along with the system's memory map to locate the bad chip(s).
Non-System Disk or Disk Error. Replace and Strike Any Key When Ready.	If you are trying to boot from the hard drive, make sure there is no disk in drive A and make sure that drive C has the necessary boot files. If you are trying to boot from the floppy drive, make sure that the floppy drive has the necessary boot files.
No ROM Basic	There is nothing to boot from. (i.e., the system cannot find an operating system). Be certain that a bootable disk is defined in the CMOS setup program and that you have the correct CMOS parameters. In addition, make sure that you have an active partition.
NVRAM Checksum Error, NVRAM Cleared	The Extended System Configuration Data (ESCD), part of the plug-and-play system, was reinitialized because of a NVRAM checksum error. Try rerunning the ISA Configuration utility (ICU). If the problem still exists, replace the NVRAM IC or replace the motherboard.
NVRAM Data Invalid, NVRAM Cleared	Invalid data has been found in the ESCD, part of the plug-and-play system and has been automatically cleared. Try rebooting the system.
Off Board Parity Error	There is a parity error with memory installed in an expansion slot at address XXXX (hex). Make sure the RAM chip is seated properly. If the problem still exists, replace the RAM chip or motherboard.
Offending Address Not Found	This message is used in conjunction with the "I/O Channel Check" and "RAM Parity Error" messages when the segment that has caused the problem cannot be isolated.
Offending Segment	This message is used in conjunction with the "I/O Channel Check" and "RAM Parity Error" messages when the segment that has caused the problem cannot be isolated.
On Board Parity Error	There is a parity error with memory on the motherboard at address XXXX (hex). ("On Board" specifies that the memory is not on an expansion board, but rather is located on the motherboard physically). Possibly correctable with software from the motherboard manufacturer. In addition, check for viruses since some viruses cause parity errors.
Override Enabled—Defaults Loaded	If the system cannot boot using the current CMOS configuration, the BIOS can override the current configuration with a set of BIOS defaults designed for the most stable, minimal-performance system operations.
Parallel Port Resource Conflict	The parallel port has requested a resource (I/O address, IRQ, DMA, or memory address) that is already in use. Trying changing the resources used by the plug-and-play system.

Table B.11 Continued

Parity Error	There is a parity error with memory somewhere in the system. Make sure the RAM chip is seated properly. If the problem still exists, replace the RAM chip or motherboard.
PCI I/O Port Conflict	Two devices requested the same I/O address. Try changing the I/O address of one of the devices.
PCI IRQ Conflict	Two devices requested the same IRQ. Try changing the IRQ of one of the devices.
PCI Memory Conflict	Two devices requested the same memory resource. Try changing the memory required by one of the devices.
Press F1 to Disable NMI, F2 to Reboot	When BIOS detects a nonmaskable interrupt condition during boot, this will allow you to disable the NMI and continue to boot, or you can reboot the system with the NMI enabled.
Primary Boot Device Not Found	The designated primary boot device (hard drive, floppy drive, CD-ROM, Zip drive, or LS-120 drive) could not be found. Check the installation and configuration of each boot device.
Primary IDE-Controller Resource Conflict	The primary IDE controller has requested a resource (I/O address, IRQ, DMA, or memory address) that is already in use. Try to free the resource.
Primary Input Device Not Found	The primary input device (usually the keyboard) could not be found. Check the installation and configuration of the input device, including making sure the input device is enabled in the CMOS setup program.
Primary Master Hard Disk Fail	Check the hard drive CMOS settings and hard drive configuration. If the problem still exists, check the hard drive cable, drive power connector, and hard drive.
Primary Slave Hard Disk Fail	Check the hard drive CMOS settings and hard drive configuration. If the problem still exists, check the hard drive cable, drive power connector, and hard drive.
RAM Parity Error—Checking for Segment	Indicates a parity error in Random Access Memory. Make sure the RAM chip is seated properly. If the problem still exists, replace the RAM chip or motherboard.
Secondary IDE-Controller Resource Conflict	The secondary IDE controller has requested a resource (I/O address, IRQ, DMA, or memory address) that is already in use. Try to free the resource.
Secondary Master Hard Disk Fail	Check the hard Drive CMOS settings and hard drive configuration. If the problem still exists, check the hard drive cable, drive power connector, hard drive.
Secondary Slave Hard Disk Fail	Check the hard drive CMOS settings and hard drive configuration. If the problem still exists, check the hard drive cable, drive power connector, and hard drive.
Should Be Empty but EISA Board Found	A valid board ID was found in a slot that was configured as having no board ID. Run the EISA Configuration utility.
Should Have EISA Board but Not Found	The board installed is not responding to the ID request, or no board ID has been found in the indicated slot. Run the EISA Configuration utility.
Static Device Resource Conflict or **System Board Device Resource Conflict**	A legacy card has requested a resource (I/O address, IRQ, DMA, or memory address) that is already in use. Try reconfiguring the expansion card or try freeing the resources needed by the card.

APPENDIX C

Operating System Error Codes

Table C.1 DOS/Command-Line Error Messages

Access denied	You or a program are trying to change a file that is read-only or is already in use by another program. If the file is read-only, you can shut off the read-only attribute by using the ATTRIB command.
Bad command or file name	You entered an invalid command at the command prompt or within a batch file. Make sure the command is spelled correctly, the executable file is present, and that you are in the directory of the executable file or that you have a correct path to the directory of the executable file.
Bad or missing command interpreter	During boot-up, the command interpreter (usually COMMAND.COM) can't be found or is corrupted. Using another disk, copy a good current version of COMMAND.COM to the boot device.
Bad or missing filename	The device driver specified in the CONFIG.SYS file was not found. Check the path specified in the CONFIG.SYS file, make sure the file name was spelled correctly, and make sure that the file is in the specified directory.
Batch file missing	A batch file was running and was either deleted, renamed, or moved.
Boot couldn't find NTLDR, please insert another disk	Your disk does not contain NTLDR, IO.SYS, or MSDOS.SYS, or a read error occurred when you started the system. If you are trying to boot from the hard drive, make sure that there is no disk in drive A and that drive C has the necessary boot files.
Current drive is no longer valid	The system prompt, which includes the current drive or the current path, could not show the drive that you asked for. For example, if you changed to a floppy drive without a floppy disk, you would eventually get a "Current Drive Is No Longer Valid" error message. At this point, you can change to a valid drive letter.
Data error reading drive x:	DOS was unable to read some of the data on the disk. Run SCANDISK on the disk. If the problem cannot be corrected, try to copy the data to another disk and throw the disk away.
Disk boot failure	During boot-up, IO.SYS or MSDOS.SYS could not be loaded. Boot with another disk and use the SYS command to recopy the files.
Disk unsuitable for system disk	When formatting a disk, FORMAT detected one or more bad sectors on the boot area of the disk.

Table C.1 Continued

Divide overflow	A program tried to divide by 0. This usually indicates a faulty software program. Contact the software manufacturer or programmer to find out if you have any other options.
Drive types or diskette types not compatible	When using DISKCOMP and DISKCOPY, you are using two disks that have different sizes and/or different densities.
Duplicate filename or file not found	When using the RENAME command, you tried to change a file name to another file name that already existed for another file.
Error in EXE file	DOS detected an error while executing the instructions in a file with an EXE file name extension. Reboot the computer and try again. If the problem persists, use another copy of the program or reinstall the program.
Error loading operating systems	This error occurs during boot-up from a hard drive. It indicates that the operating system could not be loaded. Try rebooting the computer. If the problem still persists, replace the boot files using the SYS command from a bootable floppy. In addition, check the hard drive for viruses, run SCANDISK, and check for hard drive failure.
Error reading (or writing) partition table	DOS could not read a hard drive's partition because it is corrupt. Run FDISK on the disk and then reformat the drive.
Error reading directory	This error message occurs when using the FORMAT command. DOS was unable to read the directory because of a corrupt FAT or bad sectors. If the error occurs on a floppy disk, throw it away. If it occurs on a hard drive, check for viruses, run SCANDISK, and check for hard drive failure.
Extended error	COMMAND.COM has detected an error but cannot show you the error message because COMMAND.COM is missing from the disk.
FCB unavailable reading (writing) drive X:	A program using file control blocks (FCB) attempted to open more file control blocks than were specified with the FCBS= command. The FCBS= command is needed for programs made for DOS 1.0.
File allocation table bad, drive D—abort, retry, fail?	DOS cannot read part of the file allocation table. Run SCANDISK on the drive and check for viruses.
File creation error	DOS or a program could not create a file in the location specified. If a file already exists with the same name, the file may be read-only. If the problem still occurs, check for viruses and run SCANDISK on the drive.
File not found	A command was issued and DOS can find the instructions but could not find the file specified, meaning DOS cannot find the file in the current directory or the file has an invalid character in it.
General failure reading (writing) device	An error occurred when DOS tried to read or write to a device.
General failure reading (writing) drive X:	An error occurred when DOS tried to read or write to the disk drive.
Illegal device name	DOS does not recognize the device name specified when using the MODE command.
Incorrect DOS version	The program was not made to work with the current version of DOS in RAM loaded during boot-up. Boot with the correct DOS version, use the command made for the current DOS version, or use the SETVER command to change the DOS version table.
Insert disk with \COMMAND.COM in drive D and strike any key when ready	COMMAND.COM had to be temporarily unloaded from RAM. When DOS tried to reload it, COMMAND.COM was not on the floppy disk in the startup drive. Therefore, place a disk with COMMAND.COM in the boot drive.
Insert disk with batch file and strike any key when ready	You were running a batch file from a floppy disk and the floppy disk was removed. Reinsert the disk with the batch file
Insufficient disk space	The disk does not have enough free space to hold the file being written or copied.

Table C.1 Continued

Insufficient memory	The computer does not have enough free RAM, usually conventional memory, to execute the program or command.
Internal stack overflow, system halted	Your program used all of the stacks assigned or exceeded the size of the stacks. If this problem keeps recurring, increase the number of stacks and the size of the stacks using the STACKS command in the CONFIG.SYS file.
Invalid COMMAND.COM in drive D: **or** **Invalid COMMAND.COM, system halted**	DOS tried to reload COMMAND.COM from the disk in drive D and found that the file was from a different version of DOS. Insert a disk with the correct version of COMMAND.COM or copy the correct COMMAND.COM to the correct place.
Invalid directory	The directory that you are trying to go into does not exist.
Invalid disk change—abort, retry, fail?	A floppy disk was changed while a program had open files to be written to the floppy disk. Place the correct disk in the disk drive and press R to retry.
Invalid disk change reading (writing) drive X:	You have removed a disk that the operating system needs access to. This usually occurs with removable media, such as floppy disks.
Invalid drive in search path	You specified an invalid disk drive name in the PATH command, or a disk drive you named is nonexistent.
Invalid drive specification	DOS does not know what drive you are trying to go to, such as the Z drive; if the drive does not exist, then you will get this error message.
Invalid media or track 0 bad—disk unusable	The disk that you are trying to format may be damaged. Try to perform an unconditional format. If the problem still exists, throw the disk away.
Invalid media type reading (writing) drive X:	The boot sector or the file allocation table (FAT) of the disk contains invalid information, making the disk unusable.
Invalid partition table	The operating system detected a problem in the hard drive's partition information. Try to correct the problem with FDISK.
Invalid path	The path contains illegal characters, the path name has more than 63 characters, or a directory name within the path is misspelled or does not exist.
Invalid path or file name	You gave a directory name or file name that does not exist, specified the wrong directory name, or mistyped a name.
Invalid STACK parameters	The STACK command in the CONFIG.SYS has the wrong syntax.
Lock violation reading (writing) drive X:	With a file-sharing program such as SHARE.EXE or network software loaded, a program attempted to access a locked file.
Memory allocation error. Cannot load COMMAND, system halted.	A program destroyed the area where DOS keeps track of memory. Restart DOS.
Missing operating system	The DOS hard disk partition entry is marked as active, but the DOS partition does not contain a copy of DOS. Try to use the SYS command on the drive or format the drive as a bootable drive.
No room for system on destination disk	There is not enough disk space to hold the system files, or the root directory is full.
No system on default drive	The SYS command cannot find the system files. Insert a bootable disk.
Nonsystem disk or disk error. Replace and strike any key when ready.	Your disk does not contain IO.SYS and MSDOS.SYS or a read error occurred when you started the system. If you are trying to boot from the hard drive, make sure that there is no disk in drive A and make sure that drive C has the necessary boot files. If you are trying to boot from the floppy drive, make sure that the floppy drive has the necessary boot files.
Not enough memory	The computer does not have enough free RAM, usually conventional memory, to execute the program or command.

Table C.1 Continued

Not ready reading (or writing) drive X:	An error occurred when DOS tried to read or write to the disk drive.
Not ready reading (writing) drive X:	The disk isn't inserted properly, the floppy disk drive is not closed on 5¼-inch disk drives, or there is a problem with the disk. If there is a problem with the disk, run SCANDISK on the disk or throw the disk away.
Out of environment space	There isn't enough room in the current environment to add the environment variables by using the PATH, PROMPT, and SET commands.
Out of memory	The computer does not have enough free RAM, usually conventional memory, to execute the program or command.
Parse error	COMMAND.COM has detected an error but cannot tell you the normal error message because the floppy disk containing COMMAND.COM is missing.
Path not found	A specified file or directory path does not exist. You may have misspelled the file name or directory name, or you may have omitted a path character (\) between directory names or between the final directory or the filename.
Path too long	You have given a path name that exceeds the DOS 64-character limit, or you omitted a space between a filename parameter.
Program too big to fit in memory	The computer does not have enough free RAM, usually conventional memory, to execute the program or command.
Read fault error reading drive X:	The disk isn't inserted properly, the floppy disk drive is not closed on 5¼-inch disk drives, or there is a problem with the disk. If there is a problem with the disk, run SCANDISK on the disk or throw the disk away.
Sector not found reading (writing) drive X: or **Seek error reading (writing) drive X:**	The disk drive was unable to find the requested sector on the disk. This error is usually the result of a defective spot on the disk or a defective disk drive.
Sharing violation reading (writing) drive X:	With a file-sharing program such as SHARE.EXE or network software loaded, a program attempted to access a file that is in use by another program.
Source diskette bad or incompatible	The disk you attempted to read during a copy process was damaged or in the wrong format.
Syntax error	You phrased a command improperly by omitting needed information, giving extraneous information, inserting an extra space into a file or path name, or using an incorrect switch.
Target diskette bad or incompatible or **Target diskette may be unusable** or **Target diskette unusable**	A problem exists with the target disk. The disk is not formatted properly or is defective.
This program requires Microsoft Windows	You tried to run a program at the DOS prompt that needs Microsoft Windows to execute.
Trying to recover allocation unit nnn	A bad allocation unit was found when the FORMAT command executed.
Unable to create destination	The MOVE command was unable to create the destination file. Either the destination disk is too full or the destination in the root directory is full.

Table C.1 Continued

Unable to create directory	You or a program could not create a directory because a directory with the same name already exists, the root directory is full, or the directory name has illegal characters or is a device name, such as LPT or PRN.
Unrecognized command in CONFIG.SYS. Error in CONFIG.SYS line nnn	DOS cannot find the file specified in the CONFIG.SYS on line nnn. Check the spelling of the path and file and make sure the file is in the correct directory.
Unrecognized switch	You tried to use a switch that was illegal for the particular internal command.
Unrecoverable read error on drive X side n, track n	DOS was unable to read the data at the specified location on the disk. Try to copy the files to another disk and throw the disk away.
Unrecoverable write error on drive X side n, track n	DOS was unable to write the data at the specified location on the disk. Try to format the disk or throw the disk away.
Write failure, diskette unusable	The disk you are writing to has a bad sector in the boot sector or the FAT. Use SCANDISK to fix it or throw the disk away.
Write fault error writing drive X:	The operating system was unable to write data to the drive. Check to see if the disk is inserted properly in the drive. If the problem still exists, check the disk or the floppy disk drive.
Write fault writing device dev	The operating system could not write data to the device specified. The printer is turned on or online, an external modem is not on, or the cables are not connected properly.
Write protect error writing drive X:	The operating system attempted to write to a disk that is write-protected. If it is a floppy disk, open the write-protect hole or remove the write-protect tab.

APPENDIX D

Windows Stop Errors

STOP 0x0000000A (0xA) IRQL_NOT_LESS_or_EQUAL

Parameters:

1 Memory referenced
2 IRQL
3 Value: 0 = read operation, 1 = write operation
4 Address that referenced memory

An attempt was made to touch pageable memory at a process internal request level (IRQL) that is too high. In other words, a driver is using improper memory addresses. It is usually caused by a bad device driver or by using a Windows NT 4.0 driver on a Windows NT 3.51.

To isolate the cause of the stop error, do the following:

- Make sure that you have the most current BIOS.
- Make sure that you have the newest Windows service pack.
- Turn off your PC and take out all cards except the video card and SCSI card if you are booting from the SCSI drive. After the OS is installed, shut down the computer and plug in one card at a time, boot the OS, and install the drivers for that card. If you get the error message again, try to update the driver.

STOP 0x0000001E (0x1E) KMODE_EXCEPTION_NOT_HANDLED

Parameters:

1 The exception code that was not handled
2 The address at which the exception occurred
3 Parameter 0 of the exception
4 Parameter 1 of the exception

While this is typically not a processor stop error, it is one of the most common bug codes. Usually the exception address pinpoints the driver or function that caused the problem. Other causes include bad processor, bad memory, bad cache or bad BIOS, or outdated BIOS. Always note this address as well as the link date of the driver or image that contains this address. A common error is exception code 0x80000003. This error means a hard-code breakpoint or assertion was hit, but the system was booted with the/NODEBUG switch. This problem should not occur very often. If it occurs repeatedly, make sure a debugger is connected and the system is booted with the /DEBUG switch.

To isolate the cause of the stop error, do the following:

- Make sure that you have adequate disk space, especially for new installations.
- Make sure that you have the most current BIOS.
- Make sure that you have the newest Windows service pack.
- Update the offending driver or reinstall the offending driver/software package. You may need to use Last Known Good Configuration or safe mode.
- If the motherboard and hard drive support Ultra DMA-66 or faster, enter the BIOS CMOS program, disable the Ultra DMA, and set the PIO to mode 4 for that channel. Then after Windows is installed, try the Ultra DMA to see if Windows is stable. Be sure to use the 40-pin, 80-conductor cable.
- Replace the memory.
- Replace the cache (if on motherboard).
- Replace the motherboard.
- Replace the processor.

STOP 0x00000023 AND 0x00000024 FAT_FILE_SYSTEM OR NTFS_FILE SYSTEM

This is usually caused by heavily fragmented drives, heavy file I/O, some types of drive-mirroring software, or some types of antivirus software.

To isolate the cause of the stop error:

- Temporarily disable any antivirus programs, backup programs, and defragmentation utilities.
- Check for hard drive corruption by running ScanDisk.
- Try safe mode and Last Known Good Configuration.
- Delete all partitions, then repartition and reformat your system.

STOP 0x0000002E (0x2E) DATA_BUS_ERROR

Parameters:

1 Virtual address that caused the fault
2 Physical address that caused the fault
3 Processor status register (PSR)
4 Faulting instruction register (FIR)

This bug code is normally caused by a parity error in the system memory. This error can also be caused by a driver accessing a 0x8XXXXXXX address that does not exist.

To isolate the cause of the stop error, do the following:

- Make sure that you have the most current BIOS.
- Make sure that you have the newest Windows service pack.
- Check for viruses.
- If you added a new device driver, start the computer in safe mode, uninstall the driver, and restart the computer.
- Update the offending driver.
- Run hardware system diagnostic program. Run a general test for the entire system and an extensive test for the memory.
- Replace the memory.
- Replace the video memory (or video card).
- Replace the cache.
- Replace the hard driver.
- Replace the processor.
- Replace the motherboard.

STOP 0x0000003E (0x3E) MULTIPROCESSOR_ CONFIGURATION_NOT_SUPPORTED

The system has multiple processors, but they are asymmetric in relation to one another. To be symmetric, all processors must be the same type and level (same type, cache size, and frequency with compatible stepping). In addition, make sure the processor supports multiprocessing. This information is stated in the Processor Specification Update guides.

STOP 0x0000003F NO_MORE_SYSTEM PTES

A driver is not cleaning up properly.

To isolate the cause of the stop error, do the following:

- Remove any recently installed software, including backup utilities or disk-intensive applications such as defragmenting, virus protection, and backup utilities.

STOP 0x00000058

The failure of a primary drive in a fault-tolerance set.

To isolate the cause of the stop error:

- Using a Windows 2000 Startup disk, start your computer from the mirrored (secondary) system drive.
- Try Last Known Good Configuration.
- Delete all partitions, then repartition and reformat your system.
- If you are using an older machine and the drive is over 8,057 GB, you may need to load some special software so that the system can recognize over 8 GB, or to update the BIOS.

STOP 0x00000077 (0x77) KERNEL_STACK_INPAGE_ERROR

Parameters:

1 0
2 0
3 PTE value at time of error
4 Address of signature on kernel stack

or

1 Status code
2 I/O status code
3 Page file number
4 Offset into page file

The requested page of kernel data could not be read. This error is caused by bad block in a paging file or a disk controller error, and in extremely rare cases, it is caused by running out of resources. If the first and second arguments are 0, the stack signature in the kernel stack was not found. This error is caused by bad hardware.

If the status code is 0xC000009A, it's probably the L2 cache. If 0xC000009C and 0xC000016A, you have a failing hard drive. If the status is 0xC0000185 (STATUS IO DEVICE ERROR) and the paging file is on a SCSI disk device, the cabling and termination should be checked. Other items to check would include defective L2 cache, defective memory, defective processor, defective motherboard, and defective hard drive.

STOP ERROR 0x00000079 MISMATCHED HAL

The hardware abstraction layer is incorrect for the machine. This usually occurs when one machine mixes single and dual processor configuration files.

To isolate the cause of the error in Windows NT, restart the install and when the message "Windows NT is examining the hardware" appears, press F5. Choose your computer type from the list that appears and continue with the installation. In Windows 2000, you should begin the installation process again and install a clean copy of OS. If this does not work, repartition and reformat your hard drive from scratch and install Windows. Then replace the motherboard and processors.

STOP 0x0000007B INACCESSIBLE_BOOT_DEVICE

A problem occurred during the initialization of the I/O system (usually the startup device or the file system).

To isolate the cause of the stop error, do the following:

- Make sure that you have the most current BIOS.
- Make sure that you have the newest Windows service pack.
- Check for viruses on your computer.
- Remove any newly added hard drives or controllers.
- If you are using a SCSI adapter, obtain the latest Windows driver from the adapter vendor. In addition, try to disable sync negotiation, check termination, and check the SCSI IDs of the devices.
- If you are using IDE devices, define the on-board IDE part to Primary only. Check the Master/Slave/Only settings for the IDE devices. Remove all IDE devices except for the hard disk.
- Run CHKDSK. The file system could be corrupt. If Windows cannot run CHKDSK, you might have to move the drive to another computer running Windows 2000 or Windows XP and run the CHKDSK command on that drive.
- Restart your computer. At the startup screen, press F8 for the Advanced Startup option, and select Last Known Good Configuration.

STOP 0x0000007F UNEXPECTED_KERNEL_MODE_TRAP

This error means a trap (exception) occurred in kernel mode, either a trap that the kernel is not allowed to have or catch (a bound trap) or a trap that is always instant death (double fault). This can be caused by a hardware or software problem, but is most commonly a hardware failure. The first number in the bug code parentheses is the number of the trap (8 = double fault). To learn more about what these traps are, consult the *Intel Software Developer's Manual, Volume 3: System Programming Guide,* chapter 5. Check for mismatched RAM, bad RAM, bad processor, or outdated BIOS.

To isolate the cause of the stop error, do the following:

- Make sure that you have the most current BIOS.
- Make sure that you have the newest Windows service pack.
- Run diagnostic software and test the RAM in the computer.
- Disable memory caching.
- Turn off your PC and take out all cards except the video card and SCSI card if you are booting from the SCSI drive. After the OS is installed, shut down the computer and plug in one card at a time, boot the OS, and install the drivers for that card. If you get the error message again, try to update the driver.
- Try removing or swapping out controllers, cards, or other peripherals.
- Check to see if the RAM modules are the same speed and that they are compatible with each other.
- Make sure that you have sufficient RAM to run Windows.
- Try different RAM.
- Try a different motherboard.
- Try a different processor.

STOP 0x00000080 NMI_HARDWARE_FAILURE

The HAL is supposed to report whatever specific data it has and to tell the user to call his or her hardware vendor for support.

To isolate the cause of the stop error, do the following:

- Make sure that you have the most current BIOS.
- Make sure that you have the newest Windows service pack.
- Check to make sure the system is not using nonparity memory in a parity-based system or mixing of parity/nonparity memory.
- Try different RAM.
- Try a different motherboard.
- Try a different processor.

STOP 0x0000009C MACHINE_CHECK_EXCEPTION

A fatal Machine Check Exception has occurred.

For Pentium processors, the parameters are:

1 Low 32 bits of P5_MC_TYPE MSR
2 Not Applicable
3 High 32 bit of P5_MC_ADDR MSR
4 Low 32 bits of P5_MC_ADDR MSR

For a processor with a P6 architecture, the parameters are:

1 Bank number
2 Address of field of MCi_ADDR MSR for the MCA bank that had the error
3 High 32 bits of MCi_STATUS MSR for the MCA bank that had the error
4 Low 32 bits of MCi_STATUS MSR for the MCA bank that had the error

NOTE: Machine-Check Exceptions are listed in the *Intel Architecture Software Developer's Manual, Volume 3: System Programming Guide,* chapter 12.

To isolate the cause of the stop error, do the following:

- Make sure that you have the newest Windows service pack.
- Make sure that you have the most current BIOS update.
- Replace the RAM.
- Try a different motherboard.
- Try a different processor or processors.

STOP 0x000000B4 VIDEO_DRIVER_INIT

The video driver is bad, corrupted, missing, or disabled.

To isolate the cause of the stop error, do the following:

- Try starting your computer in safe mode or Enable VGA mode and trying removing the driver and reinstalling the driver.
- Make sure that you have the newest Windows service pack.
- Make sure that you have the most current BIOS update.

STOP 0xC0000185 STATUS_IO_DEVICE_ERROR:

To isolate the cause of the stop error:

- Make sure the SCSI controller and SCSI cable are connected correctly.
- Check for Resource Conflicts for your SCSI card.

STOP 0x00000221 STATUS_IMAGE_CHECKSUM_MISMATCH

The installer program found a corrupt driver or DLL file for some hardware device.

To isolate the cause of the stop error:

- Make sure that you have the most current BIOS.
- Make sure that you have the newest Windows service pack.
- Turn off your PC and take out all cards except the video card and SCSI card if you are booting from the SCSI drive. After the OS is installed, shut down the computer and plug in one card at a time, boot the OS and install the drivers for that card. If you get the error message again, try to update the driver.

APPENDIX E

Certification Exam

COMPTIA A+ CERTIFICATION

The Computing Technology Industry Association (CompTIA) is a nonprofit organization that represents more than 8,000 computing and communications companies. The main goal is to develop vendor-neutral certifications to provide credibility, recognition of achievement, and quality assurance.

Out of all the CompTIA exams, the A+ exam is by far the most popular exam and the most recognized. The CompTIA A+ certification is the industry standard for validating vendor-neutral skills expected of an entry-level computer technician. Those holding the A+ certification have a broad base of knowledge and competency in core hardware and operating system technologies including installation, configuration, diagnosing, preventive maintenance, and basic networking.

The CompTIA A+ certification exam validates the knowledge and abilities of an entry-level technician with 6 months of on-the-job experience. Different from the other exams, there are two exams in the current A+ certification program:

- A+ Core Hardware exam
- A+ OS Technologies exam

A+ Core Exam

Domain 1 Installation, Configuration, and Upgrading	
1.1 Identify the names, purpose, and characteristics, of system modules. Recognize these modules by sight or definition.	
Examples of concepts and modules are:	
• Motherboard	Section 1.3.1, 3.2, 6.1, 6.2, and 7.1
• Firmware	Section 6.4
• Power supply	Section 8.2
• Processor/CPU	Section 1.3.1, 3.2, and Chapter 4
• Memory	Section 1.3.2, 3.2, and 5.1
• Storage devices	Section 1.3.3, 3.2, 9.1, 10.1, and 11.1
• Display devices	Section 1.3.4 and Chapter 14
• Adapter cards	Section 3.2
• Ports	Section 3.1
• Cases	Section 3.1
• Riser cards	Section 6.2 and 7.3.11
1.2 Identify basic procedures for adding and removing field-replaceable modules for desktop systems. Given a replacement scenario, choose the appropriate sequences.	
Desktop components:	
• Motherboard	Section 3.2

Continued

• Storage device	Section 3.2
• FDD	Section 10.2
• HDD	Section 9.3, 9.5, and 9.6
• CD/CDRW	Section 11.3
• DVD/DVDRW	Section 11.3
• Tape drive	Section 13.3.5
• Removable storage	Section 10.5
• Power supply	Section 8.2
• AC adapter	Section 8.2
• AT/ATX	Section 8.2
• Cooling systems	Section 4.4 and 8.2.8
• Fans	
• Heat sinks	
• Liquid cooling	
• Processor/CPU	Section 3.2 and Chapter 4
• Memory	Section 3.2 and 5.8
• Display device	Section 14.3
• Input devices	Chapter 15
• Keyboard	
• Mouse/pointer devices	
• Touch screen	
• Adapters	Section 3.2 and 7.4
• Network Interface Card (NIC)	
• Sound card	Section 16.3
• Video card	Section 14.3
• Modem	Section 17.3
• SCSI	Section 9.3 and 9.7
• IEEE 1394/FireWire	Section 7.3.10
• USB	Section 7.3.9
• Wireless	Section 25.8
1.3 Identify basic procedures for adding and removing field-replaceable modules for portable systems. Given a replacement scenario, choose the appropriate sequences.	
Portable components:	
• Storage devices	Section 3.3
• FDD	
• HDD	Section 9.5
• CD/CDRW	
• DVD/DVDRW	
• Removable storage	
• Power sources	Section 8.6
• AC adapter	
• DC adapter	
• Battery	
• Memory	Section 3.3
• Input devices	Section 3.3
• Keyboard	
• Mouse/pointer devices	
• Touch screen	
• PCMCIA/Mini PCI Adapters	Section 3.3, 7.3.7 and 7.3.8
• Network Interface Card (NIC)	
• Modem	
• SCSI	
• IEEE 1394/FireWire	
• USB	
• Storage (memory and hard drive)	
• Docking station/port replicators	Section 3.3
• LCD panel	Section 3.3 and 14.1
• Wireless	Section 25.8
• Adapter/controller	
• Antennae	

Continued

1.4 Identify typical IRQs, DMAs, and I/O addresses, and procedures for altering these settings when installing and configuring devices. Choose the appropriate installation or configuration steps in a given scenario. Content may include the following:	Section 7.2 and 7.4
• Legacy devices (e.g., ISA sound card)	Section 16.3
• Specialized devices (e.g., CAD/CAM)	Section 7.4
• Internal modems	Section 17.3
• Floppy drive controllers	Section 10.2
• Hard drive controllers	Section 9.5 and 9.6
• Multimedia devices	Section 16.4
• NICs	Section 25.3
• I/O ports	Section 17.1
• Serial	Section 18.1
• Parallel	Section 18.1
• USB ports	Section 7.3.9
• IEEE 1394/FireWire	Section 7.3.10
• Infrared	Section 15.5
1.5 Identify the names, purposes, and performance characteristics of standardized/common peripheral ports, associated cabling, and their connectors. Recognize ports, cabling, and connectors by sight. Content may include the following:	
• Port types	Section 3.1
• Serial	Section 17.1
• Parallel	Section 18.1
• USB ports	Section 7.3.9
• IEEE 1394/FireWire	Section 7.3.10
• Infrared	Section 15.5
• Cable types	
• Serial (Straight through vs. null modem)	Section 17.1
• Parallel	Section 18.1
• USB	Section 17.3
• Connector types	
• Serial	
• DB-9	Section 17.1
• DB-25	Section 17.1
• RJ-11	Section 17.3
• RJ-45	Section 25.4
• Parallel	
• DB-25	Section 18.1
• Centronics (mini, 36)	Section 18.1
• PS2/MINI-DIN	Section 15.1
• USB	Section 7.3.9
• IEEE 1394	Section 7.3.10
1.6 Identify proper procedures for installing and configuring common IDE devices. Choose the appropriate installation or configuration sequences in given scenarios. Recognize the associated cables. Content may include the following:	Section 9.5
• IDE Interface Types	
• EIDE	
• ATA/ATAPI	
• Serial ATA	
• PIO	
• RAID (0, 1 and 5)	Section 9.4
• Master/Slave/cable select	
• Devices per channel	
• Primary/Secondary	
• Cable orientation/requirements	

Continued

1.7 Identify proper procedures for installing and configuring common SCSI devices. Choose the appropriate installation or configuration sequences in given scenarios. Recognize the associated cables.
Content may include the following:
• SCSI Interface Types
  • Narrow
  • Fast
  • Wide
  • Ultra-wide
  • LVD
  • HVD
• Internal versus external
• SCSI IDs
  • Jumper block/DIP switch settings (binary equivalents)
  • Resolving ID conflicts
• RAID (0, 1 and 5)
• Cabling
  • Length
  • Type
  • Termination requirements (active, passive, auto)
	Section 9.6
	
	Section 9.4

1.8 Identify proper procedures for installing and configuring common peripheral devices. Choose the appropriate installation or configuration sequences in given scenarios. Content may include the following: • Modems and transceivers (dial-up, cable, DSL, ISDN) • External storage • Digital cameras • PDAs • Wireless access points • Infrared devices • Printers • UPS (Uninterruptible Power Supply) and suppressors • Monitors	 Section 17.3 and 17.4 Section 7.3.9, 9.6, and 10.6 Section 15.8 Section 15.9 Section 25.8 Section 15.5 Section 18.2 Section 8.4 Section 14.1 and 14.3

1.9 Identify procedures to optimize PC operations in specific situations. Predict the effects of specific procedures under given scenarios.
Topics may include:
• Cooling systems
  • Liquid
  • Air
  • Heat sink
  • Thermal compound
• Disk subsystem enhancements
  • Hard drives
  • Controller cards (e.g., RAID, ATA-100, etc.)
  • Cables
• NICs
• Specialized video cards
• Memory
• Additional processors
	
	Section 4.4
	
	Section 9.4
	
	Section 25.3
	Section 14.2
	Section 5.4
	Section 4.7

1.10 Determine the issues that must be considered when upgrading a PC. In a given scenario, determine when and how to upgrade system components. Issues may include: • Drivers for legacy devices • Bus types and characteristics • Cache in relationship to motherboards	 Section 7.4 Section 7.4 Section 4.1.10

Continued

• Memory capacity and characteristics	Section 5.8
• Processor speed and compatibility	Chapter 4
• Hard drive capacity and characteristics	Section 9.5 and 9.6
• System/firmware limitations	Section 6.5
• Power supply output capacity	Section 8.2
Components may include the following:	
• Motherboards	Chapter 6
• Memory	Section 5.8
• Hard drives	Section 9.5 and 9.6
• CPU	Chapter 4
• BIOS	Section 6.4 and 6.5
• Adapter cards	Section 7.3
• Laptop power sources	Section 8.6
• Lithium ion	
• NiMH	
• Fuel cell	
• PCMCIA Type I, II, III cards	Section 7.4

Domain 2 Diagnosing and Troubleshooting	
2.1 Recognize common problems associated with each module and their symptoms, and identify steps to isolate and troubleshoot the problems. Given a problem situation, interpret the symptoms and infer the most likely cause.	Chapter 2
Content may include the following:	
• I/O ports and cables	
• Serial	Section 17.1
• Parallel	Section 18.1
• USB ports	Section 7.3.9 and 7.5
• IEEE 1394/FireWire	Section 7.3.10 and 7.5
• Infrared	Section 15.5
• SCSI	Section 9.8
• Motherboards	Section 6.12
• CMOS/ BIOS settings	Section 6.12
• POST audible/visual error codes	Section 1.7.1
• Peripherals	Section 7.5
• Computer case	
• Power supply	Section 8.3
• Slot covers	Section 8.2.8
• Front cover alignment	Section 8.2.8
• Storage devices and cables	Chapter 9, 10 and 11 and Section 13.3
• FDD	Chapter 10
• HDD	Section 9.8
• CD/CDRW	Chapter 11
• DVD/DVDRW	Chapter 11
• Tape drive	Section 13.3
• Removable storage	Chapter 10
• Cooling systems	Section 4.4
• Fans	
• Heat sinks	
• Liquid cooling	
• Temperature sensors	
• Processor/CPU	Section 4.9
• Memory	Section 5.9

Continued

• Display device	Section 14.6
• Input devices	Chapter 15
• Keyboard	
• Mouse/pointer devices	
• Touch screen	
• Adapters	Section 7.5
• Network Interface Card (NIC)	
• Sound card	Section 16.4
• Video card	Section 14.6
• Modem	Section 17.3
• SCSI	
• IEEE 1394/FireWire	Section 7.3.10
• USB	Section 7.3.9
• Portable Systems	Section 8.6
• PCMCIA	Section 7.3.7
• Batteries	Section 8.6
• Docking Stations/Port Replicators	Section 2.3
• Portable unique storage	Section 10.5
2.2 Identify basic troubleshooting procedures and tools, and how to elicit problem symptoms from customers. Justify asking particular questions in a given scenario.	Section 2.1
Content may include the following:	
• Troubleshooting/isolation/problem determination procedures	
• Determining whether a hardware or software problem	
• Gathering information from user	
• Customer Environment	
• Symptoms/Error Codes	
• Situation when the problem occurred	

Domain 3 PC Preventive Maintenance, Safety, and Environmental Issues	
3.1 Identify the various types of preventive maintenance measures, products and procedures and when and how to use them.	
Content may include the following:	
• Liquid cleaning compounds	Section 2.6
• Types of materials to clean contacts and connections	Section 2.6
• Non-static vacuums (chassis, power supplies, fans)	Section 2.6
• Cleaning monitors	Section 2.6
• Cleaning removable media devices	Section 10.1 and 11.5
• Ventilation, dust and moisture control on the PC hardware interior	Section 2.6
• Hard disk maintenance (defragging, scan disk, CHKDSK)	Section 12.11
• Verifying UPS (Uninterruptible Power Supply) and suppressors	Section 8.4
3.2 Identify various safety measures and procedures, and when/how to use them.	
Content may include the following:	
• ESD (Electrostatic Discharge) precautions and procedures	Section 2.9
• What ESD can do, how it may be apparent, or hidden	
• Common ESD protection devices	
• Situations that could present a danger or hazard	
• Potential hazards and proper safety procedures relating to	
• High-voltage equipment	Section 2.9 and 2.10
• Power supply	Section 8.2
• CRTs	Section 14.6

Continued

3.3 Identify environmental protection measures and procedures, and when/how to use them. Content may include the following: • Special disposal procedures that comply with environmental guidelines. • Batteries • CRTs • Chemical solvents and cans • MSDS (Material Safety Data Sheet)	 Section 8.6 Section 14.6 Section 2.6 Section 2.6

Domain 4 Motherboard/Processors/Memory	
4.1 Distinguish between the popular CPU chips in terms of their basic characteristics. Content may include the following: • Popular CPU chips (Pentium class compatible) • Voltage • Speeds (actual vs. advertised) • Cache level I, II, III • Sockets/slots • VRM(s)	Chapter 4

4.2 Identify the types of RAM (Random Access Memory), form factors, and operational characteristics. Determine banking and speed requirements under given scenarios.
Content may include the following:
• Types
  • EDO RAM (Extended Data Output RAM)
  • DRAM (Dynamic Random Access Memory)
  • SRAM (Static RAM)
  • VRAM (Video RAM)
  • SDRAM (Synchronous Dynamic RAM)
  • DDR (Double Data Rate)
  • RAMBUS
• Form factors (including pin count)
  • SIMM (Single In-line Memory Module)
  • DIMM (Dual In-line Memory Module)
  • SoDIMM (Small outline DIMM)
  • MicroDIMM
  • RIMM (Rambus Inline Memory Module)
• Operational characteristics
  • Memory chips (8-bit, 16-bit, and 32-bit)
  • Parity chips versus non-parity chips
  • ECC vs. non-ECC
  • Single-sided vs. double sided
	
	Section 5.2
	
	Section 5.6
	
	Section 5.7

4.3 Identify the most popular types of motherboards, their components, and their architecture (bus structures).
Content may include the following:
• Types of motherboards:
  • AT
  • ATX
• Components:
  • Communication ports
  • Serial
	
	Section 6.2
	
	Section 3.1

Continued

• USB	
• Parallel	
• IEEE 1394/FireWire	Section 7.10
• Infrared	
• Memory	Section 3.2 and Chapter 5
• SIMM	
• DIMM	
• RIMM	
• SoDIMM	
• MicroDIMM	
• Processor sockets	Section 4.6
• Slot 1	
• Slot 2	
• Slot A	
• Socket A	
• Socket 7	
• Socket 8	
• Socket 423	
• Socket 478	
• Socket 370	
• External cache memory (Level 2)	Section 4.1.10
• Bus Architecture	Section 7.3
• ISA	Section 7.3
• PCI	Section 7.3
• PCI 32-bit	
• PCI 64-bit	
• AGP	Section 7.3
• 2X	
• 4X	
• 8X (Pro)	
• USB (Universal Serial Bus)	Section 7.3
• AMR (audio modem riser) slots	Section 7.3 and 17.3
• CNR (communication network riser) slots	Section 7.3
• Basic compatibility guidelines	Section 6.6 and Chapter 7
• IDE (ATA, ATAPI, ULTRA-DMA, EIDE)	
• SCSI (Narrow, Wide, Fast, Ultra, HVD, LVD [Low Voltage Differential])	Section 9.6
• Chipsets	Section 6.6
4.4 Identify the purpose of CMOS (Complementary Metal-Oxide Semiconductor) memory, what it contains, and how and when to change its parameters. Given a scenario involving CMOS, choose the appropriate course of action.	
CMOS Settings:	
• Default settings	Section 6.12
• CPU settings	Section 6.12
• Printer parallel port—Uni., bi-directional, disable/enable, ECP, EPP	Section 6.12
• COM/serial port—memory address, interrupt request, disable	Section 6.12
• Floppy drive—enable/disable drive or boot, speed, density	Section 6.12
• Hard drive—size and drive type	Section 6.12 and 9.3
• Memory—speed, parity, non-parity	Section 6.12
• Boot sequence	Section 6.12
• Date/Time	Section 6.12
• Passwords	Section 6.12
• Plug & Play BIOS	Section 6.12
• Disabling on-board devices	Section 6.12
• Disabling virus protection	Section 6.12
• Power management	Section 6.12
• Infrared	Section 15.5

Domain 5 Printers	
5.1 Identify printer technologies, interfaces, and options/upgrades. Technologies include: • Laser • Ink Dispersion • Dot Matrix • Solid ink • Thermal • Dye sublimation Interfaces include: • Parallel • Network • SCSI • USB • Infrared • Serial • IEEE 1394/Firewire • Wireless Options/Upgrades include: • Memory • Hard drives • NICs • Trays and feeders • Finishers (e.g., stapling, etc.) • Scanners/fax/copier	Section 18.2
5.2 Recognize common printer problems and techniques used to resolve them. Content may include the following: • Printer drivers • Firmware updates • Paper feed and output • Calibrations • Printing test pages • Errors (printed or displayed) • Memory • Configuration • Network connections • Connections • Paper jam • Print quality • Safety precautions • Preventive maintenance • Consumables • Environment	Section 18.2

Domain 6 Basic Networking	

6.1 Identify the common types of network cables, their characteristics and connectors.
Cable types include:
• Coaxial
  • RG6
  • RG8
  • RG58
  • RG59
• Plenum/PVC
• UTP
  • CAT3
  • CAT5/e
  • CAT6
• STP
• Fiber
  • Single-mode
  • Multi-mode
Connector types include:
• BNC
• RJ-45
• AUI
• ST/SC
• IDC/UDC
	Section 25.4

6.2 Identify basic networking concepts including how a network works. Concepts include:	
• Installing and configuring network cards	Section 25.3
• Addressing	Section 25.3
• Bandwidth	Section 25.3
• Status indicators	Section 25.3
• Protocols	
• TCP/IP	Section 25.9
• IPX/SPX (NWLINK)	Section 25.10
• AppleTalk	Section 25.12
• NETBEUI/NETBIOS	Section 25.11
• Full-duplex, half-duplex	Section 25.5
• Cabling—Twisted Pair, Coaxial, Fiber Optic, RS-232	Section 25.3 and 25.4

• Networking models
  • Peer-to-peer
  • Client/server
	Section 25.2

• Infrared	Section 25.8
• Wireless	Section 25.8
6.3 Identify common technologies available for establishing Internet connectivity and their characteristics. Technologies include: • LAN • DSL • Cable • ISDN • Dial-up • Satellite • Wireless Characteristic include: • Definition • Speed • Connections	Section 25.21

A+ Operating System Technologies

Domain 1 Operating System Fundamentals	
1.1 Identify the major desktop components and interfaces, and their functions. Differentiate the characteristics of Windows 9x/Me, Windows NT 4.0 Workstation, Windows 2000 Professional, and Windows XP.	
Content may include the following:	
• Contrasts between Windows 9x/Me, Windows NT 4.0 Workstation, Windows 2000 Professional, and Windows XP	Section 20.1, 21.1, and 21.2
• Major Operating System components	
• Registry	Section 21.14
• Virtual Memory	Section 21.8.1
• File System	Section 20.6 and 21.1
• Major Operating System Interfaces	
• Windows Explorer	Section 20.3 and 21.3
• My Computer	Section 20.2.1 and 21.2
• Control Panel	Section 20.9.1 and 21.8
• Computer Management Console	Section 21.9.3
• Accessories/System Tools	Section 21.9.1
• Command line	Section 19.1
• Network Neighborhood/My Network Places	Section 25.18
• Task Bar/systray	Section 20.2.1, 20.9.2, and 21.2
• Start Menu	Section 20.2.1 and 21.2
• Device Manager	Section 20.9.1 and 21.8.1
1.2 Identify the names, locations, purposes, and contents of major system files.	
Content may include the following:	
• Windows 9x–specific files	Section 19.2, 19.6, 19.7, 19.8, 20.5.1, 20.9.4, 20.9.6, 20.10, and 20.13
• IO.SYS	
• MSDOS.SYS	
• AUTOEXEC.BAT	
• COMMAND.COM	
• CONFIG.SYS	
• HIMEM.SYS	
• EMM386.exe	
• WIN.COM	
• SYSTEM.INI	
• WIN.INI	
• Registry data files	
• SYSTEM.DAT	
• USER.DAT	
• Windows NT-based specific files	Section 21.6 and 21.14
• BOOT.INI	
• NTLDR	
• NTDETECT.COM	
• NTBOOTDD.SYS	
• NTUSER.DAT	
• Registry data files	
1.3 Demonstrate the ability to use command-line functions and utilities to manage the operating system, including the proper syntax and switches.	Chapter 19
Command-line functions and utilities include:	
• Command/CMD	Section 19.1
• DIR	Section 19.4
• ATTRIB	Section 19.4
• VER	Section 19.4
• MEM	Section 19.4

Continued

• SCANDISK • DEFRAG • EDIT • XCOPY • COPY • FORMAT • FDISK • SETVER • SCANREG • MD/CD/RD • Delete/Rename • DELTREE • TYPE • ECHO • SET • PING	Section 12.11 Section 12.11 Section 19.4 Section 19.4 Section 19.4 Section 9.3 and 19.4 Section 9.3 and 12.11 Section 19.9.6 Section 20.12 Section 19.4 Section 19.4 Section 19.4 Section 19.4 Section 19.4 Section 19.6 Section 25.9.4

1.4 Identify basic concepts and procedures for creating, viewing, and managing disks, directories and files. This includes procedures for changing file attributes and the ramifications of those changes (for example, security issues).
Content may include the following:
• Disks
• Partitions
  • Active Partition
  • Primary Partition
  • Extended Partition
  • Logical partition
• Files Systems
  • FAT16
  • FAT32
  • NTFS4
  • NTFS5.x
• Directory Structures (root directory, subdirectories, etc)
  • Create folders
  • Navigate the directory structure
  • Maximum depth
• Files
  • Creating files
  • File naming conventions (Most common extensions, 8.3, maximum length)
  • File attributes—Read Only, Hidden, System, and Archive attributes
  • File Compression
  • File Encryption
  • File Permissions
  • File types (text vs binary file)
	
	Section 9.3.3 and 12.6
	
	Section 12.4, 12.6, 20.6, and 21.1
	
	Section 12.5, 19.4, 20.3, and 21.3
	
	Section 19.4.8, 20.3, and 21.3
	Section 12.5
	Section 12.5, 20.3, and 21.3
	Section 12.8
	Section 12.9
	Section 22.12
	Section 1.8

1.5 Identify the major operating system utilities, their purpose, location, and available switches.
• Disk Management Tools
  • DEFRAG.EXE
  • FDISK.EXE
  • Backup/Restore Utility (MSbackup, NTBackup, etc)
  • ScanDisk
  • CHKDSK
  • Disk Cleanup
  • Format
• System Management Tools
  • Device manager
  • System Manager
	
	Section 12.10
	Section 9.3 and 9.8
	Section 21.15
	Section 12.10, 20.12, and 21.9
	Section 12.10.2
	Section 21.9
	Section 19.4, 20.3, and 21.3
	
	Section 20.9 and 21.8
	Section 20.9 and 21.8

Continued

• Computer Manager	Section 21.9
• MSCONFIG.EXE	Section 20.13 and 21.15
• REGEDIT.EXE (View information/Backup registry)	Section 20.10, 20.12.7, and 21.14
• REGEDT32.EXE	Section 21.14
• SYSEDIT.EXE	Section 20.9.6
• SCANREG	Section 20.12
• COMMAND/CMD	Section 19.1
• Event Viewer	Section 21.9.4
• Task Manager	Section 21.7.4
• File Management Tools	
• ATTRIB.EXE	Section 19.4.6
• EXTRACT.EXE	Section 21.12.2 and 21.15
• Edit.com	Section 19.4.8
• Windows Explorer	Section 20.3 and 21.3

Domain 2 Installation, Configuration, and Upgrading	

2.1 Identify the procedures for installing Windows 9x/Me, Windows NT 4.0 Workstation, Windows 2000 Professional, and Windows XP, and bringing the operating system to a basic operational level.
Content may include the following:
• Verify hardware compatibility and minimum requirements
• Determine OS installation options
  • Installation type (typical, custom, other)
  • Network configuration
  • File system type
  • Dual Boot Support
	Section 20.4 and 21.4

• Disk preparation order (conceptual disk preparation)
  • Start the installation
  • Partition
  • Format drive
• Run appropriate set up utility
  • Setup
  • Winnt
• Installation methods
  • Bootable CD
  • Boot floppy
  • Network installation
  • Drive Imaging
• Device Driver Configuration
  • Load default drivers
  • Find updated drivers
• Restore user data files (if applicable)
• Identify common symptoms and problems
	Section 9.3

2.2 Identify steps to perform an operating system upgrade from Windows 9.x/ME, Windows NT 4.0 Workstation, Windows 2000 Professional, and Windows XP. Given an upgrade scenario, choose the appropriate next steps. Content may include the following: • Upgrade paths available. • Determine correct upgrade startup utility (e.g., WINNT32 vs WINNT)	Section 21.4 and 21.8

Continued

• Verify hardware compatibility and minimum requirements • Verify application compatibility • Apply OS service packs, patches, and updates • Install additional Windows components	

2.3 Identify the basic system boot sequences and boot methods, including the steps to create an emergency boot disk with utilities installed for Windows 9x/Me, Windows NT 4.0 Workstation, Windows 2000 Professional, and Windows XP.
Content may include the following:
• Boot Sequence
  • Files required to boot
  • Boot steps (9.x, NT-based)
• Alternative Boot Methods
  • Using a Startup disk
  • Safe/VGA-only mode
  • Last Known Good configuration
  • Command Prompt mode
  • Booting to a system restore point
  • Recovery Console
  • Boot.ini switches
  • Dual Boot
• Creating Emergency Disks with OS Utilities
• Creating emergency repair disk (ERD)
	Section 19.2, 20.5.1, 20.13.1, 21.6, and 21.15

2.4 Identify procedures for installing/adding a device, including loading, adding, and configuring device drivers, and required software.
Content may include the following:
• Device Driver Installation
  • Plug and Play (PNP) and non-PNP devices
  • Install and configure device drivers
  • Install different device drivers
  • Manually install a device driver
  • Search the Internet for updated device drivers
  • Using unsigned drivers (driver signing)
• Install Additional Windows components
• Determine if permissions are adequate for performing the task
	Section 20.5.3, 20.9.1, 21.4, 21.8.1, and 21.8.3

2.5 Identify procedures necessary to optimize the operating system and major operating system subsystems. Content may include the following: • Virtual Memory Management • Disk Defragmentation • Files and Buffers • Caches • Temporary file management	Section 12.10.4, 19.6.3, 19.7, 20.5.1, 20.9.1, 20.14, 21.8, and 22.8

Domain 3 Diagnosing and Troubleshooting	

3.1 Recognize and interpret the meaning of common error codes and startup messages from the boot sequence, and identify steps to correct the problems.
 	
Content may include the following:
• Common Error Messages and Codes
  • Boot failure and errors
    • Invalid boot disk
    • Inaccessible boot device
    • Missing NTLDR
    • Bad or missing Command interpreter
  • Startup messages
    • Error in CONFIG.SYS line XX
    • Himem.sys not loaded
    • Missing or corrupt Himem.sys
    • Device/Service has failed to start
  • A device referenced in SYSTEM.INI, WIN.INI, Registry is not found
  • Event Viewer—Event log is full
  • Failure to start GUI
  • Windows Protection Error
  • User-modified settings cause improper operation at startup
  • Registry corruption
• Using the correct Utilities
  • Dr. Watson
  • Boot Disk
  • Event Viewer
	Section 19.11, 19.12, 20.9.1, 20.10, 20.12, 20.13, 20.14, 21.8.1, 21.14, 21.15, and 21.16

3.2 Recognize when to use common diagnostic utilities and tools. Given a diagnostic scenario involving one of these utilities or tools, select the appropriate steps needed to resolve the problem.
 	
Utilities and tools may include the following:
• Startup disks
  • Required files for a boot disk
  • Boot disk with CD-ROM support
• Startup Modes
  • Safe mode
  • Safe mode with command prompt
  • Safe mode with networking
  • Step-by-Step/Single step mode
  • Automatic skip driver (ASD.exe)
• Diagnostic tools, utilities and resources
  • User/installation manuals
  • Internet/web resources
  • Training materials
  • Task Manager
  • Dr. Watson
  • Boot Disk
  • Event Viewer
  • Device Manager
  • WinMSD
  • MSD
  • Recovery CD
  • CONFIGSAFE
• Eliciting problem symptoms from customers
• Having customer reproduce error as part of the diagnostic process
• Identifying recent changes to the computer environment from the user
	Chapter 2 and Section 20.13, 20.12, 20.13, 21.6.2, 21.7, 21.9, 21.15, and 21.16

Continued

3.3 Recognize common operational and usability problems and determine how to resolve them.	
Content may include the following:	

• Troubleshooting Windows-specific printing problems
  • Print spool is stalled
  • Incorrect/incompatible driver for print
  • Incorrect parameter
	Section 18.2.7, 20.8, and 21.13

• Other Common problems
  • General Protection Faults
  • Bluescreen error (BSOD)
  • Illegal operation
  • Invalid working directory
  • System lock up
  • Option (Sound card, modem, input device) or will not function
  • Application will not start or load
  • Cannot log on to network (option—NIC not functioning)
  • Applications don't install
  • Network connection
	Section 20.13 and 21.16

• Viruses and virus types
  • What they are
  • TSR (Terminate Stay Resident) programs and virus
  • Sources (floppy, emails, etc.)
  • How to determine presence
	Section 13.2

Domain 4 Networks	
4.1 Identify the networking capabilities of Windows. Given configuration parameters, configure the operating system to connect to a network.	Chapter 25
Content may include the following:	

• Configure protocols
  • TCP/IP
  • Gateway
  • Subnet mask
  • DNS (and domain suffix)
  • WINS
  • Static address assignment
  • Automatic address assignment (APIPA, DHCP)
	Section 25.9 and 25.15

• PX/SPX (NWLink)	Section 25.10
• Appletalk	Section 25.12
• NetBEUI/ NetBIOS	Section 25.11

• Configure Client options
  • Microsoft
  • Novell
	Section 25.15

• Verify the configuration	Section 25.9

• Understand the use of the following tools
  • IPCONFIG.EXE
  • WINIPCFG.EXE
  • PING
  • TRACERT.EXE
  • NSLOOKUP.EXE
	Section 25.9

• Share resources (Understand the capabilities/limitations with each OS version)	Section 25.15, 25.16, and 25.17
• Setting permissions to shared resources	Section 25.15, 25.16, and 25.17
• Network type and network card	Section 25.3

Continued

4.2 Identify the basic Internet protocols and terminologies. Identify procedures for establishing Internet connectivity. In a given scenario, configure the operating system to connect to and use Internet resources.	
Content may include the following:	
• Protocols and terminologies	Section 25.9 and 25.21
• ISP	
• TCP/IP	
• Email (POP, SMTP, IMAP)	
• HTML	
• HTTP	
• HTTPS	
• SSL	
• Telnet	
• FTP	
• DNS	
• Connectivity technologies	Section 17.3, 17.4, and 25.21
• Dial-up networking	
• DSL networking	
• ISDN networking	
• Cable	
• Satellite	
• Wireless	
• LAN	
• Installing and Configuring browsers	Section 22.3
• Enable/disable script support	
• Configure Proxy Settings	
• Configure security settings	
• Firewall protection under Windows XP	Section 25.19

MICROSOFT CERTIFIED DESKTOP SUPPORT TECHNICIAN

The Microsoft Certified Desktop Support Technician (MCDST) certification will get you started in your IT career by ensuring you have the skills to successfully troubleshoot desktop environments running on the Microsoft Windows operating system. It consist of two exams:

- Supporting Users and Troubleshooting a Microsoft Windows XP Operating System—Microsoft Exam 70-271
- Supporting Users and Troubleshooting Desktop Applications on a Microsoft Windows XP Operating System—Microsoft Exam 70-272

Supporting Users and Troubleshooting a Microsoft Windows XP Operating System—Microsoft Exam 70-271

Installing a Windows Desktop Operating System	
Perform and troubleshoot an attended installation of a Windows XP operating system. • Answer end-user questions related to performing an attended installation of a Windows XP operating system. • Troubleshoot and complete installations in which an installation does not start. Tasks include configuring the device boot order and ascertaining probable cause of the failure to start. • Troubleshoot and complete installations in which an installation fails to complete. Tasks include reviewing setup log files and providing needed files. • Perform postinstallation configuration. Tasks include customizing installations for individual users and applying service packs.	Section 21.4

Continued

Installing a Windows Desktop Operating Systems	
Perform and troubleshoot an unattended installation of a Windows desktop operating system. • Answer end-user questions related to performing an unattended installation of a Windows XP operating system. Tasks include starting an installation, answering questions asked by an end user during an installation, and performing postinstallation tasks. • Configure a PC to boot to a network device and start installation of a Windows XP operating system. Tasks include configuring PXE compliant network cards. • Perform an installation by using unattended installation files.	Section 21.4.3
Upgrade from a previous version of Windows. • Answer end-user questions related to upgrading from a previous version of Windows. Considerations include available upgrade paths and methods for transferring user state data. • Verify hardware compatibility for upgrade. Considerations include minimum hardware and system resource requirements. • Verify application compatibility for upgrade. Tasks include ascertaining which applications can and cannot run, and using the application compatibility tools. • Migrate user state data from an existing PC to a new PC. • Install a second instance of an operating system on a computer.	Section 21.4
Managing and Troubleshooting Access to Resources	
Monitor, manage, and troubleshoot access to files and folders. • Answer end-user questions related to managing and troubleshooting access to filesand folders. • Monitor, manage, and troubleshoot NTFS file permissions. • Manage and troubleshoot simple file sharing. • Manage and troubleshoot file encryption.	Section 21.10.6, 21.12, and 25.16
Manage and troubleshoot access to shared folders. • Answer end-user questions related to managing and troubleshooting access to shared folders. • Create shared folders. • Configure access permission for shared folders on NTFS partitions. • Troubleshoot and interpret Access Denied messages.	Section 21.12 and 25.16
Connect to local and network print devices. • Answer end-user questions related to printing locally. • Configure and manage local printing. • Answer end-user questions related to network-based printing. • Connect to and manage printing to a network-based printer.	Section 21.13 and 25.17
Manage and troubleshoot access to and synchronization of offline files. • Answer end-user questions related to configuring and synchronizing offline files. • Configure and troubleshoot offline files. • Configure and troubleshoot offline file synchronization.	Section 21.16.3
Configuring and Troubleshooting Hardware Devices and Drivers	
Configure and troubleshoot storage devices. • Answer end-user questions related to configuring hard disks and partitions or volumes. • Manage and troubleshoot disk partitioning. • Answer end-user questions related to optical drives such as CD-ROM, CD-RW, DVD, and DVD-R. • Configure and troubleshoot removable storage devices such as pen drives, flash drives, and memory cards.	Chapter 11 and Section 21.11

Installing a Windows Desktop Operating Systems	
Configure and troubleshoot display devices. • Answer end-user questions related to configuring desktop display settings. • Configure display devices and display settings. • Troubleshoot display device settings. Configure and troubleshoot Advanced Configuration and Power Interface (ACPI). • Answer end-user questions related to configuring ACPI settings. • Configure and troubleshoot operating system power settings. • Configure and troubleshoot system standby and hibernate settings.	Chapter 14 and Section 21.6.2, 21.8.2, and 21.15 Section 8.7 and 21.8.6
Configure and troubleshoot I/O devices. • Answer end-user questions related to configuring I/O devices. • Configure and troubleshoot device settings. • Configure and troubleshoot device drivers for I/O devices. • Configure and troubleshoot hardware profiles.	Section 21.8.1
Configuring and Troubleshooting the Desktop and User Environments	
Configure the user environment. • Answer end-user questions related to configuring the desktop and user environment. • Configure and troubleshoot task and toolbar settings. • Configure and troubleshoot accessibility options. • Configure and troubleshoot pointing device settings. • Configure and troubleshoot fast-use switching.	Section 15.2, 21.2, 21.7, and 21.9.1
Configure support for multiple languages or multiple locations. • Answer end-user questions related to regional settings. • Configure and troubleshoot regional settings. • Answer end-user questions related to language settings. • Configure and troubleshoot language settings.	Section 21.8.5
Troubleshoot security settings and local security policy. • Answer end-user questions related to security settings. • Identify end-user issues caused by local security policies such as Local Security Settings and Security Configuration and Analysis. • Identify end-user issues caused by network security policies such as Resultant Set of Policy (RSoP) and Group Policy.	Section 21.7.9, 22.9
Configure and troubleshoot local user and group accounts. • Answer end-user questions related to user accounts. • Configure and troubleshoot local user accounts. • Answer end-user questions related to local group accounts. • Configure and troubleshoot local group accounts. Considerations include rights and permissions.	Section 21.7.1 and 21.12
Troubleshoot system startup and user logon problems. • Answer end-user questions related to system startup issues. • Troubleshoot system startup problems. • Answer end-user questions related to user logon issues. • Troubleshoot local user logon issues. • Troubleshoot domain user logon issues.	Section 21.6, 21.7, and 21.15
Monitor and analyze system performance. • Answer end-user questions related to system performance. • Use Help and Support to view and troubleshoot system performance. • Use Task Manager to view and troubleshoot system performance. • Use the Performance tool to capture system performance information.	Section 21.7.4 and 21.17

Troubleshooting Network Protocols and Services	
Troubleshoot TCP/IP. Tools include ARP; the Repair utility; connection properties; and the ping, ipconfig, pathping, and nslookup commands. • Answer end-user questions related to configuring TCP/IP settings. • Configure and troubleshoot manual TCP/IP configuration. • Configure and troubleshoot automated TCP/IP address configuration. • Configure and troubleshoot Internet Connection Firewall (ICF) settings such as enable and disable. Considerations include indications of issues related to enabling or disabling ICF.	Section 25.9 and 25.19
Troubleshoot name resolution issues. • Configure and troubleshoot host name resolution issues on a client computer. Considerations include Hosts files and DNS. • Configure and troubleshoot NetBIOS name resolution issues on a client computer. Considerations include Lm HOSTS files and WINS.	Section 25.9
Configure and troubleshoot remote connections. • Configure and troubleshoot a remote dialup connection. Tasks include client-side configuration. • Configure and troubleshoot a remote connection across the Internet. Tasks include client-side configuration.	Section 25.21
Configure and troubleshoot Internet Explorer. • Configure and troubleshoot Internet Explorer connections properties. • Configure and troubleshoot Internet Explorer security properties. • Configure and troubleshoot Internet Explorer general properties.	Section 22.3
Configure and troubleshoot end-user systems by using remote connectivity tools. • Use Remote Desktop to configure and troubleshoot an end user's desktop. • Use Remote Assistance to configure and troubleshoot an end user's desktop.	Section 22.8

Supporting Users and Troubleshooting Desktop Applications on a Microsoft Windows XP Operating System—Microsoft Exam 70-272

Configuring and Troubleshooting Applications	
Configure and troubleshoot Office applications. • Answer end-user questions related to configuring Office applications. • Set application compatibility settings. • Troubleshoot application installation problems. • Configure and troubleshoot email account settings.	Section 22.2 and 22.5
Configure and troubleshoot Internet Explorer.	Section 22.3
Configure and troubleshoot Outlook Express. • Answer end-user questions related to configuring Outlook Express. • Configure and troubleshoot newsreader account settings. • Configure and troubleshoot email account settings.	Section 22.4
Configure the operating system to support applications. • Answer end-user questions related to configuring the operating system to support an application. • Configure and troubleshoot file system access and file permission problems on multiboot computers. • Configure access to applications on multiuser computers. • Configure and troubleshoot application access on a multiple user client computer.	Section 21.12 and 22.1

Resolving Issues Related to Usability	
Resolve issues related to Office application support features. Tasks include configuring Office applications and interpreting error messages.	Section 22.2
Resolve issues related to Internet Explorer support features. Tasks include configuring Internet Explorer and interpreting error messages.	Section 22.3
Resolve issues related to Outlook Express features. Tasks include configuring Outlook Express and interpreting error messages.	Section 22.4
Resolve issues related to operating system features. Tasks include configuring operating system features and interpreting error messages.	Section 21.16
Resolving Issues Related to Application Customization	
Resolve issues related to customizing an Office application. • Answer end-user questions related to customizing Office applications. • Customize toolbars. • Configure proofing tools. • Manage Outlook data, including configuring, importing, and exporting data, and repairing corrupted data. • Personalize Office features.	Section 22.2
Resolve issues related to customizing Internet Explorer.	Section 22.3
Resolve issues related to customizing Outlook Express.	Section 22.4
Resolve issues related to customizing the operating system to support applications. • Answer end-user questions related to customizing the operating system to support an application. • Customize the Start menu and taskbar. • Customize regional settings. • Customize fonts. • Customize folder settings.	Section 21.2, 21.8.4, 21.8.5, 21.8.7, and 22.1
Configuring and Troubleshooting Connectivity for Applications	
Identify and troubleshoot name resolution problems. Indications of such problems include application errors.	Section 25.9.2
Identify and troubleshoot network adapter configuration problems. Indications of such problems include application errors.	Section 25.3 and 25.15
Identify and troubleshoot LAN and Routing and Remote Access configuration problems. Indications of such problems include application errors.	Section 25.9 and 25.21
Identify and troubleshoot network connectivity problems caused by the firewall configuration. Indications of such problems include application errors.	Section 25.19
Identify and troubleshoot problems with locally attached devices. Indications of such problems include application errors.	Section 21.8.1, 25.16, and 25.17
Configuring Application Security	
Identify and troubleshoot problems related to security permissions. • Answer end-user questions related to application security settings. • Troubleshoot access to local resources. • Troubleshoot access to network resources. • Troubleshoot insufficient user permissions and rights.	Section 21.12, 25.16, and 25.17

Identify and respond to security incidents. • Answer end-user questions related to security incidents. • Identify a virus attack. • Apply critical updates.	Section 13.2, 21.4.6, and 22.9
Manage application security settings.	Section 22.2.8

APPENDIX F

Answers to Odd-Numbered Questions

CHAPTER 1: A PC OVERVIEW

1. A
3. C
5. A
7. B
9. B
11. C
13. B
15. B
17. F
19. C
21. C
23. D

CHAPTER 2: THE PC TECHNICIAN

1. A and D
3. D
5. A
7. D
9. B
11. T
13. B
15. D
17. A
19. E
21. A
23. D
25. A
27. D
29. C
31. F

CHAPTER 3: THE DISASSEMBLY AND ASSEMBLY OF THE PC

1. D
3. A
5. A
7. A
9. B
11. D
13. C
15. A, B and C
17. Identify parts of the motherboard

CHAPTER 4: MICROPROCESSORS

1. C
3. A and B
5. A and B
7. A
9. B
11. C, E and F
13. D
15. E
17. A
19. D
21. D
23. D
25. T
27. A
29. C
31. B
33. B and D
35. D

CHAPTER 5: RAM

1. C
3. D
5. A and C
7. A
9. A
11. B
13. B
15. D
17. D
19. B
21. A
23. D
25. E
27. A

CHAPTER 6: MOTHERBOARDS

1. B
3. C
5. B
7. D
9. A
11. D
13. D and E
15. D
17. B
19. A
21. B
23. A, B and D
25. A and D
27. C, D, E and F

CHAPTER 7: THE EXPANSION SLOTS AND CARDS

1. D
3. C
5. A
7. D
9. C
11. A
13. B
15. C
17. A
19. C
21. A
23. D
25. C
27. D
29. D
31. A

CHAPTER 8: THE CASE AND POWER SUPPLY

1. C
3. B
5. B
7. C
9. E
11. A
13. B
15. A
17. E
19. C
21. B
23. D
25. A, B and F

CHAPTER 9: THE HARD DRIVE

1. D
3. A
5. B
7. D
9. B
11. A
13. D
15. A
17. C
19. B
21. B
23. A
25. A
27. C
29. C and E
31. C
33. F
35. A
37. A
39. C
41. C

CHAPTER 10: THE FLOPPY DISK DRIVE AND OTHER REMOVABLE MEDIA

1. B
3. D
5. A
7. C
9. C
11. A

CHAPTER 11: THE COMPACT DISK DRIVE

1. B
3. E
5. C
7. C
9. A and B
11. D
13. B
15. A

CHAPTER 12: THE DISK STRUCTURE

1. A
3. B
5. B
7. C
9. E
11. D
13. A
15. C
17. A
19. D
21. C
23. C
25. B
27. A

CHAPTER 13: TAPE DRIVES AND DATA PROTECTION

1. D
3. D
5. B
7. A
9. A
11. D
13. C
15. A
17. F
19. A
21. A
23. B

CHAPTER 14: THE VIDEO SYSTEM

1. B
3. D
5. D
7. E
9. D
11. C
13. A
15. D
17. C
19. D
21. B
23. C
25. A
27. A and D
29. A
31. B and C
33. C
35. A
37. B
39. A

CHAPTER 15: INPUT DEVICES

1. C and D
3. D
5. D
7. C
9. C
11. B
13. A
15. E
17. C
19. C
21. D
23. E

CHAPTER 16: SOUND CARDS

1. A and B
3. C
5. A
7. A and D
9. C
11. D
13. B, C and D

CHAPTER 17: SERIAL PORTS AND MODEMS

1. A
3. A
5. A
7. A
9. A
11. D
13. C
15. B
17. A
19. B
21. C
23. B
25. B
27. B
29. A
31. A, B and D
33. A, B, C and D
35. A
37. A

CHAPTER 18: PARALLEL PORTS AND PRINTERS

1. B
3. C
5. B
7. E
9. D
11. A
13. C
15. A
17. A
19. A
21. A and B
23. A
25. A
27. E
29. B
31. C
33. D
35. A and C
37. D
39. D
41. B
43. A
45. A
47. B
49. B

CHAPTER 19: THE DOS INTERFACE

1. A
3. C
5. C
7. A and E
9. A
11. A
13. D
15. A
17. C
19. C
21. B
23. A
25. C
27. C
29. B
31. A
33. A
35. A
37. A
39. A, B and C

CHAPTER 20: WINDOWS 9X

1. C
3. D
5. B
7. C
9. A and D
11. A
13. B
15. B
17. E
19. A
21. B
23. D
25. C
27. A and D
29. C
31. C
33. B
35. C
37. A
39. A
41. A
43. A
45. D
47. A
49. D
51. E
53. C
55. C
57. C
59. C

CHAPTER 21: WINDOWS NT FAMILY

1. F
3. D
5. D
7. D
9. F
11. B
13. A
15. E
17. B and D
19. D
21. D
23. B
25. E
27. B
29. D
31. C
33. D
35. D
37. A and D

CHAPTER 22: SUPPORTING WINDOWS AND WINDOWS APPLICATIONS

1. B
3. A
5. A
7. B
9. B
11. A
13. A, B, C and D
15. B
17. D
19. A
21. A, B and C
23. A
25. A
27. D
29. C
31. A
33. D
35. A
37. A
39. A
41. A
43. C
45. A
47. C

CHAPTER 23: INTRODUCTION TO LINUX

1. A
3. D
5. C
7. D
9. B
11. A
13. A
15. A, B and C
17. A
19. A
21. C
23. A
25. B
27. B

CHAPTER 24: ADVANCED LINUX

1. D
3. A
5. B
7. A
9. A
11. D
13. C
15. D
17. A
19. A
21. D
23. A and C
25. D
27. D
29. D

CHAPTER 25: COMPUTERS CONNECTED TO A NETWORK

1. D
3. C
5. C
7. B
9. C
11. B
13. A
15. B and D
17. C
19. D
21. D
23. C
25. E
27. A and D
29. C
31. B
33. C
35. D
37. C
39. A and C
41. A
43. C
45. B
47. B
49. C
51. C, E and F
53. C
55. D
57. D and E
59. A
61. D
63. A
65. B
67. A

CHAPTER 26: INTRODUCTION TO APPLE MACINTOSH COMPUTERS

1. D
3. C
5. A
7. C

Glossary

10Base2—One of several adaptations of the Ethernet (IEEE 802.3) standard for local area networks (LANs). The 10Base2 standard (also called thinnet) uses 50 ohm coaxial cable (RG-58 A/U) with maximum lengths of 185 meters (607 feet) and operates at 10 Mbit/s.

10Base5—The original cabling standard for Ethernet that uses coaxial cables. The name derives from the fact that the maximum data transfer speed is 10 Mbit/s, it uses baseband transmission, and the maximum length of cables is 500 meters (1640 feet). 10Base5 is also called *thick Ethernet, ThickWire,* and *ThickNet.*

10BaseT—One of several adaptations of the Ethernet (IEEE 802.3) standard for local area networks (LANs). The 10BaseT standard (also called *Twisted-Pair Ethernet*) uses a twisted-pair cable with maximum lengths of 100 meters (328 feet). The 10BaseT system operates at 10 Mbit/s and uses baseband transmission methods.

101-Key Keyboard—A keyboard with 101 keys, including 12 function keys and separate cursor control keys.

104-Key Keyboard—A keyboard with 104 keys. It is similar to the 101-key keyboard but has a few extra keys used primarily in Windows operating systems.

3D Accelerator Video Cards—Video accelerator cards that can perform many of the complicated calculations associated with three-dimensional (3D) images.

3DNow! Technology—A set of 21 new instructions that use SIMD and other microprocessor enhancements to open the performance bottleneck in the 3D graphics pipeline between the microprocessor and the 3D graphics accelerator card.

386 Protection Mechanism—A method used by all Intel and Intel-compatible processors since the 386 processor that has programs run in one of four rings. Ring 0 has access to all program and memory in all levels and ring 3 can only access program and memory in ring 3. Today, the kernel runs in ring 0 and other programs run in ring 3.

83-Key Keyboard—A keyboard with 83 keys. It was used with the IBM PC and XT and included 10 function keys on the left side of the keyboard.

80286 Microprocessor—A second-generation microprocessor used in the IBM AT computer. It has a 16-bit word size and 16-bit data bus.

80386DX Microprocessor—A third-generation microprocessor that was the first 32-bit microprocessor used in IBM PCs.

80386SX Microprocessor—A third-generation microprocessor that is a cut-down version of the 80836DX microprocessor. It uses a 32-bit word size and a 16-bit data bus.

80486DX Microprocessor—A fourth-generation microprocessor that is a 32-bit microprocessor with built-in RAM cache and math coprocessor.

80486SX Microprocessor—A fourth-generation microprocessor that is an 80486DX microprocessor without a math coprocessor.

8086 Microprocessor—A first-generation microprocessor. It has a 16-bit word size and 16-bit data bus.

8088 Microprocessor—A first-generation microprocessor used in the IBM PC and IBM XT computers. It has a 16-bit word size and 8-bit data bus.

A

A+ Certification—The CompTIA certification that is a vendor-neutral certification for computer hardware technicians.

A20—A microprocessor address line that gives access to the high memory area.

Accelerated Graphics Port (AGP)—A spinoff of the PCI slot (based on the PCI 2.1 specification) made exclusively for video cards.

Accelerated Hub Architecture—An Intel technology used on its 800-series chipsets to transfer data between the memory control hub (MCH), which is equivalent to the North Bridge, and the input/output controller hub (ICH), which is equivalent to the South Bridge.

Access Control Entry (ACE)—An entry within the ACL.

Access Control List (ACL)—A list that controls who has an access to a resource and the type of access that is allowed.

Access Time—The average amount of time it takes to move the read/write head to the requested sector. The sum of seek time and latency period, it is measured in milliseconds (ms).

Active Matrix Displays—A type of LCD display used in notebook computers.

Active Partition—A partition that is marked as the partition to boot from. Therefore, it is expected to have the necessary boot files.

Active Termination—A type of termination that acts as a voltage regulator to maintain a stable voltage through the chain by utilizing the termination power lines to compensate for voltage drops.

Active X—A set of rules for how applications should share information. Programmers can develop Active X controls and plug-ins in a variety of languages, including C, C++, Visual Basic, and Java. Unlike Java applets, however, Active X controls are downloaded and executed by a web browser (Internet Explorer) and have full access to the Windows operating system. Because Active X has full access to the Windows operating system, it constitutes the greatest potential threat.

Address—A word or number that refers to a storage location or port.

Address Bus—A bus that is used to define where the data bus signals are going to or coming from.

Adobe Acrobat—A program commonly used to store documentation on computers, computer components, and software.

Advanced Communication Riser (ACR)—An alternative to CNR that is designed to allow motherboard designers to add low-cost network capabilities to motherboards, but uses the same PCI connector used by PCI expansion cards.

Advanced Configuration and Power Interface (ACPI)—A standard developed by Intel, Microsoft, and Toshiba that is designed to implement power management functions in the operating system. ACPI is a replacement for APM.

Advanced Power Management (APM)—A standard that allows the system ROM BIOS (enabled in the CMOS setup program) or software to manage the power consumption of the system.

Advanced Systems Format (ASF)—An audio/video standard created by Microsoft, which is used by Windows Media. It can be compressed with a wide variety of codecs. In addition, ASF supports streaming with Windows Media Services or is optionally packaged with Windows Media Rights Manager.

Alert Log—A trace log used in Windows Performance Monitor that monitors counters, waits for them to exceed user-defined tolerances, and logs the event. You can even set up the alert log to send a message or run an application when a particular value is exceeded.

Aliasing—The distortion introduced when translating from an analog signal to a digital signal and back to an analog signal.

Alternating Current (AC)—Current that reverses directions in cycles. Its polarity changes from positive to negative to positive again. The number of complete cycles per second is measured in hertz (Hz).

American Standard Code for Information Interchange (ASCII) Character Set—Pronounced "ask-ee," ASCII is a code for representing English characters as numbers, with each letter assigned a number from 0 to 127. Since there are 128 different characters, it uses 7 bits for each character. *See* Extended ASCII.

American Wire Gauge (AWG)—A U.S. standard for measuring the thickness of copper and aluminum wire for electrical and data-transmission use.

Amperes (Amps)—The rate of current.

Amplitude—(1) The peak voltage of the sine wave. (2) Loudness or intensity.

Analog—Refers to a signal that can take any value within the overall allowable range.

Anode Cap—A flat, circular object resembling a suction cup located on the top of the CRT.

Answer file—a generic script file used in unattended installations of Windows NT, 2000, or XP.

Anti-aliasing—Software adjustment to make diagonal and curved lines appear smooth and continuous in computer-generated images.

Antistatic Bag—A bag designed to keep electrostatic electricity away from the electronic components inside the bag.

Antivirus Program—A program that detects and/or eliminates computer viruses.

Aperture Grill—Hundreds of fine metal strips that run vertically from the top of a CRT monitor that are used to aim and focus the electron beams.

Applet—(1) An icon. (2) A component in a distributed environment that is downloaded and executed by a web browser. Web browsers, which are designed to display text and graphics and also accept data input on forms, aren't very good at processing information locally on the client system, so applets were invented to solve this problem. Applets are also known as mobile code because they are downloaded from a server and run on a client.

Application Programming Interface (API)—A system call (routine) that gives programmers access to the services provided by the operating system. In IBM-compatible systems, the ROM BIOS and DOS together present an API that a programmer can use to control system hardware.

Application Software—Software that allows a user to input, format, and organize data to create useable information. It is this type of software that allows the user to create a letter, report, budget, chart, graph, or database.

ARC (Advanced RISC Computing) Path—Used to specify the location (partition) of an operating system. It is typically used in the Windows NT, Windows 2000, and Windows XP BOOT.INI files.

Architecture—The overall design and construction of a computer, software, or network.

ARCnet (Attached Resource Computer Network)—A simple, inexpensive, flexible design for small networks. ARCnet networks are connected with a star topology and usually with coaxial cable. ARCnet signals follow a bus design, and the computers use a token-passing scheme to access the network. A special advantage of ARCnet is that it permits various types of transmission media—twisted-pair wire, coaxial cable, and fiber-optic cable—to be mixed on the same network.

Areal Density—A term that describes the physical amount of data that can be held on an area of a disk. It is expressed in bits per square inch and is calculated by multiplying the bit density (bits per inch, or bpi) and the track density (tracks per inch, or tpi).

Arithmetic/Logical Unit (ALU)—The calculator part of the microprocessor that follows the instructions of the control unit. It performs mathematical operations such as adding, subtracting, multiplying, and dividing and logical comparisons such as NOT, AND, OR, and exclusive-OR.

ASCII File—A simple text file that contains characters from only the ASCII character set.

Aspect Ratio—The ratio of the number of horizontal pixels and the number of vertical pixels.

Assembly Language—A low-level programming language that uses mnemonic abbreviations to represent machine operations and storage locations. It makes it possible to program the microprocessor directly without having to use machine language.

Asymmetric Digital Subscriber Line (ADSL)—A high-speed transmission technology that uses existing UTP copper wires to communicate digitally at high speed between the telephone company central office (CO) and the subscriber. ADSL sends information asymmetrically, meaning it is faster one way than the other. The original ADSL speed was T-1 (1.536 Mbit/s) downstream. However, ADSL is available in a variety of configurations and speeds.

Asynchronous—A form of communication that has no synchronization or timer.

Asynchronous Transfer Mode (ATM)—A high-bandwidth, low-delay, cell relay (packetlike) switching and multiplexing technique. Usable capacity is segmented into fixed-size cells consisting of header and information fields, allocated to services on demand.

AT Attachment Interface (ATA)—An IDE disk interface standard that defines a compatible register set, a 40-pin connector, and its associated signals.

AT Attachment Packet Interface (ATAPI)—A standard associated with the enhanced IDE standard that allows for CD drives, tape drives, and other storage devices.

AT Command Set—A set of standard instructions used to activate a modem.

AT Computer—(1) A computer with a 286 microprocessor. (2) A computer with a 286 or higher microprocessor.

Athlon—An AMD sixth-generation processor comparable to the Intel Pentium III and Pentium 4 processor.

Attenuation—Refers to loss in signal strength due to resistance, absorption, capacitance, or any characteristic of the transmitting medium.

Attribute—A characteristic or property.

ATX Motherboard—Similar to the Baby AT motherboard, except the components are placed differently. The slots are parallel to the short side of the board, which allows more space for other components. The microprocessor and RAM are next to the power supply so that the airflow generated by the power supply runs over the microprocessor. Lastly, the ATX motherboard contains integrated I/O port connectors and an integrated PS/2 mouse connector and supports 3.3 volts coming from an ATX power supply.

ATX Power Supply—A type of power supply that blows air into the system directly over the microprocessor (to help cool the microprocessor) and pressurizes the inside of the case (keeping it clean). In addition, it contains software control of the power on/off signal so that it can shut down the system with software and always provides a 5 volt standby signal so that the system can be turned on with the keyboard.

ATX12V—A new version of the ATX power supply designed to supply more current.

Audio Video Interleave (AVI)—A video standard that interleaves video and audio data. AVI files will have an AVI file name extension.

Audio/Modem Riser (AMR)—An Intel-developed specification for packaging modem I/O ports and a codec chip into a small card that can be installed into an AMR slot or motherboard. CNR specification has largely replaced AMR.

Auto Update—a feature found in newer versions of Windows that automatically downloads critical security and compatibility updates.

B

Baby AT Motherboard—A motherboard that is the same size and has the same dimensions as the IBM XT motherboard.

Backbone—A portion of a network that handles the bulk of the traffic.

Backlit Light—A light used to illuminate LCD screens.

Backup *(noun)*—An extra copy of data. **Back up** *(verb)*. The process of creating a backup.

Backward Compatibility—The design of software and hardware to work with previous versions of the same software or hardware.

Backward Compatible—A computer, device, or software that is fully compatible with earlier versions.

Bad Sector—An area on a disk that cannot be used to read or store data.

Bandwidth—The capacity of a computer or communications channel.

Bank—A collection of memory chips that make up a block of memory readable by the processor in a single bus cycle.

Basic Disk—A type of disk that contains primary partitions, extended partitions, or logical disks that can be accessed by DOS and Microsoft Windows.

Basic Input/Output System (BIOS)—Instructions stored in ROM chips that control most of the computer's input/output functions, such as communicating with disks, RAM, and the monitor.

Battery—A device that supplies dc power, usually through chemical means.

Baud Rate—The modulation rate, or the number of times per second that a transmission line changes state.

BEDO RAM—Short for Burst Extended Data Output RAM.RAM faster than EDO RAM because it allows the page-access cycle to be divided into two components. To achieve faster access time, data is read from the memory array at the same time data is being transferred through the data bus. In addition, a counter on the chip is used to keep track of the next address so that sequential data can be accessed faster.

Benchmark—A test that attempts to measure hardware or software performance.

Beta Software—Software that has been released to selected users to test before its official release.

Bidirectional—(1) Refers to lines over which data can move in two directions, such as data bus or telephone lines. (2) Refers to the capability of a printer to print from right to left and from left to right alternatively.

Binary Number System—A simple number system that has only two digits, a zero (0) and a one (1).

Bit—Stands for binary digit, the smallest unit of information on a computer. A single bit can hold only one of two values: 0 or 1.

Bit Depth—The number of bits used to describe the color of each pixel on a computer display.

Bitmap Graphics—A picture that uses dots to form graphics images.

Blackouts—Total power failures.

Blue Screen of Death (BSOD)—A system crash in Windows that replaces the normal desktop with a blue screen, shows text reporting the problem, and locks up the system.

BlueTooth—An emerging short-range wireless networking standard that enables PCs, mobile phones, and PDAs to exchange data with each other.

BMP—A Windows graphics format that can be device dependent or independent. BMP files will have a BMP file name extension.

Boot Disk—A disk that can load the operating system using the A drive.

Boot Manager—A program that enables you to select which active partition to boot from.

Boot Partition—The partition that contains the Windows NT, Windows 2000, or Windows XP operating systems.

Boot Sector—A small program that is executed when a computer boots up. Typically, the MBR resides on the first sector of the hard disk.

Boot Sector Virus—A virus that hides or resides in the boot sector of a disk.

Boot-Up—Also referred to as *booting*, the process of loading or copying the operating system into RAM.

BOOT.INI—A file that provides a Boot Loader Operating System Selection menu that allows the selection between multiple operating systems. It is provided by Windows NT, Windows 2000, and Windows XP.

BOOTSECT.DOS—A file used with Windows NT, Windows 2000, and Windows XP that contains the old MBR used to boot older operating systems such as DOS and Windows 9X.

Bootstrap Loader—A small program located at the beginning of a disk that locates the first active or bootable partition.

Bridge—A device that connects two local area networks of similar topology or two segments of the same LAN and that divides traffic on a network segment. A bridge will pass information for one particular workstation to a segment but will not pass broadcast traffic.

Brouter—Acts like a router for certain protocols and acts as a bridge for all others. A brouter understands how to route specific types of packets (routable protocols). For other specified packets (nonroutable protocols), it acts as a bridge that simply forwards the packets to the other networks.

Brownouts—A drop in power that lasts longer than a sag. A brownout can force the computer to shut down, introduce memory errors, and cause unsaved work to be lost.

Browser Service—A service that allows you to find network resources easily.

BTX Form Factor—A case form factor meant to replace the ATX form factor that is designed to include PCI Express and Serial ATA devices.

Buffer—A block of memory used as a holding tank to store data temporarily.

Bug—A logical programming error or glitch in hardware or software that causes some sort of problem.

Bug Fix—A release of hardware or software that corrects one or more bugs.

Burn-in—The operating of a circuit or equipment to establish that its components are stable and to screen out defective parts or components.

Burndy Connector—The type of connector used in AT power supplies.

Burst Mode—A mode used by many RAM chips and buses by specifying the location of data using the address bus and accessing data sequentially without resetting the address bus, thereby increasing performance.

Bus—A collection of wires through which data or power is transmitted from one part of a computer to another.

Bus Controller—Device used to translate signals between the CPU and the expansion bus.

Bus Interface Unit (BIU)—The part of the microprocessor that links it to the rest of the computer.

Bus Mastering—When an expansion card with its own processor takes temporary control of data and the address bus to move information from one point to another. Consequently, the PC is faster.

Bus Port—A port that connects a mouse to an expansion card specifically made for a mouse.

Byte—A unit of storage consisting of 8 bits that can hold a single character.

C

CAB file—Short for *cabinet file,* the archive file type used by Microsoft to distribute recent versions of Windows and applications.

Cache—An intelligent buffer. By using an intelligent algorithm, a cache contains the data accessed most often between a slower peripheral device and the faster processor.

Cache Hit—The finding of requested information in the cache.

Cache Memory—A special ultrafast area of memory, usually made up of SRAM, that acts as a buffer between the microprocessor and the slower RAM.

Cache Miss—The failure of the system to find the required data in the cache.

Caliper—The thickness of paper, which is usually expressed in thousandths of an inch.

Capacitor—A device that stores electric charge (electrons). The amount of charge that a capacitor can hold is measured in farads (F).

CardBus—A 32-bit PC card or slot running at 33 MHz used in notebook computers.

Carpal Tunnel Syndrome—A wrist or hand injury caused by a person holding his or her wrist stiff for long periods. This repetitive stress injury makes the nerves in the wrist swell, causing great pain.

Carrier Detect Signal—A modem interface signal that indicates to the attached data terminal equipment (DTE) that it is receiving a signal form the distance modem.

Case—The box that most of the computer components rest in. It is designed to protect these components.

Cathode-Ray Tube (CRT)—A type of monitor that consists of an electronic screen lined with a phosphorescent material. When an electron gun shoots electrons at the phosphorescent material, the material glows as it is struck.

CD-Digital Audio (CD-DA)—Standard audio compact disks.

CD-E (Erasable)—A type of CD that can be written to more than once.

CD-ROM (Compact Disk Read-Only Memory)—Similar to a floppy disk or hard drive, a CD-ROM stores large quantities of data. The contents of a CD-ROM cannot be changed or erased.

CE Declaration of Conformity—The official marking required by the European community for all electric and electronic equipment that will be sold, or put into service for the first time, anywhere in the European community. It proves to the buyer—or user—that the product fulfills all essential safety and environmental requirements for machinery, low voltage, and electromagnetic compatibility as they are defined in the so-called European Directives.

Central Processing Unit (CPU)—*See* Microprocessor.

Centronics Connector—A standard interface for connecting printers and other parallel devices.

Challenge-Handshake Authentication Protocol (CHAP)—The most common dial-up authentication protocol, which uses an industry Message Digest 5 (MD5) hashing scheme to encrypt authentication.

Character—A representation—coded in binary digits—of a letter, number, or other symbol.

Character Set—All the letters, numbers, and characters a computer can use to represent data. The ASCII standard has 256 characters, each represented by a binary number from 1 to 255.

Checksum—A method of calculating a sum from a set of values that is used for error detection.

Chipset—Chips and other components on the motherboard that allow different PC components to communicate with each other, including the microprocessor. It consists of the bus controllers, peripheral controllers, memory controllers, cache controllers, clocks, and timers.

CHS Addressing—An addressing mode that uses the cylinders, heads, and sectors to define locations on a disk.

Circuit—The conductor, such as a wire or metal trace, that connects the voltage source (power supply or battery) and electronic components. Electrons leave the voltage source through the path of least resistance to a common return known as *ground.*

Clamping Speed—The amount of time it takes for a surge protector to respond to overvoltages.

Clamping Voltage—The voltage that causes a surge protector to react.

Client—A computer on a network that requests services.

Client for Microsoft Networks—The piece of software used to communicate with Microsoft Windows computers.

Client for NetWare Networks—The piece of software used to communicate with Novell NetWare.

Client Software—Software that allows communications with a network.

Client/Server Network—A network that has dedicated servers and clients.

Clipboard—In Windows, a temporary storage location in RAM that holds information so that it can be copied or moved (cut) from one place to another.

Clock Speed—The speed at which the microprocessor executes instructions. The faster the clock, the more instructions the CPU can execute per second. It is measured in megahertz (MHz) or gigahertz (GHz).

Clone—Hardware that is identical to the original of which it is a copy.

Cluster—The smallest amount of disk space addressable on a disk. It is made up of one or more sectors.

CMOS Battery—The battery found on the motherboard that is used to maintain the CMOS RAM.

CMOS RAM—A special form of RAM that uses a battery to maintain power while the computer is off. The CMOS RAM is used to hold important hardware configuration information, such as the size of the hard drive and the amount of the RAM.

CMOS Setup Program—Software, usually kept in the system ROM BIOS, used to change the configuration options contained in the CMOS RAM.

CMYK Color Model—A method of printing in four basic colors; cyan (greenish blue), magenta (deep purplish red), yellow, and black.

Coaxial Cable (Coax)—A wire that has a solid copper core surrounded by insulation, a braided metal shielding, and an outer cover. It is called *coaxial* cable because the copper wire and the braided metal shielding share the same axis, or center.

Coercitivity—A term that describes the strength of the magnetic field used to store data on platters. Its measurement is in oersteds.

Cold Boot—Reloading a computer's operating system by turning the power to the computer off and then back on.

Collision—In a LAN, if two computers transmit a packet of data at the same time on the network, the data can become garbled.

Color Depth—The amount of information that determines the color of a pixel.

Color Graphics Adapter (CGA)—The first color graphics video card. It supported several modes, including a 16-color 80 × 25 character text mode, and could display up to 16 colors in several resolutions (320 × 200, 640 × 200, and 160 × 200).

Command Interpreter—The operating system program that controls a computer's shell or user interface. The command interpreter for DOS is COMMAND.COM.

Command Queuing—Used in SCSI devices to accept multiple commands and execute them in an order that is more efficient, rather than in the order received. This increases the performance of computers running multitasking operating systems and makes it ideal for servers.

Common Command Set (CCS)—A set of SCSI commands specified in the ANSI SCSI-1 Standard.

Common Internet File System (CIFS)—An updated SMB protocol to provide file sharing and print sharing among Linux, Apple, and Microsoft computers.

Communication and Networking Riser (CNR)—A standard developed by Intel as replacement for the ARM. CRN enables motherboard makers to offer low-cost modem, networking, and audio features through a special expansion slot.

Compact Disk (CD)—A 4.72-inch encoded platter written to and read by a laser provided by a CD drive and similar to a CD used in a stereo system. CDs can store large amounts of information.

CompactFlash—An ATA flash memory card that is approximately one third the size of a standard PC card. ATA flash cards contain built-in disk controller circuitry to enable the card to function as a solid-state disk drive.

Compiler—A program that translates source code written in a programming language into object code.

Complementary Metal-Oxide Semiconductor (CMOS)—Widely used IC chips that require less power than TTL chips.

Complex Instruction Set Computer (CISC)—A processor architecture that includes commands of different sizes that must be determined how to be executed by a decoder.

Compressed Volume File (CVF)—A hidden file that simulates a disk in compressed format.

Compression and Decompression (codec)—A process that allows files to take up less space and perform better because there is less data to process.

Computer—A machine composed of electronic devices used to process data.

Conductor—A material in which current can flow easily. Most metals, including silver and copper, are good conductors.

Constant Angular Velocity (CAV)—The spinning of a drive at the same rate. Therefore, when reading the outside of the disk, where there is more data, the drive will have a higher transfer rate than when it is reading the inside of the disk.

Constant Linear Velocity (CLV)—A rate of speed used by compact disk drives. Because the outer tracks hold more information than the inner tracks, the platter spins faster on the inner tracks than it does on the outer tracks to keep a constant reading rate for data.

Continuity Check—The verifying by a measuring device that a conductor or similar device has no resistance (0 ohm).

Control Bus—The physical connections that carry control information between the CPU and other devices within the computer. Whereas the data bus carries actual data that is being processed, the control bus carries signals that report the status of various devices.

Control Panel—A graphical tool to configure the Windows environment and hardware devices.

Control Unit—A clocked logic circuit that is part of the microprocessor and that controls the entire chip, including the ALU. It translates and follows the instructions contained in an external program (such as the ROM BIOS, the operating system, or application software) and keeps track of which step of the program is being executed.

Controller—A device that controls the transfer of data from a computer to a peripheral device and vice versa.

Conventional Memory—The first 640 KB of RAM. It is also known as *lower memory* and *base memory.*

Convergence—A term used to describe the clarity and sharpness of each pixel. It is based on the color monitor's capability for focusing the three colored electron beams into a single point.

Cooperative Multitasking—A type of multitasking that is based on applications that cooperate with each other.

Corona Wire—A wire used to transfer a positive or negative charge. It is usually found in printers.

Counter Log—Counter logs used in Windows performance monitor to record data from local or remote computers about hardware usage and system service activity.

Crash—A malfunction that brings work to a halt. A system crash usually is caused by a software malfunction, and ordinarily you can restart the system by rebooting the machine.

Cross-Link File—A cluster used by two or more files.

Crosstalk—A disturbance caused by electromagnetic interference along a circuit or a cable pair. The electromagnetic interference is generated by current in a wire. A telecommunication signal disrupts a signal in an adjacent circuit and can cause the signals to become confused and cross over each other.

Cryptography—The art of protecting information by transforming it (*encrypting* it) into cipher text.

Current—The rate of flow of electrons (electricity), which is measured in amps (A).

Current Directory—The active directory currently being viewed.

Cursor—The small, flashing hyphen that appears onscreen to indicate the point at which any input from the keyboard will be placed.

Cyclic Redundancy Check (CRC)—An error-checking method that checks an entire block of data by performing a mathematical calculation on the data to be sent before and after.

Cylinder—Tracks stacked on top of each other.

D

Daemon—A background process or service that monitors and performs many critical system functions and services.

Daisy Chain—A hardware configuration in which devices are connected to one another in a series.

Daisy-Wheel Printers—Impact printers that use a ball or wheel imprinted with predefined characters.

Data—The raw facts, numbers, letters, or symbols that the computer processes into meaningful information. Data is normally considered the most important part of the computer.

Data Bus—A bus that carries instructions and data into and out of the CPU and other components.

Data Carrier Equipment (DCE)—A device that communicates with a data terminal equipment (DTE) device, usually through a serial port.

Data Encryption Standard (DES)—A popular symmetric-key encryption method that uses block cipher. The key used in DES is based on a 56-bit binary number, which allows for 72,057,594,037,927,936 encryption keys. Of these 72 quadrillion encryption keys, a key is chosen at random.

Data Terminal Equipment (DTE)—A device that controls data flowing to or from a computer, usually through a serial port.

Database—A program that allows users to work with files of related data. The data can be organized and retrieved quickly.

De Facto Standard—A standard for hardware or software that has been accepted by the industry just because it is the most common.

De Jure Standard—A standard that has been dictated by an appointed committee.

Decibel (dB)—A unit for measuring the loudness of sound.

Decimal Number System—The most commonly used numbering system, having 10 different possible digits (base 10).

Decryption—The process of converting data from encrypted format back to its original format.

Degausser—A special demagnetizing device that is moved over the outside surface of the CRT to eliminate magnetic fields.

Demand Paging—Information that is swapped between the RAM and disk (virtual memory) only on the demand of the microprocessor.

Demarcation Point (Demarc)—The point where the local loop ends at the customer's premises.

Designator—Keeps track of which drive designations are assigned to network devices.

Desktop—The visible elements of Windows that defines the limits of the graphic environment.

Desktop Case—A case that lies flat on the desktop.

Desktop Computers—Computers that are small enough to fit on a desk but are too big to carry around.

Desktop Management Interface (DMI)—An operating system and protocol independent standard developed by the Desktop Management Task Force for managing desktop systems and servers. DMI provides bidirectional path to interrogate all the hardware and software components within a PC, enabling hardware and software configurations to be monitored from a central station in a network.

Desktop Panel—In Linux, it provides quick access to applications by providing the Main menu or application starter and panel buttons to start your favorite applications.

Desktop Publishing—Software that allows the user to combine graphics and text to create newsletters, reports, and other documents.

Device Driver—Software that controls how an operating system and applications interact with specific items of hardware.

Device Manager—A component of Windows that allows users to view and configure the device and programs that use the device.

Differential—An electrical signaling method in which a pair of lines are used for each signal in "push-pull" fashion. In most cases, differential signals are balanced so that the same current flows on each line in opposite directions. Different signals have a large tolerance for common-mode noise and little crosstalk when used with twisted-pair wires in long cables.

Differential Backup—A backup that copies only the files created since the last full backup.

Digital—A term used to describe any device that represents values in the form of binary digits.

Digital Audio Tape (DAT)—A small tape that can store large amounts of data.

Digital Camera—A type of camera that uses a sensor and internal or removable flash memory in place of film to record still images. Digital cameras' picture quality is usually rated in megapixels.

Digital Multimeter (DMM)—A device that combines several measuring devices, including a voltmeter and an ohmmeter.

Digital Signal—A signal that consists of discrete (predetermined and constant) values.

Digital Signal Processor (DSP)—A processor specifically designed to manipulate large volumes of digital data.

Digital Storage Media (DSM)—A digital storage or transmission device or system.

Digital Subscriber Line (DSL)—A high-speed digital modem technology.

Digital Video Disk (DVD)—The newest type of compact disk, having the capability of storing massive computer applications, such as a full multimedia encyclopedia or a feature-length movie, on one compact disk.

Digital Visual Interface (DVI)—The current de facto standard for LCD displays developed by the Digital Display Working Group. DVI-D provides digital signals only, whereas DVI-I provides both digital and analog signals. A DVI-I connector can be converted to VGA with an external adapter.

Digital-to-analog Converter (DAC)—A device for converting digital signals to analog signals.

Digitizing—The process of converting a signal into data that the computer can understand.

DIP Switches—Small devices consisting of 4 to 12 on/off switches.

Direct Current (DC)—Current that flows in only one direction and has a fixed polarity (positive or negative).

Direct Memory Address (DMA)—Channels used to move large amounts of data into RAM without any direction from the microprocessor, which permits the CPU to keep working, making the system run faster.

Directory—A special kind of file used to organize other files into a hierarchical structure. It is sometimes referred to a *folder.*

DirectX—An application programming interface (API) developed by Microsoft that enables programs to write programs that access hardware features of a computer without knowing exactly what hardware is installed on the machine.

Disk Cache—A portion of RAM used to speed up access to data on a disk.

Disk Compression—A process that expands the amount of space on a disk.

Disk Drive—A device that reads and writes magnetic or optical disks.

Disk Duplexing—A hard drive duplicated on another hard drive that is connected to another controller card so that it can provide fault tolerance.

Disk Management Console—A console used in Windows 2000 and Windows XP to manage the disks and partitions.

Disk Mirroring—A hard drive duplicated on another hard drive that is usually connected to the same controller card so that it can provide fault tolerance.

Disk Quotas—Technology that track and control disk usage for an NTFS volume.

Display Power Management System (DPMS)—A standard introduced by the Video Electronics Standard Association (VESA). DPMS allows the monitor to go into standby mode (which uses less power than the normal operational state) and suspend/shut down mode (which turns the monitor off) during periods of inactivity.

Dithering—The process of creating more colors and shades from a given color palette.

Divide Error—A software glitch when a program tries to divide a number by zero.

Dolby Surround—A 3D audio standard that encodes four sound channels (left, center, right, and surround) onto the two tracks of any conventional stereo program source, either analog or digital.

Domain—A logical unit of computers and network resources that defines a security boundary. It is typically found on medium or large networks, or on networks that require a secure environment. A domain uses one database to share its common and security and user account information for all computers within the domain. Therefore, it allows centralized network administration of all users, groups, and resources on the network.

Domain Controller—A Windows server that maintains a centralized security database for a Windows domain and the network resources within the domain.

DOS—*See* Microsoft DOS.

DOS Protected Mode Interface (DPMI)—An industry-standard interface that allows DOS applications to execute program code in the protected mode of the 286 or later Intel processor.

Dot Pitch—The distance between pixels.

Dot-Matrix Printers—Impact printers that use a series of pins to form letters and images.

Double-Byte Character Set—*See* Unicode.

Downloading—A term that describes copying a file from a remote computer to one's own computer.

Dr. Watson—A program that starts automatically when a program error is detected; records the information about the system and the program failure into a log file.

DRAM—Short for *Dynamic RAM.* The storage cells consist of a tiny solid-state capacitor and a MOS transistor.

Drawer—Used in the GNOME desktop (Linux), it holds multiple launchers that are related to each other in some way, such as the various applications in GNOME Office.

Driver Signing—Data added to a driver that shows it has been tested and verified by Microsoft.

Driver Verifier—A tool used to monitor Windows kernel mode drivers and graphic drivers.

Dual In-Line Memory Module (DIMM)—A type of RAM closely resembling SIMMs. A small circuit board consisting of several soldered DIP chips. To connect to the motherboard, the SIMM has a row of tin or gold metal plates (contacts) along the bottom of the module.

Dual In-Line Package (DIP)—Chips, resembling a bug with many legs, that lie horizontally with metal leads extending down from the two long sides. The metal leads are inserted directly into the circuit board's DIP sockets.

Dvorak Layout—A keyboard layout with vowels in the home row under the left hand and the most commonly used consonants in the home row under the right hand.

Dynamic Data Exchange (DDE)—A method of data exchange that allows users to copy data between applications while maintaining a link. Whenever data is changed at the source, it is also changed at the target.

Dynamic Host Configuration Protocol (DHCP)—A protocol for assigning dynamic IP addresses to devices on a network. With dynamic addressing, a device can have a different IP address every time it connects to the network.

Dynamic Link Library (DLL)—Files that include sets of instructions and/or data that can be accessed at any time used to modularize Windows.

Dynamic Storage—A type of disk converted from a basic disk. Different from basic disks, they can contain unlimited number of volumes and can be extended to include noncontiguous space on available disks.

Dynamic Update—A feature built into newer versions of Windows that automatically checks for new drivers, compatibility updates, and security fixes during the Windows installations.

E

EDO RAM—Short for *Extended Data Output RAM.* It uses a two-stage pipeline, which lets the memory controller read data off the chip while it is being reset for the next operation.

Effective Permissions—The actual permissions when logging in and accessing a file or folder. They consist of explicit permissions plus any inherited permissions.

Electrically Erasable Programmable Read-Only Memory (EEPROM)—Pronounced "double-E PROM." A special type of programmable ROM chip that can be erased with higher voltage than normal. EEPROM chips can be erased only a set number of times.

Electricity—The flow of free electrons from one atom to another.

Electromagnetic Interference (EMI)—Any electromagnetic signal released by an electronic device that may disrupt the operation and performance of another device.

Electronic mail (email)—Messages, pictures, and files sent over the Internet, network, or telephone system.

Electrophoto (EP) Process—The process used by laser printers to form images on paper.

Electrosensitive Printers—A printer that uses special color paper coated with a thin layer of aluminum. Characters and images are formed by selectively removing the aluminum using electricity.

Electrostatic Discharge (ESD)—Electrostatic electricity easily generated by a person that could damage electronic components.

Electrostatic Electricity—An electrical charge at rest created by friction and separation.

Electrostatic Mat—A mat that absorbs static electricity, used while repairing a computer.

Emergency Repair Disk (ERD)—Contains information about your current Windows system settings. You can use this disk to repair your computer if it will not start or your system files are damaged or erased.

Enablers—External drivers that are not built into the operating system that is loaded during boot-up so that new hardware will work with the Macintosh operating system.

Encoding—The method or pattern used to represent bits.

Encryption—The process of disguising a message or data in what appears to be meaningless data (cipher text) to hide and protect the sensitive data from unauthorized access.

Enhanced 386 mode—A Windows 3.XX operating mode made for the 386 computer. It allows multiple DOS and Windows applications to run at the same time and provides direct access to extended memory and virtual memory.

Enhanced Graphics Adapter (EGA)—The first successful color video system. It included a 16-color 80 × 25 text mode and a 16-color 640 × 350 graphics mode.

Enhanced IDE—An enhanced version of the IDE interface allowing up to four devices to be connected, including hard drives, CD-ROM drives, and tape drives.

Enhanced Parallel Port (EPP)—A fast parallel port.

Enterprise WAN—A WAN that is owned by one company or organization.

Environment Subsystem—The subsystem used in Windows NT, Windows 2000, and Windows XP that provides the application programming interfaces (APIs) for the programs and converts them to the proper calls for Windows.

Environmental Audio Extension (EAX)—Developed by Creative Labs, EAX is one of the most popular audio 3D standards. It encompasses sophisticated audio technologies, both hardware and software based, that work together or independently to deliver a truly amazing audio experience across Creative Lab's products.

Erasable Programmable Read-Only Memory (EPROM)—A special type of programmable ROM that can be erased by shining ultraviolet light through a clear window at the top of the chip. Once erased, it can be reprogrammed.

Ergonomics—The science concerned with designing safe and comfortable machines for humans.

Error Checking and Correction (ECC)—A form of error control that uses extra bits to check the accuracy of the data bits. Different from parity, ECC can also correct some errors.

ESD Wrist Strap—A strap worn around the wrist to reduce electrostatic discharge by a person.

ESDI Interface—Short for *Enhanced Small Drive Interface.* An interface used by early hard drives that was designed to replace the ST-506 interface.

Ethernet—A local-area network (LAN) architecture that is the one of the most widely implemented LAN stands that uses a bus or start topology. Traditionally, it supports data transfer rates of 10 Mbit/s, yet newer versions can support 100 Mbit/s and 1 Gbit/s. The Ethernet specification served as the basis for the IEEE 802.3 standard, which specifies the physical and lower software layers. Ethernet uses the CSMA/CD access method to handle simultaneous demands.

Event Viewer—A utility used to view and manage logs of system, program, and security events on the computer. Event viewer gathers information about hardware and software problems, and monitors Windows NT, Windows 2000, and Windows XP security events.

Exception Error—Occurs when an application tries to pass an invalid parameter to another program.

Execution Unit—Part of the microprocessor that does the actual processing of data.

Expanded Memory Specification (EMS)—The first memory that allowed users to break the 1 MB boundary. The expanded memory specification is known as the LIM (Lotus/Intel/Microsoft) specification.

Expansion Card—Circuit board inserted into the motherboard to expand the PC. It is sometimes referred to as a *daughter board.*

Expansion Slot—Also known as the I/O bus, it is called an *expansion* slot because it expands the system by allowing circuit boards, called *expansion cards,* to be inserted. It extends the reach of the microprocessor so that it can communicate with peripheral devices.

Explicit Permissions—Those NTFS permissions granted directly to the folder or file.

Ext2—The native Linux file system. It is very similar to other modern UNIX file systems, but most closely resembles the Berkeley Fast File system used by BSD systems. The maximum size of an ext2 file system is 4 TB, whereas the maximum file size is currently limited to 2 GB by the Linux kernel.

Ext3—A journaling file system that is built upon the ext2 file system.

Extended ASCII—ASCSI characters based on 8 bits, so there are 256 different possible combinations of 0s and 1s, allowing 256 ($2^8 = 256$) different characters. The extra characters represent characters from foreign languages and special symbols for drawing pictures.

Extended Binary-Coded Decimal Interchange Code (EBCDIC)—Pronounced "eb-sih-dik," this was IBM code for representing characters as numbers. Similar to ASCSII, in an EBCDIC file, each alphabetic or numeric character is represented with an 8-bit binary number (a string of eight 0s or 1s). A total of 256 possible characters (letters of the alphabet, numerals, and special characters) are defined. Although it is widely used on large IBM computers, most other computers, including PCs and Macintoshes, use ASCII codes.

Extended Capabilities Port (ECP)—A fast parallel port.

Extended CHS—A form of addressing that combines the bits used in the CHS addressing to form a single numbering system for sectors on the hard drive.

Extended ISA (EISA)—A 32-bit expansion slot introduced to compete with the MCA slot. The EISA slot is no longer produced.

Extended Memory Specification (XMS)—The memory above 1 MB (FFFFFH) found on today's newer machines (386 and higher).

Extended Partition—A type of partition created after the primary partition and that can be divided into one or more logical drives.

Extended System Configuration Data (ESCD)—A format for storing information about plug-and-play (PnP) devices in the BIOS. Windows and the BIOS access the ESCD area each time you reboot your computer.

Extensible Firmware Interface (EFI)—A new firmware architecture that replaces the legacy BIOS. By providing a standard application programming interface to access hardware devices, it adds an interface between the operating system and the computer firmware (BIOS). It initializes chipset, buses, and drivers and locates OS loaders. Once the EFI firmware boots up the system, it hands over the system operation to the OS, where it runs in the background providing the system with simple runtime services such as monitoring firmware settings and system reset. It also provides interfaces with other industry standards such as ACPI and SMBIOS.

External Cache—A form of RAM cache often found on the motherboard but sometimes found in the microprocessor. External cache is sometimes referred to as *secondary cache* or *level 2* (L2) cache.

External Commands—Commands executed at the prompt that reside in files on a disk.

F

Fast Ethernet—Popular term for 100BaseT and other 100 Mbit/s versions of Ethernet.

Fast Page Mode RAM (FPM RAM)—A special form of DRAM that tries to reduce the number of wait states by accessing data in the same row (sometimes referred to as a page) as the preceding data.

FAT32—An enhanced version of the FAT structure that allows for long file names, drives up to 2 TB, and has the ability to use disk space more efficiently.

Fax—Short for *facsimile transmission.* A fax machine digitizes the text and pictures in a document and sends the data over a telephone line.

FC-PGA (Flip-Chip Pin Grid Array)—A type of chip packaging first used in the PGA370 versions of the Pentium III where the raw processor die has bumped contacts spaced on the face of the die and is mounted face down to a pin grid array carrier. The heat sink is then directly attached to the back of the raw silicon die surface.

Feature Connector—On a video adapter, a connector that enables an additional video feature card, such as a separate 3D accelerator, video capture card, or MPEG decoder, to be connected to the main video adapter and display.

Field Replaceable Unit (FRU)—Any PC component that can be replaced without any special skills or tools.

File Allocation Table (FAT)—(1) An index used to list which file is located in which cluster. (2) A type of file system used primarily with DOS.

File and Print Sharing for Microsoft Networks—Software that allows you to share drives, directories, and printers on Microsoft computers.

File Attribute—A characteristic or property of a file.

File Infector Virus—A virus that resides in or attaches to a file.

File Manager (WINFILE.EXE)—A Windows 3.XX graphical utility used to manage disks, directories, and files.

File Signature Verification—Technology used to identify unsigned (files not tested and verified by Microsoft) files on your computer.

File System Hierarchy Standard (FHS)—A standard that defines the names and contents of critical directories in a Linux file system.

File Transfer Protocol (FTP)—A common protocol (part of the TCP/IP protocol suite) that specializes in transferring files from one computer to another. It is found on the Internet.

Filtering—The process that smoothes out the ripple of rectified voltage.

Finish—Texture on the front surface of paper.

Firewall—A hardware or software system designed to prevent unauthorized access to or from a private network.

FireWire—*See* IEEE 1394.

Firmware—Software contained in a read-only memory device. A cross between hardware and software.

Flash RAM—A form of ROM chip that can be reprogrammed using the normal voltage found in the PC by running a BIOS update program.

Flatbed Scanner—A scanner that has a flat bed of glass. The paper to be scanned is laid face down on top of the glass.

Flicker—A monitor condition caused by refresh rates that are too low, in which the display flashes visibly. This can cause eyestrain or more severe physical problems.

Floating-Point Number—A number with a decimal point or a number that includes exponents. In essence, computers are integer machines and are capable of representing real numbers only by using complex codes. The most popular code for representing real numbers is called the *IEEE Floating-Point Standard.*

Floppy Disk Controller—Electronic interface used to connect the floppy drives to the rest of the computer.

Floppy Disk Drive—A drive that reads floppy disks.

Floppy Disks—Small, thin, plastic disks that are used to store files for long-term usage. They are inserted into floppy disk drives. The storage capacity of a floppy disk is very limited but it can be easily transported to another computer.

Focused Window—The active window, which is the window you are currently using, that will receive text when you type.

Font—A collection of characters (letters, numerals, symbols, and punctuation marks) that have common characteristics.

Forced Perfect Terminator (FPT)—A form of terminating resistor that attempts to remove reflections by automatically matching the line impedance, thus allowing "perfect" termination.

Form Factor—Physical dimensions and sizes, usually defined for motherboards, power supplies, and cases.

Frame Buffer—(1) A memory device that stores, pixel by pixel, the contents of an image. Frame buffers are used to refresh a raster image. Sometimes they incorporate local processing capability. The "depth" of the frame buffer is the number of bits per pixel, which determines the number of colors or intensity that can be displayed. (2) In Linux, a low-level but standardized interface between software and video hardware. X Window uses a frame buffer interface on many non-x86 computers.

Free System Resources (FSR)—The amount of memory available to Windows, usually expressed as a percentage.

Frequency—The rate of a vibration.

Full Backup—A backup that backs up all files on a disk.

Full Duplex—A form of data transfer in which data can travel in both directions at the same time.

Full-Motion Video—A video sequence displayed at full television standard resolutions and frame rates. In the United States, this equates to NTSC video at 30 frames per second.

Fully Qualified Domain Name (FQDN)—Consists of a host and domain name, including top-level domain. For example, www.microsoft.com is a fully qualified domain name. The *www* indicates the host or type of service, microsoft is the second-level domain, and *.com* is the top-level domain. An FQDN always starts with a host name and continues all the way up to the top-level domain name, so home.acme.com is also an FQDN.

Fuse—A protective device that melts when a circuit has too much current, causing an open in the circuit pathway.

Fuser—A device used in printers and copy machines to melt the toner into the paper.

G

Game Port—A port that is used to connect joysticks, paddles, and flight sticks.

Gateway—A combination of hardware and software that links two different types of networks.

General Protection Fault (GPF)—A condition signifying that something unexpected has happened within a Windows environment. It is usually caused by a program that tried to access a memory area that belongs to another program or an application trying to pass an invalid parameter to another program.

Giga (G)—A prefix indicating a billion (1,000,000,000). In computers, a giga indicates 1,024 megabytes, such as in a gigabyte (GB).

Gigahertz—One billion clock cycles.

GNOME—A popular desktop environment used in Linux machines.

GNU—Short for *GNUs not UNIX.* GNU is a Free Software Foundation project to build an entirely open-source OS that works like UNIX.

Glidepad—A pointing device in the form of a flat square pad. As a finger touches the glidepad, transducers under the pad sense the body capacitance. As the finger moves, the pad generates electrical signals, which move the mouse pointer.

Global WAN—A WAN that is not owned by any one company and usually crosses national boundaries.

Gopher—A system that predates the World Wide Web for organizing and displaying files on Internet servers. A Gopher server presents its contents as a hierarchically structured list of files. With the ascendance of the web, most gopher databases are being converted to websites that can be more easily accessed via web search engines.

Graphical User Interface (GUI)—A program interface that takes advantage of the computer's graphics capabilities to make the program easier to use. It usually uses a mouse pointer and icons.

Green PC—A PC that is made to conserve power.

Ground—A reference point in electronic circuits.

H

Half Duplex—A form of communication in which data can travel in both directions, one direction at a time.

Halftones—In printing, a method of simulating shades of gray by assembling patterns of black and white dots.

Handheld scanner—A scanner that is held in the hand and is physically moved from one end of a document to the other.

Handshake—A form of control between two devices.

Hard Card—A hard disk drive and controller on a single expansion card.

Hard Disk/Hard Drive—The principal device for storing programs and data. It usually has a large capacity and is much quicker than a floppy disk drive. Because it usually cannot be removed from the computer, the hard disk is sometimes called *fixed disk.*

Hardware—The physical components that make up the personal computer. If an item can be touched and carried, it is hardware.

Hardware Abstraction Layer (HAL)—A library of hardware manipulating routines that hide the hardware interface details. It contains the hardware-specific code that handles I/O interface, interrupt controllers, and multiprocessor operations so that it can act as the translator between hardware architectures and the rest of the Windows NT, Windows 2000, or Windows XP software. As a result, programs written for Windows can work on other architectures, making those programs portable.

Hardware Compatibility List (HCL)—A Microsoft listing that provides approved tested components that will work with Windows.

Hardware Interrupt (IRQ)—A signal sent to the Interrupt Controller to signal that a device needs the attention of the microprocessor.

Hardware Profile—A set of instructions that tells Windows 2000 which devices to start when you start your computer or what settings to use for each device.

Hayes Command Set—*See* AT Commands.

Head Actuator—The component contained within a disk drive that moves the read/write heads back and forth.

Head Crash—The unexpected collision between the read/write head and the rotating platter that usually results in damage to the platter and/or the read/write head.

Head to Disk Interference (HDI)—A small particle, such as dust or cigarette smoke, acting as a boulder between the read/write head and platter, causing physical damage to the read/write head and/or the platter and possibly a grinding noise

Heap—An area of memory reserved for data that is created at runtime.

Heat Sink—A finned piece of metal clipped or glued to the top of the processor. Since it has more surface area than a flat piece of metal, it dissipates heat faster.

Helical Scan—A method used to record data on tapes. Much like a VCR read/write head, tape backup drives with helical scan use read/write heads mounted at an angle on a cylindrical drum. The tape is partially wrapped around the drum, and as the tape slides across the drum, the read/write heads rotate. As each head approaches the tape, the heads take swipes at the tape, reading or writing the data.

Hercules Graphics Card—A monochrome video card that uses the same monochrome monitor as the MDA video system. It can display in graphics mode with a resolution of 720 × 350.

Hertz—One clock cycle.

Hexadecimal Number System—A number system that has 16 digits.

HFS+—An extended version of the HFS file system used on Apple Macintosh computers that accommodate larger hard drives.

Hierarchical File System (HFS)—An older file system used on Apple Macintosh computers.

High Color—A video system that displays 65,536 different colors. The 65,536 colors use 16 bits to define the color of the pixel.

High Memory Area (HMA)—An area of memory that is 64 KB minus 16 bytes, starting at the 1 MB boundary. High memory can be used to access a small part of extended memory while being in real mode.

High Performance File System (HPFS)—The file system made for OS/2 that supported long file names.

High Sierra Standard—The proposed standard for CD-ROM disks from which the ISO 9660 standard was derived.

High-Level Formatting—The process of writing the file system structure on the disk so that it can be used to store programs and data.

HKEY_LOCAL_MACHINE—One of the main trees in the Windows registry. It includes the HARDWARE, SECURITY, SAM, SOFTWARE, and SYSTEM subkeys.

Host—(1) A computer system that is accessed by a user who is working at a remote location. Typically, the term is used when there are two computer systems connected by modems and telephone lines. The system that contains the data is called the host, and the computer at which the user sits is called the remote terminal. (2) A network connection to a TCP/IP network, include the Internet. Each host has a unique IP address. Besides computers, hosts may also be network printers and routers. (3) Provides the infrastructure for a computer service. For example, there are many companies that host web servers, which means they provide the hardware, software, and communications lines required by the server, but the content on the server may be controlled by someone else.

Hot-Swappable—A term describing a device that can be connected or disconnected or inserted or removed while the power is on.

Hot-Swapping—The ability to add and remove devices to a computer while the computer is running and have the operating system automatically recognize the change.

Hotfix—A software patch for a Microsoft application or operating system.

HTML—Short for *Hypertext Markup Language.* A standardized hypertext language used to create a web page.

HTTP—Short for *Hypertext Transfer Protocol.* A protocol used to manage the links between one hypertext document and another.

HTTP 1.1—A version of the HTTP protocol.

Hub—A device that is a common connection point for devices in a network. Hubs, which have multiple hubs, are commonly used to connect segments of a LAN. When a packet arrives at one port, it is copied to the other ports so that all segments of the LAN can see all packets.

Hybrid Fiber Coaxial (HFC)—A network (such as that used by digital cable TV and two-way cable modems) that uses fiber-optic cabling for its backbone with coaxial cable connections to each individual computer or TV.

Hyper-Threading—An operating mode of processors that allows the processor to act as two logical processors so that it can better utilize its resources.

Hypertext—A specially marked word or words used to move to another location within the same document or to another document.

Hypertext Markup Language (HTML)—Used in web pages that utilize embedded code made of ordinary text to give the browser a general idea of how the information should be displayed.

HyperTransport—AMD's high-speed technology for connecting North Bridge and South Bridge or equivalent chips on a motherboard.

I

IA-64—Intel's 64-bit processor architecture, first used on the Itanium processor for servers.

IBM Compatible—A computer that is compatible with the IBM PC.

IBM PC—A personal computer made by IBM that set the standard for all personal computers. It consists of an 8088 microprocessor.

Iconify—A term used with Linux operating systems that means minimizing a program.

IDE—Short for *integrated drive electronics.* An interface developed as a fast, low-cost hard drive interface.

IEEE 1394—Sometimes known as FireWire, an external port that can connect up to 63 external devices and made for devices that require large amounts of data transfer, such as those related to video devices. A very fast external bus standard that supports data transfer rates of up to 400 Mbit/s. A single 1394 port can be used to connect up 63 external devices, making it ideal for devices that need to transfer high levels of data in real-time, such as video devices.

Impact Printers—A printer that transfers ink onto the paper by pressing or striking movable parts against a ribbon and a sheet of paper. Impact printers include daisy wheel or ball printers and dot-matrix printers.

Impedance—The total opposition a circuit offers to the flow of alternating current, measured in ohms.

Incremental Backup—A backup that copies only the files that have changed since the last full or incremental backup.

Inductor—A coil of wire that can transfer voltage or current using magnetic fields (without physical contact). It resists the change of current.

Industry Standard Architecture (ISA)—A 16-bit expansion first used in the IBM AT and still found on most PCs today. Also known as AT bus.

INF file—A Windows driver and device information file used to install new drivers or services.

Infrared (IR)—*See* IrDA Port.

Inherited Permissions—Permissions that flow down from the folder into the subfolders and files, indirectly giving permissions to a user or group.

Initialization Files—A text file with an INI file name extension that contains configuration information for an operating system or an application.

Initialization String—A list of modem AT commands that the communication software will use to initialize and prepare the modem for connection.

Ink-Jet Printer—A nonimpact printer that works by spraying small droplets of ionized ink onto a sheet of paper though a small hole. It is superior to the dot-matrix printer in that it has a better print quality and is much quieter.

Inode—Data structures that contain information about files in UNIX/Linux file systems that are created when a file system is created. Each file has an inode and is identified by an inode number (i-number) in the file system where it resides. Inodes provide important information on files such as user and group ownership, access mode (read, write, execute permissions), and type. There are a set number of inodes, which indicates the maximum number of files the system can hold.

Insulator—A poor conductor of electric current used to prevent current where it is not wanted.

Integral Subsystem—Part of Windows NT, Windows 2000, and Windows XP that perform essential operating system functions such as the security subsystem, the workstation service, and the server service.

Integrated Circuit (IC)—A device containing transistors, diodes, resistors, and capacitors in one miniaturized package.

Integrated Services Digital Network (ISDN)—Special transmission lines that allow voice, video, and data to be sent using digital telephone lines.

Intel 386 Microprocessor Protection Model—A method used by all Intel and Intel-compatible processors since the 386 processor that has programs run in one of four rings. Ring 0 has access to all program and memory in all levels and ring 3 can only access program and memory in ring 3. Today, the kernel runs in ring 0 and other programs run in ring 3.

Intel Comparative Microprocessor Performance Index (ICOMP)—A test to measure the performance of a PC.

Interlaced Monitor—A screen that redraws in two sweeps as it refreshes every other line. During the first sweep, it refreshes the odd-numbered lines and during the second sweep refreshes the even-numbered lines.

Interleaving—A process in which two banks work together. When one bank is getting ready for access, the other bank is being accessed.

Internal Cache—A form of RAM cache found inside the microprocessor. It is sometimes referred to as *primary cache* or *level 1 (L1) cache.* Internal cache is faster than external RAM cache because it is a physical part of the microprocessor.

Internal Commands—Commands performed at the prompt that reside in the RAM (COMMAND.COM).

Internet—A global network connecting millions of computers. More than 100 countries are linked into exchanges of data, news, and opinions. Unlike online services, which are centrally controlled, the Internet is decentralized by design. Each Internet computer, called a host, is independent. Its operators can choose which Internet services to use and which local services to make available to the global Internet community. Remarkably, this anarchy by design works exceedingly well. There are a variety of ways to access the Internet. Most online services, such as America Online, offer access to some Internet services. It is also possible to gain access through a commercial Internet service provider (ISP).

Internet Explorer (IE)—Microsoft's web browser.

Internet Protocol (IP)—A TCP/IP connectionless protocol that is primarily responsible for addressing and routing packets between hosts.

Internet Service Provider (ISP)—A company that provides connection to the Internet.

Interpreter—A program that executes instructions written in a high-level language.

Interrupt—Something that causes the CPU to stop its current task so that it can do another task. Whenever the second task is completed, it will go back to the original task to continue where it left off. Interrupts can be divided into hardware interrupts and software interrupts.

Interrupt Controller—Device that coordinates hardware interrupts (IRQs) so that another device can get the attention of the CPU.

Interrupt Sharing—The ability of devices to share the same interrupt.

Interrupt Vector Table—A table of addresses for specific software routines (interrupt handlers) contained in the RAM or BIOS.

Interruptible Power Supply (UPS)—A power supply that includes a battery to maintain power in the event of power fluctuations, including a power outage.

Invalid Page Faults—An error that occurs when a program tries to access a memory area that belongs to another program.

I/O Address—An address used to identify an I/O device. The I/O address must be unique.

I/O Bus—*See* Expansion Slot.

IP Address—An identifier for a computer or device on a TCP/IP network. Networks using the TCP/IP protocol route messages based on the IP address of the destination. The format of an IP address is a 32-bit numeric address written as four numbers separated by periods. Each number can be zero to 255. For example, 1.160.10.240 could be an IP address. Within an isolated network, you can assign IP addresses that are unique.

IPX (Internetwork Packet Exchange)—A networking protocol suite usually used by the Novell NetWare network operating system.

IrDA Port—A port that connects to a device using infrared light waves (wireless technology). Keyboards, serial port devices (mice and other pointing devices), and parallel port devices have been designed to use IrDA.

ISA Slot—Short for *Industry Standard Architecture.* An ISA slot is a standardized 16-bit slot introduced with the IBM AT.

ISO 9660 Standard—The standard used for CD-ROM disks.

ISO Latin-1—A set of characters used by many operating systems, as well as web browsers. Standardized as

ISO-8859-1, ISO Latin-1 is a standard character set developed by the International Organization for Standardization. It is a superset of the ASCII character set and is very similar to the ANSI character set used in Windows, though the two are not identical. Both the HTTP and HTML protocols used on the World Wide Web are based on ISO Latin-1. This means that to represent non-ASCII characters on a web page, you need to use the corresponding ISO Latin-1 code.

J

Java—A programmable language developed by Sun Microsystems that has a number of features that make it well suited for use on the web.

Java Applets—Self-contained Internet applications that are written in Java. Initially, Java applets are stored on a web server. When you first access a web page that contains HTML code to access the Java applet, the Java applet is downloaded onto the client computer. When the client subsequently accesses the server, the applet is already cached on the client's computer and is accessed with a download delay. The Java source code is run through a client-side engine or Java virtual machine (VM).

JavaScript—Created by Netscape Corporation, a scripting language that is not Java nor is it a lightweight version of Java, although it does share many of the structure and features of Java. Most web browsers support JavaScript, which is typically embedded inside a HTML page and read by the client browser. A SCRIPT tag inside the HTML code is used to denote the JavaScript. JavaScript is commonly used to communicate with other components or to accept user input. JavaScript can be used to open Java applets.

Joint Photographic Experts Group (JPEG)—A picture and movie standard that compresses each frame by eliminating redundant data for each individual image. JPEG offers rates acceptable for nearly full-motion video (30 fps), a compression ratio of 30:1, and easy editing.

Jumper—Sometimes called a *shunt,* a small, plastic-covered metal clip that is used to connect two pins protruding from the motherboard. The jumper (same as an On switch) connects the pins, which closes the circuit and allows current to flow.

K

Kernel—The central part of an operating system that controls and allocates the machine resources, such as memory, and runs and coordinates software applications. It is the part of the operating system that loads first, and it remains in main memory. Because it stays in memory, it is important for the kernel to be as small as possible while still providing all the essential services required by others parts of the operating system and applications. Typically, the kernel is responsible for memory management, process and task management, and disk management.

Kernel Mode—Part of Windows NT, Windows 2000, or Windows XP that run in ring 0 of the Intel 386 processor protection modem. The kernel mode components are protected by the processor. It has direct access to all hardware and all memory including the address space of all user mode processes. It includes the Windows Executive, hardware abstraction layer (HAL), and the microkernel.

Kernel Oops—A kernel error and its aftermath (such as program or system crash). These errors are most commonly caused by a bug in the kernel or a hardware problem.

Key—A string of bits used to map text into a code and a code back to text. You can think of the key as a super-decoder ring used to translate text messages to a code and back to text. There are two types of keys, public and private.

Keyboard—A device similar to a typewriter by which instructions and data are input to the computer. The keyboard is the main input device.

Keyboard Controller—A chip located on the motherboard that converts the parallel keyboard data and generates an interrupt so that the data can be serviced by the microprocessor.

Keyboard ROM BIOS—ROM BIOS chip located on the motherboard that contains instructions to control the keyboard.

Kilo (K)—A prefix indicating a thousand (1,000). In computers, a kilo indicates 1,024, such as in a kilobyte (KB).

L

Lap Link Cable—A cable used to connect two computers through the computer's parallel port or serial port.

Large Addressing—Addressing scheme used by ATA IDE drives that will translate one set of values of cylinder, heads, and sectors to another, typically used to overcome the initial 504 MB IDE limitation.

Laser Printer—A nonimpact printer that works like a photocopying machine. It transfers fine toner powder to paper and fixes it in place permanently by heating (fusing) the toner. The laser printer produces extremely high-quality print with a wide range of fonts and graphics. In addition, it is quiet and fast.

Last Mile—Also referred to as the *local loop* and *subscriber loop,* the telephone line that runs from your home or office to the phone company's central office (CO) or neighborhood switching station.

Latency Period—The time it takes after the read/write heads move to the requested track for the requested sector to spin underneath the head. The latency period is usually one-half the time of a single revolution of the disk platter. It is measured in milliseconds (ms).

LCD/LED Printer—A printer similar to a laser printer except that it uses liquid crystal or light-emitting diodes instead of laser light.

Legacy Cards—Expansion cards that are not plug-and-play.

Line Conditioner—A device used to filter out noise and to "fill in" brownouts.

Linux Loader (LILO)—A common boot manager that provides the boot code to load an operating system's boot loader so that an operating system can be loaded into memory.

Linuxconf—A graphical utility that gives you important configuration centralized in one location using a single interface. Linuxconf allows you to configure and control various aspects of your system including server configurations (DNS, Apache, mail, FTP, news), user accounts, password and account policies, Internet connections (modems, PPP, routing, NIS), LILO, system logs, shutdown options, date and time, and various services.

Liquid Crystal (LC)—An organic material that has the characteristics of both a liquid and a solid. Although it appears to be a liquid, it has the crystalline molecular structure usually found in solid objects. Essentially, the liquid crystal material is a vast array of rod-shaped molecules. In its normal state, LC is virtually clear, allowing light to pass through it.

Liquid-Crystal Display (LCD)—A type of monitor that uses liquid crystal. It is mostly used in notebook computers.

Load—(1) To install something, such as a program, from disk or CD-ROM. (2) To copy a program from a disk into RAM so that the program instructions can be executed. This is done by typing in or clicking on the name of an executable file or double-clicking on an icon. (3) In networking, *load* refers to the amount of data (traffic) being carried by the network. (4) In electronics, *load* refers to an element connected across the output terminals of a circuit that draws current from the circuit.

Local Area Network (LAN)—A network connected within a close geographical network, such as a building or a campus.

Local Bus—A bus that has the same data path size as the microprocessor and connects directly to the microprocessor and runs at the same speed.

Local Host—Usually assigned an address of 127.0.01, it represents the current computer.

Local Loop—Also referred to as a *local loop* or the *last mile,* the telephone line that runs from your home or office to the phone company's central office (CO) or neighborhood switching station.

Login (*noun*)—A process that allows a computer system or network to recognize a user, often by means of a user name or password. Also referred to as *Logon.* **Log in** (or *log on*) is the verb.

Logical Block Addressing (LBA)—An addressing mode that numbers each sector.

Logical Unit Number (LUN)—A number given to a device (a logical unit) attached to a SCSI physical unit and not directly to the SCSI bus.

Lost Clusters—Clusters that get "lost" or detached from a file when a program unexpectedly stops running or isn't shut down properly or when power fluctuations or disk system problems occur.

Low-Level Formatting (LLF)—The process that defines the tracks and sectors of the hard drive.

LPX Motherboards—A motherboard with expansion slots inserted into a riser card that protrudes from the motherboard. Consequently, these expansion boards are parallel to the motherboard rather than perpendicular, which permits cases to be smaller.

M

MAC Address—Short for *media access control* address, this is a unique hardware number assigned to network hardware, such as network cards and routers.

Mac OS X—The newest version of the Macintosh operating system based on Linux.

Macintosh—Often called "the Mac," a line of personal computers produced by Apple that was the first widely sold personal computer with a user-friendly, What-you-see-is-what-you-get (WYSIWYG) graphical user interface (GUI).

Macro—A formula language used in word processing, spreadsheets, and other application programs that is a set of instructions a program executes on command. Macros are used to group several keystrokes into one command or to perform complex menu selections. Therefore, they simplify redundant or complex tasks.

Macro Viruses—The newest strain of viruses and currently the most common. Unlike previous viruses, macro viruses are stored in a data document and spread when the infected documents are transferred.

Magneto-Optical Media Drives—Drives that use magnetic patterns to store data and a laser beam to read servo information on the platter that identifies the track.

Mainframe Computer—A very large and expensive computer capable of supporting hundreds or even thousands of users simultaneously.

Master Boot Record (MBR)—The first sector of a disk, which contains a small program that reads the partition table, checks which partition is active (marked as bootable), and reads the first sector of the bootable partition.

Master Partition Table—A table listed in the master boot record that lists all of the partitions on the hard drive.

Math Coprocessor—A chip that specializes in floating-point mathematical calculations.

Mean Time Between Failure (MTBF)—A statistically derived measure of the probable time a device will continue to operate before a hardware failure occurs.

Mega (M)—A prefix indicating a million (1,000,000). In computers, mega indicates 1,024 kilobytes, such as in the megabyte (MB).

Megahertz—One million clock cycles per second; used to measure the operating speed of a microprocessor or other PC component.

Megapixel—A unit of digital camera resolution equal to approximately 1 million pixels.

Memory Addresses—(1) A range of locations of RAM. (2) A range of locations of RAM assigned to be used by a device.

Memory Controller—Device that translates signals between the RAM and microprocessor.

Memory Stick—A Sony-developed flash memory device that's about the size of a stick of gum.

Metropolitan Area Network (MAN)—A network designed for a town or city, usually using high-speed connections such as fiber optics.

Micro (μ)—A prefix meaning one millionth.

Micro Channel Architecture (MCA)—A 32-bit expansion slot introduced with the IBM PS/2. The MCA slot is no longer produced.

Micro Kernel—A simple, smaller kernel that just manages memory and processes.

Microkernel—The central part of Windows NT, Windows 2000, or Windows XP that coordinates all I/O functions and synchronizes the activities of the Executive Services. Much like the other kernels, it determines what is to be performed and when it is to be performed, while handling interrupts and exceptions. Lastly, it is designed to keep the microprocessor(s) busy at all times.

Micron—A millionth of a meter.

Microphone—A device used to convert sound into analog electrical signals.

Microprocessor—The primary integrated chip of the computer considered the brain of the computer because all of the instructions it performs are mathematical calculations and logical comparisons. It is sometimes referred to as the central processing unit (CPU).

Microsoft DOS (MS-DOS)—The first operating system used in the IBM PC. It is a command-driven, single-tasking operating system. *DOS* stands for *disk operating system.*

Microsoft Management Console (MMC)—A fully customizable administrative console used in Windows 2000 and Windows XP, used as a common interface for most administrative tasks.

Microsoft Office—A family of products designed to help users complete common business tasks. Microsoft Office applications are available in suites, or groups of programs bundled together to address different user requirements.

Microsoft Software Update Service—A server/service that is used to distribute selected windows updates throughout an enterprise network.

MIDI—*See* Musical Instrument Digital Interface.

Milli (m)—A prefix meaning one thousandth.

Minicomputer—A midsized computer that is between a personal computer and a mainframe computer in capacity. In general, it supports 4 to about 200 users simultaneously.

MIPS—Millions of instructions per second.

MMX Technology—*MMX* stands for *multimedia extension* and consists of 57 instructions that improve the performance of multimedia tasks.

Modem—Short for *modulator/demodulator.* This device enables transmission of data through telephone lines.

Modem AT Commands—A set of commands used by most modems.

Modified Frequency Modulation (MFM)—Encoding method used on older disk drives.

Monitor—A device similar to a television. The monitor is the computer's main output device. It is also called a *display* or *video.*

Monochrome—A term describing a display or printer that displays two colors, one for the background and one for the foreground.

Monochrome Display Adapter (MDA)—A monochrome video card used in the IBM PC and XT that could display 25 rows of 80 characters (80 × 25 characters).

Monolithic Kernel—A large and complex kernel that contains a large number of tasks, manages processes, and provides a means of interprocess communication.

Motherboard—The primary circuit board, known as the system board, which is expandable using expansion cards (daughter boards). The microprocessor is inserted into the motherboard.

Motion Picture Experts Group (MPEG)—A movie standard that can compress frames up to a 200:1 ratio at high quality levels because it only stores the incremental changes. Unfortunately, because it omits full information for every frame, it does not allow for easy editing.

Mount Point—The directory you associate with a disk partition or any other device. In other words, each mount point is a disk partition, and that disk partition is mounted on the directory of the limb above it.

Mouse—A pointing device that that can move the cursor back and forth on the screen (assuming the software supports pointing devices). These devices are easy to use and can improve productivity over a keyboard alone.

Multibank DRAM (MDRAM)—A type of video RAM that breaks its memory into multiple 32 KB banks that can be accessed independently. This allows interleaving of the RAM.

Multihomed Server—A computer that contains multiple network cards that act as a router.

Multipartite Virus—A virus that has the characteristics of both boot sector viruses and file viruses.

Multiple Link Interface Driver (MLID)—A standard that allows multiple protocols to be used on the same network card.

Multistation Access Unit (MAU)—A token ring network device that physically connects network computers in a star topology while retaining the logical ring structure.

Multitasking—The ability to perform more than one task or application at the same time.

Musical Instrument Digital Interface (MIDI)—An interface and protocol for connecting musical instruments to a PC and storing musical instrument data.

My Computer—Desktop icon that represents the computer. It includes all disk drives and the Control Panel. From within the My Computer icon, you can access and manage all files on your drives.

My Documents—A directory created in Windows to store your documents.

N

Nano (n)—A prefix that means one-billionth.

National Television System Committee (NTSC)—The color television signal standard used in the United States and Japan.

NetBEUI (NetBios Enhanced User Interface)—An enhanced version of the NetBIOS protocol used by network operations. Although it does not require much software, it is not routable.

NetBIOS Enhanced User Interface (NetBEUI)—Provides the transport and network layers for the NetBIOS protocol.

Network—Two or more computers connected together to share resources.

Network Basic Input/Output System (NetBIOS)—A common program that runs on most Microsoft networks.

Network Interface Card (NIC)—An expansion card that allows a computer to connect directly to a network.

Network Neighborhood—A program found in Windows that allows for easy browsing of network resources.

Network Operating System (NOS)—An operating system that includes special functions for connecting computers and devices into a local area network (LAN), for managing the resources and services of the network, and for providing network security to multiple users.

NLX motherboard—A motherboard similar to the LPX motherboard but with several improvements. It supports larger memory modules and newer microprocessors and provides better access to motherboard components.

Nonvolatile Memory (NVRAM)—Random access memory whose data is retained when power is turned off.

North Bridge—The Intel term for the main portion of the motherboard chipset that incorporates the interface between the processor and the rest of the motherboard. The North Bridge contains the cache, main memory, and AGP controllers.

Noise—Radio frequency interference caused by telephones, motors, fluorescent lights, and radio transmitters that can introduce computer errors.

Nonimpact Printers—Instead of striking the paper, nonimpact printers use other methods of printing. Ink-jet printers, laser printers, and thermal printers are all nonimpact printers.

Noninterlaced Monitor—A screen that redraws in one sweep. A noninterlace monitor is better than an interlaced monitor.

Nonmaskable Interrupt (NMI)—An interrupt that cannot be masked or switched off in the normal operation of the system through software. It is normally used to notify the microprocessor about parity errors.

Norton SI—A measurement system used to measure the performance of a PC relative to the original IBM PC.

Notification Area—A Windows component located on the right side of the Taskbar, used for the clock and for any programs running in the background, such as printers and modems.

NSLOOKUP—A troubleshooting tool used to test name servers and services.

NTDETECT.COM—The second file loaded on Windows NT, Windows 2000, and Windows XP, which attempts to detect the bus/adapter type, serial ports, floating-point coprocessor, floppy disks, keyboard, mouse/pointing device, parallel ports, SCSI adapters, and video adapters.

NTFS—A new file system for Windows NT that supports long file names and provides enhanced security.

NTLDR—The first Windows NT, Windows 2000, or Windows XP file read during boot-up, which switches the processor from real mode to protected mode and starts the appropriate minifile system drivers so that it can read the VFAT/FAT16, FAT32, or NTFS file systems.

Null Modem Cable—Sometimes known as a *crossover cable.* A cable used to connect two DTE devices together, such as two computers.

O

Object Linking and Embedding (OLE)—An enhanced version of DDE that allows the user to create objects with one application and then link or embed them into another application. Embedded objects keep their original format and links to the application that created them.

OEM Service Release 2 (OSR2)—An updated version of the retail version of Windows 95.

Oersted—A unit for measuring magnetic strength.

Office Suite—A collection of productivity applications bundled together and sold as a single package. A suite typically consists of a word processor and spreadsheet program, and often contains other software packages such as database and presentation software.

Ohmmeter—A device that measures resistance.

Open—A break in a conductor that prevents current from flowing.

Open Architecture—A hardware or software architecture, design, or specification that is public.

Open Data-Link Interface (ODI) Architecture—A set of standards for protocols and network card drivers that allows multiple protocols to use a single network adapter card. It is usually associated with Novell NetWare.

Open System Interconnection (OSI) Reference Model—A model used to categorize network technology.

OpenGL—A 3D graphics language designed to improve performance on hardware that supports the OpenGL standard.

Operating System (OS)—The most important software in the computer. It coordinates the actions of the hardware, the software, and the user so that they can work as one.

Operating System/2 (OS/2)—A graphical operating system begun by IBM and Microsoft to replace MS-DOS.

Optical Character Recognition (OCR)—Software that converts the image of text to actual text.

Ordinary Links—Also known as hard links. In Linux, they are actually directory entries that point to an inode of a file.

Original Equipment Manufacturer (OEM)—A misleading term for a company that has a special relationship with computer producers. OEMs buy computers in bulk and customize them for a particular application. They then sell the customized computer under their own name. The term is really a misnomer because OEMs are not the original manufacturers, but are customizers.

Outline Fonts—Vector fonts that define the outlines of each character geometrically.

Overclocking—The process of running the microprocessor or bus speed at a clock speed faster than what the microprocessor or bus was designed for.

Overrun—A situation in which data moves from one device more quickly than a second device can accept it.

Ozone Filter—A filter used to absorb ozone gas, which causes various health problems.

P

Page Description Language—A programming language used by printers that describes the whole page being printed by using draw and position commands and mathematical formulas.

Page Fault—An error that occurs when the PC needs to access information that is stored in virtual memory or a program requests data that is not currently in RAM or virtual memory.

Pager—It allows you to maintain several virtual desktops and easily switch between them. Each virtual desktop can have several programs running.

Pages—A fixed amount of data.

Paper Transport Assembly—A component that moves the paper through a laser printer.

Parallel Loop-Back Plug—A device used to test the parallel port by looping the parallel port's output back into the parallel port.

Parallel Port—A female, 2-row, 25-pin D connector that communicates with up to 8 bits at a time. Today's parallel port is used primarily for printers but can also be used for a wide array of external devices, such as external hard drives, tape drives, removable disk drives, scanners, and network cards.

Parallel Recording—A method used for recording data on tapes by spreading the data throughout the different tracks.

Parity—A form of error control that uses an extra bit to check the accuracy of the data bits.

Partition Table—An area of the hard drive that contains information on how the disk is organized.

Partitioning—The process of dividing a physical drive (hard drive) into one or more logical volumes called *partitions*. Each partition functions as if it were a separate hard disk.

Passive Matrix Display—A type of LCD display used in notebook computers. Passive matrix displays are not as bright as active matrix displays.

Passive Termination—The prevention by electrical resistors acting as voltage dividers of signals from reflecting or echoing when they reach the end of a chain. The resistors help ensure that the chain has the correct impedance load.

Password Authentication Protocol (PAP)—The least secure authentication protocol because it uses clear text (plaintext) passwords.

Path—(1) The location of a file. (2) A listing of directories at the command prompt used to look for files executed at the prompt.

PC Card—A small, flat expansion card typically used in notebook computers.

PC Slot—(1) The 8-bit slot (sometimes referred to as an 8-bit ISA slot) used in the IBM PC. (2) The slot used in notebook computers (formerly known as the PCMCIA slot).

PCI Express—Formerly called third-generation I/O (3GIO), PCI Express is both a hardware interface and a transmission protocol meant to replace the PCI and AGP expansion bus. Like other emerging PC technologies, the PCI Express architecture does not use a wide parallel bus that requires complex and expensive electrical paths. Instead, it uses an individually clocked lane, each consisting of two pairs of data lines to carry data upstream and downstream.

Peer-to-Peer Network—A network that has no dedicated server. The computers on the network both provide network services and request network services.

Pentium 4 Processor—Intel's seventh-generation processor based on NetBurst architecture.

Pentium II—A sixth-generation microprocessor that includes MMX technology and L2 RAM cache.

Pentium III Processor—Intel's sixth-generation processor similar to the Pentium II processor but with Streaming SIMD Extensions (SSE) added.

Pentium Microprocessor—A fifth-generation microprocessor that has two pipelines and an enhanced math coprocessor.

Pentium Pro Microprocessor—A Pentium microprocessor that includes L2 RAM cache.

Peripheral Component Interconnect (PCI) Local Bus—A 32- or 64-bit local bus developed by Intel to eventually replace older bus designs.

Peripherals—Any external devices attached to a computer. Examples include printers, external disk drives, monitors, keyboards, mice, and external modems.

Permission—Defines the type of access that is granted to an object or object attribute.

Permission Bit—A single bit used to define whether or not a given user or class of users have a particular type of access to a file. For instance, the owner's execute permission bit determines whether the owner can run a file as a program. The permission bits together comprise the file's mode.

Permission String—A string that shows the permissions of a file or directory for the owner (user and group) of the file and everyone else.

Personal Computers—Computers that are meant to be used by one person.

Phase Alternate Line (PAL)—The color television signal standard used in many parts of Europe.

Photosensitive Drum—A drum that is sensitive to light used in laser printers.

Physical Address—An address indicating a specific storage area in RAM.

Picture Element—*See* Pixel.

Pipeline—A term referring to how a microprocessor executes instructions. Each segment of the pipeline can execute its operation concurrently with the other segments.

Pipelined Burst Cache—A type of RAM cache that uses a register to hold the next piece of data to be read. Therefore, while reading one piece of data, the RAM cache is already accessing the next piece of data.

Pipelining—A technique used in advanced microprocessors where the microprocessor begins executing a second instruction before the first has been completed. That is, several instructions are in the pipeline simultaneously, each at a different processing stage. The pipeline is divided into segments and each segment can execute its operation concurrently with the other segments. When a segment completes an operation, it passes the result to the next segment in the pipeline and fetches the next operation from the preceding segment. The final results of each instruction emerge at the end of the pipeline in rapid succession.

Piracy—*See* Software Piracy.

Pixel—Short for *picture element.* The dots used in a display to generate text, lines, and pictures.

Plastic Pin Grid Array (PPGA)—A chip packaging form factor used by Intel as an alternative to traditional ceramic packaging.

Platter—A round, rotating, magnetic plate on a hard drive that holds data.

Pluggable Authentication Modeles for Linux (Linux-PAM))—PAM allows you to change your authentication method and requirements on the fly, and encapsulate all local authentication methods without recompiling any of your programs.

Plug-and-Play (PnP)—Describes a device that upon insertion into the computer is automatically configured and for which the appropriate drivers are automatically loaded.

Plug-In—Software added to a web browser so that it can play audio files and view movies or other multimedia files.

Pointing Device—A device such as a mouse or trackball that can move the cursor back and forth on the screen (assuming the software supports pointing devices). These devices are easy to use and can improve productivity over using a keyboard alone.

Point-to-Point Protocol (PPP)—An advanced version of the SLIP protocol that is commonly used to connect to the Internet using a modem. It provides full-duplex, bidirectional operations between hosts and can encapsulate multiple network layer LAN protocols to connect to private networks.

Polling—A method by which the BIOS polls or checks to see if a device is ready to accept another character.

Polymorphic Virus—A virus that mutates or changes its code so that it cannot be as easily detected.

Portable Computers—Fully functional computers (laptops, notebooks, and subnotebooks) that can be carried about.

Portable Document Format (PDF)—A popular document format commonly used to store documentation for computers, computer components and software; read by Adobe Acrobat.

Portable Operating System Interface (POSIX)—A set of standard operating system interfaces based on the UNIX operating system.

Ports—(1) Plug sockets that enable an external device. (2) An address or range of addresses that identify a device.

POSIX—*See* Portable Operating System Interface (POSIX).

POST Card—An expansion card used to diagnose computer problems by displaying a numeric code.

PostScript—A common page description language developed by Adobe.

Power (P)—The rate of energy consumption or the amount of energy used in a certain length of time. In electronics, it is expressed in watts.

Power Scheme—A collection of power management settings that allows the user to conveniently configure power management options on a computer.

Power Supply—A device that converts ac into clean dc power.

Power-Good Signal—A signal sent to the computer from the power supply. When the signal is not being sent, the system is experiencing a short or overload, which causes the switching power supply to go into idle mode.

Preemptive Multitasking—A form of multitasking that allows the operating system to assign time slices to tasks and applications; occurs when the operating system assigns time slices to threads, tasks, and those with a higher priority get a larger time slice. At the end of the time slice, the kernel can regain control of the computer without permission from the thread or program.

Print Manager—A program that manages the print queue or print spooler (a holding area for print jobs sent to the printer).

Print Queue—A holding area for print jobs sent to the printer. Also known as *print spooler.*

Print Spooler—A holding area for print jobs sent to the printer. Also known as a *print queue.*

Printed Circuit Boards—A flat board made of glass-epoxy in which thin metal traces are embedded to connect the different electronic components.

Printer—A common output device used with computers that produces images of text and graphics on paper. Some printers can also produce color images.

Printer Control Language (PCL)—A common page description language developed by Hewlett-Packard.

Printer Controller Circuitry—The large circuit board in laser printers that converts signals from the computer into signals understood by the different components of the printer.

Process *(noun)*—An executing program. The term is used loose as a synonym of task. To perform some useful operations on data *(verb).*

Processor—The brains of the computer. Sometimes referred to simply as the *central processor* or *microprocessor,* the processor is where most calculations take place. In terms of computing power, the most important element of a computer system.

Processor Input/Output (PIO) Mode—The data transfer method used on most IDE drives, which use the microprocessor to handle data transfers.

Program—An organized list of instructions that, when executed, causes the computer to behave in a predetermined manner. Without programs, computers are useless. When you buy software, you normally buy an executable version of a program. This means that the program is already in machine language; it has already been compiled and assembled and is ready to execute.

Program Information File (PIF)—A file that contains information about a DOS program running in Windows.

Program Manager—A core component of the graphical user interface in Windows 3.XX. It usually fills most if not all of the desktop and contains the group windows and icons.

Programmer—A person who creates software by specifying the instructions that the computer will follow in a programming language such as BASIC, C++, Visual Basic, or Java.

Prompt—Characters on the screen typically showing the current directory and prompting the user to type in a command.

Proprietary System—A hardware or software architecture, design, or specification that is privately owned and controlled by a company and whose specifications have not been divulged so that other companies cannot duplicate the product.

Protected Mode—A type of memory utilization available on 286 machines or later that recognizes extended memory and that protects programs from each other.

Protocol—A set of rules or standards designed to enable computers to connect with one another, and peripheral devices to exchange information with as little error as possible.

PS/2 Mouse—A mouse that doesn't use a serial port.

Q

Quarter-Inch Tape Cartridge (QIC)—A type of tape that measures one-quarter of an inch.

Quartz Crystal—A crystal made of piezoelectric material, which vibrates in the presence of electricity. The frequency is controlled by varying the size and shape of the piezoelectric material.

QuickTime—A movie standard developed by Apple Computer. QuickTime files have a MOV file name extension.

Quota—A method that allows you to limit how much data the users can store on a drive.

QWERTY Layout—The most common keyboard layout used in keyboards and typewriters.

R

Radio Frequency Interference (RFI)—Electromagnetic signals that may interfere with other electronic devices.

RAM—*See* Random Access Memory.

RAM Cache—Ultrafast RAM used as a buffer between the microprocessor and the slower RAM.

RAM Drive—A simulated hard disk drive consisting of RAM.

RAM Shadowing—A process to speed up the computer by copying ROM instructions to the faster RAM.

Rambus DRAM (RDRAM)—A high-speed dynamic RAM technology developed by Rambus, Inc., which was supported by some Intel chipsets.

Rambus In-line Memory Module (RIMM)—A type of memory module made using RDRAM chips.

RAMDAC—Short for *RAM digital-analog converter.* A chip located on the video card that translates the digital information into the analog information used by the monitor.

Random Access Memory—Integrated chips that are used for short-term memory. RAM holds instructions and data that the microprocessor accesses directly. When the computer is shut off, the contents of the RAM are lost.

Raster Fonts—Fonts made up of bitmap pictures in dots of different sizes for specific video display resolutions.

Read-Only Memory—An integrated chip that contains instructions and data that the microprocessor accesses directly. It is sometimes referred to as the "instincts" of the computer. Unlike RAM, ROM instructions are permanent and cannot be changed or erased by normal means.

Read/Write Head—Component within drives that reads and writes data to and from a platter.

Real Audio—A technology that allows you to play video and sound files based on streaming technology.

Real Mode—A Windows 3.XX operating mode used on XT computers to run old Windows applications written before Windows 3.0. It only recognizes the first 1 MB of RAM and is available only in Windows 3.0.

Real Video—A popular video file format that supports streaming.

Real-Address Mode—When an Intel 80286 and later model processor pretends to be an 8086 processor whereas the processor can only recognize up to 1 MB of RAM.

Real-Time Clock (RTC)—The PC component that keeps track of the time and date.

Ream—500 sheets of paper.

Recordable CD—Also known as CD-WORM (write once read many) and CD-WO (write once). As the write-once name implies, the disks can be recorded only once and can't be changed after that.

Recovery Console—A command-line interface that will let you repair system problems using a limited set of commands, including enabling or disabling services, repairing a corrupted master boot record, or reading and writing data on a local drive (FAT, FAT32, or NTFS).

Rectification—The process that turns ac current into dc.

Recycle Bin—An icon in Windows that is used as a safe delete. When you delete a file using the GUI, Windows will store the file in the Recycle Bin.

Red Hat Package Manager—An open packaging system that packages all the necessary files for a software product in a single file (referred to as an RPM file). Since RPM is a package manager, you can install, remove, build, rebuild, and view your packages.

Redirector—A small section of code in the network operating system that intercepts requests in the computer and determines if they should be left alone to continue in the local computer's bus or redirected out to the network to another server.

Reduced Instruction Set Computer (RISC)—A type of microprocessor architecture whose processor commands are all the same size. One advantage of reduced instruction set computers is that they can execute their instructions very fast because the instructions are so simple. Another, perhaps more important advantage, is that RISC chips require fewer transistors, which makes them cheaper to design and produce.

Redundant Arrays of Inexpensive Disks (RAID)—The combination of two or more drives to establish a fault tolerance system, to protect against physical hard drive failure, and to increase hard drive performance.

Refresh Rate—The number of times the screen is redrawn in a second. It is measured in hertz (Hz).

Refresh Routine—The routine that takes control of the data and address buses from the microprocessor and recharges all of the storage cells in the RAM.

REGEDIT.EXE—A program used to edit the registry in Windows.

REGEDT32.EXE—A program used to edit the registry in Windows.

Register—An internal storage area that acts as the microprocessor's short-term memory and work area.

Registry—A central information database for Windows 95 and 98 and Windows NT organized into a tree-structured, hierarchical database.

Registry Editor—A program used to edit the registry in Windows. REGEDIT.EXE and REGEDT32.EXE are registry editors.

Regulated Power Supplies—A power supply whose output voltages are independent of line and load variations.

Reiser File System—A journaling file system.

Release Kernel—A kernel with an even second number, such as 2.2.17 or 2.4.3. Release kernels should have few bugs.

Remote Procedure Calls (RPCs)—Responsible for handling the requests between the client and server.

Repeater—A network device used to regenerate or replicate a signal or to move packets from one physical media to another.

Reserve Memory—RAM between 640 KB and 1 MB reserved for hardware.

Reset Button—A pushbutton located in the front of the computer used to reboot the computer when the computer "freezes up" and a soft boot (Ctr+Alt+Del) does not work.

Resistance—Opposition to current flow, measured in ohms (V).

Resolution—The number of pixels (picture elements) that can be displayed on the screen at one time. Usually expressed as the number of dots going across and down the screen.

Resolution Enhancement Technology (RET)—A method developed by Hewlett-Packard that produces smaller dots to fill some of the gaps between two normal-sized dots so that a line or curve will be smoother.

Ribbon Cable—A long, flat, gray cable.

Rich Text Format—A standard for formatting documents consisting of ASCII characters with special commands for such formatting information as fonts and margins.

Right—Authorizes a user to perform certain actions on a computer, such as logging on to a system interactively or backing up files and directories.

RISC86 Instruction—CISC instructions rebuilt out of smaller and faster RISC instructions.

RJ-11—The standard two-wire connector type used for single-line telephone connections.

RJ-45—A standard connector type used in networking with twisted-pair cabling. The RJ-45 connector resembles a RJ-11 connector, except the RJ-45 connector is larger.

Roll Back Driver—A new feature of Windows XP that gives the ability to replace a device driver with a previously installed version.

ROM BIOS Shadowing—The process of copying the contents of the ROM BIOS chips found on expansion cards into the RAM. System performance is increased by accessing the instructions in the faster RAM.

ROM Shadowing—A method where the contents of a slower ROM chip are copied into RAM. Since the information is accessed from the RAM, the PC has increased performance.

Root—In UNIX and Linux machines, often referred to as the superuser, the person who has access to everything on the system. Therefore, on the Linux machine, the root account is all powerful.

Root Directory—The starting point of any disk structure. It is considered the top of the tree structure.

Router—A router connects two local area networks (similar or disassimilar) and is considered an intelligent device because it can determine the best path to a destination computer or network.

RPM—*See* Red Hat Package Manager.

RS-232—A serial interface that provides an electrical description for connecting peripheral devices to computers.

Run Length Limited (RLL)—Encoding method used on newer disk drives.

Run Level—A number associated with a particular set of services that are being run. Changing run levels changes services or can shut down or restart the computer.

S

Sag—A very short drop in power lasting only a few milliseconds.

Sandbox—A security measure in the Java development environment. The sandbox is a set of rules that are used when creating an applet that prevents certain functions when the applet is sent as part of a web page. When a browser requests a web page with applets, the applets are sent automatically and can be executed as soon as the page arrives in the browser. If the applet is allowed unlimited access to memory and operating system resources, it can do harm in the hands of someone with malicious intent. The sandbox creates an environment in which there are strict limitations on what system resources the applet can request or access. Sandboxes are used when executable code comes from unknown or untrusted sources and allow the user to run untrusted code safely.

Scanner—A device that can scan or digitize images on paper (much like a copy machine does) and convert them to data that the computer can use. The data can then be stored in a file, displayed on the screen, added to documents, or manipulated.

Screen Saver—Software that is used to prevent burn-in of a screen. Today, screen savers also provide entertainment.

SCSI—Short for *small computer system interface.* A fast interface that can connect up to seven or more devices, including hard drives, CD-ROM drives, tape drives, and scanners.

SCSI Parallel Interface (SPI)—Alternative name for common SCSI standard.

SDRAM—Short for *synchronous dynamic RAM.* It is currently the fastest form of RAM and is synchronized to the external clock used on the motherboard.

Search Engine—A program used on the Internet that searches documents for specified keywords and returns a list of the documents where the keywords were found.

Sectors—512 byte units, which make up a track.

Security Account Manager (SAM)—A database found on Windows 2000 and XP computers that list the local accounts for the computer.

Seek Time—The average time it takes the read/write heads to move to the requested track. Usually the time it takes the read/write heads to move one-third of the way across the platter. It is measured in milliseconds (ms).

Semiconductor—A material that is neither a good conductor of electricity nor a good insulator.

Serial Attached SCSI (SAS)—A SCSI design that is similar to Serial ATA.

Serial Line Internet Protocol (SLIP)—An older protocol that allows computers to connect to the Internet using a modem.

Serial Line Protocols—Protocols that allow you to connect to a network using a modem. SLIP and PPP are serial line protocols.

Serial Loopback Plug—A device used to test serial ports that takes the output signal back into the serial port.

Serial Port Interface—A general-purpose interface that can be used for mice, external modems, and other devices. It is a two-row male D port with either 9 or 25 pins.

Serpentine Recording—A method used to record data on tapes, similar to parallel recording. Unlike parallel recording, serpentine recording writes the data onto one track and when the end of the track is reached, moves to the next track to write to the second track.

Server—A computer that is a dedicated service provider found on networks.

Server Message Block (SMB)—A protocol that defines a series of command used to pass information between networked computers using NetBIOS.

Service—A program, routine, or process that performs a specific system function to support other programs.

Service Pack—A collection of fixes bundled as a single upgrade.

SFX—A power supply form factor typically designed for small systems.

Shadow Mask—A fine metal mesh with openings that line up with the pixels and used to aim and focus the electron beams of the CRT monitor.

Shockwave—A technology developed by Macromedia, Inc. that enables web pages to include multimedia objects.

Short—A circuit with no or an abnormally low resistance path between two points, resulting in excessive current flow.

Shortcut Menu—Menu that appears when you click the mouse's secondary button (usually the left button) that varies depending on the object that you clicked on.

Simple Mail Transfer Protocol (SMTP)—A protocol used in email systems.

Simplex—(1) A form of communication in which data can travel in only one direction. (2) A term describing a printer that can print on only one side.

Single In-Line Memory Module (SIMM)—A type of RAM in the form of a small circuit board consisting of several soldered DIP chips. To connect to the motherboard, the SIMM has a row of tin or gold metal plates (contacts) along the bottom of the module.

Single In-Line Pin Package (SIPP)—A type of RAM in the form of a small circuit board that has several DIPs soldered onto it. The circuit board uses a single row of pins which are inserted into the motherboard.

Single Instruction, Multiple Data (SIMD)—Technology that allows a processor to have several values sitting in a register and have one instruction perform the same function on multiple pieces of data at the same time.

Slipstreaming—The process of adding a service pack to the operating system's distribution share/installation files.

Small-Outline DIMM (SO-DIMM)—A form of RAM that is narrower and thinner than the full-sized DIMMs and usually found in notebook computers. A small-outline DIMM is like a 72-pin SIMM in a reduced-size package.

Software—A series of instructions that are loaded into the computer's memory. Software is created by programmers.

Software Diagnostic Package—A software package that can report resources used by devices (I/O addresses, IRQs, DMAs, and memory addresses), perform hardware diagnostics, and troubleshoot and optimize software.

Software Piracy—The illegal copying, distribution, or installing of software (a theft of intellectual property).

Sound—Vibrations of compressed air. As sound starts out, it travels in all directions away from the source. When the sound reaches the human ear, it causes the eardrum to vibrate allowing the sound to be heard.

Sound Card—A device that adds music, speech, and sound effects to the PC.

Source Routing Bridge—A bridge that connects token ring networks.

South Bridge—The Intel term for the lower-speed component in the chipset that has always been a single individual chip. The South Bridge connects to the 33 MHz PCI bus and contains the IDE interface ports and the interface to the 8 MHz ISA bus (when present).

Spanning Tree Bridge—A bridge that connects Ethernet networks.

Spare Sectoring—The process by which a drive has extra sectors set aside to replace sectors that are found to be unreliable.

Spike—Sometimes known as a *transient,* a quick overvoltage, which can damage the computer.

Spindle—The component found in disk drives around which the platter rotates.

Spreadsheet—A software package that works with tables of numbers and/or financial models.

Spyware—Any software that covertly gathers user information through the user's Internet connection without his or her knowledge, usually for advertising purposes. Spyware applications are typically bundled as a hidden component of freeware or shareware programs that can be downloaded from the Internet; however, it should be noted that the majority of shareware and freeware applications do not come with spyware. Once installed, the spyware monitors user activity on the Internet and transmits that information in the background to someone else. Spyware can also gather information about email addresses and even passwords and credit card numbers.

SRAM—Short for *static RAM.* It consists of four transistors and two resistors that act as an electronic switch. SRAM is faster than DRAM chips and does not require refreshing. SRAM chips are typically used for RAM cache.

ST-506 Interface—An interface used by the hard drives in the IBM XT and early PCs.

Standard Mode—A Windows 3.XX operating mode normally used on 286 computers. It allows multiple Windows programs to run at the same time and provides direct access to the extended memory.

Standard—A definition or format approved by a recognized standards organization or accepted as a de facto standard by the industry.

Standing Power Supply (SPS)—Device that uses a battery to power the computer during power fluctuations.

Standoff—A device that prevents the motherboard from shorting against the computer case.

Start Button—A component of Windows used to start programs. Using the Start button, you can open recently accessed documents and access the Control Panel and printer folder, find files, and get help for Windows.

Stealth Virus—A virus that tries to hide itself by monitoring and intercepting a system call.

Stepper Motors—Electrical motors that move from one position to another in steps.

Stepping—The code used to identify the revision of a processor.

Sticky Bit—A special file permission that's most commonly used on directories. When set, only a file's owner may delete the file, even if the directory in which it resides can be modified by others.

Stop Error—An error that signifies that something unexpected has happened within the Windows environment.

Streaming SIMD Extension (SSE)—An update or extension to MMX consisting of 70 new instructions to enhance advanced imaging, powerful 3D graphics processor, streaming video and audio and speech recognition. One of the main benefits of SSE over MMX is that it supports single-precision floating-point operations. It was introduced with the Intel Pentium III processor.

Streaming SIMD Extension 2 (SSE2)—An extension to the SSE that encompasses 144 new instructions, which include instructions for memory and cacheability management. It was first used with the Intel Pentium 4 processor.

Streaming Technology—A technique for transferring data such that it can be processed as a steady and continuous stream.

Stripe Set—Similar to a volume set except the data is written evenly across all physical disks. Since all of the disks are being read from and written to concurrently, stripe sets provide much faster access.

Subdirectory—A directory below another directory. Every directory except the root directory is a subdirectory.

Subkey—An logical organization component of the Windows registry similar to a folder.

Subnet—Small networks that comprise a larger network.

Subnet Mask—Numbers that resemble an IP address used to define which bits describe the network number and which bits describe the host address.

Subscriber Loop—Also referred to as a *local loop* or the *last mile,* the telephone line that runs from your home or office to the phone company's central office (CO) or neighborhood switching station.

Super Computer—The fastest type of computer used for specialized applications that require immense amounts of mathematical calculations.

Superblock—Found at the beginning of the Linux disk system, the superblock contains a description of the basic size and shape of this file system. The information within it allows the file system manager to use and maintain the file system.

Superscalar—A processor architecture that supports two or more operations at the same time.

Surface Mount—Chip carriers and sockets designed to mount to the surface of a PC board.

Surge—An overvoltage, which can stretch into milliseconds and can damage the computer.

Surge Protector—A device designed to prevent most short-duration, high-intensity spikes, and surges from reaching a PC.

Swap File—A virtual memory file used in Windows 3.XX and Windows 9X.

Switch—(1) An electrical or electronic device that opens and closes a current path. (2) A command-line option to determine how the command will be executed or displayed.

Switching Hub—A fast multiported bridge, sometimes referred to as a switch, that actually reads the destination address of each packet and then forwards the packet to the correct port. A major advantage of using a switching hub is it allows one computer to open a connection to another computer). While those two computers communicate, other connections between other computers (or LAN segments) can be opened at the same time. Therefore, several computers can communicate at the same time.

Switching Power Supply—A power supply that switches on or off at very fast speeds. When the system needs more power, the switch stays on longer; when the system needs less power, the switch stays off longer. Small and efficient, the switching power supply has a unique overload characteristic that goes into idle mode when it detects a short or overload.

Symmetric Multiprocessing (SMP)—Involves a computer that uses two or more processors that use the same memory. If software is written to use the multiple processors, several programs can be executed at the same time, or multithreaded applications can be executed faster.

Synchronous Burst Cache—A type of RAM cache that accesses a memory area but then uses its own internal clock, which is in sync with the RAM, to count up and access sequential addresses. In addition, synchronous burst cache uses pipelining to access the next RAM address while transferring the current data.

Synchronous Graphics RAM (SGRAM)—A form of video RAM that increases the speed at which memory transfers take place. In addition, it incorporates specific performance-enhancing features, specifically the acceleration features built into the video card.

System Board—*See* Motherboard.

System Clock—The PC component that acts as the heartbeat of the computer.

System Management Mode (SMM)—A processor operating mode that provides an operating system with a transparent mechanism for implementing power management.

System Partition—The active partition that contains NTLDR and BOOT.INI used in Windows NT, Windows 2000, and Windows XP.

System ROM BIOS—The primary ROM BIOS chip found on the motherboard. It controls the boot-up procedures, performs a series of diagnostic tests known as the power-on self-test (POST) during boot-up, and generates hardware error codes (audio and video) if a problem is found during boot-up. In addition, the chip provides the most basic commands to control hardware and the compatibility between the operating system and the hardware. It contains the CMOS setup program.

System Routine—Many small individual programs found in ROM chips. They are low-level programs that directly manipulate the PC hardware.

System Software—Software (operating systems and compilers) that directs the entire system.

T

Tape—A long polyester substrate coated with a layer of magnetic material that is used to store data. Unlike a floppy disk, a tape stores and retrieves data sequentially. Tapes are usually used to back up data.

Tape Drive—A backup device that reads and stores data on tapes.

Tarball—Many files archived into a single large file and then compressed, originally created for tape archives (back up and restore files in a Linux system).

Task Manager—A component of Windows NT, Windows 2000, and Windows XP that provides a list of the current programs that are running and the overall CPU (including the number of threads and processes) and memory usage (including the amount of physical memory, size of the file cache, paged memory, and nonpaged memory). You can also use the Task Manager to switch between programs and to stop a program that is not responding.

Taskbar—A component of Windows located at the bottom of the screen, used to switch between different programs.

TCP/IP (Transmission Control Protocol/Internet Protocol)—An industrial suite of protocols on which the Internet is based.

TCP/IP Port Number—An endpoint to a logical connection. The ports are used to identify the upper-layer protocols and act as a switchboard to make sure the frames fight their way to the right network layer process.

Telnet—A common protocol (part of the TCP/IP suite) that allows the user to remotely log in to other machines on the Internet and work on the remote system or try software available there.

Tera (T)—A prefix indicating a trillion (1,000,000,000,000). In computers, a tera indicates 1,024 gigabytes, such as in a terabyte (TB).

Termination—A method of using resistors to prevent signals from bouncing back when they reach the end of a wire.

Thermal Printers—Inexpensive printers that press heated pins to a special heat-sensitive paper to form characters.

Thicknet—More commonly referred to as *10Base5.* The original cabling standard for Ethernet that uses coaxial cables. The name derives from the fact that the maximum data transfer speed is 10 Mbit/s, it uses baseband transmission, and the maximum length of cables is 500 meters (1640 feet).

Thinnet—More commonly referred to as *10Base2.* One of several adaptations of the Ethernet (IEEE 802.3) standard for local area networks (LANs). The 10Base2 standard (also called thinnet) uses 50 ohm coaxial cable (RG-58 A/U) with maximum lengths of 185 meters (607 feet) and operates at 10 Mbit/s.

Thread—A part of a program that can execute independently of other parts. Operating systems that support multithreading enable programmers to design programs whose threaded parts can execute concurrently. This can enhance a program by allowing multitasking, improving throughput, enhancing responsiveness, and aiding background processing.

Thunking—A process by which a 16-bit instruction is paired with the next instruction, making it 32-bit during execution.

Token Passing—An access method that uses a special authorizing packet of information to inform devices they can transmit data. These packets, called *tokens,* are passed around the network in an orderly fashion from one device to the next. Devices can transmit only if they have control of the token, which distribute the access control among all the devices.

Token Ring—A network protocol that uses some form of twisted-pair cable connected to a multiaccess unit (MAU). Although the token ring network uses a star topology, the signals follow a ring or loop. Computers on a token ring communicate only when they possess a token that is passed from one computer to another.

Toner—An extremely fine powder made of plastic resin bonded to iron particles. The iron particles react to electrical charges and the plastic resin has a low melting temperature.

Toner Cartridge—A replaceable cartridge used in laser printers to hold toner.

Topology—The arrangement or physical layout of network computers and cables.

Touch Screen—A transparent panel that covers a monitor screen. Instead of using a pointing device to select options, they can be selected by touching the screen.

Tower Case—A case that stands erect.

Trace Log—Used in Windows performance monitor, trace logs are event-driven, recording monitored data such as disk I/O or page faults. When a traced event occurs, it is recorded in the log.

Trackball—A pointing device that can move the cursor back and forth on the screen (assuming the software supports pointing devices). Unlike the mouse, the trackball protrudes from the top of its container. These devices are easy to use and can improve productivity over using a keyboard alone.

Trackpoint—A pointing device in the form of a small rubber cap found on keyboards that appears above the B key between the G and H keys. To move the mouse pointer, the rubber cap is connected to pressure transducers. The pressure transducers measure the amount of force being applied and the direction of the force. The harder it is pressed, the faster the pointer moves.

Tracks—Concentric circles that divide a platter.

Tractor Feed—A device with sprockets (placed on a wheel or belt) that are placed in the holes of fanfold paper. As the sprockets rotate around a wheel, the paper is pushed or pulled past the printhead.

Transformer—A device with two or more coil windings used to step up or step down voltage.

Transistor—A device that can amplify signals or to be used as an electronic on/off switch.

Transistor-Transistor Logic (TTL) Chips—Standard IC chips based on two transistors, which run on +5 V dc power.

Transport Control Protocol (TCP)—A TCP/IP protocol that provides a connection-oriented, reliable communications for applications that typically transfer large amounts of data at one time or that require an acknowledgment for data received.

Trojan Horse Virus—A virus that appears to be legitimate software, such as a game or useful utility.

True Color—A video system that displays 16 million colors. The 16 million colors use 24 bits to define the colors of the pixel.

TrueType Fonts—An outline font commonly used in Windows 3.1X, Windows 95 and 98, and Windows NT. TrueType fonts can be scaled to any size and rotated.

TSR (Terminate and Stay Resident)—A small program loaded into the RAM (typically with DOS) to control some hardware device or to provide some useful function. Unlike other programs, a TSR gives control back to the operating system while still functioning.

TWAIN—Short for *technology without an interesting name.* A standard that allows software to control scanners.

Twisted-Pair—A cable made of two insulated strands of copper wire twisted around each other. The twist in the cable helps reduce crosstalk.

U

Underwriters Laboratories Inc. (UL)—An independent, nonprofit organization that acts as a safety engineering consultant and certification body. UL's strict standards and solid reputation have led companies to pay UL to detect flaws and defects in their products before they hit the market.

Unicode—A character set used for representing characters as integers. Unlike ASCII, which uses 7 or 8 bits for each character, Unicode uses 16 bits, which means that it can represent more than 65,000 unique characters. Since Unicode uses 2 bytes to identify each character, it is also known as the *double-byte character set.*

Uniform Resource Locator (URL)—A location of a web page or site. The first part of the address indicates what protocol to use, and the second part specifies the IP address or the domain name where the resource is located. The last part indicates the folder and file name.

Uninterruptible Power Supply (UPS)—Device that protects the PC by using a battery to filter out power fluctuations.

Uniqueness Database File (UDF)—A file that supplies unique information during unattended installation for Windows NT, Windows 2000, and Windows XP.

Universal Asynchronous Receiver/Transmitter (UART)—A single IC chip that acts as translator between the serial port and the system bus (parallel connection). In serial ports, it is the component that processes, transmits, and receives data.

Universal Naming Convention (UNC)—A NetBIOS format for specifying the location of shared resources on a local area network (LAN). UNC uses the following format: \\servername\shared-resource-pathname.

Universal Serial Bus (USB)—An external port that allows up to 127 external PC peripherals to be connected in series (daisy chain). The USB connector will accept any USB peripheral, including mice, keyboards, printers, modems, and external disk drives. The standard 4-pin connector will connect seven devices directly, and these seven devices can be increased to 127 by connecting external hubs (each hub accommodates another seven devices) in a chain.

Upper Memory—Memory between 640 KB and 1 MB that is not used by hardware. It is used to load device drivers and TSRs to free conventional RAM.

Upper Memory Blocks (UMBs)—A division of upper memory.

UseNet Newsgroup—A set of bulletin boards on the Internet for conducting conversations on many different subjects, including computers.

User—The computer operator who is telling the computer what to do.

User Datagram Protocol (UDP)—A TCP/IP protocol that provides connectionless communications and does not guarantee that packets will be delivered. Applications that use UDP typically transfer small amounts of data at once. Reliable delivery is the responsibility of the application.

User Mode—A processing mode used in Windows NT, Windows 2000, and Windows XP that has programs running in ring 3 of the Intel 386 processor protection model. These programs are protected by the operating system. It is a less privileged processor mode that has no direct access to hardware and can only access its own address space.

User Profile—A collection of folders and data that store the user's current desktop environment and application settings including the personal registry setting and files that are specific to the user such as cookies, documents in the MY DOCUMENTS folder, web browser favorites, shortcuts to network places, and mapped drivers to shared folders on a network server.

User-friendly—A term indicating that computer equipment or software is easy to understand and operate.

V

VBScript—Short for *Visual Basic Scripting Edition.* VBScript is a scripting language developed by Microsoft and supported by Microsoft's Internet Explorer web browser. VBScript is based on the Visual Basic programming language, but is much simpler. It enables web authors to include interactive controls (such as buttons and scroll bars) on their web pages.

Vector Fonts—Fonts that are rendered using a mathematical model. Each character is defined as a set of lines drawn between points. Vector fonts can be scaled to any size but cannot be rotated.

Vector Graphics—A picture made up of lines and curves to define a graphics image.

Very Large-Scale Integration (VLSI)—A type of IC chip that has between 100,000 and 1,000,000 components per chip.

VESA Local Bus (VL Bus)—A form of local bus slot created by the Video Electronics Standards Association (VESA) originally to improve video performance.

VFAT—An enhanced version of the FAT structure that allows Windows 95 and Windows NT to support long filenames (up to 255 characters).

Vi—A popular text editor used in Linux.

Video Accelerator—Video cards that include processors to help process video data.

Video Capture Card—An expansion card that can capture a still image from a television, camcorder, or VCR.

Video Card—The component that sends the visual output from the computer to the monitor. It tells the monitor which pixels to light up, what color the pixel should be, and what intensity. The video card is an expansion card or is built into the motherboard.

Video Chipset—The logic circuit that includes the video coprocessor that controls the video card. The chipset used is a major factor in determining overall video performance.

Video Electronics Standards Association (VESA)—An organization formed by major computer, monitor, and video manufacturers. It is responsible for developing a Super VGA (SVGA) standard and created the VESA local bus.

Video Graphics Array (VGA)—A video system considered the first modern monitor and from which all of today's monitors are derived. It supports a resolution of 640 × 480 at 16 colors or a resolution of 320 × 200 at 256 colors (chosen from a palette of 262,144 colors). It was also the first analog monitor used on the PC.

Video Memory—Memory found on video cards used to hold information to be displayed on the monitor.

Video RAM—*See* VRAM.

Video ROM BIOS—ROM BIOS chip located on the video card (or on the motherboard, if the video card is built into the motherboard) that contains instructions to control video systems.

Virtual 8086 mode—The operating mode of the microprocessor that divides the RAM into several pretend 8086 machines, each consisting of 1 MB of RAM. The microprocessor then switches rapidly between the different virtual (pretend) machines so that it appears that all of the machines are working at the same time (multitasking).

Virtual Desktop—Desktops that represent completely different desktops, each displaying different windows.

Virtual File System (VFS)—A kernel software layer that handles all system calls related to the Linux file system. It must manage all of the different file systems that are mounted at any given time. It provides a common interface to several kinds of file systems including disk-based file systems, network-based file systems, and special file systems including the/proc and /dev file systems.

Virtual Machine (VM)—A self-contained operating environment that behaves as if it were a separate computer.

Virtual Memory—Hard drive space pretending to be RAM.

Virus—A program, many with destructive tendencies, designed to replicate and spread, generally without the knowledge or permission of the user.

Virus Hoax—A letter or email message warning you about a virus that does not exist.

Voice Coil Actuators—Head actuators that use electromagnetic force to move.

Voltage—The force that moves the electrons, measured in volts (V). Voltage is generated by the power supply or battery.

Voltmeter—A device that measures voltage.

Volume—A portion of a disk signified by a single drive letter. It can be a floppy disk, a partition, or several hard drives linked together (spanning).

Volume Boot Sector (VBS)—The first sector of any partition or the first sector of a floppy disk. It is created by high-level formatting.

Volume Set—The combining of 2 through 32 areas of unformatted free space (FAT or NTFS) on one or more physical drives to create a larger logical drive.

VRAM—Short for *video RAM*. It is RAM typically used in video cards that is dual ported (read and written to at the same time).

W

Wait-State—A CPU clock cycle during which the microprocessor lies idle so that slower RAM and other components can catch up with it and function properly. The fastest setting would be no wait states.

Warm Boot—A type of booting that doesn't require the computer to perform all of the hardware and memory checks associated with a cold boot. A warm boot is usually done by pressing the Ctrl+Alt+Del keys.

Waveform Audio (WAV)—A common sound file.

Web Browser—The client program/software that you run on your local machine to gain access to a web server. It receives the HTML commands, interprets the HTML, and displays the results.

Web Page—A document on the World Wide Web. Every web page is identified by a unique URL (Uniform Resource Locator).

Web Server—A computer equipped with the server software that uses Internet protocols such as hypertext transfer protocol (HTTP) and file transfer protocol (FTP) to respond to web client requests on a TCP/IP network via web browsers.

Weight—The total weight of a ream (500 sheets) of 17 × 22.5-in. paper.

Wide Area Network (WAN)—A network that uses long-range telecommunication links to connect the network computers over long distances and that often consists of two or more smaller LANs. Typically, the LANs are connected through public networks, such as the telephone system.

Widget—A GUI control, such as a button to be pressed.

Widget Set—Library routines build and form the components within a window such as scroll bars, menu bars, taskbars, popup menus, requester boxes, and so on.

Wild-Card Characters—An asterisk (*) or question mark (?) used to indicate several files at the same time.

Window—A rectangular display area in which a particular program or utility can function.

Windows 3.XX—An operating environment that provides a GUI for DOS.

Windows 95—A popular graphical operating system that replaced DOS and Windows 3.XX.

Windows 98—An upgraded version of the Windows 95 operating system.

Windows Driver Model (WDM)—A standard method used for Microsoft Windows that allows programs to build drivers that can be used across multiple Window platforms.

Windows Explorer—A component of Windows that is used to manage directories and files.

Windows File Protection (WFP)—Technology that prevents replacing critical Windows system and DLL files.

Windows NT—The most advanced version of the Windows operating system. It is a 32-bit operating system that supports preemptive multitasking.

Windows NT Family Executive—Services consisting of managers and device drivers.

Windows on Windows 64 (WOW64)—With the introduction of 64-bit versions of Microsoft Windows, WOW64 is a 32-bit subsystem that allows you to run 32-bit applications on 64-bit operating systems.

Windows RAM (WRAM)—A type of video RAM used by high-end video cards. It uses a dual-color block write to perform very fast pattern and text fills and can perform fast buffer-to-buffer transfers for video and double-buffered 3D animation.

Windows Setup Manager—A program that allows you to create unattended installation scripts (Answer file and Uniqueness Database File (UDF)) for Windows NT, 2000, or XP.

Windows Socket (WinSock)—A DLL file that is responsible for providing Windows applications with the ability to communicate over a TCP/IP network.

WINNT.EXE—The program used to install Windows NT, Windows 2000 or Windows XP.

WINNT32.EXE—The program used to upgrade Windows NT, Windows 2000, or Windows XP.

Word Processor—Software that allows a document to be created much like it would be on a typewriter. Word processoring software is the most common application software.

Workgroup—A group of computers connected together in which the computers keep track of their own user and group account information and do not share this information with other computers. In a workgroup, each computer has a local security database so that it tracks its own user and group account information. The user information is not shared with other workgroup computers.

Workstation—A computer acting as a client and attached to a network. It communicates with the operating system by means of client software called *shells* or *requesters*.

World Wide Web (WWW)—A system of Internet servers that support specially formatted documents. World Wide Web is synonymous with the Internet. The documents are formatted in a script called HTML (Hypertext Markup Language) that supports links to other documents, as well as graphics, audio, and video files. This means you can jump from one document to another simply by clicking on hot spots. Not all Internet servers are part of the World Wide Web. There are several applications called web browsers that make it easy to access the World Wide Web, two of the most popular being Netscape Navigator and Microsoft's Internet Explorer.

WRAM—*See* Windows RAM.

Write Once Read Many (WORM)—*See* Recordable CD.

WTX—A motherboard, case, and power supply form factor used in larger workstation and server systems.

WYSIWYG—An acronym for *What You See Is What You Get.*

X

X Window—A system with a platform-independent graphics protocol and interface that provides the GUI interface for Linux.

XFS—A journaling file system.

Xon/Xoff—Software handshaking.

XT Computer—A computer with an 8088 or 8086 microprocessor. XT computers typically use DIP switches to configure the computer rather than a CMOS setup program.

Z

Z-buffering—A 3D graphics technique used to determine which objects in a 3D scene will be visible to the user and which will be blocked by other objects. Z-buffering displays only the visible pixels in each object.

Zero Insertion Force (ZIF) Sockets—A chip socket that allows a chip to be inserted and removed without special tools. It usually uses a handle to lock or unlock a chip in place.

Zip Drive—A drive that uses 100 MB removable disks.

Zoned Recordings—A scheme that divides the platter into zones. The outer zones have more sectors per track than the inner zones.

Zoomed Video (ZV)—A direct connection used in notebook computers to the system's VGA controller.

Index